THINKING THINGS THROUGH

List of Features continues on inside back cover

23rd Edition

ANDERSON'S
BUSINESS LAW
and The Legal Environment

Comprehensive Volume

DAVID P. TWOMEY

Professor of Law
Carroll School of Management
Boston College
Member of the Massachusetts and Florida Bars

MARIANNE MOODY JENNINGS

Emeritus Professor of Legal and Ethical Studies
W.P. Carey School of Business
Arizona State University
Member of the Arizona Bar

STEPHANIE M. GREENE

Chair, Business Law Department
Professor of Business Law
Carroll School of Management
Boston College
Member of the Massachusetts Bar

CENGAGE
Learning·

Australia • Brazil • Mexico • Singapore • United Kingdom • United States

Anderson's Business Law and The Legal Environment: Comprehensive Volume, 23rd Edition

David P. Twomey, Marianne Moody Jennings, and Stephanie M. Greene

VP for Social Science and Qualitative Business: Erin Joyner

Product Director: Michael Worls

Sr. Product Manager: Vicky True-Baker

Sr. Content Developer: Kristen Meere

Product Assistant: Ryan McAndrews

Marketing Manager: Katie Jergens

Marketing Director: Kristen Hurd

Marketing Coordinator: Christopher Walz

Production Director: Sharon Smith

Sr. Content Project Manager: Ann Borman

Content Digitization Project Manager: James Schoenle

Manufacturing Planner: Kevin Kluck

Sr. Inventory Analyst: Terina Bradley

Sr. IP Director: Julie Geagan-Chavez

IP Analyst: Jennifer Nonenmacher

IP Project Manager: Betsy Hathaway

Sr. Art Director: Michelle Kunkler

Production Service and Compositor: MPS Limited

Interior and cover designer: Lou Ann Thesing

Cover Image: Vermont Lighthouse, york777/Shutterstock.com

Design elements: Colorful Light Effect Background: iStockPhoto.com/malija; part and chapter opener lighthouse: iStockPhoto.com/Sergiy1975; sustainability icon: Ella Sarkisyan/ShutterStock.com; cyberlaw laptop icon: graphixmania/ShutterStock.com; video and smartphone icons: Hilch/ShutterStock.com; trophy icon: HuHu/ShutterStock.com; scales icon: lana rinck/ShutterStock.com

Library of Congress Control Number: 2015953186

Student Edition ISBN: 978-1-305-57508-0

Loose-leaf Edition ISBN: 978-1-305-66385-5

Cengage Learning

20 Channel Center Street

Boston, MA 02210

USA

Cengage Learning is a leading provider of customized learning solutions with employees residing in nearly 40 different countries and sales in more than 125 countries around the world. Find your local representative at **www.cengage.com**.

Cengage Learning products are represented in Canada by Nelson Education, Ltd.

To learn more about Cengage Learning Solutions, visit **www.cengage.com**.

Purchase any of our products at your local college store or at our preferred online store **www.cengagebrain.com**.

Printed in Canada

Print Number: 01   Print Year: 2015

Brief Contents

Contents

PART 2

Contracts

PART 4

Negotiable Instruments

PART 6

Agency and Employment

PART 7

Business Organizations

PART 8

Real Property and Estates

Regardless of the day of the week, newspapers and magazines will have stories about law and business together. The dentists in North Carolina lost a challenge by the teeth whitening industry to the profession's rules prohibiting whitening except by licensed dentists. In 2015, BP, the international energy company, paid $18 billion to settle all the state and federal claims related to the explosion of its Deepwater Horizon off-shore oil rig. The problems with mortgages and foreclosures have resulted in a new federal agency and significant revisions to the requirements for the formation of credit contracts. Securities laws have changed because buying shares over the Internet, so-called crowdfundings, has become an entrepreneurial trend.

There were more insider trading convictions in the past three years than in any other era of financial growth. And now those convictions are being challenged because the definition of what is inside information requires clarification.

SAC Capital was one of the companies that had a large number of former and current employees convicted or enter guilty pleas to insider trading, but yet SAC's CEO was not charged and the company paid civil fines related to the activities of its brokers, analysts, and advisers.

Who is responsible for crimes committed by companies? If a mining company CEO closely tracks production, can he be held criminally liable when the problems at the mine result in an explosion and deaths of the miners? As major corporations have continued to experience major criminal, legal, and ethical difficulties, we can see how important it is for business managers to understand the law and the foundations of ethics. When a manager has a void in knowledge on law and ethics, running a company can be tricky business. Budweiser and Corona learned the intricacies of antitrust law as they worked out the details of their proposed merger.

When an entrepreneur is struggling with the decision of whether to incorporate or create an LLC, or the shareholders of Disney are grappling with issues about their rights when their CEO makes a bad decision, the law is there. No business or manager can hope to succeed without an understanding of the laws and legal environment of business. Students in business must be prepared with both knowledge of the law and the skill of applying it in the business setting. We learn principles and application through interaction with examples and by working our way through dilemmas, issues, and problems. This 23rd edition of *Anderson's Business Law and the Legal Environment* enhances the learning process while still providing a detailed and rigorous case approach.

New to This Edition

Enhanced Digital Content—*MindTap*™

Our goal—is for the students to learn the material. With that singular goal in mind, we have created what we feel is an extremely useful tool for both instructors and students. *MindTap*™ is a fully online, highly personalized learning experience combining readings, multimedia, activities, and assessments into a singular Learning Path. *MindTap* guides students through their course with ease and engagement. Instructors can personalize the Learning Path by customizing Cengage Learning resources and adding their own content via apps that integrate into the *MindTap* framework seamlessly with Learning Management Systems.

We understand that business law instructors want to help students **Prepare** for class, **Engage** with the course concepts to reinforce learning, **Apply** these concepts in real-world scenarios, and use legal reasoning and critical thinking to **Analyze** business law content.

Each and every item in the Learning Path is assignable and gradable. This gives instructors the knowledge of class standings and concepts that may be difficult. Additionally, students gain knowledge about where they stand—both individually and compared to the highest performers in class.

Instructors may view a demo video and learn more about *MindTap*, at **www.cengage.com/mindtap**.

Features of the Text

The features of this text make the business and law connection easy to understand and offer students clarity for grasping the often challenging complexities of law. The features are summarized in the following sections, which offer an overview of this edition.

Learning Outcomes

Students will better see and understand the relationship between legal concepts and their application in real-life situations by using the chapter Learning Outcomes. These are featured at the end of each chapter—along with the Summary and new Key Terms list—in an all-encompassing "Make the Connection" section. The Learning Outcomes also encourage students to utilize the existing text pedagogy by serving as a direct reference point for selected "For Example" call-outs, case summaries, and feature boxes.

Sports and Entertainment Law

Using pop culture, this feature teaches students about law and ethics in a way that is sure to engage them. What happens to the contract fees that Lance Armstrong earned from the U.S. Postal Service for its sponsorship of his races? What happens when sports figures have personal problems and the companies and products they endorse want to end that relationship? Can contracts be terminated because of public behavior? Was Heath Ledger's will, one that was drawn up and executed before he had a child, still valid? What happens to the personal property that actor Robin Williams failed to specify a distribution for? Who gets his *Mork & Mindy* suspenders? The New Orleans Saints and their bounty compensation program present an interesting series of ethical questions in a feature in Chapter 3. Students have the chance to explore the law through these examples of sports figures' and entertainers' brushes with the law.

Clarity

The writing style has been evolving and, once again, we have changed more passages that fell victim to the passive voice. The writing is clear and lively. The examples are student-friendly, and the discussions of law are grounded in the book's strong connection to business. The principles of law are taught in the language and examples of business. Students can relate to the examples, which provide memorable illustrations of complex but critical legal concepts.

CPA Helps

As always, the text provides coverage for all the legal topics covered on the CPA exam. Several topics have been eliminated from the content for the CPA exam as of June 2015.

However, the exam lags behind the content change, so the eliminated topics may continue to appear on the exam for 6 to 18 months. Below is the new business law/regulatory content for the CPA exam. The topics of property, bailments, insurance, and estates will be eliminated going forward with more emphasis on federal regulation, including in the areas of antitrust and employment law.

Business Law (17%–21%)

A. Agency

    1. Formation and termination

    2. Authority of agents and principals

    3. Duties and liabilities of agents and principals

B. Contracts

    1. Formation

    2. Performance

    3. Third-party assignments

    4. Discharge, breach, and remedies

C. Uniform Commercial Code

    1. Sales contracts

    2. Negotiable instruments

    3. Secured transactions

    4. Documents of title and title transfer

D. Debtor-Creditor Relationships

    1. Rights, duties, and liabilities of debtors, creditors, and guarantors

    2. Bankruptcy and insolvency

E. Government Regulation of Business

    1. Federal securities regulation

    2. Other federal laws and regulations (antitrust, copyright, patents, money laundering, labor, employment, and ERISA)

F. Business Structure (Selection of a Business Entity)

    1. Advantages, disadvantages, implications, and constraints

    2. Formation, operation, and termination

    3. Financial structure, capitalization, profit and loss allocation, and distributions

    4. Rights, duties, legal obligations, and authority of owners and management

Business organizations, now a substantial portion of the exam, remain a focus of eight chapters with up-to-date coverage of Dodd-Frank and its impact on business forms and disclosures. This edition continues to feature sample CPA exam questions at the end of those chapters that include legal areas covered on the exam. This edition still contains the questions for the topics that will be eliminated because of the transition period between content adoption and exam adaptation. Answers for the odd-numbered CPA exam questions in each of the appropriate chapters are given in the Instructor's Manual along with explanations for the answers. This edition of the book also continues to use a CPA highlight icon to alert students to those areas that are particularly critical in preparing for the law portion of the CPA exam.

Case Summaries

Specially selected case summaries appear in abundance and are still at the core of this text. Most chapters include three to five case summaries, and they have been updated to feature the most current and newsworthy topics. Landmark decisions also appear, including several from the 2014–2015 U.S. Supreme Court term.

e-Commerce and Cyberlaw

This feature covers e-mail privacy, Internet taxes, identity theft, contract formation on the Internet, e-commerce employment rules, electronic signatures, and more. Chapter 8, the criminal law chapter, includes greater detail on the new and evolving computer crimes. Chapter 9, the intellectual property chapter, features a section on Protection of Computer Software and Mask Works, covering copyright and patent protection of computer programs, restrictive licensing, semiconductor chip protection, and more. There are features in chapters throughout the book, such as an example in Chapter 2 about how social media is having an impact on jury selection because of the information lawyers can gather about potential jurors from these sources. The Edward Snowden issues are covered as both a cyber law and an ethical issue in Chapter 3. In Chapter 6, there is a discussion of net neutraility. Chapter 29 has a feature covering electronic presentment of instruments.

Thinking Things Through

This feature is designed to help students apply the law they have learned from the chapter and cases to a hypothetical scenario or another case that varies slightly from the examples in the reading. With these problems built into the reading, students have the chance to really think through what they have just read and studied with regard to the law presented in that chapter. This feature can be used to promote classroom discussion or as an assignment for analysis. For example, in Chapter 29, students get to walk through a liability question when there are forgeries on a check to determine who ultimately bears the loss on a fraudulent check. In Chapter 4, students can think about whether flashing your headlights to warn oncoming drivers of a speed trap is legal. Is this a form of protected speech? Is it against the law to warn other drivers?

Major Regulatory Reforms: USA Patriot Act, Dodd-Frank, and the JOBS Act

Businesses continue to be dramatically affected not only by laws at the federal level, but also by complex and intricate new federal regulatory schemes. Dodd-Frank has changed many things in many areas of the law from the behavior of analysts to the protection of consumers in mortgage and credit transactions. The provisions of the Affordable Health Care Act have twice been litigated to the level of the U.S. Supreme Court—cases that cover fundamental questions about our Constitution as well as the balance of state and federal power. The JOBS Act has made it easier for smaller companies to raise money by easing securities regulation requirements.

Ethical Focus

In addition to Chapter 3, which is devoted exclusively to the current issues in business ethics, each chapter continues to provide students with an ethical dilemma related to that particular area of law. The Ethics & the Law feature presents problems in each area of law. Students will be able to analyze ethical issues and problems that are very real and very challenging for anyone in business—for example, the issues involved in check cashing companies that take checks for a fee knowing that there are probably issues with those checks and then seek holder-in-due-course protection.

Critical Thinking

The American Assembly of Collegiate Schools of Business (AACSB) mandate on critical thinking is addressed by this text. The Thinking Things Through feature asks students to analyze a problem that requires application of the law and examination of slight changes in factual patterns from examples in the text and the cases. For example, in the negotiable instruments chapters, students can look at a sample instrument in one problem and apply the requirements for negotiability to determine whether the instrument is indeed negotiable. In the Ethics & the Law feature, students must connect ethical thought with law and public policy and walk through the logic of application and results. End-of-chapter problems are, for the most part, real cases that summarize fact patterns and ask the students to find the applicable laws in the chapter and determine applicability and results. The fact patterns in the chapter problems are detailed and realistic and offer students the chance to test their mastery of the chapter concepts.

For Additional Help in Teaching and Learning

For more detailed information about any of the following ancillaries, contact your local Cengage Learning Consultant or visit the *Anderson's Business Law and the Legal Environment* Web site.

MindTap

MindTap™ is a fully online, highly personalized learning experience combining readings, multimedia, activities, and assessments into a singular Learning Path. Instructors can personalize the Learning Path by customizing Cengage Learning resources and adding their own content via apps that integrate into the *MindTap* framework seamlessly with Learning Management Systems. To view a demo video and learn more about *MindTap*, please visit **www.cengage.com/mindtap**.

Instructor's Manual

The Instructor's Manual is prepared by Marianne Jennings, one of the textbook authors. It provides instructor insights, chapter outlines, and teaching strategies for each chapter. Discussion points are provided for Thinking Things Through, Ethics & the Law vignettes, and for each case referenced in the new Learning Outcomes. Also included are answers to CPA questions. Download the Instructor's Manual at the instructor's companion site online.

Cengage Learning Testing Powered by Cognero

Cognero is a flexible online system that allows instructors to author, edit, and manage test bank content from multiple Cengage Learning solutions; create multiple test versions in an instant; and deliver tests from the instructor's LMS, classroom, or wherever the instructor desires. The test bank includes thousands of true/false, multiple choice, and case questions.

Microsoft® PowerPoint® Lecture Review Slides

PowerPoint slides are available for use by instructors for enhancing their lectures. Download these slides at the instructor's companion site online.

Business Law Digital Video Library

This dynamic online video library features more than 90 video clips that spark class discussion and clarify core legal principles. The library, recently updated with new videos, is organized into five series including classic business and modern business and e-commerce scenarios, straightforward lecture-style explanations of concepts for student review, and clips from many popular films. Access for students is free when bundled with a new textbook or can be purchased for an additional charge. For more information about the Digital Video Library, visit: **www.cengage.com/blaw/dvl**.

Cengage Learning Custom Solutions

Whether you need print, digital, or hybrid course materials, Cengage Learning Custom Solutions can help you create your perfect learning solution. Draw from Cengage Learning's extensive library of texts and collections, add or create your own original work, and create customized media and technology to match your learning and course objectives. Our editorial team will work with you through each step, allowing you to concentrate on the most important thing—your students. Learn more about all our services at **www.cengage.com/custom**.

Acknowledgments

The development and revision of a textbook represents teamwork in its highest form. We thank the innumerable instructors, students, attorneys, and managers who have added to the quality of this textbook through its many editions.

Dean Alexander
Miami-Dade Community College

Robert A. Arnold
Thomas More College

John T. Ballantine
University of Colorado

Todd Barnet
Pace University

Marie F. Benjamin
Valencia Community College

Kenneth V. Bevan
Valencia Community College

Weldon M. Blake, JD
Bethune-Cookman University

Bob Blinderman
WTAMU and Amarillo College

Robert Boeke
Delta College

Billy Carson
Itawamba Community College

Norman Bradshaw
Alvin Community College

Thomas L. Brooks, Jr.
Purdue University

Myra Bruegger
Southeastern Community College

Barry Bunn
Valencia Community College

Jarrod Y. Burch, JD
Saint Leo University and American Intercontinental University

Deborah Carter
Coahoma Community College

Greg Cermigiano
Widener University

David A. Clough
Naugatuck Valley Community College

Anne Cohen
University of Massachusetts

Thomas S. Collins
Loras College

Jason Cooley
Copiah Lincoln Community College

Lawrence J. Danks
Camden County College

Shoshana Dennis
San Diego City College

Darrell Dies
Illinois State University

De Vee E. Dykstra
University of South Dakota

Adam Epstein
University of Tennessee

Phillip Evans
Kutztown University of Pennsylvania

Deborah Lynn Bundy Ferry
Marquette University

Darrel Ford
University of Central Oklahoma

Andrea Foster
John Tyler Community College

Leslie L. Francis
CUNY-York College

Edward J. Gac
University of Colorado

Teresa R. Gillespie
Northwest University

Kimberly Goudy
Central Ohio Technical College

Patrick J. Griffin, CPA, LL.M, JD
Lewis University

David Grigg
Pfeiffer University

Ronald Groeber
Ball State University

Francis A. Hatstat, MBA, JD
Bellevue College

Heidi Helgren
Delta College

Florence Elliot Howard
Stephen F. Austin University

Richard Hurley
Francis Marion University

Lawrence A. Joel
Bergen Community College

David Lewis Jordan
Emmanuel College

Michael A. Katz
Delaware State University

Thomas E. Knothe
Viterbo University

Ruth Kraft
Audrey Cohen College

Claire La Roche
Longwood College

Virginia Edgerton Law, JD
Saint Leo University

Paolo Longo, Jr.
Valencia Community College

Susan D. Looney
Mohave Community College

Linda McCarley
Bevill State Community College

Roy J. Millender, Jr.
Westmont College

Derek Mosley
Meridian Community College

Michael Murphy
Langston University – Tulsa

Steven Murray
Community College of Rhode Island

Ann Olazábal
University of Miami

Neal Orkin
Drexel University

Jeffrey D. Penley, JD
Catawba Valley Community College

Ronald Picker
St. Mary's of the Woods College

Francis Polk
Ocean County College

Robert Prentice
University of Texas at Austin

Linda Reppert
Marymount University

Richard J. Riley
Samford University

Simone I. Rosenberg
Valencia Community College – East Campus

Gary Sambol
Rutgers University School of Business

Samuel L. Schrager
University of Connecticut

Kathy Scott
Western Piedmont Community College

Janet Seggern
Lehigh Carbon Community College

Lester Smith
Eastern New Mexico University

Joseph A. Spadaro
Naugatuck Valley Community College

Michael Sugameli
Oakland University

Cathy L. Taylor
Park University and Webster University

Mike Teel
Samford University

Darrell H. Thompson
Mountain View College

Cathy Trecek
Iowa Western Community College

Bob Vicars
Bluefield State University

Thomas K. Ware
Johnson State College

James Welch
Kentucky Wesleyan College

Lisa Wilhite
Bevill State Community C

We extend our thanks to our families for their support and patience
hours to ensure that each edition is better than the last.

Professor David Twomey has been a member of the Business Law Department in the Carroll School of Management at Boston College since 1968. As department chair for over a decade, and four-term chair of the school's Education Policy Committee, Professor Twomey served as a spokesperson for a strong legal and ethical component in both the undergraduate and graduate curriculum. He is the author of some 35 editions of textbooks on labor, employment, and business law topics. His articles have appeared in journals such as *Best's Review, The American Business Law Journal, The Labor Law Journal, The Massachusetts Law Quarterly, The Florida Bar Journal*, and *The Business Law Review*. He has served as arbitrator in over two thousand labor-management disputes throughout the country. His service includes appointments by Presidents Ronald Reagan, George H. W. Bush, William J. Clinton, George W. Bush, and Barack Obama to nine Presidential Emergency Boards, whose recommendations served as the basis for the resolution of major disputes in the rail and airline industries. After service in the U.S. Marine Corps, he graduated from Boston College, earned his MBA at the University of Massachusetts, Amherst, and a JD degree at Boston College Law School. He is a member of the Massachusetts and Florida Bars and a member of the National Academy of Arbitrators.

Professor Marianne M. Jennings, Emeritus Professor of Legal and Ethical Studies, has taught at the WP Carey School of Business, Arizona State University, from 1977 through the present. She has six textbooks and four monographs in circulation in the areas of business ethics, ethical culture, and legal environment. She was director of the Lincoln Center for Applied Ethics from 1995 to 1999. She has worked with government agencies, professional organizations, colleges and universities, and Fortune 100 companies on ethics training and culture. She is a contributing editor of *Corporate Finance Review* and *Real Estate Law Journal*. Two of her books have been named *Library Journal*'s book of the year. Her books have been translated into three languages. Her book, *The Seven Signs of Ethical Collapse*, was published by St Martin's Press and has been used as both an audit tool and a primer by numerous organizations for creating and sustaining an ethical culture.

In 2011, she was named one of the Top 100 Thought Leaders by Trust Across America, and in 2012, she was named one of the 100 most influential people in business ethics by *Ethisphere* magazine.

She served on the board of directors for Arizona Public Service (now Pinnacle West), the owner of the Palo Verde Nuclear Station, from 1987 through 2000. She has served on INPO's advisory council since 2005. In 2015, she was named an affiliated scholar with the Center for the Study of Economic Liberty at Arizona State University. She conducts ethics training and ethical culture assessments for businesses, including Fortune 100 companies, government agencies, professional associations, and nonprofit organizations.

Professor Stephanie M. Greene has been a member of the faculty at the Boston College Carroll School of Management since 1995, where she currently serves as professor and chair of the Business Law Department. She served as editor-in-chief of the *American Business Law Journal* and is currently the senior articles editor for the *Journal of Legal Studies Education*. She has published numerous articles on intellectual property law, pharmaceutical regulation, and employment law with publications appearing in the *American Business Law Journal*, the *Northwestern Journal of International Law & Business*, and the *Columbia Business Law Review*. A member of the Massachusetts Bar, Professor Greene earned her undergraduate degree from Princeton University and her JD from Boston College Law School. She is a member of the Massachusetts Bar.

The Legal and Social Environment of Business

The Nature and Sources of Law

Learning Outcomes ⟨⟨⟨

After studying this chapter, you should be able to

LO.1 Discuss the nature of law and legal rights

LO.2 List the sources of law

LO.3 Describe the classifications of law

1-1 Nature of Law and Legal Rights

Why have law? If you have ever been stuck in a traffic jam or jostled in a crowd leaving a stadium, you have observed the need for order to keep those involved moving in an efficient and safe manner. The issues with bloggers' use of others' materials and continuing downloading of music and films without compensation to copyright holders illustrate the need for rules and order in this era of new technology. When our interactions are not orderly, whether at our concerts or through our e-mail, all of us and our rights are affected. The order or pattern of rules that society uses to govern the conduct of individuals and their relationships is called **law.** Law keeps society running smoothly and efficiently.

Law consists of the body of principles that govern conduct and that can be enforced in courts or by administrative agencies. The law could also be described as a collection or bundle of rights.

law–the order or pattern of rules that society establishes to govern the conduct of individuals and the relationships among them.

1-1a Legal Rights

A **right** is a legal capacity to require another person to perform or refrain from performing an act. Our rights flow from the U.S. Constitution, state constitutions, federal and state statutes, and ordinances at the local levels, including cities, counties, and boroughs. Within these sources of rights are also duties. A **duty** is an obligation of law imposed on a person to perform or refrain from performing a certain act.

Duties and rights coexist. No right exists in one person without a corresponding duty resting on some other person or persons. For example, if the terms of a lease provide that the premises will remain in a condition of good repair so that the tenant can live there comfortably, the landlord has a corresponding duty to provide a dwelling that has hot and cold running water.

right–legal capacity to require another person to perform or refrain from an action.

duty–an obligation of law imposed on a person to perform or refrain from performing a certain act.

1-1b Individual Rights

The U.S. Constitution gives individuals certain rights. Those rights include the right to freedom of speech, the right to due process or the right to have a hearing before any freedom is taken away, and the right to vote. There are also duties that accompany individual rights, such as the duty to speak in a way that does not cause harm to others. For example, individuals are free to express their opinions about the government or its officials, but they would not be permitted to yell "Fire!" in a crowded theater and cause unnecessary harm to others. The rights given in the U.S. Constitution are rights that cannot be taken away or violated by any statutes, ordinances, or court decisions. These rights provide a framework for the structure of government and other laws.

1-1c The Right of Privacy

One very important individual legal right is the right of privacy, which has two components. The first is the right to be secure against unreasonable searches and seizures by the government. The Fourth Amendment of the U.S. Constitution guarantees this portion of the **right of privacy.** A police officer, for example, may not search your home unless the officer has a reasonable suspicion (which is generally established through a warrant) that your home contains evidence of a crime, such as illegal drugs. If your home or business is searched unlawfully, any items obtained during that unlawful search could be excluded as evidence in a criminal trial because of the Fourth Amendment's exclusionary rule. **For Example,** in *Riley v. California*, 134 S. Ct. 2473 (2014), David Riley was stopped by a police officer for driving with expired registration tags. The officer discovered that Mr. Riley's license had been suspended, so his car was impounded and searched. Officers

right of privacy–the right to be free from unreasonable intrusion by others.

also found Mr. Riley's smart phone and, in going through the phone, found pictures and information related to a gang shooting, and Mr. Riley was then charged with that earlier shooting. However, the court held that evidence from the smart phone could not be used at trial because there was no warrant and Mr. Riley had a right of privacy in the data on that phone.[1]

A second aspect of the right of privacy protects individuals against intrusions by others. Your private life is not subject to public scrutiny when you are a private citizen. This right is provided in many state constitutions and exists through interpretation at the federal level through the landmark case of *Roe v. Wade*,[2] in which the U.S. Supreme Court established a right of privacy that gives women the right to choose whether to have an abortion.

These two components of the right to privacy have many interpretations. These interpretations are often found in statutes that afford privacy rights with respect to certain types of conduct. **For Example,** a federal statute provides a right of privacy to bank customers that prevents their banks from giving out information about their accounts except to law enforcement agencies conducting investigations. Some laws protect the rights of students. **For Example,** the Family Educational Rights and Privacy Act of 1974 (FERPA, also known as the *Buckley Amendment*) prevents colleges and universities from disclosing students' grades to third parties without the students' permission. From your credit information to your Social Security number, you have great privacy protections.

1-1d Privacy and Technology

Technology creates new situations that may require the application of new rules of law. Technology has changed the way we interact with each other, and new rules of law have developed to protect our rights. Today, business is conducted by computers, wire transfers of funds, e-mail, electronic data interchange (EDI) order placements, and the Internet. We still expect that our communication is private. However, technology also affords others the ability to eavesdrop on conversations and intercept electronic messages. The law has stepped in to reestablish that the right of privacy still exists even in these technologically nonprivate circumstances. Some laws now make it a crime and a breach of privacy to engage in such interceptions of communications.[3]

CASE SUMMARY

If You Shout It Out the Window or on Facebook, Is It Private?

FACTS: Gina L. Fawcett (plaintiff) and her then-minor son, John, sued Sea High School and the parents of Nicholas Altieri (defendants) to recover damages for John's eye injury that he sustained in an altercation with Nicholas during a tennis match with St. Joseph High School. The defendants made a discovery request for access to John's social media accounts, including Facebook, MySpace, Friendster, Flickr,

and others. Ms. Fawcett moved for a protective order to prevent discovery of the information on these sites because John's sites were not publicly available.

DECISION: The court held that a variety of factors must be considered before granting broad access to social media accounts, including privacy settings by the holder of the

---

[1] Police officers do not need a warrant in order to use the content of an incoming text message that is received while they are questioning the suspect because the sender does not have [access to the] suspect's smart phone's content. *State v. Varle,* 337 P.3d 904 (Or. App. 2014).

[2] 410 U.S. 113 (1973).

[3] *Luangkhot v. State,* 722 S.E.2d 193 (Ga. App. 2012).

If You Shout It Out the Window or on Facebook, Is It Private? continued

account, relevancy of the information to the litigation, and protections afforded by the various social media sites. The court's decision provides the guidelines for determining whether the litigants in cases will be able to have discovery access to each other's social media sites. The parties will have to do depositions and then renew the request once more factual information is available for the analysis of the request for access. [***Fawcett v. Altieri*, 960 N.Y.S.2d 592 (2013)]**

ETHICS & THE LAW

Maybe a Little Too "LinkedIn"

LinkedIn, the popular professional connection service, has a tool called "Reference Search." A premium service, employers and recruiters are using the tool to cull their connections to see who knows job applicants in order to get background on them. Employers are checking with references that the applicants did not list, references that may not have all good things to say about them. The service provides employers with the list of LinkedIn contacts that they have who worked at the same companies as the applicants and at the same time.*

Applicants are worried that employers are basing employment decisions on the information that they receive, information that may not be true or verified or verifiable. The applicants do not always know that the employer is checking with other sources or which ones and do not have the opportunity to respond to negative information.

Discuss the ethical issues in the use of this LinkedIn service by employers.

*Natasha Singer, "Funny, They Don't Look Like My References," *New York Times Magazine*, November 10, 2014, p. BU4.

E-COMMERCE & CYBERLAW

A University's Access to Your Computer

Scott Kennedy, a computer system administrator for Qualcomm Corporation in San Diego, California, discovered that somebody had obtained unauthorized access (or "hacked into," in popular parlance) the company's computer network. Kennedy contacted the Federal Bureau of Investigation (FBI). Working together, Kennedy and the FBI were able to trace the intrusion to a computer on the University of Wisconsin at Madison network. They contacted Jeffrey Savoy, the University of Wisconsin computer network investigator, who found evidence that someone using a computer on the university network was in fact hacking into the Qualcomm system and that the user had gained unauthorized access to the university's system as well. Savoy traced the source of intrusion to a computer located in university housing, the room of Jerome Heckenkamp, a computer science graduate student at the university. Savoy knew that Heckenkamp had been terminated from his job at the university computer help desk two years earlier for similar unauthorized activity.

While Heckenkamp was online and logged into the university's system, Savoy, along with detectives, went to Heckenkamp's room. The door was ajar, and nobody was in the room. Savoy entered the room and disconnected the network cord that attached the computer to the network. In order to be sure that the computer he had disconnected from the network was the computer that had gained unauthorized access to the university server, Savoy wanted to run some commands on the computer. Detectives located Heckenkamp, explained the situation, and asked for Heckenkamp's password, which Heckenkamp voluntarily provided. Savoy then ran tests on the computer and copied the hard drive without a warrant. When Heckenkamp was charged with several federal computer crimes, he challenged the university's access to his account and Savoy's steps that night, including the copy of the hard drive, as a breach of his privacy.

Was Heckenkamp correct? Was his privacy breached?

[*U.S. v. Heckenkamp*, 482 F.3d 1142 (9th Cir. 2007)]

1-2 Sources of Law

Several layers of law are enacted at different levels of government to provide the framework for business and personal rights and duties. At the base of this framework of laws is constitutional law.

1-2a Constitutional Law

Constitutional law is the branch of law that is based on the constitution for a particular level of government. A **constitution** is a body of principles that establishes the structure of a government and the relationship of that government to the people who are governed. A constitution is generally a combination of the written document and the practices and customs that develop with the passage of time and the emergence of new problems. In each state, two constitutions are in force: the state constitution and the federal Constitution.

constitution–a body of principles that establishes the structure of a government and the relationship of the government to the people who are governed.

1-2b Statutory Law

Statutory law includes legislative acts. Both Congress and the state legislatures enact statutory law. Examples of congressional legislative enactments include the Securities Act of 1933 (Chapter 45), the Sherman Antitrust Act (Chapter 5), the bankruptcy laws (Chapter 34), and consumer credit protection provisions (Chapter 32). At the state level, statutes govern the creation of corporations, probate of wills, and the transfer of title to property. In addition to the state legislatures and the U.S. Congress, all cities, counties, and other governmental subdivisions have some power to adopt ordinances within their sphere of operation. Examples of the types of laws found at this level of government include traffic laws, zoning laws, and pet and bicycle licensing laws.

statutory law–legislative acts declaring, commanding, or prohibiting something.

1-2c Administrative Law

Administrative regulations are rules promulgated by state and federal administrative agencies, such as the Securities and Exchange Commission (SEC) and the Environmental Protection Agency (EPA). For example, the restrictions on carbon emissions by businesses have all been promulgated by the EPA. These regulations generally have the force of statutes.

administrative regulations–rules made by state and federal administrative agencies.

1-2d Private Law

Even individuals and businesses create their own laws, or **private law.** Private law consists of the rules and regulations parties agree to as part of their contractual relationships. **For Example,** landlords develop rules for tenants on everything from parking to laundry room use. Employers develop rules for employees on everything from proper computer use to posting pictures and information on bulletin boards located within the company walls. Homeowner associations have rules on everything from your landscaping to the color of your house paint.

private law–the rules and regulations parties agree to as part of their contractual relationships.

1-2e Case Law, Statutory Interpretation, and Precede~

Law also includes principles that are expressed for the first time in court ~
form of law is called **case law.** Case law plays three very important r~
of clarifying the meaning of statutes, or providing statutory interpret~
in *King v. Burwell*, the U.S. Supreme Court interpreted the phr~

case law–law that includes principles that are expressed for the first time in court decisions.

established by the State" in the Affordable Care Act to determine whether tax credits were available to insurance exchanges operated by the federal government and not the states. The court held that "State," meant either the federal government or any of the states so that all exchanges qualified for the tax credits.[4] The second role that courts play is in creating precedent. When a court decides a new question or problem, its decision becomes a **precedent,** which stands as the law in future cases that involve that particular problem.

Using precedent and following decisions is also known as the doctrine of ***stare decisis.*** However, the rule of *stare decisis* is not cast in stone. Judges have some flexibility. When a court finds an earlier decision to be incorrect, it overrules that decision. For example, in *National Federation of Independent Business v. Sebelius*, 132 S.Ct. 2566 (2012) the U.S. Supreme Court held that the Affordable Care Act (Obama Care) was constitutional. However, in 2014, the Court held, based on new issues raised, that a portion of the act violated the First Amendment because it mandated health care coverage of certain types of birth controls that were in violation of the religious beliefs of the owners of a corporation. *Burwell v. Hobby Lobby Stores, Inc.*, 134 S. Ct. 2751 (2014).

The third role courts play is in developing a body of law that is not statutory but addresses long-standing issues. Court decisions do not always deal with new problems or make new rules. In many cases, courts apply rules as they have been for many years, even centuries. These time-honored rules of the community are called the **common law. For Example,** most of law that we still follow today in determining real property rights developed in England, beginning in 1066. Statutes sometimes repeal or redeclare the common law rules. Many statutes depend on the common law for definitions of the terms in the statutes.

precedent–a decision of a court that stands as the law for a particular problem in the future.

stare decisis–"let the decision stand"; the principle that the decision of a court should serve as a guide or precedent and control the decision of a similar case in the future.

common law–the body of unwritten principles originally based upon the usages and customs of the community that were recognized and enforced by the courts.

1-2f Other Forms of Law: Treaties and Executive Orders

Law also includes treaties made by the United States and proclamations and executive orders of the president of the United States or of other public officials. President Obama's executive order altering immigration policy is the subject of a constitutional challenge to the scope of executive orders.

1-2g Uniform State Laws

To facilitate the national nature of business and transactions, the National Conference of Commissioners on Uniform State Laws (NCCUSL), composed of representatives from every state, has drafted statutes on various subjects for adoption by the states. The best example of such laws is the Uniform Commercial Code (UCC).[5] (See Chapters 22–30, Chapter 33.) The UCC regulates the sale and lease of goods; commercial paper, such as checks; fund transfers; secured transactions in personal property; banking; and letters of credit. Having the same principles of law on contracts for the sale of goods and other commercial transactions in most of the 50 states makes doing business easier and less expensive. Other examples of uniform laws across the states include the Model Business Corporation Act (Chapter 43), the Uniform Partnership Act (Chapter 41), and the Uniform Residential Landlord Tenant Act (Chapter 50). The Uniform Computer Information Transactions Act (UCITA) as well as the Uniform Electronic Transactions Act

---

[4] *King v. Burwell*, 135 S.Ct. 2480 (2015).

[5] The UCC has been adopted in every state, except that Louisiana has not adopted Article 2, Sales. Guam, the Virgin Islands, and the District of Columbia have also adopted the UCC. The United Nations Convention on Contracts for the International Sale of Goods (CISG) has been adopted as the means for achieving uniformity in sale-of-goods contracts on an international level. Provisions of CISG were strongly influenced by Article 2 of the UCC.

(UETA) are two uniform laws that have taken contract law from the traditional paper era to the paperless computer age.

1-3   Classifications of Law

1-3a   Substantive Law vs. Procedural Law

substantive law–the law that defines rights and liabilities.

procedural law–the law that must be followed in enforcing rights and liabilities.

Substantive law creates, defines, and regulates rights and liabilities. The law that determines when a contract is formed is substantive law. **Procedural law** specifies the steps that must be followed in enforcing those rights and liabilities. For example, once that contract is formed, you have rights to enforce that contract, and the steps you take through the court system to recover your damages for a breach of contract are procedural laws. The laws that prohibit computer theft are substantive laws. The prosecution of someone for computer theft follows procedural law.

1-3b   Criminal Law vs. Civil Law

criminal laws–the laws that define wrongs against society.

civil laws–the laws that define the rights of one person against another.

Criminal laws define wrongs against society. **Civil laws** define the rights of one person against another. Criminal law violations carry fines and imprisonment as penalties. Civil laws carry damage remedies for the wronged individual.

For Example, if you run a red light, you have committed a crime and you will be punished with a fine and points on your license. If you run a red light and strike a pedestrian, you will also have committed a civil wrong of injury to another through your

SPORTS & ENTERTAINMENT LAW

When Players Break the Law and Owners Are Offensive

During 2014, professional sports had three events that resulted in a public engaged in the business decisions of the teams and their leagues. Baltimore Ravens player Ray Rice was accused of striking his fiancé (who would shortly become his wife) in an elevator. Local authorities declined to prosecute because his wife refused to cooperate with the investigation or the prosecution. Nonetheless, Roger Goodell, the NFL commissioner, suspended Mr. Rice from play indefinitely. Public opinion swung both ways, and Mr. Rice eventually won his appeal on the suspension and was reinstated. However, he lost his endorsement contracts with various companies, including Nike.

In the NBA, Donald Sterling was forced by the league to sell the LA Clippers franchise after an audio tape emerged of him making racist comments to his girlfriend. Steve Ballmer, the former CEO of Microsoft, bought the team for $2 billion. The team owners in the NBA made the decision by a vote to require Sterling to sell the team, a provision permitted under the bylaws of the corporation.

Back in the NFL, Adrian Peterson of the Minnesota Vikings was arrested for child abuse. Mr. Peterson entered a no-contest plea to the charges, which were based on his using a branch to hit his four-year-old son. The court's determination of guilt was postponed for two years as Mr. Peterson serves 80 hours of community service and pays a $4,000 fine. Under its bylaws, the NFL imposed a temporary suspension, and Mr. Peterson and the NFL are locked in a court and arbitration dispute over the suspension.

The three cases have these topics in common:

Private conduct affected business ownership and employment.

There were private bylaws involved that permitted league action against team owners and players.

There were also civil and criminal laws involved that required prosecution in two of the cases.

The law at various levels, including the authority of the leagues to do what they did, was at the center of these very public controversies.

carelessness. Civil laws provide that in addition to taking care of your wrong to society, you must take care of your wrong to the pedestrian and pay damages for the cost of her injuries (see Chapter 8 for more information about recovery of damages for accidents such as this).

1-3c Law vs. Equity

equity—the body of principles that originally developed because of the inadequacy of the rules then applied by the common law courts of England.

Equity is a body of law that provides justice when the law does not offer an adequate remedy or the application of the law would be terribly unfair. Equity courts developed in England as a means of getting to the heart of a dispute and seeing that justice was done. **For Example,** Christian Louboutin shoes have a distinctive red bottom that is their trademark. Yves Saint Laurent began producing its shoes with a red bottom. Common and statutory law provide for Louboutin to collect damages—the amount the company lost in sales through the copycat efforts of Yves Saint Laurent. However, if the Yves Saint Laurent shoes continue in production, Louboutin is never adequately compensated. Equity provides for an injunction, a court order to stop Yves Saint Laurent from making the red-soled shoes.[6]

At one time, the United States had separate law courts and equity courts, but today these courts have been combined so that one court applies principles of both law and equity. A party may ask for both legal and equitable remedies in a single court.[7] **For Example,** suppose a homeowner contracts to sell his home to a buyer. If the homeowner then refuses to go through with the contract, the buyer has the legal remedy of recovering damages. The rules of equity go further and could require the owner to convey title to the house, an equitable remedy known as *specific performance*. Equitable remedies may also be available in certain contract breaches (see Chapters 2, 11, and 19).

Make the Connection

Summary

Law provides rights and imposes duties. One such right is the right of privacy, which affords protection against unreasonable searches of our property and intrusion into or disclosure of our private affairs.

Law consists of the pattern of rules established by society to govern conduct and relationships. These rules can be expressed as constitutional provisions, statutes, administrative regulations, and case decisions. Law can be classified as substantive or procedural, and it can be described in terms of civil or criminal law. Law provides remedies in equity in addition to damages.

The sources of law include constitutions, federal and state statutes, administrative regulations, ordinances, and uniform laws generally codified by the states in their statutes. The courts are also a source of law through their adherence to case precedent under the doctrine of *stare decisis* and through their development of time-honored principles called the common law.

---

[6] *Christian Louboutin S.A. v. Yves Saint Laurent America, Inc.*, 778 F. Supp. 2d 445 (S.D.N.Y. 2011). The court eventually held that other companies could not copy the distinctive red sole. They could have colored soles but not the Louboutin trademark red sole.

[7] For example, when Jennifer Lopez and Marc Anthony were married, they filed suit against the manufacturer of a British company that produces baby carriages for using their images on its Web site and in ads without permission; they asked for $5 million in damages as well as an injunction to stop use of their photos and likenesses in the company's ads. *Lopez v. Silver Cross*, 2009 WL 481386 (C.D. Cal.). The case was settled prior to the dissolution of the Lopez and Anthony marriage. Silver Cross no longer uses the images of Lopez and Anthony in its ads.

Learning Outcomes

After studying this chapter, you should be able to clearly explain:

1-1 Nature of Law and Legal Rights

LO.1 Discuss the nature of law and legal rights

See Ethics & the Law for a discussion on the use of LinkedIn for finding more honest references about potential employees, page 6.
See E-Commerce & Cyberlaw for a discussion of a university student's privacy rights in using the university's server, page 6.

1-2 Sources of Law

LO.2 List the sources of law

See the *For Example* discussion of landlords developing rules for tenants on everything from parking to laundry room use, page 7.

See the list and explanation of uniform laws, page 8.
See the Sports & Entertainment Law discussion of leagues taking action against players for their private conduct, page 9.

1-3 Classifications of Law

LO.3 Describe the classifications of law

See the discussion of law, equity, procedural, substantive, criminal, and civil, pages 9–10.
See the Christian Louboutin example on its red-bottomed shoe being copied and footnote 8 with the discussion of the Jennifer Lopez/Marc Anthony suit. Explain uniform state laws, page 10.

Key Terms

administrative regulations	duty	right
case law	equity	right of privacy
civil law	law	*stare decisis*
common law	precedent	statutory law
constitution	private law	substantive law
criminal law	procedural law	

Questions and Case Problems

1. The Family Educational Rights and Privacy Act (FERPA) protects students' rights to keep their academic records private. What duties are imposed and upon whom because of this protection of rights? Discuss the relationship between rights and duties.

2. List the sources of law.

3. What is the difference between common law and statutory law?

4. Classify the following laws as substantive or procedural:

   a. A law that requires public schools to hold a hearing before a student is expelled.

   b. A law that establishes a maximum interest rate for credit transactions of 24 percent.

   c. A law that provides employee leave for the birth or adoption of a child for up to 12 weeks.

   d. A law that requires the county assessor to send four notices of taxes due and owing before a lien can be filed (attached) to the property.

5. What do uniform laws accomplish? Why do states adopt them? Give an example of a uniform law.

6. Cindy Nathan is a student at West University. While she was at her 9:00 A.M. anthropology class, campus security entered her dorm room and searched all areas, including her closet and drawers. When Cindy returned to her room and discovered what had happened, she complained to the dorm's senior resident. The senior resident said that this was the university's property and that Cindy had no right of privacy. Do you agree with the senior resident's statement? Is there a right of privacy in a dorm room?

7. Professor Lucas Phelps sent the following e-mail to Professor Marlin Jones: "I recently read the opinion piece you wrote for the *Sacramento Bee* on affirmative action. Your opinion is incorrect, your reasoning and analysis are poor, and I am embarrassed that you are a member of the faculty here at Cal State Yolinda." Professor Jones forwarded the note from Professor Phelps to the provost of the university and asked that

Professor Phelps be disciplined for using the university e-mail system for harassment purposes. Professor Phelps objected when the provost contacted him: "He had no right to forward that e-mail to you. That was private correspondence. And you have no right of access to my e-mail. I have privacy rights." Do you agree with Professor Phelps? Was there a breach of privacy?

8. Under what circumstances would a court disregard precedent?

9. What is the difference between a statute and an administrative regulation?

10. The Eminem ad for Chrysler that ran during the Super Bowl in February 2011 was rated as one of the best ads for the game. In May 2011, Audi ran an ad at a German auto show that had the "feel" of the Eminem Chrysler "Lose Yourself" ad. Subsequently, the German auto show ad made its way onto the Internet.

    The German ad caught the attention of Eminem and 8 Mile, Eminem's publishing company. They notified Audi that the ad constituted an unauthorized use of their intellectual property. Explain what rights Eminem and 8 Mile have and how the courts can help.

11. Give examples of areas covered by federal laws. Give examples of areas covered by city ordinances. What are the limitations on these two sources of laws? What could the laws at these two levels not do?

12. What is the principle of *stare decisis*?

13. Explain how Twitter, Facebook, and LinkedIn have resulted in the development of new laws and precedent.

14. During the 2001 baseball season, San Francisco Giants player Barry Bonds hit 73 home runs, a new record that broke the one set by Mark McGwire in 2000 (72 home runs). When Mr. Bonds hit his record-breaking home run, the ball went into the so-called cheap seats. Alex Popov was sitting in those seats and had brought along his baseball glove for purposes of catching any hits that might come into the stands.

    Everyone sitting in the area agreed that Mr. Popov's glove touched Bonds's home-run ball. Videotape also shows Mr. Popov's glove on the ball. However, the ball dropped and, following a melee among the cheap-seat fans, Patrick Hayashi ended up with Bonds's home-run ball.

    Mr. Popov filed suit for the ball, claiming it as his property. Such baseballs can be very valuable. The baseball from Mr. McGwire's record-breaking home run in 2000 sold for $3 million. List those areas of law that will apply as the case is tried and the owner of the baseball is determined.

15. Janice Dempsey has just started her own tax preparation firm. She has leased office space in a building, and she is incorporating her business as a Subchapter S corporation under the Internal Revenue Code. She has purchased desks, chairs, computers, and copiers from Staples through a line of credit they have established for her. Janice is a CPA in the state of Arizona and her license fees and continuing education hours are due within 90 days. Janice will begin with only a clerical person as an employee to serve as receptionist and bookkeeper. List all of the areas of the law that affect Janice in her new business.

CHAPTER 2

The Court System and Dispute Resolution

Learning Outcomes <<<

After studying this chapter, you should be able to

LO.1 Explain the federal and state court systems

LO.2 Describe court procedures

LO.3 List the forms of alternative dispute resolution and distinguish among them

2-1 The Court System

Despite carefully negotiated and well-written contracts and high safety standards in the workplace or in product design and production, businesses can end up in a lawsuit. **For Example,** you could hire the brightest and most expensive lawyer in town to prepare a contract with another party and believe the final agreement is "bulletproof." However, even a bulletproof contract does not guarantee performance by the other party, and you may have to file a suit to collect your damages.

Business disputes can be resolved in court or through alternative dispute resolution. This chapter covers the structure of the court system and the litigation process as well as the forms of alternative dispute resolution.

A **court** is a tribunal established by government to hear evidence, decide cases brought before it, and provide remedies when a wrong has been committed. As discussed in Chapter 1, sometimes courts prevent wrongs by issuing the equitable remedy of an injunction. **For Example,** in March 2012, a federal court issued an injunction against Cardinal Health because it was shipping too much oxycodone to its pharmacies in Florida, and the FDA had discovered that the prescriptions were fraudulent. The FDA needed to stop the flow of the drug while it pulled the prescriptions.[1]

2-1a The Types of Courts

Each type of court has the authority to decide certain types or classes of cases. The authority of courts to hear cases is called **jurisdiction.** One form of jurisdiction, **subject matter jurisdiction,** covers the type of cases the court has the authority to hear. Courts that have the authority to hear the original proceedings in a case (the trial court) are called courts of **original jurisdiction. For Example,** in a court of original jurisdiction witnesses testify, documents are admitted into evidence, and the jury, in the case of a jury trial, hears all the evidence and then makes a decision.

Other types of subject matter jurisdiction give courts the authority over particular legal topic areas. A court with **general jurisdiction** has broad authority to hear general civil and criminal cases. When a general jurisdiction trial court hears criminal cases, it serves as the trial court for those charged with crimes. General trial courts also have the authority to hear civil disputes, such as breach of contract cases and personal injury lawsuits.

A court with **limited or special jurisdiction** has the authority to hear only particular kinds of cases. **For Example,** many states have courts that can hear only disputes in which the damages are $10,000 or less. Other examples of limited or special jurisdiction courts are juvenile courts, probate courts, and domestic relations courts. States vary in the names they give these courts, but these courts of special or limited jurisdiction have very narrow authority for the types of cases they hear. In the federal court system, limited or special jurisdiction courts include bankruptcy courts and the U.S. Tax Court.

A court with **appellate jurisdiction** reviews the work of a lower court. **For Example,** a trial court may issue a judgment that a defendant in a breach of contract suit should pay $500,000 in damages. That defendant could appeal the decision to an appellate court and seek review of the decision itself or even the amount of the damages.[2] An **appeal** is a

court–a tribunal established by government to hear and decide matters properly brought to it.

jurisdiction–the power of a court to hear and determine a given class of cases; the power to act over a particular defendant.

subject matter jurisdiction–judicial authority to hear a particular type of case.

original jurisdiction–the authority to hear a controversy when it is first brought to court.

general jurisdiction–the power to hear and decide most controversies involving legal rights and duties.

limited (special) jurisdiction–the authority to hear only particular kinds of cases.

appellate jurisdiction–the power of a court to hear and decide a given class of cases on appeal from another court or administrative agency.

appeal–taking a case to a reviewing court to determine whether the judgment of the lower court or administrative agency was correct. (Parties—appellant, appellee)

---

[1] *Holiday CVS, LLC. v. Holder*, 839 F. Supp. 2d 145 (D.D.C. 2012).

[2] A case that is sent back for a redetermination of damages is remanded for what is known as *remititur*. For example, an appeal of Oracle's $1.3 billion verdict against SAP was sent back for another determination of damages, with the judge indicating $272 million was in the right range. *Oracle USA, Inc. v. SAP AG*, 2012 WL 29095 (N.D. Cal.).

reversible error–an error or defect in court proceedings of so serious a nature that on appeal the appellate court will set aside the proceedings of the lower court.

review of the trial and decision of the lower court. An appellate court does not hear witnesses or take testimony. An appellate court, usually a panel of three judges, simply reviews the transcript and evidence from the lower court and determines whether there has been **reversible error.** A reversible error is a mistake in applying the law or a mistake in admitting evidence that affected the outcome of the case. An appellate court can **affirm** or **reverse** a lower court decision or **remand** that decision for another trial or additional hearings.

CASE SUMMARY

Horseback Riding Videos and Judging Hairy Chest Contests—Good Evidence?

FACTS: Mary Kay Stanford (Stanford) was driving a truck for V.F. in late evening of February 7, 2006, when she began to feel nauseous. She pulled into a truck scale house to rest for the evening. She parked the truck, and as she attempted to climb into the sleeper compartment, she tripped over a cooler. Stanford fell into the sleeper compartment and hit her head on the bed rail; the fall knocked her unconscious. Stanford's husband, William Stanford, who was riding with her, attempted to revive her. After she regained consciousness, William offered to take her to the emergency room. Stanford declined and decided to stay in the sleeper compartment and rest until morning. Stanford contacted V.F. dispatch and made the notifications to the company about her injury. The company arranged for the two to return home.

On February 8, 2006, Mary Kay went to Dr. Allie Prater whose notes reflect that Stanford's chief complaints were blackouts, syncope, and slurred speech. Stanford told Dr. Prater that her symptoms had begun one week prior to her visit. Dr. Prater's notes do not mention Stanford's fall in the truck or that she was knocked unconscious. Dr. Prater diagnosed Stanford with benign essential hypertension and ordered blood tests, an ultrasound, and a brain MRI.

Dr. Prater referred Mary Kay to Dr. Glenn Crosby, a neurosurgeon. Before seeing Dr. Crosby, Stanford went to Dr. Johnny Mitias, an orthopedic surgeon, on March 15, 2006. There was no mention of her fall in Dr. Mitias's notes. In fact, he noted that "[t]here was no injury that started this." Dr. Mitias diagnosed Stanford with right sciatica and ordered physical therapy.

Dr. Crosby recommended and performed spinal surgeries on August 8, 2006. After surgery, Stanford began complaining of pain in her left buttock and down her left leg. Dr. Crosby ordered a lumbar MRI, which revealed a large

rupture of the lumbar spine at L4. On November 28, 2006, Dr. Crosby performed a diskectomy at the L4 level.

Dr. Crosby's notes indicate that Stanford "had a fall this past year" that may have aggravated her back. However, Dr. Crosby's notes do not mention that Stanford suffered a fall at work until her follow-up visit with Dr. Crosby on May 30, 2008. Dr. Crosby testified that prior to that visit, Stanford had not disclosed any history of an accident at work. However, he testified that the problems with her neck and back were probably related to her work injury.

A hearing was held before an administrative judge (AJ), who denied Stanford's claim for workers' compensation benefits. There was evidence submitted at the hearing that Stanford had taken a cruise despite her medical issues. In addition, there was video of her riding horses during the time of her treatment. There were also videos of Stanford at parties and bars. In one video she appeared to be having a great time as a judge in a "hairy chest contest." Stanford appealed the AJ's decision to the Commission, which affirmed the AJ's decision. Stanford appealed the Commission's decision to the Circuit Court of Union County, and the circuit court affirmed the Commission's decision denying benefits. Stanford then appealed.

DECISION: The court affirmed the denial of workers' compensation benefits because the evidence indicated clearly that Stanford did not tell the doctors about her work injury. The testimony about the cruise and the videos of horseback riding were damaging to Stanford's case, but they did not indicate bias particularly because the AJ had allowed evidence from Stanford's husband, friends, and relatives about her condition. Because evidence is damaging to one party does not mean that it should not be admitted. [**Stanford v. V.F. Jeanswear, LP, 84 So. 3d 825 (Miss. App. 2012)**]

2-1b The Federal Court System

The federal court system consists of three levels of courts. Figure 2-1 illustrates federal court structure.

Federal District Courts

The **federal district courts** are the general trial courts of the federal system. They are courts of original jurisdiction that hear both civil and criminal matters. Criminal cases in federal district courts are those in which the defendant is charged with a violation of federal law (the U.S. Code). In addition to the criminal cases, the types of civil cases that can be brought in federal district courts include (1) civil suits in which the United States is a party, (2) cases between citizens of different states that involve damages of $75,000 or more, and (3) cases that arise under the U.S. Constitution or federal laws and treaties.

Federal district courts are organized within each of the states. There are 94 federal districts (each state has at least one federal district and there are 89 federal districts in the United States with the remaining courts found in Puerto Rico, Guam, etc.). Judges and courtrooms are assigned according to the caseload in that geographic area of the state.[3] Some states, such as New York and California, have several federal districts because

| FIGURE 2-1 | The Federal Court System |

*Appeals often go directly to U.S. Courts of Appeals.

[3]For complete information about the courts and the number of judgeships, go to 28 U.S.C. §§81-144 and 28 U.S.C. §133.

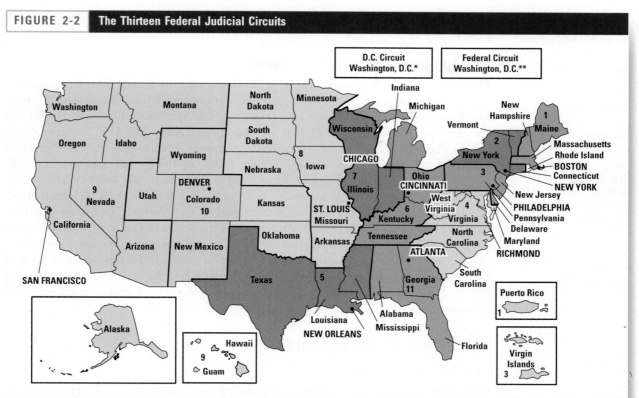

FIGURE 2-2   The Thirteen Federal Judicial Circuits

*A sizable portion of the caseload of the D.C. Circuit comes from the federal administrative agencies and offices located in Washington, D.C., such as the Securities and Exchange Commission, the National Labor Relations Board, the Federal Trade Commission, the Secretary of the Treasury, and the Labor Department, as well as appeals from the U.S. District Court of the District of Columbia.

**Rather than being defined by geography like the regional courts of appeals, the Federal Circuit is defined by subject matter, having jurisdiction over such matters as patent infringement cases, appeals from the Court of Federal Claims and the Court of International Trade, and appeals from administrative rulings regarding subject matter such as unfair import practices and tariff schedule disputes.

of the population base and the resulting caseload. Figure 2-2 shows the geographic structure of the federal court system, including the appellate circuits.

The federal system has additional trial courts with limited jurisdiction, differing from the general jurisdiction of the federal district courts. These courts include, for example, the federal bankruptcy courts, Indian tribal courts, Tax Court, Court of Federal Claims, Court of Veterans Appeals, and the Court of International Trade.

U.S. Courts of Appeals

The final decision in a federal district court can be appealed to a court with appellate jurisdiction. In the federal court system, the federal districts are grouped together geographically into 12 judicial circuits, including one for the District of Columbia. Additionally, a thirteenth federal circuit, called the *Federal Circuit*, hears certain types of appeals from all of the circuits, including specialty cases such as patent appeals. Each circuit has an appellate court called the U.S. Court of Appeals, and the judges for these courts review the decisions of the federal district courts. Generally, a panel of three judges reviews the cases. However, some decisions, called **en banc** decisions, are made by the circuit's full panel of judges. **For Example,** in 2003, the Ninth Circuit heard an appeal on a father's right to challenge the requirement that his daughter recite the Pledge of Allegiance in the public school she attended. The contentious case had so many issues that the Ninth

en banc–the term used when the full panel of judges on the appellate court hears a case.

Circuit issued three opinions and the third opinion was issued after the case was heard *en banc*.[4]

U.S. Supreme Court

The final court in the federal system is the U.S. Supreme Court. The U.S. Supreme Court has appellate jurisdiction over cases that are appealed from the federal courts of appeals as well as from state supreme courts when a constitutional issue is involved in the case or a state court has reversed a federal court ruling. The U.S. Supreme Court does not hear all cases from the federal courts of appeals but has a process called granting a **writ of *certiorari*,** which is a preliminary review of those cases appealed to decide whether a case will be heard or allowed to stand as ruled on by the lower courts.[5]

The U.S. Supreme Court is the only court expressly created in the U.S. Constitution. All other courts in the federal system were created by Congress pursuant to its Constitutional power. The Constitution also makes the U.S. Supreme Court a court of original jurisdiction. The U.S. Supreme Court serves as the trial court for cases involving ambassadors, public ministers, or consuls and for cases in which two states are involved in a lawsuit. **For Example,** the U.S. Supreme Court has served for a number of years as the trial court for a Colorado River water rights case in which California, Nevada, and Arizona are parties.

writ of *certiorari*–the U.S. Supreme Court granting a right of review by the court of a lower court decision.

2-1c State Court Systems

General Trial Courts

Most states have trial courts of general jurisdiction that may be called superior courts, circuit courts, district courts, or county courts. These courts of general and original jurisdiction usually hear both criminal and civil cases. Cases that do not meet the jurisdictional requirements for the federal district courts would be tried in these courts. Figure 2-3 illustrates a sample state court system.

Specialty Courts

Most states also have courts with limited jurisdiction, sometimes referred to as *specialty courts*. **For Example,** most states have juvenile courts, or courts with limited jurisdiction over criminal matters that involve defendants who are under the age of 18. Other specialty courts or lesser courts in state systems are probate and family law courts.

City, Municipal, and Justice Courts

Cities and counties may also have lesser courts with limited jurisdiction, which may be referred to as *municipal courts* or *justice courts*. These courts generally handle civil matters in which the claim made in the suit is an amount below a certain level, such as $5,000 or

---

[4] *Newdow v. U.S. Congress,* 292 F.3d 597 (9th Cir. 2002) *(Newdow I)*; *Newdow v. U.S. Congress,* 313 F.3d 500, 502 (9th Cir. 2002) *(Newdow II)*; and *Newdow v. U.S. Congress,* 328 F.3d 466, 468 (9th Cir. 2003) *(Newdow III)*. The U.S. Supreme Court eventually heard the case. *Elkgrove Unified School District v. Newdow,* 542 U.S. 1 (2004). Another *en banc* hearing occurred at the Ninth Circuit over the issues in the California gubernatorial recall election. The three-judge panel held that the voting methods in California violated the rights of voters and therefore placed a stay on the election. However, the Ninth Circuit then heard the case *en banc* and reversed the decision of the original three-judge panel.

[5] For example, the Supreme Court refused to grant *certiorari* in a Fifth Circuit case on law school admissions at the University of Texas. However, it granted *certiorari* in a later case involving law school admissions at the University of Michigan. *Gratz v. Bollinger,* 539 U.S. 244 (2003). A case challenging undergraduate admissions at the University of Texas *(Fisher v. University of Texas)* was heard by the U.S. Supreme Court (133 S. Ct. 2411 (2013)) and remanded, but the appellate court refused to remand the case for trial on a strict scrutiny basis. That decision of the federal court of appeals is on appeal again with *certiorari* granted. *Fisher v. University of Texas at Austin,* 2015 WL 629286.

FIGURE 2-3 | **Sample State Court System**

$10,000. These courts may also handle misdemeanor types of offenses, such as traffic violations or violations of noise ordinances, and the trials for them.

Small Claims Courts

small claims courts—
courts that resolve
disputes between parties
when those disputes do
not exceed a minimal
level; no lawyers are
permitted; the parties
represent themselves.

Most states also have **small claims courts** at the county or city level. These are courts of limited jurisdiction where parties with small amounts in dispute may come to have a third party, such as a justice of the peace or city judge, review their disputes and determine how they should be resolved. A true small claims court is one in which the parties are not permitted to be represented by counsel. Rather, the parties present their cases to the judge in an informal manner without the strict procedural rules that apply in courts of general jurisdiction. Small claims courts provide a faster and inexpensive means for resolving a dispute that does not involve a large amount of claimed damages.

State Appellate Courts

Most states also have intermediate-level courts similar to the federal courts of appeals. They are courts with appellate jurisdiction that review the decisions of lower courts in that state. Decisions of the general trial courts in a state would be appealed to these courts.

State Supreme Courts

The highest court in most states is generally known as the *state supreme court*, but a few states, such as New York, may call their highest court the *court of appeals*; Maine and Massachusetts, for example, call their highest court the *supreme judicial court*. State supreme courts primarily have appellate jurisdiction, but some states' courts do have original jurisdiction, such as in Arizona, where counties in litigation have their trial at the supreme court level. Most state supreme courts also have a screening process for cases. They are required to hear some cases, such as criminal cases in which the defendant has received the death penalty. A decision of a state supreme court is final except in those circumstances in which a federal law or treaty or the U.S. Constitution is involved. Cases with these federal subject matter issues can then be appealed to the U.S. Supreme Court.

2-2   Court Procedure

Once a party decides to use the court system for resolution of a dispute, that party enters a world with specific rules, procedures, and terms that must be used to have a case proceed.

2-2a   Participants in the Court System

plaintiff–party who initiates a lawsuit.

The **plaintiff** is the party that initiates the proceedings in a court of original jurisdiction. In a criminal case in which charges are brought, the party initiating the proceedings would be called the **prosecutor.** The party against whom the civil or criminal proceedings are brought is the **defendant.** A **judge** is the primary officer of the court and is either an elected or an appointed official who presides over the matters brought before the court. Attorneys or lawyers are representatives for the plaintiff and the defendant for purposes of presenting their cases. Lawyers and clients have a privilege of confidentiality known as the **attorney-client privilege.** Lawyers cannot disclose what their clients tell them unless the client is committing, or plans to commit, a crime.

prosecutor–party who originates a criminal proceeding.

defendant–party charged with a violation of civil or criminal law in a proceeding.

judge–primary officer of the court.

A **jury** is a body of citizens sworn by a court to reach a verdict on the basis of the case presented to them. Jurors are chosen for service based on lists compiled from voter registration and driver's license records.

attorney-client privilege–right of individual to have discussions with his/her attorney kept private and confidential.

2-2b   Which Law Applies—Conflicts of Law

jury–a body of citizens sworn by a court to determine by verdict the issues of fact submitted to them.

When a lawsuit is brought, there is not just the question of where a case will be tried but also of what law will be applied in determining the rights of the parties. The principle that determines when a court applies the law of its own state—the law of the forum—or some foreign law is called *conflict of laws*. Because there are 50 state court systems and a federal court system, as well as a high degree of interstate activity, conflicts of law questions arise frequently.

Some general rules apply. For example, the law of the state in which the court is located governs the case on procedural issues and rules of evidence. In contract litigation, the court applies the law of the state in which the contract was made for determining issues of formation. Performance disputes and damages for nonperformance are generally governed by the law of the state where the contract is to be performed. International contracts follow similar rules. **For Example,** a California court will apply Swiss law to a contract made in Switzerland that is to be performed in that country.

However, it is becoming more common for the parties to specify their choice of law in their contract.[6] In the absence of a law-selecting provision in the contract, there is a

---

[6]For example, when tourists from other countries engage in activities there, they sign a combination waiver and contract that provides in the event of an injury that they agree to be governed by the laws of that country in terms of recovery and not those of the United States. *E & H Cruises, Ltd. v. Baker*, 88 So. 3d 291 (Fla. App. 2012).

growing acceptance of the rule that a contract should be governed by the law of the state that has the most significant contacts with the transaction.

For Example, assume the buyer's place of business and the seller's plant are located in Nebraska, and the buyer is purchasing goods from the seller to resell to Nebraska customers. Many courts will hold that this is a contract governed by the law of Nebraska. In determining which state has the most significant contacts, the court considers the place of contracting, negotiating, and performing; the location of the subject matter of the contract; and the domicile (residence), states of incorporation, and principal place of business of the parties.

2-2c Initial Steps in a Lawsuit

The following steps in a lawsuit generally apply in cases brought in courts of original jurisdiction. Not every step applies in every case, but understanding litigation steps and terms is important for businesspeople.

Commencement of a Lawsuit

A lawsuit begins with the filing of a **complaint.** The complaint generally contains a description of the wrongful conduct and a request for damages, such as a monetary amount. **For Example,** a plaintiff in a contract suit would describe the contract, when it was entered into, and when the defendant stopped performance on the contract. A copy of the contract would be attached to the complaint.

Service of Process

Once the plaintiff has filed the complaint with the proper court, the plaintiff has the responsibility of notifying the defendant that the lawsuit has been filed. The defendant must be served with **process.** Process, often called a *writ, notice,* or *summons,* is delivered to the defendant and includes a copy of the complaint and notification that the defendant must appear and respond to the allegations in the complaint.

The Defendant's Response and the Pleadings

After the defendant is served with process in the case, the defendant is required to respond to or **answer** the complaint within the time provided under the court's rules. In answering the plaintiff's complaint, the defendant has several options. For example, the defendant could make a **motion to dismiss,** which is a request to the court to dismiss the lawsuit on the grounds that, even if everything the plaintiff said in the complaint were true, there is still no right of recovery. A motion to dismiss is also called a **demurrer.**

A defendant could also respond and deny the allegations. **For Example,** in a contract lawsuit, the defendant-seller could say he did not breach the contract but stopped shipment of the goods because the plaintiff-buyer did not pay for the goods in advance as the contract required. A defendant could also **counterclaim** in the answer, which is asking the court for damages as a result of the underlying dispute. The defendant-seller in the contract lawsuit might ask for damages in the counterclaim for the plaintiff-buyer's failure to pay as the contract required.

All documents filed in this initial phase of the case are referred to as the **pleadings.** The pleadings are a statement of the case and the basis for recovery if all the facts alleged can be proved.

Discovery

The Federal Rules of Civil Procedure and similar rules in all states permit one party to obtain from the adverse party information about all witnesses, documents, and any other items relevant to the case. **Discovery** requires each side to name its potential witnesses

---

complaint–the initial pleading filed by the plaintiff in many actions, which in many states may be served as original process to acquire jurisdiction over the defendant.

process–paperwork served personally on a defendant in a civil case.

answer–what a defendant must file to admit or deny facts asserted by the plaintiff.

motion to dismiss–a pleading that may be filed to attack the adverse party's pleading as not stating a cause of action or a defense.

demurrer–a pleading to dismiss the adverse party's pleading for not stating a cause of action or a defense.

counterclaim–a claim that the defendant in an action may make against the plaintiff.

pleadings–the papers filed by the parties in an action in order to set forth the facts and frame the issues to be tried, although, under some systems, the pleadings merely give notice or a general indication of the nature of the issues.

discovery–procedures for ascertaining facts prior to the time of trial in order to eliminate the element of surprise in litigation.

and to provide each side the chance to question those witnesses in advance of the trial. Each party also has the opportunity to examine, inspect, and photograph books, records, buildings, and machines. Even examining the physical or mental condition of a party is part of discovery when it has relevance in the case. The scope of discovery is extremely broad because the rules permit any questions that are likely to lead to admissible evidence.

Deposition. A **deposition** is the testimony of a witness taken under oath outside the courtroom; it is transcribed by a court reporter. Each party is permitted to question the witness. If a party or a witness gives testimony at the trial that is inconsistent with her deposition testimony, the prior inconsistent testimony can be used to **impeach** the witness's credibility at trial.

Depositions can be taken either for discovery purposes or to preserve the testimony of a witness who will not be available during the trial. Some states now permit depositions to be videotaped. A videotape is a more effective way of presenting deposition testimony than reading that testimony at trial from a reporter's transcript because jurors can see the witness and the witness's demeanor and hear the words as they were spoken, complete with inflection.

Other Forms of Discovery. Other forms of discovery include medical exams, particularly in cases in which the plaintiff is claiming damages for physical injuries. Written **interrogatories** (questions) and written **requests for production of documents** are discovery requests that can be very time consuming to the answering party and often lead to pretrial legal disputes between the parties and their attorneys as a result of the legal expenses involved.

Motion for Summary Judgment

If a case has no material facts in dispute, either party can file a **motion for summary judgment.** Using affidavits or deposition testimony obtained in discovery, the court can find that there are no factual issues and decide the case as a matter of law. **For Example,** suppose that the parties can agree that they entered into a life insurance contract but dispute whether the policy applies when there is a suicide. The facts are not in dispute; the law on payment of insurance proceeds in the event of a suicide is the issue. Such a case is one that is appropriate for summary judgment.

Designation of Expert Witnesses

In some cases, such as those involving product safety, the parties may want to designate an expert witness. An **expert witness** is a witness who has some special expertise, such as an economist who gives expert opinion on the value of future lost income or a scientist who testifies about the safety of a prescription drug. There are rules for naming expert witnesses as well as for admitting into evidence any studies or documents of the expert.[7] The purpose of these rules is to avoid the problem of what has been called *junk science*, or the admission of experts' testimony and research that has not been properly conducted or reviewed by peers.

2-2d The Trial

Selecting a Jury

Jurors drawn for service are questioned by the judge and lawyers to determine whether they are biased or have any preformed judgments about the parties in the case. Jury selection is called *voir dire* **examination. For Example,** in the trial of Martha Stewart, the multimedia home and garden diva, it took a great deal of time for the lawyers to question

---

deposition–the testimony of a witness taken out of court before a person authorized to administer oaths.

impeach–using prior inconsistent evidence to challenge the credibility of a witness.

interrogatories–written questions used as a discovery tool that must be answered under oath.

request for production of documents–discovery tool for uncovering paper evidence in a case.

motion for summary judgment–request that the court decide a case on basis of law only because there are no material issues disputed by the parties.

expert witness–one who has acquired special knowledge in a particular field as through practical experience or study, or both, whose opinion is admissible as an aid to the trier of fact.

voir dire **examination**– the preliminary examination of a juror or a witness to ascertain fitness to act as such.

---

[7] *Daubert v. Merrell Dow Pharmaceuticals, Inc.*, 509 U.S. 579 (1993).

E-COMMERCE & CYBERLAW

Google's Impact on Trials

The courts continue to struggle with the effects of the Internet on the jury selection process as well as with the jurors themselves in accessing social media sites while serving on a jury. There have been 134 cases in the past three years that involved issues with Google and jurors. In *McGaha v. Com.*, 414 S.W.3d 1 (Ky. 2013), the court held that a juror's failure to disclose being a friend of the defendant's wife on Facebook is not a presumed reason for disqualification of that juror on the basis of bias or lack of impartiality. In *People v. Levack*, 2014 WL 2118088 (Mich. App.), the jurors used Google Maps to determine whether there was a shortcut to the victim's home, as claimed in the testimony. The jurors did not consider the Google information in their deliberations and the court found that a new trial was not necessary.

The key points of these cases are that prospective jurors should disclose online connections with any of the parties in a case and that jurors should not consider any information that was not provided through the trial process. The courts follow these basic principles when evaluating whether a mistrial is necessary when the Internet has affected jurors or prospective jurors. In fact, judges often include an instruction similar to this one in turning the case over to a jury:

> *Do not visit or view any place discussed in this case, and do not use any internet maps or Google Earth or any other program or device to search for or view any place discussed in the testimony.** *

State v. Feliciano, 2014 WL 1577768 (N.J. Sup.).

---

opening statements—statements by opposing attorneys that tell the jury what their cases will prove.

admissibility—the quality of the evidence in a case that allows it to be presented to the jury.

direct examination—examination of a witness by his or her attorney.

cross-examination—the examination made of a witness by the attorney for the adverse party.

redirect examination—questioning after cross-examination, in which the attorney for the witness testifying may ask the same witness other questions to overcome effects of the cross-examination.

recross-examination—an examination by the other side's attorney that follows the redirect examination.

the potential jurors about their prior knowledge concerning the case, which had received nationwide attention and much media coverage. Lawyers have the opportunity to remove jurors who know parties in the case or who indicate they have already formed opinions about guilt or innocence. The attorneys question the potential jurors to determine if a juror should be *challenged for cause* (e.g., when the prospective juror states he is employed by the plaintiff's company). Challenges for cause are unlimited, but each side can also exercise six to eight peremptory challenges.[8] A peremptory challenge is a challenge that is used to strike (remove) a juror for any reason except on racial grounds.[9]

Opening Statements

After the jury is chosen, the attorneys for each of the parties make their **opening statements** to the jury. An opening statement, as one lawyer has explained, makes a puzzle frame for the case so jurors can follow the witnesses and place the pieces of the case—the various forms of evidence—within the frame.

The Presentation of Evidence

Following the opening statements, the plaintiff presents his case with witnesses and other evidence. A judge rules on the **admissibility** of evidence. Evidence can consist of documents, testimony, expert testimony, medical information from exams, and even physical evidence.

In the case of testimony, the attorney for the plaintiff conducts **direct examination** of his witnesses during his case, and the defense attorney conducts **cross-examination** of the plaintiff's witnesses. The plaintiff's attorney can then ask questions again of his witnesses in what is called **redirect examination.** Finally, the defense attorney may question the plaintiff's witnesses again in **recross-examination.** The defendant presents her case after the plaintiff's case concludes. During the defendant's case, the lawyer for the

---

[8] The number of peremptory challenges varies from state to state and may also vary within a particular state depending on the type of case. For example, in Arizona, peremptory challenges are unlimited in capital cases.
[9] *Felkner v. Jackson*, 562 U.S. 594 (2011).

THINKING THINGS THROUGH

Why Do We Require Sworn Testimony?

There is a difference between what people say in conversation (and even what company executives say in speeches and reports) and what they are willing to say under oath. Speaking under oath often means that different information and recollections emerge. The oath is symbolic and carries the penalty of criminal prosecution for perjury if the testimony given is false.

The *Wall Street Journal* has reported that the testimony of executives in the Microsoft antitrust trial and their statements regarding their business relationships outside the courtroom are quite different. For example, the following quotations indicate some discrepancies. Eric Benhamou, the chief executive officer (CEO) of Palm, Inc., said:

We believe that the handheld opportunity remains wide open .... Unlike the PC industry, there is no monopoly of silicon, there is no monopoly of software.

However, at the Microsoft trial, another officer of Palm, Michael Mace, offered the following testimony:

We believe that there is a very substantial risk that Microsoft could manipulate its products and its

standards in order to exclude Palm from the marketplace in the future.

Likewise, Microsoft has taken different positions inside and outside the courtroom. For example, an attorney for Microsoft stated that Microsoft had "zero deployments of its interactive TV middleware products connected to cable systems in the United States." However, Microsoft's marketing materials provide as follows:

Microsoft's multiple deployments around the world now including Charter-show Microsoft TV is ready to deploy now and set the standard for what TV can be.*

Explain why the executives had differing statements. For more information on the Microsoft antitrust cases, go to **http://www.usdoj.gov** or **http://www.microsoft.com**.

*Rebecca Buckman and Nicholas Kulish, "Microsoft Trial Prompts an Outbreak of Doublespeak," *Wall Street Journal*, April 15, 2002, B1, B3.

---

defendant conducts direct examination of the defendant's witnesses, and the plaintiff's lawyer can then cross-examine the defendant's witnesses.

Motion for a Directed Verdict

directed verdict–a direction by the trial judge to the jury to return a verdict in favor of a specified party to the action.

A motion for a **directed verdict** asks the court to grant a verdict because even if all the evidence that has been presented by each side were true, there is either no basis for recovery or no defense to recovery.

For Example, suppose that a plaintiff company presented evidence that an employee who quit working for the company posted on his Facebook page, "I just wasn't happy there." The company might not feel good about the former employee's post, but there is no false statement and no breach of privacy. The evidence is true, but there is no legal right of recovery. The defendant employee would be entitled to a directed verdict. A directed verdict means that the party has not presented enough evidence to show that there is some right of recovery under the law.

summation–the attorney address that follows all the evidence presented in court and sums up a case and recommends a particular verdict be returned by the jury.

Closing Arguments or Summation

After the witnesses for both parties have been examined and all the evidence has been presented, each attorney makes a closing argument. These statements are also called **summations;** they summarize the case and urge the jury to reach a particular verdict.

mistrial–a court's declaration that terminates a trial and postpones it to a later date; commonly entered when evidence has been of a highly prejudicial character or when a juror has been guilty of misconduct.

Motion for Mistrial

During the course of a trial, when necessary to avoid great injustice, the trial court may declare a **mistrial.** A mistrial requires a do-over, a new jury. A mistrial can be declared for jury or attorney misconduct. **For Example,** if a juror were caught fraternizing with one of the lawyers in the case, objectivity would be compromised and the court would most likely declare a mistrial. See also E-Commerce & Cyberlaw (Google's Impact on Trials) for more information on juror misconduct and case dismissals.

Jury Instructions and Verdict

instruction–summary of the law given to jurors by the judge before deliberation begins.

After the summation by the attorneys, the court gives the jurors **instructions** on the appropriate law to apply to the facts presented. The jury then deliberates and renders its verdict. After the jury verdict, the court enters a judgment. If the jury is deadlocked and unable to reach a verdict, known as a hung jury or a mistrial, the case is reset for a new trial at some future date.

Motion for New Trial; Motion for Judgment *n.o.v.*

judgment n.o.v.–or *non obstante veredicto* (notwithstanding the verdict), a judgment entered after verdict upon the motion of the losing party on the ground that the verdict is so wrong that a judgment should be entered the opposite of the verdict.

A court may grant a **judgment *non obstante veredicto*** or a **judgment *n.o.v.*** (notwithstanding the verdict) if the verdict is clearly wrong as a matter of law. The court can set aside the verdict and enter a judgment in favor of the other party. Perhaps one of the most famous judgments n.o.v. occurred in Boston in 1997 when a judge reversed the murder conviction of nanny Louise Woodward, who was charged with the murder of one of her young charges.

2-2e Post-trial Procedures

Recovery of Costs/Attorney Fees

Generally, the prevailing party is awarded costs. Costs include filing fees, service-of-process fees, witness fees, deposition transcript costs, and jury fees. Costs do not

ETHICS & THE LAW

Honesty, Lawyers, and BP Claims

Following the Deepwater Horizon oil spill in the Gulf of Mexico, BP established a $20 billion recovery fund. The purpose of the fund was to reimburse businesses and individuals who were affected by the spill, such as fishers, resorts, and boating companies that provided tours and other services.

Several lawyers and accountants were assigned to the Claims Administration Office (CAO) with the responsibilities for the receipt, evaluation, and payment of claims. In 2013, the federal judge overseeing the claims process became concerned about the conduct of those who were administering the trust. As a result, the judge appointed Louis Freeh, a former federal judge and director of the FBI, to investigate.

Among the many findings of the cases were conflicts, such as Lionel Sutton and Christine Reitano, husband and wife, two lawyers working at the CAO who had practiced law together in New Orleans as Sutton & Reitano. They referred a client, Casey Thonn, to Glen Lerner of AndryLerner, a law firm representing claimants to the CAO. Ms. Reitano then requested a referral fee from AndryLerner. The referral arrangement was never disclosed to the client, Casey Thonn,

as Louisiana's code of professional ethics requires, nor the CAO office. Mr. Sutton continued his representation of Casey Thonn in a personal injury case but did not disclose that client relationship to anyone at the CAO. Mr. Sutton also did not disclose that he had a business relationship in a reclamation company, Crown LLC, and that he was one of two equity owners of that company, with Glen Lerner, a partner at AndryLerner, being the other owner. AndryLerner had a total of $7,908,460 in claims before the CAO. Mr. Sutton approved 496 of the claims.

On November 25, 2014, the U.S. Attorney for the Middle District of Florida announced 27 indictments against individuals who are alleged to have submitted fraudulent claims for reimbursement, ranging from $11,000 to $122,000, and totaling over $1,000,000.

BP began running full-page ads in major newspaper around the country with examples of the fraudulent claims. The judge is seeking restitution from many of the claimants.

What should the lawyers have done in their situations? Why did they not do it?

include compensation spent by a party for preparing the case or being present at trial, including the time lost from work because of the case and the fee paid to the attorney, although lost wages from an injury are generally part of damages.

Attorney fees may be recovered by a party who prevails if a statute permits the recovery of attorney fees or if the complaint involves a claim for breach of contract and the contract contains a clause providing for recovery of attorney fees.

Execution of Judgment

After a judgment has been entered or all appeals or appeal rights have ended, the losing party must pay that judgment. The winning party can also take steps to execute, or carry out, the judgment. The **execution** is accomplished by the seizure and sale of the losing party's assets by the sheriff according to a writ of execution or a writ of possession.

Garnishment is a common method of satisfying a judgment. When the judgment debtor is an employee, the appropriate judicial authority in the state garnishes (by written notice to the employer) a portion of the employee's wages on a regular basis until the judgment is paid.

2-3 Alternative Dispute Resolution (ADR)

Parties can use means other than litigation to resolve disagreements or disputes. Litigation takes significant time and money, so many businesses use alternative methods for resolving disputes. Those methods include arbitration, mediation, and several other formats. Figure 2-4 provides an overall view of alternative dispute resolution procedures.

2-3a Arbitration

In **arbitration,** arbitrators (disinterested persons selected by the parties to the dispute) hear evidence and determine a resolution. Arbitration enables the parties to present the facts before trained experts familiar with the industry practices that may affect the nature and outcome of the dispute. Arbitration first reached extensive use in the field of commercial contracts and was encouraged as a means of avoiding expensive litigation and easing the workload of courts. However, over the past decade the popularity of arbitration has declined because of increasing procedural burdens and longer and more complex hearings. There have been an increasing number of cases in which arbitration clauses have been set aside as too onerous for a consumer or small business party to the agreement.[10]

A number of states have adopted the Uniform Arbitration Act.[11] Under this act and similar statutes, the parties to a contract may agree in advance that all disputes arising under it will be submitted to arbitration. In some instances, the contract will name the arbitrators for the duration of the contract. The uniform act requires a written agreement to arbitrate.[12]

The Federal Arbitration Act[13] provides that an arbitration clause in a contract relating to an interstate transaction is valid, irrevocable, and enforceable. When a contract subject to the Federal Arbitration Act provides for the arbitration of disputes, the parties are

execution–the carrying out of a judgment of a court, generally directing that property owned by the defendant be sold and the proceeds first be used to pay the execution or judgment creditor.

garnishment–the name given in some states to attachment proceedings.

arbitration–the settlement of disputed questions, whether of law or fact, by one or more arbitrators by whose decision the parties agree to be bound.

[10] *College Park Pentecostal Holiness Church v. General Steel Corp.*, 847 F. Supp. 2d 807 (D. Md. 2012).
[11] On August 3, 2000, the National Conference of Commissioners on Uniform State Laws unanimously passed major revisions to the Uniform Arbitration Act (UAA). These revisions were the first major changes in 45 years to the UAA, which is the basis of arbitration law in 49 states, although not all states have adopted it in its entirety or most current form. Only 18 states and the District of Columbia have adopted the UAA 2000 revisions. John Lande, "A Framework for Advancing Negotiation Theory: Implications from a Study of How Lawyers Reach Agreement in Pretrial Litigation," 16 *Cardozo Journal of Conflict Resolution* 1 (2014).
[12] *Minkowitz v. Israeli*, 77 A.3d 1189 (N.J. Super. 2013).
[13] 9 U.S.C. §§114 *et seq.*

FIGURE 2-4   Dispute Resolution Procedures

bound to arbitrate in accordance with the federal statute even if the agreement to arbitrate would not be binding under state law.

Mandatory Arbitration

In contrast with statutes that merely regulate arbitration when it is selected voluntarily by the parties, some statutes require that certain kinds of disputes be submitted to arbitration. In some states, by rule or statute, the arbitration of small claims is required.

Finality of Arbitration

Most parties provide, within their arbitration agreements, that the decision of the arbitrator will be final. Such a clause is binding on the parties, even when the decision seems to be wrong, and can be set aside only if there is clear proof of fraud, arbitrary conduct, or a significant procedural error.[14]

mediation—the settlement of a dispute through the use of a messenger who carries to each side of the dispute the issues and offers in the case.

2-3b Mediation

In **mediation,** a neutral person acts as a messenger between opposing sides of a dispute, carrying to each side the latest settlement offer made by the other. The mediator has no authority to make a decision, although in some cases the mediator may make suggestions that might ultimately be accepted by the disputing parties.

---

[14] *PoolRE Ins. Corp. v. Organizational Strategies, Inc.,* 2014 WL 1320188 (S.D. Tex. 2014).

The use of mediation has the advantage of keeping discussions going when the disputing parties have developed such fixed attitudes or personal animosity that direct discussion between them has become impossible.

2-3c MedArb

In this new form of alternative dispute resolution (ADR), the arbitrator is also empowered to act as a mediator. Beyond just hearing a case, the arbitrator acts as a messenger for the parties on unresolved issues.

2-3d Expert Panel

Particularly in the construction industry, one of the tools of alternative dispute resolution is the submission of a case, or perhaps a particular issue, to a panel of experts in the industry. This method has gained popularity in the construction industry where there can be technical questions about breach, including issues related to materials, process, and delays. These experts can focus on these issues and not be caught in the procedural grind of either litigation or arbitration.

2-3e Reference to a Third Person

reference to a third person–settlement that allows a nonparty to resolve the dispute.

Many types of transactions provide for **reference to a third person,** in which a third person or a committee makes an out-of-court determination of the rights of persons. **For Example,** employees and an employer may have agreed as a term of the employment contract that claims of employees under retirement plans will be decided by a designated board or committee. In a sales contract, the seller and buyer can select a third person to determine the price to be paid for goods. Construction contracts often include a provision for disputes to be referred to the architect in charge of the construction with the architect's decision being final.

These referrals often eliminate the disputes or pursuit of remedies. **For Example,** fire insurance policies commonly provide that if the parties cannot agree on the amount of the loss, each will appoint an appraiser, the two appraisers will appoint a third appraiser, and the three will determine the amount of the loss the insurer is required to pay.

2-3f Association Tribunals

association tribunal–a court created by a trade association or group for the resolution of disputes among its members.

Many disputes never reach the courts because both parties to a dispute belong to a group or an association, and the **association tribunal** created by the group or association disposes of the matter. Trade associations commonly require their members to employ out-of-court methods of dispute settlement. **For Example,** the National Association of Home Builders requires its member builders to use arbitration. The National Automobile Dealers Association provides for panels to determine warranty claims of customers. The decision of such panels is final as to the builder or dealer, but the consumer can still bring a regular lawsuit after losing before the panel. Members of an association must use the association tribunal, which means they cannot bypass the association tribunal and go directly to a law court.[15]

2-3g Summary Jury Trial

summary jury trial–a mock or dry-run trial for parties to get a feel for how their cases will play to a jury.

A **summary jury trial** is a dry-run or mock trial in which the lawyers present their claims before a jury of six persons. The object is to get the reaction of a sample jury. No evidence is presented before this jury, and it bases its opinion solely on what the lawyers state. The determination of the jury has no binding effect, but it has value in that it

[15] The securities industry follows this process as well.

gives the lawyers some idea of what a jury might think if there were an actual trial. This type of ADR has special value when the heart of a case is whether something is reasonable under all circumstances. When the lawyers and their clients see how the sample jury reacts, they may moderate their positions and reach a settlement.

2-3h Rent-A-Judge

rent-a-judge plan– dispute resolution through private courts with judges paid to be referees for the cases.

Under the **rent-a-judge plan,** the parties hire a judge to hear the case. In many states, the parties voluntarily choose the judge as a "referee," and the judge acts under a statute authorizing the appointment of referees. Under such a statute, the referee hears all evidence just as though there were a regular trial, and the rented judge's determination is binding on the parties unless reversed on appeal if such an appeal (like a court trial) is permitted under the parties' agreement.

2-3i Minitrial

minitrial–a trial held on portions of the case or certain issues in the case.

When only part of a case is disputed, the parties may stay within the framework of a lawsuit but agree that only the disputed issues will be taken to trial and submitted to a jury. **For Example,** if there is no real dispute over who is liable but the parties disagree as to the damages, the issue of damages alone may be submitted to the jury. This shortened trial is often called a **minitrial.** A minitrial may use a retired judge to make a decision on just the disputed issues. The parties may also specify whether this decision will be binding on the parties. As a practical matter, the evaluation of a case by a neutral person often brings the opposing parties together to reach a settlement.

2-3j Contract Provisions

The parties' contract may pave the way for the settlement of future disputes by including clauses that require the parties to use one of the means of ADR. Other provisions in contracts that serve to keep the parties calm with the hope of resolving differences without a lawsuit include waiting periods before a suit can be filed and obligations to continue performing even as they try to resolve differences and issues.

Make the Connection

Summary

Courts have been created to hear and resolve legal disputes. A court's specific power is defined by its jurisdiction. Courts of original jurisdiction are trial courts, and courts that review the decisions of trial courts are appellate courts. Trial courts may have general jurisdiction to hear a wide range of civil and criminal matters, or they may be courts of limited jurisdiction—such as a probate court or the Tax Court—with the subject matter of their cases restricted to certain areas.

The courts in the United States are organized into two different systems: the state and federal court systems.

There are three levels of courts, for the most part, in each system, with trial courts, appellate courts, and a supreme court in each. The federal courts are federal district courts, federal courts of appeals, and the U.S. Supreme Court.

In the states, there may be specialized courts, such as municipal, justice, and small claims courts, for trial courts. Within the courts of original jurisdiction, there are rules for procedures in all matters brought before them. A civil case begins with the filing of a complaint by a plaintiff, which is then answered by a defendant. The parties may be represented by their attorneys. Discovery is the pretrial process used by the parties to find out the evidence in the case. The parties can use depositions, interrogatories, and document requests to uncover relevant information.

The case is managed by a judge and may be tried to a jury selected through the process of *voir dire*, with the parties permitted to challenge jurors on the basis of cause or through the use of their peremptory challenges. The trial begins following discovery and involves opening statements and the presentation of evidence, including the direct examination and cross-examination of witnesses. Once a judgment is entered, the party who has won can collect the judgment through garnishment and a writ of execution.

Alternatives to litigation for dispute resolution are available, including arbitration, mediation, MedArb, reference to a third party, association tribunals, summary jury trials, rent-a-judge plans, minitrials, and expert panels. Court dockets are relieved and cases consolidated using judicial triage, a process in which courts hear the cases involving the most serious medical issues and health conditions first. Triage is a blending of the judicial and alternative dispute resolution mechanisms.

Learning Outcomes

After studying this chapter, you should be able to clearly explain:

2-1   The Court System

LO.1 Explain the federal and state court systems
See Figure 2-1 and accompanying text, page 16.
See Figure 2-3 and accompanying text, page 19.
See the *Stanford* case on page 15 for a discussion of reversible error.

2-2   Court Procedure

LO.2 Describe court procedures
See the discussion of steps in litigation, pages 21–22.
See the *For Example* discussion of the Martha Stewart *voir dire* example, page 22.

See the Google jury issues box on page 23.
See the "Why Do We Require Sworn Testimony" box on page 24.

2-3   Alternative Dispute Resolution (ADR)

LO.3 List the forms of alternative dispute resolution and distinguish among them
See the discussion of arbitration, page 26.
See the discussion of other forms of ADR, mediation, minitrials, rent-a-judge, MedArb, judicial triage, and referral to a third party, pages 27–29.
See the discussion of employee and employer referrals of disputes to a designated board or committee, page 28.

Key Terms

admissibility
affirm
answer
appeal
appellate jurisdiction
arbitration
association tribunal
attorney-client privilege
complaint
counterclaim
court
cross-examination
defendant
demurrer
deposition
direct examination
directed verdict
discovery
en banc
execution

expert witness
federal district courts
garnishment
general jurisdiction
impeach
instructions
interrogatories
judge
judgment *n.o.v.* or judgment *non obstante veredicto*
jurisdiction
jury
limited (special) jurisdiction
mediation
minitrial
mistrial
motion for summary judgment
motion to dismiss
opening statements
original jurisdiction

plaintiff
pleadings
process
prosecutor
recross-examination
redirect examination
reference to a third person
remand
rent-a-judge plan
requests for production of documents
reverse
reversible error
small claims courts
subject matter jurisdiction
summary jury trial
summations
voir dire examination
writ of *certiorari*

Questions and Case Problems

1. List the steps in a lawsuit. Begin with the filing of the complaint, and explain the points at which there can be a final determination of the parties' rights in the case.

2. Explain why a business person would want to use alternative dispute resolution methods. Discuss the advantages. What disadvantages have you learned?

3. Ralph Dewey has been charged with a violation of the Electronic Espionage Act, a federal statute that prohibits the transfer, by computer or disk or other electronic means, of a company's proprietary data and information. Ralph is curious. What type of court has jurisdiction? Can you determine which court?

4. Jerry Lewinsky was called for jury duty. When *voir dire* began, Jerry realized that the case involved his supervisor at work. Can Jerry remain as a juror on the case? Why or why not?

5. Carolyn, Elwood, and Isabella are involved in a real estate development. The development is a failure, and Carolyn, Elwood, and Isabella want to have their rights determined. They could bring a lawsuit, but they are afraid the case is so complicated that a judge and jury not familiar with the problems of real estate development would not reach a proper result. What can they do?

6. Larketta Randolph purchased a mobile home from Better Cents Home Builders, Inc., and financed her purchase through Green Tree Financial Corporation. Ms. Randolph signed a standard form contract that required her to buy Vendor's Single Interest insurance, which protects the seller against the costs of repossession in the event of default. The agreement also provided that all disputes arising from the contract would be resolved by binding arbitration. Larketta found that there was an additional $15 in finance charges that were not disclosed in the contract. She and other Green Tree customers filed a class-action suit to recover the fees. Green Tree moved to dismiss the suit because Larketta had not submitted the issue to arbitration. Larketta protests, "But I want the right to go to court!" Does she have that right? What are the rights of parties under a contract with an arbitration clause? [*Green Tree Financial Corp. v. Randolph*, 531 U.S. 79]

7. John Watson invested $5,000,000 in SmartRead, Inc., a company that was developing an electronic reading device. Within a few months, the $5,000,000 was spent but SmartRead never developed the reading device. John filed suit against the directors of SmartRead for their failure to supervise SmartRead's CEO in his operation of the company. The directors used an expert on corporate governance to testify that the directors had done all that they could to oversee the company. The expert did not disclose that he had served as a director of a company and had been found to be negligent in his role there and had been required to pay $370,000 to shareholders. The directors won the case. Is there anything Watson can do?

8. Indicate whether the following courts are courts of original, general, limited, or appellate jurisdiction:
   a. Small claims court
   b. Federal bankruptcy court
   c. Federal district court
   d. U.S. Supreme Court
   e. Municipal court
   f. Probate court
   g. Federal court of appeals

9. The Nursing Home Pension Fund filed suit against Oracle Corporation alleging that Larry Ellison, the company's CEO, misled investors in 2001 about the true financial condition of the company. During the time of the alleged misrepresentation, Mr. Ellison was working with a biographer on his life story and there are videotapes of Mr. Ellison's interviews with his biographer as well as e-mails between the two that discuss Oracle. Could the Nursing Home Pension Fund have access to the tapes and e-mails? Explain how. [*Nursing Home Pension Fund, Local 144 v. Oracle Corp.*, 380 F.3d 1226 (9th Cir.)]

10. Mostek Corp., a Texas corporation, made a contract to sell computer-related products to North American Foreign Trading Corp., a New York corporation. North American used its own purchase order form, on which appeared the statement that any dispute arising out of an order would be submitted to arbitration, as provided in the terms set forth on the back of the order. Acting on the purchase order, Mostek delivered almost all of the goods but failed to deliver the final installment. North American then demanded that the matter be arbitrated. Mostek refused to do so. Was arbitration required? [*Application of Mostek Corp.*, 502 N.Y.S.2d 181 (App. Div.)]

11. Ceasar Wright was a longshoreman in Charleston, South Carolina, and a member of the International Longshoremen's Association (AFL-CIO). Wright used the union hiring hall. The collective bargaining agreement (CBA) of Wright's union provides for arbitration of all grievances. Another clause of the CBA states: "It is the intention and purpose of all parties hereto that no provision or part of this Agreement shall be violative of any Federal or State Law."

On February 18, 1992, while Wright was working for Stevens Shipping and Terminal Company (Stevens), he injured his right heel and back. He sought permanent compensation from Stevens and settled his claims for $250,000 and another $10,000 in attorney fees. Wright was also awarded Social Security disability benefits.

In January 1995, Wright, whose doctor had approved his return to work, returned to the hiring hall and asked to be referred for work. Wright did work between January 2 and January 11, 1995, but when the companies realized that Wright had been certified as permanently disabled, they deemed him not qualified for longshoreman work under the CBA and refused to allow him to work for them.

Wright did not file a grievance under the union agreement but instead hired a lawyer and proceeded with a claim under the Americans with Disabilities Act. The district court dismissed the case because Wright had failed to pursue the grievance procedure provided by the CBA. Must Wright pursue the dispute procedure first, or can he go right to court on the basis of his federal rights under the Americans with Disabilities Act? [*Wright v. Universal Maritime Service Corp.*, 525 U.S. 70]

12. Winona Ryder was arrested for shoplifting from Saks Fifth Avenue in California. One of the members of the jury panel for her trial was Peter Guber, a Hollywood executive in charge of the production of three films in which Ms. Ryder starred, including *Bram Stoker's Dracula, The Age of Innocence*, and *Little Women*. If you were the prosecuting attorney in the case, how could you discover such information about this potential juror, and what are your options for excluding him from selection? [Rick Lyman, "For the Ryder Trial, a Hollywood Script," *New York Times*, November 3, 2002, SL-1]

13. Two doctors had a dispute over who was doing how much work at their clinic. Their dispute was submitted to arbitration and the arbitrator held in favor of the less experienced doctor. The senior doctor wants the arbitration set aside. Is it possible for the arbitrator's decision to be set aside?

14. Martha Simms is the plaintiff in a contract suit she has brought against Floral Supply, Inc., for its failure to deliver the green sponge Martha needed in building the floral designs she sells to exclusive home decorators. Martha had to obtain the sponge from another supplier and was late on seven deliveries. One of Martha's customers has been called by Martha's lawyer as a witness and is now on the witness stand, testifying about Martha's late performance and the penalty she charged. The lawyer for Floral Supply knows that Martha's customer frequently waives penalties for good suppliers. How can Floral Supply's lawyer get that information before the jury?

15. Saint Claire Adams was hired by Circuit City as a sales counselor. When he was hired he signed an employment contract that included a mandatory arbitration clause. Two years later he filed a suit against Circuit City for discrimination in the workplace. Circuit City moved to have the suit dismissed because of the arbitration requirement. Mr. Adams responded that he has certain rights under Title VII of the federal anti-discrimination laws that cannot be taken away through an arbitration clause. Is he correct? [*Circuit City Stores, Inc. v. Adams*, 532 U.S. 105]

Business Ethics, Social Forces, and the Law

Learning Outcomes ‹‹‹

After studying this chapter, you should be able to

LO.1 Define business ethics

LO.2 Discuss why ethics are important in business

LO.3 Describe how to recognize and resolve ethical dilemmas

3-1 **What Is Business Ethics?**

Much of what businesspeople do is simply a matter of their word. Executives arrive at a 9:00 A.M. meeting because they promised they would be there. An employee meets a deadline for an ad display board because she said she would. Business transactions are completed through a combination of the values of the parties and the laws that reflect those values and the importance of one's word in business.

ethics–a branch of philosophy dealing with values that relate to the nature of human conduct and values associated with that conduct.

Ethics is a branch of philosophy dealing with values that relate to the nature of human conduct and values associated with that conduct. Balancing the goal of profits with the values of individuals and society is the focus of **business ethics.** Some economists make the point that insider trading is an efficient way to run that market. To an economist, inside information allows those with the best information to make the most money. This view ignores some issues: What about those who trade stock who do not have access to that information? What will happen to the stock market if investors perceive there is not a level playing field? In the U.S. Supreme Court decision *United States v. O'Hagan*[1] on insider trading, Justice Ruth Ginsburg noted, "Investors likely wouldn't invest in a market where trading based on misappropriated nonpublic information is unchecked." The field of business ethics deals with the balance between society's values and the need for businesses to remain profitable.

business ethics–balancing the goal of profits with values of individuals and society.

3-1a **The Law as the Standard for Business Ethics**

Philosophers debate the origin of moral and ethical standards as well as which of those standards should be applied. One view of ethics is simply following what codified or **positive law** requires. The test of whether an act is legal is a common moral standard used frequently in business. Codified law, or law created by governmental authority, is used as the standard for ethical behavior. Absent illegality, all behavior is ethical under this simple standard. The phrase "AS IS," on a contract (see Chapter 24 for further discussion), means by law that there are no warranties for the goods being sold. **For Example,** if a buyer purchases a used car and the phrase "AS IS" is in the contract, the seller has no legal obligation, in most states, if the transmission falls apart the day after the buyer's purchase. Following a positive law standard only, the seller who refuses to repair the transmission has acted ethically. However, other ethical standards are different from just a legal standard. We know there was no legal obligation to fix the transmission, but was it fair that the car fell apart the day after it was purchased?

positive law–law enacted and codified by governmental authority.

3-1b **The Notion of Universal Standards for Business Ethics**

natural law–a system of principles to guide human conduct independent of, and sometimes contrary to, enacted law and discovered by man's rational intelligence.

Another view of ethics holds that standards exist universally and cannot be changed or modified by law. In many cases, universal standards stem from religious beliefs. In some countries today, the standards for business are still determined by religious tenets. **Natural law** imposes higher standards of behavior than those required by positive law and they must be followed even if those higher standards run contrary to codified law. **For Example,** in the early nineteenth century when slavery was legally permissible in the United States, a positive law standard supported slavery. However, slavery violates the natural law principle of individual freedom and would be unethical. **Civil disobedience** is the remedy natural law proponents use to change positive law.

civil disobedience–the term used when natural law proponents violate positive law.

---

[1] 521 U.S. 657 (1997). Another court explained that inside information creates a disadvantage "other investors cannot overcome with research or skill." *U.S. v. McGee*, 763 F.3d 304 (3rd Cir. 2014). See Chapter 45 for more information.

Former Supreme Court Justice Sandra Day O'Connor, who was second in her class at Stanford Law School (the late Chief Justice William Rehnquist was first), was offered a job as a receptionist for a law firm while her male classmates were hired as attorneys. At that time, no law prohibited discrimination against women, so law firms' hiring practices, using only a positive law standard, were ethical. However, if the natural law standard of equality is applied, the refusal to hire Sandra O'Connor as a lawyer, a position for which she was qualified, was a violation of the natural law principle of equality and unethical.

3-1c Ethical Theories and Standards

There are many different views about the correct theory or standard we should apply when we face ethical dilemmas. Some of those theories and standards are covered here.

The Categorical Imperative and Immanuel Kant

Kant's categorical imperative—a standard of ethics that requires that we avoid one-sided benefit for us as a result of the conduct or decision.

Philosopher Immanuel Kant does not allow any resolution of an ethical dilemma in which human beings are used as a means by which others obtain benefits. **Kant's categorical imperative** theory, reduced to simplest terms, is that you cannot use others in a way that gives you a one-sided benefit. Everyone must operate under the same usage rules. In Kant's words, "One ought only to act such that the principle of one's act could become a universal law of human action in a world in which one would hope to live." **For Example,** if you hit a car in a parking lot and damaged it but you could be guaranteed that no one saw you do it, would you leave a note on the other car with contact information? If you answered, "No, because that's happened to me 12 times before and no one left me a note," then you are unhappy with universal behaviors but are unwilling to commit to universal standards of honesty and disclosure to remedy those behaviors.

International business presents some interesting Kantian dilemmas. For example, there are some U.S. companies that use suppliers in developing nations. Those suppliers have employees in sweatshop atmospheres who work for pennies per hour. The pennies-per-hour wage seems unjust. However, suppose the company was operating under one of its universal principles: Always pay a fair wage to those who work for it. A "fair wage" in that country might be pennies, and the company owner could argue, "I would work for that wage if I lived in that country." The company owner could also argue, "But, if I lived in the United States, I would not work for that wage, would require a much higher wage, and would want benefits, and we do provide that to all of our U.S. workers."

The company has developed its own ethical standard that is universally applicable, and those who own the company could live with it if it was applied to them, but context is everything under the categorical imperative. The basic question is: Are you comfortable living in a world operating under the standards you have established, or would you deem them unfair or unjust?

There is one more part to Kant's theory: You not only have to be fair but also have to want to do it for all the right reasons. Kant wants you to adopt and accept these ethical standards because you do not want to use other people as a means to your enrichment at their expense, and not, for example, because it will be good public relations.

theory of justice—the Locke and Rawlsian standard for ethics that requires that we all agree on certain universal principles in advance.

social contract—the agreement under Locke and Rawls as to what our ethical standards will be.

The Contractarians and Justice

John Locke and John Rawls developed what is sometimes called the **theory of justice** and sometimes referred to as the **social contract.** Rawls and Locke believe that Kant was wrong in assuming that we could all have a meeting of the minds on what were the good rules for society. Locke and Rawls preferred just putting the rules into place with a social contract. Under this theory we imagine what it would be like if we had no rules or laws at all. If we started with a blank slate, or *tabula rasa* as these philosophers would say, rational people would agree—perhaps in their own self-interest, or perhaps to be fair—that certain universal rules must apply. Rational people, thinking through the results and consequences if there were not rules, would develop rules that would result in fairness. **For Example,** we would probably develop rules such as "Don't take my property without my permission" and "I would like the same rights in court that rich people have even if I am not so rich." Locke and Rawls want us to step back from the emotion of the moment and make universal principles that will survive the test of time.

Rights Theory

rights theory–Nozick's theory of ethics that we all have a set of rights that must be honored and protected by government.

The **rights theory** is also known as an **entitlement theory** and is one of the more modern theories of ethics. Robert Nozick is the key modern-day philosopher on this theory, which has two big elements: (1) everyone has a set of rights, and (2) it is up to the governments to protect those rights. **For Example,** there are rights issues related to sweatshops, abortion, slavery, property ownership and use, justice (as in court processes), animal rights, privacy, and euthanasia. Nozick dealt with all the controversial and emotional issues of ethics including everything from human dignity in suffering to third-trimester abortions.

entitlement theory–another name for Nozick's theory that we all have certain rights that must be honored and protected by government.

Ethical Egoism Theory: Ayn Rand and Atlas

ethical egoism–theory of ethics that we should all act in our own self-interest; the Ayn Rand theory that separates guilt from acting in our own self-interest.

Ethical egoism holds that we all act in our own self-interest and that all of us should limit our judgment to our own ethical egos and not interfere with the exercise of ethical egoism by others. This view holds that everything is determined by self-interest. We act as we do and decide to behave as we do because we have determined that it is in our own self-interest.

Ayn Rand, who wrote books about business and business leaders' decisions in ethical dilemmas, such as *The Fountainhead* and *Atlas Shrugged*, was an ethical egoist. These two famous books made Ms. Rand's point about ethical dilemmas: The world would be better if we did not feel so guilty about the choices we make in ethical dilemmas and just acknowledged that it is all self-interest.

The Utilitarian Theory: Bentham and Mill

utilitarians–theory of ethics based on doing the most good for the most people in making decisions.

Utilitarians resolve ethical dilemmas by doing the most good for the most people. **For Example,** suppose that the FBI has just arrested a terrorist who is clearly a leader in a movement that plans to plant bombs in the nation's trains, subways, and airports. This individual has critical information about upcoming planned attacks but refuses to speak. A utilitarian would want the greatest good for the greatest number and would feel that harsh interrogation methods would be justified to save thousands of lives. Rights theorists would disagree with using torture to obtain the information because human rights must be protected.

Moral Relativists

moral relativists–those who make decisions based on circumstances and not on the basis of any predefined standards.

Moral relativists resolve ethical dilemmas according to time and place. For example, suppose that you live in a neighborhood in which drug dealers are operating a crystal meth lab or crack house, something that is causing violence in your neighborhood. A relativist would feel justified in committing arson to get rid of the drug house. Another classic example would be a parent stealing a loaf of bread to feed a starving child. Moral relativists resolve ethical dilemmas by weighing competing factors at the moment and then taking the lesser of the evils as the solution. **For Example,** Google and other Internet service providers have agreed to do business in China despite the restrictions the Chinese government places on the use of the Internet and the content of search engines. Such restrictions in the United States would be an unconstitutional violation of our First Amendment. In China, however, government control of information is legal. Google and others testified before Congress that some entry, however restricted, was better for the Chinese people than no access at all. Their decision did not focus on the rights theory, but, rather, weighed the conflicting values and concluded that they would use the standard of honoring the law of China despite the censorship.

Plato and Aristotle: Virtue Ethics

Aristotle and Plato taught that solving ethical dilemmas requires training, that individuals solve ethical dilemmas when they develop and nurture a set of virtues. Aristotle encouraged his students to solve ethical dilemmas using virtues such as honesty, justice, and fairness.

THINKING THINGS THROUGH

Corrupt Climates: Good or Bad for Business?

As you examine the following list of countries, those in the column labeled "Least Corrupt" (countries in which government officials are least likely to accept bribes) and those in the column marked "Most Corrupt" (countries in which government officials are most likely to accept bribes), can you comment on the business climates in them? What can you conclude about following the cultural practices of paying bribes? Who is harmed when a company pays bribes?

Least Corrupt (Least Likely to Accept Bribes)

- Denmark
- New Zealand
- Finland
- Sweden
- Norway
- Switzerland
- Singapore
- Netherlands
- Luxembourg
- Canada
- Australia
- Germany

- Iceland
- United Kingdom
- Belgium
- Japan
- Barbados
- Hong Kong
- Ireland
- United States
- Chile
- Uruguay
- Austria
- Bahamas

Most Corrupt (Most Likely to Accept Bribes)

- Somalia
- Korea (North)
- Sudan
- Afghanistan
- South Sudan
- Iraq
- Turkmenistan
- Uzbekistan
- Libya
- Eritrea
- Yemen
- Venezuela
- Haiti
- Guinea Bissau
- Angola
- Syria

- Burundi
- Zimbabwe
- Myanmar
- Cambodia
- Congo, Democratic Republic of
- Chad
- Tajikstan
- Congo, Republic of
- Paraguay
- Central African Republic
- Papua New Guinea
- Laos
- Kenya
- Guinea
- Bangladesh
- Ukraine

*From 2014 Transparency International annual survey, **http://www.transparency.org**.

3-1d **The Business Stakeholder Standard of Behavior**

stakeholders–those who have a stake, or interest, in the activities of a corporation; stakeholders include employees, members of the community in which the corporation operates, vendors, customers, and any others who are affected by the actions and decisions of the corporation.

stakeholder analysis–the term used when a decision maker views a problem from different perspectives and measures the impact of a decision on various groups.

Businesses have different constituencies, referred to as **stakeholders,** often with conflicting goals for the business. Shareholders, for example, may share economists' view that earnings, and hence dividends, should be maximized. Members of the community where a business is located are also stakeholders in the business and have an interest in preserving jobs. The employees of the business itself are stakeholders and certainly wish to retain their jobs. Balancing the interests of these stakeholders is a standard used in resolving ethical dilemmas in business.

As Figure 3-1 indicates, stakeholder analysis requires a view of an issue from different perspectives in a transparent way. **Stakeholder analysis** measures the impact of a decision on various groups and then asks whether public disclosure of that decision is defensible. The questions provide insight in a variety of situations and ethical dilemmas. **For Example,** if a lender gives a loan to a debtor without checking income, the lapse seems harmless. But suppose someone purchases that loan believing the debtor met the standards and the lender verified income. The debtor defaults on the loan. The purchaser has to write down or write off the loan. If enough loans that were not documented go into default, you create the kind of ripples in the real estate and stock markets that occurred in late 2008. Stakeholder analysis helps you to see that the decisions we make in business are not made in isolation or limited in their impact. Figure 3-1 summarizes ethical analysis.

In other ethical dilemmas, a business faces the question of taking voluntary action or simply complying with the law. Some experts maintain that the shareholders' interest is paramount in resolving these conflicts among stakeholders. Others maintain that a business must assume some responsibility for social issues and their resolution. Economist Milton Friedman expresses his views on resolving the conflicts among stakeholders as follows:

> *A corporate executive's responsibility is to make as much money for the shareholders as possible, as long as he operates within the rules of the game. When an executive decides to take action for reasons of social responsibility, he is taking money from someone else—from the stockholders, in the form of lower dividends; from the employees, in the form of lower wages; or from the consumer, in the form of higher prices. The responsibility of the corporate executive is to fulfill the terms of his contract. If he can't do that in good conscience, then he should quit his job and find another way to do good. He has the right to promote what he regards as desirable moral objectives only with his own money.*[2]

FIGURE 3-1	Guidelines for Analyzing a Contemplated Action

1. Define the problem from the decision maker's point of view.
2. Identify who could be injured by the contemplated action.
3. Define the problem from the opposing point of view.
4. Would you (as the decision maker) be willing to tell your family, your supervisor, your CEO, and the board of directors about the planned action?
5. Would you be willing to go before a community meeting, a congressional hearing, or a public forum to describe the action?
6. With full consideration of the facts and alternatives, reach a decision about whether the contemplated action should be taken.

---

[2] "Interview: Milton Friedman," *Playboy*, February 1973. © 1973 *Playboy*.

ETHICS & THE LAW

Edward Snowden: Contractor with a Cause

Edward Snowden was a contractor working at the National Security Agency (NSA). During the course of his contract work at the agency, Snowden believed that the NSA engaged in global surveillance programs that were not disclosed or supervised and represented a violation of privacy rights.

Mr. Snowden leaked classified information as a way of bringing attention to the conduct. Many maintain that the leaks breached the U.S. national security.

Discuss which ethical theories and standards Snowden was following. List the stakeholders in Snowden's actions.

Many businesses feel an obligation to solve social problems because those problems affect their stakeholders. **For Example,** programs such as flextime, job sharing, and telecommuting for work are not legal requirements but voluntary options businesses offer their employees to accommodate family needs. These options are a response to larger societal issues surrounding children and their care but may also serve as a way to retain a quality workforce that is more productive without the worry of poor child care arrangements.

Some businesses are also involved in their communities through employees' volunteer work and companies' charitable donations. **For Example,** a painting company in Phoenix donates paint, and its employees work on weekends painting Habitat for Humanity homes and helping churches get their facilities painted. Apple was able to capture future customers through its donations of computers to schools. Many companies also provide support for employees to participate in volunteer programs in their communities.

3-2 Why Is Business Ethics Important?

Ethics and values represent an important part of business success. Business ethics is important for more than the simple justification that "it's the right thing to do." This section covers the significance of ethics in business success.

3-2a The Importance of Trust

Capitalism succeeds because of trust. Investors provide capital for a business because they believe the business will provide a return on their investment. Customers are willing to purchase products and services from businesses because they believe the businesses will honor their commitments to deliver quality and then stand behind their product or service. Businesses are willing to purchase equipment and hire employees on the assumption that investors will continue to honor their commitment to furnish the necessary funds and will not withdraw their promises or funds. Business investment, growth, and sales are a circle of trust. Although courts provide remedies for breaches of agreements, no economy could grow if it were based solely on positive law and court-mandated performance. It is the reliance on promises, not the reliance on litigation, that produces good business relationships.

3-2b Business Ethics and Financial Performance

Studies centering on a business's commitment to values and its financial performance suggest that those with the strongest value systems survive and do so successfully. According to the book *Building and Growing a Business Through Good Times and Bad* by Louis Grossman and Marianne Jennings,[3] an in-depth look at companies that paid 100 years

[3] Greenwood Press (2002).

of consistent dividends produced a common thread: the companies' commitment to values. All firms studied had focused on high standards for product quality, employee welfare, and customer service.

Poor value choices do have an effect on financial performance. A study of the impact of just breaches of federal law by companies showed that for five years after their regulatory or legal misstep, these companies were still struggling to recover the financial performances they had achieved prior to their legal difficulties.[4]

Over the past few years, there have been devastating stories of companies' fates after ethical lapses. For example, after the congressional hearings revealed that Goldman Sachs took positions in the market that were the opposite of recommendations to its clients, its revenue dropped 18 percent and its share price dropped 32 percent.[5] When Netflix overpromised on its number of new subscribers and then fell short, its shares dropped 26.4 percent.[6] When the subprime lender New Century Financial announced that it was finally writing down all the subprime loans it had made that had gone into default but that it had been concealing, it was forced to declare bankruptcy because it was insolvent. On January 1, 2007, New Century had $1.75 billion in market capitalization, but by the middle of March, that figure was $55 million and its stock was delisted by the New York Stock Exchange.

In 2011, MF Global had to declare bankruptcy after its risky bets on Greek bonds resulted in $1.6 billion in losses. Over 1,000 employees lost their jobs and the firm was liquidated.[7] In 2014, GM paid a $35 million fine to the National Highway Transportation Safety Administration for its failure to report a parts change in 2006 that resulted in covering up the flaws in its ignition that led to accidents, deaths, and, eventually, the recall of 17 million vehicles. Following the recall, GM took a $1.2 billion charge to earnings to cover the costs.[8]

ETHICS & THE LAW

The Veterans Affairs (VA) and the Queues

The VA put into place incentives and bonuses for administrators to "reduce the queue." That is, the goal of the VA was to reduce the amount of time it took for veterans seeking care to actually receive that care to two weeks. Staffs at VA facilities all over the United States did meet those reduction goals and earn their bonuses. However, the way they earned those bonuses was through falsified patient appointment schedules.* The real results showed that three of every five veterans did not receive their care within two weeks as the documents showed. An Inspector General's report found that the falsifications caused patients to be dropped, with many dying while awaiting calls back from VA facilities.

Thirteen percent to 62 percent of VA schedulers (depending on the facility) were instructed on how to falsify records that were submitted to central administration for purposes of awarding bonuses.** The VA used Darrell Huff's book, *How to Lie with Statistics*, in training VA staffers.

Evaluate what went wrong at the VA and discuss how employees were able to be talked into participating.

*Eric Lichtblau, "V.A. Punished Critics on Staff, Doctors Assert," *New York Times,* June 16, 2014, p. A1.
**Meghan Hoyer and Gregg Zoroya, "Fraud Masks VA Wait Times," *USA Today,* June 14, 2014, p. 1A.

[4] Melinda S. Baucus and David A. Baucus, "Paying the Piper: An Empirical Examination of Longer-Term Financial Consequences of Illegal Corporate Behavior," 40 *Academic Management Journal* 129 (1997).
[5] Susanne Craig, "Goldman's Safer Position Eats Deeply Into Its Profits," *New York Times,* July 20, 2011, p. B4.
[6] Shalini Ramachandran and Tes Stynes, "Netflix Shares Plunge As Results Fall Short," *Wall Street Journal,* October 16, 2014, p. B1.
[7] Mike Spector, Aaron Lucchetti, and Liam Pleven, "Corzine Firm's Final Struggles," *Wall Street Journal,* November 5–6, 2011, p. A1.
[8] James R. Healey, "Recall Hits the Brakes on Income," *USA Today,* July 28, 2014, p. 1B.

3-2c The Importance of a Good Reputation

Richard Teerlink, the CEO of Harley-Davidson, once said, "A reputation, good or bad, is tough to shake."[9] A breach of ethics is costly to a firm not only in the financial sense of drops in earnings and possible fines. A breach of ethics also often carries with it a lasting memory that affects the business and its sales for years to come. **For Example,** the Peanut Corporation of America had to declare bankruptcy in 2009 after government officials discovered that its plant was the source of salmonella poisonings among those customers who had eaten peanut products that used the Peanut Corporation's base in their production. Records showed that the Peanut Corporation continued to produce the product even after salmonella warnings and questions arose. The company's name and image became so damaged that it could not continue to make sales. When an ethical breach occurs, businesses lose that component of trust important to customers' decisions to buy and invest. Four employees, including the CEO, were convicted of federal felonies for falsification of records related to salmonella testing.

3-2d Business Ethics and Business Regulation: Public Policy, Law, and Ethics

When business behavior results in complaints from employees, investors, or customers, laws or regulations are often used to change the behavior. **For Example,** the bankruptcy of Lehman Brothers, the near-collapse of Bear Stearns, and the losses at Merrill Lynch and AIG in 2008–2009 all resulted from the subprime mortgage financial derivative investment market, a market that had previously been a relatively regulation-free environment. The companies had billions of dollars of exposure because of their sales and purchases of financial instruments that were tied to the subprime mortgage market that ultimately resulted in high rates of foreclosure and nearly worthless loans. Congress, the Securities and Exchange Commission (SEC), and the Federal Reserve all stepped in to regulate virtually all aspects of mortgage transactions, including the lenders and others who were involved in packaging the loans into financial products.

Confusion among consumers about car leasing and its true costs and the fees applicable at the end of the lease terms caused the Federal Reserve (now the Consumer Financial Protection Bureau) to expand its regulation of credit to car leases. Figure 3-2 depicts the relationships among ethics, the social forces of customers and investors, and the laws that are passed to remedy the problems raised as part of the social forces movement.

Businesses that act voluntarily on the basis of value choices often avoid the costs and the sometimes arbitrariness of legislation and regulation. Voluntary change by businesses is less costly and is considered less intrusive.

Businesses that respond to social forces and the movements of the cycle of societal interaction often gain a competitive advantage. Businesses that act irresponsibly and disregard society's views and desire for change speed the transition from value choice to enforceable law. Businesses should watch the cycle of social forces and follow trends there to understand the values attached to certain activities and responses. These values motivate change either in the form of voluntary business activity or legislation. All values that precipitate change have one of several basic underlying goals. These underlying goals are discussed in the following sections.

---

[9] David K. Wright, *The Harley-Davidson Motor Co.: An Official Ninety-Year History* (Milwaukee: Motorbook International, 1993).

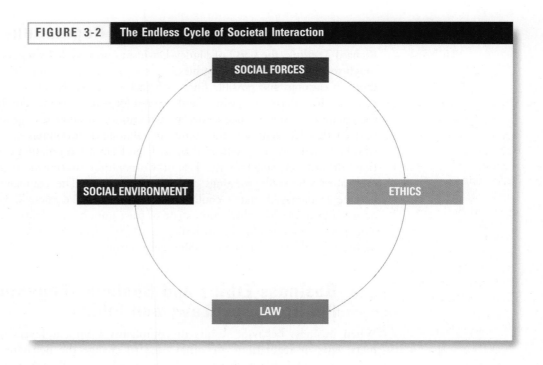

FIGURE 3-2   **The Endless Cycle of Societal Interaction**

Protection of the State

A number of laws exist today because of an underlying goal or value of protection of the state. The USA Patriot Act and airport security regulations are examples of government programs and regulations created with the protection and security of the state as the goal.

Protection of the Person

A second social force is protection of the person. Criminal laws are devoted to protection of individuals and their properties. In addition, civil suits permit private remedies for wrongful acts toward people and their property. Over time, the protection of personal rights has expanded to include the rights of privacy and the protection of individuals from defamation. Laws continue to evolve to protect the reputations, privacy, and mental and physical well-being of individuals.

Protection of Public Health, Safety, and Morals

Food-labeling regulations are an example of laws grounded in the value of protecting the safety and health of individuals. Food and restaurant inspections, mandatory inoculation, speed limits on roadways, mandatory smoke detectors and sprinkler systems in hotels, and prohibitions on the sale of alcohol to minors are all examples of laws based on the value of safety for the public. Zoning laws that prohibit the operation of adult book-stores and movie theaters near schools and churches are examples of laws based on moral values.

Protection of Property: Its Use and Title

Someone who steals another's automobile is a thief and is punished by law with fines and/or imprisonment. A zoning law that prohibits the operation of a steel mill in a residential

ETHICS & THE LAW

Ethics, Trust, and Markets

The cover of *Fortune* magazine from May 14, 2001, featured a picture of Wall Street financial analyst Mary Meeker and the words, "Can we ever trust again?"* The inside story focused on the relationship of underwriters, analysts, and brokerage houses with the high-tech companies whose stocks they were touting and selling, knowing there were questionable accounting practices and a lack of earnings at these companies. When the dot-com market bubble burst, the losses to shareholders were catastrophic. Those in the financial markets had too much at stake to be honest with investors. They did not break the law, however.

In 2002, when companies, such as Enron, WorldCom, and Tyco had to take write-downs because of years of overstating earnings, the market once again looked at analysts, wondering how they had failed to catch the accounting issues. The cover of *Fortune* read, "In Search of the Last Honest Analyst."**

During 2007, *Fortune* ran a cover with the pictures of the CEOs of the major Wall Street investment firms (such as Merrill Lynch, Bear Stearns, and Lehman Brothers) who had managed to lose trillions of investors' pension and 401(k) plans to risky investments in subprime mortgages that were marketed as low-risk investments. The cover's headline asked, "What Were They Smoking?"*** In 2011, following the collapse of Jon Corzine's MF Global hedge fund, a headline read, "Trustee Says More Cash Is Missing at MF Global." The estimated loss to investors at the firm was $1.6 billion.****

What do these headlines convey about the importance of trust and its role in markets?

*"Can We Ever Trust Again?" *Fortune*, May 14, 2001 (cover).
**"In Search of the Last Honest Analyst," *Fortune*, June 10, 2002 (cover).
***"What Were They Smoking?" *Fortune*, November 26, 2007 (cover).
****Michael J. de la Merced and Ben Protess, "Trustee Says More Cash Is Missing at MF Global," *New York Times,* November 22, 2011, p. B1.

area also provides protection for property. A civil suit brought to recover royalties lost because of another's infringement of one's copyrighted materials is based on federal laws that afford protection for property rights in nontangible or intellectual property (see Chapter 9). Laws afford protection of title for all forms of property. The deed recorded in the land record is the legal mechanism for protecting the owner's title. The copyright on a software program or a song protects the creator's rights in that intellectual property. The title documents issued by a department of motor vehicles afford protection of title for the owner of a vehicle.

Those who have title to property are generally free to use the property in any manner they see fit. However, even ownership has restrictions imposed by law. A business may operate a factory on its real property, but if the factory creates a great deal of pollution, adjoining landowners may successfully establish it as a nuisance (see Chapter 49) that interferes with their use and enjoyment of their land. Environmental laws also emerged as regulation of land use in response to concerns about legal, but harmful, emissions by companies.

Protection of Personal Rights

The desire for freedom from economic domination resulted in the free enterprise philosophy that exists in the United States today. Individual freedoms and personal rights continue as a focus of value discussions followed by legislation if those individual rights are violated.

Enforcement of Individual Intent

When we voluntarily enter into a contract, we have a responsibility to fulfill the promises made in that agreement. Principles of honesty and the honoring of commitments are the ethical values at the heart of the parties' conduct in carrying out contracts. If, however, the parties do not keep their promises, the law does enforce transactions through sets of rules governing requirements for them. **For Example,** the law will carry out the intentions of the parties to a business transaction through judicial enforcement of contract rights and damages.

Protection from Exploitation, Fraud, and Oppression

Many laws have evolved because businesses took advantage of others. Minors, or persons under legal age (see Chapter 13), are given special protections under contract laws that permit them to disaffirm their contracts so they are not disadvantaged by excessive commitments without the benefit of the wisdom of age and with the oppressive presence of an adult party.

The federal laws on disclosure in the sales of securities and shareholder relations (see Chapters 44 and 45) were developed following the 1929 stock market crash when many investors lost all they had because of the lack of candor and information by the businesses in which they were investing.

Furtherance of Trade

Some laws are the result of social forces seeking to simplify business and trade. Credit laws, regulations, and protections have made additional capital available for businesses and provided consumers with alternatives to cash purchases. The laws on checks, drafts, and notes have created instruments used to facilitate trade.

Protection of Creditors and Rehabilitation of Debtors

Mortgages, security interests, and surety relationships (see Chapters 31, 32, and 33) are mechanisms created by law to provide creditors the legal mechanisms for collecting their obligations.

When collection techniques became excessive and exploitative, new laws on debtors' rights were enacted. Debtors' prisons were abolished. Congress mandated disclosure requirements for credit contracts. The Fair Debt Collections Practices Act (see Chapter 32) limited collection techniques. The remedy of bankruptcy was afforded debtors under federal law to provide them an opportunity to begin a new economic life when their existing debts reached an excessive level and could no longer be paid in a timely fashion (see Chapter 34).

Stability and Flexibility

Because of the desire for stability, courts will ordinarily follow former decisions unless there is a strong reason to depart from them. (See Chapter 1 for more discussion of precedent.) Similarly, when no former case bears on the point involved, a court will try to reach a decision that is a logical extension of some former decision or that follows a former decision by analogy rather than strike out on a new path to reach a decision unrelated to the past.

3-3 How to Recognize and Resolve Ethical Dilemmas

Business managers often find themselves in circumstances in which they are unclear about right and wrong and are confused about how to resolve the dilemmas they face. A recent survey showed that 98 percent of all Fortune 500 companies have codes of ethics

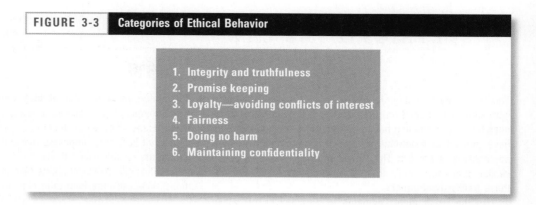

FIGURE 3-3   **Categories of Ethical Behavior**

1. Integrity and truthfulness
2. Promise keeping
3. Loyalty—avoiding conflicts of interest
4. Fairness
5. Doing no harm
6. Maintaining confidentiality

designed to help their employees recognize and resolve ethical dilemmas. Nearly 81 percent of those firms provide their employees some form of training in ethics.[10] Almost 70 percent of companies now include ethical conduct as a performance measure. These codes of ethics provide employees information about categories of behavior that constitute ethical breaches. Regardless of the industry, the type of business, or the size of the company, certain universal categories can help managers recognize ethical dilemmas. Figure 3-3 provides a list of those categories.

3-3a Categories of Ethical Behavior

Integrity and Truthfulness

A famous anonymous quote on truth is, "Circumstances beyond your control will cause the truth to come out, no matter what." As discussed earlier, trust is a key component of business relationships and of the free enterprise system. Trust begins with the belief that honesty is at the heart of relationships. Many contract remedies in law are based on the failure of the parties to be truthful with each other. **For Example,** if you purchase a home that has been certified as termite free but you discover termites in the home shortly after you move in, someone has not been truthful. If you also discover that two termite inspections were conducted and that the first one, which revealed there were termites, was concealed from you, your trust in both the sellers and their exterminators is diminished.

integrity—the adherence to one's values and principles despite the costs and consequences.

Integrity is the adherence to one's values and principles despite the costs and consequences. **For Example,** an executive contracted with a variety of companies to sell his hard-to-find computer components. When he was approached by one of his largest customers to break a contract with a small customer, the executive refused. The customer assured the executive it would be his last order with the company if he did not get more components. Despite facing the threat of losing a multimillion-dollar customer, the executive fulfilled his promises to the small purchasers. The executive kept his word on all of his contracts and demonstrated integrity.

Promise Keeping

If we examined the types of things we do in a day, we will find that most of them are based on promises. We promise to deliver goods either with or without a contract. We promise to pay the dentist for our dental work. We promise to provide someone with a

[10] Ethics Resource Center, The National Business Ethics Survey 2013, **http://www.ethics.org/downloads/2013NBESFinal-Web.pdf**.

ETHICS & THE LAW

Lying to Get into a Top School

The University of California at Berkeley has implemented a new step in its admission process. The Haas School of Business has begun running background checks on students who have applied to determine whether the information in their applications is correct. The Wharton School implemented a similar procedure and charges applicants a $35 fee for these background checks.

Of the 100 students admitted to Berkeley in the fall of 2003, 5 students were found to have offered false information on their admissions applications. The most common type of false information was the job titles they held, and the second most common type was their number of years of work experience. Haas admissions officers indicated that had the students not lied, they otherwise met the GMAT score and GPA standards for admission to Haas.

What risk do the students take in lying on their applications? What are the long-term consequences?

Source: "Cheaters Don't Make the Grade at Berkeley Business School," **http://www.azcentral.com**, March 14, 2003, AP wire reports.

ride. Keeping those promises, regardless of whether there is a legal obligation to do so, is a key component of being an ethical person and practicing ethical business. Keeping promises is also evidence of integrity for example.

Loyalty—Avoiding Conflicts of Interest

conflict of interest– conduct that compromises an employee's allegiance to that company.

An employee who works for a company owes allegiance to that company. Conduct that compromises that loyalty is a **conflict of interest. For Example,** suppose that your sister operates her own catering business. Your company is seeking a caterer for its monthly management meetings. You are responsible for these meetings and could hire your sister to furnish the lunches for the meetings. Your sister would have a substantial contract, and your problems with meal logistics would be solved. Nearly all companies have a provision in their codes of ethics covering this situation. An employee cannot hire a relative, friend, or even her own company without special permission because it is a conflict of interest. Your loyalty to your sister conflicts with the loyalty to your employer, which requires you to make the best decision at the best price.

A conflict of interest arises when a purchasing agent accepts gifts from suppliers, vendors, or manufacturers' representatives. The purchasing agent has introduced into the buy-sell relationship an element of *quid pro quo*, or the supplier's expectation that the gift will bring about a return from the agent in the form of a contract. Some companies have zero tolerance for conflicts and establish a complete prohibition on employees accepting any gifts from suppliers and manufacturers. **For Example,** Wal-Mart buyers are not permitted to accept even a cup of coffee from potential merchandise suppliers, and Amgen's buyers can go out to dinner with a supplier only if Amgen pays.

Doing No Harm

Imagine selling a product that your company's internal research shows presents significant health dangers to its users. Selling the product without disclosure of the information is unfair. There is the additional ethical breach of physical harm to your customers and users. GM sold its Cobalt and other model cars knowing that a heavy key chain or hitting a pothole could cause the ignition switch to shut down. Some drivers were on freeways when the switches shut down, bringing their cars to a sudden halt. When collisions

SPORTS & ENTERTAINMENT LAW

The Bounty Program and the New Orleans Saints

The New Orleans Saints defensive coordinator, Greg Williams, established a bounty program for the team, a program that rewarded players for injuring other players. For example, a $1,500 bonus was offered if a Saints player knocked out an opposing team player. There was $1,000 more if the player had to be carted from the field. There was an offer of $10,000 for any player who could knock Brent Favre out of the NFC Championship in 2009 when the Saints were vying for the Super Bowl. The result was that Mr. Favre was hit almost every play, many times after he had thrown the ball.*

The word around the league was that Mr. Williams rounded corners. "If you were looking at somebody to hire for an ability to coordinate defense, you would hire the guy. You have to understand what you're getting—he may take chances you may not want."** During the NFL investigation of the Saints' practices, Mr. Williams admitted that he did create the bounty program, "It was a terrible mistake, and

we knew it was wrong while we were doing it."*** And team owner Tom Benson said, "Instead of getting caught up in it, I should have stopped it."****

Why do you think everyone was so willing to go along with the bounty program? As a penalty, the Saints lost their head coach (Sean Payton) for one year, and Greg Williams was suspended indefinitely. Various other coaches were suspended, and the Saints paid a $500,000 fine. What are the flaws in thinking processes when we make decisions to go ahead with a bounty program?

*Fran Tarkenton, "Football's Bounty Hunters Must Be Clipped," *Wall Street Journal,* March 7, 2012, p. A17.
**Judy Battista, "The Man Behind the Bounties," *New York Times,* March 7, 2012, p. B11.
***Peter King, "Way Out of Bounds," *Sports Illustrated,* March 12, 2012, p. 34.
****Id.

---

occurred, the airbag protections did not deploy because the cars were off. Internal memos and e-mails from engineers at GM revealed that they were aware of the problem in 2006 but opted not to notify regulators and do the necessary recalls until 2014. The late Peter Drucker's advice on ethics for businesses is ***primum non nocere,*** or "above all, do no harm." Such a rule might have helped GM.

primum non nocere– above all, do no harm.

Maintaining Confidentiality

Often the success of a business depends on the information or technology that it holds. If the competitive edge that comes from the business's peculiar niche or knowledge is lost through disclosure, so are its profits. Employees not only owe a duty of loyalty to their employers, but they also owe an obligation of confidentiality. Employees should not use, either personally or through a competitor, information they have obtained through their employer's work or research. Providing customer lists or leads is a breach of employees' obligation of confidentiality.

In addition, managers have responsibilities regarding their employees' privacy. Performance evaluations of individual employees are private and should never be disclosed or revealed, even in one-on-one conversations outside the lines of authority and the workplace.

3-3b Resolving Ethical Dilemmas

Recognizing an ethical dilemma is perhaps the easiest part of business ethics. Resolution of that dilemma is more difficult. The earlier section on stakeholders offers one model for resolution of ethical dilemmas (see Figure 3-1). Other models have been developed to provide managers analytical methods for resolving dilemmas in a timely fashion.

E-COMMERCE & CYBERLAW

Piggybacking on Wireless Networks

A legal and ethical issue that has evolved because of technology is the practice of "piggybacking," or people tapping onto their neighbors' wireless Internet connection. The original subscriber pays a monthly fee for the service, but without security, people located in the area are able to tap into the wireless network, which bogs down the speed of the service. Once limited to geeks and hackers, the practice is now common among the ordinary folk who just want free Internet service.

One college student said, "I don't think it's stealing. I always find [p]eople out there ... aren't protecting their connection, so I just feel free to go ahead and use it."* According to a recent survey, only about 30 percent of the 4,500 wireless networks onto which the surveyors logged were encrypted, and another survey shows that 32 percent of us do engage in Wi-Fi piggybacking.

An apartment dweller said she leaves her connection wide open because "I'm sticking it to the man. I open up my network, leave it wide open for anyone to jump on." One of the users of another's wireless network said, "I feel sort of bad about it, but I do it anyway. It just seems harmless." She said that if she gets caught, "I'll just play the dumb card."

Some neighbors offer to pay those with wireless service in exchange for their occasional use rather than paying a wireless company for full-blown service. However, the original subscribers do not really want to run their own Internet service.

Do you think we need new legislation to cover this activity? What do you think of the users' statements? Is their conduct legal? Is it ethical?

*Michael Marriott, "Hey Neighbor, Stop Piggybacking on My Wireless," *New York Times,* March 5, 2006, A1, A23.

Blanchard and Peale Three-Part Test

Dr. Kenneth Blanchard, author of the books on the *One-Minute Manager,* and the late Dr. Norman Vincent Peale developed a model for evaluating ethical breaches that is widely used among Fortune 500 companies.[11] To evaluate situations, ask the following three questions: Is it legal? Is it balanced? How does it make me feel?

In answering the questions on legality, a manager should look to positive law both within and outside the company. If the proposed conduct would violate antitrust laws, the manager's analysis can stop there. If the proposed conduct would violate company policy, the manager's analysis can stop. In the field of business ethics, there is little room for civil disobedience. Compliance with the law is a critical component of a successful ethics policy in any company.

The second question on balance forces the manager to examine the ethical value of fairness. A good follow-up question is, "How would I want to be treated in this circumstance?" Perhaps the decision to downsize must be made, but couldn't the company offer the employees a severance package and outplacement assistance to ease the transition?

The final question of the Blanchard and Peale model is conscience based. Although some managers may employ any tactics to maximize profits, this final question forces a manager to examine the physical impact of a decision: Does it cause sleeplessness or appetite changes? Personalizing business choices often helps managers to see the potential harm that comes from poor ethical choices.

The Front-Page-of-the-Newspaper Test

This simple but effective model for ethical evaluation helps a manager visualize the public disclosure of proposed conduct. When he temporarily took over as the leader of Salomon

[11] Kenneth Blanchard and Norman Vincent Peale, *The Power of Ethical Management* (1986).

Brothers after its bond-trading controversy, Warren Buffett described the newspaper test as follows:

> *Contemplating any business act, an employee should ask himself whether he would be willing to see it immediately described by an informed and critical reporter on the front page of his local paper, there to be read by his spouse, children, and friends. At Salomon, we simply want no part of any activities that pass legal tests but that we, as citizens, would find offensive.*[12]

Laura Nash Model

In her work, business ethicist Laura Nash has developed a series of questions to help businesspeople reach the right decision in ethical dilemmas. These are her questions: Have you defined the problem accurately? How would you define the problem if you stood on the other side of the fence? How did this situation occur in the first place? What is your intention in making this decision? How does the intention compare with the probable results? Whom could your decision or action injure? Can you discuss your decision with the affected parties? Are you confident that your position will be as valid over a long period of time as it seems now? Could you discuss your decision with your supervisor, coworkers, officers, board, friends, and family?

The Nash model requires an examination of the dilemma from all perspectives. Defining the problem and how the problem arose provides the business assistance in avoiding the dilemma again. **For Example,** suppose that a supervisor is asked to provide a reference for a friend who works for her. The supervisor is hesitant because the friend has not been a very good employee. The ethical dilemma the manager believes she faces is whether to lie or tell the truth about the employee. The real ethical dilemma is why the supervisor never provided evaluation or feedback indicating the friend's poor performance. Avoiding the problem in the future is possible through candid evaluations. Resolving the problem requires that the supervisor talk to her friend now about the issue of performance and the problem with serving as a reference.

ETHICS & THE LAW

Pumping Up the SAT Scores for a Good Ranking

Since 2005, Claremont McKenna, ranked #9 on *U.S. News & World Report's* best liberal arts colleges in the country, has been lopping on a few points here and there to its entering students' average SAT score before reporting those numbers to *U.S. News & World Report* and rating organizations such as the Princeton Review. For example, in 2010, its combined median score was reported as 1410, rather than its actual 1400. And its 75th percentile was reported at 1510, when it was, in reality, 1480.

Claremont McKenna's vice president and dean of admissions has been removed from his job title on the college Web site. President Pamela B. Gann explained the problem and concluded, "As an institution of higher education with a deep and consistent commitment to the integrity of our academic activities, and particularly, our reporting of institutional data, we take this situation very seriously."

Robert Franek of the Princeton Review offered, "That is a pretty mild difference in a point score. That said, 10 points, 20 points to a student that isn't getting that score on the SAT could be an important distinction." Is the issue that the difference is mild? Mr. Franek also added, "I feel like so many schools have a very clear obligation to college-bound students to report this information honestly."

Evaluate the issues as well as Mr. Franek's take on the situation from an ethical perspective.

Source: Daniel E. Slotnik and Richard Pérez-Peña, "College Says It Exaggerated SAT Figures for Rating," *New York Times*, Jan. 31, 2012, p. A12.

---

[12] Janet Lowe, *Warren Buffett Speaks: Wit and Wisdom from the World's Greatest Investor* (1997).

One final aspect of the Nash model that businesspeople find helpful is a question that asks for a perspective on an issue from family and friends. The problem of group-think in business situations is very real. As businesspeople sit together in a room and discuss an ethical dilemma, they can persuade each other to think the same way. The power of consensus can overwhelm each person's concerns and values. There is a certain fear in bringing up a different point of view in a business meeting. Proper perspective is often lost as the discussion centers around numbers. Therefore, bringing in the views of an outsider is often helpful. **For Example,** when McNeil, the manufacturer of Tylenol, faced the cyanide poisonings from contaminated capsules sold in the Chicago area, it had to make a decision about the existing Tylenol inventory. It was clear to both insiders and outsiders that the poison had not been put in the capsules at McNeil but after delivery to the stores. Despite the huge numbers involved in the recall and the destruction of inventory, the McNeil managers made the decision easily because they viewed the risk to their own families, that is, from the outside. From this standpoint, the issue became a question of human life, not of numbers.[13]

Make the Connection

Summary

Business ethics is the application of values and standards to business conduct and decisions. These values originate in various sources from positive (codified) law to natural law to ethical theories and standards and on to stakeholder values. Business ethics is important because trust is a critical component of good business relationships and free enterprise. A business with values will enjoy the additional competitive advantage of a good reputation and, over the long term, better earnings. When businesses make decisions that violate basic ethical standards, they set into motion social forces and cause the area of abuse to be regulated, resulting in additional costs and restrictions for business. Voluntary value choices by businesses position them for a competitive advantage.

The categories of ethical values in business are truthfulness and integrity, promise keeping, loyalty and avoiding conflicts of interest, fairness, doing no harm, and maintaining confidentiality.

Resolution of ethical dilemmas is possible through the use of various models that require a businessperson to examine the impact of a decision before it is made. These models include stakeholder analysis, the Blanchard and Peale test, the front-page-of-the-newspaper test, and the Laura Nash model.

Learning Outcomes

After studying this chapter, you should be able to clearly explain:

3-1   What Is Business Ethics?

LO.1   Define business ethics
See the discussion of the definition and balancing the goal of profits with the values of individuals and society, page 34.

3-2   Why Is Business Ethics Important?

LO.2   Discuss why ethics are important in business
See "The Importance of Trust," page 39.
See "Business Ethics and Financial Performance," page 39.
See "The Importance of a Good Reputation," page 41.
See Ethics & the Law on market trust, page 43.
See Sports & Entertainment Law, page 47.

[13] "Brief History of Johnson & Johnson" (company pamphlet, 1992).

3-3 How to Recognize and Resolve Ethical Dilemmas

LO.3 Describe how to recognize and resolve ethical dilemmas

See "Integrity and Truthfulness," page 45.
See "Promise Keeping," page 45.
See "Loyalty—Avoiding Conflicts of Interest," page 46.
See "Doing No Harm," page 46.

See Ethics & the Law on the VA, page 40.
See "Maintaining Confidentiality," page 47.
See "Resolving Ethical Dilemmas," page 47.
See "Blanchard and Peale Three-Part Test," page 48.
See "The Front-Page-of-the-Newspaper Test," page 48.
See Ethics & the Law on pumping up SAT scores, page 49.
See "Laura Nash Model," page 49.

Key Terms

business ethics
civil disobedience
conflict of interest
entitlement theory
ethical egoism
ethics

integrity
Kant's categorical imperative
moral relativists
natural law
positive law
primum non nocere

rights theory
social contract
stakeholder analysis
stakeholders
theory of justice
utilitarians

Questions and Case Problems

1. Marty Mankamyer, the president of the United States Olympic Committee (USOC), resigned in early February 2003 following reports in *The Denver Post* that indicated she had demanded a commission from a fellow real estate broker in the Colorado Springs area, the home of the USOC, who had sold property to Lloyd Ward, the CEO of the USOC. Mr. Ward had purchased a 1.3-acre lot in Colorado Springs for $475,000 and had paid the listing broker, Brigette Ruskin, a commission.

    Ms. Mankamyer allegedly demanded a portion of the commission from Ms. Ruskin, and Ms. Ruskin sent her a check. Ms. Mankamyer had shown Mr. Ward and his wife properties in the area when they were being considered for the job and when he was considering taking the job. However, Mrs. Ward indicated that Ms. Mankamyer did not identify herself as a real estate agent and that she assumed that Ms. Mankamyer was showing the properties as a "goodwill gesture."[14] What conflicts of interest do you see here?

2. During the inauguration for President Obama in January 2013, Beyoncé was scheduled to sing the national anthem. The question arose: Did she lip-sync during her performance? No answer was forthcoming from the singer's representatives, but it was clear from those attending that the National Marine Band was not playing during her performance. Those in charge of the event felt that since she had not had an opportunity to rehearse with the band that it was best to use a tape. Are there any ethical issues involved in this choice for the performance? Was there an obligation of disclosure?

3. Fred Sanguine is a New York City produce broker. Ned Santini is a 19-year-old college student who works for Sanguine from 4:00 A.M. until 7:00 A.M. each weekday before he attends classes at Pace University. Fred has instructed Ned on the proper packing of produce as follows: "Look, put the bad and small cherries at the bottom. Do the same with the strawberries and blueberries. Put the best fruit on top and hide the bad stuff at the bottom. This way I get top dollar on all that I sell." Ned is uncomfortable about the instructions, but, as he explains to his roommate, "It's not me doing it. I'm just following orders. Besides, I need the job."

    Should Ned just follow instructions? Is the manner in which the fruit is packed unethical? Would you do it? Why or why not? Is anyone really harmed by the practice?

4. Alan Gellen is the facilities manager for the city of Milwaukee and makes all final decisions on purchasing items such as chairs, lights, and other supplies and materials. Alan also makes the final decisions for the award of contracts to food vendors at event sites. Grand Beef Franks has submitted a bid to be one of the city's vendors. Alan went to school with Grand Beef's owner, Steve Grand, who phones Alan and explains that Grand Beef owns a condominium in Maui that Alan could use. Steve's offer to Alan is: "All

[14]Richard Sandomir, "U.S. Olympic Chief Resigns in a Furor Over Ethics Issues," *New York Times*, February 5, 2003, A1, C17; Bill Briggs, *Realtor Waving Red Flag*, **http://www.denverpost.com**, February 4, 2003.

it would cost you for a vacation is your airfare. The condo is fully stocked with food. Just let me know."

Should Alan take the offer? Would you? Be sure to determine which category of ethical values this situation involves and to apply several models as you resolve the question of whether Alan should accept the invitation.

5. A Dillard's customer brought in a pair of moderately expensive dress shoes, expressing a desire to return them because they just weren't quite right. As the manager processed the order she checked inside the box to be sure that the shoes in the box were the shoes that matched the box—past experience dictated that follow-up on returns. The shoes were the correct ones for the box, but there was another issue. The shoes had masking tape on the bottom—masking tape that was dirty. When the manager returned to the customer she said, "You forgot to remove the masking tape from your shoes." The customer responded, "I only wore them once. That's all I needed them for."

From Neiman Marcus to Saks to Dillard's, managers have to stay one step ahead of customers, or lessees, who buy, or lease for free, dresses and now shoes for one use with premeditated intent to return the merchandise. Stores now place tags strategically so that the dresses cannot be worn without cutting them off and there are no returns if the tags are cut off on formal wear.

Ace Hardware and Home Depot have customers who "buy" a special tool, try to use it once, and then return it. The hardware/home improvement stores are left with opened packaging and used goods by buy-it-temporarily customers.

List some consequences for this behavior by customers.

6. Adam Smith wrote the following in *The Theory of Moral Sentiments*:

> *In the practice of the other virtues, our conduct should rather be directed by a certain idea of propriety, by a certain taste for a particular tenor of conduct, than by any regard to a precise maxim or rule; and we should consider the end and foundation of the rule, more than the rule itself.*[15]

Do you think Adam Smith adhered to positive law as his ethical standard? Was he a moral relativist? Does his quote match stakeholder analysis? What would his ethical posture be on violating the law?

7. A new phenomenon for admissions to MBA programs is hiring consultants to help applicants hone their applications. About 20 percent of those who apply to the top MBA programs have hired consultants at a cost of $150 to $200 per hour to help them say and do the right things to be admitted. The total cost for most who use a consultant is $5,000. The consultants help with personal essays and applications. One admissions officer points out that one function of the consultant is to draw out and emphasize skills that the applicant may not see as important. For example, playing the piano is looked upon favorably because it shows discipline and focus.

However, admissions committees are becoming adept at spotting the applications via consultant because, as the faculty describe it, these essays and applications have a certain "sameness" to them. The Fuqua School at North Carolina suggests that students simply call the admissions office and get comparable advice for free. Is it ethical to use an admissions consultant? When would you cross a line in using the consultant on the essay?

8. "I was very upset that there's that many dishonest people," said Andrea Reuland, the owner of Trigs Shell Station in Minocqua, Wisconsin.

She lost $3 per gallon on 586 gallons of gas sold during a 45-minute period while local residents phoned others to come and get gas because an employee had made a mistake and entered the price at 32.9 cents vs. $3.299 per gallon.

Eighty-seven percent of the people who responded to a survey about the incident said they would have done the same thing as the Minocqua residents.

Describe who is affected by what buyers did by not paying the correct price for the gas. Describe a simple test for resolving an ethical dilemma such as this where you can get something for free or very little.

9. The state of Arizona mandates emissions testing for cars before drivers can obtain updated registrations. The state hires a contractor to conduct the emissions tests in the various emissions-testing facilities around the state. In October 1999, the Arizona attorney general announced the arrest of 13 workers at one of the emissions-testing facilities for allegedly taking payoffs of between $50 and $200 from car owners to pass their cars on the emissions tests when those cars fell below emissions standards and would not have been registered. Nearly half of the staff at the emissions facility were arrested.

Why is it a crime for someone working in a government-sponsored facility to accept a payment

[15]Adam Smith, *The Theory of Moral Sentiments* (Arlington House, 1969; originally published in 1769).

for a desired outcome? Do the payoffs to the workers really harm anyone?

10. The president and athletic director at the University of California at Los Angeles (UCLA) fired the school's basketball coach because an expense form he had submitted for reimbursement had the names of two students he said had joined him for a recruiting dinner. The students had not been to the dinner. The coach was stunned because he had been at UCLA for eight years and had established a winning program. He said, "And to throw it all away on a meal?" Do you agree with the coach's assessment? Was it too harsh to fire him for one inaccurate expense form? Did the coach commit an ethical breach?

11. When some runners in the New York City Marathon hit the Queensboro Bridge, temptation sets in and, rather than finishing the last 10 miles through Harlem and the Bronx, they hop a ride on the subway and head toward the finish line at Central Park. A total of 46 runners used the subway solution to finish the race in the 2008 NYC Marathon. When one runner was questioned about his unusual time, he admitted to using the subway and said, "So I skipped a few boroughs. I didn't do anything illegal." How would you respond to his point that he did not break the law? Why should we worry about some runners?

12. David A. Vise, a Pulitzer Prize winner and a reporter for the *Washington Post*, wrote the book *The Bureau and the Mole*. When the book hit the market, Mr. Vise purchased 20,000 copies via Barnes & Noble.com, taking advantage of both free shipping offered by the publisher and a discounted initial price. Mr. Vise's book had already hit the *New York Times'* bestseller list in the week before the purchases. He used the books he purchased to conduct online sales of autographed copies of the books, and then returned 17,500 books and asked for his money back. However, that return of 17,500 books represented more books than a publisher generally runs for a book. Mr. Vise said that he did not intend to manipulate the market or profit from the transactions. He said his only intent was to "increase awareness of *The Bureau and the Mole*."

Mr. Vise's editor offered to pay Barnes & Noble for any expenses it incurred. Was it ethical to do what Mr. Vise did? Was he within his rights to return the books? What are his remedies? Does Barnes & Noble have any rights?

13. Former Enron Chief Financial Officer Andrew Fastow, in his testimony against his former bosses at their criminal trial for fraud, said, "I thought I was being a hero for Enron. At the time, I thought I was helping myself and helping Enron to make its numbers." Mr. Fastow also added, however, "I lost my moral compass."

Are you able to classify Mr. Fastow into a particular ethical standard or principle?

14. Piper High School in Piper, Kansas, a town located about 20 miles west of Kansas City, experienced national attention because of questions about students and their term papers for a botany class. Christine Pelton, a high school science teacher, had warned students in her sophomore class not to use papers posted on the Internet for their projects. When their projects were turned in, Ms. Pelton noticed that the writing in some of the papers was well above the students' usual quality and ability. She found that 28 of her 118 students had taken substantial portions of their papers from the Internet. She gave these students a zero grade on their term paper projects with the result that many of the students were going to fail the course for that semester. The students' parents protested, and the school board ordered Ms. Pelton to raise the grades.

She resigned in protest. She received a substantial number of job offers from around the country following her resignation. Nearly half of the high school faculty as well as its principal announced their plans to resign at the end of the year. Several of the parents pointed to the fact that there was no explanation in the Piper High School handbook on plagiarism. They also said that the students were unclear about what could be used, when they had to reword, and when quotations marks were necessary.

The annual Rutgers University survey on academic cheating has revealed that 15 percent of college papers turned in for grades are completely copied from the Internet.

Do you think such copying is unethical? Why do we worry about such conduct? Isn't this conduct just a function of the Internet? Isn't it accepted behavior?

15. Heinz Ketchup holds 54 percent of the ketchup market in the United States. Nine of every 10 restaurants feature Heinz ketchup. However, Heinz has learned that many restaurant owners are simply refilling Heinz Ketchup bottles with other ketchup to capture Heinz prestige without actually buying Heinz. There are no specific regulations that apply to the practice. Discuss the ethical issues. One restaurant owner has said that customers do not notice and that it is not a big deal. Evaluate the ethical issues in his comment.

C H A P T E R 4

The Constitution as the Foundation of the Legal Environment

4-1 The U.S. Constitution and the Federal System

federal system–the system of government in which a central government is given power to administer to national concerns while individual states retain the power to administer to local concerns.

The Constitution of the United States establishes the structure and powers of government but also the limitations on those powers. This Constitution forms the foundation of our legal environment. By establishing a central government to coexist with the governments of the individual states, the U.S. Constitution created a federal system. In a **federal system,** a central government has power to address national concerns while the individual states retain the power to handle local concerns.

4-1a What a Constitution Is

constitution–a body of principles that establishes the structure of a government and the relationship of the government to the people who are governed.

A **constitution** is the written document that establishes the structure of the government and its relationship to the people. The U.S. Constitution was adopted in 1789 by the 13 colonies that had won their independence from King George.[1]

4-1b The Branches of Government

tripartite–three-part division (of government).

legislative branch–the branch of government (e.g., Congress) formed to make the laws.

executive branch–the branch of government (e.g., the president) formed to execute the laws.

judicial branch–the branch of government (e.g., the courts) formed to interpret the laws.

bicameral–a two-house form of the legislative branch of government.

The U.S. Constitution establishes a **tripartite** (three-part) government: a **legislative branch** (Congress) to make the laws, an **executive branch** (the president) to execute or enforce the laws, and a **judicial branch** (courts) to interpret the laws.[2] The national legislature or Congress is a **bicameral** (two-house) body consisting of the Senate and the House of Representatives. Members of the Senate are popularly elected for a term of six years. Members of the House of Representatives are popularly elected for a term of two years. The president is elected by an electoral college whose membership is popularly elected. The president serves for a term of four years and is eligible for reelection for a second term. Judges of the United States are appointed by the president with the approval of the Senate and serve for life, subject to removal only by impeachment because of misconduct. (See Chapter 2 for a discussion of the federal court system.)

4-2 The U.S. Constitution and the States

The Constitution created certain powers within the national government that would have been exercised by the individual states, which are given their powers by the people of the state. Figure 4-1 illustrates the delegation of powers. Likewise, the states, as the power-granting authorities, reserved certain powers for themselves.

4-2a Delegated and Shared Powers

Delegated Powers

delegated powers–powers expressly granted the national government by the Constitution.

The powers given by the states to the national government are described as *delegated powers.* Some of these **delegated powers** are given exclusively to the national government. **For Example,** the national government alone may declare war or establish a currency.

---

[1] U.S. Const., Art 1, §8, cl 1. To read more of the U.S. Constitution, refer to Appendix 2, or go to **http://www.constitution.org** and click on "Founding Documents."
[2] *Free Enterprise Fund v. Public Company Accounting Oversight Board,* 561 U.S. 477 (2010).

FIGURE 4-1 | **Governments of the United States**

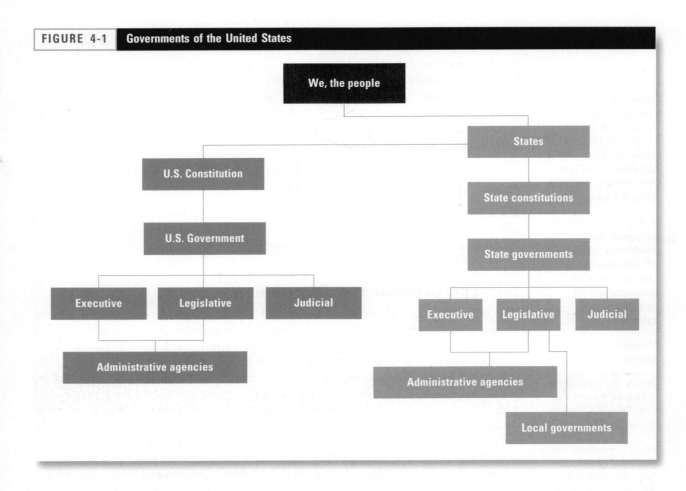

Shared Powers

shared powers–powers that are held by both state and national governments.

The powers delegated to the national government that may still be exercised by the states are **shared powers. For Example,** the grant of power to the national government to impose taxes did not destroy the state power to tax. In other cases, a state may provide regulation along with, but subject to the supremacy of, federal law. **For Example,** regulation of the use of navigable waterways within a state is an example of joint state and federal regulation.

4-2b Other Powers

Police Power of the States

police power–the power to govern; the power to adopt laws for the protection of the public health, welfare, safety, and morals.

The states possess the power to adopt laws to protect the general welfare, health, safety, and morals of the people. This authority is called the **police power. For Example,** states may require that businesses be licensed with state agencies to protect persons dealing with the business. State exercise of the police power may not unreasonably interfere with federal powers.

Prohibited Powers

***ex post facto* law**–a law making criminal an act that was lawful when done or that increases the penalty when done. Such laws are generally prohibited by constitutional provisions.

The Constitution also prohibits both states and the federal government from doing certain things. **For Example,** neither states nor the national government may adopt ***ex post facto* laws,** which make criminal an act that has already been committed but was not criminal when it was committed. Laws that increase the penalty for an act already committed above the penalty in force when the act was committed are also *ex post facto* laws.

4-2c Federal Supremacy

preemption—the federal government's superior regulatory position over state laws on the same subject area.

States cannot enact conflicting state regulation if the congressional intent to regulate exclusively can be inferred from the details of congressional regulation. **Preemption** means that the federal regulatory scheme is controlling.

Express Federal Regulation

The Constitution and statutes passed by Congress are the supreme law of the land. They cancel out any conflicting state law.[3] When a direct conflict exists between federal and state statutes, federal law prevails.

In some cases, however, no obvious conflict occurs because the federal statute covers only part of the subject matter. In such cases, the question becomes whether a state law can regulate the areas not regulated by Congress or whether the partial regulation made by Congress preempts, or takes over, the field so as to preclude state legislation.

CASE SUMMARY

Generic Preemption: Controlling Who Recovers for Pharma Injuries

FACTS: In 1978, the FDA approved an anti-inflammatory pain reliever called "sulindac" under the brand name of "Clinoril." When the patent expired, the FDA approved several generic versions of sulindac for sale, including one developed by Mutual Pharmaceutical (Petitioner). The warnings for Clinoril included the possibility of developing toxic epidermal necrolysis. Karen Bartlett (Respondent) took a generic form of sulindac in December 2004 and developed an acute case of toxic epidermal necrolysis. Sixty to sixty-five percent of Ms. Bartlett's body deteriorated, was burned off, or turned into an open wound. She spent months in a medically induced coma, underwent 12 eye surgeries, and was tube-fed for a year. She is now severely disfigured, has a number of physical disabilities, and is nearly blind.

At the time Ms. Bartlett got her sulindac prescription, the label did not refer to toxic epidermal necrolysis but warned that the drug could cause "severe skin reactions" and "fatalities." Toxic epidermal necrolysis was listed as a side effect in the package insert. After Ms. Bartlett was suffering from toxic epidermal necrolysis, the FDA did a comprehensive study and recommended that the product label include more explicit warnings about toxic epidermal necrolysis.

Ms. Bartlett sued Mutual in New Hampshire state court, and Mutual removed the case to federal court. Ms. Bartlett initially asserted both failure-to-warn and design-defect claims, but the District Court dismissed her failure-to-warn claim based on her doctor's "admi[ssion] that he had not read the box label or insert."

After a two-week trial on a design-defect claim, a jury found Mutual liable and awarded Ms. Bartlett over $21 million in damages. The Court of Appeals affirmed, and Mutual appealed. The U.S. Supreme Court granted *certiorari*.

DECISION: The court held that the federal law was clear that a generic manufacturer could not change the label, and it was the purpose of the law to provide a cheap way to get the drugs out there once the patent was expired. Generic manufacturers were to just use the same warnings provided by the brand name pharmaceutical company, without variation. Until there was a change in the label under FDA processes and standards, the generic manufacturer could not make additions or changes, and federal law preempted state laws on product liability recovery. [***Mutual Pharmaceutical Co., Inc. v. Bartlett***, 133 S. Ct. 2466 (2013)]

---

[3] U.S. Const., Art VI, cl 2 *PLIVA, Inc. v. Mensing*, 131 S. Ct. 2567 (2013).

Silence of Congress

In some situations, the silence of Congress in failing to cover a particular subject area indicates that Congress does not want any law on the matter. However, when national uniformity is essential, the silence of Congress generally means that the subject has been preempted for practical reasons by Congress and that no state law on the subject may be adopted.

Effect of Federal Deregulation

The fact that the federal government removes the regulations from a regulated industry does not automatically give the states the power to regulate that industry. If under the silence-of-Congress doctrine the states cannot regulate, they are still barred from regulating after deregulation. **For Example,** deregulation of banks in the 1980s did not mean that the states could step in and regulate those banks.[4]

4-3 Interpreting and Amending the Constitution

The Constitution as it is interpreted today has changed greatly from the Constitution as originally written. The change has been brought about by interpretation, amendment, and practice.

4-3a Conflicting Theories

Shortly after the Constitution was adopted, conflict arose over whether it was to be interpreted strictly, so as to give the federal government the least power possible, or broadly, so as to give the federal government the greatest power that the words would permit. These two views may be called the *bedrock view* and the *living-document view*, respectively.

bedrock view—a strict constructionist interpretation of a constitution.

living-document view—the term used when a constitution is interpreted according to changes in conditions.

In the **bedrock view,** or strict constructionist or originalist view, the purpose of a constitution is to state certain fundamental principles for all time. In the **living-document view,** a constitution is merely a statement of goals and objectives and is intended to grow and change with time.

Whether the Constitution is to be liberally interpreted under the living-document view or narrowly interpreted under the bedrock view has a direct effect on the Constitution. For the last century, the Supreme Court has followed the living-document view. This view has resulted in strengthening the power of the federal government, permitting the rise of administrative agencies, and expanding the protection of human rights.

One view is not selected to the exclusion of the other. As contradictory as these two views sound, the Constitution remains durable. We do not want a set of New Year's resolutions that will soon be forgotten. At the same time, we know that the world changes, and, therefore, we do not want a constitution that will hold us tied in a straitjacket of the past.

In terms of social forces that make the law, we are torn between our desire for stability and our desire for flexibility. We want a constitution that is stable. At the same time, we want one that is flexible.

---

[4]For a discussion of preemption of state regulation of airline advertising when federal regulation of air travel is so pervasive, see *New York v. Trans World Airlines,* 556 N.Y.S.2d 803 (1990) and *Pan American World Airways, Inc. v. Abrams,* 764 F. Supp. 864 (S.D.N.Y. 1991). See also footnote 3 for another case on pharmaceutical preemption and *People ex rel. Cuomo v. Greenberg,* 95 A.D.3d 474, 946 N.Y.S.2d 1 (N.Y.A.D. 2012).

FIGURE 4-2 Amending the U.S. Constitution

*Article V of the U.S. Constitution specifies the procedure for adopting amendments.

4-3b Amending the Constitution

The Constitution has been amended in three ways: (1) expressly, (2) by interpretation, and (3) by practice. Figure 4-2 illustrates these three methods of amendment.

Constitutional Method of Amending

Article V of the Constitution gives the procedure to be followed for amending the Constitution. Relatively few changes have been made to the Constitution by this formal process, although thousands of proposals have been made. Since the time of its adoption, there have been only 27 amendments to the Constitution.[5]

Amendment by Judicial Interpretation

The U.S. Supreme Court has made the greatest changes to the written Constitution by interpreting it. Generally, interpretation is used to apply the Constitution to a new situation that could not have been foreseen when the written Constitution was adopted.

Amendment by Practice

In practice, the letter of the Constitution is not always followed. Departure from the written Constitution began as early as 1793 when George Washington refused to make treaties as required by the Constitution, by and with the consent of the Senate. Washington began the practice of the president's negotiating a treaty with a foreign country and then submitting it to the Senate for approval. This practice has been followed since that time. Similarly, the electoral college was originally intended to exercise independent judgment in selecting the president, but it now automatically elects the official candidate of the party that elected the majority of the members of the electoral college.

4-3c The Living Constitution

The living Constitution has the following characteristics.

Strong Government

One of the characteristics of the new Constitution is strong government. Business enterprises are highly regulated and the economy is controlled through monetary policy.

---

[5] Gregory Watson, a University of Texas at Austin student who was doing research for a paper for a class on the U.S. Constitution, ran across a 1789 proposed amendment to the Constitution that had never been ratified by the states. Watson wrote a paper and got a "C" but through a successful letter-writing campaign was able to get the 27th Amendment passed. The amendment reads, "No law, varying the compensation for the services of the Senators and Representatives, shall take effect, until an election of Representatives shall have intervened."

Strong President

Instead of being merely an officer who carries out the laws, the president has become the political leader of a party, exerting strong influence on the lawmaking process.

Eclipse of the States

Under constitutional interpretations, all levels of government have powers that they never possessed before, but the center of gravity has shifted from the states to the nation. When the Constitution was adopted in 1789, the federal government was to have only the very limited powers specified in Article I, Section 8, of the Constitution. Whatever regulation of business was permissible was to be imposed by the states. Today, the great bulk of the regulation of business is adopted by the federal government through Congress or its administrative agencies. As the U.S. economy moved from the local community stage to the nationwide and then international stages, individual states could no longer provide effective regulation of business. Regulation migrated to the central government.

Administrative Agencies

These units of government were virtually unheard of in 1789, and the Constitution made no mention of them. The vast powers of the new Constitution are exercised to a very large degree by administrative agencies. They are in effect a fourth branch of the government, not provided for in the written Constitution. More importantly, the administrative agencies are the ones that come in contact with the majority of businesspersons and citizens.

Agencies have had a significant amount of power delegated to them. The members and heads of the agencies, boards, or commissions are not elected by the voters (see Chapter 6). They are appointed by the president and, at certain levels of appointment in the agency, must be approved by Congress.

4-4 Federal Powers

The federal government possesses powers necessary to administer matters of national concern.

4-4a The Power to Regulate Commerce

commerce clause–that section of the U.S. Constitution allocating business regulation between federal and state governments.

The desire to protect commerce from restrictions and barriers set up by the individual states was a prime factor leading to the adoption of the Constitution of 1789. To protect commerce, Congress was given Article I, Section 8, Clause 3—now known as the **commerce clause**—the power "to regulate commerce with foreign nations, and among the several states, and with the Indian tribes."[6]

Until 1937, the Supreme Court held that this provision gave Congress the power to control or regulate only that commerce crossing a state line, such as an interstate railway train or an interstate telegraph message.

The Commerce Power Becomes a General Welfare Power

In 1937, the Supreme Court began expanding the concept of interstate commerce. By 1946, the power to regulate interstate commerce had become very broad. By that year, the power had expanded to the point that it gave authority to Congress to adopt regulatory laws that were "as broad as the economic needs of the nation."[7] By virtue of this broad interpretation, Congress can regulate manufacturing, agriculture, mining, stock

[6] U.S. Const., Art 1, §8, cl 1. To read more of the U.S. Constitution, refer to Appendix 2, or go to **http://www.constitution.org** and click on "Founding Documents."
[7] *American Power & Light Co. v. Securities and Exchange Commission,* 329 U.S. 90 (1946).

exchanges, insurance, loan sharking, monopolies, and conspiracies in restraint of trade. The far reach of the interstate commerce power is seen in the Freedom of Access to Clinic Entrances Act,[8] which prohibits obstruction of entrances to clinics, as well as in the commerce clause challenges to the Affordable Health Care Act, also known as Obama Care.[9]

The case that was the beginning point in the transition of the commerce clause was *NLRB v. Jones & Laughlin Steel*, 301 U.S. 1 (1937). The "affectation" doctrine expanded the authority of the federal government under the commerce clause. At that time, the Court concluded, "If it is interstate commerce that feels the pinch, it does not matter how local the squeeze."

The Commerce Clause Today

Today, judicial review of the commerce clause typically finds some connection between the legislation and congressional authority. However, the U.S. Supreme Court has found some areas Congress may not regulate and has placed some limitations on the commerce clause. These constraints on the commerce clause focus on the nature of the underlying activity being regulated. So long as the federal regulation relates to economic/commercial activity, it is constitutional. If, however, the underlying activity is not economic and only may have an economic impact, the Supreme Court has imposed restrictions on congressional authority under the commerce clause. **For Example,** in *U.S. v. Morrison*, 529 U.S. 598 (2000), the Supreme Court held that the Violence Against Women Act was unconstitutional because the underlying activity being regulated was violence, an activity that was not economic. Regulation of economic activity is required in order to survive constitutional scrutiny under the commerce clause.

CASE SUMMARY

Mandating Health Insurance under the Commerce Clause

FACTS: Congress passed the Patient Protection and Affordable Care Act (also known as Obama Care) in order to increase the number of Americans covered by health insurance and decrease the cost of health care. One key provision in the law is the individual mandate, which requires most Americans to maintain "minimum essential" health insurance coverage. Attorneys general from several states, along with businesses, challenged this requirement (and other provisions of the law) as being unconstitutional under the commerce clause. From a series of federal court decisions below, some finding the law constitutional and others not, the affected parties appealed and the Supreme Court granted *certiorari*. Their cases were consolidated for the court's review.

DECISION: The court faced a new commerce clause issue of whether the federal government could require citizens to purchase a good or service because the lack of health insurance affected commerce. In the 5-4 decision, the court concluded, "The individual mandate, however, does not regulate existing commercial activity. It instead compels individuals to *become* active in commerce by purchasing a product, on the ground that their failure to do so affects interstate commerce. Construing the Commerce Clause to permit Congress to regulate individuals precisely *because* they are doing nothing would open a new and potentially vast domain to congressional authority. Every day individuals do not do an infinite number of things. In some cases they decide not to do something; in others they simply fail to do it. Allowing Congress to justify federal regulation by pointing to the effect of inaction on commerce would bring countless decisions an individual could *potentially* make within the scope of federal regulation, and—under the Government's theory—empower Congress to make those decisions for him." [**National Federation of Independent Business v. Sebelius,** 132 S. Ct. 2566 (2012)] (**Note: The law was still upheld.**)

---

[8] 18 U.S.C. §248.
[9] *United States v. Wilson*, 73 F.3d 675 (7th Cir. 1995), *cert. denied*, 519 U.S. 806 (1996), *Florida ex rel. National Federation of Independent Business v. Sebelius*, 132 S. Ct. 2566 (2012).

The Commerce Power as a Limitation on States

The federal power to regulate commerce not only gives Congress the power to act but also prevents states from acting in any way that interferes with federal regulation or burdens interstate commerce. **For Example,** if the federal government establishes safety device regulations for interstate carriers, a state cannot require different devices.

CASE SUMMARY

Minors in Maine and a Major Commerce Clause Decision

FACTS: Maine passed a law that prohibited anyone other than a Maine-licensed tobacco retailer from accepting an order for delivery of tobacco. The law required the retailer to arrange for delivery with a special receipt showing that someone over the age of 18 had received and signed for the tobacco products delivered. Out-of-state shippers and tobacco sellers challenged the law as one that favored Maine tobacco retailers. The state of Maine argued that its law was passed to prevent the public health hazard of minors becoming addicted to tobacco. The federal district court

granted summary judgment for the shippers, and the court of appeals affirmed. The state of Maine appealed.

DECISION: In a 9 to 0 decision, the Court held that the Maine law may have been passed with health benefits in mind, but it clearly gave Maine businesses an economic benefit. In addition, other states had managed to fight teen smoking using programs other than discrimination between in-state and out-of-state tobacco retailers. [*Rowe v. New Hampshire Motor Transport Association,* 552 U.S. 364 (2008)]

States may not use their tax power for the purpose of discriminating against interstate commerce. **For Example,** a state cannot impose a higher tax on goods imported from another state than it imposes on the same kind of goods produced in its own territory.

State regulations designed to advance local interests may conflict with the commerce clause. Such regulations are invalid. For example, suppose a state has a health concern about having milk properly processed. One way to address the concern is to require all milk to be processed in-state. Such a regulation clearly favors that state's businesses and imposes a great burden on out-of-state milk producers. Such a regulation would be an unconstitutional exercise of state power because the state could simply require all milk sellers to be licensed. Licensing would allow the state to check the milk-processing procedures of all firms and accomplish the safety goal without imposing such a burden on out-of-state firms.[10] For example, in *Granholm v. Heald,* 544 U.S. 460 (2005), both New York and Michigan statutes prohibited out-of-state wine producers from selling their wines directly to consumers there. In-state wineries could sell directly to consumers. The impact of the prohibition on the out-of-state wine producers was that they were required to pay wholesaler fees and thus could not compete with in-state wine producers on direct-to-consumer sales.

The court held that state laws violated the commerce clause because they treated in-state and out-of-state economic interests differently with the result being that one benefits and the other is burdened. The mere fact that a wine producer is not a resident of the state should not foreclose access to markets there.[11]

---

[10] *Minnesota v. Clover Leaf Creamery,* 449 U.S. 456 (1981).
[11] *Missouri v. Harris,* 58 F. Supp. 3d 1059 (E.D. Cal. 2014) – in this case a federal judge dismissed a complaint brought by egg farmers in six states who are prohibited from selling their eggs in California unless they meet the nonconfinement standards of California's Proposition 2, which requires that chickens be able to lie down, stand up, and fully extend their limbs.

4-4b The Financial Powers

The financial powers of the federal government include the powers to tax and to borrow, spend, and coin money.

The Taxing Power

The federal Constitution provides that "Congress shall have power to lay and collect taxes, duties, imposts and excises, to pay the debts and provide for the common defence and general welfare of the United States."[12] Subject to the express and implied limitations arising from the Constitution, the states may impose such taxes as they desire and as their own individual constitutions and statutes permit. In addition to express constitutional limitations, both national and local taxes are subject to the unwritten limitation that they be imposed for a public purpose. Taxes must also be apportioned. A business cannot be taxed for all of its revenues in all 50 states. There must be apportionment of taxes, and there must be sufficient connection with the state.[13] **For Example,** in *Quill v. North Dakota,* 504 U.S. 298 (1992), Quill, an office equipment and supplies seller, did business in North Dakota through catalogs and flyers, advertisements in national periodicals, and telephone calls. Quill delivered all of its merchandise to its North Dakota customers by mail or common carriers from out-of-state locations. North Dakota imposed sales tax requirements on Quill. The U.S. Supreme Court held that the exercise of the taxing authority placed an undue burden on commerce and retailers such as Quill and that the standard of a company's presence in the state through property or personnel was required to impose taxes.

CASE SUMMARY

Booking Sales Tax Revenue Against BarnesandNoble.com

FACTS: The facts of this case are not in dispute. Barnesandnoble.com LLC (Bn.com) is a Delaware corporation that sells books, movies, and other media over the Internet. In 2006, the New Mexico Taxation and Revenue Department (the Department) assessed gross receipts tax against bn.com on its sales to New Mexico residents during a period from January 1998 through July 2005. Bn.com protested the assessment, and a hearing officer granted summary judgment to bn.com, finding that it lacked a substantial nexus with the state of New Mexico, and, therefore, it could not constitutionally be required to pay the tax. The Department appealed, and the Court of Appeals held that bn.com had a substantial nexus with the state. bn.com appealed.

DECISION: The court found the following interconnected activities of the stores (Booksellers): (1) Booksellers' promotion of bn.com through sales of gift cards redeemable at bn.com and bearing bn.com's name, (2) Booksellers' policy of sharing customers' e-mail addresses with bn.com, (3) Booksellers' implicit endorsement of bn.com through the companies' shared loyalty program and Booksellers' return policy, and (4) Booksellers' in-state use of Barnes & Noble logos and trademarks, which bn.com also used. Because Booksellers' activities in New Mexico were significantly associated with bn.com's ability to establish and maintain a market here, bn.com had a substantial nexus with the state of New Mexico. Therefore, New Mexico may collect gross receipts tax on bn.com's sales in the state without offending the commerce clause of the United States Constitution. Affirmed and remanded. [*New Mexico Taxation and Revenue Department v. BarnesandNoble.com LLC,* **303 P.3d 824 (N.M. 2014)**]

---

[12] U.S. Const., Art 1, §8, cl 1. To read more of the U.S. Constitution, refer to Appendix 2, or go to **http://www.constitution.org** and click on "Founding Documents."

[13] *Polar Tankers, Inc. v. City of Valdez, Alaska,* 557 U.S. 1 (2009).

E-COMMERCE & CYBERLAW

Internet and Interstate

Collection of sales tax from Internet stores has been a stickler of an issue for businesses, state revenue officials, and the U.S. Supreme Court. All three were grappling with how to collect, what to collect, and whether anybody had any authority to collect. Internet sales represent a large, untapped source of revenue. A study from the Center for Business and Economic Research at the University of Tennessee estimated the lost tax revenue from untaxed Internet sales as $30 billion in 2011.

The merchants involved fell into different legal groups in terms of their theories on whether tax was owed and whether they should just pay it, with or without the states having the authority to tax:

1. Those stores with physical presences in states (Wal-Mart and J.C. Penney) that just collected sales tax as if they were collecting it in a store in that state where the Internet purchaser was located

2. Those stores without a physical presence (Amazon) that did collect taxes, particularly in those states known for taking a hard-line approach

3. Those stores without a physical presence that do not collect taxes and maintain that it is unconstitutional to do so

4. Those stores with or without a physical presence that have collected taxes but held them until everyone could figure out the legal status of the companies

What are the constitutional issues in this taxation question?

Amazon has negotiated with most states on sales tax issues and you can notice as a buyer that you pay some form of tax on your Amazon purchases now.

Source: Stu Woo, "Amazon Battles States Over Sales Tax," *Wall Street Journal*, August 3, 2011, p. A1.

The Spending Power

The federal government may use tax money and borrowed money "to pay the debts and provide for the common defence and general welfare of the United States."[14]

4-5 Constitutional Limitations on Government

The constitutional limitations discussed in the following sections afford protections of rights for both persons and businesses.

4-5a Due Process

The power of government is limited by both the Fifth and Fourteenth Amendments to the Constitution. Those amendments, respectively, prohibit the national government and state governments from depriving any person "of life, liberty, or property without due process of law."[15]

When Due Process Rights Arise

due process clause—a guarantee of protection against the loss of property or rights without the chance to be heard.

As a result of liberal interpretation of the Constitution, the **due process clause** now provides a guarantee of protection against the loss of property or rights without the chance to be heard. These amendments also guarantee that all citizens are given the same protections. **For Example,** the Supreme Court has extended the due process clause to protect

[14] U.S. Const., Art 1, §8, cl 1. To read more of the U.S. Constitution, refer to Appendix 2, or go to **http://www.constitution.org** and click on "Founding Documents."

[15] U.S. Const., Art 1, §8, cl 1. To read more of the U.S. Constitution, refer to Appendix 2, or go to **http://www.constitution.org** and click on "Founding Documents."

the record or standing of a student.[16] A student cannot lose credit in a course or be suspended or expelled without some form of a hearing.

Because there are so many areas in which due process rights exist and require a chance to be heard, speeding up due process has resulted in the creation of **quasi-judicial proceedings.** In these types of proceedings, the parties need not go through the complex, lengthy, and formal procedures of a trial (described in Chapter 2). Rather, these proceedings have a hearing officer or administrative law judge (see Chapter 6) who conducts an informal hearing in which the rules of evidence and procedure are relaxed.

For Example, a student taking a grade grievance beyond a faculty member's decision will generally have his case heard by a panel of faculty and students as established by college or university rules. An employer appealing its unemployment tax rate will have the appeal heard by an administrative law judge.

quasi-judicial proceedings–forms of hearings in which the rules of evidence and procedure are more relaxed but each side still has a chance to be heard.

What Constitutes Due Process?

Due process does not require a trial on every issue of rights. Shortcut procedures, such as grade grievance panels, have resulted as a compromise for providing the right to be heard along with a legitimate desire to be expeditious in resolving these issues. In *Horne v. U.S. Department of Agriculture*, 132 S. Ct. 2566 (2015), raisin farmers challenged the taking of their raisin crops by the Department of Agriculture in its efforts to stabilize the raisin market. The farmers' challenge was based on their lack of a hearing for the taking as well as compensation for the loss of their raisin crops and the imposition of penalties if they sold the raisins prohibited by the Department of Agriculture. The court held that the Fifth Amendment requires that the government pay just compensation when it takes personal property, just as when it takes real property. The government cannot make raisin growers relinquish their raisins without just compensation.

4-5b Equal Protection of the Law

The Constitution prohibits the states and the national government from denying any person the equal protection of the law.[17] This guarantee prohibits a government from treating one person differently from another when there is no reasonable ground for classifying them differently.

For Example, laws that make distinctions in the regulation of business, the right to work, and the right to use or enjoy property on the basis of race, national origin, or religion are invalid. Also invalid are laws that impose restrictions on some, but not all, persons without any justification for the distinction.[18] **For Example,** a state statute taxing out-of-state insurance companies at a higher rate than in-state insurance companies violates the equal protection clause.[19]

4-5c Privileges and Immunities

The U.S. Constitution declares that "the citizens of each state shall be entitled to all privileges and immunities of citizens in the several states."[20] The so-called **privileges and immunities clause** means that a person going into another state is entitled to make

privileges and immunities clause–a clause that entitles a person going into another state to make contracts, own property, and engage in business to the same extent as citizens of that state.

---

[16] That is, a student cannot be expelled without a chance to have his or her side of the story reviewed.

[17] U.S. Constitution, Fourteenth Amendment as to the states; modern interpretation of due process clause of the Fifth Amendment as to national government. Congress adopted the Civil Rights Act to implement the concept of equal protection.

[18] *Associated Industries of Missouri v. Lohman,* 511 U.S. 641 (1994).

[19] *Metropolitan Life Ins. Co. v. Ward,* 470 U.S. 869 (1985). But see a differing view on distinctive treatment of temporary bridge contractors vs. permanent bridge contractors, *Mabey Bridge & Shore, Inc. v. Schoch,* 666 F.3d 862 (3rd Cir. 2012).

[20] U.S. Const., Art 1, §8, cl 1. To read more of the U.S. Constitution, refer to Appendix 2, or go to **http://www.constitution.org** and click on "Founding Documents."

contracts, own property, and engage in business to the same extent as the citizens of that state. **For Example,** a state cannot bar someone who comes from another state from engaging in local business or from obtaining a hunting or fishing license merely because the person is not a resident of that state.

4-5d Protection of the Person

The Constitution has no general provision declaring that the government shall not impair rights of persons. The Constitution does not mention the phrase *unalienable right* that was part of the Declaration of Independence.[21] However, the Bill of Rights, the first 10 amendments to the Constitution, does provide protections for freedom of speech, jury trials, and freedom of religion and association.[22] The Bill of Rights provides for the due process protections discussed earlier as well as those that prohibit unlawful searches and seizures. The Second Amendment provides for the right to keep and bear arms, an issue that has resulted in some conflicting decisions that the U.S. Supreme Court has begun to address.[23]

During the last six decades, the Supreme Court has been interpreting the rights in these amendments and has been finding constitutional protection for a wide array of rights of the person that are not expressly protected by the Constitution. **For Example,** judicial interpretations have concluded that the Constitution provides for the right of privacy, the rights related to marriage,[24] protection from unreasonable zoning, protection of parental control, protection from discrimination because of poverty, and protection from gender discrimination.[25]

4-5e The Bill of Rights and Businesses as Persons

The Bill of Rights provides protections for individuals and also for corporations. **For Example,** the Fourth Amendment (see Chapter 7) provides protections against unreasonable searches. Individuals enjoy that protection in their homes, and corporations enjoy that protection with their files, offices, and business records. Businesses also enjoy freedom of speech protections under the First Amendment. The First Amendment provides that "Congress shall make no law … abridging the freedom of speech …"[26]

The U.S. Supreme Court has clarified the free speech rights of business through classification of the types of business speech. One form of business or commercial speech is advertising. This form of speech in which businesses tout their products is subject to regulation and restriction on form, content, and placement, and such regulation has been deemed constitutional. (See Chapters 24 and 32 for more information on the regulation of advertising.) However, there are other forms of commercial speech. Businesses do have the right to participate in political processes, such as creating

---

[21] The term *unalienable right* is employed in reference to natural right, fundamental right, or basic right. Apart from the question of scope of coverage, the adjective *unalienable* emphasizes the fact that the people still possess the right rather than having surrendered or subordinated it to the will of society. The word *alien* is the term of the old common law for transferring title or ownership. Today, we would say *transfer* and, instead of saying *unalienable* rights, would say *nontransferable* rights. Unalienable rights of the people were therefore rights that the people not only possessed but also could not give up even if they wanted to. Thus, these rights are still owned by everyone. It is important to note that the Declaration of Independence actually uses the word *unalienable* when describing the rights eventually placed in the Constitution as Amendments I–X, the Bill of Rights, not *inalienable*.

[22] *North Coast Women's Care Medical Group, Inc. v. San Diego County Superior Court,* 189 P.3d 959 (Ca. 2008).

[23] *District of Columbia v. Heller,* 554 U.S. 570 (2008).

[24] *U.S. v. Windsor,* 133 S. Ct. 2675 (2013).

[25] In some cases, the courts have given the due process and equal protection clauses a liberal interpretation in order to find a protection of the person; *Fisher v. University of Texas at Austin,* 133 S. Ct. 2411 (2013). *Certiorari* granted following a remand. 2015 WL 629286 (2015).

[26] For more on commercial speech, see Greater New Orleans Broadcasting Association, Inc., v. U.S., 527 U.S. 173 (1999) and *U.S. v. Philip Morris USA Inc.,* 566 F.3d 1095 (D.C. Cir. 2009). To read the full language of the First Amendment, go to Appendix 2, or to **http://www.constitution.org** and click on "Founding Documents."

political action committees and supporting or opposing ballot initiatives. Businesses often take positions and launch campaigns on ballot initiatives that will affect the taxes they will be required to pay. The courts are often balancing the power of corporate political speech, regulation of ads, and the right of corporations as citizens to speak.

CASE SUMMARY

The Case That Caused a Dust-Up between the President and a Justice

FACTS: In January 2008, Citizens United released a film entitled *Hillary: The Movie (Hillary)*, a 90-minute documentary about then-senator Hillary Clinton, who was a candidate in the Democratic Party's 2008 presidential primary elections. Most of the commentators in the film were quite critical of Senator Clinton. *Hillary* was released in theaters and on DVD, but Citizens United wanted to increase distribution by making it available through video-on-demand.

Citizens United produced two 10-second ads and one 30-second ad for *Hillary*. Each ad included a short, pejorative statement about Senator Clinton, followed by the name of the movie and the movie's Web site address. Citizens United wanted to run the advertisements on broadcast and cable television. The Federal Election Commission (FEC) wanted to stop Citizens United from running the ads and Citizens United brought suit, seeking a preliminary injunction against

the FEC. The District Court denied Citizens United a preliminary injunction and granted the FEC summary judgment. Citizens United requested and was granted *certiorari*.

DECISION: The court held that the restrictions on running ads were unconstitutional as a prior restraint on speech as well as discrimination between and among speakers. The court held that requirements on disclosure of funding for ads was constitutional, an alternative to a ban on speech that was reasonable and allowed citizens to make their own determinations about the quality/bias of the speech (ads). President Obama spoke harshly of the decision in his State of the Union address in 2011, and Justice Samuel Alito mouthed, "Not true," in response to the president's remarks. [***Citizens United v. Federal Election Commission,*** **558 U.S. 310 (2010)**]

THINKING THINGS THROUGH

Freedom of Speech and Our Headlights

Fed up with the warning signals and being outnumbered on the highways by drivers looking out for one another, police officers and state troopers began issuing tickets to those who send signals and warnings to drivers so that they can slow down and avoid being caught going above the speed limit. On November 17, 2012, a police officer pulled Michael Elli over and issued a citation for "[f]lashing lights on certain vehicles prohibited; warning of RADAR ahead."

In the case, *Elli v. City of Ellisville,* No. 4:13-CV-711 HEA (E.D. Mo. 2014), Mr. Elli was advised by the municipal judge that the standard punishment imposed in the City of Ellisville for using headlamps to communicate the presence of a speed

trap is a $1,000 fine. Mr. Elli told the judge that he wanted to plead not guilty because he did not believe flashing headlamps violated §375.100 of the Ellisville city code. The judge became agitated and asked Mr. Elli if he had ever heard of "obstruction of justice." Mr. Elli then entered a plea of not guilty, and he was ordered to return to court on February 21, 2013. However, the prosecution terminated the case by dismissing the charge prior to the hearing date. Mr. Elli, with the help of the ACLU, filed a civil rights action in federal court.

Have Mr. Elli's rights been violated? Is flashing your headlights a form of speech? What do you think the courts decided?

Make the Connection

Summary

The U.S. Constitution created the structure of our national government and gave it certain powers. It also placed limitations on those powers. It created a federal system with a tripartite division of government and a bicameral national legislature.

The national government possesses some governmental powers exclusively while both the states and the federal government share other powers. In areas of conflict, federal law is supreme.

The U.S. Constitution is not a detailed document. It takes its meaning from the way it is interpreted. In recent years, liberal interpretation has expanded the powers of the federal government. Among the powers of the federal government that directly affect business are the power to regulate commerce; the power to tax and to borrow, spend, and coin money; and the power to own and operate businesses.

Among the limitations on government that are most important to business are the requirements of due process and the requirement of equal protection of the law. In addition, government is limited by the rights given to individuals such as freedom of speech, freedom of religion, and equal protection. The equal protection concept of the U.S. Constitution prohibits both the federal government and the state governments from treating one person differently from another unless there is a legitimate reason for doing so and unless the basis of classification is reasonable.

Learning Outcomes

After studying this chapter, you should be able to clearly explain:

4-1 The U.S. Constitution and the Federal System

LO.1 Describe the U.S. Constitution and the federal system
  See the discussion of the tripartite (three-part) government, page 55.

4-2 The U.S. Constitution and the States

LO.2 Explain the relationship between the U.S. Constitution and the states
  See the discussion of the federal system, page 55.
  See Figure 4-1 for an illustration of the delegation of powers, page 56.

4-3 Interpreting and Amending the Constitution

LO.3 Discuss interpreting and amending the Constitution
  See the discussion of the bedrock and living-document views, page 58.

4-4 Federal Powers

LO.4 List and describe the significant federal powers
  See the *Bartlett* case, page 57.
  See the discussion of the commerce power. See the *Sebelius* case, page 61.
  See the discussion of the taxing power and the *Barnes & Noble* case, page 63.

4-5 Constitutional Limitations on Government

LO.5 Discuss constitutional limitations on governmental power
  See the discussion of the Bill of Rights, page 66.
  See the *Citizens United* case to understand First Amendment issues, page 67.
  See the discussion of the Fourth Amendment, page 66.
  See the discussion of due process, pages 64–65.
  See the *For Example* discussion of a student taking a grade grievance beyond a faculty member's decision, page 65.

Key Terms

bedrock view
bicameral
commerce clause
constitution
delegated powers
due process clause

executive branch
ex post facto laws
federal system
judicial branch
legislative branch
living-document view

police power
preemption
privileges and immunities clause
quasi-judicial proceedings
shared powers
tripartite

Questions and Case Problems

1. Federal law requires most interstate truckers to obtain a permit that reflects compliance with certain federal requirements. The 1965 version of the law authorized states to require proof that a truck operator had such a permit. By 1991, 39 states had demanded such proof, requiring a $10 per truck registration fee and giving each trucker a stamp to affix to a multistate "bingo card" carried in the vehicle. Finding this scheme inefficient and burdensome, Congress created the current Single State Registration System (SSRS), which allows a trucking company to fill out one set of forms in one state, thereby registering in every participating state through which its trucks travel.

   A subsection of Michigan's Motor Carrier Act imposes on truck companies operating in interstate commerce an annual fee of $100 for each self-propelled motor vehicle operated by or on behalf of the motor carrier. The American Truckers Association (ATA) and others challenged the $100 fee as preempted by the extensive federal regulation of interstate trucking and trucking companies. The ATA and others appealed to the U.S. Supreme Court. What should the U.S. Supreme Court do? Be sure to discuss what portion of the Constitution applies to this issue. [*American Trucking Associations, Inc. v. Michigan Public Service Com'n,* 545 U.S. 429]

2. J.C. Penney, a retail merchandiser, has its principal place of business in Plano, Texas. It operates retail stores in all 50 states, including 10 stores in Massachusetts, and a direct mail catalog business. The catalogs illustrated merchandise available for purchase by mail order. The planning, artwork, design, and layout for these catalogs were completed and paid for outside of Massachusetts, primarily in Texas, and Penney contracted with independent printing companies located outside Massachusetts to produce the catalogs. The three major catalogs were generally printed in Indiana, while the specialty catalogs were printed in South Carolina and Wisconsin. Penney supplied the printers with paper, shipping wrappers, and address labels for the catalogs; the printers supplied the ink, binding materials, and labor. None of these materials was purchased in Massachusetts. Printed catalogs, with address labels and postage affixed, were transported by a common carrier from the printer to a U.S. Postal Service office located outside Massachusetts, where they were sent to Massachusetts addressees via third- or fourth-class mail. Any undeliverable catalogs were returned to Penney's distribution center in Connecticut.

   Purchases of catalog merchandise were made by telephoning or returning an order form to Penney at a location outside Massachusetts, and the merchandise was shipped to customers from a Connecticut distribution center. The Massachusetts Department of Revenue audited Penney in 1995 and assessed a use tax, penalty, and interest on the catalogs that had been shipped into Massachusetts. The position of the department was that there was a tax due of $314,674.62 on the catalogs that were used by Penney's Massachusetts customers. Penney said such a tax was unconstitutional in that it had no control or contact with the catalogs in the state. Can the state impose the tax? Why or why not? [*Commissioner of Revenue v. J.C. Penney Co., Inc.,* 730 N.E.2d 266 (Mass)]

3. Alfonso Lopez, Jr., a 12th-grade student at Edison High School in San Antonio, Texas, went to school carrying a concealed .38-caliber handgun and five bullets. School officials, acting on an anonymous tip, confronted Lopez. Lopez admitted that he had the gun. He was arrested and charged with violation of federal law, the Gun-Free School Zones Act of 1990. Lopez moved to dismiss his indictment on the grounds that the provision of the Gun-Free School Zones Act with which he was charged was unconstitutional in that it was beyond the power of Congress to legislate controls over public schools. The district court found the statute to be a constitutional exercise of congressional authority.

   Lopez was found guilty and sentenced to two years in prison. He appealed and challenged his conviction on the basis of the commerce clause. The Court of Appeals agreed with Lopez, found the Gun-Free School Zones Act an unconstitutional exercise of congressional authority, and reversed the conviction. The U.S. Attorney appealed. Who should win at the U.S. Supreme Court and why? [*United States v. Lopez,* 514 U.S. 549]

4. The University of Wisconsin requires all of its students to pay, as part of their tuition, a student activity fee. Those fees are used to support campus clubs and activities. Some students who objected to

the philosophies and activities of some of the student clubs filed suit to have the fees halted. What constitutional basis do you think they could use for the suit? [*Board of Regents of Wisconsin System v. Southworth,* 529 U.S. 217]

5. The Crafts' home was supplied with gas by the city gas company. Because of some misunderstanding, the gas company believed that the Crafts were delinquent in paying their gas bill. The gas company had an informal complaint procedure for discussing such matters, but the Crafts had never been informed that such a procedure was available. The gas company notified the Crafts that they were delinquent and that the company was shutting off the gas. The Crafts brought an action to enjoin the gas company from doing so on the theory that a termination without any hearing was a denial of due process. The lower courts held that the interest of the Crafts in receiving gas was not a property interest protected by the due process clause and that the procedures the gas company followed satisfied the requirements of due process. The Crafts appealed. Were they correct in contending that they had been denied due process of law? Why or why not? [*Memphis Light, Gas and Water Division v. Craft,* 436 U.S. 1]

6. In 2002, the Williamson family, riding in their 1993 Mazda minivan, was struck head-on by another vehicle. Thanh Williamson was sitting in a rear aisle seat, wearing a lap belt; she died in the accident. Delbert and Alexa Williamson were wearing lap-and-shoulder belts; they survived. Thanh's estate brought suit in a California state court to recover from Mazda for her wrongful death. The basis of the suit was that Mazda should have installed lap-and-shoulder belts on all seats, including the rear aisle seats, and that Thanh died because Mazda equipped her seat with only a lap belt instead. Federal safety requirements do not require lap-and-shoulder belts except for seats located next to doors and windows. Middle seats (aisle) can have a lap belt only. Mazda asked for a dismissal on the grounds that allowing Thanh's estate to recover would contradict federal law and that federal law preempts state tort laws on product liability. The trial court dismissed the suit as preempted by federal law, and the Court of Appeal affirmed. The U.S. Supreme Court granted *certiorari.* What should the court decide and why? [*Williamson v. Mazda Motor of America, Inc.,* 562 U.S. 323]

7. Montana imposed a severance tax on every ton of coal mined within the state. The tax varied depending on the value of the coal and the cost of production. It could be as high as 30 percent of the price at which the coal was sold. Montana mine operators and some out-of-state customers claimed that this tax was unconstitutional as an improper burden on interstate commerce. Decide. [*Commonwealth Edison Co. v. Montana,* 453 U.S. 609]

8. Ollie's Barbecue is a family-owned restaurant in Birmingham, Alabama, specializing in barbecued meats and homemade pies, with a seating capacity of 220 customers. It is located on a state highway 11 blocks from an interstate highway and a somewhat greater distance from railroad and bus stations. The restaurant caters to a family and white-collar trade, with a take-out service for "Negroes." (Note: This term is used by the Court in its opinion in the case.) In the 12 months preceding the passage of the Civil Rights Act, the restaurant purchased locally approximately $150,000 worth of food, $69,683 or 46 percent of which was meat that it bought from a local supplier who had procured it from outside the state. Ollie's has refused to serve Negroes in its dining accommodations since opening in 1927, and since July 2, 1964, it has been operating in violation of the Civil Rights Act. A lower court concluded that if it were required to serve Negroes, it would lose a substantial amount of business. The lower court found that the Civil Rights Act did not apply because Ollie's was not involved in "interstate commerce." Will the commerce clause permit application of the Civil Rights Act to Ollie's? [*Katzenbach v. McClung,* 379 U.S. 294]

9. Ellis was employed by the city of Lakewood. By the terms of his contract, he could be discharged only for cause. After working for six years, he was told that he was going to be discharged because of his inability to generate safety and self-insurance programs, because of his failure to win the confidence of employees, and because of his poor attendance. He was not informed of the facts in support of these conclusions and was given the option to resign. He claimed that he was entitled to a hearing. Is he entitled to one? Why or why not? [*Ellis v. City of Lakewood,* 789 P.2d 449 (Colo. App.)]

10. The Federal Food Stamp Act provided for the distribution of food stamps to needy households. In 1971, section 3(e) of the statute was amended to define households as limited to groups whose

members were all related to each other. This was done because of congressional dislike for the lifestyles of unrelated hippies who were living together in hippie communes. Moreno and others applied for food stamps but were refused them because the relationship requirement was not satisfied. An action was brought to have the relationship requirement declared unconstitutional. Is it constitutional? Discuss why or why not. [*USDA v. Moreno,* 413 U.S. 528]

11. New Hampshire adopted a tax law that in effect taxed the income of nonresidents working in New Hampshire only. Austin, a nonresident who worked in New Hampshire, claimed that the tax law was invalid. Was he correct? Explain. [*Austin v. New Hampshire,* 420 U.S. 656]

12. California passed a law that prohibited the sale or rental of "violent video games." The act defined violent video games as games "in which the range of options available to a player includes killing, maiming, dismembering, or sexually assaulting an image of a human being, if those acts are depicted" in a manner that "[a] reasonable person, considering the game as a whole, would find appeals to a deviant or morbid interest of minors." The association of video game manufacturers and developers brought suit, challenging the California statute as an unconstitutional violation of their First Amendment right and a violation of their due process rights because it is so vague. What should the U.S. Supreme Court hold on the constitutionality of the statute and why? [*Brown v. Entertainment Merchants Ass'n,* 131 S. Ct. 2729]

Government Regulation of Competition and Prices

5-1 Power to Regulate Business

The federal government may regulate any area of business to advance the nation's national economic needs. Under the police power, states may regulate all aspects of business so long as they do not impose an unreasonable burden on interstate commerce or any activity of the federal government. (See Chapter 4 for a discussion of the protections and limits of the commerce clause.)

5-1a Regulation, Free Enterprise, and Deregulation

Milton Friedman, the Nobel economist, has written that government regulation of business interferes with the free enterprise system. Under a true free enterprise system, market forces would provide the necessary protections through the forces of demand and supply. Sometimes, however, the demand response, or market reaction, to problems or services is not rapid enough to prevent harm, and government regulation steps in to stop abuses. The antitrust laws step in when competitors create barriers to market entry or collude on prices or production in order to control prices.

5-1b Regulation of Unfair Competition

Each of the states and the federal government have statutes and regulations that prohibit unfair methods of competition. Unfair competition is controlled by both statutes and administrative agencies and regulations. The statutes that curb unfair competition are the Sherman Act, the Clayton Act, the Robinson-Patman Act, and the Federal Trade Commission Act.[1] Each of these statutes covers different types of anticompetitive behavior by competitors. There are horizontal restraints (those among competitors) and vertical restraints of trade (throughout the supply chain) and each is listed in Figure 5-1 and discussed in the sections that follow.

5-2 Regulation of Horizontal Markets and Competitors

Certain of the antitrust laws regulate the relationships between and among competitors, known as horizontal restraints. The goal of these laws is to be sure that firms that are

FIGURE 5-1	Types of Anticompetitive Behavior
HORIZONTAL RESTRAINTS	**VERTICAL RESTRAINTS**
Price-Fixing (Sherman Act)	Price Discrimination (Robinson-Patman Act)
Monopolization (Sherman Act)	Exclusive Dealings and Territories (Sherman Act)
Mergers among Competitors (Clayton Act)	Mergers along the Supply Chain (Clayton Act)
	Resale Price Maintenance (Sherman Act)
	Tying (Clayton Act)

[1] 15 U.S.C. §41 *et seq.* To review the Federal Trade Commission Act, go to **http://www.ftc.gov**.

gaining customers are doing so because they offer better products and better customer service and not because they are manipulating the markets or their prices.

CPA

5-2a **Regulation of Prices**

Governments, both national and state, may regulate prices. Prices in various forms are regulated, including not only what a buyer pays for goods but also through credit terms and other charges. The Sherman Act is the federal law that regulates this form of anticompetitive behavior among horizontal competitors.

CPA

Prohibition on Price-Fixing

Agreements among competitors, as well as "every contract, combination ... or conspiracy" to fix prices, violate Section 1 of the Sherman Act.[2] Known as *horizontal price-fixing*, any agreement to charge an agreed-upon price or to set maximum or minimum prices between or among competitors are *per se*—in, through, or by themselves—is a violation of the Sherman Act. Price-fixing can involve competitors agreeing to not sell below a certain price, agreeing on commission rates, agreeing on credit terms, or exchanging cost information. Price is treated as a sensitive element of competition, and discussion among competitors has also been deemed to be an attempt to monopolize. An agreement among real estate brokers to never charge below a 6 percent commission is price-fixing.[3] **For Example,** in 2014, the Justice Department filed a civil antitrust suit against Apple and various e-book publishers for conspiracy to fix e-book prices. The publishers and Apple joined forces with the hope that they could prevent Amazon from taking hold of the e-book market with what one of the CEOs of a publishing firm called "the wretched $9.99 price point."[4] The CEOs met together and discussed prices in New York City. Apple had what was called "most favored nation" clauses in its contracts with the publishers; Apple had to be given the publishers' lowest price, thus preventing the publishers from dealing with Amazon. Three publishers settled their cases. Apple went to trial and was found guilty of a conspiracy to fix prices in the e-book market.

5-2b **Monopolization**

Monopolies and combinations that restrain trade are prohibited under the federal antitrust laws.

The Sherman Act

Sherman Antitrust Act–a federal statute prohibiting combinations and contracts in restraint of interstate trade, now generally inapplicable to labor union activity.

The **Sherman Antitrust Act** includes two very short sections that control monopolistic behavior. They provide:

> *[§1] Every contract, combination in the form of trust or otherwise, or conspiracy, in restraint of trade or commerce among the several states, or with foreign nations, is declared to be illegal.*
> *[§2] Every person who shall monopolize or attempt to monopolize, or combine or conspire with any other person or persons to monopolize any part of the trade or commerce among the several states, or with foreign nations, shall be deemed guilty of a felony.*[5]

---

[2] To view the full language of Section 1 of the Sherman Act, see 15 U.S.C. §1.

[3] *McClain v. Real Estate Board of New Orleans, Inc.,* 441 U.S. 942 (1980).

[4] *U.S. v. Apple, Inc.,* 12-CV-2826 (2012). **http://online.wsj.com/news/interactive/docid=120411161455-413f968a5c71466491205e 6292975605%7Cfile=ebookssettle041112?ref=SB10001424052702304444604577337573054615152.** The other publishers also sued were Hachette Book Group, Inc., HarperCollins Publishers, The Penguin Group, and Simon & Schuster. *United States v. Apple Inc.,* 889 F. Supp. 2d 623 (S.D.N.Y. 2012), *U.S. v. Apple,* 791 F.3d 290 (2nd Cir. 2015).

[5] 15 U.S.C. §1. Free competition has been advanced by the Omnibus Trade and Competitiveness Act of 1988, 19 U.S.C. §2901 *et seq.*

CPA

The Sherman Act applies not only to buying and selling activities but also to manufacturing and production activities. Section 1 of the Sherman Act applies to agreements, conduct, or conspiracies to restrain trade, which can consist of price-fixing, tying, and monopolization. Section 2 prohibits monopolizing or attempting to monopolize by companies or individuals.

Monopolization

market power–the ability to control price and exclude competitors.

To determine whether a firm has engaged in monopolization or attempts to monopolize, the courts determine whether the firm has **market power,** which is the ability to control price and exclude competitors. Market power is defined by looking at both the geographic and product markets. **For Example,** a cereal manufacturer may have 65 percent of the nationwide market for its Crispy Clowns cereal (the product market), but it may have only 10 percent of the Albany, New York, market because of a local competitor, Crunchy Characters. Crispy Clowns may have market power nationally, but in Albany, it would not reach monopoly levels.

Having a large percentage of a market is not necessarily a monopoly.[6] The Sherman Act requires that the monopoly position be gained because of a superior product or consumer preference, not because the company has engaged in purposeful conduct to exclude competitors by other means, such as preventing a competitor from purchasing a factory. **For Example,** perhaps one of the best known monopolization cases involved Microsoft. In the case, the Justice Department alleged that because Microsoft had 90 percent of the market for operating systems, it had and used monopoly power to control and market and did so by refusing to sell its operating system to companies that installed Netscape in lieu of or in addition to the Microsoft Explorer browser.[7] Microsoft was found guilty of monopolization. Ironically, today, Microsoft has filed antitrust complaints against Google, alleging that Google drives those who use its search engine to its own specialized sites that compete with Microsoft and others.

THINKING THINGS THROUGH

Teeth Whitening and the Antitrust Laws

The market for teeth whitening began in the 1990s. North Carolina dentists grew a market for the application of concentrations of peroxide to teeth to create a chemical reaction that results in whiter teeth. In about 2003, non-dentists also started offering teeth-whitening services, often at a significantly lower price than the dentists. Day spas, chain whitening franchises, and other businesses offered the service. Shortly thereafter, dentists began complaining to the North Carolina State Board of Dental Examiners and sought to have the non-dentist whitening services shut down because allowing such services to be performed by non-dentists created public health, safety, and welfare concerns.

After receiving complaints from dentists, the Board opened an investigation into teeth-whitening services performed by non-dentists. As a result of the investigations, the Board issued 47 cease-and-desist letters to 29 non-dentist teeth-whitening providers. The letters were issued on official letterhead and noted that the companies were subject to misdemeanor charges for the unauthorized practice of dentistry if they did not cease and desist their operations. The result was that non-dentist teeth whiteners were eliminated from North Carolina.

The FTC filed a complaint against the Board charging it with unfair competition. The Board moved to dismiss the complaint. Who is correct in this situation?

[*North Carolina State Bd. of Dental Examiners v. F.T.C.,* 135 S. Ct. 1101 (2015)]

---

[6] *Bell Atlantic v. Twombly,* 550 U.S. 544 (2007).
[7] *United States v. Microsoft,* 253 F.2d 34 (D.C. Cir. 2001).

5-2c Boycotts and Refusals to Deal

Under the Sherman Act, competitors are not permitted to agree not to deal with certain buyers. Boycotts among competitors are *per se* violations of the Sherman Act, which means that there are no defenses to these kinds of controls by competitors on markets. Sometimes boycotts have the best of intentions, but they are still illegal. **For Example,** defense lawyers who went on strike in order to get a higher hourly rate for public defenders so that the indigent defendants would have quality representation still engaged in an illegal boycott.[8]

5-2d Mergers among Competitors

The Sherman Antitrust Act does not prohibit bigness. However, Section 7 of the Clayton Act provides that "no corporation ... shall acquire the whole or any part of the assets of another corporation ... where in any line of commerce in any section of the country, the effect of such acquisition may be substantially to lessen competition, or to tend to create a monopoly." If the Clayton Act is violated through ownership or control of competing enterprises, a court may order the violating defendant to dispose of such interests by issuing a decree called a **divestiture order.**[9] Courts examine market share and relevant markets to determine whether a merger would create a monopoly. **For Example,** the Justice Department filed suit to stop the proposed merger between Anheuser-Busch, InBev NV, the maker of Bud Light, and Modelo, the maker of Corona. The fears expressed in the suit were that the combination of the two companies

divestiture order—a court order to dispose of interests that could lead to a monopoly.

ETHICS & THE LAW

Toys Я Us and Horizontal/Vertical Controls on Distribution

Toys Я Us (TRU), a company that sells 20 percent of all the toys sold in the United States, coordinated informal agreements among toy manufacturers including Mattel and Hasbro that they would restrict the distribution of their products to warehouse club stores (such as Sam's and Costco). The toy market breaks out as follows:

TYPE OF RETAIL OUTLET	PRICE MARK-UP
Traditional toy and department stores	40–50%
Specialized discount toy stores (TRU)	30%
General discount (Wal-Mart/ Kmart/Target)	22%
Warehouse/club	9%

To avoid the price competition, the informal TRU agreement was that the toy manufacturers would sell their products to warehouse clubs only if they were part of a more expensive package deal. For example, a Barbie doll could be purchased individually at Toys Я Us for $10.95, but the same Barbie doll could be purchased only as part of a package deal for $15.95 at the warehouse clubs. There were also some restrictions on the toys available to warehouse clubs. For example, Hall of Fame GI Joe was never sold at warehouse clubs. Mattel and Hasbro, fearful of losing Toys Я Us as a distribution tool, went along with the arrangement.

The Federal Trade Commission (FTC) filed suit against TRU to end the agreements.*

Walk through the antitrust laws and determine whether the conduct of TRU violated any of them. Then think through the ethics of TRU's actions. What about Mattel and Hasbro agreeing to the informal arrangement? Was their conduct in violation of the antitrust laws? Was it ethical?

*_Toys "Я" Us, Inc. v. FTC_ (7th Cir. 2000). In re _Pool Products Distribution Market Antitrust Litigation_, 988 F.Supp.2d 696 (E.D. La. 2013).

---

[8] *FTC v. Superior Court Trial Lawyers Ass'n,* 493 U.S. 411 (1990).
[9] *California v. American Stores Co.,* 492 U.S. 1301 (1989).

E-COMMERCE & CYBERLAW

Steve Jobs's E-Mails in Apple's Antitrust Litigation

Apple faced its third antitrust trial related to the Internet in 2014, and the most damaging testimony against Apple came from the late Steve Jobs—through his e-mails. This third antitrust suit had been hanging around for 10 years and dealt with the issue of the workaround services that had developed to find a way to get music for the iPods loaded through sources other than Apple's iTunes. For example, in one e-mail, Mr. Jobs wrote, "We need to make sure that when Music Match launches their download music store they cannot use iPod. Is this going to be an issue?"* That would be the kind of language someone defending Apple against the antitrust allegations in this iPod case would not want to exist.

During the antitrust litigation over the e-book pricing wars, one of Mr. Jobs's e-mails read, "Throw in with Apple and see if we can all make a go of this to create a real mainstream e-books market at $12.99 and $14.99." The goal was to drive out Amazon from the market because Amazon e-book prices were cheaper.

E-mail is discoverable, admissible as evidence, and definitely not private. Employees should follow the admonition of one executive whose e-mail was used to fuel a million-dollar settlement by his company with a former employee: "If you wouldn't want anyone to read it, don't send it in e-mail."

*Brian X. Chen, "Star Witness In Apple Suit Is Still Jobs," *New York Times*, December 1, 2014, p. B1.

---

would result in their domination of the distribution chain and would result in price increases. At the time of the proposed merger, AB InBev NV held 39 percent of the beer market, Miller/Coors held 26 percent, Modelo held 7 percent, and Heineken, the last of the big four held 6 percent. Other beer makers combined hold the remaining 22 percent of the U.S. beer market. If Bud and Corona had merged as proposed, they would have held 46 percent of the country's beer market. The case was settled after Bud agreed to divestiture of certain brands that it sold that reduced its post-merger percentage of market share.

When large-size enterprises plan to merge, they must give written notice to the FTC and to the head of the Antitrust Division of the Department of Justice. This advance notice gives the department the opportunity to block the merger and thus avoid the loss that would occur if the enterprises merged and were then required to separate.[10] **For Example,** AT&T was required to notify the Justice Department when it proposed acquisition of T-Mobile because AT&T's market share was 37 percent and T-Mobile's was 16 percent. A merger (which was not approved) would have resulted in a company with a 51 percent share of the market.[11]

> **Clayton Act**–a federal law that prohibits price discrimination.

> **Robinson-Patman Act**–a federal statute designed to eliminate price discrimination in interstate commerce.

> **price discrimination**–the charging practice by a seller of different prices to different buyers for commodities of similar grade and quality, resulting in reduced competition or a tendency to create a monopoly.

5-3 Regulation of the Supply Chain and Vertical Trade Restraints

5-3a Price Discrimination

The **Clayton Act** and **Robinson-Patman Act** prohibit price discrimination.[12] **Price discrimination** occurs when a seller charges different prices to different buyers for

---

[10] Antitrust Improvement Act of 1976, 15 U.S.C. §1311 *et seq.*

[11] Thomas Catan and Spencer A. Ante, "U.S. Sues to Stop AT&T Deal," *Wall Street Journal*, September 9, 2011, p. A1.

[12] 15 U.S.C. §§1, 2, 3, 7, 8.

"commodities of like grade and quality," with the result being reduced competition or a tendency to create a monopoly.[13]

Price discrimination prohibits charging different prices to buyers as related to marginal costs. That is, volume discounts are permissible because the marginal costs are different on the larger volume of goods. However, the Robinson-Patman Act makes it illegal to charge different prices to buyers when the marginal costs of the seller for those goods are the same. Any added incentives or bonuses are also considered part of the price.

For Example, offering one buyer free advertising while not offering it to another as an incentive to buy would be a violation of the Robinson-Patman Act. The Clayton Act makes both the giving and the receiving of any illegal price discrimination a crime.

CPA   Sellers cannot sell below cost to harm competitors or sell to one customer at a secret price that is lower than the price charged other customers when there is no economic justification for the lower price.[14] Some state statutes specifically permit sellers to set prices so that they can match competitive prices, but not to undercut a competitor's prices.[15]

CASE SUMMARY

Getting a Piece of the Pie Market

FACTS: Utah Pie Company is a Utah corporation that for 30 years has been baking pies in its plant in Salt Lake City and selling them in Utah and surrounding states. It entered the frozen pie business in 1957 and was immediately successful with its new line of frozen dessert pies—apple, cherry, boysenberry, peach, pumpkin, and mince.

Continental Baking Company, Pet Milk, and Carnation, all based in California, entered the pie market in Utah. When these companies entered the Utah market, a price war began. In 1958 Utah Pie was selling pies for $4.15 per dozen. By 1961, as all the pie companies competed, it was selling the same pies for $2.75 per dozen. Continental's price went from $5.00 per dozen in 1958 to $2.85 in 1961. Pet's prices went from $4.92 per dozen to $3.46, and Carnation's from $4.82 per dozen to $3.30.

Utah Pie filed suit, charging price discrimination. The district court found for Utah Pie. The Court of Appeals reversed, and Utah Pie appealed.

DECISION: There was price discrimination. Pet was selling its pies in Utah through Safeway at prices that were lower than

its prices in other markets and also much lower than its own brand pie in the Salt Lake City market. Pet also introduced a 20-ounce economy pie under the Swiss Miss label and began selling the new pie in the Salt Lake market in August 1960 at prices ranging from $3.25 to $3.30 for the remainder of the period. This pie was at times sold at a lower price in the Salt Lake City market than it was sold in other markets. For 7 of the 44 months in question for price discrimination, Pet's prices in Salt Lake were lower than prices charged in the California markets. This was true even though selling in Salt Lake involved a 30- to 35-cent freight cost.

Also, Pet had predatory intent to injure Utah Pie. Pet admitted that it sent into Utah Pie's plant an industrial spy to seek information. Pet suffered substantial losses on its frozen pie sales during the greater part of time involved in this suit. Pet had engaged in predatory tactics in waging competitive warfare in the Salt Lake City market. Coupled with the price discrimination, Pet's behavior lessened competition and violated Robinson-Patman. [*Utah Pie Co. v. Continental Baking Co.*, **386 U.S. 685 (1967)**]

---

[13] 15 U.S.C. §13a. To read the full Clayton Act, go to **http://www.usdoj.gov** or **http://www.justice.gov** and plug in "Clayton Act" in a site search.

[14] In *Weyerhaeuser v. Ross-Simons,* 549 U.S. 212 (2007), the U.S. Supreme Court ruled that predatory bidding is also a price discrimination issue. In a monopsony, a buyer tries to control a market by overbidding all its competitors and thereby cornering the market for supplies it needs to produce goods. However, if the bidder is actually just in need of the goods and bids higher for them, there is no anticompetitive conduct.

[15] *Home Oil Company, Inc. v. Sam's East, Inc.*, 252 F. Supp. 2d 1302 (M.D. Ala. 2003).

Price discrimination is expressly permitted when it can be justified on the basis of (1) a difference in grade, quality, or quantity; (2) the cost of transportation involved in performing the contract; (3) a good-faith effort to meet competition; (4) differences in methods or quantities, that is, marginal cost differences; (5) deterioration of goods; or (6) a close-out sale of a particular line of goods. The Robinson-Patman Act[16] reaffirms the right of a seller to select customers and refuse to deal with anyone. The refusal, however, must be in good faith, not for the purpose of restraining trade.

5-3b Exclusive Dealings and Territories

Sometimes manufacturers have sole outlets. Sole outlets are not *per se* violations. For restrictions on territories and outlets to be legal, there must be enough interbrand competition to justify no intrabrand competition. **For Example,** Coca-Cola can have exclusive distributorships in cities because Pepsi will always be there providing consumers with competitive choices in soft drinks.

5-3c Resale Price Maintenance

Resale price maintenance is an attempt by manufacturers to control the prices that retailers can charge for their goods. A "suggested retail price" is just that, a suggestion, and is not a violation of the antitrust laws. However, some manufacturers have policies of terminating retailers when they charge too little or charge too much. For example, many Apple products are the same price wherever you buy them. Minimum prices are justified in a competitive sense because without them, some retailers would cut the price but not offer the customer service the manufacturer wants for its brand. Retailers who charge more can be stopped by manufacturers who do not want to gouge consumers on prices.

CASE SUMMARY

Bagging Customers for Having Sales

FACTS: Leegin Creative Leather Products, Inc., designs, manufactures, and distributes leather goods and accessories under the brand name "Brighton." The Brighton brand is sold across the United States in over 5,000 retail stores. PSKS, Inc., runs Kay's Kloset, a Brighton retailer in Lewisville, Texas, that carries about 75 different product lines but was known as the place in that area to go for Brighton.

Leegin's president, Jerry Kohl, who also has an interest in about 70 stores that sell Brighton products, believes that small retailers treat customers better, provide customers more services, and make their shopping experience more satisfactory than do larger, often impersonal retailers. In 1997, Leegin instituted the "Brighton Retail Pricing and Promotion Policy," which banished retailers that discounted Brighton goods below suggested prices.

In December 2002, Leegin discovered that Kay's Kloset had been marking down Brighton's entire line by 20 percent. When Kay's would not stop marking the Brighton products prices down, Leegin stopped selling to the store.

PSKS sued Leegin for violation of the antitrust laws. The jury awarded PSKS $1.2 million in damages and the judge trebled the damages and reimbursed PSKS for its attorney's fees and costs—for a judgment against Leegin of $3,975,000.80. The Court of Appeals affirmed. Leegin appealed.

DECISION: The Court held that the goal of providing customers with information and service through the smaller boutiques was a competitive strategy that offered consumers choices. It was not a *per se* violation for Leegin to require minimum prices. Resale price maintenance increases the choices consumers have by providing them with a full-service retailer. Each case on resale price maintenance requires examination of the market and the effect on competition, but it is not automatically anticompetitive. The decision was reversed. [*Leegin Creative Leather Products, Inc. v. PSKS, Inc.,* 551 U.S. 877 (2007)]

---

[16] 15 U.S.C. §§13, 21.

CASE SUMMARY

Fill It Up: The Price Is Right and Fixed

FACTS: Barkat U. Khan and his corporation entered into an agreement with State Oil to lease and operate a gas station and convenience store owned by State Oil. The agreement provided that Khan would obtain the gasoline supply for the station from State Oil at a price equal to a suggested retail price set by State Oil, less a margin of $3.25 per gallon. Khan could charge any price he wanted, but if he charged more than State Oil's suggested retail price, the excess went to State Oil. Khan could sell the gasoline for less than State Oil's suggested retail price, but the difference would come out of his allowed margin.

After a year, Khan fell behind on his lease payments, and State Oil gave notice of, and began, eviction proceedings. The court had Khan removed and appointed a receiver to operate the station. The receiver did so without the price constraints and received an overall profit margin above the $3.25 imposed on Khan.

Khan filed suit, alleging that the State Oil agreement was a violation of Section 1 of the Sherman Act because State Oil was controlling price. The district court held that there was no *per se* violation and that Khan had failed to demonstrate antitrust injury. The Court of Appeals reversed, and State Oil appealed.

DECISION: In what was a reversal of prior decisions, the Court held that vertical maximum prices (as in this case in which a retailer was prohibited from charging above a certain amount) are not a *per se* violation of the Sherman Act. The Court noted that benefits can come from retailers' not being able to charge above a certain amount. At a minimum, such controls on maximum prices were not an automatic violation of the Sherman Act and need to be examined in light of what happens to competition. In determining whether such prices might affect competition, the Court noted that maximum prices might have an impact on the survival of inefficient dealers, as was the case here. However, encouraging inefficiency is not the purpose of either the market or the laws on anticompetitive behavior. [*State Oil v. Khan*, 522 U.S. 3 (1997)]

5-3d Tying

tying—the anticompetitive practice of requiring buyers to purchase one product in order to get another.

It is a violation of the Sherman Act to force "tying" sales on buyers. **Tying** occurs when the seller makes a buyer who wants to purchase one product buy an additional product that he or she does not want.

The essential characteristic of a tying arrangement that violates Section 1 of the Sherman Act is the use of control over the tying product within the relevant market to compel the buyer to purchase the tied article that either is not wanted or could be purchased elsewhere on better terms.

CASE SUMMARY

If You Want Our Cartridges, You Have to Use Our Ink

FACTS: Trident, Inc., and its parent, Illinois Tool Works Inc. (petitioners), manufacture and market printing systems that include: (1) a patented piezoelectric impulse ink jet printhead, (2) a patented ink container, consisting of a bottle and valve cap, which attaches to the printhead, and (3) specially designed, but unpatented, ink. These products are sold to original equipment manufacturers (OEMs) who are licensed to incorporate the printheads and containers into printers that are in turn sold to companies for use in printing barcodes on cartons and packaging materials. The OEMs agree that they will purchase their ink exclusively from Illinois, and that neither they nor their customers will refill the patented containers with ink of any kind.

Independent Ink, Inc., has developed an ink with the same chemical composition as the ink sold by Illinois. Independent Ink filed suit, alleging that Illinois's agreements with customers constituted an illegal tying and monopolization in violation of §§ 1 and 2 of the Sherman Act. 15 U.S.C. §§1, 2.

If You Want Our Cartridges, You Have to Use Our Ink continued

The federal district court granted summary judgment for Illinois, and Independent appealed. The appellate court reversed the decision and Illinois appealed.

DECISION: The court held that tying an unpatented product to a patented one was not a *per se* violation because there needed to be proof of market power in the patented product first. On remand, to establish tying, there must be proof that Illinois Tool has market power in the sale of its cartridges—such as a percentage of market share. You can only engage in tying through a tie of an unsuccessful product to a successful one—the more successful your product and the higher the demand, the more you lose the defense to tying. [*Illinois Tool Works Inc. v. Independent Ink, Inc.*, 547 U.S. 28 (2006)]

5-3e Mergers along the Supply Chain

Vertical mergers occur between firms that have buyer and seller relationships. The Clayton Act also applies to vertical mergers. The test is whether the vertical merger will foreclose or lessen competition. **For Example,** Amazon is a retailer of both books and e-books, but it has begun its own publishing firm and has been recruiting authors. Other book publishers are watching closely as Amazon begins to obtain more power in the publishing part of the chain because of its dominance in the retail sales of books. During 2014, Amazon had a dust-up with Hachette Books because there were accusations that Amazon was holding up shipment of non-Amazon author books in order to affect sales and encourage more authors to sign with Amazon's publishing arm.

In addition to controlling business combinations, the federal government protects others. By statute or decision, associations of exporters, marine insurance associations, farmers' cooperatives, and labor unions are exempt from the Sherman Act with respect to agreements between their members. Certain pooling and revenue-dividing agreements between carriers are exempt from the antitrust law when approved by the appropriate federal agency. The Newspaper Preservation Act of 1970 grants an antitrust exemption to operating agreements entered into by newspapers to prevent financial collapse. The Soft Drink Interbrand Competition Act[17] grants the soft drink industry an exemption when it is shown that, in fact, substantial competition exists in spite of the agreements.

The general approach of the U.S. Supreme Court has been that these types of agreements should not be automatically, or *per se*, condemned as a restraint of interstate commerce merely because they create the power or potential to monopolize interstate commerce. It is only when the restraint imposed is unreasonable that the practice is unlawful. The Court applies the rule of reason in certain cases because the practice may not always harm competition.

SPORTS & ENTERTAINMENT LAW

Ticket Issues and Antitrust

The Justice Department took a very close look at whether the merger between Live Nation and Ticketmaster would be anti-competitive because the largest U.S. event promoter was proposing a merger with the largest primary and secondary ticket seller in the world. The merger was eventually approved because there were still thriving smaller ticket sellers.

---

[17] 15 U.S.C. §3501 *et seq.*

5-4 Remedies for Anticompetitive Behavior

5-4a Criminal Penalties

A violation of either section of the Sherman Act is punishable by fine or imprisonment, or both, at the discretion of the court. The maximum fine for a corporation is $100 million. A natural person can be fined a maximum of $1,000,000 or imprisoned for a maximum term of 10 years, or both.

5-4b Civil Remedies

In addition to these criminal penalties, the law provides for an injunction to stop the unlawful practices.

treble damages—three times the damages actually sustained.

Any individual or company harmed may bring a separate action for **treble damages** (three times the damages actually sustained). In addition to individual suits, there is the possibility that a state could bring a class-action suit if the antitrust violation has resulted in large numbers of buyers paying higher prices. **For Example,** Pilgrim's Pride agreed to pay $26 million in damages to dozens of poultry growers because of its closure of chicken-processing plants in order to bring down the price of chicken.

The attorney general of a state may bring a class-action suit to recover damages on behalf of those who have paid the higher prices. This action is called a *parens patriae* action on the theory that the state is suing as the parent of its people.

Make the Connection

Summary

Regulation by government has occurred primarily to protect one group from the improper conduct of another group. The police power is the basis for government regulation. Regulation is passed when the free enterprise system fails to control abuses, as when companies engage in unfair methods of competition.

There are horizontal and vertical forms of anticompetitive behavior. The Sherman Act focuses on horizontal anticompetitive behavior such as price-fixing, boycotts, refusals to deal, and monopolization achieved through means other than fair competition.

The Sherman Antitrust Act prohibits price-fixing among competitors, monopolies that do not result from superior skill or products, boycotts, and mergers that lessen competition. The Clayton Act prohibits mergers or the acquisition of the assets of another corporation when this conduct would tend to lessen competition or create a monopoly. The Justice Department requires premerger notification for proposed mergers. Violation of the federal antitrust statutes subjects the wrongdoer to criminal prosecution and possible civil liability that can include treble damages.

Vertical trade restraints include price discrimination, some exclusive dealings arrangements, resale price maintenance, and some mergers among companies positioned vertically in the supply chain.

Prices have been regulated both by prohibiting setting the exact price or a maximum price and discrimination in pricing. Price discrimination between buyers is prohibited when the effect of such discrimination could tend to create a monopoly or lessen competition. Price discrimination occurs when the prices charged different buyers are different despite the same marginal costs. Another vertical antitrust issue is resale price maintenance. Resale price maintenance is control by the manufacturer of the price of its goods as they flow through the supply chain. Resale price maintenance is not illegal *per se* if the control is for purposes of providing customer service.

Learning Outcomes

After studying this chapter, you should be able to clearly explain:

5-1   Power to Regulate Business

L0.1   Explain the powers the government has to be sure free markets are working efficiently

See the *For Example* about Crispy Clowns Cereal, page 75.

5-2   Regulation of Horizontal Markets and Competitors

L0.2   List the federal statutes that regulate horizontal markets and competition and give examples of each

See the Apple e-book pricing example, page 74.
See the Toys Я Us Ethics & the Law, page 76.
See the Thinking Things Through feature on teeth whitening, page 75.
See the Microsoft monopolization discussion, page 75.

See the Bud Light and Corona example on horizontal mergers, pages 76–77.

5-3   Regulation of the Supply Chain and Vertical Trade Restraints

L0.3   Describe the federal statutes that regulate the supply chain and vertical markets

See the *Utah Pie* case on predatory pricing, page 78.
See the *Khan* oil case on price controls, page 80.
See the *Leegin* case on resale price maintenance, page 79.
See the *Illinois Tool Works* case on tying, pages 80–81.
See the Sports & Entertainment Law feature on the merger in the event ticket market, page 81.

5-4   Remedies for Anticompetitive Behavior

L0.4   Discuss the remedies available to protect business competition

See a list of the penalties and remedies, page 82.

Key Terms

Clayton Act	price discrimination	treble damages
divestiture order	Robinson-Patman Act	tying
market power	Sherman Antitrust Act	

Questions and Case Problems

1. American Crystal Sugar Co. was one of several refiners of beet sugar in northern California, and it distributed its product in interstate commerce. American Crystal and the other refiners had a monopoly on the seed supply and were the only practical market for the beets. In 1939, all of the refiners began using identical form contracts that computed the price paid to the sugar beet growers using a "factor" common to all the refiners. As a result, all refiners paid the same price for beets of the same quality. Though there was no hard evidence of an illegal agreement, the growers brought suit under the Sherman Act against the refiners, alleging that they conspired to fix a single uniform price among themselves to hold down the cost of the beets. The growers sued for the treble damages available under the Sherman Act. Can they recover? [*Mandeville Island Farms v. American Crystal Sugar Co.*, 334 U.S. 219]

2. Penny Stafford, the owner of Belvi Coffee and Tea Exchange, located in Bellevue, Washington, brought an antitrust suit against Starbucks. She alleged that through its exclusive leases, Starbucks bans other

coffee shops from competing. Starbucks has a 73 percent market share, has $8.4 billion in annual sales in the United States, and owns 7,551 of the 21,400 coffeehouses located in the United States. However, if Dunkin' Donuts, KrispyKreme, and Tim Hortons are included in the gourmet coffee market, Starbucks holds only 43 percent of the coffee market. Starbucks purchased Seattle's Best Coffee (SBC) in 2003 and Torrefazione Italia the same year. Starbucks then closed one-half of all SBC stores and all of the Torrefazione outlets. Starbucks runs 59 stores within a two-mile radius of downtown Seattle. Stafford said that Starbucks has exclusive leases with landlords so that the landlords cannot lease space in the same building to another coffee shop. Does such an exclusive lease violate any antitrust laws, or are such clauses permitted under the law?

3. David Ungar holds a Dunkin' Donuts franchise. The terms of his franchise agreement require him to use only those ingredients furnished by Dunkin' Donuts. He is also required to buy its napkins, cups, and so on, with the Dunkin' Donuts trademark on them. Is

this an illegal tying arrangement? What if Dunkin' Donuts maintains that it needs these requirements to maintain its quality levels on a nationwide basis? [*Ungar v. Dunkin' Donuts of America, Inc.*, 429 U.S. 823]

4. During the 1980s, the NCAA, a voluntary unincorporated association of approximately 1,100 educational institutions, became concerned over the steadily rising costs of maintaining competitive athletic programs. As a way of containing those costs, the association imposed salary caps on college and university athletic coaches. The caps on salaries as well as limits on number and types of coaches were imposed pursuant to NCAA procedures and members' votes. A group of coaches filed suit, challenging the caps on salaries and hiring as being anticompetitive. The NCAA responded that it had a goal of containing athletic program costs as well as ensuring that entry-level coaching positions were available. Are the salary caps legal under the federal antitrust laws? [*Law v. National Collegiate Athletic Ass'n*, 134 F.3d 1010 (10th Cir.)]

5. Hines Cosmetic Co. sold beauty preparations nationally to beauty shops at a standard or fixed-price schedule. Some of the shops were also supplied with a free demonstrator and free advertising materials. The shops that were not supplied with them claimed that giving the free services and materials constituted unlawful price discrimination. Hines replied that there was no price discrimination because it charged everyone the same. What it was giving free was merely a promotional campaign that was not intended to discriminate against those who were not given anything free. Was Hines guilty of unlawful price discrimination? Explain.

6. Moore ran a bakery in Santa Rosa, New Mexico. His business was wholly intrastate. Meads Fine Bread Co., his competitor, engaged in an interstate business. Meads cut the price of bread in half in Santa Rosa but made no price cut in any other place in New Mexico or in any other state. This price-cutting drove Moore out of business. Moore then sued Meads for damages for violating the Clayton and Robinson-Patman Acts. Meads claimed that the price-cutting was purely intrastate and, therefore, did not constitute a violation of federal statutes. Was Meads correct? Why or why not? [*Moore v. Meads Fine Bread Co.*, 348 U.S. 115]

7. A&P Grocery Stores decided to sell its own brand of canned milk (referred to as *private label* milk). A&P asked its longtime supplier, Borden, to submit an offer to produce the private label milk. Bowman Dairy also submitted a bid, which was lower than Borden's. A&P's Chicago buyer then contacted Borden and said, "I have a bid in my pocket. You people are so far out of line it is not even funny. You are not even in the ballpark." The Borden representative asked for more details but was told only that a $50,000 improvement in Borden's bid "would not be a drop in the bucket." A&P was one of Borden's largest customers in the Chicago area. Furthermore, Borden had just invested more than $5 million in a new dairy facility in Illinois. The loss of the A&P account would result in underutilization of the plant. Borden lowered its bid by more than $400,000. The Federal Trade Commission charged Borden with price discrimination, but Borden maintained it was simply meeting the competition. Did Borden violate the Robinson-Patman Act? Does it matter that the milk was a private label milk, not its normal trade name Borden milk? [*Great Atlantic & Pacific Tea Co., Inc. v. FTC*, 440 U.S. 69]

8. Department 56 is a company that manufactures and sells collectible Christmas village houses and other replica items to allow collectors to create the whimsical "Snow Village" town or "Dickens Christmas." Department 56 has only authorized dealers. Sam's Club, a division of Wal-Mart Stores, Inc., began selling Department 56 pieces from the Heritage Village Collection. Susan Engel, president and CEO of Department 56, refused to sell Department 56 products to Wal-Mart. Does her refusal violate any antitrust laws?

9. Dr. Edwin G. Hyde, a board-certified anesthesiologist, applied for permission to practice at East Jefferson Hospital in Louisiana. An approval was recommended for his hiring, but the hospital's board denied him employment on grounds that the hospital had a contract with Roux & Associates for Roux to provide all anesthesiological services required by the hospital's patients. Dr. Hyde filed suit for violation of antitrust laws. Had the hospital done anything illegal? [*Jefferson Parish Hosp. Dist. No. 2 v. Hyde*, 466 U.S. 2]

10. BRG of Georgia, Inc. (BRG), and Harcourt Brace Jovanovich Legal and Professional Publications (HJB) are the nation's two largest providers of bar review materials and lectures. HJB began offering a Georgia bar review course on a limited basis in 1976 and was in direct, and often intense, competition

with BRG from 1977 to 1979 when the companies were the two main providers of bar review courses in Georgia. In early 1980, they entered into an agreement that gave BRG an exclusive license to market HJB's materials in Georgia and to use its trade name "Bar/Bri." The parties agreed that HJB would not compete with BRG in Georgia and that BRG would not compete with HJB outside of Georgia. Under the agreement, HJB received $100 per student enrolled by BRG and 40 percent of all revenues over $350. Immediately after the 1980 agreement, the price of BRG's course was increased from $150 to more than $400. Is their conduct illegal under federal antitrust laws? [*Palmer v. BRG of Georgia, Inc.*, 498 U.S. 46]

11. Favorite Foods Corp. sold its food to stores and distributors. It established a quantity discount scale that was publicly published and made available to all buyers. The top of the scale gave the highest discount to buyers purchasing more than 100 freight cars of food in a calendar year. Only two buyers, both national food chains, purchased in such quantities, and, therefore, they alone received the greatest discount. Favorite Foods was prosecuted for price discrimination in violation of the Clayton Act. Was it guilty?

12. Public Interest Corporation (PIC) owned and operated television station WTMV-TV in Lakeland, Florida. MCA Television Ltd. (MCA) owns and licenses syndicated television programs. In 1990, the two companies entered into a licensing contract for several first-run television shows. With respect to all but one of these shows, MCA exchanged the licenses on a "barter" basis for advertising time on WTMV. However, MCA conditioned this exchange on PIC's agreeing to license the remaining show, *Harry and the Hendersons,* for cash as well as for barter. *Harry and the Hendersons* was what some in the industry would call a "dog," a show that was not very good that attempted to capitalize on a hit movie. PIC agreed to this arrangement, although it did not want *Harry and the Hendersons.* The shows that PIC did want were *List of a Lifetime, List of a Lifetime II, Magnum P.I.,* and 17 other miscellaneous features. Is this an illegal tying arrangement? [*MCA Television Ltd. v. Public Interest Corp.,* 171 F.3d 1265 (11th Cir.)]

13. The Quickie brand wheelchair is the most popular customized wheelchair on the market. Its market share is 90 percent. Other manufacturers produce special-use wheelchairs that fold, that are made of mesh and lighter frames, and that are easily transportable. These manufacturers do not compete with Quickie on customized chairs. One manufacturer of the alternative wheelchairs has stated, "Look, it's an expensive market to be in, that Quickie market. We prefer the alternative chairs without the headaches of customizations." Another has said, "It is such a drain on cash flow in that market because insurers take so long to pay. We produce chairs that buyers purchase with their own money, not through insurers. Our sales are just like any other product." Quickie entered the market nearly 40 years ago and is known for its quality and attention to detail. Buying a Quickie custom chair, however, takes time, and the revenue stream from sales is slow but steady because of the time required to produce custom wheelchairs. Has Quickie violated the federal antitrust laws with its 90 percent market share? Discuss.

14. Gardner-Denver is the largest manufacturer of ratchet wrenches and their replacement parts in the United States. Gardner-Denver had two different lists of prices for its wrenches and parts. Its blue list had parts that, if purchased in quantities of five or more, were available for substantially less than its white list prices. Did Gardner-Denver engage in price discrimination with its two price lists? [*D. E. Rogers Assoc., Inc. v. Gardner-Denver Co.,* 718 F.2d 1431 (6th Cir.)]

15. The Aspen ski area consisted of four mountain areas. Aspen Highlands, which owned three of those areas, and Aspen Skiing, which owned the fourth, had cooperated for years in issuing a joint, multiple-day, all-area ski ticket. After repeatedly and unsuccessfully demanding an increased share of the proceeds, Aspen Highlands canceled the joint ticket. Aspen Skiing, concerned that skiers would bypass its mountain without some joint offering, tried a variety of increasingly desperate measures to re-create the joint ticket, even to the point of in effect offering to buy Aspen Highland's tickets at retail price. Aspen Highlands refused even that. Aspen Skiing brought suit under the Sherman Act, alleging that the refusal to cooperate was a move by Aspen Highlands to eliminate all competition in the area by freezing it out of business. Is there an antitrust claim here in the refusal to cooperate? What statute and violation do you think Aspen Skiing alleged? What dangers do you see in finding the failure to cooperate to be an antitrust violation? [*Aspen Skiing Co. v. Aspen Highlands Skiing Corp.,* 472 U.S. 585]

C H A P T E R 6

Administrative Agencies

6-1 **Nature of the Administrative Agency**

Late in the nineteenth century, a new type of governmental structure began to develop to meet the highly specialized needs of government regulation of business: the administrative agency. The administrative agency is now typically the instrument through which government makes and carries out its regulations.

An **administrative agency** is a government body charged with administering and implementing legislation. An agency may be a department, an independent establishment, a commission, an administration, an authority, a board, or a bureau. Agencies exist on the federal and state levels. One example of a federal agency is the Federal Trade Commission (FTC), whose structure is shown in Figure 6-1.

administrative agency—government body charged with administering and implementing legislation.

6-1a **Purpose of Administrative Agencies**

Federal administrative agencies are created to carry out general policies specified by Congress. Federal agencies include the Securities Exchange Commission (SEC), the Consumer Product Safety Commission (CPSC), and the Food and Drug Administration (FDA). The law governing these agencies is known as **administrative law.**

administrative law—law governing administrative agencies.

States also have administrative agencies that may have jurisdiction over areas of law affecting business, such as workers' compensation claims, real estate licensing, and unemployment compensation.

6-1b **Uniqueness of Administrative Agencies**

Administrative agencies differ from the legislative branch in that those who head up and operate are ordinarily appointed (in the case of federal agencies, by the president of the United States with the consent of the Senate).

In the tripartite structure of legislative, executive, and judicial branches, the judicial branch reviews actions of the executive and legislative branches to ensure that they have

FIGURE 6-1   Structure of the Federal Trade Commission

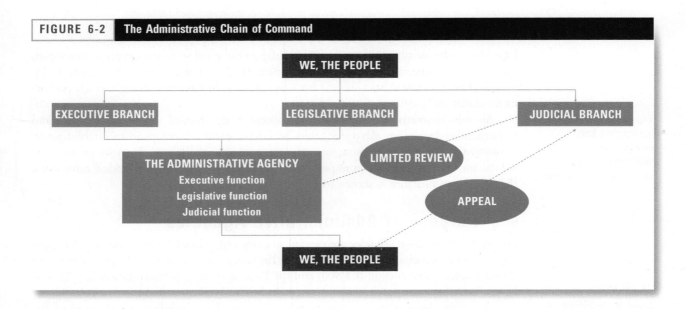

FIGURE 6-2   The Administrative Chain of Command

not exceeded their constitutional powers. However, governmental agencies combine legislative, executive, and judicial powers (Figure 6-2). These agencies make the rules, conduct inspections to see that the rules have been or are being obeyed, and determine whether there have been violations of their rules. Because agencies have such broad powers, they are subject to strict procedural rules as well as disclosure requirements (discussed in the following section).

6-1c Open Operation of Administrative Agencies

The public has ready access to the activity of administrative agencies. That access comes in three ways: (1) open records, (2) open meetings, and (3) public announcement of agency guidelines. The actions and activities of most federal agencies that are not otherwise regulated are controlled by the **Administrative Procedure Act** (APA).[1] Many states have adopted statutes with provisions similar to those of the APA.

Open Records

The **Freedom of Information Act**[2] (FOIA) provides that information contained in records of federal administrative agencies is available to citizens on proper request. The primary purpose of this statute is "to ensure that government activities be opened to the sharp eye of public scrutiny."[3] Over the past decade there has been an increasing number of FOIA requests by private groups and the media. For example, FOIA requests resulted in the release of information related to political controversies, such as the IRS targeting of certain political groups and the events that led to the death of the U.S. ambassador in Benghazi. Families and citizens also use FOIA requests to obtain information about crimes and investigations.

The Electronic Freedom of Information Act Amendments of 1996 extend the public availability of information to electronically stored data. The area of electronic government

Administrative Procedure Act–federal law that establishes the operating rules for administrative agencies.

Freedom of Information Act–federal law permitting citizens to request documents and records from administrative agencies.

---

[1] Administrative Procedures Act 5 U.S.C. §550 *et seq.*
[2] 5 U.S.C. §552 *et seq.*
[3] *Brady-Lunny v. Massey*, 185 F. Supp. 2d 928 (C.D. Ill. 2007). See also *Better Government Association v. Blagojevich*, 899 N.E.2d 382 (Ill. App. 2008).

activity has been a focus of FOIA requests. For example, in *Electronic Private Information Center v. Dept. of Homeland Security (DHS)*, 999 F. Supp. 2d 24 (2013), a private organization sought information about the authority of the DHS to shut down wireless network to prevent the detonation of explosive devices.

Because these requests can involve sensitive materials or issues of privacy, there are exceptions to this right of public scrutiny. These exceptions prevent individuals and companies from obtaining information that is not necessary to their legitimate interests and might harm the person or company whose information is being sought.[4] State statutes typically exempt from disclosure any information that would constitute an invasion of the privacy of others. **For Example,** when Sea World animal trainer, Dawn Brancheau, died as a result of an attack by a killer whale, OSHA conducted the investigation into her death because it was a workplace fatality. OSHA had taken photographs as part of the investigation and there were several FOIA requests for release of the investigation report, including the photos. Ms. Brancheau's family filed a "reverse FOI" suit to stop the disclosure of the information. However, as disturbing as the photos may have been, there is no FOIA exception for death scene materials.[5]

Freedom of information acts are broadly construed, and unless an exemption is clearly given, the information in question is subject to public inspection.[6] **For Example,** the Department of Justice is required to disclose materials related to an investigation of a member of Congress that has ended with no charges.[7] Moreover, the person claiming that there is an exemption that prohibits disclosure has the burden of proving that the exemption applies to the particular request made. Exemptions include commercial or financial information not ordinarily made public by the person or company that supplies the information to the agency as part of the agency's enforcement role.[8]

The FOIA's primary purpose is to subject agency action to public scrutiny. Its provisions are liberally interpreted, and agencies must make good-faith efforts to comply with its terms.

ETHICS & THE LAW

IRS Employees Who Snoop

In 1997, the Internal Revenue Service (IRS) disciplined employees who, out of curiosity, were looking up tax returns of famous people to see who made how much income. The IRS fired 23 employees, disciplined 349, and provided counseling for 472. In June 2013, another 349 IRS employees were disciplined, once again, for looking up tax returns of citizens without any authorization or work purpose for doing so. Is this practice so bad? What is wrong with just looking at data accessible at work?

Why are we concerned about selective research about private citizens? Does it matter that the information was not released to the public?

[4] Additional protection is provided by the Privacy Act of 1974, 5 U.S.C. §552a(b); *Doe v. U.S. Dept. of Treasury*, 706 F. Supp. 2d 1 (D.D.C. 2009) and protects government employees from disclosures about employer disciplinary actions.
[5] *Brancheau v. Secretary of Labor*, 2011 WL 4105047 (M.D. Fla.).
[6] Corporations have limited privacy rights. *FCC v. AT&T Inc.*, 562 U.S. 397 (2011).
[7] *Citizens for Responsibility and Ethics in Washington v. United States Department of Justice*, 48 F. Supp. 2d 40 (D.D.C. 2014).
[8] *Ayuda, Inc. v. Federal Trade Commission*, 70 F. Supp. 3d 247 (D.D.C. 2014); for a state law example, see *Oklahoma Public Employees Ass'n v. State ex rel. Oklahoma Office of Personnel Management*, 267 P.3d 838 (Okla. 2011).

Open Meetings

open meeting law–law
that requires advance
notice of agency meeting
and public access.

Under the Sunshine Act of 1976,[9] called the **open meeting law,** the federal government requires most meetings of major administrative agencies to be open to the public. The Sunshine Act[10] applies to those meetings involving "deliberations" of the agency or those that "result in the joint conduct or disposition of official agency business." These statutes enable the public to know what actions agencies are taking and prevent administrative misconduct by having open meetings and public scrutiny. Many states also have enacted Sunshine laws.

Public Announcement of Agency Guidelines

To inform the public of the way administrative agencies operate, the APA, with certain exceptions, requires that each federal agency publish the rules, principles, and procedures that it follows.[11]

6-2 Legislative Power of the Agency

An administrative agency has the power to make laws and does so by promulgating regulations with public input.

6-2a Agency's Regulations as Law

An agency may adopt regulations within the scope of its authority. The power of an agency to carry out a congressional program "necessarily requires the formulation of policy and the making of rules to fill any gap left by Congress."[12] If the regulation is not authorized by the law creating the agency, anyone affected by it can challenge the regulation on the basis that the agency has exceeded its authority. (See the section "Beyond the Jurisdiction of the Agency" in this chapter.)

The authority of an agency is not limited to the technology in existence at the time the agency was created or assigned jurisdiction for enforcement of laws. The sphere in which an agency may act expands with new scientific developments.[13]

CASE SUMMARY

Can an Agency Regulate Hot Air?

FACTS: On October 20, 1999, a group of 19 private organizations (Petitioners) filed a rulemaking petition asking the EPA to regulate "greenhouse gas emissions from new motor vehicles under §202 of the Clean Air Act." These organizations argued that greenhouse gas emissions have significantly accelerated climate change, and that "carbon dioxide remains the most important contributor to [man-made] forcing of climate change."

Fifteen months after the petition was filed, the EPA requested public comment on "all the issues raised in [the] petition," adding a "particular" request for comments on "any scientific, technical, legal, economic or other aspect of

---

[9] The Government in the Sunshine Act can be found at 5 U.S.C. §552b.

[10] 5 U.S.C. §552b(a)(2).

[11] APA codified at 5 U.S.C. §552. See the section "Proposed Regulations" in this chapter for a description of the *Federal Register*, the publication in which these agency rules, principles, and procedures are printed.

[12] *National Elec. Mfrs. Ass'n v. U.S. Dept. of Energy*, 654 F.3d 496 (4th Cir. 2011); *King v. Burwell*, 759 F.3d 358 (4th Cir. 2014).

[13] *United States v. Midwest Video Corp.*, 406 U.S. 649 (1972).

Can an Agency Regulate Hot Air? continued

these issues that may be relevant to EPA's consideration of this petition, including whether there was global warming due to carbon emissions." The EPA received more than 50,000 comments over the next five months.

On September 8, 2003, the EPA entered an order denying the rulemaking petition because (1) the Clean Air Act does not authorize the EPA to issue mandatory regulations to address global climate change; and (2) even if the agency had the authority to set greenhouse gas emission standards, it would be unwise to do so at this time. Massachusetts, other states, and private organizations filed suit, challenging the EPA denial as arbitrary and capricious, violative of the APA, and *ultra vires* because of statutory mandates for EPA action.

The court of appeals dismissed the appeal from the agency denial and the Supreme Court granted *certiorari*.

DECISION: The Court held that greenhouse gases were a form of pollution and that the Clean Air Act required the EPA to take steps to curb those emissions. The Court found that any justification the EPA gave for inaction was not supported by either the statutory construction or the evidence on global warming. The decision was 5 to 4 in which the dissent maintained that no matter how strongly we feel about global warming, action is left to the executive and legislative branches, not the courts. The dissent also noted that agencies should be given great deference in making their decisions on whether to regulate certain issues and that the statute did not mandate regulation—it gave the EPA broad discretion and its discretion could include lack of scientific conclusions, deference to the president, or other agencies. [*Massachusetts v. EPA*, **549 U.S. 497 (2007)**]

When an agency's proposed regulation deals with a policy question that is not specifically addressed by statute, the agency that was created or given the discretion to administer the statute may establish new policies covering such issues.[14] **For Example,** the FCC has authority to deal with cell phones and cell phone providers even though when the agency was created, there were only the traditional types of land-line telephones.[15]

6-2b Agency Adoption of Regulations

Congressional Enabling Act

Before an agency can begin rulemaking proceedings, it must be given jurisdiction by congressional enactment in the form of a statute. **For Example,** Congress has enacted broad statutes governing discrimination in employment practices and has given authority to the Equal Employment Opportunity Commission (EEOC) to establish definitions, rules, and guidelines for compliance with those laws. Sometimes an existing agency is assigned the responsibility for new legislation implementation and enforcement. **For Example,** the Department of Labor has been assigned the responsibility to handle the whistle-blower protection provisions of Sarbanes-Oxley that provide protection against retaliation and/or termination to those who report financial chicanery at their companies. The Department of Labor has been in existence for almost a century, but it was assigned a new responsibility and given new jurisdiction by Congress.

Agency Research of the Problem

After jurisdiction is established, the agency has the responsibility to research the issues and various avenues of regulation for implementing the statutory framework. As the agency does so, it determines the cost and benefit of the problems, issues, and solutions. The study may be done by the agency itself, or it may be completed by someone hired by the agency. **For Example,** before red lights were required equipment in the rear windows

---

[14] *Anglers Conservation Network v. Pritzker*, 70 F. Supp. 3d 427 (D.D.C. 2014).
[15] *Fones4All Corp. v. F.C.C.*, 550 F.3d 811 (9th Cir. 2008).

E-COMMERCE & CYBERLAW

The Open Net, Net Neutrality, and the FCC's Authority

Several subscribers to Comcast's Internet services discovered that the company was interfering with their use of peer-to-peer networking applications. The subscribers asked the FCC to regulate the Internet management practices of Comcast. However, the court held that there was no statutory authority that permitted the FCC to regulate the internal practices of communication providers. [*Comcast Corp. v. F.C.C.*, 600 F.3d 642 (C.A.D.C. 2010); see also *Verizon v. FCC*, 740 F.3d 624 (D.C. Cir. 2014)].

The case was the beginning of an ongoing legal battle for net neutrality. Net neutrality would mean that all data on the Internet would be treated equally. ISPs would not be able to charge differently depending on users, platform, etc. The ISPs claim that different treatment is necessary in order to ensure quality and access for all. The FCC has adopted a net neutrality standard, but the challenges continue.

of all cars, the Department of Transportation developed a study using taxicabs with the red lights in the rear windows and found that the accident rate for rear-end collisions with taxicabs was reduced dramatically. The study provided justification for the need for regulation as well as the type of regulation itself.

Proposed Regulations

Federal Register Act— federal law requiring agencies to make public disclosure of proposed rules, passed rules, and activities.

Federal Register— government publication issued five days a week that lists all administrative regulations, all presidential proclamations and executive orders, and other documents and classes of documents that the president or Congress direct to be published.

Following a study, the agency proposes regulations, which must be published. The **Federal Register Act**[16] requires that proposed administrative regulation be published in the *Federal Register.* This is a government publication published five days a week that lists all administrative regulations, all presidential proclamations and executive orders, and other documents and classes of documents that the president or Congress directs to be published.

The Federal Register Act provides that printing an administrative regulation in the *Federal Register* is public notice of the contents of the regulation to persons subject to it or affected by it, but in addition, the Regulatory Flexibility Act,[17] passed during the Reagan administration, requires that all proposed rules be published in the trade journals of those trades that will be affected by the proposed rules. **For Example,** any changes in federal regulations on real property closings and escrows have to be published in real estate broker trade magazines. In addition to the public notice of the proposed rule, the agency must also include a "regulatory flexibility analysis" that "shall describe the impact of the proposed rule on small entities."[18] The goal of this portion of the APA was to be certain that small businesses were aware of proposed regulatory rules and their cost impact.

Public Comment Period

Following the publication of the proposed rules, the public has the opportunity to provide input on the proposed rules. Called the *public comment period*, this time must last at least 30 days (with certain emergency exceptions)[19] and can consist simply of letters written by

---

[16] 44 U.S.C. §1505 *et seq.*

[17] 5 U.S.C. §601 *et seq.*

[18] 5 U.S.C. §603(a).

[19] An emergency exemption for the 30-day comment period was made when airport security measures and processes were changed following the September 11, 2001, attacks on the World Trade Center and the Pentagon that were carried out using domestic, commercial airliners.

those affected that are filed with the agency or of hearings conducted by the agency in Washington, D.C., or at specified locations around the country. **For Example,** when the FAA was considering allowing cell phone usage during flights, the public, flight attendants, pilots, and airlines were concerned about the negative consequences of passengers using cell phones. From air rage, to safety concerns, to noise factors, the comments were almost unanimously against the proposal. The agency responded appropriately with a no-go on usage.

Options after Public Comment

After receiving the public input on the proposed rule, an agency can decide to pass, or promulgate, *the rule.* The agency can also decide to withdraw the rule. **For Example,** the EEOC had proposed rules on handling religious discrimination in the workplace. The proposed rules, which would have required employers to police those wearing a cross or other religious symbol, met with so much public and employer protest that they were withdrawn. Finally, the agency can decide to modify the rule based on comments and then promulgate or, if the modifications are extensive or material, modify and put the proposed rule back out for public comment again. A diagram of the rulemaking process can be found in Figure 6-3.

FIGURE 6-3   Steps in Agency Rulemaking

ENABLING ACT

STUDY

DRAFT OF RULES

PUBLICATION OF PROPOSED RULES

PUBLIC COMMENT

RULES MODIFIED   RULES ADOPTED   RULES MODIFIED AND ADOPTED

6-3 Executive Power of the Agency

The modern administrative agency has the power to execute the law and to bring proceedings against violators.

6-3a Enforcement or Execution of the Law

An agency has the power to investigate, to require persons to appear as witnesses, to require witnesses to produce relevant papers and records, and to bring proceedings against those who violate the law. In this connection, the phrase *the law* embraces regulations adopted by an agency as well as statutes and court decisions.

An agency may investigate to determine whether any violation of the law or of its rules generally has occurred. An agency may also investigate to determine whether additional rules need to be adopted, to ascertain the facts with respect to a particular suspected or alleged violation, and to see whether the defendant in a proceeding before it is complying with its final order. An agency may issue subpoenas to obtain information reasonably required by its investigation.[20]

6-3b Constitutional Limitations on Administrative Investigation

Although administrative agencies have broad enforcement authority, they remain subject to the constitutional protections afforded individuals and businesses.

Inspection of Premises

Agency officials have the right to conduct inspections, pursuant to the warrant protections afforded by the Fourth Amendment (see Chapter 7). However, when violation of the law is dangerous to health and safety, a workplace inspection without advance notice or a search warrant is permitted when such a requirement could defeat the purpose of the inspection.

Production of Papers

For the most part, the constitutional guarantee against unreasonable searches and seizures does not afford much protection for the papers and records of a business being investigated by an agency. **For Example,** a subpoena to testify or to produce records cannot be opposed on the ground that it is a search and seizure. The constitutional protection is limited to cases of actual physical search and seizure rather than obtaining information by compulsion. Employers must turn over to the Occupational Health and Safety Administration (OSHA) their records on workplace injuries and lost workdays.

The protection afforded by the guarantee against self-incrimination likewise cannot be invoked when a corporate employee or officer in control of corporate records is compelled to produce those records even though he or she would be incriminated by them.[21] The privilege against self-incrimination cannot be invoked if records required to be kept by law are involved.

Inspections and Reports

To ensure that a business is obeying the law, including an agency's regulations and orders, the administrative agency may require proof of compliance through the submission of

---

[20] *EEOC v. Sidley, Austen, Brown and Wood,* 35 F.3d 696 (7th Cir. 2002).
[21] *Braswell v. United States,* 487 U.S. 99 (1988); see also *U.S. S.E.C. v. Narvett,* 16 F. Supp. 3d 979 (E.D. Wis. 2014).

periodic reports. **For Example,** OSHA requires reports on injuries and fatalities in the workplace. **For Example,** at the local level, cities require that businesses have their tax licenses on display and that those licenses be up-to-date. An agency may also require the regulated person or enterprise to file reports in a specified form.[22]

Administrative agencies also have the right of inspection or the examination either of a building or plant or documents that businesses are required to retain. The element of surprise is important in administrative agency inspections. In fact, in some industries, it is a federal crime for company officers and managers to notify employees about the presence of federal inspectors at the business. **For Example,** following the Massey Energy Company's Upper Big Branch mine disaster that killed 29 miners, several managers and executives were criminally charged for notifying miners that inspectors were on the way and ordering miners to conceal hazards that would result in shut-downs or fines.[23] Three officials have entered guilty pleas or been convicted of the charges.[24] Don Blankenship, the CEO at the time, has also been charged with conspiring to violate safety standards.

6-4 Judicial Power of the Agency

Once the investigation of an agency reveals a potential violation of the law, an agency assumes its third role of judicial arbiter to conduct hearings on violations.

6-4a The Agency as a Specialized Court

An agency, although not a court by law, may be given power to sit as a court and to determine whether any violations of the law or of agency regulations have occurred. The National Labor Relations Board (NLRB) determines whether a prohibited labor practice has been committed.[25] The Securities Exchange Commission (SEC) acts as a court for determining violations of federal securities laws.

Beginning Enforcement—Preliminary Steps

Either a private individual or company or an agency may file a written complaint alleging some violation of law or regulation that is within the agency's jurisdiction. This complaint is then served on the company or individual named in the complaint, who then has the opportunity to file an answer to the allegations. There may be other phases of pleading between the parties and the agency, but, eventually, the matter comes before the agency to be heard. After a hearing, the agency makes a decision and enters an order either dismissing the complaint or directing remedies or resolutions.

The Administrative Hearing

To satisfy the requirements of due process, an agency handling a complaint must generally give notice and hold a hearing at which all persons affected may be present. A significant difference between an agency hearing and a court hearing is that there is no right of trial by jury before an agency. **For Example,** a workers' compensation board may decide a claim without any jury. Similarly, a case in which an employer protests the

---

[22] *United States v. Morton Salt Co.*, 338 U.S. 632 (1950).

[23] The federal agency involved was the Mine Safety and Health Administration (MSHA).

[24] *U.S. v. Stover*, 499 Fed. Appx. 267 (4th Cir. 2012).

[25] One of the requirements for a valid hearing by an agency is legal appointments of the commissioners to the agency. In *N.L.R.B. v. Noel Canning*, 134 S. Ct. 2550 (2014), the U.S. Supreme Court held that a National Labor Relations Board (NLRB) order was invalid because the president's recess appointments of several members of the board was not valid, and the commissioners had to be nominated and approved by Congress before their actions would be valid.

unemployment tax rate assigned to her company by a state agency has no right to a jury trial. The lack of a jury does not deny due process (see Chapter 4). An **administrative law judge (ALJ)** hears the complaint and has the authority to swear witnesses, take testimony, make evidentiary rulings, and make a decision to recommend to the agency heads for action.

An agency hearing is ordinarily not subject to the rules of evidence. The hearing tends to be more open, with discussion, as opposed to procedural processes that exclude some evidence.

administrative law judge–judicial figure who hears administrative agency actions.

Streamlined Procedure: Consent Decrees

informal settlements–negotiated disposition of a matter before an administrative agency, generally without public sanctions.

consent decrees–informal settlements of enforcement actions brought by agencies.

Informal settlements or **consent decrees** are practical devices used to settle administrative law complaints after wrongdoer business is notified of that complaint. A consent decree is similar to a *nolo contendere* plea where there is no admission of guilt, but there are promises related to fines and cease and desists on activities.[26] The Administrative Dispute Resolution Act of 1990 encourages consent decrees and the use of other processes approaches such as alternative dispute resolution in order to expedite cases.[27] **For Example,** Kellogg's settled with the FTC on deceptive advertising charges related to health claims about its Rice Krispies®, Frosted Flakes®, and Special K® cereals. Without admitting any violation of the law, Kellogg's agreed to change the ads and package claims for the cereals. Kellogg's could no longer claim that its cereals increased the attentiveness of children.

The Hearing Process

If the parties cannot reach an agreement through a consent decree, the questions of violations and penalties will go to an administrative hearing, which is quite different from the litigation described in Chapter 2. The defendant in an administrative law hearing is the person or company accused of a violation of an administrative regulation. The judge in these hearings is called an administrative law judge (ALJ) and at other levels of government is often called a **hearing examiner** or **hearing officer.**

hearing officer (or examiner)–another name for an administrative law judge.

intervenors–in administrative actions, third parties who have an interest in the issues being determined by an ALJ.

Administrative hearings often have additional parties involved, parties with an interest in the case are permitted to participate, and are called **intervenors.** They enter the case through motions to intervene and are usually permitted to do so at any time before the start of a hearing. Typical intervenors are industry organizations. **For Example,** snowmobile manufacturers and the state of Wyoming, because of their economic interests in snowmobile activities, were intervenors in the national park cases challenging the Department of Interior snowmobile regulations for national parks.

The Administrative Agency Decision

When an administrative agency makes a decision, it usually files an opinion that sets forth findings of facts and reasons for that decision. In some instances, a statute expressly requires this type of opinion, but agencies usually file opinions so that the parties and the court (in the event of an appeal) will understand the agency's action and reasoning.[28]

---

[26] The late comedian Johnny Carson said a defense decree is when a business says, "I didn't do anything, but I promise never to do it again."
[27] 5 U.S.C. §571 *et seq.*
[28] *Jordan v. Civil Service Bd., Charlotte,* 570 S.E.2d 912 (N.C. App. 2002).

6-4b Punishment and Enforcement Powers of Agencies

Penalty

Within the last few decades, agencies have increasingly been given the power to impose a penalty and to issue orders that are binding on a regulated party unless an appeal is taken to a court, which reverses the administrative decision. **For Example,** the Occupational Safety and Health Act of 1970 provides for the assessment of civil penalties against employers who fail to end dangerous working conditions when ordered to do so by the administrative agency created by that statute.[29] **For Example,** BP paid over $150 million in fines following the explosion at its Texas City refinery because the company had failed to address over 400 previously cited OSHA violations.

Cease-and-Desist Order

Environmental protection statutes adopted by states commonly give a state agency the power to assess a penalty for violating environmental protection regulations. As an illustration of the issuance of binding orders, the FTC can issue a **cease-and-desist order** to stop a practice that it decides is improper. This order to stop is binding unless reversed on an appeal. **For Example,** the FTC can order a company to stop making claims in ads that have been determined by that agency to be deceptive.

cease-and-desist order– order issued by a court or administrative agency to stop a practice that it decides is improper.

6-4c Exhaustion of Administrative Remedies

The parties involved in an administrative agency action cannot obtain judicial review until the agency has made its final findings or decision in the case. The parties in administrative actions are required to go through the administrative process, something that is referred to the exhaustion of administrative remedies before they can take the action to court.

Exceptions to the **exhaustion of administrative remedies** requirement are: (1) available remedies that provide no genuine opportunity for adequate relief; (2) irreparable injury that could occur if immediate judicial relief is not provided; (3) an appeal to the administrative agency that would be useless; or (4) a substantial constitutional question that the plaintiff has raised.

exhaustion of administrative remedies–requirement that an agency make its final decision before the parties can go to court.

6-4d Appeal from an Administrative Agency Action

There are several bases for challenging administrative agency actions. These bases are covered in the following sections.

Procedural Issues

If the procedure that an agency is to follow is specified by law, a decision of the agency that was made without following that procedure will be set aside and the matter sent back to the agency to proceed according to the required law.[30] An agency's actions, whether enforcement or rule promulgation, can be set aside if the agency has not followed the procedures required for rulemaking or, in the case of enforcement, the due process rights of the charged business or individual.

Substantive Law or Fact Issues

When the question that an agency decides is a question of law, a court will reverse the agency if the court disagrees with the legal interpretation.[31] Courts tend to accept the

---

[29] 29 U.S.C. §651 *et seq.*
[30] *Tingler v. State Board of Cosmetology,* 814 S.W.2d 683 (Mo. App. 1991).
[31] *Wallace v. Iowa State Bd. of Educ.,* 770 N.W.2d 344 (Iowa 2009).

agency's interpretation so long as it was reasonable even though it was not the only interpretation that could have been made.

A court will not reverse an agency's decision merely because the court would have made a different decision based on the same facts.[32] Courts assume that the agency has acted properly and those who appeal an agency decision must be able to show that the agency did not act on the basis of the facts or deliberately excluded facts.

Ultra Vires or Beyond the Jurisdiction of the Agency

The action of an agency can be set aside if what the agency has done is beyond the authority granted in the enabling statute for its creation. Several groups and businesses filed suit against the EPA challenging the Transport Rule, a rule designed to limit pollution across state lines. [*EME Homer City Generation, L.P. v. EPA*, 134 S. Ct. 1584 (2014)] The rule was challenged as *ultra vires* (beyond an agency's statutory authority). The court held that the Clean Air Act gave the EPA authority to determine how to allocate responsibility for a downwind state's excess pollution and that the Transport Rule was a permissible way for the EPA to construct the good neighbor concept.

Arbitrary and Capricious

When an agency changes its prior decisions and customary actions, it must give its reasons. In the absence of such an explanation, a reviewing court can set aside the agency action.[33]

CASE SUMMARY

Drilling Down to Arbitrary and Capricious Rules

FACTS: Hornbeck and others (plaintiffs) provide services to support offshore oil and gas drilling, exploration, and production activities in the Gulf of Mexico. Kenneth Salazar is the Secretary of the Department of Interior (DOI), a federal agency that includes the Minerals Management.

Following the BP Deepwater Horizon drilling platform explosion on April 20, 2010, and the resulting devastation and unprecedented disaster, President Obama asked DOI to conduct a study to determine what steps were needed to be taken to prevent another problem with oil rigs in the Gulf.

DOI did a 30-day study, consulting respected experts from state and federal governments, academic institutions, and industry and advocacy organizations. On May 27, 2010, DOI issued a Report that recommended a six-month moratorium on permits for new wells and an immediate halt to drilling operations on the 33 permitted wells in the Gulf of Mexico. The DOI report also stated that "the recommendations contained in this report have been peer-reviewed by seven experts identified by the National Academy of

Engineering." The experts pointedly observed that this statement was misleading and called it a "misrepresentation." Although the experts agreed with the safety recommendations contained in the body of the main Report, five of the National Academy of Engineering experts and three of the other experts publicly stated that they "do not agree with the six month blanket moratorium" on floating drilling. They envisioned a more limited kind of moratorium, but a blanket moratorium was added after their final review and was never agreed to by them. The plaintiffs moved for a preliminary injunction against the moratorium.

DECISION: The court held that the experts balking at the conclusion of the report, the inconsistency of the moratorium with the report information, and the availability of alternatives made the moratorium unlikely to survive a challenge of the action being arbitrary and capricious and issued an injunction. [*Hornbeck Offshore Services, L.L.C. et al. v. Salazar*, 696 F. Supp. 2d 627 (E.D. La. 2010)]

---

[32] *Dorchester Associates LLC v. District of Columbia Bd. of Zoning Adjustment*, 976 A.2d 200 (D.C. 2009).
[33] *Lorillard Tobacco Co. v. Roth*, 786 N.E.2d 7 (N.Y. App. 2003).

Constitutional Rights

Challenges to administrative agency rules and actions can also be based in constitutional rights.[34] **For Example,** agency restrictions on language or religious freedom have been successfully challenged in court. EEOC regulations on employees wearing religious jewelry (such as necklaces with crosses) were withdrawn after the agency realized through congressional actions that the regulations could not survive a constitutional challenge.

CASE SUMMARY

The Obscenity Case That Has Been Around as Long as Cher

FACTS: In a case that has been around almost as long as Cher, the U.S. Supreme Court, once again, issued a decision related to three FCC charges against Fox and ABC Television. First, in the 2002 Billboard Music Awards, broadcast by Fox Television, the singer Cher exclaimed during an unscripted acceptance speech: "I've also had my critics for the last 40 years saying that I was on my way out every year. Right. So f * * * 'em." At the 2003 Billboard Music Awards, Nicole Richie made the following unscripted remark while presenting an award: "Have you ever tried to get cow s* * * out of a Prada purse? It's not so f * * * *ing simple." The third incident involved an episode of *NYPD Blue*, a regular television show broadcast by respondent ABC Television Network. The episode, broadcast on February 25, 2003, showed the nude buttocks of an adult female character for approximately seven seconds and for a moment the side of her breast. During the scene, in which the character was preparing to take a shower, a child portraying her boyfriend's son entered the bathroom. A moment of awkwardness followed. The FCC received indecency complaints about all three broadcasts.

After these incidents, but before the FCC issued Notices of Apparent Liability to Fox and ABC, it issued a decision sanctioning NBC for a comment made by the singer Bono during the 2003 Golden Globe Awards. Upon winning the award for Best Original Song, Bono exclaimed: "'This is really, really, f * * * *ing brilliant. Really, really great.'" The FCC found that the use of the F-word was "one of the most vulgar, graphic and explicit descriptions of sexual activity in the English language," and found that "any use of that word or a variation, in any context,

inherently" indecent. The FCC then found that both Fox and ABC had violated commission standards for decency.

The networks appealed the findings of indecency and their fines ($1.4 million each). The U.S. Supreme Court [*FCC v. Fox Television Stations, Inc.* (Fox 1), 556 U.S. 502 (2009)] held that the FCC's findings were not arbitrary nor capricious and remanded the case for findings related to the network's First Amendment challenges to the fines. On remand, the Court of Appeals found that the FCC indecency policy failed to give broadcasters sufficient notice of what would be considered indecent. The Court of Appeals found that the FCC was inconsistent as to which words it deemed patently offensive. The FCC standard was held to be void for vagueness. The FCC appealed.

DECISION: On appeal the U.S. Supreme Court held that the FCC failed to give Fox or ABC fair notice prior to the broadcasts in question that fleeting expletives and momentary nudity could be found indecent. Therefore, the FCC's standards, as applied to these broadcasts, were vague and void under the First Amendment. The Court set aside the FCC's findings as well as its orders and fines against the networks.

The FCC is free to create standards of decency for broadcasting programs. However, the standards must be established in advance of any charges of violations and those standards must be clear and applied consistently. Because the broadcasters would not have understood the standard at the time the violations occurred, the U.S. Supreme Court struck down the standards as void for vagueness. [*F.C.C. v. Fox Television Stations, Inc.*, **132 S. Ct. 2307 (2012)**]

---

[34] *CBS Corp. v. F.C.C.*, 663 F.3d 122 (3rd Cir. 2011).

Make the Connection

- -

Summary

The administrative agency is unique because it combines the three functions that are kept separate under our traditional governmental system: legislative, executive, and judicial. By virtue of legislative power, an agency adopts regulations that have the force of law, although agency members are not elected by those subject to the regulations. By virtue of the executive power, an agency carries out and enforces the regulations, makes investigations, and requires the production of documents. By virtue of the judicial power, an agency acts as a court to determine whether a violation of any regulation has occurred.

To some extent, an agency is restricted by constitutional limitations in inspecting premises and requiring the production of papers. These limitations, however, have a very narrow application in agency actions. When an agency acts as a judge, a jury trial is not required, nor must ordinary courtroom procedures be followed. Typically, an agency gives notice to the person claimed to be acting improperly, and a hearing is then held before the agency. When the agency has determined that there has been a violation, it may order that the violation stop. Under some statutes, the agency may go further and impose a penalty on the violator.

No appeal from an administrative agency's action can be made until every step available before the agency has been taken; that is, the administrative remedy must first be exhausted. An agency's actions can be reversed by a court if the agency exceeded its authority, the decision is not based in law or fact, the decision is arbitrary and capricious, the decision violates the laws or the rights of those affected by the agency's rule or actions, or, finally, the agency violated procedural steps.

Protection from secret government is provided by Sunshine laws that afford the right to know what most administrative agency records contain; by the requirement that most agency meetings be open to the public; by the invitation to the public to take part in rulemaking; and by publicity given, through publication in the *Federal Register* and trade publications, to the guidelines followed by the agency and the regulations it has adopted.

Learning Outcomes

After studying this chapter, you should be able to clearly explain:

6-1   Nature of the Administrative Agency

LO.1   Describe the nature and purpose of administrative agencies

See the discussion of the unique nature of agencies, pages 87–88.

See the discussion of obligations of administrative agencies, including APA and FOIA, page 88.

See Ethics & the Law on the IRS, page 89.

See the net neutrality Cyberlaw issue, page 92.

6-2   Legislative Power of the Agency

LO.2   Discuss the legislative or rulemaking power of administrative agencies

See the *Massachusetts v. EPA* case, pages 90–91.

6-3   Executive Power of the Agency

LO.3   Explain the executive or enforcement function of administrative agencies

See the *FCC* case, page 99.

See the Massey Energy example, page 95.

See the Kellogg's example on consent decrees, page 96.

6-4   Judicial Power of the Agency

LO.4   Discuss the judicial power of administrative agencies including the rule on exhaustion of administrative remedies

See the *Salazar* case, page 98.

Key Terms

administrative agency	consent decrees	hearing examiner
administrative law	exhaustion-of-administrative remedies	hearing officer
administrative law judge (ALJ)	*Federal Register*	informal settlements
Administrative Procedure Act	Federal Register Act	intervenors
cease-and-desist order	Freedom of Information Act	open meeting law

Questions and Case Problems

1. Following the events of September 11, 2001, in which four airplanes crashed as a result of the presence of terrorists on those flights, the FAA concluded that it needed to implement new procedures for airports and flights. The new procedures for security and flights took effect when the airports reopened five days later. Why did the FAA not need to go through the promulgation and public comment processes and time periods to have the new rules take effect?

2. The FDA was challenged by tobacco companies for its new rules that required the tobacco companies to put one of the FDA's 12 picture labels on its packaging. The tobacco companies argued that their First Amendment rights were violated by the rules, forcing them to speak in a certain way using government-mandated materials. The new labels were promulgated by both the FDA and the Department of Health and Human Services (HHS) pursuant to authority granted by Congress in 2009 under the Family Smoking Prevention and Tobacco Control Act.

   Under the law, the following nine textual statements were to be included on cigarette labels:

   > WARNING: Cigarettes are addictive.

   > WARNING: Tobacco smoke can harm your children.

   > WARNING: Cigarettes cause fatal lung disease.

   > WARNING: Cigarettes cause cancer.

   > WARNING: Cigarettes cause strokes and heart disease.

   > WARNING: Smoking during pregnancy can harm your baby.

   > WARNING: Smoking can kill you.

   > WARNING: Tobacco smoke causes fatal lung diseases in nonsmokers.

   > WARNING: Quitting smoking now greatly reduces serious risks to your health.

   The act required that these warnings and graphic labels take up 50 percent of the cigarette package label and 20 percent of all cigarette ads.

   After publishing the proposed rule and receiving more than 1,700 comments, the FDA published its final rule in June 2011. Explain how the tobacco companies could challenge the rules. Discuss whether the rules will be set aside. [In the case of *R.J. Reynolds Tobacco Company et al. v. FDA et al.*, 696 F.3d 1205 (D.C. Cir.)]

3. The Tacoma-Pierce County Health Department conducted an investigation into the quality of care provided by ambulance service providers in its jurisdiction. On the basis of that investigation, the department issued a set of temporary rules and regulations that established minimum requirements for equipment, drugs, and service availability for ambulance service providers in Pierce County. The *Tacoma News* wanted to publish an article on the matter and sought discovery of everything that had led to the adoption of the regulations, including all details of the investigation made by the health department. The health department objected to disclosing the names of the persons who had volunteered information on which the department had based its action and the names of the ambulance companies. Were the names subject to a Freedom of Information Act (FOIA) request? [*Tacoma News, Inc. v. Tacoma-Pierce County Health Dept.*, 778 P.2d 1066 (Wash. App.)]

4. Congress adopted a law to provide insurance to protect wheat farmers. The agency in charge of the program adopted regulations to govern applications for this insurance. These regulations were published in the *Federal Register*. Merrill applied for insurance, but his application did not comply with the regulations. He claimed that he was not bound by the regulations because he never knew they had been adopted. Is he bound by the regulations? [*Federal Crop Ins. Corp. v. Merrill*, 332 U.S. 380]

5. Santa Monica adopted a rent control ordinance authorizing the Rent Control Board to set the amount of rents that could be charged. At a hearing before it, the board determined that McHugh was charging his tenants a rent higher than the maximum allowed. McHugh claimed that the action of the board was improper because there was no jury trial. Is McHugh correct? Why or why not? [*McHugh v. Santa Monica Rent Control Board*, 777 P.2d 911 (Cal.)]

6. New York City's charter authorized the New York City Board of Health to adopt a health code that it declared to have the force and effect of law. The board adopted a code that provided for the fluoridation of the public water supply. A suit was brought to enjoin the carrying out of this program on the grounds that it was unconstitutional and that money

could not be spent to carry out such a program in the absence of a statute authorizing the expenditure. It was also claimed that the fluoridation program was unconstitutional because there were other means of reducing tooth decay; fluoridation was discriminatory by benefiting only children; it unlawfully imposed medication on children without their consent; and fluoridation was or may be dangerous to health. Was the code's provision valid? [*Paduano v. City of New York*, 257 N.Y.S.2d 531]

7. What is the *Federal Register*? What role does it play in rulemaking? What is the difference between the *Federal Register* and the Code of Federal Regulations?

8. The Consumer Product Safety Commission is reconsidering a rule it first proposed in 1997 that would require child-resistant caps on household products, including cosmetics. When the rule was first proposed in 1997, it was resisted by the cosmetics industry and abandoned. However, in May 2001, a 16-month-old baby died after drinking baby oil from a bottle with a pull-tab cap.

   The proposed rule would cover products such as baby oil and suntan lotion and any products containing hydrocarbons such as cleansers and spot removers. The danger, according to the commission, is simply the inhalation by children, not necessarily the actual ingestion of the products. Five children have died from inhaling such fumes since 1993, and 6,400 children under the age of five were brought into emergency rooms and/or hospitalized for treatment after breathing in hydrocarbons. There is no medical treatment for the inhalation of hydrocarbons.

   Several companies in the suntan oil/lotion industry have supported the new regulations. The head of a consumer group has said, "We know these products cause death and injury. That is all we need to know."[35]

   What process must the CPSC follow to promulgate the rules? What do you think of the consumer group head's statement? Will that statement alone justify the rulemaking?

9. The *Federal Register* contained the following provision from the Environmental Protection Agency on January 14, 2002:

   > *We, the U.S. Fish and Wildlife Service (Service), announce the re-opening of the comment period on the proposed listing of* Lomatium cookii

---

[35]Julian E. Barnes, "Safety Caps Are Considered for Cosmetics," *New York Times*, October 10, 2001, C1, C8.

(Cook's lomatium) and Limnanthes floccosa ssp. grandiflora *(large-flowered wooly meadowfoam) as endangered species under the Endangered Species Act of 1973, as amended (Act). We are re-opening the comment period to provide the public an opportunity to review additional information on the status, abundance, and distribution of these plants, and to request additional information and comments from the public regarding the proposed rule. Comments previously submitted need not be resubmitted as they will be incorporated into the public record as part of this extended comment period; all comments will be fully considered in the final rule.*

   DATES: We will accept public comments until March 15, 2002.

   What was the EPA doing and why? What could those who had concerns do at that point?

10. Macon County Landfill Corp. applied for permission to expand the boundaries of its landfill. Tate and others opposed the application. After a number of hearings, the appropriate agency granted the requested permission to expand. Tate appealed and claimed that the agency had made a wrong decision on the basis of the evidence presented. Will the court determine whether the correct decision was made? [*Tate v. Illinois Pollution Control Board*, 544 N.E.2d 1176 (Ill. App.)]

11. The planning commissioner and a real estate developer planned to meet to discuss rezoning certain land that would permit the real estate developer to construct certain buildings not allowed under the then-existing zoning law. A homeowners association claimed it had the right to be present at the meeting. This claim was objected to on the theory that the state's Open Meetings Act applied only to meetings of specified government units and did not extend to a meeting between one of them and an outsider. Was this objection valid?

12. The Michigan Freedom of Information Act declares that it is the state's policy to give all persons full information about the actions of the government and that "the people shall be informed so that they may participate in the democratic process." The union of clerical workers at Michigan State University requested the trustees of the university to give them the names and addresses of persons making monetary donations to the university. Michigan State objected because the disclosure of addresses was a violation of the right of privacy. Decide. [*Clerical-Technical*

Union of Michigan State University v. Board of Trustees of Michigan State University, 475 N.W.2d 373 (Mich.)]

13. The Department of Health and Human Services has proposed new guidelines for the interpretation of federal statutes on gifts, incentives, and other benefits bestowed on physicians by pharmaceutical companies. The areas on which the interpretation focused follow:

    • Paying doctors to act as consultants or market researchers for prescription drugs

    • Paying pharmacies fees to switch patients to new drugs

    • Providing grants, scholarships, and anything more than nominal gifts to physicians for time, information sessions, and so on, on new drugs[36]

    The Office of Inspector General is handling the new rules interpretation and has established a public comment period of 60 days. Explain the purpose of the public comment period. What ethical issues do the regulations attempt to address?

14. San Diego Air Sports (SDAS) Center operates a sports parachuting business in Otay Mesa, California. SDAS offers training to beginning parachutists and facilitates recreational jumping for experienced parachutists. It indicates that the majority of SDAS jumps occur at altitudes in excess of 5,800 feet. The jump zone used by SDAS overlaps the San Diego Traffic Control Area (TCA). Although the aircraft carrying the parachutists normally operate outside the TCA, the parachutists themselves are dropped through it. Thus, the air traffic controllers must approve each jump.

    In July 1987, an air traffic controller in San Diego filed an Unsatisfactory Condition Report with the Federal Aviation Administration (FAA), complaining of the strain that parachuting was putting on the controllers and raising safety concerns. The report led to a staff study of parachute jumping within the San Diego TCA. This was followed by a letter in March 1988 from the FAA to SDAS, informing SDAS that "[e]ffective immediately parachute jumping within or into the San Diego TCA in the Otay Reservoir Jump Zone will not be authorized." The FAA stated that the letter was final and appealable. SDAS challenged the letter in federal court on grounds that it constituted rulemaking without compliance with required Administrative Procedure Act (APA) procedures. Who is correct in this dispute and why? [*San Diego Air Sports Center, Inc. v. FAA*, 887 F.2d 966 (9th Cir.)]

15. The Endangered Species Act (ESA) charges the National Marine Fisheries Service (a federal agency) with the duty to "ensure" that any proposed action by the Council does not "jeopardize" any threatened or endangered species. The Steller sea lion is on the list of endangered species. The agency developed a North Pacific marine fishery plan that permitted significant harvest of fish by commercial fisheries in the area. Greenpeace, an environmental group, challenged the agency on the grounds that the plan was not based on a sufficient number of biological studies on the impact of the allowed fishing on the Steller sea lion. Greenpeace's biologic opinion concluded that the fishery plan would reduce the level of food for the sea lions by about 40 percent to 60 percent, if the juvenile fish were not counted in that figure. Greenpeace's expert maintained that counting juvenile fish was misleading because they were not capable of reproducing and the government agency's figure was, as a result, much lower at 22 percent. What would Greenpeace need to show to be successful in challenging the agency's fishery plan? [*Greenpeace, American Oceans Campaign v. National Marine Fisheries Service*, 237 F. Supp. 2d 1181 (W.D. Wash.)]

[36]See 67 *Federal Register* 62057, October 3, 2002. Go to **http://www.oig.hhs.gov**. See also Robert Pear, "U.S. Warning to Drug Makers Over Payments," *New York Times*, October 1, 2002, A1, A23; Julie Appleby, "Feds Warn Drugmakers: Gifts to Doctors May Be Illegal," *USA Today*, October 2, 2002, 1A.

C H A P T E R   7

Crimes

7-1 General Principles

Society sets certain standards of conduct and punishes a breach of those standards as a crime. This chapter introduces the means by which government protects people and businesses from prohibited conduct.

Detailed criminal codes and statutes define crimes and specify their punishment. Crimes vary from state to state but still show the imprint of a common law background through similar elements and structure.

7-1a Nature and Classification of Crimes

crime–violation of the law that is punished as an offense against the state or government.

misdemeanor–criminal offense with a sentence of less than one year that is neither treason nor a felony.

felony–criminal offense that is punishable by confinement in prison for more than one year or by death, or that is expressly stated by statute to be a felony.

A **crime** is conduct that is prohibited and punished by a government. Crimes are classified as *common law* or *statutory* according to their origin. Offenses punishable by less than one year in prison are called **misdemeanors.** More serious crimes are called **felonies,** including serious business crimes such as bribery and embezzlement, which are punishable by confinement in prison for more than one year. Misdemeanors include weighing goods with uninspected scales or operating without a sales tax license. An act may be a felony in one state and a misdemeanor in another.[1]

7-1b Basis of Criminal Liability

A crime generally consists of two elements: (1) a mental state (scienter or intent) and (2) an act or omission. Harm may occur as a result of a crime, but harm is not an essential element of a crime.

Mental State

Mental state, scienter, or intent, does not require an awareness or knowledge of guilt. In most crimes, the voluntary commission of the act is sufficient for proving mental state. Ignorance that a law is being broken does not mean there is not mental state. **For Example,** dumping waste without a permit is still a criminal act even when the party releasing the waste did not know about the permit requirement.

Act or Omission

Specific statutes define the conduct, or *actus reus*, that, when coupled with sufficient mental state, constitutes a crime. **For Example,** writing a check knowing you do not have the funds available is a crime. Likewise, the failure to file your annual income tax returns is also a crime.

CASE SUMMARY

Did I Know Pumping Gas Was a Crime?

FACTS: Ahmad owns a Spin-N-Market in Texas, a convenience store and gas station. One of the Spin-N-Market's gasoline tanks developed a leak. Jewel McCoy of CIT Environmental Services inspected the tank and said it needed to be drained and then pumped. McCoy gave Ahmad the cost of draining, and he suggested he would do it himself despite

---

[1] Some states further define crimes by seriousness with different degrees of a crime, such as first-degree murder, second-degree murder, and so on. Misdemeanors may be differentiated by giving special names to minor misdemeanors.

Did I Know Pumping Gas Was a Crime? continued

McCoy's warning about violations of the law. Ahmad rented a pump at the local hardware store and pumped over 5,000 gallons into a manhole near his store (4,690 of those gallons were gasoline). The gasoline made its way to the storm sewer system and then a creek as well as the city sewage treatment center. While firemen were working to divert the gasoline, the treatment center and two nearby schools had to be evacuated. Ahmad was charged with violation of the Clean Water Act and was convicted of two charges.

DECISION: The appeals court held that Ahmad did not have the intent to violate the statute, the CWA, because he thought that he was discharging water, not gasoline. There is more knowledge required for CWA violations; it is a criminal statute and there cannot be just strict liability—there still must be a showing of mental intent. [*United States v. Ahmad,* 101 F.3d 386 (5th Cir. 1996)]

7-1c Responsibility for Criminal Acts

In some cases, persons who did not necessarily commit the criminal act itself are still held criminally responsible for acts committed by others.

Corporate Liability

Corporations are held responsible for the acts of their employees. A corporation may also be held liable for crimes based on the failure of its employees to act. In the past decade, some of the nation's largest corporations have paid fines for crimes based on employees' failure to take action or for the actions they did take. **For Example,** Siemens, an international company, paid the largest fine in the history of the Foreign Corrupt Practices Act for paying bribes in order to win contracts in countries around the world, a total of $1.6 billion in fines, including $350 million in the United States.

Officers and Agents of Corporations

One of the main differences between nonbusiness and business crimes is that more people in a company can be convicted for the same business crime. For nonbusiness crimes, only those who are actually involved in the act itself can be convicted of the crime. For business crimes, however, managers of firms whose employees commit criminal acts can be held liable if the managers authorized the conduct of the employees or knew about their conduct and did nothing or failed to act reasonably in their supervisory positions to prevent the employees from engaging in criminal conduct. **For Example,** the former security chief for Massey Energy was sentenced to three years in prison after being found guilty of notifying employees in advance of the arrival of federal mine inspectors at the company's mines.[2]

CASE SUMMARY

Rats in the Warehouse and a CEO with a Fine

FACTS: Acme Markets, Inc., was a national food retail chain headquartered in Philadelphia. John R. Park was president of Acme, which, in 1970, employed 36,000 people and operated 16 warehouses.

In 1970, the Food and Drug Administration (FDA) forwarded a letter to Park describing, in detail, problems with rodent infestation in Acme's Philadelphia warehouse facility. In December 1971, the FDA found the same types

[2]Ken Maher, "Ex-Massey Official Gets Three Years," *Wall Street Journal,* March 1, 2012, p. A3.

Rats in the Warehouse and a CEO with a Fine continued

of conditions in Acme's Baltimore warehouse facility. In January 1972, the FDA's chief of compliance for its Baltimore office wrote to Park about the inspection:

> *We note with much concern that the old and new warehouse areas used for food storage were actively and extensively inhabited by live rodents. Of even more concern was the observation that such reprehensible conditions obviously existed for a prolonged period of time without any detection, or were completely ignored.*
>
> *We trust this letter will serve to direct your attention to the seriousness of the problem and formally advise you of the urgent need to initiate whatever measures are necessary to prevent recurrence and ensure compliance with the law.*

After Park received the letter, he met with the vice president for legal affairs for Acme and was assured that he

was "investigating the situation immediately and would be taking corrective action."

When the FDA inspected the Baltimore warehouse in March 1972, there was some improvement in the facility, but there was still rodent infestation. Acme and Park were both charged with violations of the federal Food, Drug and Cosmetic Act. Acme pleaded guilty. Park was convicted and fined $500; he appealed.

DECISION: Officers of a corporation can be held criminally liable for the conduct of others within the company if it can be shown that the officers knew of the issue and failed to take the steps necessary to eliminate the criminal activity. In this case, Park had been warned and had been given several opportunities to remedy the problem. Part of his responsibility as an officer is following up to be certain that tasks he has assigned are completed. Failure to follow through can be a basis for criminal liability. [***United States v. Park***, 421 U.S. 658 (1975)]

Federal Laws Targeting Officer and Director Criminal Responsibility

Following the Michael Milken and Ivan Boesky junk bond era on Wall Street in 1988, the Insider Trading and Securities Fraud Act of 1988 increased the criminal penalties for officers and directors who violated the law tenfold. In addition, the "white-collar kingpin" law imposed mandatory minimum sentences for corporate officers. Sarbanes-Oxley, which followed the 2000-era dot-com failures increased penalties for officers and directors from 5 years to 20 years, along with an increase in fines by 20 times. Under The Dodd-Frank Wall Street Reform and Consumer Protection Act, the types of white-collar executives covered under criminal laws increased to include brokers, insurers, and any financial services firms. In addition, Dodd-Frank created the Consumer Financial Protection Bureau (CFPB) that has the ability to refer cases to the Justice Department for prosecution. **For Example,** the CFPB would receive information about mortgage lenders, banks, and insurers from consumers that could then be turned over for possible criminal charges.

So-called honest services fraud has been refined by Dodd-Frank and court decisions.[3] Executives can no longer be convicted on the basis that something went wrong at their company. Proof of fraud requires something more than an officer just being an officer at the company—there must be active engagement in operations that led to the officer's committing fraud or some underlying crime, such as bribery that led to the company problems and loss in value.

Penalty for Crime: Forfeiture

When a defendant is convicted of a crime, the court may also declare that the defendant's rights in any property used or gained from a crime (an instrument of that crime) be confiscated. Some types of instruments of the crime are automatically forfeited, such as the tools of a crime. **For Example,** the U.S. government confiscated from confessed $50 billion Ponzi schemer, Bernie Madoff, everything from his yacht to his bank accounts

[3] *Skilling v. U.S.*, 561 U.S. 538 (2010).

to his seat on NASDAQ. Confiscation is, in effect, an increased penalty for the defendant's crime.

Penalties for Business and White-Collar Crimes

Most common law criminal penalties were created with "natural" persons in mind, as opposed to "artificial" or corporate persons. A $100,000 fine may be significant to an individual but to a corporation with $3 billion in assets and hundreds of millions in income, such a fine could be viewed as a minimal cost of doing business.

As a result of these fine amount realities, corporate penalties and processes have been reformed. Congress, prosecutors, and the courts are in continual processes of developing penalties for corporations and white-collar crimes so that the result is both a deterrent effect as well as changes in cultures of corporations to prevent additional violations.

Computing New Penalties for Corporations. Criminal penalties have been increased to allow judges to fine corporations according to how much a bad decision would cost. Rather than using fixed-amount fines for corporations, statutes and courts apply percentage of income, revenue, or profits penalties. **For Example,** a bad decision on a product line would cost a company 10 to 20 percent of its earnings. A criminal penalty could be imposed using that type of computation for the knowing sale of a defective product in this same percentage fashion with the idea that the company simply made a bad legal decision that should be reflected by an imposed earnings.

Corporate Integrity Agreements. Using a corporate integrity agreement (CIA), judges are able to, in effect, place corporations on probation. Under CIAs, companies are assigned monitors who are on-site and follow up to be sure the company is not committing any further violations. **For Example,** because of environmental law violations, ConEd was assigned a monitor from the National Resources Defense Council to observe the company's activities. Likewise, Apple has a monitor to prevent antitrust violations as a result of its civil charges of noncompetitive behavior. CIAs do not require an admission of guilt but generally require the payment of a fine and an agreement to "stay clean" for three to five years.

Federal Sentencing Guidelines. Another change in penalties for business and white-collar crimes has been the requirement for mandatory prison sentences for officers and directors who are convicted of crimes committed as they led their corporations. The human element of the corporation is then punished for the crimes that the business committed. The U.S. Sentencing Commission, established by Congress in 1984, has developed both federal sentencing guidelines and a carrot-and-stick approach to fighting business crime. If the managers of a company are involved and working to prevent criminal misconduct in the company and a crime occurs, the guidelines permit sentence reductions for the managers' efforts. If the managers do not adequately supervise conduct and do not encourage compliance with the law, the guidelines require judges to impose harsher sentences and fines. The guidelines, referred to as the **Federal Sentencing Guidelines** (or the *U.S. Sentencing Guidelines*), apply to federal crimes such as securities fraud, antitrust violations, racketeering, theft (embezzlement), Medicare fraud, and other business crimes. The sentencing guidelines permit a judge to place a guilty company on probation, with the length of the probation controlled by whether the company had prevention programs in place.

Federal Sentencing Guidelines—federal standards used by judges in determining mandatory sentence terms for those convicted of federal crimes.

Officer and Executive Banishment from Business Fields. One of the rapidly increasing forms of business crime punishment is barring executives and officers from working in their fields if they have a criminal conviction. **For Example,** the SEC can bar those who are convicted from the securities industry for a period of years or even for life (as in the case of junk bond king Michael Milken). In the health care field, federal agencies use the "responsible corporate officer" (RCO) doctrine to hold those who head up companies criminally responsible when their hospitals submit false Medicare claims or their drug firms misbrand prescription drugs. In addition to criminal sanctions for RCOs, agencies prosecuting the health care cases also seek to have the RCOs barred from the health care industry for periods that range from one year to life, with the typical time being 12 to 20 years.

Mandatory Sentences for Officers of Corporations Who Mastermind Crimes. The increased corporate and white-collar criminal penalties enacted under Sarbanes-Oxley (SOX) (see the next section for more discussion of SOX) also allow judges to consider the seriousness of the offense, the company's history of violations, its cooperation in the investigation, the effectiveness of its compliance program (often called an *ethics program*), and the role of senior management in the wrongdoing in determining fines and sentences. Corporate managers found to have masterminded any criminal activity must be sentenced to prison time.[4] Figure 7-1 is a summary of the current penalties for federal crimes. Under a U.S. Supreme Court decision, *U.S. v. Booker*, judges may only use the guidelines as just

FIGURE 7-1	Roster of White-Collar Criminal Charges	
COMPANY/PERSON	**ISSUE**	**STATUS**
Boeing (2003)	Charges of illicit use of competitor's proprietary documents; charges of recruiting government official	Loss of 7 government contracts worth $250 million; $615 million fine; guilty plea by official who was wooed; 9-month sentence for that official
Countrywide Mortgage (2009)	Insider trading; securities fraud	Former CEO Angelo Mozilo charged with insider trading, CFO and COO charged with failure to disclose firm's relaxed lending standards; settled case for fines
Andrew Fastow, former CFO of Enron (2004)	Multimillion-dollar earnings from serving as principal in SPEs (special purpose entities) of Enron created to keep debts off the company books	Entered guilty plea to securities and wire fraud; sentenced to 6 years; helping plaintiffs in shareholder suits
Jeffrey Skilling, former CEO of Enron (2004)	Questions about his role in the Enron fraud; resigned just prior to company's collapse	Found guilty of securities fraud and sentenced to 24.4 years; U.S. Supreme Court partially reversed his conviction on honest services fraud; sentence reduced to 14 years
Galleon Group (2011)	Insider trading charges related to hedge fund's operations	23 executives, including the CEO, convicted or entered guilty pleas; Galleon's $3.7 billion fund liquidated; CEO (Raj Rajaratnam) sentenced to 11 years; a Goldman Sachs director (Rajat Gupta) also convicted of insider trading and sentenced to 2 years in prison for feeding information to Rajaratnam
HealthSouth (2003)	$2.7 billion accounting fraud; overstatement of revenues	16 former executives indicted; 5 guilty pleas

[4] *U.S. v. Booker*, 543 U.S. 220 (2005).

FIGURE 7-1	Roster of White-Collar Criminal Charges (continued)	
COMPANY/PERSON	ISSUE	STATUS
Richard Scrushy, CEO of HealthSouth (2003)	85 federal felony counts, including violations of Sarbanes-Oxley financial certification provisions	Acquitted of financial fraud charges; found guilty of bribery and sentenced to 7 years
Martha Stewart, CEO of Martha Stewart Omnimedia and close friend of Sam Waksal, CEO of ImClone (2003)	Sold 5,000 shares of ImClone one day before public announcement of negative FDA action on Ebritux	Convicted of making false statements and conspiracy; served 5 months in prison, 5 months of home confinement, and two years of probation; fine of $30,000
KMPG (2006)	Tax shelter fraud	Settled with federal regulators by payment of $456 million penalty
Sotheby's (2003)	Price-fixing	Chairman given 1 year and 1 day in prison and a $7.5 million fine; CEO placed under house arrest for 1 year
WorldCom (2003)	Accounting issues centered on swaps—selling to other telecommunications companies and hiding expenses, thereby overstating revenue	WorldCom emerged from bankruptcy as MCI; 4 officers and managers entered guilty pleas; CEO Bernard Ebbers convicted and sentenced to 25 years
Bernie Madoff (2009)	$50 billion Ponzi scheme	Entered guilty plea to all charges; sentenced to 150 years (was 71 years old at time of sentencing); direct reports convicted
BP (2012)	Violation of Clean Air Act; willful failure to correct OSHA violations; manslaughter and obstruction	$50 million fine to EPA; $58 million fine to OSHA (largest in U.S. history) for pre–Deepwater Horizon explosion; $4 billion for crimes related to Deepwater Horizon explosion; $18 billion to settle suits
Stanford Securities (2012)	$9 billion Ponzi scheme	CEO convicted of mail, wire, and securities fraud and sentenced to 110 years; Laura Pendergest-Holt, the former chief investment officer, entered a guilty plea and was sentenced to 3 years; CFO entered a guilty plea
Massey Coal (2012)	Mine collapse resulting in the deaths of 29 miners	Three company officials entered guilty pleas and one was convicted of charges related to tipping off employees on mine inspections and destroying records to avoid government review; former CEO under indictment
Peanut Corporation of America (2013)	Indictments for producing and selling product without cleaning up salmonella issue at plant; falsifying tests that showed the salmonella was gone when it was not	Four company officers, including owner and CEO, convicted of criminal fraud and conspiracy
SAC Capital	Charges of insider trading; use of information from doctors about drug trial on new pharmaceuticals	Settled charges for $600 billion fine; 11 current and former employees convicted or entered guilty pleas

that, guidelines; the sentencing ranges are no longer mandatory for judges.[5] Going outside those ranges, however, is carefully reviewed by appellate courts.[6] Federal judges can consider evidence of prior convictions, but only if that evidence was presented at trial or if the defendant has a chance to present evidence about those convictions at the sentencing.[7]

White-Collar Crime Penalty Enhancement Act of 2002–federal reforms passed as a result of the collapses of companies such as Enron; provides for longer sentences and higher fines for both executives and companies.

Sarbanes-Oxley Reforms to Criminal Penalties. Part of SOX, passed by Congress following the collapses of Enron and WorldCom corporations, was the **White-Collar Crime Penalty Enhancement Act of 2002.**[8] This act increases penalties substantially. **For Example,** the penalties for mail and wire fraud are increased from a maximum of 5 years to a maximum of 20 years. Penalties for violation of pension laws increased from 1 year to 10 years and the fines increased from $5,000 to $100,000.[9] In addition, many federal statutes now require executives to reimburse their companies for any money earned as a result of illegal activity. **For Example,** the former CEO of UnitedHealth Group Inc. was required to pay back $448 billion in profits he had made from stock options that were granted illegally.[10]

THINKING THINGS THROUGH

Can a Pharmacy's License Be Revoked for Too Many Cash Sales of Oxycodone?

The Drug Enforcement Administration (DEA) has moved to revoke the controlled medication licenses of two pharmacies because the pharmacies were filling prescriptions for oxycodone (the painkiller) in excess of their monthly allowances for controlled substances. In addition, the DEA alleges that the pharmacies' corporate entities failed to conduct on-site inspections and failed to notice that 42 to 58 percent of all the sales of the substances were cash sales, something that is considered a red flag in the sale and distribution of controlled substances. In addition, the number of prescriptions filled continued to escalate.

The two pharmacies won an injunction against the revocation in federal district court. However, the DEA is hoping to persuade the judge to lift the injunction once it is able to show that the corporations should have known there was a problem. The rate of cash sales at these pharmacies was eight times the national rate for filling prescriptions with cash. Pharmacists at the drug stores, in interviews with the DEA agents, indicated that the customers paying cash for the oxycodone were "shady," and that they suspected that some of the prescriptions were not legitimate. One of the companies adjusted

(increased) the levels of shipment of oxycodone to the pharmacies five times. In one on-site visit by a DEA agent, the following information emerged: one of every three cars that came to the drive-thru window had a prescription for oxycodone; many patients living at the same address had the same prescriptions for oxycodone from the same doctor.

Both companies, CVS and Cardinal Health, have indicated in court filings that they have changed their practices and provided training to pharmacy personnel so that they can spot these types of illegal prescriptions and report suspicious activity. Both pharmacy companies have terminated customers, meaning that they will no longer fill prescriptions for those customers.

The DEA seeks to hold the corporations responsible because of the lack of on-site presence and the failure to follow the numbers for sales and distribution at the pharmacies. Can the corporation be held liable when it was not actually participating in the distribution of the oxycodone?

Source: Timothy W. Martin and Devlin Barrett, "Red Flags Ignored, DEA Says," *Wall Street Journal*, February 21, 2012. p. B1.

---

[5] *U.S. v. Skilling*, 554 F.3d 529 (5th Cir. 2009).
[6] *Gall v. U.S.*, 552 U.S. 38 (2007).
[7] Miriam H. Baer, "Choosing Punishment," 92 *Boston Univ. Law Rev.* 577 (2010).
[8] 18 U.S.C. §1314 *et seq.*
[9] 18 U.S.C. §§1341 and 1343; 29 U.S.C. §1131.
[10] S. Almashat et al., "Rapidly Increasing Criminal and Civil Monetary Penalties Against the Pharmaceutical Industry: 1991 to 2010," *Public Citizen's Health Research Group*, December 16, 2010, available at **http://www.citizen.org/hrg1924**.

ETHICS & THE LAW

When Addictions Are Off and On Again

In 1994, Congress passed a law that permitted nonviolent convicts to reduce their sentences by up to 12 months if they completed a drug-rehab/counseling program. When the program was first created, 3,755 inmates entered the program. In 2008, 18,000 federal prisoners were in the program and there was a waiting list of 7,000 inmates.

Dr. Sam Waksal, the former CEO of ImClone, served nine fewer months than his original seven-year sentence because he participated in a prison rehab program for inmates who have a problem with substance abuse. However, when Dr. Waksal was interviewed for the presentencing report, he told the probation officer that he was a "social drinker" and had perhaps five glasses of wine per week. One month after the interview with the probation officer, Waksal's lawyers informed a federal judge that Waksal now had a "dependence on alcohol" and requested approval for Waksal's entry into a prison rehab program.

The former mayor of Atlanta, Bill Campbell, was admitted into a federal rehab program and, as a result, got a 9-month reduction on his 30-month sentence for tax evasion. He was admitted to rehab despite the fact that his lawyers argued at his sentencing hearing that he had no substance abuse problem and that he hated the taste of alcohol, therefore urging the judge to conclude that Campbell's imprisonment was not necessary.

The Bureau of Prisons indicates that it is cracking down on admissions to the program, looking more closely at doctors' letters and past histories of the inmates.

Evaluate the ethics of the inmates who feign addiction. Evaluate the ethics of the consulting firms that help them get into the program.

Source: Kai Falkenberg, "Time Off for Bad Behavior," *Forbes*, January 12, 2009, pp. 64–65.

Creative Penalties for White-Collar Crime. Federal judges are developing new types of sentences in order to use those convicted to convince businesspeople to avoid criminal conduct. **For Example,** in 2009, a federal judge required an executive who entered a guilty plea to spend his two years of probation writing a book about what he did and offer guidance to business executives so that they can avoid his missteps. He was required to publish and distribute the book.[11] In 2010, a federal agency agreed to defer penalties if an officer agreed to travel around the country and speak to companies and executives about the mistakes he had made in order to help them understand the need for vigilance in stopping missteps that lead to crimes.

7-1d Indemnification of Crime Victims

Penalties are paid to the government. Typically, the victim of a crime does not benefit from the criminal prosecution and conviction of the wrongdoer, although courts can order that restitution be paid to victims.

The Victims of Crime Act of 1984 creates a federal Crime Victims Fund.[12] Using the fines paid into the federal courts as well as other monies, the federal government makes grants to the states to assist them in financing programs to provide assistance for victims of crime.[13] The Victim and Witness Protection Act of 1982 authorizes the sentencing judge in a federal district court to order, in certain cases, that the defendant make restitution (restoration) to the victim or pay the victim the amount of medical expenses or loss of income caused by the crime.[14]

---

[11] Natasha Singer, "Judge Orders Former Bristol-Myers Executive to Write Book," *New York Times*, June 9, 2009, p. B3.
[12] 18 U.S.C. §3771. The act was amended in 2004 to include a type of bill of rights for crime victims, including assistance through the newly created Office for Victims of Crime.
[13] 18 U.S.C. §1401 *et seq.*
[14] 18 U.S.C. §3579, as amended by 18 U.S.C. §18.18; see *Hughey v. United States*, 495 U.S. 411 (1990). In 2002, Congress passed another victims' compensation statute, with this one providing relief and assistance to the victims of terrorist attacks in the United States. 42 U.S.C. §10603b.

7-2 **White-Collar Crimes**

white-collar crimes–crimes that do not use nor threaten to use force or violence or do not cause injury to persons or property.

conspiracy–agreement between two or more persons to commit an unlawful act.

White-collar crime is generally considered business crime, the type committed generally in the course of doing business and usually involving some form of deceit used to get gains.

7-2a **Conspiracies**

The crime of conspiracy is committed before the actual crime; it is the planning of the crime. A **conspiracy** is an agreement between two or more persons to commit an unlawful act or to use unlawful means to achieve an otherwise lawful result. Some conspiracy statutes do require that those charged must have done something to carry out the agreement before the crime of conspiracy is committed. Almost all white-collar criminal charges involve a count of conspiracy, something that results from the fact that individuals work together in corporations to accomplish frauds.

7-2b **Money Laundering**

The federal government has adopted a Money Laundering Control Act (MLCA).[15] The act prohibits the knowing and willful participation in a financial transaction when the transaction is designed to conceal or disguise the source of the funds. The so-called *USA Patriot Act* that was passed on October 26, 2001, less than two months after the destruction of the World Trade Center and the damage to the Pentagon on September 11, 2001, includes a substantial number of changes and amendments to the MLCA and the Bank Secrecy Act (BSA).[16] Both statutes have been used as means to control bribery, tax evasion, and money laundering. Their changes and amendments were designed to curb the funding of terrorist activities in the United States.

The Patriot Act expands the coverage of the law from banks and financial institutions to anyone involved in financial transactions, which includes securities brokers; travel agents; those who close real estate transactions; insurance companies; loan or finance companies; casinos; currency exchanges; check-cashing firms; auto, plane, and boat dealers; and branches and agencies of foreign banks located in the United States. The amendments make even small businesses subject to the requirements of disclosure under MLCA and BSA, such as reporting cash transactions in excess of $10,000.

In addition, the types of accounts covered have been expanded. The accounts covered are not only securities accounts but also money market accounts. Furthermore, banks are now more actively involved in supervising accounts and following through on government information furnished to the bank on suspicious transactions and activities as well as individuals. Banks are required to implement new policies to prevent the types of transactions tagged by the government and conduct internal investigations for suspicious transactions. Because of the required close-watch provisions of these laws, banks and others covered under the federal statutes have developed anti-money-laundering programs. These programs must include a "Know Your Customer" training segment that teaches employees how to spot suspicious customers and transactions.

Racketeer Influenced and Corrupt Organizations (RICO) Act–federal law, initially targeting organized crime that has expanded in scope and provides penalties and civil recovery for multiple criminal offenses, or a pattern of racketeering.

7-2c **Racketeering**

Congress passed the **Racketeer Influenced and Corrupt Organizations (RICO) Act**[17] in 1970 as part of the Organized Crime Control Act. The law was designed primarily to

---

[15] 18 U.S.C. §§1956–1957 (2000). *U.S. v. Prince*, 214 F.3d 740 (6th Cir. 2000).
[16] 31 U.S.C. §531(h).
[17] 18 U.S.C. §§1961–1968.

prevent individuals involved in organized crime from investing money obtained through racketeering in legitimate businesses. However, the broad language of the act, coupled with a provision that allows individuals and businesses to sue for treble damages, has resulted in an increasing number of lawsuits against ordinary business persons not associated with organized crime.

Criminal and Civil Applications

RICO authorizes criminal and civil actions against persons who use any income derived from racketeering activity to invest in, control, or conduct an enterprise through a pattern of *racketeering activity*.[18] In criminal and civil actions under RICO, a pattern of racketeering activity must be established by proving that at least two acts of racketeering activity—so-called *predicate acts*—have been committed within 10 years.[19] For example, the former Atlanta Public Schools administrators and teachers who were involved in the cheating scandal on the state's standardized tests were convicted of racketeering because they had engaged in fraud to obtain bonuses. Conviction under RICO's criminal provisions may result in a $25,000 fine and up to 20 years' imprisonment as well as forfeiture of the property involved. A successful civil plaintiff may recover three times the actual damages suffered and attorney fees.[20]

Expanding Usage

Civil RICO actions have been successful against business entities, such as accounting firms, labor unions, insurance companies, commercial banks, and stock brokerage firms. However, under the Private Securities Litigation Reform Act of 1995, securities fraud was eliminated as a **predicate act,** or a qualifying underlying offense, for private RICO actions, absent a prior criminal conviction.[21]

predicate act–qualifying underlying offense for RICO liability.

7-2d Bribery

Bribery is the act of giving money, property, or any benefit to a particular person to influence that person's judgment in favor of the giver.[22] At common law, the crime was limited to doing such acts to influence a public official.

The giving and the receiving of a bribe constitute separate crimes. In addition, the act of trying to obtain a bribe may be a crime of solicitation of bribery in some states, while in other states bribery is broadly defined to include solicitation of bribes.

---

[18] §1961. Definitions:
(1) "Racketeering activity" means any act or threat involving murder, kidnapping, gambling, arson, robbery, bribery, extortion, dealing in obscene matter, dealing in a controlled substance or listed chemical, or sports bribery; counterfeiting; theft from interstate shipment; embezzlement from pension and welfare funds; extortionate credit transactions; fraud; wire fraud; mail fraud; procurement of citizenship or nationalization unlawfully; reproduction of naturalization or citizenship papers; obstruction of justice; tampering with a witness, victim, or an informant; retaliating against a witness, victim, or an informant; false statement in application and use of passport; forgery or false use of passport; fraud and misuse of visas, permits, and other documents; racketeering; unlawful welfare fund payments; laundering of monetary instruments; use of interstate commerce facilities in the commission of murder-for-hire; sexual exploitation of children; interstate transportation of stolen motor vehicles; interstate transportation of stolen property; trafficking in counterfeit labels of phonorecords, computer programs or computer program documentation, or packaging and copies of motion pictures or other audiovisual works; criminal infringement of a copyright; trafficking in contraband cigarettes; and white slave traffic.

[19] Brian Slocum, "RICO and the Legislative Supremacy Approach to Federal Criminal Lawmaking," 31 *Loyola Univ. Chicago Law Journal* 639 (2000).

[20] *Criminal RICO: 18 U.S.C. 1961–1968: A Manual for Federal Prosecutors.* Washington, D.C.: U.S. Dept. of Justice, Criminal Division, Organized Crime and Racketeering Section [2013].

[21] 15 U.S.C. §78(a), (n)–(t).

[22] In re *Mangone*, 923 N.Y.S.2d 679 (2011).

7-2e Commercial Bribery

Commercial bribery is a form of bribery in which an agent for another is paid or given something of value in order to make a decision on behalf of his or her principal that benefits the party paying the agent. **For Example,** a napkin supplier who pays a restaurant agent $500 in exchange for that agent's decision to award the restaurant's napkin contract to that supplier has engaged in commercial bribery.[23]

7-2f Extortion and Blackmail

Extortion and *blackmail* are crimes in which money is exchanged for either specific actions or restraint in taking action.

Extortion

When a public officer makes an illegal demand, the officer has committed the crime of **extortion. For Example,** if a health inspector threatens to close down a restaurant on a false sanitation law charge unless the restaurant pays the inspector a sum of money, the inspector has committed extortion. (If the restaurant voluntarily offers the inspector the money to prevent the restaurant from being shut down because of actual violations of the sanitation laws, the crime committed would be bribery.)

extortion–illegal demand by a public officer acting with apparent authority.

Blackmail

In jurisdictions where extortion is limited to the conduct of public officials, a nonofficial commits **blackmail** by making demands that would be extortion if made by a public official. Ordinarily, blackmail is the act of threatening someone with publicity about a matter that would damage the victim's personal or business reputation.

blackmail–extortion demands made by a nonpublic official.

7-2g Corrupt Influence

Legislative bodies have increasingly outlawed certain practices that exert a corrupting influence on business transactions.

Improper Political Influence

At the federal and state levels, it is a crime for one who holds public office to hold a financial interest in or to receive money from an enterprise that seeks to do business with the government. Such conduct is a conflict of interest between the official's duty to citizens and his or her personal financial interests. **For Example,** the former governor of Illinois, Rod Blagojevich, was convicted of seeking funds, fundraisers, and positions in exchange for political favors. To keep officials' conduct transparent, lobbyists must register in Washington, D.C.,[24] and adhere to statutory limits on gifts and contributions to political campaigns. Public officials must file annual disclosure forms about their financial positions as well as provide a disclosure of all gifts and their value.

---

[23] Connecticut's commercial bribery statute is a good example. It provides: *A person is guilty of commercial bribery when he confers, or agrees to confer, any benefit upon any employee, agent or fiduciary without the consent of the latter's employer or principal, with intent to influence his conduct in relation to his employer's or principal's affairs.* CGSA §53a-160 (2014). Other examples of commercial bribery statues can be found at Minn. Stat Ann §609.86 (Minnesota 2014); NH Rev Stat §638:8 (New Hampshire 2014); Alaska Stat §11.45.670 (Alaska 2014); and Ala. Code §13A-11-120 (Alabama 2014). Mississippi prohibits commercial bribery as well as sports bribery, which is paying the agent of a sports team in order to influence the outcome of a sporting event. Miss. Code Ann §97-9-10 (2014).

[24] Foreign Agents Registration Act, 22 U.S.C. §611 *et seq.*, as amended.

Foreign Corrupt Practices Act

The **Foreign Corrupt Practices Act (FCPA)** is a federal criminal statute that applies to businesses whose principal offices are in the United States; it is an antibribery and anticorruption statute covering these companies' international operations.[25] There is additional information on the FCPA in Chapter 10.

7-2h Counterfeiting

Counterfeiting is making, with fraudulent intent, a document or coin that appears to be genuine but is not because the person making it did not have the authority to make it. It is a federal crime to make, to possess with intent to transfer, or to transfer counterfeit coins, bank notes, or obligations or other securities of the United States. Various states also have statutes prohibiting the making and passing of counterfeit coins and bank notes. These statutes often provide, as does the federal statute, a punishment for the mutilation of bank notes or the lightening (of the weight) or mutilation of coins.

7-2i Forgery

Forgery consists of the fraudulent making or material altering of an instrument, such as a check, that attempts to create or changes a legal liability of another person.[26] Ordinarily, **forgery** consists of signing another's name with intent to defraud, but it may also consist of making an entire instrument or altering an existing one. It may also result from signing a fictitious name or using the identity of another in order to obtain funds or property. In lay language we talk about "identity theft," but it is a form of forgery because they are placing someone else's name and signature on documents.[27]

The issuing or delivery of a forged instrument to another person constitutes the crime of **uttering** a forged instrument. Sending a forged check through the channels of commerce or of bank collection constitutes an uttering of a forged instrument. The act of depositing a forged check into the forger's bank account by depositing it in an automatic teller machine constitutes uttering within the meaning of a forgery statute.[28]

7-2j Perjury

Perjury consists of knowingly giving false testimony in a judicial proceeding after having been sworn to tell the truth. Knowingly making false answers on any form filed with a government typically constitutes perjury or is subjected to the same punishment as perjury. In some jurisdictions, the false answers given in a situation other than in court or the litigation process is called the crime of *false swearing*. The penalties for perjury were increased substantially under SOX.

7-2k False Claims and Pretenses

Many statutes make it a crime to submit false claims or to obtain goods by false pretenses.

---

[25] 15 U.S.C. §78dd-1 *et seq.*

[26] Using another person's ID to obtain property or funds is a form of forgery. *Warlick v. State*, 330 P.3d 946 (Alas. App. 2014).

[27] *People v. Lloyd*, 987 N.Y.S.2d 672 (2014) (where defendants used stolen drivers' licenses and checks to forge checks and cash them).

[28] *Warren v. State*, 711 S.E.2d 108 (Ga. App. 2011).

False Claims

The federal false statement statute makes it a crime to knowingly and willfully make a false material statement about any matter within the jurisdiction of any department or agency of the United States. **For Example,** it is a crime to make false statements about income and assets on a student's application for federal financial aid.

SPORTS & ENTERTAINMENT LAW

Cycling Through Federal Funds

After cyclist Lance Armstrong admitted to doping during his cycling career, he was stripped of his seven Tour de France titles. However, the private punishment and disgrace pale in comparison to the action that the federal government is taking. The Justice Department has filed suit to collect from Mr. Armstrong the $40 million that the U.S. Postal Service paid to Mr. Armstrong's team during his career in exchange for the advertising and endorsements the USPS received. One-half of that money went to Mr. Armstrong. The suit alleges that the USPS was deceived into paying the money because Mr. Armstrong represented to the USPS that he was following the rules of cycling's governing bodies that prohibit the use of performance enhancing drugs.

A guilty verdict would mean that Mr. Armstrong would have to pay the USPS treble damages—the remedy afforded under the federal False Claims Act.

Obtaining Goods by False Pretenses

Almost all states have statutes that forbid obtaining money or goods under false pretenses.[29] An intent to defraud is an essential element of obtaining property by false pretenses.[30]

Examples of false pretense include delivering a check knowing that there is insufficient money in the bank account to cover the check.[31] False representations as to future profits in a business are also forms of false pretenses. Failing to perform on a contract is not a false pretense crime unless the contract had been entered into with the intent of not performing it.[32]

False Information Submitted to Banks

Knowingly making false statements in a loan application to a federally insured bank is a federal crime.[33] It is also a crime for a landowner to put a false value on land transferred to a bank as security for a loan.[34] **For Example,** many of the initial criminal charges in the subprime mortgage market collapse have involved mortgage brokers and appraisers who misrepresented property value or applicants' income in their mortgage applications for federally insured loans.

7-2| Bad Checks

Under a bad check statute, it is a crime to use or pass a check with the intent to defraud with the knowledge that there are insufficient funds in the bank to pay the check when it is presented for payment. Knowledge that the bad check will not be paid when presented

---

[29] *People v. Hussain*, 179 Cal. Rptr. 3d 679 (Cal. App. 2014).
[30] *U.S. v. Swisher*, 14 Cal. Daily Op. Serv. 12,314 (9th Cir. 2014)—wearing military uniform without actually having served in the military in order to obtain benefits was false pretense.
[31] *U.S. v. Tudeme*, 457 F.3d 577 (Fed. App. 2006).
[32] *Higginbotham v. State*, 356 S.W.3d 584 (Tex. App. 2011) and *People v. Headley*, 951 N.Y.S.2d 317 (2012).
[33] 18 U.S.C. §1014. See *U.S. v. Luis*, 765 F.3d 1061 (9th Cir. 2014).
[34] *U.S. v. Rizk*, 660 F.3d 1125 (9th Cir. 2011).

to the bank is an essential element of the crime. The bad check statutes typically provide that if the check is not made good within a specified number of days after payment by the bank is refused, it is presumed that the defendant acted with the intent to defraud.[35] For more information on checks, see Chapters 27 and 30.

7-2m Credit Card Crimes

It is a crime to steal a credit card and, in some states, to possess the credit card of another person without that person's consent. Using a credit card without the permission of the card owner is the crime of obtaining goods or services by false pretenses or with the intent to defraud. Likewise, a person who continues to use a credit card with the knowledge that it has been canceled is guilty of the crime of obtaining goods by false pretenses. Federal law also makes it a crime to use counterfeit credit cards for purposes of obtaining goods, services, or cash. The statute now covers the use of credit card numbers on the Internet in order to obtain goods and services.[36]

7-2n Embezzlement

embezzlement–statutory offense consisting of the unlawful conversion of property entrusted to the wrongdoer.

Embezzlement is the fraudulent conversion of another's property or money by a person to whom it has been entrusted.[37] Employees who take or sell their employer's property or funds for personal use have committed the crime of embezzlement. An agent employee commits embezzlement when he receives and keeps payments from third persons— payments the agent should have turned over to the principal. **For Example,** when an insured gives money to an insurance agent to pay the insurance company but the insurance agent uses the money to pay premiums on the policies of other persons, the agent is guilty of embezzlement. Generally, the intent to return the property or money embezzled or eventually actually returning it, is no defense.

7-2o Obstruction of Justice: Sarbanes-Oxley (SOX)

Another SOX provision clarifies what constitutes obstruction of justice and increases the penalties for such an act. The new section makes it a felony for anyone, including company employees, auditors, attorneys, and consultants,

> to alter, destroy, mutilate, conceal, cover up, falsify or make a false entry with the "intent to impede, obstruct, or influence the investigation or proper administration of any matter within the jurisdiction of any department or agency of the United States."[38]

The statute goes on to address audit records specifically and requires auditors to retain their work papers related to a client's audit for at least five years. Any destruction of documents prior to that time constitutes a felony and carries a penalty of up to 20 years. The statute was passed in response to the conduct of Arthur Andersen, the audit firm for the collapsed Enron Corporation. Many of the firm's audit papers on Enron were destroyed, but the firm and partner-in-charge escaped criminal liability because the government could not establish that the senior managers in Andersen were aware of the shredding.[39]

---

[35] *McMillan v. First Nat. Bank of Berwick,* 978 A.2d 370 (Pa. Super. 2009).

[36] 18 U.S.C. §1029. Fines for credit card fraud have been increased to between $50,000 and $100,000 per offense.

[37] *State v. Henry,* 73 So. 3d 958 (La. App. 2011); *Stern v. Epps,* 464 Fed. Appx. 388 (5th Cir. 2012).

[38] 18 U.S.C. §1519. *U.S. v. Hunt,* 526 F.3d 739 (11th Cir. 2008).

[39] *Arthur Andersen LLP v. U.S.,* 544 U.S. 696 (2005). The obstruction conviction of the firm was reversed because of insufficient proof of the firm's actual knowledge of document destruction.

7-2p **Corporate Fraud: SOX**

SOX also created a new form of mail and wire fraud. Ordinarily, mail or wire fraud consists of the use of the mail or telephones for purposes of defrauding someone of money and/or property. However, the SOX form of mail or wire fraud is based on new requirements imposed on corporate officers to certify their financial statements when they are issued. If a corporate officer fails to comply with all requirements for financial statement certification or certifies financial statements that contain false material information, the officer and company have committed corporate fraud with penalties that range from fines of $1,000,000 and/or 10 years to $5,000,000 and/or 20 years for willful violation of the certification requirements.

7-2q **The Common Law Crimes**

In contrast to white-collar crimes, *common law crimes* are crimes that involve the use of force or the threat of force or cause injury to persons or damage to property. The following sections discuss crimes of force and crimes against property that affect businesses.

Larceny

Larceny is the wrongful or fraudulent taking of the personal property of another by any person with fraudulent intent. Shoplifting is a common form of larceny. In many states, shoplifting is made a separate crime. In some states, all forms of larceny and robbery are consolidated into a statutory crime of theft. At common law, there was no crime known as theft.

Robbery

Robbery is the taking of personal property from the presence of the victim by use of force or fear. Most states have aggravated forms of robbery, such as robbery with a deadly weapon. Snatching a necklace from the neck of the victim involves sufficient force to constitute robbery. When the unlawful taking is not by force or fear, as when the victim does not know that the property is being taken, the offense is larceny, but it cannot be robbery.

Some statutes may be aimed at a particular kind of robbery. **For Example,** carjacking is a federal crime under the Anti-Car Theft Act of 1992.[40]

Burglary

At common law, *burglary* was the breaking and entering during the night into the dwelling house of another with the intent to commit a felony. Inserting the automatic teller card of another, without their knowledge or permission, into an automatic teller machine set in the wall of the bank may constitute an entry into the bank for the purpose of committing burglary.[41] Some states word their burglary *statutes*, however, so that there is no burglary in this automatic teller case. This act would be covered by other criminal statutes.

Modern statutes have eliminated many of the elements of the common law definition so that under some statutes it is now immaterial when or whether there was an entry to commit a felony. The elements of breaking and entering are frequently omitted. Under some statutes, the offense is aggravated and the penalty is increased, depending on the

---

[40] 18 U.S.C. §2119. See *U.S. v. Runyon*, 707 F.3d 475 (4th Cir. 2013).
[41] *People v. Cardwell*, 137 Cal. Rptr. 3d 525 (2012).

place where the offense was committed, such as a bank building, freight car, or warehouse. Related statutory offenses, such as the crime of possessing burglars' tools, have been created.

Arson

At common law, *arson* was the willful and malicious burning of another's dwelling. The law was originally designed to protect human life, although arson has been committed just with the burning of the building even if no one is actually hurt. In most states, arson is a felony, so if someone is killed in the resulting fire, the offense is considered a felony-murder. Under the felony-murder rule, homicide, however unintended, occurring in the commission of a felony is automatically classified as murder. Virtually every state has created a special offense of burning to defraud an insurer.

Riots and Civil Disorders

Damage to property in the course of a riot or civil disorder is ordinarily covered by other types of crimes such as the crime of larceny or arson. In addition, the act of assembling as a riotous mob and engaging in civil disorders is generally some form of crime in itself under either common law concepts of disturbing the peace or modern antiriot statutes, even without destruction or theft of property. However, statutes on civil disorders must be carefully drawn to avoid infringing on constitutionally protected free speech.

7-3 Criminal Law and the Computer

In some situations, ordinary crimes cover computer crime situations. In other situations, new criminal law statutes are required.

7-3a What Is a Computer Crime?

computer crimes–
wrongs committed using a computer or with knowledge of computers.

Generally, the term **computer crime** is used to refer to a crime that can be committed only by a person having some knowledge of the operation of a computer. Just as stealing an automobile requires knowledge of how to operate and drive a car, so the typical computer crime requires the knowledge of how the computer works.

Because the more serious and costly wrongs relating to computers do not fit into the ordinary definitions of crime, there are now computer-specific criminal statutes: Computer crimes can be committed against the computer, using the computer, or through the computer.

7-3b The Computer as Victim

A traditional crime may be committed by stealing or intentionally damaging a computer.

Theft of Hardware

When a computer itself is stolen, the ordinary law relating to theft crimes should apply. Theft of a computer is subject to the same law as the theft of a truck or a desk.

Theft of Software

When a thief takes software, whether in the form of a program written on paper or a program on a disk or memory stick, something has been taken, but it is not tangible property as larceny requires. Virtually every state makes stealing software a crime.

Intentional Damage

The computer may be the "victim" of a crime when it is intentionally destroyed or harmed. In the most elementary form of damage, the computer could be harmed if it was smashed with an ax or destroyed in an explosion or a fire. In such cases, the purpose of the intentional damage is to cause the computer's owner the financial loss of the computer and the destruction of the information that is stored in it.

Intentional damage can result from more subtle means. Gaining access to the computer and then erasing or altering the data is also the crime of intentional damage. Likewise, interfering with the air conditioning so computers are damaged or malfunction would also be covered under intentional damage statutes. Planting a bug or virus in the software, causing a program to malfunction or to give incorrect output, is a form of intentional damage. Angry employees, former employees, and competitors have all been convicted of intentional damage.

7-3c Unauthorized Use of Computers

The unlawful use of a computer belonging to someone else is also a crime in some states. There are specific statutes at the state and federal levels that make it unlawful to use government computers without permission. One of the issues that is critical in criminal prosecution is whether the use was, in fact, "unauthorized." With Wi-Fi networks, the ease of access and openness has proven to be a challenge in prosecution for unauthorized use.[42] The key to prosecution in misuse of computer cases is proof that the access was not authorized.

CASE SUMMARY

Rifling Through Videos on Your Fellow Officers

FACTS: Sergeant Kenneth Riley used videos of a fellow officer, not for training purposes, but for purposes of getting a fellow officer disciplined. He showed the videos to those within the department who would not have authorization to view them. Riley was indicted for unauthorized use of a computer and unauthorized access and disclosure of computer data. Riley moved to have the indictment dismissed.

DECISION: Riley's access and use of computer data did not constitute the crime of unauthorized use of computers. The court held that what Riley did was a violation of workplace policies but did not fit within the criminal conduct intended to be covered by the statute. The judge was concerned about arbitrary definitions and enforcement and a criminal statute being used for retaliatory purposes. [***New Jersey v. Riley**, **988 A.2d 1252 (N.J. 2009)***]

7-3d Computer Raiding

Taking information from a computer without the consent of the owner is a crime. Whether theft is accomplished by instructing the computer to make a printout of stored information or by tapping into its data bank by electronic means is not important. In some states, taking information is known as the crime of "computer trespass."[43]

---

[42] U.S.C. §1030(e)(6); for an article summarizing the issues, see Orin S. Kerr, "Cybercrime's Scope: Interpreting 'Access' and 'Authorization' in Computer Misuse Statutes," 78 *N.Y.U. L. Rev.* 1596, 1632–37 (2003).

[43] *Washington v. Riley*, 846 P.2d 1365 (Wash. 1993).

Both Congress and state legislatures have adopted statutes that make it a crime to gain unauthorized access to a computer or use information so gained to cause harm to the computer or its rightful user.[44] Again, the presence of Wi-Fi when there are unsecured users has complicated prosecutions for taking information.

7-3e Diverted Delivery by Computer

In many industries, a computer controls the delivery of goods. The person in charge of that computer or someone unlawfully gaining access to it may cause the computer to direct delivery to an improper place. That is, instead of shipping goods to the customers to whom they should go, the wrongdoer diverts the goods to a different place, where the wrongdoer or a confederate receives them.

Instructing the computer to give false directions can cause this fraudulent diversion of goods. Because the computer allows changes in delivery of goods through a mere keystroke, the depth of diversion cases is great. **For Example,** in one case, several hundred loaded freight cars disappeared. In another case, a loaded oil tanker was diverted to unload into a fleet of tank trucks operated by an accomplice of the computer operator.

7-3f Economic Espionage by Computer

Economic Espionage Act (EEA)–federal law that makes it a felony to copy, download, transmit, or in any way transfer proprietary files, documents, and information from a computer to an unauthorized person.

The **Economic Espionage Act (EEA)** is a federal law[45] passed in response to several cases in which high-level executives took downloaded proprietary information from their computers to their new employers. The EEA makes it a felony to steal, appropriate, or take a trade secret as well as to copy, duplicate, sketch, draw, photograph, download, upload, alter, destroy, replicate, transmit, deliver, send, mail, or communicate a trade secret. The penalties for EEA violations are up to $500,000 and 15 years in prison for individuals and $10 million for organizations. When employees take new positions with another

---

E-COMMERCE & CYBERLAW

They Were Bullies: Mean Girls in Cyberspace

On May 14, 2008, a federal grand jury indicted Lori Drew, 49, of Missouri, the first of what would become known as the cyber bully. Ms. Drew had created a MySpace site for Josh Evans, a fictitious teen boy she used as a means of getting information from Megan Meier, a 13-year-old girl with whom Ms. Drew's daughter had had a falling-out. Josh pretended to be interested in Megan, but then said that she was "fat" and that the world would be a better place without her. Megan hanged herself within an hour of receiving the final comments from "Josh." Ms. Drew was later charged and convicted of conspiracy and accessing computers without authorization.*

Since the time of that case, there have been a number of similar incidents in which friends, parents, and others harass individuals using the various sites available from Facebook to Instagram. States now have very specific cyberbullying statutes for prosecution. As one expert phrased it, we have to take responsibility for what we post online and the consequences that can stem from hurtful or fearsome comments. There are both civil and criminal statutes that provide curbs for victims. Civil remedies allow for injunctions, and criminal penalties are at a level that allows them to serve as a deterrent for the types of postings that began with the Drew case.

*_U.S. v. Lori Drew_, 259 F.R.D. 449 (C.D. Cal. 2009).

---

[44] The Counterfeit Access Device and Computer Fraud Act of 1984, 18 U.S.C. §1030 _et seq._; Computer Fraud and Abuse Act of 1986, 18 U.S.C. §1001; Electronic Communications Privacy Act of 1986, 18 U.S.C. §2510; Computer Fraud Act of 1987, 15 U.S.C. §§272, 278, 40 U.S.C. §759; National Information Infrastructure Protection Act, 18 U.S.C. §1030 (protecting confidentiality and integrity on the Internet).

[45] 18 U.S.C. §1831.

company, their former employers are permitted to check the departing employees' computer e-mails and hard drives to determine whether the employees have engaged in computer espionage.

7-3g Electronic Fund Transfer Crimes

The Electronic Fund Transfers Act (EFTA)[46] makes it a crime to use any counterfeit, stolen, or fraudulently obtained card, code, or other device to obtain money or goods in excess of a specified amount through an electronic fund transfer system. The EFTA also makes it a crime to ship in interstate commerce devices or goods so obtained or to knowingly receive goods that have been obtained by means of the fraudulent use of the transfer system.

7-3h Circumventing Copyright Protection Devices Via Computer

The Digital Millennium Copyright Act (DMCA)[47] makes it a federal offense to circumvent or create programs to circumvent encryption devices that copyright holders place on copyrighted material to prevent unauthorized copying. Circumventing the encryption devices on software or CDs or DVDs is a violation of the DMCA. **For Example,** Dmitry Sklyarov, a Russian computer programmer, was the first person to be charged with a violation of the DMCA. Mr. Sklyarov was arrested in early 2002 at a computer show after giving a speech in Las Vegas at the Defcon convention on his product that he had developed to permit the circumvention of security devices on copyrighted materials. His program unlocked password-protected e-books and PDF files. He gave his speech and was returned to Russia in exchange for his agreement to testify in a case that will determine the constitutionality of DMCA.

The No Electronic Theft Act makes it a federal criminal offense to willfully infringe copyrighted material worth more than $1,000 using the Internet or other electronic devices even if the infringer does not profit from others' use of the material. **For Example,** sending along copyrighted articles on the Internet to friends, without permission from the site would be a violation even though there is no profit.

7-3i Spamming

Controlling the Assault of Non-Solicited Pornography and Marketing (CAN-SPAM) Act–allows private companies to bring suit against spammers for their unauthorized use of Internet Service Providers (ISPs).

Spamming, or the practice of sending out thousands of e-mails at once to many different computer users, is an ever-increasing problem. Congress passed the **Controlling the Assault of Non-Solicited Pornography and Marketing (CAN-SPAM) Act,** which allows private companies to bring suit against spammers for their unauthorized use of Internet Service Providers (ISPs).

For example, in March 2013, security experts said that we experienced what was "the biggest cyberattack in history." At the root of it was a fight over spam. Spamhaus, a Dutch company that fights spam, added Cyberbunker to its so-called blacklist. Spamhaus's blacklist consists of companies e-mail providers use as a screen to weed out spam. Cyberbunker is a Web-hosting service that, by its own description, will host any site except "child porn and anything related to terrorism."[48] Cyberbunker wants to spam and Spamhaus wants to protect e-mail servers from spam, so there is a war in

---

[46] 15 U.S.C. §1693(n).
[47] 17 U.S.C. §512 (2010).
[48] John Markoff and Nicole Perlroth, "Dispute on Spam Stirs Big Assault on the Internet," *New York Times,* March 27, 2013, p. A1.

cyberspace. Because of the international nature of these activities, prosecution is difficult, and authorities continue to investigate the combination of spamming and hacking crimes.

7-4 Criminal Procedure Rights for Businesses

The U.S. Constitution guarantees the protection of individual and corporate rights within the criminal justice system.

7-4a Fourth Amendment Rights for Businesses

Search and Seizure: Warrants

Fourth Amendment–
privacy protection in the
U.S. Constitution;
prohibits unauthorized
searches and seizures.

search warrant–judicial
authorization for a
search of property where
there is the expectation
of privacy.

The **Fourth Amendment** of the U.S. Constitution provides that "the right of the people to be secure in their persons, houses, papers, and effects, against unreasonable searches and seizures, shall not be violated." This amendment protects individual privacy by preventing unreasonable searches and seizures. Before a government agency can seize the property of individuals or businesses, it must obtain a valid **search warrant** issued by a judge or magistrate, based on probable cause, unless an exception to this warrant requirement applies. In other words, there must be good reason to search the location named. The Fourth Amendment applies equally to individuals and corporations. If an improper search is conducted, evidence obtained during the course of that search may be inadmissible in the criminal proceedings for the resulting criminal charges.[49]

Exceptions to the Warrant Requirement

Exceptions to the warrant requirement are emergencies, such as a burning building, and the "plain-view" exception, which allows law enforcement officials to take any property that anyone can see, for no privacy rights are violated when items and property are left in the open for members of the public to see. **For Example,** you have an expectation of privacy in the garbage in your garbage can when it is in your house. However, once you move that garbage can onto the public sidewalk for pickup, you no longer have the expectation of privacy because you have left your garbage out in plain view of the public. **For Example,** in *Dow Chemical Co. v. United States*, 476 U.S. 1819 (1986), the U.S. Supreme Court held that a company does not have a right of privacy from low-flying planes of its production facilities. Pictures taken from the airplanes of plant operations were not a violation of privacy.

Another exception allows officers to enter when they are needed to give aid because of an ongoing criminal act. **For Example,** officers who are able to see a fight through the windows of a house and resulting injuries can enter to render help. Another exception would be that the person who lives in the property to be searched has given permission for the search.

Privacy and Cyber Space: Access to Our Messages and Files. One of the questions related to privacy is how much of what we post online and put on our computers at work is protected by privacy rights that would require a warrant before law enforcement could examine the content. However, if employers have access to the information on your work computer and e-mails, you do not enjoy the protection of privacy.

---

[49] See *Arizona v. Gant*, 556 U.S. 332 (2009) in which the U.S. Supreme Court held that evidence obtained searching the vehicle of a suspect who is handcuffed and locked in a police car cannot be used. A search warrant is needed when the suspect has no access to the evidence to destroy it.

CASE SUMMARY

Shared Drive + Shared Access = NO PRIVACY

FACTS: In February 2003, while serving as a civilian contractor, Michael D. King resided in a dormitory at the Prince Sultan Air Base in Saudi Arabia. During his stay in the dormitory, King kept his personal laptop computer in his room and connected it to the base network. All users of the base network signed agreements indicating that they understood their communications over and use of the base network were subject to monitoring.

An enlisted airman was searching the base network for music files when he came across King's computer on the network. The airman was able to access King's hard drive because it was a "shared" drive. The airman discovered a pornographic movie and text files "of a pornographic nature." The airman reported his discovery to a military investigator, who, in turn, referred the matter to a computer specialist. This specialist located King's computer and hard drive on the base network and verified the presence of pornographic videos and explicit text files on the computer. She also discovered a folder on the hard drive labeled "pedophilia."

Military officials seized King's computer and also found CDs containing child pornography.

Two years later, the government obtained an indictment, charging King with possession of child pornography. After his arrest, the government searched his residence pursuant to a search warrant and found additional CDs and hard drives containing over 30,000 images of child pornography.

King entered a guilty plea and was sentenced to 108 months in prison. King then appealed his conviction on the grounds that there had been an illegal search and seizure of his computer and files.

DECISION: The court held that there was no Fourth Amendment violation because the investigators did not search King's files or computer initially to discover the pornographic materials. They merely had to access the universally accessible files of the military base. King had no expectation of privacy in whatever was posted on the shared drive. The search of his home computer and files in his room was with a warrant that was based on probable cause obtained from public access to the files. [*U.S. v. King*, 509 F.3d 1338 (11th Cir. 2007)]

Business Records and Searches

In many business crimes, the records that prove a crime was committed are not in the hands of the person who committed that crime. Accountants, attorneys, and other third parties may have the business records in their possession. In addition to the Fourth Amendment issues involved in seizing these records (a warrant is still required), there may be protections for the business defendants. The next section covers those protections.

Protections for Privileged Records and Documents

All states recognize an attorney-client privilege, which means that an individual's conversations with her lawyer and the notes of those conversations are not subject to seizure unless the privilege is waived. In many of the prosecutions of companies, the Justice Department has asked companies to waive the attorney-client privilege so that it can have access to information that is then used to find other companies that may have participated in criminal activity.

Some states recognize an accountant-client privilege and other privileges, such as those between priest and parishioner or doctor and patient. A privileged relationship is one in which the records and notes resulting from the contact between individuals cannot be seized even with a warrant (with some exceptions).

7-4b Fifth Amendment Self-Incrimination Rights for Businesses

Self-Incrimination

The words "I take the Fifth" are used to invoke the constitutional protections against self-incrimination provided under the **Fifth Amendment** that prevents compelling a person to be a witness against himself. **For Example,** Mark McGwire, the former St. Louis baseball player, invoked the Fifth Amendment in his testimony during congressional hearings on steroid use. **For Example,** Edith O'Brien, an employee at the collapsed investment fund, MF Global, refused to answer questions before Congress, claiming her right against self-incrimination. Lois Lerner, a former administrator with the IRS, took the Fifth Amendment when she was subpoenaed to testify before Congress.

The Fifth Amendment protection applies only to individuals; corporations are not given Fifth Amendment protection. A corporation cannot prevent the disclosure of its books and records on the grounds of self-incrimination. The officers and employees of a corporation can assert the Fifth Amendment, but the records of the corporation belong to the corporation, not to them.

Miranda Rights

The famous **Miranda warnings** come from a case interpreting the extent of Fifth Amendment rights. In *Miranda v. Arizona*,[50] the U.S. Supreme Court ruled that certain warnings must be given to persons who face custodial interrogation for the purposes of possible criminal proceedings. The warnings consist of an explanation to individuals that they have the right to remain silent; that if they do speak, anything they say can be used against them; that they have the right to have an attorney present; and that if they cannot afford an attorney, one will be provided for them. Failure to give the *Miranda* warnings means that any statements, including a confession, obtained while the individual was being interrogated cannot be used as evidence against that individual. The prosecution will have to rely on evidence other than the statements made in violation of *Miranda*, if such evidence exists.

7-4c Due Process Rights for Businesses

Also included in the Fifth Amendment is the language of due process. **Due process** is the right to be heard, question witnesses, and present evidence before any criminal conviction can occur. Due process in criminal cases consists of an initial appearance at which the charges and the defendant's rights are outlined; a preliminary hearing or grand jury proceeding in which the evidence is determined to be sufficient to warrant a trial; an arraignment for entering a plea and setting a trial date when the defendant pleads innocent; a period of discovery for obtaining evidence; and a trial at which witnesses for the prosecution can be cross-examined and evidence presented to refute the charges. In addition to these procedural steps, the **Sixth Amendment** guarantees that the entire process will be completed in a timely fashion because this amendment guarantees a speedy trial.

Fifth Amendment—constitutional protection against self-incrimination; also guarantees due process.

Miranda warnings—warnings required to prevent self-incrimination in a criminal matter.

due process—the constitutional right to be heard, question witnesses, and present evidence.

Sixth Amendment—the U.S. constitutional amendment that guarantees a speedy trial.

[50] 384 U.S. 436 (1966).

Make the Connection

Summary

When a person does not live up to the standards set by law, this punishable conduct, called *crime*, may be common law or statutory in origin. Crimes are classified as *felonies*, which generally carry greater sentences and more long-term consequences, and *misdemeanors*.

Employers and corporations may be criminally responsible for their acts and the acts of their employees. The federal sentencing guidelines provide parameters for sentences for federal crimes and allow judges to consider whether the fact that a business promotes compliance with the law is a reason to reduce a sentence.

White-collar crimes include those relating to financial fraud. Sarbanes-Oxley reforms increased the penalties for financial fraud and added fraudulent financial statement certification as a crime. Other white-collar crimes include bribery, extortion, blackmail, and corrupt influence in politics and in business. Also included as white-collar crimes are counterfeiting, forgery, perjury, making false claims against the government, obtaining goods or money by false pretenses, using bad checks, false financial reporting, and

embezzlement. The common law crimes include those that involve injury to person and/or property, such as arson and murder.

Statutes have expanded the area of criminal law to meet situations in which computers are involved. Both federal and state statutes make the unauthorized taking of information from a computer a crime. The diversion of deliveries of goods and the transfer of funds, the theft of software, and the raiding of computers are made crimes to some extent by federal laws. Newer federal statutes that apply to computers are the Economic Espionage Act, which prohibits downloading or copying information via computer to give to a competitor, and the Digital Millennium Copyright Act that prohibits circumventing or designing programs to circumvent encryption devices.

Criminal procedure is dictated by the Fourth, Fifth, and Sixth Amendments. The Fourth Amendment protects against unreasonable searches, the Fifth Amendment protects against self-incrimination and provides due process, and the Sixth Amendment guarantees a speedy trial.

Learning Outcomes

After studying this chapter, you should be able to clearly explain:

7-1 General Principles

LO.1 Discuss the nature and classification of crimes
See the discussion of crimes and misdemeanors, page 105.

LO.2 Describe the basis of criminal liability
See the *U.S. v. Ahmad* case, pages 105–106.
See the Massey Energy example, page 106.

LO.3 Identify who is responsible for criminal acts
See *U.S. v. Park*, pages 106–107.
See the discussion of CVS in Thinking Things Through, page 111.

LO.4 Explain the penalties for crimes and the sentencing for corporate crimes
See Figure 7-1, pages 109–110.
See the example on Michael Milken, page 109.
See the discussion of the sentencing guidelines and the various cases related to them, page 108.
See the Ethics & the Law feature, page 112.

7-2 White-Collar Crimes

LO.5 List examples of white-collar crimes and their elements

See the discussion on White Collar Crimes, pages 113–120.
See the *Andersen* example of obstruction, page 118.

LO.6 Describe the common law crimes
See the discussion on Common Law Crimes, pages 119–120.
See the Sports & Entertainment Law feature on Lance Armstrong and false claims, page 117.
See the E-Commerce & Cyberlaw discussion of cyber-bullying, page 122.

7-3 Criminal Law and the Computer

LO.7 Discuss crimes related to computers
See generally the section on Computer Crimes, page 120.
See the *New Jersey v. Riley* case for unauthorized access, page 121.
See the Cyberbunker-Spamhaus example for spamming, page 123.

7-4 Criminal Procedure Rights for Businesses

LO.8 Describe the rights of businesses charged with crimes and the constitutional protections afforded them
See the *U.S. v. King* case, page 125.

Key Terms

blackmail

computer crime

conspiracy

Controlling the Assault of
   Non-Solicited Pornography and
   Marketing (CAN-SPAM) Act

crime

due process

Economic Espionage
   Act (EEA)

embezzlement

extortion

Federal Sentencing Guidelines

felonies

Fifth Amendment

Foreign Corrupt Practices
   Act (FCPA)

forgery

Fourth Amendment

Miranda warnings

misdemeanors

predicate act

Racketeer Influenced and Corrupt
   Organizations (RICO) Act

search warrant

Sixth Amendment

uttering

white-collar crime

White-Collar Crime Penalty
   Enhancement Act of 2002

Questions and Case Problems

1. Bernard Flinn operated a business known as Harvey Investment Co., Inc./High Risk Loans. Flinn worked as a loan broker, matching those who came to him with lenders willing to loan them money given their credit history and the amount involved. From 1982 through 1985, Flinn found loans for five people. Indiana requires that persons engaged in the business of brokering loans obtain a license from the state. Flinn was prosecuted for brokering loans without having a license. He raised the defense that he did not know that a license was required and that, accordingly, he lacked the criminal intent to broker loans without having a license. Does Flinn have a good defense? [*Flinn v. Indiana*, 563 N.E.2d 536 (Ind.)]

2. H. J., Inc., and other customers of Northwestern Bell Corp. alleged that Northwestern Bell had furnished cash and tickets for air travel, plays, and sporting events and had offered employment to members of the Minnesota Public Utilities Commission in exchange for favorable treatment in rate cases before the commission. A Minnesota statute makes it a felony to bribe public officials. H. J. and other customers brought suit against Northwestern for violating the criminal bribery statute. Can the customers bring a criminal action? [*H. J., Inc. v. Northwestern Bell Corp.*, 420 N.W.2d 673 (Minn. App.)]

3. Baker and others entered a Wal-Mart store shortly after 3:00 A.M. by cutting through the metal door with an acetylene torch. They had moved some of the merchandise in the store to the rear door, but the police arrived before the merchandise could be taken from the store. Baker was prosecuted for larceny. He raised the defense that he was not guilty of larceny because no merchandise had ever left the store.

Is there enough intent and action for a crime? [*Tennessee v. Baker*, 751 S.W.2d 154 (Tenn. App.)]

4. Gail drove her automobile after having had dinner and several drinks. She fell asleep at the wheel and ran over and killed a pedestrian. Prosecuted for manslaughter, she raised the defense that she did not intend to hurt anyone and because of the drinks did not know what she was doing. Was this a valid defense?

5. Dr. Doyle E. Campbell, an ophthalmologist, established his practice in southern Ohio in 1971. Many of Dr. Campbell's patients are elderly people who qualify for federal Medicare benefits and state Medicaid benefits. Under the existing financing system, a doctor who treats a Medicare patient is required to submit a "Medicare Health Insurance Claim Form" (HCFA Form 1500). The doctor is required to certify that "the services shown on this form were medically indicated and necessary for the health of the patient and were personally rendered by me or were rendered incident to my professional service by my employees." Claims Dr. Campbell submitted for his elderly patients ranged from $900 to $950, of which $530 to $680 were covered by the Medicare program. The government alleged that Dr. Campbell billed Medicare for several treatments that were either not performed or not necessary. Dr. Campbell was charged with fraud for the paperwork he submitted. Has he committed a crime? [*United States v. Campbell*, 845 F.2d 1374 (6th Cir.)]

6. In the late 1980s, Life Energy Resources, Ltd. (LER), a New York corporation, was a multilevel marketing network. LER's marketing plan provided that members of the general public could purchase its products

only through an official LER distributor or by becoming LER distributors themselves. Each potential distributor had to be sponsored by an existing distributor and was required to sign a distributorship agreement with LER stating that he or she would not make medical claims or use unofficial literature or marketing aids to promote LER products.

Ballistrea and his partner Michael Ricotta were at the top of the LER distribution network. Two products sold by LER were the REM SuperPro Frequency Generator (REM) and the Lifemax Miracle Cream (Miracle Cream). The REM, which sold for $1,350 to distributors, was a small box powered by electricity that ran currents through the feet and body of the user.

Ballistrea and Ricotta distributed literature and audiotapes to many potential downstream distributors and customers—some of whom were undercover government agents—touting the REM and the Miracle Cream. Other literature claimed that the Miracle Cream could alleviate the discomforts of premenstrual syndrome and reverse the effects of osteoporosis. The Food and Drug Administration charged Ballistrea and Ricotta with violating federal law for making medical claims concerning LER products. Their defense is that they never sold any of the products. They simply earned commissions as part of the marketing scheme and could not be held criminally liable on the charges. Are they correct? [*United States v. Ballistrea*, 101 F.3d 827 (2d Cir.)]

7. Carriage Homes, Inc. was a general contractor that built multifamily residential and land-development projects in Minnesota. John Arkell was Carriage Homes' chief executive officer, president, and sole shareholder. Carriage Homes built Southwinds, a condominium development of 38 residential units in Austin, Minnesota. The foundation elevations of some of the Southwinds units were lower than permitted under the State Building Code, causing storm water to pool in the units' driveways and garages. The city of Austin's development director sent Arkell a series of seven letters in 1999 and 2001 concerning the elevation problems, and Arkell gave the letters to the project managers, who failed to resolve the problems.

Minnesota makes a violation of the State Building Code a misdemeanor. On May 30, 2001, the state charged Carriage Homes and Arkell with three misdemeanor counts each, alleging a violation of the Uniform Building Code (UBC).

Carriage Homes pleaded guilty and was sentenced to a $1,000 fine. But Arkell pleaded not guilty, asserting that he could not be held criminally responsible for the violation. After a bench trial, the district court found Arkell guilty. He was sentenced to pay a fine, pay restitution to the condominium owners, and serve 90 days in jail, with 80 days stayed pending his compliance with sentencing conditions. Mr. Arkell appealed on the grounds that the employees and subcontractors had simply not followed his orders and he was not responsible for their failures. Is he correct? [*State v. Arkell*, 657 N.W.2d 883 (Minn. App.)]

8. James Durham runs an art gallery. He has several paintings from unknown artists that he has listed for sale. The paintings always sell at his weekly auction for $20,000 to $50,000 above what James believes them to be worth. James learns that the bidders at the auctions are employed by an olive distributor located near the shipping yards of the city. What concerns should Durham have about the art, the bidders, and the large purchase prices?

9. Jennings operated a courier service to collect and deliver money. The contract with his customers allowed him a day or so to deliver the money that had been collected. Instead of holding collections until delivered, Jennings made short-term investments with the money. He always made deliveries to the customers on time, but because he kept the profit from the investments for himself, Jennings was prosecuted for embezzlement. Was he guilty? [*New York v. Jennings*, 504 N.E.2d 1079 (N.Y.)]

10. In April 2006, a DC-9 aircraft landed in the port city of Ciudad del Carmen, located 500 miles east of Mexico City. When the plane's crew began directing security personnel away from the plane, the suspicious activity piqued the curiosity of local law enforcement officials. They decided to search the plane and found 128 suitcases packed with over 56 tons of cocaine. The cocaine was to have been delivered to Toluca, near Mexico City. In investigating the plane and individual involved, law enforcement agents discovered that the plane had been purchased with money that had been laundered through two U.S. banks, Wachovia Corp. and Bank of America Corp. Neither bank was actually aware that the money was being used to purchase a plane that would then be used for drug trafficking. Are the banks still criminally liable for breaking the rules?

Explain why or why not. What if the banks were aware of large sums of money being run through particular customers' accounts? Would that knowledge make a difference?

11. Grabert ran Beck's, an amusement center in Louisiana. He held a license for video gambling machines. Louisiana makes it illegal to allow a minor to play a video gambling machine. A mother came into Grabert's center carrying her 23-month-old baby in her arms. She sat at the video poker machine with her child on her lap and proceeded to play. State troopers witnessed the baby pushing the buttons on the machine at least three times. The Department of Public Safety and Corrections revoked Grabert's video gaming license because a minor had been allowed to play the machines, and Grabert sought judicial review. The trial court reversed, and the department appealed. Has Grabert committed the crime of allowing a minor to engage in gaming? Is this the crime of allowing a minor to gamble? [*Grabert v. Department of Public Safety & Corrections*, 680 So. 2d 764 (La. App.) *cert.* denied; *Grabert v. State through Dept. of Public Safety and Corrections*, 685 So. 2d 126 (La.)]

12. The Banco Central administered a humanitarian plan for the government of Ecuador. Fernando Banderas and his wife presented false claims that the bank paid. After the fraud was discovered, the bank sued Banderas and his wife for damages for fraud and treble damages under the Florida version of RICO. Banderas and his wife asserted that they were not liable for RICO damages because there was no proof that they were related to organized crime and because the wrong they had committed was merely ordinary fraud. They had not used any racketeering methods. Is involvement with organized crime a requirement for liability under RICO? [*Banderas v. Banco Central del Ecuador*, 461 So. 2d 265 (Fla. App.)]

13. Kravitz owned 100 percent of the stock of American Health Programs, Inc. (AHP). To obtain the Philadelphia Fraternal Order of Police as a customer for AHP, Kravitz paid money bribes to persons who he thought were officers of that organization but who in fact were federal undercover agents. He was prosecuted for violating RICO. He was convicted, and the court ordered the forfeiture of all of Kravitz's shares of AHP stock. Can a forfeiture be ordered? [*United States v. Kravitz*, 738 F.2d 102 (3d Cir.)]

14. Kathryn Erickson was the general manager of the Uintah Special Services District (USSD), an entity created to use federal-mineral-lease revenues for road projects. She, along with her secretary, Cheryl McCurdy, administered the USSD from a small office in Vernal, Utah. Ms. Erickson's authority was limited and she was not permitted to enter into or modify contracts for or to expend more than $1,000 of USSD funds, without board approval.

Mitchell Construction was a major contractor for USSD. In 1998, USSD awarded Mitchell Construction a contract to haul gravel from a site called Hamaker Bottoms and another contract to carry out small asphalt-paving projects. Both contracts were to be completed within the 1998 construction year.

During 1999 and 2000 Mitchell Construction continued to perform work on the projects covered by its 1998 contracts with USSD, despite their expiration. It submitted invoices to USSD and was paid for this work.

In June 1999 a federal grand jury began to investigate contracting irregularities at USSD and the Uintah County Road Department and issued a *subpoena duces tecum* to USSD requesting copies of "project contracts, invoices" between USSD and contractors.

While the office was preparing the response for the grand jury subpoena, Ms. McCurdy saw Ms. Erickson prepare a handwritten change order for the Hamaker Bottoms contract and saw Ms. Erickson and Gilman N. Mitchell both sign it. The change order, which was backdated to January 13, 1999, extended the contract through December 31, 2000.

Ms. McCurdy later discovered that two other change orders had been created and backdated. She spent a day copying documents for the grand jury and recording, on a handwritten list, all of the documents that she had copied. However, she left Ms. Erickson in the office while she was working on the list in order to go home for dinner. Ms. Erickson called her and told her not to come back because all the copying was done. Later, Ms. McCurdy found on Ms. Erickson's desk a photocopy of the grand jury document list and saw that two entries not in her handwriting had been added. These entries were for change orders for contracts between Mitchell Construction and USSD. Ms. McCurdy reported the change to the government.

Ms. Erickson and Mr. Mitchell were each indicted by a grand jury in the U.S. District Court for the District of Utah on three counts of obstruction of justice by knowingly falsifying a document with the knowledge and intent that the grand jury would rely on it. Are both the elements of mental intent (scienter) and action present for criminal convictions here? [*U.S. v. Erickson*, 561 F.3d 1150 (10th Cir.)]

Torts

Learning Outcomes ‹‹‹

After studying this chapter, you should be able to

LO.1 Explain the difference between torts and crimes

LO.2 Distinguish between an assault and a battery

LO.3 Explain the three different torts of invasion of privacy

LO.4 Explain the torts of defamation and defenses

LO.5 Explain the elements of negligence and defenses

LO.6 Explain the tort of strict liability and why very few defenses are available

The law of torts permits individuals and companies to recover from other individuals and companies for wrongs committed against them. Tort law provides rights and remedies for conduct that meets the elements required to establish that a wrong has occurred.

8-1   General Principles

Civil, or noncriminal, wrongs that are not breaches of contract are governed by tort law. This chapter covers the types of civil wrongs that constitute torts and the remedies available for those wrongs.

8-1a   What Is a Tort?

tort–civil wrong that interferes with one's property or person.

Tort comes from the Latin term *tortus*, which means "crooked, dubious, twisted." Torts are actions that are not straight but are crooked, or civil, wrongs. A tort is an interference with someone's person or property. **For Example,** entering someone's house without his or her permission is an interference and constitutes the tort of trespass. Causing someone's character to be questioned is a wrong against the person and is the tort of defamation. The law provides protection against these harms in the form of remedies awarded after the wrongs are committed. These remedies are civil remedies for the acts of interference by others.

8-1b   Tort and Crime Distinguished

A *crime* is a wrong that arises from a violation of a public duty, whereas a *tort* is a wrong that arises from a violation of a private duty. A crime is a wrong of such a serious nature that the appropriate level of government steps in to prosecute and punish the wrongdoer to deter others from engaging in the same type of conduct. However, whenever the act that is committed as a crime causes harm to an identifiable person, that person may recover from the wrongdoer for monetary damages to compensate for the harm. For the person who experiences the direct harm, the act is called a *tort*; for the government, the same act is called a *crime*.

When the same act is both a crime and a tort, the government may prosecute the wrongdoer for a violation of criminal law, and the individual who experiences the direct harm may recover damages. **For Example,** O. J. Simpson was charged by the state of California with the murder of his ex-wife, Nicole Brown Simpson, and her friend Ron Goldman. A criminal trial was held in which O. J. Simpson was acquitted. Simpson was subsequently sued civilly by the families of Nicole Simpson and Ron Goldman for the tort of wrongful death. The jury in the civil case found Simpson civilly liable and the court ordered him to pay nearly $20 million in damages plus interest. Only $382,000 of this judgment was paid to the families.

8-1c   Types of Torts

intentional tort–civil wrong that results from intentional conduct.

There are three types of torts: intentional torts, negligence, and strict liability. **Intentional torts** are those that occur when wrongdoers engage in intentional conduct. **For Example,** striking another person in a fight is an intentional act and would be the tort of battery and possibly also the crime of battery. Your arm striking another person's nose in a fast-moving crowd of people at a rock concert is not a tort or crime because your arm was pushed unintentionally by the force of the crowd. If you stretched out your arms in that crowd or began to swing your arms about and struck another person, you would be behaving carelessly in a crowd of people; and, although you may not have committed an intentional tort, it is possible that your careless conduct constitutes the tort of **negligence.** Careless actions, or actions taken without thinking through their consequences, constitute negligence. The harm to the other person's nose may not have been intended, but there is liability for these accidental harms under negligence. **For Example,** if you run a red light, hit another car, and injure its driver, you did not intend the result. However, your careless behavior of disregarding a traffic signal resulted in the injury, and you would have liability for your negligence to that driver.

In transmission of disease cases, depending on the facts, both intentional torts and negligence theories may apply. A person who knows or should know that he or she has herpes and fails to disclose that fact, or misrepresents that he or she is disease-free, may be liable to a sexual partner. The torts theories may include negligence, battery, intentional infliction of emotional distress, and fraud. In most cases, the three words "I have herpes" is fair notice of the danger of infection.[1] However, saying it is okay to have sex because the individual was not having an outbreak of the disease is actionable. **For Example,** Thomas R. disclosed to his girlfriend that he had herpes but nevertheless told her that it was "okay" to have sex with him because he was not then experiencing an outbreak of the disease. The jury's finding of negligence and fraudulent concealment in the transmission of the disease was upheld by the appeals court, and the plaintiff was awarded compensatory damages as well as $2.75 million in punitive damages.[2]

Strict liability is another type of tort that imposes liability without regard to whether there was any intent to harm or any negligence occurred. Strict liability is imposed without regard to fault. Strict or absolute liability is imposed because the activity involved is so dangerous that there must be full accountability. Nonetheless, the activity is necessary and cannot be prohibited. The compromise is to allow the activity but ensure that its dangers and resulting damages are fully covered through the imposition of full liability for all injuries that result. **For Example,** contractors often need to use dynamite to take a roadway through a mountainside or demolish a building that has become a hazard. When the dynamite is used, noise, debris, and possibly dangerous pieces of earth and building will descend on others' land and possibly on people. In most states, contractors are held strictly liable for the resulting damage from the use of dynamite. The activity is necessary and not illegal, but those who use dynamite must be prepared to compensate those who are injured as a result.

Other areas in which there is strict liability for activity include the storage of flammable materials and crop dusting. The federal government and the states have pure food laws that impose absolute liability on manufacturers who fail to meet the statutory standards for their products. Another area of strict liability is *product liability*, where a product is defective, and unreasonably dangerous, and has caused harm. **For Example,** Mr. Izell was awarded $6 million in compensatory damages and $18 million in punitive damages when he proved that exposure to inhalable asbestos fibers, supplied in part by Union Carbide, was a substantial factor in causing mesothelioma.[3] Product liability is covered in Chapter 24.

negligence–failure to exercise due care under the circumstances in consequence of which harm is proximately caused to one to whom the defendant owed a duty to exercise due care.

strict liability–civil wrong for which there is absolute liability because of the inherent danger in the underlying activity, for example, the use of explosives.

---

[1] *R.A.P. v. B.I.P.,* 428 N.W.2d 103, 108 (Minn. App. 1988).
[2] *Behr v. Redmond,* 123 Cal. Rptr. 3d 97 (Cal. App. 2011).
[3] *Izell v. Union Carbide Corp.,* 180 Cal. Rptr. 3d 382 (Cal. App. 2014).

8-2 Intentional Torts

8-2a Assault

An *assault* is intentional conduct that threatens a person with a well-founded fear of imminent harm coupled with the present ability to carry out the threat of harm. **For Example,** the angry assertion "I'm going to kick your butt" along with aggressive movement in the direction of the victim with the intent to carry out the threat is an assault, even though a third person intervenes to stop the intended action. Mere words, however, although insulting, are ordinarily insufficient to constitute an assault.

8-2b Battery

A *battery* is the intentional, wrongful touching of another person without that person's consent. Thus, a threat to use force is an assault, and the actual use of force is the battery. The single action of striking an individual can be both a crime and a tort. A lawsuit for the tort of battery provides a plaintiff with the opportunity to recover damages resulting from the battery. The plaintiff must prove damages, however.

CASE SUMMARY

An Exchange of Unpleasantries...

FACTS: Moore and Beye had an altercation after a public meeting regarding airport expansion. Moore owned a ranch near the airport and staunchly opposed expansion. Beye owned a flying service and avidly supports expansion. Moore and Beye exchanged unpleasantries while leaving the meeting. Beye then punched Moore on the left side of the jaw. Moore stumbled but caught himself before falling. He then exclaimed to the crowd, "You saw that. You are my witnesses. I've been assaulted. I want that man arrested." Ravalli County deputies took Beye into custody, and the state charged him with misdemeanor assault. Moore visited the hospital complaining of back and neck pain two days later and contended that he had injured his back while reeling from Beye's punch. He filed a civil complaint against Beye for damages. Moore's evidence mostly concerned his alleged

back injury. Beye did not contest that he had punched Moore. His evidence countered that Moore's back problems had existed before the altercation. The judge instructed the jury that Beye had committed a battery as a matter of law and directed that they answer the question, "Was Moore damaged as a result of the battery?" The jury voted 11 to 1 that the battery did not injure Moore, and Moore appealed.

DECISION: Judgment for Beye. Beye presented the testimony of several eyewitnesses and a medical expert that Moore had sustained no damages. Although Moore presented considerable evidence to the contrary, it was not the court's function to agree or disagree with the verdict. Beye presented sufficient evidence to uphold the jury's verdict. [***Moore v. Beye,*** **122 P.3d 1212 (Mont. 2005)**]

8-2c False Imprisonment

false imprisonment— intentional detention of a person without that person's consent; called the *shopkeeper's tort* when shoplifters are unlawfully detained.

False imprisonment is the intentional detention of a person without that person's consent.[4] The detention need not be for any specified period of time, for any detention against one's will is false imprisonment. False imprisonment is often called the *shopkeeper's tort* because so much liability has been imposed on store owners for their unreasonable detention of customers suspected of shoplifting. Requiring a customer to sit in the manager's office or not allowing a customer to leave the store can constitute the tort of false

---

[4] *Forgie-Buccioni v. Hannaford Bros. Inc., 413 F.3d 175 (1st Cir. 2005).*

shopkeeper's privilege– right of a store owner to detain a suspected shoplifter based on reasonable cause and for a reasonable time without resulting liability for false imprisonment.

imprisonment. Shop owners do, however, need the opportunity to investigate possible thefts in their stores. As a result, all states have some form of privilege or protection for store owners called a *shopkeeper's privilege.*

The **shopkeeper's privilege** permits the store owner to detain a suspected shoplifter based on reasonable suspicion for a reasonable time without resulting liability for false imprisonment to the accused customer.[5] The privilege applies even if the store owner was wrong about the customer being a shoplifter, so long as the store owner acted based on reasonable suspicions and treated the accused shoplifter in a reasonable manner.

CASE SUMMARY

A Can of Mousse: A Tote Bag of Trouble

FACTS: Patricia Holguin went to Sally's Beauty Supply Store carrying her "eco-friendly canvas shopping tote," a large bag that is conspicuous when used. Upon entering the store, there were no posted signs stating that shopping totes were not allowed. She picked up a can of mousse that was not exactly what she wanted and started to carry it in her tote toward the front counter to ask the cashier a question about it. As she walked toward the front of the store the assistant manager approached her and asked what was in the bag. She was detained by this manager, who told her that once she put the hair mousse in her tote bag, she was shoplifting. Holguin's lawsuit for false imprisonment against the store was dismissed with prejudice by the trial court. This court held that once she placed the merchandise in her bag, the store had probable cause to believe she was shoplifting and had a statutory conditional privilege to detain her, free from civil liability for false imprisonment, because she "willfully concealed merchandise." Holguin appealed.

DECISION: The court of appeals reversed the district court's decision. In general, merchants and their employees have a conditional privilege to detain a person free from civil liability based on probable cause, or reasonable grounds to believe that the individual "willfully concealed" merchandise without paying for it, provided the detention is for a reasonable time and conducted in a reasonable manner. "Willfully concealed," however, requires more than merely putting merchandise out of sight. In self-service stores customers have implied permission to pick up, handle, move, try on, replace, and carry about merchandise within the store. There must be circumstances which reflect that the purpose of the concealment is adverse to the store's right to be paid before the conclusion can be drawn that the merchandise was "willfully concealed" under the statute providing the conditional privilege to detain a customer. Placing the can of mousse in a reusable, personal canvas shopping bag to carry to the front of the store to ask a question, without more, did not constitute "willful concealment." [*Holguin v. Sally's Beauty Supply, Inc.*, 264 P.3d 732 (N. Mex. App. 2011)]

8-2d Intentional Infliction of Emotional Distress

intentional infliction of emotional distress–tort that produces mental anguish caused by conduct that exceeds all bounds of decency.

The **intentional infliction of emotional distress** (IIED) is a tort involving conduct that goes beyond all bounds of decency and produces mental anguish in the harmed individual. This tort requires proof of outrageous conduct and resulting emotional distress in the victim. **For Example,** Erica Schoen, a 16-year employee of Freightliner, returned to work on light duty after surgery for a work-related shoulder injury. She was assigned to work out of the nurse's station under two employees who intentionally worked her beyond her restrictions, assigned her to humiliating work, repeatedly called her worthless, and used her as a personal servant—ordering her to get snacks, sodas, and lunches for them and not reimbursing her. After five months of this treatment, Erica brought the matter to the human resources manager, who told her, in part, "Nobody wants you. You're

[5] *Limited Stores, Inc. v. Wilson-Robinson*, 876 S.W.2d 248 (Ark. 1994); see also *Wal-Mart Stores, Inc. v. Binns*, 15 S.W.3d 320 (Ark. 2000).

worthless. We build trucks down here...." Erica became hysterical and thereafter required psychiatric care. The jury awarded $250,000 for IIED, and the verdict was upheld on appeal because the repetitive misconduct and its duration, ratified by the human resource manager, was intolerable.[6]

8-2e Invasion of Privacy

invasion of privacy–tort of intentional intrusion into the private affairs of another.

The right to privacy is the right to be free of unreasonable intrusion into one's private affairs. The tort of **invasion of privacy** actually consists of three different torts: (1) public disclosure of private facts; (2) intrusion into the plaintiff's private affairs; and (3) appropriation of another's name, likeness, or image for commercial advantage.[7]

Public Disclosure of Private Facts

This tort involves public disclosure of a private fact, such as a business posting returned checks from customers near its cash registers in public display.

The first widely recognized call in American law for a right to privacy based on the common law and enforceable in a tort action was raised in an article by Samuel Warren and Louis Brandeis in *The Harvard Law Review* of 1890.[8] The authors recognized that the right to privacy must be subject to conditions if it is to coexist with freedom of speech, freedom of the press, and other established areas of the law. Accordingly they proposed limitations on the right such as it should not prevent publication of matters of general public interest. Or, if the person published the facts himself or consents, the facts are no longer private. The authors also speculated that the law would not grant redress for oral publications, where the injury would be so trifling that the law might well, in the interest of free speech, disregard it all together. Presently must a plaintiff in a right to privacy action produce documentation such as a writing, picture, or video to bring a common-law right-to-privacy action? The question is resolved in the *Yum! Brands, Inc.* decision.

CASE SUMMARY

Let's Get With It! The Town Crier Is No Longer the Principal Purveyor of News

FACTS: Melissa Ignat suffered from a bipolar disorder for which she was being treated with medications. Side effects of medication adjustments occasionally caused her to miss work. She alleged that after returning from one such absence her supervisor, Mary Shipma, informed her that she had told everyone in the department that Ignat was bipolar. Subsequently her coworkers avoided and shunned her, and one of them asked Shipma if Ignat was likely to "go postal" at work. Ignat brought suit for public disclosure of private facts, and the trial court granted summary judgment for Yum! Brands

on the ground that the right of privacy can be violated only by a writing, not by word of mouth.

DECISION: Judgment reversed. Limiting liability for public disclosure of private facts to those recorded in a writing is contrary to the tort's purpose, which has been since its inception to allow a person to control the kind of information about himself made available to the public—in essence, to define his public persona. While the restriction may have made sense in the 1890s—when no one dreamed of talk

---

[6] *Schoen v. Freightliner LLC*, 199 P.3d 332 (Or. App. 2008).
[7] A fourth tort of invasion of privacy also exists, known as "invasion of privacy by false light," which is very similar to defamation discussed in this chapter. Like a claim of defamation, the plaintiff cannot succeed on a claim of invasion of privacy by false light if the alleged communication is accurate or true. See *Miller v. Central Indiana Community Foundation, Inc.* 11 N.E.3d 944 (Ind. App. 2014).
[8] S. D. Warren and L. D. Brandeis, *The Right to Privacy*, 4 *Harv. L. Rev.* 193 (1890); the following analysis is derived from the *Ignat v. Yum Brands, Inc.* decision, 154 Cal. Rptr. 3d 275, 278 (Cal. App. 2013).

Let's Get With It! The Town Crier Is No Longer the Principal Purveyor of News continued

radio or confessional television—it certainly makes no sense now. Private facts can be just as widely disclosed—if not more so—through oral media as through written ones. To allow a plaintiff redress for one kind of disclosure but not the other, when both can be equally damaging to privacy, is a rule better suited to an era when the town crier was the principal purveyor of news. It is long past time to discard this outmoded rule. [***Ignat v. Yum! Brands, Inc.*** **154 Cal. Rptr. 3d 275 (Cal. App. 2013)**]

Intrusion into the Plaintiff's Private Affairs

This tort involves intrusion into the plaintiff's private affairs or seclusion. An example would be planting a microphone in the plaintiff's office or home.

Appropriation of Another's Name, Likeness, or Image for Commercial Advantage

This form of invasion of privacy is generally referred to as the *right of publicity.* The elements of this tort are (1) appropriation of the plaintiff's name or likeness for the value associated with it, and not in an incidental manner or for a newsworthy purpose, (2) identification of the plaintiff in the publication, and (3) an advantage or benefit to the defendant. The right to publicity is designed to protect the commercial interest of celebrities in their identities. **For Example,** popular and critically acclaimed rock and roll musician Don Henley, the founder and member of the band The Eagles, successfully sued a department store chain that ran an international newspaper advertisement for its Henley shirt, which stated in large letters as the focus of the ad "This is Don's Henley." The ad (1) used the value associated with the famous name Don Henley to get consumers to read it, (2) the plaintiff was identifiable in the ad, and (3) the ad was created with the belief that use of the words "Don's Henley" would help sell the product.[9] A "newsworthiness defense" protects the act of publishing or reporting factual data on public affairs or sporting activities.[10]

Some states refer to the right of publicity as a cause of action for *commercial misappropriation of a name or likeness* and provide two vehicles a plaintiff can use to protect the economic value of one's name: a common law action or a statutory remedy. The *Schlein* case involved a breach of contract action and an action for commercial misappropriation of a doctor's name.

CASE SUMMARY

The Name Game: We Are Discontinuing Your Royalty on the "Schlein Ultra," Dr. Schlein

FACTS: Orthopedic Systems, Inc. (OSI), and Dr. Schlein entered into a contract, whereby OSI would manufacture and sell an unpatented product originally designed by Dr. Schlein called the "Schlein Shoulder Positioner," to be used in arthroscopic shoulder surgery. The contract called for a 5% royalty of the list price less discounts. Over the years OSI's marketing brochures thanked "Allen P. Schlein M.D. for his assistance in the development of the

---

[9] *Henley v. Dillard Department Stores,* 46 F. Supp. 2d 587 (N.D. Tex. 1999).
[10] *Dryer v. National Football League,* 2014 WL 5106738 (D. Minn. 2014).

The Name Game: We Are Discontinuing Your Royalty on the "Schlein Ultra," Dr. Schlein continued

product." OSI paid royalty checks from January 1991 to January 2005, when OSI paid its last royalty payment for the period ending December 2004. In January 2005, OSI sent a letter to Dr. Schlein stating that in light of the fact that there was no patent protection on the product, it would be discontinuing the royalty. From January 2005 until July 29, 2005, OSI continued to market and sell the product using Dr. Schlein's name. OSI sued Dr. Schlein for declaratory relief and reformation of the royalty contract. Dr. Schlein cross-complained for breach of contract and commercial misappropriation of his name. The jury awarded Dr. Schlein $616,043 for failure to pay royalties under the contract. OSI earned $1,220,000 in profits attributed to the use of Dr. Schlein's name during the period from January 1, 2005, to July 31, 2005, after which OSI stopped using Schlein's name. The trial court declined to award the profits to Schlein, and both parties appealed.

DECISION: The statutory remedy of Section 3444(a) requires the payment of the greater of $750, or the actual damages

suffered as a result of the unauthorized use, and any profits for the unauthorized use that are attributable to use and are not taken into account in computing actual damages. The legislative history for the minimum $750 award was intended to fill the gap that existed in the common law tort of invasion of privacy as applied to noncelebrities whose names lacked commercial value on the open market. Unlike sports and entertainment stars, noncelebrities often could not prove damages under the common law; therefore, the statute established a concrete remedy for the little man with a minimum payment. An interpretation that limits damages to $750 as an alternative to all other damages would be contrary to the spirit of the statute. Judgment for Dr. Schlein, who is entitled as well to the $1,220,000 profits as a result of OSI's unauthorized use of his name. [***Orthopedic Systems, Inc. v. Schlein*, 135 Cal. Rptr. 3d 200 (Cal. App. 2011)**]

8-2f Defamation

defamation–untrue statement by one party about another to a third party.

slander–defamation of character by spoken words or gestures.

libel–written or visual defamation without legal justification.

Defamation is a false statement by one party about another to a third party. **Slander** is spoken defamation.[11] **Libel** is a false publication by writing, printing, picture, or other fixed representation to the eye, which exposes any person to hatred, contempt, or ridicule, or which has a tendency to injure the individual in his or her occupation.[12] The elements of defamation are (1) the making of defamatory statement; (2) publication of the defamatory material; and (3) damages that result from the statement.

In cases in which the victim is a public figure, such as a well-known entertainer, a professional athlete, or a political figure, another element is required: the element of *malice*, which means that the statement was made by the defendant with knowledge that it was false, or with reckless disregard for whether it was true or false.[13] **For Example,** former wrestler and governor of Minnesota and former Navy SEAL Jesse Ventura sued Chris Kyle, the author of the bestselling autobiography entitled *American Sniper*, for defamation. Kyle, also a former Navy SEAL, wrote that a character named "Scruff Face," holding court in a Coronado, California, bar said, "he hates America," that the SEALS "were killing men and women and children and murdering," and that SEALS "deserve to lose a few"; at which point Kyle "punched him out." While not naming Ventura in the book, Kyle confirmed in television, radio, and in print interviews about the book, that "Scruff

---

[11] Regarding damages, where one publishes a slander that imputes to another a communicable disease, or would adversely affect that person's fitness for the proper conduct of a lawful business, trade, or profession, the words are actionable in themselves, and the law implies compensatory damages. Once compensatory damages are established the jury will assess punitive damages to punish the party who committed the wrong and to deter others from committing similar wrongs in the future. See *Tanner v. Ebbole*, 2011 WL 4425540 (Ala. App. 2011) where the jury returned "nominal" compensatory damages of $1 and punitive damages of $100,000 against Paul Averette, the owner of a competing tattoo business, for slanderous statements to several patrons that his competitor, Chassity Ebbole, had hepatitis, syphilis, gonorrhea, and AIDS and that she used "nasty needles."

[12] See *Wong v. Jing*, 117 Cal. Rptr. 3rd (Cal. App. 2010).

[13] See *New York Times Co. v. Sullivan*, 376 U.S. 254 (1964).

Face" was Ventura. Kyle was killed by a troubled veteran, and his wife, as executor of his estate, was substituted as defendant. The case, brought by public figure Jesse Ventura, boiled down to a creditability contest, with several witnesses testifying that Ventura's version of the events was true, while several other witnesses testified that Kyle's version of the events was true. The jury decided the case for Ventura, with the court concluding that in believing Ventura's version of the facts, then Kyle's writing and telling of the story of punching out Ventura was itself a basis for the jury to make a finding of actual malice. On the defamation claim the jury awarded $500,000 in damages. Some $1,345,477 in damages was assessed for unjust enrichment for the money made in defaming Ventura in the book *American Sniper*.[14]

The defenses to defamation include truth and privilege. Also defendants may assert their free speech rights under the First Amendment to express their opinions as they see fit; and the courts are required to distinguish between statements of fact and statements of opinion.

Online Issues

Internet and mobile platforms have radically changed how society consumes and shares news, opinions, and other content. Courts are faced with an increase in Internet defamation cases, many of which involve anonymous posts, which must initially be addressed by the courts.

Unveiling Identities of Offending Anonymous Posters. Interactive Web sites are immune from liability for content created by a third-party user unless the Web site actively edits the content.[15] It thus may be necessary for a "defamed" person to seek the identity of the anonymous poster through a court subpoena in a defamation lawsuit.

The First Amendment prohibits the government from abridging the freedom of speech and it also protects anonymous speech.[16] Courts must strike a balance between the right to anonymous speech and the right of those harmed by anonymous speech to seek legal redress. Before a plaintiff can compel disclosure of the identity of an anonymous Internet speaker, the plaintiff must demonstrate to a court that he or she has a credible claim, and the anonymous speaker must be given an opportunity to defend himself before the court will order the unveiling of his or her identity.[17] **For Example,** the Leshers filed a lawsuit against anonymous posters on the Internet forum Topix, who had accused the Leshers of being sexual deviants, molesters, and drug dealers. With a credible claim established, the court ordered Topix to turn over identifying information including Internet Protocol (IP) addresses, which led to the identity of the posters and, ultimately, a jury awarding $13.78 million in damages against the posters.[18]

Vigorous Criticism Versus Defamation. Legitimate customer complaints based on opinion are not actionable defamation. And, hyperbole, figurative language, and rhetoric expression is protected opinion such as a posting claiming "the worst wedding experience of my life." However, a factual assertion that "the bridal suite was a tool shed…" in context may be actionable in some courts.[19] Other courts are less willing to interpret comments as assertions of fact. **For Example,** a defendant using a concealing screen name on an Internet discussion forum, felt free to claim that a corporate president was part of a management team of "boobs, losers, and crooks" and "has fat thighs, a fake medical

[14] *Ventura v. Kyle*, 8 F. Supp. 3d 1115 (D. Minn. 2014).
[15] Section 203(c)(1) of the Communication Decency Act of 1996.
[16] *McIntyre v. Ohio Elections Comm'n*, 514 U.S. 334, 342 (1995). "Anonymity is a shield from the tyranny of the majority." *Id.* at 357.
[17] *Doe v. Coleman*, 436 S.W.3d 207 (Ky. App. 2014).
[18] Ki Mae Heussner and Susanna Kim, *'Anonymous' Posters to Pay $13 Million for Defamatory Comments*, abcnews.com (Apr. 24, 2012), **http://abcnews.go.com/Business/jury-awards-13-million-texas-defamation-suit-anonymous/print? id=16194071**.
[19] *Neumann v. Liles*, 261 Or. App. 567 (2014).

degree, … and has poor … hygiene." The plaintiff served a subpoena on the forum's host seeking the defendant's identity, and the defendant, appearing as "Doe 6," moved to quash. The appellate court, viewing the defendant's post in the context of what was a particularly "[h]eated" discussion forum in which numerous other posts questioned the defendant's credibility, and noting the defendant's "crude, ungrammatical" language, satirical tone, and vituperative, "juvenile name-calling," concluded that the defendant's railing was nonactionable opinion and ordered the subpoena quashed.[20]

Defenses: Truth and Privilege

The defenses to defamation include the truth. If the statement is true, even if it is harmful to the victim, it is not the tort of defamation.[21]

absolute privilege—
complete defense against the tort of defamation, as in the speeches of members of Congress on the floor and witnesses in a trial.

Some statements are privileged, and this privilege provides a full or partial defense to the tort of defamation. **For Example,** members of Congress enjoy an **absolute privilege** when they are speaking on the floor of the Senate or the House because public policy requires a free dialogue on the issues pending in a legislative body. The same absolute privilege applies to witnesses in court proceedings to encourage witnesses with information to come forward and testify. Where a witness granted immunity from prosecution testifies before a governmental agency, the witness is entitled to immunity from defamation lawsuits. **For Example,** Roger Clemens sued his former trainer, Brian McNamee, for defamation, contending that McNamee falsely stated to a congressional committee that Clemens had used steroids during his professional baseball career. This defamation claim was dismissed because McNamee's statements were entitled to absolute immunity on the reasoning that the proper administration of justice requires full disclosure from witnesses without fear of retaliatory lawsuits.[22]

qualified privilege—
media privilege to print inaccurate information without liability for defamation, so long as a retraction is printed and there was no malice.

The media enjoy a **qualified privilege** for stories that turn out to be false. Their qualified privilege is a defense to defamation so long as the information was released without malice and a retraction or correction is made when the matter is brought to their attention.

A *qualified privilege* to make a defamatory statement in the workplace exists when the statement is made to protect the interests of the private employer on a work-related matter, especially when reporting actual or suspected wrongdoing. **For Example,** Neda Lewis was fired from her job at Carson Oil Company for allegedly stealing toilet paper. The employee in charge of supplies noticed that toilet paper was regularly missing from the ladies room, and one evening from a third-floor window overlooking the parking lot, she observed that the plaintiff's bag contained two rolls of toilet paper. She reported the matter to the executive secretary, who reported it to both the president and the CEO of the firm, who decided to fire her. Two other employees were also informed. The employer was able to successfully raise the defense of a qualified privilege to Ms. Lewis' defamation action for "false accusations of theft" since all of the employees involved were participants in the investigation and termination of the employee.[23]

A new statutory privilege has been evolving with respect to letters of recommendation and references given by employers for employees who are applying for jobs at other companies. Most companies, because of concerns about liability for defamation, will only confirm that a former employee did work at their firm and will provide the time period during which the person was employed. Numerous states now have statutes that provide employers a qualified privilege with respect to references and recommendations. So long

---

[20] *Krinsky v. Doe,* 72 Cal. Rptr. 3d 231 (2008).
[21] See *Stark v. Zeta Phi Beta Sorority Inc.,* 587 F. Supp. 2d 170 (D.D.C. 2008).
[22] *Clemens v. McNamee,* 608 F. Supp. 2d 811 (S.D. Tex. 2009). On June 18, 2012, Clemens was acquitted of all six counts of lying to Congress.
[23] *Lewis v. Carson Oil Co.,* 127 P.3d 1207 (Or. App. 2006).

as the employer acts in good faith in providing information, there is no liability for defamation to the former employee as a result of the information provided.

8-2g Product Disparagement

Although the comparison of products and services is healthy for competition, false statements about another's products constitute a form of slander called **slander of title** or libel called **trade libel;** collectively, these are known as **product disparagement,** which occurs when someone makes false statements about another business, its products, or its abilities.[24] The elements of product disparagement are (1) a false statement about a particular business product or about its service in terms of honesty, reputation, ability, or integrity; (2) communication of the statement to a third party; and (3) damages.

slander of title— malicious making of false statements as to a seller's title.

trade libel—written defamation about a product or service.

product disparagement— false statements made about a product or business.

contract interference— tort in which a third party interferes with others' freedom to contract.

8-2h Wrongful Interference with Contracts

The tort of **contract interference** (or tortious interference with contracts) occurs when parties are not allowed the freedom to contract without interference from third parties. While the elements required to establish the tort of contract interference are complex, a basic definition is that the law affords a remedy when a third party intentionally causes another to break a contract already in existence.[25] **For Example,** Nikke Finke, a newspaper reporter who had a contract with the *New York Post* to write stories about the entertainment industry for the *Post's* business section, wrote two articles about a lawsuit involving a literary agent and the Walt Disney Company over merchandising rights to the Winnie-the-Pooh characters. Finke reported that the trial court sanctioned Disney for engaging in "misuse of the discovery process" and acting in "bad faith" and ordered Disney to pay fees and costs of $90,000. Disney's president, Robert Iger, sent a letter to the *Post's* editor-in-chief, Col Allan, calling Finke's reporting an "absolute distortion" of the record and "absolutely false." Approximately two weeks after the Pooh articles were published, the *Post* fired Finke; her editor told her she was being fired for the Pooh articles. She sued Disney on numerous tort theories, including interference with her contract with the *Post.* Disney sought to have the complaint dismissed, which motion was denied by the court. The Court of Appeals concluded that Finke demonstrated a reasonable probability of proving that Iger's allegations that she made false statements in her article were themselves false; and it concluded that a jury could find Disney liable for intentional interference with contractual relations based on circumstantial evidence and negligent interference with contractual relations because it was reasonably foreseeable to Disney that the nature of its accusations against Finke would result in her termination from employment.[26]

8-2i Trespass

A **trespass** is an unauthorized action with respect to land or personal property. A *trespass to land* is any unpermitted entry below, on, across, or above the land of another. **For Example,** Joyce Ameral's home abuts the midway point of the 240-yard, par-4 ninth hole of the public Middlebrook Country Club. Balls sliced and hooked by golfers have damaged her windows and screens, dented her car, and made her deck too dangerous for daytime use. Her landscapers are forced to wear hard hats when cutting her lawn. In her lawsuit against the country club owner, the court ruled that the projection of golf balls onto Ameral's property constituted a continuing trespass and it enjoined the trespass.[27]

trespass—unauthorized action with respect to person or property.

---

[24] *Sannerud v. Brantz,* 879 P.2d 341 (Wyo. 1994). See *Suzuki Motor Corp. v. Consumers Union,* 230 F.3d 1110 (9th Cir. 2003), *cert. denied* 540 U.S. 983 (2003), for an example of the complexity of a product disparagement action.

[25] See *Ventas, Inc. v. HCP, Inc.,* 647 F.3d 291 (6th Cir. 2011); *ASDI, Inc. v. Beard Research, Inc.,* 11 A.3d 749 (Del. 2010).

[26] *Finke v. The Walt Disney Co.,* 2 Cal. Rptr. 3d 436 (Cal. App. 2003).

[27] *Ameral v. Pray,* 831 N.E.2d 915 (Mass. App. 2005).

A *trespass to personal property* is the invasion of personal property without the permission of the owner. **For Example,** the use of someone's car without that person's permission is a trespass to personal property.

8-3 Negligence

The widest range of tort liability today arises in the field of negligence. Accidents happen! Property is damaged and/or injuries result. The fact that an individual suffers an injury does not necessarily mean that the individual will be able to recover damages for the injury. **For Example,** Rhonda Nichols was shopping in the outdoor garden center at a Lowe's Home Center when a "wild bird" flew into the back of her head, causing injuries. Her negligence lawsuit against Lowe's was dismissed because the owner did not have a duty to protect her from a wild bird attack because it was not reasonably foreseeable.[28] Jane Costa was passively watching a Boston Red Sox baseball game at Fenway Park when a foul ball struck her in the face, causing severe and permanent injuries. Her negligence lawsuit against the Boston Red Sox was unsuccessful because it was held that the owners had no duty to warn Ms. Costa of the obvious danger of foul balls being hit into the stands.[29] Although cases involving injury to spectators at baseball games in other jurisdictions have turned on other tort doctrines, injured fans, like Ms. Costa, are left to bear the costs of their injuries. Only when an injured person can demonstrate the following four elements of negligence is a right to recover established: (1) a duty, (2) breach of duty, (3) causation, and (4) damages.[30] Several defenses may be raised in a negligence lawsuit.

8-3a Elements of Negligence

Duty to Exercise Reasonable Care

The first element of negligence is a *duty.* There is a general duty of care imposed to act as a reasonably prudent person would in similar circumstances. **For Example,** Gustavo Guzman worked for a subcontractor as a chicken catcher at various poultry farms where a Tyson Foods employee, Brian Jones, operated a forklift and worked with the catchers setting up cages to collect birds for processing at a Tyson plant. Contrary to Tyson's instructions "never to allow catchers to move behind the forklift or otherwise out of sight," Brian moved his forklift and struck Guzman, who suffered a serious spinal injury. A general contractor, Tyson Foods, owes a duty to exercise reasonable care to a subcontractor's employee, Gustavo Guzman.[31]

malpractice–when services are not properly rendered in accordance with commonly accepted standards; negligence by a professional in performing his or her skill.

Professionals have a duty to perform their jobs at the level of a reasonable professional. For a professional such as an accountant, doctor, lawyer, dentist, or architect to avoid liability for **malpractice,** the professional must perform his or her skill in the same manner as, and at the level of, other professionals in the same field.

Those who own real property have a duty of care to keep their property in a condition that does not create hazards for guests. Businesses have a duty to inspect and repair their property so that their customers are not injured by hazards, such as spills on the

---

[28] *Nichols v. Lowe's Home Center, Inc.,* 407 F. Supp. 2d 979 (S.D. Ill. 2006).
[29] *Costa v. Boston Red Sox Baseball Club,* 809 N.E.2d 1090 (Mass. App. 2004).
[30] *Alfred v. Capital Area Soccer League, Inc.,* 669 S.E.2d 277 (N.C. App. 2008).
[31] *Tyson Foods Inc. v. Guzman,* 116 S.W.3d 233 (Tex. App. 2003). But see *Pippin v. Hill-Rom Co., Inc.,* 615 F.3d 886 (8th Cir. 2010), where a shipper's failure to load cargo onto an independent truck driver's trailer, as required by the transportation contract, did not give rise to a cause of action for negligence, where the driver was injured loading the truck by himself. The shipper owed no duty to the driver, who chose to load the truck by himself.

floor or uneven walking areas. When customer safety is a concern, businesses have a duty to provide adequate security, such as security patrols in mall parking lots.

Breach of Duty

The second element of negligence is the breach of duty imposed by statute or by the application of the reasonable person standard. The defendant's conduct is evaluated against what a reasonable person would have done under the circumstances. That is, when there is sufficient proof to raise a jury question, the jury decides whether the defendant breached the duty to the injured person from a reasonable person's perspective.[32] **For Example,** the jury in Guzman's lawsuit against Tyson Foods (the *Tyson* case), after weighing all of the facts and circumstances, determined that Tyson's employee's operation of the forklift constituted a breach of Tyson's duty of care to Guzman.

Causation

A third element of negligence is *causation*, the element that connects the duty and the breach of duty to the injuries to the plaintiff. **For Example,** in Guzman's lawsuit, the forklift operator's careless conduct was the cause in fact of this worker's injuries. A "but for" test for causation is used. *But for* Tyson employee Brian Jones's negligent conduct in moving the forklift under the circumstances surrounding the accident, Guzman would not have been injured.

Once the cause in fact is established, the plaintiff must establish *proximate cause*. That is, it must establish that the harm suffered by the injured person was a foreseeable consequence of the defendant's negligent actions. Foreseeability requires only the general danger to be foreseeable. In the *Tyson* case, the court determined that while there was some evidence that a jury could possibly infer that Tyson could not foresee an accident similar to the one involving Guzman, the evidence was legally sufficient to support the jury's finding that Tyson's negligence was foreseeable and the cause in fact of Guzman's injuries.

The landmark *Palsgraf v. Long Island Rail Road Co.* case established a limitation on liability for unforeseeable or unusual consequences following a negligent act.

CASE SUMMARY

The Scales Tipped on Causation

FACTS: Helen Palsgraf lived in Brooklyn. On a summer's day, she purchased tickets to travel to Rockaway Beach on the Long Island Rail Road (LIRR) with her two daughters. She was standing on a platform on the LIRR's East New York station when two men ran to catch another train. One of the men made it onto the train, but the other man, who was carrying a package, was unsteady as the train was about to pull out of the station. The LIRR conductor pulled him up, while the LIRR platform guard pushed him into the train, but in the process, he dropped the package. It contained fireworks and exploded! The concussion from the explosion caused the scales located next to

---

[32] A breach of duty may be established by the very nature of the harm to the plaintiff. The doctrine of *res ipsa loquitur* ("the event speaks for itself") provides a rebuttable presumption that the defendant was negligent when a defendant owes a duty to the plaintiff, the nature of the harm caused the plaintiff is such that it ordinarily does not happen in the absence of negligence, and the instrument causing the injury was in the defendant's exclusive control. An example of the doctrine is a lawsuit against a surgeon after a surgical device is discovered in a former patient months after the surgery by another physician seeking the cause of the patient's continuing pain subsequent to the operation.

The Scales Tipped on Causation continued

Mrs. Palsgraf to fall over, striking and injuring her. Mrs. Palsgraf sued LIRR for the negligence of the two employees who had assisted the passenger with the package to board the train. A jury awarded her $6,000, which was upheld 3-2 by the Appellate Division. Thereafter the state's highest court considered the railroad's appeal.

DECISION: Recovery for negligence is not available unless there has been some violation of a right. Helen Palsgraf was too remote in distance from the accident for any invasion of rights. To reach a different decision would mean that there could be no end to those who might be harmed. By helping someone onto a moving train, the train employees can anticipate that the passenger himself might be injured, that other passengers might be injured, and that those around the immediate scene might be injured. But Mrs. Palsgraf was too remote for her injuries to be reasonably foreseeable as a consequence of the action of helping a passenger onto a moving train. She was 25 to 30 feet away from the scene, and the explosion cannot be called the proximate cause of her concussion and other injuries. [*Palsgraf v. Long Island R. R. Co.*, 162 N.E. 99 (N.Y. 1928)]

Damages

The plaintiff in a personal injury negligence lawsuit must establish the actual losses caused by the defendant's breach of duty of care and is entitled to be made whole for all losses. The successful plaintiff is entitled to compensation for (1) past and future pain and suffering (mental anguish), (2) past and future physical impairment, (3) past and future medical care, and (4) past and future loss of earning capacity. Life and work life expectancy are critical factors to consider in assessing damage involving permanent disabilities with loss of earning capacity. Expert witnesses are utilized at trial to present evidence based on worklife tables and present value tables to deal with these economic issues. The jury considers all of the evidence in the context of the elements necessary to prove negligence and all defenses raised, and it renders a verdict. **For Example,** in the *Tyson* case, the defendant presented evidence and argued that Gustavo Guzman was himself negligent regarding the accident. The jury found that both parties were negligent and attributed 80 percent of the fault to Tyson and 20 percent to Guzman (this is called *comparative negligence* and is discussed in the following section). The jury awarded Guzman $931,870.51 in damages ($425,000.00 for past physical pain and mental anguish, $150,000.00 for future physical pain and mental anguish, $10,000.00 for past physical impairment, $10,000.00 for future physical impairment, $51,870.51 for past medical care, $5,000.00 for future medical care, $70,000.00 for past lost earning capacity, and $210,000.00 for future lost earning capacity). After deducting 20 percent of the total jury award for Guzman's own negligence, the trial court's final judgment awarded Guzman $745,496.41.

In some situations, the independent actions of two defendants occur to cause harm. **For Example,** Penny Shipler was rendered a quadriplegic as a result of a Chevrolet S-10 Blazer rollover accident. She sued the driver Kenneth Long for negligence and General Motors for negligent design of the Blazer's roof. She was awarded $18.5 million in damages. Because two causes provided a single indivisible injury, the two defendants were held jointly and severally liable.[33] Under *joint and several liability*, each defendant may be held liable to pay the entire judgment. However, should one defendant pay the entire judgment, that party may sue the other for "contribution" for its proportionate share.

In some cases in which the breach of duty was shocking, plaintiffs may be awarded *punitive damages.* However, punitive (also called *exemplary*) damages are ordinarily applied

[33] *Shipler v. General Motors Corp.,* 710 N.W.2d 807 (Neb. 2006).

when the defendant's tortious conduct is attended by circumstances of fraud, malice, or willful or wanton conduct.[34]

8-3b Defenses to Negligence

Contributory Negligence

contributory negligence–negligence of the plaintiff that contributes to injury and at common law bars recovery from the defendant although the defendant may have been more negligent than the plaintiff.

A plaintiff who is also negligent gives the defendant the opportunity to raise the defense of **contributory negligence,** which the defendant establishes by utilizing the elements of negligence previously discussed, including the plaintiff's duty to exercise reasonable care for his or her own safety, the breach of that duty, causation, and harm. Under common law, the defense of contributory negligence, if established, is a complete bar to recovery of damages from the defendant.

CASE SUMMARY

Keep Your Eye on the Ball in Sports: Keep Your Eye on the 300-Pound Boxes in Trucking

FACTS: Lawrence Hardesty is an over-the-road tractor-trailer truck driver who picked up a load of stadium seating equipment for the NFL stadium under construction in Baltimore. The equipment was packaged in large corrugated cardboard boxes weighing several hundred pounds. The shipper, American Seating Co., loaded the trailer while Hardesty remained in the cab of his truck doing "paperwork" and napping. Considerable open space existed between the boxes and the rear door of the trailer. The evidence showed that Hardesty failed to properly examine the load bars used to secure the boxes from movement during transit. When Hardesty arrived at the Baltimore destination, he opened the rear trailer door and boxes at the end of the trailer fell out and injured him. Hardesty brought a personal injury negligence action against the shipper. American Seating Co. responded that Hardesty was contributorily negligent, thus barring his negligence claim.

DECISION: Judgment for American Seating Co. because the claim is barred by Hardesty's contributory negligence. His decision to ignore the loading process by remaining in his truck, oblivious to the manner and means of the loading of the trailer, coupled with his own failure to examine the load bars sufficiently to confirm that they would "adequately secure" the cargo, together with his decision, in the face of his prior omissions, to open the doors of the trailer upon his arrival in Baltimore while standing within the zone of danger created by the possibility (of which he negligently failed to inform himself) of injury from cargo falling out of the trailer, cohered to rise to the level of a cognizable breach of duty— contributory negligence. [*Hardesty v. American Seating Co.*, **194 F. Supp. 2d 447 (D. Md. 2002)**]

The contributory negligence defense has given way to the defense of comparative negligence in most states.[35]

Comparative Negligence

Because contributory negligence produced harsh results with no recovery of damages for an injured plaintiff, most states have adopted a fairer approach to handling situations in which both the plaintiff and the defendant are negligent; it is called *comparative*

---

[34] See *Eden Electrical, Ltd. v. Amana Co.*, 370 F.3d 824 (8th Cir. 2004); and *University of Colorado v. American Cyanamid Co.*, 342 F.3d 1298 (Fed. Cir. 2003).

[35] Alabama, the District of Columbia, Maryland, North Carolina, and Virginia are pure contributory negligence states, which hold that the damaged party cannot recover any damages even if it is just 1 percent at fault. See *RGR, LLC v. Settle*, 758 S.E.2d 215 (Va. 2014) where the Virginia Supreme Court set aside a $2.5 million judgment finding that the plaintiff was contributorily negligent as a matter of law.

negligence. Comparative negligence is a defense that permits a negligent plaintiff to recover some damages but only in proportion to the defendant's degree of fault.[36] **For Example,** in the *Tyson* case, both the defendant and the plaintiff were found to be negligent. The jury attributed 80 percent of the fault for the plaintiff's injury to Tyson and 20 percent of the fault to the plaintiff, Guzman. While Guzman's total damages were $931,870, they were reduced by 20 percent, and the final judgment awarded Guzman was $745,496.

Some comparative negligence states refuse to allow the plaintiff to recover damages if the plaintiff's fault was more than 50 percent of the cause of the harm.[37]

Assumption of the Risk

The assumption of the risk defense has two categories. *Express assumption of the risk* involves a written exculpatory agreement under which a plaintiff acknowledges the risks involved in certain activities and releases the defendant from prospective liability for personal injuries sustained as a result of the defendant's negligent conduct. Examples include ski lift tickets, white water rafting contracts, permission for high school cheerleading activities, and parking lot claim checks. In most jurisdictions these agreements are enforceable as written. However, in some jurisdictions they may be considered unenforceable because they violate public policy. **For Example,** Gregory Hanks sued the Powder Ridge Ski Resort for negligence regarding serious injuries he sustained while snowtubing at the defendant's facility. He had signed a release, which explicitly provided that the snowtuber: [*"fully] assume[s] all risks associated with [s]nowtubing, even if due to the NEGLIGENCE"* of the defendants [emphasis in original]. The Supreme Court of Connecticut found that the release was unenforceable because it violated the public policy by shifting the risk of negligence to the weaker bargainer.[38]

Implied primary assumption of the risk arises when a plaintiff has impliedly consented, often in advance of any negligence by the defendant, to relieve a defendant of a duty to the plaintiff regarding specific known and appreciated risks. It is a subjective standard, one specific to the plaintiff and his or her situation. **For Example,** baseball mom Delinda Taylor took her two boys to a Seattle Mariners baseball game and was injured during the pregame warm-up when a ball thrown by José Mesa got past Freddie Garcia, striking Taylor in the face and causing serious injuries. The defendant baseball team successfully raised the affirmative defense of implied primary assumption of the risk by showing that Mrs. Taylor had full subjective understanding of the specific risk of getting hit by a thrown baseball, and she voluntarily chose to encounter that risk.[39] However, John Coomer, a spectator at a Kansas City Royals baseball game was struck in the eye by a hotdog thrown by the team's mascot, Slugger, during a "Hotdog Launch," causing Coomer to suffer a detached retina. The Supreme Court of Missouri held that being injured by Slugger's hotdog toss was not a risk inherent in watching a Royals baseball game.[40]

A number of states have either abolished the defense of assumption of the risk, reclassifying the defense as comparative negligence so as not to completely bar a plaintiff's recovery of damages, or have eliminated the use of the assumption of the risk terminology to handle cases under the duty, breach of duty, causation, and harm elements of negligence previously discussed.[41]

---

[36] *City of Chicago v. M/V Morgan,* 375 F.3d 563 (7th Cir. 2004).

[37] *Davenport v. Cotton Hope Plantation,* 482 S.E.2d 569 (S.C. App. 1997).

[38] *Hanks v. Powder Ridge,* 885 A.2d 734 (Conn. 2005).

[39] *Taylor v. Baseball Club of Seattle,* 130 P.3d 835 (Wash. App. 2006).

[40] *Coomer v. K.C. Royals Baseball Corp.,* 437 S.W.3d 184 (Mo. 2014).

[41] See, for example, *Costa v. The Boston Red Sox Baseball Club,* 809 N.E.2d 1090 (Mass. App. 2004), where the court cites state precedent that "… the abolishment of assumption of the risk as an affirmative defense did not alter the plaintiff's burden … to prove the defendant owed [the plaintiff] a duty of care … and thus left intact the open and obvious damages rule, which operates to negate the existence of a duty to care."

SPORTS & ENTERTAINMENT LAW

Liability for Injuries under the Sports Exception Doctrine

Charles "Booby" Clark played football for the Cincinnati Bengals as a running back on offense. Dale Hackbart played defensive free safety for the Denver Broncos. As a consequence of an interception by the Broncos, Hackbart became an offensive player, threw a block, and was watching the play with one knee on the ground when Clark "acting out of anger and frustration, but without a specific intent to injure," stepped forward and struck a blow to the back of Hackbart's head and neck, causing a serious neck fracture. Is relief precluded for injuries occurring during a professional football game? The answer is no. While proof of mere negligence is insufficient to establish liability during such an athletic contest, liability must instead be premised on heightened proof of reckless or intentional conduct on the part of the defendant. In the *Hackbart* case, the court determined that if the evidence established that the injury was the result of acts of Clark that were in reckless disregard of Hackbart's safety, Hackbart is entitled to damages.* Why didn't Hackbart pursue recovery under negligence law, contending that Clark had a general duty of care to act as a reasonably prudent person

would in similar circumstances? Because football and other contact sports contain within the rules of the games inherent *unreasonable* risks of harm, a negligence theory is not applicable. What contact sports do you believe qualify under this "sports exception" doctrine for which proof of negligence is insufficient to establish liability for injuries sustained during the athletic contest? Is softball a contact sport for players? What about coaching or officiating decisions made in the middle of a fast-moving game?**

PGA golfer Walter Mallin sued PGA golfer John Paesani for injuries that Mallin sustained while competing in a PGA golf tournament when Paesani drove a golf ball that struck Mallin in the head on his right temple. Paesani contends that the "sports exception" doctrine applies and the negligence case must be dismissed. How would you decide this case?***

*Hackbart v. Cincinnati Bengals, Inc., 601 F.2d 516 (10th Cir. 1979).
**See Guillo v. DeKamp Junction, Inc., 959 N.E.2d 215 (Ill. App. 2011).
***Mallin v. Paesani, 892 A.2d 1043 (Conn. Super. 2005).

Immunity

Governments are generally immune from tort liability.[42] This rule has been eroded by decisions and in some instances by statutes, such as the Federal Tort Claims Act. Subject to certain exceptions, this act permits the recovery of damages from the United States for property damage, personal injury, or death action claims arising from the negligent act or omission of any employee of the United States under such circumstances that the United States, if a private person, would be liable to the claimant in accordance with the law of the place where the act or omission occurred. A rapidly growing number of states have abolished governmental immunity, although many still recognize it.

Until the early 1900s, charities were immune from tort liability, and children and parents and spouses could not sue each other. These immunities are fast disappearing. **For Example,** if a father's negligent driving of his car causes injuries to his minor child passenger, the child may recover from the father for his injuries.[43]

8-4 Strict Liability

The final form of tort liability is known as *strict liability*. When the standards of strict liability apply, very few defenses are available. Strict liability was developed to provide guaranteed protection for those who are injured by conduct the law deems both serious and inexcusable.

[42] *Kirby v. Macon County*, 892 S.W.2d 403 (Tenn. 1994).
[43] *Cates v. Cates*, 588 N.E.2d 330 (Ill. App. 1992); see also *Doe v. McKay*, 700 N.E.2d 1018 (Ill. 1998).

THINKING THINGS THROUGH

Torts and Public Policy

Over a decade ago, a jury awarded 81-year-old Stella Liebeck nearly $3 million because she was burned after she spilled a cup of McDonald's coffee on her lap. Based on these limited facts, a national discussion ensued about a need for tort reform, and to this day "Stella Awards" are given on Web sites for apparently frivolous or excessive lawsuits. Consider the following additional facts and the actual damages awarded Stella Liebeck. Decide whether her recovery was just.

- McDonald's coffee was brewed at 195 to 205 degrees.

- McDonald's quality assurance manager "was aware of the risk [of burns] … and had no plans to turn down the heat."

- Mrs. Liebeck spent seven days in the hospital with third-degree burns and had skin grafts. Gruesome photos of burns of the inner thighs, groin, and buttocks were entered as evidence.

- The compensatory damages were $200,000, which were reduced to $160,000 because Mrs. Liebeck was determined to be 20 percent at fault.

- The jury awarded $2.7 million in punitive damages. The trial court judge reduced this amount to $480,000.

- The total recovery at the trial court for Mrs. Liebeck was $640,000. Both parties appealed, and a settlement was reached at what is believed to be close to the $640,000 figure.

Tort remedies have evolved because of public policy incentives for the protection of individuals from physical, mental, and economic damage. Tort remedies provide economic motivation for individuals and businesses to avoid conduct that could harm others.

The amount of the compensation and the circumstances in which compensation for torts should be paid are issues that courts, juries, and legislatures review. Many legislatures have examined and continue to review the standards for tort liability and damages.

The U.S. Supreme Court devoted several decisions in recent years to dealing with excessive punitive damages in civil litigation, and it has set "guideposts" to be used by courts in assessing punitive damages.* In *State Farm Mutual Automobile Insurance Co. v. Campbell*, compensatory damages for the plaintiffs at the trial court level were $1 million, and punitive damages, based in part on evidence that State Farm's nationwide policy was to underpay claims regardless of merit to enhance profits, were assessed at $145 million. The Supreme Court concluded that the facts of *Campbell* would likely justify a punitive damages award only at or near the amount of compensatory damages. Thus, even those who act very badly as State Farm Insurance did have a constitutionally protected right under the due process clause of the Fourteenth Amendment to have civil law damages assessed in accordance with the Supreme Court's guideposts.

*__BMW of North America v. Gore__, 517 U.S. 559 (1996); __Cooper Industries v. Leatherman Tool Group, Inc.__, 532 U.S. 424 (2001); __State Farm Insurance v. Campbell__, 538 U.S. 408 (2003); __Exxon Shipping Co. v. Baker__, 544 U.S. 471 (2008).

8-4a What Is Strict Liability?

Strict liability is an absolute standard of liability imposed by the law in circumstances the courts or legislatures have determined require a high degree of protection. When strict liability is imposed, the result is that the company or person who has caused injury or damages by the conduct will be required to compensate for those damages in an absolute sense. Few, if any, defenses apply in a situation in which the law imposes a strict liability standard. **For Example,** as noted earlier in the chapter, engaging in ultrahazardous activities, such as using dynamite to excavate a site for new construction, results in strict liability for the contractor performing the demolition. Any damages resulting from the explosion are the responsibility of that contractor, so the contractor is strictly liable.

8-4b Imposing Strict Liability

Strict liability arises in a number of different circumstances, but the most common are in those situations in which a statutory duty is imposed and in product liability. **For Example,** at both the state and federal levels, there are requirements for the use, transportation, and sale of radioactive materials, as well as the disposal of biomedical materials and tools. Any violation of these rules and regulations would result in strict liability for the company or person in violation.

Product liability, while more fully covered in Chapter 24, is another example of strict liability. A product that is defective through its design, manufacture, or instructions and that injures someone results in strict liability for the manufacturer.

Make the Connection

Summary

A *tort* is a civil wrong that affords recovery for damages that result. The three forms of torts are intentional torts, negligence, and strict liability. A tort differs from a crime in the nature of its remedy. Fines and imprisonment result from criminal violations, whereas money damages are paid to those who are damaged by conduct that constitutes a tort. An action may be both a crime and a tort, but the tort remedy is civil in nature.

Selected intentional torts are false imprisonment, defamation, product disparagement, contract interference or tortious interference, and trespass. False imprisonment is the detention of another without his or her permission. False imprisonment is often called the *shopkeeper's tort* because store owners detain suspected shoplifters. Many states provide a privilege to store owners if they detain shoplifting suspects based on reasonable cause and in a reasonable manner. Defamation is slander (oral) or libel (written) and consists of false statements about another that damage the person's reputation or integrity. With an increase in Internet cases, some of which involve anonymous posts, courts may compel disclosure of identity only if the plaintiff can demonstrate a credible claim and the anonymous speaker is given the opportunity to defend before the unveiling of his or her name. Truth is an absolute defense to defamation, and there are some privileges that protect against defamation, such as those for witnesses at trial and for members of Congress during debates on the floor. There is a developing privilege for employers when they give references for former employees. Invasion of privacy is intrusion into private affairs; public disclosure of private facts; or appropriation of someone's name, image, or likeness for commercial purposes.

To establish the tort of negligence, one must show that there has been a breach of duty in the form of a violation of a statute or professional competency standards or of behavior that does not rise to the level of that of a reasonable person. That breach of duty must have caused the foreseeable injuries to the plaintiff, and the plaintiff must be able to quantify the damages that resulted. Possible defenses to negligence include contributory negligence, comparative negligence, and assumption of risk.

Strict liability is absolute liability with few defenses.

Learning Outcomes

After studying this chapter, you should be able to clearly explain:

8-1   General Principles

LO.1 Explain the difference between torts and crimes

See the discussion on wrongs that are a violation of a private duty as torts, and wrongs that are a violation of a public duty as crimes, page 132.

See the O. J. Simpson example of his acquittal of the crime of murder and his civil liability for the torts of wrongful death, page 132.

8-2   Intentional Torts

LO.2 Distinguish between an assault and a battery

See the "kick your butt" threat example of an assault, page 134.

LO.3 Explain the three different torts of invasion of privacy

See the discussion of the intrusion into a person's private affairs, public disclosure of private facts, and right of publicity torts, pages 136–137.

See the *Ignat* case, which determined that a right of privacy can be violated by word of mouth, pages 136–137.

See the *Schlein* case involving commercial misappropriation of one's name, pages 137–138.

LO.4 Explain the torts of defamation and defenses

See the discussion of slander, libel, and trade libel beginning, pages 138 and 141.

See the *Ventura* case involving the requirement of the enhanced element of malice for cases in which the victim is a public figure, page 138.

See the discussion involving unveiling the identity of offending anonymous posters of defamatory remarks on the Internet, page 139.

8-3   Negligence

LO.5 Explain the elements of negligence and defenses

See the discussion of the elements of negligence: duty, breach of duty, and causation and damages, pages 142–144.

See the discussion of the defenses of contributory negligence, comparative negligence, assumption of risk, and immunity, pages 145–147.

8-4   Strict Liability

LO.6 Explain the tort of strict liability and why very few defenses are available

See the dynamite excavation example, holding the contractor liable for any damages with no defenses because of the hazardous activity, page 148.

See the product liability example, page 149.

Key Terms

absolute privilege

contract interference

contributory negligence

defamation

false imprisonment

intentional infliction of emotional

   distress

intentional torts

invasion of privacy

libel

malpractice

negligence

product disparagement

qualified privilege

shopkeeper's privilege

slander

slander of title

strict liability

tort

trade libel

trespass

Questions and Case Problems

1. Christensen Shipyards built a 155-foot yacht for Tiger Woods at its Vancouver, Washington, facilities. It used Tiger's name and photographs relating to the building of the yacht in promotional materials for the shipyard without seeking his permission. Was this a right of publicity tort because Tiger could assert that his name and photos were used to attract attention to the shipyard to obtain commercial advantage? Did the shipyard have a First Amendment right to present the truthful facts regarding its building of the yacht and the owner's identity as promotional materials? Does the fact that the yacht was named *Privacy* have an impact on this case? Would it make a difference as to the outcome of this case if the contract for building the yacht had a clause prohibiting the use of Tiger's name or photo without his permission?

2. ESPN held its Action Sports and Music Awards ceremony in April, at which celebrities in the fields of extreme sports and popular music such as rap and heavy metal converged. Well-known musicians Ben Harper and James Hetfield were there, as were popular rappers Busta Rhymes and LL Cool J. Famed motorcycle stuntman Evel Knievel, who is commonly thought of as the "father of extreme sports," and his wife, Krystal, were photographed. The photograph depicted Evel, who was wearing a motorcycle jacket and rose-tinted sunglasses, with his right arm around Krystal and his left arm around another young woman. ESPN published the photograph on its "extreme sports" Web site with a caption that read "Evel Knievel proves that you're never too old to be a pimp." The Knievels brought suit against ESPN, contending that the photograph and caption were defamatory because they accused Evel of soliciting prostitution and implied that Krystal was a prostitute. ESPN contends that the caption was a figurative and slang usage and was not defamatory as a matter of law. Decide. [*Knievel v. ESPN*, 393 F.3d 1068 (9th Cir.)]

3. While snowboarding down a slope at Mammoth Mountain Ski Area (Mammoth), 17-year-old David Graham was engaged in a snowball fight with his 14-year-old brother. As he was "preparing to throw a snowball" at his brother, David slammed into Liam Madigan, who was working as a ski school instructor for Mammoth, and injured him. Madigan sued Graham for damages for reckless and dangerous

behavior. The defense contended that the claim was barred under the doctrine of assumption of the risk, applicable in the state, arising from the risk inherent in the sport that allows for vigorous participation and frees a participant from a legal duty to act with due care. Decide. [*Mammoth Mountain Ski Area v. Graham*, 38 Cal. Rptr. 3d 422 (Cal. App.)]

4. Following a visit to her hometown of Coalinga, Cynthia wrote "An Ode to Coalinga" (Ode) and posted it in her online journal on MySpace.com. Her last name did not appear online. Her page included her picture. The Ode opens with "The older I get, the more I realize how much I despise Coalinga" and then proceeds to make a number of extremely negative comments about Coalinga and its inhabitants. Six days later, Cynthia removed the Ode from her journal. At the time, Cynthia was a student at UC Berkeley, and her parents and sister were living in Coalinga. The Coalinga High School principal, Roger Campbell, submitted the Ode to the local newspaper, the *Coalinga Record*, and it was published in the Letters to the Editor section, using Cynthia's full name. The community reacted violently to the Ode, forcing the family to close its business and move. Cynthia and her family sued Campbell and the newspaper on the right-of-privacy theory of public disclosure of private facts. What are the essential elements of this theory? Was Cynthia and her family's right of privacy violated? [*Moreno v. Hanford Sentinel, Inc.*, 91 Cal. Rptr. 3d 858 (Cal. App.)]

5. Catherine Bosley worked as a television news anchor for WKBN Channel 27 in Youngstown, Ohio. While on vacation with her husband in Florida she participated in a "wet t-shirt" contest, which was videotaped without her consent by DreamGirls, Inc. and licensed to Marvad Corp., which runs a Web site for adult entertainment through a subscription service on the Internet. Marvad used depictions of her in advertisements to promote the materials and services it markets. Web site searches related to Catherine Bosley in 2004 were the most popular search on the World Wide Web. Due to the publicity, she resigned from her position at WKBN. Bosley sought an injunction against the defendants from using her image in any manner that promotes the sale of their goods or services. The defendants contend that an injunction would violate their First Amendment rights. What legal theory did Bosley rely on to seek the injunction? Would an injunction be in violation of the defendant's First Amendment's

rights? Decide. [*Bosley v. Wildwett.com*, 310 F. Supp. 2d 914 (N.D. Ohio)]

6. Juanita DeJesus was seriously injured when hit on the head by a foul ball at a minor league baseball game and sued the stadium operators for negligence and premises liability. The case progressed to the Indiana Supreme Court where the Indianapolis Indians urged the State Supreme Court to dispose of the premises liability and negligence claims in one fell swoop by adopting the so-called Baseball Rule, which provides that:

> *a ballpark operator that provides screening behind home plate sufficient to meet ordinary demand for protected seating has fulfilled its duty with respect to screening and cannot be subjected to liability for injuries resulting to a spectator by an object leaving the playing field.*

Should the Court adopt this clear and unambiguous rule for the national pastime? Does the Court have authority to make such a ruling? How would you decide her negligence claim? [*South Shore Baseball, LLC v. DeJesus*, 11 N.E.3d 903 (Ind.)]

7. Mallinckrodt produces nuclear and radioactive medical pharmaceuticals and supplies. Maryland Heights Leasing, an adjoining business owner, claimed that low-level radiation emissions from Mallinckrodt damaged its property and caused a loss in earnings. What remedy should Maryland Heights have? What torts are involved here? [*Maryland Heights Leasing, Inc. v. Mallinckrodt, Inc.*, 706 S.W.2d 218 (Mo. App.)]

8. An owner abandoned his van in an alley in Chicago. In spite of repeated complaints to the police, the van was allowed to remain in the alley. After several months, it was stripped of most of the parts that could be removed. Jamin Ortiz, age 11, was walking down the alley when the van's gas tank exploded. The flames from the explosion set fire to Jamin's clothing, and he was severely burned. Jamin and his family brought suit against the city of Chicago to recover damages for his injuries. Could the city be held responsible for injuries caused by property owned by someone else? Why or why not? [*Ortiz v. Chicago*, 398 N.E.2d 1007 (Ill. App.)]

9. Carrigan, a district manager of Simples Time Recorder Co., was investigating complaints of mismanagement of the company's Jackson office. He called at the home of Hooks, the secretary of that office, who expressed the opinion that part of the trouble was caused by the theft of parts and

equipment by McCall, another employee. McCall was later discharged and sued Hooks for slander. Was she liable? [*Hooks v. McCall*, 272 So. 2d 925 (Miss.)]

10. Defendant no. 1 parked his truck in the street near the bottom of a ditch on a dark, foggy night. Iron pipes carried in the truck projected nine feet beyond the truck in back. Neither the truck nor the pipes carried any warning light or flag, in violation of both a city ordinance and a state statute. Defendant no. 2 was a taxicab owner whose taxicab was negligently driven at an excessive speed. Defendant no. 2 ran into the pipes, thereby killing the passenger in the taxicab. The plaintiff brought an action for the passenger's death against both defendants. Defendant no. 1 claimed he was not liable because it was Defendant no. 2's negligence that had caused the harm. Was this defense valid? [*Bumbardner v. Allison*, 78 S.E.2d 752 (N.C.)]

11. Carl Kindrich's father, a member of the Long Beach Yacht Club before he died, expressed a wish to be "buried at sea." The Yacht Club permitted the Kindrich family the use of one of its boats, without charge, for the ceremony, and Mr. Fuller—a good friend of Carl's father—piloted the boat. Portable stairs on the dock assisted the attendees in boarding. Upon returning, Fuller asked for help to tie up the boat. The steps were not there, and Carl broke his leg while disembarking to help tie up the boat. Carl sued the Yacht Club for negligence in failing to have someone on the dock to ensure that the portable steps were available. The Yacht Club contended that it was not liable because Carl made the conscious decision to jump from the moving vessel to the dock, a primary assumption of risk in the sport of boating. The plaintiff contended that he was not involved in the sport of boating, and at most his actions constituted minimal comparative negligence, the type that a jury could weigh in conjunction with the defendant's negligence in assessing damages. Decide. [*Kindrich v. Long Beach Yacht Club*, 84 Cal. Rptr. 3d 824 (Cal. App.)]

12. Hegyes was driving her car when it was negligently struck by a Unjian Enterprises truck. She was injured, and an implant was placed in her body to counteract the injuries. She sued Unjian, and the case was settled. Two years later Hegyes became pregnant. The growing fetus pressed against the implant, making it necessary for her doctor to deliver the child 51 days prematurely by Cesarean section.

Because of its premature birth, the child had a breathing handicap. Suit was brought against Unjian Enterprises for the harm sustained by the child. Was the defendant liable? [*Hegyes v. Unjian Enterprises, Inc.*, 286 Cal. Rptr. 85 (Cal. App.)]

13. Kendra Knight took part in a friendly game of touch football. She had played before and was familiar with football. Michael Jewett was on her team. In the course of play, Michael bumped into Kendra and knocked her to the ground. He stepped on her hand, causing injury to a little finger that later required its amputation. She sued Michael for damages. He defended on the ground that she had assumed the risk. Kendra claimed that assumption of risk could not be raised as a defense because the state legislature had adopted the standard of comparative negligence. What happens if contributory negligence applies? What happens if the defense of comparative negligence applies?

14. A passenger on a cruise ship was injured by a rope thrown while the ship was docking. The passenger was sitting on a lounge chair on the third deck when she was struck by the weighted end of a rope thrown by an employee of Port Everglades, where the boat was docking. These ropes, or heaving lines, were being thrown from the dock to the second deck, and the passenger was injured by a line that was thrown too high.

The trial court granted the cruise line's motion for directed verdict on the ground there was no evidence that the cruise line knew or should have known of the danger. The cruise line contended that it had no notice that this "freak accident" could occur. What is the duty of a cruise ship line to its passengers? Is there liability here? Does it matter that an employee of the port city, not the cruise lines, caused the injury? Should the passenger be able to recover? Why or why not? [*Kalendareva v. Discovery Cruise Line Partnership*, 798 So. 2d 804 (Fla. App.)]

15. Blaylock was a voluntary psychiatric outpatient treated by Dr. Burglass, who became aware that Blaylock was violence prone. Blaylock told Dr. Burglass that he intended to do serious harm to Wayne Boynton, Jr., and shortly thereafter he killed Wayne. Wayne's parents then sued Dr. Burglass on grounds that he was liable for the death of their son because he failed to give warning or to notify the police of Blaylock's threat and nature. Was a duty breached here? Should Dr. Burglass be held liable? [*Boynton v. Burglass*, 590 So. 2d 446 (Fla. App.)]

Intellectual Property Rights and the Internet

Learning Outcomes ⟨⟨⟨

After studying this chapter, you should be able to

LO.1 Explain the spectrum of distinctiveness used to classify trademarks and explain why distinctiveness is important

LO.2 Explain how courts determine whether there is a likelihood of confusion between trademarks

LO.3 Explain how personal names can acquire trademark protection

LO.4 List the remedies available for improper use of trademarks

LO.5 Explain the difference between trademark infringement and trademark dilution

LO.6 Explain what is and is not copyrightable; explain the fair use defense

LO.7 Explain the "new and not obvious" requirement necessary to obtain a patent

LO.8 Explain what constitutes a trade secret and what steps a company must take to ensure protection

LO.9 Explain the extent of protection provided owners of software

Intellectual property comes in many forms: the writing by an author or the software developed by an employee, the new product or process developed by an inventor, the company name Hewlett-Packard, and the secret formula used to make Coca-Cola. Federal law provides rights to owners of these works, products, company names, and secret formulas that are called *copyrights, patents, trademarks*, and *trade secrets*. State laws provide protection for trade secrets. These basic legal principles are also applicable in an Internet and e-commerce context. This chapter discusses the federal and state laws governing intellectual property rights and their Internet context.

9-1 Trademarks and Service Marks

The Lanham Act is a federal law that grants a producer the exclusive right to register a trademark and prevent competitors from using that mark. This law helps ensure that the trademark holder and not an imitating competitor will reap the financial, reputation-related rewards of a desirable product. While unfair competition plays a role in trademark protection, courts are concerned with the impact that trademark infringement has on consumers. The trademark system seeks to ensure that trademarks serve their purpose of source identifiers that reduce consumers' search costs and allow consumers to make decisions that more closely coincide with their preferences.

9-1a Introduction

A mark is any word, name, symbol, device, or combination of these used to identify a product or service.[1] If the mark identifies a product, such as an automobile or soap, it is called a **trademark.** If it identifies a service, such as an airline or dry cleaner, it is called a **service mark.**

trademark–mark that identifies a product.

service mark–mark that identifies a service.

The owner of a mark may obtain protection from others using it by registering the mark in accordance with federal law at the United States Patent and Trademark Office (USPTO) in Washington, D.C.[2] To be registered, a mark must distinguish the goods or services of the applicant from those of others. Under the federal Lanham Act, a register, called the Principal Register, is maintained for recording such marks. Inclusion on the Principal Register grants the registrant the exclusive right to use the mark. Challenges may be made to the registrant's right within five years of registration, but after five years, the right of the registrant is incontestable.

A mark may be "reserved" before starting a business by filing an application for registration on the basis of the applicant's good-faith intent to use the mark. Once the mark is used in trade, then the USPTO will actually issue the registration with a priority date retroactive to the date the application was filed. The applicant has a maximum period of 36 months to get the business started and demonstrate that the mark is in "use in commerce." In the United States, the first party to use a trademark in commerce is the presumptive owner of the mark. Nevertheless, it is always preferable to register the trademark to secure legal protection.

9-1b International Registration

The Madrid Protocol is an international treaty that provides for a streamlined system of international registration of trademarks. The trademark holder can file with a single office, in one language, and pay a single fee to obtain protection in multiple countries. Changes

[1] 15 U.S.C. §1127.
[2] Lanham Act, 15 U.S.C. §§1050–1127.

in ownership of the mark as well as renewal of the mark (every 10 years) can also be effected through the Madrid Protocol. The United States became a party to the treaty in 2003. Ninety-four countries are signatories, including most of the United States' trading partners, with the exception of Canada. Before the mark can be the subject of an international application, it must have already been registered or applied for with the U.S. Patent and Trademark Office (USPTO).

9-1c Registrable Marks

distinctiveness–capable of serving the source-identifying function of a mark.

Trademark law categorizes marks along a spectrum of **distinctiveness,** based on a mark's capacity to serve a source-identifying function. A mark is classified as (1) coined or fanciful (most distinctive), (2) arbitrary, (3) suggestive, (4) descriptive, or (5) generic (least distinctive). **For Example,** the mark EXXON is fanciful because it was designed by its owner to designate petroleum and related products. The name CENGAGE is a coined creation of the owner of this trademark and has no other meaning in English, but it serves to distinguish the products of its owner from all others. The mark APPLE for computers, an arbitrary mark, consists of a word in common usage that is arbitrarily applied in such a way that it is not descriptive or suggestive. The mark COPPERTONE for suntan lotion is a suggestive mark—requiring some imagination to reach a conclusion about the nature of the product. Coined or fanciful, arbitrary, and suggestive marks may be registered on the Principal Register under the Lanham Act without producing any actual evidence of the source-identifying attribution or the public perception of these marks.

Descriptive marks are those that convey an immediate idea of the ingredients, qualities, or characteristics of the goods or service, such as SPORTS ILLUSTRATED for a sports magazine. Because descriptive marks are not inherently capable of serving as source identifiers, such marks may be registered on the Principal Register only after the owner has provided sufficient evidence to establish that the public associates the term or phrase not only with a specific feature or quality, but also with a single commercial source. When a descriptive phrase becomes associated with a single commercial source, the phrase is said to possess **"acquired distinctiveness"** or **"secondary meaning,"** and therefore functions as a trademark. **For Example,** when the public perceives the phrase SPORTS ILLUSTRATED as a particular sports magazine in addition to its primary meaning as a description of a specific feature or element, the phrase has "acquired distinctiveness" or "secondary meaning" and may receive trademark protection.

acquired distinctiveness–through advertising, use and association, over time, an ordinary descriptive word or phrase has taken on a new source-identifying meaning and functions as a mark in the eyes of the public.

secondary meaning–a legal term signifying the words in question have taken on a new meaning with the public, capable of serving a source-identifying function of a mark.

Ordinarily geographic terms are not registrable on the Principal Register. **For Example,** BOSTON BEER was denied trademark protection because it was a geographic term.[3] However, if a geographic term has acquired a secondary meaning, it would be registrable. **For Example,** the geographic term *Philadelphia* has acquired secondary meaning when applied to cream cheese products.

A personal name can acquire trademark protection if the name has acquired secondary meaning. The name must be registered as a trademark for goods or services and must be used in commerce. A name acquires secondary meaning if the buying public associates the name with a product or service. **For Example,** David Beckham has registered his name in a variety of categories from mobile phones to swim wear.

With a limited number of colors available for use by competitors, along with possible shade confusion, courts had held for some 90 years that color alone could not function as a trademark. The U.S. Supreme Court has overturned this rule, finding that if a color serves as a symbol that distinguishes a firm's goods and identifies their source without serving any other significant function, it may, sometimes at least, meet the basic legal

---

[3] *Boston Beer Co. v. Slesar Bros. Brewing Co.,* 9 F.3d 812 (1st Cir. 1994).

requirements for use as a trademark.[4] **For Example,** Owens-Corning Fiberglass Corp. has been allowed to register the color pink as a trademark for its fiberglass insulation products.

Generic terms that describe a "genus" or class of goods such as soap, car, cola, or rosé wine are never registrable because they do not have a capacity to serve as a source identifier.

CASE SUMMARY

No Hogging Generic Terms

FACTS: Beginning in the late 1960s and thereafter, the word *hog* was used by motorcycle enthusiasts to refer to large motorcycles. Into the early 1980s, motorcyclists came to use the word *hog* when referring to Harley-Davidson (Harley) motorcycles. In 1981, Harley itself began using *hog* in connection with its merchandise. In 1983, it formed Harley Owners Group, used the acronym H.O.G., and registered the acronym in conjunction with various logos in 1987. Since 1909, Harley has used variations of its bar-and-shield logo. Ronald Grottanelli opened a motorcycle repair shop under the name The Hog Farm in 1969. At some point after 1981, he sold products such as Hog Wash engine degreaser and a Hog Trivia board game. Grottanelli had used variants of Harley's bar-and-shield logo since 1979 on signs and T-shirts, dropping the name Harley-Davidson from the bar of the logo in 1982 after receiving a letter of protest from the company. He continued to use the bar and shield, however, and featured a drawing of a pig wearing sunglasses and a banner with the words "Unauthorized Dealer." From a judgment for Harley for infringement of the bar-and-shield trademark and an injunction

prohibiting the use of the word *hog* in reference to some of his products and services, Grottanelli appealed.

DECISION: *Hog* was a generic word in the language as applied to large motorcycles before segments of the public began using it to refer to Harley-Davidson motorcycles. Neither a manufacturer nor the public can withdraw from the language a generic term, already applicable to a category of products, and accord it trademark significance as long as the term retains some generic meaning. It was an error to prohibit Grottanelli from using the word *hog*. Harley must rely on a portion of its trademark to identify the brand of motorcycles, for example, Harley Hogs. Grottanelli was properly enjoined from using the bar-and-shield logo. Grottanelli's mark uses Harley's mark in a somewhat humorous manner to promote his own products, which is not a permitted trademark parody use. The use of the prefix "UN" before "AUTHORIZED DEALER" is no defense. The courts have ordinarily found the use of such disclaimers insufficient to avoid liability for infringement. [*Harley-Davidson, Inc. v. Grottanelli*, 164 F.3d 806 (2d Cir. 1999)]

9-1d Proving Trademark Infringement

To bring a successful case in trademark infringement, a plaintiff must prove that it has a valid mark, that it was the first to use the mark, and that another's use of the mark is likely to cause confusion to consumers. Courts have developed a list of factors to determine whether or not there is a likelihood of confusion. Courts consider all of the factors, with no one factor being determinative:

1. the strength of the plaintiff's mark;
2. the similarity between the two marks;
3. the similarity of the products involved;
4. the likelihood that the plaintiff will enter the defendant's market;
5. the extent of actual consumer confusion;
6. the defendant's lack of good faith in adopting the mark;
7. the quality of the defendant's product; and
8. the sophistication of the buyers

[4] *Qualitex Co. v. Jacobson Products Co., Inc.,* 514 U.S. 159 (1995).

9-1e Remedies for Improper Use of Marks

Trademark holders frequently send "cease and desist" letters to those they believe are infringing on their mark. If the alleged infringer does not cooperate, the trademark holder may seek an injunction prohibiting a competitor from imitating or duplicating the mark. If the trademark holder prevails in an infringement suit, proving the validity of its mark and the likelihood of confusion, the court will enjoin the defendant from using the particular mark.

In some cases, courts have found that there is no likelihood of confusion when marks have similar names but are used to identify different products. **For Example,** a court held that Cadillac as applied to boats, is not confusingly similar to Cadillac as applied to automobiles; therefore, its use cannot be enjoined.[5] In addition to broad injunctive relief, the prevailing party may recover lost profits and other actual damages. In cases of willful violations, the court has full discretion to award the plaintiff up to treble damages. In "exceptional cases" the court has discretion to award attorney's fees.

9-1f Abandonment of Exclusive Right to Mark

An owner who has an exclusive right to use a mark may lose that right. If other persons are permitted to use that mark, it loses its exclusive character and is said to pass into the English language and become generic. Examples of formerly enforceable marks that have made this transition into the general language are *aspirin, thermos, cellophane,* and *shredded wheat.* Nonuse for three consecutive years is prima facie evidence of abandonment.[6]

9-1g Trade Dress Protection

Firms invest significant resources to develop and promote the appearance of their products and the packages in which these products are sold so that they are clearly recognizable by consumers.

trade dress–product's total image including its overall packaging look.

Trade dress involves a product's total image and, in the case of consumer goods, includes the overall packaging look in which each product is sold.

When a competitor adopts a confusingly similar trade dress, it dilutes the first user's investment and goodwill and deceives consumers, hindering their ability to distinguish between competing brands. In 1992, the United States Supreme Court recognized that the look and feel of a place of business, such as a restaurant, may be sufficiently distinctive to receive trade dress protection.[7] Subsequently, courts have become more receptive to claims of trade dress infringement under Section 43(a) of the Lanham Act. To prevail in a case of trade dress infringement, a plaintiff must prove that its trade dress is distinctive and nonfunctional and the defendant's trade dress is confusingly similar to the plaintiff's.[8] **For Example,** a court found that Jose Cuervo International infringed upon Maker's Mark Distillery's red dripping-wax-seal trade dress element used on its bourbon bottles when it used a similar element on its tequila bottles. The court held that the wax seal was not functional because there was more than one way to seal a bottle. In cases involving trade

---

[5] *General Motors Corp. v. Cadillac Marine and Boat Co.,* 226 F. Supp. 716 (W.D. Mich. 1964). See also *Amstar Corp. v. Domino's Pizza Inc.,* 615 F.2d 252 (5th Cir. 1980), where the court held that the mark Domino as applied to pizza was not confusingly similar to Domino as applied to sugar.

[6] *Doeblers' Pennsylvania Hybrids, Inc. v. Doebler,* 442 F.3d 812 (3rd Cir. 2006).

[7] *Two Pesos, Inc. v. Taco Cabana, Inc.,* 505 U.S. 763 (1992).

[8] *Clicks Billiards v. Sixshooters, Inc.,* 251 F.3d 1252 (9th Cir. 2001); *Woodsland Furniture, LLC v. Larsen,* 124 P.3d 1016 (Idaho 2005).

dress infringement, courts use the same factors employed in trademark cases to determine likelihood of confusion.[9]

9-1h Limited Lanham Act Protection of Product Design

Trade dress originally included only the packaging and "dressing" of a product, but in recent years, federal courts of appeals' decisions have expanded trade dress to encompass the design of a product itself. Product design may include the shape, configuration, or pattern of a product such as a sofa, a handbag, or a teapot. Some manufacturers have been successful in asserting Section 43(a) Lanham Act protection against "knockoffs"— that is, copies of their designs. The Supreme Court has held that a product's design is not inherently distinctive and can meet the "distinctiveness" element required by Section 43(a) only by a showing of secondary meaning. That is, the manufacturer must show that the design has come to be known by the public as identifying the product in question and its origin.[10] A product's design, like trade dress, cannot be protected under the Lanham Act if it is functional. Functional features should be protected under patent law.

It is clear from the Supreme Court's *Wal-Mart Stores, Inc. v. Samara Bros, Inc.* decision that, ordinarily, only famous designers whose works are widely recognized by the public by their design alone, such as certain Tommy Hilfiger and Ralph Lauren garments, Dooney & Bourke handbags, and Movado watches, will be able to successfully pursue Section 43(a) trade dress protection for their designs against knockoff versions of their work. Of course if a manufacturer's design is copied along with the manufacturer's labels or logo, the makers and sellers of these counterfeit goods are always in clear violation of the Lanham Act.[11] As discussed later, design patents may protect new and nonobvious ornamental features of a product.

9-1i Prevention of Dilution of Famous Marks

The Federal Trademark Dilution Act of 1995 (FTDA)[12] provides a cause of action against the "commercial use" of another's famous mark or trade name when it results in a "dilution of the distinctive quality of the mark." The act prevents junior users from free-riding on the success of a famous mark. To prevail in an FTDA case, the plaintiff must prove: (1) that its mark is famous; (2) that another's use of the mark impacts the distinctiveness of its mark through blurring or tarnishment. Blurring is defined as the "whittling away" of the senior mark's value over time. Tarnishment involves a use that could harm the reputation of the senior mark owner. The FTDA was amended in 2006 by the Trademark Dilution Revision Act (TDRA). The TDRA makes it clear that a famous mark owner does not need to prove likelihood of confusion to prevent a junior from using its mark. The senior mark owner does not have to prove economic injury—it need only establish blurring or tarnishment. The senior mark owner is entitled to an injunction against another's use of its mark if it prevails. The act protects against discordant uses, such as Du Pont shoes, Buick aspirin, and Kodak pianos. The holder of a famous mark does not have to prove likelihood of confusion in a dilution case. The act does, however, allow truthful comparative advertising and a "fair use" defense for parodying a famous mark.[13] **For Example,** a court held that the manufacturer of a plush doggie chew toy

---

[9] *Maker's Mark Distillery, Inc. v. Jose Cuervo International*, 679 F.3d 410 (6th Cir. 2012).

[10] *Wal-Mart Stores, Inc. v. Samara Bros, Inc.*, 529 U.S. 205 (2000).

[11] See *Gucci America Inc. v. Tyrell-Miller*, 678 F. Supp. 2d 117 (S.D.N.Y. 2008), where the court assessed Ms. Miller damages of $200,000 for each of the 15 trademark violations incurred for selling counterfeit Gucci handbags on her Web site.

[12] 15 U.S.C. §1125(c)(1).

[13] Trademark Dilution Revision Act (2005).

shaped like a Louis Vuitton handbag and imitating the LV logo was not trademark dilution. The court found that the parody of the famous mark qualified as a fair use to the dilution claim.[14]

Trademark holders vigorously protect their trademarks. Holders of famous marks are sometimes accused of being "trademark bullies" when they assert their rights against small businesses. A determined small business owner, however, may use social media to gain public support for its cause. **For Example,** when Bo Muller-Moore, a Vermont silk screen artist, sought to register "Eat More Kale," Chick-Fil-A, owner of the mark "Eat Mor Chickin," opposed the registration claiming it would confuse consumers and dilute the distinctiveness of its famous mark. Muller-Moore engaged in a fierce public relations battle, using Facebook and Change.org to make his case for registering "Eat More Kale." The USPTO granted the "Eat More Kale" trademark to Muller-Moore in December 2014.

9-1j Internet Domain Names and Trademark Rights

Businesses frequently use a registered trademark in an Internet domain name, such as "Amazon.com," "Priceline.com," and the publisher of this book, "Cengage.com."

The Internet Corporation for Assigned Names and Numbers (ICANN) is a nonprofit corporation responsible for coordinating the use of domain names across the Internet. ICANN clears and delegates new generic top level domains (gTLDs). The list of gTLDs is expanding rapidly. The ubiquitous ".com" or ".org" has expanded to include ".hotel," ".apple," and many others. Trademark owners need to check the list of new gTLDs frequently for potentially infringing marks. ICANN grants a sunrise period of one or two months priority registration to trademark owners who have filed with ICANN and who are eligible to use the gTLD. **For Example,** ".bank" became available in 2015. A 30-day sunrise period grants priority to banking institutions that have registered their trademarks with ICANN. Registration of ".bank" is limited to verified members of the banking community.

Cybersquatters

cybersquatters–term for those who register and set up domain names on the Internet for resale to the famous users of the names in question.

Cybersquatters are individuals who register and set up domain names on the Internet that are identical, or confusingly similar, to existing trademarks that belong to others or are the personal names of famous persons. The cybersquatter hopes to sell or "ransom" the domain name to the trademark owner or the famous individual. New gTLDs provide new opportunities for cybersquatters.

Because the extent of the legal remedies available to famous companies or famous individuals who have been victims of cybersquatters has not always been certain, Congress passed the Federal Anticybersquatting Consumer Protection Act (ACPA)[15] in 1999 to prohibit the practice of cybersquatting and cyberpiracy and to provide clear and certain remedies. The ACPA prohibits registering, trafficking in, or using a domain name confusingly similar to, or dilutive of, a trademark. To be successful in an ACPA lawsuit, the plaintiff must prove that the name is famous and that the domain name was registered in bad faith.[16] Remedies include (1) injunctive relief preventing the use of the name, (2) forfeiture of the domain name, and (3) attorney fees and costs. In addition, trademark

---

[14] *Louis Vuitton Malletier S.A. v. Haute Diggity Dog, LLC,* 507 F.3d 252 (4th Cir. 2007).

[15] Pub. L. 106, 113 Stat. 1536, 15 U.S.C. §1051.

[16] A plaintiff must meet the burden of proof, however, that its mark is "famous," in order to come within the protection of the ACPA, with the courts requiring the marks be highly distinctive and thus well known throughout the country. Among the marks courts have ruled not to be distinctive are "Blue Man Group," the performing group; "Clue," the board game; and "Trek," for bicycles. In contrast, marks that have been ruled famous include "Nike," "Pepsi," and "Victoria's Secret." See *Philbrick v. eNom Inc.,* 593 F. Supp. 2d 352, 367 (D. N.H. 2009).

owners may obtain damages and the profits that cybersquatters made from the use of the name.

A safe harbor exists under the ACPA for defendants who "believed and had reasonable grounds to believe that the use of the domain name was fair use or otherwise lawful."[17] But a defendant who acts even partially in bad faith in registering a domain name is not entitled to the shelter of the safe harbor provision. **For Example,** Howard Goldberg, the president of Artco, is an operator of Web sites that sell women's lingerie and other merchandise. He registered a domain name **http://www.victoriassecrets.net** to divert consumers to his Web sites to try to sell them his goods. The court rejected his ACPA safe harbor defense that he intended in good faith to have customers compare his company's products with those of Victoria's Secret. The fact that Victoria's Secret is a distinctive or famous mark deserving of the highest degree of trademark protection, coupled with the fact that the defendant added a mere *s* to that mark and gave false contact information when he requested the domain name, indicates that he and his company acted in bad faith and intended to profit from the famous mark.[18]

Dispute Avoidance

To avoid the expense of trademark litigation, it is prudent to determine whether the Internet domain name selected for your new business is an existing registered trademark or an existing domain name owned by another. Commercial firms provide comprehensive trademark searches for less than $500. Determining whether a domain name is owned by another may be done online at **http://www.internic.net/whois.html.**

The Internet Corporation for Assigned Names and Numbers (ICANN) provides fast-track arbitration procedures to protect trademark owners from conflicting online domain names under the auspices of the World Intellectual Property Organization (WIPO). **For Example,** Victoria's Secret stores arbitrated the "victoriassecrets.net" domain name held by Howard Goldberg's company, and the arbitration panel transferred the ownership of the name to Victoria's Secret stores. Victoria's Secret stores subsequently brought an action against Goldberg and Artco for damages and injunctive relief under trademark law and the ACPA.

9-2 Copyrights

The United States Constitution provides that Congress has the power to "promote the progress of science and the useful arts, by securing for limited times to authors and inventors the exclusive rights to their respective writings and discoveries."[19] The Copyright Act is a federal statute that gives an author, an artist, or a creator **copyright** protection, which consists of exclusive rights to use, reproduce, and display the work. The copyright owner also has the exclusive right to make derivative works. Under the international treaty called the *Berne Convention*, members agree to protect the copyright of the works of all member nations to the same extent as copyrighted works of their own nationals.

A copyright protects the manner in which an idea is expressed but not the idea itself.[20] The Copyright Act does not apply extraterritorially. However, if the infringement is completed in the United States and the copied work is then disseminated overseas, there is liability under the act for the resulting extraterritorial damages. **For Example,** the Los Angeles News Service (LANS), an independent news organization, produced

copyright–exclusive right given by federal statute to the creator of a literary or an artistic work to use, reproduce, and display the work.

[17] U.S.C. §1125(d)(1)(B)(ii).
[18] *Victoria's Secret Stores v. Artco,* 194 F. Supp. 2d 204 (S.D. Ohio 2002).
[19] U.S. CONST. art. I, § 8.
[20] *Attia v. New York Hospital,* 201 F.3d 50 (2d Cir. 2000).

two copyrighted videotapes of the beating of Reginald Denny during the Los Angeles riots of April 1992, and LANS licensed them to NBC for use on the *Today Show* in New York. Visnews taped the works and transmitted them by satellite to Reuters in London, which provided copies to its overseas subscribers. The infringement by Visnews occurred in New York, and Visnews was liable for the extraterritorial damages that resulted from the overseas dissemination of the work.[21]

It is a violation of U.S. copyright law for satellite carriers to capture signals of network stations in the United States and transmit them abroad. **For Example,** a court held that PrimeTime's satellite retransmission of copyrighted NFL football games to satellite dish owners in Canada was a violation of U.S. copyright law, notwithstanding testimony of PrimeTime's CEO that a law firm in Washington, D.C., told him that U.S. law did not pertain to the distribution of products in Canada. The NFL was awarded $2,557,500 in statutory damages.[22]

9-2a **Duration of Copyright**

The U.S. Constitution empowers Congress to give authors the exclusive right to their writings for "limited times."

The first U.S. copyright statute, enacted in 1790, provided protection for any "book, map or chart" for 14 years, with a privilege to renew for an additional 14 years. In 1831, the initial 14-year term was extended to 28 years, with a privilege for an additional 14 years. Under the 1909 Copyright Act, the protection period was for 28 years, with a right of renewal for an additional 28 years.

The Copyright Act of 1976 set the duration of a copyright at the life of the creator of the work plus 50 years. Under the Sonny Bono Copyright Term Extension Act of 1998, the duration has been extended to the life of the creator plus 70 years.[23] If a work is a "work made for hire"—that is, a business pays an individual to create the work—the business employing the creator registers the copyright. Under the 1998 Extension Act, such a copyright has been extended by 20 years and now runs for 120 years from creation or 95 years from publication of the work, whichever period is shorter. After a copyright has expired, the work is in the public domain and may be used by anyone without cost.[24]

9-2b **Copyright Notice**

Prior to March 1, 1989, the author of an original work secured a copyright by placing a copyright notice on the work, consisting of the word *copyright* or the symbol "©," the year of first publication, and the name or pseudonym of the author. The author was also required to register the copyright with the Copyright Office. Under the Berne Convention Implementation Act of 1988,[25] a law that adjusts U.S. copyright law to conform to the Berne Convention, it is no longer mandatory that works published after March 1, 1989, contain a notice of copyright. However, placing a notice of copyright on published works is strongly recommended. This notice prevents an infringer from claiming innocent infringement of the work, which would reduce the amount of damages owed. To bring a copyright infringement suit for a work of U.S. origin, the owner must have submitted two copies of the work to the Copyright Office in Washington, D.C., for registration.

[21] *Los Angeles News Service v. Reuters*, 149 F.3d 987 (9th Cir. 1998).
[22] *National Football League v. PrimeTime 24 Joint Venture*, 131 F. Supp. 2d 458 (S.D.N.Y. 2001).
[23] P.L. 105-298, 112 Stat. 2827, 17 U.S.C. §302(b).
[24] Without the Sonny Bono Extension Act of 1998, the copyright on Mickey Mouse, created by Walt Disney Co. in 1928, was set to expire in 2003 and enter the public domain. Pluto, Goofy, and Donald Duck would have followed soon after.
[25] P.L. 100-568, 102 Stat. 2854, 17 U.S.C. §101 *et seq.*

9-2c What Is Copyrightable?

Copyrights protect literary, musical, dramatic, and artistic work. Protected are books and periodicals; musical and dramatic compositions; choreographic works; maps; works of art, such as paintings, sculptures, and photographs; motion pictures and other audiovisual works; sound recordings; architectural works; and computer programs.

The work must be original, independently created by the author, and possess at least some minimal degree of creativity.[26] **For Example,** William Darden, a Web page designer, challenged the Copyright Office's denial of a copyright registration for a series of existing maps with some changes in the nature of shading, coloring, or font. A court found that the Copyright Office acted within its discretion when it denied Darden's registration because the examiner from the Visual Arts Section concluded that the maps were "representations of the preexisting census maps in which the creative spark is utterly lacking or so trivial as to be virtually nonexistent."[27]

9-2d Copyright Ownership and the Internet

Businesses today commonly use offsite programming services to create copyrightable software, with the delivery of code over the Internet. As set forth previously, when a business pays an employee to create a copyrightable work, it is a "work for hire" and the business employing the creator owns and may register the copyright. On the other hand, if a freelancer is employed offsite to create software for a fixed fee without a contract setting forth the ownership of the work, the freelancer owns the work product and the company utilizing the freelancer has a license to use the work product but does not have ownership of it. To avoid disputes about ownership of custom software, a written contract that addresses these ownership and license questions is necessary.

9-2e Rights of Copyright Holders

A copyright holder has the exclusive right to (1) reproduce the work; (2) prepare derivative works, such as a script from the original work; (3) distribute copies of recordings of the work; (4) publicly perform the work, in the case of plays and motion pictures; and (5) publicly display the work, in the case of paintings, sculptures, and photographs.

The copyright owner may assign or license some of the rights listed and will receive royalty payments as part of the agreement. The copyright law also ensures royalty payments, which are collected by two performing rights societies, the American Society of Composers, Authors, and Publishers (ASCAP) and Broadcast Music, Inc. (BMI), which act on behalf of the copyright holders.

Copyright infringement may be intentional or unintentional and artists may deal with alleged infringement in different ways. **For Example,** Sam Smith and his co-writers agreed to share songwriting royalties for the hit *Stay With Me* (released in 2014) with Tom Petty and Jeff Lynne, who wrote *I Won't Back Down* (released in 1989). Smith agreed that there was a coincidental likeness between the songs, although he had not been familiar with the song by Petty and Lynne. In a similar case, however, the Estate of Marvin Gaye brought a copyright infringement suit against Robin Thicke and Pharrell Williams, claiming that their 2013 hit *Blurred Lines* infringed on Gaye's 1977 success *Got to Give It Up*. A jury returned a verdict for Marvin Gaye's family in the amount of $7.4 million.[28] In addition to rights

---

[26] *Feist Publications Inc. v. Rural Telephone Services Co.,* 499 U.S. 340 (1991).
[27] *Darden v. Peters,* 402 F. Supp. 2d 638 (E.D.N.C. 2005).
[28] Associated Press, *Pharrell Williams and Robin Thicke to Pay $7.4m to Marvin Gaye's Family Over Blurred Lines,* the guardian (Mar. 11, 2015), **http://www.theguardian.com/music/2015/mar/10/blurred-lines-pharrell-robin-thicke-copied-marvin-gaye.**

under the copyright law and international treaties, federal and state laws prohibit record and tape piracy.

9-2f Limitation on Exclusive Character of Copyright

A limitation on the exclusive rights of copyright owners exists under the principle of *fair use*, which allows limited use of copyrighted material in connection with criticism, news reporting, teaching, and research. The statute lists four nonexclusive factors for courts to use in assessing whether an alleged infringer is entitled to a fair use defense:

1. The purpose and character of the use, including whether such use is of a commercial nature or is for nonprofit educational purposes[29]
2. The nature of the copyrighted work
3. The amount and substantiality of the portion used in relation to the copyrighted work as a whole
4. The effect of the use on the potential market for or value of the copyrighted work[30]

First Amendment privileges of freedom of speech and the press are preserved through the doctrine of *fair use*, which allows for use of portions of another's copyrighted work for matters such as comment and criticism. Parodies and caricatures are the most penetrating forms of criticism and are protected under the fair use doctrine. Moreover, while injunctive relief is appropriate in the vast majority of copyright infringement cases because the infringements are simply piracy, in the case of parodies and caricatures where there are reasonable contentions of fair use, preliminary injunctions to prevent publication are inappropriate. The copyright owner can be adequately protected by an award of damages should infringement be found. **For Example,** Suntrust Bank, the trustee of a trust that holds the copyright to Margaret Mitchell's *Gone with the Wind*, one of the all-time best-selling books in the world, obtained a preliminary injunction preventing Houghton Mifflin Co. from publishing Alice Randall's *The Wind Done Gone*. The Randall book is an irreverent parody that turns old ideas upside down. The Court of Appeals set aside the injunction of the federal district court because Houghton Mifflin had a viable fair use defense.[31]

CASE SUMMARY

Fair Use or Not Fair Use—That Is the Question

FACTS: In 2000, Patrick Cariou, a professional photographer, published a book entitled *Yes Rasta*, containing classical photographs and portraits he took while living in Jamaica for six years. Richard Prince is a successful appropriation artist whose work has been exhibited in several prominent museums. In 2007 and 2008, Prince exhibited paintings and

---

[29] In *Princeton University Press v. Michigan Document Services, Inc.,* 99 F.3d 1381 (6th Cir. 1996), a commercial copyshop reproduced "coursepacks" and sold them to students attending the University of Michigan. The court refused to consider the "use" as one for nonprofit educational purposes because the use challenged was that of the copyshop, a for-profit corporation that had decided to duplicate copyrighted material for sale to maximize its profits and give itself a competitive edge over other copyshops by declining to pay the royalties requested by the holders of the copyrights.

[30] 17 U.S.C. §107. See fair use analysis in *Perfect 10 v. Amazon.com, Inc.,* 487 F.3d 701, 719–725 (9th Cir. 2007).

[31] *Suntrust Bank v. Houghton Mifflin Co.,* 268 F.3d 1257 (11th Cir. 2001). See also *Brownmark Films, LLC. v. Comedy Partners,* 800 F. Supp. 2d 991 (E.D. Wis. 2011), where the federal district court dismissed a copyright infringement lawsuit against the South Park defendants on the basis of fair use defense in an episode lampooning viral video crazes.

collages called *Canal Zone* at the Eden Rock Hotel in Saint Barth's and at the Gagosian Gallery in New York. The paintings and collages incorporate some of Cariou's copyrighted images from *Yes Rasta*. Prince used the photographs but altered them in various ways such as by painting "lozenges" over the faces or adding a guitar. In some paintings, Prince added works of other artists to Cariou's photographs. Cariou sued Prince and Gagosian, alleging copyright infringement. Prince and Gagosian raised the defense of fair use. The lower court held that Prince was not entitled to a fair use defense because "Prince did not intend to comment on Cariou, on Cariou's Photos, or on aspects of popular culture closely associated with Cariou or the Photos when he appropriated the Photos." The court ordered all of the infringing works to be delivered to Cariou for "impounding, destruction, or other disposition."

DECISION: Judgment for Prince. The court emphasized the transformative nature of Prince's work. Twenty-five of the thirty works appropriated by Prince manifest an aesthetic entirely different from Cariou's photographs. The serene classical photographs taken by Cariou printed in black-and-white were fundamentally different from the jarring, crude,

provocative and colorful works produced by Prince. Prince's work is transformative because it added something new to Cariou's photographs, resulting in a fundamentally different aesthetic. The transformative nature of the work impacted the four factor analysis. The first fair use factor, the purpose and character of the use, does not suggest that commercial uses are presumptively unfair. Even though Prince's use was commercial, the transformative nature of the work reduces the significance of this factor. The second statutory factor, the nature of the copyrighted work, weighs in Cariou's favor because the work is creative and published. But again the transformative nature of the work limits the usefulness of this factor. The third factor, the amount and substantiality of the portion used, weighs heavily in Prince's favor because the photographs were transformed into something new and different. The fourth factor, the effect of the secondary use on the potential market for the value of the copyrighted work, weighs in Prince's favor because Prince's work does not usurp the market for the original work. Prince's target audience and the nature of his work is distinct from that of the original. Twenty-five of the allegedly infringing works satisfied the fair use factors. Five of the works were remanded to the district court for further consideration. [*Cariou v. Prince*, **714 F.3d 694 (2d Cir. 2013)**]

9-2g Secondary Liability for Infringement

Contributory infringement and vicarious infringement are secondary forms of infringement. Contributory infringement occurs when a defendant knew of the infringing activity and participated by inducing or furthering the direct infringement. Vicarious infringement occurs when a defendant had the ability to supervise the acts of the infringer and had a direct financial interest in the exploitation of the copyrighted materials. An entity that distributes a device with the object of promoting its use to infringe copyrights as shown by clear expression or other active steps taken to foster the resulting acts of infringement is liable for these acts of infringement by third parties, regardless of the device's lawful uses. **For Example,** Grokster, Ltd., and StreamCast Networks, Inc., distributed free software products that allow all computer users to share electronic files through peer-to-peer networks, so called because users' computers communicate directly with each other, not through central servers. When these firms distributed their free software, each clearly voiced the objective that the recipients use the software to download copyrighted works. These firms derived profits from selling advertising space and streaming ads to the software users. Liability for infringement was established under the secondary liability doctrines of contributory or vicarious infringement.[32]

While copyright holders have historically chosen to litigate against the provider of new technologies rather than the users of the technology, the law is clear that copyright holders may sue individual infringers. **For Example,** Sony and other recording companies successfully sued Goucher College student Joel Tenenbaum for willfully downloading

[32] *Metro-Goldwyn-Mayer Studios, Inc. v. Grokster, Ltd.,* 545 U.S. 913 (2005).

and distributing 30 copyrighted works, and the court assessed statutory damages at $675,000.[33]

9-2h Digital Millennium Copyright Act

The Digital Millennium Copyright Act of 1998 (DMCA)[34] was enacted to curb the pirating of software and other copyrighted works, such as books, films, videos, and recordings, by creating civil and criminal penalties for anyone who circumvents encryption software. The law also prohibits the manufacture, import, sale, or distribution of circumvention devices.

Title II of the DMCA provides a "safe harbor" for Internet Service Providers (ISPs) from liability for direct, vicarious, and contributory infringement of copyrights provided the ISP (1) does not have actual knowledge of the infringing activity or expeditiously removed access to the problematic material upon obtaining knowledge of infringing activity, (2) does not receive financial benefit directly attributable to the infringing activity, and (3) responded expeditiously upon notification of the claimed infringement.

9-3 Patents

Under Article 1, Section 8, of the U.S. Constitution, the founding fathers of our country empowered Congress to promote the progress of science by securing for limited times to inventors the exclusive rights to their discoveries. Federal patent laws established under Article 1, Section 8, protect inventors just as authors are protected under copyright law authorized by the same section of the U.S. Constitution.

Thomas Jefferson was the first administrator of the United States' patent system and was the author of the Patent Act of 1793. During his time of administrating the system Jefferson saw clearly the difficulty of deciding what should be patentable. Years after drafting the 1793 act, he explained that in that act "the whole was turned over to the judiciary, to be matured into a system, under which everyone might know when his actions were safe and lawful."[35] In practice, Congress has left wide latitude for judicial construction of patent law, entrusting the courts to keep pace with advancing industrial and technological developments.

9-3a Types, Duration, and Notice

There are three types of patents, the rights to which may be obtained by proper filing with the United States Patent and Trademark Office (USPTO) in Washington, D.C. The types and duration of patents are as follows.

Utility Patents

Inventions classified as *utility* or *functional patents* grant inventors of any new and useful process, machine, manufacture, or composition of matter or any new and useful improvement of such devices the right to obtain a patent.[36] Prior to 1995, utility patents had a life of 17 years from the date of grant. Under the Uruguay Round Trade Agreement Act, effective June 8, 1995, the duration of U.S. utility patents was changed from 17 years from the date of grant to 20 years from the date of filing to be consistent with the patent law of World Trade Organization (WTO) member states.

---

[33] *Sony v. Tenenbaum*, 660 F.3d 487 (1st Cir. 2011).
[34] 17 U.S.C. §1201.
[35] See *Graham v. John Deere Co. of Kansas City*, 383 U.S. 1, 10 (1966).
[36] 35 U.S.C. §101.

Design Patents

A second kind of patent exists under U.S. patent law that protects new and nonobvious ornamental features that appear in connection with an article of manufacture.[37] These patents are called *design patents* and have a duration of 14 years. In order to establish design patent infringement, the patent holder has the difficult task of proving, by a preponderance of the evidence, that an ordinary observer (and not the eye of an expert) taking into account the prior art would believe the accused design to be the same as the patented design.[38] Design patents can be effective in combating counterfeiters. Toy manufacturers, for example, may hold design patents on game pieces, timers, and the playing board. Design patents are relatively simple in form and are issued more frequently than utility patents. The smartphone patent wars between Apple and Samsung included several design patents, including the shape of the iPhone.

Plant Patents

A third type of patent, called a *plant patent*, protects the inventors of asexually reproduced new varieties of plants. The duration is 20 years from the date of filing, the same duration applied to utility patents.

Notice

The owner of a patent is required to mark the patented item or device using the word *patent* and must list the patent number on the device to recover damages from an infringer of the patent.

The America Invents Act

Federal patent law was amended in 2011 by the America Invents Act (AIA).[39] Section 3 of the act defines the effective filing date of a claimed invention as the actual filing date of the patent or application for a patent, replacing the current "first to invent" system with a "first to file system." The purpose of this change is to provide the inventor with greater certainty regarding the scope of protection and to promote international uniformity by harmonizing the U.S. patent system with systems used in Europe and other countries with which the United States conducts trade. The AIA provides the option of an expedited patent examination process, with the goal of processing applications within 12 months, as opposed to the ordinary processing period of three to four years. The USPTO fee for this service is an extra $4,800, with a 50 percent reduction for "small entity" inventors. Under the act, the USPTO will also speed up the application process, at no additional cost, for inventions that reduce greenhouse emissions or provide energy conservation.

Challenges to patent grants can be made for up to nine months after the patent is granted. The post-grant review is made by a patent examiner.

9-3b Patentability

Section 101 of the 1952 Patent Act recognizes four categories of subject matter for patent eligibility: (1) processes, (2) machines, (3) manufactures, and (4) compositions of matter. However, even if a claim may be deemed to fit one of these categories, it may not be patent eligible. Phenomena of nature, mental processes, and abstract intellectual

---

[37] 35 U.S.C. §173.
[38] *Gorham v. White*, 81 U.S. 511 (1871).
[39] Pub. L. 112-29, H.R. 1249 enacted September 16, 2011, and effective as of March 16, 2013. Amended 35 U.S.C. §102.

concepts are not patentable because they are the basic tools of scientific and technological work.[40] **For Example,** Prometheus Laboratories Inc. patented steps for testing the proper dosage level of drug treatments for individuals with gastrointestinal diseases. When the Mayo Clinic developed a similar test to determine toxicity-risk levels, Prometheus sued Mayo for patent infringement. The Supreme Court held that the Prometheus patents were not patent eligible because they were merely instructions to apply the laws of nature.[41]

Once it is established that an invention is patent eligible, a patent may be obtained if the invention is something that is *new and not obvious* to a person of ordinary skill and knowledge in the art or technology to which the invention is related. Whether an invention is new and not obvious in its field may lead to highly technical proceedings before a patent examiner, the USPTO's Board of Patent Appeals, and the U.S. Court of Appeals for the Federal Circuit (CAFC). **For Example,** Thomas Deuel's application for a patent on complementary DNA (cDNA) molecules encoding proteins that stimulated cell division was rejected by a patent examiner as "obvious" and the rejection was affirmed by the USPTO's Board of Patent Appeals. However, after a full hearing before the CAFC, which focused on the state of research in the field as applied to the patent application, Deuel's patent claims were determined to be "not invalid because of obviousness."[42]

The novelty requirement of patent eligibility addresses actions of both the patent applicant and others. Section 102 of the Patent Act provides that a patent must be denied "if the invention was patented or described in a printed publication in this or a foreign country or in public use or on sale in this country, more than one year prior to the date of application...." In other words, if an invention is in the public domain for more than a year, either through use or publication, it must remain there. An inventor may test its invention in the market before undertaking the expense of filing for a patent but must observe the one-year time limit.

Once approved by the Patent and Trademark Office, a patent is presumed valid.[43] However, a defendant in a patent infringement lawsuit may assert a patent's invalidity as a defense to an infringement claim by showing that the invention as a whole would have been obvious to a person of ordinary skill in the art when the invention was patented. This showing is called **prior art. For Example,** Ron Rogers invented and patented a tree-trimming device that is essentially a chain saw releasably mounted on the end of a telescoping pole. Rogers sued Desa International, Inc. (DIA), for patent infringement after DIA introduced the Remington Pole Saw, a chain saw releasably mounted on the end of a telescoping pole. DIA provided evidence of prior art, citing four preexisting patents dealing with "trimming tools on extension poles" that correlated with Rogers's patent. The court nullified Rogers's patent because it concluded that the DIA had met its heavy burden of proof that releasably mounting a lightweight chain saw on the end of a telescoping pole assembly to trim trees would be obvious to a person of ordinary skill in the art.[44]

Patent law has expanded to include human-made microorganisms as patent-eligible subject matter, since such compositions are not nature's handiwork, but the inventor's own work.

prior art–a showing that an invention as a whole would have been obvious to a person of ordinary skill in the art when the invention was patented.

[40] *Gottschalk v. Benson*, 409 U.S. 63, 67 (1972).

[41] *Mayo Collaborative Services v. Prometheus Laboratories, Inc.*, 132 S. Ct. 1289, 1301 (2012).

[42] In re *Deuel*, 51 F.3d 1552 (Fed. Cir. 1995).

[43] See *Microsoft Corp. v. i4i Limited Partnership*, 131 S. Ct. 2238 (2011), where the Supreme Court determined that defenses to patent infringement claims must be proven by clear and convincing evidence.

[44] See *KRS International Co. v. Teleflex, Inc.*, 500 U.S. 398 (2007) for the Supreme Court's "obviousness" patent decision, where the Court held that mounting an available sensor on a fixed pivot point of the prior art pedal was a design step well within the grasp of a person of ordinary skill in the relevant art and that the benefit of doing so would be obvious.

CASE SUMMARY

Crude Life Forms Can Be Patented

FACTS: Chakrabarty was a microbiologist. He found a way of creating a bacterium that would break down crude oil. This could not be done by any bacteria that exist naturally. His discovery had a great potential for cleaning up oil spills. When he applied for a patent for this process, the commissioner of patents refused to grant it because what he had done was not a "manufacture" or "composition of matter" within the meaning of the federal statute and because a patent could not be obtained on something that was living. Chakrabarty appealed.

DECISION: Judgment for Chakrabarty. Discovering a way to produce a living organism that is not found in nature is within the protection of the patent laws. The fact that this kind of invention was not known when the patent laws were first adopted has no effect on the decision. The patent laws are to be interpreted according to the facts existing when an application for a patent is made. [**Diamond v. Chakrabarty**, 447 U.S. 303 (1980)]

ETHICS & THE LAW

Patenting Genes?

In *Diamond v. Chakrabarty*, the Supreme Court held that a microbiologist could patent a bacterium that breaks down crude oil. This decision spurred researchers to patent new discoveries in nature. Myriad Genetics discovered the precise location and sequence of two human genes, known as the BRCA1 and BRCA2 genes. Mutations in these genes substantially increase the risks of breast and ovarian cancer. Myriad obtained several patents based on its discovery, which, if valid, would give it the exclusive right to isolate an individual's BRCA1 and BRCA2 genes. Isolation is necessary to conduct testing. When Myriad learned that other laboratories were providing genetic testing services to women using the isolated genes, it sent letters to them stating that the genetic testing infringed its patents.

Various groups including patients, advocacy groups, and doctors filed a lawsuit claiming that Myriad's patents were invalid because they attempted to patent something that occurs in nature. The Supreme Court held that a naturally occurring DNA segment is a product of nature and not patent eligible merely because it has been isolated.* The Court

distinguished the facts in the *Myriad* case from those in *Chakrabarty*. In *Chakrabarty*, the Court stated, the bacterium was new "with markedly different characteristics from any found in nature," due to the additional plasmids and resultant "capacity for degrading oil." In *Myriad*, by contrast, the Court stated "that Myriad did not create or alter any of the genetic information encoded in the BRCA1 and BRCA2 genes."

The Court recognized that patent protection strikes a delicate balance between creating "incentives that lead to creation, invention, and discovery" and "impeding the flow of information that might permit, indeed spur, invention." The Court noted that, "Groundbreaking, innovative, or even brilliant discovery does not by itself satisfy the section 101 [novelty] inquiry."

Consider how the Court's decision impacted the cost of testing for breast cancer and ovarian cancer. Biotech companies hold patents on many genes. Do you think that the Court's decision impacts the incentive to research?

*__Association of Molecular Pathology v. Myriad Genetics, Inc.__, 133 S. Ct. 2107 (2013).

9-3c Patentable Business Methods

A 1998 Court of Appeals for the Federal Circuit (CAFC) decision recognized "business methods" as a patent-eligible "process" under Section 101 of the Patent Act.[45] A burgeoning number of business-method patents followed, with the U.S. Supreme Court referencing in

---

[45] *State Street Bank v. Signature Financial Group*, 149 F.3d 1368 (Fed. Cir. 1998).

its *eBay v. MercExchange* decision the "potential vagueness and suspect validity of some of these patents."[46] A pure business-method patent consists of a series of steps related to performing a business process. **For Example,** Patent No. 6,846,131 sets forth a method of doing business with steps for Producing Revenue from Gypsum-Based Refuse Sites. So-called junk patents have also been issued as business-method patents. **For Example,** Patent No. 4,022,227, Method of Concealing Baldness, contains a series of steps for combing one's hair that amount to what is best known as a *comb-over.* Business methods are often in the form of software programs and encompass e-commerce applications.

Such ideas are patentable only if there is some additional "inventive concept."[47] In the wake of the Supreme Court's decision in *Alice v. CLS Bank,* obtaining and enforcing software and business-method patents will be more difficult. Lower courts are increasingly invalidating such patents. Patents that recite fundamental economic principles or methods of organizing human activity will most likely be patent ineligible, even if they are trying to claim that these principles or activities are innovative because they are implemented through a computer.[48]

CASE SUMMARY

Abstract Ideas Cannot Be Monopolized

FACTS: Alice Corporation held a patent that uses a computer as a third-party intermediary to minimize the risk associated with the exchange of financial obligations. The intermediary creates and updates "shadow" records to reflect the value of each party's actual accounts held at "exchange institutions," thereby permitting only those transactions for which the parties have sufficient resources. At the end of each day, the intermediary issues irrevocable instructions to the exchange institutions to carry out the permitted transactions.

CLS Bank International operates a global network that facilitates currency transactions. It sought a declaratory judgment that Alice's patent was invalid. Section 101 of the Patent Act provides: "Whoever invents or discovers any new and useful process, machine, manufacture, or composition of matter, or any new and useful improvement thereof, may obtain a patent therefor...."

DECISION: The Court employed a two-step inquiry: 1. Whether the patent involves an abstract idea that is not patent eligible; 2. Is there anything else in the claim that transforms the abstract idea into a patent-eligible claim. A patent must be more than an abstract claim; it must include an "inventive concept." The concept of using a third-party intermediary to mitigate settlement risk is an abstract idea that is patent-ineligible. In *Bilski v. Kappos,* 561 U.S. 593 (2010), the Court held that an algorithm for a method for hedging against the financial risk of price fluctuations was not patentable because it is an abstract idea. Like the risk hedging in *Bilski,* the concept of intermediated settlement is "a fundamental economic practice long prevalent in our system of commerce." Moving to the second step, the Court concluded that requiring a generic computer implementation does not transform the idea into a patent-eligible invention. [***Alice Corporation Pty. Ltd. v. CLS Bank International,*** **134 S. Ct. 2347 (2014)]**

9-3d **Infringement**

The patent owner has the exclusive right to make, use, or sell the invention. The owner may bring suit for patent infringement for unauthorized use of a patent and obtain

---

[46] 547 U.S. 388 (2006).
[47] *Mayo Collaborative Services v. Prometheus Laboratories, Inc.,* 132 S. Ct. 1289 (2012).
[48] After *Alice v. CLS Bank,* the USPTO issued subject matter eligibility guidelines, including eight fact patterns to demonstrate the abstract idea analysis. USPTO, **http://www.uspto.gov/patents/law/exam/abstract_idea_examples.pdf.**

appropriate monetary damages and injunctive relief.[49] The Patent Act provides for the enhancement of damages upon proof of willful infringement and the award of reasonable attorney's fees in "exceptional cases."[50]

Under the act, the owner has "the right to exclude others from making, using, offering for sale or selling the invention."[51] In *eBay, Inc. v. MercExchange, LLC*, the U.S. Supreme Court dealt with the question of whether the patent holder had the right to obtain the permanent injunctive relief of stopping a business entity from "using" the patented technology in addition to obtaining damages for the patent violation. The threat of a court order may be used to seek high and often unreasonable licensing fees. Major technology companies contended that trial courts should consider multiple factors in deciding whether to issue a permanent injunction.

CASE SUMMARY

"Squeeze Play" Averted

FACTS: eBay and its subsidiary half.com operate popular Internet Web sites that allow private sellers to list goods they wish to sell at either an auction or a fixed price (its "Buy It Now" feature). MercExchange, LLC, sought to license its business-method patent to eBay, but no agreement was reached. In MercExchange's subsequent patent infringement suit, a jury found that its patent was valid, eBay had infringed the patent, and $29.5 million in damages were appropriate. However, the District Court denied MercExchange's motion for permanent injunctions against patent infringement absent exceptional circumstances. MercExchange appealed. The Federal Circuit Court of Appeals reversed, and the U.S. Supreme Court granted *certiorari*.

DECISION: Judgment against MercExchange's position. The traditional four-factor test of equity applied by courts when considering whether to award permanent injunctive relief to a prevailing plaintiff applies to disputes arising under the Patent Act. That test requires a plaintiff to demonstrate that (1) it has suffered an irreparable injury, (2) remedies

available at law are inadequate to compensate for that injury, (3) considering the balance of hardships between the plaintiff and defendant, a remedy in equity is warranted, and (4) the public interest would not be disserved by a permanent injunction. The decision to grant or deny such relief is an act of equitable discretion by the district court, reviewable on appeal for abuse of discretion. The Federal Circuit's ruling was vacated and remanded to the district court to apply the four-factor test. [A concurring opinion written by Justice Kennedy and joined by Justices Stevens, Souter, and Breyer stated that "an industry has developed in which firms use patents not as a basis for producing and selling goods but, instead, primarily for obtaining licensing fees. For these firms, an injunction, and the potentially serious sanctions arising from its violation, can be employed as a bargaining tool to charge exorbitant fees to companies that seek to buy licenses to practice the patent." Such may be considered under the four-factor test.] [***eBay, Inc. v. MercExchange, LLC,* 547 U.S. 388 (2006)**]

Under the Supreme Court's "doctrine of equivalents," infringers may not avoid liability for patent infringement by substituting insubstantial differences for some of the elements of the patented product or process. The test for infringement requires an essential inquiry: Does the accused product or process contain elements identical or equivalent to each claimed element of the patented invention?[52]

---

[49] See *Global-Tech Appliances, Inc. v. SEB S.A.,* 131 S. Ct. 2060 (2011), where the Court found that induced infringement of a patent is also actionable. Global-Tech Appliances, Inc., located in Hong Kong, developed a cool-touch deep fryer for Sunbeam Products by copying the "T-Fal" fryer in violation of SEB's U.S. patent. The Supreme Court agreed that the evidence was sufficient for a jury to find that Global-Tech willfully blinded itself to the infringing nature of the sales it encouraged Sunbeam to make.

[50] See In re *Seagate Technology, LLC,* 497 F.3d 1360 (Fed. Cir. 2007), where the CAFC set a higher "willfulness" standard, requiring at least a showing of objective recklessness on the part of the infringer.

[51] 35 U.S.C. §154(a)(1).

[52] *Warner-Jenkinson v. Hilton Davis Chemical Co.,* 520 U.S. 17 (1997). But see *Festo Corp. v. Shoketsu,* 493 F.3d 1368 (Fed. Cir. 2007).

9-4 Secret Business Information

A business may have developed information that is not generally known but that cannot be protected under federal law, or a business may want to avoid the disclosure required to obtain a patent or copyright protection of computer software. As long as such information is kept secret, it will be protected under state law relating to trade secrets.[53]

9-4a Trade Secrets

trade secret–any formula, device, or compilation of information that is used in one's business and is of such a nature that it provides an advantage over competitors who do not have the information.

A **trade secret** may consist of any formula, device, or compilation of information that is used in one's business and is of such a nature that it provides an advantage over competitors who do not have the information. It may be a formula for a chemical compound, a process of manufacturing, treating, or preserving materials. **For Example,** shortly before he departed employment with Siemens, salesman J. J. David e-mailed the wiring schematics for the company's reverse osmosis water desalination units (R.O. units) to his future co-founder of Revo Water Systems, LLC, and also requested and was allowed to observe and assist in the construction of a unit. Two years later a Siemens technician discovered that a Revo unit was a copy of the Siemens R.O. units. Siemens successfully sued David and Revo for breach of the confidentiality agreement David had signed with Siemens. The measure of damages for misappropriation of a trade secret is the profit derived from the misappropriation of the trade secret, which in this case amounted to $908,160 over a 40-month period.[54]

To a limited extent, courts will protect certain confidential customer lists. However, courts will not protect customer lists if customer identities are readily ascertainable from industry or public sources or if products or services are sold to a wide group of purchasers based on their individual needs.[55]

CASE SUMMARY

Some Companies Don't "Care Enough" To Do the Right Thing

FACTS: Hallmark Cards, Inc., hired a consulting group, Monitor Company Group, to compile research on the greeting cards market. Monitor created several PowerPoint presentations containing its findings. Hallmark and Monitor signed confidentiality agreements preventing Monitor from sharing these findings with anyone else. Monitor was closely affiliated with Clipper, a private equity firm founded by two of Monitor's original partners and headquartered in Monitor's building. Shortly after Hallmark hired Monitor, Clipper became interested in acquiring Recycled Paper Greetings (RPG), a greeting card company that competed with Hallmark. Clipper asked Monitor for the research it had compiled for Hallmark. Clipper ultimately won the auction for

RPG. Hallmark settled its claims of trade secret misappropriation with Monitor but the case against Clipper went to trial. A jury found for Hallmark and awarded it $21.3 million in compensatory and $10 million in punitive damages. Clipper appealed arguing that the PowerPoint presentations were not "trade secrets" under the Missouri Uniform Trade Secrets Act (MUTSA).

DECISION: Judgment for Hallmark. The market research qualified as trade secrets because the information compiled had economic value that gave Hallmark a competitive advantage. Hallmark took reasonable steps under the circumstances to keep the information secret. Even though

[53] Trade secrets are protected in all states either under the Uniform Trade Secrets Act or common law and under both criminal and civil statutes. The Uniform Trade Secrets Act has been adopted in all states except New York and North Carolina.

[54] *Siemens Water Technologies Corp. v. Revo Water Systems*, 74 So. 3d 824 (La. App. 2011).

[55] *Xpert Automation Systems Corp. v. Vibromatic Co.*, 569 N.E.2d 351 (Ind. App. 1990).

Some Companies Don't "Care Enough" To Do the Right Thing continued

Hallmark published some of the information from the market research, that information provided only general conclusions, not the specifics of the information compiled for Hallmark. The market research was valuable to Clipper because there was little information available about the greeting card industry. Punitive damages were appropriate because Clipper engaged in a massive cover up of its acquisition of the material with reckless disregard for the rights of Hallmark. [***Hallmark Cards, Inc. v. Monitor Clipper Partners***, 758 F.3d 1051 (8th Cir. 2014)]

9-4b Loss of Protection

When secret business information is made public, it loses the protection it had while secret. This loss of protection occurs when the information is made known without any restrictions. In contrast, there is no loss of protection when secret information is shared or communicated for a special purpose and the person receiving the information knows that it is not to be made known to others.

When a product or process is unprotected by a patent or a copyright and is sold in significant numbers to the public, whose members are free to resell to whomever they choose, competitors are free to reverse engineer or copy the article. **For Example,** Crosby Yacht Co., a boatbuilder on Cape Cod, developed a hull design that is not patented. Maine Boatbuilders, Inc. (MBI), purchased one of Crosby's boats and copied the hull by creating a mold from the boat it purchased. MBI is free to build and sell boats utilizing the copied hull.

9-4c Defensive Measures

Employers seek to avoid the expense of trade secret litigation by limiting disclosure of trade secrets to employees with a "need to know." Employers also have employees sign nondisclosure agreements, and they conduct exit interviews when employees with confidential information leave, reminding the employees of the employer's intent to enforce the nondisclosure agreement. In addition, employers have adopted industrial security plans to protect their unique knowledge from "outsiders," who may engage in theft, trespass, wiretapping, or other forms of commercial espionage.

9-4d Criminal Sanctions

Under the federal Industrial Espionage Act of 1996,[56] knowingly stealing, soliciting, or obtaining trade secrets by copying, downloading, or uploading via electronic means or otherwise with the intention that it will benefit a foreign government or agent is a crime. This act also applies to the stealing or purchasing of trade secrets by U.S. companies or individuals who intend to convert trade secrets to the economic benefit of anyone other than the owner. The definition of trade secret is closely modeled on the Uniform Trade Secrets Act and includes all forms and types of financial, business, scientific, technical, economic, and engineering information. The law requires the owner to have taken "reasonable and proper" measures to keep the information secret. Offenders are subject to fines of up to $500,000 or twice the value of the proprietary information involved, whichever is greater, and imprisonment for up to 15 years.

[56] P.L. 104–294, 18 U.S.C. §1831 *et seq.* (1996).

Corporations may be fined up to $10,000,000 or twice the value of the secret involved, whichever is greater. In addition, the offender's property is subject to forfeiture to the U.S. government, and import-export sanctions may be imposed.

9-5 Protection of Computer Software and Mask Works

Computer programs, chip designs, and mask works are protected from infringement with varying degrees of success by federal statutes, restrictive licensing, and trade secrecy.

CPA ## 9-5a Copyright Protection of Computer Programs

Under the Computer Software Copyright Act of 1980,[57] a written program is given the same protection as any other copyrighted material regardless of whether the program is written in source code (ordinary language) or object code (machine language). **For Example,** Franklin Computer Corp. copied certain operating-system computer programs that had been copyrighted by Apple Computer, Inc. When Apple sued Franklin for copyright infringement, Franklin argued that the object code on which its programs had relied was an uncopyrightable "method of operation." The Third Circuit held that computer programs, whether in source code or in object code embedded on ROM chips, are protected under the act.[58]

In determining whether there is a copyright violation under the Computer Software Copyright Act, courts will examine the two programs in question to compare their structure, flow, sequence, and organization. Courts consider whether the most *significant* steps of the program are similar rather than whether most of the program's steps are similar. To illustrate a copyright violation, substantial similarity in the structure of two computer programs for dental laboratory record-keeping was found—even though the programs were dissimilar in a number of respects—because five particularly important subroutines within both programs performed almost identically.[59]

The protection afforded software by the copyright law is not entirely satisfactory to software developers because of the distinction made by the copyright law of protecting expressions but not ideas. Also, Section 102(b) of the 1980 Computer Software Copyright Act does not provide protection for "methods of operation." A court has allowed a competitor to copy the identical menu tree of a copyrighted spreadsheet program because it was a noncopyrightable method of operation.[60]

As set forth previously, the Digital Millennium Copyright Act of 1998 was enacted to curb the pirating of a wide range of works, including software.

CPA ## 9-5b Patent Protection of Programs

Patents have been granted for computer programs; for example, a method of using a computer to translate from one language to another has been held patentable.

The disadvantage of patenting a program is that the program is placed in the public records and may thus be examined by anyone. This practice poses a potential danger that

---

[57] Act of December 12, 1980, P.L. 96–517, 94 Stat. 3015, 17 U.S.C. §§101, 117.
[58] *Apple Computer Inc. v. Franklin Computer Corp.,* 714 F.2d 1240 (3d Cir. 1983).
[59] *Whelen Associates v. Jaslow Dental Laboratory,* 797 F.2d 1222 (3d Cir. 1986).
[60] *Lotus Development Corp. v. Borland International Inc.,* 49 F.3d 807 (1st Cir. 1995), aff'd, 516 U.S. 233 (1996).

the program will be copied. To detect patent violators and bring legal action is difficult and costly.[61]

9-5c Trade Secrets

While primary protection for computer software is found in the Computer Software Copyright Act, industry also uses trade secret law to protect computer programs. When software containing trade secrets is unlawfully appropriated by a former employee, the employee is guilty of trade secret theft.

9-5d Restrictive Licensing

To retain greater control over proprietary software, it is common for the creator of the software to license its use to others rather than selling it to them. Such licensing

FIGURE 9-1   Summary Comparison of Intellectual Property Rights

TYPE OF INTELLECTUAL PROPERTY	TRADEMARKS	COPYRIGHTS	PATENTS	TRADE SECRETS
PROTECTION	WORDS, NAMES, SYMBOLS, OR DEVICES USED TO IDENTIFY A PRODUCT OR SERVICE	ORIGINAL CREATIVE WORKS OF AUTHORSHIP, SUCH AS WRITINGS, MOVIES, RECORDS, AND COMPUTER SOFTWARE	UTILITY, DESIGN, AND PLANT PATENTS	ADVANTAGEOUS FORMULAS, DEVICES, OR COMPILATION OF INFORMATION
APPLICABLE STANDARD	IDENTIFIES AND DISTINGUISHES A PRODUCT OR SERVICE	ORIGINAL CREATIVE WORKS IN WRITING OR IN ANOTHER FORMAT	NEW AND NONOBVIOUS, ADVANCED IN THE ART	NOT READILY ASCERTAINABLE, NOT DISCLOSED TO THE PUBLIC
WHERE TO APPLY	PATENT AND TRADEMARK OFFICE	REGISTER OF COPYRIGHTS	PATENT AND TRADEMARK OFFICE	NO PUBLIC REGISTRATION NECESSARY
DURATION	INDEFINITE SO LONG AS IT CONTINUES TO BE USED	LIFE OF AUTHOR PLUS 70 YEARS, OR 95 YEARS FROM PUBLICATION FOR "WORKS FOR HIRE"	UTILITY AND PLANT PATENTS, 20 YEARS FROM DATE OF APPLICATION; DESIGN PATENTS, 14 YEARS	INDEFINITE SO LONG AS SECRET IS NOT DISCLOSED TO PUBLIC

---

[61] The USPTO has adopted guidelines for the examination of computer-related inventions, 61 C.F.R. §§7478–7502.

agreements typically include restrictions on the use of the software by the licensee and give the licensor greater protection than that provided by copyright law. These restrictions commonly prohibit the licensee from providing, in any manner whatsoever, the software to third persons or subjecting the software to reverse engineering.[62]

9-5e Semiconductor Chip Protection

The Semiconductor Chip Protection Act (SCPA) of 1984[63] created a new form of industrial intellectual property by protecting mask works and the semiconductor chip products in which they are embodied against chip piracy. A **mask work** refers to the specific form of expression embodied in chip design, including the stencils used in manufacturing semiconductor chip products. A **semiconductor chip product** is a product placed on a piece of semiconductor material in accordance with a predetermined pattern that is intended to perform electronic circuitry functions. These chips operate microwave ovens, televisions, computers, robots, X-ray machines, and countless other devices. This definition of semiconductor chip products includes such products as analog chips, logic function chips like microprocessors, and memory chips like RAMS and ROMs.

Duration and Qualifications for Protection

The SCPA provides the owner of a mask work fixed in semiconductor chip products the exclusive right for 10 years to reproduce and distribute the products in the United States and to import them into the United States. The protection of the act applies only to those works that, when considered as a whole, are not commonplace, staple, or familiar in the semiconductor industry.

Limitation on Exclusive Rights

Under the SCPA's reverse engineering exemption, competitors may not only study mask works but may also use the results of that study to design their own semiconductor chip products embodying their own original masks even if the masks are substantially similar (but not substantially identical) so long as their products are the result of substantial study and analysis, not merely the result of plagiarism.

Innocent infringers are not liable for infringements occurring before notice of protection is given them and are liable for reasonable royalties on each unit distributed after notice has been given them. However, continued purchase of infringing semiconductors after notice has been given can result in penalties of up to $250,000.

Remedies

The SCPA provides that an infringer will be liable for actual damages and will forfeit its profits to the owner. As an alternative, the owner may elect to receive statutory damages of up to $250,000 as determined by a court. The court may also order destruction or other disposition of the products and equipment used to make the products. **For Example,** Altera Corporation, a manufacturer of programmable logic devices, was successful in its lawsuit against Clear Logic under the SCPA, asserting that Clear Logic had copied the layout design of its registered mask works. It was also successful in its claim that Clear Logic induced breach of software licenses with Altera customers. Damages were assessed at $36 million.[64]

mask work–specific form of expression embodied in a chip design, including the stencils used in manufacturing semiconductor chip products.

semiconductor chip product–product placed on a piece of semiconductor material in accordance with a predetermined pattern that is intended to perform electronic circuitry functions.

---

[62] See *Fonar Corp. v. Domenick*, 105 F.3d 99 (2d Cir. 1997).
[63] P.L. 98-620, 98 Stat. 3347, 17 U.S.C. §901.
[64] *Altera Corp. v. Clear Logic Inc.*, 424 F.3d 1079 (9th Cir. 2005).

Make the Connection

Summary

Property rights in trademarks, copyrights, and patents are protected by federal statutes. A trademark or service mark is any word, symbol, design, or combination of these used to identify a product (in the case of a trademark) or a service (in the case of a service mark). Terms are categorized as: (1) generic, (2) descriptive, (3) suggestive, or (4) arbitrary or fanciful. Generic terms are never registrable. Descriptive terms, geographic terms, and proper names may be registered and receive protection after they have acquired secondary meaning. Suggestive and arbitrary or fanciful marks are registrable immediately. If there is likelihood of confusion, a court will enjoin the second user from using a particular mark.

A copyright is the exclusive right given by federal statute to the creator of a literary or an artistic work to use, reproduce, or display the work for the life of the creator and 70 years after the creator's death.

A patent gives the inventor an exclusive right for 20 years from the date of application to make, use, and sell an invention that is new, useful, and nonobvious to those in the business to which the invention is related. Trade secrets that give an owner an advantage over competitors are protected under state law for an unlimited period so long as they are not made public.

Protection of computer programs and the design of computer chips and mask works is commonly obtained, subject to certain limitations, by complying with federal statutes, by using the law of trade secrets, and by requiring restrictive licensing agreements. Many software developers pursue all of these means to protect their proprietary interests in their programs.

Learning Outcomes

After studying this chapter, you should be able to clearly explain:

9-1   Trademarks and Service Marks

LO.1   Explain the spectrum of distinctiveness used to classify trademarks and explain why distinctiveness is important

See the Cengage example, a coined mark at the most distinctive end of the spectrum, page 155.

See the Sports Illustrated example, a descriptive mark with acquired distinctiveness, page 155.

See the *Harley Davidson* case where the term *hog* was found to be generic and not distinctive at all, page 156.

LO.2   Explain how courts determine whether there is a likelihood of confusion between trademarks

See the list of factors, page 156.

LO.3   Explain how personal names can acquire trademark protection

See the example involving David Beckham, page 155.

LO.4   List the remedies available for improper use of trademarks

See the applicable remedies of injunctive relief, lost profits, and attorney's fees, page 157.

LO.5   Explain the difference between trademark infringement and trademark dilution

Compare the eight factors used to determine likelihood of confusion with the requirements for proving trademark dilution, page 158.

See the example involving "Eat More Kale" and "Eat Mor Chickin," page 159.

9-2   Copyrights

LO.6   Explain what is and is not copyrightable; explain the fair use defense

See the discussion on what is copyrightable, page 162.

See the Darden example of a denial of a copyright because of lack of creativity, page 162.

See the *Cariou* case describing fair use analysis, pages 163–164.

See the *Wind Done Gone* example involving fair use parody, page 163.

9-3   Patents

LO.7   Explain the "new and not obvious" requirement necessary to obtain a patent

See the cDNA "not obvious" example, page 167.

See the mounted chainsaw "obvious" example, page 167.

See the *Alice* decision where a patent application was found to be an unpatentable abstract idea, page 169.

9-4 Secret Business Information

LO.8 Explain what constitutes a trade secret and what steps a company must take to ensure protection
See the *Hallmark* case, pages 171–172.

9-5 Protection of Computer Software and Mask Works

LO.9 Explain the extent of protection provided owners of software
See the Apple Computer example, page 173.

Key Terms

acquired distinctiveness
copyright
cybersquatters
distinctiveness

mask work
prior art
secondary meaning
semiconductor chip product

service mark
trade dress
trade secret
trademark

Questions and Case Problems

1. China is a signatory country to the Madrid Protocol on the international registration of trademarks. Starbucks opened its first café in China in 1999 and has added outlets in numerous locations including Shanghai and at the Great Wall and the imperial palace in Beijing. Xingbake Café Corp. Ltd. has imitated the designs of Starbucks' cafés in its business coffee café locations in Shanghai. *Xing* (pronounced "Shing") means star, and *bake*, or "bak kuh" is pronounced like "bucks." Does the Seattle, Washington, Starbucks Corporation have standing to bring suit in China against Xingbake Café Corp. Ltd? If so, on what theory? Decide.

2. Cable News Network with its principal place of business in Atlanta, Georgia, is the owner of the trademark CNN in connection with providing news and information services to people worldwide through cable and satellite television networks, Web sites, and news services. Its services are also available worldwide on the Internet at the domain name CNN.com. Maya Online Broadband Network (Maya HK) is a Chinese company. It registered the domain name CNNEWS.com with Network Solutions, Inc. The CNNews.com Web site was designed to provide news and information to Chinese-speaking individuals worldwide, making significant use of the terms *CNNews* and *CNNews.com* as brand names and logos that the Atlanta company contends resembles its logos. Maya HK has admitted that CNNews in fact stands for China Network News abbreviated as CNN. The Atlanta company had notified Maya HK of its legal right to the CNN mark before the Chinese company registered the CNNews.com domain name. Does the federal Anticybersquatting Consumer Protection Act apply to this case? If so, does a "safe harbor" exist under the ACPA for Maya HK in that most people who access its Web site in China have never heard of CNN? Decide. [*Cable News Network v. CNNews.com*, 177 F. Supp. 2d 506 (E.D. Va.)]

3. Sara Bostwick hired Christian Oth, Inc., to be her wedding photographer. The parties' written contract granted ownership of the copyright in all images created to Oth. Oth posted the wedding photos on its Web site. Bostwick e-mailed Oth to remove the photos from the Web site. Oth failed to do so and Bostwick sued, claiming that she had the sole and exclusive right to control her own wedding photos. Is she correct? [*Bostwick v. Christian Oth, Inc.* 936 N.Y.S.2d 176 (A.D.)]

4. A small brewery in New York called Empire Brewing Company manufactured a brand of beer called "Strikes Bock." For seven years, the brewery served the beer only on tap. With the intention of bottling and selling the beer in stores, Empire Brewing sought a trademark for "Strikes Bock." Lucasfilm opposed the trademark registration maintaining that it could cause confusion with its famous film, "The Empire Strikes Back." Should the USPTO grant the trademark to Empire Brewing? Would Lucasfilm be likely to prevail in a trademark infringement suit or a trademark dilution suit? [Natalie O'Neill, *Lucasfilm Sues Brewery over Star Wars-inspired Beer*, N.Y. POST, (Oct. 24, 2014), **http://nypost.com/2014/10/24/lucasfilm-sues-over-brewerys-empire-strikes-bock-beer/**]

5. Sullivan sold t-shirts with the name *Boston Marathon* and the year of the race imprinted on them. The Boston Athletic Association (BAA) sponsors and

administers the Boston Marathon and has used the name *Boston Marathon* since 1917. The BAA registered the name *Boston Marathon* on the Principal Register. In 1986, the BAA entered into an exclusive license with Image, Inc., to use its service mark on shirts and other apparel. Thereafter, when Sullivan continued to sell shirts imprinted with the name *Boston Marathon*, the BAA sought an injunction. Sullivan's defense was that the general public was not being misled into thinking that his shirts were officially sponsored by the BAA. Without this confusion of source, he contended, no injunction should be issued. Decide. [*Boston Athletic Ass'n v. Sullivan*, 867 F.2d 22 (1st Cir.)]

6. The Greenwich Bank & Trust Co. (GB&T) opened in 1998 and by 2008 had expanded to a total of four branches in the Greenwich, Connecticut, community of 62,000 residents. A competitor using the name Bank of Greenwich (BOG) opened in December 2006. GB&T's parent entity sued BOG for trademark violation under the Lanham Act. BOG argued that GB&T's service mark is generic and is simply not entitled to Lanham Act protection because it combines the generic term "bank" and the geographic term "Greenwich." GB&T asserted that it had been the only bank in Greenwich using the word *Greenwich* in its name and had done so exclusively for nine years. It asserted that a geographic term is entitled to protection if it acquires secondary meaning. GB&T introduced evidence regarding its advertising expenditures, sales success, and length of exclusivity of use along with evidence of actual consumer confusion. Decide. [*Connecticut Community Bank v. The Bank of Greenwich*, 578 F. Supp. 2d 405 (D. Conn.)]

7. The U.S. Polo Association (USPA) is a not-for-profit corporation that is the governing body of the sport of polo in the United States. It has been in existence since 1890 and derives the majority of its revenue from royalties obtained from licensing its trademarks. It owns more than 900 trademarks worldwide, including marks bearing the words "U.S. Polo Assn." with the depiction of two polo players for licensees on products sold in the apparel category. In 2009 it produced 10,000 units of a men's fragrance using packaging featuring its logo as used on apparel. Since 1978 PRL (Polo Ralph Lauren) and its licensee of PRL trademarks, L'Oreal, have used the mark known as the "Polo Player" logo on men's fragrances with its logo containing one player. The fragrance has been sold for 32 years and it was voted into the industry's Hall of Fame. PRL sued USPA. What must PRL establish to prevail in an action for trademark infringement? How would you decide this case? [*United States Polo Assn. v. PRL USA Holdings, Inc.*, 800 F. Supp. 2d 515 (S.D.N.Y.)]

8. Diehr devised a computerized process for curing rubber that was based on a well-known mathematical formula related to the cure time, and he devised numerous other steps in his synthetic rubber-curing process. The patent examiner determined that because abstract ideas, the laws of nature, and mathematical formulas are not patentable subject matter, the process in this case (based on a known mathematical formula) was also not patentable. Diehr contended that all of the steps in his rubber-curing process were new and not obvious to the art of rubber curing. He contended also that he did not seek an exclusive patent on the mathematical formula, except for its use in the rubber-curing process. Decide. [*Diamond v. Diehr*, 450 U.S. 175]

9. Aries Information Systems, Inc., develops and markets computer software specifically designed to meet the financial accounting and reporting requirements of such public bodies as school districts and county governments. One of Aries's principal products is the POBAS III accounting program. Pacific Management Systems Corporation was organized by Scott Dahmer, John Laugan, and Roman Rowan for marketing a financial accounting and budgeting system known as FAMIS. Dahmer, Laugan, and Rowan were Aries employees before, during, and shortly after they organized Pacific. As employees, they each gained access to Aries's software materials (including the POBAS III system) and had information about Aries's existing and prospective clients. Proprietary notices appeared on every client contract, source code list, and magnetic tape. Dahmer, Laugan, and Rowan signed an Employee Confidential Information Agreement after beginning employment with Aries. While still employees of Aries, they submitted a bid on behalf of Pacific to Rock County and were awarded the contract. Pacific's FAMIS software system is substantially identical to Aries's proprietary POBAS III system. Aries sued Pacific to recover damages for misappropriation of its trade secrets. Pacific's defense was that no "secrets" were misappropriated because many employees knew the

information in question. Decide. [*Aries Information Systems, Inc. v. Pacific Management Systems Corp.*, 366 N.W.2d 366 (Minn. App.)]

10. The plaintiff, Herbert Rosenthal Jewelry Corporation, and the defendant, Kalpakian, manufactured jewelry. The plaintiff obtained a copyright registration of a jeweled pin in the shape of a bee. Kalpakian made a similar pin. Rosenthal sued Kalpakian for infringement of copyright registration. Kalpakian raised the defense that he was only copying the idea, not the way the idea was expressed. Was he liable for infringement of the plaintiff's copyright? [*Herbert Rosenthal Jewelry Corp. v. Kalpakian*, 446 F.2d 738 (9th Cir.)]

11. Mineral Deposits, Ltd. (MD, Ltd.), an Australian company, manufactures the Reichert Spiral, a device used for recovering gold particles from sand and gravel. The spiral was patented in Australia, and MD, Ltd., had applied for a patent in the United States. Theodore Zigan contacted MD, Ltd., stating that he was interested in purchasing up to 200 devices for use in his gravel pit. MD, Ltd., agreed to lend Zigan a spiral for testing its efficiency. Zigan made molds of the spiral's components and proceeded to manufacture 170 copies of the device. When MD, Ltd., found out that copies were being made, it demanded the return of the spiral. MD, Ltd., also sought lost profits for the 170 spirals manufactured by Zigan. Recovery was sought on a theory of misappropriation of trade secrets. Zigan offered to pay for the spiral lent him by MD, Ltd. He argued that trade secret protection was lost by the public sale of the spiral. What ethical values are involved? Was Zigan's conduct a violation of trade secret law? [*Mineral Deposits, Ltd. v. Zigan*, 773 P.2d 609 (Colo. App.)]

12. Michael Cram alleged that he was the sole creator of a unique talking bottle opener. His product was very successful and he licensed the product to numerous NCAA schools, Major League Baseball, the National Football League, NASCAR, and various movie and TV studios. Cram became aware that a similar talking bottle opener, featuring McFarland's movie character "Ted," was sold with DVDs of the movie. Cram sued Seth McFarland, the creator of Ted; Universal Studios, the producer of the movie; and Target, which distributed the product, for trade dress infringement. Cram maintains that the trade dress consists of the shape of the plastic handle; the C shape of the metal opener; the no-button activator technology; the use and placement of a single image on the opener; the use and placement of the eight speaker holes; the quality of the sound; and the triggering of the sound by pressure on the metal opener. Do you think that Cram will be successful in his trade dress infringement suit? [Bryanna Cappadona, *Seth MacFarlane Is Being Sued for Plagiarizing* Ted *Bottle Openers*, BOSTON MAGAZINE, Feb. 27, 2015, **http://www.bostonmagazine.com/arts-entertainment/blog/2015/02/27/seth-macfarlane-sued-ted-bottle-openers/**]

13. The American Geophysical Union and 82 other publishers of scientific and technical journals brought a class-action lawsuit against Texaco, claiming that Texaco's unauthorized photocopying of articles from their journals constituted a copyright infringement. Texaco's defense was that the copying was fair use under Section 107 of the Copyright Act of 1976. To avoid extensive discovery, the parties agreed to focus on one randomly selected Texaco scientist, Dr. Donald Chickering, who had photocopies of eight articles from the *Journal of Catalysis* in his files. The trial court judge held that the copying of the eight articles did not constitute fair use, and Texaco appealed. [*American Geophysical Union v. Texaco, Inc.*, 60 F.3d 913 (2d Cir.)]

14. *The Column* is a sculpture of 19 stainless steel statues depicting a squad of soldiers on patrol; it is a key part of the Korean War Veterans Memorial on the National Mall in Washington, D.C. *The Column* was created by sculptor and World War II veteran Frank Gaylord. In January 1996, John Alli, an amateur photographer, visited the Memorial during a heavy snowstorm and photographed *The Column*. In 2002, the United States Postal Service issued a stamp commemorating the fiftieth anniversary of the Korean War armistice. The Postal Service selected Mr. Alli's photograph for the stamp face and paid Mr. Alli a one-time fee of $1,500 for the right to use the photo. The Postal Service did not have permission from Mr. Gaylord to feature his sculpture. Do you think that Gaylord would prevail in a copyright infringement suit? If so, how would you determine damages? [*Gaylord v. United States*, 777 F.3d 1363 (Fed. Cir.)]

CPA Questions

1. Multicomp Company wishes to protect software it has developed. It is concerned about others copying this software and taking away some of its profits. Which of the following is true concerning the current state of the law?

   a. Computer software is generally copyrightable.

   b. To receive protection, the software must have a conspicuous copyright notice.

   c. Software in human readable source code is copyrightable but machine language object code is not.

   d. Software can be copyrighted for a period not to exceed 20 years.

2. Which of the following is not correct concerning computer software purchased by Gultch Company from Softtouch Company? Softtouch originally created this software.

   a. Gultch can make backup copies in case of machine failure.

   b. Softtouch can typically copyright its software for at least 75 years.

   c. If the software consists of compiled computer databases, it cannot be copyrighted.

   d. Computer programs are generally copyrightable.

3. Using his computer, Professor Bell makes 15 copies (to distribute to his accounting class) of a database in some software he has purchased for his personal research. The creator of this software is claiming copyright. Which of the following is correct?

   a. This is an infringement of copyright, since he bought the software for personal use.

   b. This is not an infringement of copyright, since databases cannot be copyrighted.

   c. This is not an infringement of copyright because the copies were made using a computer.

   d. This is not an infringement of copyright because of the fair use doctrine.

4. Intellectual property rights included in software may be protected under which of the following?

   a. Patent law

   b. Copyright law

   c. Both of the above

   d. None of the above

The Legal Environment of International Trade

Learning Outcomes ‹‹‹

After studying this chapter, you should be able to

LO.1 List the methods of doing business abroad

LO.2 Explain which country's law will govern an international contract should a dispute arise

LO.3 Explain tariff barriers and nontariff barriers to the free movement of goods across borders

LO.4 Identify the agreements administered by the World Trade Organization

LO.5 Explain how to register and protect trademarks abroad

LO.6 Explain how trade disputes are resolved

LO.7 Explain how antidumping duties and countervailing duties operate under the WTO agreements

LO.8 Explain U.S. law regarding payment to foreign government officials

LO.9 Explain how U.S. securities laws might apply to foreign transactions

10-1 Conducting Business Internationally

10-1a Forms of International Business

The decision to participate in international business transactions and the extent of that participation depend on the financial position of the individual firm, production and marketing factors, and tax and legal considerations. There are a number of methods of conducting business abroad.

Export Sales

export sale–direct sale to customers in a foreign country.

A direct sale to customers in a foreign country is an **export sale.** A U.S. firm engaged in export selling is not present in the foreign country in such an arrangement. The export is subject to a tariff by the foreign country, but the exporting firm is not subject to local taxation by the importing country.

Agency Requirements

agent–person or firm who is authorized by the principal or by operation of law to make contracts with third persons on behalf of the principal.

A U.S. manufacturer may decide to make a limited entry into international business by appointing an agent to represent it in a foreign market. An **agent** is a person or firm with authority to make contracts on behalf of another—the **principal.** The agent will receive commission income for sales made on behalf of the U.S. principal. The appointment of a foreign agent commonly constitutes "doing business" in that country and subjects the U.S. firm to local taxation.

Foreign Distributorships

principal–person or firm who employs an agent; the person who, with respect to a surety, is primarily liable to the third person or creditor.

A **distributor** takes title to goods and bears the financial and commercial risks for the subsequent sale. To avoid making a major financial investment, a U.S. firm may decide to appoint a foreign distributor. A U.S. firm may also appoint a foreign distributor to avoid managing a foreign operation with its complicated local business, legal, and labor conditions.

distributor–entity that takes title to goods and bears the financial and commercial risks for the subsequent sale of the goods.

Licensing

licensing–transfer of technology rights to a product so that it may be produced by a different business organization in a foreign country in exchange for royalties and other payments as agreed.

U.S. firms may select licensing as a means of doing business in other countries. **Licensing** involves the transfer of technology rights in a product so that it may be produced by a different business organization in a foreign country in exchange for royalties and other payments as agreed. The technology being licensed may fall within the internationally recognized categories of patents, trademarks, and "know-how" (trade secrets and unpatented manufacturing processes outside the public domain). These intellectual property rights, which are legally protectable, may be licensed separately or incorporated into a single, comprehensive licensing contract. **Franchising,** which involves granting permission to use a trademark, trade name, or copyright under specified conditions, is a form of licensing that is now very common in international business.

franchising–granting of permission to use a trademark, trade name, or copyright under specified conditions; a form of licensing.

Wholly Owned Subsidiaries

A firm seeking to maintain control over its own operations, including the protection of its own technological expertise, may choose to do business abroad through a wholly owned subsidiary. In Europe the most common choice of foreign business organization, similar to the U.S. corporate form of business organization, is called the *société anonyme* (S.A.). In German-speaking countries, this form is called *Aktiengesellschaft* (A.G.). Small- and medium-sized companies in Europe now utilize a newly created form of business organization called the limited liability company (*Gesellschaft mit beschränkter Haftung,* or "GmbH" in Germany; *Società a responsabilità limitata,* or "S.r.l." in Spain). A wholly owned subsidiary is less complicated to form but is restrictive for accessing public capital markets.

A corporation doing business in more than one country poses many taxation problems for the governments in those countries where the firm does business. The United States has established tax treaties with many countries, granting corporations relief from double taxation. Credit is normally given by the United States to U.S. corporations for taxes paid to foreign governments.

There is a potential for tax evasion by U.S. corporations when they sell their goods to their overseas subsidiaries. Corporations could sell goods at less than the fair market value to avoid a U.S. tax on the full profit for such sales. By allowing the foreign subsidiaries located in countries with lower tax rates to make higher profits, a company as a whole would minimize its taxes. Section 482 of the Internal Revenue Code (IRC), however, allows the Internal Revenue Service (IRS) to reallocate the income between the parent and its foreign subsidiary. Intellectual property such as patent rights, internationally held and generating revenues outside the United States, provides a basis for U.S. multinational companies to legally minimize tax liability by shifting income internationally. **For Example,** global companies like Apple, Microsoft, Google, and Facebook may utilize tax avoidance techniques like the "Double Irish with a Dutch Sandwich," relying on transferring profits on international patent royalties to places like Ireland, with routing through the Netherlands, back to an Irish subsidiary, then to a Caribbean tax haven.[1]

10-1b The International Contract

What Law Applies

When there is a sale of goods within the United States, one law typically applies to the transaction. Some variation may be introduced when the transaction is between parties in different states, but for the most part, the law governing the transaction is the U.S. law of contracts and the Uniform Commercial Code (UCC). In contrast, when an international contract is made, it is necessary to determine whether it is the law of the seller's country or the law of the importer's country that will govern. The parties to an international contract often resolve that question themselves as part of their contract, setting forth which country's law will govern should a dispute arise. Such a provision is called a **choice-of-law clause. For Example,** U.S. investors Irmgard and Mitchell Lipcon provided capital to underwriters at Lloyd's of London and signed choice-of-law clauses in their investment agreements, binding them to proceed in England under English law should disputes arise. When the Lipcons realized that their investments were exposed to massive liabilities for asbestos and pollution insurance claims, they sued in U.S. district court in Florida for alleged U.S. securities acts violations. However, their complaints were dismissed based on the choice-of-law clauses in their contracts. The U.S. court of appeals stated that the Lipcons must "honor their bargains" and attempt to vindicate their claims in English courts under English law.[2]

choice-of-law clause—clause in an agreement that specifies which law will govern should a dispute arise.

CISG

The *United Nations Convention on Contracts for the International Sale of Goods* (CISG or convention) sets forth uniform rules to govern international sales contracts. National law, however, is sometimes required to fill gaps in areas not covered by the CISG. The CISG

---

[1] http://www.nytimes.com/interactive/2012/04/28/business/Double-Irish-With-A-Dutch-Sandwich.html. http://www.npr.org/blogs/money/2010/10/21/130727655/google-s-tax-tricks-double-irish-and-dutch-sandwich. See also James Barrett and Steven Hadjilogiou, "The Tax Benefits and Obstacles to U.S. Businesses in Transferring Foreign Intellectual Property to Foreign Affiliates," 89 *Fla. B. J. No.* 5, pp. 40–45 (May 2012).
[2] *Lipcon v. Underwriters at Lloyd's, London,* 148 F.2d 1285, 1299 (11th Cir. 1998).

became effective on January 1, 1988. There are currently 83 contracting states that have ratified the CISG.[3] The provisions of the CISG were strongly influenced by Article 2 of the UCC. Nevertheless, several distinct differences exist between the CISG and the UCC. The CISG does not cover the sale of goods for personal, family, or household uses and the sale of watercraft, aircraft, natural gas, or electricity; letters of credit; and auctions and securities.[4] The CISG is often viewed by foreign entities as a neutral body of law, the utilization of which can be a positive factor in successfully concluding negotiations of a contract. The parties to an international commercial contract may opt out of the CISG. However, absent an express "opt-out provision," the CISG is controlling for its signatories and preempts all national law.

The Arbitration Alternative

Traditional litigation may be considered too time consuming, expensive, and divisive to the relationships of the parties to an international venture. The parties, therefore, may agree to arbitrate any contractual disputes that may arise according to dispute resolution procedures set forth in the contract.

Pitfalls exist for U.S. companies arbitrating disputes in foreign lands. **For Example,** were a U.S. company to agree to arbitrate a contractual dispute under Chinese law, only Chinese lawyers can present an arbitration case, even if one party is a U.S. company. Consequently, it is common for parties to international ventures to agree to arbitrate their disputes in neutral countries.

An arbitration agreement gives the parties more control over the decision-making process. The parties can require that the arbitrator have the technical, language, and legal qualifications to best understand their dispute. While procedures exist for the prearbitration exchange of documents, full "discovery" is ordinarily not allowed. The decision of the arbitrator is final and binding on the parties with very limited judicial review possible.

Financing International Trade

There is no international currency. This creates problems as to which currency to use and how to make payment in international transactions. Centuries ago, buyers used precious metals, jewels, or furs in payment. Today, the parties to an international transaction agree in their sales contract on the currency to be used to pay for the goods. They commonly require that the buyer furnish the seller a **letter of credit,** which is a commercial device used to guarantee payment to a seller in an international transaction. With a letter of credit, an issuer, typically a bank, agrees to pay the drafts drawn against the buyer for the purchase price. In trading with merchants in some countries, the foreign country itself will promise that the seller will be paid.

letter of credit–
commercial device used to guarantee payment to a seller, primarily in an international business transaction.

10-2 International Trade

Today the rules of world trade are negotiated and administered by the World Trade Organization. The 160 member nations of the WTO account for 98 percent of global trade. Between World War I and World War II, world trade decreased substantially. In the 1930s, the U.S. Congress passed the Smoot-Hawley Tariff Act, a strong protectionist measure that imposed stiff tariffs on imports. Roberto Azevedo, the current Director-General of the World Trade Organization, has contrasted the trade environment during the interwar protectionist era to trade during the 2008 financial crisis. He notes that the mistakes that

[3] See CISG: Table of Contracting States, **http://www.cisg.law.pace.edu/cisg/countries/cntries.html**.
[4] C.I.S.G. art. 2(a)–(f).

were made between 1929 and 1933 were not repeated in 2008 because governments "knew that they were bound by rules and obligations that were common to all, and this gave them confidence that others were going to play by the rules as well."[5] He suggests that the commitments WTO members made to each other avoided economic catastrophe.

Before introducing the current world trading agreements, some terms in international trade are introduced.

10-2a Tariffs and Barriers to Trade

The most common barrier to the free movement of goods across borders is a tariff. A wide range of nontariff barriers also restricts the free movement of goods, services, and investments. Government export controls used as elements of foreign policy have proven to be a major barrier to trade with certain countries.

Tariff Barriers

tariff—(1) domestically—government-approved schedule of charges that may be made by a regulated business, such as a common carrier or warehouser; (2) internationally—tax imposed by a country on goods crossing its borders, without regard to whether the purpose is to raise revenue or to discourage the traffic in the taxed goods.

A **tariff** is an import or export duty or tax placed on goods as they move into or out of a country. It is the most common method used by countries to restrict foreign imports. The tariff raises the total cost, and thus the price, of an imported product in the domestic market. Thus, the price of a domestically produced product not subject to the tariff is more advantageous.

The U.S. Customs and Border Protection Service (Customs) imposes tariffs on imported goods at the port of entry. The merchandise is classified under a tariff schedule, which lists each type of merchandise and the corresponding duty rate (or percentage). Customs also determines the "computed value" of the imported goods under very precise statutory formulas.[6] The total amount of the duty is calculated by applying the duty percentage to the computed value figure.[7] Customs also has authority to investigate fraudulent schemes that seek to avoid or to underpay customs' duties.[8]

Since the Second World War, exports have grown 35-fold largely due to the fact that the average tariff rate has been reduced from around 40 percent to 4 percent under the World Trade Organization's multilateral trading rules.

Nontariff Barriers

Nontariff barriers consist of a wide range of restrictions that inhibit the free movement of goods between countries. An import quota, such as a limitation on the number of automobiles that can be imported into one country from another, is such a barrier. More subtle nontariff barriers exist in all countries. **For Example,** Japan's complex customs procedures resulted in the restriction of the sale of U.S.-made aluminum baseball bats in Japan. The customs procedures required the individual uncrating and "destruction testing" of bats at the ports of entry. Government subsidies are also nontariff barriers to trade.

---

[5] Roberto Azevedo, Speech, Regional initiatives cannot substitute for the multilateral trading system, Stockholm School of Economics, Riga, Latvia (March 24, 2015), available at **http://www.wto.org**.

[6] See Tariff Act of 1930, as amended, 19 U.S.C. §1401 a(e).

[7] It is common for importers to utilize customs brokers who research the tariff schedules to see whether a product fits unambiguously under one of the Customs Service's classifications. A broker will also research the classifications given to similar products. It may find that a fax switch may be classified as "other telephonic switching apparatus" at a tariff rate of 8.5 percent or "other telegraphic switching apparatus" with a tariff of 4.7 percent. Obviously, the importer desires to pay the lower rate, and the broker with the assistance of counsel will make a recommendation to the Customs Service for the lower rate, and Customs will make a ruling. The decisions of the Customs Service are published in the *Customs Bulletin*, the official weekly publication of the Customs Service. See *Command Communications v. Fritz Cos.*, 36 P.3d 182 (Colo. App. 2001). See also *Estee Lauder, Inc. v. United States*, 815 F. Supp. 2d 1287 (Ct. Int'l Trade 2012), where the importer successfully challenged Custom's classification of a cosmetic product and the court declined to adopt Custom's position because of the flawed analysis and application of the "rule."

[8] *U.S. v. Inn Foods, Inc.*, 560 F.3d 1338 (Fed. Cir. 2009).

One U.S. law—the Turtle Law—prohibits the importation of shrimp from countries that allow the harvesting of shrimp with commercial fishing technology that could adversely affect endangered sea turtles. **For Example,** two U.S. importers sought an exemption, representing that their Brazilian supply of shrimp was caught in the wild by vessels using turtle excluder devices (TEDs). Because Brazil had failed to comply with the U.S. Turtle Law by requiring TEDs on its commercial shrimp fleet, even though it had seven years to do so, the exemption was not granted.[9]

10-2b The World Trade Organization

The WTO is an international organization located in Geneva, Switzerland, that sets the rules for world trade. It administers several trade agreements; provides a forum for trade negotiations; monitors adherence to trade rules; and provides a mechanism for resolving trade disputes. Russia, joining in 2012, is one of the newer members of the 160 WTO nations. More than three-fourths of WTO members are developing countries. WTO agreements make special accommodations for developing countries to integrate into the global trading system.

most-favored-nation— clause in treaties between countries whereby any privilege granted to one member is extended to all members of the treaty.

The principle of nondiscrimination is one of the hallmarks of the WTO. Each member agrees to treat all WTO trading partners equally. This equal treatment among all WTO members is referred to as **most-favored-nation** treatment. Similarly, the WTO requires that its members exercise **national treatment.** In other words, a country may not discriminate between its own products and foreign products or services. The WTO favors using tariffs over other types of barriers to trade. Because tariffs are negotiated, they provide a transparent mechanism for regulating world trade.

national treatment—a WTO requirement in which a country may not discriminate between its own products and foreign products or services.

WTO agreements allow members to protect the environment, public health, and plant and animal health. In doing so, however, members must treat national and foreign businesses alike. A member cannot use the environment or public health concerns as a pretext for protectionist measures.

10-2c Agreements Administered under the WTO

The WTO is the umbrella organization that negotiates and administers several agreements.

The General Agreement on Tariffs and Trade (GATT)

The GATT existed long before the WTO. Motivated to create a more stable, peaceful world following World War II, several nations came to the Bretton Woods conference of 1944. The idea of creating an International Trade Organization was not realized at this time, but the General Agreement on Tariffs and Trade was signed in 1947. Focusing on trade in goods, the GATT seeks to liberalize world trade through multilateral negotiations. The primary goal of the GATT is to encourage trade by reducing tariffs and lowering trade barriers. Through rounds of negotiations, GATT members negotiate bound tariff rates. Thus, foreign companies, investors, and governments can be more confident in the stability and predictability of international trade.

From 1947 to 1994, GATT was the forum for trade negotiations. As a treaty GATT continues to change, as members negotiate not only tariff rates but numerous other issues including antidumping, subsidies, investment, and trade facilitation. In 1995, during the Uruguay Round of negotiations, GATT members formed the WTO to be the new administrative body to organize the rules of world trade.

---

[9] *Earth Island Institute v. Christopher*, 948 F. Supp. 1062 (Ct. Int'l Trade 1996). See *Turtle Island Restoration Network v. Evans*, 284 F.3d 1282 (Fed. Cir. 2002), on the continuing litigation on this topic and the clash between statutory enforcement and political and diplomatic considerations.

The General Agreement on Trade in Services (GATS)

The GATT pertains to trade in goods; the GATS extends the same principles of nondiscrimination to trade in services such as banks, insurance, telecommunications, and hotel chains.

Trade Related Aspects of Intellectual Property (TRIPS)

TRIPS is the WTO agreement that deals with trade rules that impact copyrights, patents, trademarks, geographical names, industrial designs, and trade secrets. As intellectual property issues became more important in trade, members were often frustrated with the variance in protection and enforcement of members' rights. TRIPS establishes minimum levels of protection that each government must provide to fellow WTO members. All members must show that their national laws are TRIPS compliant and that they have adequate standards of protection. Some exceptions to the rules are allowed to address public health problems. TRIPS also requires that governments enforce their intellectual property laws and that penalties are sufficient to deter violations.

Like all WTO agreements, TRIPS incorporates WTO principles such as national treatment and most-favored nation treatment. TRIPS also requires that intellectual property protection contribute to technical innovation and the transfer of technology. TRIPS incorporates the Paris Convention, the first international treaty addressing intellectual property. The Paris Convention covers patents, trademarks, and industrial designs.

10-2d Protecting Trademarks Worldwide

Trademarks

To protect trademarks internationally, a mark holder can either register in each country in which he seeks protection or he can use the Madrid System, which is administered by the World Intellectual Property Organization (WIPO). Members of the Paris Convention and the WTO can use the Madrid System to manage trademarks on a worldwide basis. The mark holder must register in its home country before seeking an international application. The Madrid System can also be used to manage the renewal of trademarks (usually every 10 years). Trademarks remain valid as long as they are renewed and continue to be used in commerce as a source identifier.

Trademark holders should be aware that most countries operate on a first to file basis. In the United States, although registration gives better protection, the Lanham Act recognizes the first to use the mark in commerce as the trademark owner.

If a company plans to do business in more than one country within the European Union, it can apply for a Community Trademark, which offers protection throughout the 28 countries that comprise the EU.

The Paris Convention recognizes that trademark protection is territorial. In other words, a mark registered in one country is independent of its possible registration in any other country. If a mark has been duly registered in the country of origin, members of Paris and TRIPS may not refuse to register the foreign mark unless it would infringe the rights of a third party or is otherwise objectionable as deceptive or against public morals.

Well-Known Marks

Just as U.S. law gives special protection to famous marks under the Federal Trademark Dilution Act, so international law gives special protection to **well-known marks.** The Paris Convention provides that a country may refuse to register or prohibit the use of a

well-known mark—in international law a mark that both the Paris Convention and TRIPS recognize as deserving protection even if it is not registered in the foreign country; national law determines what "well-known" means but the WIPO offers a list suggesting that the value of the mark, the extent of its use and promotion, and its recognition in the relevant sector of the public are key factors.

trademark that is well-known.[10] Under the Paris Convention, such protection was limited to cases in which the infringing use involved identical or similar goods. TRIPS extends the protection of well-known marks to infringing uses involving dissimilar goods, if such use would harm the owner of the well-known mark. Under TRIPS, WTO members are obligated to recognize well-known marks even if they are unregistered in the foreign country; to allow the holder of a well-known mark to request cancellation of an infringing mark for at least five years from the date of registration; and to have no time limit for challenging marks registered or used in bad faith.

What constitutes a well-known mark is a matter of the law of each country. The World Intellectual Property Organization has issued a list of factors to consider, and countries may use these factors for guidance. Important factors to consider include how long and how extensively the mark has been used; the extent of publicity and advertising; the record of enforcement of rights in the mark by competent authorities; and the value associated with the mark.[11] **For Example,** the Trademark Office in China has recognized JNJ (Johnson and Johnson), Bosch, and Adidas as well-known trademarks.

CASE SUMMARY

Trademarks Up in Smoke!

FACTS: Both Cubatabaco and General Cigar manufacture and distribute cigars using the COHIBA mark. General Cigar is a Delaware corporation. It owns two trademark registrations for the COHIBA mark for use in connection with cigars. Cubatabaco is a Cuban entity that owns the COHIBA mark in Cuba and supplies cigars bearing the mark throughout the world. Cubatabaco does not distribute its cigars in the United States due to import restrictions imposed by the Cuban Assets Control Regulations (CACR). An exception to the CACR allows Cuban entities to engage in transactions related to the registration and renewal of trademarks before the USPTO. Cubatabaco sought to register COHIBA for cigars and related goods. Cubatabaco also sought to cancel General Cigar's registrations. General Cigar opposed the cancellation.

DECISION: Judgment for Cubatabaco. The Lanham Act allows "any person who believes that he is or will be damaged by the registration of a mark" to petition the USPTO to cancel the mark. Cubatabaco has a legitimate commercial interest in the COHIBA mark. Because the USPTO refused Cubatabaco's registration based on a likelihood of confusion with General Cigar's Registrations, Cubatabaco has a real interest in cancelling the Registrations, a reasonable belief that the Registrations blocking its application are causing it damage. Cubatabaco must have a bona fide intent to use the mark in commerce but does not have to actually use the mark before registering it. [*Empresa Cubana del Tabaco v. General Cigar Co., Inc.,* **753 F.3d 1270 (Fed. Cir. 2014),** *cert. denied.*]

Geographical Indications

Some regions are rightfully proud of goods produced in their region. A product's geographic origin has much to do with its special characteristics. Consequently, producers of goods from a certain region seek to prohibit others from suggesting that a product comes from the famous region. **For Example,** champagne is only properly designated as champagne if it comes from Champagne, France. TRIPS requires countries to protect geographical indications. Wines and spirits receive a higher level of protection even if there is no danger of misleading the public. Negotiations continue to establish a multilateral system of notification and registration of geographical indications.

[10] Paris Convention for the Protection of Industrial Property, July 4, 1967, 21 U.S.T. 1583, T.I.A.S. No. 6295, 828 U.N.T.S. 305.
[11] World Intellectual Property Organization, Joint Recommendation Concerning Provisions on the Protection of Well-Known Marks, September 1999, **http://www.wipo.int/edocs/pubdocs/en/marks/833/pub833.pdf.**

10-2e Copyright Protection

The Berne Convention for the Protection of Literary and Artistic Works has existed since 1886 and has been amended several times.[12] The treaty is administered by the World Intellectual Property Organization. WTO members recognized that the Berne Convention provides adequate copyright protection and requires that WTO members comply with the Berne Convention. The Berne Convention requires that signatories grant protection to most copyrighted works for the life of the author plus 50 years. Note that under U.S. copyright law, authors and artists receive protection for the life of the author plus 70 years. TRIPS clarifies that the Berne Convention protects computer programs. It also covers rental rights to ensure that authors of computer programs and producers of sound recordings have the right to prohibit the commercial rental of their works to the public.

10-2f Patent Protection

TRIPS requires that WTO members provide at least 20 years of protection to patent owners and that countries recognize the rights of patent owners such as preventing unauthorized persons from using the patented process. Although the Paris Convention and TRIPS require national treatment of intellectual property, obtaining a patent in one country does not mean that another country has to grant the patent.

THINKING THINGS THROUGH

Access to Medicine versus Patent Protection

Patent protection for pharmaceutical products presents unique problems in international trade. The TRIPS agreement specifies that members may take measures to protect public health. Despite the balance that TRIPS attempts to strike between access to medicine and respect for innovators' rights, conflicts are inevitable. India's patent system raises considerable controversy. India's current patent system has been in place since 2005. Before 2005, India's patent laws allowed pharmaceutical companies to re-create another's product by making changes to the production process. This system allowed India's pharmaceutical industry to become one of the largest in the world. For example, therapy medicines for HIV/AIDS cost $10,000 per person per year in industrialized countries. An Indian company, however, makes a generic version of the drugs that it sells to its own citizens and other developing countries for less than $200 a year.*

As a member of the WTO, however, India had to become TRIPS compliant. Still, India views many of the pharmaceuticals manufactured in the United States as patent ineligible. In the United States, a company is entitled to a new patent for improvements to an existing patent. India's laws, however, make it more difficult to obtain a patent.

In 2013, the Indian Supreme Court rejected Novartis's application for a patent on its cancer drug Glivec. The court

stated that the drug was a newer version of a "known substance." Moreover, the court stated that a drug manufacturer must show that its product enhances "therapeutic efficacy" compared to its "closest prior art." A patent should not be granted for a reformulation of an existing compound. Similarly, in 2015, an Indian court rejected a patent for Gilead's Sovaldi, a drug used to treat hepatitis C.

Some organizations have praised these decisions because access to affordable medicine is problematic in India. A majority of India's population lives on less than $2 a day. Very few people in India have health insurance, with 70 percent of the population paying health care expenses out of their own pocket. A drug such as Sovaldi, usually given for three or six months, costs $84,000 for a 12-week course in the United States.**

The United States Trade Representative has demanded reform of India's patent laws to give better protection to American pharmaceutical corporations. How should the United States address such issues? Should it seek trade sanctions against India?

*David Singh Grewal and Amy Kapczynski, *Let India Make Cheap Drugs*, NYT (Dec. 11, 2014).
Summeet Chatterjee, India Rejects Hepatitis C Drug Patent Request, Reuters, Jan. 14, 2015, **http://in.reuters.com/article/2015/01/14/gilead-india-patent-idINKBN0KN20V20150114.

---

[12] The text of the Berne Convention is available at **http://www.wipo.int/treaties/en/text.jsp?file_id=283698.**

10-2g Trade Secrets

Protection of trade secrets in an increasingly global environment has become a major concern for U.S. companies. TRIPS refers to trade secrets as "undisclosed information" or "know-how." Such information is defined similarly to the definition in the United States for trade secrets. To qualify as a "trade secret," "undisclosed information," or "know-how," the information must have commercial value and the owner or organization must take reasonable steps to keep it secret. According to TRIPS, the owner of trade secret information must be able to prevent it from being disclosed to, acquired by, or used by others without his or her consent in a manner contrary to honest commercial practices. A manner contrary to honest commercial practices includes breach of contract, breach of confidence and inducement to breach, as well as the acquisition of undisclosed information by third parties who knew, or were grossly negligent in failing to know, that such practices were involved in the acquisition.

CASE SUMMARY

I hear the train a comin'
It's rollin' round the bend....*
And it ain't rollin' on cheatin' TianRui wheels!
*Johnny Cash: Folsom Prison Blues

FACTS: Amsted Industries Inc. is a domestic manufacturer of cast steel railway wheels. It owns two secret processes for manufacturing such wheels, the "ABC process" and the "Griffin process." Amsted previously practiced the ABC process at its foundry in Calera, Alabama, but it no longer uses that process in the United States. Instead, Amsted uses the Griffin process at three of its domestic foundries. Amsted licensed the "ABC process" to several firms with foundries in China. TianRui Group Company Limited, a manufacturer of cast steel railway wheels in China, hired nine employees away from one of Amsted's Chinese licensees, Datong ABC Castings Company, Limited. Datong had previously notified those employees through a written employee code of conduct that information pertaining to the ABC process was proprietary and confidential. Each employee had been advised that he had a duty not to disclose confidential information. In the proceedings brought by Amsted before the International Trade Commission (ITC), Amsted alleged that the former Datong employees disclosed information and documents to TianRui that revealed the details of the ABC process and thereby misappropriated Amsted's trade secrets. TianRui partnered with Standard Car Truck Company, Inc., to form the joint venture Barber TianRui Railway Supply, LLC, and has marketed TianRui wheels to United States customers. Other than Amsted, they are the only companies selling or attempting to sell cast steel railway wheels in the United States. The ITC determined that the importation of the articles violated the Tariff Act and issued a limited exclusion order. TianRui appealed to the United States Court of Appeals for the Federal Circuit.

DECISION: The ITC found that the wheels were manufactured using a process that was developed in the United States, protected under domestic trade secret law, and misappropriated abroad. The appeals court was asked to decide whether the ITC's statutory authority over "[u]nfair methods of competition and unfair acts in the importation of articles ... into the United States," as provided by section 337(a)(1)(A), allows it to look to conduct occurring in China in the course of a trade secret misappropriation investigation. The ITC has authority to investigate and grant relief based in part on extraterritorial conduct insofar as it is necessary to protect domestic industries from injuries arising out of unfair competition in the domestic marketplace. The imported TianRui wheels would directly compete with wheels domestically produced by the trade secret owner. Such competition constituted an injury to an "industry" within the meaning of section 337(a)(1)(A) of the Tariff Act. [*TianRui Group Co. Ltd. v. I.T.C.*, **661 F.3d 1322 (Fed. Cir. 2011)**]

10-2h The Dispute Settlement Understanding

Dispute Settlement Body (DSB)—means provided by the World Trade Organization for member nations to resolve trade disputes rather than engage in unilateral trade sanctions or a trade war.

When the WTO was formed in 1995, one of the substantial improvements it made to world trade was the creation of the **Dispute Settlement Body (DSB)** to enforce the rules of WTO agreements. Countries, not individuals or business organizations, bring disputes before panels of experts if they think their rights are infringed under a WTO agreement. Independent experts resolve the disputes by interpreting the rules of the agreements. The system encourages resolution of disputes through consultation. But dispute panels are convened if necessary and there is an appeals process.

10-2i The Doha Development Agenda

The current round of WTO trade negotiations began in Doha in 2001. For years this round of negotiations stalled as agricultural issues, including market access, subsidies, and food security, caused deadlock in negotiations. One of the critical issues that continues to be negotiated is "Implementation," which refers to how developing countries can implement the current WTO agreements. Negotiations are also addressing how WTO rules apply to members that are parties to environmental agreements. The Doha Round insists on the centrality of developing countries and ensuring that they secure a share in world trade.

One of the successes of the Doha Development Agenda (DDA) is the Trade Facilitation Agreement, which was agreed to during the Bali Conference in December 2013. By cutting red tape and streamlining customs procedures in all WTO member countries, the agreement is expected to save trillions of dollars.

10-2j Regional Trade Agreements

The slow pace and numerous complex issues involved in multilateral negotiations often lead countries to seek regional or bilateral agreements. These initiatives co-exist with the multilateral system.

EU

The *European Economic Community* (EEC) was established in 1958 by the Treaty of Rome to remove trade and economic barriers between member countries and to unify their economic policies. It changed its name and became the *European Union* (EU) after the Treaty of Maastricht was ratified on November 1, 1993. The Treaty of Rome, containing the governing principles of this regional trading group, was signed by the original six nations of Belgium, France, West Germany, Italy, Luxembourg, and the Netherlands. Membership expanded with the entry of Denmark, Ireland, and Great Britain in 1973; Greece in 1981; Spain and Portugal in 1986; and Austria, Sweden, and Finland in 1995. Ten countries joined the EU in 2004: Cyprus, the Czech Republic, Estonia, Hungary, Latvia, Lithuania, Malta, Poland, Slovakia, and Slovenia. Bulgaria and Romania joined in 2007 and Croatia in 2013.

The Single European Act eliminated internal barriers to the free movement of goods, persons, services, and capital between EU countries. The Treaty on European Union, signed in Maastricht, Netherlands (the Maastricht Treaty), amended the Treaty of Rome with a focus on monetary and political union. It set goals for the EU of (1) single monetary and fiscal policies, (2) common foreign and security policies, and (3) cooperation in justice and home affairs. The EU acts as a single body for purposes of WTO negotiations.

NAFTA

The *North American Free Trade Agreement* (NAFTA) is an agreement between Mexico, Canada, and the United States, effective January 1, 1994, that included Mexico in the arrangements previously initiated under the United States–Canada Free Trade Agreement of 1989. NAFTA eliminated all tariffs among the three countries over a 15-year period. Side agreements exist to prevent the exploitation of Mexico's lower environmental and labor standards. Products are qualified for NAFTA tariff preferences only if they originate in one or more of the three member countries. Unlike the EU members, which function as one body for WTO purposes, each NAFTA member negotiates on its own behalf.

Other Regional Trade Agreements

In addition to the EU and NAFTA, there are numerous multilateral and bilateral trade agreements. The United States has free trade agreements with 20 countries.[13] It is currently negotiating the Trans-Pacific Partnership Agreement, which involves a regional Asia-Pacific trade agreement as well as the Transatlantic Trade and Investment Partnership with the European Union.

10-2k Antidumping, Subsidies and Safeguards

WTO agreements seek to ensure the free flow of goods and services through the principles of binding tariffs and most-favored-nation treatment among all trading partners. Nevertheless, countries inevitably run afoul of the rules. The WTO recognizes three circumstances in which the WTO rules must allow exceptions.

Antidumping Actions

dumping—selling goods in another country at less than fair value.

Selling goods in a foreign market at a price lower than normally charged in the home market is referred to as **dumping.** Many governments view dumping as a form of unfair competition and have laws that prohibit and punish dumping. The WTO's Anti-Dumping Agreement does not require but allows governments to take action against dumping. The agreement requires the government to show that the dumping is causing harm to a domestic industry. If there is in fact a dumping violation, the WTO allows the injured country to deviate from its bound tariff requirements and retaliate by charging extra import duties on the product that is being dumped.

In the United States, dumping of foreign goods is prohibited under the Tariff Act of 1930. Two federal agencies examine distinct components of dumping. The International Trade Administration (ITA) of the Department of Commerce investigates whether specified foreign goods are being sold in the United States at less than fair value (LTFV). The International Trade Commission (ITC) conducts proceedings to determine if there is an injury to a domestic industry as a result of such sales. There must be both LTFV sales and injury to a domestic industry before remedial action can be taken. Remedial action might include the addition of duties to reflect the difference between the fair value of the goods and the price being charged in the United States. Decisions of the ITA and ITC may be appealed to the Court of International Trade and, if necessary, to the U.S. Court of Appeals for the Federal Circuit and then to the U.S. Supreme Court.

---

[13] According to the United States Trade Representative, the United States has free trade agreements with the following countries: Australia, Bahrain, Canada, Chile, Colombia, Costa Rica, Dominican Republic, El Salvador, Guatemala, Honduras, Israel, Jordan, Korea, Mexico, Morocco, Nicaragua, Oman, Panama, Peru, and Singapore. **https://ustr.gov/ trade-agreements/free-trade-agreements**.

Subsidies and Countervailing Duties

Government subsidies for specific products or industries may also raise concerns about unfair competition. A subsidy may take various forms. A government may require the recipient of a subsidy to meet certain export targets or to use domestic goods instead of imported goods. These types of subsidies are prohibited by the WTO because they distort trade. WTO agreements allow a country to bring claims involving subsidies before the Dispute Settlement Body. If a prohibited subsidy is found, the country impacted may impose countervailing duties. **For Example,** the United States and the European Union imposed substantial tariffs on solar panels made in China because the products were subsidized by the government and may have violated antidumping laws as well.

Safeguards

A WTO member is allowed to temporarily restrict the import of a product that is injuring or threatening to cause "serious injury" to a domestic industry. The WTO has requirements for safeguard investigations to encourage transparency and avoid arbitrary methods.

In the United States, Title II of the Trade Act of 1974[14] provides for relief for U.S. industries, communities, firms, and workers when they are substantially adversely affected by import competition. The Department of Commerce, the Secretary of Labor, and the president have roles in determining eligibility. The relief provided may be temporary import relief through the imposition of a duty or quota on the foreign goods. Workers, if eligible, may obtain readjustment allowances, job training, job search allowances, or unemployment compensation.

Section 301 and Special 301

Although the United States is likely to settle most international trade disputes through the WTO, the Omnibus Trade and Competitiveness Act of 1988 gives the United States broad authority to retaliate against "unreasonable," "unjustifiable," or "discriminatory" acts by a foreign country.[15] The authority to retaliate is commonly referred to as "Section 301 authority." The fear or actuality of the economic sting of Section 301 retaliation often leads offending foreign countries to open their markets to imports. Thus, indirect relief is provided to domestic producers and exporters adversely affected by foreign unfair trade practices.

Enforcement of the act is entrusted to the U.S. Trade Representative (USTR), who is appointed by the president. Under the 1988 act, mandatory retaliatory action is required if the USTR determines that (1) rights of the United States under a trade agreement are being denied or (2) actions or policies of a foreign country are unjustifiable and burden or restrict U.S. commerce. The overall thrust of the trade provisions of the 1988 act is to open markets and liberalize trade.

Special 301 is a provision that pertains specifically to intellectual property rights. Each year the USTR prepares an annual report assessing how U.S. trading partners have protected the intellectual property rights of U.S. rights holders. Countries that have most seriously infringed the rights of U.S. rights holders may be listed on the Priority Watch List or the Watch List.

---

[14] P.L. 93-618, 88 Stat. 1978, 19 U.S.C. §§2251, 2298.
[15] P.L. 100-418, 102 Stat. 1346, 15 U.S.C. §4727.

10-3   Issues Confronting Companies Engaged in International Business

10-3a   Export Regulations

For reasons of national security, foreign policy, or short supply of domestic products, the United States controls the export of goods and technology. The Export Administration Act imposes export controls on goods and technical data from the United States. The Bureau of Industry and Security (BIS) of the Department of Commerce issues Export Administration Regulations to enforce export controls.

The BIS may impose criminal penalties and administrative sanctions for violations of Export Administration Regulations. When an exported item could be used to threaten national security, the BIS will take action. **For Example,** in 2013, Blue Coat Systems of Sunnyvale, California, supplied Internet control devices to Computerlinks. Computerlinks resold the devices to Syria, an embargoed country. Computerlinks paid a fine of $2.8 million. Blue Coat escaped liability because its contract with Computerlinks required Computerlinks to comply with all U.S. export laws in its Middle East resales.

10-3b   The Foreign Corrupt Practices Act

Congress passed the Foreign Corrupt Practices Act (FCPA) in 1977.[16] U.S. companies, including Lockheed, Northrop, Raytheon, GTE, and Exxon, testified before the Senate Foreign Relations Committee that bribery of foreign officials was rampant. The legislation, which prohibits U.S. companies from bribing foreign officials to obtain or retain business, raised concern that U.S. companies would lose business to countries that did not punish bribery of foreign officials. In 1999, the Organization for Economic Cooperation and Development, an intergovernmental organization, passed a convention that made bribery of a foreign public official illegal. To date, 41 countries have signed the convention.[17] Today, an increasing number of countries are bringing cases for bribery committed within their borders.

What the FCPA Prohibits and Requires

The FCPA prohibits bribing a foreign official to obtain or retain business with a foreign government. It covers issuers of U.S. securities; companies organized under U.S. laws; companies with U.S. headquarters; individuals who are citizens, nationals, or residents of the United States; and non-U.S. companies if they cause a bribe to take place in the United States. Foreign issuers who are listed on a U.S. exchange are issuers for purposes of the FCPA. The FCPA prohibits paying or offering a bribe or authorizing a bribe to a foreign government official, political party, party officials, and candidates for foreign political office. Under the FCPA, the definition of foreign official includes an "instrumentality" of a foreign government. Bribes to an instrumentality of a foreign government are illegal under the FCPA. **For Example,** a court recently held that a company may be an "instrumentality" of a foreign government if the government controls an entity. The court

---

[16] 15 U.S.C. §§78dd-1, *et seq.*

[17] The current members of the Anti-Bribery Convention are Argentina, Australia, Austria, Belgium, Brazil, Bulgaria, Canada, Chile, Colombia, Czech Republic, Denmark, Estonia, Finland, France, Germany, Greece, Hungary, Iceland, Ireland, Israel, Italy, Japan, Korea, Latvia, Luxembourg, Mexico, Netherlands, New Zealand, Norway, Poland, Portugal, Russia, Slovak Republic, Slovenia, South Africa, Spain, Sweden, Switzerland, Turkey, United Kingdom, and the United States.

found that Haiti Teleco was an instrumentality of the Haitian government because Haiti's national bank owns 97 percent of Haiti Teleco and the company's director and board members are appointed by the president of Haiti. Thus, bribes to Haiti Teleco employees violated the FCPA.[18]

The FCPA also requires that companies maintain accurate books, records, and accounts and have internal controls aimed at preventing and detecting FCPA violations.

There are some exceptions to the bribery provisions. The FCPA does not cover bribes that are legal pursuant to the written law of the foreign official's home state. Most countries, however, have laws prohibiting bribery. The FCPA exempts "facilitating payments" to government officials for routine or clerical governmental actions.

Enforcement

The FCPA is enforced jointly by the Department of Justice (DOJ) and the Securities and Exchange Commission (SEC). Although enforcement was slow initially, it has increased steadily over the last years. Fines have increased dramatically, with Siemens AG paying a fine of $800 million in 2008. In settlements, the government may require the company to hire a compliance monitor or to submit periodic assessment reports to demonstrate FCPA compliance. In recent years the SEC has increased its role in FCPA enforcement through administrative procedures.

If a company promptly reports violations of the FCPA and cooperates fully with the investigation, it may be treated with leniency. **For Example,** Ralph Lauren Corporation reported that its Argentine subsidiary bribed foreign officials in Argentina to avoid inspection of its products by customs officials. The SEC and DOJ required disgorgement of profits made in connection with the bribes as well as fines. Both the SEC and DOJ entered into nonprosecution agreements with Ralph Lauren Corporation because of its prompt reporting and extensive cooperation in the investigation.

The FCPA provides no private right of action. But shareholder derivative suits and civil RICO suits may be based on harm caused by foreign corruption.

10-3c Antitrust Issues

Increased International Criminalization and Cooperation

Antitrust laws are an important regulatory area for multinational companies. For many years, most countries did not criminalize antitrust conduct. In the last 20 years, countries have increasingly passed laws prohibiting cartel-like behavior. Cartel conduct is now criminal in more than 30 countries.[19] While the United States relies heavily on criminal laws, many countries impose only administrative or civil penalties. Nevertheless, as with international bribery cases, international cooperation had grown in curbing antitrust violations. Because many foreign countries did not have laws criminalizing antitrust action, the Department of Justice could not extradite foreign executives implicated in international bribery schemes. Recently, however, as foreign countries increasingly punish antitrust activity, they have been more willing to help with foreign prosecution or extradition. **For Example,** Romano Pisciotti was the oil and gas business manager for Parker ITR srl, an Italian manufacturer of marine hoses. The company, Parker ITR, pled guilty to

---

[18] *United States v. Esquenazi,* 752 F.3d 912 (11th Cir. 2014).

[19] Mayer-Brown, The Cartel Report, Commentary on Antitrust Enforcement from Around the World (Dec. 18, 2014), available at **http://www.mayerbrown.com/files/Publication/9660c732-514e-4287-9bfb-d6e48b7fdc25/Presentation/ PublicationAttachment/7c8826b6-55d8-46d5-9cb8-3c1441b04d32/UPDATE-Antitrust_Cartel_Report_1214.pdf.**

ETHICS & THE LAW

Combating Bribery of Foreign Public Officials in International Business Transactions

Prior to 1999, German law prohibited bribery of domestic public officials but did not prohibit bribery of foreign officials. Siemens AG, headquartered in Germany, is Europe's largest engineering conglomerate; it conducts business throughout the world. Employees were allowed to withdraw up to €1 million for bribes from three "cash desks" set up at Siemens's offices to facilitate the obtaining of government contracts throughout the world. Until 1999, Siemens claimed tax deductions for these bribes, many of which were listed as "useful expenditures."

The Organization for Economic Cooperation and Development (OECD) works on global issues, endeavoring to help member countries sustain economic growth and employment. The OECD adopted its Anti-Bribery Convention in 1997 and its regulations came into effect in 1999. The Anti-Bribery Convention has legally binding standards criminalizing the bribery of foreign public officials in international business transactions. Germany joined the convention in 1999. Nevertheless, between 2001 and 2004 some $67 million was withdrawn from the Siemens "cash desks." The bribery had continued! Mark Pieth, chairman of the working group on bribery at the OECD, said, "People felt confident that they were doing nothing wrong."* With some 470,000 employee jobs at Siemens depending on the ability to obtain engineering and high-tech contracts throughout the world, were Siemens contracting agents justified in continuing to make "useful expenditures" to save jobs and their company from ruin? How could these expenditures be a bad thing?

Siemens AG was subject to the FCPA because it was listed on the New York Stock Exchange in 2001. The bribery was first discovered by Munich law enforcement. After the Munich raid, Siemens cooperated with law enforcement agencies in both Germany and the United States. Subsidiaries of Siemens engaged in systematic bribery in countries throughout the world. The DOJ characterized the bribery as "unprecedented in scale and geographic reach," involving more than $1.4 billion in bribes to government officials in Asia, Africa, Europe, the Middle East, and the Americas.** On December 11, 2008, Siemens AG, pleaded guilty to criminal violations of the United States Foreign Corrupt Practices Act and received a criminal fine of $450 million. It also reached a settlement with the U.S. Securities and Exchange Commission for violation of the FCPA's antibribery, books and records, and internal control provisions and agreed to pay $350 million in disgorgement of profits. Moreover, it agreed to fines and disgorgement of profits of $569 million to settle an investigation by the Munich Public Prosecutor's Office. Siemens's bribery involved criminal acts that allowed the corporation to have an inherently unfair competitive advantage over other contract bidders. Antibribery laws such as the OECD Convention and the FCPA strive to ensure that public works projects are awarded on the basis of sound economic judgment rather than on the basis of who offers the biggest bribe. The notoriety of the Siemens prosecutions should send a strong and clear message to all trading partners that parties to the convention must not engage in bribery to obtain business deals.** Siemens's board member Peter Solmssen believes that it is a myth that firms have to pay bribes to do business in developing countries and believes that Siemens can increase sales without paying bribes.

In 2011, the SEC brought charges against seven former Siemens AG representatives. Two of the defendants settled with the SEC in 2013 and charges against two were dismissed. In 2014, the SEC resolved charges against the former CFO of Siemens Argentina, Andres Truppel. Truppel agreed to a civil penalty of $80,000. Default judgments were entered against two defendants who were heads of major projects for Siemens. Neither defendant appeared in the case. The court ordered disgorgement and penalties of nearly $1,000,000 and $500,000 against the defendants. The SEC stated that the penalties, the largest civil penalties assessed against individual defendants under the FCPA, reflected the "extensive and egregious nature of the violations and … their utter refusal to accept any responsibility for their actions."***

*"The Siemens Scandal: Bavarian Baksheesh," *The Economist,* **http://www.economist.com/business/displaystory.cfm?story_id=12814642.**
DOJ Press Release, *Siemens AG and Three Subsidiaries Plead Guilty to Foreign Corrupt Practices Act Violations* (Dec. 15, 2008), **http://www.usdoj.gov.
***SEC v. Sharef, C.A. No 11-CIV-09073 (S.D.N.Y. 2014).

charges of participating in a global price-fixing conspiracy in 2010. Pisciotti, who resided in Italy, could not be extradited to the United States because his conduct was not criminal under Italian law. But he was arrested by German authorities in Frankfurt while waiting for a connecting flight from Nigeria to Italy. In 2014, Pisciotti entered into a plea

effects doctrine–
doctrine stating that U.S. courts will assume jurisdiction and will apply antitrust laws to conduct outside of the United States when the activity of business firms has a direct and substantial effect on U.S. commerce; the rule has been modified to require that the effect on U.S. commerce also be direct and foreseeable.

Foreign Trade Antitrust Improvements Act–the act that requires that the defendant's conduct have a "direct, substantial, and reasonably foreseeable effect" on domestic commerce.

jurisdictional rule of reason–rule that balances the vital interests, including laws and policies, of the United States with those of a foreign country.

comity–principle of international and national law that the laws of all nations and states deserve the respect legitimately demanded by equal participants.

act-of-state doctrine–doctrine whereby every sovereign state is bound to respect the independence of every other sovereign state, and the courts of one country will not sit in judgment of another government's acts done within its own territory.

agreement with the U.S. Department of Justice, agreeing to serve two years in prison and to pay a $50,000 fine.[20]

Jurisdiction

The U.S. antitrust laws have a broad extraterritorial reach. Our antitrust laws must be reconciled with the rights of other interested countries as embodied in international law.

The Effects Doctrine and the FTAIA. Judge Learned Hand's decision in *United States v. Alcoa* established the **effects doctrine**.[21] Under this doctrine, U.S. courts assume jurisdiction and apply the antitrust laws to conduct outside of the United States where the activity of the business firms has a direct and substantial effect on U.S. commerce. In 1982, Congress passed the **Foreign Trade Antitrust Improvements Act** (FTAIA),[22] to provide clarity on the extraterritorial reach of the Sherman Act. The FTAIA requires that the defendant's conduct have a "direct, substantial, and reasonably foreseeable effect" on domestic commerce. **For Example,** in a trial to determine whether the Sherman Act reached a price-fixing scheme between Taiwanese and Korean manufacturers of LCD panels, the defendants conceded that the conduct was substantial and had a reasonably foreseeable effect on United States commerce but maintained that the overseas conduct was not sufficiently "direct" under the FTAIA. In concluding that there was a direct effect, the court noted that the LCD panels were a substantial cost component of the finished product; that some panels were sold directly into the United States; that some were sold to subsidiaries of American companies and then incorporated into finished products; that the finished products were destined for the United States; and that the practical upshot of the conspiracy was increased prices to customers in the United States. The Department of Justice obtained a $500 million fine against the company and three-year sentences for its former president and vice president.[23]

The Jurisdictional Rule of Reason. The jurisdictional rule of reason applies when conduct taking place outside the United States affects U.S. commerce but a foreign state also has a significant interest in regulating the conduct in question. The **jurisdictional rule of reason** balances the vital interests, including laws and policies, of the United States with those of the foreign country involved. This rule of reason is based on **comity,** a principle of international law, that means that the laws of all nations deserve the respect legitimately demanded by equal participants in international affairs.

Defenses

Three defenses are commonly raised to the extraterritorial application of U.S. antitrust laws. These defenses are also commonly raised to attack jurisdiction in other legal actions involving international law.

Act-of-State Doctrine. By the **act-of-state doctrine,** every sovereign state is bound to respect the independence of every other sovereign state, and the courts of one country will not sit in judgment of another government's acts done within its own territory.[24] The act-of-state doctrine is based on the judiciary's concern over its possible interference with the conduct of foreign relations. Such matters are considered to be political, not judicial, questions.

---

[20] See *United States v. Pisciotti, Plea Agreement,* available at **http://www.justice.gov/atr/cases/f305500/305542.pdf**.
[21] 148 F.2d 416 (2d Cir. 1945).
[22] 15 U.S.C. 6a.
[23] See *United States v. Hui Hsiung,* 778 F.3d 738 (9th Cir. 2015).
[24] *Underhill v. Hernandez,* 108 U.S. 250, 252 (1897).

sovereign compliance doctrine–doctrine that allows a defendant to raise as an affirmative defense to an antitrust action the fact that the defendant's actions were compelled by a foreign state.

sovereign immunity doctrine–a doctrine that states that a foreign sovereign generally cannot be sued without its consent.

The Sovereign Compliance Doctrine. The **sovereign compliance doctrine** allows a defendant to raise as an affirmative defense to an antitrust action the fact that the defendant's actions were compelled by a foreign state. To establish this defense, compulsion by the foreign government is required. The Japanese government uses informal and formal contacts within an industry to establish a consensus on a desired course of action. Such governmental action is not a defense for a U.S. firm, however, because the activity in question is not compulsory.

The Sovereign Immunity Doctrine. The **sovereign immunity doctrine** states that a foreign sovereign generally cannot be sued unless an exception to the Foreign Sovereign Immunities Act of 1976 applies.[25] The most important exception covers the commercial conduct of a foreign state.[26]

10-3d Securities Fraud Regulation in an International Environment

Illegal conduct in the U.S. securities markets, whether initiated in the United States or abroad, threatens the vital economic interests of the United States. Investigation and litigation concerning possible violations of the U.S. securities laws often have an extraterritorial effect. Conflicts with the laws of foreign countries may occur.

Jurisdiction

U.S. district courts have jurisdiction over violations of the antifraud provisions of the Securities Exchange Act of 1934 when losses occur from sales to Americans living in the United States.[27] U.S. district courts also have jurisdiction when losses occur to Americans living abroad if the acts occurred in the United States. The antifraud provisions do not apply, however, to losses from sales of securities to foreigners outside the United States unless acts within the United States caused the losses.[28]

CASE SUMMARY

Extraterritorial Effect of United States Securities Law

FACTS: A federal jury convicted George Georgiou of conspiracy, securities fraud, and wire fraud for his participation in planned manipulation of the markets of four publicly traded stocks, resulting in more than $55,000,000 in actual losses. The district court sentenced him to 300 months' imprisonment, ordered him to pay restitution of $55,823,398 and also subjected him to forfeiture of $26,000,000. The four target stocks were quoted on the OTC Bulletin Board (OTCBB) or the Pink OTC Markets Inc. (Pink Sheets), which are not considered national securities exchanges. Georgiou and his co-conspirators opened brokerage accounts in Canada, the Bahamas, and Turks and Caicos. They artificially inflated the stock prices and created the false impression that there was an active market in the target stocks. In June 2006, one of Georgiou's co-conspirators began cooperating in an FBI sting. The FBI found that at least some of the manipulated trades were transacted through market makers in the United States. Georgiou maintained that his convictions were improperly based on the extraterritorial application of United States law.

---

[25] See *Verlinden B.V. v. Central Bank of Nigeria*, 461 U.S. 574 (1983).

[26] See *Dole Food Co. v. Patrickson*, 538 U.S. 468 (2003) for a limited discussion of when a foreign state can assert a defense of sovereign immunity under the Foreign Sovereign Immunities Act of 1976 (FSIA). The FSIA allows certain foreign-state commercial entities not entitled to sovereign immunity to have the merits of a case heard in federal court. The U.S. Supreme Court held in the *Dole Food* case that a foreign state must itself own a majority of the shares of a corporation if the corporation is to be deemed an instrumentality of the state under the FSIA, and the instrumentality status is determined at the time of the filing of the complaint.

[27] *Kauthar Sdn. Bhd. v. Sternberg*, 149 F.3d 659 (7th Cir. 1998).

[28] *Morrison v. National Australia Bank Ltd.*, 561 U.S. 247 (2010).

Extraterritorial Effect of United States Securities Law continued

DECISION: Judgment of Conviction Affirmed. Several of the purchases were executed by market makers operating within the United States and the stocks involved were stocks in U.S. companies. The transactions were domestic transactions because it is the place where the purchase and sale of securities occurred, not the place where the deception originated that matters. [***United States v. Georgiou***, 777 **F.3d 125 (3rd Cir. 2015)**]

secrecy laws– confidentiality laws applied to home-country banks.

blocking laws–laws that prohibit the disclosure, copying, inspection, or removal of documents located in the enacting country in compliance with orders from foreign authorities.

Impact of Foreign Secrecy Laws in SEC Enforcement

Secrecy laws are confidentiality laws applied to home-country banks. These laws prohibit the disclosure of business records or the identity of bank customers. **Blocking laws** prohibit the disclosure, copying, inspection, or removal of documents located in the enacting country in compliance with orders from foreign authorities. These laws impede, and sometimes foreclose, the SEC's ability to police its securities markets properly.

Make the Connection

Summary

U.S. firms choose to do business abroad by making export sales or contracting with a foreign distributor to take title to their goods and sell them abroad. U.S. firms may also license their technology or trademarks for foreign use. An agency arrangement or the organization of a foreign subsidiary may be required to participate effectively in foreign markets. This choice results in subjecting the U.S. firm to taxation in the host country. However, tax treaties commonly eliminate double taxation.

When contracting internationally, firms should select where they want any disputes to be resolved and which law should apply. The CISG is an international treaty that may be used instead of national law.

The World Trade Organization administers several international treaties involving trade in goods, services, and intellectual property. All WTO agreements require the 160 member nations to abide by the principles of non-discrimination and national treatment. Through rounds of negotiations, WTO members aim to reduce tariffs to liberalize world trade. The WTO also seeks to resolve issues involving dumping and government subsidies through consultation or through its Dispute Settlement Body.

Multinational corporations face numerous issues including export restrictions, antitrust laws, bribery laws, and securities laws. In some cases, U.S. law will protect or restrict the behavior of a foreign corporation. The extraterritorial reach of U.S. laws has been controversial. If Congress does not specify otherwise, the presumption is that U.S. laws do not have an extraterritorial reach. The Foreign Corrupt Practices Act prohibits the bribing of a foreign official by U.S. companies or their agents to obtain or retain business. Increasingly, other countries are criminalizing cartel activity and cooperating with U.S. authorities. U.S. securities laws do not have extraterritorial effect but courts may find that the laws do apply if the parties committed to the fraudulent activity in the United States. Antitrust laws may also have extraterritorial reach if the activity had a direct, substantial, and reasonably foreseeable effect on commerce in the United States.

Learning Outcomes

After studying this chapter, you should be able to clearly explain:

10-1 Conducting Business Internationally

LO.1 List the methods of doing business abroad

See the discussion of export sales, appointing of an agent, foreign distributorships, licensing, and subsidiaries, pages 182–183.

LO.2 Explain which country's law will govern an international contract should a dispute arise

See the discussion regarding national law, the CISG, and arbitration, pages 183–184.

See the choice of law example where the U.S. courts required the Lipcons to "honor their bargains" and vindicate their claims in an English court, page 183.

10-2 International Trade

LO.3 Explain tariff barriers and nontariff barriers to the free movement of goods across borders

See the example involving the U.S. embargo on all Brazilian shrimp because of Brazil's failure to require turtle excluder devices on its shrimp boats, page 186.

LO.4 Identify the agreements administered by the World Trade Organization

See the discussion involving the GATT, GATS, and TRIPS, pages 186–187.

LO.5 Explain how to register and protect trademarks abroad

See the discussion on the Madrid System, the European Community Trademark, and the importance of first to file regulations, page 187.

See the *Cubatabaco* case, page 188.

LO.6 Explain how trade disputes are resolved

See the discussion on the Dispute Settlement Body, page 191.

LO.7 Explain how antidumping duties and countervailing duties operate under the WTO agreements

See the discussion under the section titled "Antidumping, Subsidies and Safeguards," pages 192–193.

10-3 Issues Confronting Companies Engaged in International Business

LO.8 Explain U.S. law regarding payment to foreign government officials

See the Ethics & Law discussion regarding Siemens AG, page 196.

LO.9 Explain how U.S. securities laws might apply to foreign transactions

See the *Georgiou* case, pages 200–201.

Key Terms

act-of-state doctrine	effects doctrine	most-favored-nation
agent	export sale	national treatment
blocking laws	Foreign Trade Antitrust	principal
choice-of-law clause	Improvements Act	secrecy laws
comity	franchising	sovereign compliance doctrine
Dispute Settlement Body (DSB)	jurisdictional rule of reason	sovereign immunity doctrine
distributor	letter of credit	tariff
dumping	licensing	well-known mark

Questions and Case Problems

1. How does the selling of subsidized foreign goods in the United States adversely affect free trade?

2. Able Time Inc. imported a shipment of watches into the United States. The watches bore the mark "TOMMY," which is a registered trademark owned by Tommy Hilfiger. U.S. Customs seized the watches pursuant to the Tariff Act, which authorizes seizure of any "merchandise bearing a counterfeit mark." Tommy Hilfiger did not make or sell watches at the time of the seizure. Able argued that because Tommy Hilfiger did not make watches at the time of the seizure, the watches it imported were not counterfeit, and the civil penalty imposed by Customs was unlawful. The government argued that the mark was counterfeit and that the Tariff Act does not require the owner of the registered mark to make the

same type of goods as those bearing the offending mark. Decide. [*U.S. v. Able Time, Inc.*, 545 F.3d 824 (9th Cir.)]

3. Ronald Sadler, a California resident, owned a helicopter distribution company in West Germany, Delta Avia. This company distributed U.S.-made Hughes civilian helicopters in western Europe. Sadler's German firm purchased 85 helicopters from Hughes Aircraft Co. After export licenses were obtained in reliance on the purchaser's written assurance that the goods would not be disposed of contrary to the export license, the helicopters were exported to Germany for resale in western Europe. Thereafter, Delta Avia exported them to North Korea, which was a country subject to a trade embargo by the United States. The helicopters were converted to military use. Sadler was charged with violating the Export Administration Regulations. In Sadler's defense, it was contended that the U.S. regulations have no effect on what occurs in the resale of civilian helicopters in another sovereign country. Decide.

4. Mirage Investments Corp. (MIC) planned a tender offer for the shares of Gulf States International Corp. (GSIC). Archer, an officer of MIC, placed purchase orders for GSIC stock through the New York office of the Bahamian Bank (BB) prior to the announcement of the tender offer, making a $300,000 profit when the tender offer was made public. The Bahamas is a secrecy jurisdiction. The bank informed the SEC that under its law, it could not disclose the name of the person for whom it purchased the stock. What, if anything, may the SEC do to discover whether the federal securities laws have been violated?

5. United Overseas, Ltd. (UOL), is a U.K. firm that purchases and sells manufacturers' closeouts in Europe and the Middle East. UOL's representative, Jay Knox, used stationery listing a UOL office in New York to solicit business from Revlon, Inc., in New York. On April 1, 1992, UOL faxed a purchase order from its headquarters in England to Revlon's New York offices for the purchase of $4 million worth of shampoo. The purchase order on its face listed six conditions, none of which referred to a forum selection clause. When Revlon was not paid for the shampoo it shipped, it sued UOL in New York for breach of contract. UOL moved to dismiss the complaint because of a forum selection clause, which it stated was on the reverse side of the purchase order and provided that "the parties hereby agree to submit to the jurisdiction of the English Courts disputes arising out of the contract." The evidence did not show that the reverse side of the purchase order had been faxed with the April 1992 order. Should the court dismiss the complaint based on the "forum selection clause"? Read Chapter 31 on letters of credit and advise Revlon how to avoid similar litigation in the future. [*Revlon, Inc. v. United Overseas, Ltd.*, 1994 WL 9657 (S.D.N.Y)]

6. Reebok manufactures and sells fashionable athletic shoes in the United States and abroad. It owns the federally registered Reebok trademark and has registered this trademark in Mexico as well. Nathan Betech is a Mexican citizen residing in San Diego, California, with business offices there. Reebok believed that Betech was in the business of selling counterfeit Reebok shoes in Mexican border towns, such as Tijuana, Mexico. It sought an injunction in a federal district court in California ordering Betech to cease his counterfeiting activity and to refrain from destroying certain documents. It also asked the court to freeze Betech's assets pending the outcome of a Lanham Act lawsuit. Betech contended that a U.S. district court has no jurisdiction or authority to enter the injunction for the activities allegedly occurring in Mexico. Decide. [*Reebok Int'l, Ltd. v. Marnatech Enterprises, Inc.*, 970 F.2d 552 (9th Cir.)]

7. A complaint was filed with the U.S. Commerce Department's ITA by U.S. telephone manufacturers AT&T, Comidial Corp., and Eagle Telephones, Inc., alleging that 12 Asian manufacturers of small business telephones, including the Japanese firms Hitachi, NEC, and Toshiba and the Taiwanese firm Sun Moon Star Corp. were dumping their small business phones in the U.S. market at prices that were from 6 percent to 283 percent less than those in their home markets. The U.S. manufacturers showed that the domestic industry's market share had dropped from 54 percent in 1985 to 33 percent in 1989. They asserted that it was doubtful if the domestic industry could survive the dumping. Later, in a hearing before the ITC, the Japanese and Taiwanese respondents contended that their domestic industry was basically sound and that the U.S. firms simply had to become more efficient to meet worldwide competition. They contended that the United States was using the procedures before the ITA and ITC as a nontariff barrier to imports. How should the ITC decide the case? [*American Telephone and Telegraph Co. v. Hitachi*, 6 I.T.C. 1511]

8. Roland Staemphfli was employed as the chief financial officer of Honeywell Bull, S.A. (HB), a Swiss computer company operating exclusively in Switzerland. Staemphfli purportedly arranged financing for HB in Switzerland through the issuance of promissory notes. He had the assistance of Fidenas, a Bahamian company dealing in commercial paper. Unknown to Fidenas, the HB notes were fraudulent. The notes were prepared and forged by Staemphfli, who lost all of the proceeds in a speculative investment and was convicted of criminal fraud. HB denied responsibility for the fraudulently issued notes when they came due. Fidenas's business deteriorated because of its involvement with the HB notes. It sued HB and others in the United States for violations of U.S. securities laws. HB defended, arguing that the U.S. court did not have jurisdiction over the transactions in question. Decide. [*Fidenas v. Honeywell Bull, S.A.*, 606 F.2d 5 (2d Cir.)]

9. Marc Rich & Co., A.G., a Swiss commodities trading corporation, refused to comply with a grand jury subpoena requesting certain business records maintained in Switzerland and relating to crude oil transactions and possible violations of U.S. income tax laws. Marc Rich contended that a U.S. court has no authority to require a foreign corporation to deliver to a U.S. court documents located abroad. The court disagreed and imposed fines, froze assets, and threatened to close a Marc Rich wholly owned subsidiary that did business in the state of New York. The fines amounted to $50,000 for each day the company failed to comply with the court's order. Marc Rich appealed. Decide. [*Marc Rich v. United States*, 707 U.S. 633 (2d Cir.)]

10. U.S. Steel Corp. formed Orinoco Mining Co., a wholly owned corporation, to mine large deposits of iron ore that U.S. Steel had discovered in Venezuela. Orinoco, which was incorporated in Delaware, was subject to Venezuela's maximum tax of 50 percent on net income. Orinoco was also subject to U.S. income tax, but the U.S. foreign tax credit offset this amount. U.S. Steel purchased the ore from Orinoco in Venezuela. U.S. Steel formed Navios, Inc., a wholly owned subsidiary, to transport the ore. Navios, a Liberian corporation, was subject to a 2.5 percent Venezuelan excise tax and was exempt from U.S. income tax. Although U.S. Steel was Navios's primary customer, it charged other customers the same price it charged U.S. Steel. U.S. Steel's investment in Navios was $50,000. In seven years, Navios accumulated nearly $80 million in cash but had not paid any dividends to U.S. Steel. The IRS used IRC §482 to allocate $52 million of Navios's income to U.S. Steel. U.S. Steel challenged this action, contending that Navios's charges to U.S. Steel were at arm's length and the same it charged other customers. Decide. [*United States Steel Corp. v. Commissioner*, 617 F.2d 942 (2d Cir.)]

11. National Computers, Inc., a U.S. firm, entered into a joint venture with a Chinese computer manufacturing organization, TEC. A dispute arose over payments due the U.S. firm under the joint venture agreement with TEC. The agreement called for disputes to be arbitrated in China, with the arbitrator being chosen from a panel of arbitrators maintained by the Beijing arbitration institution, Cietac. What advantages and disadvantages exist for the U.S. firm under this arbitration arrangement? Advise the U.S. firm on negotiating future arbitration agreements with Chinese businesses.

12. Sensor, a Netherlands business organization wholly owned by Geosource, Inc., of Houston, Texas, made a contract with C.E.P. to deliver 2,400 strings of geophones to Rotterdam by September 20, 1982. The ultimate destination was identified as the USSR. Thereafter, in June 1982, the president of the United States prohibited shipment to the USSR of equipment manufactured in foreign countries under license from U.S. firms. The president had a foreign policy objective of retaliating for the imposition of martial law in Poland, and he was acting under regulations issued under the Export Administration Act of 1979. Sensor, in July and August 1982, notified C.E.P. that as a subsidiary of a U.S. corporation, it had to respect the president's embargo. C.E.P. filed suit in a district court of the Netherlands asking that Sensor be ordered to deliver the geophones. Decide. [*Compagnie Européenne des Pétroles v. Sensor Nederland*, 22 I.L.M. 66]

Contracts

C H A P T E R   11

Nature and Classes of Contracts: Contracting on the Internet

Learning Outcomes ⟨⟨⟨

After studying this chapter, you should be able to

LO.1 Explain the meaning and importance of privity of a contract

LO.2 Describe the way in which a contract arises

LO.3 Distinguish between bilateral and unilateral contracts

LO.4 Explain the reasoning behind quasi-contract recovery

LO.5 Explain how Internet contracts involve the same types of issues as offline contracts

Practically every business transaction affecting people involves a contract.

11-1   Nature of Contracts

This introductory chapter will familiarize you with the terminology needed to work with contract law. In addition, the chapter introduces quasi contracts, which are not true contracts but obligations imposed by law.

11-1a   Definition of a Contract

contract–a binding agreement based on the genuine assent of the parties, made for a lawful object, between competent parties, in the form required by law, and generally supported by consideration.

A **contract** is a legally binding agreement.[1] By one definition, "a contract is a promise or a set of promises for the breach of which the law gives a remedy, or the performance of which the law in some way recognizes as a duty."[2] Contracts arise out of agreements, so a contract may be defined as an agreement creating an obligation.

The substance of the definition of a contract is that by mutual agreement or assent, the parties create enforceable duties or obligations. That is, each party is legally bound to do or to refrain from doing certain acts.

11-1b   Elements of a Contract

The elements of a contract are (1) an agreement (2) between competent parties (3) based on the genuine assent of the parties that is (4) supported by consideration, (5) made for a lawful objective, and (6) in the form required by law, if any. These elements will be considered in the chapters that follow.

11-1c   Subject Matter of Contracts

The subject matter of a contract may relate to the performance of personal services, such as contracts of employment to work developing computer software or to play professional football. A contract may provide for the transfer of ownership of property, such as a house (real property) or an automobile (personal property), from one person to another.

11-1d   Parties to a Contract

promisor–person who makes a promise.

promisee–person to whom a promise is made.

obligor–promisor.

obligee–promisee who can claim the benefit of the obligation.

privity–succession or chain of relationship to the same thing or right, such as privity of contract, privity of estate, privity of possession.

privity of contract–relationship between a promisor and the promisee.

The person who makes a promise is the **promisor,** and the person to whom the promise is made is the **promisee.** If the promise is binding, it imposes on the promisor a duty or obligation, and the promisor may be called the **obligor.** The promisee who can claim the benefit of the obligation is called the **obligee.** The parties to a contract are said to stand in **privity** with each other, and the relationship between them is termed **privity of contract. For Example,** when the state of North Carolina and the architectural firm of O'Brien/Atkins Associates executed a contract for the construction of a new building at the University of North Carolina, Chapel Hill, these parties were in privity of contract. However, a building contractor, RPR & Associates, who worked on the project did not have standing to sue on the contract between the architect and the state because the contractor was not in privity of contract.[3]

---

[1] The Uniform Commercial Code defines *contract* as "the total legal obligation which results from the parties' agreement as affected by [the UCC] and any other applicable rules of law." U.C.C. §1–201(11).

[2] Restatement (Second) of Contracts §1.

[3] *RPR & Associates v. O'Brien/Atkins Associates, PA*, 24 F. Supp. 2d 515 (M.D.N.C. 1998). See also *Roof Techs Int Inc. v. State*, 57 P.3d 538 (Kan. App. 2002), where a layer of litigation was avoided regarding lawsuits involving the renovation of the Farrell Library at Kansas State University. The state was the only party in privity of contract with the architectural firm and would thus have to bring claims against the architectural firm on behalf of all of the contractors. Two subcontractors, the general contractor, and the owner of the library, the state of Kansas, used a settlement and liquidation agreement assigning all of the state's claims against the architect to the general contractor.

In written contracts, parties may be referred to by name. More often, however, they are given special names that better identify each party. For example, consider a contract by which one person agrees that another may occupy a house upon the payment of money. The parties to this contract are called *landlord* and *tenant*, or *lessor* and *lessee*, and the contract between them is known as a *lease*. Parties to other types of contracts also have distinctive names, such as *vendor* and *vendee* for the parties to a sales contract, *shipper* and *carrier* for the parties to a transportation contract, and *insurer* and *insured* for the parties to an insurance policy.

A party to a contract may be an individual, a partnership, a limited liability company, a corporation, or a government.[4] One or more persons may be on each side of a contract. Some contracts are three-sided, as in a credit card transaction, which involves the company issuing the card, the holder of the card, and the business furnishing goods and services on the basis of the credit card.

If a contract is written, the persons who are the parties and who are bound by it can ordinarily be determined by reading what the document says and seeing how it is signed. A contract binds only the parties to the contract. It cannot impose a duty on a person who is not a party to it. Ordinarily, only a party to a contract has any rights against another party to the contract.[5] In some cases, third persons have rights on a contract as third-party beneficiaries or assignees. A person cannot be bound, however, by the terms of a contract to which that person is not a party. **For Example,** in approximately 1995 Jeff and Mark Bass signed Marshall B. Mathers III, better known as rapper Eminem, to an exclusive record deal with FBT Productions LLC (FBT), their production company. In 2000 Aftermath Records entered into a direct contractual relationship with Eminem, transferring Eminem's recording services from FBT directly to Aftermath. Under the contract FBT became a "passive income participant," retaining a right to royalty income from Eminem's recordings. A dispute occurred regarding percentages of royalties due. Aftermath entered into an agreement with Eminem in 2009, setting the royalties for Eminem's *Recovery* and *Relapse* albums, asserting that all royalties, including royalties owed FBT were dictated by this 2009 agreement. FBT was not a party to the 2009 agreement and as such cannot be bound by it. A contract cannot bind a nonparty. Therefore, Aftermath was required to pay FBT royalties for the two albums at a higher rate in accordance with an earlier agreement.[6]

CPA

offeror–person who makes an offer.

offeree–person to whom an offer is made.

11-1e **How a Contract Arises**

A contract is based on an agreement. An agreement arises when one person, the **offeror,** makes an offer and the person to whom the offer is made, the **offeree,** accepts. There must be both an offer and an acceptance. If either is lacking, there is no contract.

11-1f **Intent to Make a Binding Agreement**

Because a contract is based on the consent of the parties and is a legally binding agreement, it follows that the parties must have an intent to enter into an agreement that is binding. Sometimes the parties are in agreement, but their agreement does not produce a contract. Sometimes there is merely a preliminary agreement, but the parties never actually make a contract, or there is merely an agreement as to future plans or intentions without any contractual obligation to carry out those plans or intentions.

---

[4] See *Purina Mills, LLC v. Less*, 295 F. Supp. 2d 1017 (N.D. Iowa 2003) in which the pig-seller plaintiff, which converted from a corporation to a limited liability company (LLC) while the contract was in effect, was a proper party in interest and could maintain a contract action against defendant buyers.

[5] *Hooper v. Yakima County*, 904 P.2d 1193 (Wash. App. 1995).

[6] *F.B.T. Productions, LLC v. Aftermath Records*, 2011 WL 5174766 (C.D. Cal. Oct. 31, 2011).

11-1g Freedom of Contract

In the absence of some ground for declaring a contract void or voidable, parties may make such contracts as they choose. The law does not require parties to be fair, or kind, or reasonable, or to share gains or losses equitably.

11-2 Classes of Contracts

formal contracts–written contracts or agreements whose formality signifies the parties' intention to abide by the terms.

Contracts may be classified according to their form, the way in which they were created, their binding character, and the extent to which they have been performed.

CPA

11-2a Formal and Informal Contracts

Contracts can be classified as formal or informal.

contract under seal– contract executed by affixing a seal or making an impression on the paper or on some adhering substance such as wax attached to the document.

Formal Contracts

Formal contracts are enforced because the formality with which they are executed is considered sufficient to signify that the parties intend to be bound by their terms. Formal contracts include (1) **contracts under seal** where a person's signature or a corporation's name is followed by a scroll, the word *seal*, or the letters *L.S.*;[7] (2) contracts of record, which are obligations that have been entered before a court of record, sometimes called a **recognizance;** and (3) negotiable instruments.

recognizance–obligation entered into before a court to do some act, such as to appear at a later date for a hearing. Also called a *contract of record.*

Informal Contracts

All contracts other than formal contracts are called **informal** (or simple) **contracts** without regard to whether they are oral or written. These contracts are enforceable, not because of the form of the transaction but because they represent agreement of the parties.

informal contract– simple oral or written contract.

11-2b Express and Implied Contracts

Simple contracts may be classified as *express contracts* or *implied contracts* according to the way they are created.

Express Contracts

express contract– agreement of the parties manifested by their words, whether spoken or written.

An **express contract** is one in which the terms of the agreement of the parties are manifested by their words, whether spoken or written.

Implied Contracts

implied contract– contract expressed by conduct or implied or deduced from the facts.

An **implied contract** (or, as sometimes stated, a *contract implied in fact*) is one in which the agreement is shown not by words, written or spoken, but by the acts and conduct of the parties.[8] Such a contract arises when (1) a person renders services under circumstances indicating that payment for them is expected and (2) the other person, knowing such circumstances, accepts the benefit of those services. **For Example,** when a building owner requests a professional roofer to make emergency repairs to the roof of a building, an obligation arises to pay the reasonable value of such services, although no agreement has been made about compensation.

---

[7] Some authorities explain L.S. as an abbreviation for *locus sigilium* (place for the seal).
[8] *Lindquist Ford, Inc. v. Middleton Motors, Inc.,* 557 F.3d 469, 481 (7th Cir. 2009). See also *Dynegy Marketing and Trade v. Multiut Corp.,* 648 F.3d 506 (7th Cir. 2011).

An implied contract cannot arise when there is an existing express contract on the same subject.[9] However, the existence of a written contract does not bar recovery on an implied contract for extra work that was not covered by the contract.

To prevail on a cause of action for breach of an implied-in-fact contract based on an idea submission, plaintiffs must show (1) they conditioned the submission of their ideas on an obligation to pay for any use of the ideas; (2) the defendants voluntarily accepted the submission of ideas; and (3) the defendants actually used these ideas, rather than their own ideas with other sources. In an idea submission case where similarities exist, it is a complete defense for the defendants to show that they independently created their product. **For Example,** in 1977, Anthony Spinner a highly regarded television producer and writer, submitted drafts of his script entitled "Lost" to ABC. ABC decided to pass on the proposal for it would be too expensive to produce. In 2004, ABC premiered a pilot for LOST in September, and the series ran for six years. Spinner's subsequent implied-in-fact idea submission lawsuit was unsuccessful because ABC demonstrated that the script for the LOST series was created independently.[10]

CPA

11-2c Valid and Voidable Contracts and Void Agreements

Contracts may be classified in terms of enforceability or validity.

Valid Contracts

A **valid contract** is an agreement that is binding and enforceable.

Voidable Contracts

A **voidable contract** is an agreement that is otherwise binding and enforceable, but because of the circumstances surrounding its execution or the lack of capacity of one of the parties, it may be rejected at the option of one of the parties. **For Example,** a person who has been forced to sign an agreement that that person would not have voluntarily signed may, in some instances, avoid the contract.

valid contract—
agreement that is binding and enforceable.

voidable contract—
agreement that is otherwise binding and enforceable but may be rejected at the option of one of the parties as the result of specific circumstances.

FIGURE 11-1	Contractual Liability

---

[9] *Pepsi-Cola Bottling Co. of Pittsburgh, Inc., v. PepsiCo, Inc.*, 431 F.3d 1241 (10th Cir. 2000).
[10] *Spinner v. American Broadcasting Companies, Inc.*, 155 Cal. Rptr. 3d 32 (Cal. App. 2013).

Void Agreements

void agreement—
agreement that cannot be enforced.

A **void agreement** is without legal effect. An agreement that contemplates the performance of an act prohibited by law is usually incapable of enforcement; hence it is void. Likewise, it cannot be made binding by later approval or ratification.

11-2d Executed and Executory Contracts

Contracts may be classified as *executed contracts* and *executory contracts* according to the extent to which they have been performed.

Executed Contracts

executed contract—
agreement that has been completely performed.

An **executed contract** is one that has been completely performed. In other words, an executed contract is one under which nothing remains to be done by either party.[11] A contract may be executed immediately, as in the case of a cash sale, or it may be executed or performed in the future.

Executory Contracts

executory contract—
agreement by which something remains to be done by one or both parties.

In an **executory contract,** something remains to be done by one or both parties.[12] **For Example,** on July 10, Mark agreed to sell to Chris his Pearl drum set for $600, the terms being $200 upon delivery on July 14, with $200 to be paid on July 21, and the final $200 being due July 28. Prior to the July 14 delivery of the drums to Chris, the contract was entirely executory. After the delivery by Mark, the contract was executed as to Mark and executory as to Chris until the final payment was received on July 28.

11-2e Bilateral and Unilateral Contracts

In making an offer, the offeror is in effect extending a promise to do something, such as pay a sum of money, if the offeree will do what the offeror requests. Contracts are classified as *bilateral* or *unilateral*. Some bilateral contracts look ahead to the making of a later contract. Depending on their terms, these are called *option contracts* or *first-refusal contracts*.

C P A

Bilateral Contracts

bilateral contract—
agreement under which one promise is given in exchange for another.

If the offeror extends a promise and asks for a promise in return and if the offeree accepts the offer by making the promise, the contract is called a **bilateral contract.** One promise is given in exchange for another, and each party is bound by the obligation. **For Example,** when the house painter offers to paint the owner's house for $3,700 and the owner promises to pay $3,700 for the job, there is an exchange of promises, and the agreement gives rise to a bilateral contract.

Unilateral Contracts

unilateral contract—
contract under which only one party makes a promise.

In contrast with a bilateral contract, the offeror may promise to do something or to pay a certain amount of money only when the offeree does an act.[13] Examples of where **unilateral contracts** commonly appear are when a reward is offered, a contest is announced, or changes are made and disseminated in an employee manual. The offeree does not accept the offer by express agreement, but rather by performance.

---

[11] *Marsh v. Rheinecker*, 641 N.E.2d 1256 (Ill. App. 1994).
[12] *DiGennaro v. Rubbermaid, Inc.*, 214 F. Supp. 2d 1354 (S.D. Fla. 2002).
[13] See *Young v. Virginia Birth-Related Neurological Injury Compensation Program*, 620 S.E.2d 131 (Va. App. 2005).

CASE SUMMARY

Unilateral Contract: Pretty Good Bonus!

FACTS: Aon Risk Services, Inc. (ARS Arkansas), and Combined Insurance Companies are subsidiaries of Aon Corporation. The parent corporation issued an "Interdependency Memo" dated February 2000, which encouraged ARS brokerage offices to place insurance business with Aon-affiliated companies. It also set up a bonus pool for revenues generated under the plan, with Combined agreeing to pay "30% of annualized premium on all life products over 15-year term plus 15% 1st year for all other products." John Meadors saw the memo in February 2000, and believed it would entitle him to this compensation over and above his employment contract. Meadors put Combined in touch with Dillard's Department Stores and on March 24, 2000, Dillard's and Combined executed a five-year agreement whereby Dillard's employees could purchase life, disability, and other insurance policies through workplace enrollment. When Meadors did not receive bonus-pool money generated by the transaction, he sued his employer for breach of a unilateral contract. The employer's defense was that the memo was not sufficiently definite to constitute an offer.

DECISION: Judgment for Meadors for $2,406,522.60. A unilateral contract is composed of an offer that invites acceptance in the form of actual performance. For example, in the case of a reward, the offeree accepts by performing the particular task, such as the capture of the fugitive for which the reward is offered. In this case the offer contained in the Interdependency Memo set out specific percentages of provisions that would go into the bonus pool, and required that the pool be distributed annually. It was sufficiently definite to constitute an offer. Meadors was responsible for the production of the Dillard's account, and was entitled to the bonus promised in the memo. [*Aon Risk Services Inc. v. Meadors*, 267 S.W.3d 603 (Ark. App. 2007)]

Option and First-Refusal Contracts

option contract–contract to hold an offer to make a contract open for a fixed period of time.

The parties may make a contract that gives a right to one of them to enter into a second contract at a later date. If one party has an absolute right to enter into the later contract, the initial contract is called an **option contract.** Thus, a bilateral contract may be made today, giving one of the parties the right to buy the other party's house for a specified amount. This is an option contract because the party with the privilege has the freedom of choice, or option, to buy or not buy. If the option is exercised, the other party to the contract must follow the terms of the option and enter into the second contract. If the option is never exercised, no second contract ever arises, and the offer protected by the option contract merely expires.

right of first refusal– right of a party to meet the terms of a proposed contract before it is executed, such as a real estate purchase agreement.

In contrast with an option contract, a contract may merely give a **right of first refusal.** This imposes only the duty to make the first offer to the party having the right of first refusal.

11-2f Quasi Contracts

quasi contract–court-imposed obligation to prevent unjust enrichment in the absence of a contract.

In some cases, a court will impose an obligation even though there is no contract.[14] Such an obligation is called a **quasi contract,** which is an obligation imposed by law.

Prevention of Unjust Enrichment

A quasi contract is not a true contract reflecting all of the elements of a contract set forth previously in this chapter. The court is not seeking to enforce the intentions of the parties contained in an agreement. Rather, when a person or enterprise receives a benefit from another, even in the absence of a promise to pay for the benefit, a court may impose an obligation to pay for the reasonable value of that benefit, to avoid *unjust enrichment*.

[14] *Thayer v. Dial Industrial Sales, Inc.*, 85 F. Supp. 2d 263 (S.D.N.Y. 2000).

| FIGURE 11-2 | Contract |

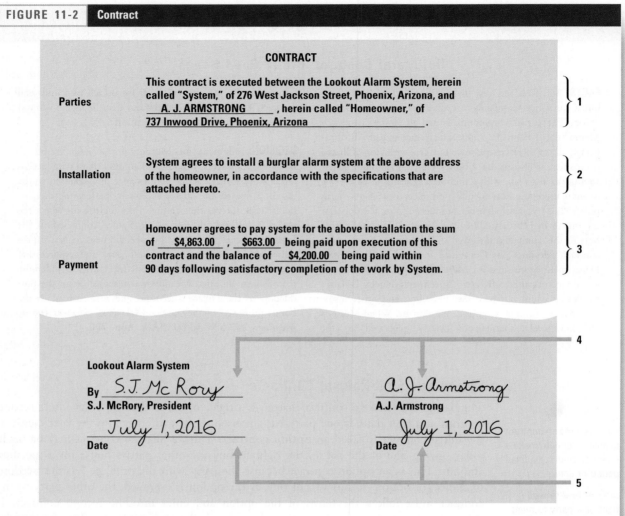

CONTRACT

Parties

This contract is executed between the Lookout Alarm System, herein called "System," of 276 West Jackson Street, Phoenix, Arizona, and ___A. J. ARMSTRONG___ , herein called "Homeowner," of 737 Inwood Drive, Phoenix, Arizona _____ .

} 1

Installation

System agrees to install a burglar alarm system at the above address of the homeowner, in accordance with the specifications that are attached hereto.

} 2

Payment

Homeowner agrees to pay system for the above installation the sum of ___$4,863.00___ , ___$663.00___ being paid upon execution of this contract and the balance of ___$4,200.00___ being paid within 90 days following satisfactory completion of the work by System.

} 3

4

Lookout Alarm System

By _S.J. Mc Rory_
S.J. McRory, President

a. J. Armstrong
A.J. Armstrong

July 1, 2016
Date

July 1, 2016
Date

5

Note that this contract includes the following important information: (1) the name and address of each party, (2) the promise or consideration of the seller, (3) the promise or consideration of the buyer, (4) the signature of the two parties, and (5) the date.

The spirit behind the law of unjust enrichment is to apply the law "outside the box" and fill in the cracks where common civil law and statutes fail to achieve justice.[15]

A successful claim for unjust enrichment usually requires (1) a benefit conferred on the defendant, (2) the defendant's knowledge of the benefit, and (3) a finding that it would be unjust for the defendant to retain the benefit without payment. The burden of proof is on the plaintiff to prove all of the elements of the claim. **For Example,** Hiram College sued Nicholas Courtad for $6,000 plus interest for tuition and other expenses. Because no evidence of a written contract was produced, the court considered it an unjust enrichment claim by the college. Courtad had attended classes for a few weeks and had not paid his tuition due to a problem with his financial aid package. Because he did not receive any credit hours toward a degree, which is the ultimate benefit

---

[15] *Hernandez v. Lopez*, 103 Cal. Rptr. 3d 376, 381 (Cal. App. 2009).

of attending college, the court found that he did not receive a benefit and that a finding of unjust enrichment was not appropriate.[16] Sometimes a contract may be unenforceable because of a failure to set forth the contract in writing in compliance with the statute of frauds or a consumer protection act.[17] In other circumstances, no enforceable contract exists because of a lack of definite and certain terms. Yet in both situations, one party may have performed services for the benefit of the other party and the court will require payment of the reasonable value of services to avoid the unjust enrichment of the party receiving the services without paying for them. These damages are sometimes referred to as *restitution damages*. Some courts refer to this situation as an action or recovery in ***quantum meruit*** (as much as he or she deserved).

quantum meruit–as much as deserved; an action brought for the value of the services rendered the defendant when there was no express contract as to the purchase price.

For Example, Arya Group, Inc. (Arya), sued the entertainer Cher for unjust enrichment. In June 1996, Cher negotiated an oral agreement with Arya to design and construct a house on her Malibu property for $4,217,529. The parties' oral agreement was set forth in a written contract with an August 1997 date and was delivered to Cher in October 1997. She never signed it. Between June 1996 and November 1997, Arya performed and received payment for a number of services discharged under the unsigned contract. In August 1997, Cher requested Arya to meet with a home designer named Bussell who had previously worked with Cher on a Florida project, and Arya showed Bussell the plans and designs for the Malibu property and introduced her to his subcontractors. In November 1997, Cher terminated her agreement with Arya without paying the balance then due, as asserted by Arya, of $415,169.41. Arya claims that Cher and Bussell misappropriated the plans and designs Arya had prepared. Cher and the other defendants demurred to Arya's unjust enrichment complaint, pointing out that construction contracts must be evidenced in a writing signed by both parties under state law in order to be enforceable in a court of law. The appeals court determined that Arya's noncompliance with the state law requiring a signed written contract did not absolutely foreclose Arya from seeking damages for unjust enrichment if he could prove the assertions in the complaint that Cher was a sophisticated homeowner with previous involvement in residential construction who had legal representation in negotiating the agreement with Arya, and that Cher would be unjustly enriched if she were not required to compensate Arya for the reasonable value of the work already performed.[18]

CASE SUMMARY

No Free Rides

FACTS: PIC Realty leased farmland to Southfield Farms. After Southfield harvested its crop, it cultivated the land in preparation for the planting in the following year. However, its lease expired, so it did not plant that crop. It then sued PIC for reimbursement for the reasonable value of the services and materials used in preparing the land because this was a benefit to PIC. There was evidence that it was customary for landlords to compensate tenants for such work.

DECISION: Southfield was entitled to recover the reasonable value of the benefit conferred upon PIC. This was necessary in order to prevent the unjust enrichment of PIC. [*PIC Realty Corp. v. Southfield Farms, Inc.*, 832 S.W.2d 610 (Tex. App. 1992)]

[16] *Hiram College v. Courtad*, 834 N.E.2d 432 (Ohio App. 2005).
[17] See *Shafer Electric & Construction v. Mantia*, 96 A.3d 989 (Pa. 2014) where the Supreme Court of Pennsylvania determined that the state's Home Improvement Consumer Protection Act did not preclude the common law equitable remedy of *quantum meruit* when a contractor fails to fully comply with the Consumer Protection Act.
[18] *Arya Group, Inc. v. Cher*, 91 Cal. Rptr. 2d 815 (Cal. App. 2000). See also *Fischer v. Flax*, 816 A.2d 1 (2003).

A situation may arise over the mistaken conference of a benefit. **For Example,** Nantucket Island has a few approved colors for houses in its historic district. Using the approved gray color, Martin Kane and his crew began painting Sheldon Adams's house in the historic district as the result of a mistaken address. Adams observed the initiation of the work from his office across the street but did nothing to stop the painters. At the end of the day when the work was done, Adams refused to pay for the work, saying, "I signed no contract and never approved this work." The law deems it inequitable that Adams should have received the benefit of this work, having observed the benefit being conferred and knowing that the painters expected payment. Adams would be unjustly enriched if he were allowed to retain the benefit without payment for the reasonable value of the work. If Adams did not have knowledge that the work was being done and thus that payment was expected, quasi-contractual liability would not be imposed.

The mistake that benefits the defendant may be the mistake of a third party.

Preclusion by an Express Contract

Courts award relief based on quasi-contractual principles, implying by law a contract where one did not exist in fact. Thus, where an express contract exists, it precludes an unjust enrichment claim.[19]

CASE SUMMARY

When in Doubt, Write It Out

FACTS: Facing financial turbulence, Philippine Airlines (PAL) sought to renegotiate its aircraft lease contract (ALC) with World Airlines (WA). WA refused to negotiate with PAL. PAL retained John Sununu, the former Governor of New Hampshire and the former Chief of Staff to President George H. W. Bush and Sununu's partner Victor Frank to represent it. Sununu and Frank sent a contract proposal to PAL, which included a proposed "success fee" of $600,000 if they persuaded WA to accept a modification of the lease contract. PAL gave Sununu and Frank a verbal go-ahead but did not sign the proposed contract. Thereafter PAL sent a contract that was different from that proposed by Sununu and Frank, containing a success fee of 4 percent of savings if they were able to reach a settlement to reduce the remaining obligation of PAL to WA in accordance with either of two very specific settlement offers. Caught up in the actual intense settlement negotiations with WA on behalf of PAL Sununu and Frank signed the contract. Thereafter, they were successful in obtaining an amendment to the lease contract, saving PAL $12.8 million. PAL refused to pay a success fee of $520,000 because the actual settlement did not meet the contractual criteria, which was

limited to just the two specific settlement offers. Sununu and Frank sued PAL for unjust enrichment and other contract theories.

DECISION: Judgment for PAL. Sununu and Frank conferred a benefit on PAL through their efforts to persuade WA to negotiate with PAL; and PAL accepted and retained the benefit for the renegotiated lease. There can be no claim, however, for unjust enrichment when an express contract exists between two parties. A court awards relief based on quasi-contractual principles, implying by law a contract, only where one did not exist in fact. The court stated:

To grant PALs summary judgment motion is not to condone its conduct. The airline can rightly be accused of stinginess for enforcing the formalistic terms of the contract in spite of the plaintiffs' earnest efforts on its behalf ... PAL may have violated Sununu and Frank's trust, but it did not violate the law.

... Sununu and Frank seem to have done their best to serve their client, but they made a reckless bet by trusting PAL. They were accustomed to

[19] However, if the parties have abandoned following the written provisions of the contract, it is proper for a court to allow recovery on the basis of *quantum meruit* on an implied contract. See *Geoscience Group Inc. v. Waters Construction Co. Inc.*, 759 S.E.2d 696 (N.C. App. 2014).

When in Doubt, Write It Out continued

handshake deals in which personal relationships count for more than legal documents, so they made little effort to put their understanding with PAL on paper. When they ran into a client who didn't play by the same rules, they paid the price.

The lesson is one that should be taught in law and business schools across America: When in doubt, write it out.
[Sununu v. Philippine Airlines, Inc., 792 F. Supp. 2d 39 (D. D.C. 2011)]

Extent of Recovery

When recovery is allowed in quasi contract, the plaintiff recovers the reasonable value of the benefit conferred on the defendant,[20] or the fair and reasonable[21] value of the work performed, depending on the jurisdiction and the circumstances of the case itself. The customary method of calculating damages in construction contract cases is actual job costs plus an allowance for overhead and profits minus amount paid.[22]

THINKING THINGS THROUGH

Twelve Years of Litigation

Brown University accepted the bid of Marshall Contractors, Inc. (Marshall), to build the Pizzitola Sports Facility on its Providence, Rhode Island, campus. The parties intended to execute a formal written contract. Brown decided to pay $7,157,051 for the project, but Marshall sought additional payment for items it deemed extras and not contemplated in its bid. Because the parties were unable to agree on the scope of the project as compared to the price Brown was willing to pay, they never executed the formal written contract. Nevertheless, in the context of this disagreement over terms and price, construction began in May 1987. When the parties could not resolve their disagreements as the project neared completion in January 1989, Marshall sued Brown University, seeking to recover the costs for what it deemed "changes." Brown asserted that an implied-in-fact contract existed for all work at the $7,157,051 figure because the contractor went ahead with the project knowing the money Brown would pay. The litigation ended up in the Supreme Court of Rhode Island, and in 1997, the court concluded that no express or implied-in-fact contract had ever been reached by the parties concerning the scope of the project and what costs were to be included in the price stipulated by Brown. The case was remanded to the trial court for a new trial. After a trial on the theories of *quantum meruit* and unjust enrichment, a jury awarded Marshall $1.2 million dollars, which was some $3.1 million less than Marshall sought. Brown University appealed, and on November 21, 2001, the Supreme Court of Rhode Island affirmed the jury verdict for the contractor, determining that the proper measure of damages on unjust enrichment and *quantum meruit* theories was "the reasonable value of the work done."*

In May 1987 when the parties could not reach agreement enabling the execution of a formal written contract, Thinking Things Through at that point in time should have exposed the potential for significant economic uncertainties to both parties in actually starting the building process under such circumstances. In the spring of 1987 when all parties were unable to reach agreement, mediation or expedited arbitration by construction experts may well have resolved the controversy and yielded an amicable written contract with little or no delay to the project. Instead, the unsettled cost issues during the building process could have had an adverse impact on the "job chemistry" between the contractor and the owner, which may have adversely affected the progress and quality of the job. The 12 years of litigation that, with its economic and human resource costs, yielded just $1.2 million for the contractor was a no-win result for both sides. A primary rule for all managers in projects of this scope is to make sure the written contracts are executed before performance begins! Relying on "implied-in-fact" or quasi-contract legal theories is simply a poor management practice.

*__*ADP Marshall, Inc. v. Brown University__, 784 A.2d 309 (R.I. 2001).*

[20] *Ramsey v. Ellis*, 484 N.W.2d 331 (Wis. 1992).
[21] *ADP Marshall, Inc. v. Brown University*, 784 A.2d 309 (R.I. 2001).
[22] *Miranco Contracting, Inc. v. Pelel*, 871 N.Y.S.2d 310 (A.D. 2008).

11-3 Contracting on the Internet

Doing business online for consumers is very similar to doing business through a catalog purchase or by phone. Before placing an order, a buyer is commonly concerned about the reputation of the seller. The basic purchasing principle of *caveat emptor* still applies: buyer beware! The Internet provides valuable tools to allow a buyer to research the reputation of the seller and its products. Online evaluations of companies and their products can be found at Web sites, such as Consumer Reports (**http://www.consumerreports.org**), Consumers Digest (**http://www.consumersdigest.com**), or the Better Business Bureau (**http://www.bbb.org**). E-consumers may have access to categorized histories of comments by other e-consumers, such as Planet Feedback ratings at **http://www.planetfeedback.com.**

The intellectual property principles set forth in Chapter 9—as well as the contractual principles, the law of sales, and privacy laws you are about to study—all apply to e-commerce transactions. When you are purchasing an item online, you must carefully read all of the terms and conditions set forth on the seller's Web site when assessing whether to make a contemplated purchase. The proposed terms may require that any disputes be litigated in a distant state or be resolved through arbitration with restricted remedies, or there may be an unsatisfactory return policy, warranty limitations, or limitation of liability. Generally, the Web site terms become the contract of the parties and are legally enforceable.

The laws you have studied that prevent deceptive advertising by brick-and-mortar businesses also apply to Internet sites.[23] If an in-state site is engaging in false advertising, you may be able to exercise consumer protection rights through your state's attorney general's office, or you may find some therapeutic relief by reporting the misconduct to the Internet Scambusters site (**http://www.scambusters.com**).

From a seller's perspective, it is exceedingly helpful to have as much information as possible on your potential customers' buying habits. Federal law prohibits the collection of personal information from children without parental consent, and some states restrict the unauthorized collection of personal information. European Union countries have strict laws protecting the privacy of consumers. Sellers intending to collect personal information should obtain the consent of their customers, make certain that children are excluded, and make sure that the information is stored in a secure environment.

Advanced encryption technology has made the use of credit card payments through the Internet very safe. No computer system connected to the Internet is totally secure, however. In the worst-case scenario, credit card issuers will not charge a user for more than the first $50 of unauthorized activity.

Internet contracts involve the same types of issues that are addressed in contracts offline but with certain technology-related nuances. The parties to the e-contracts must still negotiate their obligations in clear and unambiguous language, including such terms as quantity, quality, and price as well as warranties, indemnification responsibilities, limitations on liability, and termination procedures. The federal Electronic Signatures in Global and National Commerce Act (E-Sign) and the Uniform Electronic Transactions Act (UETA) mandate parity between paper and electronic contracts. The basic legal rules that govern contracts offline are the very same rules that govern online contracts, and basic civil procedure rules apply. **For Example,** California buyer Paul Boschetto bought a 1964 Ford Galaxy that had been advertised on eBay to be "in awesome condition" from a Milton, Wisconsin, resident, J. Hansing, for $34,106. On delivery Boschetto discovered

---

[23] See *MADCAP I, LLC v. McNamee*, 712 N.W.2d 16 (Wis. App. 2005) in which the court found genuine issues of material fact as to whether a business Web site falsely represented the size and nature of its business to induce the public to purchase products and services described on its Web site in violation of the state's fraudulent representations statute.

that the car had rust, extensive dents, and would not start. His lawsuit against Hansing in U.S. District Court in California was dismissed for lack of personal jurisdiction.[24] (The formation of a contract with a nonresident defendant was not, standing alone, sufficient to create personal jurisdiction in California.)

Boxes identifying special Internet e-commerce topics are strategically placed throughout these chapters.

Make the Connection

Summary

A contract is a binding agreement between two or more parties. A contract arises when an offer is accepted with contractual intent (the intent to make a binding agreement).

Contracts may be classified in a number of ways according to form, the way in which they were created, validity, and obligations. With respect to form, a contract may be either informal or formal, such as those under seal or those appearing on the records of courts. Contracts may be classified by the way they were created as those that are expressed by words—written or oral—and those that are implied or deduced from conduct. The question of validity requires distinguishing between contracts that are valid, those that are voidable, and those that are not contracts at all but are merely void agreements. Contracts can be distinguished on the basis of the obligations created as executed contracts, in which everything has been performed,

and executory contracts, in which something remains to be done. The bilateral contract is formed by exchanging a promise for a promise, so each party has the obligation of thereafter rendering the promised performance. In the unilateral contract, which is the doing of an act in exchange for a promise, no further performance is required of the offeree who performed the act.

In certain situations, the law regards it as unjust for a person to receive a benefit and not pay for it. In such a case, the law of quasi contracts allows the performing person to recover the reasonable value of the benefit conferred on the benefited person even though no contract between them requires any payment. Unjust enrichment, which a quasi contract is designed to prevent, sometimes arises when there was never any contract between the persons involved or when there was a contract, but for some reason it was avoided or held to be merely a void agreement.

Learning Outcomes

After studying this chapter, you should be able to clearly explain:

11-1   Nature of Contracts

LO.1   Explain the meaning and importance of privity of a contract

See the example of the subcontractor, RPR & Associates, who worked on a project but could not sue the owner for payment, pages 206–207.

See the example involving rapper Eminem, FBT, and Aftermath Records, where FBT was not a party to the contract and thus not bound by it, page 207.

LO.2   Describe the way in which a contract arises

See the discussion on offer and acceptance, page 207.

11-2   Classes of Contracts

LO.3   Distinguish between bilateral and unilateral contracts

See the example of the Nantucket painters, pages 213–214.

See the *AON Risk Services* case where an insurance agent won his case based on a unilateral contract theory, page 211.

[24] *Boschetto v. Hansing*, 539 F.3d 1011 (9th Cir. 2008).

LO.4 Explain the reasoning behind quasi-contract recovery

See the example whereby Cher had to pay a home designer for certain work even though there was no contract, page 213.

11-3   Contracting on the Internet

LO.5 Explain how Internet contracts involve the same types of issues as offline contracts

See the eBay example, page 217.

Key Terms

bilateral contract	obligee	*quantum meruit*
contract	obligor	quasi contract
contract under seal	offeree	recognizance
executed contract	offeror	right of first refusal
executory contract	option contract	unilateral contracts
express contract	privity	valid contract
formal contract	privity of contract	void agreement
implied contract	promisee	voidable contract
informal contract	promisor	

Questions and Case Problems

1. What is a contract?

2. Fourteen applicants for a city of Providence, Rhode Island, police academy training class each received from the city a letter stating that it was a "conditional offer of employment" subject to successful completion of medical and psychological exams. The 14 applicants passed the medical and psychological exams. However, these applicants were replaced by others after the city changed the selection criteria. Can you identify an offer and acceptance in this case? Can you make out a bilateral or unilateral contract? [*Ardito et al. v. City of Providence*, 213 F. Supp. 2d 358 (D.R.I.)]

3. Compare an implied contract with a quasi contract.

4. The Jordan Keys law firm represented the Greater Southeast Community Hospital of Washington, D.C., in a medical malpractice suit against the hospital. The hospital was self-insured for the first $1,000,000 of liability and the St. Paul Insurance Co. provided excess coverage up to $4,000,000. The law firm was owed $67,000 for its work on the malpractice suit when the hospital went into bankruptcy. The bankruptcy court ordered the law firm to release its files on the case to St. Paul to defend under the excess coverage insurance, and the Jordan Keys firm sued St. Paul for its legal fees of $67,000 expended prior to the bankruptcy under an "implied-in-fact contract" because the insurance company would have the benefit of all of its work. Decide. [*Jordan Keys v. St. Paul Fire*, 870 A.2d 58 (D.C.)]

5. Beck was the general manager of Chilkoot Lumber Co. Haines sold fuel to the company. To persuade Haines to sell on credit, Beck signed a paper by which he promised to pay any debt the lumber company owed Haines. He signed this paper with his name followed by "general manager." Haines later sued Beck on this promise, and Beck raised the defense that the addition of "general manager" showed that Beck, who was signing on behalf of Chilkoot, was not personally liable and did not intend to be bound by the paper. Was Beck liable on the paper? [*Beck v. Haines Terminal and Highway Co.*, 843 P.2d 1229 (Alaska)]

6. *A* made a contract to construct a house for *B*. Subsequently, *B* sued *A* for breach of contract. *A* raised the defense that the contract was not binding because it was not sealed. Is this a valid defense? [*Cooper v. G. E. Construction Co.*, 158 S.E.2d 305 (Ga. App.)]

7. Edward Johnson III, the CEO and principal owner of the world's largest mutual fund company, Fidelity Investments, Inc., was a longtime tennis buddy of Richard Larson. In 1995, Johnson asked Larson, who had construction experience, to supervise the construction of a house on Long Pond, Mount Desert Island, Maine. Although they had no written contract, Larson agreed to take on the project for $6,700 per month plus lodging. At the end of the project in 1997, Johnson made a $175,000 cash payment to Larson, and he made arrangements for

Larson to live rent-free on another Johnson property in the area called Pray's Meadow in exchange for looking after Johnson's extensive property interests in Maine. In the late summer of 1999, Johnson initiated a new project on the Long Pond property. Johnson had discussions with Larson about doing this project, but Larson asked to be paid his former rate, and Johnson balked because he had already hired a project manager. According to Johnson, at a later date he again asked Larson to take on the "shop project" as a favor and in consideration of continued rent-free use of the Pray's Meadow home. Johnson stated that Larson agreed to do the job "pro bono" in exchange for the use of the house, and Johnson acknowledged that he told Larson he would "take care" of Larson at the end of the project, which could mean as much or as little as Johnson determined. Larson stated that Johnson told him that he would "take care of" Larson if he would do the project and told him to "trust the Great Oracle" (meaning Johnson, the highly successful businessperson). Larson sought payment in March 2000 and asked Johnson for "something on account" in April. Johnson offered Larson a loan. In August during a tennis match, Larson again asked Johnson to pay him. Johnson became incensed, and through an employee, he ended Larson's participation in the project and asked him to vacate Pray's Meadow. Larson complied and filed suit for payment for work performed at the rate of $6,700 per month. Did Larson have an express contract with Johnson? What legal theory or theories could Larson utilize in his lawsuit? How would you decide this case if you believed Larson's version of the facts? How would you decide the case if you believed Johnson's version of the facts? [*Larson v. Johnson*, 196 F. Supp. 2d 38 (D. Me. 2002)]

8. While Clara Novak was sick, her daughter Janie helped her in many ways. Clara died, and Janie then claimed that she was entitled to be paid for the services she had rendered her mother. This claim was opposed by three brothers and sisters who also rendered services to the mother. They claimed that Janie was barred because of the presumption that services rendered between family members are gratuitous. Janie claimed that this presumption was not applicable because she had not lived with her mother but had her own house. Was Janie correct? [In re *Estate of Novak*, 398 N.W.2d 653 (Minn. App.)]

9. Dozier and his wife, daughter, and grandson lived in the house Dozier owned. At the request of the daughter and grandson, Paschall made some improvements to the house. Dozier did not authorize these, but he knew that the improvements were being made and did not object to them. Paschall sued Dozier for the reasonable value of the improvements, but Dozier argued that he had not made any contract for such improvements. Was he obligated to pay for such improvements?

10. When Harriet went away for the summer, Landry, a house painter, painted her house. He had a contract to paint a neighbor's house but painted Harriet's house by mistake. When Harriet returned from vacation, Landry billed her for $3,100, which was a fair price for the work. She refused to pay. Landry claimed that she had a quasi-contractual liability for that amount. Was he correct?

11. Margrethe and Charles Pyeatte, a married couple, agreed that she would work so that he could go to law school and that when he finished, she would go back to school for her master's degree. After Charles was admitted to the bar and before Margrethe went back to school, the two were divorced. She sued Charles, claiming that she was entitled to quasi-contractual recovery of the money that she had paid for Charles's support and law school tuition. He denied liability. Was she entitled to recover for the money she spent for Charles's maintenance and law school tuition? [*Pyeatte v. Pyeatte*, 661 P.2d 196 (Ariz. App.)]

12. Carriage Way was a real estate development of approximately 80 houses and 132 apartments. The property owners were members of the Carriage Way Property Owners Association. Each year, the association would take care of certain open neighboring areas, including a nearby lake, that were used by the property owners. The board of directors of the association would make an assessment or charge against the property owners to cover the cost of this work. The property owners paid these assessments for a number of years and then refused to pay any more. In spite of this refusal, the association continued to take care of the areas in question. The association then sued the property owners and claimed that they were liable for the benefit that had been conferred on them. Were the owners liable? [*Board of Directors of Carriage Way Property Owners Ass n v. Western National Bank*, 487 N.E.2d 974 (Ill. App.)]

13. When improvements or buildings are added to real estate, the real estate tax assessment is usually increased to reflect the increased value of the property. Frank Partipilo and Elmer Hallman owned neighboring tracts of land. Hallman made improvements to his land, constructing a new building and driveway on the tract. The tax assessor made a mistake about the location of the boundary line between Partipilo's and Hallman's land and thought the improvements were made on Partipilo's property. Instead of increasing the taxes on Hallman's land, the assessor wrongly increased the taxes on Partipilo's land. Partipilo paid the increased taxes for three years. When he learned why his taxes had been increased, he sued Hallman for the amount of the increase that Partipilo had been paying. Hallman raised the defense that he had not done anything wrong and that the mistake had been the fault of the tax assessor. Decide. [*Partipilo v. Hallman*, 510 N.E.2d 8 (Ill.App.)]

14. When a college student complained about a particular course, the vice president of the college asked the teacher to prepare a detailed report about the course. The teacher did and then demanded additional compensation for the time spent in preparing the report. He claimed that the college was liable to provide compensation on an implied contract. Was he correct? [*Zadrozny v. City Colleges of Chicago*, 581 N.E.2d 44 (Ill. App.)]

15. Smith made a contract to sell automatic rifles to a foreign country. Because the sale of such weapons to that country was illegal under an act of Congress, the U.S. government prosecuted Smith for making the contract. He raised the defense that because the contract was illegal, it was void and there is no binding obligation when a contract is void; therefore, no contract for which he could be prosecuted existed. Was he correct?

CPA Question

1. Kay, an art collector, promised Hammer, an art student, that if Hammer could obtain certain rare artifacts within two weeks, Kay would pay for Hammer's postgraduate education. At considerable effort and expense, Hammer obtained the specified artifacts within the two-week period. When Hammer requested payment, Kay refused. Kay claimed that there was no consideration for the promise. Hammer would prevail against Kay based on:

   a. Unilateral contract.

   b. Unjust enrichment.

   c. Public policy.

   d. Quasi contract.

Formation of Contracts: Offer and Acceptance

Learning Outcomes <<<

After studying this chapter, you should be able to

LO.1 Decide whether an offer contains definite and certain terms

LO.2 Explain the exceptions the law makes to the requirement of definiteness

LO.3 Explain all the ways an offer can be terminated

LO.4 Explain what constitutes the acceptance of an offer

LO.5 Explain the implications of failing to read a clickwrap agreement

A *contract* consists of enforceable obligations that have been voluntarily assumed. Thus, one of the essential elements of a contract is an agreement. This chapter explains how the basic agreement arises, when there is a contract, and how there can be merely unsuccessful negotiations without a resulting contract.

12-1   Requirements of an Offer

offer–expression of an offeror's willingness to enter into a contractual agreement.

An **offer** expresses the willingness of the offeror to enter into a contractual agreement regarding a particular subject. It is a promise that is conditional upon an act, a forbearance (a refraining from doing something one has a legal right to do), or a return promise.

CPA

12-1a   Contractual Intention

To make an offer, the offeror must appear to intend to create a binding obligation. Whether this intent exists is determined by objective standards.[1] This intent may be shown by conduct. **For Example,** when one party signs a written contract and sends it to the other party, such action is an offer to enter into a contract on the terms of the writing.

There is no contract when a social invitation is made or when an offer is made in obvious jest or excitement. A reasonable person would not regard such an offer as indicating a willingness to enter into a binding agreement. The test for a valid, binding offer is whether it induces a reasonable belief in the offeree that he or she can, by accepting it, bind the offeror, as developed in the *Wigod* case.

CASE SUMMARY

A Valid Offer!

FACTS: The U.S. Department of the Treasury implemented the federal Home Affordable Mortgage Program (HAMP) to help homeowners avoid foreclosure amidst the sharp decline in the nation's housing market in 2008. In 2009, Wells Fargo Bank issued Lori Wigod a four-month "trial" loan modification under a Trial Period Plan (TPP). After the trial period, if the borrower complied with all of the terms of the TPP agreement, including making all required payments and providing all required documentation, and if the borrower's representations remained true and correct, the servicer, Well Fargo, had to offer a permanent mortgage modification. Wigod alleged that she complied with these requirements and that Wells Fargo refused to grant a permanent modification. Wells Fargo contended that the TPP contained no valid offer.

DECISION: Judgment for Wigod. A person can prevent his submission from being treated as an offer by using suitable language conditioning the formation of a contract on some further step, such as approval by corporate headquarters. It is when the promisor conditions a promise on *his own* future action or approval that there is no binding offer. Here, the TTP spelled out two conditions precedent to Wells Fargo's obligation to offer a permanent modification. Wigod had to comply with the requirements of the TPP, and her financial representations had to be true and accurate. These conditions had to be satisfied by the promisee (Wigod). Here a reasonable person in Wigod's position would read the TPP as a default offer that she could accept so long as she satisfied the two conditions. [*Wigod v. Wells Fargo Bank,* **673 F.3d 547 (7th Cir. 2012)**]

Invitation to Negotiate

The first statement made by one of two persons is not necessarily an offer. In many instances, there may be a preliminary discussion or an invitation by one party to the

[1] *Glass Service Co. v. State Farm Mutual Automobile Ins. Co.,* 530 N.W.2d 867 (Minn. App. 1995).

other to negotiate or to make an offer. Thus, an inquiry by a school as to whether a teacher wished to continue the following year was merely a survey or invitation to negotiate and was not an offer that could be accepted. Therefore, the teacher's affirmative response did not create a contract.

Ordinarily, a seller sending out circulars or catalogs listing prices is not regarded as making an offer to sell at those prices. The seller is merely indicating a willingness to consider an offer made by a buyer on those terms. The reason for this rule is, in part, the practical consideration that because a seller does not have an unlimited supply of any commodity, the seller cannot possibly intend to make a contract with everyone who sees the circular. The same principle is applied to merchandise that is displayed with price tags in stores or store windows and to most advertisements. An advertisement in a newspaper is ordinarily considered an invitation to negotiate and is not an offer that can be accepted by a reader of the paper.[2] However, some court decisions have construed advertisements as offers that called for an act on the part of the customer, thereby forming a unilateral contract, such as the advertisement of a reward for the return of lost property.

Quotations of prices, even when sent on request, are likewise not offers unless the parties have had previous dealings or unless a trade custom exists that would give the recipient of the quotation reason to believe that an offer was being made. Whether a price quotation is to be treated as an offer or merely an invitation to negotiate is a question of the intent of the party giving the quotation.[3]

Agreement to Make a Contract at a Future Date

No contract arises when the parties merely agree that at a future date they will consider making a contract or will make a contract on terms to be agreed on at that time. In such a case, neither party is under any obligation until the future contract is made. Unless an agreement is reached on all material terms and conditions and nothing is left to future negotiations, a contract to enter a contract in the future is of no effect. **For Example,** Hewitt Associates provided employee benefits administrative services to Rollins, Inc., under a contract negotiated in 2001 to run through 2006. Prior to its expiration, the parties negotiated—seeking to agree to a multiyear extension of the 2001 agreement. They agreed to all of the material terms of the contract, except that Rollins balked at a $1.8 million penalty clause. Rollins's employees told Hewitt that the extension "was going to be signed." However, Rollins did not sign and the 2001 agreement expired. Hewitt's contention that the agreement was enforceable at the moment Rollins told Hewitt it was going to sign the new agreement was rejected by the court, stating that an agreement to reach an agreement is a contradiction in terms and imposes no obligation on the parties.[4]

Contracts to Negotiate

Regarding modern transactions involving significant up-front investments in deal structuring and due diligence, compelling reasons exist for parties to exchange binding promises protective of the deal-making process and why the courts may deem it socially beneficial to enforce them. Without any legal protection a counter-party may attempt to hijack the deal. Parties may wish to build in safeguards that operate early in the bargaining process to allow investing resources in a deal, but without inextricably locking themselves into a transaction that is still in a partially formulated state. *Contracts to negotiate* can satisfy this need.[5] **For Example,** David Butler, an inventor of safety technology

---

[2] *Zanakis-Pico v. Cutter, Dodge, Inc.*, 47 P.2d 1222 (Haw. 2002).
[3] Statutes prohibiting false or misleading advertising may require adherence to advertised prices.
[4] *Hewitt Associates, LLC v. Rollins, Inc.*, 669 S.E.2d 551 (Ga. App. 2008).
[5] New York, Illinois, Pennsylvania, California, and Delaware have recognized this doctrine. Mississippi and Washington have repudiated it.

for cutting tools was allowed to pursue his claim of breach of contract to negotiate against Shiraz Balolia.[6]

12-1b Definiteness

An offer, and the resulting contract, must be definite and certain so that it is capable of being enforced.[7]

CASE SUMMARY

Definite and Certain Terms

FACTS: ServiceMaster, as the general contractor hired to restore the Cleveland Brown Stadium in time for the Browns' first pre-season football game, hired subcontractor Novak to perform restoration and construction work. Novak sued for $37,158.82 for work performed on the August 2, 2007, severe rainstorm project, referred to as Loss 2. ServiceMaster contended that Novak was bound by a written but unsigned subcontractor agreement, and that Novak's alleged oral contract was lacking any definite terms to be enforceable. From a judgment for Novak, ServiceMaster appealed.

DECISION: Judgment for Novak. The record contained sufficient evidence of definite terms to enforce the oral contract. Novak V.P. Pinchot credibly testified that Novak's "time and materials" billing on the final invoice contained the hours worked at the published union rate plus the cost of materials, plus 10 percent, which method of pricing is widely understood in the construction industry. Novak is entitled to $37,158.82 plus an 18% penalty for violation of the state Prompt Payment Statute. [**Frank Novak & Sons, Inc. v. A-Team, LLC, dba ServiceMaster, 6 N.E.3d 1242 (Ohio App. 2014)**]

If an offer is indefinite or vague or if an essential provision is lacking,[8] no contract arises from an attempt to accept it. Courts are not in the business of writing contracts and will not supply terms unless the parties' obligations and intents are clearly implied. Thus, an offer to conduct a business for as long as it is profitable is too vague to be a valid offer. The acceptance of such an offer does not result in a contract that can be enforced. Statements by a bank that it was "with" the debtors and would "support" them in their proposed business venture were too vague to be regarded as a promise by the bank to make necessary loans to the debtors.

CASE SUMMARY

What Is the Meaning of an Agreement for a "Damn Good Job"?

FACTS: Larry Browneller made an oral contract with Hubert Plankenhorn to restore a 1963 Chevrolet Impala convertible. The car was not in good condition. Hubert advised the owner that his work would not yield a car of "show" quality because of the condition of the body, and he accordingly

believed that the owner merely wanted a presentable car. Larry, on the other hand, having told Hubert that he wanted a "damn good job," thought this statement would yield a car that would be competitive at the small amateur car shows he attended. When the finished car had what Larry asserted

---

[6] *Butler v. Balolia,* 736 F.3d 609 (1st Cir. 2013).
[7] *Norton v. Correctional Medicare, Inc.,* 2010 WL 4103016 (N.D.N.Y. Oct. 18, 2010).
[8] *Peace v. Doming Holdings Inc.,* 554 S.E.2d 314 (Ga. App. 2001).

What Is the Meaning of an Agreement for a "Damn Good Job"? continued

were "waves" in the paint as a result of an uneven surface on the body, Larry brought suit against Hubert for breach of the oral contract.

DECISION: There was clearly a misunderstanding between the parties over the quality of work that could and would

be obtained. *Quality* was a material term of the oral contract between the parties, on which there was no shared understanding. Accordingly, a court will not find an individual in breach of a term of the contract where the term did not exist. [**In re** *Plankenhorn*, **228 B.R. 638 (N.D. Ohio 1998)**]

The fact that minor, ministerial, and nonessential terms are left for future determination does not make an agreement too vague to be a contract.[9] **For Example,** John McCarthy executed an offer to purchase (OTP) real estate from Ana Tobin on a printed form generated by the local Real Estate Board. The OTP stated that "McCarthy hereby offers to buy" and Tobin's signature indicates that "this offer is hereby accepted". The OTP also detailed the amount to be paid and when and described the property title requirements and the time and place for closing. Above the signature line it stated: "NOTICE: This is a legal document that creates binding obligations. If not understood, consult an attorney". The OTP also required the parties to execute a standard form Purchase and Sale Agreement (PSA). Subsequently Tobin received a much higher offer for the property, which she accepted, asserting that she was free to do so because she had not signed the PSA. The court held that the OTP was a firm offer that bound Tobin to sell to McCarthy.[10]

The law does not favor the destruction of contracts because that would go against the social force of carrying out the intent of the parties.[11] Consequently, when it is claimed that a contract is too indefinite to be enforced, a court will do its best to find the intent of the parties and thereby reach the conclusion that the contract is not too indefinite. **For Example,** boxing promoter Don King had both a Promotional Agreement and a Bout Agreement with boxer Miguel Angel Gonzalez. The Bout Agreement for a boxing match with Julio Cesar Chavez gave King the option to promote the next four of Gonzalez's matches. The contract made clear that if Gonzalez won the Chavez match, he would receive at least $75,000 for the next fight unless the parties agreed otherwise, and if he lost, he would receive at least $25,000 for the subsequent fight unless otherwise agreed. The agreement did not explicitly state the purse for the subsequent match in the event of a draw. The Chavez match ended in a draw, and Gonzalez contended that this omission rendered the contract so indefinite that it was unenforceable. The court disagreed, stating that striking down a contract as indefinite and in essence meaningless is at best a last resort. The court held that although the contract was poorly drafted, the Promotional Agreement contained explicit price terms for which a minimum purse for fights following a draw may be inferred.[12] A court may not, however, rewrite the agreement of the parties in order to make it definite.

[9] *Hsu v. Vet-A-Mix, Inc.*, 479 N.W.2d 336 (Iowa App. 1991). But see *Ocean Atlantic Development Corp. v. Aurora Christian Schools, Inc.*, 322 F.3d 983 (7th Cir. 2003), where letter offers to purchase (OTP) real estate were signed by both parties, but the offers conditioned the purchase and sale of each property upon the subsequent execution of a purchase and sale agreement. The court held that the parties thus left themselves room to walk away from the deal under Illinois law, and the OTPs were not enforced.

[10] *McCarthy v. Tobin*, 706 N.E.2d 629 (Mass. 1999). But see [FN 9].

[11] *Mears v. Nationwide Mut., Inc. Co.*, 91 F.3d 1118 (8th Cir. 1996).

[12] *Gonzalez v. Don King Productions, Inc.*, 17 F. Supp. 2d 313 (S.D.N.Y. 1998); see also *Echols v. Pelullo*, 377 F.3d 272 (3rd Cir. 2004).

THINKING THINGS THROUGH

The Rules of Negotiations

Business agreements are often reached after much discussion, study, and posturing by both sides. Many statements may be made by both sides about the price or value placed on the subject of the transaction. Withholding information or presenting selective, self-serving information may be perceived by a party to the negotiations as protective self-interest. Does the law of contracts apply a duty of good faith and fair dealing in the negotiation of contracts? Does the Uniform Commercial Code provide for a general duty of good faith in the negotiation of contracts? Are lawyers under an ethical obligation to inform opposing counsel of relevant facts? The answer to all of these questions is no.

The Restatement (Second) of Contracts applies the duty of good faith and fair dealing to the performance and enforcement of contracts, not their negotiation;* so also does the UCC.** The American Bar Association's Model Rules of Professional Conduct, Rule 4.1 Comment 1, requires a lawyer to be "truthful" when dealing with others on a client's behalf, but it also states that generally a lawyer has "no affirmative duty to inform an opposing party of relevant facts."*** Comment 2 to Rule 4.1 contains an example of a "nonmaterial" statement of a lawyer as "estimates of price or value placed on the subject of a transaction."

The legal rules of negotiations state that—in the absence of fraud, special relationships, or statutory or contractual duties—negotiators are not obligated to divulge pertinent information to the other party to the negotiations. The parties to negotiations themselves must demand and analyze pertinent information and ultimately assess the fairness of the proposed transaction. Should a party conclude that the elements of a final proposal or offer are excessive or dishonest, that party's legal option is to walk away from the deal. Generally, the party has no basis to bring a lawsuit for lack of good faith and fair dealing in negotiations.

However, Thinking Things Through, the ethical standards for negotiations set forth in Chapter 3 indicate that establishing a reputation for trustworthiness, candor, and reliability often leads to commercial success for a company's continuing negotiations with its customers, suppliers, distributors, lenders, unions, and employees.****

*Restatement (Second) of Contracts §105, comment (c).
**Uniform Commercial Code §1-203.
***American Bar Association Model Rule of Professional Conduct 4.1(a) Comment 1.
****For a contrary example, consider the following story. The Atlanta Braves baseball team's general manager Frank Wren negotiated with free agent baseball player Rafael Furcal's agent Paul Kinzer. When all terms had been negotiated, Kinzer asked for a written terms-of-agreement sheet signed by the Braves, which to Wren meant an agreement had been reached. Kinzer took the sheet to the L.A. Dodgers, who then reached an agreement to sign the shortstop. Braves President John Schuerholz said, "The Atlanta Braves will no longer do business with that company—ever. I told Arn Tellem that we can't trust them to be honest and forthright." "Braves GM Blasts Furcal's Agents," Associated Press, *The Boston Globe*, December 20, 2008, C-7.

Definite by Incorporation

An offer and the resulting contract that by themselves may appear "too indefinite" may be made definite by reference to another writing. **For Example,** a lease agreement that was too vague by itself was made definite because the parties agreed that the lease should follow the standard form with which both were familiar. An agreement may also be made definite by reference to the prior dealings of the parties and to trade practices.

Implied Terms

Although an offer must be definite and certain, not all of its terms need to be expressed. Some omitted terms may be implied by law. **For Example,** an offer "to pay $400" for a certain Movado timepiece does not state the terms of payment. A court, however, would not condemn this provision as too vague but would hold that it required that cash be paid and that the payment be made on delivery of the watch. Likewise, terms may be implied from conduct. As an illustration, when borrowed money was given to the borrower by a check on which the word *loan* was written, the act of the borrower in endorsing the check constituted an agreement to repay the amount of the check.

FIGURE 12-1 | Offer and Acceptance

"Best Efforts" Clauses

While decades ago it was generally accepted that a duty defined only in terms of "best efforts" was too indefinite to be enforced, such a view is no longer widely held. **For Example,** Thomas Hinc, an inventor, executed a contract with Lime-O-Sol Company (LOS) for LOS to produce and distribute Hinc's secret ingredient Stain Remover. Under the contract, Hinc was to receive $10 per gallon sold. The contract contained a clause obligating both parties to use their "best efforts" to market the product "in a manner that seems appropriate." Ultimately, LOS never produced, marketed, or sold Stain Remover for the duration of the contract. The court rejected the defense that the "best efforts" provision was vague and unenforceable stating "[b]est efforts, as commonly understood, means, at the very least *some* effort. It certainly does not mean *zero* effort—the construction LOS urges here to escape any obligation under its contract."[13]

Divisible Contracts

divisible contract— agreement consisting of two or more parts, each calling for corresponding performances of each part by the parties.

When the agreement consists of two or more parts and calls for corresponding performances of each part by the parties, the agreement is a **divisible contract.** Thus, in a promise to buy several separate articles at different prices at the same time, the agreement may be regarded as separate or divisible promises for the articles.

Exceptions to Definiteness

The law has come to recognize certain situations in which the practical necessity of doing business makes it desirable to have a contract, yet the situation is such that it is impossible to adopt definite terms in advance. In these cases, the indefinite term is often tied to some independent factor that will be definitely ascertainable at some time in the future. The

---

[13] *Hinc v. Lime-O-Sol Company,* 382 F.3d 716 (7th Cir. 2004). See also *Olsenhaus Pure Vegan, LLC v. Electric Wonderland, Inc.,* 983 N.Y.S.2d 506 (A.D. 2014).

requirements contract–contract to buy all requirements of the buyer from the seller.

output contract–contract of a producer to sell its entire production or output to a given buyer.

indefinite term might be tied to market price, production, or sales requirements. Thus, the law recognizes binding contracts in the case of a **requirements contract**—that is, a contract to buy all requirements of the buyer from the seller.[14] **For Example,** an agreement between Honeywell International Inc. and Air Products and Chemicals Inc. whereby Air Products would purchase its total requirements of wet process chemicals from Honeywell was held to be an enforceable requirements contract.[15] The law also recognizes as binding an **output contract**—that is, the contract of a producer to sell the entire production or output to a given buyer. These are binding contracts even though they do not state the exact quantity of goods that are to be bought or sold.

CASE SUMMARY

GM—In the Driver's Seat on Quantity and Timing!

FACTS: Automodular entered into a series of purchase orders that obligated Delphi to purchase and Automodular to provide all of Delphi's requirements deliverable to the original equipment manufacturer (OEM), General Motors. Automodular receives directions from the OEM's final assembly plants, regardless of whether Automodular is under contract to the OEM or Delphi. The purchase orders ("Contracts") incorporated Delphi's terms that the Buyer, GM, could require Automodular to implement changes to the specifications or design of the goods or to the scope of any services covered by the Contracts. GM informed Automodular that it needed fewer components and directed Automodular to, among other requirements, reduce shifts, change the assembly line speed, and change the length of workers' shifts. As a result, Automodular requested a price increase per unit assembled from Delphi because Automodular believed that such an increase was warranted pursuant to the Contract's change-in-scope provision. Delphi, however, refused to negotiate any price increase and the matter was litigated.

DECISION: Judgment for Delphi. In a requirements contract, the parties do not fix a quantity term, but instead, the quantity will be the buyer's needs of a specific commodity over the contract's life. Section 2.5 of the Contract states in relevant part that "[d]eliveries will be made in the quantities, on the dates, and at the times specified by Buyer in this Contract or any subsequent releases or instructions Buyer issues under this Contract," and that "[i]f the requirements of Buyer's customers or market, economic or other conditions require changes in delivery schedules, Buyer may change the rate of scheduled shipments or direct temporary suspension of scheduled shipments without entitling [Automodular] to a price adjustment or other compensation." This provision demonstrates the intent of the parties to allow the buyer to effectively control the timing and quantity of deliveries without entitling Automodular to an adjustment in price. [**In re Delphi Corp.**, 2009 WL 803598 (S.D.N.Y. 2009)]

CPA   12-1c **Communication of Offer to Offeree**

An offer must be communicated to the offeree. Otherwise, the offeree cannot accept even though knowledge of the offer has been indirectly acquired. Internal management communications of an enterprise that are not intended for outsiders or employees do not constitute offers and cannot be accepted by them. Sometimes, particularly in the case of unilateral contracts, the offeree performs the act called for by the offeror without knowing of the offer's existence. Such performance does not constitute an acceptance. Thus, without knowing that a reward is offered for information leading to the arrest of a particular criminal, a person may provide information that leads to the arrest of the criminal. In most states, if that person subsequently learns of the reward, the reward cannot be recovered.[16]

---

[14] *Simcala v. American Coal Trade, Inc.*, 821 So. 2d 197 (Ala. 2001).
[15] *Honeywell International Inc. v. Air Products and Chemicals, Inc.*, 872 A.2d 944 (Sup. Ct. Del. 2005).
[16] With respect to the offeror, it should not make any difference, as a practical matter, whether the services were rendered with or without knowledge of the existence of the offer. Only a small number of states have adopted this view, however.

Not only must the offer be communicated but also it must be communicated by the offeror or at the offeror's direction.

CPA 12-2 Termination of Offer

An offeree cannot accept a terminated offer. Offers may be terminated by revocation, counteroffer, rejection, lapse of time, death or disability of a party, or subsequent illegality.

CPA 12-2a Revocation of Offer by Offeror

Ordinarily, an offeror can revoke the offer before it is accepted. If this is done, the offeree cannot create a contract by accepting the revoked offer. **For Example,** Bank of America (BOA) contended that it had reached a valid settlement agreement on December 17, 2010, with Jonathan Davidoff concerning his lawsuit against BOA seeking damages for slander of credit and breach of contract. At 3:08 P.M. on December 17, 2010, Davidoff revoked his offer to settle the matter. A few minutes later BOA counsel sent by e-mail the settlement agreements signed by the defendants and asked if Mr. Davidoff would "rescind his rejection." Davidoff clearly revoked the settlement offer prior to BOA's delivery of acceptance of the offer and no contract was formed.[17]

An ordinary offer may be revoked at any time before it is accepted even though the offeror has expressly promised that the offer will be good for a stated period and that period has not yet expired.

The fact that the offeror expressly promised to keep the offer open has no effect when no consideration was given for that promise.

What Constitutes a Revocation?

No particular form or words are required to constitute a revocation. Any words indicating the offeror's termination of the offer are sufficient. A notice sent to the offeree that the property that is the subject of the offer has been sold to a third person is a revocation of the offer. A customer's order for goods, which is an offer to purchase at certain prices, is revoked by a notice to the seller of the cancellation of the order, provided that such notice is communicated before the order is accepted.

Communication of Revocation

A revocation of an offer is ordinarily effective only when it is made known to the offeree.[18] Until it is communicated to the offeree, directly or indirectly, the offeree has reason to believe that there is still an offer that may be accepted, and the offeree may rely on this belief. A letter revoking an offer made to a particular offeree is not effective until the offeree receives it. It is not a revocation when the offeror writes it or even when it is mailed or dispatched. A written revocation is effective, however, when it is delivered to the offeree's agent or to the offeree's residence or place of business under such circumstances that the offeree may be reasonably expected to be aware of its receipt.

It is ordinarily held that there is a sufficient communication of the revocation when the offeree learns indirectly of the offeror's revocation. This is particularly true in a land sale when the seller-offeror, after making an offer to sell the land to the offeree, sells the land to a third person and the offeree indirectly learns of such sale. The offeree necessarily realizes that the seller cannot perform the original offer and therefore must be considered to have revoked it.

---

[17] *Davidoff v. Bank of America*, 2011 WL 999564 (S.D. Fla. Oct. 18, 2010).
[18] *MD Drilling and Blasting, Inc. v. MLS Construction, LLC*, 889 A.2d 850 (Conn. App. 2006).

If the offeree accepts an offer before it is effectively revoked, a valid contract is created.

Option Contracts

An *option contract* is a binding promise to keep an offer open for a stated period of time or until a specified date. An option contract requires that the promisor receive consideration—that is, something, such as a sum of money—as the price for the promise to keep the offer open. In other words, the option is a contract to refrain from revoking an offer.

Firm Offers

As another exception to the rule that an offer can be revoked at any time before acceptance, statutes in some states provide that an offeror cannot revoke an offer prior to its expiration when the offeror makes a firm offer. A **firm offer** is an offer that states that it is to be irrevocable, or irrevocable for a stated period of time. Under the Uniform Commercial Code, this doctrine of firm offer applies to a merchant's signed, written offer to buy or sell goods but with a maximum of three months on its period of irrevocability.[19]

firm offer–offer stated to be held open for a specified time, under the UCC, with respect to merchants.

12-2b Counteroffer by Offeree

The offeree rejects the offer when it ignores the original offer and replies with a different offer.[20] If the offeree purports to accept an offer but in so doing makes any change to the terms of the offer, such action is a **counteroffer** that rejects the original offer. An "acceptance" that changes the terms of the offer or adds new terms is a rejection of the original offer and constitutes a counteroffer.[21]

counteroffer–proposal by an offeree to the offeror that changes the terms of, and thus rejects, the original offer.

Ordinarily, if *A* makes an offer, such as to sell a used automobile to *B* for $3,000, and *B* in reply makes an offer to buy at $2,500, the original offer is terminated. *B* is in effect indicating refusal of the original offer and in its place is making a different offer. Such an offer by the offeree is known as a *counteroffer*. No contract arises unless the original offeror accepts the counteroffer.

Counteroffers are not limited to offers that directly contradict the original offers. Any departure from or addition to the original offer is a counteroffer even though the original offer was silent on the point added by the counteroffer.

CASE SUMMARY

The Counteroffer Serves as a Rejection

FACTS: While riding her motorcycle Amy Kemper was struck by a vehicle driven by Brown. She suffered serious injuries and Brown was charged with DUI. Kemper sent a demand letter to Brown's insurance claim's administrator Statewide, which stated in part:

Please send all the insurance money that Mr. Brown had under his insurance policy. In exchange, I will agree to sign a limited release.

The release must not have any language saying that I will have to pay Mr. Brown or his insurance company any of their incurred costs.

.... If you fail to meet my demand, I will be forced to hire an attorney and sue Mr. Brown and your company. Please do not contact me, or my friends[,] as this demand is very simple.

Statewide sent a letter to Kemper agreeing to settle her claims for the limits of Brown's liability insurance. Attached

[19] U.C.C. §2-205.
[20] *Bourque v. FDIC*, 42 F.3d 704 (1st Cir. 1994).
[21] *Hardy Corp. v. Rayco Industrial, Inc.*, 143 So. 3d 172 (Ala. 2013).

The Counteroffer Serves as a Rejection continued

to the letter was a $25,000 check and a two-page limited liability release form. The letter stated, in part,

> *[i]n concluding the settlement, we are entrusting that you place money in an escrow account in regards to any and all liens pending. This demand is being asserted to protect the lien's interest[.]*

Ms. Kemper rejected Statewide's "counteroffer" and filed suit. Brown filed a motion to enforce the "settlement agreement."

DECISION: Judgment for Kemper. To establish a contract the offer must be accepted unequivocally and without variance of any sort. Statewide demanded that Kemper place the settlements funds into an escrow account to protect against any pending liens. Its response was a counteroffer rather than an unconditional and unequivocal acceptance. No binding settlement agreement was formed. [*Kemper v. Brown*, **754 S.E.2d 141 (Ga. App. 2014)**]

12-2c Rejection of Offer by Offeree

If the offeree rejects the offer and communicates this rejection to the offeror, the offer is terminated. Communication of a rejection terminates an offer even though the period for which the offeror agreed to keep the offer open has not yet expired. It may be that the offeror is willing to renew the offer, but unless this is done, there is no longer any offer for the offeree to accept.

12-2d Lapse of Time

When the offer states that it is open until a particular date, the offer terminates on that date if it has not yet been accepted. This is particularly so when the offeror declares that the offer shall be void after the expiration of the specified time. Such limitations are strictly construed. **For Example,** Landry's Restaurant Minnesota Inc. extended a written, signed offer to Starlite L.P. to lease Starlite's real estate for a period of 20 years. The written offer stated that if a fully executed acceptance of the lease is not returned to Landry's Minnesota Inc. within six days of the written offer dated April 30, 1998, "the offer to lease … shall be deemed withdrawn and this lease shall be deemed null and void." Starlite signed and returned the lease agreement on May 11, 1998, five days after the May 6 deadline. Landry's Minnesota occupied the property and built a restaurant on it but vacated the property after nine years. Starlite sued the restaurant's parent corporation, Landry's Restaurants Inc., as guarantor of the lease, seeking payment for past due and ongoing rent. Starlite's lawsuit was not successful as no valid lease agreement existed because no contract could be properly formed when acceptance occurred after the written offer had expired.[22]

If the offer contains a time limitation for acceptance, an attempted acceptance after the expiration of that time has no effect and does not give rise to a contract.[23] When a specified time limitation is imposed on an option, the option cannot be exercised after the expiration of that time, regardless of whether the option was exercised within what would have been held a reasonable time if no time period had been specified.

If the offer does not specify a time, it will terminate after the lapse of a reasonable time. What constitutes a reasonable time depends on the circumstances of each case—that is, on the nature of the subject matter, the nature of the market in which it is sold, the time of

---

[22] *Starlite Limited Partnership v. Landry's Restaurants, Inc.*, 780 N.W.2d 396 (Minn. App. 2010).
[23] *Century 21 Pinetree Properties, Inc. v. Cason*, 469 S.E.2d 458 (Ga. App. 1996).

year, and other factors of supply and demand. If a commodity is perishable or fluctuates greatly in value, the reasonable time will be much shorter than if the subject matter is of a stable value. An offer to sell a harvested crop of tomatoes would expire within a very short time. When a seller purports to accept an offer after it has lapsed by the expiration of time, the seller's acceptance is merely a counteroffer and does not create a contract unless the buyer accepts that counteroffer.

12-2e Death or Disability of Either Party

If either the offeror or offeree dies or becomes mentally incompetent before the offer is accepted, the offer is automatically terminated. **For Example,** Chet Wilson offers to sell his ranch to Interport, Inc., for $2.5 million. Five days later, Chet is killed in an aviation accident. Interport, Inc., subsequently writes to Chet Wilson Jr., an adult, that his father's offer is accepted. No contract is formed because the offer made by Chet died with him.

CPA

12-2f Subsequent Illegality

If the performance of the contract becomes illegal after the offer is made, the offer is terminated. **For Example,** if an offer is made to sell six semiautomatic handguns to a commercial firing range for $550 per weapon but a new law prohibiting such sales is enacted before the offer is accepted, the offer is terminated.

CPA

12-3 Acceptance of Offer

An **acceptance** is the assent of the offeree to the terms of the offer. Objective standards determine whether there has been an agreement of the parties.

acceptance–unqualified assent to the act or proposal of another; as the acceptance of a draft (bill of exchange), of an offer to make a contract, of goods delivered by the seller, or of a gift or deed.

12-3a What Constitutes an Acceptance?

No particular form of words or mode of expression is required, but there must be a clear expression that the offeree agrees to be bound by the terms of the offer. If the offeree reserves the right to reject the offer, such action is not an acceptance.[24]

12-3b Privilege of Offeree

Ordinarily, the offeree may refuse to accept an offer. If there is no acceptance, by definition there is no contract. The fact that there had been a series of contracts between the parties and that one party's offer had always been accepted before by the other does not create any legal obligation to continue to accept subsequent offers.

CPA

12-3c Effect of Acceptance

The acceptance of an offer creates a binding agreement or contract,[25] assuming that all of the other elements of a contract are present. Neither party can subsequently withdraw from or cancel the contract without the consent of the other party. **For Example,** James Gang refused to honor an oral stock purchase agreement he made with Moshen Sadeghi under terms he assented to and that were announced on the record to a court as a mutual

[24] *Pantano v. McGowan*, 530 N.W.2d 912 (Neb. 1995).
[25] *Ochoa v. Ford*, 641 N.E.2d 1042 (Ind. App. 1994).

settlement of a dispute. Gang was not allowed subsequently to withdraw from the agreement, because it was an enforceable contract.[26]

CPA   12-3d ## Nature of Acceptance

An *acceptance* is the offeree's manifestation of intent to enter into a binding agreement on the terms stated in the offer. Whether there is an acceptance depends on whether the offeree has manifested an intent to accept. It is the objective or outward appearance that is controlling rather than the subjective or unexpressed intent of the offeree.[27]

In the absence of a contrary requirement in the offer, an acceptance may be indicated by an informal "okay," by a mere affirmative nod of the head, or in the case of an offer of a unilateral contract, by performance of the act called for.

The acceptance must be absolute and unconditional. It must accept just what is offered.[28] If the offeree changes any terms of the offer or adds any new term, there is no acceptance because the offeree does not agree to what was offered.

When the offeree does not accept the offer exactly as made, the addition of any qualification converts the "acceptance" into a counteroffer, and no contract arises unless the original offeror accepts such a counteroffer.

CPA   12-3e ## Who May Accept?

Only the person to whom an offer is directed may accept it. If anyone else attempts to accept it, no agreement or contract with that person arises.

If the offer is directed to a particular class rather than a specified individual, anyone within that class may accept it. If the offer is made to the public at large, any member of the public at large having knowledge of the existence of the offer may accept it.

When a person to whom an offer was not made attempts to accept it, the attempted acceptance has the effect of an offer. If the original offeror is willing to accept this offer, a binding contract arises. If the original offeror does not accept the new offer, there is no contract.

CASE SUMMARY

There's No Turning Back

FACTS: As a lease was about to expire, the landlord, CRA Development, wrote the tenant, Keryakos Textiles, setting forth the square footage and the rate terms on which the lease would be renewed. Keryakos sent a reply stating that it was willing to pay the proposed rate but wanted different cancellation and option terms in the renewal contract. CRA rejected Keryakos's terms, and on learning this, Keryakos notified CRA that it accepted the terms of its original letter. CRA sought to evict Keryakos from the property, claiming that no lease contract existed between it and Keryakos.

DECISION: The lease contract is governed by ordinary contract law. When the tenant offered other terms in place of those made by the landlord's offer, the tenant made a counteroffer. This had the effect of rejecting or terminating the landlord's offer. The tenant could not then accept the rejected offer after the tenant's counteroffer was rejected. Therefore, there was no contract. [*Keryakos Textiles, Inc. v. CRA Development, Inc.*, **563 N.Y.S.2d 308 (App. Div. 1990)**]

---

[26] *Sadeghi v. Gang*, 270 S.W.3d 773 (Tex. App. 2008).
[27] *Cowan v. Mervin Mewes, Inc.*, 546 N.W.2d 104 (S.D. 1996).
[28] *Jones v. Frickey*, 618 S.E.2d 29 (Ga. App. 2005).

CPA   ## 12-3f Manner and Time of Acceptance

The offeror may specify the manner and time for accepting the offer. When the offeror specifies that there must be a written acceptance, no contract arises when the offeree makes an oral acceptance. If the offeror calls for acceptance by a specified time and date, a late acceptance has no legal effect, and a contract is not formed. Where no time is specified in the offer, the offeree has a reasonable period of time to accept the offer. After the time specified in the offer or a reasonable period of time expires (when no time is specified in the offer), the offeree's power to make a contract by accepting the offer "lapses."

When the offeror calls for the performance of an act or of certain conduct, the performance thereof is an acceptance of the offer and creates a unilateral contract.

When the offeror has specified a particular manner and time of acceptance, generally, the offeree cannot accept in any other way. The basic rule applied by the courts is that the offeror is the master of the offer![29]

CPA   ## Silence as Acceptance

In most cases, the offeree's silence and failure to act cannot be regarded as an acceptance. Ordinarily, the offeror is not permitted to frame an offer in such a way as to make the silence and inaction of the offeree operate as an acceptance. Nor can a party to an existing contract effect a modification of that agreement without the other party's actual acceptance or approval. **For Example,** H. H. Taylor made a contract with Andy Stricker, a civil engineer, to design a small hotel. The parties agreed on an hourly rate with "total price not to exceed $7,200," and required that additional charges be presented to Taylor prior to proceeding with any changes. Andy was required to dedicate more hours to the project than anticipated but could not present the additional charges to Taylor because Taylor would not return his phone calls. He billed Taylor $9,035 for his services. Taylor's failure to act in not returning phone calls is not a substitute for the assent needed to modify a contract. Stricker is thus only entitled to $7,200.[30]

Unordered Goods and Tickets

Sometimes a seller writes to a person with whom the seller has not had any prior dealings, stating that unless notified to the contrary, the seller will send specified merchandise and the recipient is obligated to pay for it at stated prices. There is no acceptance if the recipient of the letter ignores the offer and does nothing. The silence of the person receiving the letter is not an acceptance, and the sender, as a reasonable person, should recognize that none was intended.

This rule applies to all kinds of goods, books, magazines, and tickets sent through the mail when they have not been ordered. The fact that the items are not returned does not mean that they have been accepted; that is, the offeree is required neither to pay for nor to return the items. If desired, the recipient of the unordered goods may write "Return to Sender" on the unopened package and put the package back into the mail without any additional postage. The Postal Reorganization Act provides that the person who receives unordered mailed merchandise from a commercial sender has the right "to retain, use, discard, or dispose of it in any manner the recipient sees fit without any obligation

---

[29] See *1-800 Contacts, Inc. v. Weigner,* 127 P.3d 1241 (Utah App. 2005).
[30] *Stricker v. Taylor,* 975 P.2d 930 (Or. App. 1999).

whatsoever to the sender."[31] It provides further that any unordered merchandise that is mailed must have attached to it a clear and conspicuous statement of the recipient's right to treat the goods in this manner.

CPA   12-3g Communication of Acceptance

Acceptance by the offeree is the last step in the formation of a bilateral contract. Intuitively, the offeror's receipt of the acceptance should be the point in time when the contract is formed and its terms apply. When the parties are involved in face-to-face negotiations, a contract is formed upon the offeror's receipt of the acceptance. When the offeror hears the offeree's words of acceptance, the parties may shake hands, signifying their understanding that the contract has been formed.

E-COMMERCE & CYBERLAW

Contract Formation on the Internet

It is not possible for an online service provider or seller to individually bargain with each person who visits its Web site. The Web site owner, therefore, as offeror, places its proposed terms on its Web site and requires visitors to assent to these terms in order to access the site, download software, or purchase a product or service.

In a written contract, the parties sign a paper document indicating their intention to be bound by the terms of the contract. Online, however, an agreement may be accomplished by the visitor-offeree simply typing the words "I Accept" in an onscreen box and then clicking a "send" or similar button that indicates acceptance. Or the individual clicks an "I Agree" or "I Accept" icon or check box. Access to the site is commonly denied those who do not agree to the terms. Such agreements have come to be known as *clickwrap* agreements and in the case of software license agreements, *SLAs*. The agreements contain fee schedules and other financial terms and may contain terms such as a notice of the proprietary nature of the material contained on the site and of any limitations on the use of the site and the downloading of software. Moreover, the clickwrap agreements may contain limitations on liability, including losses associated with the use of downloaded software or products or services purchased from the site.

To determine whether a clickwrap agreement is enforceable, courts apply traditional principles of contract law and focus on whether the plaintiffs had reasonable notice of and manifested assent to the clickwrap agreement. Failure to read an enforceable clickwrap agreement, as with any binding contract, will not excuse compliance with its terms.

In *Specht v. Netscape Communications Corp.*,* the Internet users were urged to click on a button to download free software, but the offer did not make clear to the user that clicking the download button would signify assent to restrictive contractual terms and conditions. The court, in its 2002 decision, declined to enforce this clickwrap agreement. Internet sellers and service providers generally learned from the *Specht* decision, and most clickwrap agreements now provide sufficient notice and means for clear assent. For example, in *Feldman v. Google, Inc.*,** decided in 2007, the user was unsuccessful in challenging the terms of Google's "AdWords" Program clickwrap agreement. In order to activate an AdWords account, the user had to visit a Web page that displayed the agreement in a scrollable text box. The text of the agreement was immediately visible to the user, as was a prominent admonition in boldface to read the terms and conditions carefully, and with instructions to indicate assent if the user agreed to the terms.

Unlike the impermissible agreement in *Specht*, the user here had to take affirmative action and click the "Yes, I agree to the above terms and conditions" button in order to proceed to the next step. Clicking "Continue" without clicking the "Yes" button would have returned the user to the same Web page. If the user did not agree to all of the terms, he could not have activated his account, placed ads, or incurred charges.

*306 F.3d 17 (2d Cir. 2002).
***Feldman v. Google, Inc.*, 513 F. Supp. 2d 229 (E.D. Pa. 2007). See also *A.V. v. Iparadigms, LLC*, 554 F. Supp. 2d 473 (E.D. Va. 2008).

---

[31] Federal Postal Reorganization Act §3009.

C P A   Mailbox Rule

When the parties are negotiating at a distance from each other, special rules have developed as to when the acceptance takes effect based on the commercial expediency of creating a contract at the earliest period of time and the protection of the offeree. Under the so-called *mailbox rule*, a properly addressed, postage-paid mailed acceptance takes effect when the acceptance is placed into the control of the U.S. Postal Service[32] or, by judicial extension, is placed in the control of a private third-party carrier such as Federal Express or United Parcel Service.[33] That is, the acceptance is effective upon dispatch even before it is received by the offeror.

CASE SUMMARY

When the Mailbox Bangs Shut

FACTS: The Thoelkes owned land. The Morrisons mailed an offer to the Thoelkes to buy their land. The Thoelkes agreed to this offer and mailed back a contract signed by them. While this letter was in transit, the Thoelkes notified the Morrisons that their acceptance was revoked. Were the Thoelkes bound by a contract?

DECISION: The acceptance was effective when mailed, and the subsequent revocation of the acceptance had no effect. [*Morrison v. Thoelke*, 155 So. 2d 889 (Fla. App. 1963)]

The offeror may avoid the application of this rule by stating in the offer that acceptance shall take effect upon receipt by the offeror.

C P A   Determining the Applicable Means of Communication

The modern rule on the selection of the appropriate medium of communication of acceptance is that unless otherwise unambiguously indicated in the offer, it shall be construed as inviting acceptance in any manner and by any medium reasonable under the circumstances.[34] A medium of communication is normally reasonable if it is one used by the offeror or if it is customary in similar transactions at the time and place the offer is received. Thus, if the offeror uses the mail to extend an offer, the offeree may accept by using the mail. Indeed, acceptance by mail is ordinarily reasonable when the parties are negotiating at a distance even if the offer is not made by mail.

C P A   Telephone and Electronic Communication of Acceptance

Although telephonic communication is very similar to face-to-face communication, most U.S. courts, nevertheless, have applied the mailbox rule, holding that telephoned acceptances are effective where and when dispatched.

---

[32] See *Adams v. Lindsell*, 106 Eng. Rep. 250 (K.B. 1818). Common law jurisdictions have unanimously adopted the mailbox rule, as has the Restatement (Second) of Contracts §63, and the U.C.C. [see U.C.C. §1-201(26),(38)].

[33] But see *Baca v. Trejo*, 902 N.E.2d 1108 (Ill App. 2009) whereby an Illinois court determined that a statute deeming a document to be filed with a state court on the date shown by the U.S. Postal Service cancellation mark—the mailbox rule—does not apply to documents consigned to a private carrier, UPS. The court reasoned that courts should not have the task of deciding which carriers are acceptable.

[34] Restatement (Second) of Contracts §30; U.C.C. §2-206(1) (a).

The courts have yet to address the applicability of the mailbox rule to e-mail. However, when the offeree's server is under the control of an independent entity, such as an online service provider, and the offeree cannot withdraw the message, it is anticipated that the courts will apply the mailbox rule, and acceptance will take effect on proper dispatch. In the case of companies that operate their own servers, the acceptance will take effect when the message is passed onto the Internet.

Facsimile transmissions are substantially instantaneous and could be treated as face-to-face communications. However, it is anticipated that U.S. courts, when called upon to deal with this issue, will apply the mailbox acceptance-upon-dispatch rule as they do with telephoned acceptances.

Effects of the Mailbox Rule

If an offer requires that acceptance be communicated by a specific date and the acceptance is properly dispatched by the offeree on the final date, the acceptance is timely and the contract is formed, even though the offeror actually receives the acceptance well after the specified date has passed. **For Example,** by letter dated February 18, 1999, Morton's of Chicago mailed a certified letter to the Crab House accepting the Crab House's offer to terminate its restaurant lease. The Crab House, Inc., sought to revoke its offer to terminate the lease in a certified letter dated February 18, 1999, and by facsimile transmission to Morton's dated February 19, 1999. On February 22, 1999, the Crab House received Morton's acceptance letter; and on the same date Morton's received Crab House's letter revoking the offer to terminate the lease. Acceptance of an offer is effective upon dispatch to the Postal Service, and the contract springs into existence at the time of the mailing. Offers, revocations, and rejections are generally effective only upon the offeree's receipt. Morton's dispatch of its acceptance letter on February 18 formed an agreement to terminate the lease, and the fax dispatched on February 19 was too late to revoke the offer to terminate the lease.[35]

12-3h Auction Sales

At an auction sale, the statements made by the auctioneer to draw forth bids are merely invitations to negotiate. Each bid is an offer, which is not accepted until the auctioneer indicates that a particular offer or bid is accepted. Usually, this is done by the fall of the auctioneer's hammer, indicating that the highest bid made has been accepted.[36] Because a bid is merely an offer, the bidder may withdraw the bid at any time before it is accepted by the auctioneer.

Ordinarily, the auctioneer who is not satisfied with the amounts of the bids that are being made may withdraw any article or all of the property from the sale. Once a bid is accepted, however, the auctioneer cannot cancel the sale. In addition, if it had been announced that the sale was to be made "without reserve," the property must be sold to the person making the highest bid regardless of how low that bid may be.

In an auction "with reserve," the auctioneer takes bids as agent for the seller with the understanding that no contract is formed until the seller accepts the transaction.[37]

---

[35] *Morton's of Chicago v. Crab House Inc.*, 746 N.Y.S.2d 317 (2002). *Kass v. Grais*, 2007 WL 2815498 (N.Y. Sup. Sept. 4, 2007).

[36] *Dry Creek Cattle Co. v. Harriet Bros. Limited Partnership*, 908 P.2d 399 (Wyo. 1995).

[37] *Marten v. Staab*, 543 N.W.2d 436 (Neb. 1996). Statutes regulate auctions and auctioneers in all states. For example, state of Maine law prohibits an auctioneer from conducting an auction without first having a written contract with the consignor of any property to be sold, including (1) whether the auction is with reserve or without reserve, (2) the commission rate, and (3) a description of all items to be sold. See *Street v. Board of Licensing of Auctioneers*, 889 A.2d 319 ([Me.] 2006).

Make the Connection

Summary

Because a contract arises when an offer is accepted, it is necessary to find that there was an offer and that it was accepted. If either element is missing, there is no contract.

An offer does not exist unless the offeror has contractual intent. This intent is lacking if the statement of the person is merely an invitation to negotiate, a statement of intention, or an agreement to agree at a later date. Newspaper ads, price quotations, and catalog prices are ordinarily merely invitations to negotiate and cannot be accepted.

An offer must be definite. If an offer is indefinite, its acceptance will not create a contract because it will be held that the resulting agreement is too vague to enforce. In some cases, an offer that is by itself too indefinite is made definite because some writing or standard is incorporated by reference and made part of the offer. In some cases the offer is made definite by implying terms that were not stated. In other cases, the indefinite part of the offer is ignored when that part can be divided or separated from the balance of the offer.

Assuming that there is in fact an offer that is made with contractual intent and that it is sufficiently definite, it still does not have the legal effect of an offer unless it is communicated to the offeree by or at the direction of the offeror.

In some cases, there was an offer but it was terminated before it was accepted. By definition, an attempted acceptance made after the offer has been terminated has no effect. The offeror may revoke the ordinary offer at any time. All that is required is the showing of the intent to revoke and the communication of that intent to the offeree. The offeror's power to revoke is barred by the existence of an option contract under common law or a firm offer under the Uniform Commercial Code. An offer is also terminated by the express rejection of the offer or by the making of a counteroffer, by the lapse of the time stated in the offer or of a reasonable time when none is stated, by the death or disability of either party, or by a change of law that makes illegal a contract based on the particular offer.

When the offer is accepted, a contract arises. Only the offeree can accept an offer, and the acceptance must be of the offer exactly as made without any qualification or change. Ordinarily, the offeree may accept or reject as the offeree chooses.

The acceptance is any manifestation of intent to agree to the terms of the offer. Ordinarily, silence or failure to act does not constitute acceptance. The recipient of unordered goods and tickets may dispose of the goods or use the goods without such action constituting an acceptance. An acceptance does not exist until the words or conduct demonstrating assent to the offer is communicated to the offeror. Acceptance by mail takes effect at the time and place when and where the letter is mailed or the fax is transmitted.

In an auction sale, the auctioneer asking for bids makes an invitation to negotiate. A person making a bid is making an offer, and the acceptance of the highest bid by the auctioneer is an acceptance of that offer and gives rise to a contract. When the auction sale is without reserve, the auctioneer must accept the highest bid. If the auction is not expressly without reserve, the auctioneer may refuse to accept any of the bids.

Learning Outcomes

After studying this chapter, you should be able to clearly explain:

12-1   Requirements of an Offer

LO.1   Decide whether an offer contains definite and certain terms

See the *Novak* case for an example of an oral contract with definite enforceable terms, page 224.
See the *Plankenhorn* case for the meaning of a "damn good job," page 225.

See the legal impact of a party's statement that the contract "was going to be signed" in the *Hewitt* example, page 223.
See the *Wigod* case that discusses the test for a valid, binding offer, page 222.

12-2   Termination of Offer

LO.2   Explain the exceptions the law makes to the requirement of definiteness
See the *Delphi* case on requirements contracts, page 228.

LO.3 Explain all the ways an offer can be terminated
See the discussion of revocation, counteroffer, rejection, lapse of time, death or disability of a party, or subsequent illegality, pages 229–232.
See the *Davidoff* example of a revocation communicated to the offeree prior to acceptance, page 229.
See the *Landry's Restaurants* example that illustrates the effect of an "acceptance" signed just a few days after the written offer had expired, page 231.
See the *Kemper* case showing that a counteroffer serves as a rejection, page 231.

12-3   Acceptance of Offer

LO.4 Explain what constitutes the acceptance of an offer
See the *Sadeghi* example where acceptance of an offer created a binding contract, pages 232–233.
See the *Keryakos Textiles* case on the impact of a counteroffer, page 233.

LO.5 Explain the implications of failing to read a clickwrap agreement
See the *Feldman* case as an example of an enforceable clickwrap agreement containing notice and manifested assent, page 235.

Key Terms

acceptance	firm offer	requirements contract
counteroffer	offer	
divisible contract	output contract	

Questions and Case Problems

1. Bernie and Phil's Great American Surplus store placed an ad in the *Sunday Times* stating, "Next Saturday at 8:00 A.M. sharp, 3 brand new mink coats worth $5,000 each will be sold for $500 each! First come, first served." Marsha Lufklin was first in line when the store opened and went directly to the coat department, but the coats identified in the ad were not available for sale. She identified herself to the manager and pointed out that she was first in line in conformity with the store's advertised offer and that she was ready to pay the $500 price set forth in the store's offer. The manager responded that a newspaper ad is just an invitation to negotiate and that the store decided to withdraw "the mink coat promotion." Review the text on unilateral contracts in the section titled "Bilateral and Unilateral Contracts" in Chapter 11. Decide.

2. Brown made an offer to purchase Overman's house on a standard printed form. Underneath Brown's signature was the statement: "ACCEPTANCE ON REVERSE SIDE." Overman did not sign the offer on the back but sent Brown a letter accepting the offer. Later, Brown refused to perform the contract, and Overman sued him for breach of contract. Brown claimed there was no contract because the offer had not been accepted in the manner specified by the offer. Decide. [*Overman v. Brown*, 372 N.W.2d 102 (Neb.)]

3. Katherine mailed Paul an offer with definite and certain terms and that was legal in all respects stating that it was good for 10 days. Two days later she sent Paul a letter by certified mail (time stamped by the Postal Service at 1:14 P.M.) stating that the original offer was revoked. That evening Paul e-mailed acceptance of the offer to Katherine. She immediately phoned him to tell him that she had revoked the offer that afternoon, and that he would surely receive it in tomorrow's mail. Was the offer revoked by Katherine?

4. Nelson wanted to sell his home. Baker sent him a written offer to purchase the home. Nelson made some changes to Baker's offer and wrote him that he, Nelson, was accepting the offer as amended. Baker notified Nelson that he was dropping out of the transaction. Nelson sued Baker for breach of contract. Decide. What social forces and ethical values are involved? [*Nelson v. Baker*, 776 S.W.2d 52 (Mo. App.)]

5. Lessack Auctioneers advertised an auction sale that was open to the public and was to be conducted with reserve. Gordon attended the auction and bid $100 for a work of art that was worth much more. No higher bid, however, was made. Lessack refused to sell the item for $100 and withdrew the item from the sale. Gordon claimed that because he was the highest bidder, Lessack was required to sell the item to him. Was he correct?

6. Willis Music Co. advertised a television set at $22.50 in the Sunday newspaper. Ehrlich ordered a set, but the company refused to deliver it on the grounds that the price in the newspaper ad was a mistake. Ehrlich sued the company. Was it liable? Why or why not? [*Ehrlich v. Willis Music Co.*, 113 N.E.2d 252 (Ohio App.)]

7. When a movement was organized to build Charles City College, Hauser and others signed pledges to contribute to the college. At the time of signing, Hauser inquired what would happen if he should die or be unable to pay. The representative of the college stated that the pledge would then not be binding and that it was merely a statement of intent. The college failed financially, and Pappas was appointed receiver to collect and liquidate the assets of the college corporation. He sued Hauser for the amount due on his pledge. Hauser raised the defense that the pledge was not a binding contract. Decide. What ethical values are involved? [*Pappas v. Hauser*, 197 N.W.2d 607 (Iowa)]

8. Maria Cantu was a special education teacher under a one-year contract with the San Benito School district for the 1990–1991 school year. On Saturday, August 18, just weeks before fall-term classes were to begin, she hand delivered a letter of resignation to her supervisor. Late Monday afternoon the superintendent put in the mail a properly stamped and addressed letter to Cantu accepting her offer of resignation. The next morning at 8:00, before the superintendent's letter reached her, Cantu hand delivered a letter withdrawing her resignation. The superintendent refused to recognize the attempted rescission of the resignation. Decide. [*Cantu v. Central Education Agency*, 884 S.W.2d 563 (Tex. App.)]

9. A. H. Zehmer discussed selling a farm to Lucy. After a 40-minute discussion of the first draft of a contract, Zehmer and his wife, Ida, signed a second draft stating: "We hereby agree to sell to W. O. Lucy the Ferguson farm complete for $50,000 title satisfactory to buyer." Lucy agreed to purchase the farm on these terms. Thereafter, the Zehmers refused to transfer title to Lucy and claimed they had made the contract for sale as a joke. Lucy brought an action to compel performance of the contract. The Zehmers claimed there was no contract. Were they correct? [*Lucy v. Zehmer*, 84 S.E.2d 516 (Va. App.)]

10. Wheeler operated an automobile service station, which he leased from W. C. Cornitius, Inc. The lease ran for three years. Although the lease did not contain any provision for renewal, it was in fact renewed six times for successive three-year terms. The landlord refused to renew the lease for a seventh time. Wheeler brought suit to compel the landlord to accept his offer to renew the lease. Decide. [*William C. Cornitius, Inc. v. Wheeler*, 556 P.2d 666 (Or.)]

11. Buster Cogdill, a real estate developer, made an offer to the Bank of Benton to have the bank provide construction financing for the development of an outlet mall, with funds to be provided at prime rate plus two percentage points. The bank's president Julio Plunkett thanked Buster for the proposal and said, "I will start the paperwork." Did Cogdill have a contract with the Bank of Benton? [*Bank of Benton v. Cogdill*, 454 N.E.2d 1120 (Ill. App.)]

12. Ackerley Media Group, Inc., claimed to have a three-season advertising Team Sponsorship Agreement (TSA) with Sharp Electronics Corporation to promote Sharp products at all Seattle Supersonics NBA basketball home games. Sharp contended that a valid agreement did not exist for the third season (2000–2001) because a material price term was missing, thus resulting in an unenforceable "agreement to agree." The terms of the TSA for the 2000–2001 third season called for a base payment of $144,200 and an annual increase "not to exceed 6% [and] to be mutually agreed upon by the parties." No "mutually agreed" increase was negotiated by the parties. Ackerley seeks payment for the base price of $144,200 only. Sharp contends that since no price was agreed upon for the season, the entire TSA is unenforceable, and it is not obligated to pay for the 2000–2001 season. Is Sharp correct? [*Ackerley Media Group, Inc. v. Sharp Electronics Corp.*, 170 F. Supp. 2d 445 (S.D.N.Y.)]

13. L. B. Foster invited Tie and Track Systems Inc. to submit price quotes on items to be used in a railroad expansion project. Tie and Track responded by e-mail on August 11, 2006, with prices for 9 items of steel ties. The e-mail concluded, "The above prices are delivered/Terms of Payment—to be agreed/Delivery—to be agreed/We hope you are successful with your bid. If you require any additional information please call." Just 3 of the 9 items listed in Tie and Track's price quote were "accepted" by the project. L. B. Foster demanded that Tie and Track provide the items at the price listed in the quote. Tie and Track refused. L. B. Foster sued for breach of contract. Did the August 11 e-mail constitute an offer, acceptance of which could bind the supplier to

a contract? If so, was there a valid acceptance? [*L. B. Foster v. Tie and Track Systems, Inc.*, 2009 WL 900993 (N.D. Ill.)]

14. On August 15, 2003, Wilbert Heikkila signed an agreement with Kangas Realty to sell eight parcels of Heikkila's property. On September 8, 2003, David McLaughlin met with a Kangas agent who drafted McLaughlin's offer to purchase three of the parcels. McLaughlin signed the offer and gave the agent checks for each parcel. On September 9 and 10, 2003, the agent for Heikkila prepared three printed purchase agreements, one for each parcel. On September 14, 2003, David's wife, Joanne McLaughlin, met with the agent and signed the agreements. On September 16, 2003, Heikkila met with his real estate agent. Writing on the printed agreements, Heikkila changed the price of one parcel from $145,000 to $150,000, the price of another parcel from $32,000 to $45,000, and the price of the third parcel from $175,000 to $179,000. Neither of the McLaughlins signed an acceptance of Heikkila's changes to the printed agreements before Heikkila withdrew his offer to sell. The McLaughlins learned that Heikkila had withdrawn his offer on January 1, 2004, when the real estate agent returned the checks to them. Totally shocked at Heikkila's conduct, the McLaughlins brought action to compel specific performance of the purchase agreement signed by Joanne McLaughlin on their behalf. Decide. [*McLaughlin v. Heikkila*, 697 N.W.2d 231 (Minn. App.)]

CPA Questions

1. Able Sofa, Inc., sent Noll a letter offering to sell Noll a custom-made sofa for $5,000. Noll immediately sent a telegram to Able purporting to accept the offer. However, the telegraph company erroneously delivered the telegram to Abel Soda, Inc. Three days later, Able mailed a letter of revocation to Noll, which was received by Noll. Able refused to sell Noll the sofa. Noll sued Able for breach of contract. Able:

   a. Would have been liable under the deposited acceptance rule only if Noll had accepted by mail.

   b. Will avoid liability since it revoked its offer prior to receiving Noll's acceptance.

   c. Will be liable for breach of contract.

   d. Will avoid liability due to the telegraph company's error (Law, #2, 9911).

2. On September 27, Summers sent Fox a letter offering to sell Fox a vacation home for $150,000. On October 2, Fox replied by mail agreeing to buy the home for $145,000. Summers did not reply to Fox. Do Fox and Summers have a binding contract?

   a. No, because Fox failed to sign and return Summers's letter.

   b. No, because Fox's letter was a counteroffer.

   c. Yes, because Summers's offer was validly accepted.

   d. Yes, because Summers's silence is an implied acceptance of Fox's letter (Law, #2, 0462).

3. On June 15, Peters orally offered to sell a used lawn mower to Mason for $125. Peters specified that Mason had until June 20 to accept the offer. On June 16, Peters received an offer to purchase the lawn mower for $150 from Bronson, Mason's neighbor. Peters accepted Bronson's offer. On June 17, Mason saw Bronson using the lawn mower and was told the mower had been sold to Bronson. Mason immediately wrote to Peters to accept the June 15 offer. Which of the following statements is correct?

   a. Mason's acceptance would be effective when received by Peters.

   b. Mason's acceptance would be effective when mailed.

   c. Peters's offer had been revoked and Mason's acceptance was ineffective.

   d. Peters was obligated to keep the June 15 offer open until June 20 (Law, #13, 3095).

C H A P T E R   13

Capacity and Genuine Assent

A *contract* is a binding agreement. This agreement must be made between parties who have the capacity to do so. They must also truly agree so that all parties have really consented to the contract. This chapter explores the elements of contractual capacity of the parties and the genuineness of their assent.

13-1   Contractual Capacity

Some persons lack contractual capacity, a lack that embraces both those who have a status incapacity, such as minors, and those who have a factual incapacity, such as persons who are insane.

13-1a   Contractual Capacity Defined

contractual capacity– ability to understand that a contract is being made and to understand its general meaning.

Contractual capacity is the ability to understand that a contract is being made and to understand its general meaning. However, the fact that a person does not understand the full legal meaning of a contract does not mean that contractual capacity is lacking. Everyone is presumed to have capacity unless it is proven that capacity is lacking or there is status incapacity.[1] **For Example,** Jacqueline, aged 22, entered into a contract with Sunrise Storage Co. but later claimed that it was not binding because she did not understand several clauses in the printed contract. The contract was binding. No evidence supported her claim that she lacked capacity to contract or to understand its subject. Contractual capacity can exist even though a party does not understand every provision of the contract.

Status Incapacity

Over the centuries, the law has declared that some classes of persons lack contractual capacity. The purpose is to protect these classes by giving them the power to get out of unwise contracts. Of these classes, the most important today is the class identified as minors.

Until recent times, some other classes were held to lack contractual capacity in order to discriminate against them. Examples are married women and aliens. Still other classes, such as persons convicted of and sentenced for a felony, were held to lack contractual capacity in order to punish them. Today, these discriminatory and punitive incapacities have largely disappeared. Married women have the same contractual capacity as unmarried persons.

By virtue of international treaties, the discrimination against aliens has been removed.

CASE SUMMARY

We Really Mean Equal Rights

FACTS: An Alabama statute provided that a married woman could not sell her land without the consent of her husband. Montgomery made a contract to sell land she owned to Peddy. Montgomery's husband did not consent to the sale. Montgomery did not perform the contract and Peddy sued her. The defense was raised that the contract was void and could not be enforced because of the statute. Peddy claimed that the statute was unconstitutional.

DECISION: The statute was unconstitutional. Constitutions, both federal and state, guarantee all persons the equal protection of the law. Married women are denied this equal protection when they are treated differently than married men and unmarried women. The fact that such unequal treatment had once been regarded as proper does not justify its modern continuation. [*Peddy v. Montgomery,* **345 So. 2d 988 (Ala. 1991)**]

[1] In re *Adoption of Smith,* 578 So. 2d 988 (La. App. 1991).

Factual Incapacity

A *factual incapacity* contrasts with incapacity imposed because of the class or group to which a person belongs. A factual incapacity may exist when, because of a mental condition caused by medication, drugs, alcohol, illness, or age, a person does not understand that a contract is being made or understand its general nature. However, mere mental weakness does not incapacitate a person from contracting. It is sufficient if the individual has enough mental capacity to understand, to a reasonable extent, the nature and effect of what he is doing.[2]

13-1b Minors

Minors may make contracts.[3] To protect them, however, the law has always treated minors as a class lacking contractual capacity.

Who Is a Minor?

At common law, any person, male or female, under 21 years of age was a minor. At common law, minority ended the day before the 21st birthday. The "day before the birthday" rule is still followed, but the age of majority has been reduced from 21 years to 18 years.

CPA Minor's Power to Avoid Contracts

With exceptions that will be noted later, a contract made by a minor is voidable at the election of the minor. **For Example,** Adorian Deck, a minor, created a Twitter feed titled "@OMGFacts." The feed collected and republished interesting and trivial facts from other sources on the Internet. It was subscribed to by over 300,000 Twitter users, including some celebrities. Spatz, Inc., entered into a joint venture with Deck as described in a written contract signed by both parties, under which Spatz would expand the Twitter feed into a suite of Internet products, including a Web site and a Youtube.com video channel. In an "OMG-moment" prior to his 18th birthday, Deck notified Spatz, Inc., that he wished to disaffirm the parties' agreement. This disaffirmation by a minor rescinded the entire contract, rendering it a nullity.[4] The minor may affirm or ratify the contract on attaining majority by performing the contract, by expressly approving the contract, or by allowing a reasonable time to lapse without avoiding the contract.

CPA **What Constitutes Avoidance?** A minor may avoid or *disaffirm* a contract by any expression of an intention to repudiate the contract. Any act inconsistent with the continuing validity of the contract is also an avoidance.

CPA **Time for Avoidance.** A minor can disaffirm a contract only during minority and for a reasonable time after attaining majority. After the lapse of a reasonable time, the contract is deemed ratified and cannot be avoided by the minor.

CPA **Minor's Misrepresentation of Age.** Generally, the fact that the minor has misrepresented his or her age does not affect the minor's power to disaffirm the contract. Some states hold that such fraud of a minor bars contract avoidance. Some states permit the minor

---

[2] *Fisher v. Schefers,* 656 N.W.2d 591 (Minn. App. 2003).
[3] *Buffington v. State Automobile Mut. Ins. Co.,* 384 S.E.2d 873 (Ga. App. 1989).
[4] *Deck v. Spatz, Inc.,* 2011 WL 775067 (E.D. Cal. Sept. 27, 2011).

to disaffirm the contract in such a case but require the minor to pay for any damage to the property received under the contract.

In any case, the other party to the contract may disaffirm it because of the minor's fraud.

CPA Restitution by Minor after Avoidance

When a minor disaffirms a contract, the question arises as to what the minor must return to the other contracting party.

Original Consideration Intact. When a minor still has what was received from the other party, the minor, on avoiding the contract, must return it to the other party or offer to do so. That is, the minor must put things back to the original position or, as it is called, restore the **status quo ante.**

status quo ante–original positions of the parties.

Original Consideration Damaged or Destroyed. What happens if the minor cannot return what has been received because it has been spent, used, damaged, or destroyed? The minor's right to disaffirm the contract is not affected. The minor can still disaffirm the contract and is required to return only what remains. The fact that nothing remains or that what remains is damaged does not bar the right to disaffirm the contract. In states that follow the common law rule, minors can thus refuse to pay for what has been received under a contract or can get back what had been paid or given even though they do not have anything to return or return property in a damaged condition. There is, however, a trend to limit this rule.

Recovery of Property by Minor on Avoidance

When a minor disaffirms a contract, the other contracting party must return the money received. Any property received from the minor must also be returned. If the property has been sold to a third person who did not know of the original seller's minority, the minor cannot get the property back. In such cases, however, the minor is entitled to recover the property's monetary value or the money received by the other contracting party.

CPA Contracts for Necessaries

A minor can disaffirm a contract for necessaries but must pay the reasonable value for furnished necessaries.

necessaries–things indispensable or absolutely necessary for the sustenance of human life.

What Constitutes Necessaries? Originally, **necessaries** were limited to those things absolutely necessary for the sustenance and shelter of the minor. Thus limited, the term would extend only to food, clothing, and lodging. In the course of time, the rule was relaxed to extend generally to things relating to the health, education, and comfort of the minor. Thus, the rental of a house used by a married minor is a necessary.

Liability of Parent or Guardian. When a third person supplies the parents or guardian of a minor with goods or services that the minor needs, the minor is not liable for these necessaries because the third person's contract is with the parent or guardian, not with the minor.

When necessary medical care is provided a minor, a parent is liable at common law for the medical expenses provided the minor child. However, at common law, the child can be held contractually liable for her necessary medical expenses when the parent is unable or unwilling to pay.

CASE SUMMARY

The Concussion and Legal Repercussions

FACTS: Sixteen-year-old Michelle Schmidt was injured in an automobile accident and taken to Prince George's Hospital. Although the identities of Michelle and her parents were originally unknown, the hospital provided her emergency medical care for a brain concussion and an open scalp wound. She incurred hospital expenses of $1,756.24. Ms. Schmidt was insured through her father's insurance company. It issued a check to be used to cover medical expenses. However, the funds were used to purchase a car for Ms. Schmidt. Since she was a minor when the services were rendered, she believed that she had no legal obligation to pay. After Ms. Schmidt attained her eighteenth birthday and failed to pay the hospital, it brought suit against her.

DECISION: Judgment for the hospital. The prevailing modern rule is that minors' contracts are voidable except for necessaries. The doctrine of necessaries states that a minor may be held liable for necessaries, including medical necessaries when parents are unwilling to pay. The court concluded that Ms. Schmidt's father demonstrated a clear unwillingness to pay by using the insurance money to purchase a car rather than pay the hospital. The policy behind the necessaries exception is for the benefit of minors because the procurement of such is essential to their existence, and if they were not permitted to bind themselves, they might not be able to obtain the necessaries. [*Schmidt v. Prince George's Hospital*, 784 A.2d 1112 (Md. 2001)]

CPA Ratification of Former Minor's Voidable Contract

A former minor cannot disaffirm a contract that has been ratified after reaching majority.[5]

CPA What Constitutes Ratification? Ratification consists of any words or conduct of the former minor manifesting an intent to be bound by the terms of a contract made while a minor.

CPA Form of Ratification. Generally, no special form is required for ratification of a minor's voidable contract, although in some states a written ratification or declaration of intention is required.

CPA Time for Ratification. A person can disaffirm a contract any time during minority and for a reasonable time after that but, of necessity, can ratify a contract only after attaining majority. The minor must have attained majority, or the ratification would itself be regarded as voidable.

Contracts That Minors Cannot Avoid

Statutes in many states deprive a minor of the right to avoid an educational loan;[6] a contract for medical care; a contract made while running a business; a contract approved by a court; a contract made in performance of a legal duty; and a contract relating to bank accounts, insurance policies, or corporate stock.

Liability of Third Person for a Minor's Contract

The question arises as to whether parents are bound by the contract of their minor child. The question of whether a person cosigning a minor's contract is bound if the contract is avoided also arises.

---

[5] *Fletcher v. Marshall*, 632 N.E.2d 1105 (Ill. App. 1994).
[6] A Model Student Capacity to Borrow Act makes educational loans binding on minors in Arizona, Mississippi, New Mexico, North Dakota, Oklahoma, and Washington. This act was reclassified from a uniform act to a model act by the Commissioners on Uniform State Law, indicating that uniformity was viewed as unimportant and that the matter was primarily local in character.

Liability of Parent. Ordinarily, a parent is not liable on a contract made by a minor child. The parent may be liable, however, if the child is acting as the agent of the parent in making the contract. Also, the parent is liable to a seller for the reasonable value of necessaries supplied by the seller to the child if the parent had deserted the child.

Liability of Cosigner. When the minor makes a contract, another person, such as a parent or a friend, may sign along with the minor to make the contract more acceptable to the third person.

With respect to the other contracting party, the cosigner is bound independently of the minor. Consequently, if the minor disaffirms the contract, the cosigner remains bound by it. When the debt to the creditor is actually paid, the obligation of the cosigner is discharged.

If the minor disaffirms a sales contract but does not return the goods, the cosigner remains liable for the purchase price.

13-1c **Mentally Incompetent Persons**

A person with a mental disorder may be so disabled as to lack capacity to make a contract. An individual seeking to avoid the consequences of a contract due to incompetency must demonstrate that at the time the agreement was executed he or she was suffering from a mental illness or defect, which rendered the party incapable of comprehending the nature of the transaction, or that by reason of mental illness the party was unable to control his or her conduct.[7] **For Example,** a guardian established that Ms. Brunson suffered from a mental illness at the time the challenged mortgage documents were executed, and the contract was set aside by the court.[8] However, where a guardian's evidence was insufficient to demonstrate that at the time two mortgage transactions occurred, one in 1999 for $212,000 and a second in 2003 for $7,628.08, that Mr. and Mrs. Haedrich were incompetent or that Washington Mutual Bank knew or was put on notice of their purported incapacity, the court refused to vacate the judgments of foreclosure.[9]

Effect of Incompetency

An incompetent person may ordinarily avoid a contract in the same manner as a minor. Upon the removal of the disability (that is, upon becoming competent), the formerly incompetent person can either ratify or disaffirm the contract.

A mentally incompetent person or his estate is liable for the reasonable value of all necessaries furnished that individual.

A current trend in the law is to treat an incompetent person's contract as binding when its terms and the surrounding circumstances are reasonable and the person is unable to restore the other contracting party to the status quo ante.

CASE SUMMARY

Friends Should Tell Friends about Medical Leaves

FACTS: Wilcox Manufacturing Group, Inc., did business under the name of Superior Automation Co., and Howard Wilcox served as Superior's president. As part of a loan "lease agreement" of $50,000 executed on December 5, 2000, Superior was to repay Marketing Services of Indiana (MSI) $67,213.80 over the course of 60 months. Wilcox gave a

---

[7] *Horrell v. Horrell*, 900 N.Y.S.2d 666 (2d Dept. 2010).
[8] In re *Doar*, 900 N.Y.S.2d 593 (Sup. Ct. Queens Co., Dec. 18, 2009).
[9] *JP Morgan Chase Bank v. Haedrich*, 918 N.Y.S.2d 398 (Sup. Ct. Nassau County, Oct. 15, 2010).

Friends Should Tell Friends about Medical Leaves continued

personal guarantee for full and prompt payment. Wilcox had been a patient of psychiatrist Dr. Shaun Wood since May 21, 1999, and was diagnosed as suffering from bipolar disorder during the period from June 2000 to January 2001. On June 9, 2000, Wilcox told Dr. Wood he was having problems functioning at work, and Dr. Wood determined that Wilcox was experiencing lithium toxicity, which lasted for 10 months, during which time he suffered from impaired cognitive functions that limited his capacity to understand the nature and quality of his actions and judgments. Superior made monthly payments though to October 28, 2003, and the balance owed at that time was $33,031.37. MSI sued Wilcox personally and the corporation for breach of contract. The defendants raised the defense of lack of capacity and contended that they were not liable on the loan signed by the corporate president when he was incapacitated.

DECISION: Judgment for MSI. The acts or deeds of a person of unsound mind whose condition has not been judicially ascertained and who is not under guardianship are voidable and not absolutely void. The acts are subject to ratification or disaffirmance on removal of the disability. The latest Wilcox could have been experiencing the effects of lithium toxicity was October 2001. Wilcox thus regained his capacity by that date. No attempt was made to disaffirm the contract. Rather, monthly payments continued to be made for a year and one-half before the payments ceased. The contract was thus ratified by the conduct of the president of Superior after he recovered his ability to understand the nature of the contract. [*Wilcox Manufacturing, Inc., v. Marketing Services of Indiana, Inc.*, 832 N.E.2d 559 (Ind. App. 2005)]

Appointment of Guardian

If a court appoints a guardian for the incompetent person, a contract made by that person before the appointment may be ratified or, in some cases, disaffirmed by the guardian. If the incompetent person makes a contract after a guardian has been appointed, the contract is void and not merely voidable.

13-1d Intoxicated Persons

The capacity of a party to contract and the validity of the contract are not affected by the party's being impaired by alcohol at the time of making the contract so long as the party knew that a contract was being made.

If the degree of intoxication is such that a person does not know that a contract is being made, the contract is voidable by that person. On becoming sober, the individual may avoid or rescind the contract. However, an unreasonable delay in taking steps to set aside a known contract entered into while intoxicated may bar the intoxicated person from asserting this right.[10]

Excessive intoxication is a viable defense to contracts arising between casinos and their patrons. Thus, when a casino comes to court to enforce a marker debt against a patron, it seeks to enforce a contractual debt, and the patron is entitled to raise the common law defense that his capacity to contract was impaired by voluntary intoxication.[11]

The courts treat impairment caused by the use of drugs the same as impairment caused by the excessive use of alcohol.

CPA   13-2 Mistake

The validity of a contract may be affected by the fact that one or both of the parties made a mistake. In some cases, the mistake may be caused by the misconduct of one of the parties.

---

[10] *Diedrich v. Diedrich*, 424 N.W.2d 580 (Minn. App. 1988).
[11] See *Adamar of New Jersey v. Luber*, 2011 WL 1325978 (D. N.J. Mar. 30, 2011).

13-2a Unilateral Mistake

A *unilateral mistake*—that is, a mistake by only one of the parties—as to a fact does not affect the contract when the mistake is unknown to the other contracting party.[12] When a contract is made on the basis of a quoted price, the validity of the contract is not affected by the fact that the party furnishing the quotation made a mathematical mistake in computing the price if there was no reason for the other party to recognize that there had been a mistake.[13] The party making the mistake may avoid the contract if the other contracting party knew or should have known of the mistake.

CASE SUMMARY

Bumper Sticker: "Mistakes Happen!" (or words to that effect)

FACTS: Lipton-U City, LLC (Lipton), and Shurgard Storage Centers discussed the sale of a self-storage facility for approximately $7 million. Lipton became concerned about an existing environmental condition and, as a result, the parties agreed to a lease with an option to buy rather than an outright sale. The contract specified a 10-year lease with an annual rent starting at $636,000 based on a property valuation of $7 million. Section 2.4 of the contract contained the purchase option. Shurgard representatives circulated an e-mail with a copy to Lipton representatives that a purchase option price would be based on six months of *annualized* net operating income. When the lease was submitted to Lipton, inexplicably any language regarding multiplying by 2 or annualizing the net income was omitted. Donn Lipton announced to his attorneys that the lease reflected his successful negotiation of a purchase option based on six months of *unannualized* net operating income. Eight months after signing the lease, Lipton sought to exercise the purchase option under Section 2.4 and stated a price of $2,918,103. Shurgard rejected the offer and filed suit for rescission, citing the misunderstanding about the price terms.

DECISION: Judgment for Shurgard. Under state law, if a material mistake made by one party is known to the other party or is of such a character or circumstances that the other party should know of it, the mistaken party has a right to rescission. Lipton knew or should have known of the mistake of the lessor (Shurgard) in believing that the purchase price would be based on a full year of net operating income rather than six months of net operating income. Lipton was notified by e-mail that the six-month figure was to be annualized and knew that the property was valued at approximately $7 million. [***Shurgard Storage Centers v. Lipton-U City, LLC*, 394 F.3d 1041 (8th Cir. 2005)**]

13-2b Mutual Mistake

When both parties enter into a contract under a mutually mistaken understanding concerning a basic assumption of fact or law on which the contract is made, the contract is voidable by the adversely affected party if the mistake has a material effect on the agreed exchange.[14]

A contract based on *a mutual mistake in judgment* is not voidable by the adversely affected party. **For Example,** if both parties believe that a colt is not fast enough to develop into a competitive race horse and effect a sale accordingly, when the animal later develops into the winner of the Preakness as a three-year-old, the seller cannot rescind the contract based on mutual mistake because the mutual mistake was a mistake in judgment. In contrast, when two parties to a contract believe a cow to be barren at the time they contract for its sale, but before delivery of the animal to the buyer, it is discovered that the assumption was mistaken, such is a mutual mistake of fact making the contract void.[15]

---

[12] *Truck South Inc. v. Patel*, 528 S.E.2d 424 (S.C. 2000).
[13] *Procan Construction Co. v. Oceanside Development Corp.*, 539 N.Y.S.2d 437 (App. Div. 2d 1989).
[14] See *Browning v. Howerton*, 966 P.2d 367 (Wash. App. 1998).
[15] See *Sherwood v. Walker*, 66 Mich. 568 (1887).

13-2c Mistake in the Transcription or Printing of the Contract: Reformation

In some instances, the parties make an oral agreement, and in the process of committing it to writing or printing it from a manuscript, a phrase, term, or segment is inadvertently left out of the final, signed document. The aggrieved party may petition the court to **reform** the contract to reflect the actual agreement of the parties. However, the burden of proof is heightened to clear and convincing evidence that such a mistake was made. **For Example,** Jewell Coke Co. used an illustration to explain a complex pricing formula in its negotiations with the ArcelMittal steel mill in Cleveland, Ohio, for a long-term contract for the supply of blast furnace coke. The multiplier in the illustration was the actual intent of the parties, according to ArcelMittal, but during the drafting process the multiplier was accidently inverted, resulting in an overpayment of $100,000,000 when discovered, and which potentially could result in an overpayment of over $1 billion over the life of the contract. If proven, the court will reform the contract to reflect the intentions of the parties at the time the contract was made.[16]

reformation–remedy by which a written instrument is corrected when it fails to express the actual intent of both parties because of fraud, accident, or mistake.

13-3 Deception

One of the parties may have been misled by a fraudulent statement. In such situations, there is no true or genuine assent to the contract, and it is voidable at the innocent party's option.

FIGURE 13-1   Avoidance of Contract

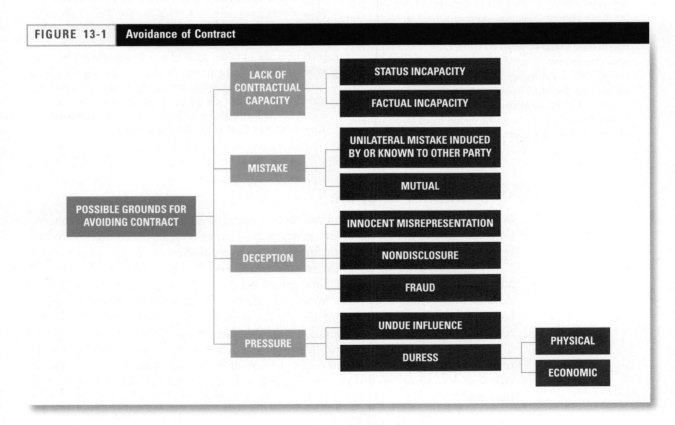

---

[16] *ArcelMittal Cleveland, Inc. v. Jewell Coke Co,* 750 F. Supp. 2d 839 (N.D. Ohio 2010).

13-3a **Intentional Misrepresentation**

Fraud is a generic term embracing all multifarious means that human ingenuity can devise and that are resorted to by one individual to get advantage over another. It is classified in the law as a *tort*. However, where a party is induced into making a contract by a material misrepresentation of fact, this form of fraudulent activity adversely affects the genuineness of the assent of the innocent party, and this type of fraud is the focus of our discussion in the chapters on contracts.

13-3b **Fraud**

fraud–making of a false statement of a past or existing fact, with knowledge of its falsity or with reckless indifference as to its truth, with the intent to cause another to rely thereon, and such person does rely thereon and is harmed thereby.

Fraud is the making of a material misrepresentation (or false statement) of fact with (1) knowledge of its falsity or reckless indifference to its truth, (2) the intent that the listener rely on it, (3) the result that the listener does so rely, and (4) the consequence that the listener is harmed.[17]

To prove fraud, there must be a material misrepresentation of fact. Such a misrepresentation is one that is likely to induce a reasonable person to assent to a contract. **For Example,** Traci Hanson-Suminski purchased a used Honda Civic from Arlington Acura for $10,899. On a test drive with salesperson Mike Dobin, Traci noticed a vibration in the steering wheel and asked if the car had been in an accident. Dobin said, "No, it's fine." The dealer put new tires on the car and Traci bought it. Traci testified that she would not have purchased the car if she had known it had been in an accident. Eight months later when she sought to trade the car for another car, she was shown a Carfax Vehicle History Report, which indicated the car had been in an accident. The dealer testified that all its sales associates are trained to respond to questions about vehicle history with "I don't know." It asserted that Dobin's statement was mere puffery. The court found that Dobin's statement was a material misrepresentation of the car's history, inducing the plaintiff to purchase the car. It rejected outright the dealer's assertion of puffery, which it defined as meaningless superlatives that no reasonable person would take seriously.[18]

Statement of Opinion or Value

Ordinarily, matters of opinion of value or opinions about future events are not regarded as fraudulent. Forecasts about the future state of financial or real estate markets must be regarded not as fact, but as predictions or speculations.

A statement of opinion may be fraudulent when the speaker knows of past or present facts that make the opinion false. **For Example,** Biff Williams, the sales manager of Abrasives International (AI), sold an exclusive dealership selling AI products to Fred Farkas for $100,000 down and a 3 percent royalty on all gross proceeds. Williams told Farkas, "You have the potential to earn $300,000 to $400,000 a year in this territory." He later added, "We have four dealerships making that kind of money today." Farkas was thus persuaded by the business potential of the territory and executed the purchase contract. He later found out that AI had a total of just four distributorships at that time, and that the actual earnings of the highest producer was $43,000. Assertions of opinions about the future profit potential alone may not amount to fraud, but the assertion of present fact—that four dealerships were presently earning $300,000 to $400,000 a year—was a material misstatement of fact that made the forecast sales potential for Farkas's territory a

---

[17] *Maack v. Resource Design & Construction, Inc.*, 875 P.2d 570 (Utah 1994); *Bortz v. Noon*, 729 A.2d 555 (Pa. 1999).
[18] *Hanson-Suminski v. Rohrman Midwest Motors Inc.*, 858 N.E.2d 194 (Ill. App. 2008).

material misstatement of fact as well. Because there were reliance and damages, Farkas can rescind the contract based on fraud and recover all damages resulting from it.[19]

CASE SUMMARY

Remember This One: Mere Opinions Are Not Actionable at All!

FACTS: In approximately July 2005 a loan broker and an appraiser working for a subsidiary of Bank of America appraised the Cansinos home at a fair market value of $620,000. Based on that appraisal and other representations by lending personnel, the Cansinos elected to refinance their home with a $496,000 adjustable rate mortgage. Lending personnel told them their home would appreciate and they would be able to sell or refinance the home at a later date before having to make higher monthly loan payments. In 2010, the Cansinos discovered that their home was valued between $350,000 and $400,000. Soon thereafter they stopped making payments on the 2005 loan. As of March 2012 the monthly payments were approximately $1,960, the balance due on the loan was approximately $626,000, and the fair market value of the home was approximately $350,000. The trial court dismissed the Cansinos fraud action against B of A, and they appealed.

DECISION: Judgment against the Cansinos. Concerning B of A's representation on the future appreciation of the Cansinos' home, such statements or predictions regarding future events are deemed to be mere opinions, which are not actionable. And, any financial market forecast must be regarded not as a fact but as prediction or speculation. While the Casinos state the home was valued between $350,000 and $400,000 in 2010, this does not support their claim that the 2005 appraisal of $620,000 was a misrepresentation. [*Cansinos v. Bank of America*, 169 Cal. Rptr. 3d 619 (Cal. App. 2014)]

Justifiable Reliance on Statement

A fraudulent statement made by one party has no importance unless the other party relies on the statement's truth. **For Example,** after making thorough tests of Nagel Company's pump, Allstate Services Company ordered 100 pumps. It later sued Nagel on the ground that advertising statements made about the pumps were false. Allstate Services cannot impose fraud liability on Nagel for the advertisements, even if they were false, because it had not relied on them in making the purchase but had acted on the basis of its own tests.

Disclaimer of reliance clauses are common in commerce these days. Trusting the honesty of salespersons or their disarming statements, an individual may knowingly or obliviously agree in a sales agreement containing a disclaimer of reliance clause that no representations have been made to him or her, while at the same time believing and relying upon representations, which in fact have been made and in fact are false and but for which the individual would not have made the agreement. Ordinarily, purchasers cannot assert justifiable reliance on statements made by sellers that directly contradict clear and specific terms of their written contracts.[20]

---

[19] The Federal Trade Commission and state agencies have franchise disclosure rules that will penalize the franchisor in this case. See Chapter 40.

[20] But see *Italian Cowboy Partners, Ltd. v. Prudential Insurance*, 341 S.W.3d 323 (Tex. 2011) where a split decision of the Texas Supreme Court determined that the following contract language was not a disclaimer of reliance to negate the "justifiable reliance" element of a fraud claim.

> Tenant acknowledges that neither Landlord nor Landlord's agents, employees or contractors have made any representations or promises with respect to the Site, the Shopping Center or this lease except as expressly set forth herein.

The court determined that the property manager's representations to the future tenant that the building was problem free; no problems had been experienced by the prior tenant; and the building was a perfect restaurant site were false statements of fact known to be false when made. Testimony indicated that the manager herself had personally experienced a sewer gas odor in the prior tenant's restaurant she described as "almost unbearable" and "ungodly."

CASE SUMMARY

Are Disclaimer of Reliance Clauses a License to Lie?

FACTS: David Sarif and seven other purchasers (Purchasers) each bought a unit at the 26-story Twelve Atlantic Station (Twelve) condominiums in 2005 and 2006. They sued the developers and the brokers for fraud in the inducement and negligent misrepresentation. They alleged that at the time of their purchases, the developers were advertising "spectacular city views" of Atlanta while they had already undertaken to develop the 46-story Atlantic Station tower directly across the street, and that their brokers were advising the Purchasers that any future development to the south of Twelve would be low- to mid-rise office buildings. Purchasers allege that they paid substantial premiums for their views of the city from the south side of the building, which is now blocked by the 46-story building. Each Purchaser signed an agreement containing a provision stating that "[t]he views from and natural light available to the Unit may change over time due to, among other circumstances, additional development and the removal or addition of landscaping"; a disclaimer at the top of the first page as required by the Georgia Condominium Act stating that "ORAL REPRESENTATIONS CANNOT BE RELIED UPON AS CORRECTLY STATING THE REPRESENTATIONS OF SELLER"; an express disclaimer in which Purchasers affirmed that they did not rely upon any representations or statements of the brokers; and a comprehensive merger clause.

DECISION: Set forth in the written contract of the parties, all of the Purchasers signed agreements that expressly stated that views may change over time, and oral representations of the sellers could not be relied on. Justifiable reliance is an essential element of a fraud or negligent misrepresentation claim. Since the Purchasers are estopped from relying on representations outside their agreements, they cannot sustain a case that requires justifiable reliance. [*Novare Group, Inc. v. Sarif,* 718 S.E.2d 304 (Ga. 2011)]

Proof of Harm

For an individual to recover damages for fraud, proof of harm to that individual is required. The injured party may recover the actual losses suffered as a result of the fraud as well as punitive damages when the fraud is gross or oppressive. The injured party has the right to have the court order the rescission or cancellation of the contract that has been induced by fraud.[21]

13-3c Negligent Misrepresentation

While fraud requires the critical element of a known or recklessly made falsity, a claim of negligent misrepresentation contains similar elements except it is predicated on a negligently made false statement. That is, the speaker failed to exercise due care regarding material information communicated to the listener but did not intend to deceive. When the negligent misrepresentation of a material fact that the listener relies on results in harm to the listener, the contract is voidable at the option of the injured party. If fraud is proven, as opposed to misrepresentation, recovery of punitive damages in addition to actual damages can occur. Because it may be difficult to prove the intentional falsity required for fraud, it is common for a lawsuit to allege both a claim of fraud and a claim of negligent misrepresentation. **For Example,** Marshall Armstrong worked for Fred Collins, owner of Collins Entertainment, Inc., a conglomerate that owns and operates video games. Collins Entertainment's core product, video poker, was hurt by a court ruling that prohibited cash payouts, which adversely affected its business and resulted in a debt of $13 to $20 million to SouthTrust bank. Chief operating officer Armstrong, on his

---

[21] *Paden v. Murray,* 523 S.E.2d 75 (Ga. App. 2000).

own time, came up with the idea of modifying bingo machines as a new venture. To exploit this idea, Collins agreed to form a corporation called Skillpins Inc., that was unencumbered by the SouthTrust debt and to give Armstrong a 10 percent ownership interest. After a period, with some 300 Skillpins machines producing income, Armstrong discovered the revenues from the new venture on the debt-laden Collins Entertainment profit and loss statement, not that of Skillpins, Inc. Armstrong's suit for both fraud and intentional misrepresentation was successful. In addition to actual damages, he received $1.8 million in punitive damages for fraud.[22]

13-3d Nondisclosure

Under certain circumstances, nondisclosure serves to make a contract voidable, especially when the nondisclosure consists of active concealment.

General Rule of Nonliability

Ordinarily, a party to a contract has no duty to volunteer information to the other party. **For Example,** if Fox does not ask Tehan any questions, Tehan is not under any duty to make a full statement of material facts. Consequently, the nondisclosure of information that is not asked for does not impose fraud liability or impair the validity of a contract.

CASE SUMMARY

Welcome to the Seesaw: Buyer versus Seller

FACTS: Dalarna Management Corporation owned a building constructed on a pier on a lake. There were repeated difficulties with rainwater leaking into the building, and water damage was visible in the interior of the building. Dalarna made a contract to sell the building to Curran. Curran made several inspections of the building and had the building inspected twice by a licensed engineer. The engineer reported there were signs of water leaks. Curran assigned his contract to Puget Sound Service Corporation, which then purchased the building from Dalarna. Puget Sound spent approximately $118,000 attempting to stop the leaks. Puget Sound then sued Dalarna for damages, claiming that Dalarna's failure to disclose the extent of the water leakage problem constituted fraud.

DECISION: Judgment for Dalarna. Curran was aware there was a water leakage problem, and therefore the burden was on the buyer to ask questions to determine the extent of the problem. There was no duty on the seller to volunteer the extent of the water damage merely because it had been a continuing problem that was more than just a simple leak. The court reached this conclusion because the law "balances the harshness of the former rule of caveat emptor [let the buyer beware] with the equally undesirable alternative of courts standing in loco parentis [in the place of a parent] to parties transacting business." [**Puget Sound Service Corp. v. Dalarna Management Corp., 752 P.2d 1353 (Wash. App. 1988)**]

Exceptions

The following exceptions to the general rule of nonliability for nondisclosure exist.

Unknown Defect or Condition. A duty may exist in some states for a seller who knows of a serious defect or condition to disclose that information to the other party where the defect or condition is unknown to the other person and is of such a nature that it is unlikely that the other person would discover it. However, a defendant who had no knowledge of the defect cannot be held liable for failure to disclose it.[23]

---

[22] *Armstrong v. Collins*, 621 S.E.2d 368 (S.C. App. 2005).
[23] *Nesbitt v. Dunn*, 672 So. 2d 226 (La. App. 1996).

confidential relationship–
relationship in which, because of the legal status of the parties or their respective physical or mental conditions or knowledge, one party places full confidence and trust in the other.

Confidential Relationship. If parties stand in a **confidential relationship,** failure to disclose information may be regarded as fraudulent. **For Example,** in an attorney-client relationship,[24] the attorney has a duty to reveal anything that is material to the client's interest when dealing with the client. The attorney's silence has the same legal consequence as a knowingly made false statement that there was no material fact to be told the client.

Active Concealment. Nondisclosure may be more than the passive failure to volunteer information. It may consist of a positive act of hiding information from the other party by physical concealment, or it may consist of knowingly or recklessly furnishing the wrong information. Such conduct constitutes fraud. **For Example,** when Nigel wanted to sell his house, he covered the wooden cellar beams with plywood to hide extensive termite damage. He sold the house to Kuehne, who sued Nigel for damages on later discovering the termite damage. Nigel claimed he had no duty to volunteer information about the termites, but by covering the damage with plywood, he committed active fraud as if he had made a false statement that there were no termites.

13-4 Pressure

What appears to be an agreement may not in fact be voluntary because one of the parties entered into it as the result of undue influence or physical or economic duress.

CPA   ### 13-4a Undue Influence

An aged parent may entrust all business affairs to a trusted child; a disabled person may rely on a nurse; a client may follow implicitly whatever an attorney recommends. The relationship may be such that for practical purposes, one person is helpless in the hands of the other. When such a confidential relationship exists, it is apparent that the parent, the disabled person, or the client is not exercising free will in making a contract suggested by the child, nurse, or attorney but is merely following the will of the other person. Because of the great possibility of unfair advantage, the law presumes that the dominating person exerts **undue influence** on the other person whenever the dominating person obtains any benefit from a contract made with the dominated person.[25] The contract is then voidable. It may be set aside by the dominated person unless the dominating person can prove that, at the time the contract was made, no unfair advantage had been taken.

undue influence–
influence that is asserted upon another person by one who dominates that person.

The class of confidential relationships is not well defined. It ordinarily includes the relationships of parent and child, guardian and ward, physician and patient, and attorney and client, and any other relationship of trust and confidence in which one party exercises a control or influence over another.

Whether undue influence exists is a difficult question for courts (ordinarily juries) to determine. The law does not regard every influence as undue.

An essential element of undue influence is that the person making the contract does not exercise free will. In the absence of a recognized type of confidential relationship, such as that between parent and child, courts are likely to take the attitude that the person who claims to have been dominated was merely persuaded and there was therefore no undue influence.

[24] In re *Boss Trust,* 487 N.W.2d 256 (Minn. App. 1992).
[25] *Ayers v. Shaffer,* 748 S.E.2d 83 (Va. 2013).

CASE SUMMARY

Cards and Small Talk Sometimes Make the Sale

FACTS: John Lentner owned the farm adjacent to the Schefers. He moved off the farm to a nursing home in 1999. In the fall of 2000, Kristine Schefers visited Lentner at the nursing home some 15 times, engaging in small talk and watching him play cards. In the spring of 2001, Lentner agreed to sell his farm to Kristine and her husband Thomas for $50,000 plus $10,000 for machinery and tools. Kristine drove Lentner to the bank to get the deed from his safe deposit box. She also took him to the abstractor who drafted the transfer documents. Soon after the sale, Earl Fisher was appointed special conservator of Lentner. Fisher sought to set aside the transaction, asserting that Kristine's repeated visits to the nursing home and her failure to involve Lentner's other family members in the transaction unduly influenced Lentner.

DECISION: Judgment for Thomas and Kristine Schefers. Undue influence is shown when the person making the contract ceased to act of his own free volition and became a mere puppet of the wielder of that influence. Mere speculation alone that Lentner was a "puppet" acting according to the wishes of Schefers is insufficient to set aside the sale. Undue influence was not established. [*Fisher v. Schefers*, **656 N.W.2d 592 (Minn. App. 2003)**]

CPA

13-4b Duress

physical duress—threat of physical harm to person or property.

economic duress—threat of financial loss.

duress—conduct that deprives the victim of free will and that generally gives the victim the right to set aside any transaction entered into under such circumstances.

A party may enter into a contract to avoid a threatened danger. The danger threatened may be a physical harm to person or property, called **physical duress,** or it may be a threat of financial loss, called **economic duress.**

Physical Duress

A person makes a contract under **duress** when there is such violence or threat of violence that the person is deprived of free will and makes the contract to avoid harm. The threatened harm may be directed either at a near relative of the contracting party or against the contracting party. If a contract is made under duress, the resulting agreement is voidable at the victim's election.

Agreements made to bring an end to mass disorder or violence are ordinarily not binding contracts because they were obtained by duress.

One may not void a contract on grounds of duress merely because it was entered into with great reluctance and proves to be very disadvantageous to that individual.[26]

Economic Duress

Economic duress is a condition in which one is induced by a wrongful act or threat of another to make a contract under circumstances that deprive one of the exercise of his own free will.[27] **For Example,** Richard Case, an importer of parts used to manufacture high-quality mountain bicycles, had a contractual duty to supply Katahdin Manufacturing Company's needs for specifically manufactured stainless steel brakes for the 2016 season. Katahdin's president, Bill Read, was in constant contact with Case about the delay in delivery of the parts and the adverse consequences it was having on Katahdin's relationship with its retailers. Near the absolute deadline for meeting orders for the 2016 season, Case called Read and said, "I've got the parts in, but I'm not sure I'll be able to send

---

[26] *Miller v. Calhoun/Johnson Co,* 497 S.E.2d 397 (Ga. App. 1998).
[27] *Hurd v. Wildman, Harrold, Allen, and Dixon,* 707 N.E.2d 609 (Ill. App. 1999).

them to you because I'm working on next year's contracts, and you haven't signed yours yet." Case's 2017 contract increased the cost of parts by 38 percent. Read signed the contract to obtain the delivery but later found a new supplier and gave notice to Case of this action. The defense of economic duress would apply in a breach of contract suit brought by Case on the 2017 contract because Case implicitly threatened to commit the wrongful act of not delivering parts due under the prior contract, and Katahdin Company had no means available to obtain parts elsewhere to prevent the economic loss that would occur if it did not receive those parts.

Make the Connection

Summary

An agreement that otherwise appears to be a contract may not be binding because one of the parties lacks contractual capacity. In such a case, the contract is ordinarily voidable at the election of the party who lacks contractual capacity. In some cases, the contract is void. Ordinarily, contractual incapacity is the inability, for mental or physical reasons, to understand that a contract is being made and to understand its general terms and nature. This is typically the case when it is claimed that incapacity exists because of insanity, intoxication, or drug use. The incapacity of minors arises because society discriminates in favor of that class to protect them from unwise contracts.

The age of majority is 18. Minors can disaffirm most contracts. If a minor received anything from the other party, the minor, on avoiding the contract, must return what had been received from the other party if the minor still has it.

When a minor disaffirms a contract for a necessary, the minor must pay the reasonable value of any benefit received.

Minors only are liable for their contracts. Parents of a minor are not liable on the minor's contracts merely because they are the parents. Frequently, an adult enters into the contract as a coparty of the minor and is then liable without regard to whether the minor has avoided the contract.

The contract of an insane person is voidable to much the same extent as the contract of a minor. An important distinction is that if a guardian has been appointed for the insane person, a contract made by the insane person is void, not merely voidable.

An intoxicated person lacks contractual capacity if the intoxication is such that the person does not understand that a contract is being made.

The consent of a party to an agreement is not genuine or voluntary in certain cases of mistake, deception, or pressure. When this occurs, what appears to be a contract can be avoided by the victim of such circumstances or conduct.

As to mistake, it is necessary to distinguish between unilateral mistakes that are unknown to the other contracting party and those that are known. Mistakes that are unknown to the other party usually do not affect the binding character of the agreement. A unilateral mistake of which the other contracting party has knowledge or has reason to know makes the contract avoidable by the victim of the mistake.

The deception situation may be one of negligent misrepresentation or fraud. The law ordinarily does not attach any significance to nondisclosure. Contrary to this rule, there is a duty to volunteer information when a confidential relationship exists between the possessor of the knowledge and the other contracting party.

When concealment goes beyond mere silence and consists of actively taking steps to hide the truth, the conduct may be classified as fraud. A statement of opinion or value cannot ordinarily be the basis for fraud liability.

The voluntary character of a contract may be lacking because the agreement had been obtained by pressure. This may range from undue influence through the array of threats of extreme economic loss (called *economic duress*) to the threat of physical force that would cause serious personal injury or damage to property (called *physical duress*). When the voluntary character of an agreement has been destroyed by deception, or pressure, the victim may avoid or rescind the contract or may obtain money damages from the wrongdoer.

Learning Outcomes

After studying this chapter, you should be able to clearly explain:

13-1   Contractual Capacity

LO.1   Define contractual capacity

See the example where Jacqueline, age 22, did not understand parts of a storage contract, page 243.

LO.2   Explain the extent and effect of avoidance of a contract by a minor

See the *Adorian Deck* example where the creator of a Twitter feed, a minor, disaffirmed his joint venture contract, page 244.

See the *Prince George's Hospital* case where a minor had to pay for medical necessaries, page 246.

13-2   Mistake

LO.3   Distinguish unilateral mistakes and mutual mistakes

See the *Shurgard Storage* case where the "other party" should have known of the unilateral mistake, page 249.

See the *Jewell Coke Co.* example of a remedy for a billion dollar mistake, page 250.

See the example of the mutual mistake of fact regarding the fertility of a cow, page 249.

13-3   Deception

LO.4   Explain the difference between intentional misrepresentation, negligent misrepresentation, and puffery

See the example of the purchase of the used Honda, where the misrepresentation was found to be fraud, not puffery, page 251.

See the *Novare Group, Inc.*, decision on the enforceability of disclaimer-of-liability clauses, page 253.

13-4   Pressure

LO.5   Explain the difference between undue influence and duress

See the *Fisher v. Schefers* undue influence litigation, page 256.

See the Katahdin bicycle example on economic duress, page 256.

Key Terms

confidential relationship
contractual capacity
duress
economic duress

fraud
necessaries
physical duress
reformation

status quo ante
undue influence

Questions and Case Problems

1. Lester purchased a used automobile from Mac-Kintosh Motors. He asked the seller if the car had ever been in a wreck. The MacKintosh salesperson had never seen the car before that morning and knew nothing of its history but quickly answered Lester's question by stating: "No. It has never been in a wreck." In fact, the auto had been seriously damaged in a wreck and, although repaired, was worth much less than the value it would have had if there had been no wreck. When Lester learned the truth, he sued MacKintosh Motors and the salesperson for damages for fraud. They raised the defense that the salesperson did not know the statement was false and had not intended to deceive Lester. Did the conduct of the salesperson constitute fraud?

2. Helen, age 17, wanted to buy a Harley-Davidson "Sportster" motorcycle. She did not have the funds to pay cash but persuaded the dealer to sell the cycle to her on credit. The dealer did so partly because Helen said that she was 22 and showed the dealer an identification card that falsely stated her age as 22. Helen drove the motorcycle away. A few days later, she damaged it and then returned it to the dealer and stated that she disaffirmed the contract because she was a minor. The dealer said that she could not because (1) she had misrepresented her age and (2) the motorcycle was damaged. Can she avoid the contract?

3. Paden signed an agreement dated May 28 to purchase the Murrays' home. The Murrays accepted Paden's offer the following day, and the sale closed on June 27. Paden and his family moved into the home on July 14, 1997. Paden had the home inspected prior to closing. The report listed four minor repairs needed by the home, the cost of which

was less than $500. Although these repairs had not been completed at the time of closing, Paden decided to go through with the purchase. After moving into the home, Paden discovered a number of allegedly new defects, including a wooden foundation, electrical problems, and bat infestation. The sales agreement allowed extensive rights to inspect the property. The agreement provided:

> *Buyer … shall have the right to enter the property at Buyer's expense and at reasonable times … to thoroughly inspect, examine, test, and survey the Property…. Buyer shall have the right to request that Seller repair defects in the Property by providing Seller within 12 days from Binding Agreement Date with a copy of inspection report(s) and a written amendment to this agreement setting forth the defects in the report which Buyer requests to be repaired and/or replaced…. If Buyer does not timely present the written amendment and inspection report, Buyer shall be deemed to have accepted the Property "as is."*

Paden sued the Murrays for fraudulent concealment and breach of the sales agreement. If Mr. Murray told Paden on May 26 that the house had a concrete foundation, would this be fraud? Decide. [*Paden v. Murray*, 523 S.E.2d 75 (Ga. App.)]

4. High-Tech Collieries borrowed money from Holland. High-Tech later refused to be bound by the loan contract, claiming the contract was not binding because it had been obtained by duress. The evidence showed that the offer to make the loan was made on a take-it-or-leave-it basis. Was the defense of duress valid? [*Holland v. High-Tech Collieries, Inc.*, 911 F. Supp. 1021 (N.D. W.Va.)]

5. Thomas Bell, a minor, went to work in the Pittsburgh beauty parlor of Sam Pankas and agreed that when he left the employment, he would not work in or run a beauty parlor business within a 10-mile radius of downtown Pittsburgh for a period of two years. Contrary to this provision, Bell and another employee of Pankas's opened a beauty shop three blocks from Pankas's shop and advertised themselves as Pankas's former employees. Pankas sued Bell to stop the breach of the noncompetition, or restrictive, covenant. Bell claimed that he was not bound because he was a minor when he had agreed to the covenant. Was he bound by the covenant? [*Pankas v. Bell*, 198 A.2d 312 (Pa.)]

6. Aldrich and Co. sold goods to Donovan on credit. The amount owed grew steadily, and finally Aldrich refused to sell any more to Donovan unless Donovan signed a promissory note for the amount due. Donovan did not want to but signed the note because he had no money and needed more goods. When Aldrich brought an action to enforce the note, Donovan claimed that the note was not binding because it had been obtained by economic duress. Was he correct? [*Aldrich & Co. v. Donovan*, 778 P.2d 397 (Mont.)]

7. James Fitl purchased a 1952 Mickey Mantle Topps baseball card from baseball card dealer Mark Strek for $17,750 and placed it in a safe deposit box. Two years later, he had the card appraised, and he was told that the card had been refinished and trimmed, which rendered it valueless. Fitl sued Strek and testified that he had relied on Strek's position as a sports card dealer and on his representations that the baseball card was authentic. Strek contends that Fitl waited too long to give him notice of the defects that would have enabled Strek to contact the person who sold him the card and obtain relief. Strek asserts that he therefore is not liable. Advise Fitl concerning possible legal theories that apply to his case. How would you decide the case? [See *Fitl v. Strek*, 690 N.W.2d 605 (Neb.)]

8. Willingham proposed to obtain an investment property for the Tschiras at a "fair market price," lease it back from them, and pay the Tschiras a guaranteed return through a management contract. Using a shell corporation, The Wellingham Group bought a commercial property in Nashville for $774,000 on December 14, and the very same day sold the building to the Tschiras for $1,985,000. The title insurance policy purchased for the Tschiras property by Willingham was for just $774,000. Willingham believes that the deal was legitimate in that they "guaranteed" a return on the investment. The Tschiras disagree. In a lawsuit against Willingham, what theory will the Tschiras rely on? Decide. [*Tschiras v. Willingham*, 133 F.3d 1077 (6th Cir.)]

9. Blubaugh was a district manager of Schlumberger Well Services. Turner was an executive employee of Schlumberger. Blubaugh was told that he would be fired unless he chose to resign. He was also told that if he would resign and release the company and its employees from all claims for wrongful discharge, he would receive about $5,000 in addition to his regular severance pay of approximately $25,000 and would

be given job-relocation counseling. He resigned, signed the release, and received about $40,000 and job counseling. Some time thereafter, he brought an action claiming that he had been wrongfully discharged. He claimed that the release did not protect the defendants because the release had been obtained by economic duress. Were the defendants protected by the release? [*Blubaugh v. Turner*, 842 P.2d 1072 (Wyo.)]

10. Sippy was thinking of buying Christich's house. He noticed watermarks on the ceiling, but the agent showing the house stated that the roof had been repaired and was in good condition. Sippy was not told that the roof still leaked and that the repairs had not been able to stop the leaking. Sippy bought the house. Some time later, heavy rains caused water to leak into the house, and Sippy claimed that Christich was liable for damages. What theory would he rely on? Decide. [*Sippy v. Christich*, 609 P.2d 204 (Kan. App.)]

11. CEO Bernard Ellis sent a memo to shareholders of his Internet-related services business some four days before the expiration of a lock-up period during which these shareholders had agreed not to sell their stock. In the memo, he urged shareholders not to sell their stock on the release date because in the event of a massive sell-off "our stock could plummet." He also stated *"I think our share price will start to stabilize and then rise as our company's strong performance continues."* Based on Ellis' "strong performance" statement, a major corporate shareholder did not sell. The price of the stock fell from $40 a share to 29 cents a share over the subsequent nine-month period. The shareholder sued Ellis for fraud, seeking $27 million in damages. Analyze the italicized statement to see if it contains an actionable misrepresentation of fact and a basis of fraud liability. [*New Century Communications v. Ellis*, 318 F.3d 1023 (11th Cir.)]

12. Office Supply Outlet, Inc., a single-store office equipment and supply retailer, ordered 100 model RVX-414 computers from Compuserve, Inc. A new staff member made a clerical error on the order form and ordered a quantity that was far in excess of what Office Supply could sell in a year. Office Supply realized the mistake when the delivery trucks arrived at its warehouse. Its manager called Compuserve and explained that it had intended to order just 10 computers. Compuserve declined to accept the return of the extra machines. Is the contract enforceable? What additional facts would allow the

store to avoid the contract for the additional machines?

13. The Printers International Union reached agreement for a new three-year contract with a large regional printing company. As was their practice, the union negotiators then met with Sullivan Brothers Printers, Inc., a small specialty shop employing 10 union printers, and Sullivan Brothers and the union agreed to follow the contractual pattern set by the union and the large printing company. That is, Sullivan Brothers agreed to give its workers all of the benefits negotiated for the employees of the large printing company. When the contract was typed, a new benefit of 75 percent employer-paid coverage for a dental plan was inadvertently omitted from the final contract the parties signed. The mistake was not discovered until six months after the contract took effect. Sullivan Brothers Printers, Inc., is reluctant to assume the additional expense. It contends that the printed copy, which does not cover dental benefits, must control. The union believes that clear and convincing evidence shows an inadvertent typing error. Decide.

14. The city of Salinas entered into a contract with Souza & McCue Construction Co. to construct a sewer. City officials knew unusual subsoil conditions (including extensive quicksand) existed that would make performance of the contract unusually difficult. This information was not disclosed when city officials advertised for bids. The advertisement for bids directed bidders to examine carefully the site of the work and declared that the submission of a bid would constitute evidence that the bidder had made an examination. Souza & McCue was awarded the contract, but because of the subsoil conditions, it could not complete on time and was sued by Salinas for breach of contract. Souza & McCue counterclaimed on the basis that the city had not revealed its information on the subsoil conditions and was thus liable for the loss. Was the city liable? [*City of Salinas v. Souza & McCue Construction Co.*, 424 P.2d 921 (Cal. App. 3d)]

15. Vern Westby inherited a "ticket" from Anna Sjoblom, a survivor of the sinking of the *Titanic*, which had been pinned to the inside of her coat. He also inherited an album of postcards, some of which related to the *Titanic*. The ticket was a one-of-a-kind item in good condition. Westby needed cash and went to the biggest antique dealer in Tacoma, operated by Alan Gorsuch and his family, doing business

as Sanford and Sons, and asked about the value of these items. Westby testified that after Alan Gorsuch examined the ticket, he said, "It's not worth nothing." Westby then inquired about the value of the postcard album, and Gorsuch advised him to come back later. On Westby's return, Gorsuch told Westby, "It ain't worth nothing." Gorsuch added that he "couldn't fetch $500 for the ticket." Since he needed money, Westby asked if Gorsuch would give him $1,000 for both the ticket and the album, and Gorsuch did so.

Six months later, Gorsuch sold the ticket at a nationally advertised auction for $110,000 and sold most of the postcards for $1,200. Westby sued Gorsuch for fraud. Testimony showed that Gorsuch was a major buyer in antiques and collectibles in the Puget Sound area and that he would have had an understanding of the value of the ticket. Gorsuch contends that all elements of fraud are not present since there was no evidence that Gorsuch intended that Westby rely on the alleged representations, nor did Westby rely on such. Rather, Gorsuch asserts, it was an arm's-length transaction and Westby had access to the same information as Gorsuch. Decide. [*Westby v. Gorsuch*, 50 P.3d 284 (Wash. App.)]

CPA Questions

1. A building subcontractor submitted a bid for construction of a portion of a high-rise office building. The bid contained material computational errors. The general contractor accepted the bid with knowledge of the errors. Which of the following statements best represents the subcontractor's liability?

   a. Not liable, because the contractor knew of the errors.

   b. Not liable, because the errors were a result of gross negligence.

   c. Liable, because the errors were unilateral.

   d. Liable, because the errors were material (5/95, Law, #17, 5351).

2. Egan, a minor, contracted with Baker to purchase Baker's used computer for $400. The computer was purchased for Egan's personal use. The agreement provided that Egan would pay $200 down on delivery and $200 thirty days later. Egan took delivery and paid the $200 down payment. Twenty days later, the computer was damaged seriously as a result of Egan's negligence. Five days after the damage occurred and one day after Egan reached the age of majority, Egan attempted to disaffirm the contract with Baker. Egan will:

   a. Be able to disaffirm despite the fact that Egan was *not* a minor at the time of disaffirmance.

   b. Be able to disaffirm only if Egan does so in writing.

   c. Not be able to disaffirm because Egan had failed to pay the balance of the purchase price.

   d. Not be able to disaffirm because the computer was damaged as a result of Egan's negligence (11/93, Law, #21, 4318).

Consideration

Will the law enforce every promise? Generally, a promise will not be enforced unless something is given or received for the promise.

14-1 General Principles

As a general rule, one of the elements needed to make an agreement binding is consideration.

14-1a Consideration Defined and Explained

consideration–promise or performance that the promisor demands as the price of the promise.

Consideration is what each party to a contract gives up to the other in making their agreement.

Bargained-for Exchange

Consideration is the bargained-for exchange between the parties to a contract. In order for consideration to exist, something of value must be given or promised in return for the performance or promise of performance of the other.[1] The value given or promised can be money, services, property, or the forbearance of a legal right.

For Example, Beth offers to pay Kerry $100 for her used skis, and Kerry accepts. Beth has promised something of value, $100, as consideration for Kerry's promise to sell the skis, and Kerry has promised Beth something of value, the skis, as consideration for the $100. If Kerry offered to *give* Beth the used skis and Beth accepted, these parties would have an agreement but not an enforceable contract because Beth did not provide any consideration in exchange for Kerry's promise of the skis. There was no *bargained-for exchange* because Kerry was not promised anything of value from Beth.

Benefit-Detriment Approach

Some jurisdictions analyze consideration from the point of view of a *benefit-detriment approach*, defining *consideration* as a benefit received by the promisor or a detriment incurred by the promisee.[2]

As an example of a unilateral contract analyzed from a benefit-detriment approach to consideration, Mr. Scully, a longtime summer resident of Falmouth, states to George Corfu, a college senior, "I will pay you $3,000 if you paint my summer home." George in fact paints the house. The work of painting the house by George, the promisee, was a legal detriment to him. Also, the painting of the house was a legal benefit to Scully, the promisor. There was consideration in this case, and the agreement is enforceable.

14-1b Gifts

Promises to make a gift are unenforceable promises under the law of contracts because of lack of consideration, as illustrated previously in the scenario of Kerry promising to give her used skis to Beth without charge. There was no bargained-for exchange because Kerry was not promised anything of value from Beth. A completed gift, however, cannot be rescinded for lack of consideration.[3]

Charitable subscriptions by which individuals make pledges to finance the construction of a college building, a church, or another structure for charitable purposes are binding to the extent that the donor (promisor) should have reasonably realized that the charity was relying on the promise in undertaking the building program. Some states require proof that the charity has relied on the subscription.[4]

[1] *Brooksbank v. Anderson*, 586 N.W.2d 789 (Minn. App. 1998).
[2] *Sullo Investments, LLC v. Moreau*, 95 A.3d 1144 (Ct. 2014).
[3] *Homes v. O'Bryant*, 741 So. 2d 366 (Miss. App. 1999).
[4] *King v. Trustees of Boston University*, 647 N.E.2d 1176 (Ma. 1995).

An agreement to give property for the consideration of love and affection does not transfer the property to the donee nor secure for the donee a right to sue to compel the completion of the contract. Love and affection alone have not been recognized as consideration for a contract.

CASE SUMMARY

What's Love Got to Do With It...

FACTS: Amber Williams and Frederick Ormsby lived together in a nonmarital relationship in a house deeded to Ormsby in 2004. The couple separated and attended couples counseling. Amber refused to move back into the house unless Frederick granted her a one-half interest in the property. On June 2, 2005, they signed a document purportedly making themselves equal partners in the home. Amber ended the relationship in September 2007, and she sought specific performance of the June 2, 2005, contract giving her a half-interest in the property. Frederick defended that "love and affection is insufficient consideration for a contract."

DECISION: Judgment for Ormsby. The only consideration offered by Amber for the June 2, 2005, agreement was her resumption of a romantic relationship with Frederick. Essentially this agreement amounts to a gratuitous promise by Frederick to give Amber an interest in property based solely on the consideration of love and affection. This June 2005 document is not an enforceable contract because it fails for want of consideration. [***Williams v. Ormsby***, **966 N.E.2d 255 (Ohio 2012)**]

14-1c Adequacy of Consideration

Ordinarily, courts do not consider the adequacy of the consideration given for a promise. The fact that the consideration supplied by one party is slight when compared with the burden undertaken by the other party is immaterial. It is a matter for the parties to decide when they make their contract whether each is getting a fair return. It is not a function of a court to review the amount of the consideration passed unless the amount is so grossly inadequate as to shock the conscience of the court.

CASE SUMMARY

A Good Neighbor Shocks the Conscience of the Court

FACTS: Dr. George Dohrmann made a contract with his very elderly childless neighbor, Mrs. Virginia Rogers, wherein she agreed to transfer to Dr. Dohrmann upon her death her valuable condominium and its contents and $4,000,000 in cash in exchange for Dohrmann incorporating the name of Rogers into the names of his two children to help perpetuate the Rogers names after her death. Dr. Dohrmann performed by taking the legal action necessary to add the Rogers name into the legal names of his two boys. From a judgment against Dohrmann on his breach of contract action against the Rogers estate, he appealed.

DECISION: Judgment against Dohrmann. He did not change the boys' surnames to Rogers, nor even change their middle names to Rogers. He merely added Rogers after their middle names. This can hardly be said to perpetuate the Rogers name after Mrs. Rogers' death. Dohrmann's argument that it is improper for a court to consider the relative value or adequacy of the consideration is rejected in this particular case. While the statement is generally true, in cases such as the one at bar it will not be applied where the consideration is so grossly inadequate as to shock the conscience of the court. [***Dohrmann v. Swaney***, **14 N.E.3d 605 (Ill. App. 2014)**]

The fact that the consideration turns out to be disappointing does not affect the binding character of the contract. Thus, the fact that a business purchased by a group of investors proves unprofitable does not constitute a failure of consideration that releases the buyers from their obligation to the seller.

14-1d **Forbearance as Consideration**

In most cases, consideration consists of the performance of an act, such as providing a service, or the making of a promise to provide a service or goods, or paying money.[5] Consideration may also consist of **forbearance,** which is refraining from doing an act that an individual has a legal right to do, or it may consist of a promise of forbearance. In other words, the promisor may desire to buy the inaction or a promise of inaction of the other party.

forbearance–refraining from doing an act.

The giving up of any legal right can be consideration for the promise of the other party to a contract. Thus, the relinquishment of a right to sue for damages will support a promise for the payment of money given in return for the promise to relinquish the right, if such is the agreement of the parties.

The promise of a creditor to forbear collecting a debt is consideration for the promise of the debtor to modify the terms of the transaction.

14-1e **Illusory Promises**

In a bilateral contract, each party makes a promise to the other. For a bilateral contract to be enforceable, there must be *mutuality of obligation.* That is, both parties must have created obligations to the other in their respective promises. If one party's promise contains either no obligation or only an apparent obligation to the other, this promise is an **illusory promise.** The party making such a promise is not bound because he or she has made no real promise. The effect is that the other party, who has made a real promise, is also not bound because he or she has received no consideration. It is said that the contract fails for lack of mutuality.

illusory promise– promise that in fact does not impose any obligation on the promisor.

Consider the example of the Jacksonville Fire soccer team's contract with Brazilian soccer star Edmundo. Edmundo signed a contract to play for the Jacksonville franchise of the new International Soccer League for five years at $25 million. The extensive document signed by Edmundo set forth the details of the team's financial commitment and the details of Edmundo's obligations to the team and its fans. On page 4 of the document, the team inserted a clause reserving the right "to terminate the contract and team obligations at any time in its sole discretion." During the season, Edmundo received a $40 million five-year offer to play for Manchester United of the English Premier League, which he accepted. Because Jacksonville had a free way out of its obligation by the unrestricted cancellation provision in the contract, it thus made its promises to Edmundo illusory. Edmundo was not bound by the Jacksonville contract as a result of a lack of mutuality and was free to sign with Manchester United.

Cancellation Provisions

Although a promise must impose a binding obligation, it may authorize a party to cancel the agreement under certain circumstances on giving notice by a certain date. Such a provision does not make this party's promise illusory, for the party does not have a free way out and is limited to living up to the terms of the **cancellation provision. For Example,** actress Zsa Zsa Gabor made a contract with Hollywood Fantasy Corporation to appear at a fantasy vacation in San Antonio, Texas, on May 2–4, for a $10,000 appearance fee plus itemized (extravagant) expenses. The last paragraph of the agreement stated: "It is agreed that if a significant acting opportunity in a film comes up, Ms. Gabor will have the right to cancel her appearance in San Antonio by advising Hollywood Fantasy in writing by April 15, 1991." Ms. Gabor sent a telegram on April 15, 1991, canceling her appearance. During the May 2 through 4 period, Ms. Gabor's only acting activity was a 14-second cameo role during the opening credits of *Naked Gun 2½.* In a lawsuit for breach of

cancellation provision– crossing out of a part of an instrument or a destruction of all legal effect of the instrument, whether by act of party, upon breach by the other party, or pursuant to agreement or decree of court.

[5] *Prenger v. Baumhoer,* 914 S.W.2d 413 (Mo. App. 1996).

contract that followed, the jury saw this portion of the movie and concluded that Ms. Gabor had not canceled her obligation on the basis of a "significant acting opportunity," and she was held liable for breach of contract.[6]

Conditional Promises

A *conditional promise* is a promise that depends on the occurrence of a specified condition in order for the promise to be binding. **For Example,** Mary Sparks, in contemplation of her signing a lease to take over a restaurant at Marina Bay, wanted to make certain that she had a highly qualified chef to run the restaurant's food service. She made a contract with John "Grumpy" White to serve as executive chef for a one-year period at a salary of $150,000. The contract set forth White's responsibilities and was conditioned on the successful negotiation of the restaurant lease with Marina Bay Management. Both parties signed it. Although the happening of the condition was within Mary's control because she could avoid the contract with Grumpy White by not acquiring the restaurant lease, she limited her future options by the contract with White. Her promise to White was not illusory because after signing the contract with him, if she acquired the restaurant lease, she was bound to hire White as her executive chef. Before signing the contract with White, she was free to sign any chef for the position. The contract was enforceable.

CPA   14-2   Special Situations

The following sections analyze certain common situations in which a lawsuit turns on whether the promisor received consideration for the promise sued on.

14-2a Preexisting Legal Obligation

Ordinarily, doing or promising to do what one is already under a legal obligation to do is not consideration.[7] Similarly, a promise to refrain from doing what one has no legal right to do is not consideration. This preexisting duty or legal obligation can be based on statute, on general principles of law, on responsibilities of an office held, or on a preexisting contract.

For Example, Officer Mary Rodgers is an undercover police officer in the city of Pasadena, California, assigned to weekend workdays. Officer Rodgers promised Elwood Farnsworth that she would diligently patrol the area of the Farnsworth estate on weekends to keep down the noise and drinking of rowdy young persons who gathered in this area, and Mr. Farnsworth promised to provide a $500 per month gratuity for this extra service. Farnsworth's promise is unenforceable because Officer Rodgers has a preexisting official duty as a police officer to protect citizens and enforce the antinoise and public drinking ordinances.

CPA   Completion of Contract

Suppose that a contractor refuses to complete a building unless the owner promises a payment or bonus in addition to the sum specified in the original contract, and the owner promises to make that payment. The question then arises as to whether the owner's promise is binding. Most courts hold that the second promise of the owner is without consideration.

---

[6] *Hollywood Fantasy Corp. v. Gabor*, 151 F.2d 203 (5th Cir. 1998).
[7] *Willamette Management Associates, Inc. v. Palczynski*, 38 A.3d 1212 (Conn. App. 2012).

CASE SUMMARY

You're Already Under Contract

FACTS: Crookham & Vessels had a contract to build an extension of a railroad for the Little Rock Port Authority. It made a contract with Larry Moyer Trucking to dig drainage ditches. The ditch walls collapsed because water would not drain off. This required that the ditches be dug over again. Larry Moyer refused to do this unless extra money was paid. Crookham & Vessels agreed to pay the additional compensation, but after the work was done, it refused to pay. Larry Moyer sued for the extra compensation promised.

DECISION: Judgment against Moyer. Moyer was bound by its contract to dig the drainage ditches. Its promise to perform that obligation was not consideration for the promise of Crookham & Vessels to pay additional compensation. Performance of an obligation is not consideration for a promise by a party entitled to that performance. The fact that performance of the contract proved more difficult or costly than originally contemplated does not justify making an exception to this rule. [*Crookham & Vessels, Inc. v. Larry Moyer Trucking, Inc.*, 699 S.W.2d 414 (Ark. App. 1985)]

If the promise of the contractor is to do something that is not part of the first contract, then the promise of the other party is binding. **For Example,** if a bonus of $5,000 is promised in return for the promise of a contractor to complete the building at a date earlier than that specified in the original agreement, the promise to pay the bonus is binding.

CPA   **Good-Faith Adjustment.** A current trend is to enforce a second promise to pay a contractor a higher amount for the performance of the original contract when there are extraordinary circumstances caused by unforeseeable difficulties and when the additional amount promised the contractor is reasonable under the circumstances.

CASE SUMMARY

"You Had a Preexisting Legal Obligation," Said the Public Guardian, Mr. Angel

FACTS: John Murray was director of finance of the city of Newport. A contract was made with Alfred Maher to remove trash. Later, Maher requested that the city council increase his compensation. Maher's costs were greater than had been anticipated because 400 new dwelling units had been put into operation. The city council voted to pay Maher an additional $10,000 a year. After two such annual payments had been made, Angel and other citizens of the city sued Murray and Maher for a return of the $20,000. They said that Maher was already obligated by his contract to perform the work for the contract sum, and there was, accordingly, no consideration for the payment of the increased compensation. From a decision in favor of the plaintiffs, the city and Maher appealed.

DECISION: Judgment for the city and Maher. When a promise modifying an original contract is made before the contract is fully performed on either side due to unanticipated circumstances that prompt the modification, and the modification is fair and equitable, such a good faith adjustment will be enforced. The unanticipated increase in the number of new units from 20 to 25 per year to 400 units in the third year of this five-year contract, which prompted the additional yearly payments of $10,000, was a voluntary good faith adjustment. It was not a "hold up" by a contractor refusing to complete an unprofitable contract unless paid additional compensation, where the preexisting duty rule would apply. [*Angel v. Murray*, 322 A.2d 630 (R.I. 1974)]

Contract for Sale of Goods. When the contract is for the sale of goods, any modification made in good faith by the parties to the contract is binding without regard to the existence of consideration for the modification.

CPA ## Compromise and Release of Claims

The rule that doing or promising to do what one is already legally bound to do is not consideration applies to a part payment made in satisfaction of an admitted or *liquidated debt*. Thus, a promise to pay part of an amount that is admittedly owed is not consideration for a promise to discharge the balance. It will not prevent the creditor from demanding the remainder later. **For Example,** John owes Mark $100,000, which was due on March 1, 2016. On March 15, John offers to pay back $80,000 if Mark will agree to accept this amount as the discharge of the full amount owed. Mark agrees to this proposal, and it is set forth in writing signed by the parties. However, Mark later sues for the $20,000 balance. Mark will be successful in the lawsuit because John's payment of the $80,000 is not consideration for Mark's promise to discharge the full amount owed because John was doing only what he had a preexisting legal duty to do.

If the debtor pays the part payment before the debt is due, there is consideration because, on the day when the payment was made, the creditor was not entitled to demand any payment. Likewise, if the creditor accepts some article (even of slight value) in addition to the part payment, consideration exists.

A debtor and creditor may have a bona fide dispute over the amount owed or whether any amount is owed. Such is called an *unliquidated debt*. In this case, payment by the debtor of less than the amount claimed by the creditor is consideration for the latter's agreement to release or settle the claim. It is generally regarded as sufficient if the claimant believes in the merit of the claim.[8]

Part-Payment Checks

When there is a good-faith dispute about the amount of a debt and the debtor tenders a check that states on its face "paid in full" and references the transaction in dispute, but the amount of the check is less than the full amount the creditor asserts is owed, the cashing of the check by the creditor discharges the entire debt.

Composition of Creditors

composition of creditors—agreement among creditors that each shall accept a part payment as full payment in consideration of the other creditors doing the same.

In a **composition of creditors,** the various creditors of one debtor mutually agree to accept a fractional part of their claims in full satisfaction of the claims. Such agreements are binding and are supported by consideration. When creditors agree to extend the due date of their debts, the promise of each creditor to forbear is likewise consideration for the promise of other creditors to forbear.

14-2b Past Consideration

past consideration—something that has been performed in the past and which, therefore, cannot be consideration for a promise made in the present.

A promise based on a party's past performance lacks consideration.[9] It is said that **past consideration** is no consideration. **For Example,** Fred O'Neal came up with the idea for the formation of the new community bank of Villa Rica and was active in its formation. Just prior to the execution of the documents creating the bank, the organizers discussed that once the bank was formed, it would hire O'Neal, giving him a three-year contract in inflation adjusted figures of $104,000 the first year, $107,000 the second year, and $110,000 the third. In a lawsuit against the bank for breach of contract, O'Neal testified that the consideration he gave in exchange for the three-year contract was his past effort to organize the bank. The court stated that past consideration generally will not support a subsequent promise and that the purported consideration was not rendered to the bank, which had not yet been established when his promotion and

---

[8] *F. H. Prince & Co. v. Towers Financial Corp.,* 656 N.E.2d 142 (Ill. App. 1995).
[9] *Smith v. Locklear,* 906 So. 2d 1273 (Fla. App. 2005).

ETHICS & THE LAW

Alan Fulkins, who owns a construction company that specializes in single-family residences, is constructing a small subdivision with 23 homes. Tretorn Plumbing, owned by Jason Tretorn, was awarded the contract for the plumbing work on the homes at a price of $4,300 per home.

Plumbing contractors complete their residential projects in three phases. Phase one consists of digging the lines for the plumbing and installing the pipes that are placed in the foundation of the house. Phase two consists of installing the pipes within the walls of the home, and phase three is installing of the surface plumbing, such as sinks and tubs. However, industry practice dictates that the plumbing contractor receive one-half of the contract amount after completion of phase one.

Tretorn completed the digs of phase one for Fulkins and received payment of $2,150. Tretorn then went to Fulkins and demanded an additional $600 per house to complete the work.

Fulkins said, "But you already have a contract for $4,300!" Tretorn responded, "I know, but the costs are killing me. I need the additional $600."

Fulkins explained the hardship of the demand, "Look, I've already paid you half. If I hire someone else, I'll have to pay them two-thirds for the work not done. It'll cost me $5,000 per house."

Tretorn responded, "Exactly. I'm a bargain because the additional $600 I want only puts you at $4,900. If you don't pay it, I'll just lien the houses and then you'll be stuck without a way to close the sales. I've got the contract all drawn up. Just sign it and everything goes smoothly."

Should Fulkins sign the agreement? Does Tretorn have the right to the additional $600? Was it ethical for Tretorn to demand the $600? Is there any legal advice you can offer Fulkins?

organization work took place.[10] The presence of a bargained-for exchange is not present when a promise is made in exchange for a past benefit.[11]

14-2c **Moral Obligation**

In most states, promises made to another based on "moral obligation" lack consideration and are not enforceable.[12] They are considered gratuitous promises and unenforceable. **For Example,** Robert Lewis and his brother Lewis Lester had an agreement under which Robert would provide help for his uncle Floyd and serve as his power of attorney and the brothers would split the uncle's estate equally. Floyd left his estate to Lewis Lester. Robert's suit against his brother to enforce their agreement failed for lack of consideration. Services performed by one family member on behalf of another family member are presumed to have been rendered in obedience to a moral obligation without expectation of compensation.[13]

14-3 **Exceptions to the Laws of Consideration**

The ever-changing character of law clearly appears in the area of consideration as part of the developing law of contracts.

14-3a **Exceptions to Consideration**

By statute or decision, traditional consideration is not required in these situations:

---

[10] *O'Neal v. Home Town Bank of Villa Rica*, 514 S.E.2d 669 (Ga. App. 1999); *Lee v. Choi*, 754 S.E.2d 371 (Ga. App. 2013).

[11] But see *United Resource Recovery Corp v. Ranko Venture Management Inc.*, 854 F. Supp. 2d 645 (S.D.N.Y. 2008) where a past work agreement was unenforceable because it was based on past consideration—however, the individual could recover under a signed consulting agreement for which no compensation had been paid. See also *Travis v. Paepke*, 3 So. 3d 131 (Miss. App. 2009).

[12] *Production Credit Ass'n of Manaan v. Rub*, 475 N.W.2d 532 (N.D. 1991). As to the Louisiana rule of moral consideration, see *Thomas v. Bryant*, 596 So. 2d 1065 (La. App. 1992).

[13] *Lewis v. Lester*, 760 N.E.2d 91 (N.C. App. 2014).

FIGURE 14-1   Consideration and Promises

Charitable Subscriptions

Where individuals made pledges to finance the construction of buildings for charitable purposes, consideration is lacking according to technical standards applied in ordinary contract cases. For public policy reasons, the reliance of the charity on the pledge in undertaking the project is deemed a substitute for consideration.

Uniform Commercial Code

In some situations, the Uniform Commercial Code abolishes the requirement of consideration. **For Example,** under the Code, consideration is not required for (1) a merchant's written, firm offer for goods stated to be irrevocable, (2) a written discharge of a claim for an alleged breach of a commercial contract, or (3) an agreement to modify a contract for the sale of goods.[14]

Promissory Estoppel

promissory estoppels—doctrine that a promise will be enforced although it is not supported by consideration when the promisor should have reasonably expected that the promise would induce action or forbearance of a definite and substantial character on the part of the promised and injustice can be avoided only by enforcement of the promise.

Under the doctrine of **promissory estoppel,** a promisor may be prevented from asserting that his or her promise is unenforceable because the promisee gave no consideration for the promise.[15] This doctrine, sometimes called the *doctrine of detrimental reliance*, is applicable when (1) the promisor makes a promise that lacks consideration, (2) the promisor intends or should reasonably expect that the promisee will rely on the promise, (3) the promisee in fact relies on the promise in some definite and substantial manner, and (4) enforcement of the promise is the only way to avoid injustice.[16]

Damages recoverable in a case of promissory estoppel are not the profits that the promisee expected, but only the amount necessary to restore the promisee to the position he or she would have been in had the promisee not relied on the promise.[17]

---

[14] U.C.C. §2-209(1).
[15] See *Weiss v. Smulders*, 96 A.3d 1175 (Conn. 2014).
[16] *Neuhoff v. Marvin Lumber and Cedar Co.*, 370 F.3d 197 (1st Cir. 2004).
[17] *Medistar Corp. v. Schmidt*, 267 S.W.3d 150 (Tex. App. 2008).

Legal difficulties often arise because parties take certain things for granted. Frequently, they will be sure that they have agreed to everything and that they have a valid contract. Sometimes, however, they do not. The courts are then faced with the problem of leaving them with their broken dreams or coming to their rescue when promissory estoppel can be established.

CASE SUMMARY

Brits Rescued by Promissory Estoppel

FACTS: Portman Lamborghini, Ltd. (Portman), was owned by Chaplake Holdings, Ltd., a United Kingdom company, which was owned by David Jolliffe and David Lakeman as equal shareholders. Between 1984 and 1987, Portman sold approximately 30 new Lamborghinis each year through its exclusive concession contract with the car maker. It was then the largest Lamborghini dealer in the world since Lamborghini's production was just 250 cars per year. These cars sold at a retail price between $200,000 and $300,000. In 1987, Chrysler Corporation bought Lamborghini, and its chairman, Lee Iacocca, presented a plan to escalate production to 5,000 units within five years. The plan included the introduction of a new model, the P140, with a retail price of $70,000. Between 1987 and 1991, *all* of the Chrysler/Lamborghini top executives with whom Jolliffe and Lakeman and their top advisors came in contact provided the same message to them: Chrysler was committed to the Expansion Plan, and in order for Portman to retain its exclusive U.K. market, it must expand its operational capacity from 35 cars in 1987 to 400 cars by 1992. Accordingly, Portman acquired additional financing, staff, and facilities and built a new distribution center. An economic downturn in the United States and major development and production problems at Lamborghini led Chrysler to reduce its expansion investment by two-thirds. Factory production delays eroded Portman's profitability and success, and it entered into receivership in April 1992. Suit was brought on behalf of the Portman and Chaplake entities on a promissory estoppel theory against Chrysler, a Delaware corporation.

DECISION: Judgment for Portman and Chaplake on the promissory estoppel theory. (1) A promise was made by Chrysler that the Lamborghini line would expand tenfold and that Portman would retain its exclusivity deal *only* if it expanded its operational capacity. (2) The promisor, Chrysler, should have reasonably expected that Portman would rely on this promise. (3) Lakeman and Jolliffe were given the same message and promise by *all* of the top executives involved, and it was therefore not unreasonable for them to rely upon the promises made by these executives and to undertake the detriment of major expansion activity that would have been unnecessary but for the Expansion Plan and the role they were promised. (4) The prevention of injustice is the "fundamental idea" underlying the doctrine of promissory estoppel, and injustice can be avoided in this case only by the enforcement of Chrysler's promise. Portman is entitled to £ 569,321 for its costs to implement its Expansion Plan, and Chaplake is entitled to £ 462,686 for its investment in Portman's expansion. [*Chrysler Corp. v. Chaplake Holdings, Ltd.*, 822 A.2d 1024 (Del. 2003)]

Make the Connection

Summary

A promise is not binding if there is no consideration for the promise. Consideration is what the promisor requires as the price for his promise. That price may be doing an act, refraining from the doing of an act, or merely promising to do or to refrain. In a bilateral contract, it is necessary to find that the promise of each party is supported by consideration. If either promise is not so supported, it is not binding, and the agreement of the parties is not a contract.

Consequently, the agreement cannot be enforced. When a promise is the consideration, it must be a binding promise. The binding character of a promise is not affected by the circumstance that there is a condition precedent to the performance promised. A promise to do what one is already obligated to do is not consideration, although some exceptions are made. Such exceptions include the rendering of a partial performance or a modified performance accepted as a good-faith adjustment to a changed situation, a compromise and release of claims, a part-payment check, and a compromise of creditors. Because consideration is the price that is given to obtain the promise, past benefits conferred on the promisor cannot be consideration.

A promise to refrain from doing an act can be consideration. A promise to refrain from suing or asserting a particular claim can be consideration. When consideration is forbearance to assert a claim, it is immaterial whether the claim is valid as long as the claim has been asserted in the good-faith belief that it was valid.

When the promisor obtains the consideration specified for the promise, the law is not ordinarily concerned with the value or adequacy of that consideration.

Under the doctrine of promissory estoppel a court may enforce a promise lacking consideration where it is the only way to avoid injustice.

Learning Outcomes

After studying this chapter, you should be able to clearly explain:

14-1   General Principles

LO.1 Explain what constitutes consideration

See the *Williams v. Ormsby* case, which determined that love and affection is not recognized as consideration, page 264.

See the "bargained for exchange" example involving Beth and Kerry, page 263.

See the "benefit-detriment" approach to consideration example, page 263.

See the discussion on forbearance as consideration, page 265.

14-2   Special Situations

LO.2 Distinguish between a "preexisting legal obligation" and "past consideration"

See the preexisting duty example involving Officer Rodgers, page 266.

See the *Angel v. Murray* case involving a good-faith adjustment exception to the preexisting duty rule, page 267.

See the example involving Fred O'Neal where he found out the past consideration is no consideration rule, page 268.

LO.3 Explain why promises based on moral obligations lack consideration

See the example of the gratuitous deeds of Robert Lewis, page 269.

14-3   Exceptions to the Laws of Consideration

LO.4 List the exceptions to the requirement of consideration

See the discussion on charitable subscriptions, the UCC, and promissory estoppel, pages 270–271.

LO.5 Explain the "fundamental idea" underlying promissory estoppel

See the *Chaplake Holdings* case where the court enforced Chrysler's promise in order to correct an injustice, page 271.

Key Terms

cancellation provision	forbearance	promissory estoppel
composition of creditors	illusory promise	
consideration	past consideration	

Questions and Case Problems

1. Sarah's house caught on fire. Through the prompt assistance of her neighbor Odessa, the fire was quickly extinguished. In gratitude, Sarah promised to pay Odessa $1,000. Can Odessa enforce this promise?

2. William E. Story agreed to pay his nephew, William E. Story II, a large sum of money (roughly equivalent to $75,000 in 2016 dollars) "if he would refrain from drinking liquor, using tobacco, swearing, and

playing cards or billiards for money until he should come to be 21 years of age." William II had been using tobacco and occasionally drank liquor but refrained from using these stimulants over several years until he was 21 and also lived up to the other requirements of his uncle's offer. Just after William II's 21st birthday, Story acknowledged that William II had fulfilled his part of the bargain and advised that the money would be invested for him with interest. Story died, and his executor, Sidway, refused to pay William II because he believed the contract between Story and William II was without consideration. Sidway asserted that Story received no benefit from William II's performance and William II suffered no detriment (in fact, by his refraining from the use of liquor and tobacco, William II was not harmed but benefited, Sidway asserted). Is there any theory of consideration that William II can rely on? How would you decide this case? [*Hamer v. Sidway*, 124 N.Y. 538]

3. Dale Dyer, who was employed by National By-Products, Inc., was seriously injured at work as the result of a job-related accident. He agreed to give up his right to sue the employer for damages in consideration of the employer's giving him a lifetime job. The employer later claimed that this agreement was not binding because Dyer's promise not to sue could not be consideration for the promise to employ on the ground that Dyer in fact had no right to sue. Dyer's only remedy was to make a claim under workers' compensation. Was the agreement binding? [*Dyer v. National By-Products, Inc.*, 380 N.W.2d 732 (Iowa)]

4. Charles Sanarwari retained Stan Gissel to prepare his income tax return for the year 2014. The parties agreed on a fee of $400. Charles had done a rough estimate based on last year's return and believed he would owe the IRS approximately $2,000. When Stan's work was completed, it turned out that Charles would receive a $2,321 tax refund. Charles paid for Stan's services and was so pleased with the work that he promised to pay Stan an additional $400 for the excellent job on the tax return when he received his tax refund. Thereafter, Charles had a falling out with Stan over a golf tournament snub. Stan was not paid the $400 promised for doing an excellent job on the tax return, and he sued Charles as a matter of principle. Decide.

5. Medistar is a real estate development company specializing in the development of medical facilities.

Dr. Schmidt, the team physician for the San Antonio Spurs basketball team, sought to develop "The Texas Center for Athletes" medical center next to the Spurs facility and urged Medistar to obtain the real estate and develop the project on his group's behalf. Medistar spent more than $1 million and thousands of man-hours on the project from 2000 to July 12, 2004, when Dr. Schmidt's new group of investors purchased the property next to the Spur's facility for the project; subsequently, Medistar was informed that it would have no role in the project. Medistar asserts that it relied on Dr. Schmidt's assurances that it would be the developer of the project—and after four years and the $1 million in time and expenses it spent, it is unconscionable to be excluded from the project. Dr. Schmidt and associates contend that Medistar has presented no contractual agreement tying it to any legal obligation to Medistar. Is there a viable legal theory available to Medistar? If so what is the remedy? [*Medistar v. Schmidt*, 267 S.W.3d 150 (Tex. App.)]

6. While on a fishing trip, Tom Snyder met an elderly couple living in near-destitute conditions in a rural area of Texas. He returned to the area often, and he regularly purchased groceries for the couple and paid for their medical needs. Some two years later, the couple's son, David, discovered what Tom had been doing and promised to reimburse Snyder for what he had furnished his parents. He failed to do so and Tom sued David for breach of his promise to reimburse Snyder. Tom has receipts for most of the purchases. What defense, if any, does David have? Decide.

7. The Aqua Drilling Company made a contract to drill a well for the Atlas Construction Company. It was expected that this would supply water for a home being constructed by Atlas. Aqua did not make any guarantee or warranty that water would be produced. Aqua drilled the well exactly as required by the contract, but no water was produced. Atlas refused to pay. It asserted that the contract was not binding on the theory that there had been a failure of consideration because the well did not produce water. Was the contract binding? [*Atlas Construction Co., Inc. v. Aqua Drilling Co.*, 559 P.2d 39 (Wyo.)]

8. Sears, Roebuck and Co. promised to give Forrer permanent employment. Forrer sold his farm at a loss to take the job. Shortly after beginning work, he was discharged by Sears, which claimed that the contract could be terminated at will. Forrer claimed

that promissory estoppel prevented Sears from terminating the contract. Was he correct? [*Forrer v. Sears, Roebuck & Co.*, 153 N.W.2d 587 (Wis.)]

9. Kemp leased a gas filling station from Baehr. Kemp, who was heavily indebted to Penn-O-Tex Oil Corp., transferred to it his right to receive payments on all claims. When Baehr complained that the rent was not paid, he was assured by the corporation that the rent would be paid to him. Baehr did not sue Kemp for the overdue rent but later sued the corporation. The defense was raised that there was no consideration for the promise of the corporation. Decide. [*Baehr v. Penn-O-Tex Corp.*, 104 N.W.2d 661 (Minn.)]

10. John Blackwell was seriously injured in an auto accident. His wife was Korean and spoke little English and needed help communicating with Blackwell's doctor. The Blackwells hired Choi as an interpreter in 1997 and over time Mr. Choi assisted with the family finances and other matters. In 2010 Blackwell's wife fired Choi and later the parties signed an agreement agreeing to pay Choi $450,000 "for the work Choi had done for Blackwell." Choi sued to obtain payment. Was he successful? [*Lee v. Choi*, 754 S.E.2d 371 (Ga. App.)]

11. Kelsoe worked for International Wood Products, Inc., for a number of years. One day Hernandez, a director and major stockholder of the company, promised Kelsoe that the corporation would give her 5 percent of the company's stock. This promise was never kept, and Kelsoe sued International for breach of contract. Had the company broken its contract? [*Kelsoe v. International Wood Products, Inc.*, 588 So. 2d 877 (Ala.)]

12. Kathy left her classic 1978 Volkswagen convertible at Freddie's Service Station, requesting a "tune-up." When she returned that evening, Freddie's bill was $374. Kathy stated that Firestone and Sears advertise tune-ups for $70, and she asked Freddie, "How can you justify this bill?" Freddie responded, "Carburator work." Kathy refused to pay the bill and left. That evening, when the station closed, she took her other set of keys and removed her car, after placing a check in the station's mail slot. The check was made out to Freddie's Service Station for $200 and stated on its face: "This check is in full payment of my account with you regarding the tune-up today on my 1978 Volkswagen convertible." Freddie cashed the check in order to meet his business expenses and then sued Kathy for the difference owed. What result?

13. On the death of their mother, the children of Jane Smith gave their interests in their mother's estate to their father in consideration of his payment of $1 to each of them and his promise to leave them the property on his death. The father died without leaving them the property. The children sued their father's second wife to obtain the property in accordance with the agreement. The second wife claimed that the agreement was not a binding contract because the amount of $1 and future gifts given for the children's interests were so trivial and uncertain. Decide.

14. Radio Station KSCS broadcast a popular music program. It announced that it would pay $25,000 to any listener who detected that it did not play three consecutive songs. Steve Jennings listened to and heard a program in which two songs were followed by a commercial program. He claimed the $25,000. The station refused to pay on the ground that there was no consideration for its promise to pay that amount. Was the station liable? [*Jennings v. Radio Station KSCS*, 708 S.W.2d 60 (Tex. App.)]

15. Hoffman wanted to acquire a franchise for a Red Owl grocery store. (Red Owl was a corporation that maintained a system of chain stores.) An agent of Red Owl informed Hoffman and his wife that if they would sell their bakery in Wautoma, acquire a certain tract of land in Chilton (another Wisconsin city), and put up $6,000, they would be given a franchise. In reliance on the agent's promise, Hoffman sold his business and acquired the land in Chilton, but he was never granted a franchise. He and his wife sued Red Owl. Red Owl raised the defense that there had been only an assurance that Hoffman would receive a franchise, but because there was no promise supported by consideration, there was no binding contract to give him a franchise. Decide. [*Hoffman v. Red Owl Stores, Inc.*, 133 N.W.2d 267 (Wis.)]

Legality and Public Policy

Learning Outcomes ⟨⟨⟨

After studying this chapter, you should be able to

LO.1 Explain the general contract principles on "illegality"

LO.2 Explain the implied obligation on all parties of good faith and fair dealing

LO.3 Understand that it is only in unusual situations that a contract provision will be unenforceable because it is unconscionable

LO.4 Explain the rationale for requiring licenses to carry on as a business, trade, or profession

LO.5 Distinguish between noncompete clauses after the sale of a business and noncompete clauses in employment contracts

A court will not enforce a contract if it is illegal, contrary to public policy, or unconscionable.

15-1 General Principles

An agreement is illegal either when its formation or performance is a crime or a tort or when it is contrary to public policy or unconscionable.

15-1a Effect of Illegality

Ordinarily, an illegal agreement is void. When an agreement is illegal, the parties are usually not entitled to the aid of the courts. Examples of illegal contracts where the courts have left the parties where they found them include a liquor store owner not being allowed to bring suit for money owed for goods (liquor) sold and delivered on credit in violation of statute and an unlicensed home improvement contractor not being allowed to enforce his contract for progress payments due him. If the illegal agreement has not been performed, neither party can sue the other to obtain performance or damages. If the agreement has been performed, neither party can sue the other to obtain damages or to set the agreement aside.[1]

CASE SUMMARY

The Illegal Paralegal

FACTS: Brian Neiman was involved in the illegal practice of law for over seven years. Having been found guilty of illegally practicing law, he sought to collect disability benefits under his disability insurance policy with Provident Life due to an alleged bipolar disorder, the onset of which occurred during the pendency of criminal and bar proceedings against him. Neiman contends that his bipolar disorder prevents him from working as a paralegal. Provident contends that Neiman should not be indemnified for the loss of income generated from his illegal practice of law.

DECISION: Because all of Neiman's income was derived from the unlawful practice of law in the seven years preceding his claim, as a matter of public policy, a court will not enforce a disability benefits policy that compensates him for his loss of income he was not entitled to earn. Neiman's own wrongdoing caused the contract to be void. Accordingly, Neiman was *in pari delicto* [equally guilty], if not more at fault than the insurance company, in causing the contract to be void and will recover neither benefits nor the premiums he paid. The court must leave the parties where it found them. [*Neiman v. Provident Life & Accident Insurance Co.,* **217 F. Supp. 2d 1281 (S.D. Fla. 2002)**]

Even if a contract appears to be legal on its face, it may be unenforceable if it was entered into for an illegal purpose. **For Example,** if zoning regulations in the special-purpose district of Washington, D.C., require that only a professional can lease space in a given building, and the rental agent suggests that two nonprofessionals take out the lease in their attorney's name but all parties realize that the premises will be used only by the nonprofessionals, then the lease in question is illegal and unenforceable.[2]

15-1b Exceptions to Effect of Illegality

To avoid hardship, exceptions are made to the rules stated previously in the section titled "Effect of Illegality."

---

[1] *Sabia v. Mattituck Inlet Marina, Inc.,* 805 N.Y.S.2d 346 (A.D. 2005).
[2] *McMahon v. A, H, & B,* 728 A.2d 656 (D.C. 1999).

Protection of One Party

When the law that the agreement violates is intended to protect one of the parties, that party may seek relief. **For Example,** when, in order to protect the public, the law forbids the issuance of securities by certain classes of corporations, a person who has purchased them may recover the money paid.

Unequal Guilt

in pari delicto—equally guilty; used in reference to a transaction as to which relief will not be granted to either party because both are equally guilty of wrongdoing.

When the parties are not *in pari delicto*—equally guilty—the least guilty party is granted relief when public interest is advanced by doing so. **For Example,** when a statute is adopted to protect one of the parties to a transaction, such as a usury law adopted to protect borrowers, the person to be protected will not be deemed to be *in pari delicto* with the wrongdoer when entering into a transaction that the statute prohibits.

15-1c Partial Illegality

An agreement may involve the performance of several promises, some of which are illegal and some legal. The legal parts of the agreement may be enforced provided that they can be separated from the parts that are illegal.

When the illegal provision of a contract may be ignored without defeating the contract's basic purpose, a court will merely ignore the illegal provision and enforce the balance of the contract. Consequently, when a provision for the payment of an attorney's fee in a car rental agreement was illegal because a local statute prohibited it, the court would merely ignore the fee provision and enforce the balance of the contract.[3]

Contracts that involve both unlawful and lawful provisions may be enforced if the illegal portion is severable from the legal. **For Example,** where two separate funds were provided to Watkins by Kyablue, one for gambling purposes and the other in the form of a loan for personal expenses, Kyablue was allowed to recover the repayment of the personal loan, which was severable from the arguably illegal portion relating to gambling-related contracts.[4]

15-1d Crimes and Civil Wrongs

An agreement is illegal, and therefore void, when it calls for the commission of any act that constitutes a crime. To illustrate, one cannot enforce an agreement by which the other party is to commit an assault, steal property, burn a house, or kill a person. A contract to obtain equipment for committing a crime is illegal and cannot be enforced. Thus, a contract to manufacture and sell illegal slot machines is void.

An agreement that calls for the commission of a civil wrong is also illegal and void. Examples are agreements to slander a third person; defraud another; infringe another's patent, trademark, or copyright; or fix prices.

15-1e Good Faith and Fairness

good faith—absence of knowledge of any defects or problems.

Every contract has an implied obligation that neither party shall do anything that will have the effect of destroying or injuring the right of the other party to receive the fruits of the contract. This means that in every contract there exists an implied covenant of **good faith** and fair dealing. **For Example,** Katy Lesser entered into a 10-year lease of retail space to operate a natural food store in South Burlington, Vermont. Her business prospered and in April 1999 she signed a lease for additional space. For five years, the

[3] *Harbour v. Arelco, Inc.,* 678 N.E.2d 381 (Ind. 1997).
[4] *Kyablue v. Watkins,* 149 Cal. Rptr. 3d 156 (Cal. App. 2012).

landlord continually rebuffed her efforts to meet and discuss plans to renovate the 1999 space to expand the grocery store, motivated solely by a desire to pressure the tenant to pay a portion of his legal fees in an unrelated zoning case. The court found that the landlord breached the obligation of good faith and fair dealing, causing the 1999 space to be essentially unusable from 1999 to 2004. The court awarded the tenant the rent she paid for this period less a storage fee adjustment.[5]

15-1f Unconscionable Clauses

Ordinarily, a court will not consider whether a contract is fair or unfair, is wise or foolish, or operates unequally between the parties. **For Example,** the Kramper Family Farm agreed to sell 17.59 acres of land to Dakota Industrial Development, Inc. (DID), for $35,000 per acre if the buyer constructed a paved road along the property by December 31. The contract also provided that if the road was not completed by the date set forth in the contract, the price per acre would be $45,000. When the road was not completed by the December 31 date, Family Farm sued DID for the additional $10,000 per acre. DID defended that to apply the contract according to its plain language would create an unconscionable result and was an unenforceable penalty provision contrary to public policy. The court refused to allow DID to escape its contractual obligations on the pretext of unconscionability and public policy arguments. The parties are at liberty to contract as they see fit, the court concluded, and, generally, a court will not inquire into the adequacy of consideration inasmuch as the value of property is a matter of personal judgment by the parties to the contract. In this case, the price consisted of either $45,000 per acre, or $35,000 per acre with the road by a certain date.[6]

However, in certain unusual situations, the law may hold a contract provision unenforceable because it is too harsh or oppressive to one of the parties. This principle may be applied to invalidate a clause providing for the payment by one party of an excessive penalty on the breaking of a contract or a provision inserted by the dominant party that it shall not be liable for the consequences of intentional torts, fraud, or gross negligence. This principle is extended in connection with the sale of goods to provide that "if the court … finds the contract or any clause of the contract to have been unconscionable at the time it was made, the court may refuse to enforce the contract, or it may enforce the remainder of the contract without the unconscionable clause, or it may so limit the application of any unconscionable clause as to avoid any unconscionable result."[7]

What Constitutes Unconscionability?

A provision in a contract that gives what the court believes is too much of an advantage over a buyer may be held void as unconscionable.

Determination of Unconscionability

Some jurisdictions analyze unconscionability as having two separate elements: procedural and substantive. Both elements must be present for a court to refuse to enforce a contract provision. Other jurisdictions analyze unconscionability by considering the doctrine of adhesion and whether the clause in question is unduly oppressive.

Procedural unconscionability has to do with matters of freedom of assent resulting from inequality of bargaining power and the absence of real negotiations and meaningful

[5] *Century Partners, LP v. Lesser Goldsmith Enterprises,* 958 A.2d 627 (Vt. 2008).
[6] *Kramper Family Farm v. Dakota Industrial Development, Inc.,* 603 N.W.2d 463 (Neb. App. 1999).
[7] U.C.C. §2-302(1).

choice or a surprise resulting from hiding a disputed term in an unduly long document or fine print. Companywide standardized form contracts imposed on a take-it-or-leave-it basis by a party with superior bargaining strength are called **contracts of adhesion,** and they may sometimes be deemed procedurally unconscionable.

Substantive unconscionability focuses on the actual terms of the contract itself. Such unconscionability is indicated when the contract terms are so one-sided as to shock the conscience or are so extreme as to appear unconscionable according to the mores and business practices of the time and place.

The U.S. Supreme Court has made clear that arbitration is an acceptable forum for the resolution of employment disputes between employees and their employers, including employment-related claims based on federal and state statutes.[8] The controlling arbitration agreement language is commonly devised and implemented by the employer. Under the Federal Arbitration Act (FAA), the employer can obtain a court order to stay court proceedings and compel arbitration according to the terms of the controlling arbitration agreement. The Supreme Court also made clear that in agreeing to arbitration of a statutory claim, a party does not forgo substantive rights afforded by the statute. In a growing number of court decisions, in effect employers are finding that courts will not enforce arbitration agreements in which the employer has devised an arbitration agreement that functions as a thumb on the employer's side of the scale.[9]

When a court finds that a contract or any clause of a contract was unconscionable at the time it was made, it may enforce the remainder of the contract without the unconscionable clause or refuse to enforce the entire agreement if the agreement is permeated by unconscionability. **For Example,** two provisions of a premarital agreement between Jeffrey and Nancy Facter waiving the right to spousal and child support upon the dissolution of the marriage were found to be unconscionable. The invalid provisions were deleted and the remainder of the agreement was enforced.[10] An arbitration agreement may be substantively unconscionable if fees and costs are so excessive as to deny the litigant the ability to pursue a claim. **For Example,** an arbitration agreement was found to be substantively unconscionable because the plaintiff John Clark, a retired senior citizen

contract of adhesion—
contract offered by a dominant party to a party with inferior bargaining power on a take-it-or-leave-it basis.

THINKING THINGS THROUGH

Legality and Public Policy

Karl Llewellyn, the principal drafter of the law that governs nearly all sales of goods in the United States—the Uniform Commercial Code (UCC)—once wrote, "Covert tools are never reliable tools." He was referring to unfairness in a contract or between the contracting parties.

The original intent of declaring certain types of contracts void because of issues of imbalance was based in equity. Courts stepped in to help parties who found themselves bound under agreements that were not fair and open in both their written terms and the communications between the parties. One contracts scholar wrote that the original

intent could be described as courts stepping in to help "presumptive sillies like sailors and heirs..." and others who, if not crazy, are "pretty peculiar."

However, as the sophistication of contracts and commercial transactions increased, the importance of accuracy, honesty, and fairness increased. Unconscionability is a contracts defense that permits courts to intervene where contracts, if enforced, would "affront the sense of decency." Unconscionability is a term of ethics or moral philosophy used by courts to prevent exploitation and fraud.

[8] *Gilmer v. Interstate/Johnson Lane Corp.,* 500 U.S. 20 (1991); *Circuit City Stores, Inc. v. Adams,* 532 U.S. 105 (2001).
[9] See *Vassi/Kouska v. Woodfield Nissan Inc.,* 830 N.E.2d 619 (Ill. App. 2005).
[10] In re *the Marriage of Facter,* 152 Cal. Rptr. 3d 79 (Cal. App. 2013).

living on a fixed income, could not afford to pay the projected $22,800 in arbitrators' fees to arbitrate his medical negligence and abuse and neglect of a vulnerable adult action against the defendant nursing home, where the arbitration agreement did not provide for a waiver/reduction of fees based on financial hardship.[11]

15-2   Agreements Affecting Public Welfare

Agreements that may harm the public welfare are condemned as contrary to public policy and are not binding. Agreements that interfere with public service or the duties of public officials, obstruct legal process, or discriminate against classifications of individuals may be considered detrimental to public welfare and, as such, are not enforceable.

15-2a   Agreements Contrary to Public Policy

A given agreement may not violate any statute but may still be so offensive to society that the courts feel that enforcing the contract would be contrary to public policy.

public policy–certain objectives relating to health, morals, and integrity of government that the law seeks to advance by declaring invalid any contract that conflicts with those objectives even though there is no statute expressly declaring such a contract illegal.

Public policy cannot be defined precisely but is loosely described as protection from that which tends to be injurious to the public or contrary to the public good or which violates any established interest of society. Contracts that may be unenforceable as contrary to public policy frequently relate to the protection of the public welfare, health, or safety; to the protection of the person; and to the protection of recognized social institutions. **For Example,** a woman entered into a services contract with a male in exchange for financial support. The record disclosed, however, that the association between the parties was one founded upon the exchange of money for sex. The court determined that the agreement for financial support in exchange for illicit sexual relations was violative of public policy and thus was unenforceable.[12] Courts are cautious in invalidating a contract on the ground that it is contrary to public policy because courts recognize that, on the one hand, they are applying a very vague standard and, on the other hand, they are restricting the freedom of the contracting parties to contract freely as they choose.[13]

15-2b   Gambling, Wagers, and Lotteries

Gambling contracts are illegal. Largely as a result of the adoption of antigambling statutes, wagers or bets are generally illegal. Private **lotteries** involving the three elements of prize, chance, and consideration (or similar affairs of chance) are also generally held illegal. In many states, public lotteries (lotteries run by a state government) have been legalized by statute. Raffles are usually regarded as lotteries. In some states, bingo games, lotteries, and raffles are legalized by statute when the funds raised are used for a charitable purpose.

lottery–any plan by which a consideration is given for a chance to win a prize; it consists of three elements: (1) there must be a payment of money or something of value for an opportunity to win, (2) a prize must be available, and (3) the prize must be offered by lot or chance.

Sales promotion schemes calling for the distribution of property according to chance among the purchasers of goods are held illegal as lotteries without regard to whether the scheme is called a *guessing contest*, a *raffle*, or a *gift*.

Giveaway plans and games are lawful so long as it is not necessary to buy anything or give anything of value to participate. If participation is free, the element of consideration is lacking, and there is no lottery.

An activity is not gambling when the result is solely or predominantly a matter of skill. In contrast, it is gambling when the result is solely a matter of luck. Rarely is any activity 100 percent skill or 100 percent luck.

[11] *Clark v. Renaissance West*, LLC, 307 P.3d 77 (Ariz. App. 2013).
[12] *Anonymous v. Anonymous*, 740 N.Y.S.2d 341 (App. Div. 2002).
[13] *Beacon Hill Civic Ass'n v. Ristorante Toscano, Inc.*, 662 N.E.2d 1015 (Mass. 1996).

ETHICS & THE LAW

Public Policy Issues Regarding Surrogacy Contracts

William Stern and his wife were unable to have children. The Sterns entered into a surrogacy contract with Mary Beth Whitehead though the Infertility Center of New York (ICNY). William Stern and the Whiteheads (husband and wife) signed a contract for Mary Beth to be artificially inseminated and carry Stern's child to term, for which Stern was to pay Mary Beth $10,000 and ICNY $7,500.

Mary Beth was successfully artificially inseminated in 1985, and "Baby M" was born on March 27, 1986. On March 30, 1986, Mary Beth turned Baby M over to the Sterns. Subsequently, Mary Beth became so emotionally distraught that the Sterns allowed her to take Baby M for one week to help her adjust. The Whiteheads fled to New Jersey with the baby, and the search and return of Baby M attracted national attention and brought forth the national discussion of the legality of surrogacy contracts. The Supreme Court of New Jersey invalidated the surrogacy contract as against public policy but affirmed the trial court's use of "the best interests of the child" analysis,* and on remand the trial court awarded the Sterns custody and visitation rights to Mary Beth Whitehead.

Assisted Reproductive Technology (ART) has created ways for people to have children regardless of their reproductive capacity, including traditional and gestational categories. The ability to create a family using ART has seemingly outpaced legislative responses to the legal questions presented. In *Rosecky v. Schissel*, the Wisconsin Supreme Court determined that a surrogacy agreement was a valid and largely enforceable contract except for the language requiring the surrogate mother to terminate her parental rights.**

Chief Justice Shirley Abrahamson in her concurring opinion disagreed with the majority opinion's authorization of people to contract out the State's traditional, statutory oversight role in the protection of children. She points out numerous public policy issues regarding the validity of surrogacy agreements including:

> *Must the agreement be in writing; should compensated agreements be allowed and what are the limits on compensation; should the availability of surrogacy be limited to married couples or to infertile intended parents; should the age of any party be limited; should a spouse be required either to consent or to be made party to the contract; must each individual involved be represented by counsel; should the State require that information about each individual's legal rights be provided; what provisions are valid regarding who makes decisions about health care and termination of the pregnancy; how and when may the agreement be terminated; and must any party to the agreement be given the opportunity to change his or her mind before or after the birth of the child.****

What is your opinion?

*Matter of Baby M., 537 A.2d 1227 (N.J. 1988).
**Rosecky v. Schissel, 833 N.W.2d 634 (Wis. 2013).
****Id.* at 126 FN.2.

15-3 Regulation of Business

Local, state, and national laws regulate a wide variety of business activities and practices.

15-3a Effect of Violation

Whether an agreement made in connection with business conducted in violation of the law is binding or void depends on how strongly opposed the public policy is to the prohibited act. Some courts take the view that the agreement is not void unless the statute expressly specifies this. In some instances, a statute expressly preserves the validity of the contract. **For Example,** if someone fails to register a fictitious name under which a business is conducted, the violator, after registering the name as required by statute, is permitted to sue on a contract made while illegally conducting business.

15-3b Statutory Regulation of Contracts

To establish uniformity or to protect one of the parties to a contract, statutes frequently provide that contracts of a given class must follow a statutory model or must contain specified provisions. **For Example,** statutes commonly specify that particular clauses must be included in insurance policies to protect the persons insured and their beneficiaries. Other statutes require that contracts executed in connection with credit buying and loans contain particular provisions designed to protect the debtor.

Consumer protection legislation gives the consumer the right to rescind the contract in certain situations. Laws relating to truth in lending, installment sales, and home improvement contracts commonly require that an installment-sale contract specify the cash price, the down payment, the trade-in value (if any), the cash balance, the insurance costs, and the interest and finance charges.

CPA   15-3c   Licensed Callings or Dealings

Statutes frequently require that a person obtain a license, certificate, or diploma before practicing certain professions, such as law and medicine.[14] A license may also be required before carrying on a particular business or trade, such as that of a real estate broker, stockbroker, hotel keeper, or pawnbroker.

If a license is required to protect the public from unqualified persons, a contract made by an unlicensed person is unenforceable. **For Example,** a corporation that does not hold a required real estate broker's license cannot sue to recover fees for services as a broker. An unlicensed insurance broker who cannot recover a fee because of the absence of a license cannot evade the statutory requirement by having a friend who is a licensed broker bill for the services and collect the payment for him.

CASE SUMMARY

How Much for a Brokerage License? How Much Commission Was Lost?

FACTS: Thompson Halbach & Associates, Inc., an Arizona corporation, entered into an agreement with Meteor Motors, Inc., the owner of Palm Beach Acura, to find a buyer for the dealership, and Meteor agreed to pay a 5 percent commission based on the closing price of the sale. Working out of Scottsdale, Arizona, Thompson solicited potential Florida purchasers for the Florida business by phone, fax, and e-mail. Among those contacted was Craig Zinn Automotive Group, which ultimately purchased Palm Beach Acura from Meteor Motors for $5,000,000. Thompson was not paid its $250,000 commission and brought suit against Meteor for breach of contract. Meteor defended that Thompson was an unlicensed broker and that a state statute declares a contract for a commission with an unlicensed broker to be invalid. Thompson responded that the Florida state statute did not apply because it worked out of Scottsdale.

DECISION: Judgment for Meteor. The Florida statute clearly applies to a foreign broker who provides brokerage activities in Florida. Thompson solicited potential Florida purchasers for the Florida business and that purchaser was a Florida corporation. [*Meteor Motors v. Thompson Halbach & Associates*, 914 So. 2d 479 (Fla. App. 2005)]

In some states an unlicensed contractor can neither enforce a home improvement contract against an owner nor seek recovery in *quantum meruit*. **For Example,** a contractor who performed work on Adam Gottbetter's apartment in New York City and was not paid for its work was barred from pursuing its claim against the owner.[15]

However, if the statute does not provide expressly that its violation will deprive the parties of their right to sue on the contract, and the denial of relief is wholly out of proportion to the requirements of public policy, the right to recover will not be denied. **For Example,** an unlicensed contractor who installed water pumps on Staten Island little

---

[14] *Hakimi v. Cantwell,* 855 N.Y.S.2d 273 (App. Div. 2008).
[15] *Orchid Construction Corp. v. Gottbetter,* 932 N.Y.S.2d 100 (A.D. 2011).

league fields was not barred from recovering $18,316.59 for the work in question, which was not home improvement work.[16]

CPA 15-3d **Contracts in Restraint of Trade**

An agreement that unreasonably restrains trade is illegal and void on the ground that it is contrary to public policy. Such agreements take many forms, such as a combination to create a monopoly or to obtain a corner on the market or an association of merchants to increase prices. In addition to the illegality of the agreement based on general principles of law, statutes frequently declare monopolies illegal and subject the parties to various civil and criminal penalties.[17]

CPA 15-3e **Agreements Not to Compete**

In the absence of a valid restrictive covenant, the seller of a business may compete with the buyer, or an ex-employee may solicit customers of the former employer. Restrictive covenants not to compete are disfavored (but not prohibited) in many states as a trade restraint because they may prevent an employee from earning a living, adversely restrain the mobility of employees, and may be overly protective of the interests of employers at the expense of employees. A noncompete provision may be enforceable, however, if (1) it is narrowly drawn to protect the employer's legitimate business interests, (2) it is not unduly burdensome on the employee's ability to earn a living, (3) the geographic restriction is not overly broad, and (4) a reasonable time limitation is given. Reasonably necessary noncompete clauses in the sale of a business are enforced in all states.

Sale of Business

When a going business is sold, it is commonly stated in the contract that the seller shall not go into the same or a similar business again within a certain geographic area or for a certain period of time, or both. In early times, such agreements were held void because they deprived the public of the service of the person who agreed not to compete, reduced competition, and exposed the public to monopoly. To modern courts, the question is whether, under the circumstances, the restriction imposed on one party is reasonably necessary to protect the other party. If the restriction is reasonable, it is valid and enforceable. **For Example,** when Scott Gaddy, the majority stockholder of GWC Insurance Brokers sold his business to Alliant for $4.1 million he agreed to refrain from competing in the insurance business in California for five years. Under California law contracts not to compete are void, except for noncompetition covenants in connection with the sale of a business. The reason for the exception is to prevent the seller from depriving the buyer of the full value of the acquisition, including the sold company's goodwill. The court enforced the covenant against Gaddy.[18]

Employment Contract

Employers rely on noncompete clauses to protect their businesses from employees who leave after receiving expensive training or engineers, scientists, or other professionals or

---

[16] *Del Carlo v. Staten Island Little League, Inc.*, 993 N.Y.S.2d 435 (A.D. 2014).

[17] Sherman Antitrust Act, 15 U.S.C. §§1–7; Clayton Act, 15 U.S.C. §§12–27; Federal Trade Commission Act, 15 U.S.C. §§41–58.

[18] Cal. Rptr. 3d 259 (Cal. App. 2008). Aside from the sale of a business, under California law, any "contract by which anyone is restrained from engaging in a lawful profession, trade or business is to that extent void." Cal B&P Code §16600. A noncompete provision is permitted, however, when "necessary to protect the employer's trade secrets." See *Lotono v. Aetna U.S. Healthcare Inc.*, 82 F. Supp. 2d 1089 (C.D. Cal. 1999), where Aetna was liable for wrongful termination when it fired a California employee for refusing to sign a noncompete agreement.

nonprofessionals who leave firms or businesses to join competitors. Employers enforce these clauses by notifying the new employer and threatening litigation,[19] or seeking a preliminary injunction prohibiting the violation of the noncompete agreement.[20] The burden of proof is on the employer to show that the provision is narrowly drawn to protect the employer's legitimate business interests as to time, place, and activities. Employers have legitimate protectable business interests including maintaining their goodwill with existing customers, their confidential information, and trade secrets. If the noncompete provision is overly broad, however, it will be unenforceable. **For Example,** Home Paramount Pest Control's noncompete clause with Justin Shaffer that prohibited him from working in the pest control industry in any capacity, barring him "in any manner whatsoever," was overly broad and unenforceable.[21] Geographic restrictions are also at issue. **For Example,** Illinois manufacturer Arcor's noncompete clause, which had a restricted area of "the United States and Canada" precluding competition by a former employee for a one-year period, was found to be unenforceable as an industry-wide ban that constituted a "blanket prohibition on competition."[22] Overly broad and unreasonable restrictive covenants will not be enforced.

CASE SUMMARY

Unreasonable and Unenforceable

FACTS: On December 12, 2012, Defendants Contreras, Senn, Verduzco, and VanderWeerd, inseminated cows at several dairy farms in Sunnyside, Washington, on behalf of their employer, Genex Cooperative, Inc. ("Genex"). The very next day, they inseminated cows at the same dairy farms—but this time on behalf of CRV USA ("CRV"), a Genex rival. Jilted by its former employees and spurned by its customers, Genex filed suit to enforce non-competition agreements against three of the defendants. Although the individual contracts varied in terms, Contreras, Senn, and Verduzco contended the agreements were unenforceable. Mr. VanderWeerd had not signed an agreement.

DECISION: Judgment against Genex. Verduzco's noncompete covenant prohibited him from contacting any dairy farm, which he had sought either new or increased business from in the last eighteen months. Under Wisconsin law, applicable to Verduzco's agreement, prohibiting an employee from soliciting any customer the employee has

tried but failed to do business with for the former employer is a violation of state law.

Senn's restrictive agreement was governed by Washington law and found to be unreasonable because it was not limited to soliciting or serving former clients. It appeared to the court that Genex actually used restrictive covenants to eliminate legitimate competition or to strong-arm employees to accept ever-dwindling wages and restrict their freedom to work.

Contreras—who cannot read or write English—was a low-level agricultural worker with an employment-at-will relationship with Genex. An at-will employee may be terminated without any cause and then be prohibited from seeking new employment in his line of work. Genex did not meet its burden to establish the reasonableness of its covenant with Contreras, and the noncompete agreement was thus unenforceable. [*Genex Cooperative, Inc. v. Contreras,* **39 IER Cases 294 (E.D. Wash. 2014)]**

---

[19] In *Socko v. Mid-Atlantic Systems of CPA, Inc.,* 99 A.3d 928 (Pa. Super. 2014), the employer notified the new employer and threatened litigation. Socko successfully challenged this action, with the court deciding that the agreement was unenforceable for lack of consideration because it was entered into after the commencement of Socko's employment with Mid-Atlantic.

[20] A motion for a preliminary injunction is heard expeditiously by the court and is ordinarily used to preserve the status quo pending a trial on the merits. However, in noncompete cases, the validity of the time limitation is "clothed with immediacy." Decisions at the preliminary injunction stage become, in effect, a determination on the merits. See *Horner International Co. v. McCoy,* 754 S.E.2d 852 (2014).

[21] *Home Paramount Pest Control Companies, Inc. v. Shaffer,* 718 S.E.2d 762 (Va. 2011).

[22] *Arcor, Inc. v. Haas,* 842 N.E.2d 265 (Ill. App. 2005).

Effect of Invalidity

When a restriction of competition agreed to by the parties is invalid because its scope as to time or geographic area is too great, how does this affect the contract? Some courts trim the restrictive covenant down to a scope they deem reasonable and require the parties to abide by that revision.[23] This rule is nicknamed the "blue-pencil rule." **For Example,** Julie Murray signed a noncompete agreement, which was validly assigned to the purchaser of the Accounting Center of Luca County, Inc. When the new owner changed from an hourly wage to commission pay for her tax preparation work, she objected and was terminated. The court found that the 24-month noncompete restriction exceeded what was reasonable to protect the employer's legitimate business interests and modified the time period to one year.[24] In the *Arcor* case, the court refused to "blue-pencil" the covenant because to render the clause reasonable, the court would in effect be writing a new agreement, which is inappropriate.[25] Other courts refuse to apply the blue-pencil rule and hold that the restrictive covenant is void or that the entire contract is void.[26] There is also authority that a court should refuse to apply the blue-pencil rule when the restrictive covenant is manifestly unfair and would virtually keep the employee from earning a living.

15-3f Usurious Agreements

usury–lending money at an interest rate that is higher than the maximum rate allowed by law.

Usury is committed when money is loaned at a higher rate of interest than the law allows. Most states prohibit by statute charging more than a stated amount of interest. These statutes provide a maximum annual contract rate of interest that can be exacted under the law of a given state. In many states, the usury law does not apply to loans made to corporations.

THINKING THINGS THROUGH

Noncompete Clauses, Cause for Concern?

Several states do not enforce noncompete clauses in employment contracts, according to the research of Matt Marx, who dedicated his doctoral studies at Harvard to this topic. The states are (from west to east): California, Nevada, Montana, North Dakota, Minnesota, Oklahoma, West Virginia, and Connecticut. (New York, Washington, and Oregon have significantly limited their applicability.) Marx had naively signed a two-year noncompete agreement out of MIT at SpeechWorks, a voice recognition start-up, and when he wanted to leave and continue in the voice recognition field, his options were to sit out the two-year noncompete period or go to work at a California firm, which he did. He is now researching whether enforcing noncompetes in a state can spur inventors, engineers, and entrepreneurs to move elsewhere to pursue development of their ideas.*

Does a state's innovation suffer when noncompete clauses handcuff employees to an employer, or force employees to take an unpaid leave for the noncompete period before continuing in their field with a new or start-up employer? Thinking Things Through, prospective employees should carefully consider the impact noncompetes would have on their lives, and if they must sign one, carefully negotiate its duration and scope.**

*See Scott Kirsner, "Why 'Noncompete' Means 'Don't Thrive,'" *Boston Globe,* December 30, 2007, E–1; Scott Kirsner, "Start-ups Stifled by Noncompetes," *Boston Globe,* June 21, 2009, G–1.
**For a comprehensive study of the strength of noncompetition enforcement rankings by state, see Norman D. Bishara, "Fifty Ways to Leave Your Employer: Relative Enforcement of Covenants Not to Compete, Trends and Implications for Employee Mobility Policy," 13 *U. Pa. J. Bus. L.* 751 (2011).

---

[23] *Keeley v. CSA, P.C.,* 510 S.E.2d 880 (Ga. App. 1999).
[24] *Murray v. Accounting Center of Lucas County, Inc.,* 898 N.E.2d 89 (Ohio App. 2008).
[25] *Arcor, Inc. v. Hass* 842 N.E.2d 265 (Ill. App. 2005).
[26] *Volcen Steel Structures, Inc. v. McCarty,* 764 S.E.2d 458 (Ga. App. 2014).

When a lender incurs expenses in making a loan, such as the cost of appraising property or making a credit investigation of the borrower, the lender will require the borrower to pay the amount of such expenses. Any fee charged by a lender that goes beyond the reasonable expense of making the loan constitutes "interest" for the purposes of determining whether the transaction is usurious.[27]

Penalites for violating usury laws vary from state to state, with a number of states restricting the lender to the recovery of the loan but no interest whatsoever; other states allow recovery of the loan principal and interest up to the maximum contract rate. Some states also impose a penalty on the lender such as the payment of double the interest paid on a usurious loan.

CASE SUMMARY

Would You Recommend Karen Canzoneri as an Investment Advisor?

FACTS: Karen Canzoneri entered into two agreements with Howard Pinchuck. Under the first agreement, Canzoneri advanced $50,000 to be repaid at 12 percent per month for 12 consecutive months "as an investment profit." The second agreement required "$36,000 to be repaid on or before 6/1/01 with an investment profit of $36,000, total being $72,000." The annualized rate of return for the first transaction was 144 percent and for the second transaction was 608 percent. The civil penalty for violating the state's maximum interest rate of 25 percent per annum is forfeiture of the entire principal amount. Canzoneri contends that the transactions were investments not subject to the usury law.

DECISION: Judgment for Pinchuck. The four elements of a usurious transaction are present: (1) the transaction was a loan, (2) the money loaned required that it be returned, (3) an interest rate higher than allowed by law was required, and (4) a corrupt intention to take more than the legal rate for the use of the money loaned exists. Even though the terms called for "profit," not "interest," the courts looked to the substance, not the form of the transaction. [**Pinchuck v. Canzoneri, 920 So. 2d 713 (Fla. App. 2006)**]

Make the Connection

Summary

When an agreement is illegal, it is ordinarily void and no contract arises from it. Courts will not allow one party to an illegal agreement to bring suit against the other party. There are some exceptions to this, such as when the parties are not equally guilty or when the law's purpose in making the agreement illegal is to protect the person who is bringing suit. When possible, an agreement will be interpreted as being lawful. Even when a particular provision is held unlawful, the balance of the agreement may be saved so that the net result is a contract minus the clause that was held illegal.

The term *illegality* embraces situations in unconscionable contract clauses in which the courts hold that contract provisions are unenforceable because they are too harsh or oppressive to one of the parties to a transaction. If the clause is part of a standard form contract drafted by the party having superior bargaining power and is presented on a take-it-or-leave-it basis (a contract of adhesion) and the substantive terms of the clause itself are unduly oppressive, the clause will be found to be unconscionable and not enforced.

[27] *Lentimo v. Cullen Center Bank and Trust Co.,* 919 S.W.2d 743 (Tex. App. 1996).

Whether a contract is contrary to public policy may be difficult to determine because public policy is not precisely defined. That which is harmful to the public welfare or general good is contrary to public policy. Contracts condemned as contrary to public policy include those designed to deprive the weaker party of a benefit that the lawmaker desired to provide, agreements injuring public service, and wagers and private lotteries. Statutes commonly make the wager illegal as a form of gambling. The private lottery is any plan under which, for a consideration, a person has a chance to win a prize.

Learning Outcomes

After studying this chapter, you should be able to clearly explain:

15-1   General Principles

LO.1   Explain the general contract principles on "illegality"

See the unenforceable illegal lease to nonprofessionals example, page 276.

See the example where a contract to manufacture and sell illegal slot machines is void, page 277.

LO.2   Explain the implied obligation on all parties of good faith and fair dealing

See the example of the Vermont landlord who deprived a tenant of her rights under a lease, page 278.

15-2   Agreements Affecting Public Welfare

LO.3   Understand that it is only in unusual situations that a contract provision will be unenforceable because it is unconscionable

See the *Kramper Family Farm* example where the court refused to consider whether the contract was fair or unfair, wise or foolish, page 278.

Illegality may consist of the violation of a statute or administrative regulation adopted to regulate business. An agreement not to compete may be illegal as a restraint of trade except when reasonable in its terms and when it is incidental to the sale of a business or to a contract of employment.

The charging by a lender of a higher rate of interest than allowed by law is usury. Courts must examine transactions carefully to see whether a usurious loan is disguised as a legitimate transaction.

But see *John Clark's* case, illustrating an unconscionable arbitration clause, page 280.

15-3   Regulation of Business

LO.4   Explain the rationale for requiring licenses to carry on as a business, trade, or profession

See the discussion requiring licenses to protect the public from unqualified persons, page 282.

LO.5   Distinguish between noncompete clauses after the sale of a business and noncompete clauses in employment contracts

See the example where the California court enforced a five-year noncompete clause against the seller of a business, page 283.

See the example involving Julie Murray's noncompete clause and why it was modified from 24 months to one year, page 285.

See the *Genex* case that illustrates a trend barring enforcement of overly broad and unreasonable non-competition clauses, page 284.

Key Terms

contracts of adhesion	*in pari delicto*	public policy
good faith	lotteries	usury

Questions and Case Problems

1. When are the parties to an illegal agreement *in pari delicto?*

2. John Iwen sued U.S. West Direct because of a negligently constructed yellow pages advertisement. U.S. West Direct moved to stay litigation and compel arbitration under the yellow pages order form, which required advertisers to resolve all controversies through arbitration, but allowed U.S. West (the publisher) to pursue judicial remedies to collect amounts due it. Under the arbitration provision, Iwen's sole remedy was a pro rata reduction or refund of the cost of the advertisement. The order

form language was drafted by U.S. West Direct on a take-it-or-leave-it basis and stated in part:

> Any controversy or claim arising out of or relating to this Agreement, or breach thereof, other than an action by Publisher for the collection of amounts due under this Agreement, shall be settled by final, binding arbitration in accordance with the Commercial Arbitration rules of the American Arbitration Association.

If forced to arbitration, Iwen would be unable to recover damages for the negligently constructed yellow pages ad, nor could he recover damages for infliction of emotional distress and punitive damages related to his many efforts to adjust the matter with the company, which were ignored or rejected. Must Iwen have his case resolved through arbitration rather than a court of law? [*Iwen v. U.S. West Direct*, 977 P.2d 989 (Mont.)]

3. Sutcliffe Banton, dba Nemard Construction, furnished labor and materials (valued at $162,895) for improving Vicky Deafeamkpor's New York City residential property. She paid only $41,718, leaving $121,987 unpaid. Banton sued her and the jury awarded $90,000 in damages. Deafeamkpor moved for an order setting aside the jury's verdict because Banton was not properly licensed by New York City. Under NYC Code an unlicensed contractor may neither enforce a home improvement contract against an owner or recover in *quantum meruit*. The jury heard all the evidence regarding the materials and labor expended on Deafeamkpor's residence and concluded that the plaintiff performed satisfactory work valued at $90,000 for which he was not paid. Should the court allow the owner to take advantage of Banton and his employees and suppliers? What public policy would support such an outcome? Decide. [*Nemard Construction Corp. v. Deafeamkpor*, 863 N.Y.S.2d 846]

4. Eugene McCarthy left his position as director of sales for Nike's Brand Jordan division in June 2003 to become vice president of U.S. footwear sales and merchandising at Reebok, one of Nike's competitors. Nike sought a preliminary injunction to prevent McCarthy from working for Reebok for a year, invoking a noncompete agreement McCarthy had signed in Oregon in 1997 when Nike had promoted him to his earlier position as a regional footwear sales manager. The agreement stated in pertinent part:

> During EMPLOYEE'S employment by NIKE… and for one (1) year thereafter, ("the Restriction Period"), EMPLOYEE will not directly or indirectly … be employed by, consult for, or be connected in any manner with, any business engaged anywhere in the world in the athletic footwear, athletic apparel or sports equipment and accessories business, or any other business which directly competes with NIKE or any of its subsidiaries or affiliated corporations.

McCarty contends that such a contract is a restraint of trade and should not be enforced. Nike contends that the agreement is fair and should be enforced. Decide. [*Nike, Inc. v. McCarthy*, 379 F.3d 576 (9th Cir.)]

5. Ewing was employed by Presto-X-Co., a pest exterminator. His contract of employment specified that he would not solicit or attempt to solicit customers of Presto-X for two years after the termination of his employment. After working several years, his employment was terminated. Ewing then sent a letter to customers of Presto-X stating that he no longer worked for Presto-X and that he was still certified by the state. Ewing set forth his home address and phone number, which the customers did not previously have. The letter ended with the statement, "I thank you for your business throughout the past years." Presto-X brought an action to enjoin Ewing from sending such letters. He raised the defense that he was prohibited only from soliciting and there was nothing in the letters that constituted a seeking of customers. Decide. What ethical values are involved? [*Presto-X-Co. v. Ewing*, 442 N.W.2d 85 (Iowa)]

6. The Minnesota adoption statute requires that any agency placing a child for adoption make a thorough investigation and not give a child to an applicant unless the placement is in the best interests of the child. Tibbetts applied to Crossroads, Inc., a private adoption agency, for a child to adopt. He later sued the agency for breach of contract, claiming that the agency was obligated by contract to supply a child for adoption. The agency claimed that it was required only to use its best efforts to locate a child and was not required to supply a child to Tibbetts unless it found him to be a suitable parent. Decide. [*Tibbetts v. Crossroads, Inc.*, 411 N.W.2d 535 (Minn. App.)]

7. Siddle purchased a quantity of fireworks from Red Devil Fireworks Co. The sale was illegal, however, because Siddle did not have a license to make the purchase, which the seller knew because it had been so informed by the attorney general of the state. Siddle did not pay for the fireworks, and Red Devil

sued him. He defended on the ground that the contract could not be enforced because it was illegal. Was the defense valid? [*Red Devil Fireworks Co. v. Siddle*, 648 P.2d 468 (Wash. App.)]

8. Justin Shaffer, while an employee of the Home Paramount Pest Control Companies Inc., signed an employment agreement providing that:

> *The Employee will not engage directly or indirectly or concern himself/herself in any manner whatsoever in the carrying on or conducting the business of exterminating, pest control, termite control and/or fumigation services as an owner, agent, servant, representative, or employee, and/or as a member of a partnership and/or as an officer, director or stockholder of any corporation, or in any manner whatsoever, in any city, cities, county or counties in the state(s) in which the Employee works and/or in which the Employee was assigned during the two (2) years next preceding the termination of the Employment Agreement and for a period of two (2) years from and after the date upon which he/she shall cease for any reason whatsoever to be an employee of [Home Paramount].*

Shaffer resigned from Home Paramount and became an employee of Connor's Termite and Pest Control Inc. Home Paramount sued Shaffer and Connor's, claiming that Shaffer's employment by Connor's violated the contract. The defendants contended that the provision was overboard and unenforceable. Decide. [*Home Paramount Pest Control Companies, Inc. v. Shaffer*, 718 S.E.2d 762 (Va.)]

9. Smith was employed as a salesman for Borden, Inc., which sold food products in 63 counties in Arkansas, 2 counties in Missouri, 2 counties in Oklahoma, and 1 county in Texas. Smith's employment contract prohibited him from competing with Borden after leaving its employ. Smith left Borden and went to work for a competitor, Lady Baltimore Foods. Working for this second employer, Smith sold in 3 counties of Arkansas. He had sold in 2 of these counties while he worked for Borden. Borden brought an injunction action against Smith and Lady Baltimore to enforce the noncompete covenant in Smith's former contract. Was Borden entitled to the injunction? [*Borden, Inc. v. Smith*, 478 S.W.2d 744 (Ark.)]

10. All new employees of Circuit City Stores were required to sign a Dispute Resolution Agreement (DRA) mandating that employees submit all employment-related disputes to arbitration. Under the DRA Circuit City was not obligated to arbitrate its claims against employees and may bring lawsuits against employees. Remedies are limited under the DRA, including a one-year back pay limit and a two-year front pay limit, with cap on punitive damages of an amount up to the greater of the amount of back pay and front pay awarded or $5,000. In a civil lawsuit under state law a plaintiff is entitled to all forms of relief. The DRA requires that employees split the cost of the arbitrator's fees with the employer. An individual is not required to pay for the services of a judge. Adams filed a sexual harassment case against his employer in state court. Circuit City filed a petition in federal court to compel arbitration. Decide. [*Circuit City Stores, Inc. v. Adams*, 274 F.3d 889 (9th Cir.)]

11. Vodra was employed as a salesperson and contracting agent for American Security Services. As part of his contract of employment, Vodra signed an agreement that for three years after leaving this employment, he would not solicit any customer of American. Vodra had no experience in the security field when he went to work for American. To the extent that he became known to American's customers, it was because of being American's representative rather than because of his own reputation in the security field. After some years, Vodra left American and organized a competing company that solicited American's customers. American sued him to enforce the restrictive covenant. Vodra claimed that the restrictive covenant was illegal and not binding. Was he correct? [*American Security Services, Inc. v. Vodra*, 385 N.W.2d 73 (Neb.)]

12. Potomac Leasing Co. leased an automatic telephone system to Vitality Centers. Claudene Cato signed the lease as guarantor of payments. When the rental was not paid, Potomac Leasing brought suit against Vitality and Cato. They raised the defense that the rented equipment was to be used for an illegal purpose—namely, the random sales solicitation by means of an automatic telephone in violation of state statute; that this purpose was known to Potomac Leasing; and that Potomac Leasing could therefore not enforce the lease. Was this defense valid? [*Potomac Leasing Co. v. Vitality Centers, Inc.*, 718 S.W.2d 928 (Ark.)]

13. The English publisher of a book called *Cambridge* gave a New York publisher permission to sell that book any place in the world except in England. The New York publisher made several bulk sales of the book to buyers who sold the book throughout the world, including England. The English publisher

sued the New York publisher and its customers for breach of the restriction prohibiting sales in England. Decide.

14. Sandra Menefee sued Geographic Expeditions, Inc. (GeoEx), for the wrongful death of her son while on a GeoEx expedition up Mount Kilimanjaro. GeoEx moved to compel arbitration under the parties' limitation of liability contract. GeoEx designed its arbitration clause to limit the plaintiffs' recovery and required them to indemnify GeoEx for its legal costs and fees if they unsuccessfully pursued any claim covered by the release agreement. Moreover, GeoEx required that plaintiffs pay half of any mediation fees and arbitrate in San Francisco, GeoEx's choice of venue, as opposed to the plaintiffs' home in Colorado. Should the court require the Menefees to arbitrate? If any component of the arbitration clause is found to be unconscionable, should the court simply sever the objectionable provision and enforce the remainder of the arbitration clause? [*Lhotka v. Geographic Expeditions, Inc.*, 104 Cal. Rptr. 3d 844 (Cal. App. 2010)]

15. Yarde Metals, Inc., owned six season tickets to New England Patriots football games. Gillette Stadium, where the games are played, had insufficient men's restrooms in use for football games at that time, which was the subject of numerous newspaper columns. On October 13, 2002, a guest of Yarde Metals, Mikel LaCroix, along with others, used available women's restrooms to answer the call of nature. As LaCroix left the restroom, however, he was arrested and charged with disorderly conduct. The Patriots organization terminated all six of Yarde's season ticket privileges, incorrectly giving as a reason that LaCroix was ejected "for throwing bottles in the seating section." Yarde sued, contending that "by terminating the plaintiff's season tickets for 2002 and for the future arbitrarily, without cause and based on false information," the Patriots had violated the implicit covenant of good faith and fair dealing of the season tickets contract. The back of each Patriots ticket states:

> *This ticket and all season tickets are revocable licenses. The Patriots reserve the right to revoke such licenses, in their sole discretion, at any time and for any reason.*

How would you decide this case? [*Yarde Metals, Inc. v. New England Patriots Ltd.*, 834 N.E.2d 1233 (Mass. App.)]

CPA Questions

1. West, an Indiana real estate broker, misrepresented to Zimmer that West was licensed in Kansas under the Kansas statute that regulates real estate brokers and requires all brokers to be licensed. Zimmer signed a contract agreeing to pay West a 5 percent commission for selling Zimmer's home in Kansas. West did not sign the contract. West sold Zimmer's home. If West sued Zimmer for nonpayment of commission, Zimmer would be:

   a. Liable to West only for the value of services rendered.

   b. Liable to West for the full commission.

   c. Not liable to West for any amount because West did not sign the contract.

   d. Not liable to West for any amount because West violated the Kansas licensing requirements (5/92, Law, #25).

2. Blue purchased a travel agency business from Drye. The purchase price included payment for Drye's goodwill. The agreement contained a covenant prohibiting Drye from competing with Blue in the travel agency business. Which of the following statements regarding the covenant is *not* correct?

   a. The restraint must be *no* more extensive than is reasonably necessary to protect the goodwill purchased by Blue.

   b. The geographic area to which it applies must be reasonable.

   c. The time period for which it is to be effective must be reasonable.

   d. The value to be assigned to it is the excess of the price paid over the seller's cost of all tangible assets (11/87, Law, #2).

Writing, Electronic Forms, and Interpretation of Contracts

Learning Outcomes >>>

After studying this chapter, you should be able to

LO.1 Explain when a contract must be evidenced by a writing

LO.2 Explain the effect of noncompliance with the statute of frauds

LO.3 Explain the parol evidence rule and the exceptions to this rule

LO.4 Understand the basic rule of contract construction that a contract is enforced according to its terms

LO.5 State the rules for interpreting ambiguous terms in a contract

When must a contract be written? What is the effect of a written contract? These questions lead to the statute of frauds and the parol evidence rule.

16-1   Statute of Frauds

A *contract* is a legally binding agreement. Must the agreement be evidenced by a writing?

16-1a   Validity of Oral Contracts

In the absence of a statute requiring a writing, a contract may be oral or written. Managers and professionals should be more fully aware that their oral communications, including telephone conversations and dinner or breakfast discussions, may be deemed legally enforceable contracts. **For Example,** suppose that Mark Wahlberg, after reviewing a script tentatively entitled *The Bulger Boys*, meets with Steven Spielberg to discuss Mark's playing mobster James "Whitey" Bulger in the film. Steven states, "You *are* Whitey, Marky! The nuns at Gate of Heaven Grammar School in South Boston—or maybe it was St. Augustine's—they don't send for the Boston Police when they are troubled about drug use in the schools; they send for you to talk to the kids. Nobody messes with you, and the kids know it. This is true stuff, I think, and this fugitive's brother Bill comes out of the Southie projects to be president of U Mass." Mark likes the script. Steven and Mark block out two months of time for shooting the film this fall. They agree on Mark's usual fee and a "piece of the action" based on a set percentage of the net income from the film. Thereafter, Mark's agent does not like the deal. He believes there are better scripts for Mark. And with Hollywood accounting, a percentage of the "net" take is usually of little value. However, all of the essential terms of a contract have been agreed on, and such an oral agreement would be legally enforceable. As set forth in the following text, no writing is required for a services contract that can be performed within one year after the date of the agreement.

Certain contracts, on the other hand, must be evidenced by a writing to be legally enforceable. These contracts are covered by the **statute of frauds.**[1]

Because many oral contracts are legally enforceable, it is a good business practice in the preliminary stages of discussions to stipulate that no binding agreement is intended to be formed until a written contract is prepared and signed by the parties.

statute of frauds–statute that, in order to prevent fraud through the use of perjured testimony, requires that certain kinds of transactions be evidenced in writing in order to be binding or enforceable.

16-1b   Contracts That Must Be Evidenced by a Writing

The statute of frauds requires that certain kinds of contracts be evidenced by a writing or they cannot be enforced. This means that either the contract itself must be in writing and signed by both parties or there must be a sufficient written memorandum of the oral contract signed by the person being sued for breach of contract. A *part performance* doctrine

---

[1] The name is derived from the original Statute of Frauds and Perjuries, which was adopted in 1677 and became the pattern for similar legislation in America. The 17th section of that statute governed the sale of goods, and its modern counterpart is §2-201 of the UCC. The 4th section of the English statute provided the pattern for U.S. legislation with respect to contracts other than for the sale of goods described in this section of the chapter. The English statute was repealed in 1954 except as to land sale and guarantee contracts. The U.S. statutes remain in force, but the liberalization by U.C.C. §2-201 of the pre-Code requirements with respect to contracts for the sale of goods lessens the applicability of the writing requirement. Additional movement away from the writing requirement is seen in the 1994 Revision of Article 8, Securities, which abolishes the statute of frauds provision of the original U.C.C. §8-319 and goes beyond by declaring that the one-year performance provision of the statute of frauds is not applicable to contracts for securities. U.C.C. §8-113 [1994 Revision].

or exception to the statute of frauds may exist when the plaintiff's part performance is "unequivocally referable" to the oral agreement.[2]

Agreement That Cannot Be Performed within One Year After the Contract Is Made

A writing is required when the contract, by its terms or subject matter, cannot be performed within one year after the date of the agreement. An oral agreement to supply a line of credit for two years cannot be enforced because of the statute of frauds.

CASE SUMMARY

Not a Good Move, Doctor

FACTS: Despite not having an executed employment agreement, Dr. William Bithoney sold his home in New York and moved to Atlanta in early October in anticipation of his October 15 start work date as an executive at Grady Memorial Hospital. But the night before his anticipated start, he was informed that Grady's governing body, the Fulton-DeKalb Hospital Authority, did not approve his hiring and would not permit him to commence work. He sued the Authority for breach of an oral contract for severance, claiming that he and Grady's CEO, Otis Story, had agreed that he would receive "a severance payment of 15 months salary if Grady terminated his employment without cause." Bithoney had received a draft employment contract from Grady, which included a provision that, in

the event Bithoney was terminated without cause, he would receive "full severance payment," which would be "payable for 15 months from the effective date of said termination."

DECISION: Judgment for the hospital. If the oral severance agreement were to be paid in a lump sum after termination, the oral agreement would not fall within the statute of frauds. Because the draft employment agreement provided that the severance "shall be payable for 15 months from the effective date of said termination," it was found to be a 15-month payment term barred by the statute of frauds. [***Bithoney v. Fulton-DeKalb Hospital Authority***, **721 S.E.2d 577 (Ga. App. 2011)**]

The year runs from the time the oral contract is made rather than from the date when performance is to begin. In computing the year, the day on which the contract was made is excluded.

No *part performance* exception exists to validate an oral agreement not performable within one year. **For Example,** Babyback's Foods negotiated a multiyear oral agreement to comarket its barbecue meat products with the Coca-Cola Co. nationwide and arranged to have several coolers installed at area grocery stores in Louisville under the agreement. Babyback's faxed to Coca-Cola a contract that summarized the oral agreement but Coca-Cola never signed it. Because Coca-Cola did not sign and no part performance exception exists for an oral agreement not performable within one year, Babyback's lawsuit was unsuccessful.[3]

When no time for performance is specified by the oral contract and complete performance could "conceivably occur" within one year, the statute of frauds is not applicable to the oral contract.[4]

When a contract may be terminated at will by either party, the statute of frauds is not applicable because the contract may be terminated within a year. **For Example,** David Ehrlich was hired as manager of Gravediggaz pursuant to an oral management agreement that was terminable at will by either Ehrlich or the group. He was entitled to

---

[2] *Carey & Associates v. Ernst*, 802 N.Y.S.2d 160 (A.D. 2005).
[3] *Coca-Cola Co. v. Babyback's International Inc.*, 841 N.E.2d 557 (Ind. 2006).
[4] *De John v. Speech Language & Communication Assoc.*, 974 N.Y.S.2d 725 (A.D. 2013).

| FIGURE 16-1 | Hurdles in the Path of a Contract |

WRITING REQUIRED

STATUTE OF FRAUDS

MORE THAN ONE YEAR TO PERFORM
SALE OF LAND
ANSWER FOR ANOTHER'S DEBT OR DEFAULT
PERSONAL REPRESENTATIVE TO PAY DEBT OF DECEDENT FROM PERSONAL FUNDS
PROMISE IN CONSIDERATION OF MARRIAGE
SALE OF GOODS FOR $500 OR MORE
MISCELLANEOUS

EXCEPTIONS

PART PERFORMANCE
PROMISOR BENEFIT
DETRIMENTAL RELIANCE

PAROL EVIDENCE RULE

EVERY COMPLETE, FINAL WRITTEN CONTRACT

EXCEPTIONS

INCOMPLETE CONTRACT
AMBIGUOUS TERMS
FRAUD, ACCIDENT, OR MISTAKE
TO PROVE EXISTENCE OR NONBINDING CHARACTER OF CONTRACT
MODIFICATION OF CONTRACT
ILLEGALITY

receive 15 percent of the gross earnings of the group and each of its members, including rap artist Robert Diggs, professionally known as RZA, for all engagements entered into while he was manager under this oral agreement. Such an at-will contract is not barred by the statute of frauds.[5]

Agreement to Sell or a Sale of an Interest in Land

All contracts to sell land, buildings, or interests in land, such as mortgages, must be evidenced by a writing.[6] Leases are also interests in land and must be in writing, except in some states where leases for one year or less do not have to be in writing.[7] **For Example,**

[5] See *Ehrlich v. Diggs*, 169 F. Supp. 2d 124 (E.D.N.Y. 2001). See also *Sterling v. Sterling*, 800 N.Y.S.2d 463 (A.D. 2005), in which the statute of frauds was no bar to an oral partnership agreement, deemed to be at will, that continued for an indefinite period of time.
[6] *Magnum Real Estate Services, Inc. v. Associates, LLC*, 874 N.Y.S.2d 435 (A.D. 2009).
[7] See, however, *BBQ Blues Texas, Ltd. v. Affiliated Business*, 183 S.W.3d 543 (Tex. App. 2006), in which Eddie Calagero of Affiliated Business and the owners of BBQ Blues Texas, Ltd., entered an oral commission agreement to pay a 10 percent commission if he found a buyer for the restaurant, and he did so. The oral agreement was held to be outside the statute of frauds because the activity of finding a willing buyer did not involve the transfer of real estate. The second contract between the buyer and seller of the restaurant, which involved the transfer of a lease agreement, was a separate and distinct agreement over which Calagero had no control.

if Mrs. O'Toole orally agrees to sell her house to the Gillespies for $250,000 and, thereafter, her children convince her that she could obtain $280,000 for the property if she is patient, Mrs. O'Toole can raise the defense of the statute of frauds should she be sued for breach of the oral agreement. Under the *part performance doctrine*, an exception exists by which an oral contract for the sale of land will be enforced by a court of equity in a suit for specific performance if the buyer has taken possession of the land under an oral contract and has made substantial improvements, the value of which cannot easily be ascertained, or has taken possession and paid part of the purchase price.

Promise to Answer for the Debt or Default of Another

If an individual *I* promises a creditor *C* to pay the debt of *D* if *D* does not do so, *I* is promising to answer for the debt of another. Such a promise is sometimes called a **suretyship** contract, and it must be in writing to be enforceable. *I*, the promisor, is obligated to pay only if *D* does not pay. *I*'s promise is a *collateral* or *secondary* promise, and such promises must be in writing under the statute of frauds.[8]

suretyship–undertaking to pay the debt or be liable for the default of another.

Main Purpose of Exception. When the main purpose of the promisor's promise to pay the debt of another is to benefit the promisor, the statute of frauds is not applicable, and the oral promise to pay the debt is binding.

For Example, an individual *I* hires a contractor *C* to repair *I*'s building, and the supplier *S* is unwilling to extend credit to *C*. In an oral promise by *I* to pay *S* what is owed for the supplies in question if *C* does not pay, *I* is promising to pay for the debt of another, *C*. However, the *main purpose* of *I*'s promise was not to aid *C* but to get his own house repaired. This promise is not within the statute of frauds.[9]

CASE SUMMARY

"I Personally Guarantee" Doesn't Mean I'm Personally Liable, Does It?

FACTS: Joel Burgower owned Material Partnerships Inc. (MPI), which supplied Sacos Tubulares del Centro, S.A. de C.V. (Sacos), a Mexican bag manufacturer, essential materials to make its products. When MPI was not paid for shipments, it insisted that Jorge Lopez, Sacos's general manager, personally guarantee all past and future obligations to MPI. In a letter to Burgower dated September 25, 1998, Lopez wrote:

> I ... want to certify you [sic] that I, personally, guaranty all outstanding [sic] and liabilities of Sacos Tubulares with Material Partnerships as well as future shipments.

Lopez drafted the letter himself and signed it over the designation "Jorge Lopez Venture, General Manager."

After receiving the September 25th letter, MPI resumed shipping product to Sacos, sending additional shipments valued at approximately $200,000. MPI subsequently received one payment of approximately $60,000 from Sacos. When Sacos did not pay for the additional shipments, MPI stopped shipping to it. The Sacos plant closed, and MPI brought suit in a Texas court against Lopez, claiming he was individually liable for the corporate debt of more than $900,000 under the terms of the personal guarantee. Lopez contended that he signed the letter in his capacity as general manager of Sacos as a corporate guarantee and that it was not an enforceable personal guarantee. MPI contended that the letter was a clear personal guarantee.

[8] See *Martin Printing, Inc. v. Sone*, 873 A.2d 232 (Conn. App. 2005), in which James Kuhe, in writing, personally guaranteed Martin Printing, Inc., to pay for printing expenses of *Pub Links Golfer Magazine*, if his corporation, Abbey Inc., failed to do so. When Abbey, Inc., failed to pay, the court enforced Kuhe's promise to pay.
[9] See *Christian v. Smith*, 759 N.W.2d 447 (Neb. 2008).

DECISION: The essential terms of a guarantee agreement required by the statute of frauds were present in this case. Lopez stated in his September 25th letter that "I, personally, guaranty," manifesting an intent to guarantee, and described the obligation being guaranteed as "all outstandings and liabilities of Sacos," as well as "future shipments." Lopez's signature over his corporate office does not render the document ambiguous because the clear intent was expressed in the word "personally." [*MPI v. Jorge Lopez Ventura,* **102 S.W.2d 252 (Tex. App. 2003)**]

Promise by the Executor or Administrator of a Decedent's Estate to Pay a Claim Against the Estate from Personal Funds

personal representative–administrator or executor who represents decedents under UPC.

executor, executrix–person (man, woman) named in a will to administer the estate of the decedent.

administrator, administratrix–person (man, woman) appointed to wind up and settle the estate of a person who has died without a will.

decedent–person whose estate is being administered.

The **personal representative (executor** or **administrator)** has the duty of handling the affairs of a deceased person, paying the debts from the proceeds of the estate and distributing any balance remaining. The executor or administrator is not personally liable for the claims against the estate of the **decedent.** If the personal representative promises to pay the decedent's debts with his or her own money, the promise cannot be enforced unless it is evidenced by a writing.

If the personal representative makes a contract on behalf of the estate in the course of administering the estate, a writing is not required. The representative is then contracting on behalf of the estate. Thus, if the personal representative employs an attorney to settle the estate or makes a burial contract with an undertaker, no writing is required.

Promises Made in Consideration of Marriage

Promises to pay a sum of money or give property to another in consideration of marriage must be in writing under the statute of frauds.

For Example, if Mr. John Bradley orally promises to provide Karl Radford $20,000 on Karl's marriage to Mr. Bradley's daughter Michelle—and Karl and Michelle marry—the agreement is not enforceable under the statute of frauds because it was not in writing.

Prenuptial or *antenuptial* agreements are entered into by the parties before their marriage. After full disclosure of each party's assets and liabilities, and in some states, income,[10] the parties set forth the rights of each partner regarding the property and, among other things, set forth rights and obligations should the marriage end in a separation or divorce. Such a contract must be in writing.

For Example, when Susan DeMatteo married her husband M. J. DeMatteo in 1990, she had a 1977 Nova and $5,000 in the bank. M. Joseph DeMatteo was worth as much as $112 million at that time, and he insisted that she sign a prenuptial agreement before their marriage. After full disclosure of each party's assets, the prenuptial agreement was signed and videotaped some five days before their marriage ceremony. The agreement gave Susan $35,000 a year plus cost-of-living increases, as well as a car and a house, should the marriage dissolve. After the couple divorced, Susan argued before the state's highest court that the agreement was not "fair or reasonable" because it gave her less than 1 percent of her former husband's wealth. The court upheld the agreement, however, pointing out that Susan was fully informed about her fiancé's net worth and was represented by counsel.[11] When there is full disclosure and representation, prenuptial agreements, like other contracts, cannot be set aside unless they are unconscionable, which in a domestic relations setting means leaving a former spouse unable to support herself or himself.

[10] See FLA. STAT. §732–702 (2).
[11] *DeMatteo v. DeMatteo,* 762 N.E.2d 797 (Mass. 2002). See also *Waton v. Waton,* 887 So. 2d 419 (Fla. App. 2004).

Sale of Goods

As will be developed in Chapter 22, Nature and Form of Sales, contracts for the sale of goods priced at $500 or more must ordinarily be in writing under U.C.C. §2-201.[12]

Promissory Estoppel

The statute of frauds may be circumvented when the party seeking to get around the statute of frauds is able to prove an enhanced promissory estoppel. While one element of a routine promissory estoppel case requires that the promisee rely on the promise in some definite and substantial manner, an enhanced level of reasonable reliance is necessary in order to have enhanced promissory estoppel, along with proof of an unconscionable injury or unjust enrichment. **For Example,** an Indiana bakery, Classic Cheesecake Inc., was able to interest several hotels and casinos in Las Vegas in buying its products. On July 27, 2004, its principals sought a loan from a local branch office of J. P. Morgan Chase Bank in order to establish a distribution center in Las Vegas. On September 17, local bank officer Dowling told Classic that the loan was a "go." When credit quality issues surfaced, Dowling continued to make assurances that the loan would be approved. On October 12, however, she told Classic that the loan had been turned down. Classic claimed that the bank's breach of its oral promise to make the loan and Classic's detrimental reliance on the promise caused it to lose more than $1 million. The Indiana statute of frauds requires agreements to lend money to be in writing. Classic contended that the oral agreement in this case must be enforced on the basis of promissory estoppel and the company's unconscionable injury. Judge Posner of the Seventh Circuit upheld the dismissal of the claim, writing (in part):

> ... For the plaintiff to treat the bank loan as a certainty because they were told by the bank officer whom they were dealing with that it would be approved was unreasonable, especially if, as the plaintiffs' damages claim presupposes, the need for the loan was urgent. Rational businessmen know that there is many a slip "twixt cup and lips," that a loan is not approved until it is approved, that if a bank's employee tells you your loan application will be approved that is not the same as telling you it has been approved, and that if one does not have a loan commitment in writing yet the need for the loan is urgent one had better be negotiating with other potential lenders at the same time....[13]

CPA   16-1c   Note or Memorandum

The statute of frauds requires a writing to evidence those contracts that come within its scope. This writing may be a note or memorandum as distinguished from a contract.[14] The statutory requirement is, of course, satisfied if there is a complete written contract signed by both parties.

Signing

The note or memorandum must be signed by the party sought to be bound by the contract. **For Example,** in the previous scenario involving Mark Wahlberg and Steven Spielberg, suppose the parties agreed to do the film according to the same terms but agreed to begin shooting the film a year from next April, and Mark wrote the essential terms on a napkin, dated it, and had Steven sign it "to make sure I got it right." Mark

---

[12] As will be presented in Chapter 22, under Revised Article 2, §2-201, the $500 amount is increased to $5,000. This revision has not yet been adopted by any state.

[13] *Classic Cheesecake Co. Inc. v. J. P. Morgan Chase Bank,* 546 F.3d 839 (7th Cir. 2008).

[14] *McLinden v. Coco,* 765 N.E.2d 606 (Ind. App. 2002).

then placed the napkin in his wallet for his records. Because the contract could not be performed within one year after the date of the agreement, a writing would be required. If Steven thereafter decided not to pursue the film, Mark could enforce the contract against him because the napkin-note had been signed by the party to be bound or "sought to be charged," Steven. However, if Mark later decided not to appear in the film, the agreement to do the film could not be enforced against Mark because no writing existed signed by Mark, the party sought to be charged. The signature may be an ordinary one or any symbol that is adopted by the party as a signature. It may consist of initials, figures, or a mark. In the absence of a local statute that provides otherwise, a signature may be made by pencil, pen, typewriter, print, or stamp. It is unlikely that a logo can constitute a legal signature. **For Example,** University of South Carolina sports fans claimed that a university brochure contained a signed writing sufficient to satisfy the statute of frauds supportive of their rights to continued premium seating at the new basketball arena. The presence or absence of the university's signature turned on whether the university logo on the brochures suffices for a legal signature. The court majority found that the logo did not constitute a legal signature. However, Justice Pleicones admonished the court majority to be more circumspect in holding that a logo can never constitute a signature for the purposes of the statute of frauds.[15]

Electronic Signature. Electronic signatures have parity with on-paper signatures under the Uniform Electronic Transactions Act (UETA).[16] The act treats e-signatures and e-records as if they were handwritten. The parties themselves determine how they will determine each other's identity such as by a credit card, a password or pin, or other secure means. Certain documents and records are exempt under the act, such as wills, trusts, and commercial law matters.

Content

The note or memorandum must contain all of the essential terms of the contract so the court can determine just what was agreed. If any essential term is missing, the writing is not sufficient. A writing evidencing a sale of land that does not describe the land or identify the buyer does not satisfy the statute of frauds. The subject matter must be identified either within the writing itself or in other writings to which it refers. A deposit check given by the buyer to the seller does not take an oral land sales contract out of the statute of frauds. This is so because the check does not set forth the terms of the sale. The note or memorandum may consist of one writing or of separate papers, such as letters, or a combination of such papers. Separate writings cannot be considered together unless they are linked. Linkage may be by express reference in each writing to the other or by the fact that each writing clearly deals with the same subject matter. An exchange of e-mails may constitute an enforceable agreement if the writings include all of the agreement's essential terms. **For Example,** three e-mails were determined to be a binding integrated fee agreement limiting the Kasowitz law firm to a flat $1 million fee and rejecting a higher success fee sought from the client. On September 8, 2006, Kasowitz (by attorney Goldberg) e-mailed a proposed fee arrangement to the client's in-house counsel, Bergman, which provided in relevant part:

> *We can do the Cardtronics case for a flat $1 million, payable over 10 months as you suggested (exclusive of disbursements), plus 20% of amounts recovered above some number, as opposed to a percentage payable from dollar one.*

---

[15] *Springolo v. University of South Carolina*, 757 S.E.2d 384 (S.C. 2014).

[16] Forty-seven states and the District of Columbia have adopted the UETA. The remaining three states, Illinois, New York, and Washington, are subject to the federal Electronic Signatures in Global and National Commerce Act (E-Sign), 15 U.S.C.§7001, which is consistent with the UETA in many respects.

> *Based on the numbers we have, which obviously are approximations, we actually think the damages could be between $10 and $11 million over the life of the contract. So I'm thinking of 20% of everything above $4 million as the success fee portion…*

On September 19, 2006, Goldberg sent an e-mail to Bergman in which he stated, in relevant part,

> *I would love to have our fee arrangement in place by then so I can just tear into these guys.*

In an e-mail response to Kasowitz that same day, Bergman wrote:

> *Go.*

The recovery amounted to $1.75 million, and no success fee was called for under the agreement evident from the e-mails.[17]

16-1d Effect of Noncompliance

The majority of states hold that a contract that does not comply with the statute of frauds is not enforceable.[18] If an action is brought to enforce the contract, the defendant can raise the defense that the alleged contract is not enforceable because it is not evidenced by a writing, as required by the statute of frauds.

Recovery of Value Conferred

In most instances, a person who is prevented from enforcing a contract because of the statute of frauds is nevertheless entitled to recover from the other party the value of any services or property furnished or money given under the oral contract. Recovery is not based on the terms of the contract but on a quasi-contractual obligation. The other party is to restore to the plaintiff what was received in order to prevent unjust enrichment at the plaintiff's expense. **For Example,** when an oral contract for services cannot be enforced because of the statute of frauds, the person performing the work may recover the reasonable value of the services rendered.

Who May Raise the Defense of Noncompliance?

Only a party to the oral contract may raise a defense that it is not binding because there is no writing that satisfies the statute of frauds. Third persons, such as an insurance company or the Internal Revenue Service, cannot claim that a contract is void because the statute of frauds was not satisfied.

16-2 Parol Evidence Rule

When the contract is evidenced by a writing, may the contract terms be changed by the testimony of witnesses?

16-2a Exclusion of Parol Evidence

The general rule is that parol or extrinsic evidence will not be allowed into evidence to add to, modify, or contradict the terms of a written contract that is fully integrated

---

[17] *Kasowitz, Benson, Torres & Friedman, LLP v. Reade*, 950 N.Y.S.2d 8 (A.D. 2012); but see *Dahan v. Weiss*, 991 N.Y.S.2d 119 (A.D. 2014), where e-mail messages failed to express the full intentions of the parties.
[18] The UCC creates several statutes of frauds of limited applicability, in which it uses the phrase "not enforceable": §1-206 (sale of intangible personal property); §2-201 (sale of goods); and §8-319 (sale of securities).

or complete on its face.[19] Evidence of an alleged earlier oral or written agreement within the scope of the fully integrated written contract or evidence of an alleged contemporaneous oral agreement within the scope of the fully integrated written contract is inadmissible as *parol evidence.*

Parol evidence is admissible, however, to show fraud, duress, or mistake and under certain other circumstances to be discussed in the following paragraphs.

The **parol evidence rule** is based on the theory that either there never was an oral agreement or, if there was, the parties abandoned it when they reached the stage in negotiations of executing their written contract. The social objective of the parol evidence rule is to give stability to contracts and to prevent the assertion of terms that did not exist or did not survive the bargaining of the parties so as to reach inclusion in the final written contract.

For Example, *L* (landlord), the owner of a new development containing a five-store mall, discusses leasing one of the stores to *T* (tenant), who is viewing the property with his sister *S*, a highly credible poverty worker on leave from her duties in Central America. *L*, in the presence of *S*, agrees to give *T* the exclusive right to sell coffee and soft drinks in the five-store mall. Soon *L* and *T* execute a detailed written lease for the store, which makes no provision for *T*'s exclusive right to sell soft drinks and coffee in the mall. Subsequently, when two of the mall's new tenants begin to sell soft drinks and coffee, *T* brings suit against *L* for the breach of the oral promise granting him exclusive rights to sell soft drinks and coffee. *T* calls *S* as his first witness to prove the existence of the oral promise. *L*, through his attorney, will object to the admission of any evidence of a prior oral agreement that would add to or amend the fully integrated written lease, which set forth all restrictions on the landlord and tenant as to uses of the premises. After study of the matter, the court, based on the parol evidence rule, will not hear testimony from either *S* or *T* about the oral promise *L* made to *T*. In order to preserve his exclusive right to sell the drinks in question, *T* should have made certain that this promise was made part of the lease. His lawsuit will not be successful.

16-2b When the Parol Evidence Rule Does Not Apply

The parol evidence rule will not apply in certain cases. The most common of these are discussed in the following paragraphs.

Ambiguity

If a written contract is **ambiguous** or may have two or more different meanings, parol evidence may generally be admitted to clarify the meaning.[20]

Parol evidence may also be admitted to show that a word used in a contract has a special trade meaning or a meaning in the particular locality that differs from the common meaning of that word.

Fraud, Duress, or Mistake

A contract apparently complete on its face may have omitted a provision that should have been included. Parol evidence may be admitted to show that a provision was omitted as the result of fraud, duress, or mistake and to further show what that provision stated. Parol evidence is admissible to show that a provision of the written contract was a mutual mistake even though the written provision is unambiguous. When one party claims to

---

parol evidence rule–rule that prohibits the introduction into evidence of oral or written statements made prior to or contemporaneously with the execution of a complete written contract, deed, or instrument, in the absence of clear proof of fraud, accident, or mistake causing the omission of the statement in question.

ambiguous–having more than one reasonable interpretation.

---

[19] *Mayday v. Grathwohl*, 805 N.W.2d 285 (Minn. App. 2011).

[20] *Berg v. Hudesman*, 801 P.2d 222 (Wash. 1990). This view is also followed by U.C.C. §2-202(a), which permits terms in a contract for the sale of goods to be "explained or supplemented by a course of dealing or usage of trade … or by course of performance." Such evidence is admissible not because there is an ambiguity but "in order that the true understanding of the parties as to the agreement may be reached." Official Code Comment to §2-202.

have been fraudulently induced by the other to enter into a contract, the parol evidence rule does not bar proof that there was a fraud. **For Example,** the parol evidence rule does not bar proof that the seller of land intentionally misrepresented that the land was zoned to permit use as an industrial park. Such evidence does not contradict the terms of the contract but shows that the agreement is unenforceable.[21]

Modification of Contract

The parol evidence rule prohibits only the contradiction of a complete written contract. It does not prohibit proof that the contract was thereafter modified or terminated.

CASE SUMMARY

All Sail and No Anchor

FACTS: On April 2, 1990, Christian Bourg hired Bristol Boat Co., Inc., and Bristol Marine Co. (defendants) to construct and deliver a yacht on July 1, 1990. However, the defendants did not live up to their promises and the contract was breached. On October 22, 1990, the defendants executed a written settlement agreement whereby Bourg agreed to pay an additional sum of $135,000 for the delivery of the yacht and to provide the defendants a loan of $80,000 to complete the construction of the vessel. Referencing the settlement agreement, the defendants at the same time executed a promissory note obliging them to repay the $80,000 loan plus interest in annual installments due on November 1 of each year, with the final payment due on November 1, 1994. The court stated in presenting the facts: "However, like the yacht itself, the settlement agreement soon proved to be just another hole in the water into which the plaintiff threw his money." Bourg sued the defendants after they failed to make certain payments on the note, and the court granted a motion for summary judgment in favor of Bourg for $59,081. The defendants appealed.

DECISION: Judgment for Bourg. Because the defendants' affidavit recites that an alleged oral side agreement was entered into at the same time as the settlement agreement and promissory note—the oral side agreement allegedly stated "that the note would be paid for by services rendered by the defendants"—the oral side agreement would have constituted a contemporaneous modification that would merge into the integrated promissory note and settlement agreement and thus be barred from admission into evidence under the parol evidence rule. Although parties to an integrated written contract can modify their understanding by a subsequent oral pact, to be legally effective, there must be evidence of mutual assent to the essential terms of the modification and adequate consideration. Here the defendants adduced no competent evidence of either mutual assent to particular terms or a specific consideration that would be sufficiently definite to constitute an enforceable subsequent oral modification to the parties' earlier written agreements. Thus, legally this alleged oral agreement was all sail and no anchor. [*Bourg v. Bristol Boat Co.*, **705 A.2d 969 (R.I. 1998)**]

16-3 Rules of Construction and Interpretation

In interpreting contracts, courts are aided by certain rules.

16-3a Intention of the Parties

When persons enter into an agreement, it is to be presumed that they intend for their agreement to have some effect. A court will strive to determine the intent of the parties and to give effect to it. A contract, therefore, is to be enforced according to its terms.[22] A court cannot remake or rewrite the contract of the parties under the pretense of interpreting.[23]

---

[21] *Edwards v. Centrex Real Estate Corp.*, 61 Cal. Rptr. 518 (Cal. App. 1997).
[22] See *Greenwald v. Kersh*, 621 S.E.2d 463 (Ga. App. 2005).
[23] *Abbot v. Schnader, Harrison, Segal & Lewis, LLP*, 805 A.2d 547 (Pa. Super. 2002).

No particular form of words is required, and any words manifesting the intent of the parties are sufficient. In the absence of proof that a word has a peculiar meaning or that it was employed by the parties with a particular meaning, a common word is given its ordinary meaning.

Meaning of Words

Ordinary words are to be interpreted according to their ordinary meaning.[24] **For Example,** when a contract requires the gasoline dealer to pay the supplier for "gallons" supplied, the term *gallons* is unambiguous and does not require that an adjustment of the gallonage be made for the temperature.[25] When a contract calls for a businessperson to pay a builder for the builder's "costs," the term *costs* is unambiguous, meaning actual costs, not a lesser amount based on the builder's bid.[26]

If there is a common meaning to a term, that meaning will be followed even though the dictionary may contain additional meanings. If technical or trade terms are used in a contract, they are to be interpreted according to the area of technical knowledge or trade from which the terms are taken.

Incorporation by Reference

The contract may not cover all of the agreed terms. The missing terms may be found in another document. Frequently, the parties executing the contract for storage will simply state that a storage contract is entered into and that the contract applies to the goods listed in the schedule attached to and made part of the contract. Likewise, a contract for the construction of a building may involve plans and specifications on file in a named city office. The contract will simply state that the building is to be constructed according to those plans and specifications that are "incorporated herein and made part of this contract." When there is such an **incorporation by reference,** the contract consists of both the original document and the detailed statement that is incorporated in it.

When a contract refers to another document, however, the contract must sufficiently describe the document or so much of it as is to be interpreted as part of the contract.

incorporation by reference–contract consisting of both the original or skeleton document and the detailed statement that is incorporated in it.

16-3b Whole Contract

The provisions of a contract must be construed as a whole in such a way that every part is given effect.

Every word of a contract is to be given effect if reasonably possible. The contract is to be construed as a whole, and if the plain language of the contract thus viewed solves the dispute, the court is to make no further analysis.[27]

CASE SUMMARY

When You Permanently Reduced the Shipping Spots to Zero, You "Terminated" the Contract, Silly

FACTS: C.A. Acquisition Newco LLC is a successor in interest to Cyphermint, Inc. ("CI"), a New York corporation specializing in software development for self-service kiosks. DHL Express (USA), Inc., is an Ohio corporation with a principal place of business in Florida. It is a division of DHL International GmBH, a Deutsche Post Company and express carrier

---

[24] *Thorton v. D.F.W. Christian Television, Inc.,* 925 S.W.2d 17 (Tex. App. 1995).
[25] *Hopkins v. BP Oil, Inc.,* 81 F.3d 1070 (11th Cir. 1996).
[26] *Batzer Construction, Inc. v. Boyer,* 125 P.3d 773 (Or. App. 2006).
[27] *Covensky v. Hannah Marine Corp.,* 903 N.E.2d 422 (Ill. App. 2009).

When You Permanently Reduced the Shipping Spots to Zero, You "Terminated" the Contract, Silly continued

of documents and freight. Until 2008, DHL provided express pick-up and delivery, including same-day air delivery of letters and packages throughout the United States.

DHL entered into an agreement with Cyphermint, hoping to expand its customer base by offering domestic shipping services in retail locations, such as Walgreens and OfficeMax, via kiosks, or "Shipping Spots." Customers were able to use the kiosks' touch screen to pay for shipping costs and print shipping labels. The contract provided for an initial three-year term (August 1, 2006, through July 31, 2009) that automatically renewed for two more years unless either party gave notice of its election not to renew 90 days before the end of the initial contract. Under the contract, Cyphermint agreed to provide interactive software, enabling customers to use DHL's services from the shipping spots. Section 10.5 of the contract governs termination fees:

> *There shall be no termination fees for any termination by either party, irrespective of the reason for such termination, except for a "Material Breach" or as provided pursuant to the "Statement of Work" (SOW).*

The SOW contains the following provision concerning termination fees:

> *Should DHL terminate this agreement for any reason other than a material breach by Cyphermint*

> *before its termination date DHL agrees to compensate CI in the amount of $50,000 per month for each month remaining in the initial term.*

In November 2008, DHL decided to end all domestic delivery service within the United States. CI requested early termination fees under Section 10.5 of the contract of $413,333.33. DHL refused to pay, contending that Section 2.8 of the contract gave DHL the discretion to control the number and placement of the shipping spots, and when it ended U.S. domestic operations, it exercised its discretion to reduce shipping spots to zero.

DECISION: Judgment for CI. In reviewing a document, a court must consider the document as a whole, rather than attempting to isolate certain parts of it. Even if the court were to accept DHL's argument that Section 2.8 gave it blanket authority to reduce or eliminate the shipping spot project altogether, the outcome would remain the same. The relevant provision in the contract provides for termination fees without regard to whether the termination was authorized. The only restriction placed on the recovery of such fees is that they will not be available in the case of a material breach by Cyphermint. DHL failed to explain how reducing the shipping spots to zero was in any way different from "terminating" the contract. [**C.A. Acquisition Newco, LLC v. DHL Express (USA), Inc.**, 795 F. Supp. 2d 140 (D. Mass. 2011)]

16-3c Contradictory and Ambiguous Terms

One term in a contract may conflict with another term, or one term may have two different meanings. It is then necessary for the court to determine whether there is a contract and, if so, what the contract really means.

CASE SUMMARY

Who Pays the Piper?

FACTS: Olander Contracting Co., developer Gail Wachter, and the City of Bismarck, North Dakota, entered into a water and sewer construction contract including, among other things, connecting a 10-inch sewer line from Wachter's housing development to the city's existing 36-inch concrete sewer main and installing a manhole at the connection, to be paid for by Wachter. Olander installed the manhole,

but it collapsed within a few days. Olander installed a second manhole, with a large base supported by pilings, but it too failed a few days after it was installed. Olander then placed a rock bedding under the city's sewer main, replaced 78 feet of the existing concrete pipe with PVC pipe, and installed a manhole a third time on a larger base. Olander sued Wachter and the City of Bismarck for damages of

Who Pays the Piper? continued

$456,536.25 for extra work it claims it was required to perform to complete its contract. Both defendants denied they were responsible for the amount sued under the contract. The jury returned a special verdict, finding that Olander performed "extra work/unforeseen work … for which it is entitled to be compensated in excess of the contract price" in the amount of $220,849.67, to be paid by the City of Bismarck. Appeals were taken.

DECISION: Judgment for Olander. The trial judge properly made the initial determination that the contract language was ambiguous. That is, the language used by the parties could support good arguments for the positions of both parties. This resolved a question of law. Once this determination had been made, the judge allowed extrinsic evidence from all parties as to what they meant when they negotiated the contract. This evidence related to the questions of fact, which were left to the jury. Testimony was taken from the parties who negotiated the contract, and testimony was also heard about the role of each of the parties in the actual construction of the manhole, the cause for the collapses, and why the contractor had to replace the city's existing concrete pipe with PVC pipe and the city's role in making this determination. The jury then fulfilled its role answering the question whether or not Olander had performed extra work in the affirmative, concluding that the city was required to pay for it. [***Olander Contracting v. Wachter*, 643 N.W.2d 29 (2002)**]

If the language within the four corners of the contract is unambiguous, the parties' intentions are determined from the plain meaning of the words, used in the contract, as a matter of law, by the judge. A contract term or provision is *ambiguous* if it is capable of more than one reasonable interpretation because of the uncertain meaning of terms or missing terms. A finding of ambiguity is justified only if the language of the contract reasonably supports the competing interpretations.[28] It is the role of the judge—a question of law—to initially determine whether a contract is ambiguous. If the contract is ambiguous, it is the role of the jury—a question of fact—to determine which party's position is correct with the aid of extrinsic evidence.

Nature of Writing

When a contract is partly a printed form or partly typewritten and partly handwritten and the written part conflicts with the printed or typewritten part, the written part prevails. When there is a conflict between a printed part and a typewritten part, the latter prevails. Consequently, when a clause typewritten on a printed form conflicts with what is stated by the print, the conflicting print is ignored and the typewritten clause controls. This rule is based on the belief that the parties had given greater thought to what they typed or wrote for the particular contract as contrasted with printed words already in a form designed to cover many transactions. Thus, a typewritten provision to pay 90 cents per unit overrode a preprinted provision setting the price as 45 cents per unit.

When there is a conflict between an amount or quantity expressed both in words and figures, as on a check, the amount or quantity expressed in words prevails. Words control because there is less danger that a word will be wrong than a number.

Ambiguity

A contract is ambiguous when the intent of the parties is uncertain and the contract is capable of more than one reasonable interpretation.[29] The background from which the contract and the dispute arose may help in determining the intention of the parties. **For Example,** when suit was brought in Minnesota on a Canadian insurance policy, the

---

[28] *QEP Energy Co. v. Sullivan*, 444 Fed. Appx. 284 (10th Cir. 2011).
[29] *Kaufman & Stewart v. Weinbrenner Shoe Co.*, 589 N.W.2d 499 (Minn. App. 1999).

question arose whether the dollar limit of the policy referred to Canadian or U.S. dollars. The court concluded that Canadian dollars were intended. Both the insurer and the insured were Canadian corporations; the original policy, endorsements to the policy, and policy renewals were written in Canada; over the years, premiums had been paid in Canadian dollars; and a prior claim on the policy had been settled by the payment of an amount computed on the basis of Canadian dollars.

Strict Construction Against Drafting Party

An ambiguous contract is interpreted strictly against the party who drafted it.[30] **For Example,** an insurance policy containing ambiguous language regarding coverage or exclusions is interpreted against the insurer and in favor of the insured when two interpretations are reasonably possible. This rule is a secondary rule that may be invoked only after all of the ordinary interpretive guides have been exhausted. The rule basically assigns the risk of an unresolvable ambiguity to the party creating it.[31]

16-3d Implied Terms

In some cases, a court will imply a term to cover a situation for which the parties failed to provide or, when needed, to give the contract a construction or meaning that is reasonable.

The court often implies details of the performance of a contract not expressly stated in the contract. In a contract to perform work, there is an implied promise to use such skill as is necessary to properly perform the work.

CASE SUMMARY

Read the Contract Your Honor. Where Did We Promise the Holguins That Their Satellite Dish Would Be Properly Installed?

FACTS: The Holguins ordered a bundle of services from AT&T and affiliates DISH California and EchoStar consisting of telephone, Internet, and satellite television services, with Deborah Holguin signing up with the AT&T sales agents. The installation process did not go as planned. The DISH technician drilled through a sewer pipe in the Holguins' wall, fed a satellite television cable through it, and patched the wall without repairing the sewer pipe. The improper installation was not discovered until 14 months later, and the damaged pipe leaked sewer water into the surrounding wall cavity and caused mold buildup in the Holguins' home. As a result, the Holguins suffered respiratory problems and other health issues. The repair efforts were a nightmare causing the Holguins to hire their own contractor to complete the remediation work. The Holguins sued AT&T, DISH, and EchoStar for breach of contract. From a judgment for the Holguins for $109,000 in

compensatory damages and attorney fees, the defendants appealed. AT&T, DISH, and EchoStar contend that the trial court erred in interpreting the Holguins' contract to contain an implied term requiring the Holguins' satellite television equipment to be properly installed.

DECISION: Judgment for the Holguins. It is a well-settled principle that express contractual terms give rise to implied duties, violations of which may themselves constitute breaches of contract. Accompanying every contract is a common-law duty to perform with care, skill, reasonable expedience, and faithfulness the thing agreed to be done, and a negligent failure to observe any of these conditions is a tort, as well as a breach of the contract. There was no error applying the implied contractual term that the equipment be properly installed. [***Holguin v. Dish Network, LLC,* 178 Cal. Rptr. 3d 100 (Cal. App. 2014)**]

---

[30] *Idaho Migrant Council, Inc. v. Warila,* 89 P.2d 39 (Wyo. 1995).
[31] *Premier Title Co. v. Donahue,* 765 N.E.2d 513 (Ill. App. 2002).

In every contract, there is an implied obligation that neither party shall do anything that will have the effect of destroying or injuring the right of the other party to receive the fruits of the contract. This means that in every contract there exists an implied covenant of **good faith** and fair dealing. When a contract may reasonably be interpreted in different ways, a court should make the interpretation that is in harmony with good faith and fair dealing. **For Example,** when a contract is made subject to the condition that one of the parties obtain financing, that party must make reasonable, good-faith efforts to obtain financing. The party is not permitted to do nothing and then claim that the contract is not binding because the condition has not been satisfied. Likewise, when a contract requires a party to obtain government approval, the party must use all reasonable means to obtain it.[32]

good faith–absence of knowledge of any defects or problems.

The Uniform Commercial Code imposes an obligation of good faith in the performance or enforcement of every contract.[33]

16-3e Conduct and Custom

The conduct of the parties and the customs and usages of a particular trade may give meaning to the words of the parties and thus aid in the interpretation of their contract.

Conduct of the Parties

The conduct of the parties in carrying out the terms of a contract is the best guide to determine the parties' intent. When performance has been repeatedly tendered and accepted without protest, neither party will be permitted to claim that the contract was too indefinite to be binding. **For Example,** a travel agent made a contract with a hotel to arrange for trips to the hotel. After some 80 trips had already been arranged and paid for by the hotel at the contract price without any dispute about whether the contract obligation was satisfied, any claim by the travel agent that it could charge additional fees must be rejected.

Custom and Usage of Trade

usage of trade–language and customs of an industry.

The customs and **usages of trade** or commercial activity to which the contract relates may be used to interpret the terms of a contract.[34] **For Example,** when a contract for the construction of a building calls for a "turn-key construction," industry usage is admissible to show what this means: a construction in which all the owner needs to do is to turn the key in the lock to open the building for use and in which all construction risks are assumed by the contractor.[35]

Custom and usage, however, cannot override express provisions of a contract that are inconsistent with custom and usage.

16-3f Avoidance of Hardship

As a general rule, a party is bound by a contract even though it proves to be a bad bargain. If possible, a court will interpret a contract to avoid hardship. Courts will, if possible, interpret a vague contract in a way to avoid any forfeiture of a party's interest.

When hardship arises because the contract makes no provision for the situation that has occurred, the court will sometimes imply a term to avoid the hardship.

---

[32] *Kroboth v. Brent,* 625 N.Y.S.2d 748 (A.D. 1995).
[33] U.C.C. §§1-201(19), 1-203.
[34] *Affiliated FM Ins. Co. v. Constitution Reinsurance Corp.,* 626 N.E.2d 878 (Mass. 1994).
[35] *Blue v. R.L. Glossen Contracting, Inc.,* 327 S.E.2d 582 (Ga. App. 1985).

Make the Connection

- -

Summary

An oral agreement may be a contract unless it is the intention of the parties that they should not be bound by the agreement without a writing executed by them. Certain contracts must be evidenced by a writing, however, or else they cannot be enforced. The statutes that declare this exception are called *statutes of frauds*. Statutes of frauds commonly require that a contract be evidenced by writing in the case of (1) an agreement that cannot be performed within one year after the contract is made, (2) an agreement to sell any interest in land, (3) a promise to answer for the debt or default of another, (4) a promise by the executor or administrator of a decedent's estate to pay a claim against the estate from personal funds, (5) a promise made in consideration of marriage, and (6) a contract for the sale of goods for a purchase price of $500 or more.

To evidence a contract to satisfy a statute of frauds, there must be a writing of all essential terms. The writing must be signed by the defendant against whom suit is brought for enforcement of the contract.

If the applicable statute of frauds is not satisfied, the oral contract cannot be enforced. To avoid unjust enrichment, a plaintiff barred from enforcing an oral contract may in most cases recover from the other contracting party the reasonable value of the benefits conferred by the plaintiff on the defendant.

When there is a written contract, the question arises whether that writing is the exclusive statement of the parties' agreement. If the writing is the complete and final statement of the contract, parol evidence as to matters agreed to before or at the time the writing was signed is not admissible to contradict the writing. This is called the *parol evidence rule*. In any case, the parol evidence rule does not bar parol evidence when (1) the writing is ambiguous, (2) the writing is not a true statement of the agreement of the parties because of fraud, duress, or mistake, or (3) the existence, modification, or illegality of a contract is in controversy.

Because a contract is based on the agreement of the parties, courts must determine the intent of the parties manifested in the contract. The intent that is to be enforced is the intent as it reasonably appears to a third person. This objective intent is followed.

In interpreting a contract, ordinary words are to be given their ordinary meanings. If trade or technical terms have been used, they are interpreted according to their technical meanings. The court must consider the whole contract and not read a particular part out of context. When different writings are executed as part of the same transaction, or one writing refers to or incorporates another, all of the writings are to be read together as the contract of the parties.

When provisions of a contract are contradictory, the court will try to reconcile or eliminate the conflict. If this cannot be done, the conclusion may be that there is no contract because the conflict makes the agreement indefinite as to a material matter. In some cases, conflict is solved by considering the form of conflicting terms. Handwriting prevails over typing and a printed form, and typing prevails over a printed form. Ambiguity will be eliminated in some cases by the admission of parol evidence or by interpreting the provision strictly against the party preparing the contract, particularly when that party has significantly greater bargaining power.

Learning Outcomes

After studying this chapter, you should be able to clearly explain:

16-1   Statute of Frauds

LO.1 Explain when a contract must be evidenced by a writing

See the discussion and examples illustrated throughout this chapter beginning on page 292.

LO.2 Explain the effect of noncompliance with the statute of frauds

See the *Bithoney* case where a doctor's oral contract for severance was barred by the statute of frauds, page 293. See the example in which an oral contract cannot be enforced because it is not in writing, but the plaintiff may recover the reasonable value of the services rendered, page 299.

16-2   Parol Evidence Rule

LO.3 Explain the parol evidence rule and the exceptions to this rule

See the example in which the tenant is not allowed to call a witness to testify about a prior oral agreement that would add to and alter the written lease, page 300. See the exceptions based on ambiguity, fraud, duress, and mistake, pages 300–301.

16-3   Rules of Construction and Interpretation

LO.4 Understand the basic rule of contract construction that a contract is enforced according to its terms

See the example of the interpretation of the word "costs," page 302.

See the *DHL Express* case that illustrates the judicial common sense of interpreting the contract as a whole rather than a strained construction contrary to the contract's intent, pages 302–303.

LO.5 State the rules for interpreting ambiguous terms in a contract

See the discussion on the nature of the writing, page 304.

Key Terms

administrator

ambiguous

decedent

executor

good faith

incorporation by reference

parol evidence rule

personal representative

statute of frauds

suretyship

usages of trade

Questions and Case Problems

1. Kelly made a written contract to sell certain land to Brown and gave Brown a deed to the land. Thereafter, Kelly sued Brown to get back a 20-foot strip of the land. Kelly claimed that before making the written contract, it was agreed that Kelly would sell all of his land to Brown to make it easier for Brown to get a building permit, but after that was done, the 20-foot strip would be reconveyed to Kelly. Was Kelly entitled to the 20-foot strip? What ethical values are involved? [*Brown v. Kelly*, 545 So. 2d 518 (Fla. App.)]

2. Martin made an oral contract with Cresheim Garage to work as its manager for two years. Cresheim wrote Martin a letter stating that the oral contract had been made and setting forth all of its terms. Cresheim later refused to recognize the contract. Martin sued Cresheim for breach of the contract and offered Cresheim's letter in evidence as proof of the contract. Cresheim claimed that the oral contract was not binding because the contract was not in writing and the letter referring to the contract was not a contract but only a letter. Was the contract binding?

3. Lawrence loaned money to Moore, who died without repaying the loan. Lawrence claimed that when he mentioned the matter to Moore's widow, she promised to pay the debt. She did not pay it, and Lawrence sued her on her promise. Does she have any defense? [*Moore v. Lawrence*, 480 S.W.2d 941 (Ark.)]

4. Jackson signed an agreement to sell 79 acres of land to Devenyns. Jackson owned 80 acres and was apparently intending to keep for himself the acre on which his home was located. The written agreement also stated that "Devenyns shall have the option to buy on property ___," but nothing was stated in the blank space. Devenyns sued to enforce the agreement. Was it binding? [In re *Jackson's Estate*, 892 P.2d 786 (Wyo.)]

5. Boeing Airplane Co. contracted with Pittsburgh–Des Moines Steel Co. for the latter to construct a supersonic wind tunnel. R.H. Freitag Manufacturing Co. sold materials to York-Gillespie Co., which subcontracted to do part of the work. To persuade Freitag to keep supplying materials on credit, Boeing and the principal contractor both assured Freitag that he would be paid. When Freitag was not paid by the subcontractor, he sued Boeing and the contractor. They defended on the ground that the assurances given Freitag were not written. Decide. What ethical values are involved? [*R.H. Freitag Mfg. Co. v. Boeing Airplane Co.*, 347 P.2d 1074 (Wash.)]

6. Louise Pulsifer owned a farm that she wanted to sell and ran an ad in the local newspaper. After Russell Gillespie agreed to purchase the farm, Pulsifer wrote him a letter stating that she would not sell it. He

sued her to enforce the contract, and she raised the defense of the statute of frauds. The letter she had signed did not contain any of the terms of the sale. Gillespie, however, claimed that the newspaper ad could be combined with her letter to satisfy the statute of frauds. Was he correct? [*Gillespie v. Pulsifer*, 655 S.W.2d 123 (Mo.)]

7. In February or March, Corning Glass Works orally agreed to retain Hanan as management consultant from May 1 of that year to April 30 of the next year for a present value fee of $200,000. Was this agreement binding? Is this decision ethical? [*Hanan v. Corning Glass Works*, 314 N.Y.S.2d 804 (A.D.)]

8. Catherine (wife) and Peter (husband) Mallen had lived together unmarried for some four years when Catherine got pregnant and a marriage was arranged. Peter asked Catherine to sign a prenuptial agreement. Although his financial statement attached to the agreement did not state his income at $560,000 per year, it showed he was wealthy, and she had lived with him for four years and knew from their standard of living that he had significant income. Catherine contends that failure to disclose Peter's income was a nondisclosure of a material fact when the agreement was drawn up and that accordingly the agreement is not valid. Peter contends that he fully disclosed his net worth and that Catherine was well aware of his significant income. Further, he contends that disparities in the parties' financial status and business experience did not make the agreement unconscionable. Decide. [*Mallen v. Mallen*, 622 S.E.2d 812 (Ga. Sup. Ct.)]

9. Panasonic Industrial Co. (PIC) created a contract making Manchester Equipment Co., Inc. (MECI), a nonexclusive wholesale distributor of its products. The contract stated that PIC reserved the unrestricted right to solicit and make direct sales of the products to anyone, anywhere. The contract also stated that it contained the entire agreement of the parties and that any prior agreement or statement was superseded by the contract. PIC subsequently began to make direct sales to two of MECI's established customers. MECI claimed that this was a breach of the distribution contract and sued PIC for damages. Decide. What ethical values are involved? [*Manchester Equipment Co. Inc. v. Panasonic Industrial Co.*, 529 N.Y.S.2d 532 (App. Div.)]

10. A contract made for the sale of a farm stated that the buyer's deposit would be returned "if for any reason the farm cannot be sold." The seller later stated that she had changed her mind and would not sell, and she offered to return the deposit. The buyer refused to take the deposit back and brought suit to enforce the contract. The seller contended that the "any reason" provision extended to anything, including the seller's changing her mind. Was the buyer entitled to recover? [*Phillips v. Rogers*, 200 S.E.2d 676 (W. Va.)]

11. Integrated, Inc., entered into a contract with the state of California to construct a building. It then subcontracted the electrical work to Alec Fergusson Electrical Contractors. The subcontract was a printed form with blanks filled in by typewriting. The printed payment clause required Integrated to pay Fergusson on the 15th day of the month following the submission of invoices by Fergusson. The typewritten part of the contract required Integrated to pay Fergusson "immediately following payment" (by the state) to the general contractor. When was payment required? [*Integrated, Inc. v. Alec Fergusson Electrical Contractors*, 58 Cal. Rptr. 503 (Cal. App.)]

12. Consolidated Credit Counseling Services, Inc. (Consolidated), sued Affinity Internet, Inc., doing business as SkyNetWEB (Affinity), for breach of its contract to provide computer and Web hosting services. Affinity moved to compel arbitration, and Consolidated argued that the contract between the parties did not contain an arbitration clause. The contract between the parties stated in part: "This contract is subject to all of SkyNetWEB's terms, conditions, user and acceptable use policies located at **http://www.skynetweb.com/company/legal/legal. php.**" An arbitration provision can be found by going to the Web site and clicking to paragraph 17 of the User Agreement. The contract itself makes no reference to an agreement to arbitrate, nor was paragraph 17 expressly referred to or described in the contract. Nor was a hard copy of the information on the Web site either signed by or furnished to Consolidated. Was Consolidated obligated to arbitrate under the clear language of paragraph 17? [*Affinity Internet v. Consolidated Credit*, 920 So. 2d 1286 (Fla. App.)]

13. Physicians Mutual Insurance Co. issued a policy covering Brown's life. The policy declared that it did not cover any deaths resulting from "mental disorder, alcoholism, or drug addiction." Brown was killed when she fell while intoxicated. The insurance company refused to pay because of the quoted provision. Her executor, Savage, sued the insurance company.

Did the insurance company have a defense? [*Physicians Mutual Ins. Co. v. Savage*, 296 N.E.2d 165 (Ind. App.)]

14. The Dickinson Elks Club conducted an annual Labor Day golf tournament. Charbonneau Buick-Pontiac offered to give a new car as a prize to anyone making "a hole in one on hole no. 8." The golf course of the club was only nine holes. To play 18 holes, the players would go around the course twice, although they would play from different tees or locations for the second nine holes. On the second time around, what was originally the eighth hole became the seventeenth hole. Grove was a contestant in the tournament. He scored 3 on the no. 8 hole, but on approaching it for the second time as the seventeenth hole, he made a hole in one. He claimed the prize car from Charbonneau. The latter claimed that Grove had not won the prize because he did not make the hole in one on the eighth hole. Decide. [*Grove v. Charbonneau Buick-Pontiac, Inc.*, 240 N.W.2d 8533 (N.D.)]

15. Tambe Electric Inc. entered into a written agreement with Home Depot to provide copper wire to Tambe at a price set forth in the writing, and allowing the contractor the option of paying for the wire over a period of time. Home Depot did not fulfill this written agreement and Tambe sued for $68,598, the additional cost it had to subsequently pay to obtain copper wire for its work. Home Depot defended that it had made an oral condition precedent requiring payment in full by Tambe at the time it accepted the price quoted in the written agreement. Decide. [*Tambe Electric v. Home Depot*, 856 N.Y.S.2d 373]

CPA Questions

1. Which of the following statements is true with regard to the statute of frauds?

    a. All contracts involving consideration of more than $500 must be in writing.

    b. The written contract must be signed by all parties.

    c. The statute of frauds applies to contracts that can be fully performed within one year from the date they are made.

    d. The contract terms may be stated in more than one document.

2. With regard to an agreement for the sale of real estate, the statute of frauds:

    a. Requires that the entire agreement be in a single writing.

    b. Requires that the purchase price be fair and adequate in relation to the value of the real estate.

    c. Does *not* require that the agreement be signed by all parties.

    d. Does *not* apply if the value of the real estate is less than $500.

3. In negotiations with Andrews for the lease of Kemp's warehouse, Kemp orally agreed to pay one-half of the cost of the utilities. The written lease, later prepared by Kemp's attorney, provided that Andrews pay all of the utilities. Andrews failed to carefully read the lease and signed it. When Kemp demanded that Andrews pay all of the utilities, Andrews refused, claiming that the lease did not accurately reflect the oral agreement. Andrews also learned that Kemp intentionally misrepresented the condition of the structure of the warehouse during the negotiations between the parties. Andrews sued to rescind the lease and intends to introduce evidence of the parties' oral agreement about sharing the utilities and the fraudulent statements made by Kemp. Will the parol evidence rule prevent the admission of evidence concerning each of the following?

	Oral agreement regarding who pays the utilities	Fraudulent statements by Kemp
a.	Yes	Yes
b.	No	Yes
c.	Yes	No
d.	No	No

Third Persons and Contracts

Learning Outcomes ⟨⟨⟨

After studying this chapter, you should be able to

LO.1 Explain the two types of intended third-party beneficiaries

LO.2 Explain why an incidental beneficiary does not have the right to sue as a third-party beneficiary

LO.3 Define an assignment

LO.4 Explain the general rule that a person entitled to receive money under a contract may generally assign that right to another person

LO.5 List the nonassignable rights to performance

17-1 Third-Party Beneficiary Contracts

Generally, only the parties to a contract may sue on it. However, in some cases a third person who is not a party to the contract may sue on the contract.

CPA

17-1a Definition

When a contract is intended to benefit a third person, such a person is an intended **third-party beneficiary** and may bring suit on and enforce the contract.

third-party beneficiary— third person whom the parties to a contract intend to benefit by the making of the contract and to confer upon such person the right to sue for breach of contract.

Creditor Beneficiary

The intended beneficiary is sometimes classified as a *creditor beneficiary* when the promisee's primary intent is to discharge a duty owed to the third party.[1] **For Example,** when Max Giordano sold his business, Sameway Laundry, to Harry Phinn, he had three years of payments totaling $14,500 owing to Davco, Inc., on a commercial Davco shirt drying and pressing machine purchased in 2006. Max (the promisee) made a contract with Harry to sell the business for a stipulated sum. A provision in this contract selling the business called for Harry (the promisor) to make the Davco machine payments when due over the next three years. Should Harry fail to make payments, Davco, Inc., as an intended creditor beneficiary under the contract between Max and Harry, would have standing to sue Harry for breach of the payment provision in the contract.

CPA

Donee Beneficiary

The second type of intended beneficiary is a *donee beneficiary* to whom the promisee's primary intent in contracting is to give a benefit. A life insurance contract is such an intended third-party beneficiary contract. An individual third-party beneficiary has a right to sue under a broad range of insurance policies.

CASE SUMMARY

Peyton Manning Can't Get the Nationwide Insurance Jingle Out of His Head
What's Prudential's Jingle, Sagarnaga?

FACTS: Dr. Garcia purchased a Prudential (Pruco) life insurance policy for a death benefit of $750,000, with his wife Margarita as the primary beneficiary and his three children as contingent beneficiaries. After Margarita's death in 2005, Dr. Garcia married Sagarnaga in 2007. In 2008, Dr. Garcia contacted Pruco and in a recorded conversation advised Pruco that he wanted to designate his wife Sagarnaga as a 50 percent beneficiary. Pruco sent him a partially completed change of beneficiary [COB] form. Dr. Garcia completed the remaining information and returned the COB request to Pruco. Thereafter the signed COB form, dated April 3, 2008, and received by Pruco on April 10, 2008, listed the beneficiaries as follows: the primary beneficiary designation stated Sagarnaga was to receive 50 percent of the Policy proceeds, 12 percent to Arturo Garcia, Jr., 13 percent to Eloisa, and 25 percent to Cecilia. Contingent beneficiaries were also listed. According to the terms of the Policy, if Pruco received a COB request,

[1] The Restatement (Second) of Contracts §302 substitutes "intended beneficiary" for the terms "creditor" and "donee" beneficiary. However, some courts continue to use the classifications of creditor and donee third-party beneficiaries. Regardless of the terminology, the law continues to be the same. See *Continental Casualty v. Zurich American Insurance*, 2009 WL 455285 (D.C. Or. 2009).

Peyton Manning Can't Get the Nationwide Insurance Jingle Out of His Head continued

Pruco would record the change and file it. The change of beneficiary would be effective as of the date the request was signed.

Dr. Garcia died in Brazil on September 22, 2009. It was discovered that Dr. Garcia's COB form received on April 10, 2008, had not been accepted or recorded because a Pruco employee saw an ambiguity regarding the contingent beneficiaries section, which had not been resolved prior to Dr. Garcia's death. Pruco stated that Sagarnaga was thus not a beneficiary under the policy. The children filed a lawsuit against Pruco seeking the entire death benefit. Pruco contended that Sagarnaga had no standing to sue and asserted that it had not breached the insurance contract. From a judgment for Sagarnaga, Prudential appealed.

DECISION: Judgment of Sagarnaga. An insurance policy is a contract between the insurer and the insured/owner of the policy. A beneficiary under such a policy has no standing to sue under the policy unless his or her interest has vested, such as the insured dies. The policy defined the right of the owner to change beneficiaries, and Dr. Garcia's primary beneficiary designation was clear and unambiguous. With the signed COB form received by Pruco on April 10, 2008, Sagarnaga became the intended beneficiary of the policy, which vested on Dr. Garcia's death. Pruco's failure to tender the 50 percent death benefit to Sagarnaga was a breach of contract. She was entitled to interest penalties and attorney's fees. [***Prudential Insurance Co. v. Durante,*** **443 S.W.2d 499 (Tex. App. 2014)**]

Necessity of Intent

A third person does not have the status of an intended third-party beneficiary unless it is clear at the time the contract was formed that the parties intended to impose a direct obligation with respect to the third person.[2] In determining whether there is intent to benefit a third party, the surrounding circumstances as well as the contract may be examined.[3] There is a strong presumption that the parties to a contract intend to benefit only themselves.[4]

CASE SUMMARY

The Pest Control Case

FACTS: Admiral Pest Control had a standing contract with Lodging Enterprises to spray its motel every month to exterminate pests. Copeland, a guest in the motel, was bitten by a spider. She sued Admiral on the ground that she was a third-party beneficiary of the extermination contract.

DECISION: Judgment against Copeland. There was no intent manifested in the contract that guests of the motel were beneficiaries of the contract. The contract was made by the motel to protect itself. The guests were incidental beneficiaries of that contract and therefore could not sue for its breach. [***Copeland v. Admiral Pest Control Co.,*** **933 P.2d 937 (Okla. App. 1996)**]

[2] *American United Logistics, Inc. v. Catellus*, 319 F.3d 921 (7th Cir. 2003).
[3] See *Becker v. Crispell-Snyder, Inc.*, 763 N.W.2d 192 (Wis. App. 2009) for an example of complex circumstances surrounding a third-party beneficiary contract. The town of Somers, Wisconsin, entered into a contract with engineering firm Crispell-Synder (C-S) because it needed an engineering firm to oversee a new subdivision to be developed by the Beckers. Under this contract C-S would submit bills to the town for overseeing the development, and the town would pay C-S through a line of credit from the Beckers. The court held that the Beckers were third-party beneficiaries entitled to sue C-S for overcharging change orders.
[4] *Barney v. Unity Paving, Inc.*, 639 N.E.2d 592 (Ill. App. 1994).

Description

It is not necessary that the intended third-party beneficiary be identified by name. The beneficiary may be identified by class, with the result that any member of that class is a third-party beneficiary. **For Example,** a contract between the promoter of an automobile stock car race and the owner of the racetrack contains a promise by the owner to pay specified sums of money to each driver racing a car in certain races. A person driving in one of the designated races is a third-party beneficiary and can sue the owner on the contract for the promised compensation.

17-1b Modification or Termination of Intended Third-Party Beneficiary Contract

Can the parties to the contract modify or terminate it so as to destroy the right of the intended third-party beneficiary? If the contract contains an express provision allowing a change of beneficiary or cancellation of the contract without the consent of the intended third-party beneficiary, the parties to the contract may destroy the rights of the intended beneficiary by acting in accordance with that contract provision.[5]

For Example, Roy obtained a life insurance policy from Phoenix Insurance Company that provided the beneficiary could be changed by the insured. Roy named his son, Harry, as the beneficiary. Later, Roy had a falling out with Harry and removed him as beneficiary. Roy could do this because the right to change the beneficiary was expressly reserved by the contract that created the status of the intended third-party beneficiary.

In addition, the rights of an intended third-party beneficiary are destroyed if the contract is discharged or ended by operation of law, for example, through bankruptcy proceedings.

17-1c Limitations on Intended Third-Party Beneficiary

Although the intended third-party beneficiary rule gives the third person the right to enforce the contract, it obviously gives no more rights than the contract provides. That is, the intended third-party beneficiary must take the contract as it is. If there is a time limitation or any other restriction in the contract, the intended beneficiary cannot ignore it but is bound by it.

If the contract is not binding for any reason, that defense may be raised against the intended third-party beneficiary suing on the contract.[6]

CPA 17-1d Incidental Beneficiaries

Not everyone who benefits from the performance of a contract between other persons is entitled to sue as a third-party beneficiary. If the benefit was intended, the third person is an intended beneficiary with the rights described in the preceding sections. If the benefit was not intended, the third person is an *incidental beneficiary.* **For Example,** real estate developer Ocean Atlantic Corp. purchased a series of bonds from American Southern Insurance Co. for the purpose of guaranteeing the performance of public improvement in a subdivision it was developing in Yorkville, Illinois. The bonds representing the surety contract between Ocean Atlantic and American Southern were issued in favor of the City

---

[5] A common form of reservation is the life insurance policy provision by which the insured reserves the right to change the beneficiary. Section 142 of the Restatement (Second) of Contracts provides that the promisor and the promisee may modify their contract and affect the right of the third-party beneficiary thereby unless the agreement expressly prohibits this or the third-party beneficiary has changed position in reliance on the promise or has manifested assent to it.

[6] *XL Disposal Corp. v. John Sexton Contractors Co.,* 659 N.E.2d 1312 (Ill. App. 1995).

right–legal capacity to require another person to perform or refrain from an action.

duty–obligation of law imposed on a person to perform or refrain from performing a certain act.

of Yorkville. Ocean Atlantic hired subcontractor Aurora Blacktop, Inc., to perform several improvements, but the project stalled and Aurora was never paid for its work. Aurora lacked standing as a third-party beneficiary to enforce the subdivision bonds against American Southern because the contractual obligations ran only to the city. Aurora was deemed an incidental beneficiary rather than a third-party beneficiary.[7]

Whether or not a third party is an *intended* or *incidental* beneficiary, therefore, comes down to determining whether or not a reasonable person would believe that the promisee intended to confer on the beneficiary an enforceable benefit under the contract in question. The intent must be clear and definite or expressed in the contract itself or in the circumstances surrounding the contract's execution.[8]

CASE SUMMARY

Third Party Must Be Identified in the Four Corners of the Contract

FACTS: Novus International, Inc., manufactures a poultry-feed supplement named Alimet at its plant in Chocolate Bayou, Texas. A key component of Alimet is the chemical MMP. Novus contracted with Union Carbide to secure MMP from Carbide's plant in Taft, Louisiana. Sometime later, Carbide entered into a major rail-transportation contract with the Union Pacific Railroad (UP). The rail contract consisted of nearly 100 pages. Exhibit 2 of the contract delineated inbound and outbound shipments to and from all of Carbide's Texas and Louisiana facilities. Among the hundreds of shipments listed in Exhibit 2 were three outbound MMP shipments from Taft, Louisiana, to Chocolate Bayou, Texas. These shipments were described as "Taft outbound liquid chemicals." Due to difficulties that arose from its merger with the Southern Pacific Railroad, UP experienced severe disruptions in its rail service over parts of two years and was unable to transport sufficient MMP to Chocolate Bayou. As a result, Novus had to utilize more expensive methods of transportation to obtain Alimet. It sued UP to recover the increased costs of premium freight resulting from UP's breach of its rail contract with Carbide. UP asserts that Novus did not have standing to sue; and Novus contends that it had standing to sue as an intended third-party beneficiary.

DECISION: Judgment for UP. Third-party beneficiary claims succeed or fail according to the provisions of the contact upon which suit is brought. The intention to confer a direct benefit on a third party must be clearly and fully spelled out in the four corners of the contract. Otherwise, enforcement of the contract by a third party must be denied. After reviewing the rail contract, no intent to confer a direct benefit on Novus is evident. Novus is never named in the contract, and all obligations flow between UP and Carbide. Nor is it stated anywhere in the contract that the parties are contracting for the benefit of Carbide's customers. Novus, thus, is an incidental beneficiary without standing to sue. [*Union Pacific Railroad v. Novus International, Inc.*, **113 S.W.3d 418 (Tex. App. 2003)**]

assignment–transfer of a right; generally used in connection with personal property rights, as rights under a contract, commercial paper, an insurance policy, a mortgage, or a lease. (Parties—assignor, assignee.)

17-2 Assignments

The parties to a contract have both rights and duties. Can rights be transferred or sold to another person or entity? Can duties be transferred to another person?

17-2a Definitions

Contracts create **rights** and **duties** between the parties to the contract. An **assignment** is a transfer of contractual rights to a third party. The party owing a duty or debt under the

[7] *City of Yorkville v. American Southern Insurance Co.,* 654 F.3d 713 (7th Cir. 2011).
[8] See *Entire Energy & Renewables, LLC v. Duncan,* 999 N.E.2d 214 (Ohio App. 2013).

| FIGURE 17-1 | Surfboard Transaction Diagram |

contract is the **obligor** or **debtor,** and the party to whom the obligation is owed is the **obligee.** The party making the assignment is the **assignor.** The third party to whom the assignment is made is the **assignee. For Example,** Randy Marshall and Marilee Menendez own Huntington Beach Board (HBB) Company, LLC, a five-employee start-up company making top-of-the line surfboards. Marilee was able to sell 100 Duke Kahanamoku–inspired "longboards" to Watersports, Inc., a large retail sporting goods chain, for $140 per board. However, the best payment terms she could obtain were payment in full in 90 days. A contract containing these terms was executed, and the goods were delivered. To meet internal cash flow needs, HBB assigned its right to receive the $14,000 payment from the buyer to West Coast Financial Associates (Associates) and received $12,800 cash from Associates on execution of the assignment documents. Notice was given at that time to Watersports, Inc., of the assignment. The right to receive the payment due in 90 days under the sales contract has thus been transferred by the seller HBB (assignor) to the third party, Associates (the assignee), to whom the buyer, Watersports, Inc. (obligor), now owes the duty of payment. Under the law of assignments, Associates, the assignee, now has direct rights against the obligor, Watersports, Inc. (See Figure 17-1.)

17-2b Form of Assignment

Generally, an assignment may be in any form. Statutes, however, may require that certain kinds of assignments be in writing or be executed in a particular form. Any words, whether written or spoken, that show an intention to transfer or assign will be given the effect of an assignment.[9]

17-2c Notice of Assignment

An assignment, if otherwise valid, takes effect the moment it is made. The assignee should give immediate notice of the assignment to the obligor, setting forth the obligor's duty to the assignee, in order to prevent improper payment.[10]

---

[9] *JBM Investments, LLC v. Callahan Industries, Inc.*, 667 S.E.2d 429 (Ga. App. 2008).
[10] In some cases, an assignee will give notice of the assignment to the obligor in order to obtain priority over other persons who claim the same right or in order to limit the defenses that the obligor may raise against the assignee. U.C.C. §9-318.

CASE SUMMARY

When You Find Yourself in a Hole, NationsBank, Stop Digging

FACTS: L & S General Contractors, LLC (L & S), purchased a book-entry certificate of deposit (CD 005) in the principal amount of $100,000 from NationsBank, N.A. L & S later assigned CD 005 to Credit General Insurance Company (Credit General) as collateral security for performance and payment bonds on a Howard Johnson construction project. Credit General forwarded to NationsBank a written notice of the assignment that stated, "Please hold this account as assigned to use until demanded or released by us." NationsBank recorded the assignment and executed a written acknowledgment. When CD 005 matured, L & S rolled over the proceeds into a short-term certificate of deposit (CD 058) and, upon maturity, rolled over the proceeds of CD 058 into another short-term certificate of deposit (CD 072).

The bank book entries of CD 058 and CD 072 recorded L & S as the only principal/payee and did not reflect Credit General's assignment interest. NationsBank admitted its failure to show Credit General as assignee on the rollover book entries for CD 058 and CD 072 was a mistake.

Upon maturity, L & S withdrew the proceeds of CD 072 without the knowledge or consent of Credit General. Later Credit General made written demand on NationsBank for the proceeds of CD 005, and NationsBank informed Credit General that CD 005 had been redeemed and refused payment. Credit General sued NationsBank for wrongful payment of proceeds. NationsBank argues that the assignment was limited in time to the completion of the Howard Johnson project.

DECISION: Judgment for the assignee, Credit General. Upon notice and acknowledgment of the assignment, NationsBank incurred a legal duty to pay the account proceeds only to the assignee, Credit General, in whom the account was vested by the terms of the assignment. The assignment was absolute and unambiguous on its face and clearly was not limited as NationsBank proposes. The assignment language controls. [*Credit General Insurance Co. v. NationsBank*, 299 F.3d 943 (8th Cir. 2002)]

If the obligor is notified in any manner that there has been an assignment and that any money due must be paid to the assignee, the obligor's obligation can be discharged only by making payment to the assignee.

If the obligor is not notified that there has been an assignment and that the money due must be paid to the assignee, any payment made by the obligor to the assignor reduces or cancels that portion of the debt. The only remedy for the assignee is to sue the assignor to recover the payments that were made by the obligor.

The Uniform Consumer Credit Code (UCCC) protects consumer-debtors making payments to an assignor without knowledge of the assignment[11] and imposes a penalty for using a contract term that would destroy this protection of consumers.[12]

17-2d Assignment of Right to Money

claim–right to payment.

cause of action–right to damages or other judicial relief when a legally protected right of the plaintiff is violated by an unlawful act of the defendant.

Assignments of contracts are generally made to raise money. **For Example,** an automobile dealer assigns a customer's credit contract to a finance company and receives cash for it. Sometimes assignments are made when an enterprise closes and transfers its business to a new owner.

A person entitled to receive money, such as payment for goods sold to a buyer or for work done under a contract, may generally assign that right to another person.[13] A **claim** or **cause of action** against another person may be assigned. Isaac Hayes, an Academy Award®–winning composer, producer, and the original voice of Chef in the television series South Park, assigned his copyright interests in several musical works in exchange for

---

[11] U.C.C.C. §2.412.
[12] U.C.C.C. §5.202.
[13] *Pravin Banker Associates v. Banco Popular del Peru*, 109 F.3d 850 (2d Cir. 1997).

royalties from Stax Records.[14] A contractor entitled to receive payment from a building's owner can assign that right to a bank as security for a loan or can assign it to anyone else.

For Example, Celeste owed Roscoe Painters $5,000 for painting her house. Roscoe assigned this claim to the Main Street Bank. Celeste later refused to pay the bank because she had never consented to the assignment. The fact that Celeste had not consented is irrelevant. Roscoe was the owner of the claim and could transfer it to the bank. Celeste, therefore, is obligated to pay the assignee, Main Street Bank.

Future Rights

By the modern rule, future and expected rights to money may be assigned. Thus, prior to the start of a building, a building contractor may assign its rights to money not yet due under an existing contract's payment on completion-phase schedule.

Purpose of Assignment

The assignment of the right to money may be a complete transfer of the right that gives the assignee the right to collect and keep the money. In contrast, the assignment may be held for security. In this case, the assignee may hold the money only as a security for some specified obligation.

Prohibition of Assignment of Rights

A clear and specific contractual prohibition against the assignment of rights is enforceable at common law. However, the UCC favors the assignment of contracts, and express contractual prohibitions on assignments are ineffective against (1) the assignment of rights to payment for goods or services, including accounts receivable,[15] and (2) the assignment of the rights to damages for breach of sales contracts.[16]

17-2e Nonassignable Rights

If the transfer of a right would materially affect or alter a duty or the rights of the obligor, an assignment is not permitted.[17]

Assignment Increasing Burden of Performance

When the assignment of a right would increase the burden of the obligor in performing, an assignment is ordinarily not permitted. To illustrate, if the assignor has the right to buy a certain quantity of a stated article and to take such property from the seller's warehouse, this right can be assigned. However, if the sales contract stipulates that the seller should deliver to the buyer's premises and the assignee's premises are a substantial distance from the assignor's place of business, the assignment would not be given effect. In this case, the seller would be required to give a different performance by providing greater transportation if the assignment were permitted.

Personal Services

Contracts for personal services are generally not assignable. **For Example,** were golf instructor David Ledbetter to sign a one-year contract to provide instruction for professional golfer Davis Love III, David Ledbetter could not assign his first assistant to provide the instruction, nor could Davis Love assign a protégé to receive instruction from Ledbetter.

---

[14] *Hayes v. Carlin America, Inc.*, 168 F. Supp. 2d 154 (S.D.N.Y. 2001).
[15] U.C.C. §9-318(4). This section of the UCC is applicable to most common commercial assignments.
[16] U.C.C. §2-210(2).
[17] *Aslakson v. Home Savings Ass'n*, 416 N.W.2d 786 (Minn. App. 1987) (increase of credit risk).

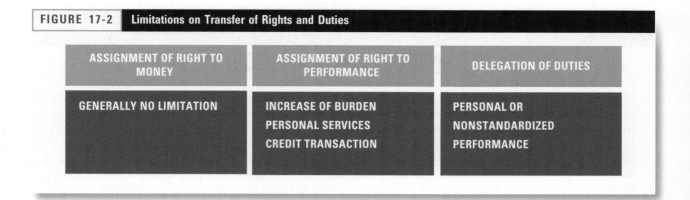

FIGURE 17-2   Limitations on Transfer of Rights and Duties

ASSIGNMENT OF RIGHT TO MONEY	ASSIGNMENT OF RIGHT TO PERFORMANCE	DELEGATION OF DUTIES
GENERALLY NO LIMITATION	INCREASE OF BURDEN PERSONAL SERVICES CREDIT TRANSACTION	PERSONAL OR NONSTANDARDIZED PERFORMANCE

Professional athletes and their agents commonly deal with assignment or trading rights of the athletes in their contracts with professional sports franchises.

There is a split among jurisdictions regarding whether employee noncompetition covenants are assignable to the new owner of a business absent employee consent. That is, some courts permit a successor employer to enforce an employee's noncompetition agreement as an assignee of the original employer. However, a majority of states that have considered this issue have concluded that restrictive covenants are personal in nature and not assignable. **For Example,** in September 2000, Philip Burkhardt signed a noncompetition agreement with his employer, NES Trench Shoring. On June 30, 2002, United Rentals Purchased NES with all contracts being assigned to United Rentals. Burkhardt stayed on with the new owner for five weeks and thereafter went to work for Traffic Control Services, a direct competitor of United. United was unsuccessful in its action to enforce the noncompetition covenant Burkhardt had signed with NES. Burkhardt's covenant with NES did not contain a clause allowing the covenant to be assigned to a new owner, and the court refused to enforce it, absent an express clause permitting assignment.[18]

Credit Transaction

When a transaction is based on extending credit, the person to whom credit is extended cannot assign any rights under the contract to another. **For Example,** Jack Aldrich contracted to sell his summer camp on Lake Sunapee to Pat Norton for $200,000, with $100,000 in cash due at the closing and the balance due on an installment basis secured by a mortgage on the property to be executed by Norton. Several days later, Norton found a more desirable property, and her sister Meg was very pleased to take over the Sunapee contract. Pat assigned her rights to Meg. Jack Aldrich, having received a better offer after contracting with Pat, refused to consent to the assignment. In this situation, the assignment to Meg is prohibited because the assignee, Meg, is a different credit risk even though the property to serve as security remained unchanged.

CPA   ### 17-2f **Rights of Assignee**

Unless restricted by the terms of the assignment or applicable law, the assignee acquires all the rights of the assignor.[19]

---

[18] *Traffic Control Sources, Inc. v. United Rentals Northwest, Inc.*, 87 P.3d 1054 (Nev. 2004).
[19] *Puget Sound National Bank v. Washington Department of Revenue*, 868 P.2d 127 (Wash. 1994).

CASE SUMMARY

An Example of An "Ironclad Contract"

FACTS: On July 7, 2006, Riviera Plaza Investments, LLC, by Haresh Shah, for value received, executed and delivered a Note by which it promised to pay Citibank the sum of $2,925,000.00 in monthly installment payments of principal plus interest. On the same date, Riviera, again by Mr. Shah, executed a Mortgage in order to secure the payment of the Note. Also on that date, Mr. Shah executed a Guaranty in favor of Citibank. Pursuant to the terms of the Guaranty, Shah guaranteed the prompt, complete, and full payment and performance of Riviera's obligations in accordance with the terms of the Note. Riviera failed to make its monthly payments and foreclosure proceedings were initiated in 2010. On February 9, 2011, Wells Fargo Bank was assigned the rights, title, and interest in the loan document and was substituted as the plaintiff in the foreclosure proceedings against Riviera and Shah in the trial court. As guarantor Shah contested litigation. From a judgment against Shah on his obligations under the Guaranty, Shah appealed.

DECISION: Judgment for Wells Fargo Bank. While it is true that guarantors are exonerated if the creditor alters the obligations of the principal without the guarantor's consent, the Guaranty expressly provided that: "this Guaranty shall follow the note and Security Instrument"… and "the holder of this Guaranty may enforce this Guaranty just as if said holder had been originally named as lender hereunder." [*Riviera Plaza Investments, LLC v. Wells Fargo Bank, N.A.,* 10 N.E.3d 541 (Ind. App. 2014)]

An assignee stands exactly in the position of the assignor. The assignee's rights are no more or less than those of the assignor. If the assigned right to payment is subject to a condition precedent, that same condition exists for the assignee. **For Example,** when a contractor is not entitled to receive the balance of money due under the contract until all bills of suppliers of materials have been paid, the assignee to whom the contractor assigns the balance due under the contract is subject to the same condition.

17-2g Continuing Liability of Assignor

The making of an assignment does not relieve the assignor of any obligation of the contract. In the absence of a contrary agreement, an assignor continues to be bound by the obligations of the original contract. **For Example,** boatbuilder Derecktor NY's assignment of obligations to a Connecticut boatbuilder did not release it from all liabilities under its boatbuilding contract with New York Water Taxi (NYWT); and NYWT was allowed to proceed against Derecktor NY for breach of contract–design and breach of contract–workmanship.[20]

When a lease is assigned, the assignee becomes the principal obligor for rent payments, and the leasee becomes a surety toward the lessor for the assignee's performance. **For Example,** Tri-State Chiropractic (TSC) held a five-year lease on premises at 6010 East Main Street in Columbus, Ohio. Without the leasor's consent, TSC assigned that lease to Dr. T. Wilson and Buckeye Chiropractic, LLC, prior to the expiration of the lease. TSC continues to be liable for rent as surety during the term of the lease, even if the leasor (owner) had consented to the assignment or accepted payment from the assignee.[21] In order to avoid liability as a surety, TSC would have to obtain a discharge of the lease by **novation,** in which all three parties agree that the original contract (the lease) would be discharged and a new lease between Dr. Wilson and the owner would

novation–substitution for an old contract with a new one that either replaces an existing obligation with a new obligation or replaces an original party with a new party.

---

[20] *New York Trans Harbor, LLC v. Derecktor Shipyards,* 841 N.Y.S.2d 821 (2007).
[21] *Schottenstein Trustees v. Carano,* 2000 WL 1455425 (Ohio App. 2000).

take effect. A novation allows for the discharge of a contractual obligation by the substitution of a new contract involving a new party.[22]

17-2h Liability of Assignee

It is necessary to distinguish between the question of whether the obligor can assert a particular defense against the assignee and the question of whether any person can sue the assignee. Ordinarily, the assignee is not subject to suit by virtue of the fact that the assignment has been made.

Consumer Protection Liability of Assignee

The assignee of the right to money may have no direct relationship to the original debtor except with respect to receiving payments. Consumer protection laws in most states, however, may subject the assignee to some liability for the assignor's misconduct.

Defenses and Setoffs

The assignee's rights are no greater than those of the assignor.[23] If the obligor could successfully defend against a suit brought by the assignor, the obligor will also prevail against the assignee.

The fact that the assignee has given value for the assignment does not give the assignee any immunity from defenses that the other party, the obligor, could have asserted against the assignor. The rights acquired by the assignee remain subject to any limitations imposed by the contract. Moreover, an assumption of obligations may be implied from an acceptance of benefits. **For Example,** Missouri Breaks, LLC, an entity formed under a bankruptcy reorganization plan that received assignment of the oil and gas leases of the now defunct entity Athens/Alpha Gas Corporation (Alpha), received the revenue from operation of the well under the leases and assumed the obligation to pay creditors. The court determined that Mission Breaks implicitly agreed to assume the liability to certain owners for unpaid royalties that were not discharged in the bankruptcy proceedings.[24]

17-2i Warranties of Assignor

When the assignment is made for a consideration, the assignor is regarded as providing an **implied warranty** that the right assigned is valid. The assignor also warrants that the assignor is the owner of the claim or right assigned and that the assignor will not interfere with the assignee's enforcement of the obligation.

implied warranty— warranty that was not made but is implied by law.

17-2j Delegation of Duties

A **delegation of duties** is a transfer of duties by a contracting party to another person who is to perform them. Under certain circumstances, a contracting party may obtain someone else to do the work. When the performance is standardized and nonpersonal, so that it is not material who performs, the law will permit the **delegation** of the performance of the contract. In such cases, however, the contracting party remains liable in the case of default of the person doing the work just as though no delegation had been made.[25]

delegation of duties— transfer of duties by a contracting party to another person who is to perform them.

delegation— transfer to another of the right and power to do an act.

---

[22] *Willamette Management Association, Inc. v. Palczynski*, 38 A.3d 1212 (Conn. App. 2012).
[23] *Shoreline Communications, Inc. v. Norwich Taxi, LLC*, 797 A.2d 1165 (Conn. App. 2002).
[24] *Van Sickle v. Hallmark & Associates, Inc.*, 840 N.W.2d 92, 105 (N.D. 2013).
[25] *Orange Bowl Corp. v. Warren*, 386 S.E.2d 293 (S.C. App. 1989).

FIGURE 17-3   **Can a Third Person Sue on a Contract?**

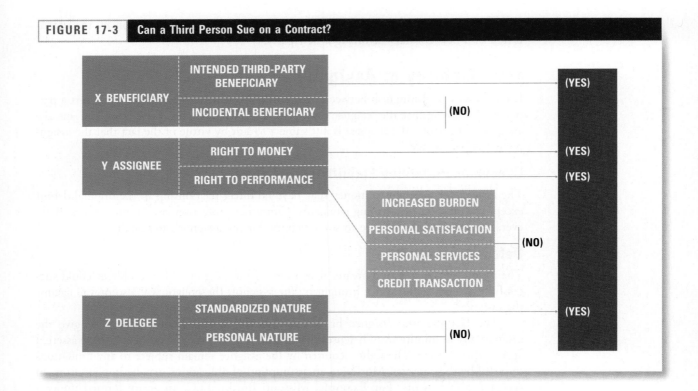

CASE SUMMARY

Who's Liable for $871,069 In Damages? Not Me. I Wasn't Even There!

FACTS: The Emersons contracted with Martin Winters, the owner of Winters Roofing Company, to install a new roof on their home. When the new roof leaked, Winters agreed to fix the problems. Without the knowledge of the Emersons, Winters hired a subcontractor, Bruce Jacobs, to perform the repair work. Jacobs's use of a propane torch in repairing the roof resulted in a fire that caused $871,069 in damages to the house and personal property. Federal Insurance Co. sued Winters to recover sums it paid the Emersons for damages resulting from the fire. Winters defended that Federal had sued the wrong party because

Winters did not participate in the repair work but had subcontracted the work out to Jacobs and was neither at the job site nor supervised Jacobs's work.

DECISION: Judgment for the plaintiff. Winters, based on his contract with the Emersons, had an implied duty under the contract to install the roof properly, skillfully, diligently, and in a workmanlike manner. The delegation of these duties to Jacobs did not serve to release Winters from liability implicit in the original content. [*Federal Insurance Co. v. Winters,* **354 S.W.3d 287 (Tenn. 2011)**]

A contract may prohibit a party owing a duty of performance under a contract from delegating that duty to another.[26] **For Example,** Tom Joyce of Patriot Plumbing Co. contracts to install a new heating system for Mrs. Lawton. A notation on the sales contract that Tom Joyce will do the installation prohibits Patriot Plumbing from delegating the installation to another equally skilled plumber or to another company if a backlog of work occurs at Patriot Plumbing.

[26] See *Physical Distribution Services, Inc. v. R. R. Donnelley,* 561 F.3d 792 (8th Cir. 2009).

If the performance of a party to a contract involves personal skill, talents, judgment, or trust, the delegation of duties is barred unless consented to by the person entitled to the performance. Examples include performance by professionals such as physicians, dentists, lawyers, consultants, celebrities, artists, and craftpersons with unusual skills.

Intention to Delegate Duties

An assignment of rights does not in itself delegate the performance of duties to the assignee. In the absence of clear language in the assignment stating that duties are or are not delegated, all circumstances must be examined to determine whether there is a delegation. When the total picture is viewed, it may become clear what was intended. The fact that an assignment is made for security of the assignee is a strong indication that there was no intent to delegate to the assignee the performance of any duty resting on the assignor.[27]

Delegation of Duties under the UCC

With respect to contracts for the sale of goods, "an assignment of 'the contract' or of 'all my rights under the contract' or an assignment in similar general terms is an assignment of rights and, unless the language or the circumstances (as in an assignment for security) indicate the contrary, it is a delegation of performance of the duties of the assignor, and its acceptance by the assignee constitutes a promise … to perform those duties. This promise is enforceable by either the assignor or the other party to the original contract."[28]

Make the Connection

- -

Summary

Ordinarily, only the parties to contracts have rights and duties with respect to such contracts. Exceptions are made in the case of third-party beneficiary contracts and assignments.

When a contract shows a clear intent to benefit a third person or class of persons, those persons are called *intended third-party beneficiaries*, and they may sue for breach of the contract. A third-party beneficiary is subject to any limitation or restriction found in the contract. A third-party beneficiary loses all rights when the original contract is terminated by operation of law or if the contract reserves the right to change the beneficiary and such a change is made.

In contrast, an incidental beneficiary benefits from the performance of a contract, but the conferring of this benefit was not intended by the contracting parties. An incidental beneficiary cannot sue on the contract.

An assignment is a transfer of a right; the assignor transfers a right to the assignee. In the absence of a local statute, there are no formal requirements for an assignment. Any words manifesting the intent to transfer are sufficient to constitute an assignment. No consideration is required. Any right to money may be assigned, whether the assignor is entitled to the money at the time of the assignment or will be entitled or expects to be entitled at some time in the future.

A right to a performance may be assigned except when (1) it would increase the burden of performance, (2) the contract involves the performance of personal services, or (3) the transaction is based on extending credit.

When a valid assignment is made, the assignee has the same rights—and only the same rights—as the assignor. The assignee is also subject to the same defenses and setoffs as the assignor had been.

[27] *City National Bank of Fort Smith v. First National Bank and Trust Co. of Rogers*, 732 S.W.2d 489 (Ark. App. 1987).
[28] U.C.C. §2-210(4).

The performance of duties under a contract may be delegated to another person except when a personal element of skill or judgment of the original contracting party is involved. The intent to delegate duties may be expressly stated. The intent may also be found in an "assignment" of "the contract" unless the circumstances make it clear that only the right to money was intended to be transferred. The fact that there has been a delegation of duties does not release the assignor from responsibility for performance. The assignor is liable for breach of the contract if the assignee does not properly perform the delegated duties. In the absence of an effective delegation or the formation of a third-party beneficiary contract, an assignee of rights is not liable to the obligee of the contract for its performance by the assignor.

Notice is not required to effect an assignment. When notice of the assignment is given to the obligor together with a demand that future payments be made to the assignee, the obligor cannot discharge liability by payment to the assignor.

When an assignment is made for a consideration, the assignor makes implied warranties that the right assigned is valid and that the assignor owns that right and will not interfere with its enforcement by the assignee.

Learning Outcomes

After studying this chapter, you should be able to clearly explain:

17-1   Third-Party Beneficiary Contracts

LO.1   Explain the two types of intended third-party beneficiaries

See the Sameway Laundry example that illustrates how the "intended creditor beneficiary" can sue the buyer, page 312.

See the *Prudential Insurance Co.* case, involving a life insurance contract and an "intended" donee third-party beneficiary's right to sue, pages 312–313.

LO.2   Explain why an incidental beneficiary does not have the right to sue as a third-party beneficiary

See the *City of Yorkville* example, in which a subcontractor was an incidental beneficiary with no standing to sue on performance bonds because the obligation ran only to the city, pages 314–315.

17-2   Assignments

LO.3   Define an assignment

See the text discussion explaining that an assignment is the transfer of contractual rights to a third party, page 315.

See the *Huntington Beach Board* example that discusses the assignee's direct rights against the obligor, page 316.

LO.4   Explain the general rule that a person entitled to receive money under a contract may generally assign that right to another person

See the example of an automobile dealer assigning a customer's credit contract to a finance company in order to raise cash to buy more inventory, page 317.

LO.5   List the nonassignable rights to performance

See the text discussion regarding increase of burden, personal services, and credit transactions, pages 318–319.

Key Terms

assignee	debtor	novation
assignment	delegation	obligee
assignor	delegation of duties	obligor
cause of action	duties	rights
claim	implied warranty	third-party beneficiary

Questions and Case Problems

1. Give an example of a third-party beneficiary contract.

2. A court order required John Baldassari to make specified payments for the support of his wife and child. His wife needed more money and applied for Pennsylvania welfare payments. In accordance with the law, she assigned to Pennsylvania her right to the support payments from her husband. Pennsylvania then increased her payments. Pennsylvania obtained a court order directing John, in accordance with the terms of the assignment from his wife, to make the support-order payments directly

to the Pennsylvania Department of Public Welfare. John refused to pay on the ground that he had not been notified of the assignment or the hearing directing him to make payment to the assignee. Was he correct? [*Pennsylvania v. Baldassari*, 421 A.2d 306 (Pa. Super.)]

3. Lee contracts to paint Sally's two-story house for $2,500. Sally realizes that she will not have sufficient money, so she transfers her rights under this agreement to her neighbor Karen, who has a three-story house. Karen notifies Lee that Sally's contract has been assigned to her and demands that Lee paint Karen's house for $2,500. Is Lee required to do so?

4. Assume that Lee agrees to the assignment of the house-painting contract to Karen as stated in question 3. Thereafter, Lee fails to perform the contract to paint Karen's house. Karen sues Sally for damages. Is Sally liable?

5. Jessie borrows $1,000 from Thomas and agrees to repay the money in 30 days. Thomas assigns the right to the $1,000 to Douglas Finance Co. Douglas sues Jessie. Jessie argues that she had agreed to pay the money only to Thomas and that when she and Thomas had entered into the transaction, there was no intention to benefit Douglas Finance Co. Are these objections valid?

6. Washington purchased an automobile from Smithville Motors. The contract called for payment of the purchase price in installments and contained the defense preservation notice required by the Federal Trade Commission regulation. Smithville assigned the contract to Rustic Finance Co. The car was always in need of repairs, and by the time it was half paid for, it would no longer run. Washington canceled the contract. Meanwhile, Smithville had gone out of business. Washington sued Rustic for the amount she had paid Smithville. Rustic refused to pay on the grounds that it had not been at fault. Decide.

7. Helen obtained an insurance policy insuring her life and naming her niece Julie as beneficiary. Helen died, and about a year later the policy was found in her house. When Julie claimed the insurance money, the insurer refused to pay on the ground that the policy required that notice of death be given to it promptly following the death. Julie claimed that she was not bound by the time limitation because she had never agreed to it, as she was not a party to the insurance contract. Is Julie entitled to recover?

8. Lone Star Life Insurance Co. agreed to make a long-term loan to Five Forty Three Land, Inc., whenever that corporation requested one. Five Forty Three wanted this loan to pay off its short-term debts. The loan was never made, as it was never requested by Five Forty Three, which owed the Exchange Bank & Trust Co. on a short-term debt. Exchange Bank then sued Lone Star for breach of its promise on the theory that the Exchange Bank was a third-party beneficiary of the contract to make the loan. Was the Exchange Bank correct? [*Exchange Bank & Trust Co. v. Lone Star Life Ins. Co.*, 546 S.W.2d 948 (Tex. App.)]

9. The New Rochelle Humane Society made a contract with the city of New Rochelle to capture and impound all dogs running at large. Spiegler, a minor, was bitten by some dogs while in her schoolyard. She sued the school district of New Rochelle and the Humane Society. With respect to the Humane Society, she claimed that she was a third-party beneficiary of the contract that the Humane Society had made with the city. She claimed that she could therefore sue the Humane Society for its failure to capture the dogs that had bitten her. Was she entitled to recover? [*Spiegler v. School District of the City of New Rochelle*, 242 N.Y.S.2d 430]

10. Zoya operated a store in premises rented from Peerless. The lease required Zoya to maintain liability insurance to protect Zoya and Peerless. Caswell entered the store, fell through a trap door, and was injured. She then sued Zoya and Peerless on the theory that she was a third-party beneficiary of the lease requirement to maintain liability insurance. Was she correct? [*Caswell v. Zoya Intl*, 654 N.E.2d 552 (Ill. App.)]

11. Henry was owed $10,000 by Jones Corp. In consideration of the many odd jobs performed for him over the years by his nephew, Henry assigned the $10,000 claim to his nephew Charles. Henry died, and his widow claimed that the assignment was ineffective so that the claim was part of Henry's estate. She based her assertion on the ground that the past performance rendered by the nephew was not consideration. Was the assignment effective?

12. Ibberson Co., the general contractor hired by AgGrow Oils, LLC, to design and build an oilseed processing plant, contracted with subcontractor Anderson International Corp. to supply critical seed

processing equipment for the project. Anderson's formal proposal to Ibberson identified the AgGrow Oils Project, and the proposal included drawings of the planned AgGrow plant. The project was a failure. Does AgGrow Oils have standing to sue Anderson under the Anderson-Ibberson contract? Explain. [*AgGrow Oils, LLC v. National Union Fire Inc.*, 420 F.2d 751 (8th Cir.)]

13. The Ohio Department of Public Welfare made a contract with an accountant to audit the accounts of health care providers who were receiving funds under the Medicaid program. Windsor House, which operated six nursing homes, claimed that it was a third-party beneficiary of that contract and could sue for its breach. Was it correct? [*Thornton v. Windsor House, Inc.*, 566 N.E.2d 1220 (Ohio)]

CPA Questions

1. On August 1, Neptune Fisheries contracted in writing with West Markets to deliver to West 3,000 pounds of lobster at $4.00 a pound. Delivery of the lobsters was due October 1, with payment due November 1. On August 4, Neptune entered into a contract with Deep Sea Lobster Farms that provided as follows: "Neptune Fisheries assigns all the rights under the contract with West Markets dated August 1 to Deep Sea Lobster Farms." The best interpretation of the August 4 contract would be that it was:

   a. Only an assignment of rights by Neptune.

   b. Only a delegation of duties by Neptune.

   c. An assignment of rights and a delegation of duties by Neptune.

   d. An unenforceable third-party beneficiary contract.

2. Graham contracted with the city of Harris to train and employ high school dropouts residing in Harris. Graham breached the contract. Long, a resident of Harris and a high school dropout, sued Graham for damages. Under the circumstances, Long will:

   a. Win, because Long is a third-party beneficiary entitled to enforce the contract.

   b. Win, because the intent of the contract was to confer a benefit on all high school dropouts residing in Harris.

   c. Lose, because Long is merely an incidental beneficiary of the contract.

   d. Lose, because Harris did not assign its contract rights to Long.

3. Union Bank lent $200,000 to Wagner. Union required Wagner to obtain a life insurance policy naming Union as beneficiary. While the loan was outstanding, Wagner stopped paying the premiums on the policy. Union paid the premiums, adding the amounts paid to Wagner's loan. Wagner died, and the insurance company refused to pay the policy proceeds to Union. Union may:

   a. Recover the policy proceeds because it is a creditor beneficiary.

   b. Not recover the policy proceeds because it is a donee beneficiary.

   c. Not recover the policy proceeds because it is not in privity of contract with the insurance company.

   d. Not recover the policy proceeds because it is only an incidental beneficiary.

Discharge of Contracts

Learning Outcomes ‹‹‹

After studying this chapter, you should be able to

LO.1 List the three types of conditions that affect a party's duty to perform

LO.2 Explain the on-time performance rule

LO.3 Explain the adequacy of performance rules

LO.4 Explain four ways a contract can be discharged by agreement of the parties

LO.5 State the effect on a contract of the death or disability of one of the contracting parties

LO.6 Explain when impossibility or impracticability may discharge a contract

In the preceding chapters, you studied how a contract is formed, what a contract means, and who has rights under a contract. In this chapter, attention is turned to how a contract is ended or discharged. In other words, what puts an end to the rights and duties created by a contract?

18-1   Conditions Relating to Performance

As developed in the body of this chapter, the ordinary method of discharging obligations under a contract is by performance. Certain promises may be less than absolute and instead come into effect only upon the occurrence of a specified event, or an existing obligation may be extinguished when an event happens. These are conditional promises.

18-1a   Classifications of Conditions

condition–stipulation or prerequisite in a contract, will, or other instrument.

When the occurrence or nonoccurrence of an event, as expressed in a contract, affects the duty of a party to the contract to perform, the event is called a **condition.** Terms such as *if, provided that, when, after, as soon as, subject to,* and *on the condition that* indicate the creation of a condition.[1] Conditions are classified as *conditions precedent, conditions subsequent,* and *concurrent conditions.*

Condition Precedent

condition precedent– event that if unsatisfied would mean that no rights would arise under a contract.

A **condition precedent** is a condition that must occur before a party to a contract has an obligation to perform under the contract. **For Example,** a condition precedent to a contractor's (MasTec's) obligation to pay a subcontractor (MidAmerica) under a "pay-if-paid" by the owner (PathNet) clause in their subcontract agreement is the receipt of payment by MasTec from PathNet. The condition precedent—payment by the owner—did not occur due to bankruptcy, and, therefore, MasTec did not have an obligation to pay MidAmerica.[2]

CASE SUMMARY

A Blitz on Offense?

FACTS: Richard Blitz owns a piece of commercial property at 4 Old Middle Street. On February 2, 1998, Arthur Subklew entered into a lease with Blitz to rent the rear portion of the property. Subklew intended to operate an auto sales and repair business. Paragraph C of the lease was a zoning contingency clause that stated, "Landlord [plaintiff] will use Landlord's best efforts to obtain a written verification that Tenant can operate [an] Auto Sales and Repair Business at the demised premises. If Landlord is unable to obtain such commitment from the municipality, then this agreement shall be deemed null and void and Landlord shall immediately return deposit monies to Tenant." The zoning board approved the location only as a general repair business. When Subklew refused to occupy the premises, Blitz sued him for breach of contract.

---

[1] *Harmon Cable Communications v. Scope Cable Television, Inc.,* 468 N.W.2d 350 (Neb. 1990).

[2] *MidAmerica Construction Management, Inc. v. MasTec North America, Inc.,* 436 F.3d 1257 (10th Cir. 2006). But see *International Engineering Services, Inc. v. Scherer Construction Co.,* 74 So. 3d 53 (Fla. App. 2011), where a "pay-when-paid" provision was found to be ambiguous, resulting in the general contractor being liable for the payment to the subcontractor.

A Blitz on Offense? continued

DECISION: Judgment for Subklew. A condition precedent is a fact or event that the parties intend must exist before there is right to a performance. If the condition is not fulfilled, the right to enforce the contract does not come into existence.

Blitz's obligation to obtain written approval of a used car business was a condition precedent to the leasing agreement. Since it was not obtained, Blitz cannot enforce the leasing agreement. [***Blitz v. Subklew*, 810 A.2d 841 (Conn. App. 2002)**]

Condition Subsequent

condition subsequent— event whose occurrence or lack thereof terminates a contract.

The parties to a contract may agree that a party is obligated to perform a certain act or pay a certain sum of money, but the contract contains a provision that relieves the obligation on the occurrence of a certain event. That is, on the happening of a **condition subsequent,** such an event extinguishes the duty to thereafter perform. **For Example,** Chad Newly served as the weekend anchor on *Channel 5 News* for several years. The station manager, Tom O'Brien, on reviewing tapes in connection with Newly's contract renewal, believed that Newly's speech on occasion was slightly slurred, and he suspected that it was from alcohol use. In the parties' contract discussions, O'Brien expressed his concerns about an alcohol problem and offered help. Newly denied there was a problem. O'Brien agreed to a new two-year contract with Newly at $190,000 for the first year and $220,000 for the second year with other benefits subject to "the condition" that the station reserved the right to make four unannounced drug-alcohol tests during the contract term; and should Newly test positive for drugs or alcohol under measurements set forth in the contract, then all of Channel 5's obligations to Newly under the contract would cease. When Newly subsequently failed a urinalysis test three months into the new contract, the happening of this event extinguished the station's obligation to employ and pay him under the contract. Conditions subsequent are strictly construed, and where ambiguous, are construed against forfeiture.[3]

SPORTS & ENTERTAINMENT LAW

Endorsement Contracts

Sports marketing involves the use of famous athletes to promote the sale of products and services in our economy. Should an athlete's image be tarnished by allegations of immoral or illegal conduct, a company could be subject to financial losses and corporate embarrassment. Endorsement contracts may extend for multiyear periods, and should a "morals" issue arise, a company would be well served to have had a broad morals clause in its contract that would allow the company at its sole discretion to summarily terminate the endorsement contract. Representatives of athletes, on the other hand, seek narrow contractual language that allows for termination of endorsement contracts only upon the indictment for a crime, and they seek the right to have an arbitrator, as opposed to the employer, make the determination as to whether the morals

clause was violated. John Daly's endorsement contract with Callaway Golf was terminated by the company when he violated his good conduct clause that restricted gambling and drinking activities; and NFL running back Adrian Peterson's endorsement contracts were canceled after he injured his four-year-old son by spanking him with a wooden switch. Nike, RadioShack, and other sponsors ended their relationships (with an estimated value of $10 million a year) with cyclist Lance Armstrong after he admitted taking performance enhancing drugs.

Can the courts be utilized to resolve controversies over whether a "morals clause" has been violated? If so, is the occurrence of a morals clause violation a condition precedent or a condition subsequent?

[3] *Cardone Trust v. Cardone*, 8 A.3d 1 (N.H. 2010).

Concurrent Condition

In most bilateral contracts, the performances of the parties are *concurrent conditions.* That is, their mutual duties of performance under the contract are to take place simultaneously. **For Example,** concerning a contract for the sale and delivery of certain goods, the buyer must tender to the seller a certified check at the time of delivery as set forth in the contract, and the seller must tender the goods to the buyer at the same time.

18-2   Discharge by Performance

When it is claimed that a contract is discharged by performance, questions arise as to the nature, time, and sufficiency of the performance.

18-2a   Normal Discharge of Contracts

A contract is usually discharged by the performance of the terms of the agreement. In most cases, the parties perform their promises and the contract ceases to exist or is thereby discharged. A contract is also discharged by the expiration of the time period specified in the contract.[4]

18-2b   Nature of Performance

Performance may be the doing of an act or the making of payment.

Tender

tender–goods have arrived, are available for pickup, and the buyer is notified.

An offer to perform is known as a **tender.** If performance of the contract requires the doing of an act, the refusal of a tender discharges the party offering to perform and is a basis for that party to bring a lawsuit.

A valid tender of payment consists of an unconditional offer of the exact amount due on the date when due. A tender of payment is not just an expression of willingness to pay; it must be an actual offer to perform by making payment of the amount owed.

Payment

When the contract requires payment, performance consists of the payment of money.

Application of Payments. If a debtor owes more than one debt to the creditor and pays money, a question may arise as to which debt has been paid. If the debtor specifies the debt to which the payment is to be applied and the creditor accepts the money, the creditor is bound to apply the money as specified.[5] Thus, if the debtor specifies that a payment is to be made for a current purchase, the creditor may not apply the payment to an older balance.

Payment by Check. Payment by commercial paper, such as a check, is ordinarily a conditional payment. A check merely suspends the debt until the check is presented for payment. If payment is then made, the debt is discharged; if not paid, the suspension terminates, and suit may be brought on either the debt or the check. Frequently, payment must be made by a specified date. It is generally held that the payment is made on time if it is mailed on or before the final date for payment.

---

[4] *Washington National Ins. Co. v. Sherwood Associates,* 795 P.2d 665 (Utah App. 1990).
[5] *Oakes Logging, Inc. v. Green Crow, Inc.,* 832 P.2d 894 (Wash. App. 1992).

CASE SUMMARY

The Mailed-Check Payment

FACTS: Thomas Cooper was purchasing land from Peter and Ella Birznieks. Cooper was already in possession of the land but was required to pay the amount owed by January 30; otherwise, he would have to vacate the property. The attorney handling the transaction for the Birznieks told Cooper that he could mail the payment to him. On January 30, Cooper mailed to the attorney a personal check drawn on an out-of-state bank for the amount due. The check arrived at the Birznieks' attorney's office on February 1. The Birznieks refused to accept the check on the grounds that it was not a timely payment and moved to evict Cooper from the property.

DECISION: Because of the general custom to regard a check mailed to a creditor as paying the bill that is owed, payment was made by Cooper on January 30 when he mailed the check. Payment was therefore made within the required time even though received after the expiration of the required time. [*Birznieks v. Cooper*, 275 N.W.2d 221 (Mich. 1979)]

18-2c Time of Performance

When the date or period of time for performance is specified in the contract, performance should be made on that date or within that time period.

No Time Specified

When the time for performance is not specified in the contract, an obligation to perform within a reasonable time is implied.[6] The fact that no time is specified neither impairs the contract on the ground that it is indefinite nor allows an endless time in which to perform. What constitutes a reasonable time is determined by the nature of the subject matter of the contract and the facts and circumstances surrounding the making of the contract.

When Time Is Essential

If performance of the contract on or within the exact time specified is vital, it is said that "time is of the essence." Time is of the essence when the contract relates to property that is perishable or that is fluctuating rapidly in value. When a contract fixes by unambiguous language a time for performance and where there is no evidence showing that the parties did not intend that time should be of the essence, failure to perform within the specified time is a breach of contract entitling the innocent party to damages. **For Example,** Dixon and Gandhi agreed that Gandhi would close on the purchase of a motel as follows: "Closing Date. The closing shall be held … on the date which is within twenty (20) days after the closing of Nomura Financing." Gandhi did not close within the time period specified, and Dixon was allowed to retain $100,000 in prepaid closing costs and fees as liquidated damages for Gandhi's breach of contract.[7]

When Time Is Not Essential

Unless a contract so provides, time is ordinarily not of the essence, and performance within a reasonable time is sufficient. In the case of the sale of property, time is not

---

[6] *First National Bank v. Clark,* 447 S.E.2d 558 (W. Va. 1994).
[7] *Woodhull Corp. v. Saibaba Corp.,* 507 S.E.2d 493 (Ga. App. 1998).

regarded as of the essence when there has not been any appreciable change in the market value or condition of the property and when the person who delayed does not appear to have done so for the purpose of speculating on a change in market price.

Waiver of Essence of Time Limitation

A provision that time is of the essence may be waived. It is waived when the specified time has expired but the party who could complain requests the delaying party to take steps necessary to perform the contract.

18-2d Adequacy of Performance

When a party renders exactly the performance called for by the contract, no question arises as to whether the contract has been performed. In other cases, there may not have been a perfect performance, or a question arises as to whether the performance satisfies the standard set by the contract.

CPA

Substantial Performance

Perfect performance of a contract is not always possible when dealing with construction projects. A party who in good faith has provided **substantial performance** of the contract may sue to recover the payment specified in the contract.[8] However, because the performance was not perfect, the performing party is subject to a counterclaim for the damages caused the other party. When a building contractor has substantially performed the contract to construct a building, the contractor is responsible for the cost of repairing or correcting the defects as an offset from the contract price.[9]

The measure of damages under these circumstances is known as "cost of completion" damages.[10] If, however, the cost of completion would be unreasonably disproportionate to the importance of the defect, the measure of damages is the diminution in value of the building due to the defective performance.

Whether there is substantial performance is a question of degree to be determined by all of the facts, including the particular type of structure involved, its intended purpose, and the nature and relative expense of repairs.

For Example, a certain building contractor (BC) and a certain owner (O) made a contract to construct a home overlooking Vineyard Sound on Martha's Vineyard according to plans and specifications that clearly called for the use of General Plumbing Blue Star piping. The contract price was $1,100,000. Upon inspecting the work before making the final $400,000 payment and accepting the building, O discovered that BC had used Republic piping throughout the house. O explained to BC that his family had made its money by investing in General Plumbing, and he, therefore, would not make the final payment until the breach of contract was remedied. BC explained that Republic pipes were of the same industrial grade and quality as the Blue Star pipes. Moreover, BC estimated that it would cost nearly $300,000 to replace all of the pipes because of the destruction of walls and fixtures necessary to accomplish such a task. BC may sue O for $400,000 for breach of contract, claiming he had substantially performed the contract, and O may counterclaim for $300,000, seeking an offset for the cost of remedying the breach. The court will find in favor of the contractor and will not allow the $300,000 offset but will allow a "nominal" offset of perhaps $100 to $1,000 for the amount by

substantial performance—equitable rule that if a good-faith attempt to perform does not precisely meet the terms of the agreement, the agreement will still be considered complete if the essential purpose of the contract is accomplished.

---

[8] *Gala v. Harris,* 77 So. 3d 1065 (La. App. 2012).

[9] Substantial performance is not a defense to a breach of contract claim, however. See *Bentley Systems Inc. v. Intergraph Corp.,* 922 So. 2d 61 (Ala. 2005).

[10] *Hammer Construction Corp. v. Phillips,* 994 So. 2d 1135 (Fla. App. 2008).

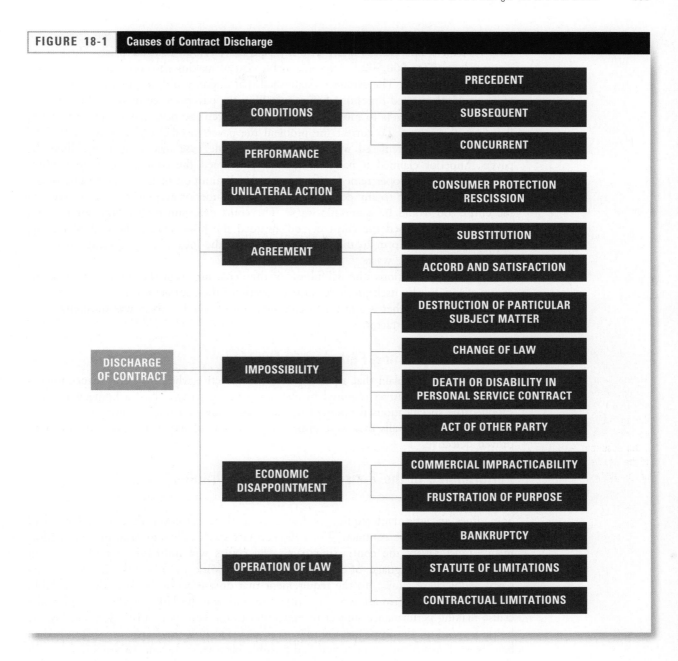

FIGURE 18-1   Causes of Contract Discharge

which the Republic pipes diminished the value of the building. To have required the pipes to be replaced would amount to economic waste.[11]

When a contractor does not substantially perform its obligations under a contract, not only will the contractor not prevail in a breach of contract claim against a homeowner for extra work beyond the contract price but the contractor is liable for the reasonable cost of making the contractor's work conform to the contract. **For Example,** Superior Wall and Paver, LLC, sued homeowners Pamela and Mark Gacek for $14,350 it claimed

[11] See *Jacob & Youngs, Inc. v. Kent,* 230 N.Y. 239 (1921).

was still owed Superior as extra work, for concrete pavers it installed in the driveway of their residence. The Gaceks had previously paid the $45,000 contract price. The Gaceks counterclaimed for $60,500 for the reasonable cost of making the contractor's work conform to the contract. The evidence established that Superior did not install a proper base of 3″ to 4″ of crushed limestone before installing the pavers as required by the contract, which caused the pavers to move, creating gaps between the pavers and causing water to flow into the garage. To correct the problem the pavers needed to be removed and the area excavated and replaced with a crushed limestone base before again installing the pavers. Superior claimed it had substantially performed the contract as a fully usable driveway, and the proper remedy, if any, was the diminution of the market value of the Gaceks' property due to any defective performance. Superior asserted the cost of redoing the entire job would be economic waste. The court determined that Superior had not substantially performed the contract and awarded the homeowners the cost of making Superior's work conform to the contract by having the job redone, rejecting Superior's assertion of economic waste.[12]

In most jurisdictions, the willfulness of the departure from the specifications of the contract does not by itself preclude some recovery for the contractor on the "cost of completion" basis but rather is a factor in consideration of whether there was substantial performance by the contractor.[13]

Fault of Complaining Party

A party cannot complain that a performance was defective when the performance follows the terms of the contract required by the complaining party. Thus, a homeowner who supplied the specifications for poured cement walls could not hold a contractor liable for damages when the walls that were poured in exact compliance with those specifications proved defective.

Performance to the Satisfaction of the Contracting Party or a Third Party

Sometimes an agreement requires performance to the satisfaction, taste, or judgment of the other party to the contract. When the contract specifically stipulates that the performance must satisfy the contracting party, the courts will ordinarily enforce the plain meaning of the language of the parties and the work must satisfy the contracting party—subject, of course, to the requirement that dissatisfaction be made in good faith. **For Example,** the Perrones' written contract to purchase the Hills' residence contained a clause making performance subject to inspection to the Perrones' satisfaction. During the house inspection, the inspector found a piece of wood in a crawl space that appeared to have been damaged by termites and had possibly been treated some 18 years before with chlordane. At the end of the inspection Mr. Perrone indicated that he would perform on the contract. Thereafter, he went on the Internet and found that chlordane is a highly toxic pesticide now banned from use as a termite treatment. As a result, the Perrones rescinded the contract under the buyer satisfaction clause. The Hills sued, believing that speculation about a pesticide treatment 18 years ago was absurd. They contended that the Perrones had breached the contract without a valid reason. The court decided for the

---

[12] *Superior Wall and Paver, LLC v. Gacek,* 73 So. 3d (Ala. App. 2011).
[13] But see *USX Corp. v. M. DeMatteo Construction Co.,* 315 F.3d 43 (1st Cir. 2002), for application of a common law rule that prohibits a construction contractor guilty of a willful breach of contract from maintaining any suit on the contract against the other party.

Perrones, since they exercised the "satisfaction clause" in good faith.[14] Good-faith personal satisfaction is generally required when the subject matter of the contract is personal, such as interior design work, tailoring, or the painting of a portrait.

With respect to things mechanical or routine performances, courts require that the performance be such as would satisfy a reasonable person under the circumstances.

When work is to be done subject to the approval of an architect, an engineer, or another expert, most courts apply the reasonable person test of satisfaction.

18-3 Discharge by Action of Parties

Contracts may be discharged by the joint action of both contracting parties or, in some cases, by the action of one party alone.

18-3a Discharge by Unilateral Action

rescission–action of one party to a contract to set the contract aside when the other party is guilty of a breach of the contract.

Ordinarily, a contract cannot be discharged by the action of either party alone. In some cases, however, the contract gives one of either party the right to cancel the contract by unilateral action, such as by notice to the other party. Insurance policies covering loss commonly provide that the insurer may cancel the policy upon giving a specified number of days' notice.

substitution–substitution of a new contract between the same parties.

Consumer Protection Rescission

A basic principle of contract law is that once made, a contract between competent persons is a binding obligation. Consumer protection legislation introduces into the law a contrary concept—that of giving the consumer a chance to think things over and to rescind the contract. Thus, the federal Consumer Credit Protection Act (CCPA) gives the debtor the right to rescind a credit transaction within three business days when the transaction would impose a lien on the debtor's home. **For Example,** a homeowner who mortgages his or her home to obtain a loan may cancel the transaction for any reason by notifying the lender before midnight of the third full business day after the loan is made.[15]

accord and satisfaction–agreement to substitute for an existing debt some alternative form of discharging that debt, coupled with the actual discharge of the debt by the substituted performance.

A Federal Trade Commission regulation gives the buyer three business days in which to cancel a home-solicited sale of goods or services costing more than $25.[16]

18-3b Discharge by Agreement

release–an instrument by which the signing party (releasor) relinquishes claims or potential claims against one or more persons (releasees) who might otherwise be subject to liability to the releasor.

A contract may be discharged by the operation of one of its provisions or by a subsequent agreement. Thus, there may be a discharge by (1) the terms of the original contract, such as a provision that the contract should end on a specified date; (2) a mutual cancellation, in which the parties agree to end their contract; (3) a mutual **rescission,** in which the parties agree to annul the contract and return both parties to their original positions before the contract had been made; (4) the **substitution** of a new contract between the same parties; (5) a novation or substitution of a new contract involving a new party;[17] (6) an **accord and satisfaction;** (7) a **release;** or (8) a **waiver.**

waiver–release or relinquishment of a known right or objection.

---

[14] *Hill v. Perrones,* 42 P.3d 210 (Kan. App. 2002).

[15] If the owner is not informed of this right to cancel, the three-day period does not begin until that information is given. Consumer Credit Protection Act §125, 15 U.S.C. §1635(a), (e), (f).

[16] C.F.R. §429.1.

[17] *Eagle Industries, Inc. v. Thompson,* 900 P.2d 475 (Or. 1995). In a few jurisdictions, the term *novation* is used to embrace the substitution of any new contract, whether between the original parties or not.

Substitution

The parties may decide that their contract is not the one they want. They may then replace it with another contract. If they do, the original contract is discharged by substitution.[18]

Accord and Satisfaction

When the parties have differing views as to the performance required by the terms of a contract, they may agree to a different performance. Such an agreement is called an *accord.* When the accord is performed or executed, there is an accord and satisfaction, which discharges the original obligation. To constitute an accord and satisfaction, there must be a bona fide dispute, a proposal to settle the dispute, and performance of the agreement.

CASE SUMMARY

A Full Court Press to No Avail

FACTS: In September 2002, La Crosse Litho Supply, LLC (La Crosse), entered into a distribution agreement with MKL Pre-Press Electronics (MKL) for the distribution of a printing system. La Crosse purchased a 7000 System unit from MKL for its end user Printing Plus. MKL technicians were to provide service and training for the unit. The 7000 System at Printing Plus failed on three occasions, and ultimately repairs were unsuccessful. On September 30, 2003, La Crosse canceled the distribution agreement. On October 2, 2003, La Crosse sent a letter to MKL's sales vice president Bill Landwer setting forth an itemized accounting of what it owed MKL Pre-Press with deductions for the purchase price of the failed 7000 System and other offsets. MKL sent a subsequent bill for repairs and services, to which La Crosse objected and stated that it would not pay. MKL's attorney sent a demand letter for $26,453.31. La Crosse's president, Randall Peters, responded by letter dated December 30, 2003, explaining that with an offset for training and warranty work it had performed, "we are sending you the final payment in the amount of $1,696.47." He added, "[w]ith this correspondence, we consider all open issues between La Crosse Litho Supply and MKL Pre-Press closed." Enclosed

with the letter was a check for $1,696.47 payable to MKL Pre-Press. In the remittance portion of the check, under the heading "Ref," was typed "FINAL PAYM." The check was endorsed and deposited on either January 26 or 27, 2004. MKL sued La Crosse for $24,756.84. La Crosse defended that the tender and subsequent deposit of the check for $1,696.47 constituted an accord and satisfaction. Jill Fleming, MKL's office manager, stated that it was her duty to process checks and that she did not read Peters' letter. From a judgment for La Crosse, MKL appealed.

DECISION: Judgment for La Crosse. There was an honest dispute as to the amount owed, as evident from the exchange of letters. La Crosse tendered an amount with the explicit understanding that it was the "final payment" of all demands, and the creditor MKL's acceptance and negotiation of a check for that amount constitutes an accord and satisfaction. Ms. Fleming had the authority to endorse checks and deposit them, and her doing so can and should be imputed to her employer, thereby constituting an accord and satisfaction. [*MKL Pre-Press Electronics v. La Crosse Litho Supply, LLC*, 840 N.E.2d 687 (Ill. App. 2005)]

Release

A release is an instrument by which the signing party (releasor) relinquishes claims or potential claims against one or more persons (releasees) who might otherwise be subject to liability to the releasor. The existence of a valid release is a complete defense to a tort action against the releasee. **For Example,** Heriberto Rodriguez, while driving a Hertz rental car, was injured in a collision with a vehicle operated by Takeshi Oto, who was

[18] See *Foti Fuels, Inc. v. Kurrle Corp.,* 90 A.3d 885 (Vt. 2013).

on company related business for his employer Toshiba of America. Heriberto settled with Hertz for $25,000.00, the limit of the Hertz coverage of the vehicle and signed a written release in favor of Hertz and Oto "and all other persons, firms, corporations, associations or partnerships." Later, Rodriquez filed a negligence action against Oto and Toshiba of America. The settlement releasing "all persons ... and corporations" applied to Oto and Toshiba and was a complete defense in this case.[19]

18-4 Discharge by External Causes

Circumstances beyond the control of the contracting parties may discharge the contract.

18-4a Discharge by Impossibility

To establish impossibility a party must show (1) the unexpected occurrence of an intervening act; (2) that the risk of the unexpected occurrence was not allocated by agreement or custom; and (3) that the occurrence made performance impossible. The doctrine of impossibility relieves nonperformance only in extreme circumstances.[20] The party asserting the defense of impossibility bears the burden of proving "a real impossibility and not a mere inconvenience or unexpected difficulty."[21] Moreover, courts will generally only excuse nonperformance where performance is objectively impossible—that is, incapable performance by anyone. Financial inability to perform a contract that a party voluntarily entered into will rarely, if ever, excuse nonperformance. **For Example,** Ms. Robinson was employed by East Capital Community Development Group under a written employment contract for one year but was terminated early for lack of funding. The contract did not reference that her continued employment was contingent on continued grant funding. The contract was objectively capable of performance. The defense of impossibility was rejected by the court.[22]

Destruction of Particular Subject Matter

When parties contract expressly for, or with reference to, a particular subject matter, the contract is discharged if the subject matter is destroyed through no fault of either party. When a contract calls for the sale of a wheat crop growing on a specific parcel of land, the contract is discharged if that crop is destroyed by blight.

On the other hand, if there is merely a contract to sell a given quantity of a specified grade of wheat, the seller is not discharged when the seller's crop is destroyed by blight. The seller had made an unqualified undertaking to deliver wheat of a specified grade. No restrictions or qualifications were imposed as to the source. If the seller does not deliver the goods called for by the contract, the contract is broken, and the seller is liable for damages.

Change of Law

A contract is discharged when its performance is made impossible, impractical, or illegal by a subsequent change in the law. A contract to construct a nonfireproof building at a particular place is discharged by the adoption of a zoning law prohibiting such a building within that area. Mere inconvenience or temporary delay caused by the new law, however, does not excuse performance.

[19] *Rodriquez v. Oto*, 151 Cal. Rptr. 3d 667 (Cal. App. 2013).
[20] *Island Development Corp. v. District of Columbia*, 933 A.2d 340, 350 (D.C. 2007).
[21] *Bergmann v. Parker*, 216 A.2d 581 (D.C. 1966).
[22] *East Capital View Community Development Corp. v. Robinson*, 941 A.2d 1036 (D.C. 2008).

CASE SUMMARY

If you're fond of sand dunes, and salty air...
... served by a window with an ocean view
You're not at the Petrozzi's house in Ocean City

FACTS: To rectify seashore protection problems, the City of Ocean City in 1989 participated in a beach replenishment and sand dunes restoration program. The Army Corps of Engineers required Ocean City to have access rights where sand was to be placed. To ease property owners' concerns over their beach front views, Ocean City proposed easements under which it would construct and maintain the dune system with height limitations of no greater than three feet above the average elevation of block bulkheads. From May 1992 to December 1995 Ocean City acquired the necessary easements. Between 1992 and 2000 natural accretion caused the dunes to grow in height and width. After 1994 the Coastal Area Facilities Review Act (CAFRA) required municipalities to receive written authorization from the Department of Environmental Protection (DEP) for dunes maintenance. Ocean City's permit applications to reduce the height of existing sand dunes was denied by the DEP. Owners of the beach front properties sued for breach of its easement agreements. From the dismissal of their claims by the trial court, certain owners appealed.

DECISION: Decision for the property owners. The 1994 CAFRA amendments rendered impossible Ocean City's performance under the easement agreements in question. Impossibility or impracticability of performance are compete defenses where a fact essential to performance is assumed by the parties but does not exist at the time of performance. Yet the fact remains that the plaintiffs gave up their rights to compensation in reliance on Ocean City's promise to protect their ocean views. The owners are entitled to damages for the loss of their ocean views. [*Petrozzi v. City of Ocean City*, 433 N.J. Super. 290 (App. Div. 2013)]

Death or Disability

When the contract obligates a party to render or receive personal services requiring peculiar skill, the death, incapacity, or illness of the party that was either to render or receive the personal services excuses both sides from a duty to perform. It is sometimes said that "the death of either party is the death of the contract."

The rule does not apply, however, when the acts called for by the contract are of such a character that (1) the acts may be as well performed by others, such as the promisor's personal representatives, or (2) the contract's terms contemplate continuance of the obligations after the death of one of the parties. **For Example,** Lynn Jones was under contract to investor Ed Jenkins to operate certain Subway sandwich shops and to acquire new franchises with funding provided by Jenkins. After Jenkins's death, Jones claimed that he was no longer bound under the contract and was free to pursue franchise opportunities on his own. The contract between Jones and Jenkins expressed that it was binding on the parties' "heirs and assigns" and that the contract embodied property rights that passed to Jenkins's widow. The agreement's provisions thus established that the agreement survived the death of Jenkins, and Jones was therefore obligated to remit profits from the franchise he acquired for himself after Jenkins's death.[23]

Act of Other Party

Every contract contains "an implied covenant of good faith and fair dealing." As a result of this covenant, a promisee is under an obligation to do nothing that would interfere with the promisor's performance. When the promisee prevents performance or otherwise makes performance impossible, the promisor is discharged from the contract. Thus, a

---

[23] *Jenkins Subway, Inc. v. Jones*, 990 S.W.2d 713 (Tenn. App. 1998).

subcontractor is discharged from any obligation when it is unable to do the work because the principal contractor refuses to deliver the material, equipment, or money required by the subcontract. When the default of the other party consists of failing to supply goods or services, the duty may rest on the party claiming a discharge of the contract to show that substitute goods or services could not be obtained elsewhere.

18-4b Developing Doctrines

Commercial impracticability and frustration of purpose may excuse performance.

Commercial Impracticability

The doctrine of *commercial impracticability* was developed to deal with the harsh rule that a party must perform its contracts unless it is absolutely impossible. However, not every type of impracticability is an excuse for nonperformance. **For Example,** I. Patel was bound by his franchise agreement with Days Inn, Inc., to maintain his 60-room inn on old Route 66 in Lincoln, Illinois, to at least minimum quality assurance standards. His inn failed five consecutive quality inspections over two years, with the inspector noting damaged guest rooms, burns in the bedding, and severely stained carpets. Patel's defense when his franchise was canceled after the fifth failed inspection was that bridge repairs on the road leading from I-55 to his inn had adversely affected his business and made it commercially impractical to live up to the franchise agreement. The court rejected his defense, determining that while the bridge work might have affected patronage, it had no effect on his duty to comply with the quality assurance standards of his franchise agreement.[24] Commercial impracticability is available only when the performance is made impractical by the subsequent occurrence of an event whose nonoccurrence was a basic assumption on which the contract was made.[25]

The defense of commercial impracticability will not relieve sophisticated business entities from their contractual obligations due to an economic downturn, even one as drastic and severe as the recent recession. **For Example,** real estate developer Beemer Associates was not excused under this doctrine of commercial impracticability from performance of its construction loan payment obligation of $5,250,000 plus interest and fees where unanticipated changes in the financial and real estate markets made it unable to secure tenants at the expected rate.[26] Economic downturns and other market shifts do not constitute unanticipated circumstances in a market economy.[27]

Frustration of Purpose Doctrine

Because of a change in circumstances, the purpose of the contract may have no value to the party entitled to receive performance. In such a case, performance may be excused if both parties were aware of the purpose and the event that frustrated the purpose was unforeseeable.[28]

For Example, National Southern Bank rents a home near Willowbend Country Club on the southeastern shore of North Carolina for $75,000 a week to entertain business guests at the Ryder Cup matches scheduled for the week in question. Storm damage

---

[24] *Days Inn of America, Inc. v. Patel,* 88 F. Supp. 2d 928 (C.D. Ill. 2000).
[25] See Restatement (Second) of Contracts §261; U.C.C. §2-615.
[26] *LSREF2 Baron, LLC v. Beemer,* 2011 WL 6838163 (M.D. Fla. Dec. 29, 2011).
[27] *Flathead-Michigan I, LLC v. Peninsula Dev., LLC,* 2011 WL 940048 (E.D. Mich. March 16, 2011).
[28] The defense of frustration of purpose, or commercial frustration, is very difficult to invoke because the courts are extremely reluctant to allow parties to avoid obligations to which they have agreed. See *Wal-Mart Stores, Inc. v. AIG Life Insurance Co.,* 872 A.2d 611 (Del. Ch. 2005), denying application of the commercial frustration doctrine when the supervening event, the invalidation of hundreds of millions in tax deductions by the IRS, was reasonably foreseeable and could have been provided for in the contract.

from Hurricane David the week before the event caused the closing of the course and the transfer of the tournament to another venue in a different state. The bank's duty to pay for the house may be excused by the doctrine of *frustration of purpose*, because the transfer of the tournament fully destroyed the value of the home rental, both parties were aware of the purpose of the rental, and the cancellation of the golf tournament was unforeseeable.

Comparison to Common Law Rule

The traditional common law rule refuses to recognize commercial impracticability or frustration of purpose. By the common law rule, the losses and disappointments against which commercial impracticability and frustration of purpose give protection are merely the risks that one takes in entering into a contract. Moreover, the situations could have been guarded against by including an appropriate condition subsequent in the contract. A condition subsequent declares that the contract will be void if a specified event occurs.[29] The contract also could have provided for a readjustment of compensation if there was a basic change of circumstances. The common law approach also rejects these developing concepts because they weaken the stability of a contract.

An indication of a wider recognition of the concept that "extreme" changes of circumstances can discharge a contract is found in the Uniform Commercial Code (UCC). The UCC provides for the discharge of a contract for the sale of goods when a condition that the parties assumed existed, or would continue, ceases to exist.[30]

Force Majeure

To avoid litigation over impossibility and impracticability issues, modern contracting parties often contract around the doctrine of impossibility, specifying the failures that will excuse performance in their contracts. The clauses in which they do this are called *force majeure*—uncontrollable event—clauses. And they are enforced by courts as written.

18-4c Temporary Impossibility

Ordinarily, a temporary impossibility suspends the duty to perform. If the obligation to perform is suspended, it is revived on the termination of the impossibility. If, however, performance at that later date would impose a substantially greater burden on the party obligated to perform, some courts discharge the obligor from the contract.

After the September 11, 2001, terrorist attack on the World Trade Center, New York City courts followed wartime precedents that had developed the law of temporary impossibility. Such impossibility, when of brief duration, excuses performance until it subsequently becomes possible to perform rather than excusing performance altogether. Thus, an individual who was unable to communicate her cancellation of travel 60 days prior to her scheduled travel as required by her contract, which needed to occur on or before September 14, 2001, could expect relief from a cancellation penalty provision in the contract based on credible testimony of attempted phone calls to the travel agent on and after September 12, 2001, even though the calls did not get through due to communication problems in New York City.[31]

Weather

Acts of God, such as tornadoes, lightning, and floods, usually do not terminate a contract even though they make performance difficult. Thus, weather conditions constitute a risk

---

[29] *Wermer v. ABI*, 10 S.W.3d 575 (Mo. App. 2000).
[30] U.C.C. §2-615.
[31] See *Bugh v. Protravel International, Inc.*, 746 N.Y.S.2d 290 (Civ. Ct. N.Y.C. 2002).

that is assumed by a contracting party in the absence of a contrary agreement. Consequently, extra expense sustained by a contractor because of weather conditions is a risk that the contractor assumes in the absence of an express provision for additional compensation in such a case. **For Example,** Danielo Contractors made a contract to construct a shopping mall for the Rubicon Center, with construction to begin November 1. Because of abnormal cold and blizzard conditions, Danielo was not able to begin work until April 1 and was five months late in completing the construction of the project. Rubicon sued Danielo for breach of contract by failing to perform on schedule. Danielo is liable. Because the contract included no provision covering delay caused by weather, Danielo bore the risk of the delay and resulting loss.

Modern contracts commonly contain a "weather clause" and reflect the parties' agreement on this matter. When the parties take the time to discuss weather issues, purchasing insurance coverage is a common resolution.

18-4d Discharge by Operation of Law

A contract is discharged by **operation of law** by (1) an alteration or a material change made by a party, (2) the destruction of the written contract with intent to discharge it, (3) bankruptcy, (4) the operation of a statute of limitations, or (5) a contractual limitation.

Bankruptcy

As set forth in the chapter on bankruptcy, even though all creditors have not been paid in full, a discharge in **bankruptcy** eliminates ordinary contract claims against the debtor.

Statute of Limitations

A **statute of limitations** provides that after a certain number of years have passed, a contract claim is barred. The time limitation provided by state statutes of limitations varies widely. The time period for bringing actions for breach of an oral contract is two to three years. The period may differ with the type of contract—ranging from a relatively short time for open accounts (ordinary customers' charge accounts) to four years for sales of goods.[32] A somewhat longer period exists for bringing actions for breach of written contracts (usually 4 to 10 years). **For Example,** Prate Installations, Inc., sued homeowners Richard and Rebecca Thomas for failure to pay for a new roof installed by Prate. Prate had sent numerous invoices to the Thomases over a four-year period seeking payment to no avail. The Thomases moved to dismiss the case under a four-year limitation period. However, the court concluded that the state's 10-year limitations period on written contracts applied.[33] The maximum period for judgments of record is usually 10 to 20 years.

A breach of contract claim against a builder begins to run when a home's construction is substantially complete. **For Example,** a breach of contract claim against home builder Stewart Brockett was time barred under a state's six-year statute of limitations for breach of contract actions inasmuch as the home in question was substantially completed in September 2001 and the breach of contract action commenced on June 17, 2008.[34] A breach of contract claim not founded upon an instrument of writing may be governed by a two-year statute of limitations.

---

[32] U.C.C. §2-725(1).
[33] *Prate Installations, Inc. v. Thomas,* 842 N.E.2d 1205 (Ill. App. 2006).
[34] *New York Central Mutual Fire Insurance Co. v. Gilder Oil Co.,* 936 N.Y.S.2d 815 (Sup. Ct. A.D. 2011).

CASE SUMMARY

Tempus Fugit: File It on Time or Loose It!

FACTS: Larry Montz and Daena Smoller, the real parties in interest (RPIs) in this case pitched a concept for a television program entitled *Ghost Expeditions Haunted* (Concepts) to NBCUniversal Media, LLC (NBC) from 1996 to 2001. The RPIs claim that, after NBC informed them they were not interested in Concepts, NBC teamed up with another company to misappropriate and exploit their concepts by producing the hit series *Ghost Hunters* without permission or compensation. The *Ghost Hunters* show premiered on the Syfy cable channel on October 6, 2004. The RPIs filed their first lawsuit on November 8, 2006. The Superior Court denied NBC's motion for summary judgment, which asserted the claims were time-barred by the applicable two-year statute of limitations, and NBC appealed this decision.

DECISION: Judgment for NBC. The statute of limitations for implied contracts in California is two years from the time the last element of a cause of action is complete. In this case a suit for breach of an implied contract not to exploit an idea without paying for it arises with the sale or exploitation of the idea. Here, the accrual date is the date on which the work is released to the general public on television on October 6, 2004. Thus RPIs had until October 5, 2006, to file their lawsuit. They did not do so until November 8, 2006, resulting in the action being time-barred. While the "discovery rule" may operate to delay accrual of a cause of action where professionals such as a doctor or lawyer breaches a duty of care, for a layperson would lack ability to observe, evaluate or detect the wrongdoing; but such a rule is inapplicable here because the offending work was publicly televised. [*NBCUniversal Media, LLC v. Superior Court*, 171 Cal. Rptr. 3d 1 (Cal. App. 2014)]

Contractual Limitations

Some contracts, particularly insurance contracts, contain a time limitation within which suit must be brought. This is in effect a private statute of limitations created by the agreement of the parties.

A contract may also require that notice of any claim be given within a specified time. A party who fails to give notice within the time specified by the contract is barred from suing on the contract.

A contract provision requiring that suit be brought within one year does not violate public policy, although the statute of limitations would allow two years in the absence of such a contract limitation.[35]

Make the Connection

Summary

A party's duty to perform under a contract can be affected by a condition precedent, which must occur before a party has an obligation to perform; a condition subsequent, that is, a condition or event that relieves the duty to thereafter perform; and concurrent conditions, which require mutual and often simultaneous performance.

Most contracts are discharged by performance. An offer to perform is called a *tender of performance*. If a tender of performance is wrongfully refused, the duty of the tenderer to perform is terminated. When the performance called for by the contract is the payment of money, it must be legal tender that is offered. In actual practice, it is

---

[35] *Keiting v. Skauge*, 543 N.W.2d 565 (Wis. App. 1995).

common to pay and to accept payment by checks or other commercial paper.

When the debtor owes the creditor on several accounts and makes a payment, the debtor may specify which account is to be credited with the payment. If the debtor fails to specify, the creditor may choose which account to credit.

When a contract does not state when it is to be performed, it must be performed within a reasonable time. If time for performance is stated in the contract, the contract must be performed at the time specified if such time is essential (is of the essence). Ordinarily, a contract must be performed exactly in the manner specified by the contract. A less-than-perfect performance is allowed if it is a substantial performance and if damages are allowed the other party.

A contract cannot be discharged by unilateral action unless authorized by the contract itself or by statute, as in the case of consumer protection rescission.

Because a contract arises from an agreement, it may also be terminated by an agreement. A contract may also be discharged by the substitution of a new contract for the original contract; by a novation, or making a new contract with a new party; by accord and satisfaction; by release; or by waiver.

A contract is discharged when it is impossible to perform. Impossibility may result from the destruction of the subject matter of the contract, the adoption of a new law that prohibits performance, the death or disability of a party whose personal action was required for performance of the contract, or the act of the other party to the contract. Some courts will also hold that a contract is discharged when its performance is commercially impracticable or there is frustration of purpose. Temporary impossibility, such as a labor strike or bad weather, has no effect on a contract. It is common, though, to include protective clauses that excuse delay caused by temporary impossibility.

A contract may be discharged by operation of law. This occurs when (1) the liability arising from the contract is discharged by bankruptcy, (2) suit on the contract is barred by the applicable statute of limitations, or (3) a time limitation stated in the contract is exceeded.

Learning Outcomes

After studying this chapter, you should be able to clearly explain:

18-1   Conditions Relating to Performance

LO.1 List the three types of conditions that affect a party's duty to perform

See the "pay-if-paid" condition-precedent example in the section titled "Condition Precedent," page 328. See the TV anchor's "failed urinalysis test" condition subsequent example, page 329.

18-2   Discharge by Performance

LO.2 Explain the on-time performance rule

See the "mailed-check payment" example, page 331. See the "time is of the essence" example, page 331.

LO.3 Explain the adequacy of performance rules

See the application of the substantial performance rule to the nonconforming new home piping example, page 332.

See the effect of failure to substantially perform a contract in the *Superior Wall and Paver* case, pages 333–334.

18-3   Discharge by Action of Parties

LO.4 Explain four ways a contract can be discharged by agreement of the parties

See the text discussion on rescission, cancellation, substitution, and novation in the section titled "Discharge by Agreement," page 335.

18-4   Discharge by External Causes

LO.5 State the effect on a contract of the death or disability of one of the contracting parties

See the Subway sandwich shops example, page 338.

LO.6 Explain when impossibility or impracticability may discharge a contract

See the Ryder Cup frustration-of-purpose example, pages 339–340.

See the *Ocean City* impossibility case, which provided a remedy, page 338.

Key Terms

accord and satisfaction	operation of law	substitution
bankruptcy	release	tender
condition	rescission	waiver
condition precedent	statute of limitations	
condition subsequent	substantial performance	

Questions and Case Problems

1. CIT entered into a sale/leaseback contract with Condere Tire Corporation for 11 tire presses at Condere's tire plant in Natchez, Mississippi. Condere ceased making payments on these presses owned by CIT, and Condere filed for Chapter 11 bankruptcy. CIT thereafter contracted to sell the presses to Specialty Tires Inc. for $250,000. When the contract was made, CIT, Condere, and Specialty Tire believed that CIT was the owner of the presses and was entitled to immediate possession. When CIT attempted to gain access to the presses to have them shipped, Condere changed its position and refused to allow the equipment to be removed from the plant. When the presses were not delivered, Specialty sued CIT for damages for nondelivery of the presses, and CIT asserted the defense of impracticability. Decide. [*Specialty Tires, Inc. v. CIT*, 82 F. Supp. 2d 434 (W.D. Pa.)]

2. Lymon Mitchell operated a Badcock Home Furnishings dealership, under which as dealer he was paid a commission on sales and Badcock retained title to merchandise on display. Mitchell sold his dealership to another and to facilitate the sale, Badcock prepared a summary of commissions owed with certain itemized offsets it claimed that Mitchell owed Badcock. Mitchell disagreed with the calculations, but he accepted them and signed the transfer documents, closing the sale on the basis of the terms set forth in the summary, and was paid accordingly. After pondering the offsets taken by Badcock and verifying the correctness of his position, he brought suit for the additional funds owed. What defense would you expect Badcock to raise? How would you decide the case? Explain fully. [*Mitchell v. Badcock Corp.*, 496 S.E.2d 502 (Ga. App.)]

3. American Bank loaned Koplik $50,000 to buy equipment for a restaurant about to be opened by Casual Citchen Corp. The loan was not repaid, and Fast Foods, Inc., bought out the interest of Casual Citchen. As part of the transaction, Fast Foods agreed to pay the debt owed to American Bank, and the parties agreed to a new schedule of payments to be made by Fast Foods. Fast Foods did not make the payments, and American Bank sued Koplik. He contended that his obligation to repay $50,000 had been discharged by the execution of the agreement providing for the payment of the debt by Fast Foods.

Was this defense valid? [*American Bank & Trust Co. v. Koplik*, 451 N.Y.S.2d 426 (A. D.)]

4. Metalcrafters made a contract to design a new earth-moving vehicle for Lamar Highway Construction Co. Metalcrafters was depending on the genius of Samet, the head of its research department, to design a new product. Shortly after the contract was made between Metalcrafters and Lamar, Samet was killed in an automobile accident. Metalcrafters was not able to design the product without Samet. Lamar sued Metalcrafters for damages for breach of the contract. Metalcrafters claimed that the contract was discharged by Samet's death. Is it correct?

5. The Tinchers signed a contract to sell land to Creasy. The contract specified that the sales transaction was to be completed in 90 days. At the end of the 90 days, Creasy requested an extension of time. The Tinchers refused to grant an extension and stated that the contract was terminated. Creasy claimed that the 90-day clause was not binding because the contract did not state that time was of the essence. Was the contract terminated? [*Creasy v. Tincher*, 173 S.E.2d 332 (W. Va.)]

6. Christopher Bloom received a medical school scholarship created by the U.S. Department of Health and Human Services to increase the number of doctors serving rural areas. In return for this assistance, Bloom agreed to practice four years in a region identified as being underserved by medical professionals. After some problem with his postgraduation assignment, Bloom requested a repayment schedule from the agency. Although no terms were offered, Bloom tendered to the agency two checks totaling $15,500 and marked "Final Payment." Neither check was cashed, and the government sued Bloom for $480,000, the value of the assistance provided. Bloom claimed that by tendering the checks to the agency, his liability had been discharged by an accord and satisfaction. Decide. [*United States v. Bloom*, 112 F.3d 200 (7th Cir.)]

7. Dickson contracted to build a house for Moran. When it was approximately 25 percent to 40 percent completed, Moran would not let Dickson work anymore because he was not following the building plans and specifications and there were many defects. Moran hired another contractor to correct the defects and finish the building. Dickson sued Moran for

breach of contract, claiming that he had substantially performed the contract up to the point where he had been discharged. Was Dickson correct? [*Dickson v. Moran*, 344 So. 2d 102 (La. App.)]

8. A lessor leased a trailer park to a tenant. At the time, sewage was disposed of by a septic tank system that was not connected with the public sewage system. The tenant knew this, and the lease declared that the tenant had examined the premises and that the landlord made no representation or guarantee as to the condition of the premises. Sometime thereafter, the septic tank system stopped working properly, and the county health department notified the tenant that he was required to connect the septic tank system with the public sewage system or else the department would close the trailer park. The tenant did not want to pay the additional cost involved in connecting with the public system. The tenant claimed that he was released from the lease and was entitled to a refund of the deposit that he had made. Was he correct? [*Glen R. Sewell Street Metal v. Loverde*, 451 P.2d 721 (Cal. App.)]

9. Oneal was a teacher employed by the Colton Consolidated School District. Because of a diabetic condition, his eyesight deteriorated so much that he offered to resign if he would be given pay for a specified number of "sick leave" days. The school district refused to do this and discharged Oneal for nonperformance of his contract. He appealed to remove the discharge from his record. Decide. What ethical values are involved? [*Oneal v. Colton Consolidated School District*, 557 P.2d 11 (Wash. App.)]

10. Northwest Construction, Inc., made a contract with the state of Washington for highway construction. Part of the work was turned over under a subcontract to Yakima Asphalt Paving Co. The contract required that any claim be asserted within 180 days. Yakima brought an action for damages after the expiration of 180 days. The defense was that the claim was too late. Yakima replied that the action was brought within the time allowed by the statute of limitations and that the contractual limitation of 180 days was therefore not binding. Was Yakima correct?

11. Farmer William Weber sued the North Loup Irrigation District for breach of contract because North Loup failed to deliver water to his farm during the 2010 season as a result of the destruction of a diversion dam caused by catastrophic flooding in June 2010. The contract between the parties stated that irrigation charges must be paid by December of the year preceding the irrigation season. At the time of the flood Weber had not yet paid his 2010 irrigation charges; and he paid the 2010 charge under protest on April 13, 2011. Weber explained, "I've never wrote a check for $10,000 in my life that I didn't get something for." Did North Loup breach its contractual duties to Weber? Was payment by December 2009 a condition precedent to North Loup's duty to deliver water? Decide. [*Weber v. North Loup River Power and Irrigation District*, 854 N.W.2d 263 (Neb.)]

12. Suburban Power Piping Corp., under contract to construct a building for LTV Steel Corp., made a subcontract with Power & Pollution Services, Inc., to do some of the work. The subcontract provided that the subcontractor would be paid when the owner (LTV) paid the contractor. LTV went into bankruptcy before making the full payment to the contractor, who then refused to pay the subcontractor on the ground that the "pay-when-paid" provision of the subcontract made payment by the owner a condition precedent to the obligation of the contractor to pay the subcontractor. Was the contractor correct? [*Power & Pollution Services, Inc. v. Suburban Power Piping Corp.*, 598 N.E.2d 69 (Ohio App.)]

13. Union Pacific Railroad's long-term coal-hauling contract with electric utility WEPCO provided that if the railroad is prevented by "an event of Force Majeure" from reloading empty coal cars (after it has delivered coal to WEPCO) with iron ore destined for Geneva, Utah, it can charge the higher rate that the contract makes applicable to shipments that do not involve backhauling. The iron ore that the railroad's freight trains would have picked up in Minnesota was intended for a steel mill in Utah. The steel company was bankrupt in 1999 when the parties signed the contract. In November 2001 the steel mill shut down and closed for good in February 2004. Thereafter, the railroad wrote WEPCO to declare "an event of Force Majeure," and that henceforth it would be charging WEPCO the higher rate applicable to shipments without a backhaul. WEPCO sued the railroad for breach of the force majeure provision in the contract, contending that the railroad waited over two plus years to increase rates. The railroad contends that the clause should be interpreted as written. Decide. [*Wisconsin Electric Power Co. v. Union Pacific Railroad Co.*, 557 F.3d 504 (7th Cir.)]

14. Beeson Company made a contract to construct a shopping center for Sartori. Before the work was

fully completed, Sartori stopped making the payments to Beeson that the contract required. The contract provided for liquidated damages of $1,000 per day if Beeson failed to substantially complete the project within 300 days of the beginning of construction. The contract also provided for a bonus of $1,000 for each day Beeson completed the project ahead of schedule. Beeson stopped working and sued Sartori for the balance due under the contract, just as though it had been fully performed. Sartori defended on the ground that Beeson had not substantially completed the work. Beeson proved that Sartori had been able to rent most of the stores in the center. Was there substantial performance of the contract? If so, what would be the measure of damages? [*J.M. Beeson Co. v. Sartori*, 553 So. 2d 180 (Fla. App.)]

15. New Beginnings provides rehabilitation services for alcohol and drug abuse to both adults and adolescents. New Beginnings entered into negotiation with Adbar for the lease of a building in the city of St. Louis and subsequently entered into a three-year lease. The total rent due for the three-year term was $273,000. After the lease was executed, the city denied an occupancy permit because Alderman Bosley and residents testified at a hearing in vigorous opposition to the presence of New Beginnings in the neighborhood. A court ordered the permit issued. Alderman Bosley thereafter contacted the chair of the state's appointment committee and asked her to pull the agency's funding. He received no commitment from her on this matter. After a meeting with the state director of Alcohol and Drug Abuse where it was asserted that the director said the funding would be pulled if New Beginnings moved into the Adbar location, New Beginnings' board decided not to occupy the building. Adbar brought suit for breach of the lease, and New Beginnings asserted that it was excused from performance because of commercial impracticability and frustration of purpose. Do you believe the doctrine of commercial impracticability should be limited in its application so as to preserve the certainty of contracts? What rule of law applies to this case? Decide. [*Adbar v. New Beginnings*, 103 S.W.2d 799 (Mo. App.)]

CPA Questions

1. Parc hired Glaze to remodel and furnish an office suite. Glaze submitted plans that Parc approved. After completing all the necessary construction and painting, Glaze purchased minor accessories that Parc rejected because they did not conform to the plans. Parc refused to allow Glaze to complete the project and refused to pay Glaze any part of the contract price. Glaze sued for the value of the work performed. Which of the following statements is correct?

   a. Glaze will lose because Glaze breached the contract by not completing performance.

   b. Glaze will win because Glaze substantially performed and Parc prevented complete performance.

   c. Glaze will lose because Glaze materially breached the contract by buying the accessories.

   d. Glaze will win because Parc committed anticipatory breach.

2. Ordinarily, in an action for breach of a construction contract, the statute of limitations time period would be computed from the date the contract is:

   a. Negotiated.

   b. Breached.

   c. Begun.

   d. Signed.

3. Which of the following will release all original parties to a contract but will maintain a contractual relationship?

	Novation	Substituted contract
a.	Yes	Yes
b.	Yes	No
c.	No	Yes
d.	No	No

Breach of Contract and Remedies

Learning Outcomes <<<

After studying this chapter, you should be able to

LO.1 Explain what constitutes a breach of contract and an anticipatory breach of contract

LO.2 Describe the effect of a waiver of a breach

LO.3 Explain the range of remedies available for breach of contract

LO.4 Explain when liquidated damages clauses are valid and invalid

LO.5 State when liability-limiting clauses and releases are valid

What can be done when a contract is broken?

19-1　What Constitutes a Breach of Contract?

The question of remedies does not become important until it is first determined that a contract has been violated or breached.

19-1a　Definition of Breach

breach–failure to act or perform in the manner called for in a contract.

A **breach** is the failure to act or perform in the manner called for by the contract. When the contract calls for performance, such as painting an owner's home, the failure to paint or to paint properly is a *breach of contract*. If the contract calls for a creditor's forbearance, the creditor's action in bringing a lawsuit is a breach of the contract.

19-1b　Anticipatory Breach

When the contract calls for performance, a party may make it clear before the time for performance arrives that the contract will not be performed. This is referred to as an **anticipatory breach.**

Anticipatory Repudiation

anticipatory breach– promisor's repudiation of the contract prior to the time that performance is required when such repudiation is accepted by the promisee as a breach of the contract.

anticipatory repudiation–repudiation made in advance of the time for performance of the contract obligations.

When a party expressly declares that performance will not be made when required, this declaration is called an **anticipatory repudiation** of the contract. To constitute such a repudiation, there must be a clear, absolute, unequivocal refusal to perform the contract according to its terms. **For Example,** Procter & Gamble (P&G) sought payment on four letters of credit issued by a Serbian bank, Investbanka. P&G presented two letters by June 8, prior to their expiration dates, with the necessary documentation for payment to Beogradska Bank New York, Investbanka's New York agent. A June 11 letter from Beogradska Bank broadly and unequivocally stated that the bank would not pay the letters of credit. Two additional letters of credit totaling $20,000 issued by Investbanka that expired by June 30 were not thereafter submitted to the New York agent bank by P&G. However, a court found that the bank had anticipatorily breached its obligations under those letters of credit by its broad renouncements in the June 11 letter, and judgments were rendered in favor of P&G.[1]

CASE SUMMARY

Splitting Tips—Contract Price Less Cost of Completion

FACTS: Hartland Developers, Inc., agreed to build an airplane hangar for Robert Tips of San Antonio for $300,000, payable in three installments of $100,000, with the final payment due upon the completion of the building and the issuance of a certificate of completion by the engineer representing Tips. The evidence shows that Tips's representative, Mr. Lavelle, instructed Hartland to cease work on the building because Tips could no longer afford to make payments. Hartland ceased work as instructed before the final completion of the building, having been paid $200,000 at the time. He sued Tips for breach of contract. On May 6, 1996, the trial court allowed Hartland the amount owing on the contract, $100,000, less the cost of completing the building according to the contract, $65,000, plus attorney fees and prejudgment interest. Tips appealed, pointing out, among other assertions, that he was required to

[1] *Procter & Gamble v. Investbanka,* 2000 WL 520630 (S.D.N.Y. 2000).

Splitting Tips—Contract Price Less Cost of Completion continued

spend $23,000 to provide electrical outlets for the hangar, which were contemplated in the contract.

DECISION: Judgment for Tips, subject to offsets. The trial judge based his damages assessment on anticipatory repudiation of contract. The evidence that Tips's representative,

Lavelle, instructed Hartland to cease work on the project because Tips no longer could afford to make payments was sufficient to support this finding. However, Tips is entitled to an offset for electrical connections of $23,000 under a breach of contract theory. [*Tips v. Hartland Developers, Inc.*, 961 S.W.2d 618 (Tex. App. 1998)]

A refusal to perform a contract that is made before performance is required, unless the other party to the contract does an act or makes a concession that is not required by the contract, is an anticipatory repudiation of the contract.[2] However, a firmly stated request for additional payment under an existing contract without refusal to perform until the additional payment is made is not a repudiation of a contract. **For Example,** Sunesis Trucking Company's August 14, 2009, letter to Thistledown Racetrack seeking additional payment for hauling straw and manure from the raceway's horse stalls stating "accept this as notice that we will haul your manure at the following fees" was held not to be a notice of termination and did not establish an anticipatory breach excusing Thistledown from its obligations under the contract.[3]

Anticipatory Repudiation by Conduct

The anticipatory repudiation may be expressed by conduct that makes it impossible for the repudiating party to perform subsequently. **For Example,** while the Town of Mammoth Lakes, California, was claiming a willingness to move forward with a hotel/condominium project under its contract with the developer, in actuality, the evidence established that town officials refused to move forward and actively sought to undermine the developer's rights under the development contract. The court affirmed a judgment of $30 million in damages and attorneys' fees.[4]

19-2   Waiver of Breach

The breach of a contract may have no importance because the other party to the contract waives the breach.

19-2a   Cure of Breach by Waiver

waiver—release or relinquishment of a known right or objection.

The fact that one party has broken a contract does not necessarily mean that there will be a lawsuit or a forfeiture of the contract. For practical business reasons, one party may be willing to ignore or waive the breach. When it is established that there has been a **waiver** of a breach, the party waiving the breach cannot take any action on the theory that the contract was broken. The waiver, in effect, erases the past breach. The contract continues as though the breach had not existed.

The waiver may be express or it may be implied from the continued recognition of the existence of the contract by the aggrieved party.[5] When the conduct of a party shows an intent to give up a right, it waives that right.[6]

---

[2] See *Black Diamond Energy, Inc. v. Encana Oil and Gas (USA) Inc.*, 326 P.3d 904 (Wyo. 2014).
[3] *Sunesis Trucking Co. v. Thistledown Racetrack, LLC,* 13 N.E.3d 727 (Ohio App. 2014).
[4] *Mammoth Lakes Land Acquisition, LLC v. Town of Mammoth Lakes,* 120 Cal. Rptr. 3d 797 (Cal. Ct. of App. 3d Dist. 2010).
[5] *Huger v. Morrison,* 809 So. 2d 1140 (La. App. 2002).
[6] *Stronghaven Inc. v. Ingram,* 555 S.E.2d 49 (Ga. App. 2001).

19-2b Existence and Scope of Waiver

It is a question of fact whether there has been a waiver.

CASE SUMMARY

Have You Driven a Ford Lately, Jennifer?

FACTS: In 1995, Northland Ford Dealers, an association of dealerships, offered to sponsor a "hole in one" contest at Moccasin Creek Country Club. A banner announced that a hole in one would win a car but gave no other details, and the local dealer parked a Ford Explorer near the banner. Northland paid a $4,602 premium to Continental Hole-In-One, Inc., to ensure the award of the contest prize. The insurance application stated in capital letters that "ALL AMATEUR MEN AND WOMEN WILL UTILIZE THE SAME TEE." And Continental established the men/women yardage for the hole to be 170 yards but did not make this known to the participants. Jennifer Harms registered for the tournament and paid her entrance fee. At the contest hole, she teed off from the amateur women's red marker, which was a much shorter distance to the pin than the 170 yards from the men's marker—and she made a hole in one. When she inquired about the prize, she was told that because of insurance requirements, all amateurs had to tee off from the amateur men's tee box, and because she had not done so, she was disqualified. Harms, a collegiate golfer at Concordia College, returned there to complete her last year of athletic eligibility and on graduation sued Northland for breach of contract. Northland contends that under NCAA rules, accepting a prize or agreeing to accept a prize would have disqualified Harms from NCAA competition. It also asserts that her continuation of her NCAA competition evinced intent to waive acceptance of the car.

DECISION: Judgment for Harms. Northland must abide by the rules it announced, not by the ones it left unannounced that disqualified all amateur women from the contest. This was a vintage unilateral contract with performance by the offeree as acceptance. Harms earned the prize when she sank her winning shot. Waiver is a volitional relinquishment, by act or word, of a known existing right conferred in law or contract. Harms could not disclaim the prize; it was not hers to refuse. She was told her shot from the wrong tee disqualified her. One can hardly relinquish what was never conferred. Northland's waiver defense is devoid of merit. [*Harms v. Northland Ford Dealers*, **602 N.W.2d 58 (S.D. 1999)**]

Existence of Waiver

A party may express or declare that the breach of a contract is waived. A waiver of a breach is more often the result of an express forgiving of a breach. Thus, a party allowing the other party to continue performance without objecting that the performance is not satisfactory waives the right to raise that objection when sued for payment by the performing party.

For Example, a contract promising to sell back a parcel of commercial property to Jackson required Jackson to make a $500 payment to Massey's attorney on the first of the month for five months, December through April. It was clearly understood that the payments would be "on time without fail." Jackson made the December payment on time. New Year's Day, a holiday, fell on a Friday, and Jackson made the second payment on January 4. He made $500 payments on February 1, March 1, and March 31, respectively, and the payments were accepted and a receipt issued on each occasion. However, Massey refused to convey title back to Jackson because "the January 4 payment was untimely and the parties' agreement had been breached." The court held that the doctrine of waiver applied due to Massey's acceptance of the late payment and the three subsequent payments without objection, and the court declared that Jackson was entitled to possession of the land.[7]

---

[7] *Massey v. Jackson*, 726 So. 2d 656 (Ala. App. 1998).

Scope of Waiver

The waiver of a breach of contract extends only to the matter waived. It does not show any intent to ignore other provisions of the contract.

Antimodification Clause

Modern contracts commonly specify that the terms of a contract shall not be deemed modified by waiver as to any breaches. This means that the original contract remains as agreed to. Either party may therefore return to, and insist on, compliance with the original contract.

In the example involving Jackson and Massey's contract, the trial court reviewed the contract to see whether the court was restricted by the contract from applying the waiver. It concluded: "In this case, the parties' contract did not contain any terms that could prevent the application of the doctrine of waiver to the acceptance of late payments."[8]

19-2c Reservation of Rights

It may be that a party is willing to accept a defective performance but does not wish to surrender any claim for damages for the breach. **For Example,** Midwest Utilities, Inc., accepted 20 carloads of Powder River Basin coal (sometimes called *Western coal*) from its supplier, Maney Enterprises, because its power plants were in short supply of coal. Midwest's requirements contract with Maney called for Appalachian coal, a low-sulfur, highly efficient fuel, which is sold at a premium price per ton. Midwest, in accepting the tendered performance with a **reservation of rights,** gave notice to Maney that it reserved all rights to pursue damages for the tender of a nonconforming shipment.

> **reservation of rights**—assertion by a party to a contract that even though a tendered performance (e.g., a defective product) is accepted, the right to damages for nonconformity to the contract is reserved.

> **remedy**—action or procedure that is followed in order to enforce a right or to obtain damages for injury to a right.

19-3 Remedies for Breach of Contract

One or more **remedies** may be available to the innocent party in the case of a breach of contract. There is also the possibility that arbitration or a streamlined out-of-court alternative dispute resolution procedure is available or required for determining the rights of the parties.

19-3a Remedies Upon Anticipatory Repudiation

When an anticipatory repudiation of a contract occurs, the aggrieved person has several options. The individual may (1) do nothing beyond stating that performance at the proper time will be required, (2) regard the contract as having been definitively broken and bring a lawsuit against the repudiating party without waiting to see whether there will be proper performance when the performance date arrives, or (3) regard the repudiation as an offer to cancel the contract. This offer can be accepted or rejected. If accepted, there is a discharge of the original contract by the subsequent cancellation agreement of the parties.

19-3b Remedies in General and the Measure of Damages

Courts provide a *quasi-contractual* or *restitution* remedy in which a contract is unenforceable because it lacked definite and certain terms or was not in compliance with the statute of frauds, yet one of the parties performed services for the other. The measure of damages in these and other quasi-contract cases is the reasonable value of the services performed, not an amount derived from the defective contract.

[8] *Id.* at 659.

FIGURE 19-1	What Follows the Breach

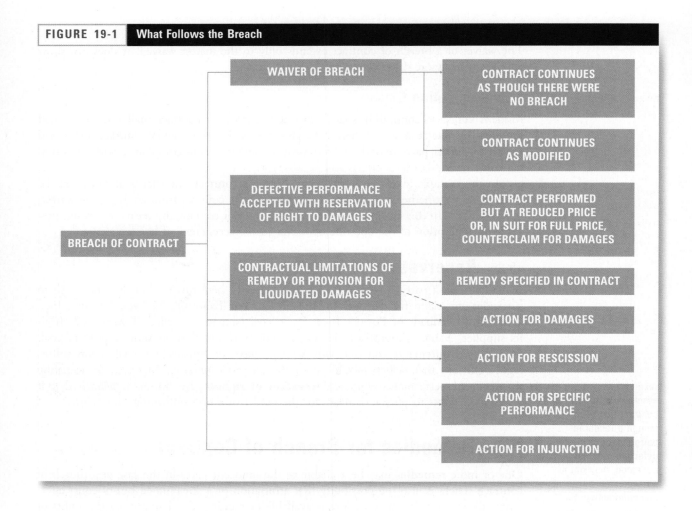

In cases when a person retains money or when a contemplated contract is not properly formed and no work is performed, the party retaining the benefit is obligated to make restitution to the person conferring the benefit. **For Example,** Kramer Associates, Inc. (KAI), a Washington D.C., consulting firm, accepted $75,000 from a Ghana-based corporation, Ikam, Ltd., to secure financing for a Ghana development project. No contract was ever executed, and KAI did virtually nothing to secure financing for the project. Restitution of the $75,000 was required.[9]

When there is a breach of contract, the regular remedy is an award of *monetary damages*. In unusual circumstances, when monetary damages are inadequate, the injured party may obtain **specific performance,** whereby the court will order that the contract terms be carried out.

specific performance— action brought to compel the adverse party to perform a contract on the theory that merely suing for damages for its breach will not be an adequate remedy.

The measure of monetary damages when there has been a breach of contract is the sum of money that will place the injured party in the same position that would have been attained if the contract had been performed.[10] That is, the injured party will be given the *benefit of the bargain* by the court. As seen in the *Tips v. Hartland Developers* case, the nonbreaching party, Hartland, was awarded the contract price less the cost of completion of the project, which had the effect of giving the builder the benefit of the bargain.

[9] *Kramer Associates, Inc. v. Ikam, Ltd.,* 888 A.2d 247 (D.C. 2005).
[10] *Leingang v. City of Mandan,* 468 N.W.2d 397 (N.D. 1991).

19-3c Monetary Damages

Monetary damages are commonly classified as compensatory damages, nominal damages, and punitive damages. **Compensatory damages** compensate the injured party for the damages incurred as a result of the breach of contract. Compensatory damages have two branches, *direct damages* and *consequential* (or *special*) *damages*.

Injured parties that do not sustain an actual loss because of a breach of contract are entitled to a judgment of a small sum of money such as $1; these damages are called **nominal damages.**

Damages in excess of actual loss, imposed for the purpose of punishing or making an example of the defendant, are known as **punitive damages** or *exemplary damages.* In contract actions, punitive damages are not ordinarily awarded.[11]

Direct and Consequential Damages

Direct damages (sometimes called *general damages*) are those that naturally flow from the given type of breach of contract involved and include *incidental damages*, which are extra expenditures made by the injured party to rectify the breach or mitigate damages.[12] **Consequential damages** (sometimes called *special damages*) are those that do not necessarily flow from the type of breach of contract involved but happen to do so in a particular case as a result of the injured party's particular circumstances.[13]

> **compensatory damages**–sum of money that will compensate an injured plaintiff for actual loss.

> **nominal damages**–nominal sum awarded the plaintiff in order to establish that legal rights have been violated although the plaintiff in fact has not sustained any actual loss or damages.

CASE SUMMARY

Who Pays the Expenses?

FACTS: Jerry Birkel was a grain farmer. Hassebrook Farm Service, Inc., made a contract with Jerry to sell to him and install a grain storage and drying bin. Jerry traded in his old dryer to the seller. The new equipment did not work properly, and Jerry had to pay other persons for drying and storing his grain. Jerry sued Hassebrook for damages and claimed the right to be repaid what he had paid to others for drying and storage.

DECISION: Jerry was entitled to recover what he had paid others for drying and storage. Because Jerry had traded in

his old dryer to the seller, it was obvious to the seller that if the new equipment did not work properly, Jerry would be forced to pay for alternative drying and storage to prevent the total loss of his crops. The cost of such an alternative was therefore within the seller's contemplation when the contract was made, and so the buyer could recover this cost as an element of damages for the seller's breach of contract. [*Birkel v. Hassebrook Farm Service, Inc.*, **363 N.W.2d 148 (Neb. 1985)**]

> **punitive damages**–damages, in excess of those required to compensate the plaintiff for the wrong done, that are imposed in order to punish the defendant because of the particularly wanton or willful character of wrongdoing; also called *exemplary damages.*

Consequential damages may be recovered only if it was reasonably foreseeable to the defendant that the kind of loss in question could be sustained by the nonbreaching party if the contract were broken.

For Example, in early August, Spencer Adams ordered a four-wheel-drive GMC truck with a rear-end hydraulic lift for use on his Aroostook County, Maine, potato farm. The contract price was $63,500. He told Brad Jones, the owner of the dealership, that he had to have the truck by Labor Day so he could use it to bring in his crop from the fields before the first frost, and Brad nodded that he understood. The truck did not arrive by

[11] A party who is not awarded actual damages but wins nominal damages can be considered a "prevailing party" for the purposes of a contractual attorney fee-shifting provision. *Brock v. King*, 629 S.E.2d 829 (Ga. App. 2006).

[12] In New York State, the courts utilize the terms *general* and *special* damages as opposed to the terms *direct* and *consequential* damages. See *Biotronik A.G. v. Connor Medsystems Ireland, Ltd.*, 988 N.Y.S.2d 527 (Ct. App. 2014).

[13] See *Powell Electrical Systems, Inc. v. Hewlett Packard Co.*, 356 S.W.3d 113 (Tex. App. 2011).

direct damages–losses that are caused by breach of a contract.

consequential damages–damages the buyer experiences as a result of the seller's breach with respect to a third party; also called *special damages*.

Labor Day as promised in the written contract. After a two-week period of gradually escalating recriminations with the dealership, Adams obtained the same model GMC truck at a dealership 40 minutes away in Houlton but at the cost of $65,500. He was also able to rent a similar truck from the Houlton dealer for $250 for the day while the new truck was being prepared. Farmhands had used other means of harvesting, but because of the lack of the truck, their work was set back by five days. As a result of the delays, 30 percent of the crop was still in the fields when the first frost came, causing damages expertly estimated at $320,000. The *direct damages* for the breach of contract in this case would be the difference between the contract price for the truck of $63,500 and the market price of $65,500, or $2,000. These direct damages naturally flow from the breach of contract for the purchase of a truck. Also, the *incidental damages* of $250 for the truck rental are recoverable direct damages. The $320,000 loss of the potato crop was a consequence of not having the truck, and this sum is arguably recoverable by Spencer Adams as *consequential* or *special damages*. Adams notified Brad Jones of the reason he needed to have the truck by Labor Day, and it should have been reasonably foreseeable to Jones that loss of a portion of the crop could occur if the truck contract was breached. However, because of Spencer Adams's obligation to mitigate damages (as discussed next), it is unlikely that Adams will recover the full consequential damages. Truck rental availability or the lack of availability within the rural area, alternative tractor usage, and the actual harvesting methods used by Adams all relate to the mitigation issue to be resolved by the jury.

Mitigation of Damages

The injured party is under the duty to mitigate damages if reasonably possible.[14] In other words, damages must not be permitted to increase if an increase can be prevented by reasonable efforts. This means that the injured party must generally stop any performance under the contract to avoid running up a larger bill. The duty to mitigate damages may require an injured party to buy or rent elsewhere the goods that the wrongdoer was obligated to deliver under the contract. In the case of breach of an employment contract by the employer, the employee is required to seek other similar employment. The wages earned from other employment must be deducted from the damages claimed. The discharged employee, however, is not required to take employment of less-than-comparable work.

Effect of Failure to Mitigate Damages. The effect of the requirement of mitigating damages is to limit recovery by the nonbreaching party to the damages that would have been sustained had this party mitigated the damages where it was possible to do so.

CASE SUMMARY

The Opposite of a Win-Win Situation

FACTS: On February 4, 2006, the Heymanns agreed to buy a condominium from Gayle Fischer for $315,000. Both parties signed a purchase and sale agreement. The Agreement authorized the Heymanns to terminate if Fischer refused to fix any "major defect" discovered upon inspection but did not permit them to terminate if Fischer refused to perform "routine maintenance" or make "minor repair[s]." On

February 10, 2006, the Heymanns demanded Fischer fix an electrical problem after an inspection report revealed that electricity was not flowing to three power outlets. The Heymanns thought this was a "major defect" under the Agreement and conditioned their purchase on Fischer's timely response. Fischer failed to timely respond to their demand—even though she eventually fixed the problem

---

[14] *West Pinal Family Health Center, Inc. v. McBryde*, 785 P.2d 66 (Ariz. App. 1989).

The Opposite of a Win-Win Situation continued

for $117 on February 20 by having an electrician push the reset button on three outlets and change a light bulb. The Heymanns tendered a mutual release to void the Agreement. Fischer refused to sign the release and sued for specific performances or damages. The case progressed to the trial court, the court of appeals, back to the trial court, and ultimately to the Supreme Court of Indiana.

After the deal fell through in 2006 Fischer attempted to mitigate damages by selling the condo but the housing market entered a major downturn. On February 13, 2007, she received an offer to purchase the condo for $240,000 but her counter-offer of $286,000 was rejected. She eventually sold the condo in November 2011 for $180,000. Fischer seeks damages for the difference between the Heymann purchase price of $315,000 and the sale in 2011 of $180,000, plus the cost of maintaining the condo from 2006 through 2011, and attorney's fees for a total of $306,616.

DECISION: Fischer's failure to respond to the Heymann's demand for electrical repairs was not a basis to void the contract. Rather the $117 repair consisting of pushing the reset button on three outlets and the change of a light bulb was not a "major defect" which would allow for the voiding of a contract. Accordingly, the Heymanns were in breach of the Purchase Agreement. The duty to mitigate damages is a common law duty independent of contract terms requiring the non-breaching party to make a reasonable effort to decrease the damage caused by the breach. Fischer acted unreasonably when she could have mitigated damages and sold the condo for $240,000, in 2007, instead of waiting until 2011. Accordingly, her compensatory damages are $75,000, the difference between $315,000 and $240,000 plus $15,109 in carrying cost to the 2007 offer date and reasonable attorney fees of $3,862 incurred up to the 2007 date for a total of $93,977. [*Fischer v. Heymann,* **12 N.E.3d 867 (Ind. 2014)**]

19-3d Rescission

When one party commits a material breach of the contract, the other party may rescind the contract; if the party in default objects, the aggrieved party may bring an action for rescission. A breach is *material* when it is so substantial that it defeats the object of the parties in making the contract.[15]

CASE SUMMARY

The Buck Doesn't Stop Here (at Slip B1)

FACTS: Edgar Buck owns *Rookie IV*, a $6 million 61-foot boat requiring a dock slip 20 feet in width. Buck's daughter Susanne owns ZAN, LCC, and Buck has authority to act on behalf of ZAN. Susanne wanted a waterfront lot to build a home, and Buck wanted a boat slip out of the Intercoastal Waterway where the boat regularly sustained damage. ZAN (Buck) agreed to purchase a slip for Buck's boat and lot 3 for Susanne. Just prior to the closing, Buck discovered that the slip designated as B1 was actually two slips, B1 and B2 and *Rookie IV* would not fit into B1. Buck was informed by Ripley Cove's agent and later its closing attorney Dan David that the sellers owned B2 and that it would be no problem to give Buck the 20 foot clearance he needed and to place two pilings in the adjoining slip. Buck then agreed to close on the property. It was later discovered that at the time of the closing, Ripley Cove no longer owned B2. Since

Rookie IV could not fit into the slip, ZAN sued for rescission of the contract for the lot and slip and damages. The trial court determined that ZAN proved its claims, awarded $10,000 for breach of contract and negligent misrepresentation but refused to rescind the contract. ZAN appealed.

DECISION: Judgment for ZAN. The main purpose of the contract was to provide Buck with a slip for *Rookie IV.* Thus ZAN was entitled to rescission of the contract *in toto*, both the slip and the land, despite the parties' lack of dispute regarding the upland parcel. A breach of contract claim warranting rescission of the contract must be so substantial and fundamental as to defeat the purpose of the contract. Such was the nature of the breach in this case. [*ZAN, LLC v. Ripley Cove, LLC,* **751 S.E.2d 664 (S.C. App. 2013)**]

[15] *Greentree Properties, Inc. v. Kissee,* 92 S.W.3d 289 (Mo. App. 2003).

An injured party who rescinds a contract after having performed services may recover the reasonable value of the performance rendered under restitutionary or quasi-contractual damages. Money paid by the injured party may also be recovered. **For Example,** the Sharabianlous signed a purchase agreement to buy a building owned by Berenstein Associates for $2 million. Thereafter the parties learned of environmental contamination on the property. Faced with uncertainty about the scope of the problem and the cost of the cleanup, the deal fell through and litigation ensued. The trial court rescinded the agreement based on mutual mistake of fact because neither party knew the full extent of the environmental hazard at the property. Damages available to parties upon mistake are more limited than those available in cases in which rescission is based on fault. The Sharabianlous were awarded $61,423.82 in expenses and an order returning their $115,000 deposit.[16]

The purpose of rescission is to restore the injured party to the position occupied before the contract was made. However, the party seeking restitutionary damages must also return what this party has received from the party in default.

For Example, Pedro Morena purchased real estate from Jason Alexander after Alexander had assured him that the property did not have a flooding problem. In fact, the property regularly flooded after ordinary rainstorms. Morena was entitled to the return of the purchase price and payment for the reasonable value of the improvements he made to the property. Alexander was entitled to a setoff for the reasonable rental value of the property during the time Morena was in possession of this property.

19-3e Action for Specific Performance

Under special circumstances, an injured party may obtain the equitable remedy of specific performance, which compels the other party to carry out the terms of a contract. Specific performance is ordinarily granted only if the subject matter of the contract is "unique," thereby making an award of money damages an inadequate remedy. Contracts for the purchase of land will be specifically enforced.[17]

Specific performance of a contract to sell personal property can be obtained only if the article is of unusual age, beauty, unique history, or other distinction. **For Example,** Maurice owned a rare Revolutionary War musket that he agreed to sell to Herb. Maurice then changed his mind because of the uniqueness of the musket. Herb can sue and win, requesting the remedy of specific performance of the contract because of the unique nature of the goods.

When the damages sustained by the plaintiff can be measured in monetary terms, specific performance will be refused. Consequently, a contract to sell a television station will not be specifically enforced when the buyer had made a contract to resell the station to a third person; the damages caused by the breach of the first contract would be the loss sustained by being unable to make the resale, and such damages would be adequate compensation to the original buyer.[18]

Ordinarily, contracts for the performance of personal services are not specifically ordered. This is because of the difficulty of supervision by the court and the restriction of the U.S. Constitution's Thirteenth Amendment prohibiting involuntary servitude except as criminal punishment.

19-3f Action for an Injunction

injunction–order of a court of equity to refrain from doing (negative injunction) or to do (affirmative or mandatory injunction) a specified act.

When a breach of contract consists of doing an act prohibited by the contract, a possible remedy is an **injunction** against doing the act. **For Example,** when the obligation in an employee's contract is to refrain from competing after resigning from the company and

---

[16] *Sharabianlou v. Karp,* 105 Cal. Rptr. 3d 300 (Cal. App. 2010).
[17] *English v. Muller,* 514 S.E.2d 195 (Ga. 1999).
[18] *Miller v. LeSea Broadcasting, Inc.,* 87 F.3d 224 (7th Cir. 1996).

the obligation is broken by competing, a court may order the former employee to stop competing. Similarly, when a vocalist breaks a contract to record exclusively for a particular label, she may be enjoined from recording for any other company. This may have the indirect effect of compelling the vocalist to record for the plaintiff.

19-3g   Reformation of Contract by a Court

At times, a written contract does not correctly state the agreement already made by the parties. When this occurs, either party may seek to have the court reform or correct the writing to state the agreement actually made.

A party seeking reformation of a contract must clearly prove both the grounds for reformation and what the agreement actually was.[19] This burden is particularly great when the contract to be reformed is written. This is so because the general rule is that parties are presumed to have read their written contracts and to have intended to be bound by them when they signed the contracts.

When a unilateral mistake is made and it is of such consequence that enforcing the contract according to its terms would be unconscionable, a court may reform the contract to correct the mistake.

CASE SUMMARY

Will a Court Correct a Huge Mistake?

FACTS: New York Packaging Corp. (NYPC) manufactured plastic sheets used by Owens Corning (OC) at its asphalt plants throughout the country as dividers to separate asphalt containers and prevent them from sticking to one another. Janet Berry, a customer service representative at Owens Corning, called and received a price from NYPC of "$172.50 per box," with a box containing 200 plastic sheets. Ms. Berry put the information into OC's computer systems, which in turn generated a purchase order. She mistakenly believed that the unit of measurement designated as "EA" on the purchase order was per box when it in fact was per sheet. As a result, the purchase orders likewise reflected a price of $172.50 per sheet rather than per box. The computer automatically calculated the total price of the purchase order and faxed it to NYPC as $1,078,195, without Ms. Berry seeing the huge total price. NYPC filled the order, which included overrun sheets, and billed OC $1,414,605.60. NYPC sought payment at the contract price of $172.50 per sheet. It points out that the purchase order contained a "no oral modification" clause and, by its terms, the order was binding when NYPC accepted. The buyer contends that NYPC is attempting to take advantage of this huge and obvious mistake and that the contract should be reformed.

DECISION: Ms. Berry made a unilateral mistake that was, or should have been, known by NYPC. OC used the sheets after its offer to return them to NYPC was refused. Therefore, the contract could not be rescinded. The drafting error in this case was so huge that to enforce the written contract would be unconscionable. Accordingly, the unit of measurement is amended to read "per box" rather than "EA"; the "Order Qty" is amended to read "41 boxes of 200 sheets per box"; and the overall price is modified to read $7,072.50, not $1,078,195. [**In re *Owens Corning et al., Debtors in Possession,* 291 B.R. 329 (2003)**]

19-4   Contract Provisions Affecting Remedies and Damages

The contract of the parties may contain provisions that affect the remedies available or the recovery of damages.

---

[19] The evidence must be "clear, unequivocal and decisive," *First Chatham Bank v. Liberty Capital, LLC,* 755 S.E.2d 219 (Ga. App. 2014).

19-4a Limitation of Remedies

The contract of the parties may limit the remedies of the aggrieved parties. **For Example,** the contract may give one party the right to repair or replace a defective item sold or to refund the contract price. The contract may require both parties to submit any dispute to arbitration or another streamlined out-of-court dispute resolution procedure.

19-4b Liquidated Damages

liquidated damages—provision stipulating the amount of damages to be paid in the event of default or breach of contract.

The parties may stipulate in their contract that a certain amount should be paid in case of a breach. This amount is known as liquidated damages and may be variously measured by the parties. When delay is possible, **liquidated damages** may be a fixed sum, such as $1,000 for each day of delay. When there is a total default, damages may be a percentage of the contract price or the amount of the down payment.

Validity

liquidated damages clause—specification of exact compensation in case of a breach of contract.

To be valid, a **liquidated damages clause** must satisfy two requirements: (1) The situation must be one in which it is difficult or impossible to determine the actual damages and (2) the amount specified must not be excessive when compared with the probable damages that would be sustained.[20] The validity of a liquidated damages clause is determined on the basis of the facts existing when the clause was agreed to.

Effect

When a liquidated damages clause is held valid, the injured party cannot collect more than the amount specified by the clause. The defaulting party is bound to pay such damages once the fact is established that there has been a default. The injured party is not required to make any proof as to damages sustained, and the defendant is not permitted to show that the damages were not as great as the liquidated sum.

Invalid Clauses

If the liquidated damages clause calls for the payment of a sum that is clearly unreasonably large and unrelated to the possible actual damages that might be sustained, the clause will be held to be void as a penalty. **For Example,** a settlement agreement between 27 plaintiffs seeking recovery for injuries resulting from faulty breast implants and the implants' manufacturer, Dow Corning Corp., called for seven $200,000 payments to each plaintiff. The agreement also called for a $100 per day payment to each plaintiff for any time when the payments were late as "liquidated damages." The court held that the $100 per day figure was not a reasonable estimate of anticipated damages. Rather, it was an unenforceable "penalty" provision.[21]

When a liquidated damages clause is held invalid, the effect is merely to erase the clause from the contract, and the injured party may proceed to recover damages for breach of the contract. Instead of recovering the liquidated damages amount, the injured party will recover whatever actual damages he can prove. **For Example,** Richard Goldblatt and his wife Valerie breached a five-year restrictive covenant in a settlement agreement with the medical devices corporation that Goldblatt had cofounded, C.P. Motion, Inc. A liquidated damages provision in the settlement agreement that obligated Goldblatt and his wife to pay $250,000 per breach of the restrictive covenant was unenforceable as a penalty clause. The appeals court set aside a $4,969,339 judgment against the Goldblatts, determining that the parties could have agreed to arrive at actual damages by

---

[20] *Southeast Alaska Construction Co. v. Alaska*, 791 P.2d 339 (Alaska 1990).

[21] *Bear Stearns v. Dow Corning Corp.*, 419 F.3d 543 (6th Or. 2005). See *Boone Coleman Construction, Inc. v. Village of Piketon*, 13 N.E.3d 1190 (Ohio App. 2014).

calculating a percentage of lost profits of specific lost clients or reclaiming any profits gained by the breaching parties. Because the liquidated damages clause was a penalty provision, C.P. Motion, Inc., may only recover the actual damages filed and proven at trial.[22]

19-4c Attorneys' Fees

Attorneys' fees are a very significant factor in contract litigation. In Medistar Corporation's suit against Dr. David Schmidt, the jury awarded it $418,069 in damages under its promissory estoppel claim and in addition thereto the trial court judge allowed Medistar to recover $408,412 for its attorneys' fees. A state statute allows recovery of attorneys' fees for the prevailing party in a breach of partnership claim. On appeal the recovery of $408,412 in attorneys' fees was reversed since the jury awarded zero damages on Medistars' breach of partnership claim. The net result after payment of attorneys' fees—and not counting attorneys' fees for the appeal—was $9,657 for Medistar, after four years of "successful" litigation.[23]

The so-called American rule states that each party is responsible for its own attorneys' fees in the absence of an express contractual or statutory provision to the contrary.[24] Even in the event of a valid contractual provision for attorneys' fees, a trial court has the discretion to exercise its equitable control to allow only such sum as is reasonable, or the court may properly disallow attorneys' fees altogether on the basis that such recovery would be inequitable. **For Example,** although Evergreen Tree Care Services was awarded some monetary damages in its breach of contract suit against JHL, Inc., it was unsuccessful in its claim for attorneys' fees under a provision for attorneys' fees in the contract because the trial court exercised its equitable discretion, finding that both parties to the litigation came to court with "unclean hands," and that Evergreen failed to sufficiently itemize and exclude fees to discovery abuses.[25]

19-4d Limitation of Liability Clauses

A contract may contain a provision stating that one of the parties shall not be liable for damages in case of breach. Such a provision is called an **exculpatory clause,** or when a monetary limit to damages for breach of contract is set forth in the contract, it may be referred to as a **limitation-of-liability clause.**

Content and Construction

If an exculpatory clause or a limitation-of-liability clause limits liability for damages caused only by negligent conduct, liability is neither excluded nor limited if the conduct alleged is found to be grossly negligent, willful, or wanton. **For Example,** Security Guards Inc. (SGI) provided services to Dana Corporation, a truck frame manufacturer under a contract that contained a limitation-of-liability clause capping losses at $50,000 per occurrence for damages "caused solely by the negligence" of SGI or its employees. When a critical alarm was activated by a fire in the paint shop at 5:39 P.M., the SGI guard on duty did not follow appropriate procedures, which delayed notification to the fire department for 15 minutes. Royal Indemnity Co., Dana's insurer, paid Dana $16,535,882 for the fire loss and sued SGI for $7 million, contending that the SGI guard's actions were grossly negligent and caused the plant to suffer increased damages. The court held that if SGI were to be found grossly negligent, the liability would not be limited to $50,000, and a jury could find damages far exceeding that amount.[26]

exculpatory clause–provision in a contract stating that one of the parties shall not be liable for damages in case of breach; also called a *limitation-of-liability clause.*

limitation-of-liability clause–provision in a contract stating that one of the parties is not liable for damages in case of breach; also called *exculpatory clause.*

[22] *Goldblatt v. C. P. Motion, Inc.,* 77 So. 3d 798 (Fla. App. 2011).
[23] *Medistar Corp. v. Schmidt,* 267 S.W.3d 150 (Tex. App. 2008).
[24] *Centimark v. Village Manor Associates, Ltd.,* 967 A.2d 550 (Conn. App. 2009).
[25] *Stafford v. JHL, Inc.,* 194 P.3d 315 (Wyo. 2008). See also *FNBC v. Jennessey Group, LLC,* 759 N.W.2d 808 (Iowa App. 2008).
[26] *Royal Indemnity Co. v. Security Guards, Inc,* 255 F. Supp. 2d 497 (E.D. Pa. 2003).

Validity

While contracts that exculpate persons from liability are not favored by the court because they encourage lack of care and are therefore strictly construed against the person or entity seeking to escape liability, nevertheless when the language of the contract and the intent of the parties are clearly exculpatory, the contract will be upheld. This principle arises out of the broad policy of the law, which accords to contracting parties' freedom to bind themselves as they see fit. **For Example,** the exculpatory clause in a rental contract that David Hyatt signed with Mini Storage On the Green, which was clearly exculpatory, relieved Mini Storage of liability for injuries Hyatt suffered when the unit door he was pulling down with some extra force came off its tracks and injured him.[27]

Releases

Release forms signed by participants in athletic and sporting events declaring that the sponsor, proprietor, or operator of the event shall not be liable for injuries sustained by participants because of its negligence are generally binding.[28]

CASE SUMMARY

How to Handle a Risky Business

FACTS: Chelsea Hamill attended Camp Cheley for three years. Before attending camp each summer her parents signed a liability/risk release form. In July 2004, when Hamill was 15 years old, she fell off a Cheley horse and broke her arm. Chelsea brought a negligence and gross negligence lawsuit against the summer camp. Hamill's mother testified at her deposition that she voluntarily signed the release after having "skimmed" it. At her deposition, the mother testified as follows:

Attorney: And, you know, you knew that someone such as Christopher Reeve had been tragically injured falling off a horse?

Ms. Hamill: Yes.

Attorney: Did you personally know Mr. Reeve?

Ms. Hamill: Yes.

Attorney: And so you were aware that there were significant risks associated with horseback riding?

Ms. Hamill: Yes.

Attorney: And you were aware that your daughter was going to be doing a significant amount of horseback riding?

Ms. Hamill: Yes.

Hamill's mother's interpretation of the release was that prospective negligent claims were not waived. The camp disagreed. The release stated in part:

> I, on behalf of myself and my child, hereby release and waive any claim of liability against Cheley … occurring to my child while he/she participates in any and all camp programs and activities.
>
> I give my permission for my child to participate in all camp activities, including those described above. I acknowledge and assume the risks involved in these activities, and for any damages, illness, injury or death … resulting from such risks for myself and my child.
>
> (Emphasis Added.)

DECISION: Judgment for Camp Cheley. The release did not need to include an exhaustive list of particularized injury scenarios to be effective. Hamill's mother had more than sufficient information to allow her to assess the extent of injury possible in horseback riding and to make an "informed" decision before signing the release. The mother was informed of the intent to release "all claims," including prospective negligence claims. While exculpatory agreements are not a bar to civil liability for gross negligence, the record is devoid of evidence of gross negligence. [**Hamill v. Cheley Colorado Camps, Inc., 262 P.3d 945 (Colo. App. 2011)**]

---

[27] *Hyatt v. Mini Storage On the Green*, 763 S.E.2d 166 (N.C. App. 2014).

[28] But see *Woodman v. Kera, LLC*, 760 N.W.2d 641 (Mich. App. 2008) where the Court of Appeals of Michigan held that a preinjury waiver signed by a parent on behalf of a five-year-old child was invalid. See also *Brooten v. Hickok Rehabilitation Services, LLC*, 831 N.W.2d 445 (Wis. App. 2013) where the court held that the release was impermissibly broad, well beyond negligence claims.

Make the Connection

Summary

When a party fails to perform a contract or performs improperly, the other contracting party may sue for damages caused by the breach. What may be recovered by the aggrieved person is stated in terms of being direct or consequential damages. Direct damages are those that ordinarily will result from the breach. Direct damages may be recovered on proof of causation and amount. Consequential damages can be recovered only if, in addition to proving causation and amount, it is shown that they were reasonably within the contemplation of the contracting parties as a probable result of a breach of the contract. The right to recover consequential damages is lost if the aggrieved party could reasonably have taken steps to avoid such damages. In other words, the aggrieved person has a duty to mitigate or reduce damages by reasonable means.

In any case, the damages recoverable for breach of contract may be limited to a specific amount by a liquidated damages clause.

In a limited number of situations, an aggrieved party may bring an action for specific performance to compel the other contracting party to perform the acts called for

by the contract. Specific performance by the seller is always obtainable for the breach of a contract to sell land or real estate on the theory that such property has a unique value. With respect to other contracts, specific performance will not be ordered unless it is shown that there was some unique element present so that the aggrieved person would suffer a damage that could not be compensated for by the payment of money damages.

The aggrieved person also has the option of rescinding the contract if (1) the breach has been made concerning a material term and (2) the aggrieved party returns everything to the way it was before the contract was made.

Although there has been a breach of the contract, the effect of this breach is nullified if the aggrieved person by word or conduct waives the right to object to the breach. Conversely, an aggrieved party may accept a defective performance without thereby waiving a claim for breach if the party makes a reservation of rights. A reservation of rights can be made by stating that the defective performance is accepted "without prejudice," "under protest," or "with reservation of rights."

Learning Outcomes

After studying this chapter, you should be able to clearly explain:

19-1   What Constitutes a Breach of Contract?

LO.1   Explain what constitutes a breach of contract and an anticipatory breach of contract

See the illustration of a painting contractor's failure to properly paint a house, page 348.
See the *Tips* case in which damages are assessed for anticipatory repudiation of a contract, pages 348–349.
See the racetrack example of a "request," not an anticipatory breach, page 349.
See the *Mammoth Lakes* example involving anticipatory repudiation by conduct, page 349.

19-2   Waiver of Breach

LO.2   Describe the effect of a waiver of a breach
See the application of the waiver doctrine as applied in the Massey example, page 350.

19-3   Remedies for Breach of Contract

LO.3   Explain the range of remedies available for breach of contract
See Figure 19-1, "What Follows the Breach," page 352.

See the Spencer Adams example involving a range of monetary damages, pages 353–354.
See the boat slip for *Rookie IV* case involving rescission of a contract, page 355.
See the rare Revolutionary War musket example of specific performance, page 356.

19-4   Contract Provisions Affecting Remedies and Damages

LO.4   Explain when liquidated damages clauses are valid and invalid
See the Dow Corning faulty breast implants settlement agreement example in which liquidated damages of a $100 per day late payment were found to be unenforceable penalty provision, page 358.

LO.5   State when liability-limiting clauses and releases are valid
See the *Cheley Camps* case that illustrates how the camp successfully raised a signed parental exculpatory release as a defense in a horseback riding injury case, page 360.

Key Terms

anticipatory breach

anticipatory repudiation

breach

compensatory damages

consequential damages

direct damages

exculpatory clause

injunction

limitation-of-liability clause

liquidated damages

liquidated damages clause

nominal damages

punitive damages

remedies

reservation of rights

specific performance

waiver

Questions and Case Problems

1. The Forsyth School District contracted with Textor Construction, Inc., to build certain additions and alter school facilities, including the grading of a future softball field. Under the contract, the work was to be completed by August 1. Various delays occurred at the outset of the project attributable to the school district, and the architect's representative on the job, Mr. Hamilton, told Textor's vice president, William Textor, not to be concerned about a clause in the contract of $250 per day liquidated damages for failure to complete the job by August 1. Textor sued the school district for breach of contract regarding payment for the grading of the softball field, and the District counterclaimed for liquidated damages for 84 days at $250 per day for failure to complete the project by the August 1 date. What legal basis exists for Textor to defend against the counterclaim for failure to complete the job on time? Was it ethical for the school district to bring this counterclaim based on the facts before you? [*Textor Construction, Inc. v. Forsyth R-III School District*, 60 S.W.3d 692 (Mo. App.)]

2. Self-described "sports nut" Gary Baker signed up for a three-year club-seat "package" that entitled him and a companion to tickets for 41 Boston Bruin hockey games and 41 Boston Celtic basketball games at the New Boston Garden Corporation's Fleet Center for approximately $18,000 per year. After one year, Baker stopped paying for the tickets thinking that he would simply lose his $5,000 security deposit. New Boston sued Baker for breach of contract, seeking the balance due on the tickets of $34,866. At trial, Baker argued to the jury that although he had breached his contract, New Boston had an obligation to mitigate damages, for example, by treating his empty seats and those of others in the same situation as "rush seats" shortly before game time and selling them at a discount. New Boston argued that just as a used luxury car cannot be returned for a refund, a season ticket cannot be canceled without consequences. Decide.

3. Rogers made a contract with Salisbury Brick Corp. that allowed it to remove earth and sand from land he owned. The contract ran for four years with provision to renew it for additional four-year terms up to a total of 96 years. The contract provided for compensation to Rogers based on the amount of earth and sand removed. By an unintentional mistake, Salisbury underpaid Rogers the amount of $863 for the months of November and December 1986. Salisbury offered this amount to Rogers, but he refused to accept it and claimed that he had been underpaid in other months. Rogers claimed that he was entitled to rescind the contract. Was he correct? [*Rogers v. Salisbury Brick Corp.*, 882 S.E.2d 915 (S.C.)]

4. Manny Fakhimi agreed to buy an apartment complex for $697,000 at an auction from David Mason. Fakhimi was obligated to put up 10 percent of the agreed-to price at the auction as a deposit. The agreement allowed Mason to keep this deposit should Fakhimi fail to come up with the remaining 90 percent of the auction price as liquidated damages for the default. Shortly after the auction, Fakhimi heard a rumor that the military base located near the apartment complex might be closing. Fakhimi immediately stopped payment on the check and defaulted on the agreement. Mason sued Fakhimi for the liquidated damages specified in the sales contract. Decide. [*Mason v. Fakhimi*, 865 P.2d 333 (Neb.)]

5. Protein Blenders, Inc., made a contract with Gingerich to buy from him the shares of stock of a small corporation. When the buyer refused to take and pay for the stock, Gingerich sued for specific performance of the contract on the ground that the value of the stock was unknown and could not be readily ascertained because it was not sold on the general market. Was he entitled to specific performance? [*Gingerich v. Protein Blenders, Inc.*, 95 N.W.2d 522 (Iowa)]

6. The buyer of real estate made a down payment. The contract stated that the buyer would be liable for damages in an amount equal to the down payment if the buyer broke the contract. The buyer refused to go through with the contract and demanded his down payment back. The seller refused to return it and claimed that he was entitled to additional damages from the buyer because the damages that he had suffered were more than the amount of the down payment. Decide. [*Waters v. Key Colony East, Inc.*, 345 So. 2d 367 (Fla. App.)]

7. Kuznicki made a contract for the installation of a fire detection system by Security Safety Corp. for $498. The contract was made one night and canceled at 9:00 the next morning. Security then claimed one-third of the purchase price from Kuznicki by virtue of a provision in the contract that "in the event of cancellation of this agreement … the owner agrees to pay 33⅓ percent of the contract price, as liquidated damages." Was Security Safety entitled to recover the amount claimed? [*Security Safety Corp. v. Kuznicki*, 213 N.E.2d 866 (Mass.)]

8. FNBC is a business brokerage firm that assists in the purchase and sale of businesses. Jennings and Hennessey were independent contractors working for FNBC. They left FNBC, and FNBC sued them for breach of their contracts with FNBC. The trial court issued a permanent injunction prohibiting the former contractors from using proprietary information and the court awarded attorneys' fees under a clause in the contract that would obligate Jennings and Hennessey to indemnify FNBC against claims "brought by persons not a party to the provision." Jennings and Hennessey appealed the decision on attorneys' fees. Decide. [*FNBC v. Jennessey Group, LLC*, 759 N.W.2d 808 (Iowa App.)]

9. Melodee Lane Lingerie Co. was a tenant in a building that was protected against fire by a sprinkler and alarm system maintained by the American District Telegraph Co. (ADT). Because of the latter's fault, the controls on the system were defective and allowed the discharge of water into the building, which damaged Melodee's property. When Melodee sued ADT, its defense was that its service contract limited its liability to 10 percent of the annual service charge made to the customer. Was this limitation valid? [*Melodee Lane Lingerie Co. v. American District Telegraph Co.*, 218 N.E.2d 661 (N.Y.)]

10. JRC Trading Corp (JRC) bought computer software and hardware from Progressive Data Systems (PDS) for $167,935, which it paid in full, to track movement of its trucks with inventory and to process transactions. The purchase agreement also called for a $7,500 per year licensing fee for an 18-year period, and it stated that in the event of default PDS could "accelerate and declare all obligations of Customer as a liquidated sum." A dispute arose between the parties, and when the case was litigated the only actual contract charges owed PDS were the license fees of $7,500 for two years. The application of the liquidated damages clause would yield an additional $120,000 cash for PDS for the future fees for 16 years without any reduction for expenses or the present cash value for the not-yet-earned fees. JRC contends that actual damages were clearly ascertainable and that the liquidated damages clause was a penalty provision that should not be enforced. Progressive argued that the court must interpret the contract as written, stating that the court has no power to rewrite the contract. Decide. [*Jefferson Randolf Corp. v. PDS*, 553 S.E.2d 304 (Ga. App.)]

11. Ken Sulejmanagic, aged 19, signed up for a course in scuba diving taught by Madison at the YMCA. Before the instruction began, Ken was required to sign a form releasing Madison and the YMCA from liability for any harm that might occur. At the end of the course, Madison, Ken, and another student went into deep water. After Ken made the final dive required by the course program, Madison left him alone in the water while he took the other student for a dive. When Madison returned, Ken could not be found, and it was later determined that he had drowned. Ken's parents sued Madison and the YMCA for negligence in the performance of the teaching contract. The defendants raised the defense that the release Ken signed shielded them from liability. The plaintiffs claimed that the release was invalid. Who was correct? [*Madison v. Superior Court*, 250 Cal. Rptr. 299 (Cal. App.)]

12. Wassenaar worked for Panos under a three-year contract stating that if the contract were terminated wrongfully by Panos before the end of the three years, he would pay as damages the salary for the remaining time that the contract had to run. After three months, Panos terminated the contract, and Wassenaar sued him for pay for the balance of the contract term. Panos claimed that this amount could not be recovered because the contract provision for the payment was a void penalty. Was this provision valid? [*Wassenaar v. Panos*, 331 N.W.2d 357 (Wis.)]

13. Soden, a contractor, made a contract to build a house for Clevert. The sales contract stated that "if either party defaults in the performance of this contract," that party would be liable to the other for attorneys' fees incurred in suing the defaulter. Soden was 61 days late in completing the contract, and some of the work was defective. In a suit by the buyer against the contractor, the contractor claimed that he was not liable for the buyer's attorneys' fees because he had made only a defective performance and because "default" in the phrase quoted meant "nonperformance of the contract." Was the contractor liable for the attorneys' fees? [*Clevert v. Soden*, 400 S.E.2d 181 (Va.)]

14. Protection Alarm Co. made a contract to provide burglar alarm security for Fretwell's home. The contract stated that the maximum liability of the alarm company was the actual loss sustained or $50, whichever was the lesser, and that this provision was agreed to "as liquidated damages and not as a penalty." When Fretwell's home was burglarized, he sued for the loss of approximately $12,000, claiming that the alarm company had been negligent.

The alarm company asserted that its maximum liability was $50. Fretwell claimed that this was invalid because it bore no relationship to the loss that could have been foreseen when the contract was made or that in fact "had been sustained." Decide.

15. Shepherd-Will made a contract to sell Emma Cousar:

> *5 acres of land adjoining property owned by the purchaser and this being formerly land of Shepherd-Will, Inc., located on north side of Highway 223. This 5 acres to be surveyed at earliest time possible at which time plat will be attached and serve as further description on property.*

Shepherd-Will owned only one 100-acre tract of land that adjoined Emma's property. This tract had a common boundary with her property of 1,140 feet. Shepherd-Will failed to perform this contract. Emma sued for specific performance of the contract. Decide. [*Cousar v. Shepherd-Will, Inc.*, 387 S.E.2d 723 (S.C. App.)]

CPA Questions

1. Master Mfg., Inc., contracted with Accur Computer Repair Corp. to maintain Master's computer system. Master's manufacturing process depends on its computer system operating properly at all times. A liquidated damages clause in the contract provided that Accur pay $1,000 to Master for each day that Accur was late responding to a service request. On January 12, Accur was notified that Master's computer system had failed. Accur did not respond to Master's service request until January 15. If Master sues Accur under the liquidated damages provision of the contract, Master will:

   a. Win, unless the liquidated damage provision is determined to be a penalty.

   b. Win, because under all circumstances liquidated damages provisions are enforceable.

   c. Lose, because Accur's breach was *not* material.

   d. Lose, because liquidated damage provisions violate public policy (5/93, Law, #25).

2. Jones, CPA, entered into a signed contract with Foster Corp. to perform accounting and review services. If Jones repudiates the contract prior to the date performance is due to begin, which of the following is *not* correct?

   a. Foster could successfully maintain an action for breach of contract after the date performance was due to begin.

   b. Foster can obtain a judgment ordering Jones to perform.

   c. Foster could successfully maintain an action for breach of contract prior to the date performance is due to begin.

   d. Foster can obtain a judgment for the monetary damages it incurred as a result of the repudiation (5/89, Law, #35).

3. Which of the following concepts affect(s) the amount of monetary damages recoverable by the nonbreaching party when a contract is breached?

	Forseeability of damages	Mitigation of damages
a.	Yes	Yes
b.	Yes	No
c.	No	Yes
d.	No	No

Sales and Leases of Goods

Personal Property and Bailments

Learning Outcomes ⟨⟨⟨

After studying this chapter, you should be able to

LO.1 Explain how title to personal property is acquired

LO.2 List and explain the various types of gifts

LO.3 Explain the legal theory whereby an owner can recover his or her property from the wrongful exclusionary retention of another

LO.4 Identify the elements necessary to create a bailment

LO.5 Explain the standard of care a bailee is required to exercise over bailed property

What is personal property? Who owns it? How is it acquired? Think of personal property as all things of value other than real estate. Many instances arise in which the owner of personal property entrusts it to another—a person checks a coat at a restaurant or leaves a watch with a jeweler for repairs; or a company rents a car to a tourist for a weekend. The delivery of personal property to another under such circumstances is a bailment.

20-1   Personal Property

20-1a   Personal Property in Context

In common usage, the term *property* refers to a piece of land or a thing or an object. As a legal concept, however, property also refers to the rights that an individual may possess in the piece of land or that thing or that object.[1] Property includes the rights of any person to possess, use, enjoy, and dispose of a thing or object of value. A right in a thing is property, without regard to whether this right is absolute or conditional, perfect or imperfect, legal or equitable.

Real property means land and things embedded in the land, such as oil tanks. It also includes things attached to the earth, such as buildings or trees, and rights in any of these things. **Personal property** is property that is movable or intangible, or rights in such things. As described in Chapter 9, rights in intellectual property, such as writings, computer programs, inventions, and trademarks, are valuable business properties that are protected by federal statutes.

Personal property then consists of (1) whole or fractional rights in things that are tangible and movable, such as furniture and books; (2) claims and debts, which are called **choses in action;** and (3) intangible property rights, such as trademarks, copyrights, and patents.

20-1b   Title to Personal Property

Title to personal property may be acquired in different ways. For example, property is commonly purchased. The purchase and sale of goods is governed by the law of sales. In this chapter, the following methods of acquiring personal property are discussed: gift, finding lost property, occupation, and escheat.

No title is acquired by theft. The thief acquires possession only, and if the thief makes a sale or gift of the property to another, the latter acquires only possession of the property. The true owner may reclaim the property from the thief or a thief's transferee. **For Example,** through a response to a classified ad, Ray purchased a Mongoose bicycle for his son from Kevin for $250, a favorable but fair price for this used bicycle. To protect himself, he obtained from Kevin a handwritten bill of sale that was notarized by a notary public. In fact, Kevin had stolen the bicycle. Its true owner, Juan, can reclaim the bike from Ray, even though Ray has a notarized bill of sale. Ray does not have legal title to the bicycle.

CPA

20-1c   Gifts

Title to personal property may be transferred by the voluntary act of the owner without receiving anything in exchange—that is, by **gift.** The person making the gift, the **donor,** may do so because of things that the recipient of the gift, the **donee,** has done in the past or is expected to do in the future. However, such things are not deemed consideration and thus do not alter the "free" character of the gift. Five types of gifts are discussed next.

---

[1] *Presley Memorial Foundation v. Clowell,* 733 S.W.2d 89 (Tenn. App. 1987).

real property–land and all rights in land.

personal property–property that is movable or intangible, or rights in such things.

chose in action–intangible personal property in the nature of claims against another, such as a claim for accounts receivable or wages.

gift–title to an owner's personal property voluntarily transferred by a party not receiving anything in exchange.

donor–person making a gift.

donee–recipient of a gift.

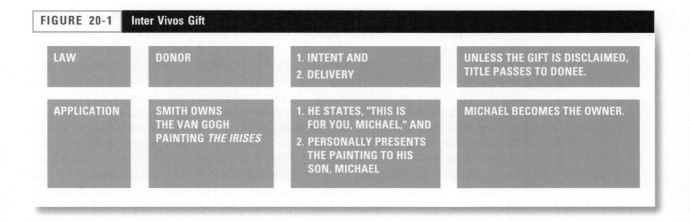

FIGURE 20-1   Inter Vivos Gift

LAW	DONOR	1. INTENT AND 2. DELIVERY	UNLESS THE GIFT IS DISCLAIMED, TITLE PASSES TO DONEE.
APPLICATION	SMITH OWNS THE VAN GOGH PAINTING *THE IRISES*	1. HE STATES, "THIS IS FOR YOU, MICHAEL," AND 2. PERSONALLY PRESENTS THE PAINTING TO HIS SON, MICHAEL	MICHAEL BECOMES THE OWNER.

Inter Vivos Gifts

inter vivos gift–any transaction that takes place between living persons and creates rights prior to the death of any of them.

The ordinary gift that is made between two living persons is an **inter vivos gift.** For practical purposes, such a gift takes effect when the donor (1) expresses an intent to transfer title and (2) makes delivery, subject to the right of the donee to disclaim the gift within a reasonable time after learning that it has been made.[2] Because there is no consideration for a gift, there is no enforceable contract, and an intended donee cannot sue for breach of contract if the donor fails to complete the gift.[3]

Intent. The intent to make a gift requires an intent to transfer title at that time. **For Example,** former ballet star Rudolf Nureyev made a valid gift when he extended deeds of gift granting ownership of his New York City apartment and its $5 million artwork collection to a nonprofit dance foundation even though he retained the right to visit the apartment and pay for its maintenance. He gave up the right to live in the apartment and executed all documents necessary to divest his domain over it.[4] In contrast, an intent to confer a benefit at a future date is not a sufficient intent to create any right in the intended donee.

A delivery of property without the intent to make a gift does not transfer title. **For Example,** Mrs. Simpson's $80,000 check to her daughter and son-in-law, Shari and Karl Goodman, to help them buy a house was not a gift if the transaction was structured as a loan, notwithstanding Shari and Karl's assertion that it was structured as a loan simply to avoid gift taxes. The legal documents setting up the loan transaction indicated that no gift was intended.[5]

symbolic delivery–delivery of goods by delivery of the means of control, such as a key or a relevant document of title, such as a negotiable bill of lading; also called constructive delivery.

Delivery. Ordinarily, the delivery required to make a gift will be an actual handing over to the donee of the thing that is given.

The delivery of a gift may also be made by a **symbolic** or **constructive delivery,** such as by the delivery of means of control of property. Such means of control might be keys to a lock or keys to a garden tractor or papers that are essential to or closely associated with the ownership of the property, such as documents of title or a ship's papers.

CPA

constructive delivery–see "symbolic delivery."

---

[2] *Bishop v. Bishop,* 961 S.W.2d 770 (Ark. 1998).
[3] *Dellagrotta v. Dellagrotta,* 873 A.2d 101 (R.I. 2005).
[4] *Rudolf Nureyev Dance Foundation v. Noureeva-Francois,* 7 F. Supp. 2d 402 (S.D.N.Y. 1998).
[5] *Simpson v. Goodman,* 727 So. 2d 555 (La. App. 1998). See also *Wright v. Mallet,* 894 A.2d 1016 (Conn. App. 2006) in which the evidence showed that a transfer of an interest in land was not intended to be a gift.

Failure to meet the "delivery" requirement will result in an ineffective gift. **For Example,** Walter Brownlee signed a bill of sale and attached a list of valuable construction equipment to it and left it with his attorney with instructions that it be passed to his son Randy after Walter's death. By leaving the bill of sale with his attorney, Walter retained control over the property and, therefore, it was never effectively delivered to Randy, resulting in an ineffective gift.[6] A completed gift is made, however, when a decedent mails a certified check to the donee prior to his death, even though the check is received after the decedent died.[7] **For Example,** Harry obtained a certified check from Colonial Bank in the amount of $80,000 on September 1, 2009, payable to Allan Foster. Harry mailed the check on September 2, 2009, and it arrived at Allan's home on September 3, 2009, several hours after Harry's death. Because the check was certified, the funds had already been subtracted from Harry's account, and Harry had relinquished all control and right over the certified check before his death, the check was a completed gift.

CPA

Donor's Death. If the donor dies before doing what is needed to make an effective gift, the gift fails.[8] An agent or the executor or administrator of the estate cannot thereafter perform the missing step on behalf of the decedent.

For Example, Mary Manning, who was in poor health, wanted to give her college-age granddaughter, Phyllis, her antique 1966 Ford Mustang convertible. She sent her daughter, Nel, to obtain the car's title from a file in the basement but was too tired to sign it on Nel's return. Mary passed away the next day without signing the document. Nel, the executrix under Mary's will, cannot complete the delivery of the gift by signing the title because it is beyond the authority of an executrix. Even though donative intent existed, no evidence of transfer of ownership and delivery to Phyllis occurred prior to Mary's death. Therefore, no valid gift was made.

Gifts Causa Mortis

gift causa mortis–gift, made by the donor in the belief that death was immediate and impending, that is revoked or is revocable under certain circumstances.

A **gift causa mortis** is made when the donor, contemplating imminent and impending death, delivers personal property to the donee with the intent that the donee shall own it if the donor dies. This is a conditional gift, and the donor is entitled to take the property back if (1) the donor does not die, (2) the donor revokes the gift before dying, or (3) the donee dies before the donor.

Gifts and Transfers to Minors

Uniform acts provide for transferring property to a custodian to hold for the benefit of a minor.[9] When a custodian holds property for the benefit of a minor under one of the uniform acts, the custodian has discretionary power to use the property "for the support, maintenance, education, and benefit" of the minor, but the custodian may not use the custodial property for the custodian's own personal benefit. The gift is final and irrevocable for tax and all other purposes on complying with the procedures of the acts.

Under the uniform acts, custodianships terminate and the property is distributed when the minor reaches age 21.

---

[6] In re *Estate of Walter Brownlee, Sr.,* 654 N.W.2d (S.D. 2002).
[7] *Foster v. Foster,* 2012 WL 29164 (Ala. App. Jan. 6, 2012).
[8] *Laverman v. Destocki,* 622 N.E.2d 1122 (Ohio App. 1994).
[9] The Uniform Gifts to Minors Act (UGMA) is in effect in South Carolina and Vermont. The Uniform Transfers to Minors Act, which expands the type of property that can be made the subject of a gift, was originally proposed in 1983. It has been adopted, often with minor variations, in all states and the District of Columbia except South Carolina and Vermont.

CASE SUMMARY

Ignorance Is No Defense

FACTS: In 1980, Larry Heath received $10,000 from his father. With interest, these funds grew to $13,381 by 1983, and in March he used this money to establish two custodian bank accounts for his minor children under the Uniform Gifts to Minors Act (UGMA). Larry was listed as custodian on each account. In August 1984, Larry closed both accounts and returned the proceeds to his mother while his father was then in Europe. The children's mother, Pamela, brought suit to recover the funds on behalf of the children, contending that the deposits were irrevocable gifts. Larry contended that the money was his father's and was never intended as a gift. Larry testified that he was a mere factory worker and was ignorant of the legal effect of his signing the signature cards for the custodian accounts.

DECISION: Judgment for Pamela on behalf of the children. To find that an inter vivos gift has been made, there must be donative intent and delivery. The UGMA expressly deals with "delivery" and provides that this element of a gift is satisfied by documentary compliance with the procedures of the statute. The issue of "donative intent" is not conclusively resolved by making a determination that there was documentary compliance with the statute. However, documentary compliance with the procedures set forth by the UGMA is highly probative on the issue of intent. Larry's testimony that he was ignorant of the legal effect of his signing the signature cards was unworthy of belief and insufficient to rebut the strong documentary showing that he had created irrevocable gifts. [**Heath v. Heath**, 493 N.E.2d 97 (Ill. App. 1986)]*

*See *Wasniewski v. Quick and Reilly, Inc.*, 940 A.2d 811 (Conn. App. 2008) where a minor's father opened a brokerage account on November 15, 1989, at Quick and Reilly in his minor son James's name funded with $30,000 in bonds. The account was closed on July 5, 2001, and all funds were transferred to a joint account in the name of the father and another son. The court determined that a contract had existed between James, the owner of the account, and the brokerage firm, and that the brokerage firm had breached its contract with James when it transferred funds to someone other than James. James was awarded principal and interest of $52,085 from Quick and Reilly.

Conditional Gifts

A gift may be made subject to a condition, such as "This car is yours when you graduate" or "This car is yours unless you drop out of school." In the first example, the gift is subject to a condition precedent—graduation. A condition precedent must be satisfied before any gift or transfer takes place. In the second example, the gift is subject to a condition subsequent—dropping out of school.

Absent a finding of an intent to create a trust, a donative transaction will be analyzed as a gift subject to conditions. **For Example,** the gift by the Tennessee United Daughters of the Confederacy (UDC) to a building fund for Peabody College expressly reserved the right to recall the gift if the college failed to comply with the conditions of placing an inscription on the 1935 building naming it Confederate Memorial Hall. Peabody College for Teachers was merged into Vanderbilt University in 1979. In 2002, Vanderbilt decided to rename Confederate Memorial Hall. The Tennessee UDC's suit for the return of its gift was successful; the court decided that it was not at liberty to relieve a party from its contractual obligations.[10]

Most courts regard an engagement ring as a conditional gift subject to the condition subsequent of a failure to marry. The inherent symbolism of the gift itself is deemed to foreclose the need to establish an express condition that there be a marriage.

Some jurisdictions require return of engagement rings only if the donor has not unjustifiably broken off the engagement. Most states now reject considerations of "fault" in the breaking of an engagement and always require the return of the ring to the donor when an engagement is broken. This "modern trend" is based on the theory that, in most cases, "fault" is impossible to determine.

[10] *Tennessee UDC v. Vanderbilt University*, 174 S.W.3d 98 (Tenn. Ct. App. 2005).

CASE SUMMARY

Your Honor, Marriages Are Not Made in Heaven, You Say?

FACTS: Dr. Barry Meyer and Robyn Mitnick became engaged on August 9, 1996, at which time Barry gave Robyn a custom-designed engagement ring that he purchased for $19,500. On November 8, 1996, Barry asked Robyn to sign a prenuptial agreement and Robyn refused. The engagement was broken during that meeting, with both Barry and Robyn contending the other party caused the breakup. Robyn did not return the ring, and Barry sued for its return. Robyn filed a countercomplaint, alleging that the ring was an unconditional gift and that because Barry broke the engagement, she was entitled to keep the ring.

DECISION: Judgment for Barry Meyer. Following the "modern trend," the court decided that an engagement ring given in contemplation of marriage is an impliedly conditional gift that is completed only upon marriage. If the engagement is called off, regardless of fault, the gift is not complete and must be returned to the donor. The court rejected the "older view" of returning the gift to the donor only when the engagement is unjustifiably broken off by the donee, or

by mutual agreement. As stated by the court in *Aronow v. Silver*, 223 N.J. Super. 344 (1987):

> *What fact justifies the breaking of an engagement? The absence of a sense of humor? Differing musical tastes? Differing political views? The painfully-learned fact is that marriages are made on earth, not in heaven. They must be approached with intelligent care and should not happen without a decent assurance of success. When either party lacks that assurance, for whatever reason, the engagement should be broken. No justification is needed. Either party may act. Fault, impossible to fix, does not count.*

[*Meyer v. Mitnick*, 625 N.W.2d 136 (Mich. App. 2001)]*

*Texas courts apply the fault-based conditional gift rule when a donee breaks the engagement. When the giver of the ring violates his promise to marry, it would seem to Texas courts that a similar result should follow; that is, he should lose, not gain, rights to the ring. **[See *Curtis v. Anderson*, 2003 WL 1832257 (Tex. App.)]**

Anatomical Gifts

Persons may make gifts of parts of their bodies, as in the case of kidney transplants. Persons may also make postdeath gifts. The Uniform Anatomical Gift Act[11] permits persons 18 years or older to make gifts of their bodies or any parts thereof. The gift takes effect on the death of the donor. The gift may be made to a school, a hospital, an organ bank, or a named patient. Such a gift may also be made, subject to certain restrictions, by the spouse, adult child, parent, adult brother or sister, or guardian of a deceased person. If a hospital misleads family members into consenting to tissue or organ donations that exceed their express wishes, such misconduct is sufficiently outrageous to support a claim for intentional infliction of emotional distress.[12]

CPA 20-1d **Finding of Lost Property**

Personal property is lost when the owner does not know where it is located but intends to retain title to or ownership of it. The person finding lost property does not acquire title but only possession. Ordinarily, the finder of lost property is required to surrender the property to the true owner when the latter establishes ownership. Meanwhile, the finder is entitled to retain possession as against everyone else.

Without a contract with the owner or a statute so providing, the finder of lost property usually is not entitled to a reward or to compensation for finding or caring for the property.

Finding in Public Place

If the lost property is found in a public place, such as a hotel, under such circumstances that to a reasonable person it would appear the property had been intentionally placed

---

[11] This act has been adopted in every state.
[12] See *Perry v. Saint Francis Hospital*, 886 F. Supp. 1551 (D. Kan. 1995).

there by the owner and the owner would be likely to recall where the property had been left and to return for it, the finder is not entitled to possession of the property. The finder must give it to the proprietor or manager of the public place to keep it for the owner. This exception does not apply if it appears that the property was not intentionally placed where it was found. In that case, it is not likely that the owner will recall having left it there.

Statutory Change

Some states have adopted statutes permitting the finder to sell the property or keep it if the owner does not appear within a stated period of time. In this case, the finder is required to give notice—for example, by newspaper publication—to attempt to reach the owner.

20-1e Occupation of Personal Property

In some cases, title to personal property may be acquired by occupation—that is, by taking and retaining possession of the property.

Wild Animals

Wild animals, living in a state of nature, are not owned by any individual. In the absence of restrictions imposed by game laws, the person who acquires dominion or control over a wild animal becomes its owner. What constitutes sufficient dominion or control varies with the nature of the animal and the surrounding circumstances. If the animal is killed, tied, imprisoned, or otherwise prevented from going at its will, the hunter exercises sufficient dominion or control over the animal and becomes its owner. If the wild animal, subsequent to its capture, should escape and return to its natural state, it resumes the status of a wild animal.

As a qualification to the ordinary rule, the following exception developed. If an animal is killed or captured on the land of another while the hunter is on the land without permission of the landowner, the animal, when killed or captured, belongs not to the hunter but to the landowner.

Abandoned Personal Property

Personal property is deemed abandoned when the owner relinquishes possession with the intention to disclaim title to it.[13] Yesterday's newspaper thrown out in the trash is abandoned personal property. Title to abandoned property may be acquired by the first person who obtains possession and control of it. A person becomes the owner at the moment of taking possession of the abandoned personal property. If, however, the owner of property flees in the face of an approaching peril, property left behind is not abandoned. An abandonment occurs only when the owner voluntarily leaves the property.

CASE SUMMARY

Not an Ordinary Bank

FACTS: Charles and Rosa Nelson owned a home in Selma, Iowa, for over one-half a century. After their death, the property was abandoned because of the substantial unpaid real estate taxes. The Selma United Methodist Church purchased the property at a tax sale. When the church razed the dwelling, it found $24,547 in cash and coins that had been buried

---

[13] See *Greenpeace, Inc. v. The Dow Chemical Co.*, 97 A.3d 1053 (D.C. Ct. of App. 2014).

Not an Ordinary Bank continued

in the ground in glass jars by Charles many years before. The heirs of the Nelson family claimed the money. The church claimed that because the real estate was abandoned by the estate, the church was now the true owner of the money.

DECISION: Judgment for the heirs. Although the real estate was abandoned, the money found by the church had not been abandoned by its owner, Charles Nelson. The fact that it was buried in glass jars indicates that the owner was trying to preserve it. Therefore, the money had not been abandoned and was owned by Nelson's heirs. [*Ritz v. Selma United Methodist Church*, 467 N.W.2d 266 (Iowa 1991)]

Conversion

The tort of conversion has its origins in the ancient common law writ of trover, created "as a remedy against the finder of lost goods who refused to return them."[14] Because of that origin, the tort of conversion was limited to property that could be lost and found (i.e., tangible personalty as opposed to real property). Wrongful dominion over a principal's tangible personal property remains a viable theory today. **For Example,** Robert Weinberg consigned a ring for auction by L. R. Bernes, LLC, and auctioneer Steven White. When the successful bidder at $2,300 failed to make payment for the ring, Bernes and White refused Weinberg's demand for the return of the ring, seeking commissions and other fees. This refusal was contrary to Bernes' and White's authority under the consignment agreement and was a wrongful exercise of dominion over the ring. Weinberg was successful in his conversion lawsuit against Bernes and White.[15]

CASE SUMMARY

Hey! That's My Stuff on the North Star Web Site!

FACTS: In 2003 Paul and Arthur Williams moved personal property from the Skinner Gallery to Smith Storage, which was operated by the Faeber family. After the death of a Faeber parent in March 2006, Smith Storage customers were notified that the business was being discontinued. Gary and Robert Faeber, sons who were not active in the business, removed property from Smith Storage in March 2006 and consigned it to North Star Auction Galleries, Inc. When Arthur Williams became aware that some of his property was listed on North Star's Web site, the Williamses sued Gary and Robert for conversion. Gary contended that he was not liable for conversion because he in good faith believed that the property consigned and sold on North Star belonged to his mother. He and Robert also asserted that the Williamses did not provide sufficient proof that the stored property belonged to them.

DECISION: Judgment for Paul and Arthur Williams. They presented documentation of their ownership interest. While the defendants assert that the property belonged to their mother, they presented no admissible evidence to support this assertion. Gary Faeber's argument that the consignment was done in "good faith" based on the belief that the property belonged to his mother is of no merit, for good faith is not a defense to conversion. The defendant's assertion that the plaintiffs did not provide sufficient evidence of ownership is irrelevant. A bailee cannot deny a bailor's title as an excuse for refusing to redeliver the property. [*Williams v. Smith Avenue Moving Co.*, 528 F. Supp. 2d 316 (N.D.N.Y. 2008)]

---

[14] Restatement, Second of Torts §242, comment d.
[15] *White v. Weinberg*, 759 S.E.2d 903 (Ga. App. 2014).

As the nature of personal property evolved to the point that tangible documents represented highly valuable rights, such as promissory notes, stock certificates, insurance policies, and bank books, common law courts expanded the tort of conversion to include such documents within its definitional scope despite their intangible aspects, which, invariably, are primary components of the document's value. The concept of conversion today, which is the wrongful exclusionary retention of an owner's physical property, applies to an electronic record as much as it does to a paper record such as valuable stock certificates and bank books. **For Example,** a computerized client/investor list created by a real estate agent is "property" protected by the law of conversion.[16]

20-1f Escheat

Who owns unclaimed property? In the case of personal property, the practical answer is that the property will probably "disappear" after a period of time, or if in the possession of a carrier, hotel, or warehouse, it may be sold for unpaid storage charges. A growing problem arises with respect to unclaimed corporate dividends, bank deposits, insurance payments, and refunds. Most states have a statute providing for the transfer of such unclaimed property to the state government. This transfer to the government is often

escheat–transfer to the state of the title to a decedent's property when the owner of the property dies intestate and is not survived by anyone capable of taking the property as heir.

called by its feudal name of **escheat. For Example,** when James Canel's 280 shares of stock in Patrick Industries were turned over to the state treasurer's office by Harris Bank because his account at the bank had been inactive for more than five years, the property was presumed to be abandoned. Once Canel claimed the property, however, he was entitled to the return of the stock and the past dividends. The state was not entitled to retain the dividends under the court's reading of the state's Unclaimed Property Act.[17] Funds held by stores for layaway items for customers who fail to complete the layaway purchases are subject to escheat to the state. To provide for unclaimed property, many states have adopted the Uniform Unclaimed Property Act (UUPA),[18] formerly called the Uniform Disposition of Unclaimed Property Act.

CASE SUMMARY

The King Is Dead! Who Gets the Unrefunded Ticket Proceeds?

FACTS: Elvis Presley contracted with the Mid-South Coliseum Board (City of Memphis) for the rental of the Coliseum and for personnel to sell tickets for concerts on August 27 and 28, 1977. Subsequently, $325,000 worth of tickets were sold. On August 16, 1977, Elvis Presley died. Refunds were given to those who returned their tickets to the coliseum board. Ten years after his death, however, $152,279 worth of ticket proceeds remained unclaimed in the custody of the board. This fund had earned $223,760 in interest. Priscilla Presley and the coexecutors of the estate of Elvis Presley brought an action claiming the unrefunded ticket proceeds for the canceled concerts. The state of Tennessee claimed that it was entitled to the proceeds under the Uniform Disposition of Unclaimed Property Act (UDUPA).

DECISION: Judgment for the state. Elvis Presley's estate has no legal claim to the ticket proceeds because his death discharged the contract represented by each ticket sold. Ticket holders would have claimed the refunds if it had not been for Presley's legendary status, and they chose to keep the tickets as memorabilia. The drafters of the UDUPA intended that windfalls such as the unrefunded proceeds in this case benefit the public rather than individuals. [*Presley v. City of Memphis*, 769 S.W.2d 221 (Tenn. App. 1988)]

---

[16] *Shmueli v. Corcoran Group,* 802 N.Y.S.2d 871 (2005).

[17] *Canel v. Topinka,* 818 N.E.2d 311 (Ill. 2004).

[18] The 1981 or 1995 version of the Act has been adopted in Alaska, Arizona, Arkansas, Colorado, Florida, Hawaii, Idaho, Illinois, Indiana, Kansas, Louisiana, Maine, Michigan, Montana, Nevada, New Hampshire, New Jersey, New Mexico, North Carolina, North Dakota, Oklahoma, Oregon, Rhode Island, South Carolina, South Dakota, U.S. Virgin Islands, Utah, Virginia, Washington, West Virginia, Wisconsin, and Wyoming.

20-1g Multiple Ownership of Personal Property

When all rights in a particular object of property are held by one person, that property is held in **severalty.** However, two or more persons may hold concurrent rights and interests in the same property. In that case, the property is said to be held in **cotenancy.** The various forms of cotenancy include (1) tenancy in common, (2) joint tenancy, (3) tenancy by entirety, and (4) community property.

Tenancy in Common

A **tenancy in common** is a form of ownership by two or more persons. The interest of a tenant in common may be transferred or inherited, in which case the taker becomes a tenant in common with the others. **For Example,** Brandt and Vincent restored an 18-foot 1940 mahogany-hulled Chris Craft runabout and own it as tenants in common. If Brandt sold his interest in the boat to Andrea, then Vincent and Andrea would be co-owners as tenants in common. If Brandt died before Vincent, a one-half interest in the boat would become the property of Brandt's heirs.

Joint Tenancy

A **joint tenancy** is another form of ownership by two or more persons, but a joint tenancy has a *right of survivorship.*[19] On the death of a joint tenant, the remaining tenants take the share of the deceased tenant. The last surviving joint tenant takes the property as a holder in severalty. **For Example,** in Brandt and Vincent's Chris Craft case, if the boat were owned as joint tenants with a right of survivorship, Vincent would own the boat outright upon Brandt's death, and Brandt's heirs would obtain no interest in it.

A joint tenant's interest may be transferred to a third person, but this destroys the joint tenancy. If the interest of one of two joint tenants is transferred to a third person, the remaining joint tenant becomes a tenant in common with the third person. **For Example,** if Brandt sold his interest to Andrea, Vincent and Andrea would be co-owners as tenants in common.

Statutes in many states have modified the common law by adding a formal requirement to the creation of a joint tenancy with survivorship. At common law, such an estate would be created by a transfer of property to "*A* and *B* as joint tenants."[20] Under these statutes, however, it is necessary to add the words "with right of survivorship" or other similar words if a right of survivorship is desired.

CASE SUMMARY

Honor Thy Mother's Wishes?

FACTS: Rachel Auffert purchased a $10,000 certificate of deposit on January 7, 1981, creating a joint tenancy in this bank deposit payable to herself or either of two children, Leo or Mary Ellen, "either or the survivor." When Rachel died, a note dated January 7, 1981, written in Rachel's handwriting and signed by her,

---

[19] *Estate of Munier v. Jacquemin,* 899 S.W.2d 114 (Mo. App. 1995).

[20] Some states have modified the common law by creating a condition that whenever two or more persons are listed as owners of a bank account or certificate of deposit, a presumption of joint tenancy with right of survivorship arises unless expressly negated by the signature card or another instrument or by extrinsic proof. Thus, when Herbert H. Herring had his bank change the designated owners of a certificate of deposit to read, "Herbert H. Herring or [his grandson] Robert J. Herring," and no words indicating survivorship upon the death of either were on the certificate, nevertheless under a 1992 Florida statute creating a presumption of survivorship, which presumption was not rebutted, grandson Robert was declared the owner of the certificate. In re *Estate of H. H. Herring,* 670 So. 2d 145 (Fla. App. 1996).

Honor Thy Mother's Wishes? continued

was found with the certificate of deposit. The note stated:

> Leo: If I die this goes to Sr. Mary Ellen,
> Wanted another name on it.
> S/Rachel Auffert
> Jan 7 1981

Mary Ellen cashed the certificate of deposit and retained the proceeds. Leo sued to recover one-half the value of the certificate.

DECISION: Judgment for Leo. There was statutory compliance when the certificate of deposit was purchased, and thus a statutory joint tenancy was created. The only means available to Rachel to alter the joint tenants' proportionate interests was to change the names on the account during her lifetime. Because Rachel failed to do so, the law presumes that Leo and Mary Ellen equally owned the certificate of deposit. [*Auffert v. Auffert,* **829 S.W.2d 95 (Mo. App. 1992)**]

If no words of survivorship are used, the transfer of property to two or more persons will be construed as creating a tenancy in common. Under such a statute, a certificate of deposit issued only in the name of "*A* or *B*" does not create a joint tenancy because it does not contain words of survivorship.

Tenancy by Entirety

tenancy by entirety or tenancy by the entireties–transfer of property to both husband and wife.

At common law, a **tenancy by entirety** or **tenancy by the entireties** was created when property was transferred to both husband and wife. It differs from joint tenancy in that it exists only when the transfer is to husband and wife. Also, the right of survivorship cannot be extinguished, and one spouse's interest cannot be transferred to a third person. However, in some jurisdictions, a spouse's right to share the possession and the profits may be transferred. This form of property holding is popular in common law jurisdictions because creditors of only one of the spouses cannot reach the property while both are living. Only a creditor of both the husband and the wife under the same obligation can obtain execution against the property.

For Example, a husband and wife, Rui and Carla Canseco, purchased a 2015 Lexus LS 460 for cash. It was titled in the names of "Rui J. *and* Carla T. Canseco." Later that year, State National Bank obtained a money judgment against Rui for $200,000, and the bank claimed entitlement to half the value of the Cansecos' car, which it asserted was Rui's share as a joint tenant. A tenancy by entirety had been created, however, so the bank could not levy against the auto. If the car had been titled "Rui *or* Carla T. Canseco," in most states the use of the word "or" would indicate that the vehicle was held in joint tenancy even if the co-owners are husband and wife. As such, Rui's half interest could be reached by the bank.

The tenancy by entirety is, in effect, a substitute for a will because the surviving spouse acquires the complete property interest on the death of the other. There are usually other reasons, however, why each spouse should make a will.

In many states, the granting of an absolute divorce converts a tenancy by the entireties into a tenancy in common.

20-1h Community Property

community property–cotenancy held by husband and wife in property acquired during their marriage under the law of some of the states, principally in the southwestern United States.

In some states, property acquired during the period of marriage is the **community property** of the husband and wife. Some statutes provide for the right of survivorship; others provide that half of the property of the deceased husband or wife shall go to the heirs of that spouse or permit such half to be disposed of by will. It is commonly

prima facie–evidence that, if believed, is sufficient by itself to lead to a particular conclusion.

bailment–relationship that exists when personal property is delivered into the possession of another under an agreement, express or implied, that the identical property will be returned or will be delivered in accordance with the agreement. (Parties—bailor, bailee)

bailor–person who turns over the possession of a property.

bailee–person who accepts possession of a property.

provided that property acquired by either spouse during the marriage is **prima facie** community property, even though title is taken in the spouse's individual name, unless it can be shown that it was obtained with property possessed by the spouse prior to the marriage.

20-2   Bailments

20-2a   Definition

A **bailment** is the relationship that arises when one person delivers possession of personal property to another under an agreement, express or implied, by which the latter is under a duty to return the property or to deliver it or dispose of it as agreed. The person who turns over the possession of the property is the **bailor.** The person who accepts is the **bailee.** Bailments may take many forms in our society. **For Example,** in commercial livestock operations, J & R Farms, the bailor, had an arrangement with Mississippi Valley Livestock, Inc. (MVI), the bailee, under which MVI would take possession and sell some of J & R's cattle to Swift & Co. and hold the proceeds for J & R's benefits, giving J & R restitution rights to the proceeds versus MVI's bankruptcy trustee.[21] Or consider the towing of bailor Robert Pelkey's car by Dan's City Used Cars (the bailee), which would imply the duties as bailee to use reasonable care while in possession of this bailed property.[22] The law of bailments also applies to the resolution of ownership and possession rights of historical documents and manuscripts.

CASE SUMMARY

Department of Cultural Resources: "Possession is nine tenths of the law." The Johnsons: "Not the law of Bailments!"

FACTS: Colonel Charles E. Johnson ("Johnson") was a descendant of former United States Supreme Court Justice James Iredell, Sr. and former North Carolina Governor James Iredell, Jr. Johnson owned the Collection, which consisted of various manuscripts and documents that belonged to his ancestors. In 1910, Johnson loaned the Collection to the North Carolina Historical Commission. In a letter to R.D.W. Connor, Secretary of the Historical Commission, dated 21 December 1910, Johnson stated: "You will remember that my position in this is that I have loaned [the Collection] to the State with the right of recall and repossession at any time if I see fit." In a letter dated 23 December 1910, Connor replied to Johnson and stated that "[i]t is thoroughly understood by the North Carolina Historical Commission that the 'Charles E. Johnson Collection' of manuscripts deposited by you with the Commission, was deposited merely as a loan, subject to your recall at any time you may see fit." In 2008, Harvey Johnson, a descendant of Johnson, discovered the 1910

correspondence and brought action for declaratory judgment under the law of bailment that he and other descendants were owners of the Collection. The state raised several defenses.

DECISION: Judgment for the descendants. Johnson's transfer of the Collection to the Historical Commission created a bailment, which continued after his death. Ownership of the Collection, including the right to recall the Collection, properly passed to Johnson's descendants through his will, which bequeathed all of his property to Mrs. Johnson, and subsequently through the residuary clause included in Mrs. Johnson's will. Plaintiffs had no viable claim against the State until after the State refused to return the Collection upon Harvey Johnson's demand in 2008. Plaintiffs timely pursued this claim, and thus, the claim was not barred by either the statute of limitations or the doctrine of laches. [*Johnson v. North Carolina Department of Cultural Resources*, 735 S.E.2d 595 (N.C. App. 2012)]

---

[21] In re *Mississippi Valley Livestock, Inc.*, 745 F.3d 299 (7th Cir. 2014).
[22] *Dan's City Used Cars, Inc. v. Pelkey*, 133 S. Ct. 1769 (2013).

20-2b Elements of Bailment

A bailment is created when the following elements are present.

Agreement

The bailment is based on an *agreement.* This agreement may be express or implied. Generally, it contains all of the elements of a contract. The bailment transaction in fact consists of (1) a contract to bail and (2) the actual bailing of the property. Ordinarily, there is no requirement that the contract of bailment be in writing. The subject of a bailment may be any personal property of which possession may be given.[23] Real property cannot be bailed.

Delivery and Acceptance

The bailment arises when, pursuant to the agreement of the parties, the property is delivered to the bailee and accepted by the bailee as subject to the bailment agreement.

In the absence of a prior agreement to the contrary, a valid delivery and acceptance generally require that the bailee be aware that goods have been placed within the bailee's exclusive possession or control. **For Example,** photography equipment belonging to Bill Bergey, the photographer of Roosevelt University's student newspaper, was stolen from the newspaper's campus office. Bergey believes that the university breached its duty as bailee because records showed that no campus police officer checked the building on the night of the theft. Bergey's case against the university on this bailment theory will fail, however, because the university did not know that the equipment was left in the office. Without this knowledge, there was neither a bailment agreement nor acceptance of delivery by the university as a bailee.

20-2c Nature of the Parties' Interests

The bailor and bailee have different legal interests in the bailed property.

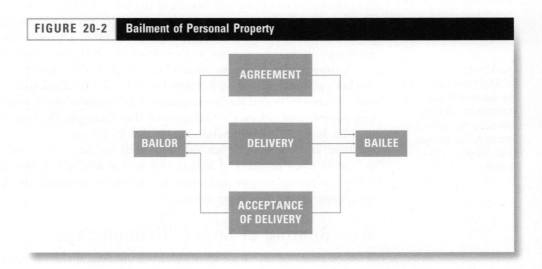

FIGURE 20-2   **Bailment of Personal Property**

---

[23] *Stone v. CDI Corp.,* 9 S.W.3d 699 (Mo. App. 1999).

Bailor's Interest

The bailor is usually the owner, but ownership by the bailor is not required. It is sufficient that the bailor have physical possession. **For Example,** Crella Magee delivered a blue fox jacket for summer storage to Walbro, Inc. When it was not returned, she sued Walbro for the replacement cost of the jacket, $3,400. Walbro's defense that Magee was not entitled to recover the replacement cost of the lost jacket because she did not prove ownership was rejected as irrelevant by the court, and the case was decided in favor of Magee.[24]

Bailee's Interest

The bailee has possession of the property only. **For Example,** the Lackawanna Chapter for the Railway & Locomotive Historical Society, Inc., and its predecessor held title to Engine No. 952, a now-rare camelback locomotive built in 1905 and retired in 1938. It was placed in the care of the St. Louis Transportation Museum in 1953 for "permanent exhibition." The Lackawanna Chapter sought the return of Engine No. 952 after more than 50 years, and the successor St. Louis Museum raised numerous defenses. Possession and control do not entitle the St. Louis Museum to continued possession that overcomes a lender's good title. The museum, as a bailee in a gratuitous bailment, has the duty to return the bailment property to the owner.[25]

Title to the property does not pass to the bailee, and the bailee cannot sell the property to a third person. If the bailee attempts to sell the property, such sale transfers only possession, and the owner may recover the property from the buyer.

20-2d Classification of Ordinary Bailments

Ordinary bailments are generally classified as being for (1) the sole benefit of the bailor, (2) the sole benefit of the bailee, or (3) the mutual benefit of both.

Bailments may or may not provide for compensation to the bailee. On the basis of compensation, bailments may be classified as (1) **bailments for mutual benefit** in which one party takes the personal property of another into her care or custody in exchange for payment or other benefit and (2) **gratuitous bailments** in which the transfer of possession and use of the bailed property is without compensation. Bailments for the sole benefit of the bailor or for the sole benefit of the bailee are sometimes described as gratuitous. The fact that no charge is made by the bailor does not necessarily make the transaction a gratuitous bailment. If the bailment is made to further a business interest of the bailor, as when something is loaned free to a customer, the bailment is not gratuitous.

A **constructive bailment** arises when one person has lawfully acquired possession of another's personal property other than by virtue of a bailment contract and holds it under such circumstances that the law imposes on the recipient of the property the obligation to keep it safely and redeliver it to the owner. **For Example,** the City of Chicago is the constructive bailee of an automobile impounded by Chicago police at the time of a driver's arrest for drunk driving. It has a duty to keep the automobile safely and turn it over to the owner upon payment of towing and storage fees. When this duty is delegated to a private contractor to tow and store, a constructive bailment for the mutual benefit of the contractor and the owner exists.

20-2e Renting of Space Distinguished

When a person rents space in a locker or building under an agreement that gives the renter the exclusive right to use that space, the placing of goods by the renter in that

bailment for mutual benefit—bailment in which the bailor and bailee derive a benefit from the bailment.

gratuitous bailment—bailment in which the bailee does not receive any compensation or advantage.

constructive bailment—bailment imposed by law as opposed to one created by contract, whereby the bailee must preserve the property and redeliver it to the owner.

---

[24] *Magee v. Walbro, Inc.,* 525 N.E.2d 975 (Ill. App. 1988).
[25] *Lackawanna Chapter v. St. Louis County,* 497 F.3d 832 (8th Cir. 2007).

space does not create a bailment, for it does not constitute a delivery of goods into the possession of the owner of the space. **For Example,** Winston Hutton entered into a rental agreement for a storage space at Public Storage Management's self-storage facility in New York City, and his stored property was stolen from the space. Hutton had procured his own lock for the storage space, and the rental agreement provided that management would not have a key. Hutton's lawsuit was unsuccessful because the defendant did not take possession of the property. The legal relationship was not a bailment.[26] Renting a safe deposit box or space in a bank vault does create a bailment, however. **For Example,** Bank of America (BOA) agreed to store the Martin Lucas law firm's file cabinets in its bank vault for a monthly fee. A water pipe burst, flooding the vault and causing significant damage to original legal documents stored in the cabinets. BOA's contention that the arrangement did not constitute a bailment because the law firm did not relinquish exclusive control over the cabinets because the bank could not open the file cabinets was rejected by the court. The relation of bailor-bailee is not disturbed by the fact that a safe deposit company does not know and is not expected to know the contents of a safe deposit box or file cabinet.[27]

20-2f Duties and Rights of the Bailee

The bailee has certain duties concerning performance, care, and return of the bailed property. The bailee must perform his part of a contract and is liable for ordinary contract damages for failure to perform the contract.

The bailee is under a duty to care for the bailed property, and the duty of care owed differs according to classification, based in terms of "benefit." A bailment may be for the sole benefit of the bailor. **For Example,** when Fred allows Mary, a college classmate from out of state, to store her books and furniture in his basement over the summer, Fred, the bailee, is liable only for gross negligence relating to damage to these stored belongings. A bailment may be for the sole benefit of the bailee, as when Mary allows Fred to borrow her Les Paul Gibson guitar. Fred, the bailee, is liable even for slight negligence in the case of any damage to the guitar. Most bailments, however, are mutual benefit bailments. **For Example,** when Harry rents for a fee a trailer from U-Haul, Inc., to transport his son's belongings to college, Harry, the bailee, is responsible for using reasonable or ordinary care under the circumstances while possessing and using the trailer. U-Haul, the bailor, has a duty to warn Harry of any known defects or defects that could be discovered on reasonable inspection.

A bailee has a right to receive payment for charges due for storage or repairs.[28] A **bailee's lien** gives the bailee the right to keep possession of the bailed property until charges are paid. A bailee who is authorized by statute to sell the bailed property to enforce a charge or claim against the bailor must give such notice as is required by the statute. A bailee who sells without giving the required notice is liable for conversion of the property.

bailee's lien—specific, possessory lien of the bailee upon the goods for work done to them. Commonly extended by statute to any bailee's claim for compensation, eliminating the necessity of retention of possession.

20-2g Breach of Duty of Care: Burden of Proof

Although a bailment is contractual in nature, an action for breach of duty of care by a bailee "sounds in tort." That is, the true nature of the liability is not contractual at all but based on tort principles.

When the bailor sues the bailee for damages to the bailed property, the bailor has the burden of proving that the bailee was at fault and that such fault was the proximate

---

[26] *Hutton v. Public Storage Management, Inc.,* 676 N.Y.S.2d 887 (N.Y. City Civ. Ct. 1998).

[27] *Martin, Lucas, Chioffi, LLP v. Bank of America,* 714 F. Supp. 2d 303 (D. Conn. 2010).

[28] See *Smith v. Lewis Auto Body,* 255 P.3d 935, 940 (Wyo. 2011). The bailee auto body shop had the right to retain possession of the 2006 Chevrolet Corvette pursuant to a valid lien until it received payment for its services. However, since it could have released the vehicle and sued for damages, it was not necessary to retain possession of the vehicle, and it thus could not accumulate storage charges of $60 a day during the period in question.

cause of the loss.[29] A prima facie right of the bailor to recover is established, however, by proof that the bailor delivered the property to the bailee in good condition and subsequently could not be returned by the bailee or was returned in a damaged condition. When this is done, the bailee has the burden of proving that the loss or damage was not caused by the bailee's failure to exercise the care required by law, which in the case of a mutual benefit bailment is that of an ordinary or due care, under all of the circumstances.

CASE SUMMARY

Towed into Court

FACTS: Mark Hadfield, a medical student in Charleston, South Carolina, went to retrieve his 1988 Lincoln Continental from a parking space on private property near the medical school where his wife had parked the car earlier that day without permission. The property owner had called Gilchrist Towing Co., and the auto had been removed. When Hadfield discovered that the car had been towed, he telephoned Gilchrist Towing and was told that he would have to wait until the next morning to retrieve the car after paying towing and storage fees. The next morning, after paying the charges, he went to the storage lot and found that his car had been extensively vandalized along with a number of other vehicles. The owner of the company, S.S. Gilchrist, refused to pay the estimated cost of repairs, $4,021.43. Hadfield brought suit, contending that a constructive bailment for the mutual benefit of Hadfield and Gilchrist had been created, and that Gilchrist breached his duty of care to Hadfield. Gilchrist contended that he towed the vehicle pursuant to Charleston Municipal Ordinances, which are for the sole benefit of the vehicle owners, intended to preserve their property. As such, the relationship created was a gratuitous bailment, which limited his duty of care. Gilchrist contended he was not liable for damages caused by unknown vandals.

DECISION: Judgment for Hadfield. Where a city ordinance is utilized as the legal justification for taking possession of a vehicle on private property, the person or entity lawfully acquiring possession of the property under the ordinance becomes a constructive bailee as a matter of law. A constructive bailment, for the mutual benefit of Hadfield and Gilchrist, was created. The burden of proof in a constructive bailment case rests upon a bailor to prove a prima facie case, and once so proven, the burden shifts to the bailee to show the use of ordinary care in the storage and safekeeping of the property. The fact that a guard was not on duty at the impound lot and the only other security for the vehicles was a chain-link fence, a reasonable basis existed to conclude that Gilchrist failed to exercise ordinary care. [*Hadfield v. Gilchrist*, 343 S.C. 88 (S.C. App. 2000)]

20-2h Liability for Defects in Bailed Property

In the case of a mutual benefit bailment, the bailor must not only inform the bailee of known defects but also make a reasonable investigation to discover defects. The bailor is liable for harm resulting from any such defects. If the bailment is for the sole benefit of the bailee, the bailor must inform the bailee of known defects.

In bailments for hire where the bailor is in the business of renting vehicles, machines, or equipment for use by bailees, such as Hertz or Avis car rental companies, Article 2A of the Uniform Commercial Code provides an implied warranty of merchantability and fitness for a particular purpose for the protection of bailee customers.[30]

20-2i Contract Modification of Liability

An ordinary bailee may limit liability (except for willful misconduct) by agreement or contract. If the bailee seeks to limit liability for its own negligence, the wording of the contract must clearly express this intention so that the other party will know what is being contracted

---

[29] *Fedrick v. Nichols*, 2008 WL 4117208 (Tex. App. 2008).
[30] U.C.C. §§2A-212, 2A-213.

away.[31] In some states, statutes prohibit certain kinds of paid bailees, such as automobile parking garages, from limiting their liability for negligence. Statutes in some states declare that a party cannot bar liability for negligent violations of common law standards of care where a public interest is involved. **For Example,** Bruce Gardner left his Porsche 911 automobile to be repaired at Downtown Porsche Auto, signing a repair order standardized adhesion contract that stated Downtown was "not responsible for loss of cars … in case of … theft." The car was stolen while in the garage for repairs due to Downtown's negligence. The California appeals court determined that because automobile repair contracts "affect the public interest," Downtown's exculpatory clause was invalid as to public policy.[32]

When a bailee attempts to limit liability by printing a limitation on a claim check, the limitation must be called to the attention of the bailor in some reasonable fashion, such as a sign at point of purchase, before it may become part of the bailment contract. **For Example,** a claim check for a coat that purports to limit liability is ineffective without a reasonably placed sign notifying customers of the limitation.

Make the Connection

Summary

Personal property consists of whole or fractional ownership rights in things that are tangible and movable as well as rights in things that are intangible.

Personal property may be acquired by purchase. Personal property may also be acquired by gift when the donor has present intent to make a gift and delivers possession to the donee or makes a constructive delivery. Personal property may be acquired by occupation and under some statutes may be acquired by finding. The state may acquire property by escheat.

All rights in a particular object of property can be held by one individual, in which case it is said to be held *in severalty*. Ownership rights may be held concurrently by two or more individuals, in which case it is said to be held in cotenancy. The major forms of cotenancy are (1) tenancy in common, (2) joint tenancy, (3) tenancy by entirety, and (4) community property.

A bailment is the relationship that exists when tangible personal property is delivered by the bailor into the possession of the bailee under an agreement, express or implied, that the identical property will be returned or delivered in accordance with the agreement. No title is transferred by a bailment. The bailee has the right of possession. When a person comes into the possession of the personal property of another without the owner's consent, the law classifies the relationship as a constructive bailment.

Bailments may be classified in terms of benefit—that is, for the (1) sole benefit of the bailor, (2) sole benefit of the bailee, or (3) benefit of both parties (mutual benefit bailment). Some courts state the standard of care required of a bailee in terms of the class of bailment. Thus, if the bailment is for the sole benefit of the bailor, the bailee is required to exercise only slight care and is liable for gross negligence only. When the bailment is for the sole benefit of the bailee, the bailee is liable for the slightest negligence. When the bailment is for the mutual benefit of the parties, as in a commercial bailment, the bailee is liable for ordinary negligence. An ordinary bailee may limit liability except for willful misconduct or where prohibited by law.

A bailee must perform the bailee's part of the contract. The bailee has a lien on the bailed property until they have paid for storage or repair charges.

In a mutual benefit bailment, the bailor is under a duty to furnish goods reasonably fit for the purposes contemplated by the parties. The bailor may be held liable for damages or injury caused by the defective condition of the bailed property.

---

[31] *Hertz v. Klein Mfg., Inc.,* 636 So. 2d 189 (Fla. App. 1994).
[32] *Gardner v. Downtown Porsche Auto,* 225 Cal. Rptr. 757 (1986).

Learning Outcomes

After studying this chapter, you should be able to clearly explain:

20-1 Personal Property

LO.1 Explain how title to personal property is acquired
See the discussion of the acquisition of property by gift, the finding of lost property, occupation, and escheat, pages 368–375.
See the example of Steam Engine No. 952, where the museum had possession and control of the locomotive for over 50 years but could not overcome the lender's good title, page 380.

LO.2 List and explain the various types of gifts
See the discussion of inter vivos gifts, gifts causa mortis, gifts and transfers to minors, conditional gifts, and anatomical gifts, pages 368–372.

LO.3 Explain the legal theory whereby an owner can recover his or her property from the wrongful exclusionary retention of another

See the example of the real estate agent who recovered her computerized client investment list from a former employer under the legal theory called "conversion," page 375.

20-2 Bailments

LO.4 Identify the elements necessary to create a bailment
See the historic documents case with its proper agreement and delivery creating a bailment and the duty to return, page 378.
See the Roosevelt University example in which there could be no bailment created because there was no agreement or acceptance of delivery, page 379.

LO.5 Explain the standard of care a bailee is required to exercise over bailed property
See the examples of duties owed according to classifications based in terms of benefits, page 381.

Key Terms

bailee	cotenancy	personal property
bailee's lien	donee	prima facie
bailment	donor	real property
bailments for mutual benefit	escheat	severalty
bailor	gift	symbolic delivery
choses in action	gift causa mortis	tenancy by entirety
community property	gratuitous bailments	tenancy by the entireties
constructive bailment	inter vivos gift	tenancy in common
constructive delivery	joint tenancy	

Questions and Case Problems

1. On March 6, Colt Manufacturing Co., a handgun manufacturer, sponsored a farewell dinner for one of its officers, Marc Fontane. At the dinner, two Colt officials presented Fontane with a .45-caliber Colt revolver. After the presentation an agent of Colt's took possession of the revolver for the purpose of improving it by installing ivory grips and adding engraving. Fontane inquired over a period of months as to when he would receive the revolver and was ultimately told that "the gun has been sold and there will be no replacement." Fontane sued Colt for the conversion of the gift with the promised improvements with a value of $8,155. The employer asserts that there was no completed gift because there was no delivery. Decide. [*Fontane v. Colt Manufacturing Co.*, 814 A.2d 433 (Conn. App.)]

2. Joe obtained a box of antique Lenox china dishes that had been left at the Mashpee town dump. He supplemented the sizable but incomplete set of dishes with other Lenox pieces found at antique dealers. At dinner parties, he proudly told of the origin of his china. When Marlene discovered that Joe had taken her dishes from the dump, she hired an attorney to obtain their return. What result?

3. Joyce Clifford gave a check for $5,000 to her nephew Carl to help with living expenses for his last year of college. The face of the check stated, "As a loan." Years later, Carl wrote to his aunt asking what he

should do about the loan. She responded on her Christmas card simply, "On money—keep it—no return." After Joyce's death, her administrator sued Carl after discovering the "As a loan" canceled check. Decide.

4. Ruth and Stella were sisters. They owned a house as joint tenants with right of survivorship. Ruth sold her half interest to Roy. Thereafter, Stella died, and Roy claimed the entire property by survivorship. Was he entitled to it?

5. Arthur Grace, a world-renowned photo-journalist, had an agreement with Sygma-Paris and Sygma-New York whereby Grace turned well over 40,000 of his photographic images to Sygma, and Sygma agreed to act as Grace's agent to license the images and administer the fee-setting process and delivery and return of the images. Grace terminated his agreement with Sygma, and Sygma was unable to return all of the photographs to Grace as obligated under the agreement. From Sygma's perspective it was a nightmare to keep track of all of the images. Identify the legal classification of this transaction and the status of the principals. Did Grace have a legal basis to sue Sygma for the value of the images it failed to return? [*Grace v. Corbis Sygma*, 403 F. Supp. 2d (S.D.N.Y.)]

6. In 1971, Harry Gordon turned over $40,000 to his son, Murray Gordon. Murray opened two $20,000 custodial bank accounts under the Uniform Gifts to Minors Act for his minor children, Eden and Alexander. Murray was listed as the custodian of both accounts. On January 9, 1976, both accounts were closed, and a single bank check representing the principal of the accounts was drawn to the order of Harry Gordon. In April 1976, Murray and his wife, Joan, entered into a separation agreement and were later divorced. Thereafter, Joan, on behalf of her children, Eden and Alexander, brought suit against Murray to recover the funds withdrawn in January 1976, contending that the deposits in both accounts were irrevocable gifts. Murray contended that the money was his father's and that it was never intended as a gift but was merely a means of avoiding taxes. Decide. [*Gordon v. Gordon*, 419 N.Y.S.2d 684 (App. Div.)]

7. New York's banking law provides that a presumption arises that a joint tenancy has been created when a bank account is opened in the names of two persons "payable to either or the survivor." While he was still single, Richard Coddington opened a savings

account with his mother, Amelia. The signature card they signed stated that the account was owned by them as joint tenants with the right of survivorship. No statement as to survivorship was made on the passbook. Richard later married Margaret. On Richard's death, Margaret claimed a share of the account on the ground that it was not held in joint tenancy because the passbook did not contain words of survivorship and because the statutory presumption of a joint tenancy was overcome by the fact that Richard had withdrawn substantial sums from the account during his life. Decide. [*Coddington v. Coddington*, 391 N.Y.S.2d 760 (Sup. Ct. App. Div.)]

8. Martin Acampora purchased a shotgun at a garage sale years ago, never used the weapon, and did not know of any defects in it. His 31-year-old son Marty borrowed the shotgun to go duck hunting. As Marty attempted to engage the safety mechanism, the shotgun fired. The force of the shotgun's firing caused it to fall to the ground and to discharge another shot, which struck Marty in the hand. Classify the bailment in this case. What duty of care was owed by the bailor in this case? Is Martin liable to his son for the injury?

9. Baena Brothers agreed to reupholster and reduce the size of the arms of Welge's sofa and chair. The work was not done according to the contract, and the furniture when finished had no value to Welge and was not accepted by him. Baena sued him for the contract price. Welge counterclaimed for the value of the furniture. Decide. [*Baena Brothers v. Welge*, 207 A.2d 749 (Conn. Cir. Ct.)]

10. Schroeder parked his car in a parking lot operated by Allright, Inc. On the parking stub given him was printed in large, heavy type that the lot closed at 6:00 P.M. Under this information, printed in smaller, lighter type, was a provision limiting the liability of Allright for theft or loss. A large sign at the lot stated that after 6:00 P.M. patrons could obtain their car keys at another location. Schroeder's car was stolen from the lot sometime after the 6:00 P.M. closing, and he sued Allright for damages. Allright defended on the basis of the limitation-of-liability provision contained in the parking stub and the notice given Schroeder that the lot closed at 6:00 P.M. Decide. [*Allright, Inc. v. Schroeder*, 551 S.W.2d 745 (Tex. Civ. App.)]

11. John Hayes and Lynn Magosian, auditors for a public accounting firm, went to lunch at the Bay View Restaurant in San Francisco. John left his

raincoat with a coatroom attendant, but Lynn took her new raincoat with her to the dining room, where she hung it on a coat hook near her booth. When leaving the restaurant, Lynn discovered that someone had taken her raincoat. When John sought to claim his raincoat at the coatroom, it could not be found. The attendant advised that it might have been taken while he was on his break. John and Lynn sued the restaurant, claiming that the restaurant was a bailee of the raincoats and had a duty to return them. Are both John and Lynn correct?

12. Rhodes parked his car in the self-service park-and-lock lot of Pioneer Parking Lot, Inc. The ticket that he received from the ticket meter stated the following: "NOTICE. THIS CONTRACT LIMITS OUR LIABILITY. READ IT. WE RENT SPACE ONLY. NO BAILMENT IS CREATED." Rhodes parked the car himself and kept the keys. There was no attendant at the lot. The car was stolen from the lot. Rhodes sued the parking lot on the theory that it had breached its duty as a bailee. Was there a bailment? [*Rhodes v. Pioneer Parking Lot, Inc.*, 501 S.W.2d 569 (Tenn.)]

13. Newman underwent physical therapy at Physical Therapy Associates of Rome, Inc. (PTAR), in Rome, Georgia, for injuries sustained in an auto accident. At a therapy session on February 6, it was necessary for Newman to take off two necklaces. She placed one of the necklaces on a peg on the wall in the therapy room, and the therapist placed the other necklace on another peg. After the session, Newman forgot to retrieve her jewelry from the wall pegs. When she called the next day for the forgotten jewelry, it could not be found. She sued PTAR for the value of the jewelry on a bailment theory. PTAR raised the defense that there was no bailment because Newman retained the right to remove the jewelry from the wall pegs. Decide. [*Newman v. Physical Therapy Associates of Rome, Inc.*, 375 S.E.2d 253 (Ga. App.)]

14. Charles and Nicolette went to Italy in November 2008, where Charles proposed marriage and presented Nicolette with a diamond ring. She accepted the proposal and the ring. On the same day, Nicolette asked Charles where he had purchased the ring. She became disappointed when he told her where he bought it, and she gave him back the ring, suggesting a different style she would like. He returned the ring to the jeweler and received a refund of $5,000. He then purchased a new ring for $12,000. Charles testified that near the end of November he "reproposed" and presented the second ring to Nicolette. The relationship soon soured and in late February 2009 Charles asked for the return of the ring. Contrary to Charles' testimony that he gave the second ring as an engagement ring in late November, Nicolette testified that he gave the second ring to her a few days before Christmas as a holiday gift. Was it an engagement ring or a holiday gift? What legal significance is there to how the gift is classified? Decide. [*Miller v. Chiaia*, 2011 WL 1367050 (Conn. Superior)]

15. Charter Apparel, Inc., supplied fabric to Marco Apparel, Inc., in December to manufacture finished articles of clothing at its Walnut Grove, Mississippi, facilities. The fabric arrived just before the Christmas holiday shutdown and was stacked on cutting tables in the old building, which was known to have a roof that leaked. The evidence showed that no precautions were taken to cover the fabric and no guard was posted at the plant during the shutdown. Severe weather and freezing rain occurred during the shutdown, and it was discovered that the rain had leaked through the roof and destroyed more than $400,000 worth of the fabric. Marco denied that it was negligent and argued that it exercised ordinary care. It offered no evidence to rebut Charter's prima facie case or to rebut Charter's evidence of negligence. It asserted, however, that as a bailee it was not an insurer of goods against severe weather conditions. Decide. [*California Union Ins. v. City of Walnut Grove*, 857 F. Supp. 515 (S.D. Miss.)]

Legal Aspects of Supply Chain Management

Learning Outcomes ⟨⟨⟨

After studying this chapter, you should be able to

LO.1 Identify and explain all of the features of a negotiable warehouse receipt

LO.2 List and explain the differences between the three types of motor carriers of goods

LO.3 Explain a common carrier's liability for loss or damage to goods

LO.4 Identify and explain the role of each of the persons or business entities involved in the sale of goods on consignment

LO.5 Describe a hotelkeeper's liability for loss of a guest's property

All bailments are not created equal. Because of the circumstances under which possession of the bailed property is transferred, the law imposes special duties in some cases on warehouses, common carriers, factors, and hotelkeepers. Documents of title facilitate the transportation, storage, and financing of goods in commerce.

21-1 Warehouses

The storage of goods in a warehouse is a special bailment.

21-1a Definitions

warehouse–entity engaged in the business of storing the goods of others for compensation.

A **warehouse** is an entity engaged in the business of storing the goods of others for compensation. **Public warehouses** hold themselves out to serve the public generally, without discrimination.

A building is not essential to warehousing. Thus, an enterprise that stores boats outdoors on land is engaged in warehousing, for it is engaged in the business of storing goods for hire.

public warehouses–entities that serve the public generally without discrimination.

21-1b Rights and Duties of Warehouses

The rights and duties of a warehouse are for the most part the same as those of a bailee under a mutual benefit bailment.[1] A warehouse is not an insurer of goods. A warehouse is liable for loss or damage to goods stored in its warehouse when the warehouse is negligent.[2]

Statutory Regulation

The rights and duties of warehouses are regulated by the UCC, Article 7. Article 7 was revised in 2003 and 32 states have adopted the revised version.[3] The purpose of revision was to provide a framework for the future development of electronic documents of title and to update the article for modern times in light of state, federal, and international developments, including the need for medium and gender neutrality. For example, the term utilized to designate a person engaged in storing goods for hire under Article 7 is *warehouseman*.[4] The revised act uses the term *warehouse*.[5] In addition, most states have passed warehouse acts defining the rights and duties of warehouses and imposing regulations. Regulations govern charges and liens, bonds for the protection of patrons, maintenance of storage facilities in a suitable and safe condition, inspections, and general methods of transacting business.

---

[1] U.C.C. §7-204.

[2] General contract principles also apply. For example, in *Williamson v. Strictland & Smith Inc.*, 673 S.E.2d 858 (Ga. App. 2009), a warehouser successfully sued an onion farmer for breach of contract when the warehouser was unable to fill a large order because the majority of the farmer's onions stored at the warehouse were rotten.

[3] Revised Article 7 (2003) has been adopted by Alabama, Arizona, Arkansas, California, Colorado, Connecticut, Delaware, Hawaii, Idaho, Illinois, Indiana, Iowa, Kansas, Maryland, Minnesota, Mississippi, Montana, Nebraska, Nevada, New Hampshire, New Jersey, New Mexico, North Carolina, North Dakota, Oklahoma, Pennsylvania, Rhode Island, Tennessee, Texas, Utah, Virginia, and West Virginia. For more modern statutory drafting, the revised edition converts subparagraph designations from numbers to letters. For example, U.C.C. §7-307(1) is designated as Rev. U.C.C. §7-307(a).

[4] U.C.C. §7-102(1)(h).

[5] Rev. U.C.C. §7-102(a)(13).

Lien of Warehouse

The public warehouse has a lien against the goods for reasonable storage charges.[6] It is a **specific lien** in that it attaches only to the property on which the charges arose and cannot be asserted against any other property of the same owner in the possession of the warehouse. However, the warehouse may make a lien carry over to other goods by noting on the receipt for one lot of goods that a lien is also claimed for charges on the other goods. The warehouse's lien for storage charges may be enforced by sale after due notice has been given to all persons who claim any interest in the stored property.

21-1c Warehouse Receipts

A **warehouse receipt** is a written acknowledgment or record of an acknowledgment by a warehouse (bailee) that certain property has been received for storage from a named person called a **depositor** (bailor). The warehouse receipt is a memorandum of the contract between the **issuer,** the warehouse that prepares the receipt, and the depositor. No particular form is required, but usually the receipt (record) will provide:

(1) the location of the warehouse where the goods are stored, (2) the date of issuance of the receipt, (3) the consecutive number of the receipt, (4) information on the negotiability of the receipt, (5) the rate of storage and handling charges, (6) a description of the goods or the packages containing them, and (7) a statement of any liabilities incurred for which the warehouse claims a lien or security interest.[7]

A warehouse receipt (as well as a bill of lading, discussed at a later point in this chapter) is considered a **document of title**—that is, a document that in the regular course of business or financing is treated as evidence that a person is entitled to receive, hold, and dispose of the document and the goods it covers.[8] Under revised Article 7 of the UCC, the term *record* is used in the definition of document of title, reflecting the present commercial reality of the use of electronic records as documents of title, in addition to traditional "written" documents of title inscribed on a tangible medium.[9] The person holding a warehouse receipt or the person specified in the receipt is entitled to the goods represented by the receipt. A warehouse receipt as a document of title can be bought or sold and can be used as security for a loan.

21-1d Rights of Holders of Warehouse Receipts

The rights of the holders of warehouse receipts differ depending on whether the receipts are nonnegotiable or negotiable.

Nonnegotiable Warehouse Receipts

A warehouse receipt in which it is stated that the goods received will be delivered to a specified person is a **nonnegotiable warehouse receipt.** A transferee of a nonnegotiable receipt acquires only the title and rights that the transferor had actual authority to transfer. Therefore, the transferee's rights may be defeated by a good-faith purchaser of the goods from the transferor of the receipt.

---

specific lien–right of a creditor to hold a particular property or assert a lien on the particular property of the debtor because of the creditor's having done work on or having some other association with the property, as distinguished from having a lien generally against the assets of the debtor merely because the debtor is indebted to the lien holder.

warehouse receipt– receipt issued by the warehouse for stored goods. Regulated by the UCC, which clothes the receipt with some degree of negotiability.

depositor–person, or bailor, who gives property for storage.

issuer–warehouse that prepares a receipt of goods received for storage.

CPA

document of title– document treated as evidence that a person is entitled to receive, hold, and dispose of the document and the goods it covers.

nonnegotiable warehouse receipt– receipt that states the covered goods received will be delivered to a specific person.

---

[6] U.C.C. §7-209(1). The warehouse's lien provision of the UCC is constitutional as a continuation of the common law lien.
[7] U.C.C. §7-202(2)(a)–(i).
[8] U.C.C. §1-201(15).
[9] Rev. U.C.C. §1-201(b)(16). An "electronic" document of title is evidenced by a record consisting of information stored in an electronic medium. A "tangible" document of title is evidenced by a record consisting of information that is inscribed on a tangible medium.

Negotiable Warehouse Receipts

negotiable warehouse receipt–receipt that states the covered goods will be delivered "to the bearer" or "to the order of."

A warehouse receipt stating that the goods will be delivered "to the bearer" or "to the order of" any named person is a **negotiable warehouse receipt.**

Negotiation. If the receipt provides for the delivery of the goods "to the bearer," the receipt may be negotiated by transfer of the document. If the receipt provides for delivery of the goods "to the order of" a named individual, the document must be indorsed[10] and delivered by that person in order for the document to be negotiated.

Due Negotiation. If a receipt is duly negotiated, the person to whom it is negotiated may acquire rights superior to those of the transferor. A warehouse receipt is "duly negotiated" when the holder purchases the document in good faith without notice of any defense to it, for value, in an ordinary transaction in which nothing appears improper or irregular.[11] The holder of a duly negotiated document acquires title to the document and title to the goods.[12] The holder also acquires the direct obligation of the issuer to hold or deliver the goods according to the terms of the warehouse receipt. The rights of a holder of a duly negotiated document cannot be defeated by the surrender of the goods by the warehouse to the depositor.[13]

It is the duty of the warehouse to deliver the goods only to the holder of the negotiable receipt and to cancel this receipt on surrendering the goods.[14]

The rights of a purchaser of a warehouse receipt by due negotiation are not cut off by the fact that (1) an original owner was deprived of the receipt in "bearer" form by misrepresentation, fraud, mistake, loss, theft, or conversion or (2) a bona fide purchaser bought the goods from the warehouse.

A purchaser of a warehouse receipt who takes by due negotiation does not cut off all prior rights. If the person who deposited the goods with the warehouse did not own the goods or did not have power to transfer title to them, the purchaser of the receipt is subject to the title of the true owner. Accordingly, when goods are stolen and delivered to a warehouse and a warehouse receipt is issued for them, the owner of the goods prevails over the due-negotiation purchaser of the warehouse receipt.

---

[10] The spelling *endorse* is commonly used in business. The spelling *indorse* is used in the UCC.

[11] U.C.C. §7-501(4).

[12] U.C.C. §7-502(1).

[13] For electronic documents of title, Revised Article 7, Section 7-106, includes a list of how a party becomes a holder, and the result is that Article 7 creates a new concept of "control." That is, a holder who has control of a document of title (as evidenced by a record that may be electronic) has all the rights of a holder. The Revised Article states:

a. A person has control of an electronic document of title if a system employed for evidencing the transfer of interests in the electronic document reliably establishes that person as the person to which the electronic document was issued or transferred,

b. A system satisfies subsection (a) and a person is deemed to have control of an electronic document of title, if the electronic document is created, stored, and assigned in such a manner that:

  1. a single authoritative copy of the document exists which is unique, identifiable, and, except as otherwise provided in paragraphs (4), (5), and (6), unalterable.

  2. the authoritative copy identifies the person asserting control as:

    A. the person to which the document was issued; or

    B. if the authoritative copy indicates that the document has been transferred, the person to which the document was most recently transferred;

  3. the authoritative copy is communicated to and maintained by the person asserting control or its designated custodian;

  4. copies or amendments that add or change an identified assignee of the authoritative copy can be made only with the consent of the person asserting control;

  5. each copy of the authoritative copy and any copy of a copy is readily identifiable as a copy that is not the authoritative copy; and

  6. any amendment of the authoritative copy is readily identifiable as authorized or unauthorized.

[14] U.C.C. §7-403(3).

Study Figure 21-1, and note all of the features of a negotiable warehouse receipt in the context of the following. **For Example,** Latham and Loud (L&L) sporting goods manufacturers' representatives in Cleveland, Ohio, hijacked a truckload of ice skates from Bartlett Shoe and Skate Company of Bangor, Maine. L&L warehoused the skates at the Northern Transfer Company warehouse and received a negotiable warehouse receipt. Jack Preston, a large sporting goods retailer who had had previous business dealings with L&L and believed it to be operated by honest individuals, made a bona fide purchase of the receipt. Bartlett, the true owner, discovered that the skates were at Northern's warehouse and informed Northern of the hijacking. Northern delivered the skates to Bartlett; Latham and Loud have fled the country. Preston believed that he was entitled to delivery of the skates because he acquired the negotiable receipt by due negotiation and

FIGURE 21-1 Negotiable Warehouse Receipt

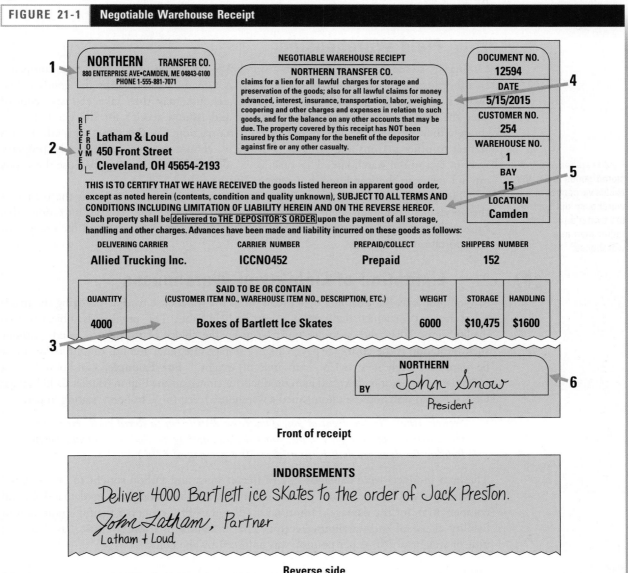

Front of receipt

Reverse side

(1) Warehouse, (2) depositor, (3) goods, (4) warehouse's lien, (5) negotiable delivery terms, (6) warehouse's authorized agent. A negotiable warehouse receipt contains a promise to deliver the goods to the bearer or to the order of the depositor, unlike a nonnegotiable warehouse receipt, which promises only to deliver them to the depositor.

informed Northern of his status before delivery of the skates to Bartlett. He contemplated legal action against Northern. Preston, however, is not entitled to the skates. Ordinarily, a purchaser of a warehouse receipt obtained by due negotiation takes title to the document and title to the goods. However, an exception exists in the case of theft. Thus, because of the theft by L&L, Preston's rights have been cut off by the true owner in this case. When conflicting claims exist, the warehouse can protect itself by instituting proceedings under UCC §7-603 to ascertain the validity of the conflicting claims.

CPA   ## Warranties

The transferor of a negotiable or nonnegotiable warehouse receipt makes certain implied warranties for the protection of the transferee. These warranties are that (1) the receipt is genuine, (2) its transfer is rightful and effective, and (3) the transferor has no knowledge of any facts that impair the validity or worth of the receipt.[15]

21-1e Field Warehousing

Ordinarily, stored goods are placed in a warehouse belonging to the warehouse company. In other instances, the owner of goods, such as a manufacturer, keeps the goods in the owner's own storage area or building. The warehouse may then take exclusive control over the area in which the goods are stored and issue a receipt for the goods just as though they were in the warehouse. Such a transaction has the same legal effect with respect to other persons and purchasers of the warehouse receipts as though the property were in fact in the warehouse. This practice is called **field warehousing** because the goods are not taken to the warehouse but remain "in the field."

field warehousing– stored goods under the exclusive control of a warehouse but kept on the owner's premises rather than in a warehouse.

The purpose of field warehousing is to create warehouse receipts that the owner of the goods may pledge as security for loans. The owner could, of course, have done this by actually placing the goods in a warehouse, but this would have involved the expense of transportation and storage.

CPA   ## 21-1f Limitation of Liability of Warehouses

A warehouse may limit liability by a provision in the warehouse receipt specifying the maximum amount for which the warehouse can be held liable. This privilege is subject to two qualifications. First, the customer must be given the choice of storing the goods without such limitation if the customer pays a higher storage rate, and, second, the limitation must be stated for each item or for each unit of weight.[16] **For Example,** Chisholm Ltd., a Canadian Corporation, delivered ham products for storage to the Fulton Market Cold Storage Co.'s Chicago warehouse. Fulton issued a warehouse receipt to Chisholm, stating in part:

> *Section 10(e): "in the event of loss, damage or destruction to stored goods for which the warehouseman is legally liable, storer declares and agrees that the warehouseman's liability for damages shall be limited to 50 ¢ per pound." (id.)*

The ham products were damaged due to freezer burn and Fulton sought to "work with" Chisholm to resolve the claim. When Chisholm would not budge off its demand for full compensation for the damage, Fulton reverted to the "fifty cents per pound" limitation of liability clause of the warehouse receipt. The limitation of liability clause based on the unit of weight of "50 ¢ per pound" was enforced by the court.[17]

---

[15] U.C.C. §7-507. These warranties are in addition to any that may arise between the parties by virtue of the fact that the transferor is selling the goods represented by the receipt to the transferee. See Chapter 24 for a discussion of seller's warranties.

[16] U.C.C. §7-204(2); *Lobel v. Samson Moving & Storage, Inc.,* 737 N.Y.S.2d 24 (A.D. 2002).

[17] *Chisholm, Ltd. v. Fulton Cold Storage Company LCC,* 2011 WL 6182347 (N.D. Ill. Dec. 13, 2011).

General contract law determines whether a limitation clause is a part of the contract between the warehouse and the customer. **For Example,** warehouse Eastern Warehousing, Inc., and customer Delavau, Inc., executed a comprehensive contract for storage of a nutritional supplement after extensive negotiations between Eastern's chief operating officer and Delavau's president. The goods were damaged due to a leaking warehouse roof. Eastern was unsuccessful in its argument that the contract was formed when the goods were subsequently delivered to the warehouse and a preprinted warehouse receipt containing a limitation-of-liability provision was given to the customer's driver. The court ruled that the terms of the receipt were not part of the contract of the parties and awarded Delavau $1,358,601 in damages.[18]

21-2 Common Carriers

The purpose of a bailment may be transportation. In this case, the bailee may be a common carrier.

21-2a Definitions

A **carrier** of goods is an individual or organization undertaking the transportation of goods regardless of the method of transportation or the distance covered. The **consignor** or shipper is the person who delivers goods to the carrier for shipment. The **consignee** is the person to whom the goods are shipped and to whom the carrier should deliver the goods.

A carrier may be classified as a common carrier, a contract carrier, or a private carrier. A **common carrier** holds itself out as willing to furnish transportation for compensation without discrimination to all members of the public who apply, assuming that the goods to be carried are proper and facilities of the carrier are available. A **contract carrier** transports goods under individual contracts, and a **private carrier** is owned and operated by the shipper. **For Example,** a truck fleet owned and operated by an industrial firm is a private carrier. Common carrier law or special bailment law applies to common carriers, ordinary bailment law to contract carriers, and the law of employment to private carriers.

The Federal Motor Carrier Safety Administration is the successor agency to the Interstate Commerce Commission and was created under the Interstate Commerce Commission Termination Act (ICCTA).[19] Under the ICCTA, Congress merged the separate classifications of common and contract carrier into one classification termed "motor carrier." The fundamental distinction between the types of carriage remains explicit in the act.

Glossary (margin)

carrier–individual or organization undertaking the transportation of goods.

consignor–(1) person who delivers goods to the carrier for shipment, (2) party with title who turns goods over to another for sale.

consignee–(1) person to whom goods are shipped, (2) dealer who sells goods for others.

common carrier–carrier that holds out its facilities to serve the general public for compensation without discrimination.

contract carrier–carrier that transports on the basis of individual contracts that it makes with each shipper.

private carrier–carrier owned by the shipper, such as a company's own fleet of trucks.

CASE SUMMARY

The Distinction Continues

FACTS: M. Fortunoff of Westbury operates a chain of department stores in New York and New Jersey. In March 1997, the company entered into a contract with Frederickson Motor Express, whereby the carrier agreed "as contract carrier and independent contractor … to transfer shipments … as authorized in Carrier's contract carrier permit … issued by the ICC." The contract further provided: "Although carrier is authorized to operate … as a common

---

[18] *Delavau v. Eastern American Trading & Warehousing, Inc.*, 810 A.2d 672 (Pa. Super. 2002).
[19] 49 U.S.C. §13906 (a)(3) (2000) (amended 2005).

The Distinction Continues continued

carrier, each and every shipment tendered to carrier by shipper ... shall be deemed to be a tender to carrier as a motor contract carrier...." Fortunoff's goods were damaged in transit, prompting it to make a claim against Frederickson. When the carrier went out of business, Fortunoff asserted the same claim against the carrier's insurer, Peerless Insurance Co., for $13,249.42 under the BMC-32 indorsement (the mandatory attachment to all common carrier insurance policies), which was part of Frederickson's insurance policy. From a judgment for Fortunoff, on the ground that the ICCTA mandated the extension of BMC-32 indorsements to all motor carriers, Peerless appealed.

DECISION: Judgment against the shipper, Fortunoff. Historically, many trucking companies obtained both a common carrier certificate and a contract carrier permit, meaning they were authorized to operate as either type of carrier. If the carrier agreed to transport a shipper's goods according to standard terms and at a fixed rate (i.e., without an individually negotiated contract) on a nonrecurring basis, the transportation was conducted under the carrier's common carrier certificate. Accordingly, common carrier rules, including the cargo liability insurance and the BMC-32 indorsement

requirement, applied. If the carrier and the shipper wished to negotiate a bilateral contract for an ongoing course of shipping services, the carrier was required to operate under its contract carrier permit, and no cargo insurance was necessary.

Requiring cargo liability insurance for common carriage but not contract carriage is not an arbitrary distinction. Instead, it makes economic sense because of the different types of services performed and the customers served by common carriage. Although the ICCTA abolished the licensing distinction between common and contract carriers, it did so in large part because most carriers had a common carrier certificate and a contract carrier permit and provided both types of service anyway. But the functional distinction between the two types of carriage survives and is still highly relevant to deciding which motor carriers must have cargo liability insurance. The administrative agency's decision to require BMC-32 cargo insurance only when performing common carriage service is consistent with the ICCTA. The district court's ruling is reversed. [*M. Fortunoff of Westbury Corp. v. Peerless Ins. Co.*, 432 F.3d 127 (2nd Cir. 2005)]

---

bill of lading–document issued by a carrier reciting the receipt of goods and the terms of the contract of transportation. Regulated by the Federal Bills of Lading Act or the UCC.

21-2b Bills of Lading

When the carrier accepts goods for shipment or forwarding, the carrier ordinarily issues to the shipper a **bill of lading** in the case of land or water transportation or an **airbill** for air transportation. This instrument is a document of title and provides rights similar to those provided by a warehouse receipt. A bill of lading is both a receipt for the goods and a memorandum of a contract stating the terms of carriage. Title to the goods may be transferred by a transfer of the bill of lading made with that intention.

Bills of lading for intrastate shipments are governed by the Uniform Commercial Code (UCC). For interstate shipments, bills of lading are regulated by the Federal Bills of Lading Act (FBLA).[20]

CPA

Contents of Bill of Lading

airbill–document of title issued to a shipper whose goods are being sent via air.

The form of the bill of lading is regulated in varying degrees by administrative agencies. Prior to the revisions to Article 7, negotiable bills of lading were printed on yellow paper, and nonnegotiable or straight bills of lading were printed on white paper. This color-coding may continue as commercial practice for those documents reduced to written form, but new commercial practices will evolve regarding the use of "records."[21]

As against the good faith transferee of the bill of lading, a carrier is bound by the recitals in the bill as to the contents, quantity, or weight of goods.[22] This means that the carrier must produce the goods that are described or pay damages for failing to do so.

---

[20] 49 U.S.C. §81 *et seq.*

[21] The UCC contains no provision regulating the form of the bill of lading and the use of records, including electronic tracking, now covered under Revised Article 7. This means that new commercial practices will evolve.

[22] U.C.C. §7-301(1).

This rule is not applied if facts appear on the face of the bill that should keep the transferee from relying on the recital.

Negotiation

negotiable bill of lading–document of title that by its terms calls for goods to be delivered "to the bearer" or "to the order of" a named person.

A bill of lading is a **negotiable bill of lading** when by its terms the goods are to be delivered "to the bearer" or "to the order of" a named person.[23] Any other bill of lading, such as one that consigns the goods to a named person, is a **nonnegotiable** or **straight bill of lading.** Like transferees of warehouse receipts who take by due negotiation, holders of bills of lading who take by due negotiation ordinarily also acquire title to the bills and title to the goods represented by them.

nonnegotiable bill of lading–see *straight bill of lading.*

Rights of a transferee are defeated by the true owner, however, when a thief delivers the goods to the carrier and then negotiates the bill of lading. The thief had no title to the goods at any time.

CASE SUMMARY

International Intrigue

FACTS: Banque de Depots, a Swiss bank, sued Bozel, a Brazilian corporation, for money owed the bank. Banque obtained a writ of attachment from the court against goods being shipped by Bozel from Rio de Janeiro through the port of New Orleans for transit to purchasers located in three states. Bozel claimed that the writ of attachment must be dissolved because the cargo was shipped under negotiable bearer bills of lading and the bills of lading had been sent to U.S. banks for collection from the purchasers.

DECISION: Judgment for Bozel. The writ of attachment must be dissolved. Goods shipped pursuant to a negotiable

bill of lading cannot be seized unless the bill of lading is surrendered to the carrier or impounded by a court. On the day of the seizure of the cargo under the writ, the negotiable bills of lading were outstanding. The bills of lading were not in the hands of the carrier, and their negotiation had not been enjoined by the court. The law protects holders of duly negotiated bills of lading from purchasing such bills and then finding out that the goods have been seized by judicial process. The holder of a duly negotiated bill of lading acquires title to the document and title to the goods described in the document. [*Banque de Depots v. Bozel*, **569 So. 2d 40 (La. App. 1990)**]

straight (or nonnegotiable) bill of lading–document of title that consigns transported goods to a named person.

Warranties

By transferring for value a bill of lading, whether negotiable or nonnegotiable, the transferor makes certain implied warranties to the transferee. The transferor impliedly warrants that (1) the bill of lading is genuine, (2) its transfer is rightful and is effective to transfer the goods represented by it, and (3) the transferor has no knowledge of facts that would impair the validity or worth of the bill of lading.[24]

21-2c Rights of Common Carrier

A common carrier of goods has the right to make reasonable and necessary rules for the conduct of its business. It has the right to charge such rates for its services to yield it a fair return on the property devoted to the business of transportation.

---

[23] U.C.C. §7-104(1)(a).

[24] U.C.C. §7-507; F.B.L.A., 49 U.S.C. §§114,116. When the transfer of the bill of lading is part of a transaction by which the transferor sells the goods represented thereby to the transferee, there will also arise the warranties that are found in other sales of goods.

As security for unpaid transportation and service charges, a common carrier has a lien on goods that it transports. The carrier's lien also secures demurrage, the costs of preservation of the goods, and the costs of sale to enforce the lien.[25]

21-2d Duties of Common Carrier

A common carrier is required (1) to receive and carry proper and lawful goods of all persons who offer them for shipment as long as the carrier has space, (2) to furnish facilities that are adequate for the transportation of freight in the usual course of business and to furnish proper storage facilities for goods awaiting shipment or awaiting delivery after shipment, (3) to follow the directions given by the shipper, (4) to load and unload goods delivered to it for shipment, but the shipper or consignee may assume this duty by contract or custom, and (5) to deliver the goods in accordance with the shipment contract.

Goods must be delivered at the usual place of delivery at the specified destination. When goods are shipped under a negotiable bill of lading, the carrier must not deliver the goods without obtaining possession of the bill, properly indorsed. When goods are shipped under a straight bill of lading, the carrier may deliver the goods to the consignee or the consignee's agent without receiving the bill of lading unless notified by the shipper to deliver the goods to someone else. If the carrier delivers the goods to the wrong person, the carrier is liable for breach of contract and for the tort of conversion.

CPA ## 21-2e Liabilities of Common Carrier

When goods are delivered to a common carrier for immediate shipment and while they are in transit, the carrier is absolutely liable for any loss or damage to the goods unless it can prove that the loss or damage was due solely to one or more of the following excepted causes: (1) an act of God, meaning a natural phenomenon that is not reasonably foreseeable, (2) an act of a public enemy, such as the military forces of an opposing government, as distinguished from ordinary robbers, (3) an act of a public authority, such as a health officer removing goods from the carrier, (4) an act of the shipper, such as fraudulent labeling or defective packing, or (5) the inherent nature of the goods, such as those naturally tending to spoil or deteriorate.

CASE SUMMARY

Landstar Learns the Hard Way

FACTS: Tempel Steel Corporation shipped a large machine press from Minster, Ohio, to Monterrey, Mexico, by Landstar Inway, Inc., a common carrier. Landstar issued Tempel a through bill of lading for this service. It then hauled the press to the U.S. border, where it hired a customs broker who utilized a local carrier, Teresa de Jesus Ortiz Obregon, to move the cargo through U.S. and Mexican customs to interchange with a Mexican carrier. It was determined that Obregon failed to secure the press properly and drove too fast, causing $300,000 damage to the press. Tempel sued Landstar to recover for this damage. Landstar defended that it was not responsible for causalities in Mexico and that the loss was the fault of Obregon.

DECISION: Landstar is financially responsible for the entire movement by having entered a competitive bid to transport goods from Ohio through to Mexico and having issued a through bill of lading. Tempel is thus entitled to hold Landstar liable for the damage, and Landstar then bears the responsibility for seeking compensation from the carrier actually

[25] U.C.C. §7-307(1); F.B.L.A., 49 U.S.C. §105.

Landstar Learns the Hard Way continued

responsible for the loss. Although Landstar had every legal right to issue a bill of lading that stopped at the U.S. border, it did not do so. Landstar must accept the legal consequences of the issuance of the through bill of lading without limitation of liability for losses. [*Temple Steel Corp. v. Landstar Inway, Inc.*, 211 F.3d 1029 (7th Cir. 2000)]

Carrier's Liability for Delay

A carrier is liable for losses caused by its failure to deliver goods within a reasonable time. **For Example,** J.B. Hunt Transport, Inc., "lost" a shipment of boxed Christmas cards specially packaged for Target Stores, Inc., by the shipper, Paper Magic, Inc. The goods were shipped on October 16, 1998, and the invoice valued them at $130,080.48. Hunt located the shipment on February 5, 1999, and Target refused the goods because it was well after Christmas and the goods were worthless to Target. The cards were worthless to Paper Magic because they were packaged with Target's private label. The court found that awarding the shipper the invoice value was a permissible award under the Carmack Amendment to the Interstate Commerce Act, which governs the liability of carriers for loss or damage in the interstate shipment of goods.[26]

The carrier, however, is not liable for every delay. The shipper assumes the risk of ordinary delays incidental to transporting goods.

Limitation of Liability of Carrier

In the absence of a constitutional or statutory prohibition, a common carrier generally has the right to limit its liability by contract.

Common carriers operating interstate may limit their liability for the negligent loss of consigned items to a stated dollar amount, such as $100 per package. Shippers, however, must be given a reasonable opportunity to select excess liability coverage for the higher value of their shipment, with payment of higher freight charges.[27] **For Example,** two transformers owned by Prolec GE International were damaged when two cars of a Kansas City Southern Railway (KCSR) train derailed near Benevides, Texas. The transformers were valued at $3,213,210, but after deducting salvage value, the loss was $2,356,066. KCSR contended that its liability was limited to $25,000 per car, a sum stated in its price quote to the logistic coordinator HLI Rail, which quote contained a reference to KCSR's Rules Publication, which in turn set forth the opportunity for full Carmack liability coverage. HLI Rail contended that it was not given proper notice of the options for full liability coverage. The court agreed, stating that the Carmack statute imposes something more than a passive, uncommunicated willingness to provide full liability terms; it mandates that the carrier actually provide those terms.[28]

The Carmack Amendment to the Interstate Commerce Act governs the liability of carriers for loss or damage in the interstate shipment of goods.[29] Shippers displeased with liability limitations permitted carriers under the Carmack Amendment may not sue a

---

[26] *The Paper Magic Group, Inc. v. J.B. Hunt Transport, Inc.*, 318 F.3d 458 (3d Cir. 2003). See also *National Hispanic Circus, Inc. v. Rex Trucking*, 414 F.3d 546 (5th Cir. 2005).

[27] In *Sassy Doll Creations Inc. v. Watkins Motor Lines Inc.*, 331 F.3d 834 (11th Cir. 2003), the carrier was held liable for the full value of a lost shipment of perfume, $28,273.60, rather than $10,000.00, the carrier's established limitation of its liability. The bill of lading prepared by the carrier contained a declared value box, which the shipper filled in. However, the document did not contain any space for requesting excess liability coverage and thus did not give the shipper a reasonable opportunity to select a higher level of coverage as required by the Carmack Amendment to the Interstate Commerce Act.

[28] *Chartis Seguros Mexico, S.A. v. HLI Rail & Rigging, LLC*, 3 F. Supp. 3d 171 (S.D.N.Y. 2014).

[29] 49 U.S.C. §11707.

carrier under any state statute if the statute in any way enlarges the responsibility of a carrier for loss or damage to the goods.[30] The Carmack Amendment provides the exclusive remedy for loss or damage, and its purpose is to provide uniformity in the disposition of claims brought under a bill of lading or waybill. An insurer, as a subrogee of the owner or shipper, has standing to sue the carrier under a bill of lading.[31]

CASE SUMMARY

Actual Damage to Cargo, $165,000: Carrier Only Has to Pay $819.71: Can That Be Right?

FACTS: On March 11, 2009, a Straight Bill of Lading (BOL) was issued by Con-way Freight, Inc., for a shipment of cargo from Canada to the United States. The BOL identified the shipper as the Tronosjet Maintenance, Inc., and the consignee as Montex Drilling, Fort Worth, Texas. The "SPECIAL AGREEMENT" box for declaring value and agreeing to pay for excess liability was blank. The BOL identified the cargo as three crates of landing gear. On March 13, 2009, the cargo was picked up in St. John, New Brunswick, Canada. On March 17, 2009, the cargo was transloaded to another trailer, carried from Canada across the border to the United States. On March 19, 2009, the cargo was transloaded to another trailer and physical damage to the crates was noted. On March 23, 2009, the damaged cargo was delivered to Montex Drilling in Fort Worth, Texas. Tronosjet seeks to recover $165,000 as full damages under the Carmack Amendment. Con-way claims that it owes just $819.71 because the claim is subject to the limitation of liability set forth in the BOL and Tariff CNWY 199.

DECISION: Judgment for Con-way. In 1995, under the ICC Termination Act, Congress required that carriers "provide to the shipper, on request of the shipper, a written or electronic copy of the rate, classification, rules, and practices upon which any rate applicable to a shipment, or agreed to between the shipper and the carrier, is based. The BOL under which the cargo shipped stated that "the shipment is received subject to Tariff CNWY–199, Carrier's pricing schedules, terms, conditions, and rules maintained at Carrier's general offices in effect on the date of issue of this Bill of Lading." Because Tronosjet does not dispute that Con-way not only maintained a tariff that incorporated both the limitation of liability at issue and a separate excess valuation charge for full liability, but also published that tariff on its Web site, and incorporated the tariff by reference into the BOL at issue, the court concluded that Con-way has presented undisputed evidence showing that Con-way had established rates for different levels of liability and would have made these rates available to Tronosjet upon request. Moreover, both the BOL and the applicable Con-way tariff clearly state that absent a declared value, Con-way's liability is limited. The court concluded that the shipper had sufficient notice of the limitation of liability and sufficient opportunity to reject that limitation by declaring the value of the shipment and agreeing to pay excess liability charges. [*Tronosjet v. Con-way Freight, Inc.*, **2011 WL 3322800 (S.D. Tex. Aug. 2, 2011)**]

Notice of Claim

The bill of lading and applicable government regulations may require that a carrier be given notice of any claim for damages or loss of goods within a specified time, generally within nine months.

COD Shipment

A common carrier transporting goods under a COD (cash on delivery) shipment may not make delivery of the goods without first receiving payment. If it does, it is liable to the shipper for any resulting loss. Thus, if a FedEx or UPS driver were to accept a bad check from a consignee on a COD shipment, the carrier would be liable to the shipper for the amount owed.

[30] *Dugan v. FedEx Corp.*, 2002 WL 31305208 (C.D. Cal. Sept. 26, 2002).
[31] *One Beacon Insurance Co. v. Haas Industries, Inc.*, 634 F.3d 1092 (9th Cir. 2011).

There are two forms of COD payments in addition to cash—certified and cashier's checks.

CASE SUMMARY

Cashier's Check Is King

FACTS: ABF Freight Systems, Inc., accepted a certified check for a COD fee owed upon delivery of 511 cartons of shoes to the location designated in the bill of lading. It turned out that the bank certification stamped on the face of the check was a forgery. The bill of lading included the specification that delivery be "COD Cashier's Check" and that ABF collect payment on behalf of Imports, Ltd. Imports sued ABF for $53,180.90, the full value of the COD payment. From a judgment for Imports for the full amount plus interest, ABF appealed.

DECISION: Judgment for Imports, Ltd. The primary difference between a bank certified check and a cashier's check is in the ease with which one can create a fraudulent instrument. To forge a cashier's check, one would need to replicate all of the other features of the bank's form. To forge a bank check, on the other hand, one need only have a writing on the check indicating that the check is "certified." Imports had a right to believe that a cashier's check is a better form of payment than a certified check. The agreement that ABF would accept only a cashier's check reflected this belief. ABF broke its contract with Imports by accepting a bank certified check rather than a cashier's check for the COD payment. [*Imports, Ltd. v. ABF Freight Systems, Inc.*, 162 F.3d 528 (8th Cir. 1998)]

Rejected Shipments

When a common carrier tenders delivery of consigned goods to a consignee that refuses to accept the delivery, the carrier is no longer a common carrier but becomes a warehouse. When the carrier-turned-warehouse receives new shipping instructions from the owner, its status again changes to that of a common carrier.

Complexities in Intercontinental and Domestic Shipping

In intercontinental ocean-to-inland shipping, carriers may or may not know whether they are dealing with an intermediary, such as a freight forwarding company rather than a cargo owner, or what legal obligations the cargo owner and intermediary have agreed upon. Moreover, the number of times goods change hands in the course of this intermodal transportation of goods adds to the complexities regarding liability limitations and other bills-of-lading issues such as forum selection clauses. **For Example,** James Kirby, Ltd, an Australian manufacturer, hired International Cargo Control (ICC) to arrange for the delivery of machinery from Australia to Huntsville, Alabama. The bill of lading that ICC issued to Kirby designated Savannah, Georgia, as the discharge port and Huntsville, Alabama, as the ultimate destination, and set ICC's liability limitation lower than the cargo's true value, using the default liability rule in the Carriage of Goods by Sea Act (COGSA) of $500 per package for the sea leg and a higher amount for the land leg. The bill also contained what is known as the "Himalaya Clause," which extends liability limitations to downstream carriers and contractors. When ICC hired a German shipping company, Hamburg Süd, to transport the containers, Hamburg Süd issued its own bill of lading to ICC. That bill of lading also adopted COGSA's default rule, extended it to any land damages, and extended it in a Himalaya Clause to "all agents … (including inland) carriers…." Hamburg Süd hired Norfolk Southern Railway (NS) to transport the machinery some 366 miles from Savannah to Huntsville. The train derailed, causing some $1.5 million in damages. Kirby sued NS for the full value of its loss, and NS, claiming the protections of the ICC and Hamburg Süd bills of lading, asserted that it owed just $500 per container. The U.S. Supreme Court held that "when it comes to liability limitations for negligence resulting in damage, an intermediary [ICC and Hamburg Süd] can negotiate reliable and enforceable agreements with the carrier it engages,"[32] thus upholding NS's limited liability of $500 per container. U.S. courts have also recognized the rule that a freight forwarder has a limited agency to bind a cargo owner to a forum selection clause by accepting a carrier's bill of lading.[33] The COGSA governs the terms of bills of lading by ocean carriers engaged in foreign trade. It does not limit the parties' ability to adopt forum-selection clauses.

CASE SUMMARY

China Cargo; Oklahoma Derailment: Tokyo Trial

FACTS: Regal-Beloit Corp. and other cargo owners delivered goods to Kawasaki Kisen Kaisha Ltd. ("K" Line) for shipping from China to inland United States destinations. "K" Line issued through bills of lading covering both the ocean and inland ports of transport. The bills of lading contained a "Himalaya Clause," which extends the bills' defenses and liability limitations to subcontractors; permitted "K" Line to subcontract to complete the journey; provided that the entire journey through to inland destinations is governed by the Carriage of Goods by Sea Act (COGSA) and contained a forum selection clause that designated a Tokyo, Japan, court as the venue for litigating any dispute. "K" Line subcontracted with Union Pacific Railroad for rail shipment to inland destinations. Upon arrival at the Port of Long Beach, the containers were loaded onto a Union Pacific train, which derailed in Tyrone, Oklahoma, destroying the cargo. The Carmack Amendment to the ICC Act governs the terms of bills of lading issued by domestic rail carriers and limits the parties' ability to choose the venue of their lawsuit. The cargo owners assert that the Tokyo forum-selection clause is thus inapplicable, and that they can bring suit against the Union Pacific in the United States under the Carmack Amendment. The district court dismissed the case, ruling that the forum-selection clause was binding. The Court of Appeals reversed, and "K" Line and Union Pacific appealed to the U.S. Supreme Court.

DECISION: Judgment for "K" Line and Union Pacific. The Carmack Amendment does not apply to a shipment originating overseas through a single bill of lading. Applying Carmack to international import shipping transport would undermine COGSA's purpose "to facilitate efficient contracting in contracts for carriage by sea." If two different bills of lading regimes applied to the same through shipments, it would seem to require rail carriers to open containers to check if damage had been done at sea, undermining international container-based transport. [*Kawasaki Kisen Kaisha Ltd. v. Regal-Beloit Corp.*, 130 S. Ct. 2433 (2010)]

21-3 Factors and Consignments

factor–bailee to whom goods are consigned for sale.

A **factor** is a special type of bailee who sells consigned goods as though the factor were the owner of those goods.

21-3a Definitions

selling on consignment–entrusting a person with possession of property for the purpose of sale.

Entrusting a person with the possession of property for the purpose of sale is commonly called **selling on consignment.**[34] The owner who consigns the goods for sale is the *consignor.* The person or agent to whom they are consigned is the factor or *consignee*; this individual may also be known as a **commission merchant.** A consignee's compensation is known as a **commission or factorage. For Example,** *consignor* Rolly Tasker Sails Co.,

commission merchant–bailee to whom goods are consigned for sale.

commission or factorage–consignee's compensation.

[32] *Norfolk Southern Ry. Co. v. Kirby*, 543 U.S. 1433 (2004). See also *Sampo Japan Insurance Co. of America v. Norfolk Southern Railway Co.*, 966 F. Supp. 2d 270 (S.D.N.Y. 2013).

[33] *Maersk Sealand v. Ocean Express Miami (Quality Print)*, 550 F. Supp. 2d 484 (S.D.N.Y. 2008).

[34] *Amoco Oil Co. v. DZ Enterprises, Inc.*, 607 F. Supp. 595 (S.D.N.Y. 1985).

Ltd. (RTS), would ship sails from Thailand to the *consignee*, Bacon & Associates of Annapolis, Maryland, with a bill of lading and an "invoice price" for each sail. Mrs. Bacon would then set her "retail fair market value price." Once a set of sails was sold, Mrs. Bacon would deposit a check to the consignor's account at Alex Brown Co. at the invoice price. Her *commission* was the difference between the retail price and the invoice price. This arrangement began in 1971 but began to unravel 27 years later. RTS was successful in its breach of *consignment agreement* lawsuit against Bacon for $345,327 in damages and $78,660 in interest.[35]

21-3b Effect of Factor Transaction

In a sale on consignment, the property remains the property of the owner-consignor, and the consignee acts as the agent of the owner to pass the owner's title to the buyer. A consignment sale is treated as a sale or return under Article 2 of the Uniform Commercial Code (UCC), and the factor-consignee has full authority to sell the goods for the consignor and can pass title to those goods. Thus, creditors of the consignee can obtain possession of the goods and have a superior right to them over the consignor. If, however, the owner-consignor complies with the security interest and perfection provisions of Article 9 of the UCC (see Chapter 33), there is public notice of the consignment, and the goods will be subject to the claims of the owner's creditors but not to those of the factor-consignee.[36]

> If the consignor is not the owner, as when a thief delivers stolen goods to the factor, a sale by the factor passes no title and is an unlawful **conversion.**

conversion–act of taking personal property by a person not entitled to it and keeping it from its true owner or prior possessor without consent.

21-4 Hotelkeepers

A hotelkeeper has a bailee's liability with respect to property specifically entrusted to the hotelkeeper's care. In addition, the hotelkeeper has special duties with respect to a guest's property brought into the hotel. The rules governing the special relationship between a hotelkeeper and a guest arose because of the special needs of travelers.

21-4a Definitions

The definitions of *hotelkeeper* and *guest* exclude lodging of a more permanent character, such as that provided by boardinghouse keepers to boarders.

Hotelkeeper

hotelkeeper–one regularly engaged in the business of offering living accommodations to all transient persons.

A **hotelkeeper** is an operator of a hotel, motel, or tourist home or anyone who is regularly engaged in the business of offering living accommodations to transient persons. In the early law, the hotelkeeper was called an *innkeeper* or a *tavernkeeper*.

---

[35] *Bacon & Associates, Inc. v. Rolly Tasker Sails Co. Ltd. (Thailand)*, 841 A.2d 53 (Md. App. 2004).

[36] For a complex case involving Articles 2 and 9 of the UCC, see *Arthur Glick Truck Sales, Inc. v. Stephen East Corp.*, 914 F. Supp. 2d 529 (S.D.N.Y. 2012) where buyers in the ordinary course of business took the consignor's truck chassis free of the consignor's security interests. Revised Article 2 (1999) modifies the rules on consignments slightly in that all transactions are treated as sales or return or sales on approval unless steps are taken to identify a transaction as a consignment and to comply with state laws on consignment. The new U.C.C. §2-326(a), (b), and (c) provides as follows:

> The provisions of this subsection are applicable even though an agreement purports to reserve title to the person making delivery until payment or resale or uses such words as "on consignment" or "on memorandum."
> However, this subsection is not applicable if the person making delivery
> a. complies with an applicable law providing for a consignor's interest or the like to be evidenced by a sign, or
> b. establishes that the person conducting the business is generally known by his creditors to be substantially engaged in selling the goods of others, or
> c. complies with the filing provisions of the Article on Second Transactions (Article 9).

Guest

guest–transient who contracts for a room or site at a hotel.

A **guest** is a transient. The guest need not be a traveler or come from a distance. A person living within a short distance of a hotel who engages a room at the hotel and remains there overnight is a guest.

In contrast, a person who enters a hotel at the invitation of a guest or attends a dance or a banquet given at the hotel is not a guest. Similarly, the guest of a registered occupant of a motel room who shares the room with the occupant without the knowledge or consent of the management is not a guest of the motel because there is no relationship between that person and the motel.

21-4b Duration of Guest Relationship

The relationship of guest and hotelkeeper does not begin until a person is received as a guest by the hotelkeeper. The guest-hotelkeeper relationship does not automatically end when the hotel bill is paid.[37]

The relationship terminates when the guest leaves or ceases to be a transient, as when the guest arranges for a more or less permanent residence at the hotel. The transition from the status of guest to the status of boarder or lodger must be clearly indicated. It is not established by the mere fact that one remains at the hotel for a long period, even though it runs into months.

Circumstances arise when a hotel assumes an obligation to deliver packages to a guest from a person who is not a guest of the hotel. The hotelkeeper has a bailee's liability for the care of such packages. **For Example,** Richard St. Angelo, vice president of sales for jewelry manufacturer Don-Linn Inc., left two boxes of jewelry prototypes at the front desk of the Westin Hotel with instructions to deliver the boxes to the hotel's guest from Dillard's Inc., a national department store. This delivery took place. Thereafter, a Dillard's representative notified St. Angelo that Dillard's review of the products was complete and he could pick up the boxes at the hotel but specified no location. St. Angelo and the Westin staff later searched for the boxes, but they were never found. The manufacturer's lawsuit against the Westin asserting a breach of bailment was not successful. St. Angelo was not a guest at the Westin, thus the obligation assumed for the care of the packages initially left at the Westin was not as a hotelkeeper but a bailee. When the Westin surrendered the packages to Dillard's group, it completed its bailment agreement. No bailment or any other legal obligation between Don-Linn and the Westin was shown to exist with regard to the return of the jewelry prototypes.[38]

21-4c Hotelkeeper's Liability for Guest's Property

With respect to property expressly entrusted to the hotelkeeper's care, the hotelkeeper has a bailee's liability. At common law, the hotelkeeper was absolutely liable for damage to, or loss of, a guest's property unless the hotelkeeper could show that the damage or loss was caused solely by an act of God, a public enemy, an act of a public authority, the inherent nature of the property, or the fault of the guest.[39]

In most states, statutes limit or provide a method of limiting the common law liability of a hotelkeeper. The statutes may limit the extent of liability, reduce the liability of a hotelkeeper to that of an ordinary bailee, or permit the hotelkeeper to limit liability by contract or by posting a notice of the limitation. Some statutes relieve the hotelkeeper from liability when the guest has not complied with directions for depositing valuables

[37] *Garrett v. Impac Hotels, LLC,* 87 S.W.3d 870 (Mo. App. 2002).
[38] *Don-Linn Jewelry Co. v. The Westin Hotel Co.,* 877 A.2d 621 (R.I. 2005).
[39] *Cook v. Columbia Sussex Corp,* 807 S.W.2d 567 (Tenn. App. 1991).

with the hotelkeeper.[40] A hotelkeeper must substantially comply with such statutes in order to obtain their protection.

CASE SUMMARY

Conspicuous Notice Necessary to Avoid Liability

FACTS: While traveling from Florida to Connecticut, Mr. and Mrs. Ippolito stopped in Walterboro, South Carolina, and paid for a room at a Holiday Inn. At the hotel, Mr. Ippolito signed a registration card on which was written, "The management is not responsible for any valuables not secured in safety deposit boxes provided at the front office." In addition to the language on the registration card, notice that the hotel had safety deposit boxes available for guests' valuables was also printed on the pouch that enclosed the key-card to the Ippolitos' room. After bringing their luggage to the room, the Ippolitos walked to a nearby restaurant, and they returned approximately 40 minutes later. Upon their return, they noticed that pieces of their luggage, which contained jewelry valued at over $500,000 and approximately $8,000 in cash, were missing. The Ippolitos sued the innkeeper, alleging that their property loss resulted from "… the negligence, gross negligence, reckless, willful, wanton and careless action …" of Innkeeper, including "… failing to post proper notices as required under South Carolina law."

The state's innkeeper statute requires the innkeeper to post notice in a "conspicuous manner" in the room occupied by the guest, and the guest must deposit money and jewels in the office safe. The Ippolitos testified that they did not see any notice of safety deposit boxes posted in their room. Police officer Sadler testified that, although he made no mention of it in his police report, he saw a notice posted on the back of the hotel room door indicating that the innkeeper had safety deposit boxes available. The jury awarded the Ippolitos $350,000 in actual damages. However, the jury found that the Ippolitos were 40 percent comparatively negligent, and reduced the award to $210,000. The hotel appealed.

DECISION: Judgment for the Ippolitos. Whether guests observed a conspicuous notice in the room regarding availability of safety deposit boxes is a question for the jury where there is a conflict in testimony. The jury believed the Ippolitos' testimony of a lack of conspicuous notice. If an innkeeper fails to post such a notice, the innkeeper's liability is not limited. [*Ippolito v. Hospitality Management Associates*, 575 S.E.2d 562 (S.C. App. 2003)]

21-4d Hotelkeeper's Lien

The hotelkeeper has a lien on the baggage of guests for the agreed charges or, if no express agreement was made, for the reasonable value of the accommodations furnished. Statutes permit the hotelkeeper to enforce this lien by selling the goods of the guests at a public sale. The lien of the hotelkeeper is terminated by (1) the guest's payment of the hotel charges, (2) any conversion of the guest's goods by the hotelkeeper, or (3) final return of the goods to the guest.

21-4e Boarders or Lodgers

The hotelkeeper owes only the duty of an ordinary bailee of personal property under a mutual benefit bailment to those persons who are permanent boarders or lodgers rather than transient guests.

A hotelkeeper has no lien on property of boarders or lodgers, as distinguished from guests, in the absence of an express agreement creating such a lien. A number of states, however, have adopted legislation giving a lien to keepers of boardinghouses or lodging houses.

---

[40] *Chappone v. First Florence Corp.*, 504 S.E.2d 761 (Ga. App. 1998). But see *World Diamond Inc. v. Hyatt Corp.*, 699 N.E.2d 980 (Ohio App. 1997), where the court held that when special arrangements have been made between the innkeeper and the guest, the innkeeper is liable for the loss of any property so received when the loss is caused by the innkeeper's negligence.

Make the Connection

Summary

A warehouse stores the goods of others for compensation and has the rights and duties of a bailee in an ordinary mutual benefit bailment. A warehouse issues a warehouse receipt to the depositor of the goods. This receipt is a document of title that ordinarily entitles the person in possession of the receipt to receive the goods. The warehouse receipt can be bought, sold, or used as security to obtain a loan. A nonnegotiable warehouse receipt states that the goods received will be delivered to a specified person. A negotiable warehouse receipt states that the goods will be delivered "to the bearer" or "to the order of" a named person. If a negotiable warehouse receipt is duly negotiated, the transferee may acquire rights superior to those of the transferor. A warehouse may limit its liability for loss or damage to goods resulting from its own negligence to an agreed valuation of the property stated in the warehouse receipt, provided the depositor is given the right to store the goods without the limitation at a higher storage rate.

A common carrier of goods is in the business of transporting goods received from the general public. It issues to the shipper a bill of lading or an airbill. Both of these are documents of title and provide rights similar to those provided by a warehouse receipt. A common carrier is absolutely liable for any loss or damage to the goods unless the carrier can show that the loss was caused solely by an act of God, an act of a public enemy, an act of a public authority, an act of the shipper, or the inherent nature of the goods. The carrier may limit its liability in the same manner as a warehouse.

A factor is a special type of bailee who has possession of the owner's property for the purpose of sale. The factor, or consignee, receives a commission on the sale.

A hotelkeeper is in the business of providing living accommodations to transient persons called guests. Subject to exceptions, at common law, hotelkeepers were absolutely liable for loss or damage to their guests' property. Most states, however, provide a method of limiting this liability. A hotelkeeper has a lien on the property of the guest for the agreed charges.

Learning Outcomes

After studying this chapter, you should be able to clearly explain:

21-1 Warehousers

LO.1 Identify and explain all of the features of a negotiable warehouse receipt

See the example of the bona fide purchase of a warehouse receipt of 4,000 pairs of ice skates. See Figure 21-1, page 391.

21-2 Common Carriers

LO.2 List and explain the differences between the three types of motor carriers of goods

See the *Fortunoff* case and distinctions made between "common" and "contract" carriers, pages 393–394.

LO.3 Explain a common carrier's liability for loss or damage to goods

See the *Tronosjet* case applying the Carmack Amendment rule on carrier liability, page 398.

See the KCSR Railway example requiring actual notice to shipper of full liability option, page 397.

21-3 Factors and Consignments

LO.4 Identify and explain the role of each of the persons or business entities involved in the sale of goods on consignment

See the Rolly Tasker Sails example involving breach of a consignment agreement, pages 400–401.

21-4 Hotelkeepers

LO.5 Describe a hotelkeeper's liability for loss of a guest's property

See the *Ippolito* case for a discussion of the common law rule on liability for loss of a guest's property and application of a statutory exemption, page 403.

Key Terms

airbill	depositor	nonnegotiable bill of lading
bill of lading	document of title	nonnegotiable warehouse receipt
carrier	factorage	private carrier
commission	factor	public warehouses
commission merchant	field warehousing	selling on consignment
common carrier	guest	specific lien
consignee	hotelkeeper	straight bill of lading
consignor	issuer	warehouse
contract carrier	negotiable bill of lading	warehouse receipt
conversion	negotiable warehouse receipt	

Questions and Case Problems

1. What social forces are involved in the rule of law governing the liability of a common carrier for loss of freight?

2. American Cyanamid shipped 7,000 vials of DPT—a vaccine for immunization of infants and children against diphtheria, pertussis, and tetanus—from its Pearl River, New York, facility to the U.S. Defense Department depot in Mechanicsburg, Pennsylvania, by New Penn Motor Express, a common carrier. Cyanamid's bill of lading included a "release value," which stated that the value of the property was declared as not exceeding $1.65 per pound. Cyanamid's shipment weighed 1,260 pounds. The bill of lading accepted by New Penn on picking up the DPT vaccine on February 6 also clearly stated that the shipment contained drugs and clearly warned to "protect from freezing." The bill further recited "rush ... must be delivered by February 8, 1989." New Penn permitted the vaccine to sit in an unheated uninsulated trailer while it gathered enough other merchandise to justify sending a truck to Mechanicsburg. The DPT vaccine was delivered on February 10 in worthless condition, having been destroyed by the cold. New Penn admitted that it owed $2,079 in damages pursuant to the bill of lading ($1.65 × 1,260 lb.). Cyanamid claimed that the actual loss was much greater, $53,936.75. It stated that because New Penn breached its contract with Cyanamid, it could not invoke the benefits of that same contract, namely, the release value clause.

   Was it ethical for New Penn to hold the vaccine while waiting for enough merchandise to justify the trip? How would you decide the case? [*American Cyanamid Co. v. New Penn Motor Express, Inc.*, 979 F.2d 301 (3d Cir.)]

3. Compare the liens of carriers, warehouses, and hotels in terms of being specific.

4. Compare the limitations of the liability of a warehouse and of a hotelkeeper.

5. Compare warehouse receipts and bills of lading as to negotiability.

6. Doyle Harms applied to his state's Public Utilities Commission for a Class B permit authorizing performance as a common carrier. Doyle testified that it was not his intention to haul in a different direction than he was already going, stating in part:

   > No way, that's not what I'm asking for. I've got enough business of my own, it's just the times when you get done with a sale at the end of the day and you've got a half load and somebody else has a half load, then you'd be able to help each other out. It's kind of the name of the game in my mind.

   He also testified that the application was so he could haul cattle for his own customers. State law defines a common carrier as "a motor carrier which holds itself out to the general public as engaged in the business of transporting persons or property in intrastate commerce which it is accustomed to and is capable of transporting from place to place in this state, for hire." Its property is "devoted to the public service." Should Doyle Harms be issued a common carrier permit? [In re *Harms*, 491 N.W.2d 760 (S.D.)]

7. Motorola manufactured cell phones for Nextel of Mexico at its facility in Plantation, Florida. Nextel used Westwind International to arrange transportation of the cell phones. Westwind utilized Transpro

Logistics to administer the transportation process and Transpro entered a Broker Transportation Agreement (BTA) with Werner Enterprises, a common carrier, to transport the phones from Florida to Texas on a regular basis. The BTA incorporated Werner's tariff, giving shippers the option of selecting Carmack Liability full-value coverage or the carrier's limitation of liability of a maximum of $200,000 per truckload shipment. In its contract with Nextel, Westwind notified Nextel that third-party carriers might limit their liability for loss and stated that it would request excess valuation coverage only upon specific written instructions from Nextel. Nextel simply relied on Westwind to handle shipping issues. On October 8, 2004, a shipment of 7,958 cell phones valued at $1,251,673 was stolen from one of Werner's trucks. Werner contended that it owed a maximum liability of $200,000 under its tariff. Nextel's insurer, Ace Seguros SA, sued Werner for the full value of the shipment, contending that contracts downstream by Westwind and Transpro cannot be imputed back to Nextel—and that the cargo owner Nextel had not been given the opportunity to choose between two or more levels of liability as required by the Carmack Amendment. Can intermediaries like Westwind and/or Transpro negotiate an enforceable agreement with a carrier it engages? Was Nextel given a reasonable opportunity to choose between two or more levels of liability? Decide. [*Werner Enterprises, Inc. v. Ace Seguros SA*, 554 F.3d 1319 (11th Cir.)]

8. Richard Schewe and others placed personal property in a building occupied by Winnebago County Fair Association, Inc. Prior to placing their property in the building, they signed a "Storage Rental Agreement" prepared by the County Fair Association, which stated: "No liability exists for damage or loss to the stored equipment from the perils of fire...." The property was destroyed by fire. Suit was brought against the County Fair Association to recover damages for the losses on the theory of negligence of a warehouse. The County Fair Association claimed that the language in the storage agreement relieved it of all liability. Decide. [*Allstate Ins. Co. v. Winnebago County Fair Ass'n, Inc.*, 475 N.E.2d 230 (Ill. App.)]

9. Buffett sent a violin to Strotokowsky by International Parcel Service (IPS), a common carrier. Buffett declared the value of the parcel at $500 on the pick-up receipt given him by the IPS driver. The receipt also stated: "Unless a greater value is declared in writing on this receipt, the shipper hereby declares and agrees that the released value of each package covered by this receipt is $100.00, which is a reasonable value under the circumstance surrounding the transportation." When Strotokowsky did not receive the parcel, Buffett sued IPS for the full retail value of the violin—$2,000. IPS's defense was that it was liable for just $100. Decide.

10. Glen Smith contracted with Dave Watson, a common carrier, to transport 720 hives of live bees along with associated equipment from Idabel, Oklahoma, to Mandan, North Dakota. At 9:00 A.M. on May 24, 1984, while en route, Watson's truck skidded off the road and tipped over, severely damaging the cargo. Watson notified Smith about what had happened, and Smith immediately set out for the scene of the accident. He arrived at 6:00 P.M. with two bee experts and a Bobcat loader. They were hindered by the turned-over truck on top of the cargo, and they determined that they could not safely salvage the cargo that evening. The next day, an insurance adjuster determined that the cargo was a total loss. The adjuster directed a bee expert, Dr. Moffat, to conduct the cleanup; Moffat was allowed to keep the salvageable cargo, valued at $12,326, as compensation. Smith sued Watson for damages. Watson denied liability and further contended that Smith failed to mitigate damages. Decide. [*Smith v. Watson*, 406 N.W.2d 685 (N.D.)]

11. Garrett and his wife checked into the St. Louis Airport North Holiday Inn on March 29, taking advantage of the hotel's "Park and Fly" package, which provided one night of lodging to individuals, provided a shuttle service to Lambert International Airport, and allowed individuals to keep a vehicle on the hotel's parking lot for up to two weeks. When the Garretts returned from their vacation on April 17, they discovered that their vehicle was stolen. They sued the hotel, contending that a special relationship of an innkeeper and guest was created by the "Park and Fly" marketing package, and that the hotel's knowledge of criminal activity on its parking lot created a duty to warn the Garretts, which it failed to do. What status did the Garretts have with the hotel regarding the protection of their vehicle after boarding the plane on their vacation trip? Was there a bailment of the vehicle under the "Park and

Fly" marketing package? [*Garrett v. IMPAC Hotels Inc.*, 87 S.W.3d 870 (Mo. App.)]

12. On March 30, Emery Air Freight Corp. picked up a shipment of furs from Hopper Furs, Inc. Hopper's chief of security filled in certain items in the airbill. In the box entitled ZIP Code, he mistakenly placed the figure "61,045," which was the value of the furs. The ZIP Code box was immediately above the Declared Value box. The airbill contained a clause limiting liability to $10 per pound of cargo lost or damaged unless the shipper makes a declaration of value in excess of the amount and pays a higher fee. A higher fee was not charged in this case, and Gerald Doane signed the airbill for the carrier and took possession of the furs. The furs were lost in transit by Emery, and Hopper sued for the value of the furs, $61,045. Emery's offer to pay $2,150, the $10-per-pound rate set forth in the airbill, was rejected. Hopper claimed that the amount of $61,045, which was mistakenly placed in the ZIP Code box, was in fact part of the contract set forth in the airbill and that Emery, on reviewing the contract, must have realized a mistake was made. Decide. [*Hopper Furs, Inc. v. Emery Air Freight Corp.*, 749 F.2d 1261 (8th Cir.)]

13. When de Lema, a Brazilian resident, arrived in New York City, his luggage consisted of three suitcases, an attaché case, and a cylindrical bag. The attaché case and the cylindrical bag contained jewels valued at $300,000. De Lema went from JFK Airport to the Waldorf Astoria Hotel, where he gave the three suitcases to hotel staff in the garage, and then he went to the lobby to register. The assistant manager, Baez, summoned room clerk Tamburino to assist him. De Lema stated, "The room clerk asked me if I had a reservation. I said, 'Yes. The name is José Berga de Lema.' And I said, 'I want a safety deposit box.' He said, 'Please fill out your registration.'" While de Lema was filling out the registration form, paying $300 in cash as an advance, and Tamburino was filling out a receipt for that amount, de Lema had placed the attaché case and the cylindrical bag on the floor. A woman jostled de Lema, apparently creating a diversion, and when he next looked down, he discovered that the attaché case was gone. De Lema brought suit against the hotel for the value of the jewels stolen in the hotel's lobby. The hotel

maintained a safe for valuables and posted notices in the lobby, garage, and rooms as required by the New York law that modifies a hotelkeeper's common law liability. The notices stated in part that the hotel was not liable for the loss of valuables that a guest had neglected to deliver to the hotel for safekeeping. The hotel's defense was that de Lema had neglected to inform it of the presence of the jewels and to deliver the jewels to the hotel. Is the hotel liable for the value of the stolen jewels? [*De Lema v. Waldorf Astoria Hotel, Inc.*, 588 F. Supp. 19 (S.D.N.Y.)]

14. Frosty Land Foods shipped a load of beef from its plant in Montgomery, Alabama, to Scott Meat Co. in Los Angeles via Refrigerated Transport Co. (RTC), a common carrier. Early Wednesday morning, December 7, at 12:55 A.M., two of RTC's drivers left the Frosty Land plant with the load of beef. The bill of lading called for delivery at Scott Meat on Friday, December 9, at 6:00 A.M. The RTC drivers arrived in Los Angeles at approximately 3:30 P.M. on Friday, December 9. Scott notified the drivers that it could not process the meat at that time. The drivers checked into a motel for the weekend, and the load was delivered to Scott on Monday, December 12. After inspecting 65 of the 308 carcasses, Scott determined that the meat was in off condition and refused the shipment. On Tuesday, December 13, Frosty Land sold the meat, after extensive trimming, at a loss of $13,529. Frosty Land brought suit against RTC for its loss. Decide. [*Frosty Land Foods v. Refrigerated Transport Co.*, 613 F.2d 1344 (5th Cir.)]

15. Tate hired Action-Mayflower Moving & Storage to ship his belongings. Action prepared a detailed inventory of Tate's belongings, loaded them on its truck, and received the belongings at its warehouse, where they would be stored until Tate asked that they be moved. Months later, a dispute arose, and Tate asked Action to release his property to a different mover. Tate had prepaid more than enough to cover all charges to this point. Action refused to release the goods and held them in storage. After allowing storage charges to build up for 15 months, Action sold Tate's property under the warehouser's public sale law. Tate sued Action for damages. Decide. [*Tate v. Action-Mayflower Moving & Storage, Inc.*, 383 S.E.2d 229 (N.C. App.)]

CPA Questions

1. A common carrier bailee generally would avoid liability for loss of goods entrusted to its care if the goods are:

   a. Stolen by an unknown person.

   b. Negligently destroyed by an employee.

   c. Destroyed by the derailment of the train carrying them due to railroad employee negligence.

   d. Improperly packed by the party shipping them.

2. Under a nonnegotiable bill of lading, a carrier who accepts goods for shipment must deliver the goods to:

   a. Any holder of the bill of lading.

   b. Any party subsequently named by the seller.

   c. The seller who was issued the bill of lading.

   d. The consignee of the bill of lading.

3. Under the UCC, a warehouse receipt:

   a. Is negotiable if, by its terms, the goods are to be delivered to bearer or to the order of a named person.

   b. Will not be negotiable if it contains a contractual limitation on the warehouse's liability.

   c. May qualify as both a negotiable warehouse receipt and negotiable commercial paper if the instrument is payable either in cash or by the delivery of goods.

   d. May be issued only by a bonded and licensed warehouser.

4. Under the Documents of Title Article of the UCC, which of the following acts may limit a common carrier's liability for damages to the goods in transit?

   a. Vandalism

   b. Power outage

   c. Willful acts of third person

   d. Providing for a contractual dollar liability limitation

Nature and Form of Sales

Learning Outcomes ⟨⟨⟨

After studying this chapter, you should be able to

LO.1 Define a sale of goods and explain when UCC Article 2 applies to contracts

LO.2 Distinguish between an actual sale of goods and other types of transactions in goods

LO.3 Describe how contracts are formed under Article 2, and list the differences in formation standards between the UCC and common law

LO.4 Explain when a contract for the sale of goods must be in writing

LO.5 List and explain the exceptions to the requirement that certain contracts be in writing

LO.6 Discuss the purpose of the United Nations Convention on Contracts for the International Sale of Goods

22-1   **Nature of the Sale of Goods**

Chapters 11 through 19 examined the common law of contracts. That source of contract law applies to contracts whose subject matter is land or services. However, there is another source of contract law, **Article 2** of the Uniform Commercial Code (UCC).

UCC Article 2 governs the sale of everything from boats to televisions to flash drives and applies to contracts for the sale of goods. Article 2 exists as a result of the work of businesspeople, commercial transactions lawyers, and legal experts who together have developed a body of contract law suitable for the fast pace of business. Article 2 continues to be refined and modified to ensure seamless laws for transactions in goods across the country.[2]

A *sale of goods* is defined under Article 2 as transfer of title to tangible personal property for a price.[3] This price may be a payment of money, an exchange of other property, or the performance of services.

The parties to a sale are the person who owns the goods, the seller or vendor, and the person to whom the title is transferred, the buyer or vendee.

> **Article 2**–section of the Uniform Commercial Code that governs contracts for the sale of goods.[1]

CPA

22-1a   **Subject Matter of Sales**

Goods, as defined under the UCC, consist of all forms of tangible personal property, including specially manufactured goods—everything from a fan to a painting to a yacht.[4] Article 2 does not cover (1) investment securities, such as stocks and bonds, the sale of which is regulated by Article 8 of the UCC; (2) insurance policies, commercial paper, such as checks, and promissory notes because they are regulated under Articles 3 and 4 of the UCC; and (3) real estate, such as houses, factories, farms, and land itself.[5]

> **goods**–anything movable at the time it is identified as the subject of a transaction.

CPA

Nature of Goods

Article 2 applies not only to contracts for the sale of familiar items of personal property, such as automobiles or chairs, but also to the transfer of commodities, such as oil, gasoline, milk, and grain.[6]

---

[1] Article 2 was revised substantially by the National Conference of Commissioners on Uniform State Laws (NCCUSL) and the American Law Institute (ALI) in August 2003. Because no state has adopted Revised Article 2, its future remains a question. Revised Article 2 is covered only briefly in this chapter and Chapters 23 through 26.

[2] The UCC Article 2 (prior to the 2003 revisions) has been adopted in 49 states plus the Virgin Islands and the District of Columbia. Louisiana adopted only Article 1.

[3] U.C.C. §2-105(1). *General Mills Operations, LLC v. Five Star Custom Foods, Ltd.*, 703 F.3d 1104 (8th Cir. 2013).

[4] *Simulados Software, Ltd. v. Photon Infotech Private, Ltd.* 40 F. Supp. 2d 1191, 83 U.C.C. Rep. Serv. 2d 528 (N.D. Cal. 2014) (mass-produced software is a good); *Nautilus Insurance Company v. Cheran Investments LLC*, 2014 WL 292809 (Neb. App. 2014), 82 U.C.C. Rep. Serv. 2d 560 (sale of bar property including kitchen equipment, television, food, and liquor was covered by the UCC); In re *Sony Gaming Networks and Customer Data Security Breach Litigation*, 996 F. Supp. 2d 942 (S.D. Cal. 2014), 82 U.C.C. Rep. Serv. 2d 493 (Internet connectivity, while it may have affected gaming, is not a good for purposes of application of the UCC); In re *Grede Foundries, Inc.*, 435 B.R. 593 (W.D. Wisc. 2010) (electricity is a good); *Leal v. Holtvogh*, 702 N.E.2d 1246 (Ohio App. 1998) (transfer of part interest in a horse is a good); *Land O'Lakes Purina Feed LLC v. Jaeger*, 976 F. Supp. 2d 1073 (S.D. Iowa 2013), 81 U.C.C. Rep. Serv. 2d 955 (weaned pigs are a good); *Bergeron v. Aero Sales*, 134 P.3d 964 (Or. App. 2006) (jet fuel is a good); *Rite Aid Corp. v. Levy-Gray*, 894 A.2d 563 (Md. 2006) (prescription drug is a good); *Shelly Materials, Inc. v. Great Lakes Crushing, Ltd.*, 2013 WL 6810660 (Ohio App. 2013), 82 U.C.C. Rep. Serv. 2d 278 (premixed cement is a good); *MWI Veterinary Supply Co. v. Wotton*, 896 F. Supp. 2d 905 (D. Idaho 2012) (patents are not goods); *Eureka Water Co. v. Nestle Waters North America, Inc.*, 690 F.3d 1139, 78 U.C.C. Rep. Serv. 2d 36 (10th Cir. 2012) (trademark is not a good); *Gladhart v. Oregon Vineyard Supply Co.*, 994 P.2d 134 (Or. App. 1999) (grape plants bought from nursery are goods); *Dantzler v. S.P. Parks, Inc.*, 40 U.C.C. Rep. Serv. 2d 955 E.D. (Pa. 1988) (purchase of ticket to amusement ride is not transaction in goods); and *Saxton v. Pets Warehouse, Inc.*, 691 N.Y.S.2d 872 (1999) (dog is a good).

[5] However, Article 2 does apply to the sale of rare coins. *Bowers and Merena Auctions, LLC, v. James Lull*, 386 B.R. 261, 65 U.C.C. Rep. Serv. 2d 194 (Haw. 2008).

[6] U.C.C. §2-105(1)—(2). *Wojtalewicz v. Pioneer Hi–Bred Intern., Inc.*, 939 F. Supp. 2d 965 (D. Neb. 2012); *Venmar Ventilation, Inc. v. Von Weise USA, Inc.*, 68 U.C.C. Serv. 2d 373 (D. Minn. 2009); *Bartlett Grain Co., LP v. Sheeder*, 829 N.W.2d 18 (Iowa 2013).

existing goods–goods that physically exist and are owned by the seller at the time of a transaction.

future goods–goods that exist physically but are not owned by the seller and goods that have not yet been produced.

bailment–relationship that exists when personal property is delivered into the possession of another under an agreement, express or implied, that the identical property will be returned or will be delivered in accordance with the agreement. (Parties—bailor, bailee)

bailee–person who accepts possession of a property.

gift–title to an owner's personal property voluntarily transferred by a party not receiving anything in exchange.

Existing and Future Goods

Goods that are already manufactured or crops already grown and owned by the seller at the time of the transaction are called **existing goods.** All other goods are called **future goods,** which include both goods that physically exist but are not owned by the seller and goods that have not yet been produced, as when a buyer contracts to purchase custom-made office furniture.

22-1b Sale Distinguished from Other Transactions

Other types of transactions in goods are not covered by Article 2 because they are not transfers of title to the goods.

Bailment

A **bailment** is not a sale because only possession is transferred to a **bailee.** Title to the property is not transferred. (For more information on bailments, their nature, and the rights of the parties, see Chapter 20.) A lease of goods, such as an automobile, is governed by Article 2A of the UCC, which is covered later in the section titled "Leases of Goods" of this chapter.

Gift

A **gift** is a gratuitous (free) transfer of the title to property. The Article 2 definition of a sale requires that the transfer of title be made for a price. Gifts are not covered under Article 2.[7]

Contract for Services

A contract for services, such as a contract for painting a home, is not a sale of goods and is not covered under Article 2 of the UCC. Contracts for services are governed by common law principles.

Contract for Goods and Services

If a contract calls for both rendering services and supplying materials to be used in performing the services, the contract is classified according to its dominant element. **For Example,** a homeowner may purchase a security system. The homeowner is paying for the equipment that is used in the system as well as for the seller's expertise and installation of that system. Is the homeowner's contract governed by Article 2, or is it a contract for services and covered under the common law of contracts?

If the service element dominates, the contract is a service contract and is governed by common law rather than Article 2. If the goods make up the dominant element of the contract, then the parties' rights are determined under Article 2.[8] In the home security system contract example, the question requires comparing the costs of the system's parts versus the costs of its installation. In some contracts, the equipment costs are minimal, and installation is key for the customer. In more sophisticated security systems, the installation is a small portion of the overall contract price, and the contract would be governed by the UCC.[9]

---

[7] The adoption of a dog from an animal shelter is not the sale of goods. *Slodov v. Animal Protective League*, 628 N.E.2d 117 (Oh. App. 1993).

[8] Trees and shrubs as part of a landscaping contract are sales of goods. *Kaitz v. Landscape Creations, Inc.*, 2000 Mass. App. Div. 140, 2000 WL 694274 (Mass. App. Div.), 42 U.C.C. Rep. Serv. 2d 691.

[9] *TK Power, Inc. v. Textron, Inc.*, 433 F. Supp. 2d 1058 (N.D. Cal. 2006); see also *Lesiak v. Central Valley Ag Co-op., Inc.*, 808 N.W.2d 67 (Neb. 2012) (a contract for the sale and application of herbicide was primarily a contract for the sale of the herbicide and was governed by the UCC).

CASE SUMMARY

When the Tire Maintenance Contract Falls Flat

FACTS: Accessory Overhaul Group, Inc. (AOG), provides commercial aircraft component testing, overhauling, and certification services. AOG had submitted a bid to Mesa Air Group, Inc. ("Mesa"), and its subsidiary, Mesa Airlines, Inc., for work on its planes, which Mesa accepted in the fall of 2007.

AOG began performing work for Mesa in October 2007, and the next month the parties executed a memorandum of understanding (MOU). The MOU provides that it "shall remain in effect until the execution of the Contract by the Parties or its termination as described herein." From 2007 to 2012, AOG serviced and maintained Mesa's wheels, tires, and brakes.

In January 2010, Mesa filed for bankruptcy protection, and the bankruptcy court deemed AOG a "critical vendor." Mesa continued its commercial relationship with AOG, and on January 14, 2010, the parties executed a critical trade agreement (CTA). The CTA broadly defined the parties' relationship during Mesa's bankruptcy case.

Sometime in 2011, after Mesa had emerged from bankruptcy, the parties resumed negotiations of a more detailed contract. AOG's president, Ron Byrd, worked with Scott Johnson, Mesa's senior director for maintenance and engineering technical administration, to draft the contract.

Byrd and Johnson exchanged several drafts of an agreement. On November 21, 2011, Johnson sent Byrd an e-mail, stating that he had updated the pricing per AOG's request and that he had included with his e-mail "a soft-copy version as well as the PDF." Johnson then stated, "If you're good, please sign and return. Then, I'll route through our contract signature process here at Mesa." Byrd signed and returned the document that day.

On January 3, 2012, Johnson informed Byrd that the document had "hit a snag" in the finance department. Mesa's senior vice president of finance had "rejected" a term dealing with late fees, and Byrd agreed to the removal of that term.

In March 2012, Johnson presented the November 21 document to Mesa's president, Michael Lotz, for his review. Lotz refused to sign the contract.

On May 9, 2012, AOG met with Mesa to discuss a rate increase. AOG unequivocally told Mesa during the meeting that if the rate did not increase, it would cease work with Mesa right away or "pretty quickly." Mesa responded that it was going to put the wheel, tire, and brake work back out for bid immediately.

That same day, Mesa issued a new request for proposals on the wheel, tire, and brake maintenance work. AOG bid on the work at its increased rate. By the end of June, Mesa had chosen a different vendor, and on June 30 Mesa removed Mesa's aircraft from AOG's servicing in August.

AOG sent Mesa invoices seeking over $3.4 million. Mesa refused to pay the invoices on the basis that the November 21 document is not a binding contract.

AOG filed suit and Mesa filed a motion for summary judgment on AOG's claims.

DECISION: Whether the UCC or common law applies depends on whether the parties' relationship predominantly involved goods or services. AOG performed repair services, and while those services may have involved goods, the primary purpose of AOG's work was to service the wheels, tires, and brakes of their aircraft.

In repair-contract cases, which typically involve goods and services, courts look to the "fundamental nature of the transaction." "The primary purpose of a repair transaction is not to sell or purchase parts, but to change or improve the item and return it to the owner. In such cases, the provision of goods is incidental, and the UCC does not apply."

Here, the parties' own words show that the primary purpose of their relationship was for AOG to provide wheel, tire, and brake services to Mesa. Beginning with the MOU, the parties characterized their relationship as a service-based one. The MOU provides that AOG would be the wheels/tire/brakes maintenance and repair and management services provider for Mesa. Thus, the MOU set forth the "terms and conditions under which AOG will provide such services to Mesa." Similarly, the CTA continued the parties' service relationship. [*Accessory Overhaul Group, Inc. v. Mesa Airlines, Inc.*, 994 F. Supp. 2d 1296 (N.D. Ga. 2014)]

CPA   22-1c **Formation of Sales Contracts**

Necessary Detail for Formation

To streamline business transactions, Article 2 of the UCC does not have standards as rigid as the formation standards of common law contracts.

THINKING THINGS THROUGH

Delivering Dirt

Paramount, a civil engineering firm and general contractor, submitted a bid to construct runway improvements at the Atlanta Hartsfield–Jackson International Airport. Paramount included DPS's quote for supplying the fill dirt for the project in its bid. DPS's written quote described its work as "furnish[ing] and haul[ing]/deliver[ing] borrow dirt from DPS's location to the job site," and specifically excluded the provision of "traffic control, dust control, security and escort services" from the scope of work. The quote provides that the dirt would be delivered for a price of "$140/Truck Load."

After Paramount was awarded the airport project, it contacted DPS about the amount of dirt and numbers of trucks that it would need for the airport project. DPS believed that the parties had a contract, and it sent a letter to Paramount confirming that it was "holding approximately 45,000 [cubic yards] of borrow dirt ready to be hauled in to your project once we receive [the] 10–day notice from you." Paramount did not respond.

Over the next two months, DPS sent other letters to Paramount, but Paramount did not respond. After executives from the two companies met, Paramount sent the following:

> [Y]ou insisted that we give commitment to you for buying the dirt before you will give us price [for other work]. This really was a surprise to us.... Also please note that we have never committed to buy all the fill materials from you. In the last meeting you were informed that we intend to purchase some materials from you and it may be through other subcontractors. Our decisions will be conveyed to you as soon as possible.

Ultimately, Paramount bought the dirt it needed from another vendor. DPS sued Paramount for breach of contract. What law governs this contract and why?

[**Paramount Contracting Co. v. DPS Industries, Inc.**, 709 S.E.2d 288 (Ga. App. 2011)]

CPA   Under the UCC, a contract can be formed even though one or more terms are left open so long as the parties clearly intend to contract.[10] The minimum terms required for formation of an agreement under the UCC are the subject matter and quantity (if there is more than one).[11] **For Example,** an agreement that described "the sale of my white Scion" would be sufficient, but an agreement to purchase "some white Scions" would require a quantity in order to qualify for formation.[12] Other provisions under Article 2 can cover any missing terms so long as the parties are clear on their intent to contract. Article 2 has provisions that cover price, delivery, time for performance, payment, and other details of performance in the event the parties agree to a sale but have not discussed or reduced to writing their desires in these areas.[13]

The Merchant versus Nonmerchant Parties

merchant–seller who deals in specific goods classified by the UCC.

Because Article 2 applies to all transactions in goods, it is applicable to sales by both **merchants** and nonmerchants,[14] including consumers. In most instances, the UCC treats all buyers and sellers alike. However, some sections in Article 2 are applicable only to merchants, and as a result, there are circumstances in which merchants are subject to different standards and rules. Generally, these areas of different treatment reflect the UCC's

---

[10] 5 U.C.C. §2-204(3); *Silicon Intern. Ore, LLC v. Monsanto Co.*, 314 P.3d 593 (Idaho 2013). Without a start date on a delivery contract, there is no contract. *Matheson Tri–Gas, Inc. v. Maxim Integrated Products, Inc.*, 444 S.W.3d 283 (Tex. App. 2014).

[11] *Brooks Peanut Co., Inc. v. Great Southern Peanut, LLC*, 746 S.E.2d 272 (Ga. App. 2013).

[12] *Dell's Maraschino Cherries Co. Inc. v. Shoreline Fruit Growers, Inc.*, 887 F. Supp. 2d 459 (E.D.N.Y. 2012).

[13] For information on terms, see U.C.C. §§2-305 (price), 2-307 to 2-308 (delivery), 2-310 (payment), and 2-311 (performance).

[14] *Merchant* is defined in U.C.C. §2-104(1). *Bev Smith, Inc. v. Atwell*, 836 N.W.2d 872 (Mich. App. 2014). An operator of a turkey farm is not a merchant with regard to heaters used on turkey farms, only for the turkeys themselves. *Jennie-O-Foods, Inc. v. Safe-Glo Prods. Corp.*, 582 N.W.2d 576 (Minn. App. 1998).

recognition that merchants are experienced, have special knowledge of the relevant commercial practices, and often need to have greater flexibility and speed in their transactions. The sections that have different rules for merchants and nonmerchants are noted throughout Chapters 23–26.

Offer

CPA

offer–expression of an offeror's willingness to enter into a contractual agreement.

firm offer–offer stated to be held open for a specified time, under the UCC, with respect to merchants.

Just as in common law, the **offer** is the first step in formation of a sales contract under Article 2.[15] The common law contract rules on offers are generally applicable in sales contract formation with the exception of the **firm offer**[16] provision, which is a special rule on offers applicable only to merchants: A firm offer by a merchant cannot be revoked if the offer (1) expresses an intention that it will be kept open, (2) is in a writing, and (3) is signed by the merchant.[17]

The period of irrevocability in a merchant's firm offer cannot exceed three months. If no specific time is given in the merchant's firm offer for its duration, it remains irrevocable only for a reasonable time. A firm offer need not have consideration to be irrevocable for a period of three months. **For Example,** a rain check given by a store on advertised merchandise is a merchant's firm offer. The rain check guarantees that you will be able to purchase two bottles of Windex at $1.99 each for a period specified in the rain check.

For nonmerchants' offers and offers in which the parties want firm offer periods that exceed three months, there must be consideration. In these situations, the parties must create an option contract just like those used in common law contracts (see Chapters 11 and 12).

Acceptance—Manner

CPA

acceptance–unqualified assent to the act or proposal of another; as the acceptance of an offer to make a contract.

Unlike the common law rules on acceptance, which control with great detail the method of acceptance, the UCC rules on acceptance are much more flexible. Under Article 2, an acceptance of an offer may be in any manner and by any medium that is reasonable under the circumstances.[18] Acceptance can occur through written communication or through performance, as when a seller accepts an offer for prompt shipment of goods by simply shipping the goods.[19] However, just as under common law, Article 2 requires that if the offer specifies the manner or medium of acceptance, the offer can be accepted only in that manner.

Acceptance—Timing

CPA

mailbox rule–timing for acceptance tied to proper acceptance.

The timing rules of the common law for determining when a contract has been formed are used to determine the formation of a contract under Article 2 with one slight modification. The **mailbox rule** applies under the UCC not just for the use of the same method of communication as that used by the offeror, but also applies when the offeree uses any reasonable method of communication. Under the common law, the offeree had to use the same method of communication in order to have the mailbox rule of acceptance apply.

---

[15] A purchase order is generally considered an offer, but it must have enough information to meet the minimum standards for an offer. *RBC Aircraft Products, Inc. v. Precise Machining & Mfg., LLC*, 26 F. Supp. 156 (D. Conn. 2014); *Whataburger Restaurants LLC v. Cardwell*, 446 S.W.3d 897 (Tex. App. 2014).

[16] Firm offers are covered in U.C.C. §2-205.

[17] A quotation is a firm offer. *Dumont Telephone Co. v. Power & Telephone Supply Co.*, 962 F. Supp. 2d 1064 (N.D. Iowa 2013); *Rich Products Corp. v. Kemutec, Inc.*, 66 F. Supp. 2d 937 (E.D. Wis. 1999); *Jerez v. JD Closeouts, LLC*, 943 N.Y.S.2d 392 (N.Y. Dist. 2012); but see *Boydstun Metal Works, Inc. v. Cottrell, Inc.*, 519 F. Supp. 2d 1119 (D. Or. 2007).

[18] U.C.C. §2-206(1) governs. See also *Ardus Medical, Inc. v. Emanuel County Hospital Authority*, 558 F. Supp. 2d 1301 (D. Ga. 2008).

[19] U.C.C. §2-206(1)(b). Shipment of coal in response to an offer is acceptance. *Central Illinois Public Service Co. v. Atlas Minerals, Inc.*, 146 F.3d 448 (7th Cir. 1998). Preliminary discussions are not offers and acceptances. *FutureFuel Chemical Co. v. Lonza, Inc.*, 756 F.3d 641 (8th Cir. 2014). However, exchanged purchase orders are. *Bro-Tech Corp. v. Purity Water Co. of San Antonio, Inc.*, 681 F. Supp. 2d 791 (W.D. Tex. 2010).

ETHICS & THE LAW

Restocking at Overstock

Cynthia Hines purchased an ElectroluxOxygen 3 Ultra Canister vacuum from Overstock.com, an online retailer that sells close-out goods. Ms. Hines returned the vacuum and was refunded her full amount, less a $30 restocking fee. She filed suit for breach of contract because she said that Overstock.com advertises that you can return merchandise at no cost and that Overstock.com did not disclose the restocking fee.

However, Overstock.com states that its Web site includes the following: "All retail purchases from Overstock are conducted through Overstock's Internet website. When an individual accesses the website, he or she accepts Overstock's terms, conditions and policies, which govern all of Overstock's customer purchases."

However, users were not required to click on the terms and conditions or to scroll all the way through the terms and conditions in order to use the site. It was possible, then, for a user to miss all the terms, such as a restocking fee.

Evaluate whether the restocking fee was part of the contract. Was it ethical for Overstock.com to impose the terms without users being aware of those terms? Discuss whether Overstock.com should have done more to disclose the restocking charge or put the notice in a different place.*

***Hines v. Overstock.com, Inc.**, **668 F. Supp. 2d 362 (E.D.N.Y. 2009)**

However, a UCC offeree can use any reasonable method for communicating acceptance and still enjoy the priority timing of the mailbox rule, something that makes an acceptance effective when it is sent. **For Example,** suppose that Feather-Light Brownies sent a letter offer to Cane Sugar Suppliers offering to buy 500 pounds of confectioner's sugar at $1 per pound. Cane Sugar Suppliers faxes back an acceptance of the letter offer. Cane Sugar Suppliers' acceptance is effective when it sends the fax.

CPA

Acceptance—Language

mirror image rule– common law contract rule on acceptance that requires language to be absolutely the same as the offer, unequivocal and unconditional.

Under the common law, the **mirror image rule** applies to acceptances. To be valid acceptances under common law, the language of the acceptance must be absolute, unconditional, and unequivocal; that is, the acceptance under common law must be the mirror image of the offer in order for a contract to be formed. However, the UCC has liberalized this rigid rule and permits formation even in circumstances when the acceptance includes terms that vary from the offer. The following sections explain the UCC rules on differing terms in acceptances.[20]

CPA

Additional Terms in Acceptance—Nonmerchants. Under Article 2, unless an offer expressly specifies that an offer to buy or sell goods must be accepted exactly as made, the offeree may accept an offer and at the same time propose an additional term or terms. The additional term or terms in the acceptance does not result in a rejection as it would under common law. A contract is formed with the terms of the original offer. The additional terms are proposals for addition to the contract and may or may not be accepted by the other party. **For Example,** Joe tells Susan, "I'll sell you my Xbox for $150," and Susan responds, "I'll take it. The 'Call of Duty' game is included." Susan has added an additional term in her acceptance. At this point, Joe and Susan have a contract for the sale of the Xbox for $150. Whether the "Call of Duty" game is included is up to Joe; Joe is free to accept Susan's proposal or reject it, but his decision does not control whether he has a contract. There is a contract because Susan has made a definite statement of acceptance.

[20] These rules for additional terms in acceptance were eliminated under Revised Article 2. However, Revised Article 2 has not been adopted widely by the states.

To avoid being bound by a contract before she is clear on the terms, Susan should make an inquiry before using the language of acceptance, such as "Would you include the 'Call of Duty' game as part of the sale?" Susan's inquiry is not an acceptance and leaves the original offer still outstanding, which she is free to accept or reject.

Additional Terms in Acceptance—Merchants. Under Article 2, the use of additional terms in acceptances by merchants is treated slightly differently. The different treatment of merchants in acceptances is the result of a commercial practice known as the **battle of the forms,** which results because a buyer sends a seller a purchase order for the purchase of goods. The seller sends back an invoice to the buyer. Although the buyer and seller may agree on the front of their documents that the subject matter of their contracts is 500 treadmills, the backs of their forms have details on the contracts, often called *boiler-plate language*, that will never match. Suppose, for example, that the seller's invoice adds a payment term of "10 days same as cash." Is the payment term now a part of the parties' agreement? The parties have a meeting of the minds on the subject matter of the contract but now have a slight difference in performance terms.

Under Article 2, in a transaction between merchants, the additional term or terms sent back in an acceptance become part of the contract if the additional term or terms do not materially alter the offer and the offeror does not object in a timely fashion.[21] **For Example,** returning to the Joe and Susan example, suppose that they are both now secondary market video game merchants negotiating for the sale and purchase of a used Xbox. They would have a contract, and the "Call of Duty" game would be included as part of the sale. Joe could, however, avoid the problem by adding a limitation to his offer, such as "This offer is limited to these terms." With that limitation, Susan would have a contract, but the contract would not include the "Call of Duty" game. Joe could also object immediately to Susan's proposal for the "Call of Duty" game and still have a contract without this additional term.[22]

If the proposed additional term in the acceptance is material, a contract is formed, but the material additional term does not become a part of the contract.[23] **For Example,** if Susan added to her acceptance the statement, "Game system carries one-year warranty," she has probably added a material term because the one-year warranty for a used game system would be unusual in the secondary market and costly for Joe.[24] Again, Joe can avoid this problem by limiting his offer so as to strike any additional terms, whether material or immaterial.

The most significant changes under Revised Article 2 dealt with §2-207. Because there were so many confusing circumstances with additional terms, the effect of the new §2-207 was to leave the issues of what is or is not included in a contract to the courts. However, the revision has not been as needed as originally believed because so many businesses and individuals are using the Internet to contract and are working out their terms through ongoing and immediate exchanges and questions.[25]

Figure 22-1 is a graphic picture of the rules on acceptance and contract terms under current Article 2 when additional terms are proposed.

[21] U.C.C. §2-207(2).

[22] *Quality Wood Designs, Inc. v. Ex–Factory, Inc.* 40 F. Supp. 2d 1137 (D.S.D. 2014). Revised UCC Article 2 makes changes in the way these additional terms operate. When there is a record of an agreement, with no objection, the terms in the record are the terms of the contract.

[23] Damage limitations clauses are considered material. *Belden Inc. v. American Electronic Components, Inc.*, 885 N.E.2d 751 (Ind. App. 2008). Forum selection clauses are immaterial. *Quality Wood Designs, Inc. v. Ex–Factory, Inc.*, 40 F. Supp. 2d 1137 (D.S.D. 2014).

[24] *Duro Textiles, LLC v. Sunbelt Corp.* 12 F. Supp. 3d 221, 83 U.C.C. Rep. Serv. 2d 347 (D. Mass. 2014).

[25] The result has been a significant reduction in the number of §2-207 cases. Francis J. Mootz III, "After the Battle of the Forms: Commercial Contracting in the Electronic Age," 4 *Journal of Law & Policy for the Information Society* 271, Summer, 2008.

FIGURE 22-1   Terms in Contracts under UCC Article §2-207

Even without all the UCC provisions on contract terms, an offeror may expressly or by conduct agree to a term added by the offeree to its acceptance of the offer. The offeror may agree orally or in writing to the additional term. There can be acceptance of the additional term by conduct of the parties if the parties just perform their obligations under the contract with knowledge that the term has been added by the offeree.[26]

CASE SUMMARY

The Inflated Acceptance on the Helium Contract

FACTS: SVC-West, L.P. (SVC), did time-share presentations at hotels and ordered helium tanks quite often for balloons. SVC placed a rush order with C9 Ventures (C9) for eight helium-filled tanks used to inflate festive balloons. C9 accepted the order and later that day delivered the tanks.

On the reverse of the invoice was an indemnification provision requiring SVC to indemnify C9 for any loss arising out of the use or possession of the helium-filled tanks. C9 later picked up the tanks, and, weeks later, SVC paid the invoice. SVC had obtained helium-filled tanks from C9 on prior occasions.

The invoice was on a single piece of paper, on the reverse side of which was a section entitled "INDEMNITY/HOLD

HARMLESS," which held C9 harmless for any injuries or damages resulting from the tanks, except for C9's "gross negligence or willful misconduct of C9." C9 had presented the same or similar invoice to SVC 10 times but had received the signature of an SVC employee only six times. SVC never attempted to substitute its own form agreement for C9's form.

C9 typically delivered the tanks in the morning when no SVC guests were present, but on July 3, C9's employee, Ernesto Roque, did not arrive at the SVC premises to make the delivery until about 5:00 P.M. Roque asked SVC employee, Zayra Renteria, where to place the eight helium-filled tanks. Renteria instructed Roque to bring the tanks up

---

[26] *Panike & Sons Farms, Inc. v. Smith,* 212 P.3d 992 (Idaho 2009).

The Inflated Acceptance on the Helium Contract continued

to the mezzanine level of the resort, at which point she would inform him where to place them. Roque wrote the following on the invoice, "[N]obody would sign all running around in lobby nobody knew who ... After accident nobody got signatures."

Roque stacked five to seven tanks against the walls next to the service elevator. He was in the process of bringing up another tank when a young boy, whose parents were attending the time-share presentation, ran up to the tanks and hugged one of them, pulling it over. The tank, which was about five feet tall and weighed 130 pounds, fell on the boy's hand. He was hospitalized and underwent surgery for his injuries.

SVC and C9 each paid the boy's family to settle a lawsuit brought to recover for his injuries. C9 filed a cross-complaint against SVC to enforce the indemnification provision on the back of the unsigned invoice. The trial court found for C9 and SVC appealed.

DECISION: The question: Is the indemnification provision on the back of the unsigned invoice enforceable against SVC? SVC and C9 entered into an oral contract when C9 accepted SVC's telephone order for eight helium-filled tanks. Under section 2-207, additional terms proposed in an acceptance or confirmation may become terms of the contract in certain situations. The oral contract between SVC and C9, however, was a lease of personal property (the helium-filled tanks) and not a sale of goods under the California Uniform Commercial Code.

The terms on the back of the unsigned invoice would have become part of the parties' oral contract only if SVC agreed to those terms. SVC did not agree to those terms by course of dealing or course of performance, or under basic contract law.

However, even if this were a transaction in goods governed by the California Uniform Commercial Code then the issue turns on whether SVC is a merchant. If SVC is not a merchant, the terms of the invoice are considered to be mere proposals for additional terms, which SVC did not accept. However, an indemnification provision is deemed a material alteration to an agreement as a matter of law, so an indemnification provision on the back of the invoice would not, under section 2-207, become part of the contract between SVC and C9.

Reversed. [*C9 Ventures v. SVC-West, L.P.*, 202 Cal. App. 4th 1483, 136 Cal. Rptr. 3d 550 (Cal. App. 2012)]

CPA   **Conflicting Terms in Acceptance.** In some situations, the offeree has not added a different term from the original offer but has instead proposed terms that contradict the terms of the offer. **For Example,** a buyer's purchase order may require the seller to offer full warranty protection, whereas the seller's invoice may include a disclaimer of all warranties. The buyer's purchase order may include a clause that provides "payment in 30 days same as cash," whereas the seller's invoice may include a term that has "10 days same as cash." Once again, it is clear that the parties intended to enter into a contract, and the subject matter is also clear. The task for Article 2 becomes one of establishing the rules that determine the terms of a contract when both sides have used different forms. However, if there are conflicting terms on the basic requirements (such as price) for formation, the courts may conclude that the parties have not met minds.[27]

When a term of an acceptance conflicts with a term of an offer but it is clear that the parties intended to be bound by a contract, the UCC still recognizes the formation of a contract. The terms that are conflicting cancel each other and are ignored. The contract then consists of the terms of the offer and acceptance that agree. **For Example,** if one party's contract form provided for full warranty protection and the other party's form provided for no warranty protection, the terms cancel each other out, and the parties' contract includes only those warranties provided under Article 2 (see Chapter 24 for a discussion of those warranties).

Defenses to Formation

Article 2 incorporates the common law defenses to formation of contracts by reference to the common law defenses in §1-103 (see Chapter 13 for a full discussion of those

---

[27] *Kolodziej v. Mason*, 774 F.3d 736 (11th Cir. 2014).

defenses). **For Example,** a party to a contract who can establish that the other party engaged in fraud to get the contract formed may cancel the contract and recover for losses that result from any damages for goods already delivered or payment already made.

Unconscionability. The UCC includes an additional contract defense for parties to a sale contract called *unconscionability*.[28] This section permits a court to refuse to enforce a sales contract that it finds to be **unconscionable,** which is generally defined as grossly unfair.[29] A court may also find a clause or portions of a contract to be unconscionable and refuse to enforce those clauses or sections.[30]

unconscionable—unreasonable, not guided or restrained by conscience and often referring to a contract grossly unfair to one party because of the superior bargaining powers of the other party.

Illegality. At common law, a contract is void if its subject matter itself is illegal, such as a contract for hire to murder someone. Under the UCC, a contract for the sale of heroin would be void. Likewise, a contract for the sale of a recalled or banned toy would be void.

The Effect of Illegal Sale. An illegal sale or contract to sell cannot be enforced. As a general rule, courts will not aid either party in recovering money or property transferred under an illegal agreement.

cost plus—method of determining the purchase price or contract price equal to the seller's or contractor's costs plus a stated percentage as the profit.

22-1d Terms in the Formed Contract

As noted earlier, contracts can be formed under Article 2 with terms of performance still missing or open. A contract is formed with just the quantity agreed on, but there are issues that must be resolved if the contract is to be completed. Article 2 has provisions for such missing terms.

CPA

Price

If the price for the goods is not expressly fixed by the contract, the price may be an open term, whereby the parties merely indicate how the price should be determined at a later time. In the absence of any reference to price, the price will be a reasonable price at the time of the delivery of the goods, which is generally the market price.[31]

Parties often use formulas for determining price in sales of goods. The price itself is missing from the contract until the formula is applied at some future time. The so-called **cost plus** formula for determining price has been used a great deal, particularly in commercial contracts. Under this formula, the buyer pays the seller the seller's costs for manufacture or obtaining the goods plus a specified percentage as profit.

output contract—contract of a producer to sell its entire production or output to a buyer.

The UCC allows contracts that expressly provide that one of the parties may determine the price. In such a case, that party must act in good faith, another requirement under the UCC that applies to merchants and nonmerchants in the formation and performance of their contracts.[32]

requirements contract—contract in which the buyer buys its needs (requirements) from the seller.

Output and Requirements Contracts

CPA

The **output contract** and the **requirements contract**[33] do not specify the quantity to be sold or purchased. Instead, the contract amount is what the seller produces or the buyer

---

[28] U.C.C. §2-302. Teri J. Dobbins, "Losing Faith: Extracting the Implied Covenant of Good Faith from (Some) Contracts," 84 *Oregon Law Rev* 227 (2005). *U.S. Welding, Inc. v. Battelle Energy Alliance, LLC*, 728 F. Supp. 2d 1110 (D. Idaho 2010).

[29] Disparity in bargaining power is an issue but is not controlling. *Petro Star, Inc. v. BP Oil Supply Co.*, 584 Fed. Appx. 709 (9th Cir. 2014).

[30] An example would be voiding exorbitant interest charges but enforcing the underlying sale. *Whirlpool Corp. v. Grigoleit Co.*, 713 F.3d 316 (6th Cir. 2013).

[31] U.C.C. §2-305(1) provides, "the price is a reasonable price at the time for delivery."

[32] Good faith requires that the party act honestly and, in the case of a merchant, also requires that the party follow reasonable commercial standards of fair dealing that are recognized in the trade. U.C.C. §§1-201(1)(a), 2-103(1)(b). *J.D. Fields & Co. v. Nucor-Yamato Steel*, 976 F. Supp. 2d 1051 (E.D. Ark. 2013).

[33] U.C.C. §2-306; *A BRC Rubber & Plastics, Inc. v. Continental Carbon Co.*, 949 F. Supp. 2d 862, 80 U.C.C. Rep. Serv. 2d 1014 (N.D. Ind. 2013).

requires. **For Example,** a homeowner may contract to purchase propane fuel for her winter heating needs. The propane company agrees to sell her the amount of propane she needs, which will vary from year to year according to the winter weather, her time at home, and other factors. Although the open quantity in contracts such as these introduces an element of uncertainty, such sales contracts are valid but subject to two limitations: (1) The parties must act in good faith and (2) the quantity offered or demanded must not be unreasonably disproportionate to prior output or requirements or to a stated estimate. With these restrictions, the homeowner will obtain all of the propane she needs for heating but could not use her particularly beneficial price under her open-quantity contract to purchase additional propane to sell to others.

Indefinite Duration Term

When the sales contract is a continuing contract, such as one calling for periodic delivery of coal, but no time is set for the life of the contract, the contract runs for a reasonable time. It may be terminated by notice from either party to the other party.

CPA
Changes in Terms: Modification of Contract

An agreement to modify a contract for the sale of goods is binding even though the modification is not supported by consideration.[34] The modification is valid so long as the agreement is voluntary. **For Example,** suppose that Chester's Drug Store has agreed to purchase 300 bottles of vitamins from Pro-Life, Inc., at a price of $3.71 per bottle. Pro-Life has experienced substantial cost increases from its suppliers and asks Chester to pay $3.74 per bottle. Chester is not required to agree to such a price increase because it has a valid contract for the lower price. If Chester agrees to the price increase, however, the agreement for the higher price is valid despite the lack of additional consideration on the part of Pro-Life. Chester may agree to the higher price because Pro-Life's price is still much lower than its competitors and Chester has a longstanding relationship with Pro-Life and values its customer service. However, Pro-Life could not threaten to cut off Chester's supply in order to obtain the price increase because that would be a breach of contract and would also be duress that would invalidate Chester's consent to the higher price. (See Chapter 13 for a discussion of duress.)

CPA
Contradicting Terms: Parol Evidence Rule

parol evidence rule–rule that prohibits the introduction in evidence of oral or written statements made prior to or contemporaneously with the execution of a complete written contract, deed, or instrument, in the absence of fraud, accident, or mistake.

The **parol evidence rule** (see Chapter 16 for a complete discussion) applies to the sale of goods, with the slight modification that a writing is not presumed to represent the entire contract of the parties unless the court specifically decides that it does.[35] If the court so decides, parol evidence is not admissible to add to or contradict the terms of the writing. **For Example,** suppose that Ralph Rhodes and Tana Preuss negotiate the sale of Ralph's 1965 Mustang to Tana. During their discussions, Ralph agrees to pay for an inspection and for new upholstery for the car. However, Tana and Ralph sign a simple sales contract that includes only a description of the Mustang and the price. Tana cannot enforce the two provisions because she failed to have them written into their final agreement. The parol evidence rule requires the parties to be certain that everything they want is in their agreement before they sign. The courts cannot referee disputes over collateral agreements the parties fail to put in writing.

If the court decides that the writing was not intended to represent the entire contract, the writing may be supplemented by additional extrinsic evidence, including the proof of

---

[34] U.C.C. §2-209(1); *J.C. Trading Ltd. v. Wal–Mart Stores, Inc.,* 947 F. Supp. 2d 449 (D. Del. 2013).
[35] U.C.C. §2-202.

additional terms as long as these terms are not inconsistent with the written terms. Parol evidence may also be admitted to interpret contract terms or show what the parties meant by their words. The parol evidence rule also does not prohibit the proof of fraud, misrepresentation, and any other defenses in formation.

Interpreting Contract Terms: Course of Dealing and Usage of Trade

course of dealing–
pattern of performance between two parties to a contract.

The patterns of doing business the parties develop through their prior contractual transactions, or **course of dealing,** become part of their contract.[36] These patterns may be used to find what was intended by the express provisions in their contract and to supply otherwise missing terms. **For Example,** if the parties had 10 previous agreements and payment was always made on the 30th day following delivery, that conduct could be used to interpret the meaning of a clause "payment due in 30 days" when the start of the 30 days is not specifically agreed to in the contract.

usage of trade–language and customs of an industry.

In addition, the customs of the industry, or **usage of trade,** are adopted by courts in their interpretation of contract terms. **For Example,** suppose that a contract provides for the sale of mohair. There are two types of mohair: adult and kid. Because adult mohair is cheaper and easier to find, industry custom provides that unless the parties specifically place the term *kid* with the term *mohair* in the contract, the contract is one for the sale of adult mohair. Under Article 2, the court need not find that a contract is ambiguous or incomplete in order to examine the parties' pattern of previous conduct as well as industry custom.[37]

22-1e Bulk Transfers

Bulk transfer law, Article 6 of the UCC, was created to deal with situations in which sellers of businesses fail to pay the creditors of the business and instead use the proceeds of the sale for their own use.

In 1989, the NCCUSL recommended that UCC Article 6 be repealed because it was obsolete and had little value in the modern business world. At the same time, the commissioners adopted a revised version of Article 6 (Alternative B) for adoption by those states that desired to retain the concept for bulk sales. Rather than relying on the bulk sales law, the trend is for suppliers to use UCC Article 9, Secured Transactions, for protection (see Chapter 33).

22-2 Form of Sales Contract

A contract for the sale of goods may be oral or written. However, under the UCC, certain types of contracts must be evidenced by a record or they cannot be enforced in court.

CPA

22-2a Amount

statute of frauds–statute that, to prevent fraud through the use of perjured testimony, requires that certain kinds of contracts be in writing to be binding or enforceable.

Whenever the sales price of goods is $500 or more, the sales contract must be evidenced by a record to be enforceable. Under Revised Article 2, this amount has been increased to $5,000.[38] The section of the UCC that establishes this requirement is known as the **statute of frauds.** (For more details on the statute of frauds and its role in common law contracts, see Chapter 16.)

---

[36] U.C.C. §2-208. Under Revised Article 2, §2-208 is eliminated for those states that have adopted Revised Article 1 because Revised Article 1 contains the definition for course of performance.

[37] Revised §2-202 provides different rules for the use of extrinsic evidence but still includes "course of performance, course of dealing, or usage of trade" as sources for interpretation of contract terms.

[38] Under Revised Article 2, the new amount of $5,000 is found at U.C.C. Rev. Art. 2, §2-201.

22-2b **Nature of the Writing Required**

The requirement for a record for a contract may be satisfied by a complete written contract signed by both parties. Under Article 2, so that the state laws will be consistent with federal laws on electronic signatures, the requirement of a writing has been changed to the requirement of a "record." Under Article 2, two merchants can reduce their agreement to a record in much simpler fashion because the detail required under common law is not required to satisfy the UCC standards.

Terms

To satisfy the UCC statute of frauds, the record must indicate that there has been a completed transaction covering certain goods. Specifically, the record must (1) indicate that a sale or contract to sell has been made and (2) state the quantity of goods involved.[39] Any other missing terms may be supplied by reference to Code sections (discussed earlier) or shown by parol evidence.

Signature

The record must be signed or authenticated by the person who is being held to the contract or by the authorized agent of that person. Whatever form of authentication is being used must be put in place in the record with the intention of authenticating the record. The authentication may consist of initials or may be a printed, a stamped, an electronic, or a typewritten signature placed with the intent to authenticate.[40] **For Example,** when you enter into a contract as part of an online transaction, you are generally asked to check a box that states that you understand you are entering into a contract. Once you check that box, a pop-up appears that explains that you are about to charge your credit card or account and that you have agreed to the purchase. These steps are used to authenticate your electronic version of a signature.

CASE SUMMARY

It's Elementary: A Crayon-Scrawled Contract Is Good Enough for the Statute of Frauds

FACTS: Michelle Rosenfeld, an art dealer, went to artist Jean-Michel Basquiat's apartment on October 25, 1982. While she was there, Basquiat agreed to sell her three paintings for $4,000 each, and she picked out three. Basquiat asked for a cash deposit of 10 percent; Rosenfeld left the loft but returned later with $1,000 in cash, which she paid to Basquiat. When she asked for a receipt, he insisted on drawing up a contract and got down on the floor and wrote it out in crayon on a large piece of paper, remarking that someday this contract would be worth money. The handwritten document listed the three paintings, bore Rosenfeld's signature and Basquiat's signature, and stated: "$12,000—$1,000 DEPOSIT ¼ Oct 25 82." Rosenfeld

later returned to Basquiat's loft to discuss delivery, but Basquiat convinced her to wait for at least two years so that he could show the paintings at exhibitions. After Basquiat's death, the estate argued that there was no contract because the statute of frauds made the agreement unenforceable. The estate contended that a written contract for the sale of goods must include the date of delivery. From a judgment in favor of the estate, Rosenfeld appealed.

DECISION: The court held that all that is required to satisfy the statute of frauds is that the writing afford a basis for believing that it confirms oral evidence of a real transaction. The writing here, though it may have been simply and in

---

[39] *Kelly-Stehney & Assoc., Inc. v. McDonald's Indus. Products, Inc.*, 693 N.W.2d 394 (Mich. 2005).
[40] U.C.C. §§1-201(39), 2-201; *CQ, Inc. v. TXU Min. Co., LP*, 565 F.3d 268 (5th Cir. 2009).

It's Elementary: A Crayon-Scrawled Contract Is Good Enough for the Statute of Frauds continued

crayon, met all the requirements for a writing: It indicated the price, the date, the specific paintings involved, and that Rosenfeld had paid a deposit. The crayon writing also had the signatures of the buyer and seller. The writing satisfied the requirements of § 2-201. [***Rosenfeld v. Basquiat*, 78 F.3d 84 (2nd Cir. 1996)**]

CPA

The UCC statute of frauds does provide an important exception to the signature requirement for merchants that enables merchants to expedite their transactions. This exception allows merchants to create a confirmation memorandum of their oral agreement as evidence of an agreement. A merchant's *confirmation memorandum* is a letter, a memo, or an electronic document signed or authenticated by one of the two merchant parties to an oral agreement.[41] This memorandum can be used by either party to enforce the contract. **For Example,** suppose that Ralph has orally agreed to purchase 1,000 pounds of T-bone steak from Jane for $5.79 per pound. Jane sends Ralph a signed memo that reads, "This is to confirm our telephone conversation earlier today. I will sell you 1,000 pounds of T-bone @ $5.79 per pound." Either Ralph or Jane can use the memo to enforce the contract.

A confirming memo, in various forms of communication, sent by one merchant to another results in a binding and enforceable contract that satisfies the statute of frauds. Such a confirmation binds the nonsigning or nonauthenticating merchant, just as if he had signed the letter or a contract. A merchant can object when he receives the confirmation memo, but he must do so immediately because the confirming memo takes effect in 10 days if there is no objection.[42] This confirmation procedure makes it necessary for merchants to watch their communications and all forms of correspondence and to act within 10 days of receiving a confirmation.

CASE SUMMARY

A Shell of a Contract for Peanut Supplies

FACTS: Brooks Peanut is a peanut shelling company operating in Samson, Alabama. Great Southern Peanut, LLC (GSP), is a competing peanut sheller. Peanut shellers and other businesses handling peanut products often use brokers to buy and sell peanuts. Typically, the broker's fee is paid by the seller. Mazur & Hockman, Inc. (M & H), is a broker used by both Brooks Peanut and GSP.

In mid-September 2010, Barrett Brooks, president of Brooks Peanut, called Richard Barnhill and Jay Strother, peanut brokers with M & H, and asked them to find peanuts for his company to buy. Brooks requested that Brooks Peanut not be identified as the buyer when M & H contacted potential sellers. M & H solicited offers from several peanut shellers, including GSP, and conveyed them to Brooks. On September 20, Brooks asked Strother to communicate a counteroffer to GSP's manager, Doug Wingate. Specifically, the counteroffer was an offer to buy 3,168,000 pounds of 2010 crop medium runner shelled peanuts for $.4675 per pound, to be delivered monthly throughout 2011.

Wingate accepted the counteroffer that same day, September 20. After Wingate accepted these terms, Strother revealed that Brooks Peanut was the buyer. According to Strother, Wingate "sighed" upon learning that a competitor was involved in the transaction; however, he did not reject the deal. Wingate testified that, although he initially accepted the deal, he declined to consummate it when he learned that Brooks Peanut was the buyer.

---

[41] *Siesta Sol, LLC v. Brooks Pharmacy, Inc.*, 617 F. Supp. 2d 38 (D. R.I. 2007); In re *Sunbelt Grain WKS, LLC*, 406 B.R. 918 (D. Kan. 2009).

[42] A confirmation memo is not effective when there is no underlying agreement or the parties did not agree on the terms. *Cargill Inc. v. Jorgenson farms*, 719 N.W.2d 226 (Minn. App. 2009).

A Shell of a Contract for Peanut Supplies Continued

On the same day, M & H prepared and then faxed to GSP and Brooks Peanut a written confirmation of the sale of peanuts. The confirmation stated: "We confirm a Sale and Purchase Transaction as described below[.]" The confirmation was printed on M & H letterhead and listed the names and addresses of the seller and the buyer, as well as terms covering price, quantity, quality, crop year, delivery schedule, and payment method. The confirmation stated that "[t]his confirmation is subject to the following condition[ ]: Seller's contract and Buyer's purchase order to follow [.]" Next to the term "Quality," the confirmation noted that the "American Peanut Shellers Association Trading Rules" applied to the transaction. The confirmation was signed by M & H's Strother.

GSP and Brooks Peanut each received the faxed confirmation from M & H. GSP did not issue a contract and Brooks Peanut did not issue a purchase order. After Strother sent the confirmation to GSP and Brooks Peanut, he continued communicating with the parties to finalize the logistics of the deliveries. For example, on September 21, he told Brooks that GSP had offered to haul the peanut loads. They also discussed increasing the monthly shipments, but Wingate stated that he wanted "to stay at 6 loads a month on the [B]rooks [Peanut] contract for right now[.]"

GSP did not raise any objection to the fax confirmation until late January 2011, almost four months after M & H sent it. Wingate testified that he "did not see the need" to object to the confirmation. Beginning in January 2011, GSP took the position that, despite the confirmation, GSP and Brooks Peanut had not entered into that particular transaction because Wingate had rejected the sale when he learned that it involved his company's competitor, that M & H was not authorized to confirm the sale or to send the confirmation, and that a condition precedent had not occurred because GSP had not issued a written contract.

M & H had routinely brokered thousands of peanut sales between other peanut companies, shellers, and manufacturers using the same form of trade confirmation. GSP had sold peanuts to Brooks Peanut in June 2009 and April 2010 and that their agreements were memorialized solely by M & H sending the parties confirmations substantially similar to the one issued this time.

The trial court concluded that GSP had a defense of the statute of frauds as a matter of law. Brooks Peanut appealed.

DECISION: The confirmation memo was sufficient to constitute evidence of a contract between the parties. The confirmation memo contained the information needed for the contract to go forward. The memo was received and there was no objection registered. Also, the parties continued to behave as if there was a contract and they were ironing out details and no one indicated any objection to the contract. You cannot continue to perform on the contract once you have not objected to a confirmation memo sent to you that confirms the existence of the contract. [***Brooks Peanut Co., Inc. v. Great Southern Peanut, LLC***, 746 S.E.2d 272 (Ga. App. 2013)]

Purpose of Execution

A writing or record can satisfy the statute of frauds even though it was not made for that purpose. For example, if a buyer writes to the seller to complain that the goods have not been delivered, there is proof of the contract because the buyer's complaint indicates that there was some kind of understanding or an acknowledgment that there was a sale of those goods.

Particular Writings

Formal contracts, bills of sale, letters, and telegrams are common forms of writings that satisfy the record requirement.[43] E-mails, faxes, EDI communications, and verifications through screen printouts will generally satisfy the requirement as to record and authentication so long as they meet minimum formation standards and comply with the requirement of the UCC to specify any quantity. Two or more records grouped together may constitute a record that will be sufficient to satisfy the UCC statute of frauds.[44]

---

[43] Contract terms can be pieced together from invoices sent over the period of the agreement and that the buyer paid. *Fleming Companies, Inc. v. Krist Oil Co.*, 324 F. Supp. 2d 933 (W.D. Wis. 2001).

[44] *ReMapp Intern. Corp. v. Comfort Keyboard Co., Inc.*, 560 F.3d 628 (7th Cir. 2009). Letters grouped together satisfy U.C.C. §2-201. *Pepsi-Cola Co. v. Steak 'N Shake, Inc.*, 981 F. Supp. 1149 (S.D. Ind. 1997). Letters and faxes also satisfy the writing requirement. In re *Walnut Associates, L.P.*, 506 B.R. 645 (E.D. Pa. 2014).

22-2c Effect of Noncompliance

A sales agreement that does not satisfy the statute of frauds cannot be enforced. However, the oral contract itself is not unlawful and may be voluntarily performed by the parties.

22-2d Exceptions to Requirement of a Writing

The absence of a writing does not always mean that a sales contract is unenforceable. Article 2 provides some exceptions for the enforceability of certain oral contracts.

C P A   **Specially Manufactured Goods**

No record is required when the goods are specially made for the buyer and are of such an unusual nature that they are not suitable for sale in the ordinary course of the seller's business. **For Example,** a manufacturer who builds a stair lift for a two-story home cannot resell the $8,000 device to someone else because it is specially built for the stairs in the buyer's home. The manufacturer could enforce the oral contract against the buyer despite the price being in excess of $500.

For this nonresellable goods exception to apply, the seller must have made a substantial beginning in manufacturing the goods or, if a distributor is the seller, in procuring them before the buyer indicates that she will not honor the oral contract.[45]

The stair lift manufacturer, for example, must have progressed to a point beyond simply ordering materials for construction of the lift because those materials could be used for any lift.

C P A   **Receipt and Acceptance**

An oral sales contract may be enforced if it can be shown that the goods were delivered by the seller and were both received and accepted by the buyer even if the amount involved is over $500 and there is no record. The receipt and acceptance of the goods by the buyer makes the contract enforceable despite the statute of frauds issue. The buyer must actually receive and accept the goods. If only part of the goods have been received and accepted, the contract may be enforced only insofar as it relates to those goods received and accepted.[46] **For Example,** suppose that Wayne ordered 700 baseball jackets at a price of $72 each from Pamela. The order was taken over the telephone, and Wayne emphasized urgency. Pamela shipped the 320 jackets she had on hand and assured Wayne that the remainder would be finished during the next two weeks. Wayne received the 320 jackets and sold them to a golf tournament sponsor. Wayne refused to pay Pamela because the contract was oral. Wayne must pay for the 320 jackets, but Pamela will not be able to recover for the remaining 380 jackets she manufactured.

C P A   **Payment**

An oral contract may be enforced if the buyer has made full payment. In the case of partial payment for divisible units of goods, a contract may be enforced only with respect to the goods for which payment has been made and accepted. In the Pamela and Wayne example, if the circumstances were changed so that Pamela agreed to ship only if Wayne sent payment, then Pamela, upon accepting the payment, would be required to perform the contract for the amount of payment received. If partial payment is made for indivisible goods, such as an automobile, a partial payment avoids the statute of frauds and is sufficient proof to permit enforcement of the entire oral contract.

---

[45] *Golden State Porcelain Inc. v. Swid Powell Design Inc.*, 37 U.C.C. Rep. Serv. 2d (N.Y. 1999). Where manufacture has not begun, this exception to the statute of frauds does not apply. *EMSG Sys. Div., Inc. v. Miltope Corp.*, 37 U.C.C. Rep. Serv. 2d 39 (E.D.N.C. 1998).

[46] In re *Tayfur*, 505 B.R. 673 (W.D. Pa. 2014).

C P A   **Admission**

An oral contract may be enforced against a party if that party admits in pleadings, testimony, or otherwise in court that a contract for sale was made. The contract, however, is not enforceable beyond the quantity of goods admitted.[47]

CASE SUMMARY

Take a Gander at This Glove Contract

FACTS: Grandoe is a family-owned manufacturer of gloves located in Gloversville, New York. In the early 2000s, Grandoe began selling winter gloves to Gander Mountain, a national retailer of outdoor sporting goods. At that time, it was customary in the glove-making industry for the manufacturer to rely on a retailer's oral commitment for the purchase of gloves. For the first few years of their relationship, Gander Mountain and Grandoe abided by this custom; Gander Mountain would orally agree to purchase a quantity of gloves, Grandoe would manufacture the gloves, and Gander Mountain would periodically issue written purchase orders for smaller shipments of gloves as the need for them arose, the sum of which was consistent with Gander Mountain's oral commitment.

In 2007, Gander Mountain attempted to change this practice by posting a document called the Vendor Buying Agreement (VBA) on its website. The VBA stated:

> Any communications from Gander Mountain in the form of forecasts, commitments, projections or other estimates provided to Vendor are for planning purposes only, do not constitute an Order and shall not be binding upon Gander Mountain unless, until and only to the extent that Gander Mountain expressly agrees in writing.

The VBA also stated that it "represent[ed] the entire and integrated Agreement between Gander Mountain and Vendor, superseding all prior negotiations, representations or agreements, written or oral" and that "by accepting [a purchase order], Vendor acknowledges and agrees to be bound by the Vendor Buying Agreement."

After posting the VBA on its website, Gander Mountain e-mailed Grandoe's vice president, asking him to "[p]lease read the attached document that explains our [purchase order] policy changes that will be effective in June." The attached memorandum explained that Gander Mountain was "updating terms and conditions" and that any manufacturer that did business with Gander Mountain would henceforth be bound by the VBA. Grandoe's vice

president did not respond to the e-mail or acknowledge in any way that he had read the memorandum or the VBA.

Subsequently, over a series of meetings in 2008, representatives from the two companies negotiated a deal whereby Grandoe would manufacture $3.05 million worth of gloves for Gander Mountain. At one of these meetings, Grandoe's president and vice president presented Gander Mountain's representative with spreadsheets detailing the quantities of gloves Grandoe would produce in each style. Gander Mountain's representative orally approved these spreadsheets. At another meeting, the parties signed a Resource Allowance Contract (RAC), which set forth certain percentage discounts and other ancillary terms for Gander Mountain's purchase of gloves from Grandoe. The parties also agreed that, consistent with their past practice, some of the logistical aspects of the deal, when and how many gloves would be shipped, would be specified in Gander Mountain purchase orders that would be sent to Grandoe.

On April 16, 2009, after Grandoe had manufactured most of the gloves, Gander Mountain told Grandoe that it would not honor the full oral commitment. Gander Mountain sent Grandoe purchase orders for approximately $940,000 worth of gloves, which Grandoe filled. Gander Mountain then ceased ordering gloves. Grandoe was able to resell some of the gloves it had manufactured for Gander Mountain, but a large number of the gloves—some $1.5 million worth—had been embroidered with Gander Mountain's logo and were largely worthless to anyone else.

Grandoe sued Gander Mountain for breach of contract. Gander Mountain asserted that the VBA and RAC voided any oral agreement the parties had allegedly reached. The court denied Gander Mountain's motion for summary judgment and submitted the case to the jury along with the VBA and RAC and instructed the jury to consider all of the evidence. The jury found that the parties had entered into a valid oral contract and awarded Grandoe $1,557,284.40 in damages.

Gander Mountain appealed.

DECISION: There was a valid oral contract and the court enforced it for the full amount. The parties did not have a

---

[47] *Delta Stat, Inc. v. Michael's Carpet World*, 666 S.E.2d 331 (Va. 2008).

Take a Gander at This Glove Contract continued

single written document that dealt with all of the issues. They had relied on oral agreements in the past and that past practice was what controlled their relationship. Their other documents did not indicate agreement and they had no purchase orders in evidence. The case was one where all the paperwork found the parties tripping over what the terms were, and the court had to go back to their past practices. Affirmed. [***Grandoe Corporation v. Gander Mountain Company*, 761 F.3d 876 (8th Cir. 2014)]**

E-COMMERCE & CYBERLAW

"I have read and understand these terms."

Sellers must make an effort to be sure that vendors and customers are aware of changes in terms that they post on their Web site. Their customers and vendors are not bound by those changes in terms unless and until they are aware of those terms. The site needs to call out changes from previous transactions. Perhaps the most effective means of notification is to require that the customer or vendor acknowledge their existence (even if they have not read them) prior to being permitted to complete a transaction. "I have read and understand these terms" is a powerful phrase for binding customers and vendors to your contract new terms.

22-2e **Bill of Sale**

bill of sale–writing signed by the seller reciting that the personal property therein described has been sold to the buyer.

Regardless of the requirement of the statute of frauds, the parties may wish to execute a writing as evidence or proof of the sale. Through custom, this writing has become known as a **bill of sale,** but it is neither a bill nor a contract. It is merely a receipt or writing signed by the seller reciting the transfer to the buyer of the title to the described property. A bill of sale can be used as proof of an otherwise oral agreement.

22-3 **Uniform Law for International Sales**

Contracts for the International Sale of Goods (CISG)–uniform international contract code contracts for international sale of goods.

The United Nations Convention on **Contracts for the International Sale of Goods (CISG)** applies to contracts between parties in the United States and parties in the other nations that have ratified the convention.[48] The provisions of this convention or international agreement have been strongly influenced by Article 2 of the UCC. The international rules of the convention automatically apply to contracts for the sale of goods if the buyer and seller have places of business in different countries that have ratified the convention. The parties may, however, choose to exclude the convention provisions in their sales contract.

22-3a **Scope of the CISG**

The CISG does not govern all contracts between parties in the countries that have ratified it. The CISG does not apply to goods bought for personal, family, or household use.[49] The CISG also does not apply to contracts in which the predominant part of the

---

[48] 52 Fed. Reg. 6262 (1987). While the list of adopting countries is always increasing, those countries involved in NAFTA, GATT, and the European Union (EU) (see Chapter 10) have adopted the CISG. For complete text, commentary, and case law on CISG, go to **http://www.cisg.law.pace.edu.**

[49] Gilles Cuniberti, "The International Market for Contracts: The Most Attractive Contract Laws," 34 *Northwestern Journal of International Law and Business* 455 (2014).

obligations of the party who furnishes the goods consists of the supply of labor or other services. The CISG has five chapters and 101 articles, and the articles have no titles to them. There is a limited body of case law interpreting the CISG because so many of the decisions under the CISG come through arbitration and other forms of dispute resolution, typical of international commercial arrangements.

22-4 Leases of Goods

Leases of goods represent a significant part of both contract law and the economy. There were more than $98 billion worth of car lease transactions in the United States in 2014.[50] One-fourth of all vehicles in the United States are leased. Article 2A of the UCC codifies the law of leases for tangible movable goods. Article 2A applies to any transaction, regardless of form, that creates a lease of personal property or fixtures. Many of the provisions of Article 2 were carried over but changed to reflect differences in style, leasing terminology, or leasing practices.[51] As a practical matter, leases will be of durable goods, such as equipment and vehicles of any kind, computers, boats, airplanes, and household goods and appliances. A **lease** is "a transfer of the right to possession and use of goods for a term in return for consideration."[52]

lease–agreement between the owner of property and a tenant by which the former agrees to give possession of the property to the latter for payment of rent. (Parties—landlord or lessor, tenant or lessee)

22-4a Types of Leases

Article 2A regulates consumer leases, commercial leases, finance leases, nonfinance leases, and subleases. These categories may overlap in some cases, such as when there is a commercial finance lease.

Consumer Lease

A **consumer lease** is made by a merchant lessor regularly engaged in the business of leasing or selling the kinds of goods involved. A consumer lease is made to a natural person (not a corporation) who takes possession of the goods primarily for personal, family, or household use. Each state places a cap on the amount considered a consumer lease. Section 2A-103(f) simply provides that the state should place its own amount in this section with the admonition to place the cap at a level that ensures that vehicle leases will be covered under the law.

consumer lease–lease of goods by a natural person for personal, family, or household use.

nonconsumer lease–lease that does not satisfy the definition of a consumer lease; also known as a *commercial lease.*

Commercial Lease

When a lease does not satisfy the definition of a consumer lease, it may be called a **nonconsumer** or a **commercial lease. For Example,** a contractor's one-year rental of a truck to haul materials is a commercial lease.

commercial lease–any nonconsumer lease.

Finance Lease

A **finance lease** is a three-party transaction involving a lessor, a lessee, and a supplier. Instead of going directly to a supplier for goods, the customer goes to a financier and tells the financier where to obtain the goods and what to obtain. The financier then acquires the goods and either leases or subleases the goods to its customer. The financier-lessor is in effect a paper channel, or conduit, between the supplier and the

finance lease–three-party lease agreement in which there is a lessor, a lessee, and a financier.

---

[50] **http://www.statista.com** (2014).

[51] Forty-nine states (Louisiana has not adopted Article 2A), the District of Columbia, and the Virgin Islands have adopted all or some portions of Article 2A. Not all states have adopted the 1997 version of Article 2A, and some have adopted only selected portions of the 1997 version.

[52] U.C.C. §2A-103(1)(j). The definition of what constitutes a lease is the subject of continuing examination by the UCC Article 2A drafters and the American Law Institute.

customer-lessee. The customer-lessee must approve the terms of the transaction between the supplier and the financier-lessor.[53]

22-4b **Form of Lease Contract**

The lease must be evidenced by a record if the total of the payments under the lease will be $1,000 or more. The record must be authenticated by the party against whom enforcement is sought. The record must describe the leased goods, state the term of the lease, and indicate that a lease contract has been formed.[54]

22-4c **Warranties**

Under Article 2A, the lessor, except in the case of finance leases, makes all usual warranties that are made by a seller in a sale of goods. In a finance lease, however, the real parties in interest are the supplier, who supplies the lessor with the goods, and the lessee, who leases the goods. The lessee looks to the supplier of the goods for warranties. Any warranties, express or implied, made by the supplier to the lessor are passed on to the lessee, who has a direct cause of action on them against the supplier regardless of the lack of privity.[55] **For Example,** if a consumer leased an auto and the auto had a defective steering mechanism that resulted in injury to the consumer, the consumer would have a cause of action against the auto manufacturer.

22-4d **Default**

The lease agreement and provisions of Article 2A determine whether the lessor or lessee is in default. If either the lessor or the lessee is in default under the lease contract, the party seeking enforcement may obtain a judgment or otherwise enforce the lease contract by any available judicial or nonjudicial procedure. Neither the lessor nor the lessee is entitled

---

E-COMMERCE & CYBERLAW

The Deal with Dell

Dell Computer customers purchased computers through the Dell Web site. There were "Terms and Conditions" on the Web site that included terms and conditions such as the requirement that contract disputes be submitted to arbitration in Illinois and the sales tax provisions related to the purchase of computers and service contracts.

Dell maintains that customers have three separate opportunities to review the terms and conditions agreement: (1) by selecting a hyperlink on the Dell Web site, (2) by reading the terms that were included in the acknowledgment/invoice that was sent to customers after they placed their orders, or (3) by reviewing the copy of the terms Dell included in the packaging of its computer products. The court found

that the terms and conditions had to be understood PRIOR to the purchase and that the "Terms and Conditions" tab was not conspicuous on the Dell Web site. From this case and other materials in the chapter, you learn that there are best practices for Internet contracting: (1) Require customers to click on terms and conditions PRIOR to buying; (2) require customers to physically scroll down through the terms before being allowed to purchase; (3) notify customers along the way as they are loading their electronic carts that there are terms and conditions and place click points for them to study those terms and conditions; and (4) posting terms and conditions on your Web site is not enough for those terms and conditions to be part of the contract.

---

[53] U.C.C. §2A-103(1)(g). One of the evolving issues in lease financing is the relationship of the parties, the use of liens, and the role of Article 9 security interests (see Chapter 33). The NCCUSL has created Uniform Certificate of Title Act (UCOTA) that makes the interrelationships of lien laws, Article 2, and Article 9 clear. UCOTA was available for adoption by the states in 2006. As of 2014, only one state had adopted the law.

[54] U.C.C. §2-201(b).

[55] U.C.C. §2A-209.

to notice of default or notice of enforcement from the other party. Both the lessor and the lessee have rights and remedies similar to those given to a seller in a sales contract.[56] If the lessee defaults, the lessor is entitled to recover any rent due, future rent, and incidental damages.[57] (See Chapter 26 for more information on remedies.)

Make the Connection

Summary

Contracts for services and real estate are governed by the common law. Contracts for the sale of goods are governed by Article 2 of the UCC. *Goods* are defined as anything movable at the time they are identified as the subject of the transaction. Goods physically existing and owned by the seller at the time of the transaction are *existing goods.*

A *sale of goods* is the transfer of title to tangible personal property for a price. A *bailment* is a transfer of possession but not title and is therefore not a sale. A *gift* is not a sale because no price is paid for the gift. A contract for services is an ordinary contract and is not governed by the UCC. If a contract calls for both the rendering of services and the supplying of goods, the contract is classified according to its dominant element.

The common law contract rules for intent to contract apply to the formation of contracts under the UCC. However, several formation rules under the UCC differ from common law contract rules. A merchant's firm offer is irrevocable without the payment of consideration. The UCC rules on additional terms in an acceptance permit the formation of a contract despite the changes. These proposals for new terms are not considered counteroffers under the UCC. The terms that are included are determined by detailed rules. If the transaction is between nonmerchants, a contract is formed without the additional terms, which the original offeror is free to accept or reject. If the transaction is between merchants, the additional terms become part of the contract if those terms do not materially alter the offer and no objection is made to them. There is no distinction between merchant and nonmerchant for additional terms under Revised Article 2 and the terms issues are left to the courts.

The same defenses available to formation under common law are incorporated in Article 2. In addition, the UCC recognizes unconscionability as a defense to formation.

The UCC does not require the parties to agree on every aspect of contract performance for the contract to be valid. Provisions in Article 2 will govern the parties' relationship in the event their agreement does not cover all terms. The price term may be expressly fixed by the parties. The parties may make no provision as to price, or they may indicate how the price should be determined later. In output or requirements contracts, the quantity that is to be sold or purchased is not specified, but such contracts are nevertheless valid. A sales contract can be modified even though the modification is not supported by consideration. The parol evidence rule applies to a sale of goods in much the same manner as to ordinary contracts. However, the UCC permits the introduction of evidence of course of dealing and usage of trade for clarification of contract terms and performance.

The UCC's statute of frauds provides that a sales contract for $500 ($5,000 under Revised Article 2) or more must be evidenced by a record. The UCC's merchant's confirmation memorandum allows two merchants to be bound to an otherwise oral agreement by a memo or letter signed by only one party that stands without objection for 10 days. Several exceptions to the UCC statute of frauds exist: when the goods are specially made or procured for the buyer and are nonresellable in the seller's ordinary market; when the buyer has received and accepted the goods; when the buyer has made either full or partial payment; and when the party against whom enforcement is sought admits in court pleadings or testimony that a contract for sale was made.

Uniform rules for international sales are applicable to contracts for sales between parties in countries that have ratified the CISG. Under the CISG, a contract for the sale of goods need not be in any particular form and can be proven by any means.

Article 2A of the UCC regulates consumer leases, commercial leases, finance leases, nonfinance leases, and subleases of tangible movable goods. A lease subject to Article 2A must be in writing if the lease payments will total $1,000 or more.

[56] U.C.C. §§2A-501, 2A-503; *Mitchell v. Ford Motor Credit Co.*, 702 F. Supp. 2d 1356 (M.D. Fla. 2010).
[57] U.C.C. §2A-529.

Learning Outcomes

After studying this chapter, you should be able to clearly explain:

22-1 Nature of the Sale of Goods

LO.1 Define a sale of goods and explain when UCC Article 2 applies to contracts

See the *Mesa Airlines* case, page 412.
See the Thinking Things Through feature, page 413.

LO.2 Distinguish between an actual sale of goods and other types of transactions in goods

See footnotes 3 and 4 for a list of examples, page 410.

LO.3 Describe how contracts are formed under Article 2, and list the differences in formation standards between the UCC and common law

See the *C9 Ventures v. SVC-West, L.P.* case, pages 417–418.
See the E-Commerce & Cyberlaw feature, pages 427, 429.
See the *Brooks* case, pages 423–424.

22-2 Form of Sales Contract

LO.4 Explain when a contract for the sale of goods must be in writing

See the *Basquiat* case, pages 422–423.

LO.5 List and explain the exceptions to the requirement that certain contracts be in writing

See the *Gander Mountain* case, pages 426–427.

22-3 Uniform Law for International Sales

LO.6 Discuss the purpose of the United Nations Convention on Contracts for the International Sale of Goods

See the discussion of the CISG, pages 427–428.

22-4 Leases of Goods

See the discussion of the types of leases on page 428.
See the discussion of warranties on page 429.

Key Terms

acceptance
Article 2
bailee
bailment
battle of the forms
bill of sale
commercial lease
consumer lease
Contracts for the International Sale of
    Goods (CISG)
cost plus
course of dealing
existing goods
finance lease
firm offer
future goods
gift
goods
lease
mailbox rule
merchants
mirror image rule
nonconsumer lease
offer
output contract
parol evidence rule
requirements contract
statute of frauds
unconscionable
usage of trade

Questions and Case Problems

1. Triple H Construction Co. contracted with Hunter's Run Stables, Inc., to erect a horse barn and riding arena on Hunter's Run's property in Big Flats, New York. Hunter's Run got a guarantee in its contract with Triple H that "such design with the span so shown will support its weight and will withstand natural forces including but not limited to snow load and wind." Hunter's Run also got the following guarantee from Rigidply, the manufacturer of the rafters: "Rigidply … hereby guarantees that the design to be used for the construction of a horse barn by Triple H … will support the weight of such barn and to snow load and wind as per drawings." The barn was completed in 1983 and collapsed under the weight of snow in 1994. Hunter's Run has sued Triple H for UCC Article 2 remedies. Does Article 2 apply? [*Hunter's Run Stables, Inc. v. Triple H, Inc.*, 938 F. Supp. 166 (W.D.N.Y.)]

2. R-P Packaging manufactured cellophane wrapping material that was used by Kern's Bakery in packaging its product. Kern's decided to change its system for packaging cookies from a tied bread bag to a tray covered with printed cellophane wrapping. R-P took measurements to determine the appropriate size for the cellophane wrapping and designed the artwork to be printed on the wrapping. After agreeing that the artwork was satisfactory, Kern placed a verbal order for the cellophane at a total cost of $13,000. When the printed wrapping material was received, Kern complained that it was too short for the trays and that the art work was not centered. The material, however, conformed exactly to the order placed by Kern. Kern returned the material to R-P by overnight express. R-P sued Kern. Kern claimed that because there was no written contract, the suit was barred by the statute of

frauds. What result? [*Flowers Baking Co. v. R-P Packaging, Inc.*, 329 S.E.2d 462 (Va.)]

3. Power & Telephone Supply Company (PTSC) put together a PowerPoint presentation for Dumont Telephone Company that showed the "head-end" system—a new phone system that would provide Dumont's customers with new video features that Dumont was not currently providing, including a TV-based Web browser with access to Internet radio, Web content, and social media. The quote purported to be a "cost estimate for Dumont Telephone." It contained the words: "For Budgetary Purposes only." It also listed a number of items of equipment. Some items were quoted at a specific quantity; others simply had "1" listed as the quantity. Some items were quoted at a specific price; others had no price listed. Is there enough between the quote and the presentation to constitute an offer? What would happen if the two companies just proceeded as if there were a contract? [*Dumont Telephone Co. v. Power & Telephone Supply Co.*, 962 F. Supp. 2d 1064 (N.D. Iowa)]

4. Mrs. Downing was fitted for dentures by a dentist, Dr. Cook. After she received her dentures, Mrs. Downing began experiencing mouth pain that she attributed to Dr. Cook's manufacture of dentures that did not fit her properly. Mrs. Downing filed suit against Dr. Cook for breach of warranty under Article 2 of the UCC. Dr. Cook defended on the grounds that his denture work was a service and therefore not covered under Article 2 warranties. The trial court found for Mrs. Downing, and Dr. Cook appealed. Is Dr. Cook correct? Are the dentures a contract for services or goods? [*Cook v. Downing*, 891 P.2d 611 (Oka. App.)] Would silicone breast implants be covered by the UCC Article 2 warranties? Does implantation of silicone gel implants constitute a sale of goods by the surgeon? [In re *Breast Implant Product Liability Litigation*, 503 S.E.2d 445 (S.C.)]

5. Meyers was under contract with Henderson to install overhead doors in a factory that Henderson was building. Meyers obtained the disassembled doors from the manufacturer. His contract with Henderson required Meyers to furnish all labor, materials, tools, and equipment to satisfactorily complete the installation of all overhead doors. Henderson felt that the doors were not installed properly and paid less than one-half of the contract price after subtracting his costs for correcting the installation. Because of a business sale and other complications, Meyers did not sue Henderson for the difference in payment until five years later. Henderson raised the defense that because the contract was for the sale of goods, it was barred by the Code's four-year statute of limitations. Meyers claimed that it was a contract for services and that suit could be brought within six years. Who is correct? Why? [*Meyers v. Henderson Construction Co.*, 370 A.2d 547 (N.J. Super.)]

6. Valley Trout Farms ordered fish food from Rangen. Both parties were merchants. The invoice that was sent with the order stated that a specified charge—a percentage common in the industry—would be added to any unpaid bills. Valley Trout Farms did not pay for the food and did not make any objection to the late charge stated in the invoice. When sued by Rangen, Valley Trout Farms claimed that it had never agreed to the late charge and therefore was not required to pay it. Is Valley Trout Farms correct? [*Rangen, Inc. v. Valley Trout Farms, Inc.*, 658 P.2d 955 (Idaho)]

7. LTV Aerospace Corp. manufactured all-terrain vehicles for use in Southeast Asia. LTV made an oral contract with Bateman under which Bateman would supply the packing cases needed for the vehicles' overseas shipment. Bateman made substantial beginnings in the production of packing cases following LTV's specifications. LTV thereafter stopped production of its vehicles and refused to take delivery of any cases. When Bateman sued for breach of contract, LTV argued that the contract could not be enforced because there was no writing that satisfied the statute of frauds. Was this a valid defense? [*LTV Aerospace Corp. v. Bateman*, 492 S.W.2d 703 (Tex. App.)]

8. Syrovy and Alpine Resources, Inc., entered into a "Timber Purchase Agreement." Syrovy agreed to sell and Alpine agreed to buy all of the timber produced during a two-year period. The timber to be sold, purchased, and delivered was to be produced by Alpine from timber on Syrovy's land. Alpine continued harvesting for one year and then stopped after making an initial payment. Syrovy sued Alpine. Alpine alleged that there was no contract because the writing to satisfy the statute of frauds must contain a quantity term. Decide. [*Syrovy v. Alpine Resources, Inc.*, 841 P.2d 1279 (Wash. App.)]

9. A subcontractor agreed to remove and dispose of cabinets from a public housing project. When a dispute arose, one party argued that the UCC applied, and the other argued that it was the common law contract. Explain who is correct and why. [*J.O. Hooker's Sons v. Roberts Cabinet*, 683 So. 2d 396]

10. Fastener Corp. sent a letter to Renzo Box Co. that was signed by Ronald Lee, Fastener's sales manager, and read as follows: "We hereby offer you 200 type #14 Fastener bolts at $5 per bolt. This offer will be

irrevocable for ten days." On the fifth day, Fastener informed Renzo it was revoking the offer, alleging that there was no consideration for the offer. Could Fastener revoke? Explain.

11. Richard, a retailer of video equipment, telephoned Craft Appliances and ordered a $1,000 videotape recorder for his business. Craft accepted Richard's order and sent him a copy of the purchase memorandum that stated the price, quantity, and model ordered and that was stamped "order accepted by Craft." Richard, however, did not sign or return the purchase memorandum and refused to accept delivery of the recorder when Craft delivered it to him three weeks later. Craft sued Richard, who raised the statute of frauds as a defense. Will Richard prevail? Why or why not?

12. REMC furnished electricity to Helvey's home. The voltage furnished was in excess of 135 volts and caused extensive damage to his 110-volt household appliances. Helvey sued REMC for breach of warranty. Helvey argued that providing electrical energy is not a transaction in goods but a furnishing of services, so that he had six years to sue REMC rather than the UCC's four-year statute of limitations, which had expired. Was it a sale of goods or a sale of services? Identify the ethical principles involved in this case. [*Helvey v. Wabash County REMC*, 278 N.E.2d 608 (Ind. App.)]

13. U.S. Surgical manufactures medical surgical instruments and markets the instruments to hospitals. The packaging for U.S. Surgical's disposable medical instruments is labeled "for single use only." As an example, one label contains the following language: "Unless opened or damaged, contents of package are sterile. DO NOT RESTERILIZE. For multiple use during a SINGLE surgical procedure. DISCARD AFTER USE."

Orris provides a service to the hospitals that purchase U.S. Surgical's disposable instruments. After the hospitals use or open the instruments, Orris cleans, resterilizes, and/or resharpens the instruments for future use and returns them to the hospitals from which they came.

U.S. Surgical filed suit asserting that reprocessing, repackaging, and reuse of its disposable instruments constituted a violation of its patent and trademark rights. Orris says that U.S. Surgical did not prohibit hospitals from reusing the instruments and that it was not doing anything that violated the contracts U.S. Surgical had with the hospitals. U.S. Surgical says the language on the packaging was an additional term that the hospitals accepted by opening the packages and using the instruments. Who is

correct? [*U.S. Surgical Corp. v. Orris, Inc.*, 5 F. Supp. 2d 1201 (D. Kan.); aff'd, 185 F.3d 885 (10th Cir.) and 230 F.3d 1382 (Fed. Cir.)]

14. Flora Hall went to Rent-A-Center in Milwaukee and signed an agreement to make monthly payments of $77.96 for 19 months in exchange for Rent-A-Center's allowing her to have a Rent-A-Center washer and dryer in her home. In addition, the agreement required Hall to pay tax and a liability waiver fee on the washer and dryer. The total amount she would pay under the agreement was $1,643.15. The agreement provided that Hall would return the washer and dryer at the end of the 19 months, or she could, at that time, pay $161.91 and own the washer and dryer as her own. Is this a sales contract? Is this a consumer lease? At the time Hall leased her washer and dryer, she could have purchased a set for about $600. What do you think about the cost of her agreement with Rent-A-Center? Is it unconscionable? Refer to Chapter 32, and determine whether any other consumer laws apply. Must this contract be in writing? [*Rent-A-Center, Inc. v. Hall*, 510 N.W.2d 789 (Wis.)]

15. Click2Boost, Inc. (C2B), entered into an Internet marketing agreement with the New York Times (NYT) on May 10, 2002, for C2B to solicit subscribers for home delivery of the New York Times newspaper through "pop up ads" at Internet Web sites with which C2B maintained "[m]arketing [a]lliances." The agreement required NYT to pay C2B a fee or commission for each home delivery subscription C2B submitted to NYT. NYT paid C2B more than $1.5 million in subscription submission fees from May 2002 to September 2003, but most of the subscriptions were ended, so NYT terminated the C2B agreement on September 16, 2003.

In October 2003, Wall Street Network (WSN) took over C2B and filed suit for breach of contract against NYT. WSN said that NYT had breached the agreement by terminating it before September 30, 2003, because the contract was one for goods and C2B had furnished those goods. WSN wanted damages under the UCC for breach of a contract because the pop-up ads were sold independently as goods. NYT argued that the contract was one for services for furnishing subscribers, something C2B did not do successfully. WSN countered that the customers generated from the pop-up ads were what was being sold, just like selling a list of names, something that would be considered a good. The trial court granted the NYT summary judgment and

WSN appealed. Should WSN win the case? Why or why not? [*Wall Street Network, Ltd. v. New York* *Times Company*, 164 Cal. App. 4th 1171, 80 Cal. Rptr. 3d 6, 66 U.C.C. Rep. Serv. 2d 261]

CPA Questions

1. Webstar Corp. orally agreed to sell Northco, Inc., a computer for $20,000. Northco sent a signed purchase order to Webstar confirming the agreement. Webstar received the purchase order and did not respond. Webstar refused to deliver the computer to Northco, claiming that the purchase order did not satisfy the UCC statute of frauds because it was not signed by Webstar. Northco sells computers to the general public, and Webstar is a computer wholesaler. Under the UCC Sales Article, Webstar's position is:

   a. Incorrect, because it failed to object to Northco's purchase order.

   b. Incorrect, because only the buyer in a sale-of-goods transaction must sign the contract.

   c. Correct, because it was the party against whom enforcement of the contract is being sought.

   d. Correct, because the purchase price of the computer exceeded $500.

2. On May 2, Lace Corp., an appliance wholesaler, offered to sell appliances worth $3,000 to Parco, Inc., a household appliances retailer. The offer was signed by Lace's president and provided that it would not be withdrawn before June 1. It also included the shipping terms: "F.O.B.—Parco's warehouse." On May 29, Parco mailed an acceptance of Lace's offer. Lace received the acceptance June 2. Which of the following is correct if Lace sent Parco a telegram revoking its offer and Parco received the telegram on May 25?

   a. A contract was formed on May 2.

   b. Lace's revocation effectively terminated its offer on May 25.

   c. Lace's revocation was ineffective because the offer could not be revoked before June 1.

   d. No contract was formed because Lace received Parco's acceptance after June 1.

3. Bond and Spear orally agreed that Bond would buy a car from Spear for $475. Bond paid Spear a $100 deposit. The next day, Spear received an offer of $575, the car's fair market value. Spear immediately notified Bond that Spear would not sell the car to Bond and returned Bond's $100. If Bond sues Spear and Spear defends on the basis of the statute of frauds, Bond will probably:

   a. Lose, because the agreement was for less than the fair market value of the car.

   b. Win, because the agreement was for less than $500.

   c. Lose, because the agreement was not in writing and signed by Spear.

   d. Win, because Bond paid a deposit.

4. Cookie Co. offered to sell Distrib Markets 20,000 pounds of cookies at $1.00 per pound, subject to certain specified terms for delivery. Distrib replied in writing as follows: "We accept your offer for 20,000 pounds of cookies at $1.00 per pound, weighing scale to have valid city certificate." Under the UCC:

   a. A contract was formed between the parties.

   b. A contract will be formed only if Cookie agrees to the weighing scale requirement.

   c. No contract was formed because Distrib included the weighing scale requirement in its reply.

   d. No contract was formed because Distrib's reply was a counteroffer.

5. Under the Sales Article of the UCC, which of the following requirements must be met for a writing to be an enforceable contract for the sale of goods?

   a. The writing must contain a term specifying the price of the goods.

   b. The writing must contain a term specifying the quantity of the goods.

   c. The writing must contain the signatures of all parties to the writing.

   d. The writing must contain the signature of the party seeking to enforce the writing.

6. Card communicated an offer to sell Card's stereo to Bend for $250. Which of the following statements is correct regarding the effect of the communication of the offer?

   a. Bend should immediately accept or reject the offer to avoid liability to Card.

   b. Card is not obligated to sell the stereo to Bend until Bend accepts the offer.

   c. Card is required to mitigate any loss Card would sustain in the event Bend rejects the offer.

   d. Bend may not reject the offer for a reasonable period of time.

Title and Risk of Loss

Learning Outcomes ⟨⟨⟨

After studying this chapter, you should be able to

LO.1 Explain when title and risk of loss pass with respect to goods

LO.2 Determine who bears the risk of loss when goods are damaged or destroyed

LO.3 Explain why it is important to know when risk of loss and title pass in transactions for the sale of goods

LO.4 Describe the passage of title and risk in special situations, such as a bailment, sale or return, or a sale on approval

LO.5 Classify the various circumstances in which title can be passed to a bona fide purchaser

23-1 Identifying Types of Potential Problems and Transactions

Problems may arise during contract performance that can result in issues of liability. For example, what if the goods are lost in transit? Must the buyer still pay for those lost goods? Can the seller's creditors take goods from the seller's warehouse when they are packed for shipment to buyers? The parties can include provisions in their contract to address these types of problems. If their contract does not cover these types of problems, however, then specific rules under Uniform Commercial Code (UCC) Article 2 apply. These rules are covered in this chapter.

Effective managers know the law and the rules of risk of loss and title so that they can negotiate risk-reducing contracts and be certain that they have all the necessary arrangements and paperwork to move goods through streams of commerce.

The types of problems that can arise in managing the contract performance aspects of supply chain management include damage to the goods in transit, claims by creditors of buyers and sellers while the goods are in transit, and questions relating to whose insurance will cover what damage and when such coverage applies.

23-1a Damage to Goods

One potential problem occurs if the goods are damaged or totally destroyed without any fault of either the buyer or the seller. With no goods and contract performance still required, the parties have questions: Must the seller bear the loss and supply new goods to the buyer? Or is it the buyer's loss so that the buyer must pay the seller the purchase price even though the goods are damaged or destroyed?[1] What liability does a carrier have when goods in its possession are damaged? The fact that there may be insurance does not avoid this question because the questions of whose insurer is liable and the extent of liability still remain.

CPA   23-1b Creditors' Claims

Another potential problem that can arise affecting the buyer's and seller's rights occurs when creditors of the seller or buyer seize the goods under the belief that their debtor has title. The buyer's creditors may seize them because they believe them to be the buyer's. The seller's creditors may step in and take goods because they believe the goods still belong to the seller, and the buyer is left with the dilemma of whether it can get the goods back from the creditors. The question of title or ownership is also important in connection with a resale of the goods by the buyer and in determining the parties' liability for, or the computation of, inventory or personal property taxes.

CPA   23-1c Insurance

insurable interest–the right to hold a valid insurance policy on a person or property.

Until the buyer has received the goods and the seller has been paid, both the seller and the buyer have an economic interest in the sales transaction. A question that can arise is whether either or both have enough of an interest in the goods to allow them to insure them; in other words, do they have an **insurable interest?** There are certain steps that must take place and timing requirements that must be met before that insurable interest can arise. Once buyers have an insurable interest in goods that are the subject matter of their contracts, they have the right to obtain insurance and can submit claims for losses on the goods.

---

[1] U.C.C. §2-509 provides for the allocation of the risk of loss in those situations where the goods are destroyed and neither party has breached the contract.

23-2 Determining Rights: Identification of Goods

identification—point in the transaction when the buyer acquires an interest in the goods subject to the contract.

The **identification** of the goods to the contract is a necessary step to provide the buyer an insurable interest. How goods that are the subject matter of a contract are identified depends on the nature of both the contract and the goods themselves.[2] Identification is also the first step for passage of title and risk of loss.

CPA

23-2a Existing Goods

existing goods—goods that physically exist and are owned by the seller at the time of a transaction.

identified—term applied to particular goods selected by either the buyer or the seller as the goods called for by the sales contract.

Existing goods are goods physically in existence at the time of the contract and owned by the seller. When particular goods have been selected by either the buyer or the seller, or both, as being the goods called for by the sales contract, the goods are **identified. For Example,** when you go into a store, point to a particular item, and tell the clerk, "I'll take that one," your sales transaction relates to existing goods that are now identified. This step of identification provides you with certain rights in those goods because of your contract as well as Article 2 protections for buyers when goods are identified.[3]

CPA

23-2b Future Goods

future goods—goods that exist physically but are not owned by the seller as well as goods that have not yet been produced.

Future goods are those not yet owned by the seller or not yet in existence. **For Example,** suppose that your company is sponsoring a 10-K run and will furnish the t-shirts for the 10,000 runners expected to participate in the race. You have contacted Sporting Tees, Inc., to produce the t-shirts with the name of the race and your company logo on the shirts. The shirts are future goods because you are contracting for goods that will be produced.

Future goods are identified when they are shipped, marked, or otherwise designated by the seller as goods to which the contract refers.[4] The t-shirts cannot be identified until Sporting Tees has manufactured them and designated them for your company. The earliest that the shirts can be identified is when they come off the production line and are designated for your company. Prior to identification of these goods, the buyer has only a future interest at the time of the contract and has few rights with respect to them.[5]

CPA

23-2c Fungible Goods

fungible goods—homogeneous goods of which any unit is the equivalent of any other unit.

Fungible goods are goods that, when mixed together, are indistinguishable. **For Example,** crops such as soybeans and dairy products such as milk are fungible goods. A seller who has 10,000 cases of cling peaches has fungible, unidentified goods. Like future goods, these fungible goods are identified when they are shipped, marked, or otherwise designated for the buyer.[6] The seller's act of tagging, marking, labeling, or in some way indicating to those responsible for shipping the goods that certain goods are associated with a particular contract or order means that identification has occurred.

---

[2] U.C.C. §2-501(1)(a). *Martini E Ricci Iamino S.P.A.—Consortile Societa Agricola v. Western Fresh Marketing Services, Inc.*, 54 F. Supp. 3d 1094 (E.D. Cal. 2014).

[3] *Duddy v. Government Employees Insurance Co., Inc.*, 23 A.3d 436 (N.J. App. 2011). *Arthur Glick Truck Sales, Inc. v. Stuphen East Corp.*, 965 F. Supp. 2d 402 (S.D.N.Y. 2013).

[4] U.C.C. §2-501(1)(b). Specially manufactured goods are fully identified when the goods are made.

[5] In re *Delta-T Corp.*, 475 B.R. 495 (E.D. Va. 2012).

[6] Farm products, such as corn, are fungible goods. However, contracts for future crops are not contracts for the sale of goods because there are no goods identified as yet for such contracts. *L & R Farm Partnership v. Cargill Inc.*, 963 F. Supp. 2d 798 (W.D. Tenn. 2013).

CPA   ### 23-2d **Effect of Identification**

Once goods that are the subject matter of a contract have been identified, the buyer holds an *insurable interest* in them. Once the buyer's economic interest in and the identity of the goods are clear, the buyer's insurance company has an obligation to provide coverage for any mishaps that could occur until the contract is performed completely.

Identification is also significant because the questions surrounding passage of title and risk of loss cannot be resolved until the goods have been identified. Identification is the first step in resolving questions about liability for damaged goods and rights of the parties and third parties, including creditors, in the goods. U.C.C. §2-401(1) provides, "Title to goods cannot pass under a contract for sale prior to their identification to the contract."

23-3   Determining Rights: Passage of Title

When title to goods passes to the buyer (following identification) depends on whether there is a document of title, whether the seller is required to ship the goods, and what the terms of that shipping agreement are. In the absence of an agreement by the parties as to when title will pass, several Article 2 rules govern the timing for passage of title.

23-3a   Passage of Title Using Documents of Title

document of title— document treated as evidence that a person is entitled to receive, hold, and dispose of the document and the goods it covers.

A **document of title** is a means whereby the parties can facilitate the transfer of title to the goods without actually moving them or provide a means for a creditor to take an interest in the goods. The use of a document of title also provides a simple answer to the question of when title to the goods passes from seller to buyer in a sales transaction. Title to the goods passes when the document of title is transferred from the seller to the buyer.[7]

CPA

Documents of title are governed under Article 7 of the UCC, the final section of the UCC to undergo major revisions in the last decade of the twentieth century. The purpose of the 2003 revisions to Article 7 was to address the issues that have arisen because of electronic filing of documents of title. The Article 7 revisions have been adopted in 48 states.[8]

bill of lading— document issued by a carrier acknowledging the receipt of goods and the terms of the contract of transportation.

Article 7 now addresses the commercial reality of electronic tracking and the use of electronic records as documents of title. Under Article 7, the definition of a document of title now includes electronic documents of title.

warehouse receipt— receipt issued by the warehouser for stored goods; regulated by the UCC, which clothes the receipt with some degree of negotiability.

The discussion of documents of title here is limited to commercial transactions, transport, and storage. Many forms of documents of title are not covered under Article 7. For example, all states have some form of title system required for the transfer of title to motor vehicles.[9] Those systems govern title passage for automobiles. The two primary forms of documents of title under Article 7 used to pass title to goods are **bills of lading** (issued by a carrier) and **warehouse receipts.**[10] Details on these documents and the rights of the parties are found in Chapter 21.

---

[7] U.C.C. §2-401(3).

[8] Wyoming and Missouri are the holds-outs. See **http://www.uniformlaws.org.**

[9] Other types of transportation, such as a boat, may not require a title document to be transferred, and title passes at the time of contracting. However, where there are title statutes, they preempt UCC provisions. *Johnson v. QFD, Inc.,* 807 N.W.2d 719 (Mich. App. 2011). See also *Bank v. Parish,* 317 P.3d 750 (Kan. 2014).

[10] U.C.C. §7-202(1) provides, "A warehouse receipt need not be in any particular form. Under Revised Article 7, it can be in electronic form."

CPA   ### 23-3b Passage of Title in Nonshipment Contracts

Unless the parties to the contract agree otherwise, UCC Article 2 does not require that the seller deliver the contracted-for goods to the buyer. In the absence of a provision in the contract, the place of delivery is the seller's place of business or the seller's residence if the seller is not a merchant. When there is no specific agreement for shipment or delivery of the goods and there is no document of title and the goods to the contract have been identified, title passes to the buyer at the time the contract is entered into by the buyer and seller.[11]

23-3c Passage of Title in Warehouse Arrangements

When the goods to a contract are in a warehouse or the possession of a third party (not the seller), the title to the goods passes from the seller to the buyer when the buyer receives the document of title or, if there is no document of title, any other paperwork required for the third party or warehouse to turn over the goods and the goods are available for the buyer to take. When goods are in the possession of a warehouse, the parties have certain duties and rights. Those rights and duties were covered in Chapter 21.

23-3d Passage of Title in Bailments and Other Forms of Possession

As a general rule, a seller can sell only what the seller owns. However, some issues of passage of title can arise in specific circumstances. Those circumstances are covered in the following sections.

CPA   ### Stolen Property

Neither those who find stolen property nor thieves can pass title to goods. A thief simply cannot pass good title to even a good-faith purchaser. Anyone who has purchased stolen goods must surrender them to the true owner. The fact that the negligence of the owner made the theft possible or contributed to losing the goods does not bar the owner from recovering the goods or money damages from the thief, the finder, or a good-faith purchaser. It does not matter that the thief may have passed the goods along through several purchasers. Title cannot be cleansed by distance between the thief and the good-faith purchaser. The good-faith purchaser always takes the goods subject to the claim by the owner. The public policy reason for this protection of true owners is to deter theft. Knowing that there is no way to sell the goods should deter those who steal and caution those who buy goods to check title and sources.

Estoppel

estoppel—principle by which a person is barred from pursuing a certain course of action or of disputing the truth of certain matters.

If an owner has acted in a way that misleads others, the owner of personal property may be prevented, or **estopped,** from asserting ownership. The owner would be barred from denying the right of another person to sell the property. **For Example,** a minor buys a car and puts it in his father's name so that he can obtain lower insurance rates. If the father then sells the car to a good-faith purchaser, the son would be estopped from claiming ownership.

CPA   ### Authorization

In certain circumstances, persons who just possess someone else's property may sell the property and pass title. Lienholders can sell property when debtors default. **For Example,**

---

[11] In re *Aleris Intern., Inc.,* 456 B.R. 35 (D. Del. 2011).

if you store your personal property in a storage locker and fail to pay rent, the owner of the storage locker holds a lien on your personal property and could sell it to pay the rent due on your storage unit. Good title passes to the buyer from such a sale. All states have some form of statute giving those who find property the authority to sell the property after certain time periods have passed or when the owner cannot be found.

Voidable Title

voidable title–title of goods that carries with it the contingency of an underlying problem.

If the buyer has a **voidable title**—for example, when the goods were obtained by fraud—the seller can rescind the sale. However, if the buyer resells the property to a good-faith purchaser before the seller has rescinded the transaction, the subsequent purchaser acquires valid title. It is immaterial whether the buyer with the voidable title had obtained title by criminal fraud.[12]

CASE SUMMARY

Fat Boy Hoodwinked by a Yacht Thief

FACTS: On August 23, 1995, Eric T. Small purchased a 37-foot (37') Sea Ray 370 Sundancer Yacht from Gulfwind Marine for $251,000.00. Sea Ray had engraved the vessel's hull identification number ("HIN") into the fiberglass on the vessel's transom. The vessel's HIN was SER4860F596 Sea Ray. Northern issued a Master Mariner yacht policy to Small, providing insurance coverage for the Sea Ray yacht for theft or loss for $200,000.00.

On February 27, 2001, Daniel Dey, a Florida resident, stole the Sea Ray yacht while it was moored at her slip at Gulfwind Marina in Venice, Florida. A police report was filed, and Northern paid Small a total loss of $200,000.00 for the vessel.

Subsequently, Dey altered the Sea Ray yacht's HIN to SERF3571C298 and made other changes to the vessel to disguise the theft and manufacture date. Dey then advertised a 1998 Sea Ray for sale on an Internet Web site. On August 5, 2002, Dey signed a bill of sale conveying the Sea Ray yacht to Fat Boy, a Delaware limited liability company, for $127,500.00. No boat dealer, retailer, distributor, or seller was involved in the transaction.

Fat Boy gave a ship mortgage on the Sea Ray yacht to Carolina First. Carolina First filed the preferred ship mortgage on the Sea Ray yacht.

George Lee and Paul Degenhart, the lawyer for and principal in Fat Boy, became concerned that the Sea Ray yacht may have been manufactured in 1996, not 1998. Lee and Degenhart confronted Dey about the incorrect model year of the Sea Ray yacht. Dey admitted the alteration to make the boat seem to be a 1998, not 1996, model.

Fat Boy and Lee then attempted to trade the Sea Ray yacht to a vessel dealer for another vessel that Lee wanted to purchase. The dealer determined that the vessel had been stolen and told Small. Small contacted Lee and Fat Boy to get back his yacht, but Lee refused.

In June 2004, the Sea Ray yacht was seized by the U.S. Marshal Service and Northern filed suit to get the yacht back. Fat Boy and Carolina First also claimed title and interest in the yacht.

DECISION: The Sea Ray yacht rightfully belongs to Northern. Small did not have knowledge of or consent to Dey's "sale" of the vessel to Fat Boy. Small did not sell the vessel to Fat Boy or Lee. Dey did not have valid title to the Sea Ray yacht when he issued a bill of sale to Fat Boy. The "sale" of the Sea Ray yacht between Dey and Fat Boy was not consummated through a boat dealer, retailer, distributor, or seller of like goods. Dey is not a boat dealer, retailer, distributor, or seller of like goods. Neither Lee nor Fat Boy ever possessed valid title to the Sea Ray yacht. A purchaser cannot obtain clear title from a thief to defeat the original owner. The most a bona fide purchaser for value can obtain from a thief is superior title to everyone except the original owner. [***Northern Insurance Company of New York v. 1996 Sea Ray Model 370DA Yacht***, 453 F. Supp. 2d 905 (D.S.C. 2006)]

---

[12] "Criminal fraud" is the language of Revised Article 2, adopted to increase the scope of the original term *larceny* and intended to encompass all forms of criminal activity that might lead to the possession or entrustment of goods.

CPA   ### Bailments or Sale by an Entrustee

A bailee can pass good title to a good-faith purchaser even when the sale was not authorized by the owner and the bailee has no title to the goods but is in the business of selling those particular types of goods.[13] **For Example,** if Gunnell's Jewelry sells and repairs watches and Julie has left her watch with Gunnell's for repair, she has created a bailment. If Gunnell's Jewelry sells Julie's watch by mistake (because Gunnell's is both a new and old watch dealer) to David, a good-faith purchaser, David has valid title to the watch. Julie will have a cause of action against Gunnell's for conversion, and in some states, if Gunnell's sold the watch knowing that it belonged to Julie, the sale could constitute a crime, such as larceny. However, all of these legal proceedings will involve Gunnell's, Julie, and possibly a government prosecution, but not David who will take good title to the watch.

In the case of an entrustee who is not a merchant, such as a prospective customer trying out an automobile, there is no transfer of title to the buyer from the entrustee. Similarly, there is no transfer of title when a mere bailee, such as a repairer who is not a seller of goods of that kind, sells the property of a customer.

23-3e Delivery and Shipment Terms

If delivery is required under the terms of the parties' agreement, the seller is normally required only to make shipment, and the seller's part of the contract is completed by placing the goods in the possession of a carrier for shipment. However, the parties may agree

---

THINKING THINGS THROUGH

Serving Up Title and Insurance at the Burned Bar

On November 12, 2008, Cheran Investments leased the premises located at "3231–3229 Harney Street, Omaha, Nebraska," to Blasini, Inc. (owned by Richard Bruno), for the purpose of operating the Attic Bar & Grill. The lease began on February 1, 2009, and Blasini was to make monthly payments. In 2011, Cheran Investments filed suit against Blasini for nonpayment of rent, taxes, and late fees from June 2010 through July 2011.

Also on December 8, 2008, Blasini entered into a "Purchase Agreement" with Dr. Raj and his wife, doing business as Chola, Inc., to purchase the "business assets" of the bar owned by the couple. The business assets of the bar that Blasini agreed to purchase under the agreement included "the furniture, Security systems, Aloha accounting system, Television, Music system, refrigerators, kitchen equipment, [and] food and liquor inventory." A handwritten ledger attached to the agreement lists the business assets and their values, totaling $150,000.

The terms of the agreement called for Blasini to pay $50,000 in the first year and the remaining $100,000 over the subsequent 24 months. Blasini failed to pay the $150,000.

On December 8, 2010, Cheran Investments executed a promissory note to Pinnacle for $379,229.23, which was

secured by the bar property at 3229 Harney Street to Pinnacle as collateral and by a security agreement granting Pinnacle a security interest in "all goods now or in the future affixed or attached to real estate" at the bar property. Pinnacle filed a "UCC Financing Statement" on December 31.

On March 28, 2011, a fire damaged the building and personal property at the Attic Bar & Grill. Nautilus Insurance Company was not sure who was entitled to the insurance proceeds and Cheran Investments, Pinnacle, Perkins, Blasini, and Bruno all claimed an interest in those proceeds. The amount due under the policy was $70,929.93 for damage to the building and $96,774.10 for damage to the business' personal property.

Who recovers for the damage to the personal property in the bar? Think about who has title to the personal property in the bar as you answer this question. Does it matter that the payments for the property were not made?

[*Nautilus Insurance Company v. Cheran Investments*, LLC, 2014 WL 292809 (Neb. App. 2014), 82 U.C.C. Rep. Serv. 2d 560]

---

[13] *Estate of Martin Luther King Jr., Inc. v. Ballou*, 856 F. Supp. 2d 860 (S.D. Miss. 2012). *Martini E Ricci Iamino S.P.A.—Consortile Societa Agricola v. Western Fresh Marketing Services, Inc.*, 54 F. Supp. 3d 1094 (E.D. Cal. 2014).

ETHICS & THE LAW

The $7 Renoir at the Flea Market

Pierre-Auguste Renoir painted "In re Paysage Bords de Seine" in 1879, a painting that was unsigned. The first recorded owner of the painting was Herbert May, a dealer in France. In 1935, Saidie May, Herbert's wife, loaned the painting to the Baltimore Museum of Art (BMA). The painting exhibition disappeared from the museum on November 17, 1951. The Baltimore Police Department investigated and the museum was paid $2,500 by its insurer for the loss.

The painting re-emerged at a flea market in West Virginia in 2008 or 2009 when Marcia Fuqua purchased it for $7. After learning of its true value, Ms. Fuqua made arrangements

to have the painting auctioned. BMA learned of the auction and notified its insurer and the FBI. The United States filed suit to have the court determine title to the painting.

Determine who has title under the UCC. What ethical issues are there when Ms. Fuqua learned of the true identity and value of the painting? What about the old adage "finders keepers"?

[In re *"Paysage Bords De Seine," 1879 Unsigned Oil Painting on Linen by Pierre-Auguste Renoir*, 991 F. Supp. 2d 740 (E.D. Va. 2014)]

---

to various shipping provisions that do affect the passage of title under Article 2.[14] Those terms are covered in the following sections, and Figure 23-1 provides a summary.

FOB Place of Shipment

FOB place of shipment–
contract that requires the
seller to arrange for
shipment only.

FOB is a shipping term that is an acronym for free on board.[15] If a contract contains a delivery term of **FOB place of shipment,** then the seller's obligation under the contract is to deliver the goods to a carrier for shipment. **For Example,** if the contract between a New York buyer and a Los Angeles seller provides for delivery as FOB Los Angeles,

FIGURE 23-1	Delivery and Shipping Terms

COD	Cash on delivery (payment term, not shipment term)
CF	Cost plus freight lump sum; price includes cost and freight
	Risk: buyer on delivery to carrier
	Title: buyer on delivery to carrier
	Cost, insurance, and freight expenses: seller pays; includes cost of freight in contract price
CIF	Lump sum; price includes cost, insurance, and freight
	Risk: buyer on delivery to carrier
	Title: buyer on delivery to carrier
	Expenses: included in contract price (seller buys insurance in buyer's name and pays freight)
FOB	Free on board
FAS	Free alongside ship (FOB for boats)

---

[14] U.C.C. §2-401(2). When a seller simply ships goods in response to a telephone order and there is no paperwork to indicate shipping terms, the contract is one of shipment (FOB place of shipment).
[15] U.C.C. §2-319.

then the seller's responsibility is to place the goods in the possession of a Los Angeles carrier and enter into a contract to have the goods shipped to New York.

CPA FOB Place of Destination

FOB place of destination–shipping contract that requires the seller to deliver goods to the buyer.

If a contract contains a delivery term of **FOB place of destination,** then the seller's responsibility is to get the goods to the buyer.

For Example, if the contract between the New York buyer and the Los Angeles seller is FOB New York, then the seller is responsible for getting the goods to New York. An FOB destination contract holds the seller accountable throughout the journey of the goods across the country.

CPA FAS

FAS–free alongside the named vessel.

FAS is a shipping term that means free alongside ship; it is the equivalent of FOB for boat transportation.[16] **For Example,** a contract between a London buyer and a Norfolk, Virginia, seller that is FAS Norfolk requires only that the seller deliver the goods to a ship in Norfolk.

CPA CF, CIF, and COD

CF–cost and freight.

CIF–cost, insurance, and freight.

COD–cash on delivery.

CF is an acronym for cost and freight, and **CIF** is an acronym for cost, insurance, and freight.[17] Under a CF contract, the seller gets the goods to a carrier, and the cost of shipping the goods is included in the contract price. Under a CIF contract, the seller must get the goods to a carrier and buy an insurance policy in the buyer's name to cover the goods while in transit. The costs of the freight and the insurance policy are included in the contract price.

Often contracts for the sale of goods provide for **COD.** The acronym stands for cash on delivery. Even though the term includes the word *delivery*, COD is not a shipping term but a payment term that requires the buyer to pay in order to gain physical possession of the goods.

23-3f Passage of Title in Shipment Contracts

When the parties have shipment and delivery terms in their contract, the type of shipment contract the parties have agreed to controls when title to the goods has passed and, as a result, the rights of creditors of the buyer and seller in those goods.

CPA Passage of Title in a Shipment-Only Contract (FOB Shipment)

Title to the goods passes from the seller to the buyer in an FOB shipment contract when the seller delivers the goods to the carrier.[18] (See Figure 23-2.) The title to the goods no longer rests with the Los Angeles seller once the goods are delivered to the carrier if the contract is a shipment contract only (an FOB Los Angeles contract). **For Example,** if the Internal Revenue Service received authorization to collect taxes by seizing the seller's property, it could not take those goods once they were delivered to the carrier. Under a shipment contract (an FOB shipment contract), the buyer owns the goods once they are in the hands of the carrier.

[16] U.C.C. §2-319.
[17] U.C.C. §§2-320 and 2-321.
[18] U.C.C. §2-401(2).

FIGURE 23-2	Passage of Title under Article 2

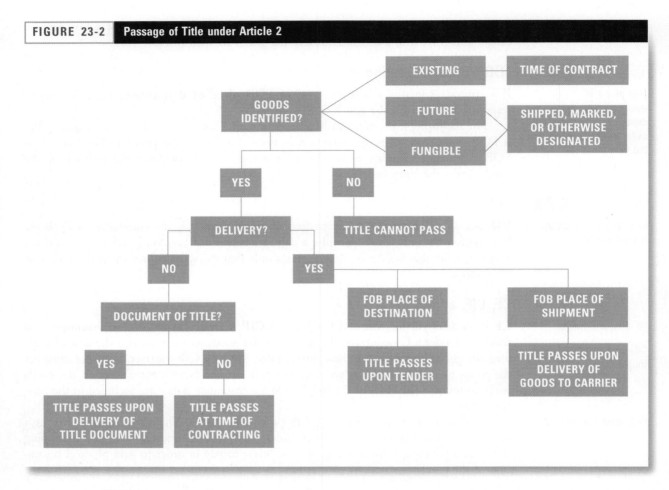

Passage of Title in a Destination Contract (FOB Place of Destination)

tender–goods have arrived, are available for pickup, and the buyer is notified.

Title to the goods passes from the seller to the buyer in an FOB destination contract when the goods are tendered to the buyer at the destination. **Tender** occurs when the goods have arrived and are available for the buyer to pick up and the buyer has been notified of their availability. **For Example,** when the contract contains an FOB destination provision requiring the seller to deliver to New York, title to the goods passes to the New York buyer when the goods have arrived in New York, they are available for pickup, and the buyer has been notified of their arrival. Thus, the IRS could seize the goods during shipment if the contract is FOB New York because title remains with the seller until actual tender. In the preceding example, the seller's obligation is complete when the goods are at the rail station in New York and the buyer has been notified that she may pick them up at any time during working hours.[19]

CPA **23-4   Determining Rights: Risk of Loss**

risk of loss–in contract performance, the cost of damage or injury to the goods contracted for.

Identification determines insurability, and title determines rights of such third parties as creditors. **Risk of loss** determines who must pay under a contract in the event the goods that are the subject of the contract are damaged or destroyed during the course of performance.

[19] In re *Sunbelt Grain WKS, LLC, Bkrtcy.*, 406 B.R. 918 (D. Kan. 2009).

23-4a Risk of Loss in Nonshipment Contracts

As noted earlier, Article 2 has no provision for delivery in the absence of an agreement. The rules for passage of risk of loss from the seller to the buyer in a nonshipment contract make a distinction between a merchant seller and a nonmerchant seller. If the seller is a merchant, the risk of loss passes to the buyer on actual receipt of the goods from the merchant.[20] If the seller is a nonmerchant, the risk of loss passes when the seller makes the goods available to the buyer or upon tender. **For Example,** if John buys a refrigerator at Kelvinator Appliances and then leaves it there while he goes to borrow a pickup truck, the risk of loss has not yet passed to John. He may have had title at the time he entered into the contract for the existing goods, and the goods are identified, but the risk of loss will not pass to John until he has actually received the refrigerator. His receipt will not occur until the refrigerator is placed in the back of his pickup truck. John is fully protected if anything happens to the refrigerator until then. If John buys the refrigerator from his neighbor at a garage sale, the risk of loss passes at the same time that title passes, or at the time of contracting.

23-4b Risk of Loss in Shipment Contracts

If the parties have agreed to delivery or shipment terms as part of their contract, the rules for risk of loss are different.[21]

C P A   Contract for Shipment to Buyer (FOB Place of Shipment)

In a contract for shipment only, or FOB place of shipment, the risk of loss passes to the buyer at the same time as title does: when the goods are delivered to the carrier, that is, at the time and place of shipment. After the goods have been delivered to the carrier, the seller has no liability for, or insurable interest in, the goods unless the seller has reserved a security interest in them. **For Example,** if the Los Angeles seller has a shipment contract (an FOB Los Angeles contract), once the goods are in the hands of the carrier, the risk belongs to the buyer or the buyer's insurer. If the goods are hijacked outside Kansas City, the New York buyer must still pay the Los Angeles seller for the goods according to the contract price and terms.

E-COMMERCE & CYBERLAW

Supply Chain and Risk Management

In today's sophisticated supplier and transportation relationships, buyers, sellers, and carriers can pinpoint exactly where goods are and when they have been delivered, and all parties have access to that information online. In many contracts, the parties can avert problems or breaches by monitoring closely the progress of the shipment. The computer interconnection of the supply chain permits faster and better communication among the parties when problems under the contract or in shipment arise. The shipment can be tracked from the time of delivery to the carrier through its route to final signature upon its arrival.

---

[20] U.C.C. §2-509. *Capshaw v. Hickman*, 880 N.E.2d 118 (Oh. App. 2007).
[21] U.C.C. §2-509. *OneBeacon Ins. Co. v. Haas Industries, Inc.*, 634 F.3d 1092 (9th Cir. 2011).

CPA   Contract for Delivery at Destination (FOB Place of Destination)

When the contract requires the seller to deliver the contract goods at a particular destination (FOB place of destination), the risk of loss does not pass to the buyer until the carrier tenders the goods at the destination. **For Example,** if the contract is FOB New York and the goods are hijacked in Kansas City, the seller is required to find substitute goods and perform under the contract because the risk of loss does not pass to the buyer until the goods arrive in New York and are available to the notified buyer.[22]

23-4c Damage to or Destruction of Goods

In the absence of a contract provision, Article 2 provides for certain rights for the parties in the event of damage to or destruction of goods that are the subject matter in a contract.

Damage to Identified Goods Before Risk of Loss Passes

Goods that were identified at the time the contract was made may be damaged or destroyed without the fault of either party before the risk of loss has passed. If so, the UCC provides, "if the loss is total the contract is avoided."[23] The loss may be partial, or the goods may have so deteriorated that they do not conform to the contract. In this case, the buyer has the option, after inspecting the goods, to either avoid the contract or accept the goods subject to an allowance or a deduction from the contract price. There is no breach by the seller, so the purpose of the law is simply to eliminate the legal remedies, allow the buyer to choose to take or not take the goods, and have the insurers involved cover the losses.[24]

CASE SUMMARY

Rotten Fruit, Rotten Carrier, Good Coverage

FACTS: Total Quality Logistics, LLC (plaintiff/TQL), hired Frye Trucking, LLC (defendant/Frye), to transport fruit to TQL's customer's facility in Georgia. Frye's driver picked up the fruit in New Jersey and Pennsylvania and transported the fruit to Georgia over a period of three days.

The driver received bills of lading for the fruit when he picked them up and, after delivery, he received the three bills of lading after they were stamped as approved by the customer. Each bill of lading has a stamp and notation from the customer that shows all cases were received, no cases were damaged, and no cases were rejected. The bills of lading also listed the pulp temperature of the fruit upon arrival.

After the driver had left the customer's premises, the customer noticed that the fruit was not in good condition and requested an inspection by the USDA. The USDA prepared three reports on March 2, 2012, the delivery date, which stated that the fruit was spoiled and evidenced decay and other issues. TQL then unsuccessfully tried to salvage the shipment of fruit, but it was determined that the fruit was in too poor of a condition to salvage. TQL filed a claim with Frye on March 13, 2012. Frye's insurance company denied an insurance claim filed for the lost fruit product because it believed that the fruit was delivered to Frye in damaged condition. TQL filed suit and both parties moved for summary judgment.

DECISION: The records showed that the temp was too high during transit with the result being that the fruit was

---

[22] *APL Co. Pte. Ltd. v. Kemira Water Solutions, Inc.*, 890 F. Supp. 2d 360 (S.D.N.Y. 2012).

[23] U.C.C. §613(a).

[24] *Great Southern Wood Preserving, Inc. v. American Home Assur. Co.*, 505 F. Supp. 2d 1287 (M.D. Ala. 2007). *CNA Ins. Co. v. Hyundai Merchant Marine Co., Ltd.*, 747 F.3d 339 (6th Cir. 2014).

Rotten Fruit, Rotten Carrier, Good Coverage continued

damaged in transit. The buyer need not pay and the seller would be able to recover from the carrier's insurer because the carrier was negligent in shipping with the high temps.

Even though the documents were signed and no damage was noted, the thorough inspection had not been done and once that was done, there was evidence of damage and the shipping records revealed that the temperature was not where it needed to be to preserve the fruit.

The plaintiff was awarded $11,925.00 plus prejudgment interest and the costs of the suit against defendant Frye Trucking. [***Total Quality Logistics, LLC v. Frye Trucking, LLC***, 997 F. Supp. 2d 384 (E.D.N.C. 2014)]

Damage to Identified Goods after Risk of Loss Passes

If partial damage or total destruction occurs after the risk of loss has passed to the buyer, it is the buyer's loss. The buyer may be able to recover the amount of the damages from the carrier, an insurer, the person in possession of the goods (such as a warehouse), or any third person causing the loss.[25] However, the carrier is permitted to limit its liability for damages on valuable goods such as artwork. Without special insurance and absent any negligence by the seller in making shipping arrangements, a buyer who holds the risk of loss will still be bound to pay the seller the full amount.

CASE SUMMARY

FedEx, Candelabras, and Damages in Shipment

FACTS: Yehouda Hanasab, president and sole shareholder of King Jewelry, Inc., bought a pair of marble and brass statues with candelabras from Elegant Reflections, a purveyor of jewelry and object d'art located in Florida, for $37,500.00. Elegant Reflections was to ship the goods to King under FOB place of shipment terms. Elegant Reflections hired Raymond Reppert, a "professional packager and crater" with 12 years' experience, to package, crate, and ship the statues and candelabras to King. Reppert packaged and crated the statues with directional markings and signs stating "Fragile—Handle with Care." Reppert paid FedEx $684.50 (transportation charge in the amount of $485.04, declared value charge in the amount of $185.00, and fuel surcharge in the amount of $14.55) to ship the candelabras. However, both candelabras were broken in transit, something King discovered when they arrived in King's offices. FedEx's airbill limits damages to $500. King sought recovery from Elegant and/or FedEx and Reppert.

DECISION: The standard airbill holding FedEx harmless for any damage to artwork was sufficiently plain and conspicuous to give reasonable notice of its meaning and, thus, effectively limited the carrier's liability for damage to the sculptures: A conspicuous notice limiting coverage for artwork appeared on the front of the airbill and directed the shipper to easily understood terms on the back; a service bill incorporated into the airbill expressly provided that the artwork was covered only up to $500; and the shipper had considerable experience in shipping goods. In an FOB place of shipment contract, the seller is not liable unless the buyer can show negligence in packing. King did not establish that Elegant or Reppert was negligent. King received $500.00. [***King Jewelry Inc. v. Federal Express Corporation***, 166 F. Supp. 2d 1280 (C.D. Cal. 2001)]

---

[25] For a discussion of parties' rights, see *Starke v. United Parcel Service, Inc.*, 898 F. Supp. 2d 560 (E.D.N.Y. 2012), *Spray-Tek, Inc. v. Robbins Motor Transp., Inc.*, 426 F. Supp. 2d 875 (W.D. Wis. 2006), and *Certain Underwriters at Interest at Lloyds of London v. United Parcel Service of America, Inc.*, 762 F.3d 332 (3rd Cir. 2014).

Damage to Unidentified Goods

As long as the goods are unidentified, no risk of loss passes to the buyer. If any goods are damaged or destroyed during this period, the loss is the seller's. The buyer is still entitled to receive the goods described by the contract. The seller is therefore liable for breach of contract if the proper goods are not delivered.

The only exceptions to these general rules on damage or destruction arise when the parties have expressly provided in the contract that the destruction of the seller's inventory, crop, or source of supply releases the seller from liability, or when it is clear that the parties contracted for the purchase and sale of part of the seller's supply to the exclusion of any other possible source of such goods. In these cases, destruction of, or damage to, the seller's supply is a condition subsequent that discharges the contract.

23-4d Effect of Seller's Breach in Risk of Loss

When the seller breaches the contract by sending the buyer goods that do not conform to the contract and the buyer rejects them, the risk of loss does not pass to the buyer. If there has been a breach, the risk of loss remains with the seller even though the risk, according to the contract terms or the Article 2 rules discussed earlier, would ordinarily have passed to the buyer.

Figure 23-3 provides a summary of all the risk provisions for parties in a sales transaction.

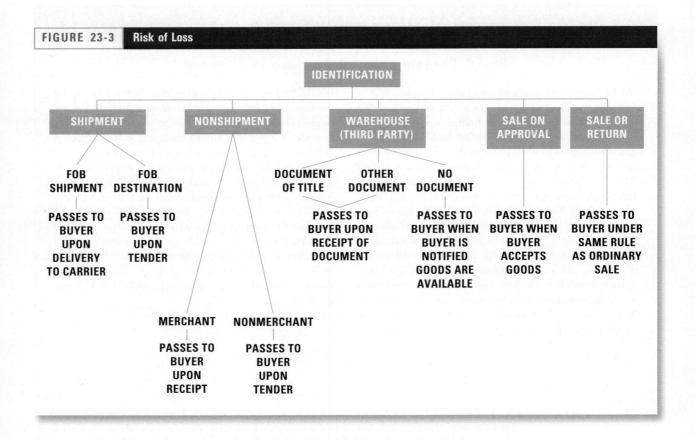

FIGURE 23-3   Risk of Loss

23-5 Determining Rights: Special Situations

23-5a Returnable Goods Transactions

The parties may agree that the goods to be transferred under the contract can be returned to the seller. This type of arrangement in which goods may be returned is classified as one of the following: (1) a sale on approval, (2) a sale or return, or (3) a consignment sale. In the first two types of transactions, the buyer is allowed to return the goods as an added inducement to purchase. The consignment sale is used when the seller is actually the owner's agent for the purpose of selling goods.[26]

CPA

sale on approval—term indicating that no sale takes place until the buyer approves or accepts the goods.

Sale on Approval

In a **sale on approval,** no sale takes place (meaning there is no transfer of title) until the buyer approves, or accepts, the goods. Title and risk of loss remain with the seller until there is an approval. Because the buyer is not the "owner" of the goods before approval, the buyer's creditors cannot attach or take the goods before the buyer's approval of the goods.

The buyer's approval may be shown by (1) express words, (2) conduct, or (3) lapse of time. Trying out or testing the goods does not constitute approval or acceptance. Any use that goes beyond trying out or testing, such as repairing the goods or giving them away as a present, is inconsistent with the seller's continued ownership. These types of uses show approval by the buyer. **For Example,** a buyer may order a home gym through a television ad. The ad allows buyers to try the room full of equipment for 30 days and then promises, "If you are not completely satisfied, return the home gym and we'll refund your money." The offer is one for a sale on approval. If the buyer does not return the home gym equipment or contact the seller within 30 days, the sale is complete.

The contract may give the buyer a fixed number of days for approval. The expiration of that period of time, without any action by the buyer, constitutes an approval. Also during this time, the buyer's creditors cannot take the goods pursuant to a judgment or lien. If no time is stated in the contract, the lapse of a reasonable time without action by the buyer constitutes an approval. If the buyer gives the seller notice of disapproval, the lapse of time thereafter has no effect.

If the buyer does not approve the goods, the seller bears the risk of and expense for their return.

sale or return—sale in which the title to the property passes to the buyer at the time of the transaction but the buyer is given the option of returning the property and restoring the title to the seller.

Sale or Return

A **sale or return** is a completed sale with an option for the buyer to return the goods. Revised Article 2 provides a new distinction between sale on approval and sale or return but with the same basic rules on title and risk of loss.

consignment—bailment made for the purpose of sale by the bailee. (Parties—consignor, consignee)

In a sale or return transaction, title and risk of loss pass to the buyer as in the case of the ordinary or absolute sale. Until the actual return of the goods is made, title and risk of loss remain with the buyer. The buyer bears the expense for and risk of return of the goods. In a sale or return, so long as the goods remain in the buyer's possession, the buyer's creditors may treat the goods as belonging to the buyer.

consignor—(1) person who delivers goods to the carrier for shipment; (2) party with title who turns goods over to another for sale.

23-5b Consignments and Factors

consignee—(1) person to whom goods are shipped; (2) dealer who sells goods for others.

Under a **consignment,** the owner of the goods entrusts them to a dealer for the purpose of selling them. The seller is the **consignor,** and the dealer is the **consignee.** The dealer-consignee is often referred to as a **factor,** a special type of bailee (see Chapter 21) who

factor—bailee to whom goods are consigned for sale.

---

[26] *Dan Cake (Portugal) S.A. v. CVS Pharmacy, Inc.,* 862 F. Supp. 2d 120 (D.R.I. 2012).

sells consigned goods just as if the goods were her own. The dealer-consignee is paid a fee for selling the goods on behalf of the seller-consignor. A consignment sale is treated as a sale or return under Article 2, and the dealer-consignee has full authority to sell the goods for the consignor and can pass title to those goods. While the goods are in the possession of the consignee, they are subject to the claims of the seller's creditors.[27]

23-5c Self-Service Stores

In the case of goods in a self-service store, the reasonable interpretation of the circumstances is that the store, by its act of putting the goods on display on its shelves, makes an offer to sell such goods for cash and confers on a prospective customer a license to carry the goods to the cashier to make payment. Most courts hold that there is no transfer of title until the buyer makes payment to the cashier. Other courts hold that a contract to sell is formed when the customer accepts the seller's offer by taking the item from the shelf. In other words, a sale actually occurs when the buyer takes the item from the shelf. Title passes at that moment to the buyer even though the goods have not yet been paid for.

CPA   ### 23-5d Auction Sales

When goods are sold at an auction in separate lots, each lot is a separate transaction, and title to each passes independently of the other lots. Title to each lot passes when the auctioneer announces by the fall of the hammer or in any other customary manner that the lot in question has been sold to the bidder.

"With reserve" auctions are those that give the auctioneer the right to withdraw the goods from the sale process if the bids are not high enough. If an auction is held "without reserve," the goods must be sold regardless of whether the auctioneer is satisfied with the levels of the bids.

Make the Connection

Summary

All along the supply chain of a business are issues of risk and title that are often complicated by additional questions about damage to goods in transit, the claims of creditors to goods that are in process under a contract, and insurance. Unless the parties specifically agree otherwise, the solution to these problems depends on the nature of the transaction between the seller and the buyer.

The first issue to be addressed in answering questions of risk, title, and loss is whether the goods are identified. Existing goods are identified at the time the contract is entered into. Future goods, or goods not yet owned by the seller or not yet in existence (as in goods to be manufactured by the seller), are identified when they are shipped, marked, or otherwise designated for the buyer. Without identification, title and risk of loss cannot pass from buyer to seller, nor can the buyer hold an insurable interest.

Once identification has occurred, the issue of title, and hence creditor's rights, can be addressed. If there are identified goods but there is no document of title associated with the goods, then title to the goods passes from the seller to the buyer at the time of the contract.

Sellers can have their goods covered by a document of title. The most common types of documents of title are bills of lading and warehouse receipts. These documents of title, if properly transferred, transfer title to both the document and the underlying goods.

---

[27] This clarification of creditors' rights in consignments came from Revised Article 9 (see Chapter 33). Revised Article 2 was changed to make the sale or return rights of creditors consistent with Revised Article 9.

While the seller has no obligation under UCC Article 2 to deliver the goods to the buyer, the parties can agree on delivery as part of their contract. Several common delivery terms are used in supply chain management. *FOB* is "free on board," and its meaning depends on the location that follows the term. *FOB place of shipment* requires the seller to deliver the goods to the carrier. In an FOB place of shipment contract, title to the goods passes from the seller to the buyer when the goods are delivered to the carrier. *FOB place of destination* requires the seller to get the goods to the buyer or a location specified by the buyer and tender the goods there. *FAS* is "free alongside ship," which means free on board for shipment by sea. *CF* is "cost and freight" and requires the seller to deliver the goods to the carrier and make a contract for their shipment. *CIF* is "cost, insurance, and freight" and requires the seller to deliver the goods to the carrier, make a contract for shipment, and purchase insurance for the goods in transit. *COD* means "cash on delivery" and requires the buyer to pay for the goods before taking possession of them.

Ordinarily, sellers cannot pass any title greater than that which they possess. In some cases, however, the law permits a greater title to be transferred even though the transferor may hold voidable title or be in possession of the goods only as in a bailment. These exceptions protect good-faith purchasers.

Risk of loss is an issue for buyers, sellers, and insurers. When the risk of loss will pass from seller to buyer is controlled, again, by the terms of the contract. In a contract in which there is no agreement on delivery, the risk of loss passes to the buyer upon receipt of the goods if the seller is a merchant and upon tender if the seller is a non-merchant. If there is an agreement for delivery and the contract provides for shipment only, or FOB place of shipment, then risk of loss passes from seller to buyer when the goods are delivered to the carrier. If the contract provides for delivery to a particular location, or FOB place of destination, then the risk of loss passes from the seller to the buyer when the goods are tendered to the buyer.

Some types of arrangements, such as sales on approval, sales or returns, and consignments or factor arrangements, have specific rules for passage of title and risk of loss. Also, if there is a breach of the contract and the seller ships goods different from those ordered, the breach prevents the risk of loss from passing from the seller to the buyer.

Learning Outcomes

After studying this chapter, you should be able to clearly explain:

23-1 Identifying Types of Potential Problems and Transactions

LO.1 Explain when title and risk of loss pass with respect to goods

See *Northern Insurance Company of New York v. 1996 Sea Ray Model 370DA Yacht*, page 440.

See "The $7 Renoir at the Flea Market" Ethics & the Law feature, page 442.

See the "Serving Up Title and Insurance at the Burned Bar" Thinking Things Through feature, page 441.

23-2 Determining Rights: Identification of Goods

LO.2 Determine who bears the risk of loss when goods are damaged or destroyed

See *King Jewelry Inc. v. Federal Express Corporation*, page 447.

23-3 Determining Rights: Passage of Title

LO.3 Explain why it is important to know when risk of loss and title pass in transactions for the sale of goods

See *Total Quality Logistics, LLC v. Frye Trucking, LLC*, pages 446–447.

23-4 Determining Rights: Risk of Loss

LO.4 Describe the passage of title and risk in special situations, such as a bailment, sale or return, or a sale on approval

See the *For Example*, discussion of Gunnell's Jewelry, page 441.

See the *For Example*, discussion of a home gymnasium that is purchased from TV, page 449.

23-5 Determining Rights: Special Situations

LO.5 Classify the various circumstances in which title can be passed to a bona fide purchaser

See the Ethics & the Law feature, "The $7 Renoir at the Flea Market," page 442.

Key Terms

bills of lading	COD	consignor
CF	consignee	document of title
CIF	consignment	estoppel

existing goods

factor

FAS

FOB place of destination

FOB place of shipment

fungible goods

future goods

identification

identified

insurable interest

risk of loss

sale on approval

sale or return

tender

voidable title

warehouse receipts

Questions and Case Problems

1. Schock, the buyer, negotiated to purchase a mobile home that was owned by and located on the sellers' property. On April 15, 1985, Schock appeared at the Ronderos' (the sellers') home and paid them the agreed-on purchase price of $3,900. Shock received a bill of sale and an assurance from the Ronderos that the title certificate to the mobile home would be delivered soon. Also on April 15 and with the permission of the sellers, Schock prepared the mobile home for removal. His preparations included the removal of skirting around the mobile home's foundation, the tie-downs, and the foundation blocks, leaving the mobile home to rest on the wheels of its chassis. Schock intended to remove the mobile home from the Ronderos' property a week later, and the Ronderos had no objection to having the mobile home remain on their premises until that time. Two days later, the mobile home was destroyed by high winds as it sat on the Ronderos' property. Schock received a clear certificate of title to the mobile home in the mail. Thereafter, Schock sued the Ronderos for return of his money on the ground that when the mobile home was destroyed, the risk of loss remained with the Ronderos. Who should win the lawsuit? [*Schock v. Ronderos*, 394 N.W.2d 697 (N.D.)]

2. John C. Clark, using the alias Thomas Pecora, rented a 1994 Lexus from Alamo Rent-A-Car on December 21, 1994. Clark did not return the car and, using falsified signatures, obtained a California so-called quick title.

    Clark advertised the car for sale in the *Las Vegas Review Journal*. Terry and Vyonne Mendenhall called the phone number in the ad and reached Clark. He told them that he lived at a country club and could not have people coming to his house to look at the car. He instead drove the car to their house for their inspection the next morning. The car title was in the name of J. C. Clark Enterprises. The Mendenhalls bought the car for $34,000 in cash. They made some improvements on the car and

registered it in Utah. On February 24, 1995, Alamo reported the car stolen. On March 21, 1995, the Nevada Department of Motor Vehicles seized the car from the Mendenhalls. The car was returned to Alamo and the Mendenhalls filed suit. The lower court found for the Mendenhalls, and Alamo appealed. Who gets the car and why? [*Alamo Rent-A-Car v. Mendenhall*, 937 P.2d 69 (Nev.)]

3. CVS Pharmacy, Inc., entered into a contract with Dan Cake, a company in Portugal, for Dan Cake to ship tins of cookies for sale at CVS pharmacies. The cookies were originally supposed to be delivered on or before September 7, 2007. There were several delays and the cookies did not arrive at CVS warehouses until between December 5 and December 15, 2007. Because of the delay, CVS proposed a new arrangement whereby it would "pay on scan," meaning that it would pay Dan Cake for all cookies sold up through December 25, 2007, but would not pay for any other cookies shipped. CVS only sold $19,000 of the cookies and the original contract had been for $197,351.08. CVS paid Dan Cake the $19,000 and sent back the remaining cookies. Dan Cake filed suit saying that CVS had taken delivery and owed Dan Cake for the cookies. What should the court do with the issues in the case? [*Dan Cake (Portugal) S.A. v. CVS Pharmacy, Inc.*, 862 F. Supp. 2d 120 (D.R.I.)]

4. Helen Thomas contracted to purchase a pool heater from Sunkissed Pools. As part of the $4,000 contract, Sunkissed agreed to install the pool heater, which was delivered to Thomas's home and left in the driveway. The heater was too heavy for Thomas to lift, and she was forced to leave it in the driveway because no one from Sunkissed responded to her calls about its installation. Subsequently, the heater disappeared from the driveway. Sunkissed maintained that the risk of loss had passed to Thomas. Thomas maintained that the failure to install the heater as promised is a breach of contract. Who should bear the risk for the

stolen pool heater? [In re *Thomas*, 182 B.R. 774 (Bankr. S.D. Fla.)]

5. Around June 2005, PPI purchased three pallets of computer wafers from Omneon Video Graphics. PPI requested that Omneon ship the wafers directly to the City University of New York, the end purchaser of the goods. Omneon and PPI agreed that Omneon would ship the wafers FOB Omneon's dock. Somewhere between the loading dock and City University, one pallet of the wafers disappeared. Who bears the loss for the lost pallet and why? [*OneBeacon Ins. Co. v. Hass Industries, Inc.*, 634 F.3d 1092 (9th Cir.)]

6. Using a bad check, B purchased a used automobile from a dealer. B then took the automobile to an auction at which the automobile was sold to a party who had no knowledge of its history. When B's check was dishonored, the dealer brought suit against the party who purchased the automobile at the auction. Was the dealer entitled to reclaim the automobile? [*Greater Louisville Auto Auction, Inc. v. Ogle Buick, Inc.*, 387 S.W.2d 17 (Ky.)]

7. Coppola, who collected coins, joined a coin club, First Coinvestors, Inc. The club would send coins to its members, who were to pay for them or return them within 10 days. What was the nature of the transaction? [*First Coinvestors, Inc. v. Coppola*, 388 N.Y.S.2d 833]

8. Would buying a car from a mechanic who works at a car dealership qualify as purchasing a car in the ordinary course of business? [*Steele v. Ellis*, 961 F. Supp. 1458 (D. Kan.)]

9. Does a pawnbroker who purchases property in good faith acquire good title to that property? Can the pawnbroker pass good title? [*Fly v. Cannon*, 813 S.W.2d 458 (Tenn. App.)]

10. Larsen Jewelers sold a necklace to Conway on a layaway plan. Conway paid a portion of the price and made additional payments from time to time. The necklace was to remain in the possession of Larsen until payment was fully made. The Larsen jewelry store was burglarized, and Conway's necklace and other items were taken. Larsen argued that Conway must bear the risk of loss. Conway sought recovery of the full value of the necklace. Decide. [*Conway v. Larsen Jewelry*, 429 N.Y.S.2d 378]

11. Future Tech International, Inc., is a buyer and distributor of Samsung monitors and other computer products. In 1993, Future Tech determined that brand loyalty was important to customers, and it sought to market its own brand of computer products. Future Tech, a Florida firm, developed its own brand name of MarkVision and entered into a contract in 1994 with Tae II Media, a Korean firm. The contract provided that Tae II Media would be the sole source and manufacturer for the MarkVision line of computer products.

The course of performance on the contract did not go well. Future Tech alleged that from the time the ink was dry on the contract, Tae II Media had no intention of honoring its commitment to supply computers and computer products to Future Tech. Future Tech alleged that Tae II Media entered into the contract with the purpose of limiting Future Tech's competitive ability because Tae II Media had its own Tech Media brand of computers and computer products.

Future Tech, through threats and demands, was able to have the first line of MarkVision products completed. Tae II Media delivered the computers to a boat but, while in transit, ordered the shipping line (Maersk Lines) to return the computers. The terms of their contract provided for delivery "FOB Pusan Korea." Future Tech filed suit, claiming that Tae II Media could not take the computer products because title had already passed to Future Tech. Is this interpretation of who has title correct? [*Future Tech Int'l, Inc. v. Tae II Media, Ltd.*, 944 F. Supp. 1538 (S.D. Fla.)]

12. Bakker Brothers of Idaho agreed to buy Charles E. Graff's 1989 onion seed crop. The contract required that the onion seeds have an 85 percent germination rate. Despite careful testing and advice from experts, Bakker Brothers could not get a germination rate on the seed tested higher than 62 to 69 percent. Bakker Brothers rejected the seed, notified Graff, and awaited instructions. Graff gave no instructions and the seed spoiled. Graff sought to recover the contract price from Bakker Brothers because the risk of loss had passed. The trial court granted summary judgment for Bakker Brothers, and Graff appealed. Was the trial court decision correct? Explain why or why not. [*Graff v. Bakker Brothers of Idaho, Inc.*, 934 P.2d 1228 (Wash. App.)]

13. Without permission, Grissom entered onto land owned by another and then proceeded to cut and sell the timber from the land. On learning that the timber had been sold, the owner of the land brought an action to recover the timber from the purchaser. The purchaser argued that he was a good-faith purchaser

who had paid value and therefore was entitled to keep the timber. Decide. [*Baysprings Forest Products, Inc. v. Wade*, 435 So. 2d 690 (Miss.)]

14. Brown Sales ordered goods from Eberhard Manufacturing Co. The contract contained no agreement about who would bear the risk of loss. There were no shipping terms. The seller placed the goods on board a common carrier with instructions to deliver the goods to Brown. While in transit, the goods were lost. Which party will bear the loss? Explain. [*Eberhard Manufacturing Co. v. Brown*, 232 N.W.2d 378 (Mich. App.)]

15. Develop a chart for when a seller's creditors can repossess goods in transit to a buyer.

CPA Questions

1. Bond purchased a painting from Wool, who is not in the business of selling art. Wool tendered delivery of the painting after receiving payment in full from Bond. Bond informed Wool that Bond would be unable to take possession of the painting until later that day. Thieves stole the painting before Bond returned. The risk of loss:

   a. Passed to Bond at Wool's tender of delivery.

   b. Passed to Bond at the time the contract was formed and payment was made.

   c. Remained with Wool, because the parties agreed on a later time of delivery.

   d. Remained with Wool, because Bond had not yet received the painting.

2. Which of the following statements applies to a sale on approval under the UCC Sales Article?

   a. Both the buyer and seller must be merchants.

   b. The buyer must be purchasing the goods for resale.

   c. Risk of loss for the goods passes to the buyer when the goods are accepted after the trial period.

   d. Title to the goods passes to the buyer on delivery of the goods to the buyer.

3. If goods have been delivered to a buyer pursuant to a sale or return contract, the:

   a. Buyer may use the goods but not resell them.

   b. Seller is liable for the expenses incurred by the buyer in returning the goods to the seller.

   c. Title to the goods remains with the seller.

   d. Risk of loss for the goods passes to the buyer.

4. Cey Corp. entered into a contract to sell parts to Deck, Ltd. The contract provided that the goods would be shipped "FOB Cey's warehouse." Cey shipped parts different from those specified in the contract. Deck rejected the parts. A few hours after Deck informed Cey that the parts were rejected, they were destroyed by fire in Deck's warehouse. Cey believed that the parts were conforming to the contract. Which of the following statements is correct?

   a. Regardless of whether the parts were conforming, Deck will bear the loss because the contract was a shipment contract.

   b. If the parts were nonconforming, Deck had the right to reject them, but the risk of loss remains with Deck until Cey takes possession of the parts.

   c. If the parts were conforming, risk of loss does not pass to Deck until a reasonable period of time after they are delivered to Deck.

   d. If the parts were nonconforming, Cey will bear the risk of loss, even though the contract was a shipment contract.

5. Under the Sales Articles of the UCC, when a contract for the sale of goods stipulates that the seller ship the goods by common carrier "FOB purchaser's loading dock," which of the parties bears the risk of loss during shipment?

   a. The purchaser, because risk of loss passes when the goods are delivered to the carrier.

   b. The purchaser, because title to the goods passes at the time of shipment.

   c. The seller, because risk of loss passes only when the goods reach the purchaser's loading dock.

   d. The seller, because risk of loss remains with the seller until the goods are accepted by the purchaser.

6. When do title and risk of loss for conforming goods pass to the buyer under a shipment contract covered by the Sales Article of the UCC?

   a. When the goods are identified and designated for shipment.

   b. When the goods are given to a common carrier.

   c. When the goods arrive at their destination.

   d. When the goods are tendered to the buyer at their destination.

Product Liability: Warranties and Torts

Learning Outcomes <<<

After studying this chapter, you should be able to

LO.1 List the theories of product liability

LO.2 Identify who may sue and who may be sued when a defective product causes harm

LO.3 Define and give examples of an express warranty

LO.4 List and explain the types of implied warranties

LO.5 Explain warranty protections under federal law

LO.6 State what constitutes a breach of warranty

LO.7 Describe the extent and manner in which implied warranties may be disclaimed under the UCC and the CISG

24-1   General Principles

What happens when goods do not work? Who can recover for injury caused by defective goods? What can you do when the goods are not as promised or pictured? When defective goods result in damages or injury to the buyer or other parties, the UCC and tort law provide remedies.

CPA

24-1a   Theories of Liability

Two centuries ago, a buyer was limited to recovery from a seller for breach of an express guarantee or for negligence or fraud. After the onset of mass production and distribution, however, these remedies had little value. A guarantee was good, but in the ordinary sales transaction no one stopped to get a guarantee. Few customers remembered to ask the manager of the supermarket to give a guarantee that the loaf of bread purchased was fit to eat. Further, negligence and fraud have become difficult to prove in a mass production world. How can one prove there was a problem in the production process for a can of soup prepared months earlier?

To give buyers protection from economic loss and personal injuries, the concept of warranty liability developed. **Warranties** are either express or implied and can be found in the UCC. There have been changes in warranty liability under the Revised UCC, but because of its limited adoption they are mentioned only briefly. Many courts have decided that still broader protection beyond the UCC contract remedies is required and have created the additional concept of **strict tort liability** (often also referred to as *product liability*) for defective goods.

There are five theories in law for what is often lumped into the term *product liability*, or the protection of buyers that also allows them recovery for injury and economic loss: express warranty, implied warranty, negligence, fraud, and strict tort liability. Any statutory remedies under consumer law or employment law are additional means of recovery. The plaintiff does not have a choice of all theories in every case; the facts of the case dictate the choices the plaintiff has available for possible theories of recovery.

warranty–promise, either express or implied, about the nature, quality, or performance of the goods.

strict tort liability– product liability theory that imposes absolute liability upon the manufacturer, seller, or distributor of goods for harm caused by defective goods.

24-1b   Nature of Harm

A defective product can cause harm to person, property, or economic interests. **For Example,** the buyer of a truck may be injured when, through a defect, the truck goes out of control and plunges down the side of a hill. Passengers in the truck, bystanders, or the driver of a car hit by the truck may also be injured. The defective truck may cause injury to a total stranger who seeks to rescue one of the victims. Property damage could occur if the buyer's truck careens off the road into a fence or even a house and causes damages. Another driver's car may be damaged. The economic interests of the buyer are affected by the discovery that the truck is defective. The defective truck is not as valuable as it would have been. If the buyer is required to rent a truck from someone else or loses an opportunity to haul freight for compensation, the fact that the truck was defective also causes commercial loss.

CPA

24-1c   Who Is Liable in Product Liability

privity of contract– relationship between a promisor and the promisee.

Until the early part of the twentieth century, only the parties to a sales contract could recover from each other on product liability issues. A seller was liable to the buyer, but the seller was not liable to others because they were not in **privity of contract** with the seller or in a direct contract relationship with the seller. This requirement of privity of contract has now been widely rejected.[1]

CPA

Who Can Recover under UCC Warranties

privity–succession or chain of relationship to the same thing or right, such as privity of contract, privity of estate, privity of possession.

Today, not only the buyer but also customers and employees of the buyer and even third persons or bystanders may recover because of harm caused by a defective product. Most states have abolished the requirement of **privity** when the person injured by a product is a member of the buyer's family or household or is a guest of the buyer and has sustained personal injury because of the product.[2] A few states require privity of contract, particularly when the plaintiff does not sustain personal injury or property damage and seeks to recover only economic loss.[3]

U.C.C. §2-318 provides alternatives for who can recover for breach of warranty. Alternative A extends warranty protection to "any individual who is in the family or household of the immediate buyer or the remote purchaser or who is a guest in the home of either…." Alternative B covers "any individual who may reasonably be expected to use, consume, or be affected by the goods." Alternative C covers the same groups as Alternative B but adds that the protections provided cannot be disclaimed.

Who Is Liable under UCC Warranties

Someone who is injured by a defective product can recover from the seller, the manufacturer of the product, and generally even the manufacturer of the component part of the product that caused the harm.[4] **For Example,** when a person is struck by an automobile because the driver has lost control because of the car's defective brakes, the person who was struck and injured may seek recovery from the seller and the manufacturer of the car. The maker of the brake assembly or system that the car manufacturer installed in the car may also be liable.

24-2 Express Warranties

A warranty may be express or implied. Both express and implied warranties operate as though the defendant had made an express promise or statement of fact. Both express and implied warranties are governed primarily by the UCC.

CPA

24-2a Definition of Express Warranty

express warranty– statement by the defendant relating to the goods, which statement is part of the basis of the bargain.

An **express warranty** is a statement of fact or promise of performance relating to the goods that becomes a basis of the buyer's bargain.[5]

---

[1] U.C.C. §2-318, Alternative A. The Code gives the states the option of adopting the provision summarized in this chapter or of making a wide abolition of the requirement of privity by adopting Alternative B or C of §2-318. As of January 2015, these states/areas had adopted the versions of §2-318 as follows: Alternative A (with modifications in many of the states) adopted in Alabama, Alaska, Arizona, Arkansas, Connecticut, District of Columbia, Florida, Georgia, Idaho, Illinois, Indiana, Kentucky, Maryland, Michigan, Mississippi, Missouri, Montana, Nebraska, Nevada, New Jersey, New Mexico, North Carolina, Ohio, Oklahoma, Oregon, Pennsylvania, Tennessee, Vermont, Washington, West Virginia, and Wisconsin. Alternative B adopted in Colorado, Delaware, Kansas, New York, South Carolina, South Dakota, Vermont, and Wyoming. Alternative C adopted in Hawaii, Iowa, Minnesota, North Dakota, Vermont, and Utah. Maine, Massachusetts, New Hampshire, Rhode Island, and Texas have their own statutes.

[2] In re *Whirlpool Corp. Front–Loading Washer Products Liability Litigation*, 45 F. Supp. 3d 706 (N.D. Ohio 2014). But see *Marshall v. Hyundai Motor America*, 51 F. Supp. 3d 451 (S.D.N.Y. 2014).

[3] *Wyman v. Ayer Properties*, 11 N.E.3d 1074 (Mass. 2014).

[4] *Benson v. Unilever U.S., Inc.*, 884 F. Supp. 2d 708 (S.D. Ill. 2012).

[5] U.C.C. §2-313; *CCB Ohio LLC v. Chemque Inc.*, 649 F. Supp. 2d 757 (S.D. Ohio 2009). *Ham v. Hain Celestial Group, Inc.*, 70 F. Supp. 3d 1188 (N.D. Cal. 2014) (claim that waffles are "all natural" was challenged because sodium acid pyrophosphate was in the waffles).

"Basis of the bargain" means that the buyer has purchased the goods because of what the seller has stated about those goods. A statement by the seller regarding the quality, capacity, or other characteristic of the goods is an express warranty. **For Example,** express warranties in sellers' statements are "This cloth is all wool," "This paint is for household woodwork," and "This engine can produce 50 horsepower." A representation that an airplane is a 2014 model is an express warranty. "This computer monitor has a glare-proof screen" is another example of an express warranty.

The manufacturer of the goods cannot isolate itself from claims that are communicated through retailers. **For Example,** WorldWide Wholesalers could purchase Pop-Tarts from Kellogg's. Kellogg's makes warranties to WorldWide Wholesalers directly through their contract relationship, one of privity. WorldWide Wholesalers then sells those Pop-Tarts to grocery stores, convenience stores, and perhaps even to commercial food distributors who then sell them to cafeterias in schools and nursing homes. WorldWide's buyers are remote purchasers. The warranty is not lost through the distribution chain.

24-2b Form of Express Warranty

No particular group of words is necessary to constitute an express warranty. A seller need not state that a warranty is being made or that one is intended. It is sufficient that the seller asserts a fact that becomes a basis of the bargain or transaction between the parties. U.C.C. §2-313(2) provides, "It is not necessary to the creation of an express warranty that the seller use formal words such as 'warrant' or 'guarantee' or that the seller have a specific intention to make a warranty."[6] If a warranty is a critical part of the bargain for the buyer, it cannot be disclaimed.

An express warranty can be written or printed as well as oral. For example, the words on the label of a can and in a newspaper ad for "boned chicken" constitute an express warranty that the can contains chicken that is free of bones.

Descriptions of goods, such as the illustrations in a seller's catalog, are express warranties. The express warranty given is that the goods will conform to the catalog illustrations.

24-2c Seller's Opinion or Statement of Value

A statement about the value of goods or the seller's opinion or commendation of the goods does not create a warranty.[7] Section 2-313(1)(b) provides, "an affirmation merely of the value of the goods or a statement purporting to be merely the seller's opinion or commendation of goods does not create a warranty."[8] A buyer cannot hold a seller liable for sales talk. **For Example,** sales talk or puffery by a seller that his cloth is "the best piece of cloth on the market" or that her glassware is "as good as anyone else's" is merely an opinion that the buyer cannot ordinarily treat as a warranty. Statements made by a cosmetics seller that its products are "the future of beauty" and are "just the product for [the plaintiff]" are sales talk arising in the ordinary course of merchandising. They do not constitute warranties.

The UCC does permit an exception to the sales talk liability exemption when the circumstances are such that a reasonable person would rely on such a statement. If the buyer has reason to believe that the seller has expert knowledge of the conditions of the market, and the buyer requests the seller's opinion as an expert, the buyer is entitled to accept as a fact the seller's statement of whether a particular good is the best obtainable. The opinion

---

[6] U.C.C. §2-313(2).
[7] *Id.*; *Giles v. Wyeth, Inc.,* 500 F. Supp. 2d 1063 (S.D. Ill. 2007); In re *Ford Motor Co. E-350 Van Products Liability Litigation,* 2008 WL 4126264, 66 U.C.C. Rep. Serv. 2d 726 (D.N.J. 2008).
[8] U.C.C. §2-313(1)(b).

statement could be reasonably regarded as forming part of the basis of the bargain. A statement by a florist that bulbs are of first-grade quality may be a warranty.[9]

CASE SUMMARY

German Beer Made in the USA

FACTS: Anheuser–Busch Companies, LLC (defendant or AB), is the brewer of Beck's beer. Beck's originated and was brewed in Germany from 1873 until 2012 when the defendant began brewing Beck's in St. Louis, Missouri.

The plaintiffs are consumers of Beck's who purchased Beck's "in reliance on representations contained on [the] packaging and Beck's history of being an imported beer from Germany." However, AB argues that the label on the beer reads, "Product of USA, Brauerei Beck & Co., St. Louis, MO." and that the words "BRAUEREI BECK & CO., BECK'S © BEER, ST. LOUIS, MO" appear on the bottom of the Beck's Beer carton.

The plaintiffs argue that it is in a font that is too small and difficult to read, its illegibility is further exacerbated by the fact that it is in metallic white print on a metallic silver background and it is blocked by the carton.

AB moved to have the consumers' complaint dismissed.

DECISION: The court found that saying a beer of a "Product of the USA" is an important fact that should have been disclosed by AB in marketing the beer as a German beer. The "Product of USA" disclaimer as printed on the actual cans and bottles themselves is difficult to read. Depending on the angle from which the viewer looks at the product, the "Product of USA" disclaimer can be obscured by overhead lighting because the disclaimer is printed in a white font against a shiny, metallic silver background. Identification is visible at any angle because the words are printed on a gray, matte background. Also, the "Product of USA" disclaimer is blocked by the carton. A consumer would have to either open the cartons of 12-pack bottles and 12-pack cans or lift the bottle from the 6-pack carton in order to see the "Product of USA" disclaimer. A reasonable consumer is not required to open a carton or remove a product from its outer packaging in order to ascertain whether representations made on the face of the packaging are misleading.

The court also held that the statement "BRAUEREI BECK & CO., BECK'S © BEER, ST. LOUIS, MO" may not be sufficiently descriptive to alert a reasonable consumer as to the location where Beck's is brewed. Although this statement contains the words "St. Louis, Mo[.]," there is nothing in the statement which discloses where Beck's is brewed. Also, "BRAUEREI BECK & CO., BECK'S © BEER, ST. LOUIS, MO" is printed underneath the carton. A reasonable consumer may not necessarily look at the underside of the carton in deciding whether to purchase a product.

The statement "Brewed under the German Purity Law of 1516" on the can was not actually true. The German Purity Law of 1516 allowed only inclusion of barley, hops, and water in beer, and Beck's actually contains yeast and other ingredients and additives. The court found that this reference to the German Purity Law was misleading.

The court also found that the phrase "German Quality" is not mere puffery when this phrase is considered in conjunction with: (1) other statements on cartons of Beck's, (2) the overall marketing campaign and efforts to maintain Beck's brand identity as a German beer, and (3) Beck's German heritage including its 139-year history of being brewed in Germany.

The court found that the allegations were sufficient to conclude that a reasonable consumer may be misled to believe that Beck's is an imported beer brewed in Germany.

The court denied AB's motion to dismiss. [*Marty v. Anheuser-Busch Companies, LLC,* 43 F. Supp. 2d 1333 (S.D. Fla. 2014)]

24-2d Warranty of Conformity to Description, Sample, or Model

When the contract is based in part on the understanding that the seller will supply goods according to a particular description or that the goods will be the same as the sample or a model, the seller is bound by an express warranty that the goods conform to the description,

---

[9] Likewise, a statement by an art gallery owner that a "painting is by Francis Bacon" is an express warranty. *Rogath v. Siebenmann,* 129 F.3d 261 (7th Cir. 1997). A promise that a washer would result in lower electricity bills is an express warranty. *Dzielak v. Whirlpool Corp.,* 26 F. Supp. 3d 304 (D.N.J. 2014).

sample, or model.[10] Section 2-313 of the UCC provides, "Any sample or model which is made part of the basis of the bargain creates an express warranty that the whole of the goods shall conform to the sample or model."[11] **For Example,** a blender sitting out in a store is a warranty that the blenders in the boxes below are the same. A model of a mobile home is an express warranty that the mobile home being sold contains the same features.

24-2e Federal Regulation of Express Warranties

A seller who makes a written express warranty for a consumer product costing more than $10 must conform to certain standards imposed by federal statute[12] and by regulations of the Federal Trade Commission (FTC).[13] The seller is not required to make any express warranty. However, if the seller does make an express warranty in a consumer sale, it must be stated in ordinary, understandable language and must be made available for inspection before purchasing so that the consumer may comparison shop.[14]

Full Warranties

If the seller or the label states that a full warranty is made, the seller is obligated to fix or replace a defective product within a reasonable time without cost to the buyer. If the product cannot be fixed or if a reasonable number of repair attempts are unsuccessful, the buyer has the choice of a cash refund or a free replacement. No unreasonable burden may be placed on a buyer seeking to obtain warranty service. **For Example,** a manufacturer offering a full warranty cannot require that the buyer pay the cost of sending the product to or from a warranty service point. A warrantor making a full warranty cannot require the buyer to return the product to a warranty service point if the product weighs over 35 pounds, to return a part for service unless it can be easily removed, or to fill out and return a warranty registration card shortly after purchase to make the warranty effective. If the manufacturer imposes any of these requirements, the warranty is not a "full warranty" under federal law and must be labeled a *limited warranty*. A **full warranty** runs with the product and lasts for its full term regardless of who owns the product.

Limited Warranties

A **limited warranty** is any warranty that does not meet the requirements for a full warranty. **For Example,** a warranty is limited if the buyer must pay any cost for repair or replacement of a defective product, if only the first buyer is covered by the warranty, or if the warranty covers only part of the product. A limited warranty must be conspicuously described as such by the seller.[15]

International Product Safety Laws in the United States

In response to quality issues related to foreign production of products sold in the United States (such as the lead paint issues in toys imported from China), Congress passed the **Consumer Product Safety Improvement Act (CPSIA),** which promulgated new

full warranty–obligation of a seller to fix or replace a defective product within a reasonable time without cost to the buyer.

limited warranty–any warranty that does not provide the complete protection of a full warranty.

Consumer Product Safety Improvement Act (CPSIA)–federal law that sets standards for the types of paints used in toys, a response to the lead paint found in toys made in China; requires tracking for international production; increases penalties.

---

[10] *Moore v. Apple, Inc.,* 73 F. Supp. 3d 1191 (N.D. Cal. 2014).

[11] U.C.C. §2-313(1)(c).

[12] The Magnuson-Moss Act, or Federal Consumer Product Warranty Law, can be found at 15 U.S.C. §2301 *et seq.*

[13] 16 C.F.R. §700.1 *et seq.*

[14] Federal warranty language rules apply only in consumer sales, or sales for personal or home use, not in business purchases. There are also state laws that can limit express warranties to the first purchaser. *Hoffman v. Daimler Trucks North America, LLC,* 940 F. Supp. 2d 347 (W.D. Va. 2013).

[15] The federal regulations here do not preempt Article 2 warranty coverage. *Wyeth v. Levine,* 555 U.S. 555 (2009). However, FDA regulations can preempt recovery against generic manufacturers of drugs who must use FDA-approved labeling only and not include additional warnings. *PLIVA, Inc. v. Mensing,* 131 S. Ct. 2567 (2011).

standards for product safety.[16] Under CPSIA, the products most affected are those for children under the age of 12. The act provides no discretion for lead levels; it prohibits lead in products for children under 12. Because of the outsourcing issues that resulted in the toys with lead paint making their way into the United States, the CPSIA requires accredited third-party laboratory testing, product tracking, labels, registration, and new warnings in ads and on Web sites about the manufacturing sources of toys. CPSIA increases to $100 million the penalties the Consumer Product Safety Commission can assess.

24-2f Effect of Breach of Express Warranty

If an express warranty is false, there is a breach of warranty. The warrantor is then liable. It is no defense that the seller or manufacturer who made the express warranty honestly believed that the warranty was true, had exercised due care in manufacturing or handling the product, or had no reason to believe that the warranty was false.

CASE SUMMARY

Fake Tiffany Lamps for $56,200 and a Disclaimer

FACTS: Richard W. La Trace attended an auction at B & B Antiques, Auction & Realty, a business owned and operated by Ray Webster, Deborah Webster, Bo Webster, and Laura Webster (collectively "the Websters"). La Trace purchased five lamps that were identified at the auction as "Tiffany" lamps and one lampshade that was also identified at the auction as a "Tiffany" product. La Trace spent a total of $56,200 on the lamps.

La Trace contacted Fontaine's Auction Gallery in Pittsfield, Massachusetts, to inquire about selling the lamps in an auction. Fontaine's sent Dean Lowry, an expert in Tiffany products, to examine La Trace's lamps and Lowry determined that the lamps were not authentic Tiffany products but were, in fact, reproductions. La Trace filed suit against the Websters and B & B for fraudulent suppression, fraudulent misrepresentation, breach of warranty, breach of contract, negligence, and wantonness.* The Websters claimed that they thought the lamps were authentic and pointed out that their sales brochure and "Conditions of Auction" document contained the following disclaimer:

1. All property is sold AS IS WHERE IS, and we make NO guarantees, warranties or representations, expressed or implied, with respect to the property or the correctness of the catalog or other description of authenticity of authorship, physical condition, size, quality, rarity, importance, provenance, exhibitions, literature or historical relevance of the property or otherwise. No statement anywhere, whether oral or written, shall be deemed such a guarantee, warranty or representation.

On a motion for summary judgment, the court found for the Websters, indicating that La Trace trusted blindly and should not have done so. La Trace appealed.

DECISION: The Websters' description of the lamps as "Tiffany" products became part of the basis of the bargain because the representations took place during the auction and were not accompanied by any qualifying statements indicating that the authenticity of the lamps was in doubt. Because it is assumed under the UCC that the object of every UCC-regulated sale is describable, the core description is nondisclaimable by a seller, being the basic foundation upon which every sales contract is made. The lamps here were sold with the core description of being Tiffany products. Although disclaimers in a sales brochure and a "Conditions of Auction" document may have been effective to prevent the formation of any express warranties that might otherwise have arisen in those documents, nothing in the language indicated that the disclaimer in the documents was effective to prevent a seller from making express warranties in the future. Judgment for La Trace. [*La Trace v. Webster*, 17 So. 3d 1210 (Ala. Civ. App. 2008)]

*B & B was dismissed from the case because it had not yet been properly formed as an LLC. See Chapter 40 for more information on forming a business entity properly.

---

[16] 15 U.S.C. §1278a.

24-3 Implied Warranties

Whenever a sale of goods is made, certain warranties are implied unless they are expressly excluded. Implied warranties differ depending on whether the seller is a merchant.

24-3a Definition of Implied Warranty

implied warranty— warranty that was not made but is implied by law.

An **implied warranty** is one that was not expressly made by the seller but that is implied in certain circumstances by law. An implied warranty arises automatically from the fact that a sale has been made regardless of the seller's conduct.

Express warranties arise because they form part of the basis on which the sale has been made. Implied warranties can exist independent of express warranties. When both express and implied warranties exist, they are interpreted as consistent, if possible. If the warranties cannot be applied together, then the express warranty prevails over any implied warranty except that an implied warranty of fitness for a particular purpose prevails over an express warranty.

24-3b Implied Warranties of Sellers

Sellers give different types of implied warranties.

Warranty of Title

Every seller, by the mere act of selling, makes an implied warranty that the seller's title to the goods is good and that the seller has the right to transfer title to the goods.[17]

warranty of title— implied warranty that title to the goods is good and transfer is proper.

The **warranty of title** may be disclaimed either by using the words, "There is no warranty of title," or by certain circumstances.[18] If a buyer has reason to know that the seller does not claim to hold the title or that the seller is limited in what can be promised, the warranty of title is disclaimed. **For Example,** no warranty of title arises when the seller makes the sale in a representative capacity, such as a sheriff, an auctioneer, or an administrator of a decedent's estate. Similarly, no warranty arises when the seller makes the sale as a creditor disposing of a debtor's collateral (security). The damages for warranty of title are often the purchase price because the buyer may have to surrender the goods to their rightful owner.[19]

Warranty against Encumbrances

warranty against encumbrances— warranty that there are no liens or other encumbrances to goods except those noted by the seller.

Every seller makes an implied **warranty against encumbrances,** that is, that the goods will be delivered free from any security interest or any other lien or encumbrance of which the buyer at the time of the sales transaction had no knowledge. If the seller sells an automobile to the buyer and then delivers a car with an outstanding lien on it that was unknown to the buyer at the time of the sale, there is a breach of the warranty against encumbrances.

Warranty of Fitness for a Particular Purpose[20]

A buyer may intend to use the goods for a particular or unusual purpose, as contrasted with the ordinary use for which they are customarily sold. If the seller states that the goods will be fit for the buyer's purpose with the buyer relying on the seller's skill or judgment to select or furnish suitable goods, and the seller, at the time of contracting, knows or has reason to know of both the buyer's particular purpose and the buyer's reliance on the seller's

---

[17] U.C.C. §2-312. The key change in the language in Revised Article 2 is that the seller warrants that the buyer will not be subjected to unreasonable litigation.

[18] *Rochester Equipment & Maintenance v. Roxbury Mountain Service, Inc.*, 891 N.Y.S.2d 781 (N.Y.A.D. 2009).

[19] *Mayberry v. Volkswagen of America, Inc.*, 692 N.W.2d 226 (Wis. 2005).

[20] U.C.C. §2-315. The warranty does not apply when there are sophisticated users. *Pike v. Trinity Industries, Inc.*, 34 F. Supp. 3rd 1193 (M.D. Fla. 2014).

E-COMMERCE & CYBERLAW

"Wii" Were Hurt

Nintendo's "Wii" video game system features games with simulation of tennis and boxing. To play the game, the players use a motion-sensitive controller in their hand. When playing the game, some players, in making the motions necessary for the sport, have lost control of their controllers. The controllers have crashed into other objects, including television sets, and then injured the players. Players who have been so injured brought a class action suit against Nintendo for a defective wrist strap on the controllers, designed to keep the controllers from flying out of control. Although the class action was not certified, the court held that there could be remedies on an individual basis for problems with the design of the physical equipment used with computers.

[*Elvig v. Nintendo of America, Inc.*, 696 F. Supp. 2d 1207 (D. Colo. 2010)]

judgment, then the seller has created an implied warranty of fitness for a particular purpose.[21] **For Example,** when the seller represents to a buyer that the two hamsters being sold are of the same gender and can safely occupy the same cage with no offspring, an implied warranty of fitness has been given. When the buyer makes the purchase without relying on the seller's skill and judgment, no warranty of fitness for a particular purpose arises.[22]

CPA   ## 24-3c Additional Implied Warranties of Merchant Sellers

A seller who deals in goods of the kind in question is classified as a merchant by the UCC and is held to a higher degree of responsibility for the product than one who is merely making a casual sale.

Warranty against Infringement

Unless otherwise agreed, every merchant seller warrants that the goods will be delivered free of the rightful claim of any third person by way of patent, copyright, or trademark infringement.

For Example, if a buyer purchases videos from a seller who is later discovered to be a bootlegger of the films on the videos, the buyer has a cause of action against the seller for any damages he experiences for perhaps renting out the bootlegged videos. Under Revised Article 2, the seller can disclaim the warranty against infringement.

implied warranty of the merchantability–group of promises made by the seller, the most important of which is that the goods are fit for the ordinary purposes for which they are sold.

Warranty of Merchantability or Fitness for Normal Use

A merchant seller makes an **implied warranty of the merchantability** of the goods sold.[23] This warranty is a group of promises, the most important of which is that the goods are fit for the ordinary purposes for which they are sold. This warranty, unless disclaimed, is given in every sale of goods by a merchant. Section 2-314 provides, "Unless excluded or modified, a warranty that the goods shall be merchantable is implied in a contract for their sale if the seller is a merchant with respect to goods of that kind."[24]

---

[21] U.C.C. §2-315. *Nationwide Agribusiness Ins. Co. v. SMA Elevator Const. Inc.*, 816 F. Supp. 2d 631 (N.D. Iowa 2011).
[22] *Berge Helene Ltd. v. GE Oil & Gas, Inc.*, 830 F. Supp. 2d 235 (S.D. Tex. 2011). Manufacturing to buyer's specifications precludes recovery for breach of the warranty of fitness for a particular purpose. *Simmons v. Washing Equipment Technologies* 857 N.Y.S.2d 412 (2008).
[23] U.C.C. §2-314; *Lawson v. Hale*, 902 N.E.2d 267 (Ind. App. 2009); *Trujillo v. Apple Computer, Inc.*, 581 F. Supp. 2d 935 (N.D. Ill. 2008); limited battery life is not a breach of the implied warranty of merchantability.
[24] U.C.C. §2-314.

CASE SUMMARY

Cell Phone Shutdowns and Merchantability: Do We Just Have to Live With It?

FACTS: Amy Rothbaum (plaintiff) and others brought suit against Samsung Telecommunications (defendant) because they alleged that Samsung knowingly sold its 4G phones with a design defect that causes the phones to shut down randomly (the Random Shutdown Defect). Rothbaum had purchased a Samsung Captivate phone from an AT&T Store in Holyoke, Massachusetts. "Within months" of her purchase, the phone "began shutting down randomly." The phone first shut down randomly in mid-December 2010. During a three-week period in December 2010, her phone shut down at least three times.

When her phone unexpectedly shut down while in sleep mode, Rothbaum was required to press and hold the "On" button to restart the phone. She did not, however, have to remove and reinsert the battery before turning the phone back on.

Rothbaum went to an AT&T service center in late December 2010 to complain about this problem. The representative performed a factory reset and gave her a phone number to call in case the problems persisted.

Rothbaum's phone again shut down on or about January 3, 2011, while "it was powered on and was in sleep mode." Rothbaum then called AT&T, which sent her a replacement battery, which she received in mid-January. Even after she replaced the battery, the phone "continued to shut down" from January 17 to January 21, 2011. She described these shutdowns as "annoying."

On March 1, 2011, Rothbaum went to the AT&T store where she had purchased the phone and reported that her problems were persisting. An AT&T representative gave her the Replacement Phone, which was the same model.

"Within a day or two" the Replacement Phone shut down randomly while in sleep mode. As with the original phone, Rothbaum only had to press the "On" button to restart the Replacement Phone. Rothbaum testified that such shutdowns occurred "no more frequently than once a month." She never needed to remove and reinsert the battery to turn the phone back on.

Rothbaum continued to use the phone for about 18 months, from March 2011 to September 2012, when she gave the Replacement Phone to her attorneys for testing in connection with this case.

Rothbaum also loaded on the Replacement Phone and used several applications ("apps") that were not created by Samsung, including Facebook, Twitter, and Words with Friends. She also used several preloaded applications, such as Gmail.

After negotiating with Rothbaum for the opportunity to test the Replacement Phone, Samsung had it inspected by one of its senior engineers in Korea. Through a variety of tests, the phone did not randomly shut down, either in sleep mode or during active use. The engineer concluded that the phone did not suffer from any shutdown defect and that the reported problems might be attributable to installed apps, such as Words with Friends.

Between July 2010 and June 2011, Samsung produced at least 985,000 i897 Samsung phones at issue in this case. In a technical service memo to AT&T, Samsung stated that "[a] small percentage of SGH–I897 handsets [the 'Captivate' model of Samsung phone] may exhibit a condition where the handset will power off after going to sleep mode." The bulletin explained that this problem occurred only in phones within a certain range of IMEI numbers. The service bulletin also explained that phone servicers should remove and replace certain capacitors to remedy the problem.

There was a steady increase in the return rate for the Samsung "Captivate" model between August 2010 and January 2011. In January 2011, 51.97 percent of returns were categorized under "Powers On/Off."

This document also stated that, "[d]ue to growing concern" about these power-related issues, Samsung sampled 200 of the returned phones to determine the cause. It found that 43 units, or 22 percent, reproduced the powering-off symptom, and that all of these units had been produced before the "corrective action" was implemented on November 6, 2010. Overall, Samsung's internal documents indicate that less than 5 percent of Samsung phones produced before November 2010 were returned for any power-related reason and that less than 1.25 percent of phones produced after the November 2010 remedy were returned for any power-related reason.

Rothbaum alleges that Samsung was aware of this defect but continued to sell the defective phones, and her suit alleged that Samsung breached its implied warranty of merchantability.

Samsung moved for summary judgment.

DECISION: Generally, courts have found that when a plaintiff has only a minor problem with his or her phone, such an inconvenience is insufficient to prove a breach of the implied warranty of merchantability. For example, in In re *Google Phone Litigation*, No. 10–CV–01177–EJD, 2012 WL 3155571 (N.D. Cal. Aug. 2, 2012), the plaintiffs alleged that their smartphones' data connections were inconsistent, leading to difficulty receiving or placing calls. The district court rejected this as a basis for a breach of the implied warranty, explaining that "[p]laintiffs' allegations that the

Cell Phone Shutdowns and Merchantability: Do We Just Have to Live With It? continued

phone drops or misses calls are insufficient to demonstrate that this alleged defect is more than inconvenience or that the Plaintiffs cannot re-initiate these calls such that the phone is unfit for its ordinary purpose."

Rothbaum claims that Samsung breached the implied warranty of merchantability under Massachusetts law by providing a defective phone. The court finds that a reasonable factfinder would have to conclude that the Replacement Phone did not have an imperfection substantial enough to

constitute a breach of the implied warranty of merchantability, and that even if the Replacement Phone did have a problem of that magnitude, the plaintiff has not shown that the defendant's proposed remedy—a fully functioning replacement phone—would fail of its essential purpose.

Accordingly, the court allowed the defendant's motion for summary judgment on this theory of liability. [*Rothbaum v. Samsung Telecommunications America, LLC*, **52 F. Supp. 3d 185 (D. Mass. 2014)**]

24-3d Implied Warranties in Particular Sales

Particular types of sales may involve special considerations in terms of the seller's liability and the buyer's rights.

Sale on Buyer's Specifications

When the buyer furnishes the seller with exact specifications for the preparation or manufacture of goods, the same warranties arise as in the case of any other sale of such goods by the particular seller. No warranty of fitness for a particular purpose can arise, however. It is clear that the buyer is purchasing on the basis of the buyer's own decision and is not relying on the seller's skill and judgment. Similarly, the manufacturer is not liable for loss caused by a product that causes an injury but that is not defective.[25]

Sale of Secondhand or Used Goods

Under the UCC, there is a warranty of merchantability in the sale of both new and used goods unless it is specifically disclaimed. However, with respect to used goods, what is considered "fit for normal use" under the warranty of merchantability will be a lower standard. Some courts still follow their pre-Code law under which no warranties of fitness arise in the sale of used goods.

CPA ### Sale of Food or Drink

The implied warranty of merchantability also applies to the purchase of food in grocery stores and restaurants. The food sold must be of average quality and fit for its ordinary purpose, which is consumption by humans.[26] **For Example,** the types of restaurant and grocery store cases brought under the warranty of merchantability include those in which the buyer or customer finds foreign substances such as grasshoppers in a can of baked beans.[27]

The application of this warranty to food cases becomes more complex when it is not a nail in a can of crabmeat, but crab shell in a can of crabmeat, or a cherry pit in the cherries of a McDonald's cherry pie. Some courts refuse to impose warranty liability if the thing in the food that caused the harm was naturally present, such as crab shell in crabmeat, prune stones in stewed prunes, or bones in canned fish. Other courts reject this foreign substance/natural substance liability test. They hold that there is liability if the seller does not deliver to the buyer goods of the character that the buyer reasonably expected. Under this view, there is a breach of the implied warranty of fitness for normal

---

[25] *Chavez v. Glock,* 144 Cal. Rptr. 3d 326 (Cal. App. 2012).
[26] *Manley v. Doe,* 849 F. Supp. 2d 594 (E.D.N.C. 2012).
[27] *Metty v. Shurfine Central Corporation,* 736 S.W.2d 527 (Mo. 1987). But see *Chambers-Johnson v. Applebee's Restaurant,* 101 So. 3d 473 (La. App. 2012).

use if the buyer reasonably expected the food to be free of harm-causing natural things, such as shells and bones that could cause harm.[28]

CASE SUMMARY

A Turkey of a Sandwich

FACTS: Stanley Pinkham consumed a hot turkey sandwich during his break as a line cook at Dysart's Truck Stop and Restaurant. Cargill, Inc., manufactured the boneless turkey product in Pinkham's sandwich, and the kitchen staff at Dysart's occasionally found pieces of bone in that turkey product. In the middle of eating the sandwich, Mr. Pinkham experienced severe and sudden pain in his upper abdominal area and thought that he might be suffering from a heart attack. He was taken by ambulance to the hospital where a doctor concluded that Mr. Pinkham's "esophageal tear or perforation" was caused by bones that were later removed from his esophagus. Mr. Pinkham brought suit against Cargill and Poultry Products of Maine for selling defective and unreasonably dangerous goods. The lower court granted summary judgment for Cargill and the Estate appealed.

DECISION: Currently, there are two tests that courts apply when faced with a defective food product claim. The traditional test is called the "foreign-natural" doctrine. The "foreign-natural" doctrine provides there is no liability if the food product is natural to the ingredients; whereas, liability exists if the substance is foreign to the ingredients, and the manufacturer can be held liable for injuries. The reasonable expectation test provides that, regardless whether a substance in a food product is natural to an ingredient thereof, liability will lie for injuries caused by the substance where the consumer of the product would not reasonably have expected to find the substance in the product. The court adopted the reasonable expectation.

The Estate presented evidence that creates a genuine issue of material fact as to whether the turkey product caused Pinkham's injury. Whether a consumer would reasonably expect to find a particular item in a food product is normally a question of fact that is left to a jury. At trial, the jury will have an opportunity to determine whether a foreign body in the turkey product caused Pinkham's injury, what the foreign body was, and whether Cargill is liable as a result. [*Estate of Pinkham v. Cargill, Inc.*, 55 A.3d 1 (Me. 2012)] Reversed.

24-3e   Necessity of Defect

To impose liability for breach of the implied warranty of merchantability, the buyer must show that the product is defective and that defect caused harm. A product may be defective because there is (1) a manufacturing defect, (2) a design defect, (3) inadequate instruction on how to use the product, or (4) inadequate warning against dangers involved in using the product.

For Example, if the manufacturer's blueprint shows that there should be two bolts at a particular place and the factory puts in only one bolt, there is a manufacturing defect. If the two bolts are put in but the product breaks because four bolts are required to provide sufficient strength, there is no manufacturing defect, but there is a design defect. A product that is properly designed and properly manufactured may be dangerous because the user is not given sufficient instructions on how to use the product. Also, a product is defective if there is a danger that is not obvious and there is no warning at all or a warning that does not describe the full danger.[29]

24-3f   Warranties in the International Sale of Goods

The warranties of both merchantability and fitness for a particular purpose exist under the Convention on Contracts for the International Sale of Goods (CISG). In most cases, the provisions are identical to those of the UCC. Sellers, however, can expressly disclaim the convention's warranties without mentioning merchantability or making the disclaimer conspicuous.

---

[28] *Parker v. Wendy's Intern., Inc.*, 41 F. Supp. 2d 487 (E.D. Va. 2014).
[29] *Houston v. Bayer Healthcare Pharmaceuticals, Inc.*, 16 F. Supp. 3d 1341 (N.D. Ala. 2014).

THINKING THINGS THROUGH

What's Foreign to You ...

Based on the discussion and the *Pinkham* case, decide which of the following would be considered a breach of the implied warranty of merchantability:

A customer ordered "pecan chicken" from T.G.I. Friday's, described on the menu as chicken with "a breaded mixture of pecans and bread crumbs." He broke a tooth when he bit into a pecan shell that was in the breading. [*Carlton v. T.G.I. Friday's*, **2006 WL 5129475 (Ohio Com. Pl.)]**

A customer suffered an injury to the throat as a result of a bone in a chicken sandwich getting stuck in his throat. [*Ruvolo v. Homovich*, **778 N.E.2d 661 (Ohio App. 2002)]**

A customer bit into a Baby Ruth candy bar, manufactured by Standard Brands, that contained a "snake bone (vertebrae)" and the customer experienced severe psychological difficulty. [*Gates v. Standard Brands Inc.*, **719 P.2d 130 (Wash. App. 1986)]**

Standard Candy manufactures the Goo Goo Cluster candy bar, featuring peanuts from Jimbo's. James Newton purchased a Goo Goo, and when he bit into it, he bit down on an undeveloped peanut. The result was a broken tooth. [*Newton v. Standard Candy Co.*, **2008 WL 752599 (D. Neb.)]**

CPA   24-4   **Disclaimer of Warranties**

The seller and the buyer may ordinarily agree that there will be no warranties. In some states, disclaimers of warranties are prohibited for reasons of public policy or consumer protection.

24-4a   **Validity of Disclaimer**

Warranties may be disclaimed by agreement of the parties, subject to the limitation that such a provision must not be unconscionable, must be conspicuous, and in certain cases must use certain language.[30]

Conspicuousness

A disclaimer provision is made conspicuous when it appears in a record under a conspicuous heading that indicates there is an exclusion or modification of warranties. A heading cannot be relied on to make such a provision conspicuous when the heading is misleading and wrongfully gives the impression that there is a warranty. **For Example,** the heading "Vehicle Warranty" is misleading if the provision that follows contains a limitation of warranties. A disclaimer that is hidden in a mass of materials or records handed to the buyer is not conspicuous and does not exclude warranties. A disclaimer of warranties under a posted notice of "Notice to Retail Buyers" has no effect. When a disclaimer of warranties is not conspicuous, the implied warranties apply to the buyer.[31]

Unconscionability and Public Policy

An exclusion of warranties made in the manner specified by the UCC is not unconscionable. In some states, warranty disclaimers are invalid because they are contrary to public policy or because they are prohibited by consumer protection laws.

---

[30] U.C.C. §2-316; In re *Rafter Seven Ranches LP*, 546 F.2d 1194 (10th Cir. 2008).
[31] A warranty disclaimer written in all caps just below the signature line is conspicuous. *Semitekol v. Monaco Coach Corp.*, 582 F. Supp. 2d 1009 (N.D. Ill. 2008).

24-4b **Particular Language for Disclaimers**

To waive the warranty of merchantability, the record must contain the following language: "The seller undertakes no responsibility for the quality of the goods except as otherwise provided in this contract."[32] The required language for waiving the warranty of fitness for a particular purpose is as follows: "The seller assumes no responsibility that the goods will be fit for any particular purpose for which you may be buying these goods, except as otherwise provided in the contract."[33]

The use of terms such as *as is* can also disclaim both of these warranties, as it does for merchant transactions, but the disclaimers must be in the record and must be conspicuously set forth in that record.

Figure 24-1 provides a summary of the warranties under Article 2 and the methods for making disclaimers.

FIGURE 24-1	UCC Warranties		
NAME OF WARRANTY	**CREATION**	**RESTRICTION**	**DISCLAIMER**
Express	Affirmation of fact, promise of performance (includes samples, models, descriptions)	Must be part of the basis of the bargain	Cannot make a disclaimer inconsistent with an express warranty
Implied warranty of merchantability	Given in every sale of goods by a merchant ("fit for ordinary purposes")	Only given by merchants	Must use statutory language disclaimer of "as is" or "with all faults"; must be conspicuous in the record
Implied warranty of fitness for a particular purpose	Seller knows of buyer's reliance for a particular use (buyer is ignorant)	Seller must have knowledge; buyer must rely on seller	(1) Must have a record (2) Must be conspicuous (3) Also disclaimed with "as is" or "with all faults"
Title	Given in every sale	Does not apply in circumstances where apparent warranty is not given	Must say "there is no warranty of title"
Magnuson-Moss (federal consumer product warranty law)	Only consumer products of $10 or more	Must label "full" or "limited"	

---

[32] U.C.C. §2-316(2). If the seller undertakes to repair the goods after their exclusion, the waiver becomes null. *Sabbath v. Martin*, 2009 WL 3449096 (La. App. 2009).

[33] *Id.*

24-4c **Exclusion of Warranties by Examination of Goods**

For an inspection of goods by the buyer to constitute a waiver, the seller must demand that the buyer inspect the goods as part of the contracting process. The seller may not use inspection as a defense to warranty issues if that demand was not made at the time the parties contracted.[34]

24-4d **Postsale Disclaimer**

Frequently, a statement purporting to exclude or modify warranties appears for the first time in a written contract sent to confirm or memorialize an oral contract made earlier. The exclusion or modification may likewise appear in an invoice, a bill, or an instruction

ETHICS & THE LAW

Executive App Promises, App Disclaimers

Former Apple executive Scott Forstall announced the launch of Apple Maps, a navigational app that could perform on any device running the then-latest version of Apple's mobile operating system (iOS 6). Apple released the iPhone 5, which used the new iOS 6 and included Apple Maps, on September 21, 2012. Apple Maps proved to be underdeveloped and lacking the amount of data necessary to provide consistently accurate mapping. Consumers complained that the application mislabeled landmarks, streets, and addresses, and led them to inaccurate locations. On September 25, 2012, Apple issued a statement saying that the company was "continuously improving" Maps and "appreciates all the customer feedback." A few days later, on September 28, 2012, Apple CEO Tim Cook posted a letter apologizing for Apple Maps' shortfalls and suggesting that customers use other applications or Web sites while Apple worked to improve the application.

The iPhone 5 includes a limited, one-year warranty (Hardware Warranty) that covers the iPhone's hardware against defects in materials and workmanship for a period of one year from the date of original retail purchase by the end-user purchaser. The Hardware Warranty does not cover any software installed on the iPhone: "This warranty does not apply to ... any software, even if packaged or sold with Apple hardware ... Apple does not warrant that the operation of the Apple Product will be uninterrupted or error-free." By using the iPhone, buyers agree to be bound by the terms of the Hardware Warranty. The warranty plainly states in capitalized typeface that it is exclusive and in lieu of all other written warranties, express or implied.

In Paragraph 7.3 of the software licensing agreement, Apple states in capitalized typeface that Maps is provided "as is," "as available," and "without warranty of any kind," and disclaims all implied warranties, including implied warranty of merchantability and fitness for particular purpose. Paragraph 7.4 states that Apple does not warrant that Maps will be "uninterrupted or error free."

Nancy Romine Minkler purchased an iPhone 5 and brought suit against Apple for breach of express warranty, breach of implied warranty, and negligent misrepresentation. The court found that Apple had disclaimed any warranties and dismissed the case. Ms. Minkler alleges that the executives told a story of a fabulous application and made promises about its performance and that the company should be held liable. She also noted that executives encouraged owners to hang on and use the iMaps program so that Apple could get feedback and get the app improved. CEO Tim Cook's September 28, 2012, letter encouraging consumers to use its products because "the more our customers use our Maps the better it will get" created an express warranty. She said she believed their promises before she bought the phone and then hung on based on statements such as Cook's with the result being that she went past the one-year limit on filing a claim on her phone. Evaluate the ethical issues in this situation.

[***Minkler v. Apple, Inc.***, 65 F. Supp. 3d 810 (N.D. Cal. 2014)]

---

[34] U.C.C. §2-316(3)(b).

manual delivered to the buyer at or after the time the goods are received. Such postsale disclaimers do not serve to disclaim warranties that arose at the time of the sale.

24-5 **Other Theories of Product Liability**

In addition to recovery for breach of an express guarantee, an express warranty, or an implied warranty, a plaintiff in a given product liability case may be able to recover for negligence, fraud, or strict tort liability.

CPA   ### 24-5a **Negligence**

negligence–failure to exercise due care under the circumstances that results in harm proximately caused to one owed a duty to exercise due care.

A person injured because of the defective condition of a product may be entitled to recover from the seller or manufacturer for the damages for **negligence.** The injured person must be able to show that the seller was negligent in the preparation or manufacture of the article or failed to provide proper instructions and warnings of dangers. An action for negligence rests on common law tort principles. Negligence does not require privity of contract.

24-5b **Fraud**

The UCC expressly preserves the pre-Code law governing fraud. A person defrauded by a distributor's or manufacturer's false statements about a product generally will be able to recover damages for the harm sustained because of such misrepresentations. False statements are fraudulent if the party who made them did so with knowledge that they were false or with reckless indifference to their truthfulness.

CPA   ### 24-5c **Strict Tort Liability**

Strict tort liability exists without regard to whether the person injured is a purchaser, a consumer, or a third person, such as a bystander.[35] It is no defense that privity of contract does not exist between the injured party and the defendant. Likewise, it is no defense that the defect was found in a component part purchased from another manufacturer.[36] **For Example,** defective tires sold on a new car were probably purchased from a tire supplier by the auto manufacturer. However, the manufacturer is not excused from liability.

Strict tort liability requires that the defect in the product exists at the time it left the control of the manufacturer or distributor. The defective condition is defined in the same way as under negligence: defective by manufacturing error or oversight, defective by design, or defective by the failure to warn.[37] There is liability if the product is defective and unreasonably dangerous and has caused harm. It is immaterial whether the seller was negligent or whether the user was contributorily negligent. Knowledge of the defect is not a requirement for liability. Assumption of risk by the injured party, on the other hand, is a defense available to the seller.[38]

---

[35] The concept of strict tort liability was judicially declared in *Greenman v. Yuba Power Products*, 377 P.2d 897 (Cal. 1963). This concept has been incorporated in the Restatement (Second) and (Third) of Torts as §402A.
[36] *Ford v. Beam Radiator, Inc.*, 708 So. 2d 1158 (La. App. 1998).
[37] *Nationwide Mut. Ins. Co. v. Barton Solvents Inc.*, 855 N.W.2d 145 (S.D. 2014).
[38] *Hilaire v. Dewalt Indus. Tool Co.*, 54 F. Supp. 3d 223 (E.D.N.Y. 2014).

24-5d Cumulative Theories of Liability

The theories of product liability are not mutually exclusive. A given set of facts may give rise to two or more theories of liability. **For Example,** suppose that a manufacturer advertises, "Coaches! Protect your players' eyes! Shatterproof sunglasses for baseball." If the glasses shattered and injured a player, an express warranty, an implied warranty, an implied warranty for a particular purpose, and a strict tort liability could apply for recovery.

CASE SUMMARY

The Toddler and the Shredder

FACTS: Amy Thomas (married to Jason Thomas) purchased the MailMate Paper Shredder online from Staples.com on November 15, 2006. The shredder was manufactured, assembled, and distributed by Executive Machines d/b/a Jeam Imports. In choosing the paper shredder, Amy Thomas said that her main considerations were that the shredder be compact and easy to use. The shredder arrived shortly after the date of purchase and was placed on a countertop in the Thomas' kitchen, routinely used there for the purpose of keeping their "junk mail" under control and securing their personal information. In using the machine, either Jason or Amy would stand in front of the counter and insert material into the machine to be shredded.

On May 25, 2008, Amy Thomas was in the process of shredding mail in the MailMate Paper Shredder when their 19-month-old daughter, Madalyn, started crying and began to pull on Amy's leg. At this point, while the shredder was still operating, Amy picked up Madalyn and placed her on her left hip. Having made no attempt to unplug or turn off the shredder, Amy turned away from Madalyn to get Madalyn some candy; as Amy turned back around to face Madalyn, she saw that Madalyn's left hand had become stuck in the shredder. Upon realizing that Madalyn's fingers were stuck in the shredder, Amy unplugged the machine.

Amy does not recall whether there was noise coming from the machine when Madalyn's fingers became stuck, whether Madalyn pulled away from her in order to reach out to the machine, or whether any portion of the envelope she had placed in the machine was still in the process of shredding. Jason was able to extract Madalyn's hand from the shredder with the use of a crowbar. Subsequently, Madalyn was transported to Wilkes–Barre Hospital for initial examination and then transported to Hershey Medical Center, where surgery was performed. Madalyn's two partially amputated fingers could not be reattached.

Mr. Thomas, on behalf of Madalyn (Plaintiffs), brought suit against Staple's and the manufacturer of the paper shredder and retailer, alleging claims for strict liability, negligence, breach of express warranty, breach of implied warranty, and compensatory and punitive damages. Staples and Executive Machines (defendants) moved for summary judgment.

DECISION: The court found that strict liability and negligence theories could be used for the case. Section 402A makes sellers liable for harm caused to consumers by unreasonably dangerous products even if the seller exercised reasonable care. A product can be defective in design when the foreseeable risks of harm posed by the product could have been reduced or avoided by the adoption of a reasonable alternative design by the seller or other distributor, or because of inadequate instructions or warnings when the foreseeable risks of harm posed by the product could have been reduced or avoided by the provision of reasonable instructions or warnings by the seller or other distributor, or a predecessor in the commercial chain of distribution, and the omission of the instructions or warnings renders the product not reasonably safe.

The court found that the small size of the shredder, the size and location of the openings and the blades, and the force of the pull made the product more dangerous and concluded that there was a jury question as to whether Staples and MailMate were negligent in designing the MailMate Paper Shredder. The case was remanded for a jury to determine these issues. [***Thomas v. Staples, Inc.*, 2 F. Supp. 3d 647 (E.D. Pa. 2014)**]

Make the Connection

Summary

Five theories protect parties from loss caused by nonconforming goods: (1) express warranty, (2) implied warranty, (3) negligence, (4) fraud, and (5) strict tort liability.

Theories of product liability are not mutually exclusive. A given set of facts may give rise to liability under two or more theories.

The requirement of privity of contract (that is, the parties to the sales contract for warranty liability) has been widely rejected. The law is moving toward the conclusion that persons harmed because of an improper product may recover from anyone who is in any way responsible. The requirement of privity has been abolished by most states, and remote buyers as well as their families, members of their households, and guests are covered under the UCC warranties.

Warranties may be express or implied. The types of implied warranties are the warranty of title, the implied warranty of merchantability, and the implied warranty of fitness for a particular purpose. The warranty of title provides that the transfer is lawful, the title is good, and there are no infringement issues. Under Revised Article 2, the warranty of title also protects the buyer against unreasonable litigation. The warranty of merchantability is given by merchants and warrants that the goods are of average quality and will do what those types of goods commonly can do. The implied warranty of fitness for a particular purpose is given in those circumstances in which the buyer relies on the seller's expertise and the seller is aware of that reliance and offers a recommendation on the types of goods.

Express warranties arise from statements of fact and promises of performance made by the seller to the buyer that become a part of the basis for the buyer contracting. Express warranties arise from samples, models, and descriptions.

Warranties may be disclaimed by agreement of the parties provided the disclaimer is not unconscionable. Merchants can have oral disclaimers, but for consumers, warranty disclaimers must be in a record and must be conspicuous. Also for consumers, certain language must be used to disclaim each type of warranty. However, for both merchants and nonmerchants, the use of terms such as *as is* or *with all faults* can disclaim both the warranty of merchantability and the implied warranty of fitness for a particular purpose (although for consumers, there must still be a record and the language must be conspicuous).

The warranties of merchantability and fitness exist under the CISG. However, disclaimers under the CISG need not mention merchantability, nor must such disclaimers be conspicuous.

The strict tort liability plaintiff must show that there was a defect in the product at the time it left the control of the defendant. No negligence need be established on the part of the defendant, nor is the plaintiff's contributory negligence a defense. If negligence is established, however, knowledge by the seller can result in punitive damages. The defendant may show that the injured party assumed the risk.

Learning Outcomes

After studying this chapter, you should be able to clearly explain:

24-1   General Principles

LO.1   List the theories of product liability
See the five theories discussed in the "Theories of Liability" section, page 456.

LO.2   Identify who may sue and who may be sued when a defective product causes harm
See the discussion of privity, page 457.

24-2   Express Warranties

LO.3   Define and give examples of an express warranty
See the *La Trace v. Webster* case, page 461.

24-3   Implied Warranties

LO.4   List and explain the types of implied warranties
See the *Marty v. Anheuser-Busch* case, page 459.
See the *Pinkham v. Cargill* case, page 466.

LO.5 Explain warranty protections under federal law

See the discussion of the Consumer Product Safety Improvement Act (CPSIA), pages 460–461.

LO.6 State what constitutes a breach of warranty

See the *Rothbaum v. Samsung* case, pages 464–465.

24-4 Disclaimer of Warranties

LO.7 Describe the extent and manner in which implied warranties may be disclaimed under the UCC and the CISG

See the Apple Ethics & the Law feature, page 469.

24-5 Other Theories of Product Liability

See the *Thomas v. Staples* case, page 471.

Key Terms

Consumer Product Safety
  Improvement Act (CPSIA)
express warranty
full warranty
implied warranty

implied warranty of the
  merchantability
limited warranty
negligence
privity

privity of contract
strict tort liability
warranties
warranty against encumbrances
warranty of title

Questions and Case Problems

1. Maria Gonzalez lived in a rental unit with her sons in Queens, New York. The hot water supplied to their apartment was heated by a Morflo water heater, which had a temperature control device on its exterior manufactured by Robertshaw and sold to Morflo. Maria Garcia, the owner of the Gonzalezes' apartment, had purchased and installed the water heater. The Morflo heater was located in the basement of the apartment house, which was locked and inaccessible to tenants.

   Extensive warnings were on the water heater itself and in the manual given to Garcia at the time of her purchase. The warning on the Robertshaw temperature device read: "CAUTION: Hotter water increases the risk of scald injury." The heater itself contained a picture of hot water coming from a faucet with the word "DANGER" printed above it. In addition, the water heater had a statement on it: "Water temperature over 120 degrees Fahrenheit can cause severe burns instantly or death from scalds. Children, disabled, and elderly are at highest risk of being scalded. Feel water before bathing or showering. Temperature limiting valves are available, see manual."

   In the Morflo manual, the following warning appeared:

   DANGER! The thermostat is adjusted to its lowest temperature position when shipped from the factory. Adjusting the thermostat past the 120 degree Fahrenheit bar on the temperature dial will increase the risk of scald injury. The normal position is approximately 120 degrees Fahrenheit.

   DANGER: WARNING: Hot water can produce first degree burns in 3 seconds at 140 degrees Fahrenheit (60 degrees Celsius), in 20 seconds at 130 degrees Fahrenheit (54 degrees Celsius), in 8 minutes at 120 degrees Fahrenheit (49 degrees Celsius).

   On October 1, 1992, 15-month-old Angel Gonzalez was being bathed by his 15-year-old brother, Daniel. When the telephone rang, Daniel left Angel alone in the bathtub. No one else was at home with the boys, and Daniel left the water running. Angel was scalded by the water that came from the tap. Angel and his mother brought suit against Morflo and Robertshaw, alleging defects in the design of the water heater and the failure to warn. Should they recover? [*Gonzalez v. Morflo Industries, Inc.*, 931 F. Supp. 159 (E.D.N.Y.)]

2. Paul Parrino purchased from Dave's Professional Wheelchair Service a wheelchair manufactured by 21st Century Scientific, Inc. The sales brochure from 21st Century Scientific stated that the wheelchair would "serve [the buyer] well for many years to come." Parrino had problems with the wheelchair within a few years and filed suit against Dave's and 21st Century for breach of express warranty. Both defended on the grounds that the statement on years of service was puffery, not an express warranty. Are they right? [*Parrino v. Sperling*, 648 N.Y.S.2d 702]

3. Jane Jackson purchased a sealed can of Katydids, chocolate-covered pecan caramel candies manufactured by NestlT. Shortly after, Jackson bit into one of the candies and allegedly broke a tooth on a pecan shell embedded in the candy. She filed a complaint,

asserting breach of implied warranty. How would you argue on behalf of the company? How would you argue on behalf of Jackson? In your answer, discuss both the reasonable expectation test and the foreign substance/natural substance test. [*Jackson v. NestlT-Beich, Inc.*, 589 N.E.2d 547 (Ill. App.)]

4. Webster ordered a bowl of fish chowder at the Blue Ship Tea Room. She was injured by a fish bone in the chowder, and she sued the tea room for breach of the implied warranty of merchantability. The evidence at trial showed that when chowder is made, the entire boned fish is cooked. Should she recover? [*Webster v. Blue Ship Tea Room*, 198 N.E.2d 309 (Mass.)]

5. Andy's Sales (owned by Andy Adams) sold a well-built trampoline to Carl and Shirley Wickers. The Wickerses later sold the trampoline to Herbert Bryant. While using the trampoline, Herbert's 14-year-old nephew, Rex, sustained injuries that left him a quadriplegic. Rex's guardian filed suit for breach of express warranty and merchantability. The sales brochure for the round trampoline described it as "safe" because it had a "uniform bounce" and "natural tendency to work the jumper toward the center." The Wickerses had purchased an oval-shaped trampoline. Discuss Rex's ability to recover. Is privity an issue? [*Bryant v. Adams*, 448 S.E.2d 832 (N.C. App.)]

6. Advent purchased ink from Borden. On the labels of the ink drums delivered to Advent, Borden had imprinted in one-sixteenth-inch type in all caps:

   SELLER MAKES NO WARRANTY, EXPRESS OR IMPLIED, CONCERNING THE PRODUCT OR THE MERCHANTABILITY OR FITNESS THEREOF FOR ANY PURPOSE CONCERNING THE ACCURACY OF ANY INFORMATION PROVIDED BY BORDEN.

   This language was printed beneath the following:

   BORDEN PRINTING INKS—"ZERO DEFECTS: THAT'S OUR GOAL"

   All of the printing was in boldface type. The disclaimer was also printed on the sales invoice and on the reverse side of the Borden form, but there was nothing on the front to call attention to the critical nature of the terms on the back because there were simply capital letters reading "SEE REVERSE SIDE." All of the terms on the back were in boldface and although the disclaimer was the first of 19

paragraphs, nothing distinguished it from the other 18 paragraphs of detailed contract terms.

Advent said that Borden failed to age the black ink that it purchased, resulting in the ink separating in Advent's printing machines. Advent refused to pay for the ink and wrote to Borden explaining that it would not tender payment because the ink was defective and demanding that Borden reimburse it for its lost profits from the downtime of printing machines. The trial court held that Borden had disclaimed any and all warranties on the ink and Advent appealed. What would you decide about the disclaimer and why? [*Borden, Inc. v. Advent Ink Co.*, 701 A.2d 255 (Pa. Sup.)]

7. John Clark purchased a paintball gun at a pawn shop and then participated in a community sport of shooting paintball guns at cars. While John and his friend were riding around their small town with their paintball guns, they spotted Chris and shot his car. Chris Rico then aimed his Brass Eagle paintball gun at the car John was riding in, but instead hit John in the eye. John required surgery on his eye that evening and filed suit against Brass Eagle under a theory of strict tort liability. Brass Eagle responded by stating that its gun was not defective and that the young men had ignored warnings about the need to wear eye protection when using the guns. John said he purchased his gun used and was not given all the packaging and instructions. Brass Eagle says that its gun was not defective and that it functioned as it was supposed to. John says the guns are inherently dangerous. Who should be responsible for the injury? Are paintball guns defective if they can harm individuals? How should the courts allocate the risk and loss on products such as these? [*Clark v. Brass Eagle, Inc.*, 866 So. 2d 456 (Miss.)]

8. James Jelinek purchased Hytest BMR Sorghum Sudan grass seed, which was produced and marketed by Land O'Lakes. Land O'Lakes warranted the seed to be free from defects and expressly warranted that by using normal farming practices and proper maintenance, Mr. Jelinek would obtain yields of 4 1/2 tons per acre. The seed resulted in reduced yields and an inferior quality crop. As a result, Mr. Jelinek was not able to sell his crop and had significant economic losses. Mr. Jelinek filed suit for breach of express warranty. Is the promise of a crop yield an express warranty? Explain your answer. [*Jelinek v. Land O'Lakes, Inc.*, 797 N.W.2d 289 (Neb. App.)]

9. Brianna Kriefall, a child, died after she ate meat at a Sizzler restaurant that was later found to contain *E. coli*. Her family brought suit against Sizzler USA to recover for the loss of their daughter. Is Sizzler liable for the death? Explain your answer. What would be the liability of Sizzler's meat supplier in the case? [*Estate of Kriefall v. Sizzler USA Franchise, Inc., 801* N.W.2d 781 (Wis. App.)]

10. Zogarts manufactured and sold a practice device for beginning golfers. According to statements on the package, the device was completely safe, and a player could never be struck by the device's golf ball. Hauter was hit by the ball while using the device. He sued Zogarts, which denied liability on the ground that the statements were merely matters of opinion, so liability could not be based on them. Was this a valid defense? [*Hauter v. Zogarts*, 534 P.2d 377 (Cal.)]

11. GE Oil & Gas, Inc., is a company that manufactures gas compressors. Berge Helene owns a large barge that it leases to oil companies for purposes of storing and producing petroleum offshore. GE Oil & Gas sold Berge Helene gas compressors that were to be used on the barge. Berge Helene representatives asked GE representatives, as they were negotiating the contract for the compressors, whether the compressors could withstand the movement and vibration that would occur on the front of the barge once it was out in the ocean. GE's representatives assured those from Berge Helene that the compressors were self-stabilizing. Once out in the ocean, the gas compressors on the hull exploded once the vibrations began. Berge Helene brought suit against GE for the resulting crew injuries and damage to the barge. Could Berge Helene recover and, if so, what theory of product liability would apply? [*Berge Helene Ltd. v. GE Oil & Gas, Inc.*, 830 F. Supp. 2d 235 (S.D. Tex.)]

12. After watching a male horse owned by Terry and Manita Darby perform at a horse show, Ashley Sheffield contacted the Darbys about buying him. The Darbys assured her that the horse had no problems and would make a good show horse for use in competition. In the presence of and in consultation with her father (who raised horses for a business), Sheffield rode the horse and decided to purchase him for $8,500.

    Within three weeks, Sheffield and her trainer discerned that the horse was lame. Sheffield sued the Darbys for fraud and for breach of express and implied warranties, and the court entered summary judgment in favor of the Darbys on all claims.

Sheffield appealed. Was the court correct in granting summary judgment? Was there a breach of an express warranty? [*Sheffield v. Darby*, 535 S.E.2d 776 (Ga. App.)]

13. On July 27, 2000, Sheldorado Aluminum Products, Inc., installed an aluminum awning on the back of Marie Villette's home for use as a carport. On January 11, 2001, the awning collapsed on top of Ms. Villette's new Mercedes automobile. Ms. Villette brought suit against Sheldorado, seeking recovery of the $3,000 she had paid to them for the awning.

    There was no formal written contract between the parties; the only writing was a one-page order/bill designated a "contract," dated July 11, 2000, and signed by Ms. Villette and apparently by Jack Finklestein, Sheldorado's salesman. No advertising or promotional material was presented by either party. Ms. Villette testified to no express warranty or representation on the transaction, and none appears in the writing. Sheldorado acknowledges that no instructions or warnings were given to Ms. Villette as to care, maintenance, or use of the awning.

    When the awning collapsed, Sheldorado took the position that the cause was an accumulation of snow and high winds and that it bore no responsibility for the loss. Its only response to the incident was to refer Ms. Villette to the insurer on their homeowner's policy.

    Does Ms. Villette have any rights that would allow her to collect damages? Apply the UCC to answer this question. [*Villette v. Sheldorado Aluminum Products, Inc.*, 2001 WL 881055 (N.Y. Supp.), 45 U.C.C. Rep Serv. 2d 470 (N.Y. Civ. Ct.)]

14. Drehman Paving & Flooring Co. installed a brick floor at Cumberland Farms that its salesman promised would be "just like" another floor Cumberland had installed several years earlier. The bricks in the new floor came loose because Drehman had failed to install expansion joints. Expansion joints were not included in the second floor contract but were part of the first. Can Cumberland recover? Under what theory? [*Cumberland Farms, Inc. v. Drehman Paving & Flooring Co.*, 520 N.E.2d 1321 (Mass. Ct. App.)]

15. Brian Felley went to the home of Tom and Cheryl Singleton on June 8 to look at a used car that the Singletons had advertised for sale in the local paper. The car was a 1991 Ford with 126,000 miles on it. Following a test drive and the Singletons' representation that the car was "in good mechanical condition," Felley purchased the car for $5,800. By June

18, 1997, Felley had the car in the shop and had paid $942.76 to have its clutch fixed. By July 9, 1997, Felley also had paid $971.18 for a new brake job. By September 16, 1997, Felley had paid another $429.09 for further brake work.

Felley brought suit for breach of express warranty. An auto expert testified that the clutch and brakes were defective when Felley bought the car. Was an express warranty breached? Why or why not? [*Felley v. Singleton*, 705 N.E.2d 930 (Ill. App.)]

CPA Questions

1. Under the UCC Sales Article, the warranty of title may be excluded by:
   a. Merchants or nonmerchants, provided the exclusion is in writing.
   b. Nonmerchant sellers only.
   c. The seller's statement that it is selling only such right or title that it has.
   d. Use of an "as is" disclaimer.

2. Which of the following factors result(s) in an express warranty with respect to a sale of goods?
   I. The seller's description of the goods is part of the basis of the bargain.
   II. The seller selects goods knowing the buyer's intended use.
      a. I only.
      b. II only.
      c. Both I and II.
      d. Neither I nor II.

3. Morgan is suing the manufacturer, wholesaler, and retailer for bodily injuries caused by a power saw Morgan purchased. Which of the following statements is correct under the theory of strict liability?
   a. The manufacturer will avoid liability if it can show it followed the custom of the industry.
   b. Morgan may recover even if he cannot show that any negligence was involved.

   c. Contributory negligence on Morgan's part will always be a bar to recovery.
   d. Privity will be a bar to recovery insofar as the wholesaler is concerned if the wholesaler did not have a reasonable opportunity to inspect.

4. On May 2, Handy Hardware sent Ram Industries a signed purchase order that stated in part: "Ship for May 8 delivery 300 Model A-X socket sets at current dealer price. Terms 2/10/ net 30." Ram received Handy's purchase order on May 4. On May 5, Ram discovered that it had only 200 Model A-X socket sets and 100 Model W-Z socket sets in stock. Ram shipped the Model A-X and Model W-Z sets to Handy without explanation concerning the shipment. The sockets were received by Handy on May 8. Assuming a contract exists between Handy and Ram, which of the following implied warranties would result?
   I. Implied warranty of merchantability
   II. Implied warranty of fitness for a particular purpose
   III. Implied warranty of title
      a. I only.
      b. III only.
      c. I and III only.
      d. I, II, and III.

Obligations and Performance

Learning Outcomes <<<

After studying this chapter, you should be able to

LO.1   List the steps that can be taken when a party to a sales contract feels insecure about the other party's performance

LO.2   Explain the obligations of the seller and the buyer in a sales contract

LO.3   Identify the types of actions and conduct that constitute acceptance

LO.4   Explain the excuses that exist for nonperformance by one party

25-1   General Principles

Contracts for the sale of goods impose both obligations and requirements for performance on the parties. Each party to a sales contract is bound to perform according to the terms of the contract. Each is likewise under a duty to exercise **good faith** in the contract's performance and to do nothing that would impair the other party's expectation that the contract will be performed.

good faith–absence of knowledge of any defects or problems.

CPA   25-1a   Obligation of Good Faith

Every contract or duty within the Uniform Commercial Code (UCC) imposes an obligation of good faith in its performance or enforcement.[1] The UCC defines good faith as "honesty in fact in the conduct or transaction concerned."[2] In the case of a merchant seller or buyer of goods, the UCC carries the concept of good faith further. The UCC imposes the additional requirement that merchants observe "reasonable commercial standards of fair dealing in the trade."[3] Section 1-203 of the UCC provides, "Every contract or duty within this Act imposes an obligation of good faith in its performance or enforcement."[4]

25-1b   Time Requirements of Obligations

In a cash sale that does not require delivery of the goods, the duties of the seller and buyer are concurrent. Each one has the right to demand that the other perform at the same time. That is, as the seller hands over the goods, the buyer hands over the purchase money. If either party refuses to act, the other party has the right to withhold performance. In self-service stores, the performance occurs simultaneously—the buyer pays as the items are bagged at checkout.

In other types of contracts, there may be blocks of time between when the parties enter into an agreement and when performance, either delivery or payment, is due. During those time periods, buyers may become concerned about the ability of a seller experiencing a labor strike to complete production of the goods ordered in the contract. A seller may feel that a buyer who is experiencing credit difficulties may not be able to pay for the goods. Article 2 covers these periods of time and the conduct of the parties after the contract is entered into but before performance is due.

25-1c   Repudiation of the Contract

repudiation–result of a buyer or seller refusing to perform the contract as stated.

anticipatory repudiation–repudiation made in advance of the time for performance of the contract obligations.

If the seller or the buyer refuses to perform the contract when the time for performance arises, a **repudiation** of the contract results. Often, before the time for performance arrives, a party to the contract may inform the other that she will not perform the terms of the contract. This repudiation made in advance of the time for performance is called an **anticipatory repudiation.**[5] Under Revised Article 2, repudiation occurs when the party furnishes a *record* (as noted in other chapters, a term that allows for e-mails) including "language that a reasonable party would interpret to mean that the other party will not or cannot make a performance still due under the contract" or when the party exhibits

---

[1] U.C.C. §1-201(20); *Druckzentrum Harry Jung GmbH & Co. KG v. Motorola Mobility LLC,* 774 F.3d 410 (7th Cir. 2014).
[2] U.C.C. §1-202; *Ergowerx International, LLC v. Maxell Corp. of America,* 18 F. Supp. 3d 430 (S.D.N.Y. 2014).
[3] U.C.C. §1-303; *Greenwood Products, Inc. v. Greenwood Forest Products, Inc.,* 273 P.3d 116 (Or. 2012); *Olsenhaus Pure Vegan, LLC v. Electric Wonderland, Inc.,* 983 N.Y.S.2d 506 (N.Y.A.D. 2014).
[4] U.C.C. §1-203.
[5] U.C.C. §2-610; *Traxys North America LLC v. Concept Min. Inc.,* 510 Fed. Appx. 262, 2013 WL 599966 (4th Cir. 2013).

"voluntary, affirmative conduct that would appear to a reasonable party to make a future performance by the other party impossible."[6]

25-1d Adequate Assurance of Performance

This time between contracting and actual performance may see some developing events that cause the parties concern about the ability of each to perform.[7] **For Example,** if the seller's warehouse is destroyed by fire, the buyer might conclude that the seller might not be able to make a delivery scheduled for the following month. Whenever a party to a sales contract has reasonable grounds to be concerned about the future performance of the other party, a demand may be made in a record for *assurance* that the contract will be performed.[8] **For Example,** a seller who is concerned about a buyer's ability to pay for goods could demand an updated credit report, financial statement, or even additional security or payment.

Form of Assurance

The person on whom demand for assurance is made must give "such assurance of due performance as is adequate under the circumstances of the particular case."[9] The UCC does not specify the exact form of assurance. If the party on whom demand is made has an established reputation, a reaffirmation of the contract obligation and a statement that it will be performed may be sufficient to assure a reasonable person that it will be performed. In contrast, if the party's reputation or economic position at the time is such that mere words and promises would not give any real assurance, it may be necessary to have a third person (or an insurance company) guarantee performance or to put up property as security for performance.

Failure to Give Assurance

If adequate assurance is not given within 30 days from the time of demand, the demanding party may treat the contract as repudiated. The party demanding assurances may then proceed as if there were a breach and may pursue damage remedies. The nonbreaching party also has the right to enter into a substitute contract with a third person to obtain goods contracted for under the now-broken contract.

CASE SUMMARY

So, Are We Good on This Contract, or What?

FACTS: On April 1, 2004, Advanced Body Care Solutions, LLC ("Advanced") and Thione International, Inc. ("Thione"), entered into an agreement that required Advanced to make minimum purchases of "Thione Antioxidant Complex," which reduces free radical damage to the body, and Thione's "Free Radical Monitor Test Kit," which is a test kit for at-home use to monitor the body's free radicals. Ampoules are small glass tubes that contain a clear liquid reagent, which tests for the presence of free radicals in a urine sample.

In exchange, Advanced received "the license and authority" "to advertise, promote, market, sell and otherwise distribute" the Dietary Supplement and the Test Kit on an

---

[6] U.C.C. §2-610. The loss of a grain dealer's license is an anticipatory repudiation of his contract to sell grains for farmers. *Timmerman v. Grain Exchange, LLC,* 915 N.E.2d 113 (Ill. App. 2009).
[7] U.C.C. §2-609.
[8] *Koursa, Inc., Plaintiff, v. manroland, Inc.,* 971 F. Supp. 2d 765 (N.D. Ill. 2013).
[9] U.C.C. §2-609(4).

So, Are We Good on This Contract, or What? continued

exclusive basis. The agreement was to remain in effect for a minimum of five years: April 1, 2004 to March 31, 2009.

On May 26, 2004, Advanced placed an order for 25,000 ampoules, for which it paid $41,250. It received about 20,000 ampoules on September 1. It was immediately apparent that 200 to 300 of the 20,000 were broken, and about 1,000 were pink, indicating that they were defective. The following day, Dr. Stephen Perry, Advanced's liaison with Thione, sent an e-mail to Dr. Mark Hersh, the CEO and chief scientist of Thione, stating that, "Carl [Pradelli, Advanced's managing member,] received some vials that are pink," and inquiring, "Do we have a production issue?"

As of March 2005, Thione had not yet identified the source of the problem with the first shipment of 20,000 ampoules, and Advanced had placed no subsequent orders. On March 18, Pradelli sent Hersh a summary of Advanced's marketing efforts. Following five pages on that subject was a section of the letter entitled "The Lingering Black Cloud" that stressed that Advanced's "biggest concern" was the defective ampoules and that it could not launch any additional marketing initiatives until satisfied that the problem was permanently solved.

During the summer of 2006, Advanced and Thione attempted to renegotiate the Licensing Agreement. The renegotiation efforts failed.

On September 26, 2006, Advanced filed suit against Thione for damages, claiming that Thione had breached the Licensing Agreement and an implied warranty by providing Advanced with defective ampoules. Thione counterclaimed for breach of the Agreement by Advanced of its minimum purchase obligations and claiming lost profits.

The district court entered judgment for Thione for $2.5 million and denied the purchaser's post-judgment motions. Advanced appealed.

DECISION: On appeal, the court held that there was sufficient evidence to support the jury's finding that Thione did not breach the installment contract as a whole. The court also held that a reasonable jury could have concluded that Advanced's e-mail inquiry to Thione and subsequent expression of marketing and quality concerns did not constitute a writing demanding adequate assurance of due performance. The e-mail was an inquiry and not an expression that the contract was hanging in the balance. Further, Advanced took no further steps to resolve the issue. Finally, the court held that the damage award was justified because Advanced had breached the contract. [***Advanced Bodycare Solutions, LLC v. Thione International, Inc.***, 615 F.3d 1352 (11th Cir. 2010)]

25-2   Duties of the Parties

The obligations of the parties to a sales contract include (1) the seller's duty to deliver the goods, (2) the buyer's duty to accept the goods, and (3) the buyer's duty to pay for the goods.

25-2a   Seller's Duty to Deliver

The seller has the duty to deliver the goods according to the terms of the contract.

Place, Time, and Manner of Delivery

The terms of the contract determine whether the seller is to send the goods or the buyer is to call for them and whether the goods are to be transported from the seller to the buyer or the transaction is to be completed by the delivery of documents without the movement of the goods. In the absence of a provision in the contract or a contrary course of performance or usage of trade, the place of delivery is the seller's place of business if the seller has one; otherwise, it is the seller's residence. (See Chapter 23 for more details on delivery and shipping terms.)[10] However, if the subject matter of the contract consists of identified goods that are known by the parties to be in some other place, that place is the

---

[10] U.C.C. §2-308.

place of delivery. If no time for shipment or delivery is stated, delivery or shipment is required within a reasonable time.

When a method of transportation called for by the contract becomes unavailable or commercially unreasonable, the seller must make delivery by means of a commercially reasonable substitute if available.

Quantity Delivered

The buyer has the right to insist that all the goods be delivered at one time. If the seller delivers a smaller or larger quantity than what is stipulated in the contract, the buyer may refuse to accept the goods.[11]

25-2b Buyer's Duty upon Receipt of Goods

The buyer must accept goods that conform to the contract, and the refusal to do so is a breach of the contract. However, the buyer has certain rights prior to acceptance.

CPA ### Right to Examine Goods—The Buyer's Right of Inspection[12]

To determine whether the goods in fact conform to the contract, the buyer has the right to examine the goods when tendered by the seller. An exception to this rule occurs when goods are sent COD. In a COD shipment, the buyer has no right to examine the goods until payment is made.

The buyer's right of inspection includes the right to remove goods from cartons and to conduct tests. **For Example,** a buyer who is purchasing potatoes for use in making potato chips has the right to peel and test a portion of the potatoes to determine whether they are the appropriate type for "chipping."

Right to Refuse or Return the Goods—The Buyer's Right of Rejection[13]

If the goods the seller has tendered do not conform to the contract in any way, the buyer can *reject* the goods. **For Example,** the buyer may reject a mobile home when it does not contain an air conditioner with the capacity specified by the contract. The buyer may reject the goods if they are not perfect.[14] The standard for rejection does not require that the defect in the goods or the breach be material. **For Example,** a small pressure mark on an ottoman is not material; the ottoman will function just as well. However, the buyer still has the right to reject the ottoman because it has a defect.

The buyer has the right to reject the full shipment, accept the full shipment and seek damages for the goods' diminished value (see Chapter 26), or accept any commercial units and reject the remainder. Commercial units are defined by trade and industry according to the customary size of cartons or containers for the goods shipped. Envelopes come in **commercial units** of boxes of 500. Bakery cookies come in packages of one dozen. Rejection by a buyer would be not of individual envelopes or cookies. **For Example,** if Donna purchased a package of 12 chocolate chip cookies and 4 of the cookies were stale, Donna would return the full package of 12 cookies for a new package. Rejection and acceptance in commercial units prevent the problems created when a seller has to open other units and mix and match goods in each. You can also see the commercial wisdom in not mixing and matching cookies after buyers have opened and touched them.

commercial unit–
standard of the trade for shipment or packaging of a good.

---

[11] U.C.C. §2-307; failure to deliver right amounts at the right time allows the buyer to repudiate the contract. *DC General Contractors, Inc. v. Slay Steel, Inc.,* 109 So. 3d 577 (Miss. App. 2013).
[12] U.C.C. §2-601.
[13] U.C.C. §2-602; *Prichard Enterprises, Inc. v. Adkins,* 858 F. Supp. 2d 576 (E.D.N.C. 2012).
[14] *Hansen–Mueller Co. v. Gau,* 838 N.W.2d 138 (Iowa 2013).

After rejecting the goods, the buyer may not exercise any right of ownership over the goods.

The buyer's rejection must be made within a reasonable time after the delivery or tender of the goods. The buyer must notify the seller of the rejection and, in transactions with merchants particularly, provide the seller with the reason for the rejection.[15]

CPA

Cure of Defective Tender or Delivery

right to cure—second chance for a seller to make a proper tender of conforming goods.

The buyer's rejection is not an end to the transaction. The seller is given a second chance, or a **right to cure,** to make a proper tender of conforming goods.[16]

This right of cure means that the buyer must give notice of rejection and the reason for that rejection, if the seller has the right, but not necessarily the intent, to cure. That is, the seller has the right to cure if the seller is able to make the cure within the time remaining under the contract. If the time for making delivery under the contract has not expired, the seller need only give the buyer **seasonable** (timely) notice of the intention to make a proper delivery within the time allowed by the contract.

seasonable—timely.

25-2c Buyer's Duty to Accept Goods

Assuming that the buyer has no grounds to reject the goods after inspection, the next step in the performance of the contract is the buyer's **acceptance** of the goods.

CPA

What Constitutes Acceptance of Goods[17]

acceptance—unqualified assent to the act or proposal of another, such as the acceptance of a draft (bill of exchange), of an offer to make a contract, of goods delivered by the seller, or of a gift or deed.

Acceptance of goods means that the buyer, pursuant to a contract, has, either expressly or by implication, taken the goods permanently. The buyer's statement of acceptance is an express acceptance. A buyer can accept goods by implication if there is no rejection after a reasonable opportunity to inspect them or within a reasonable time after the buyer has inspected them. Another form of acceptance by implication is conduct by the buyer that is inconsistent with rejection, as when a buyer uses or sells the delivered goods.[18]

A buyer accepts goods by making continued use of them and by not attempting to return them. A buyer also accepts goods by modifying them because such action is inconsistent with a rejection or with the continued ownership of the goods by the seller.[19]

CASE SUMMARY

The Pasta Ties

FACTS: Country Pasta, located in Polson, Montana, makes noodles. Viking manufactures, fabricates, and services industrial packaging equipment. In 2006, Gary Ivory, the production manager at Country Pasta, contacted Robb Leonhard, one of the owners of Viking, to discuss a quotation for a more automatic pasta bagging system. Country Pasta wanted a system in which the pasta bags would be weighed more accurately and in which the bags would be closed or tied more automatically. Ivory provided Leonhard with a sample of Country Pasta's product in the bag it was using at the time and indicated what he wanted the product to look like. Leonhard then sent Ivory photographs of a bag of Country Pasta's product with a tin-tie on it and stated, "this is basically what your look is going to be." Viking

---

[15] U.C.C. §2-602(1); *Western Dermatology Consultants, P.C. v. Vitalworks, Inc.,* 78 A.3d 167 (Conn. App. 2013).

[16] *Inter-Americas Ins. Corp., Inc. v. Imaging Solutions Co.,* 185 P.3d 963 (Kan. App. 2008).

[17] U.C.C. §2-606; *Stenzel v. Dell, Inc.,* 870 A.2d 133 (Me. 2005).

[18] *Fabrica de Tejidos Imperial v. Brandon Apparel Group, Inc.,* 218 F. Supp. 2d 974 (N.D. Ill. 2002).

[19] U.C.C. §2-606(1)(a), (b), and (c).

The Pasta Ties continued

included the photographs on the second page of the quotation.

On July 13, 2007, Country Pasta accepted Viking's quotation to purchase a pasta packaging system. The quotation shows photos of the equipment and of Country Pasta bags closed with a tin-tie. The items related to the tin-tie applicator were priced at $47,173. The total purchase price for the product packaging system was $178,074.

The quotation called for a "checkout," or a pre-shipment inspection, by Country Pasta "prior to shipment." In April 2008, Ivory and Scott Knutson went to Viking's facility to perform the checkout of the packaging system. The tin-ties on the finished bags did not regularly close up during this demonstration; however, Viking worked on the packaging system and told Country Pasta that the system was "working better." Country Pasta approved the shipment and the packaging system was delivered to Country Pasta before June 17, 2008. Ivory helped unpack and set up the equipment; he did not notice any defects.

The contract provided that "if requested by the customer, [Viking] will provide a service technician for installation of the quoted equipment." The contract did not include free installation but estimated that two days of installation and training for Country Pasta employees would cost $3,373. The contract also provided that "[a]n installation will be considered complete when all systems purchased from [Viking] perform per the Product Performance Specifications."

From June 17, 2008, through June 25, 2008, Viking technician Tim Parrish worked on installing the equipment and training Country Pasta's employees in Montana. During this visit, Parrish discovered that Country Pasta workers would drop or tap bags full of pasta on a table in order to settle the noodles to allow for a twist tie to be applied to the bag. Parrish made adjustments to the machinery, including adding a shelf to assist in the settling of the noodles. Despite these efforts, the tin-tie applicator was not functioning properly at the time he left. Viking and Country Pasta agreed to split the cost of a second visit by Parrish.

Parrish returned to Country Pasta in July 2008 with Steve Almberg, a representative from Weigh Right, the manufacturer of the scale. Parrish and Almberg improved the operation of the scale and bagger by making modifications to Country Pasta's equipment feeding the scale and bagger.

A Country Pasta memorandum regarding a meeting with Parrish on July 10, 2008, notes the improvements with the scale and bagger but states that "[t]here is no way the current tin-tie system will work with our product."

Parrish left Montana and was not asked to return to Montana to continue working on the applicator.

On December 4, 2008, five months after delivery of the packaging system, and four months after Parrish's final visit, Kellogg sent an e-mail to Viking stating that Country Pasta wanted a refund for the tin-tie applicator and the associated conveyor in the amount of $47,173. At that time, Country Pasta had outstanding invoices due to Viking in the amount of $34,110.22. Viking brought suit against Country Pasta, seeking the outstanding amount. Country Pasta counterclaimed, alleging breach of contract.

After a trial to the court, judgment for money damages was entered in favor of Viking. Country Pasta's counterclaim alleging breach of contract by Viking and alleging Country Pasta's revocation of acceptance of the tin-tie applicator and conveyor were dismissed. Country Pasta appealed.

DECISION: Country Pasta knew that the machine was not going to work when it came to getting the ties on the pasta bags as it wanted them to look. However, for five months after that, Country Pasta took no action other than to ask for a refund on the tying portion of the equipment, not for damages for a breach of contract. The machinery was one commercial unit and could not be rejected in pieces. In addition, the proposal makes it clear that the sale was for the equipment and that the installation and fine-tuning was beyond the scope of the proposal. Also, Country Pasta used the equipment for too long before deciding to revoke its acceptance. There were no grounds for rejection because there was nothing in the proposal to indicate a breach. If there were grounds for revocation, Country Pasta waited too long to revoke the acceptance.

The key elements of the decision are as follows:

1. The system did not fail to meet any identifiable product performance specifications;

2. The entire integrated system was one commercial unit;

3. The buyer's conduct constituted acceptance of goods;

4. The e-mail that the buyer's owner sent to the seller and that sought a refund for the cost of the system's tin-tie applicator was not sent within a reasonable time and, thus, did not constitute a valid rejection; and

5. The buyer did not revoke its acceptance of the system within a reasonable time.

Affirmed. [*Viking Packaging Technologies, Inc. v. Vassallo Foods, Inc.*, **804 N.W.2d 507 (Wis. App. 2011)**]

E-COMMERCE & CYBERLAW

Rejection in Cyberspace

Online retailers have their own rules for rejection. For example, Zappo's offers free returns, but the buyer must comply with the online return processes. There are also time limits placed on revocation of acceptance, such as on Amazon.

All goods must be returned within six months of purchase. The online retailers have spelled out the time limits to make rejection and revocation of acceptance requirements clear and not subject to UCC interpretation of reasonableness.

Revocation of Acceptance

Even after acceptance of the goods, the performance under the contract may not be finished if the buyer exercises the right to revoke acceptance of the goods.[20] The buyer may revoke acceptance of the goods when they do not conform to the contract, the defect is such that it substantially impairs the value of the contract to the buyer, and either the defect is such that the buyer could not discover the problem or the seller has promised to correct a problem the buyer was aware of and pointed out to the seller prior to acceptance.[21]

For Example, a buyer who purchased an emergency electric power generator found that the generator produced only about 65 percent of the power called for by the contract. This amount of power was insufficient for the operation of the buyer's electrical equipment. The seller's repeated attempts to improve the generator's output failed. The buyer, despite having used the generator for three months, could revoke his acceptance of it because its value was substantially impaired and he continued to keep it and use it only because of the seller's assurances that it would be repaired.

substantial impairment– material defect in a good.

Substantial impairment is a higher standard than the one of "fails to conform in any respect" for rejection. Substantial impairment requires proof of more than the mere fact that the goods do not conform to the contract. The buyer is not required to show that the goods are worthless but must prove that their use to the buyer is substantially different from what the contract promised.

A revocation of acceptance is not a cancellation of the contract with the seller. After revocation of acceptance, the buyer can choose from the remedies available for breach of contract or demand that the seller deliver conforming goods. (See Chapter 26 for more information on remedies for breach.)

Notification of Revocation of Acceptance

To revoke acceptance properly, the buyer must take certain steps. The buyer must give the seller notice of revocation. The revocation of acceptance is effective when the buyer notifies the seller. The buyer need not actually return the goods to make the notification or the revocation effective.

---

[20] U.C.C. §2-608; *Fode v. Capital RV Center, Inc.*, 575 N.W.2d 682 (N.D. 1998); *Barrett v. Brian Bemis Auto World*, 408 F. Supp. 2d 539 (N.D. Ill. 2005).

[21] *Bennett v. Skyline Corp.*, 52 F. Supp. 3d 796 (N.D. W. Va. 2014); *Cliffstar Corp. v. Elmar Industries, Inc.*, 678 N.Y.S.2d 222 (1998). Continued use without notification presents problems for establishing rejection. *Ferratella Bros., LLC v. Sacco*, 995 N.Y.S.2d 815 (N.Y. App. 2014).

CASE SUMMARY

Rejecting the Race Car for Its Chassis

FACTS: This case arises from the sale of a rare 1965 Dodge altered-wheelbase race car specially manufactured by Chrysler Corporation for drag racing and used as a promotional vehicle. Legendary drag racer Dave Strickler raced the Dodge during the 1965 season. The Dodge was then sold to another race car driver, Chuck McJury, who made substantial alterations to the vehicle. Among other things, McJury replaced the vehicle's original 1965 Dodge Coronet body with a 1966/1967 Dodge Charger body. McJury sold the car to Melvin Smith. Melvin Smith then sold the Dodge to David Fengel in 1979 or 1980. By that time, the vehicle was in poor condition, described as a "body shell on wheels" with "[n]o engine" and "no transmission."

Atwell (defendant) purchased the Dodge from Fengel in the early 1990s for $35,000. Fengel provided Atwell with documentation concerning the vehicle's history, alterations, and chain of title, including the vehicle's original 1965 certificate of title bearing Dave Strickler's name and address.

Atwell gathered parts and spent more than 10 years restoring the vehicle. Atwell then worked with Edward Strzelecki to sell the Dodge after he had finished restoring it. In February 2007, Strzelecki sent letters to potential buyers offering the vehicle for sale and providing certain information concerning the vehicle's history, restoration, and chain of title. In one of those letters, dated February 4, 2007, Strzelecki wrote to Nicholas Smith describing the vehicle as "Dave Strickler's 65 Dodge 'FACTORY' Altered Wheel–Base." Strzelecki explained that the Dodge was on loan to the Chrysler Museum in Auburn Hills, Michigan, where it was on "semi-permanent display." Strzelecki claimed in his letter that the Chrysler Museum had appraised the vehicle and had insured it for more than $2 million.

Nicholas Smith (who is an officer of Bev Smith, plaintiff) considered Strzelecki to be a friend. Strzelecki gave him a binder containing extensive information and documentation pertaining to the Dodge. Nicholas Smith confirmed that he had reviewed the contents of the binder before agreeing to purchase the Dodge from Atwell.

Nicholas Smith traveled to Michigan and went to the Chrysler Museum with Strzelecki to personally inspect the vehicle. He walked around the vehicle at the Chrysler Museum but remained "outside of the rails that protected the car from visitors."

Smith ultimately agreed to give the defendant $600,000 in cash, plus two other classic automobiles in exchange: (1) a 1964 Dodge Coronet Hemi Super Stock valued at $278,000, and (2) a 1964 Ford Thunderbolt valued at $250,000. The bill of sale contained the following:

Steve Atwell hereby agrees to sell and Bev Smith Ford agrees to purchase the Dave Strickler 1965 Dodge AWB ("AWB" means "altered wheelbase.") drag car, VIN W151191681. Seller represents this vehicle to be the real and authentic Strickler car, that he (Atwell) is the true owner of the car, and further that no liens or encumbrances exist against the vehicle.

After the sale, and while at a classic car event in Ohio in July 2008, a car historian informed Nicholas Smith that the Dodge had a "donor body" and was not the "real" Strickler car.

On April 20, 2010, the plaintiff's attorneys in Florida sent a letter to Atwell that stated:

[Plaintiff] has learned that the Strickler Car it purchased from you is in fact not the "real and authentic" vehicle driven by Dave Strickler in the 1960s, as you expressly represented and warranted during the sale and in the Contract. [Plaintiff] now knows that the vehicle was re-bodied and otherwise restored using predominantly non-original and reproduction parts. [Plaintiff] would never have purchased the Strickler Car if it knew the vehicle was not the "real and authentic" vehicle as promised.

As a result of your material misrepresentations regarding the authenticity and restoration of the Strickler Car, [plaintiff] has suffered and continues to suffer substantial damages.... Stated simply, you exploited the authenticity and restoration of the Strickler Car to fraudulently gain a profit from [plaintiff].

Your false misrepresentations and warranties regarding the restoration and authenticity of the Strickler Car are all actionable under the law....

Smith filed suit. The trial court granted summary judgment for Atwell.

DECISION: The court held that the defects could be discovered. The court also held that once the buyer was aware of the defects, the notification of revocation should have been given. The buyer waited two years after being aware of the problem to bring notice. The court holds that the buyer cannot recover for any losses resulting. [***Bev Smith, Inc. v. Atwell***, **836 N.W.2d 872 (Mich. App. 2013)**]

The notice of revocation of acceptance must be given within a reasonable time after the buyer discovers or should have discovered the problems with the goods. The right of revocation is not lost if the buyer gives the seller a longer period of time to correct the defects in the goods.[22] Even the lapse of a year will not cost the buyer the right of revocation of acceptance if the seller has been experimenting during that time trying to correct the problems with the goods.

Buyer's Responsibilities upon Revocation of Acceptance

After a revocation of acceptance, the buyer must hold the goods and await instructions from the seller. If the buyer revokes acceptance after having paid the seller in advance, the buyer may retain possession of the goods as security for the refund of the money that has been paid.

THINKING THINGS THROUGH

When a Court Does Not Allow Performance

The U.S. government contracted with a number of companies to furnish transportation, clothing, housing, and medical care to undocumented aliens who had entered the United States through its southern border. The program, which involved curbing deportation and admitting the aliens to the United States, was created and put into place by administrative rules drafted by the Department of Homeland Security (DHS). However, those rules were challenged by a number of state attorneys general on several grounds, including the fact that the rules had not been published for public comment, as required under the Administrative Procedures Act (APA) (see Chapter 6 for more information on this act and the process by which federal agencies make rules).

When the suit was filed, the federal judge hearing the case enjoined the implementation of the planned program until the case could be heard. The federal government then placed the program and all of the contracts on hold.

Suppose that a number of the companies under contract had set aside resources and personnel and entered into their own contracts in order to prepare for their responsibilities for the aliens under their contracts with the federal government. Suppose further that many had turned down other projects and bids in order to handle these rather large federal contracts. If they made claims against the U.S. for breach of contract, would the doctrine of commercial impracticability work as a defense for the government? Explain the reasoning behind your answer.

ETHICS & THE LAW

The Return Season

At Saks Fifth Avenue, they call it the "return season." Return season occurs within the week following a major fundraising formal dance. Women who have purchased formal evening wear return the dresses after the dance. The dresses have been worn, and the tags have been cut, but the women return the dresses with requests for a full refund. Neiman Marcus also experiences the same phenomenon of returns.

Some stores have implemented a policy that formal evening wear may not be returned if the tags are cut from it. Others require a return within a limited period of seven days. Others offer an exchange only after five days.

Are the women covered by a right of rejection under Article 2? What do you think of the conduct of the women? Is it simply revocation of acceptance? Is there good faith on the part of the women?

---

[22] A buyer who took her pop-up camper in for repairs but was then given a different camper without being told about it was entitled to revoke her acceptance. *Head v. Phillips Camper Sales & Rental, Inc.*, 593 N.W.2d 595 (Mich. Ct. App. 1999).

25-2d **Buyer's Duty to Pay**

The buyer must pay the amount stated in the sales contract for accepted goods.

Time of Payment

The sales contract may require payment in advance or may give the buyer credit by postponing the time for payment.[23]

Form of Payment

Unless otherwise agreed, payment by the buyer requires payment in cash. The seller may accept a check or a promissory note from the buyer. If the check is not paid by the bank, the purchase price remains unpaid. A promissory note payable at a future date gives the buyer credit by postponing the time for payment.

The seller can refuse to accept a check or a promissory note as payment for goods but must give the buyer reasonable time in which to obtain legal tender with which to make payment.

CASE SUMMARY

Poor Payment Pattern on Potato Contracts

FACTS: Sun Valley Potatoes, Inc. (Sun Valley) is a fresh packer of potatoes. Magic Valley Foods, Inc. (Magic Valley) is a processor of potatoes. Sun Valley and Magic Valley entered into three written contracts wherein Sun Valley agreed to sell and deliver and Magic Valley agreed to purchase potatoes. Sun Valley provided nine weekly invoices, but none of those invoices were paid according to the following term in all of the contracts: "net thirty (30) days on amounts delivered on a weekly basis." As of August 9, 1995, Sun Valley had delivered 108,169 cwt. (at the contract price of $1.13 cwt.) of potatoes to Magic Valley. Magic Valley, on the other hand, had withheld payments totaling $236,904.44.

Sun Valley ceased its deliveries because it had not been paid for a total of 24 invoices. Magic Valley had to shut down its plant for 14 days and it filed suit against Sun Valley for breach of contract. The district court concluded that because Sun Valley had not insisted on strict compliance with the 30-day payment rule, it could not unilaterally repudiate the contract due to late payments. The district court

also ruled that Magic Valley was entitled to offset the $236,904.44 it owed Sun Valley against the $231,660.60 it incurred as a result of its processing plant being down for 14 days and the loss of profits associated therewith. Sun Valley appealed.

DECISION: The court held that Sun Valley did not waive its right to timely payment under the contract. Because Magic Valley had made arrangements with other suppliers for delivery of potatoes, it was aware that its position with Sun Valley was tenuous and that it might lose the deliveries. The court also noted that if Magic Valley was worried, it should have sought assurances from Sun Valley about deliveries. However, seeking assurances would have brought the nonpayment issue to the forefront of the parties' relationship. The court found that Magic Valley was the party in breach of the agreement and that Sun Valley's response of no further deliveries was an appropriate response to a breach. [*Magic Valley Foods, Inc. v. Sun Valley Potatoes, Inc.*, **10 P.3d 734 (Idaho 2000)**]

CPA 25-2e **When Duties Are Excused**

Under Article 2, the doctrine of commercial impracticability is available as a defense to performance of a contract. The doctrine of **commercial impracticability** is the modern commercial law version of the common law doctrine of impossibility. If a party to a

[23] U.C.C. §2-310.

commercial impracticability– situation that occurs when costs of performance rise suddenly and performance of a contract will result in a substantial loss.

contract can establish that there has been an occurrence or a contingency not anticipated by the parties and not a basic assumption in their entering into a contract, the party can be excused from performance.

The standard for commercial impracticability is objective, not subjective. Additional cost alone is not grounds for application of commercial impracticability.[24]

For Example, if a farmer has contracted to sell 2 tons of peanuts to an airline and the crop fails, the farmer is not excused on the grounds of commercial impracticability. So long as peanuts are available for the farmer to buy, even at a higher price, and then sell to the buyer to satisfy their contract terms, the farmer is not excused. Commercial impracticability refers to those circumstances in which peanuts are not available anywhere because the entire peanut harvest was destroyed rather than just the individual farmer's crop.

CASE SUMMARY

A Black Day for Black Carbon

FACTS: Continental manufactures furnace-grade carbon black, a raw material filler used in tires and other rubber and plastic products. BRC Rubber & Plastics (BRC) was a longtime customer of Continental, purchasing carbon black for its rubber products it supplies to customers. Continental was BRC's exclusive supplier of carbon black at least back to 1997. From 2005 to 2008, Continental annually supplied BRC between 1.89 and 2.43 million pounds of carbon black. Continental supplied about 40 customers, and its potential annual capacity for carbon black was approximately 500 million pounds.

Thomas Nunley, a salesperson for Continental, handled the BRC account from 1997 to May 2011. Continental had instructed its sales team "to negotiate as many long-term contracts that we could convince our customer base to take" and to "get as much as we could committed long term in volume[.]"

Nunley negotiated a five-year contract to sell approximately 1.8 million pounds of carbon black to BRC, and BRC agreed to provide accurate forecasts of its needs to assist Continental in meeting BRC requirements.

If BRC purchased between 1.5 and 2.1 million pounds of carbon black a year, the price was two cents per pound. If BRC purchased more than 2.1 million pounds a year, it would receive a half-cent rebate on each pound purchased that year, and if it purchased less than 1.5 million, it would pay an additional half-cent per pound penalty. The rebate or penalty increased to one cent per pound if BRC purchased more than 2.2 million pounds or less than 1.4 million pounds.

In late 2009, Continental internally classified BRC as a "Tier 1" customer that would get its orders "filled first" if

Continental faced a shortage of supply, and Continental and BRC clicked along on their contract until 2011. The economy improved during late 2010 and early 2011, the demand for carbon black increased, and its market price began to rise. Despite this high demand, Continental was operating at a loss and had to choose between going out of business or seeking price increases from its customers.

Nunley notified BRC on April 14, 2011, that Continental was raising its two cents per pound base price to BRC effective June 1, 2011. But BRC rejected Continental's request for a price increase, first by e-mail and then by letter, and insisted that Continental provide adequate assurance that it would fill BRC's orders under the Agreement and "hold up its end of the bargain." All of Continental's other customers, however, agreed to a price increase, most ranging from four to five cents per pound.

Continental told BRC that the price was increased and "if they did not like it, they could get their carbon black someplace else." On April 29, 2011, Continental employees were instructed not to ship to 14 customers, including BRC, due to a "negative GP [gross profit]." Continental internally downgraded BRC from a "Tier 1" to a "Tier 3" customer.

On April 26, 2011, BRC sent Continental a purchase order for black carbon and asked that Continental confirm the order. When Continental failed to do so, BRC sent several additional requests for confirmation, but Continental still did not confirm the order.

By May 2011, Continental could no longer keep up with the demand for carbon black. One of Continental's production facilities was down for scheduled maintenance during this high-demand time. Because of the high demand for carbon black in the preceding months, Continental had

---

[24] U.C.C. §2-615(a).

A Black Day for Black Carbon continued

not built up inventories and began to allocate its available supply among customers.

Continental never confirmed BRC's April 26, 2011, order and did not send BRC the shipment. Continental then attempted to recall a shipment released to BRC in April, instructing Continental's plant manager that "[w]e quickly want to arrange to have this car returned to [Continental's plant] due to the failed negotiations regarding pricing increase and payment terms."

In reaction to Continental's failure to confirm orders and the missed shipment, BRC's counsel on May 16, 2011, sent a letter to Continental, demanding that it provide adequate assurance of performance under Section 2-609.

Continental responded that it had no black carbon available. But its records showed that it had supplied 1.8 million pounds of black carbon to its customers in May 2011.

Nevertheless, on the morning of May 20, Continental called BRC to tell them that the two requested shipments would be available on May 25 and June 2 but with a two-cents per pound price increase. BRC e-mailed Continental that the offer was "unacceptable" because it was "not in accordance with the terms and conditions set forth in our agreement."

Later that same day—May 20, 2011—Continental's in-house counsel confirmed to BRC's counsel that Continental would "continue producing and shipping timely at the contract prices, and w[ould] not cut off supply to BRC," and "We will continue to do our best to supply BRC and I will advise when another car will be shipped."

Continental sent a single shipment of carbon black to BRC. BRC then sent a letter to Continental, asserting that Continental had failed to adequately respond to BRC's demand for assurance, and that Continental was in breach of the Agreement. BRC informed Continental that it was terminating the Agreement "effective immediately" and, in fact, had just filed this lawsuit.

In an effort to settle the dispute, Continental sold and delivered another six railcar shipments of carbon black to BRC with the total amount of carbon black sold and delivered by Continental to BRC in 2011 reaching 1.971 million pounds. The parties ultimately could not settle the dispute, however, and BRC ceased ordering from Continental in September 2011.

BRC moved for summary judgment.

DECISION: The court found for BRC because Continental did not have the right to increase prices because although there was a market shortage, Continental was a producer and had clients to whom it owed carbon black. Further, BRC's demand for assurances of delivery of the carbon black was never answered. Some shipments followed, but the dispute as to price was an underlying issue. Continental can't get more money for what it is already obligated to do. There are no rights to increase prices. [**BRC Rubber & Plastics, Inc. v. Continental Carbon Co., 949 F. Supp. 2d 862 (N.D. Ind. 2013)**]

Make the Connection

Summary

Every sales contract imposes an obligation of good faith in its performance. Good faith means honesty in fact in the conduct or transaction concerned. For merchants, the UCC imposes the additional requirement of observing "reasonable commercial standards of fair dealing in the trade."

In the case of a cash sale where no transportation of the goods is required, both the buyer and the seller may demand concurrent performance.

A buyer's or a seller's refusal to perform a contract is called a *repudiation*. A repudiation made in advance of the time for performance is called an *anticipatory repudiation* and is a breach of the contract. If either party to a contract feels insecure about the performance of the other, that party may demand by a record adequate assurance of performance. If that assurance is not given, the demanding party may treat the contract as repudiated.

The seller has a duty to deliver the goods in accordance with the terms of the contract. This duty does not require physical transportation; it requires that the seller permit the transfer of possession of the goods to the buyer.

With the exception of COD contracts, the buyer has the right to inspect the goods upon tender or delivery. Inspection includes the right to open cartons and conduct tests. If the buyer's inspection reveals that the seller has tendered nonconforming goods, the buyer may reject them. Subject to certain limitations, the seller may then offer to replace the goods or cure the problems the buyer has noted.

The buyer has a duty to accept goods that conform to the contract, and refusal to do so is a breach of contract. The buyer is deemed to have accepted goods either expressly or by implication through conduct inconsistent with rejection or by lapse of time. The buyer must pay for accepted goods in accordance with the terms of the contract. The buyer can reject goods in commercial units, accept the goods and collect damages for their problems, or reject the full contract shipment. The buyer must give notice of rejection to the seller and cannot do anything with the goods that would be inconsistent with the seller's ownership rights. The buyer should await instructions from the seller on what to do with the goods.

Even following acceptance, the buyer may revoke that acceptance if the problems with the goods substantially impair their value and the problems were either not easily discoverable or the buyer kept the goods based on the seller's promises to repair them and make them whole. Upon revocation of acceptance, the buyer should await instructions from the seller on what steps to take.

Performance can be excused on the grounds of commercial impracticability, but the seller must show objective difficulties that have created more than cost increases.

Learning Outcomes

After studying this chapter, you should be able to clearly explain:

25-1   General Principles

LO.1   List the steps that can be taken when a party to a sales contract feels insecure about the other party's performance

See the *Advanced Bodycare Solutions, LLC v. Thione International, Inc.* case, pages 479–480.

See the *BRC Rubber & Plastics, Inc. v. Continental Carbon Co.* case, pages 488–489.

25-2   Duties of the Parties

LO.2   Explain the obligations of the seller and the buyer in a sales contract

See the *Viking Packaging Technologies v. Vassallo* case, pages 482–483.

LO.3   Identify the types of actions and conduct that constitute acceptance

See the *Bev Smith, Inc. v. Atwell*, case, page 485.

See the Thinking Things Through feature "When a Court Does Not Allow Performance," page 486.

LO.4   Explain the excuses that exist for nonperformance by one party

See the *Magic Valley Foods, Inc. v. Sun Valley Potatoes, Inc.* case, page 487.

See the *BRC Rubber & Plastics, Inc. v. Continental Carbon Co.* case, pages 488–489.

Key Terms

acceptance

anticipatory repudiation

commercial impracticability

commercial units

good faith

repudiation

right to cure

seasonable

substantial impairment

Questions and Case Problems

1. In 1992, Donna Smith telephoned Clark, the manager of Penbridge Farms, in response to an advertisement Clark had placed in the July issue of the *Emu Finder* about the availability for sale of proven breeder pairs. Clark told Smith that he had a breeder pair available. Clark sold the pair to Smith for $16,500. Some months later, after Smith had had a chance to inspect the pair, she discovered that Clark had sold her two males. Smith immediately notified Clark and revoked her acceptance of the animals. Clark said the revocation was too late. Was it?

[*Smith v. Penbridge Associates, Inc.*, 655 A.2d 1015 (Pa. Super.)]

2. On January 3, 1991, Central District Alarm (CDA) and Hal-Tuc entered into a written sales agreement providing that CDA would sell and install new security equipment described on an equipment list attached to the contract. This list included a Javelin VCR. When the system was installed, CDA installed a used JVC VCR instead of a new Javelin VCR. Hal-Tuc called CDA the day after the installation and complained that the equipment was not the Javelin brand, and that the VCR was a used JVC VCR. CDA told Hal-Tuc that the equipment was not used and that a JVC VCR was better than a Javelin. Hal-Tuc telephoned CDA personnel over a two-week period during which they denied that the equipment was used.

   After two weeks of calls, CDA's installation manager went to the store to see the equipment and admitted that it was used. No one from CDA advised Hal-Tuc in advance that it was installing used equipment temporarily until the right equipment arrived. CDA offered to replace it with a new Javelin VCR as soon as one arrived, which would take one or two months. Hal-Tuc asked CDA to return its deposit and take the equipment back, but CDA refused. Hal-Tuc put all the equipment in boxes and stored it. CDA filed a petition against Hal-Tuc for damages for breach of contract. Hal-Tuc filed a counterclaim, alleging fraud. CDA asserted it had the right to cure by tendering conforming goods after Hal-Tuc rejected the nonconforming goods. Was CDA correct? [*Central District Alarm, Inc. v. Hal-Tuc, Inc.*, 866 S.W.2d 210 (Mo. App.)]

3. Bobby Murray Chevrolet, Inc., submitted a bid to the Alamance County Board of Education to supply 1,200 school bus chassis to the district. Bobby Murray was awarded the contract and contracted with General Motors (GM) to purchase the chassis for the school board.

   Between the time of Bobby Murray's contract with GM and the delivery date, the Environmental Protection Agency (EPA) enacted new emission standards for diesel vehicles, such as school buses. Under the new law, the buses Bobby Murray ordered from GM would be out of compliance, as would the buses Bobby Murray specified in its bid to the school board.

   GM asked for several extensions to manufacture the buses within the new EPA guidelines. The school board was patient and gave several extensions, but then, because of its need for buses, purchased them from another supplier after notifying Bobby Murray of its intent to do so. The school board had to pay an additional $150,152.94 for the buses from its alternative source and sued Bobby Murray for that amount. Bobby Murray claimed that it was excused from performance on the grounds of commercial impracticability. Is Bobby Murray correct? Does the defense of commercial impracticability apply in this situation? Be sure to compare this case with other cases and examples in the chapter. [*Alamance County Board of Education v. Bobby Murray Chevrolet, Inc.*, 465 S.E.2d 306 (N.C. App.); rev. denied, 467 S.E.2d 899 (N.C.)]

4. The Home Shopping Club ordered 12,000 Care Bear lamps from Ohio International, Ltd. When the lamps arrived, they had poor painting and staining, elements were improperly glued and could come loose (a danger to the children with the lamps in their rooms), and they overheated very easily (another danger for children and a fire hazard). Home Shopping Network notified International and gave it three months to remedy the problems and provide different lamps. After three months, Home Shopping Network returned all lamps and notified International that it was pulling out of the contract. Could they do so, or had too much time passed? [*Home Shopping Club, Inc. v. Ohio International, Ltd.*, 27 U.C.C. Rep. Serv. 2d 433 (Fla. Cir. Ct.)]

5. Lafer Enterprises sold Christmas decorations to B. P. Development & Management Corp., the owners and operators of the Osceola Square Mall. The package of decorations was delivered to Osceola Square Mall prior to Thanksgiving 1986 for a total cost of $48,775, which B. P. would pay in three installments. Cathy Trivigno, a manager at B. P. who supervised the installation of the decorations, indicated that she and the Osceola Square Mall merchants were not satisfied with the quality of the decorations, but they needed to be in place for the day after Thanksgiving (the start of the holiday shopping season). B. P. complained to Lafer about the quality of the decorations but had the decorations installed. B. P. paid the first installment to Lafer but then stopped payment on the last two checks. B. P. claimed that it had rejected the decorations. Lafer claimed breach for nonpayment because B. P. had used the decorations. Did B. P. accept the decorations? [*B. P. Dev. & Management*

Corp. v. Lafer Enterprises, Inc., 538 So. 2d 1379 (Fla. App.)]

6. Westinghouse Electric Corporation entered into uranium supply contracts with 22 electric utilities during the late 1960s. The contract prices ranged from $7 to $10 per pound. The Arab oil embargo and other changes in energy resources caused the price of uranium to climb to between $45 and $75 per pound. Supply tightened because of increased demand.

   In 1973, Westinghouse wrote to the utilities and explained that it was unable to perform on its uranium sales contracts. The utilities needed uranium. Westinghouse did not have sufficient funds to buy the uranium it had agreed to supply, assuming that it could find a supply. One utility executive commented, after totaling up all 22 supply contracts, that Westinghouse could not have supplied the uranium even under the original contract terms. He said, "Westinghouse oversubscribed itself on these contracts. They hoped that not all the utilities would take the full contract amount."

   Westinghouse says it is impossible for it to perform. The utilities say that they are owed damages because they must still find uranium somewhere. What damages would the law allow? What ethical issues do you see in the original contracts and in Westinghouse's refusal to deliver? Should we excuse parties from contracts because it is so expensive for them to perform? [In re *Westinghouse Uranium Litigation*, 436 F. Supp. 990 (E.D. Va.)]

7. Steel Industries, Inc., ordered steel from Interlink Metals & Chemicals. The steel was to be delivered from a Russian mill. There were political and other issues in Russia, and the mill was shut down. Interlink did not deliver the steel to Steel Industries, claiming that it was excused from performance because it could not get the steel from the Russian mill. What would Interlink have to establish to show that it was excused from performing under the doctrine of commercial impracticability? [*Steel Industries, Inc. v. Interlink Metals & Chemicals, Inc.*, 969 F. Supp. 1046 (E.D. Mich.)]

8. Spaulding & Kimball Co. ordered from Aetna Chemical Co. 75 cartons of window washers. The buyer received them and sold about a third to its customers but later refused to pay for them, claiming that the quality was poor. The seller sued for the price. Would the seller be entitled to the contract price? Refer to the *Weil v. Murray* case described in problem 12 regarding the Degas painting for some insight. [*Aetna Chemical Co. v. Spaulding & Kimball Co.*, 126 A. 582 (Vt.)]

9. Nuco Plastics, Inc., was developing production molds for Universal Plastics, Inc. During the course of the development of the molds, Universal changed specifications and required the use of different materials. Nuco raised the price from $235 per 1,000 parts to $400 per 1,000 parts. Universal refused to pay the additional amount and ended the contract. Nuco was not paid for the molds it had produced and sued for breach of contract and damages. Universal maintained that Nuco had repudiated the contract by raising the price. Is an attempt to raise the price on a contract a repudiation of the contract? [*Nuco Plastics, Inc. v. Universal Plastics, Inc.*, 601 N.E.2d 152 (Ohio App.)]

10. Economy Forms Corp. sold concrete-forming equipment to Kandy. After using the equipment for more than six months, Kandy notified Economy that the equipment was inadequate. Economy Forms alleged that Kandy had accepted the goods. Kandy denied liability. Was there an acceptance? Why or why not? [*Economy Forms Corp. v. Kandy, Inc.*, 391 F. Supp. 944 (N.D. Ga.)]

11. Hornell Brewing Company is a supplier and marketer of alcoholic and nonalcoholic beverages, including the popular iced tea drink, Arizona. In 1992, Stephen A. Spry and Don Vultaggio, Hornell's chairman of the board, made an oral agreement for Spry to be the exclusive distributor of Arizona products in Canada. The initial arrangement was an oral agreement, and in response to Spry's request for a letter that he needed to secure financing, Hornell provided a letter that confirmed the distributorship.

   During 1993 and 1994, Hornell shipped beverages on 10-day credit terms, but between December 1993 and February 1994, Spry's credit balances grew from $20,000 to $100,000, and a $31,000 check from Spry was returned for insufficient funds.

   In March 1994, Hornell demanded that Spry obtain a line and/or letter of credit to pay for the beverages to place their relationship on a more secure footing. An actual line of credit never came about. Hornell did receive a partial payment by a wire transfer on May 9, 1994. Spry ordered 30 trailer loads of "product" from Hornell at a total purchase price of $390,000 to $450,000. Hornell learned from several sources, including its regional sales manager, Baumkel, that Spry's warehouse was empty; that he had no managerial, sales, or office staff; that he had no trucks; and that his operation was a sham.

On May 10, 1994, Hornell wrote to Spry, telling him that it would extend up to $300,000 of credit to him, net 14 days cash "based on your prior representation that you have secured a $1,500,000 U.S. line of credit." Spry did not respond to this letter. After some months of futile negotiations by counsel, Hornell filed suit. Has there been a breach? What are the parties' rights? [*Hornell Brewing Co., Inc. v. Spry*, 664 N.Y.S.2d 698 (Sup. Ct.)]

12. Mark Murray and Ian Peck are art dealers who own separate art galleries located in New York. Robert and Jean Weil reside in Montgomery, Alabama, and are art collectors. Murray and Sam Lehr, a business acquaintance of his, traveled to Montgomery to see the various paintings in the Weils' collection, including a painting by Edgar Degas titled *Aux Courses*, which Murray examined under ultraviolet light. Murray later telephoned Weil and told him that he had spoken with someone who might be interested in purchasing the Degas.

On November 3, 1997, the director of Murray's gallery, Stephanie Calman, traveled to the Weils' home in Alabama. Calman, on behalf of Murray, and Robert Weil executed an agreement that provided for consignment of the Degas to Murray's gallery "for a private inspection in New York for a period of a week" from November 3, "to be extended only with the express permission of the consignor." Calman returned to New York with the painting the same day.

Murray then showed the Degas to Peck. Peck expressed an interest in purchasing the Degas after seeing it, and the price of $1,125,000 was discussed.

On November 26, 1997, Murray signed an agreement drafted by Weil and retyped on Murray's letterhead. Weil signed the agreement on December 1, 1997.

Neither Murray nor anyone else ever paid Weil the $1 million. Nonetheless, Murray maintained possession of the Degas from November 3, 1997, through March 25, 1998, when Weil requested its return.

The Weils filed suit, seeking the price for the painting via summary judgment. Are the Weils entitled to recover? Explain why or why not. [*Weil v. Murray*, 161 F. Supp. 2d 250 (S.D.N.Y.)]

13. Trefalcon (a commercial arm of the government of Ghana) entered into a contract with Supply Commission as a purchaser of residual fuel oil (RFO). Supply Commission agreed, among other things, to supply Trefalcon with RFO at competitive prices as reserves permitted. Approximately six weeks into the agreement, on May 3, 1974, Supply Commission wrote a letter to Trefalcon proposing a method for pricing the refined fuel it would sell to Trefalcon.

A dispute arose six months later when Supply Commission first began to raise the price of RFO to account for escalations. In an effort to continue the contract, the parties orally agreed to a so-called Standstill Agreement, pursuant to which Ghana temporarily would forgo payment of escalations. By May 12, 1975, Trefalcon had paid only the base price for each of the 26 residual fuel cargoes it had received.

On May 26, 1975, J.V.L. Mensah, a representative of Supply Commission, sent a letter to Trefalcon demanding payment of $7,885,523.12 for escalation charges and declaring that no further oil would be sold until payment in full was made. After receiving the Mensah letter, Trefalcon tendered two payments to Bank of Ghana—one in the amount of $1,617,682.29 (tendered June 10, 1975), the other in the amount of $1,185,000 (tendered June 27, 1975).

With full payment still outstanding in July 1975, Supply Commission canceled the contract and sought damages for breach following the failure to provide assurances. Will Supply Commission recover? [*Reich v. Republic of Ghana*, 2002 WL 142610 (S.D.N.Y.)]

14. Harry Ulmas made a contract to buy a new car from Acey Oldsmobile. He was allowed to keep his old car until the new car was delivered. The sales contract gave him a trade-in value of $650 on the old car but specified that the car would be reappraised when it was actually brought to the dealer. When Ulmas brought the trade-in to the dealer, an Acey employee took it for a test drive and said that the car was worth between $300 and $400. Acey offered Ulmas only $50 for his trade-in. Ulmas refused to buy from Acey and purchased from another dealer, who appraised the trade-in at $400. Ulmas sued for breach of contract on the grounds of violation of good faith. Was he right? [*Ulmas v. Acey Oldsmobile, Inc.*, 310 N.Y.S.2d 147 (N.Y. Civ.)]

15. Catherine Joseph, who does business as Metro Classics, sold clothing to Jackson Hole Traders, a corporation owned by David and Elizabeth Speaks. Jackson Hole Traders is located in Jackson, Wyoming, and sells clothing for men and women through a retail store and mail-order catalog business. The clothing Joseph sold was specially manufactured for Jackson Hole Traders and had a total contract price of $50,000 with net 30 terms.

    When the clothing items were shipped between July and September 1994, approximately 900 items were sent. Elizabeth Speaks complained about the quality of some of the clothing items when they arrived and was given a credit of $1,096 for returned merchandise. However, Jackson Hole Traders did not pay $33,000 of the total Joseph bill despite its being well past the net 30-day period for payment. When Joseph demanded payment, Elizabeth Speaks boxed up approximately 350 items of the clothing and sent them back, demanding a credit for revocation of acceptance. Joseph filed suit for payment, alleging that it was too late for revocation of acceptance. The trial court found for Joseph, and the Speakses appealed. Explain what the court could decide in the case. [*Jackson Hole Traders, Inc. v. Joseph*, 931 P.2d 244 (Wyo.)]

CPA Questions

1. Under the sales article of the UCC, which of the following statements is correct?

    a. Obligations of the parties to the contract must be performed in good faith.

    b. Merchants and nonmerchants are treated alike.

    c. The contract must involve the sale of goods for a price of more than $500.

    d. None of the provisions of the UCC may be disclaimed by agreement.

2. Rowe Corp. purchased goods from Stair Co. that were shipped COD. Under the sales article of the UCC, which of the following rights does Rowe have?

    a. The right to inspect the goods before paying.

    b. The right to possession of the goods before paying.

    c. The right to reject nonconforming goods.

    d. The right to delay payment for a reasonable period of time.

3. Bibbeon Manufacturing shipped 300 designer navy blue blazers to Custom Clothing Emporium. The blazers arrived on Friday, earlier than Custom had anticipated and on an exceptionally busy day for its receiving department. They were perfunctorily examined and sent to a nearby warehouse for storage until needed. On the following Monday, upon closer examination, it was discovered that the quality of the blazer linings was inferior to that specified in the sales contract. Which of the following is correct insofar as Custom's rights?

    a. Custom can reject the blazers upon subsequent discovery of the defects.

    b. Custom must retain the blazers since it accepted them and had an opportunity to inspect them upon delivery.

    c. Custom's only course of action is rescission.

    d. Custom had no rights if the linings were merchantable quality.

4. Parker ordered 50 cartons of soap from Riddle Wholesale Company. Each carton contained 12 packages of soap. The terms were: $8.00 per carton 2/10, net/30, FOB buyer's delivery platform, delivery June 1. During transit approximately one-half the packages were damaged by the carrier. The delivery was made on May 28. Answer the following with "Yes" or "No."

    a. Riddle had the risk of loss during transit.

    b. If Parker elects to accept the undamaged part of the shipment, he will be deemed to have accepted the entire shipment.

    c. To validly reject the goods, Parker must give timely notice of rejection to Riddle within a reasonable time after delivery.

    d. If Riddle were notified of the rejection on May 28, Riddle could cure the defect by promptly notifying Parker of its intention to do so and making a second delivery to Parker of conforming goods by June 1.

    e. The statute of frauds is inapplicable to the transaction in the facts given.

Remedies for Breach of Sales Contracts

Learning Outcomes ‹‹‹

After studying this chapter, you should be able to

LO.1 List the remedies of the seller when the buyer breaches a sales contract

LO.2 List the remedies of the buyer when the seller breaches a sales contract

LO.3 Determine the validity of clauses limiting damages

26-1 Statute of Limitations

If one of the parties to a sale fails to perform the contract, the nonbreaching party has remedies under Article 2 of the Uniform Commercial Code (UCC). In addition, the parties may have included provisions on remedies in their contract as well as judicial remedies.

Judicial remedies have time limitations. After the expiration of a particular period of time, the party seeking a remedy can no longer resort to the courts. The UCC **statute of limitations** applies to actions brought for remedies on the breach of a sales contract.[1] When a suit is brought on the basis of a tort theory, such as negligence, fraud, or strict tort liability, other general statutes of limitations apply.

statute of limitations– statute that restricts the period of time within which an action may be brought.

C P A

26-1a Time Limits for Suits under the UCC

An action for breach of a sales contract must be commenced within four years after the time of the **breach.** The statute of limitations can be reduced between merchants to as little as one year but cannot be reduced in consumer contracts.

breach–failure to act or perform in the manner called for in a contract.

When a cause of action arises depends on the nature of the breach. The UCC has three measurements for determining when a breach occurs. The basic rule is that the time begins to run when the breach occurs, but that rule has exceptions that include special timing rules for repudiation, infringement, breach of warranty, and future performance.

A buyer seeking damages because of a breach of the sales contract must give the seller notice of the breach within a reasonable time after the buyer discovers or should have discovered it.[2]

C P A

26-1b Time Limits for Other Suits

When a party seeks recovery on a non-Code theory, such as on the basis of strict tort liability, fraud, or negligence, the UCC statute of limitations does not apply. The action is subject to each state's tort statute of limitations. Tort statutes of limitations are found in individual state statutes, and the time limitations vary by state. However, the tort statutes of limitations tend to be shorter than the UCC statute of limitations.

26-2 Remedies of the Seller

When the buyer breaches a sales contract, the seller has different remedies available that are designed to afford the seller compensation for the losses caused by the buyer's breach. In many cases of breach, only a combination of the various remedies can make the nonbreaching party whole again.

26-2a Seller's Lien

In the absence of an agreement for the extension of credit to the buyer for the purchase of goods, and until the buyer pays for the goods or performs whatever actions the contract requires, the seller has the right to retain possession of the goods.[3]

---

[1] U.C.C. §2-703.
[2] U.C.C. §2-607(3)(a).
[3] U.C.C. §2-703.

CPA   ## 26-2b Seller's Remedy of Stopping Shipment

When the buyer has breached the contract prior to the time the goods have arrived at their destination, the seller can stop the goods from coming into the buyer's possession. This remedy is important to sellers because it eliminates the need for sellers to try to recover goods from buyers who have indicated they cannot or will not pay.

A seller has the right to stop shipment if the buyer has received goods on credit and the seller learns that the buyer is insolvent, the buyer has not provided assurances as requested, or the seller has grounds to believe performance by the buyer will not occur.[4] Also, the right to retrieve the goods in the case of a credit buyer's insolvency continues for "a reasonable time after the buyer's receipt of the goods."

CPA   ## 26-2c Resale by Seller

When the buyer has breached the contract, the seller may resell any of the goods the seller still holds. After the resale, the seller is not liable to the original buyer on the contract and does not have to surrender any profit obtained on the resale. On the other hand, if the proceeds are less than the contract price, the seller may recover the loss from the original buyer.[5]

The seller must give reasonable notice to the breaching buyer of the intention to resell the goods. Such notice need not be given if the goods are perishable or could decline rapidly in value. The seller must conduct any method of resale under standards of commercial reasonableness.[6]

26-2d Cancellation by Seller

When the buyer materially breaches the contract, the seller may cancel the contract. Such a cancellation ends the contract and discharges all unperformed obligations on both sides. Following cancellation, the seller has any remedy with respect to the breach by the buyer that is still available.

26-2e Seller's Action for Damages under the Market Price Formula

When the buyer fails to pay for accepted goods, the seller may resell the goods, as discussed earlier, or bring a contract action to recover damages. One formula for a seller's damages is the difference between the market price at the time and place of the tender of the goods and the contract price.[7] Whether the seller chooses to resell or recover the difference between the contract price and the market price is the seller's decision.[8] The flexibility in the remedies under the UCC is provided because certain goods have very high market fluctuations. **For Example,** suppose that Sears has agreed to purchase 10 refrigerators from Whirlpool at a price of $1,000 each, but then Sears notifies Whirlpool that it will not be buying the refrigerators after all. Whirlpool determines the market price at the time of tender to be $850 per refrigerator. The best Whirlpool can find from an alternate buyer after a search is $800. Whirlpool can select the resale remedy ($1,000 – $800, or $200 in damages) to adequately compensate for the change in the market price between the time of tender and the time damages are sought.

---

[4] U.C.C. §2-705.
[5] U.C.C. §2-706(1), (6); In re *American Remnaufacturers, Inc.,* 451 B.R. 349 (D. Del. 2011).
[6] In re *Professional Veterinary Products, Ltd.,* 454 B.R. 479 (D. Neb. 2011).
[7] U.C.C. §2-708. *Stalloy Metals, Inc. v. Kennametal, Inc.,* 18 N.E.3d 1273 (Ohio App. 2014).
[8] *Peace River Seed Co–Operative, Ltd. v. Proseeds Marketing, Inc.,* 322 P.3d 531 (Or. 2014).

CPA ### 26-2f Seller's Action for Lost Profits

If the market and resale price measures of damages do not place the seller in the same position in which the seller would have been had the buyer performed, the seller is permitted to recover lost profits. The recovery of lost profits reimburses the seller for costs incurred in gearing up for contract performance.[9] **For Example,** suppose that a buyer has ordered 200 wooden rocking horses from a seller-manufacturer. Before production on the horses begins, the buyer breaches. The seller has nothing to resell, and the goods have not been identified to even permit a market value assessment. Nonetheless, the seller has geared up for production, counted on the contract, and perhaps bypassed other contracts in order to perform. An appropriate remedy for the seller of the rocking horses would be the profits it would have made had the buyer performed.

Some courts also follow the lost volume doctrine that allows sellers to recover for the profits they would have made if the buyer had completed the transaction.[10] **For Example,** suppose that Maytag has a contract to sell 10 washing machines for $600 each to Lakewood Apartment Managers. Lakewood breaches the agreement and refuses to take or pay for the washing machines. Maytag is able to resell them to Suds 'n Duds Laundromat for $600 each. The price is the same, but the theory of lost volume profits is that Maytag could have sold 20 washers, not just 10, if Lakewood had not breached. Maytag's profit on each machine is $200. Lost volume profits in this situation would be 10 times the $200, or $2,000.

CPA ### 26-2g Other Types of Damages

incidental damages— incurred by the nonbreaching party as part of the process of trying to cover (buy substitute goods) or sell (selling subject matter of contract to another); includes storage fees, commissions, and the like.

So far, the discussion of remedies has focused on the damages that result because the seller did not sell the goods. However, the seller may incur additional expenses because of the breach. Some of those expenses can be recovered as damages. U.C.C. §2-710 provides that the seller can also recover, as **incidental damages,** any commercially reasonable charges, expenses, or commissions incurred[11] in recovering damages.[12] **For Example,** the seller may recover expenses for the transportation, care, and storage of the goods after the buyer's breach, as well as any costs incurred in the return or resale of the goods. Such damages are in addition to any others that may be recovered by the seller.

CPA ### 26-2h Seller's Action for the Purchase Price

If goods are specially manufactured and the buyer refuses to take them, it is possible for the seller to recover as damages the full purchase price and keep the goods.[13] **For Example,** a printing company that has printed catalogs for a retail mail-order merchant will not be able to sell the catalogs to anyone else. The remedy for the seller is recovery of the purchase price.[14]

26-2i Seller's Nonsale Remedies

secured transaction— credit sale of goods or a secured loan that provides special protection for the creditor.

In addition to the seller's traditional sales remedies, many sellers enter into other transactions that provide protection from buyer breaches. One such protection is afforded when the seller obtains a security interest from the buyer under UCC Article 9. A **secured transaction**

---

[9] U.C.C. §2-709.

[10] *Gianetti v. Norwalk Hospital,* 43 A.3d 567 (Conn. 2012); *Collins Entertainment Corp. v. Coats and Coats Rental Amusement,* 629 S.E.2d 635 (S.C. 2006).

[11] U.C.C. §2-710.

[12] U.C.C. §2-710; *WPS, Inc. v. Expro Americas, LCC,* 369 S.W.3d 384 (Tex. App. 2012).

[13] *Hyosung America, Inc. v. Sumagh Textile Co., Ltd.,* (2nd Cir. 1998). *Barrington Group, Ltd., Inc. v. Classic Cruise Holdings S De RL,* 435 Fed. Appx. 382, 2011 WL 3364383 (5th Cir. 2011).

[14] U.C.C. §2-709(1)(a) and (b).

is a pledge of property by the buyer-debtor that enables the seller to take possession of the goods if the buyer fails to pay the amount owed. (See Chapter 33.) Figure 26-1 is a summary of the remedies available to the seller under Article 2.

FIGURE 26-1	Seller's Remedies under Article 2				
REMEDY	**STOP DELIVERY**	**RESALE PRICE**	**MARKET PRICE**	**ACTION FOR PRICE**	**LOST PROFIT**
SECTION NUMBER	2–703	2–706 2–710	2–708 2–710	2–709 2–708	2–708(2)
WHEN AVAILABLE	Insolvency* Advance breach by buyer	Buyer fails to take goods	Buyer fails to take goods	Specially manufactured goods	Anticipatory repudiation Breach
NATURE OF REMEDY	Stop delivery of any size shipment or recover goods if buyer insolvent	Contract price – Resale price + Incidental damages – Expenses saved + Consequential damages	Contract price – Market price + Incidental damages – Expenses saved + Consequential damages	Contract price + Incidental damages – Expenses saved + Consequential damages	Profits + Incidental damages – Salvage value + Consequential damages

*Insolvency is defined under UCC Article 2 as the inability to pay debts as they become due.

CASE SUMMARY

Shaving Off Damages When the Shaving Mill Sells

FACTS: James Bowen and Richard Cagle (appellants), doing business as B & C Shavings (B & C) agreed in 2009 to sell Kendall Gardner a shavings mill to produce wood shavings for poultry processors. They agreed that B & C would build an eight-foot shaving mill for Gardner. On July 13, 2009, B & C faxed an invoice to Gardner reflecting a purchase price of $86,200, a thirty percent down payment of $25,860, and a "balance due before shipment" of $60,340. Gardner sent a payment of $25,920, which included the bank's fees, via wire transfer to B & C on July 14, 2009.

In August 2009, Gardner discovered that the poultry plants with whom he had planned on doing business were no longer interested in purchasing wood shavings. Gardner called Cagle to inform him of the situation and to see if B & C could stop production of the machine.

On September 10, 2009, B & C wrote a letter to Gardner informing him that the shaving machine had been finished and that the balance of $60,340 was due. The letter further stated that Gardner had "ten days from this date ... to pay the balance due or you will lose the down payment that you paid." Gardner spoke with Cagle several times on the phone that weekend and eventually responded with a letter dated September 14, 2009, in which he explained his financial circumstances and asked B & C to help him recover part of his down payment. B & C eventually sold the machine to another company for $86,500 in November 2009. B & C never returned any of Gardner's down payment to him.

Shaving Off Damages When the Shaving Mill Sells continued

The eight-foot machine ordered by Gardner was unusual in the industry and was a special order. B & C was able to sell the machine after providing additional work to meet the new purchaser's specifications. B & C spent $10,406.67 in order to be able to sell the machine to another company.

Gardner filed a complaint seeking recovery of the down payment.

The trial court concluded that "the equitable thing here" would be for B & C to return Gardner's down payment to him, less the money that B & C spent making modifications to the machine so that it could be sold. The court therefore subtracted the $10,406 in modifications from the $25,860 down payment and concluded that

Gardner was entitled to be awarded $15,454, plus postjudgment interest. B & C appealed.

DECISION: B & C was able to resell the shaving machine for $300 more than the contract price; for that reason, there is no difference between the resale price and the contract price for B & C to "recover." B & C was, however, entitled to its incidental damages. B & C spent $10,406 in additional expenses to make the machine salable to another purchaser. As B & C had already received $25,860 from Gardner in the form of Gardner's down payment, the trial court correctly concluded that Gardner was entitled to the return of his $15,454 ($25,860 −$10,406 = $15,454). [***Bowen v. Gardner*, 425 S.W.3d 875 (Ark. App. 2013)**]

26-3   Remedies of the Buyer

When the seller breaches a sales contract, the buyer has a number of remedies under Article 2 of the UCC. Additional remedies based on contract or tort theories of product liability may also be available. (See Chapter 24.)

26-3a   Rejection of Improper Tender

As discussed in Chapter 25, if the goods tendered by the seller do not conform to the contract in some way, the buyer may reject them. However, the rejection is the beginning of the buyer's remedies. Following rejection, the buyer can proceed to recover under the various formulas provided for buyers under the UCC.

26-3b   Revocation of Acceptance

The buyer may revoke acceptance of the goods when they do not conform to the contract, the defect substantially impairs the value of the contract to the buyer, and the buyer either could not discover the problem or kept the goods because of a seller's promise of repair (see Chapter 25). Again, following revocation of acceptance, the buyer has various remedies available under the UCC.

CASE SUMMARY

Steaming Mad About the Lousy 1995 Cadillac

FACTS: On March 4, 2011, Lola Castro (of Lodge Grass, Montana) called Ernie's Auto in Billings to inquire about a used 1995 Cadillac DeVille advertised for sale in a local newspaper. The price was listed at $1,995 but Ernie's agreed to sell it to Castro for $1,500. On Friday, March 4, Castro and her husband drove to Billings to purchase the car. Upon arrival at Ernie's lot at around 5:30 P.M., Castro signed multiple purchase documents, each of which indicated in bold

Steaming Mad About the Lousy 1995 Cadillac continued

print that the car was being sold "AS IS" without any expressed or implied guarantees or warranties. Neither Castro nor her husband test drove the car before purchase.

At around 6:00 P.M., Castro and her husband left Ernie's. Castro's husband drove the Cadillac and Castro drove the family's other car. Approximately 2.5 miles from Ernie's, the Cadillac began steaming and losing fluids from the radiator. They pulled into a Town Pump service station and left the vehicle there without seeking service. Castro testified that her husband called Ernie's at that time and multiple times over the following few days but there is no record of those discussions. Castro left the Cadillac parked at the Town Pump until the following Wednesday. On that day, she and her husband returned to the Town Pump, purchased and installed a battery in the Cadillac, and drove it back to Ernie's. They parked it on the street near Ernie's lot, returned the keys to Ernie's and demanded refund of their purchase money. Ernie's refused to refund Castro's money.

On April 1, 2011, Castro filed suit. She alleged that Ernie's had breached an express warranty, violated the Montana Consumer Protection Act, and was negligent. She also alleged that she had the right to revoke her acceptance. She asked for a refund of her $1,500 purchase money, as well as $3,000 in damages, and reasonable attorney fees.

The Justice Court granted Ernie's motion for a directed verdict. Castro appealed to the District Court and the District Court affirmed the directed verdict and dismissed Castro's appeal. Castro appealed again.

DECISION: Castro had the burden of providing credible evidence that the vehicle was nonconforming but failed to do so. While she recounted the problems they had with the vehicle—the engine light came on, the car leaked fluids, and smoke or steam was emitted—she failed to establish that these problems constituted nonconformities in a 16-year-old car purchased "as is." Moreover, Castro herself testified that replacement of the battery rendered the car operable. Castro did not have the car checked by a mechanic for proof of nonconformity or to determine the actual condition of the vehicle. A purchaser of a used 1995 vehicle in 2011 "should … expect that some repairs will be necessary such as belts, hoses, battery, seals, tire balancing and alignment, etc. These sorts of things do not render a motor vehicle unsafe."

There was simply no evidence to support a ruling in favor of Castro on her "revocation of acceptance" claim. However, in an equity sense, Ernie's could not keep both the payment and the car. Ernie's either had to return the car or, if not possible, the money paid. [***Castro v. Ernie's Auto***, 2012 WL 6682134 (Mont. 2012)]

THINKING THINGS THROUGH

The Lululemon Yoga Pants That Were Lemons

Lululemon ordered Luon fabric for its famous black yoga pants from a supplier. The fabric was made into yoga pants, which were then sold as Lululemon pants, which resulted in a wave of customer complaints because the fabric was see-through. Lululemon took the pants back from customers and issued refunds. However, following this glitch in its supply chain, Lululemon began a downward spiral that saw its income and share price drop.

Lululemon also struggled to get products back onto the shelf because of difficulty in replacing the Luon fabric. What types of damages could Lululemon recover for this fabric issue?

CPA   **26-3c** **Buyer's Action for Damages for Nondelivery—Market Price Recovery**

If the seller fails to deliver the goods as required by the contract or repudiates the contract, the buyer is entitled to collect from the seller damages for breach of contract.

CPA   26-3d   # Buyer's Action for Damages for Nondelivery— Cover Price Recovery

A buyer may also choose, as a remedy for the seller's nondelivery of goods that conform to the contract, to purchase substitute goods or cover.[15] If the buyer acts in good faith, the measure of damages for the seller's nondelivery or repudiation is then the difference between the cost of cover and the contract price.[16]

The buyer need only make a reasonable cover purchase as a substitute for the contract goods. The goods purchased need not be identical to the contract goods. **For Example,** if the buyer could secure only 350 five-speed blenders when the contract called for 350 three-speed blenders, the buyer's cover would be reasonable despite the additional expense of the five-speed blenders.

CASE SUMMARY

Cashing in for the Defective Cashews

FACTS: Schutzman sells roasted and salted nuts. Nutsco is a New Jersey wholesaler of cashews that imports the nuts from Brazil and then packs and sells them in the United States.

In 2006, Nutsco used food broker Jim Warner to broker a contract between Nutsco and Schutzman, whereby Nutsco promised to deliver twelve 35,000-pound loads of super large, whole, first-quality ("SLW-1") cashews. The contract also included an option allowing Schutzman to buy four loads of large, whole, first-quality ("LW-1") cashews, if exercised by a certain date.

Schutzman later wanted to order more cashews. Warner amended the contract to add two additional loads. In March 2007, Warner sent a copy of the revised Contract Confirmation adding the two extra loads (loads 13 and 14) to both Nutsco and Schutzman.

Nutsco delivered 10 loads of SLW-1 cashews to Schutzman. After receiving the tenth load, however, Schutzman roast tested the cashews and determined that they did not qualify as "first quality" under specifications of the Association of Food Industries, Inc. (AFI), because of a high level of scorching. SLW-1 cashews must meet AFI standards for SLW-1.

At Warner's request, Schutzman provided six cases of cashews from the tenth load for evaluation by Nutsco. Nutsco concluded after its own analysis that the raw cashews did not meet AFI Specifications for first-quality cashews.

After Nutsco delivered the tenth load, it began arguing that the parties' contract only provided for 12 loads of SLW-1 cashews and that Nutsco was not responsible for providing the two additional loads because there was no signed

contract for the additional loads. Market prices for SLW-1 cashews had increased $2 per pound above the Schutzman contract price. Schutzman initially agreed to keep the load and pay the contract price on the condition that Nutsco deliver all remaining loads, including loads 13 and 14. Nutsco would not agree and Schutzman stored the tenth load in its refrigerated warehouse.

Schutzman did not pay for the rejected tenth load of SLW-1 cashews that Nutsco retrieved. Schutzman did pay all invoices for the nine preceding loads it received and accepted. Schutzman paid a reduced price on two of the invoices after Warner agreed that it could apply $1,750 and $1,284 in credit against these invoices.

Schutzman paid to purchase loads of SLW-1 cashews from other wholesalers. Schutzman paid $5.45 per pound for the additional five loads, or $367,850 more than it would have paid under the contract with Nutsco. Schutzman filed suit for damages in this amount.

DECISION: The court held that there was a contract for shipment of 14 loads of cashews. The court also held that Schutzman did not convert the below-par tenth load of cashews and that Schutzman was entitled to damages for the difference between its contract price with Nutsco and the more-than-doubled price it was required to pay for cover. The court also held that Warner, the agent, at least had apparent authority to negotiate the additional shipments of cashews. [*A. L. Schutzman Company, Inc. v. Nutsco, Inc.,* **2009 WL 5064052 (E.D. Wis. 2009)]**

---

[15] U.C.C. §2-712; *Irwin Indus. Tool Co. v. Worthington Cylinders Wisconsin, LLC*, 747 F. Supp. 2d 568 (W.D.N.C. 2010). *Santorini Cab Corp. v. Banco Popular North America*, 999 N.E.2d 46 (Ill. App. 2013).

[16] U.C.C. §2-712(1) and (2). See *New West Charter Middle School v. Los Angeles Unified School Dist.*, 114 Cal. Rptr. 3d 504 (Cal. App. 2010).

CPA   ### 26-3e **Other Types of Damages**

The buyer is also entitled to collect incidental damages in situations in which he must find substitute goods. Those incidental damages could include additional shipping expenses or perhaps commissions paid to find the goods and purchase them. Buyers often also experience **consequential damages,** which are those damages the buyer experiences with respect to a third party as a result of the seller's breach. **For Example,** a seller's failure to deliver the goods may cause the buyer's production line to come to a halt. The buyer might then breach on its sales and delivery contracts with its buyers. In the case of a government contract, the buyer may have to pay a penalty for being late. These types of damages are consequential ones and can be recovered if the seller knew about the consequences or they were foreseeable.

consequential damages–damages the buyer experiences as a result of the seller's breach with respect to a third party.

26-3f **Action for Breach of Warranty**

A remedy available to a buyer when goods are delivered but fail to conform to warranties is an action for breach of warranty.

CASE SUMMARY

A Chance of Cloudy Meatballs

FACTS: General Mills Operations, LLC, purchased "Big Meatballs Cooked Italian," which is used in General Mills' Progresso Italian–Style Wedding Soup, from Five Star Custom Foods, Ltd.

General Mills sent purchase orders to Five Star. The Purchase Order Terms and Conditions were on the back of every purchase order, including the meatball orders faxed to Five Star. General Mills also mailed a copy of the 2004 version of its Terms and Conditions to Five Star's Customer Service Manager on February 4, 2004.

The Terms and Conditions included the following:

5. GOODS: The Goods shall conform in all respects to the description on the face of this Order, and or [General Mills'] then current specifications furnished to [Five Star]. The Goods ... shall be new, of first class commercial type ... This warranty is in addition to and not in lieu of, any other warranties or guarantees made by [Five Star] or created or implied as a matter of law.

Additionally, the purchase order states that "[t]he goods must conform to all current General Mills' specifications as furnished to Seller." General Mills mailed a copy of the ingredient specifications for its meatballs to Five Star. Five Star acknowledged receipt of the specifications, which included the following:

The Beef or Beef By–Product in this ingredient must be sourced from countries or regions where USDA

recognized BSE controls are in place in accordance with the recommendations of the World Animal Health Organization.

One of Five Star's beef suppliers was Westland Meat Packing Company. Westland's beef was used in two orders of meatballs supplied to General Mills. In February 2008, the Food Safety Inspection Service (FSIS) issued a recall of all products containing beef produced by Westland between February 1, 2006, and February 15, 2008. The recall was due to Westland's supposed failure to contact FSIS when it identified nonambulatory disabled, or "downer," cows that became nonambulatory after passing inspections but before slaughter. In such situations, regulations at the time required the producer to notify FSIS and to call a public-health veterinarian to conduct an examination. Westland's alleged failure to consistently do this was deemed noncompliant, and the recall followed. There is no evidence, however, that any of the Westland beef supplied to Five Star or incorporated into General Mills' meatballs came from downer cattle.

When Five Star learned of the recall, it traced the Westland beef that it had incorporated into its products and notified General Mills of the recall on February 8, 2008. Five Star identified two purchase orders of meatballs, totaling 32,460 pounds, which contained Westland beef.

General Mills was required to identify and destroy all soup containing the recalled meatballs in its inventory as

A Chance of Cloudy Meatballs continued

well as soup that it had already sold to grocery stores and other customers. The recall cost General Mills more than $1,000,000.

General Mills filed suit in January 2010, asserting claims for breach of contract, breach of express warranties, breach of the implied warranty of merchantability, breach of the implied warranty of fitness for a particular purpose, and negligence. (Five Star filed a Third-Party Complaint asserting claims against Cattleman's Choice, Inc. d/b/a Westland.) Both General Mills and Five Star moved for summary judgment.

DECISION: There was no evidence of an actual defect in the meatball product as required to prove breach of express or implied warranties. Five Star breached the contract with

General Mills since it failed to receive the benefit of its bargain. Five Star was on notice of the terms and conditions since they had been incorporated by reference into the purchase agreement with General Mills. The contract terms were not inconspicuous, illegible, or hidden in boilerplate language; and the placement of the terms and conditions on the back of General Mills purchase order did not render terms unenforceable, under Minnesota law, since they did not materially alter the parties' agreement. General Mills was entitled to the cost of the recall ($1,000,000) plus attorneys' fees. [*General Mills Operations, LLC v. Five Star Custom Foods, LTD*, 789 F. Supp. 2d 1148 (D. Minn. 2011)]

Notice of Breach

If the buyer has accepted goods that do not conform to the contract or there has been a breach of any warranties given, the buyer must notify the seller of the breach within a reasonable time after the breach is discovered or should have been discovered.[17]

Measure of Damages

If the buyer has given the necessary notice of breach, the buyer may recover damages measured by the loss resulting in the normal course of events from the breach. If suit is brought for breach of warranty, the measure of damages is the difference between the value of the goods as they were at the time of tender and the value that they would have had if they had been as warranted.

Notice of Third-Party Action against Buyer

When a buyer elects the remedy of resale and sells the contract goods to a third party, that third party has the right of suit against the buyer for breach of warranty. In such a case, it is the buyer's option whether to give the seller notice of the action and request that the seller defend that action.

26-3g Cancellation by Buyer

The buyer may cancel or rescind the contract if the seller fails to deliver the goods, if the seller has repudiated the contract, or if the goods have been rightfully rejected or their acceptance revoked.[18] A buyer who cancels the contract is entitled to recover as much of the purchase price as has been paid, including the value of any property given as a trade-in as part of the purchase price. The fact that the buyer cancels the contract does not destroy the buyer's cause of action against the seller for breach of that contract. The buyer may recover from the seller not only any payment made on the purchase price

---

[17] *DC General Contractors, Inc. v. Slay Steel, Inc.*, 109 So. 3d 577 (Miss. App. 2013).
[18] U.C.C. §2-720.

but also damages for the breach of the contract. The damages represent the difference between the contract price and the cost of cover.[19]

The right of the buyer to cancel or rescind the sales contract may be lost by a delay in exercising the right. A buyer who, with full knowledge of the defects in the goods, makes partial payments or performs acts of ownership of the goods inconsistent with the decision to cancel may lose certain remedy provisions or be limited in recovery under Article 2.

26-3h Buyer's Resale of Goods

When the buyer has possession of the goods after rightfully rejecting them or after rightfully revoking acceptance, the buyer is treated as a seller in possession of goods after default by a buyer. When the seller has breached, the buyer has a security interest in the goods to protect the claim against the seller for breach and may proceed to resell the goods. From the proceeds of the sale, the aggrieved buyer is entitled to deduct any payments made to the seller and any expenses reasonably incurred in the inspection, receipt, transportation, care and custody, and resale of the goods.[20]

CPA ## 26-3i Action for Specific Performance

Under Article 2, specific performance is a remedy available only to buyers in those circumstances in which the goods are specially manufactured, unique, or rare, such as antiques or goods with sentimental value for the buyer. **For Example,** a buyer with a contract to buy a chair from Elvis Presley's home would be entitled to a specific performance remedy of delivery of the chair. Distributors have been granted specific performance against suppliers to deliver goods covered by supply contracts because of the unique dependence of the supply chain and the assumed continuous feeding of that chain.

Specific performance will not be granted, however, merely because the price of the goods purchased from the seller has gone up. In such a case, the buyer can still purchase the goods in the open market. The fact that it will cost more to cover can be compensated for by allowing the buyer to recover the cost increase from the seller.

26-3j Nonsale Remedies of the Buyer

In addition to the remedies given the buyer under UCC Article 2, the buyer may have remedies based on contract or tort theories of liability.

The pre-Code law on torts still applies in UCC Article 2 transactions. The seller may therefore be held liable to the buyer for any negligence, fraud, or strict tort liability that occurred in the transaction. (See Chapter 24.)

A defrauded buyer may both avoid the contract and recover damages. The buyer also has the choice of retaining the contract and recovering damages for the losses caused by the fraud.[21]

Figure 26-2 provides a summary of the remedies available to buyers under Article 2.

---

[19] U.C.C. §2-712(1), (2); *Newmar Corp. v. McCrary*, 309 P.3d 1021 (Nev. 2013).
[20] U.C.C. §2-715(1); *Whitbeck v. Champagne*, 149 So. 3d 372 (La. App. 2014).
[21] *Sherwin Alumina L.P. v. AluChem, Inc.*, 512 F. Supp. 2d 957 (S.D. Tex. 2007).

FIGURE 26-2	Buyer's Remedies under Article 2		
REMEDY	**SPECIFIC PERFORMANCE (REPLEVIN IDENTIFICATION)**	**COVER**	**MARKET PRICE**
SECTION NUMBER	2–711	2–712 2–715	2–708 2–710
WHEN AVAILABLE	Rare or unique goods	Seller fails to deliver or goods are defective (rejection) or revocation of acceptance	Seller fails to deliver or goods are defective (rejection or revocation of acceptance)
NATURE OF REMEDY	Buyer gets goods + incidental damages + consequential damages	Cover price – Contract price + Incidental damages + Consequential damages – Expenses saved	Market price – Contract price + Incidental damages + Consequential damages – Expenses saved

26-4 Contract Provisions on Remedies

The parties to a sales contract may modify the remedies provided under Article 2 or limit those remedies.

CPA 26-4a Limitation of Damages

Liquidated Damages

liquidated damages—provision stipulating the amount of damages to be paid in the event of default or breach of contract.

The parties may specify the exact amount of damages that may be recovered in case of breach. A **liquidated damages** clause in a contract can be valid if it meets the standards of Article 2. For nonconsumer contracts, the enforceability of a liquidated damages clause depends on whether the amount is reasonable in light of the anticipated or actual harm.

CASE SUMMARY

The Cost of Breaching a Jet-Set Contract

FACTS: On August 21, 1992, Miguel A. Diaz Rodriguez (Diaz) entered into a contract with Learjet to buy a Model 60 jet aircraft for $3,000,000 with a $250,000 deposit made on execution of the contract; $750,000 payment on September 18, 1992; $1,000,000 180 days before delivery of the aircraft; and the balance due on delivery of the

The Cost of Breaching a Jet-Set Contract continued

aircraft. Diaz paid the $250,000 deposit but made no other payments.

In September 1992, Diaz said he no longer wanted the aircraft and asked for the deposit to be returned. Learjet informed Diaz that the $250,000 deposit was being retained as liquidated damages because their contract provided as follows:

> *Learjet may terminate this Agreement as a result of the Buyer's failure to make any progress payment when due. If this Agreement is terminated by Learjet for any reason stipulated in the previous sentence, Learjet shall retain all payments theretofore made by the Buyer as liquidated damages and not as a penalty and the parties shall thenceforth be released from all further obligations hereunder. Such damages include, but are not limited to, loss of profit on this sale, direct and indirect costs incurred as a result of disruption in production, training expense advance and selling expenses in effecting resale of the Airplane.*

After Diaz breached the contract, Circus Circus Enterprises purchased the Learjet Diaz had ordered with some changes that cost $1,326. Learjet realized a $1,887,464 profit on the sale of the aircraft to Circus Circus, which was a larger profit than Learjet had originally budgeted for the sale to Diaz.

Diaz filed suit seeking to recover the $250,000 deposit. The district court granted summary judgment to Learjet, and Diaz appealed. The case was remanded for a determination of the reasonableness of the liquidated damages. The district court upheld the $250,000 as reasonable damages, and Diaz appealed.

DECISION: The lower court's judgment was affirmed. Diaz challenged the reasonableness of the liquidated damages clause. The $250,000 deposit as a liquidated damages clause in a contract in this price range was not unreasonable. Also, the seller was the one that lost its profits on a second sale that it would have made had Diaz not breached. The "lost volume" provision of the UCC permits nonbreaching sellers to recover the lost profits on a contract in which the other remedy sections do not compensate for the breach by the buyer. The evidence indicates that the lost profit from the Diaz contract would have been approximately $1.8 million. [***Rodriguez v. Learjet, Inc.,* 946 P.2d 1010 (Kan. App. 1997)**]

Exclusion of Damages

The sales contract may provide that in case of breach, no damages may be recovered or no consequential damages may be recovered. When goods are sold for consumer use and personal injuries are sustained, such total exclusions are unconscionable and unenforceable. Such a contract limitation is not enforceable in other types of contracts (nonconsumer) unless the party seeking to enforce it is able to prove that the limitation of liability was

ETHICS & THE LAW

The 30-Day Grace Period That Is Now 120 Days

Mondelez International, a snack and food company spun off from Kraft Foods in 2013, sent a letter to all its suppliers letting them know that it would not be paying invoices for 120 days from the time of its receipt.

Thirty days was once the accepted time frame, but companies such as Procter & Gamble have 45-day payments negotiated with its suppliers and was working to increase that time to 75 days. Merck has been asking for 90 days.

The result is that suppliers, who are dependent upon such large companies, end up carrying those amounts for the companies. The suppliers must then fund their own cash flow problems, thus increasing their costs.

There is no regulation that controls payment time, only business custom. However, consumer payments practice is that payments are due from them to their sellers within 14 to 30 days. Discuss the ethical issues in these longer payment time frames.

commercially reasonable and fair rather than oppressive and surprising. As discussed in Chapter 24, limitations on damages for personal injuries resulting from breaches of warranty are not enforceable.

CPA   ### 26-4b Limitation of Remedies

The parties may limit the remedies that are provided by the Code in the case of breach of contract. A seller may specify that the only remedy of the buyer for breach of warranty will be the repair or replacement of the goods or that the buyer will be limited to returning the goods and obtaining a refund of the purchase price, subject to the restrictions discussed in Chapter 24.

26-5 Remedies in the International Sale of Goods

The United Nations Convention on Contracts for the International Sale of Goods (CISG) provides remedies for breach of a sales contract between parties from nations that have approved the CISG.

26-5a Remedies of the Seller

Under the CISG, if the buyer fails to perform any obligations under the contract, the seller may require the buyer to pay the price, take delivery, and perform other obligations under the contract. The seller may also declare the contract void if the failure of the buyer to perform obligations under the contract amounts to a fundamental breach of contract.

26-5b Remedies of the Buyer

Under the CISG, a buyer may reject goods only if the tender is a fundamental breach of the contract. This standard of materiality of rejection is in contrast to the UCC requirement of perfect tender. Under the CISG, a buyer may also reduce the price when nonconforming goods are delivered even though no notice of nonconformity is given. However, the buyer must have a reasonable cause for failure to give notice about the nonconformity.

 E-COMMERCE & CYBERLAW

Click "Like," Waive Your Remedies

General Mills, the makers of Betty Crocker baking mixes and cereals such as Cheerios, have included language on the Facebook pages and company sites that indicates that if you click on "like," download coupons, or enter a contest sponsored by the General Mills, you lose your right to bring suit against the company. In the event of any issues with the product, the coupons, or the contest, you must go to arbitration.

Is this type of limitation on pursuit of remedies possible? Is the limitation valid?

Make the Connection

Summary

The law provides a number of remedies for the breach of a sales contract. Remedies based on UCC theories generally are subject to a four-year statute of limitations. If the remedy sought is based on a non-UCC theory, a tort or contract statute of limitations established by state statute will apply.

Remedies of the seller may include (1) a lien on the goods until the seller is paid, (2) the right to resell the goods, (3) the right to cancel the sales contract, (4) the right to recover the goods from the carrier and the buyer, and (5) the right to bring an action for damages or, in some cases, for the purchase price. The seller may also have remedies because of secured transactions.

Remedies of the buyer may include (1) the rejection of nonconforming goods, (2) the revocation of acceptance, (3) an action for damages for nondelivery of conforming goods, (4) an action for breach of warranty, (5) the cancellation of the sales contract, (6) the right to resell the

goods, (7) the right to bring an action for conversion, recovery of goods, or specific performance, and (8) the right to sue for damages and cancel if the seller has made a material breach of the contract.

The parties may modify their remedies by a contractual provision for liquidated damages, for limitations on statutory remedies, or for waiver of defenses. When consumers are involved, this freedom of contract is to some extent limited for their protection.

Under the CISG, the seller may require the buyer to pay the price, take delivery, and perform obligations under the contract, or the seller may avoid the contract if there is a fundamental breach.

A buyer may reject goods under the CISG only if there is a fundamental breach of contract. The buyer may also reduce the price of nonconforming goods.

Learning Outcomes

After studying this chapter, you should be able to clearly explain:

26-1 Statute of Limitations

26-2 Remedies of the Seller

LO.1 List the remedies of the seller when the buyer breaches a sales contract

See the *Bowen v. Gardner* case for the proper measure of damages when the seller is able to resell the goods for more money, pages 499–500.

See the discussion of the Whirlpool refrigerators, page 497.

26-3 Remedies of the Buyer

LO.2 List the remedies of the buyer when the seller breaches a sales contract

See the *Castro v. Ernie's Auto* case that deals with a damage question on revocation of acceptance by a buyer of a used car that is sold "as is," pages 500–501.
See the *Schutzman v. Nutsco* case, page 502.
See the Thinking Things Through feature about the Lululemon pants, page 501.

26-4 Contract Provisions on Remedies

LO.3 Determine the validity of clauses limiting damages
See the *Rodriguez v. Learjet, Inc.* case, pages 506–507.
See the *General Mills Operations, LLC v. Five Star Custom Foods, LTD*, case, pages 503–504.
See the E-Commerce & Cyberlaw feature on clicking on "like" as a way to limit remedies, page 508.

26-5 Remedies in the International Sale of Goods

Key Terms

breach
consequential damages

incidental damages
liquidated damages

secured transaction
statute of limitations

Questions and Case Problems

1. Firwood Manufacturing Co. had a contract to sell General Tire 55 Model 1225 postcure inflators (PCIs). PCIs are $30,000 machines used by General Tire in its manufacturing process. The contract was entered into in 1989, and by April 1990 General Tire had purchased 22 PCIs from Firwood. However, General Tire then closed its Barrie, Michigan, plant. Firwood reminded General Tire that it still had the obligation to purchase the 33 remaining PCIs. General Tire communicated to Firwood that it would not be purchasing the remaining ones. Firwood then was able, over a period of three years, to sell the remaining PCIs. Some of the PCIs were sold as units, and others were broken down and sold to buyers who needed parts. Firwood's sales of the remaining 33 units brought in $187,513 less than the General Tire contract provided, and Firwood filed suit to collect the resale price difference plus interest. Can Firwood recover? Why or why not? [*Firwood Manufacturing Co., Inc. v. General Tire, Inc.*, 96 F.3d 163 (6th Cir.)]

2. Soon after Gast purchased a used auto from a Chevrolet dealer, he experienced a series of mechanical problems with the car. Gast refused to make further payments on the bank note that had financed the purchase. The bank took possession of the automobile and sold it. Gast then brought an action against the dealer, alleging that he had revoked his acceptance. Was Gast correct? Explain your answer. [*Gast v. Rodgers-Dingus Chevrolet*, 585 So. 2d 725 (Miss.)]

3. Formetal Engineering submitted to Presto a sample and specifications for precut polyurethane pads to be used in making air-conditioning units. Formetal paid for the goods as soon as they were delivered but subsequently discovered that the pads did not conform to the sample and specifications in that there were incomplete cuts, color variances, and faulty adherence to the pad's paper backing. Formetal then informed Presto of the defects and notified Presto that it would reject the pads and return them to Presto, but they were not returned for 125 days. Presto argued that it was denied the right to cure because the goods were not returned until some 125 days after Formetal promised to do so. Was there a breach of the contract? Did the buyer (Formetal) do anything wrong in seeking its remedies? [*Presto Mfg. Co. v. Formetal Engineering Co.*, 360 N.E.2d 510 (Ill. App.)]

4. Emily Lieberman and Amy Altomondo were members of the Alpha Chi Omega (AXO) sorority at Bowling Green State University. They negotiated with Johnathan James Furlong for the purchase of custom-designed sweaters for themselves and their sorority sisters for a total price of $3,612. Lieberman and Altomondo paid Furlong a $2,000 deposit.

    When Lieberman and Altomondo saw the sweaters, they realized that Furlong had made color and design alterations in the lettering imprinted on the sweaters as part of their custom design. Altomondo, as president of AXO, called Furlong and told him that the sweaters were unacceptable and offered to return them. Furlong refused, stating that any changes were immaterial. Altomondo refused to pay the balance due and demanded the return of the $2,000 deposit. Furlong filed suit for breach of contract. What should the court do with the case and why? [*Furlong v. Alpha Chi Omega Sorority*, 657 N.E.2d 866 (Ohio Mun. Ct. 1993)]

5. McNeely entered into a contract with Wagner to pay $250,000 as a lump sum for all timber present in a given area that Wagner would remove for McNeely. The contract estimated that the volume in the area would be 780,000 board feet. Wagner also had provisions in the contract that made no warranties as to the amount of lumber and that he would keep whatever timber was not harvested if McNeely ended the contract before the harvesting was complete. The $250,000 was to be paid in three advances. McNeely paid two of the three advances but withheld the third payment and ended the contract because he said there was not enough timber. Wagner filed suit for the remaining one-third of the payment. McNeely said Wagner could not have the remaining one-third of the payment as well as the transfer; he had to choose between the two remedies. Is he correct? [*Wagner v. McNeely*, 38 U.C.C. 2d 1176 (Or.)]

6. Brown Machine Company, a division of Kvaerner U.S., Inc., entered into a contract to supply a machine and tools to Hakim Plast, a food container–producing company based in Cairo, Egypt, to enable Hakim to meet its growing demand for plastic containers. The plastic containers were for customers to use in the ice cream distribution industry. It was understood that the equipment would be ready for delivery before the busy summer ice cream season. Brown Machine was not able to meet the twice

extended deadline. It attempted to obtain another extension, but Hakim Plast refused without additional consideration. Brown refused to provide the requested consideration. Hakim Plast declared the contract breached on September 25, 1994. Brown then sold the equipment and brought suit for breach of contract, requesting damages for the loss of the sale. Hakim Plast countersued for Brown's breach seeking out-of-pocket expenses and consequential damages for loss of business. Discuss who breached the contract and determine what possible damages might be recovered. [*Kvaerner U.S., Inc. v. Hakim Plast Co.*, 74 F. Supp. 2d (E.D. Mich.)]

7. Sonya Kaminski purchased from Billy Cain's Cornelia dealership a truck that was represented to her to be a 1989 Chevrolet Silverado pickup. However, subsequent incidents involving repair of the truck and its parts, as well as a title history, revealed that the truck was a GMC rather than a Chevrolet. Sales agents at the Cornelia dealership misrepresented the truck's character and sold the truck to Kaminski as a Chevrolet.

    Kaminski filed suit for intentional fraud and deceit under the Georgia Fair Business Practices Act (FBPA) and for breach of express warranty. The jury awarded Kaminski $2,823.70 for breach of express warranty and $50,000 punitive (exemplary) damages. The judge added damages under the FBPA of $10,913.29 in actual damages and $9,295 in attorney fees and court costs. The dealership appealed. Must the dealership pay the damages? Why or why not? [*Billy Cain Ford Lincoln Mercury, Inc. v. Kaminski*, 496 S.E.2d 521 (Ga. App.)]

8. Mrs. Kirby purchased a wheelchair from NMC/ Continue Care. The wheelchair was customized for her and her home. When the wheelchair arrived, it was too wide to fit through the doorways in her home. What options does Mrs. Kirby have? [*Kirby v. NMC Continue Care*, 993 P.2d 951 (Wyo.)]

9. Wolosin purchased a vegetable and dairy refrigerator case from Evans Manufacturing Corp. When Evans sued Wolosin for the purchase price, Wolosin claimed damages for breach of warranty. The sales contract provided that Evans would replace defective parts free of charge for one year; it also stated, "This warranty is in lieu of any and all other warranties stated or inferred, and of all other obligations on the part of the manufacturer, which neither assumes nor authorizes anyone to assume for it any other obligations or liability in connection with the sale of its products." Evans claimed that it was liable only for

replacement of parts. Wolosin claimed that the quoted clause was not sufficiently specific to satisfy the limitation-of-remedies requirement of U.C.C. §2-719. Provide some insight on this issue for the parties by discussing damage limitation clauses under the UCC. [*Evans Mfg. Corp. v. Wolosin*, 47 Luzerne County Leg. Reg. 238 (Pa.)]

10. McInnis purchased a tractor and scraper as new equipment of the current model year from Western Tractor & Equipment Co. The written contract stated that the seller disclaimed all warranties and that no warranties existed except those stated in the contract. Actually, the equipment was not the current model but that of the prior year. The equipment was not new but had been used for 68 hours as a demonstrator model, after which the hour meter had been reset to zero. The buyer sued the seller for damages. The seller's defense was based on the ground that all liability for warranties had been disclaimed. Was this defense valid? [*McInnis v. Western Tractor & Equipment Co.*, 388 P.2d 562 (Wash.)]

11. Elmore purchased a car from Doenges Brothers Ford. The car had been placed with the dealership by a dealership employee as part of a consignment arrangement. Elmore was unable to obtain title to the car because the Environmental Protection Agency had issues with the car's compliance with emissions equipment requirements. Elmore was unable to drive the car. He brought suit because he was forced to sell the car for $10,300 less than he paid because of the title defect and the fact that only a salvage dealer would purchase it. Because he lost his transportation, he was out of work for eight months and experienced a $20,000 decline in income. What damages could Elmore recover under the UCC? [*Elmore v. Doenges Bros. Ford, Inc.*, 21 P.3d 65 (Okla. App.)]

12. Stock Solution is a "stock photo agency" that leases photographic transparencies produced by professional photographers for use in media advertising. Between October 1, 1994, and May 31, 1995, Stock Solution delivered Axiom 107 color transparencies to be used in Axiom's advertising. The contracts provided that in the event the transparencies were not returned by the specified "return date," Axiom would pay the following fees: (1) an initial "service charge" of $30, (2) "holding fee[s]" in the amount of "$5.00 per week per transparency", (3) "service fees" at a rate of "one and one-half percent per month" on unpaid balances of invoices beginning 30 days after

invoice date, and (4) reimbursement for loss or damage of each "original transparency" in the amount of $1,500.

Axiom failed to return 37 of the 107 transparencies in breach of the contracts. Of the 37 missing transparencies, 36 were original color transparencies and 1 was a duplicate color transparency. Stock Solution filed suit seeking damages (1) for the 36 missing original color transparencies, the agreed liquidated value of $54,000 plus sales tax of $3,294; (2) for the 1 missing duplicate color transparency, $1 plus sales tax of $0.06; (3) holding fees on the 37 missing transparencies in the amount of $23,914.83; (4) service fees and charges as provided for in the contracts; and (5) attorney fees.

Discuss whether the liquidated damage clause was enforceable under the law. [*Bair v. Axiom Design, LLC*, 20 P.3d 388 (Utah)]

13. Ramtreat Metal Technology provided for a "double your money back" remedy in its contracts for the sale of its metal drilling assemblies. A buyer filed suit seeking consequential damages and cost of replacement. Ramtreat said that its clause was a limitation of remedies. Could Ramtreat limit its remedies to "double your money back"? [*Adcock v. Ramtreat Metal Technology, Inc.*, 44 U.C.C. Rep. Serv. 2d 1026 (Wash. App.)]

14. Joseph Perna purchased a 1981 Oldsmobile at a traffic auction conducted by Locascio. The car had been seized pursuant to action taken by the New York City Parking Violation Bureau against Jose Cruz. Perna purchased the car for $1,800 plus tax and towing fees "subject to the terms and conditions of any and all chattel mortgages, rental agreements, liens, conditional bills of sale, and encumbrances that may be on the motor vehicle of the above judgment debtor." The Olds had 58,103 miles on it at the time of Perna's purchase. On May 7, 1993, Perna sold the car to Elio Marino, a coworker, for $1,200. The vehicle had about 65,000 miles on it at the time of this sale.

During his period of ownership, Marino replaced the radiator ($270), repaired the power steering and valve cover gasket ($117), and replaced a door lock ($97.45). He registered and insured the vehicle. In February 1994, Marino's son was stopped by the police and arrested for driving a stolen vehicle. The son was kept in jail until his arraignment, but the charges were eventually dropped. The Oldsmobile was never returned to Marino, who filed suit for breach of contract because he had been given a car with a defective title. He asked for damages that included the costs of getting his son out of jail and having the theft charges dropped. Is he entitled to those damages? [*Marino v. Perna*, 629 N.Y.S.2d 669 (N.Y. Cir.)]

15. Stephan's Machine & Tool, Inc., purchased a boring mill from D&H Machinery Consultants. The mill was a specialized type of equipment and was essential to the operation of Stephan's plant. The purchase price was $96,000, and Stephan's had to borrow this amount from a bank to finance the sale. The loan exhausted Stephan's borrowing capacity. The mill was unfit, and D&H agreed to replace it with another one. D&H did not keep its promise, and Stephan's sued it for specific performance of the contract as modified by the replacement agreement. Is specific performance an appropriate remedy? Discuss. [*Stephan's Machine & Tool, Inc. v. D&H Machinery Consultants, Inc.*, 417 N.E.2d 579 (Ohio App.)]

CPA Questions

1. On April 5, 1987, Anker, Inc., furnished Bold Corp. with Anker's financial statements dated March 31, 1987. The financial statements contained misrepresentations that indicated that Anker was solvent when in fact it was insolvent. Based on Anker's financial statements, Bold agreed to sell Anker 90 computers, "F.O.B.—Bold's loading dock." On April 14, Anker received 60 of the computers. The remaining 30 computers were in the possession of the common carrier and in transit to Anker. If, on April 28, Bold discovered that Anker was insolvent, then with respect to the computers delivered to Anker on April 14, Bold may:

a. Reclaim the computers upon making a demand.

b. Reclaim the computers irrespective of the rights of any third party.

c. Not reclaim the computers since 10 days have elapsed from their delivery.

d. Not reclaim the computers since it is entitled to recover the price of the computers.

CHAPTER 26: Remedies for Breach of Sales Contracts

2. On February 15, Mazur Corp. contracted to sell 1,000 bushels of wheat to Good Bread, Inc., at $6.00 per bushel with delivery to be made on June 23. On June 1, Good advised Mazur that it would not accept or pay for the wheat. On June 2, Mazur sold the wheat to another customer at the market price of $5.00 per bushel. Mazur had advised Good that it intended to resell the wheat. Which of the following statements is correct?

   a. Mazur can successfully sue Good for the difference between the resale price and the contract price.

   b. Mazur can resell the wheat only after June 23.

   c. Good can retract its anticipatory breach at any time before June 23.

   d. Good can successfully sue Mazur for specific performance.

3. Lazur Corp. entered into a contract with Baker Suppliers, Inc., to purchase a used word processor from Baker. Lazur is engaged in the business of selling new and used word processors to the general public. The contract required Baker to ship the goods to Lazur by common carrier pursuant to the following provision in the contract: "FOB Baker Suppliers, Inc., loading dock." Baker also represented in the contract that the word processor had been used for only 10 hours by its previous owner. The contract included the provision that the word processor was being sold "as is," and this provision was in a larger and different type style than the remainder of the contract. Assume that Lazur refused to accept the word processor even though it was in all respects conforming to the contract and that the contract is otherwise silent. Under the UCC Sales Article:

   a. Baker can successfully sue for specific performance and make Lazur accept and pay for the word processor.

   b. Baker may resell the word processor to another buyer.

   c. Baker must sue for the difference between the market value of the word processor and the contract price plus its incidental damages.

   d. Baker cannot successfully sue for consequential damages unless it attempts to resell the word processor.

Negotiable Instruments

Kinds of Instruments, Parties, and Negotiability

Learning Outcomes ‹‹‹

After studying this chapter, you should be able to

LO.1 Explain the importance and function of negotiable instruments

LO.2 Name the parties to negotiable instruments

LO.3 Describe the concept of negotiability and distinguish it from assignability

LO.4 List the requirements for a negotiable instrument

27-1   Types of Negotiable Instruments and Parties

commercial paper–written, transferable, signed promise or order to pay a specified sum of money; a negotiable instrument.

For convenience and as a way to facilitate transactions, businesses began to accept certain kinds of paper called **commercial paper** or negotiable instruments as substitutes for money or as a means of offering credit.[1] Negotiable commercial paper is special paper created for the special purpose of facilitating transfer of funds and payment. In addition, the use of this special paper for special purposes can create additional rights in a special party status known as a *holder in due course*. Although the details on holders in due course are covered in Chapters 28 and 29, it is important to understand that one of the purposes of the use of special paper is to allow parties to achieve the special status of holder in due course and its protections and rights. Taking each component of negotiable instruments in step-by-step sequences, from their creation to the rights associated with each, and to their transfer, helps in understanding how commercial paper is used to create rights for special persons.

Article 3 of the Uniform Commercial Code (UCC) defines the types of negotiable instruments and the parties for each.[2] Article 3 of the UCC was last amended in 2002 with those reforms adopted in some states and under consideration in others.[3] Those changes are explained in each of the relevant sections.

27-1a   Definition

negotiable instrument–drafts, promissory notes, checks, and certificates of deposit that, in proper form, give special rights as "negotiable commercial paper."

Section 3-104(a)(1) and (2) of the UCC defines a **negotiable instrument** as "an unconditional promise or order to pay a fixed amount of money, … if it (1) is payable to bearer or order…; (2) is payable on demand or at a definite time; and (3) does not state any other undertaking or instruction … to do any act in addition to the payment of money…."[4] A *negotiable instrument* is a record of a signed promise or order to pay a specified sum of money.[5] The former requirement that the instrument be in writing to be valid has been changed to incorporate requirements of UETA (Uniform Electronic Transactions Act) and E-Sign (Electronic Signatures in Global and National Commerce Act of 2000). Many lenders now use electronic promissory notes.[6] In addition, we now have electronic checks, or those check withdrawals from your account that you authorize over the phone or via the Internet.

Instruments are negotiable when they contain certain elements required by the UCC. These elements are listed and explained in the section titled "Requirements of Negotiability" of this chapter. However, even those instruments that do not meet the requirements for negotiability may still be referred to by their UCC names or classifications.

CPA   27-1b   Kinds of Instruments

There are two categories of negotiable instruments: (1) promises to pay, which include promissory notes and certificates of deposit,[7] and (2) orders to pay, including drafts and checks.

---

[1] *Carlucci v. Han*, 886 F. Supp. 2d 497 (E.D. Va. 2012).
[2] The law covering negotiable instruments has been evolving and changing. The earlier version was called UCC-Commercial Paper, and the 1990 version is called UCC-Negotiable Instruments.
[3] As of January 2015, 50 states, the District of Columbia, and the Virgin Islands had adopted the 2002 changes to Article 3.
[4] U.C.C. §3-104(a)(1) and (2).
[5] See U.C.C. §3-104.
[6] Electronic Signatures in Global and National Commerce Act, 15 U.S.C. §7001 (Supp. 2014).
[7] U.C.C. §3-104(j).

FIGURE 27-1	Promissory Note

MARCH 31, 2015

Six months after date debtor undersigned hereby promises to pay to the order of Galactic Games, Inc., three thousand six hundred dollars with interest at the rate of 5.9%. This note is secured by the Video Arcade game purchased with its funds.

In the event of default, all sums due hereunder may be collected. Debtor agrees to pay all costs of collection including, but not limited to, attorney fees, costs of repossession, and costs of litigation.

/s/ JOHN R. HALDEHAND

VIDEO ARCADE, INC.

promissory note—unconditional promise in writing made by one person to another, signed by the maker engaging to pay on demand, or at a definite time, a sum certain in money to order or to bearer. (Parties—maker, payee)

Promissory Notes

A **promissory note** is a written promise made and signed by the maker to pay a *sum certain* in money to the holder of the instrument.[8] (See Figure 27-1)

Certificates of Deposit

certificate of deposit (CD)—promise-to-pay instrument issued by a bank.

A **certificate of deposit (CD)** is a promise to pay issued by a bank.[9] Through a CD, a bank acknowledges the customer's deposit of a specific sum of money and promises to pay the customer that amount plus interest when the certificate is surrendered.

Drafts

draft, or bill of exchange—an unconditional order in writing by one person upon another, signed by the person giving it, and ordering the person to whom it is directed to pay upon demand or at a definite time a sum certain in money to order or to bearer.

A **draft, or bill of exchange,** is an order by one party to pay a sum of money to a second party. (See Figure 27-2.) The party who gives the order is called the *drawer*, and the party on whom the order to pay is drawn is the *drawee*.[10] The party to whom payment is to be made is the *payee*. The drawer may also be named as the payee, as when a seller draws a draft naming a buyer as the drawee. The draft is then used as a means to obtain payment for goods delivered to that buyer. A drawee is not bound to pay a draft simply because the drawer has placed his name on it. However, the drawee may agree to pay the draft by accepting it, which then attaches the drawee's liability for payment.

Checks

check—order by a depositor on a bank to pay a sum of money to a payee; a bill of exchange drawn on a bank and payable on demand.

Under U.C.C. §3-104(f), *check* means "a draft, other than a documentary draft, payable on demand and drawn on a bank."[11] A **check** is an order by a depositor (the drawer) on a bank or credit union (the drawee) to pay a sum of money to the order of another party (the payee).[12]

In addition to the ordinary checks just described, there are also cashier's checks, teller's checks, traveler's checks, and bank money orders. A **cashier's check** is a draft drawn by a bank on itself. U.C.C. §3-104(g) defines a cashier's check as "a draft with respect to which the drawer and drawee are the same bank or branches of the same bank."[13]

cashier's check—draft drawn by a bank on itself.

[8] *Heritage Bank v. Bruha,* 812 N.W.2d 260 (Neb. 2012).
[9] U.C.C. §3-104(j).
[10] U.C.C. §3-103(a)(2)–(3).
[11] U.C.C. §3-104(f).
[12] *Id.*
[13] U.C.C. §3-104(g).

| FIGURE 27-2 | Draft |

TO: *Topa Fabrics, Inc.*
1700 W. Lincoln
Marina Del Rey, CA

March 17, 20 *13*

Thirty days from date _____ PAY TO THE ORDER OF
Malden Mills, Inc.

THE SUM OF *sixteen thousand and no/100* _____ DOLLARS

ACCEPTED BY: _____ *Aaron Johnson*
Malden Mills, Inc.

DATE

CPA

A **teller's check** is a draft drawn by a bank on another bank in which it has an account.[14] A **traveler's check** is a check that is payable on demand, provided it is countersigned by the person whose signature was placed on the check at the time the check was purchased.[15] Money orders are issued by both banks and nonbanks. A **money order** drawn by a bank is also a check.[16]

27-1c Parties to Instruments

A note has two original parties: the *maker* and the *payee*.[17] A draft or a check has three original parties: the *drawer*, the *drawee*, and the *payee*. The names given to the parties to these instruments are important because the liability of the parties varies depending on the parties' roles. The rights and liabilities of the various parties to negotiable instruments are covered in Chapters 28 and 29.

A **party** to an instrument may be a natural person, an artificial person such as a corporation, or an unincorporated enterprise such as a government agency.

Maker

The **maker** is the party who writes or creates a promissory note, thereby promising to pay the amount specified in the note.

Drawer

The **drawer** is the party who writes or creates a draft or check.

Drawee

The **drawee** is the party to whom the draft is addressed and who is ordered to pay the amount of money specified in the draft. The bank is the drawee on a check, and the credit union is the drawee on a share draft. A drawee on a draft has no responsibility under the draft until it has accepted that instrument.

---

[14] U.C.C. §3-104(h).
[15] U.C.C. §3-104(i).
[16] *Com. v. Pantalion*, 957 A.2d 1267 (Pa. Super. 2008). Some items are held to be checks for purposes other than Article 3 negotiability. For example, in In re *Armstrong* 291 F.2d 517 (8th Cir. 2002), the court held that gambling markers were checks for purposes of the state's "bad check" law.
[17] U.C.C. §3-103(a)(5).

Payee

payee–party to whom payment is to be made.

The **payee** is the person named in the instrument to receive payment. **For Example,** on a check with the words "Pay to the order of John Jones," the named person, John Jones, is the payee.

Acceptor

acceptor–drawee who has accepted the liability of paying the amount of money specified in a draft.

When the drawee of a draft has indicated by writing or record a willingness to pay the amount specified in the draft, the drawee has accepted liability and is called the **acceptor.**[18]

Secondary Obligor (Accommodation Party)

accommodation party–person who signs an instrument to lend credit to another party to the paper.

When a party who is not originally named in an instrument allows her name to be added to it for the benefit of another party in order to add strength to the collectability of the instrument, that party becomes a secondary obligor (formerly called an **accommodation party**) and assumes a liability role.[19] Revised Article 3 now refers to drawer, indorsers, and accommodation parties as "secondary obligors."[20]

27-2 Negotiability

negotiability–quality of an instrument that affords special rights and standing.

An instrument is a form of contract that, if negotiable, affords certain rights and protections for the parties. **Negotiability** is the characteristic that distinguishes commercial paper and instruments from ordinary contracts or what makes such paper and instruments[21] special paper. That an instrument is negotiable means that certain rights and protections may be available to the parties to the instrument under Article 3. A **nonnegotiable instrument's** terms are enforceable, but the instrument is treated simply as a contract governed by contract law.[22]

CPA 27-2a Definition of Negotiability

nonnegotiable instrument–contract, note, or draft that does not meet negotiability requirements of Article 3.

If an instrument is negotiable, it is governed by Article 3 of the UCC, and it may be transferred by negotiation. This form of transfer permits the transferee to acquire rights greater than those afforded assignees of contracts under contract law. The quality of negotiability in instruments creates opportunities for transfers and financings that streamline payments in commerce. Transfers can be made with assurance of payment without the need for investigation of the underlying contract. The process of negotiation is covered in Chapter 28. For more information on the rights of assignees of contracts, refer to Chapter 17.

---

[18] U.C.C. §3-103(a)(1).

[19] U.C.C. §3-419; In re *Rust,* 510 B.R. 562 (E.D. Ky. 2014).

[20] Revised Article 3, §3-103(12), has the following definition of a secondary obligor on an instrument "an indorser, a drawer, an accommodation party, or any other party to the instrument that has a right of recourse against another party to the instrument…." This definition was changed to be consistent with the Restatement of Surety.

[21] U.C.C. §3-104.

[22] Loan-and-supply contract is not a negotiable instrument. *Quality Oil, Inc. v. Kelley Partners, Inc.,* 657 F.2d 609 (7th Cir. 2011). A note payable when "lessee is granted possession of the premises" is not a negotiable instrument, but it is an enforceable contract. *Schiffer v. United Grocers, Inc.,* 989 P.2d 10 (Or. 1999). A deed of trust may or may not be a negotiable instrument. *Arnold v. Palmer,* 686 S.E.2d 725 (W. Va. 2009); In re *Smith,* 509 B.R. 260 (N.D. Cal. 2014).

E-COMMERCE & CYBERLAW

The Check Is in the Internet

The Check Clearing for the 21st Century Act ("Check 21") allows banks to use electronic images of checks as full and complete records of transactions, the same status formerly used only for paper checks that had been canceled. You can also pay your monthly credit card bills by preauthorizing your credit card company to withdraw the amount you specify from your account. With the bank's routing number and your account number, the company can obtain payment on the due date or any date you authorize. PayPal allows you to do the same with your bank account when you purchase items on the Internet. Paperless payment is on the increase.

CPA   27-2b Requirements of Negotiability

To be negotiable, an instrument (1) must be evidenced by a record and (2) must be signed (authenticated under Revised Article 3) by the maker or the drawer, (3) must contain an unconditional promise or order to pay, (4) must pay a sum certain, (5) must be payable in money, (6) must be payable on demand or at a definite time, and (7) must be payable to order or bearer, using what are known as words of negotiability.[23]

A Record (Writing)

A negotiable instrument must be evidenced by a record. The requirement of a *record*, under Revised Article 3, is satisfied by handwriting, typing, printing, electronic record, and any other method of making a record. A negotiable instrument may be partly printed and partly typewritten. No particular form is required for an instrument to satisfy the record requirement, although customers of banks may agree to use the banks' forms as part of their contractual agreement with their banks. Telephonic checks are a complete record for purposes of Article 3 rights and obligations.

Authenticated (Signed) by the Maker or Drawer

The instrument must be authenticated (signed under old Article 3) by the maker or the drawer. When a signature is used as authentication, it usually appears at the lower right-hand corner of the face of the instrument, but there is no requirement for where the signature must be placed on the instrument.[24]

The authentication may consist of the full name or of any symbol placed with the intent to authenticate the instrument. Other means of authentication that are valid as signatures include initials, figures, and marks. Electronic security devices can be used as a means of authentication for electronic records. A person signing a trade name or an assumed name is liable just as if the signer's own name had been used.

Agent. An authentication may be made by the drawer or the maker or by his or her authorized agent. **For Example,** Eileen Smith, the treasurer of Mills Company, could sign a note for her company as an agent. No particular form of authorization for an agent to authenticate an instrument is required. An authenticating agent should disclose on the instrument (1) the identity of the principal and (2) the fact that the authentication

---

[23] U.C.C. §3-104.

[24] According to Revised U.C.C. §3-103, *authenticate* means (a) to sign or (b) to execute or otherwise adopt a symbol, or encrypt or similarly process a record in whole or in part, with the present intent of the authenticating person to identify the person and adopt or accept a record.

was done in a representative capacity. When this information appears on the face of the instrument, an authorized agent is not liable on it.

The representative capacity of an officer of an organization can be shown by the authentication of the officer along with the title of the office and the organization's name.[25] **For Example,** a signature of "James Shelton, Treasurer, NorWest Utilities, Inc.," or "NorWest Utilities, Inc., by James Shelton, Treasurer," on a note is enough to show Shelton's representative capacity. NorWest Utilities, not Shelton, would be liable on the note.

Absence of Representative Capacity or Identification of Principal. If an instrument fails to show the **representative capacity** of the person who is authenticating or fails to identify the person, then the individual who authenticates the instrument is personally liable on the instrument to anyone who acquires superior rights, such as the rights of a holder in due course (see Chapter 29). Because the instrument is a final agreement, the parol evidence rule applies, and the party who authenticated is not permitted to introduce extrinsic evidence that might clarify his or her representative capacity. The party who authenticated, in order to avoid personal liability, must indicate on the face of the instrument his or her role in the principal, such as president or vice president. (For more information about the parol evidence rule, see Chapter 16.)

However, an agent is not personally liable on a check that is drawn on the bank account of the principal and authenticated by him or her, even though the agent failed to disclose his or her representative capacity on the check. **For Example,** a check that is already imprinted with the employer's name is not the check of the employee, regardless of whether the employee only authenticates with his or her name or also adds a title such as "Payroll Clerk" or "Treasurer" near the signature.

> **representative capacity**—action taken by one on behalf of another, as the act of a personal representative on behalf of a decedent's estate, or action taken both on one's behalf and on behalf of others, as a shareholder bringing a representative action.

CASE SUMMARY

A Crushing Defeat on a Note That Had the Wrong Parties

FACTS: Green Valley Growers, Inc. (GVG) was a plant nursery owned by O. Wayne Massey and others. From 2001 until the GVG's bankruptcy, KC Crushed provided GVG raw materials and construction services, including the creation of ditches and irrigation ponds, building of rock roads, beds and loading docks, as well as the work on some of the greenhouses located on the property operated by GVG. GVG took out a loan and paid $396,527.10 of the proceeds to KC Crushed. On February 27, 2007, Massey and Hurley Ray Smith (owner of KC Crushed) executed a Promissory Note that stated: "I, Wayne Massey promise to repay Ray Smith for a Promissory Note in the amount of $400,000.00 with Interest."

Smith and Massey (defendants) contend that the Note "incorrectly listed Smith as the lender and Wayne Massey as the borrower." Smith stated that the Note was in fact between KC Crushed and GVG, not himself and Massey, "I did not draft or prepare the Promissory Note. I did not

review the Promissory Note. When the Promissory Note was presented to me, I did not read it and simply signed the note as written ... I was signing on behalf of KC Crushed Concrete, not myself individually. Wayne Massey and I agreed that [GVG] would repay KC Crushed Concrete with periodic $5,000 loan repayments, as initial interest only payments." From April 2007 until December 2008, GVG paid Smith—not KC Crushed—$80,000 toward the Note, in $5,000 monthly installments.

Smith and KC Crushed moved for summary judgment that they are not liable to Randy Williams—the bankruptcy trustee for the GVG bankruptcy.

DECISION: The Note plainly stated that Massey was the borrower and Smith was the lender. But GVG wrote the $5,000 monthly checks to Smith, not to KC Crushed. Smith's argument that he did not read the Note before he signed is

---

[25] U.C.C. §3-402. In re *Bedrock Marketing, LLC*, 404 B.R. 939 (D. Utah 2009); *Free Green Can, LLC v. Green Recycling Enterprises*, LLC, Not Reported in F. Supp. 2d, 2011 WL 5130359 (N.D. Ill.), and *Arntz v. Valdez*, 2011 WL 3433018, 163 Wash. App. 1003 (Wash. App. 2011).

A Crushing Defeat on a Note That Had the Wrong Parties continued

unavailing. Parties are presumed to know the contents of a document and have an obligation to protect themselves by reading documents prior to signing.

The parties' subjective beliefs cannot contradict the intent of the parties expressed within the four corners of the document. The rights and obligations of the parties "are determined solely from the written loan agreement, and any prior oral agreements between the parties are superseded by and merged into the loan agreement." The Note stated that the $400,000 debt ran from Massey to Smith, not from GVG to KC Crushed. The payments were not relevant because the document was clear. The payments could have been made for another purpose such as a capital contribution. [*Williams v. Houston Plants & Garden World, Inc.*, 508 B.R. 19 (S.D. Tex. 2014)]

THINKING THINGS THROUGH

When Your John Hancock Is Enough

Work through the following examples of signatures on negotiable instruments and capacity, and determine whether there would be personal liability on the part of the company executives signing the instruments.

1. Donald Schaffer owned and operated Grafton Janitorial Service, Inc. On October 6, 1998, Mr. Schaffer obtained a $25,000 line of credit for his company from First Merit Bank by executing a promissory note, which he signed both as "Donald J. Schaffer, President" and "Donald J. Schaffer, Cosigner." The note contains no guarantee provision, and Mr. Schaffer did not sign the note in the capacity as a guarantor. [*Schaffer v. First Merit Bank, N.A.*, 927 N.E.2d 15 (Ohio App. 2009)]

2. A corporate guaranty was signed as follows:

THE PRODUCERS GROUP OF FLA., INC. a Florida corporation, by the following officers solely on behalf of the corporation:

/s/ Eddie Beverly, as its President

CORPORATE PRESIDENT Eddie Beverly

/s/ Stephen Edman, as its Secretary

CORPORATE SECRETARY Steve Edman

/s/ John Bauder, as its Treasurer

CORPORATE TREASURER John Bauder

Are the officers personally liable on the guaranty?

[*Tampa Bay Economic Development Corp. v. Edman*, 598 So. 2d 172 (Fla. App. 1992)]

Promise or Order to Pay

A promissory note must contain a promise to pay money. A mere acknowledgment of a debt, such as a record stating "I.O.U.," is not a promise. A draft or check must contain an order or command to pay money.

Unconditional Promise or Order

For an instrument to be negotiable, the promise or order to pay must be unconditional.[26] **For Example,** when an instrument makes the duty to pay dependent on the completion of the construction of a building, the promise is conditional and the instrument is nonnegotiable. The instrument is enforceable as a contract, but it is not a negotiable instrument given all the rights and protections afforded under Article 3.

An order for the payment of money out of a particular fund is negotiable. The instrument can refer to a particular account or merely indicate a source of reimbursement for the drawee, such as "Charge my expense account." Nor is an instrument conditional

---

[26] U.C.C. §3-109(c). *Stancik v. Hersch*, 2012 WL 1567213 (Ohio App. 2012). A mortgage is not a negotiable instrument because it is not a promise to pay; it is a lien. *Gardner v. Quicken Loans*, 567 Fed. Appx. 362 (6th Cir. 2014).

when payment is to be made only from an identified fund if the issuer is a government or governmental unit or agency, or when payment is to be made from the assets of a partnership, an unincorporated association, a trust, or an estate.[27] However, the fund noted must in fact exist because payment from a fund to be created by a future event would be conditional. **For Example,** making an instrument "payable from the account I'll establish when the sale of my house occurs" is conditional because the fund's creation is tied to an event whose time of occurrence is unknown.

The standards for negotiability do not require that the issuer of the instrument be personally obligated pay it.[28] An instrument's negotiability is not destroyed by a reference to a related document. Section 3-106(b) provides, "A promise or order is not made conditional (i) by a reference to another writing for a statement of rights with respect to collateral, prepayment, or acceleration."[29] **For Example,** if a note includes the following phrase, "This note is secured by a mortgage on the property located at Hilding Lane," the note is still negotiable.[30]

Payment in Money

money–medium of exchange.

A negotiable instrument must be payable in money. **Money** is defined to include any medium of exchange adopted or authorized by the United States, a foreign government, or an intergovernmental organization. The parties to an instrument are free to decide which currency will be used for payment even though their transaction may occur in a different country.[31] **For Example,** two parties in the United States are free to agree that their note will be paid in pesos.

If the order or promise is not for money, the instrument is not negotiable. **For Example,** an instrument that requires the holder to take stock or goods in place of money is nonnegotiable. The instrument is enforceable as a contract, but it cannot qualify as a negotiable instrument for purposes of Article 3 rights.

Sum Certain

sum certain–amount due under an instrument that can be computed from its face with only reference to interest rates.

Negotiable instruments must include a statement of a **sum certain,** or an exact amount of money.[32] Without a definite statement as to how much is to be paid under the terms of the instrument, there is no way to determine how much the instrument is worth.

There are some minor variations from sum certain requirement. **For Example,** an instrument is not nonnegotiable because its interest rate provisions include changes in the rate at maturity or because it provides for certain costs and attorney fees to be recovered by the holder in the event of enforcement action or litigation.[33]

In most states, the sum payable under an instrument is certain even though it calls for the payment of a floating or variable interest rate. An instrument is negotiable even though it provides for an interest rate of 1 percent above the prime rate of a named bank. It is immaterial that the exact amount of interest that will be paid cannot be determined at the time the paper is issued because the rate may later change.[34]

---

[27] A check issued by a debtor in bankruptcy for payment of court-ordered obligations is not conditional because of the involvement of the court or ongoing conditions on the debtor's payments. *Ward v. Stanford*, 443 S.W.3d 334 (Tex. App. 2014).

[28] U.C.C. §3-110(c)(1)–(2) (1990); *Ocwen Loan Servicing, LLC v. Branaman*, 554 F. Supp. 2d 645 (N.D. Miss. 2008).

[29] U.C.C. §3-106(b).

[30] Reference to a bill of lading does not affect negotiability. *Regent Corp., U.S.A. v. Azmat Bangladesh, Ltd.*, 686 N.Y.S.2d 24 (1999). However, a reference to a standby agreement does affect negotiability. In re *Sabertooth, LLC*, 443 B.R. 671 (E.D. Pa. 2011).

[31] U.C.C. §3-107. *Means v. Clardy*, 735 S.W.2d 6 (Mo. App. 1987) (payment in cabinets makes a note nonnegotiable).

[32] *Heritage Bank v. Bruha*, 812 N.W.2d 260 (Neb. 2012).

[33] U.C.C. §3-106. In re *MCB Financial Group, Inc.*, 461 B.R. 914 (N.D. Ga. 2011).

[34] However, when too many documents are necessary to determine the interest rate and the interest rate floats, negotiability is affected. *Farouki v. Petra International Banking Corp.*, 63 F. Supp. 3d 84 (D.D.C. 2014).

CPA   Time of Payment

A negotiable instrument must be payable on demand or at a definite time.[35] If an instrument is payable "when convenient," it is nonnegotiable because the day of payment may never arrive. An instrument payable only upon the happening of a particular event that may or may not happen is not negotiable. **For Example,** a provision in a note to pay the sum certain when a person marries is not payable at a definite time because that particular event may never occur. It is immaterial whether the contingency in fact has happened because from an examination of the instrument alone, it still appears to be subject to a condition that might not occur.

Demand. An instrument is *payable on demand* when it expressly states that it is payable "on demand," at sight, or on presentation. U.C.C. §3-108(a) provides "A promise or order is 'payable on demand' if (i) it states that it is payable on demand or at sight, or otherwise indicates that it is payable at the will of the holder, or (ii) it does not state any time of payment."[36] Presentation occurs when a holder demands payment. Commercial paper is deemed to be payable on demand when no time for payment is stated in the instrument.[37]

definite time–time of payment computable from the face of the instrument.

Definite Time. The time of payment is a **definite time** if an exact time or times are specified or if the instrument is payable at a fixed time after sight or acceptance or at a time that is readily ascertainable.[38] The time of payment is definite even though the instrument provides for prepayment, for acceleration, or for extensions at the option of a party or automatically on the occurrence of a specified contingency.

CASE SUMMARY

Whenever... Paying When You Can Does Not a Negotiable Instrument Make

FACTS: Gary Vaughn signed a document stating that Fred and Martha Smith were loaning him $9,900. As to when the loan was to be repaid, the document stated, "when you can." Approximately 18 months later, the Smiths sued Vaughn for the entire amount, claiming default on the note as well as unjust enrichment. The Smiths moved for summary judgment. They contended that Vaughn was immediately liable for the entire amount but that they were willing to work out a repayment schedule. Vaughn also moved for summary judgment, arguing that he did not have to repay the Smiths because he did not have the ability to do so. The trial court denied the Smiths' motion and granted Vaughn's. The Smiths appealed.

DECISION: The court held the following: a promissory note that calls for a borrower to repay "when you can" was not payable on demand and was not a negotiable instrument. However, an issue of fact remained as to when a debt payable "when you can" became payable. There were other issues of fact, such as whether there was unjust enrichment and whether it was reasonable for the borrower to repay the debt. The language implied that there was an open-ended agreement. The parties might have a contract, but the Smiths could not demand payment as if the instrument were a demand negotiable instrument. Reversed for further factual determinations. [*Smith v. Vaughn*, **882 N.E.2d 941 (Ohio App. 2007)**]

CPA   **Missing Date.** An instrument that is not dated is deemed dated on the day it is issued to the payee. Any holder may add the correct date to the instrument.

---

[35] U.C.C. §3-108.
[36] U.C.C. §3-108(a).
[37] U.C.C. §3-112; *Universal Premium Acceptance Corp. v. York Bank's Trust Co.,* 69 F.3d 695 (3d Cir. 1995); *State v. McWilliams,* 178 P.3d 121 (Mont. 2008).
[38] *Gallwitz v. Novel,* 2011 WL 303253 (Ohio App. 2011).

Effect of Date on a Demand Instrument. The date on a demand instrument controls the time of payment, and the paper is not due before its date. Consequently, a check that is postdated ceases to be demand paper and is not properly payable before the date on the check. A bank making earlier payment does not incur any liability for doing so unless the drawer has given the bank a postdated check notice.

Words of Negotiability: Payable to Order or Bearer

payable to order–term stating that a negotiable instrument is payable to the order of any person described in it or to a person or order.

bearer–person in physical possession of commercial paper payable to bearer, a document of title directing delivery to bearer, or an investment security in bearer form.

An instrument that is not a check must be **payable to order** or **bearer.**[39] This requirement is met by such phrases as "Pay to the order of John Jones," "Pay to John Jones or order," "Pay to bearer," and "Pay to John Jones or bearer." The use of the phrase "to the order of John Jones" or "to John Jones or order" shows that the person executing the instrument had no intention of restricting payment of the instrument to John Jones. These phrases indicate that there is no objection to paying anyone to whom John Jones orders the paper to be paid. Similarly, if the person executing the instrument originally wrote that it will be paid "to bearer" or "to John Jones or bearer," there is no restriction on the payment of the paper to the original payee. However, if the instrument is not a check and it is payable on its face "to John Jones," the instrument is not negotiable.[40] Whether an instrument is bearer or order paper is important because the two instruments are transferred in different ways and because the liability of the transferors can be different.

CASE SUMMARY

The Goal Was a Hockey Team AND a Negotiable Instrument

FACTS: William Kidd served as managing director of Limeco Corporation. In 2001, negotiations began between Kidd/Limeco (defendants) and R.W. Whitaker and Monty Fletcher (plaintiffs) in connection with what later became a failed effort to purchase a hockey team in Tupelo. Whitaker and Fletcher loaned Limeco $750,000. Whitaker and Fletcher claim that Kidd concealed the fact that Limeco had no assets. Whitaker also loaned Kidd an additional $100,000, with the understanding that Kidd and Limeco would be responsible for paying back the loan Whitaker had taken out from the Peoples Bank & Trust Company in Tupelo in order to make the loan to Kidd.

On July 1, 2002, the parties entered into what they referred to as promissory notes (referred to as the "Fletcher note" and the "Whitaker note") to memorialize the terms of the loan agreements they had made in early 2002. Both Fletcher and Whitaker were granted a continuing lien on Limeco's monies, securities, and/or other property for the entire amount of the promissory notes (each in the amount of $375,000).

On December 11, 2003, Whitaker and Fletcher filed separate complaints against Limeco and Kidd for recovery of the more than $850,000 that had never been repaid. The trial court found that, because the suit was brought after the contracts' statute of limitations had expired, it had to be dismissed. Whitaker and Fletcher argued that the notes were negotiable instruments and their fraud claim was valid because of the six-year statute of limitations that applied with regard to negotiable instruments.

DECISION: The court held that words of negotiability are an absolute requirement for a negotiable instrument. Without those words, the note is simply a contract, and a suit on a contract required that it be filed within three years. Because Whitaker and Fletcher were over the three years, their suit had to be dismissed. If they had had the words of negotiability, then the suit could have proceeded because it was brought well within the time limits. [**Whitaker v. Limeco Corp., 32 So. 3d 429 (Miss. 2010)**]

---

[39] Guaranteed student loans have too many restrictions on transfers to be negotiable instruments. *U.S. v. Carter*, 506 Fed. Appx. 853 (11th Cir. 2013).

[40] U.C.C. §3-108.

ETHICS & THE LAW

Medicaid Eligibility and Article 3 Negotiability

Kenneth Wilson was hospitalized from January 7, 2007, until his death on February 22, 2007. During the hospitalization, Kenneth's wife, Doris, sold her 100 percent stock ownership in the Brothers Delivery Service (her husband's company) to her son. The agreement provided that Kenneth, Jr., would pay $62,531 in 60 installments of $1,041.82, starting March 1, 2007. Kenneth, Jr., did not sign the promissory note for these terms. Doris never signed the purchase agreement. Doris then applied for Medicaid benefits in order to cover the costs of her husband's hospitalization. Eligibility for Medicaid requires a determination that there are insufficient personal assets to pay the bill. The Division of Social Services concluded that Doris was the owner of a promissory note, a liquid asset, that could be sold to pay the medical bills. Coverage was denied due to excessive resources. Doris argues that there is no negotiable note because the requirements for negotiability are not met. The appellate court agreed because the underlying contract had not been signed by Doris and because there was not, as yet, a promissory note. The purchase agreement did not have words of negotiability and there was no definite time for payment because the note did not yet exist.

Discuss whether Doris attained Medicaid eligibility through a legal loophole. Does she actually have assets that could be used to pay at least part of the debt? Should legal definitions allow us to escape an obligation to pay?

[*Estate of Wilson v. Division of Social Services*, 685 S.E.2d 135 (N.C. App. 2009)]

order paper–instrument payable to the order of a party.

Order Paper. An instrument is payable to order, or **order paper,** when by its terms it is payable to the order of any person described in it ("Pay to the order of K. Read") or to a person or order ("Pay to K. Read or order").

bearer paper–instrument with no payee, payable to cash or payable to bearer.

Bearer Paper. An instrument is payable to bearer, or **bearer paper,** when it is payable (1) to bearer or the order of bearer, (2) to a specified person or bearer, or (3) to "cash," "the order of cash," or any other designation that does not purport to identify a person or when (4) the last or only indorsement is a blank indorsement (an indorsement that does not name the person to whom the instrument is negotiated). An instrument that does not identify any payee is payable to bearer.[41]

Whether an instrument is bearer or order paper is important for determining how the instrument is transferred (see Chapter 28) and what the liability of the parties under the instrument is. Review Figure 27-3 for more background.

CASE SUMMARY

I May Be a Thief, But under Article 3 Bearer Paper Rules, I Am Not a Forger

FACTS: Joshua Herrera found a purse in a dumpster near San Pedro and Kathryn Streets in Albuquerque. Herrera took the purse with him to a friend's house. Either Herrera or his friend called the owner of the purse and the owner retrieved the purse at some point. After the purse was returned to the owner, Herrera returned to the dumpster where he found a check and some other items. The check Herrera found was written out to "Cash" and he thought this meant that he "could get money for [the] check."

When he presented the check to the teller at a credit union to cash it, the teller instructed him to put his name on the payee line next to "Cash." Herrera added "to Joshua Herrera" next to the word "Cash" on the payee line of the check and indorsed the check.

Herrera had pleaded guilty to one count of forgery but moved to have the indictment dismissed on the grounds that adding his name to a bearer instrument was not forgery. He appealed the denial of the motion to dismiss the indictment.

[41] U.C.C. §3-104(d).

I May Be a Thief, But under Article 3 Bearer Paper Rules, I Am Not a Forger continued

DECISION: The court held that the instrument that Herrera originally found was bearer paper. By adding his named "to Joshua Herrera" to the "Pay to" line after "Cash" did not change the character of the instrument from bearer to order paper. At best, the addition of the words created an ambiguity and under the code interpretations should continue to be treated as bearer paper. Since he did not alter the nature of the instrument or convert it to a different instrument, he could not be charged with forgery. [*New Mexico v. Herrera*, **18 P.3d 326 (N.M. App. 2000); *cert. den.* 20 P.3d 810 (N.M. 2001)**]

FIGURE 27-3	**Bearer versus Order Paper**

"Pay to the order of ABC Corp."	ORDER
"Pay to the order of Bearer."	BEARER
"Pay to the order of ABC Corp. or Bearer"	BEARER
"Pay to the order of ABC Corp., Bearer"	ORDER
"Pay to the order of John Jones" (note)	ORDER
"Pay to the order of John Jones" (check)	ORDER
"Pay to John Jones" (note)	NONNEGOTIABLE
"Pay to John Jones" (check)	NEGOTIABLE/ORDER
"Pay to the order of John Jones or Bearer"	BEARER
"Pay to cash"	BEARER
"Pay to the order of cash"	BEARER

postdating–inserting or placing on an instrument a later date than the actual date on which it was executed.

27-2c **Factors Not Affecting Negotiability**

Omitting a date of execution or antedating or **postdating** an instrument has no effect on its negotiability.

Provisions relating to **collateral,** such as specifying the collateral as security for the debt or a promise to maintain, protect, or give additional collateral, do not affect negotiability. **For Example,** the phrase "This note is secured by a first mortgage" does not affect negotiability.

collateral–property pledged by a borrower as security for a debt.

27-2d **Ambiguous Language**

The following rules are applied when **ambiguous** language exists in words or descriptions:

ambiguous–having more than one reasonable interpretation.

1. Words control figures where conflict exists.
2. Handwriting supersedes conflicting typewritten and printed terms.
3. Typewritten terms supersede preprinted terms.
4. If there is a failure to provide for the payment of interest or if there is a provision for the payment of interest but no rate is mentioned, the judgment rate at the place of payment applies from the date of the instrument.[42]

27-2e **Statute of Limitations**

Article 3 of the UCC establishes a three-year statute of limitations for most actions involving negotiable instruments. This limitation also applies to actions for the conversion of such instruments and for breach of warranty. There is a six-year statute of limitations for suits on certificates of deposit and accepted drafts.

[42] In re *Blasco*, 352 B.R. 888 (N.D. Ala. 2006).

Make the Connection

Summary

An instrument or piece of commercial paper is a transferable, signed promise or order to pay a specified sum of money that is evidenced by a record. An instrument is negotiable when it contains the terms required by the UCC.

Negotiable instruments have two categories: (1) promises to pay and (2) orders to pay. Checks and drafts are orders to pay. Notes and certificates of deposits are promises to pay. In addition to ordinary checks, there are cashier's checks and teller's checks. A bank money order is a check even though it bears the words *money order*.

The original parties to a note are the maker and the payee. The original parties to a draft are the drawer, the drawee, and the payee. The term *party* may refer to a natural person or to an artificial person, such as a corporation. Indorsers and accommodation parties are considered secondary obligors.

The requirements of negotiability are that the instrument (1) be evidenced by a record, (2) be signed (authenticated) by the maker or the drawer, and (3) contain a promise or order (4) of an unconditional character (5) to pay in money (6) a sum certain (7) on demand or at a definite time (8) to order or bearer.

A check may be negotiable without being payable to order or bearer.

If an instrument meets the requirements of negotiability, the parties have the rights and protections of Article 3. If it does not meet the requirements of negotiability, the rights of the parties are governed under contract law.

Learning Outcomes

After studying this chapter, you should be able to clearly explain:

27-1   Types of Negotiable Instruments and Parties

LO.1 Explain the importance and function of negotiable instruments
See the discussion of negotiability that begins on page 521.
See the *New Mexico v. Herrera* case, pages 528–529.

LO.2 Name the parties to negotiable instruments
See the list of parties to instruments in the section titled "Parties to Instruments," pages 520–521.

27-2   Negotiability

LO.3 Describe the concept of negotiability and distinguish it from assignability
See *Whitaker v. Limeco Corp.* for what can happen if an instrument is not negotiable, page 527.

LO.4 List the requirements for a negotiable instrument
See the list of negotiability requirements, page 522.
See the *Williams v. Houston Plants & Garden World, Inc.* case to understand who is liable on negotiable instruments, pages 523–524.
See the *Smith v. Vaughn* case, page 526.

Key Terms

acceptor	definite time	order paper
accommodation party	draft, or bill of exchange	party
ambiguous	drawee	payable to order
bearer	drawer	payee
bearer paper	maker	postdating
cashier's check	money	promissory note
certificate of deposit (CD)	money order	representative capacity
check	negotiability	sum certain
collateral	negotiable instrument	teller's check
commercial paper	nonnegotiable instrument	traveler's check

Questions and Case Problems

1. Harold H. Heidingsfelder signed a credit agreement as vice president of J. O. H. Construction Co. for a line of credit with Pelican Plumbing Co. The credit agreement contained the following language:

   > In consideration of an open account privilege, I hereby understand and agree to the above terms.
   >
   > Should it become necessary to place this account for collection I shall personally obligate myself and my corporation, if any, to pay the entire amount due including service charges (as outlined above terms) thirty-three and one-third (33⅓%) attorney's fees, and all costs of collection, including court costs.
   >
   > Signed [Harold H. Heidingsfelder]
   > Company J. O. H. Construction Co., Inc.

   When J. O. H. Construction failed to make payment, Pelican, claiming it was a holder of a negotiable instrument, sued Heidingsfelder to hold him personally liable for his failure to indicate a representative capacity on the credit agreement. He claims that a credit application is not a negotiable instrument and that he could not be held personally liable. Is he right? [*Pelican Plumbing Supply, Inc. v. J. O. H. Construction Co., Inc.*, 653 So. 2d 699 (La.)]

2. Abby Novel signed a note with the following on it: "Glen Gallwitz 1-8-2002 loaned me $5,000 at 6% interest a total of $10,000.00." The note did not contain a payment schedule or a time for repayment.

   Abby used the $10,000 as start-up money for her business and says that she orally agreed to repay the loan out of the proceeds from her first 1,000-product sales. Abby did not make any payments. Glen passed away and his son, as executor of his estate, demanded that Abby repay the $10,000 plus 6% interest for a total of $14,958 (the amount due as of April 2010). The trial court granted judgment for the estate. Abby has appealed, alleging that she repaid the note through the care she gave for Glen. The estate maintains that the instrument was a negotiable promissory note and that it is entitled to collect the amount due in cash. Who is correct and why? [*Gallwitz v. Novel*, 2011 WL 303253 (Ohio App.)]

3. Charter Bank of Gainesville had in its possession a note containing the following provision: "This note with interest is secured by a mortgage on real estate, of even date herewith, made by the maker hereof in favor of said payee…. The terms of said mortgage are by this reference made a part hereof." When the bank sued on the note, it said that it was a holder of a negotiable instrument. Is this instrument negotiable? [*Holly Hill Acres, Ltd. v. Charter Bank of Gainesville*, 314 So. 2d 209 (Fla. App.)]

4. On October 14, 1980, United American Bank of Knoxville made a $1,700,000 loan to Frederic B. Ingram. William F. Earthman, the president of the bank and a beneficiary of the loan, had arranged for the loan and prepared the loan documents. Mr. Ingram and Mr. Earthman were old friends, and Mr. Ingram had loaned Mr. Earthman money in the past. Mr. Ingram was in jail at the time of this loan and was unable to complete the documents for the loan. Mr. Earthman says that Mr. Ingram authorized him to do the loan so long as it did not cost him anything to do it.

   Also on October 14, 1980, Mr. Earthman prepared and executed a personal $1,700,000 note to Mr. Ingram, using a standard Commerce Union Bank note form. Mr. Earthman wrote "Frederic B. Ingram" in the space for identifying the lending bank and also filled in another blank stating that the note would be due "Eighteen Months after Date." With regard to the interest, Mr. Earthman checked a box signifying that the interest would be "At the Bank's 'Prime Rate' plus % per year."

   Mr. Earthman then sold both of the notes, which ended up in the hands of third parties (holders in due course) who demanded payment. Mr. Ingram raised the defense that he had not authorized Mr. Earthman to handle the transactions. The third parties said that the notes were negotiable instruments and that they were entitled to payment without listening to Mr. Ingram's defenses. Mr. Earthman said that his note to Mr. Ingram as well as the bank note from Mr. Ingram were not negotiable and that they could both raise defenses to the third parties seeking payment.

   Who is correct? What do you think of Mr. Earthman's banking processes and procedures? What ethical issues do you see in these loan transactions? [*Ingram v. Earthman*, 993 S.W.2d 611 (Tenn.)]

5. The state of Alaska was a tenant in a large office building owned by Univentures, a partnership. The state made a lease payment of $28,143.47 to Univentures with state treasury warrant No. 21045102. Charles LeViege, the managing partner of

Univentures, assigned the warrant to Lee Garcia. A dispute then arose among the Univentures partners, and the company notified the state that it should no longer pay LeViege the rent. The state placed a stop payment order on the warrant. Garcia claimed that he was a holder of a negotiable instrument and that the state owed him the money. The state claimed that a warrant did not qualify as a negotiable instrument. The warrant was in writing, was signed by the governor of the state, provided a definite sum of $28,143.47, and stated that "it will be deemed paid unless redeemed within two years after the date of issue." The warrant stated that it was "payable to the order of Univentures." Does the warrant meet the requirements for a negotiable instrument? [*National Bank v. Univentures*, 824 P.2d 1377 (Alaska)]

6. NationWide Check Corp. sold money orders through local agents. A customer would purchase a money order by paying an agent the amount of the desired money order plus a fee. The customer would then sign the money order as the remitter or sender and would fill in the name of the person who was to receive the money following the printed words "Payable to." In a lawsuit between NationWide and Banks, a payee on some of these orders, the question was raised as to whether these money orders were checks and could be negotiable even though not payable to order or to bearer. Are the money orders negotiable instruments? [*NationWide Check Corp. v. Banks*, 260 A.2d 367 (D.C.)]

7. George S. Avery signed a letter regarding the unpaid balance on a $20,000 promissory note owed to Jim Whitworth in the form of a letter addressed to Whitworth stating: "This is your note for $45,000.00, secured individually and by our Company for your security, due February 7, 1984." The letter was signed: "Your friend, George S. Avery." It was typed on stationery with the name of Avery's employer, V & L Manufacturing Co., Inc., printed at the bottom and the words "George Avery, President" printed at the top. Avery says he is not personally liable on the note. The court granted summary judgment for Whitworth and Avery appealed. Who is liable? [*Avery v. Whitworth*, 414 S.E.2d 725 (Ga. App.)]

8. Northwest Harvest Products, Inc., fell behind on its trade account with Major Products Company, Inc., and Major requested a note for the debt. Northwest sent a $79,000 corporate note. The balance on the note was incorrect, and Northwest sent a second corporate note for $79,361.89. After further discussion between the parties, Major sent a $78,445.24 note. The Chief Executive Officer of Northwest at that time signed the note "Donald H. Eoll CEO," attached a Post-It brand fax transmittal memo indicating that the note came from Donald Eoll at Northwest, and sent the note via facsimile. The note went unpaid, and Major sued both Eoll and Northwest for the debt. Is the CEO personally liable on the note? What are the parol evidence factors in this case? [*Major Products Co., Inc. v. Northwest Harvest Products, Inc.*, 979 P.2d 905 (Wash. App. 1999)]

9. Atlas Capital, LLC's sole member and manager was Weston Wade Sleater. Mr. Sleater signed two promissory notes totaling $4,000,000 as the maker of the notes. The signature blocks of the notes read, "Weston Wade Sleater & Atlas Marketing Group, L.C.," but the signature was only that of Mr. Sleater. Mr. Sleater is referred to as the maker of the note. Mr. Sleater failed to pay the notes and a bankruptcy trustee brought suit to collect the remaining amount due. Mr. Sleater maintains that the notes are not his but those of Atlas Capital. Is he correct? Is Mr. Sleater liable on the notes? Discuss the ambiguity issues as well as the way the notes were signed. [In re *Bedrock Marketing, LLC*, 404 B.R. 929 (D. Utah)]

10. Lloyd and Mario Spaulding entered into a contract to purchase property from Richard and Robert Krajcir. The two Spaulding brothers signed a promissory note to the Krajcir brothers with the following language: "The amount of $10,000 [is] to be paid sellers at the time of the initial closing [delivery of the deed]; plus, the principal amount payable to sellers at the time of the final indorsement of the subject H.U.D. loan." In litigation over the note, the Spauldings said it was not a negotiable instrument. The lower court found it to be a negotiable promissory note and the Spaulding partners appealed. Is the note negotiable? [*Krajcir v. Egid*, 712 N.E.2d 917 (Ill. App.)]

11. Is the following instrument negotiable?

> *I, Richard Bell, hereby promise to pay to the order of Lorry Motors Ten Thousand Dollars ($10,000) upon the receipt of the final distribution from the estate of my deceased aunt, Rita Dorn. This negotiable instrument is given by me as the down payment on my purchase of a 1986 Buick to be delivered in three weeks.*
>
> *Richard Bell (signature).*

12. Smith has in his possession the following instrument:

    September 1, 2003
    I, Selma Ray, hereby promise to pay Helen
    Savit One Thousand Dollars ($1,000) one
    year after date. This instrument was given for
    the purchase of Two Hundred (200) shares of
    Redding Mining Corporation, Interest 6%.
    *   Selma Ray (signature).*

    What is this instrument? Is it negotiable?

13. Master Homecraft Co. received a promissory note with a stated face value from Sally and Tom Zimmerman. The note was payment for remodeling their home and contained unused blanks for installment payments but contained no maturity date. When Master Homecraft sued the Zimmermans on the note, the couple argued that they should not be liable on the note because it is impossible to determine from its face the amount due or the date of maturity. Decide. [*Master Homecraft Co. v. Zimmerman*, 22 A.2d 440 (Pa.)]

CPA Questions

1. A company has in its possession the following instrument:

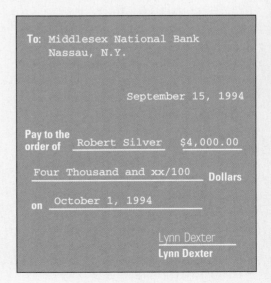

    This instrument is:

    a. Not negotiable until December 1, 1987.

    b. A negotiable bearer note.

    c. A negotiable time draft.

14. A note from Mark Johnson with HealthCo International as payee for $28,979.15 included the following language:

    [p]ayable in _____, Successive Monthly
    Installments of $ Each, and in 11 Successive
    Monthly Installments of $2,414.92 Each
    thereafter, and in a final payment of
    $2,415.03 thereafter. The first installment
    being payable on the _____ day of
    _____ 20 _____, and the remaining
    installments on the same date of each month
    thereafter until paid.

    Johnson signed the note. Is it negotiable? [*Barclays Bank, P.L.C. v. Johnson*, 499 S.E.2d 769 (N. C. App.)]

15. The text of a handwritten note stated simply that "'I Robert Harrison owe Peter Jacob $25,000 …,' /s/ Robert Harrison." Peter Jacob sought to use the handwritten note as a negotiable promissory note. Can he? [*Jacob v. Harrison*, 49 U.C.C. Rep. Serv. 2d 554 (Del. Super.)]

    d. A nonnegotiable note because it states that it is secured by a conditional sales contract.

2. The instrument shown here is a:

    a. Draft.

    b. Postdated check.

    c. Trade acceptance.

    d. Promissory note.

3. Under the commercial paper article of the UCC, for an instrument to be negotiable, it must:

   a. Be payable to order or to bearer.

   b. Be signed to the payee.

   c. Contain references to all agreements between the parties.

   d. Contain necessary conditions of payment.

4. An instrument reads as follows:

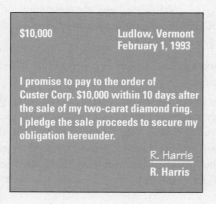

$10,000   Ludlow, Vermont
           February 1, 1993

I promise to pay to the order of Custer Corp. $10,000 within 10 days after the sale of my two-carat diamond ring. I pledge the sale proceeds to secure my obligation hereunder.

                              R. Harris
                              R. Harris

   Which of the following statements correctly describes this instrument?

   a. The instrument is nonnegotiable because it is not payable at a definite time.

   b. The instrument is nonnegotiable because it is secured by the proceeds of the sale of the ring.

   c. The instrument is a negotiable promissory note.

   d. The instrument is a negotiable sight draft payable on demand.

5. Which of the following instruments is subject to the provisions of the Negotiable Instruments Article of the UCC?

   a. A bill of lading

   b. A warehouse receipt

   c. A certificate of deposit

   d. An investment security

6. Under the Negotiable Instruments Article of the UCC, which of the following statements is correct regarding a check?

   a. A check is a promise to pay money.

   b. A check is an order to pay money.

   c. A check does not need to be payable on demand.

   d. A check does not need to be drawn on a bank.

Transfers of Negotiable Instruments and Warranties of Parties

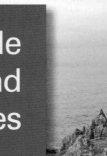

Learning Outcomes ⟨⟨⟨

After studying this chapter, you should be able to

LO.1   Explain the difference between negotiation of order paper and negotiation of bearer paper

LO.2   List the types of indorsements and describe their uses

LO.3   Determine the legal effect of forged and unauthorized indorsements

LO.4   Be familiar with the forged payee impostor exceptions

LO.5   List the indorser's warranties and describe their significance

CPA

28-1   Transfer of Negotiable Instruments

Much of the commercial importance of negotiable instruments lies in the ease with which they can be transferred. Negotiable instruments are transferred by a process known as *negotiation*.

28-1a   Effect of Transfer

When a contract is assigned, the transferee has the rights of the transferor. The transferee is entitled to enforce the contract but, as assignee, has no greater rights than the assignor. The assignee is in the same position as the original party to the contract and is subject to any defense that could be raised in a suit on an assigned contract.

When a negotiable instrument is transferred by negotiation, the transferee becomes the *holder of the paper*. A holder who meets certain additional requirements may also be a **holder in due course.** The status of holder in due course gives immunity from certain defenses that might have been asserted against the transferor (see Chapter 29 for a discussion of the rights and role of a holder in due course).

holder in due course–a holder who has given value, taken in good faith without notice of dishonor, defenses, or that instrument is overdue, and who is afforded special rights or status.

28-1b   Definition of Negotiation

Under U.C.C. §3-201(a), **negotiation** means "a transfer of possession … of an instrument by a person other than the issuer to a person who thereby becomes a holder."[1] Negotiation, then, is simply the transfer of a negotiable instrument in such a way that the transferee becomes a holder.[2] A **holder** is different from a possessor or an assignee of the paper. A holder is a transferee in possession of an instrument that runs to her. An instrument runs to a party if it is payable to her order, is indorsed to her, or is bearer paper.

negotiation–the transfer of commercial paper by indorsement and delivery by the person to whom it is then payable in the case of order paper and by physical transfer in the case of bearer paper.

holder–someone in possession of an instrument that runs to that person (i.e., is made payable to that person, is indorsed to that person, or is bearer paper).

28-1c   How Negotiation Occurs: The Order or Bearer Character of an Instrument

The order or bearer character of the paper determines how it may be negotiated. The order or bearer character of an instrument is determined according to the words of negotiability used (see Chapter 27 for a complete discussion of order and bearer words of negotiation and more examples of bearer versus order instruments). The types of instruments that qualify as bearer paper include those payable to bearer as well as those payable to the order of "Cash" or payable in blank. The character of an instrument is determined as of the time negotiation takes place even though its character originally or at the time of prior transfers may have been different.

CPA

28-2   How Negotiation Occurs: Bearer Instruments

U.C.C. §3-201(b) provides, "If an instrument is payable to bearer, it may be negotiated by transfer of possession alone."[3] If an instrument qualifies for bearer status, then it is negotiated by **delivery** to another.[4] Delivery can be accomplished by actual transfer of

delivery–constructive or actual possession.

---

[1] U.C.C. §3-201(a).
[2] U.C.C. §3-201; *Bank of New York Mellon v. Deane*, 970 N.Y.S.2d 427 (N.Y. 2013); In re *Miller*, 666 F.3d 1255 (10th Cir. 2012).
[3] U.C.C. §3-201(b). In re *Hussain*, 508 B.R. 417 (9th Cir. 2014).
[4] If no payee is named, the instrument is bearer paper and is negotiated by delivery. *DCM Ltd. Partnership v. Wang*, 555 F. Supp. 2d 808 (E.D. Mich. 2008); *Waldron v. Delffs*, 988 S.W.2d 182 (Tenn. App. 1999).

possession wherein the transferee has possession of the instrument, or constructive transfer, whereby the transferee has exclusive access. **For Example,** when mortgage lenders finance a home mortgage, they often transfer the underlying promissory note on the mortgage several times through financial streams. Many of the underlying problems in the financial market's collapse in 2008 were the large bundles of the promissory notes tied to home mortgages that were in amounts above the value of the mortgaged properties. Who held the bearer promissory notes became a critical issue in foreclosures. Bearer paper is negotiated to a person taking possession of it without regard to whether such possession is lawful. Because delivery of a bearer instrument is effective negotiation, it is possible for a thief or an embezzling officer to transfer title to a bearer instrument. Such a person's presence in the chain of transfer does not affect the rights of those who have taken the bearer instrument in good faith.[5]

CASE SUMMARY

The Blank Indorsement Draws a Blank on Wrongful Foreclosure

FACTS: On September 22, 2006, Richard and Sabrina Emmons signed an adjustable rate promissory note and deed of trust with Chevy Chase Bank (now known as Capital One) for a property located in Vancleave, Mississippi. The note indicates that "[t]he Lender or anyone who takes this Note by Transfer and who is entitled to receive payments under this Note is called the 'Note Holder.'" According to the terms of the deed of trust, "MERS (Mortgage Electronic Recording System) is the beneficiary under this Security Instrument." Based on the assignment of deed of trust, executed on April 9, 2010, MERS then assigned the Emmons' deed of trust to U.S. Bank as trustee.

The deed of trust listed MERS and MERS' successors and assigns as beneficiary and nominee. On April 9, 2010, MERS assigned the deed of trust to U.S. Bank. The Emmons defaulted on their payments. The deed of trust provides for a power of sale in the event of the borrowers'

default—a right which U.S. Bank then exercised through a nonjudicial foreclosure (power of sale). The Emmons then filed suit alleging, among other things, wrongful foreclosure because they claimed U.S. Bank was not a holder of the promissory note.

DECISION: The court held that the Emmons' promissory note was a negotiable instrument that had been indorsed in blank and was therefore bearer paper. It could be further negotiated to a holder via the simple action of delivery. So the holder of the note (in this case, Capital One) would have the right to conduct a foreclosure sale should the parties fall into default on their payments. There was no wrongful foreclosure as long as the party foreclosing was a holder of the note and there had been a default. Capital One was a holder and the Emmons had defaulted. [***Emmons v. Capital One,*** **2012 WL 773288 (S.D. Miss. 2012)**]

Even though a bearer instrument may be negotiated by a mere transfer of possession, the one to whom the instrument is delivered may require the bearer to indorse the instrument. This situation most commonly arises when a check payable to "Cash" is presented to a bank for payment. The reason a transferee of bearer paper would want an indorsement is to obtain the protection of an indorser's warranties from the bearer.[6] The bank wants an indorsement on a check made payable to "Cash" so that it can turn to the party cashing the check in the event payment issues arise.

---

[5] U.C.C. §§3-202 and 3-204; *Knight Pub. Co., Inc. v. Chase Manhattan Bank, N.A.*, 479 S.E.2d 478 (N.C. App. 1997); review denied 487 S.E.2d 548 (N.C. 1997); In re *Federal-Nogul Global, Inc.*, 319 B.R. 363 (D. Del. 2005).

[6] The Uniform Electronic Transactions Act (UETA), promulgated by the National Conference of Commissioners on Uniform State Laws in July 1999 and enacted in 46 states, provides that the transfer of a note by electronic record affords the transferee the same rights as a tangible written note.

ETHICS & THE LAW

Having Your Mortgage Set Aside

In cases such as the *Emmons v. Capital One* case, the borrowers bring suit seeking to have their mortgage obligations set aside on the basis of technicalities in the paperwork or the separation of the paperwork. Generally, these borrowers owe far more on their mortgages than their homes are worth.

In some cases, the mortgages have been deemed invalid or the courts have held there was no authority for foreclosure because of the problems with note transfers and the right of foreclosure. Evaluate the ethics of the borrowers in seeking to have their mortgages set aside.

CPA   28-3   # How Negotiation Occurs: Order Instruments

indorsement–signature of the payee on an instrument.

U.C.C. §3-201(b) provides, "if an instrument is payable to an identified person, negotiation requires transfer of possession of the instrument and its indorsement by the holder."[7] A negotiable instrument that is payable to the order of a specific party is *order paper*, which can be negotiated only through indorsement and transfer of possession of the paper. **Indorsement** and transfer of possession can be made by the payee or indorsee or by an authorized agent of that person.[8]

CASE SUMMARY

The Tax Man Cometh, but He Can't Provide Your Indorsement

FACTS: Thorton Ring was behind on his property taxes for his property in Freeport, Maine. When he received a check payable to his order from Advest, Inc., in the amount of $11,347.09, he wrote the following on the back of the check: "Payable to Town of Freeport Property Taxes 2 Main St."; he sent it along with a letter to the town offices. The letter included the following: "I have paid $11,347.09 of real estate taxes and request the appropriate action to redeem the corresponding property." Ring did nothing further and his property was then liened by the tax clerk. Ring objected because he had paid the taxes. The town argued that the check was not indorsed and Ring thus had not paid the

taxes in time to avoid the lien. The lower court found for the town and Ring appealed.

DECISION: There was no indorsement. Ring's name must be signed for there to be negotiation of the instrument to the town. The check had only the first part of the necessary indorsement for order paper; Ring had to indorse the instrument for further negotiation. Indorsements vary according to the method of signing and the words used along with the signature. The nature of an indorsement also affects the future of the instrument in terms of its requirements for further negotiation. [*Town of Freeport v. Ring*, 727 A.2d 901 (Me. 1999)]

---

blank indorsement–an indorsement that does not name the person to whom the paper, document of title, or investment security is negotiated.

28-3a   Blank Indorsement

When the indorser merely signs a negotiable instrument, the indorsement is called a **blank indorsement** (Figure 28-1). A blank indorsement does not indicate the person to whom the instrument is to be paid, that is, the transferee. A blank indorsement turns an

---

[7] U.C.C. §3-201(b). Although the modern spelling is "endorsement," the UCC has retained the British spelling of "indorsement."
[8] UCC §3-204. The UCC spellings are "indorse" and "indorser," the spellings used in this text. However, courts (including in some cases in this text) use the modern "endorse" and "endorser." *Jenkins v. Wachovia Bank*, 711 S. E.2d 80 (Ga. App. 2011).

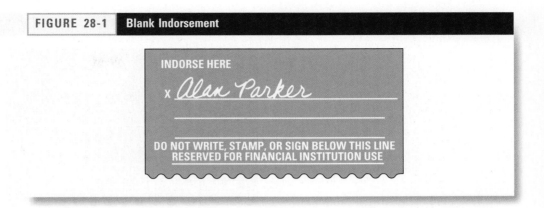

FIGURE 28-1 | **Blank Indorsement**

order instrument into a bearer instrument. A person who possesses an instrument on which the last indorsement is blank is the holder.[9] **For Example,** if a check is payable to the order of Jill Barnes and Ms. Barnes indorses the check on the back "Jill Barnes," then the check that was originally an order instrument is now a bearer instrument. The check can now be transferred as bearer paper, which requires only delivery of possession. Once Jill Barnes's signature appears as a blank indorsement on the back, the check becomes transferrable simply by delivery of possession to another party.

28-3b Special Indorsement

special indorsement—an indorsement that specifies the person to whom the instrument is indorsed.

indorsee—party to whom special indorsement is made.

A **special indorsement** consists of the signature of the indorser and words specifying the person to whom the indorser makes the instrument payable, that is, the **indorsee** (Figure 28-2).[10] **For Example,** if Jill Barnes wrote on the back of the check payable to her "Pay to Jack Barnes, /s/ Jill Barnes," the check could be negotiated further only through the signature and possession of Jack Barnes. A special indorsement in this case continues an order instrument as an order instrument. If, after receiving the check, Jack Barnes simply signed it on the back, the check would become bearer paper and could be transferred through possession only.

Although words of negotiability are required on the front of negotiable instruments, it is not necessary that indorsements contain the word *order* or *bearer*. Consequently, the

 E-COMMERCE & CYBERLAW

New Flexibility for Cyberspace Commercial Paper

The Check Clearing for the 21st Century Act (sometimes called "Check 21") allows banks to use images of checks as a substitute for paper checks. The substitute check is the legal equivalent of the paper check that has, for so long, dominated U.S. commerce. Under Check 21, the bank is also able to send you electronic copies of your canceled checks. Even if you still opt for paper summaries of your account activity each month, the bank need not return physical checks and

can send small reproductions of your checks grouped together on the statement. Recently, you have been able to secure faster credits to your accounts for deposited checks because ATMs scan the checks in, checks that are recognized immediately as deposits. All the new regulations on check substitutes are known as Regulation CC and can be found at Regulation CC, 12 C.F.R. §229.2(zz)(2).

[9] In re *Smith*, 509 B.R. 260 (N.D. Cal. 2014).
[10] U.C.C. §3-205; *Chicago Title Ins. Co. v. Allfirst Bank*, 905 A.2d 366, 60 U.C.C. Rep. Serv. 2d 864 (Md. 2006).

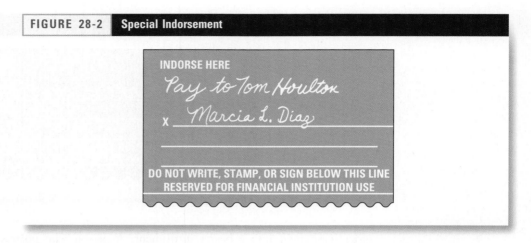

FIGURE 28-2   Special Indorsement

paper indorsed as shown in Figure 28-2 continues to be negotiable and may be negotiated further.[11]

An indorsement of "Pay to account [number]" is a special indorsement. In contrast, the inclusion of a notation indicating the debt to be paid is not a special indorsement.

28-3c   Qualified Indorsement

qualified indorsement—
an indorsement that
includes words such as
"without recourse" that
disclaims certain liability
of the indorser to a maker
or a drawee.

A **qualified indorsement** is one that qualifies the effect of a blank or a special indorsement by disclaiming certain liability of the indorser to a maker or a drawee. This disclaimer is given by using the phrase "Without recourse" as part of the indorsement (Figure 28-3). Any other words that indicate an intent to limit the indorser's secondary liability in the event the maker or the drawee does not pay on the instrument can also be used.[12]

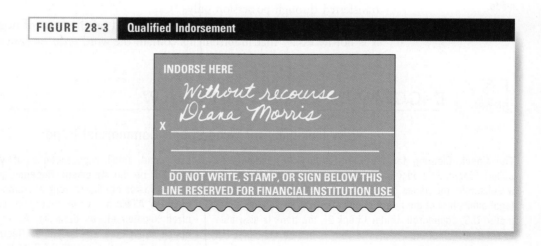

FIGURE 28-3   Qualified Indorsement

---

[11] Only a check may use the phrase "Pay to" on its face and remain negotiable. All other instruments require words of negotiability on their face. Indorsements, on all instruments, need only "Pay to." U.C.C. §3-110.

[12] *Antaeus Enterprises, Inc. v. SD-Barn Real Estate, LLC*, 480 F. Supp. 2d 734 (S.D.N.Y. 2007).

The qualification of an indorsement does not affect the passage of title or the negotiable character of the instrument. It merely disclaims certain of the indorser's secondary liabilities for payment of the instrument in the event the original parties do not pay as the instrument provides.

This qualified form of indorsement is most commonly used when the indorser is a person who has no personal interest in the transaction. **For Example,** an agent or an attorney who is merely indorsing a check of a third person to a client might make a qualified indorsement because he is not actually a party to the transaction.

28-3d Restrictive Indorsement

restrictive indorsement– an indorsement that restricts further transfer, such as in trust for or to the use of some other person, is conditional, or for collection or deposit.

A **restrictive indorsement** specifies the purpose of the indorsement or the use to be made of the instrument (Figure 28-4).[13] An indorsement is restrictive when it includes words showing that the instrument is to be deposited (such as "For deposit only"), when it is negotiated for collection or to an agent or a trustee, or when the negotiation is conditional.[14]

A restrictive indorsement does not prevent transfer or negotiation of the instrument once the initial restriction is honored. The indorsement "For deposit only" requires only that the first party who receives the instrument after the restriction is placed on it comply with that restriction. The indorsement "For deposit only" makes an instrument a bearer instrument for any bank. If the indorser's account number is added to a "For deposit only" indorsement, then the only party who can take the instrument after this restrictive indorsement is a bank with that account number. A restrictive indorsement reduces the risk of theft or unauthorized transfer by eliminating the bearer quality of a blank indorsement.

28-3e Correction of Name by Indorsement

Sometimes the name of the payee or the indorsee of an instrument is spelled improperly. **For Example,** H. A. Price may receive a paycheck that is payable to the order of "H. O. Price." If this error in Price's name was a clerical one and the check is indeed intended for

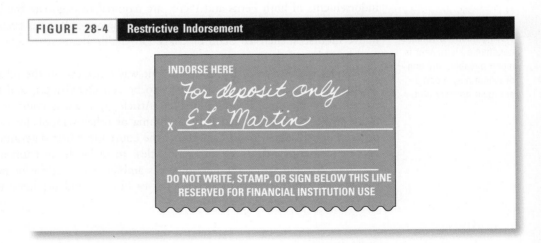

| FIGURE 28-4 | Restrictive Indorsement |

INDORSE HERE

For deposit only
X *E.L. Martin*

DO NOT WRITE, STAMP, OR SIGN BELOW THIS LINE
RESERVED FOR FINANCIAL INSTITUTION USE

[13] U.C.C. §3-206.
[14] *Travelers Cas. and Sur. Co. of America v. Bank of America*, 2009 WL 5176769 (Sup. Ct. N.Y.).

H. A. Price, the employee may ask the employer to write a new check payable to the proper name. However, under Article 3, a much simpler solution allows the payee or indorsee whose name is misspelled to indorse the wrong name, the correct name, or both. The person giving or paying value or taking it for collection for the instrument may require both forms of the signature.[15]

This correction of name by indorsement may be used only when it was intended that the instrument should be payable to the person making the corrective indorsement. If there were in fact two employees, one named H. A. Price and the other H. O. Price, it would be forgery for one to take the check intended for the other and, by indorsing it, obtain the benefit of the proceeds of the check.[16]

A fictitious, assumed, or trade name is treated the same as a wrong name. The same procedure for correction of a misspelled name with indorsement of both names applies to these forms of payee identification as well.[17]

28-3f Bank Indorsement

To simplify the transfer and collection of negotiable instruments from one bank to another, "any agreed method which identifies the transferor bank is sufficient for the item's further transfer to another bank."[18] A bank could simply indorse with its Federal Reserve System number instead of using its name.

Likewise, when a customer has deposited an instrument with a bank but has failed to indorse it, the bank may make an indorsement for the customer unless the instrument expressly requires the payee's personal indorsement. Furthermore, the mere stamping or marking on the item of any notation showing that it was deposited by the customer or credited to the customer's account is effective as an indorsement by the customer.

28-3g Multiple Payees and Indorsements

Ordinarily, one person is named as the payee in the instrument, but two or more payees may be named. In that case, the instrument may specify that it is payable to any one or more of them or that it is payable to all jointly. **For Example,** if the instrument is made payable "to the order of Ferns and Piercy," then Ferns and Piercy are joint payees. The indorsements of both Ferns and Piercy are required to negotiate the instrument.

alternative payees— those persons to whom a negotiable instrument is made payable, any one of whom may indorse and take delivery of it.

If the instrument is payable to **alternative payees** or if it has been negotiated to alternative indorsees, such as "Stahl or Glass" or "Stahl/Glass," it may be indorsed and delivered by either of them.

Under old Article 3, if the instrument was not clear on the relationship or types of multiple payees or indorsees, they were to be considered joint, and the signatures of all parties were required.[19] Under Revised Article 3, when a court is faced with two or more payees who are separated by a comma or other symbol, for example, "Pay to the order of Jeff Bridges—Susan Sarandon," the court must first determine whether the symbols or separating marks are sufficiently clear to make the instrument payable jointly. If the court concludes that the instrument is ambiguous, then the preference is for alternative payees, which means that either Jeff or Susan could negotiate the instrument with

---

[15] U.C.C. §3-204(d).
[16] *Hyatt Corp. v. Palm Beach Nat. Bank*, 840 So. 2d 300 (Fla. App. 2003).
[17] *DCM Ltd. Partnership v. Wang*, 555 F. Supp. 2d (E.D. Mich. 2008).
[18] U.C.C. §4-103.
[19] In re *Ames Dept. Stores, Inc.*, 322 B.R. 238 (S.D.N.Y. 2003).

one signature; they would not have to have the other's indorsement for negotiation. Under Revised Article 3, if the instrument is ambiguous, the payees or indorsees are considered payees in the alternative.

CASE SUMMARY

Checking Indorsements at Check City

FACTS: L & T Enterprises issued checks to one of L & T's subcontractors and one of that subcontractor's suppliers. Check City cashed the checks but did so with the indorsement of only the subcontractor, not the supplier. The subcontractor had a long, positive history with Check City. Although the reverse side of the checks contained what at cursory glance might appear to be two signatures, even minimal attention to those signatures shows they are the subcontractor's business name and the signature of a presumably authorized employee, albeit in an order that is the opposite of what is customary. Both entries are in the same handwriting, and a prudent person cashing the checks could not possibly have mistaken the two entries for proper indorsements by both the subcontractor and the subcontractor's supplier.

Check City filed suit against L & T for negligence. The trial court held that L & T owed Check City a duty and that

L & T breached that duty by failing to exercise ordinary care and substantially contributing to an alteration of an instrument or forged signature. L & T appealed.

DECISION: There is a difference between the liability for a forged indorsement and a missing indorsement. Here, Check City failed to obtain the necessary signatures for the two payees. The result is that Check City has liability for the losses. Check City cannot hold L & T liable for opening the door to forgery when it failed to ensure that the signatures were there and genuine, a duty it holds as the first party to receive the check. The judgment in favor of Check City on its complaint is reversed. The parties will bear their own costs on appeal. [*Check City, Inc. v. L & T Enterprises*, **237 P.3d 910 (Utah App. 2010)**]

28-3h Agent or Officer Indorsement

An instrument may be made payable to the order of an officeholder. **For Example,** a check may read "Pay to the order of Receiver of Taxes." Such a check may be received and negotiated by the person who at the time is the receiver of taxes. This general identification of a payee is a matter of convenience, and the drawer of the check is not required to find out the actual name of the receiver of taxes at that time.

If an instrument is drawn in favor of an officer of a named corporation, the instrument is payable to the corporation, the officer, or any successor to such officer. Any of these parties in possession of the instrument is the holder and may negotiate the instrument.[20]

28-3i Missing Indorsement

When the parties intend to negotiate an order instrument but for some reason the holder fails to indorse it, there is no negotiation. The transfer without indorsement has only the effect of a contract assignment.[21] If the transferee gave value for the instrument (see Chapter 29 for more information on what constitutes giving value), the transferee has the right to require that the transferor indorse the instrument unqualifiedly and thereby negotiate the instrument.

[20] U.C.C. §3-110(cc)(2)(li).
[21] U.C.C. §3-204(d). *Cyprus Federal Credit Union v. Cumis Ins. Soc., Inc.,* 2013 WL 7174130 (10th Cir. 2013).

THINKING THINGS THROUGH

The Minor with an Embezzling Conservator

Steven Powell died in a tragic accident at work, entitling his minor son, Cody, to approximately $252,000 in life insurance proceeds. Karen Unrue, Steven's sister, approached Elizabeth Powell, Steven's widow, and offered to manage the insurance proceeds for Cody.

The probate court appointed Karen Unrue and Travis Powell (Steven's brother) as co-conservators. The probate court also waived the bond requirement and ordered "that the funds of the minor child, [Cody], be deposited in a restricted account and that no funds be withdrawn or transferred from such account without written [o]rder of [the probate court]." The certificate of appointment and fiduciary letter included the following restriction: "No withdrawals without court order."

On Cody's behalf, Unrue received seven checks totaling $252,447.51. Three of the checks were made payable to her and Travis jointly and included the designation "Co-conservators For [Cody], A Minor" or "Co-Cn For Minor, [Cody]." The other four checks were made payable to Unrue and included the designation "As Conservator Of [Cody], A Minor." Unrue endorsed the checks without including her title as co-conservator. Unbeknownst to Travis, Unrue forged his name on the three checks made payable to her and Travis as co-conservators and took all the checks to the Pawleys Island Bank of America (BOA). Unrue had Lee Ann Yourko, a personal banker, open a certificate of deposit (CD) account titled "Karen M. Unrue Guardian [Cody]." Yourko collected the checks and took them to a teller, who processed the checks and deposited the proceeds into the CD account. Neither Yourko nor the teller questioned the conservator designation in the payee line of the checks.

A few days later, Unrue returned to the Pawleys Island BOA with a single check for $253.67 made payable to her "As Conservator For Cody A Minor." Unrue requested Meredith Lawrence, the branch manager, to open a Uniform Gift to Minors Act (UGMA) account titled, "Karen M. Unrue—cust [Cody]—UMGA [sic]." Lawrence did not question the conservator title on the payee line of the check. Lawrence also failed to notice that Unrue endorsed the check without including her title.

Approximately a month later, after the CD matured, Unrue withdrew 100 percent of the funds, $253,991.50, from the CD account. Unrue took the funds to the Pawleys Island BOA and deposited them in the UGMA savings account. Over the next several months, Unrue made seven online transfers totaling $258,500 from the UGMA savings account to her personal checking account.

Mrs. Powell brought suit against BOA for its negligence in managing the accounts and failing to notice the indorsement requirements and restrictions imposed on the conservator.

Would Bank of America be liable? Be sure to discuss what you know about indorsement requirements and restrictive indorsements in formulating your answer.

[*Cody P. v. Bank of America, N.A.*, 720 S.E.2d 473 (S.C. App. 2011)]

28-4 Problems in Negotiation of Instruments

The issues of signatures and requirements for negotiation can become quite complex when issues such as forgery, employee misconduct, and embezzlement arise.

28-4a Forged and Unauthorized Indorsements

forged or unauthorized indorsement–instrument indorsed by an agent for a principal without authorization or authority.

A **forged** or **unauthorized indorsement** is not a valid indorsement.[22] Accordingly, anyone who has possession of a forged instrument is not a holder because the indorsement of the person whose signature was forged was necessary for effective negotiation of the instrument to the possessor. However, proof of forgery requires clear proof, and a split from a pattern of payments is helpful.

If payment of an instrument is made to one claiming under or through a forged indorsement, the payor ordinarily remains liable to the person who is the rightful owner of the paper. However, if the rightful owner has been negligent and contributed to the forgery or unauthorized signature problem, there are exceptions to these general rules on

[22] U.C.C. §3-403(2); Steven B. Dow, "Imposter Rule and the Problem of Agency under the Revised Uniform Commercial Code: New Risks for Bank Customers?" 16 *Comm. L.J.* 199 (2001).

liability for forged indorsements (see Chapter 29 for more information on the rights and liabilities of the parties).

CASE SUMMARY

The Great Rite-Aid Heist

FACTS: B.D.G.S., Inc., a New York corporation with head-quarters in Washington, owns a warehouse in Utica, New York. In 1991, B.D.G.S. entered into an oral agreement with two local men, Anthony Balio and his employee, Peter Duniec, to manage the warehouse. Their responsibilities included finding tenants and collecting rent, which was then to be forwarded to B.D.G.S. and deposited into its bank account in Washington. Balio and Duniec formed the Beech-grove Warehouse Corporation and maintained a business account in that name at Savings Bank of Utica (SBU).

Between 1996 and 2000, B.D.G.S. believed that one of its tenants, Rite-Aid, had been falling behind and failing to make its rent payments. B.D.G.S. later discovered that Rite-Aid had been making the payments, but 16 checks had been indorsed to Beechgrove Warehouse and deposited into Beech-grove's SBU account. The checks had been made payable to DBGS (an apparent typographical error). There was a hand-written indorsement on the back of each check stating:

DBGS, Inc.
Pay to the order of

Beechgrove Warehouse
For Deposit [followed by Beechgrove's SBU account number]

A refund check from Niagara Mohawk for $427,781.82 had similarly been indorsed and deposited in the SBU account. B.D.G.S. filed suit against SBU, Balio, Duniec, and Beechgrove Warehouse. B.D.G.S. also brought a claim against SBU. The jury found that SBU had not followed reasonable commercial standards by accepting the checks for deposit. The appellate court affirmed and SBU appealed.

DECISION: The court affirmed noting that SBU was dealing with a payee forgery and it was SBU's responsibility to verify that the party with the checks was actually the payee and was authorized to deposit the checks. Because SBU was the one that had contact with Balio and Duniec it had a chance to prevent the embezzlement but its practices were not detailed enough to catch payee forgeries. [***B.D.G.S., Inc. v. Balio,*** **861 N.E.2d 813 (N.Y. 2006)]**

28-4b Quasi Forgeries: The Impostor Rule

impostor rule—an exception to the rules on liability for forgery that covers situations such as the embezzling payroll clerk.

The **impostor rule** provides three exceptions to the rule that a forged indorsement is not effective to validly negotiate an instrument. If one of the three impostor exceptions applies, the instrument is still effectively negotiated, even though there may have been a forgery of an indorsement.

When the Impostor Rule Applies

The impostor rule applies in cases where an indorser is impersonating a payee and in two cases where the indorser is a dummy payee.[23]

Impersonating Payee. The impersonation of a payee in the impostor rule exception includes impersonation of the agent of the person who is named as payee. **For Example,** if Jones pretends to be the agent of Brown Corporation and thereby obtains a check payable to the order of the corporation, the impostor exception applies.

Dummy Payee. Another impostor scenario arises when the preparer of the instrument intends that the named payee will never benefit from the instrument. Such a "dummy" payee may be an actual or a fictitious person. This situation arises when the owner of a checking account wishes to conceal the true purpose of taking money from the account at

[23] *State Sec. Check Cashing, Inc. v. American General Financial Services (DE)*, 972 A.2d 882 (Md. 2009).

the bank. The account owner makes out a check purportedly in payment of a debt that in fact does not exist.[24]

Dummy Payee Supplied by Employee. The third impostor situation arises when an agent or employee of the maker or the drawer has supplied the name to be used for the payee, intending that the payee should not have any interest in the paper.[25] This last situation occurs when an employee fraudulently causes an employer to sign a check made to a customer or another person, whether existing or not. The employee does not intend to send it to that person but rather intends to forge the latter's indorsement, cash the check, and keep the money. This exception to the impostor rule imposes responsibility on employers to have adequate internal controls to prevent employees from taking advantage of an accounting system with loopholes so that others are not required to bear the cost of the employer's lack of appropriate precautions.

Effect of Impostor Rule

When the impostor rule is applicable, any person may indorse the name of the payee. This indorsement is treated as a genuine indorsement by the payee and cannot be attacked on the ground that it is a forgery. This recognition of the fictitious payee's signature as valid applies even though the dummy payee of the paper is a fictitious person.[26]

Limitations on Impostor Rule

The impostor rule does not apply when there is a valid check to an actual creditor for a correct amount owed by the drawer and someone later forges the payee's name. The impostor rule does not apply in this situation even if the forger is an employee of the drawer.

Even when the unauthorized indorsement of the payee's name is effective by virtue of the impostor rule, a person forging the payee's name is subject to civil and criminal liability for making such an indorsement.

For the impostor rule to apply, the holders or the takers of the instrument must show that they took the instrument (1) in good faith and (2) for payment or collection.

CASE SUMMARY

Sorry, Charlie Walks Away with the $6.3 Million

FACTS: Won Charlie Yi solicited money from investors in the Korean–American community (plaintiffs) by representing that he would invest their money in brokerage accounts at Carlin Equities Corporation, a nationally recognized broker-dealer based in New York. Yi, however, did not invest the money he received from plaintiffs at all. Instead, Yi registered the name "Carlin Co." as a fictitious name under which he did business. He opened a bank account at Wells Fargo in the name of "Won Charlie Yi dba Carlin Co." Between January and September of 2003, Yi received eight checks, totaling $6.3 million, payable to "Carlin Co.," "Carlin Corp.," or "Carlin Corporation." Yi deposited the checks into his Wells Fargo account and absconded with plaintiffs' money. He was later apprehended by federal authorities and convicted of a variety of criminal fraud charges.

The defrauded investors filed suit against Wells Fargo to recover their losses for the bank's lack of ordinary care in

---

[24] *Schultz v. Bank of America*, 990 A.2d 1078 (Md. 2010).

[25] *Advocate Health and Hospitals Corp. v. Bank One*, 810 N.E.2d 962 (Ill. App. 2004).

[26] *Bank of Nichols Hills v. Bank of Oklahoma*, 196 P.3d 984 (Okla. App. 2008). *Advance Dental Care, Inc. v. SunTrust Bank*, 816 F. Supp. 2d 268 (D. Md. 2011); *State Sec. Check Cashing, Inc. v. American General Financial Services*, 972 A.2d 882 (Md. 2009).

Sorry, Charlie Walks Away with the $6.3 Million continued

being certain that the checks deposited were deposited with the intended payee. A jury found in favor of Wells Fargo and the investors appealed.

DECISION: The court affirmed the lower court's decision because the checks were made out to an intended payee. Although there were differing names on the check and the indorsements were not always precise, the parties intended the checks to go to Charlie's company and Charlie's account. Charlie was a fraudster and they lost their

money, but Wells Fargo is not liable for losses when customers write legitimate checks to those whom they later realize cannot be trusted. Losses are absorbed by banks when they fail to act in a commercially reasonable manner in honoring checks. In this situation, there were no signals that there was anything wrong with the checks because, indeed, the checks were written by the account holders. [***Unlimited Adjusting Group Inc. v. Wells Fargo Bank***, **94 Cal. Rptr. 3d. 672 (2009)**]

Negligence of Drawee not Required

The impostor rule applies without regard to whether the drawee bank acted with reasonable care.

28-4c Effect of Incapacity or Misconduct on Negotiation

A negotiation is effective even though (1) it was made by a minor or any other person lacking capacity; (2) it was an act beyond the powers of a corporation; (3) it was obtained by fraud, duress, or a mistake of any kind; or (4) the negotiation was part of an illegal transaction or was made in breach of duty. The rights of the parties in these types of negotiations depends on who holds the instrument (see Chapter 29).

28-4d Lost Instruments

The liability on lost instruments depends on who is demanding payment from whom and on whether the instrument was order or bearer paper when it was lost.

Order Instruments

If the lost instrument is order paper, the finder does not become the holder because the instrument has not been indorsed and delivered by the person to whom it was then payable. The former holder who lost it is still the rightful owner of the instrument.

Bearer Instruments

If the lost instrument is in bearer form when it is lost, the finder, as the possessor of a bearer instrument, is the holder and is entitled to enforce payment.

CPA 28-5 Warranties in Negotiation

When a negotiable instrument is transferred by negotiation, the transferors give certain implied warranties.

28-5a Warranties of Unqualified Indorser

When the transferor receives consideration for the indorsement and makes an unqualified indorsement, the warranties stated in this section are given by the transferor by implication.

No distinction is made between an unqualified blank indorsement and an unqualified special indorsement.

Scope of Warranties

The warranties of the unqualified indorser are found in Section 3-416 of the UCC and provide that the warrantor is a person entitled to enforce the instrument; that all signatures on the instrument are authentic and authorized; that the instrument has not been altered; that the instrument is not subject to a defense or claim; that the drawer of the draft has authorized the issuance of the item in the amount for which the item is drawn; and that the warrantor has no knowledge of any insolvency proceeding with respect to the maker or acceptor.[27]

Those who present an instrument for payment (see Chapter 29), or the last party in line before the payor, make three warranties: that the warrantor is entitled to enforce the draft or authorized to obtain payment or acceptance of the draft; that the draft has not been altered; and that the warrantor has no knowledge that the signature of the drawer of the draft is unauthorized.[28]

If a forged indorsement has appeared during the transfer of the instrument, and there is a refusal to pay because of that problem, the last party who is a holder may turn to her transferor to recover on the basis of these implied warranties. These warranties give those who have transferred and held the instrument recourse against those parties who were involved in the transfer of the instrument, although they were not parties to the original instrument.

What Is Not Warranted

The implied warranties stated here do not guarantee that payment of the instrument will be made. Similarly, the holder's indorsement of a check does not give any warranty that the account of the drawer in the drawee bank contains funds sufficient to cover the check. However, implied warranties do, for example, promise that the signatures on the instrument are not forged. Likewise, they promise that no one has altered the amount on the instrument. The warranties are not warranties of payment or solvency. They are simply warranties about the nature of the instrument. A holder may not be paid the amount due on the instrument, but if the lack of payment results from a forgery, the holder has rights against those who transferred the instrument with a forged signature.

Beneficiary of Implied Warranties

The implied warranties of the unqualified indorser pass to the transferee and any subsequent transferees. There is no requirement that subsequent transferees take the instrument in good faith to be entitled to the warranties. Likewise, the transferee need not be a holder to enjoy warranty protections.

Disclaimer of Warranties

Warranties may be disclaimed when the instrument is not a check. A disclaimer of warranties is ordinarily made by adding "Without warranties" to the indorsement.

Notice of Breach of Warranty

To enforce an implied warranty of an indorser, the party claiming under the warranty must give the indorser notice of the breach. This notice must be given within 30 days

---

[27] U.C.C. §3-416 (1990).
[28] U.C.C. §3-417. These warranties are for consumer accounts.

after the claimant learns or has reason to know of the breach and the identity of the indorser. If proper notice is not given, the warranty claim is reduced by the amount of the loss that could have been avoided had timely notice been given.

28-5b Warranties of Other Parties

Warranties are also made by the indorser who indorses "Without recourse" and by one who transfers by delivery only.

Qualified Indorser

The warranty liability of a qualified indorser is the same as that of an unqualified indorser.[29] A qualified indorsement means that the indorser does not assume liability for the payment of the instrument as written. (See §3-416(4).) However, a qualified indorsement does not eliminate the implied warranties an indorser makes as a transferor of an instrument. The implied warranty that is waived by a qualified indorsement is the fourth warranty on defenses. A qualified indorser still makes the other warranties on signatures and alteration but waives the warranty on defenses.

Transfer by Delivery

When the negotiable instrument is negotiated by delivery without indorsement, the warranty liability of the transferor runs only to the immediate transferee. In all other respects, the warranty liability is the same as in the case of the unqualified indorser. **For Example,** Thomas, a minor, gives Craig his note payable to bearer. Craig transfers the note for value and by delivery only to Walsh, who negotiates it to Hall. Payment is then refused by Thomas, who chooses to disaffirm his contract. Hall cannot hold Craig liable. Craig, having negotiated the instrument by delivery only, is liable on his implied warranties only to his immediate transferee, Walsh. Likewise, because Craig did not indorse the note, he is not secondarily liable for payment of the note.

Make the Connection

Summary

Negotiation is the transferring of a negotiable instrument in such a way as to make the transferee the holder. When a negotiable instrument is transferred by negotiation, the transferee becomes the holder of the instrument. If such a holder becomes a holder in due course, the holder will be immune to certain defenses.

An *order instrument* is negotiated by an indorsement and delivery by the person to whom it is then payable. A bearer instrument is negotiated by delivery alone. The order or bearer character of an instrument is determined by the face of the instrument as long as the instrument is

not indorsed. If the instrument has been indorsed, the character is determined by the last indorsement.

A number of different kinds of indorsements can be made on negotiable instruments. When an indorser merely authenticates the instrument, the indorsement is called a *blank indorsement*. If the last indorsement is a blank indorsement, the instrument is bearer paper, which may be negotiated by change of possession alone. A special indorsement consists of the authentication by the indorser and words specifying the person to whom the indorser makes the instrument payable. If the last

[29] U.C.C. §3-416(a).

indorsement is a special indorsement, the instrument is order paper and may be negotiated only by an indorsement and delivery. A qualified indorsement eliminates the liability of the indorser to answer for dishonor of the paper by the maker or the drawee. A restrictive indorsement specifies the purpose of the instrument or its use.

A forged or unauthorized indorsement is no indorsement, and the possessor of the instrument cannot be a holder. The impostor rule makes three exceptions to this rule: dummy payee; employee fraud; and impersonating a payee.

A negotiation is effective even though (1) it is made by a minor, (2) it is an act beyond the powers of a corporation, (3) it is obtained by fraud, or (4) the negotiation is part of an illegal transaction. However, the transferor may be able to set aside the negotiation under general legal principles apart from the UCC. The negotiation cannot be set aside if the instrument is held by a person paying it in good faith and without knowledge of the facts on which the rescission claim is based.

The warranties of the unqualified indorser are as follows: (1) the warrantor is a person entitled to enforce the instrument; (2) all signatures on the instrument are authentic and authorized; (3) the instrument has not been altered; (4) the instrument is not subject to a defense or claim in recoupment of any party that can be asserted against the warrantor; with respect to any item drawn on a consumer account, which does not bear a handwritten signature purporting to be the signature of the drawer, that the purported drawer of the draft has authorized the issuance of the item in the amount for which the item is drawn; and (5) the warrantor has no knowledge of any insolvency proceeding commenced with respect to the maker or acceptor or, in the case of an unaccepted draft, the drawer.

Learning Outcomes

After studying this chapter, you should be able to clearly explain:

28-1   Transfer of Negotiable Instruments
28-2   How Negotiation Occurs: Bearer Instruments
28-3   How Negotiation Occurs: Order Instruments

LO.1   Explain the difference between negotiation of order paper and negotiation of bearer paper
See the *Emmons v. Capital One* case, page 537.
See the Ethics & the Law issue "Having Your Mortgage Set Aside" to see that the note is separate from the mortgage, page 538.

LO.2   List the types of indorsements and describe their uses
See the *Town of Freeport v. Ring* case, page 538.
See *Check City, Inc. v. L & T Enterprises* for joint payee issues, page 543.

28-4   Problems in Negotiation of Instruments

LO.3   Determine the legal effect of forged and unauthorized indorsements
See the Thinking Things Through feature on minors affected by conservators misusing funds placed in trust with them, page 544.

LO.4   Be familiar with the forged payee impostor exceptions
See the *B.D.G.S., Inc. v. Balio* case, page 545.
See the *Unlimited Adjusting Group, Inc. v. Wells Fargo Bank* case, pages 546–547.

28-5   Warranties in Negotiation

LO.5   List the indorser's warranties and describe their significance
See the discussion of warranties, pages 547–549.

Key Terms

alternative payees
blank indorsement
delivery
forged or unauthorized
   indorsement

holder
holder in due course
impostor rule
indorsee
indorsement

negotiation
qualified indorsement
restrictive indorsement
special indorsement

Questions and Case Problems

1. Corey Brandon Bumgarner, who was separated from his wife, Crystal, had an accident caused by Donald Wood that resulted in $2,164.46 in damages to Corey's vehicle. Wood's insurance carrier mailed a draft in the amount of $2,164.46 drawn on Fleet Bank of Hartford, Connecticut, payable to Corey, to his box at P.O. Box 153, Hillsboro, North Carolina. The draft was negotiated at Community Bank and Trust, and the name, "Crystal Bumgarner," was handwritten on the back of the draft. Corey's name was written below Crystal Bumgarner's name. Crystal Bumgarner's driver's license number was handwritten on the front of the draft.

    Corey Bumgarner filed suit to have the insurer pay him the $2,164.46. The insurer indicated that it had sent order paper, that it had been delivered, and that there was, therefore, no claim against it or Wood. The trial court found that there had been no delivery and that Bumgarner was entitled to another check. Wood and his insurer appealed. Who is correct about delivery and why? [*Bumgarner v. Wood*, 563 S.E.2d 309, 47 U.C.C. Rep. Serv. 2d 1099 (N.C. App.)]

2. How could a check made out to "Joseph Klimas and his Attorney Fritzshall & Gleason & Blue Cross Blue Shield Company and Carpenters Welfare Fund" be negotiated further? What would be required? [*Chicago District Council of Carpenters Welfare Fund v. Gleason & Fritzshall*, 693 N.E.2d 412 (Ill. App.)]

3. An insurer issued a settlement check on a claim brought by an injured minor that was payable to "Trudy Avants attorney for minor child Joseph Walton, mother Dolores Carpenter 11762 S. Harrells Ferry Road #E Baton Rouge LA 70816." The lawyer indorsed the check. Two unknown individuals forged indorsements for the other two names and obtained payment of the check. The insurer sued the payor bank claiming that the instruments were not properly payable because of the forged indorsements. The court is unclear whether the indorsement required is one for an either/or payee or joint payee. What advice can you offer the court as it faces this issue? [*Coregis Insurance Co. v. Fleet National Bank*, 793 A.2d 254 (Conn. App.)]

4. ABCO (Abbott Development Company) made a note payable to Western State Bank of Midland.

The FDIC took over Western State's operations after it failed. ABCO had defaulted on the note, after which the FDIC permitted ABCO Homes to refinance the note, making its refinancing note payable to the FDIC. The FDIC indorsed its note to SMS Financial and inadvertently sent it to SMS as part of a large batch of documents. When litigation resulted on the note, SMS claimed it was the holder. Others challenged its status, saying that SMS never had the instrument delivered to it. The lower court held SMS was not a holder and SMS appealed. Is SMS a holder? Why or why not? [*SMS Financial, L.L.C v. ABCO Homes, Inc.*, 167 F.3d 235 (5th Cir.)]

5. Jerry O. Peavy, Jr., who did not have a bank account of his own, received a draft from CNL Insurance America in the amount of $5,323.60. The draft was drawn on CNL's account at Bank South, N.A., and was "payable to the order of Jerry Peavy and Trust Company Bank." Jerry O. Peavy, Sr., allowed his son Peavy, Jr., to deposit the draft in his account at Bank South, NA. Bank South accepted the draft and deposited it on December 29, 1992, with only the signature of Jerry Peavy, Jr. Both Mr. and Mrs. Peavy, Sr., then wrote checks on the amount of the draft using the full amount to benefit their son.

    On March 30, 1993, Bank South realized that it had improperly deposited the draft because it was lacking an indorsement from Trust Company Bank and reversed the transaction by debiting Mr. and Mrs. Peavy's account for the full amount of the draft. A bank officer then called Mr. and Mrs. Peavy, told them what had happened with the draft, and "threatened to send them to jail if they did not immediately deposit the sum of $5,323.60." The Peavys deposited that amount from the sale of some stock they owned and then filed suit against Bank South for its conversion of their son's draft and funds. Do the Peavys have a case? [*Peavy v. Bank South*, 474 S.E. 2d 690 (Ga. App.)]

6. Getty Petroleum distributes gasoline through dealer-owned stations. Customers who buy gas at a Getty station can pay by cash or credit card. When a customer uses a credit card, Getty processes the transactions, receives payment from the credit card company, and then issues computer-generated checks payable to dealers to reimburse them for their

credit card sales. Many checks, however, are not intended for negotiation and are never delivered to the payees. Instead, Getty uses these checks for bookkeeping purposes, voiding them and then crediting the check amount toward the dealer's future purchases of gasoline from Getty.

Lorna Lewis, a supervisor in Getty's credit processing department, stole over 130 checks, forged the indorsements of the payees by hand or rubber stamp, and then submitted the checks to American Express and other credit card companies to pay her own debts. The credit card companies then forwarded the checks through ordinary banking channels to Chemical Bank, where Getty had its checking account. Chemical Bank honored the checks Lewis had forged.

Getty, on discovering the larceny of Lewis, sought recovery of the amounts from the credit card companies. Getty sought payment on 31 of the checks from American Express (which had been paid by Chemical Bank). At trial, a judge held American Express liable to Getty for $58,841.60. The appeals court found that American Express was grossly negligent in taking and cashing the checks and also held it liable. American Express appealed. Who wins and why? [*Getty Petroleum Corp. v. American Exp. Travel Related Services Co., Inc.*, 683 N.E.2d 311 (N.Y.)]

7. Snug Harbor Realty Co. had a checking account in First National Bank. When construction work was obtained by Snug Harbor, its superintendent, Magee, would examine the bills submitted for labor and materials. He would instruct the bookkeeper which bills were approved, and the bookkeeper then prepared the checks in accordance with his instructions. After the checks were signed by the proper official of Snug Harbor, Magee picked them up for delivery. Instead of delivering certain checks, he forged the signatures of the respective payees as indorsers and cashed the checks. The drawee bank then debited the Snug Harbor account with the amount of the checks. Snug Harbor claimed that this was improper and sued the bank for the amount of the checks. The bank claimed that it was protected by the impostor rule. Will the bank be successful? Explain. [*Snug Harbor Realty Co. v. First National Bank*, 253 A.2d 581 (N.J. Super.)]

8. Benton, as agent for Savidge, received an insurance settlement check from Metropolitan Life Insurance Co. He indorsed it "For deposit" and deposited it in Bryn Mawr Trust Co. in Savidge's account. What were the nature and effect of this indorsement? [*Savidge v. Metropolitan Life Ins. Co.*, 110 A.2d 730 (Pa.)]

9. Allstate Insurance Company issued a check payable to "Chuk N. Tang & Rosa C. Tang HWJT" with "Bank of America" on the second line and the following explanation on the front of the check: "Settlement of our rental dwelling loss caused by fire on 11/21/93." The Tangs indorsed the check and forged the indorsement of Bank of America. When Bank of America objected, the Tangs claimed that only they needed to sign the instrument for further negotiations. The check was intended as a joint payment for Bank of America as the mortgagee on the Tangs' rental property because the insurance policy required that the mortgagee be paid first before any proceeds went to the property owners. Bank of America sued Allstate. Is Bank of America entitled to recover for the lack of its indorsement? Was its indorsement necessary for further negotiation? [*Bank of America Nat'l Trust & Savings Ass'n v. Allstate Insurance Co.*, 29 F. Supp. 2d 1129 (C.D. Cal.)]

10. When claims filed with an insurance company were approved for payment, they were given to the claims clerk, who would prepare checks to pay those claims and then give the checks to the treasurer to sign. The claims clerk of the insurance company made a number of checks payable to persons who did not have any claims and gave them to the treasurer with the checks for valid claims, and the treasurer signed all of the checks. The claims clerk then removed the false checks, indorsed them with the names of their respective payees, and cashed them at the bank where the insurance company had its account. The bank debited the account of the insurance company with the amount of these checks. The insurance company claimed that the bank could not do this because the indorsements on the checks were forgeries. Was the insurance company correct? [*General Accident Fire & Life Assur. Corp. v. Citizens Fidelity Bank & Trust Co.*, 519 S.W. 2d 817 (Ky.)]

11. Eutsler forged his brother Richard's indorsement on certified checks and cashed them at First National Bank. When Richard sought to recover the funds from the bank, the bank stated that it would press criminal charges against Eutsler. Richard asked the

bank to delay prosecution to give him time to collect directly from his brother. His brother promised to repay him the money but vanished some six months later without having paid any money. Richard sued the bank. What result? [*Eutsler v. First Nat'l Bank, Pawhuska*, 639 P.2d 1245 (Okla.)]

12. Michael Sykes, the president of Sykes Corp., hired Richard Amelung to handle the company's book-keeping and deal with all of its vendors.

    Amelung entered into an agreement with Eastern Metal Supply to help reduce Sykes's debt to Eastern. Whenever Sykes received a check, Amelung would sign it over to Eastern and allow it to keep 30 percent of the check amount. On 28 checks that totaled $200,000, Amelung indorsed the back as follows: "Sykes & Associates or Sykes Corporation, Richard Amelung." Amelung then turned the checks over to Eastern, and Eastern deposited them into its account at Barnett Bank. Eastern would then write one of its checks to Sykes Corp. for the 70 percent remaining from the checks. When Michael Sykes learned of the arrangement, he demanded the return of the 30 percent from Barnett Bank, claiming that it had paid over an unauthorized signature and that the indorsement was restricted and had been violated by the deposit into Eastern's account. What type of indorsement did Amelung make? Did he have the authority to do so? Should Sykes be reimbursed by Barnett? [*Sykes Corp. v. Eastern Metal Supply, Inc.*, 659 So. 2d 475 (Fla. App.)]

13. In January 1998, Allied Capital Partners, L.P., and American Factors Corporation were in the business of factoring accounts receivable for third-party clients. Allied assigned its factoring contract with Complete Design, Inc., to American but retained an interest in the factoring of Complete Design's invoices. On January 25, 1998, in payment of invoices issued by Complete Design, Clark Wilson Homes, Inc., issued a check for $6,823.15. The check was payable to:

Complete Design Allied Capital Partners, L.P. 2340 E. Trinity Mills Ste. 300 Carrollton, Texas 75006

On February 10, 1998, Clark Wilson issued another check for $26,329.32 made payable to:

Complete Design Allied Capital Partners, L.P. 2340 E. Trinity Mills Ste. 300 Carrollton, Texas 75006

Complete Design deposited both checks in its account at Bank One. However, Allied and American received none of the proceeds of the checks.

Complete Design subsequently declared bankruptcy, and Allied and American made demand on Bank One for damages resulting from Bank One's conversion of the two checks. Bank One denied all liability for conversion of the checks. Allied and American subsequently sued Bank One, asserting conversion. Bank One filed a motion for summary judgment asserting that, because it was ambiguous to whom the checks at issue were payable, they were payable upon a single indorsement. The trial court granted Bank One's motion. Allied and American appealed. Who is correct here? Were both signatures necessary for a proper indorsement, or will one do? [*Allied Capital Partners, L.P. v. Bank One, Texas, N.A.*, 68 S.W.3d 51 (Tex. App.)]

14. Would a bank be liable to a customer who indorsed a check "For deposit only into account #071698570" if that check were deposited into the wrong account? What if the customer's indorsement was "For deposit only"? Would any account qualify? Would any bank qualify? [*Qatar v. First American Bank of Virginia*, 885 F. Supp. 849 (E.D. Va.)]

15. What would happen if an employee directed funds to his or her account electronically? Would the UCC rules on fictitious payees apply? [*Koss Corp. v. American Exp. Co.*, 309 P.3d 898 (Ariz. App.)]

CPA Questions

1. Hand executed and delivered to Rex a $1,000 negotiable note payable to Rex or bearer. Rex then negotiated it to Ford and indorsed it on the back by merely signing his name. Which of the following is a correct statement?

a. Rex's indorsement was a special indorsement.

b. Rex's indorsement was necessary to Ford's qualification as a holder.

c. The instrument initially being bearer paper cannot be converted to order paper.

d. The instrument is bearer paper, and Ford can convert it to order paper by writing "pay to the order of Ford" above Rex's signature.

2. Jane Lane, a sole proprietor, has in her possession several checks that she received from her customers. Lane is concerned about the safety of the checks since she believes that many of them are bearer paper that may be cashed without endorsement. The checks in Lane's possession will be considered order paper rather than bearer paper if they were made payable (in the drawer's handwriting) to the order of:

a. Cash.

b. Ted Tint, and indorsed by Ted Tint in blank.

c. Bearer, and indorsed by Ken Kent, making them payable to Jane Lane.

d. Bearer, and indorsed by Sam Sole in blank.

3. West Corp. received a check that was originally made payable to the order of one of its customers, Ted Burns. The following indorsement was written on the back of the check:

Ted Burns, without recourse, for collection only

Which of the following describes the indorsement?

	Special	*Restrictive*
a.	Yes	Yes
b.	No	No
c.	No	Yes
d.	Yes	No

4. An instrument reads as follows:

> $250.00 Chicago, Illinois April 1, 1992
>
> Thirty days after date I promise to pay to the
>
> order of __Cash__
>
> Two hundred and fifty _____ Dollars at
>
> New York City _____
>
> Value received with interest at the rate of six percent per annum. This agreement arises out of a separate agreement.
>
> No. 20 Due May 1, 1992   Robert Smith

Answer "Yes" or "No" for the following questions about the previous item.

a. The instrument is a draft.

b. The instrument is order paper.

c. This is a negotiable instrument.

d. Robert Smith is the maker.

e. The instrument may be negotiated without indorsement.

5. Ashley needs to endorse a check that had been endorsed by two other individuals prior to Ashley's receipt of the check. Ashley does not want to have surety liability, so Ashley endorses the check "without recourse." Under the Negotiable Instruments Article of the UCC, which of the following types of endorsement did Ashley make?

a. Blank

b. Special

c. Qualified

d. Restrictive

Liability of the Parties under Negotiable Instruments

Learning Outcomes ‹‹‹

After studying this chapter, you should be able to

LO.1   Distinguish between an ordinary holder and a holder in due course

LO.2   List the requirements for becoming a holder in due course

LO.3   Explain the rights of a holder through a holder in due course

LO.4   List and explain the limited defenses not available against a holder in due course

LO.5   List and explain the universal defenses available against all holders

LO.6   Describe how the rights of a holder in due course have been limited by the Federal Trade Commission

29-1   Parties to Negotiable Instruments: Rights and Liabilities

Chapters 27 and 28 introduced the requirements for negotiable instruments and the methods for transfer of those instruments. However, the requirements of negotiability and transfer are simply preliminary steps for the discovery of the real benefit of using negotiable instruments in commerce, which is to streamline payment in commercial transactions. The rights and defenses of the parties to negotiable instruments are determined by the types of parties involved.

29-1a   Types of Parties

assignee–third party to whom contract benefits are transferred.

Parties with rights in a negotiable instrument can be **assignees** or **holders.** A holder may be an ordinary holder or a **holder in due course.** As noted in Chapter 27, a holder in due course is a special party to an instrument with special rights beyond those of the ordinary holder.

29-1b   Ordinary Holders and Assignees

holder–someone in possession of an instrument that runs to that person (i.e., is made payable to that person, is indorsed to that person, or is bearer paper).

holder in due course–a holder who has given value, taken in good faith without notice of dishonor, defenses, or that instrument is overdue, and who is afforded special rights or status.

A holder is a party in possession of an instrument that runs to him. An instrument "runs" to a party if it is payable to his order, is bearer paper, or is indorsed to him (see Chapter 28). Any holder has all of the rights given through and under the negotiable instrument. The holder may demand payment or bring suit for collection on the instrument. A holder can give a discharge or release from liability on the instrument. A holder who seeks payment of the instrument is required only to produce the instrument and show that the signature of the maker, drawer, or indorser is genuine. If the party obligated to pay under the instrument has no valid defense (such as forgery, which was discussed in Chapter 28), the holder is entitled to payment of the instrument.

The holder can recover from any of the parties who are liable on the instrument, regardless of the order of the signatures on the instrument. A holder could recover from the first indorser on an instrument or from the last party to indorse the instrument.

The rights of a holder are no different from the rights of a contract assignee (see Chapter 17). The assignee of a contract is in the same position and has the same rights as an ordinary holder. **For Example,** if a farmer who signed a note to pay for his tractor has a warranty problem with the tractor, he has a defense to payment on the note. Anyone who is assigned that note as an assignee or holder is also subject to the farmer's defense. (See Figure 29-1 and also the provisions on consumer credit protection under the discussion of the Federal Trade Commission rule in Chapter 32 and later in this chapter.)

29-1c   The Holder-in-Due-Course Protections

The law gives certain holders of negotiable instruments special rights by protecting them from certain defenses. This protection makes negotiable instruments more attractive and allows greater ease of transfer. Unlike ordinary holders or assignees, holders in due course take free of contract assignment defenses that are good against ordinary holders or assignees. Figure 29-1 shows the different rights of holders, assignees, and holders in due course.

| FIGURE 29-1 | Assignee, Holder, and Holder-in-Due-Course Rights |

Suppose that Farmer Fred signs an installment contract to purchase a tractor from John Deere for $153,000. John Deere assigns the contract to Finance Co.

Suppose that Farmer Fred signs a negotiable promissory note for $153,000 and John Deere then transfers it to Finance Co., a holder in due course.

Suppose that Farmer Fred has a roofing company replace the roof on his home, and he signs a negotiable promissory note for $5,000. Roofing Co. transfers the note to Finance Co.

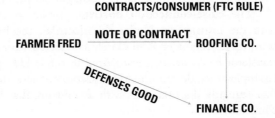

Holder in Due Course (HDC)

To obtain the preferred status of a holder in due course,[1] a person must first be a holder. However, the preferred status of HDC requires additional standards. Those holders who do not meet the standards for an HDC have all the rights of a holder. However, HDCs enjoy additional protections beyond those basic holder rights. Under U.C.C. §3-302(a), there are four requirements for becoming an HDC.[2]

[1] U.C.C. §3-302. Adam J. Levitin, "Finding Nemo: Rediscovering the Virtues of Negotiability in the Wake of Enron," 2007 *Columbia L. Rev.* 83 (2007).
[2] U.C.C. §3-302(a). *New Randolph Halsted Currency Exchange, Inc. v. Regent Title Ins. Agency, LLC*, 939 N.E.2d 1024 (Ill. App. 2010).

value–consideration or antecedent debt or security given in exchange for the transfer of a negotiable instrument or creation of a security interest.

Value. Value is similar to consideration (see Chapter 14). **For Example,** a person who receives a negotiable note as a gift does not give value because gifts are not supported by consideration or value.[3]

A transferee takes an instrument for value when (1) the holder has promised to do something in exchange (such as update a Web site); (2) the transferee takes the instrument as security for a loan (such as when a debtor transfers a promissory note payable to him to the transferee); or (3) the transferee receives the instrument as payment for a debt already due.[4] As with consideration, the courts do not consider whether the value is enough; they determine only whether some value has been given.[5]

Under Article 3, the original payee of a note is not an HDC unless that note is transferred to others and then back to the payee.[6]

A bank does not give value for a deposited check when it credits the depositor's account with the amount of the deposit. The bank gives value to the extent that the depositor is permitted to withdraw funds against that deposit.[7] **For Example,** if Janice deposits a $300 check into her account, which already has $400 in it, Janice's bank does not give value until Janice has written checks or withdrawn funds beyond the existing $400. The code follows FIFO (first in, first out) for drawing on funds. A bank that lets the customer draw on the funds deposited gives value.[8]

good faith–absence of knowledge of any defects in or problems; "pure heart and an empty head."

Good Faith. The element of **good faith** for becoming an HDC requires that a holder of a negotiable instrument act honestly in acquiring the instrument. In addition, the taker must follow reasonable standards of fair dealing.[9] Karl Llewellyn, one of the key drafters of the UCC, said that to comply with reasonable standards and good faith, the party must act with a "pure heart and an empty head."

Bad faith sometimes exists just because the transferee takes the instrument under such odd circumstances. **For Example,** if a transferee buys a note made payable to an estate from an accountant in a bar at midnight, suspicion prevents HDC status.

close-connection doctrine–circumstantial evidence, such as an ongoing or a close relationship, that can serve as notice of a problem with an instrument.

The **close-connection doctrine** applies in circumstances that indicate a problem with the instrument. Under this doctrine, the holder has taken so many instruments from its transferor or is so closely connected with the transferor that any knowledge the transferor has is deemed transferred to the holder, preventing holder-in-due-course status. Examples include consumer transactions where the holder in due course is a company that regularly does business with a company that has continual problems with consumer complaints.

---

[3] However, if the donor of the negotiable instrument were a holder in due course, it might be possible under a special Article 3 protection for the heir to also be a holder in due course despite the gift acquisition. U.C.C. §3-302(c) (iii). This protection for gift transfers by holders in due course is called the *shelter provision* (and is covered later in this chapter).

[4] U.C.C. §3-303.

[5] U.C.C. §3-303; *Ocwen Loan Servicing, LLC v. Branaman,* 554 F. Supp. 2d 645 (N.D. Miss. 2008); *Agriliance, LLC v. Farmpro Services, Inc.,* 328 F. Supp. 2d 958 (S.D. Iowa 2003).

[6] U.C.C. §3-302(c).

[7] U.C.C. §4-211.

[8] Allowing a deposit of a check with provisional credit does not make a bank a holder in due course, but on a cashier's check, when the bank becomes both the drawer and the drawee, the bank is obligated to pay on the instrument. *Flatiron Linen, Inc. v. First American State Bank,* 23 P.3d 1209 (Colo. 2011). If the bank does not impose provisional credit and makes the funds available immediately for the customer, it gives value and qualifies as a holder in due course. But see *Travelers Cas. and Sur. Co. of America v. Wells Fargo Bank N.A.,* 374 F.3d 521 (7th Cir. 2004).

[9] U.C.C. §3-103(a)(4); issue of whether a party is a holder in due course is always an issue of fact. *Pasack Community Bank, Inc. v. Universal Funding, LLP,* 16 A.3d 1097 (N.J. App. 2011).

CASE SUMMARY

Embezzling $29,000 and Having an HDC Cash Your Check

FACTS: Regent served as a settlement agent for closing real estate transactions. Regent cut checks to distribute funds to all the parties to such transactions. On December 23, 2005, New Randolph cashed a check from Regent, which was made out to Charae Pearson, for $1,945.99. Four days later, New Randolph cashed another check for Pearson, again from Regent, this time for $2,500. On January 11, 2006, Pearson brought Regent's check number 22221 for $29,588.31 to New Randolph. Unlike the prior checks, which spelled Pearson's name correctly, this check showed the payee as "CHAREA PAERSON." The check indicated that Pearson received it as a "LOAN PAYOFF." Pearson presented the check to Patrice Keys, manager of New Randolph. Pearson showed Keys her state identification card, which had been issued on December 30, 2005. Pearson told Keys that Regent issued the check to her to pay her a commission she earned from the sale of property.

PLS Check Cashers, which owned New Randolph, did not authorize Keys to cash checks in excess of $5,000 without approval from her supervisor. Keys contacted Sandra Arizaga of PLS. Arizaga authorized Keys to cash the check. Arizaga, who worked as director of operations for PLS, testified that she approved about three checks each week for amounts exceeding the amount of Regent's check number 22221. She spoke with Keys about the check, and then she looked up the phone number for Regent at Regent's Web site. Arizaga spoke with a woman who confirmed that Regent issued the check to Pearson in the amount shown. Arizaga then contacted American Chartered Bank, which confirmed that the check came from a valid account with sufficient funds to cover the check, and that Regent had not stopped payment on the check.

Regent introduced PLS's manual into evidence. The manual emphasizes that PLS earns its fees by cashing checks,

so the employee should "[s]pend * * * time proving that the check can be cashed and not looking for excuses not to cash it." The manual identifies several signs that a check might not be valid, including several of the factors present in this case. According to the manual, the employee should "verify that the check is good" by "phoning the maker."

Police arrested Pearson, charging her with check fraud. Two days later, police arrested Tatiana Auson, an employee of Regent, on the same charge. Auson had checks intended for parties to real estate transactions canceled and then issued new checks to different payees for the amounts of the original checks. Pearson admitted that Auson gave her the three checks that New Randolph cashed for Pearson. Pearson kept about $5,000 of the proceeds from the checks, and she gave the remainder to Auson. All three checks appeared to bear the signature of Karen Hendricks, who had authority to sign checks on behalf of Regent.

Regent told its bank to stop payment on the check. New Randolph sued Regent for payment of the check, claiming that its status as a holder in due course entitled it to payment, despite the evidence that Auson and Pearson conspired to defraud Regent.

New Randolph appealed.

DECISION: Notice that disqualifies a party from being an HDC is something more than a suspicion. The verification call made in this situation showed the good faith of New Randolph. It checked to be sure that the check was good and was entitled to payment regardless of the embezzlement and breaches of fiduciary duties of their respective employees in working through the transactions. [*New Randolph Halsted Currency Exchange, Inc. v. Regent Title Insurance Co.*, 939 N.E.2d 1024 (Ill. App. 2011)]

Ignorance of the Instrument's Being Overdue or Dishonored. An instrument can be negotiated even though it has been dishonored, it is overdue,[10] or it is demand paper, such as a check, that has been outstanding for more than a reasonable time.[11] These instruments can still be transferred and the transferee is still a holder. However, the fact that the instrument is circulating at a late date or after it has been dishonored is suspicious and results in notice from the circumstances that there may be some adverse claim or defense. A person who acquires title to the instrument under such circumstances can be a holder but cannot be a holder in due course. **For Example,** buying a discounted note after its due date is notice that something may be wrong with the instrument.

---

[10] *Erkins v. Alaska Trustee, LLC*, 265 P.3d 292 (Alaska 2011); *Cadle Co. v. DeVincent*, 781 N.E.2d 817 (Mass. App. 2003); *Interim Capital LLC v. Herr Law Group, Ltd.*, 2011 WL 7047062 (D. Nev. 2011).
[11] *Max Duncan Family Investments, Ltd. v. NTFN Inc.*, 267 S.W.3d 447 (Tex. 2008).

Ignorance of Defenses and Adverse Claims. Prior parties on an instrument may have defenses that entitle them to withhold payment from a holder of an instrument. **For Example,** the drawer of a check, upon demand for payment by the payee, could assert as a defense to payment that the merchandise the payee delivered under the terms of their underlying contract was defective. A person who acquires an instrument with notice or knowledge that there is a defense that a party may have or that there are claims of ownership of the instrument from different parties cannot be an HDC. In general, transferees who are aware of facts that would make a reasonable person ask questions are deemed to know what they would have learned if they had asked questions.[12] Such knowledge and the failure to ask questions will cost them their special status of holder in due course; they remain simply holders.

Knowledge acquired by a holder after the instrument was acquired does not prevent the holder from being a holder in due course. The fact that a holder, after acquiring the instrument, learns of a defense does not work retroactively to destroy the holder's character as an HDC.

CASE SUMMARY

Cashing a Postdated Check from an Embezzler: HDC?

FACTS: A check dated August 10, 2007, was made payable to one of Liccardi's employees, Charles Stallone, Jr. Liccardi withheld the check from Stallone because he suspected him of embezzlement. However, the check still disappeared from the company offices, and when the disappearance was discovered, Liccardi immediately placed a stop payment on the check. JCNB Check Cashing, Inc. (JCNB), cashed the check for Stallone before the issue date (the check was postdated) and JCNB then deposited the check in its own bank account on August 9, 2007. However, the issuing bank refused to honor the check. On February 11, 2009, Robert Triffin acquired the dishonored payroll check from JCNB and sued Liccardi and Stallone for the amount of the check plus interest. Triffin's business is buying dishonored checks and attempting to collect on them.

The trial court dismissed Triffin's complaint on the grounds that he was not a holder in due course. Triffin appealed.

DECISION: The Court held that Triffin was not a holder in due course because he had taken a check that was already dishonored. In addition, Triffin could not be a holder in due course through JCNB being a holder in due course, because JCNB did not follow reasonable commercial standards when it cashed the postdated check. New Jersey's statute that regulates check cashing services requires those services to at least examine the face of the instrument before cashing it. JCNB, thus, was not a holder in due course and Triffin could not step into its shoes as an HDC. [*Triffin v. Liccardi Ford, Inc.*, 10 A.3d 227 (N.J. Super. 2011)]

ETHICS & THE LAW

The Corner Check Cashing Company and Good Faith

Some public policy experts have argued that no check cashing company, defined as one that takes a portion of the amount of the check as a fee for cashing checks for individuals who cannot get them cashed at banks and credit unions, should ever be allowed holder-in-due-course status.

Do you agree with this argument? Are check cashing companies ethical in their behavior? Do you believe that the state laws on check cashing firms are a means of mandating ethical conduct?

[12] *Specialized Loan Servicing, LLC v. January,* 119 So. 3d 582 (La. 2013); *Jelmoli Holding, Inc. v. Raymond James Financial Services, Inc.,* 470 F.3d 14 (1st Cir. 2006).

CPA

holder through a holder in due course–holder of an instrument who attains holder-in-due-course status because a holder in due course has held it previous to him or her.

Holder Through a Holder in Due Course

Those persons who become holders of the instrument after an HDC has held it are given the same protection as the HDC, provided they are not parties to any fraud or illegality that affects the instrument. This status of **holder through a holder in due course** is given in these circumstances even if the transferee from a holder in due course does not satisfy the requirements for holder-in-due-course status. This elevated or protected status is called Article 3's "shelter rule," and it allows a person who is not an HDC to hide under the "umbrella" with a holder in due course and be sheltered from claims and defenses as if actually being an HDC. **For Example,** a person who acquires an instrument as an inheritance from an estate does not give value and is missing one of the requirements for being a holder in due course. However, if the estate was an HDC, that status does transfer to the heir. Furthermore, suppose that Avery is a holder in due course of a $5,000 promissory note due May 31, 2015. Avery gives the note to his nephew Aaron for Aaron's birthday on June 1, 2015. Aaron did not give value because the note was a gift, and he has taken the note as a holder after it has already become due. Nonetheless, because Avery was a holder in due course, Aaron assumes that status under Article 3's shelter provision.

29-2 Defenses to Payment of a Negotiable Instrument

One of the key reasons for attaining HDC status is to be able to obtain payment on the negotiable instrument free of any underlying problems between the original parties to the instrument. An HDC takes an instrument free from certain types of defenses to payment. Whether a defense may be raised against an HDC claiming under a negotiable instrument depends on the nature of the defense.

CPA

29-2a Classification of Defenses

The importance of being a holder in due course or a holder through an HDC is that such holders are not subject to certain defenses called *limited defenses*. Another class of defenses, *universal defenses*, may be asserted against any party, whether an assignee, an ordinary holder, an HDC, or a holder through an HDC.[13]

29-2b Defenses against Assignee or Ordinary Holder

Assignees of negotiable instruments are subject to every defense raised. Similarly, a holder who does not become an HDC is subject to every payment defense just as though the instrument were not negotiable.

29-2c Limited Defenses Not Available against a Holder in Due Course

HDCs are not subject to any of the following defenses.

[13] Under the pre-Code law and under the 1952 Code, the universal defense was called a *real defense*, and the limited defense was called a *personal defense*. These terms have now been abandoned, but some licensing and CPA examinations may continue to use these pre-Code terms.

CPA
Ordinary Contract Defenses

In general terms, the defenses that could be raised in a breach of contract claim cannot be raised against an HDC. The defenses of lack, failure, or illegality of consideration with respect to the instrument's underlying transaction cannot be asserted against the holder in due course. Misrepresentation about the goods underlying the contract is also not a defense.

For Example, a businessperson cannot refuse to pay a holder in due course on the note used to pay for her copy machine just because her copy machine does not have the speed she was promised.

Incapacity of Maker or Drawer

Ordinarily, the maker's or drawer's lack of capacity (except minors) may not be raised as a defense to payment to a holder in due course. Such incapacity is a defense, however, if the incapacity is at a legal level that makes the instrument a nullity. **For Example,** a promissory note made by an insane person for whom a court has appointed a guardian is void. In the case of a claim on the note by an HDC, the incapacity of the maker would be a defense.

CPA
Fraud in the Inducement

fraud in the inducement—fraud that occurs when a person is persuaded or induced to execute an instrument because of fraudulent statements.

If a person is persuaded or induced to execute the instrument because of fraudulent statements, such **fraud in the inducement** cannot be raised against a party with holder-in-due-course status. **For Example,** suppose Mills is persuaded to purchase an automobile because of Pagan's statements that the car was a demonstrator for the dealership and in good mechanical condition with a certification from the dealership's head mechanic. Mills, a car dealer, gives Pagan a note, which is negotiated until it reaches Han, who is a holder in due course. Mills meanwhile learns that the car has been in an accident and has a cracked engine block, that the head mechanic was paid to sign the certification, and that Pagan's statements were fraudulent. When Han demands payment of the note, Mills cannot refuse to pay on the ground of Pagan's fraud. Mills must pay the note because Han, as an HDC, does not take the note subject to any fraud or misrepresentation in the underlying transaction. Mills is left with the remedy of recovering from Pagan for misrepresentation or fraud.

Miscellaneous Defenses[14]

The limited defenses listed in the preceding three subsections are those most commonly raised against demands by holders in due course for payment. The following are additional limited defenses that may be asserted: (1) prior payment or cancellation of the instrument, (2) nondelivery, (3) conditional or special-purpose delivery, (4) breach of warranty, (5) duress consisting of threats, (6) unauthorized completion, and (7) theft of a bearer instrument. These defenses, however, have a very limited effect in defending against an HDC's demand for payment.

CASE SUMMARY

Fake Rolex; Good Check

FACTS: On September 23, 2011, Houston Gold Exchange issued a $3,500 check as payor to Shelly McKee as payee to buy a purported Rolex watch from her. The check was postdated September 26, 2011. McKee properly endorsed the check and presented it to RR Maloan, which cashed the check for her on September 24, 2011. On September 24, 2011,

---

[14] U.C.C. §3-305.

Fake Rolex; Good Check continued

Houston Gold Exchange issued a stop payment order on the check based on information that the watch was counterfeit. RR Maloan presented the check to Houston Gold Exchange's bank for payment. Houston Gold Exchange's bank refused to honor the check based on the stop payment order.

RR Maloan sued Houston Gold Exchange to collect on the check. RR Maloan maintained that it was a holder in due course entitled to collect on the check. Houston Gold Exchange was not present on the trial date, and the small claims court signed a default judgment in RR Maloan's favor. On appeal, the trial court found for Houston Gold Exchange, and RR Maloan appealed.

DECISION: A holder in due course takes the instrument free from all claims and all defenses of any party to the instrument with whom he has not dealt unless a defense that bars recovery by a holder in due course applies. RR Maloan took the check "for value" as required. "Good faith" is defined as "honesty in fact and the observance of reasonable

commercial standards of fair dealing." The record here conclusively establishes RR Maloan's good faith as that concept is defined for these purposes in the statute. No evidence was presented that the owner or any employee of RR Maloan had knowledge at the time the check was accepted that the watch was not authentic.

Because the fact of postdating did not impose a duty on RR Maloan to investigate the surrounding circumstances, Houston Gold Exchange cannot establish that RR Maloan failed to observe "reasonable commercial standards of fair dealing" by failing to investigate based on the postdating of the check.

UCC case law is very clear that fraud by the payee is not a defense against a holder in due course. McKee's asserted fraud in selling an allegedly fake Rolex to Houston Gold Exchange does not bar RR Maloan from collecting on the check as a holder in due course.

Reversed and remanded.

[RR Maloan Investments, Inc. v. New HGE, Inc., 428 S.W.3d 355 (Tex. App. 2014)]

29-2d Universal Defenses Available against All Holders

Certain defenses are regarded as so basic that the social interest in preserving them outweighs the social interest of giving negotiable instruments the freely transferable qualities of money. Accordingly, such defenses are given universal effect and may be raised against all holders, whether ordinary holders, HDCs, or holders through a holder in due course. These defenses are called **universal defenses.**[15]

universal defenses— defenses that are regarded as so basic that the social interest in preserving them outweighs the social interest of giving negotiable instruments the freely transferable qualities of money; accordingly, such defenses are given universal effect and may be raised against all holders.

C P A

Fraud as to the Nature or Essential Terms of the Instrument

The fact that a person signs an instrument because the person is fraudulently deceived as to its nature or essential terms is a defense available against all holders.[16] When one person induces another to sign a note by falsely representing that, for example, it is a contract for repairs or that it is a character reference, the note is invalid, and the defense of the misrepresentation of the character of the instrument can be used against a holder in due course. **For Example,** suppose that two homeowners are asked to sign a statement for a salesperson that he was in their home and did a demonstration of a new solar water heater. Just as the homeowners are about to sign the verification statement, the salesman distracts them and then switches the verification for a purchase contract and promissory note for a $5,000 solar water heating system that the owners declined to purchase. The owners would have a defense of fraud in factum against a holder in due course of this note. The difference between fraud in the inducement—a personal defense—and fraud in factum—a universal defense—is that fraud in factum involves deception as to the documents themselves, not as to the underlying goods, services, or property.

[15] *City Rentals, Inc. v. Kessler*, 946 N.E.2d 785 (Ohio App. 2010).
[16] U.C.C. §3-305(a)(1)(iii).

C P A   ## Forgery or Lack of Authority

The defense that a signature was forged or signed without authority can be raised by a drawer or maker against any HDC. The fact that the negligence of the drawer helped the wrongdoer does not prevent the drawee from raising the defense of forgery. (See Chapters 28 and 30 for more discussion of the impact of forgery on liability.)

Duress Depriving Control

A party may execute or indorse a negotiable instrument in response to a force of such a nature that, under general principles of law, duress makes the transaction void rather than merely voidable. Duress of this type and level may be raised as a defense against any holder. Economic duress, in the form of a reluctance to enter into a financially demanding instrument, is not a universal defense.[17] Duress that is attempted murder is a universal defense.

Incapacity

The fact that the defendant is a minor who under general principles of contract law may avoid the obligation is a matter that may be raised against any kind of holder. Other kinds of incapacity may be raised as a defense if the effect of the incapacity is to make the instrument void, as when there has been a formal declaration of insanity.[18]

Illegality

If an instrument is void by law when executed in connection with certain conduct, such as a note for gambling or one that involves usury, such defenses may be raised against an HDC.

C P A   ## Alteration

alteration–unauthorized change or completion of a negotiable instrument designed to modify the obligation of a party to the instrument.

An **alteration** is an unauthorized change or completion of a negotiable instrument designed to modify the obligation of a party to the instrument.[19] **For Example,** changing the amount of an instrument from $150 to $450 is an alteration.[20]

Person Making Alteration. An alteration is a change made by a party to the instrument. Recovery on the instrument is still possible under the terms of the instrument as it originally existed, if proof of the original terms is possible.

Effect of Alteration. If the alteration to the instrument was made fraudulently, the person whose obligations under the instrument are affected by that alteration is discharged from liability on the instrument. The instrument, however, can be enforced according to its original terms or its terms as completed. This right of enforcement is given to holders in due course who had no notice of such alteration.[21] While a holder in due course would come within the protected class on alteration, such status is not required for this recovery provision in the event of alteration. **For Example,** Ryan signed a negotiable demand note for $100 made payable to Long. A subsequent holder changed the amount from $100 to

[17] *JPMorgan Chase Bank, N.A. v. Asia Pulp & Paper Cp., Ltd.,* 707 F.3d 853 (7th Cir. 2013).
[18] U.C.C. §3-305(a)(1)(ii). *Erkins v. Alaska Trustee LLC,* 265 P.3d 292 (Alaska 2011).
[19] U.C.C. §3-407(a); *Stahl v. St. Elizabeth Medical Center,* 948 S.W.2d 419 (Ky. App. 1997). *Farmers Deposit Bank v. Bank One,* 2005 WL 3453979 (E.D. Ky. 2005). A material alteration made based on the parties' negotiations (a 13 percent versus an 18 percent interest rate) is not fraudulent. *Darnall v. Petersen,* 592 N.W.2d 505 (Neb. App. 1999); *Knoefler v. Wojtalewicz,* 2003 WL 21496933 (Neb. App. 2003) (difference between bank interest rate and judgment interest rate is not material).
[20] However, if an instrument, such as a note, has been altered and the maker continues to pay without objection to the alteration, the alteration does not discharge the maker's liability. *Richard v. Wells Fargo Bank, N.A.,* 2013 WL 5726009 (Mo. App. 2013).
[21] U.C.C. §3-407(b), (c).

FIGURE 29-2	Defenses to Payment of Negotiable Instrument

UNIVERSAL (Available against assignees, holders, and holders in due course) (Real)	LIMITED (Available against assignees and holders but not against holders in due course) (Personal)	MIXED (Circumstances vary the availability of these defenses)
Fraud as to the nature of the instrument (fraud in factum)	Fraud in the inducement	Duress
Forgery	Misrepresentation	Incapacity
Unauthorized signature	Lack of consideration	
Incapacity (declaration)	Breach of warranty	
Illegality	Cancellation	
Alteration	Failure of delivery	
Consumer credit contracts with FTC notice	Unauthorized completion	
	All ordinary contract defenses	

$700. A later holder in due course presented the note to Ryan for payment. Ryan would still be liable for the original amount of $100.

A summary of the universal and limited defenses is presented in Figure 29-2.

29-2e Denial of Holder-in-Due-Course Protection

In certain situations, the taker of a negotiable instrument is denied the status and protections of an HDC.

Participating Transferee

When the transferee is working with the lender or seller to obtain a negotiable instrument from the buyer/borrower, the transferee's holder-in-due-course status comes into question. This close-connection doctrine (discussed earlier in this chapter as an issue in the good-faith requirement for becoming a holder in due course) prevents a transferee with intimate knowledge of the transferor's business practices from becoming an HDC.[22]

The Federal Trade Commission Rule

In 1976, the Federal Trade Commission (FTC) adopted a rule that limits the rights of a holder in due course in a consumer credit transaction. The rule protects consumers who

---

[22] In re *Neals*, 459 B.R. 612 (D.S.C. 2011). *AIG Global Securities Lending Corp. v. Banc of America Securities LLC*, 2006 WL 1206333 (S.D.N.Y. 2006).

purchase goods or services for personal, family, or household use on credit.[23] When the note the buyer gave the seller as payment for the consumer goods is transferred to even a holder in due course, the consumer buyer may raise any defense that could have been raised against the seller. The FTC regulation requires that the following notice be included in boldface type at least 10 points in size in consumer credit contracts covered under the rule:

> *Notice*
> *Any holder of this consumer credit contract is subject to all claims and defenses which the debtor could assert against the seller of goods or services obtained with the proceeds hereof. Recovery hereunder by the debtor shall not exceed amounts paid by the debtor hereunder.*

When a notice preserving consumer defenses is included in a negotiable instrument, no subsequent person can be a holder in due course of the instrument.[24]

29-3 Liability Issues: How Payment Rights Arise and Defenses Are Used

In this chapter and in Chapters 27 and 28, issues surrounding the types of instruments, transfers, holders, and holders in due course have been covered. However, there are procedures under Article 3 for bringing together all of the parties, instruments, and defenses so that ultimate liability and, hopefully, payment can be determined and achieved.

CPA

29-3a The Roles of Parties and Liability

Every instrument has primary and secondary parties. The **primary party** is the party to whom the holder or holder in due course must turn first to obtain payment. The primary party on a note or certificate of deposit is the **maker.** The primary party on a draft is the **drawee,** assuming that the drawee has accepted the draft. Although a check must first be presented to the drawee bank for payment, the bank is not primarily liable on the instrument because the bank has the right to refuse to pay the check (see following and Chapter 30). The drawee bank on a check is the party to whom a holder or holder in due course turns first for payment despite the lack of primary-party status on the part of that drawee bank. The maker of a note is the party to whom holders and holders in due course must turn first for payment.

The **secondary parties** (or *secondary obligors*, as they are now called under Article 3) to an instrument are those to whom holders turn when the primary party, for whatever reason, fails to pay the instrument. Secondary parties on notes are **indorsers,** and secondary parties on checks and drafts are **drawers** and indorsers.

CPA

29-3b Attaching Liability of the Primary Parties: Presentment

Presentment occurs when the holder or HDC of an instrument orally, in writing, or by electronic communication to the primary party requests that the instrument be paid

---

primary party–party to whom the holder or holder in due course must turn first to obtain payment.

maker–party who writes or creates a promissory note.

drawee–person to whom the draft is addressed and who is ordered to pay the amount of money specified in the draft.

secondary parties– called secondary obligors under Revised Article 3; parties to an instrument to whom holders turn when the primary party, for whatever reason, fails to pay the instrument.

indorser–secondary party (or obligor) on a note.

drawer–person who writes out and creates a draft or bill of exchange, including a check.

presentment–formal request for payment on an instrument.

---

[23] The regulation does not cover purchases of real estate, securities, or consumer goods or services for which the purchase price is more than $25,000. *Fifth Third Bank v. Jones*, 168 P.3d 1 (Colo. App. 2007).

[24] U.C.C. §3-106(d). The rule changes the status of the parties as holders in due course. It does not change contract rights. *Pennsylvania Dept. of Banking v. NCAS of Delaware, LLC*, 931 A.2d 771 (Pa. 2007).

E-COMMERCE & CYBERLAW

Electronic Presentment: One Fell Swoop, All Rights, All Payments, New Laws

Because we now use debit cards, some of the UCC Article 3 provisions on checks are used far less, and the rights of the merchants and the buyers are covered under various federal and state laws on electronic funds transfers (covered in Chapter 30). Issues continue to evolve, such as the protections on debit cards and credit cards and increasing cyber security at banks and stores to prevent hackers from obtaining information, including card and pin numbers.

THINKING THINGS THROUGH

The Corner Check Cashing Company and Thieves—Who Wins?

Now is an ideal time to bring together all of the concepts you have learned in Chapters 26, 27, and 28. Analyzing this problem will help you integrate your knowledge about negotiable instruments. Sid's Salmon has purchased salmon from Fred's Fisheries. Sid wrote a check for $22,000 to Fred's. A thief broke into Fred's offices and took the cash on hand as well as the unindorsed check from Sid's. The thief took the check to the Corner Check Cashing Company (CCCC) and received $22,000 less the cashing fee of $2,000. Fred notified Sid, who then notified First Commerce Bank, the drawee of the check, of the theft. CCCC has presented the check for payment, and First Commerce refuses to pay. CCCC says it is a holder in due course.

Are you able to help First Commerce Bank develop its response to CCCC? Suppose that Fred had already indorsed the check when the thief stole it. Would CCCC be a holder in due course?

according to its terms. The primary party has the right to require that the presentment be made in a "commercially reasonable manner," which would include reasonable times for presentment, such as during business hours. The primary party can also require identification, authorization, and even a signature of receipt of the funds due under the instrument. In addition, the primary party can demand a valid indorsement on the instrument prior to making payment. Upon presentment, the primary party is required to pay according to the terms of the instrument unless there are defenses such as forgery, any of the other universal defenses for HDCs, or any defenses for holders.

dishonor—status when the primary party refuses to pay the instrument according to its terms.

If the primary party refuses to pay the instrument according to its terms, there has been a *dishonor*, and the holder is then left to turn to the secondary parties.

29-3c Dishonor and Notice of Dishonor

CPA

notice of dishonor— notice that an instrument has been dishonored; such notice can be oral, written, or electronic but is subject to time limitations.

Dishonor occurs when the primary party refuses to pay the instrument according to its terms. The primary party is required to give **notice of dishonor.** The notice that the instrument has been dishonored can be oral, written, or electronic. That notice is subject to time limitations. **For Example,** a bank must give notice of dishonor by midnight of the next banking day. Nonbank primary parties must give notice of dishonor within 30 days following their receipt of notice of dishonor. Returning the dishonored check is sufficient notice of dishonor. (See Chapter 30 for more discussion of liability issues on dishonor of checks.) Upon dishonor, the holder must then turn to the secondary parties for payment.

limited defenses— defenses available to secondary parties if the presenting party is a holder in due course.

The obligation of the secondary parties in these situations is to pay according to the terms of the instrument. These secondary parties will have **limited defenses** if the presenting party is a holder in due course. **For Example,** suppose that a check drawn on

First Interstate Bank is written by Ben Paltrow to Julia Sutherland as payment for Julia's Bentley auto that Ben purchased. Julia deposits Ben's check into her account at Ameri-Bank, and AmeriBank sends the check to First Interstate to present it for payment. First Interstate finds that Ben's account has insufficient funds and dishonors the check. Ameri-Bank must notify First Interstate by midnight of the next banking day that the check has been dishonored, and then First Interstate must notify Julia by midnight of the next banking day that Ben's check was dishonored. Julia then has 30 days to notify Ben and turn to him as a drawer, or secondary party, for payment on the check.

Make the Connection

Summary

A holder of a negotiable instrument can be either an ordinary holder or an HDC. The ordinary holder has the same rights that an assignee would have. Holders in due course and holders through an HDC are protected from certain defenses. To be an HDC, a person must first be a holder—that is, the person must have acquired the instrument by proper negotiation. The holder must then also take for value, in good faith, without notice that the paper is overdue or dishonored, and without notice of defenses and adverse claims. Those persons who become holders of the instrument after an HDC are given the same protection as the HDC through the shelter provision, provided they are not parties to any fraud or illegality affecting the instrument.

The importance of being an HDC is that those holders are not being subject to certain defenses when demand for payment is made. These defenses are limited defenses and include ordinary contract defenses, incapacity unless it makes the instrument void, fraud in the inducement, prior payment or cancellation, nondelivery of an instrument, conditional delivery, duress consisting of threats, unauthorized completion, and theft of a bearer instrument. Universal defenses may be asserted against

any assignee, an ordinary holder, or HDC. Universal defenses include fraud as to the nature or essential terms of the paper, forgery or lack of authority, duress depriving control, incapacity, illegality that makes the instrument void, and alteration. Alteration is only a partial defense; an HDC may enforce the instrument according to its original terms.

The Federal Trade Commission rule on consumer credit contracts limits the immunity of an HDC from defenses of consumer buyers against their sellers. Immunity is limited in consumer credit transactions if the notice specified by the FTC regulation is included in the sales contract. When a notice preserving consumer defenses is stated in a negotiable instrument, no subsequent person can be an HDC.

Holders and HDCs are required to present instruments for payment to primary parties. Primary parties are makers and drawees. If the primary party refuses to pay, or dishonors, the instrument, it must give notice of dishonor in a timely fashion. The holder can then turn to secondary parties, drawers, and indorsers (secondary obligors) for payment.

Learning Outcomes

After studying this chapter, you should be able to clearly explain:

29-1   Parties to Negotiable Instruments: Rights and Liabilities

LO.1 Distinguish between an ordinary holder and a holder in due course

See the sections titled "Ordinary Holders and Assignees" and "The Holder-in-Due-Course Protections" for examples of distinction, pages 556–561.

LO.2 List the requirements for becoming a holder in due course

See the *Triffin v. Liccardi Ford, Inc.* case, page 560.

29-2   Defenses to Payment of a Negotiable Instrument

LO.3 Explain the rights of a holder through a holder in due course

See the *New Randolph Halsted Currency Exchange, Inc. v. Regent Title Insurance Co.* case, page 559.

LO.4 List and explain the limited defenses not available against a holder in due course

See the list of defenses in Figure 29-2, page 565.
See the *RR Maloan Investments, Inc. v. New HGE, Inc.* case, pages 562–563.

LO.5 List and explain the universal defenses available against all holders

See the Thinking Things Through discussion of the Corner Check Cashing Company, page 567.
See the ethical issue on check cashing companies, page 560.

29-3   Liability Issues: How Payment Rights Arise and Defenses Are Used

LO.6 Describe how the rights of a holder in due course have been limited by the Federal Trade Commission

See the language of the rule, page 566.

Key Terms

alteration	good faith	notice of dishonor
assignees	holders	presentment
close-connection doctrine	holder in due course	primary party
dishonor	holder through a holder in due course	secondary parties
drawee	indorsers	universal defenses
drawers	limited defenses	value
fraud in the inducement	maker	

Questions and Case Problems

1. Randy Bocian had a bank account with First of America-Bank (FAB). On October 8, Bocian received a check for $28,800 from Eric Christenson as payment for constructing a pole barn on Christenson's property. Bocian deposited the check at FAB on October 9 and was permitted to draw on the funds through October 12. Bocian wrote checks totaling $12,334.21, which FAB cleared. On October 12, Christenson stopped payment on the check as the result of a contract dispute over the pole barn. Bocian's account was then overdrawn once the check was denied clearance by Christenson's bank. FAB brought suit against both Bocian and Christenson to collect its loss. Christenson counterclaimed against Bocian for his contract breach claims on the pole barn construction. FAB maintained that it had given value and was a holder in due course and that, as such, it was not required to be subject to the pole barn issues or the stop payment order. Is FAB right? [*First of America-Bank Northeast Illinois v. Bocian*, 614 N.E.2d 890 (Ill. App.)]

2. Cronin, an employee of Epicycle, cashed his final paycheck at Money Mart Check Cashing Center. Epicycle had issued a stop payment order on the check. Money Mart deposited the check through normal banking channels. The check was returned to Money Mart marked "Payment Stopped." Money Mart brought an action against Epicycle, claiming that, as a holder in due course, it was entitled to recover against Epicycle. Epicycle argued that Money Mart could not be a holder in due course because it failed to verify the check as good prior to cashing it. Is Money Mart a holder in due course? [*Money Mart Check Cashing Center, Inc. v. Epicycle Corp.*, 667 P.2d 1372 (Colo.)]

3. Halleck executed a promissory note payable to the order of Leopold. Halleck did not pay the note when due, and Leopold brought suit on the note, producing it in court. Halleck admitted that he had signed the note but claimed plaintiff Leopold was required to prove that the note had been issued for consideration and that the plaintiff was in fact the holder. Are these elements of proof required as part of the case? [*Leopold v. Halleck*, 436 N.E.2d 29 (Ill. App.)]

4. Calhoun/Johnson Company d/b/a Williams Lumber Company (Williams) sold building materials to Donald Miller d/b/a Millercraft Construction Company (Millercraft) on credit. Miller had signed a personal guaranty for the materials. Miller requested lien waivers from Williams for four of his projects

and asked for them from Fabian Boudreau, Williams's credit manager. Fabian refused to grant the waivers because Miller was $28,000 delinquent on his account. Miller agreed to bring his account current with the exception of $11,000 for which he signed a no-interest promissory note. Miller obtained the lien waivers and then defaulted on the note. Williams brought suit for payment, and Williams said there was lack of consideration and that the note was not valid. He said he must give value to be able to recover on the note. Was he correct? [*Miller v. Calhoun/Johnson Co.*, 497 S.E.2d 397 (Ga. App.)]

5. Jane bought a string of pearls from Grantham Jewelers. Jane wrote a check for $1,760 to pay for the pearls. When Jane had the pearls appraised for insurance purposes, she learned from the appraiser that the pearls were fake. Jane stopped payment on the check. However, Grantham had transferred the check to Jim Holub, who had then transferred the check back to Grantham. Is Grantham an HDC?

6. Can check cashing companies be holders in due course? What arguments can you make for and against their holder-in-due-course status? [*Dal-Tile Corp. v. Cash N' Go*, 487 S.E.2d 529 (Ga. App.)]

7. Jones, wishing to retire from a business enterprise that he had been conducting for a number of years, sold all of the assets of the business to Jackson Corp. Included in the assets were a number of promissory notes payable to the order of Jones that he had taken from his customers. Upon the maturity of one of the notes, the maker refused to pay because there was a failure of consideration. Jackson Corp. sued the maker of the note. Who should succeed? Explain.

8. Elliot, an officer of Impact Marketing, drew six postdated checks on Impact's account. The checks were payable to Bell for legal services to be subsequently performed for Impact. Financial Associates purchased them from Bell and collected on four of the checks. Payment was stopped on the last two when Bell's services were terminated. Financial argued that it was a holder in due course and had the right to collect on the checks. Impact claimed that because the checks were postdated and issued for an executory promise, Financial could not be a holder in due course. Who was correct? Why? [*Financial Associates v. Impact Marketing*, 394 N.Y.S.2d 814]

9. *D* drew a check to the order of *P*. *P* took the check postdated. *P* knew that *D* was having financial difficulties and that the particular checking account on which this check was drawn had been frequently overdrawn. Do these circumstances prevent *P* from being a holder in due course? [*Citizens Bank, Booneville v. National Bank of Commerce*, 334 F.2d 257 (10th Cir.); *Franklin National Bank v. Sidney Gotowner*, 4 U.C.C. Rep. Serv. 953 (N.Y. Supp.)]

10. Daniel, Joel, and Claire Guerrette are the adult children of Elden Guerrette, who died on September 24, 1995. Before his death, Elden purchased a life insurance policy from Sun Life Assurance Company of Canada through a Sun Life agent, Steven Hall, and named his children as his beneficiaries. Upon his death, Sun Life issued three checks, each in the amount of $40,759.35, to each of Elden's children. The checks were drawn on Sun Life's account at Chase Manhattan Bank in Syracuse, New York. The checks were given to Hall for delivery to the Guerrettes. Hall and an associate, Paul Richard, then fraudulently induced the Guerrettes to indorse the checks in blank and to transfer them to Hall and Richard, purportedly to be invested in HER, Inc., a corporation formed by Hall and Richard. Hall took the checks from the Guerrettes and turned them over to Richard, who deposited them in his account at the Credit Union on October 26, 1995. The Credit Union immediately made the funds available to Richard.

The Guerrettes quickly regretted having negotiated their checks to Hall and Richard, and they contacted Sun Life the next day to request that Sun Life stop payment on the checks. Sun Life immediately ordered Chase Manhattan to stop payment on the checks. When the checks were ultimately presented to Chase Manhattan for payment, Chase refused to pay the checks, and they were returned to the Credit Union. The Credit Union received notice that the checks had been dishonored on November 3, 1995, the sixth business day following their deposit. By the time the Credit Union received notice, however, Richard had withdrawn from his account all of the funds represented by the three checks. The Credit Union was able to recover almost $80,000 from Richard, but there remained an unpaid balance of $42,366.56.

The Credit Union filed suit against Sun Life, and all of the parties became engulfed in litigation. The Credit Union indicated it was a holder in due course and was entitled to payment on the instrument. Sun Life alleged fraud. Is the Credit Union a holder in due course? Can the parties allege the fraud defense against it? [*Maine Family Federal Credit*

Union v. Sun Life Assur. Co. of Canada, 727 A.2d 335 (Maine)]

11. G.C. Vincent was an employee of Porter County Development Corporation (PCDC). Vincent had three personal credit cards through Citibank. Vincent diverted checks to the PCDC, deposited them into his personal checking account, and issued checks drawn upon that personal account to pay part of the outstanding balance of his three Citibank-held credit card accounts. Citibank was unaware that Vincent used misappropriated funds to pay his credit card balance. PCDC filed suit to have Citibank return the embezzled funds. Citibank moved for summary judgment on the grounds that it was an HDC. The trial court granted summary judgment and PCDC appealed. Who should prevail on appeal and why? [*Porter County Development Corp. v. Citibank (South Dakota),* N.A., 855 N.E.2d 306 (Ind. App.)]

12. Sanders gave Clary a check but left the amount incomplete. The check was given as advance payment on the purchase of 100 LT speakers. The amount was left blank because Clary had the right to substitute other LT speakers if they became available and the substitution would change the price. It was agreed that in no event would the purchase price exceed $5,000. Desperate for cash, Clary wrongfully substituted much more expensive LT speakers, thereby increasing the price to $5,700. Clary then negotiated the check to Lawrence, one of his suppliers. Clary filled in the $5,700 in Lawrence's presence, showing him the shipping order and the invoice applicable to the sale to Sanders. Lawrence accepted the check in payment of $5,000 worth of overdue debts and $700 in cash. Can Lawrence recover the full amount? Why or why not?

13. GRAS is a Michigan corporation engaged in the business of buying and selling cars. Between 1997 and 2000, Katrina Stewart was employed as a manager by GRAS. During that period, Stewart wrote checks, without authority, on GRAS's corporate account payable to MBNA and sent them to MBNA for payment of her husband's MBNA credit card account. MBNA accepted the checks and credited the proceeds to Stewart's husband's credit card debt. MBNA accepted and processed the GRAS checks in its normal manner through electronic processing. When MBNA receives a check for a credit card payment, the envelope containing the check and the payment slip is opened by machine and the check and the payment slip are electronically processed and

credited to the cardholder's account balance. MBNA does not normally review checks for credit card payments. After crediting a payment check to the cardholder's account, MBNA transfers it to the bank on which it is written for collection. Pursuant to its standard practice, MBNA did not review the checks it received from Stewart. GRAS did not have a customer relationship with MBNA during the relevant time period.

GRAS sought a refund of the amounts Stewart embezzled via the MBNA application of the checks to Stewart's husband's credit card account. MBNA said it was a holder in due course. Was MBNA a holder in due course? Was MBNA subject to GRAS's defense of unauthorized instruments? [*Grand Rapids Auto Sales, Inc. v. MBNA America Bank,* 227 F. Supp. 2d 721 (W.D. Mich.)]

14. William Potts was employed by Jemoli Holdings, Inc., to liquidate assets of defunct companies. Potts had the authority to sign checks for Jemoli. Potts had a personal investment account with Raymond James Financial Services. When the stock market had its 2000 crash due to the dot-com bubble, Potts had difficulty meeting his margin calls. He began giving checks from Jemoli to Raymond James to cover the margin calls. When a representative questioned Mr. Potts about the Jemoli checks, he assured the representative that Jemoli was him, and that it was his firm. Over four months, Potts wrote checks totaling $1.5 million to Raymond James to cover loans and to make more investments. When Jemoli's principals discovered the embezzlement they brought suit to recover the funds from Raymond James. Raymond James says it was an HDC of the checks and not subject to Jemoli's claims for breach of fiduciary duty by its agent, Potts. Who is correct about the HDC status of Raymond James and why? [*Jemoli Holding, Inc. v. Raymond James Financial, Inc.,* 470 F.3d 14 (1st Cir.)]

15. Omni Trading issued two checks totaling $75,000 to Country Grain Elevators for grain it had purchased. Country Grain indorsed the checks over to the law firm of Carter & Grimsley as a retainer. Country Grain then collapsed as a business, and Omni stopped payment on the checks because all of its grain had not been delivered. Carter & Grimsley claimed it was a holder in due course and entitled to payment. However, the Department of Agriculture claimed its interest in the checks for liens and maintained that Carter & Grimsley was not a holder in due course because it had not given value.

The trial court granted summary judgment for the Department of Agriculture because the checks were indorsed as a retainer for future legal work and Carter & Grimsley had not given value. Is Carter & Grimsley a holder in due course? [*Carter & Grimsley v. Omni Trading, Inc.,* 716 N.E.2d 320 (Ill. App.)]

CPA Questions

1. Under the Commercial Paper Article of the UCC, which of the following requirements must be met for a person to be a holder in due course of a promissory note?

   a. The note must be payable to bearer.

   b. The note must be negotiable.

   c. All prior holders must have been holders in due course.

   d. The holder must be the payee of the note.

2. A maker of a note will have a real defense against a holder in due course as a result of any of the following conditions except:

   a. Discharge in bankruptcy.

   b. Forgery.

   c. Fraud in the execution.

   d. Lack of consideration.

3. Under the commercial paper article of the UCC, in a nonconsumer transaction, which of the following are real (universal) defenses available against a holder in due course?

	Material Alteration	Discharge in Bankruptcy	Breach of contract
a.	No	Yes	Yes
b.	Yes	Yes	No
c.	No	No	Yes
d.	Yes	No	No

4. A holder in due course will take free of which of the following defenses?

   a. Infancy, to the extent that it is a defense to a simple contract.

   b. Discharge of the maker in bankruptcy.

   c. A wrongful filling-in of the amount payable that was omitted from the instrument.

   d. Duress of a nature that renders the obligation of the party a nullity.

5. Mask stole one of Bloom's checks. The check was already signed by Bloom and made payable to Duval. The check was drawn on United Trust Company. Mask forged Duval's signature on the back of the check at the Corner Check Cashing Company, which in turn deposited it with its bank, Town National Bank of Toka. Town National proceeded to collect on the check from United. None of the parties mentioned were negligent. Who will bear the loss, assuming the amount cannot be recovered from Mask?

   a. Bloom

   b. Duval

   c. United Trust Company

   d. Corner Check Cashing Company

6. Robb stole one of Markum's blank checks, made it payable to himself, and forged Markum's signature to it. The check was drawn on the Unity Trust Company. Robb cashed the check at the Friendly Check Cashing Company, which in turn deposited it with its bank, Farmer's National. Farmer's National proceeded to collect on the check from Unity Trust. The theft and forgery were quickly discovered by Markum, who promptly notified Unity. None of the parties mentioned were negligent. Who will bear the loss, assuming the amount cannot be recovered from Robb?

   a. Markum

   b. Unity Trust Company

   c. Friendly Check Cashing Company

   d. Farmer's National

7. For a person to be holder in due course of a promissory note:

   a. The note must be payable in U.S. currency to the holder.

   b. The holder must be the payee of the note.

   c. The note must be negotiable.

   d. All prior holders must have been holders in due course.

Checks and Funds Transfers

Learning Outcomes ‹‹‹

After studying this chapter, you should be able to

LO.1 List and explain the duties of the drawee bank

LO.2 Explain the methods for, and legal effect of stopping payment

LO.3 Describe the liability of a bank for improper payment and collection

LO.4 Discuss the legal effect of forgeries and material alterations

LO.5 Specify the time limitations for reporting forgeries and alterations

LO.6 Describe the electronic transfer of funds and laws governing it

30-1 **Checks**

check–order by a depositor on a bank to pay a sum of money to a payee; a bill of exchange drawn on a bank and payable on demand.

As discussed in Chapter 27, a **check** is, under Uniform Commercial Code (UCC) §3-104(f), "(i) a draft ... payable on demand and drawn on a bank or (ii) a cashier's check or teller's check. An instrument may be a check even though it is described on its face by another term, such as 'money order.'"[1] The distinguishing characteristics of checks[2] and drafts are summarized in Figure 30-1. Under Article 4, the change in consumer payment patterns away from formal, signed checks is reflected with the addition of "remotely-created consumer item," which are items directing payment that are drawn on a consumer account but do not carry a handwritten signature of the drawer.[3] Consumer account is defined as a bank account used for household, family, or personal purposes.[4] These types of payments include PayPal authorizations to pay from consumer checking accounts and automatic bill payments that consumers direct via online banking.

30-1a **Nature of a Check**

Sufficient Funds on Deposit

As a practical matter, a check is drawn on the assumption that the bank has on deposit in the drawer's account an amount sufficient to pay the check. In the case of other drafts, there is no assumption that the drawee has any of the drawer's money with which to pay the instrument. In international transactions, sellers may require buyers not only to accept a draft agreeing to pay but also to back up that draft with a line of credit from the buyer's bank. That line of credit is the backup should the funds for the draft not be forthcoming from the buyer.

If a draft is dishonored, the drawer is civilly liable. If a check is drawn with intent to defraud the person to whom it is delivered, the drawer is also subject to criminal

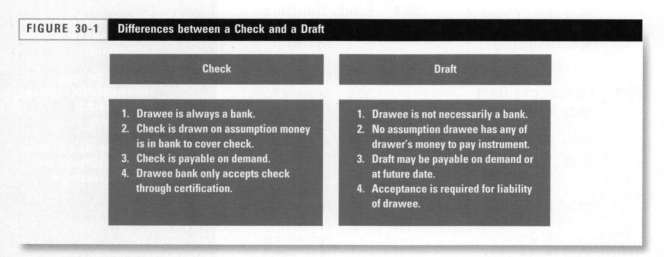

FIGURE 30-1 | **Differences between a Check and a Draft**

Check	Draft
1. Drawee is always a bank.	1. Drawee is not necessarily a bank.
2. Check is drawn on assumption money is in bank to cover check.	2. No assumption drawee has any of drawer's money to pay instrument.
3. Check is payable on demand.	3. Draft may be payable on demand or at future date.
4. Drawee bank only accepts check through certification.	4. Acceptance is required for liability of drawee.

---

[1] U.C.C. §3-104(f).
[2] Checks are governed by both Article 3 of the UCC and Article 4 governing bank deposits and collections. The 2001 and 2002 versions of Article 4 are covered in this chapter, along with notations of the changes since the 1990 version. The new versions of Article 4 incorporate most provisions of the American Bankers Association Bank Collection Code. The purpose of the code was to introduce clarity into the processing of millions of electronic and paper transactions that banks must handle and to recognize the reality of electronic payments.
[3] U.C.C. §3-104(16).
[4] U.C.C. §3-104(2).

prosecution in most states. The laws under which such drawers are prosecuted are known as **bad check laws.** Most states provide that if the check is not made good within a stated period, such as 10 days, there is a presumption that the drawer originally issued the check with the intent to defraud.

Demand Paper

A draft may be payable either on demand or at a future date. A check is a form of **demand draft.** The standard form of check does not specify when it is payable, and it is therefore automatically payable on demand.

One exception arises when a check is **postdated**—that is, when the check shows a date later than the actual date of execution. Postdating a check means that the check is not payable until the date arrives, and it changes the check from a demand draft to a **time draft.**[5] However, banks are not obligated to hold a postdated check until the time used on the check unless the drawer has filed the appropriate paperwork with the bank for such a delay. Because of electronic processing, banks are not required to examine each instrument and honor postdated instrument requests unless the hold is placed into the bank's processing system by the customer (a stop payment order).

Form of the Check

A check can be in any form of writing.[6] However, bank customers may agree, as part of the contract with their bank, to use certain forms for check writing. A remotely created consumer item need only be evidenced by a *record*, not by a written document. Under Revised U.C.C. §3-104(a)(14), a *record* is defined as "information that is inscribed on a tangible medium or which is stored in an electronic or other medium and is retrievable in perceivable form."[7]

Delivery Not Assignment

The delivery of a check is not an assignment of the money on deposit, so it does not automatically transfer the rights of the depositor against the bank to the holder of the check. A check written by a drawer on his drawee bank does not result in a duty on the part of the drawee bank to the holder to pay the holder the amount of the check. An ordinary check drawn on a customer's account is direction from a customer to the bank for payment, but it does not impose absolute primary liability on the bank at the time the check is written.[8]

Banks assume more responsibility for some types of checks than for the ordinary customer's check. **For Example,** a bank **money order** payable to John Jones is a check and has the bank as both the drawer and the drawee.[9] U.C.C. §3-104(g) defines a cashier's check as "a draft with respect to which the drawer and drawee are the same bank or branches of the same bank."[10] In other words, a **cashier's check** is a check or draft drawn by a bank again on itself. If a cashier's check is drawn on another bank in which the drawer bank has an account, it is a **teller's check.** Although the drawer and drawee may be the same on a money order or a cashier's check, the instrument does not lose its three-party character or its status as a check.

bad check laws–laws making it a criminal offense to issue a bad check with intent to defraud.

CPA

demand draft–draft that is payable upon presentment.

postdate–to insert or place on an instrument a later date than the actual date on which it was executed.

time draft–bill of exchange payable at a stated time after sight or at a definite time.

money order–draft issued by a bank or a nonbank.

cashier's check–draft drawn by a bank on itself.

teller's check–draft drawn by a bank on another bank in which it has an account.

---

[5] A bank is required to comply with a postdate on a check only if it is notified of the postdate in the same way the customer issues a stop payment order.

[6] Although not required for negotiation or presentment, a printed bank check, when the customer is using a written form, is preferable because it generally carries magnetic ink figures that facilitate sorting and posting.

[7] *Smith v. Farmers Union Mut. Ins. Co.* 260 P.3d 163 (Mont. 2011).

[8] *Sapp v. Flagstar Bank, FSB*, 12 N.E.3d 913 (Ind. App. 2014).

[9] U.C.C. §3-104(f). *Lawyer's Mut. Liability Ins. Co. of North America v. Mako*, 756 S.E.2d 809 (N.C. App. 2014).

[10] U.C.C. §3-104(g). *Golden v. Citibank, N.A.*, 23 N.Y.3d 934 (N.Y. 2014).

Under federal laws that Article 4 recognizes, there is another form of payments known as a **substitute check,** which is an electronic image or paper printout of an electronic image of a check. A substitute check has the same legal effect as a paper check. The bank that converts the paper check into electronic form, called the *reconverting bank*, has certain duties imposed by federal regulations to be certain that the electronic version or substitute check has all of the necessary legal information such as visible indorsements, magnetic bank code strip, payee, and signature of drawer.

30-1b Certified Checks

The drawee bank may *certify* or accept a check drawn on it. Under U.C.C. §3-409(d), a certified check is "a check accepted by the bank on which it is drawn."[11] While a bank is under no obligation to certify a check, if it does so, the certification has the effect of the bank accepting primary liability on the instrument. Check certification requires that the actual certification be written on the check and authenticated by the signature of an authorized representative of the bank.[12] Upon certification, the bank must set aside, in a special account maintained by the bank, the amount of the certified check taken from the drawer's account. The certification is a promise by the bank that when the check is presented for payment, the bank will make payment according to the terms of the check. Payment is made regardless of the status of the drawer's account at that time.

A holder or drawer may request that a check be certified by a bank. When certification is at the request of the holder, all prior indorsers and the drawer are released from liability. When certification is at the request of the drawer, the indorsers and drawer, as secondary parties, are not released. Unless otherwise agreed, the delivery of a certified check, a cashier's check, or a teller's check discharges the debt for which the check is given, up to the amount of that check.[13]

CASE SUMMARY

A Cashier's Check Is Only as Good as Its Signature

FACTS: On March 26, 2012, Dale M. Smith (defendant/counter-plaintiff) presented a cashier's check for $294,500.99 for deposit in his account with State Bank (plaintiff). The check appeared to be a cashier's check drawn on Chase bank. State Bank accepted the check for deposit. The following day, March 27, 2012, Smith requested that plaintiff wire approximately $275,000 from his account to an account in Japan. Before performing this transfer, State Bank contacted a local Chase branch and spoke to a representative. A Chase representative "confirmed the check number, the account number, verified the amount in the check and represented there were no stop-payment orders placed on the item." State Bank then processed Smith's wire transfer request.

On March 28, 2012, Chase returned the check to State Bank with the notation "refer to maker." State Bank then presented the check to Chase for payment a second time, and Chase again returned the check to State Bank. Elizabeth Roush, a Vice President and Reconciliation Manager for Chase, explained that the cashier's check was "different

---

[11] U.C.C. §3-409(d).

[12] Many courts treat cashier's checks and certified checks as the same because of their uniform commercial acceptability. See *Jones v. Wells Fargo Bank, N.A.,* 666 F.3d 955 (5th Cir. 2012). However, the rights of the parties are different because certification discharges all other parties to the instrument. A cashier's check does not result in the discharge of other parties on the instrument.

[13] U.C.C. §3-104(h) defines a traveler's check as "a draft drawn by a bank (i) on another bank, or (ii) payable at or through a bank."

A Cashier's Check Is Only as Good as Its Signature continued

from the form of official cashier's checks issued by Chase." The check number had an incorrect number of digits, did not include "a printed audit number to indicate its validity [,]" did not have the proper signature, and was missing a security symbol. At her deposition, Roush explained that only one authorized signature exists for all cashier's checks drawn on the account number printed on the cashier's check. This signature is electronically printed on all checks issued by Chase retail branches. Roush was immediately able to identify that the check was not issued by Chase because the signature was not an authorized signature for that account. Roush did not know who signed the check.

On May 16, 2012, State Bank filed suit against Smith and Chase. State Bank alleged that Chase wrongfully dishonored the check. The trial court granted summary judgment for Chase and State Bank appealed.

DECISION: The lack of a valid signature on a negotiable instrument is a real defense. The court held for Chase because the cashier's check did not have an authorized signature. An instrument is not valid unless it has a proper signature and no one is required to pay an instrument unless there is a valid signature. State Bank could not be an HDC of an instrument without a proper signature. And even if State Bank thought it was an HDC, the lack of an authorized signature is a real defense against an HDC seeking payment. Therefore, Chase was permitted to refuse payment because of a missing, authorized signature. [*State Bank v. Smith*, 85 U.C.C. Rep. Serv. 2d 260, 2014 WL 6088513 (Mich. App. 2014)]

E-COMMERCE & CYBERLAW

The Nigerian "I Need Your Help" E-Mails

They are quite common, those e-mails that come into our accounts asking for help in transferring funds in exchange for a percentage of those funds. They only ask that they be able to use our bank accounts in the United States so that they are able to collect the money owed to them, with your 12 to 15 percent service fee for use of your account deducted.

These are scams, accomplished by simple means. The scammers do indeed have their alleged creditors furnish large checks initially to be deposited in your account. Those checks do seem to clear. They then have you write checks in the amount deposited (less your percentage fee) to them. However, subsequent problems develop with those initially deposited checks and your bank wants you to now cover the overdraft created by the scammers cashing your check.

You end up owing the money to your bank. You have no claim based on forgery because it was your check. In short, the Nigerians win. There is no remedy under Article 3 or 4 for you, but there have been remedies under negligence by the banks in processing the transfers. Fraud is the easiest theory of recovery, but finding the scammers is a tall order. The federal government works tirelessly to alert people to the scams because it is nearly impossible for them to locate the scammers. Beware of e-mails coming your way from folks from Nigeria, Malaysia, and, well, any other country who wishes to use your bank account for processing their payments.

[*Anderson v. Branch Banking and Trust Co.*, 56 F. Supp. 3d 1345 (S.D. Fla. 2014)]

CPA 30-1c **Presentment for Obtaining Payment on a Check**

A holder of a check must take required steps to obtain payment. As discussed in Chapter 29, there are primary and secondary parties for every negotiable instrument. Primary parties are makers and drawees. Under Article 3, secondary parties are referred to as *secondary obligors* and are defined to include "an indorser, a drawer, an accommodation party, or any other party to the instrument that has a right of recourse against another party to the instrument."[14]

---

[14] U.C.C. §3-104(12).

presentment–formal
request for payment on
an instrument.

The process for a holder to be paid on an instrument involves mandatory steps with time limitations. The holder must first seek payment from the drawee through **presentment.** No secondary obligor is liable on an instrument until presentment has been made. Presentment is required for checks, and presentment is made first to the drawee bank.[15]

Presentment Requirements

Presentment occurs when the holder of a check or other consumer transaction authorization demands payment.[16] Under Revised Article 3, the party presents either the check or a record for payment. If the presentment is done in person, the party to whom presentment is made can require that the presenter exhibit identification. The holder who is presenting the instrument must present the check or record for payment in a commercially reasonable manner; banks can treat the transaction as having occurred the following day when presentment is made after *the close of the business day*.[17] In the case of electronic banking, banks are permitted to impose times after which posting will occur the next day. If a check is presented to the drawee bank for payment and paid, the drawer has no liability because payment has been made. (For more details on presentment, generally, of instruments, see Chapter 29.)

C P A   Time for Presentment of a Check for Payment[18]

Under the UCC, presentment must be made within a reasonable time after the drawers and indorsers have signed the check. What constitutes a reasonable time is determined by the nature of the instrument, by commercial usage, and by the facts of the particular case.

Failure to make timely presentment discharges all secondary obligors (prior indorsers) of the instrument. It also discharges the drawer to the extent that the drawer has lost, through the bank's failure, money that was on deposit at the bank to make the payment due under the check.[19]

The UCC establishes two presumptions as to what is a reasonable time for presentment of checks. If the check is not certified and is both drawn and payable within the United States, it is presumed that 90 days after the date of the check or the date of its issuance, whichever is later, is the reasonable period in which to make presentment for payment in order to attach secondary liability to the drawer.[20] With respect to attachment of the liability of an indorser, 30 days after indorsement is the presumed reasonable time.[21]

If a check is dated with the date of issue, it may be presented immediately for payment. If it is postdated, ordinarily it may not be presented until that date arrives. However, as noted earlier, the bank need not honor the date on the postdated instrument.[22] If the holder delays in making presentment, the delay discharges the drawer if the bank itself fails during such delay. If the holder of the check does not present it for payment or

---

[15] It is important to note that the bank is unique as a drawee because its contract as a primary party is limited by its right to dishonor a check and its right to give only provisional credit.

[16] In addition to the UCC restrictions on times for presentment, banks must comply with federally imposed time constraints. Under the Expedited Funds Availability Act, 12 U.S.C. §4001 *et seq.*, banks are required to lift provisional credits on customer accounts.

[17] U.C.C. §4-107(1). *Rogers v. Bank of America, N.A.*, 73 U.C.C. Rep. Serv. 2d 47 (S.D. Ill. 2010).

[18] U.C.C. §3-501. In re *Agriprocessors*, 490 B.R. 852 (N.D. Iowa 2013).

[19] U.C.C. §3-605.

[20] Under the previous versions of Articles 3 and 4, the time was six months.

[21] U.C.C. §3-304. *Eco-Built, Inc. v. The Nat. Bank of Indianapolis*, 683 F. Supp. 2d 892 (S.D. Ind. 2010).

[22] U.C.C. §4-208(c).

collection within 90 days after an indorsement was made, the secondary obligors (indorsers) are discharged from liability to the extent that the drawer has lost, through the bank's failure, money that was on deposit at the bank to meet the payment under the check.

Under Articles 3 and 4, agreeing to honor an instrument beyond this time limit changes the obligation of the primary obligor and, as a result, changes the obligation of the secondary obligors. Such changes in the terms and conditions of payment serve to discharge the secondary obligors, a change that brings UCC Articles 3 and 4 in line with the principles of surety law (see Chapter 32).

A bank may continue to honor checks presented for payment after the 90-day period, but it does so with understanding of the discharge of liability for the primary and secondary obligors. A bank honoring a check that is overdue subjects the bank to questions about whether it exercised good faith and reasonable care in honoring it.[23]

30-1d Dishonor of a Check

If the bank refuses to make payment, the drawer is then subject to the same secondary liability as the drawer of an ordinary draft.[24] To be able to attach that secondary liability, the holder of the instrument must notify the drawer of the dishonor by the drawee. The notice of dishonor may be oral, written, or electronic.

CPA   **Time for Notice of Dishonor**

Banks in the chain of collection for a check must give notice of dishonor by midnight of the next banking day.[25] Others, including the payee or holder of the check, must give notice of dishonor within 30 days after learning that the instrument has been dishonored. If proper notice of dishonor is not given to the drawer of the check, the drawer will be discharged from liability to the same extent as the drawer of an ordinary draft.[26]

CPA   **Overdraft**

overdraft–negative balance in a drawer's account.

If the bank pays the check but the funds in the account are not sufficient to cover the amount, the excess of the payment over the amount on deposit is an **overdraft.** This overdraft is treated as a loan from the bank to the customer, and the customer must repay that amount to the bank.

If the bank account from which the check is drawn is one held by two or more persons, the joint account holder who does not sign the check that creates an overdraft is not liable for the amount of the overdraft if she received no benefit from the proceeds of that check.[27] Additional issues on overdrafts and dishonor of checks are covered in the next section, "The Customer-Bank Relationship."

---

[23] Article 3 changed the "negligence" of the bank to the "failure to exercise ordinary are" in §3-406. A bank need not pay a check that is presented to it after 90 days (the presumptive ordinary care period) from the date of issue (except for certified checks), but it can honor such a check and charge the customer's account if it does so in good faith.

[24] U.C.C. §3-414. PayPal is not considered a bank for purposes of Articles 3 and 4. *Zepeda v. PayPal Inc.*, 777 F. Supp. 2d 1215 (N.D. Cal. 2011).

[25] The former time frame for nonbanks was midnight of the third business day. *Troy Bank and Trust Co. v. Citizens Bank*, 166 So. 3d 57 (Ala. 2014).

[26] U.C.C. §4-213. Under Federal Reserve regulations, notice of dishonor may be given by telephone. *Security Bank and Trust Co. v. Federal Nat'l Bank*, 554 P.2d 119 (Okla. Ct. App. 1976). But it must be an official notice of dishonor and not notice that there is a problem with the check prior to it being presented for payment. *City Check Cashing, Inc. v. Manufacturers Hanover Trust Co.*, 764 A.2d 411, 43 U.C.C. Rep. Serv. 2d 768 (N.J. 2001).

[27] U.C.C. §§4-214 and 4-401(b). *Sapp v. Flagstar Bank, FSB*, 12 N.E.3d 913 (Ind. App. 2014).

ETHICS & THE LAW

Getting Hit for SOOO Many Overdraft Fees

On August 28, 2008, Cortney Hassler had a balance of $112.35 in his checking account. He made a $39.58 payment in the morning and a $140.00 debit in the afternoon. Sovereign Bank did not post the transactions in the order that they occurred but, rather, rearranged the debits so that Cortney had to pay two $33 overdraft fees on his account. A provision in his checking account agreement indicated that Sovereign had the right to pay the withdrawals in any order. Cortney filed a class-action suit against the bank for unfair trade practices and unjust enrichment.

Evaluate the legal rights of the bank to post the transactions as it did. Evaluate the ethical issues in the changes in posting order so as to maximize the overdraft fees.

[*Lunsford v. Woodforest Nat. Bank,* 299 F.R.D. 695 (N.D. Ga. 2013)]

30-1e **The Customer-Bank Relationship**

The relationship between banks and customers is governed by Articles 3 and 4 of the UCC as well as by several federal statutes. These laws impose duties and liabilities on both banks and customers.

Privacy

USA Patriot Act–federal law that, among other things, imposes reporting requirements on banks.

The bank owes its customer the duty of maintaining the privacy of the information that the bank acquires in connection with its relationship with the customer. Law enforcement officers and administrative agencies cannot require the disclosure of information relating to a customer's account without first obtaining the customer's consent or a search warrant or without following the statutory procedures designed to protect customers from unreasonable invasions of privacy.[28] The **USA Patriot Act** does impose certain reporting requirements on banks, financial institutions, and businesses with regard to deposits of cash and large cash payments. These reporting requirements were imposed to be able to track money laundering efforts as well as possible funding of terrorist activities.[29] For example, checks that involve amounts of more than $10,000 generally trigger the bank reporting systems under the USA Patriot Act.

With the advent of the Internet and other electronic exchanges of information, it has become much easier for businesses, including banks, to exchange information about customers. All businesses are subject to federal constraints on the use of customer information. (See Chapter 32 for more information.)

Payment

A bank is under a general contractual duty to its customers to pay on demand all checks to the extent of the funds in a depositor's account.

CPA

stale check–a check whose date is longer than six months ago.

Stale Checks. A bank is under no obligation to a customer to pay a check (other than one that is certified) that is presented for payment more than six months after its date. This type of check is commonly called a **stale check.**[30] However, if a bank acts in good faith, it can charge a customer's account for a check that is older than six months. Establishing that "good faith" is an uphill battle, so most banks will not cash a stale check unless and until it has verified such with its customer. Regardless of the date of the check, banks are always under an obligation to use good faith and commercial reasonableness in processing all checks.

---

[28] Right to Financial Privacy Act of 1978, 12 U.S.C. §3401 *et seq.*
[29] 12 U.S.C. §5311 *et seq.* 2001.
[30] U.C.C. §§3-304 and 4-404; *Commerce Bank, N.A. v. Rickett,* 748 A.2d 111 (N.J. Super. 2000).

Do not confuse the six-month stale check rule with the 90-days overdue instrument rule. The 90-day rule in Section 3-304 is the timing provision for an HDC to take a check in good faith and without notice that it is overdue. Ninety days is not the measurement for bank processing of a customer's check and six months is not the time limit for taking as an HDC. There are two separate time frames here for two different issues.

Payment after Depositor's Death. From the time of death, the bank can continue paying items until it actually knows of the customer's death.[31] The bank has the right, even with notice of the death, to continue to pay items for 10 days unless, for example, an heir or a government agency halts the payments.[32]

CPA

30-1f Stopping Payment of a Check

stop payment order— order by a depositor to the bank to refuse to make payment of a check when presented for payment.

A drawer may stop payment of a check by notifying the drawee bank in the required manner.[33] **Stop payment orders** are often used when a check is lost or mislaid. The drawer can always write a duplicate check but wants assurance that the original lost or misplaced check will not then also be presented for payment. The drawer can stop payment on the first check to prevent double-dipping. A drawer can also use a stop payment order on a check if the payee has not kept his end of the contract or has failed to provide assurances (see Chapter 25). However, the drawer must keep in mind that if a holder in due course has the check, the holder in due course can demand payment because she would not be subject to the personal defenses of breach of contract or nonperformance of contract. (See Chapter 29 and the rights of holders in due course.)

Stop payment orders are invalid for some forms of checks even when properly executed. Neither the drawer nor a bank customer can stop payment of a **certified check.** A bank customer cannot stop payment of a cashier's check.

CPA

Form of Stop Payment Order

certified check—check for which the bank has set aside in a special account sufficient funds to pay it; payment is made when check is presented regardless of amount in drawer's account at that time; discharges all parties except certifying bank when holder requests certification.

The stop payment order may be either oral or by record (written or evidence of electronic order). If oral, however, the order is binding on the bank for only 14 calendar days unless confirmed in writing within that time. A record of the stop payment order or confirmation is effective for six months. A stop payment order can be renewed for an additional six months if the customer provides the bank a written extension.

Liability to Holder for Stopping Payment

The act of stopping payment may in some cases make the drawer liable to the holder of the check. If the drawer has no proper ground for stopping payment, the drawer is liable to the holder of the check. In any case, the drawer is liable for stopping payment with respect to any holder in due course or any other party having the rights of a holder in due course unless payment was stopped for a reason that may be asserted as a defense against a holder in due course (see Chapter 29). The fact that payment of a check has been stopped does not affect its negotiable character.[34]

30-1g Wrongful Dishonor of a Check

wrongfully dishonored— error by a bank in refusing to pay a check.

A check is **wrongfully dishonored** by the drawee bank if the bank refuses to pay the amount of the check although (1) it is properly payable and (2) the account on which it is drawn is sufficient to pay the item. Dishonor for lack of funds can be a breach of contract if the customer has an agreement with the bank that it will pay overdraft items.

---

[31] U.C.C. §4-405(2).
[32] U.C.C. §4-405(b); *Hieber v. Uptown Nat'l Bank of Chicago*, 557 N.E.2d 408 (Ill. App. 1990).
[33] U.C.C. §4-403.
[34] *Aliaga Medical Center, S.C. v. Harris Bank N.A.*, 21 N.E.3d 1203 (Ill. App. 2014).

C P A

Bank's Liability to Drawer of Check

If the bank improperly refuses to make payment, it is liable to the drawer for damages sustained by the drawer as a consequence of such dishonor.

Bank's Liability to Holder

If a check has not been certified, the holder has no claim against the bank for the dishonor of the check regardless of the fact that the bank was wrong in its dishonor. The bank that certifies a check is liable to the holder when it dishonors the check.

Holder's Notice of Dishonor of Check

When a check is dishonored by nonpayment, the holder must follow the procedure for notice to the secondary parties. Notice of dishonor need not be given to the drawer who has stopped payment on a check or to drawers and indorsers who are aware that there are insufficient funds on deposit to cover the check. In those circumstances, no party has reason to expect that the check will be paid by the bank.

30-1h Agency Status of Collecting Bank

When a customer deposits negotiable instruments in a bank, the bank is regarded as being merely an **agent,** even though the customer may be given the right to make immediate withdrawals against the deposited item. Because of the bank's **agency** status, the customer remains the owner of the item and is subject to the risks of ownership involved in its collection.

When a bank cashes a check deposited by its customer or cashes a check drawn by its customer based on an amount from a deposited check, it is a holder of the check deposited by its customer. The bank may still collect from the parties on the check even though the bank is an agent for collection and has the right to charge back the amount of the deposited check if it cannot be collected.

30-1i Bank's Duty of Care

A bank is required to exercise ordinary care in the handling of items. The liability of a bank is determined by the law of the state where the bank, branch, or separate office involved is located.

C P A

Modification of Bank Duties

The parties in the bank collection process may modify their rights and duties by agreement. However, a bank cannot disclaim liability for lack of good faith or failure to exercise ordinary care, nor can it limit the measure of damages for such lack of care.

When a bank handles checks by automated processes, the bank must use the ordinary standard of care of the industry and that standard of ordinary care does not require the bank to make a physical examination of each item.

Encoding Warranty and Electronic Presentment

In addition to transfer and presentment warranties, an **encoding warranty** is also given by those who transfer instruments. Under this warranty, anyone placing information on an item or transmitting the information electronically warrants that the information is correct. When there is an agreement for electronic presentment, the presenter warrants that the transfer is made properly for transmissions.[35]

agent–person or firm who is authorized by the principal or by operation of law to make contracts with third persons on behalf of the principal.

agency–the relationship that exists between a person identified as a principal and another by virtue of which the latter may make contracts with third persons on behalf of the principal. (Parties–principal, agent, third person)

encoding warranty–warranty made by any party who encodes electronic information on an instrument; a warranty of accuracy.

[35] U.C.C. §§4-207 to 4-209.

Counterfeit Checks

One of the problems that banks now experience is the use of counterfeit checks. Because of automated processing, these checks can sail through bank systems and seemingly are cleared. Customers, in reliance on the check clearing, use those funds only to be told later that the check was a counterfeit and the funds credited to their account are then debited. The liability for the losses resulting from counterfeit checks will depend on whether the bank acted reasonably in its processing systems in clearing checks (particularly those for large amounts) and whether it complied with the time requirements for notifying customers of a dishonor of a deposited counterfeit check.

CASE SUMMARY

The Lawyers Who Got Taken by Their Counterfeit Clients

FACTS: Greenberg, Trager & Herbst, LLP (GTH), is a law firm specializing in construction litigation law. In September 2007, a partner at GTH received an e-mail from a representative of Northlink Industrial Limited, a Hong Kong company. Northlink was looking for legal representation to assist it in the collection of debts owed by its North American customers. Through a series of e-mails GTH agreed to represent Northlink and requested a $10,000 retainer. GTH then received a Citibank check for $197,750 from a Northlink customer and was told that it could take its retainer from those funds. On Friday, September 21, 2007, GTH deposited the check into its account at HSBC.

The next business day, Monday, September 24, HSBC processed the check through the Federal Reserve Bank of Philadelphia (FRBP) and, because of the federal funds availability law, provisionally credited GTH's account for $197,750. FRBP presented an image replacement document (IRD) of the check to Citibank that same day.

Because the routing number was not recognized by Citi's processing system, the automated sorting system directed the IRD to the reject pocket.

HSBC received the IRD with the notation "sent wrong" the next day, September 25, 2007. Because the check was marked "sent wrong," HSBC assumed that there was a problem with the routing number that required sending the check to a different Federal Reserve bank. On September 26, 2007, HSBC sent the check to the Federal Reserve Bank, San Francisco (FRBS). HSBC never informed GTH of the "administrative return" of the check.

On September 27, 2007, a GTH partner called HSBC to determine whether the check had "cleared" and if the funds were available for disbursement. GTH was informed that the funds were available. Later that day, GTH wired $187,750 from its account to Hong Kong as Northlink instructed.

On October 2, 2007, HSBC received Citibank's notice that the check was being dishonored as "RTM [return to maker] Suspect Counterfeit." HSBC contacted GTH to inform them that the check had been dishonored. HSBC then revoked its provisional settlement and charged back GTH's account.

GTH filed suit against HSBC and Citibank for failure to inform GTH that the check had been returned and dishonored on September 25 and for informing GTH over the phone that the funds had "cleared" and were available for disbursement. HSBC and Citibank moved for summary judgment.

The trial court found that HSBC had no duty under the UCC to inform GTH that the check had been returned "sent wrong" on September 25, but rather that the dishonor actually took place when HSBC discovered that the check was "Suspect Counterfeit," and dismissed the complaint.

DECISION: The bank did not owe duty to GTH to have effective procedures in place to detect counterfeit checks. The bank is only required to present the check for payment to the drawee bank, and the drawee bank and its customer are charged with the duty of monitoring properly payable items. The bank's alleged oral statement that the check had "cleared" and the funds were available for transfer was not a misrepresentation because banking rules do not allow reliance on oral representations. A check is not cleared until it actually goes through the banking system. The bank exercised ordinary care in handling the check and did not breach any duty to GTH and its alleged oral representations could not be a basis for GTH's reliance. [*Greenberg, Trager & Herbst, LLP v. HSBC Bank USA*, **934 N.Y.S.2d 43 75 U.C.C. Rep. Serv. 2d 775 (Sup. Ct. 2011)**]

CPA   **30-2   Liability of a Bank**

Banks can make mistakes in the payment and collection of items presented to them by their customers. **For Example,** a check may slip through and be cashed over a customer's properly executed stop payment order. The bank would be liable for this improper payment and may also be liable for improperly collecting, paying, or refusing to pay a check.

30-2a   Premature Payment of a Postdated Check

A check may be postdated, but the bank is not liable for making payments on the check before the date stated unless the drawer has given the bank prior notice. Such a notice is similar to a stop payment order; it must provide sufficient information so that the bank is moved to action by the trigger that comes from the orderly processing of the check as it flows through its electronic processing system.[36]

30-2b   Payment over a Stop Payment Order

A bank must be given a reasonable time in which to put a stop payment order into effect. However, if the bank makes payment of a check after it has been properly notified to stop payment, and there has been sufficient time for the order to be put into the system, the bank is liable to the drawer (customer) for the loss the drawer sustains in the absence of a valid limitation of the bank's liability.[37] The bank must have complete information on a stop payment order, such as the payee, check number, and amount, to be held responsible for the failure to stop payment.

CASE SUMMARY

When Writing "Stop" Is Not Enough to Halt a Check

FACTS: Aliaga Medical Center first opened a business checking account with Harris Bank in December 2003. Upon opening the account, Aliaga acknowledged that it received the "Harris Bank Handbook for Personal and Business Deposit Accounts." The first page of the handbook included the statement that the customer "agree[s] to the terms of this Agreement when [Aliaga] sign[s] [Harris Bank's] account opening form or signature card, make[s] deposits or withdrawals, or leave[s] funds on deposit."

The handbook also required that if Aliaga wanted to stop payment on a check it had written, the following requirements would apply:

> *If you do not want us to pay a check you have written, you can order us to stop payment. Your stop payment order must include your account number, the number and date of the check, the name of the payee, and the amount. We must receive*

your stop payment order before our stop payment cut-off time, which is 10 a.m. Central Time (C.T.) on the next Business Day after the check is presented to us for payment. We will accept a stop payment order from any account owner regardless of who signed the check. Your stop payment order will be effective for six months. If you want the stop payment order to continue after six months, you must renew it.

Under the agreement, Harris Bank specifically "reserve[d] [its] right to pay * * * a stale check."

The agreement contained a number of other relevant notification provisions, including notice provisions that required customers to notify the Bank of any issues or problems with its account within 60 days of receiving a statement and that suit must be filed within one year of receiving the statement.

---

[36] Note that a "postdated check" is not a check but a time draft. U.C.C. §§4401 to 4-402.
[37] U.C.C. §4-403(c); *Lombino v. Bank of America, N.A.,* 797 F. Supp. 2d 1078 (D. Nev. 2011).

When Writing "Stop" Is Not Enough to Halt a Check continued

On July 10, 2010, Dr. Federico Aliaga, the plaintiff's president, issued a check in the amount of $50,000 (the check), payable to his wife, whom he was divorcing. The face of the check included the statement "void after 90 days" immediately above the signature line. Harris Bank honored the check on December 30, 2010. Aliaga never placed a stop payment order on the check, and, in fact, never communicated with Harris about the check anytime between July 10, 2010, and December 30, 2010.

In January 2011, Harris Bank sent and made available to Aliaga its December 2010 checking account statement, which showed that Harris Bank had honored the check on December 30, 2010. Aliaga, however, did not notify Harris Bank of the improper check payment within the 60-day notification period delineated in the parties' agreement. Additionally, Aliaga did not initiate this lawsuit within one year of the date Harris Bank sent or made available the December 2010 statement. Instead, Aliaga waited until October or November 2012, nearly two years after the December 2010 statement was made available, before disputing the check with Harris.

Harris moved to dismiss the complaint. The trial court granted the motion, and Aliaga appealed.

DECISION: Harris had the right to pay the check despite the "void after 90 days" language because Aliaga failed to properly stop payment of the check. Under the parties' agreement, if Aliaga did not want Harris Bank to pay a check it had written, then Aliaga had to comply with certain requirements.

Aliaga claims that under a UCC provision (810 ILCS 5/4–403(a) (West 2012)), it was only required to stop payment "in a time and manner that gives the bank a reasonable opportunity to comply" and that its notation on the check "certainly achieves this." However, Aliaga's contention is without merit for several reasons. First, the UCC permits that "[t]he effect of [its] provisions * * * may be varied by agreement."

Furthermore, even if Aliaga is correct that the stop payment provision of the agreement was neither exclusive nor meant to override the UCC, the "void" notation was ineffective because it did not comply with section 4–403(a) of the UCC by providing notice "at a time and in a manner that affords the bank a reasonable opportunity to act on it."

Aliaga also failed to comply with its obligation to timely notify Harris Bank of the alleged unauthorized payment of the check within 60 days after Harris Bank made Aliaga's December 2010 statement available to it.

Aliaga admitted that it did not comply with these terms of the agreement by providing timely notice to Harris Bank within 60 days of the date that it sent, or otherwise made available to Aliaga, the December 2010 statement. Aliaga further conceded that it did not contact Harris Bank about the payment within 60 days of receiving the December 2010 statement. As a result, Aliaga's claim is untimely.

Finally, Aliaga failed to timely commence this lawsuit within one year from the date that Harris Bank sent or made available the December 2010 statement.

Affirmed. [***Aliaga Medical Center, S.C. v. Harris Bank N.A.***, **21 N.E.3d 1203 (Ill. App. 2014)**]

CPA   30-2c   ## Payment on a Forged Signature of Drawer

A forgery of the signature of the drawer occurs when the name of the drawer has been signed by another person without authority to do so with the intent to defraud by making it appear that the drawer signed the check. The bank is liable to the drawer if it pays a check on which the drawer's signature has been forged because a forgery ordinarily has no effect as a signature. The risk of loss caused by the forged signature of the drawer is placed on the bank without regard to whether the bank could have detected the forgery.[38] The reasoning behind the bank's liability for a forged drawer's signature is that the bank is presumed to know its own customers' signatures even if it does not regularly review checks for authenticity of the signature.

A bank's customer whose signature has been forged may be barred from holding the bank liable if the customer's negligence substantially contributed to the making of the forgery. This preclusion rule prevents or precludes the customer from making a forgery

---

[38] *Du v. Bank of America, N.A.* Not Reported in N.E.2d, 30 Mass. L. Rptr. 337, 2012 WL 5362292 (Mass. Super. 2012). Some states allow for an action for conversion of funds by the customer. *300 Broadway Healthcare Center, LLC v. Wachovia Bank, N.A.*, 39 A.3d 248 (N.J. App. 2012), but see *DMDB Adults, Inc. v. Bank of America Corp.*, 951 N.Y.S.2d 492 (N.Y.A.D. 2012).

claim against the bank. However, to enjoy the protection of the preclusion rule, the bank, if negligent in its failure to detect the forgery or alteration, must have cashed the check in good faith or have taken it for value or collection.[39]

Article 4 of the UCC extends forgery protections and rights to alterations and unauthorized signings. When an officer with authority limited to signing $5,000 checks signs a check for $7,500, the signature is unauthorized. If the principal for the drawer account is an organization and has a requirement that two or more designated persons sign negotiable instruments on its behalf, signatures by fewer than the specified number are also classified as unauthorized signatures.

CPA   ## 30-2d Payment on a Forged or Missing Indorsement

A drawee bank that honors a customer's check bearing a forged indorsement must recredit the customer's account upon the drawer's discovery of the forgery and notification to the bank. A drawee bank is liable for the loss when it pays a check that lacks an essential indorsement.[40] In such a case, the instrument is not properly payable. Without proper indorsements for an order instrument and special indorsements, the person presenting the check for payment is not the holder of the instrument and is not entitled to demand or receive payment. However, the bank can then turn to the indorsers and transferors of the instrument for breach of warranty liability in that all signatures were not genuine or authorized and they did not have title. All transferors can turn to their previous transferor until liability ultimately rests with the party who first accepted the forged indorsement. This party had face-to-face contact and could have verified signatures.[41]

When a customer deposits a check but does not indorse it, the customer's bank may make an indorsement on behalf of the depositor unless the check expressly requires the customer's indorsement. A bank cannot add the missing indorsement of a person who is not its customer when an item payable is deposited in a customer's bank account.

30-2e Alteration of a Check

If the face of a check has been altered so that the amount to be paid has been increased, the bank is liable to the drawer for the amount of the increase when it makes payment of the greater amount.

The drawer may be barred from claiming that there was an alteration if there was negligence in writing the check or reporting its alteration. A drawer is barred from claiming alteration if the check was written negligently, the negligence substantially contributed to the making of the material alteration, and the bank honored the check in good faith and observed reasonable commercial standards in doing so. **For Example,** the drawer is barred from claiming alteration when the check was written with blank spaces that readily permitted a change of "four" to "four hundred" and the drawee bank paid out the latter sum because the alteration was not obvious. A careful drawer will write figures and words close together and run a line through or cross out any blank spaces.

30-2f Unauthorized Collection of a Check

A collecting bank, or a bank simply collecting an item for a customer, is protected from liability when it follows its customer's instructions. It is not required to inquire or verify

---

[39] U.C.C. §4-406(e); *Citizens Bank of Pennsylvania v. Reimbursement Technologies, Inc.,* 2014 WL 2738220 (E.D. Pa. 2014); *Rodgeres v. Bank of America, N.A.,* 73 U.C.C. Rep. Serv. 2d 47 (S.D. Ill. 2011).

[40] *Simi Management Corp. v. Bank of America, N.A.,* 930 F. Supp. 2d 1082 (N.D. Cal. 2013); *VIP Mortg. Corp. v. Bank of America, N.A.,* 769 F. Supp. 2d 20 (D. Mass. 2011).

[41] *Smith v. Farmers Union Mut. Ins. Co.,* 260 P.3d 163 (Mont. 2011).

that the customer had the authority to give such instructions. In contrast, instructions do not protect a payor bank. It has an absolute duty to make proper payment. If it does not do so, it is liable unless it is protected by estoppel or by the preclusion rule. The person giving wrongful instructions is liable for the loss caused by those instructions.

CASE SUMMARY

The Devil Shops at Neiman Marcus Using Her Boss's Checks

FACTS: Carol Young was employed as Brian P. Burns's secretary at a salary that never exceeded $75,000. Between 1995 and 2000, Young opened several credit card accounts with Neiman Marcus. In the three-year period prior to 2006, Young spent approximately $1 million at Neiman Marcus, and "the balance on [one] credit card, as of January 10, 2006, was in excess of $242,000." Young was offered entrée into Neiman Marcus's exclusive INCIRCLE® rewards program—a loyalty incentive program. Young had a personal shopper who knew of her annual salary of less than $75,000. However, the personal shopper repeatedly contacted and encouraged Young to make excessive purchases with her various Neiman Marcus cards.

Young would personally deliver on a regular basis fraudulent and forged checks drawn on Burns's Union Bank of California checking account to pay down her various [Neiman Marcus] credit card bills at the Customer Service Center in Neiman's San Francisco store. Young used three different methods for presenting Burns's checks: (a) stealing checks and forging Burns's signature; (b) stealing checks with no signature whatsoever; and (c) stealing checks with Burns's signature—checks that Burns presumed were for payments toward his own Neiman Marcus credit card account, but which were diverted to Young's credit card accounts.

Because Young managed all of Burns's accounts, the reconciliations she made had fake ledger entries for payment to third parties to cover her payments to Neiman Marcus. Burns did not detect Young's activities for three years because he did not see the bank statements, only Young did. A serendipitous examination of the ledger and canceled checks resulted in the discovery. Burns recovered what he could from his bank, an amount limited by UCC Article 4. Burns filed suit against Neiman Marcus, seeking to recover the funds paid on the checks and claiming that Neiman Marcus was subject to the defenses of forgery and unauthorized payments. The trial court granted Neiman Marcus's motion for demurrer and Burns appealed.

DECISION: The court affirmed the lower court's dismissal because it was unwilling to impose a broad duty on third parties to verify that every third-party check it receives is legitimate. Such a requirement would significantly slow down the flow and use of negotiable instruments and defeat both the purposes of Articles 3 and 4 as well as the well-defined rules for responsibility and liability when there are drawer and drawee forgeries. [***Burns v. Neiman Marcus Group, Inc.***, 173 Cal. App. 4th 479 (Cal. App. 1st Dist. 2009)]

30-2g Time Limitations

The liability of the bank to its depositor is subject to certain time limitations.

CPA   ### Forgery and Alteration Reporting Time

A customer must examine with reasonable care and promptness a bank statement and relevant checks that are paid in good faith and sent to the customer by the bank and must try to discover any unauthorized signature or alteration on the checks. The customer must notify the bank promptly after discovering either a forgery or an alteration. If the bank exercises ordinary care in paying a forged or an altered check and suffers a loss because the customer fails to discover and notify the bank of the forgery or alteration, the customer cannot assert the unauthorized signature or alteration against the bank.[42]

---

[42] *Crawford Supply Group, Inc. v. Bank of America, N.A.,* 2011 WL 1131292 (N.D. Ill. 2011).

Under the Check Truncation Act (CTA—which is part of the Check 21 statute covered in Chapter 27), banks now have the right to substitute electronic images of checks for customer billing statements. The CTA is largely implemented through Federal Reserve Board regulations found at 12 CFR §229.2. Banks do not need to provide the original check to their customers and can simply send copies of electronic images so long as the image provides enough clarity for the customer to see payee, encoding, indorsements, and so on.

With the use of substituted checks and online banking, consumers now have additional rights and time limits with substituted checks. Under the Check 21 statute, consumers have a new right to an expedited recredit to their account if a substitute check was charged improperly to their account. They have the right to see the original check if they can explain why it is necessary and that they are suffering a loss as a result of the improper charge of a substitute check to their account. Consumers have 40 calendar days from whichever of the following is later: (1) the delivery of their monthly bank statements or (2) that date on which the substitute check was made available to them for examination and/or review. If a consumer has been traveling or has been ill, the rules permit the extension of the deadline to challenge a substitute check. Consumers can even call their bank and challenge a payment, but they will not then get the benefit of all the rights and protections under Check 21 and its regulations if they choose to proceed without a written demand on a substitute check.[43] Once the demand is made, the bank must either recredit the consumer's account within one business day or explain why it believes the substitute check was charged properly to the consumer's account. The oral demand does not start this clock running for the consumer's protection. There are also fines and overdraft protections provided while the substitute check issue is in the dispute/investigation stage.

Some cases of forgery are the result of a customer's lack of care, such as when an employee is given too much authority and internal controls are lacking with the result that the employee is able to forge checks on a regular basis not easily detected by the bank. Referred to as the *fictitious payee and impostor exceptions*, this issue was covered in Chapter 28.

Customers are precluded from asserting unauthorized signatures or alterations if they do not report them within one year from the time the bank statement is received.[44] A forged indorsement must be reported within three years.

Unauthorized Signature or Alteration by Same Wrongdoer

If there is a series of improperly paid items and the same wrongdoer is involved, the customer is protected only as to those items that were paid by the bank before it received notification from the customer and during that reasonable amount of time that the customer has to examine items or statements and to notify the bank. If the customer failed to exercise reasonable promptness and failed to notify the bank but the customer can show that the bank failed to exercise ordinary care in paying the items, the loss will be allocated between the customer and the bank.[45]

Statute of Limitations

An action to enforce a liability imposed by Article 4 must be commenced within three years after the cause of action accrued.

---

[43] 12 C.F.R. 229.54(b)(1)(iii).
[44] U.C.C. §4-406.
[45] U.C.C. §4-406 (2012); *HH Computer Systems, Inc. v. Pacific City Bank*, 179 Cal. Rptr. 689 (Cal. App. 2014).

THINKING THINGS THROUGH

The Business Law Professor with the Lost Cashier's Check

Marianne Jennings obtained a cashier's check in order to pay off her car loan in the amount of $37,000. Professor Jennings mailed the cashier's check via Express Mail, requiring signature. An employee at the lender (an automaker financial arm) received the check and felt that because it did not have the signature of "Marianne Jennings" on it that it was invalid. The employee sent the check back to Professor Jennings via regular U.S. mail.

Professor Jennings, having received proof of receipt on the check, did not make her next car payment. She then received a notice of an overdue payment, a penalty for late payment, and that her late payment had been reported to the credit bureau.

Professor Jennings contacted the lender and was told that the check had been returned, and the late penalty would stand. Professor Jennings then went to the bank to discuss options. The bank indicated that it could issue a stop payment order if Professor Jennings would pay for a bond in the amount of $37,000, which would run about $1,200. The bank indicated that it could not issue a stop payment and that the cashier's check had been properly issued.

Discuss for Professor Jennings her rights in this situation, including any possible solutions to the situation. The cashier's check was never found. Also, be sure to discuss liability issues regarding the late payment, penalties, and effect on her credit rating.

30-3 Consumer Funds Transfers

Consumers are using electronic methods of payment at an increasing rate. From the swipe of the card at the grocery store checkout to the retrieval of funds from the local automated teller machine, *electronic funds transfers* represent a way of life for many consumers. A federal statute protects consumers making electronic funds transfers.

30-3a Electronic Funds Transfer Act

Electronic Funds Transfer Act (EFTA)– federal law that provides consumers with rights and protections in electronic funds transfers.

Congress passed the **Electronic Funds Transfer Act (EFTA)** to protect consumers making electronic transfers of funds.[46] **Electronic funds transfer (EFT)** means any transfer of funds (other than a transaction originated by check, draft, or similar paper instrument) that is initiated through an electronic terminal, a telephone, a computer, or a magnetic tape that authorizes a financial institution to debit or credit an account. The service available from an automated teller machine is a common form of EFT.[47]

electronic funds transfer (EFT)–any transfer of funds (other than a transaction originated by a check, draft, or similar paper instrument) that is initiated through an electronic terminal, a telephone, a computer, or a magnetic tape so as to authorize a financial institution to debit or credit an account.

30-3b Types of Electronic Funds Transfer Systems

Currently, five common types of EFT systems are in use. In some of these systems, the consumer has a card to access a machine. The consumer usually has a private code that prevents others who wrongfully obtain the card from using it.

Automated Teller Machine

The *automated teller machine (ATM)* performs many of the tasks once performed exclusively by bank employees. Once a user activates an ATM, he can deposit and withdraw funds from his account, transfer funds between accounts, make payments on loan accounts, and obtain cash advances from bank credit cards.

---

[46] 15 U.S.C. §1693 *et seq.*
[47] The majority of the states have adopted the 1990 version of Article 4A.

Pay-by-Phone System

This system facilitates paying telephone, mortgage, utility, and other bills without writing checks. The consumer calls the bank and directs the transfer of funds to a designated third party.

Direct Deposit and Withdrawal

Employees may authorize their employers to deposit wages directly to their accounts. A consumer who has just purchased an automobile on credit may elect to have monthly payments withdrawn from a bank account to be paid directly to the seller.

Point-of-Sale Terminal

The *point-of-sale terminal* allows a business with such a terminal to transfer funds from a consumer's account to the store's account. The consumer must be furnished in advance with the terms and conditions of all EFT services and must be given periodic statements covering account activity. Any automatic EFT from an individual's account must be authorized in writing in advance.

Financial institutions are liable to consumers for all damages proximately caused by the failure to make an EFT in accordance with the terms and conditions of an account. Exceptions include insufficient funds, funds subject to legal process, exceeding an established credit limit, or insufficient cash is available in an ATM.

Internet Banking

Internet banking is the customer use of computer access to bank systems to pay bills, balance accounts, transfer funds, and even obtain loans. Increasing in popularity, this form of banking still suffers from concerns about privacy and security. However, the revisions to Articles 3 and 4 recognize electronic records as valid proof of payment.

CPA   ## 30-3c Consumer Liability

A consumer who notifies the issuer of an EFT card within two days after learning of a loss or theft of the card can be held to a maximum liability of $50 for unauthorized use of the card. If you report the loss before the card is used, you have no liability. Failure to notify within this time (after 2 days but before 60 days) will increase the consumer's liability for losses to a maximum of $500. After 60 days, you have unlimited liability. However, by the end of 60 days, you will have been through at least two monthly statements and will have had every opportunity to provide notification. Consumers have the responsibility to examine periodic statements provided by their financial institution.

CPA   # 30-4 Funds Transfers

The funds transfers made by businesses are governed by the UCC and Federal Reserve regulations.

30-4a What Law Governs?

In states that have adopted Article 4A of the Uniform Commercial Code, that article governs funds transfers. In addition, whenever a Federal Reserve Bank is involved, the provisions of Article 4A apply by virtue of Federal Reserve regulations.

30-4b **Characteristics of Funds Transfers**

The transfers regulated by Article 4A are characteristically made between highly sophisticated parties dealing with large sums of money. Speed of transfer is often an essential ingredient. An individual transfer may involve many millions of dollars, and the national total of such transfers on a business day can amount to trillions of dollars.

30-4c **Pattern of Funds Transfers**

In the simplest form of funds transfer, both the debtor and the creditor have separate accounts in the same bank.[48] In this situation, the debtor can instruct the bank to pay the creditor a specified sum of money by subtracting that amount from the debtor's account and adding it to the creditor's account. As a practical matter, the debtor merely instructs the bank to make the transfer.

A more complex situation is involved if each party has an account in a different bank. In that case, the funds transfer could involve only these two banks and no clearinghouse. The buyer can instruct the buyer's bank to direct the seller's bank to make payment to the seller. There is direct communication between the two banks. In a more complex situation, the buyer's bank may relay the payment order to another bank, called an **intermediary bank,** and that bank, in turn, transmits the payment order to the seller's bank. Such transactions become even more complex when two or more intermediary banks or a clearinghouse is involved.

> **intermediary bank**–bank between the originator and the beneficiary bank in the transfer of funds.

30-4d **Scope of UCC Article 4A**

Article 4A applies to all funds transfers except as expressly excluded because of their nature or because of the parties involved.

EFTA and Consumer Transactions

Article 4A does not apply to consumer transaction payments to which the EFTA applies. If any part of the funds transfer is subject to the EFTA, the entire transfer is expressly excluded from the scope of UCC Article 4A.[49]

Credit and Debit Transfers

When the person making payment, such as the buyer, requests that payment be made to the beneficiary's bank, the transaction is called a **credit transfer.** If the beneficiary entitled to money goes to the bank according to a prior agreement and requests payment, the transaction is called a **debit transfer.** The latter transfer type is not regulated by Article 4A. Article 4A applies only to transfers begun by the person authorizing payment to another.

> **credit transfer**–transaction in which a person making payment, such as a buyer, requests payment be made to the beneficiary's bank.

> **debit transfer**–transaction in which a beneficiary entitled to money requests payment from a bank according to a prior agreement.

30-4e **Definitions**

Article 4A employs terms that are peculiar to that article or are used in a very different context from the contexts in which they appear elsewhere.

---

[48] The text refers to *debtor* and *creditor* in the interest of simplicity and because that situation is the most common in the business world. However, a gift may be made by a funds transfer. Likewise, a person having separate accounts in two different banks may transfer funds from one bank to another.

[49] U.C.C. §4A-108. This exclusion applies when any part of the transaction is subject to Regulation E adopted under the authority of that statute.

Funds Transfer

A **funds transfer** is more accurately described as a communication of instructions or a request to pay a specific sum of money to, or to the credit of, a specified account or person. There is no actual physical transfer or passing of money.

Originator

The person starting the funds transfer is called the **originator** of the funds transfer.[50]

Beneficiary

The **beneficiary** is the ultimate recipient of the benefit of the funds transfer. Whether the recipient is the beneficiary personally, an account owned by the beneficiary, or a third person to whom the beneficiary owes money is determined by the payment order.

Beneficiary's Bank

The **beneficiary's bank** is the final bank in the chain of transfer that carries out the transfer by making payment or application as directed by the payment order.

Payment Order

The **payment order** is the direction the originator gives to the originator's bank or by any bank to a subsequent bank to make the specified funds transfer. Although called a *payment order*, it is in fact a request. No bank is required or obligated to accept a payment order unless it is so bound by a contract or a clearinghouse rule that operates independently of Article 4A.

30-4f Manner of Transmitting Payment Order

Article 4A makes no provisions for the manner of transmitting a payment order. As a practical matter, most funds transfers under Article 4A are controlled by computers, and payment orders are electronically transmitted. Article 4A, however, applies to any funds transfer payment order even if made orally, such as by telephone, or in writing. Also, the agreement of the parties or the clearinghouse and funds transfer system rules may impose some restrictions on the methods for communicating orders.

30-4g Regulation by Agreement and Funds Transfer System Rules

Article 4A, with minor limitations, permits the parties to make agreements that modify or change the provisions of Article 4A that would otherwise govern. Likewise, the rules of a clearinghouse or a funds transfer system through which the banks operate may change the provisions of the Code.

Choice of Law

When the parties enter into an agreement for a funds transfer, they may designate the law that is to apply in interpreting the agreement.

[50] U.C.C. §4A-201.

Clearinghouse Rules

The banks involved in a particular funds transfer may be members of the same clearinghouse. In such a case, they will be bound by the lawful rules and regulations of the house.

The rights of the parties involved in a funds transfer may be determined by the rules of FedWire, a clearinghouse system operated by the Federal Reserve System, or by CHIPS, which is a similar system operated by the New York clearinghouse.

30-4h Reimbursement of the Bank

After the beneficiary's bank accepts the payment order, it and every bank ahead of it in the funds transfer chain is entitled to reimbursement of the amount paid to or for the beneficiary. This reimbursement is due from the preceding bank. By going back along the funds transfer chain, the originator's bank, and ultimately the originator, makes payment of this reimbursement amount.

30-4i Error in Funds Transfer

There may be an error in a payment order. The effect of an error depends on its nature.

Type of Error

The error in a payment order may consist of a wrong identification or a wrong amount.

Wrong Beneficiary or Account Number. The payment order received by the beneficiary's bank may contain an error in the designation of the beneficiary or in the account number. This error may result in payment being made to or for the wrong person or account.

Excessive Amount. The payment order may call for the payment of an amount that is larger than it should be. For example, the order may wrongly add an additional zero to the specified amount.

Duplicating Amount. The payment order may be issued after a similar payment order has already been transferred, so that the second order duplicates the first. This duplication would result in doubling the proper amount paid by the beneficiary's bank.

Underpayment. The payment order may call for the payment of a smaller sum than was ordered. For example, the order may drop off one of the zeros from the amount ordered by the originator.

Effect of Error

When the error falls under one of the first three classes just discussed, the bank committing the error bears the loss because it caused the item to be wrongfully paid. In contrast, when the error is merely underpayment, the bank making the mistake can cure the fault by making a supplementary order for the amount of the underpayment. If verification by the agreed-upon security procedure would disclose an error in the payment order, a bank is liable for any loss caused by the error if it failed to verify the payment order by such a procedure. In contrast, if the security procedure followed did not reveal any error, there is no liability for accepting the payment order.

When an error of any kind is made, there may be liability under a collateral agreement of the parties, a clearinghouse or funds transfer system rule, or general principles of contract law. However, these rights may be lost in certain cases by failure to notify the involved bank that the mistake has been made.

30-4j Liability for Loss

Unless otherwise regulated by agreement or clearinghouse rule, banks have little or no liability in the funds transfer chain if they have followed the agreed-upon security procedure.

Unauthorized Order

If a bank executes or accepts an unauthorized payment order, it is liable to any prior party in the transfer chain for the loss caused. If a bank acts on the basis of an unauthorized order that nevertheless is verified by the security procedure, the bank is not liable for the loss that is caused.

Failure to Act

A bank that fails to carry out a payment order is usually liable, at the most, for interest loss and expenses. There is no liability for the loss sustained by the originator or for consequential damages suffered because payment was not made to satisfy the originator's obligation to the beneficiary.

Make the Connection

Summary

A *check* is a particular kind of draft; it is drawn on a bank and is payable on demand. A delivery of a check is not an assignment of money on deposit with the bank on which it is drawn. A check does not automatically transfer the rights of the depositor against the bank to the holder of the check, and there is no duty on the part of the drawee bank to the holder to pay the holder the amount of the check.

A check may be an *ordinary check*, a *cashier's check*, or a *teller's check*. The name on the paper is not controlling. Unless otherwise agreed, the delivery of a certified check, a cashier's check, or a teller's check discharges the debt for which it is given, up to the amount of the check.

Certification of a check by the bank is the acceptance of the check—the bank becomes the primary party. Certification may be at the request of the drawee or the holder. Certification by the holder releases all prior indorsers and the drawer from liability.

Notice of nonpayment of a check must be given to the drawer of a check. If no notice is given, the drawer is discharged from liability to the same extent as the drawer of an ordinary draft.

A depositor may stop payment on a check. However, the depositor is liable to a holder in due course unless the stop payment order was for a reason that may be raised against a holder in due course. The stop payment order may be made orally (binding for 14 calendar days) or with a record (effective for six months).

The depository bank is the agent of the depositor for the purpose of collecting a deposited item. The bank may become liable when it pays a check contrary to a stop payment order or when there has been a forgery or an alteration. The bank is not liable, however, if the drawer's negligence has substantially contributed to the forgery. A bank that pays on a forged instrument must recredit the drawer's account. A depositor is subject to certain time limitations to enforce liability of the bank. Banks are subject to reporting requirements under the USA Patriot Act.

A customer and a bank may agree that the bank should retain canceled checks and simply provide the customer with a list of paid items. The customer must examine canceled checks (or their electronic images) or paid items to see whether any were improperly paid.

An *electronic funds transfer (EFT)* is a transfer of funds (other than a transaction originated by check, draft, or other commercial paper) that is initiated through an electronic terminal, a telephone, a computer, or a magnetic tape to authorize a financial institution to debit or credit an account. The Electronic Funds Transfer Act requires that a financial institution furnish consumers with specific information containing all the terms and conditions of all EFT services. Under certain conditions, the financial institution will bear the loss for unauthorized transfers. Under other circumstances, the consumer will bear the loss.

Funds transfers regulated by UCC Article 4A are those made between highly sophisticated parties that deal with large sums of money. If any part of the funds transfer is subject to the EFTA, such as consumer transactions, the entire transfer is expressly excluded from the scope of Article 4A. A funds transfer is simply a request or an instruction to pay a specific sum of money to, or to the credit of, a specified person.

Learning Outcomes

After studying this chapter, you should be able to clearly explain:

30-1   Checks

LO.1 List and explain the duties of the drawee bank
See the discussion of duties and Ethics & the Law on overdrafts, pages 579, 582–583.

LO.2 Explain the methods for, and legal effect of stopping payment
See Thinking Things Through, "The Business Law Professor with the Lost Cashier's Check," page 589. See the Ethics & the Law on overdraft fees, page 580.

30-2   Liability of a Bank

LO.3 Describe the liability of a bank for improper payment and collection
See the *State Bank v. Smith* case for a discussion of liability related to cashier's checks, pages 576–577. See the E-Commerce & Cyberlaw feature on the Nigerian e-mails, page 577.

See the Ethics & the Law feature for a discussion of overdraft fees issues, page 580.
See the *Aliaga Medical Center S.C. v. Harris Bank N.A.* case for a discussion on 90-day limits on cashing checks, pages 584–585.

LO.4 Discuss the legal effect of forgeries and material alterations
See the *Greenberg, Trager & Herbst v. HSBC Bank USA* case, page 583.

LO.5 Specify the time limitations for reporting forgeries and alterations
See the *Burns v. Neiman Marcus* case, page 587.

30-3   Consumer Funds Transfers

See the EFTA discussion, page 589.

30-4   Funds Transfers

LO.6 Describe the electronic transfer of funds and laws governing it
See the discussion of Article 4A, page 591.

Key Terms

agency
agent
bad check laws
beneficiary
beneficiary's bank
cashier's check
certified check
check
credit transfer
debit transfer

demand draft
electronic funds transfer (EFT)
Electronic Funds Transfer Act
    (EFTA)
encoding warranty
funds transfer
intermediary bank
money order
originator
overdraft

payment order
postdated
presentment
stale check
stop payment orders
substitute check
teller's check
time draft
USA Patriot Act
wrongfully dishonored

Questions and Case Problems

1. William Elias was the former owner of Direct Lending, a subprime mortgage company purchased by EA Management. Sometime after the sale, Elias

went to Chase Bank and had three cashier's checks drawn to third parties and payable out of Direct Lending accounts in the amount of $191,251.31.

When the new owners of Direct Lending checked their account balances online, they discovered the withdrawal for the three cashier's checks. The treasurer went to the bank and stopped payment on all three cashier's checks. Elias brought suit against the bank for wrongful dishonor and consequential damages to his businesses as a result of the dishonor. Can Elias recover? Be sure to explain which Article 4 provisions apply and why. [*EA Management v. JP Morgan Chase, N.A.*, 655 F.3d 573 (6th Cir.)]

2. Helen was a very forgetful person, so she had placed her bank code (PIN number) on the back of her debit card. A thief stole Helen's card and was able to take $100 from an ATM on the day of the theft. That same day, Helen realized that the card was gone and phoned her bank. The following morning, the thief withdrew another $100. For how much, if anything, is Helen responsible? Why?

3. Adam Paul Strege (APS) opened a checking account at U.S. Bank. Just below his signature card for the account, he wrote, "Call if I bounce a check." APS bounced several checks, and each time U.S. Bank covered those checks but it did not notify APS of the bounced check status. The result was that APS continued to write checks and U.S. Bank had to request funds from him to cover the overdrafts in his account. APS refused to pay the amount due because he argued that U.S. Bank had breached its agreement with him to report all bounced checks. Discuss whether U.S. Bank had the obligation to notify APS of the bounced checks. [*APS v. U.S. Bank*, 2009 WL 4723311 (D. Minn.)]

4. Arthur Odgers died, and his widow, Elizabeth Odgers (Elizabeth Salsman by remarriage), retained Breslow as the attorney for her husband's estate. She received a check payable to her drawn on First National City Bank. Breslow told her to deposit it in her husband's estate. She signed an indorsement "Pay to the order of Estate of Arthur J. Odgers." Breslow deposited this check in his trustee account in National Community Bank, which collected the amount of the check from the drawee, First City National Bank. Thereafter, Elizabeth, as administratrix of the estate of Arthur J. Odgers, sued National Community Bank for collecting this check and crediting Breslow's trustee account with the proceeds. Was National Community Bank liable? Explain. [*Salsman v. National Community Bank*, 246 A.2d 162 (N.J. Super.)]

5. Shipper was ill for 14 months. His wife did not take care of his affairs carefully, nor did she examine his bank statements as they arrived each month. One of Shipper's acquaintances had forged his name to a check in favor of himself for $10,000. The drawee bank paid the check and charged Shipper's account. Shipper's wife did not notify the bank for 13 months after she received the statement and the forged check. Can she compel the bank to reverse the charge? Why or why not?

6. Ann Weldon maintained an account at Trust Company Bank. James Weldon, her son and a garment broker, purchased textile goods from Sportswear Services for resale to another corporation known as Thicket Textiles. Sportswear demanded certified funds from James Weldon before it would ship the goods. When James Weldon requested a certified check from Trust Company, Trust Company officer Sweat informed James that if it issued a certified check, payment could not be stopped even if the merchandise delivered was not as promised under the terms of the contract.

   Ann Weldon then obtained a $16,319.29 cashier's check drawn on her account and payable to Sportswear. James had deposited his funds into her account to cover the check. The check was delivered to Sportswear, and the goods were shipped the next day, but they were defective.

   Ann Weldon went to Trust Company Bank to issue a stop payment order, and the bank, believing that the check had not yet been delivered to Sportswear, did so for $25. James Weldon then notified Sportswear of the stop payment order. After Trust Company dishonored the cashier's check, Sportswear's bank was in contact with the bank and informed it that the check had already been delivered to Sportswear. Trust Company honored the check and credited Ann Weldon's account with the $25 stop payment fee. Ann filed suit because Trust Company did not stop payment. Should payment have been stopped? Why or why not? [*Weldon v. Trust Co. Bank of Columbus*, 499 S.E.2d 393 (Ga. App.)]

7. Gloria maintains a checking account at First Bank. On the third day of January, the bank sent her a statement of her account for December accompanied by the checks that the bank had paid. One of the checks had her forged signature, which Gloria discovered on the 25th of the month when she prepared a bank reconciliation. On discovering this, Gloria

immediately notified the bank. On January 21, the bank had paid another check forged by the same party who had forged the December item. Who must bear the loss on the forged January check?

8. Dean bought a car from Cannon. As payment, Dean gave him a check drawn on South Dorchester Bank of Eastern Shore Trust Co. Cannon cashed the check at the Cambridge Bank of Eastern Shore Trust Co. The drawee bank refused payment when the check was presented on the ground that Dean had stopped payment because of certain misrepresentations made by Cannon. Will Eastern Shore Trust Co. succeed in an action against Dean for payment? [*Dean v. Eastern Shore Trust Co.*, 150 A. 797 (Md.)]

9. John G. Vowell and his wife, now deceased, had a checking account and a savings/money-market account with Mercantile Bank of Arkansas. In June 1997, Dr. Vowell and his wife allowed their daughter, Suzan Vowell, now also deceased, and her boyfriend to move in with them at their home. At that time, they knew that Suzan and her boyfriend had been involved with drugs, alcohol, writing bad checks, and stealing. They also knew that Suzan had stolen checks from them in the past and forged either Dr. Vowell's or his wife's signatures. They took precautions by hiding Mrs. Vowell's purse, which contained their checkbook, under the kitchen sink.

Beginning in June 1997, Suzan forged Mrs. Vowell's signature on 42 checks, drawn on both accounts, and committed nine unauthorized ATM withdrawals in the aggregate amount of $12,028.75. Suzan found her mother's purse hidden under the kitchen sink and stole the checkbooks and ATM card from the purse. She apparently had access to the personal identification number (PIN) for the accounts because the number was identical to the home security system code.

The Vowells received the following statements from the bank for the checking and savings accounts:

Date of Transaction	Amount	Statement date covering
July 9, 1997	$230.00	June 6–July 7, 1997
August 8, 1997	$1,235.25	July 8–August 6, 1997
August 23, 1997	$5,140.00	July 23–Aug 21, 1997
September 9, 1997	$1,423.50	Aug 7–Sept 7, 1997
September 26, 1997	$4,000.00	Aug 22–Sept 22, 1997

On September 15, 1997, Dr. Vowell had Mercantile freeze their accounts and begin investigating the alleged forgeries and other unauthorized transactions pursuant to its policy. Suzan was arrested subsequently when she tried to use the ATM card again.

The bank refused to credit the Vowells' account because it maintained that their negligence in handling their daughter caused the losses. The court found that the bank was liable for only $6,014.38, one-half of the entire sum of Suzan Vowell's unauthorized bank transactions and forgeries. The bank appealed. Can the Vowells recover? How much and why? [*Mercantile Bank of Arkansas v. Vowell*, 117 S.W.3d 603 (Ark. App.)]

10. Bogash drew a check on National Safety Bank and Trust Co. payable to the order of Fiss Corp. At the request of Fiss Corp., the bank certified the check. The bank later refused to make payment on the check because of a dispute between Bogash and the corporation over the amount due the corporation. Fiss sued the bank on the check. Can Fiss recover? [*Fiss Corp. v. National Safety Bank and Trust Co.*, 77 So. 2d 293 (N.Y. City Ct.)]

11. Rovell wrote a check to Pretty Eyes Detective Agency for $10,000 too much ($38,250). A staff member for Rovell gave a stop payment order and then issued a new check ($27,284.50). But the staff member was unsure of the check number. Pretty Eyes cashed both checks, Rovell's account was overdrawn, and he sued the bank. Is the check valid? Who gets the funds? Is it possible for Rovell to recover from the bank? [*Rovell v. American National Bank*, 232 B.R. 381, 38 U.C.C. 2d 896 (N.D. Ill. 1998)]

12. Norris, who was ill in the hospital, was visited by his sister during his last days. Norris was very fond of his sister and wrote a check to her that she deposited in her bank account. Before the check cleared, Norris died. Could the sister collect on the check even though the bank knew of the depositor's death? Explain. [In re *Estate of Norris*, 532 P.2d 981 (Colo.)]

13. Scott D. Leibling gave his bank, Mellon Bank, an oral stop payment order. Nineteen months later, the check emerged and Mellon Bank honored it. Leibling has filed suit against Mellon Bank for acting

unreasonably under the circumstances. Is Mellon Bank liable to Leibling for paying the 19-month-old check when there was an oral stop payment order? Discuss your reasons for your answer. [*Leibling, P.C. v. Mellon, PSFS (NJ) N.A.*, 710 A.2d 1067, 35 U.C.C. 2d 590 (N.J. Super.)]

14. Hixson paid Galyen Petroleum Co. money he owed by issuing three checks to Galyen. The bank refused to cash the three checks because of insufficient funds in the Hixson account to pay all three. Galyen sued the bank. What was the result? Why? [*Galyen Petroleum Co. v. Hixson*, 331 N.W.2d 1 (Neb)]

CPA Questions

1. A check has the following endorsements on the back:

   (1) Paul Frank **"without recourse"**

   (2) George Hopkins **"payment guaranteed"**

   (3) Ann Quarry **"collection guaranteed"**

   (4) Rachell Ott

   Which of the following conditions occurring subsequent to the endorsements would discharge all of the endorsers?

   a. Lack of notice of dishonor.

   b. Late presentment.

   c. Insolvency of the maker.

   d. Certification of the check.

2. Blare bought a house and provided the required funds in the form of a certified check from a bank. Which of the following statements correctly describes the legal liability of Blare and the bank?

   a. The bank has accepted; therefore, Blare is without liability.

   b. The bank has not accepted; therefore, Blare has primary liability.

   c. The bank has accepted, but Blare has secondary liability.

   d. The bank has not accepted, but Blare has secondary liability.

3. In general, which of the following statements is correct concerning the priority among checks drawn on a particular account and presented to the drawee bank on a particular day?

   a. The checks may be charged to the account in any order convenient to the bank.

   b. The checks may be charged to the account in any order provided no charge creates an overdraft.

   c. The checks must be charged to the account in the order in which the checks were dated.

   d. The checks must be charged to the account in the order of lowest amount to highest amount to minimize the number of dishonored checks.

Debtor-Creditor Relationships

Nature of the Debtor-Creditor Relationship

Learning Outcomes ‹‹‹

After studying this chapter, you should be able to

LO.1 Distinguish a contract of suretyship from a contract of guaranty

LO.2 Define the parties to a contract of suretyship and a contract of guaranty

LO.3 List and explain the rights of sureties to protect themselves from loss

LO.4 Explain the defenses available to sureties

LO.5 Explain the nature of a letter of credit and the liabilities of the various parties to a letter of credit

31-1 Creation of the Credit Relationship

This section of the book deals with all aspects of debt: the creation of the debtor-creditor relationship, the statutory requirements for disclosure in those credit contracts, the means by which creditors can secure repayment of debt, and, finally, what happens when debtors are unable to repay their debts.

A debtor-creditor relationship consists of a contract that provides for the creditor to advance funds to the debtor and requires the debtor to repay that principal amount with specified interest over an agreed-upon time. The credit contract, so long as it complies with all the requirements for formation and validity covered in Chapters 11 through 17, is enforceable just like any other contract. However, credit contracts often have additional statutory obligations and relationships that provide assurances on rights and collection for both the debtor and the creditor. Chapter 32 covers the rights of both debtors and creditors in consumer credit relationships. Chapter 33 covers the additional protection that creditors enjoy when debtors offer security interests in collateral. This chapter covers the additional relationships for securing repayment of debt known as *suretyships* and *lines of credit*.

31-2 Suretyship and Guaranty

A debtor can make a separate contract with a third party that requires the third party to pay the debtor's creditor if the debtor does not pay or defaults in the performance of an obligation. This relationship, in which a third party agrees to be responsible for the debt or other obligation, is used most commonly to ensure that a debt will be paid or that a contractor will perform the work called for by a contract. **For Example,** a third-party arrangement occurs when a corporate officer agrees to be personally liable if his corporation does not repay funds received through a corporate note. Contractors are generally required to obtain a surety bond in which a third party agrees to pay damages or complete performance of the construction project in the event the contractor fails to perform in a timely manner or according to the contract terms.

31-2a Definitions

One type of agreement to answer for the debt or default of another is called a **suretyship.** The **obligor** or third party who makes good on a debtor's obligation is called a **surety.** The other kind of agreement is called a **guaranty,** and the obligor is called a **guarantor.** In both cases, the person who owes the money or is under the original obligation to pay or perform is called the **principal, principal debtor,** or **debtor.**[1] The person to whom the debt or obligation is owed is the **obligee** or **creditor.**

As discussed in Chapters 27 and 30, the revisions to Articles 3 and 4 put accommodation parties (now secondary obligors) in the same legal status as those in a surety/guarantor relationship. The revisions place secondary obligors in the position of a surety.

Suretyship and guaranty undertakings have the common feature of a promise to answer for the debt or default of another. The terms are often used interchangeably. However, certain forms of guaranty are qualified by one distinction. A surety is liable from the moment the principal is in default. The creditor or obligee can demand performance or payment from the surety without first proceeding against the principal debtor. A **guaranty of collection** is one in which the creditor generally cannot proceed directly

---

Sidebar definitions (left margin):

suretyship–pledge or guaranty to pay the debt or be liable for the default of another.

obligor–promisor.

surety–obligor of a suretyship; primarily liable for the debt or obligation of the principal debtor.

guaranty–agreement or promise to answer for a debt; an undertaking to pay the debt of another if the creditor first sues the debtor.

guarantor–one who undertakes the obligation of guaranty. **C P A**

principal–person or firm who employs an agent; the person who, with respect to a surety, is primarily liable to the third person or creditor; property held in trust.

principal debtor–original borrower or debtor.

C P A

debtor–buyer on credit (i.e., a borrower).

obligee–promisee who can claim the benefit of the obligation.

creditor–person (seller or lender) who is owed money; also may be a secured party.

guaranty of collection–form of guaranty in which creditor cannot proceed against guarantor until after proceeding against debtor.

---

[1] Unless otherwise stated, *surety* as used in the text includes guarantor as well as surety. Often, the term *guarantee* is used for guaranty. In law, guarantee is actually one who benefits from the guaranty.

absolute guaranty—
agreement that creates the same obligation for the guarantor as a suretyship does for the surety; a guaranty of payment creates an absolute guaranty.

CPA

against the guarantor and must first attempt to collect from the principal debtor.[2] An exception is an **absolute guaranty,** which creates the same obligation as a suretyship. A **guaranty of payment** creates an absolute guaranty and requires the guarantor to pay upon default by the principal debtor.

31-2b Indemnity Contract Distinguished

guaranty of payment—
absolute promise to pay when a debtor defaults.

Both suretyship and guaranty differ from an **indemnity contract.** An indemnity contract is an undertaking by one person, for a consideration, to pay another person a sum of money in the event that the other person sustains a specified loss. **For Example,** a fire insurance policy is an indemnity contract. The insurance you obtain when you use a rental car is also an example of an indemnity contract.

indemnity contract—
agreement by one person, for consideration, to pay another person a sum of money in the event that the other person sustains a specified loss.

31-2c Creation of the Relationship

Suretyship, guaranty, and indemnity relationships are based on contract. The principles relating to capacity, formation, validity, and interpretation of contracts are applicable. Generally, the ordinary rules of offer and acceptance apply. Notice of acceptance usually must be given by the obligee to the guarantor.

In most states, the statute of frauds requires that contracts of suretyship and guaranty be evidenced by a record to be enforceable. No record is required when the promise is made primarily for the promisor's benefit.

When the suretyship or guaranty is created at the same time as the original transaction, the consideration for the original promise that is covered by the guaranty is also consideration for the promise of the guarantor. When the suretyship or guaranty contract is entered into after and separate from the original transaction, there must be new consideration for the promise of the guarantor.

CASE SUMMARY

Widowed Husband Has Rights of Subrogation Against His Ex-Wife's Ex-Husband for Her Divorce Attorney's Fees

FACTS: Ellen Marshall, an attorney, represented Laureen Moran, the late wife of William M. Burke, M.D. (plaintiff) in their divorce proceedings. Marshall and Burke were involved in litigation after Burke refused to pay her fee for the divorce case, which the trial court had awarded and for which Burke had guaranteed payment.

In early 1999 Burke arranged a meeting with Marshall and Moran to discuss Marshall's representation of Moran in a post-divorce action initiated by Moran's former husband, John Izmirlian. Earlier, Marshall had told Burke that Izmirlian was dishonest, concealing his income from both the Internal Revenue Service and Moran. In that meeting, which lasted two hours, they talked almost exclusively about

Moran's legal situation. Burke once again mentioned that Izmirlian was attempting to hide his finances and that he wanted to ensure Izmirlian paid his support obligations. Moran said she was unable to pay for Marshall's services and Marshall herself knew that Moran had no steady means of supporting herself, that Izmirlian had no money, and that Moran had previously discharged a fee obligation of approximately $15,000 in bankruptcy proceedings. Consequently, Marshall raised the issue of payment, asserting that litigation would be expensive and that she could not proceed without payment. According to Marshall, Burke assured her that he was "willing to throw some money at this, so that that little prick pays to support his kid" (a daughter who had

---

[2] On the CPA exam, the term "guarantor of collection" is used to distinguish it from a surety and the differing obligations between these two categories of backups for debtors.

Widowed Husband Has Rights of Subrogation Against His Ex-Wife's Ex-Husband for Her Divorce Attorney's Fees continued

lived with Burke and Moran). With that assurance, Marshall and Moran signed a retainer agreement and Marshall commenced work on the case, including arranging a meeting between the parties, which turned out to be unproductive.

Moran became very ill and Marshall cautioned Izmirlian (defendant) and Moran against proceeding; however, Burke urged Marshall to continue and again promised to pay, which Marshall confirmed in a letter. Although Marshall never received payment during her representation of Moran, she did not demand payment during Moran's illness because she relied on Burke's promise and by then had only represented Moran for a short period. Both Moran and Burke, on the other hand, deny that Burke agreed to pay plaintiff's legal fees and costs on behalf of Moran. Burke admits paying a forensic accountant who aided Moran in tracking down Izmirlian's assets.

At the conclusion of the suit between Marshall and Izmirlian, Izmirlian was ordered to "pay a counsel fee of $32,177.29 to Ellen Marshall, Esq. in accordance with the order filed February 22, 2000." Izmirlian did not pay.

Burke filed a suit alleging that Izmirlian's breach of court orders caused him harm, including compelling his payment of Marshall's fees. The court entered a default judgment against Izmirlian but later vacated it.

Izmirlian then moved for summary judgment in Burke's case against him. The trial court granted summary judgment because Burke was not entitled to proceed because he had paid Marshall as a volunteer.

Burke appealed.

DECISION: Burke was a surety and that entitles him to step into his wife's shoes for purposes of collection of those fees. Burke had agreed to pay his wife's attorney's fees. If he pays them, his wife would be entitled to collect those fees from someone else (her ex-husband). Burke then steps into the shoes of his wife and is entitled to exercise the right to collect payment from the debtor Izmirlian. Here, Marshall needed to be paid, an obligation that belonged to Burke's wife, Moran. If Moran did not pay, and Burke does, then he is entitled to collect from the debtor. Burke had the right to enforce the judgment his wife won against the debtor on payment of child support. The agreement Burke had with Marshall made him a surety for Moran's payment. He can then collect from Moran's debtors, and Izmirlian was one of those debtors.

Reversed and remanded.

[*Burke v. Izmirlian*, **Not Reported in A.3d, 2011 WL 1661022 (N.J. Super. A.D. 2011)**]

CPA   31-2d **Rights of Sureties**

Sureties have a number of rights to protect them from loss, to obtain their discharge because of the conduct of others that would be harmful to them, or to recover money that they were required to pay because of the debtor's breach.

Exoneration

A surety can be exonerated from liability, a means of discharging or relieving liability, if the creditor could have taken steps to stop or limit the surety's exposure for the debt. **For Example,** suppose that the surety learns that a debtor is about to leave the state, an act that makes it more difficult to collect debts. The surety may call on the creditor to take action against the debtor to provide a literal and figurative roadblock to the debtor's planned departure. If the creditor could proceed against the debtor who is about to leave and thereby protect the repayment and fails to do so, the surety is released or **exonerated** from liability to the extent that the surety has been harmed by such failure.

Subrogation

When a surety pays a claim that it is obligated to pay, it automatically acquires the claim and the rights of the creditor. This stepping into the shoes or position of another is known as **subrogation.**[3] That is, once the creditor is paid in full, the surety stands in

[3] *SFI Ltd. Partnership 8 v. Carroll*, 851 N.W.2d 82 (Neb. 2014).

the same position as the creditor and may collect from the debtor or enforce any rights the creditor had against the debtor to recover the amount it has paid. The effect is the same as if the creditor, on being paid, made an express assignment of all rights to the surety. Likewise, the surety acquires any rights the debtor has against the creditor. **For Example,** if the creditor has not complied with statutory requirements, the surety can enforce those rights against the creditor just as the original debtor could.

Indemnity

A surety that has made payment of a claim for which it was liable as surety is entitled to **indemnity** from the principal debtor; that is, it is entitled to demand from the principal reimbursement of the amount that it has paid.

Contribution

If there are two or more sureties (known as co-sureties), each is liable to the creditor or claimant for the full amount of the debt until the claim or debt has been paid in full. Between themselves, however, each co-surety is liable only for a proportionate share of the debt. Accordingly, if a surety has paid more than its share of the debt, it is entitled to demand **contribution** from its **co-sureties.** In the absence of a contrary agreement, co-sureties must share the debt repayment on a *pro rata* basis. **For Example,** Aaron and Bobette are co-sureties of $40,000 and $60,000, respectively, for Christi's $60,000 loan. If Christi defaults, Aaron owes $24,000 and Bobette owes $36,000.

CPA | ## 31-2e Defenses of Sureties

The surety's defenses include those that may be raised by a party to any contract and special defenses that are peculiar to the suretyship relationship.

Ordinary Contract Defenses

Because the relationship of suretyship is based on a contract, the surety may raise any defense that a party to an ordinary contract may raise. For example, a surety may raise the defense of lack of capacity of parties, absence of consideration, fraud, or mistake.

Fraud and **concealment** are common defenses. Fraud on the part of the principal that is unknown to the creditor and in which the creditor has not taken part does not ordinarily release the surety.

Because the risk of the principal debtor's default is thrown on the surety, it is unfair for a creditor to conceal from the surety facts that are material to the surety's risk. Under

indemnity–right of a person secondarily liable to require that a person primarily liable pay for loss sustained when the secondary party discharges the obligation that the primary party should have discharged; an undertaking to pay another a sum of money to indemnify when loss is incurred.

contribution–right of a co-obligor who has paid more than a proportionate share to demand that other obligors pay their *pro rata* share.

co-sureties–sureties for the same debt.

fraud–intentional making a false statement of fact, with knowledge or reckless indifference that it is false with resulting reliance by another.

concealment–failure to volunteer information not requested.

THINKING THINGS THROUGH

Pro Rata Shares for Co-Sureties

AFC Corporation borrowed $90,000 from First Bank and demanded three sureties for the loan. Anna Flynn agreed to be a surety for $45,000 for AFC's debt. Frank Conlan agreed to be a surety for $60,000, and Charles Aspen agreed to be a surety for $75,000. When AFC owed $64,000, it defaulted on the loan and demanded payment from the co-sureties. However, Frank Conlan was in bankruptcy.

How much would Anna and Charles have to pay to First Bank?

common law, the creditor was not required to volunteer information to the surety and was not required to disclose that the principal was insolvent. A modern view that is receiving increased support is that the creditor should be required to inform the surety of matters material to the risk when the creditor has reason to believe that the surety does not possess such information.

CPA | ## Suretyship Defenses

Perhaps the most important thing for a surety to understand is the type of defense that does not result in a discharge of her obligation in the suretyship. The insolvency or bankruptcy of the principal debtor does not discharge the surety. The financial risk of the principal debtor is the reason that a surety was obtained from the outset. The lack of enforcement of the debt by the creditor is not a defense to the surety's obligation or a discharge. The creditor's failure to give the surety notice of default is not a defense. The creditor's right, without a specific guaranty of collection, is simply to turn to the surety for payment.[4]

pledge—bailment given as security for the payment of a debt or the performance of an obligation owed to the pledgee. (Parties—pledgor, pledgee)

In some cases, the creditor may have also taken a **pledge** of collateral for the debt in addition to the commitment of a surety. It is the creditor's choice as to whether to proceed against the collateral or the surety. If, however, the creditor proceeds first against the surety, the surety then has the right of exoneration and can step into the shoes of the creditor and repossess that collateral.

Changes in the terms of the loan agreement do not discharge a compensated surety. A surety who is acting gratuitously, however, would be discharged in the event of such changes. Changes in the loan terms that would discharge a gratuitous surety's obligation include extension of the loan terms and acceptance of late payments.[5]

A surety is discharged when the principal debtor performs his obligations under the original debt contract. If a creditor refuses to accept payment from a debtor, a surety is discharged.

A surety is also discharged, to the extent of the value of the collateral, if a creditor releases back to the debtor any collateral in the creditor's possession. **For Example,** suppose that Bank One has in its possession $10,000 in gold coins as collateral for a loan to Janice in the amount of $25,000. Albert has agreed to serve as a surety for the loan to Janice in the amount of $25,000. If a Bank One manager returns the $10,000 in coins to Janice, then Albert is discharged on his suretyship obligation to the extent of that $10,000. Following the release of the collateral, the most that Albert could be held liable for in the event of Janice's default is $15,000.

A surety is also discharged from her obligation if the creditor substitutes a different debtor. A surety and a guarantor make a promise that is personal to a specific debtor and do not agree to assume the risk of an assignment or a delegation of that responsibility to another debtor. A surety also enjoys the discharge rights afforded all parties to contracts, such as the statute of limitations. If the creditor does not enforce the suretyship agreement within the time limits provided for such contract enforcement in the surety's jurisdiction, the obligation is forever discharged.[6]

Figures 31-1 and 31-2 provide summaries of the defenses and release issues surrounding suretyship and guaranty relationships.

[4] *Rossa v. D.L. Falk Const., Inc.,* 266 P.3d 1022 (Cal. 2012).
[5] In re *Chemtura Corp.,* 448 B.R. 635 (S.D.N.Y. 2011).
[6] *Travelers Cas. and Sur. Co. of America v. Caridi,* 73 A.3d 863 (Conn. App. 2013).

CASE SUMMARY

The Bank Tries to Take the Sure Thing Away From the Surety

FACTS: Five Corners Rialto, LLC, obtained a construction loan from Vineyard Bank to develop a 70-unit townhome project (Project), with guaranties from Thomas DelPonti and David Wood, the principals of Five Corners (Guarantors). Five Corners contracted with Advent, Inc., a general contractor, to build the project in two phases. Everything went according to schedule for the first 18 months. However, when Phase I of the Project was nearly complete, the Bank stopped funding approved payment applications, preventing completion and sale of the Phase I units, which, in turn, caused Five Corners to default on the loan.

The Bank reached an agreement with Five Corners, requiring Advent to finish Phase I so the units could be sold at auction and promising to pay the subcontractors if they discounted their bills and released any liens. Advent paid the subcontractors out of its own pocket in order to keep the project lien-free so the auction could proceed. However, the Bank foreclosed against Five Corners. The Bank (through its assignee California Bank and Trust), sued Five Corners and the Guarantors under various theories for the deficiency following a Trustee's Sale of the Deed of Trust, while Advent sued the developer and the Bank for restitution for the amounts it paid out of pocket.

The cases were consolidated and tried. The court awarded judgment in favor of Advent. The court found that the Bank breached the loan contract, exonerating the Guarantors. The court awarded attorneys' fees to Advent and the Guarantors.

The Bank appealed.

DECISION: The court held that the Guarantors had done everything expected of them and performed according to the new agreement to the extent the Bank permitted. The court did not agree with the Bank's argument that the Guarantors waived all of their defenses.

A guarantor cannot be held liable where a contract is unlawful or contravenes public policy. The rule against enforcement of illegal transactions is founded on considerations of public policy.

A guarantor's waiver of defenses is limited to legal and statutory defenses expressly set out in the agreement. A waiver of statutory defenses does not waive all defenses, especially *equitable defenses*, such as unclean hands, where to enforce the guaranty would allow a lender to profit by its own fraudulent conduct. In all suretyship and guaranty relations, the creditor owes the surety a duty of continuous good faith and fair dealing. This duty was not waived by the Guarantors in the agreement.

The judgment was affirmed in full. Advent and the Guarantors were awarded costs on appeal. [*California Bank & Trust v. DelPonti*, 232 Cal. App. 4th 162 (Cal. App. 2014)]

FIGURE 31-1	No Release of Surety

1. Fraud by debtor
2. Misrepresentation by debtor
3. Changes in loan terms (e.g., Extension of payment)—compensated surety only
4. Release of principal debtor
5. Bankruptcy of principal debtor
6. Insolvency of principal debtor
7. Death of principal debtor
8. Incapacity of principal debtor
9. Lack of enforcement by creditor
10. Creditor's failure to give notice of default
11. Failure of creditor to resort to collateral

FIGURE 31-2	Release of Surety

1. **Proper performance by debtor**
2. **Release, surrender, or destruction of collateral (to extent of value of collateral)**
3. **Substitution of debtor**
4. **Fraud/misrepresentation by creditor**
5. **Refusal by creditor to accept payment from debtor**
6. **Change in loan terms—uncompensated surety only**
7. **Statute of frauds**
8. **Statute of limitations**

31-3   Letters of Credit

letter of credit– commercial device used to guarantee payment to a seller, primarily in an international business transaction.

issuer–party who issues a document such as a letter of credit or a document of title such as a warehouse receipt or bill of lading.

standby letter–letter of credit for a contractor ensuring he will complete the project as contracted.

A **letter of credit** is a three-party arrangement with a payor, a beneficiary, and a party on whom the letter of credit is drawn, or **issuer.** A letter of credit is an agreement that the issuer of the letter will pay drafts drawn by the beneficiary of the letter. Letters of credit are a form of advance arrangement for financing. Sellers of goods, for example, know in advance how much money may be obtained from the issuer of the letter. A letter of credit may also be used by a creditor as a security device because the creditor knows that the drafts that the creditor draws will be accepted or paid by the issuer of the letter.[7]

The use of letters of credit arose in international trade. While international trade continues to be the primary area of use, there is a growing use of letters in domestic sales and in transactions in which the letter of credit takes the place of a surety bond. A letter of credit has been used to ensure that a borrower would repay a loan, that a tenant would pay the rent due under a lease, and that a contractor would properly perform a construction contract. This kind of letter of credit is known as a **standby letter.**

There are few formal requirements for creating a letter of credit. Although banks often use a standardized form for convenience, they may draw up individualized letters of credit for particular situations (Figure 31-3).

In international letters of credit, there are several sources of recognized standards that businesses use for the creation and execution of letters of credit. Along with the UCC, there is the Uniform Customs and Practice for Documentary Credits (or UCP), something that reflects ordinary international banking operational practices on letters of credit. The UCP is revised, generally, about every 10 years by the International Chamber of Commerce (ICC, see Chapter 7).

31-3a   Definition

A letter of credit is an engagement by its issuer that it will pay or accept drafts when the conditions specified in the letter are satisfied. The issuer is usually a bank.

Three contracts are involved in letter-of-credit transactions: (1) the contract between the issuer and the customer of the issuer, (2) the letter of credit itself, and (3) the

---

[7] *Rafool v. Evans*, 497 B.R. 312 (C.D. Ill. 2013), discussing the character and purpose of letters of credit. See also *City of Maple Grove v. Marketline Const. Capital, LLC*, 802 N.W.2d 809 (Minn. App. 2011) for discussion of fact that a document is not a letter of credit if it requires verification of an outside event, as opposed to submission of documents.

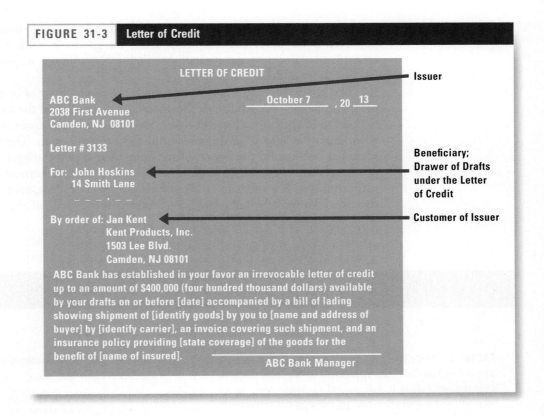

FIGURE 31-3   Letter of Credit

underlying agreement, often a contract of sale, between the beneficiary and the customer of the issuer of the letter of credit (Figure 31-4).

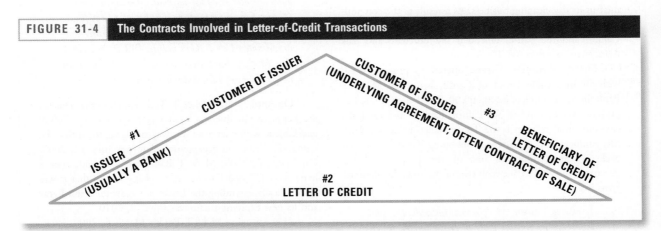

FIGURE 31-4   The Contracts Involved in Letter-of-Credit Transactions

The letter of credit is completely independent from the other two contracts. Consideration is not required to establish or modify a letter of credit.

The issuer of the letter of credit is, in effect, the obligor on a third-party-beneficiary contract made for the benefit of the beneficiary of the letter. The key to the commercial success of letters of credit is their independence. **For Example,** a bank obligated to issue payment under a letter of credit "when the goods are delivered" must honor that obligation even if the buyer has complaints about the goods. It is the terms of the letter of credit that control the payment, not the relationship, contract, or problems of the beneficiary or issuer of the letter of credit.

The key to the commercial vitality and function of a letter of credit is that the issuing bank's promise is independent of the underlying contracts and the bank should not resort to them in interpreting a letter of credit. Sometimes called *the strict compliance rule*, banks must honor the letter of credit terms using strict interpretation. The respective parties are protected by a careful description of the documents that will trigger payment. The claim of a beneficiary of a letter of credit is not subject to defenses normally applicable to third-party contracts. Known as the *independence rule*, banks cannot, except in limited circumstances, delve into the underlying contract issues; the focus of the bank is only on the terms of the letter of credit.

CASE SUMMARY

The Letter of Credit and the Shoddy Mall

FACTS: In 2007, Wood Center Properties (WCP) entered into a Purchase and Sale Agreement to buy five shopping centers from Robert B. Greene and Louisville Mall Associates, LP, and several other mall property groups (collectively, the "Mall Appellants"). While performing its due diligence, WCP discovered environmental contamination at the Crestwood Shopping Center, one of the shopping centers it intended to purchase. A prior shopping center tenant, Crestwood Coin Laundry (Tenant), spilled hazardous chemicals used in its dry cleaning business. As a result of the contamination, WCP chose not to purchase Crestwood Shopping Center, and the parties amended the Purchase and Sale Agreement to reflect WCP's decision.

Shortly thereafter, Greene offered to provide WCP with an irrevocable Letter of Credit, issued by M & T Bank, in the amount of $200,000.00. The Letter of Credit's purpose was to insulate WCP from liability and fund the environmental cleanup if the Tenant failed to do so. With that inducement, Crestwood Shopping Center was put back in the contract as one of the properties being purchased by WCP. Paragraph two of the amended contract provided:

At closing, Robert M. Greene, individually, shall deliver an irrevocable letter of credit for the benefit of Wood Center Properties, LLC in the amount of Two Hundred Thousand Dollars ($200,000.00) drawn on M & T Bank. This letter of credit shall extend for one (1) year from the date of Closing, and shall automatically renew for one (1) additional year unless Notice of non-renewal is given to [WCP] at

least 60 days prior to the expiration date on the face of the Greene Letter of Credit.

On June 13, 2007, M & T Bank issued the Letter of Credit for the benefit of WCP. The Letter of Credit contained an original expiration date of June 12, 2008, that provided:

It is a condition of this credit that it shall be deemed automatically extended without amendment for one (1) year from the expiration date hereof, or any future expiration date, unless sixty (60) days prior to any expiration date M & T Bank notifies [WCP] in writing that M & T Bank elects not to consider this credit renewed for any such additional period.

On April 7, 2008, M & T Bank automatically renewed the Letter of Credit for a second year and provided WCP and Greene with a letter of renewal, notifying them that the Letter of Credit's new expiration date was June 12, 2009. On March 6, 2009, M & T Bank sent a second renewal letter to WCP and Greene, again giving notice that it was automatically extending the Letter of Credit for a third year and its new expiration date was June 12, 2010.

After receiving M & T Bank's March 6, 2009, letter, Greene told M & T Bank his view that the Letter of Credit was only valid for two years and should expire on June 12, 2009. Greene requested that M & T not renew the credit. Despite Greene's request, M & T did not send a nonrenewal notification to WCP. WCP sought payment under the Letter of Credit and submitted the documents to M & T that were necessary for payment.

The Letter of Credit and the Shoddy Mall continued

WCP filed a declaratory judgment action seeking the court's ruling that WCP was entitled to draw on the Letter of Credit. The court entered summary declaratory judgment in WCP's favor. Greene appealed.

DECISION: A letter of credit must be interpreted on its face, independent of other contracts and the underlying transaction. The underlying contract between the customer and the beneficiary should not be considered in interpreting the letter of credit, and should not be used to supplement or amplify the terms of the letter of credit or to add obligations thereto.

The Letter of Credit itself expressly provides that its terms shall not be amplified or interpreted by reference to any outside document.

The issuer is neither expected nor entitled to look beyond the pieces of paper to determine whether the statements they contain are true, or to determine whether under its agreement with the applicant, the beneficiary has the right to make demand under the letter of credit.

M & T Bank was only required to examine the documents presented by WCP to determine if they complied with the terms and conditions of the Letter of Credit; M & T Bank was not required to look beyond the documents to determine whether WCP's statement that it complied with [the contract] was, in fact, accurate. The court properly awarded WCP summary judgment. [*Louisville Mall Associates, LP v. Wood Center Properties, LLC*, 361 S.W.3d 323 (Ky. App. 2012)]

31-3b Parties

advising bank—bank that tells beneficiary that letter of credit has been issued.

correspondent bank—will honor the letter of credit from the domestic bank of the buyer.

The parties to a letter of credit are (1) the issuer; (2) the customer who makes the arrangements with the issuer; and (3) the beneficiary, who will be the drawer of the drafts that will be drawn under the letter of credit. There may also be (4) an **advising bank**[8] if the local issuer of the letter of credit requests its **correspondent bank,** where the beneficiary is located, to notify or advise the beneficiary that the letter has been issued. **For Example,** a U.S. merchant may want to buy goods from a Spanish merchant. There may have been prior dealings between the parties so that the seller is willing to take the buyer's commercial paper as payment or to take trade acceptances drawn on the buyer. If the foreign seller is not willing to do this, the U.S. buyer, as customer, may go to a bank, the issuer, and obtain a letter of credit naming the Spanish seller as beneficiary. The U.S. bank's correspondent or advising bank in Spain will notify the Spanish seller that this has been done. The Spanish seller will then draw drafts on the U.S. buyer. Under the letter of credit, the issuer is required to accept or pay these drafts.

31-3c Duration

A letter of credit continues for any length of time it specifies. Generally, a maximum money amount is stated in the letter, so that the letter is exhausted or used up when the issuer has accepted or paid drafts aggregating that maximum. A letter of credit may be used in installments as the beneficiary chooses. The issuer or the customer cannot revoke or modify a letter of credit without the consent of the beneficiary unless that right is expressly reserved in the letter.

31-3d Form

A letter of credit must be in writing and signed by the issuer. If the credit is issued by a bank and requires a documentary draft or a documentary demand for payment[9] or if the

---

[8] See U.C.C. §5-107; *Speedway Motorsports Intern. Ltd. v. Bronwen Energy Trading, Ltd.,* 706 S.E.2d 262 (N.C. 2011).

[9] A *documentary draft* or a *documentary demand for payment* is one for which honor is conditioned on the presentation of one or more documents. A document could be a document of title, security, invoice, certificate, notice of default, or other similar paper. U.C.C. §5-103(1)(b).

credit is issued by a nonbank and requires that the draft or demand for payment be accompanied by a document of title, the instrument is presumed to be a letter of credit (rather than a contract of guaranty). Otherwise, the instrument must conspicuously state that it is a letter of credit.

31-3e Duty of Issuer

The issuer is obligated to honor drafts drawn under the letter of credit if the conditions specified in the letter have been satisfied. The issuer takes the risk that the papers submitted are the ones required by the letter. If they are not, the issuer cannot obtain reimbursement for payment made in reliance on such documents. The issuer has no duty to verify that the papers are properly supported by facts or that the underlying transaction has been performed. It is immaterial that the goods sold by the seller in fact do not conform to the contract so long as the seller tenders the documents specified by the letter of credit. If the issuer dishonors a draft without justification, it is liable to its customer for breach of contract.[10]

ETHICS & THE LAW

When the Creditors Rule the Debtor

Very often the creditors of a business can exercise a great deal of authority over the operation of the business when it has missed a payment on its debt or has experienced some business or market setbacks. Without owning any stock in a corporation, creditors will, in more than 50 percent of all cases in which they express concern about repayment, succeed in having both boards and officers replaced in part or in toto. **For Example,** Worlds of Wonder, Inc., a creative and innovative toy manufacturer that was responsible for the first talking toy, Teddy Ruxpin, was required by demands from its secured and unsecured creditors to obtain the resignation of its founder and CEO, Donald Kingsborough. Kingsborough was paid $212,500 at his departure for "emotional distress."* For example, in 2009, the federal government, as a lender, required that the CEO of General Motors resign as a condition to receiving additional funds from the government to cover debt payments. In addition, the federal government negotiated the positions of union workers, investors, and hedge funds in the Chrysler Corporation restructuring as a condition of its receipt of federal funds.

Studies show** that creditors also have input on the following corporate actions:

Type of Decision	Percentage of Creditors with Vote
Declaration of dividends	48
Increased security	73
Restructuring of debt	55
Cap on borrowing	50
Cap on capital expenses	25
Restrictions on investment	23

Is it fair to have creditors control corporate governance? What are the risks for shareholders when creditors control the management of a company?

*"Toymaker Has Financing Pact," *New York Times*, April 2, 1988, C1 (Reuters item).
See Tim Reason, "Keeping Skin in the Game," *CFO Magazine*, February 1, 2005, **http://www.cfo.com, for a discussion of why creditors are involved and what they can do to help manage a debtor.

---

[10] *CRM Collateral II, Inc. v. TriCounty Metropolitan Transp. Dist of Oregon*, 669 F.3d 963 (9th Cir. 2012). In some cases, letters of credit are so poorly drafted that payment must be made despite evolving concerns by the parties. *Nissho Iwai Europe PLC v. Korea First Bank*, 782 N.E.2d 55 (N.Y. 2002).

31-3f Reimbursement of Issuer

When the issuer of a letter of credit makes proper payment of drafts drawn under the letter of credit, it may obtain reimbursement from its customer for such payment. Examples of improper payment include payment made after the letter has expired or a payment that is in excess of the amount authorized by the letter. No reimbursement is possible if the payment is made without the proper presentation of required documents or if the payment is made in violation of a court injunction against payment.

Make the Connection

Summary

Suretyship and guaranty undertakings have the common feature of a promise to answer for the debt or default of another. The terms are used interchangeably, but a guarantor of collection is ordinarily only secondarily liable, which means that the guarantor does not pay until the creditor has exhausted all avenues of recovery. If the guarantor has made an absolute guaranty, then its status is the same as that of a surety, which means that both are liable for the debt in the event the debtor defaults, regardless of what avenues of collection, if any, the creditor has pursued.

Surety and guaranty relationships are based on contract. Sureties have a number of rights to protect them. They are exoneration, subrogation, indemnity, and contribution. In addition to those rights, sureties also have certain defenses. They include ordinary contract defenses as well as some defenses peculiar to the suretyship relationship, such as release of collateral, change in loan terms, substitution of debtor, and fraud by the creditor.

A letter of credit is an agreement that the issuer of the letter will pay drafts drawn on the issuer by the beneficiary of the letter. The issuer of the letter of credit is usually a bank. There are three contracts involved in letter-of-credit transactions: (1) the contract between the issuer and the customer of the issuer, (2) the letter of credit itself, and (3) the underlying agreement between the beneficiary and the customer of the issuer of the letter of credit.

The parties to a letter of credit are the issuer, the customer who makes the arrangement with the issuer, and the beneficiary who will be the drawer of the drafts to be drawn under the letter of credit. The letter of credit continues for any time it specifies. The letter of credit must be in writing and signed by the issuer. Consideration is not required to establish or modify a letter of credit. If the conditions in the letter of credit have been complied with, the issuer is obligated to honor drafts drawn under the letter of credit.

Learning Outcomes

After studying this chapter, you should be able to clearly explain:

31-1 Creation of the Credit Relationship

31-2 Suretyship and Guaranty

LO.1 Distinguish a contract of suretyship from a contract of guaranty
See the definitions and discussion of the terms related to surety and guaranty, pages 602–603.

LO.2 Define the parties to a contract of suretyship and a contract of guaranty
See the example on corporate officers and their relationship with company debt, page 602.
See the *Burke v. Izmirlian* case, pages 603–604.

LO.3 List and explain the rights of sureties to protect themselves from loss
See the discussion of contribution, page 605.
See the Thinking Things Through Feature, *Pro Rata Shares for Co-Sureties*, on page 605.

LO.4 Explain the defenses available to sureties
See the *California Bank & Trust v. DelPonti* case, page 607.

31-3 Letters of Credit

LO.5 Explain the nature of a letter of credit and the liabilities of the various parties to a letter of credit
See the *Louisville Mall Associates, LP v. Wood Center Properties, LLC,* case, pages 610–611.

Key Terms

absolute guaranty	fraud	obligee
advising bank	guarantor	obligor
concealment	guaranty	pledge
contribution	guaranty of collection	principal
correspondent bank	guaranty of payment	principal debtor
co-sureties	indemnity	standby letter
creditor	indemnity contract	subrogation
debtor	issuer	surety
exoneration	letter of credit	suretyship

Questions and Case Problems

1. First Interstate Bank issued a letter of credit in favor of Comdata Network. Comdata is engaged in money transfer services. It provides money to truckers on the road by way of cash advances through form checks written by truckers. When Comdata enters into a business relationship with a trucking company, it requires a letter of credit. This requirement is to secure advances made on behalf of the trucking company. One of the trucking companies defrauded the bank that issued the letter of credit. Comdata demanded that the bank make payment to it under the letter of credit for cash advances that the trucking company had not repaid. The bank, alleging fraud by the trucking company, refused. Comdata filed suit. Can Comdata force payment? [*Comdata Network, Inc. v. First Interstate Bank of Fort Dodge*, 497 N.W.2d 807 (Iowa App.)]

2. LaBarge Pipe & Steel Company agreed to sell PVF $143,613.40 of 30-inch pipe provided that PVF obtain a letter of credit for $144,000, with the letter of credit entitling LaBarge to payment if PVF did not pay for the pipe within 30 days of invoice. PVF obtained the letter of credit from First Bank but received only a facsimile copy of it. The letter of credit required LaBarge to submit the original of the letter of credit for a demand of payment.

   PVF did not pay within 30 days and LaBarge submitted a facsimile copy of the letter of credit and requested payment. First Bank denied the request for payment and LaBarge filed suit against First Bank for failure to pay. LaBarge argued that it was not disputed that PVF had not paid on the contract and First Bank was required to pay on the letter of credit. How would you explain First Bank's rights to LaBarge? [*LaBarge Pipe & Steel Co. v. First Bank*, 550 F.3d 442 (5th Cir.)]

3. On August 1, 1987, Dori Leeds signed a "guarantee of credit" with Sun Control Systems, which guaranteed "the prompt payment, when due, of every claim of [Sun Control Systems] against [Dori Leeds dba 'Blind Ambitions']." At the time she signed the guarantee of credit, Blind Ambitions was in the business of installing window treatments and installed only Faber brand blinds, which were purchased from Sun Control Systems. In 1991, Sun Control Systems sold and assigned all of its assets to Faber. Shortly thereafter, Dori assigned her interest in Blind Ambitions to David and Judith Leeds, who continued to do business as Blind Ambitions. In 1994 and 1995, Blind Ambitions made credit purchases from Faber and did not pay under the terms of those contracts. Faber brought suit against Dori Leeds as the guarantor of credit for Blind Ambitions. Dori refused to pay on the grounds that she was acting as a personal guarantor for her business, not for Blind Ambitions. Is she correct? [*Faber Industries, Ltd. v. Dori Leeds Witek*, 483 S.E.2d 443 (N.C. App.)]

4. Fern Schimke's husband, Norbert, was obligated on two promissory notes in favor of Union National Bank. Some time prior to his death, Union National Bank prepared a guaranty contract that was given to Norbert for his wife to sign. She signed the guaranty at the request of her husband without any discussion with him about the provisions of the document she was signing. On Norbert's death, the bank brought suit against Fern on the basis of the guaranty. Fern argued that because there was no consideration for the guaranty, she could not be liable. Is Fern correct? Must there be consideration for a guarantor to be responsible for payment? [*Union Nat'l Bank v. Fern Schimke*, 210 N.W.2d 176 (N.D.)]

5. In May 1989, Alma Equities Corp., owned by its sole shareholder and president, Lewis Futterman, purchased a hotel and restaurant in Vail, Colorado, from Alien for $3,900,000. Alma paid $600,000 in cash to Alien, and Alien provided a purchase money loan to Alma for the remaining amount of the sale price, with the loan secured by a deed of trust on the hotel and restaurant. The hotel and restaurant did not do well, and Futterman negotiated a friendly foreclosure on the property in 1991, whereby Alma would continue to operate the hotel and restaurant on a lease basis, with Futterman providing a personal guaranty for the lease. Alma failed to make the lease payments for the months of November and December 1991 and, following an unlawful detainer action filed by Alien for possession of the hotel and restaurant, was forced into bankruptcy. Alien turned to Futterman for satisfaction on the lease payments. Futterman said he should not have been forced to pay because Alien's unlawful detainer forced Alma into bankruptcy. Was Futterman correct? Did he have a defense? [*Alien, Inc. v. Futterman*, 924 P.2d 1063 (Colo.)]

6. Crown Corporation has borrowed $16,000,000 from Third Bank. Third Bank required four sureties for the loan. The sureties are as follows:

Andover	$4,000,0000
Busch	$8,000,0000
Chapman	$2,000,0000
Davidson	$2,000,0000

Crown has defaulted on the loan after paying back $4,000,000. How much will each surety be required to pay? What if Busch was bankrupt? How much would Andover, Chapman, and Davidson have to pay?

7. Tri County Truck & Diesel borrowed $165,000 from Security State Bank and pledged its inventory as security for the loan. In addition, Fred and Randelle Burk agreed to act as sureties for the loan. Tri County defaulted on the loan and Security Bank repossessed the collateral. The inventory was damaged while Security Bank held it, and as a result, the sale of the inventory brought only $5,257.50 at a public auction. The Burks raised the defense of the damages as a setoff to their surety amount for the remainder of the loan. Security Bank said the Burks could not raise the damages as a defense because the Burks were sureties and had guaranteed the full amount of the loan. The trial court granted summary

judgment for Security Bank, and the Burks appealed. What should the court do? [*Security State Bank v. Burk*, 995 P.2d 1272 (Wash App.)]

8. UPS Capital Business Credit agreed to loan Ashford International, Inc, an American company based in Atlanta, Georgia, for the sale of computers to the Ministry of Education in Jordan. Ashford was required to obtain a letter of credit from United California Discount Corporation (UCDC) for the loan. Ashford filed for bankruptcy and UPS submitted documentation for payment on the letter of credit. UCDC responded to the payment demand with a list of requirements for compliance with the letter of credit demands. UPS satisfied all the demands and UCDC then refused to pay because UPS did not submit original documents as required by the letter of credit. UPS maintains that UCDC waived that requirement by not listing it in its demands. Who is correct and why? [*Export-Import Bank of the U.S. v. United Cal. Discount Corp.*, 738 F. Supp. 2d 1047 (C.D. Cal.)]

9. Ribaldgo Argo Consultores entered into a contract with R. M. Wade & Co. for the purchase of irrigation equipment. Ribaldgo obtained a letter of credit from Banco General, a bank with its principal place of business in Quito, Ecuador. The letter of credit required that Wade submit certain documents to obtain payment. The documents were submitted through Citibank as correspondent bank for Banco General. However, the documents were incomplete, and Citibank demanded additional information as required under the letter of credit. By the time Wade got the documents to Citibank, more than 15 days had expired, and the letter of credit required that Wade submit all documentation within 15 days of shipping the goods to obtain payment. Citibank refused to authorize the payment. Wade filed suit. Must Citibank pay? Why or why not? [*Banco General Runinahui, S.A. v. Citibank International*, 97 F.3d 480 (11th Cir.)]

10. Hugill agreed to deliver shingles to W. I. Carpenter Lumber Co. and furnished a surety bond to secure the faithful performance of the contract on his part. After a breach of the contract by Hugill, the lumber company brought an action to recover its loss from the surety, Fidelity & Deposit Co. of Maryland. The surety denied liability on the grounds that there was concealment of (a) the price to be paid for the shingles and (b) the fact that a material advance had been made to the contractor equal to the amount of

the profit that he would make by performing the contract. Decide. [*W. I. Carpenter Lumber Co. v. Hugill*, 270 P.94 (Wash.)]

11. Donaldson sold plumbing supplies. The St. Paul-Mercury Indemnity Co., as surety for him, executed and delivered a bond to the state of California for the payment of all sales taxes. Donaldson failed to pay, and the surety paid the taxes that he owed and then sued him for the taxes. What was the result? [*St. Paul-Mercury Indemnity Co. v. Donaldson*, 83 S.E.2d 159 (S.C.)]

12. Paul owed Charles a $1,000 debt due September 1. On August 15, George, for consideration, orally promised Charles to pay the debt if Paul did not. On September 1, Paul did not pay, so Charles demanded $1,000 from George. Is George liable? Why or why not?

13. First National Bank hired Longdon as a secretary and obtained a surety bond from Belton covering the bank against losses up to $100,000 resulting from Longdon's improper conduct in the performance of his duties. Both Longdon and the bank signed the application for the bond. After one year of service, Longdon was promoted to teller, and the original bond remained in effect. Shortly after Longdon's promotion, examination showed that Longdon had taken advantage of his new position and stolen $50,000. He was arrested and charged with embezzlement. Longdon had only $5,000 in assets at the time of his arrest. (a) If the bank demands a payment of $50,000 from Belton, what defense, if any, might Belton raise to deny any obligation to the bank? (b) If Belton fully reimburses the bank for its loss, under what theory or theories, if any, may Belton attempt to recover from Longdon?

14. Jack Smith was required by his bank to obtain two sureties for his line of credit of $100,000. Ellen Weiss has agreed to act as a surety for $50,000, and Allen Fox has agreed to act as a surety for $75,000. Smith has used the full $100,000 in the line of credit and is now in bankruptcy. What is the maximum liability of Weiss and Fox if the bank chooses to collect from them for Smith's default? How should the $100,000 be allocated between Weiss and Fox?

15. Industrial Mechanical had a contract with Free Flow Cooling, Ltd., a British company. Free Flow owed Industrial $171,974.44 for work Industrial had performed on a construction project in Texas. Free Flow did not pay Industrial, and Industrial filed suit against Siemens Energy & Automation as a guarantor or surety on the debt. Industrial alleges that Siemens is a surety based on a fax it received from Siemens on January 27, 1994. The fax is handwritten and states: "We have received preliminary notices and we like [sic] to point out that the contract we have signed does not allow for such action to recourse [sic] with the customer. Please advise all subcontractors and suppliers that the only recourse that they will have is against Siemens." The fax was signed "kind regards" by Arnold Schultz, Siemens's senior project manager for the Texas construction project. Nowhere in the fax did Siemens guarantee the debt of any specified entity or state that Siemens was agreeing to indemnify anyone or pay the obligations on behalf of anyone else. The fax failed to identify the principal debtor whom Siemens purportedly agreed to indemnify and failed to state that Siemens agreed to answer for that entity's debt. Can Industrial collect the amount of Free Flow's debt from Siemens? Why or why not? [*Industrial Mechanical, Inc. v. Siemens Energy & Automation, Inc.*, 495 S.E.2d 103 (Ga. App.)]

CPA Questions

1. Marbury Surety, Inc., agreed to act as a guarantor of collection of Madison's trade accounts for one year beginning on April 30, 1980, and was compensated for same. Madison's trade debtors are in default in payment of $3,853 as of May 1, 1981. As a result:

   a. Marbury is liable to Madison without any action on Madison's part to collect the amounts due.

   b. Madison can enforce the guaranty even if it is not in writing because Marbury is a del credere agent.

   c. The relationship between the parties must be filed in the appropriate county office because it is a continuing security transaction.

   d. Marbury is liable for those debts for which a judgment is obtained and returned unsatisfied.

2. Queen paid Pax and Co. to become the surety on a loan that Queen obtained from Squire. The loan is due, and Pax wishes to compel Queen to pay Squire. Pax has not made any payments to Squire in its capacity as Queen's surety. Pax will be most successful if it exercises its right to:

   a. Reimbursement (indemnification).

   b. Contribution.

   c. Exoneration.

   d. Subrogation.

3. Which of the following defenses by a surety will be effective to avoid liability?

   a. Lack of consideration to support the surety undertaking.

   b. Insolvency in the bankruptcy sense of the debtor.

   c. Incompetency of the debtor to make the contract in question.

   d. Fraudulent statements by the principal debtor that induced the surety to assume the obligation and that were unknown to the creditor.

4. For each of the numbered words or phrases, select the one best phrase from the list a through j. Each response may be used only once.

   (1) Indemnity contract

   (2) Suretyship contract

   (3) Surety

   (4) Third-party beneficiary

   (5) Co-surety

   (6) Statute of frauds

   (7) Right of contribution

   (8) Reimbursement

   (9) Subrogation

   (10) Exoneration

   a. Relationship whereby one person agrees to answer for the debt or default of another.

   b. Requires certain contracts to be in writing to be enforceable.

   c. Jointly and severally liable to creditor.

   d. Promises to pay debt on default of principal debtor.

   e. One party promises to reimburse debtor for payment of debt or loss if it arises.

   f. Receives intended benefits of a contract.

   g. Right of surety to require the debtor to pay before surety pays.

   h. Upon payment of more than his/her proportionate share, each co-surety may compel other co-sureties to pay their shares.

   i. Upon payment of debt, surety may recover payment from debtor.

   j. Upon payment, surety obtains same rights against debtor that creditor had.

5. When a principal debtor defaults and a surety pays the creditor the entire obligation, which of the following remedies gives the surety the best method of collecting from the debtor?

   a. Exoneration

   b. Contribution

   c. Subrogation

   d. Attachment

6. Which of the following bonds are an obligation of a surety?

   a. Convertible bonds

   b. Debenture bonds

   c. Municipal bonds

   d. Official bonds

Consumer Protection

32-1 General Principles

The consumer protection movement, which began in the 1960s, continues to expand with rights for consumers in everything from ads to credit collection. Consumer protection began with the goal of protecting persons of limited means and limited knowledge. One writer described consumer protection statutes as laws that protect "the little guy."[1] Over the past 20 years, however, that protection has expanded considerably in both who is protected and the types of activities that are regulated or provide consumers with statutory remedies.

32-1a Expansion of Consumer Protection

Some statutes are worded so that consumer protections apply only to natural persons. Some statutes are interpreted to apply only to consumer transactions, not to commercial transactions. However, many consumer protection statutes, once limited to individuals, now include partnerships, corporations, banks, or government entities that use goods or services as consumers. The statutes thus go beyond providing protection only for the unsophisticated and uneducated.[2] **For Example,** in defining **consumer,** courts have held that a collector paying nearly $100,000 for jade art objects, a glass manufacturer purchasing 3 million gallons of diesel oil fuel, and the city of Boston purchasing insurance are all consumers for purposes of statutory protections. Some states, such as Arizona, Arkansas, Delaware, Illinois, Iowa, Missouri, and New Jersey, even have two separate statutes, one for the protection of individual consumers and another for the protection of businesses. In addition, the protected consumer may be a firm of attorneys.[3]

consumer—any buyer afforded special protections by statute or regulation.

Today, all 50 states and the District of Columbia have some version of what are called "Little FTC Acts" (the Federal Trade Commission Act [which created the FTC] discussed later in the chapter is the federal consumer protection statute that prohibits unfair or deceptive practices) or "unfair or deceptive acts or practices" ("UDAP") statutes. Although there are 51 versions of consumer protection statutes, they have several common threads. First, consumer protection statutes provide faster remedies for consumers. Statutory remedies under consumer protection statutes often mean that consumers need not establish that a tort has been committed or establish actual damage levels because the statute provides for both the elements for recovery and perhaps even a formula for recovery of damages. Second, the harms addressed by consumer statutes tend to affect the public generally and involve more than just one contract or even one seller. **For Example,** one area of consumer protection provides consumers control over both the release and content of their credit report information. The use of credit information, the granting of credit, and the use of credit to make purchases all have a profound impact on buyers, sellers, and national, state, and local economies. These protections provide a statutory formula for consumer damages when credit information is misused or is incorrect.

32-1b Who Is a Consumer?

A consumer claiming a violation of the consumer protection statute has the burden of proving that the statutory definition of consumer has been satisfied. The business accused

---

[1] Olha N. M. Rybakoff, "An Overview of Consumer Protection and Fair Trade Regulation in Delaware," 8 *Delaware L. Rev.* 63 (2005). This article provides a good history and summary of consumer protection laws.

[2] *Prime Ins. Co. v. Imperial Fire and Cas. Ins. Co.*, 151 So. 3d 670 (La. App. 2014). *Garden Catering-Hamilton Avenue, LLC v. Wally's Chicken Coop, LLC*, 30 F. Supp. 3d 117 (D. Conn. 2014).

[3] Statutes that broaden the protected group to protect buyers of goods and services are often called *deceptive trade practices statutes* instead of being referred to by the earlier term, *consumer protection statutes.* But see *Lifespan of Minnesota, Inc. v. Minneapolis Public Schools Independent School Dist. No. 1*, 841 N.W.2d 656 (Minn. App. 2014).

of unfair or deceptive trade practices then has the burden of showing that the statute does *not* apply as well as establishing exceptions and exemptions. **For Example,** some consumer protection statutes do not apply when a buyer is purchasing goods for resale.

32-1c Who Is Liable under Consumer Protection Statutes?

Those who are liable for violations of consumer protection situations are persons or enterprises that regularly enter into the type of transaction in which the injured consumer was involved. **For Example,** the merchant seller, the finance company, the bank, the leasing company, the home contractor, and any others who regularly enter into transactions with consumers are subject to the statutes. Some consumer protection statutes apply only to specific types of merchants and service providers such as auto repair and sale statutes, funeral home disclosure statutes and regulations, and swimming pool contractors.

32-1d When Is There Liability under Consumer Protection Statutes?

Consumer protection laws typically list the types of conduct that are prohibited as well as failures to act properly that are harmful to consumers. For example, the failure to disclose all of the charges related to a consumer loan or a credit purchase made by a consumer would be an omission that carries rights for the consumers and penalties for the business. *Deceptive advertising* is an act that is prohibited by consumer protection statutes that provide remedies for consumers who were deceived or misled by the ads. Deceptive advertising that is listed and described in detail in the consumer protection statutes is often easier for consumers to prove than a common law case of fraud. Consumer protection statutes do not require proof of intent. An ad might not have seemed deceptive to the merchant selling computers when he reviewed the ad copy for the newspaper. However, a consumer without the merchant's sophistication could be misled. **For Example,** suppose that a consumer sees the ad for a 19-inch flat-screen computer monitor for $158 after rebate that reads, "Compare this price with any 19-inch flat-screen monitor, and you will see we cannot be matched." The average consumer might not understand that speakers are not included with such monitors. The computer store, on the other hand, might have assumed that everyone understands that flat-screen monitors with speakers are in a different price category. Adding "no speakers" or "speakers not included" would have allowed the consumer the information needed to shop and compare.

Consumers enjoy a great deal of protection when there are omissions of material information or they are given misleading information, but consumer protection does not protect consumers from their own negligence. Consumers who sign contracts without reading or understanding what is in them are still bound. Moreover, when the contract signed by the consumer clearly states one thing, the consumer cannot introduce evidence about statements the merchant made if the contract terms are clear. Consumers must exercise reasonable care and cannot blindly trust consumer protection law to rescue them from their own blunders.

One of the areas where there have been many new consumer protections is in the area of subprime lending. In the subprime lending market, which includes "do-or-die" loans such as car title loans and home title loans as well as payday loans, there are now extensive disclosure requirements on interest rates, payments, and the effects of default. In addition, these laws have imposed stringent requirements on lenders who seek to foreclose on properties that secure those loans.

CASE SUMMARY

A Loan Modification that Finds you Owing More

FACTS: Robert and Sheryl Laughlin (Plaintiffs), who were having difficulty making their mortgage payments, applied for a HAMP modification with Bank of America, NA (BANA). HAMP is the federal Home Affordable Modification Program, a program that was one of several assistance programs created in an effort to stem the foreclosure crisis. HAMP is intended to lower a qualifying mortgagor's monthly payments to 31 percent of the [borrowers'] verified monthly gross income in order to make payments more affordable. After months of delay and inconsistent responses, BANA informed the Laughlins that they qualified for the HAMP program and would be placed in a trial period plan. BANA told the Laughlins that if they accepted a trial period plan under HAMP, they would be ineligible to short sell their house. The Laughlins opted out of the proposed HAMP modification plan in order to remain eligible for a short sale.*

A BANA representative then advised the Laughlins to accept a HAMP modification instead of attempting a short sale, but they were not allowed to have the previously offered HAMP Trial Plan reinstated. On April 11, 2012, the Laughlins resubmitted the necessary financial documentation required in order to be considered for a modification. On June 21, 2012, the Laughlins received a Notice of Intent to Foreclose. On that same day, the Laughlins received a phone call from a BANA representative, informing them that they were denied a loan modification and would need to make at least one monthly loan payment in order to qualify for any mortgage assistance programs. On June 25, 2012, the Laughlins made this payment.

On August 15, 2012, the Laughlins received a Federal Housing Agency ("FHA") Trial Period Plan Agreement ("TPP"). On the same day, Robert Laughlin spoke with a BANA representative about his concern regarding the calculation of the amount due under the loan. Robert Laughlin believed that a portion of the principal balance was being "doublecounted" because BANA was adding unpaid principal on top of the balance due on the loan. A BANA representative informed them that this was how the calculation was done. The Laughlins then [accepted the TPP].

Under the terms of the TPP, the Laughlins were obligated to make three monthly payments on or before September 15, 2013; October 15, 2013; and November 15, 2013. The Laughlins made the payments, and on November 30, 2012, were told that their loan modification request was under review and that they would receive a final loan modification within 30–45 days. They were advised to continue making the monthly trial payments in the meantime.

On January 2, 2013, BANA acknowledged the Laughlins' compliance with the FHA Trial Plan Agreement and advised in writing to continue making trial payments until a final loan modification was processed. They received their permanent loan modification offer on April 10, 2013.

The terms of the permanent loan modification offer had a modified principal balance of $680,042.78. Before the modification, their loan balance was $617,735.87. The proposed modified loan also extended the term of the loan for 30 years, providing that the loan would now mature on November 1, 2042. Finally, the proposed permanent loan modification included a balloon payment of $25,013.27, which BANA said reflected the "missed" payments from the period between the end of the TPP and before the permanent loan modification offer.

The Laughlins filed suit against BANA for breach of the duty of good faith and violation of the New Jersey consumer fraud statute (NJCFA). BANA made a motion to dismiss the case and the Laughlins opposed the motion.

DECISION: The court held that allegations of "unconscionable commercial practice, deception, fraud, false pretense, false promise, misrepresentation, or the knowing concealment, suppression, or omission of any material fact" during the loan modification process constitute unlawful conduct in violation of the NJCFA. The loan modification process, from negotiation to the signing of a permanent modification, effectively operates as a subsequent performance on the original mortgage. It would be disingenuous to hold that a loan servicer would be free from the ramifications of violating consumer rights if it engaged in unlawful conduct while participating in a loan modification.

The Court found that Plaintiffs' allegations that BANA breached its implied duty, based upon the contractual relationship between Plaintiffs and BANA, to diligently evaluate Plaintiffs for a permanent loan were actionable under the consumer protection statutes of New Jersey.

BANA's Motion to Dismiss was denied.
[*Laughlin v. Bank of America, N.A.*, **2014 WL 2602260 (D.N.J. 2014)**]

*A "short sale" in real estate occurs when the outstanding loans against a property are greater than what the property is worth and the lender agrees to accept less than it is owed to permit a sale of the property that secures its note.

32-1e **What Remedies Do Consumers Have?**

Although consumers have the theoretical right to bring suit for defenses to contracts or enforcement when the other party does not perform, the right to prove fraud, misrepresentation, duress, or breach is often of little practical value to consumers because both the costs of litigation and the burden of proof are high. The amount that the consumer has lost may be too small to be worth pursuing when compared with the cost of litigation. Consumer protection legislation provides special remedies for consumers so that pursuing their rights in court is cost beneficial. Class-action suits provide groups of consumers options for pursuing remedies that they might not be able to pursue (due to the cost) if they were acting alone. **For Example,** the *Laughlin v. Bank of America, N.A.,* case has resulted in several class actions around the country by homeowners who were forced into similar situations as the Laughlins and they are seeking relief. Under most consumer protection statutes class actions give homeowners a chance to recover their damages as well as the costs and attorneys' fees for pursuing recovery. Under some federal statutes debtors who bring class-action suits may be able to recover a statutorily provided percentage of the net worth of the company that has violated their rights.

In addition, consumer statutes often provide initial or alternative means for consumers to enforce their rights. Consumer statutes provide procedural steps for consumers to use to try to resolve their problems with the businesses involved and to document what has happened in their contract or relationship. **For Example,** some statutes require consumers to give the business involved written notice of the consumer's complaint. Having this notice then provides the business an opportunity to examine the consumer's complaint or concerns and possibly work out a solution.

In addition to procedural remedies other than litigation, consumer protection statutes provide other ways for consumers to seek their remedies, sometimes with the help of others who are more experienced in resolving consumer protection statutory violations.

Government Agency Action

At both the federal and state levels, administrative agencies that are responsible for the enforcement of laws and regulations also have the power to take steps to obtain relief for consumers. **For Example,** the Federal Trade Commission (FTC) can file a complaint against a company for false advertising. In settling the complaint with the company that had the false ads, the FTC could require the company to refund to the consumers affected by the ads the price of the product featured in the ad.[4] The federal Consumer Financial Protection Bureau (CFPB) (see p. 630) has the same authority to bring such complaints.

Action by Attorney General

A number of states allow their state attorneys general to bring actions on behalf of consumers who are victims of fraud or other unfair conduct. In these actions, the attorney general can request that consumers' contracts be canceled and that they be given restitution of whatever they paid. These suits by attorneys general are not criminal actions; they are civil suits in which the standard of proof is a preponderance of the evidence, not proof beyond a reasonable doubt. **For Example,** the litigation brought by state attorneys general for alleged deception by tobacco companies on the health harms of using tobacco resulted in settlements by those companies. The funds were used to compensate the states for health care costs for individuals with tobacco-related illnesses for whom the state was caring. The funds were also used to pay for educational programs and ads that caution young people not to smoke and warn them about the health hazards of using tobacco.

[4] *F.T.C. v. Affiliate Strategies, Inc.,* 849 F. Supp. 2d 1085 (D. Kan. 2011).

Many states also permit their attorneys general to bring actions for an injunction against violations of the consumer protection statute. These statutes commonly give the attorney general the authority to obtain a voluntary cease-and-desist consent decree (see Chapter 6) for improper practices before seeking an injunction from a court. The attorney general, like the agency, can impose a penalty for a violation.

Action by Consumer

Consumer protection statutes can also provide that a consumer who has been harmed by a violation of the statutes may recover by his own suit against the business that acted improperly.[5] The consumer may either seek to recover a penalty provided for in the consumer protection statute or bring an action on behalf of consumers as a class. Consumer protection statutes are often designed to rely on private litigation as an aid to enforcement of the statutory provisions. The Consumer Product Safety Act of 1972 authorizes "any interested person" to bring a civil action to enforce a consumer product safety rule and certain orders of the Consumer Product Safety Commission.[6]

Replacement or Refund

Some state consumer protection statutes require that the consumer be made whole by the replacement of the good, the refund of the purchase price, or the repair of the item within a reasonable time.[7]

Invalidation of Consumer's Contract

Other consumer protection statutes provide that when the contract made by a consumer violates the statute, the consumer's contract is void. In such a case, the seller cannot recover from the consumer buyer for any unpaid balance. Likewise, the seller cannot repossess the goods for nonpayment. The consumer keeps the goods without making any further payment.[8]

compensatory damages–sum of money that will compensate an injured plaintiff for actual loss.

punitive damages–damages, in excess of those required to compensate the plaintiff for the wrong done, that are imposed to punish the defendant because of the particularly wanton or willful character of wrongdoing; also called exemplary damages.

32-1f What Are the Civil and Criminal Penalties under Consumer Protection Statutes?

Only certain government agencies and attorneys general can seek criminal and civil penalties against those who violate consumer protection statutes. The agency or attorney general may use those penalties to provide compensation to consumers who have been victims of the violations. When consumers successfully bring individual or class-action suits against those who violate their rights as consumers, they recover damages. Some consumer protection statutes authorize the recovery of **compensatory damages** to compensate the consumer for the loss.[9] These types of statutes are designed to put the customer in as good a position as he would have been in had there not been a deception, breach, or violation of other requirements under the consumer protection statute. Other statutes authorize the recovery of **punitive damages,** which are additional damages beyond compensatory damages and may be a percentage of the company's net worth. Under antitrust statutes that prohibit anticompetitive behavior, consumers can collect treble punitive damages for a violation. Consumers cannot claim both treble damages authorized by a

---

[5] *Devlin v. Wells Fargo Bank, N.A.,* 2014 WL 1155415 (W.D.N.C. 2014).
[6] 15 U.S.C. §2051 *et seq.*
[7] Note that apart from these statutes, the buyer may have protection under a warranty to repair or replace. Likewise, a revocation of acceptance under the UCC would give the right to a refund of the purchase price.
[8] *State ex rel. King v. B & B Investment Group, Inc.,* 329 P.3d 658 (N.M. 2014).
[9] *Chow v. Chak Yam Chau,* 555 Fed. Appx. 842 (11th Cir. 2014).

statute and also punitive damages under the common law. Such double recovery would be duplicative remedies for the same wrong.

32-2 Areas of Consumer Protection

The following sections discuss important areas of consumer protection. Figure 32-1 provides an overview of these areas.

32-2a Advertising

Statutes commonly prohibit fraudulent advertising. Most advertising regulations are entrusted to an administrative agency, such as the FTC, which is authorized to issue orders to stop false or misleading advertising. Statutes prohibiting false advertising are liberally interpreted.

A store is liable for false advertising when it advertises a reduced price sale of a particular item that is out of stock when the sale begins. It is no defense that the presale demand was greater than usual.

Deception

Under consumer protection statutes, *deception* rather than *fraud* is the significant element.[10] A breach of these statutes occurs even without proof that the wrongdoer intended to defraud or deceive anyone.

FIGURE 32-1   **The Legal Environment of the Consumer**

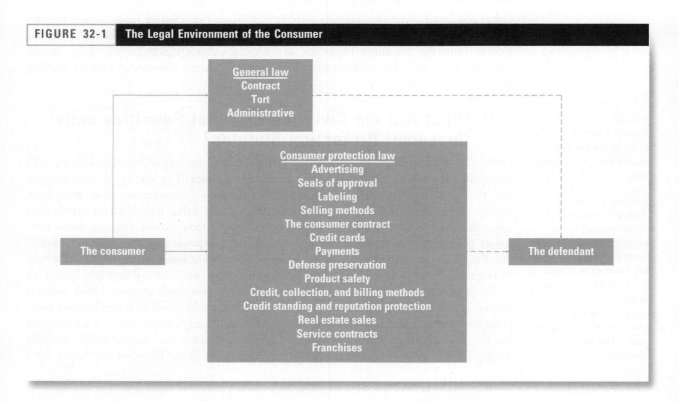

---

[10] *Michael v. Mosquera-Lacy*, 200 P.3d 695 (Wash. 2009); *Williams v. Lifestyle Lift Holdings, Inc.*, 302 P.3d 523 (Wash. App. 2013).

The deception statutes and regulations represent a shift in the law and public policy. These regulations are not laws based on fault; rather, they are based on the question of whether a buyer is likely to be misled by the ad. The good faith of an advertiser or the absence of intent to deceive is immaterial. False advertising regulation protects *consumers* regardless of the advertiser's motives.

The FTC requires advertisers to maintain records of the data used as support for statements made in ads that deal with the safety, performance, efficacy, quality, or comparative price of an advertised product. The FTC can require the advertiser to produce these data and backup material. If it is in the interest of the consumer, the FTC can make this information public except to the extent that it contains trade secrets or privileged material.

Corrective Advertising

When an enterprise has made false and deceptive statements in advertising, the FTC may require new advertising to correct the former statements so that consumers are aware of the truth. This corrective advertising required by the FTC is also called *retractive advertising*. The FTC can also halt ads that it finds to be deceptive.

CASE SUMMARY

Stringing Buyers Along on Floss

FACTS: In June 2004, Pfizer Inc. ("Pfizer") launched a consumer advertising campaign for its mouthwash, Listerine Antiseptic Mouthrinse. Print ads and hang tags on the bottles in the stores featured an image of a Listerine bottle balanced on a scale against a white container of dental floss.

The campaign also featured a television commercial called the "Big Bang." The commercial announced that "Listerine's as effective as floss at fighting plaque and gingivitis. Clinical studies prove it." There had been two studies on floss vs. mouthwash, but the studies concluded that flossing was still necessary in addition to mouthwash. The studies were suggesting that mouthwash with no flossing is better than nothing at all but still concluded that there was no substitute that brought the same results as flossing.

McNeil-PPC, Inc. ("PPC") (and a division of Johnson & Johnson), the market leader in sales of string dental floss and other interdental cleaning products, brought suit alleging that Pfizer had engaged in false advertising in its conclusions about the studies and the use of floss and asked for an injunction halting the ads.

DECISION: The court held that the ads were deceptive because the studies Pfizer was using also concluded that there was no substitute for floss. The studies recommended that flossing continue. The court concluded that the ads misled consumers and granted an injunction halting them. Ads must not misrepresent the results of scientific studies and mislead consumers into doing something that could prove harmful to their dental health. [**McNeil-PPC, Inc. v. Pfizer Inc.**, 351 F. Supp. 2d 226 (S.D.N.Y. 2005)]

32-2b Labeling

Closely related to the regulation of advertising is the regulation of labeling and marking products. Various federal statutes are designed to give consumers accurate information about a product, whereas others require warnings about dangers of use or misuse. Consumer protection regulations prohibit labeling or marking products with such terms as *jumbo, giant*, and *full*, which tend to exaggerate and mislead. **For Example,** the health foods store Eating Well sold a number of foods with the label "Fat Free." This label was false, and Eating Well knew that the foods were ordinary foods not free of fat. Eating Well violated consumer protection statutes that prohibit false labeling. Sales made on

THINKING THINGS THROUGH

The Difference in Concussions and Football Helmet Ad Claims

Riddell, Inc., and Schutt Sports, Inc., both manufacture football helmets. Together, the two companies make up 90 percent of the football helmet market. Riddell's market share is slightly higher than Schutt's.

In 2002, the University of Pittsburgh conducted a study to compare concussion and recovery rates for football players. Riddell provided a grant to underwrite the study that would include salary support for two leading authors of the study, Micky Collins and Mark R. Lovell. A third author, Mark Ide, is a Riddell employee.

The study, conducted from 2002 through 2004, focused on a subset of high school players in the Pennsylvania Interscholastic Athletic Association. For "ethical reasons," the high school students studied were allowed to choose whether to use a Riddell Revolution helmet or one of the traditional helmets. The Revolution helmets supplied in 2002 to study participants were new, but the same helmets were reused in the following years. The traditional helmets were drawn from the schools' inventories and were not necessarily new. Traditional and Revolution helmets that were not new were refurbished and recertified each year by a member of the National Athletic Equipment Reconditioners Association using standards established by the National Operating Committee on Standards for Athletic Equipment.

In 2002, the authors found that athletes wearing the Revolution helmet and athletes wearing the traditional helmets during the 2002 season had nearly identical concussion rates. The data gathered in 2003 showed that the difference in the rate of concussion between the groups of athletes wearing the Revolution helmet and the athletes wearing the traditional helmets was not statistically significant, although the difference "approached" statistical significance.

In 2004, an internal study stated that the total number of participants over the three years was 2,207, with 1,173 fitted with the Revolution helmet and 1,034 equipped with traditional helmets. The internal report showed that 5.29 percent of the athletes wearing the Revolution helmet had diagnoses of cerebral concussions, while 7.16 percent of the athletes wearing traditional helmets sustained concussions.

The final three-year study considered only 2,141 of those participants, with 1,173 fitted with the Revolution and 968 fitted with traditional helmets. Using these numbers, the concussion rates were 5.3 percent and 7.6 percent, respectively, which the authors of the study described as a "statistically significant difference." According to two authors, the results "demonstrated a trend toward a lowered incidence of concussion" but the "limited size sample precludes a more conclusive statement of findings at this time."

When the study was submitted to the journal *Neurosurgery,* the reviewers found "substantial conflicts of interest" as well as flaws in design, the unknown age of the helmets, randomness, and statistical significance. The study was published with comments on its methodological flaws.

Ridell used the study in its ads, stating, "Research has shown that players wearing the Riddell Revolution football helmet are 31% less likely to suffer a concussion than players wearing traditional football helmets." Some ads added that the study showed a reduced risk of concussion "up to 41%" and others added that the 41 percent rate was only for players who had not previously suffered a concussion. Most of the advertisements also included a reference to the *Neurosurgery* article. Riddell also sent out an ad to coaches that referenced the study and developed a PowerPoint presentation with the study included to be used by sales representatives.

The sales pitches and ads were successful and Riddell was able to convert high school and college players to wearing the Riddell Revolution helmet.

Schutt Sports filed suit for false advertising, product disparagement, and deceptive trade practices. Ridell moved for summary judgment and Schutt sought an injunction to stop Ridell from using the study in its ads. Based on the *McNeil-PPC, Inc. v. Pfizer Inc.* case, what do you think the court should do?

Make a list of the ethical issues you see in the Riddell and Schutt case.

[*Riddell, Inc. v. Schutt Sports, Inc.*, 724 F. Supp. 2d 963 (W.D.Wis. 2010)]

the basis of the false labels meant that Eating Well had misled consumers about the fat content of its products.

32-2c Selling Methods

In addition to regulating ads, consumer protection statutes regulate the methods used to sell goods and services.

SPORTS & ENTERTAINMENT LAW

The NFL and Concussion Protocol

The NFL has been the target of criticism and litigation because of problems developing in retired football players that are allegedly related to the number of concussions they experienced during their careers with the NFL, including dementia, depression, and Alzheimer's. The NFL Head, Neck, and Spine Committee has developed a list of steps and procedures that teams should use when there is an injury as well as a policy on return to play. The steps are available in pamphlet guidelines as well as reproduced on wall posters to be posted in team locker rooms so that players are aware of their rights when they sustain an injury.

One part of the protocol is that there be a third-party physician available to conduct the assessment. A third-party physician is one who is not affiliated with the team, an independent doctor who evaluates the scope of the injury, recommends necessary tests, and provides information for the return-to-play decision.

In 2013, the NFL settled a lawsuit brought by former players who said that their mental ailments were caused by blows to the head that they experienced as players. The NFL has always denied the connection, but Commissioner Roger Goodell instructed the NFL's lawyers to "do the right thing for the game and the men who played it." The NFL settled the suit for $765 million. There were 4,000 former players who were plaintiffs in the class-action suit, and the suit provided a cap of $4 million damage award per player. The protocols were developed as a result of the litigation.

Home-Solicited Sales

A sale of goods or services for $25 or more made to a buyer at home may be set aside within three business days. This consumer right of rescission may be exercised merely because the buyer does not want to go through with the contract. There is no requirement that the buyer prove any seller misconduct or defect in the goods or services.[11]

When the buyer has made an oral agreement to purchase and the seller then comes to the buyer's home to work out the details, the transaction is not a home-solicited sale and cannot be rescinded under the federal regulation.[12] A sale was also not home-solicited when the seller phoned the consumer at his or her home for permission to mail the consumer a promotional brochure, and thereafter the consumer went to the seller's place of business where the contract was made.[13]

Telemarketing Fraud

High-pressure selling by telephone has attracted sham businesses and resulted in consumer contracts that are often unconscionable. The Telephone Consumer Protection Act (TCPA) gave the FTC authority to promulgate rules that restrict telemarketing.[14] The TCPA outlaws automated marketing calls without the prior express consent of the called party and prohibits calls to emergency telephone lines or patient rooms in hospitals, health care facilities, or elderly homes. The FTC has added rules that prohibit unsolicited transmissions to fax machines as well as telemarketing calls before 8 A.M. or after 9 P.M. States have additional regulations on telemarketing, including systems that require telemarketers to register with the state.

The TCPA also resulted in a National Do Not Call Registry.[15] Consumers can register to opt out of any telemarketing, except for political and charitable calls.

[11] Federal Trade Commission Regulation, 16 CFR §429:1.
[12] *Burson v. Capps*, 102 A.3d 353 (Md. 2014).
[13] In re *Deitch*, 522 B.R. 99 (E.D. Pa. 2014).
[14] 47 U.S.C. §227.
[15] 16 C.F.R. §310.8.

E-COMMERCE & CYBERLAW

Blocking WiFi to Charge More

It all started with a guest at the Marriott's Gaylord Opryland Hotel and Convention Center in Nashville, Tennessee. The guest found that he could not use any Wi-Fi hotspots in the Marriott convention space at the hotel. He filed a complaint with the Federal Communications Commission (FCC), alleging that the hotel was "jamming mobile hotspots so that you can't use them." Under a federal law that was passed at the time radio transmissions were in the infancy, it is a crime to "willfully or maliciously interfere with radio communications of any licensed station." 47 U.S.C. §333 (2014).

The investigation bureau of the FCC found that Marriott had used features of a Wi-Fi monitoring system at the Gaylord Opryland to contain and/or de-authenticate guest-created Wi-Fi hotspot access points in the conference facilities. In some cases, Marriott employees were sending de-authentication packets to the targeted access points, which would dissociate consumers' devices from their own Wi-Fi hotspot access points and disrupt their current Wi-Fi transmissions and prevent future transmissions.

The FCC also found that the purpose of the jamming was revenue. Marriott charges conference exhibitors and other attending meetings at their convention facilities at the hotel between $250 and $1,000 per device to use the Gaylord Wi-Fi services. Convention participants were left with the choice of paying twice for access (through hot-spot services or through Marriott) or having no access at all.

The FCC brought a complaint against Marriott for violating federal law. Marriott entered into a consent decree, one that contains an admission that employees were scrambling access for convention participants. Marriott agreed to pay a $600,000 fine.

Also as part of the consent decree, Marriott agreed to submit a report and compliance plan to the FCC. The hotel chain must conduct an audit of all the facilities it owns or manages to stop any similar activity and then develop a plan to prevent such activity in the future.

Businesses need to be careful about interfering with Wi-Fi, even on their own properties. Interference is an unfair and deceptive practice in addition to a violation of the federal law on radio transmissions.

32-2d The Consumer Contract

Consumer contracts are regulated in different ways.

Form of Contract

Consumer protection laws commonly regulate the form of the contract, requiring that certain items be specifically listed, that payments under the contract be itemized, and that finance charges be clear (see Chapter 33). Generally, consumer protections require that certain portions of the contract be printed in a certain font size and that a copy of the contract be furnished the consumer.

Contracts Printed on Two Sides

To be sure that consumers see all contract disclosures required by law, contracts that have their terms printed on both the front and the back of the contract must carry the warning "NOTICE: see other side for important information." Consumers must sign the back side of each sheet.

Particular Sales and Leases

The Motor Vehicle Information and Cost Savings Act requires dealers to make certain disclosures to buyers. In addition, the act prohibits selling an automobile without informing the buyer that the odometer has been reset below the true mileage. **For Example,** if a seller knows that the real mileage on a car is 120,073 miles but rolls the odometer back to 20,073 miles, the seller has committed odometer fraud, a violation that allows the buyer to recover three times the actual loss or $1,500, whichever amount is higher.[16] This federal odometer law imposes a higher standard on auto dealers. An auto dealer who may not actually know of a roll-back cannot claim lack of knowledge that the odometer was false when that conclusion was reasonably apparent from the condition of the car.[17]

The federal government regulates particular types of leases of goods. For example, under the Consumer Leasing Act of 1976, leases of autos and other durable goods require specific contract details and disclosures such as the number of lease payments as well as the amount due at the end of the lease for the consumer to purchase the leased goods.[18]

Contract Terms

Consumer protection legislation does not ordinarily affect the right of the parties to make a contract on whatever terms they choose. It is customary, however, to prohibit the use of certain clauses that are harsh for the consumer or that have too great a potential for exploitive abuse by a creditor, such as waiving a warranty limitations disclosure. The Warranty Disclosure Act requires sellers to specify whether the provided warranty protection is full or limited, a standard defined in the act itself.

Limitations on Credit: Subprime and Predatory Lending

With the economic crisis of 2008, there have been significant additional rights for consumers in credit contracts (see discussion later in the section titled "Credit Disclosures"). Part of the reforms focused on the **subprime lending market.** This credit market makes loans to consumers who have bankruptcies, no credit history, low-to-moderate incomes, or a poor credit history. Because of the higher risk of these types of loans, these credit contracts involve lower loan amounts; higher origination costs, brokers' fees, credit insurance fees; higher interest rates; significant collateral pledges; large prepayment penalties (meaning that the consumer debtor is locked into the high interest rate); and faster repayment requirements. Subprime loans have had notoriously difficult-to-read contracts.

Part of the subprime lending market includes lenders who take advantage of less sophisticated consumers or even consumers who are just desperate for funds. These lenders use their superior bargaining positions to obtain credit terms that go well beyond compensating them for their risk. For example, title loans (loans made in exchange for title to a car or house if the borrower defaults) have been widely used in subprime markets. These types of loans, sometimes called **predatory lending,** are highly regulated by both the states and the federal government. The new wave of consumer protection on subprime loans includes limitations on interest rates, 10-day rescission periods, additional contract disclosures requirements, and the requirement of credit counseling before consumers may sign for certain types of subprime loans.

Unconscionability

The UCC has a longstanding form of consumer protection through its prohibition on "unconscionability" in contracts. The types of provisions that make contracts unconscionable include clauses that award excessive damages or the application of credit payments across purchases over time so that the consumer is never able to pay off any goods.

Some specific state statutes are aimed at activities deemed unconscionable—for example, price gouging on consumer goods or services for which the demand is abnormally greater than the supply. **For Example,** New York's statute provides: "During any abnormal disruption of the market for consumer goods and services vital and necessary for the

subprime lending market–a credit market that makes loans to high-risk consumers (those who have bankruptcies, no credit history, or a poor credit history), often loaning money to pay off other debts the consumer has due.

predatory lending–a practice on the part of the subprime lending market whereby lenders take advantage of less sophisticated consumers or those who are desperate for funds by using the lenders' superior bargaining positions to obtain credit terms that go well beyond compensating them for their risk.

[16] 15 U.S.C. §1901 *et seq.*, as amended; recodified as 49 U.S.C. §§32701–32711.
[17] *Ukegbu v. Daniels*, 438 S.W.3d 284 (Ark. App. 2014).
[18] 15 U.S.C. §1667.

health, safety, and welfare of consumers, resulting from stress of weather, convulsion of nature, failure or shortage of electric power or other source of energy … no merchant shall sell or offer to sell any such consumer goods or services for an amount which represents an unconscionably excessive price." Such a statute protects, for example, purchasers of electric generators for home use during a hurricane-caused blackout. During floods and other natural disasters, these statutes limit what sellers can charge for water and other staples.

32-2e Credit Disclosures

While general consumer statutes prohibit deception in ads and sales practices, specific federal laws require the disclosure of all interest charges, points, and fees for all types of loans and credit contracts. These laws require disclosure of an annual percentage rate (APR) so that the consumer can see just how much the transaction costs per year and can compare alternatives.[19] The Truth in Lending Act (TILA) provides the requirements for disclosures in credit contracts and consumer rights when full disclosure is not made. When a consumer sale or contract provides for payment in more than four installments, it is subject to the TILA. The application of the TILA is required even when there is no service or finance charge for the installment payments. There are additional obligations of disclosure under the Fair Credit and Charge Card Disclosure Act,[20] the Home Equity Loan Consumer Protection Act,[21] and the Credit Card Accountability, Responsibility and Disclosure (CARD) Act of 2009.[22] The CARD Act applies to all credit cards. All of these statutes and regulations, discussed in the following sections, require advance disclosures and timing mandates.

The Federal Reserve Board was originally delegated the responsibility for enforcing TILA and has promulgated regulations to carry out the details of disclosure, but the **Consumer Financial Protection Bureau** (CFPB), created under the **Dodd-Frank Wall Street Reform and Consumer Protection Act** (DFCPA), also known as the Wall Street Reform and Consumer Financial Protection Act or the Consumer Financial Protection Act (CFPA), holds that enforcement role. Housed within the Federal Reserve, the CFPB now serves the combined roles that the Federal Reserve as well as the FTC and other federal agencies played in dealing with consumer credit laws, regulations, and issues.

32-2f Credit Cards

Credit cards and credit arrangements are so readily available that consumers tell of receiving credit cards when they apply in the name of their Labrador retrievers. Because of the extensive availability of credit cards and the ease with which they are issued, there are extensive federal regulations of credit card use and the rights of consumers with credit cards.[23]

Unsolicited Credit Cards

Federal regulations prohibit the unsolicited distribution of credit cards to persons who have not applied for them. The practice of simply sending credit cards through the mail to consumers is now illegal. The problems with rising identity theft have made this

Consumer Financial Protection Bureau–consumer protection bureau located within the Federal Reserve that now has jurisdiction over all consumer credit issues and statutes.

Dodd-Frank Wall Street Reform and Consumer Protection Act–federal legislation passed following the financial markets collapse that includes consumer protections as well as market and mortgage lending reforms.

---

[19] Consumer Credit Protection Act (CCPA), 15 U.S.C. §§1605, 1606, & 1636; Regulation Z adopted by the Federal Reserve, 12 C.F.R. §226.5.

[20] 15 U.S.C. §1601 *et seq.*

[21] *Id.*

[22] PL 111-24, 2009 HR 627, 15 U.S.C. §1601, amending sections 1602, 1637, 1640, 1665, 1666b, 1666e, 1666j, 1666i-2.

[23] Heidi Mandanis Schooner, "Consuming Debt: Structuring the Federal Response to Abuses in Consumer Credit," 18 *Loyola Consumer L. Rev.* 43 (2005).

protection especially important to consumers because identity thieves were able to intercept the mail and seize the unsolicited credit cards.

Credit Cards for Those under the Age of 21

The CARD Act substantially restricts the solicitation of credit card accounts from those under the age of 21. Credit card companies must have a written application in hand from those under 21 and those applications must carry the signature of a parent, guardian, or someone over the age of 21 who has the means to repay debt. The line of credit on a co-signed card for someone under the age of 21 cannot be increased without the co-signer's permission. Colleges and universities are now restricted in their partnering with credit card companies, arrangements that allowed the colleges and universities and their alumni associations to receive funds from the credit card companies in exchange for access to their students and alumni. The CARD Act limits locations for college student credit card solicitations, requires colleges and universities to disclose their financial relationships with such credit card companies, and also requires colleges and universities to provide debt counseling for their students.

Surcharge Prohibited

Under some statutes, a seller cannot add any charge to the purchase price because the buyer uses a credit card instead of paying with cash or a check.[24]

Unauthorized Use

A cardholder is not liable for more than $50 for the unauthorized use of a credit card. To even recover the $50 amount, the credit card issuer must show that (1) the credit card was an accepted card,[25] (2) the issuer gave the holder adequate notice of possible liability in such a case, (3) the issuer furnished the holder with notification means in the event of loss or theft of the credit card, (4) the issuer provided a method by which the user of the card could be identified as the person authorized to use it,[26] and (5) unauthorized use of the card had occurred or might occur as a result of loss, theft, or some other event.

The burden of proof is on the card issuer to show that the use of the card was authorized or that the holder is liable for its unauthorized use.[27]

Unauthorized Purpose Distinguished

Unauthorized use of a credit card occurs only when it is used without the permission or approval of the cardholder. The holder may authorize use by another, but only for a limited purpose, such as purchasing office supplies or a new fax machine. If the person uses the card for any item other than the purpose specified, the use remains authorized because merchants cannot know these private restrictions.[28] The same rule is applied when an employer has cards issued to employees for making employment-related purchases but that employees use for personal purposes.

---

[24] The Truth in Lending Act, 15 U.S.C. §1666f, permits a merchant to offer a discount to cash-paying customers but not to customers using a credit card.
[25] A credit card is accepted when the cardholder has requested and received or has signed, used, or authorized another to use the card for the purpose of obtaining money, property, labor, or services on credit.
[26] Regulation Z of the Board of Governors of the Federal Reserve, 12 C.F.R. §226.13(d), as amended, provides that the identification may be by signature, photograph, or fingerprint on the credit card or by electronic or mechanical confirmation.
[27] The Fair and Accurate Credit Transactions Act (FACTA), 15 U.S.C. §1681, requires merchants to use only the last few digits of a credit card on their receipts (a truncated number) so as to reduce the likelihood of a thief finding the receipt and using the full credit card number. *Redman v. RadioShack Corp.*, 768 F.3d 622 (7th Cir. 2014).
[28] *Hayes v. Shelby County Trustee*, 971 F. Supp. 2d 717 (W.D. Tenn. 2013).

Late Payment Fee

The contract between a credit card issuer and a holder may require the holder to pay a late payment fee. The CARD Act changed substantially the law on late payments because of so much abuse by credit card companies with regard to late fees. Under CARD, all credit card companies must have bills in consumers' hands not less than 21 days before the bill is due. In addition, the CARD Act requires conspicuous disclosures about the amount of late fees as well as the impact of a late payment on the consumer's rate of interest.

Credit Card Balance Transfers

Consumers often receive competing offers from credit card companies to transfer their balances from existing cards to what seem to be lower-interest-rate credit cards. The CARD Act imposes maximum fees allowed with these transfers and time requirements for how quickly credit card companies can change the advertised terms of the transfer. The consumer must know all terms of transferring balances, such as the upfront disclosure of transfer fees as well as potential changes in the APR once the transfer has occurred. The CARD Act also places limits on how often companies can change a credit card holder's interest rate.

32-2g Gift Cards

Gift cards have become increasingly popular. During the Christmas shopping season, many retailers' gift card revenues equal their actual sales of merchandise. However, many retailers had built in hidden expiration dates and inactivity fees. Under the CARD Act, a gift card cannot have an expiration date any earlier than five years from the time it is issued and there must be a conspicuous disclosure notice about that expiration date. Inactivity fees on gift cards and cards that decline in value are now regulated under CARD. There are now controls on those declining value fees, such as when they can be charged and what must be disclosed up front.

32-2h Payments

Under the CARD Act, consumer credit card payments are tightly regulated. The due date must specify that the time is 5:00 P.M. on that date. There had been creditor abuses that resulted when they made 9:00 A.M. the cut-off time for payments, thus depriving the debtors of the possibility that their mailed bills could get in for posting by the due date. When consumers make payments in excess of the minimum payment due on their credit card bills, the creditor must apply that extra amount to that portion of the account that carries the highest interest rate.

When and how consumers can exceed their credit limits are subject to disclosure requirements, interest rate change notices, and limitations for how long increased interest rates can apply to, for example, exceeding your credit balance. These rules all affect the amount of the minimum payment and how long the additional interest and fees can apply when a consumer has been tardy on payments or delinquent on the credit card account.

32-2i Preservation of Consumer Defenses

Consumer protection laws generally prohibit a consumer from waiving or giving up any defense provided by law. In an ordinary contract situation, when goods or services purchased or leased by a consumer are not proper or are defective, the consumer is not required to pay for the goods or services or is required to pay only a reduced amount. With the modern expansion of credit transactions, sellers and lessors have used several techniques for getting paid without regard to whether the consumer had any complaint against them. To prevent this, the FTC has adopted a regulation requiring that in every sale or lease of goods or services to a consumer, there must be a contract that gives the consumer the right to assert defenses. This notice can be found in the discussion of negotiable instruments and the rights of the parties in Chapter 28. A good deal of consumer credit issues will no longer be handled by the FTC but rather by the CFPB (see the discussion under "Credit Disclosures").

32-2j Product Safety

A variety of statutes and rules of law protects the health and well-being of consumers. Most states have laws governing the manufacture of various products and establishing product safety standards. The federal Consumer Product Safety Act provides for research and setting uniform standards for products to reduce health hazards and establishes civil and criminal penalties for the distribution of unsafe products. The Consumer Product Safety Commission (CPSC) has the authority to require recalls and obtain permanent bans on the sale of products.[29] **For Example,** the CPSC banned the sale of Bucky Balls, the magnetic building blocks toys, because it established that the product could not be made safe by labeling, warnings, or age limits. Children who swallowed the powerful magnetic pieces ended up requiring surgery due to collapsed organs drawn together by the strong magnets. (See Chapters 9 and 23.)

32-2k Credit, Collection, and Billing Methods

Various laws and regulations protect consumers from discriminatory and improper credit and collection practices.

CPA Equal Credit Opportunity Act: Credit Discrimination

Under the Equal Credit Opportunity Act (ECOA), it is unlawful to discriminate against an applicant for credit on the basis of race, color, religion, national origin, gender, marital status, or age; because all or part of the applicant's income is obtained from a public assistance program; or because the applicant has in good faith exercised any right under the Consumer Credit Protection Act (CCPA). When a credit application is refused, the applicant must be furnished a written explanation. **For Example,** when Robert applied for a loan at Tradesman Bank, he was told on the phone that the loan would not be made to him because of his criminal record. Tradesman must furnish Robert with the specifics regarding that denial. Using Robert's race to decline the loan would be an ECOA violation. However, denial based on a criminal record is permitted.[30]

Fair Credit Billing Act: Correction of Errors

When a consumer believes that a credit card issuer has made a billing error, the consumer should send the creditor a written statement and explanation of the error. The creditor or card issuer must investigate and make a prompt written reply to the consumer.[31] Many credit card companies now permit consumers to file these disputes online.

[29] 15 U.S.C. §§2051–2081.
[30] *Semler v. General Elec. Capital Corp.*, 127 Cal. Rptr. 3d 794 (Cal. App. 2011).
[31] Fair Credit Billing Act, 15 U.S.C. §1601.

Improper Collection Methods

Unreasonable methods of debt collection are often expressly prohibited by statute or are held by courts to constitute an unreasonable invasion of privacy.[32] A creditor is liable for unreasonably attempting to collect a bill that in fact has been paid. This liability can arise under general principles of tort law as well as under special consumer protection legislation.

Fault of Agent or Employee. When improper collection methods are used, it is no defense to the creditor that the improper acts were performed by an agent, an employee, or any other person acting on behalf of the creditor. Under general principles of agency law, a creditor hiring an individual or an agency to collect a debt is liable to the debtor for damages for unlawful conduct by the collector.

CPA **Fair Debt Collection Practices Act (FDCPA).** The federal FDCPA prohibits improper practices in the collection by third parties of debts incurred primarily for personal, family, or household purposes. For purposes of the FDCPA, collectors are defined to include attorneys who are collecting for clients as well as those who are collecting from consumers for bad checks but it does not cover original creditors who are collecting from their original debtors.[33]

Collection Letters. Under the FDCPA, collectors must comply with restrictions on correspondence with debtors. The collector must not misrepresent its status in the letterhead, for example, by stating that the collector is a law firm or lawyer.[34] A letter from a collection agency to a consumer that gives the impression a lawsuit is about to be brought against the consumer when in fact it will not be brought is also a violation of the FDCPA.[35]

A debt collection letter sent to the debtor's place of employment that reveals the nature of the correspondence is a violation of FDCPA. For example, if the words "final demand for payment" can be read through the envelope sent to the place of employment, then the collector has violated the debtor's privacy. Postcards that revealed the purpose of the collector's contact or identity would also be FDCPA violations.

What Is Not a Defense. When a collection agency violates the FDCPA, it is liable to the debtor for damages. It is no defense that the debtor owed the money that the agency was seeking to collect. When a creditor uses improper collection methods, it is no defense that the improper acts were performed by an agent, an employee, or any other person acting on behalf of the creditor.

CPA ## 32-2l Protection of Credit Standing and Reputation

When a person purchases on credit or applies for a loan, a job, or an insurance policy, those who will extend these benefits often wish to know more about the applicant. Credit reporting agencies gather such information on borrowers, buyers, and applicants and sell the information to interested persons.

The Fair Credit Reporting Act (FCRA)[36] protects consumers from various abuses that may arise as this information is recorded and revealed. This statute governs credit reporting agencies, sometimes called *credit bureaus*.

---

[32] Fair Debt Collection Practices Act, 15 U.S.C. §1692 *et seq.*; Federal Trade Commission Regulation, 16 C.F.R. §237.
[33] *Buchanan v. Northland Group, Inc.*, 776 F.3d 393 (6th Cir. 2015) (Mich. 2015).
[34] *Plummer v. Atlantic Credit & Finance, Inc.*, 66 F. Supp. 3d 484 (S.D.N.Y. 2014).
[35] *Szczurek v. Professional Management, Inc.*, 59 F. Supp. 3d 721 (E.D. Pa. 2014).
[36] 15 U.S.C. §1681 *et seq.*

ETHICS & THE LAW

Getting Into Debt and Getting Debt Relief—from the Same Company

Howard Dvorkin is the founder and former president of Consolidated Credit Counseling Services, Inc. The company works with consumers to provide credit counseling and negotiate with lenders to help those consumers pay their debts. Mr. Dworkin has also set up companies that provide services to payday lenders. Payday lenders offer high-interest loans to consumers that are designed to be paid back once the consumers get their paychecks. Mr. Dworkin has denied any involvement in the payday firms and said that he expects the firms to "ethically operate." However, all the companies use the same mailbox or space in the office complex where Consolidated Credit Counseling Services is located.

Some of the companies that indicate an ownership interest by Mr. Dvorkin charge interest rates between 235 percent and 782 percent on 14-day loans. When asked about this conflict Mr. Dvorkin said, "There could be some people that could

say, 'Wow, that's weird.' But I don't really have any involvement whatsoever in those businesses."*

There has been a great deal of focus on the payday loan industry Congress and a number of state legislatures. There is proposed legislation that would affect everything from disclosure requirements to limitations on interest rates for payday loans. The stories on conflicts of interest such as this one continue to appear in the media and have led to proposals that would require more disclosure about the other roles that lenders and credit counselors play, including the companies that they own or operate that are also consumer lenders.

Explain what conflicts could arise when credit counselors own lending companies and debt relief companies.

*Jason Zweig and Rachel Louise Ensign, "Credit Counselor Has Ties to Payday Lenders," *Wall Street Journal*, January 13, 2015, p. A1.

consumer credit–credit for personal, family, and household use.

The FCRA applies only to **consumer credit,** which is defined as credit for "personal, family, and household" use; it does not apply to business or commercial transactions.

Privacy

Credit reporting agencies are not permitted to disclose information to persons not having a legitimate use for it. It is a federal crime to obtain or to furnish a credit report for an improper purpose. On request, a credit reporting agency must tell a consumer the names and addresses of persons to whom it has made a credit report during the previous six months. It must also tell, when requested, which employers were given such a report during the previous two years.

A store may not publicly display a list of named customers from whom it will not accept checks; such action is an invasion of the privacy of those persons.

Protection from False Information

hearsay evidence–statements made out of court that are offered in court as proof of the information contained in the statements and that, subject to many exceptions, are not admissible in evidence.

Much of the information obtained by credit bureaus is based on statements made by persons, such as neighbors, when interviewed by the bureau's investigator. Sometimes the statements are incorrect. Quite often they are **hearsay evidence** and would not be admissible in a legal proceeding. Nevertheless, such statements may go on credit records without further verification and be furnished to a client of the agency, who will tend to regard them as accurate and true.

A person has a limited right to request that a credit bureau disclose the nature and substance of the information it possesses. The right to know, however, does not extend to medical information. The bureau is also not required to identify the persons giving information to its investigators, nor is it required to give the applicant a copy of, or to permit the applicant to see, any file.

CASE SUMMARY

A Crime Online in the Credit Report

FACTS: On September 11, 2012, Tony Smith (plaintiff) applied for a job as a truck driver with Dart Transit Company through Dart's student driver training program. Dart ordered a criminal background check on Smith from E-Backgroundchecks.com (BGC). Dart ordered a U.S. One-SEARCH, which is an automated computer search of BGC's nationwide criminal database programmed to return results instantaneously. U.S. OneSEARCH reports are prepared by matching identifying information provided by the end-users to identifiers contained within the public criminal records in BGC's database, and BGC's practice is to report criminal records that match a consumer's full name and date of birth.

Dart supplied the name "Tony Willie Smith," his date of birth, the state within which he works, and his Social Security number, though the Social Security number was not required. BGC's system identified six criminal records matching plaintiff's first and last name and date of birth, and which did not contain any middle name.

BGC returned these records to Dart in a two-step process as well. First, BGC provided Dart with a summary screen showing basic information about each of the matching records. BGC's system then required Dart to indicate, based on its review of the summary records, whether any records did not match Smith. Dart did not indicate that any of the records supplied by BGC were not a match to Smith and it therefore continued on to the second step of the process, which entailed BGC providing Dart with a detailed view of the criminal records that carried over from another screen. Dart was then able to review each record individually and was required to indicate whether each record would negatively affect plaintiff's employment. Following this step, BGC then completed and electronically returned the criminal background report to Dart at 4:51 P.M. on September 12, 2012.

Because the report contained public criminal record information, BGC's system automatically generated a letter to Smith, advising him that BGC had reported public record information to Dart and enclosing a copy of the report, a summary of plaintiff's rights under the FCRA, and a dispute form. The letter was dated September 12, 2012, and was mailed to Smith, which he admits he received at his home sometime after BGC transmitted the report to Dart.

Smith contacted BGC on September 17, 2012, and disputed the contents of the report he had received from Dart. Two days later, on September 19, BGC issued a corrected report removing all of the previously reported criminal records provided on the September 12 report and showing that Smith had no matching criminal records. That same day, BGC e-mailed a notice to Dart, advising Dart that it had updated Smith's criminal background report. On September 20, 2012, Dart approved plaintiff to begin the training program, which he began on September 25.

Smith filed suit against BGC, alleging that BGC inaccurately reported his criminal history on his consumer report and that in September 2012, he applied for and was denied employment with Dart due to the inaccurate information, which included convictions for possession of a controlled substance by an unregistered person, carrying firearms without a license, and criminal conspiracy. Smith alleged that BGC "continues to publish and disseminate such inaccurate information to other third parties" in violation of the FCRA.

DECISION: BGC furnished to Dart an indisputably inaccurate report that did not match plaintiff's full name and Social Security number that Dart had provided to BGC. Since BGC had in its possession information that could have been used to demonstrate the inaccuracy of the report it furnished to Dart, there is a material dispute of fact as to whether BGC's initial search procedures were in fact reasonable in this instance because while requiring a credit reporting agency to go beyond the face of court records to determine whether those records correctly report the outcome of the underlying action may be too much to ask, requiring a CRA to correctly determine which public records belong to which individual consumers is not.

BGC returned records that only matched plaintiff's first and last name, a very common name at that, and despite having Smith's complete name and Social Security number, BGC took no steps prior to issuing its initial report to confirm whether the "Tony Smith" criminal records it provided to Dart were associated with the full name and Social Security number of plaintiff.

BGC did not have a process to confirm whether its records are in fact a match to the individual. BGC even admitted that the automated computer program had no way of differentiating between individuals with the same name and date of birth, and that after it compiled its initial matching records, it then placed the burden on employers to indicate whether any records did not match the individual.

BGC's motion for summary judgment was denied. [*Smith v. E-Backgroundchecks.com, Inc.*, **81 F. Supp. 3d 1342 (N.D. Ga. 2015)**]

When a person claims that report information is erroneous, the credit bureau must take steps within a reasonable time to determine the accuracy of the disputed item.

Adverse information obtained by investigation cannot be given to a client after three months unless it is verified to determine that it is still valid. Most legal proceedings cannot be reported by a bureau after 7 years, although a bankruptcy proceeding can be reported for 10 years.

Credit Repair Organizations

These organizations, some nonprofit and others for-profit, advertise their ability to help consumers work their way out of debt and eliminate negative credit information. Congress began regulating these groups with the Credit Repair Organization Act of 1996. Both the bankruptcy reforms (see Chapter 34) and state laws have established standards and procedures to ensure that consumers are not absorbing higher costs for services that they could do for themselves. There were additional reforms under the Consumer Financial Protection Act, including requirements for disclosures.

32-2m Other Consumer Protections

Various laws aimed at protecting purchasers of real estate, buyers of services, and prospective franchisees have been adopted in the states and at the federal level.

Real Estate Development Sales: Interstate Land Sales Full Disclosure Act

Anyone promoting the sale of a real estate development that is divided into 50 or more parcels of less than 5 acres each must file a **development statement** with the secretary of Housing and Urban Development (HUD). This statement must set forth significant details of the development as required by the federal Interstate Land Sales Full Disclosure Act (ILSFDA).[37]

Anyone buying or renting one of the parcels in the subdivision must be given a **property report,** which is a condensed version of the development statement filed with the secretary of HUD. This report must be given to the prospective customer at least 48 hours before the signing of the contract to buy or lease.

State statutes complement the ILSFDA and frequently require that particular enterprises selling property disclose certain information to prospective buyers. Some state statutes provide protection for sales of real property interests such as time-sharing condominiums that are not covered under the ILSFDA.[38]

Service Contracts

The UCCC treats a consumer service contract the same as a consumer sale of goods if (1) payment is made in installments or a credit charge is made and (2) the amount financed does not exceed $25,000. The UCCC defines *services* broadly as embracing transportation, hotel and restaurant accommodations, education, entertainment, recreation, physical culture (such as athletic clubs or bodybuilding schools), hospital accommodations, funerals, and cemetery accommodations.

In some states, it is unlawful for a repair shop to make unauthorized repairs to an automobile and then refuse to return the automobile to the customer until the customer has paid for the repairs. In some states, a consumer protection statute imposes multiple

development statement— statement that sets forth significant details of a real estate or property development as required by the federal Land Sales Act.

property report— condensed version of a property development statement filed with the secretary of HUD and given to a prospective customer at least 48 hours before signing a contract to buy or lease property.

[37] 15 U.S.C. §1701 *et seq.*
[38] *Beaver v. Tarsadia Hotels,* 29 F. Supp. 3d 1294 (S.D. Cal. 2014).

damages on a repair shop that delays unreasonably in performing a contract to repair property of the consumer.[39]

Franchises

franchisee–person to whom franchise is granted.

franchisor–party granting the franchise.

franchise–(1) a privilege or authorization, generally exclusive, to engage in a particular activity within a particular geographic area, such as a government franchise to operate a taxi company within a specified city, or a private franchise as the grant by a manufacturer of a right to sell products within a particular territory or for a particular number of years; (2) the right to vote.

To protect prospective **franchisees** from deception by **franchisors** that seek to sell interests, an FTC regulation requires that the franchisor give a prospective franchisee a disclosure statement 10 days before the franchisee signs a contract or pays any money for a **franchise.** The disclosure statement provides detailed information relating to the franchisor's finances, experience, size of operation, and involvement in litigation. The FTC enforces these disclosure requirements and can impose fines.

Automobile Lemon Laws

All states have adopted special laws for the protection of consumers buying automobiles that develop numerous defects or defects that cannot be corrected. These statutes protect only persons buying automobiles for personal, family, or household use. They generally classify an automobile as a *lemon* if it cannot be put in proper or warranted condition within a specified period of time or after a specified number of repair attempts. In general, they give the buyer greater protection than is given to other buyers by the UCC or other consumer protection statutes (see Chapter 24). In some states, the seller of a car that turns out to be a lemon is required to give the buyer a brand-new replacement car. In some states, certain agencies may also bring an action to collect civil penalties from the seller of a lemon car.

Lemon laws in most states are designed to increase the prelitigation bargaining power of consumers and reduce the greater power of manufacturers to resist complaints or suits by consumers.[40] **For Example,** Abdul, who owned a paint store, purchased two automobiles from Prime Motors, one for delivering paint to his customers and the second for his wife to use for shopping and taking their children to school. Both cars were defective and in need of constant repair. Abdul claimed that he was entitled to remedies provided by the local automobile lemon law. He was wrong with respect to the store's delivery car because lemon laws do not cover cars purchased for commercial use, but the other car was protected by the lemon law because it was clearly a family car.

Make the Connection

- -

Summary

Modern methods of marketing, packaging, and financing have reduced the ordinary consumer to a subordinate position. To protect the consumer from the hardship, fraud, and oppression that could result from being in such an inferior position, consumer protection laws, at both the state and federal levels, afford rights to consumers and impose requirements on those who deal with consumers.

When a consumer protection statute is violated, an action may sometimes be brought by the consumer against the wrongdoer. More commonly, an action is brought by an administrative agency or by the state attorney general.

Consumer protection laws are directed at false and misleading advertising; misleading or false use of labels; the methods of selling, with specific requirements on the

[39] *Raysoni v. Payless Auto Deals, LLC,* 766 S.E.2d 24 (Ga. 2014).
[40] *James Michael Leasing Co. LLC v. PACCAR, Inc.,* 772 F.3d 815 (7th Cir. 2014).

disclosure of terms and the permitting of consumer cancellation of home-solicited sales; and types of credit arrangements. The consumer is protected in a contract agreement by regulation of its form, prohibition of unconscionable terms, and limitation of the credit that can be extended to a consumer. Credit card protections include prohibition of the unauthorized distribution of credit cards and limited liability of the cardholder for the unauthorized use of a credit card. Included in consumer protection laws are the application of payments; the preservation of consumer defenses as against a transferee of the consumer's contract; product safety; the protection of credit standing and reputation; and (to some extent) real estate development sales, franchises, and service contracts. Lemon laws provide special protection to buyers of automobiles for personal, household, or family use.

Learning Outcomes

After studying this chapter, you should be able to clearly explain:

32-1   General Principles

LO.1   Explain what consumer protection laws do and the types of consumer protections

See the list of headings in this chapter to determine areas of consumer protection, page 618.

See the *Laughlin v. Bank of America* case on consumer protections in mortgage modifications, page 621.

See the *McNeil-PPC, Inc. v. Pfizer Inc.* case on page 625.

See the Thinking Things Through that deals with ads between competing football helmet manufacturers and the concussions, and a study that Ridell used in its ads that Schutt Sports says is misleading, page 626.

See the Sports & Entertainment Law feature related to the football helmet case and concussions, page 627.

32-2   Areas of Consumer Protection

LO.2   List the rights and protections consumer debtors have when a collector contacts them

See the discussion of the Fair Debt Collection Practices Act, page 634.

See the Ethics & the Law feature, "Getting Into Debt and Getting Debt Relief—from the Same Company," page 635.

See the E-Commerce & Cyberlaw feature on Marriott blocking WiFi in its hotels so that convention participants and exhibitors had to pay for WiFi, page 628.

LO.3   Give a summary of the rights of consumers with regard to credit reports

See the *Smith v. E-Backgroundchecks.com* case, page 636.

LO.4   Describe the types of protections available for consumers who have credit cards

See the discussion of the CARD Act, pages 630–632.

Key Terms

compensatory damages	Dodd-Frank Wall Street Reform and	predatory lending
consumer	Consumer Protection Act	property report
consumer credit	franchise	punitive damages
Consumer Financial Protection	franchisees	subprime lending market
Bureau	franchisors	
development statement	hearsay evidence	

Questions and Case Problems

1. The San Antonio Retail Merchants Association (SARMA) was a credit reporting agency. It was asked by one of its members to furnish information on William Douglas Thompson III. It supplied information from a file that contained data on William III and on William Daniel Thompson Jr. The agency had incorporated information related to William Jr. into the file relating to William III so that all information appeared to relate to William III. This was a negligent mistake because each William had a different Social Security number, which should have raised a suspicion that there was a mistake. In addition, SARMA should have used a number of checkpoints to ensure that incoming information would be put into the proper file. William Jr. had bad credit standing. Because of its mistake, SARMA gave a bad

report on William III, who was denied credit by several enterprises. The federal Fair Credit Reporting Act makes a credit reporting agency liable to any consumer about whom it furnishes a consumer report without following reasonable procedures to ensure maximum possible accuracy of information. William III sued SARMA for its negligence in confusing him with William Jr. Is SARMA liable? [*Thompson v. San Antonio Retail Merchants Ass'n*, 682 F.2d 509 (5th Cir.)]

2. Colgate-Palmolive Co. ran a television commercial to show that its shaving cream, Rapid Shave, could soften even the toughness of sandpaper. The commercial showed what was described as the sandpaper test. Actually, what was used was a sheet of Plexiglas on which sand had been sprinkled. The FTC claimed that this was a deceptive practice. The advertiser contended that actual sandpaper would merely look like ordinary colored paper and that Plexiglas had been used to give the viewer an accurate visual representation of the test. Could the FTC prohibit the use of this commercial? [*Federal Trade Commission v. Colgate-Palmolive Co.*, 380 U.S. 374]

3. Sharolyn Charles wrote a check for $17.93 to a Poncho's Restaurant on July 4, 1996, as payment for a meal she had there. The check was returned for insufficient funds. Poncho's forwarded the check to Check Rite for collection.

   On July 19, Check Rite sent a letter to Charles, stating that "[t]his is an attempt to collect a debt" and requesting total payment of $42.93—the amount of the check plus a service charge of $25. On August 7, Check Rite sent a second letter, requesting payment of $42.93 and advising Charles that failure to pay the total amount due might result in additional liability for damages and attorneys' fees, estimated at $242.93.

   Check Rite subsequently referred the matter to the law firm of Lundgren & Associates for collection. On September 8, Lundgren sent a letter to Charles offering to settle within 10 days for a total amount of $127.93—the amount of the check plus a settlement amount of $110. Lundgren further advised that it had made no decision to file suit, that it could later decide to do so, and that Charles's potential liability was $317.93. Charles immediately sent to Lundgren a money order in the amount of $17.93. On September 13, Lundgren sent a second letter, repeating the settlement offer made in the September 8 letter. Lundgren then returned

Charles's payment on September 14, declining to accept it as payment in full and repeating the settlement offer. On September 19, Lundgren sent a fourth letter to Charles, repeating the settlement offer.

   On October 15, 1996, Charles filed suit in federal district court alleging violations of the Fair Debt Collections Practices Act (FDCPA). Lundgren & Associates moved to dismiss the case on grounds that an attempt to collect on a check is not a "debt" governed by FDCPA. The district court dismissed the case; Charles appealed. Should Charles win? Is she protected under the FDCPA? [*Charles v. Lundgren & Associates, P.C.*, 119 F.3d 739 (9th Cir.)]

4. Thomas was sent a credit card through the mail by a company that had taken his name and address from the telephone book. Because he never requested the card, Thomas left the card lying on his desk. A thief stole the card and used it to purchase merchandise in several stores in Thomas's name. The issuer of the credit card claimed that Thomas was liable for the total amount of the purchases made by the thief. Thomas claimed that he was not liable for any amount. The court decided that Thomas was liable for $50. Who is correct? Why?

5. On May 16, 2003, Sari Smith filed a class-action lawsuit in Cook County, Illinois, against J.M. Smucker Co. on behalf of "[a]ll purchasers in the United States of America of spreadable fruit products labeled 'Simply 100% Fruit' manufactured, produced, and sold by J.M. Smucker Co. excluding its directors, officers and employees" for consumer fraud, deceptive business practices, unjust enrichment, and breach of warranty, alleging that Smucker's Simply 100% Fruit products do not contain 100 percent fruit. The premium jam's label indicates that, for example, its Strawberry jam also contains "fruit syrup, lemon juice concentrate, fruit pectin, red grape juice concentrate and natural flavors." Is the label a form of deceptive advertising?

   If you were a Smucker's executive, what would you argue in the case on deceptive ads? [*J.M. Smucker Co. v. Rudge*, 877 So. 2d 820 (Fla. App.)]

6. International Yogurt Co. (IYC) developed a unique mix for making frozen yogurt and related products. Morris and his wife purchased a franchise from the company but were not told that a franchise was not a requirement for obtaining the mix—that the company would sell its yogurt mix to anyone. The Morrises' franchise business was a failure, and they

sold it at a loss after three years. They then sued the company for fraud and for violation of the state Franchise Investment Protection Act and the state Consumer Protection Act for failing to inform them that the mix could be obtained without a franchise. IYC claimed that no liability could be imposed for failing to make the disclosure. Was it correct? [*Morris v. International Yogurt Co.*, 729 P.2d 33 (Wash.)]

7. In December 2008, Corey and Jamie Baker purchased a TV from Best Buy as well as a four-year service contract for the TV. In November 2010, Best Buy determined that the problems the Bakers were having with the TV could not be fixed, so Best Buy replaced the TV with a comparable model. Best Buy told the Bakers that if they wanted the full protection on the replacement TV, they would need to buy a new four-year policy. The Bakers and others filed suit against Best Buy for consumer fraud and false statements in advertisements because the Bakers felt that the ads depicted the service agreement as being one of full protection for four years. Under the terms of the service contract purchased by the appellants, coverage under the plan was effective from the date the product was purchased and would expire four years from the effective date. But the next paragraph of the service contract adds that "[o]ur obligations under this Plan will be fulfilled in their entirety if we replace your product." The contract further stated "Limits of Liability," defining a limit of the lesser of repair or replacements and finally stating that "[i]n the event … we replace the product, we shall have satisfied all obligations under the Plan." What should the court decide? Was there deception, or is the contract clear enough for buyers? Discuss the factors the court will consider in deciding whether there has been consumer fraud. [*Baker v. Best Buy Stores, LP*, 812 N.W.2d 177 (Minn. App.)]

8. The town of Newport obtained a corporate MasterCard that was given to the town clerk for purchasing fuel for the town hall. The town clerk used the card for personal restaurant, hotel, and gift shop debts. The town refused to pay the card charges on the grounds that they were unauthorized. Was the town correct? [*MasterCard v. Town of Newport*, 396 N.W.2d 345 (Wis. App.)]

9. Stevens purchased a pair of softball shoes manufactured by Hyde Athletic Industries. Because of a defect in the shoes, she fell and broke an ankle. She sued Hyde under the state consumer protection act, which provided that "any person who is injured in … business or property … could sue for damages sustained." Hyde claimed that the act did not cover personal injuries. Stevens claimed that she was injured in her "property" because of the money that she had to spend for medical treatment and subsequent care. Decide. [*Stevens v. Hyde Athletic Industries, Inc.*, 773 P.2d 87 (Wash. App.)]

10. A consumer made a purchase on a credit card. The card issuer refused to accept the charge, and an attorney then sued the consumer for the amount due. In the complaint filed in the lawsuit, the attorney wrongly stated that interest was owed at 18 percent per annum. This statement was later corrected by an amendment of the complaint to 5 percent. The case against the consumer was ultimately settled, but the consumer then sued the attorney for penalties under the Fair Debt Collection Practices Act, claiming that the overstatement of the interest due in the original complaint was a violation of that act. The attorney defended on the ground that the act did not apply. Did it? [*Green v. Hocking*, 9 F.3d 18 (6th Cir.)]

11. Classify each of the following activities as proper or prohibited under the various consumer statutes you have studied.

    a. Calling a hospital room to talk to a debtor who is a patient there.

    b. Calling a hospital room to sell surgical stockings.

    c. Rolling back the odometer on one's car before selling it privately.

    d. No TILA disclosures on an instant tax refund program in which the lender takes 40 percent of the tax refund as a fee for advancing the money when the taxpayer files the tax return.

12. Alpha University has an arrangement with Axis Credit Card Company to collect 1 percent on all credit card charges made by students who obtain their cards through booths on the Alpha campus. Do any consumer protection statutes apply to this relationship?

13. List three areas in consumer credit cards affected by the CARD Act.

C H A P T E R   33

Secured Transactions in Personal Property

CPA   33-1   **Creation of Secured Transactions**

Creditors can have some additional assurance of payment if the debtor pledges property as security for the loan. If the debtor does not pay, the creditor can then turn to the property and sell it or keep it as a means of satisfying the obligation.

A *secured transaction* is one means by which personal property is used to provide a backup plan or security for the creditor in the event the borrower does not pay. Secured transactions are governed by Article 9 of the Uniform Commercial Code (UCC). Article 9 has been revised several times, and its latest version (2001) has been adopted in some form by all states and the District of Columbia.[1]

33-1a   **Definitions**

> **secured transaction**–credit sale of goods or a secured loan that provides special protection for the creditor.

A **secured transaction** in personal property is created by giving the creditor a security interest in that property. A **security interest** is like a lien in personal property; it is a property right that enables the creditor to take possession of the property if the debtor does not pay the amount owed. **For Example,** if you borrow money from a bank to buy a car, the bank takes a security interest in the car. If you do not repay the loan, the bank can repossess the car and sell it to recover the money the bank has loaned you. If you purchase a side-by-side refrigerator from Kelvin's Appliances on credit, Kelvin's takes a security interest in the refrigerator. If you do not repay Kelvin's, Kelvin's can repossess the refrigerator and sell it to cover the amount you still owe.

> **security interest**–property right that enables the creditor to take possession of the property if the debtor does not pay the amount owed.

The property that is subject to the security interest is called **collateral.** In the preceding examples, the car was the bank's collateral for the loan, and the refrigerator was Kelvin's collateral.

> **collateral**–property pledged by a borrower as security for a debt.

Parties

> **creditor**–person (seller or lender) who is owed money; also may be a secured party.

The person to whom the money is owed, whether a seller or a lender, is called the **creditor** or **secured party.** The buyer on credit or the borrower is called the **debtor.**

Nature of Creditor's Interest

> **secured party**–person owed the money, whether as a seller or a lender, in a secured transaction in personal property.

The creditor does not own the collateral, but the security interest is a property right. That property right can ripen into possession and the right to transfer title by sale.

A creditor who has possession of the collateral as a means of security has a duty of care imposed under the UCC. Under the UCC, the creditor in possession must exercise reasonable care to preserve the property. The creditor is liable for any damage that results from falling short of that standard.

Nature of Debtor's Interest

> **debtor**–buyer on credit (i.e., a borrower).

A debtor who is a borrower ordinarily owns the collateral.[2] As such, the debtor has all rights of any property owner to recover damages for the loss or improper seizure of, or damage to, the collateral.[3]

---

[1] Not all states, however, have adopted verbatim versions. For example, the application of Article 9 to governmental units varies significantly among the states. See "UCC Article 9: Personal Property Secured Transactions," 60 *Bus. Lawyer* 1725 (2005).

[2] *Heartland Bank and Trust v. The Leiter Group*, 18 N.E.3d 558 (Ill.App.2014); *Farmers-Merchants Bank & Trust Co. v. Southern Structures, LLC*, 134 So. 3d 142 (La. App. 2014).

[3] Article 9 does cover consignment arrangements. The consignor continues to own the goods, and the consignee is treated as a secured creditor with a purchase money security interest in the consigned goods.

33-1b **Creation of a Security Interest**

The attachment, or the creation of a valid security interest, occurs when the following three conditions are satisfied: There is (1) a security agreement, (2) value has been given, and (3) the debtor has rights in the collateral. These three conditions can occur in any order. A security interest will attach when the last of these conditions has been met. When the security interest attaches, it is then enforceable against the debtor and the collateral.

CPA

security agreement– agreement of the creditor and the debtor that the creditor will have a security interest.

Agreement

The **security agreement** is the contract between creditor and debtor for the security interest. This required agreement must identify the parties, contain a reasonable description of the collateral, indicate the parties' intent that the creditor has a security interest in it, describe the debt or the performance that is secured thereby, and be authenticated by the debtor.[4] Electronic authentication by debtors is acceptable under Article 9.[5] Authentication can come from the debtor's actions that indicate an understanding of a credit and secured debt agreement.[6] A security interest description is valid if it "reasonably identifies what is described."[7] Examples of reasonable identification include a specific listing, category,[8] quantity, and serial numbers. "Supergeneric descriptions"[9] such as "all the debtor's personal property" are insufficient,[10] but "livestock" is a sufficient description.[11] The requirement for description of consumer goods as collateral is more stringent than for other types of collateral.[12]

If the creditor has possession of the collateral, the security agreement may be oral regardless of the amount involved.[13] **For Example,** if you pledge your stereo system to a friend as security for the loan and the friend will keep it at his home until you have repaid him, your friend has possession of the collateral, and your oral security agreement is valid and enforceable by your friend. If the creditor does not have possession of the collateral, as in the case of credit sales and most secured loans, the security agreement must be evidenced by a record that meets all requirements.

Field warehousing, covered in Chapter 21, is another form of possession of goods that permits an oral security agreement. Credit unions and banks can possess an account

---

[4] "No magic words are necessary … to create a security interest." In re *Okke,* 513 B.R. 896 (W.D. Mich. 2014).

[5] However, the debtor must be aware that a security agreement is being signed. An electronic signature on a credit card transaction does not indicate that the debtor was aware he was agreeing to a security interest by Best Buy if the terms were not reviewed or made conspicuous in the sales receipt. In re *Cunningham,* 489 B.R. 602 (D. Kan. 2013).

[6] Article 9, §9-102(a)(69) defines "record," the new substitute for "signed agreement" of old Article 9, as "information that is inscribed on a tangible medium and is retrievable in perceivable form." Authentication need not be a signature. In re *Eyerman,* 517 B.R. 800 Bankr. (S.D. Ohio. 2014). One court held that a letter between the debtor and creditor qualified as a security agreement because it contained all of the necessary elements of description, signature, etc. In re *Loop* 76, *LLC,* 578 Fed. Appx. 644 (9th Cir. 2014). Not all states follow the "collage doctrine" that allows the grouping together of documents to establish a security agreement. In re *Thrun,* 495 B.R. 861 (W.D. Wis. 2013).

[7] U.C.C. §9-110.

[8] Commercial tort claims and consumer transactions cannot be sufficiently described by type of collateral. The security agreement must give more specifics. §9-108(e)(1) and (2).

[9] U.C.C. §9-108(c).

[10] The comments to §9-108 indicate that serial numbers are not necessarily required, but an outsider must be able to tell from the description what property is or is not included under the security agreement. Official Comment, §9-108, 2. "Debtor's new trucks" is insufficient. In re *LDB Media, LLC,* 497 B.R. 332 (M.D. Fla. 2013).

[11] *Baldwin v. Castro County Feeders I, Ltd.,* 678 N.W.2d 796 (S.D. 2004). All "IP assets" is also sufficient. In re *ProvideRx of Grapevine, LLC,* 507 B.R. 132 (N.D. Tex. 2014).

[12] In re *Gracy,* 522 B.R. 686 (D. Kan. 2015). "Goods purchased on [debtor's] account is insufficient." In re *Cunningham,* 489 B.R. 602 (D. Kan. 2013).

[13] U.C.C. §9-207; In re *Rowe,* 369 B.R. 73 (Mass. 2007). If there is no record the security interest itself is destroyed when the collateral is surrendered.

pledged as security if the funds cannot be used by the account holder without permission and clearance from a bank officer.

Value

value–consideration or antecedent debt or security given in exchange for the transfer of a negotiable instrument or creation of a security interest.

The creditor gives **value** either by lending money to the debtor or by delivering goods on credit. The value may be part of a contemporaneous exchange or given previously as a loan. **For Example,** a debtor who already owes a creditor $5,000 could later pledge a water scooter as collateral for that loan and give the debtor a security interest in the scooter. In fact, creditors who become nervous about repayment often request collateral later during the course of performance of a previously unsecured loan.

Rights in the Collateral

The debtor must have rights in the collateral for a security interest to attach. For example, when goods are sent "FOB place of shipment" to a debtor, the debtor has title at the time those goods are delivered to the carrier by the seller. See Chapter 23 for more information. The buyer has rights in the collateral that allow for the collateral to be subject to the creditor's security interest.[14]

CPA 33-1c **Purchase Money Security Interest**

purchase money security interest (PMSI)–the security interest in the goods a seller sells on credit that become the collateral for the creditor/seller.

When a seller sells on credit and is given a security interest in the goods sold, that interest is called a **purchase money security interest (PMSI).** If the buyer borrows money from a third person so that the purchase can be made for cash, a security interest given in those goods to that lender is also called a purchase money security interest.[15] Certain special priority rights (discussed later in this chapter) are given in some circumstances to creditors who hold a PMSI.

CASE SUMMARY

The Best Buys on Credit

FACTS: Charles and Charity Cunningham (the Debtors) filed a joint Chapter 7 bankruptcy. The Debtors had purchased two iPods, a camera, a computer, and other items in 12 separate consumer transactions of consumer goods from Best Buy, N.A., a national retailer of consumer electronics and related products and services. Some of Debtors' purchases were made on credit provided by Capital One.

The Debtors signed a credit application, which states, "you grant the Bank a purchase money security interest in the goods purchased on your Account." Furthermore, the application states in that same section that the cardholder, the Debtors, agree to the terms and conditions of the Cardholder Agreement.

The Application has this language buried in a 16-line paragraph in a small font. A magnifying glass is necessary to find and read the language. The language appears in the ninth and tenth lines of the paragraph. The Debtors agreed, in this fine print, to the terms and conditions of the Cardholder Agreement. The Application indicates that the Cardholder Agreement would be sent to the Debtors after the Application and initial purchase of consumer products on January 16, 2010. The Cardholder Agreement is not signed. Buried in 41 numbered paragraphs in small print in the Cardholder Agreement is language that refers to Debtors granting to Capital One "a purchase money security interest in the goods purchased with your Card."

---

[14] U.C.C. §9-112.
[15] U.C.C. §9-107. In re *Marriage of Christodolou,* 2012 WL 4814606 (Tex. App. 2012).

The Best Buys on Credit continued

The cardholder agreement states in paragraph 17 entitled "Security," "you grant us a purchase money security interest in the goods purchased with your Card."

The 12 Best Buy receipts for the purchases all were signed by one of the Debtors, except for one transaction. The receipts contain basic information, such as the location of the Best Buy store, a brief description of items purchased and the price of these items, and the date and time of the sale. The receipts also state "Payment Type: BBY CARD/HSBC." The following language appears below the place of signature:

> *KEEP YOUR RECEIPT!*
>
> *I HAVE READ AND AGREE TO ALL RETURN AND REFUND POLICIES PRINTED ON THE BACK OF THIS*
>
> *RECEIPT AND POSTED IN THE STORE. I HAVE RECEIVED GOODS AND/OR SERVICES IN THE AMOUNT*
>
> *SHOWN ABOVE. BESTBUY.COM RETURN AND EXCHANGE INFORMATION AND PRICE MATCH POLICY*
>
> *MAY VARY SLIGHTLY FROM IN–STORE POLICY. PLEASE LOG ONTO WWW.BESTBUY.COM*
>
> *FOR COMPLETE DETAILS.*

The court did not have copies of the reverse side of the receipts, which were not provided. Regardless, it appears that the reverse side of the receipts only contains language pertinent to the return and refund policies of Best Buy. There is no reference on the receipts to security interests, purchase money or otherwise, retained by anyone. The receipts also do not contain a reference to the Application or the Cardholder Agreement. The Debtors requested a determination by the Court that Capital One does not hold a security interest, purchase money or otherwise, in the goods they purchased at Best Buy.

DECISION: A security agreement or financing statement must contain a description of the collateral that reasonably identifies the collateral. The use of categories or types of collateral defined under the UCC (i.e., inventory) is still permitted. However, in consumer transactions and a limited number of other situations, a description by type or class of collateral is ineffective as to after-acquired property. Article 9 permits "supergeneric" descriptions in the financing statement such as "all assets" or "all personal property" but not in the security agreement.

The Debtors argued that any security interest that Capital One may have never attached to the Consumer Goods because an insufficient description is fatal to the attachment of a security interest in consumer goods. Capital One argued that the description is sufficient if one combines the language contained in the application, the receipts, and the Cardholder Agreement. The issue before the Court was whether the description is sufficient to allow attachment and enforceability. The Capital One receipts do not contain a reference to a purchase money security interest or any other security interest. Capital One may not rely upon the description of the Debtors' goods purchased on the receipts because the receipts are not a component of a security agreement between the parties.

The security agreement is not enforceable in a consumer transaction because, excluding the receipts, the collateral is only described by type or class. Therefore, Capital One does not hold a security interest in the Debtors' goods. [In re ***Cunningham***, **489 B.R. 602, 80 U.C.C. Rep. Serv. 2d 576 (D. Kan. 2013)**]

CPA   33-1d **The Nature and Classification of Collateral**

The nature of the collateral in a credit transaction, as well as its classification under Article 9, affect the procedural obligations and rights of creditors. Article 9 contains an extensive list of the types of collateral, including the traditional types such as consumer goods, equipment, inventory, general intangibles, farm products, and fixtures,[16] but also accounts, accounts receivable, accounts receivable held because of credit card transactions or license fees, energy contracts, insurance policy proceeds, amounts due for services rendered, amounts earned from chartering a vessel, winnings in the state lottery, and health

---

[16] U.C.C. §9-102.

care insurance receivables. The general category of "account"[17] does not include commercial tort claims, deposit accounts, investment property, or letters of credit but does include insurance claims, lottery winnings, and property proceeds.[18]

Consumer Goods

consumer goods–goods used or bought primarily for personal, family, or household use.

Collateral that is classified as a **consumer good** results in different rights and obligations under Article 9, regardless of the type of property it is. Collateral is considered a consumer good if it is "used or bought for use primarily for personal, family, or household purposes."[19] The use of the good, and not its properties, controls its classification. **For Example,** a computer purchased by an architect for her office is not a consumer good. That same computer purchased by the same architect for use by her children at their home is a consumer good. A refrigerator purchased for the kitchen near an office conference center is not a consumer good. That same model refrigerator purchased for a home is a consumer good. The use of the goods controls the label that is applied to the collateral.

CPA

After-Acquired Collateral and Ongoing Credit

after-acquired goods– goods acquired after a security interest has attached.

floating lien–claim in a changing or shifting stock of goods of the buyer.

A creditor's rights can be expanded to include coverage of all future loans and funds advances as well as future acquisitions of collateral. If the security agreement so provides, the security interest attaches to **after-acquired goods** and applies to all loans to the debtor.[20] **For Example,** a security interest can cover the current inventory of the debtor and any future replenishments if a clause in the security agreement adds "after-acquired property" to the description of the inventory. Referred to in lay terms as a **floating lien,** the creditor's security interest covers the inventory regardless of its form or time of arrival in relation to attachment of the security interest.

After-acquired clauses in consumer credit contracts are restricted. An after-acquired property clause in a consumer security agreement can cover only goods acquired by the debtor within 10 days after the creditor gave value to the debtor.

Proceeds

The UCC defines proceeds as "whatever is received upon the sale, exchange, collection, or other disposition of collateral."[21] Collateral may change its form and character during the course of the security agreement. **For Example,** a debtor who has pledged its inventory of cars as collateral will be selling those cars. However, the buyers will sign credit contracts for the purchase of those cars. Article 9 considers the credit contracts and the right to payment under those contracts as proceeds. If the collateral has been insured and is damaged or destroyed, the debtor will receive money, another form of proceeds, from the insurance company. Proceeds are automatically subject to the creditor's security interest unless the security agreement provides to the contrary. The proceeds may be in any form, such as cash, checks, promissory notes, or other property.

---

[17] Deposit accounts are not considered "general intangibles" under Article 9 because of specific provisions on accounts. U.C.C. §§9-102(a)(29), 9-104, 9-109(d)(13), 9-312(b)(1), and §9-314. *ImagePoint, Inc. v. JPMorgan Chase Bank, Nat. Ass'n,* 27 F. Supp. 3d 494 (S.D.N.Y. 2014).

[18] U.C.C. §§9-102(2)(a)(5), 9-102(72), & 9-109(a)(2). A membership in a golf club can be pledged as security for a loan used to purchase the membership. *Bonem v. Golf Club of Georgia,* 591 S.E.2d 462, 52 U.C.C. Rep. Serv. 2d (West) 280 (Ga. Ct. App. 2003).

[19] U.C.C. §9-109(1).

[20] U.C.C. §9-204.

[21] U.C.C. §9-306(1).

Electronic Chattel Paper

"Electronic chattel paper" is a record of a right to funds, payment, or property that is stored in an electronic medium. **For Example,** it is possible to pledge the funds you have available in your Internet shopping account as an Article 9 security interest?[22]

CASE SUMMARY

Numismatic Nuance: Coins Are Not Money under Article 9

FACTS: On April 18, 2006, James W. Lull entered into a consignment agreement with Bowers and Merena for auction of his Standing Liberty quarter-dollar collection. On April 21, 2006, Bowers and Merena also agreed to loan to Lull $700,000, with the loan to be repaid from the auction proceeds.

The collection sold at auction for $1,119,750. After repayment of its loan to Lull and expenses of sale, Bowers held net proceeds of $455,046.11. However, Gardiner, Kapaa 382, and Yamaguchi went to Bowers and Merena and tried to claim the auction proceeds.

Gardiner's claim resulted from a March 1, 2005, loan to Lull for $3.8 million. Lull was unable to repay the loan when it became due on February 28, 2006, so in July 2006 Gardiner agreed not to take legal action to enforce the note after Lull executed a security agreement on July 19, 2006, which granted Gardiner a security interest in "all personal property and other assets" of Lull and specifically listed all commonly known categories of personal property, including goods, accounts, money, chattel paper, general intangibles, instruments, and the proceeds thereof.

Gardiner recorded a financing statement in the Bureau of Conveyances of the State of Hawaii on July 20, 2006. The financing statement described Gardiner's collateral as "All assets and all personal property of the Debtor (including, without limitations, fixtures), whether now owned or hereafter acquired or arising, and wherever located, and all proceeds and products thereof."

Kapaa 382 made short-term loans to Lull on September 20, 2005, for $933,000; on December 5, 2005, for $471,566.82; on December 15, 2005, for $165,000; and on December 19, 2005, for $400,000. On July 26, 2006, Lull executed a "Partial Settlement Agreement" in which he agreed, among other things, to "convey and transfer to [Kapaa 382] title to the Coin Collection currently consigned to Bowers and Merena Auctions, LLC for auction scheduled to occur in August 2006, by Bill of Sale[.]"

Kapaa 382 filed a financing statement with the California Secretary of State on August 22, 2006, but the financing statement listed Kapaa 382 as both the debtor and the secured party and did not mention Lull.

On July 11, 2006, Lull executed an assignment of the proceeds of the coin auction to Yamaguchi for an unpaid promissory note, dated May 16, 2006, in the amount of $700,000. The assignment was not recorded.

On December 8, 2006, Lull filed a voluntary Chapter 7 petition. Claims in the bankruptcy case exceeded $55 million, including unsecured claims of nearly $42 million. The parties involved with the coins all claimed priority.

DECISION: The coins were not money for purposes of Article 9 and could be subject to a security interest. Because the coins were collector's items they were a unique form of personal property and not used as a medium of exchange. The parties could create a security interest in the coins and be entitled to Article 9 perfection rights. **[In re *Lull*, 386 B.R. 261, 65 U.C.C. Rep. Serv. 2d 194 (D. Haw. 2008)]**

CPA 33-2 Perfection of Secured Transactions

The attachment of a security interest gives the creditor the important rights of enforcement of the debt through repossession of the collateral (see the section titled "Creditor's Possession and Disposition of Collateral" for more discussion of enforcement and repossession). *Attachment* allows the secured party to resort to the collateral to collect the debt

[22] U.C.C. §9-105.

when the debtor defaults. However, more than one creditor may hold an attached security interest in the same collateral. A creditor who obtains a **perfected security interest** enjoys priority over unperfected interests and may in some cases enjoy priority over other perfected interests. A security interest is valid against the debtor even though it is not perfected. However, perfection provides creditors with rights superior to those of other creditors with unperfected interests. Attachment provides creditors with rights; perfection gives them priority, and a creditor can obtain perfection in collateral in several ways.

perfected security interest–security interest with priority because of filing, possession, automatic, or temporary priority status.

CPA

33-2a Perfection by Creditor's Possession

If the creditor has possession of the collateral, the security interest in the possessed goods is perfected.[23] It remains perfected until that possession is surrendered. **For Example,** when a creditor has taken a security interest in 50 gold coins and has those gold coins in his vault, his possession of the coins is perfection.

A more complex example of possession as a means of perfection is found in the commercial tool of **field warehousing.** (See Chapter 21) In this arrangement, a creditor actually has an agent on site at a buyer's place of business, and the creditor's agent controls the buyer's access to, use of, and transfer of the collateral. **For Example,** an aircraft manufacturer may have an agent on site at an aircraft dealership. That agent decides when the planes can be released to buyers and who will receive the buyers' payments or notes.[24]

field warehousing–stored goods under the exclusive control of a warehouse but kept on the owner's premises rather than in a warehouse.

CPA

33-2b Perfection for Consumer Goods

A purchase money security interest in consumer goods is perfected from the moment it attaches.[25] Known as **automatic perfection,** no other action is required for perfection as against other creditors. Because so many consumer purchases are made on credit, the UCC simplifies perfection so that creditors who are merchant sellers are not overly burdened with paperwork. However, as discussed later in this chapter in the section on priorities, the automatic perfection of a PMSI in consumer goods has some limitations. It may be destroyed by the debtor consumer's resale of the goods to a consumer who does not know of the security interest.

automatic perfection–perfection given by statute without specific filing or possession requirements on the part of the creditor.

33-2c Perfection for Health Care Insurance Receivables

Article 9 has a form of collateral known as *health care insurance receivables.* The nature of this collateral requires a unique method of perfection. When a consumer gives a creditor a security interest in health insurance proceeds that are forthcoming, the creditor need not make any filing or take any further steps to have a perfected security interest in those proceeds. The perfection is automatic.[26]

33-2d Automatic Perfection

A creditor attains automatic perfection in certain circumstances under Article 9. **For Example,** a creditor has an automatic PMSI in software that is sold with a computer that is subject to a creditor's PMSI. If you buy an IBM ThinkPad® from Best Buy on credit and get Microsoft Office software as part of your package deal, Best Buy has an automatically perfected security interest not only in the consumer goods (your new

---

[23] U.C.C. §9-305; In re *Clean Burn Fuels, LLC,* 492 B.R. 445 (N.C. 2013).
[24] U.C.C. §9-312.
[25] U.C.C. §§9-301, & 9-304; In re *Saxe,* 491 B.R. 244 (W.D. Wis. 2013).
[26] Article 9, §9-309(5).

computer) but also in the software sold with it.[27] The perfection for consumer purchase money security interests that occurs when the security interest attaches is also a form of automatic perfection.

temporary perfection— perfection given for a limited period of time to creditors.

33-2e Temporary Perfection

Some creditors are given **temporary perfection** for the collateral.[28] **For Example,** a creditor is generally given four months to refile its financing statement in a state to which a debtor has relocated. During that four-month period, the interest of the creditor is temporarily perfected in the new state despite no filing of a financing statement in that state's public records. Most creditors' agreements provide that the failure of the debtor to notify the creditor of a move constitutes a default under the credit agreement. Creditors need to know of the move so that they can refile in the debtor's new state.[29] Creditors enjoy a 20-day temporary perfection in negotiable instruments taken as collateral. Following the expiration of the 20-day period, measured from the time their security interest attaches, creditors must perfect in another way, such as by filing a financing statement or by possession.

33-2f Perfection by Control

Control is a form of possession under Article 9.[30] Control is achieved when a bank or creditor is able to require the debtor account holder to clear all transactions in that account with the bank or creditor. The debtor cannot use the funds that have been pledged as collateral without permission from the party holding the control. **For Example,** a credit union member could secure a loan with the credit union by giving the credit union a security interest in her savings account. The credit union then has control of the account and is perfected by the ability to dictate what the credit union member can do with those funds.

33-2g Perfection for Motor Vehicles

In most states, a non-Code statute provides that a security interest in a noninventory motor vehicle must be noted on the vehicle title registration. When so noted, the interest is perfected.[31] States that do not have a separate motor vehicle perfection system require financing statements, as described in the next section.

financing statement— brief statement (record) that gives sufficient information to alert third persons that a particular creditor may have a security interest in the collateral described.

33-2h Perfection by Filing a Financing Statement

The **financing statement** (known as a UCC-1) is an authenticated record statement that gives sufficient information to alert third persons that a particular creditor may have a security interest in the collateral described. With technological capabilities, the paper-signed documents are no longer a requirement. The creditor must be able to show that the documents filed were "authorized" and an "authenticated record."[32] In other words,

---

[27] Article 9, §§9-102 & 9-103.

[28] U.C.C. §9-312.

[29] U.C.C. §9-316(a).

[30] U.C.C. §9-104.

[31] U.C.C. §9-303. In re *Gracy,* 522 B.R. 686 (D. Kan. 2015).

[32] The sample financing form included with U.C.C. §9-521 does not even have a place for the debtor's signature. While a signed security agreement and signed financing statement are valid for both the security agreement and financing statement, such formalities are no longer necessary. A jail detainee's filing of a financing statement against a judge was declared invalid because the judge failed to consent. Indeed, the judge was not aware of the detainee's activities or that he owed the detainee money. *Nichols v. Branton,* 995 N.Y.S.2d 450 (N.Y. Supp. 2014).

the debtor's signature is not required for the financing statement to be valid. Article 9 gives three ways for the debtor to authorize a financing statement:

1. By authenticating a security agreement.[33]

2. By becoming bound under a security agreement, the debtor agrees to allow financing statements to be filed on the collateral in the security agreement.

3. By acquiring collateral subject to a security agreement.

An unauthorized financing statement filed without meeting one of these requirements does not provide the creditor perfected creditor status.[34]

The Content of the Financing Statement

A financing statement must provide "the name of the debtor … the name of the secured party or representative of the secured party … [and an indication of] the collateral covered by the financing statement."[35] The form provided with Article 9 includes much more information. Under §9-516, additional requirements are imposed for initial financing statements that include "a mailing address for the debtor [and] … whether the debtor is an individual or organization."[36] Furthermore, §9-511 requires that the secured party of record provide an address so that there is an address for mailing notices required under other sections.

Because the filings for Article 9 perfection are electronic, the precise identification of the debtor has become critical. With electronic filings, those who will be doing searches on debtors will not find matches when the name of the debtor has not been properly entered on the financing statement. With computer technology, additional precision in debtors' names is necessary or searches are thwarted. The consequences for misspelling a debtor's name are greater in an electronic system and the risk is high. The failure to properly identify the debtor will be a loss of priority by perfection because the electronic search in the state did not uncover prior interests. Courts continue their balancing of rights, notice, and technology in dealing with proper filing and priorities that result.[37]

CASE SUMMARY

The Misplaced "9" under Article 9

FACTS: On September 8, 2005, Wells Fargo (Defendants) and the Christopher Hanson Insurance Agency entered into a promissory note and a security agreement for one million dollars. As security for the loan, Hanson assigned his interests in two separate annuity contracts, both issued by Fidelity & Guaranty Life Insurance Company ("Fidelity &

Guaranty"). The two annuity contracts were valued at one million dollars, and they were identified as "L9E00015" and "L9E00016," respectively.

That same day, Wells Fargo filed a financing statement with the Secretary of State of Missouri. The financing statement identified the "Debtor" as

---

[33] U.C.C. §9-509 permits the debtor and creditor to agree otherwise. For example, a debtor can place a requirement in the security agreement that the creditor obtain his or her signature before filing a financing statement.
[34] U.C.C. §9-510.
[35] U.C.C. §9-502(a).
[36] U.C.C. §9-516(b)(5).
[37] U.C.C. §9-506(a). In re *PTM Technologies, Inc.,* 452 B.R. 165 (M.D.N.C. 2011); In re *Webb,* 520 B.R. 748 (E.D. Ark. 2014).

The Misplaced "9" under Article 9 continued

"Christopher J. Hanson," and it describes the collateral as follows:

> All of Debtor's right, title, and interest in and to, assets and rights of Debtor, wherever located and whether now owned or hereafter acquired or arising and all proceeds and products in that certain Annuity Contract No.: LE900015 issued by Lincoln Benefit Life in the name of Debtor....

The financing statement identified the contract number as "LE900015" instead of "L9E00015," and it identified the issuer as "Lincoln Benefit Life" instead of Fidelity & Guaranty. On September 16, 2005, Wells Fargo filed an additional financing statement that correctly identified the contract number but once again mistakenly referred to the issuer of this contract as "Lincoln Benefit Life" instead of Fidelity & Guaranty.

On February 9, 2006, Hanson obtained a loan from ProGrowth Bank, Inc. As security for the loan, Hanson assigned his interests in the Fidelity & Guaranty annuity contracts to ProGrowth. On February 14, 2006, ProGrowth filed two financing statements with the Secretary of State of

Missouri that identified Hanson and the Agency as the debtor and accurately described the collateral as: "Fidelity and Guaranty Life Insurance Annuity Contracts Number L9E00015 and Number L9E00016[.]"

ProGrowth filed suit seeking a declaration that Wells Fargo and Global One were not perfected secured creditors and that it had priority to the annuity funds. The district court granted summary judgment in favor of ProGrowth Bank, Inc. Wells Fargo appealed.

DECISION: The court held that Wells Fargo had enough in the financing statements to put a subsequent creditor on notice that there were interests in the debtor's property. Further, despite the transposition of the numbers of the annuities and the misidentification of the issuer, Wells had provided enough information to warrant simple clarification. Wells Fargo was a secured, perfected creditor in first position. [***ProGrowth Bank, Inc. v. Wells Fargo Bank, N.A., 558 F.3d 809 (8th Cir. 2008)***]*

*For a case that found a financing statement insufficient in description, see In re *Harvey Goldman & Co.*, 455 B.R. 621 (E.D. Mich. 2011).

The requirements for description of the collateral in the financing statements are now more general.[38] A security agreement can be filed as a financing statement if it contains all of the aforementioned required information.

Because the financing statement is intended as notice to third parties, it must be filed in a public place.[39] The formerly complex issues of filing location were simplified as a means of encouraging electronic systems that will be statewide, accessible across state lines, and organized simply by name in any index. The general rule is central filing for financing statements for all types of collateral. Filings for fixtures and other property-related interests have also been simplified with deferral to state laws on the proper filing location.[40]

CPA   Defective Filing

When the filing of the financing statement is defective either because the statement is so erroneous or incomplete that it is seriously misleading or the filing is made in a wrong county or office, the filing fails to perfect the security interest.[41] The idea of perfection by filing is to give public notice of a creditor's interest. To the extent that the notice

[38] However, the sample financing form included with U.C.C. §9-521 includes boxes for all of the same information required under the previous versions Article 9.
[39] U.C.C. §9-401; *Official Committee of Unsecured Creditors of Motors Liquidation Co. v. JPMorgan Chase Bank, N.A.*, 103 A.3d 1010 (Del. 2014).
[40] U.C.C. §9-501.
[41] In re *Sterling*, 519 B.R. 586 (W.D.N.Y. 2014).

cannot be located or does not give sufficient information, the creditor then cannot rely on it to obtain the superior position of perfection.

33-2i Loss of Perfection

The perfection of the security interest can be lost if the creditor does not comply with the Article 9 requirements for continuing perfection.[42]

Possession of Collateral

When perfection is obtained because the creditor takes possession of the collateral, that perfection is lost if the creditor voluntarily surrenders the collateral to the debtor without any restrictions.

Consumer Goods

The perfection obtained by the automatic status of a PMSI is lost in some cases by removal of the goods to another state. The security interest may also be destroyed by resale of the goods to a consumer. To protect against these types of losses of protection, the creditor needs to file a financing statement. In the case of a PMSI, the perfection is good against other creditors but is not superior when it comes to buyers of the goods.

E-COMMERCE & CYBERLAW

Engines Are from Mars; Priorities Are from Financing Statements

In 2001, the International Association of Corporate Administrators promulgated Model Administrative Rules (MARS), a set of rules for the standards for search engines for court system, land, tax, and lien records. State and local governments will have different technology and standards that range from a liberal search engine to a strict search engine. A *liberal search engine* is similar to Google, which kicks back a corrected term and says, "Did you mean?" when you type in a name or word that is misspelled. A *strict search engine,* such as the simple one in Microsoft Word, will not find a word or phrase in a document unless you have spelled the search item exactly the way it appears in the document.

The MARS standards migrate toward the strict search engine. However, states have adopted different standards, and the result is that the electronic searches for debtors in various states can be very different. If there is a strict search engine in a state and the person doing the search types in "Ann Smythe," the correct spelling of the debtor's name, the financing statement against "Smythe" that was filed as "Ann Smith" will not be a match and the electronic system will kick out a "NO MATCH FOUND." Likewise, a creditor who files

under the name "House, Roger" when the debtor's actual name is "Roger House" has not perfected.* The same would be true of a financing statement filed under "Terry J. Kinderknecht" when the debtor's actual legal name is "Terrance Joseph Kinderknecht."**

Article 9 has standard rules for search logic that tend toward the "strict" end of the spectrum. The majority of states have now adopted some version of MARS, although many states have modified the rules in some respect (which has resulted in a great deal of inconsistency; furthermore, some states have not adopted any rule on search logic at all). Creditors should be cautious in their searches.

*_Pankratz Implement Company v. Citizens National Bank,_ 102 P.3d 1165 **(Kan. App. 2004).**

**These examples would result in a "NO MATCH FOUND" and emphasize the importance of using both the debtor's legal name and correct spelling. Furthermore, the courts in all three cases did not honor the financing statement as resulting in perfection because the names were misleading. The person doing the search is permitted to assume that the debtor has no other secured creditors. _CNH Capital America LLC v. Progreso Materials Ltd.,_ Not Reported in F. Supp. 2d, 2012 WL 5305697 (S.D. Tex. 2012). See In re _EDM Corp.,_ 431 B.R. 459 (Neb. 2010).

---

[42] In re _C.W. Min. Co.,_ 488 B.R. 715 (D. Utah. 2013).

Lapse of Time

The perfection obtained by filing a financing statement lasts five years. The perfection may be continued for successive five-year periods by filing a continuation statement within six months before the end of each five-year period.[43] Article 9 permits a "manufactured home" exception allowing financing statements on mobile homes to be effective for 30 years.

Removal from State

In most cases, the perfection of a security interest lapses when the collateral is taken by the debtor to another state unless, as noted earlier, the creditor makes a filing in that second state within the four-month period of temporary perfection.

Motor Vehicles

If the security interest is governed by a non-Code statute creating perfection by title certificate notation, the interest, if so noted, remains perfected without regard to lapse of time or removal to another state. The perfection is lost only if a state issues a new title without the security interest notation.

CPA 33-3 Rights of Parties before Default

The rights of parties to a secured transaction are different in the time preceding the debtor's default from those in the time following the default.

33-3a Statement of Account

To keep the record straight, the debtor may send the creditor a written statement of the amount the debtor thinks is due and an itemization of the collateral together with a request that the creditor approve the statement as submitted or correct and return the statement. Within two weeks after receiving the debtor's statement, the creditor must send the debtor a written approval or correction. If the secured creditor has assigned the secured claim, the creditor's reply must state the name and address of the assignee.[44]

33-3b Termination Statements

termination statement– document (record), which may be requested by a paid-up debtor, stating that a security interest is no longer claimed under the specified financing statement.

A debtor who has paid his debt in full may make a written demand on the secured creditor, or the latter's assignee if the security interest has been assigned, to send the debtor a **termination statement,**[45] which states that a security interest is no longer claimed under the specified financing statement. The debtor may present this statement to the filing officer, who marks the record terminated and returns the various papers that were filed to the secured party. The termination statement clears the debtor's record so subsequent buyers or lenders will not be subject to the now-satisfied security interest. The creditor has 20 days from receipt of a demand for a termination statement from a debtor to file a termination statement (one month for consumer goods).[46]

---

[43] U.C.C. §9-516. Failure to file with the secretary of state was fatal for a priority of secured creditor when a central filing was required, despite the filing at the county level. In re *Borden,* 361 B.R. 489 (Neb. 2007).

[44] U.C.C. §9-515.

[45] U.C.C. §9-513; In re *Hickory Printing Group, Inc.,* 479 B.R. 388 (W.D.N.C. 2012).

[46] U.C.C. §9-513(b) and (c).

33-3c **Correction Statements**

Because Article 9 permits creditors and others to simply file "authorized" financing statements, debtors are given protection for abusive filings of Article 9 interests. Under Article 9, debtors are permitted to protest filed financing statements with a filing of their own correction statements. While the security interest is not abolished by such a filing, its content does provide public notice of an underlying dispute. A debtor can also file a correction statement when a creditor fails to provide a termination statement.[47]

33-4 **Priorities**

Two or more parties may have conflicting interests in the same collateral. This section discusses the rights of creditors and buyers with respect to each other and to collateral that carries a secured interest or perfected secured interest.

CPA   33-4a **Unsecured Party versus Unsecured Party**

pro rata–proportionately, or divided according to a rate or standard.

When creditors are unsecured, they have equal priority. In the event of insolvency or bankruptcy of the debtor, all the unsecured creditors stand at the end of the line in terms of repayment of their debts (see Chapter 34 for more details on bankruptcy priorities). If the assets of the debtor are insufficient to satisfy all unsecured debtors, the unsecured debtors simply receive a *pro rata* share of their debts.

CPA   33-4b **Secured Party versus Unsecured Party**

A secured creditor has a right superior to that of an unsecured creditor because the secured creditor can take back the collateral from the debtor's assets, while an unsecured creditor simply waits for the leftovers once all secured creditors have taken back their collateral. If the collateral is insufficient to satisfy the secured creditor's debt, the secured debtor can still stand in line with the unsecured creditors and collect any additional amount not satisfied by the collateral or a pro rata share. **For Example,** suppose that Linens Galore has a security interest in Linens R Us's inventory. Linens Galore has the right to repossess the inventory and sell it to satisfy the debt Linens R Us owes. Suppose that Linens R Us owes Linens Galore $22,000, and the sale of the inventory brings $15,000. Linens Galore still has a claim as an unsecured creditor for the remaining $7,000 due.

CPA   33-4c **Secured Party versus Secured Party**

first-in-time provision–creditor whose interest attached first has priority in the collateral when two creditors have a secured interest.

If two creditors have a security interest in the same collateral, their priority is determined according to the **first-in-time provision;** that is, the creditor whose interest attached first has priority in the collateral. The secured party whose interest was last to attach must then proceed against the debtor as an unsecured creditor because the collateral was given to the creditor whose interest attached first. **For Example,** if Bob pledged his antique sign collection to Bill on January 15, 2015, with a signed security agreement in exchange for a $5,000 loan, and then pledged the same collection to Jane on February 20, 2015, with a signed security agreement, Bill has priority because his security agreement attached first.

[47] U.C.C. §9-518.

CPA   ## 33-4d Perfected Secured Party versus Secured Party

The perfected secured creditor takes priority over the unperfected secured creditor and is entitled to take the collateral. The unperfected secured party is then left to seek remedies as an unsecured creditor because the collateral has been given to the perfected creditor. **For Example,** with respect to Bob's sign collection, if Jane filed a financing statement on February 21, 2015, she would have priority over Bill because her perfected interest would be superior to Bill's unperfected interest even though Bill's interest attached before Jane's.

CASE SUMMARY

The Bank Doesn't Win: When Secured Parties Take Priority over Overdrafts

FACTS: General Motors Acceptance Corporation (GMAC) financed the inventory of Donohue Ferrill Motor Company, Inc., which gave GMAC a security interest in its vehicle inventory and all the proceeds of that inventory. The security agreement and financing statements were executed, and GMAC properly filed the financing statements.

Shortly before Donohue Ferrill's business failed, it sold six trucks and then deposited the proceeds of $124,610.80 from the sale of those trucks into its account at Lincoln National Bank. Lincoln took the deposited funds and applied them to account overdrafts that Donohue Ferrill had. For 38 of the 62 business days of September, October, and November 1991, Donohue Ferrill's account was overdrawn. Lincoln National honored 133 overdrafts during

these three months and charged Donohue Ferrill a total of $1,995 in fees. The total amount of the overdrawn balances for those 38 days was $1,943,306.25.

GMAC objected, saying that it had priority in those funds. The trial court and court of appeals found for the bank and GMAC appealed.

DECISION: GMAC's security interest takes priority over the bank's right of setoff. The bank's interest is a statutory one, but an unsecured interest, and GMAC had a duly recorded security interest, which the bank knew of or should have known of at the time it took its offset rights. [*General Motors Acceptance Corp. v. Lincoln Nat'l Bank*, **18 S.W.3d 337 (Ky. 2000)**]

first-to-perfect basis— rule of priorities that holds that first in time in perfecting a security interest, mortgage, judgment, lien, or other property attachment right should have priority.

The perfected secured party's interest as against other types of creditors, such as lienors, mortgagees, and judgment creditors, is also determined on a **first-to-perfect basis.** If the secured party perfects before a judgment lien or mortgage is recorded,[48] the perfected secured creditor has priority.[49] The perfected party takes priority over the secured party even when the perfected secured party is aware of the security interest prior to perfection.[50]

CPA   ## 33-4e Perfected Secured Party versus Perfected Secured Party

The general rule for priority among two perfected secured creditors in the same collateral is also a first-in-time rule: The creditor who perfected first is given priority. **For Example,** again with respect to Bob's sign collection, if Bill filed a financing statement on February

---

[48] U.C.C. §9-313; *Arvest Bank v. SpiritBank, N.A.*, 191 P.3d 1228 (Ok. App. 2008), and *Fifth Third Bank v. Peoples Nat. Bank*, 929 N.E.2d 210 (Ind. App. 2010).
[49] *Banner Bank v. First Community Bank*, 854 F. Supp. 2d 846 (D. Mont. 2012).
[50] *Farm Credit of Northwest Florida, ACA v. Easom Peanut Co.*, 718 S.E.2d 590 (Ga. App. 2011).

22, 2015, Jane would still have priority because she perfected her interest first. If, however, Bill filed a financing statement on January 31, 2015, he would have priority over Jane. There are, however, three exceptions to this rule of first-in-time, first-in-right for perfected secured creditors.

CPA

The Purchase Money Security Interest in Inventory[51]

If the collateral is inventory, the purchase money secured creditor must do two things to prevail even over prior perfected secured creditors. The creditor must (1) perfect before the debtor receives possession of the goods that will be inventory and (2) give notice to any other secured party who has previously filed a financing statement with respect to that inventory.[52] The other secured parties must receive this notice before the debtor receives possession of the goods covered by the purchase money security interest. Compliance with these notice requirements gives the last creditor to extend credit for the inventory the priority position, which is a rule of law based on the practical notion that a debtor must be able to replenish its inventory to stay in business and keep creditors paid in a timely fashion. With this priority for subsequently perfected creditors, debtors have the opportunity to replenish inventory. **For Example,** suppose that First Bank has financed the inventory for Roberta's Exotic Pets, taken a security interest in the inventory, and filed a financing statement covering Roberta's inventory. Two months later, Animal Producers sells reptiles on credit to Roberta, taking a security interest in Roberta's inventory. To take priority over First Bank, Animal Producers would have to file the financing statement on the inventory before Roberta receives the reptiles and notify First Bank at the same time. The commercial rationale for this priority exception is to permit businesses to replenish their inventories by giving new suppliers a higher priority.

Purchase Money Security Interest—Noninventory Collateral

If the collateral is *noninventory collateral*, such as equipment, the purchase money secured creditor prevails over all others as to the same collateral if that creditor files a financing statement within 20 days after the debtor takes possession of the collateral. **For Example,** First Bank loans money to debtor Kwik Copy and properly files a financing statement covering all of Kwik Copy's present and subsequently acquired copying equipment. Second Bank then loans money to Kwik Copy for the purchase of a new copier. Second Bank's interest in the copier will be superior to First Bank's interest if Second Bank perfects its interest by filing either before the debtor receives the copier or within 20 days thereafter.

Status of Repair or Storage Lien

What happens when the debtor does not pay for the repair or storage of the collateral? In most states, a person repairing or storing goods has a lien or right to keep possession of the goods until paid for such services. The repairer or storer also has the right to sell the goods to obtain payment if the customer fails to pay and if proper notice is given.[53] Article 9 makes a statutory lien for repairs or storage superior to a perfected security interest in the same collateral.

---

[51] U.C.C. §9-103 expands the definition of a PMSI in inventory. Consignments are treated as PMSIs in inventory.
[52] U.C.C. §9-324.
[53] U.C.C. §9-333; In re *James,* 463 B.R. 719 (M.D. Pa. 2011).

CASE SUMMARY

Stephen Tolbert and His Inconsistent Tales: A BFP of a Corvette?

FACTS: In 2003, Automotive Finance Corporation ("AFC") executed a contract to provide "floorplan financing" to R American Auto, Inc., a used car dealership, for the purchase of inventory. As collateral for the financing, AFC took a security interest in all of R American's present and future inventory. AFC filed a UCC Financing Statement to record the security interest on December 16, 2003.

On August 24, 2006, R American purchased a white 2006 Corvette for its inventory. AFC took possession of the Corvette's certificate of title. On January 31, 2007, Kip Rowley, the owner of R American, gave AFC a business check for $43,220 as payment in full for the Corvette, and AFC provided Rowley with the certificate of title to the Corvette. The check was dishonored because R American's bank account had been closed. An agent of AFC went to R American's car lot to secure possession of the Corvette and discovered that it was not on the lot. AFC filed a lien on the missing vehicle.

On March 4, 2008, Steven Tolbert filed a petition seeking a release of AFC's lien on the Corvette because he claimed to be a *bona fide* purchaser" of the Corvette from Ultimate Motor Cars, LLC, on January 21, 2007. AFC filed an answer to the petition and a counterclaim against Tolbert for conversion, seeking damages for the value of the Corvette.

Tolbert testified that he paid $52,000 to Kip Rowley on November 2, 2006, and immediately took possession of the Corvette. He gave Rowley a check made out to "R American" for $50,900 and also paid $1,100 in cash. Tolbert did not receive a bill of sale and the certificate of title to the Corvette until nearly three months later on January 21, 2007. The bill of sale, issued by "Ultimate Motor Cars, Inc.," indicated that the sale was completed on January 21, 2007, and that the purchase price was $52,099. The certificate of title indicated that R American acquired the Corvette on August 24, 2006, and then transferred the Corvette to Ultimate Motor Cars on October 20, 2006. Tolbert's name was listed both as the seller of the Corvette as agent for R American and as the buyer of the Corvette as

agent for Ultimate Motor Cars. Tolbert testified that he inadvertently signed in the wrong spot as seller on the Corvette's certificate of title. Nevertheless, Tolbert was not concerned with these discrepancies because he believed Rowley did business as both R American and Ultimate Motor Cars. Tolbert said he was unaware of AFC's security interest until February 2007, when he attempted to have the Corvette titled in his name and learned about the lien.

Jason Yount, branch manager for AFC, testified that on September 7, 2006, R American paid AFC for the Corvette, and that AFC gave R American the certificate of title to the Corvette. On December 12, 2006, R American gave the certificate of title back to AFC, AFC advanced R American credit for the Corvette, and R American "refloored" the Corvette. Before reclaiming the title, on December 12, 2006, an agent of AFC physically inspected the Corvette on R American's lot, verified the Corvette's VIN, and ensured that the Corvette's certificate of title indicated that R American owned the Corvette. Yount explained that AFC would not have advanced credit to R American and accepted the Corvette's certificate of title on December 12, 2006, if at that time the certificate of title indicated that R American had transferred the Corvette to Ultimate Motor Cars on October 20, 2006.

The court issued a judgment awarding AFC $53,904.41. Tolbert appealed the judgment.

DECISION: The court affirmed the judgment for AFC because Tolbert was not a *bona fide* purchaser (BFP). There was nothing normal about his transaction. He received no documents and when he did finally receive the documents, the documents raised questions because they had different names on them and he seemed to be confused about who was selling and who was buying. Tolbert's story about the transactions differed from the paperwork trail on the financing and when the car was actually available for sale. [*Tolbert v. Automotive Finance Corp.*, 341 S.W.3d 195 (Mo. App. 2011)]

Figure 33-1 provides a summary of the priorities of various parties with respect to secured and unsecured creditor interests.

33-4f Secured Party versus Buyer of Collateral from Debtor

The debtor may sell the collateral to a third person. How does this sale affect the secured creditor?

FIGURE 33-1	Priority of Secured Interest under Article 9

CONFLICT	PRIORITY
Secured party versus secured party	First to attach
Unsecured party versus secured party	Secured party
Perfected secured party versus secured party	Perfected secured party
Perfected secured party versus perfected secured party	Party who is first to perfect
Perfected secured party versus lienor	Party who filed (financing statement or lien) first [§ 9-307(2)] (rev. § 9-317)
EXCEPTIONS	
PMSI in fixtures versus perfected secured party	PMSI creditor if perfected before annexation or within 20 days after annexation (PMSI will have priority even over prior perfected secured party) (§ 9-313, § 9-314) (rev. § 9-317)
PMSI in equipment versus perfected secured party	PMSI is perfected within 20 days after delivery [§ 9-301(2), § 9-312(4)] (rev. § 9-317)
PMSI in inventory versus perfected secured party	PMSI is perfected before delivery and if perfected secured party given notice before delivery [§ 9-312(3)] (rev. § 9-317)
PMSI in consumer goods versus buyer	Buyer unless perfection is by filing before purchase [§ 9-302(1)(d)] (rev. § 9-317)
Perfected secured party versus buyer	Buyer in ordinary course wins even with knowledge [§ 9-306(1)(d)] (rev. § 9-320)

C P A   Sales in the Ordinary Course of Business

A buyer who buys goods from the debtor in the ordinary course of business is not subject to any creditor's security interest regardless of whether the interest was perfected or unperfected and regardless of whether the buyer had actual knowledge of the security interest. The reason for this protection of buyers in the ordinary course of business is that subjecting buyers to a creditor's reclaim of goods would cause great delay and hesitation in commercial and consumer sales transactions.[54]

[54] U.C.C. §9-320 covers the rights of buyers of goods.

C P A   **Sales Not in the Ordinary Course of Business: The Unperfected Security Interest**

A sale not in the ordinary course of business is one in which the seller is not usually a seller of such merchandise. **For Example,** if a buyer purchases a computer desk from an office supply store, the sale is in the ordinary course of business. If that same buyer purchases that same computer desk from a law firm that is going out of business, that buyer is not purchasing in the ordinary course of business. If a buyer is purchasing collateral and such purchase is not in the ordinary course of business but the security interest is unperfected, such a security interest has no effect against a buyer who gives value and buys in good faith, that is, not knowing of the security interest. A buyer who does not satisfy these conditions is subject to the security interest.

C P A   **Sales Not in the Ordinary Course of Business: The Perfected Security Interest**

If the security interest was perfected, the buyer of the collateral is ordinarily subject to the security interest unless the creditor consented to the sale.[55]

C P A   **Sales Not in the Ordinary Course of Business: The Consumer Debtor's Resale of Consumer Goods**

When the collateral constitutes consumer goods in the hands of the debtor, a resale of the goods to another consumer destroys the automatically perfected PMSI of the consumer debtor's creditor. Assuming that the buyer who purchases from the consumer debtor has no knowledge of a security interest, she will take the collateral free and clear from the creditor's security interest even though there was perfection by that creditor. Thus, the perfection without filing option afforded consumer PMSI creditors has a flaw in its coverage when it comes to a consumer debtor selling his refrigerator to a neighbor. Without a

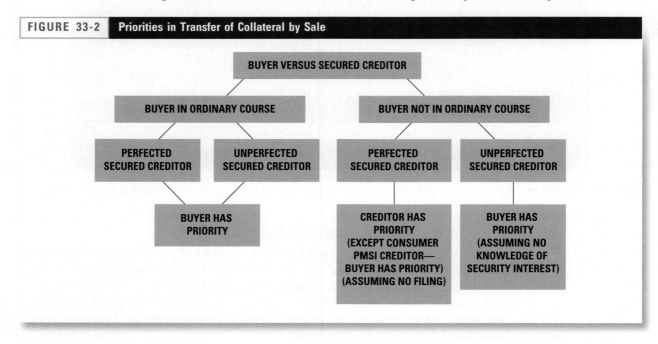

FIGURE 33-2   **Priorities in Transfer of Collateral by Sale**

---

[55] U.C.C. §1-201(9) adds that a purchase from a pawnbroker will not be considered a sale in the ordinary course of business.

filed financing statement, the neighbor buyer takes the refrigerator free and clear of the creditor's security interest in it. However, consumer creditors can avoid the loss of this perfected interest by perfecting through filing. With filing, consumer PMSI creditors enjoy continuation of their interests even when the neighbor has paid the consumer debtor for the refrigerator. Figure 33-2 offers a summary of the rights of buyers of collateral with respect to the creditors who hold security interests in that collateral.

CASE SUMMARY

The Craigslist Seller with the Fake Title

FACTS: In May 2006, Jacob J. Magish agreed to purchase a certain 2001 Harley-Davidson Motorcycle from Christine and Larry Logsdon for $14,635. Magish took out a loan at a Fifth Third Bank branch in Indianapolis with a security interest in the Motorcycle favor of Fifth Third in order to borrow $15,000 for the purchase. Magish presented to Fifth Third the Logsdons' original certificate of title. As part of the transaction, Magish executed, among other documents, an Application for Certificate of Title and a Power of Attorney. Fifth Third's Closing Representative, John Wargel, copied the Logsdon Original Title and then gave the Logsdon Original Title back to Magish. Wargel instructed Magish to apply for a new title at the Indiana Bureau of Motor Vehicles ("BMV"). Wargel kept the May 31 application and the Magish file in the loan file.

Shortly after the transaction, Magish, using deception, approached the Logsdons and requested that they sign paperwork to obtain a duplicate title. The Logsdons, who had no knowledge that Magish had financed the purchase of the Motorcycle through Fifth Third, unwittingly signed an application to obtain a duplicate title and gave the application to Magish.

Magish obtained a duplicate title from the BMV in the name of the Logsdons. The Logsdons signed the Logsdon Duplicate Title as Sellers. The Logsdon Duplicate Title inactivated the Logsdon Original Title in the BMV records.

Magish, using the Logsdon Duplicate Title, submitted an application to the BMV for a new title in his name. Magish intentionally omitted Fifth Third from the June 20 application and did not list a lienholder. Magish concurrently tendered the Logsdon Duplicate Title to the BMV and failed to notate Fifth Third as lienholder. On June 28, 2006, the BMV issued a new title in Magish's name. There was no lien notated on the First Magish Title.

On October 16, 2006, Fifth Third submitted an application for an amended title to the BMV ... Fifth Third did not have the Logsdon Original Title nor the First Magish Title in its possession and so did not tender to the BMV either with the Fifth Third application.

On October 18, 2006, the BMV issued a new title listing Magish as owner and Fifth Third as lienholder. The Second Magish Title inactivated the First Magish Title in the BMV records. The whereabouts of the Second Magish Title are unknown and Fifth Third has no record of receiving it.

In 2009, the Dawsons responded to a Magish posting on Craigslist for the sale of the Motorcycle. On June 18, 2009, Magish sold and delivered the Motorcycle to the Dawsons for $13,050.00. Magish, who was terminally ill and died in August 2009, had defaulted on the loan in 2008. Magish gave the Dawsons the certificate of title that showed it was free of any lienholders. After the sale, the Dawsons submitted an application for a new title to the Motorcycle to the BMV. The BMV advised the Dawsons that, according to the BMV records, the title the Dawsons had was not the most current title. For privacy reasons the BMV would not tell the Dawsons exactly what the issue was but said it was either there was a duplicate title or a lienholder on the title. After discussions with Magish and his wife, the Dawsons determined that Fifth Third was a lienholder. The BMV refused to issue a new title to the Motorcycle to the Dawsons.

The Dawsons filed suit against Fifth Third, arguing that Fifth Third's lien against the Motorcycle should be unenforceable because, under a theory of equitable estoppel, Fifth Third should bear the loss of Magish's fraud on the Dawsons because Fifth Third's acts and omissions made the loss possible. Fifth Third filed a counterclaim, seeking replevin of the Motorcycle.

The trial court denied the Dawsons' summary judgment motion, granted Fifth Third's summary judgment motion, awarded permanent possession of the Motorcycle to Fifth Third, and ordered that the Dawsons maintain possession of the Motorcycle pending their appeal.

DECISION: There was a perfected secured creditor (Fifth Third Bank) who had a right to replevin (take back) of the Motorcycle. The bank's lienholder status was on the title and it was the only title of public record. A buyer not in the

The Craigslist Seller with the Fake Title continued

ordinary course should check for perfected secured interests prior to buying, and the Dawsons did not check the title. The Dawsons took title subject to Fifth Third Bank's security interest. The Dawsons tried to make an equitable argument that Fifth Third Bank could have prevented the problem if it

had been more careful with the title. However, the court held that they were the parties best able to check the title and because they did not check for perfected secured interests, the equities were on Fifth Third Bank's side. [*Dawson v. Fifth Third Bank,* **965 N.E.2d 730 (Ind. App. 2012)**]

self-help repossession— creditor's right to repossess the collateral without judicial proceedings.

33-5 Rights of Parties after Default

When a debtor defaults on an obligation in a secured transaction, the secured creditor has the option to sue the debtor to enforce the debt or of proceeding against the collateral.

breach of the peace— violation of the law in the repossession of the collateral.

C P A ### 33-5a Creditor's Possession and Disposition of Collateral

Upon the debtor's default, the secured party is entitled to take the collateral from the debtor.[56] **Self-help repossession** is allowed if this can be done without causing a **breach of the peace.**[57] If a breach of the peace might occur, the seller must use court action to obtain the collateral. Breaking and entering a debtor's property is a breach of the peace.

CASE SUMMARY

I Was in My Driveway in My Underwear When They Repossessed My Car!

FACTS: Koontz entered into an agreement with Chrysler to purchase a 1988 Sundance in exchange for 60 monthly payments of $185.92. When Koontz defaulted on the contract in early 1991, Chrysler notified him that it would repossess the vehicle if he did not make up the missed payments. Koontz notified Chrysler that he would make every effort to catch up on the payments, that he did not want the vehicle to be repossessed, and that Chrysler was not to enter his private property to repossess the car. Chrysler repossessed the car, however, according to the self-help repossession statute of the UCC.

When Koontz heard the repossession in progress, he rushed outside in his underwear and hollered, "Don't take it," to the repossessor. The repossessor did not respond and proceeded to take the vehicle. Chrysler sold the car and filed a complaint against Koontz seeking a deficiency judgment

for the balance due on the loan. Koontz alleged that the repossession was a breach of the peace. From a judgment in favor of Chrysler, Koontz appealed.

DECISION: There was no breach of the peace under Article 9 standards. Koontz only yelled, "Don't take it"; there was no verbal or physical response, no threat made at the repossessor, nor was there a breach of the peace. To find otherwise would be to invite the ridiculous situation whereby a debtor could avoid a deficiency judgment by merely stepping out of his house and yelling once at those sent to repossess the collateral. Such a narrow definition of the conduct necessary to breach the peace would render the self-help repossession statute useless. [*Chrysler Credit v. Koontz,* **661 N.E.2d 1171 (Ill. App. Ct. 1996)**]

---

[56] U.C.C. §9-607.
[57] The courts are divided on what is and is not a breach of the peace. *Thompson-Young v. Wells Fargo Dealer Services, Inc.,* Not Reported in N.E.3d, 2014 WL 3726900 (Ill. App. 2014). But see *Smith v. AFS Acceptance, LLC,* Not Reported in F. Supp. 2d, 2012 WL 1969415 (N.D. Ill. 2012).

The secured creditor may sell, lease,[58] or otherwise dispose of the collateral to pay the defaulted debt.[59] The sale may be private or public, at any time and place, and on any terms provided that the sale is done in a manner that is commercially reasonable. The creditor's sale eliminates all of the debtor's interest in the collateral.

33-5b Creditor's Retention of Collateral

Instead of selling the collateral, the creditor may wish to keep it and cancel the debt owed.[60]

Notice of Intention

To retain the collateral in satisfaction of the debt, the creditor must send the debtor written notice of this intent.[61]

C P A   Compulsory Disposition of Collateral

In two situations, the creditor must dispose of the collateral. A creditor must sell the collateral if the debtor makes a written objection to retention within 21 days after the retention notice was sent. The creditor must also dispose of the collateral if it consists of consumer goods and the debtor has paid 60 percent or more of the cash price or of the loan secured by the security interest. The sale must be held within 90 days of the repossession. However, the debtor, after default, surrenders the right to require the resale.[62]

A creditor who fails to dispose of the collateral when required to do so is liable to the debtor for conversion of the collateral or for the penalty imposed by the Code for violation of Article 9.[63]

33-5c Debtor's Right of Redemption

The debtor may redeem the collateral at any time prior to the time the secured party has disposed of the collateral or entered into a binding contract for resale. To redeem, the debtor must tender the entire obligation that is owed plus any legal costs and expenses incurred by the secured party.[64]

33-5d Disposition of Collateral

Upon the debtor's default, the creditor may sell the collateral at a public or private sale or may lease it to a third party. The creditor must give any required notice and act in a commercially reasonable manner. Revised Article 9 imposes specific notice requirements and provides a form that, if used by the creditor, is deemed adequate notice of sale. There are different notice forms for consumer and other transactions, but the basic information required is the day, time, location for the sale, and a contact number for questions the debtor and other secured parties might have. The notice must be sent to the debtor and any other creditors with an interest in the property.[65]

[58] *Golden v. Prosser,* 2014 WL 4626489 (D. Minn. 2014).
[59] U.C.C. §9-611 requires the secured party to notify all other secured parties and lienholders who have filed or recorded interests in the collateral of its intent to sell the collateral. *Whitecap (U.S.) Fund I, LP v. Siemens First Capital Commercial Finance LLC,* 121 A.D.3d 584, 995 N.Y.S.2d 40 (N.Y.A.D. 2014).
[60] U.C.C. §§9-620, 9-621, and 9-624.
[61] U.C.C. §§9-620 through 9-622. If there has been no notice, repossession is a breach of the peace. *Molinski v. Chase Auto Finance Corp.,* 837 N.W.2d 166 (Wis. App. 2013).
[62] U.C.C. §9-620. *Spellman v. Independent Bankers' Bank of Florida,* 39 Fla. L. Weekly D1687 (Fla. App. 2014).
[63] U.C.C. §§9-625 through 9-627.
[64] U.C.C. §9-623.
[65] U.C.C. §§9-613 and 9-614. *Wilder v. Toyota Financial Services Americas Corp.,* 764 F. Supp. 2d 249 (D. Mass. 2011).

THINKING THINGS THROUGH

Repossessing and Replacing Tires

Les Schwab sold Mr. Reed four tires for $509.82 on credit. Between January 2008 and May 2008, Mr. Reed failed to make any payments. After notifying Mr. Reed of his default, Jacob Schreiber, a Les Schwab manager, went to Mr. Reed's residence. Mr. Reed's vehicle was parked in the driveway while Mr. Reed was at work. Mr. Schreiber, after consultation with two other members of the management team, removed the tires and wheels from the vehicle. They removed the tires from the wheels at the store and then returned the wheels to Mr. Reed's vehicle the next day. The purpose of removing the tires at the store was to prevent damage to the wheels by using the store's machine for the removal process.

Mr. Reed filed suit against Les Schwab for breach of the peace because his wheels were taken and they were owned by him. Only the tires were subject to repossession. Mr. Reed claimed damages from having his car immobilized and not being able to go to work because of the conversion of his property by Les Schwab employees.

Is Mr. Reed correct? Was this a breach of the peace? Explain your answer.

[***Reed v. Les Schwab Tire Centers, Inc.,*** **160 Wash. App. 1020 (Wash. App. 2011)**]

ETHICS & THE LAW

Women, Children, and the Repo Guys

Repossessions of autos financed on credit are at an all-time high. Lenders explain that the growth period of the past decade inspired many to overextend themselves with credit purchases, and now the repossessions are taking place.

According to the "repo industry," about 15 percent of debtors surrender their cars voluntarily. Confrontations occur about 10 percent of the time during repossession. Many debtors change the color of their cars, change the tires and rims, or cover the vehicle identification number to foil repossession companies' efforts. One auto dealer, trying to repossess a woman's car, had two male employees scale the fence of the Murfeesboro, Tennessee, Domestic Violence Program Shelter. The shelter's security cameras spotted the men and after police were notified, they were ordered off the premises. The woman who owned the car left the shelter to make the necessary payments to bring her obligations current.

The shelter director said that if the men had come through the proper administrative channels at the shelter, the shelter would have cooperated with them. The shelter director called the men's scaling of the fence at a shelter for women and children "irresponsible."

Do you think it is ethical for the debtors to do these things? Should debtors surrender their cars voluntarily?

In two incidents in 2006, cars that were repossessed had children sleeping in them. The cars were hooked to the tow vehicle and the children were transported to the tow yards. An industry spokesman said that "repo guys" have to get in and hook the cars up as quickly as possible; they do not have time to check the inside of the vehicle.

Source: Rich Beattie, "Boom Times for Repo Guys," *New York Times,* April 18, 2003, D1, D8.

CPA 33-5e **Postdisposition Accounting**

When the creditor disposes of the collateral, the proceeds are applied in the following order. Proceeds are first used to pay the expenses of disposing of the collateral. Next, proceeds are applied to the debt owed the secured creditor making the disposition. Remaining proceeds are applied to any debts owed other creditors holding security interests in the same collateral that are subordinate to the interest of the disposing creditor.[66]

[66] U.C.C. §9-615.

Distribution of Surplus

If there is any money remaining, the surplus is paid to the debtor.[67]

Liability for Deficit

If the proceeds of the disposition are not sufficient to pay the costs and the debt of the disposing creditor, the debtor is liable for the deficiency. However, the disposition of the collateral must have been conducted in the manner required by the UCC. This means that proper notice must have been given, if required, and that the disposition must have been made in a commercially reasonable manner. Factors that determine commercial reasonableness include notice, the difference between the sale price and the value of the goods, and public versus private sale according to industry practice.[68]

Make the Connection

Summary

A security interest is an interest in personal property or fixtures that secures payment or performance of an obligation. The property that is subject to the interest is called the *collateral*, and the party holding the interest is called the *secured party*. *Attachment* is the creation of a security interest. To secure protection against third parties' claims to the collateral, the secured party must perfect the security interest. *Tangible collateral* is divided into classes: consumer goods, equipment, inventory, general intangibles, farm products, and fixtures. Under Revised Article 9, intangibles have been expanded to include bank accounts, checks, notes, and health care insurance receivables.

Perfection of a security interest is not required for its validity, but it does provide the creditor certain superior rights and priorities over other types of creditors and creditors with an interest in the same collateral. Perfection can be obtained through possession, filing, automatically (as in the case of a PMSI in consumer goods), by control for accounts under Revised Article 9, or temporarily when statutory protections are provided for creditors for limited periods of time.

Priority among creditors is determined according to their status. Unperfected, unsecured creditors simply wait to see whether there will be sufficient assets remaining after priority creditors are paid. Secured creditors have the right to take the collateral on a priority basis. As between secured creditors, the first creditor's interest to attach takes priority in the event the creditors hold security interests in the same collateral. A perfected secured creditor takes priority over an unperfected secured creditor. Perfected secured creditors with interests in the same collateral take priority generally on a first-to-perfect basis. Exceptions include PMSI inventory creditors who file a financing statement before delivery and notify all existing creditors, and equipment creditors who perfect within 20 days of attachment of their interests.

A buyer in the ordinary course of business always takes priority, even over perfected secured creditors who have knowledge of the creditor's interest. A buyer not in the ordinary course of business loses out to a perfected secured creditor but extinguishes the rights of a secured creditor unless the buyer had knowledge of the security interest. A buyer from a consumer debtor takes free and clear of the debtor's creditor's perfected security interest unless the creditor has filed a financing statement and perfected beyond just the automatic PMSI consumer goods perfection.

Upon default, a secured party may repossess the collateral from the buyer if this can be done without a breach of the peace. If a breach of the peace could occur, the secured party must use court action to regain the collateral. If the buyer has paid 60 percent or more of the cash price of the consumer goods, the seller must resell them within 90 days after repossession unless the buyer, after default, has waived this right in writing. Notice to the debtor of the sale of the collateral is usually required. A debtor may redeem the collateral prior to the time the secured party disposes of it or contracts to resell it.

---

[67] U.C.C. §9-616.
[68] *Mercado v. HFC Collection Center, Inc.*, Not Reported in F. Supp. 2d, 2013 WL 645988 (M.D. Fla. 2013).

Learning Outcomes

After studying this chapter, you should be able to clearly explain:

33-1   Creation of Secured Transactions

LO.1   Explain the requirements for creating a valid security interest

See the In re *Cunningham* case, pages 645–646.
See the *ProGrowth Bank, Inc. v. Wells Fargo Bank, N.A.*, case, pages 651–652.
See the *Dawson v. Fifth Third Bank* case, pages 661–662.

LO.2   List the major types of collateral

See the In re *Lull* case, page 648.

33-2   Perfection of Secured Transactions

LO.3   Define perfection and explain its significance in secured transactions

See E-Commerce & Cyberlaw, "Engines Are from Mars; Priorities Are from Financing Statements," page 653.

33-3   Rights of Parties before Default

33-4   Priorities

LO.4   Discuss the priorities of parties with conflicting interests in collateral when default occurs

See the *General Motors Acceptance Corp. v. Lincoln* case, page 656.
See the *Tolbert v. Automotive Finance Corp.* case for priorities of buyers and secured parties, page 658.

33-5   Rights of Parties after Default

LO.5   State the rights of the parties on the debtor's default

See the *Chrysler Credit v. Koontz* case, page 662.
See the Thinking Things Through feature on repossession of tires, page 664.
See Ethics & the Law, "Women, Children, and the Repo Guys," page 664.

Key Terms

after-acquired goods	financing statement	secured party
automatic perfection	first-in-time provision	secured transaction
breach of the peace	first-to-perfect basis	security agreement
collateral	floating lien	security interest
consumer good	perfected security interest	self-help repossession
creditor	*pro rata*	temporary perfection
debtor	purchase money security interest	termination statement
field warehousing	(PMSI)	value

Questions and Case Problems

1. On October 22, 2001, Benjamin Ritchie executed a promissory note and mortgage in consideration for a $47,000 loan from WaMu. The mortgage covered both real estate located at 1790 Mount Mariah Road, Carlisle, Kentucky, and a manufactured home to be situated on the real property. The mortgage was properly filed in the Nicholas County Clerk's Office on October 31, 2001.

   Ritchie used the proceeds of the loan to purchase a manufactured home, which was subsequently rendered a total loss as a result of heavy fire damage. As the named loss payee on the insurance policy for the home, WaMu received and released the insurance proceeds to the Debtor to purchase a replacement manufactured home. WaMu failed, however, to record its lien on the certificate of title to the replacement manufactured home.

   On January 20, 2006, WaMu initiated a foreclosure action on the property. Ritchie raised the defense that WaMu no longer had a valid lien on the manufactured home. Is Ritchie correct? Explain your answer. [In re *Ritchie*, 416 B.R. 638 (6th Cir.)]

2. In 1983, Carpet Contracts owned a commercial lot and building, which it operated as a retail carpet outlet. In April of 1983, Carpet Contracts entered into a credit sales agreement with Young Electric Sign Corp. (Yesco) for the purchase of a large electronic sign for the store. The cost of the sign was $113,000, with a down payment of $25,000 and 60 monthly payments of $2,100 each.

In August 1985, Carpet Contracts agreed to sell the property to Interstate. As part of the sale, Carpet Contracts gave Interstate an itemized list showing that $64,522 of the proceeds from the sale would be used to pay for the "Electronic Sign." The property was transferred to Interstate, and the Carpet Contracts store continued to operate there, but now it paid rent to Interstate. In June 1986, Carpet Contracts asked Yesco to renegotiate the terms of the sign contract. Yesco reduced Carpet Contracts' monthly payments and filed a financing statement on the sign at the Utah Division of Corporations and Commercial Code. In December 1986, Interstate agreed to sell the property and the sign to the Webbs, who conducted a title search on the property, which revealed no interest with respect to the electronic sign. Interstate conveyed the property to the Webbs. Carpet Contracts continued its operation but was struggling financially and had not made its payments to Yesco for some time. By 1989, Yesco declared the sign contract in default and contacted the Webbs, demanding the balance due of $26,100. The Webbs then filed suit, claiming Yesco had no priority as a creditor because its financing statement was not filed in the real property records where the Webbs had done their title search before purchasing the land. Was the financing statement filed properly for perfection? [*Webb v. Interstate Land Corp.*, 920 P.2d 1187 (Utah)]

3. McLeod purchased several items from Sears, Roebuck & Co. on credit. The description of the items, in which Sears took a purchase money security interest, was as follows: "MITER SAW; LXITV-RACDC [a television, videocassette recorder, and compact disc spinner]; 25 UPRIGHT, 28 UPRIGHT [two pieces of luggage]; BRA-CELET, DIA STUDS, RING; 14K EARR, P, EARRINGS, P [diamond bracelet, ring, and earrings]; and 9-INCH E-Z-LIFT [an outdoor umbrella]." In a dispute over creditors' priorities in McLeod's bankruptcy, one creditor argued that the description of the goods was insufficient to give Sears a security interest. Does the description meet Article 9 standards? [*McLeod v. Sears, Roebuck & Co.*, 41 U.C.C. 2d (Bankr. E.D. Mich.)]

4. When Johnson Hardware Shop borrowed $20,000 from First Bank, it used its inventory as collateral for the loan. First Bank perfected its security interest by filing a financing statement. The inventory was subsequently damaged by fire. Flanders Insurance paid Johnson Hardware $5,000 for the loss, but First Bank claimed the proceeds of the insurance. Was First Bank correct? Why or why not?

5. Consider the following cases and determine whether the financing statements as filed would be valid under Article 9. Be sure to consider the standard of "seriously misleading" under Revised Article 9.

   a. In re *Thriftway Auto Supply, Inc.*, 159 B.R. 948, 22 U.C.C. Rep. Serv. 2d 605 (W.D. Okla.). The creditor used the debtor's corporate trade name, "Thriftway Auto Stores," not its legal name, "Thriftway Auto Supply, Inc."

   b. In re *Mines Tire Co., Inc.*, 194 B.R. 23, 29 U.C.C. 2d 617 (Bankr. W.D.N.Y). The creditor used the name "Mines Company Inc." instead of "Mines Tire Company, Inc."

   c. *Mountain Farm Credit Service, ACA v. Purina Mills, Inc.*, 459 S.E.2d 75 (N.C. App.). The creditor filed the financing statement under "Warren Killian and Robert Hetherington dba Grey Daw Farms" in a situation in which the two individuals were partners running Grey Daw Farms as a partnership.

   d. *B.T. Lazarus & Co. v. Christofides*, 662 N.E.2d 41 (Ohio App.). The creditor filed a financing statement in the debtor's old name when, prior to filing, the debtor had changed its name from B.T.L., Inc., to Alma Manufacturing, Inc.

   e. In re *SpecialCare, Inc.*, 209 B.R. 13, 34 U.C.C. 2d 857 (N.D. Ga). The creditor failed to refile an amended financing statement to reflect debtor's name change from "Davidson Therapeutic Services, Inc." to "SpecialCare, Inc."

   f. *Industrial Machinery & Equipment Co. Inc. v. Lapeer County Bank & Trust Co.*, 540 N.W.2d 781 (Mich. App.). The creditor filed the financing statement under the company's trade name, KMI, Inc., instead of its legal name, Koehler Machine, Inc.

   g. *First Nat'l Bank of Lacon v. Strong*, 663 N.E.2d 432 (Ill. App.). Creditor filed the financing statement using the trade name "Strong Oil Co." instead of the legal name "E. Strong Oil Company."

6. First Union Bank of Florida loaned money to Dale and Lynn Rix for their purchase of Ann's Hallmark, a Florida corporation. First Union took a security

interest in the store's equipment, fixtures, and inventory and filed the financing statement under the names of Dale and Lynn Rix. Subsequently, the Rixes incorporated their newly acquired business as Michelle's Hallmark Cards & Gifts, Inc. When Michelle's went into bankruptcy, First Union claimed it had priority as a secured creditor because it had filed its financing statement first. Other creditors said First Union had priority against the Rixes but not against the corporation. Who was correct? What was the correct name for filing the financing statement? [In re *Michelle's Hallmark Cards & Gifts, Inc.*, 36 U.C.C. 2d 225 (Bankr. M.D. Fla.)]

7. Rawlings purchased a typewriter from Kroll Typewriter Co. for $600. At the time of the purchase, he made an initial payment of $75 and agreed to pay the balance in monthly installments. A security agreement that complied with the UCC was prepared, but no financing statement was ever filed for the transaction. Rawlings, at a time when he still owed a balance on the typewriter and without the consent of Kroll, sold the typewriter to a neighbor. The neighbor, who had no knowledge of the security interest, used the typewriter in her home. Could Kroll repossess the typewriter from the neighbor?

8. Kim purchased on credit a $1,000 freezer from Silas Household Appliance Store. After she had paid approximately $700, Kim missed the next monthly installment payment. Silas repossessed the freezer and billed Kim for the balance of the purchase price, $300. Kim claimed that the freezer, now in the possession of Silas, was worth much more than the balance due and requested that Silas sell the freezer to wipe out the balance of the debt and to leave something for her. Silas claimed that because Kim had broken her contract to pay the purchase price, she had no right to say what should be done with the freezer. Was Silas correct? Explain.

9. Benson purchased a new Ford Thunderbird automobile. She traded in her old car and used the Magnavox Employees Credit Union to finance the balance. The credit union took a security interest in the Ford. Subsequently, the Ford was involved in a number of accidents and was taken to a dealer for repairs. Benson was unable to pay for the work done. The dealer claimed a lien on the car for services and materials furnished. The Magnavox Employees Credit Union claimed priority. Which claim had priority? [*Magnavox Employees Credit Union v. Benson*, 331 N.E.2d 46 (Ind. App.)]

10. Lockovich borrowed money from a bank to purchase a motorboat. The bank took a security interest in it but never filed a financing statement. A subsequent default on the loan occurred, and the debtor was declared bankrupt. The bank claimed priority in the boat, alleging that no financing statement had to be filed. Do you agree? Why? [In re *Lockovich*, 124 B.R. 660 (W.D. Pa.)]

11. In 1987, the Muirs bought a motor home. In 1988, the Muirs created and Bank of the West acquired and perfected a security interest in the motor home. In 1992, the Muirs entered into an agreement with Gateleys Fairway Motors by which Gateleys would sell the motor home by consignment. Gateleys sold the motor home to Howard and Ann Schultz. The Schultzes did not know of the consignment arrangement or of the security interest of the bank. Gateleys failed to give the sales money to the Muirs and then filed for bankruptcy.

    The Schultzes brought suit seeking a declaration that they owned the motor home free of the bank's security interest. The trial court granted the Schultzes summary judgment. Who has title to the motor home and why? [*Schultz v. Bank of the West, C.B.C.*, 934 P.2d 421 (Or.)]

12. On April 18, 2000, Philip Purkett parked his car, on which he owed $213 in payments, in his garage and locked the garage. Later that night, TWAS, Inc., a vehicle repossession company, broke into the garage and repossessed the car without notice to Purkett. To get the car back, Purkett paid a $140 storage fee and signed a document stating that he would not hold TWAS liable for any damages. Did TWAS and Key Bank violate Article 9 requirements on repossession? [*Purkett v. Key Bank USA, Inc.*, 2001 WL 503050, 45 U.C.C. Rep. Serv. 2d 1201 (N.D. Ill.)]

13. *A* borrowed money from *B* and orally agreed that *B* had a security interest in equipment that was standing in *A*'s yard. Nothing was in writing, and no filing of any kind was made. Nine days later, *B* took possession of the equipment. What kind of interest did *B* have in the equipment after taking possession of it? [*Transport Equipment Co. v. Guaranty State Bank*, 518 F.2d 373 (10th Cir.)]

14. Cook sold Martin a new tractor truck for approximately $13,000, with a down payment of approximately $3,000 and the balance to be paid in 30 monthly installments. The sales agreement provided that "on default in any payment, Cook [could] take immediate possession of the property … without

notice or demand. For this purpose vendor may enter upon any premises on which the property may be." Martin failed to pay the installments when due, and Cook notified him that the truck would be repossessed. Martin left the tractor truck attached to a loaded trailer and locked on the premises of a company in Memphis. Martin intended to drive to the West Coast with the trailer. When Cook located the tractor truck, no one was around. To disconnect the trailer from the truck (because he had no right to the trailer), Cook removed the wire screen over a ventilator hole by unscrewing it from the outside with his penknife. He next reached through the ventilator hole with a stick and unlocked the door of the tractor truck. He then disconnected the trailer and had the truck towed away. Martin sued Cook for unlawfully repossessing the truck by

committing a breach of the peace. Decide. [*Martin v. Cook*, 114 So. 2d 669 (Miss.)]

15. Kimbrell's Furniture Co. sold a new television set and tape player to Charlie O'Neil and his wife. Each purchase was on credit, and in each instance, a security agreement was executed. Later on the same day of purchase, O'Neil carried the items to Bonded Loan, a pawnbroker, and pledged the television and tape deck as security for a loan. Bonded Loan held possession of the television set and tape player as security for its loan and contended that its lien had priority over the unrecorded security interest of Kimbrell. Who had priority? [*Kimbrell's Furniture Co. v. Sig Friedman, d/b/a Bonded Loan*, 198 S.E.2d 803 (S.C.)]

CPA Questions

1. On March 1, Green went to Easy Car Sales to buy a car. Green spoke to a salesperson and agreed to buy a car that Easy had in its showroom. On March 5, Green made a $500 down payment and signed a security agreement to secure the payment of the balance of the purchase price. On March 10, Green picked up the car. On March 15, Easy filed the security agreement. On what date did Easy's security interest attach?

   a. March 1
   b. March 5
   c. March 10
   d. March 15

2. Carr Corp. sells VCRs and videotapes to the public. Carr sold and delivered a VCR to Sutter on credit. Sutter executed and delivered to Carr a promissory note for the purchase price and a security agreement covering the VCR. Sutter purchased the VCR for personal use. Carr did not file a financing statement. Is Carr's security interest perfected?

   a. No, because the VCR was a consumer good.
   b. No, because Carr failed to file a financing statement.
   c. Yes, because Carr retained ownership of the VCR.
   d. Yes, because it was perfected at the time of attachment.

3. On July 8, Ace, a refrigerator wholesaler, purchased 50 refrigerators. This comprised Ace's entire inventory and was financed under an agreement with Rome Bank that gave Rome a security interest in all refrigerators on Ace's premises, all future-acquired refrigerators, and the proceeds of sales. On July 12, Rome filed a financing statement that adequately identified the collateral. On August 15, Ace sold one refrigerator to Cray for personal use and four refrigerators to Zone Co. for its business. Which of the following statements is correct?

   a. The refrigerators sold to Zone will be subject to Rome's security interest.
   b. The refrigerators sold to Zone will not be subject to Rome's security interest.
   c. The security interest does not include the proceeds from the sale of the refrigerators to Zone.
   d. The security interest may not cover after-acquired property even if the parties agree.

4. Fogel purchased a television set for $900 from Hamilton Appliance. Hamilton took a promissory note signed by Fogel and a security interest for the $800 balance due on the set. It was Hamilton's policy not to file a financing statement until the purchaser defaulted. Fogel obtained a loan of $500 from Reliable Finance, which took and recorded a security interest in the set. A month later, Fogel

defaulted on several loans and one of his creditors, Harp, obtained a judgment against Fogel, which was properly recorded. After making several payments, Fogel defaulted on a payment due to Hamilton, who then recorded a financing statement subsequent to Reliable's filing and the entry of the Harp judgment. Subsequently, at a garage sale, Fogel sold the set for $300 to Mobray. Which of the parties has the priority claim to the set?

a. Reliable

b. Hamilton

c. Harp

d. Mobray

5. Under the Secured Transactions Article of the UCC, which of the following items can usually be excluded from a filed original financing statement?

a. The name of the debtor.

b. The address of the debtor.

c. A description of the collateral.

d. The amount of the obligation secured.

6. Under the Secured Transactions Article of the UCC, which of the following security agreements does not need to be in writing to be enforceable?

a. A security agreement collateralizing a debt of less than $500.

b. A security agreement where the collateral is highly perishable or subject to wide price fluctuations.

c. A security agreement where the collateral is in the possession of the secured party.

d. A security agreement involving a purchase money security interest.

C H A P T E R   34

Bankruptcy

Learning Outcomes 〈〈〈

After studying this chapter, you should be able to

LO.1 List the requirements for the commencement of a voluntary bankruptcy case and an involuntary bankruptcy case

LO.2 Explain the procedure for the administration of a debtor's estate

LO.3 List a debtor's duties and exemptions

LO.4 Explain the significance of a discharge in bankruptcy

LO.5 Explain when a business reorganization plan or an extended-time payment plan might be used

34-1   Bankruptcy Law

What can a person or business do when overwhelmed by debts? Bankruptcy proceedings can provide temporary and sometimes permanent relief from those debts.

Bankruptcy is a statutory proceeding with detailed procedures and requirements.

34-1a   The Federal Law

Bankruptcy law is based on federal statutes that have been refined over the years. In October 2005, Congress passed the Bankruptcy Abuse Prevention and Consumer Protection Act of 2005 (BAPCPA), the law that is still in effect.[1]

Jurisdiction over bankruptcy proceedings is in courts of special jurisdiction called **bankruptcy courts,** which operate under the umbrella of the federal district courts.

bankruptcy courts–court of special jurisdiction to determine bankruptcy issues.

34-1b   Types of Bankruptcy Proceedings

There are three types of bankruptcy proceedings.

Liquidation or Chapter 7 Bankruptcy

C P A

Chapter 7 bankruptcy–liquidation form of bankruptcy under federal law.

liquidation–process of converting property into money whether of particular items of property or of all the assets of a business or an estate.

A **Chapter 7 bankruptcy** is one in which all of the debtor's assets (with some exemptions) will be **liquidated** to pay debts. Those debts that remain unpaid or are paid only partially are discharged, with some exceptions. The debtor who declares Chapter 7 bankruptcy begins again with a nearly clean slate.

Chapter 7 bankruptcy is available to individuals, partnerships, and corporations. However, farmers, insurance companies, savings and loans, municipalities, Small Business Administration companies, and railroads are not entitled to declare Chapter 7 bankruptcy because they are specifically governed by other statutes or specialized sections of the Bankruptcy Code.[2]

Under the BAPCPA, consumers generally cannot go directly to a Chapter 7 liquidation bankruptcy because they must demonstrate that they do not have the means to repay the debts before they can do a Chapter 7 liquidation.[3] The means test, which is discussed later, considers the disposable income that is available after the bankruptcy court has deducted allowable expenses that are listed as part of the means section of the BAPCPA, including items such as health insurance and child support.

Reorganization or Chapter 11 Bankruptcy

C P A

Chapter 11 bankruptcy–reorganization form of bankruptcy under federal law.

Chapter 11 bankruptcy is a way for a debtor to reorganize and continue a business with protection from overwhelming debts and without the requirement of liquidation. Abercrombie & Fitch, Fuddruckers, the Chicago Cubs, Chrysler, General Motors, the Sharper Image, United Airlines, and Delta are all examples of companies that have gone through Chapter 11 bankruptcies. Stockbrokers, however, are not eligible for Chapter 11 bankruptcy.

---

[1] The act is codified at 11 U.S.C. §101 *et seq.*

[2] For example, the Small Business Investment Act governs the insolvency of small business investment companies, 11 U.S.C. §109(b). Municipalities' bankruptcies are governed by Chapter 9 of the Bankruptcy Code, and farmers' bankruptcies are covered under Chapter 11. Following the 2008 market collapse, there were a series of municipal bankruptcies because of excessive debt and pension obligations.

[3] 11 U.S.C. §707(C)(2)(a). There are exceptions to the requirements of establishing no means, such as those who incurred their debts while on active military service.

ETHICS & THE LAW

Bankruptcy Records

According to **http://www.bankruptcydata.com**, the following are the largest bankruptcies in the history of the United States:

Total bankruptcy filings in the United States from 2008 to 2014 were as follows. Note the spike following 2008 because of the economic crisis.

Company	Date	Amount
Lehman Brothers	09/15/2008	$640,000,000 billion
Washington Mutual (WaMu)	09/26/2008	$327,900,000 billion
WorldCom	07/21/2002	$103,900,000 billion
General Motors	06/01/2009	$91,000,000 billion
CIT	11/01/2009	$80,400,000 billion
Enron	12/02/2001	$65,500,000 billion
Conseco	12/02/2002	$61,300,000 billion
MF Global	10/31/2011	$41,000,000 billion
Chrysler	04/20/2009	$39,300,000 billion
Thornburg Mortgage	05/05/2009	$36,500,000 billion

Year	Total	Nonbusiness	Business
2014	936,795	909,812	26,983
2013	1,071,932	1,038,720	33,212
2012	1,221,091	1,181,016	40,075
2011	1,410,653	1,362,847	47,806
2010	1,593,081	1,536,799	56,282
2009	1,473,675	1,412,838	60,837
2008	1,117,641	1,074,108	43,533

Is there an ethical component to declaring bankruptcy? For example, actor Gary Busey's agent referred to bankruptcy as a business strategy. What are the risks of using bankruptcy as a business strategy?

CPA

Chapter 13 Bankruptcy or Payment Plans or Consumer Debt Adjustment Plans

Chapter 13 bankruptcy— proceeding of consumer debt readjustment plan bankruptcy.

Chapter 13 of the federal Bankruptcy Code provides consumers an individual form of reorganization. Chapter 13 works with consumer debtors to develop a plan to repay debt. To be eligible for **Chapter 13 bankruptcy,** the individual must owe unsecured debts of less than $383,175 and secured debts of less than $1,149.525 and have regular income.[4] Chapter 13 plays an expanded role in bankruptcy because reforms require debtors with the means to pay their debts to go first into Chapter 13 bankruptcy rather than automatically declaring Chapter 7 bankruptcy.

34-2 How Bankruptcy Is Declared

Bankruptcy can be declared in different ways. The federal Bankruptcy Code spells out the requirements and process for declaration.

CPA

34-2a Declaration of Voluntary Bankruptcy

voluntary bankruptcy— proceeding in which the debtor files the petition for relief.

A **voluntary bankruptcy** is begun when the debtor files a petition with the bankruptcy court. A joint petition may be filed by a husband and wife. When a voluntary case is

---

[4] 11 U.S.C. §109(e). These amounts were automatically increased in 2013 and are in effect for three years (through April 2016).

begun, the debtor must file a schedule of current income and current expenditures unless the court excuses this filing.

A court can dismiss an individual debtor's (consumer's) petition for abuse if the debtor does not satisfy the **means test,** which measures the debtor's ability to pay by computing the debtor's disposable income. Only those debtors who fall below their state's median disposable income will be able to continue in a Chapter 7 proceeding. Individual debtors who meet the means test are required to go into Chapter 13 bankruptcy because they have not qualified for Chapter 7 bankruptcy. The formula for applying the means test is as follows:

Debtor's current monthly income less
Allowable expenses under the Bankruptcy Code = Disposable income $\times$ 60

The debtor commits bankruptcy abuse if this number is not less than the lower of the following:

- 25 percent of the debtor's unsecured claims or $7,475, whichever is greater; or
- $12,475

A finding of abuse means that the debtor's Chapter 7 voluntary petition is dismissed.[5]

Under the BAPCPA, the bankruptcy judge also has the discretion to order the debtor's lawyer to reimburse the trustee for costs and attorney's fees and to assess a civil penalty against the lawyer if the court finds that the lawyer has not acted in good faith in filing the debtor's bankruptcy petition.[6] Lawyers are required to declare themselves (in public ads as well as in any individual meetings with clients) to be "debt relief agencies" or state that they "help people file for relief under the Bankruptcy Code." Debt relief organizations must disclose that bankruptcy may be part of what is required for relief from their debts. Lawyers who advertise their credit/bankruptcy expertise are subject to the laws and regulations that apply to debt relief agencies. If the agency/lawyer advises them to do something that causes the court to declare that there has been bankruptcy abuse, the lawyer/debt relief agency is responsible as well. As part of their role as debt counselors, lawyers are prohibited from advising clients to undertake more debt in contemplation of filing bankruptcy.[7]

Debtors are required to undergo credit counseling (from an approved nonprofit credit counseling agency) within the 180 days prior to declaring a bankruptcy. In addition, the court applies the means test described earlier to determine whether the debtor qualifies for bankruptcy.[8]

There is significant disagreement among the bankruptcy courts about the meaning of "projected income." The disagreement results from the differing situations of the debtors. **For Example,** how do courts deal with debtors who are about to experience a large drop in disposable income? And do courts then consider what happens when debtors'

---

means test–new standard under the Reform Act that requires the court to find that the debtor does not have the means to repay creditors; goes beyond the past requirement of petitions being granted on the simple assertion of the debtor saying, "I have debts."

---

[5] 11 U.S.C. §707(b). Debtor using bankruptcy to stall a lawsuit who filled out the bankruptcy forms inaccurately was held to have acted in bad faith. In re *Crest By The Sea,* 522 B.R. 540 (D.N.J. 2014). Debtors who failed to disclose their income from a rental property were guilty of bad faith. In re *Fox,* 521 B.R. 520 (D. Md. 2004).

[6] 11 U.S.C. §707(b)(4).

[7] 11 U.S.C. §§526-528. *Milavetz, Gallop & Milavetz, P.A. v. U.S.,* 559 U.S. 229 (2010).

[8] 11 U.S.C. §109(h)(2). There are exceptions to the counseling requirements; for example, active military duty, disability, and emergencies. 11 U.S.C. 111(a) is the counseling provision. The counseling must be completed prior to filing for bankruptcy or the petition can be dismissed, In re *Alvarado,* 496 B.R. 200 (N.D. Cal. 2013). However, being in prison is not an excuse for not going through counseling, and the petition may be dismissed. In re *Gordon,* 467 B.R. 639 (W.D. Ky. 2012) and In re *Kerr,* 2014 WL 6747112 (N.D. Ohio 2014).

incomes are expected to go up? If the projected income test used is applied, the bankruptcy could be dismissed. Debtors and creditors take different positions depending on which way the income goes, and the courts continue to debate the definition of projected income.[9]

CASE SUMMARY

Lawyer/Debtor in the Hoosegow: Still Eligible for Chapter 13?

FACTS: Topous obtained a judgment against Clarence Kenyon Gomery, a lawyer (Debtor), and his law firm, Gomery and Associates, PLLC. That case arose from Mr. Gomery's representation of Topous in various business transactions, including the purchase of property referred to as the Old Mitchell Creek Golf Course. Topous alleged that Mr. Gomery drafted an Operating Agreement creating a limited liability company, T & G Real Estate Development, LLC, to purchase and hold the Mitchell Creek property. Although Topous paid the full purchase price to acquire the property, Mr. Gomery defrauded Topous in the transaction by surreptitiously giving himself a one-half ownership interest in T & G in the Operating Agreement he drafted. The jury awarded ownership of the Mitchell Creek property to Topous and ordered Mr. Gomery to pay Topous damages in the net amount of $11,622.22 and imposed sanctions for Frivolous Defense and for Spoliation of Evidence (see Chapter 2) against Mr. Gomery and his law firm, jointly and severally, for $314,629.27.

Unable to pay the judgment, Mr. Gomery filed a voluntary petition under Chapter 13 on April 2, 2014.

In July 2014, Mr. Gomery was arrested and charged with solicitation of murder. Detective Gomez testified about a recorded conversation between Mr. Gomery and Dale Fisher. During the course of the recorded conversation, Mr. Gomery offered Mr. Fisher $20,000 to kill Christopher K. Cooke, the attorney who represented Topous. Detective Gomez also testified that Mr. Gomery paid Mr. Fisher $1,000 during the recorded conversation, purportedly to purchase the weapon that would be used in committing the crime. Mr. Gomery is currently incarcerated and awaiting trial on these criminal charges.

Mr. Gomery seeks confirmation of his Chapter 13 Plan. The Trustee and Topous have objected to the Plan on the grounds that the Plan is not feasible, and that neither the Plan nor the petition was filed in good faith. The

Trustee has also requested that Mr. Gomery's case be converted to Chapter 7 due to the Debtor's lack of good faith.

DECISION: The Debtor's schedules failed to disclose significant and valuable assets. For example, JACCK Enterprises, LLC, in which the Debtor had an interest, appeared on the Debtor's own individual tax returns for 2009 through 2013, along with the returns of JACCK itself. Those returns reflect his income from JACCK and show him as having a one-half ownership interest in the LLC. But he did not disclose JACCK.

The Debtor's Schedules did not disclose that he owned any firearms.

Chapter 13 relief is reserved for the 'honest but unfortunate debtor.'

The court found that the Debtor had not been fair in his treatment of his creditors and was not been forthright in his dealings with the Trustee, the creditors, and this Bankruptcy Court. Under the circumstances, the court found that the Debtor had not acted in good faith.

The Court held that conversion to Chapter 7, which would allow these matters to be investigated by a Chapter 7 trustee, was in the best interests of creditors in this case.

The Debtor offered no explanation, let alone evidence, of the source of the funds he proposed to use to make the $100 monthly payments required under his proposed Plan. The Debtor was incarcerated at the time of the bankruptcy proceedings and had offered no evidence of any current income. Although the Debtor's Plan proposed increasing his payments in the future, the Debtor's attorney admitted that it is unlikely that the Debtor will resume his legal practice in the future. Because the Debtor had no current income, and limited prospects for income in the future, the Court concluded that the Debtor is not eligible to be a debtor under Chapter 13. The Debtor's case was converted to a Chapter 7 proceeding. **[In re *Gomery*, 523 B.R. 773 (W.D. Mich. 2015)]**

[9] In re *Turner,* 425 B.R. 918 (S.D. Ga. 2010); In re *Hilton,* 395 B.R. 433 (E.D. Wis. 2008); In re *Anstett,* 383 B.R. 380 (D.S.C. 2008); In re *Colclasure,* 383 B.R. 463 (E.D. Ark. 2008); and In re *Justice,* 418 B.R. 342 (W.D. Mo. 2009).

CPA   34-2b **Declaration of Involuntary Bankruptcy**

Eligibility

involuntary bankruptcy– proceeding in which a creditor or creditors file the petition for relief with the bankruptcy court.

An **involuntary bankruptcy** is begun when creditors file a petition with the bankruptcy court. An involuntary case may be commenced against any individual, partnership, or corporation, except those excluded from filing voluntary petitions. Nonprofit corporations are also exempt from involuntary proceedings.[10]

CPA   **Number and Claims of Petitioning Creditors**

If there are 12 or more creditors, at least 3 of those creditors whose unsecured and undisputed claims total $15,325 or more must sign the involuntary petition.[11] If there are fewer than 12 creditors, excluding employees or insiders (that is, the debtor's relatives,

---

THINKING THINGS THROUGH

Means Test Justifying the End of Debt

The following excerpt is a hypothetical case an experienced bankruptcy attorney worked through to illustrate the application of the means test.

The Brokes, a married couple in their early 40s, have two children in private schools. They are residents of Memphis, Shelby County, Tennessee; their annual gross income is $86,496. Like many debtors, the Brokes lost their home following an unsuccessful Chapter 13 case three years ago. They now rent a house for $2,000 a month. They owe back federal taxes in the amount of $9,000. They have secured debt on two cars with remaining balances of $10,000 and $6,000 and unsecured, consumer debt totaling $28,000. They desire to seek relief under Chapter 7 of the Bankruptcy Code.

The Brokes' gross monthly income is $7,208. After deducting taxes and other mandatory payroll deductions of $1,509, the couple has $5,699 in monthly income. The means test requires several additional deductions from the Brokes' gross monthly income. Section 707(b)(A)(2)(ii) provides a deduction for living and housing expenses using National Standards and Local Standards and additional Internal Revenue Service (IRS) figures. Allowable living expenses for a family of four in Ura and Ima Brokes' income bracket, based on national standards, total $1,564, while housing and utility figures for Shelby County, Tennessee, allow $1,354. In addition, there are allowable expenses for transportation. Based on IRS figures, the Brokes can subtract national ownership costs of $475 for the first car and $338 for the second, as well as regional operating and public transportation costs of $242 and $336, respectively. They can also

deduct their reasonably necessary health insurance costs, here the sum of $600, and $250 a month for private school tuition. Subtracting all of these figures from the Brokes' monthly income leaves $540.

Under §707(b)(2)(A)(iii), the Brokes can subtract payments on secured debt. The amount contractually due on their two automobiles over the next 60 months is $16,000. After dividing this total by 60 and rounding to the nearest dollar, the monthly allowable deduction for secured debt is $267. Subtracting this amount from $540 leaves $273.

Next come priority claim deductions. The Brokes are not subject to any child support or alimony claims, but they do owe $9,000 in back taxes. Again, dividing this amount by 60 yields a deductible amount of $150. Subtracting this from $273 leaves $123 in disposable monthly income. This figure would be multiplied by 60, amounting to a total of $7,380 in disposable income over the five-year period. Abuse is thus statutorily presumed because the debtors' current monthly income reduced by allowable amounts is not less than either $7,000 (25 percent of their nonpriority unsecured claims of $28,000) or $6,000. The Brokes' Chapter 7 case will therefore be dismissed (or they will be allowed voluntarily to convert their Chapter 7 case to a case under Chapter 13).

Does the means test make it more difficult for debtors to declare bankruptcy?*

*Robert J. Landry III and Nancy Hisey Mardis, "Consumer Bankruptcy Reform: Debtors' Prison without Bars or 'Just Desserts' for Deadbeats?" 36 *Golden Gate U. L Rev.* 91 (2006). Reprinted with permission.

---

[10] 11 U.S.C. §303(a). In re *C.W. Min. Co.*, 431 B.R. 307 (Utah 2009). These amounts are adjusted periodically by statutory formulas.

[11] 11 U.S.C. §303.

partners, directors, and controlling persons), any creditor whose unsecured claim is at least $15,325 may sign the petition. In the case of involuntary consumer petitions, there is disagreement as to whether the debtor will still be required to complete the credit counseling requirement prior to the granting of the automatic stay.

bona fide–in good faith; without any fraud or deceit.

If a creditor holds security for a claim, only the amount of the claim in excess of the value of the security is counted. The holder of a claim that is the subject of a **bona fide** dispute may not be counted as a petitioning creditor.[12] **For Example,** David, a CPA, is an unsecured creditor of Arco Company for $16,000. Arco has a total of 10 creditors, all of whom are unsecured. Arco has not paid any of the creditors for three months. The debtor has fewer than 12 creditors. Any one of the creditors may file the petition if the unsecured portion of the amount due that creditor is at least $15,325. Because David is owed $16,000 in unsecured debts, he may file the petition alone.

CPA

Grounds for Relief for Involuntary Case

The mere filing of an involuntary case petition does not result in an order of relief. The debtor may contest the bankruptcy petition. If the debtor does not contest the petition, the court will enter an order of relief if at least one of the following grounds exists: (1) The debtor is generally not paying debts as they become due or (2) within 120 days before the filing of the petition, a custodian has been appointed for the debtor's property.

CPA

automatic stay–order to prevent creditors from taking action such as filing suits or seeking foreclosure against the debtor.

34-2c **Automatic Stay**

Just the filing of either a voluntary or an involuntary petition operates as an **automatic stay,** which prevents creditors from taking action, such as filing suits or foreclosure actions, against the debtor.[13] The stay freezes all creditors in their filing date positions so that no one creditor gains an advantage over other creditors. This automatic stay ends when the bankruptcy case is closed or dismissed (for example, on a finding of abuse by the debtor who has failed to survive the means-to-pay test) or when the debtor is granted a discharge. An automatic stay means that all activity by creditors with respect to collection must stop, with some exceptions incorporated for child support and other family support issues. All litigation with the debtor is halted, and any judgments in place cannot be executed.[14]

34-2d **If the Creditors Are Wrong: Rights of Debtor in an Involuntary Bankruptcy**

If an involuntary petition is dismissed other than by consent of all petitioning creditors and the debtor, the court may award costs, reasonable attorney fees, or damages to the debtor. The damages are those that were caused by taking possession of the debtor's property. The debtor may also recover damages against any creditor who filed the petition in bad faith.

Figure 34-1 provides a summary of the requirements for declaration of bankruptcy and the standards for relief.

---

[12] 11 U.S.C. §303(b)(1). *Farmers & Merchants State Bank v. Turner,* 518 B.R. 642 (N.D. Fla. 2014).
[13] 11 U.S.C. §362. In re *Taggart,* 522 B.R. 627 (D. Or. 2014). Proceeding with the foreclosure on a home after a stay is entered is a violation of the stay order. In re *Betchan,* 524 B.R. 830 (E.D. Wash. 2015).
[14] In re *Hill,* 523 B.R. 704 (D. Mont. 2014).

FIGURE 34-1	Declaration of Bankruptcy

	Chapter 7	Chapter 11	Chapter 13
Trustee	Yes	No	Yes
Eligible persons: Individuals Partnerships Corporations	Yes (consumer restrictions) Yes Yes	Yes (individual restrictions) Yes Yes	Yes (consumer restrictions) No No
Voluntary	Yes	Yes	Yes
Involuntary	Yes, except for farmers and nonprofits**	Yes, except for farmers and nonprofits	No
Exemptions	S & L's, credit unions, SBA, railroads, municipalities	Same as Chapter 7 plus stockbrokers*	Only individuals allowed
Requirements-Voluntary	Debts; means test applies to consumers	Debts; means test applies to consumers	Income plus <$383,175 unsecured debt; <$1,149,525 secured debt
Requirements-Involuntary	<12 = 1/$15,325 ≥12 = 3/$15,325	<12 = 1/$15,325 ≥12 = 3/$15,325	N/A

*Railroads are eligible
**Chapter 9 — Municipalities; Chapter 12 — Farmers

34-3 Administration of the Bankruptcy Estate

The administration of the bankruptcy estate varies according to the type of bankruptcy declared. This section of the chapter focuses on the process for liquidation or Chapter 7 bankruptcy. Figure 34-2 provides a flowchart view of the Chapter 7 liquidation process.

34-3a The Order of Relief

order of relief–the order from the bankruptcy judge that starts the protection for the debtor; when the order of relief is entered by the court, the debtor's creditors must stop all proceedings and work through the bankruptcy court to recover debts (if possible). Court finding that creditors have met the standards for bankruptcy petitions.

The **order of relief** is granted by the bankruptcy court and is the procedural step required for the case to proceed in bankruptcy court.[15] An order of relief is entered automatically in a voluntary case and in an involuntary case when those filing the petition have established that the debtor is unable to pay his, her, or its debts as they become due. In consumer cases and Chapter 11 cases that involve an individual, the bankruptcy court must apply the means test to determine whether the individual is eligible for declaring bankruptcy or whether there has been an abuse of the bankruptcy court and system.

34-3b List of Creditors

It is the debtor's responsibility to furnish the bankruptcy court with a list of creditors. Although imposing the responsibility for disclosing debts on the debtor may not seem to be effective, the debtor has an incentive for full disclosure. Those debts not disclosed by the debtor will not be discharged in bankruptcy.

[15] 11 U.S.C. §301.

SPORTS & ENTERTAINMENT LAW

From Millions to Nada: Celebrity Bankruptcies

- Michael Vick, who was one of the highest paid NFL players, filed for bankruptcy in 2008, from prison. Mr. Vick could not afford to pay his bills as well as the fines that were imposed when he entered a guilty plea on charges related to a dog-fighting operation. The fines were not discharged, but he was relieved of his other debts related to his personal property.

- MC Hammer, the "Hammer Time" mega star of the early 1990s, declared bankruptcy in 1996 with $9.6 million in assets and $13.7 million in debts. Mr. Hammer's problem was that he had salary costs of $500,000 per month in order to maintain his entourage.

- Kim Basinger, actress, had to declare bankruptcy after settling a contract suit by Main Line Pictures for $3.8 million for backing out of a movie deal with the company.

- Willie Nelson, Country Western singer, declared bankruptcy in 1990, a necessary result of his owing $16.7 million in taxes because the IRS won its case on Nelson's tax shelters, which were fraudulent. Mr. Nelson also said that he had too many hangers-on that he was supporting. Mr. Nelson was not able to get all of his tax debt discharged because not all tax debts are fully dischargeable and there is no discharge allowed for tax debts that resulted from fraud.

- Walt Disney declared bankruptcy in Kansas City before he moved to Hollywood. Mr. Disney ran a small animation studio there and when his only customer went bankrupt, Mr. Disney tried to continue on, living in his office and eating only canned beans. He eventually gave up, declared bankruptcy, and moved to Hollywood, where he founded an empire.

- Sir Elton John is the quintessential profligate spender whose purchases landed him in bankruptcy. By the time he declared bankruptcy in 2002, Sir Elton had credit card charges of $400,000 per month. His total debt per month was $2,000,000.

- Sinbad, the comedian, failed to pay taxes on his earnings from *Jingle All the Way*. California's Department of Revenue filed a $2.5 million lien on his home and he and his wife declared bankruptcy shortly after in 2009.

- Meat Loaf, singer, declared bankruptcy following a lawsuit filed by a former partner who wrote songs with him.

- Dionne Warwick, singer, filed for bankruptcy because of $10 million in back taxes and negligent financial management.

What are the causes of bankruptcy? What advice would you give to celebrities and athletes about management of their income and bills?

34-3c Trustee in Bankruptcy

trustee in bankruptcy— impartial person elected to administer the debtor's estate.

The **trustee in bankruptcy** is elected by the creditors. The court or the U.S. trustee will appoint an interim trustee if the creditors do not elect a trustee.

The trustee automatically becomes the owner of all of the debtor's property in excess of the property to which the debtor is entitled under exemption laws. The trustee holds all of the rights formerly owned by the debtor.

CPA 34-3d The Bankrupt's Estate

All of the debtor's property, with certain exceptions discussed later, is included in the *bankrupt's estate.* Property inherited by the debtor within six months after the filing of the petition also passes to the trustee.

preferences— transfers of property by a debtor to one or more specific creditors to enable these creditors to obtain payment for debts owed.

In many cases, when a debtor knows that insolvency is a problem and bankruptcy is imminent, the debtor attempts to hang onto property or reputation by making transfers of assets to friends, relatives, and creditors. However, trustees have the authority to set aside or void (1) transfers by the debtor that a creditor holding a valid claim under state law could have avoided at the commencement of the bankruptcy case, (2) **preferences,** that is, transfers of property by the debtor to a creditor, the effect of which is to enable

FIGURE 34-2   Anatomy of Bankruptcy Case

Voidable preferences

1. 2 yr. Fraud
2. 1 yr. Insolvent ** and unfair
3. 1 yr. Insider
4. 90 days—presumed insolvent**—not
   ordinary course of business
5. Security for antecedent debt

OK (not voidable)

1. Up to $600 consumer debt
2. Contemporaneous exchange
3. Regular payments
4. Up to $5,850 for non-consumer
   creditors***

*Means test for consumers
**Insolvent = "Bankruptcy" sense (liabilities > assets)
***Amounts are adjusted annually

the creditor to obtain payment of a higher percentage of the creditor's claim than the creditor would have received if the debtor's assets had been liquidated in bankruptcy, and (3) statutory liens that became effective against the debtor at the commencement of the bankruptcy.

34-3e Voidable Preferences

A debtor may not transfer property to prevent creditors from satisfying their legal claims. The trustee may void any such transfer, known as *a fraudulent transfer*, made or obligation incurred by the debtor within one year of bankruptcy when the debtor's actual intent was to hinder, delay, or defraud creditors by doing so.

The trustee may also void certain transfers of property made by a debtor merely because their effect is to make the debtor insolvent or to reduce the debtor's assets to an unreasonably low amount.[16]

insolvency–excess of debts and liabilities over assets, or inability to pay debts as they mature.

balance sheet test–comparison of assets to liabilities made to determine solvency.

preferential transfers–certain transfers of money or security interests in the time frame just prior to bankruptcy that can be set aside if voidable.

insider–full-time corporate employee or a director or their relatives.

The Insolvent Debtor

A debtor is insolvent for purposes of determining voidable transfers when the total fair value of all of the debtor's assets does not exceed the debts owed by the debtor. This test for **insolvency** under voidable transfers is commonly called the **balance sheet test** because it is merely a comparison of assets to liabilities without considering whether the debtor will be able to meet future obligations as they become due. The debtor is presumed to be insolvent in the 90 days prior to declaration of bankruptcy.

Preferential Transfers

A transfer of property by the debtor to a creditor may be set aside as **preferential transfers** and the property recovered by the debtor's trustee in bankruptcy if (1) the transfer was made to pay a debt incurred at some earlier time, (2) the transfer was made when the debtor was insolvent and within 90 days before the filing of the bankruptcy petition, and (3) the transfer resulted in the creditor receiving more than the creditor would have received in a liquidation of the debtor's estate. A debtor is presumed to be insolvent on and during the 90 days immediately preceding the date of the filing of the bankruptcy petition.[17]

Transfers made to **insiders** within the 12 months prior to the filing of the petition may be set aside.[18] **For Example,** if a building contractor transferred title to one of his model homes to the company accountant just six months before declaring bankruptcy, the transfer would be a preferential one that would be set aside. However, a transfer by an insider to a noninsider is not subject to recovery by the trustee. The sale of that same model home to a good faith buyer just three days before bankruptcy would be valid. **For Example,** the trustee in the Bernie Madoff case sought to set aside several transfers made to companies and individuals just prior to the time Mr. Madoff admitted that he had an insolvent, $50 billion Ponzi scheme. The trustee used several of the voidable preferences theories to seek a return of funds.

The trustee may not set aside certain transfers by a debtor as preferences. A transaction for present consideration, such as a cash sale, is not set aside.[19] A payment by a debtor in the ordinary course of business, such as the payment of a utility bill, will not be set aside. Under the prior bankruptcy law, a payment was not a voidable preference if it was made in the ordinary course of business and it was made according to industry terms and practices. Nonconsumer debt payments that have a value of less than $6,225 are not subject to the voidable preference standards. The expectation is that the time and effort spent by bankruptcy trustees and courts will be reduced because of the minimum amount required before a challenge can be made. In nonconsumer debts, transfers of less than $6,225 within the voidable preference period are not considered voidable preferences.

---

[16] 11 U.S.C. §548.
[17] 11 U.S.C. §547(f).
[18] 11 U.S.C. §547(b)(4)(B). In re *First Pay, Inc.*, 773 F.3d 583 (4th Cir. 2014).
[19] Payments made 50.29 days after the invoice date were not made in the ordinary course of business. In re *Quebecor World (USA), Inc.*, 518 B.R. 757 (S.D.N.Y. 2014).

CASE SUMMARY

The Honda Pilot Preference

FACTS: On July 3, 2013, Scott and Nicole Conklin (Debtors) entered into a retail installment contract with Hannigan Auto Sales, LLC, in Emmett, Idaho, to purchase a Honda Pilot. CAC agreed to finance Debtors' purchase in the amount $12,871.20. Debtors took possession of the Honda the same day.

CAC thereafter mailed a "Report of Sale and Application for Certificate of Title" to Gem County. The Application was received by Gem County on August 2, 2013, as is evidenced by a date stamp appearing on the Application. However, while the certificate of title issued for the Honda by the State of Idaho properly listed CAC as the "lienholder," it indicated that CAC's lien was "recorded" on August 6, 2013. August 2, 2013, is 30 days after July 3, 2013, the day Debtors purchased and took possession of the Honda.

Debtors filed their Chapter 7 case on September 4, 2013. On October 21, 2013, the Trustee commenced this adversary proceeding against CAC contending that because CAC's security interest in the Honda was not perfected until August 6, as evidenced by the recording date on the title, that security interest was a voidable preference.

The discrepancy between the date the Application was received by Gem County, and the lien recording date listed in the title record for the Honda occurred when the information was transmitted by Gem County to the Department to create the certificate of title. Legal Counsel for the Conklins made a request to have the date changed and, thereafter, the date in the electronic records for the Honda title certificate was changed to reflect a recording date of August 2, instead of August 6, 2013. A certified copy of a printout of the electronic record of title for the Honda, which shows August 2, 2013, as the "recorded" date for CAC's lien, was submitted in evidence.

Both parties moved for summary judgment.

DECISION: Currently under Idaho Code, there is a twenty (20) day time frame from the date of sale in which a lender can perfect a security interest. Federal bankruptcy code was amended to allow a thirty (30) day time frame to perfect a lien.

Applying the revised Idaho statute, the Court concluded Debtors and CAC had shown that the lien on the Honda was perfected under Idaho law on August 2, 2013, the 30th day after Debtors received possession of the Honda. Therefore, under §547(c)(3), Debtors' transfer of the security interest to CAC is protected from avoidance. Summary judgment for the Debtors. [**In re Conklin, 511 B.R. 688 (D. Idaho 2014)**]

Self-Settled Trust

Under the Reform Act, the trustee has the ability to set aside the transfer of property into a "self-settled" (a self-created personal trust) any time within the past 10 years if the trustee can establish that the trust was created with actual intent to hinder, delay, or defraud existing or future creditors.[20] This section was added to address the problem of the many assets of individuals being in personal trusts for which those individuals serve as trustees.

34-3f Proof of Claim

claim—creditor's right to payment.

proof of claim—written statement, signed by the creditor or an authorized representative, setting forth any claim made against the debtor and the basis for it.

Bankruptcy law regulates the manner in which creditors present their claims and the way in which the debtor's assets are distributed in payment of these claims.

After the debtor has filed a list of creditors, the court then sends a notice of the bankruptcy proceedings to listed creditors. The creditors who wish to participate in the distribution of the proceeds of the liquidation of the debtor's estate must file a proof of claim. A **claim** is a right to payment, whether liquidated (certain and not disputed), unliquidated, contingent, unmatured, disputed, legal, or equitable. A **proof of claim** is a written statement, signed by the creditor or an authorized representative, setting forth any claim

[20] 11 U.S.C. §548(e).

made against the debtor and the basis for it. It must ordinarily be filed within 90 days after the first meeting of creditors.[21] A creditor must file within that time even though the trustee in bankruptcy in fact knows of the existence of the creditor's claim.

CPA   34-3g **Priority of Claims**

Creditors who hold security for payment, such as a lien or a mortgage on the debtor's property, are less affected by the debtor's bankruptcy. Secured creditors may enforce their security interest to obtain payment of their claims up to the value of their security, the collateral in which they hold an interest. **For Example,** suppose that First Bank holds a mortgage on a company's office building. The mortgage amount is $750,000. The building is sold for $700,000. First Bank is entitled to the $700,000 from the sale. For the remaining portion of the debt, First Bank drops down in priority to wait with the other unsecured creditors for its remaining $50,000. Unsecured creditors with unsecured debts have a statutory order of priority following the secured creditors' rights in their collateral as outlined in the list that appears next.[22] Once the bottom of the priority list is reached, any remaining unsecured creditors share on *a pro rata* basis any remaining assets of the debtor. Any balance remaining after all creditors have been paid goes to the debtor. However, in 98 to 99 percent of all bankruptcies, no unsecured creditors receive any payments, so it is highly unlikely that the debtor would ever receive anything from the bankruptcy litigation of the debtor's property and funds.

The list that follows is the statutory one for priorities of the unsecured creditors following the payment to any secured creditors from the debtors' pledged property:

1. Allowed claims for debts to a spouse, former spouse, or child of the debtor and for alimony to, maintenance for, or support of such spouse or child (that were obligations at the time of the filing of the bankruptcy petition).[23]

2. Costs and expenses of administration of the bankruptcy case, including fees to trustees, attorneys, and accountants, and the reasonable expenses of creditors in recovering property transferred or concealed by the debtor.

3. Claims arising in the ordinary course of a debtor's business or financial affairs after the commencement of the case but before the order of relief (involuntary).

4. Claims for wages, salaries, or commissions, including vacation, severance, or sick leave pay earned within 180 days before the filing of the petition or the date of cessation of the debtor's business, whichever occurred first, limited, however, to $12,475 for each person.

5. Claims arising for contributions to employee benefit plans, based on services rendered within 180 days before the filing of the petition or when the debtor ceased doing business, whichever occurred first; the maximum amount is $12,475. Payments of key-employee retention plans are not permitted unless the plans are "essential" to keeping the key employee at the company that is in bankruptcy. Proving that they are essential requires the key employee actually to have a "bona fide" offer of employment from another company. In addition, there are limits on how much can be paid under key-employee retention plans.

6. Farm producers (up to $6,150) and fishers against debtors who operate grain storage facilities or fish storage or processing facilities, up to $6,150 per claim.

---

[21] 11 U.S.C. §302(c).
[22] 11 U.S.C. §507(1)–(6). Secured creditors' priority is determined by the priority rules related to Article 9, liens, and mortgages. In re *Restivo Auto Body, Inc.,* 772 F.3d 168 (4th Cir. 2014).
[23] In re *Coon,* 522 B.R. 357 (M.D. Ala. 2014).

7. Claims by consumer creditors, not to exceed $2,775 for each claimant, arising from the purchase of consumer goods or services when such property or services were not delivered or provided.

8. Certain taxes and penalties due government, such as income and property taxes (there are time limits, for example, three years is the general time limit, with exceptions for fraud).

9. All other unsecured creditors.

10. Tort claims for death or personal injury resulting from operation of a vehicle or vessel while intoxicated from alcohol, drug, and other substances.

11. Remainder (if any) to debtor.

Each claim must be paid in full before any lower claim is paid anything. If a class of claims cannot be paid in full, the claims in that case are paid on *a pro rata* basis. **For Example,** suppose that following the payment of all secured creditors, $10,000 is left to be distributed. The accountants who performed work on the bankruptcy are owed $15,000, and the lawyers who worked on it are owed $10,000. Because there is not enough to pay two parties in the same priority ranking, the $10,000 is split proportionately. The accountants will receive 15/25, or 3/5, of the $10,000, or $6,000, and the lawyers will receive 10/25, or 2/5, of the $10,000, or $4,000.

34-4   Debtor's Duties and Exemptions

Bankruptcy law imposes certain duties on the debtor and provides for specific exemptions of some of the debtor's estate from the claims of creditors.

34-4a   Debtor's Duties

A debtor must file with the court a list of creditors, a schedule of assets and liabilities, and a statement of her financial affairs. The debtor must also appear for examination under oath at the first meeting of creditors.

CPA   34-4b   Debtor's Exemptions

A debtor is permitted to claim certain property of the estate in the trustee's possession and keep it free from claims of creditors. Exemptions are provided under federal law, but state laws also provide for exemptions. Examples of exempt property from the federal code include wedding rings, property used to earn a living, one VCR, and one car. New York exemptions include "all stoves in the home, one sewing machine, the family Bible, a pew in a public house of worship, enough food for sixty days, a wedding ring, and a watch not exceeding thirty-five dollars in value."[24] California exempts tools of the trade and the family cemetery plot.[25]

The principal exemptions provided by the Bankruptcy Code are the debtor's interest in real or personal property used as a residence.[26] The homestead exemption is now greatly limited and, in effect, preempts state law on this debtor exemption. Debtors are required to have lived in the home for two years prior to bankruptcy, and the amount

[24] N.Y. C.P.L.R. §5205 (2014).
[25] Cal. Civ. Proc. Code §704.010-704.210 (2014).
[26] A married couple gets a single homestead exemption.

of the homestead exemption would be limited to $155,675.[27] To be able to use a higher state homestead exemption, the debtor must have lived in the home for 1,215 days (40 months).[28] Labeled as the most flagrant abuse of the existing bankruptcy system, debtors have used the homestead exemption to shift their assets into expensive homes to shield everything from bankruptcy. Known as the "mansion loophole," the changes in the Reform Act related to the homestead exemption were among the most debated and the most dramatic.[29] **For Example,** prior to the reforms actor Burt Reynolds declared bankruptcy in Florida and was relieved of millions in debt, but he was able to keep his $2.5 million Valhalla estate there. Corporate raider Paul Bilzerian, who was convicted of securities fraud, also declared bankruptcy in Florida but kept his mansion, the largest home in Hillsborough County, Florida. Former WorldCom CFO Scott Sullivan (who entered a guilty plea to fraud and other charges and is serving a five-year sentence) built a multimillion-dollar home in Florida to gain homestead protections. Wendy Gramm, who sat on Enron's board, purchased 200 acres of land in Texas and constructed a large home with her husband, former senator Phil Gramm, to take advantage of homestead exemptions then available in Texas. However, the Reform Act closed this corporate executive loophole by requiring that the $155,675 exemption apply to debtors who are convicted of securities fraud or bankruptcy fraud.[30]

Other exemptions include payments under a life insurance contract, alimony and child support payments, and awards from personal injury litigation.[31] Under the Reform Act, college savings accounts and IRAs are exempt property under the federal exemptions and can be used even by those debtors who are using state exemptions. The IRA exemption is limited to $1,245,475.[32]

CASE SUMMARY

Planning for Bankruptcy: Can You Stash Cash Away in College and Retirement Accounts?

FACTS: Leonard Bronk, a retiree living in Stevens Point, Wisconsin, incurred significant debts providing for his wife's medical care before her death in 2007, and he himself suffered a stroke in early 2009. With his medical debts mounting—they exceeded $345,000 by the time he filed for bankruptcy—Bronk sought the advice of an attorney about pre-bankruptcy exemption planning. His assets included his home, which he owned free and clear, and a certificate of deposit in the amount of $42,000. On the advice of counsel, Bronk sought to protect these nonexempt assets by converting them to exempt assets.

In May 2009, a few months before filing his Chapter 7 petition, Bronk borrowed $95,000 from Citizens Bank and mortgaged his previously unencumbered home. He used these funds to establish five college savings accounts for the benefit of his grandchildren under section 529 of the Internal Revenue Code.

Account owners control the funds in these accounts (known as "Edvest" accounts) and may designate and change account beneficiaries. Beneficiaries do not control account assets.

In addition to creating the college savings accounts using the equity in his home, Bronk converted the $42,000 certificate of deposit into an annuity with CM Life Insurance Company. The annuity contract was issued on May 4, 2009, and does not begin making payments until January 3, 2035, but it also includes a death benefit.

---

[27] The time requirement is at 11 U.S.C. §522(b)(3)(A), and the amount limitation is at 11 U.S.C. §522(o)(1). This amount refers to those who elect state exemptions. In the absence of state exemptions, the federal maximum is $22,975.
[28] 11 U.S.C. §522(p)(2)(B).
[29] 11 U.S.C. §522(p).
[30] 11 U.S.C. §522(q).
[31] 11 U.S.C. §522(d) (including automatic adjustments).
[32] 11 U.S.C. §522(n). There are time requirements on college savings (529) accounts in order to obtain the exemption.

Planning for Bankruptcy: Can You Stash Cash Away in College and Retirement Accounts? continued

On August 5, 2009, Bronk filed for bankruptcy under Chapter 7. The trustee objected to the college-fund and annuity transactions, arguing that Bronk had transferred his property with the intent to hinder, delay, or defraud his creditors and thus should be denied a discharge.

The judge accepted Bronk's argument about the annuity, holding that it was fully exempt as a retirement benefit as were the Edvest accounts.

Both sides appealed to the district court. The district judge agreed that Bronk was entitled to a discharge because the trustee had not proven that the asset transfers were made with intent to hinder, delay, or defraud creditors. Second, the district judge agreed with the bankruptcy judge's interpretation and upheld the decision to deny the claimed exemption for Bronk's Edvest accounts (which was reversed on remand). Finally, the judge narrowed the bankruptcy court's interpretation of "retirement benefit" and remanded the case for additional fact-finding on whether the annuity qualified under the statute.

Bronk appealed, challenging the disallowance of the exemption for his college savings accounts. The trustee filed a cross-appeal challenging the court's ruling on the annuity.

DECISION: Wisconsin's exemption statute allows debtors to exempt "[a]n interest in a college savings account" from execution by creditors. The term "interest" is not specifically defined in the statute or by regulation, but an "interest" is generally defined as "[a] legal share in something; all or part of a legal or equitable claim to or a right in property." Bronk clearly has a legal interest in each of the Edvest college savings accounts. He owned the accounts and could at any time select and change beneficiaries, transfer funds between accounts, receive distributions from the accounts, and (subject to certain limitations) remove funds from the accounts.

To qualify for full exemption, the retirement plan or contract must meet one of two additional requirements: (1) it must be employer sponsored; or (2) it must comply with the Internal Revenue Code.

The statute requires that the retirement product "provid[e] benefits" by reason of age, illness, death, etc., not that it be "purchased" by reason of age. Moreover, there is no special test for annuities.

Bronk's annuity begins paying on a fixed date—January 3, 2035—and thus does not pay benefits because of age, length of service, or the onset of an illness or disability. But the annuity also contains a death benefit. That feature brings it under the umbrella of an exemption.

To qualify for full exemption as a "retirement benefit," a retirement product must be either employer sponsored or "compl[y] with the provisions of the internal revenue code." The trustee raised this issue for the first time in the district court, and even then simply asserted—without developing an argument—that Bronk's annuity was not tax qualified. The argument was held to be waived.

The court held that the exemption statute applied to the college savings accounts. However, the court held that there were still issues about the retirement plan that required the court to make some factual findings. Because the plan was not employer-sponsored, a finding that it met the Internal Revenue Code standards was still needed. [**In re Bronk**, **775 F.3d 871 (7th Cir. 2015)**]

34-4c Debtor's Protection against Discrimination

Federal, state, and local law may not discriminate against anyone on the basis of a discharge in bankruptcy. For example, a state cannot refuse to issue a new license to an individual if the license fees on a previous one have been discharged as a debt in the individual's declaration of bankruptcy.

34-5 Discharge in Bankruptcy

The main objectives of a bankruptcy proceeding are to collect and distribute the debtor's assets and then issue a **discharge in bankruptcy** of the debtor from obligations. The decree terminating the bankruptcy proceeding is generally a discharge that releases the debtor from most debts. Under the BAPCPA, a discharge is available only once every eight years.

34-5a Denial of Discharge

The court will refuse to grant a discharge if the debtor has (1) within one year of the filing of the petition fraudulently transferred or concealed property with intent to hinder, delay,

discharge in bankruptcy– order of the bankruptcy court relieving the debtor from obligation to pay the unpaid balance of most claims.

ETHICS & THE LAW

The Skies Are Not So Friendly to Employee Pensions

As part of its Chapter 11 bankruptcy, United Airlines was relieved of its pension liabilities. Employees and unions wonder how a company can be permitted to renege on those benefits when so many protections were built into the law under ERISA. Congressional hearings revealed that there were loopholes in the accounting processes for pension fund reporting that permitted United, and many others, to report pension numbers that made the pension funds look healthy when they really were not. The loopholes were Enronesque in nature. Companies could spin the pension obligations off the books so that the existing levels of obligations of the plan looked small and the assets very rich.

Because of United's pension bailout, Congress changed the accounting for pension plans to avoid the problem of the rosy picture when the funds really need further funding. One interesting approach to protecting pension plans is to require companies to fund the pension plans according to the numbers they have reported to the SEC in their financials. If United had funded its plans when its SEC numbers indicated it needed to (e.g., in 1998), the plan would have been sufficiently funded. Under ERISA guidelines, it was not required to kick in funds until 2002 when it was grossly underfunded.

Were companies acting ethically on their pension accounting? Were they acting legally?*

*Marry Williams Walsh, "Pension Law Loopholes Helped United Hide Its Troubles," *New York Times,* June 7, 2005, C1.

---

or defraud creditors, (2) failed to keep proper financial records, (3) made a false oath or account,[33] (4) failed to explain satisfactorily any loss of assets, (5) refused to obey any lawful order of the court or refused to testify after having been granted immunity, (6) obtained a discharge within the last eight years,[34] (7) filed a written waiver of discharge that is approved by the court,[35] or (8) in the case of a consumer debtor, has failed to complete a personal financial management instructional course.[36] A discharge releases the debtor from the unpaid balance of most debts except for taxes, customs duties, child support obligations, and tax penalties.[37] Student loan obligations are not discharged in bankruptcy unless the loan first became due more than seven years before bankruptcy or unless not allowing a discharge would impose undue hardship on the debtor.

CASE SUMMARY

Your Living Expenses Are Fairly Minimal in Maximum Security

FACTS: Bryan Anthony Looper (Debtor) had over $300,000 in student loans that were used to finance his education at Mercer University where he obtained an A.B., an M.B.A, and another unspecified graduate degree as well as a large number of courses toward his J.D. degree. He did not make payments on these student loans.

In 1996, he was elected assessor for Putnam County, Tennessee, a position he held for two years

---

[33] The debtor must actually make a false statement. Obtaining a credit card under false pretenses is fraud. In re *Levasseur*, 737 F.3d 814 (1st Cir. 2013). However, just the use of a credit card for unnecessary purchases is not fraud, In re *Quinn*, 492 B.R. 341 (N.D. Ga. 2013).

[34] 11 U.S.C. §727(a)(8).

[35] 11 U.S.C. §523.

[36] 11 U.S.C. §727(a)(11). The financial management course requirement applies to both Chapter 7 and Chapter 13 consumer bankruptcies.

[37] Child support obligations enjoy additional protections and priorities in bankruptcy. 11 U.S.C §507(a).

Your Living Expenses Are Fairly Minimal in Maximum Security continued

and four months. He was then convicted of the first-degree murder of state senator Tommy Burks. He exhausted all of his appeals and is currently serving a life sentence without the possibility of parole. Looper has one dependent, a son born in August 1998. The circuit court for Putnam County, Tennessee, ordered Looper to pay child support of $161.00 per month plus $7,254.20 in medical expenses. Looper did not make any of the court-ordered child support payments and was in arrears by more than $23,515.00.

Looper asked to have his student loans discharged on the basis of his hardship.

DECISION: The court refused to discharge the student loans. Looper had all of his living expenses covered by the Tennessee Department of Corrections. Looper had made no effort to make any payments on any of his student loans and had also not made attempts to try and work with his lenders or apply to programs set up to help with student loans. The court also noted that Looper's circumstances were the result of his choices and conduct, not the result of unforeseen and uncontrollable events. He had three degrees and the capability of earning a living but, through poor choices, produced his own difficult circumstances. [**In re** *Looper*, **2007 WL 1231700 (B. E.D. Tenn. 2007)**]

In addition, the following debts are not discharged by bankruptcy: (1) loans obtained by use of a false financial statement made with intent to deceive and on which the creditor reasonably relied, (2) debts not scheduled or listed with the court in time for allowance, (3) debts arising from fraud while the debtor was acting in a fiduciary capacity or by reason of embezzlement or larceny, (4) alimony and child support, (5) a judgment for willful and malicious injury, (6) a consumer debt to a single creditor totaling more than $650 for luxury goods or services (within 90 days of the order of relief) and cash advances exceeding $925 based on consumer open-end credit, such as a credit card (within 70 days of the order of relief),[38] (7) damages arising from drunk driving or the

---

FIGURE 34-3   **Nondischargeable Debts in Bankruptcy**

1. Taxes within three years of filing bankruptcy petition
2. Liability for obtaining money or property by false pretenses
3. Willful and malicious injuries
4. Debts incurred by driving DWI*
5. Alimony, maintenance, or child support
6. Unscheduled debts (unless actual notice)
7. Debts resulting from fraud as a fiduciary (embezzlement)
8. Government fines or penalties imposed within three years prior
9. Educational loans due within seven prior years (unless hardship)
10. Prior bankruptcy debts in which debtor waived discharge
11. Presumption on luxury goods: $650 goods; $925 cash
12. Reaffirmation agreements
    - Writing
    - Filed with court
    - Not rescinded prior to discharge

*Includes vessels and aircraft

---

[38] 11 U.S.C. §523(a)(2)(c)(i). (Amounts are adjusted each year.)

operation of vessels and aircrafts by people who are inebriated,[39] (8) loans used to pay taxes (including credit cards),[40] (9) taxes not paid as a result of a fraudulent return, although other unpaid taxes beyond the past three years can be discharged,[41] (10) pre-bankruptcy fees and assessments owed to homeowners associations, and (11) debts owed to tax-qualified retirement plans. **For Example,** one of the financial concerns facing athlete Lance Armstrong is that the litigation against him may include findings of malice with the result being that those judgments cannot be discharged in bankruptcy, thus making all those judgments a lifetime obligation. Figure 34-3 has a listing of non-dischargeable debts.

34-6 **Reorganization Plans under Chapter 11**

In addition to liquidation under Chapter 7, the Bankruptcy Code permits debtors to restructure the organization and finances of their businesses so that they may continue to operate. In these rehabilitation plans, the debtor keeps all of the assets (exempt and nonexempt), continues to operate the business, and makes a settlement that is acceptable to the majority of the creditors. This settlement is binding on the minority creditors.

Individuals, partnerships, and corporations in business may all be reorganized under the Bankruptcy Code. The first step is to file a plan for the debtor's reorganization. This plan may be filed by the debtor, any party in interest, or a committee of creditors. If the debtor wishes to move from a Chapter 11 proceeding (in the case of an individual debtor), the debtor must survive the means test that is now a requirement for determining eligibility for bankruptcy.

34-6a **Contents of the Plan**

The plan divides ownership interests and debts into those that will be affected by the adoption of the plan and those that will not be. It then specifies what will be done to those interests and claims that are affected. **For Example,** when mortgage payments are too high for the income of a corporation, a possible plan would be to reduce the mortgage payments and give the mortgage holder preferred stock to compensate for the loss sustained.

All creditors, shareholders, and other interest holders within a particular class must be treated the same way. **For Example,** the holders of first mortgage bonds must all be treated similarly. The treatment of the bondholders in the Chrysler and GM bankruptcies was a point of contention and negotiation in those reorganizations.

A plan can also provide for the assumption, rejection, or assignment of executory contracts. The trustee or debtor can, under certain circumstances, suspend performance of a contract not yet fully performed. **For Example,** collective bargaining agreements may be rejected with the approval of the bankruptcy court.[42]

34-6b **Confirmation of the Plan**

After the plan is prepared, the court must approve or confirm it. A plan will be confirmed if it has been submitted in good faith and if its provisions are reasonable.[43] After the plan is confirmed, the owners and creditors of the enterprise have only the rights that are specified in the plan. They cannot go back to their original contract positions.

---

[39] 11 U.S.C. §523(a)(9).
[40] 11 U.S.C. §523(a)(14A), (14B).
[41] 11 U.S.C. §§1129(a)(9)(c), (D), 1129(b)(2)(B), 1141(d)(6)(B).
[42] 11 U.S.C. §1113.
[43] 11 U.S.C. §1129.

CPA   ## 34-7 Payment Plans under Chapter 13

The Bankruptcy Code also provides for the adoption of extended-time payment plans for individual debtors who have regular income. These debtors must owe unsecured debts of less than $383,175 and secured debts of less than $1,149,525.

An individual debtor who has a regular income may submit a plan for the installment payment of outstanding debts. If the court approves it, the debtor may then pay the debts in the installments specified by the plan even if the creditors had not originally agreed to such installment payments.

34-7a Contents of the Plan

The individual debtor plan is, in effect, a budget of the debtor's future income with respect to outstanding debts. The plan must provide for the eventual payment in full of all claims entitled to priority under the Bankruptcy Code. All creditors holding the same kind or class of claim must be treated the same way.

34-7b Confirmation of the Plan

The plan has no effect until the court approves or confirms it. A plan will be confirmed if it was submitted in good faith and is in the best interests of the creditors.[44] When the plan is confirmed, debts are payable in the manner specified in the plan.

34-7c Discharge of the Debtor

After all of the payments called for by the plan have been made, the debtor is given a discharge. The discharge releases the debtor from liability for all debts except those that would not be discharged by an ordinary bankruptcy discharge.[45] Under the bankruptcy reforms, the court cannot grant a discharge until the debtor has completed an instructional course concerning personal financial management.[46] If the debtor does not perform under the plan, the creditors can move to transfer the debtor's case to a Chapter 7 proceeding, but they would still face the means test in qualifying for this move to Chapter 7.

Make the Connection
- -

Summary

Jurisdiction over bankruptcy cases is in U.S. district courts, which may refer all cases and related proceedings to adjunct bankruptcy courts.

Three bankruptcy proceedings are available: liquidation (Chapter 7), reorganization (Chapter 11), and extended-time payment (Chapter 13). A liquidation proceeding under Chapter 7 may be either voluntary or involuntary.

A *voluntary case* is commenced by the debtor's filing a petition with the bankruptcy court. A voluntary petition is subject to the means test to determine if the debtor meets the standard for declaring bankruptcy. An involuntary case is commenced by the creditors' filing a petition with the bankruptcy court. If there are 12 or more creditors, at least 3 whose unsecured claims total $15,325 or more

[44] 11 U.S.C. §1325.
[45] 11 U.S.C. §1328.
[46] 11 U.S.C. §1328(g)(1).

must sign the involuntary petition. If there are fewer than 12 creditors, any creditor whose unsecured claim is at least $15,325 may sign the petition. If the debtor contests the bankruptcy petition, it must be shown that the debtor is not paying debts as they become due.

Eligibility for Chapters 7 and 11 bankruptcy excludes railroads, municipalities, and Small Business Administration companies. Individual debtors are restricted on Chapters 7 and 11 filings by their ability to repay. If found to have the means to pay, they go into a Chapter 13 proceeding. Chapter 13 eligibility is limited to consumers with $383,175 in unsecured debt and $1,149,525 in secured debt.

An automatic stay prevents creditors from taking legal action against the debtor after a bankruptcy petition is filed. The trustee in bankruptcy is elected by the creditors and is the successor to, and acquires the rights of, the debtor. In certain cases, the trustee can avoid transfers of property to prevent creditors from satisfying their claims. Preferential transfers may be set aside. A transfer for a present consideration, such as a cash sale, is not a preference.

Bankruptcy law regulates the way creditors present their claims and how the assets of the debtor are to be distributed in payment of the claims. Some assets of the debtor are exempt from the bankruptcy estate, such as a portion of the value of the debtor's home.

Secured claims are not affected by the debtor's bankruptcy. Unsecured claims are paid in the following order of priority:

1. Support or maintenance for a spouse, former spouse, or child.

2. Costs and expenses of administration of the bankruptcy case.

3. Claims arising in the ordinary course of a debtor's business or financial affairs after the commencement of the case but before the order of relief (involuntary).

4. Claims for wages, salaries, or commissions, including vacation, severance, or sick leave pay earned within 180 days before the filing of the petition or the date of cessation of the debtor's business, limited to $12,475 for each person.

5. Claims arising for contributions (up to $6,225) to employee benefit plans based on services rendered within 180 days before the filing of the petition or when the debtor ceased doing business.

6. Farm producers (up to $6,150) and fishers against debtors who operate grain storage facilities or fish produce storage or processing facilities, up to $6,150 per claim.

7. Claims by consumer creditors, not to exceed $2,775 for each claimant.

8. Certain taxes and penalties due government units, such as income and property taxes.

9. All other unsecured creditors.

10. Remainder (if any) to debtor.

The decree terminating bankruptcy proceedings is generally a discharge that releases the debtor from most debts. Certain debts, such as income taxes, student loans, loans obtained by use of a false financial statement, alimony, and debts not listed by the debtor, are not discharged.

Under Chapter 11 bankruptcy, individuals, partnerships, and corporations in business may be reorganized so that the business can continue to operate. A plan for reorganization must be approved by the court. Under a Chapter 13 bankruptcy proceeding, individual debtors with a regular income may adopt extended-time payment plans for the payment of debts. A plan for extended-time payment must also be confirmed by the court. Federal, state, and local law may not discriminate against anyone on the basis of a discharge in bankruptcy.

Learning Outcomes

After studying this chapter, you should be able to clearly explain:

34-1   Bankruptcy Law

34-2   How Bankruptcy Is Declared

LO.1   List the requirements for the commencement of a voluntary bankruptcy case and an involuntary bankruptcy case

See the Sports & Entertainment Law discussion of celebrity bankruptcies, page 679.

See the discussion of Chapters 7, 11, and 13 and Figure 34-1, pages 672–673, 678.

See the In re *Gomery* case for a discussion of relationships between Chapter 7 and Chapter 13, page 675.

34-3   Administration of the Bankruptcy Estate

LO.2   Explain the procedure for the administration of a debtor's estate

See the list of priorities in the section titled "Priority of Claims," pages 683–684.

See In re *Conklin* on priority positions of the creditor, page 682.

34-4   Debtor's Duties and Exemptions

LO.3   List a debtor's duties and exemptions

See the discussion of the homestead exemptions, pages 684–685.

See the In re *Bronk* case for a discussion of structuring exemptions prior to bankruptcy, pages 685–686.

34-5   Discharge in Bankruptcy

LO.4   Explain the significance of a discharge in bankruptcy

See In re *Looper* for a discussion of hardship, pages 687–688.

34-6   Reorganization Plans under Chapter 11

See Ethics & the Law, "The Skies Are Not So Friendly to Employee Pensions," page 687.

34-7   Payment Plans under Chapter 13

LO.5   Explain when a business reorganization plan or an extended-time payment plan might be used

See the Ethics & the Law discussion of United Airlines, page 687.

Key Terms

automatic stay	claim	order of relief
balance sheet test	discharge in bankruptcy	preferences
bankruptcy courts	insiders	preferential transfers
bona fide	insolvency	proof of claim
Chapter 7 bankruptcy	involuntary bankruptcy	trustee in bankruptcy
Chapter 11 bankruptcy	liquidated	voluntary bankruptcy
Chapter 13 bankruptcy	means test	

Questions and Case Problems

1. Hall-Mark regularly supplied electronic parts to Peter Lee. On September 11, 1992, Lee gave Hall-Mark a $100,000 check for parts it had received. Hall-Mark continued to ship parts to Lee. On September 23, 1992, Lee's check was dishonored by the bank. On September 25, 1992, Lee delivered to Hall-Mark a cashier's check for $100,000. Hall-Mark shipped nothing more to Lee after receipt of the cashier's check. On December 24, 1992, Lee filed a voluntary petition for bankruptcy. The trustee filed a complaint to have the $100,000 payment to Hall-Mark set aside as a voidable preference. Hall-Mark said it was entitled to the payment because it gave value to Lee. The trustee said that the payment was not actually made until the cashier's check was delivered on September 25, 1992, and that Hall-Mark gave no further value to Lee after that check was paid. Who was correct? [In re *Lee*, 108 F.3d 239 (9th Cir.)]

2. Orso, who had declared bankruptcy, received a structured tort settlement in a personal injury claim he had pending. The settlement would pay him an annuity each year for 30 years because the claim was the result of an auto accident that left him permanently and severely brain damaged with an IQ of about 70. His ex-wife had a pending claim for $48,000 in arrearages on Orso's $1,000 per month child support payments. His ex-wife wanted the annuity included in the bankruptcy estate. Would this property have been included in Orso's bankruptcy estate? [In re *Orso*, 214 F.3d 637 (5th Cir.)]

3. Harold McClellan sold ice-making machinery to Bobbie Cantrell's brother for $200,000 to be paid in installment payments. McClellan took a security interest in the ice machine but did not perfect it by filing a financing statement. The brother defaulted when he owed $100,000, and McClellan brought suit. With the suit pending, the brother "sold" the ice machine to Bobbie Cantrell for $10. Bobbie then sold the machine to someone for $160,000 and refused to explain what happened to that money. McClellan added Bobbie as a defendant in his suit against her brother. Bobbie then declared bankruptcy. McClellan sought to have the various transfers set aside. The trial court refused to do so, and McClellan appealed. Should the transfers be set aside? Why or why not? [*McClellan v. Cantrell*, 217 F.3d 890 (7th Cir.)]

4. Okamoto owed money to Hornblower & Weeks-Hemphill, Noyes (a law firm and hereafter Hornblower). Hornblower filed an involuntary bankruptcy petition against Okamoto, who moved to dismiss the petition on the ground that he had more than 12 creditors and the petition could not be filed by only 1 creditor. Hornblower replied that the other creditors' claims were too small to count and,

therefore, the petition could be filed by one creditor. Decide. [In re *Okamoto*, 491 F.2d 496 (9th Cir.)]

5. Jane Leeves declared voluntary Chapter 7 bankruptcy. The trustee included the following property in her bankruptcy estate:

- Jane's wedding ring
- Jane's computer for her consulting business that she operated from her home
- Jane's car payment from a client in the amount of $5,000 that was received 91 days after Jane filed bankruptcy

After collecting all of Jane's assets, the bankruptcy trustee was trying to decide how to distribute the assets. Jane had the following creditors:

- Mortgage company—owed $187,000 (the trustee sold Jane's house for $190,000)
- Expenses of the bankruptcy—$3,000
- Federal income taxes—$11,000
- Utility bills—$1,000
- Office supply store open account—$1,000

The trustee had $11,500 in cash, including the $3,000 additional cash left from the sale of the house after the mortgage company was paid. How should the trustee distribute this money? What if the amount were $14,500; how should that be distributed?

6. Kentile sold goods over an extended period of time to Winham. The credit relationship began without Winham's being required to furnish a financial statement. After a time, payments were not made regularly, and Kentile requested a financial statement. Winham submitted a statement for the year just ended. Kentile requested a second statement. The second statement was false. Kentile objected to Winham's discharge in bankruptcy because of the false financial statement. Should the discharge be granted? Why or why not?

7. D. Erik Von Kiel obtained loans from the U.S. Department of Health & Human Services so that he could complete his education as an osteopathic physician. He works at the International Academy of Life (IAL) in Orem, Utah, for no salary but receives gifts from IAL that total $150,000 per year, or about $12,787 per month. He pays no taxes on these "gifts" and has received them since 2005. Dr. Von Kiel pays all but $1,000 to his ex-wife and nine children for their support. He has given up his practice, taken a vow of poverty, and works at IAL to concentrate on alternative medicine. He has signed

over full authority for the management of his financial affairs to two individuals, who apparently failed to manage wisely. As a result, Dr. Von Kiel filed for bankruptcy in order to be discharged from his HHS loans. HHS says that Dr. Von Kiel should not be discharged because of bad faith. Who is correct and why? [In re *Von Kiel*, 461 B.R. 323 (E.D. Pa.)]

8. Sonia, a retailer, has the following assets: a factory worth $1 million; accounts receivable amounting to $750,000, which fall due in four to six months; and $20,000 cash in the bank. Sonia's sole liability is a $200,000 note falling due today, which she is unable to pay. Can Sonia be forced into involuntary bankruptcy under the Bankruptcy Code? [In re *35th & Morgan Development Corp.*, 510 B.R. 832 (N.D. Ill.)]

9. Samson Industries ceased doing business and is in bankruptcy proceedings. Among the creditors are five employees seeking unpaid wages. Three of the employees are owed $3,500 each, and two are owed $1,500 each. These amounts became due within 90 days preceding the filing of the petition. Where, in the priority of claims, will the employees' wage claims fall?

10. Carol Cott, doing business as Carol Cott Fashions, is worried about an involuntary bankruptcy proceeding being filed by her creditors. Her net worth, using a balance sheet approach, is $8,000 ($108,000 in assets minus $100,000 in liabilities). However, her cash flow is negative, and she has been hard pressed to meet current obligations as they mature. She is in fact some $17,000 in arrears in payments to her creditors on bills submitted during the past two months. Will the fact that Cott is solvent in the balance sheet sense result in the court's dismissing the creditors' petition if Cott objects to the petition? Explain. [*Forever Green Athletic Fields, Inc. v. Dawson*, 514 B.R. 768 (E.D. Pa.)]

11. On July 1, Roger Walsh, a sole proprietor operating a grocery, was involuntarily petitioned into bankruptcy by his creditors. At that time, and for at least 90 days prior to that time, Walsh was unable to pay current obligations. On June 16, Walsh paid the May electric bill for his business. The trustee in bankruptcy claimed that this payment was a voidable preference. Was the trustee correct? Explain.

12. Steven and Teresa Hornsby are married and have three young children. On May 25, 1993, the Hornsbys filed a voluntary Chapter 7 petition. They had by that date accumulated more than $30,000 in debt, stemming almost entirely from student loans. They wanted a discharge of their student loans on grounds of undue hardship. The Hornsbys attended

a succession of small Tennessee state colleges. Both studied business and computers, but neither graduated. Although they received several deferments and forbearances on the loans, they ultimately defaulted before making any payments. Interest had accumulated on the loans to the extent that Steven was indebted to the Tennessee Student Assistance Corporation (TSAC) for $15,058.52, and Teresa was indebted to TSAC for $18,329.15.

Steven was working for AT&T in Dallas, Texas; he made $6.53 per hour, occasionally working limited overtime hours. Teresa was employed by KinderCare Learning Center. Although she had begun work in Tennessee, she had transferred to become the director of a child care facility in Dallas. Teresa was earning $17,500 per year with medical benefits at the time of the hearing. In monthly net income, Steven earned approximately $1,083.33, and Teresa earned $1,473.33, amounting to $2,556.66 of disposable income per month. The Hornsbys' reported monthly expenses came to $2,364.90. They operated with a monthly surplus of $191.76 to $280.43, depending on whether Steven earned overtime for a particular month. Under the federal bankruptcy laws, are the Hornsbys entitled to a discharge on their student loans? Explain your answer. [In re *Hornsby*, 144 F.3d 433 (6th Cir.)]

13. TLC was an Atlanta rhythm, blues, and hip-hop band that performed at clubs in 1991. The three-woman group signed a recording contract with LaFace Records. The group's first album that LaFace produced, *Oooooooohhh on the TLC Tip*, sold almost 3 million albums in 1992. The group's second album, *Crazysexycool*, also produced by LaFace, sold 5 million albums through June 1996. The two albums together had six top-of-the-chart singles.

LaFace had the right to renew TLC's contract in 1996 following renegotiation of the contract terms. In the industry, royalty rates for unknown groups, as TLC was in 1991, are generally 7 percent of the revenues for the first 500,000 albums and 8 percent for sales on platinum albums (albums that sell over 1 million copies). The royalty rate increases to 9.5

percent for all sales on an eighth album. Established artists in the industry who renegotiate often have royalty rates of 13 percent, and artists with two platinum albums can command an even higher royalty.

The three women in TLC—Tionne Watkins (T-Boz), Lisa Lopes (Left-Eye, who has since died), and Rozonda Thomas (Chili)—declared bankruptcy in July 1995. All three listed debts that exceeded their assets, which included sums owed to creditors for their cars and to Zale's and The Limited for credit purchases. Lopes was being sued by Lloyd's of London, which claimed she owed it $1.3 million it had paid on a policy held by her boyfriend on his home that was destroyed by fire. Lopes pleaded guilty to one count of arson in the destruction of the home but denied that she intended to destroy it. She was sentenced to five years probation and treatment at a halfway house.

Lopes asked that the Lloyd's claim be discharged in her bankruptcy. All three members of TLC asked that their contract with LaFace be discharged in bankruptcy because being bound to their old contract could impede their fresh financial starts.

Did the three women meet the standards for declaring bankruptcy? Evaluate whether Lopes's Lloyd's claim should be discharged. Determine whether the record contract should be discharged.

14. Place the following in order for a bankruptcy proceeding:
    a. Order of relief
    b. Collection of bankrupt's estate
    c. List of creditors
    d. Petition
    e. Evaluation of claims
    f. Voidable preferences
    g. Discharge

15. Three general unsecured creditors are owed $45,000 as follows: *A*, $15,000; *B*, $5,000; and *C*, $25,000. After all other creditors were paid, the amount left for distribution to general unsecured creditors was $9,000. How will the $9,000 be distributed?

CPA Questions

1. Which of the following statements is correct concerning the voluntary filing of a petition of bankruptcy?
   a. If the debtor has 12 or more creditors, the unsecured claims must total at least $15,325.
   b. The debtor must be solvent.
   c. If the debtor has less than 12 creditors, the unsecured claims must total at least $15,325.
   d. The petition may be filed jointly by spouses (AICPA adapted).

2. On February 28, Master, Inc., had total assets with a fair market value of $1,200,000 and total liabilities of $990,000. On January 15, Master made a monthly installment note payment to Acme Distributors Corp., a creditor holding a properly perfected security interest in equipment having a fair market value greater than the balance due on the note. On March 15, Master voluntarily filed a petition in bankruptcy under the liquidation provisions of Chapter 7 of the federal Bankruptcy Code. One year later, the equipment was sold for less than the balance due on the note to Acme.

   If a creditor challenged Master's right to file, the petition would be dismissed:

   a. If Master had less than 12 creditors at the time of filing.

   b. Unless Master can show that a reorganization under Chapter 11 of the federal Bankruptcy Code would have been unsuccessful.

   c. Unless Master can show that it is unable to pay its debts in the ordinary course of business or as they come due.

   d. If Master is an insurance company.

3. A voluntary petition filed under the liquidation provisions of Chapter 7 of the federal Bankruptcy Code:

   a. Is not available to a corporation unless it has previously filed a petition under the reorganization provisions of Chapter 11 of the federal Bankruptcy Code.

   b. Automatically stays collection actions against the debtor except by secured creditors for collateral only.

   c. Will be dismissed unless the debtor has 12 or more unsecured creditors whose claims total at least $15,325.

   d. Does not require the debtor to show that the debtor's liabilities exceed the fair market value of assets.

4. Which following conditions, if any, must a debtor meet to file a voluntary bankruptcy petition under Chapter 7 of the federal Bankruptcy Code?

	Insolvency	*Three or More Creditors*
a.	Yes	Yes
b.	Yes	No
c.	No	Yes
d.	No	No

5. On July 15, 1988, White, a sole proprietor, was involuntarily petitioned into bankruptcy under the liquidation provisions of the Bankruptcy Code. White's nonexempt property has been converted to $13,000 cash, which is available to satisfy the following claims:

Unsecured claim for 1986 state income tax	$10,000
Fee owed to Best & Co., CPAs, for services rendered from April 1, 1988, through June 30, 1988	$6,000
Unsecured claim by Stieb for wages earned as an employee of White during March 1988	$3,000

   There are no other claims.

   What is the maximum amount that will be distributed for the payment of the 1986 state income tax?

   a. $4,000   c. $7,000

   b. $5,000   d. $10,000

6. On May 1, 1997, two months after becoming insolvent, Quick Corp., an appliance wholesaler, filed a voluntary petition for bankruptcy under the provisions of Chapter 7 of the federal Bankruptcy Code. On October 15, 1996, Quick's board of directors had authorized and paid Erly $50,000 to repay Erly's April 1, 1996, loan to the corporation. Erly is a sibling of Quick's president. On March 15, 1996, Quick paid Kray $100,000 for inventory delivered that day. Which of the following is not relevant in determining whether the repayment of Erly's loan is a voidable preferential transfer?

   a. That Erly is an insider.

   b. That Quick's payment to Erly was made on account of an antecedent debt.

   c. Quick's solvency when the loan was made by Erly.

   d. That Quick's payment to Erly was made within one year of the filing of the bankruptcy petition.

Insurance

By means of insurance, protection from loss and liability may be obtained.

35-1 The Insurance Contract

insurance–a plan of security against risks by charging the loss against a fund created by the payments made by policyholders.

Insurance is a contract by which one party for a stipulated consideration promises to pay another party a sum of money on the destruction of, loss of, or injury to something in which the other party has an interest or to indemnify that party for any loss or liability to which that party is subjected.

35-1a The Parties

insurer–promisor in an insurance contract.

underwriter–insurer.

insured–person to whom the promise in an insurance contract is made.

policy–paper evidencing the contract of insurance.

The promisor in an insurance contract is called the **insurer** or **underwriter.** The person to whom the promise is made is the **insured** or the policyholder. The promise of the insurer is generally set forth in a written contract called a **policy.**

Insurance contracts are ordinarily made through an agent or broker. The **insurance agent** is an agent of the insurance company, often working exclusively for one company. For the most part, the ordinary rules of agency law govern the dealings between this agent and the applicant for insurance.[1]

An **insurance broker** is generally an independent contractor who is not employed by any one insurance company. When a broker obtains a policy for a customer, the broker is the agent of the customer for the purpose of that transaction. Under some statutes, the broker is made an agent of the insurer with respect to transmitting the applicant's payments to the insurer.

insurance agent–agent of an insurance company.

insurance broker–independent contractor who is not employed by any one insurance company.

35-1b Insurable Interest

A person obtaining insurance must have an insurable interest in the subject matter insured. If not, the insurance contract cannot be enforced.

Insurable Interest in Property

A person has an insurable interest in property whenever the destruction of the property will cause a direct pecuniary loss to that person.[2]

It is immaterial whether the insured is the owner of the legal or equitable title, a lienholder, or merely a person in possession of the property.[3] **For Example,** Vin Harrington, a builder, maintained fire insurance on a building he was remodeling under a contract with its owner, Chestnut Hill Properties. The building was destroyed by fire before renovations were completed. Harrington had an insurable interest in the property to the extent of the amount owed him under the renovation contract.

To collect on property insurance, the insured must have an insurable interest at the time the loss occurs.

Insurable Interest in Life

A person who purchases life insurance can name anyone as beneficiary regardless of whether that beneficiary has an insurable interest in the life of the insured. A beneficiary who purchases a policy, however, must have an insurable interest in the life of the insured. Such an interest exists if the beneficiary can reasonably expect to receive

---

[1] *Tidelands Life Ins. Co. v. France,* 711 So. 2d 728 (Tex. App. 1986).
[2] *Plaisance v. Scottsdale Insurance Co.,* 2008 WL 4372888 (E.D. La. Sept. 22, 2008).
[3] See *Rydings v. Cincinnati Special Underwriters Insurance Co.,* 1 N.E.3d 40 (Ill. App. 2013) where a property insurance policy in the name of a public guardian was held to cover fire damages to certain real property included in an estate.

pecuniary gain from the continued life of the other person and, conversely, would suffer financial loss from the latter's death. Thus, a creditor has an insurable interest in the life of the debtor because he may not be paid the amount owed upon the death of the debtor.

CASE SUMMARY

She Lost Interest When He Got the House

FACTS: While Dorothy and James Morgan were still married, Dorothy purchased insurance on their home from American Security Insurance Company. The policy was issued on November 3, 1981, listing the "insured" as Dorothy L. Morgan. Shortly thereafter the Morgans entered into a separation agreement under which Dorothy deeded her interest in the house to James. The Morgans were divorced on August 26, 1982. On November 28, 1982, the house was destroyed by fire. American Security refused to pay on the policy, claiming that Dorothy had no insurable interest in the property at the time of the loss. The Morgans sued the insurer, contending that

they were entitled to payment under the policy issued to Dorothy.

DECISION: Judgment for American Security. In the case of property insurance, the insurable interest must exist at the time of the loss. If the insured parts with all interest in the property prior to the loss, that individual is not covered. Dorothy had conveyed her interest in the property prior to the loss. She did not have an insurable interest at the time of the loss and therefore could not recover on the policy. James Morgan was not insured under the policy. [*Morgan v. American Security Ins. Co.*, 522 So. 2d 454 (Fla. App. 1998)]

A partner or partnership has an insurable interest in the life of each of the partners because the death of any one of them will dissolve the firm and cause some degree of loss to the partnership. A business enterprise has an insurable interest in the life of an executive or a key employee because that person's death would inflict a financial loss on the business to the extent that a replacement might not be readily available or could not be found.

In the case of life insurance, the insurable interest must exist at the time the policy is obtained. It is immaterial that the interest no longer exists when the loss is actually sustained.[4] Thus, the fact that a husband (insured) and wife (beneficiary) are divorced after the life insurance policy was procured does not affect the validity of the policy. Also, the fact that a partnership is terminated after a life insurance policy is obtained by one partner on another does not invalidate the policy.

---

[4] One who obtains insurance on his own life may legally name a beneficiary without an insurable interest or later assign the policy to one without an insurable interest. Stranger-owned life insurance policies, or "STOLI" plans, are a growing concern for insurers in the life insurance industry. Under STOLI schemes elderly individuals are able to obtain third-party financing to purchase a life insurance policy and to fund the premiums owed under that policy, with some understanding or expectation that the policy will be assigned to an individual lacking an insurable interest, following the expiration of the policy's two-year contestability period. And, these policies may be sold on the Secondary Life Insurance Market. Although an insured may generally purchase life insurance in good faith, intending to keep it for himself and later assign it to a third party, regardless of whether the third party has an insurable interest, where a person who has an interest "lends himself to one without any, as a cloak to what is, in its inception, a wager" then the contract is void as against public policy. See *Carton v. B&B Equities Group, LLC*, 827 F. Supp. 2d 1235 (D. Nev. 2011). STOLI arrangements are in violation of public policy in most states that have addressed the issue.

In *Grabner v. James*, 963 F. Supp. 2d 938 (N.D. Cal. 2013), the adult children and co-trustees of the Trabert Family Trust purchased three viatical life settlement contracts for $475,000, where the viators afflicted with AIDS sold their life insurance policy at discounts in exchange for immediate cash. When the projected demise dates (the expected payoff dates) of two of the viators did not occur, the Traberts began to suspect that the AV Reports regarding viators' life expectancies were inaccurate and that the contracts were fraudulent. Their lawsuit was dismissed by the court for waiting longer than the statutory three-year time period before filing their lawsuit.

CASE SUMMARY

Proceeds to the Surviving Partner or the Deceased Partner's Wife?

FACTS: Jewell Norred's husband, James Norred, was the business partner of Clyde Graves for 10 years. On May 7, 1979, Graves and Norred took out life insurance policies, with Graves being the beneficiary of Norred's policy and Norred being the beneficiary of Graves's policy. Premiums were paid out of partnership funds. On February 28, 1983, Graves and Norred divided the partnership assets, but they did not perform the customary steps of dissolving and winding up the partnership. Graves became the sole owner of the business and continued to pay the premiums on both insurance policies until James Norred died on December 5, 1983.

Jewell Norred sued Graves, seeking the proceeds of the insurance policy for herself, alleging that Graves had no insurable interest in the life of James Norred at the time of his death. From a judgment on behalf of the estate, Graves appealed.

DECISION: Judgment for Graves. A partner or partnership has an insurable interest in the life of one of the partners. This interest continues even if the partnership is discontinued prior to the death of one of the partners. Thus, Graves was entitled to the proceeds of the policy. [*Graves v. Norred*, **510 So.2d 816 (Ala. 1987)**]

35-1c The Contract

The formation of a contract of insurance is governed by the general principles applicable to contracts. By statute, an insurance policy must be written. To avoid deception, many state statutes also specify the content of certain policies, in whole or in part. Some statutes specify the size and style of type to be used in printing the policies. Provisions in a policy that conflict with statutory requirements are generally void.

The Application as Part of the Contract

The application for insurance is generally attached to the policy when issued and is made part of the contract of insurance by express stipulation of the policy.

The insured is bound by all material statements in the attached application. **For Example,** insurers seek to stop the issuance of stranger-owned life insurance policies or "STOLI" plans by amending their application process to require all applicants and their brokers to fill out Policy Owner Intent Forms, requiring disclosures that, if answered honestly, will indicate a STOLI scheme and rejection of the application. And, if not answered honestly, the policy can be voided during the two-year contestability period because of the material misrepresentations.[5]

Statutory Provisions as Part of the Contract

When a statute requires that insurance contracts contain certain provisions or cover certain specified losses, a contract of insurance that does not comply with the statute will be interpreted as though it contained all the provisions required by the statute. **For Example,** Louisiana law clearly requires liability insurance coverage on all rental vehicles to protect the victims injured due to the fault of the drivers of the rental vehicles. Avis did provide liability protection for the vehicle it rented to White. However, the terms of the car rental agreement provided for termination of liability coverage in wide-ranging circumstances. White injured Terence Czop while driving intoxicated, one of the causes set forth in the rental agreement for termination of liability coverage. Because state law requires coverage on rental vehicles, the court determined that to allow termination of coverage based on a violation of the rental agreement is against public policy.[6]

[5] See *Principal Life Insurance Co. v. DeRose*, 2011 WL 4738114 (M.D. Pa. Oct. 5, 2011).
[6] *Czop v. White*, 80 So. 3d 1255 (La. App. 2011).

E-COMMERCE & CYBERLAW

Insurance Contracts & E-Sign

The Electronic Signatures in Global and National Commerce Act (E-Sign) applies broadly to the insurance business.* Thus, with consent of the consumer, contracts may be executed with electronic signatures and documents may be delivered by electronic means. E-Sign also provides protections for insurance agents against liability resulting from any deficiencies in the electronic procedures set forth in an electronic contract, provided the agent did not engage in tortious conduct and was not involved in the establishment of the electronic procedures.

Insurance providers are precluded from canceling health insurance or life insurance protection by means of electronic notices.

*15 U.S.C. §7001(i).

35-1d Antilapse and Cancellation Statutes and Provisions

If the premiums are not paid on time, the policy under ordinary contract law would lapse because of nonpayment. However, with life insurance policies, by either policy provision or statute, the insured is allowed a grace period of 30 or 31 days in which to make payment of the premium due. When there is a default in the payment of a premium by the insured, the insurer may be required by statute to (1) issue a paid-up policy in a smaller amount, (2) provide extended insurance for a period of time, or (3) pay the cash surrender value of the policy.

The contract of insurance may expressly declare that it may or may not be canceled by the insurer's unilateral act. By statute or policy provision, the insurer is commonly required to give a specific number of days' written notice of cancellation.[7]

CASE SUMMARY

Oops ... Victoria Insurance Co. didn't know that the ten-day grace period applied *after* the due date.
(My goodness. The company learns something new every day.☹)

FACTS: On September 6, 2009, Robert Vietzen was injured in an automobile accident when a car driven by Dean Mandell and owned by Paulette Henry collided with his vehicle. Victoria Automobile Insurance Company ("Victoria Insurance") had issued an insurance policy for Ms. Henry's vehicle. The parties agree that Mr. Vietzen obtained a judgment against Ms. Henry in the amount of $97,000.00. Victoria Insurance refused to satisfy the judgment based on its assertion that it had cancelled Ms. Henry's policy at 12:01 a.m. on September 6, 2009, for nonpayment of the premium. Victoria Insurance had mailed a billing statement to Ms. Henry on August 24, 2009 stating that a minimum payment of $198.39 was due on September 5, 2009, with notice that

if payment is not received on the due date, the policy cancels on September 6, at 12:01 a.m. Mr. Vietzen sued Victoria Insurance for failure to pay the judgment. From a decision for Victoria Insurance, Vietzen appealed.

DECISION: Judgment for Mr. Vietzen. State law includes a grace period of ten days during which an insured may cure her failure to pay a premium by its due date. An insurance company must wait until the insured has actually failed to pay her premium before mailing notice of cancellation of the policy, which can take place no fewer than ten days after the mailing of the notice. [*Vietzen v. Victoria Automobile Insurance Co.*, 9 N.E.3d 500 (Ohio App. 2014)]

---

[7] *Transamerican Ins. Co. v. Tab Transportation*, 906 P.2d 1341 (Cal. 1995).

35-1e Modification of Contract

As is the case with most contracts, a contract of insurance can be modified if both insurer and insured agree to the change. The insurer cannot modify the contract without the consent of the insured when the right to do so is not reserved in the insurance contract.

To make changes or corrections to the policy, it is not necessary to issue a new policy. An endorsement on the policy or the execution of a separate rider is effective for the purpose of changing the policy. When a provision of an endorsement conflicts with a provision of the policy, the endorsement controls because it is the later document.

35-1f Interpretation of Contract

A contract of insurance is interpreted by the same rules that govern the interpretation of ordinary contracts. Words are to be given their plain and ordinary meaning and interpreted in light of the nature of the coverage intended. However, an insurance policy is construed strictly against the insurer, who chooses the language of the policy, and if a reasonable construction may be given that would justify recovery, a court will do so.[8] **For Example,** Dr. Kolb consented to an elective surgical procedure on his right eye after which "something happened that caused the wound to start leaking" and resulted in loss of vision in his eye. This forced him to retire as an orthopedic surgeon. His Paul Revere Life Insurance disability income insurance policy provided income for life for a disability due to "accidental bodily injury." The policy provided benefits for a shorter duration if the disability was caused by "sickness." Dr. Kolb's vision loss was not expected and proceeded from an unidentified postsurgical cause. Applying the plain and ordinary meaning of "accidental" and "injury," the court decided that Dr. Kolb was entitled to income for life under the "injury" provision of the policy.[9]

If there is an ambiguity in the policy, the provision is interpreted against the insurer.[10] **For Example,** on August 29, 2005, the Buentes' residence in Gulfport, Mississippi, was damaged during Hurricane Katrina. Allstate tendered a check for $2,600.35 net after the deductible, under its Deluxe Homeowner's Policy. The Buentes contend that their covered losses are between $50,000 and $100,000. They brought suit against Allstate. The trial judge denied Allstate's motion to dismiss, finding that the two provisions of the policy that purport to exclude coverage for wind and rain damage were ambiguous in light of other policy provisions granting coverage for wind and rain damage and in light of the inclusion of a "hurricane deductible" as part of the policy. The court found that because the policy was ambiguous, its weather exclusion was unenforceable in the context of losses attributable to wind and rain that occur in a hurricane.[11]

35-1g Burden of Proof

When an insurance claim is disputed by the insurer, the person bringing suit has the burden of proving that there was a loss, that it occurred while the policy was in force, and that the loss was of a kind that was within the coverage or scope of the policy.[12]

A policy will contain exceptions to the coverage. This means that the policy is not applicable when an exception applies to the situation. Exceptions to coverage are generally strictly interpreted against the insurer. However, insurance policies are contracts and the

---

[8] *SWE Homes, L.P. v. Wellington Insurance Co.*, 436 S.W.3d 86 (Tex. App. 2014).
[9] *Kolb v. Paul Revere Life Insurance Co.*, 355 F.3d 1132 (8th Cir. 2004).
[10] See *Arrowood Indemnity Co. v. King*, 39 A.3d 712 (Conn. 2012); *Koziol v. Peerless Insurance Co.*, 41 A.3d 647 (R.I. 2012).
[11] *Buente v. Allstate Ins. Co.*, 422 F. Supp. 2d 690 (S.D. Miss. 2006).
[12] *Koslik v. Gulf Insurance Co.*, 673 N.W.2d 343 (Wis. App. 2003).

plain and unambiguous language of the contract will apply. **For Example,** Aroa Marketing, Inc., purchased a commercial general liability (CGL) policy from Hartford Midwest Insurance Co. The policy covered any damages that Aroa became legally obligated to pay because of "bodily injury," "property damage," or "personal and advertising injury" arising out of Aroa's business. Coverage was excluded, however, for "personal and advertising injury" arising out of "any violation of any intellectual property rights, such as copyright, patent, trademark, trade name, trade secret, service mark, or other destination of origin or authenticity." Aroa hired Tara Radcliffe to appear in and film an exercise video for its business to be used at a consumer electronics show and on a client's Internet site. Aroa used her images to sell other products, and she sued for misappropriation of her image and violation of her right of publicity. The court found that Hartford had no duty to defend or indemnify Aroa because the model's claim fell within the intellectual property exclusion.[13]

35-1h Insurer Bad Faith

As is required in the case of all contracts, an insurer must act in good faith in processing and paying claims under its policy. In some states, laws have been enacted making an insurer liable for a statutory penalty and attorney fees in case of a bad-faith failure or delay in paying a valid claim within a specified period of time.[14] A bad-faith refusal is generally considered to be any frivolous or unfounded refusal to comply with the demand of a policyholder to pay according to the policy.[15]

CASE SUMMARY

Ruining General Lafayette's* Good Name
*Check him out online.

FACTS: Don and Myna Leland owned rental property in Lake Charles, Louisiana, that was damaged by a tree falling into the building, shearing off a portion of the facade during Hurricane Rita in September 2005. By October 7, 2005, they notified their insurer, Lafayette Insurance Co., of the damages to this property. In September 2007, two years after the hurricane, the Lelands filed a lawsuit against the issuer for breach of the insurer's duty of good faith and fair dealing in adjusting losses associated with the hurricane. The jury found in favor of the Lelands, concluding that the plaintiffs sustained losses in excess of the amount paid under the defendant's policy in the amount of $144,800.00. Further, the jury concluded that the defendant: (1) failed to initiate a loss adjustment to the property within 30 days after notification of loss; (2) was arbitrary, capricious, or without probable cause in failing to pay any claim due within 60 days after receipt of satisfactory proof of loss; (3) failed to make an offer to settle the property damage within

30 days of receipt of satisfactory proof of loss; and (4) misrepresented pertinent facts or insurance policy provisions related to coverage at issue. From a judgment for the Lelands, Lafayette appealed.

DECISION: Judgment for the Lelands. The court of appeals affirmed the trial court's damages as amended as follows: $5,000 for loss of rental income, $53,000 for loss of personal income, $30,000 in interest and $45,000 each for the Lelands for mental anguish and emotional distress for a total of $178,000 in damages attributable to the insurer's breach of its duties. State law added a penalty of two times these damages, or $356,000. The insurer was also obligated to pay $144,800 in contractual damages for repairs owed under the insurance contract and $226,266 in attorneys' fees. In particular the court determined that the evidence was sufficient to support the awards for mental anguish. Mr. Leland testified extensively regarding the

[13] *Aroa Marketing, Inc. v. Hartford Insurance Co.,* 130 Cal. Rptr. 3d 466 (Cal. App. 2011).
[14] *Maslo v. Ameriprise Auto & Home Insurance,* 173 Cal. Rptr. 3d 854 (Cal. App. 2014).
[15] *Uberti v. Lincoln National Life Ins. Co.,* 144 F. Supp. 2d 90 (D. Conn. 2001).

frustrations encountered in pursuing the multiyear claim and making little progress toward a conclusion, including a record of repeated and persisted demands to the insurers regarding his property, which remained unrepaired, causing him to borrow more than $142,000 for repairs in order to avoid the city's pending action to demolish the property. Both Lelands testified to the negative impact the multiyear process had taken on their personal relationship. [***Leland v. Lafayette Insurance Co.*, 77 So.3d 1078 (La. App. 2011)**]

When it is a liability insurer's duty to defend the insured and the insurer wrongfully refuses to do so, the insurer is guilty of breach of contract and is liable for all consequential damages resulting from the breach. In some jurisdictions, an insured can recover for an excess judgment rendered against the insured when it is proven that the insurer was guilty of negligence or bad faith in failing to defend the action or settle the matter within policy limits.

If there is a reasonable basis for the insurer's belief that a claim is not covered by its policy, its refusal to pay the claim does not subject it to liability for a breach of good faith or for a statutory penalty.[16] This is so even though the court holds that the insurer is liable for the claim.

For Example, the following illustrates an insurer's bad-faith failure to pay a claim, as opposed to an insurer's reasonable basis for failure to pay. Carmela Garza's home and possessions were destroyed in a fire set by an arsonist on August 19. Carmela's husband, Raul, who was no longer living at the home, had a criminal record. An investigator for the insurer stated that while he had no specific information to implicate the Garzas in the arson, Carmela may have wanted the proceeds to finance relocation to another city. By October, however, Aetna's investigators ruled out the possibility that Garza had the motive or the opportunity to set the fire. The insurer thus no longer had a reasonable basis to refuse to pay the claim after this date. Yet it took over a year and a half and court intervention for Aetna to allow Carmela to see a copy of her policy, which had been destroyed in the fire. Two years after the fire, Aetna paid only $28,624.55 for structural damage to the fire-gutted home, which was insured for $111,000. The court held that Aetna's actions constituted a bad-faith failure to pay by the insurer.[17]

35-1i Time Limitations on Insured

The insured must comply with a number of time limitations in making a claim. For example, the insured must promptly notify the insurer of any claim that may arise, submit a proof-of-loss statement within the time set forth in the policy, and bring any court action based on the policy within a specified time period.[18]

35-1j Subrogation of Insurer

In some instances, the insured has a claim against a third person for the harm covered by the insurance policy. **For Example,** *A* sells an automobile insurance policy that provides

---

[16] *Shipes v. Hanover Ins. Co.*, 884 F.2d 1357 (11th Cir. 1989).

[17] See *Aetna Casualty & Surety Co. v. Garza*, 906 S.W.2d 543 (Tex. App. 1995).

[18] But see *Seeman v. Sterling Ins. Co.*, 699 N.Y.S.2d 542 (A.D. 1999), where the insured's four-month delay in notifying the insurer was excused because of his belief that only on-premises injuries were covered by his homeowners insurance policy and thus the policy would not cover an injury in which a paintball he fired at work struck his coworker in the eye.

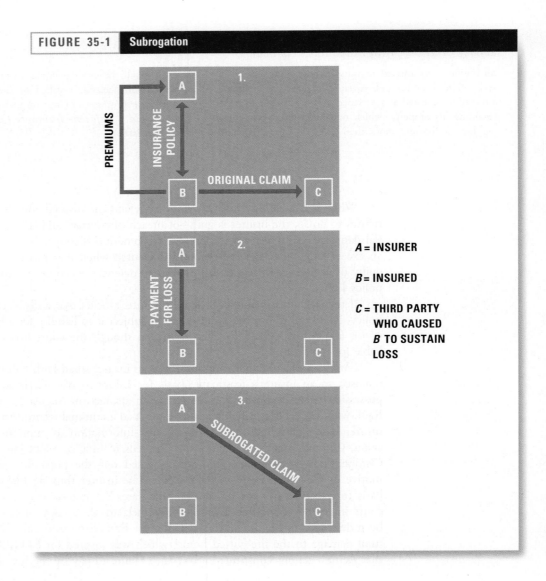

FIGURE 35-1   Subrogation

A = INSURER

B = INSURED

C = THIRD PARTY
WHO CAUSED
B TO SUSTAIN
LOSS

subrogation–right of a party secondarily liable to stand in the place of the creditor after making payment to the creditor and to enforce the creditor's right against the party primarily liable in order to obtain indemnity from such primary party.

risk–peril or contingency against which the insured is protected by the contract of insurance.

collision coverage to *B*. *C* "rear-ends" *B*'s car at a traffic rotary in the city. *A* pays *B* the full amount of the property damage repair costs. *A* is then **subrogated** to *B*'s claim against *C*, the person who caused the harm. See Figure 35-1. When the insurer is subrogated to the insured's claim, the insurer may enforce that claim against the third person.[19]

35-2 Kinds of Insurance

Businesses today have specialized **risk** managers who identify the risks to which individual businesses are exposed, measure those risks, and purchase insurance to cover those risks (or decide to self-insure in whole or in part).

Insurance policies can be grouped into certain categories. Five major categories of insurance are considered here: (1) business liability insurance, (2) marine and inland

---

[19] *Stratus Services Group, Inc. v. Kash 'N Gold Ltd.*, 935 N.Y.S.2d 302 (A.D. 2011).

marine insurance, (3) fire and homeowners insurance, (4) automobile insurance, and (5) life insurance.

35-2a Business Liability Insurance

Businesses may purchase Commercial General Liability (CGL) policies. This insurance is a broad, "all-risk" form of insurance providing coverage for mostly all sums that the insured may become legally obligated to pay as damages because of "bodily injury" or "property damage" caused by an "occurrence." The insurer is obligated to defend the insured business and pay damages under CGL policies for product liability cases, actions for wrongful termination of employees, sexual harassment cases, damages caused by business advertising or employee dishonesty, and trademark infringement suits.[20] The insurer may also be obligated to pay for damages in the form of cleanup costs imposed for contamination of land, water, and air under environmental statutes.[21]

CASE SUMMARY

The Clash Between the "Auto" Insurer and the "CGL" Insurer
The Case of the Hot Defective Deep Fryer on the Moving Food Truck

FACTS: Royal Catering Company (Royal) owned a fleet of food trucks. It leased its trucks to operators who drove from site to site selling food. Royal leased one of these trucks to Esmeragdo Gomez, who, along with his wife, Irais Gomez, operated the truck. The Gomezes' food truck had two seats and two seatbelts, for a driver and a cook. The food truck was equipped with a specially designed deep fryer, grill, steam table, oven, refrigerator, and coffee maker. That equipment was built into the truck and was not designed to be used apart from the truck. On the day of the accident, Mr. Gomez was driving the food truck. A guest sat in the truck's passenger seat, and Mrs. Gomez stood in the rear of the truck. At an intersection, Mr. Gomez swerved to avoid an approaching truck. Mr. Gomez's evasive action failed to avoid a collision. Just prior to the collision, hot oil splashed on and burned Mrs. Gomez. The Gomezes and the passenger in their truck brought an action against Royal Catering for injuries sustained in connection with the accident, including a product liability claim for a defective deep fryer basket. American States Insurance Company issued automobile insurance policies to Royal. Travelers Insurance provided commercial general liability coverage (CGL) to Royal. The automobile insurer, American States, claims that the injuries should be covered under the Traveler CGL policy that,

although excluding coverage for injuries arising out of the use of automobiles, covers "mobile equipment," defined as vehicles used for a primary purpose other than transporting persons or cargo. Travelers asserts that the primary purpose of the food truck was to transport "persons and cargo" so that it is not within the "mobile equipment" exception to the Travelers' CGL auto exclusion. From a decision by the trial court that the food truck was an "auto" obligating American States to cover the claims for injury, American States appealed.

DECISION: Judgment for American States. Although the Traveler's CGL policy excluded coverage for injuries arising out of the use of automobiles, the policy contained an exception for "mobile equipment," including vehicles "maintained primarily for purposes other than transportation of persons or cargo." The primary purpose of the food truck was to serve as a mobile kitchen and not transport persons or cargo. Like a fire truck a food truck may transport persons and cargo—that is, food, but its core functional identity emerges when it operates a mobile kitchen at specified locations. [*American State Insurance Co. v. Traveler Property Casualty Co. of America*, 167 Cal. Rptr. 3d 288 (Cal. App. 2014)]

---

[20] *Charter Oak Fire Ins. Co. v. Heedon & Cos.*, 280 F.3d 730 (7th Cir. 2002).

[21] *Chemical Leaman Tank Lines, Inc. v. Aetna Casualty Co.*, 788 F. Supp. 846 (D.N.J. 1992); *United States v. Pepper's Steel, Inc.*, 823 F. Supp. 1574 (S.D. Fla. 1993). But see *Northville Industries v. National Union Fire and Ins. Co.*, 636 N.Y.S.2d 359 (A.D. 1995); *Aydin Corp. v. First State Ins. Co.*, 62 Cal. Rptr. 2d 825 (A.D. 1997).

ETHICS & THE LAW

On September 11, 2001, terrorist attacks killed 3,119 persons, devastated the U.S. airline industry, and had a severe impact on the U.S. insurance industry. In New York City, several office buildings, including One and Two World Trade Center, were destroyed, and other businesses in lower Manhattan were forced to shut down.

Business interruption insurance coverage is usually written as part of a company's commercial property insurance package. It not only covers policyholders for their lost profits and fixed charges and expenses for interruption to their business caused by physical damage or destruction to the insured's own property, but it may also cover "contingent business interruption" resulting from suspension of operations caused by damages to the property of a key supplier, distributor, or manufacturer. Such coverage, however, contains an exclusion for "war or military action." Are the September 11, 2001, terrorist attacks an "act of war" such that insurers are not responsible for business interruption claims? Can the president's words regarding war with al Qaeda be used to prove an "act of war" exclusion?

A court called upon to interpret an "act of war" exclusion will apply the plain and ordinary meaning of the policy's terms, and any ambiguity will be construed against the insurer. In *Pan American World Airways, Inc., v. Aetna*

Casualty & Surety Co., the Second Circuit Court of Appeals held that an air carrier was entitled to recover for the destruction of its plane by terrorists in Cairo, Egypt, and the damage was not excluded under the policy's "act of war" exclusion. The court reasoned in part that there was no existing "war" between recognized sovereign states.

Pressured by historic losses as a result of "9/11," insurance companies in certain areas excluded perils resulting from "terrorism" in new commercial property insurance policies. Is it fair for insurers to exclude coverage altogether for losses due to acts of terrorism? Is it best to have the community absorb the losses? Is it best to have individuals and individual businesses cover the losses? See the Terrorism Risk Insurance Program Reauthorization Act of 2014, which extends the Terrorism Insurance Act of 2002 through December 31, 2021. This law provides a federal insurance backstop in the context of the insurance marketplace where catastrophic terrorism is an uninsurable risk. The law continues the existing $100 million "trigger level" of aggregate insured losses. The Secretary of State, in concurrence with the Attorney General of the United States has authority to certify an event as an act of terrorism.

*See **Pan American World Airways, Inc. v. Aetna Casualty & Surety Co.**, 505 F.2d 989 (2d Cir. 1974).

The insurer must defend when coverage is a "close issue" regarding whether the policy would provide indemnity. The duty to defend does not depend on the truth or falsity of the allegations made against the insured by a third party; rather, the factual allegations in the complaint that potentially support a covered claim are all that is needed to invoke the insurer's duty to defend.[22] It is common for the insurer to seek a declaratory judgment if it believes the policy does not call for either a defense or an indemnity. **For Example,** State Automobile Mutual Insurance Co. brought an action for declaratory judgment that it had no duty to defend and indemnify Flexdar, Inc., for the cost of cleanup of a chemical solvent discovered in the soil of Flexdar's manufacturing site, referencing its "pollution exclusion" language in its policies. The court found the language in the CGL policy in question was ambiguous and thus ruled against the insurer.[23]

Businesses may purchase policies providing liability insurance for their directors and officers. Manufacturers and sellers may purchase product liability insurance. Professional persons, such as accountants, physicians, lawyers, architects, and engineers, may obtain liability insurance protection against malpractice suits. **For Example,** the architects of the MCI Center, a sports arena in Washington, D.C., were entitled under their professional liability insurance coverage to be defended by their insurer in a lawsuit seeking only

---

[22] *Mid Continent Casualty Co. v. JHP Development Inc.*, 557 F.3d 207 (6th Cir. 2009).
[23] *State Automobile Mutual Insurance Co. v. Flexdar, Inc.*, 964 N.E.2d 845 (Ind. 2012). The court majority stated:

> After all, "[t]he insurance companies write the policies; we buy their forms or we do not buy their insurance." By more careful drafting State Auto has the ability to resolve any question of ambiguity. And in fact it has done so. In 2005 State Auto revised its policies to add an "Indiana Changes—Pollution Exclusion" endorsement. Id. At 852.

marine insurance–
policies that cover perils
relating to the
transportation of goods.

ocean marine–policies
that cover transportation
of goods in vessels in
international and coastal
trade.

inland marine–
insurance that covers
domestic shipments of
goods over land and
inland waterways.

hull insurance–
insurance that covers
physical damage on a
freight-moving vessel.

injunctive relief for the firm's alleged failure to comply with the Americans with Disabilities Act's enhanced sightline requirements.[24]

35-2b Marine Insurance

Marine insurance policies cover perils relating to the transportation of goods. **Ocean marine** insurance policies cover the transportation of goods in vessels in international and coastal trade. **Inland marine** insurance principally covers domestic shipments of goods over land and inland waterways.

Ocean Marine

Ocean marine insurance is a form of insurance that covers ships and their cargoes against "perils of the sea." Four classes of ocean marine insurance are generally available: (1) hull, (2) cargo, (3) liability, and (4) freight. **Hull insurance** covers physical damage to the vessel.[25] **Cargo insurance** protects the cargo owner against financial loss if the goods being shipped are lost or damaged at sea.[26]

CASE SUMMARY

This Coverage Is Worth a Hill of Beans

FACTS: Commodities Reserve Company (CRC) contracted to sell 1,008 tons of beans and 50 tons of seed to purchasers in Venezuela. CRC purchased the beans and seeds in Turkey and chartered space on the ship *MV West Lion*. The cargo was insured under an ocean marine policy issued by St. Paul Fire & Marine Insurance Company. The Sue and Labor Clause in CRC's ocean marine policy with St. Paul provided: "In case of any loss or misfortune, it shall be lawful and necessary to and for the Assured … to sue, labor and travel for, in and about the defense, safeguard and recovery of the said goods and merchandise … to the charges whereof, the [insurer] will contribute according to the rate and quantity of the sum hereby insured." While the ship was

sailing through Greek waters, Greek authorities seized the vessel for carrying munitions. CRC had to go to the expense of obtaining an order from a court in Crete to release the cargo. When St. Paul refused to pay the costs of the Cretan litigation to release the cargo, CRC brought suit against St. Paul.

DECISION: Judgment for CRC. The Sue and Labor Clause required CRC to sue for "recovery of the said goods and merchandise." The clause also requires the insurer to reimburse the insured for those expenses. [*Commodities Reserve Co. v. St. Paul Fire & Marine Ins. Co.*, 879 F.2d 640 (9th Cir. 1998)]

---

cargo insurance–
insurance that protects a
cargo owner against
financial loss if goods
being shipped are lost or
damaged at sea.

liability insurance–
covers the shipowner's
liability if the ship causes
damage to another ship
or its cargo.

freight insurance–
insures that shipowner
will receive payment for
transportation charges.

Cargo insurance does not cover risks prior to the loading of the insured cargo on board the vessel. An additional warehouse coverage endorsement is needed to insure merchandise held in a warehouse prior to import or export voyages.

Liability insurance covers the shipowner's liability if the ship causes damage to another ship or its cargo. **Freight insurance** ensures that the shipowner will receive payment for the transportation charges. "All-risk" policies consolidate coverage of all four classes of ocean marine insurance into one policy.[27]

---

[24] *Washington Sports and Entertainment, Inc. v. United Coastal Ins.*, 7 F. Supp. 2d 1 (D.D.C. 1998).
[25] *Lloyd's v. Labarca*, 260 F.3d 3 (1st Cir. 2001).
[26] *Kimta, A. S. v. Royal Insurance Co., Inc.*, 9 P.3d 239 (Wash. App. 2001).
[27] *Transamerican Leasing, Inc. v. Institute of London Underwriters*, 7 F. Supp. 2d 1340 (S.D. Fla. 1998).

Inland Marine

Inland marine insurance evolved from marine insurance. It protects goods in transit over land; by air; or on rivers, lakes, and coastal waters. Inland marine insurance can be used to insure property held by a bailee. Moreover, it is common for institutions financing automobile dealers' new car inventories to purchase inland marine insurance policies to insure against damage to the automobiles while in inventory.

35-2c Fire and Homeowners Insurance

fire insurance policy–a contract that indemnifies the insured for property destruction or damage caused by fire.

A **fire insurance policy** is a contract to indemnify the insured for property destruction or damage caused by fire. In almost every state, the New York standard fire insurance form is the standard policy. A **homeowners insurance policy** is a combination of the standard fire insurance policy and comprehensive personal liability insurance. It thus provides fire, theft, and certain liability protection in a single insurance contract.

homeowners insurance policy–combination of standard fire insurance and comprehensive personal liability insurance.

Fire Insurance

For fire insurance to cover fire loss, there must be an actual hostile fire that is the immediate cause of the loss. A *hostile fire* is one that becomes uncontrollable, burns with excessive heat, or escapes from the place where it is intended to be. To illustrate, when soot is ignited and causes a fire in the chimney, the fire is hostile. On the other hand, if a loss is caused by the smoke or heat of a fire that has not broken out of its ordinary container or become uncontrollable, the loss results from a friendly fire. The policy does not cover damage from a friendly fire.

By policy endorsement, however, the coverage may be extended to include loss by a friendly fire.

CASE SUMMARY

Excuse Me? The Fire Wasn't Hostile?

FACTS: Youse owned a ring that was insured with the Employers Fire Insurance Company against loss, including "all direct loss or damage by fire." Youse accidentally threw the ring into a trash burner, and it was damaged when the trash was burned. He sued the insurer.

DECISION: Judgment for insurer. A fire policy covers only loss caused by a hostile fire. The fire was not hostile because it burned in the area in which it was intended to burn. [*Youse v. Employers Fire Ins. Co.,* **238 P.2d 472 (Kan. 1951)**]

---

coinsurance clause–clause requiring the insured to maintain insurance on property up to a stated amount and providing that to the extent that this is not done, the insured is to be deemed a coinsurer with the insurer, so that the latter is liable only for its proportionate share of the amount of insurance required to be carried.

Coinsurance. The insurer is liable for the actual amount of the loss sustained up to the maximum amount stated in the policy. An exception exists when the policy contains a coinsurance clause. A **coinsurance clause** requires the insured to maintain insurance on the covered property up to a certain amount or a certain percentage of the value (generally 80 percent). Under such a provision, if the policyholder insures the property for less than the required amount, the insurer is liable only for the proportionate share of the amount of insurance required to be carried. **For Example,** suppose that the owner of a building with a value of $400,000 insures it against loss to the extent of $240,000. The policy contains a coinsurance clause requiring that insurance of 80 percent of the value of the property be carried (in this case, $320,000). Assume that a $160,000 loss is then sustained. The insured would receive not $160,000 from the insurer but only three-fourths of that amount, which is \$120,000, because the amount of the insurance carried (\$240,000) is only three-fourths of the amount required (\$320,000).

Some states prohibit the use of a coinsurance clause.

Assignment. Fire insurance is a personal contract, and in the absence of statute or contractual authorization, it cannot be assigned without the consent of the insurer.

Occupancy. Provisions in a policy of fire insurance relating to the use and occupancy of the property are generally strictly construed because they relate to the hazards involved.

Homeowners Insurance

In addition to providing protection against losses resulting from fire, the homeowners policy provides liability coverage for accidents or injuries that occur on the premises of the insured. Moreover, the liability provisions provide coverage for unintentional injuries to others away from home for which the insured or any member of the resident family is held responsible, such as injuries caused to others by golfing, hunting, or fishing accidents.[28] Generally, motor vehicles, including mopeds and recreational vehicles, are excluded from such personal liability coverage.

A homeowners policy also provides protection from losses caused by theft. In addition, it provides protection for all permanent residents of the household, including all family members living with the insured. Thus, a child of the insured who lives at home is protected under the homeowners policy for the value of personal property lost when the home is destroyed by fire.

35-2d **Automobile Insurance**

Associations of insurers, such as the National Bureau of Casualty Underwriters and the National Automobile Underwriters Association, have proposed standard forms of automobile insurance policies. These forms have been approved by the association members in virtually all states. The form used today by most insurers is the Personal Auto Policy (PAP).

Perils Covered

Part A of the policy provides liability coverage that protects the insured driver or owner from the claims of others for bodily injuries or damage to their property. Part B of the policy provides coverage for medical expenses sustained by a covered person or persons in an accident. Part C of the PAP provides coverage for damages the insured is entitled to recover from an *uninsured motorist*.[29] Part D provides coverage for loss or damage to the covered automobile. Coverage under Part D includes collision coverage and coverage of "other than collision" losses, such as fire and theft.

Covered Persons

Covered persons include the named insured or any family member (a person related by blood, marriage, or adoption or a ward or foster child who is a resident of the household). If an individual is driving with the permission of the insured, that individual is also covered. In any case, however, the language of the insurance policy is controlling. **For Example,** a court upheld State Farm Mutual's position that Robert Gaudina was not an insured under his wife's automobile policy. Gaudina had been asked to leave the household by his wife until he found a job, and his residence was not at his wife's home

---

[28] *American Concept Ins. Co. v. Lloyds of London,* 467 N.W.2d 480 (S.D. 1991).
[29] *Montano v. Allstate Indemnity,* 211 F.3d 1278 (10th Cir. 2002).

at the time of the accident. The policy definition was controlling, which stated: "Spouse – means your husband or wife who resides primarily with you."[30]

Use and Operation

The coverage of the PAP policy is limited to claims arising from the "use and operation" of an automobile. The term *use and operation* does not require that the automobile be in motion. Thus, the term embraces loading and unloading as well as actual travel.[31]

Notice and Cooperation

The insured is under a duty to give notice of claims, to inform, and to cooperate with the insurer. Notice and cooperation are conditions precedent to the liability of the insurer.

No-Fault Insurance

Traditional tort law (negligence law) placed the economic losses resulting from an automobile accident on the one at fault. The purpose of automobile liability insurance is to relieve the wrongdoer from the consequences of a negligent act by paying defense costs and the damages assessed. Under no-fault laws, injured persons are barred from suing the party at fault for ordinary claims. When the insured is injured while using the insured automobile, the insurer will make a payment without regard to whose fault caused the harm. However, if the automobile collision results in a permanent serious disablement or disfigurement, or death, or if the medical bills and lost wages of the plaintiff exceed a specified amount, suit may be brought against the party who was at fault.

35-2e Life Insurance

There are three basic types of life insurance: term insurance, whole life insurance, and endowment insurance.

Term insurance is written for a specified number of years and terminates at the end of that period. If the insured dies within the time period covered by the policy, the face amount is paid to the beneficiary. If the insured is still alive at the end of the time period, the contract expires, and the insurer has no further obligation. Term policies have little or no cash surrender value.

Whole life insurance (or ordinary life insurance) provides lifetime insurance protection. It also has an investment element.

Part of every premium covers the cost of insurance, and the remainder of the premium builds up a **cash surrender value** of the policy.

An **endowment insurance** policy is one that pays the face amount of the policy if the insured dies within the policy period. If the insured lives to the end of the policy period, the face amount is paid to the insured at the end of the period.

Many life insurance companies pay double the amount of the policy, called **double indemnity,** if death is caused by an accident and death occurs within 90 days afterward. A comparatively small additional premium is charged for this special protection.

In consideration of an additional premium, many life insurance companies also provide insurance against total permanent disability of the insured. **Disability** is usually defined in a life insurance policy as any "incapacity resulting from bodily injury or disease to engage in any occupation for remuneration or profit."

term insurance–policy written for a specified number of years that terminates at the end of that period.

whole life insurance–ordinary life insurance providing lifetime insurance protection.

cash surrender value–sum paid the insured upon the surrender of a policy to the insurer.

endowment insurance–insurance that pays the face amount of the policy if the insured dies within the policy period.

double indemnity–provision for payment of double the amount specified by the insurance contract if death is caused by an accident and occurs under specified circumstances.

disability–any incapacity resulting from bodily injury or disease to engage in any occupation for remuneration or profit.

[30] *Robert Gaudina v. State Farm Mutual Automobile Insurance Co.,* 8 N.E.3d 588 (Ill. App. 2014).
[31] See *American Home Insurance Co. v. First Specialty Insurance Corp.,* 894 N.E.2d 1167 (Mass. App. 2008).

Exclusions

Life insurance policies frequently provide that death is not within the protection of the policy and that a double indemnity provision is not applicable when death is caused by (1) suicide,[32] (2) narcotics, (3) the intentional act of another, (4) execution for a crime, (5) war activities, or (6) operation of aircraft.

The Beneficiary

beneficiary–person to whom the proceeds of a life insurance policy are payable, a person for whose benefit property is held in trust, or a person given property by a will; the ultimate recipient of the benefit of a funds transfer.

The recipient of life insurance policy proceeds that are payable upon the death of the insured is called the **beneficiary.** The beneficiary may be a third person or the estate of the insured, and there may be more than one beneficiary.

The beneficiary named in a policy may be barred from claiming the proceeds of the policy. It is generally provided by statute or stated by court decision that a beneficiary who has feloniously killed the insured is not entitled to receive the proceeds of the policy.

The customary policy provides that the insured reserves the right to change the beneficiary without the latter's consent. When the policy contains such a provision, the beneficiary cannot object to a change that destroys all of that beneficiary's rights under the policy and that names another person as beneficiary.

An insurance policy will ordinarily state that to change the beneficiary, the insurer must be so instructed in writing by the insured and the policy must then be endorsed by the company with the change of the beneficiary. These provisions are construed liberally. If the insured has notified the insurer but dies before the endorsement of the change by the company, the change of beneficiary is effective.[33] However, if the insured has not taken any steps to comply with the policy requirements, a change of beneficiary is not effective even though a change was intended.

Incontestability Clause

incontestability clause– provision that after the lapse of a specified time the insurer cannot dispute the policy on the ground of misrepresentation or fraud of the insured or similar wrongful conduct.

Statutes commonly require the inclusion of an **incontestability clause** in life insurance policies. Ordinarily, this clause states that after the lapse of two years, the policy cannot be contested by the insurance company.[34] The insurer is free to contest the validity of the policy at any time during the contestability period. Once the period has expired, the insurer must pay the stipulated sum upon the death of the insured and cannot claim that in obtaining the policy, the insured had been guilty of misrepresentation, fraud, or any other conduct that would entitle it to avoid the contract of insurance.[35]

Courts and legislatures have addressed the issue of "imposter fraud." In *Amex Life Assurance Co. v. Superior Court*, the California Supreme Court concluded that after the contestability period had expired, an insurer may not assert the defense that an imposter took the medical examination. Jose Morales had applied for a life insurance policy from Amex. A paramedic working for Amex met a man claiming to be Morales and took blood and urine samples, listing him as 5' 10" and weighing 172 pounds. His blood sample was HIV negative. The individual did not provide identification. Some two years later, Morales died of AIDS–related causes. Morales had listed his height as 5' 6" and his weight as 142 on his insurance application. The California Supreme Court stated that Amex, which had done nothing to protect its interest but collect premiums, could not challenge coverage based on the imposter defense.[36] Subsequent to the court's decision,

[32] *Mirza v. Maccabees Life and Annuity Co.*, 466 N.W.2d 340 (Mich. App. 1991).
[33] *Zeigler v. Cardona*, 830 F. Supp. 1395 (M.D. Ala. 1993).
[34] The two-year period runs from the policy's date of issue to the date the suit is filed in court. See *PHL Variable Insurance Co. v. The Sheldon Hathaway Family Insurance Trust*, 2011 WL 703839 (D. Utah Feb. 20, 2011).
[35] *Amica Life Insurance Co. v. Barbor*, 488 F. Supp. 2d 750 (N.D. Ill. 2007).
[36] *Amex Life Assurance Co. v. Superior Court*, 930 P.2d 1264 (Cal. 1997).

the California legislature amended state insurance law to provide for an "imposter defense" in that state. As set forth in the *Miller* case, Florida does not recognize an imposter defense to incontestability. The legislative purpose of such clauses is to protect beneficiaries from an insurer's refusal to honor policies by asserting pre-existing conditions, leaving beneficiaries in the untenable position of having to battle with powerful insurance companies in court.

CASE SUMMARY

The Impostor Defense: Dealing with Substitutes with Different Attributes

FACTS: The Allstate life insurance policy on which this case centers went into effect on September 20, 2000, insuring the life of John Miller. The policy stated that if the insured died while the policy was in force, Allstate would pay a death benefit to the policy beneficiaries upon receiving proof of death. As required by Fla. Stat. § 627.455, the policy further provided that it would become incontestable after remaining in force during the lifetime of the insured for a period of two years from its effective date. John Miller died on April 20, 2003—more than two years after the policy went into effect. The beneficiaries accordingly filed statements seeking to collect benefits under the policy. Rather than disburse the benefits, Allstate sought a declaratory judgment that the policy was void, alleging that the application was completed using fraudulent information and that an imposter had appeared at the medical exam in place of John Miller. The beneficiaries counterclaimed, alleging breach of contract based on Allstate's failure to pay benefits upon proof of death in accordance with the insurance policy's terms. Allstate appealed a judgment in favor of the beneficiaries.

DECISION: Judgment for the beneficiaries. The incontestability clause works to the mutual advantage of the insured, giving the insured a guarantee against expensive litigation to defeat the policy after it has been in effect during the lifetime of the insured for a period of two years from its date of issue and giving the company a reasonable time to ascertain whether the insurance contract should remain in force. Under Florida law where the insured's death occurred after the contestability period, Allstate could not void the policy on the ground that an imposter had undergone the precoverage physical examination in the insured's place. [*Allstate Life Ins. Co. v. Miller*, 424 F.3d 1113 (11th Cir. 2005)]

Make the Connection

Summary

Insurance is a contract called a *policy*. Under an insurance policy, the insurer provides in consideration of premium payments, to pay the insured or beneficiary a sum of money if the insured sustains a specified loss or is subjected to a specified liability. These contracts are made through an insurance agent, who is an agent for the insurance company, or through an insurance broker, who is the agent of the insured when obtaining a policy for the latter.

The person purchasing an insurance contract must have an insurable interest in the insured's life or property. An insurable interest in property exists when the damage or destruction of the property will cause a direct monetary loss to the insured. In the case of property insurance, the insured must have an insurable interest at the time of loss. An insurable interest in the life of the insured exists if the purchaser would suffer a financial loss from the insured's death. This interest must exist as of the time the policy is obtained.

Ocean marine policies insure ships and their cargoes against the perils of the sea. Inland marine policies insure goods being transported by land, by air, or on inland and coastal waterways.

For fire insurance to cover a fire loss, there must be an actual hostile fire that is the immediate cause of the loss. The insurer is liable for the actual amount of the loss sustained up to the maximum amount stated in the policy. An exception exists when the policy contains a coinsurance clause requiring the insured to maintain insurance up to a certain percentage of the value of the property. To the extent this is not done, the insured is deemed a coinsurer with the insurer, and the insurer is liable for only its proportional share of the amount of insurance required to be carried. A homeowners insurance policy provides fire, theft, and liability protection in a single contract.

Automobile insurance may provide protection for collision damage to the insured's property and injury to persons. It may also cover liability to third persons for injury and property damage as well as loss by fire or theft.

A life insurance policy requires the insurer to pay a stated sum of money to a named beneficiary upon the death of the insured. It may be a term insurance policy, a whole life policy, or an endowment policy. State law commonly requires the inclusion of an incontestability clause, whereby at the conclusion of the contestability period, the insurer cannot contest the validity of the policy.

Learning Outcomes

After studying this chapter, you should be able to clearly explain:

35-1 The Insurance Contract

LO.1 Explain the necessity of having an insurable interest to obtain an insurance policy
> See the Vin Harrington example of insurable interest in property, page 697.
> See the discussion of a creditor's insurable interest in the life of a debtor, page 698.

LO.2 Recognize that the formation of a contract is governed by the general principles of contract law
> See how insurers stop "STOLI" schemes through the application process where false answers to material questions make the insurance contract voidable by insurer, page 699.

LO.3 Explain why courts strictly construe insurance policies against insurance companies
> See the discussion and examples in which the courts awarded coverage for the insured because the insurers chose the ambiguous language of the policies, page 701.

> See the example in which a court determined a husband was not an insured under the contractual definition of "spouse," pages 709–710.

35-2 Kinds of Insurance

LO.4 List and explain the five major categories of insurance
> See the description on business liability insurance, marine and inland insurance, fire and homeowners insurance, automobile insurance, and life insurance, pages 705–712.
> See the CGL application to a food truck as "mobile" equipment, page 705.

LO.5 Explain coinsurance and its purpose
> See the example of the homeowner who underinsured his property, resulting in the insurer paying a claim at a proportionate share of the amount of insurance required, pages 708–709.

LO.6 Explain incontestability clauses
> See the example of the handling of imposter fraud after the incontestability period has run out, page 712.

Key Terms

beneficiary	endowment insurance	inland marine
cargo insurance	fire insurance policy	insurance
cash surrender value	freight insurance	insurance agent
coinsurance clause	homeowners insurance policy	insurance broker
disability	hull insurance	insured
double indemnity	incontestability clause	insurer

liability insurance

marine insurance

ocean marine

policy

risk

subrogation

term insurance

underwriter

whole life insurance

Questions and Case Problems

1. Mr. Keyes was injured on April 30, 2010, when he fell off Ms. Thibodeaux's roof. Mr. Keyes was cleaning and measuring the roof in preparation for painting when, unbeknownst to him, Ms. Thibodeaux sprayed a section of the metal roof with water. Mr. Keyes slipped on the wet roof and fell, seriously injuring himself. He filed the lawsuit under Ms. Thibodeaux's homeowners policy against Lighthouse Property Insurance. Mr. Keyes and Ms. Thibodeaux married in August of 2008 but physically separated four months into the marriage. Mr. Keyes and Ms. Thibodeaux have not divorced. Mr. Keyes testified that he lives in a home he owns with his grandmother and aunt. He stated that he lived in that house prior to marrying Ms. Thibodeaux and returned there after he was kicked out of her home 15 months prior to the accident. The homeowners policy precluded coverage for bodily injury to the named insured and relatives "who are residents of the insured's household." The definitions section of the policy states that the spouse of the name insured is treated as the named insured, if a resident of the same household. Lighthouse has refused coverage for Keyes under its reading of the policy. Keyes disagrees. Decide. [*Keyes v. Thibodeaux*, 85 So. 3d 1284 (La. App.)]

2. Cecil Usher owned Belize NY, Inc. (Belize), a small construction company doing business in New York City. Belize purchased a commercial general liability insurance policy from Mount Vernon Fire Insurance Co. The policy's first page, entitled "Policy Declarations," describes the insured as "Belize N.Y., Inc."; it classifies the "Form of Business" as "Corporation," the "Business Description" as "Carpentry," and indicates that Belize was afforded commercial liability insurance in the amount of $1,000,000 per occurrence and $2,000,000 in the aggregate for the period June 1, 1995, to June 1, 1996. Two classifications are listed under "Premium Computation" on the Declarations page: "Carpentry—Interior—001" and "Carpentry—001." The policy makes no further mention of these two terms. Belize performed some $60,000 of demolition work on the United House of Prayer's renovation project on 272 West 125th Street in New York City. Belize was thereafter hired to supervise subcontractors working on the job. During that period of time, a person entered the building, shot several people with a firearm, and started a fire. Seven people died and several others were injured. The estates of the victims sued Belize, Inc., for "negligence, carelessness and recklessness" regarding the fire, and Belize notified Mount Vernon of the lawsuit. Mount Vernon refused to defend or indemnify Belize because Belize was not engaging in its carpentry operations in the building at the time of the incident. It asserted that its risk is limited to carpentry operations in accordance with the classifications set forth in the policy. Belize contended that the language of the policy did not provide that the classification "Carpentry" defined covered risks, and exclusions should have been stated in the contract. Decide. [*Mount Vernon Fire Insurance Co. v. Belize NY, Inc.*, 227 F.3d 232 (2d Cir.)]

3. Gerhard Schillers was assisting his friend J.L. Loethen in removing a transmission from the bed of the Loethens' truck on the Loethens' property. While Schillers was carrying the transmission down the driveway, he fell and was seriously injured. J.L. was insured under his parents' automobile insurance policy with Shelter Mutual Insurance Company, which insured for liability, including "the loading and unloading" of the vehicle. Is Shelter Mutual liable to Schillers for the injury under its motor vehicle liability policy? Decide. [*American Family Mutual Ins. Co. v. Shelter Mutual Ins. Co.*, 747 S.W.2d 174 (Mo. App.)]

4. From the United Insurance Co., Rebecca Foster obtained a policy insuring the life of Lucille McClurkin and naming herself as beneficiary. McClurkin did not live with Foster, and Foster did not inform McClurkin of the existence of the policy. Foster paid the premiums on the policy and upon the death of McClurkin sued the United Insurance Co. for the amount of the insurance. At the trial, Foster testified vaguely that her father had told her that McClurkin was her second cousin on his side of the family. Was Foster entitled to recover on the

policy? [*Foster v. United Ins. Co.*, 158 S.E.2d 201 (S.C.)]

5. Dr. George Allard and his brother-in-law, Tom Rowland, did not get along after family land that was once used solely by Rowland was partitioned among family members after the death of Rowland's father. Rowland had a reputation in the community as a bully and a violent person. On December 17, Allard was moving cattle down a dirt road by "trolling" (leading the cattle with a bucket of feed, causing them to follow him). When he saw a forestry truck coming along the road, he led the cattle off the road onto Rowland's land to prevent frightening the cattle. When Rowland saw Allard, Rowland ran toward him screaming at him for being on his land. Allard, a small older man, retreated to his truck and obtained a 12-gauge shotgun. He pointed the gun toward the ground about an inch in front of Rowland's left foot and fired it. He stated that he fired the shot in this fashion to bring Rowland to his senses and that Rowland stepped forward into the line of fire. Allard claimed that if Rowland had not stepped forward, he would not have been hit and injured. Allard was insured by Farm Bureau homeowners and general liability policies, which did not cover liability resulting from intentional acts by the insured. Applying the policy exclusion to the facts of this case, was Farm Bureau obligated to pay the $100,000 judgment against Allard? [*Southern Farm Bureau Casualty Co. v. Allard*, 611 So. 2d 966 (Miss.)]

6. Arthur Katz testified for the U.S. government in a stock manipulation case. He also pled guilty and testified against three of his law partners in an insurance fraud case. He received a six-month sentence in a halfway house and a $5,000 fine. Katz was placed in the Federal Witness Protection Program. He and his wife changed their names to Kane and moved to Florida under the program. Both he and his wife obtained new driver's licenses and Social Security numbers. Using his new identity, "Kane" obtained two life insurance policies totaling $1.5 million. He named his wife beneficiary. A routine criminal background check on Kane found no criminal history.

    From 1984 to 1987, Kane invested heavily in the stock market. On October 17, 1987, the day the stock market crashed, Kane shot and wounded his stockbroker, shot and killed the office manager, and then committed suicide. The insurers refused to pay on the policies, claiming that they never insure persons with criminal records. Mrs. Kane contended that the policies were incontestable after they had been in effect for two years. Decide. [*Bankers Security Life Ins. Society v. Kane*, 885 F.2d 820 (11th Cir.)]

7. Linda Filasky held policies issued by Preferred Risk Mutual Insurance Co. Following an injury in an automobile accident and storm damage to the roof of her home, Filasky sustained loss of income, theft of property, and water damage to her home. These three kinds of losses were covered by the policies with Preferred, but the insurer delayed unreasonably in processing her claims and raised numerous groundless objections to them. Finally, the insurer paid the claims in full. Filasky then sued the insurer for the emotional distress caused by the bad-faith delay and obstructive tactics of the insurer. The insurer defended that it had paid the claims in full and that nothing was owed Filasky. Decide. [*Filasky v. Preferred Risk Mut. Ins. Co.*, 734 P.2d 76 (Ariz.)]

8. Baurer purchased a White Freightliner tractor and agreed that his son-in-law, Britton, could use it in the trucking business. In return, Britton agreed to haul Baurer's hay and cattle, thus saving Baurer approximately $30,000 per year. Baurer insured the vehicle with Mountain West Farm Bureau Insurance Company. The policy contained an exclusionary clause that provided: "We don't insure your [truck] while it is rented or leased to others…. This does not apply to the use of your [truck] on a share expense basis." When the vehicle was destroyed, Mountain West refused to pay on the policy, contending that the arrangement between Baurer and Britton was a lease of the vehicle, which was excluded under the policy. Baurer sued, contending that it was a "share expense basis" allowed under the policy. Is the insurance policy ambiguous? What rule of contract construction applies in this case? Decide. [*Baurer v. Mountain West Farm Bureau Ins.*, 695 P.2d 1307 (Mont.)]

9. Collins obtained from South Carolina Insurance Co. a liability policy covering a Piper Colt airplane he owned. The policy provided that it did not cover loss sustained while the plane was being piloted by a person who did not have a valid pilot's certificate and a valid medical examination certificate. Collins held a valid pilot's certificate, but his medical examination certificate had expired three months before. Collins was piloting the plane when it crashed, and he was killed. The insurer denied liability because Collins did not have a valid medical certificate. It was

stipulated by both parties that the crash was in no way caused by the absence of the medical certificate. Decide. [*South Carolina Ins. Co. v. Collins*, 237 S.E.2d 358 (S.C.)]

10. Marshall Produce Co. had insured its milk- and egg-processing plant against fire. When smoke from a fire near its plant permeated the environment and was absorbed into the company's egg powder products, cans of powder delivered to the U.S. government were rejected as contaminated. Marshall Produce sued the insurance company for a total loss, but the insurer contended that there had been no fire involving the insured property and no total loss. Decide. [*Marshall Produce Co. v. St. Paul Fire & Marine Ins. Co.*, 98 N.W.2d 280 (Minn.)]

11. Amador Pena, who had three insurance policies on his life, wrote a will in which he specified that the proceeds from the insurance policies should go to his children instead of to Leticia Pena Salinas and other beneficiaries named in the policies. He died the day after writing the will. The insurance companies paid the proceeds of the policies to the named beneficiaries. The executor of Pena's estate sued Salinas and the other beneficiaries for the insurance money. Decide. [*Pena v. Salinas*, 536 S.W.2d 671 (Tex. App.)]

12. Spector owned a small automobile repair garage in rural Kansas that was valued at $80,000. He purchased fire insurance coverage against loss to the extent of $48,000. The policy contained an 80 percent coinsurance clause. A fire destroyed a portion of his parts room, causing a loss of $32,000. Spector believes he is entitled to be fully compensated for this loss, as it is less than the $48,000 of fire protection that he purchased and paid for. Is Spector correct?

13. Carman Tool & Abrasives, Inc., purchased two milling machines, FOB Taiwan, from the Dah Lih Machinery Co. Carman obtained ocean marine cargo insurance on the machines from St. Paul Fire and Marine Insurance Co. and authorized Dah Lih to arrange for the shipment of the two machines to Los Angeles, using the services of Evergreen Lines. Dah Lih booked the machinery for shipment onboard Evergreen's container ship, the *M/V Ever Giant*; arranged for the delivery of the cargo to the ship; provided all of the shipping information for the bill

of lading; and was the party to whom the bill was issued. Dah Lih then delivered the bill of lading to its bank, which in turn negotiated it to Carman's bank to authorize payment to Dah Lih. After the cargo was removed from the vessel in Los Angeles but before it was delivered to Carman, the milling machines were damaged to the extent of $115,000. Is the insurer liable to Carman? Can the insurer recover from Evergreen? [*Carman Tool & Abrasives, Inc. v. Evergreen Lines*, 871 F.2d 897 (9th Cir.)]

14. Vallot was driving his farm tractor on the highway. It was struck from the rear by a truck, overturned, exploded, and burned. Vallot was killed, and a death claim was made against All American Insurance Co. The death of Vallot was covered by the company's policy if Vallot had died from "being struck or run over by" the truck. The insurance company claimed that the policy was not applicable because Vallot had not been struck; the farm tractor had been struck, and Vallot's death occurred when the overturned tractor exploded and burned. The insurance company also claimed that it was necessary that the insured be both struck and run over by another vehicle. Decide. [*Vallot v. All American Ins. Co.*, 302 So. 2d 625 (La. App.)]

15. Anderson Development Co. (ADC) manufactures organic materials at its plant in Adrian, Michigan. The Environmental Protection Agency (EPA) sent ADC a formal notification that it was considered a "potentially responsible party" (PRP) for the release of hazardous substances into the soil and groundwater. This notice was called a *PRP letter*. ADC notified its insurer Travelers of the letter, and Travelers contended that it was not prepared to defend or cover ADC in the matter. The EPA and ADC entered a consent decree wherein ADC agreed to the cleanup activities, spending more than $6 million on the cleanup. ADC brought an action against its insurer, seeking coverage under its general liability insurance policies for the cost of its defense and the cost of cleanup. Travelers responded that its policy language "defend any suit" and "damages" did not apply to this EPA action. Decide. [*Anderson Development Co. v. Travelers Indemnity Co.*, 49 F.3d 1128 (6th Cir.)]

Agency and Employment

Agency

Learning Outcomes ‹‹‹

After studying this chapter, you should be able to

LO.1 Explain the difference between an agent and an independent contractor

LO.2 Explain three methods of creating an agency relationship

LO.3 Recognize that third persons who deal with an agent are required to take notice of acts contrary to the interests of the principal

LO.4 List and explain the duties an agent owes the principal

LO.5 Explain how the Uniform Durable Power of Attorney Act changes the common law rule on incapacity of the principal

One of the most common business relationships is that of agency. By virtue of the agency device, one person can make contracts at numerous places with many different parties at the same time.

36-1   Nature of the Agency Relationship

Agency is ordinarily based on the consent of the parties and for that reason is called a *consensual relationship*. However, the law sometimes imposes an agency relationship. If consideration is present, the agency relationship is contractual.

36-1a   Definitions and Distinctions

agency–relationship that exists between a person identified as a principal and another by virtue of which the latter may make contracts with third persons on behalf of the principal. (Parties— principal, agent, third person)

agent–person or firm who is authorized by the principal or by operation of law to make contracts with third persons on behalf of the principal.

Agency is a relationship based on an express or implied agreement by which one person, the **agent,** is authorized to act under the control of and for another, the **principal,** in negotiating and making contracts with third persons.[1] The acts of the agent obligate the principal to third persons and give the principal rights against third persons. (See Figure 36-1.)

The term *agency* is frequently used with other meanings. It is sometimes used to denote the fact that one has the right to sell certain products, such as when a dealer is

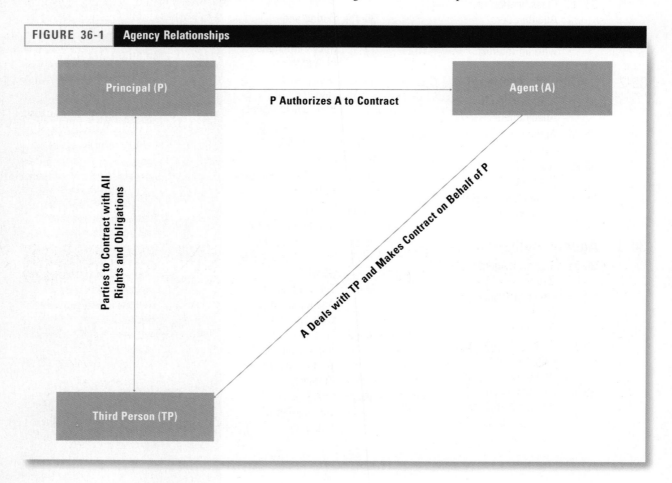

FIGURE 36-1   Agency Relationships

Principal (P)

P Authorizes A to Contract

Agent (A)

Parties to Contract with All Rights and Obligations

A Deals with TP and Makes Contract on Behalf of P

Third Person (TP)

[1] Restatement (Second) of Agency §1; *Union Miniere, S.A. v. Parday Corp.*, 521 N.E.2d 700 (Ind. App. 1988).

principal–person or firm who employs an agent; person who, with respect to a surety, is primarily liable to the third person or creditor; property held in trust.

said to possess an automobile agency. In other instances, the term is used to mean an exclusive right to sell certain articles within a given territory. In these cases, however, the dealer is not an agent in the sense of representing the manufacturer.

It is important to be able to distinguish agencies from other relationships because certain rights and duties in agencies are not present in other relationships.

Employees and Independent Contractors

Control and authority are characteristics that distinguish ordinary employees and independent contractors from agents.

Employees. An agent is distinguished from an ordinary employee who is not hired to represent the employer in making contracts with third persons. It is possible, however, for the same person to be both an agent and an employee. **For Example,** the driver for a spring water delivery service is an agent in making contracts between the company and its customers but is an employee with respect to the work of delivering products.

independent contractor–contractor who undertakes to perform a specified task according to the terms of a contract but over whom the other contracting party has no control except as provided for by the contract.

Independent Contractors. An **independent contractor** is bound by a contract to produce a certain result—for example, to build a house. The actual performance of the work is controlled by the contractor, not the owner. An agent or employee differs from an independent contractor in that the principal or employer has the right to control the agent or employee, but not the contractor, in the performance of the work. **For Example,** Ned and Tracy Seizer contract with Fox Building Company to build a new home on Hilton Head Island, South Carolina, according to referenced plans and specifications. Individuals hired by Fox to work on the home are subject to the authority and control of Fox, the independent contractor, not the Seizers. However, Ned and Tracy could decide to build the home themselves, hiring two individuals from nearby Beaufort, Ted Chase and Marty Bromley, to do the work the Seizers will direct each day. Because Ted and Marty would be employees of the Seizers, the Seizers would be held responsible for any wrongs committed by these employees within the scope of their employment. As a general rule, on the other hand, the Seizers are not responsible for the torts of Fox, the independent contractor, and the contractor's employees. A "right to control" test determines whether an individual is an agent, an employee, or an independent contractor.[2]

CASE SUMMARY

Why Some Businesses Use Independent Agents Rather than Employees!

FACTS: Patricia Yelverton died from injuries sustained when an automobile owned and driven by Joseph Lamm crossed the center line of a roadway and struck the automobile driven by Yelverton. Yelverton's executor brought suit against Lamm and Lamm's alleged employer, Premier Industrial Products Inc. The relationship between Lamm and Premier was governed by a written contract entitled "Independent Agent Agreement," in which Lamm, as

"Independent Agent," was given the right to sell Premier's products in a designated territory. The agreement provided that all orders were subject to acceptance by Premier and were not binding on Premier until so accepted. Lamm was paid by commission only. He was allowed to work on a self-determined schedule, retain assistants at his own expense, and sell the products of other companies not in competition with Premier. The executor claimed Lamm was an agent or employee of Premier. Premier stated Lamm was an independent contractor.

DECISION: Judgment for Premier. Lamm had no authority to make contracts for Premier but simply took orders.

Therefore, he was not an agent. Lamm was not an employee of Premier. Premier had no right to control the way he performed his work and did not in fact do so. Lamm was an independent contractor. [*Yelverton v. Lamm,* **380 S.E.2d 621 (N.C. App. 1989)**]

A person who appears to be an independent contractor may in fact be so controlled by the other party that the contractor is regarded as an agent of, or employee of, the controlling person. **For Example,** Pierce, who was under contract to Brookville Carriers, Inc., was involved in a tractor-trailer/car collision with Rich and others. Pierce owned the tractor involved in the accident on a lease from Brookville but could use it only to haul freight for Brookville; he had no authority to carry freight on his own, and all of his operating authority belonged to Brookville. The "owner/operator" was deemed an employee rather than independent contractor for purposes of assessing the liability of the employer.[3] The separate identity of an independent contractor may be concealed so that the public believes that it is dealing with the principal. When this situation occurs, the principal is liable as though the contractor were an agent or employee.

special agent–agent authorized to transact a specific transaction or to do a specific act.

36-1b Classification of Agents

A **special agent** is authorized by the principal to handle a definite business transaction or to do a specific act. One who is authorized by another to purchase a particular house is a special agent.

general agent–agent authorized by the principal to transact all affairs in connection with a particular type of business or trade or to transact all business at a certain place.

A **general agent** is authorized by the principal to transact all affairs in connection with a particular type of business or trade or to transact all business at a certain place. To illustrate, a person who is appointed as manager by the owner of a store is a general agent.

universal agent–agent authorized by the principal to do all acts that can lawfully be delegated to a representative.

A **universal agent** is authorized by the principal to do all acts that can be delegated lawfully to a representative. This form of agency arises when a person absent because of being in the military service gives another person a blanket power of attorney to do anything that must be done during such absence.

CPA

36-1c Agency Coupled with an Interest

interest in the authority–form of agency in which an agent has been given or paid for the right to exercise authority.

An agent has an **interest in the authority** when consideration has been given or paid for the right to exercise the authority. **For Example,** when a lender, in return for making a loan of money, is given, as security, authority to collect rents due the borrower and to apply those rents to the payment of the debt, the lender becomes the borrower's agent with an interest in the authority given to collect the rents.

interest in the subject matter–form of agency in which an agent is given an interest in the property with which that agent is dealing.

An agent has an **interest in the subject matter** when, for a consideration, she is given an interest in the property with which she is dealing. Hence, when the agent is authorized to sell property of the principal and is given a lien on such property as security for a debt owed to her by the principal, she has an interest in the subject matter.

36-2 Creating the Agency

An agency may arise by appointment, conduct, ratification, or operation of law.

[3] *Rich v. Brookville Carriers, Inc.,* 256 F. Supp. 2d 26 (D. Me. 2003).

36-2a **Authorization by Appointment**

express authorization—
authorization of an agent
to perform a certain act.

The usual method of creating an agency is by **express authorization;** that is, a person is appointed to act for, or on behalf of, another.

The authorization of the agent may be oral or in writing. **For Example,** Russell Jones, the owner of Westex, gave equipment operator Daniel Flores actual authority to sign an equipment rental agreement on behalf of Westex that acknowledged delivery of a loader to a job site.[4] However, some appointments must be made in a particular way. A majority of the states, by statute, require the appointment of an agent to be in writing when the agency is created to acquire or dispose of any interest in land. A written authorization of agency is called a **power of attorney.** An agent acting under a power of attorney is referred to as an **attorney in fact.**[5]

power of attorney—
written authorization
to an agent by the
principal.

attorney in fact—agent
authorized to act for
another under a power of
attorney.

36-2b **Authorization by Conduct**

Conduct consistent with the existence of an agency relationship may be sufficient to show authorization. The principal may have such dealing with third persons as to cause them to believe that the "agent" has authority. Thus, if the owner of a store places another person in charge, third persons may assume that the person in charge is the agent for the owner in that respect. The "agent" then appears to be authorized and is said to have *apparent authority*, and the principal is estopped from contradicting the appearance that has been created.[6]

CASE SUMMARY

The "Bulletproof Against Rust" Case. Oops! Now What?

FACTS: While constructing a hotel in Lincoln City, Oregon, the owner, Todd Taylor, became concerned about possible rusting in the exterior stucco system manufactured by ChemRex that was being installed at the hotel. The general contractor, Ramsay-Gerding, arranged a meeting with the owner, the installer, and ChemRex's territory manager for Oregon, Mike McDonald, to discuss Mr. Taylor's concerns. McDonald told those present that the SonoWall system was "bulletproof against rust," and stated that "you're getting a five-year warranty." He followed up with a letter confirming the five-year warranty on parts and labor. A year later rust discoloration appeared, and no one from ChemRex ever

fixed the problem. Taylor sued ChemRex for breach of warranty. ChemRex defended that McDonald did not have actual or apparent authority to declare such a warranty.

DECISION: Judgment for Taylor. The evidence indicated that ChemRex clothed Mike McDonald with the title of "territory manager" and gave him the actual authority to visit job sites and resolve problems. Although it denies he had actual authority, ChemRex took sufficient steps to create apparent authority to provide the five-year warranty on the stucco system. [***Taylor v. Ramsay-Gerding Construction Co.,*** 196 P.3d 532 (Or. 2008)]

The term *apparent authority* is used when there is only the appearance of authority but no actual authority, and that appearance of authority was created by the principal. The test for the existence of apparent authority is an objective test determined by the principal's outward manifestations through words or conduct that lead a third person reasonably to believe that the "agent" has authority. A principal's express restriction on authority not made known to a third person is no defense.

[4] *Jones v. Pomroy Equipment Rental, Inc.,* 438 S.W.3d 125 (Tex. App. 2014).
[5] *Lamb v. Scott,* 643 So. 2d 972 (Ala. 1994).
[6] *Intersparex Leddin KG v. AL-Haddad,* 852 S.W.2d 245 (Tenn. App. 1992).

Apparent authority extends to all acts that a person of ordinary prudence, familiar with business usages and the particular business, would be justified in believing that the agent has authority to perform. It is essential to the concept of apparent authority that the third person reasonably believe that the agent has authority. The mere placing of property in the possession of another does not give that person either actual or apparent authority to sell the property.

CPA   36-2c **Agency by Ratification**

An agent may attempt, on behalf of the principal, to do an act that was not authorized, or a person who is not the agent of another may attempt to act as such an agent. Very generally, notification may be express, where the principal explicitly approves the contract, or implied, where the principal does not object to the contract and accepts the contract's benefits. **For Example,** Morang-Kelly Investments, Inc., doing business as Farmer's Best Supermarket, denied that Mike Awdish was its authorized agent regarding the purchase and installation of used supermarket refrigerators at its Wyoming Street market. Nevertheless, by accepting the goods and services as well as the invoices for those goods and services for equipment still in use at the market it ratified Mr. Awdish's actions.[7]

Intention to Ratify

Initially, ratification is a question of intention. Just as in the case of authorization, when there is a question of whether the principal authorized the agent, there is a question of whether the principal intended to approve or ratify the action of the unauthorized agent.

The intention to ratify may be expressed in words, or it may be found in conduct indicating an intention to ratify. **For Example,** James Reiner signed a five-year lease of commercial space on 320 West Main Street in Avon, Connecticut, because his father, Calvin, was away on vacation, and the owner, Robert Udolf, told James that if he did not come in and sign the lease, his father would lose the opportunity to rent the space in question. James was aware that his father had an interest in the space, and while telling Robert several times that he had no authority, James did sign his name to the lease. In fact, his father took occupancy of the space and paid rent for three years and then abandoned the space. James is not liable on the remainder of the lease because the owner knew at the time of signing that James did not have authority to act. Although he did not sign the lease, Calvin ratified the lease signed by James by his conduct of moving into the space and doing business there for three years with full knowledge of all material facts relating to the transaction. The owner, therefore, had to bring suit against Calvin, not James.[8]

Conditions for Ratification

In addition to the intent to ratify, expressed in some instances with a certain formality, the following conditions must be satisfied for the intention to take effect as a ratification:

1. The agent must have purported to act on behalf of or as agent for the identified principal.

2. The principal must have been capable of authorizing the act both at the time of the act and at the time it was ratified.

3. The principal must have full knowledge of all material facts.

---

[7] *Bellevue Ventures, Inc. v. Morang-Kelly Investments, Inc.* 836 N.W.2d 898 (Mich. App. 2013).
[8] *Udolf v. Reiner,* 2000 WL 726953 (Conn. Super. May 19, 2000).

It is not always necessary, however, to show that the principal had actual knowledge. Knowledge will be imputed if a principal knows of other facts that would lead a prudent person to make inquiries or if that knowledge can be inferred from the knowledge of other facts or from a course of business. **For Example,** Stacey, without authorization but knowing that William needed money, contracted to sell one of William's paintings to Courtney for $298. Stacey told William about the contract that evening; William said nothing and helped her wrap the painting in a protective plastic wrap for delivery. A favorable newspaper article about William's art appeared the following morning and dramatically increased the value of all of his paintings. William cannot recover the painting from Courtney on the theory that he never authorized the sale because he ratified the unauthorized contract made by Stacey by his conduct in helping her wrap the painting with full knowledge of the terms of the sale. The effect is a legally binding contract between William and Courtney.

Effect of Ratification

When an unauthorized act is ratified, the effect is the same as though the act had been originally authorized. Ordinarily, this means that the principal and the third party are bound by the contract made by the agent.[9] When the principal ratifies the act of the unauthorized person, such ratification releases that person from the liability that would otherwise be imposed for having acted without authority.

CPA ### 36-2d Proving the Agency Relationship

The burden of proving the existence of an agency relationship rests on the person who seeks to benefit by such proof. The third person who desires to bind the principal because of the act of an alleged agent has the burden of proving that the latter person was in fact the authorized agent of the principal and possessed the authority to do the act in question.[10]

36-3 Agent's Authority

When there is an agent, it is necessary to determine the scope of the agent's authority.

36-3a Scope of Agent's Authority

The scope of an agent's authority may be determined from the express words of the principal to the agent or it may be implied from the principal's words or conduct or from the customs of the trade or business.

Express Authority

If the principal tells the agent to perform a certain act, the agent has express authority to do so. Express authority can be given orally or in writing.

Incidental Authority

incidental authority— authority of an agent that is reasonably necessary to execute express authority.

An agent has implied **incidental authority** to perform any act reasonably necessary to execute the express authority given to the agent. **For Example,** if the principal authorizes the agent to purchase goods without furnishing funds to the agent to pay for them, the agent has the implied incidental authority to purchase the goods on credit.[11]

[9] *McCurley Chevrolet v. Rutz*, 808 P.2d 1167 (Wash. App. 1991).
[10] *Cummings, Inc. v. Nelson*, 115 P.3d 536 (Alaska 2005).
[11] *Badger v. Paulson Investment Co.*, 803 P.2d 1178 (Or. 1991).

customary authority–
authority of an agent to do any act that, according to the custom of the community, usually accompanies the transaction for which the agent is authorized to act.

apparent authority–
appearance of authority created by the principal's words or conduct.

Customary Authority

An agent has implied **customary authority** to do any act that, according to the custom of the community, usually accompanies the transaction for which the agent is authorized to act. An agent who has express authority to receive payments from third persons, for example, has the implied customary authority to issue receipts.

Apparent Authority

A person has **apparent authority** as an agent when the principal's words or conduct leads a third person to reasonably believe that the person has that authority and the third person relies on that appearance.[12]

CASE SUMMARY

CSX Gets Railroaded by Albert Arillotta

FACTS: Recovery Express and Interstate Demolition (IDEC) are two separate corporations located at the same business address in Boston. On August 22, 2003, Albert Arillotta, a "partner" at IDEC, sent an e-mail to Len Whitehead, Jr., of CSX Transportation expressing an interest in buying "rail cars as scrap." Arillotta represented himself to be "from interstate demolition and recovery express" in the e-mail. The e-mail address from which he sent his inquiry was **albert@recoveryexpress.com.** Arillotta went to the CSX rail yard, disassembled the cars, and transported them away. Thereafter CSX sent invoices for the scrap rail cars totaling $115,757.36 addressed to IDEC at its Boston office shared with Recovery Express. Whitehead believed Arillotta was authorized to act for Recovery Express, based on the e-mail's domain name, recoveryexpress.com. Recovery claims that Arillotta never worked for it. Recovery's president, Thomas Trafton, allowed the "fledgling" company to use telephone, fax, and e-mail services at its offices but never shared anything—assets, funds, books of business, or financials with IDEC—CSX sued Recovery for the invoice amount on the doctrine of "apparent authority." IDEC is now defunct. Recovery claims that Arillotta never worked for it and that it is not liable.

DECISION: Judgment for Recovery. Issuance of an e-mail address with Recovery's domain name to an individual who shared office space with Recovery did not give the individual, Albert Arillotta, apparent authority to enter contracts on Recovery's behalf. No reasonable person could conclude that Arillotta had apparent authority on the basis of an e-mail domain name by itself. Given the anonymity of the Internet, the court warned businesses to take additional action to verify a purported agent's authority to make a deal. [*CSX Transportation, Inc. v. Recovery Express, Inc.*, 415 F. Supp. 2d 6 (D. Mass. 2006)]

36-3b Effect of Proper Exercise of Authority

When an agent with authority properly makes a contract with a third person that purports to bind the principal, there is by definition a binding contract between the principal and the third person. The agent is not a party to this contract. Consequently, when the owner of goods is the principal, the owner's agent is not liable for breach of warranty with respect to the goods "sold" by the agent. The owner-principal, not the agent, was the "seller" in the sales transaction.

[12] *Alexander v. Chandler*, 179 S.W.2d 385 (Mo. App. 2005).

CPA **36-3c Duty to Ascertain Extent of Agent's Authority**

A third person who deals with a person claiming to be an agent cannot rely on the statements made by the agent concerning the extent of authority.[13] If the agent is not authorized to perform the act or is not even the agent of the principal, the transaction between the alleged agent and the third person will have no legal effect between the principal and the third person. It is imperative that one who deals exclusively with an agent must recognize that it is his or her responsibility to ascertain the scope of that agent's authority. **For Example,** the Articles of Organization of limited liability company, Zions Gate R.V. Resort, provide that Zions Gate shall be managed by two managers, Jones and Sorpold, and the Articles require the consent and approval of both managers to constitute the act of the entity. Utah LLC law states that Articles of Organization filed with the state constitute notice of its content to third persons. Thus a 99-year RV lot lease to Oliphant signed only by manager Sorpold was invalid because Oliphant was deemed to have notice of the limitation on Sorpold's authority. Oliphant argued that it was unreasonable and unrealistic to expect individuals to acquire Articles of Organization to determine if the signatory to an agreement is authorized to act for the entity. The court responded that it is not its prerogative to question the statutory scheme enacted by the legislation.[14]

Third persons who deal with an agent whose authority is limited to a special purpose are bound at their peril to find out the extent of the agent's authority. An attorney is such an agent. Unless the client holds the attorney out as having greater authority than usual, the attorney has no authority to settle a claim without approval from the client.

Agent's Acts Adverse to Principal

The third person who deals with an agent is required to take notice of any acts that are clearly adverse to the interest of the principal. Thus, if the agent is obviously using funds of the principal for the agent's personal benefit, persons dealing with the agent should recognize that the agent may be acting without authority and that they are dealing with the agent at their peril.

The only certain way that third persons can protect themselves is to inquire of the principal whether the agent is in fact the agent of the principal and has the necessary authority. **For Example,** Ron Fahd negotiated the sale of a fire truck to the Edinburg Volunteer Fire Company on behalf of the manufacturer, Danko Company, at a price of $158,000. On Danko forms and letterhead Fahd drafted a "Proposal for Fire Apparatus" and it was signed by the president of the Fire Company and Fahd, as a dealer for Danko. Fahd gave a special $2,000 discount for prepayment of the cost of the chassis. Fahd directed that the prepayment check of $55,000 be made payable to "Ron Fahd Sales" in order to obtain the discount. The Fire Company's treasurer inquired of Fahd why the prepayment check was being made out to Fahd rather than Danko, and he accepted Fahd's answer without contacting Danko to confirm this unusual arrangement. Fahd absconded with the proceeds of the check. The Fire Company sued Danko, claiming Fahd had apparent authority to receive the prepayment. While there was some indicia of agency, the court found that the Fire Company had failed to make reasonable inquiry with Danko to verify Fahd's authority to receive the prepayment in Fahd's name, and it rejected the claim that Fahd had apparent authority to accept the prepayment check made out to Fahd as opposed to Danko.[15]

[13] *Breed v. Hughes Aircraft Col.*, 35 Fed. App. 864 (Fed. Cir. 2002).
[14] *Zions Gate R.V. Resort, LLC v. Oliphant*, 326 P.3d 118 (Utah App. 2014).
[15] *Edinburg Volunteer Fire Company v. Danko*, 867 N.Y.S.2d 547 (A.D. 2008).

36-3d Limitations on Agent's Authority

A person who has knowledge of a limitation on the agent's authority cannot ignore that limitation. When the third person knows that the authority of the agent depends on whether financing has been obtained, the principal is not bound by the act of the agent if the financing in fact was not obtained. If the authority of the agent is based on a writing and the third person knows that there is such a writing, the third person is charged with knowledge of limitations contained in it.

"Obvious" Limitations

In some situations, it may be obvious to third persons that they are dealing with an agent whose authority is limited. When third persons know that they are dealing with a representative of a government agency, they should recognize that such a person will ordinarily have limited authority. Third persons should recognize that a contract made with such an officer or representative may not be binding unless ratified by the principal.

The federal government places the risk on any individual making arrangements with the government to accurately ascertain that the government agent is within the bounds of his or her authority.

CASE SUMMARY

Humlen Was Had?

FACTS: The FBI approached Humlen for assistance in securing the conviction of a drug trafficker. Humlen executed an agreement with the FBI to formalize his status as an informant. The agreement he signed contained compensation figures significantly less than those he had been promised by the FBI agents with whom he was dealing. Humlen claims that five agents repeatedly assured him that he would receive the extra compensation they had discussed with him, despite the wording of the contract. It was explained that the agreement had to be "couched" in that way because it was a discoverable document in any future criminal prosecution and thus could be used to destroy his credibility. Based on the information provided by Humlen, an arrest was made, and Humlen sought the remainder of his promised monetary reward from the FBI. The FBI refused to pay him any more than the contract stipulated. When no additional payment was forthcoming, Humlen sued the U.S. government.

DECISION: Judgment for the United States. The government, unlike private parties, cannot be bound by the apparent authority of its agents. When an agent exceeds his or her authority, the government can disavow the agent's words and is not bound by an implied contract. As a general rule, FBI agents lack the requisite actual authority—either express or implied—to contractually bind the United States to remit rewards to confidential informants. Moreover, Humlen's claims directly collide with the plain language of the agreement. [*Humlen v. United States*, 49 Fed. Cl. 497 (2001)]

Secret Limitations

If the principal has clothed an agent with authority to perform certain acts but the principal gives secret instructions that limit the agent's authority, the third person is allowed to take the authority of the agent at its face value. The third person is not bound by the secret limitations of which the third person has no knowledge.

36-4 Duties and Liabilities of Principal and Agent

The creation of the principal-agent relationship gives rise to duties and liabilities.

36-4a Duties and Liabilities of Agent during Agency

While the agency relationship exists, the agent owes certain duties to the principal.

Loyalty

An agent must be loyal or faithful to the principal.[16] The agent must not obtain any secret benefit from the agency.

CASE SUMMARY

Impermissible Practices Involving Art Dealers with Russian Clients? No Way!

FACTS: On July 23, 2008, Luba Mosionzhnik, a 25 percent shareholder and vice president of the Gallery, was summoned to a meeting by Ezra Chowaiki, a 25 percent shareholder and president of the Gallery, and financial backer David Dangoor, a 50 percent shareholder. She was accused of a myriad of improprieties and fired from her employment. Section 42 of the Shareholders Agreement provided that upon termination of an employee who owned stock, he or she would be required to sell their shares to the Gallery. Mosionzhnik admitted to committing the most egregious of the alleged improper acts. She secretly opened a Swiss bank account, which she used to divert approximately $500,000 related to the Gallery's art sales, and used over $13 million of art consigned by the Gallery's clients as collateral for loans without the clients' consent. Rather than deny these allegations, at her deposition, Mosionzhnik testified that her actions were not improper and noted that "plenty of advisors take a kickback … that's not ethical but it happens because it's the art world." With respect to illegally using client art as collateral, her defense is that Chowaiki also did so and told her that such a thing was accepted practice in the industry. The Holtz accounting firm determined that Mosionzhnik shares were worth $170,000. The Gallery seeks to recover from Mosionzhnik for her improprieties. She seeks to keep the $500,000 in the Swiss bank account and believes her shares are worth $4,367,200 as valued by her experts "GMSL."

DECISION: While the Shareholder's Agreement permitted Mosionzknik to engage in private art transactions for her own benefit, the deals that led to the $500,000 secretly transferred to a Swiss bank account were all related to Gallery transactions with Russian clients. Taking a kickback on a finder's fee is legally impermissible, even if such a practice is pervasive in the art world. Consequently she must pay the $500,000 in kickbacks to the Gallery. Mosionzhnik's and Chowaiki's cross-accusations of improprieties are barred from consideration by the court by the doctrine of *in pari delicto*. The court will not intercede to resolve disputes between wrongdoers, especially with the Gallery itself benefitting from all sorts of shady practices regarding its Russian business. Mosionzhnik is nevertheless entitled to be paid the fair market valid of her shares, $170,000 as calculated by the Holtz accounting firm in accordance with the Shareholder's Agreement, because her equity is not compensation for services. [*Mosionzhnik v. Chowaiki*, 972 N.Y.S.2d 841 (A.D. 2013)]

Alternatively, the principal can approve the transaction and sue the agent for any secret profit obtained by the agent.

A contract is voidable by the principal if the agent who was employed to sell the property purchases the property, either directly or indirectly, without full disclosure to the principal.

An agent cannot act as agent for both parties to a transaction unless both know of the dual capacity and agree to it. If the agent does act in this capacity without the consent of both parties, any principal who did not know of the agent's double status can avoid the transaction.

---

[16] *Patterson Custom Homes v. Bach*, 536 F. Supp. 2d 1026 (E.D. Ill. 2008).

An agent must not accept secret gifts or commissions from third persons in connection with the agency. If the agent does so, the principal may sue the agent for those gifts or commissions. Such practices are condemned because the judgment of the agent may be influenced by the receipt of gifts or commissions.

It is a violation of an agent's duty of loyalty to make and retain secret profits or to secretly usurp the business opportunities of the principal.

CASE SUMMARY

Was Grappolini a "Bad Boy"?

FACTS: Arthur Frigo, an adjunct professor at the Kellogg Graduate School of Management, formed Lucini Italia Co. (Lucini) to import and sell premium extra virgin olive oil and other products from Italy. Lucini's officers hired Guiseppe Grappolini as their olive oil supplier. They also hired him as their consultant. Grappolini signed an exclusivity agreement and a confidentiality agreement acknowledging the confidential nature of Lucini's product development, plans, and strategies. Grappolini was "branded" as a "master cultivator" in Lucini's literature and commercials.

In 1998, Lucini and Grappolini, as his consultant, discussed adding a line of extra virgin olive oils blended with "essential oils," for example, natural extracts such as lemon and garlic. It spent more than $800,000 developing the market information, testing flavors, designing labels and packaging, creating recipes, and generating trade secrets for the new products. Vegetal-Progress s.r.l. (Vegetal) was identified as the only company in Italy that was capable of producing the superior products Lucini sought, and Grappolini was assigned responsibility to obtain an exclusive supply contract with Vegetal.

In direct contravention of his representations to Lucini, Grappolini secretly negotiated an exclusive supply contract for the Grappolini Co., not for Lucini. Moreover, Grappolini Co. began to sell flavored olive oils in the United States, which coincided with Lucini's market research and recipe development that had been disclosed to Grappolini. When Lucini officers contacted Vegetal, they acknowledged that Grappolini was a "bad boy" in procuring the contract for his own company rather than for Lucini, but they would not renege on the contract. Lucini sued Grappolini.

DECISION: Judgment for Lucini. Grappolini was Lucini's agent and owed Lucini a duty to advance Lucini's interests, not his own. When he obtained an exclusive supply agreement with Vegetal for the Grappolini Co. instead of Lucini, he was disloyal and breached his fiduciary duties. As a result, Lucini suffered lost profits and damages of $4.17 million. In addition to these damages, Grappolini was ordered to pay $1,000,000 in punitive damages to deter similar acts in the future. Additionally, a permanent injunction was issued prohibiting Grappolini from using Lucini's trade secrets. [*Lucini Italia Co. v. Grappolini*, 2003 WL 1989605 (N.D. Ill. 2003)]

An agent is, of course, prohibited from aiding the competitors of a principal or disclosing to them information relating to the business of the principal. It is also a breach of duty for the agent to knowingly deceive a principal.[17]

Obedience and Performance

An agent is under a duty to obey all lawful instructions.[18] The agent is required to perform the services specified for the period and in the way specified. An agent who does not do so is liable to the principal for any harm caused. For example, if an agent is instructed to take cash payments only but accepts a check in payment, the agent is liable for the loss caused the principal if a check is dishonored by nonpayment.

[17] *Koontz v. Rosener*, 787 P.2d 192 (Colo. App. 1990).
[18] *Stanford v. Neiderer*, 341 S.E.2d 892 (Ga. App. 1986).

Reasonable Care

It is the duty of an agent to act with the care that a reasonable person would exercise under the circumstances. **For Example,** Ethel Wilson applied for fire insurance for her house with St. Paul Reinsurance Co., Ltd., through her agent Club Services Corp. She thought she was fully covered. Unbeknown to her, however, St. Paul had refused coverage and returned her premium to Club Services, which did not refund it to Ms. Wilson or inform her that coverage had been denied. Fire destroyed her garage and St. Paul denied coverage. Litigation resulted, and St. Paul ended up expending $305,406 to settle the Wilson matter. Thereafter, St. Paul successfully sued Club Services Corp. under basic agency law principles that an agent (Club Services) is liable to its principal for all damages resulting from the agent's failure to discharge its duties.[19] In addition, if the agent possesses a special skill, as in the case of a broker or an attorney, the agent must exercise that skill.

Accounting

An agent must account to the principal for all property or money belonging to the principal that comes into the agent's possession. The agent must, within a reasonable time, give notice of collections made and render an accurate account of all receipts and expenditures. The agency agreement may state at what intervals or on what dates such accountings are to be made. An agent must keep the principal's property and money separate and distinct from that of the agent.

Information

It is the duty of an agent to keep the principal informed of all facts relating to the agency that are relevant to protecting the principal's interests.[20]

36-4b Duties and Liabilities of Agent after Termination of Agency

When the agency relationship ends, the duties of the agent continue only to the extent necessary to perform prior obligations. For example, the agent must return to the former principal any property that had been entrusted to the agent for the purpose of the agency. With the exception of such "winding-up" duties, the agency relationship is terminated, and the former agent can deal with the principal as freely as with a stranger.[21]

36-4c Duties and Liabilities of Principal to Agent

The principal must perform the contract, compensate the agent for services, make reimbursement for proper expenditures, and, under certain circumstances, must indemnify the agent for loss.

Employment According to Terms of Contract

When the contract is for a specified time, the principal is obligated to permit the agent to act as agent for the term of the contract. Exceptions are made for just cause or contract provisions that permit the principal to terminate the agency sooner. If the principal gives the agent an exclusive right to act in that capacity, the principal cannot give anyone else

---

[19] *St. Paul Reinsurance Co., Ltd. v. Club Services Corp.*, 30 Fed. Appx. 834 (10th Cir. 2002).

[20] Restatement (Second) of Agency §381; *Lumberman's Mutual Ins. Co. v. Franey Muha Alliant Ins.*, 388 F. Supp. 2d 292 (S.D.N.Y. 2005).

[21] *Corron & Black of Illinois, Inc. v. Magner*, 494 N.E.2d 785 (Ill. App. 1986).

the authority to act as agent, nor may the principal do the act to which the exclusive agent's authority relates. **For Example,** if Jill Baker gives Brett Stamos the exclusive right for six months to sell her house, she cannot give another real estate agent the right to sell it during the six-month period or undertake to sell the house herself. If the principal or another agent sells the house, the exclusive agent is entitled to full compensation just as though the act had been performed by the exclusive agent.

Compensation

The principal must pay the agent the agreed compensation.[22] If the parties have not fixed the amount of the compensation by their agreement but intended that the agent should be paid, the agent may recover the customary compensation for such services. If there is no established compensation, the agent may recover the reasonable value of the services rendered.

Repeating Transactions. In certain industries, third persons make repeated transactions with the principal. In these cases, the agent who made the original contract with the third person commonly receives a certain compensation or percentage of commissions on all subsequent renewal or additional contracts. In the insurance business, for example, the insurance agent obtaining the policyholder for the insurer receives a substantial portion of the first year's premiums and then receives a smaller percentage of the premiums paid by the policyholder in subsequent years.

Postagency Transactions. An agent is not ordinarily entitled to compensation in connection with transactions, such as sales or renewals of insurance policies, occurring after the termination of the agency even if the postagency transactions are the result of the agent's former activities. However, if the parties' employment contract calls for such compensation, it must be paid. **For Example,** real estate agent Laura McLane's contract called for her to receive $1.50 for every square foot the Atlanta Committee for the Olympic Games, Inc. (ACOG), leased at an Atlanta building; and even though she had been terminated at the time ACOG executed a lease amendment for 164,412 additional square feet, she was contractually entitled to a $246,618 commission.[23]

36-5 Termination of Agency

An agency may be terminated by the act of one or both of the parties to the agency agreement or by operation of law. When the authority of an agent is terminated, the agent loses all right to act for the principal.

36-5a Termination by Act of Parties

The duration of the agency relationship is commonly stated in the contract creating the relationship. In most cases, either party has the power to terminate the agency relationship at any time. However, the terminating party may be liable for damages to the other if the termination is in violation of the agency contract.

When a principal terminates an agent's authority, it is not effective until the agent receives the notice. Because a known agent will have the appearance of still being an agent, notice must be given to third persons of the termination, and the agent may have the power to bind the principal and third persons until this notice is given.

---

[22] *American Chocolates, Inc. v. Mascot Pecan Co., Inc.,* 592 So. 2d 93 (Miss. 1992).
[23] *McLane v. Atlanta Market Center Management Co.,* 486 S.E.2d 30 (Ga. App. 1997).

36-5b Termination by Operation of Law

The agency relationship is a personal one, and anything that renders one of the parties incapable of performing will result in the termination of the relationship by operation of law. The death of either the principal or the agent ordinarily terminates the authority of an agent automatically even if the death is unknown to the other.[24]

An agency is also terminated by operation of law on the (1) insanity of the principal or agent, (2) bankruptcy of the principal or agent, (3) impossibility of performance, such as the destruction of the subject matter, or (4) when the country of the principal is at war with that of the agent.

CASE SUMMARY

Missing Out by Minutes

FACTS: William Moore, a fire chief for the city of San Francisco, suffered severe head injuries in a fall while fighting a fire. Moore sued the building owner, Lera, for negligence. The attorneys for the parties held a conference and reached a settlement at 5:15 P.M. Unknown to them, Moore had died at 4:50 P.M. on that day. Was the settlement agreement binding?

DECISION: No. The death of either the principal or the agent terminates the agency. Thus, the death of a client terminates the authority of his agent to act on his behalf. Because Moore died at 4:50 P.M., his attorney no longer had authority to act on his behalf, and the settlement was not enforceable. [*Moore v. Lera Development Inc.*, 274 **Cal. Rptr. 658 (Cal. App. 1990)**]

36-5c Disability of the Principal under the UDPAA

The Uniform Durable Power of Attorney Act (UDPAA) permits the creation of an agency by specifying that "this power of attorney shall not be affected by subsequent disability or incapacity of the principal." Alternatively, the UDPAA permits the agency to come into existence upon the disability or incapacity of the principal. For this to be effective, the principal must designate the attorney in fact in writing. The writing must contain words showing the intent of the principal that the authority conferred shall continue notwithstanding the disability or incapacity of the principal. The UDPAA, which has been adopted by most states,[25] changes the common law and the general rule that insanity of the principal terminates the agent's authority to act for the principal. Society today recognizes that it may be in the best interest of a principal and good for the business environment for a principal to designate another as an attorney in fact to act for the principal when the principal becomes incapacitated.[26] It may be prudent to grant durable powers of attorney to different persons for property matters and for health care decisions.

---

[24] *New York Life Ins. Co. v. Estate of Haelen*, 521 N.Y.S.2d 970 (N.Y. Civ. Ct. 1987).

[25] The Uniform Durable Power of Attorney Act has been adopted in some fashion in all states except Connecticut, Florida, Georgia, Illinois, Indiana, Kansas, Louisiana, and Missouri.

[26] The Uniform Probate Code and the Uniform Durable Power of Attorney Act provide for the coexistence of durable powers and guardians or conservators. These acts allow the attorney in fact to continue to manage the principal's financial affairs while the court-appointed fiduciary takes the place of the principal in overseeing the actions of the attorney in fact. See *Rice v. Flood*, 768 S.W.2d 57 (Ky. 1989).

Durable powers of attorney grant only those powers that are specified in the instrument.[27] A durable power of attorney may be terminated by revocation by a competent principal and by the death of the principal.

CASE SUMMARY

Broad Powers ... But There Is a Limit, Lucille

FACTS: On May 31, 2000, Thomas Graham made his niece Lucille Morrison his attorney in fact by executing a durable power of attorney. It was notarized and filed at the Registry of Deeds. The power of attorney granted Lucille broad powers and discretion in Graham's affairs. However, it did not contain express authority to make gifts. On October 26, 2000, Lucille conveyed 11.92 acres of property valued at between $400,000 and $700,000 to herself based on consideration of services rendered to the principal, Thomas Graham. On June 5, 2001, Lucille, as attorney in fact for Graham, conveyed Graham's house in Charlotte to her son Ladd Morrison. On June 20, 2001, she conveyed Graham's Oakview Terrace property to her brother John Hallman for $3,000 to pay for an attorney to defend Graham in a competency proceeding. Thomas Graham died on August 7, 2001, and his estate sued to set aside the deeds, alleging Lucille's breach of fiduciary duties. After a judgment for the defendants, the estate appealed.

DECISION: Judgment for the estate regarding the 11.92-acre parcel of land Lucille conveyed to herself. When an attorney in fact conveys property to herself based on consideration of services rendered to the principal, the consideration must reflect a fair and reasonable price when compared with the market value of the property. There was no testimony regarding the value of Lucille's services compared with the value of the real property. The deed must be set aside. The conveyance of Graham's home to Ladd Morrison was a gift that was not authorized by her power of attorney and must be set aside. Lucille had authority to sell the principal's property to John Hallman to obtain funds to pay an attorney to represent the principal. The estate's claim of conversion regarding this sale was denied. [*Estate of Graham v. Morrison*, 607 S.E.2d 295 (N.C. App. 2005)]

36-5d Termination of Agency Coupled with an Interest

An agency coupled with an interest is an exception to the general rule as to the termination of an agency. Such an agency cannot be revoked by the principal before the expiration of the interest. It is not terminated by the death or insanity of either the principal or the agent.

36-5e Protection of Agent from Termination of Authority

The modern world of business has developed several methods of protecting an agent from the termination of authority for any reason.[28]

These methods include the use of an exclusive agency contract, a secured transaction, an escrow deposit, a standby letter of agreement, or a guarantee agreement.

---

[27] An attorney in fact (the holder of a power of attorney) may make decisions concerning litigation for the principal, such as deciding to settle a case, but a non-lawyer attorney in fact may not act as a lawyer to implement those decisions, nor may such an individual testify in place of an otherwise competent party in matters such as a divorce. See *Marisco v. Marisco*, 94 A.3d 947 (N.J. Super. 2013).

[28] These methods generally replace the concept of an agency coupled with an interest because of the greater protection given to the agent. Typically, the rights of the agent under these modern devices cannot be defeated by the principal, by operation of law, or by claims of other creditors.

36-5f Effect of Termination of Authority

If the principal revokes the agency, the authority to act for the principal is not terminated until the agent receives notice of revocation. As between the principal and the agent, the right of the agent to bind the principal to third persons generally ends immediately upon the termination of the agent's authority. This termination is effective without giving notice to third persons.

When the agency is terminated by the act of the principal, notice must be given to third persons. If this notice is not given, the agent may have the power to make contracts that will bind the principal and third persons. This rule is predicated on the theory that a known agent will have the appearance of still being the agent unless notice to the contrary is given to third persons.[29] **For Example,** Seltzer owns property in Boca Raton that he uses for the month of February and leases the remainder of the year. O'Neil has been Seltzer's rental agent for the past seven years, renting to individuals like Ed Tucker under a power of attorney that gives him authority to lease the property for set seasonal and off-season rates. O'Neil's right to bind Seltzer on a rental agreement ended when Seltzer faxed O'Neil a revocation of the power of attorney on March 1. A rental contract with Ed Tucker signed by O'Neil on behalf of Seltzer on March 2 will bind Seltzer, however, because O'Neil still appeared to be Seltzer's agent and Tucker had no notice to the contrary.

When the law requires giving notice in order to end the power of the agent to bind the principal, individual notice must be given or mailed to all persons who had prior dealings with the agent. In addition, notice to the general public can be given by publishing in a newspaper of general circulation in the affected geographic area a statement that the agency has been terminated.

If a notice is actually received, the power of the agent is terminated without regard to whether the method of giving notice was proper. Conversely, if proper notice is given, it is immaterial that it does not actually come to the attention of the party notified. Thus, a member of the general public cannot claim that the principal is bound on the ground that the third person did not see the newspaper notice stating that the agent's authority had been terminated.

Make the Connection

Summary

An agency relationship is created by an express or implied agreement by which one person, the agent, is authorized to make contracts with third persons on behalf of, and subject to, the control of another person, the principal. An agent differs from an independent contractor in that the principal, who controls the acts of an agent, does not

have control over the details of performance of work by the independent contractor. Likewise, an independent contractor does not have authority to act on behalf of the other contracting party.

A special agent is authorized by the principal to handle a specific business transaction. A general agent is

[29] See *Stout Street Funding, LLC v. Johnson*, 2012 WL 1994800 (E.D. Pa. June 1, 2012). TRGC terminated its contract with Mabstract to serve as TRGC's closing agent on July 12, 2010, and obtained a court injunction barring Mabstract from engaging in any business on behalf of TRGC on July 15. Stout asserts that it had no actual notice of Mabstract's termination nor were there any red flags when it transmitted $480,000 into an escrow account held by Mabstract for a July 19 real estate transaction, which funds were misappropriated by Mabstract. It asserts that apparent authority lasts until a third party has actual notice of an agent's termination or until the third party has enough information to put that individual on inquiry.

authorized by the principal to transact all business affairs of the principal at a certain place. A universal agent is authorized to perform all acts that can be lawfully delegated to a representative.

The usual method of creating an agency is by express authorization. However, an agency relationship may be found to exist when the principal causes or permits a third person to reasonably believe that an agency relationship exists. In such a case, the "agent" appears to be authorized and is said to have apparent authority.

An unauthorized transaction by an agent for a principal may be ratified by the principal.

An agent acting with authority has the power to bind the principal. The scope of an agent's authority may be determined from the express words of the principal to the agent; this is called express authority. An agent has incidental authority to perform any act reasonably necessary to execute the authority given the agent. An agent's authority may be implied so as to enable the agent to perform any act in accordance with the general customs or usages in a business or an industry. This authority is often referred to as customary authority.

The effect of a proper exercise of authority by an agent is to bind the principal and third person to a contract. The agent, not being a party to the contract, is not liable in any respect under the contract. A third person dealing with a person claiming to be an agent has a duty to ascertain the extent of the agent's authority and a duty to take notice of any acts that are clearly adverse to the principal's interests. The third person cannot claim that apparent authority existed when that person has notice that the agent's conduct is adverse to the interests of the principal. A third person who has knowledge of limitations on an agent's authority is bound by those limitations. A third person is not bound by secret limitations.

While the agency relationship exists, the agent owes the principal the duties of (1) being loyal, (2) obeying all lawful instructions, (3) exercising reasonable care, (4) accounting for all property or money belonging to the principal, and (5) informing the principal of all facts relating to the agency that are relevant to the principal's interests. An agency relationship can be terminated by act of either the principal or the agent. However, the terminating party may be liable for damages to the other if the termination is in violation of the agency contract.

Because a known agent will have the appearance of still being an agent, notice must be given to third persons of the termination, and the agent may have the power to bind the principal and third persons until this notice is given.

An agency is terminated by operation of law upon (1) the death of the principal or agent, (2) insanity of the principal or agent, (3) bankruptcy of the principal or agent, (4) impossibility of performance, caused, for example, by the destruction of the subject matter, or (5) war. In states that have adopted the Uniform Durable Power of Attorney Act (UDPAA), an agency may be created that is not affected by subsequent disability or incapacity of the principal. In UDPAA states, the agency may also come into existence upon the "disability or incapacity of the principal." The designation of an attorney in fact under the UDPAA must be in writing.

Learning Outcomes

After studying this chapter, you should be able to clearly explain:

36-1 Nature of the Agency Relationship

LO.1 Explain the difference between an agent and an independent contractor

See the Ned and Tracy Seizer example and the "right to control" test, page 721.

36-2 Creating the Agency

LO.2 Explain three methods of creating an agency relationship

See the discussion on the usual method of creating an agency (which is by express authorization), page 723.

See the *Taylor* case where actual authority to perform some tasks created apparent authority to perform other related tasks, page 723.

See the agency by ratification example of James and Calvin Reiner, page 724.

36-3 Agent's Authority

LO.3 Recognize that third persons who deal with an agent are required to take notice of acts contrary to the interests of the principal

See the example of the Fire Company that failed to verify with the principal an agent's authority to receive a prepayment check of $55,000 made out in the agent's name, page 727.

36-4 Duties and Liabilities of Principal and Agent

LO.4 List and explain the duties an agent owes the principal

See the discussion concerning an agent's duty of loyalty, obedience, reasonable care, accounting, and information, pages 729–731.

See the *Mosionzhnik* case exposing an agent's breach of her duty of loyalty, page 729.

36-5 Termination of Agency

LO.5 Explain how the Uniform Durable Power of Attorney Act changes the common law rule on incapacity of the principal

See the *Estate of Graham* case on the limits of a durable power of attorney, page 734.

Key Terms

agency
agent
apparent authority
attorney in fact
customary authority

express authorization
general agent
incidental authority
independent contractor
interest in the authority

interest in the subject matter
power of attorney
principal
special agent
universal agent

Questions and Case Problems

1. How does an agent differ from an independent contractor?

2. Compare authorization of an agent by (a) appointment and (b) ratification.

3. Ernest A. Kotsch executed a durable power of attorney when he was 85 years old, giving his son, Ernie, the power to manage and sell his real estate and personal property "and to do all acts necessary for maintaining and caring for [the father] during his lifetime." Thereafter, Kotsch began "keeping company" with a widow, Margaret Gradl. Ernie believed that the widow was attempting to alienate his father from him, and he observed that she was exerting a great deal of influence over his father. Acting under the durable power of attorney and without informing his father, Ernie created the "Kotsch Family Irrevocable Trust," to which he transferred $700,000, the bulk of his father's liquid assets, with the father as grantor and initial beneficiary and Ernie's three children as additional beneficiaries. Ernie named himself trustee. His father sued to avoid the trust. Ernie defended his action on the ground that he had authority to create the trust under the durable power of attorney. Decide. [*Kotsch v. Kotsch*, 608 So. 2d 879 (Fla. App.)]

4. Ken Jones, the number-one-ranked prizefighter in his weight class, signed a two-year contract with Howard Stayword. The contract obligated Stayword to represent and promote Jones in all business and professional matters, including the arrangement of fights. For these services, Jones was to pay Stayword

10 percent of gross earnings. After a year, when Stayword proved unsuccessful in arranging a title match with the champion, Jones fired Stayword. During the following year, Jones earned $4 million. Stayword sued Jones for $400,000. Jones defended himself on the basis that a principal has the absolute power at any time to terminate an agency relationship by discharging the agent, so he was not liable to Stayword. Was Jones correct?

5. Paul Strich did business as an optician in Duluth, Minnesota. Paul used only the products of the Plymouth Optical Co., a national manufacturer of optical products and supplies with numerous retail outlets and some franchise arrangements in areas other than Duluth. To increase business, Paul renovated his office and changed the sign on it to read "Plymouth Optical Co." Paul did business this way for more than three years—advertised under that name, paid bills with checks bearing the name of Plymouth Optical Co., and listed himself in the telephone and city directories by that name. Plymouth immediately became aware of what Paul was doing. However, because Paul used only Plymouth products and Plymouth did not have a franchise in Duluth, it saw no advantage at that time in prohibiting Paul from using the name and losing him as a customer. Paul contracted with the *Duluth Tribune* for advertising, making the contract in the name of Plymouth Optical Co. When the advertising bill was not paid, the *Duluth Tribune* sued Plymouth Optical Co. for payment. Plymouth's defense was that it

never authorized Paul to do business under the name, nor authorized him to make a contract with the newspaper. Decide.

6. Record owned a farm that was managed by his agent, Berry, who lived on the farm. Berry hired Wagner to bale the hay and told him to bill Record for this work. Wagner did so and was paid by Record. By the summer of the following year, the agency had been terminated by Record, but Berry remained in possession as tenant of the farm and nothing appeared changed. Late in the summer, Berry asked Wagner to bale the hay as he had done the previous year and bill Record for the work. He did so, but Record refused to pay on the ground that Berry was not then his agent. Wagner sued him. Decide. [*Record v. Wagner*, 128 A.2d 921 (N.H.)]

7. Gilbert Church owned Church Farms, Inc., in Manteno, Illinois. Church advertised its well-bred stallion Imperial Guard for breeding rights at $50,000, directing all inquiries to "Herb Bagley, Manager." Herb Bagley lived at Church Farms and was the only person available to visitors. Vern Lundberg answered the ad, and after discussions in which Bagley stated that Imperial Guard would remain in Illinois for at least a two-year period, Lundberg and Bagley executed a two-year breeding rights contract. The contract was signed by Lundberg and by Bagley as "Church Farms, Inc., H. Bagley, Mgr." When Gil Church moved Imperial Guard to Oklahoma prior to the second year of the contract, Lundberg brought suit for breach of contract. Church testified that Bagley had no authority to sign contracts for Church Farms. Decide. [*Lundberg v. Church Farms, Inc.*, 502 N.E.2d 806 (Ill.)]

8. The Holzmans signed an exclusive listing agreement with the Blum real estate brokerage firm. The contract provided that the Holzmans had an obligation to pay a commission "if they enter into a written agreement to sell the property to any person during the term of this exclusive listing agreement." The Holzmans entered into a written agreement to sell their house for $715,000 to the Noravians. On the advice of their attorney, the Holzmans included a default provision in this contract stating that in the event of default by the Holzmans, the Noravians' only remedy would be a refund of their deposit. Subsequently, the Sterns offered $850,000 for the property and the Holzmans canceled their contract with the Noravians and returned their deposit. After the exclusive listing period expired, the Holzmans executed a contract to sell their property to the

Sterns at the offered price of $850,000—with the contract calling for the Holzmans to pay half the real estate fee to Blum and half to a cooperating broker. Blum was paid this fee of $21,500. Blum brought suit against the Holzmans seeking the full commission for the Noravian contract under the exclusive listing agreement. Did Blum have a legal obligation or ethical duty to advise the Holzmans when considering the Sterns' offer that he believed they were obligated to him for the full commission under the Novarian contract? Decide. [*Holzman v. Blum*, 726 A.2d 818 (Md. App.)]

9. Tillie Flinn properly executed a durable power of attorney designating her nephew James C. Flanders and/or Martha E. Flanders, his wife, as her attorney in fact. Seven months later, Martha Flanders went to the Capitol Federal Savings and Loan Association office. She had the durable power of attorney instrument, five certificates of deposit, and a hand-printed letter identifying Martha as an attorney in fact and stating that Tillie wished to cash her five CDs that Martha had with her. At approximately 10:31 A.M., five checks were given to Martha in the aggregate amount of $135,791.34, representing the funds in the five CDs less penalties for early withdrawal. Some of the checks were drawn to the order of Martha individually and some to the order of James and Martha, as individuals. Tillie was found dead of heart disease later that day. The time of death stated on her death certificate was 11:30 A.M. The Flanderses spent the money on themselves. Bank IV, as administrator of Tillie's estate, sued Capitol Federal to recover the amount of the funds paid to the Flanderses. It contended that Capitol Federal breached its duty to investigate before issuing the checks. Capitol Federal contended that it did all that it had a duty to do. Decide. [*Bank IV v. Capitol Federal Savings and Loan Ass'n*, 828 P.2d 355 (Kan.)]

10. Lew owns a store on Canal Street in New Orleans. He paid a person named Mike and other individuals commissions for customers brought into the store. Lew testified that he had known Mike for less than a week. Boulos and Durso, partners in a wholesale jewelry business, were visiting New Orleans on a business trip when Mike brought them into the store to buy a stereo. While Durso finalized the stereo transaction with the store's manager, Boulos and Mike negotiated to buy 2 cameras, 3 videos, and 20 gold Dupont lighters. Unknown to the store's manager, Mike was given $8,250 in cash and was to deliver the merchandise later that evening to the

Marriott Hotel, where Boulos and Durso were staying. Mike gave a receipt for the cash, but it showed no sales tax or indication that the goods were to be delivered. Boulos testified that he believed Mike was the store owner. Mike never delivered the merchandise and disappeared. Boulos and Durso contended that Lew is liable for the acts of his agent, Mike. Lew denied that Mike was his agent, and the testimony showed that Mike had no actual authority to make a sale, to use a cash register, or even to go behind a sales counter. What ethical principle applies to the conduct of Boulos and Durso? Decide. [*Boulos v. Morrison*, 503 So. 2d 1 (La.)]

11. Martha Christiansen owns women's apparel stores bearing her name in New Seabury, Massachusetts; Lake Placid, New York; Palm Beach, Florida; and Palm Springs, California. At a meeting with her four store managers, she discussed styles she thought appropriate for the forthcoming season, advised them as always to use their best judgment in the goods they purchased for each of their respective stores, and cautioned "but no blue jeans." Later, Jane Farley, the manager of the Lake Placid store, purchased a line of high-quality blue denim outfits (designer jeans with jacket and vest options) from Women's Wear, Inc., for the summer season. The outfits did not sell. Martha refused to pay for them, contending that she had told all of her managers "no blue jeans" and that if it came to a lawsuit, she would fly in three managers to testify that Jane Farley had absolutely no authority to purchase denim outfits and was, in fact, expressly forbidden to do so. Women's Wear sued Martha, and the three managers testified for her. Is the fact that Martha had explicitly forbidden Farley to purchase the outfits in question sufficient to protect her from liability for the purchases made by Farley?

12. Fred Schilling, the president and administrator of Florence General Hospital, made a contract, dated August 16, 1989, on behalf of the hospital with CMK Associates to transfer the capacity to utilize 25 beds from the hospital to the Faith Nursing Home. Schilling, on behalf of the hospital, had previously made a contract with CMK Associates on May 4, 1987. Schilling had been specifically authorized by the hospital board to make the 1987 contract. The hospital refused to honor the 1989 contract because the board had not authorized it. CMK contended that Schilling had apparent authority to bind the hospital because he was

president and administrator of the hospital and he had been the person who negotiated and signed a contract with CMK in 1987. Thus, according to CMK, the hospital had held out Schilling as having apparent authority to make the contract. The hospital disagreed. Decide. [*Pee Dee Nursing Home v. Florence General Hospital*, 419 S.E.2d 843 (S.C. App.)]

13. Real estate broker Donald Alley Sr. had a listing contract that gave him the exclusive right to sell Wayman Ellison's farm for at least $200,000. Ellison was told that a buyer was found. The buyer, Cora Myers, who had been paid $585,000 for her small farm because the land was needed for a commercial development, agreed to pay $380,000 for the large Ellison farm. Alley told Ellison that the sale price was $200,000. The buyer paid $380,000, however, and Alley kept the difference. When Ellison later learned of these details, he sued Alley for the $180,000. From a judgment for Ellison, Alley appealed, seeking at least his commission on the sale since he procured a ready, willing, and able buyer. Decide. [*Ellison v. Alley*, 842 S.W.2d 605 (Tenn)].

14. Francis Gagnon, an elderly gentleman, signed a power of attorney authorizing his daughter, Joan, "to sell any of my real estate and to execute any document needed to carry out the sale … and to add property to a trust of which I am grantor or beneficiary." This power was given in case Gagnon was not available to take care of matters personally because he was traveling. When Joan learned that Gagnon intended to sell his Shelburne property to Cosby for $750,000, she created an irrevocable trust naming Gagnon as beneficiary and herself as trustee. Acting then on the basis of the authority set forth in the power of attorney, she conveyed the Shelburne property to herself as trustee of the irrevocable trust, thus blocking the sale to Cosby. When Gagnon learned of this, he demanded that Joan return the Shelburne property to him, but she refused, saying she had acted within the authority set forth in the power of attorney. Did Joan violate any duty owed to Gagnon? Must she reconvey the property to Gagnon? [*Gagnon v. Coombs*, 654 N.E.2d 54 (Mass. App.)]

15. Daniels and Julian were employed by the Marriott Hotel in New Orleans and were close personal friends. One day after work, Daniels and Julian went to Werlein's music store to open a credit account. Julian, with Daniels's authorization and in her

presence, applied for credit using Daniels's name and credit history. Later, Julian went to Werlein's without Daniels and charged the purchase of a television set to Daniels's account, executing a retail installment contract by signing Daniels's name. Daniels saw the new television in Julian's home and was informed that it was charged to the Werlein's account. Daniels told Julian to continue making payments. When Werlein's credit manager first contacted Daniels to inform her that her account was delinquent, she claimed that a money order for the television was in the mail. On the second call, she asked for a "payment balance." Some four months after the purchase, she informed Werlein's that she had not authorized the purchase of the television nor ratified the purchase. Werlein's sued Daniels for the unpaid balance. Decide. [*Philip Werlein, Ltd. v. Daniels*, 536 So. 2d 722 (La. App.)]

CPA Questions

1. Generally, an agency relationship is terminated by operation of law in all of the following situations except the:

   a. Principal's death.

   b. Principal's incapacity.

   c. Agent's renunciation of the agency.

   d. Agent's failure to acquire a necessary business license.

2. Able, on behalf of Pix Corp., entered into a contract with Sky Corp., by which Sky agreed to sell computer equipment to Pix. Able disclosed to Sky that she was acting on behalf of Pix. However, Able had exceeded her actual authority by entering into the contract with Sky. If Pix wishes to ratify the contract with Sky, which of the following statements is correct?

   a. Pix must notify Sky that Pix intends to ratify the contract.

   b. Able must have acted reasonably and in Pix's best interest.

   c. Able must be a general agent of Pix.

   d. Pix must have knowledge of all material facts relating to the contract at the time it is ratified.

3. Which of the following actions requires an agent for a corporation to have a written agency agreement?

   a. Purchasing office supplies for the principal's business.

   b. Purchasing an interest in undeveloped land for the principal.

   c. Hiring an independent general contractor to renovate the principal's office building.

   d. Retaining an attorney to collect a business debt owed the principal.

4. Simmons, an agent for Jensen, has the express authority to sell Jensen's goods. Simmons also has the express authority to grant discounts of up to 5 percent of list price. Simmons sold Hemple a 10 percent discount. Hemple had not previously dealt with either Simmons or Jensen. Which of the following courses of action may Jensen properly take?

   a. Seek to void the sale to Hemple.

   b. Seek recovery of $50 from Hemple only.

   c. Seek recovery of $50 from Simmons only.

   d. Seek recovery of $50 from either Hemple or Simmons.

5. Ogden Corp. hired Thorp as a sales representative for nine months at a salary of $3,000 per month plus 4 percent of sales. Which of the following statements is correct?

   a. Thorp is obligated to act solely in Ogden's interest in matters concerning Ogden's business.

   b. The agreement between Ogden and Thorp formed an agency coupled with an interest.

   c. Ogden does not have the power to dismiss Thorp during the nine-month period without cause.

   d. The agreement between Ogden and Thorp is not enforceable unless it is in writing and signed by Thorp.

6. Frost's accountant and business manager has the authority to:

   a. Mortgage Frost's business property.

   b. Obtain bank loans for Frost.

   c. Insure Frost's property against fire loss.

   d. Sell Frost's business.

Third Persons in Agency

Learning Outcomes ⟨⟨⟨

After studying this chapter, you should be able to

LO.1 Explain when an agent is and is not liable to a third person as a party to a contract

LO.2 Describe how to execute a contract as an agent on behalf of a principal

LO.3 Explain the legal effect of a payment made by a third person to an authorized agent

LO.4 Explain the doctrine of *respondeat superior*

LO.5 Distinguish between the authority of a soliciting agent and that of a contracting agent

The rights and liabilities of the principal, the agent, and the third person with whom the agent deals are generally determined by contract law. In some cases, tort or criminal law may be applicable.

37-1 Liability of Agent to Third Person

The liability of the agent to the third person depends on the existence of authority and the manner of executing the contract.

37-1a Action of Authorized Agent of Disclosed Principal

If an agent makes a contract with a third person on behalf of a disclosed principal and has proper authority to do so and if the contract is executed properly, the agent has no personal liability on the contract. Whether the principal performs the contract or not, the agent cannot be held liable by the third party. **For Example,** Lincoln Apartment Management, LP, required a vendor to sign a form before commencing work renovating Woodchase Village Apartments, which stated:

> *"Vendor understands and agrees that the legal Owner of the community is responsible for the payments of any services or materials performed or delivered, and not Lincoln, which is the property management company and Agent for the Owner of the community."*

The contractor's field manager, Jane Yang, signed the form before commencing work. After the work was performed the apartment complex was foreclosed, with the contractor still owing $59,758 for unpaid services. In a lawsuit against Lincoln by the contractor, the court determined that the owner, not the property manager, was solely liable for the debt.[1]

In speaking of an agent's action as authorized or unauthorized, it must be remembered that *authorized* includes action that, though originally *unauthorized*, was subsequently ratified by the principal. Once there is an effective ratification, the original action of the agent is no longer treated as unauthorized.

37-1b Unauthorized Action

If a person makes a contract as agent for another but lacks authority to do so, the contract does not bind the principal. When a person purports to act as agent for a principal, an implied warranty arises that that person has authority to do so. If the agent lacks authority, there is a breach of this warranty.

If the agent's act causes loss to the third person, that third person may generally hold the agent liable for the loss.

For Example, Bruce Elieff and Todd Kurtin were equal partners and owners in a series of California real estate ventures, which included a group designated as the "Joint Entities" who were independent third-party owners. Elieff signed a settlement agreement buying out Kurtin for $48.8 million in four installments "individually and on behalf of the Elieff Separate Entities and the Joint Entities." Some $23 million of the last buyout installment was not paid by the Joint Entities. As agent for the Joint Entities, Elieff

[1]*Grand Master Contracting, LLC v. Lincoln Apartment Management, LP,* 724 S.E.2d 456 (Ga. App. 2012).

misstated his authority to bind the Joint Entities and he is liable to Kurtin for breach of warranty of an agent's authority.[2]

It is no defense for the agent in such a case that the agent acted in good faith or misunderstood the scope of authority. The purported agent is not liable for conduct in excess of authority when the third person knows that she is acting beyond the authority given by the principal.

An agent with a written authorization may avoid liability on the implied warranty of authority by showing the written authorization to the third person and permitting the third person to determine the scope of the agent's authority.

37-1c Disclosure of Principal

There are three degrees to which the existence and identity of the principal may be disclosed or not disclosed. An agent's liability as a party to a contract with a third person is affected by the degree of disclosure.

Disclosed Principal

disclosed principal— principal whose identity is made known by the agent as well as the fact that the agent is acting on the principal's behalf.

When the agent makes known the identity of the principal and the fact that the agent is acting on behalf of that principal, the principal is called a **disclosed principal.** The third person dealing with an agent of a disclosed principal ordinarily intends to make a contract with the principal, not the agent. Consequently, the agent is not a party to, and is not bound by, the contract that is made.[3] **For Example,** Biefeld Jewelers was the trade name of Bie-Jewel Corp., a closely held corporation of which Margie Biefeld was one of several employees. The plaintiff sought to hold her personally liable on a contract for advertising services. While Ms. Biefeld signed a contract for advertising services without reference to holding a corporate office, the plain language of the agreement established that she was acting as an agent for a disclosed principal and that the plaintiff had notice of her status.[4]

Partially Disclosed Principal

partially disclosed principal—principal whose existence is made known but whose identity is not.

When the agent makes known the existence of a principal but not the principal's identity, the principal is a **partially disclosed principal.** Because the third party does not know the identity of the principal, the third person is making the contract with the agent, and the agent is therefore a party to the contract.

Undisclosed Principal

undisclosed principal— principal on whose behalf an agent acts without disclosing to the third person the fact of agency or the identity of the principal.

When the third person is not told or does not know that the agent is acting as an agent for anyone else, the unknown principal is called an **undisclosed principal.**[5] In this case, the third person is making the contract with the agent, and the agent is a party to that contract.

---

[2] *Kurtin v. Elieff*, 155 Cal. Rptr. 3d 573 (2013).
[3] *Robinson v. Deutsche Bank Nat'l Trust Co.*, 932 F. Supp. 2d 95, 109 (D.C. Cir. 2013).
[4] *CBS Outdoor Group, Inc. v. Biefeld*, 836 N.Y.S.2d 497 (Civ. Ct. 2007).
[5] See *Castle Cheese Inc. v. MS Produce Inc.*, 2008 WL 4372856 (W.D. Pa. Sept. 19, 2008), where the court held that an agent must disclose both the identity of the principal and the fact of the agency relationship to avoid liability under a contract. One of the defendants, CVS Foods, did not establish that it had disclosed the fact it was acting as an agent, and it was held liable for breach of contract.

CASE SUMMARY

You've Got to Tell Them You're Contracting on Behalf of the Named Principal, Silly

FACTS: In 2003, Philip Steen formed Nashville Sports Leagues, LLC, for the purpose of providing a recreational sports league for a growing demographic of active adults in Middle Tennessee. Mr. Steen served as the managing member of Nashville Sports until the LLC was administratively dissolved in 2004. Three years later, in January 2007, Mr. Steen registered TN Sports, LLC, with the Tennessee Secretary of State. TN Sports performed the same functions as Nashville Sports, and Mr. Steen continued to serve as the managing member. Mr. Steen also continued to do business under the name "Nashville Sports Leagues." In correspondence, he identified himself as an executive of Nashville Sports Leagues and used an "@nashvillesports.com" e-mail address. By spring 2007, the popularity of TN Sports had grown considerably with 11,000 members on more than 175 teams. Players had their choice of six different sports with options year-round. The success of TN Sports was due at least in part to the ease of finding willing players and forming teams on the TN Sports Web site. In addition to its essential networking function, the Web site provided users with game schedules and venue information, among other details about leagues and events. In the spring of 2007, Mr. Steen moved his TN Sports Web site to ICG Link,

Inc., and it recommended that Mr. Steen build a new Web site to improve functionality. However, problems existed with the new Web site. Mr. Steen had not paid invoices from March to October, and ICG employees were instructed to "slow walk" the TN Sports Web site. The parties were unable to resolve their differences, and ICG Link filed a lawsuit against the LLC, and Mr. Steen personally, for breach of contract. The trial court found there was quasi-contract liability, less the cost to repair defects in the new Web site. It found Mr. Steen personally liable for the judgment and he appealed.

DECISION: In order for an agent to avoid personal liability on a contract, the agent must disclose the facts of the agency and the identity of the principal. Mr. Steen is the managing member of TN Sports, LLC. However, in his transactions with ICG he failed to disclose that TN Sports, LLC, was his principal, identifying himself as an executive of Nashville Sports Leagues. Thus he is personally liable for the judgment for ICG on its quasi-contract claim in the amount of $13,952, which consists of amounts owed for Web site development and hosting services, with an offset for the cost of completion of the new Web site. [*ICG Link, Inc. v. Steen*, 363 S.W.3d 533 (Tenn. App. 2011)]

37-1d Assumption of Liability

Agents may intentionally make themselves liable on contracts with third persons.[6] This situation frequently occurs when the agent is a well-established local brokerage house or other agency and when the principal is located out of town and is not known locally.

In some situations, the agent makes a contract that will be personally binding. If the principal is not disclosed, the agent is necessarily the other contracting party and is bound by the contract. Even when the principal is disclosed, the agent may be personally bound if it was the intention of the parties that the agent assume a personal obligation even though this was done to further the principal's business.[7]

CASE SUMMARY

The Thanks I Get for Being a Nice Person

FACTS: Grant Colledge was the managing member of A.T. Masterpiece Homes, a limited liability company. The trial court concluded that Colledge had assumed personal

responsibility regarding the quality of work during the construction of the Bennetts' and the Hoefferles' homes. When the construction finished, the homes were in various stages of

---

[6] *Fairchild Publications v. Rosston*, 584 N.Y.S.2d 389 (N.Y. County Sup. 1992).
[7] See *Boros v. Carter*, 537 So. 2d 1134 (Fla. App. 1989).

The Thanks I Get for Being a Nice Person continued

disrepair and structural failure. Judgment was issued against Colledge personally for $173,250 for the Bennetts and $55,250 for the Hoefferles. On appeal, Colledge contended that he should be shielded from personal liability because he was at all times acting only as an agent on behalf of a limited liability company, A.T. Masterpiece; and, he contends, any statements attributed to him where he said "I will take care of it" or "I guarantee it" were simply figures of speech and did not amount to an express assumption of personal liability.

DECISION: Judgment against Colledge. A person acting as an agent may assume personal liability on a business contract where he voluntarily undertakes a personal responsibility. For example, Colledge's statements to the Hoefferles had the effect of personally obligating himself for the structural integrity of the dormer because he made the statements with the goal of securing the Hoefferles' continuing performance on the contract. And his statements to the Bennetts led them to believe that he would personally ensure that the completed home was built properly. [***Bennett v. A.T. Masterpiece Homes at Broadsprings, LLC,* 40 A.3d 145 (Pa. Super. 2012)**]

37-1e Execution of Contract

A simple contract that would appear to be the contract of the agent can be shown by other evidence, if believed, to have been intended as a contract between the principal and the third party.

CASE SUMMARY

If You Sign as an Agent, You Don't Have to Pay

FACTS: Audrey Walton was transferred from a hospital to Mariner Health Nursing Home on January 26, 2001. Her daughter Patricia Walton signed a 30-page document, "Resident's Agent Financial Agreement." Patricia indicated in that agreement that the only method of payment would be Medicare or Medical Assistance. Medicare assistance stopped in February 2001. On January 10, 2003, Mariner Health sued both Audrey and Patricia for unpaid monthly bills amounting to $86,235. From a judgment for Mariner Health against both the patient and her daughter, Patricia appealed.

DECISION: Judgment for Patricia. As an agent, Patricia entered into the contract only for the benefit of Audrey and is personally insulated from liability by virtue of her status as an agent. *Note:* A state Nursing Home Bill of Rights did not authorize a nursing home to bring a private cause of action against a patient's agent for breach of contract unless the agent voluntarily and knowingly agreed to pay for the care with her or his own funds. [***Walton v. Mariner Health,* 894 A.2d 584 (Md. 2006)**]

To avoid any question of interpretation, an agent should execute an instrument by signing the principal's name and either *by* or *per* and the agent's name. **For Example,** if Jane R. Craig is an agent for B. G. Gray, Craig should execute instruments by signing either "B.G. Gray, by Jane R. Craig" or "B. G. Gray, per Jane R. Craig." Such a signing is in law a signing by Gray, and the agent is therefore not a party to the contract. The signing of the principal's name by an authorized agent without indicating the agent's name or identity is likewise in law the signature of the principal.

If the instrument is ambiguous as to whether the agent has signed in a representative or an individual capacity, parol evidence is admissible as between the original parties to the transaction for establishing the character in which the agent was acting.

37-1f Torts and Crimes

Agents are liable for harm caused to third persons by the agents' fraudulent, intentional, or negligent acts.[8] The fact that persons were acting as agents at the time or that they acted in good faith under the directions of a principal does not relieve them of liability if their conduct would impose liability on them when acting for themselves.

CASE SUMMARY

Employees Are Not Personally Liable for Roadway Accidents While at Work, Are They?

FACTS: Ralls was an employee of the Arkansas State Highway Department. While repairing a state highway, he negligently backed a state truck onto the highway, causing a collision with Mittlesteadt's car. Mittlesteadt sued Ralls, who raised the defense that, because he was acting on behalf of the state, he was not liable for his negligence.

DECISION: The fact that an employee or agent is acting on behalf of someone else does not excuse or exonerate the agent or employee from liability for torts committed by the agent or employee. Ralls was therefore liable for his negligence even though it occurred within the scope of his employment by the state. [*Ralls v. Mittlesteadt*, 596 S.W.2d 349 (Ark. 1980)]

If an agent commits a crime, such as stealing from a third person or shooting a third person, the agent is liable for the crime without regard to the fact of acting as an agent. The agent is liable without regard to whether the agent acted in self-interest or sought to advance the interest of the principal.

37-2 Liability of Principal to Third Person

The principal is liable to the third person for the properly authorized and executed contracts of the agent and, in certain circumstances, for the agent's unauthorized contracts.

37-2a Agent's Contracts

The liability of a principal to a third person on a contract made by an agent depends on the extent of disclosure of the principal and the form of the contract that is executed.

CPA   **Simple Contract with Principal Disclosed**

When a disclosed principal with contractual capacity authorizes or ratifies an agent's transaction with a third person and when the agent properly executes a contract with the third person, a binding contract exists between the principal and the third person. The principal and the third person may each sue the other in the event of a breach of the contract. The agent is not a party to the contract, is not liable for its performance, and cannot sue for its breach.[9]

The liability of a disclosed principal to a third person is not discharged by the fact that the principal gives the agent money with which to pay the third person.

---

[8] *Mannish v. Lacayo,* 496 So. 2d 242 (Fla. App. 1986).
[9] *Levy v. Gold & Co., Inc.,* 529 N.Y.S.2d 133 (A.D. 1988).

ETHICS & THE LAW

Some time ago, dairy farmers owned large tracts of land in south Tempe, Arizona. The farmers used the land for grazing animals. Economic growth in this suburb of Phoenix was limited because of the state's inability at that time to attract large businesses to the area for relocation or location of new facilities.

In 1973, three farmers who owned adjoining parcels of land in the south Tempe area were approached by a local real estate agent with an offer for the purchase of their property. The amount of the offer was approximately 10 percent above the property's appraised value. The three farmers discussed the offer and concluded that with their need to retire, it was best to accept the offer and sell the land. All three signed contracts for the sale of their land.

After the contracts were entered into but before the transactions had closed, the three farmers learned that the land was being purchased by a real estate development firm from southern California. The development firm had planned, and would be proposing to the Tempe City Council, a residential community, the Lakes. The Lakes would consist of upper-end homes in a community laced with parks, lakes, and ponds, with each house in the developed area backing up to its own dock and water recreation. The development firm had begun the project because it had learned of the plans of American Express, Rubbermaid, and Dial to locate major facilities in the Phoenix area.

The three farmers objected to the sale of their land when they learned the identity of the buyer. "If we had known who was coming in here and why, we never would have sold for such a low price." Were the farmers' contracts binding?

Is it ethical to use the strategy of an undisclosed principal? What is the role of an agent in a situation in which the third party is making a decision not as beneficial to him or her as it could or should be? Can the agent say anything?

Consequently, the liability of a buyer for the purchase price of goods is not terminated by the fact that the buyer gave the buyer's agent the purchase price to remit to the seller.

Simple Contract with Principal Partially Disclosed

A partially disclosed principal is liable for a simple contract made by an authorized agent. The third person may recover from either the agent or the principal.

Simple Contract with Principal Undisclosed

An undisclosed principal is liable for a simple contract made by an authorized agent. Although the third person initially contracted with the agent alone, the third person, on learning of the existence of the undisclosed principal, may sue that principal.[10] In most jurisdictions, third persons can sue and collect judgments from the agent or principal, or both, until the judgment is fully satisfied (joint and several liability).[11]

37-2b Payment to Agent

When the third person makes payment to an authorized agent, the payment is deemed made to the principal. Even if the agent never remits or delivers the payment to the principal, the principal must give the third person full credit for the payment so long as the third person made the payment in good faith and had no reason to know that the agent would be guilty of misconduct.[12]

---

[10] *McDaniel v. Hensons, Inc.*, 493 S.E.2d 529 (Ga. App. 1997).

[11] *Crown Controls, Inc. v. Smiley*, 756 P.2d 717 (Wash. 1988).

[12] This general rule of law is restated in some states by Section 2 of the Uniform Fiduciaries Act, which is expressly extended by Section 1 of the act to agents, partners, and corporate officers. Similar statutory provisions are found in a number of other states.

CASE SUMMARY

But We Already Paid!

FACTS: E.I. duPont de Nemours & Company licensed Enjay Chemical Company (now Exxon) and Johnson & Johnson to use certain chemical processes in return for which royalty payments by check were to be made to duPont. By agreement between the companies, the royalty payments to be made to duPont were to be made by check sent to a specified duPont employee, C.H.D., in its Control Division. These checks were sent during the next nine years. C.H.D. altered some of them so that he was named thereon as the payee. He then cashed them and used the money for his own purposes. Liberty Mutual Insurance Company, which insured the fidelity of duPont's employees, and

duPont sued Enjay and Johnson & Johnson on the basis that they still owed the amounts embezzled by C.H.D.

DECISION: Judgment for Enjay and Johnson & Johnson. Payment to an authorized agent has the legal effect of payment to the principal regardless of whether the agent remits the payment to the principal or embezzles it. C.H.D. was the agent authorized to receive the royalty checks. Therefore, the defendants had effectively paid the royalties when they sent C.H.D. the checks. His misconduct did not revive the debts that were paid by sending him the checks. [*Liberty Mutual Ins. Co. v. Enjay Chemical Co.*, 316 A.2d 219 (Del. Super. 1974)]

Because apparent authority has the same legal effect as actual authority, a payment made to a person with apparent authority to receive the payment is deemed a payment to the apparent principal.

When a debtor makes payment to a person who is not the actual or apparent agent of the creditor, such a payment does not discharge the debt unless that person in fact pays the money to the creditor.

CASE SUMMARY

But We Already Paid!
No You Didn't

FACTS: Basic Research, LLC, ran advertisements on Rainbow Media Holdings' cable television networks from January to March 2008. Basic used an advertising agency named Icebox to place advertisements for its products. It paid Icebox up front for all of this advertising. Icebox went into bankruptcy, and it was discovered that Icebox had not paid Rainbow Networks for three months of advertising, worth $590,000. Rainbow Networks obtained a $132,000 payment from the Icebox bankruptcy estate. Rainbow now seeks payment from Basic for the remaining $406,000.

Basic contends that Rainbow's only remedy was through the bankruptcy estate.

DECISION: Basic Research was a disclosed principal with whom Rainbow Networks had a credit agreement. Basic chose Icebox as its agent to place its advertisements and to make payments. Icebox didn't pay. It is Basic who is liable for the actions of its agent, and Basic is responsible for the $406,000 owed Rainbow Networks. [*Basic Research v. Rainbow Media Holdings, Inc.*, 2011 WL 2636833 (D. Utah July 6, 2011)]

37-2c Agent's Statements

A principal is bound by a statement made by an agent while transacting business within the scope of authority. This means that the principal cannot later contradict the statement of the agent and show that it is not true. Statements or declarations of an agent, in order to bind the principal, must be made at the time of performing the act to which they relate or shortly thereafter.

37-2d Agent's Knowledge

The principal is bound by knowledge or notice of any fact that is acquired by an agent while acting within the scope of actual or apparent authority. When a fact is known to the agent of the seller, the sale is deemed made by the seller with knowledge of that fact.

The rule that the agent's knowledge is imputed to the principal is extended in some cases to knowledge gained prior to the creation of the agency relationship. The notice and knowledge in any case must be based on reliable information. Thus, when the agent hears only rumors, the principal is not charged with notice.

If the subject matter is outside the scope of the agent's authority, the agent is under no duty to inform the principal of the knowledge, and the principal is not bound by it. The principal is not charged with knowledge of an agent when (1) the agent is acting adversely to the principal's interest or (2) the third party acts in collusion with the agent for the purpose of cheating the principal.

37-3 Liability of Principal for Torts and Crimes of Agent

Under certain circumstances, the principal may be liable for the torts or crimes of the agent or the employee.

CPA ### 37-3a Vicarious Liability for Torts and Crimes

Assume that an agent or an employee causes harm to a third person. Is the principal or the employer liable for this conduct? If the conduct constitutes a crime, can the principal or the employer be criminally prosecuted? The answer is that in many instances, the principal or the employer is liable civilly and may also be prosecuted criminally. That is, the principal or the employer is liable although personally free from fault and not guilty of any wrong. This concept of imposing liability for the fault of another is known as **vicarious liability.**

vicarious liability–
imposing liability for the fault of another.

This situation arises both when an employer's employee or a principal's agent commits the wrong. The rules of law governing the vicarious liability of the principal and the employer are the same. In the interest of simplicity, this section is stated in terms of employees acting in the course of employment. Remember that these rules are equally applicable to agents acting within the scope of their authority. As a practical matter, some situations will arise only with agents. **For Example,** the vicarious liability of a seller for the misrepresentations made by a salesperson arises only when the seller appointed an agent to sell. In contrast, both the employee hired to drive a truck and an agent driving to visit a customer could negligently injure a third person with their vehicles. In many situations, a person employed by another is both an employee and an agent, and the tort is committed within the phase of "employee work."

respondeat superior–
doctrine that the principal or employer is vicariously liable for the unauthorized torts committed by an agent or employee while acting within the scope of the agency or the course of the employment, respectively.

The rule of law imposing vicarious liability on an innocent employer for the wrong of an employee is also known as the doctrine of *respondeat superior.* In modern times, this doctrine can be justified on the grounds that the business should pay for the harm caused in the doing of the business, that the employer will be more careful in the selection of employees if made responsible for their actions, and that the employer may obtain liability insurance to protect against claims of third persons.

Nature of Act

The wrongful act committed by an employee may be a negligent act, an intentional act, a fraudulent act, or a violation of a government regulation. It may give rise only to civil liability of the employer, or it may also subject the employer to prosecution for crime.

Negligent Act. Historically, the act for which liability would be imposed under the doctrine of *respondeat superior* was a negligent act committed within the scope of employment.

Intentional Act. Under the common law, a master was not liable for an intentional tort committed by a servant. The modern law holds that an employer is liable for an intentional tort committed by an employee for the purpose of furthering the employer's business.[13] **For Example,** Crane Brothers, Inc., drilled a well for Stephen May. When May did not pay his bill, two Crane Brothers' employees went to May's workplace, and an altercation ensued in which May was injured. Crane Brothers, Inc., was held vicariously liable for the torts of the employees, not because the employer itself committed the wrongful acts but because it was answerable for the manner in which its agents, the two employees, conducted themselves in doing the business of the employer.[14]

Fraud. Modern decisions hold the employer liable for fraudulent acts or misrepresentations. The rule is commonly applied to a principal-agent relationship. To illustrate, when an agent makes fraudulent statements in selling stock, the principal is liable for the buyer's loss. In states that follow the common law rule of no liability for intentional torts, the principal is not liable for the agent's fraud when the principal did not authorize or know of the agent's fraud.

Government Regulation. The employer may be liable because of the employee's violation of a government regulation. These regulations are most common in the areas of business and protection of the environment. In such cases, the employer may be held liable for a penalty imposed by the government. In some cases, the breach of the regulation will impose liability on the employer in favor of a third person who is injured as a consequence of the violation.

Course of Employment

The mere fact that a tort or crime is committed by an employee does not necessarily impose vicarious liability on the employer. It must also be shown that the individual was acting within the scope of authority if an agent or in the course of employment if an employee. If an employee was not acting within the scope of employment, there is no vicarious liability.[15]

---

[13] Restatement (Second) of Agency §231.

[14] *Crane Brothers, Inc. v. May*, 556 S.E.2d 865 (Ga. App. 2001).

[15] See *Ali v. State of New York*, 981 N.Y.S.2d (App. Div. 2014) where during a phone conversation a state employee working as a security guard in the New York State Workers' Compensation Office in Brooklyn was informed of his grandmother's death. In reaction to that news, he went over to the waiting area and punched a wooden bench that was in front of the claimant, Mr. Ali, causing it to fall on Mr. Ali and injure him. Because the security guard was acting solely for personal motives unrelated to state business at the time of the incident, the state was not held vicariously liable for the security guard's actions.

CASE SUMMARY

A Hard Pill to Swallow for Walgreen: $1.4 Million in Damages

FACTS: A.E.H. was engaged in an on-and-off sexual relationship with Peterson. She filled her prescriptions, including birth control pills at a Walgreen pharmacy. Peterson began dating a Walgreen pharmacist, Audra Withers. A.E.H. became pregnant with Peterson's child. Peterson learned that he had contracted genital herpes and told Withers about the baby and that he may have exposed her to herpes. Withers became terrified, and during her shift at work she looked up A.E.H.'s prescription profile in the Walgreen computer system to see if she could find any information about her sexually transmitted disease. Peterson sent a text message to A.E.H.:

> I'm not trying to start any crap but I have a printout showing that you didn't even refill ur birth control prescription for July or august. The last time you filled ur prescription was June. I know uve lied... but the printout does not lie...

A.E.H. replied in part:

> Print out. It's illegal for u to obtain any kind of information like that regarding me...

After the child was born Peterson mailed a gift to his son. By an Internet search regarding the return address A.E.H. discovered that Peterson was married to Withers and that Withers was a Walgreen pharmacist. In a lawsuit based on negligence/malpractice the jury found that Walgreen and Withers were jointly responsible for $1.4 million in damages. Walgreen appealed.

DECISION: Judgment for A.E.H. against both Withers and Walgreen. Withers was acting within the scope of her employment with Walgreen for her actions were of the same general nature as those authorized or incidental to the actions that were authorized, using the Walgreen computer system and printer to look up customer information and patient prescription histories. Withers owed A.E.H. a duty of privacy protection by virtue of her employment as a pharmacist, and she breached this duty. Her actions are imputed to Walgreen under the doctrine of *respondeat superior.* [*Walgreen Co. v. A.E.H.,* **2014 WL 6130795 (Ind. App. 2014)**]

Employee of the United States

The Federal Tort Claims Act (FTCA) declares that the United States shall be liable vicariously whenever a federal employee driving a motor vehicle in the course of employment causes harm under such circumstances that a private employer would be liable. Contrary to the general rule, the statute exempts the employee driver from liability.[16]

THINKING THINGS THROUGH

Rule No. 1: Take the Safe Course

The National Safety Council estimates that one quarter of all automobile and truck accidents involve cell phone use or texting. In fatality and injury vehicle accidents, plaintiffs' attorneys subpoena cell phone records, which often form the basis of compelling liability cases against driver-employees *and* their employers. It is a near automatic conclusion by jurors that the operator using a cell phone or texting caused the accident. Thinking Things Through, for the safety of employees and the public, as well as the extraordinary liability risks for employers, it may well be a sound business practice to ban all cell phone usage while driving on company business.

---

[16] Claims of negligent hiring are not permissible under the FTCA. See *Tonelli v. United States*, 60 F.3d 492 (8th Cir. 1995).

37-3b **Negligent Hiring and Retention of Employees**

In addition to a complaint against the employer based on the doctrine of *respondeat superior*, a lawsuit may often raise a second theory, that of negligent hiring or retention of an employee.[17] Unlike the *respondeat superior* theory by which the employer may be vicariously liable for the tort of an employee, the negligent hiring theory is based on the negligence of the employer in the hiring process. Under the *respondeat superior* rule, the employer is liable only for those torts committed within the scope of employment or in the furtherance of the employer's interests. The negligent hiring theory has been used to impose liability in cases when an employee commits an intentional tort, almost invariably outside the scope of employment, against a customer or the general public, and the employer knew or should have known that the employee was incompetent, violent, dangerous, or criminal.[18]

Need for Due Care in Hiring

An employer may be liable on a theory of negligent hiring when it is shown that the employer knew, or in the exercise of ordinary care should have known, that the job applicant would create an undue risk of harm to others in carrying out job responsibilities. Moreover, it must also be shown that the employer could have reasonably foreseen injury to the third party. Thus, an employer who knows of an employee's preemployment drinking problems and violent behavior may be liable to customers assaulted by that employee.

Employers might protect themselves from liability in a negligent hiring case by having each prospective employee fill out an employment application form and then checking into the applicant's work experience, background, character, and qualifications. This would be evidence of due care in hiring. Generally, the scope of a preemployment investigation should correlate to the degree of opportunity the prospective employee would have to do harm to third persons. A minimum investigation consisting of filling out an application form and conducting a personal interview would be satisfactory for hiring an outside maintenance person, but a full background inquiry would be necessary for hiring a security guard. However, such inquiry does not bar *respondeat superior* liability.

Employees with Criminal Records

The hiring of an individual with a criminal record does not by itself establish the tort of negligent hiring.[19] An employer who knows that an applicant has a criminal record has a duty to investigate to determine whether the nature of the conviction in relationship to the job to be performed creates an unacceptable risk to third persons.

Negligent Retention

Courts assign liability under negligent retention on a basis similar to that of negligent hiring. That is, the employer knew, or should have known, that the employee would create an undue risk of harm to others in carrying out job responsibilities.

A hospital is liable for negligent retention when it continues the staff privileges of a physician that it knew or should have known had sexually assaulted a female patient in the past.[20]

---

[17] *Medina v. Graham's Cowboys, Inc.*, 827 P.2d 859 (N.M. App. 1992).

[18] *Rockwell v. Sun Harbor Budget Suites*, 925 P.2d 1175 (Nev. 1996).

[19] *Connes v. Molalla Transportation Systems*, 831 P.2d 1316 (Colo. 1992).

[20] *Capithorne v. Framingham Union Hospital*, 520 N.E.2d 139 (Mass. 1988). A hospital may also be vicariously liable for the negligent credentialing of its physicians, as determined in *Larson v. Wasemiller*, 738 N.W.2d 300 (Minn. 2007).

CASE SUMMARY

(1) Alcohol, (2) Battery, and (3) Negligent Retention: Three Strikes and You're Out!

FACTS: Mark Livigni was manager of the National Super Markets store in Cahokia, Illinois. After drinking alcoholic beverages one evening, he stopped by the store to check the premises when he observed a 10-year-old boy's unacceptable behavior outside the store. Livigni chased the boy to a car, where he pulled another child, a 4-year-old named Farris Bryant, from the car and threw him through the air. A multicount lawsuit was brought against National and Livigni. The evidence revealed that some eight years before the incident with Farris Bryant, Livigni had thrown an empty milk crate at a subordinate employee, striking him on the arm and necessitating medical treatment, and that some two years before the incident, he threw his 13-year-old son onto a bed while disciplining him, causing the boy to sustain a broken collarbone. Livigni was promoted to store manager subsequent to the milk crate incident, and he pled guilty to aggravated battery to his child and was sentenced to two years' probation. A verdict was rendered against National for $20,000 under a *respondeat superior* theory for the battery of Farris Bryant. A verdict was also rendered against

National for $15,000 for negligent retention of Livigni and for $115,000 in punitive damages for willful and wanton retention. National appealed the trial court's denial of its motions for directed verdicts on these counts.

DECISION: Judgment for Bryant. Employers that wrongfully hire or retain unfit employees expose the public to the acts of these employees, and it is not unreasonable to hold the employer accountable when the employee causes injury to another. The principle is not *respondeat superior*; rather, it is premised on the wrongful conduct of the employer itself. In addition, the employer in this case is responsible under *respondeat superior* because Livigni was prompted to act, in part, to protect store property. A dissenting opinion stated that the decision would send the wrong message to employers on the negligent retention issue and cause them to terminate any employee who has ever had an altercation on or off company premises, which is contrary to the state's public policy of rehabilitating criminal offenders. [***Bryant v. Livigni,*** **619 N.E.2d 550 (Ill. App. 1993)**]

37-3c Negligent Supervision and Training

A separate theory of liability in addition to the doctrine of *respondeat superior* is that of negligent supervision and training that holds the principal directly liable for its negligence in regard to training and supervision of its employees and agents. **For Example,** Monadnock Training Council, Inc., certified Robert Hebert as an "authorized Monadnock instructor" and granted him actual authority to market and promote its PR-24 police baton. In a training session run by Hebert at the Cheshire County House of Corrections in New Hampshire, Charles Herman suffered severe head trauma when training with Hebert without protective headgear in a room with unpadded cement walls. Monadnock was held directly liable for Herman's injuries based on its negligent supervision and training of Hebert.[21]

37-3d Agent's Crimes

A principal is liable for the crimes of an agent committed at the principal's direction. When not authorized, however, the principal is ordinarily not liable for an agent's crime merely because it was committed while the agent was otherwise acting within the scope of the latter's authority or employment. **For Example,** the owner of the Main Tower Cafe in Hartford, Connecticut, was not vicariously liable for injuries sustained by a patron who was shot by a bouncer while attempting to enter the bar because the bouncer's intentional and willful act was motivated by his own spleen and malevolence against the victim in

---

[21] *Herman v. Monadnock PR-24 Training Council, Inc.,* 802 A.2d 1187 (N.H. 2002).

FIGURE 37-1	Liability for Torts of Agent or Employee

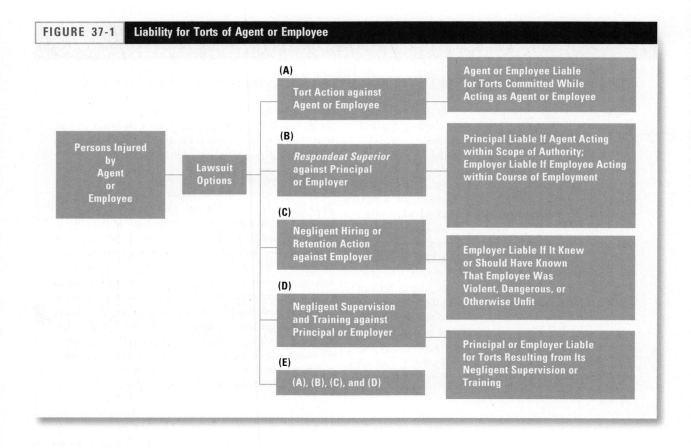

clear departure from his employment.[22] As an exception to the rule of nonliability just stated, courts now hold an employer criminally liable when the employee has in the course of employment violated environmental protection laws, liquor sales laws, pure food laws, or laws regulating prices or prohibiting false weights. **For Example,** an employer may be held criminally responsible for an employee's sale of liquor to a minor in violation of the liquor law even though the sale was not known to the employer and violated instructions given to the employee.

37-3e Owner's Liability for Acts of an Independent Contractor

If work is done by an independent contractor rather than by an employee, the owner is not liable for harm caused by the contractor to third persons or their property. Likewise, the owner is not bound by the contracts made by the independent contractor. The owner is ordinarily not liable for harm caused to third persons by the negligence of the employees of the independent contractor.[23]

---

[22] *Pruitt v. Main & Tower, Inc.*, 2002 WL 532467 (Conn. Super. March 14, 2002); see also *Burgess v. Lee Acceptance Corp.*, 2008 WL 5111905 (E.D. Mich. Dec. 4, 2008).

[23] *King v. Lens Creek, Ltd, Partnership*, 483 S.E.2d 265 (W. Va. 1996).

CASE SUMMARY

Plaintiffs' Attorneys Whine, "Why Do Courts Keep on Applying the 'Right to Control Test'?"

FACTS: Mark McLaurin was employed as a carpenter by Friede Goldman Offshore, Inc. Noble Drilling Inc. contracted with Friede Goldman (FG) to refit one of the offshore drilling rigs, the "Noble Clyde Boudreaux," at FG's Jackson County, Mississippi, facility. On July 30 and 31, 2002, McLaurin was assigned by Friede Goldman to construct scaffolding inside one of the pontoon extensions. A crane, operated by Friede Goldman employees, was in the process of lowering the roof structure of the pontoon for final placement. McLaurin was injured when he placed his hand in a "pinch point"—a space between two objects—while the roof was being lowered. McLaurin suffered a severely crushed left hand and arm. He received medical benefits and disability compensation from FG under the Longshore and Harbor Workers' Compensation Act. Maritime workers are also allowed to pursue separate claims against third parties responsible for their injuries, and McLaurin sued Noble Drilling for

negligence. Noble Drilling sought dismissal of the case asserting that it was not responsible for the negligence of the employees of an independent contractor.

DECISION: Judgment for Noble Drilling. McLaurin testified that no one from Noble instructed him to work inside the pontoon extension or how to do his work. McLaurin's supervisor testified that Noble never told any member of his crew what to do and that he had "total control over my crew." Only FG employees were involved in the fitting work at the time of McLaurin's injury. And no Noble employee was present to observe the unsafe placement of McLaurin's hand in the pontoon extension. The mere fact that Noble could observe, inspect, and make recommendations does not establish that it had substantial control over the operation. [*McLaurin v. Noble Drilling Inc.*, 2009 WL 367401 (S.D. Miss. Feb. 10, 2009)]

Exceptions to Owner's Immunity

There is a trend toward imposing liability on the owner when work undertaken by an independent contractor is inherently dangerous.[24] That is, the law is taking the position that if the owner wishes to engage in a particular activity, the owner must be responsible for the harm it causes. The owner cannot be insulated from such liability by the device of hiring an independent contractor to do the work.

Regardless of the nature of the activity, the owner may be liable for the torts and contracts of the independent contractor when the owner controls the conduct of the independent contractor.

In certain circumstances, such as providing security for a business, collecting bills, and repossessing collateral, there is an increased risk that torts may be committed by the individuals performing such duties. The trend of the law is to refuse to allow the use of an independent contractor for such work to insulate the employer.

Undisclosed Independent Contractor

In some situations, the owner appears to be doing the act in question because the existence of the independent contractor is not disclosed or apparent. This situation occurs most commonly when a franchisee does business under the name of the franchisor; when a concessionaire, such as a restaurant in a hotel, appears to be the hotel restaurant, although in fact it is operated by an independent concessionaire; or when the buyer of a business continues to run the business in the seller's name. In such cases of an undisclosed independent contractor, it is generally held that the apparent owner (that is, the franchisor, the grantor of the concession, or the seller) is liable for the torts and contracts of the undisclosed independent contractor.

[24] *Hinger v. Parker & Parsley Petroleum Co.*, 902 P.2d 1033 (N.M. App. 1995).

37-3f Enforcement of Claim by Third Person

A lawsuit may be brought by a third person against the agent or the principal if each is liable. In most states and in the federal courts, the plaintiff may sue either or both in one action when both are liable. If both are sued, the plaintiff may obtain a judgment against both, although the plaintiff is allowed to collect the full amount of the judgment only once.

37-4 Transactions with Sales Personnel

Many transactions with sales personnel do not result in a contract with the third person with whom the salesperson deals.

37-4a Soliciting and Contracting Agents

soliciting agent–
salesperson.

Giving an order to a salesperson often does not give rise to a contract. A salesperson may be a **soliciting agent,** whose authority is limited to soliciting offers from third persons and transmitting them to the principal for acceptance or rejection. Such an agent does not have authority to make a contract that will bind the principal to the third person. The employer of the salesperson is not bound by a contract until the employer accepts the order, and the third person (customer) may withdraw the offer at any time prior to acceptance.

contracting agent–agent
with authority to make
contracts; person with
whom the buyer deals.

In contrast, if the person with whom the buyer deals is a **contracting agent** with authority to make contracts, by definition a binding contract exists between the principal and the customer from the moment that the agent agrees with the customer. In other words, the contract arises when the agent accepts the customer's order.[25]

Make the Connection

Summary

An agent of a disclosed principal who makes a contract with a third person within the scope of authority has no personal liability on the contract. It is the principal and the third person who may each sue the other in the event of a breach. A person purporting to act as an agent for a principal warrants by implication that there is an existing principal with legal capacity and that the principal has authorized the agent to act. The person acting as an agent is liable for any loss caused the third person for breach of these warranties. An agent of a partially disclosed or an undisclosed principal is a party to the contract with the third person. The agent may enforce the contract

against the third person and is liable for its breach. To avoid problems of interpretation, an agent should execute a contract "Principal, by Agent." Agents are liable for harm caused third persons by their fraudulent, malicious, or negligent acts.

An undisclosed or a partially disclosed principal is liable to a third person on a simple contract made by an authorized agent. When a third person makes payment to an authorized agent, it is deemed paid to the principal.

A principal or an employer is vicariously liable under the doctrine of *respondeat superior* for the torts of an agent or an employee committed within the scope of authority

---

[25] But see the complications that developed in *Ferris v. Tennessee Log Homes, Inc.,* 2009 WL 1506724, (W.D. Ky. May 27, 2009), where Tennessee Log Homes (TLH) had a licensing agreement that explicitly granted authority to its "agent" to generate contracts for the sale of log home packages on behalf of TLH.

or the course of employment. The principal or the employer may also be liable for some crimes committed in the course of employment. An owner is not liable for torts caused by an independent contractor to third persons or their property unless the work given to the independent contractor is inherently hazardous.

A salesperson is ordinarily an agent whose authority is limited to soliciting offers (orders) from third persons and transmitting them to the principal. The principal is not bound until he or she accepts the order. The customer may withdraw an offer at any time prior to acceptance.

Learning Outcomes

After studying this chapter, you should be able to clearly explain:

37-1   Liability of Agent to Third Person

LO.1   Explain when an agent is and is not liable to a third person as a party to a contract

See the Biefeld Jewelers example in which Margie Biefeld was acting as an agent for a disclosed principal when she signed the contract and was not a party to the contract, page 743.

LO.2   Describe how to execute a contract as an agent on behalf of a principal

See the "B. G. Gray, by Jane R. Craig" example, page 745.

Learn from the mistake of Philip Steen's insufficient disclosure of his principal in the *ICG Link* case, page 744.

37-2   Liability of Principal to Third Person

LO.3   Explain the legal effect of a payment made by a third person to an authorized agent

See the discussion of a third party's payment to an authorized agent who absconds with the payment, page 747.

But see the effect of a payment by a disclosed principal to its agent who fails to pay the third party in the *Rainbow Networks* case, page 748.

37-3   Liability of Principal for Torts and Crimes of Agent

LO.4   Explain the doctrine of *respondeat superior*

See the Crane Brothers, Inc., example of employer liability for torts of the employees, page 750.

See the *Walgreen* case where the employee's negligence/malpractice was imputed to the employer under the doctrine of *respondeat superior*, page 751.

37-4   Transactions with Sales Personnel

LO.5   Distinguish between the authority of a soliciting agent and that of a contracting agent

See the discussion of the soliciting and contracting of agents, page 756.

Key Terms

contracting agent
disclosed principal
partially disclosed principal

respondeat superior
soliciting agent
undisclosed principal

vicarious liability

Questions and Case Problems

1. Richard Pawlus was an owner of Dutch City Wood Products, Inc., which did business as "Dutch City Marketing." Pawlus purchased merchandise from Rothschild Sunsystems from April 24 to June 24 using the designation "Richard Pawlus Dutch City Marketing" on orders and correspondence. In October, Rothschild was notified that Pawlus was acting on behalf of the corporation when the merchandise was purchased. Rothschild sued Pawlus for payment for the merchandise. Pawlus contended that he was an agent of the corporation and was thus not personally liable. Decide. [*Rothschild Sunsystems, Inc. v. Pawlus*, 514 N.Y.S.2d 572 (A.D.)]

2. Judith Studebaker was injured when a van owned and driven by James Ferry collided with her vehicle. On the morning of the incident, Ferry made his usual runs for the florist for whom he delivered flowers, Nettie's Flower Garden. He had made a slight detour prior to the accident to conduct personal business at a pawnshop and was returning to the flower shop at the time of the accident. Nettie's set standards for Ferry's dress and conduct, determined his territory, and set standards for his van. Studebaker brought an action against Nettie's on a *respondeat superior* theory on the belief that Ferry was Nettie's employee at the time of the accident. Nettie's defended that Ferry was an

independent contractor, not an employee. Decide. [*Studebaker v. Nettie's Flower Garden Inc.*, 842 S.W.2d 227 (Mo. App.)]

3. Lowell Shoemaker, an architect, was hired by Aff-house to work on a land development project. In September Shoemaker contacted Central Missouri Professional Services about providing engineering and surveying services for the project. Central submitted a written proposal to Shoemaker in October. About a week later, Shoemaker orally agreed that Central should proceed with the work outlined in the proposal. When the first phase of the work was completed, a bill of $5,864.00 was sent to Shoemaker. Shoemaker called Central and requested that all bills be sent directly to the owner/developer, Affhouse. When the bills were not paid, Central sued Shoemaker and Affhouse. The trial court entered a judgment against Shoemaker for $5,864 and he appealed. Shoemaker acknowledged that he did not disclose the identity of the principal to Central at the time the transaction was conducted, and explained:

> Q. You never told Mike Bates or Central Missouri Professional Services that you were an agent for Affhouse or any other undisclosed principal?
> A. That's correct. I never did.
>
> Q. Another note I wrote down was that the subject of Affhouse came up in your conversations with Mike Bates of Central Missouri Professional Services after he sent the bill to you?
> A. The early part of the year, yes.

Shoemaker contends that since he made clear to Central that he was an architect and not the developer, there was no binding oral contract between Central and him. Decide. [*Central Missouri Professional Services v. Shoemaker*, 108 S.W.3d 6 (Mo. App.)]

4. Beverly Baumann accompanied her mother to Memorial Hospital, where her mother was placed in intensive care for heart problems. A nurse asked Baumann to sign various documents, including one that authorized the hospital to release medical information and to receive the mother's insurance benefits directly. This form stated: "I understand I am financially responsible to the hospital for charges not covered by this authorization." Baumann's mother died during the course of her hospitalization. The hospital later sued Baumann to recover $19,013.42 in unpaid hospital charges based on the form she signed, which the hospital called a "guarantee of payment." Baumann contended that she signed the document as an agent for her mother and was thus not personally liable. Decide. [*Memorial Hospital v. Baumann*, 474 N.Y.S.2d 636 (A.D.)]

5. Craig Industries was in the business of manufacturing charcoal. Craig, the corporation's president, contracted in the name of the corporation to sell the company's plants to Husky Industries. Craig did not have authority from the board of directors to make the contract, and later the board of directors voted not to accept it. Husky Industries sued Craig on the theory that he, as agent for the corporation, exceeded his authority and should be held personally liable for damages. Decide. [*Huskey Industries v. Craig*, 618 S.W.2d 458 (Mo. App. 1981)]

6. Leo Bongers died intestate. Alfred Bongers and Delores Kuhl, Leo's nephew and niece, were appointed personal representatives of his estate. Leo left more than 120 antique cars, trucks, and motorcycles. The estate hired Bauer-Moravec to sell the vehicles at auction. Auctioneer Russ Moravec suggested that the vehicles be sold at an airstrip auction in May, June, or July. The estate rejected this recommendation and insisted that the sale be conducted in January on a farm owned by the estate. On January 30, the auction took place beginning at 9:30 A.M. with temperatures below freezing and some 800 people jammed into the bid barn. One auctioneer had purchased Putnam hitch balls to be used with mylar-type ropes so that small farm tractors could tow the vehicles into and out of the bid barn. One hour into the auction, Joseph Haag was seriously injured when a hitch ball came loose from the drawbar of the tractor towing an antique Studebaker truck. Haag sued the estate, claiming that Bauer-Moravec was acting as agent for the estate and that its negligence in not properly attaching the hitch ball and in using mylar-type tow rope rather than chains should be imputed to the estate under the doctrine of *respondeat superior*. The estate defended that it was not liable for the torts of the auctioneer and its employees because the auctioneer was an independent contractor. Decide. [*Haag v. Bongers*, 589 N.W.2d 318 (Neb.)]

7. On July 11, 1984, José Padilla was working as a vacation-relief route salesperson for Frito-Lay. He testified that he made a route stop at Sal's Beverage Shop, where he was told by Mrs. Ramos that she was dissatisfied with Frito-Lay service and no longer

wanted its products in the store. He asked if there was anything he could do to change her mind. She said no and told him to pick up his merchandise. He took one company-owned merchandise rack to his van and was about to pick up another rack when Mr. Ramos said that the rack had been given to him by the regular route salesperson. Padilla said the route salesperson had no authority to give away Frito-Lay racks. A confrontation occurred over the rack, and Padilla pushed Mr. Ramos against the cash register, injuring Ramos's back. Frito-Lay has a company policy, clearly communicated to all employees, that prohibits them from getting involved in any type of physical confrontation with a customer. Frito-Lay contended that Padilla was not acting within the course and scope of his employment when the pushing incident took place and that the company was therefore not liable to Ramos. Ramos contended that Frito-Lay was responsible for the acts of its employee, Padilla. Decide. [*Frito-Lay, Inc. v. Ramos*, 770 S.W.2d 887 (Tex. App.)]

8. Jason Lasseigne, a Little League baseball player, was seriously injured at a practice session when he was struck on the head by a poorly thrown baseball from a team member, Todd Landry. The league was organized by American Legion Post 38. Claude Cassel and Billy Johnson were the volunteer coaches of the practice session. The Lasseignes brought suit on behalf of Jason against Post 38, claiming that the coaching was negligent and that Post 38 was vicariously liable for the harm caused by such negligence. Post 38 contended that it had no right to control the work of the volunteer coaches or the manner in which practices were conducted and as a result should not be held vicariously liable for the actions of the coaches. Decide. [*Lasseigne v. American Legion Post 38*, 543 So. 2d 1111 (La. App.)]

9. Moritz, a guest at Pines Hotel, was sitting in the lobby when Brown, a hotel employee, dropped a heavy vacuum cleaner on her knee. When Moritz complained, the employee insulted her and hit her with his fist, knocking her unconscious. She sued the hotel for damages. Was the hotel liable? [*Moritz v. Pines Hotel, Inc.*, 383 N.Y.S.2d 704 (A.D.)]

10. Steve Diezel, an employee of Island City Flying Service in Key West, Florida, stole a General Electric Credit Corp. (GECC) aircraft and crashed the plane while attempting to take off. GECC brought suit against Island City on the theory that it had negligently hired Diezel as an employee and was therefore legally responsible for Diezel's act of theft. Diezel had a military prison record as a result of a drug offense and had been fired by Island City twice previously but had been immediately reinstated each time. Island City claimed that the evidence was insufficient to establish that it had been negligent in employing Diezel. Decide. [*Island City Flying Service v. General Electric*, 585 So. 2d 274 (Fla.)]

11. The Bay State Harness Horse Racing and Breeding Association conducted horse races at a track where music for patrons was supplied by an independent contractor hired by the association. Some of the music played was subject to a copyright held by Famous Music Corp. The playing of that music was a violation of the copyright unless royalties were paid to Famous Music. No royalties were paid, and Famous Music sued the association, which raised the defense that the violation had been committed by an independent contractor specifically instructed not to play Famous Music's copyrighted material. Decide. [*Famous Music Corp. v. Bay State Harness Horse Racing and Breeding Association, Inc.*, 554 F.2d 1213 (1st Cir.)]

12. Steven Trujillo, told by the assistant door manager of Cowboys Bar "to show up to work tonight in case we need you as a doorman," came to the bar that evening wearing a jacket with the bar logo on it. Trujillo "attacked" Rocky Medina in the parking lot of the bar, causing him serious injury. Prior to working for Cowboys, Trujillo was involved in several fights at that bar and in its parking lot, and Cowboys knew of these matters. Medina sued Cowboys on two theories of liability: (1) *respondeat superior* and (2) negligent hiring of Trujillo. Cowboys's defense was that the *respondeat superior* theory should be dismissed because the assault was clearly not within the course of Trujillo's employment. Concerning the negligent hiring theory, Cowboys asserted that Trujillo was not on duty that night as a doorman. Decide. [*Medina v. Graham's Cowboys, Inc.*, 827 P.2d 859 (N.M. App.)]

13. Neal Rubin, while driving his car in Chicago, inadvertently blocked the path of a Yellow Cab Co. taxi driven by Robert Ball, causing the taxi to swerve and hit Rubin's car. Angered by Rubin's driving, Ball got out of his cab and hit Rubin on the head and shoulders with a metal pipe. Rubin sued Yellow Cab Co. for the damages caused by this beating, contending that the employer was vicariously liable for

the beating under the doctrine of *respondeat superior* because the beating occurred in furtherance of the employer's business, which was to obtain fares without delay. The company argued that Ball's beating of Rubin was not an act undertaken to further the employer's business. Is the employer liable under *respondeat superior*? [*Rubin v. Yellow Cab Co.*, 507 N.E.2d 114 (Ill. App.)]

14. Brazilian & Colombian Co. (B&C), a food broker, ordered 40 barrels of olives from Mawer-Gulden-Annis (MGA). MGA's shipping clerk was later told to make out the bill of lading to B&C's customer Pantry Queen; the olives were shipped directly to Pantry Queen. Eight days after delivery, the president of B&C wrote MGA to give it the name of its principal, Pantry Queen, and advised MGA to bill the principal directly. Pantry Queen was unable to pay for the olives, and MGA sued B&C for payment. B&C contended that it was well known to MGA that B&C was a food broker (agent) and the olives were shipped directly to the principal by MGA. It stated that as an agent, it was not a party to the contract and was thus not liable. Decide. [*Mawer-Gulden-Annis, Inc. v. Brazilian & Colombian Coffee Co.*, 199 N.E.2d 222 (Ill. App.)]

CPA Questions

1. Frey entered into a contract with Cara Corp. to purchase televisions on behalf of Lux, Inc. Lux authorized Frey to enter into the contract in Frey's name without disclosing that Frey was acting on behalf of Lux. If Cara repudiates the contract, which of the following statements concerning liability on the contract is *not* correct?

   a. Frey may not hold Cara liable and obtain money damages.

   b. Frey may hold Cara liable and obtain specific performance.

   c. Lux may hold Cara liable upon disclosing the agency relationship with Frey.

   d. Cara will be free from liability to Lux if Frey fraudulently stated that he was acting on his own behalf.

2. A principal will *not* be liable to a third party for a tort committed by an agent:

   a. Unless the principal instructed the agent to commit the tort.

   b. Unless the tort was committed within the scope of the agency relationship.

   c. If the agency agreement limits the principal's liability for the agent's tort.

   d. If the tort is also regarded as a criminal act.

3. Cox engaged Datz as her agent. It was mutually agreed that Datz would *not* disclose that he was acting as Cox's agent. Instead, he was to deal with prospective customers as if he were a principal acting on his own behalf. This he did and made several contracts for Cox. Assuming Cox, Datz, or the customer seeks to avoid liability on one of the contracts involved, which of the following statements is correct?

   a. Cox must ratify the Datz contracts in order to be held liable.

   b. Datz has *no* liability once he discloses that Cox was the real principal.

   c. The third party can avoid liability because he believed he was dealing with Datz as a principal.

   d. The third party may choose to hold either Datz or Cox liable.

4. Which of the following statements is (are) correct regarding the relationship between an agent and a nondisclosed principal?

   I. The principal is required to indemnify the agent for any contract entered into by the agent within the scope of the agency agreement.

   II. The agent has the same actual authority as if the principal had been disclosed.

   a. I only

   b. II only

   c. Both I and II

   d. Neither I nor II

Regulation of Employment

Learning Outcomes ‹‹‹

After studying this chapter, you should be able to

LO.1 Explain the contractual nature of the employment relationship

LO.2 Explain how whistleblower protection under Sarbanes-Oxley is limited to conduct in violation of fraud or securities laws

LO.3 Explain how Dodd-Frank expands whistleblower protection to a wide range of financial services employees and provides incentives for whistleblowers

LO.4 Explain how the National Labor Relations Act prohibits employers from firing employees attempting to form a union and requires employers to bargain with certified unions in good faith over wages, hours, and working conditions

LO.5 Explain how ERISA protects employee pensions and benefits

LO.6 Explain the essentials of unemployment benefits, family and medical leaves, military leaves, and Social Security benefits

LO.7 Explain how OSHA is designed to ensure workers' safe and healthful working conditions

LO.8 Explain the three types of benefits provided by Workers' Compensation statutes

LO.9 Explain the sources of privacy rights and applications to telephone, e-mail, and property searches

LO.10 Explain an employer's verification obligations when hiring new employees

Employment law involves the law of contracts and the law established by lawmakers, courts, and administrative agencies.

38-1 The Employment Relationship

The relationship of an employer and an employee exists when, pursuant to an express or implied agreement of the parties, one person, the employee, undertakes to perform services or to do work under the direction and control of another, the employer, for compensation. In older cases, this relationship was called the *master-servant relationship*.

38-1a Characteristics of Relationship

An employee is hired to work under the control of the employer. An employee differs from an agent, who is to negotiate or make contracts with third persons on behalf of, and under the control of, a principal. However, a person may be both an employee and an agent for a party. An employee also differs from an independent contractor, who is to perform a contract independent of the control of the employer.[1]

38-1b Creation of Employment Relationship

The relationship of employer and employee can be created only with the consent of both parties.

Individual Employment Contracts

As in contracts generally, both parties must assent to the terms of an employment contract. Subject to statutory restrictions, the parties are free to make a contract on any terms they wish.

Collective Bargaining Contracts

Collective bargaining contracts govern the rights and obligations of employers and employees in many private and public areas of employment. Under collective bargaining, representatives of the employees bargain with a single employer or a group of employers for an agreement on wages, hours, and working conditions. The agreement worked out by the representatives of the employees, usually union officials, is generally subject to a ratification vote by the employees. Terms usually found in collective bargaining contracts are (1) identification of the work belonging exclusively to designated classes of employees, (2) wage and benefits clauses, (3) promotion and layoff clauses, which are generally tied in part to seniority, (4) a management's rights clause, and (5) a grievance procedure. A grievance procedure provides a means by which persons claiming that the contract was violated or that they were disciplined or discharged without just cause may have their cases decided by impartial labor arbitrators.

38-1c Duration and Termination of Employment Contract

In many instances, the employment contract does not state any time or duration. In such a case, it may be terminated at any time by either party. In contrast, the employment contract may state that it shall last for a specified period of time; an example would be an individual's contract to work as general manager for five years.

---

[1] *Ost v. West Suburban Travelers Limousine, Inc.*, 88 F.3d 435 (7th Cir. 1996).

Employment-at-Will Doctrine and Developing Exceptions

Ordinarily, a contract of employment may be terminated in the same manner as any other contract. If it is to run for a definite period of time, the employer cannot terminate the contract at an earlier date without justification. If the employment contract does not have a definite duration, it is terminable at will. Under the **employment-at-will doctrine** the employer has historically been allowed to terminate the employment contract at any time for any reason or for no reason.[2] Gradually, federal and state statutes were enacted to provide certain individual rights to workers, protecting them from workplace exploitation and discrimination by employers. And, in most states, courts have carved out narrow exceptions to the employment-at-will doctrine when the discharge violates an established public policy. **For Example,** home health care nurse Eugene Patterson continued to provide wound care to a patient after he was directed to cease the care by his employer, and he was discharged for insubordination. Patterson did so because the physician's order for the care remained in place, and he believed that state law governing the practice of nursing required him to complete the physician-directed care. The court held Patterson could sue his employer, Gentiva Health Services, for wrongful termination in violation of public policy.[3] Absent statutory protection, or a court-created contract or tort exception, the employment-at-will doctrine is still the basic default rule governing employment in the United States.

Public policy exceptions are often made to the employment-at-will doctrine when an employee is discharged in retaliation for insisting that the employer comply with the state's food and drug act or for filing a workers' compensation claim.[4] In some states, so-called whistleblower laws have been enacted to protect employees who disclose employer practices that endanger public health or safety. Also, a statutory right exists for at-will employees who are terminated in retaliation for cooperating with a federal criminal prosecution or who are terminated in violation of the public policy to provide truthful testimony.[5]

CASE SUMMARY

Pretext at the Pizzeria

FACTS: While working his nighttime cooking shift at Pizzeria Uno, Gerald Adams noticed that the restaurant's kitchen floor was saturated with a foul-smelling liquid coming from the drains. Adams left work, complaining of illness, and contacted the Department of Health about the drainage problem in the restaurant's kitchen. Upon returning to the restaurant a few days later, Adams was ordered into his manager's office. He was accused of stealing a softball shirt and taking home a work schedule. A shouting match ensued, and Adams was later arraigned on a criminal charge of disorderly conduct. The charges were eventually dropped and have since been expunged from his record. Adams contends that he was unlawfully terminated in violation of the state's whistleblower act because he notified the Board of Health regarding the unsanitary kitchen conditions. Uno contends he was fired for threatening the supervisor, which is an untenable act.

[2] *Payne v. Western & Atlantic Railroad Co.*, 82 Tenn. 507, 518–519 (1884).

[3] *Patterson v. Gentiva Health Services, Inc.*, 2011 WL 3235466 (D. S.C. July 25, 2011).

[4] *Brigham v. Dillon Companies, Inc.*, 935 P.2d 1054 (Kan. 1997).

[5] *Fitzgerald v. Salsbury Chemical, Inc.*, 613 N.W.2d 275 (Iowa 2000). In *Garcetti v. Ceballos*, 547 U.S. 410 (2006), the U.S. Supreme Court held that when public employees make statements pursuant to their official duties, the First Amendment of the Constitution does not insulate their communications from employer discipline because the employees are not speaking as citizens for First Amendment purposes. In his dissent, Justice Souter argued that a public employee should have constitutional protection when the employee acts as a whistleblower.

Pretext at the Pizzeria continued

DECISION: Judgment for Adams in the amount of $7,500. The confrontation between Adams and his employer was calculated by the employer to provoke a reaction from Adams that would serve as an excuse to fire him, a pretext for the real reason—Adam's phone call to the Board of Health. The wrongful termination and criminal charges that ensued from the verbal altercation were sufficient to establish damages for emotional distress. Adams's loss of security clearance in the National Guard, which prevented him from participating in an overseas mission in Germany, also supported the jury's finding of compensable emotional distress. [**Adams v. Uno Restaurants, Inc., 794 A.2d 489 (R.I. 2002)**]

Other courts still follow the common law at-will rule because they believe that a court should not rewrite the contract of the parties to provide employee protection that was never intended.[6]

Employer Adjustments

Employers have revised their personnel manuals and employee handbooks and have issued directives to all employees that no assurance of continued employment exists—that the employers are not obligated to have good cause to terminate employees, just as employees are free to leave their positions with the employers. While simultaneously reserving their at-will termination powers, many employers also may design specific, apparently fair termination procedures and promulgate antiharassment and antidiscrimination policies and procedures, as seen in the *Semple v. FedEx* decision.

CASE SUMMARY

It's Not Easy to Get Around the Employment-at-Will Doctrine, Mr. Semple

FACTS: John Semple was terminated from his employment with FedEx for falsification of company documents. He appealed his termination through internal FedEx procedures without success and thereafter sued the employer in federal court, contending that his termination was in violation of the "public policy exception" to the employment-at-will doctrine in that his termination resulted from his filing internal grievances regarding harassment by his superiors and that he was protected by the employee handbook exception to the at-will doctrine. The employer disagreed.

DECISION: Judgment for FedEx. When he was hired, John Semple signed an employment contract that included the following statement:

I also agree that my employment and compensation can be terminated with or without cause and without notice or liability whatsoever, at any time, at the option of either the company or myself.

The employee handbook stated in part:

The employment relationship between the Company and employee may be terminated at the will of either party as stated in the employment agreement signed upon application for employment. As described in that agreement, the policies and procedures set forth in this manual provide guidelines for management and employees during employment, but do not create contractual rights regarding termination otherwise.

Semple was an employee at-will. No public policy prevented FedEx from terminating Semple's employment. Moreover, FedEx had not surrendered its statutory right to terminate at-will employees based on its employee handbook. [**Semple v. Federal Express Corp., 2008 WL 1793481 (D.S.D. April 17, 2008); affirmed 566 F.3d 788 (8th Cir. 2009)**]

---

[6] See *Texas Farm Bureau Mutual Insurance Co. v. Sears*, 84 S.W.3d 604 (Tex. 2002).

Justifiable Discharge

An employer may be justified in discharging an employee because of the employee's (1) nonperformance of duties, (2) misrepresentation or fraud in obtaining the employment, (3) disobedience of proper directions, (4) disloyalty, (5) theft or other dishonesty, (6) possession or use of drugs or intoxicants, (7) misconduct, or (8) incompetence.

Employers generally have the right to lay off employees because of economic conditions, including a lack of work. Such actions are sometimes referred to as *reductions in force (RIFs)*.

Employers, however, must be very careful not to make layoffs based on age for that is a violation of the Age Discrimination in Employment Act.

In some states, a "service letter" statute requires an employer on request to furnish to a discharged employee a letter stating the reason for the discharge.

38-1d Whistleblower Protection under the Sarbanes-Oxley and Dodd-Frank Acts

The Sarbanes-Oxley Act (SOX) was enacted to restore investor confidence in financial markets following the exposure in 2001–2002 of widespread misconduct by directors and officers of publicly held companies. SOX contains reforms regarding corporate accountability, enhanced disclosure requirements, and enforcement and liability provisions. Title VIII of the Act contains protections for corporate whistleblowers.[7]

Protection Provided

SOX prohibits a publicly traded company or any agent of it from taking an adverse employment action against an employee who provides information, testifies, or "otherwise assists" in proceedings regarding (1) mail, wire, bank, or securities fraud, (2) any violation of an SEC rule or regulation, or (3) any federal law protecting shareholders against fraud.[8] The act sets forth the types of adverse employment actions that qualify for protection, specifically protecting employees from discharge, demotion, suspension, threats, harassment, failure to hire or rehire, blacklisting, or action otherwise discriminatory against employees in their terms and conditions of employment.

The act protects employees who provide information or assistance to supervisors, or a federal regulatory or law enforcement agency, or to members of Congress or a congressional committee. The act does not protect employees who provide information to the world, however. **For Example,** Nicholas Tides and Matthew Neumann were not protected under SOX when they provided a newspaper reporter information and documents about the questionable integrity of Boeing's data storage system and were fired for violating company confidentiality rules.[9]

Case law cautions that SOX whistleblower protection provisions do not provide "whistleblower protection for all employee complaints about how a public company spends its money and pays its bills."[10]

[7] 18 U.S.C. §1514A (2005).

[8] In *Lawson v. FMR LLC*, 134 S. Ct. 1158 (2014), the U.S. Supreme Court extended whistleblower protection under SOX to employees of private contractors and subcontractors serving public companies.

[9] *Tides v. Boeing Co.*, 644 F.3d 809 (9th Cir. 2011).

[10] *Platone v. Flyi, Inc.*, 2006 WL 3246910 (Dept. of Labor Sept. 29, 2006). See also *Welch v. Choa*, 536 F.3d 269 (4th Cir. 2008), in which CFO Welch had refused to certify an SEC quarterly report as required by SOX because of accounting irregularities and thus was fired. The court of appeals held that the conduct in question was not shown to be in violation of any fraud or securities laws listed in SOX; thus, Welch was not protected. However, in *Sylvester v. Parexel International LLC*, 2011 WL 2165854 (DOL Adm. Rev. Bd. May 25, 2011) the DOL's Administrative Review Board subsequently held that its prior ruling in *Platone v. Flyi, Inc.*—that an employee's complaint must "definitely and specifically" relate to the categories of fraud or securities violations listed in Section 806—"has evolved into an inappropriate test and is often applied too strictly."

Procedures

An individual who believes that she or he has been subject to an adverse employment action because of whistleblowing activities must file a complaint with the Department of Labor's Occupational Safety and Health Administration (OSHA) within 90 days after the asserted adverse employment action. OSHA administers 13 other federal whistleblower laws and has experienced investigators to facilitate its responsibilities under SOX.

The Dodd-Frank Expansion

The Dodd-Frank Wall Street Reform and Consumer Protection Act of 2010 (Dodd-Frank)[11] expands whistleblower protections to a wide range of financial services employees and provides expanded protections and incentives for whistleblowers.

Dodd-Frank covers almost any employee working in the financial services industry related to the extension of credit, including employees of privately held companies, and protects them from retaliation for disclosing information about fraud or unlawful conduct related to consumer financial products. It covers employees who extend credit, service loans, provide real estate settlement services, and provide financial advice, including credit counseling to consumers.[12]

Dodd-Frank requires the Securities and Exchange Commission to pay whistleblowers bounties of between 10 and 30 percent on monetary sanctions that aggregate to at least $1 million. To recover an award, a whistleblower must provide the SEC (1) voluntarily (2) with original information (3) that leads to a successful enforcement action or actions in federal court or before an agency (4) in which overall recovery totals over $1,000,000.[13]

Dodd-Frank expands on the SOX cause of action as follows:

1. Dodd-Frank expands the SOX statute of limitations from 90 to 180 days. The Dodd-Frank limitations period is six years.

2. Whistleblowers must exhaust administrative remedies under SOX at OSHA and DOL's Administrative Review Board before court review. Dodd-Frank allows an immediate lawsuit in federal district court.

3. SOX provides for actual back pay lost, as part of make whole relief, while Dodd-Frank allows recovery of double back pay as liquidated damages.

Dodd-Frank exempts whistleblower claims from predispute arbitration agreements. And it provides a burden-shifting framework for a private cause of action for employees who are retaliated against for protected activity so that once an employee has shown by a preponderance of the evidence that the protected activity was a contributing factor in an adverse employment action, the employer must show by clear and convincing evidence that it would have taken the same action in the absence of the employee's whistleblowing activities to avoid liability.

38-1e Duties of the Employee

The duties of an employee are determined primarily by the contract of employment with the employer. The law also implies certain obligations.

---

[11] The whistleblower protection provisions are codified at 15 U.S.C. §78u-6.

[12] In *Zillges v. Kenney Bank and Trust*, 24 F. Supp. 3d 795 (2014), a Dodd-Frank case was dismissed because the employee disclosure related to a violation of banking regulations, not a securities law violation.

[13] 17 C.F.R. §240.21F-1, *et seq.* To start an action a whistleblower must file a complaint with the SEC's Office of the Whistleblower, which includes a description of the misconduct, demonstrates eligibility, and declares under penalty of perjury that the information is true and accurate. Whistleblowers may submit a claim anonymously through an attorney.

Services

Employees are under the duty to perform such services as may be required by the contract of employment.

Trade Secrets

An employee may be given confidential trade secrets by the employer but must not disclose this knowledge to others. An agreement by the employee to refrain from disclosing trade secrets is binding. If the employee violates this obligation, the employer may enjoin the use of the information by the employee and by any person to whom it has been disclosed by the employee.

Former employees who are competing with their former employer may be enjoined from using information about suppliers and customers that they obtained while employees when this information is of vital importance to the employer's business. Injunctive relief is denied, however, if the information is not important or not secret.

Inventions

Employment contracts commonly provide that an employer will own any invention or discovery made by an employee, whether during work hours, after work hours, or for a period of one or two years after leaving the employment. In the absence of an express or implied agreement to the contrary, the inventions of an employee usually belong to the employee. This is true even though the employee used the time and property of the employer in the discovery. In this case, however, the employer has what is known as a **shop right** to use the invention without cost in its operations.

shop right–right of an employer to use in business without charge an invention discovered by an employee during working hours and with the employer's material and equipment.

38-1f Rights of the Employee

The rights of an employee are determined by the contract of employment and by the law as declared by courts, lawmakers, and administrative agencies.

Compensation

The rights of an employee with respect to compensation are governed in general by the same principles that apply to the compensation of an agent. In the absence of an agreement to the contrary, when an employee is discharged, whether for cause or not, the employer must pay wages to the expiration of the last pay period. State statutes commonly authorize employees to sue employers for wages improperly withheld and to recover penalties and attorney fees. In addition to hourly wages, payments due for vacations and certain bonuses are considered "wages" under state statutes.[14] **For Example,** Diane Beard worked for Summit Institute as a licensed practical nurse for 13 months when she walked off the job and terminated her employment. She requested her accrued vacation pay of $432, but Summit refused to pay her, claiming she had abandoned her job and thus forfeited her right to vacation pay under company policy. Accrued vacation qualifies as "wages," and she was entitled to the $432 vacation pay plus a penalty equal to 90 days' wages at the employee's rate of pay or $9,720, plus $2,400 in attorneys' fees for the trial and an additional $2,600 in attorneys' fees for the appeal. These statutes with their penalty provisions are designed as a coercive means to compel employers to promptly pay their employees.[15]

---

[14] *Knutson v. Snyder Industries, Inc.,* 436 N.W.2d 496 (Neb. 1989).
[15] *Beard v. Summit Institute of Pulmonary Medicine and Rehabilitation, Inc.,* 707 So. 2d 1233 (La. 1998); see also *Beckman v. Kansas Dep't. of Human Resources,* 43 P.3d 891 (Kan. App. 2002).

Federal Wage and Hour Law

Workers at enterprises engaged in interstate commerce are covered by the Fair Labor Standards Act (FLSA),[16] popularly known as the Wage and Hour Act. These workers cannot be paid less than a specified minimum wage.

CASE SUMMARY

What Is a "Willful" Violation?

FACTS: An action against an employer for violating the Fair Labor Standards Act must be brought within two years unless the violation was willful, in which case it may be brought within three years. McLaughlin, the Secretary of Labor, brought suit against Richland Shoe Company for failing to pay the minimum wage. Richland claimed that the suit was barred because more than two years had elapsed. McLaughlin claimed that the violation was willful, in which case the action was properly brought because three years had not expired. The parties disagreed as to what proof was required to establish that the violation was "willful."

DECISION: To be "willful" within the statute, the violation must be intentional or made with reckless indifference to whether the statute has been satisfied. Because the case had not been tried on the basis of this standard, the case was remanded to the lower court to determine the matter in the light of the new definition of *willful*. [**McLaughlin v. Richland Shoe Co.**, 486 U.S. 128 (1998)]

The FLSA has been amended to cover domestic service workers, including housekeepers, cooks, and nannies. Executive, administrative, and professional employees and outside salespersons are exempt from both the minimum wage and overtime provisions of the law.[17] Students "working" at internships *may* be covered by the FLSA.[18]

Subminimum Wage Provisions. The FLSA allows for the employment of full-time students at institutions of higher education at wage rates below the statutory minimum. Also, individuals whose productive capacity is impaired by age, physical or mental deficiency, or injury may be employed at less than the minimum wage to prevent the curtailment of work opportunities for these individuals. In these cases, however, a special certificate is needed by the employer from the Department of Labor's (DOL) Wage and Hour Division, which has offices throughout the United States.

Wage Issues. Deductions made from wages as a result of cash or merchandise shortages and deductions for tools of the trade are not legal if they reduce wages below the

---

[16] P.L. 75-718, 52 Stat. 1060, 29 U.S.C. §201 *et seq.*

[17] In *Christopher v. SmithKline Beecham Corp.*, 132 S. Ct. 2156 (2012), the U.S. Supreme Court determined that pharmaceutical representatives, whose primary duty is to obtain nonbinding commitments from physicians to prescribe their drugs, are "outside salesmen" excluded from overtime pay requirements of the FLSA.

[18] A developing issue in our society is the utilization of unpaid interns—generally high school or college students—and their coverage, if any, under the FLSA and other employment laws. The FLSA does not define the terms *intern* or *trainee*. The act broadly defines the word "employee" as "to suffer or permit to work." The DOL utilizes a six-factor test for determining whether an individual is a trainee (intern) or an employee under the FLSA. In *Solis v. Laurelbrook Sanitarium and School, Inc.*, 642 F.3d 518 (6th Cir. 2011), the U.S. Court of Appeals for the Sixth Circuit determined that the DOL's test was overly rigid, and applied a "primary benefit of the relationship test" deciding that the primary benefit in that case ran to the students. In *Glatt v. Fox Searchlight Pictures, Inc.*, 2 F.R.D. 516 (S.D.N.Y. 2013) the court focused on whether the company derived an immediate advantage from the interns' work, and the court decided the case for the plaintiffs, finding that they worked as paid employees worked, and the educational benefits they received were the result of having worked as any other employee worked. Unpaid interns not considered employees are not entitled to the protections of the FLSA and Title VII of the Civil Rights Act of 1964. Practically speaking, it is up to the high schools and colleges to make sure that the internships they arrange are for the primary benefit of their students and not substitutes for regular, paid employees.

minimum wage. An employer's requirement that employees provide uniforms or tools of their own is a violation of the law to the extent that the expenses for these items reduce wages below the minimum wage.[19]

Job-related training generally is compensable under the FLSA. However, an exception exists for voluntary training not directly related to an employee's job when the employee does not perform productive work. **For Example,** Hogar, Inc., operates a nursing home and required new employees to undergo two days of unpaid training before assuming paid duties as nurses' aides, maintenance/laundry workers, and kitchen workers. Little or no instruction was offered to these "trainees," and each individual would perform the regular duties of the position for the two-day period. Hogar's practices did not fall within the training exception because the trainees performed productive work with little or no actual training during a regular shift. In a lawsuit brought by the Secretary of Labor, Hogar was ordered by the court to pay 14 hours' pay (two days' pay) for each employee so "trained," plus liquidated damages of an additional 14 hours pay.[20]

A large Pennsylvania landscape contractor whose cash wages appeared to comply with all applicable laws was found to be in violation of the FLSA because his Guatemalan and Mexican seasonal workers were required to pay employment-related costs, such as point-of-hire transportation costs, visa costs, and recruiter's fees, which reduced their real wages to below the minimum wage.[21]

Overtime Pay. Overtime must be paid at a rate of one and a half times the employee's regular rate of pay for each hour worked in excess of 40 hours in a workweek.[22]

Child Labor Provisions. The FLSA child labor provisions are designed to protect educational opportunities for minors and prohibit their employment in occupations detrimental to their health and well-being. The FLSA restricts hours of work for minors under 16 and lists hazardous occupations too dangerous for minors to perform.

38-2 Labor Relations Laws

Even if employers are not presently unionized, they are subject to certain obligations under federal labor relations law. It is important to both unionized and nonunionized employers to know their rights and obligations under the National Labor Relations Act (NLRA).[23] Employee rights and obligations are also set forth in this act. The Labor-Management Reporting and Disclosure Act regulates internal union affairs.[24]

38-2a The National Labor Relations Act

The National Labor Relations Act (NLRA), passed in 1935, was based on the federal government's power to regulate interstate commerce granted in Article 1, Section 8, of the Constitution. Congress, in enacting this law, explained that its purpose was to remove

---

[19] See Gayle Cinqugrani, "Uniform Deductions, Low Commissions Lead to DOL Penalties for FLSA Violations," *107 D.L.R. A-10* (June 6, 2012), where an investigation by the Wage and Hour Division of the DOL between November 2008 and November 2010 found that Vizza Wash LP, doing business as Wash-Tub, made illegal deductions from employees' paychecks for items such as uniforms, insurance claims, and cash register shortages, which caused the employees' pay to fall below the federal minimum wage of $7.25 per hour.

[20] *Herman v. Hogar Praderas De Amor, Inc.*, 130 F. Supp. 2d 257 (S.D.P.R. 2001).

[21] *Rivera v. Brttman Group, Ltd.*, 2008 WL 81570 (E.D. Pa. Jan. 7, 2008).

[22] DOL regulations, referred to as the *white collar exemptions* from the overtime requirements of the FLSA, took effect on August 23, 2004. Generally, executive, administrative, professional, outside sales, computer professional, and certain "highly compensated employees" are exempt from the overtime requirements if they meet the "tests" set forth in the new regulations.

[23] 29 U.S.C. §§141–169.

[24] 29 U.S.C. §§401–531.

obstructions to commerce caused by employers who denied their employees the right to join unions and refused to accept collective bargaining.[25] Congress stated that these obstructions resulted in depression of wages, poor working conditions, and diminution of purchasing power.

Section 7 of the amended NLRA is the heart of the act, stating in part that "[e]mployees shall have the right to self-organization ... to bargain collectively through representatives of their own choosing and to engage in other concerted activities for the purpose of collective bargaining or other mutual aid or protection.... and shall have the right to refrain from such activities...."

Section 8 of the NLRA contains employer and union unfair labor practices, set forth in Figure 38-1, and authorizes the National Labor Relations Board to conduct proceedings to stop such practices.

The act applies to private-sector employers with gross incomes of $500,000 or more. The Railway Labor Act applies to employees of railroad and air carriers.

38-2b **National Labor Relations Board**

Administration of the NLRA is entrusted to the five-member National Labor Relations Board (NLRB, or Board) and the general counsel of the Board. The general counsel is responsible for investigating and prosecuting all unfair labor practice cases. The five-member Board's major function is to decide unfair labor practice cases brought before it by the general counsel.

The Board is also responsible for conducting representation and decertification elections. This responsibility is delegated to the regional directors of the 26 regional offices located throughout the United States who (1) determine the appropriateness of each proposed bargaining unit for the purpose of collective bargaining, (2) investigate petitions for the certification or decertification of unions, and (3) conduct elections to determine the choice of the majority of those employees voting in the election. Should a majority of the employees voting select a union, the NLRB will certify that union as the exclusive representative of all employees within the unit for the purpose of bargaining with the employer to obtain a contract with respect to wages, hours, and other conditions of employment.

38-2c **Election Conduct**

The NLRB has promulgated preelection rules restricting electioneering activities so that the election will express the true desire of employees. The NLRA prohibits employer interference or coercion during the preelection period. The act also prohibits during this period employer statements that contain threats of reprisal or promises of benefits. **For Example,** it is a violation of Section 8(c) of the NLRA for a Southern California manufacturer to make implied threats to relocate its plant to Mexico if the employees choose union representation. Furthermore, when the company announced its intent to move to Mexico one day after the union won a representation election, the Labor Board obtained an injunction against the move.[26]

The Board prohibits all electioneering activities at polling places and has formulated a "24-hour rule," which prohibits both unions and employers from making speeches to captive audiences within 24 hours of an election. The rationale is to preserve free elections and to prevent any party from obtaining undue advantage.

---

[25] N.L.R.A. §1; 29 U.S.C. §141.
[26] See *Quadrtech Corp.,* N.L.R.B., No. 21–CA–33997 (settlement Dec. 11, 2000).

FIGURE 38-1   **Employer and Union Unfair Labor Practices Charge**

UNFAIR LABOR PRACTICES CHARGES AGAINST EMPLOYERS	SECTION OF THE NLRA*
1. Restrain or coerce employees in the exercise of their rights under Section 7; threat of reprisals or promise of benefits	8(a)(1); 8(c)
2. Dominate or interfere with the formation or administration of a labor organization or contribute financial or other support to it	8(a)(2)
3. Discriminate in regard to hire or tenure of employment or any term or condition of employment in order to encourage or discourage membership in any labor organization	8(a)(3)
4. Discharge or otherwise discriminate against employees because they have given testimony under the act	8(a)(4)
5. Refuse to bargain collectively with representatives of its employees	8(a)(5)

UNFAIR LABOR PRACTICES CHARGES AGAINST UNIONS	SECTION OF THE NLRA
1. Restrain or coerce employees in the exercise of their rights under Section 7	8(b)(1)(A)
2. Restrain or coerce an employer in the selection of its representatives	8(b)(1)(B)
3. Cause or attempt to cause an employer to discriminate against an employee	8(b)(2)
4. Refuse to bargain collectively with the employer	8(b)(3)
5. Require employees to pay excessive fees for membership	8(b)(5)
6. Engage in "featherbed practices" of seeking pay for services not performed	8(b)(6)
7. Use secondary boycotts (banned, except for publicity proviso)	8(b)(4)
8. Allow recognitional and organizational picketing by an uncertified union	8(b)(7)
9. Enter into "hot cargo" agreements, except for construction and garment industries	8(e)

* 29 U.S.C. §151.

38-2d Union Activity on Private Property

Although Section 7 of the NLRA gives employees the statutory right to self-organization, employers have the undisputed right to make rules to maintain discipline in their establishments. Generally speaking, employers may prohibit union solicitation by employees during work periods. During nonworking time, employers may prohibit activity and communications only for legitimate efficiency and safety reasons and only if the prohibitions are not manifestly intended to impede employees' exercise of their rights under the law. Nonunion employers, moreover, may not refuse to interview or retain union members because of their union membership. And even if a union pays an individual working for a nonunion employer to help organize the company, that individual is still protected under the NLRA.[27]

An employer may validly post its property against all nonemployee solicitations, including distribution of union literature, if reasonable efforts by the union through other available channels of communication would enable it to reach the employees with its message.[28]

38-2e Social Media and Section 7: Protected Activity for Union and Nonunion Workers

Section 7 of the NLRA grants all employees—union and nonunion—the right to engage in protected concerted activities pertaining to self-organization, forming, joining, or assisting a union or "for other mutual aid or protection."[29] Under Section 7, employees have a right to discuss their terms and conditions of employment with coworkers. Some employers' Internet and social media policies may be overly broad in that they may tend to chill employees' exercise of their Section 7 rights. **For Example,** the NLRB determined that a nonprofit organization, Hispanics United of Buffalo, Inc., unlawfully terminated five employees under its antiharassment policy because the employees posted comments on Facebook on a nonworkday, some of which were profane and sarcastic, in response to a complaint by a coworker, Cruz-Moore, about their job performance. The activity of the five nonunion employees was "concerted" within the protections of Section 7 of the act, because "they were taking the first step towards taking group action to defend themselves against the accusations they could reasonably believe Cruz-Moore was going to make to management." And, the fact that the employer lumped the five individuals together in terminating them, established that the employer viewed them as a group and that their activity was concerted.[30]

Though employees retain the right to talk about working conditions on social media, including discussing treatment by a supervisor in blunt language, case law will develop that not only protects Section 7 rights, but also protects employer rights to make rules to maintain discipline in the workplace and to protect the employer's reputation when a Facebook conversation on a page set to allow access to "friends of friends" involves very offensive, insulting, and disrespectful comments about supervisors or managers. The latter situation is not like a conversation between employees at a water cooler, where there is an expectation of privacy, but is more like calling the boss names on the plant floor in front

---

[27] *N.L.R.B. v. Town & Country Electric, Inc.*, 516 U.S. 85 (1995).

[28] *Lechmere, Inc. v. NLRB*, 502 U.S. 527 (1992).

[29] On June 18, 2012, the NLRB announced that it has launched a Web page describing the rights of employees to engage in concerted activity, even if they do not belong to a union. It is available at **http://www.nlrb.gov/concerted-activity.**

[30] *Hispanics United of Buffalo, Inc.*, 359 N.L.R.B. No. 37 (Dec. 14, 2012). See *Richmond District Neighborhood Center and Ian Callaghan*, 361 N.L.R.B. No. 74 (Oct. 28, 2014) where the N.L.R.B. found that the employer did not violate the NLRA when it terminated two individuals for egregious insubordinate Facebook posts.

of multiple employees and the public, as there is no expectation of privacy. This conduct does not involve protected concerted activity. Although discussion of grievances in the context of "mutual aid or protection" is protected under Section 7, an individual's personal griping is not.

38-2f Firing Employees for Union Activity

Although employers and supervisors often feel betrayed by individual employees who take leadership roles in forming organizations, the NLRA prohibits discrimination against such employees because of their union activity.

The NLRB has found evidence of discrimination against active union supporters when the employer

1. Discharges on the strength of past misdeeds that were condoned;
2. Neglects to give customary warnings prior to discharge;
3. Discharges for a rule generally unenforced;
4. Applies disproportionately severe punishment to union supporters; or
5. Effects layoffs in violation of seniority status with disproportionate impact on union supporters.

The NLRA preserves the right of the employer to maintain control over the workforce in the interest of discipline, efficiency, and pleasant and safe customer relations. Employees, on the other hand, have the right to be free from coercive discrimination resulting from union activity.

At times these two rights may collide. For example, an employee may be discharged for apparently two reasons: (1) violation of a valid company rule and (2) union activity. The employer gives the former as the reason for termination; the latter remains unstated on the employer's part, causing the filing of a Section 8(a)(3) unfair labor practice charge against the employer. These are known as *dual motive cases*. The general counsel must present on behalf of the dismissed employee a prima facie case that such protected conduct as union activity was a motivating factor in the dismissal. After this showing, the burden shifts to the employer, who must prove that the employee would have been dismissed for legitimate business reasons even absent the protected conduct.

CASE SUMMARY

The Sam Santillo Story

FACTS: Prior to his discharge, Sam Santillo was a bus driver for Transportation Management Corporation. On March 19, Santillo talked to officials of the Teamsters Union about organizing the drivers who worked with him. Over the next four days, Santillo discussed with his fellow drivers the possibility of joining the Teamsters and distributed authorization cards. On the night of March 23, George Patterson, who supervised Santillo and the other drivers, told one of the drivers that he had heard of Santillo's activities. Patterson referred to Santillo as two-faced and promised to

get even with him. Later that evening, Patterson talked to Ed West, who was also a bus driver. Patterson asked, "What's with Sam and the Union?" Patterson said that he took Santillo's actions personally, recounted several favors he had done for Santillo, and added that he would remember Santillo's activities when Santillo again asked for a favor. On Monday, March 26, Santillo was discharged. Patterson told Santillo that he was being fired for leaving his keys in the bus and taking unauthorized breaks. Santillo filed charges with the Board, and the general counsel issued a complaint, contending that Santillo was discharged because of his union activities in distributing authorization cards to fellow employees. The evidence revealed that the practice of leaving keys in buses was commonplace among company employees and the company tolerated the practice of taking coffee breaks. The company had never taken disciplinary action against an employee for the behavior in question.

DECISION: Judgment for Santillo and the NLRB. The general counsel established a prima facie case by showing that Santillo was involved in union-organizing activities just prior to his discharge. The employer did not meet its burden of proving that Santillo was fired for a legitimate business reason. The infractions involved were commonplace, and no discipline had ever been issued to any employee previously. The reasons given by the company were pretextual. Santillo would not have been fired had the employer not considered his effort to establish a union. [*NLRB v. Transportation Management Corp.*, **462 U.S. 393 (1983)**]

38-2g Duty of Employer to Bargain Collectively

Once a union wins a representative election, the Board certifies the union as the exclusive bargaining representative of the employees. The employer then has the obligation under the NLRA to bargain with the union in good faith over wages, hours, and working conditions. These matters are *mandatory subjects of bargaining* and include seniority provisions, promotions, layoff and recall provisions, no-strike no-lockout clauses, and grievance procedures. Employers also have an obligation to bargain about the "effects" of the shutdown of a part of a business[31] and may have an obligation to bargain over the decision to relocate bargaining unit work to other plants.[32] Absent clearly expressed consent by a union, an employer violates its duty to bargain by changing a term or condition of employment without first bargaining to impasse with a union. **For Example,** Aramark Educational Services violated the NLRA when it unilaterally implemented a new, strict "Social Security no-match" policy of suspending employees with uncorrected discrepancies in their Social Security numbers prior to any discussion and impasse in bargaining with UNITE HERE Local 26.[33]

Permissive subjects of bargaining are those over which an employer's refusal to bargain is not a Section 8(a)(5) unfair labor practice. Examples are the required use of union labels, internal union affairs, and benefits for already retired workers.

38-2h Right to Work

right-to-work laws—laws restricting unions and employees from negotiating clauses in their collective bargaining agreements that make union membership compulsory.

The NLRA allows states to enact **right-to-work laws.** These laws restrict unions and employers from negotiating clauses in their collective bargaining agreements that make union membership compulsory.[34]

Advocates of such laws contend that compulsory union membership is contrary to the First Amendment right of freedom of association. Unions have attacked these laws as unfair because unions must represent all employees, and in right-to-work states where a majority of employees vote for union representation, nonunion employees receive all of the benefits of collective bargaining contracts without paying union dues.

---

[31] *First National Maintenance v. N.L.R.B.*, 452 U.S. 666 (1981).

[32] *Dubuque Packing Co. and UFCWIU, Local 150k*, 303 N.L.R.B. 66 (1991).

[33] *Aramark Educational Services, Inc.*, 335 N.L.R.B. No. 11 (Feb. 18, 2010).

[34] Right-to-work statutes declare unlawful any agreement that denies persons the right to work because of nonmembership in a union or the failure to pay dues to a union as a condition of employment. These laws have been adopted in Alabama, Arizona, Arkansas, Florida, Georgia, Idaho, Indiana Iowa, Kansas, Louisiana, Mississippi, Nebraska, Nevada, North Carolina, North Dakota, Oklahoma, South Carolina, South Dakota, Tennessee, Texas, Utah, Virginia, Wisconsin, and Wyoming.

38-2i Strike and Picketing Activity

If the parties reach an impasse in the negotiation process for a collective bargaining agreement, a union may call a strike and undertake picketing activity to enforce its bargaining demands. Strikers in such a situation are called **economic strikers.** Although the strike activity is legal, the employers may respond by hiring temporary or permanent replacement workers.

economic strikers– union strikers trying to enforce bargaining demands when an impasse has been reached in the negotiation process for a collective bargaining agreement.

Rights of Strikers

Economic strikers who unconditionally apply for reinstatement when their positions are filled by permanent replacements are not entitled to return to work at the end of the economic strike. They are, however, entitled to full reinstatement when positions become available.

CASE SUMMARY

Avoiding the Sack—The Pilots Returned before Their Positions Were Filled

FACTS: Striking pilots of Eastern Airlines made an unconditional offer to return to work on November 22, 1989. As of that date, some 227 new-hire replacement pilots were in training but had not obtained certificates from the Federal Aviation Administration permitting them to fly revenue flights. The striking pilots contended that the trainees were not permanent replacement pilots on the date they offered to go back to work because the trainees could not lawfully fly revenue flights. Eastern contended that the new-hire pilots were permanent employees and as such should not be displaced.

DECISION: The pilots' positions were not filled by permanent replacements at the time the striking pilots unconditionally applied to return to work. The new-hire replacement pilots were not qualified to fill the positions at that time. Giving preference to trainees over returning strikers would discourage employees from exercising their right to strike. [*Eastern Airlines Inc. v. Airline Pilots Association Int'l,* **970 F.2d 722 (11th Cir. 1990)**]

primary picketing–legal presentations in front of a business notifying the public of a labor dispute.

Strikers responsible for misconduct while out on strike may be refused reemployment by the employer.

When employees strike to protest an employer's unfair labor practice, such as firing an employee for union-organizing activity, these unfair labor practice strikers have a right to return to their jobs immediately at the end of the strike. This right exists even if the employer has hired permanent replacements.[35]

mass picketing–illegal tactic of employees massing together in great numbers to effectively shut down entrances of the employer's facility.

Picketing

Placing persons outside a business at the site of a labor dispute so that they may, by signs or banners, inform the public of the existence of a labor dispute is called **primary picketing** and is legal. Should the picketing employees mass together in great numbers in front of the gates of the employer's facility to effectively shut down the entrances, such coercion is called **mass picketing;** it is illegal. **Secondary picketing** is picketing an employer with whom a union has no dispute to persuade the employer to stop doing business with a party to the dispute. Secondary picketing is generally illegal under the NLRA. An exception exists for certain product picketing at supermarkets or other

secondary picketing– picketing an employer with which a union has no dispute to persuade the employer to stop doing business with a party to the dispute; generally illegal under the NLRA.

[35] *Poly America, Inc. v. N.L.R.B.,* 260 F.3d 465 (5th Cir. 2001).

multiproduct retail stores provided that it is limited to asking customers not to purchase the struck product at the neutral employer's store.[36]

38-2j Regulation of Internal Union Affairs

To ensure the honest and democratic administration of unions, Congress passed the Labor-Management Reporting and Disclosure Act (LMRDA).[37] Title IV of the LMRDA establishes democratic standards for all elections for union offices, including

1. Secret ballots in local union elections;
2. Opportunity for members to nominate candidates;
3. Advance notice of elections;
4. Observers at polling and at ballot-counting stations for all candidates;
5. Publication of results and preservation of records for one year;
6. Prohibition of any income from dues or assessments to support candidates for union office; and
7. Advance opportunity for each candidate to inspect the membership name and address lists.

38-3 Pension Plans and Federal Regulation

The Employee Retirement Income Security Act (ERISA)[38] was adopted in 1974 to protect employee pensions and benefits.

38-3a ERISA

The act sets forth fiduciary standards and requirements for administration, vesting, funding, and termination insurance.

Administration

Commonly a "benefits claims committee" is set up under the plan to make determinations about coverage issues, and courts will not disturb the finding of a benefits committee unless the determinations are "arbitrary and capricious." **For Example,** Joe Gustafson, who provided chauffeur services for senior executives at NYNEX for a number of years while classified as an independent contractor, sought benefits under ERISA because he asserted he was a common law employee of NYNEX. While the court determined he was in fact an employee entitled to overtime compensation under the Fair Labor Standards Act, the court was compelled to defer to the benefits committee's determination that Gustafson was not an employee under the NYNEX plan because he was not "on the payroll" as required by the plan guidelines. The court found that such a determination was not arbitrary or capricious.[39] Nevertheless, individuals may successfully challenge determinations of the plan administrators. **For Example,** Bell South denied ERISA-covered benefits to Suzanne Lee under both its Short Term Disability Plan and its Long Term Disability Plan. She suffered from chronic pain syndrome, and the

---

[36] *N.L.R.B. v. Fruit and Vegetable Packers, Local 760 (Tree Fruits, Inc.),* 377 U.S. 58 (1964); but see *N.L.R.B. v. Retail Clerks, Local 1001 (Safeco Title Ins. Co.),* 477 U.S. 607 (1980).

[37] 29 U.S.C. §§401–531.

[38] P.L. 93-406, 88 Stat. 829, 29 U.S.C. §§1001–1381.

[39] *Gustafson v. Bell Atlantic Corp.,* 171 F. Supp. 2d 311 (S.D.N.Y. 2001).

administrator determined that she had failed to submit "objective medical evidence" of her condition. The U.S. Court of Appeals reviewed the extensive medical record of pain care specialists supporting her diagnosis and determined that Bell South had acted arbitrarily and capriciously in denying Lee's claim of benefits.[40]

Fiduciary Standards and Reporting

Persons administering a pension fund must handle it to protect the interest of employees.[41]

The fact that an employer contributed all or part of the money to the pension fund does not entitle it to use the fund as though the employer still owned it. Persons administering pension plans must make detailed reports to the Secretary of Labor.

Vesting

Vesting is the right of an employee to pension benefits paid into a pension plan in the employee's name by the employer. Prior to ERISA, many pension plans did not vest accrued benefits until an employee had 20 to 25 years of service. Thus, an employee who was forced to terminate service after 18 years would have no pension rights or benefits. Under ERISA, employees' rights must be fully vested within five or seven years in accordance with the two vesting options available under the law.

In the past, it had been common for pension plans to contain break-in-service clauses, whereby employees who left their employment for a period longer than one year for any reason other than an on-the-job injury lost pension eligibility rights. Under the Retirement Equity Act of 1984,[42] an individual can leave the workforce for up to five consecutive years and still retain eligibility for pension benefits.

Funding

Pension funds may be broadly classified as "defined contribution plans" and "defined benefit plans."

A **defined contribution plan** is one that provides for an individual account for each plan participant and for benefits based solely on the amount contributed to the participant's account. It is also known as an *individual account plan.* These plans include 401(k) plans, employee stock option plans (ESOPs), profit-sharing plans, and stock bonus plans. Commonly, the employer establishes these plans and defines its own contributions to be matched by contributions from plan participants.

A **defined benefit plan** is an employer commitment to make specified future payments to participants upon retirement. The employer establishes a pension fund for this purpose, and the employer is contractually obligated to make those payments even if the assets set aside to finance the plan turn out to be inadequate. ERISA established an insurance plan, called the **Pension Benefit Guaranty Corporation (PBGC),** to protect employees covered under defined benefit plans should the employer go out of business.

In the case of defined benefit plans, the entire investment risk is on the employer who sponsors the plan. The employer must cover any underfunding that may result from the plan's poor performance. However, if the plan becomes overfunded, the employer may reduce or suspend its contributions.[43]

defined contribution plan–a plan providing individual accounts for each employee participant with benefits defined solely on the amounts contributed by each employee with matching contributions by the employer.

defined benefit plan–an employer established pension fund obligating the employer to make specified future payments to participants upon retirement.

Pension Benefit Guaranty Corporation (PBGC)–an insurance plan to protect employees covered by defined benefit plans in case an employer is unable to meet its payment obligations from the employer's pension fund.

---

[40] *Lee v. Bell South Telecommunications Inc.*, 318 Fed. Appx. 829 (11th Cir. 2009).
[41] *John Hancock Mutual Life Ins. Co. v. Harris Trust,* 510 U.S. 86 (1993).
[42] P.L. 98-397, 29 U.S.C. §1001.
[43] *Hughes Aircraft Co. v. Jacobson*, 523 U.S. 1093 (1998).

Defined contribution plans are the ones most frequently offered by employers today, in part because of the employers' risk of underfunding defined benefit plans. Defined contribution plans are not insured by the PBGC.

Enforcement

ERISA authorizes the Secretary of Labor and employees to bring court actions to compel the observance of statutory requirements.

38-4 Unemployment Benefits, Family Leaves, and Social Security

Generally, when employees are without work through no fault of their own, they are eligible for unemployment compensation benefits. Twelve-week maternity, paternity, or adoption leaves and family and medical leaves are available for qualifying employees. Social Security provides certain benefits, including retirement and disability benefits.

38-4a Unemployment Compensation

Unemployment compensation today is provided primarily through a federal-state system under the unemployment insurance provisions of the Social Security Act of 1935.[44] All states have laws that provide similar benefits, and the state agencies are loosely coordinated under the federal act. Agricultural employees, domestic employees, and state and local government employees are not covered by this federal-state system. Federal programs of unemployment compensation exist for federal civilian workers and former military service personnel. A separate federal unemployment program applies to railroad workers.

Eligibility

In most states, an unemployed person must be available for placement in a similar job and willing to take such employment at a comparable rate of pay. Full-time students generally have difficulty proving that they are available for work while they are still going to school.

If an employee quits a job without cause or is fired for misconduct, the employee is ordinarily disqualified from receiving unemployment compensation benefits. For example, stealing property from an employer constitutes misconduct for which benefits will be denied. Moreover, an employee's refusal to complete the aftercare portion of an alcohol treatment program has been found to be misconduct connected with work, disqualifying the employee from receiving benefits.

Funding

Employers are taxed for unemployment benefits based on each employer's "experience rating" account. Thus, employers with a stable workforce with no layoffs, who therefore do not draw on the state unemployment insurance fund, pay lower tax rates. Employers whose experience ratings are higher pay higher rates. Motivated by the desire to avoid higher unemployment taxes, employers commonly challenge the state's payment of unemployment benefits to individuals who they believe are not properly entitled to benefits. If an employee had good cause to resign her employment, she is eligible to receive benefits. **For Example,** Ms. Williams, a certified early childhood teacher, resigned her position at

---

44 42 U.S.C. §§301–1397e.

the Good Shepard Infant & Toddler Center because it was violating state regulations regarding child-to-staff ratios and it resisted Williams' attempt to get the matter corrected. The court found that she had good cause to resign and was eligible to receive unemployment compensation benefits.[45]

38-4b Family and Medical Leaves of Absence

The Family and Medical Leave Act of 1993 (FMLA)[46] entitles an eligible employee, whether male or female, to a total of 12 workweeks of unpaid leave during any 12-month period (1) because of the birth or adoption of the employee's son or daughter, (2) to care for the employee's spouse, son, daughter, or parent with a serious health condition, or (3) because of a serious health condition that makes the employee unable to perform the functions of his or her position. Notice should be given by the employer to an employee that the leave he or she is taking will count against FMLA entitlement in order to comply with the Secretary of Labor's regulations.[47] In the case of an employee's serious health condition or that of a covered family member, an employer may require the employee to use any accrued paid vacation, personal, medical, or sick leave toward any part of the 12-week leave provided by the act. When an employee requests leave because of the birth or adoption of a child, the employer may require the employee to use all available paid personal, vacation, and medical leave, but not sick leave, toward any FMLA leave.

To be eligible for FMLA leave, an employee must have been employed by a covered employer for at least 12 months and have worked at least 1,250 hours during the 12-month period preceding the leave. Covered employers are those that employ 50 or more employees.[48] Upon return from FMLA leave, the employee is entitled to be restored to the same or an equivalent position with equivalent pay and benefits. **For Example,** when Magda Brenlla returned to her position at LaSorsa Buick in the Bronx, New York, after quadruple bypass surgery, she was terminated by the owner, who told her that he had decided to consolidate the positions of office manager and controller, even though he had no business plan for restructuring, and soon thereafter had to hire additional help in the office. The judge upheld a jury verdict of $320,000, finding that the jury had ample evidence to conclude that the real reason for her termination was her FMLA leave.[49]

The FMLA provides specific statutory relief for violations of the provisions of the act, including pay to the employee for damages equal to lost wages and benefits or any actual monetary losses, plus interest, plus an equal amount in liquidated damages.[50]

38-4c Leaves for Military Service under USERRA

The Uniformed Services Employment and Re-Employment Rights Act (USERRA) was enacted in 1994 to encourage noncareer service in the armed services, minimize the disruption experienced in the civilian careers of reservists, and promote prompt reemployment of reservists upon return from military leave.[51] As updated in 2008, the USERRA has and will have a broad impact on U.S. employers as it provides reemployment

---

[45] *Williams v. Favored, LLC,* 443 S.W.3d 716 (Mo. App. 2014).

[46] 29 U.S.C. §§2601–2654.

[47] See *Ragsdale v. Wolverine World Wide, Inc.,* 535 U.S. 81 (2002).

[48] *Bellum v. PCE Constructors Inc.,* 407 F.3d 734 (5th Cir. 2005). Joint employers are obligated to honor FMLA-qualifying leaves. See *Grace v. USCAR,* 521 F.3d 655 (6th Cir. 2008).

[49] *Brenlla v. LaSorsa Buick,* 2002 WL 1059117 (S.D.N.Y. May 28, 2002).

[50] See *Arban v. West Publishing Co.,* 345 F.3d 390 (6th Cir. 2003), in which the U.S. Court of Appeals required the doubling of a jury verdict of $130,000 under the FMLA provision providing for liquidated damages unless the employer is able to prove that it acted "in good faith ..." and had reasonable grounds to believe it was not in violation of the FMLA. 29 U.S.C. §2617(a)(iii).

[51] 38 U.S.C. §4301.

and benefit protection rights for returning military personnel and prohibits discrimination against individuals because of their application for or performance of military service.[52]

Protections

Section 4312 of the USERRA generally requires returning reservists to be "promptly reemployed" and returned to the same or comparable positions of like seniority, status, and pay they would have had if they had not been activated. Moreover, Section 4316(c) provides that persons reemployed under the act shall not be discharged from employment within a year of their reemployment if their period of service was more than 180 days. For service of more than 30 days, the protective period is 180 days. However, the employer may terminate an individual for cause regardless of the duration of service.

Sections 4312(a)(3) and (4) provide protection for those disabled while in the service and requires employers to make reasonable efforts to accommodate each employee's disability so that each individual may return to the same or comparable positions or, if no longer qualified for the position, allow for the transfer to a position the disabled individual can perform closest to the prior position in terms of seniority, status, and pay.

Section 4323 of the act provides a full range of remedies, including back pay for loss of wages and benefits as well as liquidated damages in an amount equal to the actual damages when the employer's failure to comply with the act was willful. The act's enforcement is performed by the U.S. Justice Department's Division of Civil Rights.

CASE SUMMARY

USERRA—Because It's the Right Thing to Do!

FACTS: Michael Serricchio, an Air Force reservist, was employed as a financial advisor at Wachovia Securities and called up to active duty in the wake of September 11, 2001. Upon completion of his active duty, he sought to return to Wachovia with comparable earnings potential and opportunity for advancement. In the year prior to his activation for military duty, Mr. Serricchio was personally responsible for servicing in excess of 130 accounts, was responsible for managing in excess of $9 million dollars with his partner, and was earning $6,500 per month based on those assets. If Serricchio accepted Wachovia's reemployment offer, he would have been managing a handful of accounts, generating, according to Wachovia's own documents, a small amount in monthly commissions that had to be repaid to Wachovia to offset his monthly draw.

The employer argued that it provided the same draw and commission structure to the plaintiff and this was sufficient to fulfill its reemployment obligations under Section 4316. Serricchio contended that Wachovia's offer did not satisfy its obligation to reemploy him in a position of like pay; and the employer's failure to comply with the USERRA was willful, entitling him to double back pay as liquidated damages.

DECISION: Judgment for Serricchio. Wachovia understood that Serricchio had a right to be reinstated to his previous position as if he had never left. But even though Wachovia had a military-leave policy that expressly included that provision, the company did not offer Serricchio a position comparable to the one he held before leaving for military service. The court upheld an award of $389,453 in back pay, $389,453 in liquidated damages, $830,107 in attorneys' fees and costs, and $36,567 in interest for a total of $1.64 million. [*Serricchio v. Wachovia Securities, LLC,* **685 F.3d 169 (2d Cir. 2011)**]

---

[52] 38 U.S.C. §§4312, 4316, and 4317. For a benefits protection case, see *DeLee v. City of Plymouth, Ind.,* 773 F.3d 172 (7th Cir. 2014).

Defenses

In addition to an employer's right to terminate a reemployed service person for cause, employers may be excused from reemploying or continuing employment of persons under §4312(d)(1) of the act when the employer's circumstances have so changed as to make reemployment impossible, unreasonable, or an undue hardship. The burden of proof on the matter is on the employer.

38-4d Social Security

Employees and employers are required to pay Social Security taxes, which provide employees with four types of insurance protection: retirement benefits, disability benefits, life insurance benefits, and health insurance (Medicare). The federal Social Security Act established a federal program of aid for the aged, the blind, and the disabled. This is called the Supplemental Security Income (SSI) program. Payments are administered directly by the Social Security Administration, which became an independent government agency in 1995.

38-5 Employees' Health and Safety

The Occupational Safety and Health Act of 1970 (OSHA) was passed to assure every worker, so far as possible, safe and healthful working conditions and to preserve the country's human resources.[53] OSHA provides for (1) the establishment of safety and health standards and (2) effective enforcement of these standards and the other employer duties required by OSHA.

38-5a Standards

The Secretary of Labor has broad authority under OSHA to promulgate occupational safety and health standards.[54] Except in emergency situations, public hearings and publication in the *Federal Register* are required before the secretary can issue a new standard. Any person adversely affected may then challenge the validity of the standard in a U.S. Court of Appeals. The secretary's standards will be upheld if they are reasonable and supported by substantial evidence. The secretary must demonstrate a need for a new standard by showing that it is reasonably necessary to protect employees against a "significant risk" of material health impairment. The cost of compliance with new standards may run into billions of dollars. The secretary is not required to do a cost-benefit analysis for a new standard but must show that the standard is economically feasible.

38-5b Employer Duties

Employers have a "general duty" to furnish each employee a place of employment that is free from hazards that are likely to cause death or serious physical injuries.

OSHA requires employers to maintain records of occupational illness and injuries if they result in death, loss of consciousness, or one or more lost workdays or if they require medical treatment other than first aid. Such records have proven to be a valuable aid in recognizing areas of risk. They have been especially helpful in identifying the presence of occupational illnesses.

---

[53] 29 U.S.C. §651 *et seq.*
[54] *Martin v. OSHRC*, 499 U.S. 144 (1991).

38-5c Enforcement

The Occupational Safety and Health Administration (also identified as OSHA) is the agency within the Department of Labor that administers the act. OSHA has authority to conduct inspections and to seek enforcement action when noncompliance has occurred. Worksite inspections are conducted when employer records indicate incidents involving fatalities or serious injuries.[55] These inspections may also result from employee complaints. The act protects employees making complaints from employer retaliation. Employers have the right to require an OSHA inspector to secure a warrant before inspecting the employer's plant.

If OSHA issues a citation for a violation of workplace health or safety standards, the employer may challenge the citation before the Occupational Safety and Health Review Commission (OSHRC). Judicial review of a commission ruling is obtained before a U.S. Court of Appeals.

CASE SUMMARY

Risky Business

FACTS: On February 24, 2010, a performance was still in progress when Tilikum, a 32-year-old killer whale, seized Sea-World trainer Dawn Brancheau and pulled her off her platform into the pool causing her death. The Secretary of Labor issued citations to SeaWorld alleging two instances of "willful" violations of the general duty clause for exposing trainers to recognized hazards of drowning or injury when working with killer whales during performances. The Secretary of Labor set forth abatement procedures prohibiting trainers from working with whales unless the trainers are protected through the use of physical barriers or the use of decking systems. The Secretary proposed a penalty of $70,000. Sea-World appealed, contending that its training adequately controlled the risk. And, it asserted that trainers formally accept and control their own exposure to risks like the risks inherent in much of the sports and entertainment industries.

DECISION: Judgment for the Secretary of Labor. The general duty clause, §5(a)(1) of the Act, provides, "Each employer shall furnish to each of his employees a place of employment … free from recognized hazards … likely to cause death or serious physical harm to his employees." SeaWorld's assertion that working with killer whales is not a recognized hazard because its training controls the risk is rejected. The record of incident reports and the death of Ms. Brancheau demonstrate that a recognized hazard existed. The employer's duty to ensure a safe workplace is on the employer and not the employee. The "assumption of risk" doctrine is rejected. Moreover, the abatement procedures are feasible. [*SeaWorld of Florida, LLC v. Perez*, **748 F.3d 1202 (D.C. Cir. 2014)**]

The Occupational Safety and Health Act provides that no employer shall discharge or in any manner discriminate against employees because they filed a complaint with OSHA, testified in any OSHA proceeding, or exercised any right afforded by the act. A regulation issued by the Secretary of Labor under the act provides that if employees with no reasonable alternative refuse in good faith to expose themselves to a dangerous condition, they will be protected against subsequent discrimination. The Secretary of Labor may obtain injunctive and other appropriate relief in a U.S. district court against an employer who discriminates against employees for testifying or exercising any right under the act.

---

[55] *Chao v. Mallard Bay Drilling Co.*, 534 U.S. 235 (2002).

THINKING THINGS THROUGH

Taking Chances or Shortcuts in Violation of OSHA Standards Is Bad Management

John Carlo, Inc. (JCI), was installing a sewer line down the middle of an existing roadway in Jacksonville, Florida. The new line crossed under an existing gas line that was perpendicular to the proposed sewer line. The JCI crew worked in two stacked trench boxes, laying pipe up to the location where the pipeline crossed the trench for the sewer line. OSHA regulations require protection of employees from cave-ins; trench boxes and sloping of trench walls provide this protection. The following day, the crew removed the top trench box because both boxes would not fit under the perpendicular gas line. The crew pulled the bottom box under the perpendicular gas line and prepared the bottom of the trench to lay one joint of the sewer pipe. Project superintendent Cox had discussed this move with his foreman Jacobs. Jacobs reminded Cox that this move would leave the top portion of the trench unprotected. Cox explained that he realized the problem, but because JCI had bid the project based on 6-foot-wide trenches, they could not slope the trenches. The supervisors anticipated that just 15 minutes was needed to lay the one joint of pipe. Two crew members entered the trench to lay the pipe. The trench walls above the box (approximately 6 feet) were not sloped or otherwise protected. A large clay ball dislodged, fell into the trench, and struck one employee, who eventually died as a result.

Thinking Things Through, was it a reasonable risk for the employer to utilize the two employees in the trench for just 15 minutes to lay one joint of pipe? Of course not! The ALJ found that both supervisors "knowingly and deliberately" violated the OSHA standard because it was "more expedient to place employees in an unprotected trench ... than to take the time to adequately shore up or slope the trench to protect the employees." The $50,000 willful violation penalty was upheld by the U.S. Court of Appeals.*

In 1970, the year that OSHA became law, the American population was approximately 204,000,000; over 14,000 workers were killed in industrial accidents. In 2013, with the U.S. population at an estimated 316,500,000, some 4,405 workers were killed in work-related incidents. OSHA has drastically improved the safety and health of workers. OSHA standards are commonly devised as corrective responses to the occurrence of previous fatalities or injuries on often similarly situated work sites. Employees are empowered to refuse to expose themselves to dangerous duties under the *Whirlpool v. Marshall* U.S. Supreme Court decision.** Management and employees must always be encouraged to take the safe course!

*John Carlo, Inc. v. Secretary of Labor, 2008 CCH OSHD 1 32,929.
**445 U.S. 1 (1980).

38-5d State "Right-to-Know" Legislation

Laws that guarantee individual workers the "right to know" if there are hazardous substances in their workplaces have been enacted by many states in recent years. These laws commonly require an employer to make known to an employee's physician the chemical composition of certain workplace substances in connection with the employee's diagnosis and treatment by the physician. Furthermore, local fire and public health officials, as well as local neighborhood residents, are given the right to know if local employers are working with hazardous substances that could pose health or safety problems.

38-6 Compensation for Employees' Injuries

For most kinds of employment, workers' compensation statutes govern compensation for injuries. These statutes provide that an injured employee is entitled to compensation for accidents occurring in the course of employment from a risk involved in that employment.

38-6a Common Law Status of Employer

In some employment situations, common law principles apply. Workers' compensation statutes commonly do not apply to employers with fewer than a prescribed minimum number of employees or to agricultural, domestic, or casual employment. When an exempted area of employment is involved, it is necessary to consider the duties and defenses of employers apart from workers' compensation statutes.

Duties

The employer is under the common law duty to furnish an employee with a reasonably safe place in which to work, reasonably safe tools and appliances, and a sufficient number of competent fellow employees for the work involved. The employer is also under the common law duty to warn the employee of any unusual dangers particular to the employer's business.

Defenses

At common law, the employer is not liable to an injured employee if the employee is harmed by the act of a fellow employee. Similarly, an employer is not liable at common law to an employee harmed by an ordinary hazard of the work because the employee assumed such risks. If the employee is guilty of contributory negligence, regardless of the employer's negligence, the employer is not liable at common law to an injured employee.

38-6b Statutory Changes

The rising incidence of industrial accidents resulting from the increasing use of more powerful machinery and the growth of the industrial labor population led to a demand for statutory modification of common law rules relating to the liability of employers for industrial accidents.

Modification of Employer's Common Law Defenses

One type of change by statute was to modify the defenses that an employer could assert when sued by an employee for damages. For example, under the Federal Employer's Liability Act (FELA), which covers railroad workers, the injured employee must still bring an action in court and prove the negligence of the employer or other employees. However, the burden of proving the case is made lighter by limitations on employers' defenses. Under FELA, contributory negligence is a defense only in mitigation of damages; assumption of the risk is not a defense.[56]

Workers' Compensation

A more sweeping development was made by the adoption of workers' compensation statutes in every state. In addition, civil employees of the U.S. government are covered by the Federal Employees' Compensation Act. When an employee is covered by a workers' compensation statute and the injury is job connected, the employee's remedy is limited to that provided in the workers' compensation statute.[57]

Workers' compensation proceedings are brought before a special administrative agency or workers' compensation board. In contrast, a common law action for damages or an action for damages under an employer's liability statute is brought in a court of law.

---

[56] 45 U.S.C. §1 *et seq.*

[57] In *Fu v. Owens*, 622 F.3d 880 (8th Cir. 2010), Helen Fu's injuries, incurred when a coworker assaulted her at work at a Target-owned clinic in Minnesota, occurred because she was at the job, in touch with associations and conditions inseparable from it. The injuries occurred because she was on the job and thus she was subject to the exclusivity provision of the Workers' Compensation Act.

CASE SUMMARY

Locked in

FACTS: Bryant is the administrator of the estate of the deceased and the guardian of the deceased's minor child. Bryant sued Wal-Mart for damages following the death of the deceased based on the theory of false imprisonment. While working on the night restocking crew, the deceased suffered a stroke. Medical personnel arrived six minutes later but could not enter the store because management had locked all doors of the store for security reasons and no manager was present to open a door. By the time the medical crew entered the store to assist her, they were unable to revive her, and she died 15 hours later. Bryant contended that the false imprisonment occurred between the time the deceased became ill and the time the medical team was unable to enter the store. Wal-Mart contended that Bryant's exclusive remedy is the Workers' Compensation Act.

DECISION: Judgment for Wal-Mart. It is well settled that a claim under the Workers' Compensation Act is the sole and exclusive remedy for injury or occupational disease incurred in the course of employment. In exchange for the right to recover scheduled compensation without proof of negligence on the part of the employer, employees forgo other rights and remedies they once had. Injuries to an employee's peace, happiness, and feelings are not compensable under the act. [*Bryant v. Wal-Mart Stores, Inc.*, 417 S.E.2d 688 (Ga. Ct. App. 1992)]

For injuries arising within the course of the employee's work from a risk involved in that work, workers' compensation statutes usually provide (1) immediate medical benefits, (2) prompt periodic wage replacement, often computed as a percentage of weekly wages (ranging from 50 to 80 percent of the injured employee's wage) for a specified number of weeks, and (3) a death benefit of a limited amount.[58] In such cases, compensation is paid without regard to whether the employer or the employee was negligent. However, no compensation is generally allowed for a willful, self-inflicted injury or one sustained while intoxicated.[59]

There has been a gradual widening of the workers' compensation statutes, so compensation today is generally recoverable for both accident-inflicted injuries and occupational diseases.

38-7 Employee Privacy

Employers may want to monitor employee telephone conversations in the ordinary course of their business to evaluate employee performance and customer service; to document business transactions between employees and customers; or to meet special security, efficiency, or other needs. Employers may likewise want to monitor e-mail for what they perceive to be sound business reasons. Employers also may seek to test employees for drug use or search employee lockers for illicit drugs. Litigation may result because employees may believe that such activities violate their right to privacy.

38-7a Source of Privacy Rights

The Bill of Rights contained in the U.S. Constitution, including the Fourth Amendment, which protects against unreasonable search and seizure, provides a philosophical and legal basis for individual privacy rights for federal employees. The Fourteenth Amendment applies this privacy protection to actions taken by state and local governments that affect

---

[58] *Union Light & Power Co. v. DC Department of Employment Services*, 796 A.2d 665 (D.C. App. 2002).
[59] See *Beck v. Newt Brown Contractors, LLC*, 72 So. 3d 982 (La. App. 2011).

their employees. The privacy rights of individuals working in the private sector are not directly controlled by the Bill of Rights, however, because challenged employer actions are not government actions. Limited employee privacy rights in the private sector are provided by statute, case law, and collective bargaining agreements.

38-7b Monitoring Employee Telephone Conversations

The Federal Wiretapping Act[60] makes it unlawful to intercept oral and electronic communications and provides for both criminal liability and civil damages against the violator. There are two major exceptions, however. The first allows an employer to monitor a firm's telephones in the "ordinary course of business" through the use of extension telephones; a second exception applies when there is prior employee consent to the interception. If employer monitoring results in the interception of a business call, it is within the ordinary-course-of-business exception. Personal calls can be monitored, however, only to the extent necessary to determine that the call is personal, and the employer must then cease listening. **For Example,** Newell Spears taped all phone conversations at his store in trying to find out if an employee was connected to a store theft. He listened to virtually all 22 hours of intercepted and recorded telephone conversations between his employee Sibbie Deal and her boyfriend Calvin Lucas without regard to the conversations' relation to Spears's business interest. While Spears might well have legitimately monitored Deal's calls to the extent necessary to determine that the calls were personal and made or received in violation of store policy, the scope of the interception in this case was well beyond the boundaries of the ordinary-course-of-business exception and in violation of the act.[61]

Employer monitoring of employee phone calls can be accomplished without fear of violating the act if consent is established. Consent may be established by prior written notice to employees of the employer's monitoring policy. It is prudent, as well, for the employer to give customers notice of the policy through a recorded message as part of the employer's phone-answering system.

38-7c E-Mail Monitoring

Electronic mail (e-mail) is a primary means of communication in many of today's businesses, serving for some employers as an alternative to faxes, telephones, or the U.S. Postal Service. Employers may want to monitor employees' e-mail messages to evaluate the efficiency and effectiveness of their employees or for corporate security purposes, including the protection of trade secrets and other intangible property interests. When employees are disciplined or terminated for alleged wrongful activities discovered as a result of e-mail searches, however, the issue of privacy may be raised. The Electronic Communications Privacy Act of 1986 (ECPA)[62] amended the federal wiretap statute and was intended in part to apply to e-mail. However, ordinary-course-of-business and consent exceptions apply to e-mail, and it would appear that employers have broad latitude to monitor employee e-mail use. **For Example,** the e-mails that Gina Holmes sent to her personal attorney on a company-issued computer regarding litigation with the company were not protected by the attorney-client privilege because the company handbook stated that employees were prohibited from using the computer to send or receive personal e-mails. Moreover, the company warned that it would monitor its technology resources for compliance with its computer policy, and that employees "have no rights of privacy" with respect to information on the computers.[63] Very few cases involving e-mail and Web site issues

[60] Title III of the Omnibus Crime Control and Safe Streets Act of 1968, 28 U.S.C. §§2510–2520.
[61] *Deal v. Spears*, 580 F.2d 1153 (8th Cir. 1992); *Arias v. Mutual Central Alarm Services, Inc.*, 182 F.R.D. 407 (S.D.N.Y. 1998).
[62] 18 U.S.C. §§2510–2520.
[63] *Holmes v. Petrovich Development Co.*, 191 Cal. App. 4th 1047 (3d Dist. 2011).

have been adjudicated so far under the ECPA. It has been held that for an employee's secure Web site to be "intercepted" in violation of the wiretap act, the electronic documents acquired must be acquired during transmission, not while in electronic storage.[64]

An employer can place itself within the consent exception of the act by issuing a policy statement to all employees that informs them of the monitoring program and its purposes and justification.

38-7d Property Searches

Protected by the Fourth Amendment, public-sector employees have a reasonable expectation of privacy with respect to their desks and file cabinets. However, depending on the fact-specific purpose, justification, and scope of the search, the balance of interest should favor the public employer because its interests in supervision, control, and the efficient operation of the workplace outweigh a public employee's privacy interests.[65] Search of a postal service employee's locker was held not to be a Fourth Amendment violation because well-publicized regulations informed employees that their lockers were subject to search to combat pilferage and stealing. However, the warrantless search of the desk and files of a psychiatrist employed by a state hospital was found to be a Fourth Amendment violation, exceeding the scope of a reasonable work-related search when the search examined his private possessions, including purely personal belongings, and management sought to justify the search on false grounds.[66]

In the private sector, employers may create a reasonable expectation of privacy by providing an employee a locker and allowing the employee to provide his or her own lock. A search of that locker could be an invasion of privacy.[67] If, however, the employer provides a locker and lock but retains a master key and this is known to employees, the lockers may be subject to legitimate reasonable searches by the employer. If a private-sector employer notifies all employees of its policy on lockers, desks, and office searches and the employer complies with its own policy, employees will have no actionable invasion of privacy case.

Many businesses use overt or hidden video cameras as a security method in the workplace to enhance worker safety and to prevent and/or detect theft or other criminal conduct. To avoid state constitutional or statutory claims for invasion of privacy, employers should not set up video cameras in areas where employees have a reasonable expectation of privacy.[68] Utilizing signs to notify employees and members of the public that certain areas are under video surveillance is a common business practice not likely to initiate privacy claims. Additionally, employers should disseminate their written policy on surveillance and obtain a consent form from employees acknowledging that they received this notice to preserve their consent defense.

38-7e Drug and Alcohol Testing

Drug and alcohol testing is an additional source of privacy concerns for employees. Public-sector employees may see drug and alcohol testing as potentially infringing on their Fourth

---

[64] *Konop v. Hawaiian Airlines, Inc.*, 302 F.3d 868 (9th Cir. 2002); *Fraser v. Nationwide Mutual Insurance Co.*, 352 F.3d 107 (3d Cir. 2003) (court held that the wiretaps act was not violated because the employer did not "intercept" the e-mail but retrieved it after it had been sent and received).

[65] *O'Connor v. Ortega*, 480 U.S. 709 (1987).

[66] *Ortega v. O'Connor*, 146 F.3d 1149 (9th Cir. 1998).

[67] *Kmart Corp. v. Trotti*, 677 S.W.2d 632 (Tex. App. 1984).

[68] See *Kline v. Security Guards, Inc.*, 386 F.3d 246 (3d Cir. 2004). Some 370 employees of Dana Corporation's Reading, Pennsylvania, facility sued the corporation and its security guard company after employees learned that a new audio and video surveillance system at the entrance of the facility allowed what was said in the area where employees "punch in" for work to be observed and heard in the guard booth. The Third Circuit Court of Appeals rejected the employer's preemption claims and remanded the matter to the state court to handle the invasion of privacy and other tort claims.

and Fifth Amendment rights, although they may be subject to this testing on the basis of reasonable suspicion. In ordinary circumstances, however, random drug testing is not permissible in the public sector except for mass transit workers and some safety-sensitive positions. The Federal Omnibus Transportation Employee Testing Act,[69] which covers certain classes of employees working in the airline, railroad, and trucking industries, makes covered employees subject to random drug and alcohol testing. Random drug and alcohol testing of employees working in safety-sensitive positions in the private sector also is permissible, as is the testing of private-sector employees on the basis of reasonable suspicion.

38-8   Employment-Related Immigration Laws

The Immigration and Naturalization Act (INA), the Immigration Reform and Control Act of 1986 (IRCA), and the Immigration Act of 1990[70] are the principal employer-related immigration laws. Administration of these laws was formerly under the Immigration and Naturalization Service and is now reorganized under the Department of Homeland Security (DHS) as the United States Bureau of Citizenship and Immigration Services (USCIS).

38-8a   Employer Liability

The IRCA sets criminal and civil penalties against employers who knowingly hire aliens who have illegally entered the United States. The IRCA was designed to stop illegal immigration by eliminating job opportunities for these aliens.

38-8b   Employer Verification

Upon hiring a new employee, an employer must verify that the employee is authorized to work in the United States. USCIS has designated Form I-9, Immigration Eligibility Verification Form, as the official verification form to comply with the IRCA.

The prospective employee must complete the initial portion of Form I-9, attesting under the penalty of perjury that he or she is a U.S. citizen or is authorized to work in the United States, and that the verification document(s) presented to the employer are genuine and relate to the signer. The employer must then review the documents that support the individual's right to work in the United States.

In April 2011, USCIS issued a final rule on acceptable identity documents for the I-9 employment eligibility process, divided into three sections.[71] List A documents verify identity and employment authorization and include a U.S. passport, the new U.S. passport card, and the temporary Form I-551 (permanent resident card) or a permanent resident card that includes a machine-readable immigrant visa. List B documents verify only identity; an example is a state-issued driver's license. List C documents, such as a Social Security card or official birth certificate, verify employment authorization. The employer is prohibited from requiring other documentation.[72]

E-Verify

Employers may verify new employee eligibility status through the federal government's mostly voluntary employment verification program called E-Verify. The E-Verify system is an Internet-based voluntary system that electronically compares information on I-9

---

[69] P.L. 102-143, 105 Stat. 952, 49 U.S.C. §1301 nt.

[70] P.L. 101-649, 8 U.S.C. §1101.

[71] See *Federal Register* (Apr. 15, 2011). USCIS stated that concerns about document fraud were among the most important reasons for this rulemaking.

[72] 8 U.S.C. §1324B (a)(b).

forms with records at the Social Security Administration and the Department of Homeland Security (DHS). In 2010, DHS instituted a U.S. passport photo matching program by comparing E-Verify data with State Department records. Employers that use E-Verify must notify applicants that they use E-Verify and cannot use the program as a prescreening tool. USCIS statistics for FY 2010 on E-Verify use showed that 98.3 percent of new hires surveyed were confirmed "work authorized" in three to five seconds.

Executive Order 12989 was amended in 2008 to require federal contractors to use E-Verify to confirm the employment eligibility of their workforce.

Under the Legal Arizona Workers Act, upheld by the Supreme Court, all an Arizona employer is required to do to avoid sanctions is to use the I-9 system and E-Verify.[73]

Many technology companies are utilizing L-1 visas as an alternative to the H-1B visas. Although the H-1B visa program requires employers to pay foreign workers the prevailing U.S. wage for a particular job, the L-1 visa has no such requirement. For example, an engineer on an L-1 visa from India may be paid the same wage rate as paid in India, rather than the much higher prevailing rate for U.S. engineers. USCIS requires each transferee, or his or her employer, to demonstrate that the transferee's responsibilities are "primarily managerial."

For Example, Brazilian corporation Granite Ebenezer established a U.S.-based affiliate, Brazil Quality Stones, Inc. (BQS), as a California corporation. Eugene dos Santos, a Brazilian citizen, served as President and CEO of both entities and owned 99 percent of the corporation's stock. Citizenship and Immigration Services determined that he was not entitled to an L-1 visa. Although BQS submitted an organizational chart with him at the top supervising five employees, only three had received pay during the quarter. The USCIS determined that BQS had not reached the level of development in which dos Santos could devote his primary attention to managerial duties as opposed to operational ones.[74]

Make the Connection

Summary

The relationship of employer and employee is created by the agreement of the parties and is subject to the principles applicable to contracts. If the employment contract sets forth a specific duration, the employer cannot terminate the contract at an earlier date unless just cause exists. If no definite time period is set forth, the individual is an at-will employee. Under the employment-at-will doctrine, an employer can terminate the contract of an at-will employee at any time for any reason or for no reason. Courts in many jurisdictions, however, have carved out exceptions to this doctrine when the discharge violates public policy or is contrary to good faith and fair dealing in the employment relationship. The Fair Labor Standards Act regulates minimum wages, overtime hours, and child labor.

Under the National Labor Relations Act, employees have the right to form a union to obtain a collective bargaining contract or to refrain from organizational activities. The National Labor Relations Board conducts elections to determine whether employees in an appropriate bargaining unit desire to be represented by a union. The NLRA prohibits employers' and unions' unfair labor practices and authorizes the NLRB to conduct proceedings to stop such practices. Economic strikes have limited reinstatement rights. Federal law sets forth democratic standards for the election of union offices.

The Employees Retirement Income Security Act (ERISA) protects employees' pensions by requiring (1) high standards of those administering the funds,

---

[73] *Chamber of Commerce of the United States v. Whiting,* 131 S. Ct. 624 (2011).
[74] *Brazil Quality Stones, Inc. v. Chertoff,* 531 F.3d 1063 (9th Cir. 2008).

(2) reasonable vesting of benefits, (3) adequate funding, and (4) an insurance program to guarantee payments of earned benefits.

Unemployment compensation benefits are paid to persons for a limited period of time if they are out of work through no fault of their own. Persons receiving unemployment compensation must be available for placement in a job similar in duties and comparable in rate of pay to the job they lost. Twelve-week maternity, paternity, and adoption leaves are available under the Family and Medical Leave Act. Employers and employees pay Social Security taxes to provide retirement benefits, disability benefits, life insurance benefits, and Medicare.

The Occupational Safety and Health Act provides for the (1) establishment of safety and health standards and (2) effective enforcement of these standards. Many states have enacted "right-to-know" laws, which require employers to inform their employees of any hazardous substances present in the workplace.

Workers' compensation laws provide for the prompt payment of compensation and medical benefits to persons injured in the course of employment without regard to fault. An injured employee's remedy is generally limited to the remedy provided by the workers' compensation statute. Most states also provide compensation to workers for occupational diseases.

The Bill of Rights is the source of public-sector employees' privacy rights. Private-sector employees may obtain limited privacy rights from statutes, case law, and collective bargaining agreements. Employers may monitor employee telephone calls, although once it is determined that the call is personal, the employer must stop listening or be in violation of the federal wiretap statute. The ordinary-course-of-business and consent exceptions to the Electronic Communications Privacy Act of 1986 (ECPA) give private employers a great deal of latitude to monitor employee e-mail. Notification to employees of employers' policies on searching lockers, desks, and offices reduces employees' expectations of privacy, and a search conducted in conformity with a known policy is generally not an invasion of privacy. Drug and alcohol testing is generally permissible if it is based on reasonable suspicion; random drug and alcohol testing may also be permissible in safety-sensitive positions.

Immigration laws prohibit the employment of aliens who have illegally entered the United States.

Learning Outcomes

After studying this chapter, you should be able to clearly explain:

38-1   The Employment Relationship

LO.1   Explain the contractual nature of the employment relationship

See the *FedEx* case in which the employment contract and the employee handbook both preserved the employer's at-will termination powers, page 764.

See the example of the public policy exception to the employment-at-will doctrine protecting home health care nurse Eugene Patterson, page 763.

LO.2   Explain how whistleblower protection under Sarbanes-Oxley is limited to conduct in violation of fraud or securities laws

See the example involving whistleblowers Tides and Neumann who were not protected under SOX because they disclosed information and documents to a newspaper and not a regulatory or law enforcement agency, page 765.

LO.3   Explain how Dodd-Frank expands whistleblower protection to a wide range of financial services employees and provides incentives for whistleblowers

See what a whistleblower must do to recover a bounty under Dodd-Frank, page 766.

38-2   Labor Relations Laws

LO.4   Explain how the National Labor Relations Act prohibits employers from firing employees attempting to form a union and requires employers to bargain with unions in good faith over wages, hours, and working conditions

See the *Sam Santillo* case on wrongful termination of an employee because of his union activity, pages 773–774.

See the role that the National Labor Relations Board plays in regulating employers' overly broad social media policies that are in violation of Section 7 of the NLRA, page 772.

See the discussion of mandatory and permissive subjects of bargaining, page 774.

38-3   Pension Plans and Federal Regulation

LO.5   Explain how ERISA protects employee pensions and benefits

See the Bell South example in which Ms. Lee successfully sued for disability benefits, pages 776–777.

See the discussion of defined contribution plans and defined benefit plans, page 777.

38-4 Unemployment Benefits, Family Leaves, and Social Security

LO.6 Explain the essentials of unemployment benefits, family and medical leaves, military leaves, and Social Security benefits

38-5 Employees' Health and Safety

LO.7 Explain how OSHA is designed to ensure workers' safe and healthful working conditions

See the Thinking Things Through discussion for reasons why taking chances or shortcuts in violation of OSHA standards is bad management, page 783.

See the *SeaWorld* case concerning a willful violation of the general duty clause, page 782.

38-6 Compensation for Employees' Injuries

LO.8 Explain the three types of benefits provided by Workers' Compensation statutes

38-7 Employee Privacy

LO.9 Explain the sources of privacy rights and applications to telephone, e-mail, and property searches

38-8 Employer-Related Immigration Laws

LO.10 Explain an employer's verification obligations when hiring new employees

Key Terms

defined benefit plan

defined contribution plan

economic strikers

employment-at-will doctrine

mass picketing

Pension Benefit Guaranty Corporation (PBGC)

primary picketing

right-to-work laws

secondary picketing

shop right

Questions and Case Problems

1. Robert Evjen was a full-time employee of Boise Cascade Co. At the same time, he was a full-time student at Chemata Community College. He was laid off as part of a general economy move by the employer. He applied for unemployment compensation. His claim was opposed on the ground that he was not "available for work" because he was going to school. Testimony showed that Evjen never missed work to go to classes, that he could not afford to go to school without working, and that, in case of any conflict between work and school, work came first. The employer countered that he needed to be available for all shifts of suitable work to qualify for unemployment benefits. Decide. [*Evjen v. Employment Agency*, 539 P.2d 662 (Or. App.)]

2. Michael Smyth was an operations manager at Pillsbury Co., and his employment status was that of an employee at will. Smyth received certain e-mail messages at home, and he replied to his supervisor by e-mail. His messages contained some provocative language, including the phrase "kill the backstabbing bastards" and a reference to an upcoming company party as the "Jim Jones Koolaid affair." Later, Smyth was given two weeks' notice of his termination, and he was told that his e-mail remarks were inappropriate and unprofessional. Smyth believes that he is the victim of invasion of privacy because the e-mail messages caused his termination, and the company had promised that e-mail communications would not be intercepted and used as a basis for discipline or discharge. The company denies that it intercepted the e-mail messages and points out that Smyth himself sent the unprofessional comments to his supervisor. Is Smyth entitled to reinstatement and back pay because of the invasion of privacy? [*Smyth v. Pillsbury Co.*, 914 F. Supp. 97 (E.D. Pa.)]

3. Michael Hauck claimed that he was discharged by his employer, Sabine Pilot Service, because he refused its direction to perform the illegal act of pumping the bilges of the employer's vessel into the waterways. Hauck was an employee at will, and Sabine contends that it therefore had the right to discharge him without having to show cause. Hauck brought a wrongful discharge action against Sabine. Decide. [*Sabine Pilot Service, Inc., v. Hauck*, 687 S.W.2d 733 (Tex.)]

4. Jeanne Eenkhoorn worked as a supervisor at a business office for the New York Telephone Co. While at work, she invented a process for terminating the telephone services of delinquent subscribers. The telephone company used the process but refused to compensate her for it, claiming a shop right. Eenkhoorn then sued for damages on a quasi-contract

theory. Decide. [*Eenkhoorn v. New York Telephone Co.*, 568 N.Y.S.2d 677]

5. One Monday, a labor organization affiliated with the International Ladies Garment Workers Union, began an organizational drive among the employees of Whittal & Son. On the following Monday, six of the employees who were participating in the union drive were discharged. Immediately after the firings, the head of the company gave a speech to the remaining workers in which he made a variety of antiunion statements and threats. The union filed a complaint with the NLRB, alleging that the six employees were fired because they were engaging in organizational activity and were thus discharged in violation of the NLRA. The employer defended its position, arguing that it had a business to run and that it was barely able to survive in the global economy against cheap labor from third-world countries. It asserted that the last thing it needed was "union baloney." Was the NLRA violated?

6. David Stark submitted an application to the maintenance department of Wyman-Gordon Co. Stark was a journeyman millwright with nine years' experience at a neighboring company at the time of his application to Wyman-Gordon. Stark was vice president of the local industrial workers' union. In his preliminary interview with the company, Ms. Peevler asked if Stark was involved in union activity, and Stark detailed his involvement to her. She informed Stark that Wyman-Gordon was a nonunion shop and asked how he felt about this. Peevler's notes from the interview characterize Stark's response to this question as "seems to lean toward third-party intervention." Company officials testified that Stark's qualifications were "exactly what we were looking for," but he was not hired. Stark claimed that he was discriminated against. Wyman-Gordon denied that any discrimination had occurred. Is a job applicant (as opposed to an employee) entitled to protection from antiunion discrimination? On the facts of this case, has any discrimination taken place? [*Wyman-Gordon Co. v. N.L.R.B.*, 108 L.R.R.M. 2085 (1st Cir.)]

7. Armenda Malone and Stephen Krantz were induced to leave other employment and join ABI's CD-ROM division as national account managers in part because of a favorable commission agreement at ABI. Their employment relationship with ABI had no set duration, and as such they were employees at will. For the first two quarters of their employment, their commission reports were approved by the president of the division and paid without incident. Thereafter, a new management team took over the division. When the mid-level manager presented third quarter commission reports based on the prior practice to the new vice president, Bruce Lowry, for approval, he was told, "You got to learn how to f—these people." Lowry then utilized severable variables—some of which the mid-level manager found "ridiculous"—to reduce the commission figures. After much discourse that carried on well into the fourth quarter, Lowry announced that a new model for determining commissions would be implemented. Commissions for both the third and fourth quarters, ending in December, were then calculated based on this model. ABI asserts that because Malone and Krantz were employees at will, the employer had the right to interpret or alter how it pays employees as it sees fit. Krantz and Malone left ABI and have sued for what they believe are the full commissions earned in the third and fourth quarters. Present a legal theory on behalf of Malone and Krantz for the payment of back commissions. Assess the strengths and weaknesses of Lowry's approach to employee relations. How would you decide this case? [*Malone v. American Business Information, Inc.*, 647 N.W.2d 569 (Neb.)]

8. Jane Richards was employed as the sole crane operator of Gale Corp. and held the part-time union position of shop steward for the plant. On May 15, Richards complained to OSHA concerning what she contended were seven existing violations of the Occupational Safety and Health Act that were brought to her attention by members of the bargaining unit. On May 21, she stated to the company's general manager at a negotiating session: "If we don't have a new contract by the time the present one expires on June 15, we will strike." On May 22, an OSHA inspector arrived at the plant, and Richards told her supervisor, "I blew the whistle." On May 23, the company rented and later purchased two large electric forklifts that were used to do the work previously performed by the crane, and the crane operator's job was abolished. Under the existing collective bargaining contract, the company had the right to lay off for lack of work. The contract also provided for arbitration, and it prohibited discipline or discharge without "just cause." On May 23, Richards was notified that she was being laid off "for lack of work" within her classification of crane operator. She was also advised that the company was not planning on using the crane in the future and that, if she were smart, she would get another job. Richards claimed that her layoff violated the

National Labor Relations Act, the Occupational Safety and Health Act, and the collective bargaining agreement. Was she correct?

9. Virgil Deemer and Thomas Cornwell, employees at a Whirlpool Corporation plant, refused to comply with a supervisor's order that they perform maintenance work on certain mesh screens located some 20 feet above the plant floor. Twelve days before a fellow employee had fallen to his death from the screens. Because they refused to do the work assigned them, they were told to punch out and go home; reprimands were placed in their files. Should employees be able to pick and choose what work they will perform? Do Deemer and Cornwell have any recourse? [*Whirlpool v. Marshall*, 445 U.S. 1]

10. In May, the nurses union at Waterbury Hospital went on strike, and the hospital was shut down. In mid-June, the hospital began hiring replacements and gradually opened many units. To induce nurses to take employment during the strike, the hospital guaranteed replacement nurses their choice of positions and shifts. If a preferred position was in a unit that was not open at that time, the hospital guaranteed that the individual would be placed in that position at the end of the strike. The strike ended in October and as the striking workers returned to work, the hospital began opening units that had been closed during the strike. It staffed many of these positions with replacement nurses. The nurses who had the positions prior to the strike and were waiting to return to work believed that they should have been called to fill these positions rather than the junior replacements who had held other positions during the strike. Decide. [*Waterbury Hospital v. NLRB*, 950 F.2d 849 (2d Cir.)]

11. Buffo was employed by the Baltimore & Ohio Railroad. Along with a number of other workers, he was removing old brakes from railroad cars and replacing them with new brakes. In the course of the work, rivet heads and scrap from the brakes accumulated on the tracks under the cars. This debris was removed only occasionally when the workers had time. Buffo, while holding an air hammer in both arms, was crawling under a car when his foot slipped on scrap on the ground, causing him to strike and injure his knee. He sued the railroad for damages under the Federal Employers Liability Act. Decide. [*Buffo v. Baltimore & Ohio Railroad Co.*, 72 A.2d 593 (Pa.)]

12. Mark Phipps was employed as a cashier at a Clark gas station. A customer drove into the station and asked him to pump leaded gasoline into her 1976 Chevrolet, an automobile equipped to receive only unleaded gasoline. The station manager told Phipps to comply with the request, but he refused, believing that his dispensing leaded gasoline into the gas tank was a violation of law. Phipps stated that he was willing to pump unleaded gas into the tank, but the manager immediately fired him. Phipps sued Clark for wrongful termination. Clark contended that it was free to terminate Phipps, an employee at will, for any reason or no reason. Decide. [*Phipps v. Clark Oil & Refining Corp.*, 396 N.W.2d 588 (Minn. App.)]

13. Reno, Nevada, police officers John Bohach and Jon Catalano communicated with each other on the Alphapage computer system, typing messages on a keyboard and sending them to each other by use of a "send" key. The computer dials a commercial paging company, which receives the message by modem, and the message is then sent to the person paged by radio broadcast. When the system was installed, the police chief warned that every Alphapage message was logged on the network, and he barred messages that were critical of department policy or discriminatory. The two police officers sought to block a department investigation into their messages and prevent disclosure of the messages' content. They claimed that the messages should be treated the same as telephone calls under federal wiretap law. The department contended that the system was essentially a form of e-mail whose messages are by definition stored in a computer, and the storage was itself not part of the communication. Was the federal wiretap law violated? [*Bohach v. City of Reno*, 932 F. Supp. 1232 (D. Nev.)]

14. Michael Kittell was employed at Vermont Weatherboard. While operating a saw at the plant, Kittell was seriously injured when a splinter flew into his eye and penetrated his head. Kittell sued Vermont Weatherboard, seeking damages under a common law theory. His complaint alleged that he suffered severe injuries solely because of the employer's wanton and willful acts and omissions. The complaint stated that he was an inexperienced worker, put to work without instructions or warning on a saw from which the employer had stripped away all safety devices. Vermont Weatherboard made a motion to dismiss the complaint on the ground that the Workers' Compensation Act provided the exclusive remedy for his injury. Decide. [*Kittell v. Vermont Weatherboard, Inc.*, 417 A.2d 926 (Vt.)]

C H A P T E R   39

Equal Employment Opportunity Law

Laws of the United States reflect our society's concern that all Americans, including minorities, women, and persons with disabilities, have equal employment opportunities and that the workplace is free from discrimination and harassment. Title VII of the Civil Rights Act of 1964, as amended in 1972, 1978, and 1991, is the principal law regulating equal employment opportunities in the United States. Other federal laws require equal pay for men and women doing substantially the same work and forbid discrimination because of age or disability.

CPA 39-1 Title VII of the Civil Rights Act of 1964, as Amended

Title VII of the Civil Rights Act of 1964[1] seeks to eliminate employer and union practices that discriminate against employees and job applicants on the basis of race, color, religion, sex, or national origin. The law applies to the hiring process and to discipline, discharge, promotion, and benefits.

39-1a Theories of Discrimination

The Supreme Court has created, and the Civil Rights Act of 1991 has codified, two principal legal theories under which a plaintiff may prove a case of unlawful employment discrimination: disparate treatment and disparate impact.

A *disparate treatment* claim exists where an employer treats some individuals less favorably than others because of their race, color, religion, sex, or national origin. Proof of the employer's discriminatory motive is essential in a disparate treatment case.[2]

Disparate impact exists when an employer's facially neutral employment practices, such as hiring or promotion examinations, although neutrally applied and making no adverse reference to race, color, religion, sex, or national origin, have a significantly adverse or disparate impact on a protected group. In addition, the employment practice in question is not shown by the employer to be job related and consistent with business necessity. Under the disparate impact theory, it is not a defense for an employer to demonstrate that it did not intend to discriminate.

For Example, if plant manager Jones is heard telling the personnel director that the vacant welder's position should be filled by a male because "this is man's work," a qualified female applicant turned down for the job would prevail in a *disparate treatment* theory case against the employer because she was not hired because of her gender. Necessary evidence of the employer's discriminatory motive would be satisfied by testimony about the manager's "this is man's work" statement.

If the policy for hiring new pilots at Generic Airlines, Inc., required a minimum height of 5 feet 7 inches, and no adverse reference to gender was stated in this employment policy, nevertheless, the 5-feet-7-inch minimum height policy has an adverse or disparate impact on women because far fewer women than men reach this height. Such an employment policy would be set aside on a *disparate impact* theory, and a minimum height for the position would be established by the court based on evidence of job-relatedness and business necessity. A 5-feet-5-inch height requirement was set by one court for pilots.

---

[1] 42 U.S.C. §2000(e) *et seq.*
[2] *Woodson v. Scott Paper Co.,* 109 F.3d 913 (3d Cir. 1997).

CASE SUMMARY

Number 1 on the Charts! The Case That Created the Disparate Impact Theory

FACTS: Griggs and other black employees of the Duke Power Company's Dan River Station challenged Duke Power's requirement of a high school diploma and passing standardized general intelligence tests for transfer to more desirable "inside" jobs. The district court and Court of Appeals found no violation of Title VII because the employer did not adopt the diploma and test requirements with the purpose of intentionally discriminating against black employees. The Supreme Court granted *certiorari*.

DECISION: Judgment for Griggs. The absence of any intent on the part of the employer to discriminate was not a defense. Title VII prohibits not only overt discrimination but also practices that are fair in form but discriminatory in operation. If any employment practice, such as a diploma or testing requirement, that operates to exclude minorities at a substantially higher rate than white applicants cannot be shown to be "job-related" and consistent with "business necessity," the practice is prohibited. [***Griggs v. Duke Power Co.***, 401 U.S. 424 (1971)]

"Disparate treatment" and "disparate impact" may both be at issue in the same case. **For Example,** as required by the city charter, the city of New Haven used objective examinations to identify those firefighters best qualified for promotion to fill vacant lieutenant and captain positions. On the basis of the examinations' results, no black candidates were eligible for immediate promotion. A rancorous public debate ensued. The city threw out the results based on the statistical racial disparity to avoid potential liability in a lawsuit based on *disparate impact* against the black candidates. White and Hispanic firefighters who passed the exams but were denied a chance for promotion by the city's refusal to certify the test results, sued the city, alleging a *disparate treatment* (intentional discrimination) case—that discarding the test results discriminated against them based on their race in violation of Title VII. The Supreme Court determined that the city rejected the test results because the higher-scoring candidates were white and that without some other justification this express race-based decision making is prohibited. The Court stated that "a strong basis in evidence" standard was necessary before the city could make an employment decision based on fear of liability under Title VII—and the Court held that the city did not meet this standard. The statistical disparity by itself was insufficient to constitute a strong basis in evidence of unlawful disparate impact. The examinations were job related and consistent with business necessity. And there was no strong basis in evidence of an equally valid, less-discriminating testing alternative. Thus, in a 5-4 decision, the U.S. Supreme Court ruled that the city had violated the civil rights of the white and Hispanic firefighters and remanded the case for further proceedings.[3]

39-1b The Equal Employment Opportunity Commission

The Equal Employment Opportunity Commission (EEOC) is a five-member body appointed by the president to establish equal employment opportunity policy under the laws it administers. The EEOC supervises the agency's conciliation and enforcement efforts.

[3] *Ricci v. DeStefano*, 557 U.S. 557 (2009). Contrary to the extensive presentation in the majority decision of the detailed steps taken to develop and administer the examinations, the dissent asserted that the Court had ignored substantial evidence of multiple flaws in the tests and that the Court had failed to acknowledge that better tests used in other cities have yielded less racially skewed outcomes. The decision, the dissent, and two concurrences provide an insight into the complexities of our judicial process.

The EEOC administers Title VII of the Civil Rights Act, the Equal Pay Act (EPA), the Age Discrimination in Employment Act (ADEA), Section 501 of the Rehabilitation Act (which prohibits federal-sector discrimination against persons with disabilities), and Title I (the employment provisions) of the Americans with Disabilities Act (ADA) and the ADA Amendments Act (ADAA).

Procedure

Where a state or local EEO agency with the power to act on claims of discriminatory practices exists, the charging party must file a complaint with that agency. The charging party must wait 60 days or until the termination of the state proceedings, whichever occurs first, before filing a charge with the EEOC. If no state or local agency exists, a charge may be filed directly with the EEOC so long as it is filed within 180 days of the occurrence of the discriminatory act. The commission conducts an investigation to determine whether reasonable cause exists to believe that the charge is true. If such cause is found to exist, the EEOC attempts to remedy the unlawful practice through conciliation. If the EEOC does not resolve the matter to the satisfaction of the parties, it may decide to litigate the case when systemic or unusual circumstances exist, including a "pattern or practice of discrimination." In most instances, however, the EEOC issues the charging party a *right-to-sue letter*. Thereafter, the individual claiming a violation of EEO law has 90 days to file a lawsuit in a federal district court.[4]

Pattern-or-Practice Cases. Section 707 of Title VII permits the EEOC to sue employers when it has reasonable cause to believe they are engaged in a *pattern or practice* of unlawful employment discrimination. It must establish that intentional discrimination was the defendant employer's "standard operating procedure." A first phase focuses on the employer's policy or practice, not on individual charges. Once the pattern or practice of discrimination is established, the process moves to the individual relief phase, where individual claims may be presented. The purpose of Section 707 is to provide the government with a swift and effective weapon to eliminate unlawful practices.[5]

Systemic "Class Action" Cases. The EEOC has placed renewed focus on identifying, developing, and litigating discrimination cases involving employment policies affecting large classes of individuals in every statute enforced by the agency. When an individual files a discrimination charge with the EEOC, it now may expand its investigation into that employer's related employment practices involving similarly situated individuals. Possible statutory violations discovered during the course of the investigation of the initial individual charge may lead the EEOC to bring a "systemic" case on behalf of a number of employees against the employer under Section 706 of the act.[6]

Damages

Title VII sets damages available to victims of discrimination (Figure 39-1).

---

[4] An individual who misses the filing deadline of Title VII may be able to bring a race discrimination case under the two-year time limit allowed under Section 1981 of the Civil Rights Act of 1964, codified at 42 U.S.C. §1981, and sometimes called a *Section 1981 lawsuit*. In the *Edelman v. Lynchburg College* decision, 535 U.S. 106 (2002), the U.S. Supreme Court approved an EEOC regulation that allows certain defective charges to be cured, with the cured charge relating back to the date the EEOC first received the initial charge, which was within the 300-day filing period.

[5] See *EEOC v. Mitsubishi Motor Manufacturing of America*, 102 F.3d 869 (7th Cir. 1996).

[6] Courts currently disagree on the extent of investigation and conciliation the EEOC must conduct in systemic cases. Some courts have held that the EEOC must conduct an investigation and attempt conciliation on each individual charge. See *EEOC v. CRST Van Expedited, Inc.*, 679 F.3d 657 (8th Cir. 2012). Other courts have found that the EEOC need only give the employer adequate notice that it was investigating on a class-wide basis and that it need not conciliate on behalf of each claimant. See *Serrano v. Cintas Corp.*, 699 F.3d 884 (6th Cir. 2012). The Supreme Court has recognized that the EEOC has broad discretion in conciliating claims but has not directly addressed this issue. See *Mach Mining, LLC v. EEOC*, 135 S. Ct. 1645 (2015).

FIGURE 39-1 Unlawful Discrimination under Title VII of the Civil Rights Act of 1964 as Amended by the Civil Rights Act of 1991

DISCRIMINATORY TREATMENT IN EMPLOYMENT DECISIONS ON THE BASIS OF RACE, COLOR, RELIGION, SEX, OR NATIONAL ORIGIN

DISPARATE TREATMENT THEORY	DISPARATE IMPACT THEORY
NONNEUTRAL PRACTICE OR NONNEUTRAL APPLICATION	FACIALLY NEUTRAL PRACTICE AND NEUTRAL APPLICATION
REQUIRES PROOF OF DISCRIMINATORY INTENT	DOES NOT REQUIRE PROOF OF DISCRIMINATORY INTENT REQUIRES PROOF OF ADVERSE EFFECT ON PROTECTED GROUP AND EMPLOYER IS UNABLE TO SHOW THAT THE CHALLENGED PRACTICE IS JOB RELATED FOR THE POSITION IN QUESTION AND IS CONSISTENT WITH BUSINESS NECESSITY
EITHER PARTY HAS A RIGHT TO REQUIRE A JURY TRIAL WHEN SEEKING COMPENSATORY OR PUNITIVE DAMAGES	NO RIGHT TO A JURY TRIAL
REMEDY REINSTATEMENT, HIRING, OR PROMOTION BACK PAY LESS INTERIM EARNINGS RETROACTIVE SENIORITY ATTORNEY AND EXPERT WITNESS FEES PLUS COMPENSATORY* AND PUNITIVE DAMAGES DAMAGES CAPPED FOR CASES OF SEX AND RELIGIOUS DISCRIMINATION DEPENDING ON SIZE OF EMPLOYER:	REMEDY REINSTATEMENT, HIRING, OR PROMOTION BACK PAY LESS INTERIM EARNINGS RETROACTIVE SENIORITY ATTORNEY AND EXPERT WITNESS FEES

NUMBER OF EMPLOYEES	DAMAGES CAP
100 OR FEWER	$ 50,000
101 TO 200	100,000
201 TO 500	200,000
OVER 500	300,000
NO CAP ON DAMAGES FOR RACE CASES	

* COMPENSATORY DAMAGES INCLUDE FUTURE PECUNIARY LOSSES AND NONPECUNIARY LOSSES SUCH AS EMOTIONAL PAIN AND SUFFERING.

Section 706(k) of Title VII provides that the court in its discretion allow the prevailing party, other than the EEOC and the United States, a reasonable attorneys' fee. Thus, a court may award a prevailing individual in a Civil Rights Act lawsuit against an employer reasonable attorney fees and costs. It also may award attorneys' fees against the EEOC itself if the agency's lawsuit is without foundation. **For Example,** in *EEOC v. Peoplemark*, the federal district court awarded a temporary staffing firm, Peoplemark, the prevailing party in a lawsuit initiated by the EEOC, attorneys' fees, expert witness fees, and other expenses totaling $751,942.48, because the EEOC should have known at a certain point that there was no evidence supporting its complaint that the company maintained a policy adversely affecting a class of African Americans of denying employment to any person with a criminal record.[7]

The Arbitration Option

With the exception of transportation employees, employers can craft arbitration agreements that require employees to arbitrate any employment dispute, including statutory discrimination claims, and these mandatory arbitration clauses can be enforced in federal courts under the Federal Arbitration Act.[8] Courts do, however, require that the arbitration clauses be "fair." Moreover, a party agreeing to arbitration does not forgo substantive rights afforded by Title VII or alter federal antidiscrimination statutes. A fair arbitration clause requires adequate discovery, mandates that the arbitrator have authority to apply the same types of relief available from a court, and should not preclude an employee from vindicating statutory rights because of arbitration costs.[9]

A union may negotiate a provision in a collective bargaining agreement requiring all employment-related discrimination claims to be resolved in arbitration.[10]

39-1c Definition of "Supervisor"

Under Title VII an employer's liability for workplace harassment of employees may depend on the status of the harasser. If the harassing individual is the victim's coworker the employer is liable only if the employer was negligent in controlling working conditions. If the harasser is a "supervisor" who takes an adverse tangible employment action against the victim, the employer is strictly liable. The *Vance v. Ball State University* decision defines the word "supervisor" under Title VII of the Civil Rights Act of 1964.

CASE SUMMARY

It's About Abusing the Power Given by the Employer

FACTS: Maetta Vance sued her employer Ball State University (BSU) alleging that a fellow employee Saundra Davis created a racially hostile work environment in violation of Title VII. The trial court dismissed the case because Davis was not a "supervisor," and the matter progressed to the U.S. Supreme Court for resolution.

DECISION: Judgment for Ball State University. An employee is a "supervisor" for purposes of vicarious liability under Title VII only if the individual is empowered by the employer to take tangible employment actions against the victim, such as hiring, firing, failing to promote, reassignment with significantly different responsibilities, or a decision causing a significant change in benefits. Davis had no such authority. Moreover, there was no showing by Ms. Vance that BSU permitted harassment by a co-worker to occur. [*Vance v. Ball State University*, 133 S. Ct. 2434 (2013)]

---

[7] *EEOC v. Peoplemark*, 2010 WL 748250 (W.D. Mich. Feb. 26, 2010).

[8] *Circuit City Stores, Inc. v. Adams*, 532 U.S. 105 (2001).

[9] See *Circuit City II*, 279 F.3d 889 (9th Cir. 2002).

[10] For some 35 years it was widely understood that an individual may prospectively waive his or her own statutory right to a judicial forum and be compelled to resolve a statutory discrimination claim in arbitration, but a union may not prospectively waive that right for the individual in a collective bargaining agreement. See *Alexander v. Gardner-Denver Co.*, 485 U.S. 36 (1974) and *Gilmer v. Interstate/Johnson Lane Corp.*, 500 U.S. 20 (1991). In *14 Penn Plaza, LLC v. Pyett*, 556 U.S. 247 (2009), the U.S. Supreme Court, in a 5-4 decision, held that a provision in a collective bargaining agreement (CBA) negotiated under the National Labor Relations Act between a union and employer group that requires union members to arbitrate Age Discrimination in Employment Act (ADEA) claims is enforceable as a matter of federal law. Thus, the petitioner union members were precluded from bringing their ADEA case in federal court and the matter had to be resolved under the arbitration provisions of the CBA.

39-2 **Protected Classes and Exceptions**

To successfully pursue a Title VII lawsuit, an individual must belong to a protected class and meet the appropriate burden of proof. Exceptions exist for certain employment practices.

39-2a **Race and Color**

The legislative history of Title VII of the Civil Rights Act demonstrates that a primary purpose of the act is to provide fair employment opportunities for black Americans. The protections of the act are applied to blacks based on race or color.

The word *race* as used in the act applies to all members of the four major racial groupings: white, black, Native American, and Asian-Pacific. Native Americans can file charges and receive the protection of the act on the basis of national origin, race, or, in some instances, color. Individuals of Asian-Pacific origin may file discrimination charges based on race, color, or, in some instances, national origin. Whites are also protected against discrimination because of race and color.

For Example, two white professors at a predominately black university were successful in discrimination suits against the university when it was held that the university had discriminated against them on the basis of race and color in tenure decisions.[11]

39-2b **Religion**

Title VII requires employers to accommodate their employees' or prospective employees' religious practices. Most cases involving allegations of religious discrimination revolve around the determination of whether an employer has made reasonable efforts to accommodate religious beliefs.

If an employee's religious beliefs prohibit working on Saturday, an employer's obligation under Title VII is to try to find a volunteer to cover for the employee on Saturdays. The employer would not have an obligation to violate a seniority provision of a collective bargaining agreement or call in a substitute worker if such accommodation would require more than a *de minimis* or very small cost.

Garments Worn for Religious Reasons

Ordinarily employers have little reason to be informed or concerned about the religious practices of individual employees. However, because many Muslim women wear special clothing as part of their religious observances, which may conflict with an employer's safety or grooming standards, employers should develop appropriate and justifiable policies for their business and provide training for supervisors on how to properly handle requests for religious accommodations. **For Example,** a federal district court ruled in favor of a Muslim employee who was terminated for refusal to remove her head scarf when dealing with customers, where the employer did not strictly enforce its "company uniform policy" until after the terrorist attacks on September 11, 2001. The court did not accept the employer's argument that allowing an exception for the employee would lead to the need for many other exceptions, making its company uniform policy meaningless.[12]

---

[11] *Turgeon v. Howard University*, 571 F. Supp. 679 (D.D.C. 1983).

[12] *EEOC v. Alamo Rent-A-Car*, 432 F. Supp. 2d 1006 (D. Ariz. 2006). In a recent decision, the United States Supreme Court considered whether Abercrombie & Fitch violated Title VII when it did not hire a teenage Muslim woman who wore a headscarf because the company had a dress policy that did not allow employees to wear caps. The Court held that a job applicant does not have to show that the employer had "actual knowledge" that she was wearing the headscarf for religious reasons. She had to show only that the need for an accommodation was a motivating factor in the employer's decision not to hire her. *EEOC v. Abercrombie & Fitch Stores, Inc.*, 135 S. Ct. 2028 (2015).

Safety risks may provide a justifiable basis for a dress code. **For Example,** a court ruled that Kelly Services did not discriminate against a Muslim woman when it decided not to refer her to a client company, Nahan Printing, because she wears a khimar. She had been informed by a Kelly staffing supervisor that "you would have to take your scarf off—you cannot cover your hair," and the applicant replied that she could not remove her khimar because her religion required her to wear it. The EEOC asserted that the employer could have reasonably accommodated her by allowing her to tie her khimar back like people with long hair are allowed to do. However, the Nahan Printing executive explained that hair is permanent; a khimar is different from hair because of the risk that the khimar—like a hat—could fall off into the machinery; and the safety risk would be the worker reaching in and trying to grab it, pulling an individual into a piece of equipment or damaging equipment, or other individuals who are trying to help could potentially be hurt as well.[13]

Body Art Work Rules and Religious Beliefs

Employees have challenged employer bans on body art as religious discrimination, asserting that the employers have not made reasonable efforts to accommodate religious beliefs. EEOC's 1980 Guidelines broadly define religion "to include moral or ethical beliefs as to what is right and wrong which are sincerely held with the strength of traditional religious views."[14] The Guidelines do not limit religion to theistic practices or to beliefs professed by organized religions. **For Example,** Kimberly Cloutier was a member of the Church of Body Modification. Costco's grooming policy prohibited any "visible facial or tongue jewelry" in order to present a professional image to its customers. Ms. Cloutier wore an eyebrow ring as a religious practice. Ms. Cloutier rejected Costco's offer to return her to work if she wore a bandage or plastic retainer over the jewelry because it would violate her religious beliefs. The U.S. Court of Appeals determined that her refusal to accept an accommodation short of an exemption was an undue hardship for the employer because an exemption would negatively impact the company's policy of professionalism.[15]

Some courts, however, look for actual proof of harm to the employer in assessing whether undue hardship exists for an employer. **For Example,** the EEOC brought an action against Red Robin Gourmet Burgers, Inc., for failure to provide an exemption from its grooming policy for an employee's religious tattoos surrounding his wrists. The federal district court looked for actual proof of the restaurant's assertion that the tattoos contravened the company's "family-oriented image," such as customer complaints or other evidence, as opposed to the mere assertion. The court concluded that the employer failed to provide sufficient evidence of undue hardship in accommodating an exemption for the employee.[16]

Title VII permits religious societies to grant hiring preferences in favor of members of their religion. It also provides an exemption for educational institutions to hire employees of a particular religion if the institution is owned, controlled, or managed by a particular religious society. The exemption is a broad one and is not restricted to the religious activities of the institution.

---

[13] *EEOC v. Kelly Services, Inc.*, 598 F.3d 1022 (8th Cir. 2010).

[14] 29 C.F.R. §1605.1 (1980). The EEOC's definition of religion was derived from early Selective Service cases that moved beyond institutional religions and theistic belief structures in handling exemptions to the draft and military service. See *Welsh v. U.S.*, 398 U.S. 333, 343–44 (1970), which allows for expansion of belief systems to include nonreligious ethical or moral codes.

[15] *Cloutier v. Costco*, 390 F.3d 126 (1st Cir. 2004).

[16] *EEOC v. Red Robin Gourmet Burger, Inc.*, 2005 WL 2090677 (W.D. Wash. Aug. 29, 2005).

39-2c Sex

Employers who discriminate against female or male employees because of their sex are held to be in violation of Title VII. The EEOC and the courts have determined that the word *sex* as used in Title VII means a person's gender, not the person's sexual orientation. State and local legislation, however, may provide specific protection against discrimination based on sexual orientation.

Height, Weight, and Physical Ability Requirements

Under the *Griggs v. Duke Power* precedent, an employer must be able to show that criteria used to make an employment decision that has a disparate impact on women, such as minimum height and weight requirements, are, in fact, job related. All candidates for a position requiring physical strength must be given an opportunity to demonstrate their capability to perform the work. Women cannot be precluded from consideration just because they have not traditionally performed such work.

Pregnancy-Related Benefits

Title VII was amended by the Pregnancy Discrimination Act (PDA) in 1978. The amendment prevents employers from treating pregnancy, childbirth, and related medical conditions in a manner different from the manner in which other medical conditions are treated. Thus, women unable to work as a result of pregnancy, childbirth, or related medical conditions must be provided the same benefits as all other workers. These include temporary and long-term disability insurance, sick leave, and other forms of employee benefit programs. An employer who does not provide disability benefits or paid sick leave to other employees is not required to provide them for pregnant workers.[17]

The PDA also protects women from termination or other employment actions because of pregnancy. **For Example,** a catering manager who informed her employer that she would be taking a 12-week leave after childbirth during the busiest time of the year and was subsequently fired by her employer for "customer complaints," was able to bring suit against the employer under the PDA, where the employer's reason was a "pretext."[18] The PDA also protects women from discrimination after giving birth to a child for up to four months thereafter. **For Example,** Katherine Albin was allowed to pursue her claim against Thomas Pink clothing store that she was denied promotion to manager based on her "recent pregnancy," with the alleged discriminatory act occurring three and a half months from the date of birth of her first child.[19]

39-2d Sexual Harassment

Tangible employment action and hostile work environment are two classifications of sexual harassment.

---

[17] In *AT&T Corporation v. Hulteen*, 556 U.S. 701 (2009), the U.S. Supreme Court addressed a current effect of a pre-PDA personnel policy. Prior to the PDA of 1978, AT&T employees on "disability" leave received full-service credit toward retirement benefits for the entire period of absence. Pregnancy at that time was considered a "personal" leave of absence and women on this leave received a maximum service credit of 30 days. Upon retirement, Noreen Hulteen received seven months less service credit for the pre-PDA leave for a pregnancy than she would have had for the same leave time for a disability, and it resulted in a smaller pension benefit. The Court decided against Ms. Hulteen, determining that there was no intent to apply the PDA retroactively, and that AT&T's pre-PDA leave policy was not discriminatory when adopted.

[18] *Newman v. Deer Path Inn*, 1999 WL 1129105 (N.D. Ill. Nov. 7, 1999).

[19] *Albin v. LVMH Moet Louis Vuitton, Inc.* 2014 WL 3585492 (S.D.N.Y. July 8, 2014).

Tangible Employment Action

Sexual harassment classified as *tangible employment action* involves situations in which a supervisor performs an "official act" of the enterprise, such as discharge, demotion, or undesirable reassignment against a subordinate employee because of the employee's refusal to submit to the supervisor's demand for sexual favors. The employer is always vicariously liable for this harassment by a supervisor under the so-called aided-in-the-agency-relation standard. That is, the supervisor is aided in accomplishing the wrongful objective by the existence of the agency relationship. The employer empowered the supervisor as a distinct class of agent to make economic decisions affecting other employees under the supervisor's control. The employer can raise no affirmative defense based on the presence of an employer's antiharassment policy in such a case.

Hostile Work Environment

A second type of sexual harassment classified as *hostile work environment* occurs when a supervisor's conduct does not affect an employee's economic benefits but causes anxiety and "poisons" the work environment for the employee. Such conduct may include unwelcome sexual flirtation, propositions, or other abuses of a sexual nature, including the use of degrading words or the display of sexually explicit pictures.[20] This type of sexual harassment applies to all cases involving supervisors in which the enterprise takes no official act, including constructive discharge cases. The plaintiff must prove severe and pervasive conduct on the supervisor's part to meet the plaintiff's burden of proof.[21] The employer may raise an affirmative defense to liability for damages by proving that (1) it exercised reasonable care to prevent and promptly correct any sexually harassing behavior at its workplace and (2) the plaintiff employee unreasonably failed to take advantage of corrective opportunities provided by the employer. The existence of an employer's sexual harassment policy and notification procedures (Figure 39-2) will aid the employer in proving the affirmative defense in hostile working environment cases.

Rationale

The "primary objective of Title VII, like that of any statute meant to influence primary conduct, is not to provide redress but to avoid harm."[22] When there is no "official act" of the employer, the employer may raise an affirmative defense. This approach fosters the preventative aspect of Title VII, encouraging employers to exercise reasonable care to prevent and correct sexual harassment while providing damages only when the conduct is clearly attributed to an official action of the enterprise or when the employer has not exercised reasonable care to prevent and correct misconduct. **For Example,** Kim Ellerth alleged that she was subject to constant sexual harassment by her supervisor, Ted Slowik, at Burlington Industries. Slowik made comments about her breasts, told her to "loosen up," and warned, "You know, Kim, I could make your life very hard or very easy at Burlington." When Kim was being considered for promotion, Slowik expressed reservations that she was not "loose enough" and then reached over and rubbed her knee. She received the promotion, however. After other such incidents, she quit and filed charges

---

[20] According to EEOC Guidelines §1604.11(f), unwelcome sexual advances, requests for sexual favors, and other verbal or physical conduct of a sexual nature constitute sexual harassment when (1) submission to or rejection of such conduct has the purpose or effect of unreasonably interfering with an individual's work performance or creating an intimidating, hostile, or offensive working environment.

[21] *Oncale v. Sundowner Offshore Services, Inc.*, 523 U.S. 75 (1998). The Supreme Court stated in *Oncale* that it did not intend to turn Title VII into a civility code, and the Court set forth the standard for judging whether the conduct in question amounted to sexual harassment requiring that the conduct be judged from the perspective of a reasonable person in the plaintiff's position, considering all circumstances. The Court warned that "common sense" and "context" must apply in determining whether the conduct was hostile or abusive.

[22] *Faragher v. City of Boca Raton*, 524 U.S. 775, 805 (1998) (citing *Albemale Paper Co. v. Moody*, 422 U.S. 405, 418 (1975)).

| FIGURE 39-2 | Employer Procedure—Sexual Harassment |

A. DEVELOP AND IMPLEMENT AN EQUAL EMPLOYMENT POLICY THAT SPECIFICALLY PROHIBITS SEXUAL HARASSMENT AND IMPOSES DISCIPLINE UP TO AND INCLUDING DISCHARGE. SET FORTH SPECIFIC EXAMPLES OF CONDUCT THAT WILL NOT BE TOLERATED SUCH AS:

- UNWELCOME SEXUAL ADVANCES, WHETHER OR NOT THEY INVOLVE PHYSICAL TOUCHING

- SEXUAL EPITHETS AND JOKES; WRITTEN OR ORAL REFERENCES TO SEXUAL CONDUCT; GOSSIP REGARDING ONE'S SEX LIFE; COMMENTS ON AN INDIVIDUAL'S BODY; AND COMMENTS ABOUT AN INDIVIDUAL'S SEXUAL ACTIVITY, DEFICIENCIES, OR PROWESS

- DISPLAY OF SEXUALLY SUGGESTIVE OBJECTS, PICTURES, AND CARTOONS

- UNWELCOME LEERING, WHISTLING, BRUSHING AGAINST THE BODY, SEXUAL GESTURES, AND SUGGESTIVE OR INSULTING COMMENTS

- INQUIRIES INTO ONE'S SEXUAL EXPERIENCES

- DISCUSSION OF ONE'S SEXUAL ACTIVITIES

B. ESTABLISH ONGOING EDUCATIONAL PROGRAMS, INCLUDING ROLE-PLAYING AND FILMS TO DEMONSTRATE UNACCEPTABLE BEHAVIOR.

C. DESIGNATE A RESPONSIBLE SENIOR OFFICIAL TO WHOM COMPLAINTS OF SEXUAL HARASSMENT CAN BE MADE. AVOID ANY PROCEDURE THAT REQUIRES AN EMPLOYEE TO FIRST COMPLAIN TO THE EMPLOYEE'S SUPERVISOR, BECAUSE THAT INDIVIDUAL MAY BE THE OFFENDING PERSON. MAKE CERTAIN COMPLAINANTS KNOW THAT THERE WILL BE NO RETALIATION FOR FILING A COMPLAINT.

D. INVESTIGATE ALL COMPLAINTS PROMPTLY AND THOROUGHLY.

E. KEEP COMPLAINTS AND INVESTIGATIONS AS CONFIDENTIAL AS POSSIBLE AND LIMIT ALL INFORMATION TO ONLY THOSE WHO NEED TO KNOW.

F. IF A COMPLAINT HAS MERIT, IMPOSE APPROPRIATE AND CONSISTENT DISCIPLINE.

alleging that she was constructively discharged because of the unendurable working conditions resulting from the hostile work environment created by Slowik. She did not use Burlington's sexual harassment internal complaint procedures. Because she was not a victim of a tangible employment action involving an official act of the enterprise, because she received the promotion sought, the employer will be able to raise an affirmative defense. She will be able to prove severe and pervasive conduct on the part of a supervisor under a hostile work environment theory. However, the employer may defeat liability by proving both that it exercised reasonable care to prevent and correct sexual harassing behavior through its internal company complaint policies and that Kim unreasonably failed to take advantage of the company procedures.[23]

[23] *Burlington Industries, Inc. v. Ellerth*, 524 U.S. 742 (1998); see also *Faragher v. City of Boca Raton*, 524 U.S. 775 (1998). In *Pennsylvania v. Suders*, 542 U.S. 129 (2004), the U.S. Supreme Court reviewed a decision of the Third Circuit Court of Appeals that held that a "constructive discharge," if proved, constituted a "tangible employment action" that renders the employer liable for damages and precludes an affirmative defense. The Supreme Court disagreed with the Third Circuit's reading of its *Ellerth/Faragher* decisions and made it very clear that "an official act of the enterprise" is necessary for the plaintiff to defeat the employer's right to raise an affirmative defense.

Nonsupervisors

An employer is liable for the sexual harassment caused its employees by coworkers or customers only when it knew or should have known of the misconduct and failed to take prompt remedial action.

39-2e Protection against Retaliation

Section 704(a) sets forth Title VII's antiretaliation provision in the following terms:

> *It shall be an unlawful practice for an employer to discriminate against any of his employees or applicants for employment … because he has opposed any practice made an unlawful employment practice by this subchapter* [the opposition clause], *or because he has made a charge, testified, assisted, or participated in any manner in an investigation, proceeding, or hearing under this subchapter* [the participation clause].

Some U.S. courts of appeals had held that the retaliation provisions set forth in Section 704(a) of Title VII apply only to retaliation that takes the form of "ultimate employment actions" such as demotions, suspensions, and terminations and do not apply to ministerial matters such as reprimands and poor evaluations. The EEOC believed that the statute prohibits any adverse treatment that is based on a retaliatory motive and is reasonably likely to deter the charging party or others from engaging in protected activity. In *Burlington Northern v. White* (*Burlington*) the Supreme Court held that a plaintiff may pursue a retaliation claim under Title VII if the "employer's challenged action would have been material to a reasonable employee" and likely would have "dissuaded a reasonable worker from making or supporting a charge of discrimination."[24] By focusing on the materiality of the challenged action and the perspective of a reasonable person, this standard was designed to screen out trivial conduct while capturing those acts that are likely to dissuade employees from complaining or assisting in complaints about discrimination.

CASE SUMMARY

New Traction for the Antiretaliation Provisions Thanks to Track Laborer White

FACTS: BNSF Railway hired Shelia White as a track laborer at its Tennessee Yard. She was the only woman in the track department. When hired, she was given the job of operating forklifts as opposed to doing ordinary track labor tasks. Three months after being hired, she complained to the roadmaster that her foreman treated her differently than male employees and had twice made inappropriate remarks. The foreman was suspended without pay for 10 days and ordered to attend training on sexual harassment. Also at that time, the roadmaster reassigned the forklift duties to the former operator who was "senior" to White and assigned White to track labor duties. Six months into her employment, White refused to ride in a truck as directed by a different foreman, and she was suspended for insubordination. Thirty-seven days later, she was reinstated with full back pay, and the discipline was removed from her record. She filed a complaint with the EEOC, claiming that the reassignment to track laborer duties was unlawful gender discrimination and retaliation for her complaint about her treatment by the foreman. The 37-day suspension led to a second retaliation charge. A jury rejected her gender discrimination claim and awarded her compensatory damages for her retaliation claims. BNSF appealed, contending that Ms. White had been hired as a track laborer and it was not retaliatory to

---

[24] *Burlington Northern Santa Fe Railway Co. v. White*, 548 U.S. 133 (2006).

New Traction for the Antiretaliation Provisions Thanks to Track Laborer White continued

assign her to do the work she was hired to do. It also asserted that the 37-day suspension had been corrected and she had been made whole for her loss.

DECISION: Judgment for White. The Supreme Court held that the jury could reasonably conclude that the reassignment from forklift operator to track laborer duties would have been materially adverse to a reasonable employee, thus constituting retaliatory discrimination. Moreover, the Court held that an indefinite suspension without pay for a month, even if the employee later received back pay, could well act as a deterrent to filing a discrimination complaint. [***Burlington Northern Santa Fe Railway Co. v. White,*** **548 U.S. 53 (2006)]**

Subsequent to the *Burlington* decision, the Supreme Court has settled the broad legal issues regarding retaliation claims under federal antidiscrimination laws, including protection of an employee who speaks out about discrimination not of her own initiative, but in answering questions during an internal investigation into rumors of sexual harassment by her supervisor[25] and also providing a "zone of interest" standard for determining whether third parties' retaliation claims are protected under Title VII.[26]

The EEOC takes the position that claims can be filed for retaliation not only under Title VII but also under the Americans with Disabilities Act, the Age Discrimination in Employment Act, and the Equal Pay Act.

39-2f National Origin

Title VII protects members of all nationalities from discrimination. The judicial principles that have emerged from cases involving race, color, and gender employment discrimination are generally applicable to cases involving allegations of discrimination related to national origin. Thus, physical standards, such as minimum height requirements, that tend to exclude persons of a particular national origin because of the physical stature of the group have been found unlawful when these standards cannot be justified by business necessity.

Adverse employment action based on an individual's lack of English language skills violates Title VII when the language requirement bears no demonstrable relationship to the successful performance of the job to which it is applied. **For Example,** Flight Services & Systems Inc. (FSS) purchased the assets of FAI, and assumed FAI's contract with Southwest Airlines to provide wheel chair attendants for Southwest in Denver. FSS took over in October 2009 and by June 2010 "only a few" Ethiopians were still employed by FSS, despite the fact that nearly 200 had held positions there when FSS took over. FSS contended that Southwest requires that FSS employees "possess the ability to communicate effectively in English." On this issue the court determined that passing the written tests required a level of English proficiency beyond what was necessary to do their jobs, thus supporting the plaintiffs' claims of national origin discrimination.[27]

39-2g Title VII Exceptions

Section 703 of Title VII defines which employment activities are unlawful. This same section, however, also exempts several key practices from the scope of Title VII enforcement. The most important are the bona fide occupational qualification exception, the testing and educational requirement exception, and the seniority system exception.

[25] *Crawford v. Metropolitan Government of Nashville,* 555 U.S. 271 (2009).
[26] *Thompson v. North American Stainless, LP,* 131 S. Ct. 863 (2011).
[27] *Tuffa v. Flight Services & Systems Inc.,* 2015 WL 273730 (D. Colo. 2015).

THINKING THINGS THROUGH

Retaliation – The Number One Risk for Employers

Since the Supreme Court's adoption of a broader definition of retaliation than was used in some judicial circuits prior to the *Burlington* decision, the number of retaliation charges filed with the EEOC has risen dramatically. Management-side employment lawyers see "retaliation as the number one risk for employers today." The litigation costs involved in a single retaliation case are substantial.

The source of unlawful retaliation can emanate from a CEO and other top executives down through middle managers or first-level managers, and it can also originate from organizational tolerance of coworker retaliation. Retaliation occurs in all types and sizes of organizations in all employment sectors of society.

Need for a Comprehensive Program. Employers must develop and implement effective antiretaliation and educational policies and procedures for their top executives, middle managers, and first-level supervisors. Additionally, each organization's highest human resource (HR) officer must have authority to independently investigate and report directly to the CEO and have authority as well to report to an appropriate board of directors' committee regarding the business justification for proposed or actual employer actions with potential retaliation liability.*

Educational Discussion of Human Nature and the Costs of Retaliation. Employers must recognize that the educational effort is going to be challenging in some cases because of the "human nature" of the controversy. For instance, an employee has gone to a supervisor's supervisor, the HR department, or the EEOC, and has charged his or her supervisor with discrimination based on race, color, religion, sex, national origin, age, or disability. If the complaint is valid, the supervisor should be appropriately disciplined. It may well be that the complaint is perceived by management or coworkers as lacking merit. How can the accused supervisor

or coworkers treat the complainant as though nothing has happened? Is it not human nature for the supervisor to want to take materially adverse action against that individual? Would not the ideal solution for the supervisor be to "come up with" a business basis for terminating the complainant?

The adverse economic consequences of such an action to the employer could be severe. For example, in the Supreme Court's *Crawford v. Metropolitan Government of Nashville*** case, on remand to the district court, the employer contended that it fired Crawford for irregularities in the school system's payroll office for which Crawford was responsible. Crawford testified that she had never previously been disciplined during her 30 years of service with Metro, and local officials did not begin to investigate her job performance until after she disclosed the alleged sexual harassment by the school district's employee relations coordinator. The jury found that the reasons for firing Crawford were pretextual and awarded Crawford $420,000 in compensatory damages, $408,762 in back pay, and $727,496 in front pay, for a total monetary award of approximately $1.56 million.

Thinking Things Through, all employees at all levels should be instructed that because of the adverse impact on the complainant-victim, the potential adverse economic consequence to the employer, and the distraction and disruption to the workforce caused by ongoing litigation, violations of the employer's no-discrimination and no-retaliation policy will been enforced with major discipline—up to and including discharge!

*Some employees with poor records believe that if they have filed complaints with the EEOC, they are immune from all discipline. However, these "protected" employees are not immune from discipline or discharge. The *Burkhart v. American Railcar Industries Inc.* decision, 603 F.3d 472 (8th Cir. 2010), can be used in an educational program for executives, managers, and staff to demonstrate that employees who have engaged in protected activities under Title VII are not immune from discipline or discharge for major performance issues.
**555 U.S. 271 (2009).

Bona Fide Occupational Qualification Exception

It is not an unlawful employment practice for an employer to hire employees on the basis of religion, sex, or national origin in those certain instances where religion, sex, or national origin is a bona fide occupational qualification (BFOQ) reasonably necessary to the normal operation of a particular enterprise. **For Example,** a valid BFOQ is a men's clothing store's policy of hiring only males to do measurements for suit alterations. An airline's policy of hiring only female flight attendants is not a valid BFOQ because such a policy is not reasonably necessary to safely operate an airline.

CASE SUMMARY

It's a Woman's Choice

FACTS: Johnson Controls, Inc. (JCI), manufactures batteries. A primary ingredient in the battery-manufacturing process is lead. Occupational exposure to lead entails health risks, including the risk of harm to any fetus carried by a female employee. After eight of its employees became pregnant while maintaining blood lead levels exceeding those set by the Centers for Disease Control as dangerous for a worker planning to have a family, respondent JCI announced a policy barring all women, except those whose infertility was medically documented, from jobs involving lead exposure exceeding the OSHA standard. The United Auto Workers (UAW) brought a class action in the district court, claiming that the policy constituted sex discrimination violative of Title VII of the Civil Rights Act of 1964, as amended. The court granted summary judgment for JCI based on its BFOQ defense, and the Court of Appeals affirmed. The Supreme Court granted *certiorari*.

DECISION: Judgment for the UAW. JCI's fetal protection policy discriminated against women because the policy applied only to women and did not deal with the harmful effect of lead exposure on the male reproductive system. JCI's concerns about the welfare of the next generation do not suffice to establish a BFOQ of female sterility. Title VII, as amended, mandates that decisions about the welfare of future children be left to the parents who conceive, bear, support, and raise them rather than to the employers who hire those parents or to the courts. Moreover, an employer's tort liability for potential fetal injuries does not require a different result. If, under general tort principles, Title VII bans sex-specific fetal-protection policies, the employer fully informs the woman of the risk, and the employer has not acted negligently, the basis for holding an employer liable seems remote at best. [*UAW v. Johnson Controls*, 499 U.S. 187 (1991)]

Testing and Educational Requirements

Section 703(h) of the act authorizes the use of "any professionally developed ability test [that is not] designed, intended, or used to discriminate." Employment testing and educational requirements must be "job related"; that is, the employers must prove that the tests and educational requirements bear a relationship to job performance.

Courts will accept prior court-approved validation studies developed for a different employer in a different state or region so long as it is demonstrated that the job for which the test was initially validated is essentially the same job function for which the test is currently being used. **For Example,** a court-approved firefighters' test that has been validated in a study in California will be accepted as valid when later used in Virginia. Such application is called *validity generalization*.

The Civil Rights Act of 1991 makes it an unlawful employment practice for an employer to adjust scores or use different cutoff scores or otherwise alter the results of employment tests to favor any race, color, religion, sex, or national origin. This provision addresses the so-called race-norming issue, whereby the results of hiring and promotion tests are adjusted to ensure that a minimum number of minorities are included in application pools.

Seniority System

Section 703(h) provides that differences in employment terms based on a bona fide seniority system are sanctioned so long as the differences do not stem from an intention to discriminate. The term *seniority system* is generally understood to mean a set of rules that ensures that workers with longer years of continuous service for an employer will have a priority claim to a job over others with fewer years of service. Because such rules provide workers with considerable job security, organized labor has continually and successfully fought to secure seniority provisions in collective bargaining agreements.

39-2h Affirmative Action and Reverse Discrimination

Employers have an interest in affirmative action because it is fundamentally fair to have a diverse and representative workforce. Moreover, affirmative action is an effective means of avoiding litigation costs associated with discrimination cases while at the same time preserving management prerogatives and preserving rights to government contracts. Employers, under **affirmative action plans (AAPs),** may undertake special recruiting and other efforts to hire and train minorities and women and help them advance within the company. However, the plan may also provide job preferences for minorities and women. Such aspects of affirmative action plans have resulted in numerous lawsuits contending that Title VII of the Civil Rights Act of 1964, the Fourteenth Amendment, or collective bargaining contracts have been violated. The Supreme Court has not been able to settle the many difficult issues before it with a clear and consistent majority. The Court has decided cases narrowly, with individual justices often feeling compelled to speak in concurring or dissenting opinions.

affirmative action plan (AAP)–plan to have a diverse and representative workforce.

Affirmative Action Programs

In its 1995 *Adarand Constructors, Inc. v. Pena*[28] decision, the Supreme Court placed significant limits on the federal government's authority to implement programs favoring businesses owned by racial minorities over white-owned businesses. The decision reinstated a reverse discrimination challenge to a federal program designed to provide highway construction contracts to "disadvantaged" subcontractors in which race-based presumptions were used to identify such individuals. The Court found the program to be violative of the equal protection component of the Fifth Amendment's due process clause and announced a strict scrutiny standard for evaluating the racial classifications used in the federal government's Disadvantaged Business Enterprise (DBE) program. This standard can be satisfied only by narrowly tailored measures that further compelling governmental interests. The Court stated that programs based on disadvantage rather than race are subject only to the most relaxed judicial scrutiny. Six additional years of litigation ensued before the case involving Adarand Constructors, Inc., was finally concluded on procedural and jurisdictional grounds. *Adarand I*, as it is now called, is now the landmark Supreme Court decision setting forth the legal principles for evaluating affirmative action programs involving race and remedies.

Following the Court's *Adarand I* decision, the EEOC issued a statement on affirmative action, stating, in part:

> *Affirmative action is lawful only when it is designed to respond to a demonstrated and serious imbalance in the workforce, is flexible, is time limited, applies only to qualified workers, and respects the rights of nonminorities and men.*[29]

Reverse Discrimination

When an employer's AAP is not shown to be justified or "unnecessarily trammels" the interests of nonminority employees, it is often called *reverse discrimination*. **For Example,** a city's decision to rescore police promotional tests to achieve specific racial and gender percentages unnecessarily trammeled the interests of nonminority police officers.[30]

[28] 515 U.S. 200 (1995).
[29] *The Steelworkers v. Weber*, 443 U.S. 193 (1979), and *Johnson v. Santa Clara Transportation Agency*, 480 U.S. 617 (1987), are very important U.S. Supreme Court decisions in the developing law on permissible affirmative action plans.
[30] *San Francisco Police Officers Ass'n v. San Francisco*, 812 F.2d 1125 (9th Cir. 1987). See also *Barella v. Village of Freeport*, 16 F. Supp. 3d 144 (E.D.N.Y. 2014).

Executive Order

Presidential Executive Order 11246 regulates contractors and subcontractors doing business with the federal government. This order forbids discrimination against minorities and women and in certain situations requires affirmative action to be taken to offer better employment opportunities to minorities and women. The Secretary of Labor has established the Office of Federal Contract Compliance Programs (OFCCP) to administer the order.

39-3 Other Equal Employment Opportunity (EEO) Laws

Major federal laws require equal pay for men and women doing equal work and forbid discrimination against older people and those with disabilities.

39-3a Equal Pay

The Equal Pay Act prohibits employers from paying employees of one gender a lower wage rate than the rate paid employees of the other gender for equal work, or substantially equal work, in the same establishment for jobs that require substantially equal skill, effort, and responsibility and that are performed under similar working conditions.[31]

CASE SUMMARY

I Do the Same Job as Two Male Colleagues. Doesn't the Equal Pay Act Require That I Get Equal Pay?

FACTS: Jeannette Renstrom was the head grocery buyer at wholesale food distributor Nash Finch Co. at its St. Cloud, Minnesota, distribution center. She sued her employer under the Equal Pay Act because Nash Finch paid her less than two male employees who performed equal work—Bill Crosier, the head grocery buyer for the Omaha distribution center, and Dale Ebensteiner, the head grocery buyer for the Fargo and Minot distribution centers. Nash Finch seeks summary judgment.

DECISION: The term *establishment* refers to a distinct physical place of business rather than an entire business or enterprise, which may include several places of business. Each of Nash Finch's distribution centers is a separate "establishment." Because Renstrom did not work at the same establishment as the two comparators that she has identified (Crosier and Ebensteiner), her claim under the EPA must be dismissed.

Additionally, in order for the equal pay standard to apply, Ms. Renstrom needed to show that the Head Grocery Buyer jobs required equal skill, equal effort, and equal responsibility. There is little question that the job involved equal skill and responsibility. In light of the undisputed evidence that both Crosier and Ebensteiner had essentially "double work"—Crossier, because he handled 18 military facilities, and Ebensteiner, because he handled two distribution centers—Renstrom cannot meet her burden to show that the jobs required equal effort. Judgment for Nash Finch. [***Renstrom v. Nash Finch Co.,*** **787 F. Supp. 2d 961 (D. Minn. 2011)**]

The Equal Pay Act does not prohibit all variations in wage rates paid men and women but only those variations based solely on gender. The act sets forth four exceptions. Variances in wages are allowed where there is (1) a seniority system, (2) a merit

---

[31] 29 U.S.C. §206 (d)(1).

system, (3) a system that measures earnings by quantity or quality of production, or (4) a differential based on any factor other than gender.

39-3b Age Discrimination

The Age Discrimination in Employment Act (ADEA) forbids discrimination by employers, unions, and employment agencies against persons over 40 years of age.[32] Section 4(a) of the ADEA sets forth the employment practices that are unlawful under the act, including the failure to hire because of age and the discharge of employees because of age. Section 7(b) of the ADEA allows for doubling the damages in cases of willful violations of the act. Consequently, an employer who willfully violates the ADEA is liable not only for back wages and benefits but also for an additional amount as liquidated damages.[33]

CASE SUMMARY

Miffed at Being RIF-ed

FACTS: Calvin Rhodes began his employment with Dresser Industries in 1955 as an oil industry salesman. In the throes of a severe economic downturn, Rhodes took a job selling oil field equipment at another Dresser company that became Guiberson Oil Tools. After seven months, he was discharged and told that the reason was a reduction in force (RIF) but that he would be eligible for rehiring. At that time, he was 56 years old. Within two months, Guiberson hired a 42-year-old salesperson to do the same job. Rhodes sued Guiberson for violating the ADEA. At the trial, Lee Snyder, the supervisor who terminated Rhodes, testified in part that Jack Givens, Snyder's boss who instructed Snyder to fire Rhodes, once said that he could hire two young salesmen for what some of the older salesmen were costing.

DECISION: Judgment for Rhodes. The official reason given Rhodes, that he was being terminated under a RIF, was false. Every other reason given by the employer was countered with evidence that Rhodes was an excellent salesman. Based on all of the evidence, including the statement about hiring two young salesmen for what some of the older salesmen were costing, a reasonable jury could find that Guiberson Oil discriminated against Rhodes on the basis of age. [*Rhodes v. Guiberson Oil Tools*, **75 F.3d 989 (5th Cir. 1996)**]

The Older Workers Benefit Protection Act (OWBPA) of 1990[34] amends the ADEA by prohibiting age discrimination in employee benefits and establishing minimum standards for determining the validity of waivers of age claims. The OWBPA amends the ADEA by adopting an "equal benefit or equal cost" standard, providing that older workers must be given benefits at least equal to those provided for younger workers unless the employer can prove that the cost of providing an equal benefit would be more for an older worker than for a younger one.

Employers commonly require that employees electing to take early retirement packages waive all claims against their employers, including their rights or claims under the ADEA. The OWBPA requires that employees be given a specific period of time to evaluate a proposed package.

---

[32] 29 U.S.C. §623.

[33] In *Reeves v. Sanderson Plumbing Products Co., Inc.*, 530 U.S. 133 (2000), the Supreme Court reinstated a $98,490 judgment for Roger Reeves, which included $35,000 in back pay, $35,000 in liquidated damages, and $28,490.80 in front pay, and held that the plaintiff's evidence establishing a prima facie case and showing that the employer's stated reason for the termination was false was sufficient to prove that age was the motivation for the discharge. See also *Williams v. Asbury Automotive Group, Inc.*, 998 F. Supp. 2d 769 (E.D. Ark. 2014).

[34] 29 U.S.C. §623. This law reverses the Supreme Court's 1989 ruling in *Public Employees Retirement System of Ohio v. Betts*, 492 U.S. 158 (1989), which had the effect of exempting employee benefit programs from the ADEA.

Enforcement of the ADEA is the responsibility of the EEOC. Procedures and time limitations for filing and processing ADEA charges are the same as those under Title VII.[35] However, Title VII is materially different from the ADEA with respect to burdens of persuasion, and Supreme Court decisions construing Title VII do not control the construction of the ADEA. Rather, in all cases of disparate treatment, including mixed-motive cases, the plaintiff has to prove, by a preponderance of the evidence, that age was the "but for" cause of the challenged adverse employment action.[36]

39-3c Discrimination against Persons with Disabilities

The right of persons with disabilities to enjoy equal employment opportunities was established on the federal level with the enactment of the Rehabilitation Act of 1973.[37]

Although not specifically designed as an employment discrimination measure but as a comprehensive plan to meet many of the needs of persons with disabilities, the act contains three sections that provide guarantees against discrimination in employment. Section 501 is applicable to the federal government itself, Section 503 applies to federal contractors, and Section 504 applies to the recipients of federal funds.

Title I of the Americans with Disabilities Act of 1990 extends employment protection for disabled persons beyond the federal level to state and local governmental agencies and to all private employers with 15 or more employees. The ADA refers to the term *qualified individuals with disabilities* rather than the term *handicapped persons*, which is used in the Rehabilitation Act. In drafting the ADA, Congress relied heavily on the language of the Rehabilitation Act and its regulations. It was anticipated that the body of case law developed under the Rehabilitation Act would provide guidance in the interpretation and application of the ADA. However, protections for individuals were eroded by U.S. Supreme Court decisions in 1999 and 2002. Under these precedents, numerous claims of ADA plaintiffs were extinguished at the threshold stage of proving the plaintiff had a disability. With the cooperation and agreement of both the employer and disability communities, the ADA Amendments Act of 2008 (ADAAA) became law (effective January 1, 2009), effectively overturning the Supreme Court decisions and restoring the original congressional intent of providing broad coverage to protect individuals who face discrimination on the basis of disability.[38] Under Title I of the ADA, an employer may make preemployment inquiries into the ability of a job applicant to perform job-related functions. Under "user-friendly" EEOC guidelines on preemployment inquiries under the ADA, an employer may ask applicants whether they will need reasonable accommodations for the hiring process. If the answer is yes, the employer may ask for reasonable documentation of the disability. In general, the employer may not ask questions about whether an applicant will need reasonable accommodations to do the job. However, the employer

---

[35] In *Smith v. City of Jackson, Mississippi,* 544 U.S. 228 (2005), the U.S. Supreme Court determined that disparate impact claims of age discrimination are permitted under the ADEA. The Court relied on its Title VII *Griggs v. Duke Power Co.* precedent, which interpreted text identical to that in the ADEA, with the substitution of the word "age" for the words "race, color, religion, sex or national origin," the narrowing of the coverage of the ADEA, which permits employers to take actions that would otherwise be prohibited based on "reasonable factors other than age" (called the *RFOA provision*), and the EEOC regulations permitting disparate impact claims. The dissenting justices asserted that in the nearly four decades since the law's enactment, the Court had never read it to impose liability on an employer without proof of discriminatory intent. The *Smith v. City of Jackson* court decided the disparate impact case before it against the petitioning police officers, finding that the City's larger pay raises to younger employees were based on an RFOA that responded to the City's legitimate goal of retaining its new police officers.

[36] *Gross v. FBL Financial Services, Inc.,* 557 U.S. 167 (2009). See also *Scheick v. Tecumseh Public Schools,* 766 F.3d 523 (6th Cir. 2014).

[37] 42 U.S.C. §§701–794.

[38] 42 U.S.C. §§12101-12117; P.L. 110-325, S3406 (Sept. 25, 2008).

may make preemployment inquiries regarding the job applicant's ability to perform job-related functions.

After making a job offer (contingent upon the applicant's passing a medical examination), the employer may rescind the offer if the position in question poses a direct threat to the worker's health or safety. **For Example,** Mario Echazabal was initially offered a job at Chevron's El Segundo, California, oil refinery but the offer was rescinded when the company doctors determined that exposure to chemicals on the job would further damage his already-reduced liver functions (due to hepatitis C) and might potentially kill him. An affirmative defense then exists for employers—not only in cases where hiring an individual poses a direct threat to the health or safety of other employees in the workplace, but also when there is a direct threat to the employee in question. However, the employer must make an individualized medical risk assessment of the employee's condition.[39]

Proving a Case

The Americans with Disabilities Act, as amended in 2008, prohibits employers from discriminating "against a qualified individual on the basis of a disability." A qualified individual with a disability is one "who, with or without reasonable accommodation, can perform the essential functions of the employment position." To establish a viable claim under the act, a plaintiff must prove that (1) he or she has a disability; (2) he or she is qualified for the position; and (3) an employer has discriminated against him or her because of a disability.

The ADAAA defines the term *disability* in a three-pronged definition as follows:

1. *DISABILITY: The term "disability" means, with respect to an individual—*

   A. *a physical or mental impairment that substantially limits one or more major life activities of such individual;*
   B. *a record of such an impairment; or*
   C. *being regarded as having such an impairment.*

The ADAAA sets forth in unmistakable language that the definition of disability "shall be construed in favor of broad coverage of individuals under this Act" and mandates that the term "substantially limits" be construed accordingly. Moreover, the determination of whether an impairment substantially limits a major life activity must be made without regard to the ameliorative effects of mitigating measures (with the exception that ameliorative effects of ordinary eyeglasses or contact lenses are considered in determinations of whether an impairment substantially limits a major life activity).

The ADAAA includes an expansive compilation of major life activities to confirm the congressional purpose of providing a broad scope of protection to individuals under the ADA.[40] In addition to establishing that the plaintiff has a disability, a plaintiff must also show that he or she is qualified for the position. **For Example,** the Department of Transportation regulations disqualify any commercial motor vehicle driver with a "current clinical diagnosis of alcoholism" for service as an over-the-road trucker. Sakari Jarvela's ADA claim against Crete Carrier Corp. failed because, disqualified by DOT as a driver, he no

---

[39] *Chevron v. Echazabal,* 536 U.S. 73 (2002).
[40] Section 3(2) of the act provides:
MAJOR LIFE ACTIVITIES—

A. IN GENERAL.—For purposes of paragraph (1), major life activities include, but are not limited to, caring for oneself; performing manual tasks; seeing, hearing, eating, sleeping, walking, standing, lifting, bending, speaking, breathing, learning, reading, concentrating, thinking, communicating, and working.
B. MAJOR BODILY FUNCTIONS.—For purposes of paragraph (1), a major life activity also includes the operation of major bodily functions, included but not limited to, functions of the immune system; normal cell growth; digestive, bowel, bladder, neurological, brain, respiratory, circulatory, endocrine, and reproductive functions.

longer could perform the essential functions of his driver's job with or without reasonable accommodations.[41]

Reasonable Accommodations under the ADA

Section 101(9) of the ADA defines an employer's obligation to make "reasonable accommodations" for individuals with disabilities to include (1) making existing facilities accessible to and usable by individuals with disabilities and (2) restructuring jobs, providing modified work schedules, and acquiring or modifying equipment or devices.[42] An employer is not obligated under the ADA to make accommodations that would be an "undue hardship" on the employer.

Seniority systems provide for a fair and uniform method of treating employees whereby employees with more years of service have a priority over employees with less years of service when it comes to layoffs, job selection, and other benefits such as days off and vacation periods. Seniority rules apply not only under collective bargaining agreements but also to many nonunion job classifications and to nonunion settings. An employer's showing that a requested accommodation conflicts with seniority rules is ordinarily sufficient to show that the requested "accommodation" is not "reasonable." **For Example,** Robert Barnett, a cargo handler for U.S. Airways, Inc., sought a less physically demanding job in the mailroom due to a back injury. Because a senior employee bid the job, U.S. Airways refused Barnett's request to accommodate his disability by allowing him to work the mailroom position. Barnett filed suit under the ADA, and the case progressed to the U.S. Supreme Court, which determined that ordinarily such a requested accommodation is not "reasonable." On remand to the trial court, Barnett was given the opportunity to show that the company allowed exceptions to the seniority rules and he fit within such exceptions.[43]

Failure to Take Action

With courts applying a less-demanding standard for coverage under the amended ADA, employers are finding requests to provide "reasonable accommodations" more common. Employers are liable for failure to take appropriate action regarding requests for reasonable accommodations. **For Example,** Jane Gagliardo had been diagnosed with multiple sclerosis that began affecting her work. The most severe symptom was fatigue, which affected her ability to think, focus, and remember. All of her symptoms were subject to being exacerbated by stress. She sought a "reasonable accommodation" under the ADA of having one major client removed from her job responsibilities. The employer took no action on this request. Moreover, while she continued to seek accommodation to no avail, the employer began disciplining her for poor job performance and ultimately fired her. She was awarded $2.3 million in compensation and punitive damages.[44]

Where a disability is obvious and known to the employer, an employee is obligated to engage in an "interactive process" regarding accommodation of a disability, even when

---

[41] *Jarvela v. Crete Carrier Corp.*, 776 F.3d 822 (11th Cir. 2015).

[42] A reasonable accommodation may also include "reassignment to a vacant position." In *Duvall v. Georgia-Pacific Consumer Products LP.*, 607 F.3d 1255 (10th Cir. 2010), the Tenth Circuit Court of Appeals was called upon to decide when a position is "vacant" for the purpose of the ADA. It determined that when a disabled employee seeks the reasonable accommodation of reassignment to a vacant position, positions within the company are "vacant" for the purpose of the ADA when they would be available to similarly suited nondisabled employees to apply for and obtain. Duvall, the employee in question, did not meet his burden of showing that the jobs he sought were available within GP, as they were occupied by a contractor service, and no GP employee had been given a contractor-filled position during the time in question.

[43] *U.S. Airways v. Barnett*, 535 U.S. 391 (2002).

[44] *Gagliardo v. Connaught Laboratories, Inc.*, 311 F.3d 565 (3d Cir. 2008). See also *Tobin v. Liberty Mutual Insurance Co.*, 553 F.3d 121 (1st Cir. 2009).

a formal request for accommodation is not made. **For Example,** 19-year-old Patrick Brady, who has cerebral palsy, was hired to work as a Wal-Mart pharmacy aide. After "a few days" on the job with no training, he was transferred to the job of collecting shopping carts and garbage in the parking lot. His supervisor, Ms. Chin, regarded Brady as "too slow" and stated that "she knew there was something wrong with him." While Brady did not request reasonable accommodations because his disability was obvious and known to the employer, Wal-Mart was found to be in violation of the ADA, and a judgment of $900,000—including $300,000 in punitive damages—was upheld by the U.S. Court of Appeals.[45] Mental disabilities frequently are not obvious to employers, and it is up to the employee to disclose nonobvious disabilities and any related limitations and a need for accommodations to his or her employer. **For Example,** Ms. Walz acknowledged that she failed to inform her employer of her bipolar disorder and obtain an accommodation. The court therefore determined that her employer had no duty to accommodate her, and her discharge for erratic and disruptive behavior, aggressiveness with a coworker, and disrespect to her supervisor was upheld.[46]

Exclusions from Coverage of the Act

The act excludes from its coverage employees or applicants who are "currently engaging in the illegal use of drugs." The exclusion does not include an individual who has been successfully rehabilitated from such use or is participating in or has completed supervised drug rehabilitation and is no longer engaging in the illegal use of drugs.

Title V of the act states that behaviors such as transvestitism, transsexualism, pedophilia, exhibitionism, compulsive gambling, kleptomania, pyromania, and psychoactive substance use disorders resulting from current illegal use of drugs are not in and of themselves considered disabilities.

39-3d GINA

The Genetic Information Nondiscrimination Act (GINA) is also administered by the EEOC.[47] GINA was enacted in 2008 to prevent discrimination on the basis of genetic information in health insurance and employment. Employees requiring fitness-for-duty or post-job-offer medical examinations have to make certain that "company doctors" do not ask for DNA tests or family medical histories. It is advisable that all medical forms and questionnaires include prominently printed language that notifies individuals: "Do not give us genetic information or family medical history."

39-4 Extraterritorial Employment

The Civil Rights Act of 1991 amended both Title VII and the ADA to protect U.S. citizens employed in foreign countries by American-owned or American-controlled companies against discrimination based on race, color, religion, national origin, sex, or disability.[48] The 1991 act contains an exemption if compliance with Title VII or the ADA would cause a company to violate the law of the foreign country in which it is located.

---

[45] *Brady v. Wal-Mart Stores, Inc.*, 531 F.3d 127 (2d Cir. 2008).

[46] *Walz v. Ameriprise Financial, Inc.*, 779 F.3d 842 (8th Cir. 2015). See also the discussion of recognizing that interacting with others as a major life activity does not mean that any cantankerous person will be deemed substantially limited in a major life activity, as discussed in *Weaving v. City of Hillsboro*, 763 F.3d 1106 (9th Cir. 2014).

[47] Pub. L. 110-233, 122 Stat. 881 (May 21, 2008).

[48] Section 109 of the Civil Rights Act of 1991, P.L. 102-166, 105 Stat. 1071.

Make the Connection

Summary

Title VII of the Civil Rights Act of 1964, as amended, forbids discrimination on the basis of race, color, religion, sex, or national origin. The EEOC administers the act. Intentional discrimination is unlawful when there is disparate treatment of individuals because of their race, color, religion, gender, or national origin. Also, employment practices that make no reference to race, color, religion, sex, or national origin, but that nevertheless have an adverse or disparate impact on the protected group, are unlawful. In disparate impact cases, the fact that an employer did not intend to discriminate is no defense. The employer must show that there is a job-related business necessity for the disparate impact practice in question. Employers have several defenses they may raise in a Title VII case to explain differences in employment conditions: (1) bona fide occupational qualifications reasonably necessary to the normal operation of the business, (2) job-related professionally developed ability tests, and (3)

bona fide seniority systems. If a state EEO agency or the EEOC is not able to resolve the case, the EEOC issues a right-to-sue letter that enables the person claiming a Title VII violation to sue in a federal district court. An affirmative action plan is legal under Title VII provided there is a voluntary "plan" justified as a remedial measure and provided it does not unnecessarily trammel the interests of whites.

Under the Equal Pay Act (EPA), employers must not pay employees of one gender a lower wage rate than the rate paid to employees of the other gender for substantially equal work. Workers over 40 years old are protected from discrimination by the Age Discrimination in Employment Act (ADEA). Employment discrimination against persons with disabilities is prohibited by the Americans with Disabilities Act (ADA). Under the ADA, employers must make reasonable accommodations without undue hardship on them to enable individuals with disabilities to work.

Learning Outcomes

After studying this chapter, you should be able to clearly explain:

39-1   Title VII of the Civil Rights Act of 1964, as Amended

LO.1   Explain the difference between the *disparate treatment* theory of employment discrimination and the *disparate impact* theory of employment discrimination

See the discussion of the New Haven Firefighters case in which the city relied on a disparate impact theory and the firefighters asserted disparate treatment, page 796.

39-2   Protected Classes and Exceptions

LO.2   List and explain the categories of individuals protected against unlawful employment discrimination under Title VII

See the discussion and examples of protections under Title VII applied to the categories of race and color, religion, sex, and national origin, pages 800–802, 806.

LO.3   Recognize, and know the remedies for, sexual harassment in the workplace

See the Ellerth example and the employer's affirmative defense, pages 803–804.

See Figure 39-2 for a presentation of an employer sexual harassment policy, page 804.

39-3

LO.4   Explain the antiretaliation provision of Title VII

See the *White* case, which sets forth the elements of retaliatory discrimination and the remedy provided, pages 805–806.

See why retaliation is the number one employment liability risk for employers and the antiretaliation actions proposed for employers, page 807.

39-3   Other Equal Employment Opportunity (EEO) Laws

LO.5   List and explain the laws protecting equal pay for women and men for equal work as well as the laws forbidding discrimination on the basis of age and against individuals with disabilities

See the *Renstrom* case with the narrow meaning of the word "establishment," making her EPA case without merit, page 810.

See the *Rhodes* case with facts and a remedy applicable to age discrimination, page 811.

See the Patrick Brady example of the attention-getting judgment in a case where the employer failed to recognize its obligation to make a reasonable accommodation, page 815.

39-4   Extraterritorial Employment

LO.6   Explain how both Title VII of the Civil Rights Act and the ADA protect from discrimination U.S. citizens working in foreign countries for American-owned and American-controlled businesses

Key Term

affirmative action plans (AAPs)

Questions and Case Problems

1. List the major federal statutes dealing with the regulation of equal rights in employment.

2. The EEOC notified North American Stainless (NAS) in February 2003 that Miriam Regalado had filed a charge of sex discrimination against the company. Three weeks later NAS fired her coworker Eric Thompson, a person to whom Ms. Regalado was engaged. Thompson had worked for NAS for seven years as a metallurgical engineer. Thompson filed his own charge with the EEOC and a subsequent lawsuit under Title VII of the Civil Rights Act, claiming that NAS fired him to retaliate against Regalado for filing her charge with the EEOC.

   The employer contended that because Thompson did not "engag[e] in any statutorily protected activity, either on his own behalf or on behalf of Miriam Regalado," he is not included in the class of persons for whom Congress created a retaliation cause of action. Thompson argued that the Supreme Court adopted a broad standard in its *Burlington* decision because Title VII's antiretaliation provision is worded broadly, and that there is no textual basis for making an exception to it for third-party reprisals. Decide. [*Thompson v. North American Stainless Steel, LP*, 131 S. Ct. 863]

3. Dial Corp. implemented a "work tolerance test," which all new employees were required to pass to obtain employment in its Armour Star brand sausage-making department. Of the applicants who passed the test, 97 percent were male and 38 percent were female. The EEOC "demonstrated" that the facially neutral work tolerance test "caused" a disparate impact on women. The defending employer did not deny that the employment practice in question caused the disparate impact. Rather, the employer responded that the test was "job related" and "necessary" to reduce job-related injuries at the plant and submitted evidence that the number of job injuries

See the discussion of the exemption for employers where compliance would cause a company to violate the law of the country in which it is located, page 815.

had been reduced after implementation of the testing program. The evidence showed that the company had initiated numerous other safety initiatives that had an impact on reducing injuries at the plant. After they failed the test, 52 women were denied jobs. Decide this case. [*EEOC v. Dial Corp.*, 2005 WL 2839977 (S.D. Iowa)]

4. Continental Photo, Inc., is a portrait photography company. Alex Riley, an African American man, applied for a position as a photographer with Continental. Riley submitted an application and was interviewed. In response to a question on a written application, Riley indicated that he had been convicted for forgery (a felony) six years before the interview, had received a suspended sentence, and was placed on five-year probation. He also stated that he would discuss the matter with his interviewer if necessary. The subject of the forgery conviction was subsequently not mentioned by Continental's personnel director in his interview with Riley. Riley's application for employment was eventually rejected. Riley inquired about the reason for his rejection. The personnel director, Geuther, explained to him that the prior felony conviction on his application was a reason for his rejection. Riley contended that the refusal to hire him because of his conviction record was actually discrimination against him because of his race in violation of Title VII. Riley felt that his successful completion of a five-year probation without incident and his steady work over the years qualified him for the job. Continental maintained that because its photographers handle approximately $10,000 in cash per year, its policy of not hiring applicants whose honesty was questionable was justified. Continental's policy excluded all applicants with felony convictions. Decide. Would the result have been different if Riley had been a convicted murderer?

[*Continental Photo, Inc.*, 26 Fair Empl. Prac. Cas. (B.N.A.) 1799 (E.E.O.C.)]

5. Beth Faragher worked part-time and summers as an ocean lifeguard for the Marine Safety Section of the city of Boca Raton, Florida. Bill Terry and David Silverman were her supervisors over the five-year period of her employment. During this period, Terry repeatedly touched the bodies of female employees without invitation and would put his arm around Faragher, with his hand on her buttocks. He made crudely demeaning references to women generally. Silverman once told Faragher, "Date me or clean the toilets for a year." She was not so assigned, however. The city adopted a sexual harassment policy addressed to all employees. The policy was not disseminated to the Marine Safety Section at the beach, however. Faragher resigned and later brought action against the city, claiming a violation of Title VII and seeking nominal damages, costs, and attorneys' fees. The city defended that Terry and Silverman were not acting within the scope of their employment when they engaged in harassing conduct and that the city should not be held liable for their actions. Are part-time employees covered by Title VII? Was Silverman's threat, "Date me or clean toilets for a year," a basis for *quid pro quo* vicarious liability against the city? Decide this case. [*Faragher v. City of Boca Raton*, 524 U.S. 775]

6. Mohen is a member of the Sikh religion whose practice forbids cutting or shaving facial hair and requires wearing a turban that covers the head. In accordance with the dictates of his religion, Mohen wore a long beard. He applied for a position as breakfast cook at the Island Manor Restaurant. He was told that the restaurant's policy was to forbid cooks to wear facial hair for sanitary and good grooming reasons and that he would have to shave his beard or be denied a position. Mohen contended that the restaurant had an obligation to make a reasonable accommodation to his religious beliefs and let him keep his beard. Is he correct?

7. Sylvia Hayes worked as a staff technician in the radiology department of Shelby Memorial Hospital. On October 1, Hayes was told by her physician that she was pregnant. When Hayes informed the doctor of her occupation as an X-ray technician, the doctor advised Hayes that she could continue working until the end of April so long as she followed standard safety precautions. On October 8, Hayes told Gail Nell, the director of radiology at Shelby, that she had discovered she was two months pregnant. On October 14, Hayes was discharged by the hospital. The hospital's reason for terminating Hayes was its concern for the safety of her fetus given the X-ray exposure that occurs during employment as an X-ray technician. Hayes brought an action under Title VII, claiming that her discharge was unlawfully based on her condition of pregnancy. She cited scientific evidence and the practice of other hospitals where pregnant women were allowed to remain in their jobs as X-ray technicians. The hospital claimed that Hayes's discharge was based on business necessity. Moreover, the hospital claimed that the potential for future liability existed if an employee's fetus was damaged by radiation encountered at the workplace. Decide. [*Hayes v. Shelby Memorial Hospital*, 546 F. Supp. 259 (N.D. Ala.)]

8. Overton suffered from depression and was made sleepy at work by medication taken for this condition. Also, because of his medical condition, Overton needed a work area away from public access and substantial supervision to complete his tasks. His employer terminated him because of his routinely sleeping on the job, his inability to maintain contact with the public, and his need for supervision. Overton argued that he is a person with a disability under the ADA and the Rehabilitation Act, fully qualified to perform the essential functions of the job, and that the employer had an obligation to make reasonable accommodations, such as allowing some catnaps as needed and providing some extra supervision. Decide. [*Overton v. Reilly*, 977 F.2d 1190 (7th Cir.)]

9. A teenage female high school student named Salazar was employed part-time at Church's Fried Chicken Restaurant. Salazar was hired and supervised by Simon Garza, the assistant manager of the restaurant. Garza had complete supervisory powers when the restaurant's manager, Garza's roommate, was absent. Salazar claimed that while she worked at the restaurant, Garza would refer to her and all other females by a Spanish term that she found objectionable. According to Salazar, Garza once made an offensive comment about her body and repeatedly asked her about her personal life. On another occasion, Garza allegedly physically removed eye shadow from Salazar's face because he claimed it was unattractive. Salazar also claimed that one night she was restrained in a back room of the restaurant while Garza and another employee fondled her. Later that night,

when Salazar told a customer what had happened, she was fired. Salazar brought suit under Title VII against Garza and Church's Fried Chicken, alleging sexual harassment. Church's, the corporate defendant, maintained that it should not be held liable under Title VII for Garza's harassment. Church's based its argument on the existence of a published fair treatment policy. Decide. [*Salazar v. Church's Fried Chicken, Inc.*, 44 Fair Empl. Prac. Cas. (B.N.A.) 472 (S.D. Tex.)]

10. Manuel Fragante applied for a clerk's job with the city and county of Honolulu. Although he placed high enough on a civil service eligibility list to be chosen for the position, he was not selected because of a perceived deficiency in oral communication skills caused by his "heavy Filipino accent." The clerks are constantly dealing with the public and the ability to speak clearly is one of the most important skills required for the position according to the city. Fragante brought suit, alleging that the defendants had discriminated against him on the basis of his national origin in violation of Title VII of the Civil Rights Act. Decide. [*Fragante v. City and County of Honolulu*, 888 F.2d 591 (9th Cir.)]

11. John Chadbourne was hired by Raytheon on February 4, 1980. His job performance reviews were uniformly high. In December 1983, Chadbourne was hospitalized and diagnosed with AIDS. In January 1984, his physician informed Raytheon that Chadbourne was able to return to work. On January 20, 1984, Chadbourne took a return-to-work physical examination required by Raytheon. The company's doctor wrote the County Communicable Disease Control director, Dr. Juels, seeking a determination of the appropriateness of Chadbourne's returning to work. Dr. Juels informed the company that "contact of employees to an AIDS patient appears to pose no risk from all evidence accumulated to date." Dr. Juels also visited the plant and advised the company doctor that there would be no medical risk to other employees at the plant if Chadbourne returned to work. Raytheon refused to reinstate Chadbourne to his position until July 19, 1984. Its basis for denying reinstatement was that coworkers might be at risk of contracting AIDS. Was Raytheon entitled to bar Chadbourne from work during the six-month period of January through July? [*Raytheon v. Fair Employment and Housing Commission*, 261 Cal. Rptr. 197 (Ct. App.)]

12. Connie Cunico, a white woman, was employed by the Pueblo, Colorado, School District as a social worker. She and other social workers were laid off in seniority order because of the district's poor financial situation. However, the school board thereafter decided to retain Wayne Hunter, a black social worker with less seniority than Cunico because he was the only black on the administrative staff. No racial imbalance existed in the relevant workforce with black persons constituting 2 percent. Cunico, who was rehired over two years later, claimed that she was the victim of reverse discrimination. She stated that she lost $110,361 in back wages plus $76,000 in attorneys' fees and costs. The school district replied that it was correct in protecting with special consideration the only black administrator in the district under the general principles it set forth in its AAP. Did the employer show that its affirmative action in retaining Hunter was justified as a remedial measure? Decide. [*Cunico v. Pueblo School District No. 6*, 917 F.2d 431 (10th Cir.)]

13. Della Janich was employed as a matron at the Yellowstone County Jail in Montana. The duties of the position of matron resemble those of a parallel male position of jailer. Both employees have the responsibility of booking prisoners, showering and dressing them, and placing them in the appropriate section of the jail depending on the offender's sex. Because 95 percent of the prisoners at the jail were men and 5 percent were women, the matron was assigned more bookkeeping duties than the jailer. At all times during Janich's employment at the jail, her male counterparts received $125 more per month as jailers. Janich brought an action under the Equal Pay Act, alleging discrimination against her in her wages because of her sex. The county sheriff denied the charge. Decide. [*Janich v. Sheriff*, 29 Fair Empl. Prac. Cas. (B.N.A.) 1195 (D. Mont.)]

14. Following a decline in cigarette sales, L & M, Inc., hired J. Gfeller as vice president of sales and charged him to turn around the sales decline. After receiving an analysis of the ages of sales personnel and first-line management, Gfeller and his assistant, T. McMorrow, instituted an intensive program of personnel changes that led to the termination of many older managers and sales representatives. A top manager who sought to justify keeping an older manager was informed that he was "not getting the message." Gfeller and McMorrow emphasized that they wanted young and aggressive people and that the

older people were not able to conform or adapt to new procedures. R. E. Moran, who had been rated a first-rate division manager, was terminated and replaced by a 27-year-old employee. Gfeller and McMorrow made statements about employees with many years' experience: "It was not 20 years' experience, but rather 1 year's experience 20 times." The EEOC brought suit on behalf of the terminated managers and sales representatives. The company vigorously denied any discriminatory attitude with regard to age. Decide. [*EEOC v. Liggett and Meyers, Inc.*, 29 F.E.P. 1611 (E.D.N.C.)]

15. Mazir Coleman had driven a school bus for the Casey County, Kentucky, Board of Education for four years. After that time, Coleman's left leg had to be amputated. Coleman was fitted with an artificial leg and underwent extensive rehabilitation to relearn driving skills. When his driving skills had been sufficiently relearned over the course of four years, Coleman applied to the county board of education for a job as a school bus driver. The board refused to accept Coleman's application, saying that it had no alternative but to deny Coleman a bus-driving job because of a Kentucky administrative regulation. That regulation stated in part: "No person shall drive a school bus who does not possess both of these natural bodily parts: feet, legs, hands, arms, eyes, and ears. The driver shall have normal use of the above named body parts." Coleman brought an action under the Rehabilitation act, claiming discrimination based on his physical handicap. The county board of

education denied this charge, claiming that the reason they rejected Coleman was because of the requirement of the state regulation. Could Coleman have maintained an action for employment discrimination in light of the state regulation on natural body parts? Decide. [*Coleman v. Casey County Board of Education*, 510 F. Supp. 301 (N.D. Ky.)]

16. Marcia Saxton worked for Jerry Richardson, a supervisor at AT&T's International Division. Richardson made advances to Saxton on two occasions over a three-week period. Each time Saxton told him she did not appreciate his advances. No further advances were made, but thereafter Saxton felt that Richardson treated her condescendingly and had stopped speaking to her on a social basis at work. Four months later, Saxton filed a formal internal complaint, asserting sexual harassment, and went on "paid leave." AT&T found inconclusive evidence of sexual harassment but determined that the two employees should be separated. Saxton declined a transfer to another department, so AT&T transferred Richardson instead. Saxton still refused to return to work. Thereafter, AT&T terminated Saxton for refusal to return to work. Saxton contended that she had been a victim of hostile working environment sexual harassment. AT&T argued that while the supervisor's conduct was inappropriate and unprofessional, it fell short of the type of action necessary for sexual harassment under federal law (the *Harris* case). Decide. [*Saxton v. AT&T Co.*, 10 F.3d 526 (7th Cir.)]

Business Organizations

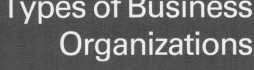

Types of Business Organizations

Learning Outcomes <<<

After studying this chapter, you should be able to

LO.1 Explain the advantages and disadvantages of the three principal forms of business organizations

LO.2 Recognize that the rules of law governing the rights and liabilities of joint ventures are substantially the same as those that govern partnerships

LO.3 Evaluate whether a business arrangement is a franchise protected under state or federal law

LO.4 Explain how the rights of the parties to a franchise agreement are determined by their contract

LO.5 Explain why freedom from vicarious liability is a reason for franchisors to use the franchise format

LO.6 Recognize the implications of the misclassifications of employees as franchisee-independent contractors

What form of legal organization should you have for your business? The answer will be found in your needs for money, personnel, control, tax and estate planning, and protection from liability.

40-1 Principal Forms of Business Organizations

The law of business organizations may be better understood if the advantages and disadvantages of proprietorships, partnerships, and corporations are first considered.

40-1a Individual Proprietorships

A **sole or individual proprietorship** is a form of business ownership in which one individual owns the business. The owner may be the sole worker of the business or employ as many others as needed to run the concern. Individual proprietorships are commonly used in retail stores, service businesses, and agriculture.

Advantages

The proprietor or owner is not required to expend resources on organizational fees. The proprietor, as the sole owner, controls all decisions and receives all profits. The net earnings of the business are not subject to corporate income taxes but are taxed only as personal income.

Disadvantages

The proprietor is subject to unlimited personal liability for the debts of the business and cannot limit this risk. The investment capital in the business is limited by the resources of the sole proprietor. Because all contracts of the business are made by the owner or in the owner's name by agents of the owner, the authority to make contracts terminates on the death of the owner, and the business is subject to disintegration.

40-1b Partnerships, LLPs, and LLCs

A **partnership** involves the pooling of capital resources and the business or professional talents of two or more individuals whose goal is to make a profit. Law firms, medical associations, and architectural and engineering firms may operate under the partnership form. Today, however, these firms are likely to convert to a **limited liability partnership (LLP).** A wide range of small manufacturing, retail, and service businesses operate as partnerships. These businesses may operate under the form of organization called **limited liability company (LLC),** which allows tax treatment as a partnership with limited liability for the owners.

Advantages

The partnership form of business organization allows individuals to pool resources and then initiate and conduct their business without the requirement of a formal organizational structure.

Disadvantages

Major disadvantages of a partnership are the unlimited personal liability of each partner and the uncertain duration of the business because the partnership is dissolved by the death of one partner. Unlimited personal liability is remedied by the LLC form of

---

sole or individual proprietorship–form of business ownership in which one individual owns the business.

partnership–pooling of capital resources and the business or professional talents of two or more individuals (partners) with the goal of making a profit.

limited liability partnership (LLP)–partnership in which at least one partner has a liability limited to the loss of the capital contribution made to the partnership.

limited liability company (LLC)–a partnership for federal tax treatment and the limited liability feature of the corporate form of business organization.

business organization. Professional partnerships that convert to an LLP shield innocent partners from personal liability beyond their investment in the firm.

40-1c Corporations

corporation–artificial being created by government grant, which, for many purposes, is treated as a natural person.

Business **corporations** exist to make a profit and are created by government grant. State statutes regulating the creation of corporations require a corporate structure consisting of shareholders, directors, and officers. The shareholders, as the owners of the business, elect a board of directors, which is responsible for managing the business. The directors employ officers, who serve as the agents of the business and run day-to-day operations. Corporations range in size from incorporated one-owner enterprises to large multinational concerns.

Advantages

The major advantage to the shareholder, or investor, is that the shareholder's risk of loss from the business is limited to the amount of capital she invested in the business or paid for shares. This factor, coupled with the free transferability of corporate shares, makes the corporate form of business organization attractive to investors.

By purchasing shares, a large number of investors may contribute the capital assets needed to finance large business enterprises. As the capital needs of a business expand, the corporate form becomes more attractive.

A corporation is a separate legal entity capable of owning property, contracting, suing, and being sued in its own name. It has perpetual life. In other words, a corporation is not affected by the death of any of its shareholders or the transfer of their shares. In contrast to the case of a partnership or proprietorship, the death of an owner has no legal effect on the corporate entity.

Disadvantages

A corporation is required to pay corporate income taxes. Shareholders are required to pay personal income taxes on the amount received from a distribution of profits from the corporation. This is a form of double taxation.

Incorporation involves the expenditure of funds for organizational expenses. Documents necessary for the formation of a corporation, which are required by state law, must be prepared, and certain filing fees must be paid. State corporation laws may also require filing an annual report and other reports.

40-2 Specialized Forms of Organizations

CPA   ## 40-2a Joint Ventures

joint venture–relationship in which two or more persons or firms combine their labor or property for a single undertaking and share profits and losses equally unless otherwise agreed.

A **joint venture,** or joint adventure, is a relationship in which two or more persons or entities combine their labor or property for a single business undertaking and share profits and losses equally or as otherwise agreed.[1] **For Example,** when a passenger died as a result of injuries sustained in a bus accident and she had purchased her bus ticket from an online ticket vendor, the plaintiff sought to recover damages for the decedent's wrongful death from both the bus company and the online ticket vendor, alleging that they were engaged in a joint venture. The court found that the elements of a joint venture were

[1] See *Abeles Inc. v. Creekstone Farms Premium Beef, LLC,* 2009 WL 2495802 (E.D.N.Y. March 30, 2009), for an in-depth discussion of the law of joint ventures. The court referenced a precedent, stating: "A joint venture has been described as a nebulous concept whose boundaries are not precisely drawn. Defining a joint venture is easier than identifying it, for each case depends upon its own facts."

satisfied: the parties manifested an intent to associate as joint venturers; they mutually contributed to the business; they each had some control over the enterprise; and they had a mechanism for sharing profits and losses.[2]

A joint venture is similar in many respects to a partnership. It differs primarily in that the joint venture typically involves the pursuit of a single limited purpose rather than an ongoing enterprise, although its accomplishment may require several years.[3] A partnership is generally a continuing business or activity but may be expressly created for a single transaction. Because the distinction is so insubstantial, most courts hold that joint ventures are subject to the same principles of law as partnerships.

CASE SUMMARY

Unilateral Action: Years of Litigation

FACTS: Prior to 1992, Drs. Kurwa and Kislinger maintained their own ophthalmologist practices in the San Gabriel Valley. They subsequently agreed to pursue a new business model at that time by creating a joint venture where, under what is called a "capitation agreement." HMOs would pay the joint venture a monthly fee based on the number of members of the HMO in exchange for their ophthalmologist services. They signed a handwritten "Agreement between Bud and Mark" in which they outlined the structure within which they would solicit business and share profits. They agreed to incorporate as a professional medical corporation to operate their joint venture business. Thus, Trans Valley Eye Associates, Inc., was formed. The joint venture had capitation agreements with three HMOs serving some 200,000 patients in the year before its demise and earned revenues of $2 million. Beginning September 26, 2003, Dr. Kurwa was suspended from the practice of medicine for 60 days and placed on five years' probation by the California Medical Board. The doctors also discovered at that time that their corporation did not contain a specific statement in its Articles of Incorporation that it was a professional medical corporation, thus making it an ordinary for-profit corporation. Dr. Kislinger unilaterally terminated the joint venture and appropriated for himself, without any compensation to Dr. Kurwa, the very successful 11-year venture. Dr. Kislinger contended that Dr. Kurwa had no standing to bring an action against him on behalf of Trans Valley. From adverse decisions in the trial court, Dr. Kurwa appealed.

DECISION: Courts in other states have recognized that joint ventures may choose to operate their venture in the corporate form without divesting themselves of the rights and obligations of joint venturers. The factual allegations in the complaint state a cause of action against Dr. Kislinger for breach of his fiduciary duty as a director of Trans Valley for misappropriating assets of the corporation. While Dr. Kurwa may have been precluded from owning shares in a professional corporation during his suspension, that does not mean Dr. Kislinger is not required to account to Dr. Kurwa for his interest in the joint enterprise or allow Dr. Kurwa to sell his shares in Trans Valley to an eligible licensed person. [***Kurwa v. Kislinger*, 138 Cal. Rptr. 3d 610 (Cal. App. 2012)]**

Duration of Joint Venture

A joint venture continues for the time specified in the agreement of the parties. In the absence of a fixed-duration provision, a joint venture is ordinarily terminable at the will of any participant. When the joint venture clearly relates to a particular transaction, such as the construction of a specified bridge, the joint venture ordinarily lasts until the particular transaction or project is completed or becomes impossible to complete.

[2] *Clarke v. Sky Express, Inc. et al.*, 118 A.D.3d 935 (N.Y. App. Div. 2014).
[3] *Ride, Inc. v. APS Technology, Inc.*, 11 F. Supp. 3d 169 (D. Conn. 2014).

Liability to Third Persons

The conclusion that persons are joint venturers is important when a suit is brought by or against a third person for personal injuries or property damage. If there is a joint venture, the fault or negligence of one venturer will be imputed to the other venturers.[4]

40-2b Unincorporated Associations

unincorporated association— combination of two or more persons for the furtherance of a common nonprofit purpose.

An **unincorporated association** is a combination of two or more persons for the furtherance of a common purpose.[5] No particular form of organization is required. Any conduct or agreement indicating an attempt to associate or work together for a common purpose is sufficient.

The authority of an unincorporated association over its members is governed by ordinary contract law. Except when otherwise provided by statute, an unincorporated association does not have any legal existence apart from its members. Thus, an unincorporated association cannot sue or be sued in its own name.

Generally, the members of an unincorporated association are not liable for the debts or liabilities of the association by the mere fact that they are members. It must usually be shown that they authorized or ratified the act in question. If either authorization or ratification by a particular member can be shown, that member has unlimited liability for the act.

CASE SUMMARY

Batters with Two Strikes Should Never Trust the Umpire, and Their Parents Should Have Little Faith That the Association Will Pay the Bills

FACTS: Golden Spike Little League was an unincorporated association of persons who joined together to promote a Little League baseball team in Ogden, Utah. They sent one of their members to arrange for credit at Smith & Edwards, a local sporting goods store. After getting credit, various members went to the store and picked up and signed for different items of baseball equipment and uniforms, at a total cost of $3,900. When Smith, the owner, requested payment, the members arranged a fundraising activity that produced only $149. Smith sued the Golden Spike Little League as an entity and the members who had picked up and signed for the equipment individually. The individual defendants denied that they had any personal liability, contending that only the Golden Spike Little League could be held responsible.

DECISION: Judgment for Smith against the individual members. The association could not be held liable because it did not have any legal existence. The persons who purchased the goods from the seller were personally liable as buyers even though they had purported to act on behalf of the unincorporated association. [*Smith & Edwards v. Golden Spike Little League*, 577 P.2d 132 (Utah 1978)]

40-2c Cooperatives

cooperative— group of two or more persons or enterprises that acts through a common agent with respect to a common objective, such as buying or selling.

A **cooperative** consists of a group of two or more independent persons or enterprises that cooperate for a common objective or function. Thus, farmers may pool their farm products and sell them. Consumers may likewise pool their orders and purchase goods in bulk.

---

[4] *Kim v. Chamberlain*, 504 So. 2d 1213 (Ala. App. 1987).
[5] The National Conference of Commissioners on Uniform State Laws has adopted a Uniform Unincorporated Nonprofit Association Act. An unincorporated nonprofit association (UNA) is a default organization. Thus, if the organization is not a charitable trust or a nonprofit corporation or any other type of statutory trust it may be considered a UNA. Such organizations are governed by a variety of common law principles and statutes. The Revised Uniform Unincorporated Nonprofit Association Act provides useful information to small informal associations that may fail to consider legal and organizational issues. The text of the act is available at **http://apps.americanbar.org/intlaw/leadership/policy/ RUUNAA_Final_08.pdf**.

Incorporated Cooperatives

Statutes commonly provide for the special incorporation of cooperative enterprises. Such statutes often provide that any excess of payments over the cost of operation shall be refunded to each participant member in direct proportion to the volume of business that the member has done with the cooperative. This system contrasts with the payment of a dividend by an ordinary business corporation in which the payment of dividends is proportional to the number of shares held by the shareholder and is unrelated to the extent of the shareholder's business activities with the enterprise.

Antitrust Law Exemption

When members of a sellers' cooperative agree to sell all products at a common price, the agreement to fix prices is basically an agreement in restraint of trade and a violation of antitrust laws. The Capper-Volstead Act of 1922 expressly exempts normal selling activities of farmers' and dairy farmers' cooperatives from the operation of the federal Sherman Antitrust Act so long as the cooperatives do not conspire with outsiders to fix prices. In recent years, the Capper-Volstead exemption has been challenged in cases involving agricultural products such as mushrooms, milk, eggs, potatoes, and cattle. Some argue that the antitrust exemption should no longer apply because farms have become larger and are vertically integrated. Others maintain that farmers need this antitrust immunity because they rely on cooperatives for market access.[6]

40-3 The Franchise Business Format

franchise–privilege or authorization, generally exclusive, to engage in a particular activity within a particular geographic area, such as a government franchise to operate a taxi company within a specified city, or a private franchise as the grant by a manufacturer of a right to sell products within a particular territory or for a particular number of years.

Franchising is a *method* of doing business, not a *form* of business organization. A franchisor or franchisee could be a sole proprietor, a partnership, a limited liability company, or a corporation. The franchise agreement is a contract that sets forth the rights and obligations of the parties. Contract law governs questions that arise under the franchise agreement. Franchises are also subject to Section 5 of the Federal Trade Commission Act and state laws prohibiting deceptive, manipulative, or unfair business practices.[7] Both the FTC and state laws impose disclosure requirements on franchises. A variety of other laws may also impact franchises, such as securities, intellectual property, antitrust violations, sales, agency, employment, and tort law.

As defined by the Federal Trade Commission (FTC) a commercial business arrangement is a **franchise** if it satisfies three definitional elements: the franchisor must (1) promise to provide a trademark or other commercial symbol; (2) promise to exercise significant control or provide significant assistance in the operation of the business; and (3) require a minimum payment of at least $540 during the first six months of operations.[8]

---

[6] See Randon W. Wilson, "The Evolution of Farmers, Their Cooperatives and the Capper-Volstead Act," ABA Antitrust Section, *Agriculture and Food Committee e-Bulletin*, 4(1) (Spring 2013), **http://www.americanbar.org/content/dam/aba/ publications/antitrust_law/at800006_newsletter_2013spring.authcheckdam.pdf**.

[7] 15 U.S.C. §45.

[8] Some business opportunities that do not meet the definition of a franchise (because they do not require a minimum payment or do not involve use of a trademark) may be subject to the FTC's "Business Opportunity Rule." Such opportunities may include work-at-home opportunities, such as stuffing envelopes or assembling crafts or running vending machines. The disclosure requirements for these business opportunities involve a one-page document. The disclosure requirement seeks to balance protection of consumers from deceptive practices against unnecessary and burdensome compliance costs on both sellers and buyers of business opportunities. 16 C.F.R. Part 437. Business opportunities may also be subject to state laws.

40-3a Definition and Types of Franchises

franchisor–party granting the franchise.

franchisee–person to whom franchise is granted.

The **franchisor** is the party granting the franchise, and the **franchisee** is the person to whom the franchise is granted. There are three principal types of franchises. The first is a *manufacturing* or *processing franchise*, in which the franchisor grants the franchisee authority to manufacture and sell products under the trademark(s) of the franchisor. The franchisor may supply an essential ingredient in a processing franchise, such as the syrup for an independent regional Coca-Cola bottling company. The second type of franchise is a *service franchise*, in which the franchisee renders a service to customers under the terms of a franchise agreement. The drain-cleaning service provided by Roto-Rooter is an example of a service franchise. The third type is a *distribution franchise*, in which the franchisor's products are sold to a franchisee, who then resells to customers in a geographical area. Exxon Mobil Oil Company's products are often sold to retail customers through independent distribution franchises.

A franchise benefits both the franchisor and the franchisee. The franchisor derives revenue from fees for its trademarks and other franchise fees while avoiding the risk and cost of running its own stores. The franchisee has an opportunity to run a store independently with "the expertise, goodwill and reputation of the franchisor."[9] The franchisor, however, assumes some risk to reputation by giving day-to-day control to the franchisee. The franchisee incurs some risk because it usually has less bargaining power than the franchisor. Recognizing the inequality in bargaining power, state laws often protect franchisees from the more powerful franchisor by providing specific requirements about how and when a franchise may be terminated. Consequently, a common issue in litigation is whether the business arrangement meets the definition of a franchise under the applicable state law.[10]

40-3b The Franchise Agreement

franchise agreement–sets forth rights of franchisee to use trademarks, etc., of franchisor.

trademark–mark that identifies a product.

trade name–name under which a business is carried on and, if fictitious, must be registered.

trade dress–product's total image including its overall packaging look.

trade secret–formula, device, or compilation of information that is used in one's business and is of such a nature that it provides an advantage over competitors who do not have the information.

The relationship between the franchisor and the franchisee is ordinarily an arm's-length relationship between two independent contractors. The respective rights of the parties are determined by the contract existing between them, called the **franchise agreement.**[11] The agreement sets forth the rights of the franchisee to use the **trademarks, trade name, trade dress,** and **trade secrets** of the franchisor. **For Example,** Burger King Corporation licenses franchisees to use the trademarks Burger King, Whopper, Croissanwich, and Whopper Jr.[12] The franchise agreement commonly requires the franchisor to provide training for the franchisee's employees, including processing or repair training. Thus, a new Chili's Bar and Grill franchise can expect to have its employees taught how to prepare and serve the food on its menu. In a distribution franchise, an Acura dealer can expect the franchisor to train its mechanics to repair the automobiles it sells. The franchise agreement also deals with terms for payment of various fees by the franchisee and sets forth compliance requirements for quality control set by the franchisor.

The duration of a franchise is a critical element of the franchise agreement. The franchise may last for as long as the parties agree. The laws in some states may require advance written notice of cancellation.[13] Franchise contracts generally specify the causes for which the franchisor may terminate the franchise, such as the franchisee's death, bankruptcy, failure to make payments, or failure to meet sales quotas.[14] Failure to comply with the franchise agreement may be grounds for termination. **For Example,** Burger King

---

[9] *Patterson v. Domino's Pizza, LLC,* 333 P.3d 723 (S. Ct. Cal. 2014).
[10] *Missouri Beverage Co., Inc. v. Shelton Brothers, Inc.,* 669 F.3d 873 (8th Cir. 2012).
[11] See *American Standard Inc. v. Meehan,* 517 F. Supp. 2d 976 (N.D. Ohio 2007).
[12] *Burger King Corp. v. Hinton, Inc.,* 203 F. Supp. 2d 1357 (S.D. Fla. 2002).
[13] See, for example, Mo. Rev. Stat. §407.405.
[14] *Smith's Sports Cycles, Inc. v. American Suzuki,* 82 So. 3d 682 (Ala. 2011).

Corp. required that a new item, value meals, "be sold in all U.S. restaurants … and failure to comply will be considered a default under the applicable franchise agreement." The Sadiks, who owned four Burger King franchises in New York City, did not comply with the value meal requirement. The court concluded that termination of the franchises was appropriate because Burger King clearly "had the power and authority under the Franchise Agreements to impose the Value Menu on its franchisees."[15]

Franchise agreements frequently contain an arbitration provision under which a neutral party is to make a final and binding determination whether there has been a breach of the contract sufficient to justify cancellation of the franchise.[16] The arbitration provision may provide that the franchisor can appoint a trustee to run the business of the franchisee while arbitration proceedings are pending.

40-3c Special Protections under Federal and State Laws

Federal and state legislation may protect franchisees in certain industries. Holders of automobile dealership franchises are protected from bad-faith termination of their dealerships by the federal Automobile Dealers' Day in Court Act (ADDCA)[17] as well as by state law. Such legislation recognizes the disparity in bargaining power between dealers and manufacturers and the fact that dealers are dependent on the manufacturer for the supply of cars. **For Example,** electric car manufacturer Tesla Motors sells its cars directly to consumers. This practice has been strongly opposed by automobile dealers. Some states had legislation in place that prohibited auto manufacturers from selling direct to consumers. Other states have proposed legislation to prohibit such sales. While Tesla does not currently pose a threat to dealership franchises, dealers fear that larger manufacturers could seek to undercut their business by following a direct sales model.[18]

State laws may also prevent franchisors from unreasonably withholding consent for sale of the franchise. Some states have laws that specifically protect motor vehicle franchises from unreasonable termination or limitations on resale. **For Example,** a California court held that Yamaha unreasonably withheld its consent for the sale of a motorcycle franchise even though the franchisee had closed the dealership. Yamaha argued that "termination of the Franchise Agreement left Powerhouse with nothing to sell and Yamaha with nothing to approve." But the court held that the law protected the franchisee's attempt to receive fair and reasonable compensation for the value of the franchised business.[19]

CASE SUMMARY

"Reputation Poisoning" is a Material and Incurable Breach

FACTS: Giuffre contracted with Hyundai Motor America to be an authorized Hyundai dealer. After a court found that Giuffre had engaged in fraudulent, illegal, and deceptive practices, including false advertising and strong-arm sales methods, Hyundai terminated the dealership. Giuffre argued that the termination was unlawful.

[15] *Burger King Corp. v. E-Z Corporations,* 572 F.3d 1306 (11th Cir. 2009).
[16] *Central New Jersey Freightliner, Inc., v. Freightliner Corp.,* 987 F. Supp. 289 (D.N.J. 1998).
[17] 15 U.S.C. §§1221-1225.
[18] See Evan Puschak, *Tesla vs. the Auto Dealers of America* (Oct. 3, 2013), **http://www.msnbc.com/the-last-word/tesla-vs-the-auto-dealers-america**.
[19] *Powerhouse Motorsports Group, Inc. v. Yamaha Motor Corp., U.S.A.,* 221 Cal. App. 4th 867 (March 12, 2014).

"Reputation Poisoning" is a Material and Incurable Breach continued

DECISION: Judgment for the franchisor. A franchisor must have due cause to terminate a franchise agreement. Due cause exists if there has been a material breach of the agreement and if the breach is not cured within a reasonable time.

In this case, the illegal practices of the franchisee created a material and incurable breach. [*Giuffre Hyundai, LTD. v. Hyundai Motor America*, **756 F.3d 204 (2d Cir. 2014)**]

The Petroleum Marketing Practices Act (PMPA) is a federal law that limits a franchisor's ability to terminate or refuse to renew a service station franchise.[20] The United States Supreme Court considered the reach of the PMPA in a case involving Shell Oil and several of its franchisees. The franchisees maintained that Shell discontinued a program of rent subsidies and then, as leases expired, Shell calculated higher annual rent payments. The franchisees signed lease renewals under protest but claimed that Shell's pricing practices constituted constructive termination of their franchise in violation of the PMPA. The Supreme Court held that the PMPA recognizes claims for constructive termination and constructive nonrenewal but that the franchisee must actually sever its relationship with the franchisor to benefit from the statute's protection. According to the Court, the PMPA regulates only "the circumstances in which franchisors may terminate a franchise or decline to renew a franchise relationship." It would contravene the purpose of the act, the Court stated, to allow a franchisee to obtain PMPA relief when a franchisor's conduct did not force the franchisee to end its franchise. The Court also stated that the PMPA does not prevent franchisors from responding to market demands by proposing new and different terms at the expiration of a franchise agreement. The Court noted that state law might protect the dealers where the PMPA does not reach.[21]

40-3d Disclosure

The offer and sale of a franchise requires compliance with both federal and state laws.

Federal Law

Franchise Rule—FTC rule requiring detailed disclosures and prohibiting certain practices.

Franchisors must comply with the FTC's amended **Franchise Rule,** which requires a franchisor to provide each prospective franchisee with a detailed franchise disclosure document (FDD) at least 14 calendar days before the prospective franchisee signs a binding agreement or makes any payment to the franchisor. This requirement ensures that prospective franchisees have sufficient time in which to review the disclosures. The FDD requires some 23 items of disclosure, including: (1) the business experience of the franchisor and its brokers, (2) any current and past litigation against the franchisor, (3) any previous bankruptcy, (4) the material terms of the franchise agreement, (5) initial and recurring payments, (6) restrictions on territories, (7) grounds for termination of the franchise, and (8) actual, average, or projected sales, profits, or earnings.[22] The FTC does not review the FDD but it may bring suit against the franchisor for false or misleading statements in the FDD.

[20] 15 U.S.C. §§2801 *et seq.*
[21] *Mac's Shell Service, Inc. v. Shell Oil Products Co., LLC*, 599 U.S. 175 (2010).
[22] See the Federal Trade Commission, *Franchise Rule Compliance Guide*, 16 C.F.R. Part 436, for details on the other disclosure items required by the FDD.

State Laws

Some 35 states require only that franchisors properly prepare FDDs. The remaining 15 states have additional requirements, including registration with a state agency. State laws may provide additional protection to franchisees, allowing them to sue for damages resulting from improper disclosure.[23]

40-3e Vicarious Liability Claims against Franchisors

In theory, a franchisor is not liable to a third person dealing with or affected by the franchise holder. This freedom from liability is one of the main reasons franchisors use franchises. If the negligence of the franchisee causes harm to a third person, the franchisor is generally not liable because the franchisee is an independent contractor. However, franchisors continue to be subject to lawsuits based on the wrongful conduct of their franchisees under the theory of either actual agency or apparent agency.[24] Plaintiffs may claim that the franchisor was the employer of persons working for the franchisee, that the franchisee was the agent of the franchisor, and, consequently, that the franchisor could be held vicariously liable for the wrongs of the franchisee's employees. Whether the franchisor stands in an employment or agency relationship with the franchisee and its employees for purposes of vicarious liability depends on the amount of control the franchisor exerts over the franchisee.[25]

CASE SUMMARY

Why Franchisors Use Franchises!

FACTS: William Roberts operated a McDonald's restaurant in Newcastle, Washington, under a franchise agreement with McDonald's Corporation. A thriving drug scene existed among employees and assistant managers at the restaurant. In May 2000, the restaurant hired 15-year-old D.L.S., and within weeks, she was part of the drug scene there. Thereafter, she left home to live with an assistant manager and use drugs. Her father, Clifford Street, and D.L.S. sued McDonald's Corp. and Roberts for introducing D.L.S. to drugs and sex. The trial court dismissed the claims against McDonald's Corp. D.L.S. and her father appealed. Mr. Street testified that "no person in their right mind would believe that McDonald's did not control what happened at the individual restaurants."

DECISION: The franchise agreement clearly provided that Roberts was not an agent of McDonald's Corporation and

that McDonald's had no control over the daily operations of the restaurant. Thus, McDonald's has no liability as Roberts' actual principal. The court next considered an apparent authority theory to determine whether McDonald's created apparent authority that it operated the Newcastle restaurant and would ensure a safe working environment for young workers there. Beyond the general impression created by advertising that McDonald's restaurants offer a wholesome environment, no representations or acts of McDonald's existed to create an apparent employment relationship between McDonald's and D.L.S. D.L.S. and her parents must pursue their claims against the franchisee. [*D.L.S. v. Maybin,* **121 P.3d 1210 (Wash. App. 2005)**]

---

[23] See *Legacy Academy, et al. v. Mamilove, LLC, et al.,* 761 S.E.2d 880 (Ga. App. 2014).
[24] *Ketterling v. Burger King Corporation,* 272 P.3d 527 (Idaho 2012).
[25] *Patterson v. Domino's Pizza, LLC,* 333 P.3d 723 (S. Ct. Cal. 2014).

To maintain uniform systems for processing or distributing goods or rendering services, franchisors often place significant controls on their franchisees' businesses. These controls are set forth in franchise agreements and operating manuals. In a lawsuit brought against a franchisor for the wrongful conduct of its franchisee, the franchise agreement and operations manuals may be used as evidence of the franchisor's right to control the franchisee and the existence of an agency relationship rather than an independent contractor relationship.[26]

To avoid negating its franchisees' independent contractor status and being liable for the wrongful conduct of a franchisee, the franchisor should make certain that the franchise agreement minimizes the number and kind of provisions that authorize the

THINKING THINGS THROUGH

Don't Finagle the Bagel!

Ken Miyamoto was president and a shareholder of Bixby's Food Systems, Inc. (Bixby's), a franchisor of bagel restaurants. The business is incorporated and provides limited liability to Miyamoto and its other corporate investors. Bixby's hired a lawyer familiar with franchise disclosure laws in Illinois and drafted a franchise offering circular (FOC) in accordance with state laws. Jan and Phillip McKay attended a meeting of existing and prospective franchisees where Miyamoto spoke and said that prospective franchisees had signed and paid for 340 development agreements; a similar statement also appeared in a Bixby's newsletter. The McKays soon thereafter executed a franchise agreement. Based on Miyamoto's view that a lease of larger retail space than recommended in Bixby's circular would bring in larger revenues, the McKays executed the larger-than-recommended lease and spent $400,000 making their restaurant operational, which was a much higher investment than projected in the FOC. When the restaurant opened, sales did not come close to the figures estimated in the FOC. After eight months of operations, Bixby's terminated the McKays' franchise for their inability to pay Bixby's franchise royalty fees. Bixby's sued the McKays for continuing to use its trademark, and the McKays counterclaimed against Bixby's, Inc., and Miyamoto as an individual for violation of the state Franchise Disclosure Act and the state Deceptive Business Practices Act.

Bixby's FOC was not shown to contain material misstatements of fact. However, the McKays listed a number of statements made by Miyamoto that were untrue concerning future events regarding costs, profitability, and financial success, like his encouraging them to rent larger-than-recommended

retail space to bring in larger revenues, which did not materialize. The court held that such statements about future events, costs, and profitability are not actionable misrepresentations under the state Franchise Disclosure Act. Corporate executives selling franchises have latitude to take the facts set forth in franchise offering circulars and project a bright future in most respects. That is, they have a legal right to put their "spin" on the facts, just as society does in governmental and personal affairs. Of course, buyers must beware and view assertions about future events, costs, and profitability with critical analysis and informed skepticism.

With his business incorporated and his circulars drafted by competent counsel, was Miyamoto immune from personal liability in this case? The answer is no. When Miyamoto told the group of prospective franchisees that some 340 development agreements had been signed and paid for and later repeated this statement in a newsletter, he was not Thinking Things Through. Through the discovery process that preceded a trial, the McKays' attorney "discovered" that Bixby's had just 15 agreements executed and paid for at the time of Miyamoto's assertion that 340 agreements were executed and paid for. Such a material misstatement of fact was a violation of the state franchising and deceptive practices laws.

The economic resources expended by Bixby's, Inc., to provide limited liability could not shield its shareholder-president from the consequences of his enormous lie. Along with Bixby's, Inc., Miyamoto was held personally liable to the McKays under the state statutes.*

*_Bixby's Food Systems, Inc. v. McKay_, 193 F. Supp. 2d 1053 (N.D. Ill. 2002).

[26] _J. M. v. Shell Oil Co._, 922 S.W.2d 759 (Mo. 1996).

franchisor to control the "means" of operating the business. For example, the franchisor should not exercise control over employment-related matters.[27]

Franchisors may also insulate themselves from liability by requiring individual franchisees to take steps to publicly maintain their own individual business identities. **For Example,** a gas station may post a sign stating that it is "dealer owned and operated," or a real estate franchise may list on its business sign the franchise name and the name of the local owner, such as Century 21, L & K Realty Co. All invoices, purchase orders, paychecks, and notices to employees should contain notice of the independent ownership and operation of the business. Finally, franchisors should require their franchisees to maintain appropriate comprehensive general liability insurance, workers' compensation insurance, and other appropriate insurance.

40-3f Franchises and Employee Misclassifications

The franchise agreement typically states that it does not create an employment relationship. Whether someone is a franchisee-independent contractor or an employee is determined by the actual relationship between the individual and the business, and not by a label or a franchise agreement. **For Example,** Coverall North American Inc. is one of the largest global commercial cleaning franchisors in North America, with over 9,000 franchise owners and 50,000 customers. Each individual who purchases a janitorial cleaning franchise must enter a standard unit agreement with Coverall. The agreement gives Coverall the exclusive rights to perform all billing and collection services provided by franchisees and to deduct fees before remitting payments. State law deals with whether an individual who is performing services is an independent contractor or an employee. Under one prong of the Massachusetts law, the burden is placed on Coverall to establish that the individual "is performing services that are part of an independent, separate, and distinct business from that of the employer." Coverall trains its franchisees and provides them with uniforms and identification badges; it contracted with all customers, with limited exceptions, until May 2009; and Coverall is the party billing all customers for cleaning services performed and receives a percentage of the revenues earned on every cleaning service. Accordingly, Coverall sells cleaning services, the same services provided by the "franchisees." Because the franchisees did not perform services outside the usual course of Coverall's business, Coverall failed to establish that franchisees were independent contractors.[28]

---

[27] Consider the degree of control exercised by McDonald's Corp. over its franchises. Only designated food and beverages may be served, and franchisees are required to use prescribed buildings and equipment. The franchisor dictates the level of quality, service, and cleanliness. All franchisees' employees must wear the uniforms designated by the franchisor with McDonald's logos. McDonald's dictates management, advertising, and personnel policies and requires that managers be trained at its "Hamburger University." The Illinois Court of Appeals held that the question of whether a franchise was an apparent agent of McDonald's was an issue of material fact that should go to a jury in a lawsuit involving a customer's slip and fall on ice in the franchised restaurant's bathroom. The court stated that the employees responsible for maintaining the bathroom wore "McDonald's uniforms" and were required to follow McDonald's standards of "quality, service, and cleanliness." *O'Banner v. McDonald's Corp.*, 653 N.E.2d 1267 (Ill. App. 1995). On further appeal to the Supreme Court of Illinois, the Court of Appeals was reversed because in order to recover on an apparent agency theory, the customer had to show that he actually relied on the apparent agency in going to the restaurant where he was injured. The customer failed to do so, thus losing the right to hold McDonald's Corp. liable for his injuries. *O'Banner v. McDonald's Corp.*, 670 N.E.2d 632 (Ill. 1996). See *Husain v. McDonald's Corp.*, 140 Cal. Rptr. 3d 370, 377 (Cal. App. 2012), where the form license agreement between McDonald's and the franchisor explains the essence of the "McDonald's system" is to ensure comprehensive control by McDonald's over every material aspect of the restaurant's operations so the uniformity of the McDonald's customer experience could be assured in every one of its locations.

[28] *Awauh v. Coverall North America, Inc.* 707 F. Supp. 2d 80 (D. Mass. 2010).

Cases raising similar issues were filed in Massachusetts and California in the summer of 2014 against the popular ride-sharing service, Uber. Some Uber drivers claim that the company has misclassified its drivers as independent contractors to avoid paying them the benefits it would have to pay employees.[29] The cases focus on whether or not the company controls the worker enough to qualify him or her as an employee.

The U.S. Labor Secretary stated that classifying workers as independent contractors rather than as employees has saved some employers as much as 20 to 30 percent on their labor costs. This practice gives employers an advantage in gaining business. Because their employment costs are lower, they are able to underbid employers who abide by the law and accurately report the status of their workers. Misclassification of employees as independent contractors depresses wages and reduces government revenues.

Make the Connection

Summary

The three principal forms of business organizations are sole proprietorships, partnerships, and corporations. A *sole proprietorship* is a form of business organization in which one person owns the business, controls all decisions, receives all profits, and has unlimited liability for all obligations and liabilities. A *partnership* involves the pooling of capital resources and talents of two or more persons whose goal is to make a profit; the partners are subject to unlimited personal liability. However, newly created forms of business organizations—the *limited liability company* and the *limited liability partnership*—allow for tax treatment as a partnership with certain limited liability for the owners.

A business *corporation* exists to make a profit. It is created by government grant. Its shareholders elect a board of directors whose members are responsible for managing the business. A shareholder's liability is limited to the capital the shareholder invested in the business or paid for shares. Corporate existence continues without regard to the death of shareholders or the transfer of stock by them.

The selection of the form of organization is determined by the nature of the business, tax considerations, the financial risk involved, the importance of limited liability, and the extent of management control desired.

A *joint venture* exists when two or more persons combine their labor or property for a single business undertaking and share profits and losses as agreed.

An *unincorporated association* is a combination of two or more persons for the pursuit of a common purpose.

A *cooperative* consists of two or more persons or enterprises, such as farmers, who cooperate to achieve a common objective such as the distribution of farm products.

In a franchise, the owner of a trademark, trade name, or copyright licenses others to use the mark or copyright to sell goods or services. To protect against fraud, the FTC requires that franchisors provide prospective franchisees with a disclosure statement 14 days prior to any transaction. The Automobile Dealers' Day in Court Act and the Petroleum Marketing Practices Act are federal laws that provide covered franchisees with protection from bad-faith terminations. State laws also protect franchisees in a wide range of businesses. A franchisor is not liable to third persons dealing with its franchisees. Liability of the franchisor may, however, be imposed on the ground of the apparent authority of the franchisee or the latter's control by the franchisor. Liability of the franchisor may also arise in cases of product liability.

---

[29] See Michael B. Farrell, "New Lawsuit Claims Uber Exploits Its Drivers," *Boston Globe* (June 26, 2014).

Learning Outcomes

After studying this chapter, you should be able to clearly explain:

40-1   Principal Forms of Business Organizations

LO.1   Explain the advantages and disadvantages of the three principal forms of business organizations

See the discussion on proprietorships, partnerships (LLPs and LLCs), and corporations, pages 824–825.

40-2   Specialized Forms of Organizations

LO.2   Recognize that the rules of law governing the rights and liabilities of joint ventures are substantially the same as those that govern partnerships

See the *Kurwa* case and the joint venture remedy while operating in the corporate form, page 826.

40-3   The Franchise Business Format

LO.3   Evaluate whether a business arrangement is a franchise protected under state or federal law

Consider the implications of Tesla's business model, page 830.

See the *Yamaha* example, page 830.

LO.4   Explain how the rights of the parties to a franchise agreement are determined by their contract

See the *Burger King* example involving cancellation of franchises, pages 829–830.

See the *Hyundai* case involving termination of a franchise for unethical behavior, pages 830–831.

LO.5   Explain why freedom from vicarious liability is a reason for franchisors to use the franchise format

See the *McDonald's* case in which only the franchisee was liable for the torts to the minor emanating from the McDonald's restaurant, page 832.

LO.6   Recognize the implications of the misclassifications of employees as franchisee-independent contractors

See the *Coverall* and *Uber* misclassification scheme, pages 834–835.

Key Terms

cooperative
corporations
franchise
franchise agreement
Franchise Rule
franchisee

franchisor
joint venture
limited liability company (LLC)
limited liability partnership (LLP)
partnership
sole or individual proprietorship

trade dress
trade name
trade secrets
trademarks
unincorporated association

Questions and Case Problems

1.   In July 2008 Miller Brewing Co. and Coors Brewing Co. formed a joint venture to better compete with the dominant beer manufacturer, Anheuser Busch. The venture was named "MillerCoors LLC." Under the joint venture agreement, Miller Brewing Co. and Coors Brewing Company have a 50 percent voting interest in the entity, and each appoints half of the directors. Moreover, the CEOs of Miller and Coors resolve disputes, and all revenues are distributed directly to Miller and Coors, with cash returned to meet the operating needs of the joint venture. Ohio law requires just cause for the termination of beer distributors but allows a "successor manufacturer" to terminate existing distributorships without proving just cause so long as the predecessor does not exercise control over the successor. In accordance with the "successor manufacturer" exception, MillerCoors LLC notified Ohio wholesale beer distributors that it was terminating their distributorships. The distributorships sought injunctive relief. MillerCoors LLC moved for summary judgment. Decide. [*Beverage Distributors, Inc. v. Miller Brewing Co.*, 690 F.3d 788 (6th Cir.)]

2.   Jerome, Sheila, Gary, and Ella agreed to purchase a tract of land and make it available for use as a free playground for neighborhood children. They called the enterprise Meadowbrook Playground. Jerome and Gary improperly hung one of the playground swings, and a child was injured. Suit was brought against Meadowbrook Playground. Can damages be recovered?

3. Morris Friedman was president of Tiny Doubles International, Inc. He sold business opportunities for Tiny Doubles Studios, which made small photographic statues of people for customers. Friedman was the primary negotiator with prospective buyers of these studio business opportunities. He advised buyers up front that the opportunities were not franchises, and, accordingly, he did not provide all of the information set forth in the disclosure rule on franchising, although he did provide full answers to all questions asked. Many businesses closed, however, because of lack of success. The FTC claims that Friedman violated its disclosure rule. Friedman disagrees. Decide. [*FTC v. Tiny Doubles Int'l, Inc.*, 1996 Bus. Franchise Guide (C.C.H.) ¶ 10,831]

4. Wolf, King, and others sold business "opportunities" in vending machines by taking out ads in newspapers throughout the country. When individuals responded, telemarketers called "fronters" would tell them of false earnings estimates, and those who could afford $16,000 to $25,000 for vending machines were turned over to "closers" who promised wonderful results. References were provided who were "shills"—they did not own vending machines but were paid to tell "stories" that were monitored by Wolf, King, and other supervisors. None of the individuals was given franchise disclosure documents. King induced one investor to mortgage her house so that she could pay $70,000 for a number of vending machines. In three years Wolf, King, and others took in some $31.3 million. The FTC alleged that the defendants violated the FTC franchise disclosure rule.

   Is there a franchise disclosure rule violation if Wolf and King were merely selling vending machines? What if Wolf and King promised exclusive territories for the machines? Why would a franchise disclosure rule be necessary in this case? Decide. [*FTC v. Wolf*, Bus. Franchise Guide ¶ 27,655 (C.C.H. D. Fla.)]

5. Katherine Apostoleres owned the rights to Dunkin' Donuts franchises in Brandon and Temple Terrace, Florida. The franchisor offered all its franchisees the right to renew their existing franchise agreements if they agreed to abide by advertising decisions favored by two-thirds of the local franchise owners in a given television market. Apostoleres refused the offer because she did not want to be bound by the two-thirds clause. Soon thereafter, Dunkin' Donuts audited her two stores. Using a "yield and usage" analysis, it concluded that gross sales were being underreported. Based on these audits and a subsequent audit, Dunkin' Donuts gave notice of immediate termination of Apostoleres's franchises, contending that the franchise agreement had been violated. Apostoleres stated that an implied obligation of good faith exists by operation of law in every contract and that the audits were in retaliation for her refusal to accept the renewal agreement. The yield and usage test used in the audit was not specified in the franchise agreement as a measure to be used to enforce the franchisor's rights, and certain accounting experts testified as to the unreliability of this test. Was Dunkin' Donuts liable for breach of its implied obligation of good faith in this case? [*Dunkin' Donuts of America v. Minerva, Inc.*, 956 F.2d 1566 (11th Cir.)]

6. A woman claimed that she was sexually harassed by a male coworker at the franchisee's pizza store. She sued not only the harasser and the franchisee but also the franchisor, Domino's, claiming that the franchisor was the employer of those working for the franchisee and that the franchisee was the agent of the franchisor. The court recognized that the franchisor exerted control through "comprehensive and meticulous standards for marketing its trademarked brand and operating its franchises in a uniform way." Was Domino's vicariously liable for the conduct of the franchisee's employee? [*Patterson v. Domino's Pizza*, 333 P.3d 723 (S. Ct. Cal.)]

7. For a five-year period, Laurie Henry worked for James Doull, the owner of four Taco Bell franchises. During that time, she had an affair with Doull. He was the father of her two illegitimate children. Enraged over a domestic matter, Doull physically assaulted her at the Taco Bell Restaurant and then fired her and ordered her off the premises. Later, on Doull's recommendation, she was hired by a "company store" in an adjoining state. Henry brought suit against Doull, his corporate entity Taco Tia, Inc., and the Taco Bell Corporation (TBC). She did not characterize her suit as a case of sexual harassment. Rather, she contended that TBC was responsible for Doull's actions because he was TBC's agent. She sought damages for the loss of romantic and material satisfactions a person might expect from a traditional courtship and wedding. TBC denied that Doull was its employee or agent. The evidence showed that Henry knew that Doull's stores differed from TBC "company" stores. Henry insisted, having worked for

four years for Doull at stores adorned with Taco-Bell signs, that Taco Bell was responsible for Doull's actions. Decide. [*Henry v. Taco Tia, Inc.*, 606 So. 2d 1376 (La. App.)]

8. The Armory Committee was composed of officers from various National Guard units. It organized a New Year's Eve dance at a charge of $2 per person to defray costs. Perry, along with others, was a member of the Armory Committee. Libby was a paying guest at the dance who was injured by slipping on frozen ruts in the immediate approaches to the steps leading to the armory building where the dance was held. He sued Perry, Turner, and the other committee members. The evidence showed that every member of the committee had taken some part in planning or running the dance with the exception of Turner. Was the Armory Committee an unincorporated association or a joint venture? Decide. [*Libby v. Perry*, 311 A.2d 527 (Me.)]

9. The Kawasaki Shop of Aurora, Illinois (dealer), advised Kawasaki Motors Corp. (manufacturer) that it intended to move its Kawasaki franchise from New York Street to Hill Avenue, which was in the same market area. The Hill Avenue location was also the site of a Honda franchise. The manufacturer's sales manager advised the dealer that he did not want the dealer to move in with Honda at the Hill Avenue site. In February, the dealer moved to the Hill Avenue location. Effective May 1, the manufacturer terminated the dealer's franchise. The dealer brought suit against the manufacturer under the state's Motor Vehicle Franchise Act, which made it unlawful to terminate franchises for site control (requiring that the dealer's site be used exclusively as a Kawasaki dealership). The manufacturer argued that it had a right to have its products sold by a dealer who was not affiliated with a competitor. Decide. [*Kawasaki Shop v. Kawasaki Motors Corp.*, 544 N.E.2d 457 (Ill. App.)]

10. Goodward, a newly hired newspaper reporter for the *Cape Cod News*, learned that the local cranberry growers had made an agreement under which they pooled their cranberry crops each year and sold them at what they determined to be a fair price. Goodward believes that such an agreement is in restraint of trade and a violation of the antitrust laws. Is he correct?

11. Food Caterers of East Hartford, Connecticut, obtained a franchise from Chicken Delight to use that name at its store. Food Caterers agreed to the product standards and controls specified by the franchisor. The franchise contract required the franchisee to maintain a free delivery service to deliver hot, freshly prepared food to customers. The franchisee used a delivery truck that bore no sign or name. Its employee, Carfiro, was driving the truck in making a food delivery when he negligently struck and killed McLaughlin. The victim's estate sued Chicken Delight on the theory that Carfiro was its agent because he was doing work that Chicken Delight required and that benefited Chicken Delight. Was Carfiro the agent of Chicken Delight? [*McLaughlin's Estate v. Chicken Delight, Inc.*, 321 A.2d 456 (Conn.)]

12. The Girl Scouts of the United States (GSUSA) is led by the National Council. Local councils are governed by their own independent board of directors and employ their own officers and professional staff and are responsible for their own financial health. For a nominal fee, GSUSA issues a charter to the local council, which grants to that council "the right to develop, manage, and maintain Girl Scouting throughout the areas of its jurisdiction, including the right to use GSUSA's names and protected marks." Each local council has exclusive territory demarcated in its charter. The councils are not subsidiaries of GSUSA, rather the national organization relates to the councils as franchisor to franchisee. It authorizes the local councils to sell cookies and other merchandise under the "Girl Scout" trademark, which it owns. Manitou Council, a local council, makes most of its money from the sale of Girl Scout cookies and generates other income from charitable donations, fees from Girl Scout camps it owns, and investments. The GSUSA, in an effort to attract more members from minority groups and to increase revenue, sought to dissolve Manitou's territory as part of a realignment of council boundaries. Manitou sued to enjoin GSUSA from taking away its territory, which would not put it out of business, but would preclude it from representing itself as a Girl Scouts organization or otherwise using Girl Scout trademarks. Manitou Council claimed that GSUSA violated the Wisconsin Fair Dealership Law (WFDL) because it did not show good cause for termination as the law required. GSUSA defended by stating that Manitou is not a "dealer" (franchise) protected by the statute. The WFDL defines a dealership agreement as one in which the grantee is authorized to use the grantor's trademark and creates "a community of interest" between the parties "in the business of offering,

selling or distributing goods or services." Do you think that Manitou Council has the characteristics of a franchise? Should it be protected by the WFDL? Does it matter that the GSUSA and the local councils are nonprofit enterprises? [*Girl Scouts of Manitou v. GSUSA*, 549 F.3d 1079 (7th Cir.)]

13. Brenner was in the scrap iron business. Almost daily, Plitt lent Brenner money with which to purchase scrap iron. The agreement of the parties was that when the scrap was sold, Plitt would be repaid and would receive an additional sum as compensation for making the loans. The loans were to be repaid in any case without regard to whether Brenner made a profit. A dispute arose over the nature of the relationship between the two men. Plitt claimed that it was a joint venture. Decide. [*Brenner v. Plitt*, 34 A.2d 853 (Md.)]

14. Donald Salisbury, William Roberts, and others purchased property from Laurel Chapman, a partner of Chapman Realty, a franchisee of Realty World. The purchasers made payments directly to Laurel Chapman at the Realty World office, and Chapman was to make payments on the property's mortgage. However, Chapman did not make the payments and absconded with the funds. Salisbury and Roberts sued the franchisor, Realty World, claiming that Realty World was liable for the wrongful acts of the apparent agent, Chapman. Realty World and Chapman Realty were parties to a franchise agreement stating that the parties were franchisor and franchisee. The agreement contained a clause that required Chapman to prominently display a certificate in the office setting forth her status as an independent franchisee. Chapman displayed such a sign, but the plaintiffs did not recall seeing it. Chapman Realty hires, supervises, and sets the compensation for all of its employees. The plaintiffs pointed out that Chapman Realty used the service mark Realty World on its signs, both outside and inside its offices. They pointed out that a Realty World manual sets forth the general standards by which franchisees must run their businesses and that this represents clear control over the franchise. They contended that, all things considered, Realty World held out Chapman Realty as having authority to bind Realty World. Realty World disagreed, stating that both were independent businesses. Decide. [*Salisbury v. Chapman and Realty World, Inc.*, 65 N.E.2d 127 (Ill. App.)]

15. H.C. Blackwell Co. held a franchise from Kenworth Truck Co. to sell its trucks. After 12 years, the franchise was nearing expiration. Kenworth notified Blackwell that the franchise would not be renewed unless Blackwell sold more trucks and improved its building and bookkeeping systems within the next 90 days. Blackwell spent $90,000 attempting to meet the demands of Kenworth but could not do so because a year was required to make the specified changes. Kenworth refused to renew the franchise. Blackwell sued Kenworth for damages under the federal Automobile Dealers' Day in Court Act. Blackwell claimed that Kenworth had refused to renew in bad faith. Decide. [*Blackwell v. Kenworth Truck Co.*, 620 F.2d 104 (5th Cir.)]

CPA Question

1. A joint venture is a(an):
   a. Association limited to no more than two persons in business for profit.
   b. Enterprise of numerous co-owners in a nonprofit undertaking.
   c. Corporate enterprise for a single undertaking of limited duration.
   d. Association of persons engaged as co-owners in a single undertaking for profit.

Partnerships

Partnerships may be created without the formality of even a written partnership agreement when two or more individuals simply operate a business for a profit as co-owners. **For Example,** in July 2008, Paula Balzer was recruited to work for Blue Flame, a firm specializing in the business of marketing and live promotions. As of October 1, 2008, she states she was made a partner. Two firm e-mails reference her as a partner; she was paid a monthly $15,000 draw; and the firm's 2008 and 2009 tax returns listed her as a partner of Blue Flame. In October 2010, the partners had a falling-out with Paula. She disengaged from the firm on November 12, 2010, upon completion of two events she was committed to staging. The partners never executed a written partnership agreement with Paula and as a result did not believe she had partnership rights. When the firm failed to pay her certain money and expenses, the court reverted to basic partnership law that a written contract of partnership is not necessary to the formation of a partnership and concluded that a partnership existed on the basis of the facts before the court.[1] Partnership relations are governed by the partnership agreement. Only when the partnership agreement does not resolve an issue does partnership law apply. In many instances, individuals do not obtain legal advice in choosing the partnership form of business organization. Properly informed individuals today will probably not choose the partnership form of organization because partners are open to unlimited personal liability; they may choose a limited liability company to insulate the members from personal liability.

41-1 Nature and Creation

Partnerships are created by agreement. States have partnership laws that apply when there is no written agreement or to fill gaps in the partnership agreement. All states except Louisiana have adopted either the Uniform Partnership Act (UPA) or the Revised Uniform Partnership Act (RUPA), which is more detailed than the UPA.[2] Certain features of the RUPA that differ from those of the UPA are identified in the text. At common law, a partnership was considered to be an aggregate of the individual partners. Under the UPA and the RUPA, the partnership may be viewed as an entity separate from the partners for certain purposes. The RUPA enhances the entity theory of partnerships.[3] Under the aggregate theory, a partnership is characterized by the collection of its individual members. Consequently, if a partner dies or withdraws, the partnership ceases to exist. Under the entity theory, the partnership continues to exist as distinct from its partners, even if a partner dies or withdraws.[4] Even under the entity theory, however, each partner remains personally liable for the obligations of the partnership.[5] The 1994 or 1997 versions of the Revised Uniform Partnership Act apply in 38 states.[6] Limited partnerships (LPs) and limited liability partnerships (LLPs) differ significantly from general partnerships and are discussed in the next chapter.

41-1a Definition

A **partnership** (also called a **general partnership**) is a relationship created by the voluntary "association of two or more persons to carry on as co-owners a business for profit."[7] The persons so associated are called **partners** or **general partners.** A partner is the agent

partnership—pooling of capital resources and the business or professional talents of two or more individuals (partners) with the goal of making a profit.

general partnership—partnership in which the partners conduct as co-owners a business for profit, and each partner has a right to take part in the management of the business and has unlimited liability.

partner—one of two or more persons who jointly own and carry on a business for profit.

general partners—partners who publicly and actively engage in the transaction of firm business.

---

[1] *Balzer v. Millward*, 2011 WL 1547211 (D. Conn. April 21, 2011).
[2] The Louisiana Civil Code has many provisions similar to those in the UPA and RUPA.
[3] See *Mission West v. Republic*, 873 A.2d 372 (Md. App. 2005).
[4] See *Robertson v. Jacobs Cattle Co.*, 830 N.W.2d 191 (Neb. 2013).
[5] The UPA or the RUPA is in effect in all states except Louisiana.
[6] The RUPA was approved in 1992 and amended in 1993, 1994, and 1997. States that have adopted the RUPA provide for a transition period after passage during which only newly created partnerships come under the new law, with all partnerships in the state eventually being governed by the RUPA (see R.U.P.A. §1206(a)).
[7] U.P.A. §6(1).

of the partnership and of each partner with respect to partnership matters. A partner is not an employee of the partnership even when doing work that would ordinarily be done by an employee.

CASE SUMMARY

A Partner Is Not an Employee

FACTS: Ford and Mitcham were partners engaged in construction. Ford was killed at work. His widow made a claim for workers' compensation against the partnership. Mitcham opposed the claim on the ground that Ford was a partner, not an employee.

DECISION: Workers' compensation denied. While a working partner does work, a partner is not an employee. The essential element of an employment relationship is the right of the employer to control the employee. Although a partner is required to act in a proper manner, a partner is not subject to the control of the partnership in the same sense as an employee and therefore is not an "employee" of the partnership for the purpose of workers' compensation. [*Ford v. Mitcham*, 298 So. 2d 34 (Ala. App. 1974)]

41-1b Characteristics of a Partnership

A partnership has distinguishing characteristics:

1. A partnership is a voluntary, consensual relationship.
2. A partnership involves partners' contributions of capital, services, or a combination of these.
3. The partners are associated as co-owners to transact the business of the firm for profit.

unincorporated association– combination of two or more persons for the furtherance of a common nonprofit purpose.

If profit is not the object, the group will commonly be an **unincorporated association.**

Under the UPA, the partnership is not an entity separate from its partners and cannot bring suit in its own name, unless a special statute or procedural rule specifically allows. In RUPA states, however, partnerships are recognized as entities and suit may be brought against the partnership. In either case, plaintiffs must name the individual partners to have access to their individual assets.

41-1c Rights of Partners

The rights of partners are determined by the partnership agreement. If written, this agreement is interpreted by the same rules that govern the interpretation of any other written document. Any matter not covered by the partnership agreement may be covered by a provision of the UPA or RUPA, depending on which version the state has adopted.

41-1d Partnership Agreement

Partnership agreements are typically written to cover numerous, complex issues. However, there is no requirement that they be in writing unless compliance with a statute of frauds is required. **For Example,** the world's highest-paid performers in the early 1990s, the New Kids on the Block, who grossed $74.1 million in one year, were a group started by promoter Maurice Starr. He obtained $60,000 from James Martorano, who was connected with organized crime, and $50,000 from businessman Jeffrey Furst to finance the initial recording and promotion of the group. Martorano and Furst testified that, ultimately, all three agreed with a handshake that 50 percent of the profits from the group would be shared between Martorano as a silent partner and Furst, who would also provide limousine service and security. They testified that Starr would keep half of the profits. Starr denied that a partnership existed because he believed that such an alleged business arrangement would have had to be reduced to writing with great detail. However, based on the evidence, which included damaging testimony that Starr tried to buy some witnesses' silence, a jury decided that a binding oral partnership agreement existed.[8]

To reduce or avoid disputes and litigation, partnership agreements should be in writing. Courts will enforce partnership agreements, under the standards of the law of contracts, according to the terms of the agreement.[9] **For Example,** dentist Steven Schwartz was terminated from a three-dentist practice "without cause" by vote of his two other partners. The partnership agreement allowed for termination of a partner as long as either party gave the other 90 days' notice. The appeals court held that the written terms of the agreement were determinative. The parties were sophisticated and highly educated professionals and the provision was not in violation of public policy.[10]

The formal document that is prepared to evidence the contract of the parties is termed a **partnership agreement, articles of partnership,** or **articles of copartnership.** The partnership agreement governs the partnership during its existence and may contain provisions relating to dissolution. (See Figure 41-1.)

partnership agreement–document prepared to evidence the contract of the parties. (Parties—partners or general partners)

articles of partnership–see *partnership agreement.*

articles of copartnership–see *partnership agreement.*

FIGURE 41-1   Partnership Agreement

PARTNERSHIP AGREEMENT
THIS IS A PARTNERSHIP AGREEMENT EXECUTED AT CINCINNATI, OHIO, THIS 9TH DAY OF SEPTEMBER, 1998, BY AND AMONG LOUIS K. HALL, SHARON B. YOUNG, AND C. LYNN MUELLER, INDIVIDUALS RESIDING IN CINCINNATI, OHIO, HEREINAFTER SOMETIMES REFERRED TO INDIVIDUALLY AS "PARTNER" AND COLLECTIVELY AS "PARTNERS."

RECITALS
THE PARTNERS TO THIS AGREEMENT DESIRE TO ACQUIRE A CERTAIN PARCEL OF REAL ESTATE AND TO DEVELOP SUCH REAL ESTATE FOR LEASE OR SALE, ALL FOR INVESTMENT PURPOSES. THIS AGREEMENT IS BEING EXECUTED TO DELINEATE THE BASIS OF THEIR RELATIONSHIP.

PROVISIONS
1. NAME; AND PRINCIPAL OFFICES. THE NAME OF THE PARTNERSHIP SHALL BE: HALL, YOUNG AND MUELLER, ASSOCIATES. ITS PRINCIPAL PLACE OF BUSINESS SHALL BE AT: 201 RIVER ROAD, CINCINNATI, OHIO 45238.
2. PURPOSE. THE PURPOSE OF THE PARTNERSHIP SHALL BE TO PURCHASE AND OWN FOR INVESTMENT PURPOSES, A CERTAIN PARCEL OF REAL ESTATE LOCATED AT 602 SIXTH STREET, CINCINNATI, OHIO, AND TO ENGAGE IN ANY OTHER TYPE OF INVESTMENT ACTIVITIES THAT THE PARTNERSHIP MAY FROM TIME TO TIME HEREINAFTER UNANIMOUSLY AGREE UPON.
3. CAPITAL CONTRIBUTIONS. THE CAPITAL OF THE PARTNERSHIP SHALL BE THE AGGREGATE AMOUNT OF CASH AND PROPERTY CONTRIBUTED BY THE PARTNERS. A CAPITAL ACCOUNT SHALL BE MAINTAINED FOR EACH PARTNER.
A. CAPITAL CONTRIBUTIONS. ANY ADDITIONAL CAPITAL WHICH MAY BE REQUIRED BY THE PARTNERSHIP SHALL BE CONTRIBUTED TO THE PARTNERSHIP BY THE PARTNERS IN THE SAME RATIO AS THAT PARTNER'S ORIGINAL CONTRIBUTION TO CAPITAL AS TO THE TOTAL OF ALL ORIGINAL CAPITAL CONTRIBUTIONS TO THE PARTNERSHIP UNLESS OTHERWISE AGREED BY THE PARTNERS.

[8] Judy Rakowsky, "New Kids' Profits on the Block," *Boston Globe*, November 18, 1995.
[9] *Krajacich v. Great Falls Clinic*, 276 P.3d 922 (Mont. 2012).
[10] *Schwartz v. Family Dental Group*, P.C., 943 A.2d 1122 (Conn. App. 2008).

CPA   41-1e **Determining the Existence of a Partnership**

If the parties agree to operate a business for profit as co-owners, a partnership is created even though the parties may not have labeled their new relationship as such.[11] The law is concerned with the substance of the relationship rather than the name. Conversely, a partnership does not arise if the parties do not agree to the elements of a partnership even though they call it one.[12]

CASE SUMMARY

The Case of the Absolutely Dumbfounded Investor (Partner)

FACTS: David Byker, an accountant, and Tom Mannes, a real estate professional, agreed to engage in an ongoing business enterprise to raise investment funds for separate real estate–related ventures and to share equally in the profits, losses, and expenses. Over the years, the parties pursued various individual limited partnerships, sharing equally in commissions, financing fees, and termination costs. Byker and Mannes then created a subsequent entity, Pier 1000, Ltd., to own and manage a marina. This venture was not successful, and they took profits from a prior entity and borrowed money to continue operations. The unsuccessful marina was later returned to its previous owners in exchange for assumption of Byker's and Mannes's direct obligations to that business. The nine-year business relationship between them ceased. Later, Byker approached Mannes and requested that he share in the payments resulting from losses that were incurred from their various entities. Mannes was, in his words, "absolutely dumbfounded" by the request, and he refused payment. Byker sued, contending that a general partnership was underlying all their business affairs. Mannes asserted that he merely invested in separate business ventures with Byker and that there were no other understandings between them.

DECISION: Judgment for David Byker. Partnership law does not require that individuals be aware of their status as "partners" to have a legal partnership. The intent to create a partnership is not required if the acts and the conduct of the parties otherwise evidence that the parties carried on as co-owners of a business for profit. No writing is needed to form a partnership. No name or tax ID number is necessary to attain legal status as a partnership, nor is it required that the parties must aggregate all entities under a general partnership tax return. Mannes filed his tax returns based on his share of the income and expense from the individual legal entities that existed with the legal status of each entity controlling his tax obligations. However, additional evidence indicated that a partnership existed, including the general agreement in principle from the beginning that they would share profits and losses together in their real estate investment business. While they should have created a legal entity to address the situation that precipitated the lawsuit, because they did not, partnership law applies. [*Byker v. Mannes*, **641 N.W.2d 210 (Mich. 2002)**]

A partnership is shown to exist when it is established that the parties have agreed to the formation of a business organization that has the characteristics of a partnership. The burden of proving the existence of a partnership is on the person who claims that one exists.[13]

When the nature of the relationship is not clear, the following rules aid in determining whether the parties have created a partnership.

CPA   **Control**

The presence or absence of control of a business enterprise is significant in determining whether there is a partnership and whether a particular person is a partner.

[11] *Swecker v. Swecker*, 360 S.W.3d 422 (Tenn. App. 2011).
[12] See *Cleland v. Thirion*, 704 N.Y.S.2d 316 (A.D. 2000).
[13] *MacArthur v. Stein*, 934 P.2d 214 (Mont. 1997).

CPA ### Sharing Profits and Losses

The fact that the parties share profits and losses is strong evidence of a partnership.[14]

CPA ### Sharing Profits

An agreement that does not provide for sharing losses but does provide for sharing profits is evidence that the parties are partners. If the partners share profits, it is assumed that they will also share losses. Sharing profits is prima facie evidence of a partnership. However, a partnership is not to be inferred when profits are received in payment (1) of a debt, (2) of wages, (3) of an annuity to a deceased partner's surviving spouse or representative, (4) of interest, or (5) for the goodwill of the business.[15] **For Example,** the fact that one doctor receives one-half of the net income does not establish that doctor as a partner of another doctor when the former was guaranteed a minimum annual amount. Also, federal income tax and Social Security contributions were deducted from the payments to the doctor, thus indicating that the relationship was that of employer and employee. If there is no evidence of the reason for receiving the profits, a partnership of the parties involved exists.

CPA ### Gross Returns

The sharing of gross returns is itself very slight, if any, evidence of a partnership.

CPA ### Contribution of Skill or Labor

The fact that all persons have not contributed capital to an enterprise does not establish that the enterprise is not a partnership. A partnership may be formed even though some of its members furnish only skill or labor.

CPA ### Fixed Payment

When a person who performs continuing services for another receives a fixed payment that does not depend on the existence of profit and is not affected by losses, that person is not a partner.

CPA ## 41-1f Partners as to Third Persons

In some instances, persons who are in fact not partners may be held liable to third persons as though they were partners. This liability arises when they conduct themselves in such a manner that others are reasonably led to believe that they are partners and to act in reliance on that belief to their injury.[16] A person who is held liable as a partner under such circumstances is termed a *nominal partner, a partner by estoppel,* or an *ostensible partner.*

Partnership liability may arise by estoppel when a person who in fact is not a partner represents herself as a partner or consents to another representing her as a partner. The person is liable to any such person to whom such representation is made. To prevail on a partnership by estoppel claim, the plaintiff must have reasonably relied on the representation of partnership or joint venture status. **For Example,** purchasers of condominiums at Las Vegas Cay Club sued those who represented that they were in a partnership with the developer. The purchasers claimed that they relied on marketing materials that indicated Cay Clubs was in a partnership with certain entities and that they bought the condominiums relying on the expertise and resources of these purported partners to develop the luxury resort. When the developers abandoned the project, the purchasers were left

---

[14] *Botsee Gates v. Houston,* 897 N.E.2d 532 (Ind. App. 2008).
[15] U.P.A. §7(4).
[16] U.P.A. §16(1); *Andrews v. Elwell,* 367 F. Supp. 2d 35 (D. Mass. 2005).

with "worthless property." The court concluded that under Nevada law partnership by estoppel applied because the purchasers reasonably relied on the representation that Cay Clubs was in a partnership with established developers.[17] Under the RUPA, an apparent partnership or partnership by estoppel is called a *purported* partnership, and a third person who relies on the partnership's representations that the purported partner had authority to bind the partnership can hold it liable as if the purported partner were an actual partner with authority.[18] Under the RUPA, a partnership can limit potential liability with a publicly recorded statement of partnership authority or limitation on partner authority.[19]

CPA ### 41-1g Partnership Property

In general, partnership property consists of all property contributed by the partners or acquired for the firm or with its funds.

There is usually no limitation on the type and amount of property that a partnership may acquire. The firm may own real as well as personal property unless it is prohibited from doing so by statute or by the partnership agreement.

The parties may agree that real estate owned by one of the partners should become partnership property. When this intent exists, the particular property constitutes partnership property even if it is still in the name of the original owner.

Article 2 of the RUPA recognizes that partnerships are "entities" that can acquire and own property in the partnership's name. If a partner desires to retain an interest in property contributed to the partnership in RUPA states, the partner must condition the transfer of the property to the partnership to reflect this interest or set forth the condition in the partnership agreement. Otherwise, the property becomes partnership property under the entity theory, and the contributing partner has no right to get it back, even in liquidation.[20]

41-1h Tenancy in Partnership

tenancy in partnership— ownership relationship that exists between partners under the Uniform Partnership Act.

Under the UPA, partners hold title to firm property by **tenancy in partnership.**[21] The characteristics of such a tenancy are as follows:

1. Each partner has an equal right to use firm property for partnership purposes in the absence of a contrary agreement.

2. A partner possesses no divisible interest in any specific item of partnership property that can be voluntarily sold, assigned, or mortgaged by a partner.

charging order—order by a court, after a business partner's personal assets are exhausted, requiring that the partner's share of the profits be paid to a creditor until the debt is discharged.

3. A creditor of a partner cannot proceed against any specific items of partnership property. The creditor can proceed only against the partner's interest in the partnership. This is done by applying to a court for a **charging order.** By this procedure, the share of any profits that would be paid to the debtor-partner is paid to a receiver on behalf of the creditor, or the court may direct the sale of the interest of the debtor-partner in the partnership.

4. Upon the death of a partner, the partnership property vests in the surviving partners for partnership purposes and is not subject to the rights of the surviving spouse of the deceased partner.

[17] In re *Cay Clubs*, 130 Nev. Adv. 14 (2014).
[18] R.U.P.A. §308.
[19] R.U.P.A. §303.
[20] R.U.P.A. §204.
[21] U.P.A. §25(1); *Krause v. Vollmar*, 614 N.E.2d 1136 (Ohio App. 1992).

CPA ### 41-1i **Assignment of a Partner's Interest**

Although a partner cannot transfer specific items of partnership property in the absence of authority to so act on behalf of the partnership, a partner's interest in the partnership may be voluntarily assigned by the partner. The assignee does not become a partner without the consent of the other partners. Without this consent, the assignee is entitled to receive only the assignor's share of the profits during the continuance of the partnership and the assignor's interest upon the dissolution of the firm. The assignee has no right to participate in the management of the partnership or to inspect the books of the partnership.

41-2 **Authority of Partners**

The scope of a partner's authority is determined by the partnership agreement and by the nature of the partnership. **For Example,** in a family farming partnership, the agreement specified that whenever there were more than two managing partners, the approval of a majority of the managing partners was required to act on behalf of the partnership. One of the managing partners entered into a series of grain contracts on behalf of the partnership, which led to substantial losses. The court found that he had no right to bind the partnership to the contracts without a majority vote of the managing partners. The consequences for the unauthorized partner were grave. Because he did not have authority and did not act in good faith, he was held personally liable for the partnership's losses.[22]

41-2a **Authority of Majority of Partners**

When there are more than two partners in a firm, the decision of the majority prevails in matters involving how the ordinary functions of the business will be conducted. Thus, if a majority of the partners of a firm decide to increase the firm's advertising and enter into a contract for that purpose, the transaction is valid and binds the firm and all of the partners.

Majority action is not binding if it contravenes the partnership agreement. For such matters, unanimous action is required.[23] Thus, the majority of the members cannot change the nature of the business against the protests of the minority.

When there is an even number of partners, an even division on a matter that requires majority approval is always a possibility. In such a case, the partnership is deadlocked. When the partners are evenly divided on any question, one partner has no authority to act.

If the division is over a basic issue and the partners persist in the deadlock so that it is impossible to continue the business, any one of the partners may petition the court to order the dissolution of the firm.

41-2b **Express Authority of Individual Partners**

express authority—
authority of an agent to perform a certain act.

An individual partner may have **express authority** to perform certain acts either because the partnership agreement provides for such authority or because a sufficient number of partners have agreed to it.

A partner's authority to act for the firm is similar to that of an agent to act for a principal. Thus, in addition to express authority, a partner has the authority to do those acts that are customary for a member of a partnership conducting the particular business of that partnership.[24] As in the case of an agent, the acts of a partner in excess of authority do not ordinarily bind the partnership.

---

[22] *Elting v. Elting*, 849 N.W.2d 444 (Neb. 2014).
[23] U.P.A. §18(h).
[24] *Ball v. Carlson*, 641 P.2d 303 (Colo. App. 1981).

41-2c Customary Authority of Individual Partners

A partner, by virtue of being a comanager of the business, customarily has certain powers necessary and proper for carrying out that business. The scope of such powers varies with the nature of the partnership and with the business customs and usages of the area in which the partnership operates.

A partner may make any contract necessary to transact the firm's business.

CASE SUMMARY

"Jerry Should Have Run It by Me," Silvio Seethed

FACTS: Silvio Giannetti and his daughter and son-in-law, Anne Marie and Jerry Pruzinsky, are partners in a general partnership known as Giannetti Investment Company (GIC), which owns and operates Brougham Manor Apartments. Jerry entered into an access agreement with Omnicom, a provider of cable television services, giving Omnicom the right to enter Brougham Manor for purposes of installing, maintaining, and promoting cable service. Some time later, when he learned of the contract, Silvio denied Omnicom access to the property. Omnicom was unable to repair a signal leakage problem and was forced to discontinue cable

service. Omnicom sued GIC for breach of contract. GIC contended that Jerry did not sign the agreement in the partnership name and thereby failed to bind GIC.

DECISION: Judgment for Omnicom. A contract executed in the name of a partner is binding on the partnership. Jerry executed the contract in the usual course of GIC's business, for it is a typical activity for an apartment complex to contract for cable television. [*Omnicom v. Giannetti Investment Co.*, 561 N.W.2d 138 (Mich. App. 1997)]

A partner can sell the firm's goods in the regular course of business, make purchases within the scope of the business, and borrow money for firm purposes. When borrowing money, a partner may execute commercial paper in the firm's name or give security such as a mortgage.[25] A partner may purchase insurance, hire employees, and adjust claims for or against the firm. Notice given to a partner is effective notice to the partnership.[26]

41-2d Limitations on Authority

The partners may agree to limit the powers of each partner. When a partner, contrary to such an agreement, executes a contract on behalf of the firm with a third person, the firm is bound if the third person was unaware of the limitation and the partner violating the agreement is liable to the other partners for any loss caused by the breach of the limitation.[27] Under the UPA, if the third person knew of the limitation, the firm would not be bound.[28] Under the RUPA, the term *knew* is confined to actual knowledge,[29] which is cognitive awareness. Under the RUPA, a partnership may file a statement of partnership authority setting forth any restrictions on a general partner's authority.[30] **For Example,** Bernard Roeger was a general partner of RNR, with three limited partners. Restrictions were clearly set forth in the partnership agreement limiting Roeger's borrowing authority to no more than $650,000 for the construction of a building on partnership property. Roeger on behalf of RNR entered a construction loan agreement with People's Bank

---

[25] *U.S. Leather v. H&W Partnership,* 60 F.3d 222 (5th Cir. 1995).
[26] *Cham, Hill, Inc., v. Block & Veatch,* 557 N.W.2d 829 (Wis. App. 1996).
[27] *Blankenship v. Smalley,* 324 P.3d 573 (Or. App. 2014).
[28] U.P.A. §9(4).
[29] R.U.P.A. §102(a).
[30] R.U.P.A. §303.

| FIGURE 41-2 | Limitations on Authority of Individual Partner to Bind Partnership |

with a note and mortgage in the amount of $990,000, and over an 18-month period, the bank disbursed an aggregate sum of $952,699. The bank did not request a written consent from any of the other partners or review the partnership agreement. When the loan was not paid, the bank foreclosed on the property. RNR defended on behalf of the partnership that the bank negligently failed to investigate and discover the limitation on Roeger's authority to borrow. The case was decided for the bank because it had no actual knowledge or notice of the restriction on the general partner's authority. The court also pointed out that the partnership could have protected itself by filing a statement of partnership authority setting forth the restrictions on the general partner under RUPA section 303.[31]

A third person must not assume that a partner has all of the authority that the partner purports to have. If there is anything that would put a reasonable person on notice that the partner's powers are limited, the third person is bound by that limitation.

The third person must be on the alert for the following prohibited transactions because they warn that the partner with whom the third person deals has either restricted authority or no authority at all. (See Figure 41-2.)

41-2e **Prohibited Transactions**

A partner cannot enter into certain transactions on behalf of the partnership unless expressly authorized to do so. A third person entering into such a transaction does so at the risk that the partner has not been authorized. The following are prohibited transactions.

Cessation of Business

A partner cannot bind the firm by a contract that would make it impossible for the firm to conduct its usual business.[32]

---

[31] *RNR Investments, Ltd. v. People's First Community Bank*, 812 So. 2d 561 (Fla. App. 2002).
[32] *Wales v. Roll*, 769 P.2d 899 (Wyo. 1989).

CASE SUMMARY

Family Feud

FACTS: The Patel family, consisting of parents and a son, was a partnership that owned and operated a motel. The parents made a contract to sell the motel, but thereafter the son refused to sell. He claimed that the contract of sale was not binding.

DECISION: Judgment for the son. The motel was not an asset held by the partnership for sale. It was an asset that was essential for the running of the partnership/business. Accordingly, neither one partner nor a majority had implied authority to sell the motel. To the contrary, the unanimous consent of all partners was required for the sale of the motel because such a sale would make it impossible to continue the partnership business. [*Patel v. Patel*, 260 Cal. Rptr. 255 (Cal. App. 1989)]

Suretyship

A partner has no implied authority to bind the firm by contracts of surety, guarantee, or indemnity for purposes other than firm business.[33]

Arbitration

A partner cannot submit controversies of the firm to arbitration "unless authorized by the other partners or unless they have abandoned the business."[34]

Confession of Judgment

All partners should have an opportunity to defend in court. Consequently, a partner cannot confess judgment against the firm on one of its obligations. Exceptions exist when the other partners consent or when they have abandoned the business.

Assignment for Creditors

A partner cannot make a general assignment of firm property for the benefit of creditors unless authorized by the other partners or unless they have abandoned the business.

Personal Obligations

A partner cannot discharge personal obligations or claims of the firm by interchanging them in any way.

41-3 Duties, Rights, and Liabilities of Partners

The rights and duties of partners are based on their dual capacity of agent and co-owner.

41-3a Duties of Partners

In many respects, the duties of a partner are the same as those of an agent.

Loyalty and Good Faith

Each partner must act in good faith toward the partnership. One partner must not take advantage of the other(s) by the slightest misrepresentation or concealment.[35] Famous

---

[33] *First Interstate Bank of Oregon v. Bergendahl*, 723 P.2d 1005 (Or. App. 1986).
[34] U.P.A. §9(3)(e).
[35] *Brosseau v. Ranzau*, 81 S.W.3d 381 (Tex. App. 2002).

language from a decision authored by Justice Cardozo describes the duty of partners and joint venturers to each other, as follows: "Not honesty alone, but the punctilio of an honor the most sensitive, is then the standard of behavior."[36] Each partner also owes a duty of loyalty to the firm. This duty requires a partner's devotion to the firm's business and bars making any secret profit at the expense of the firm.[37]

Moreover, the duty of loyalty bars the use of the firm's property for personal benefit or the exploitation of a business opportunity of the partnership for personal gain. A partner cannot promote a competing business. A partner who does so is liable for damages sustained by the partnership.

Each partner also owes a fiduciary duty of good faith to all other partners. This duty extends to any transaction connected with the formation, conduct, or liquidation of the partnership.

A breach of fiduciary duty requires the complete forfeiture of all compensation during the period of the breach. **For Example,** general partners Michael Morton and Scott DeGraff breached their fiduciary duty to their partners when they did not disclose the parts of a deal they were keeping for themselves relating to a proposed relocation of the partnership's Las Vegas nightclub, Drink. Morton and DeGraff had been paid $833,190 in management fees during the period of time they were found to be in breach of their fiduciary duty to the partnership. The court ordered them to return these funds to the partnership.[38]

Obedience

Each partner is obligated to perform all duties and to obey all restrictions imposed by the partnership agreement or by the vote of the required number of partners.[39] **For Example,** when the partnership agreement required that each partner in an insurance sales firm give his "entire time" to the business and "not engage in any other business that would work to the disadvantage of the partnership," Richard Levatino's engaging in an insurance-related business outside the firm was a breach of the partnership agreement and was a proper basis for the assessment of punitive damages.[40]

Other Duties

The RUPA states that a partner must refrain from engaging in grossly negligent or intentional misconduct in transacting firm business.[41] Partners are accountable as a fiduciary and must hold as trustee for the firm any profits derived by a partner without the consent of the other partners.[42]

CPA   41-3b Rights of Partners as Owners

Each partner, in the absence of a contrary agreement, has the following rights. These rights stem from the fact that the partner is a co-owner of the partnership business.

CPA   Management

Each partner has a right to take an equal part in transacting the business of the firm. It is immaterial that one partner contributed more than another or that one contributed only services.

---

[36] *Meinhard v. Salmon*, 164 N.E. 545, 546 (N.Y. 1928).

[37] Under R.U.P.A. 404(e), partners may pursue their own interests without automatically violating their fiduciary duties to the firm.

[38] *Caparos v. Morton*, 845 N.E.2d 773 (Ill. App. 2006).

[39] *Cobin v. Rice*, 823 F. Supp. 1419 (D. Ind. 1993).

[40] *Gates, Duncan, and VanCamp v. Levatino*, 962 S.W.2d 21 (Tenn. App. 1997).

[41] R.U.P.A. §404(c).

[42] U.P.A. §21; R.U.P.A. §404(b)(1).

Incidental to the right to manage the partnership, each partner has the right to possession of the partnership property for the purposes of the partnership.

CPA   Inspection of Books

All partners are equally entitled to inspect the books of the firm. "The partnership books shall be kept, subject to any agreement between the partners, at the principal place of business of the partnership, and every partner shall at all times have access to and may inspect and copy any of them."[43]

CPA   Share of Profits

Each partner is entitled to a share of the profits. The partners may provide, if they so wish, that profits shall be shared in unequal proportions. In the absence of such a provision in the partnership agreement, each partner is entitled to an equal share of the profits without regard to the amount of capital contributed or services performed for the partnership.

CPA   Compensation

In the absence of a contrary agreement, a partner is not entitled to compensation for services performed for the partnership. There is no right to compensation even if the services are unusual or more extensive than the services rendered by other partners. Consequently, when one partner becomes seriously ill and the other partners transact all of the firm's business, they are not entitled to compensation for those services. The sickness of a partner is considered a risk assumed in the relationship. No agreement can be inferred that the active partners are to be compensated even though the services rendered by them are such that they would ordinarily be rendered in the expectation of receiving compensation. As an exception, "a surviving partner is entitled to reasonable compensation for services performed in winding up the partnership affairs."[44]

Partners may agree that one of the partners will work full time as manager of the business and receive for such services a salary in addition to the managing partner's share of the profits.

Repayment of Loans

A partner is entitled to the return of any money advanced to or for the firm. Such amounts must be separate and distinct from original or additional contributions to the capital of the firm.

CPA   Payment of Interest

In the absence of an agreement to the contrary, contributions to capital do not draw interest. The theory is that the profits constitute sufficient compensation. Advances by a partner in the form of loans are treated as if they were made by a stranger and bear interest from the date the advance is made. When the partnership business continues after dissolution, a retiring partner is entitled to interest on the value of her interest in the partnership.[45]

CPA   Contribution and Indemnity

A partner who pays more than a proportionate share of the debts of the firm has a right to contribution from the other partners. Under this principle, if an employee of a

---

[43] U.P.A. §19. See *Smith v. Brown & Jones*, 633 N.Y.S.2d 436 (Sup. Ct. 1995).
[44] U.P.A. §18(f).
[45] *Lewis v. Edwards*, 554 S.E.2d 17 (N.C. App. 2001).

partnership negligently injures a third person while acting within the scope of employment and if the injured party collects damages from one partner, the latter may enforce contribution from the other partners to divide the loss proportionately among them.

The partnership must indemnify every partner for payments made and personal liabilities reasonably incurred in the ordinary and proper conduct of its business or for the preservation of its business or property. A partner has no right, however, to indemnity or reimbursement if the partner has (1) acted in bad faith, (2) negligently caused the necessity for payment, or (3) previously agreed to assume the expense alone.[46]

CPA ## Distribution of Capital

After the payment of all creditors and the repayment of loans made to the firm by partners, every partner is entitled to receive a share of the firm property upon dissolution. Unless otherwise stated in the partnership agreement, all partners are entitled to the return of their capital contributions.

After such distribution is made, each partner is the sole owner of the fractional part distributed to that partner rather than a co-owner of all the property as during the existence of the partnership.

CPA ## 41-3c Liability of Partners and Partnership

The liability of a partnership and of the partners for the acts of individual partners and of employees is governed by the same principles that apply to the liability of an employer or a principal for the acts of an employee or agent. A partner may be vicariously liable for the acts of his partners, even if those acts are fraudulent. **For Example,** Joseph Palilla had a common law partnership in a used auto sales business with Lowell Andrews. Andrews bought used cars, purportedly to resell them, but never delivered the money to the sellers. Even though Palilla was unaware of his partner's fraud, the court held that the embezzlement was imputed to the innocent partner.[47]

joint liability–apportions partners' responsibility for partnership debt equally.

CPA ### Nature and Extent of Partner's Liability

joint and several liability– disproportionate satisfaction of partnership debt rendering each partner liable for the entire debt with the right to contribution from other partners.

Partners are **jointly liable** on all firm contracts. They are **jointly and severally liable** for all torts committed by an employee or one of the partners in the scope of the partnership business.[48] When partners are liable for the wrongful injury caused a third person, the latter may sue all or any of the members of the firm.

Partners who have satisfied a claim against the partnership have the right to contribution from the other partners, whereby the liability is apportioned among all partners. Unlike the UPA, partners under the RUPA are jointly and severally liable for both tort and contract obligations of the firm.[49] However, the RUPA alters the traditional applications of "joint and several" liability by requiring that the creditors and tort victims satisfy their claims against the partnership before pursuing the personal assets of a partner.

---

[46] *Gramacy Equities Corp. v. DuMont,* 531 N.E.2d 629 (N.Y.A.D.1988).

[47] In re *Palilla,* 439 B.R. 248 (D. Colo. 2013).

[48] See *Wayne Smith Construction v. Wolman, Durberstein,* 604 N.E.2d 157 (Ohio 1992), where the Ohio Supreme Court described joint liability and joint and several liability as follows: Joint liability apportions responsibility for a contractual debt equally, in the absence of a partnership agreement to the contrary, among the partners and thereby limits the creditor's execution on one individual partner's personal property to a *pro rata* share of the debt. Joint and several liability, on the other hand, allows for disproportionate satisfaction of the partnership obligation by rendering each general partner responsible for the entire amount of the partnership debt.

[49] R.U.P.A. §307(d).

CASE SUMMARY

"Joint Liability" and "Joint and Several Liability": A Big Difference

FACTS: PNC Bank sued two of the eight general partners of Washington Square Enterprises, Farinacci and Gruttadauria, for the unpaid balance of their partnership's business line of credit. The trial court entered judgment in the amount of $4,190.33 plus interest against each of the two partners. The trial court determined that the eight general partners were jointly liable, not jointly and severally liable, for the debt to PNC. In addition, it issued a separate judgment against Farinacci and Gruttadauria in the amount of one-eighth each of the entire debt of $33,522. PNC appealed, contending that the trial court should have found the partners jointly and severally liable or that the trial court should have apportioned the debt according to the percentages of each partner's ownership interest in the partnership, rather than dividing the debt equally among the eight partners.

DECISION: The trial court properly decided the case, holding the two partners jointly liable. In 2007 Ohio adopted the Revised Uniform Partnership Act (RUPA) effective January 1, 2010, which provides that all partners are liable jointly and severally for all obligations of the partnership unless otherwise agreed by the claimant or provided by law. However, the new law states that the RUPA language does not apply to partnerships formed prior to January 1, 2009. The Washington Square Partnership was formed in 1978. "Joint liability" apportions responsibility for a contractual debt equally among all general partners in the absence of a partnership agreement to the contrary. PNC Bank's contention that the judgment be apportioned according to the percentage of the partners' ownership interests is without legal precedent. [*PNC Bank N.A. v. Farinacci*, 964 N.E.2d 1124 (Ohio App. 2011)]

CPA ## Liability of New Partners

A person admitted as a partner into an existing partnership has *limited liability* for all obligations of the partnership arising before such admission. The preadmission claim may be satisfied only out of partnership property and does not extend to the individual property of the newly admitted partner.[50] **For Example,** Citizens Bank was unsuccessful in its attempt to satisfy part of a $1.2 million deficiency judgment against the Parkham-Woodman Medical partnership from the individual property of Dr. Hunley, who had joined the practice after the underlying obligation leading to the deficiency judgment was assumed.[51]

Effect of Dissolution on Partner's Liability

A partner remains liable after dissolution of the partnership unless expressly released by the creditors or unless all claims against the partnership have been satisfied. The dissolution of the partnership does not of itself discharge the existing liability of any partner. The individual property of a deceased partner may be reached to satisfy obligations of the partnership that were incurred while the deceased partner was alive. However, the individual creditors of the deceased partner have priority over the partnership creditors with respect to such property.[52]

41-3d Enforcement and Satisfaction of Creditors' Claims

A firm may be sued in the name of all individual partners doing business as the partnership, such as "*Plaintiff v. A, B, C, doing business as the Ajax Warehouse.*" The partners

---

[50] U.P.A. §17; see also U.P.A. §41(1), (7).
[51] *Citizens Bank v. Parkman Woodman Medical Associates*, 874 F. Supp. 705 (D. Mass. 1995).
[52] U.P.A. §36.

named are bound by the judgment against the firm if they have been properly served in the suit.

If a debt is contractual in origin, common law requires that the partnership's assets be resorted to and exhausted before partnership creditors can reach a partner's individual assets.[53]

Personal creditors of a partner must first pursue the assets of that partner for satisfaction of their claims. After a partner's personal assets are exhausted, the creditor may enforce the unpaid portion of a judgment by obtaining a charging order against the partner's interest in the partnership. Under such an order, a court requires that the partner's share of the profits be paid to the creditor until the debt is discharged.

41-4   Dissolution and Termination

The end of a partnership's existence is marked by dissolution and termination.

CPA   ### 41-4a   Effect of Dissolution

Dissolution is the "change in the relationship of the partners caused by any partner ceasing to be associated in the carrying on as distinguished from the winding-up of the business."[54] Dissolution does not necessarily mean that the business has ended. If the partnership agreement provides that the business is to be continued by the remaining partner(s), it will continue without a winding up, and the former partner's interest will be bought out according to the partnership agreement. Also, when breach of the partnership agreement causes dissolution, innocent partners may continue the business, provided they pay the breaching partner the value of his or her interest.[55]

If no legal basis exists to continue the business, dissolution ends the right of the partnership to exist as a going concern, but it does not end the existence of the partnership.[56] Dissolution is followed by a winding-up period at the conclusion of which the partnership's legal existence terminates.

Dissolution reduces the authority of the partners. From the moment of dissolution, the partners lose authority to act for the firm "except so far as may be necessary to wind up partnership affairs or to complete transactions begun but not then finished."[57] The vested rights of the partners are not extinguished by dissolving the firm, and the existing liabilities remain.

41-4b   Dissolution by Act of the Parties

A partnership may be dissolved by action of the parties. However, certain acts of the parties do not cause a dissolution.

Agreement

A partnership may be dissolved in accordance with the terms of the original agreement of the parties. This may be by the expiration of the period for which the relationship was to continue or by the performance of the object for which the partnership was organized.[58] The relationship may also be dissolved by subsequent agreement. The partners may agree to dissolve the firm before the lapse of the time specified in the articles of partnership or before the attainment of the object for which the firm was created.

---

[53] *McCune & McCune v. Mountain Bell Tel. Co.,* 758 P.2d 914 (Utah 1988).
[54] U.P.A. §29.
[55] U.P.A. §38 (2)(b).
[56] *Sheppard v. Griffin,* 776 S.W.2d 119 (Tenn. App. 1989).
[57] U.P.A. §33.
[58] U.P.A. §31(1)(a).

Expulsion

A partnership is dissolved by the expulsion of any partner from the business, whether or not authorized by the partnership agreement.[59]

Alienation of Interest

Neither a voluntary sale of a partner's interest nor an involuntary sale for the benefit of creditors works a dissolution of the partnership.

Withdrawal

A partner has the power to withdraw from the partnership at any time. However, if the withdrawal violates the partnership agreement, the withdrawing partner becomes liable to the copartners for damages for breach of contract.[60] When the relationship is for no definite purpose or time, a partner may withdraw without liability at any time.

CASE SUMMARY

The Business School Graduate Who Should Have Taken Business Law

FACTS: Geoffrey Buehler and Antonio Gelman formed a partnership by oral agreement after they graduated from business school. They aimed to raise $600,000 to search for and acquire a business with growth potential. They planned to sell the business at a profit. When they disagreed over ownership interest in the partnership, Buehler withdrew from the partnership. Gelman sued for breach of contract, claiming that Buehler could not unilaterally terminate his obligations under the agreement.

DECISION: Judgment for Buehler. New York's version of the Uniform Partnership Act states that a partnership may be dissolved by "the express will of any partner when no definite or particular undertaking is specified" in the partnership agreement. The critical issue is whether the partnership agreement set forth a "definite term" or identified a particular objective to be achieved. The temporal framework for the partnership plan was flexible. The length of time for soliciting investors, identifying the business, and purchasing and operating the enterprise before the sale could not be determined with reasonable certainty. The plan was also too "amorphous" to meet the statutory "particular undertaking" standard. Consequently, the breach of contract claim must be dismissed. [*Gelman v. Buehler*, 986 N.E.2d 914 (N.Y. App. 2013)]

41-4c Dissolution by Operation of Law

operation of law– attaching of certain consequences to certain facts because of legal principles that operate automatically, as contrasted with consequences that arise because of the voluntary action of a party designed to create those consequences.

A partnership is dissolved by **operation of law** in the following instances.

Death

A partnership is dissolved immediately upon the death of any partner. Thus, when the executor of a deceased partner carries on the business with the remaining partner, there is legally a new firm.

Bankruptcy

Bankruptcy of the firm or of one of the partners causes the dissolution of the firm; insolvency alone does not.

---

[59] *Susman v. Cypress Venture*, 543 N.E.2d 184 (Ill. App. 1989).
[60] *BPR Group v. Bendetson*, 906 N.E.2d 956 (Mass. 2009).

Illegality

A partnership is dissolved by an event that makes it unlawful for the business of the partnership to be carried on or for the members to carry it on in partnership. For example, when a statute specifies that it is unlawful for judges to engage in the practice of law, a law firm is dissolved when one of its members becomes a judge.

41-4d Dissolution by Decree of Court

A court may decree the dissolution of a partnership for proper cause. A court will not order the dissolution for trifling causes or temporary grievances that do not involve a permanent harm or injury to the partnership.

The filing of a complaint seeking a judicial dissolution does not in itself cause a dissolution of the partnership; it is the decree of the court that has that effect.

A partner may obtain a decree of dissolution for any of the following reasons.

Insanity

A partner has been judicially declared insane or of unsound mind.

Incapacity

One of the partners has become incapable of performing the terms of the partnership agreement.

Misconduct

One of the partners has been guilty of conduct that substantially prejudices the continuance of the business. The habitual drunkenness of a partner is a sufficient cause for judicial dissolution.

Impracticability

One of the partners persistently or willfully acts in such a way that it is not reasonably practicable to carry on the partnership business. Dissolution will be granted when dissensions are so serious and persistent that continuance is impracticable or when all confidence and cooperation between the partners have been destroyed. If management of the partnership is deadlocked, a court may exercise its discretion to dissolve the partnership.[61]

CASE SUMMARY

Strategy = Squeeze Out Dyas
Ethics (Trust, Fairness, Loyalty, Doing No Harm) = None
Law = Dissociation, Dissolution

FACTS: Edward Dyas and Joseph Della Ratta were equal owners of two hotels in Ocean City, Maryland. The "old" hotel was completed in 1988 and the "new" hotel was completed in 2006, with both properties owned under their Spa Motel General Partnership (Spa). They were also developers and equal owners of the Maresol Condominium project in Ocean City, which was completed in 2004 and held under Dyas's and Della Ratta's Bay View Limited Liability Company (Bay View). Della Ratta owned the construction company that built these projects, "DRI," and he also owned

---

[61] *Maree et al. v. ROMAR Joint Venture*, 763 S.E.2d 899 (Ga. App. 2014).

Strategy = Squeeze Out Dyas Ethics (Trust, Fairness, Loyalty, Doing No Harm) = None Law = Dissociation, Dissolution continued

"CMC," the company that managed the two hotels. Dyas believed that Della Ratta was attempting to squeeze him out from ownership of Spa and Bay View. Under Dyas's analysis, Della Ratta's strategy in the general partnership, Spa, was to call for a very substantial capital contribution to pay claims asserted by CMC for alleged advances made by it to pay for operational expenses and to pay claims to DRI for the new hotel's construction costs. Dyas contended that those calls were unauthorized because the underlying claims could not be substantiated and the partnership agreement required that the developers first seek a commercial loan.

With respect to Bay View, Dyas's theory of Della Ratta's squeeze-out strategy involved two ploys. First, that Della Ratta sought personally to purchase the loan from Severn Bank and obtain from it an assignment of the security instrument, on which Della Ratta then would foreclose, so that he could buy in at the foreclosure sale. Severn Bank, however, would not assign the loan to Della Ratta. Dyas further alleged that, as an alternate squeeze-out strategy, Della Ratta wrongfully refused to sell condominium units

in Maresol. The resulting illiquidity would deprive Bay View of the cash needed to repay Severn Bank, so that Della Ratta could buy Maresol at a foreclosure sale conducted by Severn Bank. After a 10-day trial, the circuit court concluded that Dyas had proven these allegations. The ultimate findings of the trial court were that it was "no longer reasonably practicable to carry on the business" of Spa or of Bay View and that Dyas "had proved to the court's satisfaction facts sufficient for the court to grant a dissolution" of the entities. The court further ordered dissociation of Della Ratta as a partner in Spa. The court supervised the winding up of the general partnership. Della Ratta appealed.

DECISION: Judgment for Dyas. A review of Della Ratta's activities while a partner in Spa demonstrates satisfactory grounds for the dissociation and dissolution determinations of the trial court since his conduct was such that it was "not reasonably practicable to carry on the business in partnership with him." [*Della Ratta v. Dyas*, 961 A.2d 629 (Md. App. 2008)]

Lack of Success

The partnership cannot continue in business except at a loss.

Equitable Circumstances

A decree of dissolution will be granted under any other circumstances that equitably call for a dissolution. Such a situation exists when one partner was induced by fraud to enter into the partnership.

CPA   41-4e Dissociation under the RUPA

Under the RUPA and its "entity" concept, a partner can leave the firm and not disrupt the partnership's legal existence. The RUPA uses the term *dissociation* for the departure of a partner[62] and reserves the term *dissolution* for those instances when a partner's departure results in the winding up and termination of the business.[63]

A partner has the absolute power to dissociate at will, just as a partner has the power to withdraw under the UPA, even if it is wrongful.[64] If wrongful, the partner is liable for damages for breach of contract.

A partner's dissociation from a firm ends the individual's right to participate in the management of the business.[65] It also ends the duty of loyalty owed the firm, and the individual may compete with the firm once dissociated.[66] If the partnership business continues after a partner dissociates from a firm, the partnership must buy out the dissociated

---

[62] R.U.P.A. §601 cmt 1.

[63] R.U.P.A. §801.

[64] R.U.P.A. §601(1), 602(a).

[65] In a two-person partnership, when one partner withdraws, the partnership is dissolved by operation of law because there cannot be a one-person partnership. The buyout rule of RUPA §701(b) does not apply, and the dissolution procedures take over. See *Corrales v. Corrales*, 129 Cal. Rptr. 3d 428 (Cal. App. 2011).

[66] R.U.P.A. §404(2).

partner's interest based on his share of the higher of the liquidation value of the firm or the value of the firm's business as a going concern on the date of dissociation, with interest.[67]

The RUPA created "notices" to deal with lingering authority of a dissociated partner based on apparent authority. To avoid liability, notice of lack of authority or liability should be given to customers and creditors regarding the dissociation of a partner. A filing with the Secretary of State limits liability and authority to 90 days after filing.[68] If no notice is given or filed, the partnership may be bound by the acts of a dissociated partner for up to two years after dissociation based on apparent authority.[69]

CPA 41-4f **Notice of Dissolution**

Under some circumstances, one partner may continue to possess the power to make a contract that binds the partnership even though the partnership has been dissolved.

Notice to Partners

When the firm is dissolved by the act of a partner, notice must be given to the other partners unless that partner's act clearly shows an intent to withdraw from or to dissolve the firm. If the withdrawing partner acts without notice to the other partners, that partner is bound by contracts created for the firm.

When the dissolution is caused by the act, death, or bankruptcy of a partner, each partner is liable to the copartners for a share of any liability created by any other partner acting for the partnership without knowledge or notice of the act, death, or bankruptcy of the partner who caused the dissolution.

CPA Notice to Third Persons

When dissolution is caused by the act of a partner or of the partners, notice must be given to third parties. A notice should expressly state that the partnership has been dissolved. Circumstances from which a termination may be inferred are generally not sufficient notice.

Thus, the fact that the partnership checks added the abbreviation *Inc.* after the partnership name was not sufficient notice that the partnership did not exist and that the business had been incorporated.

Actual notice of dissolution must be given to persons who have dealt with the firm.

CASE SUMMARY

Notice Necessary!

FACTS: Paul Babich ran a business under the name of House of Paul. The business became a partnership between Babich, Dyson, and Schnepp but continued under the same name. The partners arranged for printing advertising material with Philipp Lithographing Company, making contracts on three separate occasions for such printing. During the course of these dealings, the House of Paul became a corporation. When the printing bills were not paid in full, Philipp sued the partners as individuals. They claimed they were not liable because the corporation had made the contracts.

---

[67] R.U.P.A. §701(b). In *Rapport v. Gelfand*, 129 Cal. Rptr. 3d 670, 680 (Cal. App. 2011), the court interpreted the term *liquidation value* as used in R.U.P.A. §701(b) to mean the sale price of the separate assets based on their market value as determined by a willing and knowledgeable buyer and a willing and knowledgeable seller, neither of whom is under any compulsion to buy or sell. Thus, for purposes of section 701, subdivision (b), "liquidation value" does not incorporate the common definition of "liquidation," which generally implies some urgency for immediate cash.

[68] R.U.P.A. §704.

[69] R.U.P.A. §702.

DECISION: Whether or not the House of Paul was a corporation with respect to a particular contract was not important because no notice had been given of its change from a partnership to a corporation. Having originally done business with the defendant as a partnership, Philipp could hold the individual persons liable as partners until notice to the contrary was given to Philipp. [***Philipp Lithographing Co. v. Babich***, 135 N.W.2d 343 (Wis. 1965)]

For persons who have had no dealings with the firm, a publication of the fact of dissolution is sufficient. Such notice may be by newspaper publication, by posting a placard in a public place, or by any similar method. Failure to give proper notice continues the power of each partner to bind the others with respect to third persons on contracts within the scope of the business.

When dissolution has been caused by operation of law, notice to third persons is not required. As between the partners, however, the UPA requires knowledge or notice of dissolution by death and bankruptcy.

41-4g Winding Up Partnership Affairs

Most established partnerships deal with the question of how to proceed with the business upon the death of a partner in the written partnership agreement. The agreement may set forth a method for establishing the value of the deceased partner's interest as of the date of death or allow for the remaining partners to purchase the deceased partner's interest. The agreement may also allow for the continuation of the business as usual while the valuation process is completed. However, in the absence of an agreement, either express or implied, permitting the surviving partners to continue the business, the partners must wind up the business and account for the share of the deceased partner.[70]

When dissolution is obtained by court decree, the court may appoint a receiver to conduct the winding up of the partnership business. This may be done in the usual manner, or the receiver may sell the business as a going concern to those partners who wish to continue its operation.

With a few exceptions, all partners have the right to participate in the winding up of the business.[71]

CPA 41-4h Distribution of Assets

Creditors of the firm have first claim on the assets of the partnership.[72] Difficulty arises when there is a contest between the creditors of the firm and the creditors of the individual partners. The general rule is that firm creditors have first claim on assets of the firm. The individual creditors share in the remaining assets, if any.

After the firm's liabilities to nonpartners have been paid, the assets of the partnership are distributed as follows: (1) each partner is entitled to a refund of advances made to or for the firm, (2) contributions to the capital of the firm are then returned, and (3) the remaining assets, if any, are divided equally as profits among the partners unless there is some other agreement. A partner who contributes only services to the partnership is not considered to have made a capital contribution, absent an agreement to the contrary.

---

[70] *Chaney v. Burdett*, 560 S.E.2d 21 (Ga. 2002); *King v. Stoddard*, 104 Cal. Rptr. 903 (Cal. App. 1972).
[71] U.P.A. §37. In *Urbain v. Beierling*, 835 N.W.2d 455 (Mich. App. 2013), the court found that a partner who was excluded from the winding up should have been given the right to participate, but she could not show that she was damaged.
[72] *Holmes v. Holmes*, 849 P.2d 1140 (Or. App. 1993).

CASE SUMMARY

Are Time and Labor Capital Contributions? Fred Ott Says They Ought to Be

FACTS: Fred Ott and Charles Corley were partners doing business as "Lakewood Associates, a general partnership." Corley provided the capital to purchase the land to be sold by the partnership, called Lakewood Estates. Corley brought suit for the dissolution of the partnership, and Ott contended that his contributions of time and labor in improving Lakewood Estates should be credited to him as capital contributions in the distribution of assets.

DECISION: Judgment for Corley. There was no evidence of any agreement between the partners that Ott's services should be credited as capital contributions. Therefore, the value of the services could not be credited as capital contributions in the distribution of assets. [***Corley v. Ott***, 485 S.E.2d 97 (S.C. 1997)]

If the partnership has sustained a loss, the partners assume it equally in the absence of a contrary agreement. Distribution of partnership assets must be made on the basis of actual value when it is clear that the book values are merely nominal or arbitrary amounts.

A provision in a partnership agreement that upon the death of a partner the interest of the partner shall pass to that partner's surviving spouse is valid. Such a provision takes effect against the contention that it is not valid because it does not satisfy the requirements applicable to wills.

41-4i Continuation of Partnership Business

As a practical matter, the business of the partnership is commonly continued after dissolution and winding up. In all cases, however, there is a technical dissolution, winding up, and termination of the life of the original partnership.

If the business continues, either with the surviving partners or with additional partners, it is a new partnership. Again, as a practical matter, the liquidation of the old partnership may in effect be merely a matter of bookkeeping entries, with all partners contributing again or relending to the new business any payment to which they would be entitled from the liquidation of the original partnership.

Make the Connection

Summary

A *partnership* is a relationship created by the voluntary association of two or more persons to carry on as co-owners a business for profit.

A partnership agreement governs the partnership during its existence and may also contain provisions relating to dissolution. The partnership agreement will generally be in writing, and this may be required by the statute of frauds. The existence of a partnership may be found from the existence of shared control in the running of the business and the fact that the parties share profits and losses. The sharing of gross returns, as opposed to profits, is slight evidence of a partnership.

Partners hold title to firm property by tenancy in partnership. A creditor of a partner cannot proceed against any specific item of partnership property but must obtain a charging order to seize the debtor-partner's share of the profits. An assignee of a partner's interest does not become a partner without the consent of the other partners and is entitled only to a share of the profits and the assignor's interest upon dissolution.

When there are more than two partners in a firm, the decisions of the majority prevail on ordinary matters relating to the firm's business unless the partnership agreement provides otherwise. A partner's authority to act for the firm is similar to that of an agent to act for a principal. A partner may not bind the firm by a contract that makes it impossible for the firm to conduct its business.

A partner's duties are the same as those of an agent. If there is no contrary agreement, each partner has the right to take an equal part in the management of the business, to inspect the books, to share in the profits, and after payment of all of the firm's debts and the return of capital, to share in the firm's property or surplus upon dissolution.

Partners have unlimited personal liability for partnership liabilities. Partners are jointly liable on all firm contracts. They are jointly and severally liable for all torts committed by one of the partners or by a firm employee within the scope of the partnership's business. A partner remains liable after dissolution unless expressly released by creditors. An incoming partner is not liable for the existing debts of the partnership unless the new partner expressly assumes those debts.

Dissolution ends the right of the partnership to exist as a going concern. Dissolution is followed by a winding-up period and the distribution of assets. A partnership may be dissolved by the parties themselves in accordance with the terms of the partnership agreement, by the expulsion of a partner, by the withdrawal of a partner, or by the bankruptcy of the firm or one of the partners. A court may order dissolution of a partnership upon the petition of a partner because of the insanity, incapacity, or major misconduct of a partner. Dissolution may be decreed because of lack of success, impracticability, or other circumstances that equitably call for dissolution. Notice of dissolution, except dissolution by operation of law, must be given. Actual notice must be given to those who have dealt with the firm as a partnership.

All partners generally have a right to participate in the winding up of the business. After the firm's liabilities to nonpartners have been paid, the assets are distributed among the partners as follows: (1) refund of advances, (2) return of contributions to capital, and (3) division of remaining assets in accordance with the partnership agreement or, if no agreement is stated, division of net assets equally among the partners.

Learning Outcomes

After studying this chapter, you should be able to clearly explain:

41-1   Nature and Creation

LO.1   Explain how partnerships are created by agreement, and understand that only when the partnership agreement does not resolve an issue does partnership law apply

See the example of the dentist who was terminated from the three-person dental partnership without cause by majority vote, where the partnership agreement allowed for such a termination, page 843.

LO.2   Understand that no writing is needed to form a partnership, nor a tax ID number, nor a partnership name. All that is needed is clear evidence that the partners carried on as co-owners of a business for profit

See the *Byker* case where one individual who carried on a business for a profit was dumbfounded to find out that he was, by law, a partner, page 844.

41-2   Authority of Partners

LO.3   Distinguish between express authority and customary authority of a partner to act for a partnership

See the discussion on the role of individual partners to act as expressly directed by a majority of partners (express authority) and to act on their own to make ordinary contracts necessary to transact the firm's business (customary authority), pages 847–848.

41-3   Duties, Rights, and Liabilities of Partners

LO.4   List the duties of partners to one another

See the discussion and examples of partners' duties of loyalty, good faith, and obedience, pages 850–851.

LO.5   Explain the nature and extent of a partner's liability on firm contracts and torts

41-4   Dissolution and Termination

LO.6   Describe how a partnership may be dissolved by the acts of partners, by operation of law, and by order of the court

See the *Della Ratta* case involving partnership dissolution by decree of court because of impracticability, pages 857–858.

See the *Gelman* case discussing unilateral termination of an oral partnership agreement, page 856.

Key Terms

articles of copartnership
articles of partnership
charging order
express authority
general partners

general partnership
jointly and severally liable
jointly liable
operation of law
partners

partnership
partnership agreement
tenancy in partnership
unincorporated association

Questions and Case Problems

1. Ray, Linda, and Nancy form a partnership. Ray and Linda contribute property and cash. Nancy contributes only services. Linda dies, and the partnership is liquidated. After all debts are paid, the surplus is not sufficient to pay back Linda's estate and Ray for the property and cash originally contributed by Linda and Ray. Nancy claims that the balance should be divided equally among Ray, Linda's estate, and Nancy. Is she correct?

2. Baxter, Bigelow, Owens, and Dailey were partners in a New York City advertising agency. Owens, who was in poor health and wanted to retire, advised the partners that she had assigned her full and complete interest in the partnership to her son, Bartholomew, a highly qualified person with 10 years of experience in the advertising business. Baxter, Bigelow, and Dailey refused to allow Bartholomew to attend management meetings and refused his request to inspect the books. Bartholomew pointed out that his mother had invested as much in the firm as any other partner. He believed, as assignee of his mother's full and complete partnership interest, that he is entitled to (a) inspect the books as he sees fit and (b) participate fully in the management of the firm. Was Bartholomew correct?

3. Amy Gargulo and Paula Frisken operated as a partnership Kiddies Korner, an infants' and children's clothing store. They operated the business very successfully for three years, with both Paula and Amy doing the buying and Paula keeping the books and paying the bills. Amy and Paula decided to expand the business when an adjoining store became vacant. At the same time, they incorporated the business. Children's Apparel, Inc., was a major supplier to the business before the expansion. After the expansion, business did not increase as anticipated, and when a nationally known manufacturer of children's apparel opened a factory outlet nearby, the business could no longer pay its bills. Children's Apparel, which had supplied most of the store's stock after expansion, sued Amy and Paula as partners for bills due for

expansion stock. Children's Apparel did not know that Amy and Paula had incorporated. Amy and Paula contended that the business was incorporated and that they therefore were not liable for business debts occurring after incorporation. Were Amy and Paula correct?

4. Calvin Johnson and Rudi Basecke did business as the Stockton Cheese Co., a partnership, which owned a building and equipment. The partners agreed to dissolve the partnership but never got around to completing the winding-up process. Calvin continued to use the building and to pay insurance on it but removed Rudi's name as an insured on the policy. When the building was later destroyed by fire, Calvin claimed the proceeds of the fire insurance policy because he and his wife were the named insureds on the policy and they had paid the premiums. Rudi claimed that although the partnership was dissolved before the fire, the winding up of the partnership was not completed at the time of the fire. He therefore claimed that he was entitled to half of the net proceeds of the policy. Decide. [*State Casualty v. Johnson*, 766 S.W.2d 113 (Mo. App.)]

5. Samuel Shaw purchased a ticket through Delta Airlines to fly a "Delta Connection" flight on SkyWest Airlines to Elko, Nevada. He was seriously injured when the SkyWest plane crashed near Elko. SkyWest's relationship with Delta was a contractual business referral arrangement, whereby Delta benefits through its charges for issuing tickets to connecting passengers to and from smaller communities, and SkyWest benefits from revenue generated by passengers sent to it by Delta. Both firms make a profit from this arrangement. SkyWest and Delta are often mentioned together by Delta in national print advertisements. Shaw believed that regardless of how the airlines characterize themselves, these airlines are in fact partners because they share profits from their combined efforts. Delta contended that it had no control over SkyWest's airplane operations and that sharing profits as compensation for services does not

create a partnership. Decide. [*Shaw v. Delta Airlines, Inc.*, 798 F. Supp. 1453 (D. Nev.)]

6. After graduating from Vanderbilt University with a degree in economics, James Pettes worked for Video Magic, a video rental business. In 1987, Dr. Gordon Yukon, a pediatrician, wanted to invest in a two-store video business called Rent-a-Flick. One store was located on Quince Road and the other in Germantown. Pettes testified that Yukon paid $42,000 for the business and that he and Yukon agreed they would be partners. Pettes would manage the two stores and earn the same amount he earned at Video Magic. Pettes testified that he worked 70 to 80 hours a week and that his "sweat equity" was a capital contribution to the partnership. He also testified that Yukon frequently referred to him as a partner. According to Pettes, in 1992, the parties agreed to divide the business, with the Germantown store going to Yukon and the Quince Road store to Pettes. In December 1992, Pettes made a written demand for an accounting. On January 5, 1993, Dr. Yukon "fired" Pettes. Sutherland, an employee, testified that when she questioned Yukon about firing a partner, Yukon did not deny that there was a partnership but stated that Pettes could not prove there was a partnership because there was no written agreement. Pettes sued for breach of an oral partnership agreement and an accounting. Decide. [*Pettes v. Yukon*, 912 S.W.2d (Tenn. App.)]

7. Two brothers, Eugene and Marlowe Mehl, formed a partnership to operate the family farm. One year, Eugene Mehl withdrew $7,200 from the partnership account and bought the Dagmar Bar. The warranty deed and the liquor license to the bar were obtained in the names of Eugene Mehl and his wife, Bonnie. In a subsequent lawsuit, Marlowe claimed that the bar was a partnership asset. Decide. [*Mehl v. Mehl*, 786 P.2d 1173 (Mont.)]

8. Summers and Dooley formed a partnership to collect trash. Summers became unable to work and he hired a third man to do his work and paid him out of his personal funds. Summers suggested to Dooley that the third man be paid from the partnership funds, but Dooley refused to do so. Summers sued Dooley for reimbursement of the money he spent to pay the third man. Decide.

9. Thomas Bartomeli decided to leave his employment to join his brother Raymond full-time in a small construction company. The brothers each contributed individual assets to the company and worked together to acquire equipment with both signing notes jointly to acquire certain equipment. Thomas considered himself a partner in the company; Raymond often referred to Thomas as his partner. It was the practice of the company to garage the equipment at Thomas's house. In 1983, the company was incorporated, but Thomas never held any shares in the company. On several occasions, Thomas's careless operation of equipment resulted in loss or damage to the company. Raymond became dissatisfied with Thomas's work performance, and on January 17, 1991, Thomas was removed as secretary of the corporation.

On April 19, 1991, Thomas went to the company office and demanded a blank check from the secretary. Raymond found out about this demand and fired him. On April 20, 1991, Thomas demanded from Raymond either 50 percent of the company or certain equipment owned by the company. On April 22, 1991, Thomas was removed as vice president of the company. Raymond attempted to reach an agreement with Thomas on a division of company assets at that point but was not successful. Thereafter, Thomas sued his brother, alleging that Raymond had breached the brothers' contract of partnership. Because the company was a corporation, is it legally inconsistent for Thomas to contend that there was a contract for partnership in the company? How would you decide this case? [*Bartomeli v. Bartomeli*, 783 A.2d 1050 (Ct. App.)]

10. Friedman, the "O" Street Carpet Shop, Inc., and Langness formed a partnership known as NFL Associates. "O" Street Carpet's net contribution to capital was $5,004; Langness contributed $14,000 in cash; and Friedman contributed his legal services, on which no value was placed by the articles of partnership. The articles stated that Friedman was entitled to 10 percent of the profits and that Langness was to receive payments of $116.66 per month. The partnership's accountant treated the payments to Langness as a return of her capital. Years later, the partnership sold the rental property owned by the partnership, and the partnership was wound up. Friedman claimed that he was entitled to 10 percent of the partnership capital upon dissolution. Langness claimed that Friedman was not entitled to a capital distribution and that the monthly payments to her should not have been treated as a return of capital. Decide. [*Langness v. "O" Street Carpet, Inc.*, 353 N.W.2d 709 (Neb.)]

11. Ross, Marcos, and Albert are partners. Ross and Marcos each contributed $60,000 to the partnership; Albert contributed $30,000. At the end of the fiscal year, distributable profits total $150,000. Ross claims $60,000 as his share of the profits. Is he entitled to this sum?

12. Leland McElmurry was one of three partners of MHS Enterprises, a Michigan partnership. Commonwealth Capital Investment Corp. sued the partnership and obtained a judgment of $1,137,285 against it, but the partnership could not pay the judgment. Commonwealth then sued McElmurry for the entire debt on the theory that, as a partner of MHS, he was liable for its debts. What, if any, is McElmurry's liability? [*Commonwealth Capital Investment Corp. v. McElmurry*, 302 N.W.2d 222 (Mich. App.)]

13. Thomas Smith and Jackie Lea were partners in the logging business. In January 1981, they joined Gordon Redd and went into business running a sawmill, calling the business Industrial Hardwood Products (IHP). Smith and Lea used their logging equipment at the mill site. Smith hauled 400 loads of gravel, worth some $26,000, from his father's land for the mill yard in the process of getting the mill operational. Smith and Lea received $300 a week compensation for their work, which was reported on federal W-2 forms. They worked up to 65 hours per week and were not paid overtime. All three discussed business decisions. Smith and Lea had the authority to write checks and to hire and fire employees. Lea left the business in 1983 and was paid $20,000 by Redd. The testimony indicated that the three individuals agreed in January 1981 that as soon as the bank was paid off and Redd was paid his investment, Lea and Smith would be given an interest in the mill. No written agreement existed. Redd invested

$410,452 in the business and withdrew $500,475 from it. As of December 31, 1986, IHP had sufficient retained earnings to retire the bank debt. In April 1987, Smith petitioned the Chancery Court for dissolution of the "partnership" and an accounting. Redd denied that any partnership agreement was formed and asserted that Smith was an employee because he was paid wages. He offered to pay Smith $50,000 for the gravel and use of his equipment. Decide. [*Smith v. Redd*, 593 So. 2d 989 (Miss.)]

14. Mason and Phyllis Ledbetter operated a business in Northbrook, Illinois, as a partnership called Ledbetters' Nurseries that specialized in the sale of garden lilies. The grounds of the nurseries were planted with numerous species of garden lilies, and hundreds of people toured the Ledbetters' gardens every day. After a tour, Sheila Clark offered to buy the facilities at a "top-notch price." Mason felt he could not refuse the high offer, and he signed a contract to sell all the facilities, including all flowers and the business name. When Phyllis refused to go along with the contract, Clark sued the Ledbetters' Nurseries partnership, seeking to obtain specific performance of the sales contract. Decide.

15. St. John Transportation Co., a corporation, made a contract with the partnership of Bilyeu and Herstel, contractors, by which the latter was to construct a ferryboat. Herstel, a member of the firm of contractors, executed a contract in the firm name with Benbow for certain materials and labor in connection with the construction of the ferryboat. In an action brought by Benbow to enforce a lien against the ferryboat, the *James Johns*, it was contended that all members of the firm were bound by the contract made by Herstel. Do you agree? [*Benbow v. The Ferryboat James Johns*, 108 P. 634 (Or.)]

CPA Questions

1. Acorn and Bean were general partners in a farm machinery business. Acorn contracted, on behalf of the partnership, to purchase 10 tractors from Cobb Corp. Unknown to Cobb, Acorn was not authorized by the partnership to make such contracts. Bean refused to allow the partnership to accept delivery of the tractors, and Cobb sought to enforce the contract. Cobb will:

   a. Lose, because Acorn's action was beyond the scope of Acorn's implied authority.

   b. Prevail, because Acorn had implied authority to bind the partnership.

   c. Prevail, because Acorn had apparent authority to bind the partnership.

   d. Lose, because Acorn's express authority was restricted, in writing, by the partnership agreement.

2. Upon dissolution of a general partnership, distributions will be made on account of:
   I.   Partners' capital accounts.
   II. Amounts owed partners with respect to profits.
   III. Amounts owed partners for loans to the partnership in the following order:

   a. III, I, II
   b. I, II, III
   c. II, III, I
   d. III, II, I

3. Which of the following statements is correct with respect to a limited partnership?

   a. A limited partner may *not* be an unsecured creditor of the limited partnership.
   b. A general partner may *not* also be a limited partner at the same time.
   c. A general partner may be a secured creditor of the limited partnership.
   d. A limited partnership can be formed with limited liability for all partners.

4. When a partner in a general partnership lacks actual or apparent authority to contract on behalf of the partnership, and the party contracted with is aware of this fact, the partnership will be bound by the contract if the other partners:

	Ratify the Contract	*Amend the Partnership Agreement*
a.	Yes	Yes
b.	Yes	No
c.	No	Yes
d.	No	No

LPs, LLCs, and LLPs

Learning Outcomes ⟨⟨⟨

After studying this chapter, you should be able to

LO.1 Explain the history of making limited liability available to general partnerships

LO.2 Explain the extent of a founding general partner's liability for the debts of the firm, and how unlimited liability can be avoided by utilization of a corporate general partner

LO.3 Explain the nature and extent of a limited partner's liability for the debts of the firm

LO.4 Explain the advantages of a limited liability company

LO.5 Understand that an LLC is not liable for the conduct of its promoters prior to organization

LO.6 Understand that unless modified in an operating agreement, managers of LLCs owe member-investors the traditional duties of loyalty and care

LO.7 Explain how a limited liability partnership "shields" innocent partners from liability to third parties

42-1 The Arrival of Partnership Limited Liability

Individuals owning businesses or professional firms are concerned about exposing their personal wealth to liability beyond that invested in their businesses or firms. As discussed previously, limited liability is not a feature of general partnership law. The concept of making limited liability available to general partnerships was considered by the RUPA Drafting Committee when it began its work to revise the Uniform Partnership Act in 1987, but the concept was rejected. A limited partnership form of business organization had existed since 1916 under the Uniform Limited Partnership Act with limited partners (investors) having limited liability, but the firm's general partners were exposed to personal liability for firm debts under this act. The concept of full limited liability for partnerships began to take hold in 1986 when businesses forming limited partnerships under the Revised Uniform Limited Partnership Act utilized corporate general partners, with the general partners avoiding personal liability by the simple expedient of incorporating.

An IRS ruling classifying a Wyoming limited liability company (LLC) as a partnership for tax purposes led to the rapid spread of LLC statutes to every state within six years of the IRS ruling.[1] As part of the limited liability trend established by the swift enactment of LLC laws throughout the country, most states have also enacted limited liability partnership (LLP) acts. Like LLCs, they provide businesses and those offering professional services the benefit of single taxation as a partnership as well as limited liability.

42-2 Limited Partnership

A limited partnership is a special kind of partnership.

42-2a Formation of Limited Partnerships

The Uniform Limited Partnership Act (ULPA) was approved by the National Conference of Commissioners on Uniform State Law in 1916. It was revised in 1976 as the Revised Uniform Limited Partnership Act (RULPA) and was amended in 1985. All states except Louisiana have adopted a version of the RULPA.

Members of a Limited Partnership

In a **limited partnership** certain members contribute capital but have limited liability for firm debts. The most these members can lose is their investment. These members are known as **limited partners.** The partners who manage the business are called **general partners.** General partners are personally liable for the firm's debts.[2] A limited partnership can be formed by "one or more general partners and one or more limited partners."[3]

Certificate of Limited Partnership

Unlike a general partnership, a limited partnership can be created only by executing a certificate of limited partnership.

Under the 1985 amendments to the RULPA, the certificate requires the following information: (1) the limited partnership's name, (2) the address of the partnership's registered office and the name and business address of its agent for service of process, (3) the name and business address of each general partner, (4) the partnership's mailing address, and (5) the latest date on which the limited partnership is to dissolve. The names of the limited partners (the investors) are not required in order to preserve the confidentiality of the investors'

---

limited partnership—partnership that can be formed by "one or more general partners and one or more limited partners."

limited partner—partner who neither takes part in the management of the partnership nor appears to the public to be a general partner.

general partner—partnership in which the partners conduct as co-owners a business for profit, and each partner has a right to take part in the management of the business and has unlimited liability; general partners publicly and actively engage in the transaction of firm business.

---

[1] Rev. Rul. 88-76, 1988—2 C.B. 360.
[2] *Brooke v. Mt. Hood Meadows, Ltd.*, 725 P.2d 925 (Or. App. 1986).
[3] R.U.L.P.A. §101(7).

names from competitors. New investors may be admitted as limited partners without the significant administrative burden involved in amending the certificate, as was required under the ULPA. The RULPA provides that the certificate should be filed with the Office of the Secretary of State, as opposed to the local filing required under the ULPA.

If a limited partnership certificate is not filed, all participants have the status and liability of general partners in a general partnership. However, technical defects in the certificate do not prevent formation of a limited partnership if there has been substantial, good-faith compliance with the filing requirements.[4]

CPA Limited Partnership Agreement

The RULPA embodies the policy of freedom of contract and maximum flexibility regarding the limited partnership agreement.[5] Most limited partnership agreements are drafted almost exclusively by their founding general partners. Courts resolve ambiguities against the drafting general partners and in favor of the reasonable expectations of the limited partners. **For Example,** when the general partners of the Nantucket Island Associates Limited Partnership unilaterally amended the limited partnership agreement to add a new class of preferred limited partnership units with superior rights to existing unit holders, the court construed the ambiguous language in the agreement against the general partners. The general partners were found to be in breach of the agreement by adding the new class of units.[6]

42-2b Characteristics of Limited Partnerships

A limited partnership has the following characteristics.

CPA Capital Contributions

Under the ULPA, a limited partner contributed either cash or property but not services. Under the RULPA, however, a limited partner may contribute services.

CPA Firm Name

With certain exceptions, a limited partner's name cannot appear in the firm name. Under the RULPA, the words *limited partnership* must appear without abbreviation in the firm name.

CPA Management and Control of the Firm

The general partners manage the business and are personally liable for firm debts. However, general partners may avoid personal liability by incorporating. Limited partners (the investors) have the right to a share of the profits and a return of capital upon dissolution; they also have limited liability. The limitation of liability is lost, however, if they participate in the control of the business.

The RULPA lists a number of "safe harbor" activities in which limited partners may engage without losing their protection from liability. These activities include:

1. Being a contractor for, or an agent or employee of, the limited partnership or of a general partner;
2. Consulting with and advising a general partner regarding the partnership business;
3. Acting as a surety for the limited partnership; and
4. Voting on partnership matters, such as dissolving and winding up the limited partnership or removing a general partner.

---

[4] R.U.L.P.A. §201(b); *Fabry Partnership v. Christensan*, 794 P.2d 719 (Nev. 1990).
[5] See *Gotham Partners, L.P. v. Hallowood Realty Partners, LP*, 817 A.2d 160 (Del. 2002).
[6] In re *Nantucket Island Associates Limited Partnership Unit Holders Litigation*, 810 A.2d 351 (Del. Ch. 2002).

Right to Sue

A limited partner may bring a derivative action on behalf of the limited partnership to enforce a claim that the limited partnership possesses against others but that the partnership refuses to enforce.[7] This derivative suit is filed in the name of the limited partner, and the partnership is named as a defendant, with the limited partnership deriving the benefits of the action.

Limited partners may sue their partnership's general partner to protect the limited partners' interest. General partners today are commonly corporations with their own boards of directors and management teams, with the limited partnership format providing investment and tax incentives for investor–limited partners and the general partners reserving to themselves broad authority to act in the general partners' sole discretion and often in the general partners' own best interest. **For Example,** Donald Weedon and others formed a limited partnership under Delaware law to raise capital for the securities broker–dealer business. The partnership agreement, as allowed by Delaware law, gave the corporate general partners and its directors the right to restrict their fiduciary duties in managing the partnership and gave the general partner broad power to act, even in conflicted situations, subject only to very loose constraints of a subjective bad-faith standard. Nonemployee limited partners referred to by the court as the "outside investors" brought suit against the corporate general partners and members of the general partner's board of directors and top management for squeezing out all nonemployee limited partners and paying less than the fair value for their units in violation of fiduciary duties and the partnership agreement. The trial court decided in favor of the plaintiffs, stating in part:

> … *Even given the wide discretion the partnership agreement gives to the defendants to issue new units without fear of liability, the defendants managed to step out of bounds in one important respect. By deciding to permit the general partner's outside directors to acquire new units at a favorable price and by denying the same opportunity to Outside Investors, the defendants breached their contractual duties. This decision, I find, was not undertaken in good faith but instead as quid pro quo for the outside directors' willing assent to the issuance of a large number of new units to management and employees.…*

The plaintiffs received a make-whole remedy from the court with monetary damages tied to fair market values.[8]

Dissolution

The dissolution and winding up of limited partnerships is governed by the same principles applicable to general partnerships.

42-3   Limited Liability Companies

Limited liability company (LLC) acts were rapidly adopted by state legislatures throughout the country following a favorable tax ruling on this form of organization by the Internal Revenue Service.[9] This corporate-sounding entity is considered in this chapter because it is a form of limited partnership.

---

[7] *Garber v. Stevens*, 941 N.Y.S.2d 127 (A.D. 2012).
[8] *Gelfman v. Weeden Investors, L.P.*, 859 A.2d 89 (Del. Ch. 2004).
[9] IRS Rev. Rul. 88-76. LLCs have been adopted by every state and the District of Columbia. A Uniform Limited Liability Company Act was approved by the National Conference of Commissioners on Uniform State Law.

CPA   42-3a **Characteristics of LLCs**

The IRS has determined that an LLC may qualify for partnership federal tax treatment. Unlike a corporation, an LLC pays no federal taxes on its income as an entity. Instead, the income (or losses, deductions, and credits) flows through to the LLC's owners (called *members*) based on their proportionate interest in the company. The members report the income on their personal tax returns. The LLC combines this tax advantage with the limited liability feature of the corporate form of business organization. The owners and managers are not personally liable for the debts and obligations of the entity, provided that these individuals fulfill their common law duty to disclose that they are acting as agents for the limited liability company.

CPA   **Formation**

As set forth previously, general partnerships may be created without the formality of a written partnership agreement when two individuals operate a business for profit as co-owners. LLCs, however, require a formal filing of articles of organization with the Secretary of State in a manner similar to a filing of articles of incorporation by a corporation or a certificate of limited partnership for a limited partnership.

The articles for an LLC must contain the name, purpose, duration, registered agent, and principal office of the LLC. An LLC must use the words *limited liability company* or *LLC* in the company's name. The LLC is a legal entity with authority to conduct business in its own name.[10] LLC acts are characterized as "flexible statutes" because they generally permit owners to engage in the private ordering of relationships, with broad freedom of contract to govern these relationships as set forth in their operating agreements.[11]

Liability of Promoters

Before the LLC is formally organized, promoters prepare for the conduct of business. Promoters may enter into contracts or seek investors for the new entity. An LLC is generally not liable for the preformation contracts of its promoters.

CASE SUMMARY

All Bottled Up!

FACTS: Clifford Hansen was an entrepreneur who sought to purchase a water bottling company in South Carolina. He approached Robert Fields for help locating investors and securing financing. Fields and Hansen worked together for some time. But Fields began to work on behalf of his own company, Fields Company LLC, as well as other LLCs. He found investors to purchase the water bottling company on behalf of these entities and cut Hansen out of the deal.

Hansen sued Fields Company LLC for breach of fiduciary duty, breach of contract, and several torts. A jury found for Hansen with damages over one million dollars. Fields Company LLC appealed.

DECISION: Judgment for Fields Company, LLC. The LLC is not liable for its promoter's preincorporation contracts unless the contract was ratified expressly or implicitly by

---

[10] An individual has a right to appear before a court and represent himself or herself. However, a member of an LLC who as such is not personally liable for the LLC's actions cannot appear before a court on behalf of the LLC entity. The LLC may appear in court only through counsel. Thus, a nonattorney member of an LLC was not allowed to represent the LLC in a court case. *Collier v. Cobalt, LLC,* 2002 WL 726640 (E.D. La. April 22, 2002). See also *Gobe Media Group, LLC v. Cisneros,* 959 A.2d 892 (N.J. Super. 2008).

[11] *Elf Atochem N. America, Inc. v. Jaffari,* 727 A.2d 286 (Del. Super. Ct. 1999).

accepting its benefits. There was no evidence that Fields LLC ratified any contract with Hansen or that it accepted any benefits of Fields' or his related entities' contracts with Hansen. The general rule regarding a corporation's liability for torts is that a promoter is not liable for torts that its promoters committed before it came into existence. An LLC is not liable for torts committed by its promoter prior to organization because (1) there is no agency relationship between a promoter and a non-existent LLC; (2) the injured party may seek recourse from the promoter directly; and (3) the potential for such liability would stifle investment. [***Hansen v. Fields Company, LLC,* 763 S.E.2d 31 (S.C. 2014)**]

C P A   Capital Contributions

An ownership interest in an LLC may be issued for cash, property, or services.

If there is no operating agreement, statutory provisions govern the relationship between the members and the operation of the company.[12] If there is an operating agreement, the members must comply with its terms, including provisions on capital contributions. **For Example,** William Eichengrun claimed that his capital contribution to the LLC was in services, not cash, because he was the LLC's managing member. However, in proceedings to dissolve the LLC and distribute its assets, Eichengrun was not allowed to participate in the distribution because the operating agreement required that "initial capital contributions" of members be in cash or the fair market value of property.[13]

C P A   Management

Management of an LLC is vested in its members. An *operating agreement*, equivalent to the bylaws of a corporation or a partnership agreement, sets forth the specific management authority of members and managers.

The operating agreement need not be in writing. All amendments must be unanimous unless otherwise agreed to by the members. Oral amendments may modify written terms unless otherwise set forth in the operating agreement. To promote certainty in management, it is recommended that the operating agreement be in writing and that it be changed only by written amendments adopted by a specified percentage or number of members.

The management structure created in the operating agreement may provide for the company to be member managed. However, members commonly delegate authority to run the entity to managers who may or may not be required to be members of the LLC. A member is not entitled to compensation for services performed for an LLC unless it is stipulated in the operating agreement. (Members receive profits and losses according to the terms of the operating agreement.)

In a member-managed company, each member has equal rights in management, with decisions made by a majority vote of the members.[14] In a manager-managed company, nonmanager members have no rights in management except for extraordinary matters, such as amending the operating agreement or consenting to merge with another entity.

Managers have the same fiduciary duties to the entity as corporate officers have to a corporation. LLC acts are characterized as "flexible statutes" allowing broad freedom of contract to govern relationships, as spelled out in detail in operating agreements. The parties are free to waive or modify the duties of loyalty and care owed by managers to

---

[12] *Germano v. Beaujean,* 997 N.E.2d 1238 (Ohio App. 2013).
[13] *KSI Rockville, LLC v. Eichengrun,* 760 N.Y.S.2d 520 (A. D. 2003).
[14] *IIC Holdings, LLC v. HR Software Acquisition Group, Inc.,* 750 N.Y.S.2d 425 (Sup. Ct. 2002).

members in the operating agreement. Unless modified by the operating agreement, however, state LLC acts may apply fiduciary duties to managers who would qualify as fiduciaries under traditional equitable principles.

CASE SUMMARY

Golf Course Owner Out of Bounds

FACTS: Minority members in a Delaware limited liability company, Peconic Bay, LLC, brought a breach of fiduciary duty action against the LLC's manager and its majority interest holder regarding the sale of the LLC at an auction, in which the LLC was purchased by the manager. The "manager" was Gatz Properties, LLC, which was managed and partially owned by William Gatz. Peconic Bay, LLC, held a long-term lease on valuable property in New York that allowed the LLC to operate a first-rate Robert Trent Jones, Jr., designed golf course, called Long Island National Golf Course. The golf management company, American Golf, held a sublease on the property after it opened in 1999, never made a profit, and let the course fall into disrepair. Gatz knew in 2004 that American Golf would exercise its early termination option in 2010, yet he did nothing to plan for its exit. Rather, Gatz made a series of decisions that placed Peconic Bay in an economically vulnerable position. Then Gatz decided to put Peconic Bay on the auction block without engaging an experienced broker to market it to golf course managers or owners. Gatz, on behalf of Gatz Properties, was the only bidder to show up. Knowing this fact before formulating his bid, Gatz purchased Peconic Bay for a nominal value over the debt and merged Peconic Bay into Gatz Properties.

DECISION: Judgment for the minority members. The LLC agreement made it clear that the manager could enter into a self-dealing transaction, such as its purchase of the LLC, only if it proved that the terms were fair. The LLC agreement essentially incorporated a core element of the traditional fiduciary duty of loyalty. The manager's defense that his voting power gave him a license to exploit the minority shareholders fundamentally misunderstands Delaware law. The manager was free not to vote his membership interest for a sale. But he was not free to create a situation of distress by failing to cause the LLC to explore its market alternatives and then buying the LLC for a nominal price. The purpose of the duty of loyalty is in large measure to prevent the exploitation by a fiduciary of his self-interest to the disadvantage of the minority. The fair price requirement of that duty, which is incorporated in the LLC agreement here, makes sure that if the conflicted fiduciary engages in self-dealing, he pays a price that is as much as an arms-length purchaser would pay. [***Auriga Capital Corp. v. Gatz Properties, LLC***, **40 A.3d 839 (Del. Ch. 2012)**]

In some states, members of manager-managed LLCs owe no fiduciary duty to the LLC unless a member exercises some or all of the authority of a manager pursuant to the operating agreement.[15]

CPA ## Distributions

Profits and losses are shared according to the terms of the operating agreement.

Liquidating distributions must first be applied to return all contributions not previously returned, and the remainder is distributed per capita to members unless members alter these rules in the operating agreement.

---

[15] In *Remora Investments, LLC v. Orr*, 673 S.E.2d 845 (Va. 2009), the Virginia Supreme Court held that nothing in the statutory provisions relating to LLCs provides for fiduciary duties between members of an LLC or between a member and a manager of an LLC. The statutory standard of conduct for a manager of an LLC is to discharge duties in accordance with his or her good-faith business judgment of the best interests of the company, rather than by imposing fiduciary duties on members. In contrast, the Uniform Limited Liability Act of 2006, which has been adopted in Idaho, Iowa, Nebraska, Utah, and Wyoming, states that members of an LLC owe each other the fiduciary duties of loyalty and care. See *Bush v. Sage Health Care, LLC*, 203 P.3d 694 (Idaho 2009). See also *Melcher v. Apollo Medical Fund Management*, 208 N.Y.S.2d 207 (A.D. 2006), referencing Delaware Code, Title 6 §18-110(c).

Any distribution made when the company is insolvent is unlawful. Each member or manager who votes to make an unlawful distribution is in violation of his or her fiduciary duty to the firm and is personally liable for the amount of distribution improperly paid.[16] However, the individual may compel contribution from all other responsible members and managers.

LLC Property

The LLC is an independent entity separate and distinct from the members. The LLC owns and holds property in its own name.[17]

Assignment

An interest in an LLC is personal property and is generally assignable. However, LLC members cannot transfer the right to participate in management without the consent of the other members of the LLC.

CASE SUMMARY

"I'm in Charge," said the Admiral's Daughter.
"No, You're Not," said the Admiral's New Wife.

FACTS: Admiral Dewey Monroe and his wife Lou Ann Monroe formed an LLC in 2003, with Dewey holding an 80% membership interest and Lou Ann a 20% membership interest, respectively. The LLC provided that Lou Ann would be the managing member. Dewey died in 2004 and bequeathed his entire estate to his daughter, Janet Ott. Janet called a meeting of the company, seeking to remove Lou Ann and elect herself as the company's new managing member, asserting that she had inherited her father's full LLC membership upon his death under his will. The LLC asserted that Janet had inherited only Dewey's right to share profits

and losses and to receive distributions but did not inherit a right to the management and control of the company.

DECISION: Judgment for the LLC and Lou Ann. Dewey Monroe was dissociated from the company upon his death by operation of law, terminating all his rights as a member to participate in the management and control of the company. Only the right to share profits and losses and to receive distributions survived to be inherited by Janet under his will. **[*Ott v. Monroe*, 719 S.E.2d 309 (Va. 2011)]**

A creditor's right against a member's interest in an LLC is limited to a *charging order*. The creditor with such an order has only the rights of an assignee of an interest in an LLC.

Dissolution

Most LLC statutes provide that an LLC will dissolve by the consent of the members or upon the death, retirement, resignation, expulsion, or bankruptcy of a member. Statutes also provide, however, that the business of the LLC may be continued with the consent of all of the remaining members. With a change in IRS regulations away from its four-factor corporate characteristics test, discussed in the following section, some states have begun to amend LLC laws to give limited liability companies the option of perpetual existence.

Situations in which it is not reasonably practicable to carry on the business in conformity with the operating agreement may arise. The LLC statute commonly permits a court

---

[16] *Florence Cement Co. v. Vitttaino*, 807 N.W.2d 461 (Mich. App. 2011).
[17] *Northeast Realty, LLC v. Misty Bayou, LLC*, 920 So. 2d 938 (La. App. 2006).

| FIGURE 42-1 | Comparison of General Partnership, Limited Partnership, Limited Liability Company, and Limited Liability Partnership |

	General Partnership	**Limited Partnership**	**Limited Liability Company (LLC)**	**Limited Liability Partnership (LLP)**
Creation	No formality required.	Filing a certificate of limited partnership with appropriate state office.	Filing articles of organization with Secretary of State.	Registration of LLP filed with state government.
Liability	Unlimited liability of each partner for firm debts.	General partners: unlimited liability for firm debts. Limited partners: no liability beyond loss of investment.	All members are liable for LLC debts to the extent of their capital contributions and equity in firm. No personal liability beyond this.	No liability for partners beyond their contributions and equity in firm, except unlimited personal liability for their own wrongful acts and those of persons whom they supervise.
Management	All partners according to their partnership agreement or the UPA or RUPA.	General partners according to their partnership agreement or the UPA or RUPA. Limited partners excluded.	By members of firm, who may delegate authority to managers.	All partners according to partnership agreement or the UPA.
Dissolution	As set forth in the partnership agreement or the UPA or RUPA.	As set forth in the partnership agreement or the ULPA or RULPA.	As set forth in LLC statute or articles of organization.	As set forth in partnership agreement or the UPA or RUPA.

to decree dissolution of the LLC when such a situation occurs.[18] **For Example,** Haley and Talcott each had a 50 percent interest in a real estate LLC. They had a falling out. The operating agreement contained an exit mechanism to buy out Haley's share, but the

[18] *Venture Sales, LLC v. Perkins*, 86 So. 3d 910 (Miss. 2012).

mechanism could not relieve Haley of his obligation as a personal guarantor for the LLC's mortgage. Because the LLC was deadlocked and the exit mechanism was not an adequate remedy, the court ordered the dissolution of the LLC and the sale of its property.[19]

Upon the winding up of an LLC, the assets are distributed according to the operating agreement. Should the agreement fail to provide for this event, the assets will be distributed according to the state's LLC statute.

Tax Classification

The IRS applied a four-factor corporate characteristics test to determine whether an LLC would be taxed as a partnership or a corporation. If the LLC had more than two of the characteristics, it would not qualify for taxation as a partnership. The factors were continuity of life, centralized management, limited liability, and free transferability of interest. The four-factor test became obsolete when the IRS implemented its so-called check-the-box entity classification election procedure available to unincorporated associations that are not publicly traded.[20] Now, if an LLC wants to be classified as a partnership, all it needs to do is make that election by checking the box on the appropriate IRS form.

Disregarding the LLC Entity

Some LLC statutes provide that courts may disregard the LLC entirely and hold the owners personally liable beyond their investments to the same extent as done in corporate law when exceptional circumstances demand.[21] Courts will disregard the corporate entity and hold individuals liable to prevent injustice, but doing so is the exception rather than the rule.[22]

CASE SUMMARY

Piercing the LLC Veil

FACTS: Kaycee Land and Livestock entered into a contract with Flahive Oil and Gas, LLC, allowing it to use the surface of its real property. Kaycee alleged that Flahive Oil and Gas caused environmental contamination of its real property. Because the LLC had no assets at the time of suit, Kaycee sought to pierce the limited liability company veil and disregard the LLC entity of Flahive Oil and Gas and hold Roger Flahive, the managing member of the LLC who directed all operations on the property, individually liable for the contamination. The question presented to the court was, "In the absence of fraud, is the remedy of piercing the veil available against a company formed under the Wyoming Limited Liability Company Act?"

DECISION: The equitable remedy of piercing the corporate veil is available under the Wyoming Limited Liability Company Act. When corporations fail to follow the statutorily mandated formalities, commingle funds, or ignore restrictions in their articles of incorporation regarding separate treatment of the corporate property, the courts deem it appropriate to disregard the separate identity and do not permit shareholders to be sheltered from liability to third parties for damages caused by the corporation's acts. No public policy exists to treat LLCs differently than corporations regarding veil piercing. [*Kaycee Land and Livestock v. Flahive*, 46 P.3d 323 (Wyo. 2002)]

---

[19] *Haley v. Talcott*, 864 A.2d 86 (Del. Ch. 2004).
[20] Treas. Reg. 301.7701 *et seq.*
[21] *Net Jets Aviation, Inc. v. LHC Communications, LLC*, 537 F.3d 168 (2d Cir. 2008); but see *Serio v. Baystate Properties, LLC*, 39 A.3d 131 (Md. App. 2012).
[22] See *Hibbs v. Berger*, 430 S.W.3d 296 (2014).

42-3b LLCs and Other Entities

LLCs are distinguishable from Subchapter S corporations and limited partnerships.

LLC Distinguished from a Subchapter S Corporation

Under a Subchapter S corporation (so named from Subchapter S of the Internal Revenue Code), shareholders of a close corporation may be treated as partners for tax purposes and retain the benefit of limited liability under the corporate form. An S corporation is limited to 100 shareholders who must be U.S. citizens or resident aliens.[23] Although partnerships and corporations may generally not be shareholders, employee stock ownership plans (ESOPs) and nonprofit entities may be. In contrast, an LLC has no limit on the number of owners, and there is no restriction on the types of entities or persons who may own an LLC. Thus, partnerships, corporations, and foreign investors may be owners of an LLC. Because substantial taxes on appreciated assets are payable on the liquidation of an S corporation, it is generally not feasible to convert an existing S corporation to an LLC.

CPA ### LLC Distinguished from a Limited Partnership

Limited partners in a limited partnership have the advantage of limited liability. However, every limited partnership must have a general partner who manages the business, and this partner can be subject to unlimited liability. This structural feature is a major disadvantage of the limited partnership form that does not exist in a limited liability company (LLC). Also, individual limited partners may lose their limited liability if they participate in the control of the business. Under an LLC, the members may actively participate in the control of the business and still receive limited liability protection. As stated previously in this chapter, a general partner may avoid unlimited liability on a sizeable limited partnership project by incorporating.

Usage

The LLC will in many instances replace general and limited partnerships as well as close corporations and S corporations. The LLC will not replace the publicly traded corporation, however, because publicly traded companies and LLCs must be classified as corporations for tax purposes.[24]

42-4 Limited Liability Partnerships

As part of the limited liability trend established by the swift enactment of LLC laws throughout the country, most states have enacted limited liability partnership (LLP) acts. Like LLCs, they provide businesses and those offering professional services the benefit of single taxation as a partnership as well as limited liability.[25]

---

[23] See IRS, S Corporations, **http://www.irs.gov/Businesses/Small-Businesses-&-Self-Employed/S-Corporations.**

[24] See IRS Notice 88-75, 1988, 1988-2 CB 386. The traditional corporation retains many advantages, such as the low corporate income tax on corporate profits, which allows accumulation of capital for expansion or the distribution of all corporate earnings as compensation as well as providing fringe benefits for employee-owners with pretax dollars (IRC §§79, 119, 162).

[25] The 1994 Revised Uniform Partnership Act (RUPA) was amended in 1996 to include two new articles: Article 10, dealing with limited liability partnerships, and Article 11, dealing with foreign limited liability partnerships. Articles 1 through 11 constitute the Uniform Limited Liability Partnership Act.

CPA   42-4a **Extent of Limited Liability**

In a general partnership, partners are jointly liable for partnership debts and jointly and severally liable for partnership torts. LLP statutes were initially drafted to shield innocent partners from vicarious negligence or malpractice liability of their partners. Some states now provide "full shields" for innocent partners that eliminate the vicarious personal liability of these partners for the obligations of the partnership and free them from any obligation to contribute personal assets beyond their investments in the partnership. However, the "liability shield" of a registered limited liability partnership applies only to a partner's liability to third parties and does not shield against breaches of the partnership's or partners' obligations to each other. In every state, however, LLP partners remain fully liable for their own negligence and continue to have unlimited liability for the wrongful acts of those whom they directly supervise and control.

CASE SUMMARY

A Limited Shield

FACTS: Phillip Kuslansky sued his former law partners for breach of contract for failure to pay him the value of his interest in the registered limited liability partnership upon his withdrawal from the partnership. His former partners moved to dismiss the complaint, contending that they were shielded from liability with respect to the plaintiff partner who had withdrawn from the partnership. From a judgment for the defendant former partners, Kuslansky appealed.

DECISION: Judgment for Kuslansky. The state LLP law does not shield general partners in registered limited liability partnerships from personal liability for breaches of the partnership's or partners' obligations to each other. [*Kuslansky v. Kuslansy, Robbins, Stechel and Cunningham, LLP*, 858 N.Y.S.2d 213 (A.D. 2008)]

Professional LLPs continue to be subject to professional regulations, and the appropriate regulating boards set the amount and type of malpractice insurance that firms must carry to operate as an LLP.

To illustrate the effects of a change from a general partnership to an LLP, consider the case of surgeons Jones, Smith, and Gray, who were partners. Jones inadvertently removed Miller's healthy kidney rather than his diseased kidney, and a jury returned a verdict of $2 million. Under general partnership law, Smith and Gray, although innocent partners, are jointly and severally liable along with Jones, and their personal assets can be reached to pay the judgment if necessary. Under an LLP, only partnership assets and the personal assets of Jones are available to pay the judgment. Smith's and Gray's personal assets cannot be reached.

CPA   42-4b **Registration and Usage**

LLP statutes are designed to permit the conversion of existing general partnerships into limited liability partnerships. The statutes require registration with the Secretary of State, and the name of the partnership must contain the term *limited liability partnership* or *LLP*.

Traditional partnership agreements, like those used by many accounting and law firms and other professional partnerships, can be converted into limited liability partnership agreements without major redrafting or renegotiating of the underlying agreements. Consequently, many professional firms organize under this form of partnership.

ETHICS & THE LAW

The S & L Crisis

When the Office of the Special Counsel concluded its work in both civil and criminal litigation against officers, directors, and consultants involved with failed savings and loan institutions in the late 1980s, it released a report on its work. On the civil side, the Office of the Special Counsel had obtained settlements from defendants in civil suits of $2.9 billion in restitution. Accounting firms, along with lawyers and consultants, comprised 71 percent of the defendants.

Because most accounting firms were organized as partnerships, the result was that many partners were required to dig into their personal assets to meet the restitution requirements imposed by the federal government. Since the creation of LLPs, all of the largest accounting firms in the United States have restructured, with most choosing the LLP for conducting business. All forms of restructuring will ensure limited personal liability for their principals.

Was the restructuring undertaken to avoid liability? Does limited liability insulate those who make decisions from liability for those decisions? Financiers attempt to determine what stake the officers in a corporation have in the corporation. Stock ownership and exposure to losses through the value of those shares are seen as a positive influence. Do liability limitations reduce the stake a principal has? Is it good to have decision makers separated from the costs of those decisions?

Make the Connection

Summary

A limited partnership consists of one or more limited partners who contribute cash, property, or services without liability for losses beyond their investment, and one or more general partners, who manage the business and have unlimited personal liability. A limited partner's protection from unlimited liability may be lost if the partner participates in the control of the business. "Safe harbor" activities for limited partners are set forth in the RULPA. General partners may avoid personal liability by incorporating. A certificate of limited partnership must be filed when the partnership is formed for the law to apply. Otherwise, general partnership law applies.

A limited liability company is a hybrid form of business organization that combines the tax advantages of a partnership with the limited liability feature of the corporation. It must be formed in accordance with state law in order to have effect, and the designation LLC must appear with the company's name. Management of an LLC is vested in its members, and members can delegate authority to run the entity to managers, the terms of which are set forth in the company's operating agreement. Members receive profits and losses according to the operating agreement. A member's interest in an LLC is assignable, but consent of the other members is needed for the assignee to participate in the firm's management.

A limited liability partnership allows existing partnerships to convert to this form without major renegotiation of the underlying partnership agreement. Innocent partners in a limited liability partnership are not personally liable for the torts of other partners beyond their investment in the firm.

Learning Outcomes

After studying this chapter, you should be able to clearly explain:

42-1   The Arrival of Partnership Limited Liability

LO.1 Explain the history of making limited liability available to general partnerships

See the presentation of the developing law of partnership limited liability, page 868.

42-2   Limited Partnership

LO.2 Explain the extent of a founding general partner's liability for the debts of the firm, and how unlimited liability can be avoided by utilization of a corporate general partner

See the discussion of general partners' avoidance of personal liability through incorporation, page 868.

LO.3 Explain the nature and extent of a limited partner's liability for the debts of the firm

42-3   Limited Liability Companies

LO.4 Explain the advantages of a limited liability company

See the discussion of the advantages of an LLC, including the tax advantages of treatment as a partnership with the limited liability feature of a corporation, page 871.

LO.5 Understand that an LLC is not liable for the conduct of its promoters prior to organization

See the *Hansen* case, pages 871–872.

LO.6 Understand that unless modified in an operating agreement, managers of LLCs owe member-investors the traditional duties of loyalty and care

See the *Auriga Capital* case, where the manager's conduct breached his fiduciary duties to minority members, page 873.

42-4   Limited Liability Partnerships

LO.7 Explain how a limited liability partnership "shields" innocent partners from liability to third parties

See the example involving Dr. Jones's removal of the wrong kidney, with innocent partners Smith's and Gray's personal assets being shielded from liability from a large judgment beyond partnership and Dr. Jones' assets, page 878.

Key Terms

general partners   limited partners   limited partnership

Questions and Case Problems

1. What is the principal advantage of an LLP over an LLC?

2. Alan Waung, a Hong Kong businessperson, purchased a golf course in Saginaw, Michigan, as an investment. As an avid golfer, Alan anticipates spending several weeks during the year at his "Northern Pines" course. He has been informed that a Subchapter S corporation would allow him and his family-member shareholders to be treated as partners for U.S. tax purposes while retaining the limited liability of the corporate form. Advise Mr. Waung on this matter. What form of business organization would you recommend?

3. Kate Haley, an experienced builder, formed a limited partnership in August 2011, along with two limited partners, Drs. Growbioski and Gailen, who each provided $100,000 to the partnership for initial capital for the construction of a medical office building near Stowe, Vermont. With the bustle of getting building and environmental permits and placating abutters to the property, as well as lining up suppliers and subcontractors and getting the job started, Kate simply did not find an opportunity to take the long drive to file the certificate of limited partnership with the Secretary of State's office in Montpelier. A confluence of bad weather, an accident causing serious personal injury, financing disappointments, labor difficulties, design problems, and some personal problems resulted in the project being stopped before completion with some $550,000 in overdue bills. Dr. Growbioski has been approached by several suppliers and craftsmen seeking payment for supplies and work performed. As a limited partner, he believes that he is not liable for firm debts beyond his investment, which was $100,000. Explain to Dr. Growbioski his obligations at this point.

4. Gilroy, Sims & Associates, Ltd., was a limited partnership engaged in real estate development. The original general partners were Richard Gilroy and William Sims. Thomas Green and John Murphy, Jr., were listed as limited partners, along with certain other individuals, on the certificate of limited partnership. Green and Murphy took an active role in the day-to-day operations of the real estate developed by the limited partnership. Financing was obtained to construct the venture's building in St. Louis in 1968, with a mortgage that was payable to American National Insurance Company over 27 years. In 1976, Green and Murphy became general partners of Gilroy, Sims. They executed a Restated Agreement and agreed to "unlimited liability for the debts of the partnership." In the fall of 1990, the partnership stopped making mortgage payments. After foreclosure by American National, a deficiency of $1,437,840 was outstanding. Green and Murphy

believed they were absolved from any personal liability beyond the assets of the firm because they were limited partners when the debt was incurred in 1968. Decide. [*American National Ins. Co. v. Gilroy, Sims & Associates, Ltd.*, 874 F. Supp. 971 (E.D. Mo.)]

5. Sabastian Hafner joined a start-up business with a business plan focused on making breads without common food allergens, such as wheat, yeast, dairy, and gluten, to be marketed in a major metropolitan area. The five founders of the business, including Sabastian, selected the limited liability company (LLC) as their form of business organization. The Articles of Organization for the limited liability company were duly filed with the Secretary of State. The Operating Agreement simply provided that founding member Jillian Lopez would be the sole manager of the firm, and it set a salary for her at $40,000 per year. She hired employees to perform production, delivery, and sales work. Sabastian and the other three members spent nights and early mornings "pitching in" at the bakery. After two months of diligent work, Sabastian, a second-year MBA student, sought back pay for the 40 hours each week he spent at the bakery during the previous eight weeks. He pointed out to the other members of the LLC that state law authorizes employees to sue for their wages. What are Sabastian's rights regarding pay for the service he performed for the LLC?

6. Hurwitz and Padden practiced law as equal partners for a short period of time before converting to an LLC. Some three years later, Padden informed Hurwitz that he intended to leave the firm. When they could not agree on how to divide $200,000 in fees relating to work acquired before the dissolution of the LLC, Hurwitz filed suit seeking an equal division of the fees under partnership principles. Padden contended that partnership principles should not apply to the dissolution of an LLC even though the state's LLC law incorporated the definition and use of the term *dissolution* from the UPA. Decide. [*Hurwitz v. Padden*, 581 N.W.2d 359 (Minn. App.)]

7. Don Mason and Beth Daley were managers and members of Pacific Beach Developers, LLC (PBD), a start-up real estate development company focusing on rehabilitating older properties for increased rental values and possible resale. Daley made a contract with San Diego Architects Associates (SDAA) to provide plans for the rehabilitation of a 60-unit building on Ingraham Street for $97,000, signing the contract "Beth Daley, manager P.B.D. LLC." Financing for the Ingraham Street property fell through, and PBD's option on the property expired. Although Daley notified SDAA that the "Ingraham Street deal was off," SDAA had nearly completed its work, and SDAA brought suit for the contract price against both the LLC and Beth Daley. At the point the lawsuit was initiated, PBD had no working capital remaining, and Don and Beth had "moved on," having taken jobs as mutual fund salespersons. Advise Beth of her legal obligations to SDAA.

8. John and Amelia have general commitments from a number of individuals to invest in their Sproondrift Cove Club golf course and distinctive residential community in Duval County. John wants to form a limited partnership. He realizes that every limited partnership must have a general partner who manages the business and is subject to unlimited liability for all debts and liabilities of the limited partnership. But he says that is no problem because the general partner can be a corporation and can limit its liability exposure by simply creating a "shell" corporation. John stated to Amelia, "As officers of the corporate general partner, you and I can operate the business without the limited partners interfering … we run the show!" Amelia responded, "John, what you propose seems so very complicated, risky, and expensive. A number of our investors are relatives who may want to be listened to, and some of our investors are professionals who could give us some valuable advice. Maybe a limited liability company would be a better entity for us." Compare the advantages and disadvantages of an LLC with a limited partnership and recommend the most appropriate form of business organization for this venture.

9. Hacienda Farms, Ltd., was organized as a limited partnership with Ricardo de Escamilla as the general partner and James L. Russell and H. W. Andrews as limited partners. The partnership raised vegetables and truck crops that were marketed principally through a produce concern controlled by Andrews. All three individuals decided which crops were to be planted. The general partner had no power to withdraw money from the partnership's two bank accounts without the signature of one of the limited partners. After operating for some seven and one-half months under these procedures, the limited partners demanded that the general partner resign as farm manager, which he did. Six weeks later, the partnership went into bankruptcy. Laurance Holzman, as trustee in bankruptcy, brought an action against Russell and Andrews, claiming that they had become liable to the creditors of the partnership as general partners because they had taken part in the control of the partnership business. How would

you decide the case under the ULPA? Would the outcome be different under the RULPA? [*Holzman v. de Escamilla*, 195 P.2d 833 (Cal. App.)]

10. Jerome Micco was a major shareholder and corporate officer of Micco and Co., Inc., which was a limited partner in Harbor Creek, Ltd., a limited partnership formed to build a condominium complex. Hommel, an electrical contractor, was the successful bidder on certain electrical work for the project. For several months, Hommel worked under the direction of the construction supervisor and was paid by the limited partnership for his work. Because of financial difficulties, the supervisor was released. Thereafter, Jerome Micco played a major role in the building of the project, directing the work to be performed. Hommel submitted payment invoices directly to Micco. When Hommel was not paid, he sued Micco, contending that Micco was a limited partner who ran the operation personally and was personally responsible for the debt. Micco argued that he was an employee or agent of a corporation (Micco and Co., Inc.) and thus could not be held liable for the debt. The evidence reveals that Micco had no occasion to tell Hommel that he was acting as a corporate officer. Is it ethical for a corporate officer and shareholder to seek to avoid individual liability in this case? How would you decide the case? [*Hommel v. Micco*, 602 N.E.2d 1259 (Ohio App.)]

11. Ralph and Maureen K. Hagan (collectively Hagan) owned the Stuart Court Apartments in Richmond, Virginia. On April 30, 1994, Hagan executed an agreement with Adams Property Associates, Inc. (Adams), giving Adams the exclusive right to sell the property for $1,600,000. The agreement provided that if the property was "sold or exchanged" within one year, with or without Adams's assistance, Hagan would pay Adams a fee of 6 percent of the "gross sales amount." Seven days before the year expired, Hagan, Roy T. Tepper, and Lynn Parsons formed a limited liability company, Hagan, Parsons, & Tepper, LLC (HPT). By deed dated April 23, 1995, Hagan transferred the property to HPT. Adams

contends it is entitled to a commission from Hagan pursuant to the April 1994 agreement. Hagan contends the transaction was just a contribution of capital to a new company, not a sale. Decide. [*Hagan v. Adams Property Associates, Inc.*, 482 S.E.2d 805 (Va. 1997)]

12. Peter Kertesz formed an LLC and operated it in South Florida under the business name "Mourning Flowers." The LLC specialized in the sale of flowers to funeral homes. Although Kertesz was initially the only member and manager, he ultimately granted ownership interests totaling 55 percent of the LLC to six individuals. In mid-2007, the members had a falling out that culminated in the majority removing Kertesz as managing member. Kertesz alleged that shortly after this, the LLC's distributors and clients "threatened to terminate their relationship with the LLC if Kertesz was not brought back into the operations of the LLC." These actions, Kertesz claimed, caused the LLC to suffer irreparable harm. Kertesz sought the judicial dissolution of the LLC on the basis of these circumstances and an alleged deadlock in management of the LLC. He sought the appointment of a receiver to protect the assets and goodwill of the LLC. What relief, if any, is Kertesz entitled to? [*Kertesz v. The Spa Floral, LLC*, 994 So. 2d 473 (Fla. App.)]

13. Thomas Banner assigned his voting rights and his right to receive distributions in the Hut at Avon, LLC, to Elizabeth Condo as part of a divorce settlement. When the other members of the Hut Group, Thomas Connors and George Roberts, learned of the unapproved assignment, they contacted Banner and expressed the view that the assignment violated the anti-assignment clause of the operating agreement, which required the primary consent of all the members. After some negotiations, Banner agreed to sell his entire rights to Connors and Roberts for $125,000. Condo sued these members in court for the destruction of the value of the assignment. The LLC defended that the assignment was in violation of the operating agreement and thus was void. Decide. [*Condo v. Connors*, 266 P.3d 1110 (Colo. 2011)]

CPA Question

1. Which of the following statements is correct with respect to a limited partnership?

   a. A limited partner may *not* be an unsecured creditor of the limited partnership.

   b. A general partner may *not* also be a limited partner at the same time.

   c. A general partner may be a secured creditor of the limited partnership.

   d. A limited partnership can be formed with limited liability for all partners.

Corporation Formation

Learning Outcomes <<<

After studying this chapter, you should be able to

LO.1 Recognize that a corporation is a separate legal entity, distinct and apart from its stockholders and that individual shareholders are not liable for claims against the corporation

LO.2 Explain the wide range of power given to corporations under modern corporate codes

LO.3 Understand that the promoter is personally liable for preincorporation contracts

LO.4 Understand that after a corporate charter has been dissolved the owners and officers may be personally responsible for contracts made in the corporate name if they knew or should have known of the dissolution

LO.5 Explain a stockholder's option when he or she objects to a proposed consolidation or merger of the corporation

LO.6 Recognize that liabilities of predecessor corporations can be imposed on successor corporations when the transaction is a de facto merger or a continuation of the predecessor

The corporation is one of the most important forms of business organization.

43-1 Nature and Classes

A *corporation* is an artificial person that is created by government action.

43-1a The Corporation as a Person

corporation–artificial being created by government grant, which for many purposes is treated as a natural person.

certificate of incorporation–written approval from the state or national government for a corporation to be formed.

A **corporation** is an artificial person created by government action and granted certain powers. It exists in the eyes of the law as a person, separate and distinct from the persons who own the corporation.

The concept that the corporation is a distinct legal person means that the corporation's property is owned not by the persons who own shares in the corporation but by the corporation itself. Debts of the corporation are debts of this artificial person, not of the persons running the corporation or owning shares of stock in it.[1] The corporation can sue and be sued in its own name, but shareholders cannot be sued or held liable for corporate actions or obligations.[2] The cardinal rule is that a corporation has a legal existence separate and apart from its officers and shareholders.[3] Consequently, even a sole shareholder is not ordinarily liable for corporate acts.[4]

CASE SUMMARY

Personal Liability versus Corporate Liability

FACTS: Thomas Sauers asked a family friend, Robert Crozier, to lend him money to expand his auto glass business. Crozier loaned $180,000 pursuant to an oral agreement. The loan was to purchase an existing auto glass company and to be a down payment on two buildings for corporate purposes. Crozier gave Sauers four checks made out to T & M Corp. The buildings were never purchased but Sauers testified that the funds were used to cover operating expenses of T & M Corp. Crozier sued for repayment of the loan amount, maintaining that Thomas Sauers was personally liable for the repayment of the loan.

DECISION: Judgment for Sauers. The parties understood that the funds were for corporate purposes, were advanced to the corporation, were deposited in the corporation's account, and were used for corporate purposes. There was no evidence that Sauers agreed to be personally responsible for repaying the loan. The complaint against Sauers must be dismissed. [*Crozier v. Sauers*, **109 A.D.3d 507 (N.Y. App. Div. 2013)**]

articles of incorporation–See *certificate of incorporation.*

charter–grant of authority from a government to exist as a corporation. Generally replaced today by a certificate of incorporation approving the articles of incorporation.

A corporation is formed by obtaining approval of a **certificate of incorporation, articles of incorporation,** or a **charter** from the state or national government.[5]

[1] *American Truck Lines, Inc. v. Albino*, 424 S.E.2d 367 (Ga. App. 1992).

[2] Also, a corporation does not have standing to pursue a claim on behalf of its sole shareholder. See *Accurate Printers, Inc. v. Stark*, 671 S.E.2d 228 (Ga. App. 2008).

[3] *Hayes v. Collins*, 538 S.E.2d 785 (Ga. App. 2000).

[4] If a court finds that a corporation is merely the alter ego of an individual shareholder, the court may "pierce the corporate veil" and hold the individual personally liable. Piercing the corporate veil is addressed in Chapter 44, Shareholders Rights in Corporations.

[5] *Charter, certificate of incorporation,* and *articles of incorporation* are all terms used to refer to the documents that serve as evidence of a government's grant of corporate existence and powers. Most state incorporation statutes now provide for a certificate of incorporation issued by the Secretary of State, but a Revised Model Business Corporation Act (RMBCA) has done away with the certificate of incorporation. Under the RMBCA, corporate existence begins when articles of incorporation are filed with the Secretary of State. An endorsed copy of the articles together with a fee, receipt, or acknowledgment replaces the certificate of incorporation. See RMBCA §§1.25 and 2.03.

43-1b Classifications of Corporations

Corporations may be classified in terms of their relationship to the public, the source of their authority, and the nature of their activities.

Public, Private, and Quasi-Public Corporations

A **public corporation** is one established for governmental purposes and for the administration of public affairs. A city is a public or municipal corporation acting under authority granted to it by the state.

A **private corporation** is one organized for charitable and benevolent purposes or for purposes of finance, industry, and commerce. Private corporations are often called *public* in business circles when their stock is sold to the public.

A **quasi-public corporation,** sometimes known as a public service corporation or a public utility, is a private corporation furnishing services on which the public is particularly dependent, such as a gas or electric company.

Public Authorities

The public increasingly demands that government perform services. Some of these are performed directly by government. Others are performed by separate corporations or **authorities** created by government. **For Example,** a city parking facility may be organized as a separate municipal parking authority, or a public housing project may be operated as an independent housing authority.

Domestic and Foreign Corporations

A corporation is called a **domestic corporation** with respect to the state under whose law it has been incorporated. Any other corporation going into that state is called a **foreign corporation.** Thus, a corporation holding a Texas charter is a domestic corporation in Texas but a foreign corporation in all other states.[6]

Special Service Corporations

Corporations formed for transportation, banking, insurance, and savings and loan operations and similar specialized functions are subject to separate codes or statutes with regard to their organization. In addition, federal and state laws and administrative agencies regulate in detail the way these businesses are conducted.

Close Corporations

A corporation whose shares are held by a single shareholder or a small group of shareholders is known as a **close corporation.** Its shares are not traded publicly. Many such corporations are small firms that are incorporated to obtain either the advantage of limited liability or a tax benefit, or both.

Many states have statutes that have liberalized corporation law as it applies to close corporations. **For Example,** a brother and sister inherited their parents' stock in a domestic close corporation, Hall's Mortuary, Inc., a prominent and successful funeral home in

---

Margin glossary:

public corporation—corporation that has been established for governmental purposes and for the administration of public affairs.

private corporation—corporation organized for charitable and benevolent purposes or for purposes of finance, industry, and commerce.

quasi-public corporation—private corporation furnishing services on which the public is particularly dependent, for example, a gas and electric company.

authorities—corporations formed by government that perform public service.

domestic corporation—corporation that has been incorporated by the state in question as opposed to incorporation by another state.

foreign corporation—corporation incorporated under the laws of another state.

close corporation—corporation whose shares are held by a single shareholder or a small group of shareholders.

---

[6] Failure of a foreign corporation to obtain a certificate of authority to do business within the state, under that state's door-closing statute, may mean that the foreign corporation cannot enforce a contract entered into in the state. For Example, TradeWinds Environmental Restoration, Inc., a New York–based company, entered into a contract with Alabama contractor BBC to do structural-drying services at a number of coastal condominiums after Hurricane Ivan in 2004. TradeWinds performed the work under the contract valued at $400,000. When TradeWinds sued for the money owed under the contract, the court determined that the "labor" performed is not an article of commerce nor is the agreement to supply it an act of commerce. The court determined that TradeWinds' business was intrastate, rather than interstate, and without a certificate of authority to perform the work, TradeWinds could not enforce the contract. *TradeWinds Environmental Restoration, Inc. v. Brown Brothers Construction, LLC*, 999 So. 2d 875 (Ala. 2008).

Louisiana. Nancy was the secretary-treasurer, a director, and the shareholder of 50 percent of the corporation's stock. Hall was president, a director, and the shareholder of the other 50 percent of the corporation's stock. The siblings had a falling out that involved Nancy demanding more participation in the management of the business. Hall maintained that he and Nancy were deadlocked in the management of corporate affairs and petitioned the court for involuntary dissolution and the appointment of a liquidator. The court applied a statute, nearly identical to the Delaware statute, "designed to obviate a deadlocked vote of two equal shareholders" of a close corporation and ordered the dissolution of the corporation.[7]

CPA   Subchapter S Corporations

Subchapter S is a subdivision of the Internal Revenue Code. If corporate shareholders meet the requirements of this subdivision, they may elect Subchapter S status, which allows the shareholders to be treated as partners for tax purposes and retain the benefit of limited liability under the corporate form. A Subchapter S corporation is limited to 100 shareholders.[8]

Professional Corporations

A corporation may be organized for the purpose of conducting a profession, such as law, medicine, accounting, architecture, or engineering. Each officer, director, and shareholder of a professional corporation must be licensed to practice the profession. Professional incorporation does not shield a practitioner from personal liability relating to the professional services rendered. State laws vary, with some states recognizing professional corporations, or P.C.s, and other states recognizing a Professional Limited Liability Company (PLLC). In addition to approval from the Secretary of State, professional corporations may need approval from the state professional licensing body.

Nonprofit Corporations

eleemosynary corporation–corporation organized for a charitable or benevolent purpose.

A *nonprofit corporation* (or an **eleemosynary corporation**), is one that is organized for charitable or benevolent purposes. Nonprofit corporations include hospitals, nursing homes, and universities.[9] Special procedures for incorporation are prescribed, and provision is made for a detailed examination of and hearing regarding the purpose, function, and methods of raising money for the enterprise. State laws vary and may require a nonprofit corporation to include a brief statement of its purpose.[10]

Benefit Corporations

benefit corporation–for-profit corporation that sets a goal to create a public benefit while still providing economic returns to its investors.

Benefit, or **B-corporations** are for-profit corporations that set a goal to create a public benefit while still providing economic returns to their investors. **For Example,** Patagonia, registered under California's benefit corporation statute, uses the benefit corporation to emphasize its commitment to the environment. State laws typically recognize that directors will take benefits to society or the environment into account when making corporate decisions and require benefit corporations to adopt independent, third-party standards to measure their success or failure. At least 26 states have benefit corporation statutes and several have legislation pending. The state of Washington recognizes a social purpose corporation, or SPC.

---

[7] *Judson v. Davis*, 916 So. 2d 1106 (La. App. 2005).
[8] See IRS, S Corporations, **http://www.irs.gov/Businesses/Small-Businesses-&-Self-Employed/S-Corporations.**
[9] The Committee on Corporate Laws of the American Bar Association has prepared a Model Nonprofit Corporation Act. A revised Model Nonprofit Corporation Act was approved in 1986.
[10] See *Peters Creek United Presbyterian Church v. Washington Presbytery of Penn.*, 90 A.3d 95 (2014).

43-1c **Corporations and Governments**

The power of governments to create and regulate corporations may involve several issues.

Power to Create

By definition a corporation is created by government. Thus, the right to be a corporation must be obtained from the proper governmental agency. The federal government may create corporations whenever appropriate to carry out the powers granted to it.

Generally, a state by virtue of its **police power** may create any kind of corporation for any purpose. Most states have a **general corporation code,** which lists certain requirements, and anyone who satisfies the requirements and files the necessary papers with the government may automatically form a corporation. In 1950, the American Bar Association (ABA) published a Model Business Corporation Act (MBCA) to assist legislative bodies in the modernization of state corporation laws. An updated version was published in 1969. Statutory language similar to that contained in the 1969 version of the MBCA has been adopted in whole or in part by 35 states. A complete revision of the model act was approved in 1984 (RMBCA).[11] Jurisdictions following the model act have made numerous modifications to reflect differing views about balancing the interests of public corporations, shareholders, and management. Caution must therefore be exercised in making generalizations about model act jurisdictions. There is no *uniform* corporation act.

police power–power to govern; the power to adopt laws for the protection of the public health, welfare, safety, and morals.

general corporation code–state's code listing certain requirements for creation of a corporation.

Power to Regulate

Subject to constitutional limitations, corporations may be regulated by statutes.

Protection of the Corporation as a Person. The Constitution of the United States prohibits the national government and state governments from depriving any person of life, liberty, or property without due process of law. Many state constitutions contain a similar limitation on their respective state governments. A corporation is regarded as a "person" within the meaning of such provisions.

The federal Constitution prohibits a state from denying to any person within its jurisdiction the equal protection of the laws. No such express limitation is placed on the federal government, although the due process clause binding the federal government is liberally interpreted so that it prohibits substantial inequality of treatment.

Recall the *Citizens United* case in Chapter 4 in which the Supreme Court held that the government may not suppress political speech on the basis of the speaker's corporate identity.[12]

Protection of the Corporation as a Citizen. For certain purposes, such as determining the right to bring a lawsuit in a federal court, a corporation is a citizen of any state in which it has been incorporated and of the state where it has its principal place of business.

43-2 **Corporate Powers**

Except for limitations in the federal Constitution or the state's own constitution, a state legislature may give corporations any lawful powers. The RMBCA contains a general provision on corporate powers granting a corporation "the same powers as an individual to do all things necessary or convenient to carry out its business and affairs."[13]

---

[11] The Revised Model Business Corporation Act (1984) was approved by the Committee on Corporate Laws Section of Business Law of the American Bar Association. Model act citations are to the 1984 Revised Model Business Corporation Act (RMBCA) unless designated otherwise.

[12] *Citizens United v. Federal Election Com'n,* 558 U.S. 310 (2010).

[13] RMBCA §3.02. State statutes generally contain similar broad catchall grants of powers.

43-2a **Particular Powers**

Modern corporation codes give corporations a wide range of powers.

Perpetual Life

One of the distinctive features of a corporation is its perpetual or continuous life—the power to continue as an entity forever or for a stated period of time regardless of changes in stock ownership or the death of any shareholders.

Corporate Name

A corporation must have a name to identify it. As a general rule, it may select any name for this purpose. Most states require that the corporate name contain some word indicating the corporate character[14] and that the name not be the same as, or deceptively similar to, the name of any other corporation. Some statutes prohibit the use of a name that is likely to mislead the public.

Corporate Seal

A corporation may have a distinctive seal. However, a corporation need not use a seal in the transaction of business unless it is required by statute or a natural person in transacting that business would be required to use a seal.

Bylaws

CPA

bylaws–rules and regulations enacted by a corporation to govern the affairs of the corporation and its shareholders, directors, and officers.

Bylaws are the rules and regulations enacted by a corporation to govern the affairs of the corporation and its shareholders, directors, and officers.

Bylaws are adopted by shareholders, although in some states they may be adopted by the directors of the corporation. Approval by the state or an amendment of the corporate charter is not required to make the bylaws effective.

The bylaws are subordinate to the general law of the state, the statute under which the corporation is formed, and the charter of the corporation.[15] Bylaws that conflict with such superior authority or that are in themselves unreasonable are invalid. Bylaws that are valid are binding on all shareholders regardless of whether they know of the existence of those bylaws or were among the majority that consented to their adoption. Bylaws are not binding on third persons, however, unless they have notice or knowledge of them.

Stock

A corporation may issue certificates representing corporate stock. Under the RMBCA, authorized, but unissued, shares may be issued at the price set by the board of directors. Under UCC Article 8 (1978 and 1994 versions), securities may be "uncertificated," or not represented by an instrument.

Making Contracts

Corporation codes give corporations the power to make contracts.

Borrowing Money

Corporations have the implied power to borrow money in carrying out their authorized business purposes.

---

[14] RMBCA §4.01(a) declares that the corporate name must contain the word *corporation, company, incorporated,* or *limited* or an abbreviation of one of these words.

[15] *Roach v. Bynum,* 403 So. 2d 187 (Ala. 1981).

Executing Negotiable Instruments

Corporations have the power to issue or indorse negotiable instruments and to accept drafts.

Issuing Bonds

A corporation may exercise its power to borrow money by issuing bonds.

Transferring Property

The corporate property may be leased, assigned for the benefit of creditors, or sold. In many states, however, a solvent corporation may not transfer all of its property without the consent of all or a substantial majority of its shareholders.

A corporation, having power to incur debts, may mortgage or pledge its property as security for those debts. This rule does not apply to public service companies, such as street transit systems and gas and electric companies.

Acquiring Property

A corporation has the power to acquire and hold such property as is reasonably necessary for carrying out its express powers.

Buying Back Stock

treasury stock— corporate stock that the corporation has reacquired.

Generally, a corporation may purchase its own stock if it is solvent at the time and the purchase does not impair capital. Stock that is reacquired by the corporation that issued it is commonly called **treasury stock.**

Although treasury stock retains the character of outstanding stock, it has an inactive status while it is held by the corporation.[16] Thus, the treasury shares cannot be voted nor can dividends be declared on them.

Doing Business in Another State

A corporation has the power to engage in business in other states. However, such power does not exempt the corporation from satisfying valid restrictions imposed by the foreign state in which it seeks to do business.

Participating in an Enterprise

Corporations may generally participate in an enterprise to the same extent as individuals. They may enter into joint ventures and partnerships. A corporation may also be a limited partner. The RMBCA authorizes a corporation "to be a promoter, partner, member, associate, or manager of any partnership, joint venture, trust, or other entity."[17]

Paying Employee Benefits

The RMBCA empowers a corporation "to pay pensions and establish pension plans, pension trusts, profit-sharing plans, share bonus plans, share option plans, and benefit or incentive plans for any or all of its current or former directors, officers, employees, and agents."[18]

---

[16] When a corporation reacquires its own shares, it has the choice of retiring them and thus restoring them to the status of authorized, but unissued, shares or of treating them as still issued and available for transfer. The latter are described as treasury shares.

[17] RMBCA §3.02(9).

[18] RMBCA §3.02(12).

Charitable Contributions

The RMBCA authorizes a corporation, without any limitation, "to make donations for the public welfare or for charitable, scientific, or educational purposes."[19] In some states, a limitation is imposed on the amount that can be donated for charitable purposes.

43-2b *Ultra Vires* Acts

ultra vires–act or contract that the corporation does not have authority to do or make.

When a corporation acts in excess of or beyond the scope of its powers, the corporation's act is described as **ultra vires.** Such an action is improper in the same way that it is improper for an agent to act beyond the scope of the authority given by the principal. It is also improper with respect to shareholders and creditors of the corporation because corporate funds have been diverted to unauthorized uses.

The modern corporation statute will state that every corporation formed under it will have certain powers unless the articles of incorporation expressly exclude some of the listed powers, and then the statute will list every possible power that is needed to run a business. In some states, the legislature makes a blanket grant of all power that a natural person running the business would possess.[20] The net result is that the modern corporation possesses such a broad scope of powers that it is difficult to find an action that is *ultra vires*. If a mining corporation should begin to manufacture television sets, that might be an *ultra vires* transaction but such an extreme departure rarely happens.

Because nonprofit corporations have a more restricted range of powers than business corporations, actions not authorized by the charters of nonprofit corporations are more likely to be found *ultra vires*.[21]

43-3 Creation and Termination of the Corporation

All states have general laws governing the creation of corporations.

43-3a Promoters

promoters–persons who plan the formation of the corporation and sell or promote the idea to others.

Corporations come into existence as the result of the activities of one or more persons known as **promoters** who bring together persons interested in the enterprise, aid in obtaining subscriptions to stock, and set in motion the machinery that leads to the formation of the corporation itself.

A corporation is not liable on a contract made by its promoter for its benefit unless the corporation takes some affirmative action to adopt the contract, such as express words of adoption or acceptance of the contract's benefits.[22] A corporation may also become bound by such contracts through assignment or novation.

The promoter is personally liable for all contracts made on behalf of the corporation before its existence unless the promoter is exempted by the terms of the agreement or by the circumstances surrounding it.[23]

---

[19] RMBCA §3.02(13).

[20] Note the broad powers granted under RMBCA §3.02; see also *MIC v. Battle Mountain Corp.*, 70 P.3d 1176 (Colo. 2003), where Colorado's *ultra vires* statute prohibits claims that a corporation is acting beyond the scope of its powers.

[21] *Lovering v. Seabrook Island Property Owners Ass'n*, 344 S.E.2d 862 (S.C. App. 1986). But see *St. Louis v. Institute of Med. Ed. & Res.*, 786 S.W.2d 885 (Mo. App. 1990).

[22] The *Hansen v. Fields Company, LLC* case, summarized in Chapter 42, addresses the distinction between an LLC's liability and that of the promoter.

[23] See *GS Petroleum, Inc. v. R and S Fuel, Inc.*, 2009 WL 1554680 (Del. Super. June 4, 2009), where the court found that the promoters were not liable on the preincorporation contract for the sale of a Shell gas station. The court reasoned that the terms of the contract did not intend promoter liability, and the business was incorporated by the buyer before taking possession of the business.

A promoter is liable for all torts committed in connection with the promoter's activities. The corporation is not ordinarily liable for the torts of the promoter, but it may become liable by its conduct after incorporation. If a promoter induces making a contract by fraud, the corporation is liable for the fraud if it assumes or ratifies the contract with knowledge or notice of such fraud.

A promoter stands in a fiduciary relation to the corporation and to stock subscribers and cannot make secret profits at their expense. Accordingly, if a promoter makes a secret profit on a sale of land to the corporation, the promoter must surrender the profit to the corporation.

The corporation is not liable in most states for the expenses and services of the promoter unless it subsequently promises to pay for them or the corporation's charter or a statute imposes such liability on it.

43-3b Incorporation

incorporator—one or more natural persons or corporations who sign and file appropriate incorporation forms with a designated government official.

One or more natural persons or corporations may act as **incorporators** of a corporation by signing and filing appropriate forms with a designated government official.[24] These papers are filed in duplicate, and a filing fee must be paid. The designated official (usually the Secretary of State), after being satisfied that the forms conform to statutory requirements, stamps "Filed" and the date on each copy. The official then retains one copy and returns the other copy, along with a filing fee receipt, to the corporation.[25]

Statutes may require incorporators to give some form of public notice, such as by advertising in a newspaper, of their intention to form a corporation, stating its name, address, and general purpose.

43-3c Application for Incorporation

In most states, the process of forming a corporation is begun by filing an application for a certificate of incorporation. This application contains or is accompanied by articles of incorporation. The instrument is filed with the Secretary of State and sets forth certain information about the new corporation. The articles of incorporation must contain (1) the name of the corporation, (2) the number of shares of stock the corporation is authorized to issue, (3) the street address of the corporation's initial registered office and the name of its initial registered agent, and (4) the name and address of each incorporator.[26] The articles of incorporation may also state the purpose or purposes for which the corporation is organized. If there is no "purpose clause," the corporation automatically has the purpose of engaging in any lawful business.[27] Also, if no reference is made to the duration of the corporation in the articles of incorporation, it will automatically have perpetual duration.[28]

43-3d The Certificate of Incorporation

Most state incorporation statutes now provide for a certificate of incorporation to be issued by the Secretary of State after articles of incorporation that conform to state requirements have been filed. The Revised Model Business Corporation Act (RMBCA) has eliminated the certificate of incorporation in an effort to reduce the volume of paperwork handled by the Secretary of State.

[24] RMBCA §2.01.
[25] RMBCA §1.25.
[26] RMBCA §2.02.
[27] RMBCA §3.01.
[28] RMBCA §3.02.

Under the RMBCA, corporate existence begins when the articles are filed with the Secretary of State.[29] In some states, corporate existence begins when the proper government official issues a certificate of incorporation. In other states, it does not begin until an organizational meeting is held by the new corporation.

43-3e Proper and Defective Incorporation

corporation de jure—corporation with a legal right to exist by virtue of law.

If the procedure for incorporation has been followed, the corporation has a legal right to exist. It is then called a **corporation de jure,** meaning that it is a corporation by virtue of law.

The law usually overlooks defects that are not material and holds that the corporation is a corporation de jure.

The RMBCA abolishes objections to irregularities and defects in incorporating. It provides that the

secretary of state's filing of the articles of incorporation is conclusive proof that the incorporators satisfied all conditions precedent to incorporation....[30]

De Facto Corporation

The defect in the incorporation may be so substantial that it cannot be ignored, and the corporation will not be accepted as a corporation de jure, yet compliance may be sufficient for recognizing that there is a corporation. When this occurs, the association is called a **de facto** corporation.

de facto—existing in fact as distinguished from as of right, as in the case of an officer or a corporation purporting to act as such without being elected to the office or having been properly incorporated.

Although conflict exists among authorities, the traditional elements of a de facto corporation are that (1) a valid law exists under which the corporation could have been properly incorporated, (2) an attempt to organize the corporation has been made in good faith, (3) a genuine attempt to organize in compliance with statutory requirements has been made, and (4) corporate powers have been used.

Corporation by Estoppel

The defect in incorporation may be so great that by law the association cannot be accepted as a de facto corporation. In such a case, there is no corporation. If the individuals involved proceed to run the business in spite of such irregularity, they may be held personally liable as partners for the business's debts.[31] This rule is sometimes not applied when a person has dealt with the business as though it were a corporation.[32] In such instances, the party is estopped from denying that the "corporation" had legal existence. In effect, there is **corporation by estoppel** with respect to that party.

corporation by estoppel—corporation that comes about when parties estop themselves from denying that the corporation exists.

Several jurisdictions that follow the 1969 MBCA have expressly retained the doctrines of corporation by estoppel and de facto corporations.[33] Other courts interpreting the language of the 1969 MBCA, however, have held that the doctrines of de facto corporation and corporation by estoppel no longer exist.

The language of the 1984 version allows some jurisdictions sufficient room for the de facto and estoppel doctrines to operate through Section 2.04 of the MBCA.

With respect to preincorporation debts, the 1984 act imposes liability only on persons who act as, or on behalf of, a corporation while knowing that no corporation

---

[29] RMBCA §2.03(a).

[30] RMBCA §2.03(b).

[31] In a minority of states, a court will not hold individuals liable as partners but will hold liable the person who committed the act on behalf of the business on the theory that that person was an agent who acted without authority and is therefore liable for breach of the implied warranties of the existence of a principal possessing capacity and of proper authorization.

[32] *Am. South Bank v. Holland*, 669 So. 2d 151 (Ala. Civ. App. 1994).

[33] See Ga. Bus. Corp Code §22-5103; Minn. Bus. Corp Act §301:08. See also *H. Rich Corp. v. Feinberg*, 518 So. 2d 377 (Fla. App. 1987).

exists.[34] Courts may allow a corporation to sue to enforce a preincorporation agreement if the corporation had a "personal stake" in the agreement.[35]

43-3f Insolvency, Bankruptcy, and Reorganization

When a corporation has financial troubles so serious that it is insolvent, the best thing may be to go through bankruptcy or reorganization proceedings. The law with respect to bankruptcy and reorganizations is discussed in Chapter 34.

43-3g Forfeiture of Charter

In states that have adopted the RMBCA, the Secretary of State may commence proceedings to administratively dissolve a corporation if (1) the corporation does not pay franchise taxes within 60 days after they are due, (2) the corporation does not file its annual report within 60 days after it is due, or (3) the corporation is without a registered agent or registered office for 60 days or more.[36] After a corporate charter has been dissolved, the owners and officers of the dissolved corporation are not shielded from personal liability by using the corporate name when making contracts if they knew or should have known of the dissolution. **For Example,** on October 2, 2004, Dinky, Inc., was involuntarily dissolved for failure to file an annual report and pay an annual franchise tax. Elaine Kostopulos, the president and sole shareholder of Dinky, Inc., had incorporated her business in 1989 and regularly purchased products manufactured by Benetton USA, Inc., since that time. During the five years after Dinky was dissolved, she continued to operate as a corporation, ordering and making payments to Benetton through June 7, 2009. Between June and November 2009, Benetton sought payment of over $200,000 owed by Dinky. Ms. Kostopulos claims she was unaware of the dissolution until late 2009, when payment problems arose. Dinky applied for reinstatement at that time. With corporate status reinstated, Ms. Kostopulos contended that she was not personally liable for the debts incurred by the dissolved corporation during the time of its dissolution. The court determined that Ms. Kostopulos could not escape personal liability by reinstating her corporation, holding that "she should have known" about the dissolution of Dinky, over such a long period of time.[37]

After a corporation is dissolved, a contract made by an officer of the dissolved corporation cannot be enforced against the other party to the contract. **For Example,** a lucrative contract with Florio Entertainment, Inc., was signed "Louis Lofredo, LL Associates as company president" using a letterhead "LL Associates, Inc." In fact, the corporation "LL Associates, Inc." had been dissolved years before the contract was negotiated and signed, and Lofredo had made no effort to reinstate the corporation. LL Associates, Inc., had no legal existence and thus could not be a party to the contract and could not enforce the contract.[38]

A corporation whose powers are suspended for nonpayment of taxes cannot sue or defend a lawsuit while its taxes remain unpaid.[39] Upon payment of taxes, however, corporate powers are revived. Thus, if a corporation filed a timely appeal while its powers were suspended, it could proceed with the appeal after paying its taxes.[40]

---

[34] RMBCA §2.04.

[35] *De La Garza v. Clean Oil Innovations, Inc.*, 2013 WL 1222109 (S.D. Tex. March 20, 2013).

[36] RMBCA §14.20.

[37] *Benetton U.S.A. Corp. v. Dinky, Inc.*, 2011 WL 5024549 (N.D. Ill. Oct. 19, 2011). But see section 2.04 of the 1984 RMBCA, which provides that all persons purporting to act for or on behalf of a corporation "knowing that there was no incorporation" under the act are jointly and severally liable for all liabilities while so acting. There would be no liability for an individual who did not and should not have known of the dissolution.

[38] *Animazing Entertainment, Inc. v. Louis Lofredo Associates, Inc.*, 88 F. Supp. 2d 265 (S.D.N.Y. 2000).

[39] *Kaufman, Inc. v. Performance Plastering, Inc.*, 39 Cal. Rptr. 3d 33 (Cal. App. 2006).

[40] See *Bourhis v. Lord*, 295 P.3d 895 (Cal. 2013).

43-3h Judicial Dissolution

Judicial dissolution of a corporation may be decreed when its management is deadlocked and the deadlock cannot be broken by the shareholders.[41] In some states, a "custodian" may be appointed for a corporation when the shareholders are unable to break a deadlock in the board of directors and irreparable harm is threatened to, or sustained by, the corporation because of the deadlock.

43-3i Voluntary Dissolution

State laws describe the requirements for voluntary dissolution of a corporation. For example, publication in a paper of general circulation may be required. Compliance with such statutes is important to protect the company from subsequent claims. A state law may state that a claim against the corporation will be barred unless the claim is brought within two years of publication of the notice of dissolution.[42]

> **consolidation (of corporations)**– combining of two or more corporations in which the corporate existence of each one ceases and a new corporation is created.

43-4 Consolidations, Mergers, and Conglomerates

Two or more corporations may be combined to form a new structure or enterprise.

CPA ### 43-4a Definitions

Enterprises may be combined by a consolidation or merger of corporations or by the formation of a conglomerate.

CPA ### Consolidation

In a **consolidation** of two or more corporations, the separate existence of the two corporations ceases, and a new corporation with the property and assets of the old corporations comes into being (Figure 43-1).

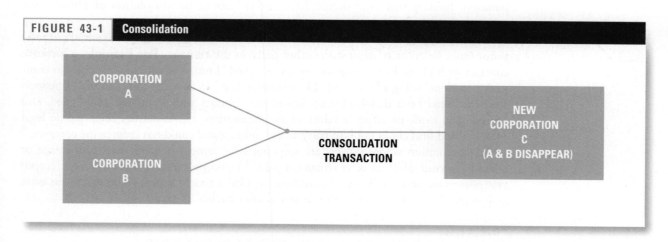

FIGURE 43-1   Consolidation

CORPORATION A

CORPORATION B

CONSOLIDATION TRANSACTION

NEW CORPORATION C (A & B DISAPPEAR)

---

[41] After a shareholder has requested dissolution of a corporation, a state statute may offer an option to the corporation or other existing shareholders to purchase shares owned by the petitioning shareholder(s) for "fair value" in lieu of dissolution. See *Dawkins v. Hickman Family Corp.*, 2010 WL 4683472 (N.D. Miss. Nov. 10, 2010).

[42] *Lewis Oil, Inc. v. Bourbon Mini-Mart, Inc.*, 16 N.E.3d (Ind. App. 2014). Lewis Oil gave reasonable notice of voluntary dissolution in a paper of general circulation. The notice stated that claims against the corporation had to be filed within two years after publication of the notice. A suit by a liquor store claiming that Lewis Oil contributed to environmental contamination on the property was dismissed because it was time-barred by the notice of dissolution.

FIGURE 43-2 Merger

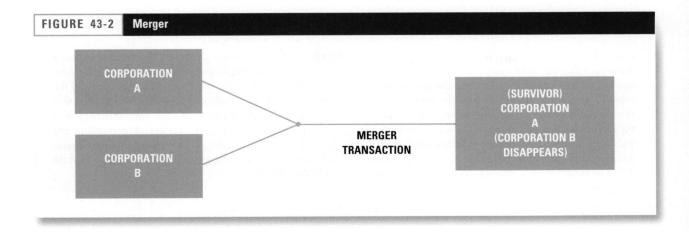

When a consolidation occurs, the new corporation ordinarily succeeds to the rights, powers, and immunities of its component parts. However, limitations may be imposed by constitution, statute, or certificate of incorporation.

CPA   Merger

merger (of corporations)– combining of corporations by which one absorbs the other and continues to exist, preserving its original charter and identity while the other corporation ceases to exist.

When two corporations **merge,** one absorbs the other. One corporation retains its original charter and identity and continues to exist; the other disappears, and its corporate existence terminates (Figure 43-2).

A stockholder who objects to a proposed consolidation or merger or who fails to convert existing shares into stock of the new or continuing corporation may apply to a court to appraise the value of the stock that she holds.[43] Should either party act arbitrarily, vexatiously, or not in good faith in the appraisal process, the courts have the right to assess court costs and attorney fees. The new or continuing corporation is then required to pay the "fair value" of the stock to the stockholder.[44]

CASE SUMMARY

The Sound of Music: $63.44 per Share

FACTS: The Trapp Family Lodge, Inc. (TFL), was incorporated in 1962 as a holding company for certain assets of the Von Trapp family, including the Trapp Family Lodge, a resort hotel complex located in Stowe, Vermont, and other assets, including certain royalty rights related to the family's story as portrayed in a Broadway musical and a movie. A majority of TFL shareholders approved a merger with a new corporation in 1994, and the merger took place on January 28, 1995. The dissenting shareholders, holding 76,529 of the corporation's 198,000 outstanding shares,

were paid $33.84 per share as fair value by the TFL board of directors. The dissenting shareholders brought suit seeking a higher price as fair value. After the trial court set the fair value of $63.44, TFL appealed.

DECISION: Judgment for the dissenting shareholders. Dissenters' rights statutes were enacted in response to the common law rule that required unanimous consent from shareholders to make fundamental changes in a corporation. Under this rule minority shareholders could block corporate

---

[43] *Delaware Open MRI Radiology v. Kessler*, 898 A.2d 290 (Del. Ch. 2006).
[44] See *Spenlinhauer v. Spencer Press Inc.*, 959 N.E.2d 436 (Mass. App. 2011), where a minority shareholder dissented to a proposed merger, and after executing a cash-out merger, the court determined the "fair value" of the minority shares as the pro rata percentage of the net selling price.

The Sound of Music: $63.44 per Share continued

change by refusing to cooperate in hope of establishing a nuisance value for their shares. In response, legislatures enacted statutes authorizing corporate changes by majority vote. To protect the interests of minority shareholders, statutes generally permit a dissenting minority to demand that the corporation buy back shares at fair value. The basic concept of fair value is that the stockholder is entitled to be paid for his or her "proportionate interest in a going concern." The trial court properly rejected the fact-specific appraisal made on behalf of the majority shareholders because it

lacked thoroughness and credibility, unjustifiably reducing the value of the lodge operations and overstating income taxes to reduce after-tax cash flows. The court accepted the appraisal made on behalf of the minority shareholders that utilized the average of a net asset value method of evaluation and a discounted cash flow method of evaluation, and yielded a value of $63.44 per share. [**In re *75,629 Shares of Common Stock of Trapp Family Lodge, Inc.*, 725 A.2d 927 (Vt. 1999)**]

Conglomerate

conglomerate–
relationship of a parent corporation to subsidiary corporations engaged in diversified fields of activity unrelated to the field of activity of the parent corporation.

Conglomerate describes the relationship of a parent corporation to subsidiary corporations engaged in diversified fields of activity unrelated to the parent corporation's field of activity. **For Example,** a wire-manufacturing corporation that owns all the stock of a newspaper corporation and of a drug-manufacturing corporation would be described as a conglomerate. In contrast, if the wire-manufacturing company owned a mill that produced the metal used in making the wire and a mine that produced the ore that was used by the mill, the relationship would probably be described as an *integrated industry* rather than as a conglomerate. This term is merely a matter of usage rather than of legal definition. Likewise, when the parent company is not engaged in production or the rendering of services, it is customary to call it a *holding company*.

Without regard to whether the enterprise is a holding company or whether the group of corporations constitutes a conglomerate or an integrated industry, each part is a distinct corporation to which ordinary corporation law applies. In some instances, additional principles apply because of the nature of the relationships existing among the several corporations involved.

43-4b Legality

Consolidations, mergers, and asset acquisitions between enterprises are prohibited by federal antitrust legislation when the effect is to lessen competition in interstate commerce. A business corporation may not merge with a charitable corporation because this combination would divert the assets of the respective corporations to purposes not intended by their shareholders.

43-4c Liability of Successor Corporations

When corporations are combined in any way, the question of who is liable for the debts and obligations of the predecessor corporation arises.

Mergers and Consolidations

Generally, the enterprise engaging in or continuing the business after a merger or consolidation succeeds to all of the rights and property of the predecessor, or disappearing, corporation.[45]

---

[45] *Corporate Express Office Products, Inc. v. Phillips*, 847 So. 2d 406 (Fla. 2003).

CASE SUMMARY

A Marshmallow of a Case for the Plaintiff Marsh USA

FACTS: The Orleans Parish School Board ("School Board") in New Orleans, Louisiana, hired Johnson & Higgins, Inc. (J&H), in 1996, creating an ongoing insurance consulting agreement between them. The terms of the agreement provided that the School Board would pay J&H, Inc., for its consulting services and would later be reimbursed by the insurance carrier eventually selected by the School Board. Pursuant to their agreement, over the next few years, J&H's Mrs. Ippolito prepared several Requests for Proposals ("RFP") on behalf of the School Board. The School Board paid its fees for this consulting work without complaint. During this time, Johnson & Higgins merged with Marsh McLennan, a company that thereafter merged into Marsh USA, Inc. In 2001, Mrs. Ippolito prepared, at the request of the School Board, two more requests for proposals. Per the terms of the RFPs, Marsh was to receive $70,000 as its consulting fee under NO. 7656 and a $5,000 consulting fee

under NO. 7657. Mrs. Ippolito and her staff spent several months working on the project for the School Board. The School Board never paid Marsh for the services and Marsh USA, Inc., sued the School Board for breach of contract, seeking payment of $75,000. The School Board asserted that Marsh USA was not a proper party to the lawsuit and that no contract had existed with it. From a judgment for Marsh USA, Inc., the School Board appealed.

DECISION: Judgment for Marsh USA, Inc. When two corporations merge or consolidate, the new successor corporation acquires all of the assets and rights of the former corporation. The minutes of a School Board meeting reflect the School Board's awareness of the merger in this case as well as its continuing contract with the firm. [*Marsh Advantage America v. Orleans Parish School Board*, 995 So. 2d 53 (La. App. 2008)]

The enterprise continuing the business is also subject to all of the debts and liabilities of the predecessor corporation.[46]

Liabilities of predecessor corporations can be imposed on a successor corporation when the transaction is a de facto merger[47] or the successor is a mere continuation of the predecessor. **For Example,** Steven Stepp manufactured pleasure boats through Thoroughbred Power Boats, Inc., until August 1996 at which time Thoroughbred Power Boats, Inc., ceased manufacturing and selling boats. In August 1996, Velocity Power Boats, Inc., began manufacturing and selling pleasure boats at the same location. Stephen Stepp and his wife were the only officers and board members of both corporations. Finding that Velocity was merely a "new hat" for Thoroughbred Power Boats, Inc., with the same or similar management and ownership, Velocity Power Boats, Inc., was held liable as a successor corporation for damages for a May 6, 1995, boating accident caused by a defective Thoroughbred Power Boats, Inc., manufactured boat.[48]

Asset Sales

In contrast with a merger or consolidation, a corporation may merely purchase the assets of another business. In that case, the purchaser does not become liable for the obligations of the predecessor business. **For Example,** Hull Corporation sold one of its operating divisions to SP Industries, Inc. (SPI), for $6 million under an asset purchase agreement (APA) that stated that the buyer SPI assumed no liability for preclosing claims against Hull. In fact as Hull and SPI were negotiating the APA, Hull was having difficulties regarding engineering and installation work the division had performed in China for Berg Chilling Systems, Inc. Berg Chilling sued SPI under the doctrine of successor liability for the payment of a

[46] *Beck v. Roper Whitney, Inc.*, 190 F. Supp. 2d 524 (W.D.N.Y. 2001).
[47] *Ulanet v. D'Artagnan, Inc.*, 170 F. Supp. 2d 356 (E.D.N.Y. 2001); see *Callahan & Sons, Inc. v. Dykeman Electric Co. Inc.*, 266 F. Supp. 2d 208 (D. Mass 2003).
[48] *Paten v. Thoroughbred Power Boats, Inc.*, 294 F.3d 640 (5th Cir. 2002).

$1,650,000 arbitration award because of the defective work done by Hull in China. The court held that SPI did not assume Hull's contractual liability to Berg under any exception to the traditional corporate rule of successor nonliability.[49]

Corporations may seek to avoid liability for the obligations of a predecessor corporation by attempting to disguise a consolidation or merger as being merely a sale of assets. Courts will not recognize such a transaction and will impose a successor's liability on the successor corporation.[50] In addition, even when the old corporate entity is not formally dissolved, a finding of a de facto merger resulting in successor liability may occur.

CASE SUMMARY

Corporate Shell Games Not Allowed

FACTS: Since 1976, McGhan/Cal. Inc., a manufacturer of prostheses used in breast augmentation surgery, and later McGhan/Del., received numerous complaints about its implants. It also received inquiries from the Food and Drug Administration. In April 1977, Mary Marks had surgery; two McGhan implants were used. Because of defects in the McGhan implants, Marks underwent three additional operations, eventually having the McGhan products replaced with implants manufactured by another company. In June 1977, McGhan/Cal. was acquired by a Delaware subsidiary of 3M, called McGhan/Del. Inc. McGhan/Del. removed the implants from the market in April 1979. On January 1, 1981, 3M's wholly owned subsidiary, McGhan/Del. Inc., was reorganized as a division of 3M and dissolved. In January 1982, following her fourth surgery, Marks brought a product liability suit against 3M. 3M contended that it was not liable for the actions of the predecessor corporation.

DECISION: The transaction between the 3M subsidiary McGhan/Del. Inc. and McGhan/Cal. Inc. amounted to a de facto merger of the seller and the purchaser. McGhan/Cal. changed its name, distributed 3M stock to its shareholders, and dissolved, and all key employees signed employment contracts to work for the purchaser. No cash was paid for the business. The transaction was not an assets sale. The second reorganization amounted to a continuation of the de facto merger. Public policy requires that 3M, having accepted the benefits of a going concern, should also assume the costs that all other going concerns must bear. It should not be allowed to avoid liability to an injured person by merely shuffling paper and manipulating corporate entities. [*Marks v. Minnesota Mining and Manufacturing Co.*, **232 Cal. Rptr. 594 (Cal. App. 1986)**]

Make the Connection

Summary

A *corporation* is an artificial person created by government action. It exists as a separate and distinct entity possessing certain powers. In most states, the corporation comes into existence when the Secretary of State issues a certificate of incorporation. The most common forms of corporations are private business corporations whose stock is sold to the public (publicly held) and close corporations, which are business firms whose shares are not traded publicly.

Corporations may be formed for purposes other than conducting a business. For example, there are nonprofit corporations, municipal corporations, and public authorities for governmental purposes.

An *ultra vires* act occurs when a corporation acts beyond the scope of the powers given it. Because states now grant broad powers to corporations, it is unlikely that a modern corporation would act beyond the scope of its powers.

[49] *Berg Chilling Systems Inc. v. Hull Corp.*, 435 F.3d 455 (3d Cir. 2006).
[50] *State v. Westwood Squibb Pharmaceutical Co., Inc.*, 981 F. Supp. 760 (W.D.N.Y. 1997).

A *promoter* is a person who brings together the persons interested in the enterprise and sets in motion all that must be done to form a corporation. A corporation is not liable on contracts made by its promoter for the corporation unless it adopts the contracts. The promoter is personally liable for contracts made for the corporation before its existence. A promoter stands in a fiduciary relation to the corporation and stockholders.

The procedures for incorporation are set forth in the statutes of each state. In most states, the corporation comes into existence on issuance of the certificate of incorporation. When all requirements have been satisfied, the corporation is a corporation de jure. When there has not been full compliance with all requirements for incorporation, a de facto corporation may be found to exist. Or when sufficient compliance for a de facto corporation does not exist, in some jurisdictions a third person may be estopped from denying the legal existence of the "corporation" with which it did business (corporation by estoppel).

A corporation has the power to continue as an entity forever or for a stated period of time regardless of changes in the ownership of the stock or the death of a shareholder. It may make contracts, issue stocks and bonds, borrow money, execute commercial paper, transfer and acquire property, acquire its own stock if it is solvent and the purchase does not impair capital, and make charitable contributions. Subject to limitations, a corporation has the power to do business in other states. A corporation may also participate in a business enterprise to the same extent as an individual; that is, it may be a partner in a partnership, or it may enter a joint venture or other enterprise. Special service corporations, such as banks, insurance companies, and railroads, are subject to separate statutes governing their organization and powers.

Two or more corporations may be combined to form a new enterprise. This combination may be a consolidation, with a new corporation coming into existence, or a merger, in which one corporation absorbs the other.

Learning Outcomes

After studying this chapter, you should be able to clearly explain:

43-1 Nature and Classes

LO.1 Recognize that a corporation is a separate legal entity, distinct and apart from its stockholders and that individual shareholders are not liable for claims against the corporation

43-2 Corporate Powers

LO.2 Explain the wide range of power given to corporations under modern corporate codes

See the RMBCA general provision granting corporations "the same powers as an individual to do all things necessary or convenient to carry out its business and affairs," page 887.

43-3 Creation and Termination of the Corporation

LO.3 Understand that the promoter is personally liable for preincorporation contracts

LO.4 Understand that after a corporate charter has been dissolved the owners and officers may be personally

responsible for contracts made in the corporate name if they knew or should have known of the dissolution

See the example where Ms. Kostopulos was personally liable for debts incurred during the time of dissolution because she should have known about the dissolution, page 893.

43-4 Consolidations, Mergers, and Conglomerates

LO.5 Explain a stockholder's option when he or she objects to a proposed consolidation or merger of the corporation

See the *Trapp Family Lodge* case, page 895.

LO.6 Recognize that liabilities of predecessor corporations can be imposed on successor corporations when the transaction is a de facto merger or a continuation of the predecessor

See the example of Velocity Power Boats, Inc., which became essentially a "new hat" for Thoroughbred Power Boats, Inc., with liability as a corporate successor for a defective Thoroughbred boat, page 897.

Key Terms

articles of incorporation
authorities
benefit corporation
bylaws
certificate of incorporation
charter
close corporation
conglomerate
consolidation
corporation
corporation by estoppel
corporation de jure
de facto
domestic corporation
eleemosynary corporation

foreign corporation
general corporation code
incorporators
merge

police power
private corporation
promoters
public corporation

quasi-public corporation
treasury stock
ultra vires

Questions and Case Problems

1. Edwin Edwards and Karen Davis owned EEE, Inc., which owned three convenience stores, all of which sold gasoline. Reid Ellis delivered to the three convenience stores $26,675.02 worth of gasoline for which he was not paid. Ellis proved that Edwards and Davis owned the business, ran it, and in fact personally ordered the gasoline. He claimed that they were personally liable for the debt owed him by EEE, Inc. Decide. [*Ellis v. Edwards*, 348 S.E.2d 764 (Ga. App.)]

2. Clinton Investors Company, as landlord, entered into a three-year lease with the Clifton Park Learning Center as tenant. The lease was executed by Bernie Watkins who represented himself as the treasurer of the Learning Center. On May 31, 1984, the day before the lease term began, Watkins signed a rider to the lease. He again signed as treasurer of the tenant, identifying the tenant as "the Clifton Park Learning Center, Inc." Watkins had not consulted an attorney regarding the formation of the corporation. He mistook the reservation of the business name with the Secretary of State for the filing of a certificate of incorporation. On February 11, 1985, a certificate of incorporation was filed. By March 1986, the Learning Center had become delinquent in rental payments and other fees in the amount of $18,103. Clinton sued Watkins and the Learning Center for the amounts due. Watkins claimed that only the corporation was liable. Decide. [*Clinton Investors Co. v. Watkins*, 536 N.Y.S. 2d 270 (A.D. 1989)]

3. Compare and contrast consolidations, mergers, and conglomerates.

4. On January 27, 1982, Joe Walker purchased a wheel-loader machine from Thompson & Green Machinery Co. (T&G). Walker signed a promissory note for $37,886.30 on behalf of "Music City Sawmill, Inc., by Joe Walker, President." When Sawmill was unable to make payments on the loader, the machine was returned to T&G. T&G brought suit against Sawmill and subsequently discovered that Sawmill had not been incorporated on January 27, 1982, when the machine was purchased but had been incorporated the next day. T&G then sued Walker individually. The lawsuit was Walker's first notice that Sawmill was not incorporated on the date of the sale. Walker's defense was that T&G dealt with Sawmill as a corporation and did not intend to bind him personally on the note and therefore was estopped to deny Sawmill's corporate existence. Decide based on the 1969 MBCA. What would be the result if the RMBCA applied? [*Thompson & Green Machinery Co. v. Music City Lumber Co., Inc., Music City Sawmill Co., Inc.*, 683 S.W.2d 340 (Tenn. App.)]

5. North Pole, Inc., approved a plan to merge with its subsidiary, Santa's Workshop, Inc. The merger plan provided that certain of Workshop's shareholders would receive $3.50 per share. The highest independent appraisal of the stock was $4.04 per share. Hirschfeld, Inc., a shareholder, claimed that the fair value was $16.80 per share. Workshop offered to make its corporate books and records available to Hirschfeld to assess the validity of the $16.80 demand. This offer was declined. Hirschfeld did not attempt to base the $16.80 demand on any recognizable method of stock valuation. Hirschfeld contended that it had a right to get the asking price. Refer to RMBCA §§13.02, 13.28, and 13.31. Could Hirschfeld have blocked the merger until Workshop paid the $16.80? Decide. [*Santa's Workshop v. Hirschfeld, Inc.*, 851 P.2d 265 (Colo. App.)]

6. Richard Ramlall was hired by CloseCall (MD) Inc. to negotiate a billing dispute with Verizon involving some $2 million in asserted overcharges. CloseCall (MD) agreed to a contingent fee "bonus" for its negotiators of 10 percent of the refund. The negotiations were successful. However, before he could collect his fee CloseCall (MD) merged with MVCC Acquisition Corp., a wholly owned subsidiary of MobilePro Corp., which was created for the express purpose of merging with CloseCall (MD). MVCC survived and CloseCall (MD) dissolved. MVCC then changed its name to CloseCall (DE). The merger agreement between CloseCall and MVCC referenced the 10 percent bonus due on the Verizon billing dispute. The surviving Delaware corporation created by the merger of CloseCall (MD) into MVCC is CloseCall (DE). Ramlall sued CloseCall (DE) for the bonus as the successor corporation of

CloseCall (MD). CloseCall (DE) contends that after the merger CloseCall (DE) did not owe any money to Ramlall. Is CloseCall (DE) a successor corporation? Is it liable to Ramlall for the "bonus fee"? [*Ramlall v. Mobile Pro Corp.*, 30 A.2d 1003 (Md. App.)]

7. The Community Youth Center (CYC) Corporation failed to pay its annual registration fee in 2000 and was automatically dissolved by the state corporation commission. CYC continued to operate and held itself out as a corporation well into 2005 when it obtained a loan from the First Community Bank to finance a swimming pool at its facility. The loan was secured by the CYC property. After the corporation defaulted on its loan payments, the bank foreclosed and subsequently purchased the property at a foreclosure sale. CYC contended that the president, vice president, and treasurer of CYC had no standing to make the 2005 loan transaction because CYC's corporate status had been terminated. The bank contended that under the doctrine of corporation by estoppel, CYC continued to exist in 2005, and, consequently, the officer-directors had authority to borrow money and grant a deed of trust, thereby giving the bank a valid lien on the property. Decide. [*First Community Bank, N.A. v. Community Youth Center*, 2010 WL 8696179 (Ca. Cir. Ct.)]

8. Emmick was a director and shareholder of Colonial Manors, Inc. (CM). He organized another corporation named Oahe Enterprises, Inc. To obtain shares of the Oahe stock, Emmick transferred CM shares arbitrarily valued by him at $19 per share to Oahe. The CM shares had a book value of $.47 per share, but Emmick believed that the stock would increase to a value of $19. The directors of Oahe approved Emmick's payment with the valuation of $19 per share. Golden sued Emmick on the ground that he had fraudulently deceived Oahe Corp. about the value of the CM shares and thus had made a secret profit when he received the Oahe shares that had a much greater value than the CM shares he gave in exchange. Emmick contended that his firm opinion was that the future potential value of CM shares would surely reach $19 per share. Decide. [*Golden v. Oahe Enterprises, Inc.*, 295 N.W.2d 160 (S.D.)]

9. Madison Associates purchased control of the majority of shares of 79 Realty Corp. from the Kimmelmans and the Zauders, who then resigned as directors. The Alpert group, which owned the remaining 26 percent of 79 Realty refused to sell their shares. Partners of Madison Associates replaced the Kimmelmans and Zauders as directors of 79 Realty Corp., and as controlling directors, they approved a plan to merge 79 Realty Corp. with the Williams Street Corp., which was owned by Madison Associates. A shareholders' meeting was called, and the merger was approved by two-thirds of the shareholders. The Alpert group's shares were then forcibly canceled, with the price paid for these shares determined at their fair market value. The Alpert group brought suit contending that the merger was unlawful because the sole purpose was to benefit the Madison Associates. Decide. [*Alpert v. 28 Williams Street Corp.*, 473 N.E.2d 19 (N.Y.)]

10. The Seabrook Island Property Owners Association, Inc., is a nonprofit corporation organized under state law to maintain streets and open spaces owned by property owners of Seabrook Island. Seabrook Island Co. is the developer of Seabrook Island and has majority control of the board of directors of the association. The association's bylaws empower the board of directors to levy an annual maintenance charge. Neither the association's charter nor its bylaws authorize the board to assess any other charges. When the board levied, in addition to the annual maintenance charge, an emergency budget assessment on all members to rebuild certain bridges and to revitalize the beach, the Loverings and other property owners challenged in court the association's power to impose the assessment. Decide. [*Lovering v. Seabrook Island Property Owners Ass'n*, 344 S.E.2d 862 (S.C. App.)]

11. Adams and two other persons were promoters for a new corporation, Aldrehn Theaters Co. The promoters retained Kridelbaugh to perform legal services in connection with the incorporation of the new business and promised to pay him $1,500. Aldrehn was incorporated through Kridelbaugh's services, and the promoters became its only directors. Kridelbaugh attended a meeting of the board of directors at which he was told that he should obtain a permit for the corporation to sell stock because the directors wished to pay him for his previous services. The promoters failed to pay Kridelbaugh, and he sued the corporation. Was the corporation liable? [*Kridelbaugh v. Aldrehn Theaters Co.*, 191 N.W. 803 (Iowa)]

12. On August 19, 1980, Joan Ioviero injured her hand when she slipped and fell while leaving the dining room at the Hotel Excelsior in Venice, Italy. This hotel was owned by an Italian corporation, Cigahotels, S.p.A. (The designation *S.p.A.* stands for *Societa per Azionean*, the Italian term for *corporation*.)

In 1973, a firm called Ciga Hotels, Inc., was incorporated in New York. Its certificate of incorporation was amended in 1979, changing the name of the firm to Landia International Services, Inc. This New York corporation was employed by the Italian corporation Cigahotels, S.p.A., to provide sales and promotional services in the United States and Canada. Ioviero sought to hold the New York corporation liable for her hand injury at the Venice hotel. She pointed to the similarity of the first corporate name used by the New York firm to the name Cigahotels, S.p.A., and the fact that the New York firm represented the interests of the Italian firm in the United States as clear evidence that the two firms were the same single legal entity. She asked that the court disregard the separate corporate entities. The New York corporation moved that the case be dismissed because it was duly incorporated in New York and did not own the Excelsior Hotel in which Ioviero was injured. Decide. [*Ioviero v. CigaHotel, Inc., aka Landia I.S., Inc.*, 475 N.Y.S.2d 880 (A.D.)]

13. William Sullivan was ousted from the presidency of the New England Patriots Football Club, Inc. Later, he borrowed $5,348,000 to buy 100 percent control of the voting shares of the corporation. A condition of the loan was that he reorganize the Patriots so that the income from the corporation could be devoted to repayment of the personal loan and the team's assets could be used as collateral. Sullivan, therefore, arranged for a cash freeze-out merger of the holders of the 120,000 shares of nonvoting stock. David Coggins, who owned 10 shares of nonvoting stock and took special pride in the fact that he was an owner of the team, refused the $15-a-share buyout and challenged the merger in court. He contended that the merger was not for a legitimate corporate purpose but to enable Sullivan to satisfy his personal loan. Sullivan contended that legitimate business purposes were given in the merger proxy statement, such as the National Football League's policy of discouraging public ownership of teams. Coggins responded that before the merger, Sullivan had 100 percent control of the voting stock and thus control of the franchise and that no legal basis existed to eliminate public ownership. Decide. [*Coggins v. New England Patriots Football Club*, 492 N.E.2d 1112 (Mass.)]

CPA Questions

1. Which of the following statements is correct concerning the similarities between a limited partnership and a corporation?

   a. Each is created under a statute and must file a copy of its certificate with the proper state authorities.

   b. All corporate stockholders and all partners in a limited partnership have limited liability.

   c. Both are recognized for federal income tax purposes as taxable entities.

   d. Both are allowed statutorily to have perpetual existence.

2. Rice is a promoter of a corporation to be known as Dex Corp. On January 1, 1985, Rice signed a nine-month contract with Roe, a CPA, which provided that Roe would perform certain accounting services for Dex. Rice did not disclose to Roe that Dex had not been formed. Prior to the incorporation of Dex on February 1, 1985, Roe rendered accounting services pursuant to the contract. After rendering accounting services for an additional period of six months pursuant to the contract, Roe was discharged without cause by the board of directors of Dex. In the absence of any agreements to the contrary, who will be liable to Roe for breach of contract?

   a. Both Rice and Dex

   b. Rice only

   c. Dex only

   d. Neither Rice nor Dex

3. In general, which of the following must be contained in articles of incorporation?

   a. The names of the states in which the corporation will be doing business

   b. The name of the state in which the corporation will maintain its principal place of business

   c. The names of the initial officers and their terms of office

   d. The classes of stock authorized for issuance

Shareholder Rights in Corporations

Learning Outcomes ‹‹‹

After studying this chapter, you should be able to

LO.1 Explain how to calculate the book value of a share of stock

LO.2 Distinguish between stocks and bonds

LO.3 Distinguish between subscriptions for and transfers of stock

LO.4 Explain the rights of shareholders

LO.5 Explain the nature of a shareholder derivative lawsuit

LO.6 Explain the exceptions to the limited liability of shareholders

The two most common instruments used to provide funds for a corporation are stocks and bonds.

44-1 Corporate Stocks and Bonds

Ownership of a corporation is represented by stock. A *bond* is a corporate debt.

44-1a Nature of Stock

An interest in a corporation is based on ownership of one or more shares of stock of the corporation. Each share represents a fractional interest in the total property of the corporation. The shareholder does not own or have an interest in any specific property of the corporation; the corporation is the owner of all of its property. The terms *share, stock*, and *share of stock* mean the same thing.

Capital and Capital Stock

outstanding–name for shares of a company that have been issued to stockholders.

Capital refers to the net assets of the corporation. Shares that have been issued to holders are said to be **outstanding. Capital stock** refers to the value received by the corporation for its outstanding stock.

capital stock–declared money value of the outstanding stock of the corporation.

Valuation of Stock

par value–specified monetary amount assigned by an issuing corporation for each share of its stock.

Corporate stock may have a specified **par value.** This means that the person subscribing to the stock and acquiring it from the corporation must pay that amount.

Shares may be issued with no par value. In that case, no amount is stated in the certificate, and the amount that the subscriber pays the corporation is determined by the board of directors. The Revised Model Business Corporation Act (RMBCA) eliminates the concept of par value, so stock issued by corporations in states following the RMBCA is always no par.

book value–value found by dividing the value of the corporate assets by the number of shares outstanding.

The value found by dividing the value of the net corporate assets by the number of shares outstanding is the **book value** of the shares. **For Example,** Roger Eggett entered a Shareholder Agreement in 1995 with Todd Cusick and Curtis Chisholm, forming the Wasatch Energy Corporation. The terms of the Shareholder Agreement provided that should a shareholder separate from the corporation, the remaining shareholders would have the option to purchase that shareholder's corporate stock. The remaining shareholders, as per the Shareholder Agreement, would either purchase the stock for book value, if the separating shareholder voluntarily left the corporation, or for par value, if the shareholder was terminated for cause. The Shareholder Agreement defined *book value* as the shareholder's net equity in the corporation, which would be determined by Wasatch's certified year-end financial statements. The Shareholder Agreement defined *par value* as the original price the shareholder paid for the stock. Egget tendered his resignation two years later and offered to sell his stock according to the Shareholder Agreement "for the audited book value of the corporation as of June 30, 1997 divided by the number of shares he owned." Wasatch Corp. responded by firing Egget, wrongly asserting the firing was for cause, and tendered him a check for the par value of his stock, $1,217, Eggett's original investment. Eggett sued and was awarded the book value of his shares, $135,671, plus $60,000 in attorney fees.[1] The **market value** of a share of stock is the price at which that stock can be voluntarily bought or sold in the open market.

market value–price at which a share of stock can be voluntarily bought or sold in the open market.

---

[1] *Eggett v. Wasatch Energy Corp.*, 29 P.3d 668 (Utah App. 2001).

There can be a substantial difference between book value and market value. If an agreement refers to book value or market value a court may construe the term strictly even if the result in interpretation yields vastly different amounts. **For Example,** a family partnership agreement provided for a buyout based on book value. The book value of the partnership was calculated at $177,808. The fair market value, however, was in excess of $30 million. The court found that the agreement was unambiguous and enforced it even though doing so resulted in a windfall to the purchaser.[2]

44-1b Certificates of Stock and Uncertificated Shares

certificate of stock–
document evidencing a shareholder's ownership of stock issued by a corporation.

A corporation ordinarily issues a **certificate of stock** or *share certificate* as evidence of the shareholder's ownership of stock. The issuance of such certificates is not essential either to the existence of a corporation or to the ownership of its stock. Many companies have stopped issuing paper stock certificates and use electronic registration to create a more secure and efficient system.[3]

In states that have adopted the 1978 and 1994 amendments to Article 8 of the UCC, uncertificated shares may be issued. Uncertificated shares are not represented by instruments. Their ownership and transfer are registered on the books maintained by, or on behalf of, the issuer corporation.[4] The registered stockholder is considered the stockholder of record. Registered owners may have either physical certificates or uncertificated ownership.

44-1c Kinds of Stock

The stock of a corporation may be divided into two or more classes.

CPA

Classification by Preferences

common stock–stock
that has no right or priority over any other stock of the corporation as to dividends or distribution of assets upon dissolution.

Common stock is ordinary stock that has no preferences. Each share usually entitles the holder to have one vote, to receive a share of the profits in the form of dividends when declared, and to participate in the distribution of capital upon dissolution of the corporation. **Preferred stock** has a priority over common stock. The priority may be with respect to either dividends or the distribution of capital upon dissolution of the corporation, or both. Preferred stock is ordinarily nonvoting.

CPA

preferred stock–stock
that has a priority or preference as to payment of dividends or upon liquidation, or both.

Cumulative Preferred Stock. The right to receive dividends depends on the declaration of dividends by the board of directors for a particular period of time. If there is no fund from which the dividends may be declared or if the directors do not declare them from an available fund, the shareholder has no right to dividends. The fact that a shareholder has not received dividends for the current year does not in itself give the right to accumulate or carry over into the next year a claim for those dividends. However, in the absence of a statement that the right to dividends is noncumulative, courts frequently hold that preferred stock has the right to accumulate dividends for each year in which there was a surplus available for dividend payment but dividends were not declared.

CPA

Participating Preferred Stock. Sometimes the preferred stock is given the right of participation. If it is, then after the common shares receive dividends or a capital distribution is made equal to that first received by the preferred stock, both kinds participate or share equally in the balance.

[2] See *Estate of Cohen v. Booth Computer*, 22 A.3d 991 (N.J. App. Div. 2011).
[3] Some stock certificates are collectors' items. Walt Disney Co. stopped issuing paper stock certificates in 2013. It was one of the last large companies to stop issuing paper stock certificates.
[4] U.C.C. §8-102(1)(b). The 1978 and 1994 amendments to Article 8 of the UCC have been adopted in all of the states except Alabama.

Duration of Shares

Ordinarily, shares continue to exist for the life of the corporation. However, any kind of share, whether common or preferred, may be made terminable at an earlier date.

Fractional Shares

A corporation may issue fractional shares or scrip or certificates representing fractional shares. These can be sold or combined for the acquisition of whole shares.

44-1d Characteristics of Bonds

A **bond** is an instrument promising to repay a loan of money to a corporation. Typically, the loan is for a relatively long period of time, generally five years or longer. A bond obligates the corporation to pay the bondholder the amount of the loan, called the *principal*, at a stated time, called the **maturity date,** and to pay a fixed amount of *interest* at regular intervals, commonly every six months. The relationship between the bondholder and the issuing corporation is that of creditor and debtor. Companies and government entities may use bonds to finance a wide variety of projects. Unlike dividends, which are discretionary, bond interest must be paid. A bond may be secured by a mortgage or lien on corporate property. A **debenture** is an unsecured bond of the corporation with no specific corporate assets pledged as security for payment.

Bonds are negotiable securities.[5] Bonds held by owners whose names and addresses are registered on the books of the corporation are called **registered bonds.**

44-1e Terms and Control

The contractual terms of a particular bond issue are set forth in an agreement called a **bond indenture** or **deed.** An **indenture trustee,** usually a commercial banking institution, represents the interests of the bondholders in making sure that the corporation meets the terms and covenants of the bond issue.[6] For example, the terms of the bond indenture may require a **sinking fund,** by which the borrowing corporation is required to set aside a fixed amount of money each year toward the ultimate payment of the bonds.

Bondholders do not vote for directors or have the right to vote on matters on which shareholders vote. However, when the debt is risky, it is highly likely that significant restraints on the corporation's freedom of action will be imposed by the terms of the indenture.

44-2 Acquisition of Shares

Shares may be acquired from the corporation or from an existing shareholder.

44-2a Nature of Acquisition

Shares of stock may be acquired (1) from the corporation by subscription, either before or after the corporation is organized, or (2) by transfer of existing shares from a shareholder or from the corporation. The transfer may be voluntary, as by a sale, gift, or bequest by will, or involuntary, as by an execution sale to pay the judgment of a creditor. The transfer may also take place by operation of law—as when the stock of a shareholder passes to the shareholder's trustee in bankruptcy.

---

[5] U.C.C. §8-105.
[6] *Lorenc v. CSX Corp.,* CCH Sec. L. Rep. 95298 (W.D. Pa. 1990).

44-2b Statute of Frauds

Under the 1978 version of Article 8, a contract for the sale of corporate shares must be evidenced by a writing, or it cannot be enforced.[7] The 1994 version of Article 8 renders the statute of frauds inapplicable to contracts for the sale or purchase of securities.[8] The commentary notes explain that the 1978 statute's potential for filtering out fraudulent claims is outweighed by the obstacles the statute presents to the development of modern commercial practices in the securities business.

No writing is required for a contract by which a broker agrees with a customer to buy or sell securities for the customer. That is an agency agreement, not a sale made between the customer and the broker.

44-2c Subscription

stock subscription– contract or agreement to buy a specific number and kind of shares when they are issued by the corporation.

A **stock subscription** is a contract or an agreement to buy a specific number and kind of shares when the corporation issues them. As in the case of any other contract, the agreement to subscribe to shares of a corporation may be avoided for fraud.

Subscription before Incorporation

In many states, a preincorporation subscription of shares is an offer to the corporation. According to this view, it is necessary for the corporation to accept the subscription offer either expressly or by conduct. A few states hold that subscriptions automatically become binding contracts when the organization of the corporation has been completed. In some states, the preincorporation subscription is irrevocable for a stated period. The RMBCA provides that "a subscription for shares entered into before incorporation is irrevocable for six months unless the subscription agreement provides a longer or shorter period or all the subscribers agree to revocation."[9]

Subscription after Incorporation

acceptance–unqualified assent to the act or proposal of another; as the acceptance of a draft (bill of exchange), of an offer to make a contract, of goods delivered by the seller, or of a gift or deed.

Subscriptions may be made after incorporation. In that event, the transaction is like any other contract with the corporation. The offer of the subscription may come from the subscriber or from the corporation. In either case, there must be an **acceptance.** Upon acceptance, the subscriber immediately becomes a shareholder with all the rights, privileges, and liabilities of a shareholder even though she has not paid any of the purchase price. Moreover, the subscriber is a shareholder even though no share certificate has been issued. In contrast with a contract for immediate subscription to shares, the contract may be one for the future issue of shares. In that case, the contracting party has only a contract and is not a shareholder as of the formation of the contract.

44-2d Transfer of Shares

In the absence of a valid restriction, a shareholder may transfer shares to anyone.

Restrictions on Transfer

Restrictions on the transfer of stock are valid if they are not unreasonable. It is lawful to require that the corporation or other stockholders be given the first right to purchase stock before a shareholder may sell stock to an outsider.

Such restrictions are widely used, particularly in close corporations, so current shareholders can control the ownership and management of the corporation and prevent outsiders from "invading the business;" also, restrictions serve to maintain parity among shareholders.

---

[7] U.C.C. §8-319(a); *Goldfinger v. Brown*, 564 N.Y.S.2d 461 (A.D. 1991).
[8] U.C.C. §8-113.
[9] RMBCA §6.20(a).

CASE SUMMARY

Restrictions on Transfer of Stock Are Legal, Morris

FACTS: In 1974 Billy Fought, Brady Morris, Clayton Strong, and John Peyton organized Vicksburg Mold and Die, Inc., for the purpose of designing and manufacturing plastic and metal products. Each individual was issued 25 shares of stock. The shareholders entered into a stock redemption agreement requiring a stockholder wishing to sell his stock to offer proportionate shares to each stockholder. Morris was elected president and Fought vice president, and all four individuals worked at the plant. Strong retired in 1979 and sold his shares in accordance with the stock redemption plan. In 1983, Peyton decided to sell his shares and agreed to sell them all to Morris, thus giving Morris control of the corporation. Fought sued Morris for breach of his fiduciary duty to Fought and for the value of Fought's pro rata share of Peyton's stock.

DECISION: Judgment for Fought. Section 2 of the stock redemption agreement was designed to maintain a balance of power in the four-person close corporation. Before stock could be sold to others, it had to be offered to each shareholder on a pro rata basis. Each individual had an opportunity to maintain the initial balance of power. By purchasing all of Peyton's stock, Morris bought control of the corporation. In doing so, he violated the stock redemption agreement and thus breached his fiduciary duty as a director, officer, and shareholder. [*Fought v. Morris*, 543 So. 2d 167 (Miss. 1989)]

A provision giving a corporation the right to purchase a shareholder's shares on the death of the shareholder is valid.[10]

A restriction on the right of a certificate's purchaser to transfer his stock is not valid unless the restriction is conspicuously noted on the certificate or the transferee had actual knowledge of the restriction. A restriction on the transfer of stock is strictly interpreted.[11]

When no restrictions exist, the issuer has a duty to register the transfer. **For Example,** Richard Jones purchased 1,000 certificated shares of International Generic Corporation (IGC) from Madison Tucker on March 30, 2016, at fair market value. Tucker properly indorsed the certificates to Jones on that date, and her signatures were duly notarized. On September 15, 2016, Jones presented the securities to IGC to register the transfer of shares and to collect dividends for the second quarter (April 1 through June 30) and the third quarter (July 1 through September 30). IGC refused to register the shares in Jones's name, believing him to be a person of questionable integrity that it did not want as an "owner" of IGC. Under either the 1978 or 1994 version of Article 8 of the UCC, it was improper for IGC to fail to register the stock that had been transferred to a bona fide purchaser, Jones. No restrictions existed on the certificate, and IGC had a duty to register the transfer and was liable for its failure to do so. Jones was entitled to the dividends from the date of presentation of the stock for transfer. Prior to that date, the issuer, IGC, was entitled to treat the registered owner, Madison Tucker, as exclusively entitled to exercise the rights of ownership, including the right to dividends. Thus, IGC was not liable to Jones for the second-quarter dividends. However, dividends declared after the date of presentment, which included the third-quarter dividend declared in October 2016 with a record date in October, must be paid to Jones by IGC.

[10] See *Puritas Metal Products v. Cook*, 972 N.E2d 615 (Ohio 2012), where a trial court incorrectly determined that the decedent's death resulted in a "transfer" under the corporation's code of regulation. In fact, the decedent's shares were in a marital trust, and upon his death the shares were retained by the trustee of the trust, his wife, to administer and vote as she saw fit.

[11] *Capano v. Wilmington Country Club, Inc.*, 2001 WL 1359254 (Del. Ch. Nov. 1, 2001).

Interest Transferred

The transfer of shares may be absolute; that is, it may divest all ownership and make the transferee the full owner. The transfer may be of only a partial interest in the stock, or the transfer may be for security, such as when stock is pledged to secure the repayment of a loan.

44-2e Mechanics of Transfer

When stock is represented by a certificate, the ownership of shares is transferred by the delivery of the certificate of stock, indorsed by its owner in blank or to a specified person. Ownership may also be transferred by the delivery of the certificate accompanied by a separate assignment or power of attorney executed by the owner.[12]

A delivery from the owner of the shares directly to the transferee is not required. It can be made to an intermediary. When there is no delivery of the share certificate to anyone, however, there is no transfer of ownership of the shares.

A physical transfer of the certificate without a necessary indorsement is effective as between the parties. Thus, a gift of shares is binding even though no indorsement has been made. An indorsement is required to make the transferee a bona fide purchaser.

44-2f Effect of Transfer

The transfer of existing shares of stock may raise questions between the parties to the transfer as well as between the parties and the corporation.

Validity of Transfer

Because a transfer of shares is a transfer of ownership, the transfer must satisfy the requirements governing any other transfer of property or agreement to transfer property.[13] As between the parties, a transfer may be set aside for any ground that would warrant similar relief under property law. If the transfer has been obtained by duress, the transferor may obtain a rescission of the transfer.

Negotiability

Under common law, the transferee of shares of stock had no greater right than the transferor because the certificate and the shares represented by the certificate were nonnegotiable. By statute, the common law rule has been changed by imparting negotiability to certificated stock. Just as various defenses cannot be asserted against the holder in due course of a commercial paper, statutory law provides that similar defenses cannot be raised against the person acquiring the certificate in good faith and for value. Against such a person, the defense cannot be raised that the transferor did not own the shares or did not have authority to deliver the certificate or that the transfer was made in violation of a restriction on transfer not known to the person and not noted conspicuously on the certificate.

Statements sent by the issuer identifying the ownership of uncertificated securities are neither certificated securities nor negotiable instruments. Although certificated securities have the quality of negotiability, they are not commercial paper within Article 3 of the UCC.

Secured Transaction

Corporate stock is frequently delivered to a creditor as security for a debt owed by the shareholder. Thus, a debtor borrowing money from a bank may deliver shares of stock

---

[12] U.C.C. §8-309. See *Kesling v. Kesling*, 967 N.E.2d 66, 68 (Ind. App. 2012), where the corporate bylaws set forth the two methods of transferring stock in the corporation.

[13] *Gallant v. Kanterman*, 294 A.D.2d 59 (N.Y. App. Div. 1998).

to the bank as collateral security for the repayment of the loan. A broker's customer purchasing stock on margin may leave the stock in the possession of the broker as security for the payment of any balance due. The delivery of the security to the creditor is a pledge. This gives rise to a perfected security interest without any filing by the creditor. In itself, the pledge does not make the pledgee of the corporate stock the owner of the stock.

Effect of Transfer on Corporation

The corporation is entitled to treat as the owner of shares the person whose name is on the corporation's books as the owner. Therefore, until there is a transfer on its books, the corporation may still treat a transferor of shares as the owner. The corporation may properly refuse to recognize a transferee when the corporation is given notice or has knowledge that the transfer is void or in breach of trust. In such a case, the corporation properly refuses to register a transfer until the rights of the parties have been determined. The corporation may also refuse to register the transfer of shares when the outstanding certificate is not surrendered to it or there is a lack of satisfactory proof that the certificate has been lost, destroyed, or stolen.

44-2g Lost, Destroyed, and Stolen Share Certificates

The owner of a lost, destroyed, or stolen share certificate is entitled to a replacement if the owner files a sufficient indemnity bond and requests the new certificate within a reasonable time before the issuer has notice that the original certificate has been acquired by a bona fide purchaser. A *share* is the actual property of the shareholder, while the *certificate* is merely the authentic evidence of the stockholder's ownership of shares.[14] If, after the new security is issued, a bona fide purchaser appears with the original certificate, the corporation must register a transfer of the security to that person and accept that person as the owner of the shares.

CPA ## 44-3 Rights of Shareholders

The rights of shareholders stem from their status as owners.

CPA ## 44-3a Ownership Rights

Shareholder control over the corporation is indirect. Periodically (ordinarily once a year), the shareholders elect directors and by this means control the corporation. At other times, however, the shareholders have no right or power to control corporate activity so long as it is conducted within lawful channels.

CPA ### Certificates of Stock

A shareholder has the right to have a properly executed certificate as evidence of ownership of shares. An exception is made when the corporation is authorized to issue uncertificated securities.

CPA ### Transfer of Shares

Unless limited by a valid restriction, a shareholder has the right to transfer her shares. The shareholder may sell the shares at any price or transfer them as a gift. The fact that the seller sells at a price higher than the market price is not unlawful even if the seller is a director or an officer.

---

[14] *Rosso v. Rosso*, 701 N.W.2d 355 (Neb. 2005).

CASE SUMMARY

It's the Real Thing, Controlling Shares in Coke-Anderson, and You Have to Pay a Premium

FACTS: Paul Warlick, Jr., was the president and chief executive officer and a stockholder of Coca-Cola Bottling Company of Anderson, S.C. (Coke-Anderson). He controlled a majority of the shares of stock of the company. Warlick agreed to sell this controlling interest in Coke-Anderson to Coke-Asheville for a price greater than the market value of the shares. Wayne Shoaf, a minority shareholder, brought suit against Warlick, contending that Warlick had violated his fiduciary duty to the corporation by receiving an unlawful premium for the sale of the majority interest in Coke-Anderson.

DECISION: Judgment for Warlick. Paying or receiving a premium for the controlling shares of stock in a corporation is not unlawful. A majority shareholder who is also a director and an officer is generally under no duty to minority shareholders to refrain from receiving a premium on the sale of the controlling stock. [*Shoaf v. Warlick,* **380 S.E.2d 865 (S.C. App. 1989)**]

C P A 44-3b ## Right to Vote

The right to vote means the right to vote at shareholders' meetings for the election of directors and on other special matters that shareholders must vote on. **For Example,** a proposal to change the capital structure of the corporation or a proposal to sell all or substantially all assets of the corporation must be approved by the shareholders.

C P A ## Who May Vote

Ordinarily, only shareholders of record—those common shareholders in whose name the stock appears on the books of the corporation—are entitled to vote. The board of directors may fix a date for closing the corporate books for this purpose.

C P A ## Number of Votes

cumulative voting– system of voting for directors in which each shareholder has as many votes as the number of voting shares owned multiplied by the number of directors to be elected, and such votes can be distributed for the various candidates as desired.

Unless there is a provision to the contrary, for each share owned, each shareholder is entitled to one vote on each matter to be voted. This procedure is called *straight voting,* and it is the normal method for shareholder voting on corporate matters. However, in the case of voting to elect directors only, **cumulative voting** is mandatory in nearly half of the states. This requirement is imposed by either state constitution or state statute. Cumulative voting is permitted by law in other states when provided for in the articles of incorporation or bylaws.

Cumulative voting is a form of voting that is designed to give proportional representation on the board of directors to minority shareholders. Under a cumulative voting plan, each shareholder has as many votes as the number of shares owned multiplied by the number of directors to be elected. A shareholder may cast all of these votes for one candidate or may divide the votes between two or more candidates. This system enables minority shareholders to cast all of their votes for a candidate who will represent their interests on the board of directors.

Under straight voting, minority shareholders would always be outvoted. **For Example,** assume that minority shareholder Tyler Feldberg owned 400 shares of stock and majority shareholder C. J. Jones controlled the remaining 600 shares. Also assume that five directors are to be elected to the board. If straight voting were used for the election of directors, C. J., with 600 shares, would always outvote Tyler's 400 shares.

However, under cumulative voting, Tyler would be allowed 2,000 votes (400 shares times five directors), and C. J. would be allowed 3,000 votes (600 shares times five directors). The five candidates with the highest number of votes will be elected. If Tyler casts 1,000 votes for each of two directors and C. J. casts 1,000 votes for each of three directors, Tyler, who owns 40 percent of the stock, is able to elect two-fifths of the board to represent his interests.

Voting by Proxy

A shareholder has the right to authorize another to vote the shares owned by the shareholder. This procedure is known as **voting by proxy.** In the absence of restrictions to the contrary, any person, even someone who is not a shareholder, may act as a proxy. The authorization from the shareholder may be made by any writing.[15] The authorization is also commonly called a **proxy.**

Voting Agreements and Trusts

Shareholders, as a general rule, are allowed to enter into an agreement by which they concentrate their voting strength for the purpose of electing directors or voting on any other matter.

A **voting trust** is created when by agreement a group of shareholders or all of the shareholders transfer their shares in trust to one or more persons as trustees. The trustees are authorized to vote the stock during the life of the trust agreement.[16] In general, such agreements are upheld if their object is lawful. In some jurisdictions, such trusts cannot run beyond a stated number of years. There are some signs of a relaxation as to time. Several states have abandoned all time limitations, several have extended the time limitation, and many provide for an extension or renewal of the agreement.

CPA   44-3c Preemptive Offer of Shares

If the capital stock of a corporation is increased, shareholders ordinarily have the **preemptive right** to subscribe to the same percentage of the new shares that their old shares represented of the former total of capital stock. This right is given to enable shareholders to maintain their relative interests in the corporation.

The existence of a preemptive right may make it impossible to conclude a transaction in which the corporation is to transfer a block of stock as consideration. Moreover, practical difficulties arise as to how stock should be allocated among shareholders of different classes.

The RMBCA provides that shareholders do not have preemptive rights unless the articles of incorporation provide for them.

CPA   44-3d Inspection of Books

A shareholder has the right to inspect the books of the shareholder's corporation. In some states, there are no limitations on this right. In most states, the inspection must be made in good faith, for proper motives, and at a reasonable time and place.[17] **For Example,** shareholders have a proper purpose to inspect the books and records of a corporation to determine whether the directors and officers engaged in self-dealing to the detriment of the corporation.[18] Some courts have even allowed shareholders to demand the production of documents that fall under the attorney-client privilege.[19] In many states, a shareholder

---

voting by proxy— authorizing someone else to vote the shares owned by the shareholder.

proxy—written authorization by a shareholder to another person to vote the stock owned by the shareholder; the person who is the holder of such a written authorization.

voting trust—transfer by two or more persons of their shares of stock of a corporation to a trustee who is to vote the shares and act for such shareholders.

preemptive right— shareholder's right upon the increase of a corporation's capital stock to be allowed to subscribe to such a percentage of the new shares as the shareholder's old shares bore to the former total capital stock.

---

[15] RMBCA §7.07.
[16] *Bettner Trust v. Bettner*, 495 N.E.2d 194 (Ind. App. 1986).
[17] RMBCA §16.02(c); *Leary v. Foley*, 884 So. 2d 655 (La. App. 2004).
[18] *Sunlitz Holding Co. v. Trading Block Holdings, Inc.*, 17 N.E.3d 715 (Ill. App. 2014).
[19] *Wal-Mart Stores, Inc. v. Indiana Electrical Workers Pension Trust Fund IBEW*, 2014 WL 3638848 (Del. July 23, 2014).

must own a certain percentage of the outstanding stock of a corporation (commonly 5 percent) or must own at least one share of stock for a minimum amount of time (commonly six months) to have the right to inspect the books. A shareholder is not relegated to accepting opinions and numbers offered by a company's auditor and may employ an expert accountant of his own to review and analyze the books and records of the corporation.[20] If a corporation unreasonably refuses inspection, a court may require the corporation to pay the shareholder's litigation costs, including reasonable attorneys' fees.[21]

A shareholder is entitled to inspect the records to determine the financial condition of the corporation, the quality of its management, and any matters relating to rights or interests in the corporate business, such as the value of stock.[22]

CASE SUMMARY

When Shareholders Investigate Bribery and a Corporate Cover-Up, Even Privileged Documents Must Be Produced

FACTS: In April 2012, the *New York Times* ran a story about bribery at WalMex, a Mexican subsidiary of Wal-Mart. The article described a scheme of illegal bribery payments made to Mexican officials at the direction of WalMex CEO, Eduardo Castro-Wright, between 2002 and 2005. The article stated that WalMex received benefits such as zoning changes and rapid and favorable processing of permits and licenses for new stores in exchange for bribes. The *NYT* article stated that Wal-Mart executives were aware of the conduct no later than September 2005. A stockholder of Wal-Mart, the Electrical Workers Pension Trust Fund IBEW (IBEW), demanded to inspect the books and records of the corporation with the purpose of investigating the bribery allegations and breaches of fiduciary duty by Wal-Mart or WalMex executives in connection with the bribery allegations. Wal-Mart produced approximately 3,000 documents, including documents regarding its compliance with the Foreign Corrupt Practices Act and minutes and materials referencing the WalMex Allegations. Wal-Mart declined to provide documents that it believed were not necessary and essential to the stated purposes or that were protected by the attorney-client privilege and work-product doctrine.

The Court of Chancery held that Wal-Mart had to produce these additional documents because they were "necessary and essential" to achieve a "proper purpose," as required by Section 220 of the Delaware Code. According to Section 220, documents are "necessary and essential" if they address

the "crux of the shareholder's purpose" and if that information "is unavailable from another source."

DECISION: Judgment for the shareholder, IBEW. There is a fiduciary exception to the attorney-client privilege. Ordinarily, a corporation may assert the privilege even when stockholders request privileged information. But when the corporation is in suit against its stockholders and is potentially acting against shareholder interests, the stockholders may show cause why the privilege should not be invoked. Section 220 of the Delaware Code requires that shareholders demonstrate that the corporate documents they request are "necessary and essential" for a legitimate shareholder purpose. The record showed that IBEW's purpose in seeking the information was to investigate the handling of the WalMex Investigation, whether a cover-up took place, and what details were shared with the Wal-Mart Board. Once a stockholder has satisfied the "necessary and essential" requirements, it must then show that there is good cause for access to the privileged documents. Good cause existed in this case because the stockholders had a "colorable claim" based on Wal-Mart's public statements about alleged illegalities in Mexico. The fact that the information would be difficult to obtain from another source also supported a good cause finding. [***Wal-Mart Stores, Inc. v. Indiana Electrical Workers Pension Trust Fund IBEW***, 2014 WL 3638848 (Del. July 23, 2014)]

A shareholder is entitled to inspect the books to obtain information needed for a lawsuit against the corporation or its directors or officers, to organize the other shareholders

[20] *Missouri v. III Investments, Inc.*, 80 S.W.3d 855 (Mo. App. 2002).
[21] *Clark v. Anjacko, Inc.*, 333 P.2d 779 (Ariz. App. 2014).
[22] *Ihrig v. Frontier Equity Exchange*, 128 P.3d 993 (Kan. App. 2006).

into an "opposition" party to remove the board of directors at the next election, or to buy the shares of other shareholders.[23]

Inspection has frequently been refused when it was sought merely from idle curiosity or for "speculative purposes." Inspection has sometimes been denied on the ground that it was sought merely to obtain a mailing list of persons who would be solicited to buy products of another enterprise. Inspection has also been refused when the object of the shareholder was to advance political or social beliefs without regard to the welfare of the corporation. Cases that deny the right of inspection do so when it would be harmful to the corporation[24] or is sought only for the purpose of annoying, harassing, or causing vexation or of aiding competitors of the corporation.

Form of Books

There are generally no requirements regarding the form of corporate books and records. The RMBCA recognizes that corporate books and records may be stored in modern data storage systems. "A corporation shall maintain its records in written form or in any other form capable of conversion into written form within a reasonable time."[25]

Financial Statements

The RMBCA requires a corporation to furnish annual financial statements. These statements include a balance sheet at the end of the fiscal year, an income statement for that year, and a statement of changes in shareholders' equity for that year.[26] A number of state statutes contain similar provisions and set forth a statutory penalty for any officer responsible for providing the financial statements who fails to perform such duties after written request.

CPA   44-3e   Dividends

A shareholder has the right to receive a proportion of dividends as they are declared, subject to the relative rights of other shareholders to preferences, accumulation of dividends, and participation. There is no absolute right that dividends be declared, but dividends, when declared, must be paid in the manner indicated.

CPA   Funds Available for Declaration of Dividends

Statutes commonly provide that no dividends may be declared unless there is an "earned surplus" for their payment. Earned surplus, also known as *retained earnings*, consists of the accumulated profits earned by the corporation since its formation less prior dividend distributions. Dividend payments are prohibited if the corporation is insolvent or would be rendered insolvent by the payment of the dividend.

As an exception to these rules, a wasting assets corporation may pay dividends out of current net profits without regard to the preservation of the corporate assets. **Wasting assets corporations** are those designed to exhaust or use up the assets of the corporation (for example, by extracting oil, coal, iron, and other ores) as compared with manufacturing

wasting assets corporation–corporation designed to exhaust or use up the assets of the corporation, such as by extracting oil, coal, iron, and other ores.

---

[23] See *Kelley Manufacturing Co. v. Martin*, 674 S.E.2d 92 (Ga. App. 2009), where the court determined that two shareholders showed a proper purpose for seeking inspection of books: to enforce the company's bylaws; to ensure proper corporate governance and to determine if corporate waste, mismanagement, and other breaches of fiduciary duty were occurring; to inspect corporate records to protect the shareholders substantial ownership interest; and to inspect records related to the shareholders' removal as trustees, directors, officers, and employees of the corporation.

[24] *Retail Property Investors, Inc., v. Skeens*, 471 S.E.2d 181 (Va. 1996).

[25] RMBCA §16.01(d).

[26] RMBCA §16.20. See *Troccoli v. Lab Contract Industries, Inc.*, 687 N.Y.S.2d 400 (A.D. 1999).

plants whose object is to preserve the plant as well as to continue to manufacture. A wasting assets corporation may also be formed for the purpose of buying and liquidating a stock of merchandise from a company that has received a discharge in bankruptcy court.

In some states, statutes provide that dividends may be declared from earned surplus or from current net profits without regard to the existence of a deficit from former years.

CPA ### Discretion of Directors

Assuming that a fund is available for the declaration of dividends, it is then a matter primarily within the discretion of the board of directors whether a dividend shall be declared. The fact that there is an earned surplus that could be used for dividends does not mean that they must be declared. This rule is not affected by the nature of the shares. Thus, the fact that the shareholders hold cumulative preferred shares does not give them any right to demand a declaration of dividends or to interfere with an honest exercise of discretion by the directors.

Maintaining an adequate cash and working capital position is an important practical consideration in determining whether to declare a cash dividend. In general, courts refuse to substitute their judgment for the judgment of the directors of the corporation and interfere with their decision on dividend declaration only when it is shown that their conduct is harmful to the welfare of the corporation or its shareholders.[27]

Form of Dividends

Customarily, a dividend is paid in money. However, it may be paid in property, such as a product manufactured by the corporation; in shares of other corporations held by the corporation; or in shares of the corporation itself.

Effect of Transfer of Shares

When a corporation declares a cash or property dividend, the usual practice is for the board of directors to declare a dividend as of a certain date—the *declaration date*—payable to shareholders of record on a stated future date—the *record date*—with a *payment date* following the record date, usually by some 30 days. The person who is the owner of the shares on the record date is entitled to the dividend even if the shares are transferred prior to the payment date.

If the dividend consists of shares in the corporation declaring the dividend, ownership of the dividend is determined by the date of distribution. Whoever is the owner of the shares when the stock dividend is distributed is entitled to the stock dividend. The reason for this variation from the cash dividend rule is that the declaration of a stock dividend has the effect of diluting the existing corporate assets among a larger number of shares. The value of the holding represented by each share is diminished as a result. Unless the person who owns the stock on the distribution date receives a proportionate share of the stock dividend, the net effect will be to lessen that person's holding.

44-3f Capital Distribution

Upon dissolution of the corporation, shareholders are entitled to receive any balance of the corporate assets that remains after the payment of all creditors. Certain classes of stock may have a preference or priority in this distribution.

---

[27] *Gabelli & Co. v. Liggett Group, Inc.*, 479 A.2d 276 (Del. Super. 1984).

CPA 44-3g **Shareholders' Actions**

derivative (secondary) action–secondary action for damages or breach of contract brought by one or more corporate shareholders against directors, officers, or third persons.

When the corporation has the right to sue its directors, officers, or third persons for damages caused by them to the corporation or for breach of contract, one or more shareholders may bring such action if the corporation refuses to do so. This is a **derivative (secondary) action** in that the shareholder enforces only the cause of action of the corporation and any money recovery is paid into the corporate treasury.

In a derivative action, when a corporation has failed to enforce a right, a shareholder bringing such a suit must show that a demand was made on the directors to enforce the right in question. The shareholder must show (1) that the directors refused to enforce the right[28] or (2) that a demand that the directors enforce the right is excused because the directors are deemed incapable of making an impartial decision regarding the pursuit of the litigation. Additionally, where a special litigation committee (SLC) is formed by the board of directors with full authority to decide what position to take with regard to a derivative lawsuit, demand on the entire board may be excused on a case-by-case basis.

CASE SUMMARY

"Curb Your Enthusiasm," Defendants Greenberg and Smith Argue

FACTS: Plaintiff stockholders sued derivatively CEO Maurice Greenberg, CFO Howard Smith, and other former officers who had served on American Insurance Group's (AIG's) board of directors. The plaintiffs took this action on behalf of the corporation for damages the former officers had caused AIG by having the corporation engage in illegal acts. In one example, the plaintiffs asserted that AIG had created a fictional reinsurance business transaction with General Reinsurance Corp. to inflate loss reserves, thus making AIG appear to be a healthier company than it actually was and inflating AIG's stock price. AIG's board of directors formed a special litigation committee (SLC) to look into the stockholder plaintiffs' allegations, giving full authority to the SLC to address the litigation. The SLC investigated all matters and decided to join this action as a direct plaintiff on behalf of the corporation, asserting breach of fiduciary duty and indemnification claims against former CEO Greenberg and former CFO Smith. The defendants, Greenberg and Smith, contended

that the stockholder plaintiffs had to make a demand on the full board. Moreover, they asserted that under procedural law, boards of directors should not be lightly bypassed by derivative plaintiffs.

DECISION: Judgment for the stockholder plaintiffs. Corporation law seeks to ensure that boards are not lightly bypassed by derivative plaintiffs and not allowed to usurp the board's right to manage the affairs of the corporation. AIG's board's primacy in decision making has been fully honored. The SLC chose to have AIG sue Greenberg and Smith itself, to seek dismissal of certain defendants, and to otherwise take no position on the plaintiffs' claims. The board gave the SLC full authority to make this decision, and through the SLC the board asserted control over the lawsuit. Demand on the full board is thus excused and the plaintiffs are free to proceed against the defendants. [*AIG, Inc. v. Greenberg*, **965 A.2d 763 (Del. Ch. 2009)**]

A special litigation committee is vested with enormous power to pursue a corporate claim or seek dismissal of a derivative suit. But courts will defer to the business judgment and conclusions of the SLC only if the directors involved possess a disinterested independence and do not have relationships that prevent an unprejudicial exercise of judgment.[29]

---

[28] *Marx. v. Akers*, 666 N.E.2d 1034 (N.Y. 1996). But see *Potter v. Hughes*, 546 F.3d 1051 (9th Cir. 2008).
[29] In re *Comverse Technology, Inc.*, 766 N.Y.S.2d 10 (A.D. 2008).

CASE SUMMARY

It's Not Good Retailing to Publicly Tout "Low Cost Manufacturing – High Retail Pricing" on Wall Street: Wall Street Abuts Main Street

FACTS: Shareholders of Abercrombie & Fitch Co. filed a derivative suit on behalf of the company against several officers and directors alleging that the defendants caused Abercrombie to make misleading public statements between June 2 and August 18, 2005, which caused stock prices to rise and then fall once the falsity of the statements were revealed. According to the complaint, Abercrombie adopted a business model of selling products with a low manufacturing cost at high retail prices, resulting in a high per-unit margin. The company sought to create such a desired brand that it could "train" its customers to not expect a sale or markdowns and instead just pay the high price. This approach manifested itself most particularly in Abercrombie's denim products. Abercrombie issued reports indicating that its denim sales were strong and that its high gross margin business strategy was working. The shareholders allege that these statements were misleading because company insiders knew that Abercrombie was amassing a large surplus of inventory such that there would have to be dramatic markdowns to clear out the inventory, causing a negative correction in the company's stock price. The stock price eventually did fall, which kicked off a spate of lawsuits and regulatory investigations. During this time, when the insiders are alleged to have known that the price would soon fall, five of the defendants—Singer, Jeffries, Bachmann, Kessler, and Griffin—sold a large number of their personally owned shares of Abercrombie stock. The corporation formed an SLC, consisting of board members Allan Tuttle and Lauren Brisky. During the investigation Mr. Tuttle recused himself from considering claims against Mr. Singer, Abercrombie's president, COO, and CFO, due to a prior relationship at the Gucci company. The SLC recommended that the corporation seek dismissal of the suit, and the district court granted a motion to dismiss. The shareholders appealed.

DECISION: The court of appeals reversed the district court, having serious doubts about Mr. Tuttle's independence because he recused himself from considering the claims against the person at the very center of the alleged improper activity. When Tuttle recused himself from considering the claims against Singer, he essentially launched a signal flare that he was not independent. Mr. Singer, as the COO, appears to have been heavily involved in the strategy of touting the success of the business model to the market. He was also alleged to have engaged in insider trading. Without a demonstration that its SLC was independent, the corporation's motion to dismiss based on the SLC's recommendation could not be granted. [*Booth Family Trust v. Jeffries,* **640 F.3d 134 (6th Cir. 2011)**]

Mere allegations that a director and other directors move in the same social circles or are characterized as close friends is not enough to negate a director's independence for presuit demand excusal purposes.

Lawsuits may be brought by minority shareholders against majority shareholders who are oppressive toward minority shareholders. Oppressive conduct may include payment of grossly excessive salaries and fringe benefits to the majority stockholders who are also officers of the corporation. Shareholders may bring a derivative action to obtain a dissolution of the corporation by judicial decree.[30]

44-4 Liability of Shareholders

A shareholder is ordinarily protected from the liabilities of the corporation. Some exceptions exist, however.

---

[30] *Miller v. Up In Smoke, Inc.,* 738 F. Supp. 2d 878 (N.D. Ind. 2010). But see *Whithorn v. Whithorn Farms, Inc.,* 195 P.3d 836 (Mont. 2008).

44-4a Limited Liability

The liability of a shareholder is generally limited. This means that the shareholder is not personally liable for the debts and liabilities of the corporation. The capital contributed by shareholders may be exhausted by the claims of creditors, but there is no personal liability for any unpaid balance.

44-4b Ignoring the Corporate Entity

Ordinarily a corporation is regarded and treated as a separate legal entity, and the law does not look behind a corporation to see who owns or controls it.

The fact that two corporations have identical shareholders does not justify a court's regarding the two corporations as one. Similarly, the fact that there is a close working relationship between two corporations does not in itself constitute any basis for ignoring their separate corporate entities when they in fact are separately run enterprises.

"Piercing the Corporate Veil"

A court may disregard the corporate entity, or figuratively "pierce the corporate veil," when exceptional circumstances warrant. The decision whether to disregard the corporate entity is made on a case-by-case basis, weighing all factors before the court. Factors that may lead to piercing the corporate veil and imposing liability on its owners (the shareholders) are (1) the failure to maintain adequate corporate records and the commingling of corporate and other funds,[31] (2) grossly inadequate capitalization,[32] (3) the diversion by shareholders of corporate funds or assets,[33] (4) the formation of the corporation to evade an existing obligation, (5) the formation of the corporation to perpetrate a fraud or conceal illegality, and (6) a determination that injustice and inequitable consequences would result if the corporate entity were recognized.[34]

CASE SUMMARY

Sometimes "Parents" Have to Pay the Rent in Business, Too

FACTS: Inter-Tel is an Arizona corporation that designs, manufactures, and sells telecommunication services primarily to businesses. Inter-Tel Technology Inc. (Technologies) operates Inter-Tel's retail division. On July 2, 1998, Technologies purchased Integrated Telecom Services Corp. (ITS), with Inter-Tel, the Arizona parent, paying for the stock. ITS was Inter-Tel's first retail branch in Kentucky, selling Inter-Tel's products from an office building in Louisville it leased from Linn Station Properties. After ITS was acquired by

Technologies, ITS no longer possessed any financial independence. ITS could not maintain a bank account, hold any funds, or pay any bills. All of ITS's regional offices were transformed from independent dealers of communications equipment into direct sales "branches" of Inter-Tel. ITS employees became employees of Inter-Tel and were paid by Inter-Tel from its headquarters in Arizona. When a customer purchased a telecommunications system from ITS the payment went directly into a "lock box" or

---

[31] *East Market v. Tycorp Pizza IV, Inc.*, 625 S.E.2d 191, 198 (N.C. App. 2006).

[32] In *Trevino v. MERSCORP, Inc.*, 583 F. Supp. 2d 521 (D. Del. 2008), the court determined that a shortage of capital is not per se a reason to pierce the corporate veil; rather, a more relevant inquiry would be "Was the entity established to defraud its creditors?" An example of grossly inadequate capitalization is found in *Klokke Corp. v. Classic Exposition, Inc.*, 912 P.2d 929 (Or. App. 1996), in which Classic's two shareholders invested $1,000 of capital to start a business and immediately took out a $200,000 loan. The business remained undercapitalized until part of it was sold. However, the two shareholders effectively withdrew all of the proceeds of the sale in October 1991, and the business was again without sufficient capital, leaving it unable to meet its financial obligations. The court held that the shareholders were personally liable up to the amount withdrawn in October 1991 after the partial sale of the business.

[33] See *Trustees of the National Elevator Industry Pension Fund v. Lutyk*, 332 F.3d 188 (3d Cir. 2003).

[34] *Barton v. Moore*, 558 N.W.2d 746 (Minn. 1997).

Sometimes "Parents" Have to Pay the Rent in Business, Too continued

depository account controlled by Inter-Tel. Once the funds were placed in this account, they belonged to Inter-Tel. Inter-Tel paid all the vendors who provided ITS with goods and services. Inter-Tel paid ITS's rent for the Linn Station Road property from the time Technologies acquired ITS until ITS abandoned the premises in 2002. Linn Properties sued ITS for unpaid rent and failure to maintain the property, and a default judgment was entered against ITS for $332,900. ITS was a defunct corporation without any assets, so Linn Properties sought to pierce the corporate veil to collect the debt from Technologies and Inter-Tel.

DECISION: Judgment for Linn Properties. Limited liability for corporate entities is described by some scholars as springing from both democratic and economic principles in the early days of the United States. The "imposition of limited liability was perceived as a means of encouraging the small-scale entrepreneur, and of keeping entry into business markets competitive and democratic," assuring that the corporate world was not dominated by industrialists who had the immense personal wealth to withstand any business risk. The economic rationale was that the public would benefit from investment by shareholders who would be willing to

take risks in industry, manufacturing, and general commercial development if personal liability could be avoided should their ventures not succeed. By the twentieth century, deliberate misuse of the corporate form by shareholders who were either individuals or other corporations had led courts to authorize piercing the corporate veil. The equitable doctrine of veil piercing cannot be thwarted by having two entities, rather than one, dominate the subsidiary and dividing the conduct between the two so that each can point the finger to some extent at the other. Inter-Tel and Technologies together exercised complete control and dominion over ITS, causing it to lose any semblance of separate corporate existence. Technologies and Inter-Tel transferred all of ITS's income and assets to themselves, thus deriving all of the benefits from the business while leaving behind a shell entity from which a legitimate creditor could recover nothing. Under these circumstances there was the requisite domination and injustice to justify piercing ITS's corporate veil to hold both Technologies and Inter-Tel responsible for the default judgment previously obtained by Linn Station against ITS. [*Inter-Tel Technologies Inc. v. Linn Station Properties, LLC*, **360 S.W.3d 152 (Ky. 2012)**]

"Alter Ego" Theory

Some courts express their reasons for disregarding the corporate entity by stating that the corporation is the "*alter ego*" of the wrongdoer. A corporation is a separate and distinct person from the person or persons who own the corporation. However, when a corporation is so dominated and controlled by a shareholder(s), officer(s), or director(s) that the separate personalities of the individual and the corporation no longer exist and there is a wrongful use of that control, the courts will disregard the corporate entity so as not to sanction a fraud or injustice.[35]

For Example, V&M Industries, Inc., owned land on which some 40,000-plus used tires caught fire. It took nearly a week to extinguish the fire and it caused severe air pollution in the St. Louis area. Vernon Leirer originally owned 99 percent of V&M corporate stock; all corporate officers other than Leirer were nonfunctioning; the corporation was inadequately capitalized; no stock certificates were issued; and corporate records were generally not kept. At a time just before the fire, when Leirer was no longer a shareholder or officer, he exercised total direction and control over the corporation and "ran the show." The court held that to adhere to the fiction of separate corporate existence would sanction fraud. It concluded that V&M, Inc., was the *alter ego* for Leirer, and Leirer was personally responsible for civil penalties under the Environmental Protection Act.[36]

Limited liability is important to our economy because it encourages investors to make investments in high-risk ventures. It should be disregarded only in exceptional circumstances. When fraud or deceit is absent, other circumstances for piercing the corporate veil must be so strong as to clearly indicate that the corporation is the alter ego of the controlling person.

---

[35] *Dishon v. Ponthie*, 918 So. 2d 1132 (La. App. 2005).
[36] *Illinois v. V&M Industries*, 700 N.E.2d 746 (Ill. App. 1998).

Obtaining Advantages of Corporate Existence

Courts will not go behind the corporate identity merely because the corporation has been formed to obtain tax savings or to obtain limited liability for its shareholders. Similarly, the corporate entity will not be ignored merely because the corporation does not have sufficient assets to pay the claims against it.

One-person, family, and other closely held corporations are permissible and entitled to all of the advantages of corporate existence. The fact that the principal shareholder runs or oversees the day-to-day operations does not justify ignoring the corporate entity.

44-4c Other Exceptions to Limited Liability

Liability may be imposed on a shareholder as though there were no corporation when the court ignores the corporate entity either because of the particular circumstances of the case or because the corporation is so defectively organized that it is deemed not to exist.

Wage Claims

Statutes sometimes provide that the shareholders shall have unlimited liability for the wage claims of corporate employees. This exception has been abandoned in some states in recent years or has been confined to corporate officers who are active in corporate decision making.[37]

Unpaid Subscriptions

Most states prohibit the issuance of par value shares for less than par or except for "money, labor done, or property actually received." Whenever shares issued by a corporation are not fully paid for, the original subscriber receiving the shares, or any transferee who does not give value or who knows that the shares were not fully paid for, is liable for the unpaid balance if the corporation is insolvent and the money is required to pay its creditors.[38]

CASE SUMMARY

You've Got to Pay for Your Stock, Silly

FACTS: On July 19, 1984, Keith and Joan Bryan incorporated Bryan's Inc. The corporation was authorized to issue 100 shares of stock with a par value of $1,000 per share. The corporation issued 50 shares to Keith and 50 shares to Joan, although it did not receive any payment in labor, services, money, or property for the stock. On August 30, 1984, Bryan's Inc. bought Hanewald's dry goods store, giving Hanewald a promissory note for part of the purchase price. The business was not successful, and after four months, Keith and Joan Bryan decided to close the store. They disbursed all of the corporation's funds in payment of all bills except for the debt owed Hanewald. No corporate funds were available to pay this debt. Hanewald sued the Bryans individually for the amount owed. The Bryans contended that they were not personally liable for the corporation's debts.

DECISION: Judgment for Hanewald. Organizing a corporation to avoid personal liability is legitimate and a primary advantage to doing business in the corporate form. But proper capitalization is the principal prerequisite for this limited liability. Keith and Joan Bryan's failure to pay for their stock makes them liable to Hanewald, the corporate creditor, to the extent that the stock was not paid for. Because the debt to Hanewald, $36,000, was less than the par value of their stock, $100,000, the Bryans are personally liable for the entire corporate debt owed to Hanewald. [*Hanewald v. Bryan's, Inc.*, 429 N.W.2d 414 (N.D. 1988)]

---

[37] *Cusimano v. Metro Auto, Inc.*, 860 P.2d 532 (Colo. App. 1993).
[38] *Frasier v. Trans-Western Land Corp.*, 316 N.W.2d 612 (Neb. 1982). But see *Brunfield v. Horn*, 547 So. 2d 415 (Ala. 1989).

If the corporation has issued the shares as fully paid for, has given them as a bonus, or has agreed to release the subscriber for the unpaid balance, the corporation cannot recover that balance. The fact that the corporation is thus barred does not prevent creditors of the corporation from bringing an action to compel payment of the balance. The same rules are applied when stock is issued as fully paid for in return for property or services that were overvalued so that the stock is not actually paid for in full. A conflict of authority exists, however, as to whether the shareholder is liable from the mere fact that the property or service given for the shares was in fact overvalued by the directors or whether it must also be shown that the directors acted in bad faith in making the erroneous valuation. The trend of modern statutes is, in the absence of proof of fraud, to prohibit disputing the valuation placed by the corporation on services or property.

Unauthorized Dividends

If dividends are improperly paid out of capital, shareholders are generally liable to creditors to the extent of such depletion of capital. In some states, the liability of a shareholder depends on whether the corporation was insolvent at the time and whether debts were existing at the time.

44-4d The Professional Corporation

The extent to which incorporation limits the liability of shareholders of a professional corporation depends on the interpretation of the statute under which the corporation was formed.

Act of Shareholder in Creating Liability

The statutes that authorize the formation of professional corporations usually require that share ownership be limited to duly licensed professionals. If a shareholder in a professional corporation, such as a corporation of physicians, negligently drives the professional corporation's automobile in going to attend a patient or is personally obligated on a contract made for the corporation or is guilty of malpractice, the physician-shareholder is liable without limit for the liability that has been created. This is the same rule of law that applies in the case of the ordinary business corporation.

Professional corporation statutes generally repeat the rule governing malpractice liability by stating that the liability of a shareholder for malpractice is not affected by the fact of incorporation.

Malpractice Liability of an Associate

The liability of a shareholder in a professional corporation for the malpractice of an associate varies from state to state depending on the language of the professional corporation statute in effect and on the court decisions under the statute.[39]

If the statute provides for limited liability, as in a business corporation, then where doctors *A*, *B*, and *C* are a professional corporation, *A* and *B* will not be liable for the malpractice of *C* beyond the extent of corporate assets. If the statute provides for vicarious personal liability, as in a partnership, and doctors *A*, *B*, and *C* are a professional corporation, each will have unlimited liability for any malpractice liability incurred by the others. Often the statutory reference to malpractice liability is not very clear, and the courts are called on to resolve the question of the liability of a professional shareholder for the malpractice of an associate.

---

[39] ABA Model Professional Corporation Act Amendments (1984) §34 offers three alternative positions regarding the liability of shareholders: (1) limited liability, as in a business corporation, (2) vicarious personal liability, as in a partnership, and (3) personal liability limited in amount and conditioned on financial responsibility in the form of insurance or a surety bond.

Make the Connection

Summary

The ownership of a corporation is evidenced by a holder's shares of stock that have been issued by the corporation. Common stock is ordinary stock that has no preferences but entitles the holder to (1) participate in the control of the corporation by exercising one vote per share of record, (2) share in the profits in the form of dividends, and (3) participate, upon dissolution, in the distribution of net assets after the satisfaction of all creditors (including bondholders). Other classes of stock exist, such as preferred stock, that have priority over common stock with regard to distribution of dividends and/or assets upon liquidation. Shares may be acquired by subscription of an original issue or by transfer of existing shares.

Bonds are debt securities, and a bondholder is a creditor rather than an owner of the corporation. Bondholders' interests are represented by an indenture trustee who is responsible for ensuring that the corporation complies with the terms of the bond indenture.

Shareholders control the corporation, but this control is indirect. Through their voting rights, they elect directors, and by this means, they can control the corporation.

Preemptive rights, if they exist, allow shareholders to maintain their voting percentages when the corporation issues additional shares of stock. Shareholders have the right to inspect the books of the corporation unless it would be harmful to the corporation. Shareholders also have the right to receive dividends when declared at the discretion of the directors. Shareholders may bring a derivative action on behalf of the corporation for damages to the corporation. Shareholders are ordinarily protected from liability for the acts of the corporation.

Ordinarily, each corporation is treated as a separate person, and the law does not look beyond the corporate identity merely because the corporation was formed to obtain tax savings or limited liability. The fact that two corporations have the same shareholders does not justify disregarding the separate corporate entities. However, when a corporation is formed to perpetrate a fraud, a court ignores the corporate form, or "pierces the corporate veil." The corporate form is also ignored to prevent injustice or because of the functional reality that the two corporations in question are one.

Learning Outcomes

After studying this chapter, you should be able to clearly explain:

44-1   Corporate Stocks and Bonds

LO.1   Explain how to calculate the book value of a share of stock

See the example in which Roger Eggett was awarded the book value of his stock, page 904.

LO.2   Distinguish between stocks and bonds

See the discussion of stocks as an ownership interest in a corporation and bonds as a corporate debt, page 904.

44-2   Acquisition of Shares

LO.3   Distinguish between subscriptions for and transfers of stock

See the discussion of stock subscriptions for new issues of stock, page 907.

See the discussion of transfers of shares and the impact of restrictions, pages 907–908.

44-3   Rights of Shareholders

LO.4   Explain the rights of shareholders

See the discussion of shareholder ownership rights, including the right to vote, inspect books and records, and receive dividends when declared, pages 911–915.

LO.5   Explain the nature of a shareholder derivative lawsuit

See the *AIG* case, where stockholder plaintiffs were excused from making a demand on the full board, page 916.

See the Abercrombie & Fitch Co. litigation where the court did not defer to the special litigation committee (SLC) because one of the two members was not "independent," page 917.

44-4   Liability of Shareholders

LO.6   Explain the exceptions to the limited liability of shareholders

See the *Inter-Tel* case where "grandparent" and "parent" corporations transferred all income and assets to themselves, and as a result the corporate entities were disregarded to accomplish justice, pages 918–919.

Key Terms

acceptance	deed	preferred stock
bond	derivative (secondary)	proxy
bond indenture	action	registered bonds
book value	indenture trustee	sinking fund
capital stock	market value	stock subscription
certificate of stock	maturity date	voting by proxy
common stock	outstanding	voting trust
cumulative voting	par value	wasting assets
debenture	preemptive right	corporations

Questions and Case Problems

1. Monica Beam, a shareholder of Martha Stewart Living Omnimedia, Inc. (MSO), filed a derivative action against Martha Stewart and the other MSO board of directors, alleging that Stewart breached her duties to MSO by illegally selling ImClone stock and mishandling media attention, thereby jeopardizing the financial future of MSO. Ms. Beam asserted that it would be a futile act to make a demand on the corporation because a majority of the outside directors were not independent of Stewart. Ms. Beam pleaded the particularized facts that director Darla Moore attended a wedding reception hosted by Stewart's personal lawyer for his daughter and was a longtime friend of Stewart; and that director Naomi Seligman made a phone call to publisher John Wiley, Inc., to express concern over a planned book critical of Stewart. Should Ms. Beam be excused from making a demand on the board of directors to pursue the derivative action because the outside directors were not independent of Stewart? [*Beam v. Stewart*, 845 A.2d 1040 (Del)]

2. Six members of the Weston family, who owned 6.8 percent of the stock of Weston Paper and Manufacturing Company, brought suit against three corporate directors and CFIS, a firm hired by the company to make the annual evaluation of the company's stock for allocating stock options to its employees. The Westons stated that their claims against the defendants were personal claims, alleging that they were injured by CFIS and the three directors who kept the price of the stock low to obtain more shares of stock through the stock option plan. From an adverse ruling on their right to maintain a direct action against the directors, the Westons appealed. How would you decide this case? [*Weston v. Weston Paper and Manufacturing Co.*, 74 Ohio 377]

3. Tomlinson and Hubbard were two of five shareholders in Multimedia Software Distributors, a corporation. The corporation was formed in 1992 and filed for bankruptcy in 1994. In 1996, Tomlinson filed a claim in his own name, alleging that Hubbard had breached his fiduciary duties to Tomlinson by diverting proceeds owned by Multimedia to another business owned by Hubbard. Hubbard contends that Tomlinson is an improper plaintiff. Decide. [*Hubbard v. Tomlinson*, 747 N.E.2d 69 (Ind. App.)]

4. Equivest, a partnership, owned 10,000 shares of Altec International, Inc. Equivest pledged these shares to secure loans by Lloyds Bank. Sometime after pledging the stock, Equivest transferred beneficial ownership of 350 shares of Altec stock to Thorn Hoffman and 350 shares to John Erikson. Thereafter, in 1988, Altec elected to be treated as a Subchapter S corporation, which necessitated that shareholders return their old stock certificates in exchange for new stock certificates. Neither Erikson nor Hoffman had certificates to return because their stock had been pledged by Equivest to Lloyds Bank. Altec had knowledge that Erikson and Hoffman were the beneficial owners of 700 shares of Altec stock. However, Altec distributed cash dividends to Equivest, the registered owner of the 10,000 shares during the period from 1988 until March 14, 1990. Equivest defaulted on its loan to Lloyds Bank and Lloyds sold all of the pledged stock, including Hoffman's and Erikson's 700 shares, at public auction. Hoffman and Erikson contend that Altec should have made all cash distributions to them as shareholders, not Equivest. Altec contends that it complied with the UCC by making distributions to the owner of record. Do you think the distribution should have gone to Hoffman and Erikson or to

Equivest? [*Hoffman v. Altec Int'l Inc.*, 546 N.W.2d 162 (Wis. App.)]

5. The stock of West End Development Co. was subject to a transfer restriction. This restriction required that any shareholder selling shares first offer every other shareholder the right to purchase a proportion of the shares being sold. The proportions were to be the same as the percentages of the outstanding shares that the other shareholders already owned. This restriction was stated in the articles of incorporation but was not stated on the stock certificate of the corporation. The Taylors owned stock in the company and sold their stock to Vroom, an officer of the corporation, without first offering any stock to the other shareholders, as required by the restriction. The other shareholders brought an action against Vroom to recover from him the percentages of the shares they would have been entitled to if the Taylors had followed the transfer restriction. Decide. [*Irwin v. West End Development Co.*, 481 F.2d 34 (10th Cir.)]

6. Siebrecht organized Siebrecht Realty Co., a corporation, and then transferred his building to the corporation in exchange for its stock. The corporation rented different parts of the building to different tenants. Elenkrieg, an employee of one of the tenants, fell and was injured because of the defective condition of a stairway. She sued Siebrecht individually on the ground that the corporation had been formed by him for the purpose of securing limited liability. Decide. [*Elenkrieg v. Siebrecht*, 144 N.E. 519 (N.Y.)]

7. U.S. Die Casting, Inc., is a closely held Ohio corporation that owns 5 percent of Security First Corporation, a Delaware corporation. David Slyman is the president of U.S. Die and its sole shareholder. The defendant, Security First, entered into a merger agreement with Mid Am, Inc., a large regional bank holding company. After the announcement of the merger, Security First's stock increased significantly. The merger agreement required Security First to pay a termination fee of $2 million plus third-party expenses not to exceed $250,000 contingent on the occurrence of certain events within one year after termination should Security First pull out of the merger. The merger did not go through, and the market price for Security First dropped significantly. According to Security First, it did not go through with the merger because it realized that Mid Am's "management philosophy and direction were fundamentally different from its own." Security First paid Mid Am $275,000 in expenses and agreed to pay an

additional $2 million if a certain event occurred within one and one-half years after termination. U.S. Die submitted a written demand to Security First pursuant to Section 220 of the Delaware Code to inspect all of its books and records related to the Mid Am merger and its termination. Security First refused to comply. The Court of Chancery granted U.S. Die's demand and Security First appealed. Should U.S. Die be allowed to inspect Security First's books? [*Security First Corp. v. U.S. Die Casting, Inc.*, 687 A.2d 563 (Del.)]

8. Ken and Charlotte Maschmeier were the majority shareholders of Southside Press; each owned 1,300 shares. Marty and Larry Maschmeier, who each owned 1,200 shares of the corporation, had a falling out with Ken and Charlotte and were terminated as employees of the business. Ken and Charlotte started a new corporation, which employed most of the employees of the old corporation and which took most of its former customers. Gross receipts of Southside Press went from $613,258 down to $18,172 two years later. The $18,172 figure was from the lease of equipment. Ken and Charlotte continued to draw from Southside annual salaries of $20,000, which were in excess of the gross receipts of the business. Marty and Larry brought suit against Ken and Charlotte, alleging "oppressive" conduct. Ken and Charlotte stated that they had paid Marty and Larry excellent salaries when they were employed by the corporation. Ken and Charlotte contended that they had a right to start a new corporation as they saw fit. Decide. [*Maschmeier v. Southside Press, Inc.*, 435 N.W.2d 377 (Iowa App.)]

9. Gladys Boles and 28 other owners of property at Hidden Valley Lakes Development sued the corporate developer, National Development Co. Inc. (NDC); NDC's parent, Sunstates Corporation; and the individual behind both corporations, Clyde Engle, for breach of contract and fraud. The centerpiece of this development, Crystal Lake, a 30-acre recreational lake, failed to hold water; and it was determined that it could never do so. Instead of having a 30-acre lake as the centerpiece, the plaintiffs had a 30-acre hole in the ground. While the controversy over NDC's breach of contract was pending, Engle made a "proposal" to the CEO of NDC to transfer $2.4 million in receivables to Sunstates in exchange for an unsecured promissory note. Evidence showed that all of Sunstates' assets thereafter were transferred to Engle, making the note NDC

held from Sunstates worthless. Sunstates purchased approximately $1.9 million of oriental art, antique jewelry, rare books, and other collectibles, which were maintained in Engle's home in Illinois. Likewise, Sunstates purchased a Rolls Royce from Libco, a corporation in which Engle was the majority shareholder. This automobile also appeared to be in Engle's possession or control. Engles regrets that the lake did not work out, a risk that the developer and the homeowners have to live with, and points out that NDC is a separate legal entity with limited liability for its shareholders. Engle asserts that he is not personally liable for damages in this case. Decide. [*Boles v. National Development Co., Inc.*, 175 N.W.3d 226 (Tenn. App.)]

10. Ed Klein was the sole shareholder, director, and chief executive officer of The Gun Exchange, Inc., a retail firearms dealership. The inventory of The Gun Exchange had been pledged as security for a $622,500 debt owed to InterFirst Bank. It also owed $231,484.60 to Sporting Goods, Inc.; this debt was unsecured. On May 20, InterFirst Bank notified Klein of its intention to foreclose on the inventory and sell it at public auction. InterFirst Bank further advised Klein that, pursuant to his personal guarantee, he would be responsible for any deficiency following the sale. Klein immediately incorporated The Gun Store, Inc., for the purpose of purchasing the assets of The Gun Exchange at the foreclosure sale. Before the foreclosure sale, Klein obtained a $650,000 line of credit from CharterBank on behalf of The Gun Store. At the sale, Klein purchased the assets of The Gun Exchange for $650,000 even though the highest prior bid was $175,000. (Had the $175,000 bid been accepted, Klein would have been personally liable for the deficiency to InterFirst Bank.)

    After the foreclosure sale, no funds existed to pay the unsecured creditors of The Gun Exchange. Following the sale, The Gun Store began operating as a retail firearms dealer with the inventory purchased from the foreclosure sale. It operated in the same location and with the same personnel as The Gun Exchange. Sporting Goods, Inc., sued Klein individually for the $231,484.60. Klein contended that the corporate form under which he did business insulated him as a shareholder from liability for corporate obligations. Decide. Is it ethical to seek limited liability under the corporate form, as Klein did in this case? [*Klein v. Sporting Goods, Inc.*, 772 S.W.2d 173 (Tex. Civ. App.)]

11. Ibanez owned shares of stock in Farmers Underwriters. He left the stock certificate lying on top of his desk in his office. Many persons continually passed through the office, and one day Ibanez realized that someone had taken the certificate from the top of his desk. Ibanez applied to Farmers Underwriters for a duplicate stock certificate. The corporation refused to issue a duplicate on the ground that it was Ibanez's own fault that the original certificate had been stolen. Ibanez claimed that he was entitled to a new certificate even though he had been at fault. Was he correct? [*Ibanez v. Farmers Underwriters Ass'n*, 534 P.2d 1336 (Cal.)]

12. On March 3, 2002, pursuant to a public offering, First All State Trucking Corp. (FAST) issued securities to investors in denominations of $1,000. The interest rate was 7 percent per year payable semiannually, and the maturity date was March 3, 2010. The rights and obligations of the issuer, FAST, and the holders of the securities were set forth in an indenture agreement. Because the securities were not secured by a mortgage or lien on corporate property, Alec believes that they are shares of preferred stock. Is Alec correct? Fully explain the type of security involved, and discuss the extent of the holders' voting rights.

13. Linhart owned shares of stock in First National Bank. She borrowed money from the bank and pledged the stock as security. She later decided to transfer 70 head of cattle and the shares of stock to her son, but she could not deliver the share certificate to him because it was held by the bank. She therefore executed a bill of sale reciting the transfer of the cattle and the stock to the son. She gave him the bill of sale, and he had the bill recorded. After her death, the son brought an action to determine the ownership of the stock. Was the son the owner of the shares?

14. Birt was a hospital patient. The doctor who treated him was a shareholder of a professional corporation organized under the Indiana Medical Professional Corporation Act. Birt claimed that the doctor who treated him was guilty of malpractice, and he sued the doctor. He also sued the professional corporation and all of its officers, directors, and shareholders. These other defendants asserted that they were not liable because the corporate entity shielded them. The plaintiff claimed that the corporation was not a shield because in fact all of the persons were rendering medical services and should be held liable as

in a partnership. The statute did not expressly regulate the matter of limited liability beyond declaring that it did not change the law between a person supplying medical services and the patient. Decide. [*Birt v. St. Mary Mercy Hospital*, 370 N.E.2d 379 (Ind. App.)]

15. Ronald Naquin, an employee of Air Engineered Systems & Services, Inc., owned one-third of its outstanding shares. After six years, he was fired and an offer was made to buy out his interest in Air Engineered at a price that Naquin thought inadequate. He then formed a competing business and made a written request to examine the corporate records of Air Engineered. This request was denied. Naquin filed suit to require Air Engineered to allow him to examine the books. Air Engineered raised the defense that he was a competitor seeking to gain unfair competitive advantage. Decide. [*Naquin v. Air Engineered Systems & Services, Inc.*, 463 So. 2d 992 (La. App.)]

CPA Questions

1. A stockholder's right to inspect books and records of a corporation will be properly denied if the stockholder:

   a. Wants to use corporate stockholder records for a personal business.

   b. Employs an agent to inspect the books and records.

   c. Intends to commence a stockholder's derivative suit.

   d. Is investigating management misconduct.

2. The limited liability of a stockholder in a closely held corporation may be challenged successfully if the stockholder:

   a. Undercapitalized the corporation when it was formed.

   b. Formed the corporation solely to have limited personal liability.

   c. Sold property to the corporation.

   d. Was a corporate officer, a director, or an employee.

3. Price owns 2,000 shares of Universal Corp.'s $10 cumulative preferred stock. During its first year of operations, cash dividends of $5 per share were declared on the preferred stock but were never paid. In the second year, dividends on the preferred stock were neither declared nor paid. If Universal is dissolved, which of the following statements is correct?

   a. Universal will be liable to Price as an unsecured creditor for $10,000.

   b. Universal will be liable to Price as a secured creditor for $20,000.

   c. Price will have priority over the claims of Universal's bond owners.

   d. Price will have priority over the claims of Universal's unsecured judgment creditors.

4. Under the Revised Model Business Corporation Act, a dissenting stockholder's appraisal right generally applies to which of the following corporate actions?

	Consolidations	Shares from mergers
a.	Yes	Yes
b.	Yes	No
c.	No	Yes
d.	No	No

Securities Regulation

Learning Outcomes ⟨⟨⟨

After studying this chapter, you should be able to

LO.1   Explain the meaning of state "blue sky laws"

LO.2   Define "security"

LO.3   Compare and distinguish between the Securities Act of 1933 and the Securities Exchange Act of 1934

LO.4   Explain the changes that the JOBS Act has had on registration exemptions

LO.5   Explain how the 1934 act's policy of fostering reliance on market integrity is served by Rule 10b-5 private investor lawsuits when investors are injured by material misstatements by the issuer

LO.6   Explain the factors that subject an individual to liability for insider trading

LO.7   Explain how the primary and secondary markets are regulated by the SEC as well as private enforcement organizations

45-1 State Regulation

To protect the public from the sale of fraudulent securities, many states have adopted statutes regulating the intrastate sale of securities.

State laws regulating securities are called **blue sky laws.** The term *blue sky* is derived from the purpose of such laws, which is to prevent the sale of speculative schemes that have no more value than the blue sky. The state statutes vary in detail. They commonly contain (1) an antifraud provision prohibiting fraudulent practices and imposing criminal penalties for violations, (2) broker-dealer licensing provisions regulating the persons engaged in the securities business, and (3) provisions for the registration of securities, including disclosure requirements, with a designated government official.

A Uniform Securities Act, covering the foregoing three categories of regulations, exists to provide guidance to states in updating their securities laws. This act also contains alternative regulations that can be adopted by states with different regulatory philosophies.

Congress reallocated responsibility between state and federal security regulators in the National Securities Markets Improvement Act (NSMIA)[1] recognizing that the dual system of state and federal regulation of securities resulted in duplicative regulation and expenses. The NSMIA allows the states to investigate and bring enforcement actions for fraud or deceit or for unlawful conduct by a broker or dealer in connection with securities transactions.[2]

45-2 History of Federal Regulation and Market Trends

The federal system for regulation of securities sales and the secondary market began following the stock market crash of 1929 and the resulting Great Depression. The Securities Act of 1933 and the Securities Exchange Act of 1934, both covered in detail in this chapter, were the beginning of the extensive federal regulatory structure for capital markets. In response to market events that revealed loopholes and gaps in regulation, Congress has continued to refine securities regulation.

In the mid-1980s there was substantial abuse of penny stocks in "pump and dump" schemes as well as "churning" of accounts. Abuse of penny stocks resulted in significant investor losses and fraudulent offerings. Penny stocks are those that are not listed on the exchanges and that trade over the counter below $5. The Securities Enforcement Remedies and Penny Stock Reform Act of 1990[3] required more regulation and increased disclosure to reduce penny stock fraud. The act imposed more stringent regulations on broker-dealers who recommend penny stocks to clients. **For Example,** the SEC charged Oppenheimer & Co. with failure to respond to red flags about the unregistered sales of billions of shares of penny stocks. Oppenheimer admitted to wrongdoing and paid fines of $10 million to the SEC and $10 million to the Treasury Department's Financial Crimes Enforcement Network.[4]

The Market Reform Act of 1990[5] was enacted to provide the SEC with powers to deal with market volatility. The act was passed in response to the savings and loan crisis

---

[1] P.L. 104-290, 110 Stat 3416, 15 U.S.C. §78a nt.
[2] The 1996 act amends §18(c) of the 1933 Securities Act to accomplish this result.
[3] P.L. 101-429, 104 Stat. 931, 15 U.S.C. §77g.
[4] Press Release, SEC, "SEC Charges Oppenheimer with Securities Law Violations Related to Improper Penny Stock Sales" (Jan. 27, 2015), **http://www.sec.gov/news/pressrelease/2015-14.html.**
[5] P.L. 101-432, 104 Stat. 963, 15 U.S.C. §78a.

in the 1980s and 1990s.[6] Under the law, the SEC has the power to suspend all trading when markets are excessively volatile. Also, the SEC may require "large traders" to identify themselves and provide information concerning their trading.

The Private Securities Litigation Reform Act (PSLRA) of 1995[7] was passed in response to increasing abuses in private securities litigation, including lawyers filing suits on behalf of plaintiff shareholders who were unaware that they were involved in those suits. The intent of the act is to reduce the number of lawsuits brought against issuers of securities and accounting firms.

Congress passed sweeping legislation in response to widespread accounting fraud that began with Enron's collapse in 2001 (Sarbanes-Oxley Act). The financial crisis in 2008 led to the Dodd-Frank Wall Street Reform and Consumer Protection Act (Dodd-Frank), which seeks to prevent another financial crisis and to restore investor confidence in the market. Because of the widespread economic impact of the 2008 crisis, Congress passed the Jumpstart Our Business Startups (JOBS) Act in 2012 to encourage investment in companies, especially smaller companies, by providing easier access to capital markets. The role of the SEC is to protect investors even as it oversees efficient operation of the markets through monitoring compliance with the law and enforcing its rules and regulations. Its role and regulations expand as market events and activities change.

45-2a The Securities Act of 1933

primary offerings–the original distribution of securities by the issuing corporations.

The 1933 act deals with the original distribution of securities by the issuing corporations, or **primary offerings.** The 1933 act is a disclosure statute designed to secure essential facts for the investor who is buying shares from the company. The 1934 act focuses on the secondary distribution of securities in the national securities exchanges and in the over-the-counter markets. That is, the 1933 act regulates the sale of securities by a corporation to the first owner, a primary offering. An offer or sale of securities to the public in interstate commerce requires that a registration statement be filed with the SEC unless an exemption applies. The exemptions are discussed later in this chapter.

Applicability and Definition of Security

securities–stocks and bonds issued by a corporation. Under some investor protection laws, the term includes any interest in an enterprise that provides unearned income to its owner.

For the securities acts to apply, the transaction must involve a "security" within the meaning of the acts.[8] Congress adopted a definition of **security** sufficiently broad to encompass virtually any instrument that might be sold as an investment.

The 1933 act applies to the sale of securities, including (1) stocks, (2) corporate bonds, and (3) any conceivable type of corporate interest or instrument that has the characteristics of an investment security, including convertible securities and variable annuities.

The definition of *security* includes not only investment instruments such as stocks and bonds but also "investment contracts." The definition of an *investment contract*, developed by the Supreme Court, is sufficiently broad to allow the securities acts to apply to a wide range of investment transactions or schemes, including the sale of bottled

---

[6] A savings and loan or "thrift" is a financial institution that accepts savings deposits and makes payments for individuals such as mortgages or car payments. During the S&L crisis 747 out of the 3,234 saving and loan associations in the United States failed. Many S&Ls became insolvent when they could not attract sufficient capital. Some CEOs invented creative accounting strategies to make the S&Ls look profitable while they were actually losing money.

[7] P.L. 104-67, 109 Stat. 737, 15 U.S.C. §78a nt.

[8] The Supreme Court has consistently held that the definition of a security set forth in §3(a)(10) of the 1934 act is identical to the definition set forth in §2(1) of the 1933 act. The definition of security under these acts is not to be confused with the narrower definition in Article 8 of the Uniform Commercial Code. See *SEC v. Infinity Group Co.*, 993 F. Supp. 321 (E.D. Pa. 1998).

registration statement–
document disclosing
specific financial
information regarding the
security, the issuer, and
the underwriter.

whiskey, cattle-breeding programs, and a limited liability partnership to operate local tele-phone companies.[9] Under the Supreme Court's definition, an investment contract exists if the following elements are present: (1) an investment of money, (2) a common enterprise, and (3) an expectation of future profits from the efforts of others. **For Example,** the sale of citrus groves to investors, coupled with the execution of service contracts to plant, har-vest, and sell the fruit and the distribution of the profits of the venture to the investors, is an investment contract. An instrument denominated as a "note" may, in fact, be a "secu-rity" subject to regulation under the 1934 act.[10]

CASE SUMMARY

10,000 Investors Wish They Had Missed This Opportunity

FACTS: "Opportunity doesn't always knock … sometimes it rings" (ETS Payphones promotional brochure). And some-times it hangs up. So it did for the 10,000 people who invested a total of $300 million in the payphone sale-and-leaseback arrangements touted by ETS under that slogan. Charles Edwards was the chairman, chief executive officer, and sole shareholder of ETS Payphones, Inc. Acting partly through a subsidiary, ETS sold payphones to the pub-lic via independent distributors. The payphones were offered packaged with a site lease, a five-year leaseback and manage-ment agreement, and a buyback agreement. The purchase price for the payphone packages was approximately $7,000. Under the leaseback and management agreement, purchasers received $82 per month, a 14 percent annual return. Purcha-sers were not involved in the day-to-day operation of the payphones they owned. ETS selected the site for the phones, installed the equipment, arranged for connection and long distance service, collected coin revenues, and maintained and repaired the phones. Under the buyback agreement, ETS promised to refund the full purchase price of the pack-age at the end of the lease or within 180 days of the purcha-ser's request. The payphones did not generate enough revenue for ETS to make the payments required by the lease-back agreements, so the company depended on funds from

new investors to meet its obligations. In September 2000, ETS filed for bankruptcy protection. The SEC brought this civil enforcement action alleging that Edwards and ETS had violated the registration requirements and antifraud provi-sions of the 1933 act. The district court concluded that the arrangement was an "investment contract" subject to the securities laws. The Court of Appeals for the Eleventh Circuit reversed the lower court because the scheme offered a con-tractual entitlement to a fixed, rather than a variable, return.

DECISION: Judgment for the SEC. Congress's purpose in enacting the securities laws was to regulate investments in whatever form they are made and by whatever name they are called. To that end, it enacted a broad definition of "secu-rity" sufficient to encompass virtually any instrument that might be sold as an investment. The U.S. Supreme Court applied the *Hovey* test for an investment contract finding (1) an investment of money, (2) a common enterprise, and (3) an expectation of future "profits" from the efforts of others, including fixed returns based on contracts. The Court determined that the ETS investment scheme can be an "investment contract" and thus a "security" under the securities laws. It reversed and remanded the case to the Court of Appeals. [*SEC v. Edwards*, **540 U.S. 389 (2004)**]

prospectus–information
provided to each
potential purchaser of
securities setting forth
the key information
contained in the
registration statement.

45-2b **The Filing Requirements: Registration Statements**

A **registration statement** is a document disclosing specific financial information regarding the security, the issuer, and the underwriter. The seller must also provide a prospectus to each potential purchaser of the securities. The **prospectus** sets forth the key information contained in the registration statement. The object is to provide the interested investor detailed information about the security and the enterprise. The SEC does not approve or disapprove the securities as being good or bad investments but only reviews the form

---

[9] *SEC v. Shiner*, 268 F. Supp. 2d 1333 (S.D. Fla. 2003).
[10] *SEC v. Wallenbrock*, 313 F.3d 532 (9th Cir. 2002).

and content of the registration statement and the prospectus to ensure full disclosure. The requirements of advance disclosure to the public through the filing of the registration statement with the SEC and the sending of a prospectus to each potential purchaser are commonly referred to as the **registration requirements** of the 1933 act.

registration requirements–provisions of the Securities Act of 1933 requiring advance disclosure to the public of a new securities issue through filing a statement with the SEC and sending a prospectus to each potential purchaser.

The JOBS Act and Dodd-Frank have made it easier for smaller reporting companies and emerging growth companies to comply with registration and disclosure rules for primary offerings. If a company qualifies as a smaller reporting company (based on equity amount or less than $50 million in annual revenue) or an emerging growth company (EGC) (total annual gross revenues of less than $1 billion during its most recent fiscal year), then the registration requirements are easier and less costly for their primary offerings. One of the helpful provisions for an ECG or smaller reporting companies is that the initial SEC filing may be made on a confidential basis. The confidential filing is a way for these companies to determine if they can meet regulatory standards without the public disclosure that the SEC has rejected their offering. They can then withdraw the offering until such time as they can meet the regulatory requirements without the taint of having been denied registration.

The Registration Process

Section 5 of the 1933 act provides for the division of the registration process into three time periods: (1) the prefiling period, (2) the waiting period or quiet period, from the date of filing with the SEC to the date the registration statement becomes effective (a minimum of 20 days but commonly extended for additional 20-day periods after each amendment by the issuer in compliance with SEC requirements for additional information), and (3) the posteffective period. The time divisions allow the public an opportunity to study the information disclosed in the registration process before a sale can be made. Permissible, required, and prohibited activities during these time periods are set forth in Figure 45-1.

CPA   Regulation A Offerings

Regulation A provides a simplified registration process for small issues of securities by small businesses. Regulation A originally allowed registration exemptions for offerings of securities up to $5 million in a 12-month period. The Jumpstart Our Business Startups (JOBS) Act, signed into law in 2012, expanded Regulation A to allow emerging enterprises to raise public capital efficiently and to allow more choices to investors through a simpler SEC registration process. The new regulation, sometimes referred to as Regulation A+, increases the amount of capital a business can raise in a Regulation A offering from $5 million to $50 million.[11] One of the primary benefits of the new regulation is that it allows companies to register only with the SEC and exempts them from registering with state financial regulators.[12] If Regulation A companies meet certain standards, they can avoid onerous reporting and disclosure requirements. The new regulation allows investment by both accredited and nonaccredited investors, with some limits on the amount a nonaccredited investor may invest.[13] One of the significant advantages of Regulation A is that it allows companies to "test the waters" through general solicitation and advertising before filing an offering statement. In other words, issuers can solicit interest in a potential offering before incurring substantial expenses either before or after filing the offering statement. Once the offering statement has been filed, the issuer must provide a

---

[11] Before the amount was increased and the state regulation requirement was changed, Regulation A offerings were rarely used.

[12] The revised Regulation A creates two tiers: a Tier 1 offering allows up to $20 million in 12 months; a Tier 2 offering allows up to $50 million in 12 months. The requirements and benefits of the tiers differ. Tier 1 offerings still require state registration, while Tier 2 offerings require registration only with the SEC.

[13] Tier 2 offerings limit a nonaccredited investor to 10 percent of the greater of annual income or net worth.

FIGURE 45-1	Registration Periods

	PROHIBITED OR REQUIRED ACTIVITIES	PERMITTED ACTIVITIES
PREFILING PERIOD	ISSUER MUST NOT SELL OR OFFER FOR SALE A SECURITY BEFORE REGISTRATION STATEMENT IS FILED.	ISSUER MAY PLAN WITH UNDERWRITERS THE DISTRIBUTION OF THE SECURITY.
WAITING PERIOD	NO FINAL SALE OF A SECURITY PERMITTED DURING THIS PERIOD.	PRELIMINARY PROSPECTUS* CONTAINING INFORMATION FROM THE REGISTRATION STATEMENT BEING REVIEWED BY THE SEC MAY BE DISTRIBUTED TO INVESTORS, WHO MAY MAKE OFFERS. ADVERTISEMENTS MAY BE PLACED IN FINANCIAL PUBLICATIONS, IDENTIFYING PARTICULARS OF THE SECURITY, FROM WHOM A PROSPECTUS CAN BE OBTAINED, AND BY WHOM ORDERS WILL BE EXECUTED.**
POSTEFFECTIVE PERIOD	MUST PROVIDE A COPY OF FINAL PROSPECTUS WITH EVERY WRITTEN OFFER, CONFIRMATION OF SALE, OR DELIVERY OF SECURITY. MUST UPDATE PROSPECTUS WHENEVER IMPORTANT NEW DEVELOPMENTS OCCUR OR AFTER NINE MONTHS.	SALES OF THE SECURITY MAY BE COMPLETED.

*The preliminary prospectus is commonly called the *red herring* prospectus because of the red ink caption required by the SEC, informing the public that a registration statement has been filed but is not yet effective and that no final sale can be made until after the effective date. A red herring prospectus does not include key details such as price and the number of shares offered.

**These advertisements are sometimes called *tombstone ads* because they are commonly framed by a black ink border.

preliminary offering circular or provide information to potential investors on where the most current preliminary offering circular can be obtained, such as a Web site.

Financial statements for a Regulation A offering are less extensive than those required for a public offering but issuers must file balance sheets and financial statements for the two previous fiscal years. Only companies that are organized in and have their principal place of business in the United States or Canada are eligible for Regulation A exemptions. Issuers considered "bad actors" by the SEC are not eligible.[14]

CPA **Regulation D Exemptions**

Certain private and limited offerings of securities are exempt from the registration requirements under Regulation D, which includes three different types of exemptions.

CPA **Rule 506 Exemption.** Regulation D is a rule that provides general permission to offer and sell to a potentially indefinite number of individuals who meet the definition of

[14] "Bad actors" would be those who have had difficulties with the SEC, such as investigations, sanctions, fines, or any types of criminal convictions.

accredited investor.[15] Regulation D is commonly referred to as the *private placement exemption*. Under the Rule 506 exemption, specific information must be provided to all buyers if any buyers are nonaccredited investors; the number of nonaccredited investors is limited to no more than 35 investors. Under Rule 506(b) a company may not use general solicitation or advertising to market the securities. Under the JOBS Act, the SEC made changes to Rule 506 that allow general solicitation if all purchasers of the securities are accredited investors and the issuer takes reasonable steps to verify that the purchasers are accredited investors. The new rule on general solicitation was a response to the need for companies to communicate more efficiently with potential investors in a market where both capital and information flow swiftly.

CPA **Rule 505 Exemption.** Rule 505 of Regulation D exempts from registration offerings of less than $5 million to no more than 35 nonaccredited purchasers over a 12-month period. No limit exists on the number of accredited investors who may participate. No general solicitation or general advertising is permitted under Rule 505. If any prospective investors are nonaccredited, the issuer must furnish all investors specific information on the issuer, its business, and the securities offered for sale.

CPA **Rule 504 Exemption.** Under Rule 504 of Regulation D, an issuer can offer and sell securities up to $1 million within a 12-month period without registration and without most of the restrictions contained in Rules 505 and 506.

CPA **Restrictions.** Securities acquired under Rules 506, 505, and 504 exemptions from registration are considered restricted securities. Their resale may require registration. Rules requiring registration of these Regulation D securities prior to resale ensure that investors purchase these securities as an investment rather than for public distribution. When there is no attempt to make public distributions, investors ordinarily fit within one of several exemptions to registration upon resale. Generally, all restrictions expire after two years. Companies do not have to register their offering of securities with the SEC if they are relying on Rule 504, 505, or 506 under Regulation D. Companies relying on these exemptions must, however, file a "Form D," which provides the names and addresses of the company's promoters, executive officers, and directors and some details about the offering.[16]

Intrastate Offerings Exemption

An intrastate offering exemption may be used to finance local business operations through local investment. SEC Rule 147 provides stringent standards for the exemption. The company must be organized in the state where it is offering securities and it must meet the so-called Triple 80 requirement.[17] All of the offerees and purchasers must be residents of the same state where the offering is made. The exemption may be lost if a sale is made to even one out-of-state person. The exemption does not limit the number of persons who may purchase the securities and there is no limit on the size of the offering.[18]

---

[15] The term *accredited investor* is defined to include virtually every type of institution that participates in the private placement market, such as banks, stock brokerage firms, insurance companies, mutual fund companies, and retirement plans with assets in excess of $5 million. A director, an executive officer, or a general partner of the company selling the securities is an accredited investor. An individual is considered an accredited investor if he or she has a net worth of at least $1 million, not including the value of his or her primary residence or if his or her income exceeds $200,000 in each of the two most recent calendar years or joint income with a spouse exceeds $300,000 for those years and there is a reasonable expectation of the same income level in the current year.

[16] A company's Form D can be accessed from the SEC's EDGAR database.

[17] 17 C.F.R. §230.147 (2015). Rule 147 offerings must meet the so-called Triple 80 requirements: 80 percent of the offeror's assets must be in one state, 80 percent of its revenue must be earned within that state, and 80 percent of the proceeds from the offering must be used within that state.

[18] Several states have enacted or proposed state crowdfunding legislation, relying on the intrastate exemption. The SEC has stated that general advertising or solicitation through the Internet does not make such local crowdfunding efforts ineligible for the exemption if there are sufficient disclaimers to ensure that offers are made only to state residents.

Crowdfunding Exemption

Crowdfunding has become a popular way to raise money by attracting relatively small individual contributions form a large number of people. The JOBS Act requires the SEC to create a crowdfunding exemption that would allow companies to raise $1 million in any 12-month period. Under the proposed rule, companies must use an intermediary that is registered with the SEC. The proposed rule also limits individual investors in the amount they can invest in crowdfunding in any 12-month period.[19]

CPA   Enforcement of the 1933 Act

Issuers, sellers, and "aiders and abettors" may be subject to civil and criminal liability under the 1933 act.

CPA   Issuer's Civil Liability for False or Misleading Statements. The Securities Act of 1933 imposes civil liability under section 11 for making materially false or misleading statements in a registration statement and for omitting any required material fact. An issuing company has virtually no defense if there has been a false statement and a loss.

CPA   Civil Liability of Sellers of Securities. Section 12 of the 1933 act applies to those who "offer or sell" securities and employ any device or scheme to defraud or obtain money by means of untrue statements of material facts. This section makes such persons or firms liable to purchasers for damages sustained.

CPA   Criminal Liability. Section 24 of the 1933 act imposes criminal penalties on anyone who willfully makes untrue statements of material facts or omits required material facts from a registration statement. Section 17 of the act makes it unlawful for any person to employ any device, scheme, or artifice to defraud in the offer or sale of securities.

CPA   45-2c The Securities Exchange Act of 1934

The 1934 Securities Exchange Act regulates the sale of securities from one owner to another, the secondary markets. Other federal laws supplement the 1934 act by regulating other market participants.[20] These laws cover holding companies in utility businesses, trustees for debt securities, mutual funds, and investment advisors.

CPA   Registration and Reporting Requirements

Exchanges, brokers, and dealers who deal in securities traded in interstate commerce or on any national security exchange must register with the SEC unless exempted by it.

---

[19] The proposed rules state that investors whose annual income or net worth is less than $100,000 may invest up to the greater of $2,000 or 5 percent of annual income or net worth. Investors whose annual income or net worth is more than $100,000 may invest up to 10 percent of annual income or net worth up to a maximum amount of $100,000. Net worth does not include the value of an investor's primary residence.

[20] The Public Utility Holding Company Act of 1935 (15 U.S.C. §79 *et seq.*) provides comprehensive regulation of holding companies and their subsidiaries in interstate gas and electric utilities businesses. The Trust Indenture Act of 1939 (15 U.S.C. §§77aaa to 77bbb) was enacted to protect the interests of the holders of bonds and other debt securities offered to the public in interstate commerce by requiring the appointment of independent institutional trustees. The Investment Company Act of 1940 (15 U.S.C. §§80a-1 to 80a-52) provides for the registration and comprehensive regulation of mutual funds and all other investment companies. The Investment Advisers Act of 1940 (15 U.S.C. §§80b-1 to 80b-21) requires registration with the Securities and Exchange Commission of all persons engaged in the business of providing investment advice in interstate commerce. In 1970, the Securities Investors Protection Act was enacted to protect investors from the business failures of brokers and dealers.

Companies whose securities are listed on a national securities exchange and unlisted companies with assets in excess of $10 million and a class of equity securities, such as common stock that is held of record by either (1) 2,000 or more persons or (2) 500 or more persons who are not accredited investors, are subject to the reporting requirements of the act. The JOBS Act requires the SEC to adopt rules permitting crowdfunding. Under such rules, companies will be able to exclude holders of securities issued under the crowdfunding exemption.

CPA **Principal Reports.** Publicly traded companies must disclose information to the SEC on an ongoing basis. Domestic issuers must submit annual reports on Form 10-K. Form 10-K provides an overview of the company's business and financial condition and must include audited financial statements. It is similar, but distinct, from the annual report to shareholders. Publicly traded companies must also file quarterly reports on Form 10-Q. Companies must report material changes or events, such as acquisitions, bankruptcy, or the resignation of directors, on Form 8-K.

CPA **Certifications and Disclosure Controls.** The Sarbanes-Oxley Act of 2002 requires written certification of the 10-K and 10-Q reports by each company's CEO and CFO. Section 302(a) of the act requires CEOs and CFOs to certify that:

(1) *the signing officer has reviewed the report;*

(2) *based on the officer's knowledge, the report does not contain any untrue statement of a material fact or omit to state a material fact necessary in order to make the statements made, in light of the circumstances under which such statements were made, not misleading;*

(3) *based on such officer's knowledge, the financial statements, and other financial information included in the report, fairly present in all material respects the financial condition and results of operations of the issuer as of, and for, the periods presented in the report;*

(4) *the signing officers—*

   (A) *are responsible for establishing and maintaining internal controls....*

A "knowing" misrepresentation in connection with the certification process is punishable by fine up to $1 million and imprisonment of up to 10 years. A "willful" misrepresentation in connection with the certification process is punishable by fine up to $5 million and imprisonment of up to 20 years.[21]

Section 304 of Sarbanes Oxley contains a clawback provision. If an issuer is required to prepare an accounting restatement due to fraudulent activity or noncompliance with financial reporting requirements, the CEO and CFO must reimburse the issuer for any bonus or incentive-based compensation received during the 12-month period following the issuance of the restated financial statements.[22] **For Example,** Carl Jasper, the CFO of semiconductor manufacturer Maxim Integrated Products, issued backdated stock options without properly expensing them. During the years 2000 to 2005, Jasper regularly backdated stock options so that options were granted at the lowest possible price to employees. He concealed millions of dollars in expenses from investors and significantly overstated the company's income. Because Jasper had certified false financial statements in 10-Ks and 10-Qs, Section 304 required that he reimburse Maxim $1.8 million in bonuses and profits from the sale of Maxim stock during the relevant period.[23]

---

[21] 18 U.S.C. §1350(c).

[22] The Dodd-Frank Act also requires the SEC to implement a rule that requires national securities exchanges to prohibit the listing of any security of a company that fails to adopt a clawback policy.

[23] *SEC v. Jasper,* 678 F.2d 1116 (9th Cir. 2012). He also paid a civil fine of $360,000 and was barred from serving as an officer or director of a publicly traded company for two years.

Before Sarbanes-Oxley was implemented, many public companies published pro forma (provided in advance) financial results in press releases before filing their official quarterly reports with the SEC. This approach allowed these companies to cast their "financials" in a favorable light. The SEC financial statements are prepared under a set of accounting conventions called *generally accepted accounting principles*, or GAAP. Pro forma financial results are not prepared using GAAP, and they may not provide a true and accurate picture of a company's financial status. Section 401 of the Sarbanes-Oxley Act instructed the SEC to issue rules requiring the presentation of pro forma financial statements in a manner that does not contain material misstatements or omit material facts and can be reconciled with financial results using GAAP. SEC Regulation G imposes a broad range of limitations on the use of pro forma results. If a company issues a press release saying that its pro forma earnings will be $5 million for the quarter when its official GAAP earnings will be just $4 million, the company will have to disclose both figures and explain what expenses were excluded from the pro forma figures and why.

CPA Antifraud Provision

Section 10(b) of the 1934 act makes it unlawful for any person to use any manipulative or deceptive device in contravention of SEC rules. Under the authority of section 10(b) of the 1934 act, the SEC has promulgated *Rule 10b-5*. This rule is the principal antifraud rule relating to the secondary distribution of securities. The rule states:

> *It shall be unlawful for any person, directly or indirectly, by use of any means or instrumentality of interstate commerce, or of the mails or of any facility of any national securities exchange,*
>
> *(a) To employ any device, scheme, or artifice to defraud,*
> *(b) To make any untrue statement of a material fact or to omit to state a material fact necessary in order to make the statements made, in the light of the circumstances under which they were made, not misleading, or*
> *(c) To engage in any act, practice, or course of business that operates or would operate as a fraud or deceit upon any person, in connection with the purchase or sale of any security.*[24]

CPA **Private Actions.** Rule 10b-5 applies to all securities, whether registered or not, as long as use is made of the mail, interstate commerce, or a national stock exchange. Subject to the safe harbor provisions of the Private Securities Litigation Reform Act as discussed in the following section, under Rule 10b-5, a civil action for damages may be brought by any private investor who purchased or sold a security and was injured because of false, misleading, or undisclosed information.[25]

CPA **Liability for "Material Misstatements or Omissions of Fact."** Rule 10b-5 prohibits the making of any untrue statement of a "material" fact or the omission of a material fact necessary to render statements made not misleading. The SEC considers information "material" if there is a substantial likelihood that it would have been viewed by a reasonable investor as having significantly altered the total mix of information made available and if a reasonable investor would have considered the fact important in making an investment decision. In every Rule 10b-5 case, the plaintiff must show "reliance" on the misrepresentation and resulting injury.

---

[24] 17 C.F.R. §240.10b-5.
[25] *Miller v. Thane International, Inc.*, 519 F.3d 879 (9th Cir. 2008).

In *Basic, Inc. v. Levinson*, the Supreme Court dealt with the question of what should be the standard of "materiality" in merger cases as well as the standard for determining whether or not the plaintiffs relied on the misrepresentation.

CASE SUMMARY

Why Silence Is Golden

FACTS: In December 1978, Combustion Engineering, Inc., and Basic, Inc., agreed to merge. During the preceding two years, representatives of the two companies had meetings regarding the possibility of a merger. During this time, Basic made three public statements denying that any merger negotiations were taking place or that it knew of any corporate developments that would account for the heavy trading activity in its stock. Certain former shareholders who sold this stock between Basic's first public denial of merger activity and the public announcement of the merger brought a section 10(b) and Rule 10b-5 action against Basic and some of its directors. The former shareholders contended that Basic had made material misrepresentations in its public statements denying merger activity. Basic raised the defense that the alleged misrepresentations were not material and

that there was no showing of reliance by the shareholders on Basic's statements.

DECISION: The standard for materiality applicable to preliminary merger discussions is to be decided on a case-by-case basis depending on the probability that the transaction will be consummated and on its significance to the issuer. There is a presumption of reliance by the shareholders on the misstatements of the corporations. This presumption is supported by the policy of the 1934 act, which is to foster reliance on market integrity. However, the presumption may be rebutted by showing that the market price was not affected by the misrepresentation. The case is remanded for further proceedings consistent with this opinion. [***Basic, Inc. v. Levinson*, 485 U.S. 224 (1988)]**

In the pharmaceutical industry "materiality" of adverse event reports is a "fact-specific" inquiry. It requires consideration of the source and content and context of the reports, as set forth in the *Matrixx Initiatives* case.

CASE SUMMARY

Rule No. 1 For Corporate Finance Executives: Be Very Careful About What You Say

FACTS: Matrixx develops, manufactures, and markets over-the-counter pharmaceutical products. Its core product, Zicam Cold Remedy, with its active ingredient, zinc gluconate, accounted for approximately 70 percent of Matrixx's sales. Individuals who purchased Matrixx securities between October 22, 2003, and February 6, 2004, filed a securities fraud class action against Matrixx under Section 10(b) of the 1934 Act. In October 2003 Matrixx made a statement to the market that Zicam was "poised for growth in the upcoming cold and cough season." It expressed its expectations that revenues would "be up in excess of 50%." In January 2004 it raised its revenue guidance, predicting an 80 percent increase.

On January 30, 2004, Dow Jones Newswires reported that the Food and Drug Administration (FDA) was "looking into complaints that an over-the-counter common-cold medicine manufactured by a unit of Matrixx Initiatives,

Inc., may be causing some users to lose their sense of smell" in light of at least three product liability lawsuits. Matrixx's stock fell from $13.55 to $11.97 per share after the report. In response, on February 2, Matrixx issued a press release that stated in part:

> *Matrixx believes statements alleging that intranasal Zicam products caused anosmia (loss of smell) are completely unfounded and misleading. In no clinical trial of intranasal zinc gluconate gel products has there been a single report of lost or diminished olfactory function (sense of smell). Rather, the safety and efficacy of zinc gluconate for the treatment of symptoms related to the common cold have been well established ...*

The day after Matrixx issued this press release, its stock price bounced back to $13.40 per share. On February 6,

Rule No. 1 For Corporate Finance Executives: Be Very Careful About What You Say continued

2004, *Good Morning America*, a nationally broadcast morning news program, reported that Dr. Jafek had discovered more than a dozen patients suffering from anosmia after using Zicam. It also noted that four lawsuits had been filed against Matrixx. The price of Matrixx stock plummeted to $9.94 per share that same day. Zicam again issued a press release largely repeating its February 2 statement.

Prior to these public statements, between October 2003 and February 2004, medical experts had revealed to Matrixx a plausible causal relationship between Zicam Cold Remedy and anosmia. For example, Dr. Linschoten sent abstracts of studies to Matrixx that had confirmed "zinc's toxicity." In September 2003 Matrixx learned of a planned national medical conference presentation by Dr. Jafek of the University of Colorado finding that 10 patients suffered loss of smell after Zicam use. The investors claim that the information the company had about the causal relationship between Zicam and anosmia were material facts necessary in order to make the statements made by Matrixx to the market not misleading. Matrixx defended that the investors had not alleged a statistically significant correlation between the use of Zicam and anosmia so as to make failure to publicly disclose complaints and the University of Colorado study a material omission.

DECISION: The "materiality" requirement of a Section 10(b) claim by investors that Matrixx made statements that were misleading as to material facts was satisfied in this case. There is a substantial likelihood that the disclosure of the omitted facts asserted in this case would have been viewed by a reasonable investor as having significantly altered the "total mix" of information made available by the company. Section 10(b) and Rule 10b-5 do not create an affirmative duty to disclose any and all material information (silence, absent a duty to disclose, is not misleading under Rule 10b-5). However, disclosure is required in order to make the statements made by Matrixx to the market not misleading. Matrixx told the market that revenues were going to rise 50 then 80 percent, yet it had information that its leading revenue product caused loss of the sense of smell. Matrixx also stated that reports its product caused anosmia were "completely unfounded and misleading," yet it had contrary information that a reasonable investor would deem material. The FDA and medical professionals do not limit the evidence considered for assessing causation to statistically significant data nor should investors be so limited. [*Matrixx Initiatives, Inc. v. Siracusano*, **131 S. Ct. 1309 (2011)**]

Reliance and the Fraud-on-the Market Theory. The United States Supreme Court has stated that to prevail in a securities fraud case under section 10(b) and Rule 10b-5, a plaintiff must prove: "(1) a material misrepresentation or omission by the defendant; (2) scienter; (3) a connection between the misrepresentation or omission and the purchase or sale of a security; (4) reliance upon the misrepresentation or omission; (5) economic loss; and (6) loss causation."[26] The Court has long recognized the difficulty of proving reliance on a material misstatement or omission. In *Basic v. Levinson*, the Supreme Court held that requiring direct proof of reliance "would place an unnecessarily unrealistic evidentiary burden on the Rule 10b-5 plaintiff who has traded on an impersonal market."[27] The **fraud-on-the-market** theory creates a presumption that securities fraud plaintiffs relied on the misrepresentation. The theory assumes that the market price of shares reflect publicly available information, including material misrepresentations. Several companies have challenged the fraud-on-the-market theory, arguing that *Basic v. Levinson* should be overruled because the premise on which it is founded—market efficiency—is no longer tenable. The Supreme Court, however, has refused to "jettison" *Basic's* fraud-on-the-market theory.[28]

fraud-on-the-market–a theory that in an open and developed securities market, the price of a stock is determined by the information on the company available to the public, and misleading statements will defraud purchasers of stock even if they do not directly rely on these statements.

[26] In *Amgen, Inc. v. Connecticut Retirement Plans and Trust Funds*, 133 S. Ct. 1184 (2013), the Court held that plaintiffs who employ the fraud-on-the-market theory of reliance do not need to establish materiality of alleged misstatements or omissions of fact at the class certification stage.

[27] *Basic v. Levinson*, 485 U.S. 224, 245 (1988).

[28] See *Halliburton Co. v. Erica P. John Fund, Inc.*, 134 S. Ct. 2398 (2014). In this case, Halliburton claimed that each securities fraud plaintiff should have to prove that he actually relied on the defendant's misrepresentation in deciding to buy or sell a company's stock. The Court disagreed, emphasizing that the fraud-on-the-market theory allows a defendant to rebut the presumption of reliance on market information. Moreover, the Court stated that even though the efficient market theory has been criticized, Halliburton did not identify a "fundamental shift in economic theory" to justify overruling *Basic*. In dissent, three justices stated that *Basic's* fraud-on-the-market theory should be abandoned based on "logic" and "economic realities."

CPA   ## Litigation Reform Act

The Private Securities Litigation Reform Act (PSLRA, or the Litigation Reform Act) of 1995 was passed because of (1) congressional concern over an excess of frivolous private securities lawsuits, (2) the financial burdens placed on accountants and other professional advisors by such litigation, and (3) concern that the investors in a class-action lawsuit have their interests fairly represented. Important features of the act are as follows.

CPA   **Safe Harbor Rules.** Issuers of securities frequently believed that lawsuits against them under Rule 10b-5 occurred simply because the corporation made a projection that failed to materialize. The Litigation Reform Act provides shelter for issuers from private liability for forward-looking statements that were not known to be false when made and that were accompanied by meaningful cautionary statements informing investors of contingencies that could cause results to differ from projected results.

To preserve the protections of the PSLRA, quarterly and annual reports to the SEC (Forms 10-Q and 10-K) and quarterly and annual reports to stockholders, as well as corporate press releases on financial matters, now commonly utilize the expression *forward-looking statements* regarding corporate statements that estimate or project the short-term and long-term outlook for a business. Moreover, these reports typically include a section entitled "Cautionary Statements" or "Risk Factors," and contain a statement such as:

> *Forward-looking statements as contained in this report involve a number of risks, including but not limited to product demand, pricing, market acceptance, supply problems, intellectual property rights and litigation, and risks in product and technology development.*

Corporations do not have to caution against every conceivable factor that may cause results to differ from the issuer's forward-looking statements. **For Example,** Ivax Corporation, a drug company, issued a press release including optimistic assumptions about future events. Attached to the release was an italicized warning that stated in specific detail the kinds of misfortunes that could befall Ivax and could cause results to differ from its forward-looking statements. This cautionary statement did not mention that a large goodwill writedown could occur; and when a writedown did occur, Ivax stock declined sharply. Harris, Wolpin, and others brought a Rule 10b-5 fraud suit against Ivax based on the omission of a warning about the writedown risk. The court held that the cautionary statements were sufficient to warn an investor of risks similar to that actually realized and the statements satisfied Ivax's burden to warn under the statute. Ivax was not required to list all risk factors, and the failure to mention one risk that in fact occurred did not "blow Ivax out of the safe harbor."[29]

CPA   **Litigation Reform.** The Litigation Reform Act places a heightened pleading requirement on plaintiffs attempting to plead fraud in securities cases and requires not only that the plaintiffs specify each statement alleged to have been false or misleading and the reason for the belief but also that the plaintiffs plead "scienter"—the mental state embracing intent to deceive, manipulate, or defraud.[30] In the *Matrixx Initiatives* case, the Supreme Court held that the investors adequately pleaded scienter, where the allegations gave rise to the compelling inference that Matrixx elected not to disclose the reports of adverse events not because it believed they were meaningless, but because it understood their likely effect on the market.[31]

[29] *Harris v. Ivax Corp.*, 182 F.3d 799 (11th Cir. 1999).

[30] See In re *Lucent Technologies Inc., Securities Litigation*, 307 F. Supp. 2d 633 (D. N.J. 2004).

[31] *Matrixx Initiatives, Inc. v. Siracusano*, 131 S. Ct. 1309, 1324 (2011); see also *Frank v. Dana Corp.*, 646 F.3d 954 (6th Cir. 2011).

The Litigation Reform Act also provides for *proportionate liability*, as opposed to joint and several liability, for defendants who are found not to have knowingly committed a violation of the security laws. In addition, securities fraud is eliminated as a predicate for private RICO actions absent a prior criminal conviction.[32] Under the act, frivolous private securities lawsuits require payment of the defendant's reasonable attorney fees.

CPA

Class-Action Reforms. Reforms were necessary to protect against "lawyer-driven lawsuits" in which a class-action counsel would direct a "professional" plaintiff to buy a security to have standing to bring a class-action lawsuit. Thereafter, the class-action counsel would race to the courthouse to file before any other plaintiff and thus be able to claim enhanced standing to represent the class. The Litigation Reform Act provides that the status of lead plaintiff must be offered to the person with the largest financial interest in the case.

Aiders and Abettors. For many years the courts and the SEC held aiders and abettors, such as banks, accountants, trustees, and attorneys, liable in private actions under section 10(b) of the Securities Exchange Act of 1934 and Rule 10b-5. The broad language of the act and the rule arguably allowed private parties to sue aiders and abettors for fraud or deceit in connection with the sale of securities. In a 1994 decision, the Supreme Court limited the liability of such aiders and abettors. In *Central Bank of Denver v. First Interstate Bank of Denver*, the Court made a distinction between primary violators who directly misstate or omit material facts that investors rely on and secondary violators or aiders and abettors.[33] Aiders and abettors are liable in private actions, the Court held, only if investors can show reliance on their material misstatements or omissions. Thus, a plaintiff who sues an attorney, an accountant, or a bank for securities fraud must sue that party as a primary violator and show reliance on that party's material misstatements or omissions.

In 2008, the Court again limited the liability of third parties in securities fraud cases. In *Stoneridge Investment Partners, LLC v. Scientific Atlanta, Inc.*, investors maintained that Scientific Atlanta and Motorola helped giant cable TV firm Charter Communications inflate its financial statements to bolster its stock price.[34] The companies allegedly helped Charter to generate $17 million in phony revenues. Investors maintained that the two companies should be treated as primary violators because they were involved in a scheme to defraud investors, even though they did not issue any public statements. The Court found that the investors had no knowledge of the companies' deceptive acts and could not show reliance "except in an indirect chain that was too remote for liability." The Court stated that the companies were subject to criminal laws preventing such fraudulent scheming and to SEC enforcement actions, but that liability did not extend to private investors.

In 2011, the Court considered whether a mutual fund investment advisor was liable to investors under section 10(b) and Rule 10b-5 for false statements included in the mutual fund prospectuses. The Court held that investment advisors cannot be sued under federal securities law for false statements made by the fund they advised.[35] The Court held that Janus Capital Group, the investment advisor, did not "make" the false statements, rather the mutual fund itself made the statements. The Court held that only a party "with ultimate authority over the statement including its content and whether and how to communicate it" is the one that "makes" the statement within the meaning of Rule 10b-5.

---

[32] The RICO Act is discussed in Chapter 7.
[33] 511 U.S. 164 (1994).
[34] 552 U.S. 148 (2008).
[35] *Janus Capital Group, Inc. v. First Derivative Traders*, 131 S. Ct. 2296 (2011).

CPA   ### 45-2d Trading on Insider Information

Illegal insider trading occurs when a person who owes a fiduciary duty to a company buys or sells a security while in possession of material nonpublic information. Enforcing insider trading laws is a high priority for the SEC. In recent years, the SEC has pursued insider trading cases against financial professionals, hedge fund managers, corporate insiders, and attorneys.

insider information— privileged information on company business known only to employees.

Section 10(b) and Rule 10b-5 form a basis for imposing sanctions for trading on **insider information.** Those accused of insider trading may face both criminal and civil actions. The Insider Trading and Securities Fraud Enforcement Act of 1988, which amended the 1934 act, gave the SEC authority to bring an action against an individual purchasing or selling a security while in possession of material inside information. Persons who "aid or abet" in the violation may also be held liable under the act.

Individuals convicted of criminal insider trading may be sentenced up to 20 years in prison per violation and can face fines of up to $5 million or twice the gain from the offense. In a civil action by the SEC, an individual may have to disgorge any profits from the offense and may have to pay fines not to exceed the greater of $1 million or three times the amount of the profit gained or loss avoided. Individuals can be barred from serving as an officer or a director of a public company, or from acting as a securities broker or an investment advisor. Attorneys and accountants may be barred from serving before the SEC. **For Example,** Mathew Martoma, formerly a portfolio manager for SAC Capital Advisors, was sentenced to nine years in prison for his role in carrying out one of the biggest insider trading schemes ever. He was convicted of using inside information about a clinical trial for an experimental Alzheimer's drug to make illegal trades in the shares of two drug companies. The information allowed SAC to generate $275 million in profits. Martoma was also ordered to forfeit a $9.38 million bonus as well as his Florida home. He was the eighth employee of SAC to be convicted or plead guilty to insider trading charges. SAC, a highly successful hedge fund, pleaded guilty to insider trading. SAC paid record fines of $1.2 billion to the federal government and $600 million to the SEC. Steven A. Cohen, the founder and owner of the hedge fund, was not charged with any criminal wrongdoing. He closed the hedge fund and reorganized it as a family office that manages his own money.[36]

Under the 1988 insider trading act, "controlling persons," including employers whose lax supervision may allow employees to commit insider trading violations, are subject to civil penalties.[37] The SEC must prove "knowing" or "reckless" behavior by the controlling person. The 1988 law establishes bounty programs that allow the SEC to reward informants giving information on insider trading activity. The reward is up to 10 percent of any penalty imposed.

Broker-dealers and investment advisors are also required to establish and maintain procedures to prevent the misuse of material nonpublic information.[38] **For Example,** in 2014, the SEC charged Wells Fargo Advisors LLC with failing to maintain adequate controls to prevent one of its employees from trading on a customer's nonpublic information. After learning confidentially from his client that Burger King was being acquired by a New York-based private equity firm, a Wells Fargo broker traded on that information.

---

[36] See Michael Bobelian, "What Does Martoma's Conviction Mean for SAC Capital's Steven Cohen," FORBES (Feb. 7, 2014), **http://www.forbes.com/sites/michaelbobelian/2014/02/07/what-does-martomas-conviction-mean-for-sac-capitals-steven-cohen/**. The SEC filed an administrative complaint against Steven A. Cohen maintaining that he failed to supervise his senior employees in a reasonable manner.

[37] P.L. 100-704, 102 Stat. 4677, 15 U.S.C. §78u-1(a)(2).

[38] Section 15(g) of the 1934 Exchange Act and Section 204A of the Investment Advisers Act of 1940 require broker-dealers and investment advisors to establish, maintain, and enforce policies and procedures to prevent the misuse of material nonpublic information.

Wells Fargo agreed to pay a $5 million penalty to settle the SEC's charges. The case was the first in which the SEC charged a broker-dealer with failure to protect a customer's material nonpublic information.[39]

Classical Theory of Insider Trading

The classical theory of insider trading states that a corporate insider, such as an officer or a director, violates section 10(b) and Rule 10b-5 by using material nonpublic information about the corporation to trade in the corporation's securities. Underlying insider liability is the concept that there is a special relationship of trust and confidence between the shareholders of a corporation and those insiders who have obtained confidential information by virtue of their position. An **insider** may be a director or corporate employee. A **temporary insider** is someone retained by the corporation for professional services, such as an attorney, accountant, or investment banker. Insiders and temporary insiders are liable for inside trading when they fail to disclose material nonpublic information before trading on it and thus make a secret profit. A **tippee** is an individual who receives information from an insider or a temporary insider. A tippee is subject to the insider's fiduciary duty to shareholders when the insider has breached the fiduciary duty to shareholders by improperly disclosing the information to the tippee and when the tippee knows or should know that there has been a breach.[40] Such a breach occurs when an insider benefits personally from her disclosure. When the insider does not breach a fiduciary duty, a tippee does not violate the securities laws. The Supreme Court has made it clear that an insider must breach a fiduciary duty in disclosing material nonpublic information and that the breach must involve a personal benefit.[41] Some courts have held that a tippee must know that the insider received a personal benefit by disclosing the material nonpublic information. What constitutes a "personal benefit" is a question that is likely to be hotly contested in litigation.[42]

insider–full-time corporate employee or a director.

temporary insider–someone retained by a corporation for professional services on an as-needed basis, such as an attorney, accountant, or investment banker.

tippee–individual who receives information about a corporation from an insider or temporary insider.

CASE SUMMARY

No Secrets from Secrist!

FACTS: On March 6, 1973, Dirks, an investment analyst, received information from Secrist, a former officer of Equity Funding of America, alleging that the assets of Equity Funding were vastly overstated as the result of fraudulent corporate practices. On investigation by Dirks, certain corporation employees corroborated the charges of fraud. Neither Dirks nor his firm owned or traded any Equity Funding stock, but

throughout his investigation, he openly discussed the information he had obtained with a number of clients and investors. The information from Dirks induced them to sell Equity Funding stock in excess of $16 million. On March 27, the New York Stock Exchange halted trading of Equity Funding stock, and a subsequent investigation revealed the vast fraud that had taken place. The SEC, investigating Dirks's role in

[39] Press Release, SEC, "Wells Fargo Advisors Admits Failing to Maintain Controls and Producing Altered document, Agrees to Pay $5 Million Penalty" (Sept. 22, 2014), **http://www.sec.gov/News/PressRelease/Detail/PressRelease/1370543012047.**

[40] *United States v. Chestman*, 974 F.2d 564 (2d Cir. 1991).

[41] *Dirks v. SEC*, 468 U.S. 646 (1983).

[42] In *United States v. Newman*, the Court of Appeals for the Second Circuit held that there was insufficient evidence that two hedge fund portfolio managers had knowledge of a breach of fiduciary duty and personal benefit by the sources of the inside information. The court found that evidence that the insiders were friends with the tippees or received "career advice" from the tippees was not enough to show they received a personal benefit. 773 F.3d 438 (2d Cir. 2014). The Justice Department sought a rehearing *en banc* of the Second Circuit's interpretation of "personal benefit."

No Secrets from Secrist! continued

the exposure of the fraud, claimed that Dirks had aided and abetted violations of the Securities Act of 1933, the Securities Exchange Act of 1934, and SEC Rule 10b-5 by repeating the allegations of fraud to members of the investment community who later sold their Equity Funding stock.

DECISION: Judgment for Dirks. Secrist, the insider, did not violate any fiduciary duty to shareholders when he disclosed

information about the fraudulent practices to the tippee, Dirks. Secrist received no monetary or personal benefit for the information but was motivated by the desire to expose the fraud. Because the insider did not breach his fiduciary duty when he gave nonpublic information to Dirks, Dirks breached no duty when he passed the information on to investors. [***Dirks v. SEC*, 463 U.S. 646 (1983)**]

Misappropriation Theory of Insider Trading

Individuals who misappropriate or steal valuable nonpublic information in breach of a fiduciary duty to their employer and trade in securities on that information are guilty of insider trading as "misappropriators." **For Example,** an employee working for a financial printing firm was found guilty of insider trading under section 10(b) and Rule 10b-5.[43] While proofreading a financial document being prepared for a client firm, he figured out the identity of tender offer targets. Soon after that, he traded on this valuable nonpublic information to his advantage.

It is no defense to a section 10(b) and Rule 10b-5 criminal charge of participating in a "scheme to defraud" that the victim of the fraud (an employer) had no economic interest in the securities traded. The convictions of a stockbroker and a columnist for the *Wall Street Journal* were upheld under section 10(b) of the 1934 act. The columnist violated his fiduciary duty to his employer by revealing prepublication information about his column to the stockbroker. The stockbroker then used the information to trade in the securities identified in the column.[44]

Where an individual misappropriates confidential information for security trading purposes in breach of a fiduciary duty owed to the source of the information rather than to the shareholders who sold securities to the individual, that individual may be convicted of security fraud in violation of section 10(b) and Rule 10b-5.

CASE SUMMARY

The Case of the Dastardly Misappropriator

FACTS: James O'Hagan was a partner in the law firm of Dorsey & Whitney in Minneapolis, Minnesota. In July 1988, Grand Metropolitan PLC, a company based in London, England, retained Dorsey & Whitney as local counsel to represent Grand Met regarding a potential tender offer for the common stock of the Pillsbury Company

headquartered in Minneapolis. O'Hagan did no work on the Grand Met representation. Dorsey & Whitney withdrew from representing Grand Met on September 9, 1988. Less than a month later, on October 4, 1988, Grand Met publicly announced its tender offer for Pillsbury stock. Previously, on August 18, 1988, while Dorsey & Whitney was

[43] *SEC v. Materia*, 745 F.2d 197 (2d Cir. 1984).
[44] *Carpenter v. United States*, 484 U.S. 19 (1987).

The Case of the Dastardly Misappropriator continued

still representing Grand Met, O'Hagan began purchasing call options for Pillsbury stock. Each option gave him the right to purchase 100 shares of Pillsbury stock by a specified date in September 1988. Later in August and September, O'Hagan purchased additional Pillsbury call options. By the end of September, he owned 2,500 unexpired Pillsbury options, apparently more than any other individual investor. O'Hagan also purchased, in September 1988, some 5,000 shares of Pillsbury common stock at a price just under $39 per share. When Grand Met announced its tender offer in October, the price of Pillsbury stock rose to nearly $60 per share. O'Hagan then sold his Pillsbury call options and common stock, making a profit of more than $4.3 million. O'Hagan was charged and convicted of securities fraud in violation of section 10(b) and Rule 10b-5. On appeal, he claimed that he was not a "misappropriator," for he had no fiduciary duty to the Pillsbury shareholders from whom he

purchased calls and stock; in fact, he had not even worked on the transaction at the law firm.

DECISION: Judgment against O'Hagan. "Misappropriation" requires that there be "deceptive" conduct "in connection with" a securities transaction. A fiduciary who pretends loyalty to the principal while secretly converting the principal's information for personal gain dupes or defrauds the principal. O'Hagan's failure to disclose his personal trading to his law firm and its client, Grand Met, was a breach of his fiduciary duty and was "deceptive" conduct "in connection with" a securities transaction. The misappropriation theory is designed to protect the integrity of the securities market against "outsiders" like O'Hagan who have access to confidential information that will affect a company's stock price when revealed but have no fiduciary or other duty to the company's shareholders. [*United States v. O'Hagan*, 521 U.S. 642 (1997)]

Regulation FD

The SEC adopted Regulation FD (Fair Disclosure) in 2000 to end the practice of selective disclosure by issuers of securities to security analysts and selected institutional investors of important nonpublic information, such as advance warnings of negative or positive earnings results, before disclosing the information to the general public. Many companies disclosed material information in meetings and during conference calls. Shareholders and the general public were at a disadvantage regarding such information. Those privy to the early release of the information were able to make a profit or avoid a loss at the expense of the uninformed general public. Regulation FD changed the way companies disclose information. As companies increasingly use social media for corporate disclosure, the SEC considered whether information provided through social media complied with Regulation FD. **For Example,** in July 2012, Netflix CEO, Reed Hastings, posted on his personal Facebook page: "Congrats to Ted Sarandos, and his amazing content licensing team. Netflix monthly viewing exceeded 1 billion hours for the first time ever in June. When House of Cards and Arrested Development debut, we'll blow these records away. Keep going Ted, we need even more!" This information arguably did not comply with Regulation FD because it was a disclosure of material information. The SEC questioned whether the posting was "private," even though Mr. Hastings had more than 200,000 Facebook followers. The SEC did not pursue the case but offered additional guidance regarding disclosures through social media. Companies that make disclosures over social media channels should give advance warning that information will be disclosed through its Web site, or through social media such as Facebook or Twitter. Companies may also use technology that provides investors with alerts that new information has been posted.

Remedy for Investors

Investors who lack the inside information possessed by the insider and sell their stock during the relevant time period may recover damages from any insider who made use of undisclosed information. Recovery is by a civil action based on Rule 10b-5.

45-2e Disclosure of Ownership and Short-Swing Profits

Corporate directors and officers owning equity securities in their corporation and any shareholder owning more than 10 percent of any class of the corporation's equity securities are statutorily defined as insiders and must file with the SEC a disclosure statement regarding such ownership and all related transactions. This disclosure is required under section 16(a) of the 1934 act. Under section 403(a) of the Sarbanes-Oxley Act, these individuals must electronically report transactions in company stock to the SEC by the second business day after the transaction. Moreover, the transaction must be posted on the SEC's and the company's Web sites within one day after the filing date.

Section 16 is designed to prevent the unfair use of information available to these corporate insiders. This section prevents insiders from participating in short-term trading in their corporation's securities.

short-swing profit–profit realized by a corporate insider from selling securities less than six months after purchase.

If such a person sells at a profit any of these securities less than six months after their purchase, the profit is called a **short-swing profit.** Under section 16(b), the corporation may sue a director, an officer, or a major stockholder for a short-swing profit.[45] The corporation may recover that profit even if the corporate insider had no fraudulent intent in acquiring and selling the securities. The corporation must bring the lawsuit within two years after the date the profit was realized.[46]

45-2f Tender Offers

A corporation or group of investors may seek to acquire control of another corporation by making a general offer to all shareholders of the target corporation to purchase their shares for cash at a specified price. This type of offer is called a **cash tender offer.** The offer to purchase is usually contingent on the tender of a fixed number of shares sufficient to ensure takeover. The bid price is ordinarily higher than the prevailing market price. Should more shares be tendered than the offeror is willing to purchase, the tender offeror must purchase shares from each shareholder on a pro rata basis.

cash tender offer–general offer to all shareholders of a target corporation to purchase their shares for cash at a specified price.

The Williams Act amended the 1934 act[47] to ensure that public shareholders have adequate information about the cash tender offer. Under section 14(d) of the Williams Act, a person making a tender offer must file appropriate SEC forms. These forms provide information about the background and identity of the person filing, the source of funds used to make stock purchases, the amount of stock beneficially owned, the purpose of the purchases, any plan the purchaser proposes to follow if it gains control over the target corporation, and any contracts or understandings that it has with other persons concerning the target corporation.[48]

Section 14(e) of the Williams Act is the antifraud section. It prohibits fraudulent, deceptive, or manipulative practices. SEC Rule 14e-1 requires any tender offer to remain open for a minimum of 20 business days from the date it is first published or given to security holders.[49] Federal and state legislation, as well as administrative regulation, is aimed at requiring disclosure of information and allowance of a reasonable length of

---

[45] *Levy v. Southbrook International Investments, Ltd.,* 263 F.3d 10 (2d Cir. 2001); *Donaghue v. Natural Microsystems Corp.,* 198 F. Supp. 2d 487 (S.D.N.Y. 2002).

[46] *Credit Suisse Securities (USA) LLC v. Simmonds,* 132 S. Ct. 1414 (2012).

[47] P.L. 90-439, 82 Stat. 454, 15 U.S.C. §78m(d), (e).

[48] Section 14(d) requires a filing by any person making a tender offer that, if successful, would result in the acquisition of 5 percent of any class of an equity security required to be registered under the 1934 Act. Section 13(d) of the act requires disclosure to the issuer, the SEC, and the appropriate stock exchange when a person acquires 5 percent of a class of equity security through stock purchases on exchanges or through private purchases. The person may have acquired the stock for investment purposes, not for control, but must still file disclosure forms under §13(d). See *SEC v. Bilzerian,* 814 F. Supp. 116 (D. D.C. 1993). Section 14(d) applies only to shares to be acquired by tender offer.

[49] For certain types of securities, under certain conditions, the SEC may allow shorter periods for tender offers.

time for consideration of the facts. These requirements are designed to make agreement to takeovers the result of voluntary action based on full knowledge of material facts.

As far as the courts are concerned, takeovers must be regarded with a neutral eye. If there is misrepresentation or other misconduct, the law will interfere. Otherwise, freedom of contract requires that courts not interfere with the judgment of the contracting parties.

CPA 45-2g SEC Enforcement under the 1934 Act

Dodd-Frank Enforcement Powers

The Dodd-Frank Act of 2010[50] contains numerous reforms and initiatives to help restore market trust and reform Wall Street to protect the economy, American consumers, investors, and businesses. To prevent another financial crisis the act created the Financial Stability Oversight Council to oversee the various government agencies responsible for regulating financial institutions. Many sections of the act require various studies to be undertaken and mandate or permit rulemaking by the Commodity Futures Trading Commission and the SEC.

Dodd-Frank further increased the SEC's power. In addition to issuing cease-and-desist orders, the SEC can seek disgorgement and civil penalties. Furthermore, the SEC can bring administrative proceedings against any person, not just regulated persons, for violations of the federal securities laws. With its new power, the SEC has substantially increased the number of administrative proceedings it brings against unregulated persons in a variety of actions including fraud and insider trading. Members of the securities industry have questioned the fairness of the SEC's new power.[51]

Enforcement and Whistleblowers

Section 922 of Dodd-Frank authorized the SEC to create a whistleblower program to encourage individuals to provide the SEC with information that would lead to the discovery and prosecution of violations of the federal securities laws. The program, implemented in 2012, allows a monetary award to whistleblowers who provide original information that leads to successful enforcement actions resulting in monetary sanctions over $1 million. It also protects the identity of the informant and prohibits retaliation by employers. In 2014, the SEC announced its largest whistleblower award since the program began. A single individual received $30 million, an amount that the SEC noted could have been higher had the whistleblower not delayed unreasonably in reporting the violation. According to the SEC, whistleblowers provide information about fraudulent activity that would otherwise be difficult to detect. The SEC has interpreted the Dodd-Frank whistleblower reward provisions to include whistleblowers from outside the United States. At least one court, however, has held that the act does not apply extraterritorially.[52]

---

[50] P.L. 111-203, 124 Stat. 1376, 15 U.S.C. §8305 (2012).

[51] The fairness of the SEC's power is questioned because the SEC brings the charges, an Administrative Law Judge within the agency hears the case, and the SEC commissioners make the final decision as to the fate of those charged. Between October 2010 and May 2015, the SEC won 90 percent of its cases against defendants before its own judges. See Jean Eaglesham, "In-House Judges Help SEC Rack Up Wins," *Wall Street Journal*, May 6, 2015, p. A1.

[52] *Liu Meng-Lin v. Siemens AG*, 763 F.3d 175 (2d Cir. 2014). The whistleblower discovered that Siemens employees were indirectly making improper payments to officials in North Korea and China in connection with the sale of medical equipment in those countries. He reported the conduct to his superiors through internal company procedures. After he was fired, he reported the payments to the SEC, suggesting that Siemens had violated the Foreign Corrupt Practices Act. The plaintiff was a citizen and resident of Taiwan, employed as a compliance officer for the health care division of Siemens China Ltd. The court held that Dodd-Frank whistleblower protection does not extend to foreign workers employed abroad by foreign corporations because "a statute is presumed in the absence of clear congressional intent to the contrary, to apply only domestically...."

Enforcement and Third–Party Market Participants

The financial crisis of 2008 triggered numerous lawsuits by institutional investors against Wall Street securities firms, claiming that securities firms misrepresented risks when advising clients about complex investments. In response, the Dodd-Frank Act directed the SEC to study the need for establishing a new, uniform federal fiduciary standard of care for broker-dealers and investment advisors. The SEC is in the comment stage of developing this uniform standard, and the standard as proposed would impose a fiduciary duty on both broker-dealers and investment advisors.

Currently, investment advisors and broker-dealers are regulated by different laws.[53] Investment advisors owe a fiduciary duty to their clients. Broker-dealers generally do not owe a fiduciary duty to their clients under federal law. An investment advisor has a duty of good faith and full and fair disclosure; a duty to recommend only securities suitable for the investor; and a duty of loyalty to serve the best interests of his client.[54] Broker-dealers are exempt from the Investment Advisers Act if the advice to clients is "solely incidental" to the conduct of business as a broker or dealer and the broker-dealer receives no "special compensation" for providing the advice.[55] Nevertheless, FINRA rules require that a broker-dealer recommend only investments that are suitable for the customer and anti-fraud provisions of the securities laws protect investors as well. Those who favor the rule maintain that the rules will strengthen investor protection against conflicted investment advice. Opponents in the financial industry say that it would significantly raise regulatory and liability costs for brokers and force them to drop middle-income clients with modest investable assets.[56]

Regulation of Attorneys and Accountants by the SEC

Accountants play a vital role in financial reporting under the federal securities laws administered by the SEC. Sections 1, 12, 17, and 24 of the 1933 act and section 10(b) of the 1934 act are the sections under which accountants may be subject to liability.

An accountant who prepares any statement, opinion, or other legal paper filed with the SEC with the preparer's consent is deemed to be practicing before the SEC. Because it relies so heavily on accountants, the SEC has promulgated Rule 2(e), which regulates and provides the basis for discipline of accountants, attorneys, and consultants who practice before the SEC.[57] Under Rule 2(e), the SEC may suspend or disbar from practice before it those who are unqualified or unethical or who have violated federal securities laws or SEC rules.[58] SEC Rules also state that "[a]ny ... person who has been convicted of a felony or a misdemeanor involving moral turpitude shall be forthwith suspended from appearing or practicing before the Commission."[59]

---

[53] Investment advisors are regulated by the Investment Advisers Act of 1940 and are subject to the antifraud provisions of the Securities Act of 1933 and the Securities Exchange Act of 1934. Broker-dealers are regulated under both the Securities Act and the Exchange Act as well as by FINRA rules and state regulations.

[54] Investment Advisers Act of 1940, §206.

[55] Investment Advisers Act of 1940 §202(a)(11)(C).

[56] In 2015, the Department of Labor proposed a revision to its regulation that redefines what it means to be a fiduciary under the Employee Retirement Income Security Act (ERISA) and the Internal Revenue Code.

[57] 17 C.F.R. §201.2e.

[58] Rule 2(e) provides: "Suspension and disbarment. (1) The Commission may deny, temporarily or permanently, the privilege of appearing or practicing before it in any way to any person who is found by the Commission after notice of an opportunity for hearing in the matter (i) not to possess the requisite qualifications to represent others, or (ii) to be lacking in character or integrity or to have engaged in unethical or improper professional conduct, or (iii) to have willfully violated, or willfully aided and abetted, the violation of any provision of the federal securities laws (15 U.S.C. §§77a to 80B-20), or the rules and regulations thereunder." 17 C.F.R. §201.2e.

[59] 15 U.S.C. §78d-3, 17 C.F.R. §201.102(e)(2).

Section 307 of the Sarbanes-Oxley Act gave authority to the SEC to establish minimum standards of professional conduct for attorneys practicing before the SEC in the representation of publicly held companies. The act and SEC rules require that attorneys report evidence of material violations of securities laws, up the chain of command, to the companies' general counsel, CEO, audit committees, or the full board of directors. Lawyers can make a quiet withdrawal; that is, they do not have to go to the SEC, but they are under a professional obligation to not represent a client in an ongoing fraud on the market.

The ABA Model Rules of Professional Conduct, which serve as a basis for most states' ethics rules for lawyers, were revised to free lawyers from their duty of confidentiality to those clients who use the lawyers' advice to commit a crime or fraud.[60] The ABA also revised its Model Rules to allow a lawyer who knows that an officer or employee of a corporation will likely harm the company to refer the matter to higher-up officials of the organization.[61]

Regulation of Corporate Officers and Auditors

Provisions of the Dodd-Frank Act impacting executives and executive compensation give the SEC additional enforcement tools in the activities of officers and directors in preparing financial statements. These tools include clawback provisions that allow for the recoupment of executive compensation and bonuses based on financial performance when that performance turns out to be falsified.

Additional provisions of the Dodd-Frank Act impacting auditors' roles in developing financial information for release to the markets are covered in Chapter 47. In addition, the Litigation Reform Act amends the 1934 act by requiring auditors who discover illegal acts to notify management and the board of directors and, in some cases, to notify the SEC if the issuer does not.[62] Auditors are relieved from liability for any such disclosure to the SEC.

45-3 Industry Self-Regulation

The Financial Industry Regulatory Authority (FINRA) is the largest independent, not-for-profit regulator for all securities firms doing business in the United States. The National Association of Securities Dealers (NASD) and the New York Stock Exchange merged their member regulation functions into this one self-regulatory organization. FINRA is authorized by Congress to protect investors by ensuring that the securities industry is fair and honest. The agency writes and enforces rules for securities firms and brokers; monitors compliance with its rules; fosters market transparency; and educates investors. FINRA administers the largest dispute resolution forum for investors and registered firms.[63] Most agreements between investors and stockbrokers include mandatory arbitration agreements. It provides a BrokerCheck system, which allows investors to check out the professional and disciplinary backgrounds of firms and brokers online.[64] FINRA also refers fraud and insider trading cases to the SEC for investigation.

---

[60] Model Rule 1.6, "Confidentiality of Information."
[61] Model Rule 1.13, "Organization as Client."
[62] P.L. 104-671, 109 Stat. 763, 15 U.S.C. §78j-l nt.
[63] FINRA oversees some 629,640 registered securities representatives. In 2014, FINRA brought 1,397 disciplinary actions against registered brokers and firms; it imposed fines totaling $134 million and ordered restitution to harmed investors of $32.3 million. See **http://www.finra.org/ABOUTFINRA**.
[64] **http://www.finra.org/brokercheck**.

ETHICS & THE LAW

Problem: Conflicts of Interest—Remedy: Commonsense Rules

An investigation into Merrill Lynch by the New York Attorney General's Office revealed that while certain Merrill analysts were publicly recommending certain technology companies that were investment banking clients of the firm, internal e-mails indicated that these analysts believed the same companies were "crap" and "junk." One wrote to a colleague questioning his "positive" recommendation of a company whose numbers seemed weak to her, and his response to her was, he had written "pos," in place of [expletive deleted].

The public and retail clients believed that the firm's analysts were independent of the investment banking function of the firm and that the recommendations were made solely with retail clients' interests in mind. The New York Attorney General's Office concluded, however, that analysts and investment bankers were closely involved in each other's work and were not independent; that the analyst department's compensation was tied to the results of the investment banking department's results; and that analysts were negotiating with investment banking clients for ratings.

The SEC has eliminated these problems with the following rules: (1) Investment banking divisions may not supervise firms' analysts, (2) compensation for analysts may not be linked to specific investment banking transactions, (3) analysts must disclose whether they own shares in a company they recommend and certify that their recommendations are their true opinions, (4) analysts appearing in public forums before the media must disclose whether they have an interest in the company being discussed, and (5) firms must make comprehensive disclosures about their rating systems and the firms they represent as investment banking clients.

45-3a Arbitration of Securities Disputes

Both NASD and securities firms with seats on the New York Stock Exchange have adopted codes of arbitration that allow customers and members to submit disputes to arbitration. The arbitration rights are contractual and are set forth in writing when opening an account with the securities firms. Investors who have agreed to arbitrate their securities disputes can be compelled to arbitrate, rather than sue, in courts. NASD and NYSE arbitrations are now administered by FINRA. Courts are very reluctant to vacate an arbitration award.

Make the Connection

Summary

State blue sky laws, which apply only to intrastate transactions, protect the public from the sale of fraudulent securities. The term *security* is defined sufficiently broadly to encompass not only stocks and bonds but also any conceivable type of corporate interest that has investment characteristics.

Two principal laws provide the basic framework for federal regulation of the sale of securities in interstate commerce. The Securities Act of 1933 deals with the issue or original distribution of securities by issuing corporations. The 1933 act requires registration of primary offering securities unless they are exempt. There are a number of exemptions that have been expanded under the JOBS Act that allow smaller offerings and offerings to accredited investors to offer securities for sale without the costs of full registration. These offerings require disclosures and may have limits on distribution and resale but allow companies to raise capital more easily. Criminal and civil penalties exist for fraudulent statements made in the registration process.

The Securities Exchange Act of 1934 regulates the secondary distribution or sale of securities on exchanges.

These acts are administered by the Securities and Exchange Commission. The 1934 act provides reporting requirements for companies whose securities are listed on a national exchange and unlisted companies that have assets in excess of $10 million and 2,000 or more holders of record or 500 or more unaccredited shareholders. The JOBS Act has made it easier for smaller reporting companies and emerging growth companies to comply with registration and disclosure requirements.

Rule 10b-5 is the principal antifraud rule under the 1934 act. Trading on "inside information" is unlawful and may subject those involved to a civil penalty of three times the profit made on the improperly disclosed information.

Under 10b-5, there can be liability on the part of individuals and companies for withholding or misrepresenting material information about the company and its financial performance. Cash tender offers are regulated by the SEC under authority of the Williams Act.

The SEC and private regulatory organizations have a wide variety of tools that are used for enforcement including fines and penalties as well as sanctions that can prohibit practice before the SEC or employment by individuals in publicly traded companies or the securities industry. The securities industry provides arbitration procedures to resolve disputes between customers and firms.

Learning Outcomes

After studying this chapter, you should be able to clearly explain:

45-1   State Regulation

LO.1   Explain the meaning of state "blue sky laws"
See the discussion of the common-content features of state securities laws such as antifraud provisions, licensing provisions, and regulation of securities, page 928.

45-2   History of Federal Regulation and Market Trends

LO.2   Define "security"
See the *Edwards* case as an example of the broad definition of *security* sufficient to encompass virtually any instrument that might be sold as an investment, page 930.

LO.3   Compare and distinguish between the Securities Act of 1933 and the Securities Exchange Act of 1934
See the discussion regarding the regulation of the original issue of securities, pages 929–934.
See the discussion regarding the secondary distribution of securities designed to prevent fraudulent and manipulative practices on the securities exchanges, page 934.

LO.4   Explain the changes that the JOBS Act has had on registration exemptions
See the discussion on Regulation D, Rule 506, referring to private placement offerings and the change that the JOBS Act made regarding general solicitation of accredited investors, pages 932–933.
See the discussion on the SEC's proposed crowdfunding exemption, page 934.

LO.5   Explain how the 1934 act's policy of fostering reliance on market integrity is served by Rule 10b-5 private investor lawsuits when investors are injured by material misstatements by the issuer
See the *Basic Inc.* case on the fraud-on-the-market theory and "materiality" in merger cases, page 937.
See the *Matrixx* case on "materiality" in the pharmaceutical industry, pages 937–938.

LO.6   Explain the factors that subject an individual to liability for insider trading
See the *Dirks* case that illustrates the rule that when the insider does not breach a fiduciary duty, a tippee does not violate securities laws, pages 942–943.
See the *O'Hagan* case regarding outsiders who have access to confidential information that will affect a company's stock price, pages 943–944.

LO.7   Explain how the primary and secondary markets are regulated by the SEC as well as private enforcement organizations
See the discussion regarding false and misleading statements in the registration process of the 1933 act, page 934.
See the SEC's enforcement powers under Dodd-Frank including its powers to bring administrative proceedings against defendants, to reward whistle-blowers, to regulate attorneys and accountants, and to regulate officers and accountants in the preparation of financial statements, pages 946–948.

45-3   Industry Self-Regulation
See the section on industry self-regulation and FINRA's role, page 948.

Key Terms

blue sky laws

cash tender offer

fraud-on-the-market

insider

insider information

primary offering

prospectus

registration requirements

registration statement

security

short-swing profit

temporary insider

tippee

Questions and Case Problems

1. Lawrence D. Polizzotto, a former vice president at First Solar Inc., spoke in one-on-one phone calls with some analysts and investors. He stated that the company was unlikely to receive a much-anticipated loan guarantee from the U.S. Department of Energy. The next morning, this information was disclosed in a press release. The stock price dropped 6 percent. Has Polizzotto violated any SEC rules or regulations? [*In the Matter of Lawrence D. Polizzotto*, Adm. Proc. File No. 3-15458 (September 6, 2013)]

2. Corporation A was involved in merger discussions with Corporation B. During this time, Corporation A made public statements denying that any merger negotiations were taking place or that it knew of any corporate developments that would account for heavy trading activity in its stock. A class of former shareholders who sold Corporation A stock after the public denial of merger activity and the announcement of the merger some six weeks later sued Corporation A, contending that it made material misrepresentations of fact in denying the merger activity. Corporation A stock increased 25 percent upon the merger announcement. Corporation A stated that at the time of its denial of merger activity it was just involved in preliminary negotiations and its actions were not material until negotiations reached an agreement in principle. Moreover, it asserted that the shareholders made no showing that they relied on the denial statement. Decide.

3. *Business Week* magazine is sent to a national distributor of magazines, Curtis Circulations Co., which sells the magazines to various wholesalers, including Hudson News. *Business Week* publishes a column entitled "Inside Wall Street," and the evidence shows that stocks discussed favorably in the column tend to increase in value after release to the public. *Business Week* has a strict confidentiality policy prior to release of the magazine to the public applicable to all employees involved in production and distribution. This policy also applies to Hudson News. Gregory

Savage, an employee of Hudson News, and the "top person" in the delivery room area, arranged to have the "Inside Wall Street" column faxed to his neighbor, a stockbroker named Larry Strath, prior to the close of the market on Thursday and prior to release to the public that evening. Strath traded on the information and passed it on to Joseph Falcone, who likewise traded on the basis of this information. While Falcone paid Strath $200 for a copy of the column each week, he contends that the information he received was too remote from the *Business Week* confidentiality policy to be actionable by the SEC. What theory do you believe the SEC pursued against Falcone? What are the elements of the theory? How would you decide this case? [*United States v. Falcone*, 257 F.3d 226 (2d Cir.)]

4. Minnesota Prostate Research Labs, Inc. (MPRL), made an initial public offering of its shares in August 1998. It stated in its prospectus that research on laboratory animals indicated that the lab may have discovered a cure for prostate cancer in humans. MPRL pointed out as well that results in animal testing did not necessarily mean that the same positive result would occur in humans. MPRL shares initially traded at $10 per share in 1999 and rose to $18 in August 2001, when the MPRL prostate cancer drug was finally approved for sale to the public. Tuttle reviewed the initial prospectus and analysts' reports on the drug and purchased 10,000 shares at $18 per share on August 18, 2001. In September 2002, an independent study of the four leading prostate medicines indicated that MPRL's product was as effective as sugar pills in curing prostate cancer and other prostate symptoms. The price of MPRL shares plummeted to $6 per share. Tuttle is contemplating a Rule 10b-5 securities fraud class-action lawsuit against MPRL. Advise him of his chances of success in this lawsuit and any expenses that he would be exposed to other than the cost of his attorney.

5. The following transactions in Heritage Cosmetics Co., Inc., stock took place: On January 21, Jones,

the corporation's vice president of marketing, purchased 1,000 shares of stock at $25 per share. On January 24, Sylvan, a local banker and director of Heritage, purchased 500 shares of stock at $26 per share. On January 30, McCarthy, a secretary at Heritage, purchased 300 shares of stock at $26.50. On February 12, Winfried, a rich investor from New England, purchased 25,000 shares at an average price of $26 per share. At that time, Heritage had a total of 200,000 shares of stock outstanding. On June 14, Winfried sold his entire holding in Heritage at an average price of $35 per share. In a local newspaper interview, Winfried was quoted regarding his reasons for selling the stock: "I have not had the pleasure of meeting any person from Heritage, but I have the highest regard for the Heritage Company, … I sold my stock simply because the market has gone too high and in my view is due for a correction." After independently reading Winfried's prediction on the stock market, Jones, Sylvan, and McCarthy sold their shares on June 15 for $33 per share. On June 20, Heritage Co. demanded that Jones, Sylvan, McCarthy, and Winfried pay the corporation the profits made on the sale of the stock. Was the corporation correct in making such a demand on each of these people?

6. Dorozhko hacked into the corporate network of Thomson Financial on October 17, 2007, at 2:15 P.M. and gained access to IMS Health's soon-to-be-released negative earnings announcement due out at 5:00 P.M. He purchased $41,670 worth of put options. IMS shares were trading at $29.56 at the close on October 17. On October 18, 2007, IMS Health's stock price plunged at the opening of trading to $21.20 per share on the negative news issued at 5:00 P.M. on October 17. Within six minutes, Dorozhko sold the put options for a net profit of $286,456. Did Dorozhko's "hacking and trading" violate either the traditional or misappropriation theories of "insider trading"?

7. Mary Dale worked in the law office of Emory Stone, an attorney practicing securities law. While proofreading Mary's keying of a document relating to the merger of two computer software companies, Emory joked to her, "If I weren't so ethical, I could make a few bucks on this info. Nomac Software stock prices are going to take off when this news hits 'The Street.'" That evening, Mary told her friend Rick Needleworth, a stockbroker, what her boss had said. Needleworth bought 500 shares of Nomac Software stock the next day and sold it three days later when the news of the merger was made public. He made a profit of $3,500. Did Dale, Stone, or Needleworth violate any securities law(s) or ethical principles with respect to the profit made by Needleworth?

8. International Advertising, Inc. (IA), would like to raise $10 million in new capital to open new offices in Eastern Europe. It believes it could raise the capital by selling shares of stock to its directors and executive officers as well as to its bank and a large insurance company whose home office is located near IA's headquarters. Opposition to the financing plan exists because of the trouble, time, and cost involved with registering with the SEC. Advise IA how best to proceed with the registration of the new issue of stock.

9. Dubois sold Hocking a condominium that included an option to participate in a rental pool arrangement. Hocking elected to participate in the arrangement. Under it, the rental pool's agent rented condominiums, pooled the income, and after deducting a management fee, distributed the income to the owners on a pro rata basis. Hocking brought a Rule 10b-5 fraud action against Dubois. Dubois contended that the sale of the condominium was not a security under the securities acts so Hocking could not bring a securities suit against her. Was Dubois correct? [*Hocking v. Dubois*, 839 F.2d 290 (9th Cir.)]

10. William Rubin, president of Tri-State Mining Co., sought a loan from Bankers Trust Co. To secure the loan, he pledged worthless stock in six companies and represented that the stock was worth $1.7 million. He also arranged for fictitious quotations to appear in an investment reporting service used by the bank to value the pledged securities. The bank loaned Rubin $475,000 and took the securities as pledged collateral. In a criminal action against Rubin under section 17(a) of the 1933 act, Rubin's defense was that the pledging of securities did not constitute an offer or sale of securities under the act. Was Rubin correct? [*Rubin v. United States*, 449 U.S. 424]

11. J. C. Cowdin, a director of Curtis-Wright Co., phoned Robert Gintel, a partner of Cady, Roberts & Co., a stock brokerage house, and advised him that Curtis-Wright's quarterly dividend had been cut. Gintel immediately entered orders selling Curtis-Wright shares for his customers' accounts. The stock was selling at over $40 a share when the orders were executed but fell to $30 soon after the dividend cut was announced to the public. The SEC contended that the firm, Cady, Roberts & Co., and Gintel

violated section 10(b) of the 1934 act, Rule 10b-5, and section 17(a) of the 1933 act. Gintel and Cady, Roberts & Co. disagreed. Decide. [In re *Cady, Roberts & Co.*, 40 SEC 907]

12. In a January 2000 prospectus for its initial public offering of shares, Apex Oil Discovery Co. (AODC) estimated a sizable volume of oil production based on the studies of two geologists and a test well at one of its Oklahoma properties. A cautionary statement advised that the projections were only estimates based on the opinion of the two experts and a test well, and that actual production could vary significantly. Lutz bought 10,000 shares of Apex in May 2000 for $20 per share. By October 2000, 12 of its 15 drilling operations under way that year turned out to be dry holes. On October 18, 2000, AODC stock fell to $6 per share. Lutz brought a private securities civil action under SEC Rule 10b-5 against AODC, alleging that the AODC oil production estimates that induced him to buy the stock were fraudulent as evidenced by the 80 percent failure rate of its drilling operations. What defense, if any, does AODC have in this case? Decide.

13. Douglas Hansen, Leo Borrell, and Bobby Lawrence were three psychiatrists who recognized the need for an inpatient treatment facility for adolescents and children in their community. They became limited partners in building a for-profit psychiatric facility. Each had a 6.25 percent interest in the partnership. Healthcare International, Inc., the general partner with a 75 percent interest, had expertise in hospital construction, management, and operation. Hansen, Borrell, and Lawrence asserted that the managerial control of the partnership was undertaken and operated by the general partner to the exclusion of the limited partners. The doctors claimed that their interest was a security—"an investment contract"—that gave them status to file a securities suit against the general partner under the 1934 act. The general partner disagreed. Decide. [*L & B Hospital Ventures, Inc. v. Health-care International, Inc.*, 894 F.2d 150 (5th Cir.)]

14. Texas International Speedway, Inc. (TIS), filed a registration statement and prospectus with the Securities and Exchange Commission offering a total of $4,398,900 in securities to the public. The proceeds of the sale were to be used to finance the construction of an automobile speedway. The entire issue was sold on the offering date. TIS did not meet with success, and the corporation filed a petition for bankruptcy. Huddleston and Bradley instituted a class-action suit in U.S. district court on behalf of themselves and other purchasers of TIS securities. Their complaint alleged violations of section 10(b) of the 1934 act. The plaintiffs sued most of the participants in the offering, including the accounting firm of Herman & MacLean. Herman & MacLean had issued an opinion concerning certain financial statements and a pro forma balance sheet that were contained in the registration statement and prospectus. The plaintiffs claimed that the defendants had engaged in a fraudulent scheme to misrepresent or conceal material facts regarding the financial condition of TIS, including the costs incurred in building the speedway. Herman & MacLean contended that the case should be dismissed because section 11 of the 1933 act provides an express remedy for a misrepresentation in a registration statement, so an action under section 10(b) of the 1934 act is precluded. Decide. [*Herman & MacLean v. Huddleston*, 459 U.S. 375]

15. Melvin J. Ford, president of International Loan Network, Inc. (ILN), promoted ILN's financial enrichment programs to ILN members and prospective members with evangelical fervor at revival-style "President's Night" gatherings. His basic philosophy was this:

> *The movement of money creates wealth. What we believe is that if you organize people and get money moving, it can actually create wealth.*

One ILN program was the Maximum Consideration Program, which, somewhat like a chain letter, provided $5,000 awards to members who sold $3,000 worth of new memberships called PRAs and made a deposit on the purchases of nonresidential real estate. According to Ford, an individual purchasing $16,000 worth of PRAs could receive an award of up to $80,000 because "all of a sudden the velocity of money increases to such a point, the ability to create wealth expands to such a degree, that we could come back and give somebody an award for up to $80,000." The SEC contended that ILN was selling unregistered investment contracts in violation of the 1933 act. ILN disagreed, contending that the program never guaranteed a return and was thus not an investment contract. Decide. Could ILN have provided full disclosure to investors concerning the program in a prospectus if required by the 1933 act? [*SEC v. ILN, Inc.*, 968 F.2d 1304 (D.C. Cir.)]

CPA Questions

1. Which of the following is least likely to be considered a security under the Securities Act of 1933?

   a. Stock options

   b. Warrants

   c. General partnership interests

   d. Limited partnership interests

2. Which of the following statements is correct regarding a common stock offering that requires registration under the Securities Act of 1933?

   a. The registration statement is automatically effective when filed with the SEC.

   b. The issuer would act unlawfully if it were to sell the common stock without providing the investor with a prospectus.

   c. The SEC will determine the investment value of the common stock before approving the offering.

   d. The issuer may make sales 10 days after filing the registration statement.

3. Hamilton Corp. is making a $4,500,000 securities offering under Rule 505 of Regulation D of the Securities Act of 1933. Under this regulation, Hamilton is:

   a. Required to provide full financial information to accredited investors only.

   b. Allowed to make the offering through a general solicitation.

   c. Limited to selling to no more than 35 nonaccredited investors.

   d. Allowed to sell to an unlimited number of investors both accredited and nonaccredited.

4. Under the liability provisions of Section 11 of the Securities Act of 1933, an auditor may help to establish the defense of due diligence if:

   I. The auditor performed an additional review of the audited statements to ensure that the statements were accurate as of the effective date of a registration statement.

   II. The auditor complied with GAAS.

   a. I only

   b. II only

   c. Both I and II

   d. Neither I nor II

5. Under the Securities Exchange Act of 1934, which of the following conditions generally will allow an issuer of securities to terminate the registration of a class of securities and suspend the duty to file periodic reports?

	The corporation has fewer than 300 shareholders	*The securities are listed on a national securities exchange*
a.	Yes	Yes
b.	Yes	No
c.	No	Yes
d.	No	No

Accountants' Liability and Malpractice

Learning Outcomes ⟨⟨⟨

After studying this chapter, you should be able to

LO.1 Define *malpractice*

LO.2 Distinguish malpractice liability from breach of contract liability

LO.3 List which third parties may recover for the malpractice liability of accountants and when they may do so

LO.4 Discuss the difference between accounting malpractice and fraud

LO.5 Explain how Sarbanes-Oxley and Dodd-Frank have affected the accounting profession and accountants' liability

46-1 General Principles of Accountants' Liability

Whether an accountant can be held liable for malpractice requires a look at what constitutes malpractice, the effect of others' conduct on liability, whether there are limitations on such liability, and whether there are damages that resulted from malpractice.

46-1a What Constitutes Malpractice?

malpractice–practice that occurs when services are not properly rendered in accordance with commonly accepted standards; negligence by a professional in performing his or her skill.

An accountant who makes a contract to perform services has a duty to exercise the skill and care that are common for the accounting profession.[1] If the services are not rendered in accordance with those standards, the result is **malpractice,** as it is commonly called, which is a tort and a form of negligence.

Accountants are not insurers of the content of financial statements they prepare and, unless they agree to do so, are not normally liable for detecting fraud.[2] Sarbanes-Oxley (SOX) (covered later in the chapter) requires accountants who perform audit work to undertake the role of certifying the internal controls of companies. This certification requirement was imposed with the hope that adequate internal controls can prevent fraud.[3] An accountant can, however, be held liable for turning a blind eye to suspicious issues and items.[4]

The standards for accountants' professional liability are found in state and federal statutes (see Chapter 45 for a discussion of federal securities issues, liabilities, and standards), court decisions, the actual contract with the client, generally accepted auditing standards (GAAS), and generally accepted accounting practices (GAAP).[5] Following GAAP and GAAS is persuasive but not conclusive evidence of meeting standards for the profession. Customs in any profession are persuasive but not conclusive evidence of professional performance.

Recovery from an accountant for malpractice requires proof of the elements of negligence (see Chapter 9 for more information). The duty and breach of duty elements are determined by the professional performance standards. The breach of professional standards must have caused the losses or damages, which must also be established.

Certified public accountants are liable for damages proximately caused by their negligence, or their failure to observe sound accounting practices. Accountants owe their clients a duty to exercise the degree of care, skill, and competence that reasonably competent members of their profession would exercise under similar circumstances.[6] Accountants are also liable if they fail to call attention to a condition that causes losses if the client could have taken preventive steps following the accountant's warning.[7]

An accountant is liable to the client if the accountant negligently fails to detect or fraudulently conceals signs that an employee of the client is embezzling or the internal audit controls of the client's business are not being observed or are lax. An accountant who prepares tax returns and acts as tax manager for the client will be liable when additional taxes or penalties are assessed against the client as a result of the accountant's

---

[1] In re *Shengdatech*, 519 B.R. 292, 2014 WL 452449 (D. Nev. 2014).

[2] In re *Puda Coal Securities Inc., Litigation*, 30 F. Supp. 3d 230 (S.D.N.Y. 2014).

[3] Section 404 of Sarbanes-Oxley has become a day-to-day term in business language as companies work to obtain their "404 certifications" from auditors. Securities and Exchange Commission, *Management's Reports on Internal Controls over Financial Reporting and Certification in Exchange Act Periodic Reports*, Securities Act Release No. 33-8283 (June 5, 2003).

[4] *USACM Liquidating Trust v. Deloitte & Touche*, 754 F.3d 645 (9th Cir. 2014).

[5] In re *Colonial Bancgroup, Inc. Securities Litigation*, 9 F. Supp. 3d 1258 (M.D. Ala. 2014). In re *CBI Holding Co.*, 419 B.R. 553 (S.D.N.Y. 2009).

[6] *Willis v. Marshall*, 401 S.W.2d 689 (Tex. App. 2013).

[7] *Klopfenstein v. Deutsche Bank Securities, Inc.*, 592 Fed. Appx. 812 (11th Cir. 2014).

negligent advice. For example, a client may recover damages from the accountant when the accountant negligently fails to inform the client of the tax consequences of selling the business.[8]

CASE SUMMARY

Suing for Your Fee and Getting Nailed for Malpractice

FACTS: We can't say exactly when the trouble started for Larry and Patricia Sumrall, but it had to be by the time they hired Dale K. Barker, Jr., and his accounting firm. The Sumralls needed professional help with past-due tax returns and other amounts they owed the IRS, and they turned to Mr. Barker. At the end of the day, though, the Sumralls found themselves having to pay the IRS over $222,000 in taxes, penalties, and interest.

Mr. Barker then filed suit against the Sumralls for failure to pay their bills in full. By this time, however, the Sumralls were convinced that Mr. Barker had contributed to their problems with the IRS. So they replied with counterclaims of their own—for breach of contract, negligence, and breach of fiduciary duty, among other things.

The district court concluded that Mr. Barker's services had been deficient and cost the Sumralls dearly. The court held that Mr. Barker's bills were unjustified; that he was entitled to no fees beyond those he'd already been paid; and that the Sumralls were entitled to compensation from Mr. Barker for their counterclaims.

Mr. Barker appealed.

DECISION: The district court awarded $70,296.91, and Mr. Barker argued that this award was speculative. In fact, however, the Sumralls ultimately paid the IRS $222,001.27 in taxes, interest, and penalties. Relying on the Sumralls' expert's testimony, the district court found that, but for Mr. Barker's misconduct, the Sumralls could have settled the claim with the IRS for $151,704.36, meaning they needlessly incurred $70,296.91.

The Sumralls' experts testified that Mr. Barker owed the Sumralls a duty to complete their civil matter "promptly after 1996," and that a resolution at that time "should have been vigorously pursued … and [the matter] settled fairly quickly." The Sumralls' experts also provided at least two estimates they believed were reasonable "starting point[s]" for use as a "frame of reference" in calculating the cost to the Sumralls of not settling earlier. Although Mr. Barker disputes the best method of estimating damages, there is no question that evidence exists in the record to support the positions the district court took. It is settled, too, that a "precise" amount of damages need not be proven; a district court may estimate damages "based upon approximations, … reasonable assumptions[,] or projections."

The Sumralls were awarded their attorneys' fees for bringing the counterclaims against Mr. Barker in his suit for payment.

Affirmed. [*Dale K. Barker Co., P.C. v. Valley Plaza,* **541 Fed. Appx. 810 (10th Cir. 2013)**]

46-1b **Choice of Remedy**

In addition to liability under tort law for malpractice, accountants may be held liable for breach of contract for their failure to meet professional standards.

Breach of Contract

An accountant breaches an audit contract if the audit work, for example, was not completed. In such a situation, the client need not pay the accountant's fee. If the work was complete, but there were minor errors, the damages caused by the error can be deducted from the fee.

Remedies for breach of contract are not available to third parties against accountants because they are not ordinarily considered third-party beneficiaries of contracts with accountants.

---

[8] *Maese v. Garrett*, 329 P.3d 713 (N.M. App. 2014).

ETHICS & THE LAW

The Feeder Fund and the Auditor

Charles Hecht was an investor in Andover, a feeder fund for Bernard L. Madoff Investment Securities. Madoff Securities purported to pursue an investment strategy on behalf of feeder funds such as Andover whereby it would purchase a basket of stocks on the S & P 100 Index and hedge those purchases with related options contracts. In reality, Madoff conducted no actual securities or options trading on behalf of its customers. Instead, Madoff deposited customer investments into a single commingled checking account and, for years, fabricated customer statements to show fictitious securities trading activity and annual returns ranging between 10 and 17 percent. Hecht and other investors filed suit against Andover and Citrin Cooperman & Co., its auditor, for accounting malpractice.

Citrin's engagement letter required it to audit the balance sheet of Andover and the related statements of operations, changes in partners' capital, and cash flows. Mr. Hecht says that Citrin Cooperman had a responsibility to confirm the existence, custody, and value of portfolio securities held by Madoff at year end and selected interim dates.

Citrin Cooperman said that it was not responsible for the investors' losses because even if it had asked Madoff for confirmation that he would have lied. Evaluate Citrin Cooperman's response in terms of its legal liability as well as its professional responsibility to the Andover investors.

[*Hecht v. Andover Associates Management Corp.,* 6 N.Y.S.3d 427 (N.Y. 2015)]

Tort Liability

A client or third party may be able to recover from an accountant on the basis of negligence, gross negligence, or fraud. These theories are covered in the remaining sections of the chapter.

Because malpractice is both a breach of contract and an independent tort, the client who is harmed has the choice of recovering for breach of contract or for the particular tort that is involved. Generally, the client will bring a tort action because there are higher damages under tort law than those afforded for a breach of contract. The statute of limitations on torts versus contracts may also influence the theory for liability. The statute of limitations begins to run on the tort of malpractice from the date the harm was discovered. The contract statute of limitations runs from the date the contract is breached. This time differential may be very important because, in some cases, the client may not realize that there has been any harm until some time after a breach of the contract occurred.

46-1c The Environment of Accountants' Malpractice Liability

Accountants have moved from being primarily clerical business participants to being essential players in business strategies. In addition, accountants have moved from being employees of one employer to being independent contractors performing accounting services for many clients. Accountants are now employed to produce data that third parties use and rely on in making decisions about loans or investments. **For Example,** accountants prepare statements submitted to banks that will use those statements to determine whether to make a loan or extend a line of credit. Auditors' certifications of financial statements become part of the documents given to potential investors in companies. As these changes in the role of accountants took place, it became natural for courts to allow third parties relying on accountants' work and certifications to recover from the accountants when the accountants' and auditors' malpractice caused damages to them.

At the same time that these changes were taking place in the nature and role of accountants, changes were also taking place in other areas of the law. Manufacturers and parts suppliers were held liable to those who purchased the final products and were injured by defects in them. The rising tide of liability to third parties has naturally influenced the law regulating accountants.[9]

46-1d **Limitation of Liability**

Can accountants protect themselves from liability for malpractice claims of clients and third parties? Influenced by the consumer protection movement and by the law governing product liability, courts have recognized some liability limitations as valid. However, such disclaimers must be (1) clear and unambiguous and (2) conspicuous. If these requirements are not met, the disclaimers are not enforceable.

Scope of Limitation

Disclaimers are valid only in certain limited circumstances.[10] **For Example,** when a client owns land in a foreign country, it is reasonable for the accountant to accept the valuation placed on the land by someone in that foreign country. The accountant should, however, include in the financial statement prepared for the client a statement that the valuation of that land was obtained from an identified person in the foreign country and that the accountant assumes no responsibility for the accuracy of that valuation.

If the accountant's work has been restricted, the accountant is protected from claims of third parties because there has been full disclosure about the accountant's limited information and ability to verify the work of others. **For Example,** when the accountant is restricted from examining accounts receivable and the accountant's certification states that no opinion was expressed as to accounts receivable, the accountant cannot be held liable if the accounts receivable turn out to be overstated.[11]

Limitations on Exculpatory Provisions

A disclaimer based on lack of knowledge does not protect the accountant from liability if the accountant knew or had reason to know that the statements made were false. If the accountant states that he had no personal knowledge, he impliedly represents that he did not have any knowledge or reason to know that the statements were not correct. A disclaimer that is made when the accountant has reason to suspect that underlying information is false would be **misrepresentation** and would result in the accountant's liability.[12]

In some states, a **limitation-of-liability** or **exculpatory clause** protects the accountant from a malpractice suit brought by a client only, not from a suit brought by a third party. In such cases, courts apply the general rule of contract law that only a party to a contract is bound by an exculpatory or limitation-of-liability clause.

misrepresentation—false statement of fact made innocently without any intent to deceive.

limitation-of-liability clause—provision in a contract stating that one of the parties is not liable for damages in case of breach; also called *exculpatory clause*.

exculpatory clause—provision in a contract stating that one of the parties is not liable for damages in case of breach; also called *limitation-of-liability clause*.

---

[9] The interplay between the various areas of malpractice liability and those of accountants is seen further in the fact that the Restatement (Second) of Torts does not contain a separate provision applicable only to accountants but deals with the subject of malpractice liability of accountants to third parties in a general section (§552). Section 552 provides that

> [O]ne who in the course of his business, profession or employment, or in any other transaction in which he has a pecuniary interest, supplies false information for the guidance of others in their business transactions, is subject to liability for pecuniary loss caused to them by their justifiable reliance on the information, if he fails to exercise reasonable care or competence in obtaining or communicating the information.

The section then defines which parties can enforce this liability.

[10] The American Institute of Certified Public Accountants has an ethics rule on liability limitations and indemnifications, and the 2014 standards on indemnification clauses in engagement letters can be found at **http://www.aicpa.org**.

[11] But disclaimers do not permit auditors to ignore fraud. *Sacher v. Beacon Associates Management Corp.*, 980 N.Y.S.2d 121 (App. Div. 2014).

[12] However, an accountant cannot disclaim liability for failure to spot grossly inflated values in financial statements. *Serino v. Lipper*, 994 N.Y.S.2d 64 (N.Y. App. 2014).

CPA   46-2 **Accountants' Liability to Third Parties: Beyond Privity**

Most accountants' malpractice litigation involves the question of whether third parties may recover from the accountants, not on what standards of conduct accountants should observe. Various issues and factors, covered in both judicial decisions and statutes, determine whether accountants will be held liable to third parties.[13]

46-2a Status of the Accountant

An accountant may be a full-time employee of a company, an independent contractor doing regular work for a client, or an independent outside auditor. What constitutes negligence is the same for all three types of accountants. The liability of the accountant to the third party, when recognized, is based on the reliance of the third party on the work of the accountant.[14]

46-2b Conflicting Theories of Accountants' Third-Party Liability

There are a number of theories that have been developed for third parties to recover for an accountant's negligence. These views may be identified as (1) the privity rule, (2) the contact rule, (3) the known user rule, (4) the foreseeable user rule, and (5) the intended user rule. In addition, some courts follow (6) a flexible rule, deciding each case as it arises. Each of these views is an attempt to draw a boundary line between the interloper and a "proper" plaintiff with sufficient connection to the accountant for recovery for the accountant's negligence. In some states, statutes define when nonprivity plaintiffs may recover for an accountant's negligence.[15]

The Privity Rule

privity rule—succession or chain of relationship to the same thing or right, such as privity of contract, privity of estate, privity of possession.

The **privity rule** precludes a negligence malpractice suit by a third party. This rule holds that only the party in privity with the accountant—that is, the accountant's client—may recover from the accountant.[16] When the privity rule is applied, a bank lending money to the accountant's client cannot recover from the accountant for malpractice.[17]

The Contact Rule

In states in which the privity rule is relaxed, a third party can recover from a negligent accountant if there was some contact between the third party and the accountant. **For Example,** an accountant may go to a bank to see what information the bank requires for the accountant's client to obtain a loan. In this case, there is a sufficient "link" or "contact" between the bank and the accountant to allow the bank to recover from the

[13] *Hanover Ins. Group v. DNH Business Consultants, P.C.,* 2012 WL 1886458 (N.D. Ill. 2012).
[14] *Seibu Corp. v. KPMG, LLP,* 2001 WL 1658130 (N.D. Tex. 2001), but see *Prospect High Income Fund v. Grant Thorton, LLP,* 203 S.W.3d 602 (Tex. App. 2006).
[15] See, e.g., *Ark. Code Ann.* §16-114-302 (2014); 225 *Ill. Comp. Stat.* 450/30.1 (2014); *Kan. Stat. Ann.* §1-402 (2014); *La. Rev. Stat. Ann.* §37:91 (2014); *Mich. Comp. Laws* §600.2962 (2014); *N.J.S.A* 2A:53A-25(b)(2) (2014); *Utah Code Ann.* §58-26a-602 (2014); *Wyo. Stat. Ann.* §33-3-201 (2014).
[16] This rule was originally known as the New York rule, *Ultramares Corp. v. Touche,* 174 N.E. 441 (N.Y. 1931). Although it has been replaced in New York by the contact rule, the privity rule is still the law in many jurisdictions. *JH Kelly, LLC v. Tianwei New Energy Holdings Co., Ltd.,* 68 F. Supp. 3d 1194 (D. Idaho 2014).
[17] *Citibank, N.A. v. McGladrey and Pullen, LLP,* 953 N.E.2d 38 (Ill. App. 2011).

accountant if it sustains a loss because of the accountant's negligence.[18] The New York *contact rule* requires that the accountant meet or communicate with the nonprivity party to establish a relationship equivalent to privity. The accountant must also know the purpose of the accounting work and foresee the nonprivity party's reliance on that work.[19]

There must be enough contact with, or dealings between, the third party and the accountant to give the accountant reason to know that the third party was relying for a particular purpose on the financial statements prepared by the accountant.[20]

The Known User Rule

Under this rule for nonprivity parties, the accountant is liable to third parties who experience a loss as a result of the accountant's negligence when the accountant knew that the third party would be using the accountant's work product. **For Example,** a shareholder may recover from an accountant for negligently preparing and certifying an annual financial report that was prepared for distribution to shareholders.[21]

Under the known user rule, the fact that the nonprivity party's reliance on a financial statement was foreseeable does not entitle the third party to recover from the accountant for negligent preparation of the statement. The third party must show that the accountant knew about the third party and his interest in the accountant's work.[22]

CASE SUMMARY

The CPA Who Let His Client Send the Tax Refund to Thailand

FACTS: Bradley Beddall, a real estate developer, and Douglas Dewar began a condominium conversion project for the Lea Hill Condominiums. When the local real estate market declined and the project floundered, Beddall owed Dewar $3,900,000 and could no longer meet his obligations. Beddall told Dewar that he wanted out of the project.

Beddall signed a quit claim deed conveying the Lea Hill property to Dewar. Dewar and Beddall signed a settlement agreement, part of which was that Beddall could obtain a large tax refund based upon his losses from the project and would turn that refund over to Dewar. The agreement gave Dewar the right of "review, evaluation, and approval" of the

tax return in his "sole and absolute discretion." Beddall signed an "irrevocable" power of attorney and appropriate IRS Form 2848 authorizing his attorney, Jonathan Hatch, to sign the tax return, receive and negotiate the refund check, and deliver the funds to Dewar.

Kenneth Smith, a CPA, had an engagement letter with Beddall that did not mention Dewar. But Smith knew the content of the settlement agreement and its purpose. During his preparation of Beddall's tax return, Smith had a copy of the agreement. Consistent with the Hatch–Beddall power of attorney and IRS forms, Smith prepared the return for Hatch's signature.

[18] *Sykes v. RFD Third Ave.*, 938 N.E.2d 325 (N.Y. 2010); *Retirement Programs for Employees of Town of Fairfield v. NEPC, LLC*, 2011 WL 6934794, 53 Conn. L. Rptr. 194 (Conn. Super. 2011). Some courts are strict on the contact rule and describe the contact rule not as a different rule but as requiring "a relationship sufficiently intimate to be equated with privity." *Empire of American v. Arthur Andersen & Co.*, 514 N.Y.S.2d 578 (N.Y. 1987). The contact rule has been adopted by a minority of states. *Idaho Bank & Trust Co. v. First Bankcorp of Idaho*, 772 P.2d 720 (Idaho 1989), but it is under constant judicial assault.

[19] *Travelers Cas. and Sur. Co. of America v. Ernst & Young LLP*, 542 F.3d 475 (5th Cir. 2008).

[20] The contact rule applies to malpractice defendants generally. It is not limited to suits against accountants. *Ossining Union Free School District v. Anderson*, 539 N.E.2d 91 (N.Y. 1989), but see *Indianapolis-Marion County Public Library v. Charlier Clark & Linard, P.C.*, 900 N.E.2d 801 (Ind. App. 2009).

[21] *Altrust Financial Services, Inc. v. Adams*, 76 So. 2d 228 (Ala. 2011).

[22] *Bank of America, N.A. v. Knight*, 875 F. Supp. 2d 837 (N.D. Ill. 2012). The rule that the nonprivity plaintiff may recover from the accountant for malpractice negligence only if the accountant's statement was furnished to that plaintiff, or the accountant knew that the client who was given the statement would in turn give the statement to the plaintiff, is often identified as "the Restatement rule." There is, however, some uncertainty as to the exact boundaries of the Restatement rule. See *Meridian Horizon Fund, LP v. KPMG (Cayman)*, 487 Fed. Appx. 636 (2d Cir. 2012).

The CPA Who Let His Client Send the Tax Refund to Thailand continued

Hatch signed the completed tax return, which had Beddall's address on it. As the settlement agreement required, Smith transmitted the return to Dewar for his review. The same day, Dewar notified Smith that, "The only change I insist on is the address change." After Smith changed the address, Hatch signed the amended return, which Smith filed the same day.

Shortly after Smith filed the return, Beddall instructed him to stop discussing the matter with Hatch and to communicate about the return only with Beddall. During a call with the IRS with Smith, Beddall asked the IRS representative to change the address on his tax return from Hatch's address to Smith's address.

Smith did not tell Dewar or Hatch that Beddall had amended the address on the return. The IRS sent four refund checks totaling $1,206,703.32 to Smith's office. Smith notified Beddall, who instructed him to deliver the checks to Beddall's son-in-law, Ron Rubin. Smith did so.

Beddall sent an e-mail to Dewar and Hatch to tell them that the tax refund money was in Thailand. When Beddall forwarded this e-mail to Smith, Smith withdrew from his engagement with Beddall.

Dewar sued Kenneth Smith for conversion, civil conspiracy, tortious interference with contractual relationship, breach of implied contract, breach of duty owed to third-party beneficiary, and breach of fiduciary duties. The trial court granted Dewar's motion for partial summary judgment to establish that Smith owed Dewar a duty of care. The court also held that Smith committed negligent misrepresentation when the address on the tax return was changed, he received the checks, and he gave them to Rubin without disclosing these actions to Dewar and Hatch. Smith appealed.

DECISION: The court held that the CPA owed a duty of care to the creditor and that the evidence supported a finding of breach of duty. The court held that there was a question of fact as to whether the CPA's action caused the resulting injuries and losses. The court also noted that the federal prohibition of disclosing tax return information did not preclude a finding that the CPA committed negligent misrepresentation. The case was remanded for trial on the issues related to conduct and causation. [*Dewar v. Smith*, 342 P.3d 328 (Wash. App. 2015)]

Under the known user rule, the accountant need not know the identity of a particular user to be held liable to that user. However, some states do indeed limit recovery to known users.[23] **For Example,** an accountant prepares a financial statement for a client with the knowledge that the client will take it to First National Bank to obtain a loan. First National Bank may recover from the accountant for negligence even though the bank never had any direct contact or dealings (that is, was never in privity) with the accountant. However, in states that restrict the expansion of known users, another lender, such as Fifth Third Bank, would not be able to recover from the accountant for negligence.

The fact that the third party was a foreseeable user does not afford a basis for recovery in states that limit their privity expansion to "known user" status. When an accountant prepares a financial statement for the client and the accountant is told nothing about further use of the statement, creditors of the client cannot recover from the accountant for negligent preparation of the statement. The client would be the only known user.

CPA   The Foreseeable User Rule

The accountant may foresee that a particular class of unknown parties will rely on her work. **For Example,** when the accountant prepares a financial statement knowing that the client is going to use it to borrow money from some bank or finance company, the accountant foresees a class of lenders. Similarly, the accountant may know that the financial statement will be used to sell the stock of the client corporation. Here again, there is a foreseeable class consisting of unknown parties.

---

[23] In re *Enron Corp. Securities, Derivatives, & ERISA Litigation*, 762 F. Supp. 2d 942 (S.D. Tex. 2010).

The *foreseeable user rule* imposes liability on the accountant for negligent malpractice when he can foresee the parties who will rely on his work in the financial statements. The foreseeable user rule allows these third parties to recover for their losses without regard to the lack of privity of contract between them and the accountant.[24]

CASE SUMMARY

The Artful Financial Statements That Cast Out Liability

FACTS: Cast Art Industries* produced and sold collectible figurines and giftware. Papel Giftware was in the same line of business as Cast Art, and in spring 2000 Cast Art explored acquiring Papel. Among the factors that made Papel so attractive to Cast Art were Papel's large number of existing customer accounts, its existing sales force, and its production facilities. Eventually, Cast Art decided on a merger, rather than an acquisition. Cast Art negotiated a loan agreement with PNC Bank for $22 million to fund the venture. PNC's conditions included that it receive audited financial statements and that Cast Art's CEO, Scott Sherman, personally guarantee $3.3 million of the loan.

KPMG (defendant) had audited Papel's financial statements since 1997. KPMG was already in the process of auditing Papel's 1998 and 1999 financial statements when Cast Art and Papel began their merger discussions. In its letter to the chairman of Papel's audit committee dated November 17, 1999, in which it agreed to undertake these audits and report the results, KPMG noted the parameters of its work:

> [T]here is a risk that material errors, fraud (including fraud that may be an illegal act), and other illegal acts may exist and not be detected by an audit performed in accordance with generally accepted auditing standards. Also, an audit is not designed to detect matters that are immaterial to the financial statements.

In September 2000, KPMG delivered to Papel the completed audits for the years 1998 and 1999. KPMG included in its accompanying opinion letter, which again was addressed to the chairman of Papel's audit committee, that Papel "was not in compliance with certain financial covenants" with its lenders, which KPMG characterized as raising "substantial doubt about the Company's ability to continue as a going concern."

Cast Art obtained copies of the completed 1998 and 1999 audits and provided copies to PNC. Three months later, in December 2000, Cast Art and Papel consummated the merger. Shortly after the merger was finalized, Cast Art began to experience difficulty in collecting some of the accounts receivable that it had believed Papel had had outstanding prior to the merger. Cast Art began its own investigation and learned that the 1998 and 1999 financial statements prepared by Papel were inaccurate and that Papel had engaged regularly in accelerating revenue.

Papel did not follow its stated policy to recognize revenue from sales when goods were shipped and invoices sent. Papel routinely booked revenue from goods that had not yet been shipped. There was also testimony that at certain points Papel would not close out its books at month's end. Rather, it would hold them open and book the improperly extended month revenue that was earned in the following period. There was also testimony that at least one transaction, referred to at trial as the "Bookman" transaction, was a fraudulent entry of a $121,244 sale that never occurred.

Although Cast Art knew at the time of the merger that Papel was carrying a significant amount of debt, it was unaware of those accounting irregularities until after the merger was complete. The surviving corporation was unable to generate sufficient revenue to carry its debt load and produce new goods, and it eventually failed.

Following a lengthy trial for KPMG's malpractice, a jury returned a verdict in favor of Cast Art and awarded damages totaling $31.8 million, which was amended to $38,096,902 by the trial court judge. The Appellate Division upheld the verdict on liability but vacated the damage award and remanded for a new trial on damages. The case was certified to the New Jersey Supreme Court.

DECISION: KPMG argued that because Cast Art had not retained it to audit Papel, Cast Art was not its client, and

---

[24] In re *Washington Mut., Inc. Securities, Derivative & ERISA Litigation*, 2010 WL 2545415 (W.D. Wash. 2010). See also *Bank of America, N.A v. BDO Seidman, LLP*, 2012 WL 806007 (Mass. Super. 2012).

The Artful Financial Statements That Cast Out Liability continued

Cast Art's claim was consequently barred by the Accountant Liability Act, NJ.SA. 2A:53A–25.

Accounting firms should no longer be permitted to hide within the citadel of privity and avoid liability for their malpractice.

However, auditor is entitled to know at the outset the scope of the work it is being requested to perform and the concomitant risk it is being asked to assume. At the outset of its engagement with Papel, KPMG was not told that a non-client would be relying on its work.

Because Cast Art failed to establish that KPMG "knew at the time of the engagement by the client" or thereafter agreed that Cast Art could rely on its work in proceeding with this merger, Cast Art failed to satisfy the requisite elements of NJ.SA. 2A:53A–25(b)(2), and KPMG was entitled to judgment.

QUESTIONS

1. Describe the types of accounting irregularities that were going on at Papel.
2. What is the significance of the term "engagement" in the opinion?
3. Where does New Jersey fit with regard to privity and the Restatement rule when it comes to auditor liability to third parties?

[*Cast Art Industries, LLC v. KPMG LLP*, **36 A.3d 1049 (N.J. 2012)**]

*The individual plaintiffs, Scott Sherman, Gary Barsellotti, and Frank Colapinto, were Cast Art's shareholders. Because the claims of Cast Art and the individual plaintiffs are inextricably intertwined, the court referred simply to Cast Art and plaintiff in the singular.

THINKING THINGS THROUGH

How Many Plaintiffs Can There Be in a Class-Action Securities Litigation? How Many Defendants?

With the collapse of companies such as Countrywide, New Century Financial, Lehman Brothers, and other firms affected by or involved in the subprime mortgage market, litigation against all of these firms' auditors is ongoing. The following is a list of all of the types of plaintiffs who have brought suit against auditors:

- Shareholders who purchased stock in the companies
- State pension funds with stock in their portfolios
- Banks and other institutions that lent money

- Banks and other institutions that accepted stock as collateral for loans
- Universities that received stock as endowment gifts
- Companies that contracted with the companies after having requested financial statements

Applying the various standards for accountant liability you have learned, discuss whether each of these groups will be able to recover from the auditors for these firms and why or why not.

The Intended User Rule

Fear that the foreseeability rule does not sufficiently restrict the number of potential claimants has led some courts to limit recovery to those nonprivity users who were not merely foreseeable but also expected or intended to rely on the work of the accountant in a particular transaction or another similar transaction.[25] In this view, the accountant must have furnished the information directly to the nonprivity user or to the client, knowing that the client would transmit the information to the nonprivity plaintiff.

[25] *D & H Autobath v. PJCS Properties I, Inc.*, 983 N.E.2d 891 (Ohio. App. 2012). Some courts regard this rule as representing the majority view. The foreseeable user rule brings the law with respect to accountants into harmony with the tort law relating to other parties and activities.

The Flexible Rule

Some courts have rejected the requirement of privity for malpractice against accountants but have not adopted any of the rules discussed in the preceding sections. These courts prefer to keep the question open and to decide each case as it arises.

Unknown User

When the accountant has no knowledge of, or reason to know of, any third party's use of the accountant's work, the third party is not able to come within any exception to the requirement of privity. Consequently, a nonprivity party cannot recover for the accountant's negligence when the accountant had no knowledge of any use that could affect the party.[26]

CPA   ### 46-2c Nonliability Parties

There are some third parties to whom accountants do not have liability.

Interlopers

No court imposes liability on the accountant to a total stranger who gets possession of the accountant's work and then sustains a loss because of a false statement in the work. This applies regardless of whether the statement was negligent or intentional. **For Example,** assume that a negligently prepared financial statement of a corporation is thrown in the wastepaper basket and is then retrieved by a security guard. If the guard thinks that the statement is a "hot tip" and invests in the stock of the corporation on the basis of the statement, the guard cannot recover from the accountant for negligence in preparing the statement. Accountants are not liable to interlopers, but courts continue to struggle with drawing the line between interlopers and rightful third parties.

CPA   ### Parties Affected by the Decision of Accountant's Client

On the basis of information furnished by the accountant to a client, the client may make a decision that affects a third party. **For Example,** a report by an independent auditor may indicate that a fiscal officer of the client has not handled funds properly. The report may indicate that it is economically unsound to enter into a contract with a third party. Assume that the client relies on the accountant's report and fires the employee or refuses to make a contract with the third party. If the report of the accountant was negligently made and the true facts would not have justified the action taken by the client, most courts hold that third parties harmed in this indirect way have no cause of action.[27]

contributory negligence—negligence of the plaintiff that contributes to injury and at common law bars recovery from the defendant although the defendant may have been more negligent than the plaintiff.

46-2d Defenses to Accountants' Liability: Contributory and Comparative Negligence of the Client or Third Party

Contributory Negligence

When an accountant has been negligent, the client's negligence may reduce the accountant's liability. To establish client **contributory negligence,** the accountant must show that the client contributed to the accountant's failure or that the client ignored the

---

[26] *Cromeans v. Morgan Keegan & Co., Inc.,* 2014 WL 1901197 (W.D. Mo. 2014).
[27] *World Radio Laboratories, Inc. v. Coopers & Lybrand,* 538 N.W.2d 501 (Neb. App. 1995).

accountant's instructions. **For Example,** when the financial statement indicates that it is merely a working examination and is not certified by the accountant, the third party is negligent in relying on the statement and has been contributorily negligent.

If those who are using a financial statement are highly sophisticated and have been warned by their advisers that the corporate assets have been overvalued, the users cannot hold the accountant who prepared the financial statement liable for negligence in overstating the value of the corporate assets. In such a case, the users are contributorily negligent, something that reduces or eliminates the accountant's liability.[28]

Some states ignore the contributory negligence of clients except in two circumstances. One is if the client interfered with the accountant's audit. Client interference with the accountant's work will excuse the accountant's liability. Another is if the client's negligence contributed to the accountant's negligence, but such contribution is not a bar to recovery by the client. **For Example,** the negligence of the accountant's client in keeping records is not a bar to the accountant's liability to the client because the liability comes from the accountant's failure to discover the true facts.[29] The issue in these circumstances becomes not whether the accountant knew, but whether the accountant should have known.

Comparative Negligence

comparative negligence–defense to negligence that allows plaintiff to recover reduced damages based on his level of fault.

Some states apply the **comparative negligence** concept and permit proof of the client's negligence.[30] Under comparative negligence standards, the accountant and the client are assessed a percentage of blame for their respective levels of negligence in the use and preparation of the financial statements, and the client's recovery is reduced by its percentage of fault. **For Example,** if a jury finds that the client was responsible for 30 percent of the resulting loss, recovery from the accountant is reduced by 30 percent.

CPA   46-2e Accountants' Fraud Malpractice Liability to Third Parties

Society in general condemns fraud more strongly than it does negligence. There is greater liability of accountants for fraudulent malpractice.

What Constitutes Fraud by Accountants

Fraud is defined as a false statement made with knowledge that it was false or with reckless indifference as to whether it was true[31] with the intent that the listener rely on it. A false statement in accounting typically occurs when the client's financial statements make it appear to be in a better financial position than is actually the case. **For Example,** the auditor for Bernie Madoff Securities signed off for years on financial statements that made the firm seem solvent when in fact the company had lost $50 billion. The auditor was sentenced to two years of home detention and supervised release.

At times, falsified financial statements are used as a means to obtain a downgrade on the ratings for the financial condition of a corporation. Such undervaluation then induces shareholders to sell their stock to a dominant group of shareholders. The false financial statement purposely undervalues the corporation's assets to make the shareholders believe that their stock has little value and that sale at the low price offered by the dominant group is a good buy.

---

[28] *Grant Thornton LLP v. Prospect High Income Fund,* 314 S.W.3d 913 (Tex. 2010).

[29] *USACM Liquidating Trust v. Deloitte & Touche,* 754 F.3d 645 (9th Cir. 2014).

[30] *American Nat'l Bank v. Touche Ross & Co.,* 659 N.E.2d 1276 (Ohio 1996).

[31] *Cannonball Fund, Ltd. v. Dutchess Capital Management, LLC,* 993 N.E.2d 350 (Mass. App. 2013); In re *Dell Securities Litigation,* 591 F. Supp. 2d 877 (W.D. Tex. 2009).

FIGURE 46-1	Theories of Accountants' Liability to Third Parties

THEORY	TYPE OF LIABILITY	THIRD PARTY LIABILITY	CLIENT LIABILITY
STATUTORY	1933 SECURITIES ACT— OMISSION OR MISSTATEMENT IN REGISTRATION STATEMENT 1934 SECURITIES EXCHANGE ACT—10b (SEE CHAPTER 45)	PURCHASERS OF SHARES

SHAREHOLDERS; PURCHASER OF SHARES | COMPANY |
CONTRACT	BREACH OF CONTRACT	NO—NOT CONSIDERED THIRD PARTY BENEFICIARIES	MATERIAL BREACH; MINOR BREACH DAMAGES
TORT	PRIVITY REQUIRED	NO RECOVERY	RECOVERY ALLOWED UNLESS DEFENSES APPLY
	CONTACT RULE	CAN RECOVER IF ACTUAL CONTACT WITH ACCOUNTANT	
	KNOWN USER RULE	CAN RECOVER IF ACCOUNTANT KNOWS THIRD PARTY WILL USE FINANCIALS/WORK	
	FORESEEABLE USER RULE	CAN RECOVER IF ACCOUNTANT CAN FORESEE UNKNOWN PERSONS RELYING ON FINANCIALS	
	INTENDED USER RULE	CAN RECOVER IF ACCOUNTANT KNOWS CLIENT WILL GIVE IT TO ANOTHER	
	UNKNOWN USER	NO RECOVERY	
FRAUD	KNOWN AND UNKNOWN	RECOVERY	RECOVERY

Accountants' Fraud Liability to Intended Victims

Fraud by an accountant typically misleads a third party or a class of parties, a group whose identity is known to the accountant. Any such victim, whether an identified party or member of a class of potential victims, may recover from the accountant for loss caused by fraud. Privity (relating to liability for negligence) is not required when the basis of the malpractice suit is fraud. The public policy of preventing fraud overrides the concern of holding accountants liable to third parties.[32]

[32] However, fraud is difficult to establish in suits against accountants and auditors. *Iowa Public Employee's Retirement System v. Deloitte & Touche LLP*, 919 F. Supp. 2d 321 (S.D.N.Y. 2013).

An accountant might certify a false financial statement for a corporate client with knowledge that it will be used to sell the corporation's securities to third parties.[33] If so, the third parties may recover from the accountant for the damages sustained. **For Example,** an accountant was held liable for disguising the true character of a hoped-for profit from the sale and resale of real estate. The accountant described the sale and resale as "deferred income," although there was little reason to believe that the transaction could ever be completed because the buyer, who was obligated to pay $5 million for the property, had assets of only $100,000. The financial statement would have shown a loss instead of a substantial profit if the true character of this risky transaction had been disclosed.

CASE SUMMARY

When the Auditor Just Does What Management Wants

FACTS: Throughout the early and mid-1990s, Xerox financial reports reflected a financially healthy company with revenues rising at a double-digit rate. By the late 1990s, however, Xerox faced increasing competition from Japanese competitors in the digital copier market and it was able to meet Wall Street's earning expectations only by engaging in massive accounting fraud.

Xerox reallocated revenues from service to the equipment portion of sales-type leases by assuming an artificial gross margin differential between the two lease components (or an assumed profit margin) that had no basis in economic reality. Equipment margins were in fact falling. Xerox used this method to pull forward $617 million of equipment revenues from 1997 to 2000. Internally, KPMG referred to this method as "half-baked revenue recognition." By relying on this methodology, from 1997 to 1999, Xerox inflated its pre-tax earnings by a net of $43 million. According to the SEC, in 1996, KPMG objected to this practice as violating GAAP but, after arguments with Xerox senior management, approved its implementation in 1998, while continuing to criticize its use.

In 1999, KPMG informed Xerox that this practice violated GAAP, but Xerox refused to follow this advice. Nevertheless, KPMG certified Xerox's 1999 and 2000 financial statements.

In November of 1999, Xerox senior managers discussed the fact that without their accounting actions, Xerox had essentially no growth through the late 1990s. In 2001, Xerox began issuing a series of earnings restatements that would total $11 billion. In late 2001, Xerox announced

that PriceWaterhouse Coopers, LLP ("PwC") was replacing KPMG as the company's new auditor for the 2001 fiscal year. Xerox paid a $10 million fine to the SEC to settle civil charges and also agreed to complete its restatement of earnings for 1997 through 2001.

Investors such as the Florida State pension plan and other individual investors (plaintiffs) brought suit against the executive officers of Xerox as well as KPMG for fraud.

KPMG moved to have the complaint against it dismissed because of its lack of scienter.

DECISION: When the factual allegations in the Complaint are viewed as a whole, the plaintiffs have at a minimum alleged facts constituting strong circumstantial evidence of recklessness on the part of KPMG.

However, the factual allegations in the Complaint portray KPMG as a "virtual pushover" in its dealings with Xerox. KPMG went along with accounting practices it knew to be clear violations of GAAP, and continued to go along even after it was clear early in 2001 that there were very serious concerns about Xerox's accounting practices. KPMG also realized that it was questionable—at best— whether Xerox took seriously its obligation to comply with applicable accounting rules. Despite all this, KPMG was intimidated into signing off on a minimal restatement of Xerox's financial statements that accounted for only a small portion of Xerox's overstatements of revenues and pre-tax earnings. The conduct on the part of KPMG was highly unreasonable and represents an extreme departure from the standards of ordinary care.

[33] In re *IMAX Securities Litigation*, 587 F. Supp. 2d 471 (S.D.N.Y. 2008).

When the Auditor Just Does What Management Wants continued

[The court denied KPMG's motion to dismiss after concluding that there was enough in the pleadings to give rise to scienter.]

QUESTIONS

1. Give some examples of "turning points" or events when KPMG should have acted differently.

2. Describe the level of accounting errors at Xerox from 1997 through 2001.

3. Why do you think the officers and KPMG auditors acted as they did?

[***Carlson v. Xerox Corp.*, 392 F. Supp. 2d 267 (D. Conn. 2005)**]

CPA   46-3 # Federal Laws on Auditors, Accounting, and Financial Reporting

Sarbanes-Oxley Act (SOX or SarBox) is legislation passed in response to the collapses of major corporations at the turn of the century (Enron, WorldCom). SOX imposes substantial requirements on auditors and the standards and practices of the audit profession. Following the market collapse in 2008, SOX was expanded through The Wall Street Reform and Consumer Protection Act, known as Dodd-Frank.[34]

CPA   46-3a ## SOX and Auditor Independence

SOX has provisions to protect the independence of auditors in conducting audits of their clients.

Public Company Accounting Oversight Board

SOX created a new Public Company Accounting Oversight Board (PCAOB) that is responsible for promoting high professional standards among auditors.[35] The board, which consists of five presidential appointees, is not a governmental body but a nonprofit organization with its own budgeting and staffing authority. No more than two members of the board can be CPAs, and members of the board operate on a full-time basis. The board has the following responsibilities:

- Operating a registration system for public accounting firms that prepare audit reports for companies that issue securities

- Enforcing and refining rules to ensure audit quality, ethics, and independence by auditors

- Conducting inspections of public accounting firms to determine their compliance with Sarbanes-Oxley requirements

- Investigating violations and imposing disciplinary sanctions where necessary for members of the profession

- Encouraging the highest professional standards among public accounting firms and auditors

---

[34] Dodd-Frank amends various existing statutes found at 12 U.S.C. and 15 U.S.C. The regulations that controlled accounting conflicts have been adapted to cover analysts and those who rate securities.

[35] In the financial industry, professionals have translated the acronym for the new board, PCAOB, as *Peekaboo* because of the board's role in shedding light on financial systems and reporting.

Registration with the PCAOB

Any public accounting firm that conducts audits for companies that issue securities must file an annual registration statement with PCAOB. That registration requires the accounting firm to disclose all companies for which it has done audits and all the fees paid by those companies—both audit fees and nonaudit fees, commonly referred to as *consulting services*. The accounting firm is also required to disclose any sanctions and pending civil or criminal proceedings against it, along with its policies and procedures for quality control in audits. PCAOB then approves the accounting firm for continued work in the audit of issuers of securities. That approval or denial must be made within 45 days following the accounting firm's annual registration filing. In addition, PCAOB also reviews the work of audit firms to determine whether they are complying with professional audit standards. These reviews are part of the input for considering audit firms for approval or renewal.

Maintaining Auditor Independence

Auditors' conflicts proved to be problematic in the financial collapses of 2001 to 2002. Auditors' judgments were tainted by close connections with their audit clients through fee structure, longstanding presence, or simply friendships that blinded professional assessments on whether the companies were viable entities. **For Example,** many of the audit firms received substantial fees from companies for management consulting services for which they were providing certified statements. Arthur Andersen received $21 million annually for its audit work with Enron and another $29 million for its consulting services. The consulting contract created a conflict that interfered with the audit firm's ability to make honest decisions in its audit work.

To help eliminate conflicts of interest, Sarbanes-Oxley prohibits certain activities by audit firms for their audit clients, including the following:

1. Bookkeeping and other services related to the accounting records or financial statements of the audit client

2. Design and implementation of financial information systems

3. Appraisal and valuation services, fairness opinions, and contribution-in-kind reports

4. Actuarial services

5. Internal audit outsourcing services

6. Management functions and human resources

7. Broker or dealer, investment adviser, and investment banking services

8. Legal services and expert services unrelated to the audit

9. Any other service that the board determines, by regulation, is impermissible[36]

All nonaudit services to be performed by the auditor for an audit client (except those listed above as expressly prohibited) require prior approval by the board.

In addition, to ensure that audit partners do not become entrenched, Sarbanes-Oxley requires audit firms to change audit partners at least once every five years.[37] The rotation of the audit partner in charge of a company account brings a new perspective to the issues in the financial systems and reports and helps to eliminate the bias of close, personal relationships that develop over longstanding working relationships.

---

[36] 15 U.S.C. §78j-1. For a discussion of the complexity of conflicting roles, see *Rhode Island Economic Development Corp. v. Wells Fargo Securities, LLC*, 2013 WL 4711306 (R.I. 2013).
[37] 15 U.S.C. §78j-1.

SOX also requires accounting firms to set up internal systems for developing and monitoring professional ethics and for the discussion of ethical issues that arise during the course of the audits of clients.

CPA 46-3b SOX and Audit Committees

SOX also addresses issues on the corporate side of the interaction between auditors and companies—the audit committee of the company's board. Under the statute, audit committees must be composed of board members who are independent, defined in the statute as directors who do not accept consulting or other fees from the company and who are not affiliated with the company, certain of its employees, or any of its subsidiaries.[38]

Members of audit committees must also be allowed to interact with auditors without management being present and also be permitted to hire independent advisors. At least one member of the audit committee must be a financial expert or someone who understands financial reporting and audit work. The audit committee is now the central point for ensuring that SOX standards are being followed.

Audit committees are required to establish procedures whereby they can be notified of problems with the company's internal controls. Audit committees need to establish the means and mechanisms for monitoring the company's internal control systems so they can verify that financial reports are based on data generated by effective company reporting systems.

CPA 46-3c SOX and Records Retention

Accounting firm Arthur Andersen was convicted of one count of obstruction of justice for its destruction of Enron records while SEC investigations were pending. The conviction was later reversed because the court held that although there may have been sufficient evidence about individual Andersen employees' willful destruction of documents, the jury instructions were flawed in attributing that knowledge to the full Andersen firm automatically without proof of actual knowledge (an element required in all criminal

E-COMMERCE & CYBERLAW

Emails: The Destruction of a Career, Destruction of a Firm

The congressional investigation into the Enron collapse uncovered the following e-mails:

- A May 28, 1999, e-mail to David Duncan from Benjamin Neuhausen, a member of Andersen's Professional Standards Group at its Chicago main office, evaluated the wisdom of having Enron's CFO Andrew Fastow as the principal in a company that was off the books and doing trades with Enron: "Setting aside the accounting, idea of a venture entity managed by CFO is terrible from a business point of view. Conflicts galore. Why would any director in his or her right mind ever approve such a scheme?"

- A June 1, 1999, e-mail from David Duncan responded: "[O]n your point 1 (i.e., the whole thing is a bad idea), I really couldn't agree more. Rest assured that I have already communicated and it has been agreed to by Andy that CEO, General [Counsel], and Board discussion and approval will be a requirement, on our part, for acceptance of a venture similar to what we have been discussing."

These e-mails are discoverable and admissible when litigation results from an auditor's work. The only protections are the privilege between lawyer and client, but these e-mails were between auditors who worked for the same audit firm.

---

[38] 15 U.S.C. §1741.

cases; see Chapter 8).[39] The statute used for prosecution in that case was not specific enough to tie the firm to individual employee conduct. Furthermore, the penalties, even with such a conviction, were minimal. As discussed in Chapter 8, SOX substantially increased both the scope of and penalties for the obstruction of justice through accountants' and auditors' destruction of records. Under Sarbanes-Oxley, those who destroy, conceal, alter, or mutilate documents when either a civil or criminal investigation is pending are subject to up to 20 years' imprisonment as well as fines.[40]

CPA   46-3d Dodd-Frank and Accountants as Whistleblowers

Under the Dodd-Frank Act (see Chapter 45 for more information), accountants who work for audit firms are not permitted to use information obtained during the court of an audit for purposes of obtaining an award that comes from their reporting information to the SEC that results in an enforcement action. Auditors and audit firm responsibilities are to report any fraud at the company to management and the audit committee. If the board takes no action, the auditor must then go to the SEC. Auditors are only eligible for whistleblower rewards if they report conduct by the company that is intended to thwart an SEC investigation.

Make the Connection

Summary

Professionals who agree to perform services for others must perform those services according to the standards of the profession. Accountants, as professionals, must perform their audit work at the levels and standards of competency and thoroughness established for their profession. If an accountant negligently fails to observe those standards, the accountant could be liable for breach of contract or negligence. This tort of negligent breach of contract constitutes malpractice, and the other party to the contract can recover from the accountant either for breach of contract or for the negligence involved.

In some circumstances, not only are accountants liable to their clients, they may also be liable for malpractice to certain third parties who have used or relied on the financial statement. States and courts differ as to when an accountant is liable to third parties. Some courts do not recognize accountant liability to third parties; these courts require privity between the parties. Most courts hold accountants liable to some third parties but differ as to which third parties and how far to extend the

accountant's liability. The various rules that determine accountant liability to third parties are the contact rule, which requires that the third party must have had some contact with the accountant before there can be liability; the known user rule in which the accountant is aware of the third party who will use the accountant's information; the foreseeability rule in which the accountant is held liable if it was possible to foresee that the third party would use the accountant's information; the intended user rule in which the client tells the accountant of the intended use of the audit work; the unknown user rule in which the accountant is not liable to third parties it could not have known would use the information or audit work; and the flexible rule that decides on a case-by-case basis.

Accountants guilty of fraud have liability to all third parties, even those not in privity of contract with the accountant.

To a limited degree, an accountant is protected from malpractice liability by a disclaimer of liability or by the contributory negligence of the plaintiff.

---

[39] *Andersen, LLP v. U.S.*, 544 U.S. 696 (2005). David Duncan, the partner in charge of the Enron account, withdrew his guilty plea on obstruction when the court reversed the firm's guilty verdict.
[40] 18 U.S.C. §1512. Persuading another to destroy documents is obstruction of justice. *People v. Alcindor*, 118 A.D.3d (N.Y. 2014); *U.S. v. Katakis*, 21 F. Supp. 3d 1018 (E.D. Cal. 2014).

Sarbanes-Oxley (SOX) increases the penalties for accountants who destroy documents when civil or criminal investigations are pending. The act also prohibits conduct by accountants that creates a conflict of interest and requires audit firms to register for authorization to do audit work on public companies. Audit committees of boards are now required to work closely with auditors to make sure that the financial systems in the company and

its reports are sound. A federal oversight board reviews the work of audit firms and is authorized to discipline audit firms and accountants for their failure to honor standards or comply with the law.

Auditors have responsibilities under Dodd-Frank to raise issues to both the audit committee and the board. However, Dodd-Frank whistleblower provisions do not apply to auditors unless the company is obstructing an investigation.

Learning Outcomes

After studying this chapter, you should be able to clearly explain:

46-1   General Principles of Accountants' Liability

LO.1   Define *malpractice*

See the section titled "What Constitutes Malpractice?" page 956.

See *Dale K. Barker Co., P.C. v. Valley Plaza* for a discussion of accountant liability for failure to reach a reasonable settlement with the IRS, page 957.

LO.2   Distinguish malpractice liability from breach of contract liability

See the section titled "Choice of Remedy," pages 957–958.

See *Cast Art Industries, LLC v. KPMG LLP*, pages 963–964.

46-2   Accountants' Liability to Third Parties: Beyond Privity

LO.3   List which third parties may recover for the malpractice liability of accountants and when they may do so

See *Dewar v. Smith* for a discussion of privity, forseeability, and liability, pages 961–962.

LO.4   Discuss the difference between accounting malpractice and fraud

See the *Carlson v. Xerox Corp* case, pages 968–969.

See Ethics & the Law on auditor for Bernie Madoff feeder fund, page 958.

46-3   Federal Laws on Auditors, Accounting, & Financial Reporting

LO.5   Explain how Sarbanes-Oxley and Dodd-Frank have affected the accounting profession and accountants' liability

See the E-Commerce & Cyberlaw feature, page 971.

Key Terms

comparative negligence	limitation-of-liability clause	privity rule
contributory negligence	malpractice	
exculpatory clause	misrepresentation	

Questions and Case Problems

1.   The auditing firm of Timm, Schmidt & Co. prepared annual financial statements for Clintonville Fire Apparatus, Inc. (CFA). CFA showed these statements to Citizens State Bank and asked for loans. On the basis of the financial statements, Citizens loaned CFA approximately $380,000. Timm later discovered that the financial statements overvalued CFA by more than $400,000. Citizens demanded repayment of the loans. CFA could not pay the balance, and Citizens sued Timm and its

malpractice liability insurer. They raised the defense that the suit was barred by lack of privity and the fact that no one in the Timm firm knew that CFA intended to use the financial statements to obtain loans from anyone. Is the lack of privity a defense? [*Citizens State Bank v. Timm, Schmidt & Co.*, 335 N.W.2d 361 (Wis.)]

2.   Parente, Randolph, Orlando & Associates (Parente) is an accounting firm that had done auditing work for Sparkomatic for nearly 20 years. On June 14,

1993, Sparkomatic entered into a Memorandum of Intent with Williams Controls to sell Williams assets from Sparkomatic's Kenco division. The sale price was to be the "audited book value" of the assets, and the book value would be based on the June 30, 1993, balance sheet (which Parente did not prepare). Sparkomatic then engaged Parente to audit the financial statements for December 31, 1990, 1991, and 1992 and to prepare an interim balance sheet for 1993.

On August 1, 1993, Sparkomatic and Williams Controls entered into an asset purchase agreement, which required that Williams be furnished financials through June 1993 as prepared by "Sparkomatic's independent public accountant." Parente was not identified by name in the agreement. Parente did review the asset purchase agreement with Williams prior to commencing its work and knew that Williams would be using the information Parente prepared.

Following the closing, additional information came to light indicating that Williams had overpaid for the assets of Kenco, and Williams filed suit against Parente for negligence, negligent misrepresentation, and breach of contract. Parente moved for summary judgment. What should the decision be and why? Discuss several possible theories. [*Williams Controls v. Parente, Randolph, Orlando, & Associates*, 39 F. Supp. 2d 517 (M.D. Pa.)]

3. David S. Talesnick served as the accountant for Kenneth Ronson and his wife as well as for Ronson's company, performing accounting and tax services for all. From 1980 to 1983, Ronson, his wife, and his company invested in the White Rim Oil & Gas, Pine Coal, and Winchester Coal limited partnerships. During those years, the Ronsons and his company were able to report losses on their income tax returns because of these investments. However, the IRS determined that the limited partnerships were not qualified investments under the tax code and disallowed the loss deductions. The Ronsons and his company all owed back taxes, interest, and penalties as a result. The Ronsons disputed the finding and asked Talesnick how they might appeal the ruling and not have the interest clock ticking on what they owed. Talesnick wrote a letter and advised them to post a bond of $91,300, the amount then due. Talesnick was incorrect in his advice on payment and accrual of interest, and by the time the final determination was made against the Ronsons and Ronson's

company, they owed $235,063 with interest. The Ronsons sued Talesnick for malpractice. Could they recover? How much? [*Ronson v. David S. Talesnick, CPA*, 33 F. Supp. 2d 347 (D.N.J.)]

4. The certified public accounting partnership of James, Guinn, and Head prepared a certified audit report of four corporations, known as the Paschal Enterprises, with knowledge that their report would be used to induce Shatterproof Glass Corp. to lend money to those corporations. The report showed the corporations to be solvent when in fact they were insolvent. Shatterproof relied on the audit report, loaned approximately $500,000 to the four corporations, and lost almost all of it because the liabilities of the companies were in excess of their assets. Shatterproof claimed that James and other accountants had been negligent in preparing the report and sued them to recover the loss on the loan. The accountants raised the defense that they had been retained not by Shatterproof but by Paschal. Was this defense valid? [*Shatterproof Glass Corp. v. James*, 466 S.W.2d 873 (Tex. App.)]

5. AUSA Life Insurance Company and others were institutional investors in the securities of JWP, Inc., a company that went belly up, resulting in nearly a 100 percent loss of their investments. Ernst & Young served as auditor for JWP from 1985 to 1992. During most of that period, JWP was in a period of rapid expansion that was financed by private placements of debt securities, and it became increasingly leveraged. By 1991, it was losing an average of $10 million per month. Ernst & Young knew of "accounting irregularities" from at least 1988 through 1991 but did not insist on their correction. Ernst & Young issued unqualified financial opinions for all of those years. One of the irregularities was recording anticipated future tax benefits of net operating loss in violation of GAAP. AUSA and its fellow investors sued Ernst & Young for their losses. The federal district court dismissed the case and AUSA appealed. Should AUSA be able to recover? Explain your answer. [*AUSA Life Insurance Co. v. Ernst & Young*, 206 F.3d 202 (2d Cir.), 119 F. Supp. 2d 394 (S.D.N.Y.), aff'd in unpublished opinion]

6. For almost 13 years, Touche Ross had prepared the annual audit of Buttes Gas and Oil Co. Buttes wanted to obtain a loan from Dimensional Credit Corp. (DCC) and showed DCC its most recent annual audit. DCC made the loan on the basis of

what it learned from the audit. The loan was not repaid, and DCC then realized that it had been misled by negligent statements about Buttes's financial condition that appeared in the annual statement prepared by Touche Ross. Would DCC be able to recover against Touche Ross for its negligence in preparing this report?

7. Henry Hatfield, CPA, was hired to prepare audited financial statements for Happy Campers, a nonprofit organization providing summer camp scholarships for inner-city, low-income children. The executive director of Happy Campers was embezzling but falsified records that Hatfield used in his audit. First Bank gave Happy Campers a $100,000 loan based on Hatfield's certified financials. The embezzlement was discovered, and Happy Campers defaulted on the loan. Can First Bank recover its loss from Hatfield?

8. What are an accountant's obligations if he or she knows a client is violating the terms of a contract with a third party?

9. Hicks, the president and manager of Intermountain Merchandising, wanted to sell the business to Montana Merchandising, Inc. To provide a basis for the transaction, he retained Bloomgren, an accountant, to conduct an audit of Intermountain. Bloomgren knew that Montana would use the audit report in making the purchase of the business from Intermountain. Bloomgren's audit report showed the Intermountain business as profitable. Thayer, Montana's president, relied on this report in agreeing to purchase the business of Intermountain and in agreeing to the terms of the purchase. Sometime later, it was discovered that the accountant had made a number of mistakes and that the business that was sold was actually insolvent. Thayer and Montana Merchandising sued Hicks and Bloomgren for damages. The suit claimed that the accountant had negligently misrepresented the facts. The accountant defended on the basis that Thayer was not in privity of contract with him and therefore could not sue him. Was he right? [*Thayer v. Hicks*, 793 P.2d 784 (Mont.)]

10. McGladrey conducted a financial audit of Subspecialty Centers of America, LLC (SCA). SCA is owned by Dr. Mark S. Weinberger, an ear, nose, and throat surgeon. The audit was for the year ending December 31, 2003. McGladrey issued its audit report in March 2004. The audit report indicated that SCA's "balance sheet presents fairly in all material respects to the financial position of SCA in conformity with generally accepted auditing standards." Citibank received the audit report and in June 2004 made a $1.4 million term loan to SCA. The term loan was a modification of a prior term loan that Citibank had made to SCA. Prior to 2004, Citibank had four outstanding loans to SCA: (1) a mortgage loan for its diagnostic surgery center; (2) a mortgage loan for its office condominium; (3) a revolving line of credit; and (4) a term loan. The 2004 term loan was an increase and an extension of the prior term loan.

Dr. Weinberger took the $1.4 million and left for Europe. Dr. Weinberger was subsequently located residing in a tent in the Italian Alps and was brought back to the United States in 2010. Hundreds of malpractice suits were filed against him, and federal prosecutors charged him with multiple counts of health care fraud.

Citibank brought suit to recover money it loaned SCA ($1.4 million term loan) from McGladrey on the grounds that it negligently audited Dr. Weinberger's surgical practice. Citibank claims that it relied on McGladrey's audit in making the $1.4 million term loan to SCA. Discuss whether Citibank would be able to recover and under what theories and standing. [*Citibank, N.A. v. McGladrey and Pullen, LLP*, 953 N.E.2d 38 (Ill. App.)]

11. Equisure, Inc., was required to file audited financial statements when it applied for a listing on the American Stock Exchange (AMEX). Stirtz, Equisure's auditor, issued a favorable audit opinion used for the AMEX application. Stirtz also issued "clean" opinions on Equisure's required SEC filings, such as its 10k.

Noram, a securities broker, loaned $900,000 in margin credit to purchasers of Equisure's stock based on the firm's audited financials. AMEX stopped trading on Equisure's stock because of allegations of insider trading and stock manipulation, and Noram was left without collateral for $2.5 million in loans. Stirtz resigned as Equisure's auditor, and Noram filed suit against Stirtz. The trial court granted Stirtz summary judgment. Noram appealed. Who is liable here? Was the court's decision correct? [*Noram Investment Services, Inc. v. Stirtz Bernards Boyden*, 611 N.W.2d 372 (Minn. App.)]

CPA Questions

1. In general, the third-party (primary) beneficiary rule as applied to a CPA's legal liability in conducting an audit is relevant to which of the following causes of action against a CPA?

	Fraud	Constructive Fraud	Negligence
a.	Yes	Yes	No
b.	Yes	No	No
c.	No	Yes	Yes
d.	No	No	Yes

2. Beckler & Associates, CPAs, audited and gave an unqualified opinion on the financial statements of Queen Co. The financial statements contained misstatements that resulted in a material overstatement of Queen's net worth. Queen provided the audited financial statements to Mac Bank in connection with a loan made by Mac to Queen. Beckler knew that the financial statements would be provided to Mac. Queen defaulted on the loan. Mac sued Beckler to recover for its losses associated with Queen's default. Which of the following must Mac prove in order to recover?

   I. Beckler was negligent in conducting the audit.

   II. Mac relied on the financial statements.

   a. I only

   b. II only

   c. Both I and II

   d. Neither I nor II

3. In a common law action against an accountant, lack of privity is a viable defense if the plaintiff:

   a. Is the client's creditor who sues the accountant for negligence.

   b. Can prove the presence of gross negligence that amounts to a reckless disregard for the truth.

   c. Is the accountant's client.

   d. Bases the action upon fraud.

4. Cable Corp. orally engaged Drake & Co., CPAs, to audit its financial statements. Cable's management informed Drake that it suspected the accounts receivable were materially overstated. Though the financial statements Drake audited included a materially overstated accounts receivable balance, Drake issued an unqualified opinion. Cable used the financial statements to obtain a loan to expand its operations. Cable defaulted on the loan and incurred a substantial loss.

   If Cable sues Drake for negligence in failing to discover the overstatement, Drake's best defense would be that Drake did *not*:

   a. Have privity of contract with Cable.

   b. Sign an engagement letter.

   c. Perform the audit recklessly or with an intent to deceive.

   d. Violate generally accepted auditing standards in performing the audit.

5. Which of the following services is a CPA generally required to perform when conducting a personal financial planning engagement?

   a. Assisting the client to identify tasks that are essential in order to take action on planning decisions.

   b. Assisting the client to take action on planning decisions.

   c. Monitoring progress in achieving goals.

   d. Updating recommendations and revising planning decisions.

6. Which of the following statements is (are) correct regarding the common law elements that must be proven to support a finding of constructive fraud against a CPA misrepresentation?

   I. The plaintiff has justifiably relied on the CPA's misrepresentation.

   II. The CPA has acted in a grossly negligent manner.

   a. I only

   b. II only

   c. Both I and II

   d. Neither I nor II

Management of Corporations

Learning Outcomes ⟨⟨⟨

After studying this chapter, you should be able to

LO.1   Explain how shareholders, as owners of the corporation, exercise limited control over management by voting at shareholders' meetings to elect directors

LO.2   Explain the qualifications and powers of directors

LO.3   Explain the liability of directors and the meaning of the business judgment rule (BJR)

LO.4   Explain the obligation of officers—who have access to corporate information and agency powers—to not violate their fiduciary duties to the corporation

LO.5   Explain the rationale for the "say-on-pay" provision of the Dodd-Frank Act

LO.6   Explain how directors, officers, and the corporation itself may be criminally liable for regulatory offenses

47-1 Shareholders

A corporation is managed, directly or indirectly, by its shareholders, board of directors, and officers.[1] As owners, the shareholders have the right to control the corporation.

47-1a Extent of Management Control by Shareholders

As a practical matter, control of the shareholders is generally limited to voting at shareholders' meetings to elect directors. In this sense, shareholders indirectly determine the management policies of the business. At shareholders' meetings, shareholders may also vote to amend bylaws, approve shareholder resolutions, or vote on so-called extraordinary corporate matters. *Extraordinary matters* include the sale of corporate assets outside the regular course of the corporation's business or the merger or dissolution of the corporation.

47-1b Meetings of Shareholders

To have legal effect, action by the shareholders must ordinarily be taken at a regular or special meeting.

Regular Meetings

The time and place of regular or stated meetings are usually prescribed by the articles of incorporation or the bylaws. Notice to shareholders of such meetings is ordinarily not required, but it is usually given as a matter of good business practice. Some statutes require that notice of all meetings be given.

Special Meetings

Generally, notice must be given specifying the subject matter of special meetings. Unless otherwise prescribed, special meetings are called by the directors. It is sometimes provided that a special meeting may be called by a certain percentage of shareholders.[2] Notice of the day, hour, and place of a special meeting must be given to all shareholders. The notice must include a statement of the nature of the business to be transacted, and no other business may be transacted at this meeting.

Quorum

quorum–minimum number of persons, shares represented, or directors who must be present at a meeting in order to lawfully transact business.

A valid meeting requires the presence of a quorum of the voting shareholders. A **quorum** is the minimum number of persons (shareholders or persons authorized to vote a stated proportion of the voting stock) required to transact business. If a quorum is present, a majority of those present may act on any matter unless there is an express requirement of a higher affirmative vote.

When a meeting opens with a quorum, the quorum is generally not broken if shareholders leave the meeting and those remaining are not sufficient to constitute a quorum.

---

[1] State corporate codes as well as federal laws such as the Securities Act of 1933 and the Securities Exchange Act of 1934, as amended by the Sarbanes Oxley Act of 2002 and the Dodd-Frank Act of 2010, impact the management of corporations. Articles of incorporation and corporate bylaws also impact corporate management. Chapter 43, Corporation Formation, and Chapter 45, Securities Regulation, provide background on these issues.
[2] N.Y. Bus. Corp. Law §603.

47-1c Action without Meeting

A number of statutes provide for corporate action by shareholders without holding a meeting. The Revised Model Business Corporation Act (RMBCA) provides that "action required or permitted by this Act to be taken at a shareholders' meeting may be taken without a meeting if the action is taken by all shareholders entitled to vote on the action."[3] The action must be evidenced by a written consent describing the action taken, signed by all shareholders entitled to vote on the action, and delivered to the corporation for inclusion in the minutes.

47-2 Directors

A state's corporate law or the articles of incorporation delegate powers to the board of directors. The board has oversight responsibility for a company's business affairs, including (1) approving strategic plans, (2) reviewing operating and financial results, (3) approving SEC filings, (4) approving the hiring of executives, (5) evaluating management's performance and approving executive compensation packages, (6) appointing and meeting with auditors, and (7) evaluating and acting on extraordinary matters, such as the merger, acquisition, or sale of the business.

Most states now permit the number of directors to be fixed by the bylaws. Many specify that the board of directors shall consist of not less than three directors; a few authorize one or more.[4] Professional corporation legislation often authorizes or is interpreted as authorizing a one- or two-person board of directors.

47-2a Qualifications

Eligibility for membership on a board of directors is determined by statute, articles of incorporation, or bylaws.[5] In the absence of a contrary provision, any person (including a nonresident, a minor, or a person who is not a shareholder) is eligible for membership. Bylaws may require that a director own stock in the corporation although this requirement is not ordinarily imposed.

CPA 47-2b Powers of Directors

The board of directors has authority to manage the corporation. Courts will not interfere with the board's discretion in the absence of (1) illegal conduct or (2) fraud harming the rights of creditors, shareholders, or the corporation.

The board of directors may enter into any contract or transaction necessary to carry out the business for which the corporation was formed. The board may appoint officers and other agents to act for the company, or it may appoint several of its own members as an executive committee to act for the board between board meetings. (See Figure 47-1.) Broad delegation of authority, however, may involve the risk of being treated as an unlawful abdication of the board's management power.

---

[3] RMBCA §7.04(a).

[4] Del. Code §141(b). See also RMBCA §8.03.

[5] In family-owned businesses, shareholder agreements are often utilized to impose restrictions on the voting of shares and eligibility standards for membership on the board of directors to maintain continuity of management, ownership, and control of a corporation. See *Miniat v. EMI*, 315 F.3d 712 (7th Cir. 2002).

CASE SUMMARY

The Case of Medoff, the Marathon Man

FACTS: The Boston Athletic Association (BAA) is a nonprofit corporation created to sponsor the annual Boston Marathon. The BAA authorized its president, William Cloney, to negotiate contracts for it. Cloney executed a contract with attorney Marshall Medoff, giving Medoff exclusive power to promote the marathon. The BAA transferred to Medoff all rights to use the marathon name and logos. The contract's financial terms were extremely favorable to Medoff, who could renew the contract from year to year. When the BAA's board members learned of the contract, they declared that it was beyond the authorization vested in Cloney. The board brought an action to have the contract set aside. Medoff contended that Cloney had authority to make the contract and that therefore the contract bound the corporation.

DECISION: Judgment for the BAA. It is the obligation of the board to direct the corporation. Consistent with this obligation, a board may delegate general managerial functions to corporate officers, but certain powers cannot be delegated. The contract made with Medoff surrendered virtually complete control of the marathon to Medoff. The board in this case improperly delegated to Cloney the authority to make such a contract, which prevented accomplishment of the BAA's corporate purpose, that of sponsoring the marathon. Authority to make such a contract was beyond the power of the board to delegate. [***Boston Athletic Association v. International Marathon, Inc.,*** 467 N.E.2d 58 (Mass. 1984)]

FIGURE 47-1   Powers of Directors

CPA   47-2c   Conflict of Interest

A director is disqualified from taking part in corporate action involving a matter in which the director has an undisclosed conflicting interest. The corporation generally may avoid any transaction because of a director's undisclosed conflict of interest.

A number of states provide by statute that a director's conflict of interest does not impair the transaction or contract entered into or authorized by the board of directors if the disqualified director disclosed the interest and if the contract or transaction is fair and reasonable with respect to the corporation. Thus, a director may lend money to a corporation if the board of directors is informed of the transaction and the terms approximate the market rate for businesses with similar credit ratings. Some states simply require notice of the conflicting interests and abstaining from all participation in the transaction. **For Example,** Delos Yancey, Jr., and Delos Yancey III were directors of State Mutual Insurance Co. Subsequently, they formed North American Services, Inc., and served as directors of both companies. State Mutual decided to sell one of its companies, Atlas Life Insurance, Inc. North American expressed an interest in purchasing Atlas, and thereafter the Yanceys recused themselves from State Mutual's decision-making process in selling the company. State Mutual sold Atlas to North American at a $5.2 million loss. Some two years later, North American resold Atlas for a $22.6 million gain, and a shareholder derivative suit was brought against the Yanceys. The court decided the case in favor of the Yanceys, holding that they complied with the state's "safe harbor" law by giving notice of their conflicting interest to State Mutual and thereafter abstaining from all participation in the corporate transaction.[6]

To prevent conflicts of interest and covert compensation schemes, section 402(a) of the federal Sarbanes-Oxley Act[7] prohibits all loans either directly or indirectly to directors and executive officers by their corporations. The act makes an exception for companies in the consumer credit business, which may make loans to directors and officers on terms no more favorable than those offered to the general public.

Prior to Sarbanes-Oxley, it was a common practice for publicly traded companies to provide low-interest loans to company officers. **For Example,** Bernard Ebbers, while CEO of WorldCom, Inc., used company stock as collateral for bank loans to buy additional shares of WorldCom stock. When WorldCom's share prices weakened in late 2000 and Ebbers needed to put up additional collateral to cover his loans, WorldCom's board of directors agreed to lend him more than $400 million at just over 2 percent interest with no fixed due date. The company rate was far below the personal loan rate at banks near company headquarters of between 9.75 percent and 16.67 percent and well below margin loan rates at 5 percent. Another scandal involved business conglomerate Tyco International Ltd. Tyco maintained a "key employee loan fund" that was used like a revolving line of credit by Tyco executives Dennis Kozlowski and Martin Swartz to fund their lavish lifestyles. Sarbanes-Oxley responded to these abuses with language that is broad and far-reaching, prohibiting all direct personal loans by public companies, such as relocation loans, tax loans, and loans to purchase securities.

47-2d Meetings of Directors

Action by directors is ordinarily taken at a meeting of the board of directors. Bylaws sometimes require the meeting to be held at a particular place. Generally, a director is not allowed to vote by proxy. Most states permit action to be taken by the board of directors without holding an actual meeting. A meeting may be required, however, if the action requires a writing signed by all directors.

47-2e Liability of Directors

In dealing with the corporation, the directors act in a fiduciary capacity. It is into their care that the stockholders have entrusted the control of the corporate property and the management of the business.

---

[6] *Fisher v. State Mutual Insurance Co.*, 290 F.3d 1256 (11th Cir. 2002).
[7] P.L. 107-204, 116 Stat. 745.

CPA

The Business Judgment Rule

Courts recognize that the decisions of corporate directors often involve weighing and balancing legal, ethical, commercial, promotional, public relations, and other factors. Accordingly, courts will not sit in judgment or second guess the wisdom of decisions made by directors. If the directors have acted in good faith on the basis of adequate information, courts will not enjoin the course of action taken by the directors.[8] Moreover, if directors' decisions cause loss to the corporation, the directors will not be held personally liable for it. This principle is called the **business judgment rule (BJR).** It is one of the most important protections against personal liability for officers and directors.

business judgment rule (BJR)–rule that allows management immunity from **CPA** liability for corporate acts where there is a reasonable indication that the acts were made in good faith with due care.

The Traditional Rule. Courts apply the business judgment rule as a presumption that in making a business decision, the directors acted (1) on an informed basis, (2) in good faith, and (3) in the honest belief that the action taken was in the best interest of the corporation. The party challenging the directors' actions has the burden of proving that the director did not act on an informed basis or in good faith or in the best interest of the corporation.[9] (See the *Disney* case.)

CASE SUMMARY

Problem: "A Mismatch of Cultures and Styles"
Solution: $140 Million Severance Payment
Shareholders: Not Happy!

FACTS: In 1995, Michael Ovitz was a founder of Creative Artists Agency (CAA), an agency with 1,400 of Hollywood's top actors, directors, writers, and musicians. Ovitz was considered one of the most powerful figures in Hollywood at that time. Because of the untimely death of Disney's prior president in a helicopter crash, Walt Disney Co. CEO Michael Eisner focused on hiring Ovitz as president. The chairman of Disney's compensation committee, Irwin Russell, in consultation with Eisner, negotiated the Ovitz employment agreement (OEA). As part of the OEA, if Disney fired Ovitz for any reason other than gross negligence or malfeasance, Ovitz would be entitled to a nonfault termination (NFT) package consisting of his remaining salary for the five-year period, bonuses, and the immediate vesting of stock options. Russell met with a compensation expert for advice on the contract and had telephone conversations with two compensation committee members, Sidney Poitier and Ignatio Lozano. CEO Eisner telephoned each member of the board of directors to inform them of his plan to hire Ovitz. On September 26, 1995, the Compensation Committee had a one-hour meeting to discuss several topics, including the OEA. Thereafter, the full board of directors met and elected Ovitz president of Disney. After he joined Disney, it soon became apparent that a "mismatch of cultures and styles" ensued and that Ovitz was not succeeding as president. The trial provided the following example:

> In January 1996, a corporate retreat was held at Walt Disney World in Orlando, Florida. At that retreat, Ovitz failed to integrate himself in the group of executives by declining to participate in group activities, insisting on a limousine, when the other executives, including Eisner, were taking a bus, and making inappropriate demands of the park employees. In short, Ovitz "was a little elitist for the egalitarian Walt Disney World cast members [employees]," and a poor fit with his fellow executives.

When it became clear that Ovitz was not working out, Eisner considered his options. Sanford Litvak, Disney's general counsel, advised Eisner and other directors that Ovitz had not been shown to have been grossly negligent or malfeasant

---

[8] In discharging their duties, directors are not individually liable if, acting in good faith, they rely upon "the opinion of counsel for the corporation" or "written reports setting forth financial data concerning the corporation and prepared by an independent public accountant or certified public accountant or firm of such accountants"—which opinions or statements turn out to be flawed. *Casey v. Brennan*, 344 N.J. Super. 83 (2002).

[9] *Huang Group v. LTI*, 760 N.E.2d 14 (Ohio App. 2002).

Problem: "A Mismatch of Cultures and Styles" continued

in his year at Disney, and no cause existed to avoid the NFT payments. Eisner decided it was necessary to terminate Ovitz on a nonfault basis and notified the board members. The board members supported this decision under the nonfault termination agreement. Ovitz was ultimately paid $140 million in severance pay. Stockholders brought a derivative suit, asserting that Eisner and the board of directors had breached their fiduciary duties in connection with Ovitz's hiring and termination. Years of litigation cumulated in a 37-day trial that ended on January 19, 2005.

DECISION: Judgment for the defendants. Eisner's actions should not serve as a model for directors and CEOs. By virtue of his imperial nature as CEO, he handicapped the board's decision-making abilities, stacking the board with his friends who, although not necessarily beholden to him in a legal sense, were more willing to support him unconditionally than truly independent directors. He failed to keep the board informed as he should have and failed to better involve the board in the process of hiring Ovitz, usurping the role for himself. Nevertheless, Eisner did not violate the law. Despite the legitimate criticisms leveled at Eisner, especially at having enthroned himself as the omnipotent and infallible monarch of his personal Magic Kingdom, Eisner's actions were taken in good faith and did not breach his fiduciary duty of care because he was not grossly negligent, nor was any other director in violation of a fiduciary duty. The redress for failures that arise from faithful management (not in violation of fiduciary duties) must come from the markets, not the courts. Corporate decisions are made, risks are taken, the results become apparent, capital flows accordingly, and shareholder value increases or decreases. [**In re Walt Disney Co. Derivative Litigation, 907 A.2d 693 (Del. Ch. 2005)**]

CPA   **Application in Corporate Control Transactions.** When a corporation receives a takeover bid, the target board of directors may tend to take actions that favor the board's interests over the interests of shareholders. Courts have recognized the potential for director self-interest in this situation. (See the *Van Gorkom* case.)

CASE SUMMARY

Directors—Independent Evaluators, Not Pawns

FACTS: Jerome Van Gorkom was chairman and chief executive officer of Trans Union Inc. On September 13, Van Gorkom arranged a meeting with Jay Pritzker, a well-known takeover specialist and a social acquaintance, to determine his interest in acquiring Trans Union. On Thursday, September 18, Pritzker made an offer of $55 per share (a price suggested by Van Gorkom). Pritzker wanted a decision to be made by the board no later than Sunday, September 21. On Friday, Van Gorkom called a special meeting of the board of directors for noon the following day; no agenda was announced. At the directors' meeting, Van Gorkom made a 20-minute oral analysis of the merger transaction. He showed that the company was having difficulty generating sufficient income to offset its increasingly large investment tax credits. Van Gorkom discussed his meeting with Pritzker and the reasons for the meeting. Copies of the proposed merger agreement were delivered too late to be studied before or during the meeting. No consultants or investment advisors were called on to support the merger price of $55 per share. The merger was approved at the end of the two-hour meeting. Certain shareholders brought a class-action suit against the directors, contending that the board's decision was not the product of informed business judgment. The directors responded that their good-faith decision was shielded by the business judgment rule.

DECISION: Judgment for the shareholders. Directors cannot claim the protection of the business judgment rule if they have been grossly negligent in exercising their judgment. The directors approved the merger based on a 20-minute oral analysis by the president, Van Gorkom, at a hastily called board meeting with no prior notice of its purpose. No investment consultants or other experts were employed to assess the intrinsic value of the company, nor were the merger documents containing the terms of the merger available for study by the directors. Deciding to sell the company without any information and deliberation was gross negligence. The directors therefore could not claim the protection of the business judgment rule when they voted to "sell" the company for $55 per share. The directors are personally liable for damages. [**Smith v. Van Gorkom, 488 A.2d 858 (Del. 1985)**]

Protection of Directors. In the wake of court decisions holding directors personally liable for damages for gross negligence and in the wake of the resulting general reluctance of individuals to serve as directors, states have passed statutes to protect directors. The aim of the various state laws is essentially the same: to reduce the risk of personal liability for directors who act in good faith when their decisions are challenged. The laws permit a corporation, by a stockholder-approved amendment to its charter or certificate of incorporation, to protect its directors from monetary liability for duty-of-care violations (gross negligence) provided they have not acted in bad faith, breached their duty of loyalty, or gained an improper personal benefit.[10] The laws provide for indemnification and advancement of expenses. **For Example,** the certificate of incorporation of Jennifer Convertibles, Inc., a Delaware corporation, includes an exculpatory clause that protects directors from liability for breach of fiduciary duty except in cases of breach of duty of loyalty, bad faith, knowing violation of the law, or improper personal benefit. Delaware's General Corporate Law, section 102(b)(7), states that a corporation may include an exculpation clause in its certificate of incorporation.[11] Statutes intended to protect directors from liability have raised questions about whether the business judgment rule applies to officers. Although most courts recognize that the business judgment rule applies to both directors and officers,[12] several courts have held that the rule applies only to independent directors, not to officers if the state statute refers only to directors.[13]

Actions against Directors

Actions against directors should be brought by the corporation. If the corporation fails to act, as is the case when the directors alleged to be liable control the corporation, shareholders may bring the action in a representative capacity for the corporation.[14] **For Example,** Risa Weinberger, a shareholder, became concerned that the president and majority shareholder of American Composting Inc., James Willits, was using corporate funds for his own personal benefit. Corporate bank statements showed payments to his ex-wife of $283,068.48, payments to the law firm that represented him in his divorce of $145,789, and a "loans to shareholders" balance that increased from $21,075 in 2004 to $444,642 by September 2011. The court determined that Ms. Weinberger could pursue the shareholder derivative suit on behalf of American Composting Inc. because Willets controlled the board of directors and a demand on the board would be futile.[15]

Removal of Director

Ordinarily, directors are removed by vote of the shareholders. In some states, the board of directors may remove a director and elect a successor on the ground that the removed director (1) did not accept office, (2) failed to satisfy the qualifications for office, (3) was continually absent from the state without a leave of absence granted by the board, generally for a period of six months or more, (4) was discharged in bankruptcy, (5) was

---

[10] See Del. Code §102(b)(7); N.Y. Bus. Corp. Law §§721–723; Ohio Gen. Corp. Law §1701.59; Ind. Bus. Corp. Law, ch. 35, §1(e); Mo. Gen. Bus. Corp. Law 351.355 §§2, 7.

[11] In *KDW Restructuring & Liquidation Services LLC v. Greenfield*, 2012 WL 2125986 (S.D.N.Y. June 12, 2012), the court found that there were sufficient facts in the complaint against Harley Greenfield, Jennifer's CEO, to support claims for breach of duty of loyalty and breach of the duty to act in good faith regarding a 2009 transaction causing a net loss of $11 million at the end of the 2009 fiscal year.

[12] See, for example, *FDIC v. Loudermilk, et al.*, 761 S.E.2d 332 (Ga. 2014).

[13] Several decisions by federal district courts in California ruled that the business judgment rule applies only to independent directors, under California law. These cases involved suits by the Federal Deposit Insurance Corporation against officers at failed banks. The FDIC sued the officers for negligence in generating and acquiring risky residential loans. See, for example, *FDIC v. Perry*, 2012 WL 589569 (C.D. Cal. 2012); *FDIC v. Faigin*, 2013 WL 3389490 (C.D. Cal. 2013).

[14] In re *Abbott Laboratories Derivative Shareholder Litigation*, 325 F.3d 795 (7th Cir. 2003).

[15] *Weinberger v. American Composting, Inc.*, 2012 WL 1190970 (E.D. Ark. Apr. 9, 2012).

convicted of a felony, (6) was unable to perform the duties of director because of any illness or disability, generally for a period of six months or more, or (7) had been judicially declared of unsound mind.[16]

The RMBCA provides for removal of directors "with or without cause" by a majority vote of the shareholders unless the articles of incorporation provide that directors may be removed only for cause.[17] **For Example,** former Conseco, Inc., director Dennis Murray, Sr., was unsuccessful in his action against the board of directors in challenging his removal from the board. The court held that the directors had unlimited authority to remove a fellow director without regard for the reasons why the other directors wished to remove him.[18] Directors may always be voted out of office at a regular meeting of shareholders held for the election of directors.

47-3   Officers, Agents, and Employees

Corporations generally have a president, at least one vice president, a secretary, a treasurer, and, frequently, a chief executive officer (CEO). The duties of these officers are generally set forth in the corporation's bylaws. The duty of the secretary to keep minutes of the proceedings of shareholders and directors is commonly included. Corporation codes generally expressly permit the same person to be both secretary and treasurer. In large corporations, there is often a recording secretary and a corresponding secretary.

Sometimes the officers are elected by the shareholders, but usually they are appointed by the board of directors. The RMBCA follows the general pattern of providing for the appointment of officers by the board of directors.[19] Ordinarily, no particular formality is required to make such appointments. Unless prohibited, a director may hold an executive office.

Officers ordinarily hire the employees and agents of the corporation.

47-3a Powers of Officers

The officers of a corporation are its agents. Consequently, their powers are controlled by the laws of agency.[20] As in the case of any other agency, a third person has the burden of proving that a particular officer had the authority he or she purported to have.

The fact that the officer or employee acting on behalf of the corporation is a major shareholder does not give either any greater agency powers. Moreover, the person dealing with the officer or employee is charged with knowledge of any limitation on authority contained in the recorded corporate charter or articles of incorporation.

When the nature of the transaction is unusual, that unusual nature should alert a third person to the necessity of specific authorization from the corporation.

President

It is sometimes held that, in the absence of some limitation on authority, the president of a corporation has by virtue of that office the authority to act as agent on behalf of the corporation within the scope of the business in which the corporation is empowered to engage. It has also been held, however, that the president has such broad powers only when the president is the general manager of the corporation. In instances in which a corporation has a president and a chief executive officer, the CEO has authority to exercise personal

---

[16] See California Corp Code §807, recognizing grounds (1), (2), (5), and (7).
[17] RMBCA §8.08(a).
[18] *Murray v. Conseco, Inc.*, 766 N.E.2d 38 (Ind. App. 2002).
[19] RMBCA §8.40(a).
[20] *Credit Corp. v. Nuova Pasta Co.*, 815 F. Supp. 268 (N.D. Ill. 1993).

judgment and discretion in the administrative and executive functions of the corporation as endowed by its bylaws and the resolutions of the board of directors. When a corporation has both a CEO and a president, the CEO is ordinarily the officer entrusted with the broader decisional powers, whereas the president is the executing officer. The president does not have authority by virtue of his office to make a contract that would require action by the board of directors or shareholders due to its unusual character.[21]

The president cannot make a contract to fix long-term or unusual contracts of employment, release a claim of the corporation, promise that the corporation will later repurchase shares issued to a subscriber, or mortgage a corporate property.[22]

It is ordinarily held that the president of a business corporation is not authorized to execute commercial paper in the name of the corporation. However, the president may do so when authorized by the board of directors to borrow money for the corporation.

Other Officers and Employees

The authority of corporate employees and other officers, such as the secretary or treasurer, is generally limited to the duties of their office. However, the authority may be extended by the conduct of the corporation in accordance with the general principles governing apparent authority based on the conduct of the principal. An unauthorized act may, of course, be ratified. The authority of the general manager of the corporation is determined by principles of ordinary agency law.

47-3b Liability Relating to Fiduciary Duties

The relationship of officers to the corporation, like that of directors, is a fiduciary one. Officers, because of their access to corporate information developed in the pursuit of their daily duties on behalf of the corporation, have an obligation to inform the directors of material information relating to the business. Officers have an obligation not to make any secret financial gain at the expense of the corporation. Because of their level of knowledge of the business, officer-directors have a high fiduciary duty to the corporation.

Corporate Opportunities

If an officer diverts a corporate opportunity, the corporation may recover from the officer the profits of which the corporation has been deprived.

CASE SUMMARY

Ruling Wisely and Decently?

FACTS: Demoulas Super Markets, Inc. (DSM), was owned by brothers George and Telemachus Demoulas, each owning an equal number of shares of stock. From 1964 through May 1971, the company grew from 5 stores to a chain of 14 supermarkets, including 2 stores in New Hampshire. George died suddenly on June 27, 1971, and, at his death, Telemachus assumed control of DSM under the terms of a voting trust. In 1990, George's son Arthur, age 22 and a shareholder of DSM, brought a shareholder derivative action on behalf of DSM, contending that since George's death, Telemachus had diverted business opportunities away from DSM into other businesses that were solely owned by Telemachus's branch of the family. The evidence showed that in the 1970s two new corporations were formed that operated

---

[21] *French v. Chosin Few, Inc.*, 173 F. Supp. 2d 451 (W.D.N.C. 2001).
[22] *Schmidt v. Farm Credit Services*, 977 F.2d 511 (10th Cir. 1992).

Ruling Wisely and Decently? continued

supermarkets in New Hampshire; DSM supplied the financing and management, but ownership was held in the name of Telemachus's sister and daughter. By 1986, these stores grew into a single supermarket chain operating under the Market Basket name and entirely owned by members of Telemachus's branch of the family. The trial court judge determined that Telemachus had diverted these corporate opportunities from DSM, and the court ordered the transfer of the assets and liabilities of the new corporations back to DSM. In her decision, the judge cited lines from *Ulysses*, by Alfred Lord Tennyson, in which Ulysses speaks lovingly of his son, Telemachus, expressing the belief that he would rule wisely and decently after his death. Telemachus denied that any acts were improper or gave rise to liability and charged that the judge was not impartial, as evidenced by her quotation from Tennyson's poem.

DECISION: Judgment against Telemachus. Judicial bias was not present, and the literary reference was simply the judge's stylistic way of stating the theme of her decision against Telemachus, based on the facts she had found. Telemachus had a fiduciary duty to DSM. A fiduciary violates his duty of loyalty by advancing the pecuniary interests of a child or a sibling in a manner that would constitute a breach if he had acted for himself. The record is clear that the New Hampshire companies were set up under Telemachus's direction and were independent in name only, with DSM managing and financing them. The return to DSM of the assets and liabilities of the diverted business was the proper remedy. [*Demoulas v. Demoulas Super Markets, Inc.*, 677 N.E.2d 159 (Mass. 1997); see also 787 N.E.2d 1059 (Mass. 2003)]

An opportunity that would be advantageous to the corporation must first be offered to the corporation before an officer or a director, who owes a fiduciary duty to the corporation, can take advantage of the opportunity. Full disclosure is required. Only if the opportunity is rejected by a majority of disinterested directors may the officer then take advantage of the opportunity. **For Example,** Nancy Harris was president of the Northeast Harbor Golf Club, Inc. In her capacity as club president, she learned of an opportunity to purchase the Gilpin property, which adjoined the golf club. Her private purchase of the property constituted the taking of a corporate opportunity and resulted in her liability to the club. Harris believed that her purchase, in a separate transaction, of the Smallidge land, which was adjacent to three of the golf club's holes and could be developed, was not usurpation of a corporate opportunity because she learned of the availability independently of the club. However, this also was a corporate opportunity because it was so closely related to the club's business. She was obligated to disclose the opportunity to the corporation and let it decide whether to pursue it.[23]

Officers may avail themselves of all opportunities lying outside the field of their duties as officers when business opportunities come to them in an individual capacity.[24]

Secret Profits

Officers are liable to the corporation for secret profits made in connection with, or at the expense of, the business of the corporation.

Duty of Loyalty

A corporate officer, while still employed by his or her firm, may be in breach of the officer's fiduciary duty of loyalty by recruiting key management employees to join a competing company. However, an officer may legally make arrangements before leaving the firm to compete in the future. The line separating mere preparation from active competition may be difficult to discern and, if misjudged, may lead to significant liability for the officer and a competitor aider and abettor, as is evidenced by the *Security Title v. Pope* case.

[23] *Northeast Harbor Golf Club v. Harris*, 725 A.2d 1018 (Me. 1999); see *Anderson v. Bellino*, 658 N.W.2d 645 (Neb. 2003).
[24] *Hill v. Southeastern Floor Covering Co.*, 596 So. 2d 874 (Miss. 1992).

CASE SUMMARY

Walkin' with Linda Pope

FACTS: Linda Pope ran one of the largest and most successful title insurance branches in the title insurance industry for Security Title Insurance. First American Title Insurance sought to regain its top position in title insurance sales through its Talon division by recruiting key people from other companies who had relationships with key customers and other key employees. Talon recruited Pope. While still employed by Security Title, Pope secretly solicited key management employees to join Talon–First American and planned to bring all 40 employees with her. Over drinks and dinner, she arranged for a Talon official to help with the recruiting by telling Security Title employees about Talon's beneficial compensation, signing bonuses, medical benefits, and superior computer system. When Security Title discovered Pope's plan to leave Security Title, it fired her and "walked her out." Thirty-five employees walked out with her. Security Title asserted that Pope's actions, aided

and abetted by Talon, resulted in $12,194,335 in lost profits. Security Title sued Pope for breach of fiduciary duty of loyalty and sued Talon–First American as an aider and abettor. Pope defended that she was merely making arrangements to compete in the future.

DECISION: Judgment for Security Title. Pope breached her fiduciary duty by improperly recruiting Security Title employees for Talon while she was still employed by Security Title. First American's argument that Pope had merely discussed her plans with the other employees and was only preparing to compete with Security Title flies in the face of a wealth of evidence presented to the jury. She secretly solicited key management employees to join a competitor and enticed employees to leave by telling them of bonuses and benefits. [*Security Title Agency, Inc. v. Pope*, 200 P.3d 977 (Ariz. App. 2008)]

47-3c Agents and Employees

The authority, rights, and liabilities of an agent or employee of a corporation are governed by the same rules as those applicable when the principal or employer is a natural person. The authority of corporate employees is also governed by general agency principles. **For Example,** R. Bryan Smith, president of Allstate Building Systems applied for a credit account with 84 Lumber Company. The first sentence of the application stated: "BY SIGNING BELOW I HEREBY CERTIFY THAT I AM THE OWNER, GENERAL PARTNER OR PRESIDENT OF THE ABOVE BUSINESS,…" The instructions on the first page of the contract state, "If the Applicant is a corporation, then President must sign the application." The language is a certification that the individual signing the contract has the authority to sign the contract in a representative capacity for the company. Immediately following this clause is the language, "I DO UNCONDITIONALLY … PERSONALLY GUARANTEE THIS CREDIT ACCOUNT AND PAYMENTS OF ANY AND ALL AMOUNTS DUE BY THE ABOVE BUSINESS." Mr. Smith signed both in a representative capacity and personally guaranteed the contract. He agreed to be personally responsible for the $27,611 owed on the account and the court enforced the agreement as written.[25]

The fact that a person is acting on behalf of a corporation does not serve as a shield from the liability that would be imposed for acts done on behalf of a natural person.

---

[25] *84 Lumber Co. v. Smith*, 356 S.W.3d 380 (Tenn. 2011); but see *Stamina Products, Inc. v. Zinctec USA Inc.*, 90 A.D.3d 1021 (A.D.2d 2011), where Anthyony Yau signed a contract on behalf of Zinctec, solely as a corporate officer, and did not bind himself individually under the agreement.

47-3d Executive Compensation under Dodd-Frank

The economic downturn in 2008 prompted many companies to take a hard look at executive compensation. There was widespread perception that executive pay practices contributed to the financial crisis. According to this view, some executives took excessive risks to realize short-term gains at the expense of long-term shareholder value and financial stability. As some CEOs pursued risky strategies or investments, boards were often complacent and failed to rein in the senior executives. Furthermore, boards approved executive compensation plans that rewarded excessive risk-taking.

Several sections of the Dodd-Frank Act require greater accountability by the board of directors to shareholders about executive compensation. The law took effect on July 21, 2010, with directions for the SEC to promulgate rules addressing issues such as executive pay, pay for performance, the independence of compensation committees, and claw-back provisions for erroneous payments to executives based on inaccurate financial statements. The following sections explain these provisions and the progress on SEC Rules.

Section 951. Say on Pay (Rule effective 2011)

This section requires that shareholders have a nonbinding vote to approve or disapprove executive compensation. Shareholders must first hold a "say-on-frequency" vote to determine how frequently shareholders will vote—every year, second year, or third year. The say-on-pay rule responds to the complaint that directors are not sufficiently accountable to shareholders when awarding executive pay packages. Boards are frequently influenced by management, especially the CEO, and may make decisions about pay that ignore their obligations to maximize shareholder value. The advisory shareholder vote is designed to increase the accountability of the board of directors to the shareholders and to encourage the board to consider shareholder interests when designing executive pay. Section 951 also requires a nonbinding vote on golden parachute payments. It is triggered whenever shareholders are asked to approve an acquisition, a merger, a consolidation, a sale, or other disposition of all or substantially all the assets of the company.

Section 952. Compensation Committee (Rule effective 2012)

This rule requires that most companies listed on the national exchanges have independent compensation committees. Compensation consultants, legal counsel, or other advisors to the compensation committee must also be independent.

Section 953. Pay for Performance: Executive Compensation Disclosures (Rule proposed)

The federal securities laws require clear disclosure about CEO compensation to enhance transparency for investors in publicly held companies. Information about executive pay is located in several sources including the company's annual proxy statement, the company's annual report on form 10-K, and registration statements to register securities for sale to the public. Annual proxy statements containing information on executive pay can be accessed easily on the SEC's Web site. The "pay for performance" section of the rule requires disclosure of "the relationship between executive compensation actually paid and the financial performance of the issuer, taking into account any change in the value of the shares of stock and dividends of the issuer and any distributions."

The SEC approved a rule that requires most public companies to state the ratio of the CEO's pay to that of the average employee. This rule will take effect in 2017. This rule and the pay for performance rule are controversial because some companies maintain that they unduly burden reporting companies without substantial benefit to shareholders.[26]

Section 954. Recovery of Erroneously Awarded Compensation (Rule proposed)

This rule would require exchanges to prohibit the listing of securities of issuers that have not developed and implemented compensation claw-back policies. A claw-back policy requires current or former executive officers to repay to the issuer any "incentive-based compensation including stock options awarded as compensation received during the three year period preceding the date on which the issuer is required to prepare an accounting restatement, based on the erroneous data, in excess of what would have been paid to the executive officer under the accounting restatement." The idea is that executives should not benefit from pay that is supposed to be related to performance when it is later discovered that it was related to fraudulent actions. Clawback provisions could curb the problem of high pay for poor performance.

47-4   Liability

Limited liability is a major reason for incorporating. Management, however, is not free from all civil and criminal liability simply because the corporate form is used.

47-4a   Liability of Management to Third Persons

Officers and managers of a corporation are not personally liable to third parties for the economic consequences of their advice so long as they acted in good faith to advance the interests of the corporation, even if they cause the corporation to refuse to deal with or break its contract with these third persons.

Ordinarily, the management of a corporation (its directors, officers, and executive employees) is not liable to third persons for the effect of its management or advice. The liability of a director or an officer for misconduct may usually be enforced only by the corporation or by shareholders bringing a derivative action on behalf of the corporation. Ordinarily, directors or officers are not liable to a third person for loss caused by the negligent performance of their duties as directors or officers even if, because of such negligence, the corporation is in turn liable to the third person to whom the corporation owed the duty to use care or was under a contract obligation to render a particular service.

However, in those rare cases when a director or an officer has in some way participated in or directed the tortious act, personal liability will attach. **For Example,** a corporate officer and director may be held personally liable for the tort of fraud in the inducement regarding a false promise to grant an insurance agency an exclusive territory selling viatical settlements, by which life insurance policies of terminally ill people are purchased at a discount in exchange for an immediate cash settlement.[27]

---

[26] There is some evidence that the financial crisis and the regulations that followed have made an impact on Wall Street. The gap between what bank CEOs take home in comparison to other bank employees has narrowed since the financial crisis. In 2014, CEOs made on average 124 times what the average worker at a bank makes, down from 273 in 2006. In 2006, the five CEOS at J.P. Morgan Chase, Goldman Sachs, Morgan Stanley, Bank of America, and Citigroup took home $173.6 million all together. In 2014, that number was down to $92.5 million. Peter Rudegeair, "Pay Gap Between Wall Street CEOs and Employees Narrows," *Wall Street Journal* (Apr. 6, 2015), available at **http://www .wsj.com/articles/a-pay-gap-narrows-on-wall-street-1428267898.**

[27] *First Financial USA, Inc. v. Steinger,* 760 So. 2d 996 (Fla. App. 2000).

ETHICS & THE LAW

Executive Compensation

Is it worth it to pay large sums of money to rock star CEOs? One study shows that the highest paid CEOs are the worst performers. According to the study, the 5 percent of CEOs who were the highest paid were running companies that performed 15 percent worse than their peers. Overconfidence is one reason that top CEOs don't have high-performing companies. The research also found that the longer CEOs stayed with a company, the more poorly the company performed. This correlation may be attributed to the fact that CEOs appoint allies to their boards who are likely to go along with the CEO's decisions—even the bad decisions.*

Consider the case of Larry Ellison, CEO of Oracle. In 2012, Ellison was paid $96.2 million; in 2013, $78.4 million. He stepped down as CEO in September 2014. Mr. Ellison received a token salary of $1 but received large stock grants. Using Dodd-Frank's say-on-pay provision, a union-affiliated group, Change to Win, urged Oracle shareholders to vote against the pay package for Mr. Ellison in 2012 and 2013. The organization noted that "Mr. Ellison's pay far outstrips that of the highest paid executives at the companies Oracle has identified as peers" (including Google and Microsoft). Oracle shareholders voted overwhelmingly against Ellison's pay package.

Despite some high-profile votes against executive compensation packages, most are not challenged.

The Wall Street Journal's annual compensation survey looked at 2013 compensation for CEOs at 300 publicly traded companies in the United States. The survey noted that CEO pay rose by a median of 5.5 percent while companies' median profit rose 8 percent. Compensation for ordinary employees in the private-sector rose an average of 1.8 percent.

Top Ten Earners in 2013

Compensation packages vary in the amount of cash, stock option grants, restricted stock grants, and performance awards.**

Oracle	Larry Ellison	$76.9
CBS	Leslie Moonves	$65.4
Liberty Global	Michael Fries	$45.5
Freeport-McMoRan	Richard Adkerson	$38.9
Viacom	Philippe Dauman	$36.8
Walt Disney	Robert Iger	$33.4
Time Warner	Jeffrey Bewkes	$32.4
Aetna	Mark Bertollini	$31.2
Estee Lauder	Fabrizio Freda	$30.9
General Electric	Jeffrey Immelt	$28.2

Do you think that say-on-pay legislation will impact CEO compensation? Will it increase directors' willingness to listen to shareholders? Will directors be likely to respond to advisory votes in order to preserve their seats on the board? Or, is say-on-pay legislation an intrusion on free enterprise?

*See Michael J. Cooper, Huseyin Gulin, and P. Raghavendra Rau, *Performance for Pay? The Relation Between CEO Incentive Compensation and Future Stock Price Performance* (October 1, 2014). Available at SSRN: **http://ssrn.com/abstract=1572085** or **http://dx.doi.org/10.2139/ssrn.1572085**.
Theo Francis and Joann S. Lublin, *CEO Pay Rises Moderately; a Few Reap Huge Rewards*, WSJ (May 27, 2014), **http://www.wsj.com/articles/ceo-pay-rises-moderately-a-few-reap-huge-rewards-1401235102.

47-4b Criminal Liability

Officers and directors, as well as the corporation itself, may be criminally accountable for business regulatory offenses.

Active Participation

Officers and directors, as in the case of agents, are personally responsible for any crimes committed by them even when they act on behalf of the corporation.[28] At the local level, they may be criminally responsible for violation of ordinances relating to sanitation, safety, and hours of closing.

At the state level, they may be criminally liable for conducting a business without obtaining necessary licenses or after the corporate certificate of incorporation has been forfeited.

---

[28] *Joy Management Co. v. City of Detroit*, 455 N.W.2d 55 (Mich. App. 1990).

At the federal level, officers and directors may be criminally liable for tax and securities law violations as well as egregious environmental protection law and worker safety law violations. International transactions may lead to potential criminal exposure. Under the Foreign Corrupt Practices Act, it is a crime for a U.S. firm to make payments or gifts to a foreign officer to obtain business. Not only is the U.S. corporation subject to a fine but also the officers and individuals involved are subject to fine and imprisonment.

Responsible Corporate Officer Doctrine

Officers and directors may be criminally liable under a number of federal and state statutes for failure to prevent the commission of a crime if they are found to be the "responsible corporate officers." These statutes include the Food, Drug and Cosmetic Act, the Federal Hazardous Substances Act, the Occupational Safety and Health Act, the Federal Water Pollution Act, and, at the state level, the California Corporate Criminal Liability Act.

For Example, Gary Lundgren was a shareholder and officer of KIE, Inc., which owned and operated a sewage treatment plant on Ketron Island. He knew of the facility's discharge of pollutants into Puget Sound without a permit. As the "responsible corporate officer," he was held personally liable for a $250,000 penalty because he controlled the

THINKING THINGS THROUGH

Responsible Corporate Officers—The Park Doctrine Revisited

Food safety violations may give rise to civil and criminal prosecution for companies as well as for corporate executives. In 2013, the United States Department of Justice brought criminal charges against five former officials and employees of Peanut Corporation of America (PCA), including the president and owner of the company, Stewart Parnell.

The charges stem from a salmonella outbreak that was traced to the PCA roasting plant in Georgia. An investigation by the FDA revealed that the processing plant was not properly cleaned. The roof leaked and there was poor ventilation and inadequate pest control. According to the FDA, at least nine people died and more than 700 became ill due to tainted peanut products. More than 100 people who were sickened settled their civil suit against PCA for $12 million. PCA went bankrupt and is no longer in business.

Parnell and his brother, who also worked for the company, were convicted on 97 felony counts, including fraud, conspiracy, and obstruction of justice. Other employees reached plea agreements with the government.

The criminal case involved a six-year conspiracy in which employees failed to notify customers that laboratory tests showed salmonella was present in the product. Employees also falsified certificates of analysis, which summarized lab results.

The government has rarely used criminal provisions to charge individual food industry executives and employees. In *United States v. Park*, 421 U.S. 658 (1975), the United States

Supreme Court decided a case that led to what is now known as the Park Doctrine, a doctrine that allows corporate executives to be prosecuted criminally, even for unintentional violations of food and drug laws by their companies.

The charges against Parnell were likely pursued because the deception was particularly callous about consumer safety. An e-mail notified PCA's president that salmonella testing was not yet available on a shipment—to which the president replied "s**t, just ship it. I cannot afford to loose (sic) another customer."

On September 19, 2014, a federal jury convicted Parnell on charges of mail and wire fraud and the introduction of misbranded food into interstate commerce with the intent to defraud or mislead. Parnell was also convicted of obstruction of justice. Parnell, who could face more than 30 years in prison, is seeking to overturn the jury's conviction.*

The case is one of the first felony convictions of a food processor under the Federal Food, Drug and Cosmetic Act. The case demonstrates the government's interest in food safety cases and its willingness to use the Park Doctrine against executives.**

*Michelle Gillette and Mina Nasseri, *Guilty Convictions in Salmonella Trial May Signify Landmark in Criminal Food-Safety Prosecutions, Consumer Product Matters* (Sept. 22, 2014), **http://www.martindale.com/products-liability-law/article_Mintz-Levin-Cohn-Ferris-Glovsky-Popeo-PC_2178980.htm**.

Press Release, "United States Department of Justice, All Defendants Convicted in Trial of Former Peanut Company Officials," *United States v. Stewart Parnell et al.*, **http://www.justice.gov/civil/current-and-recent cases.

facility with knowledge of the violations.[29] The California Corporate Criminal Liability Act requires managers in control of corporate operations who have knowledge of "serious concealed dangers" to employees or customers to notify the appropriate regulatory authority or be subject to criminal liability.[30]

Liability of the Corporation Itself

A corporation itself may be convicted of a criminal offense if its agent committed the offense acting within the scope of the agent's authority. **For Example,** Steenberg Homes, Inc., was convicted of negligent criminal homicide in the deaths of two cyclists who were killed when the company's trailer truck, loaded with timber, disengaged from the tractor. If safety chains had been properly attached, the accident would not have happened. The corporation's failure to establish and enforce safety procedures was a cause of the deaths of the cyclists.[31]

Punishment of Corporations

Under the Organizational Federal Sentencing Guidelines, organizations, including corporations, trusts, pension funds, unions, and nonprofit organizations, are subject to greatly increased fines for criminal convictions. However, corporations and other covered organizations that implement an effective compliance program designed to prevent and detect corporate crimes and voluntarily disclose such crimes to the government will be subject to much lower fines under the guidelines.[32]

47-4c Indemnification of Officers, Directors, Employees, and Agents

While performing what they believe to be their duty, officers, directors, employees, and agents of corporations may commit acts for which they are later sued or criminally prosecuted. The RMBCA broadly authorizes the corporation to indemnify these persons if they acted in good faith and in a manner reasonably believed to be in, or not opposed to, the interests of the corporation and had no reason to believe that their conduct was unlawful.[33] In some states, statutes require the corporation to indemnify directors and officers for reasonable expenses incurred by them in defending unwarranted suits brought against them by shareholders.

47-4d Liability for Corporate Debts

Because the corporation is a separate legal person, debts that it owes are ordinarily the obligations of the corporation only. Consequently, neither directors nor officers are individually liable for corporate debts, even though it may have been their acts that gave rise to the debts.

In some states, liability for corporate debts is imposed on the corporation's officers and directors when the corporation improperly engages in business.

47-4e Protection of Shareholders

Shareholders may obtain protection from misconduct by management and by the majority of the shareholders. Shareholders may protect themselves by voting at annual elections

---

[29] *State Department of Ecology v. Lundgren*, 971 P.2d 948 (Wash. App. 1999).
[30] Cal. Penal Code §387 (West 2006).
[31] *State v. Steenberg Homes, Inc.*, 859 N.W.2d 668 (Wis. App. 1998).
[32] U.S. Sentencing Commission Guidelines Manual §§8C2.5(f), 8C2.6 (2014).
[33] Subchapter 8E, added in 1980 and revised in 1994.

for new directors and for new officers. Shareholders may take remedial action at a special meeting called for that purpose. Objecting shareholders may bring a legal action when the management misconduct complained of constitutes a legal wrong.[34]

47-4f Civil Liability of the Corporation

A corporation is liable to third persons for the acts of its officers, employees, and agents to the same extent that a natural person is liable for the acts of agents and employees. The ordinary rules of agency law determine the extent to which the corporation is liable to a third person for a contract made or a tort committed by management personnel, employees, and agents.

Make the Connection

Summary

Ordinarily, stockholder action is taken at a regular or special meeting of the stockholders. The presence of a quorum of the voting shareholders is required.

Management of a corporation is under the control of a board of directors elected by the shareholders. Courts will not interfere with the board's judgment in the absence of unusual conduct such as fraud. A director is disqualified from taking part in corporate action when the director has a conflict of interest. Action by directors is usually taken at a properly called meeting of the board. Directors act in a fiduciary capacity in dealing with the corporation. Directors who act in good faith and have exercised reasonable care are not liable for losses resulting from their management decisions under the business judgment rule. Ordinarily, directors are removed by shareholders.

Officers of a corporation, including a CEO, president, vice president, secretary, and treasurer, are usually selected and removed by the board of directors. Officers are agents of the corporation, and their powers are governed by the law of agency. Their relations with the corporation are fiduciary in nature, and they are liable for any secret profits and for diverting corporate opportunities to their own advantage.

Directors and officers, as in the case of agents generally, are personally responsible for any torts or crimes they commit even if they act on behalf of the corporation. The corporation itself may be prosecuted for crimes and is subject to fines if convicted. The ordinary rules of agency law determine the extent to which a corporation is liable for a contract made or tort committed by a director, an officer, a corporate agent, or an employee.

Learning Outcomes

After studying this chapter, you should be able to clearly explain:

47-1   Shareholders

LO.1 Explain how shareholders, as owners of the corporation, exercise limited control over management by voting at shareholders' meetings to elect directors

See the discussion of shareholder voting and meetings, page 978.

47-2   Directors

LO.2 Explain the qualifications and powers of directors
See the discussion regarding the broad authority of directors to manage the corporation, page 979.

LO.3 Explain the liability of directors and the meaning of the business judgment rule (BJR)
See the *Walt Disney* case in which an unsuccessful action taken by directors was protected by the BJR, pages 982–983.

---

[34] *Christner v. Anderson, Nietzke & Co.*, 444 N.W.2d 779 (Mich. 1989).

See the *Van Gorkom* case in which directors were not protected by the BJR because they were grossly negligent in their judgment, page 983.

47-3   Officers, Agents, and Employees

LO.4   Explain the obligation of officers—who have access to corporate information and agency powers—to not violate their fiduciary duties to the corporation

See the *Demoulas Super Markets* case regarding diverting corporate opportunities, pages 986–987.

See the *Security Title v. Pope* case regarding a manager's duty of loyalty, page 988.

LO.5   Explain the rationale for the "say-on-pay" provision of the Dodd-Frank Act

See the examples of executive compensation practices leading to the financial crisis of 2008–2009, page 989.

See Ethics & the Law on Executive Pay, page 991.

47-4   Liability

LO.6   Explain how directors, officers, and the corporation itself may be criminally liable for regulatory offenses

See the Gary Lundgren example in which, as a "responsible corporate officer," Gary was held personally liable for environmental law violations, pages 992–993.

See the Thinking Things Through segment about criminal conviction of an executive under the "responsible corporate officer" doctrine, page 992.

Key Terms

business judgment rule (BJR)   quorum

Questions and Case Problems

1. Shareholders of Bear Stearns sued the directors of the corporation for damages for violation of the directors' fiduciary duties in effecting a stock-for-stock merger with J.P. Morgan Chase for an implied value of $10 per share while the company's stock had previously reached a 15-month high of $160. On March 10, 2008, information began leaking into the market that Bear Stearns had a liquidity problem. On March 13, 2008, the company was forced to seek emergency financing from the Federal Reserve and J.P. Morgan Chase. By the weekend of March 14–16, the company could no longer operate without major financing. In an effort to preserve some shareholder value while averting the uncertainty of bankruptcy (where stockholders would likely receive nothing), and represented by teams of legal and financial experts and relying on their financial advisor Lazard Freres & Co.'s opinion that the "exchange ratio is fair, from a financial point of view, to the shareholders," the board of directors approved the initial merger agreement. The shareholder plaintiffs contended that the ultimate $10 share price paid was inadequate and they presented their experts who vigorously dissected the board's decisions. What defense, if any, would you raise on behalf of the Bear Stearns board of directors? [*In re Bear Stearns Litigation*, 870 N.Y.S.2d 709]

2. In 1996, Congress offered national banks the opportunity to become Subchapter S entities.

Amboy Bancorporation was a small, highly profitable New Jersey Bank that was overcapitalized. Amboy's president and CEO utilized Bank Advisory Group, Inc. (BAG), to calculate the fair value of individual shares of Amboy stock. The board of directors approved a merger cash buyout program designed to reduce the shareholder base to below the 75 qualified shareholders necessary to obtain Subchapter S status. BAG incorrectly applied a minority and marketability discount to its evaluation of the fair value of the stock, bringing it down from $110 per share to $70.13 per share. Casey and other shareholders who cashed out under the plan at $73 per share sued the board of directors individually for damages for approving such a flawed plan. Are directors personally liable when they act in reliance on a report by an outside expert whose advice is flawed? If a public accounting firm or an attorney gave the flawed advice, would the directors be personally liable? [*Casey v. Brennan*, 344 N.J. Super. 83]

3. The majority shareholder and president of Dunaway Drug Stores, Inc., William B. Dunaway, was structuring and executing the sale of virtually all of the corporation's assets to Eckerd Drug Co. While doing this, he negotiated a side noncompete agreement with Eckerd, giving Dunaway $300,000 plus a company car in exchange for a covenant not to compete for three years. He simultaneously amended

two corporate leases with Eckerd, thereby decreasing the value of the corporation's leasehold estates. The board of directors approved the asset sale. Minority shareholders brought a derivative action against William Dunaway, claiming breach of his fiduciary duty in negotiating the undisclosed noncompete agreement, which did not require him to perform any service for buyer Eckerd Drug. Did William Dunaway make sufficient disclosure about all of the negotiations of the asset sale to Eckerd Drug? Did William Dunaway violate any fiduciary duty to the corporation? Decide. [*Dunaway v. Parker*, 453 S.E.2d 43 (Ga. App.)]

4. Larry Phillips was hired for a two-year period as executive secretary of the Montana Education Association (MEA). Six months later, he was fired. He then sued MEA for breach of contract and sued the directors and some of the other employees of MEA on the theory that they had caused MEA to break the contract with him and were therefore guilty of the tort of maliciously interfering with his contract with MEA. The evidence showed that the individual defendants, without malice, had induced the corporation to break the contract with Phillips but that this had been done to further the welfare of the corporation. Was MEA liable for breach of contract? Were the individual defendants shielded from personal liability? [*Phillips v. Montana Education Ass'n*, 610 P.2d 154 (Mont.)]

5. Christy Pontiac, a corporation, was indicted for theft by swindle and forgery involving a GM cash rebate program. Hesli, a middle-management employee of Christy Pontiac, had forged the cash rebate applications for two cars so that the rebate money was paid to Christy Pontiac instead of its customers. When confronted by a customer who should have received a rebate, the president of the dealership attempted to negotiate a settlement. The president did not contact GM headquarters until after an investigation was begun by the state attorney general. Christy Pontiac argued that it could not be held responsible for a crime involving specific intent because only natural persons, as opposed to corporations, can form such intent. Decide. [*State v. Christy Pontiac-GMC, Inc.*, 354 N.W.2d 17 (Minn.)]

6. Larry G. Snodgrass and Mark Swinnea owned equal interests in two business entities, ERI Consulting Engineers, Inc. (ERI), and Malmeba Company, Ltd., which they operated together for approximately 10 years. ERI manages asbestos abatement projects for

contractors. It leased office space from Malmeba, their partnership that owned the building. Snodgrass and ERI purchased Swinnea's interest in ERI in 2001. ERI paid Swinnea $497,500 to redeem Swinnea's ERI stock, and Snodgrass transferred his half-interest in Malmeba to Swinnea. ERI agreed to employ Swinnea for six years, and Swinnea agreed not to compete with ERI. At the same time, ERI agreed to continue leasing from Malmeba for six years. Unknown to Snodgrass, the wives of Swinnea and Chris Power, an ERI employee, had created a new company called Air Quality Associates a month before Swinnea and Snodgrass executed the buyout agreement. Air Quality Associates was created to perform mold abatement but later engaged in asbestos abatement as a contractor even though neither wife had experience in the asbestos abatement field. Swinnea did not disclose the existence of Air Quality Associates to Snodgrass during the ERI buyout negotiations. Over a 33-month period Snodgrass suffered a total loss of profits of $178,000 for business lost to Swinnea. Was Swinnea free to outmaneuver Snodgrass in their buyout agreement as part of the competitive spirit of America? Do owners have a fiduciary duty to each other in negotiating a buyout agreement with a noncompete clause? Are Swinnea's action's so contrary to our public sense of justice and propriety to merit exemplary damages? [*ERI Consulting Engineers, Inc. v. Swinnea*, 318 S.W.3d 867 (Tex.); *Swinnea v. ERI Consulting Engineers*, 364 S.W.3d 421 (Tex. App.)]

7. Discuss the power of a corporation's president to employ a sales manager and to agree that the manager should be paid a stated amount per year plus a percentage of any increase in the dollar volume of sales that might take place.

8. Richard Grassgreen was executive vice president and then president and chief operating officer of Kinder-Care, Inc., the largest proprietary provider of child care in the country. The company was restructured in 1989 and changed its name to the Enstar Group, Inc. Between 1985 and 1990, while Grassgreen served as the corporation's investment manager, he invested millions of dollars of company money in junk bond deals with Michael Milken, and he secretly retained some $355,000 in commitment fees. When the corporation discovered this, Grassgreen repaid the corporation. It sued him to recover any compensation paid him over the five-year period during which the secret payments were made, some

$5,197,663. Grassgreen defended that his conduct caused little, if any, damage to the corporation because the corporation did not lose any money on any of the investments for which he received personal fees. Decide. [*Enstar Group, Inc. v. Grassgreen*, 812 F. Supp. 1562 (M.D. Ala.)]

9. Danny Hill, the general manager of Southeastern Floor Covering Co., Inc. (SE), had full authority to run the business. His responsibilities included preparing and submitting bid proposals to general contractors for floor coverings and ceilings on construction projects. Hill prepared and submitted a bid for a job for Chata Construction Co. for asbestos encapsulation, ceramic tile, ceilings, carpets, and vinyl tile flooring. However, because SE was not licensed by the EPA, the asbestos work was withdrawn. In the past, SE had used Larry Barnes's company, which was EPA licensed, to do asbestos work under a subcontract agreement. Hill did not pursue a subcontract with Barnes for the Chata job. Rather, Hill and Barnes worked up a bid together and submitted it to Chata for the asbestos work. The bid was accepted, and Hill made $90,000 from the Chata job. Two years later, SE found out about Hill's role in the asbestos work done for Chata, and the corporation sued him for the lost profits. Hill argued that SE was not licensed by the EPA to do asbestos work and thus could not claim a lost corporate opportunity when it was not qualified to do the work. Decide. Are any ethical principles applicable to this case? [*Hill v. Southeastern Floor Covering Co.*, 596 So. 2d 874 (Miss.)]

10. A director of a corporation cannot lend money to the corporation because that would create the danger of a conflict of interest between the director's status as a director and as a creditor. Appraise this statement.

11. Hamway and other minority shareholders brought an action against majority shareholders of Libbie Rehabilitation Center, Inc., including Frank Giannotti, CEO-director; Alex Grossman, president-director; Henry Miller, vice president-director; Ernest Dervishian, secretary and corporate attorney; and Lewis Cowardin, treasurer-director. The minority shareholders contended that the corporation paid excessive salaries to these director-officers and was wasting corporate assets. Prior to coming to Libbie, Giannotti had been a carpet and tile retailer, Grossman a pharmacist, Miller a real estate developer, Dervishian a lawyer, and Cowardin a jeweler. The evidence showed that the extent of their work for the corporation was very limited. For example, Cowardin, Libbie's finance officer, who was paid $78,121, demonstrated no knowledge of the Medicare and Medicaid programs, the principal source of Libbie's income. Although he claimed to have spent 20 to 25 hours a week on corporate duties, he reported on the tax return for his jewelry business that he spent 75 percent of his working time in that business. One expert witness for the plaintiff testified that the five men were performing the management functions of one individual. The director-officers contended that the business was making a profit and that all salaries were approved by a board of directors that had extensive business experience. Were the directors within their rights to elect themselves officers and set pay for themselves as they saw fit? Did they violate any legal or ethical duty to their shareholders?

12. Anthony Yee was the president of Waipahu Auto Exchange, a corporation. As part of his corporate duties, he arranged financing for the company. Federal Services Finance Corp. drew 12 checks payable to the order of Waipahu Auto Exchange. These were then indorsed by its president, "Waipahu Auto Exchange, Limited, by Anthony Yee, President," and were cashed at two different banks. Bishop National Bank of Hawaii, on which the checks were drawn, charged its depositor, Federal Services, with the amount of the checks. Federal Services then sued Bishop National Bank to restore to its account the amount of the 12 checks on the ground that Bishop National Bank had improperly made payment on the checks because Anthony Yee had no authority to cash them. Did Yee have authority to indorse and cash the checks? [*Federal Services Finance Corp. v. BishopNatl Bank of Hawaii*, 190 F.2d 442 (9th Cir.)]

13. Klinicki and Lundgren incorporated Berlinair, Inc., a closely held Oregon corporation. Lundgren was president and responsible for developing business. Klinicki served as vice president and director responsible for operations and maintenance. Klinicki owned one-third of the stock, and Lundgren controlled the rest. They both met with BFR, a consortium of Berlin travel agents, about contracting to operate some charter flights. After the initial meeting, all contracts with BFR were made by Lundgren, who learned that there was a good chance that the BFR contract would be available. He incorporated Air Berlin Charter Co. (ABC) and was its sole owner. He presented BFR with a contract proposal, and it

awarded the contract to ABC. Although Lundgren was using Berlinair's working time and facilities, he managed to keep the negotiations a secret from Klinicki. When Klinicki discovered Lundgren's actions, he sued him for usurping a corporate opportunity for Berlinair. Lundgren contended that it was not a usurpation of corporate opportunity because Berlinair did not have the financial ability to undertake the contract with BFR. Decide. Are any ethical principles applicable to this case? Consider the applicability of Chief Justice Cardozo's statement in *Meinhard v. Salmon*, 164 N.E. 545 (N.Y. 1928), concerning the level of conduct for fiduciaries: "A trustee is held to something stricter than the morals of the marketplace. Not honesty alone, but the punctilio of an honor the most sensitive is then the standard of behavior...." [*Klinicki v. Lundgren*, 695 P.2d 906 (Or.)]

14. Rudolph Redmont, the president of Abbott Thinlite Corp., left Abbott to run Circle Corp. in competition with his former employer. It was claimed that he diverted contracts from his former employer to his new one, having gained the advantage of specific information about the deals in progress while employed by Abbott. Abbott sued Redmont and Circle Corp. to recover lost profits. Redmont contended that all of the contracts in question were made after he left Abbott, at which time his fiduciary

duty to Abbott had ceased. Decide. [*Abbott Thinlite Corp. v. Redmont*, 475 F.2d 85 (2d Cir.)]

15. William Gurtler was president and a board member of Unichem Corp., which produced and sold chemical laundry products. While president of Unichem, he encouraged his plant manager to leave to join a rival business, which Gurtler was going to join in the near future. Moreover, Gurtler sold Unichem products to his son, G. B. Gurtler, at a figure substantially below their normal price and on credit even though G. B. had no credit history. Gurtler made the sales with full knowledge that G. B. was going to start a rival business. Also at that time, Gurtler was aware that his wife was soliciting Unichem employees to join the new Gurtler Chemical Co., and he helped her design Gurtler's label so that it would look like Unichem's. Gurtler guaranteed a $100,000 bank loan for the new Gurtler Chemical Co. with funds to be disbursed after he left Unichem. One month later, he became president of Gurtler Chemical Co. Unichem sued Gurtler for breach of fiduciary duty and for the loss of profits that resulted. Gurtler contended that his sales to G. B. guaranteed needed revenue to Unichem and constituted a sound business decision that should be applauded and that was protected under the business judgment rule. Decide. Are any ethical principles applicable to this case? [*Unichem Corp. v. Gurtler*, 498 N.E.2d 724 (Ill. App.)]

CPA Questions

1. Davis, a director of Active Corp., is entitled to:
   a. Serve on the board of a competing business.
   b. Take sole advantage of a business opportunity that would benefit Active.
   c. Rely on information provided by a corporate officer.
   d. Unilaterally grant a corporate loan to one of Active's shareholders.

2. Absent a specific provision in its articles of incorporation, a corporation's board of directors has the power to do all of the following *except:*
   a. Repeal the bylaws.
   b. Declare dividends.
   c. Fix compensation of directors.
   d. Amend the articles of incorporation.

3. Which of the following statements is correct regarding fiduciary duty?
   a. A director's fiduciary duty to the corporation may be discharged by merely disclosing his or her self-interest.
   b. A director owes a fiduciary duty to the shareholders but *not* to the corporation.
   c. A promoter of a corporation to be formed owes no fiduciary duty to anyone, unless the contract engaging the promoter so provides.
   d. A majority shareholder as such may owe a fiduciary duty to fellow shareholders.

Real Property and Estates

Real Property

Learning Outcomes <<<

After studying this chapter, you should be able to

LO.1 List the types of real property interests, the rights of the parties and their liabilities

LO.2 Distinguish between liens, licenses, and easements

LO.3 Discuss the nature and form of real property ownership

LO.4 Explain the liability of landowners for injury to others on their property

LO.5 Discuss the forms of co-ownership and parties' rights

LO.6 Describe how deeds convey title to land

LO.7 Describe the characteristics and effect of a mortgages

48-1 Nature of Real Property

real property–land and all rights in land.

Real property has special characteristics of permanence and uniqueness. These characteristics have strongly influenced the rules that society has developed to resolve disputes concerning real property.

48-1a Land

land–earth, including all things embedded in or attached thereto, whether naturally or by the act of humans.

Land means more than the surface of the earth. It is composed of the soil and all things of a permanent nature affixed to the ground, such as shrubs, grass, trees, and other growing, natural products. The word also includes the waters on the ground and minerals that are embedded beneath the surface.

easement–permanent right that one has in the land of another, as the right to cross another's land or an easement of way.

Technically, land extends downward to the earth's center and upward indefinitely. The general view is that the owner of the land owns the space above that land subject to the right of flying aircraft that do not interfere with the use of the land and are not dangerous to persons or property on the land.

C P A

48-1b Easements

dominant tenement–land that is benefited by an easement.

servient tenement–land that is subject to an easement.

An **easement** is the right to use another's property, such as the right to cross another's land. Rights in another person's land also include profits, or the right to remove minerals. The easement belongs to the land that is benefited. The benefited land is called the **dominant tenement,** and the land that is subject to the easement is called the **servient tenement.**[1]

Creation of Easement

easement by implication–easement not specifically created by deed that arises from the circumstances of the parties and the land location and access.

way of necessity–grantee's right to use land retained by the grantor for going to and from the conveyed land.

prescription–acquisition of a right to use the land of another, as an easement, by making hostile, visible, and notorious use of the land, continuing for the period specified by the local law.

Because an easement is an interest in land, an oral promise to create an easement is not binding because of the statute of frauds. An oral grant of an easement would be a license (see the section titled "Licenses"). An easement created by agreement is transferred by deed. However, an easement may also be created by implication. An **easement by implication** arises when one conveys a portion the land that has been used as a dominant estate in relation to the part retained. **For Example,** if water pipes or drain pipes run from the part of the land conveyed through the part retained, there is an implied right to continue using the pipes. For an easement to be implied, the use, as in this case with the pipes, must be apparent, continuous, and reasonably necessary.

An easement by implication arises when one subdivides land and sells a portion to which no entry can be made except over the land retained or over the land of a stranger. The grantee's right to use the land retained by the grantor for the purpose of going to and from the land conveyed is known as a **way of necessity.**

An easement may be created by **prescription.** Under prescription, a person acquires an easement by adverse use, or use contrary to the landowner's use, for a statutory period. No easement is acquired by prescription if the use of the land is with the permission of the owner.

Termination of Easement

Once an easement has been granted, it cannot be destroyed by the act of the grantor. A "revocation" attempted without the easement owner's consent has no effect.

An easement may be lost by nonuse when surrounding circumstances show an intent to abandon the easement.[2] **For Example,** when a surface transit system had an easement to maintain trolley tracks but abandoned the easement when the tracks were removed and

---

[1] *Gaw v. Seldon*, 85 So. 3d 312 (Miss. App. 2012).
[2] *Howard v. U.S.*, 964 N.E.2d 779 (Ind. 2012).

all surface transportation was discontinued, the easement was lost through abandonment. Likewise, when the owner of the easement planted a flower bed on the land across the end of the path of the easement, the intent to abandon the easement was evident.

CASE SUMMARY

Freddie and Peggy's Speed Bumps on the Easement Get Bumped

FACTS: Adrian and Charline Wingate (Appellees) own and occupy a home adjoining Gloria Dianne and Freddie L. Wingate's (Appellants) property. On February 1, 1999, Appellant Freddie L. Wingate and his (now deceased) wife, Peggy Ann Wingate (now Peggy Dianne), granted an easement over and across their property, providing ingress and egress to Adrian and Charline, which was recorded. Around October 21, 2009, Freddie and Peggy placed speed bumps across a paved portion of the easement, which is used by Adrian and Charline to gain access to their residence. Freddie and Peggy also placed concrete barriers on either side of the speed bumps to prevent vehicles from going around the speed bumps. The speed bumps have proven dangerous to drivers and their passengers and have damaged vehicles passing over them. Adrian and Charline demanded summary judgment as well as a permanent injunction restraining Freddie and Peggy from keeping the speed bumps across the easement. The court granted summary judgment and ordered the removal of the speed bumps. Peggy and Freddie appealed.

DECISION: The court held that there were issues of fact about the burden that the speed bumps caused the dominant easement holders. The issues that require examination are whether there are underlying reasons for the control of ingress and egress, whether the easement language offers guidance on what the servient interest holder can do, and if there are other means for accomplishing whatever safety goals the servient interest holder may have. Dominant interest holders do not have a right of absolute prohibition of ingress and egress restrictions unless such is spelled out in the easement grant itself. The decision was reversed and the lower court was required to hold a trial on all of these issues. [***Dianne v. Wingate*, 84 So. 3d 427 (Fla. App. 2012)**]

THINKING THINGS THROUGH

The Dryer Vent That Dumped on the Doc

Danetta Garfink owns a condominium unit at The Cloisters at Charles Condominiums. Garfink purchased her unit (one of the model units) in 1991 during the development and construction phase of the project. The original construction included installed household appliances in each unit, a clothes dryer among them. As originally installed, the clothes dryer was connected and vented into the furnace room, rather than to the outside of the building, contrary to the terms of the construction contract, and in violation of prevailing building codes and regulations.

In 2000, the clothes dryer malfunctioned and Garfink purchased a replacement from Sears, Roebuck & Co. After viewing the existing vent system, however, Sears refused to install the replacement because a "fire hazzard [sic] was identified."

Garfink took it upon herself to have the venting system rerouted. The new system was routed from the dryer through the wall of the laundry room into the adjoining garage, then through the garage and then the exterior wall. Garfink's immediate neighbor, Dr. Oscar Kantt, found that the new vent was within 17 feet of the front door of his residence, and Dr. Kantt complained about the discharge. Garfink says she has an easement for the dryer vent. Analyze whether she does have an easement. Be sure to think through the types of easements.

[***Garfink v. Cloisters at Charles, Inc.*, 897 A.2d 206 (Md. 2006)**]

CPA   48-1c **Profits**

profit–right to take a part of the soil or produce of another's land, such as timber or water.

Profits are rights to take part of the soil, subsurface materials, or resources or produce from land that belongs to another. **For Example,** profits could include the right to remove coal from the land of another and the right to use the water from another's land.

CPA   48-1d **Licenses**

license–personal
privilege to do some act
or series of acts upon the
land of another, as the
placing of a sign thereon,
not amounting to an
easement or a right of
possession.

A **license** is a personal, revocable privilege to perform an act or series of acts on the land of another. Unlike an easement, a license is not an interest in land. **For Example,** the person allowed to come into the house to use the telephone has a license. The advertising company that has permission to paint a sign on the side of a building also has a license. A ticket to see a movie is a license.

A license may be terminated at the will of the licensor. It continues only as long as the licensor is the owner of the land.

SPORTS & ENTERTAINMENT LAW

The New England Patriots and Their Season License Holders

In its litigation against StubHub, Inc., over StubHub's listing of its tickets for resale, the New England Patriots alleged that StubHub was engaged in intentional interference with advantageous relations through StubHub's knowing solicitation of ticket holders to violate the terms on which their tickets for access to Patriots home football games are granted (i.e., the license restrictions on transfer of the tickets). Massachusetts' Supreme Court had already held that tickets to entertainment events are revocable licenses, which a venue owner may revoke at any time and for any reason. The Patriots argued that StubHub, by offering season ticket holders' tickets for sale online, was interfering with its license rights. StubHub argued that a ticket was not a license but more like a bearer instrument that could be transferred easily. Not surprisingly, the Patriots continued their winning streak in court. The result is, because 95 percent of the tickets held to a Patriots game are season tickets, there is no open secondary market for ticket sales to Patriots games. Fans have only the license holder options afforded for selling their tickets.

[*Yarde Metals, Inc. v. New England Patriots, LP.*, 834 N.E.2d 450 (2005); *New England Patriots, LP. and NPS LLC, Herman v. Admit One Ticket Agency*, 912 N.E.2d 450 (Mass. 2009)]

CPA   48-1e **Liens**

lien–claim or right,
against through
judgment or levy.

Real property may be subject to **liens** that arise by the voluntary act of the owner of the land. **For Example,** the lien of a mortgage is created when the owner borrows money and uses the land as security for repayment of the debt.

tax lien–lien on property
for nonpayment of taxes.

Liens may also arise involuntarily, as in the case of **tax liens, judgment liens,** and **mechanic's liens.** In the case of taxes and judgments, the liens provide a means for enforcing the obligations of the owner of the land to pay the taxes or the judgment. Mechanic's liens give persons furnishing labor and materials in the improvement of real estate the right to proceed against the real estate for the collection of the amounts due them.

judgment lien–lien
obtained through the
courts.

mechanic's lien–claim
by laborers or materials
suppliers for property
improvements.

48-1f **Fixtures**

Under the laws relating to fixtures, personal property becomes real property.

CPA   **Definition**

fixture–personal
property attached to or
adapted to real estate.

A **fixture** is personal property that is attached to the earth or placed in a building in such a way or under such circumstances that it is considered part of the real property.

A person may buy a refrigerator, an air conditioner, a furnace, or some other item that is used in a building and then have the item installed. The question of whether such an item is a fixture, and therefore part of a building, can arise in a variety of situations: (1) The real estate tax assessor assesses the building and adds in the value of the item on the theory that it is part of the building, (2) the buyer of the item owns and then sells the building, and the new owner of the building claims that the item stays with the building, (3) the buyer places a mortgage on the building, and the mortgagee claims that the item is bound by the mortgage, (4) the buyer is a tenant in the building in which the item is installed, and the landlord claims that the item must stay in the building when the tenant leaves, and (5) the buyer does not pay in full for the item, and the seller of the item has a security interest that the seller wishes to enforce against the buyer or against the landlord of the building in which the buyer installs the item. The seller of the item may also assert a claim against the mortgagee of the building or against the buyer of the building. The determination of the rights of these parties depends on the common law of fixtures, as occasionally modified by statute.

Tests of a Fixture

In the absence of an agreement between the parties, the courts apply three tests to determine whether personal property has become a fixture.

Annexation. Generally, personal property becomes a fixture if it is so attached to the realty that it cannot be removed without materially damaging the real property or destroying the personal property itself. If the property is so affixed as to lose its specific identity, such as bricks in a wall, it becomes part of the realty. When cabinets are attached to kitchen walls so as to be immovable, they are fixtures.

Adaptation. Personal property especially adapted or suited to the use made of the building may constitute a fixture such as the pipes for a church organ.

Intent. One controlling test is the intention of the person affixing the property. Intent is considered as of the time the property was affixed.[3] In the absence of direct proof of such intent, courts resort to the nature of the property, the method of its attachment, and all the surrounding circumstances to determine intent.

The fact that machinery installed in a plant would be very difficult and expensive to move or is so delicate that the moving would cause damage is significant in reaching the conclusion that the owner installed the equipment as a permanent addition and intended to make the equipment fixtures. **For Example,** when the floors in a large apartment house are made of concrete and covered with a thin sheet of plywood to which wall-to-wall carpeting is stapled, the carpeting constitutes a fixture that cannot be removed from the building. Removal would probably destroy the carpeting because it was cut to size. In addition, the carpeting is necessary to make the building livable as an apartment.

CPA   Movable Machinery and Equipment

Machinery and equipment that are movable are ordinarily held not to be fixtures even though, in order to move them, it is necessary to unbolt them from the floor or to disconnect electrical wires or water pipes. **For Example,** refrigerators, freezers, and gas and electric ranges are not fixtures. They do not lose their character as personal property when they are readily removable after disconnecting pipes or unplugging wires. A portable window air conditioner that rests on a rack that is affixed to the windowsill by screws and is connected directly to the building only by an electric cord plug is not a fixture.

The mere fact that an item may be unplugged, however, does not establish that it is not a fixture. **For Example,** a computer and its related hardware constitute fixtures when there is such a mass of wires and cables under the floor that the installation gives the impression of permanence.

---

[3] In re *Treadwell*, 520 B.R. 788 (W.D. Mo. 2014).

C P A   **Trade Fixtures**

Equipment that a tenant attaches to a rented building and uses in a trade or business is ordinarily removable by the tenant when the tenant permanently leaves the premises. Such equipment is commonly called a *trade fixture.*[4]

CASE SUMMARY

The Lake Home "Stripped" of Fixtures

FACTS: Denny Ryerson (Debtor) filed his Chapter 11 bankruptcy case on August 30, 2013, and Anaconda (mortgage creditor) asked for relief from the stay to sell the property securing the mortgage notes. The property securing the notes is located on the shore of Lake Coeur d'Alene. A residence and related structures sit on two contiguous lakefront lots, and there are two additional lots adjacent thereto. The two primary lots total 2.18 acres. The residence, a luxury custom home, is about 11,000 square feet in size. There is a separate 1,500 square foot caretaker residence and a separate 900 square foot garage with a dwelling unit over it. The court valued the lots and residences, excluding moveable personal property (i.e., extensive furniture and art), at $9,000,000.

Anaconda commenced foreclosure on the deeds of trust. There was a $7,000,000 bid that Anaconda obtained for the residence property. At a separate foreclosure sale on April 15, Anaconda obtained a $145,000 bid for the adjacent lots.

Ryerson was entitled to remove personal property such as furniture and art, but he also removed fixtures and Anaconda sought remedies for the loss of the improperly removed fixtures. Anaconda requested that the court order the Debtor, who had "stripped" over $550,000 worth of "fixtures" from the property, be required to return them.

The Debtor maintained that the items are not fixtures and sought to sell the non-fixture personal property and devote the proceeds to payment of creditors under the Chapter 11 plan.

DECISION: The court decided for the debtor with respect to some of the property and the creditor in others.

1. under Idaho law, recessed "can" lighting, in-cabinet lighting, wall sconces, installed indirect lighting, and outdoor "carriage lights" were fixtures, but suspended or hanging lighting, including large chandeliers, were not;
2. the French-made gas and electric range, though a wedding present from debtor to his wife, was "installed" in a manner that spoke objectively to the intent that it be a permanent accession, and so was a fixture;
3. the other appliances were not fixtures;
4. the house's sound system was a fixture because of its integration into the walls;
5. the house's standby generators were not fixtures because they could be removed from their concrete bases;
6. the two large bronze statues on the property were not fixtures because they could be moved from their bases without damage; and
7. the dock built for use in conjunction with the property was not a fixture because it could be detached and moved.

The decisions were based on degree of attachment, damage upon removal, relationship of the item to the property, and whether its use could be transferred elsewhere. **[In re Ryerson, 519 B.R. 275 (D. Idaho 2014)]**

---

fee simple estate–highest level of land ownership; full interest of unlimited duration.

life estate–an estate for the duration of a life.

C P A   ## 48-2 Nature and Form of Real Property Ownership

A person's interest in real property may be defined in terms of the period of time for which the person will remain the owner as (1) a **fee simple estate** or (2) a **life estate.** These estates are termed *freehold estates,* which are interests of uncertain duration. At the time of creation of a freehold estate, a termination date is not known. When a person

[4] *Steel Farms, Inc. v. Croft & Reed, Inc.,* 297 P.3d 222 (Idaho 2012); *Taco Bell of America, Inc. v. Com. Transp. Com'r,* 710 S.E.2d 478 (Va. 2011).

leasehold estate–
interest of a tenant in
rented land.

owns property for a specified period of time, this interest is not regarded as a freehold estate; it is a **leasehold estate,** subject to special rules of law.

estate in fee–largest
estate possible in which
the owner has absolute
and entire interest in the
land.

48-2a   Fee Simple Estate

An **estate in fee,** a fee simple, or a fee simple absolute lasts forever. The owner of such a land interest held in fee simple has the absolute and entire interest in the land. The important characteristics of this estate are that (1) it is alienable, or transferable, during life, (2) it is alienable by will, (3) it passes to heirs of the owner if it is not specifically devised (transferred by will), (4) it is subject to rights of the owner's surviving spouse, and (5) it can be attached or used to satisfy debts of the owner before or after death.

fee simple defeasibles–
fee simple interest that
can be lost if restrictions
on its use are violated.

There are other forms of the fee simple estate generally used for control of land use. **Fee simple defeasibles** are interests that give the grantee all the rights of a fee simple holder provided that the grantee complies with certain restrictions. **For Example,** the grant "To Ralph Watkins so long as he uses the property for school purposes" is an example of a fee simple defeasible. Watkins will have all the rights of a fee simple holder provided that he uses the property for school purposes. If Watkins ever stops using the property for school purposes, the property reverts back to the grantor.

48-2b   Life Estate

A *life estate* (or life tenancy), as its name indicates, lasts only during the life of a person (ordinarily its owner). Upon the death of the person by whose life the estate was measured, the owner of the life estate has no interest remaining to pass to heirs or by will. **For Example,** a grant of a life estate would be "To my husband, Nathan Jones, for life, and then to my children." Jones would hold title to the property only for the time he is alive. When Jones dies, he cannot give the property away by will. If Jones conveys the property while he is alive, the grantee for the property holds title to the land only until Jones's death.

48-2c   Future Interests

In several of the examples given to illustrate fee simple and life estates, interests were created in more than one person. **For Example,** in the preceding life estate example, the children of the grantor are given an interest in the land at the same time that Jones is. However, the interests of the children will not take effect until Jones dies. The children have a future interest in the land. Their interest is referred to as a **remainder interest** because they have the remaining interest in the land once the life estate ends.

remainder interest–land
interest that follows a life
estate.

possibility of reverter–
nature of the interest
held by the grantor after
conveying land outright
but subject to a condition
or provision that may
cause the grantee's
interest to become
forfeited and the interest
to revert to the grantor or
heirs.

In the Watkins fee simple defeasible example, the grantor has a future interest if Watkins violates the restriction. The grantor's interest is called a **possibility of reverter.** It is a future interest because it cannot exist unless Watkins violates the use restriction placed on his present interest.

48-3   Liability to Third Persons for Condition of Real Property

A person entering the land of another may be injured by the condition of the land. Who is liable for such harm?

CPA

48-3a Common Law Rule

trespasser—person who is on the land of another without permission or authorization.

licensee—someone on another's premises with the permission of the occupier, whose duty is to warn the licensee of nonobvious dangers.

invitee—person who enters another's land by invitation.

attractive nuisance doctrine—a rule imposing liability upon a landowner for injuries sustained by small children playing on the land when the landowner permits a condition to exist or maintains equipment that a reasonable person should realize would attract small children who could not realize the danger. The rule does not apply if an unreasonable burden would be imposed upon the landowner in taking steps to protect the children.

Under the common law, liability to a person who enters the land of another is controlled by the status of the injured person—that is, whether the person injured was a **trespasser,** a **licensee,** or an **invitee.** A different duty is owed by the owner (or occupier, as when a tenant is leasing property) of land to persons in each of these three categories.

Trespassers

For a trespasser, the landowner ordinarily owes the duty of refraining from causing intentional harm only once the presence of the trespasser is known. The landowner is not under any duty to warn of dangers or to make the premises safe to protect the trespasser from harm. The most significant exception to this rule arises in the case of small children. Even when children are trespassers, they are generally afforded greater protection through the **attractive nuisance doctrine. For Example,** the owner of a tract of land was held liable for the death of a seven-year-old child who drowned in a creek on that land. Snow had covered the ice on the creek, and children running across the land did not know of the creek's location or the danger of the ice. The landowner had a duty to fence the creek, put up warnings, or control the children's access.[5]

Licensees

Licensees are on the premises with the permission of the landowner, who owes the duty of warning of nonobvious dangers that are known to the owner. A host must warn a guest of such dangers. **For Example,** when a sliding glass door is "invisible" if the patio lights are on and the house lights are off, the owner must warn guests of the presence of the glass. The owner is liable if he has not warned guests of the danger and a guest is injured in shattering the glass. An owner, however, owes no duty to a licensee to take any steps to learn of the presence of dangers that are unknown to the owner.

Invitees

Invitees are persons who enter another's land by invitation. The entry is connected with the owner's business or with an activity the occupier conducts on the land. Business customers, for example, are invitees.

Owners have a duty to take reasonable steps to discover any danger and a duty to warn the invitee or to correct the danger. **For Example,** a store must make a reasonable inspection of the premises to determine that there is nothing on the floor that would be dangerous, such as a slippery substance that might cause a patron to fall. The store must correct the condition, appropriately rope off the danger area, or give suitable warning. If the owner of the premises fails to take the degree of care required and an invitee is harmed as a result, then the owner is liable for such harm.

In most states, the courts have expanded the concept of invitees beyond the category of customers, or those whose presence will economically benefit the occupier. Invitees now usually include members of the public who are invited onto the premises and who cannot be reasonably expected to make an inspection of the premises before using them and would not be able to make necessary repairs to dangerous conditions. Some courts have also made inroads into the prior law by treating a recurring licensee, such as a letter carrier, as an invitee. For more information on landowner liability, refer to Chapter 9 on torts.

[5] *Peguero v. Tau Kappa Epsilon Local Chapter,* 106 A.3d 565 (N.J. Super. A.D. 2015).

CASE SUMMARY

A Loose Clothes Line, a Saved Cow, and a Broken Back

FACTS: On March 10, 2006, Rodney Wrinkle (appellant/plaintiff) and his friend Raymond Lee observed four or five cows wandering loose in front of property belonging to Gene and Charlene Norman (defendants), and some of the cattle were straying toward the highway that ran between Wrinkle's and the Normans' property. Wrinkle was riding his lawn tractor, and he signaled to approaching cars to slow down. Initially riding on his lawn tractor and then going on foot, Wrinkle proceeded to herd the cattle into the Normans' yard. The Normans' gate was open, and Wrinkle herded the cows through the gate toward a pen.

A clothesline wire was attached to a pole in the Normans' yard. As Wrinkle herded the cattle across the Normans' yard toward the cow pen, one calf strayed into the clothesline wire, caught the line around its neck, and began to choke. Wrinkle grabbed the back of the clothesline and walked around to the other side, flipping the line several times in order to remove the line from the calf's neck. The calf took off running toward the gate of the pen, apparently catching the clothesline somehow, so that the clothesline caught Wrinkle from behind. Wrinkle's feet went out from under him, and he landed on his back on a concrete pad.

Wrinkle immediately experienced severe pain. Lee helped him get home, and Wrinkle eventually went to the hospital, where he was diagnosed with a broken back. He was hospitalized for 30 days. Afterward, he approached the Normans in person about the injury and later wrote a letter in which he asked that they submit to their insurance carrier a claim for $44,115.72, which was the outstanding balance on his hospital bill. The Normans refused to arrange for payment of the medical expenses.

Wrinkle then filed an action grounded in negligence alleging that the Normans had created a dangerous condition on their property that presented an unreasonable risk of harm by leaving their gate open and by leaving a clothesline wire running across the ground.

The Normans filed a motion for summary judgment. The court granted the Normans' motion for summary judgment, holding that Wrinkle was a trespasser on the Normans' property and they had breached no duty toward him. The Court of Appeals affirmed. Wrinkle appealed.

DECISION: Although the rescuer was somewhere between a licensee and invitee, the question is what to do about Samaritans who enter the property of another to help that property owner.

The duty of reasonable care is essentially the same as the duty under the theory that the Normans were negligent in the manner of storing their clothesline. Because Wrinkle asserts that the injury occurred on the Normans' property and in the course of attempting to protect the Normans' calf, it is that theory of negligence that governs the duty of care.

The court held that the Normans could be held liable under a theory of negligence and that there was a question of fact that required the case to go to a jury to make the determination of whether the Normans had exercised reasonable care in hanging their clothes.

DISSENT: A duty to remove any object from one's property that could in any fashion somehow be a factor in an injury to another person entering one's property simply increases the possibility of liability and litigation to an absurd level. [**Wrinkle v. Norman**, 301 P.3d 312 (Kan. 2013)]

48-4 Co-Ownership of Real Property

Real property may be owned by one or several persons, and the method of co-ownership determines the extent of the owners' rights.

48-4a Multiple Ownership

Several persons may have *concurrent interests* (or interests that exist at the same time) in the same real property. The forms of multiple ownership for real property are the same as those for personal property. Real property can be held by tenants in common, by joint tenants with right of survivorship, by tenants by the entirety, or under community property rights. When co-owners sell property, they hold the proceeds of sale by the same kind of tenancy as that in which they held the original property.

48-4b **Condominiums**

condominium—combination of co-ownership and individual ownership.

A **condominium** is a combination of co-ownership and individual ownership. **For Example,** persons owning an office building or an apartment house by condominium are co-owners of the land and of the halls, lobby, elevators, stairways, exits, surrounding land, incinerator, laundry rooms, and other areas used in common. Each apartment or office in the building, however, is individually owned and is transferred in the same way as other forms of real property.

Control and Expense

In some states, owners of the various units in the condominium have equal voice in its management and share an equal part of its expenses. In others, control and liability for expenses are shared by a unit owner in the same ratio that the value of the unit bears to the value of the entire condominium project. In all states, unit owners have equal rights to use the common areas. An owners' association is created by the condominium owners to operate the common areas of the condominium property and resolve any disputes among owners.

The owner of each condominium unit makes the repairs required by the owner's deed or contract of ownership. The owner is prohibited from making any major change that would impair or damage the safety or value of an adjoining unit.

Collection of Expenses from Unit Owner

When a unit owner fails to pay the owner's share of taxes, operating expenses, and repairs, the owners' association generally has the right to a lien against that owner's unit for the amount due.

Tort Liability

Most condominium projects fail to make provision for the liability of unit owners for a tort occurring in the common areas. A few states expressly provide that when a third person is injured in a common area, a suit may be brought only against the condominium association. Any judgment recovered is a charge against the association to be paid off as a common expense. When the condominium association is incorporated, the same result should be obtained by applying ordinary principles of corporation law. Under principles of corporation law, liability for torts occurring on the premises of the corporation would not be the liability of individual shareholders.

cooperative—group of two or more persons or enterprises that acts through a common agent with respect to a common objective, such as buying or selling.

deed—an instrument by which the grantor (owner of land) conveys or transfers the title to a grantee.

Cooperatives Distinguished

Ownership in a condominium is different from ownership in a **cooperative.** An apartment cooperative is typically a corporation that owns an apartment complex. The "ownership" interests of the apartment occupants are as stockholders of the corporation.

grantor—owner who transfers or conveys an interest in land to a new owner.

grantee—new owner of a land conveyance.

48-5 **Transfer of Real Property by Deed**

Although many of the technical limitations of the feudal system and earlier common law on transfer of land have disappeared, much of the law relating to the modern deed originated in those days.

CPA

transferee—buyer or vendee.

48-5a **Definitions**

A **deed** is an instrument or writing by which an owner or **grantor** transfers or conveys an interest in land to a new owner. The new owner is called a **grantee** or **transferee.** Real property may be either sold or given as a gift. A deed, however, is necessary to transfer title to land, even if it is a gift.

In contrast to the situation with a contract, no consideration is required to make a deed effective. Although consideration is not required to make a deed valid or to transfer title by deed, the absence of consideration may show that the owner makes the transfer to defraud creditors. The creditors may then be able to set aside the fraudulent transfer.

CPA

quitclaim deed–deed by which the grantor purports to give up only whatever right or title the grantor may have in the property without specifying or warranting transfer of any particular interest.

CPA

warranty deed–deed by which the grantor conveys a specific estate or interest to the grantee and makes one or more of the covenants of title.

acceptance–unqualified assent to the act or proposal of another, such as the acceptance of a draft (bill of exchange), of an offer to make a contract, of goods delivered by the seller, or of a gift or deed.

CPA

recorder–public official in charge of deeds.

race statute–statute under which the first party to record the deed holds the title.

notice statute–statute under which the last good-faith or bona fide purchaser holds the title.

48-5b Classification of Deeds

Deeds may be classified according to the interest conveyed as **quitclaim deeds** or **warranty deeds.** A quitclaim deed merely transfers whatever interest, if any, the grantor may have in the property without specifying that interest in any way. A warranty deed transfers a specified interest and warrants or guarantees that such interest is transferred. Figure 48-1 is a sample warranty deed.

48-5c Execution of Deeds

Ordinarily, the grantor must sign, by signature or mark, a deed. A deed must be executed and delivered by a person having capacity. A deed may be set aside by the grantor for fraud by the grantee if third persons have not acquired rights in the land in good faith.

48-5d Delivery and Acceptance of Deeds

A deed has no effect and title does not pass until the deed has been delivered. Delivery is a matter of intent as shown by words and conduct; no particular form of ceremony is required. The essential intent in delivering a deed is not merely that the grantor intends to hand over physical control and possession of the paper on which the deed is written but also that the grantor intends thereby to transfer the ownership of the property described in the deed. That intent can be shown by handing it to the grantee or placing the deed, addressed to the grantee, in the mail or by giving it to a third person with directions to give it to the grantee.

An effective delivery of a deed may be made symbolically, or constructively, such as by delivering to the grantee the key to a locked box and informing the grantee that the deed to the property is in the box. **For Example,** the delivery of a safe deposit box key has been held to constitute delivery of a deed that was in the box.

Generally, there must be an **acceptance** by the grantee. In all cases, an acceptance is presumed unless the grantee disclaims the transfer.

48-5e Recording of Deeds

The owner of land may record the deed in the office of a public official, sometimes called a **recorder** or *commissioner of deeds.* The recording is not required to make the deed effective to pass title, but it is done so that the public will know that the grantee is the present owner and thereby prevent the former owner from making any future transfer or transaction relating to the property.

When no document is recorded, states have statutes for determining who obtains title and who will be left to take action against the party that has conveyed the property to more than one person. **For Example,** suppose that Grant conveys a tract of land to Dee. Dee does not record her deed. Grant then conveys the same tract of land to Joe, who also does not record his deed, but Joe is unaware of Dee's acquisition. Then Grant conveys the same property to Larry who knows about Dee and Joe but records his deed. Who will hold title, and who will be left to pursue Grant for remedies? Under **race statutes,** the first party to record the deed holds title, so Larry holds title. Under **notice statutes,** the last good-faith or bona fide purchaser (BFP), someone who does not know

FIGURE 48-1   Form of Warranty Deed

THIS DEED, made the twentieth day of November, two thousand and . . . between James K. Damron, residing at 132 Spring Street in the Borough of Manhattan, City and State of New York, party of the first part, and Terrence S. Bloemker, residing at 14 Steinway Street in the Borough of Queens, City and State of New York, party of the second part,

WITNESSETH, that the party of the first part, in consideration of the sum of one dollar ($1), lawful money of the United States, and other good and valuable consideration paid by the party of the second part, does hereby grant and release unto the party of the second part, his heirs and assigns forever,

ALL that certain lot, piece, and parcel of land situated in the Borough of Manhattan, City and County of New York, and State of New York, and bounded and described as follows:

Beginning at a point on the northerly side of Spring Street, distant two hundred (200) feet westerly from the corner formed by the intersection of the northerly side of Spring Street with the westerly side of 6th Avenue, running thence northerly parallel with 6th Avenue one hundred (100) feet, thence westerly and parallel with said Spring Street one hundred (100) feet; thence southerly, again parallel with said 6th Avenue one hundred (100) feet to the northerly side of Spring Street, and thence easterly along the said northerly side of Spring Street one hundred (100) feet to the point or place of beginning.

Together with the appurtenances and all the estate and rights of the party of the first part in and to said premises.

TO HAVE AND TO HOLD the premises herein granted unto the party of the second part, his heirs and assigns forever.

AND the party of the first part covenants as follows:

First. That the party of the first part is seised of the said premises in fee simple, and has good right to convey the same;

Second. That the party of the second part shall quietly enjoy the said premises;

Third. That the said premises are free from encumbrances except as expressly stated;

Fourth. That the party of the first part will execute or procure any further necessary assurance of the title to said premises;

IN WITNESS WHEREOF, the party of the first part has hereunto set his hand and seal the day and year first above written.

JAMES K. DAMRON

(L.S.)

In presence of:

DIANA L. REILMAN

State of New York   } S.S.:*

County of New York

On the twentieth day of November in the year two thousand and . . . , before me personally came James K. Damron, to me known and known to me to be the individual described in, and who executed, the foregoing instrument, and he acknowledged that he executed the same.

DIANA L. REILMAN

Notary Public, New York County

*Acknowledgment before a notary public is not essential to the effectiveness of a deed, but it is typically required to qualify the deed for recording.

notice-race statute— statute under which the first bona fide purchaser to record the deed holds the title.

about the previous conveyances, takes title. Under notice, Joe holds title because he is the last BFP. Larry knows about the prior transactions and that fact controls title, not the recording of his deed under notice statutes. Under **notice-race** or **race-notice statutes,** the first BFP to record the deed holds title. So, if Dee records first, she holds title. If Joe records first, he will. Larry has recorded but does not meet the second requirement of

race-notice statute–see *notice-race statute*.

race-notice, which is that one must be the first BFP to record to take title in a race-notice statute. Suppose that Larry is a BFP, but Joe is not because he is aware of the conveyance to Dee. Under race, Larry holds title. Under notice, Larry holds title. Under race-notice, Larry wins again. If Dee records her deed, all of these issues are moot because recording the deed is complete notice for all subsequent purchasers.

The fact that a deed is recorded provides notice to the world about who holds title. The recording of a deed, however, is only such notice if the deed was properly executed. Likewise, the grantee of land cannot claim any protection by virtue of the recording of a deed when (1) a claim is made by one whose title is superior to that of the owner of record, (2) the grantee had notice or knowledge of the adverse claim when title was acquired, (3) a person acting under a hostile claim was then in possession of the land, (4) the grantee received the land as a gift, or (5) the transfer to the grantee was fraudulent.

CASE SUMMARY

The Double-Deeded Property to the Incurious Neighbors

FACTS: In January 1986, Norman and Mildred Dahl conveyed the disputed property (a 1.667 acre tract located in McKenzie County) to Harry and Linda Chornuk by warranty deed, but the deed was not recorded until June 24, 2010. On June 17, 2005, after Norman Dahl's death, Mildred Dahl conveyed the same property by warranty deed to the Nelsons as part of the conveyance of approximately 44.5 acres. The deed was recorded on July 5, 2005.

In 2010, the Chornuks sued the Nelsons to quiet title to the property. The district court quieted title in favor of the Chornuks. The court found that the Chornuks' actions were sufficient to put a prudent person on notice that someone else had an interest in the property and that the Nelsons

were required to conduct further inquiry before purchasing the property from Mildred Dahl. The court found the Nelsons had constructive notice of the Chornuks' interest and were not good-faith purchasers.

The Nelsons appealed.

DECISION: The Chornuks held title to the property because they were the first good-faith purchasers to record. The Nelsons recorded first, but they were not good-faith purchasers because they had seen the Chornuks on the property and never asked questions about their presence or reasons for improving and caring for the property. Judgment affirmed. [*Chornuk v. Nelson*, 857 N.W.2d 587 (N.D. 2014)]

abstract of title–history of the transfers of title to a given piece of land, briefly stating the parties to and the effect of all deeds, wills, and judicial proceedings relating to the land.

48-5f Additional Protection of Buyers

In addition to the protection given to buyers and third persons by the recorded title to property, a buyer is generally protected by procuring title insurance or an abstract of title. An **abstract of title** is a summarized report of the title to the property as shown by the records, together with a report of all judgments, mortgages, and similar recorded claims against the property.

48-5g Grantor's Warranties

The warranties of the grantor relate to the title transferred by the grantor and to the fitness of the property for use.

CPA

Warranties of Title

warranty of title–implied warranty that title to the goods is good and transfer is proper.

In the common law deed, the grantor may expressly warrant or make certain *covenants* as to the title conveyed. The statutes authorizing a short form of deed provide that, unless otherwise stated in the deed, the grantor is presumed to have made certain **warranties of title.**

covenants (or
warranties) of title–
grantor's covenants of a
deed that guarantee
such matters as the right
to make the conveyance,
to ownership of the
property, to freedom of
the property from
encumbrances, or that
the grantee will not be
disturbed in the quiet
enjoyment of the land.

covenant of seisin–
guarantee that the
grantor of an interest in
land owns the estate
conveyed to a new
owner.

covenant of right to
convey–guarantee that
the grantor of an interest
in land, if not the owner,
has the right or authority
to make the conveyance
to a new owner.

covenant against
encumbrances–
guarantee that conveyed
land is not subject to any
right or interest of a third
person.

covenant of quiet
enjoyment–covenant by
the grantor of an interest
in land to not disturb the
grantee's possession of
the land.

The more important of the **covenants (or warranties) of title** that the grantor may make are (1) **covenant of seisin,** or guarantee that the grantor owns the estate conveyed, (2) **covenant of right to convey,** or guarantee that the grantor, if not the owner as in the case of an agent, has the right or authority to make the conveyance, (3) **covenant against encumbrances,** or guarantee that the land is not subject to any right or interest of a third person, such as a lien or an easement, (4) **covenant of quiet enjoyment,** or guarantee by the grantor that the grantee's possession of the land will not be disturbed either by the grantor, in the case of a **limited covenant,** or by the grantor or any person claiming title under the grantor, in the case of a general covenant, and (5) **covenant of further assurances,** or guarantee that the grantor will execute any additional documents that may be required to perfect the title of the grantee.

Fitness for Use

Courts in most states hold that when a builder or real estate developer sells a new house to a home buyer, the buyer gets an implied warranty that the house and foundation are fit for occupancy or use. This warranty arises regardless of whether the house was purchased before, during, or after completion of construction.[6] This first buyer is not responsible for the builder warranty when the house is resold. However, there is authority that the second buyer may recover from the original contractor for breach of the implied warranty even though there is no privity of contract.[7]

48-5h Grantee's Covenants

In a deed, the grantee may agree to do or to refrain from doing certain acts. Such an agreement becomes a binding contract between the grantor and the grantee. The grantor may recover from the grantee for its breach. The right to enforce the covenant also runs with the land owned by the grantor to whom the promise was made. **For Example,** a promise not to use a tract of land for a parking lot between two adjoining landowners would be passed (conveyed) to any buyers who subsequently acquire these tracts. For more information on covenants, see Chapter 49, Environmental Law and Land Use Controls.

48-6 Other Methods of Transferring Real Property

Title to real property can also be acquired by eminent domain and by adverse possession.

CPA

limited covenant–any
covenant that does not
provide the complete
protection of a full
covenant.

covenant of further
assurances–promise
that the grantor of an
interest in land will
execute any additional
documents required to
perfect the title of the
grantee.

48-6a Eminent Domain

Under **eminent domain,** property is taken from its private owner for a public purpose. The title is then taken by a government or public authority. There are constitutionally protected rights of property owners under eminent domain. Known as the "takings clause," this portion of the Fifth Amendment to the U.S. Constitution requires compensation when private property is taken for public use. Two important issues arise under the takings clause: whether there is a taking of property and whether the property is taken for a public use. With respect to whether a taking has occurred, it is not necessary that the owner be physically deprived of the property but that normal use of the property has been

---

[6] *Richards v. Powercraft Homes, Inc.,* 678 P.2d 427 (Ariz. 1984); *Hernandez v. Chisesi Investments, L.L.C.,* 164 So. 3d 912 (La. App. 2014).
[7] Many states have passed statutes that govern the extent of the implied warranty of habitability. Although the statutes vary, the types of defects covered include defects in construction, design, and appearance. See *Corry v. Jahn,* 972 N.E.2d 907 (Ind. App. 2012).

eminent domain–power of government and certain kinds of corporations to take private property against the objection of the owner, provided the taking is for a public purpose and just compensation is made for it.

impaired or lost. Whether there is a public use for the taking is a question that continues to be challenged in court because the definition of public purpose is so broad. **For Example,** property can be taken to build a freeway as well as for the preservation of a historic site. In the eminent domain cases after 2000, much of the litigation centered on whether revitalizations of areas with urban blight were permissible takings. Eminent domain has activated a concerned public as state and local governments take more and more houses and land for purposes of economic development.

CASE SUMMARY

Little Pink Houses, for You, but Not for Me...Anymore

FACTS: In 1978, the city of New London, Connecticut, undertook a redevelopment plan for purposes of creating a redeveloped area in and around the existing park at Fort Trumball. The plan had the goals of achieving all the related ambience a state park should have, including the absence of pink cottages and other architecturally eclectic homes. Part of the redevelopment plan was the city's deal with Pfizer Corporation for the location of its research facility in the area. The preface to the city's development plan stated that it would *"create jobs increase tax and other revenues, encourage public access to and use of the city's waterfront, and eventually 'build momentum' for the revitalization of the rest of the city, including its downtown area."*

Susette Kelo, and other property owners whose homes would be razed and whose land would be taken to allow for the park, Pfizer's facility, and other redevelopment (15 total owners including Kelo), asked to be permitted to stay in the area. The city refused their request.

Kelo and the other homeowners filed suit challenging New London's legal authority to take their homes. The trial court issued an injunction preventing New London from taking certain of the properties but allowing others to be taken. Those property owners who were held subject to eminent domain appealed.

The appellate court found for New London on all claims; the landowners appealed.

DECISION: In a 5-4 decision delivered by Justice Stevens, joined by Justices Kennedy, Souter, Ginsberg, and Breyer,

the U.S. Supreme Court upheld the decision of the Connecticut Supreme Court. New London's taking of the homes of Kelo and others qualifies as a "public use." Local governments cannot take private land simply to give to a particular private party, but when the takings are part of a carefully considered economic development plan, then the takings are constitutional. Public purpose is a broad category for purposes of determining when takings are constitutional. Economic development is a legitimate and constitutionally protected public purpose. Local governments' determinations that areas are economically distressed are enough to justify a program of economic development and local authorities are entitled to make that determination. The courts will not second-guess local authorities.

AFTERMATH: Ms. Kelo's home and 15 others were razed. Pfizer merged with Wyeth in 2009 and closed all company operations in New London. The Fort Trumball area has no houses, no research park, no businesses, and is now undeveloped land. However, following Hurricane Irene, officials from the city of New London announced that the citizens of their fair city could dump their branches and fallen trees at the site where Ms. Kelo's home once sat. A new mayor of New London announced a plan in 2015 to turn the area into a park to serve as a memorial to those who lost their homes to eminent domain. Forty-five states changed their eminent domain statutes to prevent takings such as those in *Kelo.* [***Kelo v. City of New London*, 545 U.S. 469 (2005)**]

adverse possession–hostile possession of real estate, which when actual, visible, notorious, exclusive, and continued for the required time, will vest the title to the land in the person in such adverse possession.

48-6b Adverse Possession

Title to land may be acquired by possessing it adversely for a statutorily prescribed period of time. A possessor who complies with the requirements for **adverse possession** can gain title. Those who adversely possess property gain title to property even though they had no right to use the property at the beginning of their use or possession.

To acquire title by adverse possession, the possession must be (1) actual, (2) visible and notorious, (3) exclusive, (4) hostile, and (5) continuous for a required period of time.

THINKING THINGS THROUGH

Putting the Brakes on Eminent Domain

Bailey's Brake Service, a bit of an eyesore at a main intersection near a failing downtown area of Mesa, Arizona, was a family-founded, owned, and operated business that had been open in its existing location since 1970. Lenhart's True Value Hardware store was also a longstanding Mesa business with a location south and east of Bailey's and a desire for a better location. The Lenharts had purchased the property abutting Bailey's but felt that the street facing Bailey's property was necessary for its location.

The city did a taking by eminent domain and then "reissued" the property to Lenhart's for its store. The Baileys challenged the city's taking in the Superior Court as unconstitutional, but the court held that the taking was constitutional as part of the city's plan for redevelopment and revitalization of the area. The Baileys appealed the trial court decision. Should the Baileys get their property back? Was this a proper eminent domain taking?

[*Bailey v. Myers*, 76 P.3d 898 (Az. Ct. App. 2003)]

State statutes control the required time period, but the typical range is 10 to 20 years. Use or possession of land under a mistaken belief that one is the owner still qualifies for the "hostile" possession required under the fourth element listed.[8]

---

mortgage–interest in land given by the owner to a creditor as security for the payment of the creditor for a debt, the nature of the interest depending upon the law of the state where the land is located. (Parties—mortgagor, mortgagee)

CPA

48-7 Mortgages

An agreement that creates an interest in real property as security for an obligation until that obligation is repaid is a **mortgage.**

The property owner, whose interest in the property is given as security, is the *mortgagor.*

The person who receives the security is the *mortgagee.*

48-7a Characteristics of a Mortgage

A mortgage has three characteristics: (1) the termination of the mortgagee's interest on the performance of the obligation secured by the mortgage, (2) the right of the mortgagee to enforce the mortgage by foreclosure on the mortgagor's failure to perform, and (3) the mortgagor's right to redeem or regain the property.

48-7b Property Subject to Mortgage

In general, any form of property that may be sold or conveyed may be mortgaged. It is immaterial whether the right is a present right, a future interest, or merely a right in the land of another. It is not necessary that the mortgagor have complete or absolute ownership in the property. Mortgagors may mortgage any type of land interest they own.

CPA ## 48-7c Form of Mortgage

Because a mortgage of real property transfers an interest in the property, it must be in writing under the statute of frauds. As a general rule, no particular form of language is required if the language used expresses the intent of the parties to create a mortgage. Many state statutes provide a standardized form for mortgage language that may be used.

---

[8] The state with the shortest period for adverse possession is Texas, whose adverse possession period can be as short as three years. The state with the longest adverse possession period is Wyoming, with 40 years.

48-7d Creative Forms of Financing

adjustable rate mortgage (ARM)– mortgage with variable financing charges over the life of the loan.

reverse mortgage– mortgage in which the owners get their equity out of their home over a period of time and return the house to the lender upon their deaths.

In many situations in which a buyer seeks to purchase property, the conventional methods for obtaining a mortgage are not available because of affordability or qualifications required for a loan. Many creative forms of financing have been developed to help buyers purchase property. **For Example,** residential land buyers, particularly during the real estate boom in 2005–2006, could obtain an **adjustable rate mortgage (ARM),** in which the lower interest rates applied at the beginning of the mortgage help the buyer qualify for the loan. The ARM changes interest rates along with the market, going up and down, unless the ARM has a fixed minimum rate. Other buyers may have the seller finance their purchase through the use of a land or an installment contract. Some new forms of financing, such as the **reverse mortgage,** permit those who have paid off their mortgages on their property to get the value out of their property by having a mortgage company take a mortgage out on the property and pay them money over time. Many senior citizens are able to obtain the additional monthly income they may need by this form of financing, which permits them to draw on their equity in their land. Because of the collapse of the subprime mortgage market in 2007–2008, these creative forms of financing are now under extensive state and federal regulation. In addition, state and federal reforms (under Dodd-Frank) require additional disclosures about the full cost of financing a real property purchase through a mortgage, especially in the types of mortgages in which payments and interest rates fluctuate. (See Chapter 31 for more information.)

48-7e Recording or Filing of Mortgage

An unrecorded mortgage is still valid and binding between and among the parties. A mortgage cannot be set aside on the ground that it has not been recorded. However, recording the mortgage does protect the mortgagee in terms of priority as against other creditors. The recording statutes, including the problems with MERS, also apply to mortgages.

E-COMMERCE & CYBERLAW

MERS and Problems

Mortgage Electronic Registration Systems, Inc. (MERS), was the system used by most lenders for purposes of recording their mortgages for loans on residential property and, thereby, attaining their secured interest and priority. About one-half of the residential mortgages in the United States were recorded in MERS. The effect was that MERS was listed as the mortgagee on the public records. Debtors wanted to know, "Who is MERS?" The result has been litigation around the country, brought by homeowners facing foreclosure. These suits have alleged that MERS had not perfected its security interest in the mortgaged property because the note was split (and sold off in bundles that were then the foundation of collateralized debt obligations on Wall Street) from the deed of trust or mortgage. And MERS was not their mortgagee. Further, the debtors were unable to fight foreclosure because it became difficult to determine who actually was the mortgagee for purposes of determining default, rights, and redemption. The debtors have

argued that their notes were unenforceable without an accompanying mortgage and mortgagee. With the note unenforceable, the debtors argued that they could not be in default because no money was due and owing. The argument has not fared well in deed-of-trust lending, but the litigation continues around the country. Known as the "lost chain of title" cases, the result has been investigations by state attorneys general of how loan and mortgage documents were transferred (including allegations of robo-signing by transferees for transferors). As one writer noted, MERS has had a destructive effect on 400 years of recorded property rights in the United States because the chain of title has been lost in so many cases.

[*Rostami v. BAC Home Loans Servicing, L.P.,* 2013 WL 100946 (D. Nev. 2013)]

Source: David E. Woolley, "MERS: The Unreported Effects of Lost Chain of Title on Real Property Owners," 8 *Hastings Bus. L J.,* 365 (2012).

48-7f **Responsibilities of the Parties**

The mortgagor and mortgagee have the following duties and liabilities when a mortgage is placed on real property.

CPA Taxes, Assessments, and Insurance

The duty to pay taxes and assessments rests with the mortgagor. In the absence of an agreement, neither party is under a duty to insure the mortgaged property. Both parties, however, may insure their respective interests. It is common practice for the mortgagor to obtain a single policy of insurance on the property payable to the mortgagee and the mortgagor generally according to the standard mortgagee clause that pays the outstanding loan balance first.

Impairment of Security

The mortgagor is liable to the mortgagee for any damage to the property caused by the mortgagor that impairs the security of the mortgage by materially reducing the value of the property. Both the mortgagor and the mortgagee have a right of action against a third person who wrongfully injures the property.

48-7g **Transfer of Interest**

Questions arise as to transfers by the mortgagor and the mortgagee of their respective interests and of the liability of a transferee of the mortgagor.

CPA Transfer by Mortgagor

The mortgagor may ordinarily transfer the property without the consent of the mortgagee. Such a transfer passes only the interest of the mortgagor and does not divest or impair a properly recorded mortgage.

The transfer of the property by the mortgagor does not affect the liability of the mortgagor to the mortgagee. Unless the mortgagee has agreed to substitute the mortgagor's grantee for the mortgagor, the mortgagor remains liable for the mortgage debt as though no transfer had been made.[9]

CPA Liability of the Parties in a Transfer by a Mortgagor

assumption–mortgage transfers in which the transferee and mortgagor are liable and the property is subject to foreclosure by the mortgagee if payments are not made.

There are two ways to transfer mortgaged property, and each way has different results in terms of personal liability for the transferee. In the assumption of a mortgage, the transferee agrees to assume liability. In an **assumption,** the mortgagor remains liable, the transferee is liable, and the property is subject to foreclosure by the mortgagee in the event the payments are not made. **For Example,** if Bob sold his house with a $175,000 mortgage for $200,000 to Jane, Jane could pay Bob $25,000 cash and then agree to assume Bob's mortgage. Jane may get the benefit of a lower interest rate by assuming Bob's mortgage. Both Bob and Jane are personally liable, and the mortgagee may foreclose on the property if the payments are not made.

The second method of transfer is called a "subject to" transfer. In this type of transfer, the property is subject to foreclosure, but the transferee does not agree to assume the mortgage personally. The mortgagor remains liable in this type of transfer, too.

Transfer by Mortgagee

In most states, a mortgage may be transferred or assigned by the mortgagee.

---

[9] *Regan v. Jeff D.,* 339 P.3d 1162 (Idaho 2014).

48-7h Rights of Mortgagee after Default

Upon the mortgagor's default, the mortgagee in some states is entitled to obtain possession of the property and collect the rents or to have a receiver appointed for that purpose. In all states, the mortgagee may enforce the mortgage by **foreclosure,** a judicial procedure resulting in sale of the mortgaged property. Generally, upon any default under the terms of the mortgage agreement, the mortgagee has the right to accelerate the debt or declare that the entire mortgage debt is due. The mortgagee generally has this right even though the default related only to paying an installment or to doing some act, such as maintaining insurance on the property or producing receipts for taxes.

A sale resulting from the foreclosure of the mortgage ends the mortgage lien (subject to rights of redemption), and the property passes free of the mortgage to the buyer at the sale. However, the extinction of the mortgage by foreclosure does not destroy the debt that was secured by the mortgage. The mortgagor remains liable for any unpaid balance or deficiency. In many states, the mortgagor is generally given credit for the fair value of the property if it was purchased by the mortgagee.[10]

48-7i Rights of Mortgagor after Default

After default, the mortgagor may seek to stop or stay foreclosure or to redeem the mortgaged land.

Stay of Foreclosure

In certain cases authorized by statute, a **stay (or delay) of foreclosure** may be obtained by the mortgagor to prevent undue hardship.

Redemption

The right of **redemption** is the right of the mortgagor to pay off the mortgage lien and all foreclosure expenses and, by so doing, acquire title to the property. State laws vary, but the right of redemption generally runs from the time of default through to six months after the foreclosure sale.

Make the Connection

Summary

Real property includes land, buildings, fixtures, and rights in the land of another. Some land interests include the right to use the land, such as easements. Easements can be granted or arise by implication or prescription.

The interest held by a person in real property may be defined in terms of the period of time for which the person will remain the owner. The interest may be a fee simple estate, which lasts forever, or a life estate, which lasts for the life of a person. These estates are known as *freehold estates*. If the ownership interest exists for a specified number of days, months, or years, the interest is a leasehold estate.

Personal property may be attached to, or associated with, real property in such a way that it becomes real property. In such a case, it is called a *fixture*. To determine whether property has in fact become a fixture, the courts

---

[10] *BMO Harris Bank, N.A. v. Wildwood Creek Ranch, LLC,* 340 P.3d 1071 (Ariz. 2015).

look to the method of attachment, to how the property is adapted to the realty, and to the intent of the person originally owning the personal property.

Under common law, the liability of a landowner for injury to third persons on the premises depends on the status of the third persons as trespassers, licensees, or invitees. Many jurisdictions, however, are ignoring these common law distinctions in favor of an ordinary negligence standard or are giving licensees the same protection as invitees.

Real property may be the subject of multiple ownership. The forms of multiple ownership are the same as those for personal property. In addition, there are special forms of co-ownership for real property, such as condominiums and cooperatives.

A *deed* is an instrument by which a grantor transfers an interest in land to a grantee. A deed can be a quitclaim deed or a warranty deed. To be effective, a deed must be signed or sealed by the grantor and delivered to the grantee. Recording the deed is not required to make the deed effective to pass title, but recording provides notice to the public that the grantee is the present owner. The warranties of the grantor relate to the title transferred by the

grantor and to the fitness of the property for use. In the absence of any express warranty in the deed, no warranty of fitness arises under the common law in the sale or the conveyance of real estate. Most states today hold that when a builder or real estate developer sells a new home to a buyer, an implied warranty of habitability arises. Title to real estate may also be acquired by eminent domain and adverse possession.

An agreement that creates an interest in real property as security for an obligation and that ends upon the performance of the obligation is a mortgage. A mortgage must be in writing under the statute of frauds. If the mortgage is unrecorded, it is valid between the parties. The mortgage should be recorded to put good-faith purchasers on notice of the mortgage. A purchaser of the mortgaged property does not become liable for the mortgage debt unless the purchaser assumes the mortgage. The mortgagor still remains liable unless the mortgagee agrees to a substitution of parties. If the mortgagor defaults, the mortgagee may enforce the mortgage by foreclosure. Such foreclosure may be delayed because of undue hardship.

Learning Outcomes

After studying this chapter, you should be able to clearly explain:

48-1   Nature of Real Property

LO.1 List the types of real property interests, the rights of the parties and their liabilities
See *Kelo v. City of New London*, page 1015.

LO.2 Distinguish between liens, licenses, and easements
See *Dianne v. Wingate* for a discussion of easement holder rights, page 1003.
See the Sports & Entertainment Law discussion of the New England Patriots, page 1004.

48-2   Nature and Form of Real Property Ownership

LO.3 Discuss the nature and form of real property ownership
See In re *Ryerson* that covers stripping a home of property and the court's analysis as to what is a fixture and what is personal property, page 1006.

48-3   Liability to Third Persons for Condition of Real Property

LO.4 Explain the liability of landowners for injury to others on their property
See the slip-and-fall example in the section titled "Invitees," page 1008.

See the *Wrinkle v. Norman* case for coverage of the duty of landowners to Samaritans who come onto their property to help, page 1009.

48-4   Co-Ownership of Real Property

LO.5 Discuss the forms of co-ownership and parties' rights
See the example of the rights of condominium owners, page 1010.

48-5   Transfer of Real Property by Deed

LO.6 Describe how deeds convey title to land
See the *Chornuk v. Nelson* case for a discussion of multiple deed transfers and the rights of the parties, page 1013.

48-6   Other Methods of Transferring Real Property

Explain eminent domain and adverse possession.
See the *Kelo* case, page 1015.

48-7   Mortgages

LO.7 Describe the characteristics and effect of a mortgages
See the *For Example* discussion of Bob and Jane in the section titled "Liability of the Parties in a Transfer by a Mortgagor," page 1018.

Key Terms

abstract of title
acceptance
adjustable rate mortgage (ARM)
adverse possession
assumption
attractive nuisance doctrine
condominium
cooperative
covenant against encumbrances
covenant of further assurances
covenant of quiet enjoyment
covenant of right to convey
covenant of seisin
covenants (or warranties) of title
deed
dominant tenement
easement
easement by implication
eminent domain
estate in fee

fee simple defeasibles
fee simple estate
fixture
foreclosure
grantee
grantor
invitee
judgment liens
land
leasehold estate
license
licensee
liens
life estate
limited covenant
mechanic's liens
mortgage
notice statutes
notice-race statute
possibility of reverter

prescription
profits
quitclaim deeds
race statutes
race-notice statute
real property
recorder
redemption
remainder interest
reverse mortgage
servient tenement
stay (or delay) of foreclosure
tax liens
transferee
trespasser
warranties of title
warranty deeds
way of necessity

Questions and Case Problems

1. In 1972, Donald and Joyce Carnahan purchased a
   1-acre lot located on a 22-acre lake. The purchase
   included a portion of the lake bed. The Carnahans
   used the lake for recreational activity in both winter
   and summer, and their activities included motor-
   boats, jet skis, and wave runners. In 1991, the
   Moriah Property Owners Association, Inc., acquired
   title to the majority of the lots along the lake and
   imposed restrictive covenants on the use of the lake,
   including one that prohibited all motors on the lake
   except for those powered by 12-volt batteries. The
   Carnahans filed suit to establish a prescriptive easement in their right to use the lake for all their
   activities. Do you think the Carnahans acquired an
   easement by prescription? [*Carnahan v. Moriah
   Property Owners Association, Inc.*, 716 N.E.2d 437
   (Ind.)]

2. Bunn and his wife claimed that they had an easement to enter and use the swimming pool on
   neighboring land. A contract between the former
   owners of the Bunns' property and the adjacent
   apartment complex contained a provision that the
   use of the apartment complex's swimming pool
   would be available to the purchaser and his family.
   No reference to the pool was made in the contract

between the former owners and the Bunns, nor was
there any reference to it in the deed conveying the
property to the Bunns. Decide. [*Bunn v. Offutt*,
222 S.E.2d 522 (Va.)]

3. Harald Dude's real estate dealings began breaking
   bad in 2003. After securing a $1.9 million loan from
   Washington Mutual on a house he owned in Aspen,
   Mr. Dude quickly sought to borrow another
   $500,000 from Wells Fargo. The Washington
   Mutual mortgage was not yet recorded because of a
   defect in the property description. To satisfy Wells
   Fargo, Mr. Dude had to complete a form for the
   bank's title insurance company, Stewart Title. On
   that form, he was asked to disclose existing liens and
   loans on the property, at least those that hadn't
   already turned up in Stewart Title's title search.
   Knowing that the company had failed to discover the
   existence of the Washington Mutual loan and worried that disclosing it now might scotch any chance
   he had of winning a second loan from Wells Fargo,
   Mr. Dude decided to conceal its existence. The plan
   worked: Stewart Title and Wells Fargo proceeded
   with the second loan just as Mr. Dude had hoped.
   Discuss who will have priority in the land if
   Mr. Dude defaults. Does it matter that Mr. Dude

failed to disclose the loan and lien of Washington Mutual? What can we learn from situations such as this one? [*Stewart Title Guaranty Company v. Dude*, 708 F.3d 1191 (10th Cir.)]

4. After executing the various deeds, J. M. Fernandez Jr. placed them in a closet (with other valuable papers) for safekeeping until they could be physically delivered to the various grantees, including Sylvia Sheppard, when she returned to Key West. This closet was in the home that Fernandez shared with Betty DeMerritt. They were not married but lived together the final 15 years of Fernandez's life. Shortly thereafter, Fernandez was debilitated by a stroke and became a total invalid. He never regained his health and died before Sylvia Sheppard could return to Key West to receive physical delivery of the deed personally from him. When Sylvia Sheppard did arrive in Key West, Betty DeMerritt gave her the deed. This took place two or three days after the death of Fernandez. When questioned as to why she turned the deed over to Sylvia, Betty DeMerritt stated, "I knew he wanted me to do it … because he couldn't do it." She was speaking of Fernandez's physical disability. Does Sylvia have title to the property? Was there delivery? [*Kerr v. Fernandez*, 792 So. 2d 685 (Fla.)]

5. Kenneth Corson, 10, lived with his mother, Lynda Lontz, in an apartment building owned by Bruno and Carolyn Kosinski. While playing with other children who lived in the same building, Corson was drawn to a stairwell that provided access to the building's laundry room and roof. Corson and the other children climbed to the roof and discovered an area where they could jump from the roof of their building to that of the building next door. The children engaged in roof-hopping for several days. On the last day, Corson misjudged his jump and fell the three stories to the ground below. Corson and his mother filed suit against the Kosinskis to collect damages for Corson's injuries. What theory might be used to hold the Kosinskis liable? [*Corson by Lontz v. Kosinski*, 801 F. Supp. 75 (N.D. Ill.)]

6. Determine whether the following would be fixtures or personal property.

   a. Refrigerator in a home

   b. Refrigerators in an apartment complex with furnished units

   c. Refrigerators in a restaurant kitchen

   d. Refrigeration/freezer units in a grocery store

   e. Mini-refrigerator in a student dorm

7. What is the relationship between trespass and adverse possession?

8. At approximately 3:00 A.M., on February 3, 2000, Sonya Winchell was driving two of her friends through a Fort Wayne Taco Bell drive-thru. When Winchell arrived in line, there was one car in front of her at the speaker. Winchell noticed that the occupants of the car, Remco Guy and Ariel Graham, were taking a long time placing their order and then got out of their car. At that point, Winchell yelled out her window, "Can we get moving, we are hungry!" Guy approached Winchell's car, stuck his head in the window, and "started cussing everybody out." Guy removed his head from the window, stuck it back in, and asked, "You got an f-ing problem?" Winchell responded by "drill[ing] him in the nose." Guy then pulled a gun out of his pants and shot Winchell. One of Winchell's passengers and others summoned police officers who were in a nearby parking lot. Winchell survived the shooting, and Guy was convicted of attempted murder. Winchell filed a civil action against Guy and Graham, and against Taco Bell, alleging negligence. Is Taco Bell liable for the injuries that occur on its property? [*Winchell v. Guy*, 857 N.E.2d 1024 (Ind.)]

9. Miller executed a deed to real estate, naming Zieg as grantee. He placed the deed in an envelope on which was written "To be filed at my death" and put the envelope and deed in a safe deposit box in the National Bank that had been rented in the names of Miller and Zieg. After Miller's death, Zieg removed the deed from the safe deposit box. Moseley, as executor under Miller's will, brought an action against Zieg to declare the deed void. Decide. [*Moseley v. Zieg*, 146 N.W.2d 72 (Neb.)]

10. Henry Lile owned a house. When the land on which it was situated was condemned for a highway, he moved the house to the land of his daughter, Sarah Crick. In the course of construction work, blasting damaged the house. Sarah Crick sued the contractors, Terry & Wright, who claimed that Lile should be joined in the action as a plaintiff and that Sarah could not sue by herself because it was Lile's house. Were the defendants correct? [*Terry & Wright v. Crick*, 418 S.W.2d 217 (Ky.)]

11. Bradt believed that his backyard ran all the way to a fence. Actually, a strip on Bradt's side of the fence belonged to his neighbor, Giovannone, but Bradt never intended to take land away from anyone. Bradt later brought an action against Giovannone to

determine who owned the strip on Bradt's side of the fence. Who is the owner? Why? [*Bradt v. Giovannone*, 315 N.Y.S.2d 96]

12. Robert E. Long owned land in the City of Hampton that he leased to Adams Outdoor Advertising Limited Partnership. Adams had an advertising billboard placed on the property. On October 6, 1993, Long notified Adams that he was terminating the lease. Adams accepted the termination and told Long that it would have the electrical service disconnected and would schedule demolition of the billboard for the first week in November. Long wanted to use the billboard to advertise his own business and filed suit to enjoin Adams from destroying the billboard. Long maintained that the billboard was part of the land and that it belonged to him. Adams asserted that it owned the billboard as a lessee. The trial court found for Long, and Adams appealed. Decide. [*Adams Outdoor Adv., Ltd., Part. v. Long*, 483 S.E.2d 224 (Va.)]

13. The Friersons have a two-story building in Easley, South Carolina, that shares a common wall with an adjacent two-story building owned by David and Patricia Watson. An outdoor stairway located on the Watsons' property provides access to the second floor of both buildings. A dispute arose when David Watson began to construct apartments on the second floor of his building and proposed to close off a connecting indoor hallway between the two properties at the top of the stairs located inside the building. The Friersons maintained that they had an easement to use both the outdoor stairway and the indoor hallway for access.

The Friersons' predecessors-in-interest, E. C, E. O., and D. M. Frierson, purchased the building in 1929 from the "Estate of R. F. Smith, Inc." The 1929 deed, dated January 14 and recorded on January 23, expressly conveyed "an easement in a certain four foot stairway in the back of the building, with right of ingress and egress on said stairway to the second story of said building." On January 21, 1929, two days before the deed was recorded, the parties to the sale executed a "Memorandum of Agreement" that granted an easement for the use of the hallway. The memo was not recorded. The Friersons brought suit to stop Watson's construction.

The Friersons claimed that Watson's construction violated their easement by eliminating the hallway, which denied them access to the second floor of their building.

The circuit court determined that the Friersons had established an easement for use of the hallway by grant and by prescription and granted the Friersons' motion. David Watson appealed. Who is correct on this easement issue? Explain why. [*Frierson v. Watson*, 636 S.E. 2d 872 (S.C. App.)]

14. Martin Manufacturing decided to raise additional long-term capital by mortgaging an industrial park it owned. First National Loan Co. agreed to lend Martin $1 million and to take a note and first mortgage on the land and building. The mortgage was duly recorded. Martin sold the property to Marshall, who took the property and assumed the mortgage debt. Does Marshall have any personal liability on the mortgage debt? Is Martin still liable on the mortgage debt? Explain.

15. Christine and Steve Mallock buried their son in a burial plot purchased at Southern Memorial Park, Inc. Each year the Mallocks conducted a memorial service for their son at his burial plot. On the seventh anniversary of their son's death, the Mallocks went to their son's grave at 11:00 A.M. for the annual service, which generally took 30 minutes. When they arrived, they discovered that a tent and chairs set up for funeral services on the plot next to their son's grave were actually resting on his gravesite. The Mallocks asked Southern's management if the tent and chairs could be moved until they could conduct their service. The managers refused, and the Mallocks went ahead with their ceremony, cutting it to five minutes, after they moved the chairs and tents by themselves. Southern's managers called the police and had the Mallocks evicted. Southern claimed that the Mallocks had no rights on the property except for the grave and that their deed for the plot did not award an easement for access. Did the Mallocks have the right to access to the gravesite? [*Mallock v. Southern Memorial Park, Inc.*, 561 So. 2d 330 (Fla. Ct. App.)]

16. *O* conveys property to *A* on December 1, 2015. *O* conveys the same property to *B* who does not know about *A* and who records his deed on December 2, 2015. *O* then conveys the same property to *C*. Who has title to the property?

CPA Questions

The topic of insurance has been eliminated from the content outline for the CPA exam as of October 2009. However, the exam lags behind the content change, and real property questions have continued to be released as questions on the exam.

1. Which of the following statements is correct with respect to a real estate mortgage?

   a. It must be signed only by the mortgagor (borrower).

   b. It must be recorded in order to be effective between the mortgagor and the mortgagee.

   c. It does *not* have to be recorded to be effective against third parties without notice if it is a purchase money mortgage.

   d. It is effective even if *not* delivered to the mortgagee.

2. To be enforceable against the mortgagor, a mortgage must meet all the following requirements *except*:

   a. Be delivered to the mortgagee.

   b. Be in writing and signed by the mortgagor.

   c. Be recorded by the mortgagee.

   d. Include a description of the debt and land involved.

3. Ritz owned a building in which there was a duly recorded first mortgage held by Lyn and a recorded second mortgage held by Jay. Ritz sold the building to Nunn. Nunn assumed the Jay mortgage and had no actual knowledge of the Lyn mortgage. Nunn defaulted on the payments to Jay. If both Lyn and Jay foreclosed and the proceeds of the sale were insufficient to pay both Lyn and Jay, then:

   a. Jay would be paid after Lyn was fully paid.

   b. Jay and Lyn would be paid proportionately.

   c. Nunn would be personally liable to Lyn but not to Jay.

   d. Nunn would be personally liable to Lyn and Jay.

4. Which of the following deeds will give a real property purchaser the greatest protection?

   a. Quitclaim

   b. Bargain and sale

   c. Special warranty

   d. General warranty

Environmental Law and Land Use Controls

Learning Outcomes ‹‹‹

After studying this chapter, you should be able to

LO.1 List and describe the federal statutes that regulate various aspects of the environment

LO.2 Explain how environmental laws are enforced and describe the criminal penalties for violation of environmental laws

LO.3 Define *nuisance* and list the remedies available

LO.4 Explain the role and application of covenants and zoning laws

49-1 Statutory Environmental Law

As the United States changed from a rural, agricultural society to an urban, industrial one, new laws were needed to prevent the pollution of the environment.

49-1a Air Pollution Regulation

Legislative History of Air Pollution Regulation

Clean Air Act–federal legislation that establishes standards for air pollution levels and prevents further deterioration of air quality.

The first legislation that dealt with air pollution, passed in 1955, was the Air Pollution Control Act, which was simply a statutory recognition of a concern about air quality. Even the first statute regulating air pollution, the **Clean Air Act**, passed in 1963, produced no response from the states, which were charged with the responsibility of developing pollution standards and enforcement mechanisms. It was not until the 1970 amendments to the Clean Air Act that the federal law on air pollution got some teeth, for it was in those amendments that Congress established the federal agency responsible for enforcing the law, the Environmental Protection Agency (EPA). The EPA was authorized to establish national air quality standards and see that the states developed plans for the implementation of those standards.

Modern Legislation and Requirements

nonattainment areas–"dirty" areas that do not meet federal standards under the Clean Air Act.

emissions offset policy–controls whether new factories can be built in a nonattainment area.

bubble concept–method for determining total emissions in one area; all sources are considered in an area.

Under the 1970 Clean Air Act,[1] as well as the 1977 and 1990 amendments to it, states must measure sulfur dioxide, carbon monoxide, and hydrocarbons and then take appropriate steps to bring their air quality within the federal limits established for each of these. States that do not meet federal standards are called **nonattainment areas**, or *dirty areas*, and their plans for implementation are strictly reviewed by the EPA, which can halt federal highway funding in the event the implementation plan is not followed. Those states that do meet the federal standards must still have a plan to remain at that level.

For nonattainment areas, the EPA developed an **emissions offset policy**, which controls whether new factories can be built. For a new plant to obtain a permit to begin operations in a nonattainment area, the business proposing the new plant must be able to show that (1) the plant will have the greatest possible emissions controls, which means having better-than-existing emissions standards, (2) the business has all of its other plants and operations in compliance with federal emissions standards, and (3) the new plant's emissions will be offset by reductions in emissions in other facilities in the area. This last requirement is often referred to as the **bubble concept**, which requires an examination of all emissions from all sources in an area. Before any new operations with emissions can be permitted, the business seeking approval must be able to show that overall emissions in the area will not increase.

The 1990 amendments to the Clean Air Act increased the role of the bubble concept with the ability of businesses to transfer their emissions permits. Those businesses that can reduce their emissions below their allowable amounts or that can eliminate their emissions are free to transfer their permit rights to emit to someone else who can then use them without affecting total emissions in the bubble area. There is a market exchange for emissions permits because the EPA will not, under the 1990 act, issue any additional permits beyond the rights to emissions that already exist. Today, approximately 10 percent of all the emissions permit rights are owned by environmental groups.

[1] 42 U.S.C. §1857 *et seq.*

New Developments in Air Quality: The U.S. Supreme Court and the EPA

In *Environmental Defense v. Duke Energy*, 549 U.S. 561 (2007), the U.S. Supreme Court heard a case in which the EPA had brought suit against Duke Energy for implementing modifications to its coal-fired electricity plants without first filing for approval from the agency. Duke maintained that only major modifications to power plants required EPA approval, a standard the EPA had been following for years. However, the EPA based its expanded permit requirements for even minor modifications under the Prevention of Significant Deterioration (PSD) regulations. The utilities challenged the agency's authority to act on greenhouse gases and global warming issues because there was no statutory provision that covered such an expansion. The Court held that the EPA could step up its permit requirements and still be within its statutory authority in choosing which modifications to regulate via permit. The standard has now evolved to one that goes beyond best available technology (BAT) to maximum achievable control technology (MACT), a standard that is not controlled by cost alone, but under recent rulings cost must be considered and weighed.

In *Massachusetts v. EPA*, 549 U.S. 497 (2007), the Court held that the Clean Air Act mandated EPA action on greenhouse gases and global warming. In *Michigan v. EPA*, 135 S.Ct. 2699 (2015), the court held that the EPA must consider cost in researching and promulgating rules with regard to plant emissions. The court held that cost is relevant under the statutes that give the EPA its authority. The EPA efforts against primarily coal-fired plants can continue, but the agency will have to examine the costs of, for example, reducing mercury emissions vs. the benefits obtained.

One expansion of EPA authority has been the EPA rule promulgated to address downwind pollution from coal and gas-fired power plants—that is, pollution that drifts from one state to others. The EPA now requires the upwind states to reduce emissions that result in air pollution problems downwind. Upwind states (there are 28) must control sources within their borders from emitting pollution that travels across state lines in a way that prevents downwind states' attainment of their air quality levels.[2] Known as the **Transport Rule,** this regulation is also referred to as a "good neighbor" provision, and its impact has been the shutdown of coal-fired facilities.

From 2009 forward, there has been increasing expansion of EPA authority through rules that were implemented regardless of the costs to business. **For Example,** the *Michigan v. EPA* case held that the EPA had acted unreasonably under the so-called mercury rules, where the cost of power plant compliance would have been $9.6 billion a year, but the quantifiable benefits from the reduction would be only $4 million to $6 million. The Court's 5-4 holding was one that allowed EPA expansion with the caveat that the agency employ cost/benefit analysis.

Transport Rule–the rule promulgated to address downwind pollution from coal and gas-fired power plants.

49-1b Water Pollution Regulation

The first meaningful regulation in water pollution began at about the same time as effective air pollution regulation. The first legislation with enforcement power was passed in 1972 as the Federal Water Pollution Control Act and then amended and renamed in 1977 as the **Clean Water Act.**[3] Under the Clean Water Act, the EPA has developed **effluent guidelines,** which are ranges for discharges organized according to industrial groups and for

Clean Water Act–federal legislation that regulates water pollution through a control system.

effluent guidelines–EPA standards for maximum ranges of discharge into water.

---

[2] *EME Homer City Generation, L.P. v. EPA*, 134 S. Ct. 1584 (2014). The Transport Rule continues to be a subject of litigation. *Westar Energy, Inc. v. E.P.A.*, 608 Fed.Appx. 1 (C.A.D.C. 2014); Emma E. Schoedel, "The Siren's Song of a Trickle-Down Bureaucracy: The Transport Rule, The Problem of Air Contamination Crossing State Lines, and the EPA Crossing Its Line," 53 *Duquesne Law Review* 629 (2015).

[3] 33 U.S.C. §1251 *et seq*. The pollution of navigable waters had been regulated by the Rivers and Harbors Act of 1899, which required a permit for discharging into navigable rivers, streams, and lakes.

specific plants in each of these groups. The guidelines establish the maximum amounts that can be discharged, and those maximums are coupled with a permit system that requires each plant to obtain a permit from the EPA before discharging anything into any type of pool, pond, river, lake, stream, or ocean.[4] **For Example,** a plant that releases hot water from a steam generator must still have a permit just to release hot water into the stream near the plant. The EPA also has standards for the treatment of water that is used in a plant's production process before that water can be discharged.[5] **For Example,** a plant must still have a permit to discharge water even though that water is cleaner as it is discharged from the plant than it was when it was brought in to be used in production or manufacturing. However, the EPA is permitted to use cost-benefit analysis in setting the standards for the quality of the water that is released back into the river, lake, and other bodies of water. All discharges into the waterways require a **National Pollutant Discharge Elimination System (NPDES)** permit from the EPA. This type of permit is required only for direct dischargers, or **point sources,** and is not required of plants that discharge into sewer systems (although these secondary dischargers may still be required to pretreat their discharges). Obtaining a permit requires EPA and state approval as well as public hearings.

The permits also impose requirements on the permit holder. If the plant is going to release a conventional pollutant, the EPA can require the plant to pretreat the substance with the **best conventional treatment** (BCT). However, the EPA can also require the **best available treatment** (BAT) standard, which is the highest standard imposed. Until 2009, the standard for requiring BAT was solely the consideration of environmental effects and not the economic effects on the applicant. However, the U.S. Supreme Court has held that the EPA can use cost-benefit analysis to allow variances from those standards. In the *Entergy Corporation v. Riverkeeper* case, Entergy's cost of bringing cooling water intake structures to the higher level that the EPA requires for new structures would have been nine times the existing costs. The Court held that the additional benefit achieved was too small to justify the cost of bringing the cooling water facilities up to BAT standards.[6] With this decision as well as the decision in *Michigan v. EPA*, the court has held that cost is a factor in the validity of EPA rules on both air and water pollution controls.

There are other federal statutes that address water pollution issues. The **Safe Drinking Water Act** requires the EPA to establish national standards for contaminants in drinking water. The **Oil Pollution Act** is a federal law passed following the oil spill from the *Exxon Valdez* off the coast of Alaska, which resulted in damage to the waters, fish, and birds in that area. Under this law, companies are financially responsible for the cleanup of their spills that occur in U.S. waters. The act also provides for substantial penalties for failure to take action to clean up a spill, and those penalties can be as high as $25,000 per day or $3,000 per barrel if the spill is the result of negligence or willful misconduct.[7] Failure to report a spill carries penalties of up to five years in prison and/or $250,000 per individual and $500,000 for corporations. In addition, civil penalties for the failure to clean up an oil spill can cost the company up to $50,000,000 in penalties.

---

[4] Even the placement of dirt from adjoining property into a stream can be a CWA violation. *Sackett v. EPA*, 132 S. Ct. 1367 (2012).

[5] In *Coeur Alaska v. Southeast Alaska Conservation*, 557 U.S. 261 (2009), the court held that a project in an Alaskan lake under the supervision of the Army Corps of Engineers did not require an EPA permit process for the operator to obtain permission to dump fill dirt into the lake.

[6] *Entergy Corporation v. Riverkeeper, Inc.*, 556 U.S. 208 (2009).

[7] 33 U.S.C. §2701 *et seq.* The act establishes a cleanup fund for those spills in which the party to blame is unknown or is financially unable to pay the cost of cleanup. The act also requires that boats be double-hulled. The *Exxon Shipping Co. v. Baker*, 554 U.S. 471 (2008) case went through the courts several times before Exxon's initial penalty of $4.5 billion was reduced to maritime limitations of $507.5 million. *Exxon Valdez v. Exxon Mobil*, 568 F.3d 1077 (9th Cir. 2009). Following the 2010 BP Deepwater Horizon rig explosion, BP paid a criminal penalty of $4.5 billion. The civil penalty settlement, which is the settlement of all states and federal claims against BP, is $18.7 billion. Total costs, penalties, and settlements in the case resulted in BP paying out $43.7 billion.

ETHICS & THE LAW

Spreading the Manure a Little Too Thick

Mahard Egg Farm, Inc., headquartered in Texas and with operations in Oklahoma, is the country's 17th largest egg producer. Mahard's poultry operations generated significant amounts of manure—estimated to be in excess of 50,000 tons of dry manure per year. Mahard applied poultry manure to its agricultural fields, with the result being that when it rained and the soil washed into creeks and rivers, the waterways also had high levels of nutrients.

In addition, Mahard stored manure on its farms and the manure piles often resulted in what are called "inactive manure lagoons," with the resulting smells and flies as well

as seepage of the manure and the nutrients into the groundwater.

Mahard has some NPDES permits for some of its facilities, but it did not for others. In addition, Mahard did not comply with its permit requirements for grass buffers as well as control of soil flow.

Develop a list of possible environmental violations. Does it matter for purposes of EPA discharge regulations that the nutrients came from nature (i.e., the manure)? What are the risks for a business when its operations are not in compliance?

Toxic Substances Control Act (TOSCA)–first federal law to control the manufacture, use, and disposal of toxic substances.

Resource Conservation and Recovery Act (RCRA)–federal law that regulates the disposal of potentially harmful substances and encourages resource conservation and recovery.

Comprehensive Environmental Response, Compensation, and Liability Act (CERCLA)–federal law that assigns liability for cleanup of hazardous sites.

Superfund sites–areas designated by the EPA for cleanup.

Superfund Amendment and Reauthorization Act–federal law that expands scope and operation of CERCLA.

potentially responsible parties (PRPs)–those beyond actual polluters who could be responsible for cleanup costs.

49-1c Solid Waste Disposal Regulation

The disposal of solid waste (garbage) has also been regulated since the 1960s, but the initial legislation simply provided money for research by state and local governments on how to dispose of solid waste.[8] In 1970, the **Resource Recovery Act** provided federal money for cities and states with recycling programs.

After several major open-dumping problems that produced community-wide illnesses, including those in the Love Canal area near Buffalo, New York, Congress passed the **Toxic Substances Control Act (TOSCA),** which controls the manufacture, use, and disposal of toxic substances, a list of which the EPA developed. Along with TOSCA, Congress passed the **Resource Conservation and Recovery Act (RCRA),** which regulates the disposal of potentially harmful substances through a permit system and uses federal grants to encourage the restoration of damaged resources.[9] **For Example,** many strip mine locations were restored due to the RCRA.

In 1980, Congress passed the **Comprehensive Environmental Response, Compensation, and Liability Act (CERCLA),**[10] which authorizes the U.S. president to issue funds to be used for the cleanup of areas that were once disposal sites for hazardous wastes. The act set up a trust fund for cleanups, to be reimbursed by the company responsible for such hazardous wastes. The funds in the trust are available for government use but are not subject to attachment by private citizens who seek to get an area cleaned up by removing the hazardous waste. Under CERCLA, the EPA has the authority to designate **Superfund sites,** or parcels of land that are deemed to have, or potentially have, hazardous wastes that require cleanup.

The **Superfund Amendment and Reauthorization Act** authorizes the EPA to bring suit for the purpose of collecting the costs of cleanup from those who are responsible for the hazardous wastes on the site. The act and its judicial interpretations provide a very broad definition of who is responsible under CERCLA for the costs of cleanup. Four classes of parties, known as **potentially responsible parties (PRPs),** can be held liable under CERCLA. "Owners and operators" of contaminated property are liable under the statute.

[8] See the Solid Waste Disposal Act, 42 U.S.C. §3251 *et seq.*, and the Resource Recovery and Policy Act of 1970, 42 U.S.C. §3251 *et seq.*
[9] 42 U.S.C. §6901 *et seq.*
[10] 42 U.S.C. §9601 *et seq.*

Owners include present owners as well as past owners, whether or not they are responsible for the hazardous wastes being dumped on the property. *Operators* include those who are leasing the property, again regardless of whether they are responsible for the hazardous waste being dumped. **For Example,** many gas stations have been designated as Superfund sites because the underground tanks have leaks, causing gas to seep into the soil. Current and past owners of such a station are responsible under CERCLA as well as an owner who has converted the station into some other use.[11]

Other responsible parties under CERCLA include anyone who transported hazardous waste to a site and anyone who hired another or arranged to transport hazardous waste to the site. Lenders were, at one time, also held liable for cleanup costs in the event they took back property from a debtor. However, the Asset Conservation, Lender Liability, and Deposit Insurance Protection Act of 1996 provides an exclusion for lenders provided the lender does not actually participate in the management or operational affairs of the facility of the debtor.[12]

CASE SUMMARY

Don't Blame Me, I'm Only the Arranger

FACTS: In 1960, Brown & Bryant, Inc. (B & B), began operating an agricultural chemical distribution business. Using its own equipment, B & B applied its products to customers' farms. B & B opened its business on a 3.8 acre parcel of former farmland in Arvin, California, and in 1975, expanded operations onto an adjacent .9 acre parcel of land owned jointly by the Atchison, Topeka & Santa Fe Railway Company, and the Southern Pacific Transportation Company (Railroads). Waste water and chemical runoff from the facility was allowed to seep into the ground water below.

During its years of operation, B & B stored and distributed various hazardous chemicals (D-D) on its property sold by Shell Oil Company (Shell). When B & B purchased chemicals from Shell, Shell would arrange for delivery by common carrier, f.o.b. destination. When the product arrived, it was transferred from tanker trucks to a bulk storage tank located on B & B's primary parcel. During each of these transfers leaks and spills could—and often did—occur. Although the common carrier and B & B used buckets to catch spills from hoses and gaskets connecting the tanker trucks to its bulk storage tank, the buckets sometimes overflowed or were knocked over, causing chemical spills onto the ground during the transfer process.

In the late 1970s Shell took several steps to encourage the safe handling of its products. Shell provided distributors with detailed safety manuals and instituted a voluntary discount program for distributors that made improvements in their bulk handling and safety facilities. Later, Shell required distributors to obtain an inspection by a qualified engineer and provide self-certification of compliance with applicable laws and regulations. B & B's Arvin facility was inspected twice and B & B had made a number of recommended improvements to its facilities. Despite these improvements, B & B remained a "[s]loppy [o]perator." The EPA soon discovered significant contamination of soil and ground water.

By 1989, B & B was insolvent and ceased all operations, and the Arvin facility was designated as a Superfund site. By 1998, the Governments had spent more than $8 million in cleanup costs.

In 1991, EPA (Governments) ordered the Railroads to conduct certain cleanup processes. The Railroads did so, incurring expenses of more than $3 million in the process. Seeking to recover at least a portion of these costs, the Railroads brought suit against B & B.

The District Court held that both the Railroads and Shell were PRPs under CERCLA—the Railroads because they were owners of a portion of the facility, and Shell because it had "arranged for" the disposal of hazardous substances through its sale and delivery of chemicals.

---

[11] Courts do require some proof of causation between a company's conduct and the resulting toxic contamination. *NCR Corp. v. George A. Whiting Paper Co.*, 768 F.3d 682 (7th Cir. 2014).

[12] "Participating" does not include monitoring or enforcing the security agreement, monitoring or inspecting the premises, providing financial advice, mandating cleanup of hazardous materials, restructuring the loan, foreclosing, or selling or leasing the property.

Don't Blame Me, I'm Only the Arranger continued

Although the court found the parties liable, it did not impose joint and several liability on Shell and the Railroads for the entire cleanup cost. The court apportioned the Railroads' liability as 9% of the Governments' total response cost. Based on estimations of chemicals spills of Shell products, the court held Shell liable for 6% of the total site response cost.

The state and local governments appealed the District Court's apportionment, and Shell cross-appealed the court's finding of liability. Applying a theory of arranger liability, the Ninth Circuit held that Shell arranged for the disposal of a hazardous substance.

The Court of Appeals held Shell and the Railroads jointly and severally liable for the Governments' cost of responding to the contamination of the Arvin facility.

The Railroads and Shell appealed.

DECISION: The primary pollution at the Arvin facility was contained in the southeastern portion of the facility most distant from the Railroads' parcel and the spills of hazardous chemicals that occurred on the Railroad parcel contributed to no more than 10% of the total site contamination, some of which did not require cleanup.

The court reversed the Court of Appeals' conclusion that the Railroads are subject to joint and several liability for all costs arising out of the contamination of the Arvin facility.

The court held that Shell should not be held liable as an arranger under CERCLA because it did not arrange for disposal and it ran responsible programs to get distributors to comply with its standards. However, there was not intent on the part of Shell to dump the chemicals by arranging for their delivery. The court also held that the Railroads' share of the site cleanup costs was reasonably apportioned at 9% and that the parties were not joint and severally liable. The judgment was reversed. [***Burlington Northern Railway/Shell Oil Co. v. U.S.,*** **556 U.S. 599 (2009)**]

CERCLA liability has been extended to those who merge or buy corporations; these parties also buy into CERCLA liability, and liability under CERCLA cannot be avoided by a transfer of ownership. The U.S. Supreme Court has ruled in *United States v. Bestfoods*, 525 U.S. 51 (1998), that a parent corporation is not automatically liable under CERCLA for a subsidiary corporation's conduct but may be responsible if the subsidiary is simply a shell. In other words, CERCLA liability of parent corporations for the actions of their subsidiaries is governed by corporate law on piercing the corporate veil (see Chapter 3 for more information).

THINKING THINGS THROUGH

The Leaking Barrels GE Sold

For over 30 years, GE manufactured electric capacitors containing Pyranol at its plants located in New York. GE met its Pyranol needs by purchasing polychlorinated biphenyl (PCB) from Monsanto. GE then refined the PCBs it purchased until the PCBs attained the level of purity necessary for the Pyranol used in the capacitors.

Pyranol that fell short of GE purity standards was deemed "scrap Pyranol" and was stored in 55-gallon drums on site. Over time, GE accumulated a glut of scrap Pyranol and had Frederic H. Fletcher, local manufacturer, "chemical scrapper," and businessman, purchase the scrap Pyranol from GE at bargain prices for his industrial needs.

For approximately 10 years, ending in 1967, Fletcher purchased about 200,000 gallons, or 3,600 55-gallon drums,

of Pyranol from GE. Fletcher was not prompt on his payments and by August 1967, Fletcher's account was delinquent. Fletcher told GE that the scrap Pyranol he received had markedly declined and he ended his relationship with GE.

In 1987, EPA found hundreds of drums containing scrap Pyranol and other chemicals at Fletcher's business. The drums were unmarked and several had leaked. The EPA filed suit against GE to recoup costs associated with the Fletcher site's cleanup as an arranger. Explain whether GE is an arranger and whether GE should be held liable for the cost of the Fletcher cleanup.

[***U.S. v. General Elec. Co.,*** **670 F.3d 377 (1st Cir. 2012)**]

One of the new key areas for minimizing CERCLA liability is that of the self-audit, a company's internal investigation of its operations and lands to determine whether any environmental hazards are on its properties. Many companies wanted to know, for the sake of financial planning and minimizing harm, whether they had any Superfund issues. However, they did not want their voluntary investigations and cleanups to work against them. To encourage these types of internal investigations and self-reporting, the EPA developed its Incentives for Self-Policing, Disclosure, Correction, and Prevention of Violations. Under this EPA program, companies can have their penalties reduced and not waive any rights if they follow the procedures and meet the following requirements: (1) the violations were uncovered as part of a self-audit, (2) the violations were uncovered voluntarily, (3) the violations were reported to the EPA within 10 days, (4) the discovery was made independently and disclosed independently and no one was threatening disclosure, (5) the violations are corrected within 60 days, (6) there is a written agreement that the conduct will not happen again, (7) there is no history of repeat violations, (8) no serious harm came to anyone as a result of the conduct, and (9) the company cooperates completely with the EPA. If these requirements are met, the company is eligible for reductions in fines and penalties of up to 75 percent.

CERCLA has been so effective that designated Superfund sites estimates place the number of currently undeveloped brownfields at 425,000. "**Brownfields,**" are sites defined by the EPA as "real property, the expansion, redevelopment, or reuse of which may be complicated by the presence or potential presence of a hazardous substance, pollutant, or contaminant." The Small Business Liability Relief and Brownfields Revitalization Act brings together 75 federal agencies that work through the *Federal Partnership Action Agenda* to provide funding for proposals to clean up and use these brownfields (42 U.S.C.A. §9601). The EPA has a process for becoming an "innocent landowner," someone who seeks to develop the brownfield but wants an exemption from CERCLA exposure. That designation then allows the applicant to obtain federal funding for purposes of cleaning up and developing the brownfield.

49-1d Environmental Quality Regulation

The federal statutes on air, water, and solid waste pollution are directed at private parties in their use of land. However, the federal government also regulates itself in terms of its operations and impact on the environment. The **National Environmental Policy Act (NEPA)** requires federal agencies to consider the impact on the environment of their proposed projects.[13] An agency must prepare a report, called an **environmental impact statement (EIS),** that documents the impact of the proposed federal project on the environment and covers consideration of practical and feasible alternatives with a lesser impact.[14] **For Example,** the federal government was required to file an EIS for the Alaska oil pipeline, the extermination of wild horses, the construction of a post office, the implementation of a change in national park airport procedures that would permit jets to land, and highway construction.

49-1e Other Environmental Regulations

In addition to the major categories of environmental laws just covered, several other important statutes regulate specific areas of the environment. The **Noise Control Act** sets standards for noise from low-flying aircraft for the protection of landowners who are

---

brownfields–land that is a designated Superfund cleanup site but which lies fallow because no one is willing to risk liability by buying the property, even when the hazardous waste has been removed, or property no one is willing to spend the money to remove the hazardous waste.

National Environmental Policy Act (NEPA)–federal law that mandates study of a project's impact on the environment before it can be undertaken by any federal agency.

environmental impact statement (EIS)–formal report prepared under NEPA to document findings on the impact of a federal project on the environment.

Noise Control Act–federal law that controls noise emissions from low-flying aircraft.

---

[13] 42 U.S.C. §4321 *et seq.*

[14] For contrasting cases of when an EIS is required, see *Kentucky Coal Ass'n, Inc. v. Tennessee Valley Authority*, 68 F. Supp. 3d 685 (W.D. Ky. 2014), and *Confederated Tribes of Grand Ronde Community of Oregon v. Jewell*, 75 F. Supp. 3d 387 (D.D.C. 2014).

in flight paths.[15] The **Endangered Species Act (ESA)** gives the secretary of the interior the responsibility of identifying and protecting endangered terrestrial species, while the secretary of commerce is responsible for endangered marine species.[16] These cabinet-level federal officers have the authority to curtail any development, noise, or other act that threatens those species on their endangered lists.[17]

CASE SUMMARY

The Loggers and the Naturalists Can't Be Friends: Oregon—Where the Spotted Owl Comes Flying in the Trees

FACTS: Two U.S. agencies halted logging in the Pacific Northwest because it endangered the habitat of the northern spotted owl and the red-cockaded woodpecker, both endangered species. Sweet Home Chapter (respondents) is a group of landowners, logging companies, and families dependent on the forest products industries in the Pacific Northwest. They brought suit seeking clarification of the authority of the secretary of the interior and the director of the Fish and Wildlife Service (petitioners) to include habitation modification as a harm covered by the Endangered Species Act (ESA).

The federal district court found for the secretary and director and held that they had the authority to protect the northern spotted owl through a halt to logging. The court of appeals reversed. Babbitt, the secretary of the interior, appealed.

DECISION: The statutory word *harm* encompasses direct as well as indirect injuries. The broad purpose of the ESA supports the secretary's decision to extend protection against

activities that cause the precise harms Congress enacted the statute to avoid—that is, to provide a means whereby the ecosystems upon which endangered species and threatened species depend may be conserved.

When it enacted the ESA, Congress delegated broad administrative and interpretive power to the secretary. The proper interpretation of a word such as *harm* involves a complex policy choice. When Congress has entrusted the secretary with broad discretion, courts should not substitute their views of wise policy. The judgment of the Court of Appeals was reversed.* [*Babbitt v. Sweet Home Chapter of Communities for a Great Oregon*, 515 U.S. 687 (1995)]

*Following this decision, Congress passed a rider to a budget-reduction bill that suspended environmental laws in many national forests in Washington and Oregon. The logging industry, paper products processors, and environmentalists have since worked together to find mutually acceptable solutions to logging and the protection of endangered species. Known as the "Sustainable Forestry Initiative," the goal is ecofriendly logging.

Endangered Species Act (ESA)–federal law that identifies and protects species that are endangered from development or other acts that threaten their existence.

49-1f **State Environmental Regulation**

All states have some form of environmental regulation, and their environmental agencies work closely with the EPA on enforcement and standards.[18] All states have some form of hazardous waste controls that define hazardous waste differently and carry a range of penalties for violations. **For Example,** Oregon imposes a fine of $3,500 per animal killed as a result of hazardous waste dumping. Other states mandate disclosure of the history of property use before that property can be sold, transferred, or mortgaged.

49-2 **Enforcement of Environmental Laws**

Federal environmental laws can be enforced through criminal sanctions, penalties, injunctions, and suits by private citizens. In addition to federal enforcement rights, certain common law remedies exist for the protection of property rights, such as the remedies for nuisance.

[15] 42 U.S.C. §4901.
[16] 16 U.S.C. §1530 *et seq.*
[17] The authority to bring suit rests with both landowners and environmentalists. *Bennett v. Spear*, 520 U.S. 154 (1997). See also *Northwest Coalition for Alternatives to Pesticides v. U.S. E.P.A.*, 920 F. Supp. 2d 1168 (W.D. Wash. 2013).
[18] *Chico Service Station, Inc. v. Sol Puerto Rico Ltd.*, 633 F.3d 20 (1st Cir. 2011).

49-2a Parties Responsible for Enforcement

The EPA is the primary federal agency responsible for the enforcement of federal environmental laws, including those on air and water pollution, solid waste disposal, toxic substance control, and noise pollution. The EPA establishes emissions standards through regulation and then enforces them with a system of permits and sanctions for violations. The EPA works closely with state environmental agencies in enforcement.

Council on Environmental Quality (CEQ)–federal agency that establishes national policies on environmental quality and then recommends legislation to implement these policies.

The **Council on Environmental Quality (CEQ)** was established in 1966 as a part of the executive branch to establish national policy on environmental quality and then make recommendations for legislation for the implementation of that policy. Other federal agencies with responsibility for enforcement of federal environmental laws include the Department of Commerce, the Department of the Interior, the U.S. Forest Service, and the Bureau of Land Management.

Private citizens also have the right to enforce federal environmental laws through private litigation. **For Example,** a private citizen can bring a suit to halt the construction of a dam by the federal government if the agency responsible failed to conduct an environmental impact study or if the EIS is inadequate.[19]

49-2b Criminal Penalties

Most of the federal environmental laws carry criminal penalties for violations. Figure 49-1 provides a summary of those penalties to which both companies and their employees are subject.

49-2c Civil Remedies

injunction–order of a court of equity to refrain from doing (negative injunction) or to do (affirmative or mandatory injunction) a specified act.

Although criminal remedies are costly to businesses, the EPA also has the authority to have the polluting activity halted through the use of **injunction.** The EPA simply brings suit against a business and shows that it is engaged in unauthorized dumping, the release of emissions in excess of a permit, or discharge without a permit. A court can then order the business to halt the activity that is resulting in the violation. In some cases, the effect of the injunction is to shut down the business. The business is then required to negotiate with the EPA to meet certain standards before the EPA will agree to have the injunction lifted.

Private citizens can also bring suit for injunctions against companies that are in violation of federal law or not in compliance with statutory procedures. **For Example,** private citizens have filed suit against developers to stop construction when there is an issue of possible violation of the Endangered Species Act.

49-2d Private Remedies: Nuisance

nuisance–conduct that harms or prejudices another in the use of land or that harms or prejudices the public.

Conduct that unreasonably interferes with the enjoyment or use of land is a **nuisance,**[20] which may be smoke from a chemical plant that damages the paint on neighboring houses. It may be noise, dirt, or vibration from passing heavy trucks. Some conduct is clearly so great an interference that it is easy to conclude that it constitutes a nuisance, but not every interference is a nuisance. Furthermore, determining whether the interference is sufficiently great to be halted as unreasonable is frequently difficult. The fact that the activity or business is lawful and is conducted in a lawful manner does not mean that it is not a nuisance. The effect on others determines whether there is a nuisance.[21]

---

[19] *Alliance for the Wild Rockies v. Austin,* 55 F. Supp. 3d 1294 (D. Mont. 2014).
[20] *Kitsap County v. Kitsap Rifle and Revolver Club,* 337 P.3d 328 (Wash. App. 2014).
[21] A drive-in theater that affects a neighbor is not a nuisance. *Blue Ink, Ltd. v. Two Farms, Inc.,* 96 A.3d 810 (Md. App. 2014).

FIGURE 49-1	Penalties for Violations of Federal Environmental Laws

Act	Penalties	Private suit
Clean Air Act	$25,000 per day; up to 1 year of imprisonment; 15 years and/or $1,000,000 for willful or repeat violations; $10,000 rewards	Citizen suits; authorized EPA suit for injunctive relief
Clean Water Act	$25,000 per day, up to 1 year; $50,000 and/or 3 years for violations with knowledge; $100,000 and/or 6 years for subsequent violations	Citizen suits; authorized EPA suit for injunctive relief
Resource Conservation Recovery Act (Solid Waste Disposal Act)	$250,000 and/or 15 years' of imprisonment for intentional violations; $1,000,000 for corporations, $50,000 and/or 5 years for others	Citizen and negligence suits (after EPA refuses to handle)
Hazardous Substance/ Response Trust	Fund for cleanup	EPA suit for injunctive relief and reimbursement of trust funds
Oil Pollution Act	$25,000 per day, or $1,000 per barrel; $3,000 per barrel if willful or negligent; $250,000 and/or 5 years for failure to report	Private suits

A neighbor's expansion of a pond in order to attract more water fowl that then roosted in the neighbors' property is a nuisance even though no law was broken.[22]

The courts attempt to balance the social utility of the activity with the resulting harm. The mere fact that there is harm does not establish that there is a nuisance. When community welfare outweighs the harm to land and owners, the activity is not a nuisance.[23] **For Example,** courts have held that smoke, fumes, and noise from public utilities and power plants were not nuisances, although they did create harm. The interests of the community in the activity of the public utilities outweighed the interests of those affected.

Those affected by a nuisance are entitled to damages for the loss of the use of the land or for harm that is caused by the nuisance. Sometimes, an injunction that stops the conduct is necessary. If the nuisance is permanent, the damages are the loss in value of the land. If the nuisance can be stopped, the measure of damages is the reduction in value of the property during the time of the nuisance.[24]

---

[22] *Schillaci v. Sarris*, 997 N.Y.S.2d 504 (N.Y.A.D. 2014).
[23] *Hurley v. Port Blakely Tree Farms L.P.*, 332 P.3d 469 (Wash. App. 2014).
[24] *Valley Estates, Ltd. Partnership v. Pangle*, 448 S.W.3d 235 (Ark. App. 2014).

Private and Public Nuisances

private nuisance—
nuisance that affects
only one or a few
individuals.

public nuisance—
nuisance that affects the
community or public at
large.

When a nuisance affects only one or a few persons, it is called a **private nuisance.** When it affects the community or public at large, it is called a **public nuisance.** Planting trees or erecting a fence, although otherwise lawful, constitutes a public nuisance when it creates a traffic hazard by obscuring an intersection. For example, the smell and harmful pollutants from a grain processing plant near Muscatine, Iowa, were examples of public nuisances that entitled the nearby residents to some form of relief.[25] The existence of a statutory environmental protection procedure may bar or supersede the common law of nuisance.

Remedy for Nuisance

A criminal nuisance may be terminated by abatement or closure by government authority. A civil nuisance may be stopped by an injunction, and the injured person may sue for money damages for the harm caused.

When an injunction is issued, the court must exercise great care to halt the nuisance while avoiding going too far by enjoining conduct that is otherwise lawful.[26]

CASE SUMMARY

Moooving to the Nuisance

FACTS: Spur Industries operated a cattle feedlot near Youngtown and Sun City, Arizona (communities 14 to 15 miles west of Phoenix). Spur had been operating the feedlot since 1956, and the area had been agricultural since 1911.

In 1959 Del E. Webb began development of the Sun City area, a retirement community. Webb purchased the 20,000 acres of land for about $750 per acre.

In 1960 Spur began an expansion program in which its operating area grew from 5 acres to 115 acres.

At the time of the suit, Spur was feeding between 20,000 and 30,000 head of cattle, which produced 35 to 40 pounds of wet manure per head per day, or over one million pounds per day. And despite the admittedly good feedlot management and good housekeeping practices of Spur, the resulting odor and flies produced an annoying if not unhealthy situation as far as the senior citizens of southern Sun City were concerned. There is no doubt that some of the citizens of Sun City were unable to enjoy the outdoor living which Del Webb had advertised. Del Webb was faced with sales resistance from prospective purchasers as well as strong and persistent complaints from the people who had purchased homes in that area. Nearly 1,300 lots could not be sold. Webb then filed suit alleging Spur's operation was a nuisance because of the flies and odors constantly drifting over Sun City. The trial court enjoined Spur's operations and Spur appealed.

DECISION: The court held that because Del Webb had "moved to the nuisance" that Spur could not be required to shut down its operations. Rather, Spur would have to relocate because of the court's actions of balancing the interests of the important cattle industry in Arizona with the equally important housing/retirement industry. However, Del Webb would have to compensate Spur for the costs of the move—$11 million. [*Spur Industries, Inc. v. Del E. Webb Development Co.*, 494 P.2d 700 (Az. 1972)]

The Technological Environment of the Law of Nuisance

As technology changes, new ways of manufacturing, new methods of transportation, and new ways of living develop. Groups such as NIMBYs (not in my backyard) have become active in challenging everything from cell phone towers to wind turbines. The courts and legislatures are working to find ways to accommodate advancement with the impact of the

[25] *Freeman v. Grain Processing Corp.*, 848 N.W.2d 58 (Iowa 2014).
[26] *City of South Milwaukee v. Kester*, 830 N.W.2d 710 (Wis. App. 2013) (case in which an injunction was issued to stop the public nuisance of a sex offender living in close proximity to an elementary school).

E-COMMERCE & CYBERLAW

Data Barns, Nuisance, and E-Commerce

Data barns are Internet services centers that are generally located in rural areas. They are becoming increasingly important because of our increasing reliance on cloud storage technology. For example, Microsoft bought 75 acres of bean fields in Grant County, Washington, to set up a digital warehouse. The issue of nuisance arose because Microsoft installed 40 diesel generators that operate as a backup source of power when there are transmission failures. The generators, located next to an elementary school, produce smoke and noise. The emissions from the generators are now classified as a *toxic pollutant* under Washington state law. The courts are weighing the need for the data barns versus the effect on neighboring properties and those in close proximity. In these situations, the courts will use a balancing approach to find a way to accommodate e-commerce without affecting the quality of life of those who live near these facilities.

forces that allow that advancement on those who live near these new technology sites. Also, the parties affected are working together. For example, federal and local laws protect the placement of cell towers so that neighbors cannot impede progress. However, in Arizona, the towers are disguised with artificial foliage that gives the towers the appearance of tall palm trees. Aesthetics are protected as technology advances.

49-2e **Private Remedies: Due Diligence**

due diligence—process of checking the environmental history and nature of land prior to purchase.

Another method by which problems with land are remedied is through sales transactions in which the buyer demands that a situation or problem on the land be fixed before signing a contract for purchase. **Due diligence** is the process by which the buyer conducts a thorough investigation of the property and its current and former uses to determine whether any problems with respect to environmental law or nuisance exist. Due diligence is conducted through a search of public records, an inspection of the land, and, often, when problems appear in these first two steps, some soil testing. This advance determination of problems is a civil means for land cleanup because sellers will be unable to transfer their properties until they meet the buyers' standards, determined by a close examination of the property for violations.

49-3 **Land Use Controls**

In addition to environmental laws, other restrictions, both private and public, place controls and limits on how land can be used.

49-3a **Restrictive Covenants in Private Contracts**

restrictive covenants—covenants in a deed by which the grantee agrees to refrain from doing specified acts.

Real estate developers find that when there are consistent patterns in the appearance of a neighborhood's homes and buildings (for example, similarity of design instead of a hodgepodge look), the property values are enhanced. To make sure this consistency is maintained, developers place **restrictive covenants** on the land that obligate the buyers to honor limitations in their use of their property, the nature of buildings that will be maintained or constructed on the land, and so on. If a restrictive covenant is valid, it binds buyers who had actual notice or knowledge of the restrictions. The notice comes from a notation in the deed about the covenants; the covenants then are said to "run with the land." That is, all owners are subject to them and all owners in that development have the right to stop another owner from violating the covenant.

A restrictive covenant must be clearly stated to be effective. Contract rules apply in interpreting covenants. If any uncertainty exists, the covenant will be construed strictly in favor of the free use of the land. When there is no uncertainty and no reason to depart from the meaning of the words of the covenant, a court will enforce those words.

Because of property rights, courts interpret restrictive covenants narrowly to permit the greatest possible use of the land. However, courts often disagree as to what is permitted by a restrictive covenant. **For Example,** there has been a great deal of litigation over restrictive covenants that require building design such as "traditional New England fashion, with pitched roofs, clapboard siding, and double-hung windows."[27]

Restrictive covenants that violate laws or constitutional rights are not valid. For example, a restrictive covenant that discriminates against persons with disabilities is void because it violates the Fair Housing Act.[28]

A restrictive covenant that has not been enforced or observed is no longer valid. For example, if houses in a neighborhood have had their roofs replaced with materials that did not comply with the restrictive covenants but no one objects, those new materials become the standard for the neighborhood, not the covenant materials.[29]

49-3b Public Zoning

zoning–restrictions imposed by government on the use of designated land to ensure an orderly physical development of the regulated area.

By **zoning,** a governmental unit such as a city adopts an ordinance imposing restrictions on the use of the land. The object of zoning is to ensure an orderly physical development of the regulated area. In effect, zoning is the same as restrictive covenants; the difference is in the source of authority. In most cases, zoning is based on an ordinance of a local political subdivision, such as a municipality or a county. Restrictive covenants, on the other hand, are created by agreement of the parties.

The zoning power permits any regulation that is conducive to advancing public health, welfare, and safety. The object of a particular zoning regulation may be to prevent high-density population.

Some zoning ordinances may be conservation inspired. An ordinance may prohibit or regulate the extraction of natural resources from any land within the zoned area. The fact that a zoning restriction limits the owner in the use of a property does not amount to a "taking" of property for which compensation must be made.[30] If, however, the zoning law deprived the owner of use of the land in any fashion, that would be a "taking" that required compensation.

Nonconforming Use

nonconforming use–use of land that conflicts with a zoning ordinance at the time the ordinance goes into effect.

When the use of land is in conflict with a zoning ordinance at the time the ordinance goes into effect, such use is described as a **nonconforming use. For Example,** when a zoning ordinance that requires a setback of 25 feet from the boundary line is adopted, an existing building that has a 10-foot setback is a nonconforming use.

A nonconforming use has a constitutionally protected right to continue, but if the nonconforming use is discontinued, it cannot be resumed.[31] The right to a

---

[27] *Lynch v. Town of Pelham*, 104 A.3d 1047 (N.H. 2014). Generally, these design covenants are upheld, so you find McDonald's is able to secure a place in a town with restrictive covenants, but the McDonald's will look like the other business buildings in the town and not its traditional free-standing model involving red and yellow colors.

[28] *Bhogaita v. Altamonte Heights Condominium Ass'n, Inc.*, 765 F.3d 1277 (11th Cir. 2014) (issue of restriction on pets when a resident suffered from post-traumatic stress disorder).

[29] *Oakwood Meadows Homeowners Ass'n v. Urban*, 2014 WL 2935908 (Mich. App. 2014) (lax enforcement on the construction of sheds and other buildings in violation of covenants).

[30] *California-Nevada Annual Conference of the Methodist Church v. City and County of San Francisco*, 74 F. Supp. 3d 1144 (N.D. Cal. 2014).

[31] *Day v. Town of Phippsburg*, 110 A.3d 645 (Me. 2014).

SPORTS & ENTERTAINMENT LAW

The Star Wars Studio

Quietly over the years, beginning in the 1970s when the money from his films began to roll in, George "Star Wars" Lucas has been acquiring land in Marin County (6,000 acres in total) with the goal of preserving its natural beauty and stopping its development. In fact, 97 percent of the acreage cannot be developed under deed restrictions. Mr. Lucas has planted 8,000 trees on the land and restored pathways for walking and hiking.

However, Mr. Lucas always intended to build a studio complex there, a 269,000-square-foot facility that would be located on a little over 1,000 of the acres. The plan has been 27 years in the making and was canceled last week

because of what Mr. Lucas called "regulatory delay" and fierce opposition from the neighborhoods around the planned site. The neighbors opposed the facility, known as the Grady Ranch project, because it would employ 463 people and bring too much noise and traffic into the area. Neighbors indicated that regardless of county approval that they would file suits that would delay the project until their concerns were fully litigated. More details on the project can be found at Victoria Baret, "Millionaire NIMBYs 1; Billionaire Filmmaker 0," **http://www.forbes.com/sites/victoriabarret/2012/04/18/how-star-wars-george-lucas-lost-out-to-a-california-subdivision/** *Forbes*, May 2, 2012, p. 18.

---

nonconforming use may be lost by abandonment. If a garage is a nonconforming use and its owner stops using it as a garage and uses it for storing goods, a return to the use of the property as a garage will be barred by abandonment.

At times, a real estate development or building construction is only partly completed when a zoning ordinance that would prohibit such development or building is adopted. To avoid hardship for the persons involved, it is customary to exempt partly finished projects from the zoning ordinance just as though they were existing nonconforming uses.[32]

variance–permission of a landowner to use the land in a specified manner that is inconsistent with the zoning ordinance.

Variance

The administrative agency charged with the enforcement of a zoning ordinance may grant a **variance.** This permits the owner of the land to use it in a specified manner that is inconsistent with the zoning ordinance.

CASE SUMMARY

No Tattoos in My Neighborhood

FACTS: Hold Fast Tattoo (Plaintiff) wished to open a tattoo studio on North Sheridan Road in the City of North Chicago and obtained a prospective lessor at its desired location. In accordance with North Chicago's zoning ordinance, Hold Fast Tattoo applied for a special use permit to operate a tattoo studio at that location. On June 21, 2007, the Zoning Board of Appeals of North Chicago recommended approval of the permit to its city council. The proposal was discussed at two council meetings, on July 9, 2007, and July 16, 2007, and Hold Fast Tattoo's request for a special use permit was ultimately denied. The city council

informed Hold Fast that its special use permit was denied because it was "not the kind of business" the council wanted in North Chicago. Hold Fast filed suit.

DECISION: The court held that there were no First Amendment violations in prohibiting the tattoo parlor because the tattoo parlor was not speaking; its clients were the ones speaking and they were not prohibited from having tattoos. This control only related to where they could obtain tattoos. The court also held that cities are permitted to have zoning plans and regulations that restrict certain types of businesses

---

[32] See, for example, *Anderton v. City of Cedar Hill*, 447 S.W.3d 84 (Tex. App. 2014).

No Tattoos in My Neighborhood continued

as long as there is a public purpose. The city was worried about the level of traffic and congestion from the business and the court found that there was a legitimate public purpose in excluding tattoo parlors from the area. [*Hold Fast Tattoo, LLC v. City of North Chicago,* **580 F. Supp. 2d 656 (N.D. Ill. 2008)**]*

*Other states have held that tattoos are a form of protected speech and refused to allow denial of licenses and zoning permits solely based on the tattoo reasoning. *Coleman v. City of Mesa,* 284 P.3d 853 (Ariz. 2012); *Jucha v. City of North Chicago,* 63 F. Supp. 2d 820 (N.D. Ill. 2014); *Anderson v. City of Hermosa Beach,* 621 F.3d 1051 (9th Cir. 2014). The tattoo-zoning issue has a split among the federal circuits as well as in the states and may require a U.S. Supreme Court decision.

spot zoning–allowing individual variation in zoning.

Agencies ordinarily are reluctant to permit a variance when neighboring property owners object because, to the extent that variation is permitted, the basic plan of the zoning ordinance is defeated. Likewise, the allowance of an individual variation, or **spot zoning,** may result in such inequality as to be condemned by the courts.[33] In addition, there is a consideration of practical expediency. If variances are readily granted, every property owner will request a variance and flood the agency with these requests.

When the desired use of land is in harmony with the general nature of surrounding areas, a zoning variance is usually granted. A zoning variance is not granted on the ground of hardship, however, when the landowner created the hardship by purchasing land that was subject to a zoning ordinance.

Make the Connection

Summary

Public and private regulations apply to land use. The public regulations consist of environmental laws and zoning. Environmental laws exist at both the state and the federal levels. At the federal level, regulations govern air pollution through limits on emissions and permits for discharges; water pollution with permit requirements, discharge prohibitions, and treatment standards; solid waste disposal with limitations on dumping and liability for cleanup when hazardous materials are found on property; and environmental quality through the use of advance studies on projects and their impact on the environment. Other federal regulations on the environment protect endangered species, set standards for drinking water, and impose liability for oil spills as well as safety standards for oil tankers.

Environmental laws are primarily enforced at the federal level by the Environmental Protection Agency (EPA), but other federal agencies as well as state agencies work together to enforce these laws, using criminal and civil penalties and injunctions to halt pollution. Private citizens also have the right to bring suit under federal statutes to enforce the requirements imposed.

A *nuisance* is a public or private interference with the use and enjoyment of land, and individuals can bring suit to halt nuisances. Courts perform a balancing test in deciding how to handle concerns about nuisances. They seek to balance the use and enjoyment of land with the economic interests of all involved parties.

Restrictive covenants in deeds are valid land use restrictions that pass from owner to owner and are enforceable as long as they do not violate any constitutional rights. *Zoning* is a public means of regulating land use. Zoning laws are part of an overall plan for development adopted by a governmental entity. Some landowners can obtain variances from zoning laws, and some preexisting uses are permitted to continue with the protection of a nonconforming use.

[33] *City of Ocean Springs v. Psycamore, LLC,* 124 So. 3d 658 (Miss. 2013).

Learning Outcomes

After studying this chapter, you should be able to clearly explain:

49-1   Statutory Environmental Law

LO.1 List and describe the federal statutes that regulate various aspects of the environment

See the *Massachusetts v. EPA* discussion, page 1027.

See the *Environmental Defense v. Duke Energy* discussion, page 1027.

See the discussion of the liability for CERCLA cleanup in *Burlington Northern Railway/Shell Oil Co. v. U.S.*, pages 1030–1031.

49-2   Enforcement of Environmental Laws

LO.2 Explain how environmental laws are enforced and describe the criminal penalties for violation of environmental laws

See the list of penalties in Figure 49-1, page 1035.

Study the Thinking Things Through feature "The Leaking Barrels GE Sold" and GE Pyranol, page 1031. See the *Babbitt v. Sweet Home Chapter of Communities for a Great Oregon* case, page 1033.

LO.3 Define *nuisance* and list the remedies available

See the *Spur Industries v. Del Webb* case, page 1036.

See the E-Commerce & Cyberlaw feature "Data Barns, Nuisance, and E-Commerce" for a discussion of nuisance in the technology age, page 1037.

49-3   Land Use Controls

LO.4 Explain the role and application of covenants and zoning laws

See the *Hold Fast Tattoo, LLC v. City of North Chicago* case for a discussion of zoning and rights of owners, pages 1039–1040.

Key Terms

best available treatment

best conventional treatment

brownfields

bubble concept

Clean Air Act

Clean Water Act

Comprehensive Environmental Response, Compensation, and Liability Act (CERCLA)

Council on Environmental Quality (CEQ)

due diligence

effluent guidelines

emissions offset policy

Endangered Species Act (ESA)

environmental impact statement (EIS)

injunction

National Environmental Policy Act (NEPA)

National Pollutant Discharge Elimination System (NPDES)

Noise Control Act

nonattainment areas

nonconforming use

nuisance

Oil Pollution Act

point sources

potentially responsible parties (PRPs)

private nuisance

public nuisance

Resource Conservation and Recovery Act (RCRA)

Resource Recovery Act

restrictive covenants

Safe Drinking Water Act

spot zoning

Superfund Amendment and Reauthorization Act

Superfund sites

Toxic Substances Control Act (TOSCA)

Transport Rule

variance

zoning

Questions and Case Problems

1. Union Electric wishes to construct a new coal-fired plant in the northeastern corner of Arizona. Union plans to use the maximum achievement technology for the scrubbers on the plant to reduce emissions. Will Union be able to obtain a permit from the EPA to build and operate the new power plant? Discuss the issues that Union faces.

2. Federal Oil Co. was loading a tanker with fuel oil when the loading hose snapped for some unknown reason and about 1,000 gallons of oil poured into the ocean. Federal Oil was prosecuted for this water

pollution. It raised the defense that it had exercised due care, was not at fault in any way, and had not intended to pollute the water. What statutes could be used to prosecute Federal Oil? What are the potential penalties?

3. Philip Carey Co. owned a tract of land in Plymouth Township, Pennsylvania, on which it deposited a large pile of manufacturing waste containing asbestos. Carey sold the land to Celotex, and Celotex sold the land to Smith Land & Improvement Corp. The EPA notified Smith that unless it took steps to

eliminate the asbestos hazard, the EPA would do the work and pursue reimbursement. Smith cleaned up the land to the EPA's satisfaction at a cost of $218,945.44. Smith asked Celotex and Carey for reimbursement. Which firms have liability for the cleanup costs? [*Smith Land & Improvement Corp. v. Celotex*, 851 F.2d 86 (3d Cir.)]

4. The McConnells bought a home in Sherwood Estates. The land was subject to a restrictive covenant that "no building, fence, or other structure" could be built on the land without the approval of the developer of the property. The McConnells built a dog pen in their yard that consisted of a cement base with fencing surrounding the base. They claimed that approval was not required on the theory that the restrictive covenant did not apply because it showed an intent to restrict only major construction, not minor additions to the landscape. A lawsuit was brought to compel the McConnells to remove the dog pen because prior approval had not been obtained. Are restrictive covenants applied this expansively to homeowners? Must the McConnells have prior approval? [*Sherwood Estates Homes Ass'n, Inc. v. McConnell*, 714 S.W.2d 848 (Mo. App.)]

5. General Automotive operates Grand Auto Parts Stores, which receive used automotive batteries from customers as trade-ins. General's policy in disposing of these batteries had been to drive a screwdriver through each spent battery and then sell them to a battery-cracking plant operated by Morris P. Kirk & Sons, Inc., which extracted and smelted the lead. After the lead was extracted from the batteries, Kirk washed and crushed the battery casings, loaded them into a dump truck, and then dumped them. Tons of pieces of crushed batteries were dumped onto Catellus Development Corp.'s property. Under CERCLA, Catellus sought to recover from General the costs of cleaning up the hazardous battery parts from its property. General maintained that it was not liable because it sold the batteries to Kirk, and Kirk did the dumping. Was General correct? [*Catellus Development Corp. v. United States*, 34 F.3d 748 (9th Cir.)]

6. A zoning ordinance of the city of Dallas, Texas, prohibited the use of property in a residential district for gasoline filling stations. Lombardo brought an action against the city to test the validity of the ordinance. He contended that the ordinance violated the rights of the owners of property in such districts. Do you agree with this contention? [*Lombardo v. City of Dallas*, 73 S.W.2d 475 (Tex.)]

7. Taback began building a vacation home on a parcel of wooded land. It was to be a three-story house, 31 feet high. This height violated the local zoning ordinance that limited residential homes to two and one-half stories, not exceeding 35 feet. When Taback learned of this violation, he applied for a zoning variance. Because of the delay of the zoning board and because winter was approaching, Taback finished the construction of the building as a three-story house. At a later hearing before the zoning board, he showed that it would be necessary for him to rebuild the third floor to convert the house into a two and one-half story house. The zoning board recognized that Taback's violation could not be seen from neighboring properties. Was Taback entitled to a zoning variance? [*Taback v. Town of Woodstock Zoning Board of Appeals*, 521 N.Y.S.2d 838 (App. Div.)]

8. The EPA has increased its BACT standards to impose greenhouse gas emissions standards for passenger cars, light-duty trucks, and medium-duty passenger vehicles and all businesses that emit greenhouse gases. The emissions from these small businesses and vehicles are not *per se* pollutants, but, rather, greenhouse gases. Does the EPA have the authority to regulate these emissions in vehicles? What about the costs associated with additional permits? [*Utility Air Regulatory Group v. E.P.A.*, 134 S. Ct. 2427]

9. The Stallcups lived in a rural section of the state. In front of their house ran a relatively unused, unimproved public county road. Wales Trucking Co. transported concrete pipe from the plant where it was made to a lake where the pipe was used to construct a water line to bring water to a nearby city. In the course of four months, Wales made 825 trips over the road, carrying from 58,000 to 72,000 pounds of pipe per trip and making the same number of empty return trips. Because the heavy use of the road by Wales cut up the dirt and made it like ashes, the Stallcups sued Wales for damages caused by the deposit of dust on their house and for the physical annoyance and discomfort it caused. Wales defended its position on the ground that it had not been negligent and that its use of the road was not unlawful. Decide. [*Wales Trucking Co. v. Stallcup*, 465 S.E.2d 44 (Tex. App.)]

10. Some sections of the city of Manitou Springs have hills of varying degrees of slope. To protect against water drainage and erosion, the city adopted a hillside zoning ordinance that required homes on hillsides to be surrounded by more open land than in

the balance of the city. Sellon owned land on a hillside and claimed that the hillside ordinance was unconstitutional because it did not treat all homeowners equally. Was the ordinance valid? [*Sellon v. City of Manitou Springs*, 745 P.2d 229 (Colo.)]

11. Patrick Bossenberry owned a house in a planned community area. Each lot in the area was limited by a restrictive covenant to use for a single-family dwelling. The covenant defined *family* as a blood or marital relationship between most of the occupants. Bossenberry rented his building to Kay-Jan, Inc., which wanted to use the building as a care home for not more than six adult mentally retarded persons. The neighbors sought to enjoin this use as a breach of the covenant. A number of Michigan statutes had been adopted that advanced the public policy of providing care for mentally retarded persons. Could the neighbors prevent the use of the property as a care home for mentally retarded adults? [*Craig v. Bossenberry*, 351 N.W.2d 596 (Mich. App.)]

12. Kenneth and Mary Norpel purchased a house, and Kenneth attached a 35-foot flagpole to it. He did not obtain the permission of the architectural committee of the Stone Hill Community Association. This consent was required by a restrictive covenant to which the Norpel house was subject. The association objected to the flagpole from which Norpel then flew the American flag. The association brought an action to compel the removal of the pole. Norpel claimed that as a combat veteran of World War II, he had a constitutionally protected right to fly the American flag. Can he be compelled to remove the flagpole?

13. In 1997, Isbell purchased a building in San Diego with the intent to open an adult entertainment establishment there. Because this building was located within 1,000 feet of a residential area, however, a San Diego zoning ordinance precluded him from operating there. Isbell applied for a variance but was unsuccessful. He then filed suit, arguing that the city's ordinance violates the First Amendment, and that its standards for variances violate the equal protection clause. Can the city restrict the operation of this business? What must the city be able to establish? [*Isbell v. City of San Diego*, 258 F.3d 1108 (9th Cir.)]

14. Explain why a company would want to perform a self-audit to determine whether it has any environmental violations.

15. Gregory Mills lives next to Dean Kimbley. Mills kept a journal of Kimbley's activities, and even videotaped a few of the activities, including Kimbley's smoking marijuana and standing drunk in his backyard and yelling, "Hi, neighbor!" Kimbley also threw a snowball into Mills' yard and nearly hit Mills' girlfriend with it. When Mills listed his property for sale because of the issues with Kimbley, Kimbley sent a pizza delivery man to Mills' door and told him to offer $125,000 to buy Mills' home. Kimbley then hired a real estate agent and took a tour of Mills' home with that real estate agent. Kimbley also drove an All Terrain Cycle onto Mills' lawn. Is this a nuisance case? Are these the elements of nuisance? Explain why or why not. [*Mills v. Kimbley*, 909 N.E.2d 1068 (Ind. App.)]

CPA Questions

1. Which of the following remedies is available against a real property owner to enforce the provisions of federal acts regulating air and water pollution?

	Citizen Suits against the Environmental Protection Agency to Enforce Compliance	State Suits to Enforce the Laws against Violators	Citizen Suits against Violators to Enforce the Laws
a.	Yes	Yes	Yes
b.	Yes	Yes	No
c.	No	Yes	Yes
d.	Yes	No	Yes

2. Under the Comprehensive Environmental Response, Compensation, and Liability Act (CERCLA), commonly known as Superfund, which of the following parties would be liable to the Environmental Protection Agency (EPA) for the expense of cleaning up a hazardous waste disposal site?

I. The current owner or operator of the site

II. The person who transported the wastes to the site

III. The person who owned or operated the site at the time of the disposal

   a. I and II

   b. I and III

   c. II and III

   d. I, II, and III

3. The National Environment Policy Act was passed to enhance and preserve the environment. Which of the following is not true?

    a. The act applies to all federal agencies.

    b. The act requires that an environmental impact statement be provided if any proposed federal legislation may significantly affect the environment.

    c. Enforcement of the act is primarily accomplished by litigation of persons who decide to challenge federal government decisions.

    d. The act provides generous tax breaks to those companies that help accomplish national environmental policy.

4. Which of the following actions should a business take to qualify for leniency if an environmental violation has been committed?

	Conduct Environmental Audits	Report Environmental Violations to the Government
a.	Yes	Yes
b.	Yes	No
c.	No	Yes
d.	No	No

CHAPTER 50

Leases

Learning Outcomes ‹‹‹

After studying this chapter, you should be able to

LO.1 List the ways in which a lease may be terminated

LO.2 List and explain the rights and duties of the parties to a lease

LO.3 Describe a landlord's liability for a tenant's and a third person's injuries sustained on the premises

LO.4 Define *sublease* and *assignment of a lease* and distinguish between them

50-1 Creation and Termination

Leases are governed by the common law of property as modified by judicial decisions and statutes.[1]

50-1a Definition and Nature

A **lease** is the relationship in which one person is in lawful possession of real property owned by another. In common usage, *lease* also refers to the agreement that creates that relationship.

The person who owns the real property and permits the occupation of the premises is known as the **lessor, or landlord.** The **lessee, or tenant,** is the one who occupies the property. A lease establishes the relationship of landlord and tenant.

50-1b Creation of the Lease Relationship

The relationship of landlord and tenant is created by an express or implied contract. An oral lease is valid at common law, but statutes in most states require written leases for certain tenancies. Many states provide that a lease for a term exceeding one year must be in writing.

Antidiscrimination

Statutes in many states prohibit an owner who rents property for profit from discriminating against prospective tenants on the basis of race, color, religion, or national origin. Also, the federal *Fair Housing Act* prohibits such discrimination. In addition, landlords are subject to the Americans with Disabilities Act (ADA) and must make reasonable accommodations for tenants with disabilities. **For Example,** a tenant whose physician has prescribed a comfort pet must be allowed to have that pet in his or her apartment even if the complex does not allow pets.[2] However, the use of medical marijuana in leased premises is not protected under the ADA.[3]

Unconscionability

At common law, the parties to a lease had freedom to include such terms as they chose. However, that freedom has been curbed in some states that require that leases follow the pattern of UCC section 2-302 and not include terms and conditions that are unconscionable. **For Example,** a provision in a residential lease stating that the landlord cutting off heat or water will not constitute an eviction is unconscionable. Such a clause does not prevent the tenant from recovering on the grounds of unconscionability or for breach of the implied warranty of habitability when there has been no heat or water.

50-1c Classification of Tenancies

Tenancies are classified by duration as tenancies for years, from year to year, at will, and by sufferance.

---

lease–agreement between the owner of property and a tenant by which the former agrees to give possession of the property to the latter in consideration of the payment of rent. (Parties—landlord or lessor, tenant or lessee)

lessor–one who conveys real or personal property by a lease; a landlord.

landlord–one who leases real property to another.

lessee–one who has a possessory interest in real or personal property under a lease; a tenant.

tenant–one who holds or possesses real property by any kind of right or title; one who pays rent for the temporary use and occupation of another's real property under a lease.

---

[1] A uniform act, the Uniform Residential Landlord and Tenant Act (URLTA), has been adopted in some form, often just in sections, in 21 states. URLTA does not apply to dorm rooms, fraternities, homeless shelters, or halfway houses. *Picken v. Multnomah County*, 2012 WL 1151037 (D. Or. 2012).

[2] *Bhogaita v. Altamonte Heights Condominium Ass'n, Inc.*, 765 F.3d 1277 (11th Cir. 2014).

[3] *Forest City Residential Management, Inc. ex rel. Plymouth Square Ltd. Dividend Housing Ass'n v. Beasley*, 71 F. Supp. 3d 715 (E.D. Mich. 2014).

tenancy for years–
tenancy for a fixed period of time, even though the time is less than a year.

periodic tenancy–
tenancy that continues indefinitely for a specified rental period until terminated; often called a month-to-month tenancy.

tenancy at will–holding of land for an indefinite period that may be terminated at any time by the landlord or by the landlord and tenant acting together.

tenancy at sufferance–lease arrangement in which the tenant occupies the property at the discretion of the landlord.

Tenancy for Years

A **tenancy for years** is one under which the tenant has a lease that runs for a definite duration. The expression "for years" is used to describe such a tenancy whether the duration of the tenancy is for only six months or as long as 10 years.

Periodic Tenancy

A **periodic tenancy** is one under which a tenant has a lease that has an indefinite duration and under which the tenant pays annual, monthly, or weekly rent. This tenancy does not terminate at the end of a year, month, or week except with proper notice. Proper notice, in most states, means giving notice for at least one period before ending the lease.[4] **For Example,** on a month-to-month tenancy, the notice must be at least one month prior to ending the lease.

In almost all states, a periodic tenancy is implied if the tenant, with the consent of the landlord, stays in possession of property after a tenancy for years. Consent exists when there is an express statement or by conduct, such as when a landlord continues to accept rent.[5]

Tenancy at Will

When a lease runs for an indefinite period, which may be terminated at any time by the landlord or the tenant, a **tenancy at will** exists. A person who possesses land for an indefinite period with the owner's permission but without any agreement as to rent is a tenant at will. Statutes in some states and decisions in others require advance notice of termination of this kind of tenancy.

Tenancy at Sufferance

When a tenant remains in possession after the termination of the lease without permission of the landlord, the landlord may treat the tenant as either a trespasser or a tenant.[6] Until the landlord elects to do one or the other, a **tenancy at sufferance** exists. **For Example,** if John's one-year lease expired on January 31, 2016, and John remained in the apartment for a week, he would be a tenant at sufferance during that week. If John's landlord accepted a rental payment at the end of the first week, John would be a *periodic* or *month-to-month tenant*. In this situation, John was a tenant for years, a tenant at sufferance, and then a periodic tenant.[7]

50-1d Termination of Lease

A lease is generally not terminated by the death, insanity, or bankruptcy of either party except in the case of a tenancy at will. Leases may be terminated in the following ways.

Termination by Notice

Unless prohibited by statute, a lease may give the landlord the power to terminate it by giving notice to the tenant. In states that follow the common law on termination by notice, it is immaterial why the landlord terminates. A provision in a lease giving the landlord the right to terminate the lease by notice is strictly construed against the landlord.

Expiration of Term in a Tenancy for Years

A tenancy for years ends upon the expiration of the term. There is no requirement that one party give the other any notice of termination. However, a lease may require express

---

[4] *Meek v. Mallory and Evans, Inc.,* 734 S.E.2d 109 (Ga. App. 2012). URLTA §1.303.
[5] In re *2408 W. Kennedy, LLC,* 512 B.R. 708 (M.D. Fla. 2014).
[6] *Coinmach Corp. v. Aspenwood Apartment Corp.,* 417 S.W.3d 909 (Tex. 2013).
[7] *Brittany Sobery Family Ltd. Partnership v. Coinmach Corp.,* 392 S.W.3d 46 (Mo. App. 2013).

notice in this type of lease with a specified term except when a statute prohibits the land-lord from imposing such a requirement.

Notice in a Periodic Tenancy

In the absence of an agreement of the parties, notice for termination of a periodic tenancy is now usually governed by statute. It is common practice for the parties to require 30 or 60 days' notice to end a tenancy from year to year.

Destruction of Property

By either an express provision in a lease or under a statutory provision, tenants are released from their liability to pay rent if the leased premises are destroyed. Alternatively, the amount of rent may be reduced in proportion to the loss. **For Example,** a tenant may only be able to use one-half of the property, so the rent would be cut in half. Such sta-tutes do not require the landlord to repair or restore the property to its former condition. When the lease covers rooms or an apartment in a building, a destruction of the leased premises terminates the lease.

Fraud

Because a lease is based on a contract, a lease agreement is subject to the contract defense of fraud. (See Chapter 13.)

Transfer of the Tenant

Residential leases may contain a provision for termination if there is a change in the tenant's circumstances, such as the tenant's being transferred by an employer to another city or on the tenant's being called into active military service. Such provisions are strictly construed against the tenant. Tenants should be certain to request personal circumstances provisions in their leases that are broad enough to cover these types of job events and military duty.

50-1e Notice of Termination

When notice of termination is required, no particular words are necessary to constitute a sufficient notice so long as the words used clearly indicate the intention of the party. The notice, whether given by the landlord or the tenant, must be definite. Statutes sometimes require that the notice be in writing. In the absence of such a provision, however, oral notice is generally sufficient.

50-1f Renewal of Lease

When a lease terminates for any reason, the landlord and the tenant ordinarily enter into a new agreement if they wish to extend or renew the lease. The power to renew the lease may be stated in the original lease by declaring that the lease runs indefinitely, as from year to year, subject to being terminated by either party's giving written notice of a speci-fied number of days or months before the termination date. Renewal provisions are strictly construed against the tenant.

The lease may require the tenant to give written notice of intention to renew the lease. In such a case, there is no renewal if the tenant does not give the required notice but merely remains on the premises after the expiration of the original term.[8]

---

[8] *Faison v. RTFX, Inc.,* 6 N.E.3d 376 (Ill. App. 2014).

50-2   **Rights and Duties of Parties**

The rights and duties of the landlord and tenant are based on principles of real estate law and contract law. There is an increasing tendency to treat the residential lease like any other type of consumer contract and to govern the rights and duties of the parties by general principles of contract law.

50-2a   **Possession**

possession–exclusive dominion and control of property.

The tenant has the right to acquire **possession** of the property and to remain in possession of that property until the term of the lease has expired or he or she is removed according to legal proceedings provided to landlords for removal of tenants in breach of the lease.

Right of Possession

By making a lease, the lessor or landlord agrees to give possession of the premises to the tenant at the time specified in the lease. If the landlord rents a building that is being constructed, there is an implied promise in the contract that the leased premises will be ready for occupancy on the date specified in the lease for the beginning of the lease term.

If the landlord interferes with the tenant's possession, the landlord has breached the lease agreement, and legal remedies are available to the tenant. *Interference* is generally defined to be an eviction that occurs by judicial proceedings or when the landlord prevents access by the tenant, as when the locks are changed and the tenant does not have a key. If the landlord wrongfully deprives the tenant of the use of one room when the tenant is entitled to use an entire apartment or building, there is a partial eviction. An eviction in violation of the lease or law entitles the tenant to collect damages from the landlord for interference with possession of the leased premises.

Covenant of Quiet Enjoyment

covenant of quiet enjoyment–covenant by the grantor of an interest in land to not disturb the grantee's possession of the land.

Most written leases today contain an express promise by the landlord called a **covenant of quiet enjoyment.** Such a provision protects the tenant from interference with possession by the landlord or the landlord's agent, but it does not impose liability on the landlord for the unlawful acts of third persons.[9]

Constructive Eviction

constructive eviction–act or omission of the landlord that substantially deprives the tenant of the use and enjoyment of the premises.

A **constructive eviction** occurs when some act or omission of the landlord substantially deprives the tenant of the use and enjoyment of the premises.

To establish a constructive eviction, the tenant must show that the condition of the property is such that it is impossible for the tenant to remain in possession. In addition, constructive eviction is not established unless the tenant actually leaves the premises. If the tenant continues to occupy the premises for more than a reasonable time after what is claimed to be a constructive eviction, the tenant waives or loses the right to object to the landlord's conduct. The definition of constructive eviction requires the establishment of conditions so awful that a tenant is forced to leave. The tenant's remaining behind in the leased premises contradicts one of the elements required for establishing constructive eviction.[10] **For Example,** a condition of constructive eviction would be sewage backing up

---

[9] *Haslam-James v. Lawrence*, 39 A.3d 1121 (Conn. 2012).

[10] Some states prohibit a landlord of residential property from willfully turning off the utilities of a tenant for the purpose of evicting the tenant. *City and County of San Francisco v. Sainez*, 77 Cal. App. 4th 1302, 92 Cal. Rptr. 2d 418 (Cal. App. 2009) (imposing civil penalty of $663,000 for shutting off utilities for 530 days). Such conduct is also a violation of URLTA §§2.104 and 4.105. *Mik v. Federal Home Loan Mortgage Corp.*, 743 F.3d 149 (6th Cir. 2014).

through the bathtub. The tenant could claim that the sewage in the apartment constituted constructive eviction, but the tenant would also need to move out of the apartment.

50-2b Use of Premises

The lease generally specifies those uses authorized for the tenant. In the absence of express or implied restrictions, a tenant is entitled to use the premises for any lawful purpose for which they are adapted or for which they are ordinarily employed or in a manner contemplated by the parties in executing the lease. A provision specifying the use to be made of the property is strictly construed against the tenant.

Change of Use

If the tenant uses the property for any purpose other than the one specified, the landlord has the option to declare the lease terminated.

Continued Use of Property

A tenant is ordinarily required to give the landlord notice of nonuse or vacancy of the premises. This notice is a practical issue; landlords need to be aware when premises are vacant because there is an increased danger of damage to the premises by vandalism or fire. Also, there is commonly a provision in the landlord's fire insurance policy making it void if a vacancy continues for a specified time.

Rules

The modern lease generally contains a blanket agreement by the tenant to abide by the provisions of rules and regulations adopted by the landlord. These rules are generally binding on the tenant whether they exist at the time the lease was made or are adopted afterward.

Prohibition of Pets

A lease restriction prohibiting pet ownership is valid, as are cleaning fees for violations of the restriction.

50-2c Rent

The tenant is under a duty to pay rent as compensation to the landlord. The amount of rent agreed to by the parties may be subject to government regulation, as when a city or county has enacted rent control laws.

Time of Payment

The time of payment of rent is ordinarily fixed by the lease. However, statutes or custom may require rent to be paid monthly or may require a substantial deposit before the lease begins.

CPA

Assignment

If the lease is assigned (the tenant's entire interest is transferred to a third person), the assignee is liable to the landlord for the rent. However, the assignment does not in itself discharge the tenant from the duty to pay the rent. If the assignee of the lease does not make the lease payments, the landlord may bring an action for the rent against either the original tenant or the assignee, or both, but is entitled to payment of only what is due under the lease, not a double amount as collected from each party. A **sublessee** (a person

sublessee–person with lease rights for a period of less than the term of the original lease (also *subtenant*).

to whom part of a tenant's interest is transferred) ordinarily is not liable to the original lessor for rent unless that liability has been expressly assumed or is imposed by statute.

Rent Escalation

escalation clause– provision for the automatic increase of the rent at periodic intervals.

When property is rented for a long term, it is common to include some provision for the automatic increase of the rent at periodic intervals. Such a provision is often tied to increases in the cost of living or in the landlord's operating costs and is called an **escalation clause.** There may, however, also be rent controls that would prohibit such rent increases.[11]

50-2d Repairs and Condition of Premises

In the absence of an agreement to the contrary, the tenant has no duty to make repairs. When the landlord makes repairs, reasonable care must be exercised to make them in a proper manner. The tenant is liable for any damage to the premises caused by his or her willful or negligent acts.

Inspection of Premises

Under the URLTA, the landlord has the right to enter the leased premises for emergency purposes or with notice to the tenant for repairs, evaluations, and estimates.

Housing Laws

Various laws protect tenants by requiring landlords to observe specified safety, health, and fire prevention standards. Some statutes require a landlord who leases a building for dwelling purposes to keep it in a condition fit for habitation. Leases commonly require the tenant to obey local ordinances and laws relating to the care and use of the premises.

Landlords must comply with the ADA. Compliance means that landlords cannot discriminate on the basis of disability in deciding whether to rent to a particular tenant.[12] Also, landlords are required to make reasonable modifications to accommodate tenants with disabilities, which can include everything from making sure that sidewalks on the property are smooth enough for operation of wheelchairs to permitting guide dogs to live with their sight-impaired owners.

THINKING THINGS THROUGH

The Rotting Balcony

Cayetano Giron stepped out onto the balcony of the apartment that he and his wife Robin leased from Jane Bailey. After taking four steps onto the balcony, Cayetano's foot sank into the soft floorboards and he fell toward the railing. He tried to grab the railing, but the railing broke off in his hand and he fell from the balcony to the street below (a two-story fall) and was injured. Robin had notified Mrs. Bailey, shortly after moving into the apartment, that the wooden balcony was "a little lopped." No repair attempts were made. Cayetano brought suit to recover for his injuries. Can he recover from Mrs. Bailey? Why or why not? [*Giron v. Bailey,* **985 A.2d 1003 (2009)**]

In the summer of 2015, six students were killed and seven were injured when a balcony collapsed during one of the student's 21st birthday celebration. Would the landlord be liable? What if the balcony had passed inspection less than one year ago?

---

[11] *Fisher v. City of Berkeley, California,* 475 U.S. 260 (1986); N.Y. Comp. Codes R. & Regs. tit. 9, §2520.1 (2014).
[12] *Short v. Manhattan Apartments, Inc.,* 915 F. Supp. 2d 375 (S.D.N.Y. 2012).

One of the developing areas of landlord-tenant law involves landlords' rights with regard to leasing to convicts and those who are registered as sex offenders. About 600,000 inmates are released from prisons each year, and their housing choices generally involve leasing.[13] The federal government requires public housing authorities to screen and evict tenants for drug-related or "safety-threatening" behavior. Public housing authorities that receive federal funds must include a lease clause that requires automatic lease termination for any drug or violent criminal activity, even if the activity does not occur on the landlord's property.

CASE SUMMARY

But I'm Innocent!!!

FACTS: Several young men, grandsons of William Lee and Barbara Hill, both of whom were residents on leases of the Oakland Housing Authority (OHA), were caught in the apartment complex parking lot smoking marijuana. The daughter of Pearlie Rucker, who resided with her and was listed on the OHA lease as a resident, was found with cocaine and a crack cocaine pipe three blocks from Rucker's apartment. On three instances within a two-month period, Herman Walker's, another OHA resident, caregiver and two others were found with cocaine in Walker's apartment.

After OHA initiated the eviction proceedings in state court against the Hills, Rucker, and Walker (respondents), they commenced actions against OHA in federal district court, challenging the Department of Housing and Urban Development's (HUD's) interpretation of the federal statute requiring eviction of tenants for criminal activity or the failure to control criminal activity in their apartments. The tenants of OHA argued that the federal statute and HUD regulations result in the eviction of "innocent" tenants and are unconstitutional.

The district court issued a preliminary injunction, enjoining OHA from terminating the leases of the tenants. A panel of the court of appeals reversed, and the full court of appeals reversed the panel and reinstated the district court's injunction. HUD appealed to the U.S. Supreme Court.

DECISION: Congress, wanting to ensure the safety of public housing, allowed the eviction for criminal activity in leased property even when the tenants were not involved. There are no constitutional issues as long as the proper processes under state law for eviction are followed. [***Department of Housing and Urban Development v. Rucker***, 535 U.S. 125 (2002)]

ETHICS & THE LAW

Screening Tenants for Criminal Records

There are several suits pending around the country against landlords who refuse to rent to tenants who have criminal records. The suits are brought by nonprofit groups that seek to help ex-cons with rehabilitation by getting them housing and jobs. However, the landlords note that once they are aware of criminal history and rent to that tenant, then they can be held liable for any crimes that individual might commit against tenants in their rental properties. San Francisco and Newark have ordinances that prohibit landlords from asking about criminal history. Many landlords have an individual review of applicants, not a blanket policy where they consider the nature of the crime, the time spent in prison, and the time since being released from prison. Discuss the ethical issues in setting policies on screening applicants with criminal records.

[13] Meghan L. Schneider, "From Criminal Confinement to Social Confinement: Helping Ex-Offenders Obtain Public Housing with a Certificate of Rehabilitation," 36 *New. Eng. J. on Crim. & Civil Confinement*, 335 (2010).

Warranty of Habitability

At common law, a landlord was not bound by any obligation that the premises be fit for use unless the lease contained an express warranty to that effect. Most jurisdictions now reject this view and have created a **warranty of habitability** to protect tenants. The warranty of habitability requires, in most states, that the premises have running water, have heat in winter, and be free from structural defects and infestation. If the landlord breaches a warranty of habitability, the tenant is entitled to damages. These damages may be offset against the rent that is due, or if no rent is due, the tenant may bring an independent lawsuit to recover damages from the landlord.[14]

warranty of habitability– implied warranty that the leased property is fit for dwelling by tenants.

CASE SUMMARY

Don't Let the Bedbugs Bite

FACTS: Geoffrey Green lived in a rent-control apartment in New York City. Bedbugs in his apartment forced him and his partner, Dana Shapiro, to sleep with the lights on, and rotate between sleeping in the bedroom, the kitchen, and the living room. They did not use the bedroom between May and August in 2005 and 2006.

Mr. Green testified that from April 2005 through July 2008, he did not have a single full night's sleep during the summer months. Lack of sleep affected Mr. Green's relationship with Ms. Shapiro and his ability to get to work on time.

Mr. Green withheld rent from October 2005 through January 2007, but only for the prime bedbug months, that is, non-winter months, during this period for a total amount of $5,665.84. His landlord (Petitioner) brought a forcible detainer action to have him evicted. Mr. Green counterclaimed for his damages from the bedbugs. Mr. Green offered into evidence two zip-loc bags containing dead bedbugs.

The exterminator for the complex had come to spray the building but said he never saw any live or dead bedbugs in the Green/Shapiro apartment except the specimens that Mr. Green had shown him, in a zip lock bag.* The exterminator believed Green and Shapiro (Respondents) may have brought the bedbugs with them from their previous apartment. Theresa Lonng, a neighbor, testified that she had bedbugs in her apartment, but that she also had them in her apartment in the building next door, where she had lived until moving next to Mr. Green and Ms. Shapiro.

DECISION: The presence of bedbugs was a breach of the warranty of habitability, regardless of where the bugs came from. As the court noted, those who travel run the risk of bedbugs and landlords must be prepared to eliminate the bugs, wherever and however they land.

The court did question the credibility of tenants who would stay in a bug-infested place for three years without some more diligent form of action. However, the court awarded the tenants a rent abatement to cover September 2005 through December 2006. The first documented notification to the landlord regarding the alleged condition was in September 2005. That was the first documented phone call to the exterminator, and the tenants withheld their rent in September and October of 2005. Based on the log of bites that was kept by the tenants for January 2007 forward, the court found that the tenants had failed to establish the presence of bedbugs from January 2007 forward, and that the bites documented were in all likelihood other insect bites.

The tenants received a 12 percent abatement in rent, for the period of September 2005 through December 2006, totaling $2724.21. [**Bender v. Green, 874 N.Y.S.2d 786 (N.Y. Civ. Ct. 2009)**]

*The court used the terms "zip lock" and "zip-loc" rather than the registered term, "Ziploc."

Abatement and Escrow Payment of Rent

To protect tenants from unsound living conditions, statutes sometimes provide that a tenant is not required to pay rent as long as the premises are not fit to live in. As a compromise, some statutes require the tenant to continue to pay the rent but require that it be paid into an escrow or agency account. The money in the escrow account is paid to the landlord only upon proof that the necessary repairs have been made to the premises.

[14] *Erlach v. Sierra Asset Servicing, LLC,* 173 Cal. Rptr. 3d 159 (Cal. App. 2014).

50-2e **Improvements**

In the absence of a special agreement, neither the tenant nor the landlord is under a duty to make improvements, as contrasted with repairs.[15] Either party may, as a term of the original lease, agree to make improvements, in which case a failure to perform will result in liability in an action for damages for breach of contract brought by the other party. In the absence of an agreement to the contrary, improvements become part of the realty and belong to the landlord.

50-2f **Taxes and Assessments**

In the absence of an agreement to the contrary, the landlord, not the tenant, is usually under a duty to pay taxes and/or assessments. The lease may provide for an increase in rent if taxes on the rented property are increased.[16]

If taxes or assessments are increased because of improvements made by the tenant, the landlord is liable for such increases if the improvements remain with the property. If the improvements can be removed by the tenant, the amount of the increase must be paid by the tenant.

50-2g **Tenant's Deposit**

A landlord may require a tenant to make a deposit to protect the landlord from any default on the part of the tenant.[17] There may be statutory limits on the amount of the deposit. Some states provide tenants with protections on these deposits. For example, the landlord may have to hold the deposits in a trust fund or be responsible for paying interest for the period the deposit is held. The landlord may be subject to a penalty if the money is used before the lease would allow for its use.

50-2h **Protection from Retaliation**

The URLTA and most state laws protect tenants from retaliation by the landlord for the tenants' exercise of their lawful rights or reporting the landlord for violations of housing and sanitation codes. The types of retaliation from which reporting tenants are protected include refusing to renew a lease and evicting the tenant.

50-2i **Remedies of Landlord**

If a tenant fails to pay rent, the landlord may bring an ordinary lawsuit to collect the amount due and in some states may seize and hold the property of the tenant.

Landlord's Lien

In the absence of an agreement or a statute, the landlord does not have a lien on the personal property or crops of the tenant for money due for rent. The parties may create, by express or implied contract, a lien in favor of the landlord for rent and also for advances, taxes, or damages for failure to make repairs. In the absence of a statutory provision, the lien of the landlord is superior to the claims of all other persons except prior lienors and good-faith purchasers.

---

[15] The Americans with Disabilities Act requires commercial landlords and tenants to comply with legal requirements for access by the disabled. Shopping centers, medical offices, banks, and professional buildings must be in compliance. *Brooks Shopping Centers, LLC v. DCHWWC Restaurants, Inc.*, 929 N.Y.S.2d 354 (N.Y. App. 2012). *Anderson v. Little League Baseball, Inc.*, 794 F. Supp. 342 (D. Ariz. 1992).

[16] *Reach Community Development v. Stanley*, 274 P.3d 211 (Or. App. 2012).

[17] URLTA §2.101.

Suit for Rent

Whether or not the landlord has a lien for unpaid rent, the landlord may collect rent from the tenant as specified in the lease. In some states, the landlord is permitted to bring a combined action against the tenant to recover the possession of the premises and the over-due rent at the same time.

Recovery of Possession

A lease commonly provides that on the breach of any of its provisions by the tenant, such as the failure to pay rent, the lease terminates or the landlord may exercise the option to declare the lease terminated. When the lease is terminated for any reason, the landlord then has the right to evict the tenant and retake possession of the property.

A landlord cannot lock out a tenant for overdue rent. The landlord must employ legal process to regain possession even if the lease expressly gives the landlord the right to self-help.

The landlord may resort to legal process to evict the tenant to enforce the right to possession of the premises. Statutes in many states provide a summary remedy to recover possession that is much more efficient than the slow common law remedies. Often referred to as a **forcible entry and detainer,** this action restores the property to the land-lord's possession unless the tenant complies with payment requirements.

Landlord's Duty to Mitigate Damages

If the tenant leaves the premises before the expiration of the lease, is the landlord under any duty to rent the premises again to reduce the rent or damages for which the departing tenant will be liable? By common law and majority rule, a tenant holds a possessory estate in land, and if the tenant abandons it, there is no duty on the landlord to find a new tenant for the premises. But a growing minority view places greater emphasis on the contractual aspects of a lease. Under this view, when the tenant abandons the property, thereby defaulting on the contract, the landlord has a duty to seek to mitigate the damages caused by the tenant's breach and make a reasonable effort to rent the abandoned property.

50-3 Liability for Injury on Premises

When the tenant, a member of the tenant's family, or a third person is injured because of the condition of the premises, the question of who is liable for the damages sustained by the injured person arises.

50-3a Landlord's Liability to Tenant

At common law, in the absence of a covenant to keep the premises in repair, the landlord was not liable for the tenant's personal injuries caused by the defective condition of the premises that, by the lease, are placed under the control of the tenant. However, recent cases have imposed liability on landlords for their failure to keep leased premises in repair, even when there is no covenant of repair. Tenants must still take reasonable precautions when they are aware of a defect. Giving the landlord notice, avoiding the broken step, and even stepping carefully are required when the tenant becomes aware of a dangerous condition and the landlord has not had an opportunity to make repairs.[18]

forcible entry and detainer–action by the landlord to have the tenant removed for nonpayment of rent.

---

[18] *Mauskopf v. 1528 Owners Corp.*, 958 N.Y.S.2d 759 (N.Y.A.D. 2013).

Crimes of Third Persons

Ordinarily, the landlord is not liable to the tenant for crimes committed on the premises by third persons, such as when a third person enters the premises and commits larceny or murder.[19] The landlord is not required to establish a security system to protect the tenant from crimes of third persons.

In contrast, when the criminal acts of third persons are reasonably foreseeable, the landlord may be held liable for the harm caused a tenant. **For Example,** when a tenant has repeatedly reported that the deadbolt on the apartment door is broken, the landlord is liable for the tenant's loss when a thief enters through the door because such criminal conduct was foreseeable. Likewise, when the landlord of a large apartment complex does not take reasonable steps to prevent repeated criminal acts, the landlord is liable to the tenant for the harm caused by the foreseeable criminal act of a third person.

CASE SUMMARY

Parking Outside the Gate and Living in a Gated Community: High Risk

FACTS: Arnel Management Company manages the Pheasant Ridge Apartments. Pheasant Ridge is a 620-unit, multibuilding apartment complex with over 1,000 residents, situated on 20.59 acres in Rowland Heights, California. Before the gated entrance to the complex are two parking lots; one is a visitor lot, and the other is the parking lot for the leasing office, located on the other side of the road. There are two security gates just past the parking lot. The gates are remote-control operated. Most of the property's parking spaces lie behind these gates by the apartments.

Yu Fang Tan and his wife, Chun Kuei Chang, and their child moved into Pheasant Ridge in July 2002 and received one assigned parking space. Tenants could pay an additional fee for a garage, but Tan chose not to rent one. Tenants with a second car could park in unassigned parking spaces located throughout the complex, or in one of the two lots—as long as the car was removed from the leasing office lot before 7:00 A.M.

At around 11:30 P.M. on December 28, 2002, Tan returned home and tried to find an unassigned open parking space because his wife had parked the family's other car in their assigned space. Unable to locate an available space, he parked in the leasing office parking lot outside the gated area. As Tan was parking his car, an unidentified man

approached him and asked for help. When Tan opened his window, the man pointed a gun and told him to get out of the car because the man wanted it. Tan responded, "Okay. Let me park my car first." But then the car rolled a little, and at that point, the assailant shot Tan in the neck. The incident rendered Tan a quadriplegic. Tan and Chang filed suit against Arnel for their negligent management of the complex as well as its policy of not providing sufficient parking inside the gated area and of charging more for such additional spaces. The trial court granted judgment on the pleadings for Arnel, and Tan and Chang appealed.

DECISION: Judgment for Tan. There had been a chain of events at the apartment complex and, particularly, in the parking lots that put the landlord on notice that there was a need for additional precautions. An expert had recommended various solutions that did not require a great deal of expense such as (1) moving the existing security gates from the back of the access road, and (2) installing "very similar" gates before the visitor and leasing office parking lots. The expert also noted that you don't get much more foreseeability in a property situation than was present in this situation. Reversed. [*Yu Fang Tan v. Arnel Management Co.,* 170 Cal. App. 4th 1087, 88 Cal. Rptr. 3d 754 (2009)]

Limitation of Liability

A number of courts, however, have restricted the landlord's power to limit liability in the case of residential, as distinguished from commercial, leasing. A provision in a residential lease excusing a landlord from liability for damage caused by water, snow, or ice is void.

---

[19] *Galanis v. CMA Management Co.,* _____ So. 3d _____, 2014 WL 5556196 (Miss. App. 2014). A co-tenant's application revealing credit-card fraud criminal history does not result in liability of landlord for tenant's murder.

Indemnification of Landlord

The modern lease commonly contains a provision declaring that the tenant will indemnify the landlord for any liability of the landlord to a third person that arises from the tenant's use of the rented premises.

50-3b **Landlord's Liability to Third Persons**

A landlord is ordinarily not liable to third persons injured because of the condition of any part of the rented premises that is in the possession of a tenant by virtue of a lease. If the landlord retains control over a portion of the premises, such as hallways or stairways, however, a landlord's liability exists for injuries to third persons caused by failure to exercise proper care in connection with that part of the premises. Most courts impose liability on the landlord for harm caused to a third person when the landlord was obligated, under a contract with the tenant, to correct the condition that caused the harm or to keep the premises in repair.

CPA 50-3c **Tenant's Liability to Third Persons**

A tenant in possession has control of the property and is liable when his or her failure to use due care under the circumstances causes harm to (1) licensees, such as a person allowed to use a telephone, and (2) invitees, such as customers entering a store. For both classes, the liability is the same as that of an owner in possession of property. It is likewise immaterial whether the property is used for residential or business purposes.

The liability of the tenant to third persons is not affected by the fact that the landlord may have contracted in the lease to make repairs that, if made, would have avoided the injury. The tenant can be protected, however, in the same manner that the landlord can be protected: by procuring liability insurance for indemnity against loss from claims of third persons.

SPORTS & ENTERTAINMENT LAW

The Quarter Pipe 360 Liability Issue

Timothy Lucier, two days shy of his thirteenth birthday, went with his father and several of his friends to Impact (a commercial skate park located in East Providence, Rhode Island) to skateboard to celebrate his birthday. At the skate park, Timothy's father signed the waiver that was required of all who used the park. Timothy donned a helmet, kneepads, and elbow pads, and then he and his friends used the skate park half pipes and quarter pipes. At one point, Timothy climbed on top of the quarter pipe, and as he pushed forward to go down the ramp, the front wheel of his skateboard caught inside a "nub" or "little tiny hole" in the ramp, causing the tail of his skateboard to swing around in a clockwise direction. Timothy twisted off the skateboard and fell on his right leg, causing a spiral fracture in his right leg. Timothy said that after he fell, he looked back at the ramp and saw that there was a split in the wood covering the ramp.

Timothy's parents filed suit against Impact Recreation, Ltd., the operator of the skateboard facility, and Eugene Voll, Impact's landlord. They alleged that there had been a failure by the landlord to ensure that the commercial tenant was not engaging in an activity that was inherently dangerous to the public at large.

Voll required Impact to have insurance, obtain signed waivers from all participants, and obtain his approval prior to the installation of any equipment. Do you believe the landlord is liable to the Luciers? Why or why not?

[*Lucier v. Impact Recreation, LTD.*, 864 A.2d 635 (R.I. 2005)]

50-4 **Transfer of Rights**

Both the landlord and the tenant have property and contract rights with respect to the lease. Can they be transferred or assigned? A landlord who sells his property transfers the rights in the leased premises to the buyer. The tenant also has transfer rights that are covered next.

50-4a Tenant's Assignment of Lease and Sublease

assignment–transfer of a right. Generally used in connection with personal property rights, as rights under a contract, commercial paper, an insurance policy, a mortgage, or a lease. (Parties—assignor, assignee)

sublease–a transfer of the premises by the lessee to a third person, the sublessee or subtenant, for a period of less than the term of the original lease.

An **assignment** of a lease is a transfer by the tenant of the tenant's entire interest in the premises to a third person. A tenancy for years may be assigned by the tenant unless the tenant is restricted from making such an assignment by the terms of the lease or by a statute. A **sublease** is a transfer to a third person, the *sublessee*, of less than the tenant's entire interest, or full lease term.

Limitations on Rights

The lease may contain provisions denying or limiting the right to assign or sublet. Such restrictions protect the landlord from new tenants who might damage the property or be financially irresponsible.

Restrictions in the lease are construed liberally in favor of the tenant. No violation of a provision prohibiting assignment or subleasing occurs when the tenant merely permits someone else to use the premises.

Effect of Assignment or Sublease

An assignee or a sublessee has no greater rights than the original lessee.[20] An assignee becomes bound by the obligations of the lease by the act of taking possession of the premises.

Neither the act of subletting nor the landlord's agreement to it releases the original tenant from liability under the terms of the original lease. When a lease is assigned, the original tenant remains liable for the rent that becomes due thereafter.

The tenant should require the sublessee to perform all obligations under the original lease and to indemnify the tenant for any loss caused if the sublessee defaults. Such liability on the part of the sublessee requires an express covenant. The fact that the sublease is made "subject to" the terms of the original lease merely recognizes the superiority of the original lease but does not impose any duty on the sublessee to perform the tenant's obligation under the original lease. If the sublessee promises to assume the obligations of the original lease, the landlord, as a third-party beneficiary, may recover from the sublessee for breach of the provisions of the original lease.

Make the Connection

Summary

The agreement between a lessor and a lessee by which the latter holds possession of real property owned by the former is a lease. Statutes in many states prohibit discrimination by an owner who rents property. Statutes in some states require that the lease not be unconscionable.

Tenancies are classified according to duration as tenancies for years, from year to year, at will, and at sufferance.

A lease is generally not terminated by the death, insanity, or bankruptcy of either party except for a tenancy at will. Leases are usually terminated by the expiration of the

---

[20] *First Hudson Capital LLC v. Seaborn*, 862 N.Y.S.2d 501 (N.Y.A.D. 2008).

specified term, notice, surrender, forfeiture, or destruction of the property or because of fraud. A tenant has the right to acquire possession at the beginning of the lease and has the right to retain possession until the lease is ended. Evictions may be either actual or constructive. The tenant is under a duty to pay rent as compensation to the landlord.

An assignment of a lease by the tenant is a transfer of the tenant's entire interest in the property to a third person; a sublease is a transfer of less than an entire interest—in either space or time. A lease may prohibit both an assignment and a sublease. If the lease is assigned, the assignee is liable to the landlord for the rent. Such an assignment, however, does not discharge the tenant from the duty to pay rent. In a sublease, the sublessee is not liable to the original lessor for rent unless that liability has been assumed or is imposed by statute.

The tenant need not make repairs to the premises, absent an agreement to the contrary. A warranty of habitability was not implied at common law, but most states now reject this view and imply in residential leases a warranty that the premises are fit for habitation.

A landlord is usually liable to the tenant only for injuries caused by latent defects or by defects that are not apparent but of which the landlord had knowledge. The landlord is not liable to the tenant for crimes of third persons unless they are reasonably foreseeable.

Learning Outcomes

After studying this chapter, you should be able to clearly explain:

50-1 Creation and Termination

LO.1 List the ways in which a lease may be terminated
See the discussion of the types of tenancies, page 1047.
See the Ethics & the Law feature on screening tenants for criminal records, page 1052.
See *Department of Housing and Urban Development v. Rucker* for a discussion of federal housing policy on eviction for drug use, page 1052.

50-2 Rights and Duties of Parties

LO.2 List and explain the rights and duties of the parties to a lease
See the *Bender v. Green* case, page 1053.

See the Thinking Things Through feature about the rotting balcony, page 1051.

50-3 Liability for Injury on Premises

LO.3 Describe a landlord's liability for a tenant's and a third person's injuries sustained on the premises
See the *Yu Fang Tan v. Arnel Management Co.* case, page 1056.
See the Sports & Entertainment Law discussion of the quarter pipe, page 1057.

50-4 Transfer of Rights

LO.4 Define *sublease* and *assignment of a lease* and distinguish between them
See the discussion of transfer of rights, pages 1057–1058.

Key Terms

assignment
constructive eviction
covenant of quiet enjoyment
escalation clause
forcible entry and detainer
landlord

lease
lessee
lessor
periodic tenancy
possession
sublease

sublessee
tenancy at sufferance
tenancy at will
tenancy for years
tenant
warranty of habitability

Questions and Case Problems

1. Johnny C. Carpenter and Harvey E. Hill died of asphyxiation when a fire broke out in their Hattiesburg, Mississippi, apartment on the morning of February 20, 1983. There were no smoke detectors in the apartment at the time of the fire, as required under Hattiesburg City Ordinance 2021. The administrators of the estates of Carpenter and Hill filed suit against London, Stetelman, and Kirkwood, the owners and managers of the apartment complex. Who is liable? [*Hill v. London,*

Stetelman, and Kirkwood, Inc., 906 F.2d 204 (5th Cir.)]

2. Petra Valoma and her three roommates rented an apartment in New York City with a security deposit of $2,850, two months of rent for $5,700, and a property loss payment of $800. Less than a month after the group of four took possession of the property, they found bedbugs. The manager sent an exterminator each week for six weeks, with no effective results. The four had to move out and lost most of their furniture because it was infected with bedbugs. The four sought to recover the rent that they had paid as well as damages for their lost furniture. What can they recover? [*Valoma v. G-Way Management, LLC*, 918 N.Y.S.2d 401 (N.Y. Cir. Ct.)]

3. Rod had a five-year lease in a building owned by Darwood and had agreed to pay $800 a month rent. After two years, Rod assigned his rights under the lease to Kelly. Kelly moved in and paid the rent for a year and then, owing two months' rent, moved out without Darwood's knowledge or consent. Darwood demanded that Rod pay him the past-due rent. Must Rod do so? Why or why not?

4. Sue A. Merrill injured her right shoulder when she fell as she was ascending the front steps leading to the porch and front door of the mobile home that her daughter, Sherri Pritchard, rented from Alvina Jansma. The step became loose during the time Ms. Pritchard rented the home. Prior to the fall, Ms. Pritchard had attempted to repair the step by securing it with nails. When that failed, she informed the manager of the property that the step was loose. The manager suggested that Ms. Pritchard try using screws to secure the step. Ms. Pritchard told the manager that she did not have a screw gun. The manager had one and said she would screw the step into place. Subsequently, and without Ms. Pritchard's knowledge, the manager attempted to repair the step. Apparently, that effort was unsuccessful and Ms. Merrill fell when the step separated from the porch as she stepped on it. Ms. Merrill filed a negligence claim against Ms. Jansma to recover for her medical expenses, lost wages, and damages for emotional distress and pain and suffering. Could Ms. Merrill recover? [*Merrill v. Jansma*, 86 P.3d 270 (Wyo.)]

5. Jennifer Sanchez and her three children lived in a two-story townhome operated by CAA (the Cincinnati Community Action Agency). CAA is a nonprofit entity that provides housing for single mothers in financial need. Sanchez requested maintenance on an area behind her toilet on the second floor of the townhome. Josh Hill, a maintenance employee for CAA, came to fix the area. Hill's plan was to simply plaster over the moist area. However, Ms. Sanchez's boyfriend and the father of her children, Ruben, was present and offered his expertise as someone who earned a living doing drywall work. He loaned Hill a box cutter to cut out the moist portion of the wall and Ruben walked Hill through the repair. As Hill finished the work, Ms. Sanchez called Ruben downstairs and Hill left.

The two- and four-year-olds ended up in the bathroom near the repair area and found the box cutter. In a fight over the box cutter, the four-year-old (V.R.) sliced her finger trying to seize it from the two-year-old. V.R. had to have several surgeries for nerve and tendon damage. Ms. Sanchez, Ruben, and V.R. sued CAA alleging that it had breached its duty as a landowner and caused the injury for their failure to maintain the premises. Can they recover? [In re *V.R.*, 2014 WL 6090396 (Ohio App.)]

6. On June 21, 1997, Julio Ramos was helping his cousin move out of a second-floor apartment. He positioned himself on the outer side of the second-floor balcony railing, his feet between its spindles, to pass furniture to a friend on the ground below. While perched in this precarious position, Ramos held onto the railing with one hand and used his other hand to move the furniture. The reason for this method of removing the furniture was that many pieces were too large to be taken down the stairs. After approximately an hour of moving furniture in this manner, Ramos heard some cracking and felt the railing giving way. He released the furniture and attempted to grab onto the railing with both hands, but the spindles broke, and Ramos fell to the ground.

Ramos brought suit against the landlord to recover for his injuries. How does this case compare to the *Tan* case? Should the landlord in this case be held liable? [*Ramos v. Granajo*, 822 A.2d 936 (R.I.)]

7. A tenant leased an apartment in which so much noise emanated from surrounding apartments late at night and in the wee hours of the morning that he could not get much sleep. The tenant brought suit against the landlord, alleging that the landlord had breached the implied warranty of habitability. Is the tenant correct? Can noise be a breach of the warranty

of habitability? [*Nostrand Gardens Co-op v. Howard*, 634 N.Y.S.2d 505]

8. James Santelli was staying at a motel owned by Abu Rahmatullah for several months as he worked at a nearby construction project.

   Joseph Pryor had been previously employed at the motel as a general maintenance man. There was no criminal background check done on Pryor. Pryor had a prior conviction and was wanted at the time he was hired for probation violations. When he left his job at the motel, Pryor kept his master keycard. Pryor used the keycard to enter Santelli's room and later confessed to robbing and killing him, with a resulting sentence of 85 years. Mr. Santelli's widow brought suit against Rahmatullah for his negligence in hiring Pryor. Can Rahmatullah be held liable for Mr. Santelli's death? [*Santelli v. Rahmatullah*, 966 N.E.2d 661 (Ind. App.)]

9. During the remodeling of an apartment building, tenants had so much dust from the construction settle in their apartment that they experienced damage to their expensive sound and recording equipment. They had rented the very specialized and large apartment because it was suitable to use as a recording studio. Would the presence of the dust be grounds for constructive eviction? Would it be a breach of the warranty of habitability? [*Minjak Co. v. Rudolph*, 528 N.Y.S.2d 554]

10. Cantanese leased a building for the operation of his drugstore from Saputa. He moved his drugstore from Saputa's building to another location but continued to pay rent to Saputa. Saputa, fearing that he was losing his tenant, entered the premises without Cantanese's permission and made extensive alterations to the premises to suit two physicians who had agreed to rent the premises from Saputa. Cantanese informed Saputa that he regarded the making of the unauthorized repairs as grounds for canceling the lease. Saputa then claimed that Cantanese was liable for the difference between the rent that Cantanese had agreed to pay and the rent that the doctors would pay for the remainder of the term of the Cantanese lease. Was Cantanese liable for such rent? [*Saputa v. Cantanese*, 182 So. 2d 826 (La. App.)]

11. Sargent rented a second-floor apartment in a building owned by Ross. Anna, Sargent's four-year-old daughter, fell from an outdoor stairway and was killed. Sargent brought suit against Ross for her daughter's death. Ross contended that she did not have control over the stairway and therefore was not liable for its condition. Was this defense valid? [*Sargent v. Ross*, 308 A.2d 528 (N.H.)]

12. Charles leased a house from Donald for four years. The rent agreed on was $850 per month. After two years, Charles assigned his rights under the lease to Smith, who moved in and paid rent regularly for a year. Owing rent, Smith moved out sometime later without Donald's knowledge or consent. Donald demanded that Charles pay the rent. Is Charles liable?

13. Green rented an apartment from Stockton Realty. The three-story building had a washroom and clothesline on the roof for use by the tenants. The clothesline ran very near the skylight, and there was no guard rail between the clothesline and the skylight. Green's friend, who was 14 years old, was helping Green remove clothes from the line when she tripped on an object and fell against the skylight. The glass was too weak to support her weight, and she fell to the floor below, sustaining serious injuries. Is the landlord responsible for damages for the injury sustained? Decide. [*Reiman v. Moore*, 180 P.2d 452 (Cal.)]

14. Suzanne Andres was injured when she fell from the balcony of her second-floor apartment in the Roswell-Windsor Village Apartments. Andres was leaning against the railing on the balcony when it gave out, and she and the railing fell to the ground. Andres filed suit against Roswell-Windsor for its failure to maintain the railing. Roswell-Windsor maintains that the railing was not in a common area and was in Andres's exclusive possession and that she was responsible for its maintenance or at least letting the manager know the railing needed repairs. Should Andres recover from the landlord for her injuries? [*Andres v. Roswell-Windsor Village Apartments*, 777 F.2d 671 (11th Cir.)]

15. Williams, an elderly man who was sensitive to heat, rented an apartment in the Parker House. His apartment was fully air-conditioned, which enabled him to stand the otherwise unbearable heat of the summer. The landlord was dissatisfied with the current rent, and although the lease had a year to run, insisted that Williams agree to an increase. Williams refused. The landlord attempted to force Williams to pay the increase by turning off the electricity and thereby stopping the apartment's air conditioners. He also sent up heat on the hot days. After one week of such treatment, Williams, claiming that he had been evicted, moved out. Has there been an eviction? Explain.

CPA Questions

1. Which of the following provisions must be included to have an enforceable written residential lease?

	A Description of the Leased Premises	A Due Date for the Payment of Rent
a.	Yes	Yes
b.	Yes	No
c.	No	Yes
d.	No	No

2. Bronson is a residential tenant with a 10-year written lease. In the absence of specific provisions in the lease to the contrary, which of the following statements is correct?

   a. The premises may not be sublet for less than the full remaining term.

   b. Bronson may not assign the lease.

   c. The landlord's death will automatically terminate the lease.

   d. Bronson's purchase of the property will terminate the lease.

3. Which of the following provisions must be included in a residential lease agreement?

   a. A description of the leased premises.

   b. The due date for payment of rent.

   c. A requirement that the tenant have public liability insurance.

   d. A requirement that the landlord will perform all structural repairs to the property.

Decedents' Estates and Trusts

Learning Outcomes

After studying this chapter, you should be able to

LO.1 Define *testamentary capacity* and *testamentary intent*

LO.2 Discuss how a valid will is created

LO.3 Explain how a will may be modified or revoked

LO.4 Describe briefly the probate and contest of a will

LO.5 Describe the ordinary pattern of distribution by intestacy

LO.6 Explain the nature of a trust

51-1 **Wills**

What happens to your property after you die? There is a process for estate administration that is governed by state statutes and judicial decisions. There is wide variation in state law and there are only 17 states that have adopted the **Uniform Probate Code (UPC).**[1]

When a **decedent** has died with a valid will, he or she is said to have died **testate,** and the will determines who is entitled to receive the estate property after creditors have been paid. If the decedent did not make a valid will, laws for **intestate** distribution determine the distribution.

51-1a **Definitions**

Testate distribution describes the distribution that is made when the decedent leaves a valid will. A **will** is ordinarily a writing that provides for a distribution of property upon death but that confers no rights prior to that time. A man who makes a will is called a **testator;** a woman, a **testatrix.**

A gift of personal property by will is a **legacy** or **bequest,** in which case the beneficiary may also be called a **legatee.** A gift of real property by will is a **devise,** and the beneficiary may be called a **devisee.**

51-1b **Parties to Will**

Each state has variations on the qualifications of persons who wish to make a will. The following requirements are typical.

Testator

Generally, the right to make a will is limited to persons 18 or older. The testator must have **testamentary capacity,**[2] which means that a person must have sufficient mental capacity to understand that the writing that is being executed is a will—that is, that it disposes of the person's property after death. The testator must also have a reasonable appreciation of who the beneficiaries of his will are as well as a grasp of the identity of relatives and friends and the nature and extent of the property that will be given and to whom upon death.

Testamentary capacity is challenged by surviving relatives quite often. Eccentric behavior does not mean that the individual lacks capacity. The excessive and continued use of alcohol or multiple medications, producing mental deterioration, may be sufficient to justify the conclusion that the decedent lacked testamentary capacity. However, there can be lucid periods even among those who suffer from addictions. Expert testimony, the observations of friends and relatives, and the conduct of the decedent prior to death are all relevant factors in determining whether there was testamentary capacity.[3]

Uniform Probate Code (UPC)–uniform statute on wills and administration of estates.

decedent–person whose estate is being administered.

testate–condition of leaving a will upon death.

intestate–condition of dying without a will as to any property.

testate distribution–distribution of an estate in accordance with the will of the decedent.

will–instrument executed with the formality required by law by which a person makes a disposition of his or her property to take effect upon death.

testator, testatrix–man, woman who makes a will.

legacy–gift of money made by will.

bequest–gift of personal property by will.

legatee–beneficiary who receives a gift of personal property by will.

devise–gift of real estate made by will.

devisee–beneficiary of a devise.

testamentary capacity–sufficient mental capacity to understand that a writing being executed is a will and what that entails.

---

[1] The Uniform Probate Code has been adopted in Alaska, Arizona, Colorado, Florida, Hawaii, Idaho, Maine, Massachusetts, Michigan, Minnesota, Montana, Nebraska, New Mexico, North Dakota, South Carolina, South Dakota, and Utah. Other states have adopted portions or select provisions of the UPC. The predominant form of the UPC continues to be the 1969 version, but the 1990 and 2003 versions have been integrated into existing UPC states' statutes.
[2] In re *Estate of Rosen*, 23 N.E.3d 116 (Mass. App. 2014).
[3] *Parish v. Parish*, 704 S.E.2d 99 (Va. 2011).

CASE SUMMARY

Paranoia, Dementia, and Alzheimer's: Enough to Void a Will?

FACTS: Patricia Watson, the decedent, was raised in Missouri, but taught elementary school in California where she had three marriages and one daughter who was murdered in 1980. Ms. Watson retained close ties with her half siblings, Richard Ivie, Jimmie Ivie, Ladonna Small, and Bernard Ivie ("the Ivies").

When Watson retired from teaching in February 2002, and she married Smith. At the time of their marriage, Watson was 70 years old and Smith was 60 years old. Watson had substantial income and approximately $1 million in assets, including her home in California, real estate in Missouri, a pension from the California State Teachers' Retirement System (CALSTRS), and several bank accounts, retirement accounts, and vehicles. Smith had filed for bankruptcy in 1997 and had minimal income and assets. Watson created her original trust on May 9, 2002, about three months after marrying Smith. At the same time, Watson also created a will with a provision "pouring over" all of her estate's assets into the trust. Watson's Missouri attorney, Reginald Young, prepared the documents. All of Watson's property was conveyed into the trust. They moved to Missouri in 2004.

The Ivies were the sole beneficiaries of the trust. The trust provided "It is expressly the Grantor's intention that her husband, Arnold L. Smith, not receive any part of the Trust Estate."

Watson began showing signs that her mental health was progressively deteriorating. She saw a doctor who wrote in his report: "She thinks her husband is trying to poison her with rat poison. She denies hallucinations, but apparently gets very angry quickly on questioning.... At this time the patient seems to have paranoia."

According to her sister, Watson wanted a divorce from Smith because he had ruined her life. Watson also told one of her brothers that she thought she was losing her mind, that she was afraid of Smith, and that she thought he was trying to poison her.

Watson had a neuro-psychological evaluation at the Mayo Clinic in October 2005. Test results showed "a mild to moderate degree of cognitive impairment." The Mayo Clinic physician concluded that Watson's diagnosis was vascular dementia.

A second physician stated without qualification in November 2006 that the diagnosis was Alzheimer's dementia.

Before Watson executed the first trust amendment, she was no longer able to care for herself. She needed help with all of her daily living activities. By May 2007, at a family gathering, Watson did not recognize the children of one of her brothers and other previously known family members.

Roughly one month after leaving the hospital following a hospitalization, on July 27, 2007, Watson signed the first trust amendment decreasing the Ivies' share of her property and granting Smith a share. The amendment also added a "no-contest" clause, the purpose of which was to cause anyone challenging the trust to lose his or her share.

Watson's mental health continued to worsen. At some point after July 2007, she visited one of her neighbors and took off her own clothes in the neighbor's living room. In-home nurses' reports reflect that Watson's dementia was uncontrolled, she was paranoid and experienced forgetfulness and mood swings.

From early December 2007 to mid-January 2008, Watson retitled her checking account and money market account from the trust to her own name individually and signed documents to "pay on death" to Smith. Watson removed the Ivies from all accounts and beneficiary status.

The in-home nursing staff noted that her forgetfulness continued and that she had bouts of confusion. In late January, she asked Smith, "Am I still your wife? Are we married?" In late March, she was disoriented in her home and could not find the bathroom. In April, she wanted her lawn hand-pulled instead of mowed. In May, she was hospitalized after falling, and hospital reports repeatedly showed that she was "Confused/Disoriented/Senile/Irrational/Non–Compliant." On June 5, back at home, Watson said that she saw a baby while staring at the ceiling and that she was hearing voices.

Watson lived in a nursing home until July 2, 2008, which was the day she signed the second trust amendment. The second trust amendment further reduced the Ivies' shares in the trust estate and increased Smith's share. Because Reginald Young recognized that Watson's mental health had deteriorated and because he anticipated controversy over the changes to Watson's estate plan, he prepared a memorandum for his file stating that he believed she understood what she was doing.

Watson died April 10, 2009. After Watson's death, the Ivies filed to set aside the trust amendments, beneficiary designations, and various property transfers. The court entered judgment for the Ivies. The court found that Watson lacked testamentary capacity with regard to her estate plan. Smith appealed.

DECISION: There was substantial evidence to support a finding that Watson lacked testamentary capacity to make the

Paranoia, Dementia, and Alzheimer's: Enough to Void a Will? continued

changes to her estate plan. Although the testamentary capacity standard takes into account the ability of persons who have been diagnosed with some form of mental defect to make a valid will or trust, it remains a factual issue of whether a person had testamentary capacity at the particular time of execution. Lower courts are in the best position to

decide precisely when a person has testamentary capacity, and the bizarre and declining behaviors of the Testator indicate that she did not understand what she was doing through the changes and to whom.

Affirmed. [***Ivie v. Smith*, 439 S.W.3d 189 (Mo. 2014)**]

Beneficiary

beneficiary–person to whom the proceeds of a life insurance policy are payable, a person for whose benefit property is held in trust, or a person given property by a will; the ultimate recipient of the benefit of a funds transfer.

Generally, the capacity of the **beneficiary** is not an issue. However, when part of a decedent's estate passes to a minor, a guardian may be appointed to administer that interest for the minor. If a will directs that any share payable to a minor be held by a particular person as trustee for the minor, the minor's interest will be so held, and a guardian is not required. Statutes often provide that if the estate or interest of the minor is not large, it may be paid directly to the minor or to the parent or person by whom the minor is maintained.

51-1c Testamentary Intent

testamentary intent– designed to take effect at death, as by disposing of property or appointing a personal representative.

To execute a valid will, testators must demonstrate an intent to transfer property upon their deaths. This mental state is called **testamentary intent.**[4] This is the testator's intent that certain persons become the owners of certain property upon his or her death. However, there is still testamentary intent when the testator designates an executor only and does not make any disposition of property.

51-1d Form

Because the privilege of disposing of property by will is purely statutory, the will must be executed in the manner required by state statutes. Unless statutory requirements are met, the will is invalid, and the testator is considered to have died intestate. In such a case, the decedent's property will be distributed according to the laws of intestacy of the particular state.

Writing

Ordinarily, a will must be in writing. Some state statutes, however, permit oral wills in limited circumstances, and the use of videotaped wills is gaining some legal ground.

Signature

A written will must be signed by the testator. In case of physical incapacity, the testator may be assisted in signing the will.[5] Witnesses to the will can then verify that simple marks were indeed made by the testator while experiencing a physically debilitating condition.

Generally, a will must be signed at the bottom or end. The purpose of this requirement is to prevent unscrupulous persons from taking a will that has been validly signed and writing or typing additional provisions in the space below the signature.

[4] In re *Estate of Tyler*, 80 A.3d 797 (Pa. Super. 2013).
[5] In re *Estate of Shapiro*, 995 N.Y.S.2d 805 (N.Y. App. 2014).

E-COMMERCE & CYBERLAW

Where There's a Video, Is There a Will?

With technology, wills are no longer always just written but may be supplemented with electronic verification. The American Bar Association's Web site (**http://www.abanet.org**) offers the following thoughts on the new trend in video wills:

> More and more people are preparing a video in which they read the will and explain why certain gifts were made and others not made. The video recording might also show the execution of the will. Should a disgruntled relative decide to

challenge the will, the video can provide compelling proof that the person making the will was mentally competent and observed the formalities of execution.

> Keep in mind that videos do not last forever and are subject to damage. You should consult a lawyer before making such a video to find out about your state's laws on video wills. Generally, such a video would supplement the will and is not always a substitute for a validly executed will.

Attestation

Attestation is the act of witnessing the execution of a will. Generally, attestation consists of a witness signing the will following a clause that declares that the witness either saw the testator sign the will or that the testator told the witness that he or she did indeed sign the will. The clause that describes what the witness saw or knows is called an **attestation clause.** Statutes often require that attestation be made by the witnesses in the presence of the testator and in the presence of each other. Most states and the Uniform Probate Code (UPC) require two witnesses; a few states require three.

Self-proved wills are wills that carry a presumption that they are valid if executed according to the requirements set forth by statute. The UPC recognizes self-proved wills. A will may be simultaneously executed, attested, and made self-proving by acknowledgment by the testator and by affidavits of the witnesses.

The **acknowledgment** and **affidavits** must each be made before an officer authorized to administer oaths under state law, such as a notary. The acknowledgement and affidavits must carry an official seal, such as a notary's seal, which must be evidenced by the officer's certificate under official seal.

The self-proving provisions attached to the will are not a part of the will. Self-proving provisions allow a will to be admitted to probate without requiring the testimony of the witnesses to the will. The will itself must still meet the requirements of the law. The execution of a valid will is a condition precedent to use of the self-proving provisions.

In some states, a witness cannot be a beneficiary under the will. In those states, use of a beneficiary as a witness will not affect the will, but the witness's share is limited to whatever his or her intestate share would have been if there had been no will. Under the UPC, a will can be validly witnessed by an interested person.

Date

There is generally no requirement that a testator date a will, but a dated will does reduce confusion. When there are several wills, the most recent one will control when there are conflicting provisions between and among the wills.

51-1e Modification of Will

A will may be modified by executing a *codicil*, a separate writing that amends a will. The will, except as changed by the codicil, remains the same. The effect is that the provisions

attestation clause–clause that indicates a witness has observed either the execution of the will or the testator's acknowledgment of the writing as the testator's will.

self-proved wills–wills that eliminate some formalities of proof by being executed according to statutory requirements.

acknowledgment–admission or confirmation, generally of an instrument and usually made before a person authorized to administer oaths, such as a notary public.

affidavit–statement of facts under oath; executed before a notary public or anyone authorized to administer oaths.

of the codicil are substituted for those provisions of the will that are inconsistent with the codicil. A codicil must be executed with all the formality of a will and is treated in all other respects the same as a will.

A will cannot be modified merely by crossing out a clause and writing in what the testator wishes. Such an **interlineation** is not operative unless it is executed with the same formality required of a will or, in some states, unless the will is republished in its interlineated form.

interlineation–writing between the lines or adding to the provisions of a document, the effect thereof depending upon the nature of the document.

revoke–testator's act of taking back his or her will and its provisions.

51-1f Revocation of Will

At any time during the testator's life, the testator may **revoke** the will made or make changes in its terms. It may be revoked by act of the testator or by operation of law. A testator must have the same degree of mental capacity to revoke a will as is required to make one.

Revocation by Act of Testator

A will or a codicil is revoked when the testator destroys, burns, or tears it or crosses out the provisions of the will or codicil with the intention to revoke them. The revocation may be in whole or in part.[6]

CASE SUMMARY

When Wife #2 Finds Wife #1's Will with a Lot of Lines Through It

FACTS: On June 15, 1982, Shirley Joyce Speers signed a "Last Will and Testament." It named her husband, Ralph Speers, as her executor. It also gave her daughter, Sherr Arlene Ross, her household furnishings and appliances, and her son, Daniel Eugene Speers, her livestock. Her husband was named the beneficiary of the rest of the estate, provided he paid the estate's expenses. If he failed to do so, his share went to their children and grandsons. The will was probably witnessed and signed, but not notarized. The witnesses did not see any lines or strikeouts in the will when they signed it. Shirley died on April 20, 1997, and the will was not probated at the time of her death.

After his wife's death, Ralph married Ann Speers. Ralph died some time before June 2005, and Ann then discovered a copy of Shirley's will with lines through it and cross-outs. She filed a petition seeking to admit the will to probate. The will she submitted contained several handwritten strikeouts and interlineations. Shirley's children objected to the admission of the will, arguing that it was invalid because the original will was destroyed. The court found for Ann and the children appealed. The Court of Appeals reversed and Ann appealed.

DECISION: The court affirmed, holding that the original will was not self-proving because of the lack of a notary seal and because its strike-outs indicated that Shirley had revoked its provisions. The result was a completely different distribution of property under state intestacy law for Shirley's estate and, as a result, for Ralph's. Whether the will was admitted determined whether Ann or the children inherited Ralph's property. A dissent in the case concluded that the will should be admitted and that the witnesses' testimony had been clouded by the cross-outs and lines in the copy of the will. [**In re Estate of Speers**, 179 P.3d 1265 (Okl. 2008)]

Revocation by Operation of Law

In certain instances, statutes provide that a change of circumstances has the effect of a revocation. **For Example,** when a person marries after executing a will, the will is revoked or is presumed revoked unless it was made in contemplation of marriage or unless it provided for the future spouse. In some states, the revocation is not total but is effective only

[6] In re *Estate of Irvine*, 264 P.3d 127 (Mont. 2011).

to the extent of allowing the spouse to take such share of the estate as that to which the spouse would have been entitled had there been no will.

The birth or adoption of a child after the execution of a will commonly works a revocation or partial revocation of the will as to that child. In the case of a partial revocation, the child is entitled to receive the same share as if the testator had died intestate.

The divorce of the testator does not in itself work a revocation. However, the majority of courts hold that if a property settlement is carried out on the basis of the divorce, a prior will of the testator is revoked, at least to the extent of the legacy given to the divorced spouse.

51-1g Election to Take against the Will

To protect the husband or wife of a testator, the surviving spouse may generally ignore the provisions of a will and elect to take against the will. In such a case, the surviving spouse receives the share of the estate he or she would have received had the testator died without leaving a will or receives a fractional share specified by statute.

The right to take against the will is generally barred by certain kinds of misconduct by the surviving spouse. If a spouse is guilty of desertion or nonsupport that would have justified the decedent's obtaining a divorce, the surviving spouse usually cannot elect to take against the will.

51-1h Disinheritance

disinherited—excluded from sharing in the estate of a decedent.

With some exceptions, any person may be **disinherited** or excluded from sharing in the estate of a decedent.[7] A person who would inherit if there were no will is excluded from

SPORTS & ENTERTAINMENT LAW

Wills, Estates, & Probate Mistakes of the Rich and Famous

Philip Seymour Hoffman's sudden death offered some insights into the importance of effective estate planning, even by those who are young. For example, from Heath Ledger's estate we learn that it is important to keep your will updated. Mr. Ledger had not updated his will following the birth of his daughter. Mr. Hoffman's will only mentioned his first child, not the two who were born following the will's execution. While courts can step in and include the other children, there is always the chance of misunderstandings, challenges, and, perhaps most importantly, how the children's inheritance and care is to be handled.

When there are partners who are not married, there are complications. Who will manage any inheritance the children receive? Is the partner to be the trustee? Also, part of estate planning could include marriage because marriage does save estate taxes. For example, Mr. Hoffman gave his $35 million estate to the mother of his three children, Marianne O'Donnell. If the two had been married, there would be no estate tax.

Because they were not married, there is a personal exemption of $5.34 million and the remainder of the estate is taxes, at about 50 percent, so $15 million of Mr. Hoffman's estate will go to the federal government.

If Mr. Hoffman had established a trust for his children and partner, his estate would have simply "poured over" into the trust and his probate would have been completely private.

James Gandolfini's untimely death resulted in a payment of $30 million in taxes of his $70 million estate. He had likewise not structured his estate to minimize taxes. His young daughter will receive the bulk of the estate when she turns 21.

Robin Williams' death has resulted in a probate battle over his personal property items between his third wife and his children. The children want to have personal items, such as Mr. Williams' suspenders from his hit television series, "Mork and Mindy." While Mr. Williams had taken care with trusts and appropriate planning for his major property interests, the little items have proven to be a source of contention in probate.

---

[7] One exception, for example, is a surviving spouse. A surviving spouse has marital property rights and cannot be disinherited completely.

receiving any part of a decedent's estate if the decedent has left a will giving everything to other persons.

51-1i Special Types of Wills

In certain situations, special types of wills are used.

Holographic Wills

holographic will—unwitnessed will written by hand.

A **holographic will** is an unwitnessed will that is written by the testator entirely by hand. Some states make no distinction between holographic and other wills. Other states apply the general law of wills to holographic wills, with certain variations. Some states require that a holographic will be dated. Under the UPC, a holographic will is valid, whether witnessed or not, if the signatures and the material provisions are in the handwriting of the testator.[8]

Living Wills

living will—document by which individuals may indicate that if they become unable to express their wishes and are in an irreversible, incurable condition, they do not want life-sustaining medical treatments.

Living wills are documents that individuals use to decide in advance what level of life-sustaining medical treatments that want if they become unable to express their wishes and are in an irreversible, incurable condition (Figure 51-1). Living wills are legal in most states. Such personal wishes are entitled to constitutional protection as long as they are expressed clearly.

51-2 Administration of Decedents' Estates

A decedent's estate consists of the assets the decedent owned at death, and the administration of the estate requires a determination of who is entitled to receive that property. If the decedent owed debts, those debts must be paid first. After those payments, any balance must be distributed according to the terms of the will or by the intestate law if the decedent did not leave a valid will.

51-2a Definitions

executor, executrix—man, woman named in a will to administer the estate of the decedent.

administrator, administratrix—person (man, woman) appointed to wind up and settle the estate of a person who has died without a will.

personal representatives—administrators and executors who represent decedents under the UPC.

The decedent has the privilege of naming the person who will administer the estate. A man named in a will to administer the estate of the decedent is an **executor;** a woman, an **executrix.** If the decedent failed to name an executor or executrix or did not leave a will, the law permits another person, usually a close relative, to be appointed to wind up the estate. This person is an **administrator** or **administratrix.** Administrators and executors are referred to generally under the UPC as **personal representatives** of the decedents because they represent the decedents or stand in their place.

51-2b Probate of Will

probate—procedure for formally establishing or proving that a given writing is the last will and testament of the person who purportedly signed it.

Probate is the act by which the proper court or official accepts a will and declares that the instrument satisfies the statutory requirements as the will of the testator. Until a will is probated, it has no legal effect.

When witnesses have signed a will, generally they must appear and state that they saw the testator sign the will (unless the will is self-proving). If those witnesses cannot be found, have died, or are outside the jurisdiction, the will may be probated nevertheless.

---

[8] Determination of the validity of a holographic will requires the court to examine the nature of the document submitted for probate. In re *Succession of Duskin,* 153 So. 3d 567 (La. App. 2014).

FIGURE 51-1   Living Will

Living Will

INSTRUCTIONS:

This is an important legal document It sets forth your directions regarding medical treatment. You have the right to refuse treatment you do not want. You may make changes in any of these directions, or add to them, to conform them to your personal wishes.

I, _John Jones_ , being of sound mind, make this statement as a directive to be followed if I become permanently unable to participate in decisions regarding my medical care. These instructions reflect my firm and settled commitment to decline medical treatment under the circumstances indicated below:

I direct my attending physician to withhold or withdraw treatment that serves only to prolong the process of my dying, if I should be in an incurable or irreversible mental or physical condition with no reasonable expectation of recovery.

These instructions apply if I am (a) in a terminal condition; (b) permanently unconscious; or (c) if I am conscious but have irreversible brain damage and will never regain the ability to make decisions and express my wishes.

I direct that treatment be limited to measures to keep me comfortable and to relieve pain, including any pain that might occur by withholding or withdrawing treatment.

While I understand that I am not legally required to be specific about future treatments, if I am in the condition(s) described above I feel especially strongly about the following forms of treatment:

I do not want cardiac resuscitation.
I do not want mechanical respiration.
I do not want tube feeding.
I do not want antibiotics.
I do want maximum pain relief.

Other directions (insert personal instructions): _NONE_

These directions express my legal right to refuse treatment, under the law of [name of state]. I intend my instructions to be carried out, unless I have rescinded them in a new writing or by clearly indicating that I have changed my mind.

Sign and date here in the presence of two adult witnesses, who should also sign.

Keep the signed original with your personal papers at home. Give copies of the signed original to your doctor, family, lawyer, and others who might be involved in your care.

Signed: _John Jones_
Witness: _Earl Hummel_
  Address: _7852 Bailey Avenue_
           Buffalo, New York
Witness: _Ramona Yaley_
  Address: _8921 Clinton Street_
           Buffalo, New York

When no witnesses are required, it is customary to require two or more persons to identify the signature of the testator at the time of probate.

After the probate witnesses have made their statements under oath, the official or court will ordinarily admit the will to probate in the absence of any circumstances indicating that the writing should not be probated. A certificate or decree that officially declares that the will is the will of the testator and has been admitted to probate is then issued.

Any qualified person who wishes to object to the probate of the will on the ground that it is not a proper will may appear before the official or court prior to the entry of the decree of probate. A person may petition after probate to have the probate of the will set aside.

51-2c Will Contest

The probate of a will may be refused or set aside on the ground that the will is not the free expression of the intention of the testator. It may be attacked on the ground of (1) a lack of mental capacity to execute a will, (2) undue influence, duress, fraud, or mistake existing at the time of the execution of the will that induced or led to its execution, or (3) forgery.[9] With the exception of mental capacity, these terms consist of the same elements they do in contract law.

If any one of these problems exists, the probate court can refuse to admit the will for probate. The decedent's estate is then distributed as if there had been no will unless an earlier will can be probated.

CASE SUMMARY

There's a Melody in the Heirs

FACTS: John C. Ramsey Sr. (Senior) executed a will in the last months of his life that left the bulk of his estate to Melody Taylor, his paramour. Senior's relationships with his son and grandsons were strained, and his will included the following clause:

I have intentionally provided significant, yet smaller amounts for my son and grandsons because they have for several years alienated my affections by being irresponsible, contentious, and constantly seeking financial support from me rather than providing for themselves.

I have made provisions for MELODY J. TAYLOR because MELODY J. TAYLOR provides me care and support.

Senior was suffering from cancer and renal failure, and his pain was extraordinary. His doctors prescribed high doses of morphine that Melody administered. Senior died from an overdose of morphine.

John Ramsey Jr. (Junior), Senior's son, challenged the validity of the will on the grounds of undue influence as well as felonious killing of a testator by a beneficiary. The trial court found there was undue influence and refused to admit the will to probate. Melody appealed.

DECISION: Judgment for Melody. There was a long history of bad blood between Junior and Senior. Further, Senior had disinherited Junior long before Melody came into the picture. The clear statement in the will that he knew he was leaving out Junior and why was indicative of clear thinking and lack of duress from Melody. Senior also had independent advice on his will and took his time in executing it. Melody's administration of the fatal drug dose was pursuant to physician's instructions, and she was still entitled to inherit under the valid will that was admitted to probate. [*Ramsey v. Taylor*, **999 P.2d 1178 (Or. App. 2000)**]

51-2d When Administration Is Not Necessary

No administration is required when the decedent did not own any property at the time of death. In some states, special statutes provide for a simplified administration when the decedent leaves only a small estate. Likewise, when all property owned by the decedent

[9] *Shoaf v. Shoaf*, 727 S.E.2d 301 (N.C. App. 2012).

was owned with another person as joint tenants with right of survivorship, no administration is required.

51-2e Appointment of Personal Representative

Both executors and administrators must be appointed to their roles by a court or an officer designated by law. The appointment is made by granting to the personal representative **letters testamentary,** in the case of an executor, or **letters of administration,** in the case of an administrator.

51-2f Proof of Claims against the Estate

State statutes vary widely on how **claims** against a decedent's estate are presented. In very general terms, statutes provide for some form of public notice of the grant of letters testamentary or letters of administration. Creditors are then required to give notice of their claims within a period specified by either statute or a court order (for example, within six months). In most states, failure to present a claim within the specified time bars the claim.

51-2g Construction of a Will

The will of a decedent is interpreted according to the ordinary or plain meaning evidenced by its words. The court will strive to give effect to every provision of the will to avoid concluding that any part of the decedent's estate was not disposed of by the will.[10]

> **letters testamentary–** written authorization given to an executor of an estate as evidence of appointment and authority.
>
> **letters of administration–** written authorization given to an administrator of an estate as evidence of appointment and authority.
>
> **claims–** right to payment.

ETHICS & THE LAW

Preparing Your Client's Will When You're the Beneficiary

John Richard Tomlan, an attorney, befriended Katherine Rice, a 90-year-old nursing home resident, shortly after she was admitted to the home in 1993. Ms. Rice, unmarried and childless, had Parkinson's disease as well as dementia. Mr. Tomlan handled several legal items for her, including the sale of her cabin and the necessary legal paperwork for its closing. In 1998, Tomlan prepared a will that left her substantial estate to a niece and nephew, with the remainder of the estate to various philanthropic organizations.

Later, Ms. Rice told Mr. Tomlan that she wanted to leave the bulk of her estate to him. He explained that he could not ethically prepare such a will. Ms. Rice never contacted another attorney to make the change in the will. After that point, Mr. Tomlan began transferring Ms. Rice's assets into accounts that were joint and survivorship accounts with him. He was then able to convince her to give him a durable power of attorney so that he had control over all of her assets, including investment accounts, property, and bank

accounts. Using that power, he had $1,000,000 in shares of stock transferred solely to him.

Mr. Tomlan maintained that everything was a gift that Ms. Rice had directed be given to him. When Ms. Rice died at the age of 99, Mr. Tomlan failed to probate her estate despite questions and demands from Ms. Rice's niece. Eventually, the estate was processed and had just over $200,000 left. However, with the property that had been gifted to Mr. Tomlan, the estate was valued at over $2.1 million. Ms. Rice's niece reported Mr. Tomlan to the state bar of Ohio and he was given an indefinite suspension of his license to practice law. Clients are dependent upon absolute trust and arms-length relationships with their lawyers. When friendship and gifting enter the picture, the power of lawyer over client is one that dissipates estates.

[***Disciplinary Counsel v. Tomlan,*** **885 N.E.2d 895 (Ohio 2008)]**

---

[10] In re *Estate of Nalaschi,* 90 A.3d 8 (Pa. Super. 2014).

51-2h Testate Distribution of an Estate

general legacies—
certain sums of money bequeathed to named persons by the testator; to be paid out of the decedent's assets generally without specifying any particular fund or source from which the payment is to be made.

specific legacies—
identified property bequeathed by a testator; also called *specific devises*.

abate—put a stop to a nuisance; reduce or cancel a legacy because the estate of the decedent is insufficient to make payment in full.

adeemed—canceled; as in a specifically bequeathed property being sold or given away by the testator prior to death, thus canceling the bequest.

antilapse statutes—
statutes providing that the children or heirs of a deceased beneficiary may take the legacy in the place of the deceased beneficiary.

The last phase of the administration of the estate by the decedent's personal representative is the distribution of property remaining after the payment of all debts and taxes in accordance with the provisions of the will or by intestacy rules if there was no valid will.

There are various types of gifts under a will. A testator can bequeath to named persons certain sums of money called **general legacies,** or gifts in which no particular money is specified. The testator may also bequeath identified property called **specific legacies** or *specific devises.* **For Example,** a testator may give "$1,000 to *A*; $1,000 to *B*; my automobile to *C*." The first two bequests are general; the third is specific. After such specific bequests, the testator may make a bequest of everything remaining, called a *residuary bequest,* such as "the balance of my estate to *D*."

Abatement of Legacies

Assume in the preceding example that after all debts are paid, and only $1,500 and the automobile remain. What disposition is to be made?

Legacies **abate** or bear loss in the following order: (1) residuary, (2) general, (3) specific. The law also holds that legacies of the same class abate proportionately. **For Example,** in the hypothetical case, *C*, the specific legatee, would receive the automobile; *A* and *B*, the general legatees, would each receive $750; and *D*, the residuary legatee, would receive nothing.

Ademption of Property

When specifically bequeathed property is sold or given away by the testator prior to death, the bequest is considered **adeemed,** or canceled. The specific legatee in this instance is not entitled to receive any property or money. *Ademption* has the same consequence as though the testator had formally canceled the bequest. **For Example,** if Aunt Claire left her 2011 Honda Accord to her niece, Helen, but Aunt Claire sold the Honda Accord in 2014 and died in 2015, Helen receives nothing from Aunt Claire's estate because the bequest of the Honda is adeemed or canceled.

Antilapse Statutes

If the beneficiary named in the testator's will died before the testator and the testator did not make any alternate provision applicable in such a case, the gift ordinarily does not lapse. **Antilapse statutes** commonly provide that the gift to the deceased beneficiary

THINKING THINGS THROUGH

Close Enough for a Will?

Gloria Waterloo had difficulty with her handwriting. When Rabbi Zimmerman and his wife came to visit her at a hospice facility, she asked his wife, Sandie, to take dictation and write out her will, a resulting one-page document that listed five provisions. One of the provisions left $3,000,000 to Rabbi Zimmerman and appointed him guardian of her estate. After the provisions were dictated, Gloria went through and signed them all and then signed her name. No one witnessed the will. Gloria died less than a month later. Her heirs moved to set aside the will. Give a list of the possible theories her heirs could use to challenge the will.

[In re *Estate of Waterloo*, 250 P.3d 558 (Ariz. App. 2011)]

shall not lapse but that the children or heirs of that beneficiary may take the legacy in the place of the deceased beneficiary. An antilapse statute does not apply if the testator specified a disposition that should be made of the gift if the original legatee had died.

51-2i Intestate Distribution of an Estate

If the decedent does not effectively dispose of all property by will or does not have a will, the decedent's property is distributed to certain relatives. Because such persons acquire or succeed to the rights of the decedent and because the circumstances under which they do so is the absence of an effective will, it is said that they acquire title by **intestate succession.**

The right of intestate succession or inheritance is not a basic right of the citizen or an inalienable right. It exists only because the state legislature so provides. It is within the power of the state legislature to modify or destroy the right to inherit property.

Although wide variations exist among the statutory provisions of the states, a common pattern of intestate distribution exists.

Spouses

The surviving spouse of the decedent, whether husband or wife, shares in the estate. Generally, the amount received is a fraction that varies with the number of children. If no children survive, the spouse is generally entitled to take the entire estate. Otherwise, the surviving spouse ordinarily receives a one-half or one-third share of the estate.

Lineals

Lineals, or lineal descendants, are blood descendants of the decedent. Lineal descendants include children and grandchildren. That portion of the estate that is not distributed to the surviving spouse is generally distributed to lineals.

Parents

If the estate has not been fully distributed by this time, the remainder is commonly distributed to the decedent's parents.

Collateral Heirs

These are persons who are not descendants of the decedent but are related through a common ancestor. Generally, brothers and sisters and their descendants share any part of the estate that has not already been distributed. Statutes vary as to how far distribution will be made to the descendants of brothers and sisters. Under some statutes, a degree of relationship is specified, such as first cousins, and no person more remotely related to the decedent is permitted to share in the estate.

If the entire estate is not distributed within the permitted degree of relationship, the property that has not been distributed is given to the state government. This right of the state to take the property is the **right of escheat.** Under some statutes, the right of escheat arises only when there is no relative of the decedent, however remotely related.

Distribution *Per Capita* and *Per Stirpes*

The fact that different generations of distributees may be entitled to receive the estate creates a problem of determining the proportions in which distribution is to be made (Figure 51-2). When all the distributees stand in the same degree of relationship to the decedent, distribution is made *per capita,* each receiving the same share. **For Example,** if the decedent is survived by three children—*A, B,* and *C*—each of them is entitled to receive one-third of the estate.

---

intestate succession– distribution, made as directed by statute, of a decedent's property not effectively disposed of by will.

lineals–relationship that exists when one person is a direct descendant of the other; also called *lineal descendants*.

right of escheat–right of the state to take the property of a decedent that has not been distributed.

per capita–method of distributing estate assets on an equal-per-person basis.

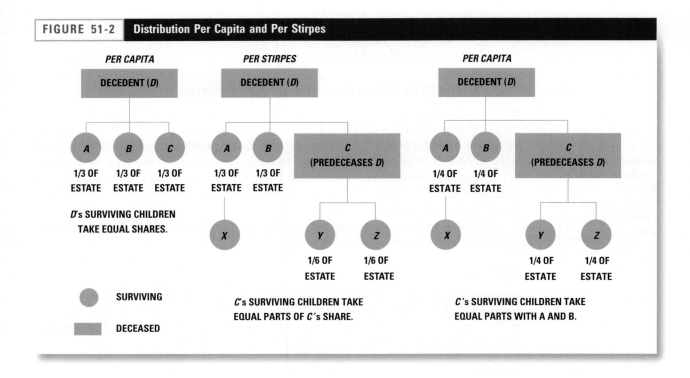

FIGURE 51-2   **Distribution Per Capita and Per Stirpes**

If the distributees stand in different degrees of relationship, distribution is made in as many equal parts as there are family lines, or *stirpes*, represented in the nearest generation. Parents take to the exclusion of their children or subsequent descendants, and when members of the nearest generation have died, their descendants take by way of representation. This is called **distribution *per stirpes***, or *stirpital distribution*. **For Example,** Thomas dies leaving two living children, *A* and *B*, and one child, *C*, who predeceased him but left two children (Thomas's grandchildren, *D* and *E*). *A* and *B* would each take one-third of Thomas's estate, and *D* and *E* would, under a ***per stirpes*** distribution, split a one-third interest, each receiving one-sixth of the estate.

distribution *per stirpes*—distribution of an estate made in as many equal parts as there are family lines represented in the nearest generation; also known as *stirpital distribution.*

per stirpes—method for distribution of an estate that divides property equally down family lines.

Murder of Decedent

Statutes generally provide that a person who murders the decedent cannot inherit from the victim by intestacy. In the absence of such a statute, courts are divided over whether the heir may inherit.

CASE SUMMARY

When Mother and Daughter Die: The Son-in-Law's Rights

FACTS: Deanna Edwards Palladino and Brandon Palladino were high school sweethearts who married in 2007. On December 17, 2008, Brandon killed his mother-in-law, Dianne Edwards (hereinafter the decedent), by strangling her to death. The decedent's will bequeathed her entire estate to Deanna, her only child. In October 2009, Brandon was indicted for the crime of murder in the second degree for causing the death of the decedent. Deanna, who was not criminally charged in connection with the decedent's death, stood by Brandon and believed in his innocence.

When Mother and Daughter Die: The Son-in-Law's Rights continued

In February 2010, approximately 14 months after her mother's death, Deanna died intestate of an accidental drug overdose. Although the decedent's will had been admitted to probate in October 2009, none of the decedent's estate had been distributed to Deanna prior to Deanna's death. Deanna was survived by one distributee, Brandon. Brandon designated his mother, Donna DiRusso, as the administrator of Deanna's estate. According to DiRusso's petition for letters of administration, Deanna's estate consisted only of funds received as the beneficiary of the decedent's retirement plan and the expected inheritance from the decedent.

On October 12, 2010, approximately 10 months after Deanna's death, Brandon pleaded guilty to manslaughter in the first degree, in connection with the death of the decedent. During the plea proceeding, Brandon admitted to entering the decedent's home on December 17, 2008, for the purpose of taking her jewelry. While Brandon was in the decedent's bedroom taking jewelry from her jewelry box, the decedent returned home and the two got into a physical fight. Brandon placed the decedent in a choke hold and squeezed as the decedent was resisting and scratching him. Brandon admitted that he intended to cause the decedent serious physical injury but asserted that he did not intend to kill her. However, Brandon subsequently moved for leave to file a late notice of appeal from the judgment of conviction, and his motion was granted by this Court by decision and order dated April 4, 2012.

The decedent's estranged sister, Donna Larsen, submitted objections to the account arguing that Brandon forfeited his interest in any property that would pass to him from the decedent's estate through Deanna's estate, due to his conviction for causing the decedent's death.

DiRusso moved to dismiss the objections, and Larsen cross-moved for summary judgment on the objections. In a decision and order dated March 28, 2012, the Surrogate's Court denied DiRusso's motion and granted Larsen's motion in part. DiRusso appealed.

DECISION: The issue here is whether a wrongdoer should be prevented from indirectly profiting from his or her own wrongdoing. May Brandon inherit assets of the decedent's estate indirectly through Deanna's estate?

There is a clear causal link between the wrongdoing and the benefits sought. But for Brandon's killing of the decedent, the estate of Deanna would not likely include any assets from the decedent's estate. Deanna's "intervening estate" should not be used to allow Brandon to profit from his unlawful killing of the decedent.

Allowing Brandon to inherit the assets of the decedent's estate through Deanna's estate would be rewarding Brandon's criminal behavior.

Affirmed. **[In re *Edwards*, 991 N.Y.S.2d 431 (N.Y.A.D. 2014)]**

Uniform Simultaneous Death Act–law providing that when survivorship cannot be established, the property of each person shall be disposed of as though he or she had survived the other.

trust–transfer of property by one person to another with the understanding or declaration that such property be held for the benefit of another; the holding of property by the owner in trust for another, upon a declaration of trust, without a transfer to another person. (Parties—settlor, trustee, beneficiary)

Death of Distributee after Decedent

The persons entitled to distribution of a decedent's estate are determined as of the date of death. If a distributee dies after that, the rights of the distributee are not lost but pass from the original decedent's estate to the deceased distributee's estate.

Simultaneous Death

The **Uniform Simultaneous Death Act**[11] provides that when survivorship cannot be established, the property of each person shall be disposed of as if he or she had survived the other.

51-3 Trusts

A **trust** is a legal device by which property, real or personal, is held by one person for the benefit of another. Legal problems in the area of trusts invariably require a determination of the nature of the relationship created by the trust and the rights and obligations of the parties with respect to that relationship.

---

[11] The 1940 version of this act has been adopted in all states except Louisiana and Ohio. The newest version of the act (1993) has been adopted in one-third of the states.

51-3a **Definitions**

The property owner who creates the trust is the **settlor.** (The word *settlor* is taken from the old legal language of "settling the property in trust.") The settlor is sometimes called the **donor** or **trustor.** The person to whom the property is transferred in trust is the **trustee.** The person for whose benefit the trustee holds the property is the beneficiary (or ***cestui que trust***).

Property held in trust is sometimes called the **trust corpus,** *trust fund, trust estate,* or *trust res.* A distinction is made between the **principal,** or the property in trust, and the **income** that is earned by the principal and distributed by the trustee.

If the trust is created to take effect within the lifetime of the settlor, it is a **living trust,** or an *inter vivos trust.* If the trust is provided for in the settlor's will and is to become effective only when the will takes effect after death, the trust is called a **testamentary trust.**

51-3b **Creation of Trusts**

The requirements for creating a trust are not uniform, but there are certain typical requirements.

Capacity of Beneficiary

The capacity of the beneficiary of the trust to hold property or to contract is immaterial. Many trusts are created because the beneficiary lacks legal or actual capacity to manage the property. The trustee, as the holder of legal title, must have capacity.

Formality

In creating a trust, it is common practice to execute a writing, called a **trust agreement** or *deed of trust.* No particular form of language is necessary to create a trust as long as the property, the trust purpose, and the beneficiaries are designated. If an *inter vivos* trust relates to an interest in land, the statute of frauds requires that the trust be in writing with the details of the trust included. A writing signed by the trustee and referring to a deed from the trustor can satisfy this requirement. When the trust depends on a transfer of title to land, there must be a valid transfer of the title to the trustee. If a trust is created by the will of the settlor, there must be a writing that meets the requirements of a will.

Intention

The settler must express some intention to place property in trust. It is not necessary, however, that the word *trust* or *trustee* be used. The settlor will ordinarily name a trustee, but failure to do so is not fatal to the trust because a trustee will be appointed by the court.

Identity of Beneficiary

Every trust must have a beneficiary. In a private trust, the beneficiaries must be identified by name, description, or designation of the class to which the beneficiaries belong. In a charitable trust, it is sufficient that the beneficiaries be members of the public at large or a general class of the public.

51-3c **Nature of Beneficiary's Interest**

When property is transferred to a trust, the trustee has **legal title** and the beneficiary has **equitable title.** The beneficiary may transfer or assign such interest in the trust. The beneficiary's creditors may reach that interest in satisfaction of their claims. However, the trustor can protect beneficiaries from creditors by creating a **spendthrift trust,** which does not allow creditors of the beneficiary to attach the beneficial interest, nor is the beneficiary permitted to assign or pledge that interest.[12]

[12] However, see In re *Marriage of Beevers,* 2013 WL 3872784 (Ill. App. 2013).

Margin glossary:

settlor–one who settles property in trust or creates a trust.

donor–person making a gift.

trustor–donor or settlor who is the owner of property.

trustee–party who has legal title to estate and manages it.

cestui que trust–beneficiary of the trust.

trust corpus–fund or property that is transferred to the trustee also called *trust fund, trust estate,* and *trust res.*

principal–property held in trust.

income–money earned by the principal, or property in trust, and distributed by the trustee.

living trust–trust created to take effect within the lifetime of the settlor; also called *inter vivos* trust.

testamentary trust–trust that takes effect upon the settlor's death.

trust agreement–instrument creating a trust; also called *deed of trust.*

legal title–title held by the trustee in a trust situation.

equitable title–beneficial interest in a trust.

spendthrift trust–a trust that, prevents creditors of the beneficiary from reaching the principal or income held by the trustee and precludes beneficiary assignments.

51-3d Powers of Trustee

A trustee can exercise only those powers that are given by law or the trust instrument or those that the court will construe as being given by implication. Modern trusts commonly give the trustee discretion to make decisions on matters that could not be foreseen by the settlor. **For Example,** the trustee may be authorized to expend principal as well as income when, in the trustee's opinion, it is necessary for the education or medical care of a beneficiary.

51-3e Duties of Trustee

The duty of a trustee is to administer the trust. The trustee who accepts the appointment must take all necessary steps to carry out the trust in a proper manner.

Performance

A trustee is under a duty to carry out the trust according to its terms and is personally liable for any loss sustained from an unjustified failure to perform such duties. A trustee cannot delegate the performance of personal duties.

Due Care

The trustee is under a duty to use reasonable skill, prudence, and diligence in the performance of trust duties. More simply stated, the trustee must use the care that would be exercised by a reasonable person under the circumstances.

Loyalty

A trustee is entitled to compensation but is not permitted to profit personally from the position of trustee.[13]

Possession and Preservation of Trust Property

The trustee has a duty to take possession of trust property and to preserve it from loss or damage. If the property includes accounts receivable or outstanding debts, the trustee is responsible for collecting them.

Production of Income

By either express or implied direction, the trustee is required to invest the money or property in enterprises or transactions that will yield an income to the estate. A trustee must invest the trust property as a reasonable and prudent investor would.

Accounting and Information

A trustee must keep accurate records so that it can be determined whether the trust has been properly administered. On request by a beneficiary, the trustee must furnish information about the trust. Periodically or at certain times, as determined by the law in each state, a trustee must file an account in court. At such time, the court examines the stewardship of the trust.

In some trusts, the trustee must balance the interests of the life beneficiary (the party entitled to the income from the trust while he or she is alive) with those of the eventual recipients of the trust *res*. **For Example,** a testator might put this provision in her will: "To my husband in trust for his life, and upon his death in fee simple to my children." How does the trustee account for rental income? What if the rental properties need

---

[13] *Whitman v. Whitman*, 2012 WL 367055 (Ohio App. 2012).

FIGURE 51-3 **Trust Principal/Income Allocation**

PRINCIPAL	PAYABLE FROM PRINCIPAL	INCOME	PAYABLE FROM INCOME
Original trust property	Loans (principal)	Rent	Loans (interest)
Proceeds and gains from sale	Litigation expenses	Interest	Taxes
Insurance payments	Permanent improvements	Cash	Insurance premiums
New property purchased with principal	Costs of purchase	Dividends	Repairs
Stock dividends		Royalties	
Stock splits			

---

repairs? Do the repairs come from the income, or are they taken from principal? There are clear rules for the allocation of income and principal and the expenses of operation of the trust and the trust properties. These rules are summarized in Figure 51-3.

51-3f Remedies for Breach of Trust

A breach of trust may occur in a variety of ways. The manner in which a trust is breached affects the remedies available. These remedies include the following: (1) A money judgment against the trustee for losses, (2) an injunction, (3) criminal prosecution for misconduct, (4) recovery of trust property, (5) removal of the trustee for misconduct, and (6) recovery from any third parties who participated in a breach of trust.

51-3g Termination of Trust

A trust may be terminated (1) by its own terms—for example, the trust is an education fund that has a termination date of college graduation, (2) because of the impossibility of attaining the object of the trust—for example, the trust is for the trustor's grandchild and his only child has died before having any children, (3) via revocation by the settlor when allowed by the terms of the trust, but trusts are presumed irrevocable unless the trust document permits revocation, (4) by merger of all interests in the same person (as when there is only one trustee and one beneficiary and they are the same person), or (5) upon the request of all the beneficiaries, as approved by a court, when there is no express purpose that requires continuation of the trust.

Make the Connection

Summary

A *will* is a writing that provides for a disposition of property to take effect upon death. A man who makes a will is called a *testator*; a woman, a *testatrix*. The person to whom

property is left by will is a *beneficiary*. A *legacy* is a gift of personal property by will; a gift of real property by will is a *devise*. A testator must have testamentary capacity to make a will and must manifest some intention that the will is to be effective only upon death. The will must be signed by the testator and be witnessed.

A will may be modified by a codicil or revoked either by the act of the testator or by operation of law.

Probate is the process by which a proper court official accepts a will. Probate may be refused or set aside on grounds that the will is not the free expression of the testator.

A *holographic* will is an unwitnessed will written entirely in the handwriting of the testator. A *self-proved will* may be admitted to probate without the testimony of subscribing witnesses. A *living will* allows a person to make wishes known regarding life-sustaining medical treatment.

If there is a valid will, the last phase of administration of the estate is the distribution of property after the payment of all debts and taxes. *General legacies* are bequests of money, whereas *specific legacies* or *specific devises* are gifts of identified personal or real property. Legacies abate in the following order: residuary, general, and specific. If a beneficiary named in the will has died before the testator and no alternate provision has been made for that beneficiary, antilapse statutes provide that the gift will not lapse. In that event, the children or heirs of the beneficiary may take the legacy in the place of the deceased beneficiary.

If the decedent does not dispose of all property by will or does not have a will, the property will be distributed according to state intestacy statutes. A surviving spouse may generally elect to take the statutory allocation instead of that provided in the will.

The estate of the testator will be administered by the person appointed in the will (the *executor*) or, if there is no will, by a person appointed by the court (an *administrator*). Creditors who have claims against the estate are required to give notice of their claims to the personal representative; otherwise, the claims will be barred.

A *trust* is a legal device by which property is held by one person for the benefit of another. The settlor creates the trust, and the person for whose benefit the trustee holds the property is the beneficiary. Property held in trust is called the *trust corpus, trust fund, trust estate*, or *trust res*.

A trust is usually created by a trust agreement or deed of trust. No particular form or language is required. A trust is not created unless an active duty is placed on the trustee to manage the property in some manner. A trustee's acceptance of duties is presumed.

Legal title to trust property is given to the trustee, and the beneficiary holds equitable title. A beneficiary may transfer an interest in the trust except in the case of a spendthrift trust.

The trustee can exercise only those powers that are given by law or the trust instrument. The trustee must administer the trust and carry out the trust in a proper manner. A trustee is liable for breach of the terms of the trust agreement. A trust comes to an end when its terms so provide or when it becomes impossible to attain the object of the trust.

Learning Outcomes

After studying this chapter, you should be able to clearly explain:

51-1 Wills

LO.1 Define *testamentary capacity* and *testamentary intent*

See *Ivie v. Smith* for a case discussion of a testator who lacks capacity, pages 1065–1066.

See the Sports & Entertainment feature on the mistakes that the rich and famous make in their estate plans and wills, page 1069.

LO.2 Discuss how a valid will is created

See the discussion of the *Ramsey v. Taylor* case, page 1072.

LO.3 Explain how a will may be modified or revoked

See the In re *Estate of Speers* case, page 1068.

51-2 Administration of Decedents' Estates

LO.4 Describe briefly the probate and contest of a will

See the Ethics & the Law discussion of a lawyer's duties, page 1073.

LO.5 Describe the ordinary pattern of distribution by intestacy

See Figure 51-2, page 1076.

See the In re *Edwards* case for a discussion of a son-in-law inheriting his mother-in-law's estate after confessing to killing her, pages 1076–1077.

51-3 Trusts

LO.6 Explain the nature of a trust

See the sections titled "Creation of Trusts," "Nature of Beneficiary's Interest," and "Powers of Trustee" on trust terminology and creation, pages 1078–1079.

Key Terms

abate
acknowledgment
adeemed
administrator
administratrix
affidavits
antilapse statutes
attestation clause
beneficiary
bequest
cestui que trust
claims
decedent
devise
devisee
disinherited
distribution *per stirpes*
donor
equitable title
executor
executrix

general legacies
holographic will
income
interlineations
intestate
intestate succession
legacy
legal title
legatee
letters of administration
letters testamentary
lineal
living trust
living wills
per capita
per stirpes
personal representatives
principal
probate
revoke
right of escheat

self-proved wills
settlor
specific legacies
spendthrift trust
testamentary capacity
testamentary intent
testamentary trust
testate
testate distribution
testator
testatrix
trust
trust agreement
trust corpus
trustee
trustor
Uniform Probate Code (UPC)
Uniform Simultaneous Death Act
will

Questions and Case Problems

1. After an eleven-month struggle with esophageal cancer, Leonard R. Brener died on December 8, 2001, at age 85. He had never married. He had no children. He had a long and successful career as a stockbroker. The value of his estate approximated $8 million. Several nieces and nephews survived him. He had originally left nearly all of his estate to The Carroll Center for the Blind, the Perkins School for the Blind, and Beth Israel Deaconess Medical Center, Inc. The gifts to these nonprofit organizations during Brener's life and through his will were complicated and made through detailed living, testamentary, and pour-over trusts. During the last five weeks of his life he was hospitalized and drafted and executed the final version of his will, which made one niece and her husband the primary beneficiaries of his estate. The nonprofit organizations sought to have the will set aside for lack of testamentary capacity.

   During those five weeks of terminal illness, Brener spoke of suicide by jumping out of the window, complained of depression, and often complained to his lawyer that he did not understand all the estate planning tools that were being used in his

will. The staff at the hospital testified that Brener did not seem confused and was aware that he was dying and wanted to be sure his affairs were in order. [*Maimonides School v. Coles,* 881 N.E.2d 778 (Mass. App.)]

2. Gerald "Pat" Arrington was diagnosed with a brain tumor. At the time of the diagnosis, he was married to Brenda Arrington, but they were separated pending their divorce. Brenda and Pat had no children, but Pat had five children from a previous marriage. Patricia Daley had lived with Pat since she was born. Pat referred to her as his only "stable" child. After Patricia married David Daley, the two stayed with Pat at his ranch and helped him with the cattle and working the land.

   Pat executed a new will one year before his death and following the brain tumor diagnosis that left everything to Patricia because Pat felt that Brenda would just sell his ranch and he did not want it to be sold. After Pat died, Patricia, as executrix of the estate, had the will admitted to probate. Brenda challenged the admission of the will to probate because she said that he gave his property to someone who was not legally his child and that showed he lacked capacity. The will was witnessed by two employees of a bank and both testified that Pat seemed to be his usual self and that he had done business at the bank for 20 years. What should the court do with the will and the challenge to it and why? [In re *Estate of Arrington*, 365 S.W.3d 463 (Tex. App.)]

3. Iona wrote her will. The following year, she wrote another will that expressly revoked the earlier will. Later, while cleaning house, she came across the second will. She mistakenly thought that it was the first will and tore it up because the first will had been revoked. Iona died shortly thereafter. The beneficiaries named in the second will claimed that the second will should be probated. The beneficiaries named in the first will claimed that the second will had been revoked when it was torn up. Had the second will been revoked?

4. Logsdon, who had three children, disliked one of them without any reason. In his will, he left only a small amount to the child he disliked and gave the bulk of his estate to the remaining two. On his death, the disliked child claimed that the will was void and had been obtained by undue influence. Do you agree? [*Logsdon v. Logsdon*, 104 N.E.2d 622 (Ill.)]

5. Field executed a will. On her death, the will was found in her safe deposit box, but the part of it containing the fifth bequest had been torn from the will. This torn fragment was also found in the box. There was no evidence that anyone other than Field had ever opened the box. A proceeding was brought to determine whether the will was entitled to be probated. Had the will been revoked? Was the will still valid with a portion torn from it? [*Flora v. Hughes*, 228 S.W.2d 27 (Ky.)]

6. Miller wrote a will that was 11 pages long and enclosed it in an envelope, which she sealed. She then wrote on the envelope "My last will & testament" and signed her name below this statement. This was the only place where she signed her name on any of the papers. Was this signature sufficient to allow this writing to be admitted to probate as her will? [*Miller's Executor v. Shannon*, 299 S.W.2d 103 (Ky.)]

7. Ms. Lingenfelter's will was offered for probate and was opposed. Ms. Lingenfelter (the testatrix) was sick, highly nervous, and extremely jealous, and she committed suicide a week after executing the will. She had, however, seemed to understand the will when she discussed it with an attorney. The will

disinherited her husband because she feared he was not faithful to her despite the fact that he was seriously ill when she wrote the will. He died the day after she executed the will, and she grieved his death terribly for one week before committing suicide. Did she have the capacity to make a will? Should it be admitted to probate? [In re *Lingenfelter's Estate*, 241 P.2d 990 (Cal.)]

8. Copenhaver wrote a will in ink, which was found with her other papers in her bedroom at her death. Pencil lines had been drawn through every provision of the will and the signature. There was no evidence as to the circumstances under which this had been done. Was the will revoked? Why or why not? [*Franklin v. Maclean*, 66 S.E.2d 504 (Va.)]

9. George Baxter executed a will that left the bulk of his estate to the Church of Christ in New Boston, Texas. Two members of the church served as the witnesses for the will. Is the will valid? [In re *Estate of Gordon*, 519 S.W.2d 902 (Tex.)]

10. Jeanette Wall worked for D. J. Sharron for many years. Sharron executed a will, leaving his entire estate to Jeanette. He re-executed the same will sometime thereafter with the same provisions. Sharron's children contested the will, offering evidence that Sharron was a very sick man, physically as well as mentally, and that Wall was active in Sharron's business as well as his personal life. They offered no evidence that Wall had any involvement in the procurement of the original or the re-executed will. Who is entitled to the estate? Why? [*Wall v. Hodges*, 465 So. 2d 359 (Ala. App.)]

11. In 1984, Alexander Tolin executed a will under which the residue of his estate was to be devised to his friend Adair Creaig. The will was prepared by Steven Fine, Tolin's attorney, and executed in Fine's office. Fine retained the original will and gave a blue-backed photocopy to Tolin. In 1989, Tolin executed a codicil to the will that changed the residuary beneficiary from Creaig to Broward Art Guild, Inc. Fine prepared the codicil, and retained the original, giving Tolin a blue-backed photocopy of the original executed codicil.

   Tolin died in 1990. Six months before his death, he told his neighbor Ed Weinstein, who was a retired attorney, that he made a mistake and wished to revoke the codicil and reinstate Creaig as the residuary beneficiary. Weinstein told Tolin he could do this by tearing up the original codicil. Tolin handed Weinstein a blue-backed document that

Tolin said was the original codicil. Weinstein looked at the document; it appeared to him to be the original, and gave it back to Tolin. Tolin then tore up and destroyed the document with the intent and for the purpose of revocation.

Some time after Tolin's death, Weinstein spoke with Fine and found out for the first time that Fine had the original will and codicil. Creaig filed a petition to determine if there had been a revocation of the codicil. From a judgment that Tolin's destruction of a copy of the codicil was not an effective revocation of the codicil, Creaig appealed. Who is correct about the revocation and why? [In re *Estate of Tolin*, 622 So. 2d 988 (Fla.)]

12. Valerie and Flora are the beneficiaries of a trust left to them by their mother upon her death. Their mother named Art Casanelli, a family friend, as the trustee. Flora has seen Art driving a new car and has learned that he just purchased a new and rather large home. She is concerned about the trust funds and Art's unfettered access to them. How can she determine whether Art is using trust funds? What happens if she finds that he is?

13. Can a murderer inherit property from his victim? Why or why not?

14. James Horne's will provides that his estate is to be distributed to his heirs *per capita*. Upon his death, two of his three children are surviving and his deceased child left two children (James's grandchildren). His will provides that all his property is to be distributed *per capita* to these children and grandchildren. How will the property be distributed? How would it be distributed if he had provided for a *per stirpes* distribution?

15. Justin Whitman is the adult son of Jeffrey Whitman, an attorney who has served as the trustee for a trust of which Justin is the beneficiary. The trust was established for Justin by his grandfather, Jeffrey's father. Justin asked his father/trustee for an accounting of the principal and income of the trust. Jeffrey asked for the accounting in 2007 and received nothing by 2008 and filed suit for the accounting. Is Jeffrey entitled to receive the accounting? What could a court do in order to obtain the accounting? [*Whitman v. Whitman*, 2012 WL 367055 (Ohio App.)]

How to Find the Law

In order to determine what the law on a particular question or issue is, it may be necessary to examine (1) compilations of constitutions, treaties, statutes, executive orders, proclamations, and administrative regulations; (2) reports of state and federal court decisions; (3) digests of opinions; (4) treatises on the law; and (5) loose-leaf services. These sources can be either researched traditionally or using fee and/or non-fee-based computerized legal research, accessed through the World Wide Web.

Compilations

In the consideration of a legal problem in business it is necessary to determine whether the matter is affected or controlled by a constitution, national or state; by a national treaty; by an Act of Congress, a state legislature, or a city ordinance; by a decree or proclamation of the President of the United States, a governor, or a mayor; or by a regulation of a federal, state, or local administrative agency.

Each body or person that makes laws, regulations, or ordinances usually compiles and publishes at the end of each year or session all of the matter that it has adopted. In addition to the periodical or annual volumes, it is common to compile all the treaties, statutes, regulations, or ordinances in separate volumes. To illustrate, the federal Anti-Injunction Act may be cited as the Act of March 23, 1932, 47 Stat. 70, 29 U.S.C. § 101 et seq. This means that this law was enacted on March 23, 1932, and that it can be found at page 70 in Volume 47 of the reports that contain all of the statutes adopted by the Congress.

The second part of the citation, 29 U.S.C. § 101 et seq., means that in the collection of all of the federal statutes, which is known as the United States Code, the full text of the statute can be found in the sections of the 29th title beginning with Section 101.

Court Decisions

For complicated or important legal cases or when an appeal is to be taken, a court will generally write an opinion, which explains why the court made the decision. Appellate courts as a rule write opinions. The great majority of these decisions, particularly in the case of the appellate courts, are collected and printed. In order to avoid confusion, the opinions of each court are ordinarily printed in a separate set of reports, either by official reporters or private publishers.

In the reference "*Pennoyer v. Neff*, 95 U.S. 714, 24 L.Ed. 565," the first part states the names of the parties. It does not necessarily tell who was the plaintiff and who was the defendant. When an action is begun in a lower court, the first name is that of the plaintiff and the second name that of the defendant. When the case is appealed, generally the name of the person taking the appeal appears on the records of the higher court as the first one and that of the adverse party as the second. Sometimes, therefore, the original order of the names of the parties is reversed.

The balance of the reference consists of two citations. The first citation, 95 U.S. 714, means that the opinion which the court filed in the case of *Pennoyer v. Neff* may be found on page 714 of the 95th volume of a series of books in which are printed officially the opinions of the United States Supreme Court. Sometimes the same opinion is printed in two different sets of volumes. In the example, 24 L.Ed. 565 means that in the 24th volume of another set of books, called Lawyer's Edition, of the United States Supreme Court Reports, the same opinion begins on page 565.

In opinions by a state court there may also be two citations, as in the case of *Morrow v. Corbin*, 122 Tex. 553, 62 S.W.2d 641. This means that the opinion in the lawsuit between Morrow and Corbin may be found in the 122nd volume of the reports of the highest court of Texas, beginning on page 553; and also in Volume 62 of the Southwestern Reporter, Second Series, at page 641.

The West Publishing Company publishes a set of sectional reporters covering the entire United States. They are called "sectional" because each reporter, instead of being limited to a particular court or a particular state, covers the decisions of the courts of a particular section of the country. Thus the decisions of the courts of Arkansas, Kentucky, Missouri, Tennessee, and Texas are printed by the West Publishing company as a group in a sectional reporter called the Southwestern Reporter.[1] Because of the large number of decisions involved, generally only the opinions of the state appellate courts are printed. A number of states[2] have discontinued publication of the opinions of their courts, and those opinions are now found only in the West reporters.

The reason for the "Second Series" in the Southwestern citation is that when there were 300 volumes in the original series, instead of calling the next volume 301, the publisher called it Volume 1, Second Series. Thus 62 S.W.2d Series really means the 362nd volume of the Southwestern Reporter. Six to eight volumes appear in a year for each geographic section.

In addition to these state reporters, the West Publishing Company publishes a Federal Supplement, which primarily reports the opinions of the Federal District Courts; the Federal Reporter, which primarily reports the decisions of the United States Courts of Appeals; and the Supreme Court Reporter, which reports the decisions of the United States Supreme Court. The Supreme Court decisions are also reported in a separate set called the Lawyers' Edition, published by the Lawyers Cooperative Publishing Company.

The reports published by the West Publishing Company and Lawyers Cooperative Publishing Company are unofficial reports, while those bearing the name or abbreviation of the United States or of a state, such as "95 U.S. 714" or "122 Tex. 553" are official reports. This means that in the case of the latter, the particular court, such as the United States Supreme Court, has officially authorized that its decisions be printed and that by federal statute such official printing is made. In the case of the unofficial reporters, the publisher prints the decisions of a court on its own

initiative. Such opinions are part of the public domain and not subject to any copyright or similar restriction.

Digests of Opinions

The reports of court decisions are useful only if one has the citation, that is, the name and volume number of the book and the page number of the opinion one is seeking. For this reason, digests of the decisions have been prepared. These digests organize the entire field of law under major headings, which are then arranged in alphabetical order. Under each heading, such as "Contracts," the subject is divided into the different questions that can arise with respect to that field. A master outline is thus created on the subject. This outline includes short paragraphs describing what each case holds and giving its citation.

Treatises and Restatements

Very helpful in finding a case or a statute are the treatises on the law. These may be special books, each written by an author on a particular subject, such as Williston on Contracts, Bogert on Trusts, Fletcher on Corporations, or they may be general encyclopedias, as in the case of *American Jurisprudence, American Jurisprudence, Second*, and *Corpus Juris Secundum*.

Another type of treatise is found in the restatements of the law prepared by the American Law Institute. Each restatement consists of one or more volumes devoted to a particular phase of the law, such as the Restatement of the Law of Contracts, Restatement of the Law of Agency, and Restatement of the Law of Property. In each restatement, the American Law Institute, acting through special committees of judges, lawyers, and professors of law, has set forth what the law is; and in many areas where there is no law or the present rule is regarded as unsatisfactory, the restatement specifies what the Institute deems to be the desirable rule.

Loose-Leaf Services

A number of private publishers, notably Commerce Clearing House and Prentice-Hall, publish loose-leaf books devoted to particular branches of the law. Periodically, the publisher sends to the purchaser a number of pages that set forth any decision, regulation, or statute made or adopted since the prior set of pages was prepared. Such services are unofficial.

---

[1] The sectional reporters are: Atlantic—A. (Connecticut, Delaware, District of Columbia, Maine, Maryland, New Hampshire, New Jersey, Pennsylvania, Rhode Island, Vermont); Northeastern—N.E. (Illinois, Indiana, Massachusetts, New York, Ohio); Northwestern—N.W. (Iowa, Michigan, Minnesota, Nebraska, North Dakota, South Dakota, Wisconsin); Pacific—P. (Alaska, Arizona, California, Colorado, Hawaii, Idaho, Kansas, Montana, Nevada, New Mexico, Oklahoma, Oregon, Utah, Washington, Wyoming); Southeastern—S.E. (Georgia, North Carolina, South Carolina, Virginia, West Virginia); Southwestern—S.W. (Arkansas, Kentucky, Missouri, Tennessee, Texas); and Southern—So. (Alabama, Florida, Louisiana, Mississippi). There is also a special New York State reporter known as the New York Supplement and a special California State reporter known as the California Reporter.

[2] See, for example, Alaska, Florida, Iowa, Kentucky, Louisiana, Maine, Mississippi, Missouri, North Dakota, Oklahoma, Texas, and Wyoming.

Computerized Legal Research

National and local computer services are providing constantly widening assistance for legal research. The database in such a system may be opinions, statutes, or administrative regulations stored word for word; or the later history of a particular case giving its full citation and showing whether the case has been followed by other courts; or the text of forms and documents. By means of a terminal connected to the system, the user can retrieve the legal information at a great saving of time and with the assurance that it is up-to-date.

There are two leading, fee-based systems for computer-aided research. Listed alphabetically, they are LEXIS and WESTLAW.

A specialized service of legal forms for business is provided by Shepard's BUSINESS LAW CASE MANAGEMENT SYSTEM. A monthly fee is required for usage.

Numerous free, private sites offer a lot of legal resources. The federal government offers a variety of case law, regulations, and code enactments, either pending or newly promulgated. To find the most comprehensive source of government-maintained legal information, go to **http://www.house.gov**. The United States Supreme Court has information about both its current term and past terms at **www.supremecourt.gov**. Another website that provides excellent information about current controversies that reach the United States Supreme Court is **www.scotusblog.com**.

State governments provide access to regulations and codes online. As an example, go to the State of California's site, **http://www.leginfo.ca.gov**. You can access an array of information about both state and federal government through links at **www.USA.gov**.

The Constitution of the United States

We the people of the United States of America, in order to form a more perfect union, establish justice, insure domestic tranquility, provide for the common defense, promote the general welfare, and secure the blessings of liberty to ourselves and our posterity, do ordain and establish this Constitution for the United States of America.

Article I

SECTION 1

All legislative powers herein granted shall be vested in a Congress of the United States, which shall consist of a Senate and House of Representatives.

SECTION 2

1. The House of Representatives shall be composed of members chosen every second year by the people of the several States, and the electors in each State shall have the qualifications requisite for electors of the most numerous branch of the State legislature.

2. No person shall be a representative who shall not have attained to the age of twenty-five years, and been seven years a citizen of the United States, and who shall not, when elected, be an inhabitant of that State in which he shall be chosen.

3. Representatives and direct taxes shall be apportioned among the several States which may be included within this Union, according to their respective numbers, which shall be determined by adding to the whole number of free persons, including those bound to service for a term of years, and excluding Indians not taxed, three fifths of all other persons.[1] The actual enumeration shall be made within three years after the first meeting of the Congress of the United States, and within every subsequent term of ten years, in such manner as they shall by law direct. The number of representatives shall not exceed one for every thirty thousand, but each State shall have at least one representative; and until such enumeration shall be made, the State of New Hampshire shall be entitled to choose three, Massachusetts eight, Rhode Island and Providence Plantations one, Connecticut five, New York six, New Jersey four, Pennsylvania eight, Delaware one, Maryland six, Virginia ten, North Carolina five, South Carolina five, and Georgia three.

4. When vacancies happen in the representation from any State, the executive authority thereof shall issue writs of election to fill such vacancies.

5. The House of Representatives shall choose their speaker and other officers; and shall have the sole power of impeachment.

SECTION 3

1. The Senate of the United States shall be composed of two senators from each State, chosen by the legislature thereof, for six years; and each senator shall have one vote.

2. Immediately after they shall be assembled in consequence of the first election, they shall be divided as equally as may be into three classes. The seats of the senators of the first class shall be vacated at the expiration of the second year, of the second class at the expiration of the fourth year, and of the third class at the expiration of the sixth year, so that one third may be chosen every second year; and if vacancies happen by resignation, or otherwise, during the recess of the legislature of any State, the executive thereof may make temporary appointments until the next meeting of the legislature, which shall then fill such vacancies.[2]

3. No person shall be a senator who shall not have attained to the age of thirty years, and been nine years a citizen of the United States, and who shall not, when elected, be an inhabitant of that State for which he shall be chosen.

4. The Vice President of the United States shall be President of the Senate, but shall have no vote, unless they be equally divided.

---

[1] See the 14th Amendment.

[2] See the 17th Amendment.

5. The Senate shall choose their other officers, and also a president pro tempore, in the absence of the Vice President, or when he shall exercise the office of the President of the United States.

6. The Senate shall have the sole power to try all impeachments. When sitting for that purpose, they shall be on oath or affirmation. When the President of the United States is tried, the chief justice shall preside: and no person shall be convicted without the concurrence of two thirds of the members present.

7. Judgment in cases of impeachment shall not extend further than to removal from office, and disqualification to hold and enjoy any office of honor, trust or profit under the United States: but the party convicted shall nevertheless be liable and subject to indictment, trial, judgment and punishment, according to law.

SECTION 4

1. The times, places, and manner of holding elections for senators and representatives, shall be prescribed in each State by the legislature thereof; but the Congress may at any time by law make or alter such regulations, except as to the places of choosing senators.

2. The Congress shall assemble at least once in every year, and such meeting shall be on the first Monday in December, unless they shall by law appoint a different day.

SECTION 5

1. Each House shall be the judge of the elections, returns and qualifications of its own members, and a majority of each shall constitute a quorum to do business; but a smaller number may adjourn from day to day, and may be authorized to compel the attendance of absent members, in such manner, and under such penalties as each House may provide.

2. Each House may determine the rules of its proceedings, punish its members for disorderly behavior, and, with the concurrence of two thirds, expel a member.

3. Each House shall keep a journal of its proceedings, and from time to time publish the same, excepting such parts as may in their judgment require secrecy; and the yeas and nays of the members of either House on any question shall, at the desire of one fifth of those present, be entered on the journal.

4. Neither House, during the session of Congress, shall, without the consent of the other, adjourn for more than three days, nor to any other place than that in which the two Houses shall be sitting.

SECTION 6

1. The senators and representatives shall receive a compensation for their services, to be ascertained by law, and paid out of the Treasury of the United States. They shall in all cases, except treason, felony, and breach of the peace, be privileged from arrest during their attendance at the session of their respective Houses, and in going to and returning from the same; and for any speech or debate in either House, they shall not be questioned in any other place.

2. No senator or representative shall, during the time for which he was elected, be appointed to any civil office under the authority of the United States, which shall have been created, or the emoluments whereof shall have been increased during such time; and no person holding any office under the United States shall be a member of either House during his continuance in office.

SECTION 7

1. All bills for raising revenue shall originate in the House of Representatives; but the Senate may propose or concur with amendments as on other bills.

2. Every bill which shall have passed the House of Representatives and the Senate, shall, before it becomes a law, be presented to the President of the United States; if he approves he shall sign it, but if not he shall return it, with his objections to that House in which it shall have originated, who shall enter the objections at large on their journal, and proceed to reconsider it. If after such reconsideration two thirds of that House shall agree to pass the bill, it shall be sent, together with the objections, to the other House, by which it shall likewise be reconsidered, and if approved by two thirds of that House, it shall become a law. But in all such cases the votes of both Houses shall be determined by yeas and nays, and the names of the persons voting for and against the bill shall be entered on the journal of each House respectively. If any bill shall not be returned by the President within ten days (Sundays excepted) after it shall have been presented to him, the same shall be a law, in like manner as if he had signed it, unless the Congress by their adjournment prevent its return, in which case it shall not be a law.

3. Every order, resolution, or vote to which the concurrence of the Senate and the House of Representatives may be necessary (except on a question of adjournment) shall be presented to the President of the United States; and before the same shall take effect, shall be approved

by him, or being disapproved by him, shall be repassed by two thirds of the Senate and House of Representatives, according to the rules and limitations prescribed in the case of a bill.

SECTION 8

The Congress shall have the power

1. To lay and collect taxes, duties, imposts, and excises, to pay the debts and provide for the common defense and general welfare of the United States; but all duties, imposts, and excises shall be uniform throughout the United States;

2. To borrow money on the credit of the United States;

3. To regulate commerce with foreign nations, and among the several States, and with the Indian tribes;

4. To establish a uniform rule of naturalization, and uniform laws on the subject of bankruptcies throughout the United States;

5. To coin money, regulate the value thereof, and of foreign coin, and fix the standard of weights and measures;

6. To provide for the punishment of counterfeiting the securities and current coin of the United States;

7. To establish post offices and post roads;

8. To promote the progress of science and useful arts, by securing for limited times to authors and inventors the exclusive rights to their respective writings and discoveries;

9. To constitute tribunals inferior to the Supreme Court;

10. To define and punish piracies and felonies committed on the high seas, and offenses against the law of nations;

11. To declare war, grant letters of marque and reprisal, and make rules concerning captures on land and water;

12. To raise and support armies, but no appropriation of money to that use shall be for a longer term than two years;

13. To provide and maintain a navy;

14. To make rules for the government and regulation of the land and naval forces;

15. To provide for calling forth the militia to execute the laws of the Union, suppress insurrections and repel invasions;

16. To provide for organizing, arming, and disciplining the militia, and for governing such part of them as may be employed in the service of the United States, reserving to the States respectively, the appointment of the officers, and the authority of training the militia according to the discipline prescribed by Congress;

17. To exercise exclusive legislation in all cases whatsoever, over such district (not exceeding ten miles square) as may, by cession of particular States, and the acceptance of Congress, become the seat of the government of the United States, and to exercise like authority over all places purchased by the consent of the legislature of the State in which the same shall be, for the erection of forts, magazines, arsenals, dockyards, and other needful buildings; and

18. To make all laws which shall be necessary and proper for carrying into execution the foregoing powers, and all other powers vested by this Constitution in the government of the United States, or in any department or officer thereof.

SECTION 9

1. The migration or importation of such persons as any of the States now existing shall think proper to admit, shall not be prohibited by the Congress prior to the year one thousand eight hundred and eight, but a tax or duty may be imposed on such importation, not exceeding ten dollars for each person.

2. The privilege of the writ of habeas corpus shall not be suspended, unless when in cases of rebellion or invasion the public safety may require it.

3. No bill of attainder or ex post facto law shall be passed.

4. No capitation, or other direct, tax shall be laid, unless in proportion to the census or enumeration hereinbefore directed to be taken.[3]

5. No tax or duty shall be laid on articles exported from any State.

6. No preference shall be given by any regulation of commerce or revenue to the ports of one State over those of another: nor shall vessels bound to, or from, one State be obliged to enter, clear, or pay duties in another.

7. No money shall be drawn from the treasury, but in consequence of appropriations made by law; and a regular statement and account of the receipts and expenditures of all public money shall be published from time to time.

[3] See the 16th Amendment.

8. No title of nobility shall be granted by the United States: and no person holding any office of profit or trust under them, shall, without the consent of the Congress, accept of any present, emolument, office, or title, of any kind whatever, from any king, prince, or foreign State.

SECTION 10

1. No State shall enter into any treaty, alliance, or confederation; grant letters of marque and reprisal; coin money; emit bills of credit; make anything but gold and silver coin a tender in payment of debts; pass any bill of attainder, ex post facto law, or law impairing the obligation of contracts, or grant any title of nobility.

2. No State shall, without the consent of the Congress, lay any imposts or duties on imports or exports, except what may be absolutely necessary for executing its inspection laws: and the net produce of all duties and imposts laid by any State on imports or exports, shall be for the use of the treasury of the United States; and all such laws shall be subject to the revision and control of the Congress.

3. No State shall, without the consent of the Congress, lay any duty of tonnage, keep troops, or ships of war in time of peace, enter into any agreement or compact with another State, or with a foreign power, or engage in war, unless actually invaded, or in such imminent danger as will not admit of delay.

Article II

SECTION 1

1. The executive power shall be vested in a President of the United States of America. He shall hold his office during the term of four years, and, together with the Vice President, chosen for the same term, be elected as follows:

2. Each State shall appoint, in such manner as the legislature thereof may direct, a number of electors, equal to the whole number of senators and representatives to which the State may be entitled in the Congress: but no senator or representative, or person holding an office of trust or profit under the United States, shall be appointed an elector.

The electors shall meet in their respective States, and vote by ballot for two persons, of whom one at least shall not be an inhabitant of the same State with themselves. And they shall make a list of all the persons voted for, and of the number of votes for each; which list they shall sign and certify, and transmit sealed to the seat of the government of the United States, directed to the president of the Senate. The president of the Senate shall, in the presence of the Senate and House of Representatives, open all the certificates, and the votes shall then be counted. The person having the greatest number of votes shall be the President, if such number be a majority of the whole number of electors appointed; and if there be more than one who have such majority, and have an equal number of votes, then the House of Representatives shall immediately choose by ballot one of them for President; and if no person have a majority, then from the five highest on the list the said House shall in like manner choose the President. But in choosing the President, the votes shall be taken by States, the representation from each State having one vote; a quorum for this purpose shall consist of a member or members from two thirds of the States, and a majority of all the States shall be necessary to a choice. In every case, after the choice of the President, the person having the greatest number of votes of the electors shall be the Vice President. But if there should remain two or more who have equal votes, the Senate shall choose from them by ballot the Vice President.[4]

3. The Congress may determine the time of choosing the electors, and the day on which they shall give their votes; which day shall be the same throughout the United States.

4. No person except a natural born citizen, or a citizen of the United States, at the time of the adoption of this Constitution, shall be eligible to the office of President; neither shall any person be eligible to that office who shall not have attained to the age of thirty-five years, and been fourteen years a resident within the United States.

5. In the case of removal of the President from office, or of his death, resignation, or inability to discharge the powers and duties of the said office, the same shall devolve on the Vice President, and the Congress may by law provide for the case of removal, death, resignation, or inability, both of the President and Vice President, declaring what officer shall then act as President, and such officer shall act accordingly, until the disability be removed, or a President shall be elected.

6. The President shall, at stated times, receive for his services a compensation, which shall neither be

[4] Superseded by the 12th Amendment.

increased nor diminished during the period for which he shall have been elected, and he shall not receive within that period any other emolument from the United States, or any of them.

7. Before he enter on the execution of his office, he shall take the following oath or affirmation:—"I do solemnly swear (or affirm) that I will faithfully execute the office of President of the United States, and will to the best of my ability, preserve, protect and defend the Constitution of the United States."

SECTION 2

1. The President shall be commander in chief of the army and navy of the United States, and of the militia of the several States, when called into the actual service of the United States; he may require the opinion, in writing, of the principal officer in each of the executive departments, upon any subject relating to the duties of their respective office, and he shall have power to grant reprieves and pardons for offenses against the United States, except in cases of impeachment.

2. He shall have power, by and with the advice and consent of the Senate, to make treaties, provided two thirds of the senators present concur; and he shall nominate, and by and with the advice and consent of the Senate, shall appoint ambassadors, other public ministers and consuls, judges of the Supreme Court, and all other officers of the United States, whose appointments are not herein otherwise provided for, and which shall be established by law: but the Congress may by law vest the appointment of such inferior officers, as they think proper, in the President alone, in the courts of law, or in the heads of departments.

3. The President shall have power to fill up all vacancies that may happen during the recess of the Senate, by granting commissions which shall expire at the end of their next session.

SECTION 3

He shall from time to time give to the Congress information of the state of the Union, and recommend to their consideration such measures as he shall judge necessary and expedient; he may, on extraordinary occasions, convene both Houses, or either of them, and in case of disagreement between them with respect to the time of adjournment, he may adjourn them to such time as he shall think proper; he shall receive ambassadors and other public ministers; he shall take care that the laws be faithfully executed, and shall commission all the officers of the United States.

SECTION 4

The President, Vice President, and all civil officers of the United States, shall be removed from office on impeachment for, and conviction of, treason, bribery, or other high crimes and misdemeanors.

Article III

SECTION 1

The judicial power of the United States shall be vested in one Supreme Court, and in such inferior courts as the Congress may from time to time ordain and establish. The judges, both of the Supreme and inferior courts, shall hold their offices during good behavior, and shall, at stated times, receive for their services, a compensation, which shall not be diminished during their continuance in office.

SECTION 2

1. The judicial power shall extend to all cases, in law and equity, arising under this Constitution, the laws of the United States, and treaties made, or which shall be made, under their authority;—to all cases affecting ambassadors, other public ministers and consuls;—to all cases of admiralty and maritime jurisdiction;—to controversies to which the United States shall be a party;—to controversies between two or more States; between a State and citizens of another State;[5]—between citizens of different States;—between citizens of the same State claiming lands under grants of different States, and between a State, or the citizens thereof, and foreign States, citizens or subjects.

2. In all cases affecting ambassadors, other public ministers and consuls, and those in which a State shall be party, the Supreme Court shall have original jurisdiction. In all the other cases before mentioned, the Supreme Court shall have appellate jurisdiction, both as to law and to fact, with such exceptions, and under such regulations as the Congress shall make.

3. The trial of all crimes, except in cases of impeachment, shall be by jury; and such trial shall be held in the State where the said crimes shall have been committed; but when not committed within any State, the trial shall be at such place or places as the Congress may by law have directed.

[5] See the 11th Amendment.

SECTION 3

1. Treason against the United States shall consist only in levying war against them, or in adhering to their enemies, giving them aid and comfort. No person shall be convicted of treason unless on the testimony of two witnesses to the same overt act, or on confession in open court.

2. The Congress shall have power to declare the punishment of treason, but no attainder of treason shall work corruption of blood, or forfeiture except during the life of the person attainted.

Article IV

SECTION 1

Full faith and credit shall be given in each State to the public acts, records, and judicial proceedings of every other State. And the Congress may by general laws prescribe the manner in which such acts, records and proceedings shall be proved, and the effect thereof.

SECTION 2

1. The citizens of each State shall be entitled to all privileges and immunities of citizens in the several States.[6]

2. A person charged in any State with treason, felony, or other crime, who shall flee from justice, and be found in another State, shall on demand of the executive authority of the State from which he fled, be delivered up to be removed to the State having jurisdiction of the crime.

3. No person held to service or labor in one State under the laws thereof, escaping into another, shall in consequence of any law or regulation therein, be discharged from such service or labor, but shall be delivered up on claim of the party to whom such service or labor may be due.[7]

SECTION 3

1. New States may be admitted by the Congress into this Union; but no new State shall be formed or erected within the jurisdiction of any other State, nor any State be formed by the junction of two or more States, or parts of States, without the consent of the legislatures of the States concerned as well as of the Congress.

2. The Congress shall have power to dispose of and make all needful rules and regulations respecting the territory or other property belonging to the United States; and nothing in this Constitution shall be so construed as to prejudice any claims of the United States, or of any particular State.

SECTION 4

The United States shall guarantee to every State in this Union a republican form of government, and shall protect each of them against invasion; and on application of the legislature, or of the executive (when the legislature cannot be convened) against domestic violence.

Article V

The Congress, whenever two thirds of both Houses shall deem it necessary, shall propose amendments to this Constitution, or, on the application of the legislature of two thirds of the several States, shall call a convention for proposing amendments, which in either case, shall be valid to all intents and purposes, as part of this Constitution when ratified by the legislatures of three fourths of the several States, or by conventions in three fourths thereof, as the one or the other mode of ratification may be proposed by the Congress; provided that no amendment which may be made prior to the year one thousand eight hundred and eight shall in any manner affect the first and fourth clauses in the ninth section of the first article; and that no State, without its consent, shall be deprived of its equal suffrage in the Senate.

Article VI

1. All debts contracted and engagements entered into, before the adoption of this Constitution, shall be as valid against the United States under this Constitution, as under the Confederation.[8]

2. This Constitution, and the laws of the United States which shall be made in pursuance thereof; and all treaties made, or which shall be made, under the authority of the United States, shall be the supreme law of the land; and the judges in every State shall be bound thereby, anything in the Constitution or laws of any State to the contrary notwithstanding.

3. The senators and representatives before mentioned, and the members of the several State legislatures, and all executive and judicial officers, both of the United States and of the several States, shall be bound by oath or affirmation to support this Constitution; but no

---

[6] See the 14th Amendment, Sec. 1.
[7] See the 13th Amendment.

[8] See the 14th Amendment, Sec. 4.

religious test shall ever be required as a qualification to any office or public trust under the United States.

Article VII

The ratification of the conventions of nine States shall be sufficient for the establishment of this Constitution between the States so ratifying the same.

Done in Convention by the unanimous consent of the States present the seventeenth day of September in the year of our Lord one thousand seven hundred and eighty-seven, and of the independence of the United States of America the twelfth. In witness whereof we have hereunto subscribed our names.

Amendments

First Ten Amendments passed by Congress Sept. 25, 1789.

Ratified by three-fourths of the States December 15, 1791.

Amendment I

Congress shall make no law respecting an establishment of religion, or prohibiting the free exercise thereof; or abridging the freedom of speech, or of the press; or the right of the people peaceably to assemble, and to petition the government for a redress of grievances.

Amendment II

A well regulated militia, being necessary to the security of a free State, the right of the people to keep and bear arms, shall not be infringed.

Amendment III

No soldier shall, in time of peace be quartered in any house, without the consent of the owner, nor in time of war, but in a manner to be prescribed by law.

Amendment IV

The right of the people to be secure in their persons, houses, papers, and effects, against unreasonable searches and seizures, shall not be violated, and no warrants shall issue, but upon probable cause, supported by oath or affirmation, and particularly describing the place to be searched, and the person or things to be seized.

Amendment V

No person shall be held to answer for a capital, or otherwise infamous crime, unless on a presentment or indictment of a grand jury, except in cases arising in the land or naval forces, or in the militia, when in actual service in time of war or public danger; nor shall any person be subject for the same offense to be twice put in jeopardy of life or limb; nor shall be compelled in any criminal case to be a witness against himself, nor be deprived of life, liberty, or property, without due process of law; nor shall private property be taken for public use without just compensation.

Amendment VI

In all criminal prosecutions, the accused shall enjoy the right to a speedy and public trial, by an impartial jury of the State and district wherein the crime shall have been committed, which district shall have been previously ascertained by law, and to be informed of the nature and cause of the accusation; to be confronted with the witnesses against him; to have compulsory process for obtaining witnesses in his favor, and to have the assistance of counsel for his defense.

Amendment VII

In suits at common law, where the value in controversy shall exceed twenty dollars, the right of trial by jury shall be preserved, and no fact tried by a jury shall be otherwise reexamined in any court of the United States, then according to the rules of the common law.

Amendment VIII

Excessive bail shall not be required, nor excessive fines imposed, nor cruel and unusual punishments inflicted.

Amendment IX

The enumeration in the Constitution of certain rights shall not be construed to deny or disparage others retained by the people.

Amendment X

The powers not delegated to the United States by the Constitution, nor prohibited by it to the States, are reserved to the States respectively, or to the people.

Amendment XI

Passed by Congress March 5, 1794. Ratified January 8, 1798.

The judicial power of the United States shall not be construed to extend to any suit in law or equity, commenced or prosecuted against one of the United States by citizens of another State, or by citizens or subjects of any foreign State.

Amendment XII

Passed by Congress December 12, 1803. Ratified September 25, 1804.

The electors shall meet in their respective States, and vote by ballot for President and Vice President, one of whom, at least, shall not be an inhabitant of the same State with themselves; they shall name in their ballots the person voted for as President, and in distinct ballots, the person voted for as Vice President, and they shall make distinct lists of all persons voted for as President and of all persons voted for as Vice President, and of the number of votes for each, which lists they shall sign and certify, and transmit sealed to the seat of the government of the United States, directed to the President of the Senate;—The President of the Senate shall, in the presence of the Senate and House of Representatives, open all the certificates and the votes shall then be counted;—The person having the greatest number of votes for President, shall be the President, if such number be a majority of the whole number of electors appointed; and if no person have such majority, then from the persons having the highest numbers not exceeding three on the list of those voted for as President, the House of Representatives shall choose immediately, by ballot, the President. But in choosing the President, the votes shall be taken by States, the representation from each State having one vote; a quorum for this purpose shall consist of a member or members from two thirds of the States, and a majority of all the States shall be necessary to a choice. And if the House of Representatives shall not choose a President whenever the right of choice shall devolve upon them, before the fourth day of March next following, then the Vice President shall act as President, as in the case of the death or other constitutional disability of the President. The person having the greatest number of votes as Vice President shall be the Vice President, if such number be a majority of the whole number of electors appointed, and if no person have a majority, then from the two highest numbers on the list, the Senate shall choose the Vice President; a quorum for the purpose shall consist of two thirds of the whole number of Senators, and a majority of the whole number shall be necessary to a choice. But no person constitutionally ineligible to the office of President shall be eligible to that of Vice President of the United States.

Amendment XIII

Passed by Congress February 1, 1865. Ratified December 18, 1865.

SECTION 1

Neither slavery nor involuntary servitude, except as punishment for crime whereof the party shall have been duly convicted, shall exist within the United States, or any place subject to their jurisdiction.

SECTION 2

Congress shall have power to enforce this article by appropriate legislation.

Amendment XIV

Passed by Congress June 16, 1866. Ratified July 23, 1868.

SECTION 1

All persons born or naturalized in the United States, and subject to the jurisdiction thereof, are citizens of the United States and of the State wherein they reside. No State shall make or enforce any law which shall abridge the privileges or immunities of citizens of the United States; nor shall any State deprive any person of life, liberty, or property, without due process of law; nor deny to any person within its jurisdiction the equal protection of the laws.

SECTION 2

Representatives shall be apportioned among the several States according to their respective numbers, counting the whole number of persons in each State, excluding Indians not taxed. But when the right to vote at any election for the choice of electors for President and Vice President of the United States, representatives in Congress, the executive and judicial officers of a State, or the members of the legislature thereof, is denied to any of the male inhabitants of such State, being twenty-one years of age, and citizens of the United States, or in any way abridged, except for participation in rebellion, or other crime, the basis of representation therein shall be reduced in the proportion which the number of such male citizens shall bear to the whole number of male citizens twenty-one years of age in such State.

SECTION 3

No person shall be a senator or representative in Congress, or elector of President and Vice President, or hold any office, civil or military, under the United States, or under any State, who having previously taken an oath, as a member of Congress, or as an officer of the United States, or as a member of any State legislature, or as an executive or judicial officer of any State, to support the Constitution of the United States, shall have engaged in insurrection or rebellion against the same, or given aid or comfort to the enemies thereof. But Congress may by a vote of two thirds of each House, remove such disability.

SECTION 4

The validity of the public debt of the United States, authorized by law, including debts incurred for payment of pensions and bounties for services in suppressing insurrection or rebellion, shall not be questioned. But neither the United States nor any State shall assume or pay any debt or obligation incurred in aid of insurrection or rebellion against the United States, or any claim for the loss or emancipation of any slave; but all such debts, obligations, and claims shall be held illegal and void.

SECTION 5

The Congress shall have power to enforce, by appropriate legislation, the provisions of this article.

Amendment XV

Passed by Congress February 27, 1869. Ratified March 30, 1870.

SECTION 1

The right of citizens of the United States to vote shall not be denied or abridged by the United States or by any State on account of race, color, or previous condition of servitude.

SECTION 2

The Congress shall have power to enforce this article by appropriate legislation.

Amendment XVI

Passed by Congress July 12, 1909. Ratified February 25, 1913.

The Congress shall have power to lay and collect taxes on incomes, from whatever source derived, without apportionment among the several States, and without regard to any census or enumeration.

Amendment XVII

Passed by Congress May 16, 1912. Ratified May 31, 1913.

The Senate of the United States shall be composed of two senators from each State, elected by the people thereof, for six years; and each senator shall have one vote. The electors in each State shall have the qualifications requisite for electors of the most numerous branch of the State legislature.

When vacancies happen in the representation of any State in the Senate, the executive authority of such State shall issue writs of election to fill such vacancies: Provided, That the legislature of any State may empower the executive thereof to make temporary appointments until the people fill the vacancies by election as the legislature may direct.

This amendment shall not be so construed as to affect the election or term of any senator chosen before it becomes valid as part of the Constitution.

Amendment XVIII

Passed by Congress December 17, 1917. Ratified January 29, 1919.

After one year from the ratification of this article, the manufacture, sale, or transportation of intoxicating liquors within, the importation thereof into, or the exportation thereof from the United States and all territory subject to the jurisdiction thereof for beverage purposes is hereby prohibited.

The Congress and the several States shall have concurrent power to enforce this article by appropriate legislation.

This article shall be inoperative unless it shall have been ratified as an amendment to the Constitution by the legislatures of the several States, as provided in the Constitution, within seven years from the date of the submission hereof to the States by Congress.

Amendment XIX

Passed by Congress June 5, 1919. Ratified August 26, 1920.

The right of citizens of the United States to vote shall not be denied or abridged by the United States or by any State on account of sex.

The Congress shall have power by appropriate legislation to enforce the provisions of this article.

Amendment XX

Passed by Congress March 3, 1932. Ratified January 23, 1933.

SECTION 1

The terms of the President and Vice President shall end at noon on the 20th day of January, and the terms of Senators and Representatives at noon on the 3d day of January, of the years in which such terms would have ended if this article had not been ratified; and the terms of their successors shall then begin.

SECTION 2

The Congress shall assemble at least once in every year, and such meeting shall begin at noon on the 3d day of January, unless they shall by law appoint a different day.

SECTION 3

If, at the time fixed for the beginning of the term of the President, the President-elect shall have died, the Vice President-elect shall become President. If a President shall not have been chosen before the time fixed for the beginning of his term, or if the President-elect shall have failed to qualify, then the Vice President-elect shall act as President until a President shall have qualified; and the Congress may by law provide for the case wherein neither a President-elect nor a Vice President-elect shall have qualified, declaring who shall then act as President, or the manner in which one who is to act shall be selected, and such person shall act accordingly until a President or Vice President shall have qualified.

SECTION 4

The Congress may by law provide for the case of the death of any of the persons from whom the House of Representatives may choose a President whenever the right of choice shall have devolved upon them, and for the case of the death of any of the persons from whom the Senate may choose a Vice President whenever the right of choice shall have devolved upon them.

SECTION 5

Sections 1 and 2 shall take effect on the 15th day of October following the ratification of this article.

SECTION 6

This article shall be inoperative unless it shall have been ratified as an amendment to the Constitution by the legislatures of three-fourths of the several States within seven years from the date of its submission.

Amendment XXI

Passed by Congress February 20, 1933. Ratified December 5, 1933.

SECTION 1

The eighteenth article of amendment to the Constitution of the United States is hereby repealed.

SECTION 2

The transportation or importation into any State, Territory, or possession of the United States for delivery or use therein of intoxicating liquors in violation of the laws thereof, is hereby prohibited.

SECTION 3

This article shall be inoperative unless it shall have been ratified as an amendment to the Constitution by conventions in the several States, as provided in the Constitution, within seven years from the date of the submission thereof to the States by the Congress.

Amendment XXII

Passed by Congress March 24, 1947. Ratified February 26, 1951.

SECTION 1

No person shall be elected to the office of the President more than twice, and no person who has held the office of President, or acted as President, for more than two years of a term to which some other person was elected President shall be elected to the office of the President more than once. But this article shall not apply to any person holding the office of President when this article was proposed by the Congress, and shall not prevent any person who may be holding the office of President, or acting as President, during the term within which this article becomes operative from holding the office of President or acting as President during the remainder of such term.

SECTION 2

This article shall be inoperative unless it shall have been ratified as an amendment to the Constitution by the legislatures of three-fourths of the several States within seven years from the date of its submission to the States by the Congress.

Amendment XXIII

Passed by Congress June 16, 1960. Ratified April 3, 1961.

SECTION 1

The District constituting the seat of Government of the United States shall appoint in such manner as the Congress may direct:

A number of electors of President and Vice President equal to the whole number of Senators and

Representatives in Congress to which the District would be entitled if it were a State, but in no event more than the least populous State; they shall be in addition to those appointed by the States, but they shall be considered, for the purposes of the election of President and Vice President, to be electors appointed by a State; and they shall meet in the District and perform such duties as provided by the twelfth article of amendment.

SECTION 2

The Congress shall have power to enforce this article by appropriate legislation.

Amendment XXIV

Passed by Congress August 27, 1962. Ratified February 4, 1964.

SECTION 1

The right of citizens of the United States to vote in any primary or other election for President or Vice President, for electors for President or Vice President, or for Senator or Representative in Congress, shall not be denied or abridged by the United States or any State by reason of failure to pay any poll tax or other tax.

SECTION 2

The Congress shall have power to enforce this article by appropriate legislation.

Amendment XXV

Passed by Congress July 6, 1965. Ratified February 23, 1967.

SECTION 1

In case of the removal of the President from office or of his death or resignation, the Vice President shall become President.

SECTION 2

Whenever there is a vacancy in the office of the Vice President, the President shall nominate a Vice President who shall take office upon confirmation by a majority vote of both Houses of Congress.

SECTION 3

Whenever the President transmits to the President pro tempore of the Senate and the Speaker of the House of Representatives his written declaration that he is unable to discharge the powers and duties of his office, and until he transmits to them a written declaration to the contrary, such powers and duties shall be discharged by the Vice President as Acting President.

SECTION 4

Whenever the Vice President and a majority of either the principal officers of the executive departments or of such other body as Congress may by law provide, transmit to the President pro tempore of the Senate and the Speaker of the House of Representatives their written declaration that the President is unable to discharge the powers and duties of his office, the Vice President shall immediately assume the powers and duties of the office as Acting President.

Thereafter, when the President transmits to the President pro tempore of the Senate and the Speaker of the House of Representatives his written declaration that no inability exists, he shall resume the powers and duties of his office unless the Vice President and a majority of either the principal officers of the executive department or of such other body as Congress may by law provide, transmit within four days to the President pro tempore of the Senate and the Speaker of the House of Representatives their written declaration that the President is unable to discharge the powers and duties of his office. Thereupon Congress shall decide the issue, assembling within forty-eight hours for that purpose if not in session. If the Congress, within twenty-one days after receipt of the latter written declaration, or, if Congress is not in session, within twenty-one days after Congress is required to assemble, determines by two-thirds vote of both Houses that the President is unable to discharge the powers and duties of his office, the Vice President shall continue to discharge the same as Acting President; otherwise, the President shall resume the powers and duties of his office.

Amendment XXVI

Passed by Congress March 23, 1971. Ratified July 5, 1971.

SECTION 1

The right of citizens of the United States, who are eighteen years of age or older, to vote shall not be denied or abridged by the United States or by any State on account of age.

Amendment XXVII

Passed by Congress September 25, 1789. Ratified May 18, 1992.

No law, varying the compensation for the services of the Senators and Representatives, shall take effect, until an election of Representatives shall have intervened.

Uniform Commercial Code (Selected Sections)

(Adopted in fifty-two jurisdictions; all fifty States, although Louisiana has adopted only Articles 1, 3, 4, 7, 8, and 9; the District of Columbia; and the Virgin Islands.)

Articles

1. General Provisions
2. Sales
   2A. Leases
3. Negotiable Instruments
4. Bank Deposits and Collections
   4A. Funds Transfers
5. Letters of Credit
6. Repealer of Article 6—Bulk Transfers and [Revised] Article 6—Bulk Sales
7. Warehouse Receipts, Bills of Lading and Other Documents of Title
8. Investment Securities
9. Secured Transactions

Article 1 General Provisions

Part 1 Short Title, Construction, Application and Subject Matter of the Act

* * * *

§1—103. SUPPLEMENTARY GENERAL PRINCIPLES OF LAW APPLICABLE

Unless displaced by the particular provisions of this Act, the principles of law and equity, including the law merchant and the law relative to capacity to contract, principal and agent, estoppel, fraud, misrepresentation, duress, coercion, mistake, bankruptcy, or other validating or invalidating cause shall supplement its provisions.

* * * *

§1—201. GENERAL DEFINITIONS
* * * *

(3) "Agreement" means the bargain of the parties in fact as found in their language or by implication from other circumstances including course of dealing or usage of trade or course of performance as provided in this Act (Sections 1—205 and 2—208). Whether an agreement has legal consequences is determined by the provisions of this Act, if applicable; otherwise by the law of contracts (Section 1—103). (Compare "Contract".)

(4) "Bank" means any person engaged in the business of banking.

(5) "Bearer" means the person in possession of an instrument, document of title, or certificated security payable to bearer or indorsed in blank.

(6) "Bill of lading" means a document evidencing the receipt of goods for shipment issued by a person engaged in the business of transporting or forwarding goods, and includes an airbill. "Airbill" means a document serving for air transportation as a bill of lading does for marine or rail transportation, and includes an air consignment note or air waybill.

* * * *

(9) "Buyer in ordinary course of business" means a person that buys goods in good faith, without knowledge that the sale violates the rights of another person in the goods, and in the ordinary course from a person, other than a pawnbroker, in the business of selling goods of that kind. A person buys goods in the ordinary course if the sale to the person comports with the usual or customary practices in the kind of business in which the seller is engaged or with the seller's own usual or customary practices. A person that sells oil, gas, or other minerals at the wellhead or minehead is a person in the business of selling goods of that kind. A buyer in ordinary course of business may buy for cash, by exchange of other property, or on secured or unsecured credit, and may acquire goods or documents of title under a pre-existing contract for sale. Only a buyer that takes

possession of the goods or has a right to recover the goods from the seller under Article 2 may be a buyer in ordinary course of business. A person that acquires goods in a transfer in bulk or as security for or in total or partial satisfaction of a money debt is not a buyer in ordinary course of business.

(10) "Conspicuous": A term or clause is conspicuous when it is so written that a reasonable person against whom it is to operate ought to have noticed it. A printed heading in capitals (as: NON-NEGOTIABLE BILL OF LADING) is conspicuous. Language in the body of a form is "conspicuous" if it is in larger or other contrasting type or color. But in a telegram any stated term is "conspicuous". Whether a term or clause is "conspicuous" or not is for decision by the court.

(11) "Contract" means the total legal obligation which results from the parties' agreement as affected by this Act and any other applicable rules of law. (Compare "Agreement".)

* * * *

(15) "Document of title" includes bill of lading, dock warrant, dock receipt, warehouse receipt or order for the delivery of goods, and also any other document which in the regular course of business or financing is treated as adequately evidencing that the person in possession of it is entitled to receive, hold and dispose of the document and the goods it covers. To be a document of title a document must purport to be issued by or addressed to a bailee and purport to cover goods in the bailee's possession which are either identified or are fungible portions of an identified mass.

* * * *

(17) "Fungible" with respect to goods or securities means goods or securities of which any unit is, by nature or usage of trade, the equivalent of any other like unit. Goods which are not fungible shall be deemed fungible for the purposes of this Act to the extent that under a particular agreement or document unlike units are treated as equivalents.

* * * *

(19) "Good faith" means honesty in fact in the conduct or transaction concerned.

(20) "Holder" with respect to a negotiable instrument, means the person in possession if the instrument is payable to bearer or, in the cases of an instrument payable to an identified person, if the identified person is in possession. "Holder" with respect to a document of title means the person in possession if the goods are deliverable to bearer or to the order of the person in possession.

* * * *

(23) A person is "insolvent" who either has ceased to pay his debts in the ordinary course of business or cannot pay his debts as they become due or is insolvent within the meaning of the federal bankruptcy law.

(24) "Money" means a medium of exchange authorized or adopted by a domestic or foreign government and includes a monetary unit of account established by an intergovernmental organization or by agreement between two or more nations.

(25) A person has "notice" of a fact when

(a) he has actual knowledge of it; or

(b) he has received a notice or notification of it; or

(c) from all the facts and circumstances known to him at the time in question he has reason to know that it exists.

* * * *

(37) "Security interest" means an interest in personal property or fixtures which secures payment or performance of an obligation. The term also includes any interest of a consignor and a buyer of accounts, chattel paper, a payment intangible, or a promissory note in a transaction that is subject to Article 9. The special property interest of a buyer of goods on identification of those goods to a contract for sale under Section 2—401 is not a "security interest", but a buyer may also acquire a "security interest" by complying with Article 9. Except as otherwise provided in Section 2—505, the right of a seller or lessor of goods under Article 2 or 2A to retain or acquire possession of the goods is not a "security interest", but a seller or lessor may also acquire a "security interest" by complying with Article 9. The retention or reservation of title by a seller of goods notwithstanding shipment or delivery to the buyer (Section 2—401) is limited in effect to a reservation of a "security interest".

Whether a transaction creates a lease or security interest is determined by the facts of each case; however, a transaction creates a security interest if the consideration the lessee is to pay the lessor for the right to possession and use of the goods is an obligation for the term of the lease not subject to termination by the lessee, and

(a) the original term of the lease is equal to or greater than the remaining economic life of the goods,

(b) the lessee is bound to renew the lease for the remaining economic life of the goods or is bound to become the owner of the goods,

(c) the lessee has an option to renew the lease for the remaining economic life of the goods for no additional consideration or nominal additional consideration upon compliance with the lease agreement, or

(d) the lessee has an option to become the owner of the goods for no additional consideration or nominal additional consideration upon compliance with the lease agreement.

A transaction does not create a security interest merely because it provides that

(a) the present value of the consideration the lessee is obligated to pay the lessor for the right to possession and use of the goods is substantially equal to or is greater than the fair market value of the goods at the time the lease is entered into,

(b) the lessee assumes risk of loss of the goods, or agrees to pay taxes, insurance, filing, recording, or registration fees, or service or maintenance costs with respect to the goods,

(c) the lessee has an option to renew the lease or to become the owner of the goods,

(d) the lessee has an option to renew the lease for a fixed rent that is equal to or greater than the reasonably predictable fair market rent for the use of the goods for the term of the renewal at the time the option is to be performed, or

(e) the lessee has an option to become the owner of the goods for a fixed price that is equal to or greater than the reasonably predictable fair market value of the goods at the time the option is to be performed.

* * * *

(39) "Signed" includes any symbol executed or adopted by a party with present intention to authenticate a writing.

(40) "Surety" includes guarantor.

* * * *

(43) "Unauthorized" signature means one made without actual, implied or apparent authority and includes a forgery.

(44) "Value". Except as otherwise provided with respect to negotiable instruments and bank collections (Sections 3—303, 4—210 and 4—211) a person gives "value" for rights if he acquires them

(a) in return for a binding commitment to extend credit or for the extension of immediately available credit whether or not drawn upon and whether or not a chargeback is provided for in the event of difficulties in collection; or

(b) as security for or in total or partial satisfaction of a pre-existing claim; or

(c) by accepting delivery pursuant to a preexisting contract for purchase; or

(d) generally, in return for any consideration sufficient to support a simple contract.

(45) "Warehouse receipt" means a receipt issued by a person engaged in the business of storing goods for hire.

(46) "Written" or "writing" includes printing, typewriting or any other intentional reduction to tangible form.

* * * *

§1—203. OBLIGATION OF GOOD FAITH

Every contract or duty within this Act imposes an obligation of good faith in its performance or enforcement.

§1—204. TIME; REASONABLE TIME; "SEASONABLY"

(1) Whenever this Act requires any action to be taken within a reasonable time, any time which is not manifestly unreasonable may be fixed by agreement.

(2) What is a reasonable time for taking any action depends on the nature, purpose and circumstances of such action.

(3) An action is taken "seasonably" when it is taken at or within the time agreed or if no time is agreed at or within a reasonable time.

§1—205. COURSE OF DEALING AND USAGE OF TRADE

(1) A course of dealing is a sequence of previous conduct between the parties to a particular transaction which is fairly to be regarded as establishing a common basis of understanding for interpreting their expressions and other conduct.

(2) A usage of trade is any practice or method of dealing having such regularity of observance in a place, vocation or trade as to justify an expectation that it will be observed with respect to the transaction in question. The existence and scope of such a usage are to be proved as facts. If it is established that such a usage is embodied in a written trade code or similar writing the interpretation of the writing is for the court.

(3) A course of dealing between parties and any usage of trade in the vocation or trade in which they are engaged or of which they are or should be aware give particular meaning to and supplement or qualify terms of an agreement.

(4) The express terms of an agreement and an applicable course of dealing or usage of trade shall be construed wherever reasonable as consistent with each other; but

when such construction is unreasonable express terms control both course of dealing and usage of trade and course of dealing controls usage trade.

(5) An applicable usage of trade in the place where any part of performance is to occur shall be used in interpreting the agreement as to that part of the performance.

(6) Evidence of a relevant usage of trade offered by one party is not admissible unless and until he has given the other party such notice as the court finds sufficient to prevent unfair surprise to the latter.

* * * *

Article 2 Sales

§2—102. SCOPE; CERTAIN SECURITY AND OTHER TRANSACTIONS EXCLUDED FROM THIS ARTICLE

Unless the context otherwise requires, this Article applies to transactions in goods; it does not apply to any transaction which although in the form of an unconditional contract to sell or present sale is intended to operate only as a security transaction nor does this Article impair or repeal any statute regulating sales to consumers, farmers or other specified classes of buyers.

§2—103. DEFINITIONS AND INDEX OF DEFINITIONS

(1) In this Article unless the context otherwise requires

 (a) "Buyer" means a person who buys or contracts to buy goods.

 (b) "Good faith" in the case of a merchant means honesty in fact and the observance of reasonable commercial standards of fair dealing in the trade.

 (c) "Receipt" of goods means taking physical possession of them.

 (d) "Seller" means a person who sells or contracts to sell goods.

§2—104. DEFINITIONS: "MERCHANT"; "BETWEEN MERCHANTS"; "FINANCING AGENCY"

(1) "Merchant" means a person who deals in goods of the kind or otherwise by his occupation holds himself out as having knowledge or skill peculiar to the practices or goods involved in the transaction or to whom such knowledge or skill may be attributed by his employment of an agent or broker or other intermediary who by his occupation holds himself out as having such knowledge or skill.

§2—105. DEFINITIONS: TRANSFERABILITY; "GOODS"; "FUTURE" GOODS; "LOT"; "COMMERCIAL UNIT"

(1) "Goods" means all things (including specially manufactured goods) which are movable at the time of identification to the contract for sale other than the money in which the price is to be paid, investment securities (Article 8) and things in action. "Goods" also includes the unborn young of animals and growing crops and other identified things attached to realty as described in the section on goods to be severed from realty (Section 2—107).

(2) Goods must be both existing and identified before any interest in them can pass. Goods which are not both existing and identified are "future" goods. A purported present sale of future goods or of any interest therein operates as a contract to sell.

(3) There may be a sale of a part interest in existing identified goods.

(4) An undivided share in an identified bulk of fungible goods is sufficiently identified to be sold although the quantity of the bulk is not determined. Any agreed proportion of such a bulk or any quantity thereof agreed upon by number, weight or other measure may to the extent of the seller's interest in the bulk be sold to the buyer who then becomes an owner in common.

(5) "Lot" means a parcel or a single article which is the subject matter of a separate sale or delivery, whether or not it is sufficient to perform the contract.

(6) "Commercial unit" means such a unit of goods as by commercial usage is a single whole for purposes of sale and division of which materially impairs its character or value on the market or in use. A commercial unit may be a single article (as a machine) or a set of articles (as a suite of furniture or an assortment of sizes) or a quantity (as a bale, gross, or carload) or any other unit treated in use or in the relevant market as a single whole.

* * * *

§2—107. GOODS TO BE SEVERED FROM REALTY: RECORDING

(1) A contract for the sale of minerals or the like (including oil and gas) or a structure or its materials to be removed from realty is a contract for the sale of goods within this Article if they are to be severed by the seller but until severance a purported present sale thereof which is not effective as a transfer of an interest in land is effective only as a contract to sell.

(2) A contract for the sale apart from the land of growing crops or other things attached to realty and capable of severance without material harm thereto but not described in subsection (1) or of timber to be cut is a contract for the sale of goods within this Article whether the subject matter is to be severed by the buyer or by the seller even though it forms part of the realty at the time of contracting, and the parties can by identification effect a present sale before severance.

(3) The provisions of this section are subject to any third party rights provided by the law relating to realty records, and the contract for sale may be executed and recorded as a document transferring an interest in land and shall then constitute notice to third parties of the buyer's rights under the contract for sale.

§2—201. FORMAL REQUIREMENTS; STATUTE OF FRAUDS

(1) Except as otherwise provided in this section a contract for the sale of goods for the price of $500 [some states have increased this amount to $5,000] or more is not enforceable by way of action or defense unless there is some writing sufficient to indicate that a contract for sale has been made between the parties and signed by the party against whom enforcement is sought or by his authorized agent or broker. A writing is not insufficient because it omits or incorrectly states a term agreed upon but the contract is not enforceable under this paragraph beyond the quantity of goods shown in such writing.

(2) Between merchants if within a reasonable time a writing in confirmation of the contract and sufficient against the sender is received and the party receiving it has reason to know its contents, it satisfies the requirements of subsection (1) against such party unless written notice of objection to its contents is given within ten days after it is received.

(3) A contract which does not satisfy the requirements of subsection (1) but which is valid in other respects is enforceable

(a) if the goods are to be specially manufactured for the buyer and are not suitable for sale to others in the ordinary course of the seller's business and the seller, before notice of repudiation is received and under circumstances which reasonably indicate that the goods are for the buyer, has made either a substantial beginning of their manufacture or commitments for their procurement; or

(b) if the party against whom enforcement is sought admits in his pleading, testimony or

otherwise in court that a contract for sale was made, but the contract is not enforceable under this provision beyond the quantity of goods admitted; or

(c) with respect to goods for which payment has been made and accepted or which have been received and accepted (Sec. 2—606).

§2—202. FINAL WRITTEN EXPRESSION: PAROL OR EXTRINSIC EVIDENCE

Terms with respect to which the confirmatory memoranda of the parties agree or which are otherwise set forth in a writing intended by the parties as a final expression of their agreement with respect to such terms as are included therein may not be contradicted by evidence of any prior agreement or of a contemporaneous oral agreement but may be explained or supplemented

(a) by course of dealing or usage of trade (Section 1—205) or by course of performance (Section 2—208); and

(b) by evidence of consistent additional terms unless the court finds the writing to have been intended also as a complete and exclusive statement of the terms of the agreement.

* * * *

§2—204. FORMATION IN GENERAL

(1) A contract for sale of goods may be made in any manner sufficient to show agreement, including conduct by both parties which recognizes the existence of such a contract.

(2) An agreement sufficient to constitute a contract for sale may be found even though the moment of its making is undetermined.

(3) Even though one or more terms are left open a contract for sale does not fail for indefiniteness if the parties have intended to make a contract and there is a reasonably certain basis for giving an appropriate remedy.

§2—205. FIRM OFFERS

An offer by a merchant to buy or sell goods in a signed writing which by its terms gives assurance that it will be held open is not revocable, for lack of consideration, during the time stated or if no time is stated for a reasonable time, but in no event may such period of irrevocability exceed three months; but any such term of assurance on a form supplied by the offeree must be separately signed by the offeror.

§2—206. OFFER AND ACCEPTANCE IN FORMATION OF CONTRACT

(1) Unless other unambiguously indicated by the language or circumstances

(a) an offer to make a contract shall be construed as inviting acceptance in any manner and by any medium reasonable in the circumstances;

(b) an order or other offer to buy goods for prompt or current shipment shall be construed as inviting acceptance either by a prompt promise to ship or by the prompt or current shipment of conforming or non-conforming goods, but such a shipment of non-conforming goods does not constitute an acceptance if the seller seasonably notifies the buyer that the shipment is offered only as an accommodation to the buyer.

(2) Where the beginning of a requested performance is a reasonable mode of acceptance an offeror who is not notified of acceptance within a reasonable time may treat the offer as having lapsed before acceptance.

§2—207. ADDITIONAL TERMS IN ACCEPTANCE OR CONFIRMATION

(1) A definite and seasonable expression of acceptance or a written confirmation which is sent within a reasonable time operates as an acceptance even though it states terms additional to or different from those offered or agreed upon, unless acceptance is expressly made conditional on assent to the additional or different terms.

(2) The additional terms are to be construed as proposals for addition to the contract. Between merchants such terms become part of the contract unless:

(a) the offer expressly limits acceptance to the terms of the offer;

(b) they materially alter it; or

(c) notification of objection to them has already been given or is given within a reasonable time after notice of them is received.

(3) Conduct by both parties which recognizes the existence of a contract is sufficient to establish a contract for sale although the writings of the parties do not otherwise establish a contract. In such case the terms of the particular contract consist of those terms on which the writings of the parties agree, together with any supplementary terms incorporated under any other provisions of this Act.

§2—208. COURSE OF PERFORMANCE OR PRACTICAL CONSTRUCTION

(1) Where the contract for sale involves repeated occasions for performance by either party with knowledge of the nature of the performance and opportunity for objection to it by the other, any course of performance accepted or acquiesced in without objection shall be relevant to determine the meaning of the agreement.

(2) The express terms of the agreement and any such course of performance, as well as any course of dealing and usage of trade, shall be construed whenever reasonable as consistent with each other; but when such construction is unreasonable, express terms shall control course of performance and course of performance shall control both course of dealing and usage of trade (Section 1—205).

(3) Subject to the provisions of the next section on modification and waiver, such course of performance shall be relevant to show a waiver or modification of any term inconsistent with such course of performance.

§2—209. MODIFICATION, RESCISSION AND WAIVER

(1) An agreement modifying a contract within this Article needs no consideration to be binding.

(2) A signed agreement which excludes modification or rescission except by a signed writing cannot be otherwise modified or rescinded, but except as between merchants such a requirement on a form supplied by the merchant must be separately signed by the other party.

(3) The requirements of the statute of frauds section of this Article (Section 2—201) must be satisfied if the contract as modified is within its provisions.

(4) Although an attempt at modification or rescission does not satisfy the requirements of subsection (2) or (3) it can operate as a waiver.

(5) A party who has made a waiver affecting an executory portion of the contract may retract the waiver by reasonable notification received by the other party that strict performance will be required of any term waived, unless the retraction would be unjust in view of a material change of position in reliance on the waiver.

§2—210. DELEGATION OF PERFORMANCE; ASSIGNMENT OF RIGHTS

* * * *

(5) An assignment of "the contract" or of "all my rights under the contract" or an assignment in similar general terms is an assignment of rights and unless the language or the circumstances (as in an assignment for security) indicate the contrary, it is a delegation of performance of the duties of the assignor and its acceptance by the assignee constitutes a promise by him to perform those duties. This promise is enforceable by either the assignor or the other party to the original contract.

§2—301. GENERAL OBLIGATIONS OF PARTIES

The obligation of the seller is to transfer and deliver and that of the buyer is to accept and pay in accordance with the contract.

§2—302. UNCONSCIONABLE CONTRACT OR CLAUSE

(1) If the court as a matter of law finds the contract or any clause of the contract to have been unconscionable at the time it was made the court may refuse to enforce the contract, or it may enforce the remainder of the contract without the unconscionable clause, or it may so limit the application of any unconscionable clause as to avoid any unconscionable result.

(2) When it is claimed or appears to the court that the contract or any clause thereof may be unconscionable the parties shall be afforded a reasonable opportunity to present evidence as to its commercial setting, purpose and effect to aid the court in making the determination.

§2—303. ALLOCATIONS OR DIVISION OF RISKS

Where this Article allocates a risk or a burden as between the parties "unless otherwise agreed", the agreement may not only shift the allocation but may also divide the risk or burden.

§2—304. PRICE PAYABLE IN MONEY, GOODS, REALTY, OR OTHERWISE

(1) The price can be made payable in money or otherwise. If it is payable in whole or in part in goods each party is a seller of the goods which he is to transfer.

(2) Even though all or part of the price is payable in an interest in realty the transfer of the goods and the seller's obligations with reference to them are subject to this Article, but not the transfer of the interest in realty or the transferor's obligations in connection therewith.

§2—305. OPEN PRICE TERM

(1) The parties if they so intend can conclude a contract for sale even though the price is not settled. In such a case the price is a reasonable price at the time for delivery if

(a) nothing is said as to price; or

(b) the price is left to be agreed by the parties and they fail to agree; or

(c) the price is to be fixed in terms of some agreed market or other standard as set or recorded by a third person or agency and it is not so set or recorded.

(2) A price to be fixed by the seller or by the buyer means a price for him to fix in good faith.

(3) When a price left to be fixed otherwise than by agreement of the parties fails to be fixed through fault of one party the other may at his option treat the contract as cancelled or himself fix a reasonable price.

(4) Where, however, the parties intend not to be bound unless the price be fixed or agreed and it is not fixed or agreed there is no contract. In such a case the buyer must return any goods already received or if unable so to do must pay their reasonable value at the time of delivery and the seller must return any portion of the price paid on account.

§2—306. OUTPUT, REQUIREMENTS AND EXCLUSIVE DEALINGS

(1) A term which measures the quantity by the output of the seller or the requirements of the buyer means such actual output or requirements as may occur in good faith, except that no quantity unreasonably disproportionate to any stated estimate or in the absence of a stated estimate to any normal or otherwise comparable prior output or requirements may be tendered or demanded.

(2) A lawful agreement by either the seller or the buyer for exclusive dealing in the kind of goods concerned imposes unless otherwise agreed an obligation by the seller to use best efforts to supply the goods and by the buyer to use best efforts to promote their sale.

§2—307. DELIVERY IN SINGLE LOT OR SEVERAL LOTS

Unless otherwise agreed all goods called for by a contract for sale must be tendered in a single delivery and payment is due only on such tender but where the circumstances give either party the right to make or demand delivery in lots the price if it can be apportioned may be demanded for each lot.

§2—308. ABSENCE OF SPECIFIED PLACE FOR DELIVERY

Unless otherwise agreed

(a) the place for delivery of goods is the seller's place of business or if he has none his residence; but

(b) in a contract for sale of identified goods which to the knowledge of the parties at the time of contracting are in some other place, that place is the place for their delivery; and

(c) documents of title may be delivered through customary banking channels.

§2—309. ABSENCE OF SPECIFIC TIME PROVISIONS; NOTICE OF TERMINATION

(1) The time for shipment or delivery or any other action under a contract if not provided in this Article or agreed upon shall be a reasonable time.

§2—310. OPEN TIME FOR PAYMENT OR RUNNING OF CREDIT; AUTHORITY TO SHIP UNDER RESERVATION

Unless otherwise agreed

(a) payment is due at the time and place at which the buyer is to receive the goods even though the place of shipment is the place of delivery; and

(b) if the seller is authorized to send the goods he may ship them under reservation, and may tender the documents of title, but the buyer may inspect the goods after their arrival before payment is due unless such inspection is inconsistent with the terms of the contract (Section 2—513).

* * * *

§2—312. WARRANTY OF TITLE AND AGAINST INFRINGEMENT; BUYER'S OBLIGATION AGAINST INFRINGEMENT

(1) Subject to subsection (2) there is in a contract for sale a warranty by the seller that

(a) the title conveyed shall be good, and its transfer rightful; and

(b) the goods shall be delivered free from any security interest or other lien or encumbrance of which the buyer at the time of contracting has no knowledge.

(2) A warranty under subsection (1) will be excluded or modified only by specific language or by circumstances which give the buyer reason to know that the person selling does not claim title in himself or that he is purporting to sell only such right or title as he or a third person may have.

(3) Unless otherwise agreed a seller who is a merchant regularly dealing in goods of the kind warrants that the goods shall be delivered free of the rightful claim of any third person by way of infringement or the like but a buyer who furnishes specifications to the seller must hold the seller harmless against any such claim which arises out of compliance with the specifications.

§2—313. EXPRESS WARRANTIES BY AFFIRMATION, PROMISE, DESCRIPTION, SAMPLE

(1) Express warranties by the seller are created as follows:

(a) Any affirmation of fact or promise made by the seller to the buyer which relates to the goods and becomes part of the basis of the bargain creates an express warranty that the goods shall conform to the affirmation or promise.

(b) Any description of the goods which is made part of the basis of the bargain creates an express warranty that the goods shall conform to the description.

(c) Any sample or model which is made part of the basis of the bargain creates an express warranty that the whole of the goods shall conform to the sample or model.

(2) It is not necessary to the creation of an express warranty that the seller use formal words such as "warrant" or "guarantee" or that he have a specific intention to make a warranty, but an affirmation merely of the value of the goods or a statement purporting to be merely the seller's opinion or commendation of the goods does not create a warranty.

§2—314. IMPLIED WARRANTY: MERCHANTABILITY; USAGE OF TRADE

(1) Unless excluded or modified (Section 2—316), a warranty that the goods shall be merchantable is implied in a contract for their sale if the seller is a merchant with respect to goods of that kind. Under this section the serving for value of food or drink to be consumed either on the premises or elsewhere is a sale.

(2) Goods to be merchantable must be at least such as

(a) pass without objection in the trade under the contract description; and

(b) in the case of fungible goods, are of fair average quality within the description; and

(c) are fit for the ordinary purposes for which such goods are used; and

(d) run, within the variations permitted by the agreement, of even kind, quality and quantity within each unit and among all units involved; and

(e) are adequately contained, packaged, and labeled as the agreement may require; and

(f) conform to the promises or affirmations of fact made on the container or label if any.

(3) Unless excluded or modified (Section 2—316) other implied warranties may arise from course of dealing or usage of trade.

§2—315. IMPLIED WARRANTY: FITNESS FOR PARTICULAR PURPOSE

Where the seller at the time of contracting has reason to know any particular purpose for which the goods are required and that the buyer is relying on the seller's skill or judgment to select or furnish suitable goods, there is unless excluded or modified under the next section an implied warranty that the goods shall be fit for such purpose.

§2—316. EXCLUSION OR MODIFICATION OF WARRANTIES

(1) Words or conduct relevant to the creation of an express warranty and words or conduct tending to negate or limit warranty shall be construed wherever reasonable as consistent with each other; but subject to the provisions of this Article on parol or extrinsic evidence (Section 2—202) negation or limitation is inoperative to the extent that such construction is unreasonable.

(2) Subject to subsection (3), to exclude or modify the implied warranty of merchantability or any part of it the language must mention merchantability and in case of a writing must be conspicuous, and to exclude or modify any implied warranty of fitness the exclusion must be by a writing and conspicuous. Language to exclude all implied warranties of fitness is sufficient if it states, for example, that "There are no warranties which extend beyond the description on the face hereof."

(3) Notwithstanding subsection (2)

(a) unless the circumstances indicate otherwise, all implied warranties are excluded by expressions like "as is", "with all faults" or other language which in common understanding calls the buyer's attention to the exclusion of warranties and makes plain that there is no implied warranty; and

(b) when the buyer before entering into the contract has examined the goods or the sample or model as fully as he desired or has refused to examine the goods there is no implied warranty with regard to defects which an examination ought in the circumstances to have revealed to him; and

(c) an implied warranty can also be excluded or modified by course of dealing or course of performance or usage of trade.

(4) Remedies for breach of warranty can be limited in accordance with the provisions of this Article on liquidation or limitation of damages and on contractual modification of remedy (Sections 2—718 and 2—719).

§2—317. CUMULATION AND CONFLICT OF WARRANTIES EXPRESS OR IMPLIED

Warranties whether express or implied shall be construed as consistent with each other and as cumulative, but if such construction is unreasonable the intention of the parties shall determine which warranty is dominant. In ascertaining that intention the following rules apply:

(a) Exact or technical specifications displace an inconsistent sample or model or general language of description.

(b) A sample from an existing bulk displaces inconsistent general language of description.

(c) Express warranties displace inconsistent implied warranties other than an implied warranty of fitness for a particular purpose.

§2—318. THIRD PARTY BENEFICIARIES OF WARRANTIES EXPRESS OR IMPLIED

Note: If this Act is introduced in the Congress of the United States this section should be omitted. (States to select one alternative.)

Alternative A

A seller's warranty whether express or implied extends to any natural person who is in the family or household of his buyer or who is a guest in his home if it is reasonable to expect that such person may use, consume or be affected by the goods and who is injured in person by breach of the warranty. A seller may not exclude or limit the operation of this section.

Alternative B

A seller's warranty whether express or implied extends to any natural person who may reasonably be expected to use, consume or be affected by the goods and who is injured in person by breach of the warranty. A seller may not exclude or limit the operation of this section.

Alternative C

A seller's warranty whether express or implied extends to any person who may reasonably be expected to use, consume or be affected by the goods and who is injured by breach of the warranty. A seller may not exclude or limit the operation of this section with respect to injury to the person of an individual to whom the warranty extends.

§2—319. F.O.B. AND F.A.S. TERMS

(1) Unless otherwise agreed the term F.O.B. (which means "free on board") at a named place, even though used only in connection with the stated price, is a delivery term under which

(a) when the term is F.O.B. the place of shipment, the seller must at that place ship the goods in the manner provided in this Article (Section 2—504) and bear the expense and risk of putting them into the possession of the carrier; or

(b) when the term is F.O.B. the place of destination, the seller must at his own expense and risk transport the goods to that place and there tender delivery of them in the manner provided in this Article (Section 2—503);

(c) when under either (a) or (b) the term is also F.O.B. vessel, car or other vehicle, the seller must in addition at his own expense and risk load the goods on board. If the term is F.O.B. vessel the buyer must name the vessel and in an appropriate case the seller must comply with the provisions of this Article on the form of bill of lading (Section 2—323).

(2) Unless otherwise agreed the term F.A.S. vessel (which means "free alongside") at a named port, even though used only in connection with the stated price, is a delivery term under which the seller must

(a) at his own expense and risk deliver the goods alongside the vessel in the manner usual in that port or on a dock designated and provided by the buyer; and

(b) obtain and tender a receipt for the goods in exchange for which the carrier is under a duty to issue a bill of lading.

(3) Unless otherwise agreed in any case falling within subsection (1)(a) or (c) or subsection (2) the buyer must seasonably give any needed instructions for making delivery, including when the term is F.A.S. or F.O.B. the loading berth of the vessel and in an appropriate case its name and sailing date. The seller may treat the failure of needed instructions as a failure of cooperation under this Article (Section 2—311). He may also at his option move the goods in any reasonable manner preparatory to delivery or shipment.

(4) Under the term F.O.B. vessel or F.A.S. unless otherwise agreed the buyer must make payment against tender of the required documents and the seller may not tender nor the buyer demand delivery of the goods in substitution for the documents.

§2—320. C.I.F. AND C. & F. TERMS

(1) The term C.I.F. means that the price includes in a lump sum the cost of the goods and the insurance and freight to the named destination. The term C. & F. or C.F. means that the price so includes cost and freight to the named destination.

(2) Unless otherwise agreed and even though used only in connection with the stated price and destination, the term C.I.F. destination or its equivalent requires the seller at his own expense and risk to

(a) put the goods into the possession of a carrier at the port for shipment and obtain a negotiable bill or bills of lading covering the entire transportation to the named destination; and

(b) load the goods and obtain a receipt from the carrier (which may be contained in the bill of lading) showing that the freight has been paid or provided for; and

(c) obtain a policy or certificate of insurance, including any war risk insurance, of a kind and on terms then current at the port of shipment in the usual amount, in the currency of the contract, shown to cover the same goods covered by the bill of lading and providing for payment of loss to the order of the buyer or for the account of whom it may concern; but the seller may add to the price the amount of the premium for any such war risk insurance; and

(d) prepare an invoice of the goods and procure any other documents required to effect shipment or to comply with the contract; and

(e) forward and tender with commercial promptness all the documents in due form and with any indorsement necessary to perfect the buyer's rights.

(3) Unless otherwise agreed the term C. & F. or its equivalent has the same effect and imposes upon the seller the same obligations and risks as a C.I.F. term except the obligation as to insurance.

(4) Under the term C.I.F. or C. & F. unless otherwise agreed the buyer must make payment against tender of the required documents and the seller may not tender nor the buyer demand delivery of the goods in substitution for the documents.

* * * *

§2—322. DELIVERY "EX-SHIP"

(1) Unless otherwise agreed a term for delivery of goods "ex-ship" (which means from the carrying vessel) or in equivalent language is not restricted to a particular ship and requires delivery from a ship which has reached a place at the named port of destination where goods of the kind are usually discharged.

(2) Under such a term unless otherwise agreed

(a) the seller must discharge all liens arising out of the carriage and furnish the buyer with a direction which puts the carrier under a duty to deliver the goods; and

(b) the risk of loss does not pass to the buyer until the goods leave the ship's tackle or are otherwise properly unloaded.

* * * *

§2—324. "NO ARRIVAL, NO SALE" TERM

Under a term "no arrival, no sale" or terms of like meaning, unless otherwise agreed,

(a) the seller must properly ship conforming goods and if they arrive by any means he must tender them on arrival but he assumes no obligation that the goods will arrive unless he has caused the non-arrival; and

(b) where without fault of the seller the goods are in part lost or have so deteriorated as no longer to conform to the contract or arrive after the contract time, the buyer may proceed as if there had been casualty to identified goods (Section 2—613).

* * * *

§2—326. SALE ON APPROVAL AND SALE OR RETURN; RIGHTS OF CREDITORS

(1) Unless otherwise agreed, if delivered goods may be returned by the buyer even though they conform to the contract, the transaction is

(a) a "sale on approval" if the goods are delivered primarily for use, and

(b) a "sale or return" if the goods are delivered primarily for resale.

(2) Goods held on approval are not subject to the claims of the buyer's creditors until acceptance; goods held on sale or return are subject to such claims while in the buyer's possession.

(3) Any "or return" term of a contract for sale is to be treated as a separate contract for sale within the statute of frauds section of this Article (Section 2—201) and as contradicting the sale aspect of the contract within the provisions of this Article or on parol or extrinsic evidence (Section 2—202).

§2—327. SPECIAL INCIDENTS OF SALE ON APPROVAL AND SALE OR RETURN

(1) Under a sale on approval unless otherwise agreed

(a) although the goods are identified to the contract the risk of loss and the title do not pass to the buyer until acceptance; and

(b) use of the goods consistent with the purpose of trial is not acceptance but failure seasonably to notify the seller of election to return the goods is acceptance, and if the goods conform to the contract acceptance of any part is acceptance of the whole; and

(c) after due notification of election to return, the return is at the seller's risk and expense but a merchant buyer must follow any reasonable instructions.

(2) Under a sale or return unless otherwise agreed

(a) the option to return extends to the whole or any commercial unit of the goods while in substantially their original condition, but must be exercised seasonably; and

(b) the return is at the buyer's risk and expense.

§2—328. SALE BY AUCTION

(1) In a sale by auction if goods are put up in lots each lot is the subject of a separate sale.

(2) A sale by auction is complete when the auctioneer so announces by the fall of the hammer or in other customary manner. Where a bid is made while the hammer is falling in acceptance of a prior bid the auctioneer may in his discretion reopen the bidding or declare the goods sold under the bid on which the hammer was falling.

(3) Such a sale is with reserve unless the goods are in explicit terms put up without reserve. In an auction with reserve the auctioneer may withdraw the goods at any time until he announces completion of the sale. In an auction without reserve, after the auctioneer calls for bids on an article or lot, that article or lot cannot be withdrawn unless no bid is made within a reasonable time. In either case a bidder may retract his bid until the auctioneer's announcement of completion of the sale, but a bidder's retraction does not revive any previous bid.

(4) If the auctioneer knowingly receives a bid on the seller's behalf or the seller makes or procures such a bid, and notice has not been given that liberty for such bidding is reserved, the buyer may at his option avoid the sale or take the goods at the price of the last good faith bid prior to the completion of the sale. This subsection shall not apply to any bid at a forced sale.

§2—401. PASSING OF TITLE; RESERVATION FOR SECURITY; LIMITED APPLICATION OF THIS SECTION

Each provision of this Article with regard to the rights, obligations and remedies of the seller, the buyer, purchasers or other third parties applies irrespective of title to the goods except where the provision refers to such title. Insofar as situations are not covered by the other provisions of this Article and matters concerning title became material the following rules apply:

(1) Title to goods cannot pass under a contract for sale prior to their identification to the contract

(Section 2—501), and unless otherwise explicitly agreed the buyer acquires by their identification a special property as limited by this Act. Any retention or reservation by the seller of the title (property) in goods shipped or delivered to the buyer is limited in effect to a reservation of a security interest. Subject to these provisions and to the provisions of the Article on Secured Transactions (Article 9), title to goods passes from the seller to the buyer in any manner and on any conditions explicitly agreed on by the parties.

(2) Unless otherwise explicitly agreed title passes to the buyer at the time and place at which the seller completes his performance with reference to the physical delivery of the goods, despite any reservation of a security interest and even though a document of title is to be delivered at a different time or place; and in particular and despite any reservation of a security interest by the bill of lading

    (a) if the contract requires or authorizes the seller to send the goods to the buyer but does not require him to deliver them at destination, title passes to the buyer at the time and place of shipment; but

    (b) if the contract requires delivery at destination, title passes on tender there.

(3) Unless otherwise explicitly agreed where delivery is to be made without moving the goods,

    (a) if the seller is to deliver a document of title, title passes at the time when and the place where he delivers such documents; or

    (b) if the goods are at the time of contracting already identified and no documents are to be delivered, title passes at the time and place of contracting.

(4) A rejection or other refusal by the buyer to receive or retain the goods, whether or not justified, or a justified revocation of acceptance revests title to the goods in the seller. Such revesting occurs by operation of law and is not a "sale".

* * * *

§2—403. POWER TO TRANSFER; GOOD FAITH PURCHASE OF GOODS; "ENTRUSTING"

(1) A purchaser of goods acquires all title which his transferor had or had power to transfer except that a purchaser of a limited interest acquires rights only to the extent of the interest purchased. A person with voidable title has power to transfer a good title to a good faith purchaser for value. When goods have been delivered under a transaction of purchase the purchaser has such power even though

    (a) the transferor was deceived as to the identity of the purchaser, or

    (b) the delivery was in exchange for a check which is later dishonored, or

    (c) it was agreed that the transaction was to be a "cash sale", or

    (d) the delivery was procured through fraud punishable as larcenous under the criminal law.

(2) Any entrusting of possession of goods to a merchant who deals in goods of that kind gives him power to transfer all rights of the entruster to a buyer in ordinary course of business.

(3) "Entrusting" includes any delivery and any acquiescence in retention of possession regardless of any condition expressed between the parties to the delivery or acquiescence and regardless of whether the procurement of the entrusting or the possessor's disposition of the goods have been such as to be larcenous under the criminal law.

(4) The rights of other purchasers of goods and of lien creditors are governed by the Articles on Secured Transactions (Article 9), Bulk Transfers (Article 6) and Documents of Title (Article 7).

§2—501. INSURABLE INTEREST IN GOODS; MANNER OF IDENTIFICATION OF GOODS

(1) The buyer obtains a special property and an insurable interest in goods by identification of existing goods as goods to which the contract refers even though the goods so identified are non-conforming and he has an option to return or reject them. Such identification can be made at any time and in any manner explicitly agreed to by the parties. In the absence of explicit agreement identification occurs

    (a) when the contract is made if it is for the sale of goods already existing and identified;

    (b) if the contract is for the sale of future goods other than those described in paragraph (c), when goods are shipped, marked or otherwise designated by the seller as goods to which the contract refers;

    (c) when the crops are planted or otherwise become growing crops or the young are conceived if the contract is for the sale of unborn young to be born within twelve months after contracting or for the sale of crops to be harvested within twelve months or the next normal harvest season after contracting whichever is longer.

(2) The seller retains an insurable interest in goods so long as title to or any security interest in the goods

remains in him and where the identification is by the seller alone he may until default or insolvency or notification to the buyer that the identification is final substitute other goods for those identified.

(3) Nothing in this section impairs any insurable interest recognized under any other statute or rule of law.

§2—502. BUYER'S RIGHT TO GOODS ON SELLER'S INSOLVENCY

(1) Subject to subsections (2) and (3) and even though the goods have not been shipped a buyer who has paid a part or all of the price of goods in which he has a special property under the provisions of the immediately preceding section may on making and keeping good a tender of any unpaid portion of their price recover them from the seller if:

(a) in the case of goods bought for personal, family, or household purposes, the seller repudiates or fails to deliver as required by the contract; or

(b) in all cases, the seller becomes insolvent within ten days after receipt of the first installment on their price.

(2) The buyer's right to recover the goods under subsection (1)(a) vests upon acquisition of a special property, even if the seller had not then repudiated or failed to deliver.

(3) If the identification creating his special property has been made by the buyer he acquires the right to recover the goods only if they conform to the contract for sale.
As amended in 1999.

§2—503. MANNER OF SELLER'S TENDER OF DELIVERY

(1) Tender of delivery requires that the seller put and hold conforming goods at the buyer's disposition and give the buyer any notification reasonably necessary to enable him to take delivery. The manner, time and place for tender are determined by the agreement and this Article, and in particular

(a) tender must be at a reasonable hour, and if it is of goods they must be kept available for the period reasonably necessary to enable the buyer to take possession; but

(b) unless otherwise agreed the buyer must furnish facilities reasonably suited to the receipt of the goods.

(2) Where the case is within the next section respecting shipment tender requires that the seller comply with its provisions.

(3) Where the seller is required to deliver at a particular destination tender requires that he comply with subsection (1) and also in any appropriate case tender

documents as described in subsections (4) and (5) of this section.

(4) Where goods are in the possession of a bailee and are to be delivered without being moved

(a) tender requires that the seller either tender a negotiable document of title covering such goods or procure acknowledgment by the bailee of the buyer's right to possession of the goods; but

(b) tender to the buyer of a non-negotiable document of title or of a written direction to the bailee to deliver is sufficient tender unless the buyer seasonably objects, and receipt by the bailee of notification of the buyer's rights fixes those rights as against the bailee and all third persons; but risk of loss of the goods and of any failure by the bailee to honor the non-negotiable document of title or to obey the direction remains on the seller until the buyer has had a reasonable time to present the document or direction, and a refusal by the bailee to honor the document or to obey the direction defeats the tender.

(5) Where the contract requires the seller to deliver documents

(a) he must tender all such documents in correct form, except as provided in this Article with respect to bills of lading in a set (subsection (2) of Section 2—323); and

(b) tender through customary banking channels is sufficient and dishonor of a draft accompanying the documents constitutes non-acceptance or rejection.

§2—504. SHIPMENT BY SELLER

Where the seller is required or authorized to send the goods to the buyer and the contract does not require him to deliver them at a particular destination, then unless otherwise agreed he must

(a) put the goods in the possession of such a carrier and make such a contract for their transportation as may be reasonable having regard to the nature of the goods and other circumstances of the case; and

(b) obtain and promptly deliver or tender in due form any document necessary to enable the buyer to obtain possession of the goods or otherwise required by the agreement or by usage of trade; and

(c) promptly notify the buyer of the shipment. Failure to notify the buyer under paragraph (c) or to make a proper contract under paragraph (a) is a ground for rejection only if material delay or loss ensues.

* * * *

§2—506. RIGHTS OF FINANCING AGENCY

(1) A financing agency by paying or purchasing for value a draft which relates to a shipment of goods acquires to the extent of the payment or purchase and in addition to its own rights under the draft and any document of title securing it any rights of the shipper in the goods including the right to stop delivery and the shipper's right to have the draft honored by the buyer.

(2) The right to reimbursement of a financing agency which has in good faith honored or purchased the draft under commitment to or authority from the buyer is not impaired by subsequent discovery of defects with reference to any relevant document which was apparently regular on its face.

§2—507. EFFECT OF SELLER'S TENDER; DELIVERY ON CONDITION

(1) Tender of delivery is a condition to the buyer's duty to accept the goods and, unless otherwise agreed, to his duty to pay for them. Tender entitles the seller to acceptance of the goods and to payment according to the contract.

(2) Where payment is due and demanded on the delivery to the buyer of goods or documents of title, his right as against the seller to retain or dispose of them is conditional upon his making the payment due.

§2—508. CURE BY SELLER OF IMPROPER TENDER OR DELIVERY; REPLACEMENT

(1) Where any tender or delivery by the seller is rejected because non-conforming and the time for performance has not yet expired, the seller may seasonably notify the buyer of his intention to cure and may then within the contract time make a conforming delivery.

(2) Where the buyer rejects a non-conforming tender which the seller had reasonable grounds to believe would be acceptable with or without money allowance the seller may if he seasonably notifies the buyer have a further reasonable time to substitute a conforming tender.

§2—509. RISK OF LOSS IN THE ABSENCE OF BREACH

(1) Where the contract requires or authorizes the seller to ship the goods by carrier

   (a) if it does not require him to deliver them at a particular destination, the risk of loss passes to the buyer when the goods are duly delivered to the carrier even though the shipment is under reservation (Section 2—505); but

   (b) if it does require him to deliver them at a particular destination and the goods are there duly tendered while in the possession of the carrier, the risk of loss passes to the buyer when the goods are there duly so tendered as to enable the buyer to take delivery.

(2) Where the goods are held by a bailee to be delivered without being moved, the risk of loss passes to the buyer

   (a) on his receipt of a negotiable document of title covering the goods; or

   (b) on acknowledgment by the bailee of the buyer's right to possession of the goods; or

   (c) after his receipt of a non-negotiable document of title or other written direction to deliver, as provided in subsection (4)(b) of Section 2—503.

(3) In any case not within subsection (1) or (2), the risk of loss passes to the buyer on his receipt of the goods if the seller is a merchant; otherwise the risk passes to the buyer on tender of delivery.

(4) The provisions of this section are subject to contrary agreement of the parties and to the provisions of this Article on sale on approval (Section 2—327) and on effect of breach on risk of loss (Section 2—510).

§2—510. EFFECT OF BREACH ON RISK OF LOSS

(1) Where a tender or delivery of goods so fails to conform to the contract as to give a right of rejection the risk of their loss remains on the seller until cure or acceptance.

(2) Where the buyer rightfully revokes acceptance he may to the extent of any deficiency in his effective insurance coverage treat the risk of loss as having rested on the seller from the beginning.

(3) Where the buyer as to conforming goods already identified to the contract for sale repudiates or is otherwise in breach before risk of their loss has passed to him, the seller may to the extent of any deficiency in his effective insurance coverage treat the risk of loss as resting on the buyer for a commercially reasonable time.

§2—511. TENDER OF PAYMENT BY BUYER; PAYMENT BY CHECK

(1) Unless otherwise agreed tender of payment is a condition to the seller's duty to tender and complete any delivery.

(2) Tender of payment is sufficient when made by any means or in any manner current in the ordinary course of business unless the seller demands payment in legal tender and gives any extension of time reasonably necessary to procure it.

(3) Subject to the provisions of this Act on the effect of an instrument on an obligation (Section 3—310), payment by check is conditional and is defeated as between the parties by dishonor of the check on due presentment.

As amended in 1994.

§2—512. PAYMENT BY BUYER BEFORE INSPECTION

(1) Where the contract requires payment before inspection non-conformity of the goods does not excuse the buyer from so making payment unless

(a) the non-conformity appears without inspection; or

(b) despite tender of the required documents the circumstances would justify injunction against honor under this Act (Section 5—109(b)).

(2) Payment pursuant to subsection (1) does not constitute an acceptance of goods or impair the buyer's right to inspect or any of his remedies.

§2—513. BUYER'S RIGHT TO INSPECTION OF GOODS

(1) Unless otherwise agreed and subject to subsection (3), where goods are tendered or delivered or identified to the contract for sale, the buyer has a right before payment or acceptance to inspect them at any reasonable place and time and in any reasonable manner. When the seller is required or authorized to send the goods to the buyer, the inspection may be after their arrival.

(2) Expenses of inspection must be borne by the buyer but may be recovered from the seller if the goods do not conform and are rejected.

(3) Unless otherwise agreed and subject to the provisions of this Article on C.I.F. contracts (subsection (3) of Section 2—321), the buyer is not entitled to inspect the goods before payment of the price when the contract provides

(a) for delivery "C.O.D." or on other like terms; or

(b) for payment against documents of title, except where such payment is due only after the goods are to become available for inspection.

(4) A place or method of inspection fixed by the parties is presumed to be exclusive but unless otherwise expressly agreed it does not postpone identification or shift the place for delivery or for passing the risk of loss. If compliance becomes impossible, inspection shall be as provided in this section unless the place or method fixed was clearly intended as an indispensable condition failure of which avoids the contract.

* * * *

§2—601. BUYER'S RIGHTS ON IMPROPER DELIVERY

Subject to the provisions of this Article on breach in installment contracts (Section 2—612) and unless otherwise agreed under the sections on contractual limitations of remedy (Sections 2—718 and 2—719), if the goods or the tender of delivery fail in any respect to conform to the contract, the buyer may

(a) reject the whole; or

(b) accept the whole; or

(c) accept any commercial unit or units and reject the rest.

§2—602. MANNER AND EFFECT OF RIGHTFUL REJECTION

(1) Rejection of goods must be within a reasonable time after their delivery or tender. It is ineffective unless the buyer seasonably notifies the seller.

(2) Subject to the provisions of the two following sections on rejected goods (Sections 2—603 and 2—604),

(a) after rejection any exercise of ownership by the buyer with respect to any commercial unit is wrongful as against the seller; and

(b) if the buyer has before rejection taken physical possession of goods in which he does not have a security interest under the provisions of this Article (subsection (3) of Section 2—711), he is under a duty after rejection to hold them with reasonable care at the seller's disposition for a time sufficient to permit the seller to remove them; but

(c) the buyer has no further obligations with regard to goods rightfully rejected.

(3) The seller's rights with respect to goods wrongfully rejected are governed by the provisions of this Article on Seller's remedies in general (Section 2—703).

§2—603. MERCHANT BUYER'S DUTIES AS TO RIGHTFULLY REJECTED GOODS

(1) Subject to any security interest in the buyer (subsection (3) of Section 2—711), when the seller has no agent or place of business at the market of rejection a merchant buyer is under a duty after rejection of goods in his possession or control to follow any reasonable instructions received from the seller with respect to the goods and in the absence of such instructions to make reasonable efforts to sell them for the seller's account if they are perishable or threaten to decline in value speedily. Instructions are not reasonable if on demand indemnity for expenses is not forthcoming.

(2) When the buyer sells goods under subsection (1), he is entitled to reimbursement from the seller or out of the proceeds for reasonable expenses of caring for and selling them, and if the expenses include no selling commission then to such commission as is usual in the trade or if there is none to a reasonable sum not exceeding ten per cent on the gross proceeds.

(3) In complying with this section the buyer is held only to good faith and good faith conduct hereunder is neither acceptance nor conversion nor the basis of an action for damages.

§2—604. BUYER'S OPTIONS AS TO SALVAGE OF RIGHTFULLY REJECTED GOODS

Subject to the provisions of the immediately preceding section on perishables if the seller gives no instructions within a reasonable time after notification of rejection the buyer may store the rejected goods for the seller's account or reship them to him or resell them for the seller's account with reimbursement as provided in the preceding section. Such action is not acceptance or conversion.

§2—605. WAIVER OF BUYER'S OBJECTIONS BY FAILURE TO PARTICULARIZE

(1) The buyer's failure to state in connection with rejection a particular defect which is ascertainable by reasonable inspection precludes him from relying on the unstated defect to justify rejection or to establish breach

  (a) where the seller could have cured it if stated seasonably; or

  (b) between merchants when the seller has after rejection made a request in writing for a full and final written statement of all defects on which the buyer proposes to rely.

(2) Payment against documents made without reservation of rights precludes recovery of the payment for defects apparent on the face of the documents.

§2—606. WHAT CONSTITUTES ACCEPTANCE OF GOODS

(1) Acceptance of goods occurs when the buyer

  (a) after a reasonable opportunity to inspect the goods signifies to the seller that the goods are conforming or that he will take or retain them in spite of their non-conformity; or

  (b) fails to make an effective rejection (subsection (1) of Section 2—602), but such acceptance does not occur until the buyer has had a reasonable opportunity to inspect them; or

  (c) does any act inconsistent with the seller's ownership; but if such act is wrongful as against the seller it is an acceptance only if ratified by him.

(2) Acceptance of a part of any commercial unit is acceptance of that entire unit.

§2—607. EFFECT OF ACCEPTANCE; NOTICE OF BREACH; BURDEN OF ESTABLISHING BREACH AFTER ACCEPTANCE; NOTICE OF CLAIM OR LITIGATION TO PERSON ANSWERABLE OVER

(1) The buyer must pay at the contract rate for any goods accepted.

(2) Acceptance of goods by the buyer precludes rejection of the goods accepted and if made with knowledge of a non-conformity cannot be revoked because of it unless the acceptance was on the reasonable assumption that the non-conformity would be seasonably cured but acceptance does not of itself impair any other remedy provided by this Article for non-conformity.

(3) Where a tender has been accepted

  (a) the buyer must within a reasonable time after he discovers or should have discovered any breach notify the seller of breach or be barred from any remedy; and

  (b) if the claim is one for infringement or the like (subsection (3) of Section 2—312) and the buyer is sued as a result of such a breach he must so notify the seller within a reasonable time after he receives notice of the litigation or be barred from any remedy over for liability established by the litigation.

(4) The burden is on the buyer to establish any breach with respect to the goods accepted.

(5) Where the buyer is sued for breach of a warranty or other obligation for which his seller is answerable over

  (a) he may give his seller written notice of the litigation. If the notice states that the seller may come in and defend and that if the seller does not do so he will be bound in any action against him by his buyer by any determination of fact common to the two litigations, then unless the seller after seasonable receipt of the notice does come in and defend he is so bound.

  (b) if the claim is one for infringement or the like (subsection (3) of Section 2—312) the original seller may demand in writing that his buyer turn over to him control of the litigation including settlement or else be barred from any remedy over and if he also agrees to bear all expense and to satisfy any adverse judgment, then unless the buyer after seasonable receipt of the demand does turn over control the buyer is so barred.

(6) The provisions of subsections (3), (4) and (5) apply to any obligation of a buyer to hold the seller harmless against infringement or the like (subsection (3) of Section 2—312).

§2—608. REVOCATION OF ACCEPTANCE IN WHOLE OR IN PART

(1) The buyer may revoke his acceptance of a lot or commercial unit whose non-conformity substantially impairs its value to him if he has accepted it

(a) on the reasonable assumption that its non-conformity would be cured and it has not been seasonably cured; or

(b) without discovery of such non-conformity if his acceptance was reasonably induced either by the difficulty of discovery before acceptance or by the seller's assurances.

(2) Revocation of acceptance must occur within a reasonable time after the buyer discovers or should have discovered the ground for it and before any substantial change in condition of the goods which is not caused by their own defects. It is not effective until the buyer notifies the seller of it.

(3) A buyer who so revokes has the same rights and duties with regard to the goods involved as if he had rejected them.

§2—609. RIGHT TO ADEQUATE ASSURANCE OF PERFORMANCE

(1) A contract for sale imposes an obligation on each party that the other's expectation of receiving due performance will not be impaired. When reasonable grounds for insecurity arise with respect to the performance of either party the other may in writing demand adequate assurance of due performance and until he receives such assurance may if commercially reasonable suspend any performance for which he has not already received the agreed return.

(2) Between merchants the reasonableness of grounds for insecurity and the adequacy of any assurance offered shall be determined according to commercial standards.

(3) Acceptance of any improper delivery or payment does not prejudice the party's right to demand adequate assurance of future performance.

(4) After receipt of a justified demand failure to provide within a reasonable time not exceeding thirty days such assurance of due performance as is adequate under the

circumstances of the particular case is a repudiation of the contract.

§2—610. ANTICIPATORY REPUDIATION

When either party repudiates the contract with respect to a performance not yet due the loss of which will substantially impair the value of the contract to the other, the aggrieved party may

(a) for a commercially reasonable time await performance by the repudiating party; or

(b) resort to any remedy for breach (Section 2—703 or Section 2—711), even though he has notified the repudiating party that he would await the latter's performance and has urged retraction; and

(c) in either case suspend his own performance or proceed in accordance with the provisions of this Article on the seller's right to identify goods to the contract notwithstanding breach or to salvage unfinished goods (Section 2—704).

§2—611. RETRACTION OF ANTICIPATORY REPUDIATION

(1) Until the repudiating party's next performance is due he can retract his repudiation unless the aggrieved party has since the repudiation cancelled or materially changed his position or otherwise indicated that he considers the repudiation final.

(2) Retraction may be by any method which clearly indicates to the aggrieved party that the repudiating party intends to perform, but must include any assurance justifiably demanded under the provisions of this Article (Section 2—609).

(3) Retraction reinstates the repudiating party's rights under the contract with due excuse and allowance to the aggrieved party for any delay occasioned by the repudiation.

§2—612. "INSTALLMENT CONTRACT"; BREACH

(1) An "installment contract" is one which requires or authorizes the delivery of goods in separate lots to be separately accepted, even though the contract contains a clause "each delivery is a separate contract" or its equivalent.

(2) The buyer may reject any installment which is non-conforming if the non-conformity substantially impairs the value of that installment and cannot be cured or if the non-conformity is a defect in the required documents; but if the non-conformity does not fall within subsection (3) and the seller gives adequate assurance of its cure the buyer must accept that installment.

(3) Whenever non-conformity or default with respect to one or more installments substantially impairs the value of the whole contract there is a breach of the whole. But the aggrieved party reinstates the contract if he accepts a non-conforming installment without seasonably notifying of cancellation or if he brings an action with respect only to past installments or demands performance as to future installments.

§2—613. CASUALTY TO IDENTIFIED GOODS

Where the contract requires for its performance goods identified when the contract is made, and the goods suffer casualty without fault of either party before the risk of loss passes to the buyer, or in a proper case under a "no arrival, no sale" term (Section 2—324) then

    (a) if the loss is total the contract is avoided; and

    (b) if the loss is partial or the goods have so deteriorated as no longer to conform to the contract the buyer may nevertheless demand inspection and at his option either treat the contract as voided or accept the goods with due allowance from the contract price for the deterioration or the deficiency in quantity but without further right against the seller.

§2—614. SUBSTITUTED PERFORMANCE

(1) Where without fault of either party the agreed berthing, loading, or unloading facilities fail or an agreed type of carrier becomes unavailable or the agreed manner of delivery otherwise becomes commercially impracticable but a commercially reasonable substitute is available, such substitute performance must be tendered and accepted.

(2) If the agreed means or manner of payment fails because of domestic or foreign governmental regulation, the seller may withhold or stop delivery unless the buyer provides a means or manner of payment which is commercially a substantial equivalent. If delivery has already been taken, payment by the means or in the manner provided by the regulation discharges the buyer's obligation unless the regulation is discriminatory, oppressive or predatory.

§2—615. EXCUSE BY FAILURE OF PRESUPPOSED CONDITIONS

Except so far as a seller may have assumed a greater obligation and subject to the preceding section on substituted performance:

    (a) Delay in delivery or non-delivery in whole or in part by a seller who complies with paragraphs (b) and (c) is not a breach of his duty under a contract for sale if performance as agreed has been made impracticable by the occurrence of a contingency the nonoccurrence of which was a basic assumption on which the contract was made or by compliance in good faith with any applicable foreign or domestic governmental regulation or order whether or not it later proves to be invalid.

    (b) Where the causes mentioned in paragraph (a) affect only a part of the seller's capacity to perform, he must allocate production and deliveries among his customers but may at his option include regular customers not then under contract as well as his own requirements for further manufacture. He may so allocate in any manner which is fair and reasonable.

    (c) The seller must notify the buyer seasonably that there will be delay or non-delivery and, when allocation is required under paragraph (b), of the estimated quota thus made available for the buyer.

* * * *

§2—702. SELLER'S REMEDIES ON DISCOVERY OF BUYER'S INSOLVENCY

(1) Where the seller discovers the buyer to be insolvent he may refuse delivery except for cash including payment for all goods theretofore delivered under the contract, and stop delivery under this Article (Section 2—705).

(2) Where the seller discovers that the buyer has received goods on credit while insolvent he may reclaim the goods upon demand made within ten days after the receipt, but if misrepresentation of solvency has been made to the particular seller in writing within three months before delivery the ten day limitation does not apply. Except as provided in this subsection the seller may not base a right to reclaim goods on the buyer's fraudulent or innocent misrepresentation of solvency or of intent to pay.

(3) The seller's right to reclaim under subsection (2) is subject to the rights of a buyer in ordinary course or other good faith purchaser under this Article (Section 2—403). Successful reclamation of goods excludes all other remedies with respect to them.

§2—703. SELLER'S REMEDIES IN GENERAL

Where the buyer wrongfully rejects or revokes acceptance of goods or fails to make a payment due on or before delivery or repudiates with respect to a part or the whole, then with respect to any goods directly affected and, if the breach is of the whole contract

(Section 2—612), then also with respect to the whole undelivered balance, the aggrieved seller may

(a) withhold delivery of such goods;

(b) stop delivery by any bailee as hereafter provided (Section 2—705);

(c) proceed under the next section respecting goods still unidentified to the contract;

(d) resell and recover damages as hereafter provided (Section 2—706);

(e) recover damages for non-acceptance (Section 2—708) or in a proper case the price (Section 2—709);

(f) cancel.

§2—704. SELLER'S RIGHT TO IDENTIFY GOODS TO THE CONTRACT NOTWITHSTANDING BREACH OR TO SALVAGE UNFINISHED GOODS

(1) An aggrieved seller under the preceding section may

(a) identify to the contract conforming goods not already identified if at the time he learned of the breach they are in his possession or control;

(b) treat as the subject of resale goods which have demonstrably been intended for the particular contract even though those goods are unfinished.

(2) Where the goods are unfinished an aggrieved seller may in the exercise of reasonable commercial judgment for the purposes of avoiding loss and of effective realization either complete the manufacture and wholly identify the goods to the contract or cease manufacture and resell for scrap or salvage value or proceed in any other reasonable manner.

§2—705. SELLER'S STOPPAGE OF DELIVERY IN TRANSIT OR OTHERWISE

(1) The seller may stop delivery of goods in the possession of a carrier or other bailee when he discovers the buyer to be insolvent (Section 2—702) and may stop delivery of carload, truckload, planeload or larger shipments of express or freight when the buyer repudiates or fails to make a payment due before delivery or if for any other reason the seller has a right to withhold or reclaim the goods.

(2) As against such buyer the seller may stop delivery until

(a) receipt of the goods by the buyer; or

(b) acknowledgment to the buyer by any bailee of the goods except a carrier that the bailee holds the goods for the buyer; or

(c) such acknowledgment to the buyer by a carrier by reshipment or as warehouseman; or

(d) negotiation to the buyer of any negotiable document of title covering the goods.

(3) ****

(a) To stop delivery the seller must so notify as to enable the bailee by reasonable diligence to prevent delivery of the goods.

(b) After such notification the bailee must hold and deliver the goods according to the directions of the seller but the seller is liable to the bailee for any ensuing charges or damages.

(c) If a negotiable document of title has been issued for goods the bailee is not obliged to obey a notification to stop until surrender of the document.

(d) A carrier who has issued a non-negotiable bill of lading is not obliged to obey a notification to stop received from a person other than the consignor.

§2—706. SELLER'S RESALE INCLUDING CONTRACT FOR RESALE

(1) Under the conditions stated in Section 2—703 on seller's remedies, the seller may resell the goods concerned or the undelivered balance thereof. Where the resale is made in good faith and in a commercially reasonable manner the seller may recover the difference between the resale price and the contract price together with any incidental damages allowed under the provisions of this Article (Section 2—710), but less expenses saved in consequence of the buyer's breach.

(2) Except as otherwise provided in subsection (3) or unless otherwise agreed resale may be at public or private sale including sale by way of one or more contracts to sell or of identification to an existing contract of the seller. Sale may be as a unit or in parcels and at any time and place and on any terms but every aspect of the sale including the method, manner, time, place and terms must be commercially reasonable. The resale must be reasonably identified as referring to the broken contract, but it is not necessary that the goods be in existence or that any or all of them have been identified to the contract before the breach.

(3) Where the resale is at private sale the seller must give the buyer reasonable notification of his intention to resell.

(4) Where the resale is at public sale

(a) only identified goods can be sold except where there is a recognized market for a public sale of futures in goods of the kind; and

(b) it must be made at a usual place or market for public sale if one is reasonably available and except in the case of goods which are perishable or threaten to decline in value speedily the seller must give the buyer reasonable notice of the time and place of the resale; and

(c) if the goods are not to be within the view of those attending the sale the notification of sale must state the place where the goods are located and provide for their reasonable inspection by prospective bidders; and

(d) the seller may buy.

(5) A purchaser who buys in good faith at a resale takes the goods free of any rights of the original buyer even though the seller fails to comply with one or more of the requirements of this section.

(6) The seller is not accountable to the buyer for any profit made on any resale. A person in the position of a seller (Section 2—707) or a buyer who has rightfully rejected or justifiably revoked acceptance must account for any excess over the amount of his security interest, as hereinafter defined (subsection (3) of Section 2—711).

* * * *

§2—708. SELLER'S DAMAGES FOR NON-ACCEPTANCE OR REPUDIATION

(1) Subject to subsection (2) and to the provisions of this Article with respect to proof of market price (Section 2—723), the measure of damages for non-acceptance or repudiation by the buyer is the difference between the market price at the time and place for tender and the unpaid contract price together with any incidental damages provided in this Article (Section 2—710), but less expenses saved in consequence of the buyer's breach.

(2) If the measure of damages provided in subsection (1) is inadequate to put the seller in as good a position as performance would have done then the measure of damages is the profit (including reasonable overhead) which the seller would have made from full performance by the buyer, together with any incidental damages provided in this Article (Section 2—710), due allowance for costs reasonably incurred and due credit for payments or proceeds of resale.

§2—709. ACTION FOR THE PRICE

(1) When the buyer fails to pay the price as it becomes due the seller may recover, together with any incidental damages under the next section, the price

(a) of goods accepted or of conforming goods lost or damaged within a commercially reasonable time after risk of their loss has passed to the buyer; and

(b) of goods identified to the contract if the seller is unable after reasonable effort to resell them at a reasonable price or the circumstances reasonably indicate that such effort will be unavailing.

(2) Where the seller sues for the price he must hold for the buyer any goods which have been identified to the contract and are still in his control except that if resale becomes possible he may resell them at any time prior to the collection of the judgment. The net proceeds of any such resale must be credited to the buyer and payment of the judgment entitles him to any goods not resold.

(3) After the buyer has wrongfully rejected or revoked acceptance of the goods or has failed to make a payment due or has repudiated (Section 2—610), a seller who is held not entitled to the price under this section shall nevertheless be awarded damages for non-acceptance under the preceding section.

§2—710. SELLER'S INCIDENTAL DAMAGES

Incidental damages to an aggrieved seller include any commercially reasonable charges, expenses or commissions incurred in stopping delivery, in the transportation, care and custody of goods after the buyer's breach, in connection with return or resale of the goods or otherwise resulting from the breach.

§2—711. BUYER'S REMEDIES IN GENERAL; BUYER'S SECURITY INTEREST IN REJECTED GOODS

(1) Where the seller fails to make delivery or repudiates or the buyer rightfully rejects or justifiably revokes acceptance then with respect to any goods involved, and with respect to the whole if the breach goes to the whole contract (Section 2—612), the buyer may cancel and whether or not he has done so may in addition to recovering so much of the price as has been paid

(a) "cover" and have damages under the next section as to all the goods affected whether or not they have been identified to the contract; or

(b) recover damages for non-delivery as provided in this Article (Section 2—713).

(2) Where the seller fails to deliver or repudiates the buyer may also

(a) if the goods have been identified recover them as provided in this Article (Section 2—502); or

(b) in a proper case obtain specific performance or replevy the goods as provided in this Article (Section 2—716).

(3) On rightful rejection or justifiable revocation of acceptance a buyer has a security interest in goods in his possession or control for any payments made on their price and any expenses reasonably incurred in their inspection, receipt, transportation, care and custody and may hold such goods and resell them in like manner as an aggrieved seller (Section 2—706).

§2—712. "COVER"; BUYER'S PROCUREMENT OF SUBSTITUTE GOODS

(1) After a breach within the preceding section the buyer may "cover" by making in good faith and without unreasonable delay any reasonable purchase of or contract to purchase goods in substitution for those due from the seller.

(2) The buyer may recover from the seller as damages the difference between the cost of cover and the contract price together with any incidental or consequential damages as hereinafter defined (Section 2—715), but less expenses saved in consequence of the seller's breach.

(3) Failure of the buyer to effect cover within this section does not bar him from any other remedy.

§2—713. BUYER'S DAMAGES FOR NON-DELIVERY OR REPUDIATION

(1) Subject to the provisions of this Article with respect to proof of market price (Section 2—723), the measure of damages for non-delivery or repudiation by the seller is the difference between the market price at the time when the buyer learned of the breach and the contract price together with any incidental and consequential damages provided in this Article (Section 2—715), but less expenses saved in consequence of the seller's breach.

(2) Market price is to be determined as of the place for tender or, in cases of rejection after arrival or revocation of acceptance, as of the place of arrival.

§2—714. BUYER'S DAMAGES FOR BREACH IN REGARD TO ACCEPTED GOODS

(1) Where the buyer has accepted goods and given notification (subsection (3) of Section 2—607) he may recover as damages for any non-conformity of tender the loss resulting in the ordinary course of events from the seller's breach as determined in any manner which is reasonable.

(2) The measure of damages for breach of warranty is the difference at the time and place of acceptance between the value of the goods accepted and the value they would have had if they had been as warranted, unless special circumstances show proximate damages of a different amount.

(3) In a proper case any incidental and consequential damages under the next section may also be recovered.

§2—715. BUYER'S INCIDENTAL AND CONSEQUENTIAL DAMAGES

(1) Incidental damages resulting from the seller's breach include expenses reasonably incurred in inspection, receipt, transportation and care and custody of goods rightfully rejected, any commercially reasonable charges, expenses or commissions in connection with effecting cover and any other reasonable expense incident to the delay or other breach.

(2) Consequential damages resulting from the seller's breach include

(a) any loss resulting from general or particular requirements and needs of which the seller at the time of contracting had reason to know and which could not reasonably be prevented by cover or otherwise; and

(b) injury to person or property proximately resulting from any breach of warranty.

§2—716. BUYER'S RIGHT TO SPECIFIC PERFORMANCE OR REPLEVIN

(1) Specific performance may be decreed where the goods are unique or in other proper circumstances.

(2) The decree for specific performance may include such terms and conditions as to payment of the price, damages, or other relief as the court may deem just.

(3) The buyer has a right of replevin for goods identified to the contract if after reasonable effort he is unable to effect cover for such goods or the circumstances reasonably indicate that such effort will be unavailing or if the goods have been shipped under reservation and satisfaction of the security interest in them has been made or tendered. In the case of goods bought for personal, family, or household purposes, the buyer's right of replevin vests upon acquisition of a special property, even if the seller had not then repudiated or failed to deliver.

§2—717. DEDUCTION OF DAMAGES FROM THE PRICE

The buyer on notifying the seller of his intention to do so may deduct all or any part of the damages resulting from any breach of the contract from any part of the price still due under the same contract.

§2—718. LIQUIDATION OR LIMITATION OF DAMAGES; DEPOSITS

(1) Damages for breach by either party may be liquidated in the agreement but only at an amount which is reasonable in the light of the anticipated or actual harm caused by the breach, the difficulties of proof of loss, and the inconvenience or nonfeasibility of otherwise obtaining an adequate remedy. A term fixing unreasonably large liquidated damages is void as a penalty.

(2) Where the seller justifiably withholds delivery of goods because of the buyer's breach, the buyer is entitled to restitution of any amount by which the sum of his payments exceeds

(a) the amount to which the seller is entitled by virtue of terms liquidating the seller's damages in accordance with subsection (1), or

(b) in the absence of such terms, twenty per cent of the value of the total performance for which the buyer is obligated under the contract or $500, whichever is smaller.

(3) The buyer's right to restitution under subsection (2) is subject to offset to the extent that the seller establishes

(a) a right to recover damages under the provisions of this Article other than subsection (1), and

(b) the amount or value of any benefits received by the buyer directly or indirectly by reason of the contract.

(4) Where a seller has received payment in goods their reasonable value or the proceeds of their resale shall be treated as payments for the purposes of subsection (2); but if the seller has notice of the buyer's breach before reselling goods received in part performance, his resale is subject to the conditions laid down in this Article on resale by an aggrieved seller (Section 2—706).

§2—719. CONTRACTUAL MODIFICATION OR LIMITATION OF REMEDY

(1) Subject to the provisions of subsections (2) and (3) of this section and of the preceding section on liquidation and limitation of damages,

(a) the agreement may provide for remedies in addition to or in substitution for those provided in this Article and may limit or alter the measure of damages recoverable under this Article, as by limiting the buyer's remedies to return of the goods and repayment of the price or to repair and replacement of non-conforming goods or parts; and

(b) resort to a remedy as provided is optional unless the remedy is expressly agreed to be exclusive, in which case it is the sole remedy.

(2) Where circumstances cause an exclusive or limited remedy to fail of its essential purpose, remedy may be had as provided in this Act.

(3) Consequential damages may be limited or excluded unless the limitation or exclusion is unconscionable. Limitation of consequential damages for injury to the person in the case of consumer goods is prima facie unconscionable but limitation of damages where the loss is commercial is not.

§2—720. EFFECT OF "CANCELLATION" OR "RESCISSION" ON CLAIMS FOR ANTECEDENT BREACH

Unless the contrary intention clearly appears, expressions of "cancellation" or "rescission" of the contract or the like shall not be construed as a renunciation or discharge of any claim in damages for an antecedent breach.

§2—721. REMEDIES FOR FRAUD

Remedies for material misrepresentation or fraud include all remedies available under this Article for non-fraudulent breach. Neither rescission or a claim for rescission of the contract for sale nor rejection or return of the goods shall bar or be deemed inconsistent with a claim for damages or other remedy.

§2—722. WHO CAN SUE THIRD PARTIES FOR INJURY TO GOODS

Where a third party so deals with goods which have been identified to a contract for sale as to cause actionable injury to a party to that contract

(a) a right of action against the third party is in either party to the contract for sale who has title to or a security interest or a special property or an insurable interest in the goods; and if the goods have been destroyed or converted a right of action is also in the party who either bore the risk of loss under the contract for sale or has since the injury assumed that risk as against the other;

(b) if at the time of the injury the party plaintiff did not bear the risk of loss as against the other party to the contract for sale and there is no arrangement between them for disposition of the recovery, his suit or settlement is, subject to his own interest, as a fiduciary for the other party to the contract;

(c) either party may with the consent of the other sue for the benefit of whom it may concern.

§2—723. PROOF OF MARKET PRICE: TIME AND PLACE

(1) If an action based on anticipatory repudiation comes to trial before the time for performance with respect to some or all of the goods, any damages based on market price (Section 2—708 or Section 2—713) shall be determined according to the price of such goods prevailing at the time when the aggrieved party learned of the repudiation.

(2) If evidence of a price prevailing at the times or places described in this Article is not readily available the price prevailing within any reasonable time before or after the time described or at any other place which in commercial judgment or under usage of trade would serve as a reasonable substitute for the one described may be used, making any proper allowance for the cost of transporting the goods to or from such other place.

(3) Evidence of a relevant price prevailing at a time or place other than the one described in this Article offered by one party is not admissible unless and until he has given the other party such notice as the court finds sufficient to prevent unfair surprise.

§2—724. ADMISSIBILITY OF MARKET QUOTATIONS

Whenever the prevailing price or value of any goods regularly bought and sold in any established commodity market is in issue, reports in official publications or trade journals or in newspapers or periodicals of general circulation published as the reports of such market shall be admissible in evidence. The circumstances of the preparation of such a report may be shown to affect its weight but not its admissibility.

§2—725. STATUTE OF LIMITATIONS IN CONTRACTS FOR SALE

(1) An action for breach of any contract for sale must be commenced within four years after the cause of action has accrued. By the original agreement the parties may reduce the period of limitation to not less than one year but may not extend it.

(2) A cause of action accrues when the breach occurs, regardless of the aggrieved party's lack of knowledge of the breach. A breach of warranty occurs when tender of delivery is made, except that where a warranty explicitly extends to future performance of the goods and discovery of the breach must await the time of such performance the cause of action accrues when the breach is or should have been discovered.

(3) Where an action commenced within the time limited by subsection (1) is so terminated as to leave available a remedy by another action for the same breach such other action may be commenced after the expiration of the time limited and within six months after the termination of the first action unless the termination resulted from voluntary discontinuance or from dismissal for failure or neglect to prosecute.

(4) This section does not alter the law on tolling of the statute of limitations nor does it apply to causes of action which have accrued before this Act becomes effective.

Article 2 Amendments (Excerpts)

Part 1 Short Title, General Construction and Subject Matter

* * * *

§2—103. DEFINITIONS AND INDEX OF DEFINITIONS

(1) In this article unless the context otherwise requires

* * * *

(b) "Conspicuous", with reference to a term, means so written, displayed, or presented that a reasonable person against which it is to operate ought to have noticed it. A term in an electronic record intended to evoke a response by an electronic agent is conspicuous if it is presented in a form that would enable a reasonably configured electronic agent to take it into account or react to it without review of the record by an individual. Whether a term is "conspicuous" or not is a decision for the court. Conspicuous terms include the following:

  (i) for a person:

    (A) a heading in capitals equal to or greater in size than the surrounding text, or in contrasting type, font, or color to the surrounding text of the same or lesser size;

    (B) language in the body of a record or display in larger type than the surrounding text, or in contrasting type, font, or color to the surrounding text of the same size, or set off from surrounding text of the same size by symbols or other marks that call attention to the language; and

  (ii) for a person or an electronic agent, a term that is so placed in a record or display that the person or electronic agent cannot proceed without taking action with respect to the particular term.

(c) "Consumer" means an individual who buys or contracts to buy goods that, at the time of contracting, are intended by the individual to be used primarily for personal, family, or household purposes.

(d) "Consumer contract" means a contract between a merchant seller and a consumer.

* * * *

(j) "Good faith" means honesty in fact and the observance of reasonable commercial standards of fair dealing.

(k) "Goods" means all things that are movable at the time of identification to a contract for sale. The term includes future goods, specially manufactured goods, the unborn young of animals, growing crops, and other identified things attached to realty as described in Section 2—107. The term does not include information, the money in which the price is to be paid, investment securities under Article 8, the subject matter of foreign exchange transactions, and choses in action.

* * * *

(m) "Record" means information that is inscribed on a tangible medium or that is stored in an electronic or other medium and is retrievable in perceivable form.

(n) "Remedial promise" means a promise by the seller to repair or replace the goods or to refund all or part of the price upon the happening of a specified event.

* * * *

(p) "Sign" means, with present intent to authenticate or adopt a record,

(i) to execute or adopt a tangible symbol; or

(ii) to attach to or logically associate with the record an electronic sound, symbol, or process.

* * * *

Part 2 Form, Formation, Terms and Readjustment of Contract; Electronic Contracting

§2—201. FORMAL REQUIREMENTS; STATUTE OF FRAUDS

(1) A contract for the sale of goods for the price of $5,000 or more is not enforceable by way of action or defense unless there is some record sufficient to indicate that a contract for sale has been made between the parties and signed by the party against whom which enforcement is sought or by the party's authorized agent or broker. A record is not insufficient because it omits or incorrectly states a term agreed upon but the contract is not enforceable under this subsection beyond the quantity of goods shown in the record.

(2) Between merchants if within a reasonable time a record in confirmation of the contract and sufficient against the sender is received and the party receiving it has reason to know its contents, it satisfies the requirements of subsection (1) against such party the recipient unless notice of objection to its contents is given in a record within 10 days after it is received.

(3) A contract which does not satisfy the requirements of subsection (1) but which is valid in other respects is enforceable

(a) if the goods are to be specially manufactured for the buyer and are not suitable for sale to others in the ordinary course of the seller's business and the seller, before notice of repudiation is received and under circumstances which reasonably indicate that the goods are for the buyer, has made either a substantial beginning of their manufacture or commitments for their procurement; or

(b) if the party against whom which enforcement is sought admits in the party's pleading, or in the party's testimony or otherwise under oath that a contract for sale was made, but the contract is not enforceable under this paragraph beyond the quantity of goods admitted; or

(c) with respect to goods for which payment has been made and accepted or which have been received and accepted (Sec. 2—606).

(4) A contract that is enforceable under this section is not rendered unenforceable merely because it is not capable of being performed within one year or any other applicable period after its making.

* * * *

§2—207. TERMS OF CONTRACT; EFFECT OF CONFIRMATION

If (i) conduct by both parties recognizes the existence of a contract although their records do not otherwise establish a contract, (ii) a contract is formed by an offer and acceptance, or (iii) a contract formed in any manner is confirmed by a record that contains terms additional to or different from those in the contract being confirmed, the terms of the contract, subject to Section 2—202, are:

(a) terms that appear in the records of both parties;

(b) terms, whether in a record or not, to which both parties agree; and

(c) terms supplied or incorporated under any provision of this Act.

* * * *

Part 3 General Obligation and Construction of Contract
* * * *

§2—312. WARRANTY OF TITLE AND AGAINST INFRINGEMENT; BUYER'S OBLIGATION AGAINST INFRINGEMENT

(1) Subject to subsection (2) there is in a contract for sale a warranty by the seller that

(a) the title conveyed shall be good, good and its transfer rightful and shall not, because of any colorable claim to or interest in the goods, unreasonably expose the buyer to litigation; and

(b) the goods shall be delivered free from any security interest or other lien or encumbrance of which the buyer at the time of contracting has no knowledge.

(2) Unless otherwise agreed a seller that is a merchant regularly dealing in goods of the kind warrants that the goods shall be delivered free of the rightful claim of any third person by way of infringement or the like but a buyer that furnishes specifications to the seller must hold the seller harmless against any such claim that arises out of compliance with the specifications.

(3) A warranty under this section may be disclaimed or modified only by specific language or by circumstances that give the buyer reason to know that the seller does not claim title, that the seller is purporting to sell only the right or title as the seller or a third person may have, or that the seller is selling subject to any claims of infringement or the like.

§2—313. EXPRESS WARRANTIES BY AFFIRMATION, PROMISE, DESCRIPTION, SAMPLE; REMEDIAL PROMISE

(1) In this section, "immediate buyer" means a buyer that enters into a contract with the seller.

* * * *

(4) Any remedial promise made by the seller to the immediate buyer creates an obligation that the promise will be performed upon the happening of the specified event.

§2—313A. OBLIGATION TO REMOTE PURCHASER CREATED BY RECORD PACKAGED WITH OR ACCOMPANYING GOODS

(1) This section applies only to new goods and goods sold or leased as new goods in a transaction of purchase in the normal chain of distribution. In this section:

(a) "Immediate buyer" means a buyer that enters into a contract with the seller.

(b) "Remote purchaser" means a person that buys or leases goods from an immediate buyer or other person in the normal chain of distribution.

(2) If a seller in a record packaged with or accompanying the goods makes an affirmation of fact or promise that relates to the goods, provides a description that relates to the goods, or makes a remedial promise, and the seller reasonably expects the record to be, and the record is, furnished to the remote purchaser, the seller has an obligation to the remote purchaser that:

(a) the goods will conform to the affirmation of fact, promise or description unless a reasonable person in the position of the remote purchaser would not believe that the affirmation of fact, promise or description created an obligation; and

(b) the seller will perform the remedial promise.

(3) It is not necessary to the creation of an obligation under this section that the seller use formal words such as "warrant" or "guarantee" or that the seller have a specific intention to undertake an obligation, but an affirmation merely of the value of the goods or a statement purporting to be merely the seller's opinion or commendation of the goods does not create an obligation.

(4) The following rules apply to the remedies for breach of an obligation created under this section:

(a) The seller may modify or limit the remedies available to the remote purchaser if the modification or limitation is furnished to the remote purchaser no later than the time of purchase or if the modification or limitation is contained in the record that contains the affirmation of fact, promise or description.

(b) Subject to a modification or limitation of remedy, a seller in breach is liable for incidental or consequential damages under Section 2—715, but the seller is not liable for lost profits.

(c) The remote purchaser may recover as damages for breach of a seller's obligation arising under subsection (2) the loss resulting in the ordinary course of events as determined in any manner that is reasonable.

(5) An obligation that is not a remedial promise is breached if the goods did not conform to the affirmation of fact, promise or description creating the obligation when the goods left the seller's control.

§2—313B. OBLIGATION TO REMOTE PURCHASER CREATED BY COMMUNICATION TO THE PUBLIC

(1) This section applies only to new goods and goods sold or leased as new goods in a transaction of purchase in the normal chain of distribution. In this section:

(a) "Immediate buyer" means a buyer that enters into a contract with the seller.

(b) "Remote purchaser" means a person that buys or leases goods from an immediate buyer or other person in the normal chain of distribution.

(2) If a seller in advertising or a similar communication to the public makes an affirmation of fact or promise that relates to the goods, provides a description that relates to the goods, or makes a remedial promise, and the remote purchaser enters into a transaction of purchase with knowledge of and with the expectation that the goods will conform to the affirmation of fact, promise, or description, or that the seller will perform the remedial promise, the seller has an obligation to the remote purchaser that:

(a) the goods will conform to the affirmation of fact, promise or description unless a reasonable person in the position of the remote purchaser would not believe that the affirmation of fact, promise or description created an obligation; and

(b) the seller will perform the remedial promise.

(3) It is not necessary to the creation of an obligation under this section that the seller use formal words such as "warrant" or "guarantee" or that the seller have a specific intention to undertake an obligation, but an affirmation merely of the value of the goods or a statement purporting to be merely the seller's opinion or commendation of the goods does not create an obligation.

(4) The following rules apply to the remedies for breach of an obligation created under this section:

(a) The seller may modify or limit the remedies available to the remote purchaser if the modification or limitation is furnished to the remote purchaser no later than the time of purchase. The modification or limitation may be furnished as part of the communication that contains the affirmation of fact, promise or description.

(b) Subject to a modification or limitation of remedy, a seller in breach is liable for incidental or consequential damages under Section 2—715, but the seller is not liable for lost profits.

(c) The remote purchaser may recover as damages for breach of a seller's obligation arising under subsection (2) the loss resulting in the ordinary course of events as determined in any manner that is reasonable.

(5) An obligation that is not a remedial promise is breached if the goods did not conform to the affirmation of

fact, promise or description creating the obligation when the goods left the seller's control.

* * * *

§2—316. EXCLUSION OR MODIFICATION OF WARRANTIES.

* * * *

(2) Subject to subsection (3), to exclude or modify the implied warranty of merchantability or any part of it in a consumer contract the language must be in a record, be conspicuous and state "The seller undertakes no responsibility for the quality of the goods except as otherwise provided in this contract," and in any other contract the language must mention merchantability and in case of a record must be conspicuous. Subject to subsection (3), to exclude or modify the implied warranty of fitness the exclusion must be in a record and be conspicuous. Language to exclude all implied warranties of fitness in a consumer contract must state "The seller assumes no responsibility that the goods will be fit for any particular purpose for which you may be buying these goods, except as otherwise provided in the contract," and in any other contract the language is sufficient if it states, for example, that "There are no warranties which extend beyond the description on the face hereof." Language that satisfies the requirements of this subsection for the exclusion and modification of a warranty in a consumer contract also satisfies the requirements for any other contract.

(3) Notwithstanding subsection (2):

(a) unless the circumstances indicate otherwise, all implied warranties are excluded by expressions like "as is", "with all faults" or other language which in common understanding calls the buyer's attention to the exclusion of warranties, makes plain that there is no implied warranty, and in a consumer contract evidenced by a record is set forth conspicuously in the record; and

(b) when the buyer before entering into the contract has examined the goods or the sample or model as fully as desired or has refused to examine the goods after a demand by the seller there is no implied warranty with regard to defects which an examination ought in the circumstances to have revealed to the buyer; and

(c) an implied warranty can also be excluded or modified by course of dealing or course of performance or usage of trade.

* * * *

§2—318. THIRD PARTY BENEFICIARIES OF WARRANTIES EXPRESS OR IMPLIED

(1) In this section:

   (a) "Immediate buyer" means a buyer that enters into a contract with the seller.

   (b) "Remote purchaser" means a person that buys or leases goods from an immediate buyer or other person in the normal chain of distribution.

Alternative A to subsection (2)

(2) A seller's warranty whether express or implied to an immediate buyer, a seller's remedial promise to an immediate buyer, or a seller's obligation to a remote purchaser under Section 2—313A or 2—313B extends to any natural person who is in the family or household of the immediate buyer or the remote purchaser or who is a guest in the home of either if it is reasonable to expect that the person may use, consume or be affected by the goods and who is injured in person by breach of the warranty, remedial promise or obligation. A seller may not exclude or limit the operation of this section.

Alternative B to subsection (2)

(2) A seller's warranty whether express or implied to an immediate buyer, a seller's remedial promise to an immediate buyer, or a seller's obligation to a remote purchaser under Section 2—313A or 2—313B extends to any natural person who may reasonably be expected to use, consume or be affected by the goods and who is injured in person by breach of the warranty, remedial promise or obligation. A seller may not exclude or limit the operation of this section.

Alternative C to subsection (2)

(2) A seller's warranty whether express or implied to an immediate buyer, a seller's remedial promise to an immediate buyer, or a seller's obligation to a remote purchaser under Section 2—313A or 2—313B extends to any person that may reasonably be expected to use, consume or be affected by the goods and that is injured by breach of the warranty, remedial promise or obligation. A seller may not exclude or limit the operation of this section with respect to injury to the person of an individual to whom the warranty, remedial promise or obligation extends.

* * * *

Part 5 Performance
* * * *

§2—502. BUYER'S RIGHT TO GOODS ON SELLER'S INSOLVENCY

(1) Subject to subsections (2) and (3) and even though the goods have not been shipped a buyer who that has paid a part or all of the price of goods in which the buyer has a special property under the provisions of the immediately preceding section may on making and keeping good a tender of any unpaid portion of their price recover them from the seller if:

   (a) in the case of goods bought by a consumer, the seller repudiates or fails to deliver as required by the contract; or

   (b) in all cases, the seller becomes insolvent within ten days after receipt of the first installment on their price.

(2) The buyer's right to recover the goods under subsection (1) vests upon acquisition of a special property, even if the seller had not then repudiated or failed to deliver.

(3) If the identification creating the special property has been made by the buyer, the buyer acquires the right to recover the goods only if they conform to the contract for sale.

* * * *

§2—508. CURE BY SELLER OF IMPROPER TENDER OR DELIVERY; REPLACEMENT

(1) Where the buyer rejects goods or a tender of delivery under Section 2—601 or 2—612 or except in a consumer contract justifiably revokes acceptance under Section 2—608(1)(b) and the agreed time for performance has not expired, a seller that has performed in good faith, upon seasonable notice to the buyer and at the seller's own expense, may cure the breach of contract by making a conforming tender of delivery within the agreed time. The seller shall compensate the buyer for all of the buyer's reasonable expenses caused by the seller's breach of contract and subsequent cure.

(2) Where the buyer rejects goods or a tender of delivery under Section 2—601 or 2—612 or except in a consumer contract justifiably revokes acceptance under Section 2—608(1)(b) and the agreed time for performance has expired, a seller that has performed in good faith, upon seasonable notice to the buyer and at the seller's own expense, may cure the breach of contract, if the cure is appropriate and timely under the

circumstances, by making a tender of conforming goods. The seller shall compensate the buyer for all of the buyer's reasonable expenses caused by the seller's breach of contract and subsequent cure.

§2—509. RISK OF LOSS IN THE ABSENCE OF BREACH

(1) Where the contract requires or authorizes the seller to ship the goods by carrier

(a) if it does not require the seller to deliver them at a particular destination, the risk of loss passes to the buyer when the goods are delivered to the carrier even though the shipment is under reservation (Section 2—505); but

(b) if it does require the seller to deliver them at a particular destination and the goods are there tendered while in the possession of the carrier, the risk of loss passes to the buyer when the goods are there so tendered as to enable the buyer to take delivery.

(2) Where the goods are held by a bailee to be delivered without being moved, the risk of loss passes to the buyer

(a) on the buyer's receipt of a negotiable document of title covering the goods; or

(b) on acknowledgment by the bailee to the buyer of the buyer's right to possession of the goods; or

(c) after the buyer's receipt of a non-negotiable document of title or other direction to deliver in a record, as provided in subsection (4)(b) of Section 2—503.

(3) In any case not within subsection (1) or (2), the risk of loss passes to the buyer on the buyer's receipt of the goods.

* * * *

§2—513. BUYER'S RIGHT TO INSPECTION OF GOODS
* * * *

(3) Unless otherwise agreed, the buyer is not entitled to inspect the goods before payment of the price when the contract provides

(a) for delivery on terms that under applicable course of performance, course of dealing, or usage of trade are interpreted to preclude inspection before payment; or

(b) for payment against documents of title, except where such payment is due only after the goods are to become available for inspection.

* * * *

Part 6 Breach, Repudiation and Excuse
* * * *

§2—605. WAIVER OF BUYER'S OBJECTIONS BY FAILURE TO PARTICULARIZE

(1) The buyer's failure to state in connection with rejection a particular defect or in connection with revocation of acceptance a defect that justifies revocation precludes the buyer from relying on the unstated defect to justify rejection or revocation of acceptance if the defect is ascertainable by reasonable inspection

(a) where the seller had a right to cure the defect and could have cured it if stated seasonably; or

(b) between merchants when the seller has after rejection made a request in a record for a full and final statement in record form of all defects on which the buyer proposes to rely.

(2) A buyer's payment against documents tendered to the buyer made without reservation of rights precludes recovery of the payment for defects apparent on the face of the documents.

* * * *

§2—607. EFFECT OF ACCEPTANCE; NOTICE OF BREACH; BURDEN OF ESTABLISHING BREACH AFTER ACCEPTANCE; NOTICE OF CLAIM OR LITIGATION TO PERSON ANSWERABLE OVER
* * * *

(3) Where a tender has been accepted

(a) the buyer must within a reasonable time after the buyer discovers or should have discovered any breach notify the seller; however, failure to give timely notice bars the buyer from a remedy only to the extent that the seller is prejudiced by the failure and

(b) if the claim is one for infringement or the like (subsection (3) of Section 2—312) and the buyer is sued as a result of such a breach the buyer must so notify the seller within a reasonable time after the buyer receives notice of the litigation or be barred from any remedy over for liability established by the litigation.

* * * *

§2—608. REVOCATION OF ACCEPTANCE IN WHOLE OR IN PART
* * * *

(4) If a buyer uses the goods after a rightful rejection or justifiable revocation of acceptance, the following rules apply:

(a) Any use by the buyer that is unreasonable under the circumstances is wrongful as against the seller and is an acceptance only if ratified by the seller.

(b) Any use of the goods that is reasonable under the circumstances is not wrongful as against the seller and is not an acceptance, but in an appropriate case the buyer shall be obligated to the seller for the value of the use to the buyer.

* * * *

§2—612. "INSTALLMENT CONTRACT"; BREACH
* * * *

(2) The buyer may reject any installment which is non-conforming if the non-conformity substantially impairs the value of that installment to the buyer or if the non-conformity is a defect in the required documents; but if the non-conformity does not fall within subsection (3) and the seller gives adequate assurance of its cure the buyer must accept that installment.

(3) Whenever non-conformity or default with respect to one or more installments substantially impairs the value of the whole contract there is a breach of the whole. But the aggrieved party reinstates the contract if the party accepts a non-conforming installment without seasonably notifying of cancellation or if the party brings an action with respect only to past installments or demands performance as to future installments.

* * * *

Part 7 Remedies

§2—702. SELLER'S REMEDIES ON DISCOVERY OF BUYER'S INSOLVENCY
* * * *

(2) Where the seller discovers that the buyer has received goods on credit while insolvent the seller may reclaim the goods upon demand made within a reasonable time after the buyer's receipt of the goods. Except as provided in this subsection the seller may not base a right to reclaim goods on the buyer's fraudulent or innocent misrepresentation of solvency or of intent to pay.

* * * *

§2—705. SELLER'S STOPPAGE OF DELIVERY IN TRANSIT OR OTHERWISE

(1) The seller may stop delivery of goods in the possession of a carrier or other bailee when the seller discovers the buyer to be insolvent (Section 2—702) or when the buyer repudiates or fails to make a payment due before delivery or if for any other reason the seller has a right to withhold or reclaim the goods.

* * * *

§2—706. SELLER'S RESALE INCLUDING CONTRACT FOR RESALE

In an appropriate case involving breach by the buyer, the seller may resell the goods concerned or the undelivered balance thereof. Where the resale is made in good faith and in a commercially reasonable manner the seller may recover the difference between the contract price and the resale price together with any incidental or consequential damages allowed under the provisions of this Article (Section 2—710), but less expenses saved in consequence of the buyer's breach.

* * * *

§2—708. SELLER'S DAMAGES FOR NON-ACCEPTANCE OR REPUDIATION

(1) Subject to subsection (2) and to the provisions of this Article with respect to proof of market price (Section 2—723)

(a) the measure of damages for non-acceptance by the buyer is the difference between the contract price and the market price at the time and place for tender together with any incidental or consequential damages provided in this Article (Section 2—710), but less expenses saved in consequence of the buyer's breach; and

(b) the measure of damages for repudiation by the buyer is the difference between the contract price and the market price at the place for tender at the expiration of a commercially reasonable time after the seller learned of the repudiation, but no later than the time stated in paragraph (a), together with any incidental or consequential damages provided in this Article (Section 2—710), but less expenses saved in consequence of the buyer's breach.

(2) If the measure of damages provided in subsection (1) or in Section 2—706 is inadequate to put the seller in as good a position as performance would have done then the measure of damages is the profit (including reasonable overhead) which the seller would have made from full performance by the buyer, together with any incidental or consequential damages provided in this Article (Section 2—710).

§2—709. ACTION FOR THE PRICE

(1) When the buyer fails to pay the price as it becomes due the seller may recover, together with any incidental or consequential damages under the next section, the price

(a) of goods accepted or of conforming goods lost or damaged within a commercially reasonable time after risk of their loss has passed to the buyer; and

(b) of goods identified to the contract if the seller is unable after reasonable effort to resell them at a reasonable price or the circumstances reasonably indicate that such effort will be unavailing.

* * * *

§2—710. SELLER'S INCIDENTAL AND CONSEQUENTIAL DAMAGES

(1) Incidental damages to an aggrieved seller include any commercially reasonable charges, expenses or commissions incurred in stopping delivery, in the transportation, care and custody of goods after the buyer's breach, in connection with return or resale of the goods or otherwise resulting from the breach.

(2) Consequential damages resulting from the buyer's breach include any loss resulting from general or particular requirements and needs of which the buyer at the time of contracting had reason to know and which could not reasonably be prevented by resale or otherwise.

(3) In a consumer contract, a seller may not recover consequential damages from a consumer.

* * * *

§2—713. BUYER'S DAMAGES FOR NON-DELIVERY OR REPUDIATION

(1) Subject to the provisions of this Article with respect to proof of market price (Section 2—723), if the seller wrongfully fails to deliver or repudiates or the buyer rightfully rejects or justifiably revokes acceptance

(a) the measure of damages in the case of wrongful failure to deliver by the seller or rightful rejection or justifiable revocation of acceptance by the buyer is the difference between the market price at the time for tender under the contract and the contract price together with any incidental or consequential damages provided in this Article (Section 2—715), but less expenses saved in consequence of the seller's breach; and

(b) the measure of damages for repudiation by the seller is the difference between the market price at the expiration of a commercially reasonable time after the buyer learned of the repudiation, but no later than the time stated in paragraph (a), and the contract price together with any incidental or consequential damages provided in this Article (Section 2—715), but less expenses saved in consequence of the seller's breach.

* * * *

§2—725. STATUTE OF LIMITATIONS IN CONTRACTS FOR SALE

(1) Except as otherwise provided in this section, an action for breach of any contract for sale must be commenced within the later of four years after the right of action has accrued under subsection (2) or (3) or one year after the breach was or should have been discovered, but no longer than five years after the right of action accrued. By the original agreement the parties may reduce the period of limitation to not less than one year but may not extend it; however, in a consumer contract, the period of limitation may not be reduced.

(2) Except as otherwise provided in subsection (3), the following rules apply:

(a) Except as otherwise provided in this subsection, a right of action for breach of a contract accrues when the breach occurs, even if the aggrieved party did not have knowledge of the breach.

(b) For breach of a contract by repudiation, a right of action accrues at the earlier of when the aggrieved party elects to treat the repudiation as a breach or when a commercially reasonable time for awaiting performance has expired.

* * * *

Article 2A Leases

§2A—102. SCOPE

This Article applies to any transaction, regardless of form, that creates a lease.

§2A—103. DEFINITIONS AND INDEX OF DEFINITIONS

* * * *

(e) "Consumer lease" means a lease that a lessor regularly engaged in the business of leasing or selling makes to a lessee who is an individual and who takes under the lease primarily for a personal, family, or household purpose [, if the total payments to be made under the lease contract, excluding payments for options to renew or buy, do not exceed $___].

* * * *

(g) "Finance lease" means a lease with respect to which:

(i) the lessor does not select, manufacture or supply the goods;

(ii) the lessor acquires the goods or the right to possession and use of the goods in connection with the lease; and

(iii) one of the following occurs:

(A) the lessee receives a copy of the contract by which the lessor acquired the goods or the right to possession and use of the goods before signing the lease contract;

(B) the lessee's approval of the contract by which the lessor acquired the goods or the right to possession and use of the goods is a condition to effectiveness of the lease contract;

(C) the lessee, before signing the lease contract, receives an accurate and complete statement designating the promises and warranties, and any disclaimers of warranties, limitations or modifications of remedies, or liquidated damages, including those of a third party, such as the manufacturer of the goods, provided to the lessor by the person supplying the goods in connection with or as part of the contract by which the lessor acquired the goods or the right to possession and use of the goods; or

(D) if the lease is not a consumer lease, the lessor, before the lessee signs the lease contract, informs the lessee in writing (a) of the identity of the person supplying the goods to the lessor, unless the lessee has selected that person and directed the lessor to acquire the goods or the right to possession and use of the goods from that person, (b) that the lessee is entitled under this Article to any promises and warranties, including those of any third party, provided to the lessor by the person supplying the goods in connection with or as part of the contract by which the lessor acquired the goods or the right to possession and use of the goods, and (c) that the lessee may communicate with the person supplying the goods to the lessor and receive an accurate and complete statement of those promises and warranties, including any disclaimers and limitations of them or of remedies.

* * * *

(h) "Goods" means all things that are movable at the time of identification to the lease contract, or are fixtures (Section 2A—309), but the term does not include money, documents, instruments, accounts, chattel paper, general intangibles, or minerals or the like, including oil and gas, before extraction. The term also includes the unborn young of animals.

(i) "Installment lease contract" means a lease contract that authorizes or requires the delivery of goods in separate lots to be separately accepted, even though the lease contract contains a clause "each delivery is a separate lease" or its equivalent.

(j) "Lease" means a transfer of the right to possession and use of goods for a term in return for consideration, but a sale, including a sale on approval or a sale or return, or retention or creation of a security interest is not a lease. Unless the context clearly indicates otherwise, the term includes a sublease.

(k) "Lease agreement" means the bargain, with respect to the lease, of the lessor and the lessee in fact as found in their language or by implication from other circumstances including course of dealing or usage of trade or course of performance as provided in this Article. Unless the context clearly indicates otherwise, the term includes a sublease agreement.

(l) "Lease contract" means the total legal obligation that results from the lease agreement as affected by this Article and any other applicable rules of law. Unless the context clearly indicates otherwise, the term includes a sublease contract.

* * * *

(o) "Lessee in ordinary course of business" means a person who in good faith and without knowledge that the lease to him [or her] is in violation of the ownership rights or security interest or leasehold interest of a third party in the goods, leases in ordinary course from a person in the business of selling or leasing goods of that kind but does not include a pawnbroker. "Leasing" may be for cash or by exchange of other property or on secured or unsecured credit and includes receiving goods or documents of title under a pre-existing lease contract but does not include a transfer in bulk or as security for or in total or partial satisfaction of a money debt.

(p) "Lessor" means a person who transfers the right to possession and use of goods under a lease. Unless the context clearly indicates otherwise, the term includes a sublessor.

(q) "Lessor's residual interest" means the lessor's interest in the goods after expiration, termination, or cancellation of the lease contract.

* * * *

§2A—104. LEASES SUBJECT TO OTHER LAW

(1) A lease, although subject to this Article, is also subject to any applicable:

(a) certificate of title statute of this State: (list any certificate of title statutes covering automobiles, trailers, mobile homes, boats, farm tractors, and the like);

(b) certificate of title statute of another jurisdiction (Section 2A—105); or

(c) consumer protection statute of this State, or final consumer protection decision of a court of this State existing on the effective date of this Article.

§2A—105. TERRITORIAL APPLICATION OF ARTICLE TO GOODS COVERED BY CERTIFICATE OF TITLE

Subject to the provisions of Sections 2A—304(3) and 2A—305(3), with respect to goods covered by a certificate of title issued under a statute of this State or of another jurisdiction, compliance and the effect of compliance or noncompliance with a certificate of title statute are governed by the law (including the conflict of laws rules) of the jurisdiction issuing the certificate until the earlier of (a) surrender of the certificate, or (b) four months after the goods are removed from that jurisdiction and thereafter until a new certificate of title is issued by another jurisdiction.

* * * *

§2A—108. UNCONSCIONABILITY

(1) If the court as a matter of law finds a lease contract or any clause of a lease contract to have been unconscionable at the time it was made the court may refuse to enforce the lease contract, or it may enforce the remainder of the lease contract without the unconscionable clause, or it may so limit the application of any unconscionable clause as to avoid any unconscionable result.

(2) With respect to a consumer lease, if the court as a matter of law finds that a lease contract or any clause of a lease contract has been induced by unconscionable conduct or that unconscionable conduct has occurred in the collection of a claim arising from a lease contract, the court may grant appropriate relief.

(3) Before making a finding of unconscionability under subsection (1) or (2), the court, on its own motion or that of a party, shall afford the parties a reasonable opportunity to present evidence as to the setting, purpose, and effect of the lease contract or clause thereof, or of the conduct.

(4) In an action in which the lessee claims unconscionability with respect to a consumer lease:

(a) If the court finds unconscionability under subsection (1) or (2), the court shall award reasonable attorney's fees to the lessee.

(b) If the court does not find unconscionability and the lessee claiming unconscionability has brought or maintained an action he [or she] knew to be groundless, the court shall award reasonable attorney's fees to the party against whom the claim is made.

(c) In determining attorney's fees, the amount of the recovery on behalf of the claimant under subsections (1) and (2) is not controlling.

§2A—109. OPTION TO ACCELERATE AT WILL

(1) A term providing that one party or his [or her] successor in interest may accelerate payment or performance or require collateral or additional collateral "at will" or "when he [or she] deems himself [or herself] insecure" or in words of similar import must be construed to mean that he [or she] has power to do so only if he [or she] in good faith believes that the prospect of payment or performance is impaired.

(2) With respect to a consumer lease, the burden of establishing good faith under subsection (1) is on the party who exercised the power; otherwise the burden of establishing lack of good faith is on the party against whom the power has been exercised.

Part 2 Formation and Construction of Lease Contract

§2A—201. STATUTE OF FRAUDS

(1) A lease contract is not enforceable by way of action or defense unless:

(a) the total payments to be made under the lease contract, excluding payments for options to renew or buy, are less than $1,000; or

(b) there is a writing, signed by the party against whom enforcement is sought or by that party's authorized agent, sufficient to indicate that a lease contract has been made between the parties and to describe the goods leased and the lease term.

(2) Any description of leased goods or of the lease term is sufficient and satisfies subsection (1)(b), whether or not it is specific, if it reasonably identifies what is described.

(3) A writing is not insufficient because it omits or incorrectly states a term agreed upon, but the lease

contract is not enforceable under subsection (1)(b) beyond the lease term and the quantity of goods shown in the writing.

(4) A lease contract that does not satisfy the requirements of subsection (1), but which is valid in other respects, is enforceable:

(a) if the goods are to be specially manufactured or obtained for the lessee and are not suitable for lease or sale to others in the ordinary course of the lessor's business, and the lessor, before notice of repudiation is received and under circumstances that reasonably indicate that the goods are for the lessee, has made either a substantial beginning of their manufacture or commitments for their procurement;

(b) if the party against whom enforcement is sought admits in that party's pleading, testimony or otherwise in court that a lease contract was made, but the lease contract is not enforceable under this provision beyond the quantity of goods admitted; or

(c) with respect to goods that have been received and accepted by the lessee.

(5) The lease term under a lease contract referred to in subsection (4) is:

(a) if there is a writing signed by the party against whom enforcement is sought or by that party's authorized agent specifying the lease term, the term so specified;

(b) if the party against whom enforcement is sought admits in that party's pleading, testimony, or otherwise in court a lease term, the term so admitted; or

(c) a reasonable lease term.

§2A—202. FINAL WRITTEN EXPRESSION: PAROL OR EXTRINSIC EVIDENCE

Terms with respect to which the confirmatory memoranda of the parties agree or which are otherwise set forth in a writing intended by the parties as a final expression of their agreement with respect to such terms as are included therein may not be contradicted by evidence of any prior agreement or of a contemporaneous oral agreement but may be explained or supplemented:

(a) by course of dealing or usage of trade or by course of performance; and

(b) by evidence of consistent additional terms unless the court finds the writing to have been intended also as a complete and exclusive statement of the terms of the agreement.

* * * *

§2A—205. FIRM OFFERS

An offer by a merchant to lease goods to or from another person in a signed writing that by its terms gives assurance it will be held open is not revocable, for lack of consideration, during the time stated or, if no time is stated, for a reasonable time, but in no event may the period of irrevocability exceed 3 months. Any such term of assurance on a form supplied by the offeree must be separately signed by the offeror.

§2A—206. OFFER AND ACCEPTANCE IN FORMATION OF LEASE CONTRACT

(1) Unless otherwise unambiguously indicated by the language or circumstances, an offer to make a lease contract must be construed as inviting acceptance in any manner and by any medium reasonable in the circumstances.

(2) If the beginning of a requested performance is a reasonable mode of acceptance, an offeror who is not notified of acceptance within a reasonable time may treat the offer as having lapsed before acceptance.

§2A—207. COURSE OF PERFORMANCE OR PRACTICAL CONSTRUCTION

(1) If a lease contract involves repeated occasions for performance by either party with knowledge of the nature of the performance and opportunity for objection to it by the other, any course of performance accepted or acquiesced in without objection is relevant to determine the meaning of the lease agreement.

(2) The express terms of a lease agreement and any course of performance, as well as any course of dealing and usage of trade, must be construed whenever reasonable as consistent with each other; but if that construction is unreasonable, express terms control course of performance, course of performance controls both course of dealing and usage of trade, and course of dealing controls usage of trade.

(3) Subject to the provisions of Section 2A—208 on modification and waiver, course of performance is relevant to show a waiver or modification of any term inconsistent with the course of performance.

§2A—208. MODIFICATION, RESCISSION AND WAIVER

(1) An agreement modifying a lease contract needs no consideration to be binding.

(2) A signed lease agreement that excludes modification or rescission except by a signed writing may not be otherwise modified or rescinded, but, except as between merchants, such a requirement on a form supplied by a merchant must be separately signed by the other party.

(3) Although an attempt at modification or rescission does not satisfy the requirements of subsection (2), it may operate as a waiver.

(4) A party who has made a waiver affecting an executory portion of a lease contract may retract the waiver by reasonable notification received by the other party that strict performance will be required of any term waived, unless the retraction would be unjust in view of a material change of position in reliance on the waiver.

* * * *

§2A—216. THIRD-PARTY BENEFICIARIES OF EXPRESS AND IMPLIED WARRANTIES

Alternative A

A warranty to or for the benefit of a lessee under this Article, whether express or implied, extends to any natural person who is in the family or household of the lessee or who is a guest in the lessee's home if it is reasonable to expect that such person may use, consume, or be affected by the goods and who is injured in person by breach of the warranty. This section does not displace principles of law and equity that extend a warranty to or for the benefit of a lessee to other persons. The operation of this section may not be excluded, modified, or limited, but an exclusion, modification, or limitation of the warranty, including any with respect to rights and remedies, effective against the lessee is also effective against any beneficiary designated under this section.

Alternative B

A warranty to or for the benefit of a lessee under this Article, whether express or implied, extends to any natural person who may reasonably be expected to use, consume, or be affected by the goods and who is injured in person by breach of the warranty. This section does not displace principles of law and equity that extend a warranty to or for the benefit of a lessee to other persons. The operation of this section may not be excluded, modified, or limited, but an exclusion, modification, or limitation of the warranty, including any with respect to rights and remedies, effective against

the lessee is also effective against the beneficiary designated under this section.

Alternative C

A warranty to or for the benefit of a lessee under this Article, whether express or implied, extends to any person who may reasonably be expected to use, consume, or be affected by the goods and who is injured by breach of the warranty. The operation of this section may not be excluded, modified, or limited with respect to injury to the person of an individual to whom the warranty extends, but an exclusion, modification, or limitation of the warranty, including any with respect to rights and remedies, effective against the lessee is also effective against the beneficiary designated under this section.

* * * *

§2A—219. RISK OF LOSS

(1) Except in the case of a finance lease, risk of loss is retained by the lessor and does not pass to the lessee. In the case of a finance lease, risk of loss passes to the lessee.

(2) Subject to the provisions of this Article on the effect of default on risk of loss (Section 2A—220), if risk of loss is to pass to the lessee and the time of passage is not stated, the following rules apply:

(a) If the lease contract requires or authorizes the goods to be shipped by carrier

(i) and it does not require delivery at a particular destination, the risk of loss passes to the lessee when the goods are duly delivered to the carrier; but

(ii) if it does require delivery at a particular destination and the goods are there duly tendered while in the possession of the carrier, the risk of loss passes to the lessee when the goods are there duly so tendered as to enable the lessee to take delivery.

(b) If the goods are held by a bailee to be delivered without being moved, the risk of loss passes to the lessee on acknowledgment by the bailee of the lessee's right to possession of the goods.

(c) In any case not within subsection (a) or (b), the risk of loss passes to the lessee on the lessee's receipt of the goods if the lessor, or, in the case of a finance lease, the supplier, is a merchant; otherwise the risk passes to the lessee on tender of delivery.

§2A—220. EFFECT OF DEFAULT ON RISK OF LOSS

(1) Where risk of loss is to pass to the lessee and the time of passage is not stated:

(a) If a tender or delivery of goods so fails to conform to the lease contract as to give a right of rejection, the risk of their loss remains with the lessor, or, in the case of a finance lease, the supplier, until cure or acceptance.

(b) If the lessee rightfully revokes acceptance, he [or she], to the extent of any deficiency in his [or her] effective insurance coverage, may treat the risk of loss as having remained with the lessor from the beginning.

(2) Whether or not risk of loss is to pass to the lessee, if the lessee as to conforming goods already identified to a lease contract repudiates or is otherwise in default under the lease contract, the lessor, or, in the case of a finance lease, the supplier, to the extent of any deficiency in his [or her] effective insurance coverage may treat the risk of loss as resting on the lessee for a commercially reasonable time.

* * * *

§2A—304. SUBSEQUENT LEASE OF GOODS BY LESSOR

(1) Subject to Section 2A—303, a subsequent lessee from a lessor of goods under an existing lease contract obtains, to the extent of the leasehold interest transferred, the leasehold interest in the goods that the lessor had or had power to transfer, and except as provided in subsection (2) and Section 2A—527(4), takes subject to the existing lease contract. A lessor with voidable title has power to transfer a good leasehold interest to a good faith subsequent lessee for value, but only to the extent set forth in the preceding sentence. If goods have been delivered under a transaction of purchase the lessor has that power even though:

(a) the lessor's transferor was deceived as to the identity of the lessor;

(b) the delivery was in exchange for a check which is later dishonored;

(c) it was agreed that the transaction was to be a "cash sale"; or

(d) the delivery was procured through fraud punishable as larcenous under the criminal law.

(2) A subsequent lessee in the ordinary course of business from a lessor who is a merchant dealing in goods of that kind to whom the goods were entrusted by the existing lessee of that lessor before the interest of the subsequent lessee became enforceable against that lessor obtains, to the extent of the leasehold interest transferred, all of that lessor's and the existing lessee's rights to the goods, and takes free of the existing lease contract.

(3) A subsequent lessee from the lessor of goods that are subject to an existing lease contract and are covered by a certificate of title issued under a statute of this State or of another jurisdiction takes no greater rights than those provided both by this section and by the certificate of title statute.

§2A—305. SALE OR SUBLEASE OF GOODS BY LESSEE

(1) Subject to the provisions of Section 2A—303, a buyer or sublessee from the lessee of goods under an existing lease contract obtains, to the extent of the interest transferred, the leasehold interest in the goods that the lessee had or had power to transfer, and except as provided in subsection (2) and Section 2A—511(4), takes subject to the existing lease contract. A lessee with a voidable leasehold interest has power to transfer a good leasehold interest to a good faith buyer for value or a good faith sublessee for value, but only to the extent set forth in the preceding sentence. When goods have been delivered under a transaction of lease the lessee has that power even though:

(a) the lessor was deceived as to the identity of the lessee;

(b) the delivery was in exchange for a check which is later dishonored; or

(c) the delivery was procured through fraud punishable as larcenous under the criminal law.

(2) A buyer in the ordinary course of business or a sublessee in the ordinary course of business from a lessee who is a merchant dealing in goods of that kind to whom the goods were entrusted by the lessor obtains, to the extent of the interest transferred, all of the lessor's and lessee's rights to the goods, and takes free of the existing lease contract.

(3) A buyer or sublessee from the lessee of goods that are subject to an existing lease contract and are covered by a certificate of title issued under a statute of this State or of another jurisdiction takes no greater rights than those provided both by this section and by the certificate of title statute.

* * * *

§2A—501. DEFAULT: PROCEDURE

(1) Whether the lessor or the lessee is in default under a lease contract is determined by the lease agreement and this Article.

(2) If the lessor or the lessee is in default under the lease contract, the party seeking enforcement has rights and remedies as provided in this Article and, except as limited by this Article, as provided in the lease agreement.

(3) If the lessor or the lessee is in default under the lease contract, the party seeking enforcement may reduce the party's claim to judgment, or otherwise enforce the lease contract by self-help or any available judicial procedure or nonjudicial procedure, including administrative proceeding, arbitration, or the like, in accordance with this Article.

(4) Except as otherwise provided in Section 1—106 (1) or this Article or the lease agreement, the rights and remedies referred to in subsections (2) and (3) are cumulative.

(5) If the lease agreement covers both real property and goods, the party seeking enforcement may proceed under this Part as to the goods, or under other applicable law as to both the real property and the goods in accordance with that party's rights and remedies in respect of the real property, in which case this Part does not apply.

§2A—502. NOTICE AFTER DEFAULT

Except as otherwise provided in this Article or the lease agreement, the lessor or lessee in default under the lease contract is not entitled to notice of default or notice of enforcement from the other party to the lease agreement.

§2A—503. MODIFICATION OR IMPAIRMENT OF RIGHTS AND REMEDIES

(1) Except as otherwise provided in this Article, the lease agreement may include rights and remedies for default in addition to or in substitution for those provided in this Article and may limit or alter the measure of damages recoverable under this Article.

(2) Resort to a remedy provided under this Article or in the lease agreement is optional unless the remedy is expressly agreed to be exclusive. If circumstances cause an exclusive or limited remedy to fail of its essential purpose, or provision for an exclusive remedy is unconscionable, remedy may be had as provided in this Article.

(3) Consequential damages may be liquidated under Section 2A—504, or may otherwise be limited, altered, or excluded unless the limitation, alteration, or exclusion is unconscionable. Limitation, alteration, or exclusion of consequential damages for injury to the person in the case of consumer goods is prima facie unconscionable but limitation, alteration, or exclusion of damages where the loss is commercial is not prima facie unconscionable.

(4) Rights and remedies on default by the lessor or the lessee with respect to any obligation or promise collateral or ancillary to the lease contract are not impaired by this Article.

As amended in 1990.

§2A—504. LIQUIDATION OF DAMAGES

(1) Damages payable by either party for default, or any other act or omission, including indemnity for loss or diminution of anticipated tax benefits or loss or damage to lessor's residual interest, may be liquidated in the lease agreement but only at an amount or by a formula that is reasonable in light of the then anticipated harm caused by the default or other act or omission.

(2) If the lease agreement provides for liquidation of damages, and such provision does not comply with subsection (1), or such provision is an exclusive or limited remedy that circumstances cause to fail of its essential purpose, remedy may be had as provided in this Article.

(3) If the lessor justifiably withholds or stops delivery of goods because of the lessee's default or insolvency (Section 2A—525 or 2A—526), the lessee is entitled to restitution of any amount by which the sum of his [or her] payments exceeds:

(a) the amount to which the lessor is entitled by virtue of terms liquidating the lessor's damages in accordance with subsection (1); or

(b) in the absence of those terms, 20 percent of the then present value of the total rent the lessee was obligated to pay for the balance of the lease term, or, in the case of a consumer lease, the lesser of such amount or $500.

(4) A lessee's right to restitution under subsection (3) is subject to offset to the extent the lessor establishes:

(a) a right to recover damages under the provisions of this Article other than subsection (1); and

(b) the amount or value of any benefits received by the lessee directly or indirectly by reason of the lease contract.

§2A—505. CANCELLATION AND TERMINATION AND EFFECT OF CANCELLATION, TERMINATION, RESCISSION, OR FRAUD ON RIGHTS AND REMEDIES

(1) On cancellation of the lease contract, all obligations that are still executory on both sides are discharged, but any right based on prior default or performance

survives, and the cancelling party also retains any remedy for default of the whole lease contract or any unperformed balance.

(2) On termination of the lease contract, all obligations that are still executory on both sides are discharged but any right based on prior default or performance survives.

(3) Unless the contrary intention clearly appears, expressions of "cancellation," "rescission," or the like of the lease contract may not be construed as a renunciation or discharge of any claim in damages for an antecedent default.

(4) Rights and remedies for material misrepresentation or fraud include all rights and remedies available under this Article for default.

(5) Neither rescission nor a claim for rescission of the lease contract nor rejection or return of the goods may bar or be deemed inconsistent with a claim for damages or other right or remedy.

§2A—506. STATUTE OF LIMITATIONS

(1) An action for default under a lease contract, including breach of warranty or indemnity, must be commenced within 4 years after the cause of action accrued. By the original lease contract the parties may reduce the period of limitation to not less than one year.

(2) A cause of action for default accrues when the act or omission on which the default or breach of warranty is based is or should have been discovered by the aggrieved party, or when the default occurs, whichever is later. A cause of action for indemnity accrues when the act or omission on which the claim for indemnity is based is or should have been discovered by the indemnified party, whichever is later.

(3) If an action commenced within the time limited by subsection (1) is so terminated as to leave available a remedy by another action for the same default or breach of warranty or indemnity, the other action may be commenced after the expiration of the time limited and within 6 months after the termination of the first action unless the termination resulted from voluntary discontinuance or from dismissal for failure or neglect to prosecute.

(4) This section does not alter the law on tolling of the statute of limitations nor does it apply to causes of action that have accrued before this Article becomes effective.

* * * *

§2A—508. LESSEE'S REMEDIES

(1) If a lessor fails to deliver the goods in conformity to the lease contract (Section 2A—509) or repudiates the lease contract (Section 2A—402), or a lessee rightfully rejects the goods (Section 2A—509) or justifiably revokes acceptance of the goods (Section 2A—517), then with respect to any goods involved, and with respect to all of the goods if under an installment lease contract the value of the whole lease contract is substantially impaired (Section 2A—510), the lessor is in default under the lease contract and the lessee may:

(a) cancel the lease contract (Section 2A—505(1));

(b) recover so much of the rent and security as has been paid and is just under the circumstances;

(c) cover and recover damages as to all goods affected whether or not they have been identified to the lease contract (Sections 2A—518 and 2A—520), or recover damages for nondelivery (Sections 2A—519 and 2A—520);

(d) exercise any other rights or pursue any other remedies provided in the lease contract.

(2) If a lessor fails to deliver the goods in conformity to the lease contract or repudiates the lease contract, the lessee may also:

(a) if the goods have been identified, recover them (Section 2A—522); or

(b) in a proper case, obtain specific performance or replevy the goods (Section 2A—521).

(3) If a lessor is otherwise in default under a lease contract, the lessee may exercise the rights and pursue the remedies provided in the lease contract, which may include a right to cancel the lease, and in Section 2A—519(3).

(4) If a lessor has breached a warranty, whether express or implied, the lessee may recover damages (Section 2A—519(4)).

(5) On rightful rejection or justifiable revocation of acceptance, a lessee has a security interest in goods in the lessee's possession or control for any rent and security that has been paid and any expenses reasonably incurred in their inspection, receipt, transportation, and care and custody and may hold those goods and dispose of them in good faith and in a commercially reasonable manner, subject to Section 2A—527(5).

(6) Subject to the provisions of Section 2A—407, a lessee, on notifying the lessor of the lessee's intention to do so, may deduct all or any part of the damages resulting from any default under the lease contract

from any part of the rent still due under the same lease contract.

§2A—509. LESSEE'S RIGHTS ON IMPROPER DELIVERY; RIGHTFUL REJECTION

(1) Subject to the provisions of Section 2A—510 on default in installment lease contracts, if the goods or the tender or delivery fail in any respect to conform to the lease contract, the lessee may reject or accept the goods or accept any commercial unit or units and reject the rest of the goods.

(2) Rejection of goods is ineffective unless it is within a reasonable time after tender or delivery of the goods and the lessee seasonably notifies the lessor.

* * * *

§2A—512. LESSEE'S DUTIES AS TO RIGHTFULLY REJECTED GOODS

(1) Except as otherwise provided with respect to goods that threaten to decline in value speedily (Section 2A—511) and subject to any security interest of a lessee (Section 2A—508(5)):

(a) the lessee, after rejection of goods in the lessee's possession, shall hold them with reasonable care at the lessor's or the supplier's disposition for a reasonable time after the lessee's seasonable notification of rejection;

(b) if the lessor or the supplier gives no instructions within a reasonable time after notification of rejection, the lessee may store the rejected goods for the lessor's or the supplier's account or ship them to the lessor or the supplier or dispose of them for the lessor's or the supplier's account with reimbursement in the manner provided in Section 2A—511; but

(c) the lessee has no further obligations with regard to goods rightfully rejected.

(2) Action by the lessee pursuant to subsection (1) is not acceptance or conversion.

§2A—513. CURE BY LESSOR OF IMPROPER TENDER OR DELIVERY; REPLACEMENT

(1) If any tender or delivery by the lessor or the supplier is rejected because non-conforming and the time for performance has not yet expired, the lessor or the supplier may seasonably notify the lessee of the lessor's or the supplier's intention to cure and may then make a conforming delivery within the time provided in the lease contract.

(2) If the lessee rejects a non-conforming tender that the lessor or the supplier had reasonable grounds to believe would be acceptable with or without money allowance, the lessor or the supplier may have a further reasonable time to substitute a conforming tender if he [or she] seasonably notifies the lessee.

* * * *

Revised Article 3 Negotiable Instruments

Part 1 General Provisions and Definitions

§3—102. SUBJECT MATTER

(a) This Article applies to negotiable instruments. It does not apply to money, to payment orders governed by Article 4A, or to securities governed by Article 8.

(b) If there is conflict between this Article and Article 4 or 9, Articles 4 and 9 govern.

(c) Regulations of the Board of Governors of the Federal Reserve System and operating circulars of the Federal Reserve Banks supersede any inconsistent provision of this Article to the extent of the inconsistency.

§3—103. DEFINITIONS

(a) In this Article:

(1) "Acceptor" means a drawee who has accepted a draft.

(2) "Drawee" means a person ordered in a draft to make payment.

(3) "Drawer" means a person who signs or is identified in a draft as a person ordering payment.

(4) "Good faith" means honesty in fact and the observance of reasonable commercial standards of fair dealing.

(5) "Maker" means a person who signs or is identified in a note as a person undertaking to pay.

(6) "Order" means a written instruction to pay money signed by the person giving the instruction. The instruction may be addressed to any person, including the person giving the instruction, or to one or more persons jointly or in the alternative but not in succession. An authorization to pay is not an order unless the person authorized to pay is also instructed to pay.

(7) "Ordinary care" in the case of a person engaged in business means observance of reasonable

commercial standards, prevailing in the area in which the person is located, with respect to the business in which the person is engaged. In the case of a bank that takes an instrument for processing for collection or payment by automated means, reasonable commercial standards do not require the bank to examine the instrument if the failure to examine does not violate the bank's prescribed procedures and the bank's procedures do not vary unreasonably from general banking usage not disapproved by this Article or Article 4.

(8) "Party" means a party to an instrument.

§3—104. NEGOTIABLE INSTRUMENT

(a) Except as provided in subsections (c) and (d), "negotiable instrument" means an unconditional promise or order to pay a fixed amount of money, with or without interest or other charges described in the promise or order, if it:

(1) is payable to bearer or to order at the time it is issued or first comes into possession of a holder;

(2) is payable on demand or at a definite time; and

(3) does not state any other undertaking or instruction by the person promising or ordering payment to do any act in addition to the payment of money, but the promise or order may contain (i) an undertaking or power to give, maintain, or protect collateral to secure payment, (ii) an authorization or power to the holder to confess judgment or realize on or dispose of collateral, or (iii) a waiver of the benefit of any law intended for the advantage or protection of an obligor.

(b) "Instrument" means a negotiable instrument.

(c) An order that meets all of the requirements of subsection (a), except paragraph (1), and otherwise falls within the definition of "check" in subsection (f) is a negotiable instrument and a check.

(d) A promise or order other than a check is not an instrument if, at the time it is issued or first comes into possession of a holder, it contains a conspicuous statement, however expressed, to the effect that the promise or order is not negotiable or is not an instrument governed by this Article.

(e) An instrument is a "note" if it is a promise and is a "draft" if it is an order. If an instrument falls within the definition of both "note" and "draft," a person entitled to enforce the instrument may treat it as either.

(f) "Check" means (i) a draft, other than a documentary draft, payable on demand and drawn on a bank or (ii) a

cashier's check or teller's check. An instrument may be a check even though it is described on its face by another term, such as "money order."

(g) "Cashier's check" means a draft with respect to which the drawer and drawee are the same bank or branches of the same bank.

(h) "Teller's check" means a draft drawn by a bank (i) on another bank, or (ii) payable at or through a bank.

(i) "Traveler's check" means an instrument that (i) is payable on demand, (ii) is drawn on or payable at or through a bank, (iii) is designated by the term "traveler's check" or by a substantially similar term, and (iv) requires, as a condition to payment, a countersignature by a person whose specimen signature appears on the instrument.

(j) "Certificate of deposit" means an instrument containing an acknowledgment by a bank that a sum of money has been received by the bank and a promise by the bank to repay the sum of money. A certificate of deposit is a note of the bank.

* * * *

§3—106. UNCONDITIONAL PROMISE OR ORDER

(a) Except as provided in this section, for the purposes of Section 3—104(a), a promise or order is unconditional unless it states (i) an express condition to payment, (ii) that the promise or order is subject to or governed by another writing, or (iii) that rights or obligations with respect to the promise or order are stated in another writing. A reference to another writing does not of itself make the promise or order conditional.

(b) A promise or order is not made conditional (i) by a reference to another writing for a statement of rights with respect to collateral, prepayment, or acceleration, or (ii) because payment is limited to resort to a particular fund or source.

(c) If a promise or order requires, as a condition to payment, a countersignature by a person whose specimen signature appears on the promise or order, the condition does not make the promise or order conditional for the purposes of Section 3—104(a). If the person whose specimen signature appears on an instrument fails to countersign the instrument, the failure to countersign is a defense to the obligation of the issuer, but the failure does not prevent a transferee of the instrument from becoming a holder of the instrument.

(d) If a promise or order at the time it is issued or first comes into possession of a holder contains a statement, required by applicable statutory or administrative law, to the effect that the rights of a holder or transferee are subject to claims or defenses that the issuer could assert against the original payee, the promise or order is not thereby made conditional for the purposes of Section 3—104(a); but if the promise or order is an instrument, there cannot be a holder in due course of the instrument.

§3—107. INSTRUMENT PAYABLE IN FOREIGN MONEY

Unless the instrument otherwise provides, an instrument that states the amount payable in foreign money may be paid in the foreign money or in an equivalent amount in dollars calculated by using the current bank-offered spot rate at the place of payment for the purchase of dollars on the day on which the instrument is paid.

§3—108. PAYABLE ON DEMAND OR AT DEFINITE TIME

(a) A promise or order is "payable on demand" if it (i) states that it is payable on demand or at sight, or otherwise indicates that it is payable at the will of the holder, or (ii) does not state any time of payment.

(b) A promise or order is "payable at a definite time" if it is payable on elapse of a definite period of time after sight or acceptance or at a fixed date or dates or at a time or times readily ascertainable at the time the promise or order is issued, subject to rights of (i) prepayment, (ii) acceleration, (iii) extension at the option of the holder, or (iv) extension to a further definite time at the option of the maker or acceptor or automatically upon or after a specified act or event.

(c) If an instrument, payable at a fixed date, is also payable upon demand made before the fixed date, the instrument is payable on demand until the fixed date and, if demand for payment is not made before that date, becomes payable at a definite time on the fixed date.

§3—109. PAYABLE TO BEARER OR TO ORDER

(a) A promise or order is payable to bearer if it:

(1) states that it is payable to bearer or to the order of bearer or otherwise indicates that the person in possession of the promise or order is entitled to payment;

(2) does not state a payee; or

(3) states that it is payable to or to the order of cash or otherwise indicates that it is not payable to an identified person.

(b) A promise or order that is not payable to bearer is payable to order if it is payable (i) to the order of an identified person or (ii) to an identified person or order. A promise or order that is payable to order is payable to the identified person.

(c) An instrument payable to bearer may become payable to an identified person if it is specially indorsed pursuant to Section 3—205(a). An instrument payable to an identified person may become payable to bearer if it is indorsed in blank pursuant to Section 3—205(b).

§3—110. IDENTIFICATION OF PERSON TO WHOM INSTRUMENT IS PAYABLE

(a) The person to whom an instrument is initially payable is determined by the intent of the person, whether or not authorized, signing as, or in the name or behalf of, the issuer of the instrument. The instrument is payable to the person intended by the signer even if that person is identified in the instrument by a name or other identification that is not that of the intended person. If more than one person signs in the name or behalf of the issuer of an instrument and all the signers do not intend the same person as payee, the instrument is payable to any person intended by one or more of the signers.

(b) If the signature of the issuer of an instrument is made by automated means, such as a check-writing machine, the payee of the instrument is determined by the intent of the person who supplied the name or identification of the payee, whether or not authorized to do so.

(c) A person to whom an instrument is payable may be identified in any way, including by name, identifying number, office, or account number.

§3—111. PLACE OF PAYMENT

Except as otherwise provided for items in Article 4, an instrument is payable at the place of payment stated in the instrument. If no place of payment is stated, an instrument is payable at the address of the drawee or maker stated in the instrument. If no address is stated, the place of payment is the place of business of the drawee or maker. If a drawee or maker has more than one place of business, the place of payment is any place of business of the drawee or maker chosen by the person entitled to enforce the instrument. If the drawee or maker has no place of business, the place of payment is the residence of the drawee or maker.

§3—112. INTEREST

(a) Unless otherwise provided in the instrument, (i) an instrument is not payable with interest, and (ii) interest on an interest-bearing instrument is payable from the date of the instrument.

(b) Interest may be stated in an instrument as a fixed or variable amount of money or it may be expressed as a fixed or variable rate or rates. The amount or rate of interest may be stated or described in the instrument in any manner and may require reference to information not contained in the instrument. If an instrument provides for interest, but the amount of interest payable cannot be ascertained from the description, interest is payable at the judgment rate in effect at the place of payment of the instrument and at the time interest first accrues.

§3—113. DATE OF INSTRUMENT

(a) An instrument may be antedated or postdated. The date stated determines the time of payment if the instrument is payable at a fixed period after date. Except as provided in Section 4—401(c), an instrument payable on demand is not payable before the date of the instrument.

(b) If an instrument is undated, its date is the date of its issue or, in the case of an unissued instrument, the date it first comes into possession of a holder.

§3—114. CONTRADICTORY TERMS OF INSTRUMENT

If an instrument contains contradictory terms, typewritten terms prevail over printed terms, handwritten terms prevail over both, and words prevail over numbers.

§3—115. INCOMPLETE INSTRUMENT

(a) "Incomplete instrument" means a signed writing, whether or not issued by the signer, the contents of which show at the time of signing that it is incomplete but that the signer intended it to be completed by the addition of words or numbers.

(b) Subject to subsection (c), if an incomplete instrument is an instrument under Section 3—104, it may be enforced according to its terms if it is not completed, or according to its terms as augmented by completion. If an incomplete instrument is not an instrument under Section 3—104, but, after completion, the requirements of Section 3—104 are met, the instrument may be enforced according to its terms as augmented by completion.

(c) If words or numbers are added to an incomplete instrument without authority of the signer, there is an alteration of the incomplete instrument under Section 3—407.

(d) The burden of establishing that words or numbers were added to an incomplete instrument without authority of the signer is on the person asserting the lack of authority.

§3—116. JOINT AND SEVERAL LIABILITY; CONTRIBUTION

(a) Except as otherwise provided in the instrument, two or more persons who have the same liability on an instrument as makers, drawers, acceptors, indorsers who indorse as joint payees, or anomalous indorsers are jointly and severally liable in the capacity in which they sign.

(b) Except as provided in Section 3—419(e) or by agreement of the affected parties, a party having joint and several liability who pays the instrument is entitled to receive from any party having the same joint and several liability contribution in accordance with applicable law.

(c) Discharge of one party having joint and several liability by a person entitled to enforce the instrument does not affect the right under subsection (b) of a party having the same joint and several liability to receive contribution from the party discharged.

* * * *

§3—118. STATUTE OF LIMITATIONS

(a) Except as provided in subsection (e), an action to enforce the obligation of a party to pay a note payable at a definite time must be commenced within six years after the due date or dates stated in the note or, if a due date is accelerated, within six years after the accelerated due date.

(b) Except as provided in subsection (d) or (e), if demand for payment is made to the maker of a note payable on demand, an action to enforce the obligation of a party to pay the note must be commenced within six years after the demand. If no demand for payment is made to the maker, an action to enforce the note is barred if neither principal nor interest on the note has been paid for a continuous period of 10 years.

(c) Except as provided in subsection (d), an action to enforce the obligation of a party to an unaccepted draft to pay the draft must be commenced within three years after dishonor of the draft or 10 years after the date of the draft, whichever period expires first.

(d) An action to enforce the obligation of the acceptor of a certified check or the issuer of a teller's check, cashier's check, or traveler's check must be commenced within three years after demand for payment is made to the acceptor or issuer, as the case may be.

(e) An action to enforce the obligation of a party to a certificate of deposit to pay the instrument must be commenced within six years after demand for payment is made to the maker, but if the instrument states a due date and the maker is not required to pay before that date, the six-year period begins when a demand for payment is in effect and the due date has passed.

(f) An action to enforce the obligation of a party to pay an accepted draft, other than a certified check, must be commenced (i) within six years after the due date or dates stated in the draft or acceptance if the obligation of the acceptor is payable at a definite time, or (ii) within six years after the date of the acceptance if the obligation of the acceptor is payable on demand.

(g) Unless governed by other law regarding claims for indemnity or contribution, an action (i) for conversion of an instrument, for money had and received, or like action based on conversion, (ii) for breach of warranty, or (iii) to enforce an obligation, duty, or right arising under this Article and not governed by this section must be commenced within three years after the [cause of action] accrues.

* * * *

Part 2 Negotiation, Transfer, and Indorsement

§3—201. NEGOTIATION

(a) "Negotiation" means a transfer of possession, whether voluntary or involuntary, of an instrument by a person other than the issuer to a person who thereby becomes its holder.

(b) Except for negotiation by a remitter, if an instrument is payable to an identified person, negotiation requires transfer of possession of the instrument and its indorsement by the holder. If an instrument is payable to bearer, it may be negotiated by transfer of possession alone.

* * * *

§3—203. TRANSFER OF INSTRUMENT; RIGHTS ACQUIRED BY TRANSFER

(a) An instrument is transferred when it is delivered by a person other than its issuer for the purpose of giving to the person receiving delivery the right to enforce the instrument.

(b) Transfer of an instrument, whether or not the transfer is a negotiation, vests in the transferee any right of the transferor to enforce the instrument, including any

right as a holder in due course, but the transferee cannot acquire rights of a holder in due course by a transfer, directly or indirectly, from a holder in due course if the transferee engaged in fraud or illegality affecting the instrument.

(c) Unless otherwise agreed, if an instrument is transferred for value and the transferee does not become a holder because of lack of indorsement by the transferor, the transferee has a specifically enforceable right to the unqualified indorsement of the transferor, but negotiation of the instrument does not occur until the indorsement is made.

(d) If a transferor purports to transfer less than the entire instrument, negotiation of the instrument does not occur. The transferee obtains no rights under this Article and has only the rights of a partial assignee.

§3—204. INDORSEMENT

(a) "Indorsement" means a signature, other than that of a signer as maker, drawer, or acceptor, that alone or accompanied by other words is made on an instrument for the purpose of (i) negotiating the instrument, (ii) restricting payment of the instrument, or (iii) incurring indorser's liability on the instrument, but regardless of the intent of the signer, a signature and its accompanying words is an indorsement unless the accompanying words, terms of the instrument, place of the signature, or other circumstances unambiguously indicate that the signature was made for a purpose other than indorsement. For the purpose of determining whether a signature is made on an instrument, a paper affixed to the instrument is a part of the instrument.

(b) "Indorser" means a person who makes an indorsement.

(c) For the purpose of determining whether the transferee of an instrument is a holder, an indorsement that transfers a security interest in the instrument is effective as an unqualified indorsement of the instrument.

(d) If an instrument is payable to a holder under a name that is not the name of the holder, indorsement may be made by the holder in the name stated in the instrument or in the holder's name or both, but signature in both names may be required by a person paying or taking the instrument for value or collection.

§3—205. SPECIAL INDORSEMENT; BLANK INDORSEMENT; ANOMALOUS INDORSEMENT

(a) If an indorsement is made by the holder of an instrument, whether payable to an identified person or payable to bearer, and the indorsement identifies a person to whom it makes the instrument payable, it is a "special indorsement." When specially indorsed, an instrument becomes payable to the identified person and may be negotiated only by the indorsement of that person. The principles stated in Section 3—110 apply to special indorsements.

(b) If an indorsement is made by the holder of an instrument and it is not a special indorsement, it is a "blank indorsement." When indorsed in blank, an instrument becomes payable to bearer and may be negotiated by transfer of possession alone until specially indorsed.

(c) The holder may convert a blank indorsement that consists only of a signature into a special indorsement by writing, above the signature of the indorser, words identifying the person to whom the instrument is made payable.

(d) "Anomalous indorsement" means an indorsement made by a person who is not the holder of the instrument. An anomalous indorsement does not affect the manner in which the instrument may be negotiated.

§3—206. RESTRICTIVE INDORSEMENT

(a) An indorsement limiting payment to a particular person or otherwise prohibiting further transfer or negotiation of the instrument is not effective to prevent further transfer or negotiation of the instrument.

(b) An indorsement stating a condition to the right of the indorsee to receive payment does not affect the right of the indorsee to enforce the instrument. A person paying the instrument or taking it for value or collection may disregard the condition, and the rights and liabilities of that person are not affected by whether the condition has been fulfilled.

(c) If an instrument bears an indorsement (i) described in Section 4—201(b), or (ii) in blank or to a particular bank using the words "for deposit," "for collection," or other words indicating a purpose of having the instrument collected by a bank for the indorser or for a particular account, the following rules apply:

   (1) A person, other than a bank, who purchases the instrument when so indorsed converts the instrument unless the amount paid for the instrument is received by the indorser or applied consistently with the indorsement.

   (2) A depositary bank that purchases the instrument or takes it for collection when so indorsed converts the instrument unless the amount paid

by the bank with respect to the instrument is received by the indorser or applied consistently with the indorsement.

   (3) A payor bank that is also the depositary bank or that takes the instrument for immediate payment over the counter from a person other than a collecting bank converts the instrument unless the proceeds of the instrument are received by the indorser or applied consistently with the indorsement.

   (4) Except as otherwise provided in paragraph (3), a payor bank or intermediary bank may disregard the indorsement and is not liable if the proceeds of the instrument are not received by the indorser or applied consistently with the indorsement.

(d) Except for an indorsement covered by subsection (c), if an instrument bears an indorsement using words to the effect that payment is to be made to the indorsee as agent, trustee, or other fiduciary for the benefit of the indorser or another person, the following rules apply:

   (1) Unless there is notice of breach of fiduciary duty as provided in Section 3—307, a person who purchases the instrument from the indorsee or takes the instrument from the indorsee for collection or payment may pay the proceeds of payment or the value given for the instrument to the indorsee without regard to whether the indorsee violates a fiduciary duty to the indorser.

   (2) A subsequent transferee of the instrument or person who pays the instrument is neither given notice nor otherwise affected by the restriction in the indorsement unless the transferee or payor knows that the fiduciary dealt with the instrument or its proceeds in breach of fiduciary duty.

(e) The presence on an instrument of an indorsement to which this section applies does not prevent a purchaser of the instrument from becoming a holder in due course of the instrument unless the purchaser is a converter under subsection (c) or has notice or knowledge of breach of fiduciary duty as stated in subsection (d).

(f) In an action to enforce the obligation of a party to pay the instrument, the obligor has a defense if payment would violate an indorsement to which this section applies and the payment is not permitted by this section.

§3—207. REACQUISITION

Reacquisition of an instrument occurs if it is transferred to a former holder, by negotiation or otherwise. A former holder who reacquires the instrument may cancel indorsements made after the reacquirer first became a holder of the instrument. If the cancellation causes the instrument to be payable to the reacquirer or to bearer, the reacquirer may negotiate the instrument. An indorser whose indorsement is canceled is discharged, and the discharge is effective against any subsequent holder.

Part 3 Enforcement of Instruments

§3—301. PERSON ENTITLED TO ENFORCE INSTRUMENT

"Person entitled to enforce" an instrument means (i) the holder of the instrument, (ii) a nonholder in possession of the instrument who has the rights of a holder, or (iii) a person not in possession of the instrument who is entitled to enforce the instrument pursuant to Section 3—309 or 3—418(d). A person may be a person entitled to enforce the instrument even though the person is not the owner of the instrument or is in wrongful possession of the instrument.

§3—302. HOLDER IN DUE COURSE

(a) Subject to subsection (c) and Section 3—106(d), "holder in due course" means the holder of an instrument if:

> (1) the instrument when issued or negotiated to the holder does not bear such apparent evidence of forgery or alteration or is not otherwise so irregular or incomplete as to call into question its authenticity; and

> (2) the holder took the instrument (i) for value, (ii) in good faith, (iii) without notice that the instrument is overdue or has been dishonored or that there is an uncured default with respect to payment of another instrument issued as part of the same series, (iv) without notice that the instrument contains an unauthorized signature or has been altered, (v) without notice of any claim to the instrument described in Section 3—306, and (vi) without notice that any party has a defense or claim in recoupment described in Section 3—305(a).

(b) Notice of discharge of a party, other than discharge in an insolvency proceeding, is not notice of a defense under subsection (a), but discharge is effective against a person who became a holder in due course with notice of the discharge. Public filing or recording of a document does not of itself constitute notice of a defense, claim in recoupment, or claim to the instrument.

(c) Except to the extent a transferor or predecessor in interest has rights as a holder in due course, a person does not acquire rights of a holder in due course of an instrument taken (i) by legal process or by purchase in an execution, bankruptcy, or creditor's sale or similar proceeding, (ii) by purchase as part of a bulk transaction not in ordinary course of business of the transferor, or (iii) as the successor in interest to an estate or other organization.

(d) If, under Section 3—303(a)(1), the promise of performance that is the consideration for an instrument has been partially performed, the holder may assert rights as a holder in due course of the instrument only to the fraction of the amount payable under the instrument equal to the value of the partial performance divided by the value of the promised performance.

(e) If (i) the person entitled to enforce an instrument has only a security interest in the instrument and (ii) the person obliged to pay the instrument has a defense, claim in recoupment, or claim to the instrument that may be asserted against the person who granted the security interest, the person entitled to enforce the instrument may assert rights as a holder in due course only to an amount payable under the instrument which, at the time of enforcement of the instrument, does not exceed the amount of the unpaid obligation secured.

(f) To be effective, notice must be received at a time and in a manner that gives a reasonable opportunity to act on it.

(g) This section is subject to any law limiting status as a holder in due course in particular classes of transactions.

§3—303. VALUE AND CONSIDERATION

(a) An instrument is issued or transferred for value if:

> (1) the instrument is issued or transferred for a promise of performance, to the extent the promise has been performed;

> (2) the transferee acquires a security interest or other lien in the instrument other than a lien obtained by judicial proceeding;

> (3) the instrument is issued or transferred as payment of, or as security for, an antecedent claim against any person, whether or not the claim is due;

> (4) the instrument is issued or transferred in exchange for a negotiable instrument; or

> (5) the instrument is issued or transferred in exchange for the incurring of an irrevocable obligation to a third party by the person taking the instrument.

(b) "Consideration" means any consideration sufficient to support a simple contract. The drawer or maker of an instrument has a defense if the instrument is issued without consideration. If an instrument is issued for a promise of performance, the issuer has a defense to the extent performance of the promise is due and the promise has not been performed. If an instrument is issued for value as stated in subsection (a), the instrument is also issued for consideration.

§3—304. OVERDUE INSTRUMENT

(a) An instrument payable on demand becomes overdue at the earliest of the following times:

(1) on the day after the day demand for payment is duly made;

(2) if the instrument is a check, 90 days after its date; or

(3) if the instrument is not a check, when the instrument has been outstanding for a period of time after its date which is unreasonably long under the circumstances of the particular case in light of the nature of the instrument and usage of the trade.

(b) With respect to an instrument payable at a definite time the following rules apply:

(1) If the principal is payable in installments and a due date has not been accelerated, the instrument becomes overdue upon default under the instrument for nonpayment of an installment, and the instrument remains overdue until the default is cured.

(2) If the principal is not payable in installments and the due date has not been accelerated, the instrument becomes overdue on the day after the due date.

(3) If a due date with respect to principal has been accelerated, the instrument becomes overdue on the day after the accelerated due date.

(c) Unless the due date of principal has been accelerated, an instrument does not become overdue if there is default in payment of interest but no default in payment of principal.

§3—305. DEFENSES AND CLAIMS IN RECOUPMENT

(a) Except as stated in subsection (b), the right to enforce the obligation of a party to pay an instrument is subject to the following:

(1) a defense of the obligor based on (i) infancy of the obligor to the extent it is a defense to a simple contract, (ii) duress, lack of legal capacity, or illegality of the transaction which, under other law, nullifies the obligation of the obligor, (iii) fraud that induced the obligor to sign the instrument with neither knowledge nor reasonable opportunity to learn of its character or its essential terms, or (iv) discharge of the obligor in insolvency proceedings;

(2) a defense of the obligor stated in another section of this Article or a defense of the obligor that would be available if the person entitled to enforce the instrument were enforcing a right to payment under a simple contract; and

(3) a claim in recoupment of the obligor against the original payee of the instrument if the claim arose from the transaction that gave rise to the instrument; but the claim of the obligor may be asserted against a transferee of the instrument only to reduce the amount owing on the instrument at the time the action is brought.

(b) The right of a holder in due course to enforce the obligation of a party to pay the instrument is subject to defenses of the obligor stated in subsection (a)(1), but is not subject to defenses of the obligor stated in subsection (a)(2) or claims in recoupment stated in subsection (a)(3) against a person other than the holder.

(c) Except as stated in subsection (d), in an action to enforce the obligation of a party to pay the instrument, the obligor may not assert against the person entitled to enforce the instrument a defense, claim in recoupment, or claim to the instrument (Section 3—306) of another person, but the other person's claim to the instrument may be asserted by the obligor if the other person is joined in the action and personally asserts the claim against the person entitled to enforce the instrument. An obligor is not obliged to pay the instrument if the person seeking enforcement of the instrument does not have rights of a holder in due course and the obligor proves that the instrument is a lost or stolen instrument.

(d) In an action to enforce the obligation of an accommodation party to pay an instrument, the accommodation party may assert against the person entitled to enforce the instrument any defense or claim in recoupment under subsection (a) that the accommodated party could assert against the person entitled to enforce the instrument, except the defenses of discharge in insolvency proceedings, infancy, and lack of legal capacity.

§3—306. CLAIMS TO AN INSTRUMENT

A person taking an instrument, other than a person having rights of a holder in due course, is subject to a claim of a property or possessory right in the instrument or its proceeds, including a claim to rescind a negotiation and to recover the instrument or its proceeds. A person having rights of a holder in due course takes free of the claim to the instrument.

§3—307. NOTICE OF BREACH OF FIDUCIARY DUTY

(a) In this section:

(1) "Fiduciary" means an agent, trustee, partner, corporate officer or director, or other representative owing a fiduciary duty with respect to an instrument.

(2) "Represented person" means the principal, beneficiary, partnership, corporation, or other person to whom the duty stated in paragraph (1) is owed.

(b) If (i) an instrument is taken from a fiduciary for payment or collection or for value, (ii) the taker has knowledge of the fiduciary status of the fiduciary, and (iii) the represented person makes a claim to the instrument or its proceeds on the basis that the transaction of the fiduciary is a breach of fiduciary duty, the following rules apply:

(1) Notice of breach of fiduciary duty by the fiduciary is notice of the claim of the represented person.

(2) In the case of an instrument payable to the represented person or the fiduciary as such, the taker has notice of the breach of fiduciary duty if the instrument is (i) taken in payment of or as security for a debt known by the taker to be the personal debt of the fiduciary, (ii) taken in a transaction known by the taker to be for the personal benefit of the fiduciary, or (iii) deposited to an account other than an account of the fiduciary, as such, or an account of the represented person.

(3) If an instrument is issued by the represented person or the fiduciary as such, and made payable to the fiduciary personally, the taker does not have notice of the breach of fiduciary duty unless the taker knows of the breach of fiduciary duty.

(4) If an instrument is issued by the represented person or the fiduciary as such, to the taker as payee, the taker has notice of the breach of fiduciary duty if the instrument is (i) taken in payment of or as security for a debt known by the taker to be the personal debt of the fiduciary, (ii) taken in a transaction known by the taker to be for the personal benefit of the fiduciary, or (iii) deposited to an account other than an account of the fiduciary, as such, or an account of the represented person.

§3—308. PROOF OF SIGNATURES AND STATUS AS HOLDER IN DUE COURSE

(a) In an action with respect to an instrument, the authenticity of, and authority to make, each signature on the instrument is admitted unless specifically denied in the pleadings. If the validity of a signature is denied in the pleadings, the burden of establishing validity is on the person claiming validity, but the signature is presumed to be authentic and authorized unless the action is to enforce the liability of the purported signer and the signer is dead or incompetent at the time of trial of the issue of validity of the signature. If an action to enforce the instrument is brought against a person as the undisclosed principal of a person who signed the instrument as a party to the instrument, the plaintiff has the burden of establishing that the defendant is liable on the instrument as a represented person under Section 3—402(a).

(b) If the validity of signatures is admitted or proved and there is compliance with subsection (a), a plaintiff producing the instrument is entitled to payment if the plaintiff proves entitlement to enforce the instrument under Section 3—301, unless the defendant proves a defense or claim in recoupment. If a defense or claim in recoupment is proved, the right to payment of the plaintiff is subject to the defense or claim, except to the extent the plaintiff proves that the plaintiff has rights of a holder in due course which are not subject to the defense or claim.

§3—309. ENFORCEMENT OF LOST, DESTROYED, OR STOLEN INSTRUMENT

(a) A person not in possession of an instrument is entitled to enforce the instrument if (i) the person was in possession of the instrument and entitled to enforce it when loss of possession occurred, (ii) the loss of possession was not the result of a transfer by the person or a lawful seizure, and (iii) the person cannot reasonably obtain possession of the instrument because the instrument was destroyed, its whereabouts cannot be determined, or it is in the wrongful possession of an unknown person or a person that cannot be found or is not amenable to service of process.

(b) A person seeking enforcement of an instrument under subsection (a) must prove the terms of the instrument and the person's right to enforce the instrument. If that proof is made, Section 3—308 applies to the case as if the person seeking enforcement had produced the instrument. The court may not enter judgment in favor of the person seeking enforcement unless it finds that the person required to pay the instrument is adequately protected against loss that might occur by reason of a claim by another person to enforce the instrument. Adequate protection may be provided by any reasonable means.

§3—310. EFFECT OF INSTRUMENT ON OBLIGATION FOR WHICH TAKEN

(a) Unless otherwise agreed, if a certified check, cashier's check, or teller's check is taken for an obligation, the obligation is discharged to the same extent discharge would result if an amount of money equal to the amount of the instrument were taken in payment of the obligation. Discharge of the obligation does not affect any liability that the obligor may have as an indorser of the instrument.

(b) Unless otherwise agreed and except as provided in subsection (a), if a note or an uncertified check is taken for an obligation, the obligation is suspended to the same extent the obligation would be discharged if an amount of money equal to the amount of the instrument were taken, and the following rules apply:

(1) In the case of an uncertified check, suspension of the obligation continues until dishonor of the check or until it is paid or certified. Payment or certification of the check results in discharge of the obligation to the extent of the amount of the check.

(2) In the case of a note, suspension of the obligation continues until dishonor of the note or until it is paid. Payment of the note results in discharge of the obligation to the extent of the payment.

(3) Except as provided in paragraph (4), if the check or note is dishonored and the obligee of the obligation for which the instrument was taken is the person entitled to enforce the instrument, the obligee may enforce either the instrument or the obligation. In the case of an instrument of a third person which is negotiated to the obligee by the obligor, discharge of the obligor on the instrument also discharges the obligation.

(4) If the person entitled to enforce the instrument taken for an obligation is a person other than the obligee, the obligee may not enforce the obligation to the extent the obligation is suspended. If the obligee is the person entitled to enforce the instrument but no longer has possession of it because it was lost, stolen, or destroyed, the obligation may not be enforced to the extent of the amount payable on the instrument, and to that extent the obligee's rights against the obligor are limited to enforcement of the instrument.

(c) If an instrument other than one described in subsection (a) or (b) is taken for an obligation, the effect is (i) that stated in subsection (a) if the instrument is one on which a bank is liable as maker or acceptor, or (ii) that stated in subsection (b) in any other case.

* * * *

§3—312. LOST, DESTROYED, OR STOLEN CASHIER'S CHECK, TELLER'S CHECK, OR CERTIFIED CHECK.

(1) "Check" means a cashier's check, teller's check, or certified check.

(2) "Claimant" means a person who claims the right to receive the amount of a cashier's check, teller's check, or certified check that was lost, destroyed, or stolen.

(3) "Declaration of loss" means a written statement, made under penalty of perjury, to the effect that (i) the declarer lost possession of a check, (ii) the declarer is the drawer or payee of the check, in the case of a certified check, or the remitter or payee of the check, in the case of a cashier's check or teller's check, (iii) the loss of possession was not the result of a transfer by the declarer or a lawful seizure, and (iv) the declarer cannot reasonably obtain possession of the check because the check was destroyed, its whereabouts cannot be determined, or it is in the wrongful possession of an unknown person or a person that cannot be found or is not amenable to service of process.

(4) "Obligated bank" means the issuer of a cashier's check or teller's check or the acceptor of a certified check.

* * * *

Part 4 Liability of Parties

§3—401. SIGNATURE

(a) A person is not liable on an instrument unless (i) the person signed the instrument, or (ii) the person is represented by an agent or representative who signed the instrument and the signature is binding on the represented person under Section 3—402.

(b) A signature may be made (i) manually or by means of a device or machine, and (ii) by the use of any name, including a trade or assumed name, or by a word, mark, or symbol executed or adopted by a person with present intention to authenticate a writing.

§3—402. SIGNATURE BY REPRESENTATIVE

(a) If a person acting, or purporting to act, as a representative signs an instrument by signing either the name of the represented person or the name of the signer, the represented person is bound by the signature to the same extent the represented person would be bound if the signature were on a simple contract. If the represented person is bound, the signature of the representative is the "authorized signature of the represented person" and the represented person is liable on the instrument, whether or not identified in the instrument.

(b) If a representative signs the name of the representative to an instrument and the signature is an authorized signature of the represented person, the following rules apply:

> (1) If the form of the signature shows unambiguously that the signature is made on behalf of the represented person who is identified in the instrument, the representative is not liable on the instrument.

> (2) Subject to subsection (c), if (i) the form of the signature does not show unambiguously that the signature is made in a representative capacity or (ii) the represented person is not identified in the instrument, the representative is liable on the instrument to a holder in due course that took the instrument without notice that the representative was not intended to be liable on the instrument. With respect to any other person, the representative is liable on the instrument unless the representative proves that the original parties did not intend the representative to be liable on the instrument.

(c) If a representative signs the name of the representative as drawer of a check without indication of the representative status and the check is payable from an account of the represented person who is identified on the check, the signer is not liable on the check if the signature is an authorized signature of the represented person.

§3—403. UNAUTHORIZED SIGNATURE

(a) Unless otherwise provided in this Article or Article 4, an unauthorized signature is ineffective except as the signature of the unauthorized signer in favor of a person who in good faith pays the instrument or takes it for value. An unauthorized signature may be ratified for all purposes of this Article.

(b) If the signature of more than one person is required to constitute the authorized signature of an organization, the signature of the organization is unauthorized if one of the required signatures is lacking.

(c) The civil or criminal liability of a person who makes an unauthorized signature is not affected by any provision of this Article which makes the unauthorized signature effective for the purposes of this Article.

§3—404. IMPOSTORS; FICTITIOUS PAYEES

(a) If an impostor, by use of the mails or otherwise, induces the issuer of an instrument to issue the instrument to the impostor, or to a person acting in concert with the impostor, by impersonating the payee of the instrument or a person authorized to act for the payee, an indorsement of the instrument by any person in the name of the payee is effective as the indorsement of the payee in favor of a person who, in good faith, pays the instrument or takes it for value or for collection.

(b) If (i) a person whose intent determines to whom an instrument is payable (Section 3—110(a) or (b)) does not intend the person identified as payee to have any interest in the instrument, or (ii) the person identified as payee of an instrument is a fictitious person, the following rules apply until the instrument is negotiated by special indorsement:

> (1) Any person in possession of the instrument is its holder.

> (2) An indorsement by any person in the name of the payee stated in the instrument is effective as the indorsement of the payee in favor of a person who, in good faith, pays the instrument or takes it for value or for collection.

(c) Under subsection (a) or (b), an indorsement is made in the name of a payee if (i) it is made in a name substantially similar to that of the payee or (ii) the instrument, whether or not indorsed, is deposited in a depository bank to an account in a name substantially similar to that of the payee.

(d) With respect to an instrument to which subsection (a) or (b) applies, if a person paying the instrument or taking it for value or for collection fails to exercise ordinary care in paying or taking the instrument and that failure substantially contributes to loss resulting from payment of the instrument, the person bearing the loss may recover from the person failing to exercise ordinary care to the extent the failure to exercise ordinary care contributed to the loss.

§3—405. EMPLOYER'S RESPONSIBILITY FOR FRAUDULENT INDORSEMENT BY EMPLOYEE

(a) In this section:

(1) "Employee" includes an independent contractor and employee of an independent contractor retained by the employer.

(2) "Fraudulent indorsement" means (i) in the case of an instrument payable to the employer, a forged indorsement purporting to be that of the employer, or (ii) in the case of an instrument with respect to which the employer is the issuer, a forged indorsement purporting to be that of the person identified as payee.

(3) "Responsibility" with respect to instruments means authority (i) to sign or indorse instruments on behalf of the employer, (ii) to process instruments received by the employer for book-keeping purposes, for deposit to an account, or for other disposition, (iii) to prepare or process instruments for issue in the name of the employer, (iv) to supply information determining the names or addresses of payees of instruments to be issued in the name of the employer, (v) to control the disposition of instruments to be issued in the name of the employer, or (vi) to act otherwise with respect to instruments in a responsible capacity. "Responsibility" does not include authority that merely allows an employee to have access to instruments or blank or incomplete instrument forms that are being stored or transported or are part of incoming or outgoing mail, or similar access.

(b) For the purpose of determining the rights and liabilities of a person who, in good faith, pays an instrument or takes it for value or for collection, if an employer entrusted an employee with responsibility with respect to the instrument and the employee or a person acting in concert with the employee makes a fraudulent indorsement of the instrument, the indorsement is effective as the indorsement of the person to whom the instrument is payable if it is made in the name of that person. If the person paying the instrument or taking it for value or for collection fails to exercise ordinary care in paying or taking the instrument and that failure substantially contributes to loss resulting from the fraud, the person bearing the loss may recover from the person failing to exercise ordinary care to the extent the failure to exercise ordinary care contributed to the loss.

(c) Under subsection (b), an indorsement is made in the name of the person to whom an instrument is payable if (i) it is made in a name substantially similar to the name of that person or (ii) the instrument, whether or not indorsed, is deposited in a depositary bank to an account in a name substantially similar to the name of that person.

§3—406. NEGLIGENCE CONTRIBUTING TO FORGED SIGNATURE OR ALTERATION OF INSTRUMENT

(a) A person whose failure to exercise ordinary care substantially contributes to an alteration of an instrument or to the making of a forged signature on an instrument is precluded from asserting the alteration or the forgery against a person who, in good faith, pays the instrument or takes it for value or for collection.

(b) Under subsection (a), if the person asserting the preclusion fails to exercise ordinary care in paying or taking the instrument and that failure substantially contributes to loss, the loss is allocated between the person precluded and the person asserting the preclusion according to the extent to which the failure of each to exercise ordinary care contributed to the loss.

(c) Under subsection (a), the burden of proving failure to exercise ordinary care is on the person asserting the preclusion. Under subsection (b), the burden of proving failure to exercise ordinary care is on the person precluded.

§3—407. ALTERATION

(a) "Alteration" means (i) an unauthorized change in an instrument that purports to modify in any respect the obligation of a party, or (ii) an unauthorized addition of words or numbers or other change to an incomplete instrument relating to the obligation of a party.

(b) Except as provided in subsection (c), an alteration fraudulently made discharges a party whose obligation is affected by the alteration unless that party assents or is precluded from asserting the alteration. No other alteration discharges a party, and the instrument may be enforced according to its original terms.

(c) A payor bank or drawee paying a fraudulently altered instrument or a person taking it for value, in good faith and without notice of the alteration, may enforce rights with respect to the instrument (i) according to its original terms, or (ii) in the case of an incomplete instrument altered by unauthorized completion, according to its terms as completed.

§3—408. DRAWEE NOT LIABLE ON UNACCEPTED DRAFT

A check or other draft does not of itself operate as an assignment of funds in the hands of the drawee available for its payment, and the drawee is not liable on the instrument until the drawee accepts it.

§3—409. ACCEPTANCE OF DRAFT; CERTIFIED CHECK

(a) "Acceptance" means the drawee's signed agreement to pay a draft as presented. It must be written on the draft and may consist of the drawee's signature alone. Acceptance may be made at any time and becomes effective when notification pursuant to instructions is given or the accepted draft is delivered for the purpose of giving rights on the acceptance to any person.

(b) A draft may be accepted although it has not been signed by the drawer, is otherwise incomplete, is overdue, or has been dishonored.

(c) If a draft is payable at a fixed period after sight and the acceptor fails to date the acceptance, the holder may complete the acceptance by supplying a date in good faith.

(d) "Certified check" means a check accepted by the bank on which it is drawn. Acceptance may be made as stated in subsection (a) or by a writing on the check which indicates that the check is certified. The drawee of a check has no obligation to certify the check, and refusal to certify is not dishonor of the check.

§3—410. ACCEPTANCE VARYING DRAFT

(a) If the terms of a drawee's acceptance vary from the terms of the draft as presented, the holder may refuse the acceptance and treat the draft as dishonored. In that case, the drawee may cancel the acceptance.

(b) The terms of a draft are not varied by an acceptance to pay at a particular bank or place in the United States, unless the acceptance states that the draft is to be paid only at that bank or place.

(c) If the holder assents to an acceptance varying the terms of a draft, the obligation of each drawer and indorser that does not expressly assent to the acceptance is discharged.

§3—411. REFUSAL TO PAY CASHIER'S CHECKS, TELLER'S CHECKS, AND CERTIFIED CHECKS

(a) In this section, "obligated bank" means the acceptor of a certified check or the issuer of a cashier's check or teller's check bought from the issuer.

(b) If the obligated bank wrongfully (i) refuses to pay a cashier's check or certified check, (ii) stops payment of a teller's check, or (iii) refuses to pay a dishonored teller's check, the person asserting the right to enforce the check is entitled to compensation for expenses and loss of interest resulting from the nonpayment and may recover consequential damages if the obligated bank refuses to pay after receiving notice of particular circumstances giving rise to the damages.

(c) Expenses or consequential damages under subsection (b) are not recoverable if the refusal of the obligated bank to pay occurs because (i) the bank suspends payments, (ii) the obligated bank asserts a claim or defense of the bank that it has reasonable grounds to believe is available against the person entitled to enforce the instrument, (iii) the obligated bank has a reasonable doubt whether the person demanding payment is the person entitled to enforce the instrument, or (iv) payment is prohibited by law.

§3—412. OBLIGATION OF ISSUER OF NOTE OR CASHIER'S CHECK

The issuer of a note or cashier's check or other draft drawn on the drawer is obliged to pay the instrument (i) according to its terms at the time it was issued or, if not issued, at the time it first came into possession of a holder, or (ii) if the issuer signed an incomplete instrument, according to its terms when completed, to the extent stated in Sections 3—115 and 3—407. The obligation is owed to a person entitled to enforce the instrument or to an indorser who paid the instrument under Section 3—415.

§3—413. OBLIGATION OF ACCEPTOR

(a) The acceptor of a draft is obliged to pay the draft (i) according to its terms at the time it was accepted, even though the acceptance states that the draft is payable "as originally drawn" or equivalent terms, (ii) if the acceptance varies the terms of the draft, according to the terms of the draft as varied, or (iii) if the acceptance is of a draft that is an incomplete instrument, according to its terms when completed, to the extent stated in Sections 3—115 and 3—407. The obligation is owed to a person entitled to enforce the draft or to the drawer or an indorser who paid the draft under Section 3—414 or 3—415.

(b) If the certification of a check or other acceptance of a draft states the amount certified or accepted, the obligation of the acceptor is that amount. If (i) the certification or acceptance does not state an amount, (ii) the amount of the instrument is subsequently raised, and (iii) the instrument is then negotiated to a holder in due course, the obligation of the acceptor is the amount of the instrument at the time it was taken by the holder in due course.

§3—414. OBLIGATION OF DRAWER

(a) This section does not apply to cashier's checks or other drafts drawn on the drawer.

(b) If an unaccepted draft is dishonored, the drawer is obliged to pay the draft (i) according to its terms at the time it was issued or, if not issued, at the time it first came into possession of a holder, or (ii) if the drawer signed an incomplete instrument, according to its terms when completed, to the extent stated in Sections 3—115 and 3—407. The obligation is owed to a person entitled to enforce the draft or to an indorser who paid the draft under Section 3—415.

(c) If a draft is accepted by a bank, the drawer is discharged, regardless of when or by whom acceptance was obtained.

(d) If a draft is accepted and the acceptor is not a bank, the obligation of the drawer to pay the draft if the draft is dishonored by the acceptor is the same as the obligation of an indorser under Section 3—415(a) and (c).

(e) If a draft states that it is drawn "without recourse" or otherwise disclaims liability of the drawer to pay the draft, the drawer is not liable under subsection (b) to pay the draft if the draft is not a check. A disclaimer of the liability stated in subsection (b) is not effective if the draft is a check.

(f) If (i) a check is not presented for payment or given to a depositary bank for collection within 30 days after its date, (ii) the drawee suspends payments after expiration of the 30-day period without paying the check, and (iii) because of the suspension of payments, the drawer is deprived of funds maintained with the drawee to cover payment of the check, the drawer to the extent deprived of funds may discharge its obligation to pay the check by assigning to the person entitled to enforce the check the rights of the drawer against the drawee with respect to the funds.

§3—415. OBLIGATION OF INDORSER

(a) Subject to subsections (b), (c), and (d) and to Section 3—419(d), if an instrument is dishonored, an indorser is obliged to pay the amount due on the instrument (i) according to the terms of the instrument at the time it was indorsed, or (ii) if the indorser indorsed an incomplete instrument, according to its terms when completed, to the extent stated in Sections 3—115 and 3—407. The obligation of the indorser is owed to a person entitled to enforce the instrument or to a subsequent indorser who paid the instrument under this section.

(b) If an indorsement states that it is made "without recourse" or otherwise disclaims liability of the indorser, the indorser is not liable under subsection (a) to pay the instrument.

(c) If notice of dishonor of an instrument is required by Section 3—503 and notice of dishonor complying with that section is not given to an indorser, the liability of the indorser under subsection (a) is discharged.

(d) If a draft is accepted by a bank after an indorsement is made, the liability of the indorser under subsection (a) is discharged.

(e) If an indorser of a check is liable under subsection (a) and the check is not presented for payment, or given to a depositary bank for collection, within 30 days after the day the indorsement was made, the liability of the indorser under subsection (a) is discharged.

As amended in 1993.

§3—416. TRANSFER WARRANTIES

(a) A person who transfers an instrument for consideration warrants to the transferee and, if the transfer is by indorsement, to any subsequent transferee that:

(1) the warrantor is a person entitled to enforce the instrument;

(2) all signatures on the instrument are authentic and authorized;

(3) the instrument has not been altered;

(4) the instrument is not subject to a defense or claim in recoupment of any party which can be asserted against the warrantor; and

(5) the warrantor has no knowledge of any insolvency proceeding commenced with respect to the maker or acceptor or, in the case of an unaccepted draft, the drawer.

(b) A person to whom the warranties under subsection (a) are made and who took the instrument in good faith may recover from the warrantor as damages for breach of warranty an amount equal to the loss suffered as a result of the breach, but not more than the amount of the instrument plus expenses and loss of interest incurred as a result of the breach.

(c) The warranties stated in subsection (a) cannot be disclaimed with respect to checks. Unless notice of a claim for breach of warranty is given to the warrantor within 30 days after the claimant has reason to know of the breach and the identity of the warrantor, the liability of the warrantor under subsection (b) is discharged to the extent of any loss caused by the delay in giving notice of the claim.

(d) A [cause of action] for breach of warranty under this section accrues when the claimant has reason to know of the breach.

§3—417. PRESENTMENT WARRANTIES

(a) If an unaccepted draft is presented to the drawee for payment or acceptance and the drawee pays or accepts the draft, (i) the person obtaining payment or acceptance, at the time of presentment, and (ii) a previous transferor of the draft, at the time of transfer, warrant to the drawee making payment or accepting the draft in good faith that:

(1) the warrantor is, or was, at the time the warrantor transferred the draft, a person entitled to enforce the draft or authorized to obtain payment or acceptance of the draft on behalf of a person entitled to enforce the draft;

(2) the draft has not been altered; and

(3) the warrantor has no knowledge that the signature of the drawer of the draft is unauthorized.

(b) A drawee making payment may recover from any warrantor damages for breach of warranty equal to the amount paid by the drawee less the amount the drawee received or is entitled to receive from the drawer because of the payment. In addition, the drawee is entitled to compensation for expenses and loss of interest resulting from the breach. The right of the drawee to recover damages under this subsection is not affected by any failure of the drawee to exercise ordinary care in making payment. If the drawee accepts the draft, breach of warranty is a defense to the obligation of the acceptor. If the acceptor makes payment with respect to the draft, the acceptor is entitled to recover from any warrantor for breach of warranty the amounts stated in this subsection.

(c) If a drawee asserts a claim for breach of warranty under subsection (a) based on an unauthorized indorsement of the draft or an alteration of the draft, the warrantor may defend by proving that the indorsement is effective under Section 3—404 or 3—405 or the drawer is precluded under Section 3—406 or 4—406 from asserting against the drawee the unauthorized indorsement or alteration.

(d) If (i) a dishonored draft is presented for payment to the drawer or an indorser or (ii) any other instrument is presented for payment to a party obliged to pay the instrument, and (iii) payment is received, the following rules apply:

(1) The person obtaining payment and a prior transferor of the instrument warrant to the person making payment in good faith that the warrantor is, or was, at the time the warrantor transferred the instrument, a person entitled to enforce the instrument or authorized to obtain payment on behalf of a person entitled to enforce the instrument.

(2) The person making payment may recover from any warrantor for breach of warranty an amount equal to the amount paid plus expenses and loss of interest resulting from the breach.

(e) The warranties stated in subsections (a) and (d) cannot be disclaimed with respect to checks. Unless notice of a claim for breach of warranty is given to the warrantor within 30 days after the claimant has reason to know of the breach and the identity of the warrantor, the liability of the warrantor under subsection (b) or (d) is discharged to the extent of any loss caused by the delay in giving notice of the claim.

(f) A [cause of action] for breach of warranty under this section accrues when the claimant has reason to know of the breach.

§3—418. PAYMENT OR ACCEPTANCE BY MISTAKE

(a) Except as provided in subsection (c), if the drawee of a draft pays or accepts the draft and the drawee acted on the mistaken belief that (i) payment of the draft had not been stopped pursuant to Section 4—403 or (ii) the signature of the drawer of the draft was authorized, the drawee may recover the amount of the draft from the person to whom or for whose benefit payment was made or, in the case of acceptance, may revoke the acceptance. Rights of the drawee under this subsection are not affected by failure of the drawee to exercise ordinary care in paying or accepting the draft.

(b) Except as provided in subsection (c), if an instrument has been paid or accepted by mistake and the case is not covered by subsection (a), the person paying or accepting may, to the extent permitted by the law governing mistake and restitution, (i) recover the payment from the person to whom or for whose benefit payment was made or (ii) in the case of acceptance, may revoke the acceptance.

(c) The remedies provided by subsection (a) or (b) may not be asserted against a person who took the instrument in good faith and for value or who in good faith changed position in reliance on the payment or acceptance. This subsection does not limit remedies provided by Section 3—417 or 4—407.

(d) Notwithstanding Section 4—215, if an instrument is paid or accepted by mistake and the payor or acceptor recovers payment or revokes acceptance under subsection (a) or (b), the instrument is deemed not to have been paid or accepted and is treated as dishonored, and the person from whom payment is recovered has rights as a person entitled to enforce the dishonored instrument.

§3—419. INSTRUMENTS SIGNED FOR ACCOMMODATION

(a) If an instrument is issued for value given for the benefit of a party to the instrument ("accommodated party") and another party to the instrument ("accommodation party") signs the instrument for the purpose of incurring liability on the instrument without being a direct beneficiary of the value given for the instrument, the instrument is signed by the accommodation party "for accommodation."

(b) An accommodation party may sign the instrument as maker, drawer, acceptor, or indorser and, subject to subsection (d), is obliged to pay the instrument in the capacity in which the accommodation party signs. The obligation of an accommodation party may be enforced notwithstanding any statute of frauds and whether or not the accommodation party receives consideration for the accommodation.

* * * *

(e) An accommodation party who pays the instrument is entitled to reimbursement from the accommodated party and is entitled to enforce the instrument against the accommodated party. An accommodated party who pays the instrument has no right of recourse against, and is not entitled to contribution from, an accommodation party.

§3—420. CONVERSION OF INSTRUMENT

(a) The law applicable to conversion of personal property applies to instruments. An instrument is also converted if it is taken by transfer, other than a negotiation, from a person not entitled to enforce the instrument or a bank makes or obtains payment with respect to the instrument for a person not entitled to enforce the instrument or receive payment. An action for conversion of an instrument may not be brought by (i) the issuer or acceptor of the instrument or (ii) a payee or indorsee who did not receive delivery of the instrument either directly or through delivery to an agent or a co-payee.

(b) In an action under subsection (a), the measure of liability is presumed to be the amount payable on the instrument, but recovery may not exceed the amount of the plaintiff's interest in the instrument.

(c) A representative, other than a depositary bank, who has in good faith dealt with an instrument or its proceeds on behalf of one who was not the person entitled to enforce the instrument is not liable in conversion to that person beyond the amount of any proceeds that it has not paid out.

§3—501. PRESENTMENT

(a) "Presentment" means a demand made by or on behalf of a person entitled to enforce an instrument (i) to pay the instrument made to the drawee or a party obliged to pay the instrument or, in the case of a note or accepted draft payable at a bank, to the bank, or (ii) to accept a draft made to the drawee.

(b) The following rules are subject to Article 4, agreement of the parties, and clearing-house rules and the like:

(1) Presentment may be made at the place of payment of the instrument and must be made at the place of payment if the instrument is payable at a bank in the United States; may be made by any commercially reasonable means, including an oral, written, or electronic communication; is effective when the demand for payment or acceptance is received by the person to whom presentment is made; and is effective if made to any one of two or more makers, acceptors, drawees, or other payors.

(2) Upon demand of the person to whom presentment is made, the person making presentment must (i) exhibit the instrument, (ii) give reasonable identification and, if presentment is made on behalf of another person, reasonable evidence of authority to do so, and (…) sign a receipt on the instrument for any payment made or surrender the instrument if full payment is made.

(3) Without dishonoring the instrument, the party to whom presentment is made may (i) return the instrument for lack of a necessary indorsement, or (ii) refuse payment or acceptance for failure of the presentment to comply with the terms of the instrument, an agreement of the parties, or other applicable law or rule.

(4) The party to whom presentment is made may treat presentment as occurring on the next business day after the day of presentment if the party to whom presentment is made has established a

cut-off hour not earlier than 2 P.M. for the receipt and processing of instruments presented for payment or acceptance and presentment is made after the cut-off hour.

§3—502. DISHONOR

(a) Dishonor of a note is governed by the following rules:

(1) If the note is payable on demand, the note is dishonored if presentment is duly made to the maker and the note is not paid on the day of presentment.

(2) If the note is not payable on demand and is payable at or through a bank or the terms of the note require presentment, the note is dishonored if presentment is duly made and the note is not paid on the day it becomes payable or the day of presentment, whichever is later.

(3) If the note is not payable on demand and paragraph (2) does not apply, the note is dishonored if it is not paid on the day it becomes payable.

(b) Dishonor of an unaccepted draft other than a documentary draft is governed by the following rules:

(1) If a check is duly presented for payment to the payor bank otherwise than for immediate payment over the counter, the check is dishonored if the payor bank makes timely return of the check or sends timely notice of dishonor or nonpayment under Section 4—301 or 4—302, or becomes accountable for the amount of the check under Section 4—302.

(2) If a draft is payable on demand and paragraph (1) does not apply, the draft is dishonored if presentment for payment is duly made to the drawee and the draft is not paid on the day of presentment.

(3) If a draft is payable on a date stated in the draft, the draft is dishonored if (i) presentment for payment is duly made to the drawee and payment is not made on the day the draft becomes payable or the day of presentment, whichever is later, or (ii) presentment for acceptance is duly made before the day the draft becomes payable and the draft is not accepted on the day of presentment.

(4) If a draft is payable on elapse of a period of time after sight or acceptance, the draft is dishonored if presentment for acceptance is duly made and the draft is not accepted on the day of presentment.

(c) Dishonor of an unaccepted documentary draft occurs according to the rules stated in subsection (b)(2), (3),

and (4), except that payment or acceptance may be delayed without dishonor until no later than the close of the third business day of the drawee following the day on which payment or acceptance is required by those paragraphs.

(d) Dishonor of an accepted draft is governed by the following rules:

(1) If the draft is payable on demand, the draft is dishonored if presentment for payment is duly made to the acceptor and the draft is not paid on the day of presentment.

(2) If the draft is not payable on demand, the draft is dishonored if presentment for payment is duly made to the acceptor and payment is not made on the day it becomes payable or the day of presentment, whichever is later.

(e) In any case in which presentment is otherwise required for dishonor under this section and presentment is excused under Section 3—504, dishonor occurs without presentment if the instrument is not duly accepted or paid.

(f) If a draft is dishonored because timely acceptance of the draft was not made and the person entitled to demand acceptance consents to a late acceptance, from the time of acceptance the draft is treated as never having been dishonored.

§3—503. NOTICE OF DISHONOR

(a) The obligation of an indorser stated in Section 3—415 (a) and the obligation of a drawer stated in Section 3—414 (d) may not be enforced unless (i) the indorser or drawer is given notice of dishonor of the instrument complying with this section or (ii) notice of dishonor is excused under Section 3—504(b).

(b) Notice of dishonor may be given by any person; may be given by any commercially reasonable means, including an oral, written, or electronic communication; and is sufficient if it reasonably identifies the instrument and indicates that the instrument has been dishonored or has not been paid or accepted. Return of an instrument given to a bank for collection is sufficient notice of dishonor.

(c) Subject to Section 3—504(c), with respect to an instrument taken for collection by a collecting bank, notice of dishonor must be given (i) by the bank before midnight of the next banking day following the banking day on which the bank receives notice of dishonor of the instrument, or (ii) by any other person within 30 days following the day on which the person receives notice of dishonor. With respect to any other instrument, notice of dishonor must be given within 30 days following the day on which dishonor occurs.

* * * *

§3—601. DISCHARGE AND EFFECT OF DISCHARGE

(a) The obligation of a party to pay the instrument is discharged as stated in this Article or by an act or agreement with the party which would discharge an obligation to pay money under a simple contract.

(b) Discharge of the obligation of a party is not effective against a person acquiring rights of a holder in due course of the instrument without notice of the discharge.

§3—602. PAYMENT

(a) Subject to subsection (b), an instrument is paid to the extent payment is made (i) by or on behalf of a party obliged to pay the instrument, and (ii) to a person entitled to enforce the instrument. To the extent of the payment, the obligation of the party obliged to pay the instrument is discharged even though payment is made with knowledge of a claim to the instrument under Section 3—306 by another person.

(b) The obligation of a party to pay the instrument is not discharged under subsection (a) if:

    (1) a claim to the instrument under Section 3—306 is enforceable against the party receiving payment and (i) payment is made with knowledge by the payor that payment is prohibited by injunction or similar process of a court of competent jurisdiction, or (ii) in the case of an instrument other than a cashier's check, teller's check, or certified check, the party making payment accepted, from the person having a claim to the instrument, indemnity against loss resulting from refusal to pay the person entitled to enforce the instrument; or

    (2) the person making payment knows that the instrument is a stolen instrument and pays a person it knows is in wrongful possession of the instrument.

§3—603. TENDER OF PAYMENT

(a) If tender of payment of an obligation to pay an instrument is made to a person entitled to enforce the instrument, the effect of tender is governed by principles of law applicable to tender of payment under a simple contract.

(b) If tender of payment of an obligation to pay an instrument is made to a person entitled to enforce the instrument and the tender is refused, there is discharge, to the extent of the amount of the tender, of the obligation of an indorser or accommodation party having a right of recourse with respect to the obligation to which the tender relates.

(c) If tender of payment of an amount due on an instrument is made to a person entitled to enforce the instrument, the obligation of the obligor to pay interest after the due date on the amount tendered is discharged. If presentment is required with respect to an instrument and the obligor is able and ready to pay on the due date at every place of payment stated in the instrument, the obligor is deemed to have made tender of payment on the due date to the person entitled to enforce the instrument.

§3—604. DISCHARGE BY CANCELLATION OR RENUNCIATION

(a) A person entitled to enforce an instrument, with or without consideration, may discharge the obligation of a party to pay the instrument (i) by an intentional voluntary act, such as surrender of the instrument to the party, destruction, mutilation, or cancellation of the instrument, cancellation or striking out of the party's signature, or the addition of words to the instrument indicating discharge, or (ii) by agreeing not to sue or otherwise renouncing rights against the party by a signed writing.

(b) Cancellation or striking out of an indorsement pursuant to subsection (a) does not affect the status and rights of a party derived from the indorsement.

§3—605. DISCHARGE OF INDORSERS AND ACCOMMODATION PARTIES

(a) In this section, the term "indorser" includes a drawer having the obligation described in Section 3—414(d).

(b) Discharge, under Section 3—604, of the obligation of a party to pay an instrument does not discharge the obligation of an indorser or accommodation party having a right of recourse against the discharged party.

(c) If a person entitled to enforce an instrument agrees, with or without consideration, to an extension of the due date of the obligation of a party to pay the instrument, the extension discharges an indorser or accommodation party having a right of recourse against the party whose obligation is extended to the extent the indorser or accommodation party proves that the extension caused loss to the indorser or accommodation party with respect to the right of recourse.

(d) If a person entitled to enforce an instrument agrees, with or without consideration, to a material modification of the obligation of a party other than an extension of the due date, the modification discharges the obligation of an indorser or accommodation party having a right of recourse against the person whose obligation is modified to the extent the modification causes loss to the indorser or accommodation party with respect to the right of recourse. The loss suffered by the indorser or accommodation party as a result of the modification is equal to the amount of the right of recourse unless the person enforcing the instrument proves that no loss was caused by the modification or that the loss caused by the modification was an amount less than the amount of the right of recourse.

(e) If the obligation of a party to pay an instrument is secured by an interest in collateral and a person entitled to enforce the instrument impairs the value of the interest in collateral, the obligation of an indorser or accommodation party having a right of recourse against the obligor is discharged to the extent of the impairment. The value of an interest in collateral is impaired to the extent (i) the value of the interest is reduced to an amount less than the amount of the right of recourse of the party asserting discharge, or (ii) the reduction in value of the interest causes an increase in the amount by which the amount of the right of recourse exceeds the value of the interest. The burden of proving impairment is on the party asserting discharge.

(f) If the obligation of a party is secured by an interest in collateral not provided by an accommodation party and a person entitled to enforce the instrument impairs the value of the interest in collateral, the obligation of any party who is jointly and severally liable with respect to the secured obligation is discharged to the extent the impairment causes the party asserting discharge to pay more than that party would have been obliged to pay, taking into account rights of contribution, if impairment had not occurred. If the party asserting discharge is an accommodation party not entitled to discharge under subsection (e), the party is deemed to have a right to contribution based on joint and several liability rather than a right to reimbursement. The burden of proving impairment is on the party asserting discharge.

* * * *

(h) An accommodation party is not discharged under subsection (c), (d), or (e) unless the person entitled to enforce the instrument knows of the accommodation or has notice under Section 3—419(c) that the instrument was signed for accommodation.

(i) A party is not discharged under this section if (i) the party asserting discharge consents to the event or conduct that is the basis of the discharge, or (ii) the instrument or a separate agreement of the party provides for waiver of discharge under this section either specifically or by general language indicating that parties waive defenses based on suretyship or impairment of collateral.

* * * *

Revised Article 4 Bank Deposits and Collections

Part 1 General Provisions and Definitions

§4—103. VARIATION BY AGREEMENT; MEASURE OF DAMAGES; ACTION CONSTITUTING ORDINARY CARE

(a) The effect of the provisions of this Article may be varied by agreement, but the parties to the agreement cannot disclaim a bank's responsibility for its lack of good faith or failure to exercise ordinary care or limit the measure of damages for the lack or failure. However, the parties may determine by agreement the standards by which the bank's responsibility is to be measured if those standards are not manifestly unreasonable.

(b) Federal Reserve regulations and operating circulars, clearing-house rules, and the like have the effect of agreements under subsection (a), whether or not specifically assented to by all parties interested in items handled.

* * * *

§4—104. DEFINITIONS AND INDEX OF DEFINITIONS

(1) "Account" means any deposit or credit account with a bank, including a demand, time, savings, passbook, share draft, or like account, other than an account evidenced by a certificate of deposit;

* * * *

(3) "Banking day" means the part of a day on which a bank is open to the public for carrying on substantially all of its banking functions;

(4) "Clearing house" means an association of banks or other payors regularly clearing items;

* * * *

(7) "Draft" means a draft as defined in Section 3—104 or an item, other than an instrument, that is an order;

(8) "Drawee" means a person ordered in a draft to make payment;

* * * *

(10) "Midnight deadline" with respect to a bank is midnight on its next banking day following the banking day on which it receives the relevant item or notice or from which the time for taking action commences to run, whichever is later;

* * * *

§4—105. "BANK"; "DEPOSITARY BANK"; "PAYOR BANK"; "INTERMEDIARY BANK"; "COLLECTING BANK"; "PRESENTING BANK"

In this Article:

(1) "Bank" means a person engaged in the business of banking, including a savings bank, savings and loan association, credit union, or trust company;

(2) "Depositary bank" means the first bank to take an item even though it is also the payor bank, unless the item is presented for immediate payment over the counter;

(3) "Payor bank" means a bank that is the drawee of a draft;

(4) "Intermediary bank" means a bank to which an item is transferred in course of collection except the depositary or payor bank;

(5) "Collecting bank" means a bank handling an item for collection except the payor bank;

(6) "Presenting bank" means a bank presenting an item except a payor bank.

§4—106. PAYABLE THROUGH OR PAYABLE AT BANK: COLLECTING BANK

(a) If an item states that it is "payable through" a bank identified in the item, (i) the item designates the bank as a collecting bank and does not by itself authorize the bank to pay the item, and (ii) the item may be presented for payment only by or through the bank.

Alternative A

(b) If an item states that it is "payable at" a bank identified in the item, the item is equivalent to a draft drawn on the bank.

Alternative B

(b) If an item states that it is "payable at" a bank identified in the item, (i) the item designates the bank as a collecting bank and does not by itself authorize the bank to pay the item, and (ii) the item may be presented for payment only by or through the bank.

(c) If a draft names a nonbank drawee and it is unclear whether a bank named in the draft is a co-drawee or a collecting bank, the bank is a collecting bank.

§4—107. SEPARATE OFFICE OF BANK

A branch or separate office of a bank is a separate bank for the purpose of computing the time within which and determining the place at or to which action may be taken or notices or orders shall be given under this Article and under Article 3.

§4—108. TIME OF RECEIPT OF ITEMS

(a) For the purpose of allowing time to process items, prove balances, and make the necessary entries on its books to determine its position for the day, a bank may fix an afternoon hour of 2 P.M. or later as a cutoff hour for the handling of money and items and the making of entries on its books.

(b) An item or deposit of money received on any day after a cutoff hour so fixed or after the close of the banking day may be treated as being received at the opening of the next banking day.

§4—109. DELAYS

(a) Unless otherwise instructed, a collecting bank in a good faith effort to secure payment of a specific item drawn on a payor other than a bank, and with or without the approval of any person involved, may waive, modify, or extend time limits imposed or permitted by this [act] for a period not exceeding two additional banking days without discharge of drawers or indorsers or liability to its transferor or a prior party.

(b) Delay by a collecting bank or payor bank beyond time limits prescribed or permitted by this [act] or by instructions is excused if (i) the delay is caused by interruption of communication or computer facilities, suspension of payments by another bank, war, emergency conditions, failure of equipment, or other circumstances beyond the control of the bank, and (ii) the bank exercises such diligence as the circumstances require.

§4—110. ELECTRONIC PRESENTMENT

(a) "Agreement for electronic presentment" means an agreement, clearing-house rule, or Federal Reserve regulation or operating circular, providing that presentment of an item may be made by transmission of an image of an item or information describing the item ("presentment notice") rather than delivery of the item itself. The agreement may provide for procedures governing retention, presentment, payment, dishonor, and other matters concerning items subject to the agreement.

* * * *

§4—111. STATUTE OF LIMITATIONS

An action to enforce an obligation, duty, or right arising under this Article must be commenced within three years after the [cause of action] accrues.

§4—201. STATUS OF COLLECTING BANK AS AGENT AND PROVISIONAL STATUS OF CREDITS; APPLICABILITY OF ARTICLE; ITEM INDORSED "PAY ANY BANK"

(a) Unless a contrary intent clearly appears and before the time that a settlement given by a collecting bank for an item is or becomes final, the bank, with respect to an item, is an agent or sub-agent of the owner of the item and any settlement given for the item is provisional. This provision applies regardless of the form of indorsement or lack of indorsement and even though credit given for the item is subject to immediate withdrawal as of right or is in fact withdrawn; but the continuance of ownership of an item by its owner and any rights of the owner to proceeds of the item are subject to rights of a collecting bank, such as those resulting from outstanding advances on the item and rights of recoupment or setoff. If an item is handled by banks for purposes of presentment, payment, collection, or return, the relevant provisions of this Article apply even though action of the parties clearly establishes that a particular bank has purchased the item and is the owner of it.

(b) After an item has been indorsed with the words "pay any bank" or the like, only a bank may acquire the rights of a holder until the item has been:

(1) returned to the customer initiating collection; or

(2) specially indorsed by a bank to a person who is not a bank.

§4—202. RESPONSIBILITY FOR COLLECTION OR RETURN; WHEN ACTION TIMELY

(a) A collecting bank must exercise ordinary care in:

(1) presenting an item or sending it for presentment;

(2) sending notice of dishonor or nonpayment or returning an item other than a documentary draft to the bank's transferor after learning that the item has not been paid or accepted, as the case may be;

(3) settling for an item when the bank receives final settlement; and

(4) notifying its transferor of any loss or delay in transit within a reasonable time after discovery thereof.

(b) A collecting bank exercises ordinary care under subsection (a) by taking proper action before its midnight deadline following receipt of an item, notice, or settlement. Taking proper action within a reasonably longer time may constitute the exercise of ordinary care, but the bank has the burden of establishing timeliness.

(c) Subject to subsection (a)(1), a bank is not liable for the insolvency, neglect, misconduct, mistake, or default of another bank or person or for loss or destruction of an item in the possession of others or in transit.

* * * *

§4—205. DEPOSITARY BANK HOLDER OF UNINDORSED ITEM

If a customer delivers an item to a depositary bank for collection:

(1) the depositary bank becomes a holder of the item at the time it receives the item for collection if the customer at the time of delivery was a holder of the item, whether or not the customer indorses the item, and, if the bank satisfies the other requirements of Section 3—302, it is a holder in due course; and

(2) the depositary bank warrants to collecting banks, the payor bank or other payor, and the drawer that the amount of the item was paid to the customer or deposited to the customer's account.

* * * *

§4—207. TRANSFER WARRANTIES

(a) A customer or collecting bank that transfers an item and receives a settlement or other consideration warrants to the transferee and to any subsequent collecting bank that:

(1) the warrantor is a person entitled to enforce the item;

(2) all signatures on the item are authentic and authorized;

(3) the item has not been altered;

(4) the item is not subject to a defense or claim in recoupment (Section 3—305(a)) of any party that can be asserted against the warrantor; and

(5) the warrantor has no knowledge of any insolvency proceeding commenced with respect to the

maker or acceptor or, in the case of an unaccepted draft, the drawer.

(b) If an item is dishonored, a customer or collecting bank transferring the item and receiving settlement or other consideration is obliged to pay the amount due on the item (i) according to the terms of the item at the time it was transferred, or (ii) if the transfer was of an incomplete item, according to its terms when completed as stated in Sections 3—115 and 3—407. The obligation of a transferor is owed to the transferee and to any subsequent collecting bank that takes the item in good faith. A transferor cannot disclaim its obligation under this subsection by an indorsement stating that it is made "without recourse" or otherwise disclaiming liability.

(c) A person to whom the warranties under subsection (a) are made and who took the item in good faith may recover from the warrantor as damages for breach of warranty an amount equal to the loss suffered as a result of the breach, but not more than the amount of the item plus expenses and loss of interest incurred as a result of the breach.

(d) The warranties stated in subsection (a) cannot be disclaimed with respect to checks. Unless notice of a claim for breach of warranty is given to the warrantor within 30 days after the claimant has reason to know of the breach and the identity of the warrantor, the warrantor is discharged to the extent of any loss caused by the delay in giving notice of the claim.

(e) A cause of action for breach of warranty under this section accrues when the claimant has reason to know of the breach.

§4—208. PRESENTMENT WARRANTIES

(a) If an unaccepted draft is presented to the drawee for payment or acceptance and the drawee pays or accepts the draft, (i) the person obtaining payment or acceptance, at the time of presentment, and (ii) a previous transferor of the draft, at the time of transfer, warrant to the drawee that pays or accepts the draft in good faith that:

> (1) the warrantor is, or was, at the time the warrantor transferred the draft, a person entitled to enforce the draft or authorized to obtain payment or acceptance of the draft on behalf of a person entitled to enforce the draft;
>
> (2) the draft has not been altered; and
>
> (3) the warrantor has no knowledge that the signature of the purported drawer of the draft is unauthorized.

(b) A drawee making payment may recover from a warrantor damages for breach of warranty equal to the amount paid by the drawee less the amount the drawee received or is entitled to receive from the drawer because of the payment. In addition, the drawee is entitled to compensation for expenses and loss of interest resulting from the breach. The right of the drawee to recover damages under this subsection is not affected by any failure of the drawee to exercise ordinary care in making payment. If the drawee accepts the draft (i) breach of warranty is a defense to the obligation of the acceptor, and (ii) if the acceptor makes payment with respect to the draft, the acceptor is entitled to recover from a warrantor for breach of warranty the amounts stated in this subsection.

(c) If a drawee asserts a claim for breach of warranty under subsection (a) based on an unauthorized indorsement of the draft or an alteration of the draft, the warrantor may defend by proving that the indorsement is effective under Section 3—404 or 3—405 or the drawer is precluded under Section 3—406 or 4—406 from asserting against the drawee the unauthorized indorsement or alteration.

(d) If (i) a dishonored draft is presented for payment to the drawer or an indorser or (ii) any other item is presented for payment to a party obliged to pay the item, and the item is paid, the person obtaining payment and a prior transferor of the item warrant to the person making payment in good faith that the warrantor is, or was, at the time the warrantor transferred the item, a person entitled to enforce the item or authorized to obtain payment on behalf of a person entitled to enforce the item. The person making payment may recover from any warrantor for breach of warranty an amount equal to the amount paid plus expenses and loss of interest resulting from the breach.

(e) The warranties stated in subsections (a) and (d) cannot be disclaimed with respect to checks. Unless notice of a claim for breach of warranty is given to the warrantor within 30 days after the claimant has reason to know of the breach and the identity of the warrantor, the warrantor is discharged to the extent of any loss caused by the delay in giving notice of the claim.

(f) A cause of action for breach of warranty under this section accrues when the claimant has reason to know of the breach.

* * * *

§4—211. WHEN BANK GIVES VALUE FOR PURPOSES OF HOLDER IN DUE COURSE

For purposes of determining its status as a holder in due course, a bank has given value to the extent it has a security interest in an item, if the bank otherwise complies with the requirements of Section 3—302 on what constitutes a holder in due course.

As amended in 1990.

§4—212. PRESENTMENT BY NOTICE OF ITEM NOT PAYABLE BY, THROUGH, OR AT BANK; LIABILITY OF DRAWER OR INDORSER

(a) Unless otherwise instructed, a collecting bank may present an item not payable by, through, or at a bank by sending to the party to accept or pay a written notice that the bank holds the item for acceptance or payment. The notice must be sent in time to be received on or before the day when presentment is due and the bank must meet any requirement of the party to accept or pay under Section 3—501 by the close of the bank's next banking day after it knows of the requirement.

(b) If presentment is made by notice and payment, acceptance, or request for compliance with a requirement under Section 3—501 is not received by the close of business on the day after maturity or, in the case of demand items, by the close of business on the third banking day after notice was sent, the presenting bank may treat the item as dishonored and charge any drawer or indorser by sending it notice of the facts.

* * * *

§4—214. RIGHT OF CHARGE-BACK OR REFUND; LIABILITY OF COLLECTING BANK: RETURN OF ITEM

(a) If a collecting bank has made provisional settlement with its customer for an item and fails by reason of dishonor, suspension of payments by a bank, or otherwise to receive settlement for the item which is or becomes final, the bank may revoke the settlement given by it, charge back the amount of any credit given for the item to its customer's account, or obtain refund from its customer, whether or not it is able to return the item, if by its midnight deadline or within a longer reasonable time after it learns the facts it returns the item or sends notification of the facts. If the return or notice is delayed beyond the bank's midnight deadline or a longer reasonable time after it learns the facts, the bank may revoke the settlement, charge back the credit, or obtain refund from its customer, but it is liable for any loss resulting from the delay. These rights to revoke, charge back, and obtain refund terminate if and when a settlement for the item received by the bank is or becomes final.

(b) A collecting bank returns an item when it is sent or delivered to the bank's customer or transferor or pursuant to its instructions.

(c) A depositary bank that is also the payor may charge back the amount of an item to its customer's account or obtain refund in accordance with the section governing return of an item received by a payor bank for credit on its books (Section 4—301).

(d) The right to charge back is not affected by:

(1) previous use of a credit given for the item; or

(2) failure by any bank to exercise ordinary care with respect to the item, but a bank so failing remains liable.

(e) A failure to charge back or claim refund does not affect other rights of the bank against the customer or any other party.

(f) If credit is given in dollars as the equivalent of the value of an item payable in foreign money, the dollar amount of any charge-back or refund must be calculated on the basis of the bank-offered spot rate for the foreign money prevailing on the day when the person entitled to the charge-back or refund learns that it will not receive payment in ordinary course.

§4—215. FINAL PAYMENT OF ITEM BY PAYOR BANK; WHEN PROVISIONAL DEBITS AND CREDITS BECOME FINAL; WHEN CERTAIN CREDITS BECOME AVAILABLE FOR WITHDRAWAL

(a) An item is finally paid by a payor bank when the bank has first done any of the following:

(1) paid the item in cash;

(2) settled for the item without having a right to revoke the settlement under statute, clearing- house rule, or agreement; or

(3) made a provisional settlement for the item and failed to revoke the settlement in the time and manner permitted by statute, clearing-house rule, or agreement.

(b) If provisional settlement for an item does not become final, the item is not finally paid.

* * * *

§4—216. INSOLVENCY AND PREFERENCE

(a) If an item is in or comes into the possession of a payor or collecting bank that suspends payment and the item has not been finally paid, the item must be returned by the receiver, trustee, or agent in charge of the closed bank to the presenting bank or the closed bank's customer.

(b) If a payor bank finally pays an item and suspends payments without making a settlement for the item with its customer or the presenting bank which settlement is or becomes final, the owner of the item has a preferred claim against the payor bank.

(c) If a payor bank gives or a collecting bank gives or receives a provisional settlement for an item and thereafter suspends payments, the suspension does not prevent or interfere with the settlement's becoming final if the finality occurs automatically upon the lapse of certain time or the happening of certain events.

(d) If a collecting bank receives from subsequent parties settlement for an item, which settlement is or becomes final and the bank suspends payments without making a settlement for the item with its customer which settlement is or becomes final, the owner of the item has a preferred claim against the collecting bank.

§4—301. DEFERRED POSTING; RECOVERY OF PAYMENT BY RETURN OF ITEMS; TIME OF DISHONOR; RETURN OF ITEMS BY PAYOR BANK

(a) If a payor bank settles for a demand item other than a documentary draft presented otherwise than for immediate payment over the counter before midnight of the banking day of receipt, the payor bank may revoke the settlement and recover the settlement if, before it has made final payment and before its midnight deadline, it

> (1) returns the item; or
>
> (2) sends written notice of dishonor or nonpayment if the item is unavailable for return.

(b) If a demand item is received by a payor bank for credit on its books, it may return the item or send notice of dishonor and may revoke any credit given or recover the amount thereof withdrawn by its customer, if it acts within the time limit and in the manner specified in subsection (a).

(c) Unless previous notice of dishonor has been sent, an item is dishonored at the time when for purposes of dishonor it is returned or notice sent in accordance with this section.

(d) An item is returned:

> (1) as to an item presented through a clearing house, when it is delivered to the presenting or last collecting bank or to the clearing house or is sent or delivered in accordance with clearing-house rules; or
>
> (2) in all other cases, when it is sent or delivered to the bank's customer or transferor or pursuant to instructions.

§4—302. PAYOR BANK'S RESPONSIBILITY FOR LATE RETURN OF ITEM

(a) If an item is presented to and received by a payor bank, the bank is accountable for the amount of:

> (1) a demand item, other than a documentary draft, whether properly payable or not, if the bank, in any case in which it is not also the depositary bank, retains the item beyond midnight of the banking day of receipt without settling for it or, whether or not it is also the depositary bank, does not pay or return the item or send notice of dishonor until after its midnight deadline; or
>
> (2) any other properly payable item unless, within the time allowed for acceptance or payment of that item, the bank either accepts or pays the item or returns it and accompanying documents.

(b) The liability of a payor bank to pay an item pursuant to subsection (a) is subject to defenses based on breach of a presentment warranty (Section 4—208) or proof that the person seeking enforcement of the liability presented or transferred the item for the purpose of defrauding the payor bank.

§4—303. WHEN ITEMS SUBJECT TO NOTICE, STOP-PAYMENT ORDER, LEGAL PROCESS, OR SETOFF; ORDER IN WHICH ITEMS MAY BE CHARGED OR CERTIFIED

(a) Any knowledge, notice, or stop-payment order received by, legal process served upon, or setoff exercised by a payor bank comes too late to terminate, suspend, or modify the bank's right or duty to pay an item or to charge its customer's account for the item if the knowledge, notice, stop-payment order, or legal process is received or served and a reasonable time for the bank to act thereon expires or the setoff is exercised after the earliest of the following:

> (1) the bank accepts or certifies the item;
>
> (2) the bank pays the item in cash;
>
> (3) the bank settles for the item without having a right to revoke the settlement under statute, clearing-house rule, or agreement;
>
> (4) the bank becomes accountable for the amount of the item under Section 4—302 dealing with the payor bank's responsibility for late return of items; or
>
> (5) with respect to checks, a cutoff hour no earlier than one hour after the opening of the next banking day after the banking day on which the bank received the check and no later than the close of that next banking day or, if no cutoff hour is fixed,

the close of the next banking day after the banking day on which the bank received the check.

(b) Subject to subsection (a), items may be accepted, paid, certified, or charged to the indicated account of its customer in any order.

§4—401. WHEN BANK MAY CHARGE CUSTOMER'S ACCOUNT

(a) A bank may charge against the account of a customer an item that is properly payable from the account even though the charge creates an overdraft. An item is properly payable if it is authorized by the customer and is in accordance with any agreement between the customer and bank.

(b) A customer is not liable for the amount of an overdraft if the customer neither signed the item nor benefited from the proceeds of the item.

(c) A bank may charge against the account of a customer a check that is otherwise properly payable from the account, even though payment was made before the date of the check, unless the customer has given notice to the bank of the postdating describing the check with reasonable certainty. The notice is effective for the period stated in Section 4—403(b) for stop-payment orders, and must be received at such time and in such manner as to afford the bank a reasonable opportunity to act on it before the bank takes any action with respect to the check described in Section 4—303. If a bank charges against the account of a customer a check before the date stated in the notice of postdating, the bank is liable for damages for the loss resulting from its act. The loss may include damages for dishonor of subsequent items under Section 4—402.

(d) A bank that in good faith makes payment to a holder may charge the indicated account of its customer according to:

(1) the original terms of the altered item; or

(2) the terms of the completed item, even though the bank knows the item has been completed unless the bank has notice that the completion was improper.

§4—402. BANK'S LIABILITY TO CUSTOMER FOR WRONGFUL DISHONOR; TIME OF DETERMINING INSUFFICIENCY OF ACCOUNT

(a) Except as otherwise provided in this Article, a payor bank wrongfully dishonors an item if it dishonors an item that is properly payable, but a bank may dishonor an item that would create an overdraft unless it has agreed to pay the overdraft.

(b) A payor bank is liable to its customer for damages proximately caused by the wrongful dishonor of an item. Liability is limited to actual damages proved and may include damages for an arrest or prosecution of the customer or other consequential damages. Whether any consequential damages are proximately caused by the wrongful dishonor is a question of fact to be determined in each case.

(c) A payor bank's determination of the customer's account balance on which a decision to dishonor for insufficiency of available funds is based may be made at any time between the time the item is received by the payor bank and the time that the payor bank returns the item or gives notice in lieu of return, and no more than one determination need be made. If, at the election of the payor bank, a subsequent balance determination is made for the purpose of reevaluating the bank's decision to dishonor the item, the account balance at that time is determinative of whether a dishonor for insufficiency of available funds is wrongful.

§4—403. CUSTOMER'S RIGHT TO STOP PAYMENT; BURDEN OF PROOF OF LOSS

(a) A customer or any person authorized to draw on the account if there is more than one person may stop payment of any item drawn on the customer's account or close the account by an order to the bank describing the item or account with reasonable certainty received at a time and in a manner that affords the bank a reasonable opportunity to act on it before any action by the bank with respect to the item described in Section 4—303. If the signature of more than one person is required to draw on an account, any of these persons may stop payment or close the account.

(b) A stop-payment order is effective for six months, but it lapses after 14 calendar days if the original order was oral and was not confirmed in writing within that period. A stop-payment order may be renewed for additional six-month periods by a writing given to the bank within a period during which the stop-payment order is effective.

(c) The burden of establishing the fact and amount of loss resulting from the payment of an item contrary to a stop-payment order or order to close an account is on the customer. The loss from payment of an item contrary to a stop-payment order may include damages for dishonor of subsequent items under Section 4—402.

§4—404. BANK NOT OBLIGED TO PAY CHECK MORE THAN SIX MONTHS OLD

A bank is under no obligation to a customer having a checking account to pay a check, other than a certified check, which is presented more than six months after its date, but it may charge its customer's account for a payment made thereafter in good faith.

§4—405. DEATH OR INCOMPETENCE OF CUSTOMER

(a) A payor or collecting bank's authority to accept, pay, or collect an item or to account for proceeds of its collection, if otherwise effective, is not rendered ineffective by incompetence of a customer of either bank existing at the time the item is issued or its collection is undertaken if the bank does not know of an adjudication of incompetence. Neither death nor incompetence of a customer revokes the authority to accept, pay, collect, or account until the bank knows of the fact of death or of an adjudication of incompetence and has reasonable opportunity to act on it.

(b) Even with knowledge, a bank may for 10 days after the date of death pay or certify checks drawn on or before the date unless ordered to stop payment by a person claiming an interest in the account.

§4—406. CUSTOMER'S DUTY TO DISCOVER AND REPORT UNAUTHORIZED SIGNATURE OR ALTERATION

(a) A bank that sends or makes available to a customer a statement of account showing payment of items for the account shall either return or make available to the customer the items paid or provide information in the statement of account sufficient to allow the customer reasonably to identify the items paid. The statement of account provides sufficient information if the item is described by item number, amount, and date of payment.

(b) If the items are not returned to the customer, the person retaining the items shall either retain the items or, if the items are destroyed, maintain the capacity to furnish legible copies of the items until the expiration of seven years after receipt of the items. A customer may request an item from the bank that paid the item, and that bank must provide in a reasonable time either the item or, if the item has been destroyed or is not otherwise obtainable, a legible copy of the item.

(c) If a bank sends or makes available a statement of account or items pursuant to subsection (a), the customer must exercise reasonable promptness in examining the statement or the items to determine whether any payment was not authorized because of an alteration of an item or because a purported signature by or on behalf of the customer was not authorized. If, based on the statement or items provided, the customer should reasonably have discovered the unauthorized payment, the customer must promptly notify the bank of the relevant facts.

(d) If the bank proves that the customer failed, with respect to an item, to comply with the duties imposed on the customer by subsection (c), the customer is precluded from asserting against the bank:

> (1) the customer's unauthorized signature or any alteration on the item, if the bank also proves that it suffered a loss by reason of the failure; and

> (2) the customer's unauthorized signature or alteration by the same wrongdoer on any other item paid in good faith by the bank if the payment was made before the bank received notice from the customer of the unauthorized signature or alteration and after the customer had been afforded a reasonable period of time, not exceeding 30 days, in which to examine the item or statement of account and notify the bank.

(e) If subsection (d) applies and the customer proves that the bank failed to exercise ordinary care in paying the item and that the failure substantially contributed to loss, the loss is allocated between the customer precluded and the bank asserting the preclusion according to the extent to which the failure of the customer to comply with subsection (c) and the failure of the bank to exercise ordinary care contributed to the loss. If the customer proves that the bank did not pay the item in good faith, the preclusion under subsection (d) does not apply.

(f) Without regard to care or lack of care of either the customer or the bank, a customer who does not within one year after the statement or items are made available to the customer (subsection (a)) discover and report the customer's unauthorized signature on or any alteration on the item is precluded from asserting against the bank the unauthorized signature or alteration. If there is a preclusion under this subsection, the payor bank may not recover for breach or warranty under Section 4—208 with respect to the unauthorized signature or alteration to which the preclusion applies.

§4—407. PAYOR BANK'S RIGHT TO SUBROGATION ON IMPROPER PAYMENT

If a payor has paid an item over the order of the drawer or maker to stop payment, or after an account has been closed, or otherwise under circumstances giving a basis for objection by the drawer or maker, to prevent unjust enrichment and only to the extent necessary to prevent loss to the bank by reason of its payment of the item, the payor bank is subrogated to the rights

(1) of any holder in due course on the item against the drawer or maker;

(2) of the payee or any other holder of the item against the drawer or maker either on the item or under the transaction out of which the item arose; and

(3) of the drawer or maker against the payee or any other holder of the item with respect to the transaction out of which the item arose.

* * * *

Article 4A Funds Transfers

Part 1 Subject Matter and Definitions

§4A—104. FUNDS TRANSFER—DEFINITIONS

(a) "Funds transfer" means the series of transactions, beginning with the originator's payment order, made for the purpose of making payment to the beneficiary of the order. The term includes any payment order issued by the originator's bank or an intermediary bank intended to carry out the originator's payment order. A funds transfer is completed by acceptance by the beneficiary's bank of a payment order for the benefit of the beneficiary of the originator's payment order.

(b) "Intermediary bank" means a receiving bank other than the originator's bank or the beneficiary's bank.

(c) "Originator" means the sender of the first payment order in a funds transfer.

(d) "Originator's bank" means (i) the receiving bank to which the payment order of the originator is issued if the originator is not a bank, or (ii) the originator if the originator is a bank.

§4A—105. OTHER DEFINITIONS

(1) "Authorized account" means a deposit account of a customer in a bank designated by the customer as a source of payment of payment orders issued by the customer to the bank. If a customer does not so designate an account, any account of the customer is an authorized account if payment of a payment order from that account is not inconsistent with a restriction on the use of that account.

(2) "Bank" means a person engaged in the business of banking and includes a savings bank, savings and loan association, credit union, and trust company. A branch or separate office of a bank is a separate bank for purposes of this Article.

(3) "Customer" means a person, including a bank, having an account with a bank or from whom a bank has agreed to receive payment orders.

(4) "Funds-transfer business day" of a receiving bank means the part of a day during which the receiving bank is open for the receipt, processing, and transmittal of payment orders and cancellations and amendments of payment orders.

(5) "Funds-transfer system" means a wire transfer network, automated clearing house, or other communication system of a clearing house or other association of banks through which a payment order by a bank may be transmitted to the bank to which the order is addressed.

(6) "Good faith" means honesty in fact and the observance of reasonable commercial standards of fair dealing.

(7) "Prove" with respect to a fact means to meet the burden of establishing the fact (Section 1—201(8)).

* * * *

§4A—106. TIME PAYMENT ORDER IS RECEIVED

(a) The time of receipt of a payment order or communication cancelling or amending a payment order is determined by the rules applicable to receipt of a notice stated in Section 1—201(27). A receiving bank may fix a cut-off time or times on a funds-transfer business day for the receipt and processing of payment orders and communications cancelling or amending payment orders. Different cut-off times may apply to payment orders, cancellations, or amendments, or to different categories of payment orders, cancellations, or amendments. A cut-off time may apply to senders generally or different cut-off times may apply to different senders or categories of payment orders. If a payment order or communication cancelling or amending a payment order is received after the close of a funds-transfer business day or after the appropriate cut-off time on a funds-transfer business day, the receiving bank may treat the payment order or communication as received at the opening of the next funds-transfer business day.

(b) If this Article refers to an execution date or payment date or states a day on which a receiving bank is required to take action, and the date or day does not fall on a funds-transfer business day, the next day that is a funds- transfer business day is treated as the date or day stated, unless the contrary is stated in this Article.

* * * *

§4A—108. EXCLUSION OF CONSUMER TRANSACTIONS GOVERNED BY FEDERAL LAW

This Article does not apply to a funds transfer any part of which is governed by the Electronic Fund Transfer Act of 1978 (Title XX, Public Law 95—630, 92 Stat. 3728, 15 U.S.C. §1693 et seq.) as amended from time to time.

* * * *

Revised Article 9 Secured Transactions

§9—102. DEFINITIONS AND INDEX OF DEFINITIONS

(1) "Accession" means goods that are physically united with other goods in such a manner that the identity of the original goods is not lost.

(2) "Account", except as used in "account for", means a right to payment of a monetary obligation, whether or not earned by performance, (i) for property that has been or is to be sold, leased, licensed, assigned, or otherwise disposed of, (ii) for services rendered or to be rendered, (iii) for a policy of insurance issued or to be issued, (iv) for a secondary obligation incurred or to be incurred, (v) for energy provided or to be provided, (vi) for the use or hire of a vessel under a charter or other contract, (vii) arising out of the use of a credit or charge card or information contained on or for use with the card, or (viii) as winnings in a lottery or other game of chance operated or sponsored by a State, governmental unit of a State, or person licensed or authorized to operate the game by a State or governmental unit of a State. The term includes health-care insurance receivables. The term does not include (i) rights to payment evidenced by chattel paper or an instrument, (ii) commercial tort claims, (iii) deposit accounts, (iv) investment property, (v) letter-of-credit rights or letters of credit, or (vi) rights to payment for money or funds advanced or sold, other than rights arising out of the use of a credit or charge card or information contained on or for use with the card.

* * * *

(5) "Agricultural lien" means an interest, other than a security or

(A) which secures payment or performance of an obligation for:

(i) goods or services furnished in connection with a debtor's farming operation; or

(ii) rent on real property leased by a debtor in connection with its farming operation;

(B) which is created by statute in favor of a person that:

(i) in the ordinary course of its business furnished goods or services to a debtor in connection with a debtor's farming operation; or

(ii) leased real property to a debtor in connection with the debtor's farming operation; and

(C) whose effectiveness does not depend on the person's possession of the personal property.

(6) "As-extracted collateral" means:

(A) oil, gas, or other minerals that are subject to a security interest that:

(i) is created by a debtor having an interest in the minerals before extraction; and

(ii) attaches to the minerals as extracted; or

(B) accounts arising out of the sale at the wellhead or minehead of oil, gas, or other minerals in which the debtor had an interest before extraction.

(7) "Authenticate" means:

(A) to sign; or

(B) to execute or otherwise adopt a symbol, or encrypt or similarly process a record in whole or in part, with the present intent of the authenticating person to identify the person and adopt or accept a record.

* * * *

(11) "Chattel paper" means a record or records that evidence both a monetary obligation and a security interest in specific goods, a security interest in specific goods and software used in the goods, a security interest in specific goods and license of software used in the goods, a lease of specific goods, or a lease of specific goods and license of software used in the goods. In this paragraph, "monetary obligation" means a monetary obligation secured by the goods or owed under a lease of the goods and includes a monetary obligation with respect to software used in the goods. The term does not include (i) charters or other contracts involving the use or hire of a vessel or (ii) records that evidence a right to payment arising out of the use of a credit or charge card or information contained on or for use with the card. If a transaction is evidenced by records that include an instrument or

series of instruments, the group of records taken together constitutes chattel paper.

(12) "Collateral" means the property subject to a security interest or agricultural lien. The term includes:

(A) proceeds to which a security interest attaches;

(B) accounts, chattel paper, payment intangibles, and promissory notes that have been sold; and

(C) goods that are the subject of a consignment.

(13) "Commercial tort claim" means a claim arising in tort with respect to which:

(A) the claimant is an organization; or

(B) the claimant is an individual and the claim:

(i) arose in the course of the claimant's business or profession; and

(ii) does not include damages arising out of personal injury to or the death of an individual.

* * * *

(19) "Consignee" means a merchant to which goods are delivered in a consignment.

(20) "Consignment" means a transaction, regardless of its form, in which a person delivers goods to a merchant for the purpose of sale and:

(A) the merchant:

(i) deals in goods of that kind under a name other than the name of the person making delivery;

(ii) is not an auctioneer; and

(iii) is not generally known by its creditors to be substantially engaged in selling the goods of others;

(B) with respect to each delivery, the aggregate value of the goods is $1,000 or more at the time of delivery;

(C) the goods are not consumer goods immediately before delivery; and

(D) the transaction does not create a security interest that secures an obligation.

(21) "Consignor" means a person that delivers goods to a consignee in a consignment.

(22) "Consumer debtor" means a debtor in a consumer transaction.

(23) "Consumer goods" means goods that are used or bought for use primarily for personal, family, or household purposes.

(24) "Consumer-goods transaction" means a consumer transaction in which:

(A) an individual incurs an obligation primarily for personal, family, or household purposes; and

(B) a security interest in consumer goods secures the obligation.

(25) "Consumer obligor" means an obligor who is an individual and who incurred the obligation as part of a transaction entered into primarily for personal, family, or household purposes.

(26) "Consumer transaction" means a transaction in which (i) an individual incurs an obligation primarily for personal, family, or household purposes, (ii) a security interest secures the obligation, and (iii) the collateral is held or acquired primarily for personal, family, or household purposes. The term includes consumer-goods transactions.

(27) "Continuation statement" means an amendment of a financing statement which:

(A) identifies, by its file number, the initial financing statement to which it relates; and

(B) indicates that it is a continuation statement for, or that it is filed to continue the effectiveness of, the identified financing statement.

(28) "Debtor" means:

(A) a person having an interest, other than a security interest or other lien, in the collateral, whether or not the person is an obligor;

(B) a seller of accounts, chattel paper, payment intangibles, or promissory notes; or

(C) a consignee.

(29) "Deposit account" means a demand, time, savings, passbook, or similar account maintained with a bank. The term does not include investment property or accounts evidenced by an instrument.

(30) "Document" means a document of title or a receipt of the type described in Section 7—201(2).

(31) "Electronic chattel paper" means chattel paper evidenced by a record or records consisting of information stored in an electronic medium.

(32) "Encumbrance" means a right, other than an ownership interest, in real property. The term includes mortgages and other liens on real property.

(33) "Equipment" means goods other than inventory, farm products, or consumer goods.

(34) "Farm products" means goods, other than standing timber, with respect to which the debtor is engaged in a farming operation and which are:

(A) crops grown, growing, or to be grown, including:

    (i) crops produced on trees, vines, and bushes; and

    (ii) aquatic goods produced in aquacultural operations;

(B) livestock, born or unborn, including aquatic goods produced in aquacultural operations;

(C) supplies used or produced in a farming operation; or

(D) products of crops or livestock in their unmanufactured states.

(35) "Farming operation" means raising, cultivating, propagating, fattening, grazing, or any other farming, livestock, or aquacultural operation.

* * * *

(39) "Financing statement" means a record or records composed of an initial financing statement and any filed record relating to the initial financing statement.

(40) "Fixture filing" means the filing of a financing statement covering goods that are or are to become fixtures and satisfying Section 9—502(a) and (b). The term includes the filing of a financing statement covering goods of a transmitting utility which are or are to become fixtures.

(41) "Fixtures" means goods that have become so related to particular real property that an interest in them arises under real property law.

(42) "General intangible" means any personal property, including things in action, other than accounts, chattel paper, commercial tort claims, deposit accounts, documents, goods, instruments, investment property, letter-of-credit rights, letters of credit, money, and oil, gas, or other minerals before extraction. The term includes payment intangibles and software.

* * * *

(44) "Goods" means all things that are movable when a security interest attaches. The term includes (i) fixtures, (ii) standing timber that is to be cut and removed under a conveyance or contract for sale, (iii) the unborn young of animals, (iv) crops grown, growing, or to be grown, even if the crops are produced on trees, vines, or bushes, and (v) manufactured homes.

The term also includes a computer program embedded in goods and any supporting information provided in connection with a transaction relating to the program if (i) the program is associated with the goods in such a manner that it customarily is considered part of the goods, or (ii) by becoming the owner of the goods, a person acquires a right to use the program in connection with the goods. The term does not include a computer program embedded in goods that consist solely of the medium in which the program is embedded. The term also does not include accounts, chattel paper, commercial tort claims, deposit accounts, documents, general intangibles, instruments, investment property, letter-of-credit rights, letters of credit, money, or oil, gas, or other minerals before extraction.

* * * *

(46) "Health-care-insurance receivable" means an interest in or claim under a policy of insurance which is a right to payment of a monetary obligation for health-care goods or services provided.

(47) "Instrument" means a negotiable instrument or any other writing that evidences a right to the payment of a monetary obligation, is not itself a security agreement or lease, and is of a type that in ordinary course of business is transferred by delivery with any necessary indorsement or assignment. The term does not include (i) investment property, (ii) letters of credit, or (iii) writings that evidence a right to payment arising out of the use of a credit or charge card or information contained on or for use with the card.

(48) "Inventory" means goods, other than farm products, which:

(A) are leased by a person as lessor;

(B) are held by a person for sale or lease or to be furnished under a contract of service;

(C) are furnished by a person under a contract of service; or

(D) consist of raw materials, work in process, or materials used or consumed in a business.

(49) "Investment property" means a security, whether certificated or uncertificated, security entitlement, securities account, commodity contract, or commodity account.

* * * *

(51) "Letter-of-credit right" means a right to payment or performance under a letter of credit, whether or not the beneficiary has demanded or is at the time entitled to demand payment or performance. The term does not include the right of a beneficiary to demand payment or performance under a letter of credit.

(52) "Lien creditor" means:

(A) a creditor that has acquired a lien on the property involved by attachment, levy, or the like;

(B) an assignee for benefit of creditors from the time of assignment;

(C) a trustee in bankruptcy from the date of the filing of the petition; or

(D) a receiver in equity from the time of appointment.

* * * *

(55) "Mortgage" means a consensual interest in real property, including fixtures, which secures payment or performance of an obligation.

(56) "New debtor" means a person that becomes bound as debtor under Section 9—203(d) by a security agreement previously entered into by another person.

(57) "New value" means (i) money, (ii) money's worth in property, services, or new credit, or (iii) release by a transferee of an interest in property previously transferreed to the transferee. The term does not include an obligation substituted for another obligation.

* * * *

(61) "Payment intangible" means a general intangible under which the account debtor's principal obligation is a monetary obligation.

* * * *

(64) "Proceeds", except as used in Section 9—609 (b), means the following property:

(A) whatever is acquired upon the sale, lease, license, exchange, or other disposition of collateral;

(B) whatever is collected on, or distributed on account of, collateral;

(C) rights arising out of collateral;

(D) to the extent of the value of collateral, claims arising out of the loss, non-conformity, or interference with the use of, defects or infringement of rights in, or damage to, the collateral; or

(E) to the extent of the value of collateral and to the extent payable to the debtor or the secured party, insurance payable by reason of the loss or non-conformity of, defects or infringement of rights in, or damage to, the collateral.

* * * *

(69) "Record", except as used in "for record", "of record", "record or legal title", and "record owner", means information that is inscribed on a tangible medium or which is stored in an electronic or other medium and is retrievable in perceivable form.

* * * *

(72) "Secured party" means:

(A) a person in whose favor a security interest is created or provided for under a security agreement, whether or not any obligation to be secured is outstanding;

(B) a person that holds an agricultural lien;

(C) a consignor;

(D) a person to which accounts, chattel paper, payment intangibles, or promissory notes have been sold;

(E) a trustee, indenture trustee, agent, collateral agent, or other representative in whose favor a security interest or agricultural lien is created or provided for; or

(F) a person that holds a security interest arising under Section 2—401, 2—505, 2—711(3), 2A—508(5), 4—210, or 5—118.

(73) "Security agreement" means an agreement that creates or provides for a security interest.

* * * *

(78) "Tangible chattel paper" means chattel paper evidenced by a record or records consisting of information that is inscribed on a tangible medium.

(79) "Termination statement" means an amendment of a financing statement which:

(A) identifies, by its file number, the initial financing statement to which it relates; and

(B) indicates either that it is a termination statement or that the identified financing statement is no longer effective.

* * * *

§9—103. PURCHASE-MONEY SECURITY INTEREST; APPLICATION OF PAYMENTS; BURDEN OF ESTABLISHING

(a) In this section:

(1) "purchase-money collateral" means goods or software that secures a purchase-money obligation incurred with respect to that collateral; and

(2) "purchase-money obligation" means an obligation of an obligor incurred as all or part of the price of the collateral or for value given to enable the debtor to acquire rights in or the use of the collateral if the value is in fact so used.

(b) A security interest in goods is a purchase-money security interest:

(1) to the extent that the goods are purchase-money collateral with respect to that security interest;

(2) if the security interest is in inventory that is or was purchase-money collateral, also to the extent that the security interest secures a purchase-money obligation incurred with respect to other inventory in which the secured party holds or held a purchase-money security interest; and

(3) also to the extent that the security interest secures a purchase-money obligation incurred with respect to software in which the secured party holds or held a purchase-money security interest.

(c) A security interest in software is a purchase-money security interest to the extent that the security interest also secures a purchase-money obligation incurred with respect to goods in which the secured party holds or held a purchase-money security interest if:

(1) the debtor acquired its interest in the software in an integrated transaction in which it acquired an interest in the goods; and

(2) the debtor acquired its interest in the software for the principal purpose of using the software in the goods.

(d) The security interest of a consignor in goods that are the subject of a consignment is a purchase-money security interest in inventory.

(e) In a transaction other than a consumer-goods transaction, if the extent to which a security interest is a purchase-money security interest depends on the application of a payment to a particular obligation, the payment must be applied:

(1) in accordance with any reasonable method of application to which the parties agree;

(2) in the absence of the parties' agreement to a reasonable method, in accordance with any intention of the obligor manifested at or before the time of payment; or

(3) in the absence of an agreement to a reasonable method and a timely manifestation of the obligor's intention, in the following order:

(A) to obligations that are not secured; and

(B) if more than one obligation is secured, to obligations secured by purchase-money security interests in the order in which those obligations were incurred.

(f) In a transaction other than a consumer-goods transaction, a purchase-money security interest does not lose its status as such, even if:

(1) the purchase-money collateral also secures an obligation that is not a purchase-money obligation;

(2) collateral that is not purchase-money collateral also secures the purchase-money obligation; or

(3) the purchase-money obligation has been renewed, refinanced, consolidated, or restructured.

(g) In a transaction other than a consumer-goods transaction, a secured party claiming a purchase-money security interest has the burden of establishing the extent to which the security interest is a purchase-money security interest.

(h) The limitation of the rules in subsections (e), (f), and (g) to transactions other than consumer-goods transactions is intended to leave to the court the determination of the proper rules in consumer-goods transactions. The court may not infer from that limitation the nature of the proper rule in consumer-goods transactions and may continue to apply established approaches.

§9—104. CONTROL OF DEPOSIT ACCOUNT

(a) A secured party has control of a deposit account if:

(1) the secured party is the bank with which the deposit account is maintained;

(2) the debtor, secured party, and bank have agreed in an authenticated record that the bank will comply with instructions originated by the secured party directing disposition of the funds in the deposit account without further consent by the debtor; or

(3) the secured party becomes the bank's customer with respect to the deposit account.

(b) A secured party that has satisfied subsection (a) has control, even if the debtor retains the right to direct the disposition of funds from the deposit account.

§9—105. CONTROL OF ELECTRONIC CHATTEL PAPER

A secured party has control of electronic chattel paper if the record or records comprising the chattel paper are created, stored, and assigned in such a manner that:

(1) a single authoritative copy of the record or records exists which is unique, identifiable and, except as otherwise provided in paragraphs (4), (5), and (6), unalterable;

(2) the authoritative copy identifies the secured party as the assignee of the record or records;

(3) the authoritative copy is communicated to and maintained by the secured party or its designated custodian;

(4) copies or revisions that add or change an identified assignee of the authoritative copy can be made only with the participation of the secured party;

(5) each copy of the authoritative copy and any copy of a copy is readily identifiable as a copy that is not the authoritative copy; and

(6) any revision of the authoritative copy is readily identifiable as an authorized or unauthorized revision.

§9—106. CONTROL OF INVESTMENT PROPERTY

(a) A person has control of a certificated security, uncertificated security, or security entitlement as provided in Section 8—106.

(b) A secured party has control of a commodity contract if:

(1) the secured party is the commodity intermediary with which the commodity contract is carried; or

(2) the commodity customer, secured party, and commodity intermediary have agreed that the commodity intermediary will apply any value distributed on account of the commodity contract as directed by the secured party without further consent by the commodity customer.

(c) A secured party having control of all security entitlements or commodity contracts carried in a securities account or commodity account has control over the securities account or commodity account.

§9—107. CONTROL OF LETTER-OF-CREDIT RIGHT

A secured party has control of a letter-of-credit right to the extent of any right to payment or performance by the issuer or any nominated person if the issuer or nominated person has consented to an assignment of proceeds of the letter of credit under Section 5—114(c) or otherwise applicable law or practice.

§9—108. SUFFICIENCY OF DESCRIPTION

(a) Except as otherwise provided in subsections (c), (d), and (e), a description of personal or real property is sufficient, whether or not it is specific, if it reasonably identifies what is described.

(b) Except as otherwise provided in subsection (d), a description of collateral reasonably identifies the collateral if it identifies the collateral by:

(1) specific listing;

(2) category;

(3) except as otherwise provided in subsection (e), a type of collateral defined in [the Uniform Commercial Code];

(4) quantity;

(5) computational or allocational formula or procedure; or

(6) except as otherwise provided in subsection (c), any other method, if the identity of the collateral is objectively determinable.

(c) A description of collateral as "all the debtor's assets" or "all the debtor's personal property" or using words of similar import does not reasonably identify the collateral.

(d) Except as otherwise provided in subsection (e), a description of a security entitlement, securities account, or commodity account is sufficient if it describes:

(1) the collateral by those terms or as investment property; or

(2) the underlying financial asset or commodity contract.

(e) A description only by type of collateral defined in [the Uniform Commercial Code] is an insufficient description of:

(1) a commercial tort claim; or

(2) in a consumer transaction, consumer goods, a security entitlement, a securities account, or a commodity account.

§9-109 SCOPE

* * * *

This article does not apply to:

(1) a landlord's lien, other than an agricultural lien;

(2) a lien, other than an agricultural lien, given by statute or other rule of law for services or materials, but Section 9—333 applies with respect to priority of the lien;

(3) an assignment of a claim for wages, salary, or other compensation of an employee;

(4) a sale of accounts, chattel paper, payment intangibles, or promissory notes as part of a sale of the business out of which they arose;

(5) an assignment of accounts, chattel paper, payment intangibles, or promissory notes which is for the purpose of collection only;

(6) an assignment of a right to payment under a contract to an assignee that is also obligated to perform under the contract;

(7) an assignment of a single account, payment intangible, or promissory note to an assignee in full or partial satisfaction of a preexisting indebtedness;

(8) a transfer of an interest in or an assignment of a claim under a policy of insurance, other than an

assignment by or to a health-care provider of a health-care-insurance receivable and any subsequent assignment of the right to payment, but Sections 9—315 and 9—322 apply with respect to proceeds and priorities in proceeds;

(9) an assignment of a right represented by a judgment, other than a judgment taken on a right to payment that was collateral;

(10) a right of recoupment or set-off, but:

(A) Section 9—340 applies with respect to the effectiveness of rights of recoupment or set-off against deposit accounts; and

(B) Section 9—404 applies with respect to defenses or claims of an account debtor;

(11) the creation or transfer of an interest in or lien on real property, including a lease or rents thereunder, except to the extent that provision is made for:

(A) liens on real property in Sections 9—203 and 9—308;

(B) fixtures in Section 9—334;

(C) fixture filings in Sections 9—501, 9—502, 9—512, 9—516, and 9—519; and

(D) security agreements covering personal and real property in Section 9—604;

(12) an assignment of a claim arising in tort, other than a commercial tort claim, but Sections 9—315 and 9—322 apply with respect to proceeds and priorities in proceeds; or

(13) an assignment of a deposit account in a consumer transaction, but Sections 9—315 and 9—322 apply with respect to proceeds and priorities in proceeds.

* * * *

§9—201. GENERAL EFFECTIVENESS OF SECURITY AGREEMENT

(a) Except as otherwise provided in [the Uniform Commercial Code], a security agreement is effective according to its terms between the parties, against purchasers of the collateral, and against creditors.

(b) A transaction subject to this article is subject to any applicable rule of law which establishes a different rule for consumers and [insert reference to (i) any other statute or regulation that regulates the rates, charges, agreements, and practices for loans, credit sales, or other extensions of credit and (ii) any consumer-protection statute or regulation].

(c) In case of conflict between this article and a rule of law, statute, or regulation described in subsection (b),

the rule of law, statute, or regulation controls. Failure to comply with a statute or regulation described in subsection (b) has only the effect the statute or regulation specifies.

(d) This article does not:

(1) validate any rate, charge, agreement, or practice that violates a rule of law, statute, or regulation described in subsection (b); or

(2) extend the application of the rule of law, statute, or regulation to a transaction not otherwise subject to it.

§9—202. TITLE TO COLLATERAL IMMATERIAL

Except as otherwise provided with respect to consignments or sales of accounts, chattel paper, payment intangibles, or promissory notes, the provisions of this article with regard to rights and obligations apply whether title to collateral is in the secured party or the debtor.

§9—203. ATTACHMENT AND ENFORCEABILITY OF SECURITY INTEREST; PROCEEDS; SUPPORTING OBLIGATIONS; FORMAL REQUISITES

(a) A security interest attaches to collateral when it becomes enforceable against the debtor with respect to the collateral, unless an agreement expressly postpones the time of attachment.

(b) Except as otherwise provided in subsections (c) through (i), a security interest is enforceable against the debtor and third parties with respect to the collateral only if:

(1) value has been given;

(2) the debtor has rights in the collateral or the power to transfer rights in the collateral to a secured party; and

(3) one of the following conditions is met:

(A) the debtor has authenticated a security agreement that provides a description of the collateral and, if the security interest covers timber to be cut, a description of the land concerned;

(B) the collateral is not a certificated security and is in the possession of the secured party under Section 9—313 pursuant to the debtor's security agreement;

(C) the collateral is a certificated security in registered form and the security certificate has been delivered to the secured party under Section 8—301 pursuant to the debtor's security agreement; or

(D) the collateral is deposit accounts, electronic chattel paper, investment property, or letter-of-credit rights, and the secured party has control under Section 9—104, 9—105, 9—106, or 9—107 pursuant to the debtor's security agreement.

(c) Subsection (b) is subject to Section 4—210 on the security interest of a collecting bank, Section 5—118 on the security interest of a letter-of-credit issuer or nominated person, Section 9—110 on a security interest arising under Article 2 or 2A, and Section 9—206 on security interests in investment property.

(d) A person becomes bound as debtor by a security agreement entered into by another person if, by operation of law other than this article or by contract:

(1) the security agreement becomes effective to create a security interest in the person's property; or

(2) the person becomes generally obligated for the obligations of the other person, including the obligation secured under the security agreement, and acquires or succeeds to all or substantially all of the assets of the other person.

(e) If a new debtor becomes bound as debtor by a security agreement entered into by another person:

(1) the agreement satisfies subsection (b)(3) with respect to existing or after-acquired property of the new debtor to the extent the property is described in the agreement; and

(2) another agreement is not necessary to make a security interest in the property enforceable.

(f) The attachment of a security interest in collateral gives the secured party the rights to proceeds provided by Section 9—315 and is also attachment of a security interest in a supporting obligation for the collateral.

(g) The attachment of a security interest in a right to payment or performance secured by a security interest or other lien on personal or real property is also attachment of a security interest in the security interest, mortgage, or other lien.

(h) The attachment of a security interest in a securities account is also attachment of a security interest in the security entitlements carried in the securities account.

(i) The attachment of a security interest in a commodity account is also attachment of a security interest in the commodity contracts carried in the commodity account.

§9—204. AFTER-ACQUIRED PROPERTY; FUTURE ADVANCES

(a) Except as otherwise provided in subsection (b), a security agreement may create or provide for a security interest in after-acquired collateral.

(b) A security interest does not attach under a term constituting an after-acquired property clause to:

(1) consumer goods, other than an accession when given as additional security, unless the debtor acquires rights in them within 10 days after the secured party gives value; or

(2) a commercial tort claim.

(c) A security agreement may provide that collateral secures, or that accounts, chattel paper, payment intangibles, or promissory notes are sold in connection with, future advances or other value, whether or not the advances or value are given pursuant to commitment.

§9—205. USE OR DISPOSITION OF COLLATERAL PERMISSIBLE

(a) A security interest is not invalid or fraudulent against creditors solely because:

(1) the debtor has the right or ability to:

(A) use, commingle, or dispose of all or part of the collateral, including returned or repossessed goods;

(B) collect, compromise, enforce, or otherwise deal with collateral;

(C) accept the return of collateral or make repossessions; or

(D) use, commingle, or dispose of proceeds; or

(2) the secured party fails to require the debtor to account for proceeds or replace collateral.

(b) This section does not relax the requirements of possession if attachment, perfection, or enforcement of a security interest depends upon possession of the collateral by the secured party.

§9—206. SECURITY INTEREST ARISING IN PURCHASE OR DELIVERY OF FINANCIAL ASSET

(a) A security interest in favor of a securities intermediary attaches to a person's security entitlement if:

(1) the person buys a financial asset through the securities intermediary in a transaction in which the person is obligated to pay the purchase price to the securities intermediary at the time of the purchase; and

(2) the securities intermediary credits the financial asset to the buyer's securities account before the buyer pays the securities intermediary.

(b) The security interest described in subsection (a) secures the person's obligation to pay for the financial asset.

* * * *

§9—207. RIGHTS AND DUTIES OF SECURED PARTY HAVING POSSESSION OR CONTROL OF COLLATERAL

(a) Except as otherwise provided in subsection (d), a secured party shall use reasonable care in the custody and preservation of collateral in the secured party's possession. In the case of chattel paper or an instrument, reasonable care includes taking necessary steps to preserve rights against prior parties unless otherwise agreed.

(b) Except as otherwise provided in subsection (d), if a secured party has possession of collateral:

(1) reasonable expenses, including the cost of insurance and payment of taxes or other charges, incurred in the custody, preservation, use, or operation of the collateral are chargeable to the debtor and are secured by the collateral;

(2) the risk of accidental loss or damage is on the debtor to the extent of a deficiency in any effective insurance coverage;

(3) the secured party shall keep the collateral identifiable, but fungible collateral may be commingled; and

(4) the secured party may use or operate the collateral:

(A) for the purpose of preserving the collateral or its value;

(B) as permitted by an order of a court having competent jurisdiction; or

(C) except in the case of consumer goods, in the manner and to the extent agreed by the debtor.

(c) Except as otherwise provided in subsection (d), a secured party having possession of collateral or control of collateral under Section 9—104, 9—105, 9—106, or 9—107:

(1) may hold as additional security any proceeds, except money or funds, received from the collateral;

(2) shall apply money or funds received from the collateral to reduce the secured obligation, unless remitted to the debtor; and

(3) may create a security interest in the collateral.

(d) If the secured party is a buyer of accounts, chattel paper, payment intangibles, or promissory notes or a consignor:

(1) subsection (a) does not apply unless the secured party is entitled under an agreement:

(A) to charge back uncollected collateral; or

(B) otherwise to full or limited recourse against the debtor or a secondary obligor based on the nonpayment or other default of an account debtor or other obligor on the collateral; and

(2) subsections (b) and (c) do not apply.

§9—208. ADDITIONAL DUTIES OF SECURED PARTY HAVING CONTROL OF COLLATERAL

(a) This section applies to cases in which there is no outstanding secured obligation and the secured party is not committed to make advances, incur obligations, or otherwise give value.

(b) Within 10 days after receiving an authenticated demand by the debtor:

(1) a secured party having control of a deposit account under Section 9—104(a)(2) shall send to the bank with which the deposit account is maintained an authenticated statement that releases the bank from any further obligation to comply with instructions originated by the secured party;

(2) a secured party having control of a deposit account under Section 9—104(a)(3) shall:

(A) pay the debtor the balance on deposit in the deposit account; or

(B) transfer the balance on deposit into a deposit account in the debtor's name;

(3) a secured party, other than a buyer, having control of electronic chattel paper under Section 9—105 shall:

(A) communicate the authoritative copy of the electronic chattel paper to the debtor or its designated custodian;

(B) if the debtor designates a custodian that is the designated custodian with which the authoritative copy of the electronic chattel paper is maintained for the secured party, communicate to the custodian an authenticated record releasing the designated custodian from any further obligation to comply with instructions originated by the secured party and instructing the custodian to comply with instructions originated by the debtor; and

(C) take appropriate action to enable the debtor or its designated custodian to make copies of or revisions to the authoritative copy which add or change an identified assignee of the authoritative copy without the consent of the secured party;

(4) a secured party having control of investment property under Section 8—106(d)(2) or 9—106 (b) shall send to the securities intermediary or commodity intermediary with which the security entitlement or commodity contract is maintained an authenticated record that releases the securities intermediary or commodity intermediary from any further obligation to comply with entitlement orders or directions originated by the secured party; and

(5) a secured party having control of a letter-of-credit right under Section 9—107 shall send to each person having an unfulfilled obligation to pay or deliver proceeds of the letter of credit to the secured party an authenticated release from any further obligation to pay or deliver proceeds of the letter of credit to the secured party.

§9—209. DUTIES OF SECURED PARTY IF ACCOUNT DEBTOR HAS BEEN NOTIFIED OF ASSIGNMENT

(a) Except as otherwise provided in subsection (c), this section applies if:

(1) there is no outstanding secured obligation; and

(2) the secured party is not committed to make advances, incur obligations, or otherwise give value.

(b) Within 10 days after receiving an authenticated demand by the debtor, a secured party shall send to an account debtor that has received notification of an assignment to the secured party as assignee under Section 9—406(a) an authenticated record that releases the account debtor from any further obligation to the secured party.

* * * *

§9—301. LAW GOVERNING PERFECTION AND PRIORITY OF SECURITY INTERESTS

Except as otherwise provided in Sections 9—303 through 9—306, the following rules determine the law governing perfection, the effect of perfection or nonperfection, and the priority of a security interest in collateral:

(1) Except as otherwise provided in this section, while a debtor is located in a jurisdiction, the local law of that jurisdiction governs perfection, the effect of perfection or nonperfection, and the priority of a security interest in collateral.

(2) While collateral is located in a jurisdiction, the local law of that jurisdiction governs perfection, the effect of perfection or nonperfection, and the priority of a possessory security interest in that collateral.

(3) Except as otherwise provided in paragraph (4), while negotiable documents, goods, instruments, money, or tangible chattel paper is located in a jurisdiction, the local law of that jurisdiction governs:

(A) perfection of a security interest in the goods by filing a fixture filing;

(B) perfection of a security interest in timber to be cut; and

(C) the effect of perfection or nonperfection and the priority of a nonpossessory security interest in the collateral.

(4) The local law of the jurisdiction in which the wellhead or minehead is located governs perfection, the effect of perfection or nonperfection, and the priority of a security interest in as-extracted collateral.

* * * *

§9—309. SECURITY INTEREST PERFECTED UPON ATTACHMENT

The following security interests are perfected when they attach:

(1) a purchase-money security interest in consumer goods, except as otherwise provided in Section 9—311(b) with respect to consumer goods that are subject to a statute or treaty described in Section 9—311(a);

(2) an assignment of accounts or payment intangibles which does not by itself or in conjunction with other assignments to the same assignee transfer a significant part of the assignor's outstanding accounts or payment intangibles;

(3) a sale of a payment intangible;

(4) a sale of a promissory note;

(5) a security interest created by the assignment of a health-care-insurance receivable to the provider of the health-care goods or services;

(6) a security interest arising under Section 2—401, 2—505, 2—711(3), or 2A—508(5), until the debtor obtains possession of the collateral;

(7) a security interest of a collecting bank arising under Section 4—210;

(8) a security interest of an issuer or nominated person arising under Section 5—118;

(9) a security interest arising in the delivery of a financial asset under Section 9—206(c);

(10) a security interest in investment property created by a broker or securities intermediary;

(11) a security interest in a commodity contract or a commodity account created by a commodity intermediary;

(12) an assignment for the benefit of all creditors of the transferor and subsequent transfers by the assignee thereunder; and

(13) a security interest created by an assignment of a beneficial interest in a decedent's estate; and

(14) a sale by an individual of an account that is a right to payment of winnings in a lottery or other game of chance.

§9—310. WHEN FILING REQUIRED TO PERFECT SECURITY INTEREST OR AGRICULTURAL LIEN; SECURITY INTERESTS AND AGRICULTURAL LIENS TO WHICH FILING PROVISIONS DO NOT APPLY

(a) Except as otherwise provided in subsection (b) and Section 9—312(b), a financing statement must be filed to perfect all security interests and agricultural liens.

(b) The filing of a financing statement is not necessary to perfect a security interest:

(1) that is perfected under Section 9—308(d), (e), (f), or (g);

(2) that is perfected under Section 9—309 when it attaches;

(3) in property subject to a statute, regulation, or treaty described in Section 9—311(a);

(4) in goods in possession of a bailee which is perfected under Section 9—312(d)(1) or (2);

(5) in certificated securities, documents, goods, or instruments which is perfected without filing or possession under Section 9—312(e), (f), or (g);

(6) in collateral in the secured party's possession under Section 9—313;

(7) in a certificated security which is perfected by delivery of the security certificate to the secured party under Section 9—313;

(8) in deposit accounts, electronic chattel paper, investment property, or letter-of-credit rights which is perfected by control under Section 9—314;

(9) in proceeds which is perfected under Section 9—315; or

(10) that is perfected under Section 9—316.

(c) If a secured party assigns a perfected security interest or agricultural lien, a filing under this article is not required to continue the perfected status of the security interest against creditors of and transferees from the original debtor.

§9—311. PERFECTION OF SECURITY INTERESTS IN PROPERTY SUBJECT TO CERTAIN STATUTES, REGULATIONS, AND TREATIES

(a) Except as otherwise provided in subsection (d), the filing of a financing statement is not necessary or effective to perfect a security interest in property subject to:

(1) a statute, regulation, or treaty of the United States whose requirements for a security interest's obtaining priority over the rights of a lien creditor with respect to the property preempt Section 9—310(a);

(2) [list any certificate-of-title statute covering automobiles, trailers, mobile homes, boats, farm tractors, or the like, which provides for a security interest to be indicated on the certificate as a condition or result of perfection, and any non Uniform Commercial Code central filing statute]; or

(3) a certificate-of-title statute of another jurisdiction which provides for a security interest to be indicated on the certificate as a condition or result of the security interest's obtaining priority over the rights of a lien creditor with respect to the property.

* * * *

§9—312. PERFECTION OF SECURITY INTERESTS IN CHATTEL PAPER, DEPOSIT ACCOUNTS, DOCUMENTS, GOODS COVERED BY DOCUMENTS, INSTRUMENTS, INVESTMENT PROPERTY, LETTER-OF-CREDIT RIGHTS, AND MONEY; PERFECTION BY PERMISSIVE FILING; TEMPORARY PERFECTION WITHOUT FILING OR TRANSFER OF POSSESSION

(a) A security interest in chattel paper, negotiable documents, instruments, or investment property may be perfected by filing.

(b) Except as otherwise provided in Section 9—315 (c) and (d) for proceeds:

(1) a security interest in a deposit account may be perfected only by control under Section 9—314;

(2) and except as otherwise provided in Section 9—308(d), a security interest in a letter-of-credit

right may be perfected only by control under Section 9—314; and

(3) a security interest in money may be perfected only by the secured party's taking possession under Section 9—313.

(c) While goods are in the possession of a bailee that has issued a negotiable document covering the goods:

(1) a security interest in the goods may be perfected by perfecting a security interest in the document; and

(2) a security interest perfected in the document has priority over any security interest that becomes perfected in the goods by another method during that time.

(d) While goods are in the possession of a bailee that has issued a nonnegotiable document covering the goods, a security interest in the goods may be perfected by:

(1) issuance of a document in the name of the secured party;

(2) the bailee's receipt of notification of the secured party's interest; or

(3) filing as to the goods.

(e) A security interest in certificated securities, negotiable documents, or instruments is perfected without filing or the taking of possession for a period of 20 days from the time it attaches to the extent that it arises for new value given under an authenticated security agreement.

(f) A perfected security interest in a negotiable document or goods in possession of a bailee, other than one that has issued a negotiable document for the goods, remains perfected for 20 days without filing if the secured party makes available to the debtor the goods or documents representing the goods for the purpose of:

(1) ultimate sale or exchange; or

(2) loading, unloading, storing, shipping, transshipping, manufacturing, processing, or otherwise dealing with them in a manner preliminary to their sale or exchange.

(g) A perfected security interest in a certificated security or instrument remains perfected for 20 days without filing if the secured party delivers the security certificate or instrument to the debtor for the purpose of:

(1) ultimate sale or exchange; or

(2) presentation, collection, enforcement, renewal, or registration of transfer.

(h) After the 20-day period specified in subsection (e), (f), or (g) expires, perfection depends upon compliance with this article.

§9—313. WHEN POSSESSION BY OR DELIVERY TO SECURED PARTY PERFECTS SECURITY INTEREST WITHOUT FILING

(a) Except as otherwise provided in subsection (b), a secured party may perfect a security interest in negotiable documents, goods, instruments, money, or tangible chattel paper by taking possession of the collateral. A secured party may perfect a security interest in certificated securities by taking delivery of the certificated securities under Section 8—301.

(b) With respect to goods covered by a certificate of title issued by this State, a secured party may perfect a security interest in the goods by taking possession of the goods only in the circumstances described in Section 9—316(d).

(c) With respect to collateral other than certificated securities and goods covered by a document, a secured party takes possession of collateral in the possession of a person other than the debtor, the secured party, or a lessee of the collateral from the debtor in the ordinary course of the debtor's business, when:

(1) the person in possession authenticates a record acknowledging that it holds possession of the collateral for the secured party's benefit; or

(2) the person takes possession of the collateral after having authenticated a record acknowledging that it will hold possession of collateral for the secured party's benefit.

(d) If perfection of a security interest depends upon possession of the collateral by a secured party, perfection occurs no earlier than the time the secured party takes possession and continues only while the secured party retains possession.

(e) A security interest in a certificated security in registered form is perfected by delivery when delivery of the certificated security occurs under Section 8—301 and remains perfected by delivery until the debtor obtains possession of the security certificate.

(f) A person in possession of collateral is not required to acknowledge that it holds possession for a secured party's benefit.

(g) If a person acknowledges that it holds possession for the secured party's benefit:

(1) the acknowledgment is effective under subsection (c) or Section 8—301(a), even if the

acknowledgment violates the rights of a debtor; and

(2) unless the person otherwise agrees or law other than this article otherwise provides, the person does not owe any duty to the secured party and is not required to confirm the acknowledgment to another person.

(h) A secured party having possession of collateral does not relinquish possession by delivering the collateral to a person other than the debtor or a lessee of the collateral from the debtor in the ordinary course of the debtor's business if the person was instructed before the delivery or is instructed contemporaneously with the delivery:

(1) to hold possession of the collateral for the secured party's benefit; or

(2) to redeliver the collateral to the secured party.

(i) A secured party does not relinquish possession, even if a delivery under subsection (h) violates the rights of a debtor. A person to which collateral is delivered under subsection (h) does not owe any duty to the secured party and is not required to confirm the delivery to another person unless the person otherwise agrees or law other than this article otherwise provides.

§9—314. PERFECTION BY CONTROL

(a) A security interest in investment property, deposit accounts, letter-of-credit rights, or electronic chattel paper may be perfected by control of the collateral under Section 9—104, 9—105, 9—106, or 9—107.

(b) A security interest in deposit accounts, electronic chattel paper, or letter-of-credit rights is perfected by control under Section 9—104, 9—105, or 9—107 when the secured party obtains control and remains perfected by control only while the secured party retains control.

(c) A security interest in investment property is perfected by control under Section 9—106 from the time the secured party obtains control and remains perfected by control until:

(1) the secured party does not have control; and

(2) one of the following occurs:

(A) if the collateral is a certificated security, the debtor has or acquires possession of the security certificate;

(B) if the collateral is an uncertificated security, the issuer has registered or registers the debtor as the registered owner; or

(C) if the collateral is a security entitlement, the debtor is or becomes the entitlement holder.

§9—315. SECURED PARTY'S RIGHTS ON DISPOSITION OF COLLATERAL AND IN PROCEEDS

(a) Except as otherwise provided in this article and in Section 2—403(2):

(1) a security interest or agricultural lien continues in collateral notwithstanding sale, lease, license, exchange, or other disposition thereof unless the secured party authorized the disposition free of the security interest or agricultural lien; and

(2) a security interest attaches to any identifiable proceeds of collateral.

(b) Proceeds that are commingled with other property are identifiable proceeds:

(1) if the proceeds are goods, to the extent provided by Section 9—336; and

(2) if the proceeds are not goods, to the extent that the secured party identifies the proceeds by a method of tracing, including application of equitable principles, that is permitted under law other than this article with respect to commingled property of the type involved.

(c) A security interest in proceeds is a perfected security interest if the security interest in the original collateral was perfected.

(d) A perfected security interest in proceeds becomes unperfected on the 21st day after the security interest attaches to the proceeds unless:

(1) the following conditions are satisfied:

(A) a filed financing statement covers the original collateral;

(B) the proceeds are collateral in which a security interest may be perfected by filing in the office in which the financing statement has been filed; and

(C) the proceeds are not acquired with cash proceeds;

(2) the proceeds are identifiable cash proceeds; or

(3) the security interest in the proceeds is perfected other than under subsection (c) when the security interest attaches to the proceeds or within 20 days thereafter.

(e) If a filed financing statement covers the original collateral, a security interest in proceeds which remains perfected under subsection (d)(1) becomes unperfected at the later of:

(1) when the effectiveness of the filed financing statement lapses under Section 9—515 or is terminated under Section 9—513; or

(2) the 21st day after the security interest attaches to the proceeds.

§9—316. CONTINUED PERFECTION OF SECURITY INTEREST FOLLOWING CHANGE IN GOVERNING LAW

(a) A security interest perfected pursuant to the law of the jurisdiction designated in Section 9—301(1) or 9—305(c) remains perfected until the earliest of:

(1) the time perfection would have ceased under the law of that jurisdiction;

(2) the expiration of four months after a change of the debtor's location to another jurisdiction; or

(3) the expiration of one year after a transfer of collateral to a person that thereby becomes a debtor and is located in another jurisdiction.

(b) If a security interest described in subsection (a) becomes perfected under the law of the other jurisdiction before the earliest time or event described in that subsection, it remains perfected thereafter. If the security interest does not become perfected under the law of the other jurisdiction before the earliest time or event, it becomes unperfected and is deemed never to have been perfected as against a purchaser of the collateral for value.

(c) A possessory security interest in collateral, other than goods covered by a certificate of title and as-extracted collateral consisting of goods, remains continuously perfected if:

(1) the collateral is located in one jurisdiction and subject to a security interest perfected under the law of that jurisdiction;

(2) thereafter the collateral is brought into another jurisdiction; and

(3) upon entry into the other jurisdiction, the security interest is perfected under the law of the other jurisdiction.

(d) Except as otherwise provided in subsection (e), a security interest in goods covered by a certificate of title which is perfected by any method under the law of another jurisdiction when the goods become covered by a certificate of title from this State remains perfected until the security interest would have become unperfected under the law of the other jurisdiction had the goods not become so covered.

(e) A security interest described in subsection (d) becomes unperfected as against a purchaser of the goods for value and is deemed never to have been perfected as against a purchaser of the goods for value if the applicable requirements for perfection under Section 9—311(b) or 9—313 are not satisfied before the earlier of:

(1) the time the security interest would have become unperfected under the law of the other jurisdiction had the goods not become covered by a certificate of title from this State; or

(2) the expiration of four months after the goods had become so covered.

(f) A security interest in deposit accounts, letter-of-credit rights, or investment property which is perfected under the law of the bank's jurisdiction, the issuer's jurisdiction, a nominated person's jurisdiction, the securities intermediary's jurisdiction, or the commodity intermediary's jurisdiction, as applicable, remains perfected until the earlier of:

(1) the time the security interest would have become unperfected under the law of that jurisdiction; or

(2) the expiration of four months after a change of the applicable jurisdiction to another jurisdiction.

(g) If a security interest described in subsection (f) becomes perfected under the law of the other jurisdiction before the earlier of the time or the end of the period described in that subsection, it remains perfected thereafter. If the security interest does not become perfected under the law of the other jurisdiction before the earlier of that time or the end of that period, it becomes unperfected and is deemed never to have been perfected as against a purchaser of the collateral for value.

§9—317. INTERESTS THAT TAKE PRIORITY OVER OR TAKE FREE OF SECURITY INTEREST OR AGRICULTURAL LIEN

(a) A security interest or agricultural lien is subordinate to the rights of:

(1) a person entitled to priority under Section 9—322; and

(2) except as otherwise provided in subsection (e), a person that becomes a lien creditor before the earlier of the time:

(A) the security interest or agricultural lien is perfected; or

(B) one of the conditions specified in Section 9—203(b)(3) is met and a financing statement covering the collateral is filed.

(b) Except as otherwise provided in subsection (e), a buyer, other than a secured party, of tangible chattel paper, documents, goods, instruments, or a security certificate takes free of a security interest or agricultural lien if the buyer gives value and receives delivery of the collateral without knowledge of the security interest or agricultural lien and before it is perfected.

(c) Except as otherwise provided in subsection (e), a lessee of goods takes free of a security interest or agricultural lien if the lessee gives value and receives delivery of the collateral without knowledge of the security interest or agricultural lien and before it is perfected.

(d) A licensee of a general intangible or a buyer, other than a secured party, of accounts, electronic chattel paper, general intangibles, or investment property other than a certificated security takes free of a security interest if the licensee or buyer gives value without knowledge of the security interest and before it is perfected.

(e) Except as otherwise provided in Sections 9—320 and 9—321, if a person files a financing statement with respect to a purchase-money security interest before or within 20 days after the debtor receives delivery of the collateral, the security interest takes priority over the rights of a buyer, lessee, or lien creditor which arise between the time the security interest attaches and the time of filing.

§9—318. NO INTEREST RETAINED IN RIGHT TO PAYMENT THAT IS SOLD; RIGHTS AND TITLE OF SELLER OF ACCOUNT OR CHATTEL PAPER WITH RESPECT TO CREDITORS AND PURCHASERS

(a) A debtor that has sold an account, chattel paper, payment intangible, or promissory note does not retain a legal or equitable interest in the collateral sold.

(b) For purposes of determining the rights of creditors of, and purchasers for value of an account or chattel paper from, a debtor that has sold an account or chattel paper, while the buyer's security interest is unperfected, the debtor is deemed to have rights and title to the account or chattel paper identical to those the debtor sold.

§9—319. RIGHTS AND TITLE OF CONSIGNEE WITH RESPECT TO CREDITORS AND PURCHASERS

(a) Except as otherwise provided in subsection (b), for purposes of determining the rights of creditors of, and purchasers for value of goods from, a consignee, while the goods are in the possession of the consignee, the consignee is deemed to have rights and title to the goods identical to those the consignor had or had power to transfer.

(b) For purposes of determining the rights of a creditor of a consignee, law other than this article determines the rights and title of a consignee while goods are in the consignee's possession if, under this part, a perfected security interest held by the consignor would have priority over the rights of the creditor.

§9—320. BUYER OF GOODS

(a) Except as otherwise provided in subsection (e), a buyer in ordinary course of business, other than a person buying farm products from a person engaged in farming operations, takes free of a security interest created by the buyer's seller, even if the security interest is perfected and the buyer knows of its existence.

(b) Except as otherwise provided in subsection (e), a buyer of goods from a person who used or bought the goods for use primarily for personal, family, or household purposes takes free of a security interest, even if perfected, if the buyer buys:

(1) without knowledge of the security interest;

(2) for value;

(3) primarily for the buyer's personal, family, or household purposes; and

(4) before the filing of a financing statement covering the goods.

(c) To the extent that it affects the priority of a security interest over a buyer of goods under subsection (b), the period of effectiveness of a filing made in the jurisdiction in which the seller is located is governed by Section 9—316(a) and (b).

(d) A buyer in ordinary course of business buying oil, gas, or other minerals at the wellhead or minehead or after extraction takes free of an interest arising out of an encumbrance.

(e) Subsections (a) and (b) do not affect a security interest in goods in the possession of the secured party under Section 9—313.

* * * *

§9—322. PRIORITIES AMONG CONFLICTING SECURITY INTERESTS IN AND AGRICULTURAL LIENS ON SAME COLLATERAL

(a) Except as otherwise provided in this section, priority among conflicting security interests and agricultural liens in the same collateral is determined according to the following rules:

(1) Conflicting perfected security interests and agricultural liens rank according to priority in time of filing or perfection. Priority dates from the earlier of the time a filing covering the collateral is first made or the security interest or agricultural lien is first perfected, if there is no period thereafter when there is neither filing nor perfection.

(2) A perfected security interest or agricultural lien has priority over a conflicting unperfected security interest or agricultural lien.

(3) The first security interest or agricultural lien to attach or become effective has priority if conflicting security interests and agricultural liens are unperfected.

(b) For the purposes of subsection (a)(1):

(1) the time of filing or perfection as to a security interest in collateral is also the time of filing or perfection as to a security interest in proceeds; and

(2) the time of filing or perfection as to a security interest in collateral supported by a supporting obligation is also the time of filing or perfection as to a security interest in the supporting obligation.

(c) Except as otherwise provided in subsection (f), a security interest in collateral which qualifies for priority over a conflicting security interest under Section 9—327, 9—328, 9—329, 9—330, or 9—331 also has priority over a conflicting security interest in:

(1) any supporting obligation for the collateral; and

(2) proceeds of the collateral if:

(A) the security interest in proceeds is perfected;

(B) the proceeds are cash proceeds or of the same type as the collateral; and

(C) in the case of proceeds that are proceeds of proceeds, all intervening proceeds are cash proceeds, proceeds of the same type as the collateral, or an account relating to the collateral.

(d) Subject to subsection (e) and except as otherwise provided in subsection (f), if a security interest in chattel paper, deposit accounts, negotiable documents, instruments, investment property, or letter-of-credit rights is perfected by a method other than filing, conflicting perfected security interests in proceeds of the collateral rank according to priority in time of filing.

(e) Subsection (d) applies only if the proceeds of the collateral are not cash proceeds, chattel paper, negotiable documents, instruments, investment property, or letter-of-credit rights.

(f) Subsections (a) through (e) are subject to:

(1) subsection (g) and the other provisions of this part;

(2) Section 4—210 with respect to a security interest of a collecting bank;

(3) Section 5—118 with respect to a security interest of an issuer or nominated person; and

(4) Section 9—110 with respect to a security interest arising under Article 2 or 2A.

(g) A perfected agricultural lien on collateral has priority over a conflicting security interest in or agricultural lien on the same collateral if the statute creating the agricultural lien so provides.

§9—323. FUTURE ADVANCES

(a) Except as otherwise provided in subsection (c), for purposes of determining the priority of a perfected security interest under Section 9—322(a)(1), perfection of the security interest dates from the time an advance is made to the extent that the security interest secures an advance that:

(1) is made while the security interest is perfected only:

(A) under Section 9—309 when it attaches; or

(B) temporarily under Section 9—312(e), (f), or (g); and

(2) is not made pursuant to a commitment entered into before or while the security interest is perfected by a method other than under Section 9—309 or 9—312(e), (f), or (g).

(b) Except as otherwise provided in subsection (c), a security interest is subordinate to the rights of a person that becomes a lien creditor to the extent that the security interest secures an advance made more than 45 days after the person becomes a lien creditor unless the advance is made:

(1) without knowledge of the lien; or

(2) pursuant to a commitment entered into without knowledge of the lien.

(c) Subsections (a) and (b) do not apply to a security interest held by a secured party that is a buyer of accounts, chattel paper, payment intangibles, or promissory notes or a consignor.

(d) Except as otherwise provided in subsection (e), a buyer of goods other than a buyer in ordinary course of business takes free of a security interest to the extent that it secures advances made after the earlier of:

    (1) the time the secured party acquires knowledge of the buyer's purchase; or

    (2) 45 days after the purchase.

(e) Subsection (d) does not apply if the advance is made pursuant to a commitment entered into without knowledge of the buyer's purchase and before the expiration of the 45-day period.

(f) Except as otherwise provided in subsection (g), a lessee of goods, other than a lessee in ordinary course of business, takes the leasehold interest free of a security interest to the extent that it secures advances made after the earlier of:

    (1) the time the secured party acquires knowledge of the lease; or

    (2) 45 days after the lease contract becomes enforceable.

(g) Subsection (f) does not apply if the advance is made pursuant to a commitment entered into without knowledge of the lease and before the expiration of the 45 day period.

§9—324. PRIORITY OF PURCHASE-MONEY SECURITY INTERESTS

(a) Except as otherwise provided in subsection (g), a perfected purchase-money security interest in goods other than inventory or livestock has priority over a conflicting security interest in the same goods, and, except as otherwise provided in Section 9—327, a perfected security interest in its identifiable proceeds also has priority, if the purchase-money security interest is perfected when the debtor receives possession of the collateral or within 20 days thereafter.

(b) Subject to subsection (c) and except as otherwise provided in subsection (g), a perfected purchase-money security interest in inventory has priority over a conflicting security interest in the same inventory, has priority over a conflicting security interest in chattel paper or an instrument constituting proceeds of the inventory and in proceeds of the chattel paper, if so provided in Section 9—330, and, except as otherwise provided in Section 9—327, also has priority in identifiable cash proceeds of the inventory to the extent the identifiable cash proceeds are received on or before the delivery of the inventory to a buyer, if:

    (1) the purchase-money security interest is perfected when the debtor receives possession of the inventory;

    (2) the purchase-money secured party sends an authenticated notification to the holder of the conflicting security interest;

    (3) the holder of the conflicting security interest receives the notification within five years before the debtor receives possession of the inventory; and

    (4) the notification states that the person sending the notification has or expects to acquire a purchase-money security interest in inventory of the debtor and describes the inventory.

(c) Subsections (b)(2) through (4) apply only if the holder of the conflicting security interest had filed a financing statement covering the same types of inventory:

    (1) if the purchase-money security interest is perfected by filing, before the date of the filing; or

    (2) if the purchase-money security interest is temporarily perfected without filing or possession under Section 9—312(f), before the beginning of the 20-day period thereunder.

(d) Subject to subsection (e) and except as otherwise provided in subsection (g), a perfected purchase-money security interest in livestock that are farm products has priority over a conflicting security interest in the same livestock, and, except as otherwise provided in Section 9—327, a perfected security interest in their identifiable proceeds and identifiable products in their unmanufactured states also has priority, if:

    (1) the purchase-money security interest is perfected when the debtor receives possession of the livestock;

    (2) the purchase-money secured party sends an authenticated notification to the holder of the conflicting security interest;

    (3) the holder of the conflicting security interest receives the notification within six months before the debtor receives possession of the livestock; and

    (4) the notification states that the person sending the notification has or expects to acquire a purchase-money security interest in livestock of the debtor and describes the livestock.

(e) Subsections (d)(2) through (4) apply only if the holder of the conflicting security interest had filed a financing statement covering the same types of livestock:

    (1) if the purchase-money security interest is perfected by filing, before the date of the filing; or

(2) if the purchase-money security interest is temporarily perfected without filing or possession under Section 9—312(f), before the beginning of the 20-day period thereunder.

(f) Except as otherwise provided in subsection (g), a perfected purchase-money security interest in software has priority over a conflicting security interest in the same collateral, and, except as otherwise provided in Section 9—327, a perfected security interest in its identifiable proceeds also has priority, to the extent that the purchase-money security interest in the goods in which the software was acquired for use has priority in the goods and proceeds of the goods under this section.

(g) If more than one security interest qualifies for priority in the same collateral under subsection (a), (b), (d), or (f):

> (1) a security interest securing an obligation incurred as all or part of the price of the collateral has priority over a security interest securing an obligation incurred for value given to enable the debtor to acquire rights in or the use of collateral; and

> (2) in all other cases, Section 9—322(a) applies to the qualifying security interests.

§9—325. PRIORITY OF SECURITY INTERESTS IN TRANSFERRED COLLATERAL

(a) Except as otherwise provided in subsection (b), a security interest created by a debtor is subordinate to a security interest in the same collateral created by another person if:

> (1) the debtor acquired the collateral subject to the security interest created by the other person;

> (2) the security interest created by the other person was perfected when the debtor acquired the collateral; and

> (3) there is no period thereafter when the security interest is unperfected.

(b) Subsection (a) subordinates a security interest only if the security interest:

> (1) otherwise would have priority solely under Section 9—322(a) or 9—324; or

> (2) arose solely under Section 2—711(3) or 2A—508(5).

§9—326. PRIORITY OF SECURITY INTERESTS CREATED BY NEW DEBTOR

(a) Subject to subsection (b), a security interest created by a new debtor which is perfected by a filed financing statement that is effective solely under Section 9—508 in collateral in which a new debtor has or acquires rights is subordinate to a security interest in the same collateral which is perfected other than by a filed financing statement that is effective solely under Section 9—508.

(b) The other provisions of this part determine the priority among conflicting security interests in the same collateral perfected by filed financing statements that are effective solely under Section 9—508. However, if the security agreements to which a new debtor became bound as debtor were not entered into by the same original debtor, the conflicting security interests rank according to priority in time of the new debtor's having become bound.

* * * *

§9—330. PRIORITY OF PURCHASER OF CHATTEL PAPER OR INSTRUMENT

(a) A purchaser of chattel paper has priority over a security interest in the chattel paper which is claimed merely as proceeds of inventory subject to a security interest if:

> (1) in good faith and in the ordinary course of the purchaser's business, the purchaser gives new value and takes possession of the chattel paper or obtains control of the chattel paper under Section 9—105; and

> (2) the chattel paper does not indicate that it has been assigned to an identified assignee other than the purchaser.

(b) A purchaser of chattel paper has priority over a security interest in the chattel paper which is claimed other than merely as proceeds of inventory subject to a security interest if the purchaser gives new value and takes possession of the chattel paper or obtains control of the chattel paper under Section 9—105 in good faith, in the ordinary course of the purchaser's business, and without knowledge that the purchase violates the rights of the secured party.

(c) Except as otherwise provided in Section 9—327, a purchaser having priority in chattel paper under subsection (a) or (b) also has priority in proceeds of the chattel paper to the extent that:

> (1) Section 9—322 provides for priority in the proceeds; or

> (2) the proceeds consist of the specific goods covered by the chattel paper or cash proceeds of the specific goods, even if the purchaser's security interest in the proceeds is unperfected.

(d) Except as otherwise provided in Section 9—331 (a), a purchaser of an instrument has priority over a security interest in the instrument perfected by a method other than possession if the purchaser gives value and takes possession of the instrument in good faith and without knowledge that the purchase violates the rights of the secured party.

(e) For purposes of subsections (a) and (b), the holder of a purchase-money security interest in inventory gives new value for chattel paper constituting proceeds of the inventory.

(f) For purposes of subsections (b) and (d), if chattel paper or an instrument indicates that it has been assigned to an identified secured party other than the purchaser, a purchaser of the chattel paper or instrument has knowledge that the purchase violates the rights of the secured party.

* * * *

§9—333. PRIORITY OF CERTAIN LIENS ARISING BY OPERATION OF LAW

(a) In this section, "possessory lien" means an interest, other than a security interest or an agricultural lien:

> (1) which secures payment or performance of an obligation for services or materials furnished with respect to goods by a person in the ordinary course of the person's business;
>
> (2) which is created by statute or rule of law in favor of the person; and
>
> (3) whose effectiveness depends on the person's possession of the goods.

(b) A possessory lien on goods has priority over a security interest in the goods unless the lien is created by a statute that expressly provides otherwise.

§9—334. PRIORITY OF SECURITY INTERESTS IN FIXTURES AND CROPS

(a) A security interest under this article may be created in goods that are fixtures or may continue in goods that become fixtures. A security interest does not exist under this article in ordinary building materials incorporated into an improvement on land.

(b) This article does not prevent creation of an encumbrance upon fixtures under real property law.

(c) In cases not governed by subsections (d) through (h), a security interest in fixtures is subordinate to a conflicting interest of an encumbrancer or owner of the related real property other than the debtor.

(d) Except as otherwise provided in subsection (h), a perfected security interest in fixtures has priority over a conflicting interest of an encumbrancer or owner of the real property if the debtor has an interest of record in or is in possession of the real property and:

> (1) the security interest is a purchase-money security interest;
>
> (2) the interest of the encumbrancer or owner arises before the goods become fixtures; and
>
> (3) the security interest is perfected by a fixture filing before the goods become fixtures or within 20 days thereafter.

(e) A perfected security interest in fixtures has priority over a conflicting interest of an encumbrancer or owner of the real property if:

> (1) the debtor has an interest of record in the real property or is in possession of the real property and the security interest:
>
>> (A) is perfected by a fixture filing before the interest of the encumbrancer or owner is of record; and
>>
>> (B) has priority over any conflicting interest of a predecessor in title of the encumbrancer or owner;
>
> (2) before the goods become fixtures, the security interest is perfected by any method permitted by this article and the fixtures are readily removable:
>
>> (A) factory or office machines;
>>
>> (B) equipment that is not primarily used or leased for use in the operation of the real property; or
>>
>> (C) replacements of domestic appliances that are consumer goods;
>
> (3) the conflicting interest is a lien on the real property obtained by legal or equitable proceedings after the security interest was perfected by any method permitted by this article; or
>
> (4) the security interest is:
>
>> (A) created in a manufactured home in a manufactured-home transaction; and
>>
>> (B) perfected pursuant to a statute described in Section 9—311(a)(2).

(f) A security interest in fixtures, whether or not perfected, has priority over a conflicting interest of an encumbrancer or owner of the real property if:

> (1) the encumbrancer or owner has, in an authenticated record, consented to the security interest or disclaimed an interest in the goods as fixtures; or

(2) the debtor has a right to remove the goods as against the encumbrancer or owner.

(g) The priority of the security interest under paragraph (f)(2) continues for a reasonable time if the debtor's right to remove the goods as against the encumbrancer or owner terminates.

(h) A mortgage is a construction mortgage to the extent that it secures an obligation incurred for the construction of an improvement on land, including the acquisition cost of the land, if a recorded record of the mortgage so indicates. Except as otherwise provided in subsections (e) and (f), a security interest in fixtures is subordinate to a construction mortgage if a record of the mortgage is recorded before the goods become fixtures and the goods become fixtures before the completion of the construction. A mortgage has this priority to the same extent as a construction mortgage to the extent that it is given to refinance a construction mortgage.

(i) A perfected security interest in crops growing on real property has priority over a conflicting interest of an encumbrancer or owner of the real property if the debtor has an interest of record in or is in possession of the real property.

* * * *

§9—336. COMMINGLED GOODS

(a) In this section, "commingled goods" means goods that are physically united with other goods in such a manner that their identity is lost in a product or mass.

(b) A security interest does not exist in commingled goods as such. However, a security interest may attach to a product or mass that results when goods become commingled goods.

(c) If collateral becomes commingled goods, a security interest attaches to the product or mass.

(d) If a security interest in collateral is perfected before the collateral becomes commingled goods, the security interest that attaches to the product or mass under subsection (c) is perfected.

(e) Except as otherwise provided in subsection (f), the other provisions of this part determine the priority of a security interest that attaches to the product or mass under subsection (c).

(f) If more than one security interest attaches to the product or mass under subsection (c), the following rules determine priority:

(1) A security interest that is perfected under subsection (d) has priority over a security interest that is unperfected at the time the collateral becomes commingled goods.

(2) If more than one security interest is perfected under subsection (d), the security interests rank equally in proportion to the value of the collateral at the time it became commingled goods.

* * * *

§9—501. FILING OFFICE

(a) Except as otherwise provided in subsection (b), if the local law of this State governs perfection of a security interest or agricultural lien, the office in which to file a financing statement to perfect the security interest or agricultural lien is:

(1) the office designated for the filing or recording of a record of a mortgage on the related real property, if:

(A) the collateral is as-extracted collateral or timber to be cut; or

(B) the financing statement is filed as a fixture filing and the collateral is goods that are or are to become fixtures; or

(2) the office of [ ] [or any office duly authorized by [ ]], in all other cases, including a case in which the collateral is goods that are or are to become fixtures and the financing statement is not filed as a fixture filing.

(b) The office in which to file a financing statement to perfect a security interest in collateral, including fixtures, of a transmitting utility is the office of [ ]. The financing statement also constitutes a fixture filing as to the collateral indicated in the financing statement which is or is to become fixtures.

Legislative Note: The State should designate the filing office where the brackets appear. The filing office may be that of a governmental official (e.g., the Secretary of State) or a private party that maintains the State's filing system.

§9—502. CONTENTS OF FINANCING STATEMENT; RECORD OF MORTGAGE AS FINANCING STATEMENT; TIME OF FILING FINANCING STATEMENT

(a) Subject to subsection (b), a financing statement is sufficient only if it:

(1) provides the name of the debtor;

(2) provides the name of the secured party or a representative of the secured party; and

(3) indicates the collateral covered by the financing statement.

(b) Except as otherwise provided in Section 9—501 (b), to be sufficient, a financing statement that covers as-extracted collateral or timber to be cut, or which is filed as a fixture filing and covers goods that are or are to become fixtures, must satisfy subsection (a) and also:

(1) indicate that it covers this type of collateral;

(2) indicate that it is to be filed [for record] in the real property records;

(3) provide a description of the real property to which the collateral is related [sufficient to give constructive notice of a mortgage under the law of this State if the description were contained in a record of the mortgage of the real property]; and

(4) if the debtor does not have an interest of record in the real property, provide the name of a record owner.

(c) A record of a mortgage is effective, from the date of recording, as a financing statement filed as a fixture filing or as a financing statement covering as-extracted collateral or timber to be cut only if:

(1) the record indicates the goods or accounts that it covers;

(2) the goods are or are to become fixtures related to the real property described in the record or the collateral is related to the real property described in the record and is as-extracted collateral or timber to be cut;

(3) the record satisfies the requirements for a financing statement in this section other than an indication that it is to be filed in the real property records; and

(4) the record is [duly] recorded.

(d) A financing statement may be filed before a security agreement is made or a security interest otherwise attaches.

Legislative Note: Language in brackets is optional. Where the State has any special recording system for real property other than the usual grantor-grantee index (as, for instance, a tract system or a title registration or Torrens system) local adaptations of subsection (b) and Section 9—519(d) and (e) may be necessary. See, e.g., Mass. Gen. Laws Chapter 106, Section 9—410.

§9—503. NAME OF DEBTOR AND SECURED PARTY

(a) A financing statement sufficiently provides the name of the debtor:

(1) if the debtor is a registered organization, only if the financing statement provides the name of the debtor indicated on the public record of the debtor's jurisdiction of organization which shows the debtor to have been organized;

(2) if the debtor is a decedent's estate, only if the financing statement provides the name of the decedent and indicates that the debtor is an estate;

(3) if the debtor is a trust or a trustee acting with respect to property held in trust, only if the financing statement:

(A) provides the name specified for the trust in its organic documents or, if no name is specified, provides the name of the settlor and additional information sufficient to distinguish the debtor from other trusts having one or more of the same settlors; and

(B) indicates, in the debtor's name or otherwise, that the debtor is a trust or is a trustee acting with respect to property held in trust; and

(4) in other cases:

(A) if the debtor has a name, only if it provides the individual or organizational name of the debtor; and

(B) if the debtor does not have a name, only if it provides the names of the partners, members, associates, or other persons comprising the debtor.

(b) A financing statement that provides the name of the debtor in accordance with subsection (a) is not rendered ineffective by the absence of:

(1) a trade name or other name of the debtor; or

(2) unless required under subsection (a)(4)(B), names of partners, members, associates, or other persons comprising the debtor.

(c) A financing statement that provides only the debtor's trade name does not sufficiently provide the name of the debtor.

(d) Failure to indicate the representative capacity of a secured party or representative of a secured party does not affect the sufficiency of a financing statement.

(e) A financing statement may provide the name of more than one debtor and the name of more than one secured party.

§9—504. INDICATION OF COLLATERAL

A financing statement sufficiently indicates the collateral that it covers if the financing statement provides:

(1) a description of the collateral pursuant to Section 9—108; or

(2) an indication that the financing statement covers all assets or all personal property.

As amended in 1999.

* * * *

§9—506. EFFECT OF ERRORS OR OMISSIONS

(a) A financing statement substantially satisfying the requirements of this part is effective, even if it has minor errors or omissions, unless the errors or omissions make the financing statement seriously misleading.

(b) Except as otherwise provided in subsection (c), a financing statement that fails sufficiently to provide the name of the debtor in accordance with Section 9—503(a) is seriously misleading.

(c) If a search of the records of the filing office under the debtor's correct name, using the filing office's standard search logic, if any, would disclose a financing statement that fails sufficiently to provide the name of the debtor in accordance with Section 9—503(a), the name provided does not make the financing statement seriously misleading.

(d) For purposes of Section 9—508(b), the "debtor's correct name" in subsection (c) means the correct name of the new debtor.

* * * *

§9—509. PERSONS ENTITLED TO FILE A RECORD

(a) A person may file an initial financing statement, amendment that adds collateral covered by a financing statement, or amendment that adds a debtor to a financing statement only if:

(1) the debtor authorizes the filing in an authenticated record or pursuant to subsection (b) or (c); or

(2) the person holds an agricultural lien that has become effective at the time of filing and the financing statement covers only collateral in which the person holds an agricultural lien.

(b) By authenticating or becoming bound as debtor by a security agreement, a debtor or new debtor authorizes the filing of an initial financing statement, and an amendment, covering:

(1) the collateral described in the security agreement; and

(2) property that becomes collateral under Section 9—315(a)(2), whether or not the security agreement expressly covers proceeds.

(c) By acquiring collateral in which a security interest or agricultural lien continues under Section 9—315(a)(1), a debtor authorizes the filing of an initial financing statement, and an amendment, covering the collateral and property that becomes collateral under Section 9—315(a)(2).

(d) A person may file an amendment other than an amendment that adds collateral covered by a financing statement or an amendment that adds a debtor to a financing statement only if:

(1) the secured party of record authorizes the filing; or

(2) the amendment is a termination statement for a financing statement as to which the secured party of record has failed to file or send a termination statement as required by Section 9—513(a) or (c), the debtor authorizes the filing, and the termination statement indicates that the debtor authorized it to be filed.

(e) If there is more than one secured party of record for a financing statement, each secured party of record may authorize the filing of an amendment under subsection (d).

§9—510. EFFECTIVENESS OF FILED RECORD

(a) A filed record is effective only to the extent that it was filed by a person that may file it under Section 9—509.

(b) A record authorized by one secured party of record does not affect the financing statement with respect to another secured party of record.

(c) A continuation statement that is not filed within the six-month period prescribed by Section 9—515(d) is ineffective.

* * * *

§9—513. TERMINATION STATEMENT

(a) A secured party shall cause the secured party of record for a financing statement to file a termination statement for the financing statement if the financing statement covers consumer goods and:

(1) there is no obligation secured by the collateral covered by the financing statement and no commitment to make an advance, incur an obligation, or otherwise give value; or

(2) the debtor did not authorize the filing of the initial financing statement.

(b) To comply with subsection (a), a secured party shall cause the secured party of record to file the termination statement:

(1) within one month after there is no obligation secured by the collateral covered by the financing statement and no commitment to make an advance, incur an obligation, or otherwise give value; or

(2) if earlier, within 20 days after the secured party receives an authenticated demand from a debtor.

(c) In cases not governed by subsection (a), within 20 days after a secured party receives an authenticated demand from a debtor, the secured party shall cause the secured party of record for a financing statement to send to the debtor a termination statement for the financing statement or file the termination statement in the filing office if:

(1) except in the case of a financing statement covering accounts or chattel paper that has been sold or goods that are the subject of a consignment, there is no obligation secured by the collateral covered by the financing statement and no commitment to make an advance, incur an obligation, or otherwise give value;

(2) the financing statement covers accounts or chattel paper that has been sold but as to which the account debtor or other person obligated has discharged its obligation;

(3) the financing statement covers goods that were the subject of a consignment to the debtor but are not in the debtor's possession; or

(4) the debtor did not authorize the filing of the initial financing statement.

(d) Except as otherwise provided in Section 9—510, upon the filing of a termination statement with the filing office, the financing statement to which the termination statement relates ceases to be effective. Except as otherwise provided in Section 9—510, for purposes of Sections 9—519(g), 9—522(a), and 9—523(c), the filing with the filing office of a termination statement relating to a financing statement that indicates that the debtor is a transmitting utility also causes the effectiveness of the financing statement to lapse.

* * * *

§9—515. DURATION AND EFFECTIVENESS OF FINANCING STATEMENT; EFFECT OF LAPSED FINANCING STATEMENT

(a) Except as otherwise provided in subsections (b), (e), (f), and (g), a filed financing statement is effective for a period of five years after the date of filing.

(b) Except as otherwise provided in subsections (e), (f), and (g), an initial financing statement filed in connection with a public-finance transaction or manufactured-home transaction is effective for a period of 30 years after the date of filing if it indicates that it is filed in connection with a public-finance transaction or manufactured-home transaction.

(c) The effectiveness of a filed financing statement lapses on the expiration of the period of its effectiveness unless before the lapse a continuation statement is filed pursuant to subsection (d). Upon lapse, a financing statement ceases to be effective and any security interest or agricultural lien that was perfected by the financing statement becomes unperfected, unless the security interest is perfected otherwise. If the security interest or agricultural lien becomes unperfected upon lapse, it is deemed never to have been perfected as against a purchaser of the collateral for value.

(d) A continuation statement may be filed only within six months before the expiration of the five-year period specified in subsection (a) or the 30-year period specified in subsection (b), whichever is applicable.

(e) Except as otherwise provided in Section 9—510, upon timely filing of a continuation statement, the effectiveness of the initial financing statement continues for a period of five years commencing on the day on which the financing statement would have become ineffective in the absence of the filing. Upon the expiration of the five-year period, the financing statement lapses in the same manner as provided in subsection (c), unless, before the lapse, another continuation statement is filed pursuant to subsection (d). Succeeding continuation statements may be filed in the same manner to continue the effectiveness of the initial financing statement.

(f) If a debtor is a transmitting utility and a filed financing statement so indicates, the financing statement is effective until a termination statement is filed.

(g) A record of a mortgage that is effective as a financing statement filed as a fixture filing under Section 9—502(c) remains effective as a financing statement filed as a fixture filing until the mortgage is released or satisfied of record or its effectiveness otherwise terminates as to the real property.

* * * *

§9—601. RIGHTS AFTER DEFAULT; JUDICIAL ENFORCEMENT; CONSIGNOR OR BUYER OF ACCOUNTS, CHATTEL PAPER, PAYMENT INTANGIBLES, OR PROMISSORY NOTES

(a) After default, a secured party has the rights provided in this part and, except as otherwise provided in Section 9—602, those provided by agreement of the parties.

A secured party:

(1) may reduce a claim to judgment, foreclose, or otherwise enforce the claim, security interest, or agricultural lien by any available judicial procedure; and

(2) if the collateral is documents, may proceed either as to the documents or as to the goods they cover.

(b) A secured party in possession of collateral or control of collateral under Section 9—104, 9—105, 9—106, or 9—107 has the rights and duties provided in Section 9—207.

(c) The rights under subsections (a) and (b) are cumulative and may be exercised simultaneously.

(d) Except as otherwise provided in subsection (g) and Section 9—605, after default, a debtor and an obligor have the rights provided in this part and by agreement of the parties.

(e) If a secured party has reduced its claim to judgment, the lien of any levy that may be made upon the collateral by virtue of an execution based upon the judgment relates back to the earliest of:

(1) the date of perfection of the security interest or agricultural lien in the collateral;

(2) the date of filing a financing statement covering the collateral; or

(3) any date specified in a statute under which the agricultural lien was created.

(f) A sale pursuant to an execution is a foreclosure of the security interest or agricultural lien by judicial procedure within the meaning of this section. A secured party may purchase at the sale and thereafter hold the collateral free of any other requirements of this article.

(g) Except as otherwise provided in Section 9—607 (c), this part imposes no duties upon a secured party that is a consignor or is a buyer of accounts, chattel paper, payment intangibles, or promissory notes.

* * * *

§9—604. PROCEDURE IF SECURITY AGREEMENT COVERS REAL PROPERTY OR FIXTURES

(a) If a security agreement covers both personal and real property, a secured party may proceed:

(1) under this part as to the personal property without prejudicing any rights with respect to the real property; or

(2) as to both the personal property and the real property in accordance with the rights with respect to the real property, in which case the other provisions of this part do not apply.

(b) Subject to subsection (c), if a security agreement covers goods that are or become fixtures, a secured party may proceed:

(1) under this part; or

(2) in accordance with the rights with respect to real property, in which case the other provisions of this part do not apply.

(c) Subject to the other provisions of this part, if a secured party holding a security interest in fixtures has priority over all owners and encumbrancers of the real property, the secured party, after default, may remove the collateral from the real property.

(d) A secured party that removes collateral shall promptly reimburse any encumbrancer or owner of the real property, other than the debtor, for the cost of repair of any physical injury caused by the removal. The secured party need not reimburse the encumbrancer or owner for any diminution in value of the real property caused by the absence of the goods removed or by any necessity of replacing them. A person entitled to reimbursement may refuse permission to remove until the secured party gives adequate assurance for the performance of the obligation to reimburse.

* * * *

§9—607. COLLECTION AND ENFORCEMENT BY SECURED PARTY

(a) If so agreed, and in any event after default, a secured party:

(1) may notify an account debtor or other person obligated on collateral to make payment or otherwise render performance to or for the benefit of the secured party;

(2) may take any proceeds to which the secured party is entitled under Section 9—315;

(3) may enforce the obligations of an account debtor or other person obligated on collateral and exercise the rights of the debtor with respect to the obligation of the account debtor or other person obligated on collateral to make payment or otherwise render performance to the debtor, and with respect to any property that secures the obligations of the account debtor or other person obligated on the collateral;

(4) if it holds a security interest in a deposit account perfected by control under Section 9—104(a)(1), may apply the balance of the deposit

account to the obligation secured by the deposit account; and

(5) if it holds a security interest in a deposit account perfected by control under Section 9—104(a)(2) or (3), may instruct the bank to pay the balance of the deposit account to or for the benefit of the secured party.

(b) If necessary to enable a secured party to exercise under subsection (a)(3) the right of a debtor to enforce a mortgage nonjudicially, the secured party may record in the office in which a record of the mortgage is recorded:

(1) a copy of the security agreement that creates or provides for a security interest in the obligation secured by the mortgage; and

(2) the secured party's sworn affidavit in recordable form stating that:

(A) a default has occurred; and

(B) the secured party is entitled to enforce the mortgage nonjudicially.

(c) A secured party shall proceed in a commercially reasonable manner if the secured party:

(1) undertakes to collect from or enforce an obligation of an account debtor or other person obligated on collateral; and

(2) is entitled to charge back uncollected collateral or otherwise to full or limited recourse against the debtor or a secondary obligor.

(d) A secured party may deduct from the collections made pursuant to subsection (c) reasonable expenses of collection and enforcement, including reasonable attorney's fees and legal expenses incurred by the secured party.

(e) This section does not determine whether an account debtor, bank, or other person obligated on collateral owes a duty to a secured party.

§9—608. APPLICATION OF PROCEEDS OF COLLECTION OR ENFORCEMENT; LIABILITY FOR DEFICIENCY AND RIGHT TO SURPLUS

(a) If a security interest or agricultural lien secures payment or performance of an obligation, the following rules apply:

(1) A secured party shall apply or pay over for application the cash proceeds of collection or enforcement under Section 9—607 in the following order to:

(A) the reasonable expenses of collection and enforcement and, to the extent provided for by

agreement and not prohibited by law, reasonable attorney's fees and legal expenses incurred by the secured party;

(B) the satisfaction of obligations secured by the security interest or agricultural lien under which the collection or enforcement is made; and

(C) the satisfaction of obligations secured by any subordinate security interest in or other lien on the collateral subject to the security interest or agricultural lien under which the collection or enforcement is made if the secured party receives an authenticated demand for proceeds before distribution of the proceeds is completed.

(2) If requested by a secured party, a holder of a subordinate security interest or other lien shall furnish reasonable proof of the interest or lien within a reasonable time. Unless the holder complies, the secured party need not comply with the holder's demand under paragraph (1)(C).

(3) A secured party need not apply or pay over for application noncash proceeds of collection and enforcement under Section 9—607 unless the failure to do so would be commercially unreasonable. A secured party that applies or pays over for application noncash proceeds shall do so in a commercially reasonable manner.

(4) A secured party shall account to and pay a debtor for any surplus, and the obligor is liable for any deficiency.

(b) If the underlying transaction is a sale of accounts, chattel paper, payment intangibles, or promissory notes, the debtor is not entitled to any surplus, and the obligor is not liable for any deficiency.

§9—609. SECURED PARTY'S RIGHT TO TAKE POSSESSION AFTER DEFAULT

(a) After default, a secured party:

(1) may take possession of the collateral; and

(2) without removal, may render equipment unusable and dispose of collateral on a debtor's premises under Section 9—610.

(b) A secured party may proceed under subsection (a):

(1) pursuant to judicial process; or

(2) without judicial process, if it proceeds without breach of the peace.

(c) If so agreed, and in any event after default, a secured party may require the debtor to assemble the collateral and make it available to the secured party at a place to be designated by the secured party which is reasonably convenient to both parties.

§9—610. DISPOSITION OF COLLATERAL AFTER DEFAULT

(a) After default, a secured party may sell, lease, license, or otherwise dispose of any or all of the collateral in its present condition or following any commercially reasonable preparation or processing.

(b) Every aspect of a disposition of collateral, including the method, manner, time, place, and other terms, must be commercially reasonable. If commercially reasonable, a secured party may dispose of collateral by public or private proceedings, by one or more contracts, as a unit or in parcels, and at any time and place and on any terms.

(c) A secured party may purchase collateral:

(1) at a public disposition; or

(2) at a private disposition only if the collateral is of a kind that is customarily sold on a recognized market or the subject of widely distributed standard price quotations.

(d) A contract for sale, lease, license, or other disposition includes the warranties relating to title, possession, quiet enjoyment, and the like which by operation of law accompany a voluntary disposition of property of the kind subject to the contract.

(e) A secured party may disclaim or modify warranties under subsection (d):

(1) in a manner that would be effective to disclaim or modify the warranties in a voluntary disposition of property of the kind subject to the contract of disposition; or

(2) by communicating to the purchaser a record evidencing the contract for disposition and including an express disclaimer or modification of the warranties.

(f) A record is sufficient to disclaim warranties under subsection (e) if it indicates "There is no warranty relating to title, possession, quiet enjoyment, or the like in this disposition" or uses words of similar import.

§9—611. NOTIFICATION BEFORE DISPOSITION OF COLLATERAL

(a) In this section, "notification date" means the earlier of the date on which:

(1) a secured party sends to the debtor and any secondary obligor an authenticated notification of disposition; or

(2) the debtor and any secondary obligor waive the right to notification.

(b) Except as otherwise provided in subsection (d), a secured party that disposes of collateral under Section 9—610 shall send to the persons specified in subsection (c) a reasonable authenticated notification of disposition.

(c) To comply with subsection (b), the secured party shall send an authenticated notification of disposition to:

(1) the debtor;

(2) any secondary obligor; and

(3) if the collateral is other than consumer goods:

(A) any other person from which the secured party has received, before the notification date, an authenticated notification of a claim of an interest in the collateral;

(B) any other secured party or lienholder that, 10 days before the notification date, held a security interest in or other lien on the collateral perfected by the filing of a financing statement that:

(i) identified the collateral;

(ii) was indexed under the debtor's name as of that date; and

(iii) was filed in the office in which to file a financing statement against the debtor covering the collateral as of that date; and

(C) any other secured party that, 10 days before the notification date, held a security interest in the collateral perfected by compliance with a statute, regulation, or treaty described in Section 9—311(a).

(d) Subsection (b) does not apply if the collateral is perishable or threatens to decline speedily in value or is of a type customarily sold on a recognized market.

(e) A secured party complies with the requirement for notification prescribed by subsection (c)(3)(B) if:

(1) not later than 20 days or earlier than 30 days before the notification date, the secured party requests, in a commercially reasonable manner, information concerning financing statements indexed under the debtor's name in the office indicated in subsection (c)(3)(B); and

(2) before the notification date, the secured party:

(A) did not receive a response to the request for information; or

(B) received a response to the request for information and sent an authenticated notification of disposition to each secured party or other lienholder named in that response whose financing statement covered the collateral.

§9—612. TIMELINESS OF NOTIFICATION BEFORE DISPOSITION OF COLLATERAL

(a) Except as otherwise provided in subsection (b), whether a notification is sent within a reasonable time is a question of fact.

(b) In a transaction other than a consumer transaction, a notification of disposition sent after default and 10 days or more before the earliest time of disposition set forth in the notification is sent within a reasonable time before the disposition.

* * * *

§9—615. APPLICATION OF PROCEEDS OF DISPOSITION; LIABILITY FOR DEFICIENCY AND RIGHT TO SURPLUS

(a) A secured party shall apply or pay over for application the cash proceeds of disposition under Section 9—610 in the following order to:

(1) the reasonable expenses of retaking, holding, preparing for disposition, processing, and disposing, and, to the extent provided for by agreement and not prohibited by law, reasonable attorney's fees and legal expenses incurred by the secured party;

(2) the satisfaction of obligations secured by the security interest or agricultural lien under which the disposition is made;

(3) the satisfaction of obligations secured by any subordinate security interest in or other subordinate lien on the collateral if:

(A) the secured party receives from the holder of the subordinate security interest or other lien an authenticated demand for proceeds before distribution of the proceeds is completed; and

(B) in a case in which a consignor has an interest in the collateral, the subordinate security interest or other lien is senior to the interest of the consignor; and

(4) a secured party that is a consignor of the collateral if the secured party receives from the consignor an authenticated demand for proceeds before distribution of the proceeds is completed.

(b) If requested by a secured party, a holder of a subordinate security interest or other lien shall furnish reasonable proof of the interest or lien within a reasonable time.

Unless the holder does so, the secured party need not comply with the holder's demand under subsection (a)(3).

(c) A secured party need not apply or pay over for application noncash proceeds of disposition under Section 9—610 unless the failure to do so would be commercially unreasonable. A secured party that applies or pays over for application noncash proceeds shall do so in a commercially reasonable manner.

(d) If the security interest under which a disposition is made secures payment or performance of an obligation, after making the payments and applications required by subsection (a) and permitted by subsection (c):

(1) unless subsection (a)(4) requires the secured party to apply or pay over cash proceeds to a consignor, the secured party shall account to and pay a debtor for any surplus; and

(2) the obligor is liable for any deficiency.

(e) If the underlying transaction is a sale of accounts, chattel paper, payment intangibles, or promissory notes:

(1) the debtor is not entitled to any surplus; and

(2) the obligor is not liable for any deficiency.

(f) The surplus or deficiency following a disposition is calculated based on the amount of proceeds that would have been realized in a disposition complying with this part to a transferee other than the secured party, a person related to the secured party, or a secondary obligor if:

(1) the transferee in the disposition is the secured party, a person related to the secured party, or a secondary obligor; and

(2) the amount of proceeds of the disposition is significantly below the range of proceeds that a complying disposition to a person other than the secured party, a person related to the secured party, or a secondary obligor would have brought.

(g) A secured party that receives cash proceeds of a disposition in good faith and without knowledge that the receipt violates the rights of the holder of a security interest or other lien that is not subordinate to the security interest or agricultural lien under which the disposition is made:

(1) takes the cash proceeds free of the security interest or other lien;

(2) is not obligated to apply the proceeds of the disposition to the satisfaction of obligations secured by the security interest or other lien; and

(3) is not obligated to account to or pay the holder of the security interest or other lien for any surplus.

* * * *

§9—617. RIGHTS OF TRANSFEREE OF COLLATERAL

(a) A secured party's disposition of collateral after default:

1) transfers to a transferee for value all of the debtor's rights in the collateral;

2) discharges the security interest under which the disposition is made; and

3) discharges any subordinate security interest or other subordinate lien [other than liens created under [cite acts or statutes providing for liens, if any, that are not to be discharged]].

(b) A transferee that acts in good faith takes free of the rights and interests described in subsection (a), even if the secured party fails to comply with this article or the requirements of any judicial proceeding.

(c) If a transferee does not take free of the rights and interests described in subsection (a), the transferee takes the collateral subject to:

(1) the debtor's rights in the collateral;

(2) the security interest or agricultural lien under which the disposition is made; and

(3) any other security interest or other lien.

* * * *

§9—620. ACCEPTANCE OF COLLATERAL IN FULL OR PARTIAL SATISFACTION OF OBLIGATION; COMPULSORY DISPOSITION OF COLLATERAL

(a) Except as otherwise provided in subsection (g), a secured party may accept collateral in full or partial satisfaction of the obligation it secures only if:

(1) the debtor consents to the acceptance under subsection (c);

(2) the secured party does not receive, within the time set forth in subsection (d), a notification of objection to the proposal authenticated by:

(A) a person to which the secured party was required to send a proposal under Section 9—621; or

(B) any other person, other than the debtor, holding an interest in the collateral subordinate to the security interest that is the subject of the proposal;

(3) if the collateral is consumer goods, the collateral is not in the possession of the debtor when the debtor consents to the acceptance; and

(4) subsection (e) does not require the secured party to dispose of the collateral or the debtor waives the requirement pursuant to Section 9—624.

(b) A purported or apparent acceptance of collateral under this section is ineffective unless:

(1) the secured party consents to the acceptance in an authenticated record or sends a proposal to the debtor; and

(2) the conditions of subsection (a) are met.

(c) For purposes of this section:

(1) a debtor consents to an acceptance of collateral in partial satisfaction of the obligation it secures only if the debtor agrees to the terms of the acceptance in a record authenticated after default; and

(2) a debtor consents to an acceptance of collateral in full satisfaction of the obligation it secures only if the debtor agrees to the terms of the acceptance in a record authenticated after default or the secured party:

(A) sends to the debtor after default a proposal that is unconditional or subject only to a condition that collateral not in the possession of the secured party be preserved or maintained;

(B) in the proposal, proposes to accept collateral in full satisfaction of the obligation it secures; and

(C) does not receive a notification of objection authenticated by the debtor within 20 days after the proposal is sent.

(d) To be effective under subsection (a)(2), a notification of objection must be received by the secured party:

(1) in the case of a person to which the proposal was sent pursuant to Section 9—621, within 20 days after notification was sent to that person; and

(2) in other cases:

(A) within 20 days after the last notification was sent pursuant to Section 9—621; or

(B) if a notification was not sent, before the debtor consents to the acceptance under subsection (c).

(e) A secured party that has taken possession of collateral shall dispose of the collateral pursuant to Section 9—610 within the time specified in subsection (f) if:

(1) 60 percent of the cash price has been paid in the case of a purchase-money security interest in consumer goods; or

(2) 60 percent of the principal amount of the obligation secured has been paid in the case of a non-purchase-money security interest in consumer goods.

(f) To comply with subsection (e), the secured party shall dispose of the collateral:

(1) within 90 days after taking possession; or

(2) within any longer period to which the debtor and all secondary obligors have agreed in an agreement to that effect entered into and authenticated after default.

(g) In a consumer transaction, a secured party may not accept collateral in partial satisfaction of the obligation it secures.

* * * *

§9—623. RIGHT TO REDEEM COLLATERAL

(a) A debtor, any secondary obligor, or any other secured party or lienholder may redeem collateral.

(b) To redeem collateral, a person shall tender:

(1) fulfillment of all obligations secured by the collateral; and

(2) the reasonable expenses and attorney's fees described in Section 9—615(a)(1).

(c) A redemption may occur at any time before a secured party:

(1) has collected collateral under Section 9—607;

(2) has disposed of collateral or entered into a contract for its disposition under Section 9—610; or

(3) has accepted collateral in full or partial satisfaction of the obligation it secures under Section 9—622.

* * * *

§9—625. REMEDIES FOR SECURED PARTY'S FAILURE TO COMPLY WITH ARTICLE

(a) If it is established that a secured party is not proceeding in accordance with this article, a court may order or restrain collection, enforcement, or disposition of collateral on appropriate terms and conditions.

(b) Subject to subsections (c), (d), and (f), a person is liable for damages in the amount of any loss caused by a failure to comply with this article. Loss caused by a failure to comply may include loss resulting from the debtor's inability to obtain, or increased costs of, alternative financing.

(c) Except as otherwise provided in Section 9—628:

(1) a person that, at the time of the failure, was a debtor, was an obligor, or held a security interest in

or other lien on the collateral may recover damages under subsection (b) for its loss; and

(2) if the collateral is consumer goods, a person that was a debtor or a secondary obligor at the time a secured party failed to comply with this part may recover for that failure in any event an amount not less than the credit service charge plus 10 percent of the principal amount of the obligation or the time-price differential plus 10 percent of the cash price.

(d) A debtor whose deficiency is eliminated under Section 9—626 may recover damages for the loss of any surplus. However, a debtor or secondary obligor whose deficiency is eliminated or reduced under Section 9—626 may not otherwise recover under subsection (b) for noncompliance with the provisions of this part relating to collection, enforcement, disposition, or acceptance.

(e) In addition to any damages recoverable under subsection (b), the debtor, consumer obligor, or person named as a debtor in a filed record, as applicable, may recover $500 in each case from a person that:

(1) fails to comply with Section 9—208;

(2) fails to comply with Section 9—209;

(3) files a record that the person is not entitled to file under Section 9—509(a);

(4) fails to cause the secured party of record to file or send a termination statement as required by Section 9—513(a) or (c);

(5) fails to comply with Section 9—616(b)(1) and whose failure is part of a pattern, or consistent with a practice, of noncompliance; or

(6) fails to comply with Section 9—616(b)(2).

(f) A debtor or consumer obligor may recover damages under subsection (b) and, in addition, $500 in each case from a person that, without reasonable cause, fails to comply with a request under Section 9—210. A recipient of a request under Section 9—210 which never claimed an interest in the collateral or obligations that are the subject of a request under that section has a reasonable excuse for failure to comply with the request within the meaning of this subsection.

(g) If a secured party fails to comply with a request regarding a list of collateral or a statement of account under Section 9—210, the secured party may claim a security interest only as shown in the list or statement included in the request as against a person that is reasonably misled by the failure.

* * * *

§9—627. DETERMINATION OF WHETHER CONDUCT WAS COMMERCIALLY REASONABLE

(a) The fact that a greater amount could have been obtained by a collection, enforcement, disposition, or acceptance at a different time or in a different method from that selected by the secured party is not of itself sufficient to preclude the secured party from establishing that the collection, enforcement, disposition, or acceptance was made in a commercially reasonable manner.

(b) A disposition of collateral is made in a commercially reasonable manner if the disposition is made:

(1) in the usual manner on any recognized market;

(2) at the price current in any recognized market at the time of the disposition; or

(3) otherwise in conformity with reasonable commercial practices among dealers in the type of property that was the subject of the disposition.

(c) A collection, enforcement, disposition, or acceptance is commercially reasonable if it has been approved:

(1) in a judicial proceeding;

(2) by a bona fide creditors' committee;

(3) by a representative of creditors; or

(4) by an assignee for the benefit of creditors.

(d) Approval under subsection (c) need not be obtained, and lack of approval does not mean that the collection, enforcement, disposition, or acceptance is not commercially reasonable.

A

abate—put a stop to a nuisance; reduce or cancel a legacy because the estate of the decedent is insufficient to make payment in full.

absolute guaranty—agreement that creates the same obligation for the guarantor as a suretyship does for the surety; a guaranty of payment creates an absolute guaranty.

absolute privilege—complete defense against the tort of defamation, as in the speeches of members of Congress on the floor and witnesses in a trial.

abstract of title—history of the transfers of title to a given piece of land, briefly stating the parties to and the effect of all deeds, wills, and judicial proceedings relating to the land.

acceptance—unqualified assent to the act or proposal of another, such as the acceptance of an offer to make a contract; the acceptance of a draft (bill of exchange); the acceptance of goods delivered by a seller, or a gift of a deed.

acceptor—drawee who has accepted the liability of paying the amount of money specified in a draft.

accommodation party—person who signs an instrument to lend credit to another party to the paper.

accord and satisfaction—agreement to substitute for an existing debt some alternative form of discharging that debt, coupled with the actual discharge of the debt by the substituted performance.

acknowledgment—admission or confirmation, generally of an instrument and usually made before a person authorized to administer oaths, such as a notary public.

acquired distinctiveness—through advertising, use and association, over time, an ordinary descriptive word or phrase has taken on a new source-identifying meaning and functions as a mark in the eyes of the public.

act-of-state doctrine—doctrine whereby every sovereign state is bound to respect the independence of every other sovereign state, and the courts of one country will not sit in judgment of another government's acts done within its own territory.

adeemed—canceled; as in a specifically bequeathed property being sold or given away by the testator prior to death, thus canceling the bequest.

adjustable rate mortgage (ARM)—mortgage with variable financing charges over the life of the loan.

administrative agency—government body charged with administering and implementing legislation.

administrative law—law governing administrative agencies.

administrative law judge—judicial figure who hears administrative agency actions.

Administrative Procedure Act—federal law that establishes the operating rules for administrative agencies.

administrative regulations—rules made by state and federal administrative agencies.

administrator, administratrix—person (man, woman) appointed to wind up and settle the estate of a person who has died without a will.

admissibility—the quality of the evidence in a case that allows it to be presented to the jury.

adverse possession—hostile possession of real estate, which when actual, visible, notorious, exclusive, and continued for the required time, will vest the title to the land in the person in such adverse possession.

advising bank—bank that tells beneficiary that letter of credit has been issued.

affidavit—statement of facts under oath; executed before a notary public or anyone authorized to administer oaths.

affirm—action taken by an appellate court that approves the decision of the court below.

affirmative action plan (AAP)—plan to have a diverse and representative workforce.

after-acquired goods—goods acquired after a security interest has attached.

agency—the relationship that exists between a person identified as a principal and another by virtue of which the latter may make contracts with third persons on behalf of the principal. (Parties–principal, agent, third person)

agent—person or firm who is authorized by the principal or by operation of law to make contracts with third persons on behalf of the principal.

airbill—document of title issued to a shipper whose goods are being sent via air.

alteration—unauthorized change or completion of a negotiable instrument designed to modify the obligation of a party to the instrument.

alternative payees—those persons to whom a negotiable instrument is made payable, any one of whom may indorse and take delivery of it.

ambiguous—having more than one reasonable interpretation.

answer—what a defendant must file to admit or deny facts asserted by the plaintiff.

anticipatory breach—promisor's repudiation of the contract prior to the time that performance is required when such repudiation is accepted by the promisee as a breach of the contract.

anticipatory repudiation—repudiation made in advance of the time for performance of the contract obligations.

antilapse statutes—statutes providing that the children or heirs of a deceased beneficiary may take the legacy in the place of the deceased beneficiary.

apparent authority—appearance of authority created by the principal's words or conduct.

appeal—taking a case to a reviewing court to determine whether the judgment of the lower court or administrative agency was correct. (Parties—appellant, appellee)

appellate jurisdiction—the power of a court to hear and decide a given class of cases on appeal from another court or administrative agency.

arbitration—the settlement of disputed questions, whether of law or fact, by one or more arbitrators by whose decision the parties agree to be bound.

Article 2—section of the Uniform Commercial Code that governs contracts for the sale of goods.

articles of copartnership—see *partnership agreement*.

articles of incorporation—see *certificate of incorporation*.

articles of partnership—see *partnership agreement*.

assignee—third party to whom contract benefits are transferred.

assignment—transfer of a right. Generally used in connection with personal property rights, as rights under a contract, commercial paper, an insurance policy, a mortgage, or a lease. (Parties—assignor, assignee)

assignor—party who assigns contract rights to a third party.

association tribunal—a court created by a trade association or group for the resolution of disputes among its members.

assumption—mortgage transfers in which the transferee and mortgagor are liable and the property is subject to foreclosure by the mortgagee if payments are not made.

attestation clause—clause that indicates a witness has observed either the execution of the will or the testator's acknowledgment of the writing as the testator's will.

attorney in fact—agent authorized to act for another under a power of attorney.

attorney-client privilege—right of individual to have discussions with his/her attorney kept private and confidential.

attractive nuisance doctrine—a rule imposing liability upon a landowner for injuries sustained by small children playing on the land when the landowner permits a condition to exist or maintains equipment that a reasonable person should realize would attract small children who could not realize the danger. The rule does not apply if an unreasonable burden would be imposed upon the landowner in taking steps to protect the children.

authorities—corporations formed by government that perform public service.

automatic perfection—perfection given by statute without specific filing or possession requirements on the part of the creditor.

automatic stay—order to prevent creditors from taking action such as filing suits or seeking foreclosure against the debtor.

B

bad check laws—laws making it a criminal offense to issue a bad check with intent to defraud.

bailee—person who accepts possession of a property.

bailee's lien—specific, possessory lien of the bailee upon the goods for work done to them. Commonly extended by statute to any bailee's claim for compensation, eliminating the necessity of retention of possession.

bailment—relationship that exists when personal property is delivered into the possession of another under an agreement, express or implied, that the identical property will be returned or will be delivered in accordance with the agreement. (Parties—bailor, bailee)

bailment for mutual benefit—bailment in which the bailor and bailee derive a benefit from the bailment.

bailor—person who turns over the possession of a property.

balance sheet test—comparison of assets to liabilities made to determine solvency.

bankruptcy—procedure by which one unable to pay debts may surrender all assets in excess of any exemption claim to the court for administration and distribution to creditors, and the debtor is given a discharge that releases him from the unpaid balance due on most debts.

bankruptcy courts—court of special jurisdiction to determine bankruptcy issues.

battle of the forms—merchants' exchanges of invoices and purchase orders with differing boilerplate terms.

bearer—person in physical possession of commercial paper payable to bearer, a document of title directing delivery to bearer, or an investment security in bearer form.

bearer paper—instrument with no payee, payable to cash or payable to bearer.

bedrock view—a strict constructionist interpretation of a constitution.

beneficiary—person to whom the proceeds of a life insurance policy are payable, a person for whose benefit property is held in trust, or a person given property by a will; the ultimate recipient of the benefit of a funds transfer.

benefit corporation—for-profit corporation that sets a goal to create a public benefit while still providing economic returns to its investors.

beneficiary's bank—the final bank, which carries out the payment order, in the chain of a transfer of funds.

bequest—gift of personal property by will.

best available treatment—a water treatment that is the most current and best available through research, even though it may not be the treatment used most frequently.

best conventional treatment—a water treatment that is generally used among industries; not always the best treatment available.

bicameral—a two-house form of the legislative branch of government.

bilateral contract—agreement under which one promise is given in exchange for another.

bill of lading—document issued by a carrier acknowledging the receipt of goods and the terms of the contract of transportation.

bill of sale—writing signed by the seller reciting that the personal property therein described has been sold to the buyer.

blackmail—extortion demands made by a nonpublic official.

blank indorsement—an indorsement that does not name the person to whom the paper, document of title, or investment security is negotiated.

blocking laws—laws that prohibit the disclosure, copying, inspection, or removal of documents located in the enacting country in compliance with orders from foreign authorities.

blue sky laws—state statutes designed to protect the public from the sale of worthless stocks and bonds.

bona fide—in good faith; without any fraud or deceit.

bond—a debt investment; a loan to a corporation or government entity usually for a defined period of time at a fixed interest rate.

bond indenture—agreement setting forth the contractual terms of a particular bond issue.

book value—value found by dividing the value of the corporate assets by the number of shares outstanding.

breach—failure to act or perform in the manner called for in a contract.

breach of the peace—violation of the law in the repossession of the collateral.

brownfields—land that is a designated Superfund cleanup site but which lies fallow because no one is willing to risk liability by buying the property, even when the hazardous waste has been removed, or property no one is willing to spend the money to remove the hazardous waste.

bubble concept—method for determining total emissions in one area; all sources are considered in an area.

business ethics—balancing the goal of profits with values of individuals and society.

business judgment rule (BJR)—rule that allows management immunity from liability for corporate acts where there is a reasonable indication that the acts were made in good faith with due care.

bylaws—rules and regulations enacted by a corporation to govern the affairs of the corporation and its shareholders, directors, and officers.

C

cancellation provision—crossing out of a part of an instrument or a destruction of all legal effect of the instrument, whether by act of party, upon breach by the other party, or pursuant to agreement or decree of court.

capital stock—declared money value of the outstanding stock of the corporation.

cargo insurance—insurance that protects a cargo owner against financial loss if goods being shipped are lost or damaged at sea.

carrier—individual or organization undertaking the transportation of goods.

case law—law that includes principles that are expressed for the first time in court decisions.

cash surrender value—sum paid the insured upon the surrender of a policy to the insurer.

cash tender offer—general offer to all shareholders of a target corporation to purchase their shares for cash at a specified price.

cashier's check—draft drawn by a bank on itself.

cause of action—right to damages or other judicial relief when a legally protected right of the plaintiff is violated by an unlawful act of the defendant.

cease-and-desist order—order issued by a court or administrative agency to stop a practice that it decides is improper.

certificate of deposit (CD)—promise-to-pay instrument issued by a bank.

certificate of incorporation—written approval from the state or national government for a corporation to be formed.

certificate of stock—document evidencing a shareholder's ownership of stock issued by a corporation.

certified check—check for which the bank has set aside in a special account sufficient funds to pay it; payment is made when check is presented regardless of amount in drawer's account at that time; discharges all parties except certifying bank when holder requests certification.

cestui que trust—beneficiary of the trust.

CF—cost and freight.

Chapter 7 bankruptcy—liquidation form of bankruptcy under federal law.

Chapter 11 bankruptcy—reorganization form of bankruptcy under federal law.

Chapter 13 bankruptcy—proceeding of consumer debt readjustment plan bankruptcy.

charging order—order by a court, after a business partner's personal assets are exhausted, requiring that the partner's share of the profits be paid to a creditor until the debt is discharged.

charter—grant of authority from a government to exist as a corporation. Generally replaced today by a certificate of incorporation approving the articles of incorporation.

check—order by a depositor on a bank to pay a sum of money to a payee; a bill of exchange drawn on a bank and payable on demand.

choice-of-law clause—clause in an agreement that specifies which law will govern should a dispute arise.

chose in action—intangible personal property in the nature of claims against another, such as a claim for accounts receivable or wages.

CIF—cost, insurance, and freight.

civil disobedience—the term used when natural law proponents violate positive law.

civil laws—the laws that define the rights of one person against another.

claim—creditor's right to payment.

Clayton Act—a federal law that prohibits price discrimination.

Clean Air Act—federal legislation that establishes standards for air pollution levels and prevents further deterioration of air quality.

Clean Water Act—federal legislation that regulates water pollution through a control system.

close corporation—corporation whose shares are held by a single shareholder or a small group of shareholders.

close-connection doctrine—circumstantial evidence, such as an ongoing or a close relationship, that can serve as notice of a problem with an instrument.

COD—cash on delivery.

coinsurance clause—clause requiring the insured to maintain insurance on property up to a stated amount and providing that to the extent that this is not done, the insured is to be deemed a coinsurer with the insurer, so that the latter is liable only for its proportionate share of the amount of insurance required to be carried.

collateral—property pledged by a borrower as security for a debt.

comity—principle of international and national law that the laws of all nations and states deserve the respect legitimately demanded by equal participants.

commerce clause—that section of the U.S. Constitution allocating business regulation between federal and state governments.

commercial impracticability— situation that occurs when costs of performance rise suddenly and performance of a contract will result in a substantial loss.

commercial lease—any nonconsumer lease.

commercial paper—written, transferable, signed promise or order to pay a specified sum of money; a negotiable instrument.

commercial unit—standard of the trade for shipment or packaging of a good.

commission merchant—bailee to whom goods are consigned for sale.

commission or factorage—consignee's compensation.

common carrier—carrier that holds out its facilities to serve the general public for compensation without discrimination.

common law—the body of unwritten principles originally based upon the usages and customs of the community that were recognized and enforced by the courts.

common stock—stock that has no right or priority over any other stock of the corporation as to dividends or distribution of assets upon dissolution.

community property—cotenancy held by husband and wife in property acquired during their marriage under the law of some of the states, principally in the southwestern United States.

comparative negligence—defense to negligence that allows plaintiff to recover reduced damages based on his level of fault.

compensatory damages—sum of money that will compensate an injured plaintiff for actual loss.

complaint—the initial pleading filed by the plaintiff in many actions, which in many states may be served as original process to acquire jurisdiction over the defendant.

composition of creditors—agreement among creditors that each shall accept a part payment as full payment in consideration of the other creditors doing the same.

Comprehensive Environmental Response, Compensation, and Liability Act (CERCLA)—federal law that assigns liability for cleanup of hazardous sites.

computer crimes—wrongs committed using a computer or with knowledge of computers.

concealment—failure to volunteer information not requested.

condition—stipulation or prerequisite in a contract, will, or other instrument.

condition precedent—event that if unsatisfied would mean that no rights would arise under a contract.

condition subsequent—event whose occurrence or lack thereof terminates a contract.

condominium—combination of co-ownership and individual ownership.

confidential relationship—relationship in which, because of the legal status of the parties or their respective physical or mental conditions or knowledge, one party places full confidence and trust in the other.

conflict of interest—conduct that compromises an employee's allegiance to that company.

conglomerate—relationship of a parent corporation to subsidiary corporations engaged in diversified fields of activity unrelated to the field of activity of the parent corporation.

consent decrees—informal settlements of enforcement actions brought by agencies.

consequential damages—damages the buyer experiences as a result of the seller's breach with respect to a third party; also called *special damages.*

consideration—promise or performance that the promisor demands as the price of the promise.

consignee—(1) person to whom goods are shipped; (2) dealer who sells goods for others.

consignment—bailment made for the purpose of sale by the bailee. (Parties—consignor, consignee)

consignor—(1) person who delivers goods to the carrier for shipment; (2) party with title who turns goods over to another for sale.

consolidation (of corporations)—combining of two or more corporations in which the corporate existence of each one ceases and a new corporation is created.

conspiracy—agreement between two or more persons to commit an unlawful act.

constitution—a body of principles that establishes the structure of a government and the relationship of the government to the people who are governed.

constructive bailment—bailment imposed by law as opposed to one created by contract, whereby the bailee must preserve the property and redeliver it to the owner.

constructive delivery—See *"symbolic delivery."*

constructive eviction—act or omission of the landlord that substantially deprives the tenant of the use and enjoyment of the premises.

consumer—any buyer afforded special protections by statute or regulation.

consumer credit—credit for personal, family, and household use.

Consumer Financial Protection Bureau—consumer protection bureau located within the Federal Reserve that now has jurisdiction over all consumer credit issues and statutes.

consumer goods—goods used or bought primarily for personal, family, or household use.

consumer lease—lease of goods by a natural person for personal, family, or household use.

Consumer Product Safety Improvement Act (CPSIA)—federal law that sets standards for the types of paints used in toys, a response to the lead paint found in toys made in China; requires tracking for international production; increases penalties.

contract—a binding agreement based on the genuine assent of the parties, made for a lawful object, between competent parties, in the form required by law, and generally supported by consideration.

contract carrier—carrier that transports on the basis of individual contracts that it makes with each shipper.

contract interference—tort in which a third party interferes with others' freedom to contract.

contract of adhesion—contract offered by a dominant party to a party with inferior bargaining power on a take-it-or-leave-it basis.

contract under seal—contract executed by affixing a seal or making an impression on the paper or on some adhering substance such as wax attached to the document.

contracting agent—agent with authority to make contracts; person with whom the buyer deals.

Contracts for the International Sale of Goods (CISG)—uniform international contract code contracts for international sale of goods.

contractual capacity—ability to understand that a contract is being made and to understand its general meaning.

contribution—right of a co-obligor who has paid more than a proportionate share to demand that other obligors pay their *pro rata* share.

contributory negligence—negligence of the plaintiff that contributes to injury and at common law bars recovery from the defendant although the defendant may have been more negligent than the plaintiff.

Controlling the Assault of Non-Solicited Pornography and Marketing (CAN-SPAM) Act—allows private companies to bring suit against spammers for their unauthorized use of Internet Service Providers (ISPs).

conversion—act of taking personal property by a person not entitled to it and keeping it from its true owner or prior possessor without consent.

cooperative—group of two or more persons or enterprises that acts through a common agent with respect to a common objective, such as buying or selling.

copyright—exclusive right given by federal statute to the creator of a literary or an artistic work to use, reproduce, and display the work.

corporation—artificial being created by government grant, which for many purposes is treated as a natural person.

corporation by estoppel—corporation that comes about when parties estop themselves from denying that the corporation exists.

corporation de jure—corporation with a legal right to exist by virtue of law.

correspondent bank—will honor the letter of credit from the domestic bank of the buyer.

cost plus—method of determining the purchase price or contract price equal to the seller's or contractor's costs plus a stated percentage as the profit.

co-sureties—sureties for the same debt.

cotenancy—when two or more persons hold concurrent rights and interests in the same property.

Council on Environmental Quality (CEQ)—federal agency that establishes national policies on environmental quality and then recommends legislation to implement these policies.

counterclaim—a claim that the defendant in an action may make against the plaintiff.

counteroffer—proposal by an offeree to the offeror that changes the terms of, and thus rejects, the original offer.

course of dealing—pattern of performance between two parties to a contract.

court—a tribunal established by government to hear and decide matters properly brought to it.

covenant against encumbrances—guarantee that conveyed land is not subject to any right or interest of a third person.

covenant of further assurances—promise that the grantor of an interest in land will execute any additional documents required to perfect the title of the grantee.

covenant of quiet enjoyment—covenant by the grantor of an interest in land to not disturb the grantee's possession of the land.

covenant of right to convey—guarantee that the grantor of an interest in land, if not the owner, has the right or authority to make the conveyance to a new owner.

covenant of seisin—guarantee that the grantor of an interest in land owns the estate conveyed to a new owner.

covenants (or warranties) of title—grantor's covenants of a deed that guarantee such matters as the right to make the conveyance, to ownership of the property, to freedom of the property from encumbrances, or that the grantee will not be disturbed in the quiet enjoyment of the land.

credit transfer—transaction in which a person making payment, such as a buyer, requests payment be made to the beneficiary's bank.

creditor—person (seller or lender) who is owed money; also may be a secured party.

crime—violation of the law that is punished as an offense against the state or government.

criminal laws—the laws that define wrongs against society.

cross-examination—the examination made of a witness by the attorney for the adverse party.

cumulative voting—system of voting for directors in which each shareholder has as many votes as the number of voting shares owned multiplied by the number of directors to be elected, and such votes can be distributed for the various candidates as desired.

customary authority—authority of an agent to do any act that, according to the custom of the community, usually accompanies the transaction for which the agent is authorized to act.

cybersquatters—term for those who register and set up domain names on the Internet for resale to the famous users of the names in question.

D

de facto—existing in fact as distinguished from as of right, as in the case of an officer or a corporation purporting to act as such without being elected to the office or having been properly incorporated.

debenture—unsecured bond of a corporation, with no specific corporate assets pledged as security for payment.

debit transfer—transaction in which a beneficiary entitled to money requests payment from a bank according to a prior agreement.

debtor—buyer on credit (i.e., a borrower).

decedent—person whose estate is being administered.

deed—instrument by which the grantor (owner of land) conveys or transfers the title to a grantee.

defamation—untrue statement by one party about another to a third party.

defendant—party charged with a violation of civil or criminal law in a proceeding.

defined benefit plan—an employer established pension fund obligating the employer to make specified future payments to participants upon retirement.

defined contribution plan—a plan providing individual accounts for each employee participant with benefits defined solely on the amounts contributed by each employee with matching contributions by the employer.

definite time—time of payment computable from the face of the instrument.

delegated powers—powers expressly granted the national government by the Constitution.

delegation—transfer to another of the right and power to do an act.

delegation of duties—transfer of duties by a contracting party to another person who is to perform them.

delivery—constructive or actual possession.

demand draft—draft that is payable upon presentment.

demurrer—a pleading to dismiss the adverse party's pleading for not stating a cause of action or a defense.

deposition—the testimony of a witness taken out of court before a person authorized to administer oaths.

depositor—person, or bailor, who gives property for storage.

derivative (secondary) action—secondary action for damages or breach of contract brought by one or more corporate shareholders against directors, officers, or third persons.

development statement—statement that sets forth significant details of a real estate or property development as required by the federal Land Sales Act.

devise—gift of real estate made by will.

devisee—beneficiary of a devise.

direct damages—losses that are caused by breach of a contract.

direct examination—examination of a witness by his or her attorney.

directed verdict—a direction by the trial judge to the jury to return a verdict in favor of a specified party to the action.

disability—any incapacity resulting from bodily injury or disease to engage in any occupation for remuneration or profit.

discharge in bankruptcy—order of the bankruptcy court relieving the debtor from obligation to pay the unpaid balance of most claims.

disclosed principal—principal whose identity is made known by the agent as well as the fact that the agent is acting on the principal's behalf.

discovery—procedures for ascertaining facts prior to the time of trial in order to eliminate the element of surprise in litigation.

dishonor—status when the primary party refuses to pay the instrument according to its terms.

disinherited—excluded from sharing in the estate of a decedent.

Dispute Settlement Body (DSB)—means provided by the World Trade Organization for member nations to resolve trade disputes rather than engage in unilateral trade sanctions or a trade war.

distinctiveness—capable of serving the source-identifying function of a mark.

distribution *per stirpes*—distribution of an estate made in as many equal parts as there are family lines represented in the nearest generation; also known as *stirpital distribution*.

distributor—entity that takes title to goods and bears the financial and commercial risks for the subsequent sale of the goods.

divestiture order—a court order to dispose of interests that could lead to a monopoly.

divisible contract—agreement consisting of two or more parts, each calling for corresponding performances of each part by the parties.

document of title—document treated as evidence that a person is entitled to receive, hold, and dispose of the document and the goods it covers.

Dodd-Frank Wall Street Reform and Consumer Protection Act—federal legislation passed following the financial markets collapse that includes consumer protections as well as market and mortgage lending reforms.

domestic corporation—corporation that has been incorporated by the state in question as opposed to incorporation by another state.

dominant tenement—land that is benefited by an easement.

donee—recipient of a gift.

donor—person making a gift.

double indemnity—provision for payment of double the amount specified by the insurance contract if death is caused by an accident and occurs under specified circumstances.

draft, or bill of exchange—an unconditional order in writing by one person upon another, signed by the person giving it, and ordering the person to whom it is directed to pay upon demand or at a definite time a sum certain in money to order or to bearer.

drawee—person to whom the draft is addressed and who is ordered to pay the amount of money specified in the draft.

drawer—person who writes out and creates a draft or bill of exchange, including a check.

due diligence—process of checking the environmental history and nature of land prior to purchase.

due process—the constitutional right to be heard, question witnesses, and present evidence.

due process clause—a guarantee of protection against the loss of property or rights without the chance to be heard.

dumping—selling goods in another country at less than fair value.

duress—conduct that deprives the victim of free will and that generally gives the victim the right to set aside any transaction entered into under such circumstances.

duty—obligation of law imposed on a person to perform or refrain from performing a certain act.

E

easement—permanent right that one has in the land of another, as the right to cross another's land or an easement of way.

easement by implication—easement not specifically created by deed that arises from the circumstances of the parties and the land location and access.

economic duress—threat of financial loss.

Economic Espionage Act (EEA)—federal law that makes it a felony to copy, download, transmit, or in any way transfer proprietary files, documents, and information from a computer to an unauthorized person.

economic strikers—union strikers trying to enforce bargaining demands when an impasse has been reached in the negotiation process for a collective bargaining agreement.

effects doctrine—doctrine stating that U.S. courts will assume jurisdiction and will apply antitrust laws to conduct outside of the United States when the activity of business firms has a direct and substantial effect on U.S. commerce; the rule has been modified to require that the effect on U.S. commerce also be direct and foreseeable.

effluent guidelines—EPA standards for maximum ranges of discharge into water.

electronic funds transfer (EFT)—any transfer of funds (other than a transaction originated by a check, draft, or similar paper instrument) that is initiated through an electronic terminal, a telephone, a computer, or a magnetic tape so as to authorize a financial institution to debit or credit an account.

Electronic Funds Transfer Act (EFTA)—federal law that provides consumers with rights and protections in electronic funds transfers.

eleemosynary corporation—corporation organized for a charitable or benevolent purpose.

embezzlement—statutory offense consisting of the unlawful conversion of property entrusted to the wrongdoer.

eminent domain—power of government and certain kinds of corporations to take private property against the objection of the owner, provided the taking is for a public purpose and just compensation is made for it.

emissions offset policy—controls whether new factories can be built in a nonattainment area.

employment-at-will doctrine—doctrine in which the employer has historically been allowed to terminate the employment contract at any time for any reason or for no reason.

en banc—the term used when the full panel of judges on the appellate court hears a case.

encoding warranty—warranty made by any party who encodes electronic information on an instrument; a warranty of accuracy.

Endangered Species Act (ESA)—federal law that identifies and protects species that are endangered from development or other acts that threaten their existence.

endowment insurance—insurance that pays the face amount of the policy if the insured dies within the policy period.

entitlement theory—another name for Nozick's theory that we all have certain rights that must be honored and protected by government.

environmental impact statement (EIS)—formal report prepared under NEPA to document findings on the impact of a federal project on the environment.

equitable title—beneficial interest in a trust.

equity—the body of principles that originally developed because of the inadequacy of the rules then applied by the common law courts of England.

escalation clause—provision for the automatic increase of the rent at periodic intervals.

escheat—transfer to the state of the title to a decedent's property when the owner of the property dies intestate and is not survived by anyone capable of taking the property as heir.

estate in fee—largest estate possible in which the owner has absolute and entire interest in the land.

estoppel—principle by which a person is barred from pursuing a certain course of action or of disputing the truth of certain matters.

ethical egoism—theory of ethics that we should all act in our own self-interest; the Ayn Rand theory that separates guilt from acting in our own self-interest.

ethics—a branch of philosophy dealing with values that relate to the nature of human conduct and values associated with that conduct.

***ex post facto* law**—a law making criminal an act that was lawful when done or that increases the penalty when done. Such laws are generally prohibited by constitutional provisions.

exculpatory clause—provision in a contract stating that one of the parties is not liable for damages in case of breach; also called *limitation-of-liability clause*.

executed contract—agreement that has been completely performed.

execution—the carrying out of a judgment of a court, generally directing that property owned by the defendant be sold and the proceeds first be used to pay the execution or judgment creditor.

executive branch—the branch of government (e.g., the president) formed to execute the laws.

executor, executrix—person (man, woman) named in a will to administer the estate of the decedent.

executory contract—agreement by which something remains to be done by one or both parties.

exhaustion of administrative remedies—requirement that an agency make its final decision before the parties can go to court.

existing goods—goods that physically exist and are owned by the seller at the time of a transaction.

exoneration—agreement or provision in an agreement that one party shall not be held liable for loss; the right of the surety to demand that those primarily liable pay the claim for which the surety is secondarily liable.

expert witness—one who has acquired special knowledge in a particular field as through practical experience or study, or both, whose opinion is admissible as an aid to the trier of fact.

export sale—direct sale to customers in a foreign country.

express authority—authority of an agent to perform a certain act.

express authorization—authorization of an agent to perform a certain act.

express contract—agreement of the parties manifested by their words, whether spoken or written.

express warranty—statement by the defendant relating to the goods, which statement is part of the basis of the bargain.

extortion—illegal demand by a public officer acting with apparent authority.

F

factor—bailee to whom goods are consigned for sale.

false imprisonment—intentional detention of a person without that person's consent; called the *shopkeeper's tort* when shoplifters are unlawfully detained.

FAS—free alongside the named vessel.

federal district court—a general trial court of the federal system.

Federal Register—government publication issued five days a week that lists all administrative regulations, all presidential proclamations and executive orders, and other documents and classes of documents that the president or Congress direct to be published.

Federal Register Act—federal law requiring agencies to make public disclosure of proposed rules, passed rules, and activities.

Federal Sentencing Guidelines—federal standards used by judges in determining mandatory sentence terms for those convicted of federal crimes.

federal system—the system of government in which a central government is given power to administer to national concerns while individual states retain the power to administer to local concerns.

fee simple defeasibles—fee simple interest that can be lost if restrictions on its use are violated.

fee simple estate—highest level of land ownership; full interest of unlimited duration.

felony—criminal offense that is punishable by confinement in prison for more than one year or by death, or that is expressly stated by statute to be a felony.

field warehousing—stored goods under the exclusive control of a warehouse but kept on the owner's premises rather than in a warehouse.

Fifth Amendment—constitutional protection against self-incrimination; also guarantees due process.

finance lease—three-party lease agreement in which there is a lessor, a lessee, and a financier.

financing statement—brief statement (record) that gives sufficient information to alert third persons that a particular creditor may have a security interest in the collateral described.

fire insurance policy—a contract that indemnifies the insured for property destruction or damage caused by fire.

firm offer—offer stated to be held open for a specified time, under the UCC, with respect to merchants.

first-in-time provision—creditor whose interest attached first has priority in the collateral when two creditors have a secured interest.

first-to-perfect basis—rule of priorities that holds that first in time in perfecting a security interest, mortgage, judgment, lien, or other property attachment right should have priority.

fixture—personal property attached to or adapted to real estate.

floating lien—claim in a changing or shifting stock of goods of the buyer.

FOB place of destination—shipping contract that requires the seller to deliver goods to the buyer.

FOB place of shipment—contract that requires the seller to arrange for shipment only.

forbearance—refraining from doing an act.

forcible entry and detainer—action by the landlord to have the tenant removed for nonpayment of rent.

foreclosure—procedure for enforcing a mortgage resulting in the public sale of the mortgaged property and, less commonly, in merely barring the right of the mortgagor to redeem the property from the mortgage.

foreign corporation—corporation incorporated under the laws of another state.

Foreign Corrupt Practices Act (FCPA)—federal law that makes it a felony to influence decision makers in other countries for the purpose of obtaining business, such as contracts for sales and services; also imposes financial reporting requirements on certain U.S. corporations.

Foreign Trade Antitrust Improvements Act—the act that requires that the defendant's conduct have a "direct, substantial, and reasonably foreseeable effect" on domestic commerce.

forged or unauthorized indorsement—instrument indorsed by an agent for a principal without authorization or authority.

forgery—fraudulently making or altering an instrument that apparently creates or alters a legal liability of another.

formal contracts—written contracts or agreements whose formality signifies the parties' intention to abide by the terms.

Fourth Amendment—privacy protection in the U.S. Constitution; prohibits unauthorized searches and seizures.

franchise—privilege or authorization, generally exclusive, to engage in a particular activity within a particular geographic area, such as a government franchise to operate a taxi company within a specified city, or a private franchise as the grant by a manufacturer of a right to sell products within a particular territory or for a particular number of years.

franchise agreement—sets forth rights of franchisee to use trademarks, etc., of franchisor.

Franchise Rule—FTC rule requiring detailed disclosures and prohibiting certain practices.

franchisee—person to whom franchise is granted.

franchising—granting of permission to use a trademark, trade name, or copyright under specified conditions; a form of licensing.

franchisor—party granting the franchise.

fraud—intentional making a false statement of fact, with knowledge or reckless indifference that it is false with resulting reliance by another.

fraud in the inducement—fraud that occurs when a person is persuaded or induced to execute an instrument because of fraudulent statements.

fraud-on-the-market—a theory that in an open and developed securities market, the price of a stock is determined by the information on the company available to the public, and misleading statements will defraud purchasers of stock even if they do not directly rely on these statements.

Freedom of Information Act—federal law permitting citizens to request documents and records from administrative agencies.

freight insurance—insures that shipowner will receive payment for transportation charges.

full warranty—obligation of a seller to fix or replace a defective product within a reasonable time without cost to the buyer.

funds transfer—communication of instructions or requests to pay a specific sum of money to the credit of a specified account or person without an actual physical passing of money.

fungible goods—homogeneous goods of which any unit is the equivalent of any other unit.

future goods—goods that exist physically but are not owned by the seller and goods that have not yet been produced.

G

garnishment—the name given in some states to attachment proceedings.

general agent—agent authorized by the principal to transact all affairs in connection with a particular type of business or trade or to transact all business at a certain place.

general corporation code—state's code listing certain requirements for creation of a corporation.

general jurisdiction—the power to hear and decide most controversies involving legal rights and duties.

general legacies—certain sums of money bequeathed to named persons by the testator; to be paid out of the decedent's assets generally without specifying any particular fund or source from which the payment is to be made.

general partner—partnership in which the partners conduct as co-owners a business for profit, and each partner has a right to take part in the management of the business and has unlimited liability; general partners publicly and actively engage in the transaction of firm business.

general partners—managers of a partnership who have personal liability for the partnership debts.

gift—title to an owner's personal property voluntarily transferred by a party not receiving anything in exchange.

gift causa mortis—gift, made by the donor in the belief that death was immediate and impending, that is revoked or is revocable under certain circumstances.

good faith—absence of knowledge of any defects or problems; "pure heart and an empty head."

goods—anything movable at the time it is identified as the subject of a transaction.

grantee—new owner of a land conveyance.

grantor—owner who transfers or conveys an interest in land to a new owner.

gratuitous bailment—bailment in which the bailee does not receive any compensation or advantage.

guarantor—one who undertakes the obligation of guaranty.

guaranty—agreement or promise to answer for a debt; an undertaking to pay the debt of another if the creditor first sues the debtor.

guaranty of collection—form of guaranty in which creditor cannot proceed against guarantor until after proceeding against debtor.

guaranty of payment—absolute promise to pay when a debtor defaults.

guest—transient who contracts for a room or site at a hotel.

H

hearing officer (or examiner)—another name for an administrative law judge.

hearsay evidence—statements made out of court that are offered in court as proof of the information contained in the statements and that, subject to many exceptions, are not admissible in evidence.

holder—someone in possession of an instrument that runs to that person (i.e., is made payable to that person, is indorsed to that person, or is bearer paper).

holder in due course—a holder who has given value, taken in good faith without notice of dishonor, defenses, or that instrument is overdue, and who is afforded special rights or status.

holder through a holder in due course—holder of an instrument who attains holder-in-due-course status because a holder in due course has held it previous to him or her.

holographic will—unwitnessed will written by hand.

homeowners insurance policy—combination of standard fire insurance and comprehensive personal liability insurance.

hotelkeeper—one regularly engaged in the business of offering living accommodations to all transient persons.

hull insurance—insurance that covers physical damage on a freight-moving vessel.

I

identification—point in the transaction when the buyer acquires an interest in the goods subject to the contract.

identified—term applied to particular goods selected by either the buyer or the seller as the goods called for by the sales contract.

illusory promise—promise that in fact does not impose any obligation on the promisor.

impeach—using prior inconsistent evidence to challenge the credibility of a witness.

implied contract—contract expressed by conduct or implied or deduced from the facts.

implied warranty—warranty that was not made but is implied by law.

implied warranty of the merchantability—group of promises made by the seller, the most important of which is that the goods are fit for the ordinary purposes for which they are sold.

impostor rule—an exception to the rules on liability for forgery that covers situations such as the embezzling payroll clerk.

in pari delicto—equally guilty; used in reference to a transaction as to which relief will not be granted to either party because both are equally guilty of wrongdoing.

incidental authority—authority of an agent that is reasonably necessary to execute express authority.

incidental damages—incurred by the nonbreaching party as part of the process of trying to cover (buy substitute goods) or sell (selling subject matter of contract to another); includes storage fees, commissions, and the like.

income—money earned by the principal, or property in trust, and distributed by the trustee.

incontestability clause—provision that after the lapse of a specified time the insurer cannot dispute the policy on the ground of misrepresentation or fraud of the insured or similar wrongful conduct.

incorporation by reference—contract consisting of both the original or skeleton document and the detailed statement that is incorporated in it.

incorporator—one or more natural persons or corporations who sign and file appropriate incorporation forms with a designated government official.

indemnity—right of a person secondarily liable to require that a person primarily liable pay for loss sustained when the secondary party discharges the obligation that the primary party should have discharged; an undertaking to pay another a sum of money to indemnify when loss is incurred.

indemnity contract—agreement by one person, for consideration, to pay another person a sum of money in the event that the other person sustains a specified loss.

indenture trustee—usually a commercial banking institution, to represent the interests of the bondholders and ensure that the terms and covenants of the bond issue are met by the corporation.

independent contractor—contractor who undertakes to perform a specified task according to the terms of a contract but over whom the other contracting party has no control except as provided for by the contract.

indorsee—party to whom special indorsement is made.

indorsement—signature of the payee on an instrument.

indorser—secondary party (or obligor) on a note.

informal contract—simple oral or written contract.

informal settlements—negotiated disposition of a matter before an administrative agency, generally without public sanctions.

injunction—order of a court of equity to refrain from doing (negative injunction) or to do (affirmative or mandatory injunction) a specified act.

inland marine—insurance that covers domestic shipments of goods over land and inland waterways.

insider—full-time corporate employee or a director or their relatives.

insider information—privileged information on company business known only to employees.

insolvency—excess of debts and liabilities over assets, or inability to pay debts as they mature.

instruction—summary of the law given to jurors by the judge before deliberation begins.

insurable interest—the right to hold a valid insurance policy on a person or property.

insurance—a plan of security against risks by charging the loss against a fund created by the payments made by policyholders.

insurance agent—agent of an insurance company.

insurance broker—independent contractor who is not employed by any one insurance company.

insured—person to whom the promise in an insurance contract is made.

insurer—promisor in an insurance contract.

integrity—the adherence to one's values and principles despite the costs and consequences.

intentional infliction of emotional distress—tort that produces mental anguish caused by conduct that exceeds all bounds of decency.

intentional tort—civil wrong that results from intentional conduct.

inter vivos gift—any transaction that takes place between living persons and creates rights prior to the death of any of them.

interest in the authority—form of agency in which an agent has been given or paid for the right to exercise authority.

interest in the subject matter—form of agency in which an agent is given an interest in the property with which that agent is dealing.

interlineation—writing between the lines or adding to the provisions of a document, the effect thereof depending upon the nature of the document.

intermediary bank—bank between the originator and the beneficiary bank in the transfer of funds.

interrogatories—written questions used as a discovery tool that must be answered under oath.

intervenors—in administrative actions, third parties who have an interest in the issues being determined by an ALJ.

intestate—condition of dying without a will as to any property.

intestate succession—distribution, made as directed by statute, of a decedent's property not effectively disposed of by will.

invasion of privacy—tort of intentional intrusion into the private affairs of another.

invitee—person who enters another's land by invitation.

involuntary bankruptcy—proceeding in which a creditor or creditors file the petition for relief with the bankruptcy court.

issuer—party who issues a document such as a letter of credit or a document of title such as a warehouse receipt or bill of lading.

J

joint and several liability—disproportionate satisfaction of partnership debt rendering each partner liable for the entire debt with the right to contribution from other partners.

joint liability—apportions partners' responsibility for partnership debt equally.

joint tenancy—estate held jointly by two or more with the right of survivorship as between them unless modified by statute.

joint venture—relationship in which two or more persons or firms combine their labor or property for a single undertaking and share profits and losses equally unless otherwise agreed.

judge—primary officer of the court.

judgment lien—lien obtained through the courts.

judgment n.o.v. (or *non obstante veredicto*, "notwithstanding the verdict")—a judgment entered after verdict upon the motion of the losing party on the ground that the verdict is so wrong that a judgment should be entered the opposite of the verdict.

judicial branch—the branch of government (e.g., the courts) formed to interpret the laws.

jurisdiction—the power of a court to hear and determine a given class of cases; the power to act over a particular defendant.

jurisdictional rule of reason—rule that balances the vital interests, including laws and policies, of the United States with those of a foreign country.

jury—a body of citizens sworn by a court to determine by verdict the issues of fact submitted to them.

K

Kant's categorical imperative—a standard of ethics that requires that we avoid one-sided benefit for us as a result of the conduct or decision.

L

land—earth, including all things embedded in or attached thereto, whether naturally or by the act of humans.

landlord—one who leases real property to another.

law—the order or pattern of rules that society establishes to govern the conduct of individuals and the relationships among them.

lease—agreement between the owner of property and a tenant by which the former agrees to give possession of the property to the latter for payment of rent. (Parties—landlord or lessor, tenant or lessee)

leasehold estate—interest of a tenant in rented land.

legacy—gift of money made by will.

legal title—title held by the trustee in a trust situation.

legatee—beneficiary who receives a gift of personal property by will.

legislative branch—the branch of government (e.g., Congress) formed to make the laws.

lessee—one who has a possessory interest in real or personal property under a lease; a tenant.

lessor—one who conveys real or personal property by a lease; a landlord.

letter of credit—commercial device used to guarantee payment to a seller, primarily in an international business transaction.

letters of administration—written authorization given to an administrator of an estate as evidence of appointment and authority.

letters testamentary—written authorization given to an executor of an estate as evidence of appointment and authority.

liability insurance—covers the shipowner's liability if the ship causes damage to another ship or its cargo.

libel—written or visual defamation without legal justification.

license—personal privilege to do some act or series of acts upon the land of another, as the placing of a sign thereon, not amounting to an easement or a right of possession.

licensee—someone on another's premises with the permission of the occupier, whose duty is to warn the licensee of nonobvious dangers.

licensing—transfer of technology rights to a product so that it may be produced by a different business organization in a foreign country in exchange for royalties and other payments as agreed.

lien—claim or right, against through judgment or levy.

life estate—an estate for the duration of a life.

limitation-of-liability clause—provision in a contract stating that one of the parties is not liable for damages in case of breach; also called *exculpatory clause*.

limited covenant—any covenant that does not provide the complete protection of a full covenant.

limited defenses—defenses available to secondary parties if the presenting party is a holder in due course.

limited liability company (LLC)—a partnership for federal tax treatment and the limited liability feature of the corporate form of business organization.

limited liability partnership (LLP)—partnership in which at least one partner has a liability limited to the loss of the

capital contribution made to the partnership.

limited partner—partner who neither takes part in the management of the partnership nor appears to the public to be a general partner.

limited partnership—partnership that can be formed by "one or more general partners and one or more limited partners."

limited (special) jurisdiction—the authority to hear only particular kinds of cases.

limited warranty—any warranty that does not provide the complete protection of a full warranty.

lineals—relationship that exists when one person is a direct descendant of the other; also called *lineal descendants*.

liquidated damages—provision stipulating the amount of damages to be paid in the event of default or breach of contract.

liquidated damages clause—specification of exact compensation in case of a breach of contract.

liquidation—process of converting property into money whether of particular items of property or of all the assets of a business or an estate.

living trust—trust created to take effect within the lifetime of the settlor; also called *inter vivos* trust.

living will—document by which individuals may indicate that if they become unable to express their wishes and are in an irreversible, incurable condition, they do not want life-sustaining medical treatments.

living-document view—the term used when a constitution is interpreted according to changes in conditions.

lottery—any plan by which a consideration is given for a chance to win a prize; it consists of three elements: (1) there must be a payment of money or something of value for an opportunity to win, (2) a prize must be available, and (3) the prize must be offered by lot or chance.

M

mailbox rule—timing for acceptance tied to proper acceptance.

maker—party who writes or creates a promissory note.

malpractice—when services are not properly rendered in accordance with commonly accepted standards; negligence by a professional in performing his or her skill.

marine insurance—policies that cover perils relating to the transportation of goods.

market power—the ability to control price and exclude competitors.

market value—price at which a share of stock can be voluntarily bought or sold in the open market.

mask work—specific form of expression embodied in a chip design, including the stencils used in manufacturing semiconductor chip products.

mass picketing—illegal tactic of employees massing together in great numbers to effectively shut down entrances of the employer's facility.

maturity date—date that a corporation is required to repay a loan to a bondholder.

means test—new standard under the Reform Act that requires the court to find that the debtor does not have the means to repay creditors; goes beyond the past requirement of petitions being granted on the simple assertion of the debtor saying, "I have debts."

mechanic's lien—claim by laborers or materials suppliers for property improvements.

mediation—the settlement of a dispute through the use of a messenger who carries to each side of the dispute the issues and offers in the case.

merchant—seller who deals in specific goods classified by the UCC.

merger (of corporations)—combining of corporations by which one absorbs the other and continues to exist, preserving its original charter and identity while the other corporation ceases to exist.

minitrial—a trial held on portions of the case or certain issues in the case.

Miranda warnings—warnings required to prevent self-incrimination in a criminal matter.

mirror image rule—common law contract rule on acceptance that requires language to be absolutely the same as the offer, unequivocal and unconditional.

misdemeanor—criminal offense with a sentence of less than one year that is neither treason nor a felony.

misrepresentation—false statement of fact made innocently without any intent to deceive.

mistrial—a court's declaration that terminates a trial and postpones it to a later date; commonly entered when evidence has been of a highly prejudicial character or when a juror has been guilty of misconduct.

money—medium of exchange.

money order—draft issued by a bank or a nonbank.

moral relativists—those who make decisions based on circumstances and not on the basis of any predefined standards.

mortgage—interest in land given by the owner to a creditor as security for the payment of the creditor for a debt, the nature of the interest depending upon the law of the state where the land is located. (Parties— mortgagor, mortgagee)

most-favored-nation—clause in treaties between countries whereby any privilege granted to one member is extended to all members of the treaty.

motion for summary judgment—request that the court decide a case on basis of law only because there are no material issues disputed by the parties.

motion to dismiss—a pleading that may be filed to attack the adverse party's pleading as not stating a cause of action or a defense.

N

National Environmental Policy Act (NEPA)—federal law that mandates study of a project's impact on the environment before it can be undertaken by any federal agency.

National Pollutant Discharge Elimination System (NPDES)—EPA system for regulating point source emissions into water.

national treatment—a WTO requirement in which a country may not discriminate between its own products and foreign products or services.

natural law—a system of principles to guide human conduct independent of, and sometimes contrary to, enacted law and discovered by man's rational intelligence.

necessaries—things indispensable or absolutely necessary for the sustenance of human life.

negligence—failure to exercise due care under the circumstances that results in harm proximately caused to one owed a duty to exercise due care.

negotiability—quality of an instrument that affords special rights and standing.

negotiable bill of lading—document of title that by its terms calls for goods to be delivered "to the bearer" or "to the order of" a named person.

negotiable instrument—drafts, promissory notes, checks, and certificates of deposit that, in proper form, give special rights as "negotiable commercial paper."

negotiable warehouse receipt—receipt that states the covered goods will be delivered "to the bearer" or "to the order of."

negotiation—the transfer of commercial paper by indorsement and delivery by the person to whom it is then payable in the case of order paper and by physical transfer in the case of bearer paper.

Noise Control Act—federal law that controls noise emissions from low-flying aircraft.

nominal damages—nominal sum awarded the plaintiff in order to establish that legal rights have been violated although the plaintiff in fact has not sustained any actual loss or damages.

nonattainment areas—"dirty" areas that do not meet federal standards under the Clean Air Act.

nonconforming use—use of land that conflicts with a zoning ordinance at the time the ordinance goes into effect.

nonconsumer lease—lease that does not satisfy the definition of a consumer lease; also known as a *commercial lease*.

nonnegotiable bill of lading—See *straight bill of lading*.

nonnegotiable instrument—contract, note, or draft that does not meet negotiability requirements of Article 3.

nonnegotiable warehouse receipt—receipt that states the covered goods received will be delivered to a specific person.

notice of dishonor—notice that an instrument has been dishonored; such notice can be oral, written, or electronic but is subject to time limitations.

notice statute—statute under which the last good-faith or bona fide purchaser holds the title.

notice-race statute—statute under which the first bona fide purchaser to record the deed holds the title.

novation—substitution for an old contract with a new one that either replaces an existing obligation with a new obligation or replaces an original party with a new party.

nuisance—conduct that harms or prejudices another in the use of land or that harms or prejudices the public.

O

obligee—promisee who can claim the benefit of the obligation.

obligor—promisor.

ocean marine—policies that cover transportation of goods in vessels in international and coastal trade.

offer—expression of an offeror's willingness to enter into a contractual agreement.

offeree—person to whom an offer is made.

offeror—person who makes an offer.

Oil Pollution Act—federal law that assigns cleanup liability for oil spills in U.S. waters.

open meeting law—law that requires advance notice of agency meeting and public access.

opening statements—statements by opposing attorneys that tell the jury what their cases will prove.

operation of law—attaching of certain consequences to certain facts because of legal principles that operate automatically as contrasted with consequences that arise because of the voluntary action of a party designed to create those consequences.

option contract—contract to hold an offer to make a contract open for a fixed period of time.

order of relief—the order from the bankruptcy judge that starts the protection for the debtor; when the order of relief is entered by the court, the debtor's creditors must stop all proceedings and work through the bankruptcy court to recover debts (if possible). Court finding that creditors have met the standards for bankruptcy petitions.

order paper—instrument payable to the order of a party.

original jurisdiction—the authority to hear a controversy when it is first brought to court.

originator—party who originates the funds transfer.

output contract—contract of a producer to sell its entire production or output to a given buyer.

outstanding—name for shares of a company that have been issued to stockholders.

overdraft—negative balance in a drawer's account.

P

par value—specified monetary amount assigned by an issuing corporation for each share of its stock.

parol evidence rule—rule that prohibits the introduction in evidence of oral or written statements made prior to or contemporaneously with the execution of a complete written contract, deed, or instrument, in the absence of fraud, accident, or mistake.

partially disclosed principal—principal whose existence is made known but whose identity is not.

partner—one of two or more persons who jointly own and carry on a business for profit.

partnership—pooling of capital resources and the business or professional talents of two or more individuals (partners) with the goal of making a profit.

partnership agreement—document prepared to evidence the contract of the parties. (Parties—partners or general partners)

party—person involved in a legal transaction; may be a natural person, an artificial person (e.g., a corporation), or an unincorporated enterprise (e.g., a governmental agency).

past consideration—something that has been performed in the past and which, therefore, cannot be consideration for a promise made in the present.

payable to order—term stating that a negotiable instrument is payable to the order of any person described in it or to a person or order.

payee—party to whom payment is to be made.

payment order—direction given by an originator to his or her bank or by any bank to a subsequent bank to make a specified funds transfer.

Pension Benefit Guaranty Corporation (PBGC)—an insurance plan to protect employees covered by defined benefit plans in case an employer is unable to meet its payment obligations from the employer's pension fund.

per capita—method of distributing estate assets on an equal-per-person basis.

perfected security interest—security interest with priority because of filing, possession, automatic, or temporary priority status.

periodic tenancy—tenancy that continues indefinitely for a specified rental period until terminated; often called a month-to-month tenancy.

personal property—property that is movable or intangible, or rights in such things.

personal representative—administrator or executor who represents decedents under UPC.

per stirpes—method for distribution of an estate that divides property equally down family lines.

physical duress—threat of physical harm to person or property.

plaintiff—party who initiates a lawsuit.

pleadings—the papers filed by the parties in an action in order to set forth the facts and frame the issues to be tried, although, under some systems, the pleadings merely give notice or a general indication of the nature of the issues.

pledge—bailment given as security for the payment of a debt or the performance of an obligation owed to the pledgee. (Parties–pledgor, pledgee)

point sources—direct discharges into bodies of water.

police power—the power to govern; the power to adopt laws for the protection of the public health, welfare, safety, and morals.

policy—paper evidencing the contract of insurance.

positive law—law enacted and codified by governmental authority.

possession—exclusive dominion and control of property.

possibility of reverter—nature of the interest held by the grantor after conveying land outright but subject to a condition or provision that may cause the grantee's interest to become forfeited and the interest to revert to the grantor or heirs.

postdate—to insert or place on an instrument a later date than the actual date on which it was executed.

postdating—inserting or placing on an instrument a later date than the actual date on which it was executed.

potentially responsible parties (PRPs)—those beyond actual polluters who could be responsible for cleanup costs.

power of attorney—written authorization to an agent by the principal.

precedent—a decision of a court that stands as the law for a particular problem in the future.

predatory lending—a practice on the part of the subprime lending market whereby lenders take advantage of less sophisticated consumers or those who are desperate for funds by using the lenders' superior bargaining positions to obtain credit terms that go well beyond compensating them for their risk.

predicate act—qualifying underlying offense for RICO liability.

preemption—the federal government's superior regulatory position over state laws on the same subject area.

preemptive right—shareholder's right upon the increase of a corporation's capital stock to be allowed to subscribe to such a percentage of the new shares as the shareholder's old shares bore to the former total capital stock.

preferences—transfers of property by a debtor to one or more specific creditors to enable these creditors to obtain payment for debts owed.

preferential transfers—certain transfers of money or security interests in the time frame just prior to bankruptcy that can be set aside if voidable.

preferred stock—stock that has a priority or preference as to payment of dividends or upon liquidation, or both.

prescription—acquisition of a right to use the land of another, as an easement, by making hostile, visible, and notorious use of the land, continuing for the period specified by the local law.

presentment—formal request for payment on an instrument.

price discrimination—the charging practice by a seller of different prices to different buyers for commodities of similar grade and quality, resulting in reduced competition or a tendency to create a monopoly.

prima facie—evidence that, if believed, is sufficient by itself to lead to a particular conclusion.

primary offerings—the original distribution of securities by the issuing corporations.

primary party—party to whom the holder or holder in due course must turn first to obtain payment.

primary picketing—legal presentations in front of a business notifying the public of a labor dispute.

primum non nocere—above all, do no harm.

principal—person or firm who employs an agent; the person who, with respect to a surety, is primarily liable to the third person or creditor; property held in trust.

principal debtor—original borrower or debtor.

prior art—a showing that an invention as a whole would have been obvious to a person of ordinary skill in the art when the invention was patented.

private carrier—carrier owned by the shipper, such as a company's own fleet of trucks.

private corporation—corporation organized for charitable and benevolent purposes or for purposes of finance, industry, and commerce.

private law—the rules and regulations parties agree to as part of their contractual relationships.

private nuisance—nuisance that affects only one or a few individuals.

privileges and immunities clause—a clause that entitles a person going into another state to make contracts, own property, and engage in business to the same extent as citizens of that state.

privity—succession or chain of relationship to the same thing or right, such as privity of contract, privity of estate, privity of possession.

privity of contract—relationship between a promisor and the promisee.

privity rule—succession or chain of relationship to the same thing or right, such as privity of contract, privity of estate, privity of possession.

pro rata—proportionately, or divided according to a rate or standard.

probate—procedure for formally establishing or proving that a given writing is the last will and testament of the person who purportedly signed it.

procedural law—the law that must be followed in enforcing rights and liabilities.

process—paperwork served personally on a defendant in a civil case.

product disparagement—false statements made about a product or business.

profit—right to take a part of the soil or produce of another's land, such as timber or water.

promisee—person to whom a promise is made.

promisor—person who makes a promise.

promissory estoppels—doctrine that a promise will be enforced although it is not supported by consideration when the promisor should have reasonably expected that the promise would induce action or forbearance of a definite and substantial character on the part of the promised and injustice can be avoided only by enforcement of the promise.

promissory note—unconditional promise in writing made by one person to another, signed by the maker engaging to pay on demand, or at a definite time, a sum certain in money to order or to bearer. (Parties—maker, payee)

promoters—persons who plan the formation of the corporation and sell or promote the idea to others.

proof of claim—written statement, signed by the creditor or an authorized representative, setting forth any claim made against the debtor and the basis for it.

property report—condensed version of a property development statement filed with the secretary of HUD and given to a prospective customer at least 48 hours before signing a contract to buy or lease property.

prosecutor—party who originates a criminal proceeding.

prospectus—information provided to each potential purchaser of securities setting forth the key information contained in the registration statement.

proxy—written authorization by a shareholder to another person to vote the stock owned by the shareholder; the person who is the holder of such a written authorization.

public corporation—corporation that has been established for governmental purposes and for the administration of public affairs.

public nuisance—nuisance that affects the community or public at large.

public policy—certain objectives relating to health, morals, and integrity of government that the law seeks to advance by declaring invalid any contract that conflicts with those objectives even though there is no statute expressly declaring such a contract illegal.

public warehouses—entities that serve the public generally without discrimination.

punitive damages—damages, in excess of those required to compensate the plaintiff for the wrong done, that are imposed in order to punish the defendant because of the particularly wanton or willful character of wrongdoing; also called *exemplary damages.*

purchase money security interest (PMSI)—the security interest in the goods a seller sells on credit that become the collateral for the creditor/seller.

Q

qualified indorsement—an indorsement that includes words such as "without recourse" that disclaims certain liability of the indorser to a maker or a drawee.

qualified privilege—media privilege to print inaccurate information without liability for defamation, so long as a

retraction is printed and there was no malice.

quantum meruit—as much as deserved; an action brought for the value of the services rendered the defendant when there was no express contract as to the purchase price.

quasi contract—court-imposed obligation to prevent unjust enrichment in the absence of a contract.

quasi-judicial proceedings—forms of hearings in which the rules of evidence and procedure are more relaxed but each side still has a chance to be heard.

quasi-public corporation—private corporation furnishing services on which the public is particularly dependent, for example, a gas and electric company.

quitclaim deed—deed by which the grantor purports to give up only whatever right or title the grantor may have in the property without specifying or warranting transfer of any particular interest.

quorum—minimum number of persons, shares represented, or directors who must be present at a meeting in order to lawfully transact business.

R

race statute—statute under which the first party to record the deed holds the title.

race-notice statute—see *notice-race statute.*

Racketeer Influenced and Corrupt Organizations (RICO) Act—federal law, initially targeting organized crime that has expanded in scope and provides penalties and civil recovery for multiple criminal offenses, or a pattern of racketeering.

real property—land and all rights in land.

recognizance—obligation entered into before a court to do some act, such as to appear at a later date for a hearing. Also called a *contract of record.*

recorder—public official in charge of deeds.

recross-examination—an examination by the other side's attorney that follows the redirect examination.

redemption—buying back of one's property, which has been sold because of a default, upon paying the amount that

had been originally due together with interest and costs.

redirect examination—questioning after cross-examination, in which the attorney for the witness testifying may ask the same witness other questions to overcome effects of the cross-examination.

reference to a third person—settlement that allows a nonparty to resolve the dispute.

reformation—remedy by which a written instrument is corrected when it fails to express the actual intent of both parties because of fraud, accident, or mistake.

registered bonds—bonds held by owners whose names and addresses are registered on the books of the corporation to ensure proper payment.

registration requirements—provisions of the Securities Act of 1933 requiring advance disclosure to the public of a new securities issue through filing a statement with the SEC and sending a prospectus to each potential purchaser.

registration statement—document disclosing specific financial information regarding the security, the issuer, and the underwriter.

release—an instrument by which the signing party (releasor) relinquishes claims or potential claims against one or more persons (releasees) who might otherwise be subject to liability to the releasor.

remainder interest—land interest that follows a life estate.

remand—term used when an appellate court sends a case back to trial court for additional hearings or a new trial.

remedy—action or procedure that is followed in order to enforce a right or to obtain damages for injury to a right.

rent-a-judge plan—dispute resolution through private courts with judges paid to be referees for the cases.

representative capacity—action taken by one on behalf of another, as the act of a personal representative on behalf of a decedent's estate, or action taken both on one's behalf and on behalf of others, as a shareholder bringing a representative action.

repudiation—result of a buyer or seller refusing to perform the contract as stated.

request for production of documents—discovery tool for uncovering paper evidence in a case.

requirements contract—contract to buy all requirements of the buyer from the seller.

rescission—action of one party to a contract to set the contract aside when the other party is guilty of a breach of the contract.

reservation of rights—assertion by a party to a contract that even though a tendered performance (e.g., a defective product) is accepted, the right to damages for nonconformity to the contract is reserved.

Resource Conservation and Recovery Act (RCRA)—federal law that regulates the disposal of potentially harmful substances and encourages resource conservation and recovery.

Resource Recovery Act—early federal solid waste disposal legislation that provided funding for states and local governments with recycling programs.

respondeat superior—doctrine that the principal or employer is vicariously liable for the unauthorized torts committed by an agent or employee while acting within the scope of the agency or the course of the employment, respectively.

restrictive covenants—covenants in a deed by which the grantee agrees to refrain from doing specified acts.

restrictive indorsement—an indorsement that restricts further transfer, such as in trust for or to the use of some other person, is conditional, or for collection or deposit.

reverse—the term used when the appellate court sets aside the verdict or judgment of a lower court.

reverse mortgage—mortgage in which the owners get their equity out of their home over a period of time and return the house to the lender upon their deaths.

reversible error—an error or defect in court proceedings of so serious a nature that on appeal the appellate court will set aside the proceedings of the lower court.

revoke—testator's act of taking back his or her will and its provisions.

right—legal capacity to require another person to perform or refrain from an action.

right of escheat—right of the state to take the property of a decedent that has not been distributed.

right of first refusal—right of a party to meet the terms of a proposed contract before it is executed, such as a real estate purchase agreement.

right of privacy—the right to be free from unreasonable intrusion by others.

right to cure—second chance for a seller to make a proper tender of conforming goods.

right-to-work laws—laws restricting unions and employees from negotiating clauses in their collective bargaining agreements that make union membership compulsory.

rights theory—Nozick's theory of ethics that we all have a set of rights that must be honored and protected by government.

risk—peril or contingency against which the insured is protected by the contract of insurance.

risk of loss—in contract performance, the cost of damage or injury to the goods contracted for.

Robinson-Patman Act—a federal statute designed to eliminate price discrimination in interstate commerce.

S

Safe Drinking Water Act—a federal law that establishes national standards for contaminants in drinking water.

sale on approval—term indicating that no sale takes place until the buyer approves or accepts the goods.

sale or return—sale in which the title to the property passes to the buyer at the time of the transaction but the buyer is given the option of returning the property and restoring the title to the seller.

search warrant—judicial authorization for a search of property where there is the expectation of privacy.

seasonable—timely.

secondary meaning—a legal term signifying the words in question have taken on a new meaning with the public, capable of serving a source-identifying function of a mark.

secondary parties—called secondary obligors under Revised Article 3; parties to an instrument to whom holders turn when the primary party, for whatever reason, fails to pay the instrument.

secondary picketing—picketing an employer with which a union has no dispute to persuade the employer to stop doing business with a party to the dispute; generally illegal under the NLRA.

secrecy laws—confidentiality laws applied to home-country banks.

secured party—person owed the money, whether as a seller or a lender, in a secured transaction in personal property.

secured transaction—credit sale of goods or a secured loan that provides special protection for the creditor.

securities—stocks and bonds issued by a corporation. Under some investor protection laws, the term includes any interest in an enterprise that provides unearned income to its owner.

security agreement—agreement of the creditor and the debtor that the creditor will have a security interest.

security interest—property right that enables the creditor to take possession of the property if the debtor does not pay the amount owed.

self-help repossession—creditor's right to repossess the collateral without judicial proceedings.

self-proved wills—wills that eliminate some formalities of proof by being executed according to statutory requirements.

selling on consignment—entrusting a person with possession of property for the purpose of sale.

semiconductor chip product—product placed on a piece of semiconductor material in accordance with a predetermined pattern that is intended to perform electronic circuitry functions.

service mark—mark that identifies a service.

servient tenement—land that is subject to an easement.

settlor—one who settles property in trust or creates a trust.

severalty—ownership of property by one person.

shared powers—powers that are held by both state and national governments.

Sherman Antitrust Act—a federal statute prohibiting combinations and contracts in restraint of interstate trade, now generally inapplicable to labor union activity.

shop right—right of an employer to use in business without charge an invention discovered by an employee during working hours and with the employer's material and equipment.

shopkeeper's privilege—right of a store owner to detain a suspected shoplifter based on reasonable cause and for a reasonable time without resulting liability for false imprisonment.

short-swing profit—profit realized by a corporate insider from selling securities less than six months after purchase.

sinking fund—fixed amount of money set aside each year by the borrowing corporation toward the ultimate payment of bonds.

Sixth Amendment—the U.S. constitutional amendment that guarantees a speedy trial.

slander—defamation of character by spoken words or gestures.

slander of title—malicious making of false statements as to a seller's title.

small claims courts—courts that resolve disputes between parties when those disputes do not exceed a minimal level; no lawyers are permitted; the parties represent themselves.

social contract—the agreement under Locke and Rawls as to what our ethical standards will be.

sole or individual proprietorship—form of business ownership in which one individual owns the business.

soliciting agent—salesperson.

sovereign compliance doctrine—doctrine that allows a defendant to raise as an affirmative defense to an antitrust action the fact that the defendant's actions were compelled by a foreign state.

sovereign immunity doctrine—a doctrine that states that a foreign sovereign generally cannot be sued without its consent.

special agent—agent authorized to transact a specific transaction or to do a specific act.

special indorsement—an indorsement that specifies the person to whom the instrument is indorsed.

specific legacies—identified property bequeathed by a testator; also called *specific devises*.

specific lien—right of a creditor to hold a particular property or assert a lien on the particular property of the debtor because of the creditor's having done work on or having some other association with the property, as distinguished from having a lien generally against the assets of the debtor merely because the debtor is indebted to the lien holder.

specific performance—action brought to compel the adverse party to perform a contract on the theory that merely suing for damages for its breach will not be an adequate remedy.

spendthrift trust—a trust that, prevents creditors of the beneficiary from reaching the principal or income held by the trustee and precludes beneficiary assignments.

spot zoning—allowing individual variation in zoning.

stakeholder analysis—the term used when a decision maker views a problem from different perspectives and measures the impact of a decision on various groups.

stakeholders—those who have a stake, or interest, in the activities of a corporation; stakeholders include employees, members of the community in which the corporation operates, vendors, customers, and any others who are affected by the actions and decisions of the corporation.

stale check—a check whose date is longer than six months ago.

standby letter—letter of credit for a contractor ensuring he will complete the project as contracted.

stare decisis—"let the decision stand"; the principle that the decision of a court should serve as a guide or precedent and control the decision of a similar case in the future.

status quo ante—original positions of the parties.

statute of frauds—statute that, in order to prevent fraud through the use of perjured testimony, requires that certain kinds of transactions be evidenced in writing in order to be binding or enforceable.

statute of limitations—statute that restricts the period of time within which an action may be brought.

statutory law—legislative acts declaring, commanding, or prohibiting something.

stay (or delay) of foreclosure—delay of foreclosure obtained by the mortgagor to prevent undue hardship.

stock subscription—contract or agreement to buy a specific number and kind of shares when they are issued by the corporation.

stop payment order—order by a depositor to the bank to refuse to make payment of a check when presented for payment.

straight (or nonnegotiable) bill of lading—document of title that consigns transported goods to a named person.

strict liability—civil wrong for which there is absolute liability because of the inherent danger in the underlying activity, for example, the use of explosives.

strict tort liability—product liability theory that imposes absolute liability upon the manufacturer, seller, or distributor of goods for harm caused by defective goods.

subject matter jurisdiction—judicial authority to hear a particular type of case.

sublease—a transfer of the premises by the lessee to a third person, the sublessee or subtenant, for a period of less than the term of the original lease.

sublessee—person with lease rights for a period of less than the term of the original lease (also *subtenant*).

subprime lending market—a credit market that makes loans to high-risk consumers (those who have bankruptcies, no credit history, or a poor credit history), often loaning money to pay off other debts the consumer has due.

subrogation—right of a party secondarily liable to stand in the place of the creditor after making payment to the creditor and to enforce the creditor's right against the party primarily liable in order to obtain indemnity from such primary party.

substantial impairment—material defect in a good.

substantial performance—equitable rule that if a good-faith attempt to perform does not precisely meet the terms of the agreement, the agreement will still be considered complete if the essential purpose of the contract is accomplished.

substantive law—the law that defines rights and liabilities.

substitute check—electronic image of a paper check that a bank can create and that has the same legal effect as the original instrument.

substitution—substitution of a new contract between the same parties.

sum certain—amount due under an instrument that can be computed from its face with only reference to interest rates.

summary jury trial—a mock or dry-run trial for parties to get a feel for how their cases will play to a jury.

summation—the attorney address that follows all the evidence presented in court and sums up a case and recommends a particular verdict be returned by the jury.

Superfund Amendment and Reauthorization Act—federal law that expands scope and operation of CERCLA.

Superfund sites—areas designated by the EPA for cleanup.

surety—obligor of a suretyship; primarily liable for the debt or obligation of the principal debtor.

suretyship—undertaking to pay the debt or be liable for the default of another.

symbolic delivery—delivery of goods by delivery of the means of control, such as a key or a relevant document of title, such as a negotiable bill of lading; also called constructive delivery.

T

tariff—(1) domestically—government-approved schedule of charges that may be made by a regulated business, such as a common carrier or warehouser; (2) internationally—tax imposed by a country on goods crossing its borders, without regard to whether the purpose is to raise revenue or to discourage the traffic in the taxed goods.

tax lien—lien on property for nonpayment of taxes.

teller's check—draft drawn by a bank on another bank in which it has an account.

temporary insider—someone retained by a corporation for professional services on an as-needed basis, such as an attorney, accountant, or investment banker.

temporary perfection—perfection given for a limited period of time to creditors.

tenancy at sufferance—lease arrangement in which the tenant occupies the property at the discretion of the landlord.

tenancy at will—holding of land for an indefinite period that may be terminated at any time by the landlord or by the landlord and tenant acting together.

tenancy by entirety or tenancy by the entireties—transfer of property to both husband and wife.

tenancy for years—tenancy for a fixed period of time, even though the time is less than a year.

tenancy in common—relationship that exists when two or more persons own undivided interests in property.

tenancy in partnership—ownership relationship that exists between partners under the Uniform Partnership Act.

tenant—one who holds or possesses real property by any kind of right or title; one who pays rent for the temporary use and occupation of another's real property under a lease.

tender—goods have arrived, are available for pickup, and the buyer is notified.

term insurance—policy written for a specified number of years that terminates at the end of that period.

termination statement—document (record), which may be requested by a paid-up debtor, stating that a security interest is no longer claimed under the specified financing statement.

testamentary capacity—sufficient mental capacity to understand that a writing being executed is a will and what that entails.

testamentary intent—designed to take effect at death, as by disposing of property or appointing a personal representative.

testamentary trust—trust that takes effect upon the settlor's death.

testate—condition of leaving a will upon death.

testate distribution—distribution of an estate in accordance with the will of the decedent.

testator, testatrix—man, woman who makes a will.

theory of justice—the Locke and Rawlsian standard for ethics that requires that we all agree on certain universal principles in advance.

third-party beneficiary—third person whom the parties to a contract intend to benefit by the making of the contract and to confer upon such person the right to sue for breach of contract.

time draft—bill of exchange payable at a stated time after sight or at a definite time.

tippee—individual who receives information about a corporation from an insider or temporary insider.

tort—civil wrong that interferes with one's property or person.

Toxic Substances Control Act (TOSCA)—first federal law to control the manufacture, use, and disposal of toxic substances.

trade dress—product's total image including its overall packaging look.

trade libel—written defamation about a product or service.

trade name—name under which a business is carried on and, if fictitious, must be registered.

trade secret—formula, device, or compilation of information that is used in one's business and is of such a nature that it provides an advantage over competitors who do not have the information.

trademark—mark that identifies a product.

transferee—buyer or vendee.

Transport Rule—the rule promulgated to address downwind pollution from coal and gas-fired power plants.

traveler's check—check that is payable on demand provided it is countersigned by the person whose specimen signature appears on the check.

treasury stock—corporate stock that the corporation has reacquired.

treble damages—three times the damages actually sustained.

trespass—unauthorized action with respect to person or property.

trespasser—person who is on the land of another without permission or authorization.

tripartite—three-part division (of government).

trust—transfer of property by one person to another with the understanding or declaration that such property be held for the benefit of another; the holding of property by the owner in trust for another, upon a declaration of trust, without a transfer to another person. (Parties—settlor, trustee, beneficiary)

trust agreement—instrument creating a trust; also called *deed of trust.*

trust corpus—fund or property that is transferred to the trustee also called *trust fund, trust estate,* and *trust res.*

trustee—party who has legal title to estate and manages it.

trustee in bankruptcy—impartial person elected to administer the debtor's estate.

trustor—donor or settlor who is the owner of property.

tying—the anticompetitive practice of requiring buyers to purchase one product in order to get another.

U

ultra vires—act or contract that the corporation does not have authority to do or make.

unconscionable—unreasonable, not guided or restrained by conscience and often referring to a contract grossly unfair to one party because of the superior bargaining powers of the other party.

underwriter—insurer.

undisclosed principal—principal on whose behalf an agent acts without disclosing to the third person the fact of agency or the identity of the principal.

undue influence—influence that is asserted upon another person by one who dominates that person.

Uniform Probate Code (UPC)—uniform statute on wills and administration of estates.

Uniform Simultaneous Death Act—law providing that when survivorship cannot be established, the property of each person shall be disposed of as though he or she had survived the other.

unilateral contract—contract under which only one party makes a promise.

unincorporated association—combination of two or more persons for the furtherance of a common nonprofit purpose.

universal agent—agent authorized by the principal to do all acts that can lawfully be delegated to a representative.

universal defenses—defenses that are regarded as so basic that the social interest in preserving them outweighs the social interest of giving negotiable instruments the freely transferable qualities of money; accordingly, such defenses are given universal effect and may be raised against all holders.

USA Patriot Act—federal law that, among other things, imposes reporting requirements on banks.

usage of trade—language and customs of an industry.

usury—lending money at an interest rate that is higher than the maximum rate allowed by law.

utilitarians—theory of ethics based on doing the most good for the most people in making decisions.

uttering—crime of issuing or delivering a forged instrument to another person.

V

valid contract—agreement that is binding and enforceable.

value—consideration or antecedent debt or security given in exchange for the transfer of a negotiable instrument or creation of a security interest.

variance—permission of a landowner to use the land in a specified manner that is inconsistent with the zoning ordinance.

vicarious liability—imposing liability for the fault of another.

void agreement—agreement that cannot be enforced.

voidable contract—agreement that is otherwise binding and enforceable but may be rejected at the option of one of the parties as the result of specific circumstances.

voidable title—title of goods that carries with it the contingency of an underlying problem.

voir dire **examination**—the preliminary examination of a juror or a witness to ascertain fitness to act as such.

voluntary bankruptcy—proceeding in which the debtor files the petition for relief.

voting by proxy—authorizing someone else to vote the shares owned by the shareholder.

voting trust—transfer by two or more persons of their shares of stock of a corporation to a trustee who is to vote the shares and act for such shareholders.

W

waiver—release or relinquishment of a known right or objection.

warehouse—entity engaged in the business of storing the goods of others for compensation.

warehouse receipt—receipt issued by the warehouser for stored goods; regulated by the UCC, which clothes the receipt with some degree of negotiability.

warranty—promise, either express or implied, about the nature, quality, or performance of the goods.

warranty against encumbrances—warranty that there are no liens or other encumbrances to goods except those noted by the seller.

warranty deed—deed by which the grantor conveys a specific estate or interest to the grantee and makes one or more of the covenants of title.

warranty of habitability—implied warranty that the leased property is fit for dwelling by tenants.

warranty of title—implied warranty that title to the goods is good and transfer is proper.

wasting assets corporation—corporation designed to exhaust or use up the assets of the corporation, such as by extracting oil, coal, iron, and other ores.

way of necessity—grantee's right to use land retained by the grantor for going to and from the conveyed land.

well-known mark—in international law a mark that both the Paris Convention and TRIPS recognize as deserving protection even if it is not registered in the foreign country; national law determines what "well-known" means but the WIPO offers a list suggesting that the value of the mark, the extent of its use and promotion, and its recognition in the relevant sector of the public are key factors.

White-Collar Crime Penalty Enhancement Act of 2002—federal reforms passed as a result of the collapses of companies such as Enron; provides for longer sentences and higher fines for both executives and companies.

white-collar crimes—crimes that do not use nor threaten to use force or violence or do not cause injury to persons or property.

whole life insurance—ordinary life insurance providing lifetime insurance protection.

will—instrument executed with the formality required by law by which a person makes a disposition of his or her property to take effect upon death.

writ of *certiorari*—the U.S. Supreme Court granting a right of review by the court of a lower court decision.

wrongfully dishonored—error by a bank in refusing to pay a check.

Z

zoning—restrictions imposed by government on the use of designated land to ensure an orderly physical development of the regulated area.

Case Index

Summarized cases are shown in boldface italic; cited cases are shown in nonbold italic.

deceptive advertising, 216, 620, 624–625
declaration dates, 915
deeds, 906, 1010–1014, 1037–1038
deeds of trust, 1078
defamation, 138–141
defendants, 20
deficiencies, 665
defined benefit plans, 777
defined contribution plans, 777–778
definite time, 526–527
delays of foreclosure, 1019
delegated powers, 55–56
delegation, 321–323
delegation of duties, 321–323
delivery, 536–537
demand, payable on, 526
demand drafts, 575
demurrer, 21
Department of Homeland Security (DHS), 789
depositions, 22
depositors, 389
deregulation, 58
derivative actions, 870, 916–917, 984
descriptive marks, 155
design patents, 166
detrimental reliance, 270–271
development statements, 637
devise, 1064
devisees, 1064
DHS (Department of Homeland Security), 789
Digital Millennium Copyright Act (DMCA), 123, 165
direct damages, 353
direct deposit, 590
direct examination, 23
direct withdrawal, 590
directed verdicts, 24
directors
    actions against, 984
    conflicts of interest, 980–981
    liability of, 981–985
    meetings of, 981
    powers of, 979–980
    qualifications of, 978
    removal of, 984–985
    short-swing profits by, 945
dirty areas, 1026
disability
    capacity to contract, 247–248
    contract offers and, 232
    defined, 710
    discharge of contracts, 338
    discrimination against people with, 812–815

partnerships, 857
    of principals in agency, 733–734
    SSI and, 781
discharge in bankruptcy, 686–689
discharge of contracts
    accord and satisfaction, 335–336
    by action of parties, 335–337
    commercial impracticability, 339
    conditions and, 328–330
    force majeure, 340
    frustration of purpose, 339–340
    illegality, 337
    impossibility, 337, 340–341
    by operation of law, 341–342
    overview, 333
    by performance, 330–335
    personal satisfaction contracts, 334–335
    releases, 335–337
    by substitution, 335–336
disclosed principals, 743
discovery, 21–22
discrimination. *See also* equal protection; Title VII
    bankruptcy protections, 686
    credit applicants, 633
    genetic information, 815
    leases, 1046
    military members, 779–781
    OSHA complaints and, 782
    union activities, 773
dishonor, 567–568, 579
disinheritance, 1069–1070
dismissal motions, 21
Disney, Walt, 679
disparate impact, 795–796
disparate treatment, 795–796
Dispute Settlement Body (DSB), 191
dissociation, 858–859
dissolution
    defined, 855
    limited partnerships, 870
    LLCs, 874–876
    partnerships, 853, 854
distinctiveness of marks, 155
distribution franchises, 829
distribution per capita, 1075–1076
distribution per stirpes, 1076
distributors, 182
diverted delivery by computer, 122
divestiture orders, 76–77
dividends, 914–915, 921
divisible contracts, 227
DMCA (Digital Millennium Copyright Act), 123, 165

doctrine of detrimental reliance, 270–271
doctrine of equivalents, 170
documentary demands for payment, 611–612
documentary drafts, 611–612
documents of title, 389, 438
Dodd-Frank Wall Street Reform and Consumer Protection Act
    enactment of, 630
    enforcement, 946–947
    executive compensation, 989–990
    honest services fraud, 107
    overview, 929
    registration requirements, 931
    say-on-pay, 989
    whistleblowers, 766, 946, 972
Doha Round, 191
domestic corporations, 885
dominant tenements, 1002
donee beneficiaries, 312
donees, 368
donors, 368, 1078
double indemnity, 710
drafts, 519–520, 529, 574
drawees, 519–520, 566
drawers, 519–520, 566
dress codes, 800–801
Drew, Lori, 122
drinks, 465–466
drug and alcohol testing, 787–788
DSB (Dispute Settlement Body), 191
dual motive cases, 773
due care, duty of, 582–583, 1079
due diligence, 1037
due process, 64–65, 126
due process clause, 64–65
dummy payees, 545–546
dumping, 192
durable powers of attorney, 733–734
duress, 256–257, 300–301, 564
duties, 4, 315, 321–323
duty of due care, 582–583, 1079
duty of loyalty, 729–730, 850–851, 987–988, 1079
duty of obedience, 730, 851
duty of performance, 730, 1079
duty of possession, 1079
duty of production of income, 1079
duty of reasonable care, 731

E

earned surplus, 914
easements, 1002–1003
easements by implication, 1002
ECOA (Equal Credit Opportunity Act), 633

e-commerce and cyberlaw. *See also* privacy
  blocking wifi to charge more, 628
  check clearing, 522, 539
  click waivers, 508
  contract formation, 235
  contract issues, 429
  data barns, 1037
  defamation, 139–140
  electronic checks, 522, 539, 567
  electronic signatures, 298, 700
  e-mail and discovery, 77
  e-mail in litigation, 77
  Google impact on trials, 23
  mean girls, 122
  MERS, 1017
  net neutrality, 92
  piggybacking, 48
  record keeping, 971
  rejection issues, 484
  sales tax, 64
  scams, 577
  search engines, 653
  supply chains, 445
  taxes on Internet purchases, 64
  terms and conditions, 429
  University access to computers, 6
  university access to computers, 6
  video wills, 1067
  Wii injuries, 463
economic duress, 256–257
Economic Espionage Act (EEA), 122–123
economic strikers, 775
ECPA (Electronic Communication Privacy
  Act), 786–787
EEA (Economic Espionage Act),
  122–123
EEOC (Equal Employment Opportunity
  Commission), 796–799
effects doctrine, 197
effluent guidelines, 1027–1028
EIS (environmental impact statements),
  1032
election conduct (unions), 770
electronic chattel paper, 648
Electronic Communication Privacy Act
  (ECPA), 786–787
Electronic Freedom of Information Act
  Amendments of 1996, 88–89
Electronic Fund Transfers Act (EFTA),
  123, 589
electronic funds transfer (ETF), 589–590
Electronic Signatures in Global and
  National Commerce Act (E-sign),
  216–217, 518, 700
eleemosynary corporations, 886
Ellison, Larry, 991

e-mail, 77, 123–124, 236–237, 786–787.
  See also e-commerce and cyberlaw
embezzlement, 118
eminent domain, 1014–1015
emissions offset policy, 1026
Employee Retirement Income Security Act
  (ERISA), 776–778
employee stock ownership plans (ESOPs),
  777, 871
employees, 785–788, 988
employers
  criminal liability of, 753–754
  negligent hiring and retention, 752
  negligent supervision and training, 753
  vicarious liability of, 749–751, 803
employment. *See also* labor relations; Title
  VII
  agency compared, 721,
    762
  characteristics of, 762
  creation of relationships, 762
  equal employment opportunity,
    810–815
  family and medical leave, 779
  health and safety of employees,
    781–783
  immigration laws, 788–789
  military leaves, 779–781
  pension plans, 776–778
  unemployment compensation,
    778–779
  whistleblowers, 763–764, 765–766
  workers' compensation, 783–785
employment contracts. *See also* labor
    relations
  arbitration clauses, 279, 799
  creation of, 762
  duration and termination of, 762–765
  employee duties under, 766–767
  employee rights, 767–769
  noncompetition agreements, 283–285
employment testing, 808
employment-at-will doctrine, 763–764
en banc decisions, 17–18
encoding warranties, 582
encryption, 123
Endangered Species Act (ESA), 1033
endorsement contracts, 329
endorsements. *See* indorsements
endowment insurance, 710
entitlement theory, 36
entrustees, 441
environmental impact statements (EIS),
  1032
environmental law
  air pollution, 1026–1027

  enforcement of, 1033–1037
  land use controls, 1037–1040
  nuisance, 1034–1037
  regulation of government, 1032–1033
  solid waste disposal, 1029–1032
  state regulation, 1033
  water pollution, 1027–1028
Environmental Protection Agency (EPA),
  1026. *See also* environmental law
Equal Credit Opportunity Act (ECOA),
  633
equal employment opportunity, 810–815.
  See also Title VII
Equal Employment Opportunity
  Commission (EEOC), 796–799
Equal Pay Act, 806, 810–811
equal protection, 65, 809
equitable title, 1078
equity, 10
ERISA (Employee Retirement Income
  Security Act), 776–778
ESA (Endangered Species Act), 1033
escalation clauses, 1051
escheat, 375, 1075
E-sign, 216–217, 518, 700
ESOPs (employee stock ownership plans),
  777, 871
estates, 1070–1077
estates in fee, 1007
estoppel
  corporations by estoppel, 892–893
  defined, 439
  partnerships by, 845–846
  promissory estoppel, 270–271, 297
ETF (electronic funds transfer), 589–590
ethical dilemmas, 44–50
ethical egoism, 36
ethics. *See also* business ethics
  addictions, 112
  admission application lies, 46
  analyst honesty, 43
  Apple warranties, 469
  attorney conflict of interest, 25
  attorneys as beneficiaries, 1073
  bankruptcy, 673
  bribery, 196
  business interruption insurance, 706
  check cashing companies, 560
  conflicts of interest, 949
  contract modifications, 269
  creditor pressure on debtors, 612,
    634–635
  debt relief, 635
  defined, 34
  distribution controls, 76
  executive compensation, 991

feeder funds, 958

grace periods for payments, 507

IRS snooping, 89

land sales, undisclosed principal, 747

LinkedIn, 6

LLPs, 879

Medicaid eligibility, 528

mortgage foreclosures, 538

overdraft fees, 580

patents for genes, 168

pensions, 687

poultry manure, 1029

repossession, 664

restocking fees, 415

returned goods, 486

SAT score lies, 49

savings and loan crisis, 879

Snowden, Edward, 39

stolen art, 442

surrogate mothers, 281

tenant screening, 1052

theories of, 35–37

Veteran's Affairs queues, 40

European Economic Community (EEC), 191

European Union (EU), 191

E-Verify, 788–789

evictions, 1055

evidence, 23, 77, 378, 635. *See also* parol evidence rule

ex post facto laws, 56–57

exculpatory clauses, 359–360, 959

executed contracts, 210

execution of judgment, 26

executive branch, 55

Executive Order 11246, 810

Executive Order 12989, 789

executive orders, as source of law, 8

executors, 296, 1070

executory contracts, 210

executrix, 1070

exemplary damages, 144–145, 148, 623–624

exemptions, 684–686

exhaustion of administrative remedies, 97

existing goods, 411, 437

exoneration, 604

expert witnesses, 22

Export Administration Act, 194

export sales, 182

express assumption of risk, 146

express authority, 724–725, 847

express authorization, 723

express contracts, 208

extortion, 115

extraordinary matters, 978

F

factorage, 400

factors, 400–401, 449–450

factual incapacity, 244

Fair Credit and Charge Card Disclosure Act, 630

Fair Credit Billing Act, 633

Fair Credit Reporting Act (FCRA), 634–635

Fair Debt Collection Practices Act (FDCPA), 634

Fair Housing Act, 1046

Fair Labor Standards Act (FLSA), 768–769

fair use, 163–164

false advertising, 216, 620, 624–625

false claims, 116–117

false imprisonment, 134–135

false pretenses, 116–117

false swearing, 116

Family and Medical Leave Act (FMLA), 779

fanciful marks, 155

FAS, 443

Fastow, Andrew, 109

FBLA (Federal Bills of Lading Act), 394

FCPA (Foreign Corrupt Practices Act), 116, 194–195, 992

FCRA (Fair Credit Reporting Act), 634–635

FDCPA (Fair Debt Collection Practices Act), 634

FDD (franchise disclosure documents), 831–832

Federal Anticybersquatting Consumer Protection Act (ACPA), 159–160

Federal Arbitration Act, 26–27, 279

Federal Bills of Lading Act (FBLA), 394

Federal Circuit, 17

federal court system, 16–18

federal district courts, 16–17

Federal Employees' Compensation Act, 784–785

Federal Employer's Liability Act (FELA), 784

Federal Omnibus Transportation Employee Testing Act, 788

Federal Register, 92–93

Federal Register Act, 92–93

Federal Sentencing Guidelines, 108

federal supremacy, 57–58

federal system, 55

Federal Tort Claims Act (FTCA), 147, 751

Federal Trade Commission (FTC), 460–461, 565–566. *See also* consumer protection; franchises

Federal Trademark Dilution Act (FTDA), 158

Federal Wiretapping Act, 786

FedWire, 593

fee simple defeasibles, 1007

fee simple estates, 1006

feeder funds, 958

FELA (Federal Employer's Liability Act), 784

felonies, 105

fictitious paper, 588

fiduciaries, 777, 986–987. *See also headings starting with "duty"*

field warehousing, 392, 644, 649

Fifth Amendment

equal protection, 65, 809

as limit on government, 64–65

self-incrimination, 126

takings, 1014–1015

finance leases, 428–429

Financial Industry Regulatory Authority (FINRA), 948–949

financial statements, 914

financing statements, 650–653, 654–655

fire insurance, 708–709

firm offers, 230, 414

First Amendment, 67, 139, 163

first-in-time provisions, 655

first-to-perfect basis, 656

529 accounts, 685

fixtures, 1004–1005

floating liens, 647

FLSA (Fair Labor Standards Act), 768–769

FMLA (Family and Medical Leave Act), 779

FOB place of destination, 443–444, 446

FOB place of shipment, 442–443

FOIA (Freedom of Information Act), 88–89

food, 465–466

forbearance, 265

force majeure, 340

forcible entry and detainer, 1055

foreclosure, 1019

foreign corporations, 885

Foreign Corrupt Practices Act (FCPA), 116, 194–195, 992

Foreign Trade Antitrust Improvements Act (FTAIA), 197

foreseeable user rule, 962–963

forfeiture, 107–108

forged indorsements, 544–547, 585–586

forgery

checks and, 585–586

defined, 116

forgery (*Continued*)
    indorsements, 544–547,
        585–586
    negotiable instrument defense, 564
Form 10-K, 935
Form I-9, 788–789
formal contracts, 208
formation of contracts. *See* contract
    formation
forward-looking statements, 939
Fourteenth Amendment, 64–65, 785–786
Fourth Amendment, 4–5, 124, 785.
        See also search and seizure
franchise disclosure documents (FDD),
        831–832
Franchise Rule, 831
franchisees, 638
franchises
    defined, 638, 828
    disclosure for, 831–832
    employee misclassification and,
        834–835
    franchise agreements, 829–830
    protections for, 830–831
    types of, 829
    vicarious liability and, 832–834
franchising, 182
franchisors, 638, 829
fraud
    accountants' liability, 966–968
    in contracts, 251–253
    defined, 251, 966
    imposter fraud, 711
    mail and wire fraud, 119
    parol evidence rule and, 300–301
    product liability and, 470
    securities regulation, 936–938
    suretyships, 605
fraud as to the nature or terms of the
        instrument, 563
fraud in the inducement, 562
fraud-on-the-market doctrine, 938
fraudulent transfers, 680–682
free enterprise system, 73
Freedom of Information Act (FOIA),
        88–89
freight insurance, 707
Friedman, Milton, 38
friendly fires, 708
front-page-of-the-newspaper test, 48–49
frustration of purpose, 339–340
FTAIA (Foreign Trade Antitrust
        Improvements Act), 197
FTC (Federal Trade Commission),
        460–461, 565–566
FTCA (Federal Tort Claims Act), 147, 751

FTDA (Federal Trademark Dilution Act),
        158
full warranties, 460
functional patents, 165
funds transfers, business, 590–594
funds transfers, consumer, 589–590
funds transfers, defined, 592
fungible goods, 437
future goods, 411, 437
future interests, 1007

G

GAAP (generally accepted accounting
        principles), 936, 956
Galleon Group, 109
gambling, 280
Gandolfini, James, 1069
garbage, 1029–1032
garnishment, 26
gas stations, 831
GATS (General Agreement on Trade in
        Services), 187
GATT (General Agreement on Tariffs and
        Trade 1994), 186
gender discrimination, 802
general agents, 722
General Agreement on Tariffs and Trade
        1994 (GATT), 186
General Agreement on Trade in Services
        (GATS), 187
general corporation codes, 887
general damages, 353
general jurisdiction, 14
general legacies, 1074
general partners, 841, 868
general partnerships, 841. *See also*
        partnerships
generally accepted accounting principles
        (GAAP), 936, 956
generic marks, 155
Genetic Information Nondiscrimination
        Act (GINA), 815
Gesellschaft mit beschränkter Haftung
        (GmbH), 182
gift cards, 632
gifts, 263–264, 368–372, 411
gifts causa mortis, 370
GINA (Genetic Information
        Nondiscrimination Act), 815
global warming, 1027
good cause discharge, 764–765
good faith
    defined, 478, 558
    discharge of contracts and, 338–339
    in every contract, 277–278, 306
    for holders in due course, 558

good faith purchasers, 439, 441
goods, 410–411. *See also* sale of goods
Google, impact on trials, 23
government regulation
    family and medical leave, 779
    health and safety of employees, 781–783
    of horizontal markets and competitors,
        73–77
    immigration laws, 788–789
    military leaves, 779–781
    pension plans, 776–778
    power to, 73
    remedies for anticompetitive behavior,
        82
    of supply chains, 77–82
    unemployment compensation,
        778–779
    vicarious liability of employer for
        employee violation of, 750
    workers' compensation, 783–785
governmental immunity, 147
grantees, 1010
grantors, 1010
gratuitous bailments, 380
greenhouse gases, 1027
Grossman, Louis, 39–40
groupthink, 50
guaranties, 602. *See also* suretyships
guaranties of collection, 602–603
guaranties of payment, 603
guarantors, 602
guardians, capacity of ward to contract,
        248
guests, 402

H

H-1B visas, 789
Hammer, MC, 679
harassment, sexual, 802–805
hazardous materials, 783
health care insurance receivables, 649
HealthSouth, 109–110
hearings officers, 96
hearsay evidence, 635
height requirements, 802, 806
hiring and retention, 752
Hoffman, Philip Seymour, 1069
holders, 536, 556–557, 561
holders in due course
    defined, 536, 556
    limited defenses not available against,
        561–562
    requirements for, 556–561
holders through holders in due course, 561
holding companies, 896
holographic wills, 1070

Home Equity Loan Consumer Protection Act, 630
homeowners insurance, 708–709
home-solicited sales, 627
homestead exemption, 684–685
honest services fraud, 107
horizontal price-fixing, 74
hostile fires, 708
hostile work environments, 803
hotelkeepers, 401–403
hotelkeepers liens, 403
hull insurance, 707

I

I-9 forms, 788–789
ICANN (Internet Corporation for Assigned Names and Numbers), 159–160
ICCTA (Interstate Commerce Commission Termination Act), 397–398
ICRA (Immigration Reform and Control Act), 788–789
identification of goods, 437–438
identified, 437
illegality
    of contracts, 276–280, 419
    discharge of contracts, 337
    negotiable instrument defense, 564
    offers, 232
    partnerships, 857
illusory promises, 265–266
ILSFDA (Interstate Land Sales Full Disclosure Act), 637
Immigration Eligibility Verification Form, 788–789
immigration laws, 788–789
Immigration Reform and Control Act (ICRA), 788–789
immunity, 147, 198
impeachment, 22
implied contract terms, 226, 305–306
implied contracts, 208–209
implied primary assumption of risk, 146–147
implied warranties, assignment, 321
implied warranty of merchantability, 463–465, 468
impossibility, 337, 340–341
imposter fraud, 711
imposter rule, 545–547, 588
impracticability, 339, 488
in pari delicto, 277
incapacity. *See* capacity
Incentives for Self-Policing, Disclosure, Correction, and Prevention of Violations, 1032

incidental authority, 725
incidental beneficiaries, 314–315
incidental damages, 353, 498
income, 1078
incontestability clauses, 711–712
incorporation by reference, 302
incorporation into contracts, 226, 302
incorporators, 891
indemnification, 984, 993, 1057
indemnity, 605, 852–853
indemnity contracts, 603
indenture trustees, 906
independence rule, 610
independent contractors, 721–722, 754–755, 834–835
India, 189
individual account plans, 777
individual proprietorship, 824
indorsees, 539
indorsements
    agents or officers, 543
    bank, 542
    of bearer paper, 537
    blank, 538–539
    defined, 538
    forged, 544–547, 585–586
    missing, 543
    multiple payees or indorsements, 542–543
    qualified, 540–541, 549
    restrictive, 541
    special, 539–540
    time for presentment, 578–579
    unauthorized, 544–547
indorsers, 566
Industrial Espionage Act, 172
informal contracts, 208
informal settlements, 96
inheritance. *See* decedents
injunctions, 10, 356–357, 1034
inland marine insurance, 708
innocent landowners, 1032
insanity. *See* disability
insider information, 941–944
Insider Trading and Securities Fraud Act, 107, 941
insiders, 681, 942
insolvency, 681
inspection right, 481, 852, 912–914
insurable interests, 436, 697–698
insurance
    antilapse provisions, 700
    automobiles, 709–710
    bad faith, 702–703
    burdens of proof in, 701–702
    business liability, 705–707

coinsurance, 708
    contracts for, 699–700
    defined, 697
    fire and homeowners, 708–709
    insurable interest requirement, 436, 697–698
    interpretation of contracts for, 701
    life, 697–698, 710–712
    marine, 707–708
    modifications of contracts, 701
    mortgages and, 1018
    parties to, 697
    subrogation, 703–704
    terrorism and, 706
    time limitations, 703
insurance agents, 697
insurance brokers, 697
insureds, 697
insurers, 697
integrated industries, 896
integrity, 45. *See also* business ethics; ethics
intellectual property rights. *See also* trademarks
    copyright, 123, 160–165, 173
    international trade and, 187–190, 193
    mask works, 175
    overview, 154, 174
    patents, 165–170, 173–174, 767
    secret business information, 171–173, 174, 767, 829
    tax issues, 183
    trade dress, 157–158, 829
intended beneficiaries. *See* third-party beneficiary contracts
intended user rule, 964
intent, criminal, 105
intentional infliction of emotional distress (IIED), 135–136
intentional torts
    assault, 134
    battery, 134
    contract interference, 141
    conversion, 374–375
    defamation, 138–141
    defined, 132–133
    false imprisonment, 134–135
    intentional infliction of emotional distress, 135–136
    invasion of privacy, 136–138, 787
    product disparagement, 141
    trespass, 122, 141–142, 373
inter vivos gifts, 369–370
interest in the authority, 722
interest in the subject matter, 722
interest rates, 285–286, 525, 906
interference by landlords, 1049

interlineations, 1068
interlopers, 965
intermediary banks, 591
internal controls, 956
international trade
    anticompetitive behavior, 195–198
    antidumping, subsidies and safeguards,
        192–193
    common carriers, 399–400
    Dispute Settlement Body, 191
    Doha Round, 191
    forms of international business,
        182–183
    international contracts, 183–184
    issues confronting companies engaged
        in, 194–199
    lines of credit for, 574
    regional trade agreements, 191–192
    sale of goods, 427–428, 508
    tariffs and barriers to trade, 185–186
    trademark registration, 154–155
    World Trade Organization, 184–187
Internet. *See also* e-commerce and cyberlaw
    bullying and, 122
    clickwrap agreements, 235
    contracts on, 216–217
    cybersquatting, 159–160
    piggybacking, 48
    privacy and, 5
    search engines, 653
    taxes on purchases via, 64
Internet banking, 590
Internet Corporation for Assigned Names
    and Numbers (ICANN), 159–160
Internet Service Providers (ISP), 165
interns, 768
interrogatories, 22
interstate commerce, 60–62
Interstate Commerce Commission
    Termination Act (ICCTA),
    397–398
Interstate Land Sales Full Disclosure Act
    (ILSFDA), 637
intervenors, 96
intervivos trusts, 1078
intestate, 1064
intestate succession, 1075–1077
intoxication, 248
intrusion into private affairs, 137
invasion of privacy, 136–138
inventions. *See* patents
inventory, priorities, 657
investment banking, 949
investment contracts, 929–930
invitations to negotiate, 222–223
invitees, 1008

involuntary bankruptcy, 676–677
ISP (Internet Service Providers), 165
issuers, 389, 608

J

Jefferson, Thomas, 165
Jennings, Marianne, 39–40
JOBS (Jumpstart Our Business Startups)
    Act of 2012, 929, 931, 933, 934
Jobs, Steve, 77
John, Elton, 679
joint and several liability, 144, 853–854
joint liability, 853–854
joint tenancy, 376–377
joint ventures, 825–827
judges, 20
judgment liens, 1004
judicial branch, 55
judicial triage, 30
Jumpstart Our Business Startups (JOBS)
    Act of 2012, 929, 931, 934
juries, 20, 22–23, 28, 95–96
jurisdiction, 14
jurisdictional rule of reason, 197
jury instructions, 25
justice courts, 18–19

K

Kant's categorical imperative theory, 35
knockoffs, 158
know-how, 190
known user rule, 961–962
KPMG, 110

L

L-1 visas, 789
labeling, 625–626
labor relations
    collective bargaining, 774
    National Labor Relations Act,
        769–770
    right-to-work laws, 774
    strikes and picketing, 775–776
    union activity, 772–774
Labor-Management Reporting and
    Disclosure Act (LMRDA), 776
land, 1002. *See also* real property
landlords, 1046. *See also* leases of real
    property
Lanham Trademark Act, 154, 187. *See also*
    trademarks
larceny, 119
law
    agency regulations as, 90–91
    business ethics and, 34

    classifications of, 9–10
    defined, 4
    equity compared, 10
    nature of, 4–6
    social forces influencing, 41–44
    sources of, 7–9
lawsuits, steps to, 21–22
lawyers, 947–948, 1073
leasehold estates, 1006–1007
leases of goods, 380–381, 428–430, 629,
    632–633
leases of real property
    assignment of, 1050–1051,
        1057–1058
    classifications of, 1046–1047
    creation of, 1046–1047
    defined, 1046
    deposits, 1054
    improvements, 1054
    injuries on premises and, 1055–1057
    landlord remedies, 1054–1055
    possession, 1049–1050
    renewal of, 1048
    rent for, 1050–1051, 1053
    repairs and condition, 1051–1053
    retaliation, 1054
    subleases, 1058
    taxes and assessments, 1054
    termination of, 1047–1048
    use of premises, 1050
Ledger, Heath, 1069
legacies, 1064
Legal Arizona Workers Act, 789
legal title, 1078
legatees, 1064
legislative branch, 55
lemon laws, 638
lessees, 1046
lessors, 1046
letters of administration, 1073
letters of credit, 184, 608–613
letters testamentary, 1073
liability insurance, 707
libel, 138
liberal search engines, 653
licensees, 1008
licenses, 1004
licensing, 174–175, 182, 282–283
Liebeck, Stella, 148
liens
    bailee's liens, 381
    floating liens, 647
    hotelkeepers liens, 403
    landlords, 1054
    overview, 1004
    repair liens, 657

National Securities Markets Improvement Act (NSMIA), 928
national treatment, 186
natural law, 34
NCCUSL (National Conference of Commissioners on Uniform State Laws), 8
necessaries, 245
negligence
    defenses, 145–147
    defined, 133
    elements of, 142–145
    hiring and retention, 752
    overview, 142–147
    product liability and, 470
    sports exception doctrine, 147
    supervision and training, 753
negligent misrepresentation, 253–254
negotiability
    ambiguous language and, 529
    authentication requirement, 522–524
    defined, 521
    factors not affecting, 529
    payable to order or bearer requirement, 527–528
    payment of sum certain in money, 525
    record requirement, 522
    of stock, 909
    time of payment requirement, 526–527
    unconditional promise or order requirement, 524–525
negotiable bills of lading, 395
negotiable instruments. *See also* checks; negotiability
    defenses to payment of, 561–566
    defined, 518
    holders, 536, 556
    holders in due course, 536, 556–561
    liability issues, 566–568
    parties to, 520–521
    presentment, 566–567
    statutes of limitations, 529
    types of, 518–520
negotiable warehouse receipts, 390–392
negotiation
    of bearer paper, 536–537
    of bills of lading, 395
    defined, 536
    imposter rule, 545–547, 588
    of order paper, 538
    problems with, 544–547
    of warehouse receipts, 390–392
    warranties in, 547–549
negotiation rules, 226
Nelson, Willie, 679

NEPA (National Environmental Policy Act), 1032
net neutrality, 92
New Orleans Saints, 47
new trial motions, 25
New York contact rule, 961
NLRA (National Labor Relations Act), 769–770
NLRB (National Labor Relations Board), 770
No Electronic Theft Act, 123
no-fault insurance, 710
Noise Control Act, 1032–1033
nominal damages, 353
nominal partners, 845–846
non obstante veredicto judgments, 25
nonattainment areas, 1026
noncompetition agreements, 283–285
nonconforming uses, 1038–1039
nonconsumer leases, 428
nondischargeable debts, 686–689
nondisclosure agreements, 172
nondisclosure in contract, 254–255
noninventory collateral, 657
nonnegotiable bills of lading, 395
nonnegotiable instruments, 521
nonnegotiable warehouse receipts, 389
nonprofit corporations, 886
North American Free Trade Agreement (NAFTA), 192
notice (process), 21
notice of dishonor, 567–568, 579
notice statutes, 1011
notice-race statutes, 1012–1013
novation, 320–321
Nozick, Robert, 36
NPDES (National Pollutant Discharge Elimination System) permits, 1028
NSMIA (National Securities Markets Improvement Act), 928
nuisance, 1034–1037

O

obedience, duty of, 730, 851
obligees, 206, 316, 602
obligors, 206, 316, 602
occupancy requirements, 709
Occupational Safety and Health Act (OSHA), 781–783
Occupational Safety and Health Administration (OSHA), 782–783
ocean marine insurance, 707
O'Connor, Sandra Day, 35
odometer fraud, 628–629
offerees, 207
offering statements, 931–932

offerors, 207
offers. *See also* acceptance of offers
    communication to offeree, 228–229
    contractual intention requirement, 222–224
    counteroffers, 230–231
    defined, 222, 414
    definiteness requirement, 224–228
    firm offers, 230
    negotiation rules, 226
    overview, 227
    revocation, 229–230
    termination of, 229–232
officers (corporate), 985–990
Oil Pollution Act, 1028
Older Workers Benefit Protection Act (OWBPA), 811
Omnibus Trade and Competitiveness Act, 193
open meeting laws, 90
open records laws, 88–89
opening statements, 23
operating agreements, 872
operation of law, 341–342, 856
operators, Superfund, 1029–1030
opinions, 251–252, 458–459
oppressive conduct, 917
option contracts, 211, 230
oral contract validity, 292, 425–426
order paper, 528, 538, 547
orders of relief, 678
Organization for Economic Cooperation and Development, 194, 196
Organizational Federal Sentencing Guidelines, 993
original jurisdiction, 14
originators, 592
OSHA (Occupational Safety and Health Act), 781–783
OSHA (Occupational Safety and Health Administration), 782–783
ostensible partners, 845–846
output contracts, 228, 419–420
outstanding stock, 904
overdrafts, 579
overtime pay, 769
OWBPA (Older Workers Benefit Protection Act), 811
owners, Superfund, 1029–1030

P

par value, 904
parens patriae actions, 82
parents, contract liability for children, 245–247
Paris Convention, 187–188

statements of account, 654

states, U.S. Constitution and, 55–58

status incapacity, 243

status quo ante, 245

Statute of Frauds
   defined, 292
   noncompliance, effects of, 299
   notes or memorandum, when sufficient, 297–299
   oral contract validity, 292
   sale of goods, 421–425
   stock and, 907
   writing, when required, 292–297

statutes of limitations
   accountants' malpractice, 958
   bank liability for checks, 588
   breach of sale of goods, 496
   discharge of contracts by, 341–342
   negotiable instruments, 529

statutory law, 7

stays of bankruptcy, 677

stays of foreclosure, 1019

Stewart, Martha, 110

stirpes, 1076

stock. *See also* securities regulation
   acquisition of, 906–910
   certificates of, 905, 910
   defined, 904
   nature of, 904–905
   overview, 888–889
   shareholder liability, 917–921
   shareholder rights, 910–917
   types of, 905–906
   unpaid subscriptions, 920–921

stock subscriptions, 907, 920–921

stolen property, title not acquired by, 368, 439

STOLI (stranger-owned life insurance policies), 698

stop payment orders, 581, 584

storage liens, 657

straight bills of lading, 395

straight voting, 911

stranger-owned life insurance policies (STOLI), 698

strict compliance rule, 610

strict liability, 133, 147–149, 456. *See also* product liability

strict search engines, 653

strikes, 775–776

Subchapter S corporations, 877, 886

subject matter jurisdiction, 14

subleases, 1058

sublessees, 1050–1051

subminimum wages, 768

subpoenas, 94

subprime lending, 620, 629

subrogation, 604–605, 703–704

subscriptions, 907

subsidies, 193

substantial impairment, 484

substantial performance, 332–334

substantive law, 9

substantive unconscionability, 279

substitute checks, 576, 588

substitution of contracts, 335–336

suggestive marks, 155

sum certain, 525

summary judgment motions, 22

summary jury trials, 28

summation, 24

summons, 21

Sunshine Act of 1976, 90

Superfund Amendment and Reauthorization Act, 1029

Superfund sites, 1029

Supplemental Security Income (SSI), 781

supply chain management. *See* common carriers; sale of goods; title

supply chains, 77–82

suretyships, 295, 602–608, 850

surplus, 665

sworn testimony, 24

symbolic delivery, 369

systemic class action cases, 797

T

takings, 1014–1015, 1038

tangible employment actions, 803

tariffs, 185–186

tax liens, 1004

taxes
   international trade and fraud, 183
   Internet purchases, 64
   leases and, 1054
   LLCs, 876
   mortgages and, 1018
   sales tax on Internet purchases, 64
   Social Security, 781
   unemployment compensation, 778–779

taxing power, 63–64

telemarketing, 627

Telephone Consumer Protection Act (TCPA), 627

telephone monitoring, 786

teller's checks, 520, 575

temporary insiders, 942

temporary perfection, 650

10-K forms, 935, 989

10-Q reports, 935

tenancy at sufferance, 1047

tenancy at will, 1047

tenancy by entirety, 377

tenancy for years, 1047

tenancy in common, 376

tenancy in partnership, 846

tenants, 1046. *See also* leases of real property

tender, 330, 444

tender offers, 945–946

tenements, 1002

term insurance, 710

termination statements, 654

terrorism, 706

Terrorism Risk Insurance Program Reauthorization Act, 706

testamentary capacity, 1064

testamentary intent, 1066

testamentary trusts, 1078

testate, 1064

testate distribution, 1064

testators, 1064

testatrix, 1064

theft, 120, 368, 439

theory of justice, 35

third-party beneficiary contracts, 312–315

Thirteenth Amendment, 356

three-part test, 48

TILA (Truth in Lending Act), 630

time drafts, 575

time is of the essence clauses, 331–332

tippees, 942

title
   bailments and, 441
   bills of lading, 394–395
   equitable title, 1078
   escheat, 375
   finding of lost personal property, 372–373
   gifts, 368–372
   legal title, 1078
   multiple ownership of personal property, 376–377
   occupation of personal property, 373–375
   passage in sale of goods, 438–444
   personal property generally, 368
   slander of title, 141
   stolen property, 368, 439
   warehouse receipts, 389–392

title abstracts, 1013

Title VII. *See also* equal employment opportunity
   affirmative action, 809–810
   exceptions to, 806–808
   extraterritorial issues, 815
   national origin, 806

E-COMMERCE & CYBERLAW

SPORTS & ENTERTAINMENT LAW